Funk & Wagnalls

STANDARD DICTIONARY

Funk & Wagnalls

STANDARD DICTIONARY

Second Edition

HarperPaperbacks
A Division of HarperCollinsPublishers

HarperPaperbacks   *A Division of* HarperCollins*Publishers*
10 East 53rd Street, New York, NY 10022

First HarperPaperbacks printing: August 1993

Printed in the United States of America

HarperPaperbacks and colophon are trademarks of HarperCollins*Publishers*

1 0 9 8 7 6 5

CONTENTS

GUIDE TO THE DICTIONARY

General vocabulary words and phrases, prefixes, suffixes, combining forms, and foreign terms are grouped together in the main A through Z section of this dictionary.

MAIN ENTRY

The main entry is a word, phrase, prefix, suffix, combining form, or foreign term that together with related entries make up an entry block in this dictionary. The main entry in the entry block is set so that it juts out into the margin of the column. These main entries are printed in an order based on letter-by-letter alphabetizing, a system in which phrases and hyphenated words are treated as if they were solid words. Therefore, **night school** follows **nightmare**, not **night**, and **go-go** follows **goggle.**

When several main entry words have the same spellings but differ in origin and meaning, each is made into a separate entry block, and the main terms are set off with superscripts. For example, **lark**[1] (bird) and **lark**[2] (a good time).

The main entry word is not repeated when a new part of speech is introduced within an entry block. Instead, a boldface dash is added before the new part of speech, and it stands for the main entry word. For example:

> **nov•el** (NOV əl) *adj.* new, strange, or unusual. —*n.* a fictional prose narrative of considerable length. . . .

The *n.pl.* designation following the pronunciation of some main entry nouns means that the main entry word is given in the plural. For example:

> **folk•ways** (FOHK wayz) *n.pl Sociol.* the traditional habits, customs, and behavior of a group, tribe, or nation.

When no singular form of the noun is shown, the entry word is usually used only in the plural and it takes a plural verb. If the plural entry word takes a singular verb, the reader will find a note, which is: (*construed as sing.*). If the plural entry can take either a singular or plural verb, the note is: (*construed as sing. or pl.*).

Some plural nouns have been made entry titles even though they have singular forms, because the plural form is far more common than the singular. In such cases the singular form is shown in the entry as follows:

al•gae (AL jee) *n. pl., sing.* **al•ga** (AL gə)

Related Entries

Entries related to the main entry are printed in boldface within the main entry block. A common phrase, such as **know the ropes**, which cannot be understood from the definitions of the separate words in the phrase, is one type of such an entry. Phrases such as these are placed in the entry block of the key word in the phrase, in this case, **rope**.

Within the definitions themselves, there may be boldface entries whose definitions are easily understood in context. For example,

> **dai•sy** (DAY zee) *n. pl.* **•sies** a plant of the composite family; esp., the **oxeye daisy** of the U.S., having a yellow disk and white rays, and the **English daisy,** having a small yellow disk and white or rose rays.

At the end of some entries there are forms of the main entry made by the addition of familiar suffixes. These derivative forms are not defined, since their meanings are readily understood from the meanings of the main entry. Such entries begin with a dash, and each ends with the part of speech label. An example of this type of run-on entry is:

> **—key'punch'er** *n.*

which appears at the end of the entry for the noun **keypunch.** When two derivative forms of the same part of speech have the same sense, they are separated by commas. For example,

> **—cap'tain•cy, cap'tain•ship** *n.*

Following some main entries, there are lists of compound words or phrases formed with the main entry word. These self-explanatory words or phrases are undefined but are offered to give the dictionary reader guidance in spelling and capitalization. See, for example, the lists at **non-** and **self.**

Syllable Division

A centered dot divides the main entry into syllables. These syllable divisions are the points at which a hyphen may be used when the full word will not fit at the end of a line and must be broken. Words in phrases are divided into syllables only when the words are not found as main entries in the dictionary. For example, **senior citizen** is not divided into syllables, because both **senior** and **citizen** are entries themselves, **senior** being entered and divided in the S's and **citizen** in the C's. However, **Achilles** in the **A·chil·les' heel** entry is divided into syllables because **Achilles** does not have a separate entry.

Prefixes, suffixes, and combining forms are not divided into syllables because their syllable breaks vary with the compound word formed by employing them.

Plurals of Nouns

Since the plurals of most nouns are formed by adding -*s*, the dictionary shows plurals only when they are formed in a different way or when the plurals are spelled in a way that might not be expected. Some examples:

> **ech·o** (EK oh) *n. pl.* **ech·oes**
> **ar·my** (AHR mee) *n. pl.* **·mies**
> **jock·ey** (JOK ee) *n. pl.* **·eys**
> **wolf** (wuulf) *n. pl.* **wolves** (wuulvz)
> **ap·pa·ra·tus** (AP ə RAT əs) *n. pl.* **·tus** or **·tus·es**
> **mon·goose** (MONG goos) *n. pl.* **·goos·es**

In most cases only the syllables that change in spelling are shown.

Comparison of Adjectives and Adverbs

Entries for adjectives and adverbs do not show the comparative and superlative forms when these forms are regular: that is, when they are made by adding -*er* or -*est* or, for adverbs, when they are made by supplying the words *more* or *most* (**cold**, **colder**, **coldest**; **slowly**, **more slowly**, **most slowly**). Frequently, only the affected syllables are shown. Some examples:

> **nut·ty** (NUT ee) *adj.* **·ti·er**, **·ti·est**
> **grim** (grim) *adj.* **grim·mer**, **grim·mest**
> **bad** (bad) *adj.* **worse**, **worst**
> **well** (wel) *adv.* **bet·ter**, **best**

Past Tense, Past Participle, and Present Participle of Verbs

When an entry for a verb does not show the past tense or the participles, these forms of the verb are constructed regularly: that is, by adding -*ed* to form the past tense and the past participle and by adding -*ing* to form the present participle (jump, jumped, jumping). Parts of the verb not formed this way are shown. For example,

> **de·fy** (də FĪ) *v.t.* **·fied**, **·fy·ing**
> **in·clude** (in KLOOD) *v.t.* **·clud·ed**, **·clud·ing**
> **eat** (eet) *v.* **ate**, **eat·en**, **eat·ing**

Pronunciation

Pronunciations are shown in parentheses after each main entry and are added after other boldface entries within an entry block when the pronunciation of these related entries differs significantly from that of the main entry in sound or stress. Using the pronunciation key, which appears on pages xiv–xv, the reader will be able to produce a pronunciation acceptable to any educated American. However, educated speakers pronounce words acceptably in different ways, and this dictionary does not usually provide variant pronunciations.

In many places, the first pronunciation is followed by a partial pronunciation, which is a pronunciation for the part that varies. Hyphens in these partial pronunciations stand for the parts not printed, parts pronounced the same as shown in the first full pronunciation. For example, in the pronunciation of

> **mu·tu·al** (MYOO choo əl) *adj.* —**mu′tu·al′i·ty** (-AL i tee) *adj.*

the first two syllables remain the same, but the third syllable changes, and the two additional syllables are shown.

This system is followed for any partial pronunciation within an entry block. For example, consider the pronunciation of the first syllable, **phle**, in **phlebitic** in the following entry:

> **phle·bi·tis** (fli BĪ tis) *n. Pathol.* inflammation of the inner membrane of a vein. —**phle·bit′ic** (-BIT ik) *adj.*

Because the pronunciation is the same as that of the first syllable of the main entry, that syllable is not repeated in the pronunciation.

Syllable breaks in pronunciations may not match those in boldface entries. Syllable breaks in pronunciation are based on the sound of speech; syllable breaks in boldface entries are based on the parts or roots that make up the entry words.

Stress

Stress within a pronounced entry is shown by the use of capital letters. Consider the entry word **candle**, which has only one stress. CAPITAL LETTERS are used to indicate the stress: (KAN dəl). In the word **candlelight**, there are two stressed syllables. The principal stress is shown by CAPITAL LETTERS: (KAN dl LĪT), the secondary stress by SMALL CAPITAL LETTERS: (KAN dl LĪT).

Stress marks are used for subordinate entries that are not pronounced. There are two stress marks. Consider the word **can′cel·a·ble**, found as a subordinate entry under **cancel**. The bold mark (′) represents the primary stress, the strongest syllable in the word. A lighter mark indicates a syllable receiving a stress of lesser intensity (′).

Consider the entry word **canonize**. Under it is found the subordinate entry **can′on•i•za′tion**. Note that the stress mark follows the syllable to which it applies.

When two syllables in a pronunciation are marked with capital letters (WEL GROOMD), both syllables receive equal stress.

Parts of Speech

The abbreviations for part of speech, the grammatical description of the *use* of a word in a sentence, are printed in italic before the definition to which each applies or before other information that applies to that part of speech only. Part of speech labels follow undefined words found at the end of some entries. The abbreviations used in this dictionary for the parts of speech are:

> *n.* noun
> *v.* verb (further differentiated into *v.t.* for transitive verb, *v.i.* for intransitive verb)
> *adj.* adjective
> *adv.* adverb
> *prep.* preposition
> *conj.* conjunction
> *interj.* interjection
> *pron.* pronoun

Every part of speech for a word is defined within one entry block; none is made a separate main entry.

Definitions

The definitions within each part of speech are grouped so that their related meanings are together. There is, otherwise, no significance to their order; the first definition is not necessarily for the earliest use, nor is it the most frequently used.

Definitions never consist of a single synonym. One-word definitions are cross references to fully defined forms.

Variations in Spelling

Acceptable spellings that vary from the spelling of the main entry are cited following the definition.

> **lar•gess** (lahr JES) *n.* liberal giving; also, something liberally given. Also **lar•gesse′**.
> **e•on** (EE ən) *n.* **1.** an incalculable period of time. **2.** *Geol.* a time interval including two or more eras. Also spelled *aeon*.

Variants are printed either in italic or boldface. The italic variant indicates that the entry referred to, *aeon* in the above example, may be found at its alphabetical position should the reader wish to check its syllabification or pronunciation. Boldface variants, which have no pronunciation, are pronounced the same as the main entry.

Since more than one spelling of the plural of nouns or the participles or past tense of verbs may be acceptable, variants are given in boldface immediately following the first form:

> **bus** (bus) *n. pl.* **bus•es** or **bus•ses**

Usage and Labels

Aids to usage, in several forms, have been offered to supplement definitions that might not be adequate to give the reader confidence in using a word or phrase. The aids easiest to spot are italic labels, but helpful information is often found just after the definition proper, and set off from it with a colon. Sometimes these are phrases or sentences directly illustrating the use of a term:

> **one-horse** (WUN HORS) *adj. Informal* small, unimportant: a *one-horse* town.
> **na•ture** (NAY chər) *n.* **1.** the essential character of something: the *nature* of democracy. **2.** . . . .

and sometimes there are notes about specific applications, cautions, etc., as:

> :said of a disease
> :used contemptuously
> :considered vulgar
> :distinguished from
> :opposed to
> :with *from* or *of*

Labels preceding definitions serve several functions. Style labels include *Informal, Dial.* (for dialectal), *Slang,* and *Illit.* (for illiterate). The label *Informal* indicates that the term is acceptable in the casual conversation of educated people but should be used only for special effect in a formal context such as a speech, a business report, a scholarly paper, etc. *Dial.* indicates a nonstandard term that is regularly used by people in specific regions, though it may be known to a wider audience. *Slang* labels a use that is intentionally outside standard English. Much slang is ephemeral, but some of it may become standard English, and some standard English words have slang applications. *Slang* is not to be confused with the label *Illit.*, which designates a usage that is regarded as incorrect by those who are educated.

Rare, Archaic, and *Obs.* (for obsolete) are currency labels. *Rare* labels words that were never in frequent use but are included because of their significant occurrence in literature. *Archaic* labels very old words, once common, that are now used only in well-defined circumstances, such as a church service. *Obs.* labels words of the more recent past that would not be used in any current context because they seem old-fashioned. Words that refer to objects no longer in use or concepts or ideas not commonly heard today are not labeled archaic or obsolete. The definitions for these terms explain that the object or idea was popular in earlier times.

Field labels identify definitions that apply especially to specific areas of study or activity. However, some of the fields of learning overlap, such as physics and chemistry, and the labeled terms may be used in more than one discipline. Examples of field labels are *Math.* (for mathematics), *Printing, Econ.* (for economics), *Eccl.* (for ecclesiastical). Field labels are usually abbreviated, as listed on pages xv–xvi.

Foreign language labels are applied to words that despite familiarity in English retain a foreign pronunciation. A *Brit.* (for British) label or a *Canadian* label is applied to words or phrases that may be known to Americans but are used primarily in Great Britain or in Canada.

Collateral Adjectives

A feature unique to the Funk & Wagnalls dictionaries is the addition at some noun entries of adjectival forms of the noun so remote in spelling that they may not be brought to mind by the noun. For example: *canine* at the **dog** entry and *thermal* at the **heat** entry. These collateral adjectives are marked by a diamond, ♦, in the noun entry.

Cross References

Cross references are directions to see another entry for additional information. The entry to look for is generally indicated in small capital letters, as

> **tsar** . . . See CZAR.
> **feet** . . . Plural of FOOT.
> **Old English** . . . See under ENGLISH.

Cross references are also used to indicate where more information may be found, or when an important distinction might otherwise be missed, as

> **petit mal** . . . :distinguished from *grand mal.*

Word Origins

The origin (etymology) of an entry word is given in square brackets following the definition. The only symbols used are <, meaning "derived from"; +, meaning "added on" or "combined with"; and a question mark, ?, meaning "perhaps." Language abbreviations are found on pages xv–xvi.

The abbreviation Cf. indicates that the word given in the etymology is not necessarily the origin of the entry but is a word from another language that descended from the same root. Nonlinguistic information appears in the etymology for words derived from names or coined for a special purpose. Words set in small capital letters in etymologies are cross references. The origin of the entry word or phrase can be found in the etymology of the word or words referred to.

PRONUNCIATION KEY

a	add, map
ah	palm, father
ahr	ark, dark
air	care, fair
aw	all, order, paw
ay	ail, pay, same
b	bat, rub
ch	check, catch
d	dog, rod
e	end, pet
ee	easy, tree
eer	beer, ear
f	fit, half
g	go, log
h	hope, hate
i	it, give
ī	ice, write
j	joy, judge
k	cool, take
kh	(initial consonant of) chutzpah
l	look, rule
m	move, seem
n	nice, tin
French final *n*	garçon, vin
ng	ring, song
o	odd, hot
oh	open, so
oi	oil, boy
oo	pool, food
oor	poor, tour
ow	out, now
p	pit, stop
r	run, poor
s	see, pass
sh	sure, rush

t	talk, sit
th	thin, both
th	this, bathe
u	up, done
ur	urn, term
uu	took, full
v	vain, eve
w	win, away
y	yet, yearn
yoo	use, few
z	zest, muse
zh	vision, pleasure
ə	the schwa, representing the vowel in unstressed syllables, represents the sound spelled
a	in *above*
e	in *sicken*
i	in *clarity*
o	in *melon*
u	in *focus*

In a few words, such as *button* (BUT n) and *sudden* (SUD n), no vowel appears in the unstressed syllable because the (n) constitutes the whole syllable.

ABBREVIATIONS USED IN THIS BOOK

A.D. year of our Lord
adj. adjective
adv. adverb
Aeron. Aeronautics
AF Anglo-French
Agric. Agriculture
Alg. Algebra
alter. alteration
Am.Ind. American Indian
Am.Sp. American Spanish
Anat. Anatomy
Anthropol. Anthropology
appar. apparently
Archeol. Archeology
Archit. Architecture
assoc. association
Astron. Astronomy
aug. augmentative

Austral. Australian
Bacteriol. Bacteriology
B.C. Before Christ
Biochem. Biochemistry
Biol. Biology
Bot. Botany
Brit. British
c. century
cap. capitalized
cf. compare
Chem. Chemistry
Chron. Chronicles
compar. comparative
conj. conjunction
contr. contraction
Crystall. Crystallography
Dan. Danish
def. definition

Dent. Dentistry
Deut. Deuteronomy
Dial. Dialect, Dialectal
dim. diminutive
Du. Dutch
E. English
Eccl. Ecclesiastical
Eccles. Ecclesiastes
Ecol. Ecology
Econ. Economics
Electr. Electricity
Engin. Engineering
Entomol. Entomology
esp. especially
est. estimate
Esth. Esther
Ex. Exodus
Ezek. Ezekiel
F, Fr. French
fem. feminine
freq. frequentative

G, Ger. German
Gen. Genesis
Geog. Geography
Geol. Geology
Geom. Geometry
Gk. Greek
Gmc. Germanic
Govt. Government
Gram. Grammar
HG High German
Hind. Hindustani
Hung. Hungarian
Icel. Icelandic
Illit. Illiterate
imit. imitative
infl. influence, influenced
intens. intensive
interj. interjection
Ital. Italian
Jap. Japanese
L, Lat. Latin
Lev. Leviticus
LG Low German
LGk. Late Greek
Ling. Linguistics
lit. literally
LL Late Latin
M Middle
masc. masculine
Math. Mathematics
MDu. Middle Dutch
ME Middle English
Mech. Mechanics
Med. Medicine, Medieval
Med.Gk. Medieval Greek
Med.L. Medieval Latin
Metall. Metallurgy
Meteorol. Meteorology
MF Middle French
MHG Middle High German
Mil. Military

Mineral. Mineralogy
MLG Middle Low German
n. noun
Nah. Nahum
N.Am.Ind. North American Indian
Naut. Nautical
NE Northeast
neut. neuter
NL New Latin
Norw. Norwegian
Num. Numbers
NW Northwest
O Old
Obs. Obsolete
ODan. Old Danish
OE Old English
OF Old French
OHG Old High German
OIrish Old Irish
ON Old Norse
orig. original, originally
Ornithol. Ornithology
OS Old Saxon
Paleontol. Paleontology
Pathol. Pathology
Pg. Portuguese
Phil. Philippians
Philos. Philosophy
Phonet. Phonetics
Photog. Photography
Physiol. Physiology
pl. plural
pop. population
pp. past participle, pages
ppr. present participle
pr. pronounced
prep. preposition
prob. probably
pron. pronoun
pronun. pronunciation
Prov. Proverbs

Ps. Psalms
Psychoanal. Psychoanalysis
Psychol. Psychology
pt. preterit
ref. reference
Rom. Romans
Russ. Russian
S.Am.Ind. South American Indian
Scand. Scandinavian
Scot. Scottish
SE Southeast
sing. singular
Skt. Sanskrit
Sociol. Sociology
S. of Sol. Song of Solomon
Sp. Spanish
Stat. Statistics
superl. superlative
Surg. Surgery
SW Southwest
Sw. Swedish
Telecom. Telecommunication
Theol. Theology
trans. translation
Trig. Trigonometry
ult. ultimately
U.S. United States
usu. usually
v. verb
var. variant
Vet. Veterinary medicine
v.i. intransitive verb
v.t. transitive verb
WGmc. West Germanic
Zool. zoology
< from
+ plus
? possibly

A

a, A (ay) *n. pl.* **a's, A's 1.** the first letter of the English alphabet. **2.** any sound represented by the letter *a.* —*symbol* **1.** primacy in class. **2.** *Music* the sixth tone in the diatonic scale of C.

a¹ (ə) *indefinite article or adj.* in each; to each; for each: one dollar *a* bushel. [ME]

a² (ə, *stressed* ay) *indefinite article or adj.* one; any; some; each: expressing singleness, unity, etc., more or less indefinitely. It is used: **1.** before a noun expressing an individual object or idea: *a* bird; *a* hope. **2.** before an abstract noun used concretely: show *a* kindness. **3.** before a collective noun: *a* crowd. **4.** before a proper noun denoting a type: He is *a* Hercules. **5.** before plural nouns: with *few, great many,* or *good many: a* few books. **6.** after *on, at,* or *of,* denoting oneness, sameness: birds of *a* feather. ♦ Before vowel sounds the form becomes *an.*

aard·vark (AHRD vahrk) *n.* a burrowing, ant-eating African mammal. [< Afrikaans < Du. *aarde* earth + *vark* pig]

a·back (ə BAK) *adv. Naut.* back against the mast: said of sails so blown by the wind. — **taken aback** disconcerted; surprised. [ME *abak*]

ab·a·cus (AB ə kəs) *n. pl.* **·cus·es** or **·ci** (-sī) a calculator with sliding counters. [< NL]

ab·a·lo·ne (AB ə LOH nee) *n.* an edible mollusk having a shell lined with mother-of-pearl. [< Am. Sp.]

a·ban·don (ə BAN dən) *v.t.* **1.** give up wholly; desert; forsake. **2.** surrender or give over: with *to.* **3.** yield (oneself) without restraint, as to an emotion. —*n.* surrender to one's feelings or impulses. [ME *abandonen*] —**a·ban'don·ment** *n.*

a·ban·doned (ə BAN dənd) *adj.* **1.** deserted; forsaken. **2.** unrestrained. **3.** profligate; shameless.

a·base (ə BAYS) *v.t.* **a·based, a·bas·ing** lower in position, rank, prestige, or estimation; cast down; humble. [ME *abassen*] —**a·base'ment** *n.*

a·bash (ə BASH)) *v.t.* deprive of self-possession; make ashamed. [ME *abaishen* put down] —**a·bash'ed·ly** (-id lee) *adv.* —**a·bash'·ment** *n.*

a·bate (ə BAYT) *v.* **a·bat·ed, a·bat·ing** *v.t.* **1.** make less in quantity or intensity. **2.** end by legal action. —*v.i.* **3.** become less. **4.** end. [ME] —**a·bate'ment** *n.*

ab·ba·cy (AB ə see) *n. pl.* **·cies** the office of an abbot.

ab·bé (a BAY) *n.* in France, a title of a priest or other cleric. [< F]

ab·bess (AB is) *n.* the female superior of a community of nuns. [ME *abbesse*]

ab·bey (AB ee) *n. pl.* **·beys 1.** a monastery or convent under the rule of an abbot or abbess. **2.** an abbey church. [ME *abbeye*]

ab·bot (AB ət) *n.* the superior of a community of monks. [ME] —**ab'bot·cy** *n.*

ab·bre·vi·ate (ə BREE vee ayt) *v.t.* **·at·ed, ·at·ing 1.** make briefer. **2.** shorten, as a word. [ME *abbreviaten*] —**ab·bre'vi·a'tor** *n.*

ab·bre·vi·a·tion (ə BREE vee AY) *n.* **1.** a shortened form of a word or phrase. **2.** the act of abbreviating.

ABC (AY BEE SEE) *n. pl.* **ABC's** or **ABCs 1.** *usu. pl.* the alphabet. **2.** *usu. pl.* the rudiments.

ab·di·cate (AB də KAYT) *v.t. & v.i.* **·cat·ed, ·cat·ing** give up formally, as a throne. [< L *abdicare* renounce] —**ab·di·ca·tion** (AB di KAY shən) *n.*

ab·do·men (AB də mən) *n.* **1.** in mammals, the body cavity between the diaphragm and pelvis, containing the viscera. **2.** in arthropods, the hindmost of the main body divisions. [< L, belly] —**ab·dom·i·nal** (AB DOM ə nəl) *adj.*

ab·duct (ab DUKT) *v.t.* carry away (a person) by force; kidnap. [< L *abducere* lead away] —**ab·duc'tion** *n.* —**ab·duc'·tor** (-tər) *n.*

ab·er·ra·tion (AB ə RAY shən) *n.* deviation from the normal or expected. [< L *aberrare* deviate] —**ab·er·rance** (AB ər əns) *n.* —**ab·er·rant** (AB ər ənt) *adj.*

a·bet (ə BET) *v.t.* **a·bet·ted, a·bet·ting** encourage and incite, esp. wrongdoing. [ME *abette* bait] —**a·bet'·ment** *n.* — **a·bet'tor** or **a·bet'ter** *n.*

a·bey·ance (ə BAY əns) *n.* suspension or temporary inaction. [< AF] —**a·bey'ant** *adj.*

ab·hor (ab HOR) *v.t.* **·horred, ·hor·ring** regard with repugnance; loathe. [ME]

ab·hor·rence (ab HOR əns) *n.* **1.** a feeling of loathing. **2.** something repugnant.

ab·hor·rent (ab HOR ənt) *adj.* **1.** repugnant or detestable. **2.** opposed: with *to.*

a·bide (ə BĪD) *v.* **a·bode** or **a·bid·ed, a·bid·ing** *v.i.* **1.** remain in a place. —*v.t.* **2.** wait for. **3.** put up with. —**abide by** behave in accordance with. [ME *abiden* await] — **a·bi'dance** *n.* —**a·bid'ing·ly** *adv.*

a·bil·i·ty (ə BIL ə tee) *n. pl.* **·ties 1.** the state or quality of being able; capacity. **2.** a talent or skill. [ME *habilite* aptitude]

ab·ject (AB jekt, ab JEKT) *adj.* sunk to a low condition; helpless or hopeless. [ME thrown away] —**ab·ject'ness, ab·jec' tion** *n.*

ab·jure (ab JUUR) *v.t.* **·jured, ·jur·ing 1.** renounce under oath. **2.** retract, as an opinion. [ME] —**ab·ju·ra·tion** (ab jə RAY shən) *n.* —**ab·jur'er** *n.*

ab·la·tive (AB lə tiv) *adj. Gram.* in some languages, as Latin, designating a case expressing separation, position, motion from, etc. [ME] —*n.* the ablative case or a word in this case.

a·blaze (ə BLAYZ) *adv.* on fire. —*adj.* **1.** flaming. **2.** zealous.

a·ble (AY bəl) *adj.* **a·bler, a·blest 1.** having adequate power. **2.** having superior abilities. [ME] —**a'bly** *adv.*

-able *suffix* **1.** likely to: *changeable.* **2.** capable of; worthy of: *eatable, salable.* Also **-ble, -ible.** [ME]

ab·lu·tion (ə BLOO shən) *n.* a cleansing of the body, esp. as a ceremony. [ME]

-ably *suffix* in the manner of: *peaceably.*

ab·ne·gate (AB nə gayt) *v.t.* **·gat·ed, ·gat·ing** deny; renounce. [< L *abnegare* deny] —**ab'ne·ga'tion** *n.* —**ab'ne· ga'tor** *n.*

ab·nor·mal (ab NOR məl) *adj.* different from the normal. [< Med.L *anormalus*] — **ab·nor'mal·ly** *adv.*

ab·nor·mal·i·ty (AB nor MAL i tee) *n. pl.* **·ties 1.** the state of being abnormal. **2.** an abnormal thing.

a·board (ə BORD) *adv.* **1.** into, in, or on a ship, train, etc. **2.** alongside. —**a·board'** *prep.*

a·bode (ə BOHD) past tense and past participle of ABIDE. —*n.* **1.** a dwelling; home. **2.** an extended stay in a place. [ME *abood* stay]

a·bol·ish (ə BOL ish) *v.t.* do away with. [ME] —**a·bol'ish·ment** *n.*

ab·o·li·tion (AB ə LISH ən) *n.* **1.** the act of abolishing. **2.** *sometimes cap.* the abolishing of slavery in the United States. —**ab'o·li' ·tion·ism** *n.* —**ab'o·li'tion·ist** *n.*

A-bomb (AY bom) *n.* an atomic bomb.

a·bom·i·na·ble (ə BOM in ə bəl) *adj.* **1.** detestable; loathsome. **2.** very ·disagreeable; bad. [ME] —**a·bom'i·na·bly** *adv.*

abominable snowman a legendary manlike animal said to inhabit the Himalayas: also called *yeti.*

a·bom·i·nate (ə BOM ə nayt) *v.t.* **·nat·ed, ·nat·ing** regard with loathing; abhor. [< L *abominari* abhor] —**a·bom'i·na'tion** *n.*

ab·o·rig·i·nal (AB ə RIJ ə nəl) *adj.* **1.** of or pertaining to aborigines. **2.** native; indigenous.

ab·o·rig·i·ne (AB ə RIJ ə nee) *n.* one of the original inhabitants of an area. [< L *ab origine* from the beginning]

a·bort (ə BORT) *v.t. & v.i.* **1.** undergo or cause the abortion of a fetus. **2.** fail or cause to fail of completion. [< L *aboriri* miscarry] —**a·bor'tive** *adj.* —**a·bor'tive·ly** *adv.*

a·bor·tion (ə BOR shən) *n.* **1.** the premature expulsion of a fetus; miscarriage. **2.** such expulsion produced artificially. **3.** the defective result of a premature birth. **4.** partial or complete arrest of development.

a·bor·tion·ist (ə BOR shə nist) *n.* one who performs an abortion.

a·bound (ə BOWND) *v.i.* **1.** be plentiful. **2.** be full; teem. [ME *abounden* overflow]

a·bout (ə BOWT) *adv.* **1.** approximately; nearly. **2.** nearby; in the vicinity. **3.** to a reversed position. **4.** astir; active. **5.** on every side; around. —*prep.* **1.** on every side of. **2.** near; close to. **3.** concerning; in reference to. **4.** nearly ready; with *to.* [ME *abouten* outside of]

a·bout-face (ə BOWT FAYS) *n.* **1.** *Mil.* a turn to the rear when halted. **2.** any reversal, as of opinion. —*v.i.* **-faced, -fac·ing** perform an about-face.

a·bove (ə BUV) *adv.* **1.** in or to a higher place. **2.** superior in rank or position. **3.** in preceding text. —*adj.* written or named before. —*n.* that which precedes in text. — *prep.* **1.** higher than; over. **2.** more than; beyond. **3.** superior to; beyond the influence of. [ME *aboven*]

Above as a combining form having the meaning earlier in order:

above-captioned	**above-mentioned**
above-cited	**above-given**
above-named	**above-written**

a•bove•board (ə BUV bord) *adj. & adv.* without concealment or trickery.

ab•ra•ca•dab•ra (AB rə kə DAB rə) *n.* 1. a mystical word or expression. 2. jargon; nonsensical words. [< LL]

a•brade (ə BRAYD) *v.t.* a•brad•ed, a•brad•ing rub or wear off by friction. [< L *abradere* scrape away] —a•bra′dant *adj. & n.*

a•bra•sion (ə BRAY zhən) *n.* 1. a wearing or rubbing away. 2. an abraded area.

a•bra•sive (ə BRAY siv) *adj.* 1. wearing away. 2. emotionally irritating. —*n.* an abrading substance.

a•breast (ə BREST) *adv. & adj.* side by side. —abreast of (or with) 1. side by side with. 2. informed of recent developments.

a•bridge (ə BRIJ) *v.t.* a•bridged, a•bridg•ing 1. make shorter, as in words or time. 2. curtail, as rights. [ME *abreggen* shorten] — a•bridg′a•ble or a•bridge′a•ble *adj.*

a•bridg•ment (ə BRIJ mənt) *n.* 1. the act of abridging. 2. t condensation, as of a book. Also a•bridge′ment.

a•broad (ə BRAWD) *adv.* 1. in or to foreign lands. 2. at large; in circulation. [ME]

ab•ro•gate (AB rə gayt) *v.t.* •gat•ed, •gat•ing annul by authority, as a law. [< L *abrogatus* repealed] —ab′ro•ga′tion *n.*

a•brupt (ə BRUPT) *adj.* 1. beginning, ending, or changing suddenly. 2. cutting short amenities; brusque. 3. steep, as a cliff. [< L *abrumptus* broken off] —a•brupt′ly *adv.* —a•brupt′ness *n.*

ab•scess (AB ses) *Pathol. n.* a collection of pus in inflamed tissue. —*v.i.* form an abscess. [< L *abscessus*] —ab′scessed *adj.*

ab•scis•sa (ab SIS ə) *n. pl.* ab•scis•sas or ab•scis•sae (SIS ee) *Math.* the distance of any point from the vertical or Y-axis in a coordinate system, measured on a line parallel to the horizontal or X-axis. [< L *abscindere* sever]

ab•scis•sion (ab SIZH ən) *n.* the act of cutting off or removing.

ab•scond (ab SKOND) *v.i.* depart suddenly and secretly, esp. escape the law. [< L *abscondere* stow away] —ab•scond′er *n.*

ab•sence (AB səns) *n.* 1. the state of being absent. 2. the period of being away. 3. lack. [ME]

ab•sent (AB sənt) *adj.* 1. not present; away. 2. lacking; nonexistent. 3. inattentive; absent-minded. —*v.t.* (ab SENT) take or keep (oneself) away. [ME]

ab•sen•tee (AB sən TEE) *n.* one who is ab-

sent, as from a job. —*adj.* temporarily absent. —ab′sen•tee′ism *n.*

ab•sent-mind•ed (AB sənt MIN did) *adj.* lost in thought and inattentive to one's surroundings or business; forgetful. —ab′sent-mind′ed•ness *n.*

absent without leave *Mil.* absent without authorization but not intending to desert; AWOL.

ab•sinthe (AB sinth) *n.* 1. a green, bitter liqueur having the flavor of licorice and wormwood. 2. wormwood. [< F]

ab•so•lute (AB sə loot) *adj.* 1. free from restriction; unlimited; unconditional. 2. complete; perfect. 3. not relative to anything else; independent. 4. positive; certain. [ME] —ab′so•lute′ly *adv.*

absolute pitch *Music* the ability to produce or name the pitch of any note: also *perfect pitch.*

absolute zero the hypothetical temperature at which a body contains no heat, equal to about −273.16°C. or −459.7°F.

ab•so•lu•tion (ab sə LOO shən) *n.* 1. the act of absolving, as from guilt. 2. *Eccl.* a remission of sin and its penalties pronounced by a priest. [ME *absolucion*]

ab•so•lut•ism (AB sə loo TIZ əm) *n.* in government, the doctrine or practice of unlimited authority and control; despotism.

ab•solve (ab ZOLV) *v.t.* •solved, •solv•ing 1. free from the penalties or consequences of an action. 2. release, as from an obligation. 3. *Eccl.* grant a remission of sin. [< L *absolvere* loosen]

ab•sorb (ab ZORB) *v.t.* 1. drink in or suck up, as through or into pores. 2. engross completely. 3. take up or in by chemical or molecular action, as gases, heat, liquid, light, etc. 4. take in and incorporate. 5. receive the force or action of. [< L *absorbere* suck in]

ab•sor•bent (ab SOR bənt) *adj.* absorbing or tending to absorb: *absorbent* cotton. — *n.* a substance that absorbs. —ab•sor′ben•cy *n.*

ab•sorp•tion (ab SORB shən) *n.* 1. the act or process of absorbing or being absorbed. 2. assimilation, as by digestion. 3. preoccupation of the mind. —ab•sorp′tive *adj.*

ab•stain (ab STAYN) *v.i.* keep oneself back; refrain voluntarily: with *from.* [ME *absteinen* hold back] —ab•stain′er *n.*

ab•ste•mi•ous (ab STEE mee əs) *adj.* eating and drinking sparingly; abstinent;

temperate. [< L *abstemius*] —**ab•ste′mi•ous•ness** *n.*

ab•sten•tion (ab STEN shən) *n.* an abstaining. —**ab•sten′tious** *adj.*

ab•sti•nence (AB stə nəns) *n.* the act or practice of abstaining from some or all food, liquor, etc. [ME] —**ab′sti•nent** *adj.*

ab•stract (ab STRAKT) *adj.* **1.** considered apart from matter or from specific examples; not concrete. **2.** theoretical; ideal, as opposed to practical. **3.** abstruse. **4.** considered or expressed without reference to particular example, as numbers, attributes, or qualities. **5.** in art, generalized; nonrepresentational. —*n.* (AB strakt) **1.** a summary or epitome, as of a document. **2.** the essence of some larger object or whole. —*v.t.* (ab STRAKT) **1.** take away; remove. **2.** withdraw (the attention, interest, etc.). **3.** (AB strakt) make an abstract of; summarize. [ME] —**ab•stract′ness** *n.*

ab•stract•ed (ab STRAK tid) *adj.* **1.** lost in thought; absentminded. **2.** separated from all else; apart. —**ab•stract′ed•ly** *adv.*

ab•strac•tion (ab STRAK shən) *n.* **1.** the process of abstracting. **2.** a product of this process; concept. **3.** preoccupation. **4.** an art form or work of art in which the qualities are abstract. —**ab•strac′tive** *adj.* —**ab•strac′tive•ness** *n.*

ab•struse (ab STROOS) *adj.* hard to understand. [< L *abstrudere* thrust away] —**ab•struse′ly** *adv.* —**ab•struse′ness** *n.*

ab•surd (ab SURD) *adj.* irrational; ridiculous. [< L *absurdus* uncouth] —**ab•surd′ly** *adv.* —**ab•surd′ness** *n.*

ab•surd•i•ty (ab SUR də tee) *n. pl.* **•ties 1.** the quality of being absurd. **2.** something absurd.

a•bun•dance (ə BUN dəns) *n.* **1.** a plentiful or overflowing supply. **2.** wealth; affluence. [ME]

a•bun•dant (ə BUN dənt) *adj.* **1.** existing in plentiful supply; ample. **2.** abounding. [ME] —**a•bun′dant•ly** *adv.*

a•buse (ə BYOOZ) *v.t.* **a•bused, a•bus•ing 1.** use improperly or injuriously; misuse **2.** hurt by treating wrongly; injure. **3.** speak in coarse or bad terms of or to; revile. —*n.* (ə BYOOS) **1.** Improper or injurious use; misuse. **2.** ill-treatment; injury. **3.** abusive language; slander. [ME *abusen* misuse] —**a•bus′er** *n.*

a•bu•sive (ə BYOO siv) *adj.* **1.** mistreating. **2.** insulting; vituperative. —**a•bu′sive•ly** *adv.* —**a•bu′sive•ness** *n.*

a•but (ə BUT) *v.t. & v.i.* **a•but•ted, a•but•ting** touch, join, or adjoin; border. [ME]

a•but•ment (ə BUT mənt) *n.* **1.** the act of abutting. **2.** a supporting or buttressing structure.

a•bys•mal (ə BIZ məl) *adj.* unfathomable; immeasurable; extreme: an *abysmal* ignorance.

a•byss (ə BIS) *n.* **1.** a bottomless gulf; chasm. **2.** any profound depth or void. [ME *abissus* bottomless] —**a•bys′sal** *adj.*

AC, A.C. alternating current.

-ac *suffix* **1.** having; affected by: *insomniac.* **2.** pertaining to; of: *cardiac.* [< Gk. *-akos* or L *-acus*]

a•ca•cia (ə KAY shə) *n.* any of various flowering, leguminous trees and shrubs of the tropics and warm temperate regions. [< L]

ac•a•dem•ic (AK ə DEM ik) *adj.* **1.** pertaining to an academy, college, or university; scholarly. **2.** having to do with liberal arts rather than technical studies. **3.** theoretical, as opposed to practical. **4.** pedantic. [< L *academicus*] —*n.* a college student or faculty member.

a•cad•e•mi•cian (ə KAD ə MISH ən) *n.* a member of an academy of art, science, or literature.

a•cad•e•my (ə KAD ə mee) *n. pl.* **•mies 1.** a secondary school, usually a private one. **2.** a learned society for the advancement of arts or sciences. [< L *academia*]

A•ca•di•a (ə KAY dee ə) a former name for a region in eastern Canada, including Nova Scotia and New Brunswick.

A•ca•di•an (ə KAY dee ən) *adj.* of or pertaining to Acadia or Nova Scotia. —*n.* one of the early French settlers of Acadia or their descendants. See CAJUN.

a cap•pel•la (AH kə PEL ə) *Music* sung without accompaniment. [< Ital., in chapel style]

ac•cede (ak SEED) *v.i.* **•ced•ed, •ced•ing 1.** agree; assent: with *to.* **2.** come into or enter upon an office: with *to.* [ME]

ac•cel•er•ate (ak SEL ə rayt) *v.* **•at•ed, •at•ing** *v.t.* **1.** cause to act or move faster. **2.** hasten the natural or usual course of. **3.** cause a change in rate of velocity. —*v.i.* **5.** move or become faster. [< L *acceleratus* sped up]

ac•cel•er•a•tion (ak SEL ə RAY shən) *n.* the act of accelerating or being accelerated.

ac•cel•er•a•tor (ak SEL ə RAY tər) *n.* **1.** one who or that which accelerates. **2.** *Physics* a device for accelerating the velocity of atomic particles. **3.** *Mech.* the foot throttle of an automobile.

ac·cent (AK sent) *n.* **1.** the emphasis given in speech, poetry, music, etc., to a particular sound, syllable, or word. **2.** a mark used to indicate the place of accent in a word. The **primary accent** notes the chief stress, and the **secondary accent** a weaker stress. **3.** a mark used to show the quality of a vowel. **4.** mode of utterance; pronunciation: a Southern *accent*. —*v.t.* **1.** accent; stress. **2.** accentuate. [< L *accentus* speech tone] — **ac·cen·tu·al** (ak SEN choo əl) *adj.*

ac·cen·tu·ate (ak SEN choo ayt) *v.t.* **·at·ed, ·at·ing** accent; emphasize.

ac·cept (ak SEPT) *v.t.* **1.** receive with favor, willingness, or consent. **2.** give an affirmative answer to. **3.** receive as satisfactory. **4.** resign oneself to; submit to. **5.** believe in. [ME *accepten*]

ac·cept·a·ble (ak SEP tə bəl) *adj.* worthy of acceptance. —**ac·cept'a·bil'i·ty** *n.* — **ac·cept'a·bly** *adv.*

ac·cep·tance (ak SEP təns) *n.* **1.** the act of accepting. **2.** the state of being accepted or acceptable. **3.** favorable reception. **4.** assent; belief.

ac·cept·ed (ak SEP tid) *adj.* commonly recognized, believed, or approved; popular.

ac·cess (AK ses) *n.* **1.** the act of coming to or near. **2.** a passage; path. **3.** the state or quality of being approachable; accessibility. **4.** an outburst of emotion, etc. [ME *accesse* approach]

ac·ces·si·ble (ak SES ə bəl) *adj.* **1.** approachable. **2.** attainable; obtainable. **3.** open to the influence of. —**ac·ces'·si·bil' i·ty** *n.*

ac·ces·sion (ak SESH ən) *n.* **1.** the act of attaining an office, dignity, or right. **2.** an increase by addition; something added. **3.** assent; agreement.

ac·ces·so·ry (ak SES ər ee) *n.* *pl.* **·ries 1.** something added for convenience, display, etc., as to an automobile or to one's attire. **2.** *Law* a person who aids or encourages another to commit a crime. [ME *accessorie*] —**ac·ces'so·ry** *adj.*

ac·ci·dent (AK si dənt) *n.* **1.** an unintended happening. **2.** a mishap involving injury, loss, etc. **3.** chance; fortune. [ME] — **ac·ci·den·tal** (ak si DEN təl) *adj.*

ac·claim (ə KLAYM) *v.t.* **1.** proclaim with applause; hail. **2.** shout approval of. —*v.i.* **3.** applaud; shout approval. —*n.* a shout of applause. [< L *acclamare* shout]

ac·cla·ma·tion (AK lə MAY shən) *n.* **1.** the act of acclaiming or of being acclaimed. **2.** a shout of applause or welcome. **3.** an oral vote of approval, as in a public assembly. — **ac·clam·a·to·ry** (ə KLAM ə TOR ee) *adj.*

ac·cli·mate (AK lə MAYT) *v.t. & v.i.* **·mat·ed, ·mat·ing** adapt to a new climate or environment. [< F *acclimater*] — **ac'cli·ma'tion** *n.*

ac·cli·ma·tize (ə KLĪ mə TĪZ) *v.t. & v.i.* **·tized, ·tiz·ing** acclimate. —**ac·cli' ma·ti·za'tion** *n.*

ac·cliv·i·ty (ə KLIV i tee) *n.* *pl.* **·ties** an upward slope. [< L *acclivitās* steep hill]

ac·co·lade (AK ə LAYD) *n.* a conferring of praise; an honor. [< F]

ac·com·mo·date (ə KOM ə dayt) *v.* **·dat·ed, ·dat·ing** *v.t.* **1.** do a favor for; oblige; help. **2.** provide for; give lodging to. **3.** be suitable for; contain comfortably. **4.** adapt or modify, as to new conditions. —*v.i.* **5.** be or become adjusted. [< L *accommodatus* adjusted] —**ac·com'mo·da'tive** *adj.*

ac·com·mo·dat·ing (ə KOM ə DAY ting) *adj.* obliging.

ac·com·mo·da·tion (ə KOM ə DAY shən) *n.* **1.** the act of accommodating, or the state of being accommodated; adjustment; adaptation. **2.** reconciliation; compromise. **3.** anything that meets a need; convenience. **4.** *Usu. pl.* lodging, board, etc.

ac·com·pa·ni·ment (ə KUM pə ni mənt) *n.* **1.** anything that accompanies something. **2.** *Music* A subordinate part supporting a leading voice, instrument, etc. —**ac·com' ·pa·nist** *n.*

ac·com·pa·ny (ə KUM pə nee) *v.t.* **·nied, ·ny·ing 1.** go with; attend; escort. **2.** be or coexist with. **3.** play a musical accompaniment to or for. [ME *accompanye*]

ac·com·plice (ə KOM plis) *n.* a partner in crime. [ME *complice*]

ac·com·plish (ə KOM plish) *v.t.* bring to pass or to completion. [ME] —**ac·com' plish·a·ble** *adj.*

ac·com·plished (ə KOM plisht) *adj.* **1.** completed; done. **2.** proficient; skilled.

ac·com·plish·ment (ə KOM plish mənt) *n.* **1.** the act of accomplishing. **2.** something accomplished; achievement.

ac·cord (ə KORD) *v.t.* **1.** render as due; grant. **2.** make harmonize or agree. —*v.i.* **3.** agree; harmonize. —*n.* **1.** harmony, as of sentiment, colors, sounds, etc.; agreement. **2.** a settlement of any difference, as between governments. —**of one's own accord** by one's own choice. [ME *accorden*] —**ac•cord′ance** *n.* —**ac•cord′ant** *adj.*

ac•cord•ing (ə KOR ding) *adj.* being in accord or agreement; harmonizing. — **according to 1.** in accordance with. **2.** as stated by; on the authority of.

ac•cord•ing•ly (ə KOR ding lee) *adv.* **1.** in accord; correspondingly. **2.** consequently; so.

ac•cor•di•on (ə KOR dee ən) *n.* a portable musical wind instrument with metallic reeds, a keyboard, and bellows. [< Ital. *accordare* harmonize] —**ac•cor′di•on•ist** *n.*

ac•cost (ə KAWST) *v.t.* **1.** to address; greet. **2.** of prostitutes, solicit for sexual purposes. [< LL *accostare* place side by side]

ac•count (ə KOWNT) *v.t.* **1.** hold to be; consider; estimate. —*v.i.* **2.** provide a reckoning, as of funds paid or received: with *to* or *with* (someone), *for* (something). **3.** give a rational explanation: with *for.* **4.** be responsible; answer: with *for.* —*n.* **1.** a record of events; narrative; description. **2.** an explanation. **3.** a record of monetary transactions: charge *account.* **4.** a company that is a client or customer. **5.** worth; importance. **6.** profit; advantage. —**on account of** because of. —**on no account** under no circumstances. [ME *acounten*]

ac•count•a•ble (ə KOWN tə bəl) *adj.* **1.** liable to be called to account; responsible. **2.** capable of being explained. —**ac• count′a•bil′i•ty** *n.*

ac•count•ing (ə KOWN ting) *n.* the system of recording, classifying, and summarizing business and financial transactions. — **ac•count′an•cy** *n.* —**ac•count′ant** *n.*

ac•cou•ter (ə KOO tər) *v.t.* furnish with dress or trappings; equip, as for military service. —**ac•cou′ter•ment, ac•cou′ tre•ment.** *n.* [< F *accoutrer*]

ac•cred•it (ə KRED it) *v.t.* **1.** give credit to as the owner, author, or creator of; attribute to. **2.** accept as true; believe. **3.** certify as fulfilling official requirements. [< MF *acrediter* believe] —**ac•cred•i•ta•tion** (ə KRED ə TAY shən) *n.*

ac•cre•tion (ə KREE shən) *n.* growth by external additions or by adhesion or inclusion. [< L]

ac•crue (ə KROO) *v.i.* •**crued,** •**cru•ing 1.** come as a natural result or increment, as by growth: with *to.* **2.** accumulate, as the interest on money. [ME *acrewen* increase] — **ac•cru′al** *n.*

ac•cu•mu•late (ə KYOOM yə layt) *v.* •**lat•ed,** •**lat•ing** *v.t.* **1.** heap or pile up; amass; collect. —*v.i.* **2.** become greater in quantity or number; increase. [< L *accumulare* heap up] **ac•cu′mu•la′tion** *n.* — **ac•cu′mu•la′tive** *adj.*

ac•cu•rate (AK yər it) *adj.* being without error; precise; exact. [< L *accuratus* prepared with care] —**ac′cu•ra•cy** *n.*

ac•curs•ed (ə KUR sid) *adj.* **1.** lying under a curse; doomed. **2.** deserving a curse; detestable. —**ac•curs′ed•ness** *n.*

ac•cu•sa•tion (AK yuu ZAY shən) *n.* **1.** the act of accusing, or the state of being accused. **2.** the crime or act charged. [ME *accusacion*] —**ac•cu•sa•to•ry** (ə KYOO zə TOR EE) *adj.*

ac•cu•sa•tive (ə KYOO zə tiv) *Gram. adj.* denoting the case that signifies the direct object of a verb or preposition; objective. —*n.* the objective case in English or another language. [ME]

ac•cuse (ə KYOOZ) *v.t.* •**cused,** •**cus•ing 1.** charge with fault or error; blame; censure. **2.** bring charges against, as of a crime. [ME *accusen* call to account] —**ac•cus′er** *n.* — **ac•cused** (ə KYOOZD) *n. Law* the defendant or defendants in a criminal case.

ac•cus•tom (ə KUS təm) *v.t.* familiarize by custom or use; habituate or inure. — **ac•cus•tomed** (ə KUS təmd) *adj.*

ac•er•bate (AS ər bayt) *v.t.* •**bat•ed,** •**bat•ing 1.** make sour; embitter. **2.** exasperate. [< L *acerbatus* made bitter]

a•cer•bi•ty (ə SUR bi tee) *n. pl.* •**ties 1.** sourness or bitterness, as that of unripe fruit. **2.** severity; harshness.

ac•e•tate (AS i tayt) *n.* **1.** *Chem.* a salt or ester of acetic acid. **2.** cellulose acetate, or one of its products.

a•ce•tic (ə SEE tik) *adj.* pertaining to or like vinegar; sour.

acetic acid *Chem.* a colorless, pungent liquid, occurring in a dilute form in vinegar.

ac•e•tone (AS i tohn) *n. Chem.* a clear, flammable liquid, used as a solvent for fats, camphor, and resins.

a•cet•y•lene (ə SET i leen) *n. Chem.* a colorless hydrocarbon gas, used as an illuminant and for cutting metals.

ache (ayk) *v.i.* ached, ach•ing 1. suffer dull, continuing pain. 2. yearn; be eager. —*n.* a local, dull, and protracted pain. [ME *aken*]

a•chieve (ə CHEEV) *v.* a•chieved, a•chiev•ing *v.t.* **1.** accomplish; do successfully. **2.** win or attain, as by effort or skill. —*v.i.* **3.** accomplish something. [ME *acheven* finish] —**a·chiev'a·ble** *adj.* — **a·chieve'ment** ( ) *n.*

A·chil·les' heel (ə KIL eez) a vulnerable point. [after the Greek hero *Achilles*, vulnerable only in his right heel]

Achilles' tendon *Anat.* the tendon connecting the calf muscles to the heel bone.

ach·ro·mat·ic (AK rə MAT ik) *adj.* transmitting light without separating it into its constituent colors, as a lens. —**a·chro·ma·tism** (ə KROH mə TIZ əm) *n.*

ac·id (AS id) *adj.* **1.** sharp to the taste, as vinegar; sour. **2.** *Chem.* pertaining to or like an acid. **3.** sharp-tempered; biting. —*n.* **1.** any sour substance. **2.** *Chem.* a water-soluble compound, sour to the taste, that dissolves certain metals, reacts with bases to form salts, and reddens litmus. [< L *acidus*]

a·cid·ic (ə SID ik) *adj.* **1.** *Geol.* containing a high percentage of silica: said of rocks. **2.** *Chem.* acid. —**a·cid'i·ty** *n.*

a·cid·i·fy (ə SID ə FI) *v.t. & v.i.* •**fied,** •**fy·ing** make or become acid; change into an acid. —**a·cid'i·fi·ca'tion** *n.*

a·cid·u·lous (ə SIJ ə ləs) *adj.* **1.** slightly acid; sour. **2.** bitter or rancorous. [< L *acidulus* slightly sour]

ac·knowl·edge (ak NOL ij) *v.t.* •**edged,** •**edg·ing 1.** admit the truth or fact of; confess. **2.** recognize as or avow to be. **3.** admit the validity of, as a claim or right. **4.** express thanks for. **5.** report receipt or arrival of. — **ac·knowl·edg·ment** *n.*

ac·me (AK mee) *n.* the highest point. [< Gk. *akmē* point]

ac·ne (AK nee) *n. Pathol.* A skin disease marked by pimples, chiefly on the face. [< Gk. *akmē* point]

ac·o·lyte (AK ə līt) *n.* **1.** an attendant or assistant. **2.** an altar boy. [ME *acolite* follower]

a·corn (AY korn) *n.* the fruit or nut of the oak. [ME *acorne*]

a·cous·tic (ə KOOS tik) *adj.* **1.** pertaining to hearing, heard sound, or the science of sound. **2.** adapted for conveying sound or aiding hearing. [< Gk. *akoustikós*]

a·cous·tics (ə KOOS tiks) *n.pl.* (*construed as sing. in def. 1*) **1.** the branch of physics dealing with sound. **2.** the sound-transmitting qualities of an auditorium, room, etc.

ac·quaint (ə KWAYNT) *v.t.* **1.** make familiar or conversant. **2.** inform. —**ac·quaint·ed** (ə KWAYN tid) *adj.* [ME *aqueinten* make known]

ac·quain·tance (ə KWAYN təns) *n.* **1.** knowledge of any person or thing. **2.** a person with whom one is acquainted.

ac·qui·esce (AK wee ES) *v.i.* •**esced,** •**esc·ing** consent or concur tacitly; assent; comply. [< L *acquiescere* find rest in]

ac·qui·es·cence (AK wee ES əns) *n.* compliance; passive consent. —**ac'qui·es'·cent** *adj.*

ac·quire (ə KWIR) *v.t.* •**quired,** •**quir·ing 1.** obtain by one's own endeavor or action. **2.** come to possess; receive.[< L *acquirere*]

ac·qui·si·tion (AK wə ZISH ən) *n.* **1.** the act of acquiring. **2.** anything gained or acquired.

ac·quis·i·tive (ə KWIZ ə tiv) *adj.* able or inclined to acquire (money, property, etc.); grasping. —**ac·quis'i·tive·ness** *n.*

ac·quit (ə KWIT) *v.t.* •**quit·ted,** •**quit·ting 1.** free or clear, as from an accusation. **2.** relieve, as of an obligation. **3.** conduct (oneself); behave. [ME *aquiten* settle obligations] —**ac·quit'tal** *n.*

a·cre (AY kər) *n.* **1.** a measure of land, equal to 43,560 square feet or 4,047 square meters. **2.** *pl.* lands. —**a·cre·age** (AY kər ij) *n.* [ME *aker* field]

ac·rid (AK rid) *adj.* **1.** cutting or burning to the taste or smell. **2.** sharp and satirical. [< L *acer* sharp] —**a·crid·i·ty** (ə KRID i tee) *n.*

ac·ri·mo·ny (AK rə MOH nee) *n. pl.* •**nies** sharpness or bitterness of speech or temper. [< L *acrimonia* sharpness] — **ac'ri·mo'ni·ous** *adj.*

ac·ro·bat (AK rə bat) *n.* one skilled in feats requiring muscular coordination, as in tumbling etc.; a gymnast. [< F *acrobate*] —**ac'ro·bat'ic** *adj.*

ac·ro·nym (AK rə nim) *n.* a word formed by combining initial letters (*NATO, laser*) or syllables and letters (*radar, sonar*) of a series of words or a compound term. [< *acro-* at the tip of + -*nym* name]

a·crop·o·lis (ə KROP ə lis) *n.* the citadel of an ancient Greek city. —**the Acropolis** the citadel of Athens. [< Gk. *akros* at the top + *polis* city]

a·cross (ə KRAWS) *adv.* **1.** from one side to the other. **2.** on or at the other side. —*prep.* **1.** on, to, or from the other side of. **2.** through or over the surface of.

a·cros·tic (ə KRAW stik) *n.* a poem etc. in which initial or other letters, taken in order, form a word or phrase. [< Gk. *akrostichís*] —**a·cros'tic** *adj.*

a·cryl·ic (ə KRIL ik) *n.* **1.** a thermoplastic resin used in castings, adhesives, and coatings. Also **acrylic resin. 2.** a paint (**acrylic paint**) made from acrylic resin. **3.** a synthetic fiber (**acrylic fiber**).

acrylic acid *Chem.* any of a series of acids having a sharp, acrid odor, and used in plastics.

act (akt) *v.t.* **1.** play the part of; impersonate, as in a drama. **2.** perform as if on a stage; feign the character of. —*v.i.* **3.** behave or conduct oneself. **4.** carry out a purpose or function; perform. **5.** produce an effect. **6.** serve temporarily or as a substitute, as in some office or capacity. **7.** perform on the stage; be an actor. **8.** pretend; play a part so as to appear. —**act up** behave mischievously; appear troublesome. —*n.* **1.** the exertion of mental or physical power; a doing: taken in the very *act.* **2.** a law; edict. **3.** one of the main divisions of a play or opera. **4.** *Informal* something feigned; a pose. [ME *acte* something done]

act·ing (AK ting) *adj.* **1.** operating or officiating, especially in place of another: *acting secretary.* **2.** functioning. —*n.* **1.** the occupation of an actor. **2.** pretense or simulation.

ac·tion (AK shən) *n.* **1.** the process of acting, doing, or working; operation. **2.** the result of putting forth power; a deed; act. **3.** *pl.* habitual behavior; conduct. **4.** activity; energy. **5.** the exertion of power; influence. **6.** *Law* a lawsuit. **7.** in literature, the series of connected events that form the plot in a story or play. [< L]

ac·tion·a·ble (AK shən ə bəl) *adj.* affording ground for prosecution, as a trespass or a libel.

ac·ti·vate (AK tə vayt) *v.t.* **·vat·ed, ·vat·ing 1.** make active. **2.** organize (a military unit) for its assigned function. **3.** *Chem.* promote or hasten a reaction in, as by heat. —**ac'ti·va'·tion** *n.*

ac·tive (AK tiv) *adj.* **1.** abounding in or exhibiting action; busy. **2.** being in or pertaining to a state of action; not extinct or quiescent. **3.** agile; nimble. **4.** characterized by much activity; brisk; lively. **5.** bearing interest: *active* investments. **6.** In business, productive: *active* accounts. **7.** *Gram.* designating a voice of the verb that indicates that the subject of the sentence is performing the action. —*n. Gram.* the active voice. [ME *actif*]

ac·tiv·i·ty (ak TIV i tee) *n. pl.* **·ties 1.** the state of being active; action. **2.** brisk or vigorous movement or action; liveliness; energy. **3.** a particular action or sphere of action.

act of God *Law* an event caused by the operations of nature and not due to human action or negligence.

ac·tor (AK tər) *n.* **1.** a player on the stage, in film, etc. **2.** one who does something. —**ac·tress** (AK tris) *n.*

ac·tu·al (AK choo əl) *adj.* **1.** existing in fact; real. **2.** being in existence or action now; existent; present. [< LL *actualis*] —**ac·tu·al·i·ty** (AK choo AL i tee) *n. pl.* **·ties**

ac·tu·al·ize (AK choo əe LIZ) *v.t.* **·ized, ·iz·ing 1.** make real; realize in action. **2.** represent realistically.

ac·tu·al·ly (AK choo ə lee) *adv.* as a matter of fact; really.

ac·tu·ar·y (AK choo ER ee) *n. pl.* **·ar·ies** a statistician who calculates and states risks, premiums, etc., for insurance purposes. [< L *actuarius* clerk] —**ac·tu·ar·i·al** (AK choo AIR ee əl) *adj.*

ac·tu·ate (AK choo AYT) *v.t.* **·at·ed, ·at·ing 1.** set into action or motion, as a mechanism. **2.** influence to action. [< Med.L *actuatus* reduced to action]

a·cu·i·ty (ə KYOO i tee) *n.* acuteness; sharpness. [ME *acuite* sharpness]

ac·u·men (ə KYOO mən) *n.* quickness of discernment. [< L, sharpness]

ac·u·punc·ture (AK yuu PUNGK chər) *n.* the practice, orig. Chinese, of puncturing the body at certain points with fine needles as a medical treatment.

a·cute (ə KYOOT) *adj.* **1.** coming to a crisis quickly; violent: said of a disease: opposed to *chronic.* **2.** of the greatest importance; crucial. **3.** affecting keenly; poignant; intense. **4.** keenly sensitive. [< L *acutus* sharpened]

acute angle *Geom.* an angle of less than 90°.

ad·age (AD ij) *n.* a maxim; proverb. [< F]

a·da·gio (ə DAH joh) *Music adj. & adv.* in slow time. —*n.* a composition in adagio time. [< Ital.]

ad·a·mant (AD ə mənt) *adj.* unyielding. [ME]

a·dapt (ə DAPT) *v.t.* **1.** fit for a new use; make suitable. **2.** adjust (oneself or itself) to a new situation. —*v.i.* **3.** become adjusted

to a circumstance. [< L *adaptare* adjust]
—a·dapt'a·bil'i·ty *n*.

ad·ap·ta·tion (AD əp TAY shən) *n*. **1.** the act
of adapting or the state of being adapted. **2.**
anything produced by adapting.

a·dap·tive (ə DAP tiv) *adj*. capable of, fit for,
or manifesting adaptation.

add (ad) *v.t.* **1.** join or unite, so as to increase
the importance, size, quantity, or scope:
with *to*. **2.** find the sum of, as a column of
figures. **3.** say or write further. —*v.i.* **4.**
make or be an addition: with *to*. **5.** perform
arithmetical addition. [ME *adden*]

ad·dend (AD end) *n*. a number that is to be
added to another.

ad·den·dum (ə DEN dəm) *n. pl.* **·da** (-də) a
thing added; a supplement, as to a book. [<
L, gerundive of *addere* add]

ad·der (AD ər) *n*. **1.** a viper, esp. the common European viper. **2.** any of various
other snakes, as the puff adder. [ME, mis-
construed from *a nadder* < OE. *næddre*]

ad·dict (ə DIKT) *v.t.* devote (one) habitually: with *to*. —*n*. (AD ikt) one who is given
to some habit, esp. to the use of drugs. [<
L *addictus* surrendered] —ad·dic'tion
n. —ad·dic'tive *adj*.

ad·di·tion (ə DISH ən) *n*. **1.** the act of adding. **2.** that which is added. —ad·di'tional *adj*.

ad·di·tive (AD i tiv) *n*. something added or
to be added to a product or device.

ad·dle (AD əl) *v.t. & v.i.* **·dled, ·dling 1.**
become or cause to become confused. **2.**
spoil, as eggs. [ME *adel* rotten]

ad·dle-brained (AD əl BRAYND) *adj*. confused; mixed up.

ad·dress (ə DRES) *v.t.* **dressed,
·dress·ing 1.** speak to. **2.** devote (oneself):
with *to*: address oneself to a task. **3.** mark
with a destination, as a letter. —*n*. **1.** a formal speech. **2.** one's residence or other
place to receive communications, as mail.
[ME *adressen* adorn]

ad·dress·ee (AD re SEE) *n*. one to whom
mail, etc., is addressed.

ad·duce (ə DOOS) *v.t.* **·duced, ·duc·ing**
present for proof or consideration. [< L
adducere lead into]

ad·e·noid (AD n OID) *adj*. of or like a gland.
—*n. Usu. pl. Pathol.* an enlarged lymphoid
growth behind the pharynx. [< Gk. *ade-
noeidés*]

a·dept (ə DEPT) *adj*. highly skilled; proficient. [< Med.L *adeptus* alchemist] —
a·dept (AD ept) *n*.

ad·e·quate (AD i kwit) *adj*. **1.** equal to what
is required; fully sufficient. **2.** barely sufficient. [< L *adaequatus* matched] —ad'
e·qua·cy *n*.

ad·here (ad HEER) *v.i.* **·hered, ·her·ing
1.** stick fast or together. **2.** be devoted, as to
a cause. **3.** follow closely or without deviation. [< Med.L *adherere* stick to] —
ad·her'ence *n*. —ad·her'ent *n*.

ad·he·sion (as HEE zhən) *n*. **1.** the state of
being joined. **2.** firm attachment, as to a
cause. **3.** *Med.* abnormal surface union of
dissimilar tissues. < Med.L]

ad·he·sive (ad HEE siv) *adj*. tending to adhere. —ad·he'sive *n*.

ad hoc (ad HOK) *Latin* for this purpose.

ad·i·pose (AD ə pohs) *adj*. of or pertaining
to fat; fatty. [< L *adeps* lard] —
ad·i·pos·i·ty (AD ə POS i tee) *n*.

ad·ja·cent (ə JAY sənt) *adj*. lying near or
close at hand; adjoining; contiguous. [ME]
—ad·ja'cen·cy *n*.

ad·jec·tive (AJ ik tiv) *n. Gram.* any of a
class of words used to limit or qualify a
noun. [ME] —ad·jec·ti·val (AJ ik TĪ vəl)
adj.

ad·join (ə JOIN) *v.t.* **1.** border on. —*v.i.* **2.**
lie close together. [ME *adjoinen*]

ad·journ (ə JURN) *v.t.* **1.** put off to another
time. —*v.i.* **2.** come to a close. [ME
ajournen]

ad·judge (ə JUJ) *v.t.* **·judged, ·judg·ing 1.**
decide judicially. **2.** condemn or sentence.
3. consider. [ME *ajugen* judge]

ad·ju·di·cate (ə JOO di kayt) *v.t. & v.i.*
·cat·ed, ·cat·ing determine judicially. [<
L *adjudicare*] —ad·ju'di·ca'tion *n*.

ad·junct (AJ ungkt) *n*. something joined in a
subordinate position. [< L *adjunctus*
joined to] —ad'·junct *adj*.

adjunct professor one employed, usually part-time, to teach in a college or university.

ad·jure (ə JOOR) *v.t.* **·jured, ·jur·ing**
charge or entreat solemnly. [ME] —
ad·ju·ra·tion (AJ uu RAY shən) *n*.

ad·just (ə JUST) *v.t.* **1.** arrange so as to fit or
match. **2.** settle, as differences, claims, or
figures. **3.** regulate or make accurate. —*v.i.*
4. adapt oneself. [ME *ajusten* make con-
form]

ad·ju·tant (AJ uu tənt) *n. Mil.* a staff officer
who assists a commanding officer in administrative duties. [< L]

ad-lib (AD LIB) *v.t. & v.i.* **·libbed, -lib·bing**
improvise in performance. [< L *ad libitum*

at one's pleasure] —**ad′lib′ber** n. —**ad-lib** adv. & adv.

ad·min·is·ter (ad MIN is tər) v.t. **1.** direct or manage. **2.** apply, as treatment. **3.** inflict. **4.** tender, as an oath. [< L administrare carry out] —**ad·min′·is·tra·ble** adj.

ad·min·is·tra·tion (ad MIN is TRAY shən) n. **1.** the act of administering or the state of being administered. **2.** the executive personnel of a government etc.; also, their policies. —**ad·min′is·tra′tor** n.

ad·mi·ra·ble (AD mər ə bəl) adj. worthy of admiration; excellent. [< L admirabilis]

ad·mi·ral (AD mər əl) n. **1.** the supreme commander of a navy or fleet. **2.** a naval rank above commodore. [ME]

ad·mi·ral·ty (AD mər əl tee) n. pl. **·ties 1.** the office of an admiral. **2.** Law maritime law or courts.

ad·mire (ad MIR) v.t. **·mired, ·mir·ing 1.** regard with wonder, pleasure, and approbation. **2.** have respect for. [< L admirari wonder at] —**ad·mi·ra·tion** (AD mə RAY shən) n.

ad·mis·si·ble (ad MIS ə bəl) adj. worthy of being considered; allowable. [< F] —**ad·mis′si·bil′·i·ty** n.

ad·mis·sion (ad MISH ən) n. **1.** the act of admitting. **2.** authority to enter. **3.** an entrance fee. **4.** anything conceded. [ME]

ad·mit (ad MIT) v. **·mit·ted, ·mit·ting** v.t. **1.** allow to enter. **2.** allow to join. **3.** have room or possibility for. **4.** concede or avow. —v.i. **5.** afford possibility or opportunity: This problem admits of several solutions. [< L admittere send to]

ad·mix·ture (ad MIKS chər) n. **1.** the state of being mixed. **2.** anything added in mixing.

ad·mon·ish (ad MON ish) v.t. **1.** administer mild reproof to. **2.** caution against. [ME] —**ad·mo·ni·tion** (AD mə NISH ən) n. —**ad·mon′i·to′ry** adj.

ad nau·se·am (ad NAW zee əm) Latin to the point of nausea or disgust.

ad·o·les·cence (AD ə LES əns) n. the period of growth from puberty to adulthood. [ME]

ad·o·les·cent (AD ə LES ənt) adj. **1.** approaching adulthood. **2.** characteristic of or pertaining to youth. —n. someone in the period of adolescence.

a·dopt (ə DOPT) v.t. **1.** take into one's family or as one's child. **2.** follow as one's own, as a course of action. **3.** put into effect. [< MF

adopter] —**a·dop′·tion** n. —**a·dop′tive** adj.

a·dor·a·ble (ə DOR ə bəl) adj. **1.** worthy of adoration. **2.** delightful; lovable.

a·dore (ə DOR) v.t. **·dored, ·dor·ing 1.** worship. **2.** love or honor with intense devotion. **3.** to like especially. [< L adorare speak to] —**ad·o·ra·tion** (AD ə RAY shən) n.

a·dorn (ə DORN) v.t. decorate with or as with ornaments. [ME adornen] —**a·dorn′ ment** n.

ad·re·nal (ə DREEN l) Physiol. adj. of or from the adrenal glands. [< L ad- near + renes kidneys]

adrenal gland one of a pair of ductless glands near the kidneys, secreting epinephrine and certain steroids.

a·droit (ə DROIT) adj. skillful; expert. [< F]

ad·sorb (ad SORB) v.t. Chem. hold molecules on the surface of (a solid) by electrochemical attraction. —**ad·sorp·tion** (ad SORP shən) n.

ad·u·late (AJ uu layt) v.t. **·lat·ed, ·lat·ing** flatter or praise extravagantly. [ME] —**ad·u·la·to·ry** (AJ uu lə TOR ee) adj.

a·dult (ə DULT) n. **1.** a person who has attained the age of maturity or legal majority. **2.** Biol. a fully developed animal or plant. [< L adultus grown]

a·dul·ter·ant (ə DUL tər ənt) n. an adulterating substance.

a·dul·ter·ate (ə DUL tə rayt) v.t. **·at·ed, ·at·ing** make impure or inferior by admixture of other ingredients. —adj. (ə DUL tər it) corrupted; debased. [< L adulteratus adulterated]

a·dul·ter·y (ə DUL tər ee) n. pl. **·ter·ies** the voluntary sexual intercourse of a married person with someone not the spouse. [< L adulterium] —**a·dul′ter·ous** adj.

ad·um·brate (a DUM brayt) v.t. **·brat·ed, ·brat·ing 1.** outline sketchily. **2.** overshadow; darken. [< L adumbratus shaded]

ad·vance (ad VANS) v. **·vanced, ·vanc·ing** v.t. **1.** move forward or upward. **2.** offer; propose. **3.** further; promote. **4.** make occur earlier. **5.** raise (a price etc.). **6.** pay, as money or interest, before legally due. **7.** lend, as money. —v.i. **8.** move or go forward. **9.** make progress. —adj. **1.** being before in time. **2.** being or going before. —n. **1.** the act of going forward. **2.** improvement; promotion. **3.** an increase or rise, as of prices. **4.** pl. personal approaches; overtures. **5.** money supplied on credit. [ME *avauncen*] —**ad·vance′ment** *n.*

ad·vanced (ad VANST) *adj.* **1.** in advance of others, as in progress or thought. **2.** in front; moved forward. **3.** at a late or forward stage.

ad·van·tage (ad VAN tij) *n.* **1.** any circumstance favoring success. **2.** benefit or gain. **3.** a better state or position; superiority. [ME *avauntage*]

ad·van·ta·geous (AD vəb TAY jəs) *adj.* profitable; favorable; beneficial.

ad·vent (AD vent) *n.* a coming or arrival. [ME]

Ad·vent *n.* **1.** the birth of Christ. **2.** the Second Coming of Christ as promised in scripture.

Ad·vent·ist (AD ven tist) *n.* a member of any denominations that believe the Second Coming of Christ is imminent.

ad·ven·ti·tious (AD ven TISH əs) *adj.* **1.** not inherent; accidentally acquired. **2.** *Biol.* occurring abnormally in development or habitat. [< L *adventicius* coming from abroad]

ad·ven·ture (ad VEN chər) *n.* **1.** a hazardous undertaking. **2.** a stirring experience. [ME *aventure*] —**ad·ven′ture** *v.i. & v.t.* **·tured, ·tur·ing** —**ad·ven·tur·ous** (ad VEN chər əs) *adj.*

ad·ven·tur·er (ad VEN chər ər) *n.* **1.** one who seeks after or takes part in adventures. **2.** a person who seeks advancement by questionable means.

ad·verb (AD vurb) *n. Gram.* any of a class of words used to modify the meaning of a verb, adjective, or other adverb. [< L *adverbium*] —**ad·ver·bi·al** (ad VUR bee əl) *adj.*

ad·ver·sar·y (AD vər SER ee) *n. pl.* **·sar·ies** one actively opposed to another. [ME *adversarie*]

ad·verse (ad VURS) *adj.* **1.** opposed; antagonistic. **2.** unpropitious; detrimental. **3.** opposite. [ME]

ad·ver·si·ty (ad VUR sə tee) *n. pl.* **·ties** a condition of hardship or affliction.

ad·vert (ad VURT) *v.i.* call attention; refer: with *to*. [ME *adverten* pay attention]

ad·ver·tent (ad VUR tənt) *adj.* giving attention; heedful. —**ad·ver′tence** *n.*

ad·ver·tise (AD vər TIZ) *v.t.* **·tised, ·tis·ing** make known by public notice. [< L *advertere* direct one's attention to]

ad·ver·tise·ment (AD vər TIZ mənt) *n.* a public notice, usually seeking to sell.

ad·ver·tis·ing (AD vər TI zing) *n.* **1.** adver-

tisements collectively. **2.** the business of preparing advertisements.

ad·vice (ad VIS) *n.* counsel given to encourage or dissuade. [ME *advise*]

ad·vis·a·ble (ad VI zə bəl) *adj.* proper to be recommended. —**ad·vis′a·bil′i·ty** *n.*

ad·vise (ad VIZ) *v.* **·vised, ·vis·ing** *v.t.* **1.** give advice to; counsel. **2.** recommend. **3.** notify; inform: with *of.* —*v.i.* **4.** take counsel: with *with* [ME] —**ad·vis′er** or **ad·vis′or** *n.*

ad·vised (ad VIZD) *adj.* planned; deliberate: chiefly in *ill-advised, well-advised.* —**ad·vis′ed·ly** *adv.*

ad·vi·so·ry (ad VI zər ee) *adj.* **1.** having power to advise. **2.** given as advice; not mandatory.

ad·vo·cate (AD və KAYT) *v.t.* **·cat·ed, ·cat·ing** speak or write in favor of; defend; recommend. —*n.* (AD və kit) one who pleads the cause of another; an intercessor. [< L *advocatus* legal counselor] —**ad·vo·ca·cy** (AD və kə see) *n.*

ae·gis (EE jis) *n.* a protecting influence; sponsoring agency or power. [< L, shield of Zeus]

ae·o·li·an (ee OH lee ən) *adj.* pertaining to or caused by the winds. [< L *Aeolius*, pertaining to Aeolus, god of the winds]

ae·on (EE ən) see EON.

aer·ate (AIR ayt) *v.t.* **·at·ed, ·at·ing 1.** supply or charge with air or gas. **2.** purify by exposure to air. —**aer·a′tion** *n.*

aer·i·al (AIR ee əl) *adj.* **1.** of or in the air. **2.** of, by, or pertaining to aircraft. —*n.* an antenna, as in television. [< L *aerius* of the air]

aer·i·al·ist (AIR ee əl ist) *n.* one who performs on a trapeze etc.

aer·ie (AIR ee) *n.* a high nest, as of an eagle. Also spelled *aery, eyrie.* [< AF, nest]

aer·obe (AIR ohb) *n.* a microorganism that requires free oxygen. —**aer·o′bic** *adj.*

aer·o·bics (air OH biks) *n. (construed as sing.)* a program of exercises emphasizing increased oxygen consumption without muscle strain.

aer·o·dy·nam·ics (AIR oh dī NAM iks) *n. (construed as sing.)* the branch of physics dealing with the laws of motion of gases.

aer·o·nau·tics (AIR ə NAW tiks) *n. (construed as sing.)* the science or art of flight. [< NL *aeronautica*]

aer·o·sol (AIR ə SAWL) *n.* **1.** a suspension of solid or liquid particles in a gas. **2.** formerly, a gas-charged dispenser of aerosol.

aer·o·space (AIR oh spays) *n.* the earth's atmosphere and outer space. —*adj.* designating the technology of aviation and space flight.

aes·thete (ES theet) *n.* 1. one who is very responsive to beauty in art. 2. one who affects such sensitivity. [< Gk. *aisthētes* one who perceives] —**aes·thet·ic** or **esthetic** (es THET ik) *adj.*

aes·thet·ics (es THET iks) *n.* (*used with a sing. v.*) a branch of philosophy relating to the nature and forms of beauty in art, nature, etc., and to mental and emotional responses to it. Also **esthetics**.

a·far (ə FAHR) *adv.* at, from, or to a distance.

af·fa·ble (AF ə bəl) *adj.* easy to approach; friendly. [< L *affabilis* courteous] —**af·fa·bil·i·ty** *n.*

af·fair (ə FAIR) *n.* 1. anything done or to be done. 2. *pl.* matters of business or concern. 3. a party or entertainment. 4. a love affair. [< F *affaire*]

af·fect[1] (ə FEKT) *v.t.* 1. have an effect upon. 2. move emotionally. —*n.* (AF ekt) *Psychol.* emotion; feeling. [ME]

af·fect[2] *v.t.* (ə FEKT) 1. adopt as one's style. 2. imitate. [ME]

af·fec·ta·tion (AF ek TAY shən) *n.* a studied pretense; artificiality.

af·fect·ed (ə FEK tid) *adj.* 1. artificial; feigned. 2. showing affectation.

af·fect·ing (ə FEK ting) *adj.* stirring tender emotions.

af·fec·tion (ə FEK shən) *n.* fond attachment or kind feeling.

af·fec·tion·ate (ə FEK shən it) *adj.* having affection; loving.

af·fi·ance (ə FĪ əns) *v.t.* •**anced**, •**anc·ing** promise in marriage; betroth. [ME]

af·fi·da·vit (AF ə DAY vit) *n. Law* a sworn, written declaration. [< Med. L, he has stated on oath]

af·fil·i·ate (ə FIL ee ayt) *v.t. & v.i.* •**at·ed**, •**at·ing** associate, as a member or branch; with *to* or *with.* —*n.* (ə FIL ee it) an affiliated person, company, etc. [< L *affiliatus* adopted]

af·fin·i·ty (ə FIN ə tee) *n. pl.* •**ties** 1. a natural attraction. 2. any close relationship. [ME *affinite* related by marriage]

af·firm (ə FURM) *v.t.* 1. declare or state positively. 2. confirm or ratify. —*v.i.* 3. *Law* make a formal declaration, but not under oath. [< L *affirmare* make firm] —**af·fir·ma·tion** (AF ər MAY shən) *n.*

af·firm·a·tive (ə FUR mə tiv) *adj.* 1. asserting that the fact is so. 2. asserting positive ideas. —*n.* an expression of assent.

af·fix (ə FIKS) *v.t.* 1. attach; fasten. 2. assign, as blame. —*n.* (AF iks) *Gram.* a prefix, suffix, or infix to a word. [< L *affigere* fasten]

af·fla·tus (ə FLAY təs) *n.* any creative inspiration. [< L, a breathing on]

af·flict (ə FLIKT) *v.t.* cause to suffer. [ME *afflicten*] —**af·flic·tion** *n.*

af·flu·ent (AF loo ənt) *adj.* 1. abounding; abundant. 2. wealthy; opulent. [ME] —**af·flu·ence** *n.*

af·ford (ə FORD) *v.t.* 1. have sufficient means for. 2. incur without detriment. 3. provide or furnish. [ME *aforthen* promote] —**af·ford·a·ble** *adj.*

af·front (ə FRUNT) *v.t.* 1. insult openly. 2. confront in defiance. —*n.* an insult. [ME *afrounten* strike in the face]

af·ghan (AF gan) *n.* a wool coverlet, knitted or crocheted in colors.

a·fi·cio·na·do (ə FISH ə NAH doh) *n. pl.* •**dos** an avid follower; devotee. [< Sp.]

a·fore·thought (ə FOR thawt) *adj.* intended beforehand: malice *aforethought.*

a·foul (ə FOWL) *adv. & adj.* entangled. — **run afoul of** get into difficulties with.

a·fraid (ə FRAYD) *adj.* 1. filled with fear. 2. regretful to say: I'm *afraid* you are wrong.

Af·ri·can (AF ri kən) *adj.* of or pertaining to Africa or its inhabitants. —*n.* 1. a native inhabitant of Africa. 2. a member of one of the African peoples. —**African American** a black American. —**African-American** *adj.*

Af·ri·kaans (AF ri KAHNS) *n.* one of the official languages of South Africa.

Af·ro-A·mer·i·can *adj.* of or pertaining to Americans of black African descent. — **Af·ro-A·mer·i·can** *n.*

af·ter (AF tər) *prep.* 1. following in position or time. 2. in search or pursuit of: strive *after* wisdom. 3. concerning: inquire *after* one's health. 4. in conformity with: a man *after* my own heart. 5. in honor of: named *after* him. —*adv.* following in position or time. —*adj.* following in time or place: in *after* years. —*conj.* following the time that: *After* I went home, I ate. [ME]

af·ter·birth (AF tər BURTH) *n.* the placenta and fetal membranes expelled from the uterus after childbirth.

af·ter·ef·fect (AF tər ə FEKT) *n.* an effect succeeding its cause after an interval.

af·ter·math (AF tər MATH) *n.* result; consequence. [AFTER + OE *mæth* mowing]

af·ter·taste (AF tər TAYST) *n.* a taste persisting after eating or drinking.

af·ter·ward (AF tər wərd) *adv.* in time following. Also **af·ter·wards.** [ME]

a·gain (ə GEN) *adv.* **1.** once more; anew. **2.** once repeated. **3.** to the same place; over the same course; back. **4.** further; moreover. **5.** on the other hand. [ME *agayn*]

a·gainst (ə GENST) *prep.* **1.** in the opposite direction to. **2.** in contact or collision with; upon. **3.** in opposition to; contrary to. **4.** in preparation for. [ME *agens*]

a·gape (ə GAYP) *adv. & adj.* gaping.

ag·ate (AG it) *n.* **1.** a quartz with usually banded colors. **2.** a playing marble. [ME *acchate*] —**ag'ate** *adj.*

age (ayj) *n.* **1.** the period of existence of a person, thing, nation, etc. **2.** the time of maturity, when full civil rights are attained. **3.** the closing period of life. **4.** any notable period in history. **5.** a long time. —*v.t. & v.i.* **aged, ag·ing** or **age·ing 1.** make or become old. **2.** undergo or subject to, as a food or beverage, so as to bring to a ripe or usable state. [ME]

a·ged (AY jid) *adj.* **1.** advanced in years; old. **2.** characteristic of old age. **3.** at the age of: a child *aged* six. **4.** treated by aging.

age·ism (AY jiz əm) *n.* social discrimination against the elderly.

age·less (AYJ lis) *adj.* **1.** not seeming to grow old. **2.** having no limits of duration; eternal.

a·gen·cy (AY jən see) *n. pl.* **·cies 1.** means; instrumentality. **2.** an establishment where business is done for others. **3.** the office or function of an agent. [< Med.L *agentia*]

a·gen·da (ə JEN də) *n.* a list of things to be done, esp. a program for a meeting. [< L, pl. of *agendum* that which is to be done]

a·gent (AY jənt) *n.* **1.** one who or that which acts. **2.** one who acts for another. **3.** a means by which something is done. [< L *agere* do]

a·gent pro·vo·ca·teur (AY jənt prə VOK ə TUR) *pl.* **a·gents pro·vo·ca·teurs** (AY jənts prə vok ə TUR) *French* a secret agent employed to incite a person or group to actions that will incur punishment.

ag·glom·er·ate (ə GLOM ə rayt) *v.t. & v.i.* **·at·ed, ·at·ing** gather, form, or grow into a mass. —*adj.* (ə GLOM ər it) gathered into a mass. —*n.* (ə GLOM ər it) a mass of varied things. [< L *agglomerare* gather into a ball] —**ag·glom'er·a'tive** *adj.*

ag·glu·ti·nate (ə GLOO tə nayt) *v.t. & v.i.* **·nat·ed, ·nat·ing 1.** join by adhesion. **2.** *Physiol.* mass together, as bacteria. —*adj.* (ə GLOO tə nit) joined by adhesion. [< L *agglutinare* glue together] —**ag·glu'ti·na'tive** *adj.*

ag·gran·dize (ə GRAN dīz) *v.t.* **·dized, ·diz·ing 1.** make greater. **2.** make appear greater; exalt. [< F *aggrandir* magnify] —**ag·gran·dize·ment** (ə GRAN diz mənt) *n.*

ag·gra·vate (AG rə vayt) *v.t.* **·vat·ed, ·vat·ing 1.** make worse, as an illness. **2.** exasperate. [ME] —**ag'gra·va'tion** *n.*

ag·gre·gate (AG rə gayt) *v.t.* **·gat·ed, ·gat·ing 1.** bring together, into a whole. **2.** form a whole. —*adj.* (AG ri git) collected into a whole. —*n.* (AG ri git) the whole of anything. [ME] —**ag'gre·ga'tion** *n.*

ag·gres·sion (ə GRESH ən) *n.* **1.** an unprovoked attack. **2.** hostile behavior. [< L *aggressio*] —**ag·gres'sor** (-GRES ər) *n.*

ag·gres·sive (ə GRES iv) *adj.* **1.** attacking. **2.** boldly assertive.

ag·grieve (ə GREEV) *v.t.* **·grieved, ·griev·ing 1.** cause sorrow to. **2.** give cause for complaint. [ME *agreven* worsen]

a·ghast (ə GAST) *adj.* struck with horror. [ME *agast* frightened]

ag·ile (AJ əl) *adj.* able to move quickly and easily. [< L *agilis*] —**a·gil·i·ty** (ə JIL i tee) *n.*

ag·i·tate (AJ i TAYT) *v.* **·tat·ed, ·tat·ing** *v.t.* **1.** shake or stir vigorously. **2.** excite or perturb. —*v.i.* **3.** excite, or endeavor to excite, public interest and action. [< L *agitare* set in motion] —**ag'i·ta'tor** *n.*

ag·nos·ti·cism (ag NOS tə SIZ əm) *n.* the doctrine that people cannot know ultimate truth. —**ag·nos'tic** *adj. & n.* [< Gk. *agnōtōs* not known]

a·gog (ə GOG) *adv. & adj.* in a state of eager curiosity. [< MF *en gogues* in a merry mood]

ag·o·nize (AG ə nīz) *v.i.* **·nized, ·niz·ing 1.** suffer extreme anguish. **2.** make convulsive efforts. [< Med.L *agonizare* contend]

ag·o·ny (AG ə nee) *n. pl.* **·nies 1.** intense suffering. **2.** any intense emotion. **3.** violent striving. [< Gk. *agōn* contest]

a·grar·i·an (ə GRAIR ee ən) *adj.* **1.** pertaining to land or its use. **2.** concerning farming. [< L *agrarius*] —**a·grar'i·an·ism** *n.*

a·gree (ə GREE) *v.i.* **a·greed, a·gree·ing 1.** give consent. **2.** be in harmony. **3.** be of one mind. **4.** be acceptable; suit. **5.** be consistent with. **6.** *Gram.* correspond in person, number, case, or gender. [.MEL *agre*]

a·gree·a·ble (ə GREE ə bəl) *adj.* **1.** pleasant to the senses. **2.** suitable. **3.** ready to consent. —**a·gree'a·ble·ness** *n.* —**a·gree'a·bly** *adv.*

a·gree·ment (ə GREE mənt) *n.* **1.** the act of coming into accord. **2.** the state of being in accord; conformity. **3.** a contract.

ag·ri·cul·ture (AG ri KUL chər) *n.* the cultivation of crops and raising of livestock. [ME] —**ag'ri·cul'tur·al** *adj.*

a·gron·o·my (ə GRON ə mee) *n.* the application of scientific principles to the cultivation of land. —**a·gron'o·mist** *n.*

a·ground (ə GROWND) *adv. & adj.* on the shore or bottom, as a vessel; stranded.

a·head (ə HED) *adv.* **1.** at the front. **2.** in advance. **3.** onward; forward. —**ahead of** in advance of, as in time, achievement, etc. —**get ahead** improve one's lot.

aid (ayd) *v.t. & v.i.* render assistance (to); help. —*n.* **1.** assistance; help. **2.** one who or that which affords assistance. [ME *ayde*]

aide (ayd) *n.* **1.** an aide-de-camp. **2.** an assistant. [< F]

aide-de-camp (AYD də KAMP) *n. pl.* **aides-de-camp** a military officer serving a superior officer as confidential assistant: also *aide.* [< F *aide de camp,* lit., field assistant]

AIDS (aydz) *n. Pathol.* a(cquired) i(mmune) d(eficiency) s(yndrome), a disease characterized by increased susceptibility to infection.

ail (ayl) *v.t.* **1.** cause uneasiness or pain to. —*v.i.* **2.** be ill; feel pain. [ME]

aim (aym) *v.t.* **1.** direct, as a weapon or act, toward some object or person. —*v.i.* **2.** have a purpose; try: with *to.* —*n.* **1.** the direction of anything aimed. **2.** design; purpose. [ME *aimen* estimate]

aim·less (AYM lis) *adj.* wanting in aim or purpose. —**aim'less·ness** *n.*

ain't (aynt) *Nonstandard* am not: also used for *are not, is not, has not,* and *have not.*

air (air) *n.* **1.** the mixture of gases surrounding the earth. **2.** a light wind; breeze. **3.** characteristic manner. **4.** *pl.* affectation: put on airs. **5.** a melody; tune. —**in the air** prevalent; abroad, as gossip. —*v.t.* **1.** expose to the air; ventilate. **2.** make public. [ME *eir*]

Air as a combining form has the meanings: **1.** by means of air:

air-cured	air-dried

2. conducting, confining, or regulating air:

air compressor	air filter

3. filled with air:

air chamber	air mattress

4. operated by compressed air:

air brake	air gun

5. done by or suitable for aircraft:

air attack	air race

air bag a plastic bag that inflates automatically in automobile crashes to protect passengers.

air·borne (AIR BORN) *adj.* carried by or through the air.

air-con·di·tion (AIR kən DISH ən) *v.t.* equip with a system that controls temperature and humidity of indoor air. —**air'·con·di'tioned** *adj.*

air-cooled (AIR KOOLD) *adj.* cooled, as an engine, directly by flow of air.

air·craft (AIR KRAFT) *n. pl.* **·craft** any form of craft designed for flight through the air.

air·drop (AIR DROP) *n.* delivery of supplies from an aircraft in flight. —*v.t.* **·dropped, ·drop·ping** drop (supplies, etc.) from an aircraft.

air·foil (AIR FOIL) *n.* a surface, as an airplane wing, designed to respond to air movement.

air·ing (AIR ing) *n.* **1.** an exposure to air, as for drying. **2.** public exposure or discussion. **3.** exercise out of doors.

air lane a route regularly used by airplanes.

air·lift (AIR LIFT) *n.* an emergency supply line by aircraft. —*v.t.* move by airlift.

air lock an airtight chamber for maintaining air pressure.

air·mail (AIR MAYL **1.** mail carried by airplane. **2.** a system of carrying mail by airplane. —*adj. & v.t.*

air·plane (AIR PLAYN) *n.* a heavier-than-air, powered flying craft having wings.

air pocket a sinking mass of cooled air that causes an aircraft to make a sudden drop.

air·port (AIR PORT) *n.* a field laid out as a base for aircraft, including all appurtenances.

air·ship (AIR SHIP) *n.* a lighter-than-air, powered flying craft.

air·sick·ness (AIR SIK nis) *n.* motion sickness caused by air travel.

air space *n.* that portion of the atmosphere overlying a designated area.

air·strip (AIR STRIP) *n.* a flat surface used as an airfield.

air·tight (AIR TITT) *adj.* **1.** not allowing air to

pass. 2. having no weak points: an *airtight* case.

air·wor·thy (AIR wur *thee*) *adj.* fit to fly: said of aircraft. **—air'wor'thi·ness** *n.*

air·y (AIR ee) *adj.* **air·i·er, air·i·est 1.** of or pertaining to the air. **2.** thin or light as air; delicate. **3.** lively. **4.** unsubstantial as air. **5.** open to the air; breezy. **—air'i·ly** *adv.* **—air'i·ness** *n.*

aisle (īl) *n.* **1.** a passageway between rows of seats. **2.** a division of a church at the side of a nave. [ME *ele* wing]

a·jar (ə JAHR) *adv. & adj.* partly open, as a door. [ME *on char* on the turn]

a·kim·bo (ə KIM boh) *adv. & adj.* with hands on hips. [ME *in kenebowe* in a sharp bow]

a·kin (ə KIN) *adj.* **1.** related by blood. **2.** of similar nature.

à la (AH lah) in the style of. Also **a la.** [< F]

al·a·bas·ter (AL ə BAS tər) *n.* **1.** a white or tinted fine-grained gypsum. **2.** a banded variety of calcite. **—***adj.* made of or like alabaster; smooth and white: also **al'a·bas'·trine** (-trin). [< Gk. *alábastros* alabaster box]

à la carte (AH lə KAHRT) each item having a separate price. [< F, according to the menu]

a·lac·ri·ty (ə LAK ri tee) *n.* cheerful promptness. [< L *alacritas* lively]

à la king (AH lə KING) cooked in cream sauce.

à la mode (AH lə MOHD) **1.** in style; fashionable. **2.** in cookery: **a** served with ice cream: said of pie. **b** braised with vegetables. [< F]

a·lar (AY lər) *adj.* **1.** of a wing. **2.** wing-shaped. [< L *alaris*]

a·larm (ə LAHRM) *n.* **1.** sudden fear or apprehension. **2.** any signal intended to awaken or apprise of danger. **—***v.t.* **1.** strike with sudden fear. **2.** give warning to. [ME *alarme* to arms]

a·larm·ist (ə LAHR mist) *n.* **1.** one who needlessly excites or alarms. **2.** one who is easily alarmed. **—a·larm'ist** *adj.*

al·ba·tross (AL bə TRAWS) *n.* a large, web-footed sea bird. [< Pg. *alcatraz* pelican]

al·be·it (awl BEE it) *conj.* even though. [ME *al be it* although it be]

al·bi·no (al BĪ noh) *n. pl.* **·nos 1.** a person lacking pigment in the skin, hair, and eyes. **2.** any plant or animal lacking normal pigmentation. [< Pg.] **—al·bin·ism** (AL bə NIZ əm) *n.*

al·bum (AL bəm) *n.* **1.** a booklike container for stamps, pictures, etc. **2.** a phonograph record or set of records. [< L, blank tablet]

al·bu·men (al BYOO mən) *n.* **1.** the white of an egg. **2.** albumin. [< LL]

al·bu·min (al BYOO mən) *n. Biochem.* Any of a class of water-soluble proteins found in animal and vegetable tissues. [< ALBU-MEN]

al·cáz·ar (AL kə ZAHR) *n.* a Moorish castle or fortress in Spain. [< Sp.]

al·che·my (AL kə mee) *n.* **1.** the chemistry of the Middle Ages, concerned primarily with the transmutation of base metals into gold. **2.** any process of transmutation. [< Med.L *alchymia*] **—al'che·mist** *n.*

al·co·hol (AL kə HAWL) *n.* **1.** a colorless, flammable, volatile liquid that is the intoxicating agent in liquors. **2.** drinks containing alcohol. **3.** methanol. [< NL]

al·co·hol·ic (AL kə HAW lik) *adj.* **1.** containing or using alcohol. **2.** suffering from alcoholism. **—***n.* one who suffers from alcoholism.

al·co·hol·ism (AL kə haw LIZ əm) *n.* **1.** alcoholic poisoning. **2.** an abnormal craving for alcohol.

al·cove (AL kohv) *n.* **1.** a recess at the side of a room. **2.** any secluded spot. [< F *alcôve*]

al·der·man (AWL dər mən) *n. pl.* **·men** a member of a city governing body. [ME]

ale (ayl) *n.* a fermented malt flavored with hops, resembling beer. [ME]

a·le·a·tor·y (AY lee ə TOR ee) *adj.* dependent on chance. [< L *aleatorius* gambler]

a·lem·bic (ə LEM bik) *n.* anything that tests, purifies, or transforms. [ME]

a·lert (ə LURT) *adj.* **1.** keenly watchful. **2.** lively; nimble. **3.** intelligent. **—***n.* a warning against attack. **—***v.t.* warn, as of a threatened attack. [< Ital. *all'erta* on the watch]

Al·e·ut (ə LOOT) *n.* **1.** a native of the Aleutian Islands. **2.** the language of the Aleuts. **—A·leu·tian** (ə LOO shən) *adj.*

Al·ex·an·drine (AL ig ZAN DRIN) *n.* in prosody, a line of six iambic feet.

al·fal·fa (al FAL fə) *n.* a cloverlike plant of the bean family, used as forage. [< Sp.]

al·fres·co (al FRES koh) *adv. & adj.* occurring outdoors, as a meal. [< Ital., in the open air]

al·gae (AL jee) *n.pl., sing.* **al·ga** (AL gə) a group of primitive, chlorophyll-bearing plants widely distributed in fresh and salt water. [< NL, seaweed] **—al·gal** (AL gəl) *adj.*

al·ge·bra (AL jə brə) *n.* the branch of mathematics dealing with quantity and relations of numbers in the abstract by means of letters and symbols. [< Med.L] — **al·ge·bra·ic** (AL jə BRAY ik) *adj.*

Al·gon·qui·an (al GONG kee ən) *n. pl.* **·qui·ans** 1. a family of North American Indian languages. 2. a member of an Algonquian-speaking tribe.

al·go·rithm (AL gə *rith* əm) *n.* a step-by-step problem-solving procedure, as with a computer. [after *al-Khwarizmi*, 9th c. Arabian mathematician]

a·li·as (AY lee əs) *n. pl.* **·as·es** an assumed name. —*adv.* called by an assumed name: Miller, *alias* Brown. [< L, at another time]

al·i·bi (AL ə BI) *n. pl.* **·bis** 1. *Law* a defense that the suspect was elsewhere during the crime. 2. an excuse. —*v.i.* **·bied, ·bi·ing** *Informal* make excuses. [< L, elsewhere]

al·ien (AYL yən) *adj.* 1. of another country; foreign. 2. not one's own; strange. 3. not consistent with: with *to*. —*n.* 1. a foreign resident who is not a citizen. 2. a member of a foreign people. 3. one estranged or excluded. [ME]

al·ien·a·ble (AYL yə nə bəl) *adj. Law* capable of being transferred in ownership.

al·ien·ate (AYL yə NAYT) *v.t.* **·at·ed, ·at·ing** 1. make indifferent or unfriendly; estrange. 2. turn away: *alienate* the affections. [ME] —**al'ien·a'tion** *n.*

al·i·form (AL ə FORM) *adj.* wing-shaped. [< F *ala* wing]

a·light (ə LIT) *v.i.* **a·light·ed** or **a·lit, a·light·ing** 1. descend and come to rest. 2. come by accidentally: with *on* or *upon*. [ME *alighten*]

a·lign (ə LIN) *v.t.* 1. bring into a straight line. 2. put (oneself, one's party, etc.) on one side of an issue. —*v.i.* 3. fall into line. [< F *aligner* place in a line] —**a·lign·ment** (ə LIN mənt) *n.*

a·like (ə LIK) *adj.* having precise or close resemblance. —*adv.* In the same or like manner. [ME *alykē*]

al·i·men·ta·ry (AL ə MEN tə ree) *adj.* 1. supplying nourishment. 2. relating to nourishment or nutrition.

alimentary canal the food canal between the mouth and the anus, including esophagus, stomach, and intestines.

al·i·men·ta·tion (AL ə men TAY shən) *n.* 1. the act or process of supplying or receiving nourishment. 2. maintenance; support.

al·i·mo·ny (AL ə MOH nee) *n.* the allowance made from one spouse to the other after a divorce. [< L *alimonia* nourishment]

a·live (ə LIV) *adj.* 1. in a living or functioning state. 2. continuing: keep hope *alive.* 3. animated: *alive* with enthusiasm. [ME]

al·ka·li (AL kə LI) *n. pl.* **·lis** or **·lies** *Chem.* 1. a hydroxide of a metal, capable of neutralizing acids and of turning red litmus paper blue; base. 2. any of various basic salts found in soil and ground water. [ME *alkaly*] —**al·ka·line** (AL kə LIN) *adj.* — **al·ka·lin·i·ty** (AL kə LIN ə tee) *n.*

all (awl) *adj.* 1. the whole of: *all* Europe. 2. the entire number of: known to *all* men. 3. the greatest possible: in *all* haste. 4. any whatever: beyond *all* doubt. —*n.* everything that one has: give one's *all.* —*pron.* every part or person: *All* failed. —**after all** everything else being considered. —**all told** with everything included. —**at all** in any way or degree: no luck *at all.* —**for all** to the degree that: *For all* I care, you can go. —**in all** including everything; all told: ten books *in all.* —*adv.* 1. wholly; entirely: fallen *all* to bits. 2. for each; on each side: a score of three *all.* —**all but** almost; on the verge of. —**all in** wearied. —**all out** making every effort. — **all the** (**better, more,** etc.) so much the (better, more, etc.). [ME *al*]

All as a combining form has the meanings: 1. wholly or totally:

all-colored	**all-inclusive**
all-encompassing	
all-powerful	
all-forgiving	**all-wood**

2. representing the whole or the best of the whole:

all-American	**all-star**

Al·lah (AL ə) *n.* in Islam, the one supreme being; God. [< Arabic]

al·lay (ə LAY) *v.t.* **·layed, ·lay·ing** 1. reduce the intensity of. 2. pacify; calm [ME *aleyen* put down]

al·lege (ə LEJ) *v.t.* **·leged, ·leg·ing** 1. assert to be true before proving. 2. plead as an excuse, in support of a position. [ME *allegen*] —**al·leged** (ə LEJD) *adj.* —**al·leg'ed·ly** (-LEJ id lee) *adv.*

al·le·giance (ə LEE jəns) *n.* 1. an obligation of loyalty to a government or sovereign. 2. fidelity, as to a principle. [ME *aliegiaunce*]

al·le·go·ry (AL ə GOR ee) *n. pl.* **·ries** a story or other artistic representation in which characters and events represent ideals or principles. [ME *allegorie* spoken figuratively] —al′le•gor′ic or •i•cal *adj.*

al•lele (ə LEEL) *n. Genetics* **1.** either of a pair or one of a number of mutually exclusive hereditary characteristics. **2.** the gene occurring at a given location on a chromosome. [< G *Allel*]

al•ler•gen (AL ər jən) *n.* any substance capable of producing allergy. —al′ler•gen′ ic (JEN ik) *adj.*

al•ler•gy (AL ər jee) *n. pl.* •gies *Med.* a pathological condition of heightened sensitivity to a substance. [< Gk. *allos* other + *ergon* work] —al•ler•gic (ə LUR jik) *adj.* —al•ler•gist (AL ər jist) *n.*

al•le•vi•ate (ə LEE vee ayt) *v.t.* •at•ed, •at•ing make easier to bear. [ME *alleviaten*]

al•ley (AL ee) *n. pl.* •leys **1.** a narrow street. **2.** a bowling alley. [ME *aley* walk]

al•li•ance (ə LĪ əns) *n.* **1.** any union, coalition, or agreement between persons, nations, etc. **2.** relationship in characteristics. [ME *aliance*]

al•lied (ə LĪD) *adj.* **1.** united, confederated, or leagued. **2.** closely related: *allied* interests.

al•li•ga•tor (AL i GAY tər) *n.* a large reptile of the southern U.S. and the Yangtze River, China, having a shorter, blunter snout than the crocodile. [< Sp. *el lagarto* the lizard]

alligator pear avocado.

al•lit•er•a•tion (ə LIT ə RAY shən) *n.* the occurrence of two or more words having the same initial sound, as in "a fair field full of flowers." [< Med.L] —al•lit•er•a•tive (ə LIT ər ə tiv) *adj.*

al•lo•cate (AL ə kayt) *v.t.* •cat•ed, •cat•ing set apart or assign, as funds. [< Med.L *allocatus* placed] —al•lo•ca•ble (AL ə kə bəl) *adj.*

al•lot (ə LOT) *v.t.* •lot•ted, •lot•ting assign or apportion. [ME *alotten*] —al•lot′ment *n.*

all-out (AWL OWT) *adj.* complete and entire.

al•low (ə LOW) *v.t. & v.i.* **1.** permit to occur or do. **2.** concede; admit. **3.** make provision for. **4.** make concession of: *allow* a month to pay. [ME *alowen* place] —al•low′a•ble *adj.*

al•low•ance (ə LOW əns) *n.* **1.** that which is allowed. **2.** a sum of money given at regular intervals. **3.** the act of allowing; toleration; sanction. **4.** admission; acceptance.

al•loy (AL oi) *n.* **1.** *Metall.* a mixture formed by fusion of two or more metals or of a metal and a nonmetal. **2.** anything that reduces purity. —*v.t.* (ə LOI) **1.** mix (metals) so as to form an alloy. **2.** modify or debase, as by mixture. [< MF *aloi* combine]

all right **1.** satisfactory. **2.** correct. **3.** uninjured. **4.** certainly. **5.** yes. —all-right (AWL rīt) *Informal adj.*

all-round (AWL rownd) *adj.* **1.** of comprehensive range of scope. **2.** excelling in all or many aspects. Also *all-around.*

All Saints' Day November 1, in some Christian churches a festival commemorative of all saints.

All Souls' Day November 2, in some Christian churches a day of commemoration for the souls of all deceased.

al•lude (ə LOOD) *v.i.* •lud•ed, •lud•ing make indirect or casual reference: with *to.* [< L *alludere* play beside] —al•lu•sion (ə LOO zhən) *n.* —al•lu•sive (ə LOO siv) *adj.*

al•lure (ə LUUR) *v.t. & v.i.* •lured, •lur•ing attract; entice. —*n.* fascination, charm. [ME *aluren*]

al•lu•vi•um (ə LOO vee əm) *n. pl.* •vi•ums or •vi•a a deposit, as of sand or mud, transported and laid down by flowing water. [< L] —al•lu′vi•al *adj. & n.*

al•ly (ə LĪ) *v.t. & v.i.* •lied, •ly•ing unite by some relationship: with *to* or *with.* —*n. pl.* •lies **1.** a person, country, or organization associated with another. **2.** any friendly helper. [ME *alien* bind to]

al•ma ma•ter (AL mə MAH tər) the school one has attended. [< L, nourishing mother]

al•ma•nac (AWL mə nak) *n.* a publication giving information under headings dated for the year. [ME *almenak* calendar]

al•might•y (awl MĪ tee) *adj.* able to do all things. —the Almighty God; the Supreme Being. [ME]

al•mond (AH mənd) *n.* **1.** a small tree of the rose family, widely cultivated for its nuts. **2.** the kernel of the fruit of the almond tree. [ME *almande*]

al•most (AWL mohst) *adv.* approximately; very nearly; all but. [ME]

alms (ahms) *n. sing. & pl.* A gift for the poor. ◆ Collateral adjective: *eleemosynary.* [ME *almes*]

a•lo•ha (ə LOH ə) *n. & interj.* Hawaiian love: used as a salutation and a farewell.

a•lone (ə LOHN) *adv. & adj.* **1.** without company; solitary. **2.** excluding all others; only: He *alone* survived. [ME *al one* all one]

a·long (ə LAWNG) *adv.* **1.** progressively on-ward in a course: The years roll *along* quickly. **2.** in company; together. **3.** advanced in its natural course. —*prep.* throughout or over the length of. [ME]

a·long·side (ə LAWNG SĪD) *adv.* close to the side. —*prep.* side by side with.

a·loof (ə LOOF) *adj.* distant, esp. in manner; unsympathetic. —*adv.* apart: stand *aloof.*

alp (alp) *n.* a lofty mountain. [Back formation < Alps]

al·pac·a (al PAK ə) *n.* **1.** a domesticated ruminant of South America. **2.** its wool, or cloth made of this wool. [< Sp.]

al·pen·stock (AL pən STOK) *n.* an iron-pointed staff used by mountain climbers. [< G]

al·pha (AL fə) *n.* **1.** the first letter in the Greek alphabet (A, α), corresponding to English *a.* **2.** the first of anything.

al·pha·bet (AL fə bet) *n.* the letters that form a written language, in an order fixed by custom. [ME *alphabete*] — **al·pha·bet·i·cal** (AL fə BET i kəl) *adj.*

al·pha·bet·ize (AL fə bə TĪZ) *v.t.* •ized, •iz·ing put in alphabetical order. — **al·pha·bet·i·za·tion** (AL fə BET ə ZAY shən) *n.*

al·pha·nu·mer·ic (AL fə noo MER ik) *adj.* consisting of the letters of the alphabet and numerals, as a computer code.

alpha rhythm *Physiol.* a form of brain wave associated with awake relaxation: also **al-pha wave.**

al·pine (AL pīn) *adj. Biol.* inhabiting or growing in mountain regions.

Al·pine (AL pīn) *adj.* pertaining to or char-acteristic of the Alps. [< L *Alpinus*]

al·read·y (awl RED ee) *adv.* before or by the time mentioned.

al·so (AWL soh) *adv.* in addition; besides; likewise. [ME, all so]

al·so-ran (AWL soh RAN) *n. Informal* an un-successful competitor.

al·tar (AWL tər) *n.* a raised place or struc-ture regarded as the center of worship. [ME *alter*]

altar boy an attendant at the altar; acolyte.

al·tar·piece (AWL tər PEES) *n.* a work of art over and behind an altar.

al·ter (AWL tər) *v.t.* **1.** cause to be different. **2.** castrate or spay. —*v.i.* **3.** change. [< L, other] —**al·ter·a·tion** (AWL tə RAY shən) *n.*

al·ter·ca·tion (AWL tər KAY shən) *n.* a heated dispute.

al·ter e·go (AWL tər EE goh) **1.** another self; a double. **2.** an intimate friend. [< L, lit., other I]

al·ter·nate (AWL tər nayt) *v.t. & v.i.* •nat·ed, •nat·ing follow or make to follow by turns, as in place, condition, etc. —*adj.* (AWL tər nit) **1.** occurring or following by turns. **2.** referring to every other of a series. —*n.* (AWL tər nit) a substitute or second. [< L *alternatus*] —**al'ter·na'tion** *n.*

alternating current *Electr.* a current that reverses its direction of flow at regular in-tervals.

al·ter·na·tive (awl TUR nə tiv) *n.* **1.** a choice between two things. **2.** one of two or more things to be chosen. —**al·ter'na·tive** *adj.*

al·ter·na·tor (AWL tər NAY tər) *n. Electr.* a generator giving an alternating current.

al·though (awl THOH) *conj.* notwithstand-ing the fact that. [ME *al thogh*]

al·tim·e·ter (al TIM ə tər) *n.* an instrument for measuring altitude.

al·ti·tude (AL tə tood) *n.* **1.** elevation above any given point, esp. above mean sea level; height. **2.** *Astron.* angular elevation above the horizon. **3.** *Geom.* the vertical distance from the base of a figure to its highest point. [ME]

al·to (AL toh) *Music n. pl.* •tos **1.** a musical part for the lower range of the female voice. **2.** a voice or instrument that performs this part. [< Ital.]

al·to·geth·er (AWL tə GETH ər) *adv.* **1.** completely; wholly. **2.** with everything in-cluded; without exception. —**in the alto-gether** *Informal* nude.

al·tru·ism (AL troo IZ əm) *n.* selfless devo-tion to the welfare of others. [< F *altru-isme*] —**al'tru·ist** *n.* —**al'tru·is'tic** *adj.*

a·lu·mi·num (ə LOO mə nəm) *n.* a light, bluish white, malleable, ductile metallic el-ement found only in combination.

a·lum·na (ə LUM nə) *n. pl.* •nae (-nee) a female graduate of a school. [< L, foster daughter]

a·lum·nus (ə LUM nəs) *n. pl.* •ni (-nī) a male graduate of a school. [< L, foster son]

al·ways (AWL wayz) *adv.* **1.** perpetually; for all time. **2.** at every time. [ME *always*]

Alz·hei·mer's disease (AHLTS HIM mərz) a form of dementia beginning late in mid-dle age, characterized by lapses of memory and progressive loss of mental ability. [named after Alois Alzheimer, the neurolo-gist who first described it]

am (am, *unstressed* əm) present indicative, first person singular, of BE [ME]

a·mah (AH mə) *n.* in India and the Orient, a female attendant for children; esp., a wet nurse. [< Pg. *ama* nurse]

a·mal·gam (ə MAL gəm) *n.* **1.** an alloy of mercury with another metal. **2.** any combination of two or more things. [ME *amalgame* softener]

a·mal·ga·mate (ə MAL gə mayt) *v.t. & v.i.* **·mat·ed, ·mat·ing 1.** form an amalgam. **2.** unite or combine. —**a·mal'ga·ma'tion** *n.*

a·man·u·en·sis (ə MAN yoo EN sis) *n. pl.* **·ses** (-seez) one who copies manuscript or takes dictation; secretary. [< L *(servus) amanuensis* hand (servant)]

am·a·ryl·lis (AM ə RIL is) *n.* a bulbous plant, producing large, lilylike flowers. [< L, fem. personal name]

a·mass (ə MAS) *v.t.* accumulate, as riches. [< F *amasser* pile up]

am·a·teur (AM ə CHUUR) *n.* **1.** one who practices an art, sport, or science for pleasure, without pay. **2.** one who is not expert. [< F] —**am'a·teur·ism** (AM ə chuu RIZ əm) *n.*

am·a·teur·ish (AM ə CHUUR ish) *adj.* lacking the skill of an expert or professional.

am·a·to·ry (AM ə TOR ee) *adj.* pertaining to or exciting sexual love. [< L *amatorius*]

a·maze (ə MAYZ) *v.t.* **a·mazed, a·maz·ing** overwhelm, as by wonder; astonish. [ME *amasen*] —**a·maze'·ment** *n.*

Am·a·zon (AM ə zon) *n.* **1.** in Greek mythology, one of a race of female warriors. **2.** any physically strong and aggressive woman or girl: also **amazon.** [< L]

am·bas·sa·dor (am BAS ə dər) *n.* **1.** a diplomat of the highest rank, representing one government to another. **2.** a personal representative. [ME *ambassadour*] —**am·bas'sa·do'ri·al** *adj.*

am·ber (AM bər) *n.* **1.** a brownish yellow fossilized vegetable resin, used in jewelry, etc. **2.** the color of amber. [ME *ambre* ambergris]

am·ber·gris (AM bər GREES) *n.* a secretion of the sperm whale, used in perfumery. [< MF *ambre gris* gray amber]

am·bi·ance (AM bee əns) *n.* surroundings, esp. the pervading atmosphere. Also **am'bi·ence.** [< F]

am·bi·dex·trous (AM bə DEK strəs) *adj.* able to use both hands equally well. [< L *ambi-* both + *dexter* right (hand)] —

am·bi·dex·ter·i·ty (AM bi dek STER i tee) *n.*

am·bi·ent (AM bee ənt) *adj.* surrounding; compassing. [< L *ambiens* going around]

am·big·u·ous (am BIG yoo əs) *adj.* **1.** capable of being understood in more senses than one. **2.** doubtful or uncertain. [< L *ambiguus* uncertain] —**am'bi·gu'i·ty** *n.*

am·bi·tion (am BISH ən) *n.* **1.** eager desire to succeed. **2.** the object of aspiration. [ME *ambicioun*]

am·bi·tious (am BISH əs) *adj.* **1.** actuated or characterized by ambition. **2.** challenging: an *ambitious* project.

am·biv·a·lent (am BIV ə lənt) *adj.* experiencing or marked by contradictory emotions. [< L *ambi-* both + *valere* be strong] —**am·biv'a·lence** *n.*

am·ble (AM bəl) *v.i.* **·bled, ·bling** walk or proceed leisurely. —*n.* a certain easy gait, esp. of a horse. [ME] —**am'bler** *n.*

am·bro·sia (am BROH zhə) *n.* **1.** in classical mythology, the food of the gods. **2.** any delicious food or drink. [< L] —**am·bro'sial** *adj.*

am·bu·lance (AM byə ləns) *n.* a vehicle equipped for conveying the sick and wounded. [< F]

am·bu·lant (AM byə lənt) *adj.* walking or moving about.

am·bu·la·to·ry (AM byə lə TOR ee) *adj.* **1.** of or for walking. **2.** able to walk, as an invalid. [< L *ambulatorius*]

am·bus·cade (AM bəs KAYD) *n.* an ambush. —*v.t.* **·cad·ed, ·cad·ing** ambush. [< MF *embouscade*]

am·bush (AM buush) *n.* **1.** an attack from hiding. **2.** a position for surprise attack. —*v.t.* attack from hiding. [ME *enbusshen*]

a·me·ba (ə MEE bə) *n. pl.* **·bas** or **·bae** (-bee) a unicellular protozoan found in soil and stagnant water, of indefinite and changing shape, and reproducing by division: also spelled *amoeba.* [< NL *amoeba*] —**a·me·boid** (ə MEE boid) *adj.* also **amoeboid.**

a·mel·io·rate (ə MEEL yə rayt) *v.t. & v.i.* **·rat·ed, ·rat·ing** make or become better. [< L *ad-* to + *meliorare* better] —**a·mel'io·ra·ble** (-yər ə bəl) *adj.* —**a·mel'io·ra·tive** (-yə rə tiv) *adj.*

a·men (AY MEN) *interj.* expressing solemn affirmation, usu. at the end of a prayer. [ME]

a·me·na·ble (ə MEE nə bəl) *adj.* **1.** capable

of being persuaded. **2.** liable to be called to account. [< AF]

a·mend (ə MEND) *v.t.* **1.** change for the better; improve. **2.** change or alter by authority. [ME *amenden* correct]

a·mend·ment (ə MEND mənt) *n.* **1.** a removal of faults; correction. **2.** a changing, as of a law. **3.** the statement of such a change.

a·mends (ə MENDS) *n.pl.* reparation: make *amends* for. [ME *amendes*]

a·men·i·ty (ə MEN i tee) *n. pl.* •ties **1.** agreeableness; pleasantness. **2.** *Usu. pl.* an act or expression of courtesy; civility. **3.** *pl.* comforts; conveniences. [ME *amenite*]

A·mer·i·can (ə MER i kən) *adj.* **1.** pertaining to the United States of America. **2.** pertaining to North or South America. —*n.* **1.** a citizen of the United States. **2.** an inhabitant of America.

A·mer·i·ca·na (ə MER i KAN ə) *n.pl.* American artifacts, literary papers, etc., esp. in a historical collection.

A·mer·i·can·ism (ə MER i kə NIZ əm) *n.* **1.** a trait, custom, or tradition especially characteristic of the United States. **2.** a usage characteristic of American English.

A·mer·i·can·ize (ə MER i kə NIZ) *v.t. & v.i.* •ized, •iz·ing make or become American in spirit, methods, speech, etc.

am·e·thyst (AM ə thist) *n.* a purple quartz or corundum used as a gem. [< L *amethystus*]

a·mi·a·ble (AY mee ə bəl) *adj.* **1.** pleasing in disposition; kindly. **2.** free from irritation; friendly: an *amiable* rivalry. [ME] — **a'mi·a·bil'i·ty** *n.*

am·i·ca·ble (AM ikə bəl) *adj.* friendly; peaceable. [ME] —**am'i·ca·bil'i·ty** *n.*

a·mid (ə MID) *prep.* in the midst of; among. Also *amidst, midst.* [ME *amidde*]

a·miss (ə MIS) *adj.* out of order; improper: used predicatively: Something is *amiss.* —*adv.* erroneously. [ME *amis*]

am·i·ty (AM i tee) *n.* peaceful relations, as between nations. [ME *amite*]

am·mo·nia (ə MOHN yə) *n.* a colorless, pungent, suffocating gas, obtained chiefly by synthesis from nitrogen and hydrogen. [< NL]

am·mu·ni·tion (AM yə NISH ən) *n.* **1.** any of various articles used in the discharge of firearms and ordnance, as cartridges, shells, etc. **2.** any resources for attack or defense. [< MF *amonitions* military supplies]

am·ne·sia (am NEE zhə) *n.* partial or total loss or impairment of memory. [< NL, oblivion]

am·nes·ty (AM nəs tee) *n. pl.* •ties a general pardon by which a government absolves offenders. [MF *amnestie* forgetting] —**am' nes·ty** *v.t.* •tied, •ty·ing pardon.

am·ni·o·cen·te·sis (AM nee oh sen TEE sis) *n. pl.* •ses (-seez) *Med.* the insertion of a hollow needle into the amnion and the withdrawal of fluid in order to diagnose disorders of the fetus or determine its sex.

am·ni·on (AM nee ən) *n. pl.* •ni·ons or •ni·a (-nee ə) *Biol.* a membraneous sac, filled with a fluid (**amniotic fluid**), and enclosing the embryo or fetus of mammals, birds, and reptiles. [< Gk.] —**am'ni·ot'ic** *adj.*

a·moe·ba (ə MEE bə) see AMEBA.

a·mok (ə MUK) see AMUCK.

a·mong (ə MUNG) *prep.* **1.** in the midst of. **2.** in or by the class, number, or group of: He was *among* the dead. **3.** in portions for each of: Divide it *among* you. **4.** reciprocally between: disputes *among* friends. [ME]

a·mor·al (ay MOR əl) *adj.* not subject to or concerned with moral or ethical values. — **a·mo·ral·i·ty** (AY mə RAL i tee) *n.*

am·o·rous (AM ər əs) *adj.* **1.** tending to fall in love; loving. **2.** of or related to sexual love. **3.** in love; enamored; often with *of: amorous* of the truth. [ME]

a·mor·phous (ə MOR fəs) *adj.* without definite form or character. [< Gk. *ámorphos* formless]

am·or·tize (AM ər tīz) *v.t.* •tized, •tiz·ing extinguish gradually, as a debt or liability, by installment payments or by a sinking fund. [ME *amortisen* extinguish] —**am·or·ti·za·tion** (AM ər tə ZAY shən) *n.*

a·mount (ə MOWNT) *n.* **1.** a sum total of two or more quantities. **2.** the value of the principal with the interest upon it, as in a loan. **3.** the entire significance, value, or effect. **4.** quantity: a considerable *amount* of discussion. —*v.i.* **1.** reach in number or quantity: with *to: amount* to ten dollars. **2.** be equivalent in effect or importance: with *to:* It *amounts* to treason. [ME *amounten* ascend]

a·mour (ə MOOR) *n.* a love affair, esp. a secret or illicit one. [< F]

am·per·sand (AM pər SAND) *n.* the character &, meaning *and.* [< *and per se and,* lit., & by itself and]

am·phet·a·mine (am FET ə meen) *n.* an acrid liquid compound, or one of its derivatives, used as a stimulant.

am•phib•i•an (am FIB ee ən) *adj.* **1.** *Zool.* of or pertaining to a class of cold-blooded, chiefly egg-laying vertebrates adapted for life both on land and in water, as frogs. **2.** amphibious. —*n.* **1.** an amphibian animal or plant. **2.** an airplane capable of operating from land or water. **3.** a vehicle capable of self-propulsion on land or water.

am•phib•i•ous (am FIB ee əs) *adj.* **1.** adapted to life on land or in water. **2.** capable of operating on or from land or water. [< L *amphibius*, lit., leading a double life]

am•phi•the•a•ter (AM fə THEE ə tər) *n.* an oval or round structure having tiers of seats around an arena. [< L *amphitheatrum*]

am•pho•ra (AM phə rə) *n. pl.* •rae (-ree) in ancient Greece and Rome, a tall, two-handled earthenware jar, narrow at the neck and the base. [ME]

am•ple (AM pəl) *adj.* **1.** of great dimension, capacity, amount, degree, etc.; large. **2.** more than enough; abundant. [ME, large]

am•pli•fy (AM plə FI) *v.* •fied, •fy•ing *v.t.* **1.** enlarge or increase in scope, significance, or power. **2.** add to so as to make more complete, as by illustrations. **3.** exaggerate; magnify. —*v.i.* **4.** make additional remarks. [ME *amplifyen* increase] —**am'pli•fi•ca'tion** *n.*

am•pli•tude (AM pli TOOD) *n.* **1.** greatness of extent; largeness; breadth. **2.** fullness; abundance. [< L *amplitudo*]

am•pule (AM pyool) *n. Med.* a sealed vial used as a container for one dose of a hypodermic solution. Also **ampoule.** [< F]

am•pu•tate (AM pyuu TAYT) *v.t. & v.i.* •tat•ed, •tat•ing cut off (a limb, etc.) by surgery. [< L *amputatus* trimmed] —**am'pu•ta'tion** *n.*

am•pu•tee (AM pyuu TEE) *n.* one who has had a limb or limbs amputated.

a•muck (ə MUK) *adv.* in a murderous frenzy: only in the phrase **to run amuck.** Also **amok.** [< Malay *amoq* furious attack]

am•u•let (AM yə lit) *n.* anything worn as a charm against danger. [< MF *amulete*]

a•muse (ə MYOOZ) *v.t.* **a•mused, a•mus•ing 1.** occupy pleasingly. **2.** cause to laugh or smile. [< MF *amuser*] **a•mus'ing** *adj.*

an (an, *unstreesed* ən) *indefinite article or adj.* equivalent to the article *a,* but used before words beginning with a vowel sound, as *an* eagle, and sometimes before words beginning with *h* in an unstressed syllable, as *an* historian. [ME]

a•nab•o•lism (ə NAB ə LIZ əm) *n. Biol.* the process by which food is converted into protoplasm: opposed to *catabolism.* —**an•a•bol•ic** (AN ə BOL ik) *adj.*

anabolic steroid a synthetic derivative of the male sex hormone used by some athletes to increase their weight and strength.

a•nach•ro•nism (ə NAK rə NIZ əm) *n.* **1.** the assigning of an event, person, etc., to a wrong, esp. an earlier, date. **2.** something out of its proper time. [< L *anachronismus*] —**a•nach'ro•nis'tic** *adj.*

an•aer•o•bic (AN ə ROH bik) *adj.* living or functioning in the absence of free oxygen.

an•aes•the•sia (AN is THEE *zh*ə) see ANESTHESIA.

an•a•gram (AN ə gram) *n.* **1.** a word or phrase formed by transposing the letters of another word or phrase. **2.** *pl. (construed as sing.)* a game in which the players make words by transposing or adding letters.

a•nal (AYN l) *adj. Anat.* of, pertaining to, or situated in the region of the anus.

an•al•ge•sic (AN əl JEE zik) *n.* a drug for the alleviation of pain. —*adj.* of or pertaining to a drug having this effect.

a•nal•o•gous (ə NAL ə gəs) *adj.* **1.** resembling or comparable in certain respects. **2.** *Biol.* having a similar function but differing in origin and structure, as the wings of birds and insects: distinguished from *homologous.* [< L *analogus* proportionate]

an•a•logue (AN ə lawg) *n.* anything analogous to something else. Also **analog.** [< F]

a•nal•o•gy (ə NAL ə jee) *n. pl.* •gies **1.** agreement or resemblance in certain aspects. **2.** *Logic* inference that items showing some resemblances will show others. [< L *analogia*]

a•nal•y•sis (ə NAL ə sis) *n. pl.* •ses (-seez) **1.** the separation of a whole into its parts or elements: opposed to *synthesis.* **2.** a statement of the results of this. **3.** a method of determining or describing the nature of a thing by separating it into its parts. **4.** psychoanalysis [< NL] —**an•a•lyt•ic** (AN ə LIT ik) or •**i•cal** *adj.*

an•a•lyst (AN ə list) *n.* **1.** one who analyzes or is skilled in analysis. **2.** a psychoanalyst.

an•a•lyze (AN l IZ) *v.t.* •lyzed, •lyz•ing **1.** separate into constituent parts or elements, esp. determine the nature, form, etc., of the whole. **2.** examine critically or minutely. **3.** psychoanalyze.

an•a•pest (AN ə pest) *n.* **1.** in prosody, a metrical foot consisting of two short or unaccented syllables followed by one long or accented syllable. **2.** a line of verse made up of such feet. [< L *anapaestus* struck back] —**an'a•pes'tic** *adj.*

an•ar•chism (AN ər KIZ əm) *n.* **1.** the theory that all forms of government are incompatible with individual and social liberty and should be abolished. **2.** the methods of anarchists. —**an'ar•chist** *n.*

an•ar•chy (AN ər kee) *n.* **1.** absence of government. **2.** lawless confusion and political disorder. **3.** general disorder. [< MF *anarchie* lawlessness] —**an•ar•chic** (an AR kik) *adj.*

a•nath•e•ma (ə NATH ə mə) *n. pl.* **•mas 1.** a formal ban or curse, as excommunication. **2.** one who or that which is cursed or shunned. [< L, a thing cursed]

a•nath•e•ma•tize (ə NATH ə mə TIZ) *v.t.* **•TIZED, •TIZ•ING** pronounce an anathema against; curse.

a•nat•o•mize (ə NAT ə mīz) *v.t.* **•mized, •miz•ing 1.** dissect (an animal or plant) to investigate its structure. **2.** examine minutely; analyze.

a•nat•o•my (ə NAT ə mee) *n. pl.* **•mies 1.** the structure of a plant or animal, or of any of its parts. **2.** the science of the structure of plants or animals. [ME] —**an•a•tom•i•cal** (AN ə TOM i kəl) *adj.*

an•ces•tor (AN ses tər) *n.* **1.** one from whom a person or other organism is biologically descended. **2.** anything considered as a forerunner of a later thing. [ME *ancestre*]

an•ces•try (AN ses tree) *n. pl.* **•tries** a line or body of ancestors; ancestors collectively. —**an•ces'tral** *adj.*

an•chor (ANG kər) *n.* **1.** a heavy implement, usu. of iron or steel, with hooks or flukes to grip the bottom, attached to a cable and dropped from a ship or boat to hold it in place. **2.** anything that makes stable or secure. **3.** anchorperson. —*v.t.* **1.** secure by an anchor. **2.** fix firmly. —*v.i.* **3.** lie at anchor, as a ship. [ME *anker*]

an•chor•age (ANG kər ij) *n.* a place for anchoring.

an•cho•rite (ANG kə RIT) *n.* one who has withdrawn from the world for religious reasons; hermit. [ME]

an•chor•per•son (ANG kər PUR sən) *n.* a broadcaster who coordinates and comments on reports by other broadcasters.

an•cho•vy (AN choh vee) *n. pl.* **•vies** a very small, herringlike fish inhabiting warm seas, valued as a delicacy. [< F *anchois*]

an•cient (AYN shənt) *adj.* **1.** existing or oc-

curring in times long past, esp. before the fall of the Western Roman Empire, in A.D. 476. **2.** very old. —*n.* **1.** one who lived in ancient times. **2.** an aged or venerable person. [ME *auncien*]

an•cil•lar•y (AN sə LER ee) *adj.* subordinate; auxiliary. [< L *ancilla* female slave]

and (and, *unstressed* ənd, ən, n) *conj.* **1.** also; added to; as well as: a particle denoting addition, emphasis, or union, used as a connective between words, phrases, clauses, and sentences. **2.** as a result or consequence: Make one move *and* you are dead! **3.** to: with *come, go, try,* etc.: Try *and* stop me. [ME]

and•i•ron (AND I ərn) *n.* one of two metal supports for holding wood in an open fireplace. [ME *aundyrne*]

and/or (AND OR) either *and* or or, according to the meaning intended.

an•dro•gen (AN drə jən) *n. Biochem.* any of various hormones that control the development of masculine characteristics.

an•drog•y•nous (an DROJ ə nəs) *adj.* having the characteristics of both sexes; hermaphroditic. [< L *androgynus* hermaphrodite] —**an•drog'y•ny** *n.*

an•droid (AN droid) *n.* an automaton in the form of a human being. [< NL *androides*]

an•ec•dote (AN ik DOHT) *n.* a brief story of an interesting or entertaining nature. [< NL *anecdota* unpublished things] —**an'ec•dot'al** *adj.* **an'ec•dot'ist** *n.*

a•ne•mi•a (ə NEE mee ə) *n. Pathol.* a deficiency in hemoglobin or the number of red corpuscles in the blood. [< NL] —**a•ne'mic** *adj.*

an•e•mom•e•ter (AN ə MOM ə tər) *n. Meteorol.* an instrument for measuring the velocity and direction of the wind.

a•nem•o•ne (ə NEM ə nee) *n.* **1.** a plant having flowers with no petals but showy, multicolored sepals. **2.** *Zool.* the sea anemone. [< L, daughter of the wind]

an•es•the•sia (AN is THEE zhə) *n.* partial or total loss of physical sensation, particularly of pain, due to disease or certain drugs: also spelled *anaesthesia.* [< NL]

an•es•the•si•ol•o•gy (AN əs THEE zee OL ə jee) *n. Med.* the science of using anesthetics. —**an'es•the•si•ol'o•gist** *n.*

an•es•thet•ic (AN is THET ik) *n.* a drug, gas, etc., that causes anesthesia. —*adj.* producing anesthesia. —**an•es•the•tist** (ə NES thə tist) *n.* —**an•es•the•tize** (ə NES thə TIZ) *v.t.* **•tized, •tiz•ing**

an•eu•rysm (AN yə RIZ əm) *n. Pathol.* a swelling of the wall of an artery, forming a sac. Also **an′eu•rism.** [< Gk. *anaeurysma* dilation]

a•new (ə NOO) *adv.* **1.** again. **2.** over again in a different way. [ME *onew*]

an•gel (AYN jəl) *n.* **1.** *Theol.* a spiritual being attendant upon the Deity; a heavenly messenger. **2.** a person likened to an angel in qualities of goodness, beauty, etc. **3.** *Informal* a financial backer, as of a play, etc. [ME *aungel*]

an•gel•ic (an JEL ik) *adj.* **1.** oertaining to, of, or consisting of angels; celestial. **2.** like an angel; pure; beautiful.

an•ge•lus (AN jə ləs) *n. Eccl.* **1.** a prayer used to commemorate the Annunciation. **2.** a bell rung at morning, noon, and night as a call to recite this prayer. [< L]

an•ger (ANG gər) *n.* a feeling of strong displeasure and antagonism directed against the cause of an assumed wrong or injury. — *v.t. & v.i.* make or become angry or enraged. [ME]

an•gi•na (an JĪ nə) *n. Pathol.* **1.** any disease characterized by spasmodic suffocation, as croup. **2.** angina pectoris. [< L, quinsy]

angina pec•to•ris (PEK tə ris) *Pathol.* a defect of coronary circulation, characterized by paroxysmal pain below the breast bone. [< NL, angina of the chest]

an•gi•o•sperm (AN jee ə SPURM) *n.* any of a class of plants having the seeds in a closed seed vessel.

an•gle[1] (ANG gəl) *v.i.* **•gled, •gling 1.** fish with a hook and line. **2.** try to get something slyly or artfully: with *for.* —*n.* **1.** a selfish motive. **2.** a devious method for achieving a purpose. [ME]

an•gle[2] *n.* **1.** *Geom.* **a** the figure or space made by the meeting of two straight lines or two plane surfaces. **b** the arc of rotation between these lines or surfaces, measured in degrees. **2.** a projecting corner, as of a building. **3.** the direction from which a thing is seen. —*v.t. & v.i.* **•gled, •gling** move or turn at an angle or by angles. [ME]

An•gle *n.* a member of a Germanic tribe that migrated to Britain in the 5th c. [< OE]

angle of incidence *Physics* the angle relative to the perpendicular drawn from the point at which an object, beam of light, etc., strikes a surface.

an•gler (ANG glər) *n.* **1.** one who fishes with rod, hook, and line. **2.** one who schemes to obtain something.

An•gli•can (ANG glə kən) *adj.* of the Church of England, or of the churches that agree with it in faith and order. —*n.* a member of an Anglican Church. [< Med.L *Anglicanus*]

Anglican Church 1. the Church of England. **2.** a body of churches mostly derived from the Church of England and in communion with it. —**An′gli•can•ism** *n.*

An•gli•cism (ANG glə SIZ əm) *n.* an idiom or turn of phrase peculiar to the English language.

An•gli•cize (ANG glə SĪZ) *v.t.* **•cized, •ciz•ing** give an English form, style, or idiom to. —**An′gli•ci•za′tion** *n.*

an•gling (ANG gling) *n.* the act or art of fishing with a hook, line, and rod.

An•glo•phile (ANG glə FĪL) *n.* an admirer of England or its people, customs, institutions, or manners.

An•glo•pho•bi•a (ANG glə FOH bee ə) *n.* hatred or dread of England or its customs, people, or institutions. —**An′glo•phobe** *n.*

An•glo-Sax•on (ANG gloh SAK sən) *n.* **1.** a member of one of the Germanic tribes (Angles, Saxons, and Jutes) that dominated England from the 5th to 12th c. **2.** their West Germanic language; Old English. See under ENGLISH. **3.** a person of English nationality or descent. —**An′glo-Sax′on** *adj.*

an•go•ra (ang GOR ə) *n.* **1.** a goat having long, silky hair. **2.** its wool, or yarn or cloth made of its wool: Also **Angora. 3.** a variety of cat (**Angora cat**) with long, silky hair.

an•gry (ANG gree) *adj.* **an•gri•er, an•gri•est** feeling or showing anger; wrathful. —**an•gri•ly** (ANG grə lee) *adv.*

ang•strom (ANG strəm) *n.* a linear unit equal to 10^{-8} centimeter, used for minute measurements, as of wavelengths of light. [after A.J. *Angström*, 1814–75, Swedish physicist]

an•guish (ANG gwish) *n.* excruciating mental or bodily pain; agony. —*v.i.* suffer anguish. [ME *anguisse* difficulty] —**an′guished** *adj.*

an•gu•lar (ANG gyə lər) *adj.* **1.** having, forming, or constituting an angle; sharp-cornered. **2.** measured by an angle. **3.** pertaining to angles. **4.** bony; gaunt. [< L *angularis*] —**an′gu•lar′i•ty** (-LAR i tee) *n.*

an•hy•drous (an HĪ drəs) *adj.* without water. [< Gk. *ánydros* waterless]

an•i•mad•ver•sion (AN ə mad VUR *zh*ən) *n.* a censorious comment or reflection. [< L]

an·i·mad·vert (AN ə mad VURT) *v.i.* comment critically, usu. in an adverse sense: with *on* or *upon*. [< L *animadvertere* heed]

an·i·mal (AN ə məl) *n.* **1.** a sentient living organism typically capable of voluntary motion and sensation: distinguished from *plant*. **2.** any such creature as distinguished from a human being. **3.** a bestial human being. —*adj.* **1.** of or resembling animals. **2.** carnal; sensual: *animal* appetites. [ME]

an·i·mal·ism (AN ə mə LIZ əm) *n.* **1.** bestial sensuality. **2.** the doctrine that a human being is entirely animal, having no soul. — **an'i·mal·is'tic** *adj.*

animal kingdom animal organisms collectively, as distinguished from plants.

an·i·mate (AN ə MAYT) *v.t.* •**mat·ed,** •**mat·ing 1.** impart life to; make alive. **2.** move to action. **3.** produce the illusion of motion in (a projected film) by a series of drawings. —*adj.* (AN ə mit) **1.** possessing animal life; living. **2.** full of life; vivacious; lively: also **an'i·mat'ed.** [ME *animat*]

an·i·ma·tion (AN ə MAY shən) *n.* **1.** the act of imparting life, or the state of possessing life. **2.** the quality of being lively or quick; vivacity. **3.** the making of animated films.

an·i·mism (AN ə MIZ əm) *n.* the doctrine that natural objects and phenomena possess souls. —**an'i·mist** *n.*

an·i·mos·i·ty (AN ə MOS í tee) *n. pl.* •**ties** active and vehement enmity; hatred. [ME *animosite*]

an·i·mus (AN ə məs) *n.* hostile feeling; animosity. [< L]

an·i·on (AN I ən) *n. Chem.* a negative ion: opposed to *cation*. [< Gk.]

an·ise (AN is) *n.* a small South European and North African plant that furnishes a fragrant seed (**aniseed**) used for flavoring. [ME *anis*]

an·i·sette (AN ə SET) *n.* a cordial made from or flavored with aniseed. [< F]

an·kle (ANG kəl) *n.* **1.** the joint connecting the foot and the leg. **2.** the part of the leg between the foot and the calf near the ankle joint. [ME *ankel*]

an·kle·bone (ANG kəl BOHN) *n.* the talus.

an·klet (ANG klit) *n.* **1.** an ornament or fetter for the ankle. **2.** a short sock reaching just above the ankle.

an·nals (AN əlz) *n.pl.* **1.** a record of events in their chronological order, year by year. **2.** history or records. **3.** a periodical publication of discoveries, transactions, etc. [< L *annales* yearly] —**an'nal·ist** *n.*

an·neal (ə NEEL) *v.t.* **1.** reduce the brittleness of, as glass and various metals, by heating and then slowly cooling. **2.** toughen, as the will. [ME *anelen* kindle]

an·ne·lid (AN ə lid) *Zool. n.* any segmented worm, including the earthworm and the leech.

an·nex (ə NEKS) *v.t.* **1.** append, as an addition. **2.** incorporate (territory) into a larger political unit. —*n.* (AN eks) an addition to a building. [ME]

an·ni·hi·late (ə NI ə LAYT) *v.t.* •**lat·ed,** •**lat·ing** destroy utterly. [ME *adnichilate* destroyed] —**an·ni'hi·la'tion** *n.*

an·ni·ver·sa·ry (AN ə VUR sər ee) *n. pl.* •**ries 1.** a date on which an event occurred in some preceding year. **2.** a celebration on such occasion. [ME *anniversarie*]

an·no Dom·i·ni (AN oh DOM ə nee) in the (designated) year of the Christian era. [< L, in the year of the Lord] *Abbr. A.D.*

an·no·tate (AN ə TAYT) *v.t. & v.i.* •**tat·ed,** •**tat·ing** provide (a text, etc.) with explanatory or critical notes. [< L *annotatus* noted down] —**an'no·ta'tion** *n.*

an·nounce (ə NOWNS) *v.t.* •**nounced,** •**nounc·ing 1.** make known publicly or officially; proclaim. **2.** give notice of the approach or arrival of. [< MF *anoncer*] —**an·nounce'ment** *n.*

an·nounc·er (ə NOWNS ər) *n.* **1.** one who announces. **2.** a person who identifies the station, introduces programs, etc., on radio or television.

an·noy (ə NOI) *v.t.* be troublesome to; bother; irritate. [ME *annoien*]

an·noy·ance (ə NOI əns) *n.* **1.** one who or that which annoys. **2.** the act of annoying or the state of being annoyed.

an·noy·ing (ə NOI ing) *adj.* irritating; irksome.

an·nu·al (AN yoo əl) *adj.* **1.** returning, performed, or occurring every year. **2.** reckoned by the year. —*n.* **1.** a publication issued once a year. **2.** a plant living for one year or season. [< LL *annualis* yearly] —**an'nu·al·ly** *adv.*

an·nu·i·ty (ə NOO i tee) *n. pl.* •**ties 1.** an income other than salary, paid yearly. **2.** an investment plan that provides yearly payments. [< Med.L *annuitas*] —**an·nu·i·tant** (ə NOO i tnt) *n.*

an·nul (ə NUL) *v.t.* •**nulled,** •**nul·ling** put an end to; nullify, esp. a marriage. [ME] —**an·nul'ment** *n.*

an·nu·lar (AN yə lər) *adj.* ring-shaped.

an·nu·late (AN yə lit) *adj.* furnished with rings; ringed.

an·nu·lus (AN yə ləs) *n. pl.* **·li** (-lī) or **·lus·es** a ringlike body or space. [< L, ring]

an·nun·ci·ate (ə NUN see AYT) *v.t.* **·at·ed, ·at·ing** announce. [< Med.L *annunciatus* made known]

an·nun·ci·a·tion (ə NUN see AY shən) *n.* the act of announcing, or that which is announced; proclamation. —**the Annunciation** the announcement of the Incarnation to the Virgin Mary by an angel (*Luke* i 28–38); also, the festival (March 25) commemorating this event.

an·nun·ci·a·tor (ə NUN see AY tər) *n.* **1.** an announcer. **2.** an electrical indicator used in hotels, etc., that shows the source of calls.

an·ode (AN ohd) *n. Electr.* **1.** the positive electrode in an electrolytic cell. **2.** the plate of an electron tube toward which electrons are attracted. [< Gk. *ánodos* a way up]

an·o·dyne (AN ə dīn) *n. Med.* anything that relieves pain or soothes. [< L *anodynus* painless] —**an'o·dyne** *adj.*

a·noint (ə NOINT) *v.t.* apply oil or ointment to, esp. in a religious ceremony. [ME *anoynten*]

a·nom·a·lous (ə NOM ə ləs) *adj.* exceptional; abnormal. [< Med.L *anomalus* irregular]

a·nom·a·ly (ə NOM ə lee) *n. pl.* **·lies 1.** deviation from rule, type, or form; irregularity. **2.** anything anomalous.

a·non (ə NON) *adv.* **1.** in a little while; soon. **2.** at another time; again. [ME]

a·non·y·mous (ə NON ə məs) *adj.* **1.** having or bearing no name. **2.** of unknown authorship. [< L *anonymus*] —**an·o·nym·i·ty** (AN ə NIM i tee) *n.*

a·noph·e·les (ə NOF ə leez) *n.* a mosquito carrying the malaria parasite. [< NL]

an·o·rex·i·a (AN ə REK see ə) *n. Med.* loss of appetite. [< NL]

an·oth·er (ə NUTH ər) *adj. & pron.* **1.** an additional; one more. **2.** not the same; a different one. [ME]

an·swer (AN sər) *v.i.* **1.** reply or respond. **2.** be responsible or accountable: with *for* or *to.* **3.** serve the purpose. **4.** correspond or match, as in appearance: with *to.* —*v.t.* **5.** speak, write, or act in response or reply to. **6.** be sufficient for; fulfill. **7.** conform or correspond to; match. —*n.* **1.** a reply. **2.** any action in return or in kind; retaliation. **3.** a solution to a problem. [ME *andswarien*]

an·swer·a·ble (AN sər ə bəl) *adj.* **1.** accountable; responsible. **2.** that may be answered.

ant (ant) *n.* any of a family of small, usu. wingless insects that live in colonies. [ME *amete*]

ant·ac·id (ant AS id) *n.* a neutralizing remedy for stomach acidity.

ant·ag·o·nism (an TAG ə NIZ əm) *n.* active opposition or resistance; hostility. —**an·tag'o·nist** (-ə nist) *n.* —**an·tag'o·nis'tic** *adj.*

an·tag·o·nize (an TAG ə nīz) *v.t.* **·nized, ·niz·ing 1.** make unfriendly; make an enemy of. **2.** struggle against; oppose. [< Gk. *antagōnizesthai* contend]

Ant·arc·tic (ant AHRK tik) *adj.* of or relating to the South Pole, or the regions within the Antarctic Circle. [< L *antarcticus*]

an·te (AN tee) *v.t. & v.i.* **·ted** or **·teed, ·te·ing** in poker, put up (one's stake). —*n.* in poker, the stake put up before receiving the hand. [< L, before]

ante- *prefix* before in time, order, or position. [< L *ante* before]

Some self-explanatory words beginning with *ante-*:

ante-Christian	antenatal
antelocation	anteroom
antemarital	ante-Victorian

ant·eat·er (ANT EE tər) *n.* any of several mammals that feed on ants, as the aardvark.

an·te·bel·lum (AN tee BEL əm) *adj.* before the war; esp., before the Civil War in the United States. [< L *ante bellum*]

an·te·ce·dent (AN tə SEED nt) *adj.* prior; preceding. —*n.* **1.** one who or that which precedes. **2.** *Gram.* the word, phrase, or clause to which a pronoun refers. **3.** *pl.* one's past life, ancestry, etc. [ME] —**an'te·cede'** *v.t. & v.i.* **·ced·ed, ·ced·ing** —**an'te·ce'·dence** *n.*

an·te·cham·ber (AN ti CHAYM bər) *n.* a small room that leads to a larger or main room.

an·te·date (AN ti DAYT) *v.t.* **·dat·ed, ·dat·ing 1.** precede in time. **2.** assign to a date earlier than the actual one.

an·te·di·lu·vian (AN ti di LOO vee ən) *adj.* **1.** before the Biblical flood. **2.** antiquated; primitive. [< L *ante + diluvium* deluge]

an·te·lope (AN tl OHP) *n. pl.* **·lopes** or **·lope** any of various swift, hollow-horned animals, as the gazelle; also, leather made from its hide. [ME *antelop*]

an·te me·rid·i·em (AN tee mə RID ce əm) *Latin* before noon. Abbr. *a.m., A.M.*

an·ten·na (an TEN ə) *n. pl.* **·ten·nae** (-TEN ee) *for def. 1,* **·ten·nas** *for def. 2* **1.** *Entomol.* one of the paired sense organs on the head of an insect or other arthropod. **2.** *Telecom.* a system of wires, etc., for transmitting or receiving electromagnetic waves. [< L, sail yard]

an·te·pe·nult (AN ti PEE nult) *n.* the third syllable from the end of a word. [< L] —**an'te·pe·nul'ti·mate** (-pi NUL tə mit) *adj. & n.*

an·te·ri·or (an TEER ee ər) *adj.* **1.** earlier; prior. **2.** farther front or forward. [< L, compar. of *ante* before] —**an·te'ri·or·ly** *adv.*

an·them (AN thəm) *n.* **1.** a song or hymn of gladness or praise. **2.** a musical composition, usu. set to words from the Bible. [ME *antem*]

an·thol·o·gy (an THOL ə jee) *n. pl.* **·gies** a collection of literary pieces. [< L *anthologia*] —**an·thol'o·gize'** *v.t. & v.i.* **·gized, ·giz·ing**

an·thra·cite (AN thrə SĪT) *n.* coal that burns slowly and with great heat: also called *hard coal.*

an·thrax (AN thraks) *n. Pathol.* an infectious disease of cattle and sheep, sometimes fatal to people. [ME *antrax* boil]

anthropo- *combining form* man. Also, before vowels, **anthrop-.** [< Gk. *ánthrōpos* man]

an·thro·po·cen·tric (AN thrə poh SEN trik) *adj.* interpreting the universe in terms of human values.

an·thro·poid (AN thrə poid) *adj.* like a human being in form or other characteristics, as the gorilla and chimpanzee. —*n.* an ape.

an·thro·pol·o·gy (AN thrə POL ə jee) *n.* the science treating of the physical, social, material, and cultural development of man. —**an·thro·po·log·i·cal** (AN thrə pə LOJ i kəl) *adj.* —**an'thro·pol'o·gist** *n.*

an·thro·po·mor·phism (AN thrə pə MOR fiz əm) *n.* the ascription of human form or characteristics to a deity, or to any being or thing not human. —**an'thro·po·mor'phic** *adj.*

anti- *prefix*
1. against; opposed to:
anti-American	antinoise
antifeminism	antipollution

2. opposite to; reverse:
anticlockwise	antilogic
anticyclic	antipole

3. rivaling; spurious:
antiemperor	anti-Messiah

4. counteracting; curative; neutralizing:
antibacterial	anticolic
anticoagulant	antivirus

Also, before vowels, **ant-.** [< Gk. *anti* against]

an·ti·air·craft (AN tee AIR KRAFT) *adj.* used for defense against aircraft.

an·ti·bal·lis·tic missile (AN tee bə LIS tik) a missile designed to intercept and destroy a ballistic missile in flight.

an·ti·bi·ot·ic (AN ti bī OT ik) *n. Biochem.* any of a large class of substances derived from molds and soil bacteria, having the power of destroying or arresting the growth of microorganisms. —**an'ti·bi·ot'ic** *adj.*

an·ti·bod·y (AN ti BOD ee) *n. pl.* **·bod·ies** *Biochem.* any of a class of proteins serving to immunize the body against specific antigens.

an·tic (AN tik) *n.* **1.** *Usu. pl.* a prank; caper. **2.** a clown; buffoon. —*adj.* odd; fantastic; ludicrous. [< Ital. *antico* old, grotesque]

an·ti·christ (AN ti krīst) *n. Often cap.* a disbeliever in Christ or Christianity.

An·ti·christ *n.* the blasphemous antagonist of Christ. I *John* ii 18.

an·tic·i·pate (an TIS ə PAYT) *v.t.* **·pat·ed, ·pat·ing 1.** experience or realize beforehand. **2.** look forward to. **3.** act or arrive sooner than, esp. forestall. **4.** foresee and fulfill beforehand. [< L *anticipatus* anticipated] —**an·tic'i·pa·to·ry** (an TIS ə pə TOR ee) *adj.*

an·ti·cler·i·cal (AN tee KLER i kəl) *adj.* opposed to clerical influence in political and civic affairs.

an·ti·cli·max (AN ti KLĪ maks) *n.* **1.** in rhetoric, a ludicrous decrease in the importance or impressiveness of what is said. **2.** any similar descent or fall. —**an'ti·cli·mac'tic** *adj.*

an·ti·dote (AN ti DOHT) *n.* **1.** anything that will counteract the effects of poison. **2.** anything that similarly counteracts (something). [ME]

an·ti·freeze (AN ti FREEZ) *n.* a liquid of low freezing point, used in combustion-engine radiators to prevent freezing.

an·ti·gen (AN ti jen) *n. Biochem.* a toxin or other substance that causes the development of antibodies.

an·ti·his·ta·mine (AN ti HIS tə MEEN) *n. Med.* a drug that neutralizes the action of histamine, used to treat hay fever, asthma, etc.

an·ti·ma·cas·sar (AN ti mə KAS ər) *n.* a covering to protect the backs and arms of furniture.

an·ti·mo·ny (AN tə MOH nee) *n.* a silver-white, crystalline, metallic element (symbol Sb). [< Med.L *antimonium*]

an·ti·pas·to (AN ti PAH stoh) *n. pl.* •**tos** or •**pas·ti** (-PAHS tee) a course served as an appetizer. [< Ital.]

an·tip·a·thy (an TIP ə thee) *n. pl.* •**thies** 1. an instinctive feeling of aversion or dislike. 2. the object of such a feeling. [< L *antipathia*] —**an·ti·pa·thet·ic** (AN ti pə THET ik) *adj.*

an·ti·phon (AN tə FON) *n.* a verse of a psalm or hymn said or chanted in response to another. [< Med.L *antiphona* responsive singing] —**an·tiph·o·nal** (an TIF ə nəl) *adj.*

an·ti·pode (AN ti POHD) *n.* an exact opposite.

an·tip·o·des (an TIP ə DEEZ) *n.* (*construed as pl.*) 1. regions opposite one another, or their inhabitants. [ME] —**an·tip·o·dal** (an TIP ə dl) *adj.*

an·ti·quar·i·an (AN ti KWAIR ee ən) *adj.* pertaining to antiques or antiquaries. —*n.* an antiquary.

an·ti·quar·y (AN ti KWER ee) *n. pl.* •**quar·ies** one who collects, deals in, or studies antiques or antiquities.

an·ti·quate (AN ti KWAYT) *v.t.* •**quat·ed,** •**quat·ing** make old or out-of-date. [ME *antiquat* old]

an·ti·quat·ed (AN ti KWAY tid) *adj.* 1. out-of-date; old-fashioned; obsolete. 2. ancient; very old.

an·tique (an TEEK) *adj.* 1. of or pertaining to ancient times. 2. of an earlier period: an *antique* chair. 3. old-fashioned; out-of-date. —*n.* any old object, usu. one prized for its rarity, style or craft, etc. —*v.t.* **an·tiqued,** **an·ti·quing** give the appearance of an antique to. [< L *antiiquus* ancient]

an·tiq·ui·ty (an TIK wi tee) *n. pl.* •**ties** 1. the quality of being ancient. 2. ancient times, esp. before the Middle Ages. 3. *Usu. pl.* an ancient relic.

an·ti-Sem·i·tism (AN tee SEM i TIZ əm) *n.* discrimination against or intolerance of Jews, Jewish culture, etc. —**an'ti-Sem'ite** (-SEM it) *n.* —**an'ti-Se·mit'ic** (-sə MIT ik) *adj.*

an·ti·sep·tic (AN tə SEP tik) *adj.* 1. preventing or counteracting infection by destruction or inhibition of pathogenic microorganisms. 2. free of pathogenic microorganisms; aseptic. —*n.* any antiseptic substance.

an·ti·so·cial (AN tee SOH shəl) *adj.* 1. unsociable. 2. opposed to or disruptive of society.

an·tith·e·sis (an TITH ə sis) *n. pl.* •**ses** (-seez) 1. the balancing of two contrasted words, ideas, or phrases against each other. Example: *My prayers go up; my thoughts remain below.* 2. the direct opposite. [< L] —**an·ti·thet·i·cal** (AN tə THET i kəl) *adj.*

an·ti·tox·in (AN ti TOK sin) *n. Biochem.* an antibody formed in living tissues that neutralizes a specific toxin; also, serum containing this.

ant·ler (ANT lər) *n. Usu. pl.* either of the branched horns on the head of members of the deer family. [ME *aunteler*] —**ant'lered** *adj.*

an·to·nym (AN tə nim) *n.* a word that is the opposite of another in meaning: opposed to *synonym.*

a·nus (AY nəs) *n. Anat.* the excretory opening at the lower extremity of the alimentary canal. [< L, orig., ring]

an·vil (AN vil) *n.* 1. a heavy block of iron or steel on which metal may be forged. 2. *Anat.* the incus. [ME *anvelt*]

anx·i·e·ty (ang ZĪ ə tee) *n. pl.* •**ties** 1. disturbance of mind regarding some event; worry. 2. *Psychiatry* a tense emotional state characterized by fear and apprehension without apparent cause.

anx·ious (ANGK shəs) *adj.* 1. troubled in mind. 2. causing anxiety; distressing. 3. both eager and concerned: with *for* or *to.* [< L *anxius* distressed]

an·y (EN ee) *adj.* 1. one, no matter which; a or an, or (plural) some: Have we *any* choice? 2. some, however much or little: Did he eat *any* supper? 3. every: *Any* fool knows that. —*pron.* one or more of a number: Have *any* of the guests arrived? —*adv.* at all; to any extent: Are they *any* nearer? [ME *eni*]

an·y·bod·y (EN ee BOD ee) *pron.* any person whatever; anyone.

an·y·how (EN ee HOW) *adv.* 1. by whatever means. 2. notwithstanding; whatever the case.

an·y·one (EN ee wun) *pron.* any person.

an·y·thing (EN ee thing) *pron.* any object, event, or matter whatever.

an•y•way (EN ee WAY) *adv.* **1.** in any manner. **2.** nevertheless; anyhow.

an•y•where (EN ee HWAIR) *adv.* in, at, or to any place.

an•y•wise (EN ee WIZ) *adv.* in any manner.

a•or•ta (ay OR tə) *n. pl.* **•tas** or **•tae** (-tee) *Anat.* the main artery that carries blood from the heart. [< Gk. *aeirein* raise, heave] —**a•or′tal** *adj.*

a•pace (ə PAYS) *adv.* rapidly; quickly. [ME *a pas* at a good pace]

a•pache (ə PASH) *n.* a ruffian or gangster of Paris. [< F]

A•pach•e (ə PACH ee) *n. pl.* **A•pach•es** or **A•pach•e** one of a group of Indians, inhabiting the southern and SW U.S.

a•part (ə PAHRT) *adv.* **1.** separated; not together. **2.** one from another. **3.** separately for some use or purpose. **4.** aside; to one side. **5.** in pieces or to pieces. —*adj.* separate; distinct. [ME]

a•part•heid (ə PAHR tayt) *n.* in the Republic of South Africa, the official policy of segregation formerly enforced against nonwhites. [< Afrikaans, separateness]

a•part•ment (ə PAHRT mənt) *n.* a room or suite of rooms in a building, equipped for housekeeping. [< F *appartement*]

ap•a•thy (AP ə thee) *n. pl.* **•thies 1.** lack of emotion. **2.** indifference. [< L *apathia* without feeling] —**ap•a•thet•ic** (AP ə THET ik) *adj.*

ape (ayp) *n.* **1.** a large, tailless, Old World primate, as a gorilla or chimpanzee. **2.** loosely, any monkey. —*v.t.* **aped, ap•ing** imitate; mimic. [ME]

a•per•i•tif (ə per ə TEEF) *n. French* a drink of liquor or wine taken as an appetizer.

ap•er•ture (AP ər chuur) *n.* an opening; orifice. [ME]

a•pex (AY peks) *n. pl.* **a•pex•es** or **a•pi•ces** (AY pə SEEZ) **1.** the highest point; peak. **2.** climax. [< L]

a•pha•sia (ə FAY zhə) *n.* partial or total loss of the power of speech. [< Gk., speechlessness] —**a•pha•sic** (ə FAY zik) *adj. & n.*

a•phe•li•on (ə FEE lee ən) *n. pl.* **•li•a** *Astron.* the point in an orbit, as of a planet, farthest from the sun: opposed to *perihelion.* [< NL *aphelium*]

a•phid (AY fid) *n.* a small, juice-sucking insect, injurious to plants. —**a•phid•i•an** (ə FID ee ən) *adj.*

aph•o•rism (AF ə RIZ əm) *n.* **1.** a brief statement of a truth or principle. **2.** a proverb;

maxim. [< F *aphorisme*] —**aph′o•rist** *n.* —**aph′o•ris′tic** *adj.*

aph•ro•dis•i•ac (AF rə DIZ ee ak) *adj.* arousing or increasing sexual desire or potency. —*n.* a supposed aphrodisiac drug, food, etc. [< Gk. *aphrodisiakós* relating to love]

a•pi•a•ry (AY pee ER ee) *n. pl.* **•ar•ies** a place where bees are kept; a set of hives with bees, etc. [< L *apiarium* beehive] —**a•pi•ar•ist** (AY pee ə rist) *n.*

a•pi•cul•ture (AY pi KUL chər) *n.* the raising and care of bees. —**a′pi•cul′tur•ist** *n.*

a•piece (ə PEES) *adv.* for or to each one; each.

ap•ish (AY pish) *adj.* like an ape; servilely imitative; foolish and tricky.

a•plomb (ə PLOM) *n.* assurance; self-confidence. [< F *à plomb* straight up and down]

a•poc•a•lypse (ə POK ə lips) *n.* **1.** a prophecy or revelation. **2.** *cap.* the book of Revelation, the last book of the New Testament. [ME] —**a•poc′a•lyp′tic** or **•ti•cal** *adj.*

A•poc•ry•pha (ə POK rə fə) *n.pl. (often construed as sing.)* those books of the Septuagint included in the Vulgate but rejected by Protestants and Hebrews as uncanonical. [ME]

a•poc•ry•phal (ə POK rə fəl) *adj.* having little or no authenticity.

ap•o•gee (AP ə gee) *n.* **1.** *Astron.* that point in the orbit of an object or celestial body which is farthest from the earth: opposed to *perigee.* **2.** the highest point; climax. [< F *apogée*]

A•pol•lo (ə POL oh) *n.* a handsome young man. [after *Apollōn* Apollo, Greek god of music, poetry, and sunlight]

a•pol•o•get•ic (ə POL ə JET ik) *adj.* **1.** of the nature of an apology; excusing. **2.** defending or explaining. [ME *apologetik* speech in defense]

ap•o•lo•gi•a (AP ə LOH jee ə) *n.* a justification or defense. [< LL]

a•pol•o•gist (ə POL ə jist) *n.* one who argues in defense of any person or cause.

a•pol•o•gize (ə POL ə jīz) *v.i.* **•gized, •giz•ing** acknowledge, with regret, an offense.

a•pol•o•gy (ə POL ə jee) *n. pl.* **•gies** a statement or explanation expressing regret for some error or offense. [ME *apologe* speech in defense]

ap•o•plex•y (AP ə PLEK see) *n. Pathol.* sudden paralysis and loss of sensation caused by a blood clot or hemorrhage in the brain. [ME *apoplexie*] —**ap′o·plec′tic** *adj.*

a·pos·ta·sy (ə POS tə see) *n. pl.* **·sies** desertion of one's faith, religion, party, or principles. [ME *apostasye*] —**a·pos′tate** (-tate) *adj. & n.*

a pos·te·ri·o·ri (AY po STEER ee OR ī) **1.** *Logic* reasoning from facts to principles or from effect to cause. **2.** inductive; empirical. [< L, from the latter]

a·pos·tle (ə POS əl) *n.* **1.** one of the twelve disciples originally commissioned by Christ to preach the gospel (*Matt.* x 2–4). **2.** one of a class of missionaries in the early church (I *Cor.* xii 28). **3.** the earliest or foremost advocate of a cause. [ME]

ap·os·tol·ic (AP ə STOL ik) *adj.* **1.** of or pertaining to an apostle, the apostles, or their times. **2.** according to the doctrine or practice of the apostles. **3.** *Often cap.* papal.

a·pos·tro·phe[1] (ə POS trə fee) *n.* a symbol (′) written above the line to mark the omission of a letter or letters from a word, to indicate the possessive case, or to denote certain plurals: Cross your *t's.* [< MF] — **a·pos′tro·phize′** (-fīz) *v.t. & v.i.* **·phized, ·phiz·ing**

a·pos·tro·phe[2] *n.* a digression from a discourse; esp., a turning aside to speak to an absent person. —**a·pos′tro·phize** *v.t. & v.i.* **·phized, ·phiz·ing** [< LL]

a·poth·e·car·y (ə POTH ə KER ee) *n. pl.* **·car·ies** a druggist; a pharmacy. [ME]

ap·o·thegm (AP ə THEM) *n.* a terse, instructive, practical saying; maxim. [< Gk. *apóphthegma* speaking out]

a·poth·e·o·sis (ə POTH ee OH sis) *n. pl.* **·ses** (-seez) deification; supreme exaltation of any person, principle, etc. [< LL] — **a·poth·e·o·size** (ə POTH ee ə sīz) *v.t.* **·SIZED, ·SIZ·ING**

ap·pall (ə PAWL) *v.t.* fill with dismay or horror; shock. [ME] —**ap·pal′ling** *adj.*

ap·pa·ra·tus (AP ə RAT əs) *n. pl.* **·tus** or **·tus·es 1.** a device, machine, or assembly of tools, instruments, materials, equipment, etc., for a particular purpose. **2.** an organization of political activists. [< L, equipment]

ap·par·el (ə PAR əl) *n.* clothing; attire. — *v.t.* **·eled, ·el·ing** clothe; dress. [ME *appareillen* fit out]

ap·par·ent (ə PAR ənt) *adj.* **1.** readily perceived by the mind; obvious. **2.** easily seen; visible. **3.** seeming, in distinction from real or actual. [< L *apparere* be seen]

ap·pa·ri·tion (AP ə RISH ən) *n.* **1.** an appearance, esp. an eerie or unexpected one. **2.** phantom; ghost. [ME *apparicioun*]

ap·peal (ə PEEL) *n.* **1.** an earnest entreaty for aid, sympathy, or the like. **2.** the quality of being attractive. **3.** *Law* **a** the carrying of a case to a higher tribunal for a rehearing. **b** a case so carried. —*v.t.* **1.** *Law* refer or remove, as a case, to a higher court. —*v.i.* **2.** make a plea or request, as for sympathy or aid. **3.** awaken a favorable response; be interesting. **4.** *Law* remove a case, or request that a case be moved, to a higher court. **5.** resort or have recourse: with *to.* [ME *appelen* address] —**ap·peal′ing** *adj.*

ap·pear (ə PEER) *v.i.* **1.** come into view. **2.** seem. **3.** be clear to the mind; be obvious. **4.** come before the public. **5.** *Law* come formally into court. [ME *apperen*]

ap·pear·ance (ə PEER əns) *n.* **1.** the act of appearing or coming into view. **2.** external or physical aspect; presence: a commanding *appearance.* **3.** *pl.* circumstances or indications: *Appearances* are against him. **4.** outward show; pretense.

ap·pease (ə PEEZ) *v.t.* **·peased, ·peas·ing 1.** placate by making concessions or yielding to demands. **2.** satisfy or allay. [ME *apesen*] —**ap·pease′ment** *n.* —**ap·peas′er** *n.*

ap·pel·lant (ə PEL ənt) *adj. Law* of or pertaining to an appeal. —*n.* one who appeals, in any sense.

ap·pel·late (ə PEL it) *adj. Law* pertaining to or having jurisdiction of appeals: an *appellate* court. [< L *apellatus* named]

ap·pel·la·tion (AP ə LAY shən) *n.* **1.** a name or title. **2.** the act of naming. [ME *appelacion*]

ap·pend (ə PEND) *v.t.* **1.** add, as something subordinate or supplemental. **2.** hang or attach. [< L *appendere* hang on]

ap·pend·age (ə PEN dij) *n.* **1.** anything appended. **2.** *Zool.* any part joined to or diverging from the axial trunk, as a limb.

ap·pen·dec·to·my (AP ən DEK tə mee) *n. pl.* **·mies** *Surg.* the removal of the vermiform appendix.

ap·pen·di·ci·tis (ə PEN də SĪ tis) *n. Pathol.* inflammation of the vermiform appendix.

ap·pen·dix (ə PEN diks) *n. pl.* **·dix·es** or **·di·ces** (-də seez) **1.** an addition or appendage, as of supplementary matter at the end of a book. **2.** the vermiform appendix. [< L, appendage]

ap·per·cep·tion (AP ər SEP shən) *n.*

conscious perception. [< F] —**ap'per•cep'tive** adj.

ap•per•tain (AP ər TAYN) v.i. pertain or belong as by right or fitness; relate: with to. [ME apperteynen belong to]

ap•pe•tite (AP ə TĪT) n. 1. a desire for food or drink. 2. any physical craving or natural desire. 3. a strong liking. [ME appetit]

ap•pe•tiz•er (AP ə TĪ zər) n. anything that excites appetite, esp. food or drink served before a meal.

ap•pe•tiz•ing (AP ə TĪ zing) adj. stimulating to the appetite.

ap•plaud (ə PLAWD) v.t. & v.i. 1. express approval (of) by clapping the hands. 2. commend; praise. [< L applaudere]

ap•plause (ə PLAWZ) n. approval, esp. as shown by clapping the hands.

ap•ple (AP əl) n. 1. the fleshy, edible, usu. roundish fruit of a widely distributed tree of the rose family. 2. the similar fruit of several allied species, as the crab apple. [ME appel]

ap•ple•jack (AP əl JAK) n. brandy made from cider.

ap•pli•ance (ə PLĪ əns) n. a device or instrument; esp., an electrically powered device for household work.

ap•pli•ca•ble (AP li kə bəl) adj. capable of application; relevant; fitting. [< MF] —**ap'pli•ca•bil'i•ty** n.

ap•pli•cant (AP li kənt) n. one who applies, as for a job.

ap•pli•ca•tion (AP li KAY shən) n. 1. the act of applying. 2. that which is applied. 3. a use for a special purpose. 4. capacity of being used; relevance. 5. close attention. 6. a formal, written request, esp. for employment.

ap•pli•ca•tor (AP li KAY tər) n. an instrument or utensil for applying medication etc.

ap•pli•ca•tive (AP li KAY tiv) adj. fit for application; practical.

ap•plied (ə PLĪD) adj. put in practice; utilized: said of sciences, fields of study, etc.

ap•pli•qué (AP li KAY) adj. applied: said of ornaments, as in needlework, sewn to the surface of cloth. —n. decoration so applied. —v.t. •quéd, •qué•ing (-KAY ing) decorate by appliqué work. [< F]

ap•ply (ə PLĪ) v. •plied, •ply•ing v.t. 1. bring into contact with something; put on or to. 2. devote or put to a particular use. 3. connect, as an epithet, with a particular person or thing. 4. give (oneself) wholly to; devote. —v.i. 5. make a request or petition; ask: with for. 6. be relevant. [ME applien]

ap•point (ə POINT) v.t. 1. name or select, as a person, a time and place, etc. 2. ordain, as by decree; command. 3. fit out; equip: used chiefly in combination in the past participle: a well-appointed home.

ap•point•ee (ə poin TEE) n. one appointed to an office.

ap•poin•tive (ə POIN tiv) adj. filled by appointment.

ap•point•ment (ə POINT mənt) n. 1. the act of appointing or placing in office. 2. a position held by someone appointed. 3. an agreement to meet or to be somewhere; engagement. 4. Usu. pl. furnishings.

ap•por•tion (ə POR shən) v.t. divide and assign proportionally; allot. [< MF apportionner] —**ap•por'tion•ment** n.

ap•pose (ə POHZ) v.t. •posed, •pos•ing arrange side by side. [< L apponere put nearby]

ap•po•site (AP ə zit) adj. fit for or appropriate. [< L appositus added to] —**ap'po•site•ness** n.

ap•po•si•tion (AP ə ZISH ən) n. 1. the placing of one noun or noun phrase next to another so that the second explains the first, as Joan, president of the class. 2. the act of opposing or the state of being opposed. —**ap'po•si'tion•al** adj.

ap•pos•i•tive (ə POZ ə tiv) adj. of or in apposition. —n. a word or phrase in apposition.

ap•praise (ə PRAYZ) v.t. •praised, •prais•ing 1. make an official valuation of; set a price or value on. 2. estimate the amount, quality, or worth of; judge. [ME apraysen] —**ap•prais'er** n.

ap•pre•ci•a•ble (ə PREE shee ə bəl) adj. capable of being valued or estimated.

ap•pre•ci•ate (ə PREE shee AYT) v. •at•ed, •at•ing v.t. 1. be aware of the value, importance, or magnitude of. 2. esteem adequately or highly. 3. show gratitude for. 4. raise in value. —v.i. 5. rise in value. [< Med.L appreciatus valued] —**ap•pre'ci•a'tion** n.

ap•pre•ci•a•tive (ə PREESH ə tiv) adj. showing appreciation.

ap•pre•hend (AP ri HEND) v.t. 1. lay hold of or grasp mentally; understand. 2. expect with anxious foreboding; dread. 3. arrest; take into custody. —v.i. 4. understand. [ME apprehenden grasp] —**ap'pre•hen'sion** (-HEN shən) n.

ap•pre•hen•si•ble (AP ri HEN sə bəl) adj. capable of being apprehended.

ap·pre·hen·sive (AP ri HEN siv) *adj.* fearful; anxious. **—ap'pre·hen'sive·ness** *n.*

ap·pren·tice (ə PREN tis) *n.* **1.** one who is bound by a legal agreement to serve another for a fixed period of time in order to learn a trade or business. **2.** any learner or beginner. **—v.t. ·ticed, ·tic·ing** bind or take as an apprentice. [ME *apprentis*] **—ap·pren'tice·ship** *n.*

ap·prise (ə PRĪZ) *v.t.* **·prised, ·pris·ing** notify; inform. [< F *appris* informed]

ap·proach (ə PROHCH) *v.i.* **1.** come near or nearer in time or space. **—v.t. 2.** come near or nearer to. **3.** come close to; approximate. **4.** make advances to; offer a proposal or bribe to. **5.** start to deal with: *approach* a problem. **—n. 1.** the act of approaching; a coming near. **2.** an approximation; nearness. **3.** a way or means of approaching; access. **4.** a method of beginning or accomplishing something. **5.** *Often pl.* an overture of friendship, etc.; advance. [ME *approochen*] **—ap·proach'a·bil'i·ty** *n.* **—ap·proach'a·ble** *adj.*

ap·pro·ba·tion (AP rə BAY shən) *n.* **1.** the act of approving; approval. **2.** sanction. [ME] **—ap·pro·ba·tive** (AP rə BAY tiv *adj.*

ap·pro·pri·ate (ə PROH pree it) *adj.* suitable; proper; relevant. **—v.t.** (ə PROH pree AYT) **·at·ed, ·at·ing 1.** set apart for a particular use. **2.** take for one's own use. **3.** take or use without authority. [< LL *appropriatus* made one's own] **—ap·pro'pri·ate·ness** *n.*

ap·pro·pri·a·tion (ə PROH pree AY shən) *n.* **1.** the act of appropriating. **2.** money, set apart by formal action for a special use.

ap·prov·al (ə PROO vəl) *n.* **1.** the act of approving; approbation. **2.** official consent; sanction. **3.** favorable opinion; praise. **—on approval** for (a customer's) examination without obligation to purchase.

ap·prove (ə PROOV) *v.* **·proved, ·prov·ing** *v.t.* **1.** regard as worthy, proper, or right. **2.** confirm formally or authoritatively. **—v.i. 3.** show or state approval: often with *of.* [ME *approven*] **—ap·prov'ing·ly** *adv.*

ap·prox·i·mate (ə PROK sə mit) *adj.* **1.** nearly exact, accurate, or complete. **2.** like; resembling. **3.** near; close together. **—v.** (ə PROK sə MAYT) **·mat·ed, ·mat·ing** *v.t.* **1.** come close to, as in quality, degree, or quantity. **2.** cause to come near. **—v.i. 3.**

come near in quality, degree, etc. [ME] **—ap·prox'i·ma'tion** *n.*

ap·pur·te·nance (ə PUR tn əns) *n.* **1.** something attached to another, more important thing. **2.** *pl.* apparatus. [ME]

a·pri·cot (AP ri KOT) *n.* **1.** a yellow fruit, similar to a peach. **2.** the tree bearing this fruit. **3.** a pinkish yellow color. [< MF *abricot*]

A·pril (AY prəl) *n.* the fourth month of the year, containing 30 days. [ME]

a pri·o·ri (AY prī OR ī) **1.** *Logic* proceeding from cause to effect, or from an assumption to its logical conclusion. **2.** based on theory rather than on experience or examination. [< L, from the one before]

a·pron (AY prən) *n.* **1.** a garment worn to protect or adorn the front of a person's clothes. **2.** *Engin.* **a** the platform at the entrance to a dock. **b** the platform below a dam or in a sluiceway. **3.** *Aeron.* a hard-surfaced area in front of and around a hangar or aircraft shelter. **4.** the part of a theater stage in front of the curtain. [< misconstrual of ME *a napron* as *an apron*]

ap·ro·pos (AP rə POH) *adj.* suitable; opportune: an *apropos* remark. **—adv. 1.** with reference or regard to: with *of: apropos* of spring. **2.** to the purpose; pertinently. [< F *à propos,* lit., to purpose]

apse (aps) *n.* *Archit.* an extending portion of an edifice, usually semicircular with a half dome, esp. the eastern or altar end of a church. [< L *apsis* arch]

apt (apt) *adj.* **1.** inclined; liable; likely. **2.** quick to learn; intelligent. **3.** pertinent; relevant. [ME] **—apt'ness** *n.*

ap·ti·tude (AP ti TOOD) *n.* **1.** natural or acquired ability or bent. **2.** quickness of understanding. **3.** the state or quality of being apt or fitting. [ME]

aq·ua·ma·rine (AK wə mə REEN) *n.* **1.** a sea-green variety of precious beryl. **2.** a bluish green color. **—adj.** bluish green. [< L *aqua marina* sea water]

aq·ua·naut (AK wə nawt) *n.* **1.** an undersea explorer **2.** a skin-diver. [After *astronaut*]

aq·ua·plane (AK wə PLAYN) *n.* a board on which one stands while being towed by a motorboat. **—aq'ua·plane** *v.i.* **·planed, ·plan·ing**

a·quar·i·um (ə KWAIR ee əm) *n. pl.* **a·quar·i·ums** or **a·quar·i·a 1.** a tank, pond, or the like for the exhibition or study of aquatic animals or plants. **2.** a building containing such an exhibition. [< L *aquarius* for water]

A·quar·i·us (ə KWAIR ee əs) *n.* a constellation, the Water Bearer; also, a sign of the zodiac. [< L]

a·quat·ic (ə KWAT ik) *adj.* 1. living or growing in or near water. 2. performed on or in water. —*n.* 1. an aquatic animal or plant. 2. *pl.* water sports. [< L *aquaticus* of water]

aq·ua·vit (AH kwə VEET) *n.* a clear Scandinavian liquor, flavored with caraway seeds. [< Scand. *akvavit*]

aq·ua vi·tae (VĪ tee) 1. alcohol. 2. spirit; brandy. [< L, water of life]

aq·ue·duct (AK wi DUKT) *n.* a water conduit, esp. one for supplying water to a community from a distance. [< Med.L *aquaductus*]

a·que·ous (AY kee əs) *adj.* 1. of or like water; watery. 2. made from or with water.

aqueous humor a clear fluid filling the space in the eye between the cornea and the lens.

aq·ui·line (AK wi LIN) *adj.* 1. of or like an eagle. 2. curving or hooked: an *aquiline* nose. [< L]

Ar·ab (AR əb) *n.* 1. a native or inhabitant of Arabia. 2. any of a Semitic-speaking people inhabiting Arabia. —**A·ra·bi·an** (ə RAY bee ən) *adj. & n.*

ar·a·besque (AR ə BESK) *n.* 1. a design, as used in Moorish architecture, of intertwined lines forming scrollwork, leaves, or flowers. 2. in ballet, a position in which the dancer extends one leg straight backward, one arm forward, and the other arm backward. —*adj.* relating to, executed in, or resembling arabesque; fanciful; ornamental.

Ar·a·bic (AR ə bik) *adj.* of or pertaining to Arabia, the Arabs, their language, culture, etc. —*n.* the Southwest Semitic language of the Arabs.

Arabic numerals the symbols 1, 2, 3, 4, 5, 6, 7, 8, 9, and 0.

ar·a·ble (AR ə bəl) *adj.* capable of being plowed. [< L *arabilis*]

a·rach·nid (ə RAK nid) *n.* any of a class of arthropods, including the spiders, scorpions, etc. [< NL *Arachnida* spider]

Ar·a·ma·ic (ar ə MAY ik) *n.* any of a group of Semitic languages of Biblical times.

ar·bi·ter (AHR bi tər) *n.* 1. a chosen or appointed judge or umpire. 2. an absolute and final judge. [ME *arbitour*]

ar·bi·tra·ble (AHR bi trə bəl) *adj.* subject to, capable of, or suitable for arbitration.

ar·bi·trar·y (AHR bi TRER ee) *adj.* 1. based on or subject to opinion. 2. absolute; despotic. 3. capricious; not based on reason. [ME] —**ar′bi·trar′i·ly** *adv.*

ar·bi·trate (AHR bi TRAYT) *v.t. & v.i.* ·**trat·ed, ·trat·ing** 1. act or decide as arbitrator. 2. submit (a dispute) to arbitration. [< L *arbitratus* judged] —**ar·bi·tra·tion** (AHR bi TRAY shən) *n.*

ar·bi·tra·tor (AHR bi TRAY tər) *n.* a person chosen to decide a dispute. [ME *arbitratour*]

ar·bor¹ (AHR bər) *n.* a bower, as of latticework, supporting vines or trees. [ME *herber* plot of grass]

ar·bor² *n.* a shaft, spindle, or axle in certain machines. [< L, tree]

ar·bo·re·al (ahr BOR ee əl) *adj.* 1. of or like a tree. 2. inhabiting trees, or adapted to life in trees. [< L *arboreus* of trees]

ar·bo·re·tum (AHR bə REE təm) *n. pl.* ·**tums** or ·**ta** (-tə) a place for study and display of trees. [< L, a planting of trees]

arc (ahrk) *n.* 1. anything in the shape of an arch, a curve, or a part of a circle. 2. *Geom.* a part of any curve. 3. the flame formed by passage of electric current across the gap between two conductors. —*v.i.* **arced** (ahrkt) or **arcked, arc·ing** (AHR king) or **arck·ing** form an arc. [< L *arcus* bow, arch]

ar·cade (ahr KAYD) *n.* 1. a series of arches with supporting columns or piers. 2. a roofed passageway or street, esp. one lined with shops. [ME *ark* arch]

Ar·ca·di·a (ahr KAY dee ə) any region of ideal rustic simplicity and contentment. —**Ar·ca·di·an** (ahr KAY dee ən) *adj.* rural or simple; pastoral.

ar·cane (ahr KAYN) *adj.* secret; esoteric. [< L *arcanus* hidden]

arch¹ (ahrch) *n.* 1. a curved structure spanning an opening. 2. any similar structure or object. 3. a bowlike curve. 4. a curved or archlike part, as of the foot. —*v.t.* 1. cause to form an arch or arches. 2. furnish with an arch or arches. 3. span; extend over, as an arch. —*v.i.* 4. form an arch or arches. [ME *arche*]

arch² *adj.* 1. cunning; sly. 2. most eminent; chief. 3. cute; playful. —**arch′ly** *adv.*

arch- *prefix* 1. chief; principal. 2. very great; extreme. [ME]

ar·chae·ol·o·gy (AHR kee OL ə jee) *n.* the science or study of history from the remains of early human cultures. Also spelled *ar-*

chaeology. —**ar•che•o•log•i•cal** (AHR kee ə LOJ i kəl) *adj.* —**ar'che•ol'o•gist** *n.*

ar•cha•ic (ahr KAY ik) *adj.* **1.** antiquated. **2.** characterizing a word or language no longer in current use. [< F]

ar•cha•ism (AHR kee IZ əm) *n.* an archaic word, idiom, or style.

arch•an•gel (AHRK AYN jəl) *n.* an angel of highest rank. [ME *arcangel*]

arch•bish•op (AHRCH BISH əp) *n.* a chief bishop.

arch•di•o•cese (AHRCH DĪ ə sees) *n.* the diocese or jurisdiction of an archbishop.

archeo- *combining form* ancient: *Archeozoic.* Also **archaeo-.** [< Gk. *archaios* ancient]

arch•er•y (AHR chər ee) *n.* the art or sport of shooting with bow and arrows. [ME]

ar•che•type (AHR kə tīp) *n.* an original or standard pattern or model; a prototype. [< L *archetypum* original] —**ar'che•typ'i•cal** (AHR ki TIP i kəl) *adj.*

ar•chi•pel•a•go (AHR kə PEL ə goh) *n. pl.* **•gos** or **•goes 1.** a sea with many islands. **2.** the islands in such a sea. [< Ital. *arcipelago* chief sea]

ar•chi•tect (AHR ki TEKT) *n.* **1.** one whose profession is to design and draw up the plans for building, etc., and supervise their construction. [< L *architectus* chief craftsman] **2.** one who devises or creates anything. [< L *architectus* chief craftsman]

ar•chi•tec•ture (AHR ki TEK chər) *n.* **1.** the science, art, or profession of designing and constructing buildings or other structures. **2.** a style or system of building. **3.** construction or structure generally. —**ar'chi•tec'tur•al** *adj.*

ar•chives (AHR kīvz) *n.pl.* **1.** a place where public records and historical documents are kept. **2.** public records, documents, etc., as kept in such a depository. [< F]

ar•chi•vist (AHR kə vist) *n.* a keeper of archives.

arch•way (AHRCH way) *n.* a passage under an arch.

-archy *combining form* rule; government. [ME *-archie*]

arc•tic (AHRK tik) *adj.* **1.** characteristic of the region of the Arctic Circle. **2.** extremely cold. [< L *arcticus* northern]

ar•den•cy (AHR dən see) *n.* ardor.

ar•dent (AHR dənt) *adj.* **1.** passionate; intense. **2.** hot; burning. [< L *ardere* burn]

ar•dor (AHR dər) *n.* **1.** warmth or intensity of feelings; eagerness; zeal. **2.** great heat. [ME]

ar•du•ous (AHR joo əs) *adj.* **1.** involving great labor or hardship; difficult. **2.** toiling strenuously; energetic. **3.** hard to climb or surmount. [< L *arduus* steep]

are[1] (ahr) *v.* the plural, present indicative and second person singular, of BE. [ME *aren*]

are[2] (air) *n.* in the metric system, a surface measure equal to one hundred square meters. [< F]

ar•e•a (AIR ee ə) *n.* **1.** a region. **2.** the surface included within a boundary line. **3.** the extent or scope of anything. **4.** a space having a particular function. [< L, open space] —**ar'e•al** *adj.*

a•re•na (ə REE nə) *n.* **1.** the oval space in a Roman amphitheater, where contests and shows were held. **2.** any place of this nature: a football *arena.* **3.** a scene or sphere of action: the political *arena.* [< L, sandy place]

aren't (ahrnt) are not.

a•re•o•la (ə REE ə lə) *n. pl.* **•lae** (-lee) or **•las 1.** *Bot.* an interstice in a network of leaf veins. **2.** *Anat.* the colored circle about a nipple or about a vesicle. [< L]

ar•go•sy (AHR gə see) *n. pl.* **•sies 1.** a large merchant ship. **2.** a fleet of merchant vessels. [Earlier *ragusy,* after *Ragusa,* Italian name of Dubrovnik, Yugoslavia]

ar•got (AHR goh) *n.* the specialized vocabulary or jargon of any class or group, as that of the underworld. [< F]

ar•gue (AHR gyoo) *v.* **•gued, •gu•ing** *v.i.* **1.** present reasons to support or contest a measure or opinion. **2.** contend in argument; quarrel. —*v.t.* **3.** present reasons for or against; discuss, as a proposal. **4.** contend or maintain, by reasoning. [ME] —**ar'gu•a•ble** *adj.*

ar•gu•ment (AHR gyə mənt) *n.* **1.** a discussion in which there is disagreement; debate. **2.** a quarrel. **3.** a reason or reasons offered for or against something. **4.** discourse intended to persuade or to convince. [ME]

ar•gu•men•ta•tion (AHR gyə men TAY shən) *n.* **1.** reasoning to a conclusion. **2.** discussion; debate. [ME *argumentacioun*]

ar•gu•men•ta•tive (AHR gyə MEN tə tiv) *adj.* given to argumentation; disputatious. —**ar'gu•men'ta•tive•ness** *n.*

a•ri•a (AHR ee ə) *n.* a solo vocal piece, as in an opera or oratorio, often with instrumental accompaniment. [< Ital.]

ar•id (AR id) *adj.* **1.** dry. **2.** lacking interest or feeling; dull. [< L *aridus* dry] —**a•rid•i•ty** (ə RID i tee) n.

Ar•ies (AIR eez) n. a constellation, the Ram; also, a sign of the zodiac. [< L]

a•rise (ə RĪZ) v.i. **a•rose, a•ris•en** (ə RIZ ən), **a•ris•ing 1.** get up. **2.** rise; ascend. **3.** come into being; originate; issue. **4.** result; proceed. [ME *arisen*]

ar•is•toc•ra•cy (AR ə STOK rə see) n. pl. •**cies 1.** a hereditary nobility or privileged class. **2.** any preeminent group: the *aristocracy* of talent. [< MF *aristocratie*] —**a•ris•to•crat** (ə RIS tə KRAT) n. —**a•ris•to•crat•ic** (ə RIS tə KRAT ik) adj.

a•rith•me•tic (ə RITH mə tik) n. the science of computing with numbers by addition, subtraction, multiplication, and division. [< L *arithmetica* of numbers] —**a•rith•me•tic** (AR ith MET ik) adj.

ark (ahrk) n. **1.** in the Bible: **a** the ship of Noah. *Gen.* vi–viii. **b** the chest containing the tablets bearing the Ten Commandments: also called **ark of the covenant.** *Ex.* xxv 10. **2.** a place of protection. [ME *arke* chest]

arm[1] (ahrm) n. **1.** an upper limb of the human body, from the shoulder to the hand or wrist. **2.** the forelimb of certain other vertebrates. **3.** an armlike part or appendage. [ME] —**at arm's length** at a distance. —**with open arms** cordially.

arm[2] n. **1.** a weapon. **2.** a distinct branch of the military service: the air *arm.* —v.t. & v.i. supply or equip (oneself) with weapons. [ME *armen*]

ar•ma•da (ahr MAH də) n. a fleet of war vessels. [< Sp., navy]

ar•ma•dil•lo (AH mə DIL oh) n. pl. •**los** a burrowing nocturnal mammal having an armorlike covering of jointed plates. [< Sp.]

Ar•ma•ged•don (AHR mə GED n) n. in Biblical prophecy, the scene of a great battle between the forces of good and evil, to occur at the end of the world. *Rev.* xvi 16.

ar•ma•ment (AHR mə mənt) n. **1.** Often pl. guns and other military equipment. **2.** the act of arming or equipping for war. < L *armamenta* fittings]

ar•ma•ture (AHR mə chuur) n. **1.** a piece of soft iron joining the poles of a magnet to prevent the loss of magnetic power. **2.** *Electr.* in a motor, the iron core carrying the coils of insulated wire to be revolved through the magnetic field. **3.** in sculpture, a framework to support the clay or other substance in modeling. [< MF]

arm•ful (AHRM fuul) n. pl. •**fuls** as much as can be held in one's arm or arms.

ar•mi•stice (AHR mə stis) n. a temporary cessation of hostilities by mutual agreement; truce. [< F]

arm•let (AHRM lit) n. a band worn around the arm.

ar•moire (ahrm WAHR) n. a large, movable, often ornate cabinet or cupboard. [< F]

ar•mor (AHR mər) n. **1.** a defensive covering, as of metallic plates. **2.** the armored vehicles of an army. **3.** any protective covering. —v.t. & v.i. furnish with or put on armor. [ME *armour*] —**ar•mor•er** (AHR mər ər) n.

ar•mor•y (AHR mə ree) n. pl. •**mor•ies 1.** a place where arms are kept; arsenal. **2.** a building for the use of a body of militia, including storage for arms and equipment, drill rooms, etc. [ME *armerie*]

arm•pit (AHRM PIT) n. the cavity under the arm at the shoulder; axilla. [ME]

arms (ahrmz) n.pl. **1.** weapons. **2.** warfare. —**up in arms** aroused and ready to fight. [< L *arma* weapons]

ar•my (AHR mee) n. pl. •**mies 1.** a large organized body of soldiers. **2.** the total military land forces of a country. **3.** the largest administrative and tactical unit of the U.S. land forces. **4.** any large body of people, animals, etc. [ME *armee*]

a•ro•ma (ə ROH mə) n. fragrance, as from appetizing food etc.; agreeable odor. [< L] —**ar•o•mat•ic** (AR ə MAT ik) adj. & n.

a•rose (ə ROHZ) past tense of ARISE.

a•round (ə ROWND) adv. **1.** on all sides; in various directions. **2.** in the opposite direction: turn *around.* **3.** from place to place; here and there: walk *around.* **4.** in the vicinity. **5.** in or to a particular place: Come *around* to see us. —prep. **1.** about the circumference or circuit of. **2.** on all sides of; surrounding or enveloping. **3.** here and there in or about. **4.** somewhere near or within. **5.** somewhere near in time, amount, etc.; about. [ME]

a•rouse (ə ROWZ) v.t. **a•roused, a•rous•ing 1.** awaken. **2.** excite. —**a•rous•al** (ə ROW zəl) n.

ar•raign (ə RAYN) v.t. **1.** call into court and cause to answer to an indictment. **2.** call upon for an answer; accuse. [ME *arrainen* call to account] —**ar•raign′ment** n.

ar•range (ə RAYNJ) v. •**ranged, •rang•ing** v.t. **1.** put in definite or proper order. **2.** plan the details of; prepare for. **3.** adjust, as a conflict or dispute. **4.** *Music* change or adapt for other instruments or voices. —*v.i.* **5.** come to an agreement. **6.** see about the details; make plans. [ME *arayngen*] —**ar·range′ment** *n.*

ar·rant (AR ənt) *adj.* notoriously bad; unmitigated. [ME]

ar·ras (AR əs) *n.* **1.** a tapestry. **2.** a wall hanging of tapestry. [ME, after *Arras,* France]

ar·ray (ə RAY) *n.* **1.** regular or proper order, esp. of troops. **2.** the persons or things arrayed. **3.** clothing; fine dress. **4.** a large number; an imposing collection. —*v.t.* **1.** set in order, as troops for battle. **2.** adorn; dress. [ME *arrayen prepare*]

ar·rears (ə REERZ) *n.pl.* that which is or overdue. —**in arrears** behind in meeting payment, completing work, etc. [ME *arere* behind]

ar·rest (ə REST) *v.t.* **1.** stop suddenly; check. **2.** take into legal custody. **3.** attract and fix, as the attention. —*n.* **1.** the act of arresting, or the state of being arrested. **2.** a device for arresting motion. [ME *aresten* stop]

ar·ri·val (ə RĪ vəl) *n.* **1.** the act of arriving. **2.** one who or that which arrives or has arrived.

ar·rive (ə RĪV) *v.i.* **·rived, ·riv·ing** **1.** reach a place. **2.** come to a desired object, state, etc.: often with *at.* **3.** attain success or fame. [ME *ariven* come to shore]

ar·ro·gant (AR ə gənt) *adj.* overbearing; haughty. [ME] —**ar′ro·gance** *n.*

ar·ro·gate (AR ə GAYT) *v.t.* **·gat·ed, ·gat·ing** claim or take without right. [< L *ad-* to + *rogare* ask]

ar·row (AR oh) *n.* **1.** a slender shaft, generally feathered at one end and with a pointed head at the other, to be shot from a bow. **2.** anything resembling an arrow, as a sign in the shape of an arrow, used to indicate directions. [ME *arewe*]

ar·row·head (AR oh HED) *n.* the pointed head of an arrow.

ar·roy·o (ə ROI oh) *n. pl.* **·os** **1.** a deep, dry gully. **2.** a brook. [< Sp.]

ar·se·nal (AHR sə nl) *n.* **1.** a government facility for manufacturing and storing arms and munitions. **2.** a store of arms. **3.** a store; collection; supply. [< Ital. *arsenale* shipyard]

ar·se·nic (AHR sə nik) *n.* a metallic element, forming many poisonous compounds. [ME *arsenicum*] —**ar·sen·i·cal** (ahr SEN i kəl) *adj.*

ar·son (AHR sən) *n.* the malicious burning of a building or other property. [< AF]

art[1] (ahrt) *n.* **1. a** the production of aesthetically pleasing artifacts. **b** works resulting from this activity. **2.** literature, music, and esp. painting, sculpture, drawing, etc. **3.** practical skill; dexterity. [ME]

art[2] *Archaic* second person singular present tense of BE: used with *thou.* [ME]

art de·co (DEK oh) a style of decoration of the late 1920's and the 1930's characterized by geometric shapes. [< F *Art Déco* modern decorative arts]

ar·te·ri·o·scle·ro·sis (ahr TEER ee oh sklə ROH sis) *n. Pathol.* the thickening and hardening of the walls of an artery.

ar·ter·y (AHR tə ree) *n. pl.* **·ter·ies** **1.** any of a large number of muscular vessels conveying blood away from the heart to every part of the body. **2.** any main channel or route. [ME] —**ar·te·ri·al** (ahr TEER ee əl) *adj.*

ar·te·sian well (ahr TEE zhən) a well at a level lower than the source of the water supply, from which the water flows out under pressure.

art·ful (AHRT fəl) *adj.* **1.** crafty; cunning. **2.** skillful; ingenious.

ar·thri·tis (ahr THRĪ tis) *n. Pathol.* inflammation of a joint or joints. [< NL] —**ar·thrit·ic** (ahr THRIT ik) *adj. & n.*

ar·thro·pod (AHR thrə pod) *n. Zool.* any of a large group of invertebrate animals having jointed legs and segmented body parts, including insects, spiders, and crabs. [< NL *Arthropoda*]

ar·ti·choke (AHR tə chohk) *n.* a thistlelike garden plant, having an edible flower head. [< Ital. *articiocco*]

ar·ti·cle (AHR ti kəl) *n.* **1.** a particular object or substance; a thing. **2.** an individual item in a class: an *article* of clothing. **3.** a literary piece in a newspaper, magazine, etc. **4.** a separate section in a document, as in a treaty. **5.** *Gram.* an auxiliary word inserted before a noun to limit or modify it in some way, as English *a,* an (**indefinite article**) and *the* (**definite article**). [ME]

ar·tic·u·late (ahr TIK yə lit) *adj.* **1.** able to speak, esp. well or expressively. **2.** coherent; well presented. **3.** jointed; segmented, as limbs. —*v.* **·lat·ed, ·lat·ing** (ahr TIK yə layt) *v.t.* **1.** utter distinctly; enunciate. **2.** express in words. **3.** joint together; unite by joints. —*v.i.* **4.** speak distinctly. [< L *articulatus* divided into parts] —**ar·tic·u·late·ness** (ahr TIK yə lit nis) *n.*

ar·tic·u·la·tion (ahr TIK yə LAY shən) *n.* **1.** a jointing or being jointed together. **2.** the utterance of speech sounds; enunciation.

ar·ti·fact (AHR tə FAKT) *n.* anything made by human work or skill. [< L *arte factum* made with skill]

ar·ti·fice (AHR tə fis) *n.* **1.** an ingenious stratagem; maneuver. **2.** trickery. **3.** skill; ingenuity. [< MF]

ar·tif·i·cer (ahr TIF ə sər) *n.* **1.** a skilled craftsman. **2.** an inventor.

ar·ti·fi·cial (AHR tə FISH əl) *adj.* **1.** produced by human art. **2.** made in imitation of something natural. **3.** not genuine. [ME] — **ar·ti·fi·ci·al·i·ty** (AHR tə FISH ee AL i tee) *n.*

artificial insemination impregnation of the female without direct sexual contact.

artificial respiration stimulation of breathing by forcing breath into the lungs, through the mouth, or by applying pressure to the chest cavity at regular intervals.

ar·til·ler·y (ahr TIL ə ree) *n.* **1.** guns of larger caliber than machine guns. **2.** military units armed with such guns. **3.** a branch of the U.S. Army. [ME *artillerie* armaments]

ar·ti·san (AHR tə zən) *n.* a skilled workman. [< F]

ar·tist (AHR tist) *n.* **1.** one skilled in any of the fine arts, esp. painting, drawing, etc. **2.** one whose work shows skill. [< MF *artiste*]

ar·tis·tic (ahr TIS tik) *adj.* **1.** of or pertaining to art or artists. **2.** conforming to the principles of art; tastefully executed. **3.** fond of or sensitive to art.

art·ist·ry (AHR ti stree) *n.* **1.** artistic workmanship or ability. **2.** the pursuits or occupation of an artist.

art·less (AHRT lis) *adj.* **1.** lacking craft or deceit; guileless. **2.** natural; simple. **3.** devoid of art or skill; clumsy. —**art′less·ness** *n.*

art nou·veau (AHRT noo VOH) a style of decoration dating from the 1890's, characterized by sinuous plant shapes. [< F, lit., new art]

Ar·y·an (AR ee ən) *n.* **1.** a member or descendant of a prehistoric people who spoke Indo-European. **2.** in Nazi ideology, a Caucasian gentile, esp. one of Nordic stock. [< Skt. *ārya* aristocrat]

as (az, *unstressed* əz) *adv.* to the same degree; equally. —*conj.* **1.** to the same degree or extent that: *as* fair *as* the sun. **2.** in the way that: Do *as* I do. **3.** to the degree in which: He became gentler *as* he grew older. **4.** at the same time that; while. **5.** because; since. **6.** for instance: Some animals are cunning, *as* the fox. **7.** though; however: Bad *as* it was, it might have been worse. — **as for** (or **as to**) in the matter of; concerning. —**as if** (or **as though**) the same, or in the same manner, that it would be if. — *pron.* **1.** that; who; which: after *same* and *such*: He lived in the same city *as* I did. **2.** a fact that: He is dead, *as* can be seen. — *prep.* **1.** in the role or character of: act *as* umpire. **2.** in the manner of; like: use a board *as* a hammer. [ME]

as·bes·tos (as BES təs) *n.* a white or light gray mineral that may be woven or shaped into acid-resisting, nonconducting, and fireproof articles. [< L]

as·cend (ə SEND) *v.i.* **1.** go or move upward; rise. —*v.t.* **2.** mount; climb. **3.** succeed to (a throne). [ME *ascenden* climb]

as·cen·dan·cy (ə SEN dən see) *n.* the quality, fact, or state of being in the ascendant; domination.

as·cen·dant (ə SEN dənt) *adj.* **1.** ascending; rising. **2.** superior; dominant. **3.** *Astron.* coming to or above the horizon. —*n.* a position of preeminence; domination. —**be in the ascendant** approach or occupy an influential position.

as·cen·sion (ə SEN shən) *n.* the act of ascending. —**the Ascension** *Theol.* the bodily ascent of Christ into heaven after the Resurrection.

as·cent (ə SENT) *n.* **1.** the act of ascending; a rising, soaring, or climbing. **2.** a rise in status; advancement. **3.** a way or means of ascending; upward slope.

as·cer·tain (AS ər TAYN) *v.t.* learn with certainty; find out. [ME] —**as′cer·tain′a·ble** *adj.*

as·cet·ic (ə SET ik) *n.* one who leads an austere and self-denying life, esp. for religious purposes. —*adj.* **1.** pertaining to ascetics or asceticism. **2.** rigidly abstinent; austere. [< Gk. *askētikós* hardworking] — **as·cet·i·cism** (ə SET ə sɪz əm) *n.*

as·cot (AS kət) *n.* a scarflike necktie. [after *Ascot*, England.]

as·cribe (ə SKRĪB) *v.t.* •**cribed**, •**crib·ing** **1.** attribute or impute, as to a cause or source: I *ascribe* his conduct to insanity. **2.** consider or declare as belonging (to). [ME] —**as·crib′a·ble** *adj.*

as·crip·tion (ə SKRIP shən) *n.* **1.** the act of ascribing. **2.** a staement that ascribes.

a·sep·tic (ə SEP tik) *adj.* free of pathogenic organisms.

a·sex·u·al (ay SEK shoo əl) *adj. Biol.* 1. having no distinct sexual organs; without sex. 2. occurring or performed without union of male and female gametes.

ash¹ (ash) *n. pl.* ash·es 1. the powdery, whitish gray residue of a substance that has been burned. 2. *pl.* the remains of the human body after cremation or disintegration. [ME *aisshe*]

ash² *n.* 1. a tree of the olive family. 2. the light, tough, elastic wood of this tree. [ME *asshe*]

a·shamed (ə SHAYMD) *adj.* 1. feeling shame. 2. deterred by fear of shame. [ME]

ash·en¹ (ASH ən) *adj.* 1. of, pertaining to, or like ashes. 2. pale in color; gray. [ME]

ash·en² *adj.* pertaining to or made of ash wood. [ME]

a·shore (ə SHOR) *adv. & adj.* 1. to or on the shore. 2. on land.

ash·ram (ASH rəm) *n.* 1. a secluded place for mediatation by Hindus. 2. a retreat or commune. [< Skt. *aśrama* religious experience]

Ash Wednesday the first day of Lent: from the application of ashes to the heads of penitents.

A·sian (AY zhən) *adj.* of or characteristic of Asia or its peoples. —A'sian *n.*

A·si·at·ic (AY zhee AT ik) *adj. & n.* Asian: considered offensive in referring to people.

a·side (ə SĪD) *adv.* 1. on or to one side; apart. 2. out of thought or use: put grief *aside.* —aside from 1. apart from. 2. excepting. —*n.* 1. a remark that is not addressed to everyone present. 2. a remark that digresses from the subject. [ME]

as·i·nine (AS ə nīn) *adj.* silly; stupid; obstinate. [< L *asininus* asslike] —as·i·nin·i·ty (AS ə NIN ə tee) *n.*

ask (ask) *v.t.* 1. put a question to. 2. put a question about: *ask* the time. 3. make a request of or for; solicit. 4. need or require. 5. state the price of; demand. 6. invite. —*v.i.* 7. make inquiries: with *for, after,* or *about.* 8. make a request: often with *for.* [ME *asken*]

a·skance (ə SKANS) *adv.* 1. with a side glance; sidewise. 2. disdainfully; distrustfully.

a·skew (ə SKYOO) *adj.* oblique. —*adv.* in an oblique position or manner; awry.

a·slant (ə SLANT) *adj.* slanting; oblique. —*adv.* at a slant; obliquely. —*prep.* slantingly across or over. [ME *on slant,* aslant]

a·sleep (ə SLEEP) *adj.* 1. in a state of sleep; sleeping. 2. dormant; inactive. 3. benumbed, as an arm or leg. —*adv.* into a sleeping condition: fall *asleep.* [ME]

a·so·cial (ay SOH shəl) *adj.* 1. avoiding society; not gregarious. 2. selfish; self-centered.

asp (asp) *n.* the common European viper. [ME *aspis* snakes]

as·par·a·gus (ə SPAR ə gəs) *n.* the edible shoots of a cultivated variety of an herb of the lily family. [< L]

as·pect (AS pekt) *n.* 1. facial expression. 2. appearance to the eye; look. 3. appearance presented to the mind: all *aspects* of a problem. 4. the side or surface facing in a certain direction. [ME]

as·pen (AS pən) *n.* a species of poplar with leaves that tremble in the slightest breeze. —*adj.* 1. of the aspen. 2. trembling, like aspen leaves. [ME, trembling]

as·per·i·ty (ə SPER i tee) *n. pl.* ·ties 1. roughness or harshness, as of surface, sound, etc. 2. sharpness of temper; acrimony. [ME *asperite* rough]

as·per·sion (ə SPUR zhən) *n.* 1. a slandering; defamation. 2. a slanderous or damaging report; calumny. [< MF]

as·phalt (AS fawlt) *n.* 1. a solid, brownish black, combustible mixture of bituminous hydrocarbons. 2. a mixture of this with sand or gravel, used for paving, etc. —*v.t.* pave with asphalt. [< L]

as·phyx·i·a (as FIK see ə) *n. Pathol.* unconsciousness caused by too little oxygen and too much carbon dioxide in the blood. [< NL]

as·phyx·i·ate (as FIK see AYT) *v.t. & v.i.* ·at·ed, ·at·ing cause or undergo asphyxia; suffocate. —as·phyx'i·a'tion *n.*

as·pic (AS pik) *n.* a jelly of meat or vegetable juices. [< F]

as·pir·ant (ə SPĪR ənt) *n.* one who aspires.

as·pi·rate (AS pə RAYT) *v.t.* ·rat·ed, ·rat·ing 1. utter with a puff of breath or as if preceded by an *h* sound. 2. follow with a puff of breath, as (p) when before a vowel. 3. *Med.* draw out with an aspirator. —*n.* (AS pər it) an aspirated sound. —*adj.* (AS pər it) *Phonet.* uttered with an aspirate: also as'pi·rat'ed. [< L *aspiratus* breathed upon]

as·pi·ra·tion (AS pə RAY shən) *n.* 1. exalted desire; high ambition. 2. the act of breathing; breath. **3.** *Med.* the use of an aspirator. **4.** *Phonet.* an aspirate.

as·pi·ra·tor (AS pə RAY tər) *n. Med.* a device for drawing off fluid or gases from the body by suction.

as·pire (ə SPĪR) *v.i.* **·spired, ·spir·ing** have an earnest desire or ambition. [ME] — **as·pir'ing** *adj.*

as·pi·rin (AS pər in) *n.* a white crystalline compound, salicylic acid, used for the relief of fever, pain, etc.

ass (as) *n. pl.* **ass·es 1.** a long-eared quadruped related to the horse; donkey. **2.** a stupid person; fool. [ME *asse*]

as·sail (ə SAYL) *v.t.* attack violently, as by force, argument, etc. [ME *asaylen* leap] — **as·sail·ant** (ə SAY lənt) *n.*

as·sas·sin (ə SAS in) *n.* one who kills; esp., one who murders a political figure. [< Arabic *hashshāshīn* users of hashish]

as·sas·si·nate (ə SAS ə NAYT) *v.t.* **·nat·ed, ·nat·ing 1.** kill by secret or surprise assault. **2.** destroy or injure by treachery, as a reputation. —**as·sas'si·na'tion** *n.*

as·sault (ə SAWLT) *n.* **1.** any violent attack by act or words. **2.** *Law* an unlawful attempt or threat to do bodily injury to another. **3.** a rape. [ME *asaut* leap] —**as·sault'** *v.t. & v.i.*

as·say (AS ay) *n.* **1.** the analysis or testing of an alloy or ore to ascertain its ingredients and proportions. **2.** any examination or testing. —*v.* (ə SAY) *v.t.* **1.** subject to chemical analysis. **2.** prove; test. *v.i.* **3.** show by analysis a certain value or proportion, as of a precious metal. [ME, test] —**as·say'er** *n.*

as·sem·blage (ə SEM blij) *n.* **1.** the act of assembling, or the state of being assembled. **2.** any gathering; collection; group. **3.** a fitting together, as of the parts of a machine. **4.** a work of art created by assembling materials and objects; also, the technique of making such works. [< F]

as·sem·ble (ə SEM bəl) *v.t. & v.i.* **·bled, ·bling 1.** come or bring together; collect or congregate. **2.** fit or join together, as parts. [ME]

as·sem·bly (ə SEM blee) *n. pl.* **·blies 1.** the act of assembling, or the state of being assembled. **2.** a number of persons met together for a common purpose. **3.** the act or process of fitting together the parts of a machine, etc.; also, the parts themselves. [ME *assemblee*]

as·sent (ə SENT) *v.i.* express agreement:

usu. with *to.* —*n.* **1.** mental agreement. **2.** consent; sanction. [ME *asenten*]

as·sert (ə SURT) *v.t.* **1.** state positively; declare. **2.** maintain as a right or claim, as by words or force. —**assert oneself** put forward and defend one's own rights or claims. [< L *assertus* bound]

as·ser·tion (ə SUR shən) *n.* **1.** the act of asserting. **2.** a positive declaration without attempt at proof.

as·ser·tive (ə SUR tiv) *adj.* confident; aggressive. —**as·ser'tive·ness** *n.*

as·sess (ə SES) *v.t.* **1.** charge with a tax, fine, or other payment. **2.** determine the amount of, as a tax on a person or property. **3.** evaluate for taxation. [ME *assessen*] —**as·ses'sor** *n.*

as·sess·ment (ə SES mənt) *n.* **1.** the act of assessing. **2.** an amount assessed.

as·set (AS et) *n.* **1.** an item of property. **2.** a useful or valuable thing or quality. [< AF, enough]

as·sets (AS ets) *n.pl.* all the property and resources of a person, business, etc., that may be used to pay debts or other obligations: opposed to *liabilities.*

as·sev·er·ate (ə SEV ə RAYT) *v.t.* **·at·ed, ·at·ing** affirm or declare emphatically or solemnly. [< L *asseveratus* spoken earnestly] —**as·sev'er·a'tion** *n.*

as·si·du·i·ty (AS ə DOO i tee) *n. pl.* **·ties** close application or effort; diligence. [< L *assiduitas*]

as·sid·u·ous (ə SIJ oo əs) *adj.* **1.** devoted; attentive. **2.** persistent: *assiduous* study. [< L *assiduus* sitting near]

as·sign (ə SĪN) *v.t.* **1.** set apart, as for a particular function; designate. **2.** appoint, as to a duty. **3.** allot as a task. **4.** ascribe or attribute. **5.** *Law* transfer, as personal property, rights, or interests. [ME *assignen* make a sign] —**as·sign'a·ble** *adj.* — **as·sign'er** *n.* —*Law* **as·sign·or** (ə SĪ NOR) *n.*

as·sig·na·tion (AS ig NAY shən) *n.* **1.** an appointment for meeting, esp. a secret one made by lovers. **2.** assignment. [ME *assignacioun*]

as·sign·ee (ə sī NEE) *n. Law* a person to whom property, rights, or powers are transferred.

as·sign·ment (ə SĪN mənt) *n.* **1.** the act of assigning. **2.** anything assigned, as a lesson or task. **3.** *Law* the transfer of a claim, right, or property; the instrument or writing of transfer.

as•sim•i•late (ə SIM ə layt) *v.t. & v.i.*
•lat•ed, •lat•ing 1. *Biol.* take up and incorporate or be incorporated into living organisms, as food. **2.** take or be taken in; absorb or be absorbed. **3.** make or become alike or similar. [< L *assimilatus* made like] —
as•sim′i•la′tion *n.*

as•sist (ə SIST) *v.t. & v.i.* help. —*n.* **1.** an act of helping. **2.** a play (in baseball) that helps to put out a runner or (in hockey and basketball) helps to score a goal. [< L *assistere* stand by]

as•sis•tance (ə SIS təns) *n.* the act of helping, or the help given; aid; support.

as•sis•tant (ə SIS tənt) *n.* one who assists; a subordinate or helper. —*adj.* **1.** subordinate or auxiliary. **2.** helping; assisting.

as•so•ci•ate (ə SOH shee it) *n.* **1.** a companion. **2.** a partner or colleague. **3.** one admitted to partial membership in an association, society, or institution. **4.** *cap.* a degree given by a junior college. —*adj.* **1.** joined with another or others in a common pursuit or office. **2.** having subordinate or secondary status. **3.** existing or occurring together; concomitant. —*v.* (ə SOH shee AYT) **•at•ed, •at•ing** *v.t.* **1.** ally; unite. **2.** combine. **3.** connect mentally. —*v.i.* **4.** unite for a common purpose. **5.** keep or be in company: with *with.* [ME]

as•so•ci•a•tion (ə soh SEE AY shən) *N.* **1. the act of associating, or the state of being associated. 2.** a body of persons associated for some common purpose; society. [< MF]

as•so•ci•a•tive (ə SOH shee AY tiv) *adj.* **1.** of or characterized by association. **2.** causing association.

as•sort (ə SORT) *v.t.* distribute into groups according to kinds; classify. [< MF *assorter*] —**as•sort•ed** (ə SOR tid) *adj.*

as•sort•ment (ə SORT mənt) *n.* **1.** the act of assorting; classification. **2.** a varied collection; miscellany.

as•suage (ə SWAYJ) *v.t.* **•suaged, •suag•ing 1.** make less harsh or severe; alleviate. **2.** satisfy, as thirst. **3.** calm; pacify. [ME *aswagen* sweeten] —**as•suage′ment** *n.*

as•sume (ə SOOM) *v.t.* **•sumed, •sum•ing 1.** take on or adopt, as a style of dress, aspect, or character. **2.** undertake, as an office or duty. **3.** usurp, as powers of state. **4.** take for granted. [ME]

as•sump•tion (ə SUMP shən) *n.* **1.** the act of assuming, or that which is assumed. **2.** that which is taken for granted; a supposition. **3.** Presumption; arrogance. —**the Assumption** a church feast, observed on August 15, commemorating the bodily ascent of the Virgin Mary into heaven.

as•sur•ance (ə SHUUR əns) *n.* **1.** the act of assuring, or the state of being assured. **2.** a positive statement, intended to give confidence, encouragement, etc. **3.** self-confidence; boldness. [ME *assuraunce*]

as•sure (ə SHUUR) *v.t.* **•sured, •sur•ing 1.** make sure or secure; establish firmly. **2.** make (something) certain; guarantee. **3.** cause to feel certain; convince. **4.** promise. **5.** insure, as against loss. [ME *assuren* secure]

as•sured (ə SHUURD) *adj.* **1.** made certain; guaranteed. **2.** self-possessed; confident. **3.** insured. [ME] —**as•sur′ed•ly** *adv.*

as•ter (AS tər) *n.* a composite plant having flowers with white, purple, or blue rays and a yellow disk. [< L, star]

as•ter•isk (AS tə risk) *n. Printing* a starlike figure (°) used to indicate omissions, references; etc. [ME].

as•ter•oid (AS tə ROID) *n. Astron.* any of several hundred small planets between Mars and Jupiter: also called *planetoid.* [< Gk. *asteroeides* starry]

asth•ma (AZ mə) *n. Pathol.* a chronic respiratory disorder characterized by recurrent paroxysmal coughing and constriction of the chest. [ME] —**asth•mat•ic** (az MAT ik) *adj. & n.*

as•tig•mat•ic (AS tig MAT ik) *adj.* of, having, or correcting astigmatism. [< *a-* without + Gk. *stigma* mark]

a•stig•ma•tism (ə STIG mə TIZ əm) *n.* a defect of the eye or of a lens causing imperfect focusing.

a•stir (ə STUR) *adv. & adj.* stirring; moving about.

as•ton•ish (ə STON ish) *v.t.* affect with wonder and surprise; amaze. [ME *astonyen* thunder]

as•ton•ish•ment (ə STON ish mənt) *n.* **1.** the state of being astonished. **2.** a cause of such emotion.

as•tound (ə STOWND) *v.t.* overwhelm with wonder; amaze. [ME *astouned*] —**a•stound′•ing** *adj.*

as•tral (AS trəl) *adj.* of, pertaining to, coming from, or like the stars; starry. [< MF]

a•stray (ə STRAY) *adv. & adj.* away from the right path; wandering. [ME *astraye* strayed]

a•stride (ə STRĪD) *adv. & adj.* **1.** with one

leg on each side. **2.** with the legs far apart. —*prep.* With one leg on each side of: *astride* a horse.

as·trin·gent (ə STRIN jənt) *adj.* **1.** *Med.* tending to contract tissues; binding. **2.** harsh; stern; austere. —*n.* an astringent substance. [< L *astringere* bind fast]

astro- *combining form* **1.** star. **2.** of, pertaining to, occurring in, or characteristic of outer space. [< Gk. *ástron* star]

as·tro·labe (AS trə LAYB) *n.* an instrument formerly used for obtaining the altitudes of planets and stars. [ME]

as·trol·o·gy (ə STROL ə jee) *n.* the study professing to interpret the influence of heavenly bodies on human destiny. [ME] —**as·trol′o·ger** *n.*

as·tro·naut (AS trə nawt) *n.* one who travels in space. [< F *astronaute*]

as·tro·nau·tics (AS trə NAW tiks) *n.* (*construed as sing.*) the science and art of space travel.

as·tro·nom·i·cal (AS trə NOM i kəl) *adj.* **1.** of or pertaining to astronomy. **2.** enormously or inconceivably large.

astronomical unit a unit of length for expressing the distances of the stars, equal to the mean distance of the earth from the sun, about 93 million miles.

as·tron·o·my (ə STRON ə mee) *n.* the science treating of the heavenly bodies, their motions, magnitudes, distances, and constitution. [ME *astronomie*] —**as·tron′o·mer** *n.*

as·tro·phys·ics (AS troh FIZ iks) *n.* (*construed as sing.*) the branch of astronomy treating of the physical constitution and properties of the heavenly bodies. —**as·tro·phys·i·cist** (AS troh FIZ ə sist) *n.*

as·tute (ə STOOT) *adj.* keen in discernment; shrewd. [< L *astutus* cunning] —**as·tute′ness** *n.*

a·sun·der (ə SUN dər) *adv. & adj.* **1.** apart; into pieces. **2.** in or into a different place or position. [ME]

a·sy·lum (ə SI ləm) *n.* **1.** an institution for the care of the mentally ill, the destitute, etc. **2.** a place of refuge. **3.** an inviolable shelter from arrest or punishment, as a temple or church in ancient times. [ME]

a·sym·met·ric (AY si ME trik) *adj.* not symmetrical. —**a·sym·me·try** (ay SIM ə tree) *n.*

as·ymp·tote (AS im toht) *n. Math.* a straight line that an indefinitely extended curve continually approaches as a tangent. [< Gk.

asymptotos falling together] —**as·ymp·tot·ic** (AS im TOT ik) *adj.*

at (at) *prep.* **1.** in or on the position of: at the center. **2.** of time, on or upon the point or stroke of: *at* noon. **3.** during the course of: *at* night. **4.** in contact with; upon: *at* sea. **5.** to or toward: Look *at* that! **6.** within the limits or region of: *at* home. **7.** engaged in: *at* work. **8.** attending: *at* a party. **9.** in the state or condition of: *at* war. **10.** in connection with: cringe *at* the thought. **11.** in the manner of: *at* a trot. **12.** dependent on: *at* one's mercy. **13.** according to: Act *at* your discretion. **14.** amounting to: a loan *at* five percent. [ME]

at·a·vism (AT ə VIZ əm) *n.* occurrence in an individual of a trait from a remote ancestor; also, such an individual. [< L *atavus* remote ancestor] —**at′a·vis′tic** *adj.*

ate (ayt) past tense of EAT.

at·el·ier (AT l YAY) *n.* a workshop, esp. of an artist; studio. [< F]

a·the·ist (AY thee ist) *n.* one who denies or disbelieves in the existence of God. [< Gk. *átheos* godless] —**a′the·ism** *n.*

ath·e·nae·um (ATH ə NEE əm) *n.* **1.** an institution for the promotion of learning. **2.** a reading room, library, etc. Also **ath′e·ne′um.** [< L]

ath·er·o·scle·ro·sis (ATH ər oh sklə ROH sis) *n. Pathol.* hardening of the arteries, accompanied by the deposit of fat in the inner arterial walls. [< G. *Atherosklerose*]

ath·lete (ATH leet) *n.* one trained in acts of physical strength and agility. [< L *athleta* contender]

athlete's foot ringworm of the foot.

ath·let·ic (ath LET ik) *adj.* **1.** of, pertaining to, or befitting an athlete or athletics. **2.** strong; vigorous. —**ath·let·i·cism** (ath LET ə SIZ əm) *n.*

ath·let·ics (ath LET iks) *n.pl.* games and exercises requiring physical strength, skill, endurance, and agility; sports.

At·lan·tic (at LAN tik) *adj.* of, near, in, or pertaining to the Atlantic Ocean. —*n.* the Atlantic Ocean. [ME]

at·las (AT ləs) *n.* **1.** a volume of maps. **2.** any book of tables or charts.

at·mos·phere (AT məs FEER) *n.* **1.** the body of gases surrounding the earth or a celestial body. **2.** the particular climatic condition of any place or region. **3.** any surrounding or pervasive element or influence. **4.** *Physics* a unit of pressure, equal to 14.69 pounds per square inch. [< NL

atmosphaera, lit., vapor sphere] —
at′mos·pher′ic (-FER ik) *adj.*

at·mos·pher·ics (AT məs FER iks) *n.* **1.**
(construed as sing.) in radio transmission,
static. **2.** *(construed as pl.)* mood or atmosphere.

at·oll (AT awl) *n.* a ring-shaped coral island
and its associated reef, nearly or completely
enclosing a lagoon. [< F]

at·om (AT əm) *n.* **1.** the smallest unit of an
element; one of the particles of which all
matter is formed, regarded as a system of
electrons organized around a nucleus. **2.** a
hypothetical minute entity thought to be
indivisible. **3.** the smallest quantity or particle; iota. [ME *attomos* undivided]

a·tom·ic (ə TOM ik) *adj.* **1.** of or pertaining
to an atom or atoms. **2.** of or pertaining to
atomic energy. **3.** minute; infinitesimal.

atomic bomb a bomb of immense destructive power using the energy released by the
fission of atomic nuclei: also called *atom
bomb.*

atomic clock a high-precision instrument
for the measurement of time by the vibration rate of an atomic system.

atomic energy the energy contained within
the nucleus of the atom, which can be released by fission or fusion.

atomic number *Physics* a number equal to
the positive charges (protons) in the atomic
nucleus of an element.

atomic weight *Chem.* the average weight of
an atom of an element relative to that of
carbon, taken as 12.

at·om·ize (AT ə MIZ) *v.t.* **·ized, ·iz·ing 1.**
reduce to atoms. **2.** spray or reduce to a
spray, as by an atomizer.

at·om·iz·er (AT ə MI zər) *n.* an apparatus for
producing a spray.

a·to·nal (ay TOH nəl) *adj. Music* without
tonality; lacking key or tonal center. —
a·to·nal·i·ty (AY toh NAL i tee) *n.*

a·tone (ə TOHN) *v.i.* **a·toned, a·ton·ing**
make expiation, as for sin or wrongdoing.
[back formation from ATONEMENT]

a·tone·ment (ə TOHN mənt) *n.* **1.** satisfaction, reparation, or expiation made for
wrong or injury. **2.** *Christian Theol.* the reconciliation between God and man affected
by Christ. [< earlier adverbial phrase *at
one*, in harmony + suffix *-ment*, instrument
of]

a·tri·um (AY tree əm) *n. pl.* **a·tri·a** (AY tree
ə) or **a·tri·ums 1.** the entrance hall or central open court of an ancient Roman house.
2. a court or hall. **3.** *Anat.* one of the upper
chambers of the heart: also called *auricle.*
[< NL] —**a′tri·al** *adj.*

a·tro·cious (ə TROH shəs) *adj.* **1.** very
wicked, cruel, etc. **2.** very bad, or in bad
taste. —**a·tro′cious·ness** *n.*

a·troc·i·ty (ə TROS i tee) *n. pl.* **·ties 1.** the
state or quality of being atrocious. **2.** an
atrocious deed or act. [< L *atrocitas*]

at·ro·phy (A trə fee) *n. Pathol.* a wasting or
failure in development of the body or any of
its parts. —*v.t. & v.i.* **·phied, ·phy·ing**
cause or undergo atrophy. [< MF *atrophie*]

at·tach (ə TACH) *v.t.* **1.** make fast to something; fasten on; affix. **2.** add or append, as a
signature. **3.** connect by personal ties, as of
affection. **4.** appoint officially; assign. **5.**
Law seize by legal process. —*v.t.* **6.** be attached; connect. [ME *atachen* seize]

at·ta·ché (a ta SHAY) *n.* a person officially
attached to a diplomatic mission or staff in a
specified capacity: military *attaché.* [< F,
attached]

attaché case a boxlike briefcase.

at·tach·ment (ə TACH mənt) *n.* **1.** the act
of attaching, or state of being attached. **2.**
something attached, as an accessory part
for a machine. **3.** a bond, as of affection. **4.**
Law seizure of a person or property.

at·tack (ə TAK) *v.t.* **1.** set upon violently;
begin to battle. **2.** to criticize violently; condemn. **3.** begin work on. **4.** harm; injure. —
v.i. **5.** make an attack; begin battle. —*n.* **1.**
an act of attacking; assault. **2.** an approach;
beginning. **3.** a seizure, as by disease. [<
MF *attacquer* attack]

at·tain (ə TAYN) *v.t.* **1.** gain by exertion of
body or mind; achieve. **2.** come to, as in
time; arrive at. [ME *ateinen* touch] —
at·tain′a·ble *adj.*

at·tain·der (ə TAYN dər) *n.* the loss of all
civil rights following a sentence of death or
of outlawry for a capital offense. [ME]

at·tain·ment (ə TAYN mənt) *n.* **1.** the act of
attaining. **2.** that which is attained, esp. a
skill.

at·tar (AT ər) *n.* the fragrant essential oil
extracted from the petals of flowers, esp.
roses. [< Arabic *itr* perfume]

at·tempt (ə TEMPT) *v.t.* make an effort to
do or accomplish; try. —*n.* a putting forth of
effort; endeavor. [ME]

at·tend (ə TEND) *v.t.* **1.** be present at, as a
meeting. **2.** wait upon as an attendant. **3.**
visit or minister to (a sick person). **4.** accompany. **5.** give heed to; listen to. —*v.i.* **6.** be

attendance

present. **7.** give heed; listen. [ME *atenden* notice]

at·ten·dance (ə TEN dəns) *n.* **1.** the act of attending. **2.** those who attend, collectively.

at·ten·dant (ə TEN dənt) *n.* **1.** one who attends, esp. as a servant. **2.** a concomitant; consequence. —*adj.* following or accompanying.

at·ten·tion (ə TEN shən) *n.* **1.** close or earnest attending. **2.** the power or faculty of mental concentration. **3.** practical consideration; care. **4.** *Usu. pl.* courteous behavior, esp. by a suitor.

at·ten·tive (ə TEN tiv) *adj.* **1.** observant. **2.** courteous or gallant. —**at·ten'tive·ness** *n.*

at·ten·u·ate (ə TEN yoo ayt) *v.* **·at·ed, ·at·ing** *v.t.* **1.** make thin, small, or fine; draw out, as a wire. **2.** weaken; lessen. —*v.i.* **3.** become thin or less. [< L *attenuatus* reduced] —**at·ten'u·a'tion** *n.*

at·test (ə TEST) *v.t.* **1.** confirm as accurate, true, or genuine; vouch for. **2.** certify, as by signature or oath. **3.** be proof of. —*v.i.* **4.** bear witness; testify. [< MF *attester* bear witness] —**at·tes·ta·tion** (AT e STAY shən) *n.*

at·tic (AT ik) *n.* a low story beneath the roof of a building; a garret. [< F *attique*]

At·tic (AT ik) *adj.* **1.** of Attica, a region surrounding ancient Athens. **2.** of or characteristic of Athens or its people. **3.** simple and graceful; also **at·tic**. [< L *Atticus*, Attica]

at·tire (ə TĪR) *v.t.* **·tired, ·tir·ing** dress; array. —*n.* dress or clothing. [ME *atiren* adorn]

at·ti·tude (AT i TOOD) *n.* **1.** position of the body, as suggesting some thought or feeling. **2.** state of mind, behavior, or conduct regarding some matter. [< F] —**at'ti·tu'di·nal** *adj.*

at·ti·tu·di·nize (AT ə TOOD n ĪZ) *v.i.* **·nized, ·niz·ing** assume an attitude for effect.

at·tor·ney (ə TUR nee) *n.* a person empowered by another to act in his or her stead; esp., a lawyer. [ME] —**attorney at law** a lawyer.

attorney general *pl.* **attorneys general, attorney generals** the chief law officer of a government.

at·tract (ə TRAKT) *v.t.* **1.** draw to or cause to come near by some physical force, as magnetism. **2.** appeal to. —*v.i.* **3.** exert attractive influence. [ME]

at·trac·tion (ə TRAK shən) *n.* **1.** the act or power of attracting. **2.** something that attracts.

at·trac·tive (ə TRAK tiv) *adj.* **1.** pleasing; charming. **2.** having the power to attract.

at·trib·ute (ə TRIB yoot) *v.t.* **·ut·ed, ·ut·ing** ascribe as belonging to or resulting from: *attribute* wisdom to old age. —*n.* (AT rə BYOOT) a quality or characteristic of a person or thing. [ME]

at·tri·bu·tion (A trə BYOO shən) *n.* **1.** the act of attributing. **2.** an ascribed characteristic or quality; attribute. [ME]

at·trib·u·tive (ə TRIB yə tiv) *adj.* **1.** pertaining to or of the nature of an attribute. **2.** *Gram.* designating an adjective or its equivalent that stands before the noun it modifies. —*n. Gram.* an attributive word or phrase. [< MF *attributif*]

at·tri·tion (ə TRISH ən) *n.* **1.** a rubbing out or grinding down, as by friction. **2.** a gradual reduction or weakening, as of strength or personnel. [ME]

at·tune (ə TOON) *v.t.* **·tuned, ·tun·ing 1.** bring into accord; harmonize. **2.** tune.

a·typ·i·cal (ay TIP i kəl) *adj.* not typical. —**a·typ'i·cal·ly** *adv.*

au·burn (AW bərn) *adj. & n.* reddish brown. [ME *abourne* blond]

au cou·rant (OH kuu RAHN) *French* up-to-date; well informed.

auc·tion (AWK shən) *n.* a public sale conducted by bidding, at which the highest bidder becomes the purchaser. [< L *auctio* increase] —**auc·tion** *v.t.* sell at auction.

auc·tion·eer (AWK shə NEER) *n.* one who conducts an auction.

au·da·cious (aw DAY shəs) *adj.* **1.** showing no fear; daring; bold. **2.** shameless; impudent. —**au·dac·i·ty** (aw DAS i tee) *n.* [ME]

au·di·ble (AW də bəl) *adj.* loud enough to be heard. [< LL *audibilis* able to be heard] —**au'di·bil'i·ty** *n.*

au·di·ence (AW dee əns) *n.* **1.** those who hear or see a performance or communication, esp. when assembled for the purpose. **2.** a formal interview. [ME]

au·di·o (AW dee oh) *adj.* relating to sound waves or to their transmission, reproduction, frequency range, etc. [< AUDIO-]

audio- *combining form* pertaining to hearing. Also **audi-**.

au·di·o·phile (AW dee ə FIL) *n.* an enthusiast for high-fidelity sound reproduction.

au·di·o·vis·u·al (AW dee oh VIZH oo əl)

adj. relating to presentation of information by recorded sound and pictures.

au·dit (AW dit) *v.t.* **1.** examine and certify financial accounts. **2.** attend (a college course) without credit. —*v.i.* **3.** make an audit. —*n.* an examination, certification, or final statement of an account. [ME *audite* hearing]

au·di·tion (aw DISH ən) *n.* a test performance, as of an actor. [< L *auditio* hearing] —*v.t. & v.i.* try or compete in an audition.

au·di·tor (AW di tər) *n.* **1.** one who audits accounts. **2.** a listener. [ME *auditour*]

au·di·to·ri·um (AW di TOR ee əm) *n.* a room or building for the assembly of an audience. [< L, lecture hall]

au·di·to·ry (AW di TOR ee) *adj.* of or pertaining to hearing or the organs or sense of hearing. [ME]

au·ger (AW gər) *n.* a tool for boring wood. [ME *a nauger* taken as *an auger*]

aught[1] (awt) *n.* anything; any part or item. —*adv.* by any chance; at all. [ME]

aught[2] *n.* the figure O; a naught; nothing. [*a naught* taken as *an aught*]

aug·ment (awg MENT) *v.t. & v.i.* make or become greater, as in size, number, or amount; intensify. [ME *augmenten* increase] —**aug′men·ta′tion** *n.*

au·gur (AW gər) *n.* a prophet; soothsayer. —*v.t. & v.i.* **1.** prophesy. **2.** be an omen of. [< L, soothsayer]

au·gu·ry (AW gyə ree) *n. pl.* **·ries 1.** the art or practice of divination. **2.** a portent or omen. [ME]

au·gust (aw GUST) *adj.* inspiring admiration or reverence; majestic. [< L *augustus* grand]

Au·gust (AW gəst) *n.* the eighth month of the year. [< L *Augustus Caesar*]

auk (awk) *n.* a short-winged, web-footed diving bird of northern seas. [< Scand.]

aunt (ant) *n.* a sister of one's father or mother, or the wife of one's uncle. [ME *aunte*]

au pair (oh PAIR) a person who receives room and board in a foreign household in exchange for doing certain chores, as caring for children. [< F, lit., equal]

au·ra (OR ə) *n. pl.* **au·ras 1.** an invisible emanation or exhalation. **2.** a distinctive air or quality. **3.** *Pathol. pl.* **au·rae** (OR ee) sensation preceding an epileptic attack or other neurological disorder. [ME]

au·ral (OR əl) *adj.* pertaining to the ear or the sense of hearing. [< L *auris* ear + *-al* pertaining to]

au·re·ate (OR ee it) *adj.* **1.** of the color of gold; golden. **2.** ornate; dazzling. [ME *aureat* decorated with gold]

au·re·ole (OR ee OHL) *n.* **1.** in art, a halo. **2.** any radiance or halo around a body. Also **au·re·o·la** (aw REE ə lə). [ME]

au·ri·cle (OR i kəl) *n.* **1.** *Anat.* **a** an atrium of the heart. **b** the external ear. **2.** an ear-shaped part. [< L *auricula* ear lobe]

au·ric·u·lar (aw RIK yə lər) *adj.* **1.** of or pertaining to the ear or the sense of hearing. **2.** ear-shaped. **3.** told into the ear; told privately.

au·rif·er·ous (aw RIF ər əs) *adj.* containing gold. [< L *aurifer* gold-bearing]

au·ro·ra (aw ROR ə) *n.* **1.** *Meteorol.* a display of arcs, bands, streamers, etc., of light occasionally seen in the skies of polar latitudes. **2.** the dawn. [ME] —**au·ro·ral** (aw ROR əl) *adj.*

aurora aus·tra·lis (aw STRAY lis) *Meteorol.* the aurora seen in far southern latitudes: also called *southern lights.* [< NL, southern aurora]

aurora bo·re·al·is (BOR ee AL is) *Meteorol.* the aurora seen in high northern latitudes: also called *northern lights.* [< NL, northern aurora]

aus·cul·tate (AW skəl TAYT) *v.t. & v.i.* **·tat·ed, ·tat·ing** *Med.* examine by listening, as with a stethoscope.

aus·pice (AW spis) *n. pl.* **aus·pi·ces** (AW spə siz) **1.** *Usu. pl.* patronage. **2.** an omen, or sign. [< F]

aus·pi·cious (aw SPISH əs) *adj.* **1.** of good omen; propitious. **2.** prosperous; fortunate. [< L *auspicium* auspice]

aus·tere (aw STEER) *adj.* **1.** severe, grave, or stern. **2.** morally strict; ascetic. **3.** sour. **4.** severely simple; unadorned. [ME, bitter] —**aus·ter·i·ty** (aw STER i tee) *n.*

aus·tral (AW strəl) *adj.* southern; torrid. [ME]

au·tar·chy (AW tar chee) *n. pl.* **·chies 1.** absolute rule or sovereignty, or a country under such rule. **2.** autarky. [< Gk. *autarchía* self-rule]

au·tar·ky (AW tar kee) *n.* national economic self-sufficiency. [< Gk. *autárkeia* self-sufficiency]

au·then·tic (aw THEN tik) *adj.* **1.** authoritative; reliable. **2.** of undisputed origin; genuine. [< LL *authenticus* original]

au·then·ti·cate (aw THEN ti KAYT) *v.t.*

•cat•ed, •cat•ing 1. make authentic or authoritative. 2. give legal validity to. 3. establish the authenticity of. —au•then'ti•ca'tion n.

au•then•tic•i•ty (AW then TIS i tee) n. the state or quality of being authentic, authoritative, or genuine.

au•thor (AW thər) n. 1. the writer of a book, treatise, etc.; also, one who writes as a profession. 2. one who begins or originates; creator. —v.t. be the author of; write. [< L auctor writer]

au•thor•i•tar•i•an (ə THOR i TAIR ee ən) adj. favoring subjection to authority as opposed to individual freedom. —au•thor'i•tar'i•an•ism n.

au•thor•i•ta•tive (ə THOR i TAY tiv) adj. 1. possessing or proceeding from proper authority; duly sanctioned. 2. exercising authority; commanding.

au•thor•i•ty (ə THOR i tee) n. pl. •ties 1. the right to command and to enforce obedience. 2. delegated right or power; authorization. 3. pl. those having the power to govern or command. 4. a person, citation, etc., appealed to in support of action or belief. 5. an expert. 6. an authoritative opinion, decision, or precedent. [ME autorite]

au•thor•ize (AW thə RĪZ) v.t. •ized, •iz•ing 1. confer authority upon; empower; commission. 2. warrant; justify. 3. sanction. [ME autorisen] —au'thor•i•za'tion n.

au•tism (AW tiz əm) n. Psychol. self-absorption, as daydreaming, introspection, fantasizing, etc., in which external reality is ignored. —au•tis•tic (aw TIS tik) adj.

au•to•bi•og•ra•phy (AW tə bī OG rə fee) n. pl. •phies the story of a person's life written by that person. —au•to•bi•o•graph•i•cal (AW tə BĪ ə GRAF i kəl) adj.

au•toc•ra•cy (aw TOK rə see) n. pl. •cies 1. absolute government by an individual. 2. a state ruled by an autocrat. [< Gk. autokráteia power over oneself]

au•to•crat (AW tə krat) n. 1. a supreme ruler. 2. an arrogant, dictatorial person. [< Gk. autokrates ruling alone] —au'to•crat'ic adj.

au•to-da-fé (AW toh də FAY) n. pl. au•tos-da-fé the public announcement and execution of a sentence of the Inquisition; esp., the burning of heretics at the stake. [< Pg., act of the faith]

au•to•graph (AW tə GRAF) n. 1. one's signature or handwriting. 2. a manuscript in the author's handwriting. —v.t. 1. write one's name in or on. 2. write in one's own handwriting. —adj. written by one's own hand, as a will. [< L autographum written with one's own hand]

au•to•in•tox•i•ca•tion (AW toh in TOK sə KAY shən) n. poisoning by a toxin secreted by one's own body.

au•to•mate (AW tə MAYT) •mat•ed, •mat•ing v.t. adapt, as a machine, factory, or process, for automation. [Back formation < AUTOMATION]

au•to•mat•ic (AW tə MAT ik) adj. 1. acting from forces inherent in itself; self-moving. 2. self-acting and self-regulating, as machinery; mechanical. 3. of firearms, using the force of recoil to extract and eject the used shell and move the next round to the chamber. —n. an automatic device, pistol, etc. [< Gk. autómatos self-moving]

au•to•ma•tion (AW tə MAY shən) n. 1. the use of sophisticated, automatic machines to do work. 2. conversion to such a system.

au•tom•a•ton (aw TOM ə TON) n. pl. •tons or •ta (-tə) 1. an apparatus that functions automatically. 2. a figure, as of a person, operated by a concealed mechanism; esp., a robot. 3. a robotlike being or person. [< L, automatic device]

au•to•mo•bile (AW tə mə BEEL) n. a four-wheeled passenger vehicle that carries its own source of power and travels on roads or streets. [< F]

au•to•mo•tive (AW tə MOH tiv) adj. 1. self-propelling. 2. of or for automobiles.

au•to•nom•ic (AW tə NOM ik) adj. 1. autonomous. 2. Physiol. pertaining to the autonomic nervous system.

autonomic nervous system a network of nerve tissue originating in the spinal column and acting to control the involuntary functions of the body, as the heart, stomach, etc.

au•ton•o•mous (aw TON ə məs) adj. independent; self-governing. [< Gk. autónomos independent]

au•ton•o•my (aw TON ə mee) n. pl. •mies 1. the condition or quality of being autonomous; esp., the power or right of self-government. 2. a self-governing community or group. [< Gk. autonomía independence]

au•top•sy (AW top see) n. pl. •sies examination of a human corpse, esp. to determine cause of death. [< MF autopsie]

au•tumn (AW təm) n. 1. the season of the

year occurring between summer and winter; fall. **2.** a time of maturity and incipient decline. [< L *autumnus*] —**au·tum·nal** (aw TUM nəl) *adj.*

autumnal equinox see under EQUINOX.

aux·il·ia·ry (awg ZIL yə ree) *adj.* **1.** giving or furnishing aid. **2.** subsidiary; accessory. **3.** supplementary; reserve. —*n. pl.* •**ries 1.** an assistant or associate. **2.** *Gram.* a verb that helps to express tense, mood, etc., as *have* in *We have gone:* also **auxiliary verb.** [< L *auxiliarius* helping]

a·vail (ə VAYL) *v.t. & v.i.* assist or aid; benefit. —**avail oneself of** utilize. —*n.* advantage; benefit; good. [ME *availe* be worthwhile]

a·vail·a·ble (ə VAY lə bəl) *adj.* **1.** capable of being used; usable. **2.** at hand; readily obtainable. —**a·vail′a·bil′i·ty** *n.*

av·a·lanche (AV ə LANCH) *n.* **1.** a large mass of snow, rocks, etc. falling down a slope. **2.** something like an avalanche, as in power or destructiveness. —*v.t. & v.i.* •**lanched,** •**lanch·ing** fall or slide upon like an avalanche. [< F]

a·vant-garde (ə VAHNT GAHRD) *n.* the vanguard; esp., in art, the group regarded as most advanced or daring in technique and ideas. [< F, lit., advance guard] —**a·vant-garde** *adj.*

av·a·rice (AV ə ris) *n.* greed; miserliness. [ME]

av·a·ri·cious (AV ə RISH əs) *adj.* greedy; grasping; miserly. [ME]

av·a·tar (AV ə TAHR) *n.* in Hinduism, the incarnation of a god. [< Skt. *avatāra* descent]

A·ve Ma·ri·a (AH vay mə REE ə) a Roman Catholic prayer to the Virgin Mary: also called *Hail Mary.* [ME]

a·venge (ə VENJ) *v.t. & v.i.* **a·venged, a·veng·ing** take vengeance or to punish for or in behalf of. [ME *avengen*]

av·e·nue (AV ə NYOO) *n.* **1.** a broad street, esp. one bordered with trees. **2.** a mode of access or attainment. [< F]

a·ver (ə VUR) *v.t.* **a·verred, a·ver·ring** declare as fact; affirm. [ME]

av·er·age (AV ər ij) *n.* **1.** *Math.* an arithmetic mean. **2.** a mean, ratio, etc., showing a specific standing or accomplishment: batting *average.* **3.** the ordinary rank, degree, or amount; general type. —*adj.* **1.** obtained by calculating the mean of several. **2.** medium; ordinary. —*v.* •**aged,** •**ag·ing** *v.t.* **1.** fix or calculate as the mean. **2.** amount to or ob-

tain an average of. —*v.i.* **3.** be or amount to an average. [< MF *avarie* damaged cargo]

a·verse (ə VURS) *adj.* opposed; unfavorable; reluctant: with *to.* [< MF] —**a·verse′ness** *n.*

a·ver·sion (ə VUR zhən) *n.* **1.** extreme dislike; opposition. **2.** something disliked.

a·vert (ə VURT) *v.t.* **1.** turn or direct away or aside. **2.** prevent or ward off, as a danger. [ME]

a·vi·ar·y (AY vee ER ee) *n. pl.* •**ar·ies** an enclosure or large cage for live birds. [< L *aviarium*]

a·vi·a·tion (AY vee AY shən) *n.* the act, science, or art of flying heavier-than-air aircraft. [< F]

a·vi·a·tor (AY vee AY tər) *n.* an airplane pilot.

av·id (AV id) *adj.* very desirous; eager; greedy. [< L *avidus*] —**a·vid·i·ty** (ə VID i tee) *n.*

a·vi·on·ics (AY vee ON iks) *n.pl.* the electronic devices used in aviation, space vehicles, etc.

av·o·ca·do (AV ə KAH doh) *n. pl.* •**dos 1.** the pear-shaped fruit of a West Indian tree: also called *alligator pear.* **2.** the tree bearing this fruit. [< Mexican Sp. *aguacato* < Nahuatl, testicle]

av·o·ca·tion (AV ə KAY shən) *n.* an occasional occupation; hobby. [< L *avocatio* calling away]

a·void (ə VOID) *v.t.* keep away from; shun; evade. [ME *avoiden* empty] —**a·void′ ance** (ə VOID ns) *n.*

av·oir·du·pois (AV ər də POIZ) *n.* **1.** the ordinary system of weights of the U.S. and Great Britain in which 16 ounces avoirdupois make a pound. **2.** *Informal* body weight. [ME *avoir de pois*, lit., property of weight]

a·vouch (ə VOWCH) *v.t.* **1.** vouch for; guarantee. **2.** affirm positively; proclaim. [ME *avouchen*]

a·vow (ə VOW) *v.t.* declare openly, as facts; frankly acknowledge. [ME *avowen*] —**a·vowed′** *adj.* —**a·vow′ed·ly** (ə VOW id lee) *adv.*

a·vun·cu·lar (ə VUNG kyə lər) *adj.* of, pertaining to, or like an uncle. [< L *avunculus* maternal uncle]

a·wait (ə WAYT) *v.t.* **1.** wait for; expect. **2.** be ready or in store for. [ME *awaiten*]

a·wake (ə WAYK) *adj.* not asleep; alert. —*v.* **a·woke** or **a·waked, a·woke** or **a·waked** or **a·wo·ken, a·wak·ing** *v.t.* **1.** arouse from sleep. **2.** stir up; excite. —*v.i.* **1.** cease to sleep; become awake. **2.** become alert or aroused. [ME *awaken*]

a·wak·en (ə WAY kən) *v.t. & v.i.* awake. [ME *awakenen*]

a·wak·en·ing (ə WAY kə ning) *n.* **1.** the act of waking. **2.** a rousal, as of interest.

a·ward (ə WORD) *v.t.* **1.** adjudge as due, as by legal decision. **2.** bestow, as a prize. —*n.* **1.** a decision, as by a judge or arbitrator. **2.** that which is awarded, as a medal. [ME *awarden* decide]

a·ware (ə WAIR) *adj.* conscious; cognizant: often with *of.* [ME, watchful]

a·wash (ə WOSH) *adv. & adj.* **1.** tossed or washed about by waves. **2.** at or just above the surface of the water. **3.** covered, as if by water: *awash* with demonstrators.

a·way (ə WAY) *adv.* **1.** from a given place; off. **2.** far; at or to a distance. **3.** in another direction; aside. **4.** out of existence: waste *away.* **5.** continuously: He droned *away.* **6.** from one's keeping: give food *away.* **7.** at once, without hesitation: Fire *away!* —*adj.* at a distance: three blocks *away.* —*interj.* begone! [ME]

awe (aw) *n.* reverential fear; dread mingled with veneration. —*v.t.* awed, aw·ing inspire with awe. [ME *aghe* fear] — **awe·some** (-səm) *adj.*

aw·ful (AW fəl) *adj.* **1.** very bad or unpleasant. **2.** inspiring awe. **3.** causing fear or dread. —**aw'ful·ly** *adv.*

a·while (ə HWĪL) *adv.* for a brief time. [ME]

awk·ward (AWK wərd) *adj.* **1.** ungraceful in bearing. **2.** clumsy or bungling. **3.** embarrassing or perplexing. **4.** difficult to deal with. **5.** inconvenient. [ME, perverse]

awl (awl) *n.* a pointed instrument for making small holes. [ME *al*]

awn·ing (AW ning) *n.* a rooflike cover, as of canvas, for protection from sun or rain.

a·woke (ə WOHK) a past tense and past participle of AWAKE.

AWOL (AY wawl) *Mil.* absent without leave. Also **A.W.O.L.**

a·wry (ə RĪ) *adj. & adv.* **1.** askew. **2.** amiss; wrong. [ME *on wry*]

ax (aks) *n. pl.* **ax·es** (AK siz) a tool with a bladed head mounted on a handle, used for

chopping, hewing, etc. —*v.t.* cut or trim with an ax. Also **axe.** [ME]

ax·i·al (AK see əl) *adj.* **1.** of, pertaining to, or forming an axis. **2.** situated on or along an axis. —**ax'i·al·ly** *adv.*

ax·il (AK sil) *n. Bot.* the cavity or angle formed by the junction of the upper side of a leafstalk, branch, etc., with a stem or branch. [< L *axilla* armpit]

ax·il·la (ak SIL ə) *n. pl.* **ax·il·lae** (ak SIL ee) **1.** *Anat.* the armpit. **2.** an axil.

ax·il·lar·y (AK sə LER ee) *adj.* **1.** *Bot.* of, pertaining to, or situated in an axil. **2.** *Anat.* pertaining to the axilla: *axillary* hair.

ax·i·om (AK see əm) *n.* **1.** a self-evident truth. **2.** *Logic & Math.* a self-evident proposition accepted as true without proof. [< L *axioma* worthy thing] —**ax'i·o·mat'ic** *adj.*

ax·is (AK sis) *n. pl.* **ax·es** (AK seez) **1.** a line around which a turning body rotates or may be supposed to rotate. **2.** *Geom.* **a** a straight line through the center of a plane or solid figure. **b** a fixed line, as in a graph, along which distances are measured or to which positions are referred. **3.** the central line about which the parts of a body or thing are symmetrically arranged. **4.** an alliance of two or more nations. [< L, axle]

ax·le (AK səl) *n.* a crossbar on which a wheel or wheels turn. [ME *axel*]

a·yah (AH yə) *n.* in India, a nurse or lady's maid. [< Hind. *āyā*]

aye (ī) *n.* an affirmative vote or voter. —*adv.* yes; yea. Also **ay.**

a·zal·ea (ə ZAYL yə) *n.* a flowering shrub of the heath family. [< NL]

az·i·muth (AZ ə məth) *n.* **1.** the angular distance in a horizontal plane measured clockwise from true north to a given course or celestial object. **2.** *Astron.* the angle measured at the zenith, clockwise from true south to a vertical plane passing through a heavenly body. [ME *azimut* direction] — **az·i·muth·al** (AZ ə MUTH əl) *adj.*

AZT (AY ZEE TEE) *n.* azidothymidine: an antiviral drug used in the treatment of AIDS: a trade name.

az·ure (AZH ər) *n.* a clear, sky-blue color or pigment. [ME *asure*] —*adj.* having this color.

B

b, B (bee) n. pl. **b's** or **bs, B's** or **Bs 1.** the second letter of the English alphabet. **2.** the sound represented by the letter *b*. — *symbol* **1.** *Music* the seventh tone in the diatonic scale of C. **2.** the second in a series.

baa (ba) v.i. **baaed, baa•ing** bleat, as a sheep. [Imit.] —**baa** n.

Ba•al (BAY əl) n. pl. **Ba•al•im** (BAY ə,lim) **1.** any of several ancient Semitic gods of fertility and flocks. **2.** an idol or false god. [< Hebrew *ba'al* lord]

Bab•bitt (BAB it) n. a type of conventional American businessman; a smug, middle-class philistine. [after title character of the Sinclair Lewis novel (1922)]

bab•ble (BAB əl) v. **•bled, •bling** v.i. **1.** utter inarticulate or meaningless sounds; prattle, as a baby. **2.** make a murmuring or rippling sound, as a stream. **3.** talk foolishly. —v.t. **4.** utter inarticulately. **5.** blurt out thoughtlessly. —n. **1.** inarticulate or confused speech. **2.** a murmuring sound. [ME *babelen*] —**bab'bler** n.

ba•bel (BAY bəl) n. a confusion of many voices or languages; tumult. Also **Ba'bel.** [after Tower of *Babel*, intended to reach to heaven but abandoned when God made the builders speak many strange languages (*Gen. xi* 9)]

ba•boon (ba BOON) n. a large terrestrial monkey of Africa and Asia, having a doglike muzzle and usu. a short tail. [ME *baboyne*]

ba•bush•ka (bə BUUSH kə) n. a woman's scarf, worn over the head. [< Russ., grandmother]

ba•by (BAY bee) n. pl. **•bies 1.** a very young child; an infant. **2.** the youngest or smallest member of a family or group. **3.** one who looks or acts like a child. —adj. **1.** for a baby. **2.** like a baby. **3.** small; miniature. —v.t. **•bied, •by•ing** treat as a baby; pamper. [ME] —**ba'by•ish** adj.

baby sitter a person who takes care of children in the absence of parents: also called *sitter*. —**ba'by-sit** v.i. **-sat, -sit•ting** act as a baby sitter.

bac•ca•lau•re•ate (BAK ə LOR ee it) n. **1.** the degree of a bachelor of arts, bachelor of science, etc. **2.** an address to a graduating class at commencement. [< Med.L *baccalaureatus* advanced student, bachelor]

bac•ca•rat (BAH kə RAH) n. a gambling game in which winnings are decided by comparing cards held by the banker with those held by the players. [< F *baccara*]

bac•cha•nal (BAH kə NAHL) n. **1.** a drunken reveler. **2.** a drunken orgy. [< L *Bacchanal*]

bac•cha•na•li•a (BAK ə NAY lee ə) n. pl. **•li•a, •li•as** drunken revelries; orgies. [< L] —**bac'cha•na'li•an** adj.

bach•e•lor (BACH ə lər) n. **1.** an unmarried man. **2.** one who has taken his first university or college degree. [ME *bacheler*]

ba•cil•lus (bə SIL əs) n. pl. **•cil•li** (-SIL ī) *Bacteriol.* any of a large class of rod-shaped bacteria, including both beneficial and pathogenic species. [< LL, little walking stick]

back¹ (bak) n. **1.** the part of the body nearest the spine; in people the rear, in quadrupeds the upper part, extending from the neck to the base of the spine. ♦ Collateral adj.: *dorsal*. **2.** the backbone. **3.** the rear or posterior part of anything. **4.** the farther or other side; the reverse. **5.** the part behind or opposite to the part used: the *back* of a knife. **6.** in football, a player in a position behind the line of scrimmage. —**behind one's back 1.** secretly. **2.** treacherously. —**turn one's back on 1.** show contempt toward by ignoring. **2.** renounce. —v.t. **1.** cause to move backward; reverse the action of. **2.** furnish with a back. **3.** support, as by financing or by endorsing. **4.** bet on. —v.i. **5.** move backward. —**back down** withdraw from a position; give in. —**back off** retreat. —**back out (of)** withdraw from. —adj. **1.** in the rear; behind. **2.** distant; remote: the *back* country. **3.** of or for an earlier date: a *back* issue. **4.** in arrears; overdue: *back* taxes. [ME *bak*]

back² adv. **1.** at, to, or toward the rear. **2.** in, to, or toward a former time, place, or condition. **3.** in return or retort. **4.** in reverse or concealment. **5.** in check or hindrance. **6.** in withdrawal or repudiation. —**go back on 1.** fail to keep (an engagement, promise, etc.). **2.** desert or betray.

back•bite (BAK bīt) v.t. & v.i. **•bit, •bit•ten, •bit•ing** revile behind one's back; slander. [ME]

back·board (BAK BORD) *n.* a board forming, supporting, or at the back of something.

back·bone (BAK BOHN) *n.* **1.** the spine or vertebral column. **2.** something likened to a backbone in function or appearance. **3.** strength of character. *strength of character.*

back·break·ing (BAK BRAY king) *adj.* physically exhausting.

back·door (BAK DOR) *adj.* clandestine; underhand.

back·er (BAK ər) *n.* **1.** one who supports with money. **2.** one who bets on a contestant.

back·field (BAK FEELD) *n.* in football, the players behind the line of scrimmage.

back·fire (BAK FIR) *n.* **1.** a premature explosion of gases in the cylinder of an internal combustion engine, or in the muffler. **2.** a fire built to check a forest or prairie fire by creating a clear area in its path. —*v.i.* **·fired, ·fir·ing 1.** explode in a backfire. **2.** have an unexpected and unwelcome result: *His plan backfired.*

back·gam·mon (BAK GAM ən) *n.* a board game for two persons, with the moves of pieces being determined by dice throws.

back·ground (BAK GROWND) *n.* **1.** that part in a picture against which principal subjects are represented. **2.** a subordinate position; obscurity. **3.** the sum of one's experiences; one's history. **4.** the events leading up to a situation. **5.** music or sounds subordinate to the action in a movie, television show, etc.

back·hand (BAK HAND) *n.* **1.** handwriting that slopes toward the left. **2.** a stroke of the arm made with the back of the hand forward.

back·hand·ed (BAK HAN did) *adj.* **1.** delivered with a backhand stroke. **2.** insincere; equivocal: *a backhanded* compliment. **3.** sloping to the left, as handwriting.

back·ing (BAK ing) *n.* **1.** support, assistance, or endorsement. **2.** the back of anything; esp., something added as a support.

back·lash (BAK LASH) *n.* **1.** a jarring recoil. **2.** in fishing, the tangling of line when the reel overruns the cast. **3.** a negative reaction to political or social change.

back·log (BAK LAWG) *n.* **1.** a large log at the back of an open fireplace. **2.** a reserve supply or an accumulation.

back·pack (BAK PAK) *n.* a bag worn on the back to carry supplies on walking trips. —*v.i.* take a walking trip wearing a backpack.

back·rest (BAK REST) *n.* a support for the back.

back·side (BAK SID) *n.* the rump.

back·slide (BAK SLID) *v.i.* **·slid, ·slid** or **·slid·den, ·slid·ing** return to wrong or sinful ways. —**back'slid'er** *n.*

back·spin (BAK SPIN) *n.* rotation of a ball that tends to retard its forward motion.

back·stop (BAK STOP) *n.* *Sports* a screen or the like, behind home plate, a goal, etc. to stop the ball or puck.

back talk insolent answering back.

back·track (BAK TRAK) *v.i.* **1.** retrace one's steps. **2.** withdraw from a position, undertaking, etc.

back·up (BAK UP) *n.* that which is kept available as a replacement. —**back'up** *adj.*

back·ward (BAK wərd) *adv.* **1.** toward the back; to the rear. **2.** with the back foremost. **3.** in reverse order. **4.** from better to worse. **5.** to or into time past. Also **back'wards.** —*adj.* **1.** turned to the back or rear; reversed. **2.** done the reverse or wrong way. **3.** behind in growth or development; retarded. **4.** hesitating; bashful. [ME *bakwarde*]

back·wa·ter (BAK WAW tər) *n.* **1.** water turned or held back, as by a dam, a current, etc. **2.** any place or condition regarded as stagnant, backward, etc. [ME *bakwateres*]

ba·con (BAY kən) *n.* the salted and dried or smoked back and sides of the hog. —**bring home the bacon** bring home money, food, etc. [ME *bacoun* ham]

bac·te·ri·a (bak TEER ee ə) plural of BAC·TERIUM.

bac·te·ri·ol·o·gy (bak TEER ee OL ə jee) *n.* the branch of biology and medicine that deals with bacteria. —**bac·te'ri·ol'o·gist** *n.*

bac·te·ri·um (bak TEER ee əm) *n. pl.* **·ri·a** any of numerous unicellular microorganisms ranging from the harmless and beneficial to those that cause disease. [< NL]

bad (bad) *adj.* **worse, worst 1.** not good in any manner or degree. **2.** evil; immoral. **3.** defective; worthless. **4.** faulty; incorrect or unsound. **5.** not sufficient; inadequate. **6.** lacking skill or proficiency: *a bad* poet. **7.** distressing; unfavorable: *bad* news. **8.** disagreeable: *a bad* taste. **9.** harmful. **10.** rotted; spoiled. **11.** severe: *a bad* storm. **12.** sick; in ill health. **13.** sorry; regretful: He felt *bad* about it. —**not bad** rather good: also **not half bad, not so bad.** —*n.* **1.** that which is bad. **2.** those who are bad: with *the.* **3.** wickedness. [ME *badde*] —**bad'ness** *n.*

bade (bad) past tense of BID.

badge (baj) n. **1.** any device worn to indicate rank, membership, an award, etc. **2.** any distinguishing mark or insigne. [ME *bagge*]

badg•er (BAJ ər) n. **1.** a small, burrowing, nocturnal, carnivorous mammal, with a broad body, short legs, and long-clawed toes. **2.** the fur of a badger. —v.t. harass; nag at.

bad•i•nage (BAD n AHZH) n. playful raillery; banter. —v.t. •naged, •nag•ing tease with badinage. [< F]

bad•lands (BAD LANDZ) n.pl. a barren area characterized by numerous ridges, peaks, and mesas cut by erosion.

bad•ly (BAD lee) adv. **worse, worst** in a bad manner; improperly, imperfectly, or grievously.

bad•min•ton (BAD min tn) n. a game played by batting a shuttlecock back and forth over a high, narrow net with a light racket. [after *Badminton*, an estate in England]

bad-tem•pered (BAD TEM pərd) adj. cross; irritable.

Bae•de•ker (BAY di kər) n. **1.** any of a series of travelers' guidebooks. **2.** any guidebook for travelers. [after Karl *Baedeker*, 1801—59, German publisher who issued them]

baf•fle (BAF əl) v. •fled, •fling v.t. **1.** confuse mentally; perplex. **2.** foil or frustrate. —v.i. **3.** struggle to no avail. —n. a partition used to control and direct sounds, fluids, etc. —**baf′fle•ment** n.

bag (bag) n. **1.** a sack or pouch, used as a receptacle. **2.** the amount a bag will hold. **3.** a woman's purse. **4.** a suitcase or satchel. **5.** the amount of game caught or killed in hunting. **6.** a bulging or baggy part, as of a sail. **7.** in baseball, a base. —**in the bag** *Informal* assured; certain. —**be left holding the bag** *Informal* be left to assume full blame. —v. **bagged, bag•ging** v.t. **1.** put into a bag. **2.** cause to fill out or bulge like a bag. **3.** capture or kill, as game. —v.i. **4.** bulge or swell like a bag. **5.** hang loosely. [ME *bagge* bundle]

bag and baggage 1. with all one's possessions: He cleared out *bag and baggage*. **2.** entirely; completely.

bag•a•telle (BAG ə TEL) n. **1.** a trifle. **2.** a pinball game. [< F]

ba•gel (BAY gəl) n. a doughnut-shaped roll of yeast dough simmered in water and baked. [< Yiddish *beygl*]

bag•gage (BAG ij) n. the trunks, packages, etc., of a traveler. [ME *bagage*]

bagn•io (BAN yoh) n. pl. •ios **1.** a brothel. **2.** esp. in Turkey, a bath house. [< Ital. *bagno*]

bag•pipe (BAG PĪP) n. *Often pl.* a reed musical instrument having several pipes, the air being forced through them from an inflated leather bag.

ba•guette (ba GET) n. **1.** a gem or crystal cut in long, narrow, rectangular form. **2.** a narrow loaf French bread. [< F]

bail¹ (bayl) n. a scoop or bucket for dipping out fluids, as from a boat. —v.t. & v.i. **1.** dip (water) from a boat with a bail. **2.** clear (a boat) of water by dipping out. —**bail out** jump with parachute from an aircraft; save a failing enterprise; abandon a difficult situation. [ME *beyl*]

bail² n. **1.** one who becomes surety for the debt or default of another, esp. of a person under arrest. **2.** the security given or agreed upon. **3.** release, or the privilege of release, on bail. —v.t. obtain the release of (an arrested person) by giving bail: often with *out*. [ME *bayle* custody]

bail•iff (BAY lif) n. **1.** a court officer having custody of prisoners under arraignment. **2.** a sheriff's deputy. [ME *baillif*]

bail•i•wick (BAY lə WIK) n. **1.** the office, jurisdiction, or district of a bailiff. **2.** a person's own area of authority or competence. [ME]

bait (bayt) n. **1.** food or any lure placed in a trap, on a hook, etc. **2.** any allurement or enticement. —v.t. **1.** put food or some other lure on or in: *bait* a trap. **2.** set dogs upon for sport: *bait* a bear. **3.** harass; torment. **4.** lure; entice. [ME]

baize (bayz) n. a plain woolen feltlike fabric, usu. dyed green, used for the tops of pool tables etc. [< F *baies*]

bake (bayk) v. **baked, bak•ing** v.t. **1.** cook (bread etc.) by dry heat, as in an oven. **2.** harden by heat, as bricks or pottery. —v.i. **3.** bake bread, pastry, etc. **4.** become baked or hardened by heat. —n. a baking, or the amount baked. [ME *baken*]

baker's dozen thirteen.

bak•er•y (BAY kə ree) n. pl. •er•ies **1.** a place for baking bread, cake, etc. **2.** a shop where bread, cake, etc., are sold.

bal•a•lai•ka (BAL ə LĪ kə) n. a Russian stringed instrument of the guitar family. [< Russ.]

bal•ance (BAL əns) n. **1.** *Sometimes pl.* an instrument for weighing; esp., a bar that pivots on a central point as weights are placed in the pans suspended from each end. **2.** figuratively, the scale by which deeds and principles are weighed and destinies determined. **3.** the power or authority to decide and determine. **4.** a state of equilibrium or equal relationship. **5.** bodily poise. **6.** mental or emotional stability. **7.** harmonious proportion, as in the arrangement of parts in a whole. **8.** something used to produce an equilibrium. **9.** in bookkeeping: **a** equality between the debit and credit totals of an account. **b** a difference between such totals. **10.** remainder. **11.** a balance wheel. —**strike a balance** find or take an intermediate position; compromise. —*v.* **•anced, •anc•ing** *v.t.* **1.** bring into or keep in equilibrium; poise. **2.** weigh in a balance. **3.** weigh (alternatives) in the mind. **4.** offset or counteract. **5.** place or keep in proportion. **6.** be equal or in proportion to. **7.** in bookkeeping, compute or adjust the difference between the debit and credit sides of (an account). —*v.i.* **8.** be equal or come into equilibrium. **9.** be equal. [ME *balaunce*]

balance of power a distribution of power among nations or people such that none may acquire a degree of strength dangerous to the others.

balance sheet a statement in tabular form to show assets and liabilities, profit and loss, etc., of a business.

balance wheel the oscillating wheel of a watch, which determines its rate of motion.

bal•co•ny (BAL kə nee) *n. pl.* **•nies 1.** a platform projecting from a wall of a building. **2.** a projecting gallery in a theater or public building. [< Ital. *balcone*]

bald (bawld) *adj.* **1.** without hair on the head. **2.** without natural covering or growth. **3.** unadorned. **4.** without disguise; forthright. [ME *balld* white spot] —**bald'ly** *adv.* —**bald'ness** *n.*

bal•der•dash (BAWL dər DASH) *n.* nonsense.

bald•pate (BAWLD payt) *n.* a baldheaded person.

bale (bayl) *n.* a large package of bulky goods, usu. corded. —*v.t.* **baled, bal•ing** make into a bale or bales. [ME]

ba•leen (bə LEEN) *n.* whalebone. [ME *balene* whale]

bale•ful (BAYL fəl) *adj.* **1.** hurtful; malignant. **2.** ominous. [ME]

balk (bawk) *v.i.* **1.** stop short and refuse to

proceed or take action. —*v.t.* **2.** render unsuccessful; thwart. —*n.* **1.** a hindrance or check; disappointment. **2.** an error or blunder. **3.** in baseball, an illegal motion made by the pitcher, resembling a checked pitch. [ME]

balk•y (BAW kee) *adj.* **balk•i•er, balk•i•est** given to balking.

ball¹ (bawl) *n.* **1.** a spherical or nearly spherical body. **2.** any such object used in a number of games. **3.** in sports, a ball moving, thrown, or struck in a specified manner. **4.** in baseball, a pitch in which the ball fails to pass over the home plate between the batter's armpits and knees and is not struck at by the batter. **5.** a roundish part of something. —**be on the ball** be alert or competent. —**have something on the ball** have ability. —**play ball 1.** begin or resume playing a ball game or some other activity. **2.** cooperate. —*v.t. & v.i.* form, gather, or wind into a ball. [ME *bal*]

ball² *n.* **1.** a formal social dance. **2.** a good time. [< F *bal*]

bal•lad (BAL əd) *n.* **1.** a narrative poem or song of popular origin in short stanzas, often with a refrain. **2.** a sentimental song of several stanzas, in which usu. the melody is repeated for each stanza. [ME *balade*] —**bal'lad•eer'** *n.*

bal•last (BAL əst) *n.* **1.** any heavy substance, as sand, stone, etc. used to steady a ship or other vessel. **2.** gravel or broken stone laid down as a stabilizer for a rail bed. **3.** that which gives stability. —*v.t.* **1.** provide or fill with ballast. **2.** stabilize. [< ODan. *barlast* bare load]

bal•le•ri•na (BAL ə REE nə) *n.* a female ballet dancer. [< Ital.]

bal•let (ba LAY) *n.* **1.** an elaborate dramatic group dance using conventionalized movements, often for narrative effect. **2.** a troupe of ballet dancers. [< F] —**bal•let•ic** (ba LET ik) *adj.*

bal•let•o•mane (ba LET ə MAYN) *n.* a ballet enthusiast.

ballistic missile a missile controlled to the apex of its trajectory, falling free thereafter.

bal•lis•tics (bə LIS tiks) *n.* (*usu. construed as sing.*) the science that deals with the motion of projectiles. —**bal•lis'tic** *adj.*

bal•loon (bə LOON) *n.* **1.** a large, impermeable bag inflated with gas lighter than air, designed to rise and float in the atmosphere, and often equipped to carry passengers, instruments, etc. **2.** a small, inflatable rubber bag, used as a toy. —*v.i.* **1.** increase quickly in scope or magnitude. **2.** swell out like a balloon, as a sail. **3.** ascend or travel in a balloon. —*v.t.* **4.** inflate or distend with air. [< Ital. *ballone*] —**bal·loon'ist** *n.*

bal·lot (BAL ət) *n.* **1.** a written or printed slip or ticket used in casting a secret vote. **2.** the total number of votes cast in an election. **3.** the system of voting secretly by ballots or by voting machines. **4.** a list of candidates for office. —*v.i.* **·lot·ed, ·lot·ing** cast a ballot in voting. [< MF *ballotte*]

balm (bahm) *n.* **1.** an aromatic, resinous exudation from various trees or shrubs, used as medicine; balsam. **2.** any similar substance. **3.** a pleasing fragrance. **4.** anything that soothes. [ME *basme* balsam tree]

balm·y (BAH mee) *adj.* **balm·i·er, balm·i·est 1.** mild and soothing; soft. **2.** having the fragrance of balm; aromatic.

bal·sa (BAWL sə) *n.* **1.** a tree of tropical America and the West Indies. **2.** the very light wood of this tree. [< Sp., boat]

bal·sam (BAWL səm) *n.* **1.** any of a group of fragrant oleoresins obtained chiefly from the exudations of various trees. **2.** any tree yielding such a substance. **3.** any fragrant ointment. [ME *balsamum*] —**bal·sam·ic** (bawl SAM ik) *adj.*

bal·us·ter (BAL ə stər) *n.* ane of a set of small pillars supporting a handrail. [< F *balustre* pillar]

bal·us·trade (BAL ə STRAYD) *n.* a handrail supported by balusters.

bam·bi·no (bam BEE noh) *n. pl.* **·nos** or **·ni** (-nee) **1.** a little child; a baby. **2.** an image of the child Jesus. [< Ital., childish]

bam·boo·zle (bam BOO zəl) *v.* **·zled, ·zling** *v.t.* **1.** mislead; cheat. **2.** perplex. —*v.i.* **3.** practice trickery or deception.

ban (ban) *v.t.* **banned, ban·ning** proscribe or prohibit; outlaw. —*n.* **1.** an official proclamation, especially of prohibition. **2.** *Eccl.* an edict of excommunication or interdiction. [ME *bannen* proclaim]

ba·nal (bə NAL) *adj.* hackneyed; trite. [< F] —**ba·nal·i·ty** (bə NAL i tee) *n.*

band¹ (band) *n.* **1.** a flat flexible strip of any material, often used for binding or securing. **2.** a strip of fabric used to finish, strengthen, or trim an article of dress: often in combination: *hatband.* **3.** any broad stripe. **4.** *Telecom.* a range of frequencies or wavelengths between two stated limits. —*v.t.* **1.** unite or tie with a band; encircle. **2.** mark by attaching a band to. [< MF]

band² *n.* **1.** a company of persons associated for a common purpose; a troop or gang. **2.** a group organized to play musical instruments. —*v.t. & v.i.* unite in a band. [< MF *bande*]

band·age (BAN dij) *n.* a strip of material used in dressing wounds, etc. —*v.t.* **·aged, ·ag·ing** bind or cover with a bandage. [< MF]

ban·dan·na (ban DAN ə) *n.* a large, brightly colored handkerchief. [< Hind. *bādhnū,* a method of dyeing]

band·box (BAND BOKS) *n.* **1.** a light round box, usu. used for carrying hats. **2.** a structure smaller in size than usual.

ban·dit (BAN dit) *n.* a robber; outlaw. [< Ital. *banditi* outlaws] —**ban'dit·ry** *n.*

ban·do·leer (BAN dl EER) *n.* a broad belt fitted with loops or cases for holding cartridges, and worn over the shoulder. Also **ban'do·lier'.** [< MF *bandoulliere*]

band shell a bandstand having a concave hemispherical rear wall.

band·stand (BAND STAND) *n.* a platform for a band of musicians.

band·wag·on (BAND WAG ən) *n.* a high, decorated wagon used to carry a band in a parade. —**climb (hop, get,** etc.**) on the bandwagon** support a principle or candidate apparently sure of success.

ban·dy (BAN dee) *v.t.* **·died, ·dy·ing 1.** give and take; exchange, as blows or words. **2.** pass along; circulate: *bandy* stories.

ban·dy-leg·ged (BAN dee LEG id) *adj.* bowlegged.

bane (bayn) *n.* **1.** anything destructive or ruinous. **2.** poison: now only in combination: *wolfsbane.* [ME] —**bane'ful** *adj.*

bang¹ (bang) *n.* **1.** a heavy, noisy blow or thump. **2.** a sudden, loud noise. **3.** *Informal* a sudden spurt of activity. **4.** *Informal* thrill; enjoyment. —*v.t.* **1.** strike heavily and noisily. —*v.i.* **2.** make a loud sound. **3.** strike noisily; crash. —*adv.* abruptly and loudly. [< ON *banga* hammer]

bang² *n. Usu. pl.* a fringe of hair cut straight across the forehead.

ban·gle (BANG gəl) *n.* a bracelet or anklet. [< Hind. *banglī*]

ban·ish (BAN ish) *v.t.* **1.** compel to leave a country by political decree; exile. **2.** expel; drive away. [ME *banishen*] —**ban'ish·ment** *n.*

ban·is·ter (BAN ə stər) *n.* **1.** *Often pl.* a balustrade. **2.** loosely, a baluster.

ban·jo (BAN joh) *n. pl.* **·jos** or **·joes** a long-necked, usu. five-stringed musical instrument having a drumlike body and played by plucking the strings.

bank¹ (bangk) *n.* **1.** any moundlike formation or mass; ridge. **2.** a steep slope. **3.** *Often pl.* the slope of land at the edge of a watercourse or channel. **4.** a raised portion of the ocean floor, a river bed, etc. **5.** *Aeron.* the controlled sidewise tilt of an airplane in a turn. —*v.t.* **1.** enclose, cover, or protect by a bank, dike, or border; embank. **2.** heap up into a bank or mound. **3.** give an upward lateral slope to, as the curve of a road. **4.** tilt (an airplane) laterally in flight. **5.** cause (a billiard ball) to rebound at an angle from a cushion. —*v.i.* **6.** form or lie in banks. **7.** tilt laterally in flight. [ME *banke*]

bank² *n.* **1.** an institution for lending, borrowing, exchanging, issuing, or safeguarding money. **2.** an office or building used for such purposes. **3.** the funds of a gambling house. **4.** a reserve supply: blood *bank.* —*v.t.* **1.** deposit in a bank. —*v.i.* **2.** do business as or with a bank or banker. —**bank on** rely on; be sure about. [ME]

bank³ *n.* **1.** a set of like articles arranged in a row. **2.** *Naut.* a tier of oars in a galley. —*v.t.* arrange in a bank. [ME]

bank note a promissory note of a bank, serving as currency.

bank·roll (BANGK rohl) *v.t.* **·rolled,** **·roll·ing** finance. —*n.* a supply of money.

bank·rupt (BANGK rupt) *n.* **1.** *Law* one who is judicially declared insolvent, his or her property being administered by a trustee. **2.** any person unable to pay his or her debts. **3.** one ruined in some way: a spiritual *bankrupt.* —*adj.* **1.** subject to the conditions of a bankruptcy law; insolvent. **2.** destitute; ruined. —*v.t.* make bankrupt. [< Med.L *banca rupta* broken bank] — **bank·rupt·cy** (BANGK rəp see) *n.*

ban·ner (BAN ər) *n.* **1.** a flag or standard bearing a motto or device. **2.** a headline extending across a newspaper page. —*adj.* leading; outstanding. [ME *banere*]

banns (banz) *n.pl. Eccl.* a public announcement in church of a proposed marriage. Also **bans.** [pl. of BAN]

ban·quet (BANG kwit) *n.* **1.** a sumptuous feast. **2.** a formal or ceremonial dinner. —*v.t. & v.i.* entertain or feast at a banquet. [< MF]

ban·quette (bang KET) *n.* an upholstered bench, as along a wall. [< F]

ban·shee (BAN shee) *n.* in Gaelic folklore, a female spirit whose wailing foretells a death. Also **ban'shie.** [< Irish *bean* woman + *sīdhe* fairy]

ban·tam (BAN təm) *n.* **1.** *Often cap.* any of various breeds of very small domestic fowl, characterized by combativeness. **2.** a small, pugnacious person. —*adj.* small and combative. [after *Bantam,* Java]

ban·tam·weight (BAN təm WAYT) *n.* a boxer or wrestler who weighs up to 118 pounds.

ban·ter (BAN tər) *n.* good-humored ridicule; raillery. —*v.t.* **1.** tease good-naturedly. —*v.i.* **2.** exchange good-natured repartee. —**ban'ter·er** *n.*

ban·yan (BAN yən) *n.* an East Indian fig-bearing tree whose branches send down roots that develop into new trunks. [< Pg.]

ban·zai (bahn ZĪ) *Japanese* (may you live) ten thousand years: used as a cheer, battle cry, etc.

bap·tism (BAP tiz əm) *n.* **1.** the act of baptizing or of being baptized; esp., the Christian sacrament of initiation into the Church. **2.** any initiatory or purifying experience. [ME] —**bap·tis'mal** *adj.*

bap·tize (BAP tīz) *v.t.* **·tized,** **·tiz·ing 1.** immerse in water or sprinkle water on in Christian baptism. **2.** christen. **3.** cleanse or initiate. [ME]

bar (bahr) *n.* **1.** a piece of wood, metal, etc., evenly shaped and long in proportion to its width and thickness, used as a fastening, lever, etc. **2.** an oblong block of solid material, as of soap or a precious metal. **3.** any barrier or obstacle. **4.** a bank, as of sand, at the entrance to a harbor or river. **5.** the railing about the place in a court occupied by the judge and lawyers, or where prisoners are brought to trial. **6.** a court of law. **7.** lawyers collectively; also, the legal profession. **8.** *Music* **a** the vertical line that divides a staff into measures. **b** a measure. **9.** a counter or establishment serving drinks and food, esp. alcoholic drinks. **10.** a stripe, as of color. —*v.t* **barred, bar·ring 1.** fasten or secure with a bar. **2.** prevent, prohibit, or obstruct. **3.** exclude. —*prep.* excepting: *bar* none. [ME *barre* rod]

barb (bahrb) *n.* **1.** a point projecting backward on a sharp weapon, as on a fishhook or spear. **2.** any similar sharp point, as on barbed wire. **3.** a stinging remark. [ME *barbe*] —**barb** v.t. —**barbed** adj.

bar·bar·i·an (bahr BAIR ee ən) n. **1.** one who belongs to a people, group, or tribe characterized by a primitive civilization. **2.** a rude, coarse, or brutal person. —adj. of or resembling a barbarian; uncivilized. [< L *barbaria* barbarous country]

bar·bar·ic (bahr BAR ik) adj. **1.** of or befitting barbarians; uncivilized. **2.** coarse; unrestrained.

bar·ba·rism (BAHR bə RIZ əm) n. **1.** the use of words or forms not standard in a language. **2.** such a word or form. **3.** a primitive stage of civilization. **4.** a primitive or crude trait, condition, or act.

bar·bar·i·ty (bahr BAR i tee) n. pl. **·ties 1.** barbaric conduct. **2.** a barbaric act. **3.** crudity in style or taste.

bar·ba·rize (BAHR bə RIZ) v.t. & v.i. **·RIZED, ·RIZ·ING make or become barbarous or corrupt, as a language.**

bar·ba·rous (BAHR bər əs) adj. **1.** uncivilized; primitive. **2.** lacking in refinement; coarse. **3.** cruel; brutal. **4.** rude or harsh in sound. [ME]

bar·be·cue (BAHR bi KYOO) n. **1.** a social gathering, usu. outdoors, at which meat is roasted over an open fire. **2.** an animal carcass or any meat roasted over an open fire. **3.** a grill or pit for roasting meat in this fashion. —v.t. **·cued, ·cu·ing** roast (usu. beef or pork) over an open fire, often using a highly seasoned sauce. [< Sp. *barbacoa* framework of sticks]

barbed wire fence wire having barbs.

bar·ber (BAHR bər) n. one who cuts hair, shaves beards, etc., as a business. ◆ Collateral adjective: *tonsorial*. —v.t. cut or dress the hair of; shave or trim the beard of. [ME *barbour*]

bar·ber·shop (BAHR bər SHOP) n. the place of business of a barber.

bar·bi·can (BAHR bi kən) n. an outer fortification. [ME *barbecan*]

bar·bit·u·rate (bahr BICH ər it) n. Chem. a salt or ester of barbituric acid, esp. one used as a sedative or sleeping pill.

bar·bi·tu·ric acid (BAHR bi TUUR ik) Chem. a crystalline powder, from which several sedative and hypnotic drugs are derived.

bar·ca·role (BAHR kə ROHL) n. **1.** a Venetian gondolier's song. **2.** a musical composition imitating this. [< Ital. *barcarola* boatman's song]

bard (bahrd) n. **1.** a Celtic poet and minstrel. **2.** a poet. [ME] —**bard'ic** adj

bare (bair) adj. **1.** without clothing or covering; naked. **2.** open to view; exposed. **3.** without the usual furnishings or equipment; empty. **4.** unadorned; plain. **5.** just sufficient; mere. —v.t. **bared, bar·ing** make or lay bare; reveal; expose. [ME]

bare·back (BAIR BAK) adj. riding a horse without a saddle. —adv. without a saddle.

bare·foot (BAIR FUUT) adj. & adv. with the feet bare.

bare·hand·ed (BAIR HAN did) adj. & adv. **1.** with the hands uncovered. **2.** without a weapon, tool, etc.

bare·head·ed (BAIR HED id) adj. & adv. with the head bare.

bare·leg·ged (BAIR LEG id) adj. & adv. with the legs bare.

bare·ly (BAIR lee) adv. **1.** only just; scarcely. **2.** openly; plainly.

bar·gain (BAHR gən) n. **1.** a mutual agreement between persons, esp. one to buy or sell goods. **2.** that which is agreed upon or the terms of the agreement. **3.** an article bought or offered at a low price. —**into the bargain** in addition; besides. —**strike a bargain** come to an agreement. —v.i. **1.** discuss terms for selling or buying. **2.** negotiate. —v.t. **3.** trade or arrange by bargaining. —**bargain for** expect; count on: more than I *bargained for*. [ME *bargaynen*]

barge (bahrj) n. **1.** a flat-bottomed freight boat or lighter for harbors and inland waters. **2.** a large boat for pleasure, pageants, or state occasions. —v. **barged, barg·ing** v.t. **1.** transport by barge. —v.i. **2.** move clumsily and slowly. **3.** collide: with *into*. **4.** enter or intrude rudely or awkwardly: with *in* or *in on*. [ME]

bar·i·tone (BAR i TOHN) n. **1.** a male voice of a register higher than bass and lower than tenor. **2.** a person having such a voice. **3.** an instrument having a similar range. —adj. of or pertaining to a baritone. [< Ital. *baritono* low voice]

bark¹ (bahrk) n. **1.** the short, explosive cry of a dog. **2.** any sound like this. —v.i. **1.** utter a bark, as a dog; make a sound like a bark. **2.** speak sharply. **3.** Informal solicit customers at the entrance to a show. —v.t. **4.** say roughly and curtly. —**bark up the wrong tree** be mistaken as to one's object or the means of attaining it. [ME *berken*]

bark² n. the rind or covering of a woody stem

or root. —*v.t.* **1.** remove the bark from; scrape. **2.** rub off the skin of. [ME]

bark•er (BAHR kər) *n.* one who advertises a show etc. at its entrance.

bar•ley (BAHR lee) *n.* **1.** a hardy cereal grass. **2.** the grain borne by this grass. [ME]

Bar•ley•corn, John a personification of malt liquor, or of liquors in general.

bar•maid (BAHR MAYD) *n.* a female bartender.

bar mitz•vah (bahr MITS və) in Judaism, a boy commencing his thirteenth year, the age of religious duty; also, the ceremony celebrating this. [< Hebrew, son of the commandment]

barn (bahrn) *n.* a building for storing hay, stabling livestock, etc. [ME *bern*]

bar•na•cle (BAHR nə kəl) *n.* a marine shellfish that attaches itself to rocks, ship bottoms, etc.

barn•storm (BAHRN storm) *v.i.* tour rural districts, giving shows, political speeches, exhibitions of stunt flying, etc.

barn•yard (BAHRN yahrd) *n.* a yard adjoining a barn. —*adj.* smutty.

ba•rom•e•ter (bə ROM i tər) *n.* **1.** an instrument for measuring atmospheric pressure. **2.** anything that indicates changes. — **bar•o•met•ric** (BAR ə ME trik) *adj.*

bar•on (BAR ən) *n.* **1.** a member of the lowest order of hereditary nobility. **2.** one who has great power in a commercial field. [ME] —**ba•ro•ni•al** (bə ROH nee əl) *adj.*

bar•o•ness (BAR ə nis) *n.* **1.** the wife or widow of a baron. **2.** a woman holding a barony in her own right. [ME *baronnesse*]

bar•on•et (BAR ə nit) *n.* **1.** a hereditary English title, below that of baron and not part of the nobility. **2.** a bearer of the title. — **bar′on•et•cy** *n.* [ME]

bar•o•ny (BAR ə nee) *n. pl.* **•nies** the rank, dignity, or domain of a baron. [ME *baronie*]

ba•roque (bə ROHK) *adj.* **1.** of or characteristic of a style of art and architecture developed in Europe in the late 16th and 17th centuries, characterized by extravagantly contorted classical forms and curvilinear ornament. **2.** *Music* of a style prevalent esp. in the 17th century, characterized by rich harmonies, ornamentation, and brilliant effects. **3.** fantastic in style; elaborately ornamented. —*n.* the baroque style in art. [< F]

bar•racks (BAR əks) *n.* (*construed as sing. or pl.*) a building or group of buildings for the housing of soldiers. [< F *baraques*]

bar•ra•cu•da (BAR ə KOO də) *n. pl.* **•da** or **•das** a voracious fish of tropical seas. [? < Am.Sp.]

bar•rage (bə RAHZH) *n.* **1.** *Mil.* a curtain of artillery fire. **2.** any overwhelming attack, as of words or blows. —*v.t. & v.i.* **•raged, •rag•ing** lay down or subject to a barrage. [< F]

bar•rel (BAR əl) *n.* **1.** a large, usu. bulging vessel usu. of wood, flat at the base and top. **2.** as much as a barrel will hold. **3.** something resembling or having the form of a barrel, as the tube of a gun. —*v.* **bar•reled, bar•rel•ing** *v.t.* **1.** put or pack in a barrel. —*v.i.* **2.** *Informal* move fast. [ME *barell*]

bar•ren (BAR ən) *adj.* **1.** not producing or incapable of producing offspring; sterile. **2.** not productive; unfruitful; unprofitable. **3.** lacking in interest; dull. **4.** empty; devoid. —*n. Usu. pl.* a tract of level, scrubby land. [ME *bareyne*]

bar•ri•cade (BAR i KAYD) *n.* **1.** a barrier hastily built for obstruction or defense. **2.** any barrier or obstruction. —*v.t.* **•cad•ed, •cad•ing** enclose, obstruct, or defend with a barricade. [< F]

bar•ri•er (BAR ee ər) *n.* **1.** a fence, wall, etc., erected to bar passage. **2.** any obstacle or obstruction. [ME]

barrier reef a long, narrow ridge of rock or coral parallel to the coast and close to or above the surface of the sea.

bar•ring (BAHR ing) *prep.* excepting; apart from.

bar•ri•o (BAHR ee OH) *n. pl.* **•ri•os 1.** a district of a city in Spanish-speaking countries. **2.** in the U.S., a district of a city inhabited by Spanish-speaking people. [< Sp.]

bar•ris•ter (BAR ə stər) *n.* in England, a member of the legal profession who argues cases in the courts.

bar•room (BAHR ROOM) *n.* a room where alcoholic liquors are served.

bar•row[1] (BAR oh) *n.* **1.** a frame or tray with handles at either end, used for transporting loads. **2.** a wheelbarrow. **3.** the load carried on a barrow. [ME *barewe*]

bar•row[2] *n.* a mound of earth or stones built over a grave. [ME *barowe*]

bar•tend•er (BAHR TEN dər) *n.* one who mixes and serves alcoholic drinks over a bar.

bar•ter (BAHR tər) *v.i.* **1.** trade by exchange of goods or services without use of money. —*v.t.* **2.** trade (goods or services) for something of equal value. —*n.* the act of bartering; exchange of goods. [ME]

ba·sal (BAY səl) *adj.* 1. of, at, or forming the base. 2. basic; fundamental.

basal metabolism *Physiol.* the minimum energy required by the body at rest in maintaining essential vital activities, measured by the rate (**basal metabolic rate**) of oxygen intake and heat discharge.

ba·salt (bə SAWLT) *n.* a dense, dark volcanic rock. [< L *basaltes* touchstone]

base¹ (bays) *n.* 1. the lowest or supporting part of anything; bottom. 2. an underlying principle or foundation. 3. the essential or fundamental ingredient. 4. any point, line, or quantity from which an inference, measurement, or reckoning is made. 5. *Geom.* the side of a polygon or solid figure on which it rests. 6. *Mil.* a locality or installation from which operations are projected or supported. 7. *Chem.* a compound capable of so uniting with an acid as to neutralize it and form a salt. 8. in baseball, any of the four points of the diamond, or the bag or plate marking one of these. —**off base** *Informal* thinking, speaking, etc. erroneously. —*v.t.* **based, bas·ing** 1. place on a foundation or basis; ground; establish: with *on* or *upon.* 2. form a base for. —*adj.* 1. serving as a base. 2. situated at or near the base. [ME]

base² *adj.* **bas·er, bas·est** 1. morally low; vile; contemptible. 2. menial; degrading: *base* flattery. 3. low in value: said of metals. 4. debased, as money; counterfeit. [ME *bas* low]

base·ball (BAYS BAWL) *n.* 1. a game played with a bat and a hard ball by two teams of nine players each, one team being at bat and the other in the field, alternately. 2. the ball used in this game.

base·board (BAYS BORD) *n.* a board along an interior wall, next to the floor.

base·born (BAYS BORN) *adj.* 1. of humble birth. 2. born out of wedlock. 3. vile.

base hit in baseball, a batted ball that enables the batter to reach a base unaided by a defensive error and without a force play: also called *hit.*

base·less (BAYS lis) *adj.* without foundation in fact; groundless.

base·line (BAYS LIN1. in baseball, a path connecting successive bases. 2. a line, value, etc., taken as a base for measurement or comparison.

base·ment (BAYS mənt) *n.* the lowest story of a building, usu. wholly or partly underground.

base runner in baseball, a member of the team at bat who has reached a base.

bash (bash) *v.t.* strike heavily; smash in. —*n.* 1. a smashing blow. 2. a lively party.

bash·ful (BASH fəl) *adj.* 1. shy; timid. 2. characterized by timid modesty: a *bashful* glance.

ba·sic (BAY sik) *adj.* 1. essential; fundamental. 2. *Chem.* of, pertaining to, or producing a base. —**ba′si·cal·ly** *adv.*

bas·il (BAZ əl) *n.* a plant of the mint family, used in cooking. [ME *basile*]

ba·sil·i·ca (bə SIL i kə) *n.* 1. in ancient Rome, a rectangular building divided by columns into a nave and two side aisles, used as a place of assembly. 2. a building of this type used as a Christian church. [< L *basilicus* royal]

bas·i·lisk (BAS ə lisk) *n.* 1. a fabled reptile whose breath and look were said to be fatal. 2. a tropical American lizard having an erectile crest on the head. [ME]

ba·sin (BAY sən) *n.* 1. a round, wide, shallow vessel, often with sloping sides, used for holding liquids. 2. any vessel or depression resembling this. 3. the amount a basin will hold. 4. a sink or washbowl. 5. *Geog.* a any large depression in the earth's surface, as the bed of a lake or ocean. b the region drained by a river. [ME *bacin* bowl]

ba·sis (BAY sis) *n. pl.* **·ses** (-seez) 1. that on which anything rests; foundation; base. 2. fundamental principle; groundwork. 3. the chief component of a thing. [< L, step]

bask (bask) *v.i.* 1. lie in and enjoy a pleasant warmth, as of the sun or a fire. 2. enjoy or benefit from compliments, a favorable opinion, etc.: with *in.* [ME, bathe oneself]

bas·ket (BAS kit) *n.* 1. a container made of interwoven rushes, strips of wood, etc. 2. something like a basket in form or use. 3. the amount a basket will hold. 4. in basketball: **a** one of the goals, a metal ring with a cord net suspended from it. **b** a score made by throwing the ball through the basket. [ME *baskette*]

bas·ket·ball (BAS kit BAWL) *n.* 1. a game played by two teams on a court, in which the object is to throw the ball through an elevated goal (basket). 2. the ball used in this game.

bas·ket·ry (BAS ki tree) *n.* 1. baskets collectively; basketwork. 2. the art of making baskets.

bas·ket·work (BAS kit WURK) *n.* work done in basket weave or resembling it.

Basque (bask) *n.* **1.** one of a people of unknown origin living in the western Pyrènees in Spain and France. **2.** the language of the Basque people. —*adj.* of the Basques.

bas·re·lief (BAH ri LEEF) *n.* sculpture in which the figures project only slightly from the background. [< F]

bass¹ (bas) *n. pl.* **bass** or **bass·es** any of various spiny-finned marine and freshwater food fishes. [ME]

bass² (bays) *Music n.* **1.** the lowest-pitched male singing voice. **2.** the notes in the lowest register of the piano, pipe organ, etc. **3.** the lowest part in vocal or instrumental music. **4.** one who sings or an instrument that plays such a part. —*adj.* **1.** low in pitch; having a low musical range. **2.** of or for a bass or basses. [ME *bas*]

bas·set (BAS it) *n.* a hound characterized by a long, low body, long ears, and short, crooked forelegs. Also **basset hound**. [< F]

bas·si·net (BAS i NET) *n.* a basket used as a baby's cradle, usu. with a hood over one end. [< F]

bas·so (BAS oh) *n. pl.* **·sos** (-sohz), *Ital.* **·si** (-see) **1.** a bass singer. **2.** the bass part. [< Ital.]

bas·soon (ba SOON) *n. Music* a large, low-pitched woodwind instrument. [< F *basson*]

bas·tard (BAS tərd) *n.* **1.** an illegitimate child. **2.** any irregular, inferior, or counterfeit thing. **3.** *Slang* a worthless or cruel person. —*adj.* **1.** born out of wedlock. **2.** spurious. **3.** abnormal or irregular in size, shape, etc. [ME] —**bas'tard·y** *n.*

bas·tard·ize (BAS tər DIZ) *v.t.* **·ized,** **·iz·ing 1.** prove to be or proclaim to be a bastard. **2.** make degenerate; debase.

baste¹ (bayst) *v.t.* **bast·ed, bast·ing** sew loosely together, esp. with long stitches. [ME *basten*]

baste² *v.t.* **bast·ed, bast·ing** moisten (meat or fish) with drippings, butter, etc., while cooking. [ME *basten*]

baste³ *v.t.* **bast·ed, bast·ing 1.** beat; thrash. **2.** attack verbally; abuse.

Bas·tille (ba STEEL) a prison in Paris, stormed and captured in the French Revolution on July 14, 1789.

bas·ti·na·do (BAS tə NAY doh) *n. pl.* **·does 1.** a beating with a stick, usu. on the soles of the feet. **2.** a stick or cudgel. [< Sp. *bastonada*]

bas·tion (BAS chən) *n.* **1.** in fortifications, a projecting part of a rampart. **2.** any fortified position. [< MF]

bat¹ (bat) *n.* **1.** in baseball and similar games: **a** a stick or club for striking the ball. **b** the act of batting. **c** one's turn for batting. **2.** any heavy cudgel or club. **3.** *Informal* a blow, as with a bat. **4.** *Slang* a drunken spree. —**go to bat for** *Informal* speak up for. —*v.* **bat·ted, bat·ting** *v.i.* **1.** in baseball and other games, use a bat or club. —*v.t.* **2.** strike with or as with a bat. [ME, cudgel]

bat² *n.* a nocturnal flying mammal with elongated forelimbs and digits that support a thin wing membrane. —**have bats in the belfry** *Informal* be crazy. [ME *bakke*]

bat³ *v.t.* **bat·ted, bat·ting** wink. —**not bat an eye** not show surprise.

batch (bach) *n.* **1.** a quantity or number taken together. **2.** the amount of bread produced at one time. **3.** any set of things made, done, etc., at one time. [ME *bache*]

bate (bayt) *v.t. & v.i.* **bat·ed, bat·ing** restrain; decrease. —**with bated breath** in a state of fear, suspense, expectation, etc. [ME]

bath (bath) *n. pl.* **baths** (bathz) **1.** a washing or immersing of something, esp. the body, in water or other liquid. **2.** the liquid used for this. **3.** the container for such a liquid; a bathtub. **4.** a bathroom. **5.** *Often pl.* an establishment or resort where bathing is part of a health treatment. [ME]

bathe (bayth) *v.* **bathed, bath·ing** *v.t.* **1.** place in liquid; immerse. **2.** wash; wet; apply liquid to. —*v.i.* **3.** wash oneself; take a bath. **4.** be covered or suffused as if with liquid: *bathe* in sunshine. [ME *bathien*]

bath·house (BATH HOWS) *n.* **1.** a building with facilities for bathing. **2.** a building used for changing into or out of bathing suits.

bath·ing suit (BAYTH ing) a garment worn for swimming.

ba·thos (BAY thos) *n.* **1.** a descent from the lofty to the commonplace in discourse; anticlimax. **2.** insincere pathos; sentimentality. [< Gk., depth]

bath·robe (BATH ROHB) *n.* a long, loose garment for wear before and after bathing.

bath·room (BATH ROOM) *n.* **1.** a room in which to bathe. **2.** a toilet.

bath·tub (BATH TUB) *n.* a vessel in which to bathe.

bath·y·sphere (BATH ə SFEER) *n.* a spherical diving bell equipped with windows for deep-sea observations. [< Gk. *bathy* deep + -*sphere*]

ba·tik (bə TEEK) *n.* **1.** a process for coloring fabrics, in which the parts not to be dyed are covered with wax. **2.** the fabric so colored. [< Javanese]

bat mitzvah (baht MITS və) in some branches of Judaism, a girl commencing her twelfth year; also, the ceremony celebrating this. [< Hebrew, daughter of the commandment]

ba·ton (bə TON) *n.* **1.** a short staff or truncheon borne as an emblem of authority. **2.** *Music* a slender stick used by a conductor. [< MF *baton* club]

ba·tra·chi·an (bə TRAY kee ən) *adj.* of or pertaining to a former class of amphibians, esp. to frogs and toads; amphibian. —*n.* a frog or toad. [< NL *Batrachia*]

bat·tal·ion (bə TAL yən) *n.* **1.** *Mil.* **a** a unit consisting of a headquarters and two or more companies, batteries, or comparable units. **b** a body of troops. **2.** *Often pl.* a large group or number. [< MF *bataillon*]

bat·ten¹ (BAT n) *v.i. & v.t.* grow or make fat, as cattle. [< ON *batna* improve]

bat·ten² *n.* **1.** a light strip of wood, as for covering a joint between boards. **2.** *Naut.* a thin strip of wood placed in a sail to keep it flat or for fastening a tarpaulin over a hatch. —*v.t.* fasten with battens: with *down*. [ME *bataunt* board]

bat·ter¹ (BAT ər) *v.t.* **1.** strike with repeated, violent blows. **2.** damage or injure with blows or with hard usage. —*v.i.* **3.** pound or beat with blows. [ME *bateren*]

bat·ter² *n.* in baseball, the player whose turn it is to bat.

bat·ter³ *n.* a mixture, as of eggs, flour, and milk, beaten for use in cookery. [ME *batour* beating]

battering ram *n.* a long, stout beam, used in ancient warfare for battering down walls.

bat·ter·y (BAT ə ree) *n. pl.* **·ter·ies** **1.** any unit, apparatus, or grouping in which a set of parts or components is assembled to serve a common end. **2.** *Electr.* one or more cells operating together as a single source of direct current. **3.** *Mil.* **a** an artillery unit equivalent to an infantry company. **b** a group of guns, rockets, or related equipment forming an artillery unit. **4.** *Naval* the guns of a warship, or a specific group of them. **5.** *Law* the illegal beating or touching of another person. [< MF *batterie*]

bat·ting (BAT ing) *n.* wadded cotton or wool prepared in sheets or rolls, used for interlining, stuffing mattresses, etc.

bat·tle (BAT l) *n.* **1.** a combat between hostile armies or fleets. **2.** any fighting, conflict, or struggle. —*v.* **·tled, ·tling** *v.i.* **1.** contend in or as in battle; struggle; strive. —*v.t.* **2.** fight. [ME *bataile*]

bat·tle-ax (BAT l AKS) *n.* **1.** a large ax formerly used in battle. **2.** *Slang* a formidable, disagreeable person, esp. a woman. Also **bat'tle-axe'**.

battle cry **1.** a shout uttered by troops in battle. **2.** a slogan or distinctive phrase used in any conflict or contest.

bat·tle·field (BAT l FEELD) *n.* the terrain on which a battle is fought. Also **bat'tle·ground'**.

bat·tle·ship (BAT l SHIP) *n.* a warship of great size, with heavy armor and armament.

bau·ble (BAW bəl) *n.* a worthless, showy trinket. [ME *babel*]

baux·ite (BAWK sīt) *n.* a claylike substance containing aluminum oxide or hydroxide, the principal ore of aluminum. [after *Les Baux*, France]

bawd (bawd) *n.* **1.** a prostitute. **2.** a madam. [ME *bawde*]

bawd·y (BAW dee) *adj.* **bawd'·i·er, bawd·i·est** obscene; indecent. —**bawd'·i·ness** *n.*

bawd·y·house (BAW dee HOWS) *n.* a brothel.

bawl (bawl) *v.t.* **1.** call out noisily; bellow. —*v.i.* **2.** cry or sob noisily. —**bawl out** *Informal* berate; scold. [ME, bark]

bay¹ (bay) *n.* a body of water partly enclosed by land; an inlet of the sea. [ME *baye*]

bay² *n.* *Archit.* **a** a bay window. **b** an extension or wing of a building. **2.** any opening or recess in a wall. **3.** *Aeron.* a compartment in an aircraft: weapons *bay*. [ME]

bay³ *adj.* reddish brown: said esp. of horses. —*n.* **1.** a reddish brown color. **2.** a horse (or other animal) of this color. [ME]

bay⁴ *n.* a deep bark or cry, as of dogs in hunting. —**at bay 1.** unable to escape; cornered. **2.** kept off, as by one's quarry. —*v.i.* **1.** utter a deep-throated cry, as a hound. —*v.t.* **2.** utter with or as with such a cry. [ME]

bay·o·net (BAY ə nit) *n.* a daggerlike weapon attachable to the muzzle of a firearm, used in close fighting. —*v.t.* **·net·ed, ·net·ing** stab or pierce with a bayonet. [< F *baïonnette*]

bay·ou (BI oo) *n.* a marshy inlet or outlet of a lake, river, etc. [< Louisiana F]

bay window a window structure projecting

from the wall of a building and forming a recess within.

ba·zaar (bə ZAHR) n. 1. an Oriental market or street of shops. 2. a store for the sale of miscellaneous wares. 3. a sale of miscellaneous articles, as for charity. [< Ital.]

ba·zoo·ka (bə ZOO kə) n. Mil. a tubular, portable weapon that fires an explosive rocket. [from bazooka, a comical musical instrument]

be (bee) v.i. **been, be·ing** present indicative: **I am,** he, she, it **is,** we, you, they **are;** past indicative: I, he, she, it **was,** we, you, they **were;** present subjunctive: **be;** past subjunctive: **were;** archaic forms: thou **art** (present), thou **wast** or **wert** (past) 1. as a substantive verb, be is used to mean: **a** have existence, truth, or actuality: There are bears in the zoo. **b** take place; happen: The party is today. **c** stay or continue: She was here for a day. 2. as a copulative verb between the subject and predicate noun or adjective: Anne is my daughter; He is sick. 3. as an auxiliary verb, be is used: **a** with the present participle of other verbs to express continuing action: I am working. **b** with the past participle of transitive verbs to form the passive voice: He was injured. **c** with the past participle of intransitive verbs to form the perfect tense: I am finished. **d** with the infinitive or present participle to express purpose, duty, possibility, futurity, etc.: We are to start on Monday.

be- prefix forms words meaning: 1. around; throughout: bespatter. 2. completely; thoroughly: bedrench. 3. off; away: behead. 4. about; over; against: bestraddle. 5. provide with; cover with; affect by: bewhisker. 6. conspicuously furnished with: bespectacled. [ME]

beach (beech) n. the sloping shore of a body of water, esp. a sandy shore. —v.t. & v.i. drive or haul up (a boat or ship) on a beach; strand.

beach·comb·er (BEECH kohm ər) n. 1. a vagrant living on what he or she can find or beg around wharves and beaches. 2. a long wave rolling upon a beach.

beach·head (BEECH hed) n. Mil. an area on a hostile shore established by an advance force for the landing of troops etc.

bea·con (BEE kən) n. 1. a signal, esp. a signal fire or light on a hill, building, etc., intended as a warning or guide. 2. a light, lighthouse, etc. set on a shore, shoal, or similar place to guide or warn mariners. 3.

anything that warns or signals. 4. Aeron. a radio transmitter used to plot flight courses. —v.t. 1. furnish with or guide by a beacon. —v.i. 2. shine as a beacon. [ME beken signal]

bead (beed) n. 1. a small, usually round, piece of glass, wood, etc. pierced for stringing on thread or attaching to fabric as decoration. 2. pl. a string of beads; necklace. 3. pl. a rosary. 4. a drop of liquid. —**draw a bead on** take careful aim at. —v.t. 1. decorate with beads or beading. —v.i. 2. collect in drops. [ME bede prayer]

bea·dle (BEED l) n. in the Church of England, a lay officer who ushers or keeps order. [ME bedel herald]

bead·work (BEED wurk) n. decorative work made with or of beads.

bead·y (BEE dee) adj. **bead·i·er, bead·i·est** 1. small and glittering: beady eyes. 2. covered with beads.

bea·gle (BEE gəl) n. a small, short-haired hound with short legs and drooping ears.

beak (beek) n. 1. the horny, projecting mouth parts of birds. 2. a beaklike part or organ, as the horny jaws of turtles. 3. something resembling a bird's beak, as the spout of a pitcher. [ME bec]

beak·er (BEE kər) n. 1. a large, widemouthed drinking cup or goblet. 2. a cylindrical, flat-bottomed vessel with a lip for pouring, used in chemical analysis, etc. 3. the contents of a beaker. [ME biker]

beam (beem) n. 1. a long, heavy piece of wood, metal, or stone, shaped for use. 2. a horizontal piece forming part of the frame of a building or other structure. 3. Naut. **a** one of the heavy pieces of timber or iron set across a vessel to support the decks and stay the sides. **b** the greatest width of a vessel. 4. a ray of light, or a group of nearly parallel rays. 5. Aeron. a radio beam. 6. the widest part of anything. —**off the beam** on the wrong track; wrong. —**on the beam** in the right direction; just right; correct. —v.t. 1. send out in beams or rays. 2. Telecom. aim or transmit (a signal) in a specific direction. —v.i. 3. emit light. 4. smile radiantly. [ME beem tree]

beam·ing (BEE ming) adj. radiant; smiling; cheerful.

bean (been) n. 1. the edible seed of any of various leguminous plants. 2. a plant that bears beans. 3. any of several beanlike seeds or plants. 4. an immature bean pod, used as a vegetable. 5. Slang the head. —*v.t. Slang* hit on the head. [ME *bene*]

bear[1] (bair) *v.* **bore** (*Archaic* **bare**), **borne** or **born, bear·ing** *v.t.* **1.** support; hold up. **2.** carry; convey. **3.** show visibly. **4.** conduct or guide. **5.** spread; disseminate. **6.** hold in the mind; maintain or entertain. **7.** suffer or endure; undergo. **8.** accept or acknowledge; assume, as responsibility. **9.** produce; give birth to. ◆ In this sense, the participial form in the passive is **born,** except when followed by *by.* **10.** conduct, manage, or carry (oneself or a part of oneself). **11.** move by pressing against; drive. **12.** render; give: *bear* witness. **13.** be able to withstand: *bear* investigation. **14.** have or stand in (comparison or relation): with *to.* **15.** possess as a right or power. —*v.i.* **16.** rest heavily; lean; press. **17.** produce fruit or young. **18.** move or lie in a certain direction; be pointed or aimed. **19.** be relevant; have reference: with *on* (or *upon*). **—bear down 1.** force down; overpower. **2.** exert oneself. **—bear down on** (or **upon**) **1.** put pressure on. **2.** approach, esp. forcefully. — **bear out** support; confirm. **—bear up** keep up strength and spirits. [ME *beren* carry]

bear[2] *n.* **1.** a large mammal having a massive, thickly furred body and a very short tail, as the polar bear etc. ◆ Collateral adjective: *ursine.* **2.** any of various other animals resembling the bear: koala *bear.* **3.** a gruff, ill-mannered, or clumsy person. **4.** an investor in the stock market who sells in the belief that a decline in prices is likely: opposed to *bull.* —*adj.* of, pertaining to, or caused by a decline in prices in the stock market. [ME *beare*]

bear·a·ble (BAIR ə bəl) *adj.* endurable.

beard (beerd) *n.* **1.** the hair on a man's face, esp. on the chin. **2.** any similar growth, as on the chin of an animal. —*v.t.* **1.** take by the beard; pull the beard of. **2.** defy courageously. [ME *berd*] **—beard'ed** *adj.*

bear·ing (BAIR ing) *n.* **1.** manner of conducting or carrying oneself; deportment. **2.** the act, capacity, or period of producing. **3.** that which is produced; crops; yield. **4.** *Mech.* a part on which something rests, or in which a pin, journal, etc. turns. **5.** the position or direction of an object or point. **6.** *Often pl.* the situation of an object relative to that of another. **7.** reference or relation. [ME *beryng*]

bear·ish (BAIR ish) *adj.* **1.** like a bear; rough; surly. **2.** tending toward, counting on, or causing low prices of stocks.

beast (beest) *n.* **1.** any animal except man; esp., any large quadruped. **2.** animal characteristics or animal nature. **3.** a cruel, rude, or filthy person. [ME *beeste*]

beast·ly (BEEST lee) *adj.* **·li·er, ·li·est 1.** resembling a beast; bestial. **2.** *Informal* disagreeable or nasty. **—beast'li·ness** *n.*

beat (beet) *v.* **beat, beat·en** or **beat, beat·ing** *v.t.* **1.** strike repeatedly; pound. **2.** punish by blows; thrash; whip. **3.** dash or strike against. **4.** make, as one's way by or as by blows. **5.** flap; flutter, as wings. **6.** stir or mix rapidly so as to make lighter or frothier: *beat* eggs. **7.** mark or measure as with a baton: *beat* time. **8.** sound (a signal), as on a drum. **9.** hunt over; search. **10.** subdue or defeat. **11.** surpass; be superior to. **12.** baffle: *beats* me. —*v.i.* **13.** strike repeated blows or as if with blows. **14.** throb; pulsate. **—beat about** search. **—beat about the bush** approach a subject in a roundabout way. **—beat down** get (a seller) to accept a lower price. **—beat it** *Informal* depart hastily. **—beat up** (**on**) thrash thoroughly. —*n.* **1.** a stroke or blow. **2.** regular stroke, or its sound; pulsation; throb. **3.** *Music* a regular pulsation; the basic unit of musical time. **4.** the measured sound of verse; rhythm. **5.** a round or district regularly traversed, as by a police officer or reporter. **6.** in journalism, a scoop. —*adj.* **1.** *Informal* fatigued; worn out. **2.** of or pertaining to members of the Beat Generation. [ME *beten*]

be·a·tif·ic (BEE ə TIF ik) *adj.* blissful; blessed. [< LL *beatificus* making happy]

be·at·i·fy (bee AT i FI) *v.t.* **·fied, ·fy·ing 1.** make supremely happy. **2.** in the Roman Catholic Church, declare as blessed and worthy of public honor. [< MF *beatifier*] — **be·at'i·fi·ca'tion** *n.*

beat·ing (BEE ting) *n.* **1.** the act of one who or that which beats. **2.** flogging. **3.** pulsation; throbbing, as of the heart. **4.** a defeat.

be·at·i·tude (bee AT i TOOD) *n.* supreme blessedness or felicity. **—the Beatitudes** eight declarations made by Jesus in the Sermon on the Mount. *Matt.* v 3–11 [ME]

beat·nik (BEET nik) *n.* a nonconformist, esp. a member of the Beat Generation.

beau (boh) *n. pl.* **beaus** or **beaux** (bohz) a sweetheart or lover of a girl or woman. [< F]

beau monde (BOH MOND) *French* the fashionable world.

beau·te·ous (BYOO tee əs) *adj.* beautiful.

beau·ti·cian (byoo TISH ən) *n.* one who works in or operates a beauty parlor.

beau·ti·ful (BYOO tə fə) *adj.* possessing the qualities or presenting an appearance of beauty, as in form or grace.

beau·ti·fy (BYOO tə FI) *v.t. & v.i.* **·fied, ·fy·ing** make or grow beautiful.

beau·ty (BYOO tee) *n. pl.* **·ties 1.** the quality of objects, sounds, ideas, etc. that pleases and gratifies, as by their harmony, pattern, excellence, or truth. **2.** one who or that which is beautiful, esp. a woman. **3.** a special grace or charm. [ME *beaute*]

beauty parlor an establishment where women may go for hairdressing or other cosmetic treatment. Also **beauty salon, beauty shop.** —**beauty mark** a mole or similar natural mark. Also **beauty spot.**

beaux·arts (boh ZAHR) *n.pl. French* the fine arts.

bea·ver (BEE vər) *n.* **1.** an amphibious rodent with a scaly, flat, oval tail and webbed hind feet, which builds dams in streams. **2.** the fur of the beaver. **3.** a high silk hat. [ME *bever*]

bea·ver·board (BEE vər BORD) *n.* a light, stiff building material made of compressed or laminated wood pulp.

be·calm (bi KAHM) *v.t.* **1.** *Naut.* make (a sailing vessel) motionless for lack of wind. **2.** make calm; quiet.

be·came (bi KAYM) past tense of BECOME.

be·cause (bi KAWZ) *conj.* for the reason that; on account of the fact that; since. — **because of** by reason of. [ME *bi cause*]

beck (bek) *n.* a nod or other gesture of summons. —**at one's beck and call** subject to one's slightest wish. [ME *becken* beckon]

beck·on (BEK ən) *v.t. & v.i.* **1.** signal or summon by sign or gesture. **2.** entice or lure. [ME *beknen*]

be·cloud (bi KLOWD) *v.t.* obscure with or as with clouds; darken; confuse.

be·come (bi KUM) *v.* **·came, ·come, ·com·ing** *v.i.* **1.** come to be; grow to be. — *v.t.* **2.** be appropriate to; befit. **3.** be suitable to; show to advantage. —**become of** be the condition or fate of: What *became of* him? [ME *becumen* come about]

be·com·ing (bi KUM ing) *adj.* **1.** appropriate; suitable. **2.** pleasing; attractive.

bed (bed) *n.* **1.** an article of furniture to rest or sleep on. **2.** any place or thing used for resting or sleeping. **3.** a lodging, esp. for the night. **4.** a heap or mass resembling a bed.

5. a plot of ground prepared for planting; also, the plants themselves. **6.** the ground at the bottom of a body of water. **7.** a part of surface that serves as a foundation or support. **8.** a layer in a mass of stratified rock. —*v.* **bed·ded, bed·ding** *v.t.* **1.** furnish with a bed. **2.** put or take to bed. **3.** make a bed for; provide with litter: often with *down*: *bed* down cattle. —*v.i.* **4.** go to bed. [ME]

bed and board lodging and meals.

be·daub (bi DAWB) *v.t.* smear or daub; besmirch.

be·daz·zle (bi DAZ əl) *v.t.* **·zled, ·zling** confuse or blind by dazzling.

bed·bug (BED BUG) *n.* a bloodsucking insect, infesting esp. beds.

bed·clothes (BED KLOHZ) *n.pl.* covering for a bed, as sheets, blankets, etc.

bed·ding (BED ing) *n.* **1.** a mattress and bedclothes. **2.** litter for animals to sleep on. **3.** that which forms a bed or foundation.

be·deck (bi DEK) *v.t.* adorn.

be·dev·il (bi DEV əl) *v.t.* **·iled** or **·illed, ·il·ing** or **·il·ling 1.** harass or torment. **2.** worry or bewilder. **3.** possess with or as with a devil; bewitch. —**be·dev'il·ment** *n.*

bed·fel·low (BED FEL oh) *n.* **1.** one who shares a bed. **2.** a companion; associate.

bed·lam (BED ləm) *n.* **1.** a place or scene of noisy confusion. **2.** formerly, a lunatic asylum. [after *Bedlam*, an old London hospital for the insane]

Bed·ou·in (BED oo in) *n.* one of the nomadic Arabs of Arabia etc. [ME *bedoyn* desert-dweller]

bed·pan (BED PAN) *n.* a shallow vessel to be used as a toilet by someone confined to bed.

be·drag·gle (bi DRAG əl) *v.t.* **·gled, ·gling** make wet, soiled, or untidy.

bed·rid·den (BED RID n) *adj.* confined to bed. [ME]

bed·rock (BED ROK) *n.* **1.** *Geol.* the solid rock underlying the looser materials of the earth's surface. **2.** the lowest level; bottom. **3.** fundamental principles; foundation.

bed·sore (BED SOR) *n.* a sore caused by prolonged contact with a bed or bedclothes.

bed·spread (BED SPRED) *n.* an ornamental covering for a bed.

bed·stead (BED STED) *n.* a framework for supporting the springs and mattress of a bed. Also **bedspring.**

bee (bee) *n.* **1.** a four-winged insect feeding largely on nectar and pollen, esp. the honeybee. **2.** a social gathering for work, competition, etc.: quilting *bee*. [ME *be*]

beef (beef) *n.* **1.** the flesh of a slaughtered adult bovine animal. **2.** *Informal* brawn. **3.** *Slang* a complaint. —*v.i. Slang* complain. [ME]

beef·eat·er (BEEF ee tər) *n.* a yeoman of the guard, or one of the similarly uniformed watchmen of the Tower of London.

bee·hive (BEE hɪv) *n.* **1.** a hive for a colony of bees. **2.** a place full of activity.

bee·keep·er (BEE kee pər) *n.* an apiarist.

bee·line (BEE lɪn) *n.* the shortest route from one place to another. **—make a bee-line for** go straight toward.

Be·el·ze·bub (bee EL zə BUB) the prince of the demons; the devil. [< Hebrew *ba'al-zebūb* lord of flies]

been (bin) past participle of BE.

beer (beer) *n.* **1.** an alcoholic fermented beverage made from malt and hops. **2.** a beverage made from various plants: ginger *beer*. [ME *bere*]

beer·y (BEER ee) *adj.* **beer·i·er, beer·i·est 1.** of or like beer. **2.** tipsy.

bees·wax (BEEZ wAKS) *n.* a yellow fatty solid secreted by honeybees for honeycombs.

beet (beet) *n.* **1.** the fleshy, edible root of a plant of the goosefoot family, esp. the red beet or the sugar beet. **2.** the plant itself. [ME *bete*]

bee·tle (BEET l) *n.* an insect having biting mouth parts and hard, horny front wings. —*adj.* jutting; overhanging: a *beetle* brow. —*v.i.* **·tled, ·tling** jut out; overhang. [ME *betylle*]

bee·tle-browed (BEET l BROWD) *adj.* **1.** having jutting eyebrows. **2.** scowling; frowning.

be·fall (bi FAWL) *v.* **·fell, ·fall·en, ·fall·ing** *v.i.* **1.** come about; happen; occur. —*v.t.* **2.** happen to. [ME *befallen*]

be·fit (bi FIT) *v.t.* **·fit·ted, ·fit·ting** be suited to; be appropriate for.

be·fog (bi FOG) *v.t.* **·fogged, ·fog·ging 1.** envelop in fog. **2.** confuse; obscure.

be·fore (bi FOR) *adv.* **1.** in front; ahead. **2.** preceding in time; previously. —*prep.* **1.** in front of; ahead of. **2.** earlier or sooner than. **3.** in advance of in development, rank, etc. **4.** in preference to; rather than. **5.** in the presence of. **6.** under the consideration of: the issue *before* us. —*conj.* **1.** previous to the time when. **2.** rather than. [ME *beforen*]

be·fore·hand (bi FOR hAND) *adv. & adj.* in anticipation or advance; ahead of time. [ME *bifor-hand*]

be·foul (bi FOWL) *v.t.* make foul or dirty; sully. [ME *bifor-foulen*]

be·friend (bi FREND) *v.t.* act as a friend to; help.

be·fud·dle (bi FUD l) *v.t.* **·dled, ·dling** confuse, as with liquor.

beg (beg) *v.* **begged, beg·ging** *v.t.* **1.** ask for in charity: *beg* alms. **2.** ask for or of humbly; beseech: *beg* forgiveness. —*v.i.* **3.** ask alms or charity. **4.** ask humbly. **—beg off** ask to be excused or released (from an engagement, obligation, etc.). [ME *beggen*]

be·gan (bi GAN) past tense of BEGIN.

be·get (bi GET) *v.t.* **·got** (*Archaic* **·gat**), **·got·ten** or **·got, ·get·ting 1.** be the father of. **2.** cause to be; initiate. [ME *begeten*]

beg·gar (BEG ər) *n.* **1.** one who lives by begging. **2.** a poor person; pauper. —*v.t.* **1.** impoverish. **2.** exhaust the resources of: It *beggars* analysis. [ME *beggare*]

be·gin (bi GIN) *v.* **·gan, ·gun, ·gin·ning** *v.i.* **1.** start to do something. **2.** come into being; arise. —*v.t.* **3.** do the first act or part of; start to do. **4.** originate. [ME *beginnen*]

be·gin·ner (bi GIN ər) *n.* one beginning to learn a trade, study a subject, etc.; a novice. **2.** founder; originator.

be·gin·ning (bi GIN ing) *n.* **1.** the act of starting. **2.** source or first cause; origin. **3.** the first part. **4.** *Often pl.* the first or rudimentary stage. —*adj.* elementary; introductory: a *beginning* course in physics.

be·gon·ia (bi GOHN yə) *n.* a plant having showy leaves and flowers. [after Michel *Bégon*, 1638—1710, French botanist]

be·got (bi GOT) past tense, past participle of BEGET.

be·got·ten (bi GOT n) alternative past participle of BEGET.

be·grime (bi GRĪM) *v.t.* **·grimed, ·grim·ing** soil.

be·grudge (bi GRUJ) *v.t.* **·grudged, ·grudg·ing 1.** envy one the possession or enjoyment of (something). **2.** give or grant reluctantly.

be·guile (bi GĪL) *v.t.* **·guiled, ·guil·ing 1.** deceive; mislead by guile. **2.** while away pleasantly, as time. **3.** charm; divert. [ME *bigilen*]

be·gun (bi GUN) past participle of BEGIN.

be·half (bi HAF) *n.* the interest, part, or defense: usu. preceded by *in* or *on* and followed by *of*. [ME]

be•have (bi HAYV) v. •haved, •hav•ing v.i.
1. act; conduct oneself or itself. 2. comport
oneself properly. —v.t. 3. conduct (oneself), esp. in a proper or suitable manner.
[ME *behaven*]

be•hav•ior (bi HAYV yər) n. 1. manner of
conducting oneself. 2. the way a person,
substance, machine, etc., acts under given
circumstances. —**be•hav'ior•al** adj.

be•hav•ior•ism (bi HAYV yə RIZ əm) n. Psychol. the theory that the behavior of animals
and man is determined by measurable external and internal stimuli. —**be•hav'ior-
ist** n.

be•head (bi HED) v.t. decapitate. [ME *be-
hefden*]

be•held (bi HELD) past tense, past participle of BEHOLD.

be•he•moth (bi HEE məth) n. 1. cap. in the
Bible, a huge beast. Job xl 15. 2. anything
very large. [< Hebrew *běhēmāh* beast]

be•hest (bi HEST) n. an authoritative request; command. [ME *biheste* promise]

be•hind (bi HĪND) adv. 1. in, at, or toward
the rear. 2. in a place, condition, or time
previously passed or departed from. 3. in
arrears; late. 4. slow, as a watch. —prep. 1.
at the back or rear of. 2. toward the rear of.
3. in a place or time previously passed. 4.
after (a set time). 5. not so well advanced as;
inferior to. 6. hidden by: What is *behind*
your actions? 7. backing up; supporting: be
behind a venture. —n. Informal the buttocks. [ME *behinden*]

be•hold (bi HOHLD) v.t. •held, •hold•ing
look at or upon; observe. —interj. look! see!
[ME *beholden* keep] —**be•hold'er** n.

be•hold•en (bi HOHL dən) adj. indebted;
obligated.

be•hoove (bi HOOV) v.t. •hooved,
•hoov•ing be necessary or right for: It *be-
hooves* me to leave. [ME *behoven*]

beige (bayzh) n. grayish tan. [< F] —adj. of
this color.

be•ing (BEE ing) n. 1. existence, as opposed
to nonexistence. 2. essential nature; substance: His whole *being* is musical. 3. a living thing. 4. a human individual; person.
[ME]

be•la•bor (bi LAY bər) v.t. 1. beat soundly;
assail with blows. 2. assail verbally.

be•lat•ed (bi LAY tid) adj. late, or too late.

belch (belch) v.i. 1. eject wind noisily from
the stomach through the mouth; burp. 2.
issue forth in a burst or bursts; gush. 3. emit
material violently, as a volcano. —v.t. 4.

eject or throw forth violently. [ME *belchen*]
—n. 1. an instance of belching. 2. any
strong emittance of smoke etc.

be•lea•guer (bi LEE gər) v.t. 1. surround or
shut in with an armed force. 2. surround;
beset.

bel•fry (BEL free) n. pl. •fries 1. a tower in
which a bell is hung. 2. the part of a tower or
steeple containing the bell. [ME *belfray*]

be•lie (bi LĪ) v.t. •lied, •ly•ing 1. misrepresent; disguise. 2. prove false; contradict. 3.
fail to fulfill: *belie* hopes. [ME *belyen*]

be•lief (bi LEEF) n. 1. acceptance of the
truth or actuality of anything. 2. something
held to be true or actual. 3. trust in another;
confidence. 4. a doctrine; creed. [ME *bil-
eve*]

be•lieve (bi LEEV) v. •lieved, •liev•ing v.t.
1. accept as true. 2. credit (a person) with
veracity. 3. think; assume. —v.i. 4. accept
the truth, existence, worth, etc., of something: with *in: believe* in freedom. 5. have
confidence; place one's trust: with *in.* 6.
have religious faith. 7. think. [ME *bileven*]
—**be•liev'a•ble** adj.

be•lit•tle (bi LIT l) v.t. •tled, •tling cause to
seem small or less; disparage.

bell (bel) n. 1. a hollow metallic instrument,
usu. cup-shaped, that rings when struck. 2.
anything in the shape of or suggesting a
bell, as a flower. 3. Naut. a stroke on a bell
every half hour to mark the periods of the
watch; also, each of these periods. —v.t. 1.
put a bell on. 2. shape like a bell. —v.i. 3.
take the shape of a bell. [ME]

bel•la•don•na (BEL ə DON ə) n. 1. an herb
with purple-red flowers and black berries:
also called *deadly nightshade.* 2. a poisonous substance used in medicine. [< Ital.
bella donna, beautiful lady]

belle (bel) n. a beautiful and charming
woman or girl. [< F]

belles-let•tres (bel LE tr) n.pl. literature
having aesthetic appeal, rather than instructional or informational value; poetry,
drama, fiction, etc. [< F, fine letters] —
bel•let•rist (bel LE trist) n. —
bel•le•tris•tic (BEL li TRIS tik) adj.

bell•hop (BEL hop) n. a person employed
by a hotel to answer calls for service, carry
suitcases, etc. Also **bell'boy'.**

bel•li•cose (BEL i KOHS) adj. pugnacious;
warlike. [ME] —**bel•li•cos•i•ty** (BEL i
KOS i tee) n.

bel•lig•er•ence (bə LIJ ər əns) n. 1. the
state of being warlike. 2. belligerency.

bel·lig·er·en·cy (bə LIJ ər ən see) n. the condition of being at war.

bel·lig·er·ent (be LIJ ər ənt) adj. 1. warlike; bellicose. 2. engaged in or pertaining to warfare. —n. a person or nation engaged in warfare or fighting. [< L belliger waging war]

bel·low (BEL oh) v.i. 1. utter a loud, hollow cry, as a bull. 2. roar; shout. —v.t. 3. utter with a loud, roaring voice. [ME belwen] —n. the act or an instance of bellowing.

bel·lows (BEL ohz) n. (construed as sing. or pl.) an instrument with an air chamber and flexible sides, for drawing in air and expelling it through a nozzle or tube, used for blowing fires, filling the pipes of an organ, etc. [ME belowes]

bell·weth·er (BEL WETH ər) n. 1. a ram with a bell about its neck that leads a flock of sheep. 2. one who leads a group. 3. a person or thing that sets a trend. [ME]

bel·ly (BEL ee) n. pl. ·lies 1. the abdomen in vertebrates, or the underpart of other animals. 2. the stomach. 3. the protuberance of a bulging muscle. 4. the front or underpart of anything. 5. a deep, interior cavity: belly of a ship. —v.t. & v.i. ·lied, ·ly·ing swell out or fill, as a sail. [ME bely]

bel·ly·ache (BEL ee AYK) n. a pain in the stomach. —v.i. ·ached, ·ach·ing Informal complain.

be·long (bi LAWNG) v.i. 1. be the property of someone: with to. 2. be a part of or an appurtenance to something: with to. 3. have a proper place; be suitable. 4. have relation or be a member. [ME belongen]

be·long·ing (bi LAWNG ing) n. 1. that which belongs to a person or thing. 2. pl. possessions. 3. affinity; a good relationship.

be·lov·ed (bi LUV id) adj. deeply loved. [ME biloved] —be·loved (bi LUVD) n.

be·low (bi LOH) adv. 1. in, on, or to a lower place. 2. farther down or on. 3. in a lower rank or authority. —prep. lower than in place, grade, degree, etc. [ME bilooghe]

belt (belt) n. 1. a band of flexible material worn about the waist to support clothing, tools, etc. 2. any band resembling a belt. 3. a distinctive region or zone: storm belt. — **tighten one's belt** practice thrift. —v.t. 1. gird or fasten with a belt. 2. mark with belts or bands. 3. Slang hit hard. [ME]

belt·way (BELT way n. 1. a highway around a large city. 2. cap. the highway around Washington, D.C., thought of as separating the preoccupations of government from those of the rest of the nation.

be·lu·ga (bə LOO gə) n. 1. a sturgeon, esp. of the Caspian Sea, a prime source of caviar. 2. a dolphin of Arctic and sub-Arctic seas: also called white whale. [< Russ. beluga]

be·mire (bi MĪR) v.t. ·mired, ·mir·ing 1. soil with mud or mire. 2. sink or stall in mud.

be·moan (bi MOHN) v.t. 1. lament, as a loss. 2. express sympathy or pity for. [ME bimenen]

be·muse (bi MYOOZ) v.t. ·mused, ·mus·ing bewilder or preoccupy.

bench (bench) n. 1. a long seat of wood, marble, etc., with or without a back. 2. a table for mechanical work. 3. the seat for judges in a court. 4. the judge, or judges collectively. 5. the office or dignity of a judge. 6. a seat for persons sitting in an official capacity. —v.t. in sports, remove (a player) from a game. [ME]

bench·mark (BENCH MAHRK) n. a standard of comparison. —adj. serving as a standard of reference or comparison: a benchmark court decision.

bend (bend) v. bent, bend·ing v.t. 1. cause to take the form of a curve; crook; bow. 2. direct or turn, as one's course, in a certain direction; deflect. 3. subdue or cause to yield. —v.i. 4. assume the form of a curve. 5. take a certain direction. 6. bow in submission or respect. —n. 1. an act of bending, or the state of being bent. 2. something curved or bent. [ME benden]

bends (bendz) n. decompression sickness, caisson disease.

be·neath (bi NEETH) adv. 1. in a lower place; below. 2. underneath; directly below. —prep. 1. under; underneath; below. 2. under the power or sway of; subdued by. 3. lower in rank or station. 4. unworthy of. [ME benethe]

ben·e·dic·tion (BEN i DIK shən) n. 1. the act of blessing. 2. the invocation of divine favor upon a person. [ME]

ben·e·fac·tion (BEN ə FAK shən) n. 1. the act of conferring a benefit. 2. a charitable deed. [< LL]

ben·e·fac·tor (BEN ə FAK tər) n. one who gives help or confers a benefit.

ben·e·fice (BEN ə fis) n. 1. a church office endowed with funds or property. 2. the revenue of such an office. —v.t. ·ficed, ·fic·ing invest with a benefice. [ME]

be·nef·i·cence (bə NEF ə səns) n. 1. the

quality of being beneficent. **2.** a beneficent act or gift. [ME]

be·nef·i·cent (bə NEF ə sənt) *adj.* **1.** bringing about or doing good. **2.** resulting in benefit.

ben·e·fi·cial (BEN ə FISH əl) *adj.* producing benefit; advantageous; helpful. [ME]

ben·e·fi·ci·ar·y (BEN ə FISH ee ER ee) *n. pl.* **·ar·ies 1.** one who receives benefits or advantages. **2.** *Eccl.* the holder of a benefice. **3.** *Law* one entitled to income from a trust, insurance policy, etc. [< L *beneficiarius* pertaining to a benefice]

ben·e·fit (BEN ə fit) *n.* **1.** that which is helpful; advantage; profit. **2.** a charitable deed. **3.** a public performance given to raise funds for a cause. **4.** a payment made by an insurance company, etc. —*v.* **·fit·ed**, **·fit·ing** *v.t.* **1.** be helpful or useful to. —*v.i.* **2.** profit; gain advantage. [ME *benefytt*]

be·nev·o·lence (bə NEV ə ləns) *n.* **1.** disposition to do good; kindliness. **2.** any act of kindness.

be·nev·o·lent (bə NEV ə lənt) *adj.* disposed to do good; kindly. [ME]

be·night·ed (bi NĪ) tid *adj.* ignorant; unenlightened.

be·nign (bi NĪN) *adj.* **1.** of a kind disposition; kindly. **2.** gentle; mild. **3.** favorable. **4.** *Med.* nonmalignant. [ME *benigne* kind]

be·nig·ni·ty (bi NIG ni tee) *n. pl.* **·ties 1.** the quality of being benign. Also **be·nig′nan·cy** (-nən see). **2.** a gracious action or influence.

bent (bent) past tense, past participle of BEND. —*adj.* **1.** not straight; crooked. **2.** set on a course; resolved. —*n.* **1.** state of being bent or turned. **2.** a personal inclination or penchant.

be·numb (bi NUM) *v.t.* **1.** make numb; deaden. **2.** stupefy. [ME *benomen* taken away]

ben·zene (BEN zeen) *n. Chem.* a colorless, flammable, liquid hydrocarbon, obtained chiefly from coal tar, used as a solvent and in organic synthesis.

ben·zine (BEN zeen) *n.* a colorless, flammable liquid derived from crude petroleum, used as a solvent, cleaner, and fuel.

be·queath (bi KWEETH) *v.t.* **1.** *Law* give by a will. **2.** hand down. [ME *bequethen*]

be·quest (bi KWEST) *n.* the act of bequeathing, or something bequeathed. [ME *biqueste*]

be·rate (bi RAYT) *v.t.* **·rat·ed**, **·rat·ing** scold severely.

be·reave (bi REEV) *v.t.* **·reaved** or **·reft**, **·reav·ing 1.** deprive, as of hope or happiness. **2.** leave saddened through death. [ME *bereven*] —**be·reave′ment** *n.*

be·reft (bi REFT) alternative past tense and past participle of BEREAVE.

be·ret (bə RAY) *n.* a soft, flat cap, usu. of wool. [< F]

ber·i·ber·i (BER ee BER ee) *n. Pathol.* a disease of the peripheral nerves resulting from the absence of certain vitamins in the diet. [< Sinhalese *beri* weakness]

berm (burm) *n.* a narrow ledge, shelf, or shoulder, as on the side of a road. [< F *berme*]

ber·ry (BER ee) *n. pl.* **·ries 1.** any small, succulent fruit, as a blueberry. **2.** *Bot.* a simple fruit with the seeds in a juicy pulp, as the grape. **3.** the dry seed of certain plants, as a coffee bean, etc. —*v.i.* **·ried**, **·ry·ing 1.** form or bear berries. **2.** gather berries. [ME *berie*]

ber·serk (bər SURK) *adj.* crazed; frenzied. [< ON *berserkr* warrior]

berth (burth) *n.* **1.** a bunk or bed in a vessel, sleeping car, etc. **2.** *Naut.* an anchorage. **3.** situation or employment on a vessel. —**give a wide berth to** avoid. —*v.t.* **1.** *Naut.* bring to a berth. **2.** provide with a berth. —*v.i.* **3.** *Naut.* come to a berth. [Origin uncertain]

be·seech (bi SEECH) *v.t.* **·sought**, **·seech·ing 1.** implore. **2.** beg for. [ME *bisechen*]

be·seem (bi SEEM) *v.i. Archaic.* be fitting or appropriate: It ill *beseems* you to speak thus.

be·set (bi SET) *v.t.* **·set**, **·set·ting 1.** assail; harass. **2.** hem in; encircle. [ME *besetten*]

be·side (bi SĪD) *prep.* **1.** at the side of; in proximity to. **2.** in comparison with. **3.** away or apart from: *beside* the point. **4.** other than; over and above. —**beside oneself** out of one's senses, as from anger, fear, etc. [ME]

be·sides (bi SĪDZ) *adv.* **1.** in addition; as well. **2.** moreover; furthermore. **3.** apart from that mentioned; otherwise; else. —*prep.* **1.** in addition to; other than. **2.** beyond; apart from: I care for nothing *besides* this.

be·siege (bi SEEJ) *v.t.* **·sieged**, **·sieg·ing 1.** lay siege to. **2.** crowd around. **3.** assail. [ME *bysegen*]

be·smear (bi SMEER) *v.t.* smear over; sully.

be•smirch (bi SMURCH) v.t. 1. soil; stain. 2. sully; dim the luster of.

be•sot (bi SOT) v.t. •sot•ted, •sot•ting 1. stupefy, as with drink. 2. infatuate.

be•sought (bi SAWT) past tense and past participle of BESEECH.

be•span•gle (bi SPAN gəl) v.t. •gled, •gling decorate with or as with spangles.

be•speak (bi SPEEK) v.t. •spoke (Archaic •spake), •spo•ken or •spoke, •speak•ing 1. ask or arrange for in advance. 2. give evidence of; expend. 3. foretell. [ME bespeken]

be•spoke (bi SPOHK) past tense, alternative past participle of BESPEAK.

best (best) superlative of GOOD, WELL². —adj. 1. excelling all others; of the highest quality. 2. most advantageous or desirable. 3. most; largest: the best part of a day. —adv. 1. in the most excellent way; most advantageously. 2. to the utmost degree; most thoroughly. —n. 1. the best thing, part, etc. 2. best condition or quality; utmost: Do your best. —at best under the most favorable circumstances. —make the best of adapt oneself to the disadvantages of. —v.t. defeat; surpass. [ME beste]

bes•tial (BES chəl) adj. 1. of or pertaining to beasts. 2. brutish; depraved. [ME] —bes•ti•al•i•ty (BES chee AL i tee) n.

be•stir (bi STUR) v.t. •stirred, •stir•ring rouse to activity.

be•stow (bi STOH) v.t. 1. present as a gift. 2. apply; expend, as time. 3. give in marriage.

be•strew (bi STROO) v.t. •strewed, •strewed or •strewn, •strew•ing scatter over (a surface).

be•stride (bi STRĪD) v.t. •strode, •strid•den, •strid•ing 1. sit or stand astride of; straddle. 2. stride across.

bet (bet) n. 1. an agreement to risk something, on the chance of winning something else; a wager. 2. that which is risked in a bet, as a sum of money. —v. bet, bet•ting v.t. 1. stake or pledge (money, etc.) in a bet. 2. declare as in a bet: I bet he doesn't come. —v.i. 3. place a bet.

be•ta (BAY tə) n. the second letter of the Greek alphabet (B, ß), corresponding to English b.

be•take (bi TAYK) v.t. •took, •tak•en, •tak•ing go; take (oneself). [ME bitaken]

be•tel nut (BEET l) n. the seed of an East Indian palm, the betel palm used for chewing with betel leaves and lime.

bête noire (BAYT NWAHR) pl. bêtes

noires (BAYT NWAHRZ) an object of hate or dread. [< F, black beast]

be•tide (bi TĪD) v.t. & v.i. •tid•ed, •tid•ing happen (to) or befall. [ME bitiden]

be•times (bi TĪMZ) adv. early; also, soon. [ME betimes by time]

be•took (bi TUUK) past tense of BETAKE.

be•tray (bi TRAY) v.t. 1. aid an enemy of; be a traitor to. 2. prove faithless to. 3. disclose, as a secret. 4. reveal unwittingly. 5. seduce and desert. [ME bitraien] —be•tray'al n.

be•troth (bi TRAWTH) v.t. engage to marry. [ME betrouthe]

be•troth•al (bi TROH thəl) n. an engagement, or contract to marry.

be•trothed (bi TROTHD) adj. engaged to be married; affianced. —n. a person engaged to be married.

bet•ter¹ (BET ər) comparative of GOOD, WELL². —adj. 1. superior in quality. 2. more advantageous or desirable. 3. larger; greater: the better part of the cake. 4. improved in health. —adv. 1. more advantageously. 2. to a larger degree; more thoroughly. 3. more: better than a week. —better off in a better condition. —v.t. 1. make better; improve. 2. surpass; excel. —n. 1. Usu. pl. one's superiors. 2. advantage. [ME bettre]

bet•ter² n. see BETTOR.

bet•ter•ment (BET ər mənt) n. improvement or an improvement.

bet•tor (BET ər) n. one who bets: also better.

be•tween (bi TWEEN) prep. 1. in the space that separates (two places or objects). 2. intermediate in relation to, as times, qualities, etc. 3. from one to another of; connecting. 4. by the joint action of. 5. in the joint possession of. 6. regarding one or the other of: choose between two offers. 7. being one alternative over another: judge between right and wrong. —adv. in intervening time, space, position, or relation: few and far between. [ME betwene]

be•twixt (bi TWIKST) adv. & prep. between. —betwixt and between in an intermediate or indecisive state. [ME betwix]

bev•el (BEV əl) n. 1. any inclination of two surfaces other than 90°, as at the edge of a timber. 2. an adjustable instrument for measuring angles: also bevel square. —adj. oblique; slanting. —v. bev•eled or •elled, bev•el•ing or •el•ing v.t. 1. cut or bring to a bevel. —v.i. 2. slant. [< MF]

bev•er•age (BEV ər ij) n. any drink. [ME]

bev•y (BEV ee) n. pl. bev•ies 1. a flock, esp.

of quail, grouse, or larks. **2.** a group. [ME *bevey*]

be•wail (bi WAYL) *v.t. & v.i.* lament.

be•ware (bi WAIR) *v.t. & v.i.* **•wared, •war•ing** be wary (of). [ME]

be•wil•der (bi WIL dər) *v.t.* confuse utterly; perplex.

be•witch (bi WICH) *v.t.* **1.** gain power over by magic. **2.** charm; fascinate. [ME *biwicchen*] —**be•witch'ing** *adj.* charming; captivating.

be•yond (bee OND) *prep.* **1.** on or to the far side of; farther on than. **2.** later than. **3.** outside the reach or scope of. **4.** surpassing; superior to: lovely *beyond* description. **5.** more than; over and above. —*adv.* farther on or away; at a distance. [ME *beyonden*]

bi•an•nu•al (bī AN yoo əl) *adj.* occurring every two years; biennial.

bi•as (BĪ əs) *n. pl.* **bi•as•es 1.** a line running obliquely across a fabric: to cut on the *bias.* **2.** a mental tendency, preference, or prejudice. —*adj. & adv.* on a slant or diagonal. —*v.t.* **bi•ased** or **•assed, bi•as•ing** or **•as•sing** influence or affect unduly or unfairly. [< MF *biais* oblique]

bib (bib) *n.* **1.** a cloth worn under a child's chin, esp. at meals. **2.** the upper front part of an apron or of overalls. [ME *bibben* drink]

bi•be•lot (BIB loh) *n.* a small, decorative and often rare object or trinket. [< F]

Bi•ble (BĪ bəl) *n.* **1.** in Christianity, the Old Testament and the New Testament. **2.** in Judaism, the Old Testament. [ME] —**Bib•li•cal** (BIB li kəl) *adj.*

bib•li•og•ra•phy (BIB lee OG rə fee) *n. pl.* **•phies 1.** a list of the works of an author, or of the literature bearing on a subject. **2.** a list of books or other sources mentioned or consulted by an author. —**bib•li•o•graph•ic** (BIB lee ə GRAF ik) *adj.*

bib•li•o•phile (BIB lee ə FĪL) *n.* one who loves books.

bib•u•lous (BIB yə ləs) *adj.* **1.** tending to drink to excess. **2.** absorbent. [< L *bibulus*]

bi•cam•er•al (bī KAM ər əl) *adj.* consisting of two chambers, houses, or branches.

bi•cen•ten•ni•al (BĪ sen TEN ee əl) *adj.* **1.** occurring once in 200 years. **2.** lasting or consisting of 200 years. —*n.* a 200th anniversary. Also **bi•cen•ten•ar•y** (BĪ sen TEN ə ree).

bi•ceps (BĪ seps) *n. pl.* **bi•ceps** *Anat.* **1.** the large front muscle of the upper arm. **2.** the large flexor muscle at the back of the thigh. [< L, two-headed]

bick•er (BIK ər) *v.i.* **1.** dispute petulantly; wrangle. **2.** glitter. —*n.* a petty quarrel. [ME *bikeren*]

bi•cus•pid (bī KUS pid) *n.* any of eight teeth in the human jaw having two cusps or points.

bi•cy•cle (BĪ si kəl) *n.* a two-wheeled vehicle driven by pedals. —*v.i.* **•cled, •cling** ride a bicycle. [< F] —**bi'cy•clist** *n.*

bid (bid) *n.* **1.** an offer to pay a price; also, the amount offered. **2.** in card games, the number of tricks or points that a player engages to make; also, a player's turn to bid. **3.** an effort to acquire, win, or attain. —*v.* **bid** *for defs. 1, 2, 5* or **bade** *for defs. 3, 4,* **bid•den** or **bid, bid•ding** *v.t.* **1.** make an offer of (a price). **2.** in card games, declare (the number of tricks or points one will engage to make). **3.** command; order. **4.** say to, as a greeting or farewell. —*v.i.* **5.** make a bid. [ME *bidden* ask]

bid•ding (BID ing) *n.* **1.** a command or summons. **2.** bids, or the making of bids.

bid•dy¹ (BID ee) *n. pl.* **•dies** a hen.

bid•dy² *n. pl.* **•dies** a gossipy, usu. old woman. [< *Bridget,* fem. name]

bide (bīd) *v.* **bid•ed, bid•ing** *v.t.* **1.** endure; withstand. —*v.i.* **2.** dwell; abide; stay. —**bide one's time** await the best opportunity. [ME *biden* trust]

bi•en•ni•al (bī EN ee əl) *adj.* **1.** occurring every second year. **2.** lasting or living for two years. —*n. Bot.* a plant that produces flowers and fruit in its second year, then dies. —**bi•en'ni•al•ly** *adv.*

bier (beer) *n.* a framework for carrying a corpse to the grave; also, a coffin. [ME *bere*]

bi•fo•cal (bī FOH kəl) *adj. Optics* having two foci: said of a lens ground for both near and far vision. —**bi•fo•cals** *n. pl.* eyeglasses with bifocal lenses.

bi•fur•cate (BĪ fər KAYT) *v.t. & v.i.* **•cat•ed, •cat•ing** divide into two branches or stems; fork. —*adj.* forked: also **bi'fur•cat'ed** [< Med.L *bifurcatus* forked]

big (big) *adj.* **big•ger, big•gest 1.** of great size, extent, etc. **2.** pregnant: usu. with *with.* **3.** grown. **4.** pompous; pretentious. **5.** important; prominent. **6.** loud. **7.** generous; magnanimous. —*adv. Informal* pompously; extravagantly: talk *big.* [ME *bigge*]

big•a•my (BIG ə mee) *n. Law* the criminal offense of marrying any other person while

binary

having a legal spouse living. [ME *bigamie*] —**big·a·mist** *n.*

big bang theory *Astron.* a theory that the universe began with a huge explosion and will eventually contract again.

big-heart·ed (BIG HAHR tid) *adj.* generous.

big·ot (BIG ət) *n.* an intolerant, prejudiced person. [< *MF*] —**big·ot·ed** *adj.* —**big·ot·ry** (BIG ə tree) *n. pl.* ·**ries** bigoted behavior; intolerance.

big·wig (BIG wig) *n. Informal* someone of importance.

bi·jou (BEE zhoo) *n. pl.* **bi·joux** (-zhooz) a jewel or finely made trinket. [< F]

bi·ki·ni (bi KEE nee) *n. pl.* ·**nis** a scanty two-piece bathing suit.

bi·lat·er·al (bī LAT ər əl) *adj.* **1.** pertaining to or having two sides; two-sided. **2.** on two sides. **3.** mutually binding.

bil·bo (BIL boh) *n. pl.* ·**boes** a restraint consisting of two sliding shackles attached to an iron bar. [after *Bilbao*, Spain, noted for its ironworks.]

bile (bīl) *n.* **1.** *Physiol.* a secretion from the liver that aids digestion. **2.** anger; peevishness. [< F]

bilge (bilj) *n.* **1.** *Naut.* the rounded part of a ship's bottom. **2.** bilge water. **3.** *Slang* stupid or trivial talk or writing.

bilge water foul water that collects in the bilge of a ship.

bi·lin·gual (bī LING gwəl) *adj.* **1.** written or expressed in or using two languages. **2.** able to speak two languages. [< L *bilinguis*]

bil·ious (BIL yəs) *adj.* **1.** affected or caused by an excess of bile. **2.** of or containing bile. **3.** ill-tempered. **4.** of a sickly color. [< L *biliosus*]

bilk (bilk) *v.t.* cheat or swindle.

bill[1] (bil) *n.* **1.** a statement of charges for goods delivered or services rendered. **2.** a piece of paper money; a bank note. **3.** a bill of exchange; also, loosely, a promissory note. **4.** a draft of a proposed law. **5.** any list of items or program of particulars. **6.** *Law* a formal statement of a case or a complaint. —*v.t.* **1.** enter in a bill or list. **2.** present a bill to. [ME *bille*]

bill[2] *n.* a beak, as of a bird. —*v.i.* join bills, as doves; caress. —**bill and coo** caress and speak lovingly. [ME *bile*]

bil·let[1] (BIL it) *n.* **1.** lodging for troops in private or nonmilitary buildings. **2.** an order for such lodging. **3.** a place assigned as quarters. **4.** a job. —*v.t.* lodge (soldiers etc.) by billet. [ME *bylet* official register]

bil·let[2] *n.* **1.** a short, thick stick, as of firewood. **2.** *Metall.* a mass of iron or steel drawn into a small bar. [ME *bylet* log]

bil·let-doux (BIL ay DOO) *n. pl.* **bil·lets-doux** (BIL ay DOOZ) a love letter. [< F, lit., sweet note]

bil·liards (BIL yərdz) *n. (construed as sing.)* any of various games played with hard balls (**billiard balls**) hit by cues on an oblong, cloth-covered table (**billiard table**) having cushioned edges. [< F *billard* cue]

bill·ing (BIL ing) *n.* the relative importance assigned to an actor or an act on a theater marquee, poster, etc.

bil·lings·gate (BIL ingz GAYT) *n.* vulgar or abusive language. [after *Billingsgate*, London fish market]

bil·lion (BIL yən) *n.* **1.** a thousand millions, written as 1,000,000,000. **2.** *Brit.* a million millions, written as 1,000,000,000,000: called a *trillion* in the U.S. —**bil·lion·aire** (BIL yə NAIR) *n.* one whose wealth totals a billion or more.

bill of fare a menu (def. 1).

bill of rights 1. a formal declaration of the fundamental rights of individuals. **2. Bill of Rights** the first ten amendments to the U.S. Constitution.

bill of sale an instrument attesting the transfer of property.

bil·low (BIL oh) *n.* **1.** a great wave or swell of the sea. **2.** any wave or surge, as of sound. —*v.t. & v.i.* rise or cause to rise or roll in billows; surge; swell. [< ON *bylgja* wave]

bil·low·y (BIL oh ee) *adj.* ·**low·i·er,** ·**low·i·est** swelling with or as with billows.

bil·ly (BIL ee) *n. pl.* ·**lies** a short club, esp. a policeman's. [< *Billy,* a nickname for William]

billy goat a male goat.

bi·me·tal·lic (bī mə TAL ik) *adj.* **1.** consisting of or relating to two metals. **2.** of or using bimetallism

bi·met·al·lism (bī MET l iz əm) *n.* the concurrent use of both gold and silver as the standard of currency.

bi·month·ly (bī MUNTH lee) *adj.* occurring every two months. —*n.* a bimonthly publication. —*adv.* every two months.

bin (bin) *n.* an enclosed place or large receptacle for holding coal etc. [ME *binne*]

bi·na·ry (BĪ nə ree) *adj.* **1.** pertaining to, characterized by, or made up of two; double; paired. **2.** permitting two possibilities only, as in a computer bit. **3.** designating a method of representing numbers using two digits, 0 and 1, with each digital position representing a successive power of 2. —*n. pl.* **•ries 1.** a combination of two things. **2.** *Astron.* a binary star. [ME]

binary star *Astron.* a pair of stars revolving about a common center of gravity.

bin•au•ral (bī NOR əl) *adj.* **1.** hearing with both ears. **2.** *Electronics* stereophonic (def. 2).

bind (bīnd) *v.* **bound, bind•ing** *v.t.* **1.** tie or fasten with a band, cord, etc. **2.** fasten around; gird. **3.** bandage; swathe: often with *up*. **4.** constrain or obligate, as by law. **5.** enclose between covers, as a book. **6.** cause to cohere; cement. **7.** constipate. **8.** apprentice or indenture: often with *out* or *over*. —*v.i.* **9.** tie up anything. **10.** cohere; stick together. **11.** have binding force; be obligatory. **12.** stiffen or harden; jam, as gears. —**bind over** *Law* hold on bail or under bond for future appearance in court. —*n. Informal* a difficult situation. [ME *binden*]

bind•er (BĪN dər) *n.* **1.** one who binds; esp., a bookbinder. **2.** anything used to bind, as glue. **3.** a cover in which sheets of paper may be fastened. **4.** *Law* a written statement binding parties to an agreement.

bind•er•y (BĪN də ree) *n. pl.* **•er•ies** a place where books are bound.

bind•ing (BĪN ding) *n.* **1.** the act of one who binds. **2.** anything that binds; binder. **3.** a strip sewn over an edge for protection. —*adj.* **1.** tying; restraining. **2.** obligatory.

binge (binj) *n. Informal* a drunken spree.

bin•go (BING goh) *n.* a gambling game resembling lotto.

bin•na•cle (BIN ə kəl) *n. Naut.* a stand or case for a ship's compass.

bin•oc•u•lar (bə NOK yə lər) *adj.* using or for both eyes at once. —*n. Usu. pl.* an optical instrument for use by both eyes.

bi•no•mi•al (bī NOH mee əl) *adj.* consisting of two names or terms. —*n. Math.* an algebraic expression consisting of two terms joined by a plus or minus sign. [< LL *binomius* having two names]

bio- *combining form* life: *biology.* [< Gk. *bios*]

bi•o•chem•is•try (BĪ oh KEM ə stree) *n.* the branch of chemistry relating to the processes and physical properties of living organisms. —**bi'o•chem'i•cal** *adj.* —**bi'o•chem'ist** *n.*

bi•o•de•grad•a•ble (BĪ oh di GRAY də bəl) *adj.* capable of being decomposed by microorganisms, esp. into substances considered harmless to the environment.

bi•o•feed•back (BĪ oh FEED bak) *n.* a process of bringing unconscious functions, such as brain waves, under conscious control for healing, tranquility, etc.

bi•og•ra•pher (bī OG rə fər) *n.* a writer of biography.

bi•o•graph•i•cal (bī ə GRAF i kəl) *adj.* **1.** of or concerning a person's life. **2.** pertaining to biography. Also **bi'o•graph'ic.**

bi•og•ra•phy (bī OG rə fee) *n. pl.* **•phies** an account of a person's life; also, such accounts as a form of literature. [< Gk. *biographía*]

bi•o•log•i•cal (bī ə LOJ i kəl) *adj.* **1.** of or pertaining to biology. **2.** used for or produced by biological research or practice.

biological warfare warfare that employs bacteria and other biological agents.

bi•ol•o•gy (bī OL ə jee) *n.* the science of life in all its manifestations. Its two main divisions are botany and zoology. [< G *Biologie*] —**bi•ol'o•gist** *n.*

bi•on•ics (bī ON iks) *n. (construed as sing.)* the application of data from the functioning of biological systems to engineering problems. —**bi•on'ic** *adj.*

bi•o•phys•ics (BĪ oh FIZ iks) *n. (construed as sing.)* the study of biological organisms and processes, using the methods of physics. —**bi'o•phys'i•cist** *n.*

bi•op•sy (BĪ op see) *n. pl.* **•sies** *Med.* the examination of tissue from a living subject.

bi•o•rhythm (BĪ oh RITH əm) *n.* theoretical cyclical patterns in biological activity or behavior.

bi•par•ti•san (bī PAHR tə zən) *adj.* advocated by or consisting of members of two parties. —**bi•par'ti•san•ship'** *n.*

bi•ped (BĪ ped) *n.* an animal having two feet. [< L *bipes* two-footed]

bi•po•lar (bī POH lər) *adj.* **1.** of or having two poles. **2.** of or belonging to both polar regions. **3.** containing two contradictory qualities, opinions, etc. —**bi'po•lar'i•ty** *n.*

birch (burch) *n.* **1.** a tree or shrub having the outer bark separable in thin layers: also called *white birch.* **2.** a rod from this tree, used as a whip. **3.** the wood of the birch. —*v.t.* whip with a birch rod. [ME *birche*]

bird (burd) *n.* **1.** a warm-blooded, feathered, egg-laying vertebrate having the forelimbs modified as wings. ♦ Collateral adjective:

avian. **2.** *Slang* a person, esp. one who is peculiar. [ME *byrd*]

bird·ie (BUR dee) *n.* in golf, one stroke less than par on a given hole.

bird of passage a migratory bird.

bird of prey a predatory bird, as a hawk.

bird's-eye (BURDZ I) *adj.* **1.** marked with spots resembling birds' eyes. **2.** seen from above or from afar: a *bird's-eye* view. —*n.* a pattern or fabric having eyelike markings.

bi·ret·ta (bə RET ə) *n.* a stiff, square cap with three upright projections, worn by Roman Catholic clerics. [< Ital. *berretta*]

birth (burth) *n.* **1.** the fact or act of being born. **2.** the bringing forth of offspring. **3.** beginning; origin. **4.** ancestry or descent. [ME *byrthe*]

birth·day (BURTH DAY) *n.* the day of one's birth or its anniversary.

birth·mark (BURTH MAHRK) *n.* a mark or stain existing on the body from birth.

birth·place (BURTH PLAYS) *n.* **1.** place of birth. **2.** place where something originates.

birth rate the number of births per a given number of individuals (usually 1,000), in a given area and in a given time period.

birth·right (BURTH RĪT) *n.* a privilege or possession into which one is born.

birth·stone (BURTH STOHN) *n.* a gem identified with the month of one's birth.

bis (bis) *adv.* twice; again. [< Ital.]

bis·cuit (BIS kit) *n.* **1.** a kind of shortened bread baked in small cakes, raised with baking powder or soda. **2.** in ceramics, pottery baked once but not glazed. [ME *bysquyte*]

bi·sect (BĪ SEKT) *v.t.* **1.** cut or divide into two parts; halve. —*v.i.* **2.** fork, as a road.

bi·sex·u·al (bī SEK shoo əl) *adj.* **1.** of both sexes. **2.** having the organs of both sexes; hermaphrodite. **3.** sexually attracted to both sexes. —*n.* **1.** a hermaphrodite. **2.** a person physically attracted to both sexes. —**bi·sex'u·al'i·ty** *n.*

bish·op (BISH əp) *n.* **1.** a prelate in the Christian church; esp., the head of a diocese. **2.** a miter-shaped chess piece. [ME]

bish·op·ric (BISH əp rik) *n.* the office or the diocese of a bishop. [ME *bisshoprike*]

bi·son (BĪ sən) *n. pl.* **bi·son** a bovine ruminant, closely related to the true ox; esp., the North American buffalo. [ME *bisontes* wild oxen]

bisque (bisk) *n.* **1.** a thick, rich soup, esp. one made from shellfish. **2.** a kind of ice cream containing crushed macaroons or nuts. [< F]

bis·tro (BIS troh) *n.* a small bar, tavern, or night club. [< F]

bit¹ (bit) *n.* **1.** a small piece or quantity. **2.** a short time. **3.** a small part, as in a play or movie. **4.** an amount worth 12½ cents: usu. in the expression *two bits* (a quarter). —**do one's bit** make one's contribution; do one's share. —*adj.* small; minor. [ME *bite* bite]

bit² *n.* **1.** a sharp-edged tool for boring or drilling, used with a drill press etc. **2.** the sharp or cutting part of a tool. **3.** the metallic mouthpiece of a bridle. [ME *bite*]

bit³ past tense, alternative past participle of BITE.

bit⁴ *n.* a unit of computer information equivalent to the result of a choice between two possibilities. [< *bi*nary + dig*it*]

bitch (bich) *n.* **1.** the female of the dog or other canine animal. **2.** *Slang* a malicious or promiscuous person, esp. a woman. —*v.i.* *Slang* complain. [ME *bicche*] —**bitch'i·ness** *n.* —**bitch'y** *adj.*

bite (bīt) *v.* **bit, bit·ten** or **bit, bit·ing** *v.t.* **1.** seize, tear, or wound with the teeth. **2.** cut or tear off with or as with the teeth: usually with *off*. **3.** puncture the skin of with a sting or fangs. **4.** cut, pierce, or corrode. **5.** grip; take hold of. **6.** cheat; deceive: usually *passive*. —*v.i.* **7.** seize or cut into something with the teeth. **8.** smart; sting. **9.** take hold; grip. **10.** take bait, as a fish. —*n.* **1.** the act of biting. **2.** a wound inflicted by biting. **3.** a smart; sting. **4.** a morsel of food; mouthful. **5.** a light meal; snack. **6.** the grip or hold taken by a tool, etc. [ME *biten*] —**bit·ing** *adj.* **1.** sharp; stinging. **2.** sarcastic; caustic.

bit·ten (BIT n) past participle of BITE.

bit·ter (BIT ər) *adj.* **1.** having an acrid, disagreeable taste. **2.** unpleasant to accept; distasteful; painful. **3.** feeling or showing intense animosity. —*n.* that which is bitter. [ME]

bit·ters (BIT ərz) *n.* (construed as pl.) a liquor, usu. alcoholic, made from bitter herbs, roots, etc. for use in mixed drinks or as a tonic.

bit·ter·sweet (BIT ər SWEET) *adj.* **1.** bitter and sweet. **2.** pleasant and unpleasant.

bi·tu·men (bī TOO mən) *n.* any mixture of natural substances, as asphalt. [< L] —**bi·tu·mi·nous** (bī TOO mə nəs) *adj.*

bituminous coal a mineral coal low in carbon: also called *soft coal.*

bi·va·lent (bī VAY lənt) *adj. Chem.* **a** having a valence of two. **b** having two valences.

Also *divalent.* **—bi·va′lence, bi·va′len·cy** *n.*

bi·valve (BĪ VALV) *n. Zool.* a mollusk having a shell of two lateral valves hinged together, as the oyster or clam.

biv·ou·ac (BIV oo AK) *n.* a temporary encampment, esp. for soldiers in the field. [< F] **—biv′ou·ac** *v.i.* **·acked, ·ack·ing** assemble in a bivouac.

bi·week·ly (bī WEEK lee) *adj.* occurring once every two weeks. *—n.* a biweekly publication. **—bi·weekly** *adv.*

bi·zarre (bi ZAHR) *adj.* odd; fantastic; grotesque. [< F]

blab (blab) *v.t. & v.i.* **blabbed, blab·bing** 1. disclose indiscreetly. 2. prattle. *—n.* 1. one who blabs. 2. idle chatter. Also **blab′ber.** [ME *blabbe* idle talker]

blab·ber·mouth (BLAb ər MOWTH) *n.* one who talks too much and cannot keep secrets.

black (blak) *adj.* 1. having no brightness or color; reflecting no light. 2. destitute of light. 3. gloomy; dismal; forbidding. 4. belonging to a racial group characterized by dark skin. 5. of or pertaining to black people. 6. soiled; stained. 7. indicating disgrace or censure. 8. angry; threatening. 9. evil; wicked; malignant. 10. characterized by grotesque, savage, or morbid satire: *black* humor. 11. of coffee, without cream or milk. *—n.* 1. the absence of light; the darkest of all colors. 2. something black, as soot. 3. a person with dark skin. *—v.t.* 1. make black; blacken. 2. put blacking on and polish (shoes). *—v.i.* 3. become black. — **black out** 1. suffer a temporary loss of vision or consciousness. 2. extinguish or screen all lights. [OE *blæc*]

black-and-blue (BLAK ən BLOO) *adj.* discolored: said of skin that has been bruised.

black art necromancy; magic.

black·ball (BLAK bawl) *n.* a negative vote. *—v.t.* 1. vote against. 2. ostracize; exclude.

black belt 1. a rating of expert in a martial art such as judo or karate. 2. one who holds such a rating.

black·board (BLAK bord) *n.* a blackened surface, often of slate, for drawing and writing upon with chalk.

black box a self-contained electronic device that can be inserted into a system.

Black Death an exceptionally virulent plague, epidemic in Asia and Europe during the 14th century: also called *plague.*

black·en (BLAK ən) *v.* **·ened, ·en·ing** *v.t.* 1. make black or dark. 2. slander; defame. *—v.i.* 3. become black; darken. [ME]

Black English a dialect of English spoken by some African Americans.

black eye 1. an eye with a black iris. 2. an eye having the adjacent surface discolored by a bruise. 3. a bad reputation.

black·guard (BLAG ahrd) *n.* a vile scoundrel; rogue.

black·head (BLAK hed) *n.* a plug of dried, fatty matter in a pore of the skin.

black hole a theoretical astronomical body, held to be a collapsed star, small, and with an intense gravitational field.

black·jack (BLAK JAK) *n.* 1. a small bludgeon with a flexible handle. 2. a pirate's flag. 3. twenty-one, a card game. *—v.t.* strike with a blackjack.

black·list (BLAK LIST) *n.* a list of censured persons or groups to be penalized or discriminated against.

black lung a lung disease caused by inhaling coal dust, *pneumoconiosis.*

black magic witchcraft.

black·mail (BLAK MAYL) *n.* extortion by threat of exposure of something secret; also, that which is so extorted, as money. — *v.t.* 1. level blackmail upon 2. force (to do something), as by threats: with *into.*

black market a system for selling goods in violation of official prices, quotas, etc.

Black Muslim a member of a sect (**Nation of Islam**) of African Americans in the U.S.

black·out (BLAK OWT) *n.* 1. the extinguishing or screening of lights, esp. as a precaution against air raids. 2. widespread loss of light caused by electric power failure. 3. partial or complete loss of vision or consciousness. 4. a ban, as on news.

black sheep one regarded as a disgrace by his or her family.

black·smith (BLAK SMITH) *n.* 1. one who shoes horses. 2. one who works iron on an anvil and uses a forge. [ME]

black tie 1. a black bow tie. 2. a tuxedo and its correct accessories.

black widow a North American spider, esp. the venomous female.

blad·der (BLAD ər) *n.* 1. *Anat.* an expandable membranous sac in the pelvic cavity, for the temporary retention of urine. 2. an inflatable object resembling a bladder. [ME]

blade (blayd) *n.* 1. the flat cutting part of any edged tool or weapon. 2. the thin, flat part of an oar, plow, etc. 3. the leaf of grasses or certain other plants. 4. a sword. 5. a dashing young man. [ME] **—blad′ed** adj.

blam•a•ble (BLAY mə bəl) adj. deserving blame; culpable. Also **blame′a•ble.**

blame (blaym) v.t. **blamed, blam•ing 1.** hold responsible; accuse. 2. find fault with; reproach. 3. place the responsibility for (an action or error). **—be to blame** be at fault. **—n. 1.** expression of censure; reproof. 2. responsibility for something wrong; culpability. [ME *blamen* revile, reproach] **blame′less** adj. **—blame•wor•thy** (BLAYM WUR thee) adj. deserving of blame.

blanch (blanch) v.t. **1.** remove the color from; bleach. 2. cause to turn pale. 3. scald, esp. to remove the skin of. **—v.i. 4.** turn or become white or pale. [ME *blaunchen* whiten]

bland (bland) adj. **1.** gentle and soothing. 2. mild; insipid. [< L *blandus* soothing]

blan•dish (BLAN dish) v.t. wheedle; flatter. [ME *blandisshen* soothe] **—blan′dish•ment** n. something that attempts to flatter, entice. etc.

blank (blangk) adj. **•er, •est 1.** not written on. 2. not completed or filled out, as a check. 3. showing no expression or interest; vacant. 4. lacking variety or interest. 5. bewildered. 6. empty or void; also, fruitless. **—n. 1.** an empty space; void. 2. a blank space in a printed document, to be filled in. 3. a paper or document with such spaces. 4. a partially prepared piece ready for forming into a finished object. 5. a cartridge filled with powder but having no bullets: also **blank cartridge.** **—v.t.** delete; invalidate: often with *out.* [ME]

blank check 1. a check bearing a signature but no specified amount. 2. unlimited authority or freedom.

blan•ket (BLANG kit) n. **1.** a covering of wool or other fabric, used for warmth. 2. anything that covers, conceals, or protects: a *blanket* of fog. **—adj.** covering a wide range of conditions, items, etc.: a *blanket* indictment. **—v.t.** cover with or as with a blanket. [ME]

blank verse verse without rhyme.

blare (blair) v.t. & v.i. **blared, blar•ing 1.** sound loudly, as a trumpet. 2. exclaim noisily. **—n. 1.** a loud, brazen sound. 2. brightness or glare, as of color. [ME *bleren*]

blar•ney (BLAHR nee) n. **1.** wheedling flattery; cajolery. 2. nonsense. [see BLARNEY STONE]

Blarney stone a stone in a castle in Blarney, Ireland, that reputedly endows one who kisses it with skill in flattery.

bla•sé (blah ZAY) adj. wearied or bored, as from overindulgence in pleasure. [< F]

blas•pheme (blas FEEM) v. **•phemed, •phem•ing** v.t. **1.** speak in an impious manner of (God or sacred things). 2. speak ill of; malign. **—v.i. 3.** utter blasphemy. [ME] **blas•phem′er** n.

blas•phe•my (BLAS fə mee) n. pl. **•mies** impious or profane speaking of God, or of sacred persons or things. [ME *blasphemie*] **—blas′phe•mous** adj.

blast (blast) v.t. **1.** rend in pieces by or as by explosion. 2. cause to wither or shrivel; destroy. **—blast off** *Aerospace* begin an ascent by means of rocket or jet propulsion. **—n. 1.** a strong wind; gust. 2. a loud, sudden sound, as of a trumpet. 3. a rush of air, steam, etc. 4. an explosion of dynamite etc. 5. a blight. 6. *Slang* a big, enjoyable party. **—at full blast** at capacity operation or maximum speed. [ME]

blast•ed (BLAS tid) adj. **1.** withered or destroyed. 2. damned.

blast•off (BLAST AWF) n. *Aerospace* the series of events immediately before and after a rocket leaves its launching pad; also the moment of leaving.

bla•tant (BLAYT nt) adj. **1.** offensively loud or noisy; clamorous. 2. obvious; obtrusive: *blatant* stupidity. [Coined by Edmund Spenser, 16th c.]

blath•er (BLATH ər) v.t. & v.i. speak foolishly. [ME] **—blath′er•er** n.

blaze¹ (blayz) v.i. **blazed, blaz•ing 1.** burn brightly. 2. burn as with emotion. 3. shine. **—n. 1.** a vivid glowing flame; fire. 2. brilliance; glow. 3. sudden activity; outburst, as of anger. [ME]

blaze² v.t. **blazed, blaz•ing 1.** mark (a tree) by or as by chipping off bark. 2. indicate (a trail) by this means. **—n. 1.** a white spot on the face of a horse. 2. a mark to indicate a trail. [Akin to ON *blesi* white spot on a horse's face]

blaz•er (BLAY zər) n. **1.** a lightweight jacket for informal wear. 2. something that blazes brightly. [ME]

bla•zon (BLAY zən) v.t. **1.** inscribe or adorn, as with names or symbols. 2. proclaim; publish. **—n.** ostentatious display. [ME *blasoun* coat of arms]

bleach (bleech) v.t. & v.i. make or become colorless or white; whiten. **—n. 1.** the act of bleaching. **2.** a bleaching agent. [ME *blechen* whiten]

bleach•ers (BLEECH ərz) *n. pl.* tiered, benchlike seats, esp. at a ball park.

bleak (bleek) *adj.* **1.** exposed; bare; barren. **2.** cold; cutting. **3.** cheerless; dreary. [ME *bleke* pale]

blear (bleer) *v.t.* **1.** dim (the eyes) with or as with tears. **2.** blur or make dim. [ME *bleri*]

blear•y (BLEER ee) *adj.* **•i•er, •i•est** made dim, as by tears. **—blear′i•ness** *n.*

bleat (bleet) *v.i.* **1.** utter the cry of a sheep, goat, or calf. **2.** speak or complain with a similar sound. **—v.t. 3.** utter with a bleat. [ME *bleten*] **—bleat** *n.*

bleed (bleed) *v.* **bled, bleed•ing** *v.i.* **1.** lose or shed blood. **2.** feel grief or sympathy. **3.** exude sap or other fluid. **4.** *Printing* extend to or beyond the edge of a page, as an illustration. **—v.t. 5.** draw blood from; leech. **6.** *Slang* extort money or valuables from. [ME *bleden*]

bleed•er (BLEE dər) *n.* one who bleeds profusely; esp., a hemophiliac.

blem•ish (BLEM ish) *v.t.* mar the perfection of; sully. **—n. 1.** a defect, esp. of the skin. **2.** a moral fault. [ME, make livid]

blench[1] (blench) *v.i.* shrink back; flinch. [ME *blenchen*]

blench[2] *v.t. & v.i.* blanch. [Var. of BLANCH]

blend (blend) *v.t.* **1.** mingle, combine, or mix thoroughly. **—v.i. 2.** mix; intermingle. **3.** pass or shade imperceptibly into each other, as colors. **4.** harmonize. [ME *blenden* mix] **—blend** *n.*

bless (bles) *v.t.* **blessed** or **blest, bless•ing 1.** consecrate; make holy. **2.** honor and exalt; glorify. **3.** invoke God's favor upon (a person or thing). **4.** bestow prosperity upon; make happy. **5.** endow, as with a gift. **6.** guard; protect: *Bless* me! [ME *blessen* consecrate]

bless•ed (BLES id) *adj.* **1.** (blest) made holy. **2.** enjoying the happiness of heaven. **3.** blissful; happy. **4.** causing happiness. Also spelled *blest.* **—bless′ed•ness** *n.*

blessed event the birth of a baby.

bless•ing (BLES ing) *n.* **1.** an invocation or benediction; grace. **2.** the bestowal of divine favor. **3.** that which makes happy or prosperous.

blest (blest) alternative past participle of BLESS. **—adj.** blessed.

blew (bloo) past tense of BLOW.

blight (blīt) *n.* **1.** any of a number of destructive plant diseases. **2.** anything that withers hopes, destroys prospects, or impairs growth. **—v.t. 1.** cause to decay; blast. **2.** ruin; frustrate.

blimp (blimp) *n.* a nonrigid dirigible.

blind (blīnd) *adj.* **1.** unable to see. **2.** lacking in perception or judgment. **3.** acting or done without intelligent control; random. **4.** unreasoning; heedless: *blind* prejudice. **5.** concealed: a *blind* test. **6.** closed at one end: a *blind* alley. **7.** having no opening or outlet: a *blind* wall. **8.** done without the aid of visual reference: *blind* flying. **—n. 1.** something that obstructs vision or shuts off light; esp., a window shade. **2.** a hiding place, as for a hunter. **3.** something intended to deceive. **—adv. 1.** to the stage of insensibility: *blind* drunk. **2.** by the aid of instruments only: fly *blind*. **—v.t. 1.** make blind. **2.** dazzle. **3.** deprive of judgment or discernment. [ME]

blind date a date with a person one has not previously met.

blind•fold (BLĪND FOHLD) *v.t.* **1.** cover or bandage the eyes of. **2.** hoodwink; mislead. **—n.** a bandage over the eyes. [ME *blindfellen* strike blind]

blind spot 1. *Anat.* a small area on the retina of the eye that is insensible to light because of the entrance of the optic nerve. **2.** a subject about which one is ignorant, or incapable of objective thought.

blind trust a method of administering financial holdings in which the beneficiary is deprived of all decisions so as to avoid conflict of interest.

blink (blingk) *v.i.* **1.** wink rapidly. **2.** squint. **3.** twinkle; flash on and off. **—v.t. 4.** cause to wink. **—blink at** see but ignore. **—n. 1.** a blinking; wink. **2.** a gleam. **3.** a glance or glimpse. [ME *blinken*]

blintze (blints) *n.* a thin pancake folded about a filling of cottage cheese, fruit, etc. Also **blintz**. [< Yiddish, *blintse*]

blip (blip) *v.t.* **blipped, blip•ping** excise (sound, as a taboo word) from a videotape, leaving a noticeable gap in performance. **—n. 1.** a signal recorded on a radar screen. **2.** the interruption in a television show, resulting from blipping.

bliss (blis) *n.* gladness; joy. [ME *blisse* joyous] **—bliss′ful** *adj.*

blis•ter (BLIS tər) *n.* **1.** a thin vesicle, esp. on the skin, containing watery matter, as from rubbing etc. **2.** any similar swelling. **—v.t. 1.** produce a blister or blisters upon. **2.** re-

bloodsucker

buke severely. —*v.i.* **3.** become blistered. [ME]

blithe (blīth) *adj.* cheerful; gay. [ME] — **blithe·ly** *adv.*

blithe·some (BLĪTH səm) *adj.* showing or imparting gladness.

blitz (blits) *n. Mil.* a sudden attack; blitzkrieg. —**blitz** *v.t.*

blitz·krieg (BLITS KREEG) *n.* **1.** *Mil.* a swift, sudden attack by tanks, aircraft, etc.; also, warfare so waged. **2.** any sudden attack or assault. [< G *Blitz* lightning + *Krieg* war]

bliz·zard (BLIZ ərd) *n.* a severe snowstorm.

bloat (bloht) *v.t. & v.i.* swell or cause to swell, as with fluid. [ME *blout* soft]

blob (blob) *n.* **1.** a soft, globular mass; a viscous drop. **2.** a daub or spot, as of color. **3.** something shapeless or vague.

bloc (blok) *n.* a group, as of politicians or nations, joined to foster special interests. [< F]

block (blok) *n.* **1.** a solid piece of wood, metal, etc., usu. with one or more flat surfaces. **2.** a support or form on which something is shaped or displayed. **3.** a stand from which articles are sold at auction. **4.** a set or section, as of tickets etc., handled as a unit. **5.** an area bounded, usu. on four sides, by streets; also, one side of such an area. **6.** a pulley, or set of pulleys, in a frame with a hook or the like at one end. **7.** an obstacle or hindrance. **8.** *Psychol.* an inability to think or act in certain situations. —*v.t.* **1.** shape into blocks. **2.** shape with a block, as a hat. **3.** support or strengthen with blocks. **4.** obstruct; hinder; stop. —**block out 1.** plan broadly without details. **2.** obscure from view. [ME *blok*]

block·ade (blo KAYD) *n.* **1.** the closing by hostile ships or forces of a coast etc. to traffic or communication. **2.** the ships or forces used for this. —**run a blockade** elude a blockade. —*v.t.* **·ad·ed, ·ad·ing** subject to a blockade.

block·bust·er (BLOK BUS tər) *n.* **1.** a powerful aerial bomb. **2.** something very powerful, large, or successful. **3.** one who practices blockbusting.

block·bust·ing (BLOK BUS ting) *n.* the practice of inducing owners to sell homes quickly and at a loss, by inciting fears that a minority group will take over a neighborhood, deflating values.

block·head (BLOK HED) *n.* a stupid person; dolt.

block·house (BLOK HOWS) *n.* **1.** a fortification, formerly of logs and heavy timbers, having loopholes from which to fire. **2.** a house made of hewn logs set square.

block letter 1. printing type cut from wood. **2.** a style of letters without serifs.

blond (blond) *adj.* **1.** having fair hair with light eyes and skin. **2.** flaxen or golden, as hair. —*n.* a blond person. [< MF *blonde*]

blood (blud) *n.* **1.** *Physiol.* the red fluid that circulates through the bodies of animals, delivering oxygen and nutrients to the cells and tissues. **2.** a similar fluid, as the sap of plants. **3.** the shedding of blood; murder. **4.** temperament: hot *blood.* **5.** vitality; lifeblood. **6.** descent from a common ancestor; kinship. **7.** noble descent. **8.** a dashing young man. **9.** people considered a source of new ideas or energy: new *blood.* [ME *blod*] —**bad blood** enmity. —**in cold blood 1.** deliberately; without passion. **2.** cruelly; without mercy.

blood bath wanton killing; a massacre.

blood count *Med.* the number and proportion of red and white cells in a sample of blood.

blood·cur·dling (BLUD KURD ling) *adj.* terrifying.

blood·ed (BLUD id) *adj.* **1.** having temper of a specified character: *hot-blooded.* **2.** thoroughbred.

blood·less (BLUD lis) *adj.* **1.** devoid of blood; pale. **2.** without bloodshed. **3.** lacking vigor; listless. **4.** coldhearted.

blood·let·ting (BLUD LET ing) *n.* **1.** bleeding for a therapeutic purpose. **2.** bloodshed.

blood money 1. money obtained at the cost of another's life, welfare, etc. **2.** money paid to a hired murderer. **3.** compensation paid to the kin of a murdered person.

blood plasma *Physiol.* the liquid part of the blood, without its cellular components.

blood poisoning *Pathol.* deterioration of the blood caused by bacterial substances: also called *toxemia.*

blood pressure *Physiol.* the pressure of the blood on the walls of the arteries.

blood·shed (BLUD SHED) *n.* the shedding of blood; slaughter.

blood·shot (BLUD SHOT) *adj.* suffused or shot with blood; inflamed: said of the eye.

blood·stream (BLUD STREEM *n.* the blood coursing through a living body.

blood·suck·er (BLUD SUK ər) *n.* **1.** an animal that sucks blood, as a leech. **2.** one who extorts or sponges.

bloodthirsty

blood·thirst·y (BLUD THUR stee) *adj.* murderous; cruel.

blood transfusion *Med.* the transfer of blood from one person or animal into another.

blood vessel any tubular canal, as an artery, vein, or capillary, through which the blood circulates.

blood·y (BLUD ee) *adj.* **blood·i·er, blood·i·est** 1. stained with blood. 2. of, like, or containing blood. 3. involving bloodshed. 4. bloodthirsty. —*v.t.* **blood·ied, blood·y·ing** 1. stain with blood. 2. cause to bleed.

bloom (bloom) *n.* 1. the flower of a plant; blossom. 2. the state of being in flower. 3. a prime condition, as of health or freshness. 4. the rosy tint of the cheeks or skin; glow. —*v.i.* 1. bear flowers; blossom. 2. glow with health; flourish. [ME *blom* blossom]

bloo·mers (BLOO mərz) *n. pl.* formerly, loose, wide trousers gathered at the knee, worn by women as a gymnasium costume; also, an undergarment resembling these. [after Amelia Jenks *Bloomer*, 1818—94, U.S. feminist]

bloom·ing (BLOO ming) *adj.* 1. in flower; blossoming. 2. flourishing.

blos·som (BLOS əm) *n.* 1. a flower, esp. one of a plant yielding edible fruit. 2. the state or period of flowering; bloom. —*v.i.* 1. come into blossom. 2. prosper; thrive. [ME *blosme*]

blot (blot) *n.* 1. a spot or stain, as of ink. 2. a defect or blemish. —*v.* **blot·ted, blot·ting** *v.t.* 1. spot, as with ink; stain. 2. disgrace; sully. 3. obscure: usually with *out.* 4. dry, as with blotting paper. —*v.i.* 5. spread in a blot or blots, as ink. 6. absorb. [ME *blotte*]

blotch (bloch) *n.* 1. a spot or blot. 2. an eruption on the skin. —*v.t. & v.i.* mark or become marked with blotches. —**blotch'y** *adj.* **blotch·i·er, blotch·i·est**

blot·ter (BLOT ər) *n.* 1. a sheet or pad of blotting paper. 2. the daily record of arrests in a police station.

blotting paper unsized paper for absorbing excess ink.

blouse (blows) *n.* 1. a garment for women or children extending from the neck to the waist or just below. 2. a loose, knee-length smock, usu. belted at the waist. 3. a military jacket. —*v.t. & v.i.* **bloused, blous·ing** drape loosely or fully. [< F]

blow¹ (bloh) *v.* **blew, blown, blow·ing** *v.i.* 1. be in motion: said of wind or air. 2. move in a current of air. 3. emit a current

or jet of air, steam, etc. 4. produce sound by blowing or being blown. 5. pant; gasp for breath. 6. fail or become useless, as a fuse, tire, etc.: often with *out.* —*v.t.* 7. drive or impel by a current of air. 8. direct a current of air upon. 9. sound by blowing into, as a bugle. 10. sound (a signal): *blow* taps. 11. emit, as air or smoke, from the mouth. 12. put out of breath, as a horse. 13. form by inflating a material: *blow* bubbles. 14. break, shatter, or destroy by explosion: usu. with *up, down,* etc. 15. melt (a fuse). 16. *Informal* spend (money) lavishly on; also, treat or entertain. —**blow over** 1. pass, as a storm; subside. 2. pass without bad result. —*n.* 1. a blowing, as of wind. 2. a storm or gale. [ME *blowen*]

blow² *n.* 1. a sudden stroke dealt with the fist, a weapon, etc. 2. a sudden disaster. 3. a hostile act; assault. —**come to blows** start fighting. [ME *blaw*]

blow·gun (BLOH GUN) *n.* a long tube through which a missile, as a dart, may be blown.

blow·hole (BLOH HOHL) *n.* 1. *Zool.* a nasal opening in the head, as of certain whales. 2. a vent for gas and bad air, as in mines. 3. a hole in the ice to which seals etc. come to breathe.

blown (blohn) past participle of BLOW¹ — *adj.* 1. out of breath. 2. inflated; swollen, esp. with gas.

blow·pipe (BLOH PĪP) *n.* 1. a tube for blowing air or gas through a flame to direct and intensify its heat. 2. blowgun.

blow·torch (BLOH TORCH) *n.* an apparatus that produces a strong jet of intensely hot flame.

blow·up (BLOH UP) *n.* 1. an explosion. 2. a loss of self-control; also, a fight. 3. an enlargement, as of a photograph.

blowz·y (BLOW zee) *adj.* **blowz·i·er, blowz·i·est** 1. disheveled; slovenly. 2. fat and red-faced.

blub·ber (BLUB ər) *v.i.* 1. weep and sob noisily. —*v.t.* 2. utter with sobs. —*n.* 1. *Zool.* the fat of a whale or other cetacean, used as a source of oil. 2. noisy crying. [ME *bluber* bubble]

blu·cher (BLOO kər) *n.* a shoe in which there is no front seam, the upper meeting above in two projecting flaps. [after G.L. *Blücher,* 1742—1819, a Prussian field marshal]

bludg·eon (BLUJ ən) *n.* a short club, weighted at one end, used as a weapon. —

v.t. **1.** strike with or as with a bludgeon. **2.** coerce; bully.

blue (bloo) *adj.* **blu•er, blu•est 1.** having the color of the clear sky seen in daylight. **2.** livid, as the skin from bruising or cold. **3.** depressed or depressing; melancholy. **4.** puritanical; strict. **—once in a blue moon** seldom. **—n. 1.** the color of the clear sky; azure. **2.** any pigment or dye used to impart a blue color. **—out of the blue** suddenly and unexpectedly. **—the blue 1.** the sky. **2.** the sea. **—v.t. blued, blu•ing 1.** make blue. **2.** treat with bluing. [< OF *bleu*]

blue baby an infant born with bluish skin resulting esp. from a congenital heart defect.

blue blood 1. aristocratic descent. **2.** a member of an aristocratic family.

blue chip 1. in finance, the stock of a well-known company with a record of high dividends, earnings, etc. **2.** a gambling chip of the highest value.

blue-col•lar (BLOO KOL ər) *adj.* of or relating to manual laborers or their jobs.

blue•grass[1] (BLOO GRAS) *n.* one of various grasses having bluish-green stems; esp., the Kentucky bluegrass.

blue•grass[2] *n.* country music of the upper South played by a string band and usu. unamplified. [after *Blue Grass Boys* < *Bluegrass State*, nickname of Kentucky]

blue law a law prohibiting entertainment, business, sale of liquor, etc. on Sunday.

blue•nose (BLOO NOHZ) *n.* a puritanical person.

blue•pen•cil (BLOO PEN səl) *v.t.* **•ciled, •cil•ing** edit or cancel with or as with a blue pencil.

blue•print (BLOO PRINT) *n.* **1.** a plan or drawing made by printing on sensitized paper, the drawing showing in white lines on a blue ground. **2.** any detailed plan.

blue ribbon the highest award; first prize.

blue-rib•bon (BLOO RIB ən) *adj.* selected for special qualifications: a *blue-ribbon* jury.

blues (blooz) *n.pl.* **1.** depression of spirits; melancholy. **2.** (*sing.*) a style of music originating among African Americans and characterized by minor melodies and melancholy subjects; also, the songs sung to this music.

blue•stock•ing (BLOO STOK ing) *n.* a learned, pedantic, or literary woman. [from the blue woolen stockings worn by some literary figures in 18th c. London]

bluff[1] (bluf) *v.t. & v.i.* **1.** deceive by putting on a bold front. **2.** frighten with empty threats. **—n. 1.** the act of bluffing. **2.** one who bluffs. [< LG *bluffen* frighten]

bluff[2] *n.* a steep headland or bank. **—adj. 1.** rough and hearty in manner. **2.** having a broad, steep appearance. [< MLG *blaff* smooth] **—bluff′ness** *n.*

blu•ing (BLOO ing) *n.* a blue coloring matter used in laundering to whiten.

blu•ish (BLOO ish) *adj.* somewhat blue. Also **blue′ish.**

blun•der (BLUN dər) *n.* a stupid mistake. **—v.i. 1.** act or move awkwardly; stumble. **2.** make a stupid mistake. **—v.t. 3.** utter stupidly or confusedly. **4.** bungle. [ME *blunderen* confuse]

blunt (blunt) *adj.* **1.** having a dull end or edge. **2.** abrupt in manner; brusque. **3.** slow of wit; dull. **—v.t. & v.i.** make or become dull or less hurtful. [ME]

blur (blur) *v.t. & v.i.* **blurred, blur•ring 1.** make or become vague and indistinct in outline. **2.** dim. **3.** smear; smudge. **—n. 1.** a smear; smudge. **2.** something indistinct.

blurb (blurb) *n.* a brief, laudatory description, esp. on a book jacket. [Coined by Gelett Burgess, 1866—1951, U.S. humorist]

blurt (blurt) *v.t.* utter abruptly or impulsively: often with *out*.

blush (blush) *v.i.* **1.** become red in the face from modesty or confusion; flush. **2.** become red or rosy, as flowers. **3.** feel shame or regret: usually with *at* or *for*. **—n. 1.** a reddening of the face from modesty, etc. **2.** a red or rosy tint. **—adj.** reddish. [ME *bluschen* redden]

blus•ter (BLUS tər) *v.i.* **1.** blow gustily with violence and noise, as the wind. **2.** talk loudly and aggressively. **—v.t. 3.** utter noisily and threateningly. **—n. 1.** boisterous talk or swagger. **2.** a noisy blowing of the wind; blast. **—blus′ter•y** *adj.*

bo•a (BOH ə) *n. pl.* **bo•as 1.** any of several nonvenomous snakes having great crushing power, esp. the **boa constrictor** of South America. **2.** a long feather or fur scarf for women. [< L]

boar (bor) *n. pl.* **boars** or **boar. 1.** a male swine. **2.** the wild boar. [ME *boor*]

board (bord) *n.* **1.** a flat, thin slab of sawed wood longer than it is wide. **2.** a piece of wood or other material for a specific purpose: an ironing *board*. **3.** a table set for serving food. **4.** food or meals; esp. meals furnished for pay and often including lodging. **5.** an organized official body. —**across the board** affecting all members or categories in the same degree: said of changes in salary, taxes, etc. —**on board** on or in a vessel or other conveyance. —**go by the board** fall into ruin, disuse, etc. —*v.t.* **1.** cover or enclose with boards: often with *up*. **2.** furnish with meals, or meals and lodging, for pay. **3.** place where meals and lodging are provided. **4.** get on, as a ship or train. —*v.i.* **5.** take meals, or meals and lodging. [ME]

board·er (BORD ər) *n.* one who pays for regular meals, or meals and lodging.

board foot *pl.* **board feet** the volume of a board 1 foot square and 1 inch thick, equal to 144 cubic inches or 2359.8 cubic centimeters.

board·ing·house (BORD ing HOWS) a house where meals, or meals and lodging, can be had regularly for pay. —**boarding school** a school in which pupils are boarded.

board·walk (BORD WAWK) *n.* a promenade along a beach, usually of boards.

boast (bohst) *v.i.* **1.** talk in a vain or bragging manner. **2.** speak or possess with pride: with *of*. —*v.t.* **3.** be proud to possess; take pride in. —*n.* **1.** a boastful speech. **2.** that which is boasted about. [ME *bost*] —**boast'ful** *adj.*

boat (boht) *n.* **1.** a small, open watercraft. **2.** any watercraft. **3.** a boat-shaped object. —**in the same boat** in the same situation or condition; equally involved. —*v.i.* travel or go out in a boat. [ME *boot*]

boat·house (BOHT HOWS) *n.* a building for storing boats.

boat·load (BOHT LOHD) *n.* **1.** the amount a boat can hold. **2.** the load carried.

boat·swain (BOH sən) *n.* a warrant officer of a naval ship, or a subordinate officer of a merchant vessel, who is in charge of the rigging, anchors, etc. Also spelled *bosun*, *bo's'n*. [ME *bote-swayn*]

bob[1] (bob) *v.t. & v.i.* **bobbed, bob·bing** move up and down with an irregular, jerky motion. —**bob up** appear or emerge suddenly. —*n.* **1.** a short, jerky movement. **2.** a quick bow or curtsy. **3.** in fishing, a float or cork. [ME *bobben*]

bob[2] *n.* **1.** a short haircut for a woman or child. **2.** the docked tail of a horse. **3.** a small, pendant object, as the weight on a plumb line. —*v.* **bobbed, bob·bing** *v.t.* **1.**

cut short, as hair. —*v.i.* **2.** fish with a bob. [ME *bobbe* cluster]

bob·bin (BOB in) *n.* a spool or reel holding thread for spinning, weaving, or machine sewing. [< F *bobine*]

bob·sled (BOB sled) *n.* a long racing sled with a steering wheel. [Origin unknown] —*v.i.* **·sled·ded, ·sled·ding**

bob·tail (BOB TAYL) *n.* **1.** a short tail or a tail cut short. **2.** an animal with such a tail.

boc·cie (BOCH ee) *n.* a bowling game usu. played on a long clay court [< Ital. *bocce*]

bock beer (bok) a dark, strong beer brewed in winter and served in early spring. [< G *Bockbier*]

bode (bohd) *v.t.* **bod·ed, bod·ing** foretell; presage. [ME *boden* announce]

bod·ice (BOD is) *n.* **1.** the upper portion of a woman's dress. **2.** a woman's vest.

bod·ied (BOD eed) *adj.* having a (specified kind of) body: used in combination: **able-bodied, big-bodied**.

bod·i·less (BOD ee lis) *adj.* having no body; incorporeal.

bod·i·ly (BOD l ee) *adj.* of or pertaining to the body. —*adv.* in the flesh; in person.

bod·kin (BOD kin) *n.* **1.** a pointed instrument for piercing holes in cloth etc. **2.** a blunt needle for drawing tape through a hem. **3.** a long pin for fastening the hair. [ME *badeken* dagger]

bod·y (BOD ee) *n. pl.* **bod·ies** **1.** the entire physical part of a human being, animal, or plant. **2.** a corpse; carcass. **3.** the torso; trunk. **4.** the principal part of anything. **5.** a collection of persons or things taken as a whole. **6.** a distinct mass or portion: a *body* of water. **7.** density or consistency: a wine with *body*. **8.** a person. —*v.t.* **bod·ied, bod·y·ing** furnish with or as with a body. [ME]

bod·y·guard (BOD ee GAHRD) *n.* **1.** a guard responsible for the physical safety of an individual. **2.** a retinue; escort.

body language unconscious gestures and postures considered as indications of mental and emotional states.

body stocking a snug, one-piece, knit undergarment, usu. for women, covering the torso.

Boer (bor) *n.* a Dutch colonist or person of Dutch descent in South Africa. [< Du., farmer]

bog (bog) *n.* wet and spongy ground; marsh. —*v.i.* **bogged, bog·ging** sink or be impeded in or as in a bog: often with *down*. [<

Irish *bogach* soft ground] —**bog′gy** *adj.*
•**gi•er, •gi•est**

bo•gey (BOH gee) *n. pl.* •**geys** in golf, one
stroke over par on a hole. Also **bo′gie.** —
bo′gey *v.t. & v.i.* •**geyed, •gey•ing**

bog•gle (BOG əl) *v.* •**gled, •gling** *v.i.* 1.
bewilder; overwhelm: *boggle* the mind. 2.
hesitate, as from doubt or scruples: often
with *at.* 3. start with fright. 4. equivocate;
dissemble. 5. work clumsily. —*v.t.* 6. bungle.

bo•gus (BOH gəs) *adj.* counterfeit; fake.

bo•gy (BOH gee) *n. pl.* •**gies** a goblin; bug-
bear: also spelled *bogey, bogie.*

Bo•he•mi•an (boh HEE mee ən) *adj.* 1. of
or pertaining to Bohemia, Czechoslovakia.
2. leading the life of a bohemian; unconventional. —*n.* 1. an inhabitant of Bohemia. 2. a gypsy. 3. **bohemian** a person,
usu. of artistic or literary tastes, who lives in
an unconventional manner.

boil¹ (boil) *v.i.* 1. bubble with escaping gas,
usu. from the effect of heat: said of liquids.
2. reach the boiling point. 3. undergo the
action of a boiling liquid. 4. seethe like boiling water. 5. be stirred by rage or passion.
—*v.t.* 6. bring to the boiling point. 7. cook,
cleanse, etc., by boiling. —**boil down** 1.
reduce in bulk by boiling. 2. condense;
summarize. —*n.* the act or state of boiling.
[ME *boillen*]

boil² (boil) *n.* a painful, pus-filled nodule
beneath the skin. [ME *bile*]

boil•er (BOI lər) *n.* 1. a closed vessel in
which steam is generated for heating or
power. 2. a tank for hot water.

boiling point the temperature at which
a liquid boils, for water usu. 212°F.
or 100°C.

bois•ter•ous (BOI stər əs) *adj.* 1. noisy and
unrestrained; uproarious. 2. stormy; violent. [ME *boistrous*]

bold (bohld) *adj.* •**er, •est** 1. having courage;
fearless. 2. showing or requiring courage;
daring. 3. brazen; forward. 4. vigorous; unconventional. 5. abrupt; steep, as a cliff.
[ME *bald*]

bold•face (BOHLD FAYS) *n. Printing* a type
having thick black lines.

bole (bohl) *n.* the trunk of a tree. [ME]

bo•le•ro (bə LAIR oh) *n. pl.* •**ros** 1. a short
jacket open at the front. 2. a Spanish dance,
usu. accompanied by castanets. 3. the music for this dance. [< Sp.]

boll (bohl) *n.* a round pod or seed capsule. —
v.i. form pods. [ME *bolle*]

boll weevil a beetle that destroys cotton
bolls.

bo•lo (BOH loh) *n. pl.* •**los** a large, single-
edged knife of the Philippines. [< Philippine Sp.]

Bol•she•vik (BOHL shə vik) *n.* 1. a member
of the dominant branch of the Russian Social Democratic Party, which seized power
in November 1917. 2. loosely, any Communist or radical. [< Russian *bol'shevik*]

Bol•she•vism (BOHL shə VIZ əm) *n.* the
Marxian doctrines and policies of the Bol-
sheviks; also, any practice, government, etc.
based on them.

bol•ster (BOHL stər) *n.* 1. a narrow, long
pillow. 2. a pad used as a support or for
protection. 3. anything shaped like a bolster
or used as a support. —*v.t.* prop or reinforce: often with *up.* [ME *bolstre*]

bolt¹ (bohlt) *n.* 1. a sliding bar or piece for
fastening a door etc. 2. a pin or rod for
holding something in place, usu. having a
head at one end and threaded at the other.
3. the part of a lock that is shot or withdrawn by turning the key. 4. a sliding mechanism that closes the breech of some small
firearms. 5. an arrow, esp. for a crossbow. 6.
a stroke of lightning; thunderbolt. 7. a sudden start or spring: He made a *bolt* for the
door. 8. a roll of cloth. —**a bolt from the
blue** a sudden and unexpected event. —
v.i. 1. move, go, or spring suddenly out or
away. —*v.t.* 2. fasten or lock with or as with
a bolt or bolts. 3. break away from, as a
political party. 4. gulp, as food. —**bolt upright** stiffly erect. [ME]

bolt² *v.t.* sift: *bolted* flour. [ME *bulten* sift]

bo•lus (BOH ləs) *n. pl.* •**lus•es** 1. a large pill.
2. any rounded lump or mass. [< LL, a
lump of earth]

bomb (bom) *n.* 1. *Mil.* a projectile containing explosive, incendiary, or chemical material to be discharged by concussion or by
a time fuse. 2. any sudden or unexpected
event. 3. *Slang* a complete failure. —*v.t.*
1. attack with or as with bombs. —*v.i.* 2.
Slang fail utterly. [< Sp. *bomba* ball of
fire]

bom•bard (bom BAHRD) *v.t.* 1. attack with
bombs or shells. 2. attack as with bombs.
[ME] —**bom•bard′ment** *n.*

bom•bar•dier (BOM bər DEER) *n. Mil.* the
member of the crew of a bomber who operates the bombsight and releases bombs. [<
MF]

bom•bast (BOM bast) *n.* grandiloquent or

pompous language. [< MF, padding] —
bom·bas'tic adj.

bomb·er (BOM ər) n. **1.** an airplane designed to carry and drop bombs. **2.** one who bombs.

bomb·shell (BOM SHEL) n. **1.** a bomb. **2.** a surprise.

bomb·sight (BOM SĪT) n. Mil. an instrument on an aircraft for aiming bombs.

bo·na fide (BOH nə FĪD) made in good faith; authentic; genuine. [< L]

bo·nan·za (bə NAN za) n. **1.** a rich mine or find of ore. **2.** a source of great wealth. [< Sp., smooth sea]

bon·bon (BON BON) n. a sugared candy. [< F, lit., good-good]

bond (bond) n. **1.** that which binds or holds together; a band; tie. **2.** a uniting force or influence. **3.** a substance that cements or unites; also, the union itself. **4.** Law an obligation in writing under seal. **5.** in finance, an interest-bearing certificate of debt. **6.** in insurance, a policy covering losses suffered through the acts of an employee. **7.** in commerce, the condition of goods stored in a bonded warehouse until duties are paid. **8.** a bondsman; also, bail; surety. **9.** Chem. a unit of combining power between the atoms of a molecule. — **bottled in bond** bottled under government supervision and stored in a warehouse for a stated period, as certain whiskeys. —v.t. **1.** put a certified debt upon; mortgage. **2.** furnish bond for; be surety for (someone). **3.** place, as goods or an employee, under bond. **4.** unite, as with glue, etc. —v.i. **5.** interlock or cohere. [ME]

bond·age (BON dij) n. **1.** involuntary servitude; slavery; serfdom. **2.** subjection to any influence or domination. [ME]

bond·ed (BON did) adj. **1.** secured or pledged by a bond or bonds. **2.** stored in a warehouse; placed in bond.

bonds·man (BONDZ mən) n. pl. **·men** one who provides bond for another.

bone (bohn) n. **1.** Anat. **a** a hard, dense porous material forming the skeleton of vertebrates. **b** a piece of this material. **2.** pl. the skeleton as a whole. **3.** a substance resembling bone. **4.** something made of bone or similar material. —**have a bone to pick** have a complaint. —**make no bones about** be direct or straightforward about. —v. **boned, bon·ing** v.t. remove the bones from. —v.i. Informal study in-

tensely and quickly: often with up. [ME bon]

bone meal pulverized bone, used as feed and fertilizer.

bon·er (BOH nər) n. a foolish error; blunder.

bon·fire (BON FĪR) n. a large fire built in the open air.

bon·gos (BONG gohz) a pair of connected drums played with the hands. Also **bongo drums**.

bon mot (BON MOH) pl. **bons mots** (BON MOHZ) a clever saying; witticism. [< F, lit., good word]

bon·net (BON it) n. a hat for women or children, typically tied under the chin. [ME bonet]

bon·ny (BON ee) adj. **·ni·er, ·ni·est 1.** handsome or beautiful. **2.** fine; good. **3.** robust; healthy. [ME bonie good]

bon·sai (bon SĪ) n. pl. **·sai 1.** a dwarfed tree or shrub trained into a pleasing design. **2.** the art of creating such trees or shrubs. [< Japanese]

bo·nus (BOH nəs) n. pl. **·nus·es** something paid or given in addition to a usual or stipulated amount. [< L, good]

bon vi·vant (BON vee VAHNT) pl. **bons vi·vants** (-VAHNTS) French one who enjoys luxurious living.

bon vo·yage (BON voi AHZH) French pleasant trip.

bon·y (BOH nee) adj. **bon·i·er, bon·i·est 1.** of, like, or full of bone or bones. **2.** having prominent bones; thin; gaunt.

boob (boob) n. Slang a simpleton; booby.

boo·by (BOO bee) n. pl. **·bies** a stupid person; dunce.

booby prize a mock award for a worst score or performance.

booby trap 1. a concealed bomb etc., placed so as to be detonated by the victim. **2.** any device for taking someone unawares.

book (buuk) n. **1.** a bound set of printed sheets of paper, usually between covers. **2.** a literary composition of some length. **3.** a ledger, register, etc. **4.** a main division of a literary composition: a book of the Bible. **5.** a libretto. **6.** a booklike packet, as of matches. **7.** a record of bets, especially on a horse race. **8.** in cards, a specific number of tricks or cards won. —**by the book** according to rule. —**like a book** thoroughly. — **make book** bet or accept bets. —v.t. **1.** arrange for beforehand, as accommodations or seats. **2.** engage for performance. **3.**

make a record of charges against (someone) on a police blotter. [ME]

Book is used to make many self-explanatory words and phrases, as:

bookbinder   **bookseller**
book collector   **bookselling**

book·bind·ing (BUUK BIN ding) *n.* the art and trade of binding books.

book·case (BUUK KAYS) *n.* a case with shelves for books.

book·end (BUUK END) a support or prop used to hold books upright.

book·ie (BUUK ee) *n.* a bookmaker (def. 2).

book·ish (BUUK ish) *adj.* 1. fond of books; studious. 2. pedantic.

book·keep·ing (BUUK KEE ping) *n.* the practice of recording business transactions systematically.

book·let (BUUK lit) *n.* a pamphlet.

book·mak·er (BUUK MAY kər) *n.* 1. one who compiles, prints, or binds books. 2. one who makes a business of accepting bets.

book·mark (BUUK MAHRK) *n.* any object inserted in a book to mark a place.

Book of Common Prayer the book of ritual used in the Anglican church.

book·rack (BUUK RAK) *n.* 1. a frame to hold an open book. 2. a rack to hold books.

book·stall (BUUK STAWL) *n.* a stall or stand where books are sold.

book·worm (BUUK WURM) *n.* 1. one who spends much time reading and studying. 2. any insect destructive to books.

boom[1] (boom) *v.i.* 1. emit a deep, resonant sound. 2. grow rapidly; flourish. —*v.t.* 3. utter or sound in a deep, resonant tone: often with *out.* —*n.* 1. a deep, reverberating sound. 2. a sudden increase; spurt. —*adj.* caused by a boom: *boom* conditions. [ME *bombon* buzz]

boom[2] *n.* 1. *Naut.* a spar used to extend the bottom of certain sails. 2. a long arm of a derrick, from which the objects to be lifted are suspended. [< Du., beam]

boom·e·rang (BOO mə RANG) *n.* 1. a curved, wooden missile originated in Australia, one form of which will return to the thrower. 2. a plan, statement, etc., that recoils upon the originator. —*v.i.* react harmfully upon the originator. [< native Australian name]

boon[1] (boon) *n.* a good thing bestowed; blessing. [ME *bone* prayer]

boon[2] *adj.* convivial; merry: now only in the phrase **boon companion.** [ME *bone* good]

boon·docks (BOON DOKS) *n.pl.* an unciv-

ilized or backwoods area: with *the.* [< Tagalog *bundok* mountain]

boon·dog·gle (BOON DOG əl) *v.i.* **·gled, ·gling** work on wasteful or unnecessary projects.

boor (buur) *n.* an awkward or rude person. [< Du. *boer* farmer] —**boor'ish** *adj.*

boost (boost) *v.t.* 1. raise by pushing from beneath or behind. 2. increase: *boost* prices. 3. advance by speaking well of; promote. —*n.* 1. a lift; help. 2. an increase.

boost·er (BOO stər) *n.* 1. any device or substance for increasing power. 2. an enthusiastic supporter.

boot[1] (boot) *n.* 1. a covering for the foot and part or most of the leg. 2. a kick. 3. in the Navy and Marine Corps, a recruit. — **get a boot** *Informal* enjoy: I always *get a boot* out of her jokes. —*v.t.* 1. put boots on. 2. kick or punt. 3. *Slang* dismiss; fire. [ME *bote*]

boot[2] *Obs. n.* advantage. —**to boot** in addition; over and above. [ME *bote* profit]

boot·black (BOOT BLAK) *n.* one whose business is shining boots and shoes.

booth (booth) *n.* 1. a small compartment or cubicle. 2. a seating compartment, as in a restaurant. 3. a small stall for the display or sale of goods. [ME *bothe*]

boot·leg (BOOT LEG) *v.t. & v.i.* **·legged, ·leg·ging** make, sell, or carry for sale (liquor, etc.) illegally; smuggle. —**boot'leg'ger** *n.*

boot·less (BOOT lis) *adj.* profitless; useless; unavailing.

boot·lick (BOOT LIK) *v.t. & v.i.* flatter servilely; toady. —**boot'lick'er** *n.*

boo·ty (BOO tee) *n. pl.* **·ties** 1. the spoil of war or any violence; plunder. 2. any prize or gain. [ME *botye*]

booze (booz) *Informal n.* 1. alcoholic drink. 2. a drunken spree. —*v.i.* **boozed, booz·ing** drink to excess.

bop[1] (bop) *v.t.* **bopped, bop·ping** *Slang* hit.

bop[2] *n.* a variety of jazz.

Bor·deaux (bor DOH) *n.* a white or red wine produced in the vicinity of Bordeaux, France.

bor·der (BOR dər) *n.* 1. a margin, edge, or brink. 2. the frontier line or district of a country or state; boundary. 3. a decorative edging. —*adj.* of, on, or forming the border. —*v.t.* 1. put a border or edging on. 2. lie along the border of; bound. —**border on** (or **upon**) 1. lie adjacent to. 2.

approach; verge on: The activity *borders on* piracy. [ME *bordure*]

bor·der·line (BOR dər LIN) *n.* a line of demarcation. —*adj.* difficult to classify; doubtful.

bore[1] (bor) *v.* **bored, bor·ing** *v.t.* **1.** make a hole in or through, as with a drill. **2.** make (a tunnel etc.) by or as by drilling. **3.** force (one's way). **4.** weary by being dull etc.; tire. —*v.i.* **5.** make a hole etc. by or as by drilling. **6.** force one's way. —*n.* **1.** a hole made by or as by boring. **2.** the interior diameter of a firearm or cylinder; caliber. **3.** an uninteresting, tiresome person or thing. [ME *boren*]

bore[2] past tense of BEAR[1].

bo·re·al (BOR ee əl) *adj.* of the north or the north wind. [ME *boriall* northern]

bore·dom (BOR dəm) *n.* the condition of being bored; tedium.

bor·er (BOR ər) *n.* **1.** a tool used for boring. **2.** a beetle, moth, or worm that burrows in plants, wood, etc.

born (born) *adj.* **1.** brought forth, as offspring. **2.** natural; by birth: a *born* musician. [ME]

born-a·gain (BORN ə GEN) *adj.* of a Christian, having received spiritual life, or being renewed spiritually, esp. by a personal conversion to the teachings of Christ.

borne (born) past participle of BEAR[1].

bor·ough (BUR oh) *n.* **1.** an incorporated village or town. **2.** one of the five administrative divisions of New York, N.Y. [ME *burwe* town]

bor·row (BOR oh) *v.t.* **1.** take or obtain (something) with the promise or understanding that one will return it. **2.** adopt for one's own use, as ideas. —*v.i.* **3.** borrow something. [ME *borowen*]

borscht (borsht) *n.* a Russian beet soup, eaten hot or cold. [< Yiddish. *borsht*]

bor·zoi (BOR zoi) *n.* a breed of Russian hound, having a long, silky coat: also called *Russian wolfhound.* [< Russ., swift]

bosh (bosh) *n.* empty words; nonsense. [< Turkish *bos* empty]

bo's'n (BOH sən) see BOATSWAIN.

bos·om (BUUZ əm) *n.* **1.** the breast of a human being, esp. of a woman. **2.** the breast as the seat of thought and emotion. **3.** inner circle; midst. —*adj.* close; intimate. [ME]

boss[1] (baws) *n.* **1.** one who controls and directs, as an employer, manager, etc. **2.** a professional politician who controls a political organization. —*v.t.* **1.** supervise; direct.

2. order in a high-handed manner. —*v.i.* **3.** act as boss. [< Du. *baas* master]

boss[2] *n.* a circular prominence; knob or projecting ornament. —*v.t.* ornament with bosses. [ME *boce* lump]

boss·y (BAW see) *adj.* **boss·i·er, boss·i·est** tending to boss; domineering.

bo·sun (BOH sən) see BOATSWAIN.

bo·tan·i·cal (bə TAN i kəl) *adj.* of or pertaining to botany or to plants. [< Med.L *botanicus* of plants]

bot·a·ny (BOT n ee) *n.* the division of biology dealing with plants, their structure, functions, classification, etc. —**bot'a·nist** *n.*

botch (boch) *v.t.* do or make in an inept way; bungle. [ME *bocchen*] —**botch** *n.*

both (bohth) *adj. & pron.* the two together: *Both* girls laughed. *Both* laughed. —*conj. & adv.* equally; alike; as well: with *and.* [ME *bothe*]

both·er (BOTH ər) *v.t.* **1.** pester; give trouble to. **2.** confuse; fluster. —*v.i.* **3.** trouble or concern oneself. —*n.* **1.** a state of vexation. **2.** one who or that which bothers.

both·er·some (BOTH ər səm) *adj.* causing bother.

bot·tle (BOT l) *n.* **1.** a vessel, usu. of glass, for holding liquids, having a neck and a narrow mouth that can be stopped. **2.** as much as a bottle will hold: also **bot'tle·ful'.** —**hit the bottle** *Slang* drink liquor to excess. —*v.t.* **·tled, ·tling 1.** put into a bottle or bottles. **2.** restrain: often with *up* or *in.* [ME *botel*] —**bot'tler** *n.*

bot·tle·neck (BOT l NEK) *n.* **1.** a narrow or congested passageway. **2.** anything that retards progress.

bot·tom (BOT əm) *n.* **1.** the lowest part of anything. **2.** the underside or undersurface. **3.** the ground beneath a body of water. **4.** *Informal* the buttocks. —**at bottom** fundamentally. —*adj.* lowest; fundamental. —*v.t.* **1.** provide with a bottom. **2.** fathom; comprehend. —*v.i.* **3.** touch or rest on the bottom. —**bottom out** of a security market, decline to a point where demand exceeds supply and prices rise. [ME *botme*]

bottom land lowland along a river.

bot·tom·less (BOT əm lis) *adj.* **1.** having no bottom. **2.** unfathomable; limitless; endless. **3.** nude. —**the bottomless pit** hell.

bottom line 1. a figure reflecting profit or loss, usu. the last line of a financial statement. **2.** any important result, judgment, conclusion, etc.

bot·u·lism (BOCH ə LIZ əm) *n.* poisoning caused by a toxin produced by a bacillus sometimes present in improperly preserved food. [< G *Botulismus*]

bou·doir (BOO dwahr) *n.* a lady's private sitting room or bedroom. [< F, lit., a pouting room]

bouf·fant (boo FAHNT) *adj.* puffed-out; flaring. [< F, lit., swelling]

bough (bow) *n.* a large branch of a tree. [ME *bogh*]

bought (bawt) past tense, past participle of BUY.

bouil·la·baisse (BOOL yə BAYS) *n.* a seafood chowder. [< F]

bouil·lon (BUUL yon) *n.* clear soup from beef or other meats. [< F]

boul·der (BOHL dər) *n.* a large, rounded rock. [ME *bulderston*]

boul·e·vard (BUUL ə VAHRD) *n.* a broad avenue, often lined with trees. [< F]

bounce (bowns) *v.* **bounced, bounc·ing** *v.i.* **1.** move with a bound or bounds, as a ball; rebound. **2.** move suddenly; spring. **3.** fail to be honored by a bank as worthless: said of a check. —*v.t.* **4.** cause to bounce. **5.** *Slang* eject (a person) forcibly. —*n.* **1.** a bound or rebound. **2.** a sudden spring or leap. **3.** vivacity; verve; spirit. [ME *buncin* thump] —**bounc'i·ly** *adv.* —**bounc'ing** *adj.* strong; active: a *bouncing* baby boy.

bounc·er (BOWN sər) *n.* one employed, as in a bar, to eject disorderly persons.

bound[1] (bownd) *v.i.* **1.** strike and spring back from a surface, as a ball. **2.** leap; move by a series of leaps. —*n.* a leap or spring; also, a rebound. [< MF *bond* leap]

bound[2] *n.* **1.** *Usu. pl.* a boundary; limit: out of *bounds.* **2.** *pl.* the area near or within a boundary. —*v.t.* **1.** set limits to; restrict. **2.** form the boundary of. —*v.i.* **3.** adjoin; abut. [ME *bounde*]

bound[3] past tense, past participle of BIND. —*adj.* **1.** made fast; tied with bonds. **2.** having a cover or binding. **3.** morally or legally obligated. **4.** certain; sure: It's *bound* to rain.

bound[4] *adj.* being on course for; on the way: *bound* for home. [ME *boun* ready]

bound·a·ry (BOWN də ree) *n. pl.* **·ries** anything indicating a limit or confine.

bound·less (BOWND lis) *adj.* having no limit; vast.

boun·te·ous (BOWN tee əs) *adj.* **1.** generous. **2.** abundant; plentiful. [ME *boun-tevous*] —**boun'te·ous·ness** *n.*

boun·ti·ful (BOWN tə fəl) *adj.* **1.** generous. **2.** plentiful.

boun·ty (BOWN tee) *n. pl.* **·ties 1.** liberality in giving. **2.** gifts or favors. **3.** a reward from a government, as for the killing of predatory animals. [ME *bounte* goodness]

bou·quet (boh KAY) *n.* **1.** a bunch of flowers. **2.** (boo KAY) delicate aroma, esp. of a wine. [< F]

bour·bon (BUR bən) *n.* a straight whiskey distilled from a fermented mash containing at least 51 percent corn. Also **bourbon whiskey.** [after *Bourbon* County, Kentucky, where first made]

bour·geois (buur ZHWAH) *n. pl.* **·geois 1.** a member of the middle class, esp. a tradesman. **2.** *pl.* the middle class. —*adj.* of or characteristic of the middle class: often used disparagingly. [< MF]

bour·geoi·sie (BUUR *zh*wah ZEE) *n.* the middle class of society, esp. in France.

bout (bowt) *n.* **1.** a contest; trial. **2.** a fit or spell, as of illness.

bou·tique (boo TEEK) *n.* a small retail shop. [< F]

bo·vine (BOH vīn) *adj.* **1.** of or pertaining to oxen, cows, etc. **2.** stolid; dull. —*n.* a bovine animal. [< LL *bovinus* pertaining to oxen]

bow[1] (bow) *n.* the forward part of a ship, boat, etc. [< LG or Scand.]

bow[2] *v.* **bowed, bow·ing** *v.i.* **1.** bend the body or head, as in reverence or assent. **2.** bend or incline downward. **3.** submit; yield. —*v.t.* **4.** bend (the body, head, etc.). **5.** cause to bend or stoop. —**bow out** withdraw; resign. —*n.* an inclination of the body or head. [ME *bowen* bend]

bow[3] (boh) *n.* **1.** a weapon made from a strip of wood or other pliable material, bent by a string and used to project an arrow. **2.** something bent or curved; a bend. **3.** a knot with a loop or loops, as of ribbon etc. **4.** a rod with fibers, as horsehair, stretched between raised ends, used for playing a stringed instrument. —*adj.* bent; curved; bowed. —*v.t. & v.i.* **bowed, bow·ing 1.** bend into the shape of a bow. **2.** play (a stringed instrument) with a bow. [ME *bowe*]

bowd·ler·ize (BOHD lə RĪZ) *v.t.* **·ized, ·iz·ing** expurgate or edit prudishly. [after Dr. Thomas *Bowdler's* expurgated edition of Shakespeare (1818)] —**bowd'ler·i·za'tion** *n.*

bow·el (BOW əl) *n.* **1.** an intestine. **2.** *pl.* the inner part of anything: *bowels* of the earth. [ME *bouel* sausage]

bowl[1] (bohl) *n.* **1.** a deep, round dish. **2.** the amount a bowl will hold. **3.** an amphitheater. **4.** something shaped like a bowl: the *bowl* of a pipe. [ME *bolle*]

bowl[2] *n.* **1.** a large ball used in bowling or bowls. **2.** a throw of the ball in bowling. —*v.i.* **1.** play at bowls, bowling, etc. **2.** move smoothly and swiftly: usually with *along.* —*v.t.* **3.** roll or throw, as a ball. —**bowl over** cause to be shocked or astounded. [ME *bowle* ball]

bow·leg (BOH LEG) *n.* a leg with an outward curvature at or · below the knee. — **bow·leg·ged** (BOH LEG id) *adj.*

bowl·ing (BOH ling) *n.* a game played by rolling a ball down a bowling alley in an attempt to knock down ten pins set up at the other end.

bowling alley a long, narrow wooden lane for bowling, or the building containing it.

box[1] (boks) *n.* **1.** a receptacle or case, usu. having a lid. **2.** the amount contained in a box. **3.** something resembling a box in form or use. **4.** a space partitioned off for seating, as in a theater. **5.** in baseball, any of several designated spaces, as for the pitcher. —*v.t.* place in a box. —**box in** confine in, or as in, a small space. [ME]

box[2] *v.t.* **1.** strike with the hand; cuff. **2.** fight (another) in a boxing match. —*v.i.* **3.** fight with one's fists. —*n.* a blow; cuff. [ME, *blow*]

box·car (BOKS KAHR) *n.* **1.** an enclosed freight car. **2.** *pl.* in craps, a pair of sixes

box·er[1] (BOK sər) *n.* prizefighter; pugilist.

box·er[2] *n.* a breed of dog, related to the bulldog.

box·ing (BOK sing) *n.* the art or practice of prizefighting with the fists.

boxing glove a padded mitten used for boxing.

box office 1. the ticket office of a theater, etc. **2.** receipts at the box office.

box seat a seat in a box of a theater, stadium, etc.

box spring a mattress foundation consisting of an upholstered frame set with coil springs.

boy (boi) *n.* a male child; lad; youth. [ME *boye*] —**boy'ish** *adj.*

boy·cott (BOI kot) *v.t.* **1.** combine together in refusing to deal or associate with, so as to punish or coerce. **2.** refuse to use or buy. [after Capt. C. *Boycott,* 1832—97, Irish

landlord's agent, said to have been the first victim] —**boy'cott** *n.*

boy·friend (BOI FREND *n.* a preferred male companion.

boy·hood (BOI huud) *n.* the state or period of being a boy.

boy scout a member of the **Boy Scouts of America,** an organization stressing self-reliance and good citizenship.

bra (brah) *n.* a brassiere.

brace (brays) *v.* **braced, brac·ing** *v.t.* **1.** make firm or steady; strengthen by or as by braces. **2.** make ready to withstand pressure, shock, etc. **3.** stimulate; enliven. —*v.i.* **4.** strain against pressure. —**brace up** *Informal* rouse one's courage or resolution. —*n.* **1.** a support, as of wood or metal, that steadies or strengthens. **2.** a clasp or clamp for fastening, connecting, etc. **3.** a cranklike handle for holding and turning a bit or other boring tool. **4.** a pair; couple. **5.** *Often pl. Dent.* a wire or wires fastened on irregular teeth and gradually tightened to align them. **6.** *Med.* any of various devices for supporting a joint, limb, or other part. **7.** a double curved line, { }, used to enclose words in a text. [ME]

brace·let (BRAYS lit) *n.* **1.** an ornamental band worn around the wrist or arm. **2.** *pl. Slang* handcuffs. [ME]

brac·ing (BRAY sing) *adj.* strengthening; invigorating.

brack·en (BRAK ən) *n.* **1.** a coarse, hardy fern with very large fronds: also called *brake.* **2.** a clump of such ferns. [ME *braken*]

brack·et (BRAK it) *n.* **1.** a piece of wood, metal, etc. projecting from a wall, used to support a shelf, lamp, etc. **2.** a brace used to strengthen an angle. **3.** a classification according to income for tax purposes. **4.** one of two marks [ ] used to enclose any part of a text. —*v.t.* **1.** support with a bracket. **2.** enclose within brackets. **3.** categorize together.

brack·ish (BRAK ish) *adj.* **1.** somewhat saline; briny. **2.** distasteful. [< Du. *brak* salty] —**brack'ish·ness** *n.*

brag (brag) *v.t. & v.i.* **bragged, brag·ging** boast (about oneself, one's abilities, etc.). —*n.* **1.** boastful language; boasting. **2.** one who brags. [ME] —**brag'ger** *n.*

brag·ga·do·ci·o (BRAG ə DOH shee OH) *n. pl.* **·ci·os 1.** pretentious boasting. **2.** one who boasts; a swaggerer. [after *Brag-*

gadocchio, a boastful character in Spenser's
Faerie Queene (1590)]

brag•gart (BRAG ərt) *n.* a boastful person;
bragger.

Brah•man (BRAH mən) *n. pl.* **•mans 1.** a
member of the highest Hindu caste, the
priestly caste: also spelled *Brahmin.* **2.** a
breed of cattle originating in India. [< Skt.,
praise, worship]

Brah•min (BRAH min) *n.* **1.** Brahman (def.
1). **2.** a person of an old, socially prominent
family.

braid (brayd) *v.t.* **1.** intertwine several
strands of hair, etc. **2.** bind or ornament
with ribbons, etc. **3.** form by braiding. —*n.*
1. a narrow, flat tape or strip for binding or
ornamenting fabrics. **2.** anything braided or
plaited. [ME *braiden*]

Braille (brayl) *n.* a system of printing or writing for the blind in which the characters
consist of raised dots to be read by the fingers; also, the characters themselves. Also
braille. [after Louis *Braille,* 1809–52, the
inventor]

brain (brayn) *n.* **1.** *Anat.* the large organ of
the central nervous system contained in the
cranium of vertebrates. **2.** *Often pl.* mind;
intellect. **3.** an electronic device that controls an automatic system. —*v.t.* **1.** dash out
the brains of. **2.** *Slang* hit (someone) on the
head. [ME]

brain•child (BRAYN CHILD) *n.* that which
one has created or originated, as an
idea.

brain death the condition in which brain
waves are not detectable, usu. as indicated
by flat tracings on an electroencephalograph.

brain•less (BRAYN lis) *adj.* lacking intelligence; senseless; stupid.

brain•storm (BRAYN storm) *n.* a sudden
inspiration.

brain•wash (BRAYN wosh) *v.t.* alter the
convictions, beliefs, etc. of by means of intensive, coercive indoctrination.

brain wave *Physiol.* a rhythmical fluctuation
of electrical potential in the brain.

brain•y (BRAY nee) *adj.* **brain•i•er, brain•
i•est** *Informal* intelligent; smart.

braise (brayz) *v.t.* **braised, brais•ing** cook
by searing till brown and then simmering in
a covered pan. [< F *braiser*]

brake[1] (brayk) *n.* a device for slowing or
stopping a vehicle or wheel, esp. by friction.
—*v.t. & v.i.* **braked, brak•ing** apply a
brake to or operate a brake. [ME]

brake[2] *n.* bracken, a kind of fern. [ME,
thicket]

brake[3] *n.* an area covered with brushwood,
brambles, etc.; thicket.

bram•ble (BRAM bəl) *n.* any prickly plant.
[ME]

bran (bran) *n.* the husks of cereals, separated
from the flour by sifting. [ME]

branch (branch) *n.* **1.** a woody outgrowth
from the trunk of a tree or other large plant;
limb. **2.** an offshoot, as of a deer's antlers. **3.**
any separate part or division of a system,
subject, etc. **4.** a subordinate or local store,
office, etc. **5.** a division of a family, tribe,
nation, etc. **6.** a tributary stream of a river.
—*v.i.* **1.** put forth branches. **2.** separate
into branches or subdivisions. —*v.t.* **3.** divide into branches. —**branch out** extend
or expand, as one's business. [ME *braunche*
paw]

brand (brand) *n.* **1.** a distinctive name or
trademark identifying the product of a
manufacturer. **2.** the kind or make of a
product: *a brand* of coffee. **3.** a mark made
with a hot iron, as on cattle. **4.** any mark of
disgrace; stigma. **5.** a branding iron. **6.** a
burning piece of wood or a torch. —*v.t.* **1.**
mark with a brand. **2.** stigmatize. [ME]

branding iron an iron for burning a brand.

bran•dish (BRAN dish) *v.t.* wave or flourish
triumphantly, menacingly, or defiantly.
[ME *braundisshen*]

bran•dy (BRAN dee) *n. pl.* **•dies** an alcoholic liquor distilled from wine or other fermented fruit juice. —*v.t.* **•died, •dy•ing**
mix, flavor, strengthen, or preserve with
brandy. [< Du. *brandewijn*, lit., distilled
wine]

brash (brash) *adj.* **•er, •est 1.** acting hastily;
rash; impetuous. **2.** impudent; saucy. [ME
brassche crash] —**brash'ness** *n.*

brass (bras) *n.* **1.** an alloy essentially of copper and zinc, both ductile and malleable. **2.**
Sometimes pl. Music the brass instruments
of an orchestra or band collectively. **3.** *Informal* effrontery; insolence. **4.** *Informal*
high-ranking military officers; also any high
officials. —*adj.* made of brass; brazen. [ME
bras]

bras•siere (brə ZEER) *n.* a woman's undergarment to support or shape the breasts;
also **bra.** [< F]

brass•y (BRAS ee) *adj.* **brass•i•er, brass•i•
est 1.** of or ornamented with brass. **2.** like
brass, as in sound or color. **3.** cheap and
showy. **4.** insolent; brazen.

brat (brat) *n.* a nasty child.

bra·va·do (brə VAH doh) *n. pl.* **·does** or **·dos** boastful defiance; affectation of bravery. [< Sp. *bravada* brave]

brave (brayv) *adj.* **brav·er, brav·est 1.** having or showing courage; intrepid. **2.** making a fine display. —*v.t.* **braved, brav·ing 1.** meet with courage and fortitude. **2.** defy; challenge. —*n.* **1.** a man of courage. **2.** a North American Indian warrior. [< MF] —**brave′er·y** *n.*

bra·vo (BRAH voh) *interj.* good! well done! —*n. pl.* **·vos** a shout of "bravo!" [< Ital.]

bra·vu·ra (brə VYUUR ə) *n.* **1.** *Music* a brilliant or showy passage. **2.** any brilliant or daring performance. [< Ital., spirit] —**bra·vu′ra** *adj.*

brawl (brawl) *n.* a noisy quarrel; fight. [ME *braule*] —**brawl** *v.i.* —**brawl′er** *n.*

brawn (brawn) *n.* **1.** firm or well-developed muscles. **2.** muscular power. [ME *brawne* slice of flesh] —**brawn′y** *adj.* **brawn·i·er, brawn·i·est**

bray (bray) *n.* **1.** the cry of an ass, mule, etc. **2.** any loud, harsh sound. [ME *brayen* cry out] —**bray** *v.t. & v.i.*

braze¹ (brayz) *v.t.* **brazed, braz·ing 1.** make of brass. **2.** make like brass in hardness or appearance. **3.** ornament with or as with brass. [ME *brasen*]

braze² *v.t.* **brazed, braz·ing** *Metall.* join the surfaces of (metals) with a layer of a soldering alloy applied under very high temperature. [< F *braser* solder]

bra·zen (BRAY zən) *adj.* **1.** made of or resembling brass. **2.** impudent; shameless. —*v.t.* face with effrontery or impudence: with *out.* [ME *brasen*] —**bra′zen·ness** *n.*

bra·zier¹ (BRAY zhər) *n.* a worker in brass. [ME *brasier*]

bra·zier² *n.* an open pan for holding live coals. [< F]

breach (breech) *n.* **1.** violation of a legal obligation, promise, etc. **2.** a gap or break in a dike, wall, etc. **3.** a breaking up of friendly relations; estrangement. —*v.t.* break through. [ME *breche*]

bread (bred) *n.* **1.** a food made with flour or meal, commonly leavened with yeast and baked. **2.** food in general. **3.** the necessities of life. **4.** *Slang* money. —*v.t.* roll in bread crumbs before cooking. [ME *breed*] —**bread′ed** *adj.*

breadth (bredth) *n.* **1.** distance from side to side; width. **2.** extent or scope. **3.** broadmindedness. [ME]

bread·win·ner (BRED WIN ər) *n.* one whose earnings are the principal support of a family.

break (brayk) *v.* **broke, bro·ken, break·ing** *v.t.* **1.** separate into pieces or fragments, as by a blow; shatter. **2.** crack. **3.** part the surface of; pierce: *break* ground. **4.** disable; render useless. **5.** destroy the order, continuity, or completeness of: *break* ranks. **6.** diminish the force or effect of: *break* a fall. **7.** overcome by opposing; end: *break* a strike. **8.** interrupt the course of, as a journey. **9.** violate: *break* one's promise. **10.** reduce in spirit or health, as by toil. **11.** tame, as a horse. **12.** demote. **13.** give or obtain smaller units for: *break* a dollar. **14.** make bankrupt or short of money. **15.** force (a way), as through a barrier. **16.** escape from. **17.** surpass; excel: *break* a record. **18.** make known; tell, as news. **19.** cause to discontinue a habit. **20.** *Law* invalidate (a will) by court action. —*v.i.* **21.** become separated into pieces or fragments; shatter; crack; snap. **22.** appear; come into being or evidence: The sun *broke* through the clouds. **23.** start or move suddenly: He *broke* from the crowd. **24.** exhibit a breach of continuity. **25.** change tone, as a boy's voice. **26.** in baseball, curve: said of a pitch. —**break down 1.** undergo mechanical failure. **2.** suffer physical or mental collapse. **3.** cause to yield. **4.** analyze or be analyzed. **5.** decompose. —**break in** train or make malleable. —**break into** (or **in**) **1.** interrupt or intervene. **2.** enter by force. —**break off 1.** stop or cease, as from speaking. **2.** sever (relations); discontinue. **3.** become separate or detached. —**break out 1.** start unexpectedly or suddenly, as a fire or plague. **2.** have an eruption or rash. **3.** escape, as from prison. —**break out into** (or **forth in, into,** etc.) begin to do or perform: The birds *broke* out into song. —**break up 1.** disperse; end. **2.** distress: Her death *broke up* the old man. **3.** sever relations. —**break with** sever relations with. —*n.* **1.** the act or result of breaking; fracture; rupture. **2.** a starting or opening: *break* of day. **3.** a dash or run; esp., an attempt to escape. **4.** a breach of continuity. **5.** *Informal* a chance or opportunity. **6.** a rupture in friendship; quarrel. **7.** a sudden decline or change. [ME *breken*] —**break′a·ble** *adj.*

break·age (BRAY kij) *n.* **1.** a breaking or being broken. **2.** articles broken. **3.** compensation for articles broken.

break·down (BRAYK DOWN) *n.* **1.** a collapse or failure. **2.** an analysis or summary.

break·er (BRAY kər) *n.* **1.** one that breaks. **2.** a wave that breaks on rocks etc.

break·fast (BREK fəst) *n.* the morning meal. —*v.i.* eat breakfast. [ME *brekfast*]

break·neck (BRAYK NEK) *adj.* dangerous.

break·through (BRAYK THROO) *n.* **1.** *Mil.* an attack that penetrates through an enemy's defenses. **2.** any sudden, important advance.

break·up (BRAYK UP) *n.* **1.** a dissolution or separation. **2.** an ending.

break·wa·ter (BRAYK WAW tər) *n.* a barrier against the force of waves.

breast (brest) *n.* **1.** the front of the chest from the neck to the abdomen. **2.** one of the mammary glands. **3.** the breast as the seat of the emotions. —**make a clean breast of** confess. —*v.t.* meet boldly. [ME *brest*]

breast·feed (BREST FEED) *v.t. & v.i.* **-fed, -feed·ing** suckle.

breast·stroke (BREST STROHK *n.* in swimming, a stroke made by thrusting the arms forward simultaneously from the breast and sweeping them back.

breath (breth) *n.* **1.** air inhaled and exhaled in respiration. **2.** power or ability to breathe. **3.** the act of breathing; also; life; existence: while *breath* remains. **4.** a single respiration. **5.** a slight movement of air. **6.** a murmur; whisper. —**out of breath** breathless; gasping. —**take one's breath away** awe or produce sudden emotion in. —**under one's breath** in a whisper or mutter. [ME *breth* odor]

breathe (breeth) *v.* **breathed, breath·ing** *v.i.* **1.** inhale and exhale air. **2.** be alive; live. **3.** pause for breath; rest. **4.** murmur; whisper. **5.** move gently, as breezes. —*v.t.* **6.** inhale and expel from the lungs, as air; respire. **7.** inject or infuse: *breathe* life into a statue. **8.** express; manifest: *breathe* confidence. **9.** allow a rest to, as for breath. [ME *brethen* breathe]

breath·er (BREE thər) *n.* **1.** a brief rest period. **2.** one who breathes in a particular manner: heavy *breather.*

breath·less (BRETH lis) *adj.* **1.** gasping for breath. **2.** that takes the breath away: *breathless* speed. **3.** devoid of breath; dead.

breath·tak·ing (BRETH TAY king) *adj.* thrilling; overawing.

bred (bred) past tense, past participle of BREED.

breech (breech) *n.* **1.** the posterior and lower part of the body; the buttocks. **2.** the part of a gun, cannon, etc., that is behind the bore or barrel. [ME *breeche*]

breech·es (BRICH iz) *n.pl.* **1.** a man's garment covering the hips and thighs. **2.** *Informal* trousers. [ME]

breed (breed) *v.* **bred, breed·ing** *v.t.* **1.** produce (offspring). **2.** cause. **3.** propagate (plants or animals). **4.** bring up; train. —*v.i.* **5.** procreate. **6.** increase and spread. —*n.* **1.** a race or strain of animals. **2.** a sort or kind. [ME *breden* nourish] —**breed'er** *n.*

breeder reactor a nuclear reactor that generates atomic energy in which the fuel is converted into more fissionable material than is consumed.

breed·ing (BREE ding) *n.* **1.** the act of bearing young. **2.** the rearing of the young. **3.** good manners. **4.** the scientific production of varieties of plants, animals, etc.

breeze (breez) *n.* **1.** a moderate current of air; a gentle wind. **2.** *Informal* something easily done. —*v.i.* **breezed, breez·ing** go or act quickly and blithely. [< Du. *bries* wind]

breez·y (BREE zee) *adj.* **breez·i·er, breez·i·est** **1.** having breezes; windy. **2.** brisk or carefree. —**breez'i·ly** *adv.*

breth·ren (BRETH rin) *n.pl.* **1.** brothers. **2.** members of a brotherhood.

bre·vi·ar·y (BREE vee er ee) *n. pl.* **·ar·ies** *Eccl.* in the Roman Catholic and Eastern Orthodox churches, a book of daily prayers. [< L *breviarium* abridgment]

brev·i·ty (BREV i tee) *n.* **1.** shortness of duration. **2.** conciseness. [< AF *brevite*]

brew (broo) *v.t.* **1.** make, as beer or ale, by steeping, boiling, and fermenting malt, hops, etc. **2.** prepare (any beverage) as by boiling or mixing. **3.** plot; devise. —*v.i.* **4.** make ale, beer, or the like. **5.** commence to form, as a storm. —*n.* something brewed. [ME *brewen*]

brew·er·y (BROO ər ee) *n. pl.* **·er·ies** an establishment for brewing.

bri·ar (BRĪ ər) see BRIER[1].

bri·ar·root (BRĪ ər ROOT) see BRIERROOT.

bribe (brīb) *n.* any gift or payment used corruptly to influence a person. —*v.* **bribed, brib·ing** *v.t.* **1.** give a bribe to. **2.** gain or influence by means of bribery. —*v.i.* **3.** give bribes. [ME, piece of bread given to a beggar] —**brib'a·ble** *adj.*

brib·er·y (BRĪ bər ee) *n. pl.* **·er·ies** the giving, offering, or accepting of a bribe.

bric-a-brac (BRIK ə BRAK) *n.* small objects

of curiosity or decoration. [< F, odds and ends]

brick (brik) n. **1.** a molded block of baked clay, used for building, etc. **2.** bricks collectively. **3.** any object shaped like a brick. —v.t. **1.** build or line with bricks. **2.** cover with bricks: with *up* or *in*. [ME *brike*]

brick·bat (BRIK BAT) n. **1.** a piece of a brick, esp. when used as a missile. **2.** an insulting remark.

brick·lay·er (BRIK LAY ər) n. one who builds with bricks.

bri·dal (BRĪD l) adj. pertaining to a bride or a wedding; nuptial. [ME *bridale* wedding feast]

bride (brīd) n. a newly married woman, or a woman about to be married. [ME]

bride·groom (BRĪD GROOM) n. a man newly married or about to be married. [ME *brydgrome*]

brides·maid (BRĪDZ MAYD) n. a young, usu. unmarried woman who attends a bride at her wedding.

bridge¹ (brij) n. **1.** a structure erected across a waterway, ravine, road, etc. to afford passage. **2.** something that serves as a transition or connection. **3.** a structure on a ship from which it is navigated and controlled. **4.** the upper bony ridge of the nose. **5.** the central part of a pair of spectacles. **6.** in some string instruments, a thin piece of wood that raises the strings above the soundboard. **7.** *Music* a transitional passage. **8.** *Dent.* a mounting for false teeth. —v.t. **bridged, bridg·ing 1.** construct a bridge over. **2.** make a passage over. [ME *brigge*]

bridge² n. a card game, derived from whist.

bri·dle (BRĪD l) n. **1.** the head harness, including bit and reins, used to guide or restrain a horse. **2.** anything that restrains or limits. —v. **·dled, ·dling** v.t. **1.** put a bridle on. **2.** check or control. —v.i. **3.** show resentment, esp. by tossing one's head. [ME *bridel*]

bridle path a path for saddle horses.

brief (breef) adj. **1.** short in time or extent; quickly ending. **2.** oncise. —n. **1.** a short statement or summary. **2.** *Law* a memorandum of the material facts, points of law, precedents, etc. of a case. **3.** pl. short underpants. —v.t. **1.** summarize. **2.** give a briefing to. [ME *bref* short]

brief·case (BREEF kays) n. a case, often of leather, for carrying documents etc.

brief·ing (BREE fing) n. a short lecture explaining an operation or procedure.

bri·er¹ (BRĪ ər) n. **1.** a prickly bush or shrub, esp. one of the rose family. **2.** a growth of such prickly bushes. **3.** a thorny or prickly twig. Also spelled *briar*. [ME *brer*]

bri·er² n. **1.** a shrub of southern Europe whose root is used in making pipes. **2.** a pipe made of brierroot. [< F *bruyère* heath]

bri·er·root (BRĪ ər ROOT) n. the root of the brier. Also spelled *briarroot*.

brig (brig) n. a place of confinement, esp. on shipboard.

bri·gade (bri GAYD) n. **1.** *Mil.* a unit of two or more groups or regiments. **2.** any body of persons more or less organized: a fire *brigade.* [< F]

brig·a·dier general (BRIG ə deer) In the U.S. Army an officer ranking above a colonel and next below a major general.

brig·and (BRIG ənd) n. a bandit. [ME *brigaunt*]

bright (brīt) adj. **1.** emitting or reflecting much light; full of light; shining. **2.** of brilliant color; vivid. **3.** glorious; illustrious. **4.** intelligent; quick-witted. **5.** lively; vivacious. **6.** hopeful; auspicious. —adv. in a bright manner; brightly. [ME] —**bright'ly** adv.

bright·en (BRĪT n) v.t. & v.i. make or become bright or brighter.

bril·liant (BRIL yənt) adj. **1.** sparkling or glowing with light; very bright. **2.** splendid; illustrious. **3.** having great intellect or talent. [< F *brillant* shining] —**bril'liance** n.

brim (brim) n. **1.** the rim or upper edge of a cup, bowl, etc. **2.** a projecting rim, as of a hat. **3.** an edge or margin. —v.t. & v.i. **brimmed, brim·ming** fill or be full to the brim. [ME *brimme* brink]

brim·stone (BRIM stohn) n. sulfur. [ME *brinston*]

brin·dle (BRIN dl) adj. brindled. —n. a brindled color, or a brindled animal.

brin·dled (BRIN dld) adj. tawny or grayish with irregular streaks or spots.

brine (brīn) n. **1.** water saturated with salt. **2.** sea water; the ocean. —v.t. **brined, brin·ing** treat with or steep in brine. [ME] —**brin'y** adj. **brin·i·er, brin·i·est**

bring (bring) v.t. **brought, bring·ing 1.** convey or cause (a person or thing) to come with oneself to or toward a place. **2.** cause to come about; involve as a consequence. **3.**

cause (a person or oneself) to adopt or admit, as a course of action. **4.** sell for: The house *brought* a good price. **5.** *Law* **a** prefer, as a charge. **b** institute: *bring* suit. **c** set forth, or as evidence or an argument. —**bring about** accomplish; cause to happen. — **bring forth 1.** give birth or produce. **2.** give rise to. —**bring off** do successfully. — **bring on** cause; lead to. —**bring out** reveal; cause to be evident. —**bring to** revive; restore to consciousness. —**bring up 1.** rear; educate. **2.** suggest or call attention to, as a subject. [ME *bringen*]

brink (bringk) *n.* the edge or verge, as of a steep place. [ME]

brink·man·ship (BRINGK mən SHIP) *n.* the act or policy of taking major risks in order to achieve some end. Also **brinks·man·ship** (BRINGKS mən SHIP.

bri·oche (BREE ohsh) *n.* a soft roll. [< F]

bri·quette (bri KET) *n.* a block of compressed coal dust or charcoal, used for fuel. [< F]

brisk (brisk) *adj.* **·er, ·est 1.** quick; lively; energetic. **2.** sharp or stimulating.

bris·ket (BRIS kit) *n.* the breast of an animal, or a cut of meat from it. [ME *brusket*]

bris·tle (BRIS əl) *n.* coarse, stiff hair or fiber. —*v.i.* **·tled, ·tling 1.** erect the bristles in anger or excitement. **2.** show anger or irritation. **3.** stand or become erect, like bristles. **4.** be thickly set as if with bristles. [ME *bristel*] —**bris·tly** (BRIS lee) *adj.*

britch·es (BRICH iz) *n.pl.* breeches.

Brit·i·cism (BRIT ə SIZ əm) *n.* an idiom or turn of phrase peculiar to the British.

Brit·ish (BRIT ish) *adj.* pertaining to Great Britain or the United Kingdom. —*n.* the people of Great Britain: preceded by *the.* [ME *Brittische*]

British Isles Great Britain, Ireland, the Isle of Man, and the Channel Islands.

British thermal unit *Physics* the quantity of heat required to raise the temperature of one pound of water one degree Fahrenheit. Abbr. *BTU.*

brit·tle (BRIT l) *adj.* liable to break or snap; fragile. [ME *britel*]

broach (brohch) *v.t.* **1.** mention or suggest for the first time; introduce. **2.** pierce, as a barrel, so as to withdraw a liquid. —*n.* **1.** a pointed, tapering tool for boring; a reamer. **2.** a spit for roasting. [ME *broche* spike]

broad (brawd) *adj.* **1.** extended from side to side; wide. **2.** of great extent; vast or spacious. **3.** full; clear: *broad* daylight. **4.** of wide scope or application. **5.** liberal in spirit; tolerant. **6.** not detailed; general. **7.** obvious; clear: a *broad* hint. **8.** vulgar; unrefined. —*adv.* completely; fully. [ME *brood*]

Broad forms words meaning wide or extensive, as in :

broad-based	**broad-leaved**
broad-chested	**broad-shouldered**

broad·cast (BRAWD KAST) *v.* **·cast** or (*esp. for defs. 1 & 4*) **·cast·ed, ·cast·ing** *v.t.* **1.** send or transmit by radio or television. **2.** scatter, as seed, over a wide area. **3.** disseminate; make public. —*v.i.* **4.** make a radio or television broadcast. —*n.* **1.** the act of broadcasting. **2.** a radio or television program.

broad·en (BRAWD n) *v.t. & v.i.* make or become broad.

broad·mind·ed (BRAWD MĪN did) *adj.* liberal; tolerant.

broad·side (BRAWD SĪD) *n.* **1.** all the guns on one side of a man-of-war, or their simultaneous discharge. **2.** a volley of abuse or denunciation. **3.** a wide printed sheet, formerly used esp. for political news and argument. —*adv.* with the broadside exposed.

bro·cade (broh KAYD) *n.* a fabric interwoven with a raised design. —*v.t.* **·cad·ed, ·cad·ing** weave (a cloth) with a raised design. [< Ital. *broccato* embossed]

broc·co·li (BROK ə lee) *n.* a variety of cauliflower, having green buds. [< Ital., pl. of *broccolo*]

bro·chure (broh SHUUR) *n.* a pamphlet or similar publication. [< F]

brogue[1] (brohg) *n.* an Irish accent.

brogue[2] *n.* an oxford shoe, decorated with perforations. [< Irish *brōg* shoe]

broil (broil) *v.t.* **1.** cook, as meat, by subjecting to direct heat. **2.** expose to great heat; scorch. —*v.i.* **3.** be exposed to great heat; cook. [ME *brulen* burn]

broil·er (BROI lər) *n.* **1.** a device for broiling. **2.** a young chicken suitable for broiling. [ME]

broke (brohk) past tense of BREAK. —*adj.* having no money.

bro·ken (BROH kən) past participle of BREAK. —*adj.* **1.** forcibly separated into pieces; fractured. **2.** violated; transgressed: *broken* vows. **3.** interrupted; disturbed. **4.** incomplete; fragmentary. **5.** rough; uneven, as terrain. **6.** humbled; crushed. **7.** weakened or infirm. **8.** bankrupt. **9.** trained or made malleable: often with *in.*

bro·ken·heart·ed (BROH kən HAHR tid) *adj.* crushed in spirit, as by grief.

bro·ker (BROH kər) *n.* **1.** one who buys and sells for another; esp., a stockbroker. **2.** an agent or mediator. [ME *brocour* wine merchant]

bro·ker·age (BROH kər ij) *n.* the business or commission of a broker.

bro·mid·ic (broh MID ik) *adj.* commonplace; trite. **—bro·mide** (BROH mīd) *n.* a platitude.

bron·co (BRONG koh) *n. pl.* **·cos** a small, wild or partly broken horse of the West. [< Mexican Sp., untamed horse]

bron·to·saur (BRON tə sOR) *n. Paleontol.* a huge, herbivorous dinosaur. Also **bron'·to·sau'rus** [< NL]

bronze (bronz) *n.* **1.** *Metall.* **a** a reddish brown alloy essentially of copper and tin. **b** a similar alloy of copper and some other metal, as aluminum. **2.** a reddish brown color or pigment. **3.** a statue, bust, etc. done in bronze. **—v.t. & v.i. bronzed, bronz·ing** make or become bronze in color. [< F]

brooch (brohch) *n.* an ornamental pin with a clasp. [ME *broche*]

brood (brood) *n.* **1.** the young of animals, esp. of birds, produced at one time. **2.** all the young of the same mother. **3.** kind or species. **—v.i. 1.** meditate moodily: usu. with *on* or *over.* **2.** sit on eggs. **—v.t. 3.** sit upon or incubate (eggs). **4.** protect (young) by covering with the wings. [ME]

brood·er (BROO dər) *n.* **1.** a warmed structure for artificially rearing young fowl. **2.** one who or that which broods.

brook¹ (bruuk) *n.* a natural stream, smaller than a river or creek. [ME]

brook² *v.t.* put up with; tolerate. [ME *brouken* enjoy]

broom (broom) *n.* **1.** a brush attached to a long handle for sweeping. **2.** any of various shrubs with yellow flowers and stiff green branches. **—v.t.** sweep. [ME *brome*]

broth (brawth) *n.* **1.** the water in which meat, vegetables, etc., have been boiled. **2.** a thin soup. [ME]

broth·el (BROTH əl) *n.* a house of prostitution. [ME, harlot]

broth·er (BRUTH ər) *n. pl.* **broth·ers** (*Archaic* **breth·ren**) **1.** a male individual having the same parents as another. **2.** a fellow member of a fraternity, ethnic group, etc. **3.** a comrade. **4.** one of a male religious order who is not a priest. [ME] **—broth'er·ly** *adj.* **—broth'er·li·ness** *n.*

broth·er·hood (BRUTH ər HUUD) *n.* **1.** the relationship of or state of being brothers, esp. by blood. **2.** an association of men sharing a common enterprise, profession, etc. **3.** harmony among persons of differing races or creeds.

broth·er·in·law (BRUTH ər in LAW) *n. pl.* **broth·ers·in·law 1.** a brother of one's husband or wife. **2.** the husband of one's sister. **3.** the husband of one's spouse's sister.

brought (brawt) past tense, past participle of BRING.

brou·ha·ha (BROO hah HAH) *n.* hubbub; uproar. [< F]

brow (brow) *n.* **1.** the forehead. **2.** the eyebrow. **3.** the countenance in general. **4.** the upper edge of a steep place: the *brow* of a hill. [ME *browe*]

brow·beat (BROW BEET) *v.t.* **·beat, ·beat·en, ·beat·ing** intimidate; bully.

brown (brown) *adj.* **1.** of a dark color combining red, yellow, and black. **2.** darkcomplexioned; tanned. **—n.** a brown color or pigment. **—v.t. & v.i.** make or become brown. [ME]

brown·bag (BROWN BAG) *v.i.* **·bagged, ·bag·ging** take one's lunch to work, esp. in a brown paper bag. **—brown'·bag'ger** *n.*

brown·ie (BROW nee) *n.* **1.** a small goblin or sprite, supposed to do useful work at night. **2.** a small, flat chocolate cake with nuts.

Brown·ie *n.* a junior girl scout of the age group seven through nine.

brown·stone (BROWN STOHN) *n.* a brownish red sandstone used for building; also, a house with a front of brownstone.

browse (browz) *v.* **browsed, brows·ing** *v.i.* **1.** feed on leaves, shoots, etc. **2.** inspect books or merchandise casually. **—v.t. 3.** nibble at or graze on. **—n.** growing shoots or twigs used as fodder. [ME *browsen*] **—brows'er** *n.*

bru·in (BROO in) *n.* a bear; esp., a brown bear. [< MDu. *bruym,* lit., brown one]

bruise (brooz) *v.* **bruised, bruis·ing** *v.t.* **1.** injure, as by a blow, without breaking the surface of the skin. **2.** dent or mar the surface of. **3.** hurt or offend slightly. **4.** crush, as in a mortar. **—v.i. 5.** become discolored as from a blow. **—n.** an injury caused by bruising. [ME *broosen* break]

bruit (broot) *v.t.* noise abroad; talk about: usu. in the passive. [< AF *bruire* roar]

brunch (brunch) *n.* a meal combining breakfast and lunch.

bru·net (broo NET) *adj.* dark-hued; having dark complexion, hair, and eyes. —*n.* a brunet man or boy. [< F]

bru·nette (broo NET) *adj.* brunet: feminine form. —*n.* a brunette woman or girl. [< F]

brunt (brunt) *n.* the main force or strain of a blow, attack, etc. [ME]

brush¹ (brush) *n.* **1.** an implement having bristles, wires, or the like, fixed in a handle or a back, and used for sweeping, painting, smoothing the hair, etc. **2.** the act of brushing. **3.** a light, grazing touch. **4.** a brief encounter, esp. a skirmish. **5.** *Electr.* a conductor for carrying current from a dynamo or through a motor. —*v.t.* **1.** sweep, paint, etc. with a brush. **2.** remove with or as with a brush. **3.** touch lightly in passing. —*v.i.* **4.** move lightly and quickly. —**brush off** dismiss or refuse abruptly. —**brush up** refresh one's knowledge. [ME *brusshe* brush]

brush² *n.* **1.** a growth of small trees and shrubs. **2.** wooded country sparsely settled. **3.** brushwood. [ME *brusshe* underbrush]

brush·off (BRUSH AWF) *n.* an abrupt refusal or dismissal.

brush·wood (BRUSH wuud) *n.* **1.** bushes or branches cut or broken off. **2.** a thicket.

brusque (brusk) *adj.* rude or curt; blunt. Also **brusk.** [< MF] —**brusque'ness** *n.*

brut (broot) *adj.* dry (def. 6): said of wines, esp. of champagne. [< F, raw]

bru·tal (BROOT l) *adj.* **1.** like a brute; cruel; savage. **2.** rude; coarse. —**bru·tal·i·ty** (broo TAL i tee) *n. pl.* **·ties** —**bru'tal·ize** (BROOT l IZ) *v.t.* **·ized, ·iz·ing**

brute (broot) *n.* **1.** any animal other than man. **2.** a brutal person. —*adj.* **1.** incapable of reasoning. **2.** dominated by animal appetites. [ME]

brut·ish (BROO tish) *adj.* characteristic of a brute; stupid; gross. —**brut'ish·ness** *n.*

bub·ble (BUB əl) *n.* **1.** a liquid globule filled with air or other gas. **2.** a globule of air or other gas in a liquid or solid substance. **3.** anything unsubstantial; a delusion. **4.** the process or sound of bubbling. **5.** something like a bubble, as a glass dome. —*v.* **·bled, ·bling** *v.i.* **1.** form or emit bubbles; rise in bubbles. **2.** flow with a gurgling sound. **3.** express delight in an irrepressible manner. —*v.t.* **4.** cause to bubble. **5.** burp (a baby). [ME *bobel*] —**bub'bly** *adj.*

bu·bo (BYOO boh) *n. pl.* **bu·boes** *Pathol.* an inflammatory swelling of a lymph gland in the groin or armpit. [ME] —**bu·bon·ic** (byoo BON ik) *adj.*

bubonic plague *Pathol.* a contagious, epidemic disease, usually fatal, transmitted to man by fleas from infected rats.

buc·cal (BUK əl) *adj. Anat.* **1.** of or pertaining to the cheek. **2.** pertaining to the mouth. [< L *bucca* cheek]

buc·ca·neer (BUK ə NEER) *n.* a pirate. [< F *boucanier*, barbecuer]

buck¹ (buk) *n.* **1.** the male of certain animals, as of antelopes or deer. **2.** a young man. —*v.i.* **1.** leap upward suddenly with the back arched, as a horse. **2.** move with jerks and jolts. —*v.t.* **3.** throw by bucking. **4.** defy. **5.** in football, charge into (the opponent's line). —**buck for** try hard to obtain (a promotion, raise, etc.). —**buck up** encourage or take courage. [ME *bukke* he-goat]

buck² *n.* **1.** a sawhorse. **2.** a padded frame like a sawhorse, used for vaulting, etc.

buck³ *n. Slang* a dollar.

buck·et (BUK it) *n.* **1.** a deep cylindrical vessel, with a rounded handle; pail. **2.** as much as a bucket will hold: also **buck'et·ful.** [ME *buket*]

buck·le¹ (BUK əl) *n.* **1.** a device for fastening together two loose ends, as of a strap. **2.** an ornament resembling a buckle. —*v.t. & v.i.* **·led, ·ling** fasten or be fastened with or as with a buckle. —**buckle down** apply oneself. [ME *bocle*]

buck·le² *v.t. & v.i.* **·led, ·ling** bend under pressure; warp; crumple. —*n.* a bend or twist.

buck·ram (BUK rəm) *n.* a coarse cotton fabric sized with glue, used for stiffening garments, in bookbinding, etc. [ME *bukeram*]

buck·skin (BUK skin) *n.* **1.** the skin of a buck. **2.** a soft, strong leather, now chiefly made from sheepskins. **3.** *pl.* clothing made of such skin.

buck·wheat (BUK hweet) *n.* **1.** a plant yielding triangular seeds used as fodder and for flour. **2.** its seeds. **3.** the flour.

bu·col·ic (byoo KOL ik) *adj.* pastoral; rustic. —*n.* a pastoral poem. [< L *bucolicus* rustic] —**bu·col'i·cal·ly** *adv.*

bud (bud) *n.* **1.** *Bot.* **a** an undeveloped stem, branch, or shoot of a plant, with rudimentary leaves or unexpanded flowers. **b** the act or stage of budding. **2.** *Zool.* a budlike projection or part. —**nip in the bud** stop in the initial stage. —*v.* **bud·ded, bud·ding** *v.i.* **1.** put forth buds. **2.** begin to grow or develop. —*v.t.* **3.** cause to bud. **4.** graft to another type of tree or plant. —**bud'ding** *adj.* just beginning. [ME]

Bud·dhism (BOO diz əm) *n.* a mystical and ascetic religious faith of eastern Asia, which teaches that the ideal state of nirvana is reached by right living and through meditation. —**Bud'dhist** *adj. & n.*

budge (buj) *v.t. & v.i.* **budged, budg·ing** move or stir slightly. [< AF *bouger* stir]

budg·er·i·gar (BUJ ə ree GAHR) *n.* a small Australian parrot, popular as a pet. Also *budgie.*

budg·et (BUJ it) *n.* **1.** a plan for adjusting expenditures to income. **2.** a collection or stock. —*v.t.* **1.** determine in advance the expenditure of (time, money, etc.). **2.** provide for according to a budget. —*v.i.* **3.** make a budget. [ME *bowgett* bag] —**budg·et·ar·y** (BUJ i TER ee) *adj.*

budg·ie (BUJ ee) *n.* see BUDGERIGAR.

buff (buf) *n.* **1.** a thick, soft, flexible leather made from the skins of buffalo, oxen, etc. **2.** its color, a light brownish yellow. **3.** *Informal* the bare skin; the nude. **4.** a stick or wheel covered with soft material, used for polishing. **5.** an enthusiast or devotee. —*adj.* **1.** made of buff. **2.** light, brownish yellow. —*v.t.* clean or polish with or as with a buff.

buf·fa·lo (BUF ə LOH) *n. pl.* **·loes** or **·los 1.** any of various large Old World oxen. **2.** the North American bison. —*v.t.* **·loed, ·lo·ing** *Informal* **1.** baffle. **2.** intimidate; hoodwink. [< LL *bufalus* buffalo]

buff·er[1] (BUF ər) *n.* one who or that which buffs or polishes.

buff·er[2] *n.* **1.** one who or that which diminishes shock or conflict. **2.** a substance that stabilizes the degree of acidity or alkalinity of a solution.

buf·fet[1] (bə FAY) *n.* **1.** a sideboard for china, glassware, etc. **2.** a counter or table for serving meals or refreshments. **3.** a meal set out on a buffet table. [< F]

buf·fet[2] (BUF it) *v.t.* **1.** strike or cuff, as with the hand. **2.** strike repeatedly; knock about. —*v.i.* **3.** fight; struggle. —*n.* a blow or cuff. [< F, slap] —**buf'fet·er** *n.*

buf·foon (bə FOON) *n.* **1.** a clown. **2.** one given to jokes, coarse pranks, etc. [< F *buffon*] —**buf·foon'er·y** *n.*

bug (bug) *n.* **1.** any crawling insect with sucking mouth parts, wingless or with two pairs of wings. **2.** loosely, any insect or small arthropod. **3.** *Informal* a virus or germ. **4.** *Informal* an enthusiast. **5.** *Informal* a minor

defect, as in a machine. **6.** *Informal* a miniature electronic microphone, used in wiretapping, etc. —*v.* **bugged, bug·ging** *v.i.* **1.** stick out: said of eyes. —*v.t.* **2.** annoy; pester. **3.** *Informal* fit (a room, telephone circuit, etc.) with a concealed listening device. —**bug out** *Slang* quit.

bug·bear (BUG BAIR) *n.* **1.** a real or imaginary object of dread. **2.** a hobgoblin. Also **bug·a·boo** (BUG ə BOO).

bug-eyed (BUG ID) *adj.* with the eyes bulging.

bug·gy[1] (BUG ee) *n. pl.* **·gies 1.** a light, four-wheeled carriage. **2.** a baby carriage.

bug·gy[2] *adj.* **·gi·er, ·gi·est 1.** infested with bugs. **2.** *Slang* crazy.

bu·gle (BYOO gal) *n.* a brass wind instrument resembling a trumpet, usu. without keys or valves. —*v.t. & v.i.* **·gled, ·gling** signal with or sound a bugle. [ME] —**bu'gler** *n.*

build (bild) *v.* **built, build·ing** *v.t.* **1.** construct, erect, or make by assembling separate parts or materials. **2.** establish and increase. **3.** found; make a basis for. —*v.i.* **4.** construct or erect a house, etc. **5.** base or develop an idea, theory, etc.: with *on* or *upon.* —**build up 1.** create or build by degrees. **2.** renew or strengthen; also, to increase. —*n.* **1.** the manner or style of construction. **2.** a person's figure; physique. [ME *bilden*]

build·ing (BIL ding) *n.* **1.** a structure, as a house or barn. **2.** the occupation, act, or art of constructing.

build·up (BILD UP) *n.* **1.** an increase or strengthening. **2.** extravagant publicity or praise.

built-in (BILT IN) *adj.* **1.** built as a part of the structure. **2.** inherent: *built-in* reflexes.

bulb (bulb) *n.* **1.** *Bot.* a leaf bud comprising a cluster of thickened leaves growing usu. underground and sending forth roots, as the onion or lily. **2.** any plant growing from a bulb. **3.** a rounded protuberance, as at the end of a tube. **4.** an incandescent lamp. [< L *bulbus* onion]

bulge (bulj) *n.* a protuberant, rounded part. —*v.t. & v.i.* **bulged, bulg·ing** swell out. [ME, bag]

bulk (bulk) *n.* **1.** magnitude, volume, or size. **2.** the greater or principal part. **3.** a large body or mass. —*v.i.* appear large or important; loom. [ME *bulke* heap]

bulk·head (BULK HED) *n.* **1.** *Naut.* an upright partition in a vessel, separating compartments. **2.** a partition or wall to keep back earth, gas, etc. **3.** a small structure built over an elevator shaft.

bulk·y (BUL kee) *adj.* **bulk·i·er, bulk·i·est** large; massive; also, unwieldy. —**bulk′i·ness** *n.*

bull[1] (buul) *n.* **1.** the male of a bovine animal. **2.** the male of some other animals, as of the elephant, whale, etc. **3.** one likened to a bull, as in strength or manner. **4.** a speculator who buys so as to profit from a rise in prices: opposed to *bear*[2]. —*v.t.* **1.** push or force (a way). —*v.i.* **2.** go or push ahead. —*adj.* **1.** male; masculine. **2.** like a bull; large. **3.** marked by rising prices: *bull* market. [ME *bule*] —**bull′ish** *adj.*

bull[2] *n.* a papal edict. [ME *bulle* sealed document]

bull·dog (BUUL DAWG) *n.* a medium-sized, short-haired, powerful dog with strong jaws. —*adj.* resembling a bulldog; tenacious. —*v.t. & v.i.* **·dogged, ·dog·ging** throw (a steer) by gripping its horns and twisting its neck.

bull·doze (BUUL DOHZ) *v.t.* **·dozed, ·doz·ing 1.** intimidate; bully. **2.** clear, dig, scrape, etc., with a bulldozer.

bull·doz·er (BUUL DOH zər) *n.* a tractor with a heavy steel blade, used for moving earth, clearing wooded areas, etc.

bul·let (BUUL it) *n.* **1.** a small projectile for a firearm. **2.** any small ball. [< MF *boullette* small ball]

bul·le·tin (BUUL i tn) *n.* **1.** a brief, usu. unscheduled news report, as on radio. **2.** a periodical publication, as of the proceedings of a society. [< F]

bull·fight (BUUL FĪT) *n.* a combat in an arena between men and a bull or bulls.

bull·frog (BUUL FROG) *n.* a large frog with a deep bass croak.

bull·head·ed (BUUL HED id) *adj.* stubborn.

bull·horn (BUUL HORN) *n.* an electronic device to amplify the voice.

bul·lion (BUUL yən) *n.* gold or silver uncoined or in mass, as in bars, plates, etc. [ME]

bul·lock (BUUL ək) *n.* a gelded bull; a steer or ox. [ME *bullok*]

bull pen 1. an enclosure for bulls. **2.** *Informal* a place for temporary detention of prisoners. **3.** in baseball, a place where pitchers practice during a game.

bull·ring (BUUL RING) *n.* a circular enclosure for bullfights.

bull session *Informal* an informal discussion.

bull's-eye (BUULZ Ī) *n.* **1.** the central disk on a target; also, a shot that hits this disk. **2.** something resembling a bull's-eye.

bull·whip (BUUL HWIP) *n.* a long, heavy whip. —*v.t.* **·whipped, ·whip·ping** strike with a bullwhip.

bul·ly (BUUL ee) *n. pl.* **·lies** a swaggering, quarrelsome person who terrorizes weaker people. —*v.t. & v.i.* **·lied, ·ly·ing** intimidate or terrorize (a person or animal). —*adj. Informal* excellent. —*interj. Informal* well done!

bul·rush (BUUL RUSH) *n.* **1.** a tall, rushlike plant growing in water or damp ground. **2.** in the Bible, papyrus. [ME *bulrish* papyrus]

bul·wark (BUUL wərk) *n.* **1.** a defensive wall or rampart. **2.** any safeguard or defense. **3.** *Usu. pl. Naut.* the raised side of a ship, above the upper deck. —*v.t.* surround and fortify with a bulwark. [ME *bulwerk*]

bum (bum) *n.* a worthless or dissolute loafer; tramp. —**the bum's rush** forcible ejection. —*adj. Slang* bad; inferior. —*v. Informal* **bummed, bum·ming** *v.i.* **1.** live by sponging. **2.** live idly and in dissipation. —*v.t.* **3.** get by begging: *bum* a cigarette.

bum·ble (BUM bəl) *v.t. & v.i.* **·bled, ·bling** bungle, esp. in an officious manner. —**bum′bling** *adj. & n.*

bum·ble·bee (BUM bəl BEE) *n.* any of various large, hairy bees.

bump (bump) *v.t.* **1.** come into contact with; knock into. **2.** cause to knock into or against. **3.** *Informal* displace, as from a position or seat. —*v.i.* **4.** strike heavily or with force: often with *into* or *against*. **5.** move with jerks and jolts. —**bump off** *Slang* murder. —*n.* **1.** an impact or collision; jolt. **2.** a protuberance or uneven place. —**bump′y** *adj.* **bump·i·er, bump·i·est**

bump·er[1] (BUM pər) *n.* the horizontal bar at the front or rear of an automobile to absorb the shock of collision.

bump·er[2] *n.* a cup or glass filled to the brim. —*adj.* unusually full or large: a *bumper* crop.

bump·kin (BUMP kin) *n.* an awkward rustic; a lout. [< MDu. *bommekijn* little barrel]

bump·tious (BUMP shəs) *adj.* aggressively self-assertive. —**bump′tious·ness** *n.*

bun (bun) *n.* **1.** a small bread roll, sometimes sweetened or spiced. **2.** a roll of hair shaped like a bun. [ME *bunne*]

bunch (bunch) *n.* **1.** a number of things of the same kind growing, occurring, or fastened together; a cluster. **2.** *Informal* a group of people. —*v.t. & v.i.* **1.** form bunches or groups. **2.** gather, as in folds. [ME *bunche*]

bun·combe (BUNG kəm) *n.* see BUNKUM.

bun·dle (BUN dl) *n.* **1.** a number of things or a quantity of anything bound together. **2.** a package. **3.** a group; collection. —*v.* •dled, •dling *v.t.* **1.** tie, roll, etc., in a bundle. **2.** send or put *hastily and unceremoniously: with *away, off, out,* or *into.* —*v.i.* **3.** go hastily; hustle. **4.** lie or sleep in the same bed without undressing, formerly a courting custom in Wales and New England. —**bundle up** dress warmly. [ME *bundel*]

bung (bung) *n.* **1.** a stopper for the hole through which a cask is filled. **2.** bunghole. —*v.t.* close with or as with a bung. [ME *bunge*]

bun·ga·low (BUNG gə LOH) *n.* a small house or cottage. [< Hind. *banglā*]

bung·hole (BUNG HOHL) *n.* a hole in a cask from which liquid is tapped.

bun·gle (BUNG gəl) *v.t. & v.i.* •gled, •gling work, make, or do (something) clumsily. —**bun′gler** *n.*

bun·ion (BUN yən) *n.* a painful swelling of the foot, usu. at the base of the great toe. [ME *bony* swelling]

bunk[1] (bungk) *n.* **1.** a narrow, built-in bed or shelf for sleeping; a berth. **2.** *Informal* a bed. —*v.i. Informal* sleep in a bunk.

bunk[2] *n. Informal* nonsense.

bun·ker (BUNG kər) *n.* **1.** a large bin, as for coal on a ship. **2.** in golf, a mound of earth serving as an obstacle. **3.** *Mil.* a steel and concrete fortification.

bun·kum (BUNG kəm) **1.** empty speechmaking for political effect. **2.** empty talk; humbug. Also spelled *buncombe.* [after *Buncombe* County, N.C., whose congressman (1919–21) insisted on making unimportant speeches "for Buncombe"]

bun·ny (BUN ee) *n. pl.* •nies a rabbit: a pet name.

bunt (bunt) *v.t. & v.i.* **1.** butt. **2.** in baseball, bat (the ball) lightly into the infield, without swinging the bat. —*n.* **1.** a push or a butt. **2.** in baseball: **a** the act of bunting. **b** a ball that has been bunted.

bunt·ing (BUN ting) *n.* **1.** a light fabric used for flags, etc. **2.** flags, banners, etc., collectively. **3.** a type of sleeping bag for infants.

buoy (BOO ee) *n.* **1.** a warning float moored on a hazard or marking a channel. **2.** a device for keeping a person afloat; a life buoy. —*v.t.* **1.** keep from sinking; keep afloat. **2.** cheer; encourage: usu. with *up.* [ME *boye* float]

buoy·an·cy (BOI ən see) *n.* **1.** the tendency or ability to keep afloat. **2.** the power of a fluid to keep an object afloat. **3.** cheerfulness. —**buoy′ant** *adj.*

bur (bur) *n.* **1.** *Bot.* a rough or prickly flower head or seedcase. **2.** a plant that bears burs; also spelled *burr.* **3.** a person or thing that clings like a bur. [ME *burre*]

bur·den (BUR dn) *n.* **1.** something carried; a load. **2.** something that weighs heavily, as responsibility. —*v.t.* load or overload. [ME]

bur·den·some (BUR dn səm) *adj.* heavy or hard to bear; oppressive.

bu·reau (BYUUR oh) *n. pl.* **bu·reaus** or **bu·reaux** (BYUUR ohz) **1.** a chest of drawers for clothing. **2.** a government department. **3.** an office for transacting business. [< F, desk]

bu·reau·cra·cy (byuu ROK rə see) *n. pl.* •cies **1.** government by bureaus; also, the governing officials. **2.** the undue extension of government departments and the power of their officials. **3.** rigid adherence to administrative routine. [< F *bureaucratie*]

bu·reau·crat (BYUUR ə KRAT) *n.* **1.** a member of a bureaucracy. **2.** an official who narrowly adheres to a rigid routine. —**bu′reau·crat′ic** *adj.*

bur·geon (BUR jən) *v.i.* **1.** flourish; grow. **2.** bud; sprout. —*v.t.* **3.** put forth (buds, etc.). —*n.* a bud; sprout. [ME *burjon*]

bur·glar (BUR glər) *n.* one who commits burglary. [ME]

bur·gla·ry (BUR glə ree) *n. pl.* •ries the breaking and entering of a dwelling with intent to commit a crime. —**bur′glar·ize** *v.t.* •ized, •iz·ing

bur·i·al (BER ee əl) *n.* the burying of a dead body; interment. —*adj.* of or pertaining to burial. [ME *buriel*]

burl (burl) *n.* **1.** a knot or lump in cloth, or thread. **2.** a large wartlike growth on the trunk of a tree. —*v.t.* dress (cloth) by removing burls. [ME *burle*]

bur·lap (BUR lap) *n.* a coarse fabric made of jute or hemp.

bur·lesque (bər LESK) *n.* **1.** a satire or ludicrous imitation; parody. **2.** a theatrical entertainment marked by• low comedy, striptease, etc. —*v.t. & v.i.* **•lesqued,** **•les•quing** satirize, esp. with broad caricature. [< F]

bur•ly (BUR lee) *adj.* **•li•er, •li•est** husky; stout. [ME *borli*]

burn (burn) *v.* **burned** or **burnt, burn•ing** *v.t.* **1.** destroy or consume by fire. **2.** set afire; ignite. **3.** injure or kill by fire. **4.** injure or damage by friction, steam, etc. **5.** produce, as a hole, by fire. **6.** brand or cauterize. **7.** finish or harden by intense heat; fire. **8.** use a light, oven, etc. **9.** cause a feeling of heat in. —*v.i.* **10.** be on fire; blaze. **11.** be destroyed or scorched by fire. **12.** give off light, heat, etc.; shine. **13.** appear or feel hot. **14.** be excited or inflamed. —**burn down** raze or be razed by fire. —**burn out a** become extinguished through lack of fuel. **b** destroy or wear out by heat, friction, etc. **c** wear out; exhaust —**burn up a** consume by fire. **b** *Informal* make or become enraged. —*n.* **1.** a burned place. **2.** *Pathol.* a lesion caused by heat, corrosive chemicals, radiation, etc. **3.** *Aerospace* the firing of a rocket engine. [ME *bernen*]

burn•er (BUR nər) *n.* **1.** one who or that which burns. **2.** that part of a stove, lamp, etc., from which the flame comes.

burn•ing (BUR ning) *adj.* **1.** consuming or being consumed by or as if by fire. **2.** causing intense feeling; urgent.

bur•nish (BUR nish) *v.t. & v.i.* polish; make or become shiny. —*n.* polish; luster. [ME *burnissh* polish]

bur•noose (bər NOOS) *n.* an Arab hooded cloak. Also **bur•nous'.** [< F *burnous*]

burn•out (BURN owt) *n.* **1.** a destruction or failure due to burning or to excessive heat. **2.** *Aerospace* the cessation of operation in a jet or rocket engine. **3.** exhaustion.

burnt (burnt) alternative past tense and past participle of BURN.

burp (burp) *n. Informal* a belch. —*v.t. & v.i.* belch or cause to belch.

burr[1] (bur) *n.* **1.** a rough edge or spot, esp. one left on metal in casting or cutting. **2.** any of several tools for cutting, reaming, etc. **3.** a dentist's drill with a rough head. **4.** a protuberant knot on a tree. —*v.t.* **1.** form a rough edge on. **2.** remove a rough edge from.

burr[2] *n.* **1.** a rough guttural sound of *r*, as pronounced in the Scottish dialect. **2.** a dialectical pronunciation, esp. the Scottish one, featuring such a sound.

bur•ro (BUR oh) *n. pl.* **•ros** a small donkey. [< Sp.]

bur•row (BUR oh) *n.* **1.** a hole made in the ground, as by a rabbit. **2.** any similar place of refuge. —*v.i.* **1.** live or hide in a burrow. **2.** dig a burrow. **3.** dig into, under, or through something. —*v.t.* **4.** dig a burrow in. **5.** make by burrowing. **6.** hide (oneself) in a burrow. [ME *borow*]

bur•sa (BUR sə) *n. pl.* **•sae** (-see) or **•sas** *Anat.* a pouch or saclike cavity; esp. one containing a lubricating fluid and located at joints of the body. [< NL]

bur•sar (BUR sər) *n.* a treasurer, as of a college. [< Med.L, *bursarius* purse-keeper]

bur•si•tis (bər SĪ tis) *n. Pathol.* inflammation of a bursa.

burst (burst) *v.* **burst, burst•ing** *v.i.* **1.** break open or apart suddenly and violently. **2.** be full to the point of breaking open; bulge. **3.** appear or enter suddenly or violently. **4.** become audible or evident. **5.** give sudden expression to emotion. —*v.t.* **6.** cause to break open suddenly or violently. —*n.* **1.** a sudden exploding or breaking forth. **2.** a sudden effort or spurt; rush. **3.** a sudden expression: a *burst* of eloquence. [ME *bersten*]

bur•y (BER ee) *v.t.* **bur•ied, bur•y•ing 1.** put (a dead body) in a grave, tomb, or the sea; inter. **2.** put underground; conceal, as by covering. **3.** embed; sink. **4.** occupy (oneself) entirely. [ME *berien*]

bus (bus) *n. pl.* **bus•es** or **bus•ses** a large passenger vehicle usu. following a prescribed route. —*v.t.* **bused** or **bussed, bus•ing** or **bus•sing 1.** transport by bus. **2.** transport students by bus, as to achieve racially balanced school populations. —*v.i.* **3.** go by bus. **4.** work as a busboy or busgirl. [Short form of OMNIBUS]

bus•boy (BUS boi) *n.* an employee in a restaurant who clears tables, assists the waiters, etc. Also **bus'girl.**

bush (buush) *n.* **1.** a low, treelike or thickly branching shrub. **2.** a clump of shrubs; undergrowth. **3.** wild, scrubby land; also, any rural or unsettled area. **4.** something resembling a bush, as a fox's tail. —*v.i.* **1.** grow or branch like a bush. **2.** be or become bushy. [ME *busshe*]

bushed (buushd) *adj. Informal* exhausted.

bush•el (BUUSH əl) *n.* **1.** a unit of dry measure. **2.** a container holding this amount. [ME *buisshel*]

bush•ing (BUUSH ing) n. 1. Mech. a metallic lining for a hole, designed to insulate or to prevent abrasion between moving parts. 2. Electr. a lining in a socket to insulate an electric current.

bush league in baseball, a minor league. — **bush-league** (BUUSH LEEG) adj. — **bush leaguer** n.

bush•man (BUUSH mən) n. pl. •men 1. Austral. a dweller or farmer in the bush. 2. a member of a race of nomadic hunters of southern Africa.

bus•i•ly (BIZ ə lee) adv. in a busy manner; industriously.

busi•ness (BIZ nis) n. 1. an occupation, trade, or profession. 2. any of the operations or details of trade or commerce. 3. a commercial enterprise or establishment. 4. the amount or volume of trade. 5. a proper interest or concern. 6. a matter or affair. — **give someone the business** Informal deal with harshly or summarily. —**mean business** have a serious intention. [ME]

busi•ness•man (BIZ nis MAN) n. pl. •men one engaged in business. —**busi′ness•wom′an** n.fem. pl. •wom•en

buss (bus) n., v.t. & v.i. kiss. [ME]

bust¹ (bust) n. 1. the bosom of a woman. 2. a sculpture representing the human head, shoulders, and breast. [< F buste]

bust² Informal v.t. 1. burst. 2. tame; train, as a horse. 3. bankrupt. 4. demote. 5. punch. 6. Slang arrest. —v.i. 7. burst. 8. become bankrupt. —n. 1. a failure; bankruptcy. 2. a spree. 3. Slang an arrest. 4. Informal a punch.

bus•tle¹ (BUS əl) n. excited activity; fuss. — v. •tled, •tling hurry or cause to hurry. [ME bustelen hurry]

bus•tle² n. a frame or pad formerly worn under a skirt just above the buttocks.

bus•tling (BUS ling) adj. active; busy.

bus•y (BIZ ee) adj. bus•i•er, bus•i•est 1. actively engaged in something; occupied. 2. constantly active. 3. meddling; prying. 4. temporarily engaged, as a telephone line. —v.t. bus•ied, bus•y•ing make busy. [ME busi] —bus′y•ness (BIZ ee nis) n. meaningless activity

bus•y•bod•y (BIZ ee BOD ee) n. pl. •bod•ies one who meddles in the affairs of others.

bus•y•work (BIZ ee WURK) n. nonproductive work performed to keep one occupied.

but (but) conj. 1. on the other hand; yet. 2. without the result that: It never rains but it

pours. 3. other than; otherwise than. 4. except: anything but that. 5. with the exception that; Nothing will do but I must leave. 6. that: We don't doubt but he is there. 7. that . . . not: He is not so ill but exercise will benefit him. 8. who . . . not; which . . . not: Few sought his advice but were helped by it. —prep. with the exception of. —adv. only; just: She is but a child. —all but almost; nearly. —but for were it not for. —n. an objection or condition; exception: no ifs or buts. [ME buten without]

butch•er (BUUCH ər) n. 1. one who slaughters or dresses animals for market; also, a dealer in meats. 2. one guilty of needless bloodshed. —v.t. 1. slaughter or dress for market. 2. kill cruelly or indiscriminately. 3. bungle. [ME bocher]

butch•er•y (BUUCH ə ree) n. pl. •er•ies 1. wanton slaughter. 2. a slaughterhouse. 3. the butcher's trade.

but•ler (BUT lər) n. a manservant, usu. the head servant in a household. [ME buteler]

butt¹ (but) v.t. 1. strike with the head or horns; ram. 2. push or bump, as with the head. —v.i. 3. strike or attempt to strike something with the head or horns. 4. move or drive head foremost. 5. project; jut. — **butt in** interrupt; meddle. —**butt out** cease meddling. —n. a blow or push with the head. [ME butten strike]

butt² n. a person or thing subjected to ridicule, criticism, etc. [ME, target]

butt³ n. 1. the larger or thicker end of anything. 2. an end or extremity. 3. an unused end, as of a cigar. 4. Slang the buttocks. [ME bott end]

but•ter (BUT ər) n. 1. the fatty constituent of milk churned and prepared for cooking and table use. 2. any of several substances having a semisolid consistency. —v.t. 1. put butter on. 2. Informal flatter: usu. with up. [ME] —but′ter•y adj.

but•ter•fin•gers (BUT ər FING gərz) n. Informal one who drops things easily or often.

but•ter•fly (BUT ər FLI) n. pl. •flies an insect with large, often brightly colored wings and a slender body. [ME boterflye]

but•ter•milk (BUT ər MILK) n. 1. a form of milk made by adding bacterial cultures to skim milk.

but•tock (BUT ək) n. 1. Anat. either of the two fleshy prominences that form the rump. 2. pl. the rump. [Dim. of BUTT³]

but•ton (BUT n) n. 1. a knob or disk sewn to a garment etc., serving as a fastening or for ornamentation. **2.** anything resembling a button, as the knob for operating an electric bell. **3.** *Informal* the point of the chin. **—on the button** *Informal* exactly; precisely. —*v.t. & v.i.* fasten or be capable of being fastened with a button. [ME *boton*]

but·ton·hole (BUT n HOHL) *n.* a slit or loop to receive and hold a button. —*v.t.* •**holed,** •**hol·ing 1.** work buttonholes in. **2.** seize as by the buttonhole so as to detain.

but·tress (BU tris) *n.* **1.** *Archit.* a structure built against a wall to strengthen it. **2.** any support or prop. —*v.t.* **1.** support with a buttress. **2.** prop up; sustain. [ME *butres*]

bux·om (BUK səm) *adj.* **1.** characterized by health and vigor; pleasantly plump: said of women. **2.** large-bosomed. [ME, pliant]

buy (bī) *v.* **bought, buy·ing** *v.t.* **1.** acquire with money; purchase. **2.** obtain by some exchange or sacrifice: *buy* wisdom with experience. **3.** bribe; corrupt. **4.** *Informal* accept; believe. —*v.i.* **5.** make purchases; be a purchaser. —**buy off** bribe. —**buy out** purchase the stock, interests, etc. of. —**buy up** purchase the entire supply of. —*n.* **1.** anything bought or about to be bought. **2.** a bargain. [ME *byen*]

buy·er (BĪ ər) *n.* **1.** one who makes purchases. **2.** a purchasing agent, as for a department store.

buzz (buz) *v.i.* **1.** make the humming, vibrating sound of the bee. **2.** talk or gossip excitedly. **3.** bustle. —*v.t.* **4.** cause to buzz. **5.** signal with a buzz. **6.** fly an airplane very close to (something). **7.** *Informal* telephone. —*n.* **1.** a vibrating hum. **2.** a low murmur, as of many voices. **3.** *Informal* a phone call. [ME *busse*]

buz·zard (BUZ ərd) *n.* one of several large, slow-flying hawks. [ME *busard*]

buzz·word (BUZ WURD *n.* a term with little meaning, used chiefly to impress or mystify.

by (bī) *prep.* **1.** next to; near. **2.** past and beyond: The train roared *by* us. **3.** through the agency of or by means of. **4.** by way of: Come *by* the nearest road. **5.** on the part of: a loss felt *by* all. **6.** according to: *by* law. **7.** in

the course of; during: travel *by* night. **8.** not later than. **9.** after: day *by* day. **10.** according to as a standard: work *by* the day. **11.** to the extent or amount of: insects *by* the thousands. **12.** in multiplication or measurement with: Multiply 6 *by* 8. **13.** with reference to: do well *by* one's friends. **14.** in the name of: *by* all that's holy. **—by the way** incidentally. —*adv.* **1.** at hand; near. **2.** up to and beyond something; past: The years go *by.* **3.** apart; aside: lay something *by.* **—by and by** after a time; before long. **—by and large** on the whole; generally. [ME]

by-and-by (BĪ ən BĪ) *n.* a future time.

bye (bī) *n.* in a tournament, an automatic advance to the next round.

by·gone (BĪ GAWN) *adj.* gone by; past.

by·law (BI LAW) *n.* a law adopted by an organization, and subordinate to a constitution or charter. [ME]

by·pass (BĪ PAS) *n.* a road or route connecting two points in a course other than that normally used; a detour. —*v.t.* **1.** go around or avoid (an obstacle). **2.** *Med.* circumvent by surgical means.

by-prod·uct (BĪ PROD əkt) *n.* a secondary product or result.

by·road (BĪ ROHD) *n.* a side road.

by·stand·er (BĪ STAN dər) *n.* one present but not taking part; an onlooker.

byte (bīt) *n.* a group of binary digits, usu. eight, that a computer stores and treats as a unit.

by·way (BĪ WAY) *n.* a side road or activity.

by·word (BĪ WURD) *n.* **1.** a proverb or pet phrase. **2.** a person, institution, etc. that proverbially represents a type.

Byz·an·tine (BIZ ən TEEN) *adj.* **1.** of or pertaining to Byzantium or its civilization, culture, etc. **2.** pertaining to the style of architecture of Byzantium in the 5th and 6th c. **3.** intricate, complex: his *Byzantine* argument. **4.** devious and surreptitious: *Byzantine* office politics. —*n.* a native or inhabitant of Byzantium. [< LL *Byzantinus* of Byzantium, the ancient city]

C

c, C (see) *n. pl.* **c's** or **cs, C's** or **Cs 1.** the third letter of the English alphabet. **2.** any sound represented by the letter *c.* —*symbol* **1.** the Roman numeral for 100. **2.** *Chem.* carbon (symbol C). **3.** *Music* the first tone in the diatonic scale of C. **4.** the third in sequence or class.

cab (kab) *n.* **1.** a taxicab. **2.** the operator's compartment in a truck or locomotive.

ca·bal (kə BAL) *n.* **1.** a number of persons secretly united for some private purpose. **2.** a plot. —*v.i.* **·balled, ·bal·ling** form a cabal; plot. [< Med.L *cabbala*]

cab·al·le·ro (KAB əl YAIR oh) *n. pl.* **·ros 1.** a Spanish cavalier. **2.** a horseman. [< Sp.]

ca·ban·a (kə BAN ə) *n.* a shelter near a beach or swimming pool, used as a bathhouse. [< Sp.]

cab·a·ret (KAB ə RAY) *n.* **1.** a restaurant that provides entertainment. **2.** the entertainment provided. [< F]

cab·in (KAB in) *n.* **1.** a small, rude house; a hut. **2. a** a private room on a ship. **b** an enclosed compartment on a boat. **c** a compartment for passengers on an airplane. [ME *cabane*]

cab·i·net (KAB ə nit) *n.* **1.** a case or container, usually fixed to a wall and fitted with shelves and doors. **2.** a piece of furniture having shelves or drawers. **3.** *Often cap.* a body of official advisers serving a head of state. [< MF]

cab·i·net·mak·er (KAB ə nit MAY kər) *n.* one who does fine woodwork, as for furniture.

ca·ble (KAY bəl) *n.* **1.** a heavy rope, now usu. of steel wire. **2.** a length of cable. **3.** *Electr.* **a** an insulated electrical conductor or group of conductors. **b** an underwater telegraph line. **4.** a cablegram. —*v.t. & v.i.* **·bled, ·bling** send (a cablegram). [ME]

ca·ble·gram (KAY bəl GRAM) *n.* a telegraphic message sent by underwater cable.

cable TV television transmission via cables, to paying subscribers.

ca·boose (kə BOOS) *n.* a car, usu. at the rear of a freight or work train, for use by the train crew. [< Du. *cabuse* galley]

ca·ca·o (kə KAH oh) *n. pl.* **·ca·os 1.** a small evergreen tree of tropical America. **2.** its seeds, used in making chocolate. [< Sp.]

cac·cia·to·re (KAH chə TOR ee) *adj.* cooked with tomatoes and herbs. [< Ital., hunter]

cache (kash) *v.t.* **cached, cach·ing** store in a concealed place. —*n.* a concealed place for storage; the things stored. [< F]

ca·chet (ka SHAY) *n.* **1.** a seal, as for a letter. **2.** a sign of distinction, conferring prestige. **3.** a mark, slogan, etc., printed on mail. [< F]

cack·le (KAK əl) *v.* **·led, ·ling** *v.i.* **1.** make a shrill, broken cry, as a hen that has laid an egg. **2.** laugh or talk with a similar sound. —*v.t.* **3.** utter in a cackling manner.

ca·coph·o·ny (kə KOF ə nee) *n. pl.* **·nies** disagreeable or discordant sound. [< NL *cacaphonia*] —**ca·coph'o·nous** *adj.*

cac·tus (KAK təs) *n. pl.* **·tus·es** or **·ti** (-tī) any of various green, fleshy, mostly leafless and spiny plants, found in dry regions. [< L]

cad (kad) *n.* a despicable fellow.

ca·dav·er (kə DAV ər) *n.* a dead body; esp., a human body for dissection; a corpse. [ME]

ca·dav·er·ous (kə DAV əR əs) *adj.* resembling or characteristic of a corpse; pale; ghastly; gaunt.

cad·die (KAD ee) *n.* one paid to carry clubs for golf players. —*v.i.* **·died, ·dy·ing** act as a caddie. Also spelled **caddy**.

cad·dy (KAD ee) *n. pl.* **·dies** a small box or case, as for tea.

ca·dence (KAYD ns) *n.* **1.** rhythmic or measured flow, as of poetry. **2.** the measure or beat of music, marching, etc. **3.** intonation. **4.** *Music* a harmonic progression signaling the end of a phrase, movement, etc. [ME]

ca·den·za (kə DEN zə) *n. Music* a passage, often improvised, displaying the virtuosity of a soloist. [< Ital.]

ca·det (kə DET) *n.* **1.** a student at a military or naval school. **2.** a younger son or brother. [< F]

cadge (kaj) *v.t.* **cadged, cadg·ing** get by begging.

cad·re (KAD ree) *n.* a group of trained personnel capable of continuing an organization by training others. [< F, frame]

cae·sar·e·an (si ZAIR ee ən) see CESAREAN.

cae·su·ra (si ZHUUR ə) *n. pl.* **·su·ras** or **·su·rae** (-ZHUUR ee) in prosody, a pause usu. near the middle of a line, indicated by two vertical lines (‖). [< L]

ca·fé (ka FAY) n. an informal eating place, often with a bar. [< F]

ca·fé au lait (KAF ay oh LAY) French coffee with scalded milk.

caf·e·te·ri·a (KAF i TEER ee ə) n. a restaurant where patrons serve themselves from counters. [< Am.Sp., café]

cage (kayj) n. **1.** a boxlike structure with openwork of wires or bars, for confining birds or beasts. **2.** any cagelike structure or framework. —v.t. **caged, cag·ing** shut up in a cage; confine; imprison. [ME]

cage·y (KAY jee) adj. **cag·i·er, cag·i·est** wary of being duped; shrewd and careful. Also **cag'y.** —**cag'i·ness** n.

ca·hoot (kə HOOT) n. Informal shady partnership, as in the phrase **in cahoots.**

cais·son (KAY sən) n. **1.** a large watertight chamber within which work is done under water, as on a bridge pier. **2.** a watertight device used to raise sunken ships. **3.** a two-wheeled vehicle carrying artillery ammunition. [< F]

caisson disease a painful, sometimes fatal disorder caused by too rapid a transition from the compressed air of caissons, diving bells, etc. to normal atmospheric pressure. Also called *the bends.*

ca·jole (kə JOHL) v.t. & v.i. **·joled, ·jol·ing** coax with flattery or false promises; wheedle. [< F cajoler] —**ca·jol'er** n.

Ca·jun (KAY jən) n. **1.** a reputed descendant of the Acadian French in Louisiana. **2.** their French dialect. [Alter. of ACADIAN]

cake (kayk) n. **1.** a mixture of flour, milk, sugar, etc. baked in various forms and generally sweeter and richer than bread. **2.** a small, usu. thin mass of dough, or other food, baked or fried: fish *cake.* **3.** a mass of matter compressed or hardened into a compact form: a *cake* of soap. —v.t. & v.i. **caked, cak·ing** form into a hardened mass. [ME]

cal·a·bash (KAL ə BASH) n. **1.** a tropical American tree with a gourdlike fruit. **2.** the gourd fruit of this tree, used for making pipes, bowls, etc. [< MF calabasse gourd]

cal·a·boose (KAL ə BOOS) n. Slang a jail. [< Sp. calabozo]

ca·lam·i·ty (kə LAM i tee) n. pl. **·ties 1.** a disaster. **2.** a state of great distress. [ME calamite] —**ca·lam'i·tous** adj.

cal·ci·fy (KAL sə FI) v.t. & v.i. **·fied, ·fy·ing** make or become stony by the de-

posit of lime salts. —**cal·ci·fi·ca·tion** (KAL sə fi KAY shən) n.

cal·ci·um (KAL see əm) n. a silver-white, malleable, metallic element, found in chalk etc.

cal·cu·la·ble (KAL kyə lə bəl) adj. **1.** capable of being calculated. **2.** dependable.

cal·cu·late (KAL kyə LAYT) v.t. & v.i. **·lat·ed, ·lat·ing 1.** compute. **2.** form an estimate of. **3.** think; expect. [< LL calculatus reckoned]

cal·cu·lat·ing (KAL kyə LAY ting) adj. using shrewd schemes, esp. for one's own interests.

cal·cu·la·tion (KAL kyə LAY shən) n. **1.** the act, process, or result of computing. **2.** an estimate; forecast. **3.** forethought; prudence.

cal·cu·la·tor (KAL kyə LAY tər) n. **1.** one who calculates. **2.** a machine that performs computations

cal·cu·lus (KAL kyə ləs) n. pl. **·li** (-lī) or **·lus·es 1.** Pathol. a stonelike mass, as in the bladder. **2.** Math. a method of calculating by the use of a system of algebraic symbols. —**differential calculus** the branch of analysis that investigates the changes of varying quantities when the relations between the quantities are given. —**integral calculus** the branch of analysis that, from the relations among the variations of quantities, deduces relations among the quantities themselves. [< L, pebble (used in counting)]

cal·de·ra (KAL DER ə) n. a crater of a volcano formed by collapse of the cone or by a great explosion. [< Sp., lit., cauldron]

cal·en·dar (KAL ən dər) n. **1.** any of various systems of fixing the order, length, and subdivisions of the years and months. **2.** a table showing the days, weeks, and months of a year. **3.** a schedule or list, esp. one arranged in chronological order: a court *calendar.* —v.t. place on a calendar; schedule. [ME calender account book]

calf¹ (kaf) n. pl. **calves** (kafz) **1.** the young of the cow or various other bovine animals. **2.** the young of various mammals, as the elephant, whale, etc. **3.** calfskin. [ME]

calf² n. pl. **calves** (kafz) the muscular rear part of the human leg below the knee. [ME]

calf·skin (KAF SKIN) n. **1.** the skin or hide of a calf. **2.** leather made from this.

cal·i·ber (KAL ə bər) n. **1.** the inner diameter of a tube. **2. a** the innner diameter of the barrel of a gun, cannon, etc. **b** the diameter of a bullet. **3.** degree of personal excellence. Also *esp. Brit.* **cal'i·bre.** [< MF]

cal·i·brate (KAL ə BRAYT) *v.t.* **·brat·ed, ·brat·ing 1.** graduate, correct, or adjust the scale of (a measuring instrument) into appropriate units. **2.** determine the reading of (such an instrument). —**cal'i·bra'tion** *n.*

cal·i·co (KAL i KOH) *n. pl.* **·coes** or **·cos** cotton cloth printed in a figured pattern of bright colors. —*adj.* **1.** made of calico. **2.** dappled or streaked: a *calico* cat. [after *Calicut,* India, where first obtained]

cal·i·per (KAL ə pər) *n. Usu. pl.* an instrument consisting of two hinged legs, used for measuring diameters. —*v.t. & v.i.* measure by using calipers.

ca·liph (KAY lif) *n.* the spiritual and civil head of a Muslim state. [ME *caliphe*]

cal·i·phate (KAL ə FAYT) *n.* the office, dominion, or reign of a caliph.

cal·is·then·ics (KAL əs THEN iks) *n.pl.* light, repeated exercises.

calk (kawk) see CAULK.

call·(kawl) *v.t.* **1.** say in a loud voice. **2.** summon. **3.** convoke; convene: *call* a meeting. **4.** arouse, as from sleep. **5.** telephone to. **6.** lure (birds or animals) by imitating their cry. **7.** name, designate or characterize. **8.** bring to action or consideration: *call* a case to court. **9.** demand payment of. **10.** in baseball: **a** stop or suspend (a game). **b** designate a pitch as (a ball or strike). **c** declare (a player) out, safe, etc. **11.** in poker, demand a show of hands by a bet equal to that of (another). —*v.i.* **12.** raise one's voice; speak loudly. **13.** make a brief visit, stop, or stay: with *at, on,* or *upon.* **14.** communicate by telephone. —**call back a** summon back; recall. **b** call in return, as by telephone. — **call down a** invoke from heaven. **2.** rebuke; reprimand. —**call for a** stop so as to obtain. **b** require; need. —**call in a** collect, as debts. **b** retire, as currency, from circulation. **c** summon, as for consultation. —**call off a** summon away. **b** say or read aloud. **c** cancel. —**call up a** recollect. **b** summon. **c** telephone. —*n.* **1.** a shout or cry. **2.** a summons or invitation. **3.** a demand; claim: *call* of duty. **4.** a communication by telephone. **5.** an inward urge to a religious vocation. **6.** a brief, often formal, visit. **7.** the cry of an animal, esp. of a bird. **8.** a whistle etc., with which to imitate such a cry. **9.** a need; occasion: You've no *call* to do that. **10.** in sports, a decision by a referee, umpire, or judge. —

on call a payable on demand. **b** available when sent for. [ME *callen*]

call·back (KAWL BAK) *n.* **1.** the recall by a manufacturer of a product to correct a defect. **2.** the product so recalled. **3.** a request to return for a second audition.

call girl a prostitute who accepts appointments principally by telephone.

cal·lig·ra·phy (kə LIG rə fee *n.* **1.** beautiful penmanship. **2.** handwriting in general. [< Gk. *kalligraphia* beautiful writing] — **cal·lig'ra·pher** *n.* —**cal·li·graph·ic** (KAL i GRAF ik) *adj.*

call·ing (KAW ling) *n.* **1.** the act of speaking or crying aloud. **2.** a vocation or profession. **3.** an inner urge toward a vocation.

cal·li·o·pe (kə LĪ ə pee) *n.* a musical instrument consisting of a series of steam whistles and a keyboard. [after *Calliope,* Greek Muse of eloquence.]

cal·lous (KAL əs) *adj.* **1.** thickened and hardened, as a callus. **2.** hardened in feelings; insensible. —*v.t. & v.i.* make or become callous. [ME]

cal·low (KAL oh) *adj.* inexperienced; immature. [ME]

cal·lus (KAL əs) *n. pl.* **·lus·es 1.** a thickened, hardened part of the skin. **2.** the new tissue around the ends of a broken bone in the process of reuniting. **3.** the tissue that forms over a cut on a plant stem. —*v.i.* **·lused, ·lus·ing** form a callus. [< L, hard skin]

calm (kahm) *adj.* **1.** free from agitation; still or nearly still. **2.** not excited by passion or emotion. —*n.* **1.** lack of wind or motion; stillness. **2.** serenity. —*v.t. & v.i.* make or become quiet or calm: often with *down.* [ME *calme*]

ca·lor·ic (kə LOR ik) *adj.* **1.** of or pertaining to heat. **2.** of or relating to calories. —*n.* heat. [< F *calorique*]

cal·o·rie (KAL ə ree) *n.* **1.** one of two recognized units of heat. The **large** or **great calorie** is the amount of heat required to raise the temperature of one kilogram of water 1°C. The **small calorie** is the amount of heat required to raise one gram of water 1°C. **2.** *Physiol.* the large calorie, a measure of the energy value of foods or the heat output of organisms. [< F]

cal·u·met (KAL yə MET) *n.* a tobacco pipe with a long, ornamented stem: also called *peace pipe.* [< F, pipe]

ca·lum·ni·ate (kə LUM nee AYT) *v.t. & v.i.*

•at•ed, •at•ing accuse falsely; defame; slander. [< L *calumniatus* slandered]

cal•um•ny (KAL əm nee) *n. pl.* **•nies** a false and malicious accusation or report. [ME]

calve (kav) *v.t. & v.i.* **calved, calv•ing** give birth to (a calf). [ME *calven*]

calves (kavz) plural of CALF.

ca•lyp•so (kə LIP soh) *n.* a West Indian ballad, often topical and humorous, and usu. improvised.

ca•lyx (KAY liks) *n. pl.* **ca•lyx•es** or **cal•y•ces** (-seez) *Bot.* the outermost series of leaflike parts of a flower; the sepals. [< L husk]

cam (kam) *n. Mech.* an irregularly shaped rotating piece that imparts reciprocating or variable motion to another piece bearing on it. [< Du., tooth]

ca•ma•ra•de•rie (KAH mə RAH də ree) *n.* comradeship. [< F]

cam•bi•um (KAM bee əm) *n. Bot.* a layer of tissue in trees, from which new wood and bark are formed. [< ME, exchange]

cam•el (KAM əl) *n.* a large Asian or African ruminant with a humped back, used in the desert. [ME]

camel's hair 1. the hair of the camel. **2.** a soft, warm, usu. tan cloth made of camel's hair, sometimes mixed with wool. — **cam•el•hair** (KAM əl HAIR *adj.*

Cam•em•bert (KAM əm BAIR) *n.* a rich, creamy, soft cheese.

cam•e•o (KAM ee OH) *n. pl.* **•os 1.** a gem having a design carved in relief, often contrasting in color with the background. **2.** a small part in a play or movie performed by a well-known person. [< Ital. *cammeo*]

cam•er•a (KAM ər ə) *n.* **1.** an apparatus for recording an image by light focused through a lens onto a film. **2.** *Telecom.* an enclosed unit containing the light-sensitive electron tube that converts optical images into electrical impulses for television transmission. —**in camera** *Law* not in public court; privately. [< L, vaulted room]

cam•ou•flage (KAM ə FLAHZH) *n.* **1.** *Mil.* measures or material used to conceal or misrepresent the identity of installations, ships, etc. **2.** any disguise or pretense. — *v.t. & v.i.* **•flaged, •flag•ing** hide or obscure, as with disguises. [< F]

camp¹ (kamp) *n.* **1.** a temporary shelter, esp. a group of tents for soldiers or vacationers; also, the ground or area so employed. **2.** the persons occupying such tents. **3.** a body of persons supporting a policy, theory, or doctrine; also, the position so upheld. —*v.i.* set up or live in a camp; encamp. —**camp out** sleep in a tent; live in the open. [< MF, field]

camp² *n.* **1.** exaggerated effeminacy. **2.** something so outrageous, anachronistic, etc., as to be considered amusing. —**camp** *adj.* —**camp'y** *adj.* **•i•er, •i•est**

cam•paign (kam PAYN) *n.* **1.** a series of connected military operations conducted for a common objective, in a particular area. **2.** an organized series of activities designed to obtain a definite result. —*v.i.* serve in, conduct, or go on a campaign. [< F *campagne* field]

cam•pa•ni•le (KAM pə NEEL lee) *n. pl.* **•les** or **•li** (-lee) a bell tower. [< Ital. *campana* bell]

camp•er (KAM pər) *n.* **1.** one who sojourns in a recreational camp. **2.** a vehicle affording sleeping facilities.

camp follower 1. a prostitute who operates near military camps. **2.** a person who exploits military personnel. **3.** a person who joins an organization, movement, etc. for personal gain.

camp meeting a series of religious meetings usu. held in a tent; also, one such meeting.

camp•site (KAMP SIT) *n.* a place suitable for or used for a camp.

cam•pus (KAM pəs) *n.* the grounds of a school or college. [< L, field]

cam•shaft (KAM SHAFT) *n.* a shaft with one or more cams on it.

can¹ (kan) *v.* present **can**; past **could**; used as an auxiliary with the following senses: **1.** be able to. **2.** know how to. **3.** have the right to. **4.** be permitted to; may. [ME]

can² *n.* **1.** a vessel, usu. of tinned steel or aluminum, for holding or carrying liquids, garbage, etc. **2.** a container in which fruits, tobacco, etc. are hermetically sealed; also the contents of such a container. **3.** *Slang* a jail. **b** the buttocks. —*v.t.* **canned, can•ning 1.** put in cans, jars, etc.; preserve. **2.** *Slang* **a** dismiss. **b** cease: *Can it!* [ME, cup] —**can'ner** *n.*

Canadian English the English language as spoken and written in Canada.

Canadian French the French language as spoken and written in Canada.

Ca•na•di•an•ism (kə NAY dee ə NIZ əm) *n.* **1.** a trait, custom, or tradition characteristic of the people of Canada or some of them. **2.** a word, phrase, etc. characteristic of Canadian English or French.

ca·nal (kə NAL) n. 1. an artificial waterway for inland navigation, irrigation, etc. 2. *Anat.* a passage or duct; tube: the auditory *canal.* —v.t. **ca·nalled, ca·nal·ling** dig a canal through, or provide with canals. [ME, waterpipe]

can·a·pé (KAN ə pee) n. a thin piece of toast or a cracker spread with cheese, caviar, etc. [< F]

ca·nard (kə NAHRD) n. a false or absurd story or rumor; a hoax. [< F, lit., duck]

ca·nar·y (kə NAIR ee) n. pl. **·nar·ies** 1. a small bird popular as a cage bird. 2. a bright yellow color: also **canary yellow**. [< Sp.]

ca·nas·ta (kə NAS tə) n. a card game for two to six players, based on rummy. [< Sp., lit., basket]

can·can (KAN KAN) n. an exhibition dance with high kicking performed by women. [< F]

can·cel (KAN səl) v. **can·celed, can·cel·ing** v.t. 1. mark out or off, as by drawing lines through. 2. render null and void; annul. 3. withdraw; call off. 4. mark (a postage stamp) to show use. 5. make up for; neutralize. 6. *Math.* eliminate (a common factor) from the numerator and denominator of a fraction, or from both sides of an equation. —v.i. 7. neutralize one another: with *out.* —n. 1. the deletion of a part. 2. the part omitted. [ME *cancellen* cross out] —**can'cel·a·ble** adj. —**can·cel·la·tion** (KAN sə LAY shən) n.

can·cer (KAN sər) n. 1. any of a group of often fatal diseases characterized by abnormal cellular growth and by malignancy. 2. a malignant tumor. 3. any dangerous and spreading evil. [ME] —**can'cer·ous** adj.

can·did (KAN did) adj. honest and open; sincere; frank. [< F *candide*]

can·di·da·cy (KAN di də see) n. pl. **·cies** the state or position of being a candidate.

can·di·date (KAN di DAYT) n. one who seeks, or is nominated for, an office, honor, or privilege. [< L *candidatus* dressed in white]

can·died (KAN deed) adj. 1. cooked with or in sugar. 2. crystallized or granulated. 3. flattering; honeyed.

can·dle (KAN dl) n. a cylinder of tallow, wax, or other solid fat, containing a wick, that gives light when burning. —**hold a candle to** compare with favorably: usu. used in the negative. —v.t. **·dled, ·dling** test, as eggs, by holding between the eye and a light. [ME *candel*]

can·dle·light (KAN dl LĪT) n. 1. light given by a candle; artificial light. 2. twilight.

can·dle·pow·er (KAN dl POW ər) n. the illuminating power of a standard candle, used as a measure.

can·dle·stick (KAN dl STIK) n. a holder with sockets or spikes for a candle or candles.

can·dor (KAN dər) n. 1. openness; frankness. 2. impartiality; fairness. [ME]

can·dy (KAN dee) n. pl. **·dies** any confection consisting chiefly of sugar. —v.t. **·died, ·dy·ing** 1. cause to form into crystals of sugar. 2. preserve by boiling or coating with sugar. 3. render pleasant; sweeten. [ME *candi* made of sugar]

cane (kayn) n. 1. a walking stick. 2. the jointed, woody stem of bamboo, rattan, etc., used as a weaving material in chairs, etc. 3. sugarcane. 4. the stem of a raspberry or allied plant. 5. any rod, especially one used for flogging. —v.t. **caned, can·ing** 1. strike or beat with a cane. 2. make or repair with cane, as a chair. [ME, reed]

ca·nine (KAY nīn) adj. 1. of or like a dog. 2. *Zool.* of the dog family. 3. of or pertaining to a canine tooth. —n. 1. a dog or other canine animal. 2. *Anat.* one of the four pointed teeth on either side of the upper and lower incisors. [ME, canine tooth]

can·is·ter (KAN ə stər) n. a covered container for tea, spices, etc. [< L *canistrum* wicker basket]

can·ker (KANG kər) n. 1. *Pathol.* an ulceration, chiefly of the mouth and lips. 2. anything that causes corruption, evil, decay, etc. 3. a disease of trees. [ME] —**can'ker·ous** adj.

can·na·bis (KAN ə bis) n. 1. hemp (def. 1). 2. the dried flowering tops of the female hemp plant. [< NL, hemp]

canned (kand) adj. 1. preserved in a can or jar. 2. *Informal* recorded: *canned* music.

can·ner·y (KAN ə ree) n. pl. **·ner·ies** a place where foods are canned.

can·ni·bal (KAN ə bəl) n. 1. one who eats human flesh. 2. an animal that devours its own species. [< Sp. *canibal*] —**can·ni·bal·ism** (KAN ə bəl IZ əm) n.

can·ni·bal·ize (KAN ə bə LĪZ) v.t. **·ized, ·iz·ing** take parts from (damaged tanks etc.) in order to repair others.

can·ning (KAN ing) n. the act, process, or business of preserving foods in hermetically sealed metal cans, glass jars, etc.

can·non (KAN ən) n. pl. **·nons** or **·non** *Mil.* a large tubular weapon, usu. mounted on a fixed or mobile carriage, that discharges a projectile by the use of an explosive. —*v.i.* **1.** fire cannon. —*v.t.* **2.** attack with cannon shot. [ME *canon* tube]

can·not (KAN ot) the negative of the auxiliary verb CAN.

can·ny (KAN ee) *adj.* **·ni·er, ·ni·est 1.** cautiously shrewd. **2.** frugal; thrifty. **3.** skillful. —*adv.* in a canny manner. —**can'ni·ly** *adv.*

ca·noe (kə NOO) *n.* a small, long, narrow boat, pointed at both ends, and propelled by paddles. —*v.t & v.i.* **·noed, ·noe·ing** convey or travel by canoe. [< F] — **ca·noe'ist** *n.*

can·on[1] (KAN ən) *n.* **1.** a rule or law; esp., a rule or body of rules of faith and practice enacted by a church council. **2.** an established rule; principle. **3.** a standard; criterion. **4.** the books of the Bible or other sacred books. **5.** a list, as of canonized saints. **6.** *Often cap. Eccl.* the main portion of the Mass. **7.** the works of an author that have been accepted as genuine. —**ca·non·i·cal** (kə NON i kəl) *adj.* [ME]

can·on[2] *n.* a cleric affiliated with a cathedral or collegiate church. [ME]

can·on·ize (KAN ə NIZ) *v.t.* **·ized, ·iz·ing 1.** declare (a deceased person) to be a saint. **2.** glorify. —**can'on·i·za'tion** *n.*

canon law the ecclesiastical laws of a Christian church.

can·o·py (KAN ə pee) *n. pl.* **·pies 1.** a covering suspended over a throne, bed, etc., or held over a person. **2.** any covering overhead, as the sky. —*v.t.* **·pied, ·py·ing** cover with or as with a canopy. [ME *canope* bed with netting]

cant[1] (kant) *n.* **1.** an inclination from the vertical or horizontal; a slope or tilt. **2.** a sudden motion that tilts or overturns. **3.** an outer corner or angle. **4.** a slant surface. — *v.t.* **1.** set slantingly; tilt. **2.** give a bevel to. **3.** throw out or off. —*v.i.* **4.** tilt; slant. —*adj.* oblique; slanting. [ME, side]

cant[2] *n.* **1.** insincere talk, esp. of a religious or moralistic nature. **2.** expressions peculiar to a sect, class, or calling; jargon; argot. —*v.i.* use cant. —*adj.* hypocritical. [< L *canere* sing]

can't (kant) contraction of cannot.

can·tank·er·ous (kan TANG kər əs) *adj.* quarrelsome; ill-natured; perverse. — **can·tank'er·ous·ness** *n.*

can·ta·ta (kən TAH tə) *n. Music* a narrative or dramatic vocal composition, to be sung but not acted. [< Ital.]

can·teen (kan TEEN) *n.* **1.** a small flask for carrying water or other liquids. **2.** a shop at a military camp where soldiers can buy provisions, refreshments, etc. **3.** a place for refreshments. [< F *cantine* cellar]

can·ter (KAN tər) *n.* a moderate, easy gallop. —**can'ter** *v.t. & v.i.*

can·ti·cle (KAN ti kəl) *n.* a nonmetrical hymn, said or chanted in church. [ME, song]

can·ti·lev·er (KAN tl EE vər) *n.* **1.** *Engin.* a long structural member, as a truss, beam, or slab, lying across a support with the projecting arms in balance. **2.** *Archit.* any structural part projecting horizontally and anchored at one end only. —*v.t. & v.i.* project (a building member) outward and in balance beyond the base.

can·to (KAN toh) *n. pl.* **·tos** a division of a long poem. [< Ital.]

can·ton (KAN tn) *n.* a district; esp., one of the states of Switzerland. **1.** divide into cantons or districts. **2.** assign quarters to, as troops. [< MF]

can·tor (KAN tor) *n.* the chief liturgical singer in a synagogue. [< L, singer]

can·vas (KAN vəs) *n.* **1.** a heavy, closely woven cloth of hemp, flax, or cotton, used for sails, tents, etc. **2.** a piece of such material on which to paint, esp. in oils. **3.** a painting on canvas. **4.** sails collectively. [ME *canevas* hemp]

can·vass (KAN vəs) *v.t. & v.i.* go about (a region) or among (persons) to solicit votes, opinions, etc. —*n.* **1.** the process of canvassing. **2.** a survey or poll.

can·yon (KAN yən) *n.* a deep gorge or ravine, with steep sides. [< Sp. *cañón*]

cap (kap) *n.* **1.** a covering for the head, usu. snug, brimless, and of soft material. **2.** any headgear designed to denote rank, function, membership, etc. **3.** something suggesting a cap in form, function, or position as a bottle top, an artificial covering for a tooth, etc. **4.** a container holding an explosive charge. —**set one's cap for** try to win as a suitor or husband. —*v.t.* **capped, capping 1.** put a cap on; cover. **2.** serve as a cap or cover to. **3.** add the final touch to. **4.** excel. [ME *cappe*]

ca·pa·bil·i·ty (KAY pə BIL i tee) *n. pl.* **·ties 1.** the quality of being capable; capacity or ability. **2.** *Usu. pl.* qualities that may be used or developed; potentialities.

ca·pa·ble (KAY pə bəl) *adj.* able; competent. —**capable of** having the capacity or qualities needed for. [< LL *capabilis* roomy] —**ca′pa·bly** *adv.*

ca·pa·cious (kə PAY shəs) *adj.* roomy. —**ca·pa′cious·ness** *n.*

ca·pac·i·tance (kə PAS i təns) *n. Electr.* the property of a circuit that enables it to store an electrical charge.

ca·pac·i·tor (kə PAS i tər) *n. Electr.* a device used to increase the capacitance of an electric circuit. Also called *condenser.*

ca·pac·i·ty (kə PAS i tee) *n. pl.* **·ties 1.** ability to receive, contain, or absorb. **2.** maximum volume or content. **3.** aptitude or ability. **4.** specific position or office. **5.** maximum output or production. [ME *capacite* roominess]

cape[1] (kayp) *n.* a point of land extending into the sea or a lake. [ME *cap* head]

cape[2] *n.* a sleeveless garment fastened at the neck and hanging loosely from the shoulders. [ME]

ca·per[1] (KAY pər) *n.* **1.** a playful leap; a skip. **2.** a wild prank; antic. —*v.i.* leap playfully; frolic. [< L *caper* goat]

ca·per[2] *n.* **1.** the flower bud of a Mediterranean shrub, pickled and used as a relish. **2.** the shrub itself. [ME *caperes*]

cap·il·lar·i·ty (KAP ə LAR i tee) *n. pl.* **·ties 1.** the state of being capillary. **2.** *Physics* a form of surface tension between the molecules of a liquid and those of a solid. When the adhesive force is stronger (**capillary attraction**) the liquid will tend to rise in a capillary tube; when cohesion dominates (**capillary repulsion**), the liquid tends to fall.

cap·il·lar·y (KAP ə LER ee) *adj.* **1.** of, pertaining to, or like hair; fine. **2.** having a hairlike bore, as a tube or vessel. —*n. pl.* **·lar·ies 1.** *Anat.* a very small blood vessel, as one connecting an artery and vein. **2.** any tube with a fine bore. [< L *capillaris* pertaining to hair]

cap·i·tal[1] (KAP i tl) *n.* **1.** the city or town that is the seat of government of a country, state, etc. **2.** a capital letter. **3.** the total amount of money or property owned or used by an individual or corporation. **4.** wealth applicable to the production of more wealth. **5.** in accounting, net worth after the deduction of all liabilities. **6.** possessors of wealth as a class. —**make capital of** turn to advantage. —*adj.* **1.** chief, as comprising the seat of government. **2.** standing at the head;

principal. **3.** of or pertaining to funds or capital. **4.** of the first quality. **5.** punishable by or involving the death penalty: *capital crimes.* [ME, of the head]

cap·i·tal[2] *n. Archit.* the upper member of a column or pillar. [ME *capitale* head]

cap·i·tal·ism (KAP i tl iz əm) *n.* an economic system in which the means of production and distribution are mostly privately owned and operated for private profit.

cap·i·tal·ist (KAP i tl ist) *n.* **1.** an owner of capital, esp. one who invests it in enterprises expected to make profits. **2.** a supporter of capitalism. —**cap′i·tal·is′tic** *adj.*

cap·i·tal·i·za·tion (KAP i tl ə ZAY shən) *n.* **1.** the act or process of capitalizing. **2.** a sum arrived at by capitalizing. **3.** the total capital employed in a business.

cap·i·tal·ize (KAP i tl iz) *v.* **·ized, ·iz·ing** *v.t.* **1.** print or write in capital letters. **2.** convert into capital. **3.** provide capital for. **4.** estimate the worth of (a business or stock) from earnings or potential earnings. —*v.i.* **5.** acquire an advantage; profit: with *on* or *by.*

capital letter the form of a letter used at the beginning of a sentence, with proper names, etc., as the A in Africa.

capital punishment the death penalty.

cap·i·tol (KAP i tl) *n.* **1.** the building in which a state legislature convenes; a statehouse. **2.** *Cap.* the building in which the U.S. Congress convenes. [< L *capitolium* temple of Jupiter on Capitoline hill in Rome]

ca·pit·u·late (kə PICH ə layt) *v.i.* **·lat·ed, ·lat·ing 1.** surrender on stipulated terms. **2.** acquiesce. [< Med.L *capitulatus* drawn up in chapters]

ca·pit·u·la·tion (kə PICH ə LAY shən) *n.* **1.** the act of surrendering conditionally; also, the instrument containing the terms of surrender. **2.** a surrender. **3.** a summary of a subject.

ca·pon (KAY pon) *n.* a gelded rooster. [ME]

cap·puc·ci·no (KAP uu CHEE noh) *n.* hot espresso coffee with cream or steamed milk, often flavored with cinnamon. [< Ital., lit., Capuchin, from the color of a Capuchin monk's habit]

ca·price (kə PREES) *n.* **1.** a sudden, impulsive change; whim. **2.** a tendency to make such changes; capriciousness. [< F]

ca·pri·cious (kə PRISH əs) *adj.* characterized by or resulting from caprice; fickle; whimsical.

cap·size (KAP sīz) *v.t. & v.i.* **·sized, ·siz·ing** upset or overturn.

cap·stan (KAP stən) *n. Naut.* a drumlike apparatus, turned by bars or levers, for hoisting anchors. [ME]

cap·sule (KAP səl) *n.* **1.** a small container, usu. made of gelatin, for a dose of medicine. **2.** a detachable part of an airplane, rocket, etc., containing the pilot, instruments, etc. **3.** a thin covering or seal. —*adj.* in concise form; condensed. [< L *capsula* small box] —**cap′su·lize′** *v.t.* **·ized, ·iz·ing**

cap·tain (KAP tən) *n.* **1.** one at the head or in command; a chief; leader. **2.** the master or commander of a vessel. **3.** *Mil.* a commissioned officer ranking below a major and above a first lieutenant. **4.** *Naval* a commissioned officer ranking below a rear admiral. **5.** a team leader. —*v.t.* act as captain to; command; lead. [ME *capitain* chief] —**cap′tain·cy, cap′tain·ship** *n.*

cap·tion (KAP shən) *n.* **1.** a heading, as of a document. **2.** the title and descriptive matter for an illustration. **3.** a subtitle in a motion picture. [ME *capcioun* seizure] —**cap′tion** *v.t.*

cap·tious (KAP shəs) *adj.* **1.** apt to find fault; critical. **2.** designed to ensnare or perplex. [ME *capcious* deceptive] —**cap′tious·ness** *n.*

cap·ti·vate (KAP tə vayt) *v.t.* **·vat·ed, ·vat·ing** enthrall; fascinate; charm. [< LL *captivatus* taken captive] —**cap′ti·va′tor** *n.*

cap·tive (KAP tiv) *n.* **1.** a prisoner. **2.** one enthralled by beauty, passion, etc. —*adj.* **1.** taken or held prisoner, as in war. **2.** held in restraint; confined. **3.** captivated. **4.** of or pertaining to a captive or captivity. [ME]

cap·tiv·i·ty (kap TIV i tee) *n. pl.* **·ties** the state of being held captive; confinement.

cap·tor (KAP tər) *n.* one who takes or holds captive.

cap·ture (KAP chər) *v.t.* **·tured, ·tur·ing** **1.** take by force, stratagem, etc., as in war. **2.** gain or win. —*n.* **1.** the act of capturing; seizure. **2.** the person or thing captured. [< MF]

car (kahr) *n.* **1.** an automobile. **2.** any of various wheeled vehicles. **3.** the enclosed platform of an elevator. [ME *carre* vehicle]

ca·ra·ba·o (KAHR ə BAH oh) *n. pl.* **·ba·os** or **·ba·o** a Philippine water buffalo. [< Philippine Sp.]

ca·rafe (kə RAF) *n.* a glass water bottle. [< F]

car·a·mel (KAR ə məl) *n.* **1.** a chewy candy made of sugar, butter, milk, etc. **2.** burnt sugar, used to flavor foods. [< F]

car·a·mel·ize (KAR ə mə līz) *v.t. & v.i.* **·ized, ·iz·ing** convert or be converted into caramel.

car·at (KAR ət) *n.* **1.** a unit of weight for gems, one metric carat being 200 milligrams. **2.** karat. [< Med.L *carratus* a weight]

car·a·van (KAR ə VAN) *n.* **1.** a company of traders, pilgrims, or the like, traveling together, esp. across deserts. **2.** a number of vehicles traveling together. [< Ital. *caravana*]

car·a·way (KAR ə WAY) *n.* an herb of the parsley family whose seeds (**caraway seeds**) are used for flavoring. [ME]

car·bine (KAR been) *n.* a light, semiautomatic rifle [< MF, small gun]

car·bo·hy·drate (KAHR boh HĪ drayt) *n. Biochem.* any of a group of compounds containing carbon combined with hydrogen and oxygen, and including sugars, starches, and cellulose.

car·bon (KAHR bən) *n.* **1.** a nonmetallic element found in all organic substances. **2.** *Electr.* **a** a rod of carbon, used as an electrode in an arc light. **b** the negative electrode of a primary cell. **3.** a piece of carbon paper. **4.** a copy made with carbon paper. —*adj.* **1.** of, pertaining to, or like carbon. **2.** treated with carbon. [< F *carbone*]

carbon dioxide *Chem.* a heavy, odorless, noncombustible gas taken from the atmosphere in photosynthesis and returned to it by respiration and combustion.

car·bon·ize (KAHR bə NĪZ) *v.t.* **·ized, ·iz·ing** **1.** reduce to carbon. **2.** coat with carbon, as paper. **3.** charge with carbon.

carbon monoxide *Chem.* a colorless, odorless gas formed by the incomplete oxidation of carbon, highly poisonous when inhaled.

carbon paper thin paper coated with carbon or the like, used for making copies of typewritten or handwritten material.

car·bun·cle (KAHR bung kəl) *n.* an inflammation of the subcutaneous tissue, resembling a boil but larger. [ME] —**car·bun·cu·lar** (kahr BUNG kyə lər) *adj.*

car·bu·re·tor (KAHR bə RAY tər) *n.* in an internal-combustion engine, a device used to charge air or gas with volatile hydrocarbons.

car·cass (KAHR kəs) n. **1.** the dead body of an animal. **2.** the human body, living or dead: a contemptuous or humorous use. [< MF *carcasse*]

car·cin·o·gen (kahr SIN ə jən) n. *Pathol.* a substance that causes cancer. —**car·ci·no·gen·ic** (KAHR sə nə JEN ik) adj.

car·ci·no·ma (KAHR sə NOH mə) n. pl. **·mas** or **·ma·ta** (-mə tə) *Pathol.* a malignant eipthelial tumor; cancer. [< L, ulcer] —**car′ci·no′ma·tous** adj.

card¹ (kahrd) n. **1.** a small, usu. rectangular piece of thin pasteboard or stiff paper, used for a variety of purposes. **2.** one of a pack of such pieces with figures, numbers, or other symbols, used for various games. **3.** pl. games played with such cards. **4.** a greeting card. **5.** a card certifying the identity of its owner or bearer. **6.** *Informal* a witty person. —**in the cards** likely to happen. —**put one's cards on the table** reveal one's intentions frankly. [ME *carde* leaf of paper]

card² n. a wire-toothed brush for combing and cleaning wool, etc. [ME *carde* thistle] —**card** v.t. & v.i. —**card′er** n.

card·board (KAHRD bord) n. a thin, stiff pasteboard used for making cards, boxes, etc.

car·di·ac (KAHR dee AK) adj. *Med.* pertaining to, situated near, or affecting the heart. [ME]

car·di·gan (KAHR di gən) n. a jacket or sweater opening down the front. [after the seventh Earl of *Cardigan*, 1797–1868]

car·di·nal (KAHR dn l) adj. **1.** most important; chief; principal. **2.** of a deep scarlet color. **3.** of or relating to a cardinal or cardinals. —n. **1.** in the Roman Catholic Church, a member of the College of Cardinals. **2.** a bright red, crested finch of the eastern U.S. **3.** a deep scarlet. **4.** a cardinal number. [ME]

cardinal number *Math.* any number that expresses a quantity and is used in counting, as 1, 2, 3, etc.: distinguished from *ordinal number.*

car·di·o·gram (KAHR dee ə GRAM) n. the record produced by a cardiograph.

car·di·o·graph (KAHR dee ə GRAF) n. an instrument for tracing and recording the force and character of heart movements. —**car·di·og·ra·phy** (KAHR dee OG rə fee) n.

car·di·ol·o·gy (KAHR dee OL ə jee) n. the branch of medicine dealing with the heart and heart disease. —**car′di·ol′o·gist** n.

card·sharp (KAHRD SHAHRP) n. one who cheats at cards, esp. as a livelihood.

care (kair) n. **1.** a feeling of anxiety or concern; worry. **2.** a cause of worry or anxiety. **3.** watchful regard or attention; heed. **4.** charge or guardianship; custody; supervision. —v.i. **cared, car·ing 1.** have or show regard, interest, or concern. **2.** be inclined; desire: with *to.* —**care for 1.** look after or provide for. **2.** feel interest concerning; also, have a fondness for; like. [ME]

ca·reen (kə REEN) v.i. **1.** lurch or twist from side to side while moving. **2.** lean sideways. —v.t. **3.** turn (a ship, etc.) on one side, as for cleaning or repairing. [< MF *carine* keel]

ca·reer (kə REER) n. **1.** the course or progress of events, esp. in a person's life. **2.** one's lifework; profession. **3.** a rapid course; progress at full speed. —adj. making one's profession a lifework: *career* diplomat. —v.i. move with a swift, free motion. [< MF *carriere*, lit., road]

care·free (KAIR FREE) adj. free of troubles.

care·ful (KAIR fəl) adj. **1.** exercising care; painstaking. **2.** done with care. **3.** watchful; cautious. —**care′ful·ly** adv.

care·less (KAIR lis) adj. **1.** not attentive; reckless. **2.** not done with care; neglectful. **3.** without care or concern; indifferent: with *about, in,* or *of.* —**care′less·ly** adv.

ca·ress (kə RES) n. an affectionate touch or gesture. [< F *caresse* dear] —**ca·ress′** v.t.

car·et (KAIR it) n. a sign () placed below a line to indicate where something should be inserted. [< L, there is lacking]

care·tak·er (KAIR TAY kər) n. ane who takes care of a place, thing, or person; a custodian.

care·worn (KAIR worn) adj. showing the effects of care and anxiety.

car·fare (KAHR FAIR) n. the fare for a ride on a bus, etc.

car·go (KAHR goh) n. pl. **·goes** or **·gos** goods and merchandise carried by a vessel, aircraft, etc.; freight; load. [< Sp., load]

car·hop (KAHR HOP) n. a waiter or waitress at a drive-in restaurant.

Car·ib·be·an (KAR ə BEE ən) adj. of or pertaining to the Caribbean Sea.

car·i·bou (KAR ə BOO) n. pl. **·bou** or **·bous** a North American reindeer. [< Canadian F]

car·i·ca·ture (KAR i kə chər) n. **1.** a picture or description in which features are exaggerated or distorted so as to produce an amusing or derisive effect. **2.** the act or art of caricaturing. **3.** a poor imitation. —*v.t.* **•tured, •tur•ing** represent so as to make ridiculous; burlesque. [< Ital. *caricato* distorted] —**car'i•ca•tur'ist** *n.*

car•ies (KAIR eez) *n. Pathol.* decay of a bone or of a tooth. [< L, decay] —**car'i•ous** (KAIR ee əs) *adj.*

car•il•lon (KAR ə LON) *n.* **1.** a set of stationary bells rung by hammers operated from a keyboard or by a mechanism. **2.** a melody rung on a carillon. —*v.i.* **•lonned, •lon•ning** play a carillon. **car•il•lon•neur** (KAR ə lə NUR) *n.* [< F, set of four bells]

car•i•ole (KAR ee OHL) *n.* **1.** a small, open carriage. **2.** a light cart. **3.** *Canadian* a dog sled for one person lying down. [< F *cariole* vehicle]

car•load (KAHR LOHD) *n.* the load carried in a car or freight car; also, the capacity of a car or freight car.

car•min•a•tive (kahr MIN ə tiv) *adj. Med.* tending to, or used to relieve flatulence. [< LL *carminatus* purified] —**car•min'a•tive** *n.*

car•mine (KAHR min) *n.* **1.** a deep red or purplish red color. **2.** a crimson pigment obtained from cochineal; rouge. [< F *carmin*] —**car'mine** *adj.*

car•nage (KAHR nij) *n.* extensive and bloody slaughter, as in war; massacre. [< MF]

car•nal (KAHR nl) *adj.* **1.** relating to bodily appetites; sensual. **2.** sexual. **3.** not spiritual; worldly. [ME]

car•ni•val (KAHR nə vəl) *n.* **1.** a traveling amusement show, usu. presented outdoors. **2.** any merry festival. **3.** a period of festivity immediately preceding Lent. [< Ital. *carnevale*]

car•ni•vore (KAHR nə VOR) *n.* a flesh-eating mammal, as a cat, dog, etc. < L *carnivorus*, carnivorous]

car•niv•o•rous (kahr NIV ər əs) *adj.* **1.** eating or living on flesh. **2.** of or pertaining to carnivores.

car•ol (KAR əl) *n.* a song of joy or praise; esp., a Christmas song. [ME *carole* song] —*v.t. & v.i.* **•oled, •ol•ing** —**car'ol•er** *n.*

car•om (KAR əm) *n.* **1.** in billiards, a shot in which the cue ball strikes against two other balls in succession. **2.** any impact followed by a rebound. [< F] —**car'om** *v.t. & v.i.*

ca•rou•sal (kə ROW zəl) *n.* **1.** a revel. **2.** boisterous merrymaking.

ca•rouse (kə ROWZ) *v.i.* **•roused,**

•rous•ing drink freely and boisterously. —*n.* a carousal. [< G *gar aus (trinken)* drink fully] —**ca•rous'er** *n.*

car•ou•sel (KAR ə SEL) *n.* **1.** a merry-go-round (def. 1). **2.** a continuously moving belt for boxes, suitcases, etc. [< F, a type of tournament]

carp¹ (kahrp) *v.i.* find-fault unreasonably. [ME *carpen* speak] —**carp'•ing** *n. & adj.*

carp² *n. pl.* **carp** or **carps 1.** a freshwater food fish of Europe and America. **2.** any of various related fishes, as goldfish. [ME *carpe*]

car•pal (KAHR pəl) *adj. Anat.* of, pertaining to, or near the wrist. [< NL *carpalis*]

car•pe di•em (KAHR pe DEE əm) *Latin* enjoy the present; lit., seize the day.

car•pen•ter (KAHR pən tər) *n.* a person who builds and repairs wooden structures, as houses, ships, etc. [ME] —**car'pen•try** *n.*

car•pet (KAHR pit) *n.* **1.** a heavy covering for floors; also, the fabric used for it. **2.** a surface or covering suggesting this. Also **car'pet•ing.** —**on the carpet** subjected to reproof or reprimand. [ME *carpete* cloth covering] —**car'pet** *v.t.*

car•pet•bag•ger (KAHR pit BAG ər) *n.* one of the Northern adventurers who sought advantages in the South after the Civil War.

car•pus (KAHR pəs) *n. pl.* **•pi** (-pī) *Anat.* the wrist, or the wrist bones collectively. [< NL]

car•rel (KAR əl) *n.* a small space, as among the stacks in a library, for solitary study.

car•riage (KAR ij) *n.* **1.** a wheeled, usu. horse-drawn vehicle for carrying persons. **2.** posture; bearing. **3.** a moving portion of a machine carrying another part. **4.** the act of carrying; transportation. [ME *cariage*]

car•ri•er (KAR ee ər) *n.* **1.** one who or that which carries. **2.** a person or company that carries persons or goods for hire. **3.** *Med.* a person who is immune to a disease but transmits it to others. [ME]

car•ri•on (KAR ee ən) *n.* dead and putrefying flesh. —*adj.* feeding on carrion. [ME *caroyne*]

car•rot (KAR ət) *n.* a long, reddish yellow root grown as a vegetable. —**car'rot•y** *adj.* [< MF *carotte*]

car•ry (KAR ee) *v.* **•ried, •ry•ing** *v.t.* **1.** bear from one place to another; transport; convey. **2.** serve as medium of conveyance for; transmit. **3.** have or bear upon or about one's person. **4.** bear the weight, burden, or responsibility of. **5.** be pregnant with. **6.** bear (the body or a part of it) in a specified manner. **7.** conduct or comport (oneself). **8.** take by force or effort; capture; win. **9.** gain victory or acceptance for; also, to achieve success in. **10.** extend; continue. **11.** have or keep for sale. **12.** transfer, as a number or figure, to another column. **13.** maintain on one's account books for a future settlement. **14.** sing (a part or melody). —*v.i.* **15.** act as bearer or carrier. **16.** gain victory or acceptance: *The motion carried.* —**carry away** move the feelings greatly; enchant. — **carry forward** in bookkeeping, transfer (an item etc.) to the next column or page. — **carry off 1.** cause to die. **2.** win, as a prize. **3.** succeed, as in a bluff. **4.** abduct. —**carry on 1.** keep up; continue. **2.** behave wildly or foolishly. **3.** engage in. —**carry out** accomplish; bring to completion. —**carry through** carry to completion or success. — *n. pl.* **•ries 1.** range, as of a gun; also, the distance covered by a projectile, golf ball, etc. **2.** a portage, as between streams. **3.** act of carrying. [ME *carien*]

car•ry•all (KAR ee AWL) *n.* a large bag, handbag, etc.

carrying charge in installment buying, the interest charged on the unpaid balance.

car•ry•o•ver (KAR ee OH vər) *n.* **1.** something left over or kept until later. **2.** in bookkeeping, a sum carried forward.

car•sick (KAHR SIK) *adj.* nauseated from riding in a car.

cart (kahrt) *n.* **1.** a two-wheeled vehicle, for carrying loads. **2.** a light, two-wheeled vehicle with springs, used for business or pleasure. —*v.t.* carry in or as in a cart. [ME *carte*]

carte blanche (KAHRT BLAHNCH) **1.** a signed paper granting its possessor the freedom to write his or her own conditions. **2.** unrestricted authority. [< F, lit., white card]

car•tel (kahr TEL) *n.* a syndicate that exercises, or seeks to exercise, monopolistic control over a particular market. [< MF]

car•ti•lage (KAHR tl ij) *n. Zool.* **1.** a tough, elastic form of connective tissue in man and animals; gristle. **2.** a part consisting of cartilage. [ME] —**car'ti•lag'i•nous** *adj.*

car•tog•ra•phy (kahr TOG rə fee) *n.* the art of making maps or charts. —**car•tog'ra•pher** *n.*

car•ton (KAHR tn) *n.* **1.** a cardboard box. **2.** a paper or plastic container. [< F]

car•toon (kahr TOON) *n.* **1.** a humorous or satirical drawing or caricature. **2.** a comic strip. **3.** a motion-picture film (**animated cartoon**) made from a series of drawings. —*v.t. & v.i.* make a caricature or cartoon of (a subject). [< Ital. *cartone* pasteboard]

car•tridge (KAHR trij) *n.* **1.** a casing of metal, pasteboard, or the like, containing a charge of powder for a firearm and, usu., the projectile or shot and the primer. **2.** any small container or case. [< MF *cartouche* cartridge]

carve (kahrv) *v.t. & v.i.* **carved, carv•ing 1.** make (a design, figure, etc.) by cutting, or as if by cutting. **2.** cut up (cooked meat). [ME *kerven*]

carv•ing (KAHR ving) *n.* **1.** the act of one who carves. **2.** carved work; a carved figure or design.

cas•cade (kas KAYD) *n.* **1.** a fall of water over steep rocks, or one of a series of such falls. **2.** anything resembling a waterfall. — *v.i.* **•cad•ed, •cad•ing** fall in the form of a waterfall. [< F]

case¹ (kays) *n.* **1.** a particular instance or occurrence: *a case of mistaken identity.* **2.** the actual circumstance or state of affairs: *Such is not the case.* **3.** an instance of disease or injury; also, a patient. **4.** a set of arguments, reasons, etc.: *the case for capital punishment.* **5.** a question or problem. **6.** *Law* **a** an action or suit at law. **b** the set of facts offered in support of a claim. **7.** *Gram.* the syntactical relationship of a noun, pronoun, or adjective to other words in a sentence. —**in any case** no matter what; regardless. —**in case** in the event that; if. —*v.t.* **cased, cas•ing** *Slang* look over carefully, esp. with intent to rob. [ME *cas* event]

case² *n.* **1.** a box etc. for containing something. **2.** a box and its contents. **3.** a set or pair. **4.** an outer or protective part, as of a watch. —*v.t.* **cased, cas•ing** put into or cover with a case. [ME *cas* box]

case history a record of a case or cases for use in medical, sociological, or similar studies. Also **case study.**

case law law based on judicial decisions: distinguished from *common law* or *statute law.*

case•ment (KAYS mənt) *n.* **1.** the sash of a window that opens on hinges at the side, or a window having such sashes. **2.** a case; covering. [ME]

case•work (KAYS wurk) *n.* the investigative

and counseling tasks of a social worker or the like. **—case'work'er** n.

cash (kash) n. **1.** money in hand or readily available. **2.** currency; bills and coins. —v.t. convert into ready money, as a check. — **cash in** in gambling, turn in one's chips and receive cash. —**cash in on** profit from or turn to advantage.

cash•ew (KASH oo) n. **1.** a tropical American tree that yields a gum. **2.** its small, edible fruit: also **cashew nut.** [< Pg. *cajú*]

cash•ier¹ (ka SHEER) n. **1.** one employed to collect cash payments. **2.** a bank officer responsible for the bank's assets. [< MF *caissier* guard of a money box]

cash•ier² v.t. dismiss in disgrace, as a military officer. [< MDu. *kasseren* annul]

cash•mere (KAZH meer) n. **1.** a fine wool obtained from goats of India and Tibet. **2.** a soft fabric made from this. [after *Kashmir*, India]

cas•ing (KAY sing) n. **1.** a protective case or covering. **2.** a framework, as about a door.

ca•si•no (ka SEE noh) n. pl. **•nos 1.** a place for dancing, gambling, etc. **2.** a card game for two to four players; also *cassino*. [< Ital., small house]

cask (kask) n. **1.** a barrel-shaped wooden vessel, bound with hoops. **2.** the quantity a cask will hold. [ME]

cas•ket (KAS kit) n. a coffin. [ME]

Cas•san•dra (ka SAN dra) n. one whose predictions of disaster are disregarded. [after *Cassandra*, of Greek mythology, whose prophecies were fated to be true but not believed]

cas•sa•va (ka SAH va) n. **1.** a tropical American shrub or herb, cultivated for the edible roots. **2.** a starch made from these roots, the source of tapioca. [< Sp. *cazabe*]

cas•se•role (KAS ə ROHL) n. **1.** a dish in which food is baked and served. **2.** any food so prepared and served. [< F, type of pan]

cas•sette (ka SET) n. a container of photographic film or magnetic tape wound on internal spools. Also **cas•ette'.** [< F, lit., small box]

cas•si•no (ka SEE noh) see CASINO.

cas•sock (KAS ək) n. *Eccl.* a close-fitting vestment, usu. black, reaching to the feet, and worn by clergymen. [< MF *casaque*]

cast (kast) v. **cast, cast•ing** v.t. **1.** fling. **2.** cause to fall upon or over or in a particular direction: *cast* a shadow. **3.** direct, as a glance of the eyes. **4.** let down; drop: *cast* anchor. **5.** throw off; lose; also, shed; molt.

6. throw aside; reject or dismiss. **7.** deposit; give: She *cast* her vote. **8.** throw, as dice. **9.** in the theater, movies, etc., assign the parts of or a part in a play to (an actor). **10.** compute astrologically: *cast* a horoscope. **11.** arrange by some system. **12.** *Metall.* shape in a mold. —v.i. **13.** make a throw, as with a fishing line etc. **14.** make arithmetical calculations; add. **15.** *Metall.* take shape in a mold. —**cast about** consider ways and means; scheme. —**cast away 1.** discard. **2.** shipwreck or maroon. —**cast off 1.** reject or discard. **2.** let go, as a ship from a dock. —n. **1.** the act of casting or throwing; a throw. **2.** the distance to which a thing may be thrown. **3.** *Surg.* a rigid dressing or bandage to prevent movement of fractured bones. **4.** the performers in a play, movie, etc. **5.** the act of casting or founding. **6.** an impression made of anything; a mold. **7.** a tinge; shade. **8.** a twist to one side; squint. [ME *casten* throw]

cas•ta•nets (KAS tə NETS) n.pl. two small concave disks of wood or plastic, clapped together with the fingers, as a rhythmical accompaniment to song or dance. [< Sp. *castaña* chestnut]

cast•a•way (KAST ə WAY) adj. **1.** adrift; shipwrecked. **2.** thrown away. —n. one who is shipwrecked.

caste (kast) n. **1.** in India, one of the hereditary social classes into which Hindus were traditionally divided. **2.** any rigid social class. [< Pg. *casta* race]

cast•er (KAS tər) n. **1.** one who or that which casts. **2.** one of a set of small, swiveling wheels or rollers, fastened under furniture, luggage, etc. to facilitate moving. **3.** a cruet for condiments; also, a stand for such cruets. Also (for **2** and **3**) *castor.*

cas•ti•gate (KAS ti GAYT) v.t. **•gat•ed, •gat•ing** rebuke or chastise severly; criticize. [< L *castigatus* purified] —**cas'ti•ga'tion** n.

cast•ing (KAS ting) n. **1.** the act of one who or that which casts. **2.** that which is cast or formed in a mold.

cas•tle (KAS əl) n. **1.** in feudal times, the fortified dwelling of a prince or noble. **2.** any large, imposing house. **3.** in chess, a rook. —v.t. & v.i. **•tled, •tling** in chess, move a rook to the square passed over by the king. [ME]

cast•off (KAST awf) adj. laid aside; rejected. —n. one who or that which is no longer wanted or used.

cas·tor[1] (KAS tər) *n.* **1.** an oily, odorous secretion of beavers, used in medicine and perfumery. **2.** a hat of beaver or other fur. [ME, beaver]

cas·tor[2] see CASTER (defs. 2 and 3).

castor bean the seed of the castor-oil plant.

castor oil a viscid oil extracted from castor beans and used as a cathartic and lubricant.

cas·tor-oil plant (KAS tər OIL) a plant native to India, yielding the castor bean.

cas·trate (KAS trayt) *v.t.* **·trat·ed, ·trat·ing 1.** remove the testicles from; emasculate; geld. **2.** remove the ovaries from; spay. [< L *castratratus* gelded] —**cas·tra′tion** *n.*

cas·u·al (KAZH oo əl) *adj.* **1.** accidental. **2.** without intention or plan; offhand: a *casual* question. **3.** negligent; nonchalant: a *casual* manner. **4.** designed for informal wear: *casual* clothes. [ME *casualte*]

cas·u·al·ty (KAZH oo əl tee) *n. pl.* **·ties 1.** one who or that which is destroyed, injured, or otherwise made ineffective by an accident. **2.** *Mil.* a soldier who is killed, wounded, captured, or otherwise lost through combat action. **3.** an accident, esp. a fatal or serious one. [ME *casualte*]

cas·u·ist·ry (KAZH oo ə stree) *n. pl.* **·ries 1.** a method of dealing with ambiguous cases of conscience or questions of right and wrong. **2.** deceptive or ambiguous reasoning, esp. in cases of conscience. —**cas′oo·ist** *n.* —**cas′u·is′tic** *adj.*

ca·sus bel·li (KAY səs BEL ī) *Latin* an event or action taken to justify a war. [< NL, occasion of war]

cat (kat) *n.* **1.** a domesticated carnivorous mammal having retractile claws. **2.** any other animal of the cat family, as a lion, tiger, lynx, etc. ◆ Collateral adjective: *feline.* **3.** a gossiping or backbiting woman. — **let the cat out of the bag** divulge a secret. —*v.t.* **cat·ted, cat·ting** strike with a cat-o′-nine-tails; flog. [ME]

ca·tab·o·lism (kə TAB ə LIZ əm) *n. Biol.* the process by which living tissue breaks down into simpler and more stable substances; destructive metabolism: opposed to *anabolism.* [< Gk. *katabolé* throwing down] —**cat·a·bol·ic** (KAT ə BOL ik) *adj.*

cat·a·clysm (KAT ə KLIZ əm) *n.* **1.** any violent upheaval or change, as a war, revolution, etc. **2.** a deluge. [< LL *cataclysmos* flood] —**cat′a·clys′mic** *adj.*

cat·a·comb (KAT ə KOHM) *n. Usu. pl.* an underground place of burial, consisting of passages, small rooms, and recesses for tombs. [ME *catacombe*]

cat·a·falque (KAT ə FAWK) *n.* a structure supporting a coffin during a funeral. [< F]

cat·a·log (KAT l AWG) *n.* **1.** a list or enumeration of names, objects, etc., usu. in alphabetical order. **2.** a publication containing such a list, as of articles for sale. —*v.t. & v.i.* **·loged, ·log·ing** make a catalog (of); enter (items) in a catalog. Also **cat′a·logue.** [ME *cataloge* enumeration]

ca·tal·y·sis (kə TAL ə sis) *n. pl.* **·ses** (-SEEZ) *Chem.* an increase in the rate of a chemical reaction, caused by addition of a substance that remains unchanged. [< NL, dissolution] —**cat·a·lyt·ic** (KAT l IT ik) *adj. & n.*

cat·a·lyst (KAT l ist) *n.* **1.** *Chem.* any substance that causes catalysis. **2.** one who or that which acts as a stimulus causing something to happen. —**cat·a·lyze** (KAT l IZ) *v.t.* **·lyzed, ·lyz·ing**

cat·a·ma·ran (KAT ə mə RAN) *n. Naut.* **1.** a long, narrow raft of logs, often with an outrigger. **2.** a boat having twin hulls. [< Tamil *kattamaram* tied wood]

cat·a·pult (KAT ə PULT) *n.* **1.** an ancient military device for throwing stones, arrows, etc. **2.** *Aeron.* a device for launching an airplane at flight speed, as from the deck of a ship. —*v.t.* **1.** hurl from or as from a catapult. —*v.i.* **2.** hurtle through the air. [< L *catapulta*]

cat·a·ract (KAT ə RAKT) *n.* **1.** a waterfall. **2.** a downpour. **3.** *Pathol.* opacity of the lens of the eye, causing partial or total blindness. [ME *cataracte* waterfall]

ca·tas·tro·phe (kə TAS trə fee) *n.* a great and sudden disaster; calamity. [< Gk. *katastrophé* overturning] —**cat·a·stroph·ic** (KAT ə STROF ik) *adj.*

cat·call (KAT KAWL) *n.* a shrill, discordant call or whistle expressing impatience or derision. —*v.t. & v.i.* deride or show contempt for (a person, performance, etc.) with catcalls.

catch (kach) *v.* **caught, catch·ing** *v.t.* **1.** take or seize, and hold; grasp; grip. **2.** trap; capture; ensnare. **3.** surprise in the act. **4.** stop the motion of and grasp; grab in mid-flight. **5.** grip; entangle. **6.** gather and retain: *catch* rain water in a barrel. **7.** overtake. **8.** reach in time: *catch* a train. **9.** strike. **10.** become affected with: *catch* cold. **11.** take; get: *catch* fire. **12.** apprehend or perceive; also, reproduce accurately: The artist has not *caught* her expression. **13.** see (a film, television program, etc.). —*v.i.* **14.** make a movement of grasping or seizing. **15.** in baseball, act as catcher. **16.** become entangled or fastened. **17.** be communicated or communicable, as a disease. **18.** take fire; ignite. —**catch on 1.** understand. **2.** become popular or fashionable. —**catch up 1.** regain lost ground. **2.** absorb: *caught up* in one's work. —**catch up with** (or **up to**) overtake. —*n.* **1.** the act of catching; a grasping and holding. **2.** that which catches; a fastening. **3.** that which is caught. **4.** an artful or hidden condition; trick: What's the *catch?* **5.** a scrap or fragment: *catches* of song. **6.** a stoppage; break, as in the voice. —*adj.* **1.** attracting or meant to attract attention: a *catch* phrase. **2.** tricky. [ME *cacchen* chase]

catch·all (KACH awl) *n.* **1.** a bag or the like to hold odds and ends. **2.** anything that covers a wide range of situations etc.

catch·er (KACH ər) *n.* **1.** one who or that which catches. **2.** in baseball, the player stationed behind home plate.

catch·ing (KACH ing) *adj.* **1.** infectious. **2.** attractive; catchy.

catch·word (KACH wurd) *n.* **1.** a word or phrase taken up and often repeated, esp. as a political slogan. Also *catch phrase.* **2.** a word at the head of a page or column, identifying the first or last item on the page. Also *headword.*

catch·y (KACH ee) *adj.* **catch·i·er, catch·i·est 1.** attractive; also, easily remembered: *catchy* tunes. **2.** deceptive; tricky. —**catch′i·ness** *n.*

cat·e·chism (KAT ə KIZ əm) *n.* **1.** a short manual giving, in the form of questions and answers, an outline of the principles of a religious creed. **2.** any similar instructional manual. [< LL *catechismus* instruction]

cat·e·gor·i·cal (KAT i GOR i kəl) *adj.* **1.** without qualification; absolute; unequivocal. **2.** of, pertaining to, or included in a category. —**cat′e·gor′i·cal·ly** *adv.*

cat·e·go·rize (KAT ə gə RIZ) *v.t.* **·rized, ·riz·ing** put into a category; classify.

cat·e·go·ry (KAT ə GOR ee) *n. pl.* **·ries** a division in any system of classification; a class. [< LL *categoria* predication]

ca·ter (KAY tər) *v.i.* **1.** furnish food or entertainment. **2.** provide for the gratification of any need or taste. —*v.t.* **3.** furnish food for: *cater* a party. [ME *catour* buyer of provisions] —**ca′ter·er** *n.*

cat·er·cor·nered (KAT i KOR nərd) *adj.* diagonal. —*adv.* diagonally. Also *catty-cornered.* [< L *quattuor* four + CORNERED]

cat·er·pil·lar (KAT ə PIL ər) *n.* the larva of a butterfly or moth, or of certain other insects, resembling a worm. —*adj.* moving or fitted with treads mounted on endless belts. [ME *catyrpel,* lit., hairy cat]

cat·er·waul (KAT ər WAWL) *v.i.* **1.** utter the discordant cry of cats at mating time. **2.** make any discordant screeching. [ME *caterwawen*] —**cat′er·waul** *n.*

cat·fish (KAT FISH) *n. pl.* **·fish** or **·fish·es** any of numerous scaleless fishes having whiskerlike feelers around the mouth.

cat·gut (KAT GUT) *n.* a tough cord made usu. from the intestines of sheep.

ca·thar·sis (kə THAR sis) *n. pl.* **·ses** (-seez) **1.** *Med.* purgation, esp. of the alimentary canal. **2.** a purifying or purging of the emotions. [< NL, purification]

ca·thar·tic (kə THAR tik) *adj.* purgative; purifying. —*n.* a laxative. [< LL *catharticus* fit for cleaning]

ca·the·dral (kə THEE drəl) *n.* **1.** the church containing the throne of a bishop. **2.** loosely, any large or important church. [ME]

cath·e·ter (KATH i tər) *n. Med.* a slender, flexible tube, esp. one to draw urine from the bladder. [< LL] —**cath′e·ter·ize′** *v.t.* **·ized, ·iz·ing**

cath·ode (KATH ohd) *n. Electr.* the negatively charged electrode that receives cations during electrolysis. [< Gk. *káthodos* way down]

cathode rays *Physics* a stream of electrons emitted by a cathode.

cathode-ray tube *Electr.* an electron tube in which a beam of electrons is focused and then deflected onto a sensitized screen, forming an image, as in a television receiver.

cath·o·lic (KATH ə lik) *adj.* **1.** broadminded, as in belief or tastes; liberal; comprehensive; large. **2.** universal in reach; general. [ME] —**cath·o·lic·i·ty** (KATH ə LIS i tee) *n.*

Cath·o·lic (KATH ə lik) *adj.* since the Reformation: **a** of or pertaining to the Roman Catholic Church. **b** designating those churches that claim to have the apostolic doctrine and sacraments of the ancient, undivided church, and including the Anglican, Old Catholic, Orthodox, and Roman

Catholic churches. —n. a member of any Catholic church.

Ca·thol·i·cism (kə THOL i SIZ əm) n. the doctrine, system, and practice of a Catholic church, esp. the Roman Catholic Church.

cat·i·on (KAT I ən) n. Chem. a positive ion: opposed to anion. [< Gk. katión going]

cat·kin (KAT kin) n. Bot. a spike of flowers, as in the willow. [< Du. katteken small cat]

cat·nap (KAT NAP) n. a short, light sleep — v.i. •napped, •nap·ping

cat·nip (KAT nip) n. an aromatic herb of the mint family, of which cats are fond.

cat-o'-nine-tails (KAT ə NĪN TAYLZ) n. a whip with nine knotted lines fastened to a handle.

cat's-paw (KATS paw) n. a person used as a tool or dupe.

cat·tail (KAT TAYL) n. a marsh plant having flowers in cylindrical terminal spikes.

cat·tle (KAT l) n. domesticated bovine animals, as cows, bulls, and steers. [ME catel property]

cat·ty (KAT ee) adj. •ti·er, •ti·est 1. like or pertaining to cats. 2. slyly malicious; spiteful. —cat'ti·ness n.

cat·ty-cor·nered (KAT ee KOR nərd) adj. cater-cornered.

Cau·ca·sian (kaw KAY ZHən) adj. of or belonging to a major ethnic division of the human species loosely called the white race. —n. a member of this division of the human race..

cau·cus (KAW kəs) n. a meeting of members of a political party. —v.i. cau·cused, cau·cus·ing meet in or hold a caucus.

caught (kawt) past tense, past participle of CATCH.

caul (kawl) n. a membrane that sometimes envelops the head of a child at birth. [ME calle cap]

caul·dron (KAWL drən) n. a large kettle: also spelled caldron. [ME]

cau·li·flow·er (KAW lə FLOW ər) n. 1. the fleshy, edible head of a variety of cabbage. 2. the plant bearing this.

cauliflower ear an ear deformed by blows.

caulk (kawk) v.t. make tight, as a boat's seams etc., by plugging with soft material, such as oakum. Also spelled calk. [< L calcare tread] —caulk'ing n.

cau·sal (KAW zəl) adj. pertaining to or involving a cause. [< L causalis] —caus'al·ly adv.

cau·sal·i·ty (kaw ZAL i tee) n. pl. •ties 1. the relation of cause and effect. 2. causal character or agency.

cau·sa·tion (kaw ZAY shən) n. 1. the act of causing. 2. that which produces an effect; cause. 3. the relation of cause and effect.

cause (kawz) n. 1. the agent or force producing an effect or a result. 2. sufficient ground; good reason. 3. an aim, object, or principle. 4. a matter under discussion or in dispute. —v.t. caused, caus·ing be the cause of; produce; effect. [ME]

cause cé·lè·bre (KAWZ sə LEB rə) French a famous legal case or well-known controversy.

caus·tic (KAW stik) adj. 1. corrosive; burning, as acid or lye. 2. sarcastic; biting. —n. a caustic substance. [ME, burning]

cau·ter·ize (KAW tə RĪZ) v.t. •ized, •iz·ing sear with a caustic agent or heated iron. — cau'ter·i·za'tion n.

cau·tion (KAW shən) n. 1. care to avoid injury or misfortune; prudence; wariness; discretion. 2. an admonition or warning. 3. Informal one who or that which alarms, astonishes, etc. —v.t. advise to be prudent; warn. [ME caucion] —cau·tion·ary (KAW shə NER ee) adj. urging caution.

cau·tious (KAW shəs) adj. using great care or prudence; wary.

cav·al·cade (KAV əl KAYD) n. 1. a company of horsemen on the march or in procession. 2. a procession; parade. [< MF]

cav·a·lier (KAV ə LEER) n. 1. a horseman; knight. 2. a courtly gentleman. —adj. 1. haughty; supercilious. 2. free and easy; offhand. [< MF, horseman]

cav·al·ry (KAV əl ree) n. pl. •ries troops trained to fight on horseback or, more recently, in armored motor vehicles.

cave (kayv) n. a chamber beneath the earth, in a mountainside, etc. —cave in 1. fall in or down, as when undermined; cause to fall in. 2. Informal give in; surrender. [ME]

ca·ve·at (KAV ee AT) n. a caution or warning. [< L, let him beware]

cave-in (KAYV in) n. a collapse or falling in, as of a mine.

cav·ern (KAV ərn) n. a cave, esp. one that is large or extensive. [ME caverne] —cav'er·nous adj.

cav·i·ar (KAV ee AHR) n. the salted roe of sturgeon or other fish.

cav·il (KAV əl) v.i. •iled, •il·ing raise trivial objections; carp: with at or about. [< L cavillari jeer] —cav'il n. —cav'il·er n.

cav·i·ty (KAV i tee) n. pl. •ties 1. a hollow or

sunken space; hole. **2.** a natural hollow in the body. **3.** a decayed place in a tooth. [< MF *cavite* hollowness]

ca•vort (kə VORT) *v.i.* prance about.

cay (kay) *n.* a coastal reef or sandy islet; key. [< Sp. *cayo* shoal]

cease (sees) *v.* **ceased, ceas•ing** *v.t.* **1.** leave off or discontinue, as one's own actions. — *v.i.* **2.** come to an end; stop; desist. [ME *cessen*] —**cease′less** *adj.*

cease-fire (SEES FĪR) *n.* an armistice; truce.

cede (seed) *v.t.* **ced•ed, ced•ing 1.** yield or give up. **2.** surrender title to; transfer: *cede land.* [< L *cedere* yield]

ce•dil•la (si DIL ə) *n.* a mark put under the letter *c* (ç) in some French words to indicate that it is to be sounded as (s). [< Sp.]

ceil•ing (SEE ling) *n.* **1.** the overhead covering or lining of a room. **2.** an upper limit; maximum. [ME]

cel•e•brate (SEL ə BRAYT) *v.* **•brat•ed, •brat•ing** *v.t.* **1.** observe, as a festival, with rejoicing. **2.** make known or famous; extol. **3.** perform (a ceremony) publicly and as ordained. —*v.i.* **4.** observe or commemorate a day or event. [ME] —**cel′e•brant** (SEL ə brənt) *n.* —**cel•e•bra•to•ry** (SEL ə brə TOR ee) *adj.*

ce•leb•ri•ty (sə LEB ri tee) *n. pl.* **•ties 1.** a famous or celebrated person. **2.** fame or renown. [ME]

ce•ler•i•ty (sə LER i tee) *n.* speed; rapidity. [< MF *celerite*]

ce•les•tial (sə LES həl) *adj.* **1.** of or pertaining to the sky or heavens. **2.** of heaven; divine. [ME]

cel•i•ba•cy (SEL ə bə see) *n.* the state of being unmarried or maintaining chastity, esp. as a religious vow. [< L *caelebs* unmarried]

cel•i•bate (SEL ə bit) *n.* one who remains unmarried or chaste, esp. by vow. —**cel′ i•bate** *adj.*

cell (sel) *n.* **1.** a small room, as for a prisoner or monk. **2.** a small compartment, receptacle, or cavity. **3.** a body of persons forming a single unit in an organization of similar groups. **4.** *Biol.* the fundamental structural unit of plant and animal life. **5.** *Electr.* the unit composing all or part of a battery, consisting of electrodes in contact with an electrolyte and in which a current is generated. [< L *cella* cell, small room]

cel•lar (SEL ər) *n.* **1.** a space wholly or partly underground and usu. beneath a building, used for storage, etc. **2.** a wine cellar; also, a stock of wines. —*v.t.* put or keep in a cellar. [ME *celle* monastery cell]

cell•block (SEL BLOK) *n.* in prisons, a unit of cells.

cel•lo (CHEL oh) *n. pl.* **•los** a bass instrument of the violin family: also called *violoncello.* [Short for VIOLONCELLO] —**cel′list** *n.*

cel•lu•lar (SEL yə lər) *adj.* **1.** of or like a cell or cells. **2.** consisting of cells: *cellular* telephone.

Cel•si•us scale (SEL see əs) a temperature scale in which the freezing point of water at normal atmospheric pressure is 0° and the boiling point is 100°; the centigrade scale. [after Anders *Celsius,* 1701–44, Swedish astronomer]

Celt (kelt) *n.* a person of Celtic linguistic stock, esp. the Irish, Welsh, and Bretons. — **Celt′ic** *adj.*

ce•ment (si MENT) *n.* **1.** a mixture, usu. of burned limestone and clay, which hardens when dried and is used as an ingredient of mortar and concrete. **2.** any material, as glue, that will bind objects together. **3.** something that unites. **4.** an adhesive material used in dental work. —*v.t.* **1.** unite or join with or as with cement. **2.** cover or coat with cement. —*v.i.* **3.** become united by means of cement; cohere. [ME *cyment*]

cem•e•ter•y (SEM i TER ee) *n. pl.* **•ter•ies** a place for burying the dead; graveyard. [ME]

cen•o•taph (SEN ə TAF) *n.* a monument erected to the dead but not containing the remains. [< L *cenotaphium* empty tomb]

cen•ser (SEN sər) *n.* a vessel for burning incense. [ME]

cen•sor (SEN sər) *n.* **1.** an official examiner of manuscripts, plays, movies, etc. empowered to suppress them, wholly or in part, if objectionable. **2.** an official who examines dispatches, letters, etc. in time of war. **3.** anyone who censures. —*v.t.* act as censor of. [< L, judge] —**cen•so•ri•al** (sen SOR ee əl), **cen•so•ri•ous** (sen SOR ee əs) *adj.* given to censure; faultfinding.

cen•sor•ship (SEN sər SHIP) *n.* the action or system of censoring.

cen•sure (SEN shər) *n.* the expression of disapproval or blame; reprimand. —*v.t.* **•sured, •sur•ing** express disapproval of; condemn. [ME] —**cen′sur•a•ble** *adj.*

cen•sus (SEN səs) *n. pl.* **•sus•es** an official count of a population, with statistics as to age, sex, employment, etc. [< L, assessment]

cent (sent) *n.* **1.** the hundredth part of a standard monetary unit, as the dollar; also, a coin of this value: symbol ¢. **2.** a hundred: used only in *percent.* [ME]

cen·taur (SEN tor) *n.* in Greek mythology, one of a race of monsters, half man and half horse. [ME]

cen·te·nar·y (sen TEN ə ree) *n. pl.* **·nar·ies 1.** a period of 100 years. **2.** a centennial. [< L *centenarius* hundred]

cen·ten·ni·al (sen TEN ee əl) *adj.* **1.** of or marking a period of 100 years or its completion. **2.** occurring every 100 years. —*n.* a 100th anniversary or its celebration.

cen·ter (SEN tər) *n.* **1.** the point equally distant from the extremities or sides of anything. **2.** a point about which a thing revolves. **3.** a place or point at which activity is concentrated. **4.** a point from which proceed effects, influences, etc. **5.** a group, party, etc. having moderate views or tendencies. **6.** in football, basketball, etc., a player who occupies a middle position. —*v.t.* **1.** place in or at the center. **2.** direct toward one place; concentrate. **3.** determine the center of. —*v.i.* **4.** be at the center of. —*adj.* central; middle. [ME *centre* point]

cen·ter·fold (SEN tər FOHLD) *n.* a large, usu. folded illustration, esp. of a nude, bound into the center of a magazine.

center of gravity *Physics* the point about which a body acted upon by gravity is in equilibrium in all positions.

cen·ter·piece (SEN tər PEES) *n.* a piece at the center of anything; esp., a table ornament.

cen·ti·grade (SEN ti GRAYD) *adj.* graduated to a scale of a hundred. [< F]

centigrade scale the Celsius scale.

cen·ti·me·ter (SEN tə MEE tər) *n.* the hundredth part of a meter, equal to .3937 inch.

cen·ti·pede (SEN tə PEED) *n.* a wormlike animal having many pairs of legs. [< L *centipeda*]

cen·tral (SEN trəl) *adj.* **1.** at, in, or near the center. **2.** of or constituting the center. **3.** exercising a controlling influence; dominant. **4.** most important; principal; chief. [< L *centralis*] —**cen·tral·i·ty** (sen TRAL i tee) *n.*

cen·tral·ize (SEN trə LIZ) *v.* **·ized, ·iz·ing** *v.t.* **1.** bring to a central place or under a

central authority. —*v.i.* **2.** come to a center; concentrate. —**cen'tral·i·za'tion** *n.*

central nervous system *Anat.* that part of the nervous system consisting of the brain and spinal cord.

cen·trif·u·gal (sen TRIF yə gəl) *adj.* **1.** directed or tending away from a center; radiating. **2.** employing centrifugal force: a *centrifugal* pump. —*n.* a centrifuge. [< NL *centrifugalis* center-fleeing]

centrifugal force *Physics* the force impelling a body to move outward from the center of rotation.

cen·tri·fuge (SEN trə FYOOJ) *n.* a machine using centrifugal force to separate substances of different densities. —*v.t.* **·fuged, ·fug·ing** subject to the action of a centrifuge. [< F]

cen·trip·e·tal (sen TRIP i tl) *adj.* **1.** directed, tending, or drawing toward a center. **2.** acting by drawing toward a center. [< NL *centripetus* center-seeking]

centripetal force *Physics* a force attracting a body toward the center of rotation.

cen·trist (SEN trist) *n.* one who takes a moderate position in politics.

cen·tu·ri·on (sen TUUR ee ən) *n.* in the Roman army, a captain of a group of 100 soldiers. [ME]

cen·tu·ry (SEN chə ree) *n. pl.* **·ries** a period of 100 years in any system of chronology, esp. in reckoning from the first year of the Christian era. [< L *centuria* a group made up of a hundred parts]

ce·phal·ic (sə FAL ik) *adj.* **1.** of or pertaining to the head. **2.** at, on, in, or near the head. [< L *cephalicus* of the head]

cephalic index *Anat.* the ratio of the width of the human head, multiplied by 100, to the greatest length.

ce·ram·ics (sə RAM iks) *n.* **1.** *(construed as sing.)* **1.** the art of modeling and baking in clay. **2.** *(construed as pl.)* objects made of fired and baked clay. [< Gk. *kéramos* potter's clay] —**ce·ram'ic** *adj.* —**ce·ram'ist** *n.*

ce·re·al (SEER ee əl) *n.* **1.** an edible, starchy grain, as rice, wheat, rye, oats, etc. **2.** any grain-bearing plant. **3.** a breakfast food made from such a grain. [< L *Cerealis*, of Ceres, pre-Roman goddess of agriculture]

cer·e·bel·lum (SER ə BEL əm) *n. pl.* **·bel·lums** or **·bel·la** (-BEL ə) *Anat.* that part of the brain serving as the coordination center of voluntary movements and equilibrium. [< L, brain]

ce·re·bral (sə REE brəl) *adj.* **1.** of or pertaining to the cerebrum or the brain. **2.** appealing to or involving the intellect; intellectual. [< NL *cerebralis*]

cerebral palsy *Pathol.* any paralysis affecting the ability to control movement and caused by brain damage before or at birth.

cer·e·brate (SER ə BRAYT) *v.i.* **·brat·ed, ·brat·ing** think. —**cer'e·bra'tion** *n.*

ce·re·brum (sə REE brəm) *n. pl.* **·brums** or **·bra** (-brə) *Anat.* the upper anterior part of the brain, constituting the seat of conscious processes. [< L]

cere·ments (SEER mənts) *n.pl.* a shroud; graveclothes.

cer·e·mo·ni·al (SER ə MOH nee əl) *adj.* of, pertaining to, or characterized by ceremony. —*n.* **1.** a prescribed set of ceremonies for some particular occasion; ritual. **2.** a rite; ceremony.

cer·e·mo·ni·ous (SER ə MOH nee əs) *adj.* **1.** studiously or overly polite. **2.** characterized by ceremony; formal.

cer·e·mo·ny (SER ə MOH nee) *n. pl.* **·nies 1.** a formal act or ritual, or a series of them, performed in a prescribed manner. **2.** formal observances collectively; ritual. **3.** an empty ritual. **4.** adherence to ritual forms; formality. **5.** an act of formal courtesy. —**stand on** (or **upon**) **ceremony** insist upon formalities. [ME *cerimonie* sacred rite]

ce·rise (sə REES) *n. & adj.* moderate to deep red. [< F, cherry]

cer·tain (SUR tn) *adj.* **1.** absolutely confident. **2.** fated; destined. **3.** beyond doubt; indisputable. **4.** dependable; also, unerring. **5.** fixed; determined. **6.** not explicitly stated or identified: *certain* persons. **7.** some: a *certain* improvement. —*n.* an indefinite number or quantity. [ME]

cer·tain·ly (SUR tn lee) *adv.* without doubt; surely.

cer·tain·ty (SUR tn tee) *n. pl.* **·ties 1.** the state, quality, or fact of being certain. **2.** a known fact.

cer·tif·i·cate (sər TIF i kit) *n.* an official or sworn document stating something to be a fact. —*v.t.* (sər TIF i KAYT) **·cat·ed, ·cat·ing** furnish with or attest by a certificate. [ME *certificat* made certain]

cer·ti·fi·ca·tion (SUR tə fi KAY shən) *n.* **1.** the act of certifying or guaranteeing. **2.** the state of being certified. **3.** a certificate.

cer·ti·fied (SUR tə FID) *adj.* **1.** vouched for in writing; endorsed. **2.** affirmed or guaran-

teed by a certificate. **3.** legally declared insane; committed to a mental institution.

certified check a check issued by a bank that certifies it to be good.

cer·ti·fy (SUR tə FI) *v.* **·fied, ·fy·ing** *v.t.* **1.** give certain information of; attest. **2.** testify to in writing; vouch for. **3.** endorse as meeting set standards or requirements. **4.** guarantee in writing on the face of (a check) that it is good. **5.** commit to a mental institution. —*v.i.* **6.** make attestation; vouch (*for*) or testify (*to*). [ME *certifien* make certain] —**cer'ti·fi'a·ble** *adj.*

cer·ti·tude (SUR tə TOOD) *n.* complete confidence.

ce·ru·le·an (sə ROO lee ən) *adj. & n.* sky blue; vivid blue. [< L *caeruleus* dark blue]

ce·ru·men (si ROO mən) *n.* earwax. [< NL]

cer·vix (SUR viks) *n. pl.* **cer·vix·es** or **cer·vi·ces** (-və seez) *Anat.* **1.** the neck. **2.** the constricted neck of the uterus. **3.** a necklike part. [ME] —**cer·vi·cal** (SUR vi kəl) *adj.*

ce·sar·e·an (si ZAIR ee ən) *n. Surg.* the birth of a child by surgical incision of the abdominal walls and uterus. Also called **cesarean section.** Also *caesarean.* —**ce·sar'e·an** *adj.*

ces·sa·tion (se SAY shən) *n.* a ceasing; stop; pause. [ME *cessacioun* inactivity]

ces·sion (SESH ən) *n.* the act of ceding; a giving up, as of territory or rights, to another. [ME]

cess·pool (SES POOL) *n.* **1.** a covered well or pit for sewage, etc. **2.** any repository of filth.

ces·ta (SES tə) *n.* in jai alai, a curved basket used as a racket. [< Sp.]

ce·ta·cean (si TAY shən) *adj.* of or belonging to the aquatic mammals, including the whales, dolphins, and porpoises. Also **ce·ta'ceous.** [< NL *Cetacia* the order of cetaceans] —**ce·ta'cean** *n.*

Cha·blis (sha BLEE) *n.* a dry, white wine.

chafe (chayf) *v.* **chafed, chaf·ing** *v.t.* **1.** abrade or make sore by rubbing. **2.** make warm by rubbing. **3.** irritate; annoy. —*v.i.* **4.** rub. **5.** be irritated; fret; fume: *chafe* under the abuse. —*n.* **1.** soreness or wear from rubbing; friction. **2.** irritation or vexation. [ME *chaufen* heat]

chaff¹ (chaf) *n.* **1.** the husks of grain. **2.** any trivial or worthless matter. [ME *chaf*]

chaff² *v.t. & v.i.* poke fun (at). —*n.* **1.** good-natured raillery. **2.** *Mil.* strips of foil dropped from an airplane to confuse enemy radar.

chafing dish a vessel with a heating

apparatus to cook or keep food warm at the table.

cha·grin (shə GRIN) *n.* distress or vexation caused by disappointment, failure, etc. —*v.t.* cause to feel chagrin. [< F]

chain (chayn) *n.* **1.** a series of connected rings or links, usu. of metal, serving to bind, drag, hold, or ornament. **2.** *pl.* anything that confines or restrains; shackles. **3.** *pl.* bondage. **4.** any connected series. **5.** a series of chain stores. —*v.t.* **1.** fasten or connect with a chain. **2.** fetter; bind. [ME *chayne* fetter]

chain gang a group of convicts chained together while doing hard labor.

chain letter a letter intended to be sent on from one to another in a series of recipients.

chain mail flexible armor consisting of interlinked metal chains, rings, or scales.

chain reaction 1. *Physics* the self-sustaining fission of atomic nuclei, as in a nuclear reactor. **2.** any causally linked succession of reactions or events.

chain-smoke (CHAYN SMOHK) *v.t. & v.i.* **-smoked, -smok·ing** smoke (cigarettes) without interruption.

chain store one of a number of retail stores under the same ownership and selling similar merchandise.

chair (chair) *n.* **1.** a seat, usu. having four legs and a back, for one person. **2.** a seat of office, authority, etc., as that of a professor or bishop. **3.** the office or dignity of one who presides or is in authority. **4.** a presiding officer; chairperson. **5.** the electric chair; also, execution in the electric chair. —**take the chair** preside at or open a meeting. —*v.t.* **1.** seat in a chair. **2.** install in office. **3.** preside over (a meeting). [ME *chaiere*]

chair lift a group of chairs suspended from a power-driven cable, used to transport people, esp. skiers, up or down mountains.

chair·per·son (CHAIR PUR sən) *n.* one who presides over an assembly, committee, etc.: also **chair′man** & **chair′wom′an** *n.*

chaise longue (SHAYZ LAWNG) a couchlike chair capable of supporting the sitter's outstretched legs. [< F, lit., long chair]

cha·let (sha LAY) *n.* a cottage in the Swiss style, with a gently sloping, projecting roof. [< F]

chal·ice (CHAL is) *n.* **1.** a drinking cup or goblet. **2.** *Eccl.* in the Eucharist, a cup in which the wine is consecrated. **3.** a cup-shaped flower. [ME]

chalk (chawk) *n.* **1.** a soft, grayish white lime-stone, largely composed of the shells of marine animals. **2.** a piece of limestone or similar material, used for marking, etc. **3.** a score or tally. —*v.t.* **1.** mark, write, or draw with chalk. **2.** treat or dress with chalk. **3.** make pale. —**chalk up** score; credit. —*adj.* made with chalk. [ME *chalke*] — **chalk′y** *adj.* **chalk·i·er, chalk·i·est**

chalk·board (CHAWK BORD) *n.* a writing slate, as a blackboard, on which chalk is used.

chal·lenge (CHAL inj) *v.* **·lenged, ·leng·ing** *v.t.* **1.** demand a contest with. **2.** call in question; dispute. **3.** *Law* object to. **4.** claim as due; demand. **5.** *Mil.* stop (someone) and demand identification from. **6.** arouse interest or excitement in. —*v.i.* **7.** present a challenge. —*n.* **1. a** an invitation or dare to participate in a contest. **b** an invitation to compete in a sport. **2.** *Mil.* a sentry's demand for a password or identification. **3.** a calling in question; dispute. **4.** *Law* a formal objection, as to a juror. [ME *chalenge* accusation] —**chal′lenge·a·ble** *adj.*

cham·ber (CHAYM bər) *n.* **1.** a room in a house; esp., a bedroom. **2.** *pl.* an office or suite of rooms, as of a judge. **3.** a hall where an assembly meets; also, the assembly itself. **4.** a council; board. **5.** an enclosed space or cavity, as in a gun. —*v.t.* **1.** provide with a chamber. **2.** fit into or as into a chamber. [ME *chambre* room]

chamber music music composed for a small group of instruments, as a string quartet.

cha·me·le·on (kə MEE lee ən) *n.* **1.** a lizard capable of changing color. **2.** a person of changeable disposition or habits. [ME *camelion*]

cham·ois (SHAM ee) *n. pl.* **·ois** (-eez) **1.** a mountain antelope of Europe and western Asia. **2.** a soft leather prepared from the skin of the chamois, sheep, etc. —*v.t.* dress (leather or skin) like chamois. [< MF]

champ[1] (champ) *v.t.* **1.** chew noisily; munch. **2.** bite restlessly. —*v.i.* **3.** be impatient because of delay, usu. in the expression *champ at the bit.*

champ[2] *n. Informal* champion.

cham·pagne (sham PAYN) *n.* **1.** a sparkling white wine made in the area of Champagne, France; also, any wine made in imitation of this. **2.** a pale or greenish yellow.

cham·pi·on (CHAM pee ən) *n.* **1.** one who has defeated all opponents and is ranked first, esp. in a sport. **2.** anything awarded first place. 3. one who fights for another or defends a principle or cause. —*adj.* having won first prize or rank; superior to all others. —*v.t.* fight in behalf of; defend; support. [ME] —**cham'pi•on•ship'** *n.*

chance (chans) *n.* 1. fortune; luck. 2. an unusual and unexplained event. 3. the probability of anything happening. 4. an opportunity. 5. a risk or gamble; hazard. 6. a ticket in a lottery. —*v.* **chanced, chancing** *v.i.* 1. occur accidentally; happen. —*v.t.* 2. take the chance of; risk. —**chance upon** (or **on**) find or meet unexpectedly. —*adj.* occurring by chance. [ME]

chan•cel (CHAN səl) *n.* the space near the altar of a church for the clergy and choir. [ME]

chan•cel•lor (CHAN sə lər) *n.* 1. in some European countries, a chief minister of state. 2. the chief secretary of an embassy. 3. a secretary, as of a nobleman or ruler. 4. the head of some universities. 5. a judge of a court of chancery or equity. [ME *chanceler*]

chan•cer•y (CHAN sə ree) *n. pl.* **•cer•ies** 1. a court of equity. 2. equity, or proceedings in equity. [ME *chancerie*]

chan•cre (SHANG kər) *n. Pathol.* a primary syphilitic lesion. [< MF, cancer]

chanc•y (CHAN see) *adj.* **chanc•i•er, chanc•i•est** risky.

chan•de•lier (SHAN dl EER) *n.* a branched light fixture, suspended from a ceiling. [< F, lit., something that holds candles]

change (chaynj) *v.* **changed, chang•ing** *v.t.* 1. make different; alter. 2. exchange: *change* places. 3. give or obtain the equivalent of, as money. 4. put other garments, coverings, etc., on: *change* the baby. —*v.i.* 5. become different. 6. make a change or exchange. 7. transfer from one train, etc., to another. 8. put on other garments. —**change hands** pass from one possessor to another. —*n.* 1. the act or fact of changing. 2. a substitution of one thing for another. 3. something new or different; variety. 4. a clean or different set of clothes. 5. the amount returned when cash of greater value than the sum due has been tendered. 6. money of lower denomination given in exchange for higher. 7. small coins. [ME *chaungen* exchange]

change•a•ble (CHAYN jə bəl) *adj.* 1. likely to change or vary; inconstant. 2. capable of being changed. —**change'a•bil'i•ty** *n.*

change•less (CHAYNJ lis) *adj.* free from change; enduring.

change•ling (CHAYNJ ling) *n.* a child secretly left in place of another.

change of life the menopause.

chan•nel (CHAN l) *n.* 1. the bed of a stream. 2. a wide strait. 3. *Naut.* the deep part of a river, harbor, etc. 4. a tubular passage, as for liquids. 5. the course through which anything passes. 6. *pl.* the official or proper routes of communication. 7. *Telecom.* a band of frequencies assigned for radio or television transmission. 8. a groove or furrow. —*v.t.* **chan•neled, chan•nel•ing** 1. cut or wear channels in. 2. direct or convey through or as through a channel. [ME *chanel* waterpipe]

chant (chant) *n.* 1. a simple melody in which a varying number of syllables are sung or intoned on each note. 2. a psalm or canticle so sung or intoned. 3. a song; melody. 4. any repeated singing or shouting of words, as from a mob. 5. a singing intonation in speech. —*v.t. & v.i.* 1. sing to a chant. 2. celebrate in song. 3. recite or say in the manner of a chant. [ME *chanten* sing]

chan•teuse (shan TOOS) *n. French* a woman singer, esp. of popular songs.

chant•ey (SHAN tee) *n. pl.* **•eys** a rhythmical working song of sailors: also **chan'ty.** [Alter. of F *chanter* sing]

cha•os (KAY os) *n.* 1. utter disorder and confusion. 2. the supposed unformed original state of the universe. [ME, abyss] —**cha•ot•ic** (kay OT ik) *adj.* —**cha•ot'i•cal•ly** *adv.*

chap[1] (chap) *n. Informal* a fellow; lad. [Short for *chapman* peddler]

chap[2] *v.t. & v.i.* **chapped, chap•ping** split, crack, or roughen. —*n.* a crack or roughened place in the skin. [ME *chappen* cut]

chap•ar•ral (SHAP ə RAL) *n.* a thicket of low, thorny shrubs in southwestern U.S. [< Sp.]

cha•peau (sha POH) *n. pl.* **•peaux** or **•peaus** (*both* -POHZ) a hat. [< F]

chap•el (CHAP əl) *n.* 1. a place of worship smaller than a church. 2. a part of a church, for special services. 3. a place in a college, school, etc., for religious services; also, the services. [ME *chapele* cloak]

chap•er•on (SHAP ə ROHN) *n.* a person who accompanies and supervises a group of young people. Also **chap'er•one'.** [ME] —**chap'er•on'** *v.t.*

chap•lain (CHAP lin) *n.* a clergyman who conducts religious services in a legislative assembly, for a military unit, etc. [ME *chapelain* custodian of St. Martin's cloak]

chaps (chaps) *n. (construed as pl.)* leather leggings without a seat, worn over trousers by cowboys to protect the legs.

chap·ter (CHAP tər) *n.* 1. a main division of a book or long essay, usually numbered. 2. a branch of a society or fraternity. 3. *Eccl.* an assembly of the canons; also, the canons collectively. 4. a period of time: an important *chapter* in history. —*v.t.* divide into chapters, as a book. [ME *chapiter* little head]

char (chahr) *v.* **charred, char·ring** *v.t.* 1. burn or scorch the surface of. 2. convert into charcoal by incomplete combustion. —*v.i.* 3. become charred.

char·ac·ter (KAR ik tər) *n.* 1. the combination of qualities or traits that distinguishes an individual or group. 2. any distinguishing attribute. 3. moral force; integrity. 4. a good reputation. 5. status; capacity. 6. a person in a play, novel, etc. 7. *Informal* an eccentric or humorous person. 8. a mark; letter. —**in** (or **out of**) **character** in keeping (or not in keeping) with the general character. [< L]

char·ac·ter·is·tic (KAR ik tə RIS tik) *adj.* distinguishing; typical. —*n.* a distinctive feature or trait. —**char'ac·ter·is'ti·cal·ly** *adv.*

char·ac·ter·ize (KAR ik tə RĪZ) *v.t.* **·ized, ·iz·ing** 1. distinguish as a characteristic of. 2. describe the quality of. —**char'ac·ter·i·za'tion** *n.*

cha·rade (shə RAYD) *n.* 1. a pretense 2. *pl. (construed as sing.)* a game in which words and phrases are to be guessed from their representation in pantomime. [< F]

char·coal (CHAHR kohl) *n.* 1. a black, porous substance obtained by imperfect combustion of organic matter, as wood, used as a fuel, adsorbent, filter, etc. 2. a drawing pencil made of charcoal. 3. a drawing made with such a pencil. —*v.t.* write, draw, mark, or blacken with charcoal. [ME *charcole*]

charge (chahrj) *v.* **charged, charg·ing** *v.t.* 1. place a burden or responsibility upon. 2. load or fill. 3. diffuse something throughout, as water with carbon dioxide. 4. supply (a storage battery) with reuired electricity. 5. accuse; impute something to. 6. command or exhort: *charge* a jury. 7. set or state as a price. 8. make financially liable. 9. set down or record as a debt to be paid: *charge* a purchase. 10. attack forcefully. —*v.i.* 11. make an attack; rush violently. 12. demand

or fix a price. —**charge off** regard as a loss. —*n.* 1. a load or burden. 2. the amount of anything that an apparatus or receptacle can hold at one time. 3. the amount of explosive to be detonated at one time. 4. the amount of electrical energy present in a storage battery. 5. care and custody. 6. a person or thing entrusted to one's care; responsibility. 7. an accusation; allegation. 8. an instruction or admonition given by a judge to a jury. 9. any cost or expense. 10. a debt or charged purchase, or an entry recording it. 11. an onslaught or attack; also, the signal for this. 12. *Slang* a thrill. —**in charge of** having responsibility for or control of. [ME *chargen*] —**charge·a·ble** (CHAHR jə bəl) *adj.*

charg·er (CHAHR jər) *n.* 1. one who or that which charges. 2. a horse trained for use in battle; war horse. 3. an apparatus for charging storage batteries.

char·i·ot (CHAR ee ət) *n.* an ancient two-wheeled vehicle used in war, racing, etc. —*v.t. & v.i.* convey, ride, or drive in a chariot. [ME]

cha·ris·ma (kə RIZ mə) *n.* 1. *Theol.* an extraordinary grace or gift, as of healing. 2. extraordinary personal magnetism, esp. in a political leader. [< LL, favor]

char·is·mat·ic (KAR iz MAT ik) *adj.* 1. of or pertaining to charisma. 2. *Theol.* of a Christian movement emphasizing spiritual charisma.

char·i·ta·ble (CHAR i tə bəl) *adj.* 1. generous in giving gifts to the poor. 2. inclined to judge others leniently. 3. of or concerned with charity.

char·i·ty (CHAR i tee) *n. pl.* **·ties** 1. the giving of help to the needy. 2. alms. 3. an institution, organization, or fund to help those in need. 4. tolerance; leniency. 5. an act of good will. 6. brotherly love. [ME *charite* dear]

char·la·tan (SHAHR lə tn) *n.* one who makes false claim to skill and knowledge; quack. [< MF, babbler] —**char'la·tan·ism** *n.*

charm (chahrm) *n.* 1. the power to allure or delight; fascination. 2. any fascinating quality or feature. 3. a small ornament worn on a necklace, bracelet, etc. 4. something worn to ward off evil or ensure good luck; an amulet. 5. any formula or action supposed to have magic power. —*v.t. & v.i.* 1. attract irresistibly; delight; fascinate. 2. influence by or as if by a spell; bewitch. 3. protect by or as by magic power. [ME *charme* incantation]

charm•ing (CHAHR ming) *adj.* delightful; very attractive.

chart (chahrt) *n.* 1. a map, esp. one for the use of mariners. 2. an outline map on which climatic data, military operations, etc., can be shown. 3. a sheet showing facts graphically or in tabular form. 4. a graph or table. —*v.t.* lay out on a chart; map out. [< MF *charte*]

char•ter (CHAHR tər) *n.* 1. a document of incorporation of a municipality, institution, or the like. 2. a formal document by which a sovereign or government grants rights or privileges to a person, company, or the people. 3. an authorization to establish a branch or chapter of some larger organization. 4. a contract for the lease of a bus, airplane, etc. —*v.t.* 1. hire (an airplane, train, etc.). 2. give a charter to. [ME *chartre* little paper]

charter member an original member of a corporation, order, or society.

char•treuse (shahr TROOZ) *n.* 1. a yellow, pale green, or faintly green liqueur. 2. a yellowish green color. —*adj.* of the color chartreuse. [after *La Grande Chartreuse*, a monastery in France]

char•y (CHAIR ee) *adj.* **char•i•er, char•i•est** 1. cautious; wary. 2. fastidious; particular. 3. sparing; frugal. [ME] —**char′i•ly** *adv.*

chase[1] (chays) *v.* **chased, chas•ing** *v.t.* 1. pursue with intent to catch or harm. 2. follow persistently; run after. 3. put to flight; drive. —*v.i.* 4. follow in pursuit. 5. go hurriedly.—*n.* 1. the act of chasing or pursuing. 2. the sport of hunting: preceded by *the.* 3. that which is pursued; prey; quarry.—**give chase** pursue. [ME *chacen* hunt]

chase[2] *n.* a groove or slot. —*v.t.* **chased, chas•ing** 1. indent or groove. 2. ornament by embossing. [ME *chas* box]

chas•er (CHAY sər) *n.* 1. one who chases or pursues. 2. water, etc., drunk after strong liquor.

chasm (KAZ əm) *n.* 1. a deep crack in the earth's surface; a gorge. 2. an abrupt interruption; a gap. 3. any deep difference of opinion. [< L *chasma*]

chas•sis (CHAS ee) *n. pl.* **chas•sis** (-eez) the flat, rectangular frame that supports the body of a vehicle and includes the wheels and springs. [< F *châssis* frame]

chaste (chayst) *adj.* 1. free of sexual intercourse regarded as immoral; virtuous. 2. celibate. 3. pure in character or conduct. 4. pure in artistic or literary style; simple. [ME]

chas•ten (CHAY sən) *v.t.* 1. discipline by punishment or affliction; chastise. 2. moderate; soften; temper. [ME *chastien* castigate]

chas•tise (chas TĪZ) *v.t.* **•tised, •tis•ing** 1. punish, esp. by beating. 2. scold or criticize severely. [ME *chastisen*] —**chas•tise•ment** (CHAS tiz mənt) *n.*

chas•ti•ty (CHAS ti tee) *n.* 1. the state or quality of being chaste. 2. virginity or celibacy. [ME *chastitte*]

chat (chat) *v.i.* **chat•ted, chat•ting** converse in an easy, informal manner. —*n.* easy, informal conversation. [ME]

cha•teau (sha TOH) *n. pl.* **•teaus, •teaux** (both -TOHZ) 1. a French castle. 2. a house on a country estate. [< F]

chat•tel (CHAT l) *n.* 1. *Law* an article of movable personal property. 2. any article of tangible property. [ME *chatel*]

chat•ter (CHAT ər) *v.i.* 1. click together rapidly, as the teeth in shivering. 2. talk rapidly and trivially. 3. utter a rapid series of short, inarticulate sounds, as a squirrel. —*v.t.* 4. utter in a trivial or chattering manner. —*n.* 1. idle or foolish talk; prattle. 2. jabbering, as of a monkey. 3. a rattling of the teeth. [ME *chateren*]

chat•ter•box (CHAT ər BOKS) *n.* an incessant talker.

chat•ty (CHAT ee) *adj.* **•ti•er, •ti•est** 1. talkative. 2. familiar; informal: a *chatty* style of writing.

chauf•feur (SHOH fər) *n.* one who drives an automobile for hire. —*v.t.* serve as driver for. [< F]

chau•vin•ism (SHOH və NIZ əm) *n.* an unreasoning, often fanatical pride in, attachment to, or support for one's own nation, race, sex, etc. [after Nicholas *Chauvin*, an overzealous supporter of Napoleon Bonaparte] —**chau′vin•ist** *n.*

cheap (cheep) *adj.* 1. low in price. 2. charging low prices, as a store. 3. inexpensive in proportion to its value. 4. obtained with little trouble. 5. of poor quality; inferior. 6. mean; miserly. —*adv.* at a low price: sells *cheap.* [ME *cheep*]

cheap•en (CHEE pən) *v.t. & v.i.* make or become cheap or cheaper.

cheap·skate (CHEEP skayt) *n. Informal* a miserly person.

cheat (cheet) *v.t.* 1. swindle or defraud. 2. mislead or delude; trick. 3. elude or escape; foil. —*v.i.* 4. practice fraud or act dishonestly. 5. *Informal* be unfaithful in marriage. —*n.* 1. a fraud; swindle. 2. one who cheats or defrauds. [ME *chet*]

check (chek) *n.* 1. a break in progress or advance; a halt. 2. one who or that which stops or controls. 3. control or supervision. 4. a test, examination, or comparison. 5. a mark to show that something has been verified or investigated. 6. a written order on a bank to pay a designated sum. 7. a bill in a restaurant. 8. a square in a checkered surface. 9. a fabric having a checkered pattern. 10. in chess, the position of a king open to capture if it is not protected or moved. —*v.t.* 1. bring to a stop suddenly or sharply. 2. curb; restrain. 3. test or verify; also, investigate. 4. mark with a check. 5. mark with squares or crossed lines; checker. 6. deposit or accept for temporary safekeeping. 7. in chess, put (an opponent's king) in check. 8. cause to crack. —*v.i.* 9. come to a stop; pause. 10. agree item for item; correspond accurately. —**check in** register as a guest at a hotel etc. —**check on** (or **up on**) investigate. —**check out** 1. pay one's bill and leave, as from a hotel. 2. investigate or confirm. 3. be verified. —*interj.* in chess, an exclamation proclaiming that an opponent's king is in check. [ME *chek*]

checked (chekt) *adj.* 1. marked with squares. 2. kept in check; restrained. 3. stopped.

check·er (CHEK ər) *n.* 1. a small disk used in the game of checkers. 2. one of the squares in a checkered surface; also, a pattern of such squares. 3. one who checks, esp. one who inspects, counts, or supervises the disposal of merchandise. 4. a cashier in a supermarket. —*v.t.* 1. mark with squares or crossed lines. 2. fill with variations or vicissitudes. [ME]

check·er·board (CHEK ər bord) *n.* a board divided into 64 squares, used in checkers or chess. Also *chessboard*.

check·ered (CHEK ərd) *adj.* 1. divided into squares. 2. marked by light and dark patches. 3. marked by alternations.

check·ers (CHEK ərz) *n. (construed as sing.)* a game played by two persons on a checkerboard, each player starting with twelve pieces.

check·mate (CHEK mayt) *v.t.* •**mat·ed,** •**mat·ing** 1. in chess, put (an opponent's king) in check from which no escape is possible, thus winning the game. 2. defeat by a skillful maneuver. —*n.* 1. in chess: **a** the move that checkmates a king. **b** the condition of a king when checkmated. 2. utter defeat. [ME *chek mat*]

check·out (CHEK owt) *n.* 1. the procedure or time of checking out of a hotel. 2. the itemization of goods and payment for purchases. 3. the place of payment.

check·up (CHEK up) *n.* an examining or inspection: a medical *checkup*.

cheek (cheek) *n.* 1. either side of the face below the eye and above the mouth. 2. a side or part analogous to the side of the face. 3. impudent self-assurance. [ME *cheke*]

cheek·y (CHEE kee) *adj.* **cheek·i·er, cheek·i·est** impudent; brazen. —**cheek'i·ness** *n.*

cheep (cheep) *v.t. & v.i.* make, or utter with, a faint, shrill sound, as a young bird. —*n.* a weak chirp or squeak. [Imit.]

cheer (cheer) *n.* 1. a shout of acclamation. 2. gladness or gaiety. 3. state of mind; mood. 4. that which promotes happiness or joy; encouragement. —*v.t.* 1. make cheerful; gladden: often with *up.* 2. acclaim with cheers. 3. urge; incite: often with *on.* —*v.i.* 4. become cheerful or glad: often with *up.* 5. utter cries of encouragement, approval, etc. [ME *chere* face] —**cheer·ful** (CHEER fəl) *adj.*

cheer·less (CHEER lis) *adj.* gloomy.

cheer·y (CHEER ee) *adj.* **cheer·i·er, cheer·i·est** abounding in cheerfulness. —**cheer'i·ly** *adv.*

cheese (cheez) *n.* 1. the pressed curd of milk, prepared and flavored. 2. any of various substances like cheese in consistency or shape. [ME *chese*]

chef (shef) *n.* a head cook; also, any cook. [< F *chef (de cuisine)* head (of the kitchen)]

chem·i·cal (KEM i kəl) *adj.* of or pertaining to chemistry or its phenomena, laws, operations, or results. —*n.* a substance obtained by or used in a chemical process.

chemical warfare the use of gases, incendiary materials, etc. in warfare.

che·mise (shə MEEZ) *n.* 1. a woman's loose undergarment resembling a short slip. 2. a dress hanging straight from the shoulders. [ME, shirt]

chem·ist (KEM ist) *n.* one trained in chemistry.

chem·is·try (KEM ə stree) *n. pl.* **·tries 1.** the science that deals with the structure, composition, properties, and transformations of substances. **2.** chemical composition or processes. **3.** sympathetic understanding: good *chemistry* between us.

chem·o·ther·a·py (KEE moh THER ə pee) *n. Med.* the treatment of disease, esp. cancer, by chemical means.

che·nille (shə NEEL) *n.* **1.** a soft, fuzzy cord, used for embroidery, fringes, etc. **2.** a fabric made with this cord. [< F, lit., caterpillar]

cher·ish (CHER ish) *v.t.* **1.** hold dear; treat with tenderness. **2.** entertain fondly, as a hope or an idea. [ME *cherisshen* hold dear]

cher·ry (CHER ee) *n. pl.* **·ries 1.** any of various trees of the rose family, bearing small, round or heart-shaped fruit enclosing a smooth pit; also, its wood or fruit. **2.** a bright red color resembling that of certain cherries: also **cherry red.** —*adj.* **1.** bright red. **2.** made of or with cherries. **3.** made of cherry wood. [ME *cheri*]

cher·ub (CHER əb) *n.* **1.** *pl.* **cherubs** a representation of a beautiful winged child. **2.** *pl.* **cherubs** a beautiful child; also, an innocent-looking adult. **3.** *pl.* **cherubim** (CHER ə bim) in Scripture, a celestial being. [ME] —**che·ru·bic** (chə ROO bik) *adj.*

chess (ches) *n.* a game of skill played on a chessboard by two persons, with 16 pieces on each side. [ME *ches*]

chess·board (CHES bord) see CHECKERBOARD.

chess·man (CHES MAN) *n. pl.* **·men** (-MEN) any of the pieces used in chess.

chest (chest) *n.* **1.** the part of the body enclosed by the ribs. **2.** a box or cabinet for storing or protecting articles. **3.** the treasury of a public institution; also, the funds contained there. [ME, box]

chest·nut (CHES NUT) *n.* **1.** the usually edible nut of various trees; also, a tree that bears this nut. **2.** a reddish brown color. **3.** a horse of this color. **4. a** a stale joke. **b** anything trite, as a story, song, etc. —*adj.* reddish brown. [ME *chesten* chestnut tree]

chest·y (CHES tee) *adj.* **chest·i·er, chest·i·est 1.** self-assertive. **2.** large in the chest or bosom.

chev·ron (SHEV rən) *n.* an emblem worn on a uniform sleeve to indicate rank, length of service, etc., used by military, naval, and police forces. [ME *cheveroun* rafter]

chew (choo) *v.t. & v.i.* **1.** crush or grind with the teeth; masticate. **2.** meditate upon; consider carefully. —**chew out** *Slang* reprimand severely; berate. —*n.* **1.** the act of chewing. **2.** that which is chewed. [ME *chewen*]

chew·ing gum (CHOO ing GUM) a preparation of natural gum, usu. chicle, flavored for chewing.

chew·y (CHOO ee) *adj.* **chew·i·er, chew·i·est** soft and requiring chewing: *chewy* candy.

chi·an·ti (kee AHN tee) *n.* a dry red wine.

chi·a·ro·scu·ro (kee AHR ə SKYUUR oh) *n. pl.* **·ros 1.** the distribution and treatment of light and shade in a picture. **2.** a kind of painting or drawing using only light and shade. [< Ital.]

chic (sheek) *n.* originality, elegance, and taste, esp. in dress. [< F] —**chic** *adj.*

chi·can·er·y (shi KAY nər ee) *n. pl.* **·er·ies** trickery and subterfuge. [< F *chicanerie*]

Chi·ca·no (chi KAH noh) *n. pl.* **·nos** a Mexican-American.

chi·chi (SHEE SHEE) *adj.* ostentatiously stylish or elegant. [< F]

chick·en (CHIK ən) *n.* **1.** the young of domestic fowl. **2.** a rooster or hen of any age. **3.** the flesh of the chicken, used as food. —*adj. Slang* cowardly. —*v.i. Slang* lose one's nerve: often with *out.* [ME *chiken*]

chick·en-heart·ed (CHIK ən HAHR tid) *adj.* timid, cowardly.

chicken pox *Pathol.* a contagious disease, principally of children, characterized by skin eruptions and fever.

chic·le (CHIK əl) *n.* the milky juice or latex of the *sapodilla*, a tropical tree, used as the basic ingredient of chewing gum. [< Mexican Sp.]

chic·o·ry (CHIK ə ree) *n. pl.* **·ries 1.** an herb, used in salads. **2.** its dried, roasted, and ground roots, used with or as a substitute for coffee. [< MF *chicoree*]

chide (chīd) *v.t. & v.i.* **chid·ed** or **chid** (chid), **chid·ed** or **chid** or **chid·den** (CHID n), **chid·ing** speak reprovingly (to); scold. [ME *chiden*]

chief (cheef) *n.* the person highest in rank or authority, as the head of a tribe, police force, etc. —**in chief** having the highest authority: commander *in chief.* —*adj.* **1.**

highest in rank or authority. **2.** most important or eminent; leading. [ME]

chief justice the presiding judge of a court composed of several justices.

chief·ly (CHEEF lee) *adv.* mainly; primarily; especially. —*adj.* of or like a chief.

chief of staff the principal staff officer of a division or higher level.

chief·tain (CHEEF tən) *n.* the head of a clan or tribe. [ME *cheftayne*]

chig·ger (CHIG ər) *n.* the larva of various mites of the southern U.S. that attaches itself to the skin, causing intense itching.

chi·gnon (SHEEN yon) *n.* a knot or roll of hair worn at the back of the head by women. [< F]

Chi·hua·hua (chi WAH wah) *n.* a small, smooth-coated dog with large, pointed ears. [after *Chihuahua*, Mexico]

chil·blain (CHIL blayn) *n. Pathol.* an inflammation of the hands or feet caused by exposure to cold.

child (chīld) *n. pl.* **chil·dren 1.** an offspring of human parents. **2.** a boy or girl, most commonly one between infancy and youth. **3.** a descendant. **4.** a childish person. **5.** a product of a specified condition, quality, time, etc. —**with child** pregnant. [ME]

child·bear·ing (CHĪLD BAIR ing) *n.* the bringing forth of children.

child·birth (CHĪLD BURTH) *n.* the act of giving birth to offspring.

child·hood (CHĪLD huud) *n.* the state or time of being a child. [ME *childhode*]

child·ish (CHĪL dish) *adj.* **1.** of, like, or proper to a child. **2.** unduly like a child; immature; puerile; weak. [ME *childisch*]

child·like (CHĪLD līk) *adj.* like, characteristic of, or appropriate to a child; artless, docile, etc.

chil·dren (CHIL drən) plural of CHILD.

child's play something easy to do.

chil·i (CHIL ee) *n. pl.* **chil·ies 1.** the acrid pod or fruit of the red pepper, used as a seasoning. **2.** chili con carne. [< Mexican Sp. *chile*]

chili con car·ne (kon KAHR nee) a highly seasoned dish made with meat, chili, and often beans. [< Sp., chili with meat]

chill (chil) *n.* **1.** a sensation of cold, often with shivering. **2.** a moderate degree of coldness. **3.** a check to enthusiasm, joy, etc. **4.** a numbing sensation of dread or anxiety. —*v.t.* **1.** reduce to a low temperature. **2.** affect with cold. **3.** check, as ardor; dispirit. **4.** harden the surface of (metal) by sudden

cooling. —*v.i.* **5.** become cold. **6.** be stricken with a chill. **7.** become hard by sudden cooling, as metal. —*adj.* **1.** moderately or unpleasantly cold. **2.** affected by or shivering with cold. **3.** cold in manner; distant. **4.** discouraging. [ME *chile*]

chill·er (CHIL ər) *n.* **1.** that which chills. **2.** a horror story or movie.

chill·y (CHIL ee) *adj.* **chill·i·er, chill·i·est 1.** causing chill; cold or chilling. **2.** feeling cold; affected by chill. **3.** disheartening; unfriendly.

chime (chīm) *n.* **1.** *Often pl.* a set of bells, as in a bell tower, tuned to a scale. **2.** a single bell: the *chime* of a clock. **3.** *Often pl.* the sounds or music produced by a chime. **4.** agreement; accord. —*v.* **chimed, chim·ing** *v.t.* **1.** cause to sound musically by striking; ring. **2.** announce (the hour) by the sound of bells. **3.** say rhythmically. —*v.i.* **4.** sound musically. **5.** ring chimes. **6.** harmonize; agree: with *with.* —**chime in 1.** join in harmoniously. **2.** join, and so interrupt, a conversation. [ME *chymbe* cymbal]

chi·me·ra (ki MEER ə) *n.* **1.** an absurd creation of the imagination. **2.** in painting etc., a grotesque monster. [ME, she-goat]

chi·mer·i·cal (ki MER i kəl) *adj.* **1.** of the nature of a chimera; fantastic; imaginary. **2.** given to fanciful dreams; visionary.

chim·ney (CHIM nee) *n.* **1.** a flue to conduct gases and smoke from a fire to the outer air. **2.** a structure containing such a flue, usu. vertical and rising above the roof of a building. **3.** a tube, usually of glass, for enclosing the flame of a lamp. [ME *chimenai*]

chim·pan·zee (CHIM pan ZEE) *n.* an arboreal ape of equatorial Africa.

chin (chin) *n.* the lower part of the face, between the mouth and the neck. —*v.t. & v.i.* **chinned, chin·ning** lift (oneself) while grasping an overhead bar until the chin is level with the hands. [ME]

chi·na (CHĪ nə) *n.* **1.** fine porcelain or ceramic ware. **2.** any crockery. Also **chi′na·ware′.**

chin·chil·la (chin CHIL ə) *n.* **1.** a small rodent native to the Andes. **2.** the fur of the chinchilla. **3.** a closely woven, twilled fabric having a tufted surface. [< Sp.]

chink (chingk) *n.* a small, narrow cleft; crevice. —*v.t.* **1.** make cracks or fissures in. **2.** fill the cracks of, as a wall; plug up. [ME]

chintz (chints) *n.* a cotton fabric usu. glazed and printed in bright colors. [< Hindi *chit*]

chintz•y (CHINT see) *adj.* **chintz•i•er,
chintz•i•est 1.** stingy. **2.** cheap; gaudy.
chip (chip) *n.* **1.** a small piece cut or broken
off. **2.** a small counter used in certain
games, as in poker. **3.** a crack or imperfection caused by chipping. **4.** a thinly sliced
morsel: potato *chip.* **5.** *Electronics* an integrated circuit. **—a chip off (or of) the old
block** one who resembles either parent in
behavior, appearance, etc. **—a chip on
one's shoulder** a hostile manner. —*v.*
chipped, chip•ping *v.t.* **1.** break off small
pieces of, as china. —*v.i.* **2.** become
chipped. **—chip in** contribute, as to a fund.
[ME]
chip•per (CHIP ər) *adj.* **1.** brisk; cheerful.
2. smartly dressed.
chi•rop•o•dy (ki ROP ə dee) *n.* the branch
of medicine that deals with ailments of the
foot; also called *podiatry.* **—chi•rop'
o•dist** *n.*
chi•ro•prac•tic (KĪ rə PRAK tik) *n.* a therapy based on the manipulation of bodily
structures, esp. the spinal column. **—chi'
ro•prac'tor** *n.*
chirp (churp) *v.i.* **1.** give a short, acute cry, as
a sparrow or locust. **2.** talk in a quick and
shrill manner. —*v.t.* **3.** utter with a quick,
sharp sound. **—chirp** *n.*
chis•el (CHIZ əl) *n.* a cutting tool with a
beveled edge, used on metal, stone, or
wood. —*v.t. & v.i.* **chis•eled, chis•el•ing
1.** cut, engrave, or carve with or as with a
chisel. **2.** cheat; swindle. [ME] **—chis'
el•er** *n.*
chit (chit) *n.* a voucher of a sum owed, as for
food. [< Hind. *chitthī* note]
chit•chat (CHIT CHAT) *n.* **1.** small talk. **2.**
gossip. **—chit'chat'** *v.i.* **•chat•ted,
•chat•ting**
chit•ter•lings (CHIT linz) *n.pl.* the small
intestines of pigs, esp. as used for food: also
chit•lins. [ME *cheterling*]
chiv•al•ric (shi VAL rik) *adj.* chivalrous.
chiv•al•rous (SHIV əl rəs) *adj.* **1.** having the
qualities of the ideal knight; gallant, courteous, generous, etc. **2.** pertaining to chivalry. [ME *chevalrous*]
chiv•al•ry (SHIV əl ree) *n.* **1.** the feudal
system of knighthood. **2.** the ideal qualities
of knighthood, as courtesy, valor, skill in
arms, etc. **3.** a body of knights. [ME *chival-
rie*]
chive (chīv) *n.* an herb allied to the leek and
onion, used in cooking. [ME *cive*]
chlo•rin•ate (KOOR ə NAYT) *v.t.* **•at•**

ed, **•at•ing** *Chem.* treat or cause to combine with chlorine, as in purifying water,
whitening fabrics, etc. **—chlo'rin•a'tion**
n.
chlo•rine (KLOR een) *n.* a greenish yellow,
poisonous, gaseous element, widely used as
a bleach and disinfectant.
chlo•ro•form (KLOR ə FORM) *n.* *Chem.* a
colorless, volatile liquid compound, used as
an anesthetic and solvent. —*v.t.* anesthe-
tize or kill with chloroform.
chlo•ro•phyll (KLOR ə fil) *n.* *Biochem.* the
green pigment found in plants, essential to
photosynthesis. [< Gk. *chloros* green +
phyllon leaf]
chock (chok) *n.* a block or wedge, so placed
as to prevent or limit motion. —*v.t.* make
fast or fit with a chock or chocks. —*adv.* as
fully or as close as possible. [ME, log]
chock-full (CHOK FUUL) *adj.* completely
full; stuffed. [ME *chokke-fulle*]
choc•o•late (CHAWK lit) *n.* **1.** a preparation of cacao nuts roasted and ground and
usu. sweetened. **2.** a beverage or confection
made from this. **3.** a dark, reddish-brown
color. —*adj.* **1.** flavored with or made with
chocolate. **2.** reddish-brown. [< Sp.]
choice (chois) *n.* **1.** the act of choosing; selection. **2.** the right or privilege of choosing;
option. **3.** the person or thing chosen. **4.** a
number or variety from which to choose. **5.**
an alternative. **6.** the best or preferred part
of anything. —*adj.* **choic•er, choic•est 1.**
select; excellent. **2.** chosen with care. [ME
chois]
choir (kwīr) *n.* **1.** an organized body of
singers, esp. in a church. **2.** the part of a
church occupied by such singers. —*v.t. &
v.i.* sing in chorus. [ME *quer* chorus]
choke (chohk) *v.* **choked, chok•ing** *v.t.* **1.**
stop the breathing of by obstructing the
windpipe; strangle. **2.** suppress or hinder;
retard the progress of. **3.** obstruct by filling; clog. **4.** lessen the air intake of the
carburetor in order to enrich the fuel mixture of (a gasoline engine). —*v.i.* **5.** become suffocated or stifled. **6.** become
obstructed. **—choke up 1.** be overcome
by emotion. **2.** perform poorly because of
tension, agitation, etc. —*n.* **1.** the act or
sound of choking. **2.** a device to control
the flow of air, as to a gasoline engine.
[ME *choken* suffocate]
chok•er (CHOH kər) *n.* **1.** one who or that
which chokes. **2.** a neckcloth or necklace
worn high around the throat.

chol·er (KOL ər) *n.* anger; hastiness of temper. [ME *colera* cholera] —**chol'er·ic** *adj.*

chol·er·a (KOL ər ə) *n. Pathol.* an acute, infectious disease characterized principally by serious intestinal disorders. [ME]

cho·les·ter·ol (kə LES tə ROHL) *n. Biochem.* a fatty, crystalline substance derived principally from bile, widely distributed in animal fats and tissues.

choose (chooz) *v.* **chose, cho·sen, choos·ing** *v.t.* **1.** select as most desirable; take by preference. **2.** prefer (to do something); decide. —*v.i.* **3.** make a choice. [ME *chosen*]

choos·y (CHOO zee) *adj.* **choos·i·er, choos·i·est** particular or fussy in one's choices.

chop (chop) *v.* **chopped, chop·ping** *v.t.* **1.** cut or make by strokes of a sharp tool. **2.** cut up in small pieces. **3.** make a cutting, downward stroke at (the ball), as in tennis. —*v.i.* **4.** make cutting strokes. **5.** move with sudden or violent motion. —*n.* **1.** the act of chopping. **2.** a cut of meat, usu. lamb, pork, or veal. **3.** a sharp, downward blow or stroke, as in karate, tennis, etc. [ME *choppen*]

chop·per (CHOP ər) *n.* **1.** one who or that which chops, esp. a device that chops food. **2.** *pl. Slang* teeth. **3.** *Slang* a helicopter. **4.** *Slang* a customized motorcycle.

chop·py (CHOP ee) *adj.* **·pi·er, ·pi·est 1.** full of short, rough waves. **2.** shifting; variable.

chop·sticks (CHOP stiks) *n.pl.* slender sticks of ivory or wood, used in pairs in China, Japan, etc., to convey food to the mouth. [< Chinese Pidgin English *chop* quick + STICK]

chop su·ey (CHOP SOO ee) a Chinese-American dish made with bits of meat and vegetables, served with rice. [< Chinese *tsa-sui,* lit., mixed pieces]

cho·ral (KOR əl) *adj.* pertaining to, written for, or sung by a chorus or choir. [< Med.L *choralis*]

cho·rale (kə RAL) *n.* **1.** a hymn marked by a simple melody, often sung in unison. **2.** a chorus or choir. [< G *Choral*]

chord¹ (kord) *n. Music* a combination of three or more tones sounded together, usu. in harmony. [ME *cord*]

chord² *n.* **1.** a string of a musical instrument. **2.** an emotional reaction. **3.** *Geom.* **a** a straight line connecting the extremities of an arc. **b** the portion of a straight line contained by its intersections with a curve. **4.** any of various chordlike things, as a tendon. [ME]

chore (chor) *n.* **1.** a small or minor job. **2.** an unpleasant or hard task. [ME *char*]

cho·re·o·graph (KOR ee ə GRAF) *v.t.* devise (ballet and other dance compositions). —**cho·re·og·ra·pher** (KOR ee OG rə fər) *n.*

cho·re·og·ra·phy (KOR ee OG rə fee) *n.* **1.** the devising of ballets and incidental dances, esp. for the stage. **2.** the written representation of figures and steps of dancing. **3.** the art of dancing; ballet. —**cho·re·o·graph·ic** (KOR ee ə GRAF ik) *adj.*

chor·tle (CHOR tl) *v.t. & v.i.* **·tled, ·tling** utter with chuckles of glee. [Blend of CHUCKLE and SNORT; coined by Lewis Carroll]

cho·rus (KOR əs) *n.* **1.** a musical composition to be sung by a large group. **2.** a group of singers who perform such works. **3.** a body of singers and dancers who perform together in opera, musical comedy, etc. **4.** a group of persons singing or speaking something simultaneously. **5.** a simultaneous utterance by many individuals. **6.** a refrain, as of a song. **7.** in Greek drama, a body of actors who comment upon and sometimes take part in the main action of a play. —*v.t. & v.i.* **cho·rused, cho·rus·ing** sing or speak all together in unison. [< L]

chorus girl a woman in the chorus of a musical comedy, etc. —**chorus boy** *masc.*

chose (chohz) past tense of CHOOSE.

cho·sen (CHOH zən) past participle of CHOOSE. —*adj.* **1.** made an object of choice; selected. **2.** marked or selected for special favor.

chow·der (CHOW dər) *n.* a dish usu. made of clams or fish stewed with vegetables, often in milk. [< F *chaudière* kettle]

chow mein (CHOW MAYN) a Chinese-American dish made of shredded meat and vegetables, served with fried noodles. [< Chinese *ch'ao* fry + *mein* flour]

Christ (krīst) *n.* Jesus of Nazareth, regarded by Christians as the Messiah foretold by the Hebrew prophets. [< Gk. *Christos* anointed]

chris·ten (KRIS ən) *v.t.* **1.** name in baptism. **2.** administer Christian baptism to. **3.** give a name to. **4.** use for the first time. [ME *cristenen*]

Chris·ten·dom (KRIS ən dəm) *n.* **1.** the Christian world. **2.** Christians collectively.

Chris·tian (KRIS chən) *adj.* **1.** professing or following the religion of Christ; esp., affirming the divinity of Christ. **2.** relating to or derived from Christ or his doctrine. **3.** characteristic of Christianity or Christendom. **4.** humane; civilized. —*n.* one who believes in or professes belief in the teachings of Christ; a member of any of the Christian churches.

Chris·ti·an·i·ty (KRIS chee AN i tee) *n.* **1.** the Christian religion. **2.** Christians collectively. **3.** the state of being a Christian.

Christian Science a religion and system of healing, founded in 1866 by Mary Baker Eddy: officially called the *Church of Christ, Scientist.* —**Christian Scientist**

Christ·mas (KRIS məs) *n.* December 25, held as the anniversary of the birth of Jesus Christ and widely observed as a holy day or a holiday. Also **Christmas Day.**

chro·mat·ic (kroh MAT ik) *adj.* **1.** pertaining to color. **2.** *Music* of or pertaining to a chromatic scale, or to an instrument that can play such a scale.

chromatic scale *Music* a scale proceeding by semitones.

chro·mo·some (KROH mə sohm) *n. Biol.* a complex body found in the cell nucleus, consisting of DNA and protein molecules, containing the genes, and serving to transmit hereditary information. [< Gk. *chrōma* color + -SOME[2]] —**chro′mo·so′mal** *adj.*

chron·ic (KRON ik) *adj.* **1.** prolonged; lingering; also, recurrent: said of a disease: opposed to *acute.* **2.** given to a habit; confirmed. [< L *chronicus* of time]

chron·i·cle (KRON i kəl) *n.* a register of events in the order in which they occurred. —*v.t.* •**cled,** •**cling** record in, or in the manner of, a chronicle. [ME *chronicle*] —**chron′i·cler** *n.*

chron·o·graph (KRON ə GRAF) *n.* an instrument for measuring and recording exact time intervals.

chron·o·log·i·cal (KRON l OJ i kəl) *adj.* **1.** arranged according to sequence in time. **2.** pertaining to chronology.

chro·nol·o·gy (krə NOL i jee) *n. pl.* •**gies 1.** the science of determining the proper sequence of historical events. **2.** arrangement or relationship according to order of occurrence. **3.** a chronological list or table.

chro·nom·e·ter (krə NOM i tər) *n.* a timekeeping instrument of high precision. —**chron·o·met·ric** (KRON ə ME trik) *adj.*

chrys·a·lis (KRIS ə lis) *n. pl.* **chrys·a·lis·es**

or **chry·sal·i·des** (kri SAL i DEEZ) **1.** *Entomol.* the capsule-enclosed pupa from which a butterfly or moth develops. **2.** anything in an undeveloped stage. [< L]

chrys·an·the·mum (kri SAN thə məm) *n.* **1.** any of a number of cultivated varieties of plants with large heads of showy flowers. **2.** the flower. [< L]

chub·by (CHUB ee) *adj.* •**bi·er,** •**bi·est** plump; rounded. —**chub′bi·ness** *n.*

chuck[1] (chuk) *v.t.* **1.** pat or tap affectionately, esp. under the chin. **2.** throw or pitch. **3.** *Informal* discard. **4.** *Informal* eject forcibly: with *out.* **5.** *Slang* vomit, upchuck. —*n.* **1.** a playful pat under the chin. **2.** a throw; toss.

chuck[2] *n.* **1.** the cut of beef extending from the neck to the shoulder blade. **2.** a clamp or wedge used to hold a tool or work, as in a lathe.

chuck·le (CHUK əl) *v.i.* •**led,** •**ling** laugh quietly and with satisfaction.

chuck wagon a wagon fitted with cooking equipment and provisions for cowboys.

chug (chug) *n.* a dull, explosive sound, as of the exhaust of an engine. —*v.i.* **chugged, chug·ging 1.** move or operate with a series of such sounds. **2.** move laboriously. [Imit.]

chum (chum) *n.* an intimate companion. —*v.i.* **chummed, chum·ming 1.** associate very closely with another. **2.** share the same room. **chum′my** *adj.* •**mi·er,** •**mi·est**

chump (chump) *n. Informal* a stupid or foolish person.

chunk (chungk) *n.* **1.** a thick mass or piece of anything, as wood. **2.** a considerable quantity of something. [Var. of CHUCK[2]]

chunk·y (CHUNG kee) *adj.* **chunk·i·er, chunk·i·est 1.** short and thickset; stocky. **2.** in chunks.

church (church) *n.* **1.** a building for Christian worship. **2.** regular religious services; public worship. **3.** a congregation of Christians. **4.** *Usu. cap.* a distinct body of Christians having a common faith and discipline; a denomination. **5.** all Christian believers collectively. **6.** ecclesiastical authority: separation of *church* and state. [ME *chiriche*]

church·go·er (CHURCH GOH ər) *n.* one who goes regularly to church.

Church of Christ, Scientist See CHRISTIAN SCIENCE.

Church of England the national church of England: also called *Anglican Church.*

Church of Jesus Christ of Latter-day

Saints the Mormon Church: its official name.

church·yard (CHURCH YAHRD) *n.* the ground surrounding or adjoining a church, often used as a cemetery.

churl (churl) *n.* **1.** a rude or surly person. **2.** a rustic. [ME *cherl* man] —**churl'ish** *adj.*

churn (churn) *n.* **1.** a vessel in which milk or cream is agitated to make butter. **2.** a state of unrest or agitation. —*v.t.* **1.** stir or agitate (cream or milk), as in a churn. **2.** make in a churn, as butter. **3.** agitate violently. **4.** produce mechanically in large amount: with *out.* **5.** subject (the account of a stockbroker's client) to excessive buying and selling. —*v.i.* **6.** work a churn. **7.** move with violent agitation; seethe. [ME *chirne*]

chute (shoot) *n.* **1.** an inclined trough or vertical passage down which water, coal, etc., may pass. **2.** a steep, narrow watercourse; a rapid. **3.** a narrow pen for branding or controlling cattle. **4.** a slide, as for toboggans. **5.** a parachute. [< F]

chut·ney (CHUT nee) *n.* a piquant relish of fruit, spices, etc. [< Hind. *chatni*]

chutz·pah (KHUUT spə) *n. Slang* brazen effrontery; gall. [< Yiddish *khutspa*]

ciao (chow) *interj.* used in greeting and parting. [< Ital.]

ci·ca·da (si KAY də) *n. pl.* **·das** a large winged insect, the male of which has vibrating membranes that produce a loud, shrill sound: often called *locust.* [ME]

cic·a·trix (SIK ə TRIKS) *n. pl.* **cic·a·tri·ces** (SIK ə TRĪ seez) a scar left by the healing of a wound, the fall of a leaf, etc. [ME]

cic·e·ro·ne (SIS ə ROH nee) *n.* a guide for tourists. [< Ital. < L *Ciceronem,* accusative of *Cicero,* the Roman orator]

ci·der (SĪ dər) *n.* the expressed juice of apples used to make vinegar, and as a beverage before fermentation (**sweet cider**) or after fermentation (**hard cider**). [ME *sidre* strong drink]

ci·gar (si GAHR) *n.* a small roll of tobacco leaves prepared for smoking. [< Sp. *cigarro*]

cig·a·rette (SIG ə RET) *n.* a small roll of finely cut tobacco for smoking, enclosed in thin paper. Also **cig'a·ret'·** [< F]

cil·i·um (SIL ee əm) *n. pl.* **cil·i·a** (-ee ə) **1.** *Biol.* a microscopic, hairlike process on the surface of a cell, organ, plant, etc. **2.** an eyelash. [< NL, eyelash]

cinch (sinch) *n.* **1.** a pack or saddle girth. **2.** a tight grip. **3.** *Informal* something easy or

sure. —*v.t.* **1.** fasten a saddle girth around. **2.** *Informal* get a tight hold upon. **3.** *Informal* make sure of. —*v.i.* **4.** tighten a saddle girth. [< Sp. *cincha* girdle]

cin·der (SIN dər) *n.* **1.** any partly burned substance, not reduced to ashes; esp. a tiny particle of such a substance. **2.** a bit of wood, coal, etc., that can burn but without flame. **3.** *pl.* ashes. **4.** slag. **5.** a fragment of volcanic lava. —*v.t.* burn or reduce to a cinder. [ME *synder*]

cin·e·ma (SIN ə mə) *n.* a movie house. —**the cinema** movies collectively; also, the art or business of making them.

cin·e·ma·tog·ra·phy (SIN ə mə TOG rə fee) *n.* the art and process of making motion pictures.

cin·na·mon (SIN ə mən) *n.* **1.** the aromatic inner bark of any of several tropical trees, used as a spice. **2.** any tree that yields this bark. **3.** a shade of light reddish brown. [< L]

ci·pher (SĪ fər) *n.* **1.** the figure 0; zero. **2.** a person or thing of no value or importance. **3.** any system of secret writing that uses a prearranged scheme or key. **4.** a message in cipher; also, its key. **5.** any Arabic number. —*v.t.* **1.** calculate arithmetically. **2.** write in characters of hidden meaning. —*v.i.* **3.** work out arithmetical examples. [ME *siphre* empty]

cir·ca (SUR kə) *prep.* about; around: used before approximate date or figures. [< L]

cir·ca·di·an (sur KAY dee ən) *adj.* having a rhythmic biological cycle of approximately daily periods. [< CIRCA + L *dies* day]

cir·cle (SUR kəl) *n.* **1.** a plane figure bounded by a curved line every point of which is equally distant from the center. **2.** the circumference of such a figure. **3.** something like a circle, as a halo or ring. **4.** a round or spherical body; an orb. **5.** a group of persons united by some common interest or pursuit. **6.** the domain or scope of a special influence or action. **7.** a gallery or tier of seats in a theater. **8.** a series or process that finishes at its starting point or that repeats itself without end: the *circle* of the seasons. —*v.* **·cled, ·cling** *v.t.* **1.** enclose in a circle; encompass. **2.** move around, as in a circle. —*v.i.* **3.** move in a circle. [< L *circulus*]

cir·cuit (SUR kit) *n.* **1.** a circular route or course. **2.** a periodic journey from place to place, as by a judge or minister. **3.** the territory visited in such a journey. **4.** a group of associated theaters presenting plays, films, etc., in turn. **5.** the distance around an area; circumference; also, the area enclosed. **6.** *Electr.* the entire course traversed by an electric current. **7.** *Telecom.* a transmission and reception system. —*v.t. & v.i.* go or move (about) in a circuit. [ME]

circuit breaker *Electr.* a switch or relay for interrupting a circuit under specified or abnormal conditions of current flow.

circuit court a court of law that sits in various districts under its jurisdiction.

cir·cu·i·tous (sər KYOO i təs) *adj.* roundabout; indirect. [< Med.L *circuitosus*]

circuit rider a minister who preaches at churches on a circuit or district route.

cir·cuit·ry (SUR ki tree) *n. Electr.* the design and components of an electric circuit.

cir·cu·i·ty (sər KYOO i tee) *n. pl.* **·ties** roundabout procedure or speech; indirectness.

cir·cu·lar (SUR kyə lər) *adj.* **1.** shaped like a circle; round. **2.** moving in a circle. **3.** of or referring to a circle. **4.** roundabout: *circular* reasoning. **5.** addressed to several persons, or intended for general circulation. —*n.* a notice or advertisement printed for general distribution. [ME] — **cir′cu·lar′i·ty** *n.*

cir·cu·lar·ize (SUR kyə lə RIZ) *v.t.* **·ized, ·iz·ing 1.** make circular. **2.** distribute circulars to.

cir·cu·late (SUR kyə LAYT) *v.* **·lat·ed, ·lat·ing** *v.i.* **1.** move by a circuitous course back to the starting point, as the blood. **2.** pass from place to place or person to person: Rumors *circulate* quickly. **3.** be in free motion, as air. —*v.t.* **4.** cause to circulate. [ME] —**cir′cu·la·to′ry** *adj.*

cir·cu·la·tion (SUR kyə LAY shən) *n.* **1.** free movement or flow, as air. **2.** motion in a circuit, esp. the motion of the blood through the arteries and veins. **3.** a transmission or spreading from one person or place to another; dissemination. **4.** the extent of distribution of a periodical; also, the number of copies distributed.

cir·cum·am·bi·ent (SUR kəm AM bee ənt) *adj.* encompassing; surrounding. [< LL]

cir·cum·cise (SUR kəm SIZ) *v.t.* **·cised, ·cis·ing** cut off the prepuce (of a male). [ME *circumcisen* cut around] — **cir′cum·ci′sion** (-sizh ən) *n.*

cir·cum·fer·ence (sər KUM fər əns) *n.* **1.** the boundary line of any area; esp., the boundary of a circle. **2.** the length of such a line. [ME] —**cir·cum·fer·en·tial** (sər KE M fə REN shəl) *adj.* —**cir·cum′fer·en′ tial·ly** *adv.*

cir·cum·flex (SUR kəm FLEKS) *n.* the mark ˆ written over certain letters, usu. to mark a long vowel, contraction, etc. —*adj.* **1.** pronounced or marked with the circumflex accent. **2.** *Physiol.* bent or curving around, as certain nerves. [< L *circumflexus* bent around]

cir·cum·lo·cu·tion (SUR kəm loh KYOO shən) *n.* an indirect, verbose way of expressing something; also, an example of this. [ME] —**cir′cum·loc′u·to′ry** (-LOK yə TOR ee) *adj.*

cir·cum·nav·i·gate (SUR kəm NAV ə GAYT) *v.t.* **·gat·ed, ·gat·ing** go completely around, esp. to sail around. [< L *circumnavigatus* sailed around] —**cir′cum·nav′i·ga′tion** *n.*

cir·cum·scribe (SUR kəm SKRIB) *v.t.* **·scribed, ·scrib·ing 1.** mark out the limits of; define. **2.** draw a line or figure around. [ME]

cir·cum·spect (SUR kəm SPEKT) *adj.* attentive to everything; cautious. [ME] — **cir′cum·spec′tion** *n.*

cir·cum·stance (SUR kəm STANS) *n.* **1.** a factor connected with an act, event, or condition, either as an accessory or as a determining element. **2.** *Often pl.* the conditions, influences, etc. affecting persons or actions. **3.** *pl.* financial condition in life. **4.** an occurrence. **5.** formal display: pomp and *circumstance.* —**under no circumstances** never; under no conditions. —**under the circumstances** since such is (or was) the case. —*v.t.* **·stanced, ·stanc·ing** place in or under limiting circumstances or conditions. [ME]

cir·cum·stan·tial (SUR kəm STAN shəl) *adj.* **1.** pertaining to or dependent on circumstances. **2.** incidental; not essential. **3.** full of details.

circumstantial evidence *Law* evidence that furnishes reasonable ground for inferring the existence of a fact.

cir·cum·vent (SUR kəm VENT) *v.t.* **1.** surround or entrap. **2.** gain an advantage over; outwit. **3.** go around or avoid. [< L *circumventus* surrounded] —**cir′cum·ven′tion** *n.*

cir·cus (SUR kəs) *n.* **1.** a traveling show of acrobats, clowns, etc.; also, a performance of such a show. **2.** a circular, usu. tented area used for such shows. **3.** in ancient Rome, an oblong enclosure used for races, games, etc. **4.** an uproarious or disorderly exhibition. [ME]

cir·rho·sis (sə ROH sis) *n. Pathol.* a degenerative disease of the liver. [< Gk. *kirrhos* tawny + -OSIS] —**cir·rhot·ic** (sə ROT ik) *adj.*

cir·rus (SIR əs) *n. pl.* **cir·rus** *Meteorol.* a type of white, wispy cloud, seen in tufts or feathery beards across the sky. [< L, ringlet]

cis·tern (SIS tərn) *n.* an artificial reservoir, as a tank, for holding water or other liquids. [ME *cisterne*]

cit·a·del (SIT ə dl) *n.* **1.** a fortress commanding a city. **2.** any fortress or stronghold. [< MF *citadelle*]

ci·ta·tion (sī TAY shən) *n.* **1.** a citing or quoting; also, a passage or authority so cited. **2.** a public commendation for outstanding achievement. **3.** a summons, as to appear in court. [ME *citacioun*]

cite (sīt) *v.t.* **cit·ed, cit·ing 1.** quote as authority or illustration. **2.** bring forward or refer to as proof or support. **3.** *Mil.* commend or praise, esp. for bravery. **4.** mention or enumerate. **5.** summon to appear in court. [ME, summon]

cit·i·zen (SIT ə zən) *n.* **1.** a native or naturalized person owing allegiance to, and entitled to protection from, a government. **2.** a resident of a city or town. **3.** a civilian, as distinguished from a public officer, soldier, etc. [ME *citisein*]

cit·i·zen·ry (SIT ə zən ree) *n. pl.* **·ries** citizens collectively.

Citizens Band a range of radio frequencies allocated for two-way communication between private individuals by low-powered sets. Abbr. *CB*

cit·i·zen·ship (SIT ə zən SHIP) *n.* the status of a citizen, with its rights, privileges, and duties.

cit·ric (SI trik) *adj.* of or derived from citrus fruits.

cit·rus (SI tras) *adj.* of or pertaining to trees bearing oranges, lemons, etc., or to their fruits. [< NL]

cit·y (SIT ee) *n. pl.* **cit·ies 1.** a place inhabited by a large, permanent community. **2.** in the U.S., a state-chartered municipality, larger than a town. **3.** the people of a city, collectively. [ME *cite*]

cit·y-state (SIT ee STAYT) *n.* a state consisting of a city and its contiguous territories, as ancient Athens.

civ·et (SIV it) *n.* **1.** a substance of musklike odor, secreted by the civet cat, used in per-

fumery. **2.** the civet cat or its fur. [< MF *civette*]

civet cat a feline carnivore of Africa.

civ·ic (SIV ik) *adj.* of or pertaining to a city, a citizen, or citizenship. [< L *civicus*]

civ·ics (SIV iks) *n. (construed as sing.)* the division of political science dealing with the rights and duties of citizens.

civ·il (SIV əl) *adj.* **1.** of or pertaining to community life rather than military or ecclesiastical affairs. **2.** of or pertaining to citizens and their government: *civil* affairs. **3.** occurring within the state; domestic: *civil* war. **4.** of, proper to, or befitting a citizen. **5.** civilized. **6.** proper; polite. **7.** *Law* related to the rights of citizens. [ME] —**civ'il·ly** *adv.*

civil disobedience a nonviolent refusal to comply with certain civil laws.

civil engineer a professional engineer trained to design, build, and maintain public works, as roads, bridges, etc. —**civil engineering**

ci·vil·ian (si VIL yən) *n.* one who is not in the military service. [ME, student of civil law]

ci·vil·i·ty (si VIL i tee) *n. pl.* **·ties 1.** the quality of being civil; courtesy; politeness. **2.** a polite act or speech. [ME *civilite* courtesy]

civ·i·li·za·tion (SIV ə lə ZAY shən) *n.* **1.** a state of human society characterized by a high level of intellectual, social, and cultural development. **2.** the countries and peoples considered to have reached this stage. **3.** the cultural development of a specific people, country, or region. **4.** the act of civilizing, or the process of becoming civilized.

civ·i·lize (SIV ə LIZ) *v.t.* **·lized, ·liz·ing** bring into a state of civilization; bring out of savagery. [< F *civiliser*]

civil law the body of laws dealing with personal rights.

civil liberty a liberty guaranteed to the individual by the laws of a government.

civil marriage a marriage solemnized by a government official rather than by a clergyman.

civil rights certain rights of citizens, esp. the right to vote, exception from servitude, and the right to equal treatment under the law.

civil service 1. the administrative branches of governmental service that are not military, legislative, or judicial. **2.** such governmental branches to which appointments are made as a result of competitive examinations. **3.** the persons employed in these branches. **—civil servant**

civil war war between parties or sections of the same country.

clad (klad) alternative past tense and past participle of CLOTHE.

claim (klaym) *v.t.* **1.** demand as one's right or due; assert ownership or title to. **2.** hold to be true; assert. **3.** require or deserve: The problem *claims* our attention. *—n.* **1.** a demand or an assertion of a right. **2.** an assertion of something as true. **3.** a ground for claiming something. **4.** that which is claimed, as land. [ME *claimen* cry out]

claim·ant (KLAYM ənt) *n.* one who makes a claim.

clair·voy·ance (klair VOI əns) *n.* the alleged ability to see or know things beyond the area of normal perception. [< MF] **—clair·voy'·ant** *n. & adj.*

clam (klam) *n.* **1.** any of various bivalve mollusks, usu. edible. **2.** *Informal* a close-mouthed person. *—v.i.* **clammed, clam·ming** hunt for or dig clams. **—clam up** *Slang* become or keep silent. [ME]

clam·bake (KLAM bayk) *n.* **1.** a picnic where clams and other foods are baked. **2.** any noisy gathering.

clam·ber (KLAM bər) *v.t. & v.i.* climb, mount, or descend with difficulty. [ME *clambren* climb]

clam·my (KLAM ee) *adj.* **·mi·er, ·mi·est** stickily soft and damp, and usu. cold. [ME] **—clam'mi·ness** *n.*

clam·or (KLAM ər) *n.* **1.** a loud, repeated outcry. **2.** a vehement protest or demand. **3.** any loud and continuous noise; din. *—v.i. & v.t.* make or utter with loud outcries, demands, or complaints. [ME] **—clam'or·ous** *adj.*

clamp (klamp) *n.* a device for holding objects together, securing a piece in position, etc. *—v.t.* hold or bind with or as with a clamp. **—clamp down** become more strict. [ME]

clan (klan) *n.* **1.** a united group of relatives, or families, claiming a common ancestor and having the same surname. **2.** a clique; fraternity; club. [ME]

clan·des·tine (klan DES tin) *adj.* kept secret for a purpose; furtive. [< L *clandestinus* secretly]

clang (klang) *v.t. & v.i.* make or cause to make a loud, ringing, metallic sound. **—clang** *n.*

clan·gor (KLANG ər) *n.* repeated clanging; clamor; din. *—v.i.* ring noisily. [< L, noise]

clank (klangk) *n.* a short, harsh, metallic sound. [< Du. *klank* sound] **—clank** *v.t. & v.i.*

clan·nish (KLAN ish) *adj.* **1.** of or characteristic of a clan. **2.** disposed to cling together, or bound by family prejudices, traditions, etc. **—clan'nish·ness** *n.*

clans·man (KLANZ mən) *n. pl.* **·men** a member of a clan. **—clans'wom·an** *n. fem. pl.* **·wom·en**

clap¹ (klap) *v.i.* **clapped, clap·ping** *v.i.* **1.** strike the hands together, as in applauding. **2.** make a sound, as of two boards striking together. *—v.t.* **3.** bring (the hands) together sharply and with an explosive sound. **4.** strike with the open hand, as in greeting. **5.** put or fling quickly or suddenly: They *clapped* him into jail. *—n.* **1.** the act or sound of clapping the hands. **2.** a loud, explosive sound, esp. of thunder. **3.** a blow with the open hand. [ME *clappen*]

clap² *n. Vulgar Slang* gonorrhea. [< MF *clapoir* bubo]

clap·board (KLAB ərd) *n.* a narrow board having one edge thinner than the other, used as siding on frame buildings. *—v.t.* cover with clapboards. [< MDu. *klaphout* barrel stave]

clap·trap (KLAP trap) *n.* pretentious language; nonsense.

claque (klak) *n.* a group of hired applauders. [< F]

clar·et (KLAR it) *n.* **1.** any dry red wine. **2.** ruby to deep purplish red. [ME]

clar·i·fy (KLAR ə FI) *v.t. & v.i.* **·fied, ·fy·ing** **1.** make or become clear or free from impurities. **2.** make or become understandable; explain. [ME] **—clar'i·fi·ca'tion** *n.*

clar·i·net (KLAR ə NET) *n.* a cylindrical woodwind instrument having a single-reed mouthpiece, finger holes, and keys. [< F *clarinette*] **—clar'i·net'ist** *n.*

clar·i·on (KLAR ee ən) *adj.* clear and resounding. [ME, clear]

clar·i·ty (KLAR i tee) *n.* clearness; lucidity. [ME *clarite*]

clash (klash) *v.t.* **1.** strike together with a harsh, metallic sound. **2.** collide with loud and confused noise. **3.** conflict; be in opposition. *—n.* **1.** a resounding, metallic noise. **2.** a conflict.

clasp (klasp) *n.* **1.** a fastening, as a hook, used to hold things or parts together. **2.** a firm grasp of the hand or embrace. —v.t. 1. embrace. 2. fasten with or as with a clasp. 3. grasp firmly in or with the hand. [ME]

class (klas) n. 1. a number of persons or things grouped together by shared characteristics. 2. the division of society by relative standing. 3. a category of objects, persons, etc., based on quality or rank: of the first *class*. 4. a group of students pursuing a study together; also, a meeting of such a group. 5. a group of students in a school or college graduating together. 6. *Biol.* a group of plants or animals standing below a phylum and above an order. 7. *Informal* superiority; elegance. —v.t. assign to a class; classify. [< L *classis*]

class action a legal action on behalf of all persons suffering the same alleged wrong.

clas·sic (KLAS ik) adj. 1. belonging to the first class or highest rank; recognized as a standard of excellence. 2. of, or in the style of, ancient Greece and Rome or their literature or art. 3. typical: a *classic* example. 4. of or having a style that is formal, balanced, restrained, regular, etc. —n. an author, artist, or work generally recognized as a standard of excellence. —**the classics** ancient Greek and Roman literature. [< L *classicus* of a class]

clas·si·cal (KLAS i kəl) adj. 1. generally accepted as being standard and authoritative; traditional. 2. of ancient Greece and Rome: *classical* civilization. 3. versed in the Greek and Roman classics: a *classical* scholar. 4. *Music* loosely, serious as distinguished from popular.

clas·si·cism (KLAS ə SIZ əm) n. 1. a group of esthetic principles (simplicity, restraint, balance, etc.) as manifested in classical art and literature: distinguished from *romanticism*. 2. adherence to these principles. 3. classical scholarship.

clas·si·cist (KLAS ə sist) n. 1. one versed in the classics. 2. an adherent or imitator of classic style.

clas·si·fi·ca·tion (KLAS ə fi KAY shən) n. the act, process, or result of classifying.

clas·si·fy (KLAS ə FI) v.t. **-fied, -fy·ing** 1. arrange by class or category. 2. restrict as to circulation or use, as a government document. [< L *classis* class + -FY] —**clas'si·fi'er** n.

class·mate (KLAS MAYT) n. a member of the same class in school or college.

class·room (KLAS ROOM) n. a room in a school in which classes are held.

clat·ter (KLAT ər) v.i. 1. make or give out short, sharp noises rapidly or repeatedly. 2. move with a rattling noise. 3. talk noisily; chatter. —v.t. 4. cause to clatter. —n. 1. a rattling or clattering sound. 2. a disturbance or commotion. 3. noisy talk; chatter. [ME *clateren* rattle]

clause (klawz) n. 1. a distinct part of a document, as an article in a statute, treaty, etc. 2. *Gram.* a sequence of words containing a subject and a predicate, forming part of a sentence. [ME *claus*]

claus·tro·pho·bi·a (KLAW strə FOH bee ə) n. *Psychiatry* fear of enclosed or confined places. [< L *claustrum* bolt + -PHOBIA] —**claus'tro·pho'bic** adj.

claw (klaw) n. 1. a sharp, usu. curved, horny nail on the toe of a bird, mammal, or reptile. 2. a pincer of certain insects and crustaceans. 3. anything sharp and hooked. —v.t. & v.i. tear, scratch, dig, pull, etc., with or as with claws. [ME]

clay (klay) n. 1. a fine-grained, variously colored earth, pliable when wet, used in the making of bricks, pottery, etc. 2. earth. 3. the human body. —v.t. mix or treat with clay. [ME]

clay pigeon in trapshooting, a saucer-shaped disk, as of baked clay, used as a flying target.

clean (kleen) adj. **-er, -est** 1. free from dirt or stain; unsoiled. 2. morally pure; wholesome. 3. without obstructions, encumbrances, or restrictions. 4. thorough; complete: a *clean* getaway. 5. trim; not ornate: *clean* lines. 6. neat in habits. 7. producing an explosion relatively free of radioactive fallout: said of nuclear weapons. 8. fair: a *clean* fight. 9. *Slang* **a** free from drug addiction. **b** having no illegal drugs in one's possession. —v.t. 1. render free of dirt or other impurities. 2. prepare (fowl, game, etc.) for cooking. —v.i. 3. undergo or perform the act of cleaning. —**clean out** 1. clear of trash or rubbish. 2. empty (a place) of contents or occupants. 3. leave without money. —**clean up** 1. clean thoroughly. 2. *Informal* make a large profit. —adv. **-er, -est** 1. in a clean manner; cleanly. 2. wholly; completely. [ME *clene* pure]

clean-cut (KLEEN KUT) adj. 1. cut with smooth edge or surface; well-made. 2. sharply defined; clear. 3. neat in appearance.

clean·er (KLEE nər) n. 1. a person whose

work is cleaning, esp. clothing. **2.** any substance or device that cleans.

clean·ly (KLEN lee) *adj.* **·li·er, ·li·est** habitually and carefully clean; neat; tidy. — *adv.* (KLEEN lee) in a clean manner. — **clean·li·ness** (KLEN lee nis) *n.*

cleanse (klenz) *v.t.* **cleansed, cleans·ing** free from dirt; purify. [ME *clensen* clean]

cleans·er (KLEN zər) *n.* one who or that which cleanses; esp., a soap or detergent.

clean·up (KLEEN UP) *n.* **1.** a complete cleaning. **2.** *Slang* a large profit; gain.

clear (kleer) *adj.* **·er, ·est 1.** bright; unclouded. **2.** without impurity or blemish. **3.** of great transparency. **4.** free from obstructions or restrictions. **5.** understandable. **6.** plain to the eye, ear, etc. **7.** able to discern; keen: a *clear* mind. **8.** free from uncertainty; sure. **9.** free from guilt or blame. **10.** free from a financial obligation. **11.** not in contact: usu. with *of.* **12.** without deductions; net: a *clear* $5,000. —*adv.* **·er, ·est 1.** in a clear manner. **2.** all the way: *clear* through the day. —*v.t.* **1.** make clear; brighten. **2.** free from foreign matter or impurities. **3.** remove (obstacles, obstructions, etc.). **4.** free from blame or guilt. **5.** make plain. **6.** pass or get under or over without touching. **7.** free from debt by payment. **8.** settle (a debt). **9.** obtain or give clearance for. **10.** gain over and above expenses. **11.** pass (a check) through a clearinghouse. —*v.i.* **12.** become free from fog, rain, etc. —**clear away** (or **off**) remove out of the way. —**clear out 1.** go away. **2.** empty of contents. —**clear the air** dispel tensions; settle differences. —**clear up 1.** make clear. **2.** grow fair, as the weather. **3.** free from confusion or mystery. **4.** put in order; tidy. —*n.* **1.** an unobstructed space. **2.** clearance. —**in the clear 1.** free from limitations or obstructions. **2.** free from guilt or blame. [ME *clere*]

clear·ance (KLEER əns) *n.* **1.** the act or instance of clearing. **2.** the space by which a moving object clears something. **3.** permission for a ship, airplane, etc., to proceed.

clear-cut (KLEER KUT) *adj.* **1.** distinctly and sharply outlined. **2.** plain; evident; obvious. **3.** with all trees cut down: said of timberland. —*v.t.* **-cut, -cut·ting** cut down all trees in (a tract).

clearhead·ed (KLEER HED id) *adj.* not confused; sensible. —**clear′head′ed· ness** *n.*

clear·ing (KLEER ing) *n.* **1.** a making or

becoming clear. **2.** that which is clear or cleared, as a tract of land.

clear·ing·house (KLEER ing HOWS) *n.* **1.** an office where bankers exchange checks and adjust balances. **2.** a center for the storage and exchange of information.

clear-sight·ed (KLEER SĪ tid) *adj.* **1.** having accurate perception and good judgment; discerning. **2.** having keen vision. — **clear′-sight′ed·ness** *n.*

cleat (kleet) *n.* **1.** a strip of wood or metal fastened across or projecting from a surface to strengthen, support, or provide a grip. **2.** a piece of metal or wood with arms on which to wind or secure a rope. —*v.t.* furnish or strengthen with a cleat or cleats. [ME *clete* wedge]

cleav·age (KLEE vij) *n.* **1.** a cleaving or being cleft. **2.** a split or cleft. **3.** *Mineral.* a tendency in certain rocks or crystals to split in certain directions. **4.** the area between a woman's breasts.

cleave¹ (kleev) *v.* **cleft** or **cleaved, cleft** or **cleaved** or **cloven, cleav·ing** *v.t.* **1.** split or sunder. **2.** make or achieve by cutting: to *cleave* a path. **3.** pass through; penetrate. — *v.i.* **4.** part or divide along natural lines of separation. **5.** make one's way; pass: with *through.* [ME *cleven*]

cleave² *v.i.* **cleaved, cleaved, cleav·ing 1.** stick fast; adhere: with *to.* **2.** be faithful: with *to.* [ME *cleven*]

cleav·er (KLEE vər) *n.* **1.** one who or that which cleaves. **2.** a butcher's heavy, axlike knife. [ME *clevere*]

clef (klef) *n. Music* a symbol placed on the staff to show the pitch of the notes. [< L *clavis* key]

cleft (kleft) a past tense, past participle of CLEAVE¹. —*adj.* divided partially or completely. —*n.* a fissure; crevice; rift. [ME *clift*]

cleft palate a congenital longitudinal fissure in the roof of the mouth.

clem·en·cy (KLEM ən see) *n. pl.* **·cies 1.** leniency; mercy. **2.** mildness of weather. [ME]

clem·ent (KLEM ənt) *adj.* **1.** lenient or merciful in temperament; compassionate. **2.** mild: said of weather. [ME, gentle]

clench (klench) *v.t.* **1.** grasp or grip firmly. **2.** close tightly, as the fist or teeth. **3.** clinch, as a nail. —*n.* **1.** a tight grip. **2.** a device that clenches or grips. [ME *clenchen* hold fast]

clere·sto·ry (KLER STOR ee) *n. pl.* **·ries 1.** *Archit.* the highest story of the nave and choir of a church, with windows opening above the aisle roofs, etc. **2.** a similar part in other structures. [ME]

cler•gy (KLUR jee) *n. pl.* **•gies** the whole body of individuals authorized to conduct religious services. [ME *clerge* priestly office] **—cler•gy•man** (-mən) *n. pl.* **•men.** **—cler•gy•wom•an** *n.fem. pl.* **•wom•en**

cler•ic (KLER ik) *adj.* clerical. —*n.* a member of the clergy. [< L *clericus*]

cler•i•cal (KLER i kəl) *adj.* **1.** of or related to clerks or office workers or their work. **2.** belonging to or characteristic of the clergy.

cler•i•cal•ism (KLER i kə LIZ əm) *n.* clerical influence in politics, or support for such influence.

clerk (klurk) *n.* **1.** a worker in an office who attends to accounts etc. **2.** an official or employee of a court, legislative body, or the like, charged with the care of records, etc. **3.** a salesperson. —*v.i.* work or act as clerk. [ME]

clev•er (KLEV ər) *adj.* **1.** mentally keen; quick-witted. **2.** physically adroit, esp. with the hands. **3.** ingeniously made, said, done, etc. [ME *cliver* adroit]

clew (kloo) *n.* **1.** in legends, a ball of thread that guides through a maze. **2.** a clue. [ME *clewe*]

cli•ché (klee SHAY) *n.* a trite or hackneyed expression, action, etc. [< F]

click (klik) *n.* **1.** a short, sharp, nonresonant metallic sound. **2.** *Phonet.* a speech sound made by clicking the tongue, characteristic of certain African languages. —*v.t.* **1.** cause to make a click or clicks. —*v.i.* **2.** produce a click or clicks. **3.** *Informal* succeed. — **click′er** *n.*

cli•ent (KLĪ ənt) *n.* **1.** one who engages the services of a lawyer or any professional adviser. **2.** a customer. [ME, person seeking protection]

cli•en•tele (KLĪ ən TEL) *n.* a body of clients, customers, etc. [< F *clientèle*]

cliff (klif) *n.* a high, steep face of rock; a precipice. [ME *clif*]

cliff•hang•er (KLIF HANG ər) *n.* **1.** a situation marked by suspense or uncertainty of outcome. **2.** a serialized drama marked by suspense at the end of each episode.

cli•mac•ter•ic (klī MAK tər ik) *n.* **1.** an age or period of life characterized by marked physiological change, as the menopause. **2.** any critical year or period. [< L *climactericus* rung of a ladder]

cli•mac•tic (klī MAK tik) *adj.* pertaining to or constituting a climax.

cli•mate (KLĪ mit) *n.* **1.** the temperature, precipitation, winds, etc., characteristic of a region. **2.** a region in reference to its characteristic weather. **3.** a prevailing trend or condition in human affairs: *climate* of opinion. [ME *climat* zone] **—cli•mat•ic** (klī MAT ik) or **•i•cal** *adj.*

cli•ma•tol•o•gy (klī mə TOL ə jee) *n.* the branch of science dealing with the phenomena of climate.

cli•max (KLĪ maks) *n.* **1.** the point of greatest intensity or fullest development; culmination; acme. **2.** in drama etc., the scene or moment of action that determines the final outcome. **3.** an orgasm. —*v.t. & v.i.* reach or bring to a climax. [< LL]

climb (klīm) *v.* **climbed, climb•ing** *v.t.* **1.** ascend or mount (something), esp. by means of the hands and feet. —*v.i.* **2.** rise or advance in status, rank, etc. **3.** incline or slope upward. **4.** grow upward. **—climb down** descend, esp. by using the hands and feet. —*n.* **1.** the act or process of climbing; ascent. **2.** a place ascended by climbing. [ME *climben*]

clinch (klinch) *v.t.* **1.** fasten together or secure, as a driven nail or staple, by bending down the protruding point. **2.** make sure; settle. —*v.i.* **3.** grapple, as combatants. **4.** *Slang* embrace, as lovers. —*n.* **1.** the act of clinching. **2.** a clamp. **3.** a grip or struggle at close quarters, as in boxing. **4.** *Slang* a close embrace. [Var. of CLENCH]

clinch•er (KLIN chər) *n.* **1.** one who or that which clinches. **2.** a nail made for clinching. **3.** a deciding statement, point, etc.

cling (kling) *v.i.* **clung, cling•ing** hold fast or resist separation, either physically or emotionally. [ME *clingen*]

clinging vine *Informal* a person who displays extreme dependence on others.

clin•ic (KLIN ik) *n.* **1.** an infirmary, usu. connected with a hospital or medical school, for the treatment of outpatients. **2.** the teaching of medicine by treating patients in the presence of a class; also, the class itself. **3.** a place where patients are studied and treated by specialists. **4.** a cooperative medical group. **5.** an organization that offers advice on specific problems. [< F *clinique*]

clin•i•cal (KLIN i kəl) *adj.* **1.** of or pertaining to a clinic. **2.** concerned with the obser-

vation and treatment of patients in clinics.
3. coldly scientific or detached.

cli·ni·cian (kli NISH ən) *n.* a physician trained in clinical methods, or one who gives instruction in clinics.

clink[1] (klingk) *v.t. & v.i.* make or cause to make a short, slight, ringing sound. [ME *clinken*] —**clink** *n.*

clink[2] *n. Slang* a prison. [After *Clink* prison in London]

clink·er (KLING kər) *n.* **1.** the fused residue left by coal, etc., in burning. **2.** *Slang* a mistake. [< Du. *klinker* slag]

clip[1] (klip) *n.* **1.** a device that clasps, grips, or holds articles together, as letters or papers. **2.** a device that holds cartridges for a rifle, or ammunition for insertion into firearms. —*v.t.* **clipped, clip·ping** fasten with or as with a clip. [ME *clippen* embrace]

clip[2] *v.* **clipped, clip·ping** *v.t.* **1.** cut with shears or scissors, as hair or fleece; trim. **2.** cut short; curtail. **3.** *Informal* strike with a sharp blow. **4.** *Slang* cheat or defraud. **5.** in football, block illegally. —*v.i.* **6.** cut or trim. **7.** run or move swiftly. —**clip the wings of** check the aspirations or ambitions of. —*n.* **1.** the act of clipping, or that which is clipped off. **2.** the wool yielded at one shearing or during one season. **3.** a sharp blow; punch. **4.** a quick pace. **5.** in football, an illegal block. [ME *clippen* cut]

clip·per (KLIP ər) *n.* **1.** *pl.* an instrument or tool for clipping or cutting. **2.** a sailing vessel of the mid-19th century, built for speed: also **clipper ship. 3.** one who clips.

clip·ping (KLIPing) *n.* **1.** the act of one who or that which clips. **2.** that which is cut off or out by clipping: a newspaper *clipping*.

clique (kleek) *n.* an exclusive or clannish group of people. —*v.i.* **cliqued, cli·quing** unite in a clique. [< F] —**cli'quish** *adj.*

cli·to·ris (KLIT ər is) *n. Anat.* a small erectile organ at the upper part of the vulva. [< Gk. *kleitoris* shut] —**clit'o·ral** *adj.*

cloak (klohk) *n.* **1.** a loose outer garment. **2.** something that covers or hides. —*v.t.* **1.** cover with a cloak. **2.** conceal; disguise. [ME *cloke* cape]

cloak·room (KLOHK ROOM) *n.* a room where hats, coats, luggage, etc., are left temporarily, as in a theater.

clob·ber (KLOB ər) *v.t.* **1.** beat severely; trounce. **2.** defeat utterly.

clock[1] (klok) *n.* an instrument for measuring time; esp., a mechanism that shows the hour and minute on a dial or as a digital display. —*v.t.* ascertain the speed or the time of with a stopwatch or other device. [ME *clokke*]

clock[2] *n.* a decoration on a stocking or sock.

clock·wise (KLOK WIZ) *adj. & adv.* going in the direction traveled by the hands of a clock.

clock·work (KLOK WURK) *n.* the machinery of a clock, or any similar mechanism. —**like clockwork** with regularity and precision.

clod (klod) *n.* **1.** a lump of earth, clay, etc. **2.** a dull, stupid person. [ME *clodde*] —**clod'dish** *adj.*

clod·hop·per (KLOD HOP ər) *n.* **1.** a rustic; hick; lout. **2.** *pl.* large, heavy shoes.

clog (klog) *n.* **1.** anything that impedes motion; an obstruction. **2.** a block or weight attached, as to a horse, to hinder movement. **3.** a wooden-soled shoe. —*v.* **clogged, clog·ging** *v.t.* **1.** choke up or obstruct. **2.** impede; hinder. **3.** fasten a clog to; hobble. —*v.i.* **4.** become clogged or choked. **5.** adhere in a mass; coagulate. [ME]

cloi·son·né (KLOI zə NAY) *n.* **1.** a type of decorative enamel work. **2.** the ware in this style. [< F, partitioned]

clois·ter (KLOI stər) *n.* **1.** a covered walk along the inside walls of buildings in a quadrangle, as in a monastery or college. **2.** a monastery; convent. **3.** any place of quiet seclusion. **4.** monastic life. —*v.t.* seclude; confine, as in a cloister. [ME *cloistre* enclosed place] —**clois'tered** *adj.*

clone (klohn) *n.* **1.** a group of organisms derived from a single individual by asexual means. **2.** one of the organisms so derived. [< Gk. *klōn* twig] —**clone** *v.t.* **cloned, clon·ing**

clon·ing (KLOH ning) *n.* the production of progeny genetically identical with a progenitor.

clop (klop) *v.i.* **clopped, clop·ping** produce a hollow percussive sound, as of a horse's hoof on pavement. [Imit.] —**clop** *n.*

close (klohs) *adj.* **clos·er, clos·est 1.** near or together in space, time, etc. **2.** dense; compact: a *close* weave. **3.** near to the surface; short: a *close* haircut. **4.** near to the mark: a *close* shot. **5.** nearly even or equal: said of contests. **6.** fitting tightly. **7.** conforming to an original: a *close* resemblance. **8.** thorough; rigorous. **9.** bound by strong affection, loyalty, etc.: a *close* friend. **10.** confined in space; cramped: *close* quarters.

11. strictly guarded; exclusive. 12. uncommunicative. 13. close-fisted; stingy. 14. stifling and humid; stuffy. —*v.* (klohz) **closed, clos•ing** *v.t.* 1. shut. 2. obstruct, as an opening or passage. 3. bring to an end; terminate. —*v.i.* 4. become shut or closed. 5. come to an end. 6. grapple; come to close quarters. 7. come to an agreement. 8. be worth at the end of a business day: Stocks *closed* three points higher. —**close down** cease operations, as a factory. —**close in** advance from all sides so as to prevent escape. —**close out** sell all of, usu. at reduced prices. —**close up** 1. close completely. 2. come nearer together, as troops. —*n.* (klohz) 1. the end; conclusion. 2. an enclosed place, esp. about a cathedral or building. —*adv.* (klohs) in a close manner; nearly; closely. [ME *clos*]

close call (klohs) a narrow escape.

closed circuit (klohzd) *Telecom.* a form of television in which broadcasts are transmitted by cable to a restricted number of receivers.

closed shop (klohzd) an establishment where only union members are hired, by agreement with the union.

close-fist•ed (KLOHS FIS tid) *adj.* stingy; miserly.

close-mouthed (KLOHS MOWTHD) *adj.* not given to idle speaking; reserved.

close quarters (KLOHS) 1. in fighting, an encounter at close range or hand-to-hand. 2. a small, confined space.

close shave (klohs) *Informal* a narrow escape.

clos•et (KLOZ it) *n.* 1. a small room or recess for storing clothes, linen, etc. 2. a small, private room. 3. a ruler's council chamber. —*v.t.* 1. shut up or conceal in or as in a closet: usu. reflexive. 2. take (someone) into a room for a private interview. —*adj.* private; confidential. [ME]

close•up (KLOHS UP) *n.* 1. a picture taken at close range, or with a telescopic lens. 2. a close look or view.

clo•sure (KLOH zhər) *n.* 1. a closing or shutting up. 2. that which closes or shuts. 3. an end; conclusion. 4. cloture. —*v.t. & v.i.* •**sured,** •**sur•ing** cloture. [ME]

clot (klot) *n.* a thick or coagulated mass, as of blood. —*v.t. & v.i.* **clot•ted, clot•ting** form into clots; coagulate. [ME]

cloth (klawth) *n. pl.* **cloths** (klawthz) 1. a woven, knitted, or felted fabric; also, a piece of such fabric. 2. a piece of cloth for a spe-

cial use, as a tablecloth. 3. professional attire, esp. of the clergy. —**the cloth** the clergy. [ME]

clothe (klohth) *v.t.* **clothed** or **clad, cloth•ing** 1. cover or provide with clothes; dress. 2. cover as if with clothing. [ME *clothen*]

clothes (klohz) *n.pl.* garments; clothing. [ME]

cloth•ier (KLOHTH yər) *n.* one who sells clothing.

cloth•ing (KLOH thing) *n.* 1. dress; apparel. 2. a covering.

clo•ture (KLOH chər) *n.* a parliamentary device to stop debate in a legislative body in order to secure a vote. [< F *clôture*] —**clo' ture** *v.t.* •**tured,** •**tur•ing** close a debate by cloture.

cloud (klowd) *n.* 1. a mass of visible vapor or an aggregation of watery or icy particles floating in the atmosphere. 2. any visible collection of particles in the air. 3. a cloudlike mass of things in motion; swarm. 4. something that darkens, obscures, or threatens. —**in the clouds** fanciful or impractical. —**on cloud nine** *Informal* in a transport of delight; elated. —**under a cloud** 1. overshadowed by reproach or distrust. 2. troubled or depressed. —*v.t.* 1. cover with or as with clouds; dim; obscure. 2. render gloomy or troubled. 3. disgrace; sully, as a reputation. —*v.i.* 4. become overcast: often with *up* or *over.* [ME] —**cloud' less** *adj.*

cloud•burst (KLOWD BURST) *n.* a sudden, heavy downpour.

cloud•y (KLOW dee) *adj.* **cloud•i•er, cloud•i•est** 1. overspread with clouds. 2. of or like a cloud or clouds. 3. marked with cloudlike spots. 4. not limpid or clear. 5. vague; confused: *cloudy* thinking. 6. full of foreboding; gloomy. [ME *cloudi*] —**cloud' i•ness** *n.*

clout (klowt) *n.* 1. a heavy blow or cuff with the hand. 2. *Informal* influence or power; esp., political weight. 3. in baseball, a long hit. —*v.t.* hit or strike, as with the hand. [ME]

clove[1] (klohv) *n.* a dried flower bud of a tree of the myrtle family, used as a spice. [ME *clowe*]

clove[2] a segment of a bulb, as of garlic. [ME]

clo•ven (KLOH vən) alternative past participle of CLEAVE[1]. —*adj.* parted; split.

clo•ven-hoofed (KLOH vən HUUFT) *adj.* 1. having the foot cleft, as cattle. 2. satanic.

clo·ver (KLOH vər) n. any of several plants having dense flower heads and 3-parted leaves. —**in clover** in a prosperous condition. [ME *clovere*]

clo·ver·leaf (KLOH vər LEEF) n. pl. **·leafs**, **·leaves** a type of highway intersection resembling a four-leaf clover.

clown (klown) n. 1. a professional comic performer in a play or circus; jester. 2. a coarse or vulgar person. —v.i. behave like a clown. [Earlier *cloyne*]

cloy (kloi) v.t. 1. gratify beyond desire; surfeit. —v.i. 2. cause a feeling of surfeit. [ME *acloyen* nail in] —**cloy'ing** adj.

club[1] (klub) n. 1. a stout stick or staff. 2. a stick or bat used in games. 3. a playing card bearing a black figure shaped like a three-leaf clover. —v.t. **clubbed, club·bing** beat, as with a club. [ME *clubbe*]

club[2] n. 1. a group of persons organized for some mutual aim or pursuit, esp. a group that meets regularly. 2. the meeting place of such a group. —v. **clubbed, club·bing** v.t. 1. contribute for a common purpose: to *club* resources. —v.i. 2. combine or unite: often with *together*. [Special use of CLUB[1]]

club·foot (KLUB FUUT) n. Pathol. 1. congenital distortion of the foot. 2. pl. **·feet** a foot so affected. —**club'foot'ed** adj.

club·house (KLUB HOWS) n. 1. the building occupied by a club. 2. dressing rooms for an athletic team.

cluck (kluk) v.i. 1. give the cry of a hen calling her chicks. 2. utter any similar sound. —v.t. 3. call by clucking. 4. express with a like sound: *cluck* disapproval. [ME *clokken*] —**cluck** n.

clue (cloo) n. something that leads to the solution of a problem or mystery. —v.t. **clued, clu·ing** give (someone) information. [Var. sp. of CLEW]

clump (klump) n. 1. a thick cluster. 2. a heavy, dull sound, as of tramping. 3. an irregular mass; a lump. —v.i. 1. walk clumsily and noisily. 2. form clumps. —v.t. 3. place or plant in a clump. [< OE *clympre* metal lump]

clum·sy (KLUM zee) adj. **·si·er, ·si·est** 1. lacking skill, ease, or grace. 2. Ungainly or unwieldy. 3. ill-contrived: a *clumsy* excuse. [ME *clumsen* be numb with cold] —**clum'si·ly** adv.

clung (klung) past tense, past participle of CLING.

clus·ter (KLUS tər) n. 1. a collection of similar objects growing or fastened together. 2.

a group of persons or things close together. [ME]

clutch[1] (kluch) v.t. 1. snatch, as with hands or talons. 2. grasp and hold firmly. —v.i. 3. attempt to seize, snatch, or reach: with *at*. —n. 1. a tight grip; grasp. 2. pl. power or control. 3. Mech. **a** a device for coupling two working parts, as the engine and driveshaft of an automobile. **b** a lever or pedal for operating such a device. 4. a critical or crucial situation. [ME *clucchen* clench]

clutch[2] n. 1. the number of eggs laid at one time. 2. a brood of chickens. —v.t. hatch. [< ON *klekja* hatch].

clut·ter (KLUT ər) n. 1. a disordered state or collection; litter. 2. a clatter. —v.t. 1. litter, heap, or pile in a confused manner. — v.i. 2. make a clatter. [Var. of earlier *clotter*]

coach (kohch) n. 1. a large, four-wheeled closed carriage. 2. a passenger bus. 3. a railroad passenger car or section of an airplane offering the most economical accommodations. 4. a private tutor. 5. a trainer or director in athletics, dramatics, etc. —v.t. 1. tutor or train; act as coach to. —v.i. 2. act as coach. [< Hung. *kocsi (szeker)* (wagon) of Kocs, the village where first used]

co·ag·u·lant (koh AG yə lənt) n. a coagulating agent, as rennet.

co·ag·u·late (koh AG yə LAYT) v.t. & v.i. **·lat·ed, ·lat·ing** change from a liquid into a clot or mass. [ME, curdle] —**co·ag'u·la' tion** n.

coal (kohl) n. 1. a solid, dark brown to black, combustible mineral found in the earth and used as fuel. 2. a piece of coal. 3. a glowing or charred fragment of wood or other fuel; an ember. —**carry coals to Newcastle** provide something already in abundant supply. —**haul (rake,** etc.) **over the coals** criticize severely; reprimand. —v.t. 1. supply with coal. —v.i. 2. take on coal. [ME *cole*]

co·a·lesce (KOH ə LES) v.i. **·lesced, ·lesc·ing** grow or come together into one; blend. [< L *coalescere* nourish] — **co'a·les'cence** n.

co·a·li·tion (KOH ə LISH ən) n. 1. an alliance of persons, parties, or states. 2. a fusion into one mass. [< L]

coarse (kors) adj. **coars·er, coars·est** 1. lacking refinement; vulgar. 2. inferior; base; common. 3. composed of large parts or particles. [Earlier *corse*]

coars·en (KOR sən) v.t. & v.i. make or become coarse.

coast (kohst) n. 1. the land next to the sea; the seashore. 2. a slope suitable for sliding, as on a sled; also, a slide down it. **—the Coast** the part of the United States bordering on the Pacific Ocean. **—the coast is clear** there is no danger or difficulty now. —v.i. 1. slide down a slope by force of gravity alone, as on a sled. 2. continue moving on acquired momentum alone. 3. sail along a coast. —v.t. 4. sail along, as a coast; skirt. [ME *coste* rib] **—coast'al** adj.

coast·er (KOH stər) n. 1. one who or that which coasts. 2. a sled or toboggan. 3. a small disk set under a drinking glass to protect the surface beneath.

coast guard naval or military coastal patrol and police. **—United States Coast Guard** a force set up to protect life and property at sea and to enforce customs, immigration, and navigation laws.

coast·line (KOHST LIN) n. the contour or boundary of a coast.

coat (koht) n. 1. a sleeved outer garment. 2. a natural covering, as the fur of an animal. 3. any layer covering a surface, as paint, ice, etc. —v.t. 1. cover with a surface layer, as of paint. 2. provide with a coat. [ME *cote*]

coat·ing (KOH ting) n. 1. a covering layer; coat. 2. cloth for coats.

coat of arms 1. a shield marked with the insignia of a person or family. 2. a representation of such insignia.

coat of mail pl. **coats of mail** a defensive garment made of chain mail.

coat·tail (KOHT TAYL) n. the loose, back part of a coat below the waist; also, either half of this in a coat split at the back. **—on (one's) coattails** dependent on another, esp. for success in an election.

coax (kohks) v.t. 1. seek to persuade by gentleness, flattery, etc. 2. obtain by coaxing. — v.i. 3. use persuasion or cajolery. [< earlier *cokes* a fool]

co·ax·i·al (koh AK see əl) adj. 1. having a common axis or coincident axes. 2. describing a cable consisting of two or more insulated conductors capable of transmitting radio or television signals or multiple telegraph or telephone messages.

cob (kob) n. 1. a corncob. 2. a male swan. 3. a thickset horse with short legs. [ME *cobbe* male swan]

cob·ble¹ (KOB əl) n. a cobblestone. —v.t. **·bled, ·bling** pave with cobblestones.

cob·ble² v.t. **·bled, ·bling** repair, as shoes. 2. put goether clumsily.

cob·bler¹ (KOB lər) n. one who repairs shoes.[ME *cobolere*]

cob·bler² n. a deep-dish fruit pie with no bottom crust.

cob·ble·stone (KOB əl STOHN) n. a naturally rounded stone, used for paving.

co·bra (KOH brə) n. a venomous snake of Asia and Africa that when excited can dilate its neck into a broad hood.

cob·web (KOB WEB) n. 1. the network of fine thread spun by a spider; also, a single thread of this. 2. something flimsy or entangling like a cobweb. —v.t. **·webbed, ·web·bing** cover with or as with cobwebs. [ME *coppeweb* spiderweb]

co·ca (KOH kə) n. 1. the dried leaves of a South American shrub, yielding cocaine etc. 2. the shrub itself. [< Sp.]

co·caine (koh KAYN) n. a bitter substance used as a local anesthetic and as a narcotic.

coc·cyx (KOK siks) n. pl. **coc·cy·ges** (kok SI jeez) Anat. the small triangular bone at the base of the spine. [< NL]

coch·le·a (KOK lee ə) n. pl. **·le·ae** (-lee EE), **·le·as** Anat. a spiral tube in the inner ear, forming an essential part of the mechanism of hearing. [< L]

cock¹ (kok) n. 1. a full-grown male domestic fowl; a rooster. 2. any male bird. 3. in a firearm, the hammer; also, the condition of readiness for firing. 4. a jaunty tip or upward turn, as of a hat brim. 5. a faucet or valve. —v.t. 1. set the mechanism of (a firearm) so as to be ready for firing. 2. turn up or to one side alertly, jauntily, or inquiringly, as the head. 3. bring to a position of readiness. —v.i. 4. cock a firearm. 5. stick up prominently. [ME, rooster]

cock² n. a conical pile of straw or hay. —v.t. arrange in piles or cocks, as hay. [ME]

cock·a·trice (KOK ə tris) n. a fabulous serpent, said to be hatched from a cock's egg, deadly to those who felt its breath or met its glance. [ME]

cock·chaf·er (KOK CHAY fər) n. a large European beetle destructive to vegetation.

cocked hat a tricorn. **—knock into a cocked hat** demolish; ruin.

cock·fight (KOK FIT n. a fight between specially trained cocks.

cock·horse (KOK HORS) n. a rocking horse or hobbyhorse.

cock·le (KOK əl) n. 1. a European bivalve mollusk, esp. an edible species, with ridged shells. 2. any of various similar mollusks. **—the cockles of one's heart**

the depths of one's heart or feelings. [ME *cokille* mussel]

cock·le·shell (KOK əl SHEL) n. the shell of a cockle.

cock·ney (KOK nee) n. **1.** *Often cap.* a resident of the East End of London. **2.** the dialect or accent of East End Londoners. [ME *cokeney* foolish person]

cock·pit (KOK PIT) n. **1.** a compartment in an airplane for the pilot and copilot. **2.** a pit or ring for cockfighting.

cock·roach (KOK ROHCH) n. any of a large group of chiefly nocturnal insects, many of which are household pests. [< Sp. *cucaracha*]

cock·sure (KOK SHUUR) adj. **1.** absolutely sure. **2.** overly self-confident.

cock·tail (KOK TAYL) n. **1.** any of various chilled, usually mixed alcoholic drinks. **2.** an appetizer, as chilled diced fruits or seafood seasoned with sauce.

cock·y (KOK ee) adj. **cock·i·er, cock·i·est** swaggeringly self-confident; conceited. — **cock′i·ness** n.

co·co (KOH KOH) n. pl. **·cos 1.** the coconut palm. **2.** the fruit of the coconut palm. —adj. made of coconut fiber. [< Pg., grimace]

co·coa (KOH KOH) n. **1.** a powder made from the roasted, husked seed kernels of the cacao; chocolate. **2.** a beverage made from this. **3.** a reddish brown color. [Earlier CACAO]

co·co·nut (KOH kə NUT) n. the fruit of the coconut palm, having white meat enclosed in a hard shell.

coconut milk a milky fluid inside the coconut.

coconut palm a tropical palm tree bearing coconuts.

co·coon (kə KOON) n. the fibrous envelope spun by the larvae of certain insects. [< F *cocon*]

cod (kod) n. pl. **cod** or **cods** a food fish of the North Atlantic. [ME]

co·da (KOH də) n. *Music* a passage at the end of a work or movement. [< Ital., lit., tail]

cod·dle (KOD l) v.t. **·dled, ·dling 1.** simmer in water. **2.** baby; pamper.

code (kohd) n. **1.** a systematized body of law. **2.** any system of principles or regulations. **3.** a set of signals, characters, or symbols used in communication. **4.** a set of words, letters, or numbers, used for secrecy or brevity in sending messages. —v.t. **cod·ed,**

cod·ing 1. systematize, as laws. **2.** put into the symbols of a code. [ME]

co·dex (KOH deks) n. pl. **co·di·ces** (KOH də SEEZ) an ancient manuscript volume, as of Scripture. [< L, writing tablet]

codg·er (KOJ ər) n. an eccentric or testy man, esp. an old one.

cod·i·cil (KOD ə səl) n. **1.** *Law* a supplement to a will. **2.** an appendix; addition. [ME]

cod·i·fy (KOD ə FI) v.t. **·fied, ·fy·ing** systematize, as laws. —**cod′i·fi·ca′tion** n.

cod-liver oil (KOD LIV ər) oil from the liver of cod, a source of vitamins A and D.

co·ed (KOH ED) n. a woman student at a coeducational institution. —adj. coeducational.

co·ed·u·ca·tion (KOH ej uu KAY shən) n. the education of both sexes in the same school. —**co′ed·u·ca′tion·al** adj.

co·ef·fi·cient (KOH ə FISH ənt) n. **1.** *Math.* a number or letter before an algebraic expression that multiplies it. **2.** *Physics* a number showing the change in a substance, body, or process under given conditions.

co·erce (koh URS) v.t. **·erced, ·erc·ing 1.** compel by force, authority, or fear. **2.** restrain or repress by superior force. **3.** bring about by force. [ME] —**co·er′cive** adj.

co·er·cion (koh UR shən) n. **1.** forcible constraint or restraint, moral or physical. **2.** government by force.

co·ex·ist (KOH ig ZIST) v.i. exist together, in, or at the same place or time. —**co′ex·ist′ ence** n.

cof·fee (KAW fee) n. **1.** a beverage made from the roasted and ground beans of a tropical evergreen shrub. **2.** the seeds or beans of this shrub: also **coffee beans. 3.** the shrub itself. **4.** the brown color of coffee with cream. [< Ital. *caffé*]

cof·fee·house (KAW fee HOWS) n. a place where coffee is featured and people meet to talk, play chess, etc.

cof·fer (KAW fər) n. **1.** a chest or box, esp. one for valuables. **2.** pl. financial resources; a treasury. **3.** a decorative, sunken panel in a ceiling, dome, etc. **4.** a lock in a canal. **5.** a cofferdam. [ME *cofre* basket]

cof·fer·dam (KAW fər DAM) n. **1.** a temporary enclosure built in water and pumped dry to permit work on bridge piers and the like. **2.** a watertight structure attached to a ship's side for repairs made below the water line.

cof·fin (KAW fin) *n.* a box or case in which a corpse is buried. [ME *cofin*]

cog (kog) *n.* **1.** *Mech.* a tooth or one of a series of teeth projecting from the surface of a wheel or gear to impart or receive motion. **2.** one who plays a minor but necessary part in a large or complex process. [ME *cogge*]

co·gent (KOH jənt) *adj.* compelling assent; forcible; convincing. [< L *cogentus* driven together] —**co'gen·cy** *n.*

cog·i·tate (KOJ i TAYT) *v.t. & v.i.* **·tat·ed, ·tat·ing** ponder; meditate. [< L *cogitatus* thought about] —**cog'i·ta'tion** *n.*

co·gnac (KON yak) *n.* a kind of brandy, esp. one produced in the Cognac region of France. [< F]

cog·nate (KOG nayt) *adj.* **1.** allied by blood; kindred. **2.** allied by having the same source: said esp. of words in different languages. **3.** allied by having like characteristics; similar. [< L *cognatus* related by birth] —**cog'nate** *n.*

cog·ni·tion (kog NISH ən) *n.* **1.** the act or faculty of knowing or perceiving. **2.** a thing known; a perception. [ME *cognicioun*] —**cog'ni·tive** *adj.*

cog·ni·zance (KOG nə zəns) *n.* apprehension or perception of fact; knowledge; notice. —**take cognizance of** acknowledge; recognize. [ME *conisaunce*]

cog·ni·zant (KOG nə zənt) *adj.* having knowledge; aware: with *of.*

cog·wheel (KOG HWEEL) *n.* a wheel with cogs, used to transmit or receive motion.

co·hab·it (koh HAB it) *v.i.* live together as husband and wife, esp. without sanction of marriage. [< LL *cohabitare* have joint possession] —**co·hab'i·ta'tion** *n.*

co·here (koh HEER) *v.i.* **·hered, ·her·ing 1.** stick or hold firmly together. **2.** be logically connected, as the parts of a story. [< L *cohaerere* stick together]

co·her·ence (koh HEER əns) *n.* **1.** the act or state of sticking or holding together; cohesion. **2.** logical connection or consistency. Also **co·her'en·cy.**

co·her·ent (koh HEER ənt) *adj.* **1.** sticking together, as particles of the same substance. **2.** logical; consistent. **3.** intelligible or articulate, as speech.

co·he·sion (koh HEE zhən) *n.* **1.** the act or state of cohering. **2.** *Physics* the force by which molecules of the same kind or the same body are held together. —**co·he'sive** (-siv) *adj.*

co·hort (KOH hort) *n.* **1.** the tenth of an ancient Roman legion, 300 to 600 men. **2.** a band or group, esp. of warriors. **3.** a companion or follower. [< MF *cohorte* armed force]

coif (koif) *n.* **1.** a close-fitting cap or hood, as that worn by nuns under the veil. **2.** a hairdo. —*v.t.* **1.** cover with or as with a coif. **2.** (kwahf) style (hair). [ME *coyfe* cap]

coif·feur (kwah FUR) *n. French* a hairdresser.

coif·fure (kwah FYUUR) *n.* **1.** a style of arranging the hair. **2.** a headdress. —*v.t.* dress (the hair). Also **coif.** [< F]

coil (koil) *n.* **1.** a series of concentric rings or spirals, as that formed by winding a rope. **2.** a single ring or spiral of such a series. **3.** any of several electrical devices containing a coiled wire, as an induction coil. —*v.t. & v.i.* wind spirally or in rings.

coin (koin) *n.* **1.** a piece of metal stamped by government authority for use as money. **2.** metal currency collectively. —*v.t.* **1.** stamp (coins) from metal. **2.** make into coins. **3.** originate or invent, as a word or phrase. [ME *coyne* wedge]

coin·age (KOI nij) *n.* **1.** the act or right of making coins. **2.** the coins made. **3.** the system of coins of a country; currency. **4.** the act of inventing a word, phrase, etc. **5.** the word, phrase, etc. itself.

co·in·cide (KOH in SĪD) *v.i.* **·cid·ed, ·cid·ing 1.** have the same dimensions and position in space. **2.** occur at the same time. **3.** agree exactly; accord. [< Med.L *coincidere* befall together]

co·in·ci·dence (koh IN si dəns) *n.* **1.** the condition of coinciding; correspondence. **2.** a remarkable concurrence of events, ideas, etc.

co·in·ci·dent (koh IN si dənt) *adj.* **1.** having the same position and extent. **2.** occurring at the same time. **3.** in exact agreement: with *with.*

co·in·ci·den·tal (koh IN si DEN tl) *adj.* characterized by or involving coincidence. —**co·in'ci·dent'tal·ly** *adv.*

co·i·tus (KOH i təs) *n.* sexual intercourse. Also **co·i·tion** (koh ISH ən). [< L, a coming together]

coke (kohk) *n.* **1.** a solid fuel obtained by heating coal to remove its gases. **2.** *Slang* cocaine. —*v.t. & v.i.* **coked, cok·ing** change into coke. [ME *colke*]

co·la (KOH lə) *n.* **1.** a small tropical tree bearing seeds (**cola nuts**) used in making soft drinks. **2.** a carbonated soft drink made from cola nuts.

col·an·der (KUL ən dər) *n.* a perforated vessel for draining off liquids. [ME *colyndore* strainer]

cold (kohld) *adj.* **1.** having little or no heat. **2.** having a relatively low temperature: *cold* hands. **3.** feeling little or no warmth; chilled. **4.** dead. **5.** detached; objective: *cold* reason. **6.** lacking in affection or passion; unfriendly. —**cold feet** *Informal* loss of courage; timidity. —*adv.* thoroughly; with certainty: know something *cold.* —*n.* **1.** lack of heat. **2.** the sensation caused by loss or lack of heat. **3.** an acute viral infection of the upper respiratory tract, characterized by sneezing, coughing, etc. —**out in the cold** ignored; neglected. —**catch** (or **take**) **cold** become infected with a cold. [ME]

cold-blood·ed (KOHLD BLUD id) *adj.* **1.** unsympathetic; heartless. **2.** sensitive to cold. **3.** *Zool.* having a blood temperature that varies with that of the environment, as in reptiles.

cold duck a blend of sparkling Burgundy and Champagne. [< G *Kalte Ente,* a blend of wines]

cold front *Meteorol.* the forward edge of an advancing cold air mass.

cold-heart·ed (KOHLD HAHR tid) *adj.* without sympathy; unkind.

cold shoulder a deliberate slight.

cold sore an eruption about the mouth or nostrils, often accompanying a cold or fever.

cold turkey *Informal* abrupt and total withdrawal from a drug by an addict.

cold war an intense rivalry between nations, falling short of armed conflict.

cole·slaw (KOHL SLAW) *N. a salad of shredded raw cabbage.* [< Du. *koolsla* cabbage salad]

col·ic (KOL ik) *n.* acute abdominal pain resulting from muscular spasms. —*adj.* pertaining to, near, or affecting the colon. [ME *colike*] —**col'ick·y** *adj.*

col·i·se·um (KOL i SEE əm) *n.* a large building or stadium for exhibitions, sports events, etc. [after the *Colosseum,* a Roman amphitheater]

co·li·tis (kə LĪ tis) *n.* inflammation of the colon.

col·lab·o·rate (kə LAB ə RAYT) *v.i.* •**rat·ed,** •**rat·ing 1.** work or cooperate with another, esp. in literary or scientific pursuits. **2.** be a

collaborationist. [< LL *collaboratus* worked together] —**col·lab'o·ra'tion** *n.* —**col·lab'o·ra'tive** *adj.*

col·lab·o·ra·tion·ist (kə LAB ə RAY shən ist) *n.* a citizen of an occupied country who cooperates with the enemy.

col·lage (kə LAHZH) *n.* an artistic composition consisting of or including flat materials pasted on a surface. [< F]

col·lapse (kə LAPS) *v.* •**lapsed,** •**laps·ing** *v.i.* **1.** give way; cave in. **2.** fail utterly; come to naught. **3.** assume a more compact form, as by being folded. **4.** lose health, strength, etc., suddenly. —*v.t.* **5.** cause to collapse. —*n.* **1.** the act or process of collapsing. **2.** extreme prostration. **3.** utter failure; ruin. [< L *collapsus* fallen] —**col·laps'i·ble** *adj.*

col·lar (KOL ər) *n.* **1.** the part of a garment at the neck, often folded over. **2.** a band of leather or metal for the neck of an animal. **3.** *Mech.* any of various devices encircling a rod or shaft, to form a connection, etc. —*v.t.* **1.** provide with a collar. **2.** grasp by the collar; capture. [ME *coler*]

col·late (kə LAYT) *v.t.* •**lat·ed,** •**lat·ing 1.** compare critically, as writings or facts. **2.** assemble (pages, etc.) in their correct order. [< L *collatus* brought together]

col·lat·er·al (kə LAT ər əl) *adj.* **1.** lying or running side by side; parallel. **2.** concomitant. **3.** tending to the same conclusion; corroborative. **4.** subordinate; secondary. **5.** guaranteed by stocks, property, etc.: a *collateral* loan. **6.** descended from a common ancestor, but in a different line. —*n.* security pledged for a loan or obligation. [ME]

col·la·tion (kə LAY shən) *n.* **1.** the act or process of collating. **2.** any light, informal meal. [ME *collacion*]

col·league (KOL eeg) *n.* a fellow member of a profession, association, etc.; an associate. [< MF *collegue*]

col·lect[1] (kə LEKT) *v.t.* **1.** gather together; assemble. **2.** bring together as a hobby: *collect* stamps. **3.** request and obtain (payments of money). **4.** regain control: *collect* one's wits. —*v.i.* **5.** assemble or congregate. **6.** accumulate. **7.** gather payments or donations. —*adj. & adv.* to be paid for by the receiver. [ME] —**col·lect'i·ble** *adj.*

col·lect[2] (KOL ekt) *n. Eccl.* a short, formal prayer used in several Western liturgies. [ME *collecte*]

col·lect·ed (kə LEK tid) *adj.* **1.** gathered together. **2.** composed; self-possessed.

col·lec·tion (kə LEK shən) *n.* **1.** the act or process of collecting. **2.** that which is collected. **3.** an accumulation. **4.** a soliciting of money; also, the money obtained.

col·lec·tive (kə LEK tiv) *adj.* **1.** formed or gathered together by collecting. **2.** of, relating to, or proceeding from a number of persons or things together. **3.** *Gram.* denoting in the singular number an aggregate of individuals: *collective* noun. —*n.* a collective enterprise, body, or noun.

collective bargaining negotiation between organized workers and employers on wages, hours, etc.

col·lec·tor (kə LEK tər) *n.* one who or that which collects.

col·leen (KOL een) *n.* a girl. [< Irish *cailín*]

col·lege (KOL ij) *n.* **1.** a school of higher learning that grants a bachelor's degree. **2.** any of the undergraduate divisions of a university. **3.** a school for instruction in a special field or a profession. **4.** a building or buildings used by a college or university. **5.** an association having certain rights and duties: the electoral *college*. [ME] — **col·le·giate** (kə LEE jit) *adj.*

College of Cardinals in the Roman Catholic Church, the body of cardinals who elect and advise the Pope.

col·le·gi·al·i·ty (kə LEE jee AL i tee) *n.* cordial cooperation between colleagues.

col·lide (kə LĪD) *v.i.* **·lid·ed, ·lid·ing 1.** come together with violent impact; crash. **2.** come into conflict; clash. [< L *collidere* strike together]

col·lie (KOL ee) *n.* large sheep dog with a long, narrow head and full, long-haired coat.

col·lier (KOL yər) *n.* a vessel for carrying coal. [ME *coliere*]

col·lier·y (KOL yər ee) *n. pl.* **·lier·ies** a coal mine.

col·li·mate (KOL ə MAYT) *v.t.* **·mat·ed, ·mat·ing 1.** bring into line or make parallel, as refracted rays of light. **2.** adjust the line of sight of (a telescope etc.). [< L *collimatus* directed in a straight line] — **col·li·ma·tor** (KOL i MAY tər) *n. Optics.* a device used to obtain parallel rays of light.

col·li·sion (kə LIZH ən) *n.* **1.** the act of colliding; a crash. **2.** a clash; conflict. [ME]

col·lo·qui·al (kə LOH kwee əl) *adj.* of speech or writing, informal; conversational. —**col·lo′·qui·al·ly** *adv.*

col·lo·qui·al·ism (kə LOH kwee ə LIZ əm)

n. **1.** a colloquial expression or form of speech. **2.** informal, conversational style.

col·lo·qui·um (kə LOH kwee əm) *n. pl.* **·qui·ums** or **·qui·a** (-kwee ə) a seminar, esp. one with several lecturers.

col·lo·quy (KOL ə kwee) *n. pl.* **·quies** a conversation or conference, esp. a formal one. [< L *colloquium*]

col·lude (kə LOOD) *v.i.* **·lud·ed, ·lud·ing** conspire. [< L *colludere* play together]

col·lu·sion (kə LOO zhən) *n.* secret agreement for a wrongful purpose; conspiracy. [ME] —**col·lu′·sive** (-siv) *adj.*

co·logne (kə LOHN) *n.* a toilet water consisting of alcohol scented with aromatic oils: also called *eau de Cologne.* [after *Cologne,* Germany]

co·lon[1] (KOH lən) *n.* a punctuation mark (:), used after a word introducing a quotation, list of items, etc., after the salutation in a formal letter, and in mathematical proportions. [< L]

co·lon[2] *n. Anat.* a portion of the large intestine. [ME] —**co·lon·ic** (kə LON ik) *adj.*

colo·nel (KUR nl) *n. Mil.* a commissioned officer ranking next above a lieutenant colonel and next below a brigadier general. [< MF] —**colo′·nel·cy** *n.*

co·lo·ni·al (kə LOH nee əl) *adj.* **1.** of, pertaining to, or living in a colony or colonies. **2.** of or referring to the thirteen original colonies of the U.S. —*n.* a citizen or inhabitant of a colony.

co·lo·ni·al·ism (kə LOH nee ə LIZ əm) *n.* the policy of a nation seeking to acquire, extend, or retain overseas dependencies.

col·o·nist (KOL ə nist) *n.* **1.** a member or inhabitant of a colony. **2.** a settler or founder of a colony.

col·o·nize (KOL ə NĪZ) *v.* **·nized, ·niz·ing** *v.t.* **1.** set up a colony in; settle. **2.** establish as colonists. —*v.i.* **3.** establish or unite in a colony or colonies. —**col′·o·ni·za′tion** *n.*

col·o·ny (KOL ə nee) *n. pl.* **·nies 1.** a body of emigrants living in a land apart from, but under the control of, the parent country. **2.** the region thus settled. **3.** any territory politically controlled by a distant state. **4.** a group of persons from the same country, of the same occupation, etc. living in a particular area. **5.** the area itself. **6.** *Ecol.* a group of similar plants or animals living in a particular locality. —**the Colonies** the British colonies that became the original thirteen states of the United States. [ME *colonie*]

col·or (KUL ər) *n.* **1.** a visual attribute of

bodies or substances that depends on the wavelengths of light reflected from their surfaces. **2.** a paint, dyestuff, or pigment. **3.** complexion; hue of the skin. **4.** ruddy complexion; also, a blush. **5.** pl. the ensign or flag of a nation, military or naval unit, etc. **6.** a color, ribbon, etc. used for identification: college colors. **7.** a pretext; disguise: under color or religion. **8.** liveliness or vividness, esp. in literary work. **9.** in art and literature, the use of characteristic details to produce a realistic effect: local color. —**show one's (true) colors** show one's real nature, beliefs, etc. —v.t. **1.** apply or give color to, as by painting. **2.** misrepresent or change (facts), as by exaggeration. —v.i. **3.** take on or change color. **4.** blush. [ME colour]

col·or·a·tion (KUL ə RAY shən) n. arrangement of colors, as in an animal or plant; coloring.

col·or·a·tu·ra (KUL ər ə TUUR ə) n. **1.** in vocal music, runs, trills, or other florid decoration. **2.** music characterized by this. **3.** a coloratura soprano. [< Ital., coloration]

color blindness the inability to perceive chromatic color or, more commonly, to distinguish one of the three primary colors. —**col·or-blind** adj.

col·ored (KUL ərd) adj. **1.** having color. **2.** Offensive of a dark-skinned race. **3.** misrepresented or distorted; biased.

col·or·ful (KUL ər fəl) adj. **1.** full of colors. **2.** full of variety; vivid: a colorful story. **3.** picturesque.

col·or·ing (KUL ər ing) n. **1.** the act or manner of applying colors. **2.** a substance used to impart color. **3.** appearance of anything as to color. **4.** false appearance.

col·or·ist (KUL ər ist) n. one who uses color skillfully, esp. in art.

col·or·less (KUL ər lis) adj. **1.** without color. **2.** weak in color; pallid. **3.** lacking vividness or variety; dull.

co·los·sal (kə LOS əl) adj. of immense size or extent; enormous; huge. [< COLOSSUS]

co·los·sus (kə LOS əs) n. pl. **·los·si** (- LOS ī) or **·los·sus·es 1.** a gigantic statue. **2.** something of great size or statue. [ME]

colt (kohlt) n. a young male horse. [ME] —**colt'ish** adj.

col·umn (KOL əm) n. **1.** Archit. a post or pillar, esp. consisting of base, shaft, and capital. **2.** something suggesting a column: the spinal column. **3.** a section of printed matter on a page, usu. narrow and enclosed by a rule or blank space. **4.** a feature article

that appears regularly in a newspaper or periodical. **5.** Mil. & Naval a formation in which elements of troops, vehicles, etc., are placed one behind another. [ME columne] —**co·lum·nar** (kə LUM nər) adj.

col·um·nist (KOL əm nist) n. one who writes or conducts a special column in a newspaper or periodical.

co·ma (KOHM ə) n. pl. **·mas 1.** Pathol. a condition of profound unconsciousness. **2.** stupor. [< Gk. kōma deep sleep]

co·ma·tose (KOM ə TOHS) adj. **1.** relating to or affected with coma or unconsciousness. **2.** lethargic; torpid.

comb (kohm) n. **1.** a toothed strip of hard, often flexible material, used for smoothing, dressing, or fastening the hair. **2.** a thing resembling this. **3.** the fleshy crest on the head of a fowl. **4.** honeycomb. —v.t. **1.** dress or smooth with or as with a comb. **2.** search carefully. —v.i. **3.** crest and break: said of waves. [ME]

com·bat (KOM bat) n. a battle or fight; struggle. —v. **·bat·ted, ·bat·ting** (kom BAT) **1.** fight or contend with; oppose in battle. **2.** resist. —v.i. **3.** do battle; struggle: with with or against. [< MF combattre fight] —**com·bat·ant** (kəm BAT nt) n. & adj.

com·bat·ive (kəm BAT iv) adj. apt or eager to fight. —**com·bat'ive·ness** n.

com·bi·na·tion (KOM bə NAY shən) n. **1.** the act of joining together or the state of being joined; union. **2.** that which is formed by combining. **3.** an alliance, as of persons. **4.** the series of numbers or letters which when dialed on the face of a lock (**combination lock**) will open the lock.

com·bine (kəm BĪN) v. **·bined, ·bin·ing** v.t. **1.** bring together into close union; blend; merge; unite. —v.i. **2.** become one, or parts of a whole. **3.** associate for a purpose. —n. (KOM bīn) **1.** a combination. **2.** a group of persons united in pursuit of selfish commercial or political ends. **3.** a farm machine that reaps, threshes, and cleans grain while harvesting it. [ME combinen]

combining form the stem of a word, usu. of Greek or Latin origin, as tele- and -phone in telephone, or an English word unchanged, as over in overeat, used in combination with other forms to create compounds.

com·bo (KOM boh) n. Informal **1.** combination. **2.** a small jazz or dance band.

com·bus·ti·ble (kəm BUS tə bəl) adj. capable of burning easily. —n. any substance that will burn easily, as paper or wood. [< LL *combustibilis*]

com•bus•tion (kəm BUS chən) *n.* **1.** the action or operation of burning. **2.** *Chem.* oxidation. [ME]

come (kum) *v.i.* **came, come, com•ing 1.** move to or toward the speaker; approach. **2.** arrive as the result of motion or progress. **3.** advance or move into view. **4.** arrive in due course or in an orderly progression: when your turn *comes.* **5.** occur in time. **6.** reach or extend. **7.** arrive at some state or condition: *come* to harm. **8.** happen; occur. **9.** emanate or proceed; be derived. **10.** become: The wheel *came* loose. **11.** turn out or prove to be: His prediction *came* true. **12.** be offered or produced: The car *comes* in many colors. **13.** act as the speaker wishes: used in the imperative and expressing impatience, anger, protest, etc. — **come about 1.** take place; happen. **2.** *Naut.* turn to the opposite tack. —**come across 1.** meet with or find by chance. **2.** *Informal* give or do what is requested. — **come around (or round) 1.** recover or revive. **2.** change or turn, as in direction or opinion. **3.** pay a visit. —**come back 1.** return. **2.** make a comeback. **3.** reply sharply. —**come by 1.** visit. **2.** acquire; get. —**come into 1.** inherit. **2.** enter into; join. —**come of 1.** be descended from. **2.** result from. —**come off 1.** become detached. **2.** happen; occur. —**come on 1.** meet by chance. **2.** make progress; develop. **3.** enter, as on stage. **4.** *Slang* project a certain style: He *comes* on tough. **5.** *Slang* make sexual advances: with *to.* —**come out 1.** be made public; be published. **2.** make one's debut. **3.** declare oneself. **4.** result; end. — **come through 1.** be successful (in). **2.** survive. **3.** wear through. **4.** give or do what is required. —**come to 1.** recover; revive. **2.** amount to. **3.** result in. —**come up to 1.** equal; rival. **2.** reach. —**come up with** propose or produce: *come up with* an idea. [ME *comen*]

come•back (KUM BAK) *n.* **1.** a return, as to health or lost position. **2.** a smart retort.

co•me•di•an (kə MEE dee ən) *n.* **1.** a performer who specializes in comedy. **2.** a person who writes comedy. [< F *comédien*]

come•down (KUM DOWN) *n.* a humiliating or disappointing setback.

com•e•dy (KOM i dee) *n. pl.* **•dies 1.** a light, humorous drama or narrative having a happy ending. **2.** the branch of drama in which themes are humorously treated. [ME *comedye*]

come•ly (KUM lee) *adj.* **•li•er, •li•est 1.** pleasing in person. **2.** suitable; becoming. [ME *cumli* lovely] —**come'li•ness** *n.*

com•er (KUM ər) *n.* **1.** one who comes or arrives. **2.** *Informal* one who or that which shows great promise.

co•mes•ti•ble (kə MES tə bəl) *n. Usu. pl.* food. [< LL *comestibilis* eaten up]

com•et (KOM it) *n. Astron.* a celestial body orbiting the sun and consisting of a nucleus of condensed material and a tail that points away from the sun. [ME *comete*]

come•up•pance (KUM UP əns) *n. Informal* the punishment one deserves.

com•fort (KUM fərt) *n.* **1.** a state of mental or physical ease. **2.** relief from sorrow, pain, etc. **3.** one who or that which brings ease. —*v.t.* **1.** cheer in time of trouble; console. **2.** *Law* aid; help. [ME *confortien* strengthen] —**com'fort•ing** *adj.*

com•fort•a•ble (KUMF tə bəl) *adj.* **1.** imparting comfort and satisfaction. **2.** free from distress; at ease. **3.** moderate; adequate: a *comfortable* income.

com•fort•er (KUM fə tər) *n.* **1.** one who comforts. **2.** a quilt; a woolen scarf.

com•ic (KOM ik) *adj.* **1.** of or pertaining to comedy. **2.** humorous; funny. —*n.* **1.** a comic actor or entertainer. **2.** the humorous element in art, life, etc. **3.** *pl.* comic strips or a book of comic strips. [ME]

com•i•cal (KOM i kəl) *adj.* humorous; funny.

comic strip a strip of cartoons printed in a newspaper etc.

com•ing (KUM ing) *adj.* **1.** approaching, esp. in time. **2.** on the way to fame or distinction. —*n.* an approach; arrival; advent.

com•i•ty (KOM i tee) *n. pl.* **•ties** courtesy; civility. [< L *comitas* affability]

com•ma (KOM ə) *n.* a punctuation mark (,) indicating a slight separation in ideas or in grammatical construction within a sentence. [< LL]

com•mand (kə MAND) *v.t.* **1.** order or require with authority. **2.** control or direct. **3.** overlook, as from a height. **4.** exact: *command* respect. —*v.i.* **5.** be in authority; rule. **6.** overlook something from above. — *n.* **1.** the act of commanding. **2.** the authority or power to command. **3.** that which is commanded; an order. **4.** ability to control; mastery. **5.** *Mil. & Naval* the unit or units under the command of one person. [ME *comaunden* order]

com·man·dant (KOM ən DANT) *n.* a commanding officer, as of a military school. [< F]

com·man·deer (KOM ən DEER) *v.t.* 1. force into military service. 2. seize for public use, esp. under military necessity.

com·mand·er (kə MAN dər) *n.* 1. one who commands or is in command. 2. *Naval* a commissioned officer ranking next above a lieutenant commander and next below a captain.

commander in chief *pl.* **commanders in chief** 1. *Often cap.* the supreme commander of the armed forces of a nation. 2. the commander of a major force.

com·mand·ing (kə MAN ding) *adj.* 1. exercising command. 2. impressive; imperious. 3. dominating, as from a height.

com·mand·ment (kə MAND mənt) *n.* 1. an edict; order; law. 2. *Sometimes cap.* one of the Ten Commandments.

com·man·do (kə MAN doh) *n. pl.* •dos or •does 1. a fighting force trained for raids into enemy territory. 2. a member of such a unit. [< Afrikaans *kommando* raiding party]

com·mem·o·rate (kə MEM ə RAYT) *v.t.* •rat·ed, •rat·ing celebrate the memory of. [< L *commemoratus* remembered] — **com·mem′o·ra′tion** *n.*

com·mem·o·ra·tive (kə MEM ər ə tiv) *adj.* serving to commemorate.

com·mence (kə MENS) *v.t. & v.i.* •menced, •menc·ing start; begin; originate. [ME *commencen*]

com·mence·ment (kə MENS mənt) *n.* 1. a beginning; origin. 2. a graduation ceremony at a college or school.

com·mend (kə MEND) *v.t.* 1. express approval of; praise. 2. recommend. 3. present the regards of. 4. commit with confidence. [ME *commenden*] — **com·mend′a·ble** *adj.* — **com·men·da·tion** (KOM ən DAY shən) *n.*

com·men·su·rate (kə MEN sər it) *adj.* 1. having the same measure or extent. 2. in proper proportion; adequate. 3. [< LL *commensuratus* measured]

com·ment (KOM ent) *n.* 1. a note of explanation, illustration, or criticism. 2. a remark made in observation or criticism. 3. talk; conversation. —*v.i.* make a comment or comments. [ME *coment*]

com·men·tar·y (KOM ən TER ee) *n. pl.*

•tar·ies 1. a series of comments. 2. *Usu. pl.* a historical narrative or memoir. [ME *commentaries* commentaries]

com·men·ta·tor (KOM ən TAY tər) *n.* 1. one who writes commentaries. 2. one who discusses or analyzes news events.

com·merce (KOM ərs) *n.* the exchange of materials, products, etc., esp. on a large scale between states of nations; extended trade. [< MF]

com·mer·cial (kə MUR shəl) *adj.* 1. of, relating to, or engaged in commerce; mercantile. 2. having financial gain as an object. — *n.* in radio and television, an advertisement.

com·mer·cial·ism (kə MUR shə LIZ əm) *n.* the spirit or methods of commerce.

com·mer·cial·ize (kə MUR shə līz) *v.t.* •ized, •iz·ing put on a commercial basis. —**com·mer′cial·i·za′tion** *n.*

com·min·gle (kə MING gəl) *v.t. & v.i.* •gled, •gling mix, mingle.

com·mis·er·ate (kə MIZ ə RAYT) *v.* •at·ed, •at·ing *v.t.* 1. feel or express sympathy for; pity. —*v.i.* 2. express sympathy: with *with*. [< L *commiseratus* pitied] —**com·mis′er·a′tion** *n.*

com·mis·sar (KOM ə sahr) *n.* formerly, a Soviet official in charge of a major department of the government. [< Russ. *Komissar*]

com·mis·sar·y (KOM ə SER ee) *n. pl.* •sar·ies 1. a store selling food, equipment, etc., as at a camp or military post. 2. an authority delegated for a special duty. [ME *commissarie*]

com·mis·sion (kə MISH ən) *n.* 1. the act of committing. 2. a matter committed or entrusted; a charge. 3. authorization or command to act as specified. 4. a written warrant conferring a particular authority. 5. *Mil.* a a document conferring rank and authority. b the rank or authority conferred. 6. a body of persons authorized to perform certain duties. 7. the fee or percentage given an agent or salesman. —**in commission** in active service or use. —**out of commission** not in active service or use. —*v.t.* 1. give rank or authority to. 2. *Naval* put into active service, as a ship. 3. appoint; delegate. [ME]

com·mis·sion·er (kə MISH ə nər) *n.* 1. one who holds a commission. 2. a member of a commission. 3. a public official in charge of a department. 4. the administrator in charge of a professional sport.

com·mit (kə MIT) *v.t.* •mit·ted, •mit·ting

1. do; perpetrate. 2. place in trust or charge; consign. 3. consign for preservation. 4. devote (oneself) unreservedly. [ME *committen* connect]

com·mit·ment (kə MIT mənt) *n.* 1. the act of committing, or the state of being committed. 2. an engagement or pledge to do something. 3. a consignment to a prison, mental institution, etc. Also **com·mit′tal.**

com·mit·tee (kə MIT ee) *n.* a group of people chosen to investigate, report, or act on a matter. **—in committee** under consideration by a committee. [ME]

com·mode (kə MOHD) *n.* 1. a low chest of drawers. 2. a covered washstand. 3. a toilet. [< F]

com·mo·di·ous (kə MOH dee əs) *adj.* roomy; spacious. [ME]

com·mod·i·ty (kə MOD i tee) *n. pl.* **·ties** 1. something bought and sold. 2. anything of use or profit. [ME *commoditie* convenience]

com·mo·dore (KOM ə DOR) *n.* 1. formerly, in the U.S. Navy, an officer next below a rear admiral. 2. a title given to the presiding officer of a yacht club.

com·mon (KOM ən) *adj.* 1. frequent or usual; unexceptional. 2. widespread; general. 3. shared equally. 4. pertaining to the entire community; public. 5. habitual; notorious. 6. of low rank; ordinary. 7. vulgar; low. 8. *Gram.* **a** of gender, applied to either sex, as *parent.* **b** of a noun, applicable to any individual of a class, as *boat, dog.* 9. *Math.* referring to a number or quantity belonging equally to two or more quantities: *common* denominator. **—n.** public land open to use by all in a community. **—in common** equally with another or others; jointly. [ME *comun*]

com·mon·al·i·ty (KOM ə NAL i tee) *n. pl.* **·ties** 1. the common people. 2. the entire mass; whole.

com·mon·er (KOM ən ər) *n.* one of the common people.

common fraction *Math.* a fraction expressed by a denominator and a numerator.

common law a system of jurisprudence based on custom and precedent.

common-law marriage a marriage in which both members consent to live as husband and wife without undergoing a religious or civil ceremony.

common market 1. any of several associations of nations having mutually beneficial tariff arrangements. 2. *cap.* a common market, established in 1958, which now is called the *European Community.*

common people ordinary people, as distinguished from the nobility, the rich, etc.

com·mon·place (KOM ən PLAYS) *adj.* not remarkable; ordinary. **—n.** 1. a trite remark. 2. something common.

com·mons (KOM ənz) *n.* 1. (*construed as sing.*) the dining hall of a college. 2. (*construed as sing. or pl.*) the British House of Commons.

common sense practical understanding; sound judgment. **—com·mon-sense** (KOM ən SENS) *adj.*

com·mon·wealth (KOM ən WELTH) *n.* 1. the whole people of a state or nation. 2. a state in which sovereignty is vested in the people. [ME *commun welthe*]

com·mo·tion (kə MOH shən) *n.* a violent agitation; excitement.

com·mu·nal (kə MYOON l) *adj.* of, pertaining to, or belonging to a community or commune. **—com·mu′nal·ly** *adv.*

com·mune[1] (kə MYOON) *v.i.* **·muned**, **·mun·ing** 1. converse intimately. 2. partake of the Eucharist. [ME *comunen* share]

com·mune[2] (KOM yoon) *n.* 1. the smallest political division of France, Belgium, etc. 2. any small, self-governing political unit. 3. any community. 4. a group of persons, not forming a single family, sharing a home or land in common. [< F]

com·mu·ni·ca·ble (kə MYOO ni kə bəl) *adj.* capable of being communicated, as a disease.

com·mu·ni·cant (kə MYOO ni kənt) *n.* 1. one who communicates. 2. one who partakes or has a right to partake of the Eucharist.

com·mu·ni·cate (kə MYOO ni KAYT) *v.* **·cat·ed**, **·cat·ing** *v.t.* 1. cause another or others to share in; impart. 2. transmit, as a disease. **—v.i.** 3. transmit or exchange thought or knowledge. 4. be connected. 5. partake of the Eucharist. [< L *communicatus* imparted] **—com·mu′·ni·ca′ tor** *n.*

com·mu·ni·ca·tion (kə MYOO ni KAY shən) *n.* 1. the act of communicating. 2. a message. 3. a means of communicating. 4. *pl.* the communicating of ideas, information, etc. **—com·mu·ni·ca·tive** (kə MYOO ni KAY tiv) *adj.*

com·mun·ion (kə MYOON yən) *n.* 1. mutual participation or sharing. 2. religious fellowship; also, a religious denomination.

3. *Usu. cap.* the Eucharist; Holy Communion. [ME]

com·mu·ni·qué (kə MYOO ni KAY) *n.* an official announcement or bulletin. [< F]

com·mu·nism (KOM yə NIZ əm) *n.* **1.** a social system characterized by the communal sharing of goods and services. **2.** *Often cap.* Marxist socialism, advocating a classless society and public ownership of almost all productive property; also, the system in force in any state based on this theory. [< F *communisme*]

com·mu·nist (KOM yə nist) *n.* **1.** *Often cap.* a member of a Communist party. **2.** one who advocates communism.

com·mu·ni·ty (kə MYOO ni tee) *n. pl.* **·ties** **1.** a group of people living together or in one locality and having common customs, interests, etc. **2.** the district in which they live. **3.** people having specified interests in common: the scientific *community.* **4.** the public; society in general. **5.** common ownership or participation. **6.** identity or likeness. **7.** *Ecol.* a group of plants or animals in an area living under similar conditions. [< L *communitas* fellowship]

community college a nonresidential junior college supported by public funds.

com·mu·ta·tion (KOM yə TAY shən) *n.* **1.** a substitution, as of one kind of payment for another. **2.** a payment or service substituted. **3.** the act of commuting to work. **4.** *Law* a reduction of a penalty or sentence. [ME *commutacioun* change]

com·mute (kə MYOOT) *v.* **·mut·ed,** **·mut·ing** *v.t.* **1.** interchange. **2.** exchange for something less severe. **3.** pay in gross at a reduced rate. —*v.i.* **4.** serve as a substitute. **5.** make regular trips of some distance to and from work. —*n.* a trip, usu. long in time or distance, between home and work: an hour's *commute.* [ME] —**com·mut′er** *n.*

com·pact¹ (kəm PAKT) *adj.* **1.** closely united; pressed together. **2.** brief; terse. **3.** packed into a small space. —*v.t.* (KOM pakt) pack closely; compress. —*n.* (KOM pakt) **1.** a small, hinged box with a mirror, for face powder. **2.** a small car. [ME]

com·pact² (KOM pakt) *n.* a covenant; agreement. [< L *compactum* agreement]

com·pan·ion (kəm PAN yən) *n.* **1.** a comrade; associate. **2.** a person employed to live with or assist another. **3.** one of a pair; a mate. —*v.t.* be a companion to. [ME *compainoun* fellow diner]

com·pan·ion·a·ble (kəm PAN yə nə bəl) *adj.* friendly; sociable.

com·pan·ion·ate (kəm PAN yə nit) *adj.* **1.** of or characteristic of companions. **2.** agreed upon; shared.

com·pa·ny (KUM pə nee) *n. pl.* **·nies 1.** a group of people. **2.** a gathering of persons for social purposes. **3.** a guest or guests; visitors. **4.** a business. **5.** a troupe. **6.** *Mil.* a body of soldiers larger than a platoon and smaller than a battalion. **7.** *Naut.* the entire crew of a ship, including the officers. —**keep company (with)** **1.** associate (with). **2.** *Informal* court, as lovers. —**part company (with)** end friendship or association (with). [ME]

com·pa·ra·ble (KOM pər ə bəl) *adj.* **1.** capable of comparison. **2.** worthy of comparison. —**com′pa·ra·bil′i·ty** *n.*

com·par·a·tive (kəm PAR ə tiv) *adj.* **1.** pertaining to, resulting from, or making use of comparison. **2.** not absolute; relative. **3.** *Gram.* expressing a degree of an adjective or adverb higher than the positive and lower than the superlative. —*n. Gram.* the comparative degree, or a word or form by which it is expressed: *Better* is the *comparative of good.*

com·pare (kəm PAIR) *v.* **·pared, ·par·ing** *v.t.* **1.** represent as similar or equal: with *to.* **2.** examine for similarity or dissimilarity: with *with.* **3.** *Gram.* form the degrees of comparison of (an adjective or adverb). —*v.i.* **4.** be worthy of comparison: with *with.* —*n.* comparison: in the phrase **beyond compare.** [ME *comparen* place together]

com·par·i·son (kəm PAR ə sən) *n.* **1.** a comparing or being compared. **2.** similarity. **3.** *Gram.* the inflection of adjectives or adverbs that indicates the three differences of degree, as *short, shorter, shortest.*

com·part·ment (kəm PAHRT mənt) *n.* **1.** a part or subdivision of an enclosed space. **2.** any separate section. [< MF *compartiment*]

com·pass (KUM pəs) *n.* **1.** an instrument for determining direction, having a magnetic needle that points toward the magnetic north. **2.** area or range; scope. **3.** an enclosing boundary; circumference. **4.** *Sometimes pl.* an instrument having two usu. pointed legs hinged at one end, used for taking measurements, describing circles, etc. —*v.t.* **1.** go round. **2.** surround; encompass. **3.** comprehend. **4.** attain or accomplish. **5.** plot; devise. [ME *compassen* measure]

com·pas·sion (kəm PASH ən) n. pity, with the desire to help. [ME] —**com·pas'sion·ate** (-it) adj.

com·pat·i·ble (kəm PAT ə bəl) adj. capable of existing together in harmony: usu. with *with*. [ME] —**com·pat'i·bil'i·ty** n.

com·pa·tri·ot (kəm PAY tree ət) n. a fellow countryman. —adj. of the same country. [< LL *compatriota* countryman]

com·pel (kəm PEL) v.t. **·pelled, ·pel·ling** 1. force; constrain. 2. obtain by force; exact. [ME *compellen*] —**com·pel'la·ble** adj.

com·pen·di·ous (kəm PEN dee əs) adj. succinct; concise.

com·pen·di·um (kəm PEN dee əm) n. pl. **·di·ums** or **·di·a** (-dee ə) a summary; abridgment. [< L, abridgment]

com·pen·sate (KOM pən SAYT) v. **·sat·ed, ·sat·ing** v.t. 1. make amends to or for; requite; reimburse. 2. make up for; offset. —v.i. 3. make amends: often with *for*. [< L *compensatus* balanced] —**com'pen·sa'tion** n. —**com·pen·sa·to·ry** (kəm PEN sə TOR ee) adj.

com·pete (kəm PEET) v.i. **·pet·ed, ·pet·ing** contend with another or others; engage in a contest. [< L *competere* suffice] —**com·pet·i·tor** (kəm PET i tər) n.

com·pe·tence (KOM pi təns) n. 1. the state of being competent; ability. 2. sufficient means for comfort. Also **com'pe·ten·cy.**

com·pe·tent (KOM pi tənt) adj. 1. able; capable. 2. sufficient; adequate. [ME]

com·pe·ti·tion (KOM pi TISH ən) n. 1. a striving against another or others for some object; rivalry. 2. a contest.

com·pet·i·tive (kəm PET i tiv) adj. of, pertaining to, or characterized by competition.

com·pile (kəm PĪL) v.t. **·piled, ·pil·ing** 1. put together from various sources. 2. gather (various materials) into a volume. 3. amass; collect. [ME, plunder] —**com·pi·la·tion** (KOM pə LAY shən) n. —**com·pil'er** n.

com·pla·cen·cy (kəm PLAY sən see) n. pl. **·cies** self-satisfaction; smugness. [< Med.L *complacentia*] —**com·pla'cent** adj.

com·plain (kəm PLAYN) v.i. 1. express dissatisfaction, pain, etc. 2. make a formal accusation. [ME *compleinen*]

com·plaint (kəm PLAYNT) n. 1. an expression of pain, grief, or dissatisfaction. 2. a cause for complaining; grievance. 3. an ailment. 4. *Law* a formal charge. [ME *compleynte*]

com·ple·ment (KOM plə mənt) n. 1. that which fills up or completes a thing. 2. complete number, allowance, or amount. 3. one of two parts that mutually complete each other. 4. *Geom.* an angle that when added to another angle equals 90°. 5. *Gram.* a word or phrase used after a verb to complete predication. —v.t. make complete. [ME] —**com'·ple·men'ta·ry** (-MEN tə ree) adj.

complementary color either of a pair of spectrum colors that when combined give a white or nearly white light.

com·plete (kəm PLEET) adj. 1. having all needed or normal parts; entire; full. 2. finished; concluded. 3. perfect. —v.t. **·plet·ed, ·plet·ing** 1. make whole or perfect. 2. finish; end. [ME] —**com·ple'tion** n.

com·plex (kəm PLEKS) adj. 1. consisting of various connected parts; composite. 2. complicated; involved; intricate. —n. (KOM pleks) 1. a whole made up of connected parts. 2. a group of structures or facilities designed for related activities: a sports *complex*. 3. *Psychoanal.* a group of interrelated feelings and ideas, which, when repressed, lead to abnormal behavior. 4. loosely, an excessive concern; obsession. [< LL *complexus* included]

complex fraction *Math.* a fraction in which either the numerator or the denominator is a fraction.

com·plex·ion (kəm PLEK shən) n. 1. the color and appearance of the skin, esp. of the face. 2. aspect; appearance. [ME]

com·plex·i·ty (kəm PLEK si tee) n. pl. **·ties.** 1. the state of being complex. 2. something complex.

com·pli·ance (kəm PLĪ əns) n. 1. the act of complying or yielding. 2. a disposition to comply. Also **com·pli'an·cy.** —**in compliance with** in agreement with.

com·pli·ant (kəm PLĪ ənt) adj. ready or willing to comply.

com·pli·cate (KOM pli KAYT) v. **·cat·ed, ·cat·ing** v.t. 1. make complex or difficult. 2. twist; intertwine. —v.i. 3. become complex or difficult. [< L *complicatus* folded together] —**com'pli·ca'tion** n.

com·pli·cat·ed (KOM pli KAY tid) adj. difficult to separate or understand; intricate.

com·plic·i·ty (kəm PLIS i tee) n. pl. **·ties** 1. the state of being an accomplice, as in a wrong act. 2. complexity.

com·pli·ment (KOM plə mənt) n. 1. an expression of praise or congratulation. 2. *Usu. pl.* a formal greeting or remembrance. — *v.t.* pay a compliment to. [< F]

com·pli·men·ta·ry (KOM plə MEN tə ree) *adj.* 1. conveying, using, or like a compliment. 2. given free.

com·ply (kəm PLĪ) *v.i.* •plied, •ply·ing conform; consent; obey: with *with.* [< Ital. *complire* fulfill] —**com·pli′er** *n.*

com·po·nent (kəm POH nənt) *n.* a constituent part. —*adj.* forming a part or ingredient. [< L *componere* put together]

com·port (kəm PORT) *v.t.* 1. conduct or behave (oneself). —*v.i.* 2. be compatible; agree: with *with.* [ME] —**com·port′ment** *n.*

com·pose (kəm POHZ) *v.* •posed, •pos·ing *v.t.* 1. constitute; form. 2. make of parts; fashion. 3. create (a literary or musical work). 4. calm; quiet. 5. reconcile or settle, as differences. 6. *Printing* arrange (type) in lines; set. —*v.i.* 7. create, as music. 8. *Printing* set type. [ME]

com·posed (kəm POHZD) *adj.* free from agitation; calm.

com·pos·er (kəm POH zər) *n.* one who composes; esp., one who writes music.

com·pos·ite (kəm POZ it) *adj.* 1. made up of separate parts or elements. 2. *Bot.* characteristic of or pertaining to a family of plants whose flowers are composed of dense clusters of small flowers. —*n.* 1. that which is composed or made up of parts. 2. *Bot.* a composite plant. [ME]

com·po·si·tion (KOM pə ZISH ən) *n.* 1. the act of forming a whole from parts, ingredients, etc. 2. that which is so formed. 3. constitution; make-up. 4. the act or art of creating a literary, musical, or artistic work. 5. the work so created, or its structure. 6. a short essay. 7. *Printing* the setting of type.

com·pos·i·tor (kəm POZ i tər) *n.* one who sets type.

com·post (KOM pohst) *n.* a fertilizing mixture of decomposed organic matter. [ME]

com·po·sure (kəm POH zhər) *n.* calmness.

com·pote (KOM poht) *n.* 1. fruit stewed or preserved in syrup. 2. a dish for holding fruits, etc. [< F]

com·pound¹ (KOM pownd) *n.* 1. a combination of two or more elements or parts. 2. *Gram.* a word composed of two or more words, as *shoestring.* 3. *Chem.* a substance resulting from the union of specific elements or radicals in fixed proportions. —*v.t.* (kəm POWND) 1. make by

combining various elements or ingredients. 2. mix (elements). 3. compute (interest) on both the principal and accrued interest. 4. settle for less than the sum due, as a debt. 5. add to; increase. —*adj.* (KOM pownd) composed of two or more elements or parts. [ME *compounen* put together]

com·pound² *n.* an enclosure containing buildings. [< Malay *kampung* village]

com·pre·hend (KOM pri HEND) *v.t.* 1. understand. 2. take in or embrace; include. — *v.i.* 3. understand. [ME *comprehenden* grasp] —**com′pre·hen′si·ble** *adj.*

com·pre·hen·sion (KOM pri HEN shən) *n.* 1. understanding. 2. an including or taking in; comprehensiveness.

com·pre·hen·sive (KOM pri HEN siv) *adj.* 1. large in scope or content; broad. 2. understanding; comprehending. — **com′pre·hen′sive·ness** *n.*

com·press (kəm PRES) *v.t.* press together or into smaller space; reduce in volume; condense; compact. —*n.* (KOM pres) 1. *Med.* a pad for applying moisture, cold, heat, or pressure to the body. 2. an apparatus for compressing bales of cotton, etc. [ME] —**com·pres′·sion** (kəm PRESH ən) *n.*

com·prise (kəm PRĪZ) *v.t.* •prised, •pris·ing consist of or contain; include. [ME *comprisen*]

com·pro·mise (KOM prə MĪZ) *n.* 1. an adjustment or settlement by means of concessions. 2. the result of such concessions. 3. something between, or combining the qualities of, two different things. 4. an imperiling, as of reputation. —*v.* •mised, •mis·ing *v.t.* 1. adjust by concessions, 2. expose to risk or disrepute. —*v.i.* 3. make a compromise. [ME]

com·pul·sion (kəm PUL shən) *n.* 1. the act of compelling, or the state of being compelled. 2. *Psychol.* an irresistible impulse or tendency. [ME] —**com·pul·sive** (kəm PUL siv) *adj.*

com·pul·so·ry (kəm PUL sə ree) *adj.* 1. employing compulsion; coercive. 2. required; obligatory: *compulsory* education.

com·punc·tion (kəm PUNGK shən) *n.* 1. a sense of guilt or remorse. 2. a feeling of slight regret or pity. [ME *compunccion* pricking severely]

com·pute (kəm PYOOT) *v.t. & v.i.* •put·ed, •put·ing ascertain (an amount or number) by calculation; reckon. [< L *computare* reckon.] —**com•pu•ta•tion** (KOM pyuu TAY shən) n.

com•put•er (kəm PYOO tər) n. 1. one who or that which computes. 2. an electronic machine for the high-speed performance of mathematical and logical operations, or for the processing of large masses of coded information.

com•put•er•ize (kəm PYOO tə RĪZ) v.t. •ized, •iz•ing 1. control (an operation) by means of a computer. 2. adopt the use of computers in.

com•rade (KOM rad) n. 1. a companion or friend. 2. a person who shares one's occupation, interests, etc. [< MF *camarade*] — **com'rade•ship** n.

con¹ (KON) v.t. conned, con•ning study or memorize. [ME *cunnen* become acquainted with]

con² adj. *Informal* confidence: *con* man. — v.t. conned, con•ning defraud; swindle.

con³ n. *Slang* a convict.

con•cave (kon KAYV) adj. hollow and curving inward, as the interior of a sphere or bowl. —n. (KON kayv) a concave surface; hollow. —v.t. •caved, •cav•ing (kon KAYV) make concave. [ME]

con•ceal (kən SEEL) v.t. keep from sight or discovery; hide. [ME *concelen*] — **con•ceal'a•ble** adj.

con•cede (kən SEED) v. •ced•ed, •ced•ing v.t. 1. acknowledge as correct; admit. 2. grant; yield, as a right or privilege. —v.i. 3. make a concession; yield. [< L *concedere* yield]

con•ceit (kən SEET) n. 1. overweening self-esteem. 2. an ingenious, fanciful thought or expression. 3. in poetry, an elaborate, extended metaphor. 4. imagination; fancy. [ME *conceyte*]

con•ceit•ed (kən SEE tid) adj. vain.

con•ceive (kən SEEV) v. •ceived, •ceiv•ing v.t. 1. become pregnant with. 2. form a concept of; imagine. 3. understand. 4. express in a particular way. —v.i. 5. form a mental image; think: with *of*. 6. become pregnant. [ME] —**con•ceiv'a•ble** adj.

con•cen•trate (KON sən TRAYT) v. •trat•ed, •trat•ing v.t. 1. direct to a common point; focus. 2. intensify or purify; condense. —v.i. 3. converge. 4. become compacted, intensified, or more pure. 5. direct one's entire attention: often with *on* or *upon*. —n. a product of concentration.

con•cen•tra•tion (KON sən TRAY shən) n. 1. the act of concentrating, or the state of being concentrated. 2. a concentrate. 3. complete attention.

concentration camp an enclosed camp for the confinement of political prisoners, aliens, etc.

con•cen•tric (kən SEN trik) adj. having a common center, as circles. —**con•cen'tri•cal•ly** adv.

con•cept (KON sept) n. a mental image; esp., an abstract idea; also, a thought or opinion. [< L *conceptum* something conceived]

con•cep•tion (kən SEP shən) n. 1. the act of conceiving or becoming pregnant, or the state of being conceived. 2. fertilization. 3. a beginning. 4. the act of forming concepts or ideas. 5. a concept, plan, or design.

con•cep•tu•al (kən SEP choo əl) adj. of or pertaining to conception or concepts.

con•cern (kən SURN) v.t. 1. be of interest or importance to. 2. occupy the attention of; engage: often used as a reflexive or in the passive. 3. worry; trouble: often in the passive. —n. 1. that which concerns or affects one. 2. anxiety or interest; care. 3. relation or bearing. 4. a business firm. [ME *concernen* distinguish]

con•cern•ing (kən SUR ning) prep. in relation to; regarding; about.

con•cert (KON surt) n. 1. a musical performance. 2. agreement; harmony. —**in concert** in unison; all together. —v.t. & v.i. (kən SURT) make or become unified; do together; combine. —adj. (KON surt) of or for concerts. [< F]

con•cert•ed (kən SUR tid) adj. arranged or done together; combined.

con•cer•to (kən CHER toh) n. pl. •tos, •ti (-tee) *Music* a composition for a solo instrument or instruments accompanied by an orchestra. [< Ital.]

con•ces•sion (kən SESH ən) n. 1. the act of conceding. 2. anything so yielded. 3. a right or privilege granted by a government. 4. the right to operate a subsidiary business on certain premises.

con•ces•sion•aire (kən SESH ə NAIR) n. one who holds or operates a concession. [< F]

con•ci•erge (KON see AIRZH) n. 1. a doorkeeper of a building, esp. in France. 2. a hotel emplyee who arranges for services for guests. [< F]

con•cil•i•ate (kən SIL ee AYT) v.t. •at•ed, •at•ing 1. placate. 2. secure by favorable measures; win. [< L *conciliatus* brought together] —**con·cil'i·a'tion** n.

con·cil·i·a·to·ry (kən SIL ee ə TOR ee) adj. tending to reconcile or conciliate.

con·cise (kən SĪS) adj. terse; expressed in brief form. [< L *concisus* cut short]

con·clave (KON klayv) n. a private or secret meeting. [ME]

con·clude (kən KLOOD) v. **·clud·ed, ·clud·ing** v.t. 1. end; terminate. 2. settle finally. 3. form a judgment about; decide. 4. resolve (to do); determine. —v.i. 5. come to an end. 6. come to a decision or agreement. [ME]

con·clu·sion (kən KLOO zhən) n. 1. the end or termination of something. 2. a closing part, as of a speech. 3. a result; outcome. 4. a judgment or opinion. 5. a final decision; resolve. 6. a final settlement, as of a treaty. —**in conclusion** as a final statement.

con·clu·sive (kən KLOO siv) adj. putting an end to a question; decisive.

con·coct (kon KOKT) v.t. 1. make by mixing ingredients, as a drink. 2. make up; devise. [< L *concoctus* cooked together] — **con·coc'tion** n.

con·com·i·tant (kon KOM i tənt) adj. existing or occurring together; attendant. —n. an attendant circumstance, state, or thing. [< L *concomitari* accompany] — **con·com'i·tant·ly** adv.

con·cord (KON kord) n. 1. unity; agreement; accord. 2. peace. 3. a peace treaty. [ME *concorde* harmony]

con·cor·dance (kon KOR dns) n. 1. agreement; concord. 2. an alphabetical index of the important words in a book as they occur in context: a Bible *concordance*. — **con·cor'dant** (-dənt) adj.

con·course (KON kors) n. 1. convergence. 2. a gathering. 3. a place for the assembling or passage of crowds. [ME *concours* assembly]

con·crete (KON kreet) adj. 1. specific, as opposed to general. 2. physically perceptible; real. 3. constituting a composite mass; solid. 4. made of concrete. —n. 1. a building material of sand and gravel or broken rock united by cement. 2. that which is concrete: often preceded by *the*. —v. **·cret·ed, ·cret·ing** v.t. 1. bring together in one mass or body. 2. cover with concrete. —v.i. 3. coalesce; solidify. [ME *concret* grown together]

con·cu·bine (KONG kyə BĪN) n. 1. a woman who cohabits with a man without

being married to him. 2. in certain polygamous societies, a secondary wife. [ME] — **con·cu·bi·nage** (kon KYOO bə nij) n.

con·cu·pis·cence (kon KYOO pi səns) n. 1. sexual desire; lust. 2. any immoderate desire. [ME] —**con·cu'pis·cent** adj.

con·cur (kən KUR) v.i. **·curred, ·cur·ring** 1. agree or approve. 2. cooperate. 3. happen at the same time. [ME] — **con·cur·rent** (kən KUR ənt) adj. — **con·cur'rent·ly** adv.

con·cus·sion (kən KUSH ən) n. 1. a violent shaking; shock. 2. *Pathol.* a violent shock to some organ, esp. to the brain. [ME]

con·demn (kən DEM) v.t. 1. hold to be wrong; censure. 2. pronounce judicial sentence against. 3. show the guilt of; convict. 4. declare to be unfit for use, usu. by official order. 5. appropriate for public use. [ME *condempnen*] —**con·dem·na·tion** (KON dem NAY shən) n. —**con·dem·na·to·ry** (kən DEM nə tor ee) adj.

con·dense (kən DENS) v. **·densed, ·dens·ing** v.t. 1. compress; make dense; consolidate. 2. abridge; make concise. 3. change from a gas to a liquid, or from a liquid to a solid. —v.i. 4. become condensed. [< MF *condenser* thicken] — **con·den·sa·tion** (KON den SAY shən) n. —**con·den·sate** (KON dən SAYT) n.

con·de·scend (KON də SEND) v.i. 1. lower oneself (to do something); deign. 2. behave in a patronizing manner. [ME *condescenden*] —**con'de·scen'sion** (-SEN shən) n. —**con'de·scend'ing** adj.

con·di·ment (KON də mənt) n. a seasoning, as a relish, spice, etc. [ME]

con·di·tion (kən DISH ən) n. 1. the state or mode of existence of a person or thing. 2. state of health. 3. *Informal* an ailment. 4. something necessary to the occurrence or existence of something else; prerequisite. 5. *Usu. pl.* the circumstances affecting an activity or a mode of existence: poor living *conditions*. 6. social status. 7. in a will, contract, etc., a proviso. —**in (or out of) condition** fit (or unfit), esp. for some physical activity. —**on condition that** provided that; if. —v.t. 1. be a condition or prerequisite of. 2. specify as a condition; stipulate. 3. render in good condition. 4. train, as to a conditioned response. 5. accustom (someone) to. [ME *condicioun* agreement]

con·di·tion·al (kən DISH ə nl) adj. 1. not absolute; tentative. 2. expressing a condition.

con·dole (kən DOHL) v.i. **·doled, ·dol·ing** grieve or express sympathy with: with *with*. [< LL *condolere* feel pain] —**con·do'lence** n.

con·dom (KON dəm) n. a sheath for the penis, for preventing conception or transmission of disease.

con·do·min·i·um (KON də MIN ee əm) n. **1.** joint sovereignty or ownership. **2.** a multiple-unit dwelling in which the units are owned separately; also, a unit in such a dwelling. [< NL]

con·done (kən DOHN) v.t. **·doned, ·don·ing** overlook (an offense); pardon. [< L *condonare* absolve]

con·duce (kən DOOS) v.i. **·duced, ·duc·ing** help or tend toward a result; contribute: with *to*. [ME] —**con·du·cive** (kən DOO siv) adj.

con·duct (kən DUKT) v.t. **1.** accompany and show the way; guide; escort. **2.** manage or control. **3.** direct and lead, as an orchestra. **4.** convey; transmit. **5.** act or behave: used reflexively. —v.t. **6.** serve as a conductor. **7.** direct or lead. —n. (KON dukt) **1.** behavior. **2.** management. [ME]

con·duc·tor (kən DUK tər) n. **1.** one who or that which conducts. **2.** one who has charge of a railroad car, bus, etc. **3.** the director of an orchestra or chorus. **4.** any substance or medium that conducts electricity, heat, etc.

con·duit (KON dwit) n. a channel, pipe, etc., for conveying water, electric wires, etc. [ME]

cone (kohn) n. **1.** *Geom.* a solid figure having a circle as its base and tapering evenly on all surfaces to a point. **2.** anything cone-shaped. **3.** *Bot.* a dry multiple fruit, as of the pine, composed of scales arranged symmetrically around an axis and enclosing seeds. —v.t. **coned, con·ing** shape conically. [< L *conus*]

con·fab·u·late (kən FAB yə LAYT) v.i. **·lat·ed, ·lat·ing** chat; gossip; converse. [< L *confabulari* talk together]

con·fed·er·a·cy (kən FED ər ə see) n. pl. **·cies 1.** a union of states or persons; a league; alliance. **2.** an unlawful combination; conspiracy. —**the Confederacy** a league of eleven southern states that seceded from the U.S. in 1860 or 1861: also **Confederate States of America.**

con·fed·er·ate (kən FED ər it) n. an associate or accomplice. —adj. associated in a confederacy. —v.t. & v.i. (kən FED ə RAYT **·at·ed, ·at·ing** form or join in a confederacy. [ME *confederat* unite in a league]

con·fed·er·a·tion (kən FED ə RAY shən) n. **1.** the act of confederating, or the state of being confederated. **2.** an association of states.

con·fer (kən FUR) v. **·ferred, ·fer·ring** v.t. **1.** grant or bestow. —v.i. **2.** hold a conference; consult together. [ME *conferen* consult with] —**con·fer'ment** n.

con·fer·ee (KON fə REE) n. one who takes part in a conference.

con·fer·ence (KON fər əns) n. **1.** a consultation on an important matter; also, a formal meeting for this. **2.** a league or association, as of athletic teams.

con·fess (kən FES) v.t. **1.** acknowledge or admit, as a fault or sin. **2.** concede or admit to be true. **3.** acknowledge belief or faith in. **4.** *Eccl.* **a** make known (one's sins), esp. to a priest. **b** hear the confession of: said of a priest. —v.i. **5.** make acknowledgment, as of fault or crime: with *to*. **6.** make confession to a priest. [ME *confessen*]

con·fes·sion (kən FESH ən) n. **1.** the act of confessing. **2.** that which is confessed. **3.** a statement in which something is confessed. **4.** *Eccl.* the acknowledgment of one's sins.

con·fes·sion·al (kən FESH ə nl) adj. of, pertaining to, or like confession. —n. a small enclosure where a priest hears confessions.

con·fes·sor (kən FES ər) n. **1.** a priest who hears confessions. **2.** one who confesses.

con·fi·dant (KON fi DANT) n. a person to whom secrets are confided. Also **confidante** fem.

con·fide (kən FĪD) v. **·fid·ed, ·fid·ing** v.t. **1.** reveal in trust or confidence. **2.** entrust. —v.i. **3.** have trust; impart secrets trustingly: with *in*. [< L *confidere* entrust] —**con·fid'ing** trusting adj.

con·fi·dence (KON fi dəns) n. **1.** a feeling of trust; faith. **2.** a relationship of trust. **3.** self-assurance; also, fearlessness. **4.** a feeling of certainty. **5.** a secret. —**take into one's confidence** trust with one's secrets.

confidence game a swindle in which the victim is defrauded after placing confidence in the perpetrator: *Slang, con game.*

confidence man a swindler in a confidence game. Also *con man.*

con·fi·dent (KON fi dənt) adj. **1.** having confidence; assured. **2.** self-assured; bold.

con·fi·den·tial (KON fi DEN shəl) adj. **1.** secret; private. **2.** enjoying another's confidence; trusted. **3.** of or pertaining to the confiding of secrets. **—con′fi•den′ti•al′ i•ty** *n.*

con•fig•u•ra•tion (kən FIG yə RAY shən) *n.* the arrangement of the parts of a thing; form; contour. [< LL]

con•fine (kən FĪN) *v.t.* **•fined, •fin•ing 1.** shut in; imprison. **2.** restrain or oblige to stay within doors. **3.** restrict: to *confine* remarks. **—n.** (KON fin *Usu.* pl. a boundary or border. [ME] **—con•fin′a•ble** *adj.*

con•fine•ment (kən FĪN mənt) *n.* **1.** the act of confining, or the state of being confined. **2.** childbirth.

con•firm (kən FURM) *v.t.* **1.** verify; substantiate. **2.** strengthen. **3.** render valid by formal approval. **4.** administer the rite of confirmation. [< L *confirmare* strengthen] **—con•firm′a•to′ry** *adj.*

con•fir•ma•tion (KON fər MAY shən) *n.* **1.** the act of confirming. **2.** proof. **3.** a religious rite in which a person is admitted to all the privileges of a church or synagogue.

con•firmed (kən FURMD) *adj.* **1.** firmly established; ratified. **2.** inveterate; habitual. **3.** having received religious confirmation.

con•fis•cate (KON fə SKAYT) *v.t.* **•cat•ed, •cat•ing 1.** seize for public use, usu. as a penalty. **2.** appropriate by or as by authority. [< L *confiscatus* seized for government use] **—con•fis•ca•to•ry** (kən FIS kə TOR ee) *adj.*

con•fla•gra•tion (KON flə GRAY shən) *n.* a great or extensive fire. [< L, burned up]

con•flict (KON flikt) *n.* **1.** a struggle; battle. **2.** mutual antagonism, as of ideas. **3.** a clash between contradictory impulses. **—v.i.** (kən FLIKT) **1.** come into collision or opposition; clash. **2.** battle; struggle. [ME] **—con•flic′tive** *adj.*

con•flu•ence (KON floo əns) *n.* **1.** a flowing together of streams; also, the place where they meet. **2.** the body or stream of water so formed. **3.** a coming together; crowd. [ME] **—con′flu•ent** *adj.*

con•form (kən FORM) *v.i.* **1.** show identity or resemblance; correspond: with *to.* **2.** adhere to conventional behavior. **—v.t. 3.** make the same or similar: with *to.* **4.** bring (oneself) into harmony or agreement: with *to.* [ME *conformen* shape]

con•for•ma•tion (KON for MAY shən) *n.* **1.** form; structure or outline. **2.** the arrangement of parts. **3.** the act of conforming, or the state of being conformed.

con•form•ist (kən FOR mist) *n.* one who conforms in behavior.

con•form•i•ty (kən FOR mi tee) *n. pl.* **•ties 1.** correspondence; agreement. **2.** the act or habit of conforming; acquiescence. Also **con•form′ance.**

con•found (kon FOWND) *v.t.* **1.** confuse or amaze. **2.** confuse with something else. **3.** confuse or mingle indistinguishably. **4.** (KON FOWND) damn: used as an oath. [ME *confounden* mix] **—con•found′ed** *adj.*

con•front (kən FRUNT) *v.t.* **1.** stand face to face with; face defiantly. **2.** put face to face: with *with.* **—con•fron•ta•tion** (KON frən TAY shən) *n.* [< Med.L *confrontari* bound]

con•fuse (kən FYOOZ) *v.t.* **•fused, •fus•ing 1.** perplex or perturb; bewilder. **2.** jumble. **3.** mistake one for the other. [< L *confundere* confuse!

con•fu•sion (kən FYOO zhən) *n.* **1.** the act of confusing, or the state of being confused. **2.** disarray; disorder. **3.** perplexity of mind. **4.** embarrassment.

con game *Slang* a confidence game.

con•geal (kən JEEL) *v.t. & v.i.* **1.** make or become solid, as by freezing or curdling. **2.** clot or coagulate, as blood. [ME *congelen* freeze]

con•gen•ial (kən JEEN yəl) *adj.* **1.** having similar character or tastes; sympathetic. **2.** agreeable: a *congenial* job. **—con•ge•ni•al•i•ty** (kən JEE nee AL i tee) *n.*

con•gen•i•tal (kən JEN i tl) *adj.* **1.** existing prior to or at birth: distinguished from *hereditary.* **2.** disposed as if by birth. [< L *congenitus* inborn]

con•gest (kən JEST) *v.t.* **1.** overcrowd. **2.** *Pathol.* burden (an organ or part) with an excess of fluid. **—v.i. 3.** become congested. [< L *congestus* brought together] **—con•ges′tion** *n.* **—con•ges′tive** *adj.*

con•glom•er•ate (kən GLOM ər it) *adj.* **1.** massed or clustered. **2.** *Geol.* consisting of loosely cemented heterogeneous material. **—n. 1.** a heterogeneous collection; cluster. **2.** a large corporation formed by merging a number of companies, often in unrelated fields. **—v.t. & v.i.** (kən GLOM ə RAYT) **•at•ed, •at•ing** gather into a cohering mass. [< L *conglomeratus* rolled together]

con•grat•u•late (kən GRACH ə LAYT) *v.t.* **•lat•ed, •lat•ing** express pleasure in or otherwise acknowledge the achievement or good fortune of (another). [< L *congratulatus* wished joy] **—con·grat′ u·la·to′ry** *adj.* **—con·grat·u·la·tion** (-ə LAY shən)

con·gre·gate (KONG gri GAYT) *v.t. & v.i.* **·gat·ed, ·gat·ing** gather into a crowd; assemble. [< L *congregare* flock together]

con·gre·ga·tion (KONG gri GAYT) *n.* **1.** the act of congregating. **2.** an assemblage. **3.** a group of people worshiping together or who worship in a local church or synagogue.

con·gress (KONG gris) *n.* **1.** an assembly or conference. **2.** a meeting. **3.** the legislature of various nations, esp. of a republic. [ME] **4. Con·gress** the legislative body of the U.S., consisting of the Senate and the House of Representatives. **—con· gres·sion·al** *adj.* **—con·gress·man, -wom·an** *n.* a member of a congress, esp. of the U.S. House of Representatives. [ME]

con·gru·ent (KONG groo ənt) *adj.* **1.** agreeing or conforming; congruous. **2.** *Geom.* exactly coinciding when superimposed. [ME] **—con′gru·ence** *n.*

con·gru·ous (KONG groo əs) *adj.* **1.** agreeing; harmonious. **2.** appropriate; fit. **— con·gru·i·ty** (kən GROO i tee) *n.*

con·ic (KON ik) *adj.* **1.** cone-shaped. **2.** of or formed by or upon a cone. Also **con′i·cal.** [< Gk. *kōnikos*]

con·i·fer (KON ə fər) *n.* any of a widely distributed family of evergreen shrubs and trees, as the pines, spruces, etc. [ME *confere*] **—co·nif·er·ous** (koh NIF ər əs) *adj.*

con·jec·ture (kən JEK chər) *v.t. & v.i.* **·tured, ·tur·ing** guess; infer. **—n. 1.** inference from incomplete evidence. **2.** a guess; surmise. [ME]

con·ju·gal (KON jə gəl) *adj.* pertaining to marriage; connubial. [< L *conjugalis* yoked together] **—con·ju·gal·i·ty** (KON jə GAL i tee) *n.*

con·ju·gate (KON jə GAYT) *v.* **·gat·ed, ·gat·ing** *v.t.* **1.** *Gram.* give the inflections of (a verb). **—v.i. 2.** unite; join together. **— adj.** (-jə git) **1.** joined in pairs; coupled. **2.** kindred in origin and, usu., meaning: said of words. **—n.** (-jə git) **1.** a conjugate word. **2.** a member of any conjugate pair. [ME]

con·ju·ga·tion (KON jə GAY shən) *n.* **1.** a joining or being joined together. **2.** *Gram.* **a** the inflection of verbs. **b** a presentation of the entire inflection of a verb. **c** a class of verbs that are inflected in the same manner.

con·junc·tion (kən JUNGK shən) *n.* **1.** the act of joining together, or the state of being so joined. **2.** a coincidence. **3.** *Astron.* **a** the

position of two celestial bodies when they are in the same celestial longitude. **b** the position of a planet when it is on a direct line with the earth and the sun. **4.** *Gram.* a word used to connect words, phrases, clauses, or sentences. [ME *conjunccioun*] **—con·junc′tive** *adj.*

con·jure (KON jər) *v.* **·jured, ·jur·ing** *v.t.* **1.** call on or appeal to solemnly; adjure. **2.** summon by magic, as a devil. **3.** accomplish by or as by magic. **—v.i. 4.** practice magic. [ME *conjuren* swear together]

con·jur·er (KON jər ər) *n.* a magician.

con man *Slang* a confidence man.

con·nect (kə NEKT) *v.t.* **1.** join or fasten together; link. **2.** associate as in thought. **— v.i. 3.** join or fit. **4.** meet so that passengers can transfer: said of trains, buses, etc. [ME] **—con·nec′tor** *n.*

con·nec·tion (kə NEK shən) *n.* **1.** the act of connecting, or the state of being connected. **2.** that which joins or relates; a link. **3.** logical sequence; coherence. **4.** context. **5.** family relationship. **6.** influential friend or associate. **7.** *Often pl.* a transfer or continuation from one route or vehicle to another.

con·nec·tive (kə NEK tiv) *adj.* capable of connecting, or serving to connect. **—n. 1.** that which connects. **2.** *Gram.* a connecting word or particle, as a conjunction.

con·nive (kə NĪV) *v.i.* **·nived, ·niv·ing 1.** encourage or assent to a wrong by silence or feigned ignorance: with *at.* **2.** be in collusion: with *with.* [< F *conniver* pretend not to see] **—con·niv′ance** *n.*

con·nois·seur (KON ə SUR) *n.* an expert, esp. in matters of art and taste. [< F]

con·no·ta·tion (KON ə TAY shən) *n.* **1.** the secondary significance of an expression. **2.** the act of connoting. **—con′no·ta′tive** *adj.*

con·note (kə NOHT) *v.t.* **·not·ed, ·not·ing** suggest or imply. [< Med.L *connotare* note together]

con·nu·bi·al (kə NOO bee əl) *adj.* pertaining to marriage or to the married state. [< Med.L *connubialis*]

con·quer (KONG kər) *v.t.* **1.** overcome by or as by force; vanquish; surmount. **—v.i. 2.** be victorious. [ME *conqueren*] **—con′ quer·or** *n.*

con·quest (KON kwest) *n.* **1.** the act of conquering. **2.** the thing conquered. **3.** a winning of another's favor or love. **4.** one whose favor or love has been won.

con·quis·ta·dor (kon KWIS tə DOR) *n.* a

conqueror; esp., any of the 16th c. Spanish conquerors of Mexico and Peru. [< Sp.]

con·science (KON shəns) n. the faculty by which distinctions are made between moral right and wrong. [ME, awareness]

con·sci·en·tious (KON shee EN shəs) adj. 1. scrupulous. 2. painstaking.

conscientious objector one who, on grounds of religious or moral convictions, refuses to perform military service.

con·scious (KON shəs) adj. 1. aware of one's own existence or of external objects and conditions. 2. aware of some object or fact. 3. deliberate; intentional. [< L conscius sharing information with]

con·scious·ness (KON shəs ˈnis) n. 1. awareness of oneself and one's surroundings. 2. awareness of some object, influence, etc. 3. the mental and emotional awareness of an individual, or of a group.

con·script (KON skript) n. one who is compulsorily enrolled for some service. —adj. conscripted. —v.t. (kən SKRIPT) force into military or other service. [< L conscriptus enrolled]

con·se·crate (KON si KRAYT) v.t. •crat·ed, •crat·ing 1. set apart as sacred. 2. dedicate; devote. 3. make revered; hallow. [ME consecraten] —**con'se·cra'tion** n.

con·sec·u·tive (kən SEK yə tiv) adj. 1. following in uninterrupted succession; successive. 2. characterized by logical sequence.

con·sen·sus (kən SEN səs) n. a collective opinion; general agreement. [< L]

con·sent (kən SENT) v.i. give assent; agree or acquiesce. —n. 1. a voluntary yielding; compliance. 2. agreement; harmony. [ME consenten]

con·se·quence (KON si kwens) n. 1. that which naturally follows from a preceding action or condition; result. 2. a logical conclusion. 3. importance. [ME, that which follows]

con·se·quen·tial (KON si KWEN shəl) adj. 1. following as an effect or conclusion. 2. of consequence; important.

con·se·quent·ly (KON si kwent lee) adv. as a result; therefore.

con·ser·va·tion (KON sər VAY shən) n. 1. the act of keeping or protecting from loss or injury. 2. the preservation of natural resources, as forests, fisheries, etc. [ME conservacioun] —**con'ser·va'tion·ist** n.

con·ser·va·tism (kən SUR və TIZ əm) n.

devotion to the existing order; opposition to change.

con·ser·va·tive (kən SUR və tiv) adj. 1. inclined to preserve the existing order of things; opposed to change. 2. moderate; cautious: a conservative estimate. 3. conserving; preservative. —n. a conservative person. —**con·ser'va·tive·ness** n.

con·ser·va·to·ry (kən SUR və TOR ee) n. pl. •ries 1. a small greenhouse or glass-enclosed room for plants. 2. a school of music.

con·serve (kən SURV) v.t. •served, •serv·ing 1. keep from loss or decay; maintain. 2. preserve with sugar. —n. (KON surv) Often pl. a kind of jam made of several fruits. [ME]

con·sid·er (kən SID ər) v.t. 1. think about or deliberate on. 2. look upon or regard (as). 3. believe. 4. take into account: consider the feelings of others. —v.i. 5. think carefully; deliberate. [ME consideren examine]

con·sid·er·a·ble (kən SID ər ə bəl) adj. 1. somewhat large in amount, extent, etc. 2. worthy of consideration. —**con·sid'er·a·bly** adv.

con·sid·er·ate (kən SID ər it) adj. thoughtful of others; kind.

con·sid·er·a·tion (kən SID ə RAY shən) n. 1. the act of considering; deliberation. 2. a circumstance to be taken into account. 3. thoughtful or kindly feeling or treatment. 4. something given for a service. 5. high regard; esteem. —**in consideration of** in view of, or in return for.

con·sid·er·ing (kən SID ə ring) prep. in view of; taking into account. —adv. Informal taking all the facts into account.

con·sign (kən SĪN) v.t. 1. entrust to the care of another. 2. give up or turn over. 3. forward or deliver, as merchandise. 4. set apart, as for a specific use. [ME] —**con·sign'a·ble** adj.

con·sign·ment (kən SĪN mənt) n. 1. the act of consigning something. 2. that which is consigned. —**on consignment** of goods, payable by the retailer only after they have been sold.

con·sist (kən SIST) v.i. 1. be made up or constituted: with of. 2. have as source or basis: with in. [< L consistere stand together]

con·sis·ten·cy (kən SIS tən see) n. pl. •cies 1. agreement between things, acts, or statements. 2. firmness or thickness.

con·sis·tent (kən SIS tənt adj. 1. not

contradictory or self-contradictory. **2.** conforming to a single set of principles or to previous action or belief. **—con·sis'tent·ly** adv.

con·sole[1] (kən SOHL) v.t. **•soled, •sol·ing** comfort (a person) in grief or sorrow; cheer. [< F consoler] **—con·sol'a·ble** adj. **—con·so·la·tion** (KON sə LAY shən) n.

con·sole[2] (KON sohl) n. **1.** the portion of an organ containing the keyboard and stops. **2.** a cabinet, as for a television set, that rests on the floor. **3.** an instrument panel, esp. for controlling electronic devices. [< F]

con·sol·i·date (kən SOL i DAYT) v. **•dat·ed, •dat·ing** v.t. **1.** make solid or coherent; strengthen. **2.** combine in one. **—v.i. 3.** become united, solid, or firm. [< L consolidatus made solid] **—con·sol'i·da'tion** n.

con·som·mé (KON sə MAY) n. a clear soup made of meat and sometimes vegetables. [< F, completed]

con·so·nance (KON sə nəns) n. **1.** agreement; accord. **2.** correspondence of sounds, esp. of consonants. **3.** *Music* a combination of tones regarded as stable and not requiring resolution. **—con'so·nant** adj. **—n. 1.** *Phonet.* a sound produced by complete or partial blockage of the breath stream, as the sounds of *b, f, k, s, t,* etc. **2.** a letter representing such a sound. [ME]

con·sort (KON sort) n. **1.** a husband or wife; spouse. **2.** a companion or partner. **—v.t. &** v.i. (kən SORT) associate; join. [ME]

con·sor·ti·um (kən SOR shee əm) n. pl. **•ti·a** (-shee ə) a coalition, as of banks or corporations, for a large venture. [< L, fellowship]

con·spic·u·ous (kən SPIK yoo əs) adj. clearly visible; easily seen; striking. [< L conspicuus visible] **—con·spic'u·ous·ly** adv.

con·spir·a·cy (kən SPIR ə see) n. pl. **•cies** the act of conspiring secretly; also, the plan so made. **—con·spir'a·tor** n. **—con·spir'a·to'ri·al** adj.

con·spire (kən SPIR) v. **•spired, •spir·ing** v.i. **1.** combine secretly in an evil or unlawful enterprise. **2.** act together. **—v.t. 3.** plan secretly; plot. [ME]

con·stan·cy (KON stən see) n. **1.** steadiness or faithfulness. **2.** unchanging quality. [< constantia firmness]

con·stant (KON stənt) adj. **1.** long-continuing, or continually recurring; persistent. **2.** unchanging; invariable. **3.** steady

in purpose, action, etc.; faithful. **—n. 1.** that which is permanent or invariable. **2.** *Math.* a quantity that retains a fixed value. **3.** in the sciences, any numerical expression of a characteristic that remains the same under specified conditions. [ME]

con·stel·la·tion (KON stə LAY shən) n. **1.** *Astron.* any of various groups of stars imagined to represent a being or thing, usu. mythological. **2.** any group of persons or things, esp. one regarded as brilliant. [ME constellacioun]

con·ster·na·tion (KON stər NAY shən) n. sudden fear or amazement; panic. [< F] **—con'ster·nate** v.t. **•nat·ed, •nat·ing** fill with consternation.

con·sti·pate (KON stə PAYT) v.t. **•pat·ed, •pat·ing** cause numerical expression of [ME, crowded] **—con'sti·pat'ed** adj.

con·sti·pa·tion (KON stə PAY shən) n. a condition of the bowels characterized by suppressed or difficult evacuation.

con·stit·u·en·cy (kən STICH oo ən see) n. pl. **•cies 1.** a body of voters who elect a representative; also, the district represented. **2.** any body of supporters.

con·stit·u·ent (kən STICH oo ənt) adj. **1.** forming; constituting. **2.** entitled to elect a representative. **3.** having the power to frame or modify a constitution. **—n. 1.** a voter or client. **2.** a necessary part or component.

con·sti·tute (KON sti TOOT) v.t. **•tut·ed, •tut·ing 1.** be the substance or elements of; make up; compose. **2.** enact (a law, etc.). **3.** establish, as a school or an assembly, in legal form. **4.** empower; appoint. **5.** make by combining elements or parts; frame. [< L constituere establish]

con·sti·tu·tion (KON sti TOO shən) n. **1.** the act of constituting. **2.** the composition or make-up of a thing. **3.** the fundamental laws and principles governing a state or association; also, a document recording such laws and principles.

con·sti·tu·tion·al (KON sti TOO shə nl) adj. **1.** of or inherent in the constitution of a person or thing. **2.** consistent with or pertaining to the constitution of a state. **3.** controlled by a constitution. **—n.** exercise taken for one's health. **—con'sti·tu'tion·al'i·ty** n.

con·sti·tu·tive (KON sti TOO tiv) adj. **1.** forming an essential element; basic. **2.** having power to enact or establish.

con·strain (kən STRAYN) v.t. **1.** compel;

coerce. **2.** confine, as by bonds. **3.** restrain. [ME *constrainen* constrict]

con·strained (kən STRAYND) *adj.* forced; unnatural: a *constrained* smile.

con·straint (kən STRAYNT) *n.* **1.** the use of force; coercion. **2.** confinement; restriction. **3.** unnaturalness of manner; awkwardness.

con·strict (kən STRIKT) *v.t.* draw together by force; cause to shrink or contract; bind; cramp. [< L *constrictus* bound together] —**con·stric′tion** *n.*

con·stric·tor (kən STRIK tər) *n.* **1.** that which constricts. **2.** a serpent that coils about and crushes its prey.

con·struct (kən STRUKT) *v.t.* **1.** form by combining materials or parts; build; erect. **2.** devise; form systematically. —*n.* (KON strukt) something constructed. [ME]

con·struc·tion (kən STRUK shən) *n.* **1.** the act of constructing; also, the business of building. **2.** something constructed; a structure or building. **3.** manner of construction. **4.** interpretation. **5.** *Gram.* the arrangement of forms syntactically, as in sentences.

con·struc·tive (kən STRUK tiv) *adj.* tending to build, improve, or advance. —**con·struc′tive·ness** *n.*

con·strue (kən STROO) *v.t.* •**strued,** •**stru·ing 1.** analyze the grammatical structure of; parse. **2.** interpret; deduce by inference. **3.** *Gram.* use syntactically: The noun "physics" is *construed* as singular. [< L *construere* put together]

con·sul (KON səl) *n.* **1.** an officer residing in a foreign city to protect his or her country's commercial interests and the welfare of its citizens. **2.** either of the two chief magistrates in the Roman republic. [< L] —**con·su·lar** (KON sə lər) *adj.*

con·su·late (KON sə lit) *n.* **1.** the office or term of a consul. Also **con′sul·ship. 2.** the official place of business of a consul. **3.** government by consuls. [ME]

con·sult (kən SULT) *v.t.* **1.** ask the advice of. **2.** have regard for in deciding or acting; consider. —*v.i.* **3.** ask advice. **4.** take counsel: with *with.* **5.** give professional advice. [< L *consultare* deliberate]

con·sult·ant (kən SUL tnt) *n.* **1.** a person who gives expert advice. **2.** one who consults.

con·sul·ta·tion (KON səl TAY shən) *n.* **1.** the act of consulting. **2.** a meeting of consultants. —**con·sul·ta·tive** (kən SUL tə tiv) *adj.*

con·sume (kən SOOM) *v.* •**sumed,** •**sum·ing** *v.t.* **1.** destroy, as by burning. **2.** eat, drink, or use up. **3.** engross. —*v.i.* **4.** be wasted or destroyed. [< L *consumere* take up] —**con·sum′a·ble** *adj.*

con·sum·er (kən SOO mər) *n.* **1.** one who or that which consumes. **2.** one who buys or uses an article or service.

con·sum·mate (KON sə mayt) *v.t.* •**mat·ed,** •**mat·ing 1.** complete or perfect. **2.** fulfill (a marriage) by sexual intercourse. —*adj.* (kən SUM it) perfect; complete. [< L *consummare* complete] —**con′sum·ma′tion** *n.*

con·sump·tion (kən SUMP shən) *n.* **1.** the act or process of consuming. **2.** the amount consumed. **3.** *Econ.* the using up of goods and services.

con·tact (KON takt) *n.* **1.** a coming together or touching. **2.** a potentially helpful acquaintance. —*v.t.* **1.** bring or place in contact; touch. **2.** get in touch with (someone). —*v.i.* **3.** be or come in contact; touch: with *with.* [< L *contactus* a touching]

con·ta·gion (kən TAY jən) *n.* **1.** the communication of disease by contact. **2.** a communicable disease. **3.** the communication of mental states, ideas, etc. [ME]

con·ta·gious (kən TAY jəs) *adj.* **1.** transmissible by contact, as a disease. **2.** spreading contagion. **3.** exciting or tending to excite similar feelings, etc. in others; catching. —**con·ta′gious·ness** *n.*

con·tain (kən TAYN) *v.t.* **1.** hold or enclose. **2.** include or comprise. **3.** be capable of holding. **4.** keep within bounds; restrain. [ME *conteynen* hold together]

con·tam·i·nate (kən TAM ə nayt) *v.t.* •**nat·ed,** •**nat·ing** make impure by contact or admixture; taint; pollute. [< L *contaminatus* spoiled]

con·tem·plate (KON təm playt) *v.* •**plat·ed,** •**plat·ing** *v.t.* **1.** look at attentively; gaze at. **2.** consider thoughtfully; meditate on. **3.** intend or plan. —*v.i.* **4.** meditate; muse. [< L *contemplatus* observed] —**con·tem·pla·tive** (kən TEM plə tiv) *adj.* & *n.*

con·tem·po·ra·ne·ous (kən TEM pə RAY nee əs) *adj.* living or occurring at the same time. [< L *contemporaneus*]

con·tem·po·rar·y (kən TEM pə RER ee) *adj.* **1.** contemporaneous. **2.** of the same age. **3.** current; modern. —*n. pl.* •**rar·ies** a contemporary person or thing.

con·tempt (kən TEMPT) *n.* **1.** a feeling that

contemptible **154**

something is vile and worthless; scorn. **2.** the state of being despised. **3.** *Law* willful disrespect of authority. [ME]

con·tempt·i·ble (kən TEMP ti bəl) *adj.* deserving of contempt; despicable. [ME]

con·temp·tu·ous (kən TEMP choo əs) *adj.* showing or feeling contempt; scornful.

con·tend (kən TEND) *v.i.* **1.** strive in competition; vie. **2.** argue; debate. **3.** struggle. —*v.t.* **4.** assert. [ME *contenden* compete] —**con·tend′er** *n.*

con·tent¹ (KON tent) *n.* **1.** *Usu. pl.* that which a thing contains: the *contents* of a box. **2.** subject matter or meaning. **3.** the quantity of a specified part. [ME]

con·tent² (kən TENT) *adj.* satisfied with what one has. —*n.* ease of mind; satisfaction. —*v.t.* satisfy. [ME] —**con·tent′ed** *adj.*

con·ten·tion (kən TEN shən) *n.* **1.** controversy; argument. **2.** competition; rivalry. **3.** a point asserted in argument. —**in contention** being contended over. [ME] —**con·ten′tious** *adj.* given to contention; quarrelsome. —**con·ten′tious·ness** *n.*

con·test (KON test) *n.* **1.** a struggling against one another; conflict. **2.** a dispute. **3.** a competition, game, etc. —*v.* (kən TEST) *v.t.* **1.** fight to keep or win. **2.** call in question; challenge. —*v.i.* **3.** contend with *with* or *against.* [< L *contestari* call as a witness] —**con·test′ant** *n.*

con·text (KON tekst) *n.* **1.** any phrase, sentence, or passage so closely connected to a word or words as to affect their meaning. **2.** something that surrounds and influences, as environment or circumstances. [ME] —**con·tex·tu·al** (kən TEKS choo əl) *adj.*

con·tig·u·ous (kən TIG yoo əs) *adj.* **1.** touching at the edge. **2.** close, but not touching. [< L *contiguus* bordering] —**con·ti·gu·i·ty** (KON ti GYOO i tee) *n.*

con·ti·nence (KON tn əns) *n.* self-restraint, esp. sexual abstinence. [ME]

con·ti·nent (KON tn ənt) *n.* one of the large land masses of the earth. —*adj.* **1.** self-restrained; moderate. **2.** abstinent, esp. sexually; chaste. [ME]

con·ti·nen·tal (KON tn EN tl) *adj.* **1.** of, or of the proportions of, a continent. **2.** *Often cap.* European. —*n. Usu. cap.* European.

con·tin·gen·cy (kən TIN jən see) *n. pl.* **·cies 1.** uncertainty of occurrence; dependence on chance or accident. **2.** an unforeseen but possible occurrence. **3.** something incidental.

con·tin·gent (kən TIN jənt) *adj.* **1.** liable to happen; possible. **2.** accidental; chance. **3.** dependent on an uncertain event or condition: with *on* or *upon.* —*n.* **1.** a contingency. **2.** a proportionate quota of something to be furnished, as of troops. **3.** a representative group in an assemblage. [ME, befalling]

con·tin·u·al (kən TIN yoo əl) *adj.* renewed frequently; often repeated. [< L *continualis*] —**con·tin′u·al·ly** *adv.*

con·tin·u·ance (kən TIN yoo əns) *n.* **1.** a continuing, as of an action, or a remaining, as in a place. **2.** continuation, as of a novel. **3.** duration. **4.** *Law* adjournment to a future time.

con·tin·u·a·tion (kən TIN yoo AY shən) *n.* **1.** the act of continuing or the state of being continued. **2.** the extension or a carrying to a further point. **3.** addition; sequel. [ME *continuacioun*]

con·tin·ue (kən TIN yoo) *v.* **·tin·ued, ·tin·u·ing** *v.i.* **1.** go on in some action or condition; persist. **2.** resume after an interruption. **3.** remain in the same place, condition, or capacity. **4.** last; endure. —*v.t.* **5.** persevere in; carry forward. **6.** take up again after interruption. **7.** extend or prolong. **8.** cause to remain; also, keep on, as in office. **9.** *Law* postpone. [ME]

con·ti·nu·i·ty (KON) tn OO i tee *n. pl.* **·ties 1.** the state or quality of being continuous. **2.** an unbroken series; succession. **3.** a scenario; also, a script. [ME *continuite*]

con·tin·u·ous (kən TIN yoo əs) *adj.* uninterrupted. [< L *continuus*] —**con·tin′u·ous·ly** *adv.*

con·tin·u·um (kən TIN yoo əm) *n. pl.* **·tin·u·a** (-TIN yoo ə) something continuous, with no discernible separate parts. [< L]

con·tort (kən TORT) *v.t. & v.i.* twist violently; wrench out of shape or place. [< L *contortus* twisted together] —**con·tor′tion** *n.*

con·tor·tion·ist (kən TOR shə nist) *n.* a performer who twists into unnatural positions.

con·tour (KON tuur) *n.* the outline of a figure or body, or a line representing it. —*v.t.* draw the contour lines of. —*adj.* **1.** *Agric.* following the contours of land in such a way in plowing as to minimize erosion. **2.** shaped to fit the contour of something. [< F]

con·tra·band (KON trə BAND) *n.* **1.** goods that, by law or treaty, may not be imported or exported. **2.** smuggled goods.

[< Ital. *contrabbando*] —**con'tra·band** *adj.*

con·tra·cep·tion (KON trə SEP shən) *n.* the deliberate prevention of fertilization of the human ovum. —**con'tra·cep'tive** *n. & adj.*

con·tract (kən TRAKT; for *v.* def. 2, KON trakt) *v.t.* **1.** cause to draw together; reduce in size. **2.** enter upon or settle by contract. **3.** acquire or become affected with, as a disease. **4.** *Gram.* shorten by contraction. —*v.i.* **5.** become smaller; shrink. **6.** make a contract. —*n.* (KON trakt) **1.** a formal agreement between two or more parties, esp. one that is legally binding. **2.** the document containing such an agreement. **3.** in bridge, the highest and final bid of a hand, stating a denomination and the number of tricks to be made. [ME] —**con·trac·tu·al** (kən TRAK choo əl) *adj.*

con·trac·tion (kən TRAK shən) *n.* **1.** the act of contracting, or the state of being contracted. **2.** *Gram.* the shortening of a word or phrase by the omission of letters, as in *don't* for *do not*; also, the new word formed. [ME]

con·trac·tor (KON trak tər) *n.* **1.** one who agrees to supply materials or perform services for a sum, esp. for the construction of buildings. **2.** that which contracts, as a muscle.

con·tra·dict (KON trə DIKT) *v.t.* **1.** maintain or assert the opposite of (a statement). **2.** deny a statement of (a person). **3.** be contrary to or inconsistent with. **4.** utter a contradiction. [< L *contradictus* denied]

con·tra·dic·tion (KON trə DIK shən) *n.* **1.** a denial. **2.** obvious inconsistency; discrepancy. [ME *contradiccioun*] —**con·tra·dic·to·ry** (-DIK tə ree) *adj.*

con·tra·in·di·cate (KON trə IN di kayt) *v.t. Med.* indicate the danger of. —**con'tra·in'di·ca'tion** *n.*

con·tral·to (kən TRAL toh) *n. pl.* **·tos 1.** the lowest female singing voice. **2.** one having such a voice. [< Ital.]

con·trar·y (KON trer ee) *adj.* **1.** opposed in essence, purpose, etc. **2.** opposite as to position or direction. **3.** adverse; unfavorable. **4.** (kən TRAIR ee) inclined to oppose and contradict; perverse. —*n. pl.* **·trar·ies 1.** one of two contrary things. **2.** the opposite. —**on the contrary** as opposed to the previous statement; quite the opposite. —**to the contrary** to the opposite effect. —*adv.*

in a contrary manner. [ME *contrarie*] —**con'trar·i·ness** *n.*

con·trast (kən TRAST) *v.t.* **1.** place in opposition so as to set off differences. —*v.i.* **2.** reveal differences when set in opposition. —*n.* (KON trast) **1.** the act of contrasting, or the state of being contrasted. **2.** a dissimilarity revealed by contrasting. **3.** one who or that which shows unlikeness to another. [< MF *contraster* contest]

con·tra·vene (KON trə VEEN) *v.t.* **·vened, ·ven·ing 1.** run counter to. **2.** oppose or contradict. [< LL *contravenire* come against] —**con·tra·ven·tion** (KON trə VEN shən) *n.*

con·trib·ute (kən TRIB yoot) *v.* **·ut·ed, ·ut·ing 1.** give with others for a common purpose. **2.** furnish (an article, story, etc.) to a publication. —*v.i.* **3.** share in effecting a result. **4.** make a contribution. [< L *contribuere* bring together] —**con·trib'u·tor** *n.*

con·tri·bu·tion (KON trə BYOO shən) *n.* **1.** the act of contributing. **2.** something contributed. **3.** an article, story, etc., furnished to a periodical. [ME *contribucioun*]

con·trite (kən TRĪT) *adj.* penitent; remorseful. [ME *contrit* worn down] —**con·tri·tion** (kən TRISH ən) *n.*

con·triv·ance (kən TRĪ vəns) *n.* **1.** the act or manner of contriving; also, the ability to do this. **2.** a device. **3.** an ingenious plan.

con·trive (kən TRĪV) *v.* **·trived, ·triv·ing** *v.t.* **1.** plan or plot. **2.** invent. **3.** manage, as by a scheme. —*v.i.* **4.** plan; plot. [ME *contreven* invent]

con·trol (kən TROHL) *v.t.* **·trolled, ·trol·ling 1.** exercise authority over. **2.** restrain; curb. **3.** regulate or verify, as an experiment. —*n.* **1.** power to regulate and direct. **2.** a restraining influence. **3.** a standard of comparison against which to check the results of an experiment. **4.** *Often pl. Mech.* a device for operating an airplane, automobile, etc. [ME *controllen*] —**con·trol'la·ble** *adj.*

con·trol·ler (kən TROHL ər) *n.* **1.** one who or that which controls, regulates, or directs. **2.** an officer appointed to examine and verify accounts. [ME *controllour*]

con·tro·ver·sy (KON trə VUR see) *n. pl.* **·sies 1.** dispute regarding a matter on which opinions differ. **2.** a dispute; argument; debate. [ME *controversie* turned against] —**con·tro·ver·sial** (KON trə VUR shəl) *adj.*

con·tro·vert (KON trə VURT) v.t. 1. contradict; oppose. 2. argue about. —**con'tro·vert'i·ble** adj.

con·tu·me·ly (KON tuu mə lee) n. pl. •lies 1. insulting rudeness; insolence. 2. an insult. [ME contumelie] —**con·tu·me·li·ous** (KON too MEE lee əs) adj.

con·tu·sion (kən TOO zhən) n. a bruise. [ME] —**con·tuse** (kən TOOZ) v.t. •tused, •tus·ing bruise.

co·nun·drum (kə NUN drəm) n. 1. a riddle of which the answer depends on a pun. 2. any problem or puzzle.

con·va·lesce (KON və LES) v.i. •lesced, •lesc·ing recover after illness. [< L convalescere grow strong] —**con'va·les'cence** n. —**con'va·les'cent** adj. & n.

con·vene (kən VEEN) v. •vened, •ven·ing v.t. 1. cause to assemble; convoke. 2. summon to appear, as by judicial authority. —v.i. 3. assemble. [ME]

con·ven·ience (kən VEEN yəns) n. 1. the quality of being convenient; suitability. 2. personal comfort. 3. anything that saves work. [ME] —**at one's convenience** at a time one prefers.

con·ven·ient (kən VEEN yənt) adj. 1. well suited to one's purpose or needs; conducive to ease or comfort. 2. within easy reach; handy. [ME]

con·vent (KON vent) n. 1. a religious community, esp. of nuns. 2. the building or buildings of such a community. [< Med.L conventus assembly]

con·ven·tion (kən VEN shən) n. 1. a formal meeting of delegates or members, as for political or professional purposes. 2. the persons attending such a meeting. 3. a custom or usage. 4. conventionality. 5. an agreement or contract. [ME convencioun]

con·ven·tion·al (kən VEN shən əl) adj. 1. established by custom or general agreement. 2. following approved or established practice. 3. formal; stylized. [< LL conventionalis agreeable]

con·ven·tion·al·i·ty (kən VEN shə NAL i tee) n. pl. •ties 1. adherence to established forms, customs, or usages. 2. a conventional act, principle, custom, etc.

con·verge (kən VURJ) v.t. & v.i. •verged, •verg·ing move or cause to move toward one point. [< LL convergere bend together] —**con·ver·gence** (kən VUR jəns) n.

con·ver·sant (kən VUR sənt) adj. well acquainted or familiar, as by study. [ME conversaunt associated with]

con·ver·sa·tion (KON vər SAY shən) n. 1. an informal talk with another or others. 2. intimate association or social intercourse. [ME conversacioun] —**con'ver·sa'tion·al** adj.

con·ver·sa·tion·al·ist (KON vər SAY shən nl ist) n. one who enjoys or excels in conversation.

conversation piece something, as a piece of furniture, that arouses comment.

con·verse¹ (kən VURS) v.i. •versed, •vers·ing speak together informally. [ME conversen associate with]

con·verse² (kən VURS) adj. turned about; reversed; contrary. —n. (KON vurs) that which is in a converse relation; opposite. [ME convers turned around] —**con·verse·ly** (kən VURS lee) adv.

con·ver·sion (kən VUR zhən) n. 1. the act of converting, or the state of being converted. 2. a change in which one adopts new opinions, esp. a new religious faith. [ME conversioun]

con·vert (kən VURT) v.t. 1. change; transform. 2. apply or adapt to a new purpose. 3. change from one belief, religion, or course of action to another. 4. exchange for an equivalent value, or for value of another form. 5. assume possession of illegally. —v.i. 6. become changed in character. —n. (KON vurt) a person who has been converted, as from one religion to another. [ME converten change completely]

con·vert·i·ble (kən VUR tə bəl) adj. capable of being converted. —n. 1. a convertible thing. 2. an automobile with a top that folds back.

con·vex (kon VEKS) adj. curving outward, as the exterior of a globe. [< L convexus curved] —**con·vex'i·ty** n.

con·vey (kən VAY) v.t. 1. carry; transport. 2. transmit. 3. make known; impart. 4. transfer ownership of. [ME conveyen] —**con·vey'a·ble** adj.

con·vey·ance (kən VAY əns) n. 1. the act of conveying; communication; transportation. 2. something used for conveying, as a truck or bus. 3. Law the transfer of title to property; also, the document transferring title.

con·vey·or (kən VAY ər) n. 1. one who or that which conveys. 2. any mechanical contrivance for conveying articles, as a series of rollers.

con·vict (kən VIKT) v.t. find guilty after a judicial trial. —n. (KON vikt) 1. one serving a sentence in prison. **2.** one found guilty of a crime. [ME *convicten*]

con•vic•tion (kən VIK shən) *n.* **1.** the state of being convinced. **2.** a firm belief. **3.** the act of convincing. **4.** a pronouncement of guilt. [ME]

con•vince (kən VINS) *v.t.* •vinced, •vinc•ing cause to believe something, as by proof; bring to belief: often with *of.* [< L *convincere* prove untrue]

con•vinc•ing (kən VIN sing) *adj.* **1.** tending to convince. **2.** credible or believable.

con•viv•i•al (kən VIV ee əl) *adj.* **1.** fond of feasting and good fellowship; jovial. **2.** festive. [< LL *convivialis* festive] — **con•viv•i•al•i•ty** (kən VIV ee AL i tee) *n.*

con•vo•ca•tion (KON və KAY shən) *n.* **1.** the act of convoking. **2.** a meeting, esp. an ecclesiastical one. [ME *convocacioun*]

con•voke (kən VOHK) *v.t.* •voked, •vok•ing call together; summon to meet. [< MF *convoquer* call together]

con•vo•lut•ed (KON və LOO tid) *adj.* **1.** twisted or coiled up. **2.** complex; intricate. [< L *convolutus* rolled up] — **con•vo•lu•tion** (KON və LOO shən) *n.*

con•voy (KON voi) *n.* **1.** a protecting escort, as for ships at sea. **2.** a formation of ships, military vehicles, etc., traveling together. **3.** the act of convoying, or the state of being convoyed. —*v.t.* act as convoy to; escort. [ME *convoyen* convey]

con•vul•sion (kən VUL shən) *n.* **1.** *Often pl. Pathol.* a violent and involuntary contraction or series of contractions of the voluntary muscles. **2.** any violent fit or disturbance. [< L] —**con•vul'sive** (-siv) *adj.*

cook (kuuk) *v.t.* **1.** prepare (food) for eating by the action of heat. **2.** apply heat to. —*v.i.* **3.** act as a cook. **4.** undergo cooking. — **cook up** *Informal* concoct. —*n.* one who prepares food for eating. [ME *coke* cook]

cook•ie (KUUK ee) *n.* a small, flat, dry cake, usu. sweetened. [< Du. *koekie* small cake]

cool (kool) *adj.* •er, •est **1.** moderately cold; lacking warmth. **2.** producing a feeling of coolness: a *cool* suit. **3.** calm; composed. **4.** not cordial; chilling. **5.** suggesting coolness: said of colors. **6.** *Informal* not exaggerated; actual: a *cool* million. **7.** *Slang* excellent. — *v.t. & v.i.* **1.** make or become less warm. **2.** make or become less angry, ardent, or zealous. —**cool it** *Slang* calm down. —*n.* **1.** any that is cool: the *cool* of morning. **2.** composure. [ME *cole*] —**cool'ly** *adv.*

coop (koop) *n.* an enclosure or box, as for fowl. —*v.t.* put into a coop.

co-op (KOH op) *n.* a cooperative.

co•op•er•ate (koh OP ə RAYT) *v.i.* •at•ed, •at•ing work together for a common objective; act in combination. [< LL *cooperatus* worked with] —**co•op'er•a'tion** *n.*

co•op•er•a•tive (koh OP ə rə tiv) *adj.* **1.** cooperating or willing to cooperate. **2.** of or organized for mutual economic benefit. — *n.* a business enterprise, association, or property organized or owned by a group for its common economic benefit. —**co•op'er•a•tive•ness** *n.*

co-opt (koh OPT) *v.t.* **1.** elect as a fellow member of a committee, etc. **2.** appoint. **3.** incorporate within the established order. [< L *cooptare* choose together] —**co-op'tion, co'-op•ta'tion** *n.*

co•or•di•nate (koh OR dn it) *adj.* **1.** of equal importance or rank. **2.** of or pertaining to coordinates or coordination. —*n.* **1.** one who or that which is of the same order, rank, power, etc. **2.** *Math.* any of a set of magnitudes by means of which a position is determined with reference to fixed elements. —*v.* (koh OR dn AYT) •nat•ed, •nat•ing *v.t.* **1.** put in the same rank, class, or order. **2.** bring into harmonious relation or action; adjust. —*v.i.* **3.** become coordinate. **4.** act harmoniously. —**co•or'di•na'tor** *n.*

co•or•di•na•tion (koh OR dn AY shən) *n.* **1.** the act of coordinating, or the state of being coordinated. **2.** harmonious, integrated action or interaction.

cop (kop) *n. Informal* a policeman. —*v.t.* copped, cop•ping *Informal* **1.** steal. **2.** catch. —**cop out** back down; renege.

cope (kohp) *v.i.* coped, cop•ing contend or strive, esp. successfully: often with *with.* [ME *coupen* strike]

cop•i•er (KOP ee ər) *n.* **1.** an imitator. **2.** a machine that reproduces printed or written matter.

co•pi•lot (KOH PI lət) *n.* an assistant pilot.

co•pi•ous (KOH pee əs) *adj.* **1.** abundant; plentiful. **2.** diffuse; wordy. [ME] —**co'pi•ous•ness** *n.*

cop•per[1] (KOP ər) *n.* **1.** a reddish metallic element that is one of the best conductors of heat and electricity. **2.** a coin of copper, or of bronze. **3.** a lustrous, reddish brown. — *adj.* of, or of the color of, copper. [ME *coper*] —**cop'per•y** *adj.*

cop•per[2] *n. Slang* a police officer.

cop•ra (KOH prə) n. the dried kernel of the coconut, yielding coconut oil. [< Pg.]

copse (kops) n. a thicket of bushes or small trees. Also **cop•pice** (KOP is).

cop•u•late (KOP yə LAYT) v.i. •lat•ed, •lat•ing unite in sexual intercourse. [ME] —**cop•u•la′tion** n. —**cop•u•la•to•ry** (KOP yə lə TOR ee) adj.

cop•u•la•tive (KOP yə lə tiv) adj. 1. serving to join. 2. Gram. connecting words or clauses in a coordinate relationship. 3. copulatory. —n. Gram. a copulative word. [ME copulatif joining]

cop•y (KOP ee) n. pl. **cop•ies** 1. a reproduction or imitation; duplicate. 2. a single specimen of a book, print, etc. 3. written matter, as in advertising. 4. something to be set in type or otherwise reproduced. 5. in journalism, subject matter for an article, etc. —v. **cop•ied, cop•y•ing** v.t. 1. make a copy of. 2. imitate. —v.i. 3. make a copy. [ME copie] —**cop′y•ist** n.

cop•y•read•er (KOP ee REE dər) n. a person who edits work intended for publication.

cop•y•right (KOP ee RIT) n. the exclusive statutory right of authors, composers, etc., to publish and dispose of their works for a specifi d period of time. —v.t. secure copyright for. —adj. of or protected by copyright.

cop•y•writ•er (KOP ee RI tər) n. one who writes copy for advertisements.

cor•al (KOR əl) n. 1. the skeleton secreted in or by the tissues of various marine animals; also, a mass of these skeletons forming an island, reef, etc. 2. the reddish ovaries of the lobster. 3. a pinkish or yellowish red. [ME] —**coral reef** a reef formed by coral skeletons.

cord (kord) n. 1. a string or small rope; twine. 2. a flexible, insulated electric wire, usu. with a plug at one end. 3. a measure for wood, equaling 128 cubic feet. 4. a raised rib in fabric; also, fabric with such ribs, esp. corduroy. 5. Anat. a cordlike structure: vocal cord. —v.t. bind or decorate with cord. [ME coorde gut]

cor•dial (KOR jəl) adj. warm and hearty; sincere. —n. a liqueur. [ME] —**cor•di•al•i•ty** (KOR jee AL ə tee)

cor•don (KOR dn) n. 1. a line, as of people or ships, stationed so as to guard an area. 2. a ribbon or cord worn as an insignia of honor. [ME] —**cor′don** v.

cor•du•roy (KOR də ROI) n. 1. a cotton fabric having a ribbed pile. 2. pl. trousers made of corduroy. —**cor′du•roy** adj.

core (kor) n. 1. the central or innermost part of a thing. 2. the fibrous central part of a fruit, containing the seeds. —v.t. **cored, cor•ing** remove the core of. [ME]

co•re•lig•ion•ist (KOH ri LIJ ə nist) n. an adherent of the same religion, church, or sect as another.

co•re•spon•dent (KOH ri SPON dənt) n. Law in divorce action, one charged with having committed adultery with the defendant.

cork (kork) n. 1. the light, porous outer bark of the cork oak. 2. something made of cork, esp. a bottle stopper; also, a stopper made of other material. —v.t. stop with a cork. [ME corke]

cork oak an evergreen oak of southern Europe and North Africa, from whose bark cork is produced.

cork•screw (KORK skROOI) n. an instrument for drawing corks from bottles. —v.t. & v.i. move or twist spirally. —adj. shaped like a corkscrew; twisted; spiral.

corn[1] (korn) n. 1. a tall, extensively cultivated cereal plant bearing seeds on a large ear or cob; also, the seeds of this plant: also called Indian corn, maize. 2. Informal anything trite or sentimental. —v.t. preserve in salt or in brine: corn or corned beef. [ME]

corn[2] n. a horny thickening of the skin, commonly on a toe. [ME corne horn]

corn•cob (KORN kob) n. the woody spike of corn on which the kernels grow.

cor•ne•a (KOR nee ə) n. Anat. the transparent part of the coat of the eyeball covering the iris and pupil. [ME] —**cor′ne•al** adj.

cor•ner (KOR nər) n. 1. the point formed by the meeting of two lines or surfaces. 2. the place where two streets meet. 3. a threatening or embarrassing position. 4. a region or place: in every corner of the land. 5. Econ. a scheme in which a commodity or security is bought up by one or more persons or companies with a view to forcing higher prices. —**cut corners** reduce expenditures. —v.t. 1. force into a corner; place in a dangerous or embarrassing position. 2. form a corner in (a stock or commodity). —v.i. 3. turn a corner. —adj. 1. located on a corner. 2. designed for a corner. [ME] —**cor′nered** adj.

cor•ner•stone (KOR nər STOHN n. 1. a stone uniting two walls at the corner of a building. 2. such a stone ceremoniously laid into the foundation of an edifice. **3.** something of primary importance.

cor·net (kor NET) *n.* a small wind instrument of the trumpet class. [ME] — **cor·net'ist** *n.*

cor·nu·co·pi·a (KOR nə KOH pee ə) *n.* a symbol of prosperity, represented as a curved horn overflowing with fruit, vegetables, grains, etc. Also called *horn of plenty.* [< L *cornu* + *copiae* horn of plenty]

corn·y (KOR nee) *adj.* **corn·i·er, corn·i·est** *Informal* trite, banal, or sentimental.

cor·ol·lar·y (KOR ə LER ee) *n. pl.* **·lar·ies 1.** a proposition following so obviously from another that it requires little or no proof. **2.** a natural consequence; result. [ME]

co·ro·na (kə ROH nə) *n. pl.* **·nas** or **·nae** (-nee) **1.** a crownlike part, as the top of the head, the upper part of a tooth, etc. **2.** *Astron.* **a** a luminous circle around one of the heavenly bodies, as when seen through mist. **b** the luminous envelope of ionized gases visible during a total eclipse of the sun. **3.** *Electr.* the luminous discharge from an electrical conductor under high voltage. [< L, crown]

cor·o·nar·y (KOR ə NER ee) *adj. Anat.* designating either of two arteries rising from the aorta and supplying blood to the heart muscle. —*n.* coronary thrombosis. [< L *coronarius*]

coronary thrombosis *Pathol.* the formation of a thrombus, or blood clot, in one of the coronary arteries.

cor·o·na·tion (KOR ə NAY shən) *n.* the act or ceremony of crowning a monarch.

cor·o·ner (KOR ə nər) *n.* a public officer whose principal duty is the investigation of deaths not clearly due to natural causes. [ME]

cor·po·ral[1] (KOR pər əl) *adj.* belonging or related to the body. [ME *corporall* bodily]

cor·po·ral[2] *n. Mil.* a noncommissioned officer of the lowest rank. [< MF *caporal*]

corporal punishment physical punishment given an offender, as flogging.

cor·po·rate (KOR pər it) *adj.* **1.** of or related to a corporation; incorporated. **2.** collective. [ME *corporaten* incoporate]

cor·po·ra·tion (KOR pə RAY shən) *n.* **1.** a body of persons recognized by law as an individual entity, with rights, privileges, and liabilities distinct from those of its members. **2.** any group of persons acting as one body. [ME]

cor·po·re·al (kor POR ee əl) *adj.* **1.** bodily; mortal. **2.** material; physical.

corps (kor) *n. pl.* **corps** (korz) **1.** *Mil.* **a** a tactical unit, intermediate between a division and an army. **b** a special department. **2.** a number of persons acting together. [ME, body]

corpse (korps) *n.* a dead body, usu. of a human being. [ME *corps* body]

corps·man (KOR mən) *n. pl.* **·men** *Mil.* an enlisted person trained to give medical treatment.

cor·pu·lence (KOR pyə ləns) *n.* an excess of fat in the body; obesity. [ME] —**cor'pu·lent** *adj.*

cor·pus (KOR pəs) *n. pl.* **·po·ra** (-pər ə) **1.** a collection of writings, usu. on one subject or by one author. **2.** the main part of anything. [< L, body]

cor·pus·cle (KOR pə səl) *n.* **1.** *Biol.* any protoplasmic granule of distinct shape or function, esp. one of the particles forming part of the blood of vertebrates. **2.** any minute piece. [< L *corpusculum* small body]

cor·pus de·lic·ti (KOR pəs di LIK tī) *Law* the essential fact of the commission of a crime, as, in a case of murder, the body of the victim. [< NL, lit., the body of the offense]

cor·ral (kə RAL) *n.* an enclosed space or pen for livestock. —*v.t.* **·ralled, ·ral·ling** drive into and enclose in a corral. [< Sp.]

cor·rect (kə REKT) *v.t.* **1.** make free from error or mistake. **2.** remedy or counteract. **3.** punish or rebuke so as to improve. **4.** adjust, as to a standard. —*adj.* **1.** true or exact; accurate. **2.** right or proper: *correct* behavior. —**politically correct** inoffensive to any group that might object. [ME *correcten* make straight]

cor·rec·tion (kə REK shən) *n.* **1.** the act of correcting. **2.** that which is offered or used as an improvement; an emendation. **3.** discipline or punishment. —**cor·rec'tion·al** *adj.*

cor·re·late (KOR ə LAYT) *v.* **·lat·ed, ·lat·ing** *v.t.* **1.** place or put in reciprocal relation. —*v.i.* **2.** be mutually or reciprocally related. —*adj.* having a mutual or reciprocal relation. —*n.* (KOR ə lit) either of two things mutually related. —**cor're·la'tion** *n.*

cor·rel·a·tive (kə REL ə tiv) *adj.* **1.** having correlation or mutual relation. **2.** mutually related in grammatical or logical significance: *Either . . . or* are *correlative* conjunctions. —*n.* **1.** a correlate. **2.** a correlative term.

cor•re•spond (KOR ə SPOND) *v.i.* **1.** conform in fitness or appropriateness; be in agreement; suit: often with *with* or *to*. **2.** be similar: with *to*. **3.** communicate by letters. [< MF *corresponder* reply] —**cor•re•spon•dence** (KOR ə SPON dəns) *n.*

cor•re•spon•dent (KOR ə SPON dəns) *n.* **1.** one who communicates by letters. **2.** a person employed to report news etc. from a distant place. **3.** a thing that corresponds; a correlative. —*adj.* corresponding; conforming. [ME]

cor•ri•dor (KOR i dər) *n.* **1.** a passageway, usu. having rooms opening upon it. **2.** a strip of land across a foreign country, as one affording a landlocked nation access to the sea. [< MF]

cor•ri•gi•ble (KOR i jə bəl) *adj.* capable of being corrected or reformed. [ME]

cor•rob•o•rate (kə ROB ə RAYT) *v.t.* •**rat•ed,** •**rat•ing** strengthen or support, as conviction; confirm. [< L *corroboratus* strengthened] —**cor•rob′o•ra′tive** *adj.*

cor•rode (kə ROHD) *v.* •**rod•ed,** •**rod•ing** *v.t.* **1.** eat away or destroy gradually, as by chemical action. **2.** destroy, consume, or impair. —*v.i.* **3.** be eaten away. [ME]

cor•ro•sion (kə ROH zhən) *n.* **1.** the act or process of corroding. **2.** a product of this, as rust. [ME]

cor•ro•sive (kə ROH siv) *adj.* having the power of corroding. —*n.* a corroding substance. [ME]

cor•ru•gate (KOR ə GAYT) *v.t. & v.i.* •**gat•ed,** •**gat•ing** contract into alternate ridges and furrows; wrinkle. [ME, wrinkle] —**cor′ru•ga′tion** *n.*

cor•rupt (kə RUPT) *adj.* **1.** open to bribery; dishonest. **2.** immoral or perverted. **3.** rotting; putrid. **4.** debased by changes or errors, as a text. [ME *corrupten* break] —**cor•rupt′** *v.t. & v.i.*

cor•rupt•i•ble (kə RUP tə bəl) *adj.* capable of being corrupted. —**cor•rupt′i•bil′i•ty** *n.*

cor•rup•tion (kə RUP shən) *n.* **1.** the act of corrupting, or the state of being corrupt. **2.** dishonesty; also, bribery. [ME *corrupcioun*]

cor•sage (kor SAZH) *n.* a small bouquet of flowers for a woman to wear. [< MF, bust]

cor•set (KOR sit) *n.* a close-fitting undergarment, usu. designed to support the abdomen and back, worn chiefly by women —*v.t.* enclose or dress in a corset. [ME]

cor•tege (kor TEZH) *n.* **1.** a train of attendants. **2.** a ceremonial procession. [< F *cortège* retinue]

cor•ti•sone (KOR tə ZOHN) *n.* a hormone, used in treating arthritis. [Short for *corticosterone*]

cor•vine (KOR vīn) *adj.* of or pertaining to a crow. [< L *corvinus* crowlike]

cos•met•ic (koz MET ik) *adj.* used or done to beautify or improve the appearance. —*n.* a cosmetic preparation. [< Gk. *kosmetikós* pertaining to adornment]

cos•mic (KOZ mik) *adj.* **1.** of or relating to the cosmos. **2.** limitless; vast. [< Gk. *kosmikós* worldly]

cosmic rays *Physics* streams of high-energy atomic particles from outer space.

cos•mol•o•gy (koz MOL ə jee) *n. pl.* •**gies** the general philosophy and science of the universe. [< NL *cosmologia*] —**cos′mol′o•gist** *n.*

cos•mo•naut (KOZ mə NAWT) *n.* an astronaut, esp. from the former USSR.

cos•mo•pol•i•tan (KOZ mə POL i tn) *adj.* **1.** common to all the world. **2.** at home in all parts of the world. —*n.* a cosmopolitan person.

cos•mos (KOZ məs) *n.* **1.** the world or universe considered as an orderly system. **2.** any complete system. **3.** *Bot.* a plant related to the dahlia. [ME]

cost (kawst) *v.* **cost** (*for def. 3,* **cost•ed**), **cost•ing** *v.i.* **1.** be acquirable for a specified price. **2.** be gained by the expenditure of a specified thing, as health. —*v.t.* **3.** estimate the amount spent for the production of. —*n.* **1.** the price paid for anything. **2.** loss; suffering. **3.** *pl. Law* the expenses of a lawsuit in court. —**at all costs** (*or* **at any cost**) regardless of cost; by any means. [ME *costen*]

cost•ly (KAWST lee) *adj.* •**li•er,** •**li•est 1.** expensive. **2.** extravagant.

cos•tume (KOS toom) *n.* **1.** the mode of dress of a given region, time, or class. **2.** such dress as worn by actors, dancers, etc. **3.** a set of garments for some occasion or activity: tennis *costume*. —*v.t.* •**tumed,** •**tum•ing** furnish with costumes. [< F] —**cos′tum•er**

cot (kot) *n.* a light, narrow bed, commonly of canvas stretched on a folding frame. [< Hind. *khāt*]

co•te•rie (KOH tə ree) *n.* an exclusive group

of persons who share certain interests. [< F]

co·til·lion (kə TIL yən) n. **1.** an elaborate dance marked by frequent change of partners. **2.** a formal ball at which young ladies are presented to society. [< F *cotillon* type of dance]

cot·tage (KOT ij) n. a small house, esp. in the country.

cot·ton (KOT n) n. **1.** the fibrous, white or yellowish material attached to the seeds of the cotton plant and used as a textile. **2.** the plant itself. **3.** cotton cloth or thread; also, a garment of cotton cloth. —*adj.* woven or composed of cotton cloth or thread. — **cotton to** *Informal* take a liking to. [ME *coton*] —**cot′ton·y** adj.

cotton gin a machine used to separate the seeds from the fiber of cotton.

cot·y·le·don (KOT l EED n) n. *Bot.* a seed leaf, or one of a pair of the first leaves from a sprouting seed. [< NL, cup-shaped flower]

couch (kowch) n. a piece of furniture, usu. upholstered and having a back, on which several may sit. —*v.t. & v.i.* **1.** put into words. **2.** recline. [ME *couchen* put in place]

cough (kawf) *v.i.* **1.** expel air from the lungs in a noisy or spasmodic manner. —*v.t.* **2.** expel by a cough. —**cough up 1.** expel by coughing. **2.** *Slang* produce or hand over. —*n.* **1.** a sudden, harsh expulsion of breath. **2.** an illness in which there is frequent coughing. [ME *coughen*]

could (kuud) past tense of CAN[1]. [ME *coude*]

could·n't (KUUD nt) contraction of could not.

coun·cil (KOWN səl) n. **1.** an assembly convened for consultation or deliberation. **2.** a body of persons elected or appointed to act in an administrative, legislative, or advisory capacity. [ME *councile* church]

coun·ci·lor (KOWN sə lər) n. a member of a council.

coun·sel (KOWN səl) n. **1.** mutual exchange of advice, opinions, etc.; consultation. **2.** advice; guidance. **3.** a lawyer or lawyers. — *v.* **coun·seled, coun·sel·ing** *v.t.* **1.** give advice to. **2.** recommend. —*v.i.* **3.** give or take counsel. [ME *counseil* debate]

coun·se·lor (KOWN sə lər) n. **1.** an adviser. **2.** a lawyer. **3.** a supervisor at a children's camp.

count[1] (kownt) *v.t.* **1.** list or call off one by one to ascertain the total. **2.** list numerals in sequence up to: *count* ten. **3.** consider to

be; judge. **4.** take note of. —*v.i.* **5.** list numbers in sequence. **6.** be of importance. **7.** be accounted or included. —**count on** (or **upon**) rely on. —*n.* **1.** the act of counting. **2.** the number arrived at by counting; total. **3.** *Law* a charge, as in an indictment. [ME *counten* reckon]

count[2] n. a nobleman of a rank corresponding to that of an earl in England. [< ME *counte*]

coun·te·nance (KOWN tn əns) n. **1.** the face or features. **2.** facial expression. **3.** an encouraging look; also, approval; support. —*v.t.* **·nanced, ·nanc·ing** approve; encourage. [ME *cuntenaunce* behavior]

coun·ter[1] (KOWN tər) n. **1.** something opposite or contrary. **2.** a blow, thrust, or the like given in return for a similar attack. — *v.t.* **1.** return, as a blow. **2.** oppose; contradict. —*v.i.* **3.** give a blow while receiving or parrying one. **4.** make a countermove. — *adj.* opposing; opposite; contrary. —*adv.* contrary. [ME *countre* against]

coun·ter[2] n. **1.** a board, table, etc., for showing goods, transacting business, or serving refreshments. **2.** a piece of wood, ivory, etc., used in a game, esp. to keep score. **3.** an imitation coin. [ME *countour* computing place]

counter- *combining form*

1. opposing; contrary; acting in response:

counteragent	**countermeasure**
countercharge	**countersuggestion**

2. done in reciprocation or exchange:

counterassurance	**counterplea**
counteroffer	**counterquestion**

3. complementing; duplicating:

countercheck	**counterseal**

4. opposite in direction or position:

countercurrent	**counterpressure**

[< *contra-* against]

coun·ter·act (KOWN tər AKT) *v.t.* act in opposition to; check.

coun·ter·at·tack (KOWN tər ə TAK) n. an attack designed to offset another attack. — *v.t. & v.i.* (KOWN tər ə TAK) make a counterattack against (an enemy fortification etc.)

coun·ter·bal·ance (KOWN tər BAL əns) *v.t.* **·anced, ·anc·ing** oppose with an equal weight or force; offset. —*n.* (KOWN tər BAL əns) **1.** any counterbalancing power. **2.** a weight that balances another. **3.** a state of equilibrium. Also *counterpoise.*

coun·ter·cul·ture (KOWN tər KUL chər) n.

a subculture, esp. among youth, hostile to many prevailing social values.

coun·ter·es·pi·o·nage (KOWN tər ES pee ə NAZH) *n.* measures intended to counteract enemy spying.

coun·ter·feit (KOWN tər FIT) *v.t. & v.i.* 1. make an imitation of (money, stamps, etc.), with the intent to defraud. 2. copy; also, feign: *counterfeit* sorrow. —*adj.* 1. made to resemble some genuine thing; forged. 2. pretended; feigned. —*n.* an imitation, esp. one made for fraudulent purposes. [ME *contrefet* forged]

coun·ter·in·tel·li·gence (KOWN tər in TEL i jəns) *n.* activities to oppose espionage, subversion, and sabotage.

coun·ter·mand (KOWN tər MAND) *v.t.* 1. revoke or reverse (an order). 2. recall or order back. —*n.* an order contrary to or revoking one previously issued. [ME *countermaunden* order]

coun·ter·of·fen·sive (KOWN tər ə FEN siv) *n.* a large-scale attack designed to stop an enemy offensive and seize the initiative.

coun·ter·part (KOWN tər PAHRT) *n.* someone or something resembling another.

coun·ter·point (KOWN tər POINT) *n.* Music the technique or practice of composing two or more melodic parts to be heard simultaneously. [ME]

coun·ter·poise (KOWN tər POIZ) *v.t.* ·poised, ·pois·ing balance by opposing with an equal weight, power, or force. —*n.* counterbalance. [ME *countrepeis*]

coun·ter·pro·duc·tive (KOWN tər prə DUK tiv) *adj.* working against a desired end.

coun·ter·sign (KOWN tər SIN) *v.t.* sign (a document already signed by another), as in authenticating. —*n.* *Mil.* a password. [< MF *contresigne*]

coun·ter·vail (KOWN tər VAYL) *v.t.* counteract or offset. [ME *contrevailen*]

coun·ter·weight (KOWN tər WAYT) *n.* any counterbalancing weight, force, or influence.

count·ess (KOWN tis) *n.* 1. the wife or widow of a count, or, in Great Britain, of an earl. 2. a woman equal in rank to a count or earl. [ME *countesse*]

count·less (KOWNT lis) *adj.* that cannot be counted; innumerable.

coun·tri·fied (KUN trə FID) *adj.* having the appearance, manner, etc., associated with the country or with country people; provincial; rustic.

coun·try (KUN tree) *n. pl.* ·tries 1. a land under a particular government, inhabited by a certain people, or within definite geographical limits. 2. rhe district outside cities and towns; rural areas. 3. a region of a specified character: sheep *country.* 4. the people of a nation. —*adj.* rustic. [ME *cuntree*]

country music American popular music sung in a style associated with rural areas and usu. accompanied by plucked instruments.

coun·try·side (KUN tree SID) *n.* a rural district.

coun·ty (KOWN tee) *n. pl.* ·ties an administrative division of a state or kingdom. [ME *counte*] —**county seat** the seat of government of a county.

coup (koo) *n. pl.* **coups** (kooz) a sudden, telling blow; a masterstroke. [< F, lit., a blow]

coup d'é·tat (KOO day TAH) *French* a sudden seizure of government.

coupe (koop) *n.* a small, closed automobile with two doors: also *coupé.* [< COUPÉ]

cou·pé (koo PAY) *n.* 1. a low, four-wheeled, closed carriage for two, with an outside seat for the driver. 2. a coupe. [< F, lit., cut]

cou·ple (KUP əl) *n.* 1. two of a kind; a pair. 2. two persons of opposite sex, wedded or otherwise paired. 3. a small number: a *couple* of weeks. 4. something joining two things together. —*v.t. & v.i.* **·led, ·ling** join, as one thing or person to another; link; connect; pair. [ME]

coup·let (KUP lit) *n.* 1. two successive lines of verse, usu. rhymed. 2. a pair.

coup·ling (KUP ling) *n.* 1. the act of one who or that which couples. 2. a linking device, as for joining railroad cars.

cou·pon (KOO pon) *n.* 1. one of a number of dated certificates attached to a bond, representing interest accrued. 2. a section of a ticket, advertisement, etc., entitling the holder to something. [< F]

cour·age (KUR ij) *n.* that quality of spirit enabling one to face danger. [ME *corage*] —**cou·ra·geous** (kə RAY jəs) *adj.*

cou·ri·er (KUUR ee ər) *n.* a messenger, esp. one on urgent official business. [< MF *courrier*]

course (kors) *n.* 1. onward movement in a certain direction; progress. 2. the path or ground passed over. 3. direction. 4. passage or duration in time. 5. natural or usual development: ran its *course.* 6. a series of actions, events, etc. 7. a prescribed curriculum of studies; also, any unit of study in a curriculum: a history *course.* **8.** a portion of a meal served at one time. **9.** a horizontal row or layer, as of stones in a wall. **—in due course** at the right time; eventually. **—of course 1.** as might be expected; naturally. **2.** certainly. —*v.* **coursed, cours·ing** *v.t.* **1.** run through or over. **2.** pursue. **3.** cause (hounds) to chase game. —*v.i.* **4.** race. **5.** hunt with hounds. [ME *cours*]

court (kort) *n.* **1.** a courtyard. **2.** a short street, esp. a dead end. **3.** the residence of a sovereign. **4.** a sovereign together with his or her council and retinue. **5.** a formal assembly held by a sovereign. **6.** a place where justice is administered; also, the judge or judges. **7.** the regular session of a judicial tribunal. **8.** a level space laid out for a game, as basketball. **9.** flattering attention. **10.** wooing; courtship. —*v.t.* **1.** try to gain the favor of. **2.** woo. **3.** seek or invite: *court* danger. —*v.i.* **4.** engage in courtship. —*adj.* of or pertaining to a court. [ME]

cour·te·ous (KUR tee əs) *adj.* showing courtesy; polite. [ME *courteis*]

cour·te·san (KOR tə zən) *n.* a prostitute. [< MF *courtisane* court lady]

cour·te·sy (KUR tə see) *n. pl.* **·sies 1.** politeness; good manners. **2.** a courteous favor or act. [ME *curteisie*]

court·i·er (KOR tee ər) *n.* a member of a sovereign's court.

court·ly (KORT lee) *adj.* **·li·er, ·li·est** pertaining to or befitting a court; elegant. — **court′li·ness** *n.*

court-mar·tial (KORT MAHR shəl) *n. pl.* **courts-mar·tial 1.** a military court. **2.** a trial by such a court. —*v.t.* **-mar·tialed, -mar·tial·ing** try by court-martial.

court·yard (KORT YAHRD) *n.* an enclosed yard adjoining a building or surrounded by buildings or walls.

cous·in (KUZ ən) *n.* one collaterally related by descent from a common ancestor, but not a brother or sister. Children of brothers and sisters are **first cousins.** [ME *cosin*]

cou·tu·rier (koo TUUR ee AY) *n.* a male dress designer. [< F] **—cou·tu·rière** (koo TUUR ee ER) *n.fem.*

cove (kohv) *n.* **1.** a small bay or baylike recess in a shoreline. **2.** *Archit.* a concave part, as a vault or molding. —*v.t.* **coved, cov·ing** curve inward or over. [ME]

cov·e·nant (KUV ə nənt) *n.* an agreement; a formal compact. [ME] —*v.t. & v.i.* pledge.

cov·er (KUV ər) *v.t.* **1.** place something over or upon, as to protect or conceal. **2.** provide or overlay with a cover or covering. **3.** hide; conceal: often with *up.* **4.** treat of; include. **5.** be sufficient to pay, defray, or offset. **6.** protect or guarantee (life, property, etc.) with insurance. **7.** travel over: *cover* a mile. **8.** aim directly at, as with a firearm. **9.** *Mil.* provide protective fire for (another person, unit, etc.). **10.** in journalism, report the details of. **11.** in sports, guard (an opponent); also, protect (an area or position). —*v.i.* **12.** spread over, as a liquid does. **13.** protect, as with a false story: with *for.* **14.** act as a substitute: with *for.* —*n.* **1.** that which covers or is laid over something else. **2.** shelter; protection; concealment. **3.** a pretense or pretext. **4.** the table articles, as plate, silverware, etc., for one person. **—break cover** come from hiding. **—cover up 1.** cover or overlay with something. **2.** conceal, as a crime. **—under cover 1.** protected. **2.** secret or secretly. [ME *coveren* hide]

cov·er·age (KUV ər ij) *n.* the extent to which anything is covered, included, or reported.

cov·er·let (KUV ər lit) *n.* a bedspread.

cov·ert (KOH vərt) *adj.* concealed; secret; sheltered. —*n.* (KUV ərt) **1.** a covering. **2.** a shelter or hiding place, esp. for game. [ME] —**cov′ert·ly** *adv.*

cov·er-up (KUV ər UP) *n.* the act of concealing a crime, scandal, etc.; also, a means of doing this.

cov·et (KUV it) *v.t. & v.i.* long for (esp. something belonging to another). [ME *coveiten*]

cov·et·ous (KUV i təs) *adj.* excessively desirous (of something); greedy. [ME *coveitous*] **—cov′et·ous·ness** *n.*

cov·ey (KUV ee) *n. pl.* **·eys 1.** a flock of quails or partridges. **2.** a company; set. [ME]

cow¹ (kow) *n. pl.* **cows** (*Archaic* **kine**) **1.** the mature female of a bovine animal, esp. of the domesticated species. **2.** the mature female of some other animals, as of the whale. [ME *cou*]

cow² *v.t.* overawe; intimidate; daunt. [< ON *kūga* oppress]

cow·ard (KOW ərd) *n.* one who yields unworthily to fear. [< ME] **—cow·ard·ice** (KOW ər dis) *n.* **—cow·ard·ly** (KOW ərd lee) *adj. & adv.*

cow·boy (KOW boi) *n.* a ranch worker who

herds and tends cattle. **—cow·girl** (KOW GURL) n.fem.

cow·catch·er (KOW KACH ər) n. an iron frame on the front of a locomotive or street-car for clearing the track.

cow·er (KOW ər) v.i. crouch, as in fear; tremble; quail. [ME couren]

cow·hide (KOW KID) n. 1. the skin of a cow, esp. after tanning. 2. a heavy leather whip. **—v.t. ·hid·ed, ·hid·ing** whip as with a cowhide.

cowl (kowl) n. 1. a monk's hood; also, a hooded cloak. 2. Aeron. a cowling. 3. the part of an automobile body to which the windshield, the instrument board, and the rear end of the hood are attached. [ME couele hood]

cow·lick (KOW LIK) n. a tuft of hair turned up.

cowl·ing (KOW ling) n. Aeron. the covering over or around the engine or any component of an aircraft.

cox·swain (KOK sən) n. one who steers or has charge of a small boat or a racing shell. [ME cokeswayne]

coy (koi) adj. ·er, ·est 1. shy. 2. feigning shyness to attract attention. [ME]

coy·o·te (kī OH tee) n. a small wolf of western North America. [< Mexican Sp.]

co·zy (KOH zee) adj. ·zi·er, ·zi·est snugly comfortable. **—n.** a padded cover for a tea-pot to keep it hot: also called tea cozy. [< Scot.]

crab¹ (krab) n. 1. a crustacean having four pairs of legs, a pair of pincers, and a flat shell. 2. the hermit crab. 3. the horseshoe crab. 4. the crab louse. **—v.t. crabbed, crab·bing** take or hunt crabs. [ME crabbe]

crab² n. an ill-tempered person. **—v.i. crabbed, crab·bing** Informal complain. [ME]

crab apple 1. a kind of small, sour apple. 2. a tree bearing crab apples.

crab·bed (KRAB id) adj. 1. sour-tempered; surly. 2. irregular in form. [ME]

crab·by (KRAB ee) adj. ·bi·er, ·bi·est ill-tempered; peevish. **—crab'bi·ness** n.

crab louse a louse that infests body hair, esp. pubic hair.

crack (krak) v.i. 1. break without separation of parts; also, break apart or to pieces. 2. make a sharp snapping sound, as in breaking. 3. change tone abruptly to a higher register: said of the voice. **—v.t. 4.** break partially or completely. 5. cause to give forth a short, sharp sound. 6. Informal

break into; open. 7. find the solution of. 8. tell (a joke). **—crack down** take severe repressive measures: also, with on. **— crack up** Informal 1. crash or be in a crash. 2. have a breakdown. 3. become convulsed with laughter. **—crack wise** Slang wise-crack. **—n.** 1. a partial break, in which parts are not completely separated; a fissure. 2. a narrow space. 3. a sudden sharp sound. 4. a resounding blow. 5. Informal an opportunity. 6. Informal a wisecrack. **—adj.** excellent: a crack shot. [ME crakken resound]

cracked (krakd) adj. 1. having a crack or cracks. 2. broken to pieces. 3. Informal deranged. 4. uneven in tone: said of the voice.

crack·er (KRAK ər) n. 1. a thin, crisp biscuit. 2. a firecracker. 3. a party favor that makes a popping noise. 4. Offensive Slang a poor white person of the southern U.S.

crack·er·jack (KRAK ər JAK) adj. Informal exceptional; excellent. **—n.** an exceptional person or thing.

crack·le (KRAK əl) v. ·led, ·ling v.i. 1. make a succession of light, sharp sounds. **—v.t.** 2. crush with such sounds. 3. cover, as china, with a delicate network of cracks. **—n.** 1. a sound of crackling. 2. a network of fine cracks.

crack·ling (KRAK ling) n. 1. the giving forth of small sharp sounds. 2. the crisp browned skin of roasted pork. 3. pl. the crisp remains of fat after rendering.

crack·up (KRAK UP) n. 1. a crash, as of an airplane or automobile. 2. a collapse.

-cracy combining form government or authority: democracy. [< MF -cracie power]

cra·dle (KRAYD l) n. 1. a small bed for an infant, usu. on rockers. 2. a place of origin. 3. a framework for supporting something under construction or repair. 4. any frame for support or protection. 5. the holder for the receiver of a telephone. **—v.t. ·dled, ·dling** 1. put into or rock in or as in a cradle; soothe. 2. place or support in a cradle. [ME cradel]

craft (kraft) n. 1. skill or proficiency, esp. in handwork; loosely, art. 2. skill in deception. 3. an occupation or trade, usu. one calling for manual skill. 4. the membership of a particular trade. 5. a vessel or an aircraft: also used collectively. [ME]

crafts·per·son (KRAFTS PUR sən) n. one skilled in a craft or art. **—crafts'man, crafts'wom'man, crafts'man·ship** n.

craft union a labor union limited to workers who perform the same type of work.

craft·y (KRAF tee) *adj.* **craft·i·er, craft·i·est** skillful in deceiving; cunning. [ME] **—craft'i·ness** *n.*

crag (krag) *n.* a rough, steep, or prominently projecting rock. [ME] **—crag·gy** (KRAG ee) *adj.* **·gi·er, ·gi·est**

cram (kram) *v.* **crammed, cram·ming** *v.t.* **1.** force into an inadequate space; stuff. **2.** fill or pack tightly. **3.** feed to excess. **4.** force (information) into the mind. **—v.t. 5.** eat greedily. **6.** study hurriedly. [ME *crammen* stuff] **—cram'·mer** *n.*

cramp[1] (kramp) *n.* **1.** an involuntary, sudden, painful muscular contraction. **2.** a paralysis of local muscles caused by overexertion. **3.** *pl.* acute abdominal pains. **—v.t. & v.i.** suffer or cause to suffer a cramp. [ME *crampe* constipate]

cramp[2] *n.* an iron bar bent at both ends, used to bind two timbers etc. together. **—v.t. 1.** fasten with a cramp. **2.** restrain or confine; hamper. **3.** jam (a wheel) by turning too short. [ME *crampe* hook.]

crane (krayn) *n.* **1.** one of a family of large, long-necked, long-legged birds, as the **whooping crane. 2.** a hoisting machine, usually having a projecting movable arm, by which a heavy object can be raised and moved. **—v.t. & v.i. craned, cran·ing 1.** stretch out one's neck, as a crane does. **2.** lift or move by or as if by a crane. [ME]

cra·ni·um (KRAY nee əm) *n. pl.* **·ni·ums** or **·ni·a** (-nee ə) the skull, esp. the part enclosing the brain. [ME *craneum* skull] **—cra'ni·al** *adj.*

crank (krangk) *n.* **1.** a device for transmitting motion, usu. a handle attached at right angles to a shaft. **2.** *Informal* an eccentric, hostile, or grouchy person. **—v.t. 1.** start or operate by a crank. **—v.i. 2.** turn a crank. [ME *cranke*]

crank·y (KRANG kee) *adj.* **crank·i·er, crank·i·est 1.** irritable; peevish. **2.** eccentric; queer. **—crank'i·ness** *n.*

cran·ny (KRAN ee) *n. pl.* **·nies** a narrow crevice, as in a wall. [ME *crany* notch] **—cran'nied** *adj.*

crap (krap) *n.* **1.** the game of craps. **2.** in craps, a losing throw (2, 3, or 12). **3.** *Slang* anything worthless. [See CRAPS]

crape (krayp) see CREPE.

craps (kraps) *n.* (construed as sing.) a gambling game, played with two dice. **— crap·shoot·er** (KRAP shoo tər) *n.*

crash (krash) *v.i.* **1.** break to pieces with a loud noise. **2.** suffer damage or destruction,

as by falling or striking something. **3.** make a loud noise of breaking. **4.** move with such a noise. **5.** fail or come to ruin. **6.** *Slang* return to normal from a drug-induced state. **—v.t. 7.** dash to pieces; smash. **8.** cause (an airplane, automobile, etc.) to crash. **9.** *Informal* enter without invitation or without paying admission. **—n. 1.** a loud noise, as of things being violently broken. **2.** a sudden failure or collapse. **3.** the act of crashing. **—adj.** done with intensive effort, as a project or program. [ME *crasche* break]

crass (kras) *adj.* **1.** grossly vulgar or stupid. **2.** coarse or thick. [< L *crassus* thick] **—crass'ness** *n.*

crate (krayt) *n.* **1.** a case or framework of slats in which to pack something for shipment. **2.** *Informal* a decrepit vehicle or airplane. **—v.t. crat·ed, crat·ing** pack in a crate. [ME]

cra·ter (KRAY tər) *n.* **1.** a bowl-shaped depression at the outlet of a volcano. **2.** any similar cavity. [< L, bowl]

cra·vat (krə VAT) *n.* **1.** a necktie. **2.** a scarf. [< F *cravate* neckcloth]

crave (krayv) *v.* **craved, crav·ing** *v.t.* **1.** long for; desire greatly. **2.** need; require. **3.** beg for. **—v.i. 4.** desire or long; with *for* or *after.* [ME *craven*]

craven (KRAY vən) *adj.* cowardly. **—n.** a coward. [ME *cravant* defeated] **—cra'ven·ness** *n.*

craw (kraw) *n.* **1.** the crop of a bird. **2.** the stomach of any animal. [ME *crawe*]

crawl (krawl) *v.i.* **1.** move along slowly with the body on or close to the ground, esp. on hands and knees. **2.** move slowly or feebly. **3.** be covered with things that crawl. **4.** feel as if covered with crawling things. **—n. 1.** the act of crawling. **2.** an overarm swimming stroke. [ME *crawlen*]

cray·fish (KRAY FISH) *n. pl.* **·fish** or **·fish·es** a freshwater crustacean resembling the lobster. Also **craw·fish** (KRAW FISH). [ME *crevis* crab]

cray·on (KRAY on) *n.* a stick of colored wax, chalk, etc., for use in drawing. **—v.t. & v.i.** sketch or draw with crayons. [< F, chalk]

craze (krayz) *v.t. & v.i.* **crazed, craz·ing 1.** make or become insane. **2.** cover or become covered with minute cracks, as the glaze of pottery. **—n. 1.** a fad. **2.** an extravagant enthusiasm. **3.** a minute flaw or crack. [ME *crasen* crush] **—crazed** *adj.*

cra·zy (KRAY zee) *adj.* **·zi·er, ·zi·est 1.**

disordered in mind; insane; mad. **2.** *Informal* enthusiastic or excited. **3.** *Informal* unpredictable or strange. **4.** *Slang* wonderful; exciting. —*n. pl.* •**zies 1.** *Usu. pl.* a radical youth group using violent acts of protest. **2.** an eccentric. **3.** a crazy person.

creak (kreek) *n.* **1.** a sharp, squeaking sound, as from friction. —*v.t. & v.i.* produce or cause to produce a creak. [ME *creken* croke] — **creak′y** *adj.* **creak•i•er, creak•i•est**

cream (kreem) *n.* **1.** an oily, yellowish substance contained in milk. **2.** the best part. **3.** the color of cream. **4.** something made with or resembling cream. **5.** an oily lotion for the skin. —*v.t.* **1.** skim cream from. **2.** take the best part from. **3.** add cream to, as coffee. **4.** beat, as butter and sugar, to a creamy consistency. **5.** cook or prepare (food) with cream or cream sauce. **6.** *Slang* defeat decisively. —*v.i.* **7.** froth or foam. —**cream•y** *adj.* **cream•i•er, cream•i•est** [ME *creme*]

cream•er (KREE mər) *n.* **1.** a pitcher for cream. **2.** a device for separating cream.

crease (krees) *n.* **1.** a mark or line made by folding or wrinkling. **2.** in ice hockey, the marked area in front of a goal. —*v.* **creased, creas•ing** *v.t.* **1.** make a crease or creases in. **2.** graze, as with a bullet. —*v.i.* **3.** become wrinkled. [ME *creeste* crest]

cre•ate (kree AYT) *v.t.* •**at•ed, •at•ing 1.** cause to come into existence; originate. **2.** be the cause of; occasion. **3.** invest with new office, rank, etc.; appoint. [ME *creat* created]

cre•a•tion (kree AY shən) *n.* **1.** the act of creating, or the fact of being created. **2.** anything created. **3.** *Usu. cap.* God's bringing of the universe into existence. **4.** the universe. [ME *creacioun*]

Cre•a•tion•ism (kree AY shə NIZ əm) *n.* the doctrine that God created all things at once as they now exist.

cre•a•tive (kree AY tiv) *adj.* **1.** having the power or ability to create. **2.** characterized by originality of thought and execution. — **cre•a•tiv•i•ty** (KREE ay TIV i tee) *n.*

cre•a•tor (kree AY tər) *n.* one who or that which creates. —**the Creator** God.

crea•ture (KREE chər) *n.* **1.** a living being; esp., an animal. **2.** a person. **3.** one who is dependent on something or someone; puppet; tool. [ME]

crèche (kresh) *n.* a representation of the scene in the stable at the Nativity. [< F, crib]

cre•dence (KREED ns) *n.* belief, esp. as based on the evidence of others. [ME]

cre•den•tial (kri DEN shəl) *n.* **1.** that which entitles one to authority or confidence. **2.** *Usually pl.* a document giving evidence of one's authority or identity. [ME *credencial*]

cre•den•za (kri DEN zə) *n.* a sideboard or buffet. [< Ital.]

cred•i•ble (KRED ə bəl) *adj.* **1.** believable. **2.** trustworthy; reliable. [ME] —**cred′ i•bil′i•ty** *n.*

cred•it (KRED it) *n.* **1.** belief in someone or something; trust; faith. **2.** a good reputation. **3.** a source of honor: a *credit* to one's family. **4.** approval; praise. **5.** *Usu. pl.* acknowledgment of work done on a book, film, etc. **6.** confidence in the ability of an individual, firm, etc., to fulfill financial obligations: buy on *credit.* **7.** the time extended for payment of a liability. **8.** in bookkeeping, the entry of any amount paid by a debtor. **9.** in an account, the balance in one's favor. **10.** official certification that a student has passed a course of study; also, a unit of academic study. —*v.t.* **1.** accept as true. **2.** ascribe: with *with.* **3.** in bookkeeping, give credit for or enter as credit to. [< MF, loan]

cred•it•a•ble (KRED i tə bəl) *adj.* deserving credit or esteem; praiseworthy. —**cred′ it•a•bly** *adv.*

cred•i•tor (KRED i tər) *n.* one to whom money is owed.

cre•do (KREE doh) *n. pl.* •**dos** a set of beliefs; a creed. [< L, I believe]

cre•du•li•ty (krə DOO li tee) *n.* readiness to believe; gullibility. [ME *credulite*]

cred•u•lous (KREJ ə ləs) *adj.* **1.** disposed to believe on slight evidence. **2.** arising from credulity. [< L *credulus* believing]

creed (kreed) *n.* **1.** a formal statement of religious belief or doctrine. **2.** any organized system or statement of beliefs, principles, etc. [< L *credo* I believe]

creek (kreek) *n.* a stream intermediate in size between a brook and a river. [ME *creke*]

creep (kreep) *v.i.* **crept, creep•ing 1.** crawl. **2.** move slowly or stealthily. **3.** grow along a surface or support, as a vine. **4.** have a sensation of being covered with creeping things. —*n.* **1.** the act of creeping. **2.** *pl. Informal* A feeling of apprehension. **3.** *Slang* an unattractive person. [ME *crepen*] —**creep•ing** *adj.* developing slowly: *creeping* socialism.

creep·y (KREE pee) *adj.* **creep·i·er, creep·i·est 1.** eerie; repugnant. **2.** characterized by a creeping motion. —**creep′i·ness** *n.*

cre·mate (KREE mayt) *v.t.* •**mat·ed,** •**mat·ing** burn (a dead body) to ashes. [< L *crematus* burned] —**cre·ma′tion** *n.*

cre·ma·to·ry (KREE mə TOR ee) *adj.* related to cremation. —*n. pl.* •**ries** a furnace or establishment for cremating dead bodies: also **cre′ma·to′ri·um.**

Cre·ole (KREE ohl) *n.* **1.** a native of Spanish America or the West Indies but of European descent. **2.** a descendant of the French settlers of the southern U.S., esp. of Louisiana. **3.** the speech of the Louisiana Creoles. [< F]

crepe (krayp) *n.* **1.** a thin, crinkled fabric. **2.** black crepe used as a sign of mourning: in this sense usu. *crape.* **3.** tissue paper resembling crepe: also **crepe paper. 4.** a thin pancake. Also **crêpe.** [< F]

crêpes su·zette (KRAYP soo ZET) *pl.* **su·zettes** thin pancakes usu. served aflame in a liqueur.

crept (krept) past tense of CREEP.

cres·cen·do (kri SHEN doh) *Music n. pl.* •**di** (-dee), •**dos** a gradual increase in volume: opposed to *diminuendo.* [< Ital., growing]

cres·cent (KRES ənt) *n.* **1.** the visible part of the moon in its first or last quarter, having one concave edge and one convex edge. **2.** something crescent-shaped. —*adj.* **1.** increasing: said of the moon in its first quarter. **2.** shaped like the moon in its first quarter. [ME *cressaunt*]

crest (krest) *n.* **1.** a comb, tuft, or projection on the head of an animal, esp. of birds. **2.** the top of a wave. **3.** the highest point or stage; top. **4.** *Heraldry* a device placed above the shield in a coat of arms. —*v.t.* **1.** furnish with a crest. **2.** reach the crest of. —*v.i.* **3.** come to a crest, as a wave. [ME *creste* tuft]

crest·fall·en (KREST FAW lən) *adj.* dejected.

cre·tin (KREET n) *n.* a person afflicted with cretinism. [< F *crétin*] —**cre′tin·ous** *adj.*

cre·tin·ism (KREET n IZ əm) *n. Pathol.* a congenital condition associated with thyroid deficiency, marked by arrested physical development, goiter, and mental retardation.

cre·vasse (kreə VAS) *n.* **1.** a deep fissure or chasm, as in a glacier. **2.** a breach in a levee.

—*v.t.* •**vassed,** •**vass·ing** split with crevasses. [< F]

crev·ice (KREV is) *n.* a fissure or crack; cleft. [ME *crevace* crack]

crew¹ (kroo) *n.* **1.** the company belonging to one ship, aircraft, etc. **2.** a group organized for a particular job: repair *crew.* —*v.i.* act as a member of a crew. [ME *crewe* increase]

crew² a past tense of CROW.

crew cut a closely cropped haircut.

crew·el (KROO əl) *n.* a slackly twisted worsted yarn, used in embroidery.

crib (krib) *n.* **1.** a child's bed, with side railings. **2.** a storage place for grain, having slat or openwork sides. **3.** a rack or manger for fodder. **4.** a stall for cattle. **5.** a small house or room. **6.** a framework of wood or metal, used to retain or support something, as in mines. **7.** *Informal* a translation or other unauthorized aid employed by students. —*v.* **cribbed, crib·bing** *v.t.* **1.** enclose in or as in a crib. **2.** retain or support with a crib. **3.** *Informal* plagiarize. —*v.i.* **4.** *Informal* use a crib in translating, etc. [ME *cribbe*]

crib·bage (KRIB ij) *n.* a game of cards for two, three, or four players, with the score kept on a pegboard.

crib death the sudden death, usu. during sleep, of a healthy baby for unknown reasons. Also *sudden infant death syndrome (SIDS).*

crick (krik) *n.* a muscle cramp, as in the neck. [ME *crikke*]

crick·et¹ (KRIK it) *n.* a leaping insect, the male of which makes a chirping sound. [ME *criket* insect]

crick·et² *n.* **1.** an outdoor game played with bats, a ball, and wickets, between two sides of eleven each. **2.** fair play; sportsmanship. [< MF *criquet* goal post] —**crick′et·er** *n.*

cried (krīd) past tense, past participle of CRY.

crime (krīm) *n.* **1.** *Law* an act or omission in violation of public law; esp., a felony. **2.** any grave offense. [ME]

crim·i·nal (KRIM ə nl) *adj.* **1.** implying or involving crime. **2.** *Law* pertaining to the administration of penal law. **3.** guilty of crime. —*n.* one who has committed a crime. [ME] —**crim′i·nal′i·ty** (KRIM ə NAL I TEE) *n.*

crim·i·nol·o·gy (KRIM ə NOL ə jee) *n.* the scientific study of crime and criminals. —**crim′i·nol′o·gist** *n.*

crimp (krimp) *v.t.* **1.** bend or press into ridges or folds; corrugate; flute. **2.** curl or wave. —*n.* something that has been crimped. —**put a crimp in** hinder or obstruct. [ME *crympen* curl]

crim·son (KRIM zən) *n.* a deep red color. [ME]

cringe (krinj) *v.i.* **cringed, cring·ing 1.** shrink or crouch in fear. **2.** fawn. —*n.* a servile crouching. [ME *crengen*]

crin·kle (KRING kəl) *v.t. & v.i.* **·kled, ·kling 1.** form or cause to form wrinkles. **2.** rustle or crackle. —*n.* a wrinkle or fold. [ME *crinklen* curl up] —**crin'kly** *adj.* **·kli·er, ·kli·est**

crin·o·line (KRIN l in) *n.* **1.** a stiff fabric, originally of horsehair and linen. **2.** a petticoat of this fabric. **3.** a hoop skirt. [< F]

crip·ple (KRIP əl) *n. Offensive* a lame or disabled person or animal. —*v.t.* **·pled, ·pling 1.** make lame. **2.** impair or disable. [ME *cripel*]

cri·sis (KRĪ sis) *n. pl.* **·ses** (-seez) **1.** a crucial turning point. **2.** a critical moment. **3.** any decisive change in the course of a disease. [ME]

crisp (krisp) *adj.* **·er, ·est 1.** brittle; easily crumbled. **2.** fresh and firm. **3.** brisk; invigorating. **4.** terse; curt. —*v.t. & v.i.* make or become crisp. [ME] —**crisp·y** (KRIS pee) *adj.* **crisp·i·er, crisp·i·est** crisp. —**crisp' i·ness** *n.*

criss·cross (KRIS KRAWS) *v.t.* **1.** cross with interlacing lines. —*v.i.* **2.** move in crisscrosses. —*adj.* marked by crossings. —*n.* a group of intersecting lines. —*adv.* crosswise. [Alter. of *Christcross*]

cri·te·ri·on (krī TEER ee ən) *n. pl.* **·ons, ·ri·a** (-ə) a standard or rule by which a judgment can be made. [< Gk. *kritérion* standard]

crit·ic (KRIT ik) *n.* **1.** one who judges the merits of anything, esp. books, plays, movies, etc., professionally. **2.** one who • judges severely. [< L *criticus* able to judge]

crit·i·cal (KRIT i kəl) *adj.* **1.** given to fault-finding or severe judgments. **2.** exhibiting careful judgment; analytical. **3.** of the nature of a crisis; decisive; crucial.

crit·i·cism (KRIT ə SIZ əm) *n.* **1.** the act of criticizing. **2.** a severe or unfavorable judgment. **3.** the art of making discriminating judgments. **4.** the occupation or profession of a critic.

crit·i·cize (KRIT i SIZ) *v.t. & v.i.* **1.** judge severely. **2.** evaluate.

cri·tique (kri TEEK) *n.* a critical review, esp. of a work of art or literature. [< F]

croak (krohk) *v.i.* **1.** utter a hoarse, low-pitched cry, as a frog or crow. **2.** speak in a low, hoarse voice. **3.** *Slang* die. —*v.t.* **4.** utter with a croak. — *v.t.* **5.** *Slang* kill. —*n.* a hoarse vocal sound, as of a frog.

cro·chet (kroh SHAY) *n.* needlework having looped stitches formed with a hooked needle. [< F, knitting] —**cro·chet'** *v.t. & v.i.* **·cheted** (-SHAYD) **·chet·ing** (-SHAY ing)

crock (krok) *n.* an earthenware pot or jar. [ME *crokke*] —**crock·er·y** (KROK ə ree) *n.* earthen vessels collectively.

croc·o·dile (KROK ə DIL) *n.* a large amphibious reptile of tropical regions, with long jaws and armored skin. [< L *crocodilus*] —**croc·o·dil·i·an** (KROK ə DIL ee ən) *n. & adj.*

crocodile tears hypocritical grief.

crone (krohn) *n.* a withered old woman. [ME]

cro·ny (KROH nee) *n. pl.* **·nies** a friend. [ME]

crook (kruuk) *n.* **1.** a bend or curve. **2.** the curved or bent part of a thing. **3.** something with a crook in it, as a shepherd's staff. **4.** a thief. —*v.t. & v.i.* bend. — **crook·ed** (KRUUK id) *adj.*

croon (kroon) *v.t. & v.i.* **1.** sing or hum in a low tone. **2.** sing (popular songs) in a soft and sentimental manner. —*n.* a low humming or singing. [ME *cronen* lament]

crop (krop) *n.* **1.** the cultivated produce of the land, as grain or vegetables. **2.** the product of a particular kind, place, or season. **3.** a collection or quantity of anything. **4.** a cropping, esp. of the hair. **5.** an enlargement of the gullet, as in birds; the craw. **6.** the handle of a whip. **7.** a riding whip. —*v.t.* **cropped, crop·ping 1.** cut or eat off the stems of, as grass. **2.** reap. **3.** trim or clip (the hair, ears, tail, etc.) of. —**crop up** develop or happen unexpectedly. [ME]

crop·per (KROP ər) *n.* a bad fall, as over a horse's head. —**come a cropper** fail.

cro·quet (kroh KAY) *n.* an outdoor game played with wooden balls, mallets, and wickets. [< F, hockey stick]

cro·quette (kroh KET) *n.* a cake of minced food, fried in deep fat. [< F]

cross (kraws) *n.* **1.** an ancient instrument of execution, an upright with a horizontal piece near the top, upon which the condemned persons were fastened. **2.** *Cap.* the emblem of Christianity, a representation of the cross upon which Christ died. **3.** anything in the form of a cross. **4.** any severe trial, affliction, or suffering: bear one's *cross.* **5.** the mark of one who cannot write. **6.** anything that resembles or is intermediate between two other things. **7.** a hybrid. —*v.t.* **1.** move, extend, or pass from one side to the other side of; go across; traverse. **2.** intersect. **3.** make the sign of the cross upon or over. **4.** lay or place across or over: *cross* the legs, fingers, etc. **5.** meet and pass. **6.** obstruct or hinder; thwart. **7.** *Biol.* crossbreed (plants or animals). —*v.i.* **8.** pass, move, or extend from side to side. **9.** intersect. **10.** *Biol.* crossbreed. —*adj.* **1.** ill-humored. **2.** lying across each other: *cross* streets. **3.** reciprocal. **4.** contrary; adverse: at *cross* purposes. **5.** hybrid. —*adv.* **1.** across; crosswise. **2.** adversely; contrarily. [ME]

cross•bones (KRAWS bohnz) *n.* a representation of two bones crossing each other, usu. surmounted by a skull, and used as a symbol of death.

cross•breed (KRAWS breed) *v.t. & v.i.* **•bred, •breed•ing** *Biol.* produce (a strain or animal) by interbreeding two varieties. —*n.* a hybrid.

cross-ex•am•ine (KRAWS ig ZAM in) *v.t. & v.i.* **•ined, •in•ing** **1.** question anew (a witness called by the opposing party) for the purpose of testing the reliability of previous testimony of that witness. **2.** question carefully.

cross-eye (KRAWS I) *n.* strabismus in which one or both eyes are turned inward. —**cross'-eyed'** *adj.*

cross-fer•ti•li•za•tion (KRAWS FUR tl ə ZAY shən) *n.* **1.** *Bot.* the fertilization of one plant or flower by the pollen from another. **2.** mutually beneficial interchange between two activities or cultures. —**cross'-fer' ti•lize** *v.t.* **•lized, •liz•ing**

cross•hatch (KRAWS hach) *v.t.* shade, as a picture, by crossed lines.

cross•ing (KRAWS ing) *n.* **1.** the act of going across. **2.** the act of hindering; opposition. **3.** the place where something, as a road, may be crossed. **4.** an intersection.

cross-pur•pose (KRAWS PUR pəs) *n.* a purpose or aim in conflict with another. —**be at cross-purposes** misunderstand or act counter to each other's purposes.

cross-ref•er•ence (KRAWS REF ər əns) *n.* a note or statement directing a reader from one part of a book, index, etc., to another part.

cross•road (KRAWS rohd) *n.* the place where roads meet. —**at the crossroads** at any critical point or moment.

cross section 1. a plane section of any object cut at right angles to its length. **2.** a sampling meant to be characteristic of the whole.

cross•wise (KRAWS wiz) *adv.* **1.** across. **2.** in the form of a cross. **3.** contrarily. Also **cross•ways** (KRAWS wayz).

crotch (kroch) *n.* **1.** the fork or angle formed by two diverging parts, as by the branches of a tree. **2.** the region of the human body where the legs separate from the pelvis.

crouch (krowch) *v.i.* **1.** stoop or bend low, as an animal ready to spring. **2.** cringe; cower. [ME *crouchen* lie down] —**crouch** *n.*

crou•pi•er (KROO pee AY) *n.* one who collects the stakes lost and pays out those won at a gaming table. [< F]

crou•ton (KROO ton) *n.* a small cube of toasted bread used esp. in soups. [< F]

crow[1] (kroh) *n.* a raucous bird having glossy black plumage. ♦ Collateral adjective: *corvine.* —**as the crow flies** in a straight line. —**eat crow** *Informal* recant; suffer humiliation. [ME *crowe*]

crow[2] *v.i.* **crowed** or (*for def.* 1) **crew, crowed, crow•ing 1.** utter the shrill cry of a rooster. **2.** exult; boast. **3.** utter sounds of delight, as an infant. —*n.* **1.** the cry of a rooster. **2.** any sound resembling this. [ME *crowen*]

crow•bar (KROH bahr) *n.* a straight steel bar with a flattened point, used as a lever.

crowd (krowd) *n.* **1.** a large number of persons gathered closely together. **2.** the populace; mob. **3.** a particular set of people; a clique. —*v.t.* **1.** shove or push. **2.** fill to overflowing. **3.** cram together. —*v.i.* **4.** gather in large numbers. **5.** force one's way. [ME *crowden* hurry]

crown (krown) *n.* **1.** a circlet, often of precious metal set with jewels, worn on the head as a mark of sovereign power. **2.** any similar circlet. **3.** a former British coin, worth five shillings. **4.** the top part of the head. **5.** the head itself. **6.** the top or summit of something. **7.** *Dent.* the part of a tooth that is covered with enamel or an artificial substitute for it. —*v.t.* **1.** place a crown, garland, etc. on the head of. **2.** make a monarch of. **3.** endow with honor or dignity. **4.** form the crown, ornament, or top to. **5.** finish or make complete. **6.** *Informal* strike on the head. [ME *coroune*]

crow's-foot (KROHZ fuut) *n. pl.* **-feet** one

of the wrinkles near the outer corner of the
eye.

crow's-nest (KROHZ NEST) *n.* an observation platform near the top of a ship's mast.

cru·cial (KROO shəl) *adj.* **1.** critical or decisive. **2.** difficult; severe. [< L *crux* cross] —
cru'cial·ly *adv.*

cru·ci·fix (KROO sə fiks) *n.* **1.** a cross bearing an effigy of Christ crucified. **2.** the cross
as a Christian emblem. [ME]

cru·ci·fix·ion (KROO sə FIK shən) *n.* **1.** the
act of crucifying, or the state of being crucified. **2.** a representation of the Crucifixion.
—**the Crucifixion** the putting to death of
Jesus on the cross.

cru·ci·form (KROO sə FORM) *adj.* cross-
shaped.

cru·ci·fy (KROO sə FI) *v.t.* **·fied, ·fy·ing 1.**
put to death by fastening to a cross. **2.** torture; destroy. [ME *crucifien*]

crude (krood) *adj.* **crud·er, crud·est 1.** unrefined; raw: *crude* oil. **2.** immature; unripe. **3.** roughly made; unfinished. **4.**
lacking tact, refinement, or taste. [ME] —
crude'ness *n.*

cru·di·ty (KROO di tee) *n. pl.* **·ties 1.** the
state or quality of being crude. **2.** a crude
act, remark, etc. [ME *crudite*]

cru·el (KROO əl) *adj.* **cru·el·er, cru·el·est
1.** indifferent to or enjoying the suffering of
others. **2.** causing suffering. [ME] —**cru'
el·ly** *adv.*

cru·el·ty (KROO əl tee) *n. pl.* **·ties 1.** the
quality or condition of being cruel. **2.** that
which causes suffering.

cru·et (KROO it) *n.* a small glass bottle for
vinegar, oil, etc. [ME]

cruise (krooz) *v.* **cruised, cruis·ing** *v.i.* **1.**
sail about, esp. for pleasure. **2.** travel about
at a moderate speed. **3.** move at the optimum speed for sustained travel: said of aircraft, etc. **4.** *Informal* go about, seeking a
sexual partner in a public place. —*v.t.* **5.**
cruise over. **6.** *Informal* move slowly
through a (public place) seeking a sexual
partner: *cruise* the midtown bars. —*n.* a
cruising trip, esp. a voyage at sea. [< Du.
kruisen cross]

cruis·er (KROO zər) *n.* **1.** one who or that
which cruises. **2.** a fast, maneuverable warship. **3.** a small power vessel equipped with
living facilities: also called *cabin cruiser.*

crumb (krum) *n.* **1.** a tiny fragment of bread,
cake, or the like. **2.** a bit or scrap of anything. **3.** *Slang* a contemptible person. —
v.t. **1.** crumble. **2.** in cooking, to dress or

cover with bread crumbs. [ME *crome*] —
crumb'y *adj.* **crumb·i·er, crumb·i·est**

crum·ble (KRUM bəl) *v.* **·bled, ·bling** *v.t.*
1. break into tiny parts. —*v.i.* **2.** fall to small
pieces; disintegrate. [ME *kremelen*]

crum·ple (KRUM pəl) *v.* **·pled, ·pling** *v.t.*
1. press into wrinkles; rumple. —*v.i.* **2.** become wrinkled; shrivel. **3.** collapse. [ME]

crunch (krunch) *v.t. & v.i.* **1.** chew with a
crushing or crackling sound. **2.** move or
crush with a crackling sound. —*n.* **1.** a
crunching, or its sound. **2.** a critical point or
situation.

cru·sade (kroo SAYD) *n.* **1.** *Usu. cap.* any of
the military expeditions in the 11th–13th c.,
undertaken by Christians to recover the
Holy Land from the Muslims. **2.** any expedition against heathens or heretics. **3.** any
vigorous movement or cause. [< Sp.
cruzada] —**cru·sade'** *v.i* **·sad·ed, ·sad·
ing** —**cru·sad'er** *n.*

crush (krush) *v.t.* **1.** press out of shape;
mash. **2.** smash or grind into fine particles.
3. extract by pressure. **4.** crowd. **5.** subdue;
conquer. —*v.i.* **6.** become broken or misshapen by pressure. **7.** move ahead by
pressing. —*n.* **1.** the act of crushing, or the
state of being crushed. **2.** a crowd; jam. **3.** a
substance obtained by crushing: orange
crush. **4.** *Informal* an infatuation. [ME
cruschen crush]

crust (krust) *n.* **1.** the hard outer part of
bread. **2.** a dry, hard piece of bread. **3.** the
pastry shell of a pie etc. **4.** any hard, crisp
surface, as of snow. **5.** *Slang* insolence; impertinence. **6.** *Geol.* the exterior shell of the
earth. —*v.t. & v.i.* cover with, acquire, or
form a crust. [ME] —**crus'tal** *adj.*

crus·ta·cean (kru STAY shən) *n.* one of a
class of animals having crustlike shells, and
generally aquatic, including lobsters, crabs,
etc. [< NL *Crustacea*] —**crus·ta·cean**
adj.

crust·y (KRUST ee) *adj.* **crust·i·er,
crust·i·est 1.** like or having a crust. **2.** curt;
surly. —**crust'i·ly** *adv.*

crutch (kruch) *n.* **1.** a staff used by the lame
as a support, esp. one fitting under the armpit. **2.** anything that gives support. [ME
crucche crook]

crux (kruks) *n. pl.* **crux·es** or **cru·ces**
(KROO seez) **1.** a pivotal, fundamental, or
vital point. **2.** a baffling problem. [< L,
cross]

cry (krī) *v.* **cried, cry·ing** *v.i.* **1.** utter sobbing sounds of grief, pain, etc., usu. accom-

panied by tears. **2.** shed tears. **3.** call out; shout: often with *out.* **4.** make characteristic calls: said of animals. —*v.t.* **5.** shout out. —*n. pl.* **cries 1.** a loud or emotional utterance; shout; call. **2.** a spell of weeping. **3.** an appeal; entreaty. **4.** a rallying call; battle cry. **5.** a demand; clamor. **6.** the characteristic call of a bird or animal. —**a far cry 1.** a long distance away. **2.** something very unlike. —**in full cry** in full pursuit, as a pack of hounds. [ME *crien* cry out]

cry·o·gen·ics (KRĪ ə JEN iks) *n. (construed as sing.)* the branch of physics dealing with very low temperatures. —**cry'o·gen'ic** *adj.*

crypt (kript) *n.* a chamber or vault, esp. one beneath a church, used as a place of burial. [ME *cripte* hidden place]

crypt·a·nal·y·sis (KRIP tə NAL ə sis) *n. pl.* **·ses** (-seez) the study of codes to which the key is not known. —**crypt·an·a·lyst** (krip TAN l ist) *n.*

cryp·tic (KRIP tik) *adj.* **1.** secret or hidden; occult. **2.** puzzling; mystifying. [< LL *crypticus* hidden]

cryp·to·gram (KRIP tə GRAM) *n.* a message written in code.

cryp·tog·ra·phy (krip TOG rə fee) *n.* **1.** the art or process of writing in or reconverting cipher. **2.** any system of writing in secret characters. —**cryp·tog'ra·pher** *n.* —**cryp·to·graph·ic** (KRIP tə GRAF ik) *adj.*

crys·tal (KRIS tl) *n.* **1.** colorless transparent quartz, or rock crystal. **2.** *Physics* a homogeneous solid body, exhibiting a symmetrical structure, with geometrically arranged planes and faces. **3.** any fine clear glass; also, articles made of such glass. **4.** a glass or plastic covering over the face of a watch. —*adj.* **1.** composed of crystal. **2.** like crystal; extremely clear. [ME *cristalle*] **crys·tal·line** (KRIS tl in) *adj.*

crys·tal·lize (KRIS tl Īz) *v.* **·lized,** **·liz·ing** *v.t.* **1.** cause to form crystals or become crystalline. **2.** bring to definite and permanent form. **3.** coat with sugar. —*v.i.* **4.** assume the form of crystals. **5.** assume definite and permanent form. —**crys'tal·li·za'tion** *n.*

cub (kub) *n.* the young of the bear, fox, and certain other animals; a whelp.

cube (kyoob) *n.* **1.** a solid bounded by six equal squares and having all its angles right angles. **2.** *Math.* the third power of a quantity: the *cube* of 3 is 27, or $3^3 = 3 \times 3 \times 3 = 27$. —*v.t.* **cubed, cub·ing 1.** raise to the

third power. **2.** find the cubic capacity of. **3.** form or cut into cubes. [ME *cubus* cube]

cube root the number that, taken three times as a factor, produces a number called its cube: 4 is the *cube root* of 64.

cu·bic (KYOO bik) *adj.* **1.** shaped like a cube. **2.** having three dimensions, or pertaining to three-dimensional content: a *cubic* foot. **3.** *Math.* of the third power or degree. —**cu·bi·cal** (KYOO bi kəl) *adj.*

cu·bi·cle (KYOO bi kəl) *n.* any small partitioned area, used for sleep, study, work, etc. [ME]

cub·ism (KYOO biz əm) *n.* a movement in early 20th c. art concerned with the abstract and geometric interpretation of form. —**cu'bist** *adj. & n.*

cuck·old (KUK əld) *n.* the husband of an unfaithful wife. —*v.t.* make a cuckold of. [ME *cukeweld*] —**cuck'old·ry** *n.*

cud (kud) *n.* food forced up into the mouth from the first stomach of a ruminant and chewed over again. [ME]

cud·dle (KUD l) *v.* **·dled,** **·dling** *v.t.* **1.** caress and embrace fondly; fondle. —*v.i.* **2.** lie close; nestle. —*n.* a caress or hug. [ME *cudliche* affectionate]

cudg·el (KUJ əl) *n.* a short, thick club. —**take up the cudgels** enter into a contest or controversy. —*v.t.* **cudg·eled, cudg·el·ing** beat with or as with a cudgel. [ME *cuggel*]

cue¹ (kyoo) *n.* a long, tapering rod, used in billiards or pool. —*v.t.* **cued, cu·ing** strike with a cue. [< F *queue* tail]

cue² *n.* **1.** in plays, movies, etc., any action or sound that signals the start of another action, speech, etc. **2.** any similar signal. **3.** a hint or suggestion. —*v.t.* **cued, cu·ing** call a cue to (an actor); prompt. [the letter *q*, as an abbreviation of L *quando* when]

cuff¹ (kuf) *n.* **1.** a band or fold at the lower end of a sleeve. **2.** a turned-up fold on the bottom of a trouser leg. **3.** a detachable band of fabric worn about the wrist. **4.** a handcuff. —**off the cuff** *Informal* spontaneously. —**on the cuff** *Slang* on credit. [ME *cuffe* mitten]

cuff² *v.t.* strike, as with the open hand; buffet. —*n.* a blow, esp. with the open hand.

cui·sine (kwi ZEEN) *n.* **1.** the style or quality of cooking. **2.** the food prepared. [< F]

cul-de-sac (KUL də SAK) *n. pl.* **culs-de-sac** (KULZ-) a passage open only at one end; dead end. [< F, lit., bottom of the bag]

cu·li·nar·y (KYOO lə NER ee) *adj.* of or

pertaining to cookery or the kitchen. [< L *culinarius* of the kitchen]

cull (kul) *v.t.* **1.** pick or sort out; select. **2.** gather. —*n.* something picked or sorted out, esp. something rejected as inferior. [ME *coilen* gather]

cul·mi·nate (KUL mə NAYT) *v.i.* **·nat·ed, ·nat·ing** reach the highest point or degree; come to a final result: with *in*. [< LL *culminatus* reached the top] —**cul'mi·na'tion** *n.*

cul·pa·ble (KUL pə bəl) *adj.* deserving of blame or censure. [ME] —**cul'pa·bil'i·ty** *n.*

cul·prit (KUL prit) *n.* **1.** one guilty of some offense or crime. **2.** one charged with a crime. [< AF *cul* guilty + *prest* ready]

cult (kult) *n.* **1.** a system of religious rites and observances. **2.** zealous devotion to a person, ideal, or thing. **3.** the followers of a cult. [< L *cultus* worship]

cul·ti·vate (KUL tə VAYT) *v.t.* **·vat·ed, ·vat·ing** **1.** make fit for raising crops, as by plowing, fertilizing, etc.; till. **2.** raise or care for (plants etc.). **3.** improve or develop by study, attention, or training; refine: *cultivate* one's mind. **4.** court the friendship of. [< Med.L *cultivatus* tilled] —**cul·ti·va·ble** (KUL tə və bəl) *adj.*

cul·ti·va·tion (KUL tə VAY shən) *n.* **1.** the act of cultivating, or the state of being cultivated. **2.** culture; refinement.

cul·ture (KUL chər) *n.* **1.** the cultivation of plants or animals, esp. to improve the breed. **2.** the development and refinement of mind, morals, or taste. **3.** cultivation of the soil. **4.** *Anthropol.* the sum total of the attainments and learned behavior patterns of any specific period or people. **5.** *Biol.* **a** the development of microorganisms in artificial media. **b** the organisms so developed. —*v.t.* **·tured, ·tur·ing 1.** cultivate (plants or animals). **2.** *Biol.* **a** develop or grow (microorganisms) in an artificial medium. **b** inoculate with a prepared culture. [ME] —**cul'tur·al** *adj.*

cul·tured (KUL chərd) *adj.* **1.** possessing or manifesting culture. **2.** created or grown by cultivation.

cul·vert (KUL vərt) *n.* a conduit for water, as under a road.

cum·ber·some (KUM bər səm) *adj.* **1.** unwieldy; clumsy. **2.** vexatious; burdensome. [ME *cummyrsum*]

cu·mu·la·tive (KYOO myə lə tiv) *adj.* **1.** gathering volume, strength, or value. **2.**

gained by accumulation. **3.** increasing or accruing.

cu·ne·i·form (kyoo NEE ə FORM) *adj.* wedge-shaped, as the characters in some ancient Sumerian, Assyrian, Babylonian, and Persian inscriptions. —*n.* cuneiform writing. [< L *cuneus* wedge + *-form*]

cun·ning (KUN ing) *n.* **1.** skill in deception; craftiness. **2.** skill; dexterity. —*adj.* **1.** crafty or shrewd. **2.** executed with skill; ingenious. **3.** cute; amusing. [ME, knowing]

cup (kup) *n.* **1.** a small, open vessel, often with a handle, used chiefly for drinking from. **2.** the contents of a cup; a cupful: as a measure, equal to 8 ounces. **3.** one's lot in life. **4.** a cup-shaped object or part, as of a flower. **5.** a cup-shaped vessel given as a prize, esp. in sports. **6.** in golf, a hole, or the metal receptacle within it. —**in one's cups** drunk. —*v.t.* **cupped, cup·ping 1.** shape like a cup. **2.** place in or as in a cup. **3.** one's lot in life. [ME]

cup·board (KUB ərd) *n.* **1.** a closet or cabinet with shelves, as for dishes. **2.** any small cabinet or closet.

cup·ful (KUP fuul) *n. pl.* **·fuls** the amount held by a cup.

Cu·pid (KYOO pid) *n.* **1.** a representation of the god of love, Cupid, as a naked, winged boy with a bow and arrow. **2.** one who helps arrange meetings between lovers; chiefly in the phrase **play Cupid.** [< L *Cupido* the personification of love]

cu·pid·i·ty (kyoo PID i tee) *n.* avarice; greed. [ME *cupidite*]

cu·pre·ous (KYOO pree əs) *adj.* of or pertaining to copper. [< LL *cupreus*]

cur (kur) *n.* **1.** a mongrel dog. **2.** a despicable person. [ME *curre*]

cur·a·ble (KYOOR ə bəl) *adj.* capable of being cured.

cu·ra·çoa (KYUUR ə SOH) *n.* an orange-flavored liqueur. [after *Curaçao*, an island in the Caribbean]

cu·ra·re (kyuu RAHR ee) *n.* **1.** an extract of certain South American trees that acts to paralyze motor nerves; used as an arrow poison and, in medicine, as a muscle relaxant. **2.** a plant from which this is extracted. [< Pg.]

cu·rate (KYUUR it) *n.* a member of the clergy assisting a parish priest, rector, or vicar. [ME *curat* take care]

cur·a·tive (KYUUR ə tiv) *adj.* having the power to cure. —*n.* a remedy.

cu·ra·tor (kyuu RAY tər) *n.* a person in

charge of a museum or similar institution. [ME *curatour* caretaker]

curb (kurb) *n.* **1.** anything that restrains or controls. **2.** a border of concrete or stone along the edge of a street. —*v.t.* **1.** control or check. **2.** provide with a curb. **3.** lead (a dog) off a curb for defecation in the street. [ME]

curd (kurd) *n. Often pl.* the coagulated portion of milk, of which cheese is made. —*v.t. & v.i.* form into or become curd. [ME]

cur·dle (KUR dl) *v.t. & v.i.* **·dled, ·dling** make or become curdy; coagulate.

cure (kyuur) *n.* **1.** restoration to a sound or healthy condition. **2.** that which restores health or removes an evil. **3.** a process of preserving food or other products. —*v.t.* **cured, cur·ing** **1.** restore to health. **2.** remedy or eradicate. **3.** preserve, as by salting, smoking, or aging. [ME *curen* take care of]

cure-all (KYUUR awl) *n.* panacea.

cur·few (KUR fyoo) *n.* **1.** a regulation requiring persons or certain persons to keep off the streets after a designated hour. **2.** a medieval regulation requiring fires, or lights, to be put out at the tolling of a bell. **3.** the bell itself; also the hour at which it was rung. [ME]

cu·ri·o (KYUUR ee oh) *n. pl.* **·os** a rare or curious object. [Short for CURIOSITY]

cu·ri·os·i·ty (KYUUR ee OS i tee) *n. pl.* **·ties** **1.** eager desire for knowledge of something. **2.** interest in the private affairs of others. **3.** that which excites interest by its strangeness or rarity. [ME *curiosite*]

cu·ri·ous (KYUUR ee əs) *adj.* **1.** eager for information or knowledge. **2.** given to prying or meddling. **3.** rare or novel; odd; strange. [ME]

curl (kurl) *v.t.* **1.** twist into ringlets or curves, as the hair. **2.** form into a curved or spiral shape. —*v.t.* **3.** form ringlets, as the hair. **4.** become curved; take a spiral shape. **5.** play at the game of curling. —*n.* **1.** something coiled or spiral, as a ringlet of hair. **2.** a curled or circular shape or mark. **3.** the act of curling, or the state of being curled. [ME] —**curl'y** *adj.* **curl·i·er, curl·i·est**

curl·er (KUR lər) *n.* **1.** one who or that which curls. **2.** one who plays the game of curling.

curl·i·cue (KUR li kyoo) *n.* any fancy curl or twist, as a flourish with a pen.

curl·ing (KUR ling) *n.* a game played on ice in which the opposing players slide heavy,

smooth, stones (**curling stones**) toward a goal at either end.

cur·mudg·eon (kər MUJ ən) *n.* a gruff person, esp. an old man.

cur·ren·cy (KUR ən see) *n. pl.* **·cies** **1.** a medium of exchange; money. **2.** general acceptance or circulation. [< Med.L *currentia*]

cur·rent (KUR ənt) *adj.* **1.** belonging to the immediate present: the *current* year. **2.** passing from person to person; circulating, as money or news. **3.** generally accepted; prevalent. —*n.* **1.** a continuous onward movement, as of water. **2.** the part of any body of water or air that has a more or less steady flow in a definite direction. **3.** a course or trend. **4.** *Electr.* a movement or flow of electricity. [ME *curraunt* running]

cur·ric·u·lum (kə RIK yə ləm) *n. pl.* **·la** (-lə) or **·lums** **1.** all the courses of study offered at a university or school. **2.** a regular or particular course of study. [< L, a race] — **cur·ric·u·lar** *adj.*

cur·ry¹ (KUR ee) *v.t.* **·ried, ·ry·ing** **1.** rub down and clean with a currycomb. **2.** dress (tanned hides) by soaking, smoothing, etc. —**curry favor** seek favor by flattery etc. [ME *corrayen* prepare]

cur·ry² *n. pl.* **·ries** **1.** a pungent sauce of East Indian origin. **2.** a dish cooked with this sauce. **3.** curry powder. [< Tamil *kari* sauce]

cur·ry·comb (KUR ee KOHM) *n.* a comb for grooming horses etc. —*v.t.* comb with a currycomb.

curry powder a condiment used in making curried dishes.

curse (kurs) *n.* **1.** an appeal to or as to God for evil or injury to happen to another. **2.** the evil or injury so invoked. **3.** any profane oath. **4.** a source of calamity or evil. —*v.* **cursed** (kurst) or **curst, curs·ing** *v.t.* **1.** invoke evil or injury upon; damn. **2.** swear at. **3.** cause evil or injury to; afflict. —*v.i.* **4.** utter curses; swear. [ME *curs*] —**curs·ed** (KUR sid) *adj.*

cur·sive (KUR siv) *adj.* running; flowing; said of writing in which the letters are joined. [< Med.L *cursivus* flowing]

cur·so·ry (KUR sə ree) *adj.* rapid and superficial. [< LL *cursorius* running]

curt (kurt) *adj.* brief and abrupt; esp., rudely brief: a *curt* nod. [< L *curtus* shortened]

cur·tail (kər TAYL) *v.t.* cut off or cut short; reduce. [ME *curtailen* restrict]

cur·tain (KUR tn) *n.* **1.** a piece or pieces of

cloth, hanging in a window, doorway, etc. **2.** something that conceals or separates like a curtain: the *curtain* of darkness. **3.** *pl. Slang* ruin; death. —*v.t.* provide, shut off, or conceal with or as with a curtain. [ME *courtine*]

curt·sy (KURT see) *n. pl.* **·sies** a bending of the knees and lowering of the body as a gesture of civility or respect, performed by girls and women. [Var. of COURTESY] — **curt'sy** *v.i.* **·sied, ·sy·ing**

cur·va·ceous (kur VAY shəs) *adj. Informal* having voluptuous curves: said of a woman.

cur·va·ture (KUR və chər) *n.* the act of curving, or the state of being curved. [ME]

curve (kurv) *n.* **1.** a line continuously bent, as the arc of a circle. **2.** a curving, or something curved. **3.** an instrument for drawing curves. **4.** in baseball, a ball pitched with a spin that causes it to veer to one side. —*v.t. & v.i.* **curved, curv·ing 1.** assume or cause to assume the form of a curve. **2.** move in the path of a curve. —*adj.* curved. [< L *curvus* bent]

cush·ion (KUUSH ən) *n.* **1.** a bag or casing filled with some soft or elastic material, used for lying or resting on. **2.** anything resembling a cushion in appearance or use; esp., any device to deaden an impact. —*v.t.* **1.** provide with a cushion. **2.** absorb the shock or effect of. [ME *cusshin*]

cusp (kusp) *n.* **1.** a point or pointed end. **2.** either point of a crescent moon. [< L *cuspis* a point]

cus·pid (KUS pid) *n.* in people, a canine tooth.

cus·tard (KUS tərd) *n.* a dessert of milk, eggs, sugar, and flavoring, either boiled or baked. [ME]

cus·to·di·an (ku STOH dee ən) *n.* a guardian; caretaker. [< L *custodia* watchman] — **cus·to'di·an·ship'** *n.*

cus·to·dy (KUS tə dee) *n. pl.* **·dies 1.** guardianship. **2.** restraint or confinement under guard. [ME *custodye*] —**cus·to·di·al** (ku STOH dee əl) *adj.*

cus·tom (KUS təm) *n.* **1.** the habitual practice of a community or a people. **2.** an ordinary or usual manner of doing or acting; habit. **3.** habitual patronage, as of a hotel, store, etc. **4.** *pl.* a tariff or duty on imported or, rarely, exported goods; also, the agency of the government that collects such duties (**custom house**). —*adj.* **1.** made to order. **2.** specializing in made-to-order goods. [ME *custume*]

cus·tom·ar·y (KUS tə MER ee) *adj.* according to custom; usual; habitual.

cus·tom·er (KUS tə mər) *n.* **1.** one who buys something; esp., one who deals regularly at a given establishment. **2.** *Informal* one to be dealt with: a tough *customer.*

cut (kut) *v.* **cut, cut·ting** *v.t.* **1.** open or penetrate with a sharp edge; gash; pierce. **2.** divide with a sharp edge. **3.** make or shape by cutting, as gems. **4.** fell or hew: often with *down.* **5.** wound with or as with a sharp edge. **6.** pretend not to know; snub. **7.** absent oneself from: *cut* a class. **8.** shorten or trim, as hair, grass, etc. **9.** shorten or edit by removing parts. **10.** mow or reap (wheat etc.) **11.** reduce or lessen: *cut* prices. **12.** dilute or weaken, as whiskey. **13.** dissolve or break down: *cut* grease. **14.** have (a new tooth) grow through the gum. **15.** in certain games, hit a ball so that it takes on a particular spin or is deflected. **16.** divide (a pack of cards), as before dealing. **17.** make (a recording). —*v.i.* **18.** make an incision. **19.** act as a sharp edge. **20.** penetrate like a knife. **21.** go by or be the shortest and most direct route: with *across, through,* etc. **22.** divide a pack of cards. **23.** in motion pictures, television, etc., make a quick transition from one scene to another. —**be cut out for** be suited for. —**cut back 1.** reduce or curtail. **2.** reverse one's direction. —**cut in 1.** move into a line abruptly or out of turn. **2.** interrupt a dancing couple so as to take the place of one partner. **3.** interrupt. —**cut off 1.** remove or detach by cutting. **2.** put an end to; stop. **3.** intercept. **4.** disinherit. —**cut out 1.** remove by cutting; excise. **2.** shape by cutting. **3.** oust. **4.** *Slang* stop doing; cease. —**cut up 1.** cut in pieces. **2.** affect deeply; distress. **3.** misbehave. — *n.* **1.** a severing, slashing, or piercing stroke: a clean *cut.* **2.** the opening made by such a stroke; gash; cleft. **3.** a part cut off; esp. the part of a meat animal. **4.** a deletion or excision of a part. **5.** a passage or channel that has been cut or dug out. **6.** a snub. **7.** the manner in which a thing is cut; fashion; style. **8.** a reduction in prices, wages, etc. **9.** *Informal* a share or commission. **10.** an absence from a class at school. **11.** *Printing* an engraved block or plate; also, an impression made from this. **12.** a stroke imparting spin to a ball. **13.** a cutting of a deck of cards. **14.** a phonograph recording. —**a cut above** a degree better than. —*adj.* **1.** that has been cut off, into, or through: a *cut* finger. **2.**

dressed or finished by a tool, as stone or glass. **3.** reduced, as rates or prices. **4.** diluted, as whiskey. **—cut and dried 1.** prepared or arranged according to formula. **2.** lacking interest or suspense; predictable. [ME *cutten*]

cute (kyoot) *adj.* **cut·er, cut·est 1.** pretty or attractive. **2.** pert; appealing. **3.** clever. [Var. of ACUTE]

cu·ti·cle (KYOO ti kəl) *n.* the crescent of toughened skin around the base of a fingernail or toenail. [< L *cuticula* the skin]

cut·lass (KUT ləs) *n.* a short, swordlike weapon, often curved. [< MF *coutelas*]

cut·ler·y (KUT lə ree) *n.* cutting instruments collectively, esp. those for use at the table.

cut·let (KUT lit) *n.* **1.** a thin piece of meat for frying or broiling, usu. veal or mutton. **2.** a flat croquette of chopped meat, fish, etc. [< F *côtelette* rib]

cut·off (KUT AWF) *n.* **1.** a termination or limit. **2.** a short cut.

cut·out (KUT OWT) *n.* something cut out or intended to be cut out.

cut-rate (KUT RAYT) *adj.* sold or selling at reduced prices.

cut·ter (KUT ər) *n.* **1.** one who cuts, esp. one who shapes or fits by cutting. **2.** a device that cuts. **3.** *Naut.* **a** a single-masted, fast-sailing vessel of narrow beam and deep draft. **b** a small, swift, armed vessel. **c** a ship's boat, used to discharge passengers, transport stores, etc. [ME *kittere*]

cut·throat (KUT THROHT) *adj.* **1.** bloodthirsty. **2.** ruinous; merciless. **—n.** a murderer.

cut·ting (KUT ing) *adj.* **1.** adapted to cut; edged. **2.** sharp; chilling. **3.** unkind; sarcastic. **—n. 1.** the act of one who or that which cuts. **2.** something obtained or made by cutting, as a recording.

cut·up (KUT UP) *n. Informal* a person who tries to seem funny, as a practical joker.

cy·a·no·sis (sī ə NOH sis) *n. Pathol.* a disordered condition due to inadequate oxygenation of the blood, causing the skin to look blue. [< NL] **—cy·a·not·ic** (sī ə NOT ik) *adj.*

cy·ber·net·ics (sī bər NET iks) *n. (construed as sing.)* the science that treats of the principles of control and communication as they apply both to the operation of complex machines and the functions of organisms. [< Gk. *kybernetēs* steersman] **—cy′·ber·net′ic** *adj.*

cy·cle (SĪ kəl) *n.* **1.** a recurring period within which certain events occur in a definite sequence. **2.** a completed round of events in which there is a final return to the original state. **3.** a pattern of regularly recurring events. **4.** a complete series of variations or changes in electromagnetic waves of a given frequency or of alternating current; also the number of such changes per unit of time. **5.** a body of poems or stories relating to the same character or subject. **—v.i. ·cled, ·cling 1.** pass through cycles. **2.** ride a bicycle, tricycle, etc. [ME *cicle* circle]

cy·clic (SĪ klik) *adj.* pertaining to or characterized by cycles; recurring in cycles. Also **cy′·cli·cal.**

cy·clist (SĪ klist) *n.* one who rides a bicycle, tricycle, etc.

cy·clone (SĪ klohn) *n.* **1.** *Meteorol.* a system of winds circulating about a center of relatively low barometric pressure, and advancing at the earth's surface with clockwise rotation in the Southern Hemisphere, counterclockwise in the Northern. **2.** loosely, any violent storm. **—cy·clon·ic** (sī KLON ik) *adj.*

cy·clo·tron (SĪ klə TRON) *n. Physics* an accelerator that obtains high-energy electrified particles by whirling them at very high speeds in a strong magnetic field.

cyg·net (SIG nit) *n.* a young swan. [ME *signet*]

cyl·in·der (SIL in dər) *n.* **1.** *Geom.* a solid figure generated by one side of a rectangle rotated about the opposite fixed side, the ends of the figure being equal, parallel circles. **2.** any object or container resembling a cylinder in form. **3.** *Mech.* the piston chamber of an engine. **4.** in a revolver, the rotating part that holds the cartridges. [< L *cylindrus* roller] **—cy·lin·dri·cal** (si LIN dri kəl) *adj.*

cym·bal (SIM bəl) *n.* one of a pair of concave metal plates struck together to produce a musical ringing sound. [ME]

cyn·ic (SIN ik) *n.* one who believes that all people are motivated by selfishness. [< L *Cynicus*] **—cyn·i·cism** (SIN ə SIZ əm) *n.*

Cyn·ic (SIN ik) *n.* one of a sect of ancient Greek philosophers who held that virtue was the goal of life. Their doctrine eventually came to represent contemptuous self-righteousness.

cy·no·sure (SĪ nə SHUUR) *n.* **1.** an object of notice and admiration. **2.** something that guides. [< L *Cynosura* former name of the constellation Ursa Minor, the dog star]

cy·press (SĪ prəs) *n.* 1. an evergreen tree of the pine family, having flat, scalelike foliage. 2. the wood of these trees. [ME]

Cy·ril·lic alphabet (si RIL ik) a Slavic alphabet based mainly on that of the Greeks, ascribed traditionally to Saint Cyril, used for Russian and a few other languages.

cyst (sist) *n.* 1. *Pathol.* any abnormal sac or vesicle in which matter may collect and be retained. 2. *Biol.* any saclike organ. [< NL *cystis* bag] —**cys'tic** *adj.*

cystic fibrosis a disease, appearing usu. in childhood, characterized by respiratory disorders and pancreatic deficiency.

cys·ti·tis (si STĪ tis) *n. Pathol.* inflammation of the bladder.

cy·to·plasm (SĪ tə PLAZ əm) *n. Biol.* all the protoplasm of a cell except that in the nucleus.

czar (zahr) *n.* 1. an emperor or king; esp., one of the former emperors of Russia. 2. a despot. Also *tsar, tzar.* [< Russ. *tsar'*]

cza·ri·na (zah REE nə) *n.* the wife of a czar; an empress of Russia: also *tsarina, tzarina.* [< G *Zarin* empress]

D

d, D (dee) *n. pl.* **d's** or **ds, D's** or **Ds 1.** the fourth letter of the English alphabet. **2.** a sound represented by the letter *d.* —*symbol* **1.** the Roman numeral for 500. **2.** *Music* the second tone in the diatonic scale of C. **3.** *Math.* differential. **4.** the fourth in a series or group.

dab (dab) *n.* **1.** a soft, moist patch: a *dab* of paint. **2.** a little bit. —*v.t. & v.i.* **dabbed, dab·bing 1.** strike softly; tap. **2.** pat with something soft and damp. **3.** apply (paint, etc.) with light strokes. [ME *dabben*]

dab·ble (DAB əl) *v.* **·bled, ·bling** *v.i.* **1.** play in a liquid; splash gently. **2.** engage oneself slightly or superficially: *dabble* in art. —*v.t.* **3.** wet slightly; bespatter. —**dab′bler** *n.*

da·cha (DAH chə) *n.* a Russian country villa, esp. a summer house. [< Russ. *dácha*, originally, allotment of land]

dachs·hund (DAHKS huund) *n.* a breed of dog having a long body, short legs, and a short coat. [< G *Dachs* badger + *Hund* dog]

dac·tyl (DAK til) *n.* in prosody, a metrical foot consisting of one long or accented syllable followed by two short or unaccented ones. [ME] —**dac·tyl·ic** (dak TIL ik) *adj.*

da·do (DAY doh) *n. pl.* **·does** the lower part of an interior wall, often ornamented. [< Ital., cube]

dag·ger (DAG ər) *n.* **1.** a short, pointed and edged weapon for stabbing. **2.** *Printing* a reference mark (†). [ME]

da·guerre·o·type (də GAIR ə tīp) *n.* **1.** an early photographic process using light-sensitive, silver-coated copper plates. **2.** a picture made by this process. [after Louis *Daguerre*, 1789–1851, French inventor]

dahl·ia (DAL yə) *n.* a perennial plant having tuberous roots and showy flowers; also, the flowers. [after Anders *Dahl*, 18th c., Swedish botanist]

dai·ly (DAY lee) *adj.* of, occurring, or appearing every day or every weekday. —*n. pl.* **·lies** a daily publication. —*adv.* day after day; on every day. [ME]

dain·ty (DAYN tee) *adj.* **·ti·er, ·ti·est 1.** delicately pretty or graceful. **2.** fastidious; also, too fastidious. **3.** delicious; choice. —

n. pl. **·ties** a delicacy. [ME *deintie* worthiness] —**dain′ti·ness** *n.*

dai·qui·ri (DĪ kə ree) *n.* a cocktail made of rum, lime or lemon juice, and sugar. [after *Daiquirí*, Cuba]

dair·y (DAIR ee) *n. pl.* **·ies 1.** a commercial establishment that sells milk products. **2.** a room or building on a farm where milk and cream are kept and processed. **3.** a dairy farm. [ME *daierie* dairymaid]

da·is (DAY is) *n.* a raised platform in a room or hall for a speaker, eminent guests, etc. [ME *deis*]

dai·sy (DAY zee) *n. pl.* **·sies** a plant of the composite family; esp., the **oxeye daisy**, of the U.S., having a yellow disk and white rays, and the **English daisy**, having a small yellow disk and numerous white or rose rays. [ME *dayesye*, lit., day's eye]

Da·lai La·ma (DAH lī LAH mə) the spiritual leader of Tibetan Lamaism, and traditional chief of state.

dale (dayl) *n.* a small valley. [ME *dal*]

dal·ly (DAL ee) *v.* **·lied, ·ly·ing** *v.i.* **1.** make love playfully; flirt or fondle. **2.** play; trifle. **3.** waste time. —*v.t.* **4.** waste (time): with *away.* [ME *dalien* chat] —**dal′li·ance** *n.*

dam¹ (dam) *n.* **1.** a barrier to obstruct or control the flow of water. **2.** the water held back by such a barrier. **3.** any obstruction. —*v.t.* **dammed, dam·ming 1.** erect a dam in. **2.** keep back; restrain: with *up* or *in.* [ME]

dam² *n.* a female parent: said of animals. [ME]

dam·age (DAM ij) *n.* **1.** injury to person or property. **2.** *pl. Law* money to compensate for an injury or wrong. —*v.t. & v.i.* **·aged, ·ag·ing** cause damage to or suffer damage. [ME]

dam·ask (DAM əsk) *n.* **1.** a rich, reversible, elaborately patterned fabric, used for table linen, etc. **2.** a deep pink or rose color. —*adj.* deep pink or rose colored. [ME *damaske*]

dame (daym) *n.* **1.** a mature woman; matron. **2.** *Offensive Slang* a woman. **3.** in Great Britain: **a** a title conferred on women, equivalent to that of knight. **b** the legal title of the wife of a knight or baronet. [ME]

damn (dam) *v.t.* **1.** condemn. **2.** curse or

damnable

swear at. **3.** *Theol.* condemn to eternal punishment. —*v.i.* **4.** swear; curse. —*n.* **1.** the saying of "damn" as an oath. **2.** the smallest, most contemptible bit. —*interj.* an oath expressive of irritation, disappointment, etc. —*adj. & adv.* damned. [ME *dampnen* condemn]

dam·na·ble (DAM nə bəl) *adj.* meriting damnation; detestable; outrageous. [ME *dampnable*] —**dam'na·bly** *adv.*

dam·na·tion (dam NAY shən) *n.* **1.** the act of damning, or the state of being damned. **2.** *Theol.* condemnation to eternal punishment; also, the punishment suffered. —*interj.* damn.

damned (damd) *adj.* **1.** doomed; condemned, esp. to eternal punishment. **2.** deserving damnation. —*adv. Informal* very: *damned* funny.

damned·est (DAM dist) *Informal n.* utmost; best: Do your *damndest*.

damn·ing (DAM ing) *adj.* inculpating: *damning* evidence.

damp (damp) *adj.* somewhat wet; moist. —*n.* **1.** moisture or moistness; vapor; mist. **2.** foul air or poisonous gas, esp. in a mine. —*v.t.* **1.** make damp; moisten. **2.** stifle, check, reduce, etc. [ME]

damp·en (DAM pən) *v.t.* **1.** make damp; moisten. **2.** check; depress. —*v.i.* **3.** become damp.

damp·er (DAM pər) *n.* **1.** one who or that which depresses or checks. **2.** a plate in the flue of a stove, furnace, etc., for controlling the draft.

dam·sel (DAM zəl) *n.* a young unmarried woman; maiden. [ME *damisel* lady]

dance (dans) *v.* **danced, danc·ing** *v.i.* **1.** move the body and feet rhythmically, esp. to music. **2.** move about lightly or excitedly; leap or bob about. —*v.t.* **3.** perform the steps of (a waltz, tango, etc.). **4.** cause to dance. —**dance attendance** wait upon another constantly. —*n.* **1.** a series of regular rhythmic steps or movements, usu. performed to music. **2.** a musical composition for dancing. **3.** a gathering of people for dancing; a ball. [ME *dauncen*]

dan·de·li·on (DAN dl I ən) *n.* a plant having yellow flowers and toothed, edible leaves. [< MF *dent de lion*, lit., lion's tooth]

dan·der (DAN dər) *n. Informal* ruffled temper; anger. —**get one's dander up** become angry. [Alt. of DANDRUFF]

dan·di·fy (DAN də FI) *v.t.* **·fied, ·fy·ing** cause to resemble a dandy or fop.

dan·dle (DAN dl) *v.t.* **·dled, ·dling 1.** move up and down lightly on the knees or in the arms, as an infant or child. **2.** fondle; caress.

dan·druff (DAN drəf) *n.* a fine scurf that forms on the scalp and comes off in small scales.

dan·dy (DAN dee) *n. pl.* **·dies 1.** a man who is excessively interested in an elegant appearance; a fop. **2.** *Informal* something particularly fine. —*adj.* **1.** like a dandy; foppish. **2.** *Informal* excellent; fine. —**dan'dy·ish** *adj.*

dan·ger (DAYN jər) *n.* **1.** exposure to evil, injury, or loss; peril; risk. **2.** a cause or instance of peril or risk. [ME *daunger*] —**dan·ger·ous** (DAYN jər əs) *adj.* perilous; unsafe.

dan·gle (DANG gəl) *v.* **·gled, ·gling** *v.i.* **1.** hang loosely; swing to and fro. **2.** follow or hover near. **3.** *Gram.* lack clear or proper connection in a sentence. —*v.t.* **4.** hold so as to swing loosely. **5.** leave in an uncertain state.

dank (dangk) *adj.* cold and damp. [ME] —**dank'ly** *adv.*

dap·per (DAP ər) *adj.* **1.** smartly dressed. **2.** small and active. [ME *daper* nimble]

dap·ple (DAP əl) *v.t.* **·pled, ·pling** make spotted or variegated in color. —*adj.* spotted; variegated: also **dap'pled.** —*n.* **1.** a spot or dot, as on the skin of a horse. **2.** an animal marked with spots.

dare (dair) *v.* **dared, dar·ing** *v.t.* **1.** have the courage or boldness to undertake. **2.** challenge (someone) to attempt something. —*v.i.* **3.** have the courage or boldness to do or attempt something; venture. —*n.* a challenge; taunt. [ME *dar*]

dare·dev·il (DAIR DEV əl) *n.* one who is recklessly bold. —*adj.* rash; reckless.

dar·ing (DAIR ing) *n.* adventurous courage; bravery; boldness. —*adj.*

dark (dahrk) *adj.* **1.** having or reflecting little or no light; dim. **2.** of a deep shade; black, or almost black. **3.** swarthy in complexion. **4.** cheerless or disheartening. **5.** sullen; dour. **6.** unenlightened; ignorant. **7.** evil or sinister: a *dark* deed. **8.** mysterious or secret; obscure. —*n.* **1.** lack of light. **2.** a place or condition of little or no light. **3.** night. **4.** obscurity; secrecy. **5.** ignorance. **6.** a dark shadow or color. —**in the dark** ignorant; uninformed. [ME *derk*]

Dark Ages the period in European history between the fall of the Western Roman

Empire (A.D. 476) and the Italian Renaissance.

dark·en (DAHR kən) v.t. **1.** make dark or darker; deprive of light. **2.** make dark in color. **3.** sadden. **4.** obscure; confuse. —v.i. **5.** grow dark or darker; become obscure. **6.** grow clouded.

dark horse one who unexpectedly wins a race, contest, nomination, etc.

dark·room (DAHRK ROOM) n. Photog. a room equipped to exclude light rays harmful in developing films, etc.

dar·ling (DAHR ling) n. **1.** a person tenderly loved: often a term of address. **2.** a person in great favor. —adj. **1.** beloved; very dear. **2.** charming; attractive. [ME *derling*]

darn[1] (dahrn) v.t. & v.i. repair (a garment or a hole) by filling the gap with interlacing stitches. —n. a place mended by darning.

darn[2] v.t., adj., n., & interj. Informal damn: a euphemism.

dart (dahrt) n. **1.** a thin, pointed weapon to be thrown or shot. **2.** anything like a dart in appearance or effect. **3.** a sudden, rapid motion. **4.** a tapering tuck made in a garment to make it fit. —v.i. **1.** move suddenly; rush. —v.t. **2.** throw or emit suddenly or swiftly. [ME]

Dar·win·ism (DAHR wə NIZ əm) n. the biological doctrine of the origin of species through descent by natural selection with variation, advocated by Charles Darwin. —**Dar·win'i·an** n. & adj.

dash (dash) v.t. **1.** strike, throw, or thrust with violence, esp. so as to break or shatter. **2.** bespatter. **3.** do, write, etc. hastily: with *off* or *down*. **4.** frustrate; confound: *dash* hopes. **5.** put to shame; abash. —v.i. **6.** strike or hit with violence. **7.** rush or move impetuously. —n. **1.** a splashing or splash. **2.** a small amount of some ingredient. **3.** a hasty stroke, as with a pen. **4.** a short rush. **5.** a short race: the 100-yard *dash*. **6.** vigor of style; verve. **7.** a horizontal line (—) used as a mark of punctuation to set off words or phrases in a sentence. [ME *dasshen*]

dash·board (DASH BORD) n. the instrument panel of an automobile.

da·shi·ki (də SHEE kee) n. a one-piece garment that hangs loosely from the shoulders, adapted from an African garment for men. [< Yoruba *danshiki*]

dash·ing (DASH ing) adj. **1.** spirited; bold. **2.** showy or gay.

das·tard (DAS tərd) n. a base coward; a sneak. [ME] —**das'·tard·ly** adj.

da·ta (DAY tə) n.pl. of **datum** facts or figures from which conclusions may be drawn. [< L, things given]

data bank a collection of information computerized for swift access.

data processing the operations involved in handling and storing information, using computers and other machines.

date[1] (dayt) n. **1.** a particular point of time when something occurs. **2.** an inscription giving a date, esp. when something was written or made. **3.** the age or period to which a thing belongs. **4.** the day of the month. **5.** a social appointment for a specified time. **6.** a person with whom such an appointment is made. —**to date** till now. —v. **dat·ed, dat·ing** v.t. **1.** furnish or mark with a date. **2.** ascertain the time or era of; assign a date to. **3.** make an appointment or frequent appointments with (a member of the opposite sex); go out with. —v.i. **4.** have origin in an era or time: usually with *from*: This coin *dates* from the Revolution. **5.** have social engagements with members of the opposite sex. [ME] —**dat'a·ble** adj.

date[2] n. **1.** the sweet fruit of a palm. **2.** a palm bearing this fruit: also **date palm.** [ME]

dat·ed (DAY tid) adj. **1.** marked with a date. **2.** antiquated; old-fashioned.

date·less (DAYT lis) adj. **1.** bearing no date. **2.** without end or limit. **3.** of permanent interest.

date·line (DAYT LIN) n. the line containing the date and place of issue of a publication or of any contribution printed in it. —**date' line'** v.t. **·lined, ·lin·ing**

da·tive (DAY tiv) n. Gram. the case of a noun, pronoun, or adjective in certain languages, in English denoted by the indirect object. [ME *datif*]

da·tum (DAY təm) singular of DATA.

daub (dawb) v.t. & v.i. **1.** smear or coat (something). **2.** paint without skill. —n. **1.** any sticky application, as of plaster. **2.** a smear or spot. **3.** a poor painting. **4.** an instance or act of daubing. [ME *dauben* whiten]

daugh·ter (DAW tər) n. **1.** a female child, considered in relationship to either or both of her parents. **2.** a female descendant. [ME *doughter*]

daugh·ter·in·law (DAW tər in LAW) n. pl. **daugh·ters·in·law** the wife of one's son.

daunt (dawnt) v.t. dishearten or intimidate; cow. [ME *daunten* tame]

daunt·less (DAWNT lis) adj. fearless; intrepid.

dav·it (DAV it) n. Naut. one of a pair of small cranes on a ship's side for hoisting its boats, stores, etc. [ME *daviot*]

Da·vy Jones's lock·er (DAY vee JOHN ziz) the bottom of the ocean, esp. as the grave of the drowned.

daw·dle (DAWD l) v.t. & v.i. •dled, •dling waste (time); idle: often with *away*. —**daw'·dler** n.

dawn (dawn) n. 1. daybreak. 2. a beginning or unfolding. —v.i. 1. begin to grow light in the morning. 2. begin to be understood: with *on* or *upon*. 3. begin to expand or develop. [ME *dawen*]

day (day) n. 1. the period of light from dawn to dark; daylight. 2. the interval represented by one rotation of the earth; twenty-four hours. ♦ Collateral adjective: *diurnal*. 3. a portion of a day spent in a particular way or place: a shopping *day*. 4. the hours of a day devoted to work: a seven-hour *day*. 5. a time or period; epoch. 6. *Usu. cap.* a particular day: Labor *Day*. 7. *Often pl.* a lifetime. 8. a period of success: Our *day* is past. —**day after day** every day. —**day by day** each day. —**day in, day out** every day. [ME]

day·break (DAY brayk) n. the time each morning when daylight replaces darkness.

day·care (DAY kair) adj. of or relating to a facility for preschool children during the day.

day·dream (DAY dreem) n. a dreamlike thought; reverie. —**day'dream'** v.i.

day·light (DAY līt) n. 1. the light received from the sun; the light of day. 2. insight into something; understanding. 3. exposure to view; publicity. 4. the period of light during the day.

day·long (DAY lawng) adj. lasting all day. —adv. through the entire day.

Day of Atonement Yom Kippur.

day·time (DAY tīm) n. the time of daylight.

daze (dayz) v.t. dazed, daz·ing stupefy or bewilder; stun. —n. the state of being dazed. [ME *dasen*]

daz·zle (DAZ əl) v. •zled, •zling v.t. 1. blind or dim the vision of by excess of light. 2. bewilder or charm, as with magnificence. —v.i. 3. be blinded by lights or glare. 4. excite admiration. —n. 1. the act of daz-

zling, or the state of being dazzled. 2. brightness; brilliance. [< DAZE]

D-day (DEE DAY) n. in military operations, the unspecified date of the launching of an attack.

de- prefix 1. away; off: *deflect, decapitate.* 2. down: *decline.* 3. completely; utterly: *denude.* 4. the undoing, reversing, or ridding of (the action, condition or substance expressed by the main element): *decode, decentralization.* [ME]

dea·con (DEE kən) n. 1. a lay church officer or subordinate minister. 2. a member of the clergy ranking next below a priest. [ME *deken* servant]

de·ac·ti·vate (dee AK tə vayt) v.t. •vat·ed, •vat·ing 1. render inactive or ineffective, as an explosive, chemical, etc. 2. *Mil.* release (a military unit, ship, etc.) from active duty; demobilize. —**de·ac'ti·va'tion** n.

dead (ded) adj. 1. having ceased to live; lifeless. 2. deathlike; inanimate; insensible. 3. lacking sensation; numb. 4. extinct: a *dead* language. 5. no longer in force: a *dead* law. 6. not functioning: *dead* battery. 7. very tired. 8. lacking activity, excitement, etc.: a *dead* town. 9. dull: said of colors. 10. muffled: said of sounds. 11. without elasticity. 12. complete; utter: *dead* silence. 13. perfect; exact. 14. in certain games, out of play: said of the ball. —n. 1. a dead person, or dead persons collectively: preceded by *the*. 2. the coldest, darkest, or most intense part: the *dead* of winter. —adv. 1. completely: stop *dead*. 2. directly: *dead* ahead. [ME *deed*]

dead·beat (DED BEET) n. one who avoids paying debts.

dead·en (DED n) v.t. 1. diminish the sensitivity, force, or intensity of. 2. render soundproof. 3. make dull or less brilliant.

dead end 1. a passage, street, etc. having no outlet. 2. a point from which no progress can be made.

dead·head (DED HED) *Informal* n. 1. one who is admitted, entertained, or accommodated free of charge. 2. a dull, stupid person. —v.t. & v.i. treat or go as a deadhead. —adj. of a train, truck, etc., operating without cargo.

dead heat a race in which two or more competitors tie.

dead·line (DED LIN) n. a time limit, as for the completion of newspaper copy.

dead·lock (DED LOK) n. a standstill or stoppage of activity resulting from the unrelenting opposition of equally powerful forces. —*v.t. & v.i.* cause or come to a deadlock.

dead·ly (DED lee) *adj.* **·li·er, ·li·est 1.** likely or certain to cause death. **2.** implacable; mortal: a *deadly* enemy. **3.** resembling death: *deadly* pallor. **4.** ruinous; destructive. **5.** excessive. —*adv.* **1.** as in death; deathly. **2.** completely.

dead·wood (DED wuud) *n.* **1.** wood dead on the tree. **2.** a worthless person or thing.

deaf (def) *adj.* **1.** partly or completely lacking the power to hear. **2.** unwilling to listen. [ME *deef*]

deaf·en (DEF ən) *v.t.* **1.** make deaf. **2.** overwhelm, as with noise. **3.** make soundproof. —**deaf'en·ing** *adj. & n.*

deaf-mute (DEF MYOOT) *n.* a deaf person who cannot speak, usu. because of deafness from early life.

deal[1] (deel) *v.* **dealt** (delt), **deal·ing** *v.t.* **1.** distribute or portion out. **2.** apportion to (a person). **3.** deliver or inflict, as a blow. —*v.i.* **4.** conduct oneself: with *with*. **5.** be concerned: with *in* or *with*: deal in facts. **6.** consider, discuss, or take action: with *with*. **7.** do business: with *in, with,* or *at*. **8.** in card games, act as dealer. —*n.* **1.** the act of dealing. **2.** in card games: **a** the distribution of the cards to the players. **b** the right or turn to distribute the cards. **c** the cards distributed; a hand. **3.** an indefinite amount, degree, extent, etc.: a great *deal* of time. **4.** a business transaction. **5.** a secret arrangement, as in politics. **6.** *Informal* a plan, agreement, or treatment: a rough *deal*. [ME *delen*]

deal[2] *n.* a fir or pine plank. [ME *dele* plank] —**deal** *adj.*

deal·er (DEE lər) *n.* **1.** one engaged in buying and selling; a car *dealer*. **2.** in card games, one who distributes the cards. [ME *delere*]

deal·ing (DEE ling) *n.* **1.** the act of distributing. **2.** *Usu. pl.* transactions or relations with others.

dealt (delt) past tense, past participle of DEAL.

dean (deen) *n.* **1.** an officer of a college or university, having jurisdiction over a particular group of students or area of study, or acting as head of a faculty. **2.** the senior member of a group. **3.** the chief ecclesiastical officer of a cathedral or of a collegiate church. [ME *deen*]

dear (deer) *adj.* **1.** beloved; precious. **2.** highly esteemed: used in letter salutations.

3. expensive; costly. **4.** intense; earnest: our *dearest* wish. —*n.* a darling. —*interj.* an exclamation of regret, surprise, etc. [ME *dere*]

dearth (durth) *n.* scarcity; lack. [ME *derthe*]

death (deth) *n.* **1.** the permanent cessation of all vital functions in an animal or plant. **2.** the condition of being dead. **3.** the extinction of anything; destruction. **4.** the cause or manner of dying. ♦ Collateral adjectives: *lethal, mortal.* —**put to death** kill; execute. [ME *deeth*]

death·bed (DETH BED) *n.* **1.** the bed on which a person dies. **2.** the last hours of life.

death·blow (DETH BLOH) *n.* that which causes the death or the end of a person or thing.

death·less (DETH lis) *adj.* not liable to die; perpetual; immortal.

death·ly (DETH lee) *adj.* **1.** resembling or suggesting death. Also **death'like. 2.** causing death; fatal. —*adv.* **1.** in a deathlike manner. **2.** extremely: *deathly* ill.

death rate the number of persons per thousand of population who die within a given time.

death rattle the rattling sound of the breath of one dying.

death's-head (DETHS HED) *n.* a human skull, or a representation of it, as a symbol of death.

death·watch (DETH woch) *n.* **1.** a vigil kept at the side of one who is dying or has recently died. **2.** a guard set over a condemned person before execution. **3.** a beetle that makes a ticking sound.

de·ba·cle (day BAH kəl) *n.* **1.** a sudden and disastrous breakdown or collapse. **2.** the breaking up of ice in a river. **3.** a violent flood. [< F *débâcle*]

de·bar (di BAHR) *v.t.* **·barred, ·bar·ring** bar or shut out: usu. with *from*. [ME].

de·bark (di BAHRK) *v.t. & v.i.* put or go ashore from a ship. [< F *débarquer*] —**de·bar·ka·tion** (DEE bahr KAY shən) *n.*

de·base (di BAYS) *v.t.* **·based, ·bas·ing** lower in character or worth; degrade. —**de·base'ment** *n.*

de·bate (di BAYT) *n.* **1.** a discussion of any question; argument; dispute. **2.** a formal contest in argumentation. —*v.t. & v.i.* **·bat·ed, ·bat·ing 1.** argue; discuss. **2.** consider; deliberate, as upon alternatives. **3.** discuss (a question) in formal debate. [ME *debaten*] —**de·bat'a·ble** *adj.*

de·bauch (di BAWCH) *v.t.* **1.** corrupt in

morals; seduce; deprave. —*v.i.* **2.** indulge in debauchery; dissipate. —*n.* an act or period of debauchery. [< F *débaucher* lure from work] —**de•bauch'er** *n.*

de•bauch•er•y (di BAW chə ree) *n. pl.* **•er•ies** gross indulgence of one's sensual appetites.

de•bil•i•tate (di BIL i TAYT) *v.t.* **•tat•ed, •tat•ing** make feeble or languid; weaken. [< L *debilitatus* weakened] —**de•bil'i•ta' tive** *adj.*

de•bil•i•ty (di BIL i tee) *n. pl.* **•ties** abnormal weakness. [ME *debylite*]

deb•it (DEB it) *n.* **1.** an item of debt recorded in an account. **2.** an entry of debt in an account, or the sum of such entries. —*v.t.* **1.** enter (a debt) in an account. **2.** charge (someone) with a debt. [ME]

deb•o•nair (DEB ə NAIR) *adj.* **1.** pleasantly gracious. **2.** cheerful; lively; gay. [ME *deboneire*]

de•bris (də BREE) *n.* **1.** scattered remains, as of something destroyed; ruins; rubble. **2.** *Geol.* an accumulation of rock fragments. [< F *débris*]

debt (det) *n.* **1.** that which one owes, as money, goods, or services. **2.** the obligation to pay or render something. **3.** the condition of owing something. [ME *dette*]

debt•or (DET ər) *n.* one who is in debt.

de•bug (dee BUG) *v.t.* **•bugged, •bugging 1.** eliminate flaws in (a mechanism or system) by testing and use. **2.** rid of a hidden listening device (*bug*).

de•bunk (di BUNGK) *v.t.* expose as false or pretentious.

de•but (day BYOO) *n.* **1.** a first public appearance. **2.** a formal introduction to society. **3.** the beginning, as of a career. [< F *début*] —**de•but'** *v.i.*

deb•u•tante (DEB yuu TAHNT) *n.* a young woman making a debut in society. —**deb' u•tant** *n. masc.* [< F *débutant*]

dec•ade (DEK ayd) *n.* a period of ten years.

dec•a•dence (DEK ə dəns) *n.* **1.** a process of deterioration; decay. **2.** a condition or period of decline, as in morals. [< MF] —**dec'a•dent** *adj. & n.*

Dec•a•logue (DEK ə LAWG) *n.* the Ten Commandments. [ME *decalog*]

de•camp (di KAMP) *v.i.* **1.** break camp. **2.** leave suddenly or secretly; run away. —**de•camp'ment** *n.*

de•cant (di KANT) *v.t.* **1.** pour off (a liquid) without disturbing its sediment. **2.** pour

from one container into another. [< NL *decantare*]

de•cant•er (di KAN tər) *n.* a vessel for decanting; esp. a decorative bottle.

de•cap•i•tate (di KAP i TAYT) *v.t.* **•tat•ed, •tat•ing** cut off the head of; behead. [< LL *decapitatus* beheaded]

de•cath•lon (di KATH lon) *n.* an athletic contest consisting of ten different track and field events in all of which each contestant participates. [< DEC(A)- ten + Gk. *âthlon* contest]

de•cay (di KAY) *v.i.* **1.** fail slowly as in health, strength, etc. **2.** decompose; rot. **3.** *Physics* change, disintegrate, or reduce radioactivity spontaneously. —*n.* **1.** deterioration. **2.** decomposition. [ME *decayen*]

de•cease (di SEES) *v.i.* **•ceased, •ceas•ing** die. —*n.* death. [ME *deces* death] —**de•ceased** (di SEEST) *adj.* dead. —**the deceased** the dead person or persons.

de•ce•dent (di SEED nt) *n. Law* a person deceased.

de•ceit (di SEET) *n.* **1.** the act of deceiving. **2.** an instance of deception or a device that deceives; a trick. **3.** the quality of being deceptive; falseness. [ME *deceite*] —**de•ceit'ful** *adj.*

de•ceive (di SEEV) *v.t. & v.i.* **•ceived, •ceiv•ing** mislead by deceit; delude. [ME *deceiven*] —**de•ceiv'er** *n.*

de•cel•er•ate (dee SEL ə RAYT) *v.t. & v.i.* **•at•ed, •at•ing** diminish in velocity. —**de•cel'er•a'•tion** *n.*

De•cem•ber (di SEM bər) *n.* the twelfth month of the year, having 31 days. [ME *decembre* tenth month; December was the tenth month in the Roman calendar]

de•cen•cy (DEE sən see) *n. pl.* **•cies** the quality or state of being decent; propriety. **2.** *Usu. pl.* those things that are proper or decent.

de•cen•ni•al (di SEN ee əl) *adj.* **1.** of or continuing for ten years. **2.** occurring every ten years. —*n.* an anniversary observed every ten years.

de•cent (DEE sənt) *adj.* **1.** characterized by propriety of conduct, speech, or dress; respectable. **2.** adequate; satisfactory. **3.** generous; kind. **4.** *Informal* adequately or properly clothed. [< L *decere* be fitting, proper]

de•cen•tral•ize (di SEN trə LIZ) *v.t.* **•ized, •iz•ing** reorganize into smaller and more autonomous parts. —**de•cen'tral•i•za' tion** *n.*

de·cep·tion (di SEP shən) n. 1. the act of deceiving; deceit. 2. the state of being deceived. 3. anything that deceives or is meant to deceive; a delusion. [ME *decepcioun*]

de·cep·tive (di SEP tiv) adj. having the power or tendency to deceive. —**de·cep'tive·ness** n.

dec·i·bel (DES ə BEL) n. *Physics* a measure of sound intensity.

de·cide (di SĪD) v. ·cid·ed, ·cid·ing v.t. 1. determine; settle, as a controversy. 2. determine the outcome of. 3. bring (someone) to a decision. —v.i. 4. make a decision or render a verdict. [ME *deciden*]

de·cid·ed (di SĪ did) adj. 1. certain; definite. 2. determined; emphatic. —**de·cid'ed·ly** adv.

de·cid·u·ous (di SIJ oo əs) adj. 1. *Biol.* falling off or shed at maturity or at specific seasons, as leaves or antlers. 2. shedding foliage annually; distinguished from *evergreen*. [< L *deciduus* falling]

dec·i·mal (DES ə məl) adj. 1. pertaining to or founded on the number 10. 2. proceeding by tens. —n. a decimal fraction or one of its digits. [< Med.L *decimalis* of tenths]

decimal system a system of reckoning by tens or tenths.

dec·i·mate (DES ə MAYT) v.t. ·mat·ed, ·mat·ing 1. destroy or kill a large proportion of. 2. kill one out of every ten of. [< L *decimatus* having punished every tenth man] —**dec'i·ma'tion** n.

de·ci·pher (di SĪ fər) v.t. 1. determine the meaning of (something obscure, illegible, etc.) 2. decode. —**de·ci'pher·a·ble** adj.

de·ci·sion (di SIZH ən) n. 1. the act of deciding (an issue, question, etc.). 2. a conclusion or judgment reached by deciding. 3. firmness in judgment, action, or character. [ME *decisioun*]

de·ci·sive (di SĪ siv) adj. 1. ending uncertainty or dispute; conclusive. 2. firm; determined. 3. unquestionable; unmistakable. —**de·ci'sive·ness** n.

deck (dek) n. 1. *Naut.* a a platform covering or extending horizontally across a vessel, and serving as both floor and roof. b the space between two such platforms. 2. any similar flat surface, as a porch. 3. a pack of playing cards. —v.t. 1. dress or decorate elegantly; adorn. 2. *Slang* knock to the ground. [ME *dekke* covering material]

de·claim (di KLAYM) v.i. 1. speak loudly and rhetorically. 2. give a formal, set speech. 3. attack verbally and vehemently: with *against*. —v.t. 4. utter rhetorically. [ME *declamen* shout] —**de·clam·a·to·ry** (di KLAM ə TOR ee) adj.

dec·la·ra·tion (DEK lə RAY shən) n. 1. the act of declaring or proclaiming. 2. that which is declared. 3. a statement of goods liable to taxation. 4. in bridge, a contract.

de·clar·a·tive (di KLAR ə tiv) adj. making a declaration or statement.

de·clare (di KLAIR) v.t. ·clared, ·clar·ing 1. make known or clear; esp. to announce formally. 2. say emphatically; assert. 3. reveal; prove. 4. make full statement of, as goods liable to duty. [ME *declaren* make clear]

dé·clas·sé (DAY kla SAY) adj. *French* fallen or lowered in social status, class, etc.

de·clen·sion (di KLEN shən) n. 1. *Gram.* the inflection of nouns, pronouns, and adjectives according to case, number, and gender. 2. a sloping downward; descent. 3. a decline. [ME *declenson* inflection]

dec·li·na·tion (DEK lə NAY shən) n. 1. the act of inclining or bending downward. 2. deviation, as in direction or conduct. 3. the angle formed between the direction of a compass needle and true north. 4. *Astron.* the angular distance of a heavenly body north or south from the celestial equator. 5. a polite refusal. [ME *declinacioun* turning aside]

de·cline (di KLĪN) v. ·clined, ·clin·ing v.i. 1. refuse politely to accept or do something. 2. lessen or fail gradually, as in health. 3. draw to an end. 4. bend or incline downward or aside. —v.t. 5. refuse politely to accept or do. 6. cause to bend or incline downward or aside. 7. *Gram.* give the inflected forms of (a noun, pronoun, or adjective). —n. 1. the act or result of declining; deterioration. 2. a period of declining. 3. mental or physical weakening or deterioration. 4. a downward slope. [ME *declinen* lean down]

de·cliv·i·ty (di KLIV i tee) n. pl. ·ties a downward slope. [< L *declivitas* slope] —**de·cliv'i·tous** adj.

de·code (dee KOHD) v.t. ·cod·ed, ·cod·ing convert from code into plain language. —**de·cod'er** n.

dé·colle·té (DAY kol TAY) adj. 1. cut low in the neck, as a gown. 2. wearing a low-necked garment. [< F] —**dé·colle·tage** (DAY kol TAZH) n.

de·com·pose (DEE kəm POHZ) v.t. & v.i.

•posed, •pos•ing 1. separate into constituent parts. 2. decay. —de•com•po•si•tion (DEE kom pə ZISH ən) n.

de•com•press (DEE kəm PRES) v.t. free of pressure; reduce or remove the pressure on (divers, etc.).

decompression sickness caisson disease.

de•con•tam•i•nate (DEE kən TAM ə NAYT) v.t. •nat•ed, •nat•ing make (a contaminated object or area) safe.

de•con•trol (DEE kən TROHL) v.t. •trolled, •trol•ling remove from control. —n. the removal of controls.

dé•cor (day KOR) n. the scheme or style of decoration, as of a room. Also de•cor. [< F]

dec•o•rate (DEK ə RAYT) v.t. •rat•ed, •rat•ing 1. embellish or furnish with things beautiful; adorn. 2. confer a decoration or medal upon. [< L decoratus embellished] —dec•o•ra•tive (DEK ər ə TIV) adj.

dec•o•ra•tion (DEK ə RAY shən) n. 1. the act, process, or art of decorating. 2. a thing or group of things that decorate; ornamentation. 3. a badge, ribbon, or medal awarded for merit.

dec•o•rous (DEK ər əs) adj. marked by decorum; seemly; proper. [< L decorus graceful] —dec•o•rous•ness n.

de•co•rum (di KOR əm) n. conformity to the requirements of good taste or social convention; propriety in manners. [< L]

de•coy (DEE koi) n. 1. a person or thing that lures into danger, deception, etc. 2. a bird or animal, or the likeness of one, used to lure game. 3. an enclosed place into which game may be lured. —v.t. & v.i. (di KOI) lure or be lured into danger or a trap. [Earlier coy < Du. de kooi, lit. the cage]

de•crease (di KREES) v.t. & v.i. •creased, •creas•ing grow, or cause to grow, gradually less or smaller; diminish. —n. (DEE krees) 1. the act, process, or state of decreasing. 2. the amount or degree of decreasing. [ME decres]

de•cree (di KREE) n. a formal and authoritative order or decision. —v. •creed, •cree•ing v.t. 1. order, adjudge, or appoint by law or edict. —v.i. 2. issue an edict or decree. [ME decre]

dec•re•ment (DEK rə mənt) n. 1. the act or process of decreasing. 2. the amount lost by decrease.

de•crep•it (di KREP it) adj. enfeebled or worn out by old age or excessive use. [ME] —de•crep'i•tude n.

de•crim•i•nal•ize (di KRIM ə nl IZ) v.t. •ized, •iz•ing remove from regulation by criminal laws: the state decriminalized marijuana use.

de•cry (di KRI) v.t. •cried, •cry•ing condemn or disparage openly. [< F décrier] —de•cri•al (di KRI əl) n.

ded•i•cate (DED i KAYT) v.t. •cat•ed, •cat•ing 1. set apart for any special use, duty, or purpose. 2. inscribe (a work of literature etc.) to someone. 3. commit (oneself) to a certain course of action or thought. 4. open or unveil (a bridge, statue, etc.) to the public. [ME] —ded•i•ca•tion (DED i KAY shən) n. —ded•i•ca•to•ry (DED i kə TOR ee) adj.

de•duce (di DOOS) v.t. •duced, •duc•ing 1. derive as a conclusion by reasoning. 2. trace, as origin. [< L deducere lead down]

de•duct (di DUKT) v.t. take away or subtract. [ME] —de•duct'i•ble adj.

de•duc•tion (di DUK shən) n. 1. the act of deducing. 2. Logic reasoning from the general to the particular; also, reasoning from stated premises to logical conclusions. 3. the act of deducting; also, the amount deducted. —de•duc'tive adj.

deed (deed) n. 1. anything done; an act. 2. a notable achievement; feat. 3. action in general, as opposed to words. 4. Law any written, sealed instrument of bond, contract, transfer, etc., esp. of real estate conveyance. —in deed in fact; in truth; actually. —v.t. transfer by deed. [ME dede]

deem (deem) v.t. & v.i. judge; think; believe. [ME demen judge]

deep (deep) adj. •er, •est 1. extending or situated far below a surface. 2. extending far inward or backward, or to either side. 3. having a (specified) depth or dimension: six feet deep. 4. rising to the level of: used in combination: knee-deep. 5. coming from or penetrating to a depth: a deep sigh. 6. difficult to understand. 7. learned; wise. 8. profound; extreme. 9. of intense or dark hue. 10. of low, sonorous tone. 11. absorbed: deep in thought. —n. 1. a place or thing of great depth; an abyss. 2. the most intense or profound part. —the deep the sea or ocean. —adv. 1. to great depth. 2. far along in time. 3. Sports farther than normal from the center of play: the outfield played deep for the slugger. [ME dep]

deep•en (DEE pən) v.t. & v.i. make or become deep or deeper.

deep-fry (DEEP FRĪ) *v.t.* **-fried, -fry·ing** fry in deep fat.

deep-root·ed (DEEP ROO tid) *adj.* **1.** having roots far below the surface. **2.** based deep within; deep-seated.

deep-seat·ed (DEEP SEE tid) *adj.* established far within; difficult to remove.

deep-set (DEEP SET) *adj.* deeply placed, as eyes.

deer (deer) *n. pl.* **deer** a ruminant animal having deciduous antlers, usu. in the male only, as the moose, elk, and reindeer. [ME *der*]

de·face (di FAYS) *v.t.* **·faced, ·fac·ing** mar the surface or appearance of; disfigure. [ME *defacen*]

de fac·to (dee FAK toh) actually or really existing: distinguished from *de jure*. [< L]

de·fal·cate (di FAL kayt) *v.i.* **·cat·ed, ·cat·ing** embezzle. [< Med.L *defalcatus* cut off] —**de·fal·ca·tion** (DEE fal KAY shən) *n.*

de·fame (di FAYM) *v.t.* **·famed, ·fam·ing** attack the good name or reputation of; slander; libel. [ME *defamen* slander] —**def·a·ma·tion** (DEF ə MAY shən) *n.* —**de·fam·a·to·ry** (di FAM ə TOR ee) *adj.*

de·fault (di FAWLT) *n.* a failure or neglect to fulfill an obligation or requirement, as to pay money due or finish a contest or game. [ME *defaulte*] —**de·fault'** *v.t. & v.i.*

de·feat (di FEET) *v.t.* **1.** overcome in any conflict or competition; beat. **2.** prevent the success of; frustrate. —*n.* **1.** the act or result of defeating; an overthrow; failure. **2.** frustration; bafflement. [ME *defeten* destroy]

de·feat·ism (di FEE tiz əm) *n.* the practice of those who accept defeat as inevitable. —**de·feat'ist** *n. & adj.*

def·e·cate (DEF i KAYT) *v.* **·cat·ed, ·cat·ing** *v.i.* **1.** eliminate wastes from the bowels. —*v.t.* **2.** refine; purify. [< L *defaecatus* cleansed] —**def'e·ca'tion** *n.*

de·fect (DEE fekt) *n.* **1.** lack of something necessary for perfection or completeness. **2.** a blemish; failing; fault. —*v.i.* (di FEKT) desert. [ME] —**de·fec'tion** *n.*

de·fec·tive (di FEK tiv) *adj.* having a defect; imperfect; faulty. —*n.* one who or that which is imperfect.

de·fend (di FEND) *v.t.* **1.** shield from danger, attack, or injury; protect. **2.** justify or support. **3.** *Law* **a** act in behalf of (an accused). **b** contest (a charge or suit). [ME *defenden* protect]

de·fend·ant (di FEN dənt) *n. Law* one against whom an action is brought. —*adj.* defending.

de·fense (di FENS) *n.* **1.** the act of defending against danger or attack. **2.** anything that serves to defend. **3.** a plea or argument in justification or support of something. **4.** *Law* **a** the defendant's denial of the truth of a complaint. **b** a defendant and the defendant's legal counsel, collectively. **5.** the act or science of protecting oneself or a goal, as in sports. [ME]

de·fen·si·ble (di FEN sə bəl) *adj.* capable of being defended, maintained, or justified.

de·fen·sive (di FEN siv) *adj.* **1.** intended or suitable for defense. **2.** carried on for the purpose of defense. **3.** having an attitude of defense. —*n.* an attitude or position of defense. —**de·fen'sive·ness** *n.*

de·fer¹ (di FUR) *v.t. & v.i.* **·ferred, ·fer·ring** delay or put off to some other time; postpone. [ME *deferren*] —**de·fer'ral** *n.*

de·fer² *v.i.* **·ferred, ·fer·ring** yield to the opinions or decisions of another: with *to.* [ME *deferren*]

def·er·ence (DEF ər əns) *n.* **1.** yielding to the will, opinions, etc. of another. **2.** respectful regard. —**def·er·en·tial** (DEF ə REN shəl) *adj.*

de·ferred (di FURD) *adj.* **1.** postponed. **2.** with benefits or payments held back for a specific time: *deferred* stock. **3.** temporarily exempted from military draft.

de·fi·ance (di FĪ əns) *n.* **1.** bold opposition or resistance. **2.** a challenge. —**de·fi'ant** *adj.*

de·fi·cien·cy (di FISH ən see) *n. pl.* **·cies 1.** the state of being deficient. **2.** a lack; insufficiency.

de·fi·cient (di FISH ənt) *adj.* lacking some essential; incomplete or defective.

def·i·cit (DEF ə sit) *n.* the amount by which an expected or required sum of money falls short. [< L, it lacks]

de·file¹ (di FĪL) *v.t.* **·filed, ·fil·ing 1.** make foul or dirty. **2.** corrupt the purity of; sully or profane. [ME *defilen* violate]

de·file² *v.i.* **·filed, ·fil·ing** march in a line. —*n.* **1.** a long, narrow pass, as between mountains. **2.** a marching in file. [< F *défilé* march]

de·fine (di FĪN) *v.t.* **·fined, ·fin·ing 1.** state the meaning of (a word etc.). **2.** describe the nature or properties of; explain. **3.** determine the boundary or extent of. **4.**

bring out the outline of; show clearly. **5.** specify, as the limits of power. —*v.i.* **6.** make a definition. [ME *deffinen*] —**de·fin'a·ble** *adj.*

def·i·nite (DEF ə nit) *adj.* **1.** having precise limits, quantity, etc.: a *definite* sum. **2.** known for certain; positive. **3.** clearly defined; precise. [< L *definitus* limited]

definite article *Gram* see under ARTICLE.

def·i·ni·tion (DEF ə NISH ən) *n.* **1.** the act of stating what a word, set of terms, etc., means. **2.** a statement of the meaning of a word, phrase, etc. **3.** the determining of the outline or limits of anything. **4.** the state of being clearly outlined or determined; distinctness.

de·fin·i·tive (di FIN i tiv) *adj.* **1.** sharply defining or limiting; explicit. **2.** conclusive and unalterable; final. **3.** most nearly accurate and complete: a *definitive* edition of Chaucer.

de·flate (di FLAYT) *v.t. & v.i.* **·flat·ed, ·flat·ing 1.** collapse by letting out air or gas. **2.** reduce in self-esteem. **3.** *Econ.* reduce or restrict (money or spending) so that prices decline. [< L *deflatus* blown off] —**de·fla'tion** *n.*

de·flect (di FLEKT) *v.t. & v.i.* turn aside; swerve. [< L *deflectere* bend down]

de·flec·tion (di FLEK shən) *n.* **1.** the act of deflecting, or the state of being deflected. **2.** the amount of deviation.

de·flow·er (di FLOW ər) *v.t.* **1.** despoil of flowers. **2.** deprive (a woman) of virginity. **3.** violate; rob of beauty, etc. [ME *deflouren*] —**def·lo·ra·tion** (DEF lə RAY shən) *n.*

de·fog (dee FOG) *v.t.* **·fogged, ·fog·ging** remove condensed moisture from, as a windshield.

de·fo·li·ant (dee FOH lee ənt) *n.* a chemical spray that causes growing plants to lose their leaves.

de·fo·li·ate (dee FOH lee AYT) *v.* **·at·ed, ·at·ing** *v.t.* **1.** deprive or strip of leaves. — *v.i.* **2.** lose leaves. [< Med. L *defoliatus* stripped of leaves] —**de·fo'li·a'tion** *n.*

de·form (di FORM) *v.t.* **1.** distort the form of; render misshapen. **2.** mar the beauty or excellence of. —*v.i.* **3.** become deformed. [ME *deformen*]

de·form·a·tion (def ər MAY shən) *n.* **1.** the act of deforming, or the state of being deformed. **2.** a change in form or condition for the worse. **3.** an altered form.

de·form·i·ty (di FOR mi tee) *n. pl.* **·ties 1.** a

deformed condition. **2.** anything deformed. [ME *deformite*]

de·fraud (di FRAWD) *v.t.* take or withhold from by fraud; cheat; swindle. [ME *defrauden* cheat]

de·fray (di FRAY) *v.t.* pay (the costs, expenses, etc.). [< MF *défrayer* pay costs] —**de·fray'al** *n.*

de·frock (di FROK) *v.t.* unfrock.

de·frost (di FRAWST) *v.t.* remove ice or frost from. —**de·frost'er** *n.*

deft (deft) *adj.* neat and skillful in action; adroit. [ME] —**deft'ness** *n.*

de·funct (di FUNGKT) *adj.* dead or inactive. [< L *defunctus* dead]

de·fuse (dee FYOOZ) *v.t.* **1.** remove a fuse from, as a bomb. **2.** remove the danger or potency from, as from a situation or argument.

de·fy (di FĪ) *v.t.* **·fied, ·fy·ing 1.** resist, challenge, or confront openly and boldly. **2.** resist or withstand successfully. [ME *defien*]

de·gen·er·a·cy (di JEN ər ə see) *n.* **1.** the process of degenerating; deterioration. **2.** the state of being degenerate.

de·gen·er·ate (di JEN ə RAYT) *v.i.* **·at·ed, ·at·ing 1.** become worse, or more debased; deteriorate. **2.** revert to a lower or less functional condition. —*adj.* (di JEN ər it) having become worse; degraded. —*n.* **1.** a deteriorated or degraded being. **2.** a morally degraded person. [< L *degeneratus* degenerated] —**de·gen'er·a·tive** *adj.*

de·grade (di GRAYD) *v.t.* **·grad·ed, ·grad·ing 1.** debase or lower in character, quality, etc. **2.** bring into contempt; dishonor. **3.** (di GRAYD) reduce in rank. [ME *degraden*] —**deg·ra·da·tion** (DEG rə DAY shən) *n.*

de·grad·ing (di GRAY ding) *adj.* debasing; humiliating.

de·gree (di GREE) *n.* **1.** one of a succession of steps or stages. **2.** relative extent, amount, or intensity. **3.** relative dignity, rank, or position. **4.** relative condition, manner, or respect. **5.** an academic title conferred by an institution of learning upon completion of a course of study, or as an honorary distinction. **6.** a division or unit of a scale, as of a thermometer. **7.** *Law* measure of culpability: murder in the first *degree.* **8.** *Geom.* one 360th of the circumference of a circle. **9.** *Geog.* a line or point of the earth's surface defined by its angular distance from a standard meridian or the equator. **10.** *Gram.* one of the forms of comparison (positive, comparative, or superlative) of an adjective or adverb. **—by degrees** little by little; gradually. **—to a degree** somewhat. [ME *degre*]

de·hu·man·ize (dee HYOO mə NĪZ) *v.t.* **·ized, ·iz·ing** deprive of human qualities; make mechanical.

de·hu·mid·i·fi·er (DEE hyoo MID ə FĪ ər) *n.* an apparatus that removes moisture from the air. **—de·hu·mid·i·fy** *v.t.* **·fied, ·fy·ing**

de·hy·drate (dee HĪ drayt) *v.t. & v.i.* **·drat·ed, ·drat·ing** lose or cause to lose water; dry out. **—de'hy·dra'tion** *n.*

de·ice (dee ĪS) *v.t.* **·iced, ·ic·ing** free from ice.

de·i·fy (DEE ə FĪ) *v.t.* **·fied, ·fy·ing 1.** make a god of. **2.** regard or worship as a god. **3.** glorify or idealize. [ME *deifien*] **—de'i·fi·ca'tion** *n.*

deign (dayn) *v.t. & v.i.* think it befitting oneself (to do something); condescend. [ME *deinen* judge worthy]

de·ism (DEE iz əm) *n.* belief in the existence of God, based solely on reason and denying the power of revelation. [< F *déisme*] **—de'ist** *n.*

de·i·ty (DEE i tee) *n. pl.* **·ties 1.** a god, goddess, or divine person. **2.** divine nature or status; divinity. **—the Deity** God. [ME *deite*]

de·ject (di JEKT) *v.t.* depress in spirit; dishearten. [ME *dejecten* throw down] **—de·jec'tion** *n.*

de ju·re (di JUUR ee) *Latin* by right; rightfully or legally, lit., by law: distinguished from *de facto*.

de·lay (di LAY) *v.t.* **1.** put off to a future time; postpone. **2.** make late; detain. **—v.i. 3.** linger; procrastinate. **—n. 1.** the act of delaying or state of being delayed. **2.** the amount of time of delay. [ME *delaien*]

de·lec·ta·ble (di LEK tə bəl) *adj.* giving great pleasure; delightful. [ME] **—de·lec'ta·bil'i·ty** *n.*

de·lec·ta·tion (DEE lek TAY shən) *n.* delight; enjoyment.

del·e·gate (DEL i git) *n.* a person sent with authority to represent or act for another or others. [ME] **—v.t.** (DEL i GAYT **·gat·ed, ·gat·ing 1.** send as a representative, with authority to act. **2.** commit or entrust (powers, authority, etc.) to another as an agent.

del·e·ga·tion (DEL i GAY shən) *n.* **1.** the act

of delegating, or the state of being delegated; deputation. **2.** a person or persons appointed to represent others; delegates collectively.

de·lete (di LEET) *v.t.* **·let·ed, ·let·ing** take out (written or printed matter); cancel. [< L *deletus* destroyed] **—de·le'tion** *n.*

del·e·te·ri·ous (DEL i TEER ee əs) *adj.* causing moral or physical injury. [< Gk. *dēlētērios* destructive]

de·lib·er·ate (di LIB ə RAYT) *v.* **·at·ed, ·at·ing** *v.i.* **1.** consider carefully and at length. **2.** take counsel together so as to reach a decision. **—v.t. 3.** consider carefully; weigh. **—adj.** (di LIB ər it) **1.** carefully thought out; intentional. **2.** slow and cautious. **3.** leisurely. [ME]

de·lib·er·a·tion (di LIB ə RAY shən) *n.* **1.** careful and prolonged consideration. **2.** *Often pl.* examination and discussion of the arguments for and against a measure. **3.** slowness and care in decision or action. **—de·lib·er·a·tive** (di LIB ər ə tiv) *adj.*

del·i·ca·cy (DEL i kə see) *n. pl.* **·cies 1.** the quality of being delicate. **2.** frailty or weakness of body. **3.** refinement of feeling. **4.** consideration for the feelings of others. **5.** nicety of touch or execution. **6.** sensitivity in reaction, as of instruments. **7.** need for cautious, tactful treatment: a subject of great *delicacy.* **8.** something choice and dainty, as an item of food.

del·i·cate (DEL i kit) *adj.* **1.** exquisite and fine, as in workmanship. **2.** daintily pleasing, as in taste, aroma, or color. **3.** fragile; frail. **4.** requiring tactful treatment. **5.** gentle or considerate. **6.** sensitive and subtle, as in perception or expression. **7.** refined; fastidious. **8.** sensitively accurate: a *delicate* thermometer. [ME *delicat* pleasing]

del·i·ca·tes·sen (DEL i kə TES ən) *n.* **1.** ready-to-serve foods, as cooked meats, cheeses, etc. **2.** a store that sells such food. [< G, pl. of *Delikatesse* dainty]

de·li·cious (di LISH əs) *adj.* extremely pleasant or enjoyable, esp. to the taste. [ME]

de·light (di LĪT) *n.* **1.** great pleasure; gratification; joy. **2.** that which gives extreme pleasure. **—v.t. & v.i.** give or take great pleasure. [ME *deliten*] **—de·light'ful** *adj.*

de·lin·e·ate (di LIN ee AYT) *v.t.* **·at·ed, ·at·ing 1.** draw in outline. **2.** represent by a drawing. **3.** portray verbally; describe. [< L *delineatus* delineated] **—de·lin'e·a'tion** *n.*

de·lin·quen·cy (di LING kwən see) *n. pl.*
·cies 1. neglect of duty. **2.** a fault; offense.
3. juvenile delinquency.

de·lin·quent (də LING kwənt) *adj.* **1.** neglectful or failing in duty or obligation;
guilty of an offense. **2.** due and unpaid, as
taxes. **—n. 1.** one who fails to perform a
duty or commits a fault. **2.** a juvenile delinquent. [< L *delinquere* fail]

de·lir·i·ous (di LEER ee əs) *adj.* **1.** suffering from or caused by delirium. **2.** wildly
excited.

de·lir·i·um (di LEER ee əm) *n.* **1.** a temporary mental disturbance associated with fever, etc., and marked by excitement,
hallucinations, and incoherence. **2.** wild
emotion or excitement. [< L, frenzy]

delirium tre·mens (TREE mənz) a violent
delirium associated with alcoholism.

de·liv·er (di LIV ər) *v.t.* **1.** hand over; surrender. **2.** carry and distribute: *deliver*
newspapers. **3.** give forth; deal: *deliver* a
blow. **4.** utter. **5.** throw or pitch, as a ball. **6.**
free, as from danger. **7.** assist in the birth of
(offspring). **—v.i. 8.** produce as expected or
promised. **—be delivered of** give birth to.
[ME *delivren* set free] **—de·liv′er·ance**
n.

de·liv·er·y (di LIV ə ree) *n. pl.* **·er·ies 1.** the
act of delivering or distributing something.
2. that which is distributed, as mail. **3.** liberation; release. **4.** transference; a handing
over. **5.** the bringing forth of offspring. **6.**
manner of utterance. **7.** the act or manner
of discharging a ball, a blow, etc.

del·ta (DEL tə) *n.* **1.** the fourth letter in the
Greek alphabet (Δ δ), corresponding to English *d.* **2.** *Geog.* a typically triangular silt
deposit at or in the mouth of a river. [ME
deltha]

de·lude (di LOOD) *v.t.* **·lud·ed, ·lud·ing**
mislead the mind or judgment of; deceive.
[ME *deluden*]

del·uge (DEL yooj) *v.t.* **·uged, ·ug·ing 1.**
flood with water. **2.** overwhelm; destroy.
—n. 1. a great flood or inundation.
2. something that overwhelms or engulfs.
[ME]

de·lu·sion (di LOO zhən) *n.* **1.** the act of
deluding or state of being deluded. **2.** a
false belief, held in spite of evidence to the
contrary. **—de·lu·sive** (di LOO siv), **de·
lu·so·ry** (di LOO sə ree) *adj.*

de·luxe (də LUKS) *adj.* elegant and expensive; of the highest quality. [< F *de luxe*, lit.,
of luxury]

delve (delv) *v.i.* **delved, delv·ing** investigate or research carefully. [ME *delven*]

dem·a·gogue (DEM ə GOG) *n.* one who
leads the populace by appealing to prejudices and emotions. [< Gk. *dēmagogós*
leader of the people] **—dem′a·gog′ic**
(DEM ə GOJ ik) *adj.*

dem·a·gogu·er·y (DEM ə GOG ə ree) *n.*
the spirit, method, or conduct of a demagogue.

dem·a·go·gy (DEM ə GOH jee) *n.* **1.** dema-
goguery. **2.** the rule of a demagogue. **3.**
demagogues collectively.

de·mand (di MAND) *v.t.* **1.** ask for boldly or
preemptorily. **2.** claim as due. **3.** have need
for; require. **—v.i. 4.** make a demand. **—n.**
1. the act of demanding. **2.** that which is
demanded. **3.** a claim or requirement: *demands* on one's time. **4.** *Econ.* the desire to
possess combined with the ability to purchase. **—in demand** desired; sought after.
[ME *demaunden*]

de·mar·cate (di MAHR kayt) *v.t.* **·cat·ed,**
·cat·ing 1. mark the limits of. **2.** differentiate; separate.

de·mar·ca·tion (DEE mahr KAY shən) *n.* **1.**
the fixing or marking of boundaries or
limits. **2.** the limits or boundaries fixed. **3.** a
limiting or separating. [< Sp. *demarcación*
boundary line]

de·mean[1] (di MEEN) *v.t.* behave or conduct (oneself). [ME *demeinen* to conduct]

de·mean[2] *v.t.* lower in dignity or reputation;
debase; degrade.

de·mean·or (di MEEN ər) *n.* the manner in
which one behaves or bears oneself.

de·ment·ed (di MEN tid) *adj.* insane.

de·men·tia (di MEN shə) *n.* loss or impairment of mental powers. [< L, madness]

de·mer·it (di MER it) *n.* **1.** a defect; fault. **2.**
in schools, etc., a mark for failure or misconduct. [ME]

dem·i·god (DEM ee GOD) *n.* **1.** a minor
deity. **2.** a man who is the offspring of a god.
3. a man regarded as godlike.

de·mil·i·ta·rize (dee MIL i tə RIZ) *v.t.*
·rized, ·riz·ing free from military control.

dem·i·mon·daine (DEM ee mon DAYN) *n.*
a woman of the demimonde. [< F]

dem·i·monde (DEM ee MOND) *n.* **1.** the
class of people, esp. courtesans, who have
lost social position because of sexual promiscuity. **2.** any group of doubtful respectability. [< F]

de·mise (di MIZ) *n.* **1.** death. **2.** *Law* a transfer of rights or an estate. [ME *demisse*]

dem·i·tasse (DEM i TAS) *n*. **1.** a small cup in which after-dinner coffee is served. **2.** coffee served in such a cup. [< F, lit., half a cup]

de·mo·bi·lize (dee MOH bə LIZ) *v.t.* **·lized, ·liz·ing** disband (an army or troops). —**de·mo′bi·li·za′tion** *n*.

de·moc·ra·cy (di MOK rə see) *n. pl.* **·cies 1.** a form of government in which political power resides in all the people and is exercised by them directly or is given to elected representatives. **2.** a state so governed. **3.** the spirit or practice of political, legal, or social equality. [< MF *démocratie*]

dem·o·crat (DEM ə KRAT) *n*. **1.** one who favors a democracy. **2.** one who believes in political and social equality. **3.** *cap*. a member of the Democratic Party.

dem·o·crat·ic (DEM ə KRAT ik) *adj*. **1.** characterized by the principles of democracy. **2.** existing or provided for the benefit or enjoyment of all. **3.** practicing social equality. **4.** *cap*. pertaining to or belonging to the Democratic Party.

Democratic Party one of the two major political parties in the United States.

de·moc·ra·tize (di MOK rə TIZ) *v.t. & v.i.* **·tized, ·tiz·ing** make or become democratic. —**de·moc′ra·ti·za′tion** *n*.

de·mog·ra·phy (di MOG rə fee) *n*. the study of vital and social statistics, as of births, deaths, etc. —**de·mog′ra·pher** *n*. —**dem·o·graph·ic** (DEM ə GRAF ik) *adj*.

de·mol·ish (di MOL ish) *v.t.* **1.** tear down, as a building. **2.** destroy utterly; ruin. [< MF *démolire* destroy]

dem·o·li·tion (DEM ə LISH ən) *n*. **1.** the act or result of demolishing; destruction. **2.** *pl*. explosives.

demolition derby a contest in which drivers try to eliminate competing cars by crashing into them.

de·mon (DEE mən) *n*. **1.** an evil spirit; devil. **2.** a very wicked or cruel person. **3.** a person of great skill or zeal. [ME]

de·mon·ic (di MON ik) *adj*. **1.** of or like a demon. **2.** inspired, as by a demon.

de·mon·ism (DEE mə NIZ əm) *n*. **1.** belief in demons. **2.** worship of demons. **3.** demonology.

de·mon·ol·o·gy (DEE mə NOL ə jee) *n*. the study of demons or of belief in demons. —**de′mon·ol′o·gist** *n*.

de·mon·stra·ble (di MON strə bəl) *adj*. capable of being proved.

dem·on·strate (DEM ən STRAYT) *v*. **·strat·ed, ·strat·ing** *v.t.* **1.** explain or describe, as by use of examples. **2.** prove or show by reasoning. **3.** show feelings clearly. —*v.i.* **4.** take part in a public demonstration. [< L *demonstratus* shown]

dem·on·stra·tion (DEM ən STRAY shən) *n*. **1.** the act of making known or evident. **2.** undeniable proof or evidence. **3.** an explanation or showing of how something works, as a product. **4.** a show or expression. **5.** a display of public feeling, as a mass meeting or parade.

de·mon·stra·tive (di MON strə tiv) *adj*. **1.** serving to demonstrate or point out. **2.** convincing and conclusive. **3.** inclined to strong expression, esp. of emotions.

demonstrative pronoun *Gram*. a pronoun that indicates the person or thing referred to, as *this, those*.

de·mor·al·ize (di MOR ə LIZ) *v.t.* **·ized, ·iz·ing 1.** corrupt or deprave. **2.** lower the morale of. **3.** throw into disorder. —**de·mor′al·i·za′tion** *n*.

de·mote (di MOHT) *v.t.* **·mot·ed, ·mot·ing** lower in grade or rank. —**de·mo′tion** *n*.

de·mur (di MUR) *v.i.* **·murred, ·mur·ring 1.** offer objections; take exception. **2.** *Law* interpose a demurrer. [ME *demuren* linger]

de·mure (di MYUUR) *adj*. **·mur·er, ·mur·est 1.** grave; reserved. **2.** prim; coy. [ME *demeure* well-mannered]

de·mur·rer (di MUR ər) *n*. **1.** *Law* a pleading that allows the truth of the facts stated by the opposite party, but denies that they are sufficient to constitute a good cause of action or defense in law. **2.** any objection or exception taken. **3.** one who demurs.

den (den) *n*. **1.** the cave of a wild animal; a lair. **2.** a hiding place or dwelling: *den* of thieves. **3.** a small, private room for relaxation or study. [ME]

de·na·ture (dee NAY chər) *v.t.* **·tured, ·tur·ing 1.** change the nature of. **2.** adulterate (alcohol, fat, etc.) so as to make unfit for drinking or eating without destroying other useful properties.

de·ni·a·ble (di NĪ ə bəl) *adj*. that can be denied.

de·ni·al (di NĪ əl) *n*. **1.** a contradiction, as of a statement. **2.** a disowning or disavowal. **3.** refusal to grant, give, or allow.

de·ni·er (di NĪ ər) *n*. one who makes denial.

den·im (DEN əm) *n*. **1.** a strong, twilled

cotton used for sportswear, etc. 2. *pl.* garments made of this material. [< F *(serge) de Nimes* (serge) of Nimes]

den•i•zen (DEN ə zən) *n.* 1. an inhabitant. 2. a person, animal, or thing at home or naturalized in a region or condition not native to it. [ME *denisein*]

de•nom•i•na•tion (di NOM ə NAY shən) *n.* 1. the act of naming or calling by name. 2. a name. 3. any specifically named class or group of things or people. 4. a religious group; a sect.

de•nom•i•na•tion•al (di NOM ə NAY shə nl) *adj.* of, pertaining to, or supported by a religious denomination or sect; sectarian.

de•nom•i•na•tor (di NOM ə NAY tər) *n. Math.* the term below the line in a fraction indicating the number of equal parts into which the unit is divided.

de•no•ta•tion (DEE noh TAY shən) *n.* 1. the specific meaning of a word. 2. the act of denoting.

de•note (di NOHT) *v.t.* •not•ed, •not•ing 1. point out or make known; mark. 2. signify; indicate. 3. designate; mean: said of words, symbols, etc. [< MF *dénoter* mark out] —**de•no•ta•tive** (DEE noh TAY tiv) *adj.*

de•nounce (di NOWNS) *v.t.* •nounced, •nounc•ing 1. attack or condemn openly. 2. inform against; accuse. 3. give formal notice of the termination of (a treaty, etc.). [ME *denouncen*]

dense (dens) *adj.* dens•er, dens•est 1. compact; thick; close. 2. hard to penetrate. 3. stupid. [< L *densus* thick]

den•si•ty (DEN si tee) *n. pl.* •ties 1. the state or quality of being dense. 2. *Sociol.* the number of specified units, as persons, families, or dwellings, per unit of area. [< L *densitas* thickness]

dent (dent) *n.* a small depression made by striking or pressing. —*v.t.* 1. make a dent in. —*v.i.* 2. become dented. [ME *dente*]

den•tal (DEN tl) *adj.* 1. of or pertaining to the teeth. 2. of or pertaining to dentistry. [< Med.L *dentalis* of a tooth]

den•tine (DEN teen) *n. Anat.* the hard, calcified substance forming the body of a tooth.

den•tist (DEN tist) *n.* one who practices dentistry.

den•tist•ry (DEN tə stree) *n.* 1. the branch of medicine concerned with the health and care of the teeth. 2. the work or profession of a dentist.

den•ti•tion (den TISH ən) *n.* 1. the teething process. 2. the kind, number, and arrangement of teeth in man and other animals.

den•ture (DEN chər) *n.* 1. a set of teeth. 2. a set of artificial teeth.

de•nude (di NOOD) *v.t.* •nud•ed, •nud•ing 1. strip the covering from; make naked. 2. *Geol.* expose by erosion. [< L *denudare* strip] —**den•u•da•tion** (DEN yuu DAY shən) *n.*

de•nun•ci•ate (di NUN see AYT) *v.t. & v.i.* •at•ed, •at•ing denounce. [< L *denuntiatus* announced] —**de•nun′ci•a•to′ry** (di NUN see ə TOR ee) *adj.*

de•nun•ci•a•tion (di NUN see AY shən) *n.* 1. open disapproval or condemnation. 2. an accusation. 3. formal notice that a treaty is to be terminated.

de•ny (di NI) *v.t.* •nied, •ny•ing 1. declare to be untrue; contradict. 2. refuse to believe, as a doctrine. 3. refuse to give or grant; withhold. 4. refuse to acknowledge; disown. [ME *denien*]

de•o•dor•ant (dee OH dər ənt) *adj.* destroying or disguising bad odors. —**de•o′ dor•ant** *n.* —**de•o•dor•ize** (-də RIZ) *v.t.* •ized, •iz•ing —**de•o′dor•iz′er** *n.*

de•ox•y•ri•bo•nu•cle•ic acid (dee OK see RI boh noo KLEE ik) *Biochem.* an acid forming the principal constituent of the genes and known to play an important role in the genetic action of the chromosomes. Abbr. *DNA.*

de•part (di PAHRT) *v.i.* 1. go away; leave. 2. deviate: *depart* from tradition. 3. die. [ME *departen*]

de•part•ed (di PAHR tid) *adj.* 1. gone; past. 2. dead. —**the departed** the dead person, or the dead collectively.

de•part•ment (di PAHRT mənt) *n.* a distinct part, division, or administrative unit of something, as of a business, college, or government. [< F *département*] —**de•part•men•tal** (di pahrt MEN tl) *adj.* —**de•part•men•tal•ize** (di pahrt MEN tl IZ) *v.t. & v.i.* •ized, •iz•ing divide into departments.

de•par•ture (di PAHR chər) *n.* 1. the act of going away. 2. deviation, as from an accepted method.

de•pend (di PEND) *v.i.* 1. rely; trust; with *on* or *upon.* 2. be contingent: with *on* or *upon.* 3. hang down. [ME *dependen*]

de•pend•a•ble (di PEN də bəl) *adj.* reliable; trustworthy.

de•pen•dence (di PEN dəns) *n.* 1. the state

of relying on something or someone. **2.** tel-iance or trust. **3.** contingency. **4.** an addiction.

de•pen•den•cy (di PEN dən see) *n. pl.* •cies **1.** dependence. **2.** a territory or state separate from but subject to another state or country.

de•pen•dent (di PEN dənt) *adj.* **1.** contingent on something else. **2.** subordinate. **3.** relying on someone or something for support. **4.** hanging down. —*n.* one who depends on another.

de•pict (di PIKT) *v.t.* **1.** portray by or as by drawing etc. **2.** portray in words. [< L *depictus* painted] —**de•pic′tion** *n.*

de•plete (di PLEET) *v.t.* •plet•ed, •plet•ing **1.** reduce or lessen, as by use or waste. **2.** empty completely or partially. [< L *depletus* empty] —**de•ple′tion** *n.*

de•plor•a•ble (di PLOR ə bəl) *adj.* **1.** to be deplored; lamentable. **2.** wretched; sad. [< F *déplorable*]

de•plore (di PLOR) *v.t.* •plored, •plor•ing have or show regret or sadness over; lament. [< L *deplorare* complain]

de•ploy (di PLOY) *v.t. & v.i.* place or position (forces etc.) according to a plan. [< F *déployer*] —**de•ploy′ment** *n.*

de•po•nent (di POH nənt) *n. Law* one who gives sworn testimony, especially in writing.

de•port (di PORT) *v.t.* **1.** expel from a country. **2.** behave or conduct (oneself). [< MF *déporter* carry away] —**de•port•ment** (di PORT mənt) *n.* conduct or behavior; demeanor; bearing. —**de•por•ta•tion** (DEE por TAY shən) *n.*

de•pose (di POHZ) *v.* •posed, •pos•ing *v.t.* **1.** deprive of rank or office; oust. **2.** *Law* declare under oath. —*v.i.* **3.** *Law* give testimony under oath. [ME *deposen* put down]

de•pos•it (di POZ it) *v.t.* **1.** set down; put. **2.** put down in a layer, as silt. **3.** entrust (money etc.) for safekeeping, as in a bank. **4.** give as partial payment or security; pledge. —*v.i.* **5.** be collected; become deposited. —*n.* **1.** something entrusted for safekeeping, esp. money placed in a bank. **2.** anything given as partial payment or security. **3.** that which is deposited, as sediment. **4.** *Geol.* a mass of iron, coal, etc. [< L *depositus* laid down] —**de•pos′i•tor** *n.*

de•pos•i•tar•y (di POZ i TER ee) *n. pl.* •tar•ies **1.** one entrusted with anything for safekeeping. **2.** a depository.

dep•o•si•tion (DEP ə ZISH ən) *n.* **1.** the act of deposing, as from an office. **2.** the act of

depositing; also, that which is deposited. **3.** *Law* the written testimony of a witness who is under oath.

de•pos•i•to•ry (di POZ i TOR ee) *n. pl.* •ries **1.** a place where anything is deposited. **2.** a depositary.

de•pot (DEE poh) *n.* **1.** a warehouse or storehouse. **2.** a railroad station. **3.** *Mil.* (DEP oh) **a** an installation that manufactures, procures, stores, or repairs military materiel. **b** an installation for assembling and processing personnel. [< F *dépôt*]

de•prave (di PRAYV) *v.t.* •praved, •prav•ing corrupt; pervert. [ME *depraven* pervert]

de•prav•i•ty (di PRAV i tee) *n. pl.* •ties **1.** the state of being depraved; wickedness. **2.** a depraved act or habit.

dep•re•cate (DEP ri KAYT) *v.t.* •cat•ed, •cat•ing express disapproval or disparagement of. [< L *deprecatus* prayed against] —**dep•re•ca•to•ry** (DEP ri kə TOR ee) *adj.*

de•pre•ci•ate (di PREE shee AYT) *v.* •at•ed, •at•ing *v.t.* **1.** lessen the value or price of. **2.** disparage. —*v.i.* **3.** become less in value, etc. [< LL *depretiatus* undervalued]

dep•re•da•tion (DEP ri DAY shən) *n.* a pillaging or plundering. [< LL *depraedatio* a plundering]

de•press (di PRES) *v.t.* **1.** lower the spirits of; sadden. **2.** lessen in force or energy. **3.** lower in price or value. **4.** press or push down. [ME *depressen* press down]

de•pres•sant (di PRES ənt) *Med. adj.* tending to lessen nervous or functional activity. —*n.* a sedative.

de•pressed (di PREST) *adj.* **1.** sad; dejected. **2.** pressed down; flattened. **3.** lowered even with or below the surface. **4.** reduced in power, amount, value, etc.

de•pres•sion (di PRESH ən) *n.* **1.** the act of depressing, or the state of being depressed. **2.** a low or depressed place or surface. **3.** a severe decline in business, accompanied by unemployment, falling prices, etc. **4.** *Psychiatry* deep dejection characterized by withdrawal, lack of response to stimulation etc.

de•prive (di PRĪV) *v.t.* •prived, •priv•ing **1.** take something away from; divest. **2.** keep from acquiring, using, or enjoying something. [ME *depriven*] —**dep•ri•va•tion** (DEP rə VAY shən)

depth (depth) *n.* **1.** the state or degree of

being deep. **2.** extent or distance downward, inward, or backward. **3.** profundity of thought or feeling. **4.** *Usu. pl.* an extremely remote, deep, or distant part. **5.** *Usu. pl.* an intense state of being or feeling. **6.** richness or intensity of color, sound, etc. **7.** lowness of pitch. [ME *depthe*]

dep·u·ta·tion (DEP yə TAY shən) *n.* **1.** a person or persons acting for another or others; a delegation. **2.** the act of deputing, or the state of being deputed.

de·pute (də PYOOT) *v.t.* **·put·ed, ·put·ing** delegate. [ME *deputen* assign]

dep·u·tize (DEP yə TĪZ) *v.t.* **·tized, ·tiz·ing** appoint as a deputy.

dep·u·ty (DEP yə tee) *n. pl.* **·ties 1.** one appointed to act for another: sheriff's *deputy.* **2.** a member of a legislative assembly in certain countries. [ME *depute*] —*adj.* acting as deputy.

de·range (di RAYNJ) *v.t.* **·ranged, ·rang·ing 1.** disturb, as the working or order of. **2.** unbalance the reason of; render insane. [< F *déranger* disturb] —**de·ranged′** *adj.*

der·by (DUR bee) *n. pl.* **·bies** a stiff felt hat with a curved, narrow brim and round crown.

Der·by (DUR bee) *n.* an annual horse race for three-year-olds run at Louisville, Kentucky: the Kentucky Derby.

der·e·lict (DER ə likt) *adj.* **1.** neglectful of obligation; remiss. **2.** deserted or abandoned. —*n.* **1.** that which is abandoned, as a ship at sea. **2.** a social outcast. [< L *derelictus* abandoned] —**der·e·lic·tion** (DER ə LIK shən) *n.*

de·ride (di RĪD) *v.t.* **·rid·ed, ·rid·ing** ridicule. [< L *deridere* mock]

de ri·gueur (də ri GUR) *French* necessary according to rules or custom.

de·ri·sion (di RIZH ən) *n.* ridicule; mockery. —**de·ri·sive** (di RĪ siv) —**de·ri·so·ry** (di RĪ sə ree) *adj.*

der·i·va·tion (DER ə VAY shən) *n.* **1.** the act of deriving, or the condition of being derived. **2.** that which is derived. **3.** origin or descent.

de·riv·a·tive (di RIV ə tiv) *adj.* **1.** obtained or characterized by derivation. **2.** not original. —*n.* that which is derived.

de·rive (di RĪV) *v.* **·rived, ·riv·ing** *v.t.* **1.** draw or receive, as from a source. **2.** deduce. **3.** trace the source of (a word, etc.). —*v.i.* **4.** originate; proceed. [ME *diriven* flow from]

der·ma·tol·o·gy (DUR mə TOL ə jee) *n.* the branch of medical science that relates to the skin and its diseases. —**der′ma·tol′o·gist** *n.*

der·o·gate (DER ə GAYT) **·gat·ed, ·gat·ing** *v.t. & v.i.* **1.** take or cause to take away; detract: with *from.* **2.** become or cause to become inferior: with *from.* [ME] —**der′o·ga′tion** *n.*

de·rog·a·to·ry (di ROG ə TOR ee) *adj.* belittling; disparaging: also **de·rog′a·tive.**

der·rick (DER ik) *n.* **1.** an apparatus for hoisting and swinging heavy weights, usu. consisting of a tackle at the end of a boom or mast. **2.** the framework over the mouth of an oil well. [after *Derrick,* 17th c. London hangman]

der·rin·ger (DER in jər) *n.* a pistol having a short barrel and a large bore. [after Henry *Deringer,* 19th c. U.S. gunsmith]

der·vish (DUR vish) *n.* a member of any of various Muslim orders, some of whom express their devotion in whirling, howling, etc. [< Turkish]

de·scend (di SEND) *v.i.* **1.** move from a higher to a lower point. **2.** slope downward. **3.** lower oneself; stoop. **4.** be inherited. **5.** *Biol.* be derived by heredity. **6.** arrive or attack in great numbers. —*v.t.* **7.** go down, as stairs. [ME *descenden*]

de·scend·ant (di SEN dənt) *n.* one who is descended lineally from another; offspring.

de·scend·ent (di SEN dənt) *adj.* moving or directed downward.

de·scent (di SENT) *n.* **1.** the act of descending. **2.** a decline or deterioration. **3.** a slope. **4.** ancestral derivation; lineage. [ME]

de·scribe (di SKRĪB) *v.t.* **·scribed, ·scrib·ing 1.** present or depict in words. **2.** draw the figure of; outline. [ME *describen*] —**de·scrib′a·ble** *adj.*

de·scrip·tion (di SKRIP shən) *n.* **1.** the act or technique of describing. **2.** an account that describes. **3.** a drawing or tracing, as of an arc. **4.** sort; variety: birds of that *description.*

de·scrip·tive (di SKRIP tiv) *adj.* characterized by or containing description.

des·e·crate (DES i KRAYT) *v.t.* **·crat·ed, ·crat·ing** treat sacrilegiously; profane. —**des′e·cra′tion** *n.*

de·seg·re·gate (dee SEG ri GAYT) *v.t. & v.i.* **·gat·ed, ·gat·ing** eliminate racial segregation in. —**de′seg·re·ga′tion** *n.*

de·sen·si·tize (dee SEN si TĪZ) *v.t.* **·tized,**

•tiz•ing make less sensitive. **—de•
sen′si•ti•za′tion** n.

des•ert[1] (DEZ ərt) n. **1.** a region greatly
lacking in rainfall, moisture, and vegetation. **2.** any region that is uncultivated and
desolate. —adj. of or like a desert; uninhabited. [ME]

de•sert[2] (di ZURT) v.t. **1.** forsake or abandon. **2.** forsake in violation of one's oath or
orders, as a post. —v.i. **3.** abandon one's
post, duty, etc. [< MF *déserter*] **—de•ser′
tion** n.

de•sert[3] (di ZURT) n. Often pl. that which is
deserved or merited: get one's just *deserts*.
[ME]

de•serve (di ZURV) v.t. & v.i. **•served,
•serv•ing** be worthy of; merit. [ME *de-
serven*] **—de•served** (di ZURVD) adj. —
de•serv′ed•ly (di ZUR vid lee) adv.

de•serv•ing (di ZUR ving) adj. worthy; meritorious: *deserving* of praise.

des•ic•cate (DES i KAYT) v.t. & v.i. **•cat•ed,
•cat•ing** dry thoroughly; dehydrate. [<L
desiccatus dried up]

de•sign (di ZĪN) v.t. **1.** draw or prepare preliminary plans or sketches of. **2.** plan and
make with skill, as a work of art. **3.** form or
make (plans, schemes, etc.); conceive; invent. **4.** intend; purpose. —v.i. **5.** be a designer. **6.** plan; conceive. —n. **1.** the arrangement and coordination of the parts or
details of any object: the *design* of a jet
airplane. **3.** a visual pattern or composition.
4. a plan or project. **5.** an object or purpose.
6. Often pl. a sinister scheme or plot. **7.**
intelligent, purposeful, or discoverable pattern. [ME *designen*]

des•ig•nate (DEZ ig NAYT) v.t. **•nat•ed,
•nat•ing 1.** indicate or specify. **2.** name or
entitle; characterize. **3.** select or appoint for
a specific purpose, duty, etc. —adj. (DEZ ig
nit) designated; selected: ambassador *designate.* [< L *designatus* marked out]

des•ig•na•tion (DEZ ig NAY shən) n. **1.** a
distinctive mark or title. **2.** the act of pointing out something. **3.** appointment or nomination.

de•sign•ing (di ZĪ ning) n. **1.** the act or art of
making designs. **2.** the act of plotting or
scheming. —adj. scheming, plotting, or
contriving.

de•sir•a•ble (di ZĪR ə bəl) adj. worthy of or
exciting desire. **—de•sir′a•bil′i•ty** n.

de•sire (di ZĪR) v.t. **•sired, •sir•ing 1.** wish
or long for; crave. **2.** ask for; request. —n.

1. a longing or craving. **2.** a request or wish.
3. an object desired. **4.** sexual passion; lust.
[ME *desiren* long for] **—de•sir•ous** (di
ZĪR əs) adj.

de•sist (di ZIST) v.i. cease, as from an action.
[ME]

desk (desk) n. **1.** a table or case adapted for
writing or studying. **2.** a department or post
in an organization: the service *desk*, the
copy *desk.* [ME *deske*]

des•o•late (DES ə lit) adj. **1.** destitute of
inhabitants or dwellings; deserted. **2.** made
unfit for habitation. **3.** gloomy; dreary. **4.**
without friends; forlorn. —v.t. (DES ə LAYT
•lat•ed, •lat•ing 1.** deprive of inhabitants.
2. lay waste; devastate. **3.** make sorrowful
or forlorn. [ME]

des•o•la•tion (DES ə LAY shən) n. **1.** the act
of making desolate; a laying waste. **2.** the
condition of being ruined or deserted. **3.**
loneliness. **4.** a desolate region.

de•spair (di SPAIR) v.i. lose or abandon
hope: with *of.* —n. **1.** utter hopelessness.
2. that which causes despair. [ME *des-
peir*]

des•per•ate (DES pər it) adj. **1.** without
care for danger; reckless, as from despair. **2.**
resorted to in desperation. **3.** regarded as
almost hopeless; critical. **4.** extreme; very
great. **—des•per•a•tion** (DES pə RAY
shən) n.

des•pi•ca•ble (DES pi kə bəl) adj. that is to
be despised; contemptible; vile. [< LL *de-
spicabilis*] **—des′pi•ca•bly** adv.

de•spise (di SPĪZ) v.t. **•spised, •spis•ing**
regard as contemptible or worthless. [ME
despisen]

de•spite (di SPĪT) prep. in spite of; notwithstanding. —n. **1.** contemptuous defiance.
2. an act of defiance, malice, or injury. [ME
despit]

de•spoil (di SPOIL) v.t. deprive of possessions; rob. [ME *despoilen*] **—de•spoil′er**
n.

de•spond (di SPOND) v.i. lose spirit, courage, or hope. [< L *despondere* give up] —
de•spon′dent adj.

de•spon•den•cy (di SPON dən see) n. dejection of spirits from loss of hope or courage.

des•pot (DES pət) n. **1.** an absolute monarch; autocrat. **2.** a tyrant; oppressor. [<
Gk. *despotēs* master] **—des•pot•ic** (di
SPOT ik) adj. **—des•pot•ism** (DES pə TIZ
əm) n.

des•sert (di ZURT) n. a serving of fruit, ice

cream, etc., as the last course of a meal. [< F]

des·ti·na·tion (DES ti NAY shən) n. 1. the point or place set for a journey's end, or to which something is directed. 2. the purpose for which anything is created.

des·tine (DES tin) v.t. •tined, •tin·ing 1. design for or appoint to a distinct purpose. 2. determine the future of, as by destiny. [ME *destinen* predetermine] —**des'·tined** adj.

des·ti·ny (DES tə nee) n. pl. •nies 1. the fate to which a person or thing is destined. 2. the predetermined ordering of events. 3. the power that is thought to predetermine the course of events. [ME *destinee*]

des·ti·tute (DES ti TOOT) adj. 1. lacking: with *of*. 2. extremely poor. [ME] —**des'ti·tu'tion** n.

de·stroy (di STROI) v.t. 1. ruin utterly; consume. 2. tear down; demolish. 3. put an end to. 4. kill. 5. make ineffective or useless. [ME *destroyen*]

de·stroy·er (di STROI ər) n. 1. one who or that which destroys. 2. a war vessel, smaller than a cruiser.

de·struct (di STRUKT) n. Aerospace the act of destroying a defective or dangerous missile or rocket after launch. —v.t. & v.i. destroy or be destroyed. —**de·struc'ti·ble** adj.

de·struc·tion (di STRUK shən) n. 1. the act of destroying, or the state of being destroyed; demolition; ruin. 2. that which destroys.

de·struc·tive (di STRUK tiv) adj. 1. causing destruction; ruinous: with *of* or *to*. 2. tending to damage or discredit.

des·ue·tude (DES wi TOOD) n. a condition of disuse. [ME]

des·ul·to·ry (DES əl TOR ee) adj. 1. passing from one thing to another; unmethodical. 2. occurring by chance. [< L *desultorius* one who leaps down] —**des'ul·to'ri·ly** adv.

de·tach (di TACH) v.t. 1. unfasten and separate; disconnect. 2. send off for special duty, as a regiment. [< MF *détacher* untie] —**de·tach'a·ble** adj. —**de·tached** (di TACHT) adj. 1. separated; disconnected. 2. unconcerned; impartial.

de·tach·ment (di TACH mənt) n. 1. the act of detaching or the state of being detached. 2. lack of interest in surroundings or worldly affairs. 3. absence of prejudice or partiality. 4. Mil. a part of a unit separated from its parent organization for duty.

de·tail (di TAYL) n. 1. a separately considered part or item; particular. 2. particulars or items collectively; also, the process of dealing with particulars: go into *detail*. 3. in art, architecture, etc., a minor or secondary part. 4. Mil. (DEE tayl) a small detachment designated for a particular task. —**in detail** item by item. —v.t. 1. report or narrate minutely. 2. Mil. select and send off for a special service, duty, etc. [< F *détail*]

de·tain (di TAYN) v.t. 1. keep from proceeding; stop; delay. 2. hold in custody; confine. [ME *deteynen*]

de·tect (di TEKT) v.t. 1. perceive or find, as an error. 2. expose or uncover, as a crime. [ME] —**de·tect'a·ble** adj.

de·tec·tive (di TEK tiv) n. a person whose work is to investigate crimes. —adj. 1. pertaining to detectives or their work. 2. fitted for or used in detection.

dé·tente (day TAHNT) n. an easing, as of discord between nations. [< F]

de·ten·tion (di TEN shən) n. the act of detaining, or the state of being detained. [ME]

de·ter (di TUR) v.t. •terred, •ter·ring prevent or discourage (someone) from acting by arousing fear, uncertainty, etc. [< L *deterrere* hinder]

de·ter·gent (di TUR jənt) n. a cleansing agent. [< F *détergent*]

de·te·ri·o·rate (di TEER ee ə RAYT) v.t. & v.i. •rat·ed, •rat·ing make or become worse; depreciate. [< LL *deterioratus* made worse] —**de·te'ri·o·ra'tion** n.

de·ter·mi·na·tion (di TUR mə NAY shən) n. 1. the act of reaching a decision; also, the decision reached. 2. firmness in purpose or action; resoluteness. 3. the act of determining or fixing anything; also, the result of this.

de·ter·mi·na·tive (di TUR mə NAY tiv) adj. tending or having power to determine. —n. that which determines.

de·ter·mine (di TUR min) v.t. •mined, •min·ing 1. settle or decide, as an argument. 2. ascertain or fix. 3. cause to reach a decision. 4. fix or give definite form to. 5. set bounds to; limit. [ME *determinen* limit] —**de·ter'mi·na·ble** adj.

de·ter·mined (di TUR mind) adj. resolute; firm. —**de·ter'mined·ly** adv.

de·ter·min·ism (di TUR mə NIZ əm) n. Philos. the doctrine that every event is the inevitable result of previous conditions, and that human beings do not have free will.

de·ter·rence (di TUR əns) *n.* **1.** the act of deterring. **2.** maintenance of superior military power on the belief that it will deter war.

de·ter·rent (di TUR ənt) *adj.* tending or serving to deter. —*n.* something that deters.

de·test (di TEST) *v.t.* dislike with intensity; hate; abhor. [< MF *detester* loathe] — **de·tes·ta·tion** (DEE tes TAY shən) *n.*

det·o·nate (DET n AYT) *v.t. & v.i.* **·nat·ed, ·nat·ing** explode or cause to explode. [< L *detonatus* thundered forth] —**det'o·na'tion** *n.*

de·tour (DEE tuur) *n.* a deviation from a direct route or course of action; esp., a by-road used when a main road is impassable. —*v.t. & v.i.* go or cause to go by a round-about way. [< F *détour*]

de·tox·i·fy (dee TOK si FI) *v.i.* **·fied, ·fy·ing** remove the poison or effect of poison from. —**de·tox'i·fi·ca'tion** *n.*

de·tract (di TRAKT) *v.t. & v.i.* take away (a part); diminish: with *from.* [ME] — **de·trac'tor** *n.*

det·ri·ment (DE trə mənt) *n.* **1.** damage or loss. **2.** something that impairs, injuries, or causes loss. [ME] —**det·ri·men·tal** (DE trə MEN tl) *adj.*

de·tri·tus (di TRĪ təs) *n.* **1.** loose fragments separated from masses of rock by erosion, glacial action, etc. **2.** debris [< F *détritus*]

de trop (də TROH) *French* too much; superfluous.

de·tu·mes·cence (DEE too MES əns) *n.* the act or process of being less swollen, as an organ. [< L *detumescere* cease swelling]

deuce[1] (doos) *n.* **1.** two; esp., a card or side of a die having two spots. **2.** in tennis, a score tied at 40 or at five or more games each. [ME *deus*]

deuce[2] *n.* the devil; bad luck: a mild oath.

Deu·ter·on·o·my (DOO tə RON ə mee) the fifth book of the Old Testament. [< LL *Deuteronomium*]

de·val·ue (dee VAL yoo) *v.t.* **·ued, ·u·ing** reduce the value or worth of. Also **de·val·u·ate** (dee VAL yoo AYT).

dev·as·tate (DEV ə STAYT) *v.t.* **·tat·ed, ·tat·ing 1.** lay waste, as by war, fire, etc. **2.** confound; crush. [< L *devastatus* laid waste] —**dev'as·ta'tion** *n.*

de·vel·op (di VEL əp) *v.t.* **1.** expand or bring out the potentialities, capabilities,

etc., of. **2.** enlarge upon: *develop* an idea. **3.** bring into existence: *develop* patience. **4.** *Photog.* **a** make visible (the hidden image) upon a sensitized plate that has been exposed to the action of light. **b** subject (a plate or film) to a developer. —*v.i.* **5.** increase in capabilities, maturity, etc. **6.** advance to a higher stage; evolve. **7.** be disclosed; as events, a plot, etc. **8.** come into existence; grow. [< MF *développer* wrap up]—**de·vel'op·er** *n.*

de·vel·op·ment (di VEL əp mənt) *n.* **1.** the act of developing. **2.** the state or condition of that which has been developed. **3.** a result or product of developing. **4.** an event or occurrence: a political *development.* — **de·vel'·op·men'tal** *adj.*

de·vi·ant (DEE vee ənt) *adj.* being different, esp. from the norm. —*n.* a deviate. [ME]

de·vi·ate (DEE vee it) *n.* one whose actions and beliefs differ considerably from the standards of society. —*v.i.* (DEE vee AYT) **·at·ed, ·at·ing 1.** turn aside from an appointed course. **2.** differ, as in belief. [< LL *deviatus* turned from the straight path]

de·vi·a·tion (dee vee AY shən) *n.* **1.** the act of deviating, or its result. **2.** *Stat.* the difference between a value in a series of observations and the arithmetic mean of the series.

de·vice (di VĪS) *n.* **1.** something devised or constructed for a specific purpose. **2.** a scheme or plan, esp. a crafty or evil one. **3.** an ornamental design. **4.** an emblem or motto. —**leave (a person) to his or her own devices** allow (someone) to do as he or she wishes. [ME *divis* division]

dev·il (DEV əl) *n.* **1.** *Sometimes cap.* in theology, the ruler of the kingdom of evil; Satan. **2.** any evil spirit; a demon. **3.** a wicked person. **4.** a wretched person. **5.** a person of great energy or daring. —*v.t.* **dev·iled, dev·il·ing 1.** season highly. **2.** annoy or harass. [ME *devel*]

dev·il·ish (DEV ə lish) *adj.* **1.** having the qualities of the devil; diabolical. **2.** excessive. —*adv.* excessively.

dev·il-may-care (DEV əl may KAIR) *adj.* careless; reckless.

dev·il's advocate 1. in the Roman Catholic Church, an official appointed to argue against a candidate for canonization. **2.** one who advocates the opposite side for argument's sake.

dev·il·try (DEV əl tree) *n. pl.* **·tries 1.** wanton mischief. **2.** wickedness or cruelty.

de·vi·ous (DEE vee əs) *adj.* **1.** winding or leading away from the direct course; rambling. **2.** straying from the proper way; erring. **3.** deliberately misleading; deceitful. [< L *devius* erratic]

de·vise (di VĪZ) *v.* **·vised, ·vis·ing** *v.t.* **1.** form in the mind; invent; contrive; plan. **2.** *Law* transmit (real estate) by will. —*v.i.* **3.** form a plan. —*n. Law* **1.** the act of bequeathing lands. **2.** a gift of lands by will. **3.** a will, or clause in a will, conveying real estate. [ME *divisen* design] —**de·vis′er** *n.*

de·vi·see (di vī ZEE) *n. Law* the person to whom a devise is made.

de·vi·sor (di VĪ zər) *n. Law* one who devises property.

de·vi·tal·ize (dee VĪT l Īz) *v.t.* **·ized, ·iz·ing** destroy the vitality of; make weak.

de·void (di VOID) *adj.* not possessing; destitute; empty: with *of.* [ME]

de·volve (di VOLV) *v.t. & v.i.* **·volved, ·volv·ing** pass or cause (authority, duty, etc.) to pass to a successor: with *on, upon,* or *to.* [ME *devolven*] —**dev·o·lu·tion** (DEV ə LOO shən) *n.*

de·vote (di VOHT) *v.t.* **·vot·ed, ·vot·ing 1.** apply (attention, time, or oneself) completely to some activity, purpose, etc. **2.** dedicate. [< L *devotus* vowed]

de·vot·ed (di VOH tid) *adj.* **1.** feeling or showing devotion; devout. **2.** set apart, as by a vow; consecrated. —**de·vot′ed·ly** *adv.*

dev·o·tee (DEV ə TEE) *n.* **1.** one who is deeply devoted to anything; an enthusiast. **2.** one who is marked by religious ardor.

de·vo·tion (di VOH shən) *n.* **1.** strong attachment or affection, as to a person or cause. **2.** religious ardor or zeal. **3.** *Usu. pl.* an act of worship or prayer. **4.** the act of devoting, or the state of being devoted.

de·vour (di VOWR) *v.t.* **1.** eat up greedily. **2.** destroy; waste. **3.** take in greedily with the senses or the intellect. **4.** engross. **5.** engulf; absorb. [ME *devouren*]

de·vout (di VOWT) *adj.* **1.** pious. **2.** heartfelt; sincere. **3.** containing or expressing devotion. [ME]

dew (doo) *n.* **1.** moisture condensed from the atmosphere in small drops on cool surfaces. **2.** anything moist, pure, or refreshing, as dew. —*v.t.* wet with or as with dew. [ME] —**dew′y** *adj.* **dew·i·er, dew·i·est**

dew point the temperature at which dew forms or condensation of vapor occurs.

dex·ter·i·ty (dek STER i tee) *n.* **1.** skill in

using the hands or body. **2.** mental adroitness. [< L *dexteritas* readiness]

dex·ter·ous (DEK strəs) *adj.* **1.** possessing dexterity; adroit. **2.** done with dexterity. Also **dex·trous.** [*dexter* right hand]

di·a·be·tes (DĪ ə BEE tis) *n. Pathol.* a disease, **diabetes mel·li·tus** (mə LĪ təs), associated with deficient insulin secretion, leading to excess sugar in the blood and urine. [< NL] —**di·a·bet·ic** (DĪ ə BET ik) *adj. & n.*

di·a·bol·ic (DĪ ə BOL ik) *adj.* **1.** of or pertaining to the devil; satanic. **2.** atrociously wicked or cruel; fiendish. Also **di′a·bol′i·cal.** [ME *diabolik*]

di·a·crit·ic (DĪ ə KRIT ik) *n.* a diacritical mark. —*adj.* diacritical. [< Gk. *diakritikós* distinctive]

di·a·crit·i·cal (DĪ ə KRIT i kəl) *adj.* serving to mark a distinction, as in pronunciation of a letter.

diacritical mark a mark, usu. placed over a letter to indicate its pronunciation, or to distinguish it from another letter: also called *diacritic.*

di·a·dem (DĪ ə DEM) *n.* **1.** a crown or headband worn as a symbol of royalty or honor. **2.** regal power. [ME *diademe*]

di·ag·nose (DĪ əg NOHS) *v.t. & v.i.* **·nosed, ·nos·ing** make a diagnosis.

di·ag·no·sis (DĪ əg NOH sis) *n. pl.* **·ses** (-seez) **1.** *Med.* **a** the act or process of recognizing diseases by their characteristic symptoms. **b** the conclusion arrived at. **2.** any similar examination, summary, and conclusion. [< NL] —**di·ag·nos·tic** (DĪ əg NOS tik) *adj.* —**di·ag·nos·ti·cian** (DĪ əg no STISH ən) *n.*

di·ag·o·nal (dī AG ə nl) *adj.* **1.** having an oblique direction from corner to corner or from side to side. **2.** marked by oblique lines, ridges, etc. —*n.* **1.** *Geom.* a diagonal line or plane. **2.** anything running diagonally. [< L *diagonalis*]

di·a·gram (DĪ ə GRAM) *n.* **1.** an outline, drawing, or plan intended to represent an object or area, show the relation between parts or places, etc. **2.** a graph or chart. —*v.t.* **di·a·gramed, di·a·gram·ing** represent or illustrate by a diagram. [< L *diagramma*] —**di·a·gram·mat·ic** (DĪ ə grə MAT ik) *or* **·i·cal** *adj.*

di·al (DĪ əl) *n.* **1.** any graduated circular plate or face upon which pressure, temperature, time, etc. is indicated by means of a pointer or needle. **2.** a knob on a radio or television set, used to tune in stations. 3. a rotating disk, used to make connections in an automatic telephone system. —v. **di·aled, di·al·ing** v.t. 1. turn to or indicate by means of a dial. 2. call by means of a dial telephone. 3. adjust a radio or television set to (a station, program, etc.). —v.i. 4. use a dial, as in telephoning. [ME]

di·a·lect (DĪ ə LEKT) n. a regional form of a spoken language: Southern *dialect*. [< L *dialectus* language] —**di'a·lec'tal** adj.

di·a·lec·tic (DĪ ə LEK tik) n. Often pl. the art or practice of examining statements logically, as by question and answer, to establish validity. —adj. pertaining to or using dialectic: also **di'a·lec'ti·cal.**

di·a·logue (DĪ ə LAWG) n. 1. a conversation in which two or more take part. 2. the conversation in a play, novel, etc. 3. an exchange of ideas; discussion. —v. •**logued, •logu·ing** v.t. 1. express in dialogue form. —v.i. 2. carry on a dialogue. Also **di'a·log.** [ME]

di·al·y·sis (dī AL ə sis) n. pl. •**ses** (seez) *Chem.* the separating of solutions by means of their unequal diffusion through moist membranes. [< LL]

di·am·e·ter (dī AM ə tər) n. Math. 1. a straight line passing through the center of a circle or sphere and terminating at the circumference or surface. 2. the length of such a line. [ME *diametre*]

di·a·met·ri·cal (DĪ ə ME tri kəl) adj. 1. of, pertaining to, or coinciding with a diameter. 2. directly opposite: *diametrical* motives.

dia·mond (DĪ mənd) n. 1. a mineral of great hardness and refractive power, consisting of crystallized carbon; also, this mineral when used as a gem. 2. a figure bounded by four equal straight lines, having two of the angles acute and two obtuse. 3. a playing card bearing a red, diamond-shaped spot. 4. in baseball, the infield of a baseball field; also, the entire field. —adj. made of or like diamonds. —v.t. adorn with or as with diamonds.

diamond anniversary a 60th or 75th anniversary.

dia·per (DĪ ə pər) n. 1. a folded piece of soft, absorbent fabric placed between the legs and fastened around the waist of a baby. 2. a decorative pattern of repeated figures or designs. —v.t. 1. put a diaper on (a baby). 2. decorate with a repeated figure or similar figures. [ME *diapre*]

di·aph·a·nous (dī AF ə nəs) adj. transpar-

ent; translucent. [< Med.L *diaphanus* transparent]

di·a·phragm (DĪ ə FRAM) n. 1. *Anat.* a muscular wall separating the chest and abdominal cavities in mammals. 2. the thin, vibrating disk of a telephone receiver. 3. *Optics* a disk with an adjustable aperture that can control the amount of light passing through the lens of a camera, telescope, etc. 4. a thin, disk-shaped contraceptive, usu. of rubber, that fits over the uterine cervix. [ME *diafragma*]

di·ar·rhe·a (dī ə REE ə) n. *Pathol.* a disorder of the intestine marked by abnormally frequent and fluid evacuation of the bowels. [< LL *diarrhoea* a flowing through]

di·a·ry (DĪ ə ree) n. pl. •**ries** 1. a record of daily events; esp., a personal journal. 2. a book for keeping such a record. [< L *diarium* daily allowance] —**di'a·rist** n.

di·as·to·le (dī AS tl EE) n. *Physiol.* the usual rhythmic dilatation of the heart, after each contraction. Compare SYSTOLE. [< Gk. *diastolé* dilation] —**di·as·tol·ic** (DĪ ə STOL ik) adj.

di·a·ther·my (DĪ ə THUR mee) n. *Med.* the generation of heat in the body tissues by use of high-frequency electric currents. [< G. *Diathermie*]

di·a·ton·ic (DĪ ə TON ik) adj. *Music* pertaining to a major or minor scale of eight tones without the chromatic intervals. [< LL *diatonicus*]

di·a·tribe (DĪ ə TRĪB) n. a bitter or malicious criticism or denunciation. [< L *diatriba* pastime]

dice (dīs) n. pl. of **die** 1. small cubes having the sides marked with spots from one to six. 2. a game of chance played with such cubes. —v. **diced, dic·ing** v.t. 1. cut into small cubes. —v.i. 2. play at dice. [ME *dees*] — **dic'er** n.

dic·ey (DĪ see) adj. *Informal* involving high risk.

di·chot·o·my (dī KOT ə mee) n. pl. •**mies** 1. division into two parts. 2. *Logic* the division of a class into two mutually exclusive or opposing subclasses. [< Gk. *dichotomía*] —**di·chot'o·mous** adj.

dick·er (DIK ər) v.i. work toward a deal; bargain; haggle.

dic·tate (DIK tayt) v.t. & v.i. •**tat·ed, •tat·ing** 1. utter or read aloud (something) to be recorded. 2. give (orders) authoritatively. —n. an authoritative suggestion, rule, or command: the *dictates* of reason. [< L *dictatus* said]

dic·ta·tion (dik TAY shən) *n.* **1.** the act of dictating material. **2.** that which is dictated.

dic·ta·tor (DIK tay tər) *n.* **1.** a person having absolute powers of government, esp. one considered to be an oppressor. **2.** a person who rules, prescribes, or suggests authoritatively: a *dictator* of fashion. **3.** one who dictates words to be recorded.

dic·ta·to·ri·al (DIK tə TOR ee əl) *adj.* **1.** overbearing. **2.** of or pertaining to a dictator; autocratic.

dic·ta·tor·ship (dik TAY tər SHIP) *n.* **1.** the office or term of office of a dictator. **2.** a state under the rule of a dictator. **3.** supreme or despotic control.

dic·tion (DIK shən) *n.* **1.** the use, choice, and arrangement of words in writing and speaking. **2.** the manner of speaking; enunciation. [ME *diccion*]

dic·tion·ar·y (DIK shə NER ee) *n.* *pl.* **·ar·ies 1.** a reference work containing alphabetically arranged words together with their definitions, pronunciations, etymologies, etc.; a lexicon. **2.** a lexicon whose words are given in one language together with their equivalents in another. **3.** a reference work containing information relating to a special branch of knowledge and arranged alphabetically. [< Med.L *dictionarium*]

dic·tum (DIK təm) *n.* *pl.* **·ta** (-tə) **1.** an authoritative statement; a pronouncement. **2.** a popular saying; maxim. [< L, something said]

did (did) past tense of DO[1].

di·dac·tic (dī DAK tik) *adj.* **1.** intended to instruct. **2.** morally instructive. **3.** overly inclined to teach or moralize; pedantic. [< Gk. *didaktikós* skilled at teaching]

di·do (DĪ doh) *n.* *pl.* **·dos** or **·does** *Informal* a caper; antic.

die[1] (dī) *v.i.* **died, dy·ing 1.** suffer death; expire. **2.** suffer the pains of death: The coward *dies* many times. **3.** pass gradually: with *away*, *down*, or *out*. **4.** become extinct: often with *out*. **5.** desire exceedingly: with *to* or *for*. **6.** stop functioning, as an engine. **—die off** be removed one after another by death. [ME *dien*]

die[2] *n.* *pl.* **dies** for def. 1; **dice** for def. 2. **1.** *Mech.* a hard metal device for stamping, shaping, or cutting out some object. **2.** a small marked cube. See DICE. **—the die is cast** the choice or course of action is irrevocable. [ME *de*]

die-hard (DĪ HAHRD) *n.* one who obstinately refuses to modify his or her views; esp., a political conservative.

di·er·e·sis (dī ER ə sis) *n.* *pl.* **·ses** (-SEEZ) two dots placed over the second of two adjacent vowels to indicate that they are to be pronounced separately, as in *Noël*. Also spelled *diaeresis*. [< LL *diaeresis* division]

die·sel engine (DEE zəl) an internal-combustion engine in which fuel oil is sprayed directly into the cylinder, where it is ignited by the high temperature of the air held within the cylinder at a constant pressure. Also **Diesel engine.** [after Rudolf *Diesel*, 1858–1913, German inventor]

di·et[1] (DĪ it) *n.* **1.** a regulated course of food and drink, esp. one prescribed for reasons of health. **2.** the daily fare. **3.** food, as regards its nutritive value. **—v.i.** take food and drink according to a regimen. [ME *diete*]

di·et[2] *n.* a legislative assembly: the Japanese *diet*. [ME]

di·e·tar·y (DĪ ə TER ee) *adj.* pertaining to diet.

di·e·tet·ic (DĪ ə TET ik) *adj.* relating to diet or the regulation of diet. **—di·e·tet'ics** *n.* (construed as sing.) the branch of hygiene that treats of diet and dieting. **—di·e·ti·tian** (DĪ i TISH ən) or **di'e·ti'cian** *n.*

dif·fer (DIF ər) *v.i.* **1.** be unlike in quality, degree, etc.: often with *from*. **2.** disagree: often with *with*. **3.** quarrel. [ME *differren*]

dif·fer·ence (DIF ər əns) *n.* **1.** the state, quality, or degree of being unlike or different. **2.** a specific instance of such unlikeness. **3.** a distinguishing characteristic or peculiarity. **4.** a disagreement or controversy; dispute. **5.** a discrimination. **6.** *Math.* the amount by which one quantity differs from another. **—make a difference** affect or change the case or situation. **—v.t.** **·enced, ·enc·ing** make or mark as different.

dif·fer·ent (DIF ər ənt) *adj.* **1.** marked by a difference; unlike. **2.** not the same; separate; other. **3.** not ordinary; unusual. [ME]

dif·fer·en·tial (DIF ə REN shəl) *adj.* **1.** relating to, indicating, or exhibiting difference. **2.** *Math.* pertaining to or involving differentials or differentiation. **—n.** **1.** the amount, factor, or degree in which things differ. **2.** *Math.* an infinitesimal increment of a quantity: symbol *d*.

dif·fer·en·ti·ate (DIF ər EN shee AYT) *v.* **·at·ed, ·at·ing** *v.t.* **1.** constitute the difference between. **2.** perceive and indicate the differences in or between. **3.** *Biol.* develop differences in, as a species. —*v.i.* **4.** acquire a distinct character; become specialized. **5.** discriminate. [< L *differentiatus* distinguished]

dif·fi·cult (DIF i KULT) *adj.* **1.** hard to do, accomplish, or deal with. **2.** not easy to understand; perplexing. **3.** hard to please, persuade, etc.

dif·fi·cul·ty (DIF i KUL tee) *n. pl.* **·ties 1.** the state, fact, or quality of being difficult. **2.** that which is difficult to do, overcome, or understand. **3.** a dispute. **4.** a trouble; worry. [ME *difficulte*]

dif·fi·dent (DIF ə dənt) *adj.* lacking confidence in oneself; timid. [ME] —**dif'fi·dence** *n.*

dif·fract (di FRAKT) *v.t.* **1.** separate into parts. **2.** subject to diffraction.

dif·frac·tion (di FRAK shən) *n. Physics* **1.** a deflection of light rays by an obstacle or when passing near the edges of an opening or through a minute hole. **2.** an analogous modification of other kinds of wave motion, as of sound, electricity, X-rays, etc. [< NL, a breaking up]

dif·fuse (di FYOOZ) *v.t. & v.i.* **·fused, ·fus·ing** pour or send out so as to spread in all directions. —*adj.* (di FYOOS) **1.** wordy or verbose. **2.** widely spread out; dispersed. [ME]

dif·fu·sion (di FYOO zhən) *n.* **1.** the act or process of diffusing, or the state of being diffused. **2.** *Physics* **a** the intermingling of molecules of fluids, gases, or solids, dependent on temperature. **b** the scattering of light rays, producing general illumination.

dig (dig) *v.* **dug, dig·ging** *v.t.* **1.** break up, turn up, or remove (earth, etc.). **2.** make or form by or as by digging. **3.** obtain by digging: *dig* clams. **4.** discover by careful effort or study: often with *up* or *out*. **5.** *Slang* understand or like. —*v.i.* **6.** break or turn up earth, etc. **7.** force or make a way by or as by digging. —**dig in 1.** entrench (oneself). **2.** begin to work intensively. **3.** begin eating. —*n.* **1.** a thrust; poke. **2.** a sarcastic remark; slur. **3.** an archeological excavation or its site. [ME *diggen*]

di·gest (di JEST) *v.t.* **1.** *Physiol.* change (food) chemically in the body into material

suitable for assimilation by the body. **2.** take in or assimilate mentally. **3.** arrange in systematic form, usu. by condensing. —*v.i.* **4.** be assimilated, as food. **5.** assimilate food. —*n.* (DĪ jest) a systematically arranged collection or summary of literary, scientific, legal, or other material; a synopsis. [ME *digesten* separate] —**di·gest'i·ble** *adj.*

di·ges·tant (di JES tənt) *n. Med.* any agent that assists digestion.

di·ges·tion (di JES chən) *n.* **1.** *Physiol.* the process or function of digesting. **2.** mental assimilation. [ME *digestioun*]

di·ges·tive (di JES tiv) *adj.* pertaining to or promoting digestion: *digestive* tract. —*n.* a medicine to aid digestion.

dig·gings (DIG ingz) *n.pl.* **1.** a place of excavation; esp., a mining region. **2.** the materials dug out of such a region. **3.** an archeological site.

dig·it (DIJ it) *n.* **1.** a finger or toe. **2.** any one of the ten Arabic numeral symbols, 0 to 9. [ME]

dig·i·tal (DIJ i tl) *adj.* **1.** relating to fingers or toes. **2.** relating to numbers or calculation by numbers. **3.** providing a readout or display in numbers: a *digital* watch. —**dig'i·tal·ly** *adv.*

digital computer a computing machine that receives problems and processes the answers in digital form.

dig·i·tal·is (DIJ i TAL is) *n.* a drug used as a heart stimulant. [< NL]

dig·ni·fied (DIG nə FID) *adj.* characterized by or invested with dignity; stately.

dig·ni·fy (DIG nə FI) *v.t.* **·fied, ·fy·ing 1.** impart or add dignity to. **2.** give a high-sounding name to. [ME *dignifien* make worthy]

dig·ni·tar·y (DIG ni TER ee) *n. pl.* **·tar·ies** one having high official position.

dig·ni·ty (DIG ni tee) *n. pl.* **·ties 1.** stateliness and nobility of manner; gravity. **2.** the state or quality of being excellent, worthy, or honorable. **3.** relative importance or position. **4.** a high rank, title, or office, esp. in the church. [ME *dignite* worthiness]

di·gress (di GRES) *v.i.* turn aside from the main subject in speaking or writing. [< L *digressus* departed] —**di·gres·sion** (di GRESH ən) *n.*

dike (dīk) *n.* an embankment to protect low land from being flooded. —*v.t.* **diked, dik·ing** surround or furnish with a dike. [ME *dik*]

di·lap·i·date (di LAP i DAYT) *v.t. & v.i.*

•**dat•ed**, •**dat•ing** fall or cause to fall into partial ruin or decay. [< Med.L *dilapidatus* squandered]

dil•a•ta•tion (DIL ə TAY shən) *n.* **1.** the process of dilating, or the state of being dilated. **2.** that which is dilated. **3.** *Pathol.* an excessive enlargement of an organ etc. [ME]

di•late (dī LAYT) *v.* •**lat•ed**, •**lat•ing** *v.t.* **1.** make wider or larger. —*v.i.* **2.** become larger or wider. **3.** speak or write diffusely: with *on* or *upon.* [ME *dilaten* spread out] —**di•lat'a•ble** *adj.*

di•la•tion (dī LAY shən) *n.* **1.** dilatation. **2.** *Med.* the expanding of an abnormally small canal or orifice.

dil•a•to•ry (DIL ə TOR ee) *adj.* **1.** given to delay; tardy; slow. **2.** tending to cause delay. [ME] —**dil'a•to'ri•ness** *n.*

di•lem•ma (di LEM ə) *n.* a situation requiring a choice between equally undesirable alternatives. [< LL]

dil•et•tan•te (DIL i TAHNT) *n.* one who interested in a subject superficially or for amusement; a dabbler. [< Ital.] —**dil'et•tant'ism** *n.*

dil•i•gent (DIL i jənt) *adj.* **1.** showing perseverance and application in whatever is undertaken; industrious. **2.** pursued with painstaking effort: *diligent* search. [ME] —**dil'i•gence** *n.*

di•lute (di LOOT) *v.t.* •**lut•ed**, •**lut•ing 1.** make weaker or more fluid by adding a liquid, as water. **2.** reduce the intensity, strength, or purity of. —*adj.* weak; diluted. [< L *dilutus* washed away]

dim (dim) *adj.* **dim•mer**, **dim•mest 1.** obscured or darkened from lack of light. **2.** not clear to the senses; indistinct: a *dim* figure. **3.** not clear to the mind; vague. **4.** pessimistic. —*v.t. & v.i.* **dimmed**, **dim•ming** render or grow dim. [ME]

dime (dīm) *n.* a coin of the United States and Canada, equal to a tenth of a dollar. [ME]

di•men•sion (di MEN shən) *n.* **1.** any measurable extent, as length or thickness. **2.** *Usu. pl.* extent or magnitude: the *dimensions* of the crisis. [ME *dimensioun* a measuring] —**di•men'sion•al** *adj.*

di•min•ish (di MIN ish) *v.t.* **1.** make smaller or less, as in size or degree. **2.** reduce, as in rank or authority. —*v.i.* **3.** dwindle; decrease. [ME] —**dim•i•nu•tion** (DIM ə NOO shən) *n.*

di•min•u•en•do (di MIN yoo EN doh) *Music n. pl.* •**does** a gradual lessening in volume: opposed to *crescendo.* [< Ital.]

di•min•u•tive (di MIN yə tiv) *adj.* **1.** of relatively small size. **2.** *Gram.* expressing diminished size: said of certain suffixes. —*n.* **1.** *Gram.* a word formed from another to express diminished size, familiarity, affection, etc. **2.** anything very small. [ME]

dim•ple (DIM pəl) *n.* a slight depression, esp. one in the cheek or chin. —*v.t. & v.i.* •**pled**, •**pling** mark with or form dimples. [ME *dimpel*]

din (din) *n.* a loud, continuous noise or clamor. —*v.* **dinned**, **din•ning** *v.t.* **1.** urge or press with repetition or insistence. —*v.i.* **2.** make a din. [ME *dine*]

dine (dīn) *v.* **dined**, **din•ing** *v.i.* **1.** eat dinner. **2.** eat; feed: with *on* or *upon.* —*v.t.* **3.** entertain at dinner. [ME *dinen*]

din•er (DĪ nər) *n.* **1.** one who dines. **2.** a railroad dining car. **3.** an inexpensive restaurant.

din•ghy (DING gee) *n. pl.* •**ghies** a small boat, usu. a rowboat. [< Hind. *dīngī*]

din•go (DING goh) *n. pl.* •**goes** the native wild dog of Australia. [native name]

din•gy (DIN jee) *adj.* •**gi•er**, •**gi•est** darkened or discolored, as if soiled; dull. —**din'gi•ness** *n.*

dining car formerly, a railway car in which meals were served en route.

dining room a room in which meals are served.

din•ner (DIN ər) *n.* **1.** the principal meal of the day. **2.** a banquet in honor of a person or event. [ME *diner*]

di•no•saur (DĪ nə SOR) *n. Paleontol.* one of a group of extinct vertebrates of the Mesozoic period, including the largest known land animals, usu. classed as reptiles but considered by some warm-blooded mammals and ancestors of birds. [< NL *Dinosaurus*]

dint (dint) *n.* means; force: win by *dint* of effort. [ME]

di•oc•e•san (dī OS ə sən) *n.* a bishop having jurisdcition over a diocese. [ME]

di•o•cese (DĪ ə sis) *n.* the territory or the churches under a bishop's jurisdiction. [ME *diocise*] —**di•oc•e•san** (dī OS ə sən) *adj.*

di•ode (DĪ ohd) *n. Electronics* a device that permits current to pass in one direction only.

di•oe•cious (dī EE shəs) *adj. Bot.* having the male and female organs borne by different plants. [< NL *Dioecia*]

di•o•ra•ma (DĪ ə RAM ə) *n.* an exhibit consisting of modeled figures, etc., set in a naturalistic foreground. [< F]

di·ox·ide (dī OK sīd) n. *Chem.* an oxide containing two atoms of oxygen to the molecule.

dip (dip) v. **dipped, dip·ping** v.t. **1.** put or let down into a liquid momentarily. **2.** obtain or lift up and out by scooping etc. **3.** lower and then raise, as a flag in salute. **4.** plunge (animals) into a disinfectant. **5.** make (candles) by repeatedly immersing wicks in wax or tallow. —v.i. **6.** plunge into and quickly come out of water or other liquid. **7.** reach into a container, esp. so as to take something out: often figuratively, as *dip* into savings. **8.** sink or go down suddenly. **9.** incline downward; go down; decline. **10.** engage in or read something superficially. —n. **1.** an act of dipping; a brief immersion or plunge. **2.** a liquid sauce etc. into which something is to be dipped. **3.** the quantity of something taken up at a dipping; also, the object used for dipping. **4.** a sloping downward; also, the degree of such a sloping. **5.** a hollow or depression. [ME *dippen*]

diph·the·ri·a (dif THEER ee ə) n. *Pathol.* an acute contagious disease, characterized by the formation of a false membrane in the air passages, fever, and weakness. [< NL]

diph·thong (DIF thawng) n. *Phonet.* a blend of two vowel sounds in one syllable, as *oi* in *coil*. [ME *diptonge*]

di·plo·ma (di PLOH mə) n. a certificate given by a school, college, or university testifying that a student has completed a course of study. [< L]

di·plo·ma·cy (di PLOH mə see) n. pl. **·cies** **1.** the art, science, or practice of conducting negotiations between nations. **2.** skill or tact in dealing with others. —**dip·lo·mat** (DIP lə MAT) n. **dip·lo·mat·ic** (DIP lə MAT ik) adj. [< F *diplomatie*]

diplomatic corps the corps of ambassadors and envoys who are assigned to represent their country in another country.

diplomatic immunity exemption of the members of a diplomatic corps from the ordinary processes of local law.

dip·per (DIP ər) n. **1.** one who dips. **2.** a long-handled cup used to dip liquids. **3.** *Cap.* either of two northern constellations, the Big Dipper or the Little Dipper.

dip·so·ma·ni·a (DIP sə MAY nee ə) n. uncontrollable craving for alcoholic drink. [< NL] —**dip'so·ma'ni·ac** n.

dire (dīr) adj. **dir·er, dir·est** calamitous; dreadful; terrible. [< L *dirus* fearful]

di·rect (di REKT) v.t. **1.** control or conduct the affairs of; manage. **2.** order; command. **3.** *Music* lead as a conductor. **4.** tell (someone) the way. **5.** cause to move in a desired direction: *direct* one's gaze. **6.** indicate the destination of, as a letter. **7.** intend, as remarks, for a certain person; address. **8.** guide or supervise (the performance of a play, film, etc.). —v.i. **9.** give commands or guidance. **10.** act as a director of a play, film, etc. —adj. **1.** having or being the straightest course; shortest. **2.** free from intervening agencies or conditions. **3.** straightforward; candid; plain. **4.** complete; absolute. **5.** in a continuous line of descent. **6.** in the exact words of the speaker or writer: a *direct* quote. —adv. in a direct line or manner; directly. [ME] —**di·rect'ness** n.

direct current *Electr.* a current flowing in one direction.

di·rec·tion (di REK shən) n. **1.** the act of directing. **2.** the course or position of an object or point in relation to another object or point: in the *direction* of Chicago. **3.** *Usu. pl.* instructions about how to do or use something. **4.** an order, command, or regulation. **5.** management, control, or administration. **6.** supervision and organization of a play, film, etc. **7.** tendency or movement. [ME *direccioun*]

di·rec·tion·al (di REK shə nl) adj. **1.** pertaining to direction in space. **2.** *Telecom.* **a** adapted for indicating from which of several directions signals are received. **b** receiving radio waves more effectively from some directions than from others. **3.** indicating direction: *directional* signals.

di·rec·tive (di REK tiv) n. an order or regulation; esp., a governmental or military pronouncement. —adj. acting to direct.

di·rect·ly (di REKT lee) adv. **1.** in a direct line or manner. **2.** without medium, agent, or go-between. **3.** as soon as possible; immediately. [ME *directli*]

direct object see under OBJECT.

di·rec·tor (di REK tər) n. one who directs, as the head member of a corporation, the conductor of an orchestra, etc.

di·rec·tor·ate (di REK tər it) n. **1.** a body of directors. **2.** the office or power of a director.

di·rec·to·ry (di REK tə ree) n. pl. **·ries 1.** an alphabetical or classified list: a telephone *directory*. **2.** a directorate.

dire·ful (DĪR fəl) *adj.* dreadful; terrible.

dirge (durj) *n.* **1.** a song or melody expressing mourning. **2.** a funeral hymn. [ME *dirige*]

dir·i·gi·ble (DIR i jə bəl) *n.* a self-propelled, steerable, lighter-than-air aircraft. [< L *dirigere* direct]

dirt (durt) *n.* **1.** any foul or filthy substance, as mud, dust, excrement, etc. **2.** loose earth or soil. **3.** something contemptible, mean, or of small worth. **4.** obscene speech, pictures, or writing. **5.** gossip. —*adj.* made of earth: a *dirt* road. [ME *drit*]

dirt-cheap (DURT CHEEP) *adj.* very inexpensive. —*adv.* at a very low price.

dirt·y (DUR tee) *adj.* **dirt·i·er, dirt·i·est 1.** soiled with or as with dirt; unclean. **2.** imparting dirt; making filthy. **3.** indecent; obscene. **4.** despicable; mean. **5.** not clear in color. —*v.t. & v.i.* **dirt·ied, dirt·y·ing** make or become dirty. —**dirt'i·ness** *n.*

dis- *prefix* **1.** away from; apart: *disembody.* **2.** the reverse of or the undoing of (what is expressed in the rest of the word): *disconnect.* **3.** deprivation of some quality, power, rank, etc.: *disable.* **4.** not: *disloyal.* Also: *di-* before *b, d, l, m, n, r, s, v,* and usu. before *g,* as in *digress; dif-* before *f,* as in *differ.* [< L]

dis·a·bil·i·ty (DIS ə BIL i tee) *n. pl.* **·ties 1.** that which disables. **2.** legal incapacity to act.

dis·a·ble (dis AY bəl) *v.t.* **·bled, ·bling 1.** incapacitate. **2.** render legally incapable. —**dis·a'ble·ment** *n.*

dis·a·buse (DIS ə BYOOZ) *v.t.* **·bused, ·bus·ing** free from false or mistaken ideas. [< F *désabuser*]

dis·ad·van·tage (DIS əd VAN tij) *n.* **1.** that which produces an unfavorable condition or situation; drawback; handicap. **2.** loss, injury, or detriment. —**at a disadvantage** in an unfavorable condition or situation. —*v.t.* **·taged, ·tag·ing** subject to a disadvantage.

dis·ad·van·taged (DIS əd VAN tijd) *adj.* having less than is needed for decent living.

dis·ad·van·ta·geous (dis AD vən TAY jəs) *adj.* attended with disadvantage; detrimental; inconvenient.

dis·af·fect (DIS ə FEKT) *v.t.* destroy or weaken the affection or loyalty of; alienate; estrange. —**dis'af·fec'tion** *n.*

dis·a·gree (DIS ə GREE) *v.i.* **·greed, ·gree·ing 1.** vary in opinion; differ. **2.** quarrel; argue. **3.** fail to agree or harmonize, as facts. **4.** be unacceptable or harmful: with *with.*

dis·a·gree·a·ble (DIS ə GREE ə bəl) *adj.* **1.** repugnant or offensive; unpleasant. **2.** quarrelsome; bad-tempered.

dis·a·gree·ment (DIS ə GREE mənt) *n.* **1.** failure to agree; difference. **2.** difference in views; dissent. **3.** a quarrel; dispute.

dis·al·low (DIS ə LOW) *v.t.* **1.** refuse to allow. **2.** reject as untrue or invalid.

dis·ap·pear (DIS ə PEER) *v.i.* **1.** pass from sight; fade away; vanish. **2.** cease to exist. —**dis'ap·pear'ance** *n.*

dis·ap·point (DIS ə POINT) *v.t.* **1.** fail to fulfill the expectation, hope, or desire of (a person). **2.** prevent the fulfillment of (a hope or plan). —**dis·ap·point·ed** (DIS ə POIN tid) *adj.* frustrated in expectations or hopes.

dis·ap·point·ment (DIS ə POINT mənt) *n.* **1.** the act of disappointing. **2.** the feeling of being disappointed. **3.** one who or that which disappoints.

dis·ap·pro·ba·tion (DIS ap rə BAY shən) *n.* disapproval.

dis·ap·prove (DIS ə PROOV) *v.* **·proved, ·prov·ing 1.** regard with disfavor or censure. **2.** refuse to approve; reject. —*v.i.* **3.** have or express an unfavorable opinion: often with *of.* —**dis'ap·prov'al** *n.*

dis·arm (dis AHRM) *v.t.* **1.** deprive of weapons. **2.** allay or reduce (suspicion, antagonism, etc.). —*v.i.* **3.** reduce or eliminate one's military forces, equipment, etc. [ME]

dis·ar·ma·ment (dis AHR mə mənt) *n.* the act of disarming; esp., the elimination, reduction, or limitation of armed forces, military equipment, etc.

dis·arm·ing (dis AHR ming) *adj.* tending to overcome suspicion, etc. —**dis·arm'ing·ly** *adv.*

dis·ar·range (DIS ə RAYNJ) *v.t.* **·ranged, ·rang·ing** disturb the arrangement of; disorder.

dis·ar·ray (DIS ə RAY) *n.* **1.** disorder; confusion. **2.** disorder of clothing. —*v.t.* throw into disarray. [ME]

dis·as·sem·ble (DIS ə SEM bəl) *v.t.* **·bled, ·bling** take apart. —**dis'as·sem'bly** *n.*

dis·as·so·ci·ate (DIS ə SOH shee AYT) *v.t.* **·at·ed, ·at·ing** break association with.

dis·as·ter (di ZAS tər) *n.* an event causing great distress or ruin. [< MF *desastre*] —**dis·as·trous** (di ZAS trəs) *adj.*

dis·a·vow (DIS ə VOW) *v.t.* disclaim responsibility for or approval of. —**dis′a‧vow′al** n.

dis‧band (dis BAND) v.t. **1.** break up the organization of; dissolve. —v.i. **2.** become disbanded. [< MF *desbander*]

dis‧bar (dis BAHR) v.t. **•barred, •bar‧ring** expel officially from the legal profession. —**dis‧bar′ment** n.

dis‧be‧lief (DIS bi LEEF) n. lack of belief.

dis‧be‧lieve (DIS bi LEEV) v.t. & v.i. **•lieved, •liev‧ing** refuse to believe. —**dis′be‧liev′er** n.

dis‧burse (dis BURS) v.t. **•bursed, •burs‧ing** pay out; expend. [< MF *desbourser*] —**dis‧burse′ment** n.

disc (disk) n. see DISK.

dis‧card (di SKAHRD) v.t. **1.** cast aside as useless or undesirable; reject. **2.** in card games, throw out (a card or cards) from one's hand; also, play (a card, other than a trump, not of the suit led). —v.i. **3.** in card games, throw out a card or cards. —n. (DIS kahrd) **1.** the act of discarding, or the state of being discarded. **2.** a card or cards discarded. **3.** one who or that which is discarded.

dis‧cern (di SURN) v.t. **1.** perceive, as with the eyes or mind. **2.** recognize as separate and different. —v.i. **3.** distinguish or discriminate something. [ME] —**dis‧cern′i‧ble** adj.

dis‧cern‧ing (di SUR ning) adj. showing insight; discriminating. —**dis‧cern′ment** n.

dis‧charge (dis CHAHRJ) v. **charged, •charg‧ing** v.t. **1.** remove the contents of; unload. **2.** remove by unloading. **3.** emit (fluid). **4.** shoot or fire, as a gun. **5.** dismiss from office or employment. **6.** set at liberty. **7.** relieve of duty or obligation. **8.** perform the duties of (a trust, office, etc.). **9.** pay (a debt) or satisfy (an obligation or duty). **10.** *Electr.* free of an electrical charge. —v.i. **11.** get rid of a load, burden, etc. **12.** go off, as a cannon. **13.** give or send forth contents. —n. **1.** the act of discharging or the state of being discharged. **2.** the firing of a weapon or missile. **3.** an issuing forth; emission. **4.** release or dismissal from service, employment, or custody. **5.** something that discharges, as a certificate separating one from military service. **6.** *Electr.* the flow of electricity between the terminals of a condenser when placed in very near contact. [ME *deschargen*] —**dis‧charge′a‧ble** adj.

dis‧ci‧ple (di SĪ pəl) n. **1.** one who accepts and follows a teacher or a doctrine. **2.** one of the twelve apostles of Jesus Christ. [ME]

dis‧ci‧pli‧nar‧i‧an (DIS ə plə NAIR ee ən) n. one who administers or advocates discipline.

dis‧ci‧pli‧nar‧y (DIS ə plə NER ee) adj. of or relating to discipline; used for discipline.

dis‧ci‧pline (DIS ə plin) n. **1.** training of the mental, moral, and physical powers by instruction, control, and exercise. **2.** the state or condition resulting from such training. **3.** punishment or corrective action for the sake of training. **4.** a system of rules, or method of practice, as of a church. **5.** a branch of knowledge or instruction. —v.t. **•plined, •plin‧ing 1.** train to obedience or subjection. **2.** drill; educate. **3.** punish. [ME]

dis‧claim (dis KLAYM) v.t. **1.** disavow any claim to, or responsibility for. **2.** reject or deny the authority of. —v.i. **3.** *Law* renounce a legal claim. [ME]

dis‧claim‧er (dis KLAY mər) n. **1.** one who disclaims. **2.** a denial.

dis‧close (di SKLOHZ) v.t. **•closed, •clos‧ing 1.** expose to view; uncover. **2.** make known. [ME *disclosen*]

dis‧clo‧sure (di SKLOH zhər) n. **1.** the act or process of disclosing. **2.** that which is disclosed.

dis‧col‧or (dis KUL ər) v.t. **1.** change or destroy the color of; stain. —v.i. **2.** become discolored. [ME *discolouren*] —**dis‧col′or‧a′tion** n.

dis‧com‧bob‧u‧late (DIS kəm BOB yə LAYT) v.t. **•lat‧ed, •lat‧ing** throw into confusion.

dis‧com‧fort (dis KUM fərt) n. **1.** lack of ease or comfort. **2.** that which interferes with comfort. —v.t. make uneasy; distress. [ME *discomforten* discourage]

dis‧com‧pose (DIS kəm POHZ) v.t. **•posed, •pos‧ing 1.** disturb the calm of; make uneasy. **2.** disorder or disarrange. —**dis‧com‧po‧sure** (DIS kəm POH zhər) n.

dis‧con‧cert (DIS kən SURT) v.t. **1.** disturb the composure of; confuse; upset. **2.** frustrate, as a plan. —**dis′con‧cert′ed** adj.

dis‧con‧nect (DIS kə NEKT) v.t. break the connection of or between.

dis‧con‧nect‧ed (DIS kə NEK tid) adj. **1.** not connected; disjointed. **2.** incoherent; rambling.

dis‧con‧so‧late (dis KON sə lit) adj. **1.** inconsolable; dejected. **2.** producing or marked by gloominess; cheerless. [ME]

dis·con·tent (DIS kən TENT) *n.* lack of contentment; dissatisfaction; uneasiness. —**dis'con·tent'ed** *adj.*

dis·con·tin·ue (DIS kən TIN yoo) *v.* •tin·ued, •tin·u·ing *v.t.* 1. break off or cease from; stop. 2. cease using, receiving, etc. —*v.i.* 3. come to an end; cease. —**dis·con·tin·u·ous** (DIS kən TIN yoo əs) *adj.*

dis·con·ti·nu·i·ty (DIS kon tn OO i tee) *n. pl.* •ties 1. lack of continuity. 2. a gap or break.

dis·cord (DIS kord) *n.* 1. lack of agreement; conflict; strife. 2. a harsh or disagreeable mingling of noises; din. 3. *Music* dissonance. [ME *descorde*] —**dis·cor'dant** *adj.*

dis·co·theque (DIS kə TEK) *n.* a night club offering recorded music for dancing and usu. refreshments. [< F *discothèque*, lit., record library]

dis·count (dis KOWNT) *v.t.* 1. deduct (an indicated sum or percent) from the full amount; also, reduce the cost or value of. 2. buy, sell, or lend money on (a bill, note, or other negotiable paper), less the amount of interest to be accumulated before maturity. 3. allow for exaggeration; minimize. —*n.* (DIS kownt) 1. a deduction of a particular sum or percent. 2. the interest deducted beforehand in buying, selling, or lending money on negotiable notes, etc. —**at a discount** below the amount regularly charged.

dis·coun·te·nance (dis KOWN tn əns) *v.t.* •nanced, •nanc·ing 1. disapprove of. 2. embarrass; disconcert.

dis·cour·age (di SKUR ij) *v.t.* •aged, •ag·ing 1. weaken the courage or lessen the confidence of; dishearten. 2. deter or dissuade: with *from.* 3. attempt to repress or prevent by disapproval. [ME *discoragen*]

dis·course (DIS kors) *n.* a formal, extensive, oral or written treatment of a subject. —*v.i.* (dis KORS) •coursed, •cours·ing 1. set forth one's ideas concerning a subject: with *on* or *upon.* 2. converse; confer. [ME *discours*]

dis·cour·te·ous (dis KUR tee əs) *adj.* not courteous; impolite.

dis·cour·te·sy (dis KUR tə see) *n. pl.* •sies 1. lack of courtesy. 2. a discourteous act.

dis·cov·er (di SKUV ər) *v.t.* find out, get knowledge of, or come upon, esp. for the first time. [ME] —**dis·cov'er·er** *n.*

dis·cov·er·y (di SKUV ə ree) *n. pl.* •er·ies

1. the act of discovering. 2. something discovered.

dis·cred·it (dis KRED it) *v.t.* 1. harm the credibility or reputation of. 2. refuse to believe (something asserted). —*n.* 1. the state of being discredited. 2. something that discredits. —**dis·cred'it·a·ble** *adj.*

dis·creet (di SKREET) *adj.* tactful and judicious, esp. in dealing with others. [ME *discret*] —**dis·creet'ly** *adv.*

dis·crep·an·cy (di SKREP ən see) *n. pl.* •cies 1. lack of agreement or consistency. 2. an instance of this. [< L *discrepantia* discordant sound] —**dis·crep'ant** *adj.*

dis·crete (di SKREET) *adj.* 1. distinct or separate. 2. made up of distinct parts. [ME, separated] —**dis·crete'ly** *adv.*

dis·cre·tion (di SKRESH ən) *n.* 1. the quality of being discreet; tactfulness; prudence. 2. freedom or power to make one's own judgments. [ME *discrecioun*]

dis·cre·tion·ar·y (di SKRESH ə NER ee) *adj.* left to or determined by one's discretion: *discretionary* income.

dis·crim·i·nate (di SKRIM ə NAYT) *v.* •nat·ed, •nat·ing *v.i.* 1. act toward someone or something with partiality or prejudice. 2. draw a clear distinction. —*v.t.* 3. draw or constitute a clear distinction between; differentiate. —*adj.* (di SKRIM ə nit) discriminating. [< L *discriminatus* separated] —**dis·crim'i·na'tion** *n.*

dis·crim·i·nat·ing (di SKRIM ə NAY ting) *adj.* 1. able to draw clear distinctions; discerning. 2. fastidious; particular. 3. serving to distinguish; differentiating.

dis·crim·i·na·to·ry (di SKRIM ə nə TOR ee) *adj.* showing prejudice or bias.

dis·cur·sive (di SKUR siv) *adj.* passing quickly or disjointedly from one subject to another; digressive. [< Med.L *discursivus*] —**dis·cur'sive·ness** *n.*

dis·cus (DIS kəs) *n. pl.* **dis·cus·es** or **dis·ci** (DIS ī) 1. a flat, heavy disk, as of metal or wood, hurled for distance in athletic contests. 2. such a contest. [< L]

dis·cuss (di SKUS) *v.t.* talk or write about. [ME] —**dis·cus·sion** (di SKUSH ən) *n.*

dis·dain (dis DAYN) *v.t.* 1. consider unworthy of regard or notice. 2. refuse scornfully. —*n.* scorn; contempt. [ME *disdainen* scorn] —**dis·dain'ful** *adj.*

dis·ease (di ZEEZ) *n.* 1. a condition of ill health or malfunctioning in a living organism. 2. any unwholesome condition. [ME *disese*]

dis·em·bark (DIS em BAHRK) *v.t. & v.i.*
put or go ashore from a ship.

dis·em·bod·y (DIS em BOD ee) *v.t.*
·bod·ied, ·bod·y·ing free from the body
or from physical existence. —
dis′em·bod′i·ment *n.*

dis·en·gage (DIS en GAYJ) *v.t. & v.i.*
·gaged, ·gag·ing free or become free
from entanglement, obligation, occupation, etc.

dis·es·tab·lish (DIS i STAB lish) *v.t.* 1. deprive of fixed or established status or character. 2. take away government support
from (a state church). —**dis′es·tab′lish·
ment** *n.*

dis·fa·vor (dis FAY vər) *n.* 1. lack of favor;
disapproval; dislike. 2. the state of being
frowned upon or disliked.

dis·fig·ure (dis FIG yər) *v.t.* **·ured, ·ur·ing**
mar or destroy the appearance of; deform.

dis·fran·chise (dis FRAN chīz) *v.t.*
·chised, ·chis·ing 1. deprive (a citizen) of
a right, esp. of the right to vote. 2. deprive of
a franchise, privilege, or right. Also *disen-
franchise.*

dis·gorge (dis GORJ) *v.* **·gorged,
·gorg·ing** *v.t.* 1. throw up; vomit. 2. pour
forth; discharge. 3. give up unwillingly. —
v.i. 4. discharge something; empty. [< MF
desgorger]

dis·grace (dis GRAYS) *n.* 1. a condition of
shame or dishonor. 2. anything that brings
about dishonor or shame. 3. a state of being
out of favor. —*v.t.* **·graced, ·grac·ing**
bring reproach or shame upon. [< MF]

dis·grace·ful (dis GRAYS fəl) *adj.* characterized by or causing disgrace; shameful. —
dis·grace′ful·ly *adv.*

dis·grun·tle (dis GRUN tl) *v.t.* **·tled, ·tling**
make dissatisfied; put out of humor.

dis·guise (dis GĪZ) *v.t.* **·guised, ·guis·ing**
1. alter the appearance of so as to make
unrecognizable. 2. conceal the actual nature of. —*n.* 1. the act of disguising or the
state of being disguised. 2. something that
disguises, as a mask or costume. [ME *dis-
guisen*]

dis·gust (dis GUST) *v.t.* cause a deep aversion or loathing in; sicken. —*n.* strong aversion. [< MF *desgouster* disgust]

dish (dish) *n.* 1. an open, concave, usu. shallow container, typically used for holding or
serving food. 2. a particular preparation of
food. 3. a portion of food served in a dish. 4.
a hollow or depression like that in a dish. —
v.t. 1. put (food etc.) into a dish; serve: usu.

with *up* or *out.* 2. hollow out (a surface).
[ME]

dis·ha·bille (DIS ə BEEL) *n.* 1. a state of
being partially or negligently dressed. 2.
the garments worn in this state. Also *de-
shabille.* [< F *déshabillé* undressed]

dis·heart·en (dis HAHR tn) *v.t.* discourage.

di·shev·el (di SHEV əl) *v.t.* **·eled, ·el·ing**
muss up or disarrange (the hair or clothing).
—**di·shev′eled** *adj.* [ME *discheveled*]

dis·hon·est (dis ON ist) *adj.* 1. not honest;
not trustworthy. 2. marked by a lack of honesty; deceitful. [ME *dishoneste*] —
dis·hon′es·ty *n.*

dis·hon·or (dis ON ər) *v.t.* 1. deprive of
honor; disgrace. 2. decline or fail to pay, as a
note. —*n.* 1. lack or loss of honor or of
honorable character. 2. an insult, indignity,
taint, etc. 3. refusal or failure to pay a note,
etc., when due. [ME *dishonour*] —
dis·hon′or·a·ble *adj.*

dis·il·lu·sion (DIS i LOO zhən) *v.t.* free
from illusion; disenchant. —**dis′il·lu′
sion·ment** *n.*

dis·in·cline (DIS in KLĪN) *v.t. & v.i.*
·clined, ·clin·ing make or be unwilling or
averse. —**dis·in·cli·na·tion** (dis IN klə
NAY shən) *n.*

dis·in·fect (DIS in FEKT) *v.t.* cleanse of disease germs; sterilize. —**dis′in·fec′tant** *n.
& adj.*

dis·in·gen·u·ous (DIS in JEN yoo əs) *adj.*
lacking simplicity, frankness, or sincerity;
not straightforward; crafty. —**dis′in·gen′
u·ous·ness** *n.*

dis·in·te·grate (dis IN tə GRAYT) *v.t. & v.i.*
·grat·ed, ·grat·ing break up or become
reduced into parts or particles. —
dis·in′te·gra′tion *n.*

dis·in·ter (DIS in TUR) *v.t.* **·terred,
·ter·ring** 1. remove from a grave; exhume.
2. bring to light; unearth. —**dis′in·ter′
ment** *n.*

dis·in·ter·est (DIS in tər ist) *n.* freedom
from self-seeking and bias; impartiality:
also **dis·in′ter·est·ed·ness.** —**dis·in′
ter·est·ed** *adj.*

dis·joint (dis JOINT) *v.t.* 1. take apart at the
joints; dismember. 2. put out of joint; dislo-
cate. 3. upset or destroy the coherence,
connection, or sequence of. —*v.i.* 4. come
apart at the joints; fall apart.

dis·joint·ed (dis JOIN tid) *adj.* 1. separated;
dismembered. 2. disconnected; out of order; incoherent. —**dis·joint′ed·ness** *n.*

disk (disk) *n.* 1. a fairly flat, circular plate. 2.

Anat. any flat, circular outgrowth, organ, or structure, as of cartilage. **3.** a phonograph record. **4.** a discus. Also spelled *disc.* [< L *discus* discus]

disk jockey a radio announcer and commentator who presents recorded music.

dis·like (dis LĪK) *v.t.* **·liked, ·lik·ing** regard with aversion; feel repugnance for. —*n.* a feeling of repugnance or distaste.

dis·lo·cate (DIS loh KAYT) *v.t.* **·cat·ed, ·cat·ing 1.** put out of proper place or order. **2.** *Med.* displace (a bone) from its normal position. —**dis'lo·ca'tion** *n.*

dis·lodge (dis LOJ) *v.t.* **·lodged, ·lodg·ing** remove or drive out, as from a firm position.

dis·mal (DIZ məl) *adj.* **1.** cheerless and depressing. **2.** devoid of joy. [ME *dismale* unlucky period] —**dis'mal·ly** *adv.*

dis·man·tle (dis MAN tl) *v.t.* **·tled, ·tling 1.** strip of furniture or equipment. **2.** take apart. [< MF *desmanteler*]

dis·may (dis MAY) *v.t.* fill with consternation or apprehension; dishearten and depress. [ME *desmayen*] —*n.* sudden loss of courage; perturbation.

dis·mem·ber (dis MEM bər) *v.t.* **1.** cut off or pull off the limbs or members of; tear asunder. **2.** divide forcibly into pieces; mangle. [ME *dismembren*] —**dis·mem'ber·ment** *n.*

dis·miss (dis MIS) *v.t.* **1.** discharge, as from a job. **2.** tell or allow to go or disperse. **3.** have done with quickly. **4.** *Law* put out of court without further hearing. [ME] —**dis·miss'al** *n.*

dis·mount (dis MOWNT) *v.i.* **1.** get off, as from a horse; alight. —*v.t.* **2.** remove from a setting, support, etc. **3.** disassemble. **4.** knock off, as from a horse; unseat.

dis·o·be·di·ence (DIS ə BEE dee əns) *n.* refusal or failure to obey. —**dis'o·be'di·ent** *adj.*

dis·o·bey (DIS ə BAY) *v.t. & v.i.* refuse or fail to obey.

dis·or·der (dis OR dər) *n.* **1.** lack of order; disarrangement or confusion. **2.** disturbance of proper civic order; riot. **3.** a sickness; ailment. —*v.t.* **1.** put out of order; disarrange. **2.** disturb or upset the normal health or functions of.

dis·or·der·ly (dis OR dər lee) *adj.* **1.** devoid of order; disarranged. **2.** undisciplined and unruly: a *disorderly* mob. **3.** violating public order or decency. —**dis·or'der·li·ness** *n.*

dis·o·ri·ent (dis OR ee ENT) *v.t.* confuse;

esp., cause to lose one's sense of direction, place, or time. [< F *désorienter*] —**dis·o'ri·en·ta'tion** *n.*

dis·own (dis OHN) *v.t.* refuse to acknowledge or to admit responsibility for; repudiate.

dis·par·age (di SPAR ij) *v.t.* **·aged, ·ag·ing 1.** treat or speak of with disrespect; belittle. **2.** bring discredit upon. [ME] —**dis·par'age·ment** *n.*

dis·pa·rate (DIS pər it) *adj.* essentially different. [< L *disparatus* separated] —**dis'pa·rate·ness** *n.*

dis·par·i·ty (di SPAR i tee) *n. pl.* **·ties** lack of similarity or equality, as in age or rank. [< MF *desparite*]

dis·pas·sion·ate (dis PASH ə nit) *adj.* free from passion or bias. —**dis·pas'sion** *n.*

dis·patch (di SPACH) *v.t.* **1.** send off, as a messenger, to a particular destination. **2.** dispose of quickly, as a business matter. **3.** kill summarily. —*n.* **1.** the act of dispatching. **2.** efficient quickness; promptness. **3.** a message, usu. in writing, sent with speed. **4.** a news story sent to a newspaper. [< Ital. *dispacciare* hasten]—**dis·patch'er** *n.*

dis·pel (di SPEL) *v.t.* **·pelled, ·pel·ling** drive away by or as by scattering. [< L *dispellere* drive apart]

dis·pen·sa·ble (di SPEN sə bəl) *adj.* **1.** that can be relinquished or dispensed with. **2.** that can be removed by dispensation.

dis·pen·sa·ry (di SPEN sə ree) *n. pl.* **·ries** a place where medicines or medical advice are given out.

dis·pen·sa·tion (DIS pən SAY shən) *n.* **1.** the act of dispensing; distribution. **2.** that which is distributed. **3.** a specific system of administering. **4.** a special exemption, as from a law or obligation. [ME *dispensacioun* pardon]

dis·pense (di SPENS) *v.t.* **·pensed, ·pens·ing 1.** give or deal out in portions. **2.** compound and give out (medicines). **3.** administer, as laws. **4.** excuse or exempt, as from an obligation, esp. a religious obligation. —**dispense with 1.** get along without. **2.** dispose of. [ME *dispensen* pardon]

dis·perse (di SPURS) *v.* **·persed, ·pers·ing** *v.t.* **1.** cause to scatter in various directions. **2.** drive away; dispel. **3.** spread abroad; diffuse. —*v.i.* **4.** scatter in various directions. [ME *dispersen* scatter] —**dis·per'sal** *n.*

dis·per·sion (di SPUR zhən) *n.* **1.** the act of dispersing, or the state of being dispersed.

2. *Physics* the separation of light into different colors by passing it through a prism. **3.** *Stat.* the arrangement of a series of values around the average of a distribution.

dis·pir·it·ed (di SPIR i tid) *adj.* downhearted; depressed. **—dis·pir′it** *v.t.*

dis·place (dis PLAYS) *v.t.* **·placed, ·plac·ing 1.** remove or shift from the usual or proper place. **2.** take the place of; supplant. **3.** remove from a position or office; discharge.

displaced person someone made homeless by war and forced to live in a foreign country.

dis·place·ment (dis PLAYS mənt) *n.* **1.** the act of displacing, or the state of being displaced. **2.** *Astron.* an apparent change of position, as of a star. **3.** *Physics* the weight of a fluid displaced by a floating body, being equal to the weight of the body.

dis·play (di SPLAY) *v.t.* **1.** make evident or noticeable; reveal. **2.** expose to the sight; exhibit. **3.** make a prominent or ostentatious show of. **—n. 1.** the act of displaying. **2.** that which is displayed. **3.** ostentatious show. [ME *desplayen* unfold]

dis·please (dis PLEEZ) *v.t. & v.i.* **·pleased, ·pleas·ing** cause displeasure or annoyance; offend.

dis·pleas·ure (dis PLEZH ər) *n.* the state of being displeased.

dis·port (di SPORT) *v.t.* **1.** divert or amuse (oneself). **—v.i. 2.** frisk about playfully. [ME *disporten* carry]

dis·pos·a·ble (dis SPOH zə bəl) *adj.* **1.** capable of being disposed of; esp., designed to be discarded after use. **2.** free to be used: *disposable funds.* **—dis·pos′a·ble** *n.*

dis·po·sal (dis SPOH zəl) *n.* **1.** a particular ordering or arrangement; disposition. **2.** a particular way of managing or settling something, as business affairs. **3.** transfer, as by gift or sale. **4.** a getting rid of something. **5.** liberty to deal with or dispose of in any way.

dis·pose (di SPOHZ) *v.t.* **·posed, ·pos·ing 1.** put into a receptive frame of mind for. **2.** make susceptible. **3.** put or set in a particular arrangement or position. **—dispose of 1.** deal with; settle. **2.** transfer to another, as by gift or sale. **3.** throw away. [ME]

dis·posed (di SPOHZD) *adj.* having a particular frame of mind or mood: *disposed* to lie.

dis·po·si·tion (DIS pə ZISH ən) *n.* **1.** one's usual frame of mind; temperament. **2.** a

tendency or inclination. **3.** a particular ordering or distribution, as of troops. **4.** management, as of business affairs. **5.** transfer, as by gift or sale. **6.** a getting rid of something. [ME *disposicioun*]

dis·pos·sess (DIS pə ZES) *v.t.* deprive of possession of something, as a house or land; oust.

dis·proof (dis PROOF) *n.* **1.** the act of disproving. **2.** something that disproves.

dis·pro·por·tion (DIS prə POR shən) *n.* lack of proportion or symmetry. **—dis′pro·por′tion·ate** (-shə nit) *adj.*

dis·prove (dis PROOV) *v.t.* **·proved, ·prov·ing** prove to be false, invalid, or erroneous. [ME]

dis·put·a·ble (di SPYOO tə bəl) *adj.* open to dispute; debatable. **—dis·put′a·bil′i·ty** *n.*

dis·pu·tant (di SPYOOT nt) *n.* one who disputes; a debater.

dis·pu·ta·tion (DIS pyuu TAY shən) *n.* **1.** the act of disputing. **2.** a formal debate. **—dis′pu·ta′tious** (-shəs) *adj.*

dis·pute (di SPYOOT) *v.* **·put·ed, ·put·ing** *v.t.* **1.** argue about. **2.** question the validity, etc., of. **—v.i. 3.** argue. **—n. 1.** a debate. **2.** a quarrel. [ME]

dis·qual·i·fy (dis KWOL ə FI) *v.t.* **·fied, ·fy·ing 1.** make or pronounce unqualified or unfit. **2.** in sports, bar from competition because of rule infractions etc. **—dis·qual′i·fi·ca′tion** *n.*

dis·qui·si·tion (DIS kwə ZISH ən) *n.* a formal treatise or discourse. [< L]

dis·re·gard (DIS ri GAHRD) *v.t.* pay no attention to; ignore. **—n.** lack of notice or due regard.

dis·rep·u·ta·ble (dis REP yə tə bəl) *adj.* not in good repute; not respectable.

dis·re·spect (DIS ri SPEKT) *n.* lack of courtesy or respect. **—dis′re·spect′ful** *adj.*

dis·robe (dis ROHB) *v.t. & v.i.* **·robed, ·rob·ing** undress.

dis·rupt (dis RUPT) *v.t.* **1.** throw into disorder; upset. **2.** halt or impede the movement of, procedure of, etc. [< L *disruptus* broken apart] **—dis·rup′tive** *adj.*

dis·sat·is·fy (di SAT is FI) *v.t.* **·fied, ·fy·ing** fail to satisfy; disappoint; displease. **—dis·sat·is·fac·tion** (DIS sat is FAK shən) *n.*

dis·sect (di SEKT) *v.t.* **1.** cut apart or divide in order to examine the structure. **2.** analyze in detail. [< L *dissectus* cut up] **—dis·sec′tion** *n.*

dis·sem·ble (di SEM bəl) *v.* **·bled, ·bling** *v.t.* **1.** conceal or disguise the actual nature of (intentions etc.). **2.** feign. —*v.i.* **3.** conceal one's true intentions, etc. [ME *dissimulen* pretend] —**dis·sem′bler** *n.*

dis·sem·i·nate (di SEM ə NAYT) *v.t.* **·nat·ed, ·nat·ing** scatter, as if sowing: *disseminate* knowledge. [< L *disseminatus* sown]

dis·sen·sion (di SEN shən) *n.* difference of opinion, esp. arising from anger; discord. [ME *dissensioun*]

dis·sent (di SENT) *v.i.* **1.** differ in thought or opinion: often with *from.* **2.** refuse adherence to an established church. —*n.* **1.** difference of opinion. **2.** refusal to conform to an established church. [ME *dissenten* feel apart] —**dis·sen·tient** (di SEN shənt) *adj. & n.*

dis·ser·ta·tion (DIS ər TAY shən) *n.* an extended formal treatise or discourse; esp., a written treatise required of a doctoral candidate. [< L]

dis·ser·vice (di SUR vis) *n.* injury; a harmful action. —**dis·serve′** *v.t.* **·served, ·serv·ing**

dis·si·dent (DIS i dənt) *adj.* dissenting; differing. —*n.* one who dissents. [< L]

dis·sim·i·lar (di SIM ə lər) *adj.* different. **dis·sim·i·lar·i·ty** (di SIM ə LAR i tee) *n. pl.* **·ties 1.** lack of similarity; difference. **2.** an example of this.

dis·sim·u·late (di SIM yə LAYT) *v.t. & v.i.* **·lat·ed, ·lat·ing** conceal (feelings, etc.) by pretense. [< L *dissimulatus* pretended] —**dis·sim′u·la′tion** *n.*

dis·si·pate (DIS ə PAYT) *v.* **·pat·ed, ·pat·ing** *v.t.* **1.** disperse or drive away; dispel. **2.** squander. —*v.i.* **3.** become dispersed. **4.** engage in excessive or dissolute pleasures. [< L *dissipatus* scattered] —**dis′si·pa′tion** *n.*

dis·so·ci·ate (di SOH shee AYT) *v.t.* **·at·ed, ·at·ing 1.** break the association or connection between. **2.** regard as separate in concept or nature. —**dis·so′ci·a′tion** *n.*

dis·so·lute (DIS ə LOOT) *adj.* not governed by moral restraints. [ME] —**dis′·so·lute· ness** *n.*

dis·so·lu·tion (DIS ə LOO shən) *n.* **1.** separation into parts; disintegration. **2.** the breaking up of a formal or legal union, bond, or tie. **3.** dismissal of a meeting or assembly. **4.** termination or destruction. **5.** end of life; death. [ME *dissolucioun*]

dis·solve (di ZOLV) *v.* **·solved, ·solv·ing** *v.t.* **1.** cause to pass into solution. **2.** overcome, as by emotion. **3.** put an end to: *dis-*

solve a partnership. **4.** dismiss (a meeting or assembly). —*v.i.* **5.** pass into solution. **6.** be overcome: *dissolve* in tears. **7.** come to an end; break up. **8.** in motion pictures and television, change gradually from one scene to another. [ME]

dis·so·nance (DIS ə nəns) *n.* **1.** a discordant mingling of sounds. **2.** harsh disagreement; incongruity. **3.** *Music* a simultaneous combination of tones that seem to clash and require resolution. —**dis′so·nant** (-nənt) *adj.* [< LL *dissonantia*]

dis·suade (di SWAYD) *v.t.* **·suad·ed, ·suad·ing** alter the intentions of (someone) by persuasion or advice: with *from.* [< L *dissuadere*]

dis·tance (DIS təns) *n.* **1.** the extent of spatial separation between things, places, or locations. **2.** the state or fact of being separated from something else in space, time, or condition. **3.** remoteness; esp., reserve or aloofness. **4.** a far-off point or location. [ME]

dis·tant (DIS tənt) *adj.* **1.** far away or apart in space or time. **2.** at, from, or to a distance. **3.** not closely related; remote, as to similarity, kinship, etc. **4.** reserved or unapproachable. [ME *distaunt*] —**dis′tant·ly** *adv.*

dis·taste (dis TAYST) *n.* dislike; aversion.

dis·taste·ful (dis TAYST fəl) *adj.* causing dislike; offensive; disagreeable.

dis·tem·per (dis TEM pər) *n.* **1.** *Vet.* any of several infectious diseases of animals; esp., a virus disease of puppies. **2.** a bad disposition; ill humor.

dis·tend (di STEND) *v.t. & v.i.* expand by or as by pressure from within; swell. [ME] —**dis·ten′si·ble** (-TEN sə bəl) *adj.*

dis·till (di STIL) *v.t. & v.i.* **·tilled, ·till·ing 1.** subject to or undergo distillation. **2.** give forth or let fall in drops. [ME *distillen* drip down] —**dis·til′ler** *n.*

dis·til·late (DIS tl it) *n.* the condensed product separated by distillation. [< L *distillatus* trickled down]

dis·til·la·tion (DIS tl AY shən) *n.* **1.** the act or process of heating a substance, and collecting and condensing the vapors thus formed to purify or separate the substance into its component parts. **2.** the essential or abstract quality of anything.

dis·till·er·y (di STIL ə ree) *n. pl.* **·ler·ies** an establishment for distilling, esp. alcoholic liquors.

dis·tinct (di STINGKT) *adj.* **1.** recognizably

not the same; clearly different. **2.** differentiated by individualizing features. **3.** sharp and clear to the senses or mind. [ME] — **dis·tinc′tive** (-tiv) *adj.*

dis·tinc·tion (di STINGK shən) *n.* **1.** the act of distinguishing; discrimination. **2.** a difference that may be distinguished. **3.** a characteristic difference or distinctive quality. **4.** a mark of honor. **5.** a distinguishing superiority or preeminence.

dis·tin·gué (DIS tang GAY) *adj.* of distinguished appearance or bearing. [< F]

dis·tin·guish (di STING gwish) *v.t.* **1.** indicate the differences of or between. **2.** be an outstanding characteristic of. **3.** bring fame or credit upon. **4.** perceive with the senses. —*v.i.* **5.** make or discern differences: often with *among* or *between.* [ME *distinguen* separate]

dis·tin·guished (di STING gwisht) *adj.* **1.** conspicuous for qualities of excellence; eminent. **2.** dignified in appearance or demeanor.

dis·tort (di STORT) *v.t.* **1.** twist or bend out of shape. **2.** twist the meaning of; misrepresent. **3.** reproduce (sound) improperly. [< L *distortus* distorted] —**dis·tor′tion** *n.*

dis·tract (di STRAKT) *v.t.* **1.** draw or divert (the mind or eye) from something claiming attention. **2.** bewilder; confuse. **3.** make frantic; craze. [ME] —**dis·tract′ed** *adj.* — **dis·trac′tion** *n.*

dis·traught (di STRAWT) *adj.* **1.** worried, tense, and bewildered. **2.** driven insane; crazed. [ME]

dis·tress (di STRES) *v.t.* inflict suffering upon; cause agony or worry to. —*n.* **1.** extreme suffering or its cause. **2.** a state of extreme need. [ME *destresse*] — **dis·tress′ful** *adj.*

dis·trib·ute (di STRIB yoot) *v.t.* **·ut·ed, ·ut·ing** **1.** divide and deal out in shares. **2.** divide and classify; arrange. **3.** scatter or spread out. [ME]

dis·tri·bu·tion (DIS trə BYOO shən) *n.* **1.** the act of distributing or the state of being distributed. **2.** the manner in which something is distributed. **3.** in commerce, the system of distributing goods among consumers. **4.** *Stat.* the frequency of occurrence of the values of a variable. — **dis·trib·u·tive** (di STRIB yə tiv) *adj.*

dis·trib·u·tor (di STRIB yə tər) *n.* **1.** one who or that which distributes or sells merchandise. **2.** in a gasoline engine, a device

that directs the electric current to the spark plugs.

dis·trict (DIS trikt) *n.* **1.** an area, as within a city or state, set off for administrative or judicial purposes. **2.** a region or locality having a distinct character or set apart for a particular purpose: business *district.* —*v.t.* divide into districts. [< F]

dis·trust (dis TRUST) *v.t.* doubt; suspect. —*n.* doubt; suspicion. —**dis·trust′ful** *adj.*

dis·turb (di STURB) *v.t.* **1.** destroy the composure or peace of. **2.** agitate the mind of; trouble. **3.** upset the order or system of. **4.** interrupt; break in on. **5.** inconvenience. [ME *distourben* upset]

dis·tur·bance (di STUR bəns) *n.* **1.** the act of disturbing, or the state of being disturbed. **2.** something that disturbs. **3.** a tumult or commotion; esp., a public disorder.

dis·turbed (di STURBD) *adj.* **1.** characterized by disturbance. **2.** troubled emotionally or mentally; neurotic.

dis·u·nite (DIS yoo NĪT) *v.* **·nit·ed, ·nit·ing** *v.t.* **1.** separate; part. —*v.i.* **2.** come apart.

dis·use (dis YOOS) *n.* the state of not being used; out of use.

ditch (dich) *n.* a long, narrow trench dug in the ground. —*v.t.* **1.** make a ditch in. **2.** surround with a ditch. **3.** *Slang* get rid of. — *v.i.* **4.** make a forced landing on water. [ME *dich*]

dit·to (DIT oh) *n. pl.* **·tos** **1.** the same (as written above or mentioned before), usually symbolized by ditto marks. **2.** a duplicate or copy. —*adv.* as above or before; likewise. —*v.t.* **·toed, ·to·ing** repeat or duplicate. [< Ital. *detto* said]

ditto marks two small marks (″) placed beneath an item to indicate that it is to be repeated.

dit·ty (DIT ee) *n. pl.* **·ties** a short, simple song. [ME *dite*]

di·ur·nal (dī UR nl) *adj.* **1.** of, belonging to, or occurring each day; daily. **2.** of or occurring during the daytime; not nocturnal. [ME] —**di·ur′nal·ly** *adv.*

di·va (DEE və) *n. pl.* **·vas, ·ve** (-ve) a celebrated female operatic singer; a prima donna. [< Ital., lit., goddess]

di·va·lent (dī VAY lənt) *adj. Chem.* bivalent.

dive (dīv) *v.* **dived** or **dove, dived, div·ing** *v.i.* **1.** plunge, esp. headfirst, as into water. **2.** go underwater; submerge. **3.** plunge downward at a sharp angle. **4.** dart away or leap into something. **5.** rush into and

become deeply engrossed in something. —
v.i. **6.** cause to plunge; esp., cause (an airplane) to move swiftly downward at a sharp
angle. —*n.* **1.** a plunge, as into water. **2.** a
sharp, swift descent. **3.** *Informal* a cheap,
disreputable place, as a bar. [ME *diven*
dive]

di·verge (di VURJ) *v.i.* •**verged,** •**verg·ing**
1. move or extend in different directions
from a common point or from each other. **2.**
deviate. **3.** differ. [< Med.L *divergere*] —
di·ver′gence *n.*

di·verse (di VURS) *adj.* **1.** different. **2.** varied; diversified. [ME]

di·ver·si·fy (di VUR sə FĪ) *v.t.* •**fied,** •**fy·ing**
1. make diverse; vary. **2.** make (investments) among different types of securities
so as to minimize risk. [ME] —
di·ver′si·fi·ca′tion *n.*

di·ver·sion (di VUR zhən) *n.* **1.** the act of
diverting. **2.** that which diverts or entertains.

di·ver·si·ty (di VUR si tee) *n. pl.* •**ties 1.**
unlikeness; difference. **2.** variety. [ME *di-
versite*]

di·vert (di VURT) *v.t.* **1.** turn aside, as from a
set course; deflect. **2.** distract the attention
of. **3.** amuse; entertain. [ME]

di·vest (di VEST) *v.t.* **1.** strip, as of clothes.
2. deprive, as of rights or possessions. [<
Med.L *divestire*]

di·vest·i·ture (di VES ti chər) *n.* the act of
divesting, or the state of being divested.

di·vide (di VĪD) *v.* •**vid·ed,** •**vid·ing** *v.t.*
1. separate into pieces or portions, as by
cutting. **2.** distribute the pieces or portions of. **3.** separate into groups; classify.
4. split up into opposed sides; cause dissent in. **5.** cause to be apart. **6.** *Math.*
subject to the process of division. —*v.i.* **7.**
become separated into parts; diverge. **8.**
be at variance. **9.** perform mathematical
division. —*n.* a mountain range separating
one drainage system from another; watershed. [ME]

div·i·dend (DIV i DEND) *n.* **1.** *Math.* a number or quantity to be divided. **2.** a sum of
money to be distributed to stockholders,
etc. **3.** the portion of such a sum given to
each individual. [< L *dividendum* thing to
be divided]

di·vid·er (di VĪ dər) *n.* **1.** one who or that
which divides. **2.** *pl.* a pair of compasses
used for measuring short intervals.

div·i·na·tion (DIV ə NAY shən) *n.* **1.** the act
or art of knowing the future or that which is

hidden or unknown. **2.** a prophecy. [ME
divinacioun]

di·vine (di VĪN) *adj.* **1.** of, from, or pertaining to God or a god. **2.** directed or devoted
to God or a god; sacred. **3.** extraordinarily
perfect. **4.** *Informal* altogether delightful.
—*n.* **1.** a clergyman. **2.** a theologian. —*v.*
•**vined,** •**vin·ing** *v.t.* **1.** foretell or find out
by occult means. **2.** locate (water, etc.) by
means of a divining rod. **3.** surmise by in-
stinct. —*v.i.* **4.** practice divination. **5.**
guess. [ME]

divining rod a forked branch popularly asserted to indicate underground water or
metal: also called *dowsing rod.*

di·vin·i·ty (di VIN i tee) *n. pl.* •**ties 1.** the
state or quality of being divine. **2.** a deity. **3.**
theology. —**the Divinity** God. [ME *divin-
ite*]

di·vis·i·ble (di VIZ ə bəl) *adj.* **1.** capable of
being divided. **2.** *Math.* that can be divided
and leave no remainder.

di·vi·sion (di VIZH ən) *n.* **1.** the act of dividing, or the state of being divided. **2.** one of
the parts into which a thing is divided. **3.**
something that divides or separates. **4.** disagreement; discord. **5.** *Math.* the operation
of finding how many times a number or
quantity is contained in another number or
quantity. **6.** *Mil.* a major unit larger than a
regiment and smaller than a corps. [ME
divisioun]

di·vi·sive (di VĪ siv) *adj.* creating division,
dissension, or strife.

di·vi·sor (di VĪ zər) *n. Math.* a number by
which another number is divided.

di·vorce (di VORS) *n.* **1.** dissolution of a
marriage bond by legal process or by accepted custom. **2.** any radical or complete
separation. —*v.* •**vorced,** •**vorc·ing** *v.t.* **1.**
free oneself from (one's spouse) by divorce.
2. separate. —*v.i.* **3.** get a divorce. [ME]

di·vor·cée (di vor SAY) *n.* a divorced
woman. [< F] —**di·vor′cé′** *n.masc.*

di·vulge (di VULJ) *v.t.* •**vulged,** •**vulg·ing**
tell, as a secret; disclose; reveal. [ME]

Dix·ie·land (DIK see LAND) *n.* a style of
jazz originally played in New Orleans.

diz·zy (DIZ ee) *adj.* •**zi·er,** •**zi·est 1.** having
a feeling of whirling or unsteadiness. **2.**
causing giddiness. **3.** *Informal* silly; stupid.
—*v.t.* •**zied,** •**zy·ing** make giddy; confuse.
[ME *dysy* foolish] —**diz′zi·ly** *adv.* —**diz′
zi·ness** *n.*

DNA *Biochem.* deoxyribonucleic acid.

do¹ (doo) *v.* **did, done, do·ing** *v.t.* **1.** perform, as an action; produce, as a piece of work. **2.** fulfill; complete; accomplish. **3.** cause; bring about: *do* no harm. **4.** put forth: He *did* his best. **5.** render: *do* homage. **6.** work at. **7.** work out; solve. **8.** present (a play etc.). **9.** enact the part of. **10.** cover (a distance); travel. **11.** be sufficient for; suit. **12.** *Informal* serve, as a term in prison. **13.** put in order; attend to. **14.** decorate or arrange. —*v.i.* **15.** exert onself; be active: *do* or die. **16.** conduct oneself. **17.** fare; get along. **18.** serve the purpose; suffice. —**do away with** kill; destroy. —**do by** act toward: Please *do* well *by* us. —**do for 1.** provide for; care for. **2.** ruin; kill. —**do in** *Informal* kill. —**do over 1.** do again. **2.** redecorate. —**do up** wrap or tie up. —**do without** get along without. —**have to do with** be involved with. —**make do** get along with (whatever is available). — *auxiliary* as an auxiliary, *do* is used: **1.** without specific meaning in negative, interrogative, and inverted constructions: I *do* not want it; *Do* you want to leave? **2.** to add force to imperatives: *Do* hurry. **3.** to express emphasis: I *do* believe you. **4.** to substitute for another verb to avoid repetition: I will not hesitate, as some *do.* —*n. pl.* **dos** or **do's 1.** *Informal* festivity; celebration. **2.** *pl.* that which ought to be done: used chiefly in the expression **do's and don'ts.** [ME]

do² (doh) *n. Music* the first tone of the diatonic scale.

doc·ile (DOS əl) *adj.* easy to manage or train. [< L *docilis* easily taught]

dock¹ (dok) *n.* **1.** the water space between two adjoining piers or wharves where ships can remain for loading, repair, etc. **2.** a wharf or pier. **3.** *Often pl.* a group of wharves or piers. **4.** a shipping or loading platform, as for trucks. —*v.t.* **1.** bring (a vessel, truck, etc.) into or next to a dock. —*v.i.* **2.** come into a dock. **3.** of spacecraft, be brought together in orbit and mechanically joined. [< MDu. *docke*]

dock² *n.* **1.** the fleshy part of an animal's tail. **2.** the stump of a clipped tail. —*v.t.* **1.** cut off the end of (a tail etc.), or clip short the tail of. **2.** take a part from (wages etc.), or take from the wages etc. of. [ME *dok* stump]

dock³ *n.* an enclosed space for the defendant in a criminal court.

dock·et (DOK it) *n.* **1.** a written summary. **2.** *Law* **a** a record of court judgments. **b** the book in which such a record is kept. **c** a court calendar of cases pending. **3.** any calendar of things to be done. **4.** a tag or label attached to a parcel, listing contents, directions, etc. —*v.t.* **1.** enter in a docket. **2.** put a tag or label on. [ME *doggette*]

doc·tor (DOK tər) *n.* **1.** a licensed practitioner of medicine or any of certain other healing arts, as a dentist, veterinarian, etc. **2.** a person who has received a diploma of the highest degree, as in literature. —*v.t.* **1.** treat medically. **2.** repair. **3.** falsify or alter, as evidence. [ME *doctour* teacher] —**doc′tor·al** *adj.*

doc·tor·ate (DOK tər it) *n.* the degree of doctor.

doc·tri·naire (DOK trə NAIR) *adj.* **1.** theoretical. **2.** dogmatic. —*n.* an impractical, rigid theorist. [< F]

doc·trine (DOK trə nl) *n.* **1.** teachings, as of a religious group. **2.** a particular principle or tenet that is taught. [ME]

doc·u·ment (DOK yə mənt) *n.* something written or printed that furnishes conclusive information or evidence, as an official paper or record. —*v.t.* support by conclusive information or evidence. [ME]

doc·u·men·ta·ry (DOK yə MEN tə ree) *adj.* **1.** pertaining to, consisting of, or based upon documents. **2.** that presents factual material without fictionalizing. —*n.* *pl.* **·ries** a documentary motion picture or television show.

dod·der (DOD ər) *v.i.* tremble or totter, as from age. [ME *doder*]

dodge (doj) *v.* **dodged, dodg·ing** *v.t.* **1.** avoid, as a blow, by a sudden turn. **2.** evade, as a duty or issue. —*v.i.* **3.** avoid something, esp. by moving suddenly. **4.** practice trickery. —*n.* **1.** an act of dodging. **2.** a trick to deceive.

doe (doh) *n.* the female of the deer, antelope, rabbit, kangaroo, and certain other animals. [ME *do*]

does (duz) present tense, third person singular, of DO¹.

does·n't (DUZ ənt) does not.

doff (dof) *v.t.* **1.** take off, as a hat or clothing. **2.** discard. [ME]

dog (dawg) *n.* **1.** a domesticated, carnivorous mammal of many varieties; esp., the male of any of these. ♦ Collateral adjective: *canine.* **2.** a despicable person. **3.** *Mech.* one of several devices for gripping or holding logs etc. —**go to the dogs** *Informal* go to ruin. —**put on the dog** *Informal* make a pretentious display. —

v.t. **dogged, dog·ging** pursue persistently; hound. [ME *dogge*]

dog days the hot days of July and early August. [after the *Dog Star, Sirius*, which rises and sets with the sun in this period]

doge (dohj) *n.* the elective chief magistrate in the former republics of Venice and Genoa. [< Ital.]

dog·ear (DAWG EER) *n.* a turned-down corner of a book page. —*v.t.* turn down the corner of (a page).

dog·fight (DAWG FIT) *n.* **1.** a fight between or as between dogs. **2.** *Mil.* an aerial battle between planes.

dog·ger·el (DAW gər əl) *n.* trivial, awkwardly written verse, usu. comic. [ME]

dog·house (DAWG HOWS) *n.* a small house for a dog. —**in the doghouse** *Slang* in disfavor with someone.

dog·ma (DAWG mə) *n. pl.* **·mas** a doctrine or system of doctrine, esp. one maintained by a religious body as true and necessary of belief. [< L]

dog·mat·ic (dawg MAT ik) *adj.* marked by authoritative, often arrogant, assertion of opinions or beliefs.

dog·ma·tism (DAWG mə TIZ əm) *n.* positive assertion, as of beliefs.

dog·watch (DAWG WOCH) *n. Naut.* either of two short watches aboard ship, from 4 to 6 or 6 to 8 P.M.

doi·ly (DOI lee) *n. pl.* **·lies** a small, ornamental piece of lace, etc., used to protect surfaces. [after a 17th-c. English merchant]

Dol·by (DOHL bee) *adj.* designating electronic devices that eliminate noise from recorded sound: a trade name.

dol·drums (DOHL drəmz) *n.pl.* **1.** those parts of the ocean near the equator where calms or baffling winds prevail. **2.** a becalmed state. **3.** a depressed or bored condition. [from obs. *dold* stupid]

dole (dohl) *n.* **1.** that which, as food or money, is distributed, esp. in charity. **2.** a giving out of something. **3.** a sum paid to an unemployed person. —**on the dole** receiving relief payments from the government. —*v.t.* **doled, dol·ing** dispense in small quantities; distribute: usually with *out.* [ME *dol*]

dole·ful (DOHL fəl) *adj.* melancholy. [ME *dolful*]

doll (dol) *n.* **1.** a child's toy made to resemble the human figure. **2.** *Slang* a pretty but superficial woman. **3.** a cute child. **4.** *Slang* an attractive or charming person of either sex.

—*v.t. & v.i. Informal* adorn or dress smartly: with *up.*

dol·lar (DOL ər) *n.* **1.** the standard monetary unit of the United States, Canada, and certain other countries, equivalent to 100 cents. **2.** a coin or a piece of paper currently worth one dollar. [< earlier *daler* < G *Taler*]

dol·lop (DOL əp) *n.* a small serving, as of a soft substance or liquid.

dol·ly (DOL ee) *n. pl.* **·lies 1.** a doll: a child's term. **2.** a low, flat frame set on small wheels or rollers, used for moving heavy loads. —*v.i.* **·lied, ·ly·ing** move a motion-picture or television camera toward or away from the action.

dol·men (DOHL mən) *n.* a prehistoric monument made of a large stone set on upright stones. [< F]

do·lor·ous (DOL ər əs) *adj.* sad; mournful. —**do'lor·ous·ly** *adv.*

do·main (doh MAYN) *n.* **1.** a territory under a sovereign or one government. **2.** a field of action, knowledge, etc. **3.** a landed estate. [< F *domaine*]

dome (dohm) *n.* **1.** a roof resembling an inverted cup or hemisphere. **2.** something shaped like this. **3.** *Slang* the head. —*v.t.* **domed, dom·ing 1.** furnish or cover with a dome. **2.** shape like a dome. [< L *domus* house]

domes·day (DOOMZ DAY) *n.* see DOOMS-DAY.

do·mes·tic (də MES tik) *adj.* **1.** of or pertaining to the home or family. **2.** fond of things concerning the home or family. **3.** tame; domesticated. **4.** of, produced in, or pertaining to one's own country. —*n.* a household servant. [< Med.L *domesticus* of the home]

do·mes·ti·cate (də MES ti kayt) *v.t.* **·cat·ed, ·cat·ing 1.** tame. **2.** cause to become home-loving. —**do·mes'ti·ca'tion** *n.*

do·mes·tic·i·ty (DOH me STIS i tee) *n. pl.* **·ties 1.** life at home or with one's family. **2.** devotion to home and family.

dom·i·cile (DOM ə SIL) *n.* **1.** a home, house, or dwelling. **2.** the place of one's legal home. —*v.* **·ciled, ·cil·ing** *v.t.* **1.** establish in a place of abode. —*v.i.* **2.** dwell. [< MF] —**dom·i·cil·i·ar·y** (DOM ə SIL ee ER ee) *adj.*

dom·i·nant (DOM ə nənt) *adj.* **1.** dominating; ruling. **2.** conspicuously prominent. **3.** *Genetics* designating one of a pair of hereditary characters that, appearing in hybrid offspring, masks a contrasting character: opposed to *recessive*. —*n. Music* the fifth tone of a diatonic scale, a perfect fifth above the tonic. [< L *dominari* control] —**dom'i·nance** n.

dom·i·nate (DOM ə NAYT) v. **·nat·ed, ·nat·ing** v.t. **1.** control; govern. **2.** tower above. —v.i. **3.** be dominant, as in power. [< L *dominatus* controlled]

dom·i·na·tion (DOM ə NAY shən) n. **1.** the act of dominating, or the state of being dominated. **2.** control; authority.

dom·i·neer (DOM ə NEER) v.t. & v.i. rule arrogantly. [< Du. *domineren* lord over] —**dom'i·neer'ing** adj.

do·min·ion (də MIN yən) n. **1.** sovereign or supreme authority. **2.** a country under a particular government. [ME]

dom·i·no[1] (DOM ə NOH) n. pl. **·noes** or **·nos 1.** a small mask for the eyes. **2.** a loose robe, hood, and mask worn at masquerades. [< Ital. hood and mask worn by clerics]

dom·i·no[2] n. pl. **·noes 1.** a small, oblong piece of wood, plastic, etc., with the upper side marked with dots. **2. dominos** (construed as sing.) a game usu. played with a set of 28 of these pieces.

domino theory the idea that one event, allowed to happen, will precipitate a series of like events.

don[1] (don) n. a Spanish gentleman or nobleman. **2.** *Brit.* a head, fellow, or tutor of a college. [< Sp.]

don[2] v.t. **donned, don·ning** put on, as a garment. [Contraction of *do on*]

do·nate (doh NAYT) v.t. **·nat·ed, ·nat·ing** give, as to a charity; contribute. —**do·na·tion** (doh NAY shən) n. **1.** the act of giving. **2.** a gift. [ME]

done (dun) past participle of DO[1]. —adj. **1.** completed; finished; ended; agreed. **2.** cooked sufficiently. —**done for** *Informal* **1.** ruined; finished; exhausted. **2.** dead or about to die. —**done in** *Informal* **1.** utterly exhausted. **2.** killed; destroyed.

do·nee (doh NEE) n. one who receives a gift.

Don Juan (don WAHN) a seducer of women.

don·key (DONG kee) n. the ass.

don·ny·brook (DON ee BRUUK) n. a brawl; free-for-all. [after *Donnybrook Fair*, in Ireland, known for its brawls]

do·nor (DOH nər) n. **1.** one who gives. **2.** *Med.* one who furnishes blood, organs, etc. [ME *donour*]

don't (dohnt) do not.

doom (doom) v.t. **1.** pronounce sentence upon; condemn. **2.** destine to an unhappy fate. —n. **1.** an unhappy fate. **2.** an adverse judicial sentence. **3.** death or ruin. [ME *dome*]

dooms·day (DOOMZ day) n. the day of the Last Judgment; the end of the world. Also spelled *domesday*. [< OE *dōm* doom + *dæg* day]

door (dor) n. **1.** a hinged, sliding, folding, or turning structure, used for closing or opening an entrance to a house, vehicle, etc. **2.** a doorway. **3.** any means of entrance or exit. [ME *dore*]

door·mat (DOR MAT **1.** a mat placed at an entrance for wiping the shoes. **2.** one who is the uncomplaining object of abuse by others.

door·way (DOR WAY) n. **1.** the passage for entering and leaving a room, hall, etc. **2.** any means of access: *doorway* to happiness.

dope (dohp) n. **1.** a usu. liquid substance having a specific purpose, as a lubricant, medication, etc. **2.** *Slang* a drug or narcotic. **3.** *Informal* a stupid person. **4.** *Slang* information. —v.t. **doped, dop·ing 1.** apply dope to. **2.** *Slang* drug: often with *up*. —**dope out** *Slang* plan or solve.

dop·e·y (DOH pee) adj. **·pi·er, ·pi·est** *Informal* **1.** lethargic from or as from narcotics. **2.** stupid. Also **dop'y.**

dor·mant (DOR mənt) adj. **1.** asleep or as if asleep. **2.** not active; inoperative. **3.** *Biol.* marked by partial suspension of vital processes, as many animals and plants in winter. [ME *dormaunt*] —**dor'man·cy** n.

dor·mer (DOR mər) n. a vertical window set in a small gable that projects from a sloping roof. Also **dormer window.** [< MF *dormoir* dormitory]

dor·mi·to·ry (DOR mi TOR ee) n. pl. **·ries 1.** a large room with sleeping accommodations for many persons. **2.** a building with sleeping and living accommodations, esp. at a school. [< L *dormitorium*]

dor·sal (DOR səl) adj. *Anat.* of, pertaining to, on, or near the back. [< Med.L *dorsalis*]

do·ry (DOR ee) n. pl. **·ries** a deep, flat-bottomed rowboat with a sharp prow.

dos·age (DOH sij) n. **1.** the administering of a dose of medicine. **2.** a dose.

dose (dohs) n. **1.** a particular quantity of medicine given or prescribed to be given at one time. **2.** a particular amount of something, usu. disagreeable. —*v.t.* **dosed, dos•ing** give medicine etc. to in doses. [< LL *dosis*]

do•sim•e•ter (doh SIM i tər) *n. Med.* an instrument for measuring the total amount of radiation absorbed in a given time. [< Gk. *dosis* dose + -METER]

dos•si•er (DOS ee AY) *n.* a collection of documents etc. relating to a particular matter or person. [< F, bundle of papers]

dost (dust) do: archaic or poetic second person singular, present tense of DO[1]: used with *thou.*

dot (dot) *n.* **1.** a tiny, usu. round, mark; a spot or point. **2.** a small amount. **3.** a signal in Morse code that is of shorter duration than the dash. —**on the dot** at exactly the specified time. —*v.* **dot•ted, dot•ting** *v.t.* **1.** mark with a dot or dots. **2.** be scattered thickly over or about. —*v.i.* **3.** make a dot or dots. —**dot one's i's and cross one's t's** be exact or correct. [OE *dott* head of a boil]

dot•age (DOH tij) *n.* **1.** feebleness of mind as a result of old age. **2.** excessive affection. [ME]

do•tard (DOH tərd) *n.* a foolish old person. [ME]

dote (doht) *v.i.* **dot•ed, dot•ing** **1.** lavish extreme fondness: with *on* or *upon.* **2.** be feeble-minded as a result of old age. [ME *doten* be foolish] —**dot'ing** *adj.*

doth (duth) does: archaic or poetic third person singular, present tense of DO[1]

dot•ty (DOT ee) *adj.* **•ti•er, •ti•est 1.** consisting of or marked with dots. **2.** *Informal* slightly demented.

dou•ble (DUB əl) *adj.* **1.** combined with another usu. identical one; two together: a *double* scoop of ice cream. **2.** twofold. **3.** more than one; not single. **4.** consisting of two layers. **5.** made for two. **6.** twice as great, as large, as many, etc. —*n.* **1.** something that is twice as much. **2.** a duplicate. **3.** a person, animal, or thing that closely resembles another. **4.** a fold or pleat. **5.** *pl.* in tennis etc., a game having two players on each side. **6.** in baseball, a fair hit that enables the batter to reach second base. **7.** in bridge, the act of challenging an opponent's bid by increasing its value and thus the penalty if the contract is not fulfilled. —**on the double 1.** in double time. **2.** *Informal* quickly. —*v.* **•led, •ling** *v.t.* **1.** make twice as great in number, size, value, force, etc. **2.** be twice the quantity or number of. **3.** fold

or bend one part of upon another: usu. with *over, up, back.* **4.** clench (the fist): often with *up.* **5.** in bridge, challenge (an opponent) by announcing a double. —*v.i.* **6.** become double; increase by an equal amount. **7.** turn and go back on a course: often with *back.* **8.** act or perform in two capacities. **9.** in baseball, make a two-base hit. **10.** in bridge, announce a double. —**double in brass** *Informal* be useful in another capacity apart from one's (or its) specialty. —**double up 1.** bend over, as from pain or laughter. **2.** share one's quarters, bed, etc., with another. —*adv.* in pairs; two-fold; doubly. [ME]

double boiler a cooking utensil consisting of two pots, one fitting into the other: food in the upper pot is cooked by the heat from water boiling in the lower pot.

dou•ble-breast•ed (DUB əl BRES tid) *adj.* having two rows of buttons and fastening so as to provide a double thickness of cloth across the breast: said of a coat or vest.

dou•ble-cross (DUB əl KRAWS) *v.t. Informal* betray by failing to act as promised. —**doub'le cross'** *n.*

dou•ble-date (DUB əl DAYT) *v.i.* **-dat•ed, -dat•ing** *Informal* make or go out on a social engagement of two couples. —**double date** *n.*

dou•ble-deck•er (DUB əl DEK ər) *n.* **1.** a bus etc. having two levels. **2.** a sandwich made with three slices of bread and two layers of filling.

dou•ble-edged (DUB əl EJD) *adj.* **1.** having two cutting edges. **2.** applicable two ways.

dou•ble en•ten•dre (DUB əl ahn TAHN drə) *n.* a word or phrase of double meaning. [Alter. of F *double entente*]

dou'ble expo'sure *Photog.* the act of exposing the same film or plate twice; also, a print developed from a film or plate so exposed.

dou•ble-head•er (DUB əl HED ər) *n.* in sports, two games played on the same day by the same two teams.

double jeopardy the peril under which a defendant is placed when tried more than once for the same offense.

dou•ble-joint•ed (DUB əl JOIN tid) *adj.* having very flexible joints in one's limbs, fingers, etc.

double knit a two-ply fabric knitted so that its two layers are interlocked by stitches.

double play in baseball, a play in which two

base runners are put out during one continuous play of the ball.

double pneumonia pneumonia affecting both lungs.

double standard a set of principles that permits one group greater freedom than another, esp. in sexual behavior.

dou·ble-talk (DUB əl TAWK) *n.* **1.** a flow of actual words and meaningless syllables, made to sound like talk. **2.** ambiguous talk meant to deceive.

doub·le·think (DUB əl THINGK) *n.* the holding of two contradictory views at the same time.

double time 1. in the U.S. Army, a fast marching step at the rate of 180 three-foot steps per minute. **2.** a wage rate that is twice one's normal pay.

dou·bly (DUB lee) *adv.* **1.** in twofold degree; twice. **2.** in pairs. **3.** in twice the quantity. [ME]

doubt (dowt) *v.t.* **1.** hold the truth, validity, or reliability of as uncertain; hesitate to accept. —*v.i.* **2.** be unconvinced or mistrustful. [ME *douten*] —*n.* **1.** lack of certainty. **2.** a state of affairs giving rise to uncertainty: The outcome was in *doubt*. —**beyond doubt** unquestionably; certainly. —**no doubt 1.** certainly. **2.** probably. —**without doubt** certainly. —**doubt'er** *n.*

doubt·ful (DOWT fəl) *adj.* **1.** subject to or causing doubt; uncertain; unsettled. **2.** having doubt; undecided. **3.** vague; ambiguous. **4.** of questionable character.

doubt·less (DOWT lis) *adv.* **1.** unquestionably. **2.** probably. Also **doubt'less·ly.** —*adj.* free from uncertainty.

douche (doosh) *n.* **1.** a jet of water, etc., directed into or onto some part of the body. **2.** a cleansing or medicinal treatment of this kind. **3.** a syringe or other device for administering a douche. —*v.t. & v.i.* **douched, douch·ing** treat with or take a douche. [< F]

dough (doh) *n.* **1.** a soft mass of moistened flour or meal and other ingredients, mixed for making bread, pastry, etc. **2.** any soft, pasty mass. **3.** *Slang* money. [ME *dogh*] —**dough'y** *adj.* **dough·i·er, dough·i·est**

dough·nut (DOH nət) *n.* a small cake of usu. leavened and sweetened dough, fried in deep fat, and often having a hole in the center.

dough·ty (DOW tee) *adj.* **·ti·er, ·ti·est** valiant; brave. [ME] —**dough'ti·ness** *n.*

dour (duur) *adj.* forbidding and surly; morosely stern. [ME] —**dour'ly** *adv.*

douse¹ (dows) *v.* **doused, dous·ing** *v.t.* **1.** plunge into water or other liquid; duck. **2.** drench. —*v.i.* **3.** become drenched or immersed. Also spelled *dowse*.

douse² *v.t.* **doused, dous·ing** extinguish.

dove¹ (duv) *n.* **1.** any bird of the pigeon family. **2.** a symbol of peace. **3.** one who urges negotiation and compromise in a dispute: opposed to *hawk*. **4.** a gentle, innocent person. [ME]

dove² (dohv) alternative past tense of DIVE.

dove·cote (DUV KOHT) *n.* a box used for breeding pigeons. Also **dove·cot** (DUV KOT). [ME]

dove·tail (DUV TAYL) *n.* **1.** a tenon shaped like a wedge and designed to interlock with a mortise of similar shape. **2.** a joint thus formed. —*v.t. & v.i.* join by or as by dovetails.

dow·a·ger (DOW ə jər) *n.* **1.** a widow holding property or title derived from her deceased husband. **2.** an elderly, dignified woman. [< OF *douagiere*]

dow·dy (DOW dee) *adj.* **·di·er, ·di·est** not smart in dress; frumpish. —*n. pl.* **·dies** a dowdy woman. [ME *doude* unattractive woman] —**dow'di·ness** *n.*

dow·el (DOW əl) *n.* a pin or peg fitted tightly into adjacent holes of two pieces so as to hold them together. —*v.t.* **dow·eled, dow·el·ing** furnish or fasten with dowels. [ME *dowle*]

dow·er (DOW ər) *n.* **1.** the part of a deceased man's estate that is assigned by law to his widow for life. **2.** a dowry. —*v.t.* provide with a dower. [ME *dowere*]

down¹ (down) *adv.* **1.** from a higher to a lower place. **2.** in or on a lower place, level, etc. **3.** on or to the ground. **4.** to or toward the south. **5.** from an upright to a prone or prostrate position. **6.** to lesser bulk, amount, etc.: The mixture boiled *down*. **7.** to less activity, intensity, etc.: Things quieted *down*. **8.** to a lower amount, rate, etc. **9.** in or into subjection or control: Put the rebels *down*. **10.** in or into a depressed or prostrate physical or mental state: He came *down* with a cold. **11.** from an earlier time or individual. **12.** as partial payment. **13.** in writing. —**down with** let us do away with or overthrow. —*adj.* **1.** directed downward. **2.** downcast; depressed. **3.** given as a partial amount. **4.** in games, behind an opponent by a specified number of points, strokes,

etc. **5.** ill. **6.** not working or operable. —
down and out in a completely miserable
state, as of poverty or desolation. —**down
on** *Informal* annoyed with or hostile to. —
prep. **1.** in a descending direction along,
upon, or in. **2.** during the course of: *down
the years.* —*v.t.* **1.** knock, throw, or put
down. **2.** swallow quickly; gulp. —*n.* **1.** a
downward movement; descent. **2.** a reverse
of fortune: chiefly in the phrase **ups and
downs. 3.** in football, any of the four consecutive plays during which a team must
advance the ball at least ten yards to keep
possession of it. [ME *doune*]

down² *n.* **1.** the fine, soft plumage of birds
under the feathers. **2.** any similar substance. [ME *downe*]

down³ *n.* Usu. pl. turf-covered, undulating
tracts of upland. [ME]

down•cast (DOWN KAST) *adj.* **1.** directed
downward. **2.** low in spirits; depressed.

down•fall (DOWN FAWL) *n.* **1.** ruin; collapse. **2.** a sudden fall of rain, etc.

down•grade (DOWN GRAYD) *n.* a descending slope, as of a hill or road. —*adj.* downhill. —*v.t.* •**grad•ed,** •**grad•ing** reduce in
status etc.

down•heart•ed (DOWN HAHR tid) *adj.*
dejected; discouraged.

down•hill (DOWN HIL) *adv.* in a downward direction; toward the bottom of a hill.
—**go downhill** decline, as in success or
health. —*adj.* descending.

down•home (DOWN HOHM) *adj.* having
the earthy simplicity attributed to rural
dwellers, esp. in the U.S. South.

down•pour (DOWN POR) *n.* a heavy fall of
rain.

down•right (DOWN RĪT) *adj.* **1.** thorough;
utter. **2.** straightforward. —*adv.* thoroughly; utterly.

down•stairs (DOWN STAIRZ) *adv.* **1.**
down the stairs. **2.** on or to a lower floor. —
adj. situated on a lower floor. —*n.* the
downstairs part of a house or other building.

down•stream (DOWN STREEM) *adv.*
down the stream. —*adj.* in the direction of
the current.

Down syndrome a congenital disorder
characterized by a broad, flat face and skull
and obliquely set, narrow eyes. [after the
British physician who first described it]

down•time (DOWN TĪM) *n.* time when a
machine, factory, etc. is shut down for
maintenance.

down-to-earth (DOWN too URTH) *adj.*
realistic; practical; unaffected.

down•trod•den (DOWN TROD n) *adj.* **1.**
trampled. **2.** subjugated; oppressed.

down•ward (DOWN wərd) *adv.* **1.** from a
higher to a lower level, position, etc. **2.** from
an earlier or more remote time, place, etc.
Also **down′wards.** —*adj.* **1.** descending
from a higher to a lower level. **2.** descending from that which is more remote.

down•y (DOW nee) *adj.* **down•i•er, down•
i•est** of, like, or covered with down.

dow•ry (DOW ree) *n. pl.* •**ries** the money or
property a wife brings to her husband at
marriage. [ME *dowerie*]

dowse¹ (dows) see DOUSE¹.

dowse² (dowz) *v.i.* **dowsed, dows•ing**
search with a divining rod. —**dows′er** *n.*

dows•ing rod (DOWZ ing) a divining rod.

dox•ol•o•gy (dok SOL ə jee) *n. pl.* •**gies** a
hymn or verse of praise to God. [< Med.L
doxologia]

doze (dohz) *v.i.* **dozed, doz•ing** sleep
lightly; nap. —**doze off** fall into a light,
brief sleep. —*n.* a light, brief sleep; nap.
[ME *dosnyt* dazed]

doz•en (DUZ ən) *n. pl.* **doz•ens;** *when preceded by a number,* **doz•en** a group or set of
twelve things. Abbr. **doz.** [ME *dozeine*]

drab¹ (drab) *adj.* **drab•ber, drab•best 1.**
lacking brightness; dull and monotonous. **2.**
of the color of drab. **3.** made of drab. —*n.* **1.**
a thick, woolen, yellowish brown cloth. **2.**
the color of this cloth. [< MF *drap* length
of cloth] —**drab′ness** *n.*

drab² *n.* **1.** an untidy woman. **2.** a prostitute;
slut.

drach•ma (DRAK mə) *n. pl.* •**mas** or •**mae**
(-mee) **1.** an ancient Greek silver coin. **2.**
the standard monetary unit of Greece. **3.** an
ancient Greek unit of weight. [< L]

draft (draft) *n.* **1.** the act or process of selecting an individual for some duty or purpose;
esp. for compulsory military service; conscription. **2.** a current of air. **3.** a device for
controlling the airflow, as in a furnace. **4.** a
written order, directing the payment of
money. **5.** a sketch, plan, or design of something to be made. **6.** a preliminary version
of a writing. **7.** the act of drinking; also, the
liquid taken at one drink. **8.** the drawing of
liquid from its container; also a quantity
drawn for drinking. **9.** the act of drawing air,
smoke, etc. into the lungs; also, the air etc.
taken in. **10.** the pulling of something, as a
loaded wagon; also, the load pulled. **11.**

Naut. the depth of water required for a ship to float, esp. when loaded. **—on draft** ready to be drawn, as beer from a keg. — *v.t.* **1.** draw up in preliminary form, esp. in writing. **2.** select, as for military service. **3.** draw off or away. **—adj. 1.** suitable to be used for pulling heavy loads: a *draft* animal. **2.** not bottled, as beer. [ME *draght* draw]

draft board an official board of civilians that selects candidates for compulsory service in the U.S. armed forces.

draft dodger one who avoids or attempts to avoid conscription into military service.

draft·ee (draf TEE) *n.* a person drafted for service in the armed forces.

drafts·man (DRAFTS mən) *n. pl.* **·men 1.** one who draws or prepares designs or plans of buildings, machinery, etc. **2.** an artist skilled in drawing. Also **drafts'per'son**.

draft·y (DRAF tee) *adj.* **draft·i·er, draft· i·est** having or exposed to drafts of air. — **draft'i·ness** *n.*

drag (drag) *v.* **dragged, drag·ging** *v.t.* **1.** pull along by main force; haul. **2.** sweep or search the bottom of (a body of water); dredge. **3.** draw along heavily and wearily. **4.** continue tediously: often with *on* or *out.* —*v.i.* **5.** be pulled or hauled along. **6.** move heavily or slowly. **7.** lag behind. **8.** pass slowly. **—drag one's feet** act with deliberate slowness. —*n.* **1.** the act of dragging. **2.** the resistance encountered in dragging. **3.** a slow, heavy, usu. impeded, motion or movement. **4.** something that slows down movement. **5.** something heavy that is dragged. **6.** a contrivance for dragging a river, lake, etc. **7.** anything that hinders. **8.** *Slang* influence; pull. **9.** a puff on a cigarette etc. **10.** *Slang* one who or that which is tedious or boring. **11.** a drag race. **12.** women's dress when worn by a man. [ME]

drag·net (DRAG NET) *n.* **1.** a net used in dragging a body of water. **2.** an organized widespread search for a criminal.

drag·o·man (DRAG ə mən) *n. pl.* **·mans** or **·men** an interpreter or guide for travelers in the Near East. [ME *drogman*]

drag·on (DRAG ən) *n.* a mythical, serpentlike, winged monster. [ME]

drag·on·fly (DRAG ənFLI) *n. pl.* **·flies** a predatory insect having a slender body, four wings, and strong jaws.

dra·goon (drə GOON) *n.* in some European armies, a cavalryman. —*v.t.* **1.** harass by dragoons. **2.** coerce; browbeat. [< F *dragon* dragon]

drag race a race between cars accelerating from a standstill, usu. held on a straight course (**drag strip**).

drain (drayn) *v.t.* **1.** draw off (liquid) gradually. **2.** draw liquid from. **3.** empty by drinking. **4.** use up gradually; exhaust. **5.** filter. —*v.i.* **6.** flow off gradually. **7.** become dry by the flowing off of liquid. **8.** discharge waters contained: The region *drains* into the lake. —*n.* **1.** a device for draining. **2.** a continuous outflow, expenditure, or depletion. **3.** the act of draining. [ME *dreynen*]

drain·age (DRAY nij) *n.* **1.** the act or method of draining. **2.** a system of drains. **3.** that which is drained off. **4.** a drainage basin.

drainage basin a large surface area whose waters are drained off into a principal river system.

drake (drayk) *n.* a male duck. [ME]

dram (dram) *n.* **1.** an apothecaries' weight equal to 60 grains, 3.89 grams, or one-eighth of an ounce. **2.** an avoirdupois measure equal to 27.34 grains, 1.77 grams, or one-sixteenth of an ounce. **3.** a fluid dram. **4.** a small portion, esp. of alcoholic liquor. [ME *dramme*]

dra·ma (DRAH mə) *n.* **1.** a literary composition written to be performed upon a stage; a play. **2.** stage plays as a branch of literature. **3.** the art or profession of writing, acting, or producing plays. **4.** the quality of being dramatic. [< LL]

dra·mat·ic (drə MAT ik) *adj.* **1.** of, connected with, or like the drama. **2.** characterized by the spirit of the drama; theatrical. **—dra·mat'i·cal·ly** *adv.*

dra·mat·ics (drə MAT iks) *n.* **1.** (*construed as sing. or pl.*) dramatic performance, esp. by amateurs. **2.** (*construed as sing.*) the art of staging or acting plays.

dram·a·tis per·so·nae (DRAM ə tis pər SOH nee) *Latin* the characters of a play; a list of these.

dram·a·tist (DRAM ə tist) *n.* one who writes plays.

dram·a·tize (DRAM ə TIZ) *v.t.* **·tized, ·tiz·ing 1.** present in dramatic form; adapt for performance, as a play. **2.** represent or interpret (events etc.) in a theatrical manner. **—dram'a·ti·za'tion** *n.*

drape (drayp) *v.* **draped, drap·ing** *v.t.* **1.** cover or adorn in a graceful fashion, as with drapery or clothing. **2.** arrange in graceful folds. —*v.t.* **3.** hang in folds. —*n.* **1.** pl.

drapery. **2.** the way in which cloth hangs, as in clothing. [ME]

dra·per·y (DRAY pə ree) n. pl. **·per·ies 1.** attire hanging in folds. **2.** Often pl. hangings or curtains arranged in loose folds. **3.** cloth. [ME draperie]

dras·tic (DRAS tik) adj. vigorous; extreme. [< Gk. drastikós active] —**dras'ti·cal·ly** adv.

draughts (drafts) n. (construed as sing.) Brit. the game of checkers.

draw (draw) v. **drew, drawn, draw·ing** v.t. **1.** cause to move toward or to follow behind an agent exerting physical force; pull. **2.** obtain, as from a receptacle: draw water. **3.** cause to flow forth, as blood. **4.** bring forth; elicit: draw praise. **5.** take or pull off, on, or out, as a sword. **6.** portray with lines or words; sketch; delineate. **7.** deduce or extract by a mental process: draw a conclusion. **8.** attract; entice. **9.** pull tight, as a rope. **10.** make by stretching or hammering, as wire or dies. **11.** take in, as air or a liquid, by inhaling or sucking. **12.** close or shut, as curtains. **13.** shrink or wrinkle. **14.** select or obtain, as by chance; also, win (a prize) in a lottery. **15.** receive; earn, as a salary or interest. **16.** withdraw, as money from a bank. **17.** write out (a check). **18.** Naut. of a vessel, sink to (a specified depth) in floating. — v.i. **19.** practice the art of drawing; sketch. **20.** exert a pulling or drawing force. **21.** approach or retreat: draw near or away. **22.** exert an attracting influence. **23.** obtain by making an application to some source: with on or upon: draw on one's experience. **24.** produce a current of air: My chimney draws well. **25.** end a contest without a decision; tie. —**draw a blank 1.** be unsuccessful **2.** forget something. —**draw on** approach. —**draw oneself up** straighten up, as in indignation. —**draw out 1.** prolong. **2.** cause (someone) to talk freely. —**draw the line** fix a limit and refuse to go further. —**draw up 1.** write out in proper form. **2.** bring or come to a standstill, as horses. **3.** come alongside. — n. **1.** the act of drawing. **2.** the act of drawing out a weapon for action. **3.** something drawn, as a hand in cards. **4.** something that attracts a large audience. **5.** a stalemate; tie. [ME drawen]

draw·back (DRAW bak) n. anything that hinders progress, success, etc.

draw·bridge (DRAW brij) n. a bridge of which the whole or a part may be raised, let down, or drawn aside.

draw·er (dror) n. **1.** a sliding receptacle, as in a desk, that can be drawn out. **2.** (DRAW ər) one who draws.

draw·ers (drorz) n.pl. underpants covering all or part of each leg.

draw·ing (DRAW ing) n. **1.** the act of one who or that which draws. **2.** the art of representing something with lines and often shading, by pen, pencil, etc. **3.** the picture, sketch, or design produced by this art. **4.** a lottery.

drawing card something that attracts a large audience.

drawing room 1. a room in which visitors are received and entertained. **2.** a private compartment in a sleeping car on a train.

drawl (drawl) v.t. & v.i. speak or pronounce slowly, esp. with a drawing out of the vowels. —**drawl** n.

drawn (drawn) past participle of DRAW.

dray (dray) n. a low cart with removable sides. —v.t. transport by dray. [ME draye sledge]

dread (dred) v.t. anticipate with great fear or anxiety. —adj. **1.** causing great fear; terrible. **2.** exciting awe. —n. **1.** a terrifying anticipation, as of evil or danger. **2.** awe. [ME dreden fear]

dread·ful (DRED fəl) adj. **1.** inspiring dread; terrible. **2.** disgusting; very bad. — **dread'ful·ly** adv.

dream (dreem) n. **1.** a series of images passing through the mind in sleep. **2.** a daydream; reverie. **3.** a cherished or vain hope. **4.** anything of dreamlike quality. —v. **dreamed** or **dreamt** (dremt), **dream·ing** v.t. **1.** see or imagine in or as in a dream. **2.** spend (time) in idle reverie: with away. — v.i. **3.** have a dream or dreams. **4.** daydream. —**dream up** create, as by ingenuity. [ME dreem]

dream·y (DREE mee) adj. **dream·i·er, dream·i·est 1.** of, pertaining to, or causing dreams. **2.** given to dreams; visionary. **3.** Informal wonderful. —**dream'i·ly** adv.

drear·y (DREER ee) adj. **drear·i·er, drear·i·est 1.** causing or manifesting sadness or gloom. **2.** dull or monotonous. [ME drery sad] —**drear'i·ly** adv.

dredge¹ (drej) n. **1.** a large, powerful scoop or suction apparatus for removing mud or gravel from the bottoms of channels, harbors, etc. **2.** any similar, smaller device. — v. **dredged, dredg·ing** v.t. **1.** clear or widen by means of a dredge. **2.** catch with a dredge. —*v.i.* **3.** use a dredge. [ME]

dredge² *v.t.* **dredged, dredg·ing** dust with a powdered substance, esp. flour. [< ME *drage*]

dregs (dregz) *n.pl.* **1.** the sediment of liquids, esp. of beverages; lees. **2.** coarse, worthless residue. [ME]

drench (drench) *v.t.* **1.** wet thoroughly; soak. **2.** *Vet.* administer a potion to by force. —*n. Vet.* a liquid medicine administered by force. [ME *drenchen*]

dress (dres) *v.* **dressed** or **drest, dress·ing** *v.t.* **1.** put clothes on; clothe. **2.** trim or decorate, as a store window. **3.** treat medicinally, as a wound. **4.** comb and arrange (hair). **5.** prepare (stone, timber, etc.) for use or sale. **6.** clean (fowl, game, etc.) for cooking. —*v.i.* **7.** put on or wear clothing, esp. formal clothing. —**dress down** rebuke severely; scold. —**dress up** put on or wear one's best. —*n.* **1.** an outer garment for a woman or child, usu. in one piece with a skirt. **2.** clothing collectively. **3.** external adornment or appearance. —*adj.* **1.** of or pertaining to dress or a dress. **2.** to be worn on formal occasions. [ME *dressen*]

dres·sage (drə SAHZH) *n.* the guiding of a trained horse through a set of maneuvers by imperceptible movements of the rider. [< F]

dress·er¹ (DRES ər) *n.* **1.** one who dresses something. **2.** one who assists another in dressing. **3.** one who dresses in a particular way.

dress·er² *n.* a chest of drawers for articles of clothing. [ME *dressour* sideboard]

dress·ing (DRES ing) *n.* **1.** the act of one who or that which dresses. **2.** that with which something is dressed, as medicated bandages for a wound. **3.** a stuffing for poultry or roasts. **4.** a sauce for salads etc.

dress·ing-down (DRES ing DOWN) *n.* a severe scolding.

dress rehearsal a final rehearsal of a play, done with costumes, lighting, etc.

dress·y (DRES ee) *adj.* **dress·i·er, dress·i·est** elegant; stylish. —**dress'i·ness** *n.*

drew (droo) past tense of DRAW.

drib (drib) *n.* driblet. —**dribs and drabs** small quantities.

drib·ble (DRIB əl) *v.t. & v.i.* **·bled, ·bling 1.** fall or let fall in drops. **2.** drool. **3.** in sports, propel (the ball) by successive bounces or kicks. —*n.* **1.** a small quantity of

a liquid falling in drops. **2.** the act of dribbling. —**drib'bler** *n.*

drib·let (DRIB lit) *n.* **1.** a small drop of liquid. **2.** a tiny quantity.

dried (drīd) past tense, past participle of DRY.

dri·er (DRĪ ər) comparative of DRY. —*n.* **1.** one who or that which dries. **2.** a substance added to paint, etc., to make it dry more quickly. **3.** dryer.

dri·est (DRĪ ist) superlative of DRY.

drift (drift) *n.* **1.** the act of moving along, or the fact of being carried along, in or as in a current of water, air, etc. **2.** a force or influence that drives something along. **3.** a course, tendency, or intent: conversational *drift*. **4.** the rate at which a current of water moves. **5.** the direction of a current of water. **6.** something driven along or heaped up by air or water currents; snow *drift*. **7.** the distance a ship, aircraft, etc. is driven from its course by wind, sea, etc. —*v.i.* **1.** move along in or as in a current. **2.** become heaped up by air currents or water currents. —*v.t.* **3.** cause to drift. [ME]

drift·age (DRIF tij) *n.* **1.** the act or process of drifting. **2.** deviation caused by drifting. **3.** something drifting or drifted.

drift·wood (DRIFT wuud) *n.* wood floated by water; esp., wood washed up on a seashore.

drill¹ (dril) *n.* **1.** a tool used for boring holes in hard substances. **2.** a process of training marked by fixed procedures and much repetition, as in arithmetic etc. **3.** the act of teaching through such training; also, a particular exercise. —*v.t. & v.i.* **1.** pierce with a drill. **2.** teach (someone) or learn by drill. [< Du. *drillen* bore]

drill² *Agric. n.* a machine for planting seed in rows. —*v.t. & v.i.* sow or plant in rows.

drill·mas·ter (DRIL MAS tər) *n.* one who trains by drilling.

drill press a machine tool used in drilling holes.

dri·ly (DRĪ lee) *adv.* in a dry manner.

drink (dringk) *v.* **drank, drunk, drink·ing** *v.t.* **1.** take into the mouth and swallow (a liquid). **2.** soak up or absorb. **3.** swallow the contents of (a glass etc.). —*v.i.* **4.** swallow a liquid. **5.** drink alcoholic liquors, esp. to excess. **6.** drink a toast: with *to*. —**drink the health of** offer good wishes to by a toast. —*n.* **1.** a beverage. **2.** a portion of liquid swallowed. **3.** alcoholic liquor. **4.** the practice of drinking alcoholic liquor to excess. [ME *drinken*]

drip (drip) n. **1.** the falling of liquids in drops. **2.** liquid falling in drops; also, the sound so made. **3.** melted fat exuded from meat being roasted or fried: also **drip'pings. 4.** *Slang* an insipid or inept individual. —*v.t. & v.i.* **dripped** or **dript, drip·ping** fall or cause to fall in drops. [ME *dryppe*]

drip-dry (DRIP DRĪ) *adj.* of a garment or fabric treated to dry quickly and retain its shape after being hung while wet. —*v.i.* **-dried, -dry·ing** dry in such a manner.

drive (drīv) v. **drove, driv·en, driv·ing** *v.t.* **1.** push or propel onward with force. **2.** force to work or activity. **3.** goad by force or compulsion. **4.** cause to penetrate by force. **5.** cause to go rapidly by striking. **6.** control the operation of (a vehicle). **7.** transport in a vehicle. **8.** provide the motive power for. —*v.i.* **9.** move along rapidly. **10.** strike or impel a ball etc. with force. **11.** drive or ride in a vehicle. —**drive home 1.** force in all the way, as a nail. **2.** make evident with force or emphasis. —*n.* **1.** the act of driving. **2.** a road for driving. **3.** a journey in a vehicle. **4.** the gathering together of cattle, logs, etc. **5.** an organized campaign. **6.** energy; aggressiveness. **7.** *Psychol.* a strong, motivating power or stimulus. **8.** *Mech.* a means of transmitting power, as from the motor of an automobile to the wheels. [ME *driven*]

drive-in (DRĪV IN) *n.* an outdoor motion-picture theater, restaurant, etc., for patrons in cars.

driv·el (DRIV əl) v. **·eled, ·el·ing** *v.i.* **1.** let saliva flow from the mouth. **2.** flow like saliva. **3.** talk foolishly. —*v.t.* **4.** let flow from the mouth. —*n.* **1.** a flow of saliva from the mouth. **2.** senseless talk. [ME *dryvelen*] — **driv'el·er** *n.*

driv·en (DRIV ən) past participle of DRIVE.

driv·er (DRĪ vər) *n.* **1.** one who drives a vehicle, animals, etc. **2.** in golf, a club for driving from the tee.

driz·zle (DRIZ əl) *v.t. & v.i.* **·zled, ·zling** rain steadily in fine drops. —*n.* a light rain. —**driz'zly** *adj.*

drogue (drohg) n. **1.** a bucket used as a sea anchor. **2.** a small parachute used to slow down or stabilize a satellite or spacecraft upon reentering earth's atmosphere. [< *drug,* alter. of DRAG]

droll (drohl) *adj.* humorously odd; comical; funny. [< MF *drolle* jolly rascal] —**droll'ly** *adv.*

droll·er·y (DROH lə ree) n. pl. **·er·ies 1.** the quality of being droll; humor. **2.** something droll.

drone[1] (drohn) v. **droned, dron·ing** *v.i.* **1.** make a dull, humming sound. **2.** speak monotonously. —*v.t.* **3.** utter in a monotonous tone. —*n.* a dull humming sound, as of a bee. [ME *droun* roar]

drone[2] n. **1.** the male of the bee, esp. of the honeybee, having no sting and gathering no honey. **2.** a lazy loafer. **3.** *Aeron.* an unmanned airplane piloted by remote control. [ME]

drool (drool) *v.t. & v.i.* drivel; slaver. —*n.* spittle.

droop (droop) *v.i.* **1.** sink down; hang downward. **2.** lose vigor; languish. —*v.t.* **3.** let hang or sink down. [ME *drupen* drop] — **droop'y** *adj.* **droop·i·er, droop·i·est**

drop (drop) n. **1.** a small quantity of liquid, shaped like a tiny ball. **2.** a very small amount of anything. **3.** pl. a liquid medicine given in drops. **4.** something resembling a drop in shape, size, etc. **5.** something designed to fall, slide, or hang down, as a curtain. **6.** a place for dropping or leaving something, as a slot in a mailbox. **7.** the act of falling or dropping. **8.** a sudden or quick downward movement or decrease. **9.** the vertical distance from a higher to a lower level. **10.** a falling off or away. **11.** a parachuting of people or supplies. —**have** (or **get**) **the drop on** have (or get) the advantage over. —*v.* **dropped** or **dropt, drop·ping** *v.i.* **1.** fall in drops, as a liquid. **2.** fall or descend rapidly. **3.** fall down exhausted, injured, or dead. **4.** decline or decrease. **5.** fall into some state or condition. —*v.t.* **6.** let fall by letting go of. **7.** let fall in drops. **8.** give birth to: said of animals. **9.** utter (a hint etc.) in a casual way. **10.** write and send (a note etc.). **11.** cause to fall, as by striking. **12.** have no more to do with. **13.** let out or deposit at a particular place. **14.** parachute (soldiers, supplies, etc.). **15.** omit, as a word, line, or stitch. **16.** move down; lower. —**drop in** (or **by**) make a casual visit. —**drop off 1.** decline or decrease. **2.** go to sleep. — **drop out** withdraw, as from membership. [ME *drope*]

drop-kick (DROP KIK) *v.t. & v.i.* **1.** in football, to kick (the ball) after dropping it on the ground. **2.** in soccer, to drop and kick (the ball). —**drop kick** n.

drop·let (DROP lit) n. a tiny drop.

drop•out (DROP owt) *n.* a person who drops out, esp. a student who leaves school.

dross (draws) *n.* **1.** *Metall.* impurity in melted metal. **2.** waste matter; refuse. [ME *drosse* dregs]

drought (drowt) *n.* long-continued dry weather; lack of rain. [ME]

drove¹ (drohv) past tense of DRIVE.

drove² *n.* **1.** a number of animals driven or herded for driving. **2.** a moving crowd of human beings. —*v.t.* **droved, drov•ing** drive (cows, etc.) for some distance. [ME] —**drov'er** *n.*

drown (drown) *v.i.* **1.** die by suffocation with a liquid. —*v.t.* **2.** kill by suffocation with a liquid. **3.** flood; inundate. **4.** lessen, extinguish, or muffle. [ME *drounnen*]

drowse (drowz) *v.i.* **drowsed, drows•ing** be only half awake. —*n.* the state of being half asleep. [OE *drūsian* become sluggish]

drow•sy (DROW zee) *adj.* •si•er, •si•est **1.** heavy with sleepiness; dull. **2.** making sleepy; soporific. —**drow'•si•ness** *n.*

drub (drub) *v.t.* **drubbed, drub•bing 1.** beat, as with a stick. **2.** vanquish; overcome. —*n.* a blow; thump.

drudge (druj) *v.i.* **drudged, drudg•ing** work at drudgery. [OE *drēogan* labor] —*n.* one who performs drudgery.

drudg•er•y (DRUJ ə ree) *n. pl.* •er•ies dull, wearisome, or menial work.

drug (drug) *n.* **1.** any chemical or biological substance, other than food, intended for use in the treatment, prevention, or diagnosis of disease. **2.** a narcotic, stimulant, hallucinogen, etc. —*v.t.* **drugged, drug•ging 1.** mix drugs with (food, drink, etc.). **2.** administer drugs to. **3.** stupefy or poison with or as with drugs. [ME *drogge*]

drug•gist (DRUG ist) *n.* **1.** one who compounds prescriptions and sells drugs; a pharmacist. **2.** one who operates a drugstore.

drug•store (DRUG stor) *n.* a place where prescriptions are compounded, and drugs and miscellaneous merchandise are sold; pharmacy.

dru•id (DROO id) *n. Often cap.* one of an order of priests or teachers of an ancient Celtic religion. [< L *druides*] —**dru'id•ism** *n.*

drum (drum) *n.* **1.** a hollow percussion instrument, typically shaped like a cylinder or hemisphere, having a membrane stretched tightly over one or both ends, and played by beating the membrane with sticks, the hands, etc. **2.** a sound produced by or as by a drum. **3.** something resembling a drum in shape; as: **a** a metal cylinder around which cable is wound. **b** a cylindrical metal container, as for oil. **4.** *Anat.* the tympanic membrane. —*v.* **drummed, drum•ming** *v.i.* **1.** beat a drum. **2.** tap or thump continuously. —*v.t.* **3.** force upon by constant repetition. **4.** work up (business or trade) by advertising, canvassing, etc.: usu. with *up.* **5.** expel in disgrace: usu. with *out.* [Prob. < MDu. *tromme*]

drum•stick (DRUM stik) *n.* **1.** a stick for beating a drum. **2.** the lower joint of the leg of a cooked fowl.

drunk (drungk) past participle of DRINK. — *adj.* intoxicated. —*n.* **1.** one who is drunk. **2.** a drunkard. **3.** a binge.

drunk•ard (DRUNG kərd) *n.* one who habitually drinks alcoholic beverages to excess. [ME]

drunk•en (DRUNG kən) *adj.* **1.** habitually drunk. **2.** relating to or caused by a drunken state. —**drunk'en•ness** *n.*

dry (drī) *adj.* **dri•er, dri•est 1.** devoid of moisture; not wet, damp, or liquid. **2.** marked by little or no rainfall. **3.** not lying under water: *dry* land. **4.** having all or nearly all the water or other liquid drained away, exhausted or evaporated. **5.** thirsty. **6.** lacking sweetness: said esp. of wines. **7.** dull; boring. **8.** crisp; quietly shrewd: *dry* humor. **9.** opposing or prohibiting the sale of or indulgence in alcoholic beverages: a *dry* state. —*v.* **dried, dry•ing** *v.t.* **1.** make dry. **2.** preserve (meat, fish, etc.) by removing moisture. —*v.i.* **3.** become dry. [ME *drie*]

dry•ad (DRĪ əd) *n.* in classical mythology, a nymph dwelling in or presiding over woods and trees. [< Gk. *Dryádes*]

dry-clean (DRĪ KLEEN) *v.t.* clean (clothing etc.) with solvents other than water. —**dry cleaner** *n.* —**dry cleaning** *n.*

dry dock a floating or stationary structure from which water can be removed, used for repairing and cleaning ships.

dry•er (DRĪ ər) *n.* a mechanical device for drying. Also spelled *drier.*

dry-eyed (DRĪ ID) *adj.* not weeping; tearless.

dry rot 1. a disease of timber, caused by fungi. **2.** a disease of potatoes and other vegetables.

dry run 1. *Mil.* a combat exercise done without live ammunition. **2.** any trial run.

dual

du·al (DOO əl) *adj.* **1.** denoting or relating to two. **2.** composed of two; twofold; double; binary. [< L *dualis* having two] — **du·al·i·ty** (doo AL i tee) *n.*

du·al·ism (DOO ə LIZ əm) *n. Philos.* the theory that the universe is composed of two principles, as mind and matter.

dub[1] (dub) *v.t.* **dubbed, dub·bing 1.** confer knighthood upon by tapping on the shoulder with a sword. **2.** name or style. [ME *dubben*]

dub[2] *v.t.* **dubbed, dub·bing 1.** rerecord (a record, tape, etc.) in order to make changes. **2.** insert a new sound track into (a film).

du·bi·e·ty (doo BI i tee) *n. pl.* **·ties 1.** the state of being dubious. **2.** something doubtful. [< L *dubietas*]

du·bi·ous (DOO bee əs) *adj.* **1.** unsettled in judgment or opinion; doubtful. **2.** causing doubt; equivocal. **3.** open to criticism, objection, or suspicion: a *dubious* reputation. [< L *dubius* doubtful]

du·cal (DOO kəl) *adj.* pertaining to a duke or a duchy. [< LL *ducalis* of a leader]

duch·ess (DUCH is) *n.* **1.** the wife or widow of a duke. **2.** the female sovereign of a duchy. [ME *duchesse*]

duch·y (DUCH ee) *n. pl.* **duch·ies** the territory of a duke or duchess; dukedom. [ME *duche*]

duck[1] (duk) *n.* **1.** any of various aquatic birds, with webbed feet and broad bills. **2.** the female of this bird; the male is called a *drake*. [ME *duk*]

duck[2] *v.t.* **1.** thrust suddenly under water. **2.** lower quickly; bob, as the head. **3.** dodge; evade; avoid. —*v.i.* **4.** submerge suddenly under water. **5.** move quickly; bob; dodge. —*n.* the act of ducking. [ME *duken* dive]

duck[3] *n.* **1.** a strong linen or cotton fabric similar to canvas. **2.** *pl.* trousers made of duck. [< Du. *doek* cloth]

duct (dukt) *n.* **1.** any tube, canal, or passage by which a liquid, gas, etc., is conveyed. **2.** *Anat.* a tubular passage by which a secretion is carried away. [< L *ductus* led]

duc·tile (DUK tl) *adj.* **1.** capable of being drawn out into wire or otherwise subjected to stress without breaking, as certain metals. **2.** easily molded or shaped; plastic. **3.** ready to obey; easily led. [ME] —**duc·til'i·ty** *n.*

dud (dud) *n.* **1.** *Mil.* a bomb or shell that fails to explode. **2.** a failure; flop.

dude (dood) *n.* **1.** a fop. **2.** a city person; esp.,

an Easterner vacationing on a ranch. **3.** *Slang* a fellow.

dude ranch a ranch operated as a resort.

dudg·eon (DUJ ən) *n.* sullen displeasure; anger; resentment. [ME]

duds (dudz) *n.pl.* clothes; personal belongings.

due (doo) *adj.* **1.** subject to demand for payment, esp. because of the arrival of a stipulated date. **2.** that should be rendered or given; proper. **3.** adequate; sufficient. **4.** appointed or expected to arrive, be present, or be ready: The bus is *due.* **5.** that may be charged or attributed; ascribable: with *to.* —**due to** because of; on account of. —*n.* **1.** that which is owed or rightfully required; a debt. **2.** *pl.* charge or fee. —*adv.* directly: *due* east. [ME]

du·el (DOO əl) *n.* a prearranged combat between two persons, usu. fought with deadly weapons. —*v.t. & v.i.* **du·eled, du·el·ing** fight in a duel. [< Med.L *duellum* war] —**du'el·er** or **du'el·ist** *n.*

du·en·na (doo EN ə) *n.* **1.** in Spain and Portugal, an elderly woman who serves as a companion and protector to a young girl. **2.** a chaperon. [< Sp.]

du·et (doo ET) *n.* a musical composition for two performers. [< Ital. *duetto*]

duf·fel (DUF əl) *n.* **1.** a coarse woolen fabric. **2.** equipment or supplies. [after *Duffel*, a town near Antwerp]

duffel bag a sack used to carry clothing and personal possessions.

dug[1] (dug) past tense and past participle of DIG.

dug[2] *n.* a teat or udder.

dug·out (DUG owt) *n.* **1.** a canoe made by hollowing out a log. **2.** an excavated shelter for protection against storms, bombs, etc. **3.** in baseball, a structure in which team members sit when not at bat or in the field.

duke (dook) *n.* **1.** in Great Britain and certain other European countries, a nobleman ranking immediately below a prince and above a marquis. **2.** a European prince ruling over a duchy. [ME] —**duke·dom** (DOOK dəm) *n.*

dul·cet (DUL sit) *adj.* pleasing to the ear; soothing. [ME *doucet* sweet]

dul·ci·mer (DUL sə mər) *n.* a stringed instrument played with two padded hammers or plucked with the fingers. [ME *dowcemere*]

dull (dul) *adj.* **1.** lacking in intelligence or understanding; stupid. **2.** without spirit;

listless. **3.** having a blunt edge or point. **4.** exciting little or no interest; boring. **5.** not acute or intense. **6.** cloudy; gloomy. **7.** not bright, clear, or vivid. —*v.t. & v.i.* make or become dull. [ME]

dull·ard (DUL ərd) *n.* a stupid person; dolt.

du·ly (DOO lee) *adv.* **1.** in due or proper manner; fitly. **2.** at the proper time. **3.** to an adequate degree.

dumb (dum) *adj.* **1.** having no power of speech; mute. **2.** temporarily speechless; silent. **3.** stupid. [OE]

dumb·bell (DUM bel.) *n.* **1.** a gymnastic hand instrument used for exercising, consisting of a handle with a weighted ball at each end. **2.** a stupid person.

dumb·found (dum FOWND) *v.t.* strike dumb; confuse; amaze. Also **dum·found′.** [Blend of DUMB and CONFOUND]

dum·my (DUM ee) *n. pl.* **•mies 1.** a figure representing the human form; also, a large doll used by a ventriloquist. **2.** an imitation object. **3.** *Informal* a stupid person. **4.** one who seems to be acting for his own interests while secretly representing another. **5.** *Printing* **a** a sample book or magazine, usu. blank. **b** a model page form, made up of proofs pasted into position. **6.** in certain card games, esp. bridge, an exposed hand played in addition to that of a person sitting opposite it. —*adj.* sham; counterfeit.

dump (dump) *v.t.* **1.** drop or throw down. **2.** empty out, as from a container. **3.** empty (a container), as by overturning. **4.** throw away, as rubbish. **5.** put up (goods) for sale cheaply and in large quantities, esp. in a foreign market. —**dump on** *Informal* speak disparagingly of or to. —*n.* **1.** a dumping area, as for rubbish. **2.** *Mil.* a temporary storage place for ammunition and supplies. **3.** *Informal* a shabby place. [ME]

dump·ling (DUMP ling) *n.* **1.** a ball of dough filled with fruit, ground meat, etc. and baked, steamed, or fried. **2.** a small mass of dough dropped into boiling soup or stew.

dump·y (DUM pee) *adj.* **dump·i·er, dump·i·est** short and thick; squat. —**dump′i·ness** *n.*

dun[1] (dun) *v.t. & v.i.* **dunned, dun·ning** press (a debtor) for payment. —*n.* a demand for payment.

dun[2] *adj.* of a grayish brown or reddish brown color. [ME *dunne*] —*n.* this color.

dunce (duns) *n.* a stupid or ignorant person.

—**dunce cap** a conical cap, formerly placed on the head of a dull student.

dune (doon) *n.* a hill of loose sand heaped up by the wind. [< F]

dung (dung) *n.* **1.** animal excrement; manure. **2.** anything foul. [ME]

dun·ga·ree (DUNG gə REE) *n.* **1.** a coarse cotton cloth used for work clothes, tents, etc. **2.** *pl.* trousers or overalls made of this fabric. [< Hind. *dungri*]

dun·geon (DUN jən) *n.* a dark confining prison or cell, esp. one underground. [ME *dungeoun*]

dung·hill (DUNG hil) *n.* a heap of manure.

dunk (dungk) *v.t. & v.i.* dip (bread etc.) into tea, coffee, etc. [< G *tunken* dip]

du·o·de·num (DOO ə DEE nəm) *n. pl.* **•na** (-nə) *Anat.* the first section of the small intestine extending below the stomach. [ME] —**du′o·de′nal** *adj.*

dupe (doop) *n.* one who is easily deceived or misled. —*v.t.* **duped, dup·ing** make a dupe of; deceive. [< F]

du·plex (DOO pleks) *adj.* having two parts; twofold. —*n.* a two-floor apartment, or a two-family house. [< L, twofold]

du·pli·cate (DOO pli kit) *adj.* **1.** made like or corresponding exactly to an original: a *duplicate* key. **2.** growing or existing in pairs. —*n.* **1.** an exact copy. **2.** a double or counterpart. —*v.t.* (DOO pli kayt) **•cat·ed, •cat·ing 1.** copy exactly; reproduce. **2.** do a second time. [ME]

du·pli·ca·tor (DOO pli kay tər) *n.* a mechanical device for making duplicates.

du·plic·i·ty (doo PLIS i tee) *n. pl.* **•ties** tricky deceitfulness. [ME *duplicite*]

du·ra·ble (DUUR ə bəl) *adj.* able to withstand decay or wear. [ME] —**du′ra·bil′i·ty** *n.*

dur·ance (DUUR əns) *n.* forced imprisonment. [ME]

du·ra·tion (duu RAY shən) *n.* **1.** the period of time during which anything lasts. **2.** continuance in time. [ME]

du·ress (duu RES) *n.* **1.** constraint by force or fear; compulsion. **2.** *Law* **a** coercion. **b** imprisonment without full legal sanction. [ME *duresse* harshness]

dur·ing (DUUR ing) *prep.* **1.** throughout the time, existence, or action of. **2.** in the course of; at some period in. [ME]

dusk (dusk) *n.* the partial darkness between day and night, usu. considered darker than twilight. —*adj.* somewhat dark or dim; shadowy.

dusk·y (DUS kee) *adj.* **dusk·i·er, dusk·i·est** 1. dim; obscure. 2. rather dark in shade or coloring; swarthy. 3. gloomy. —**dusk'i·ness** *n.*

dust (dust) *n.* 1. earthy matter reduced to particles so fine as to be easily borne in the air. 2. any fine powder. 3. earth, esp. as the receptacle of the dead. 4. the disintegrated remains of a human body. —**bite the dust** be killed or injured. —**throw dust in someone's eyes** deceive. —*v.t.* 1. wipe or brush dust from. 2. sprinkle with powder, insecticide, etc. 3. sprinkle (powder etc.) over something. —*v.i.* 4. wipe or brush dust from furniture, etc. [ME]

dust storm a windstorm of arid regions that carries clouds of dust with it.

dust·y (DUS tee) *adj.* **dust·i·er, dust·i·est** 1. covered with or as with dust. 2. like dust; powdery. 3. having a grayish or dull cast: *dusty* pink. —**dust'i·ness** *n.*

Dutch (duch) *adj.* of or relating to the Netherlands, its people, culture, or language. —*n.* 1. the people of the Netherlands: preceded by *the.* 2. the language of the Netherlands. 3. Pennsylvania Dutch. —**in Dutch** in trouble or disgrace. —**go Dutch** have all participants in a meal or entertainment pay their own expenses. [ME *Duch* Germanic]

Dutch door a door divided horizontally in the middle.

Dutch oven a heavy pot with a tight-fitting cover, used for meats, stews, etc.

Dutch treat an entertainment or meal at which guests pay their own bills.

Dutch uncle a frank and severe adviser.

du·te·ous (DOO tee əs) *adj.* obedient; dutiful.

du·ti·ful (DOO tə fəl) *adj.* 1. performing one's duties; obedient. 2. expressive of a sense of duty; respectful.

du·ty (DOO tee) *n. pl.* **·ties** 1. that which one is morally, professionally, or legally bound to do; obligation. 2. specific obligatory service, esp. of military personnel. 3. a tax on imported or exported goods. —**off duty** temporarily not at work. [ME *duete*]

dwarf (dworf) *n.* a human being, animal, or plant that is stunted in its growth. —*v.t.* 1. prevent the natural development of; stunt. 2. cause to appear small or less by comparison. —*adj.* diminutive; stunted. [ME *dwerf*]

dwell (dwel) *v.i.* **dwelt** or **dwelled, dwelling** 1. have a fixed home; reside. 2. linger, as on a subject: with *on* or *upon.* 3. continue in a state or place. [ME *dwellen* hinder]

dwell·ing (DWEL ing) *n.* a place of residence.

dwin·dle (DWIN dl) *v.t. & v.i.* **·dled, ·dling** diminish or become less; make or become smaller. [ME]

dye (dī) *v.* **dyed, dye·ing** *v.t.* 1. fix a color in (cloth, hair, etc.), esp. by soaking in liquid coloring matter. —*v.i.* 2. take or give color. —*n.* a coloring matter used for dyeing; also, the color so produced. [ME *dien*] —**dy'er** *n.*

dyed-in-the-wool (DĪD n thə WUUL) *adj.* 1. dyed before being woven. 2. thoroughgoing.

dye·ing (DĪ ing) *n.* the act of fixing colors in cloth etc.

dye·stuff (DĪ stuf) *n.* any material used for dyeing.

dy·ing (DĪ ing) *adj.* 1. near death; expiring. 2. coming to a close; destined to end. 3. given, uttered, or manifested just before death. —*n.* death.

dyke (dīk) *n. Offensive Slang* a lesbian, esp. one perceived as having masculine characteristics.

dy·nam·ic (dī NAM ik) *adj.* 1. of or pertaining to forces not in equilibrium, or to motion as the result of force: opposed to *static.* 2. pertaining to dynamics. 3. characterized by energy or forcefulness. [< F *dynamique*] —**dy·nam'i·cal·ly** *adv.*

dy·nam·ics (dī NAM iks) *n.* 1. *(construed as sing.)* the branch of physics that treats of the motion of bodies and the effects of forces in producing motion. 2. *(contrued as pl.)* the forces at work in any field.

dy·na·mite (DĪ nə MĪT) *n.* 1. an explosive composed of nitroglycerin held in some absorbent substance. 2. anything wonderful. —*v.t.* **·mit·ed, ·mit·ing** blow up or shatter with or as with dynamite. [< Sw. *dynamit*]

dy·na·mo (DĪ nə MOH) *n. pl.* **·mos** a generator for the conversion of mechanical energy into electrical energy.

dy·nas·ty (DĪ nə stee) *n. pl.* **·ties** a succession of sovereigns in one line of descent; also, the length of time during which one family is in power. [ME] —**dy·nas·tic** (dī NAS tik) *adj.*

dys·en·ter·y (DIS ən TER ee) *n. Pathol.* a painful inflammation of the large intestine, attended with bloody evacuations and some fever. [< Med.L *dysenteria*]

dys·lex·i·a (dis LEK see ə) *n.* any of certain

reading disorders characterized, for example, by letter and syllable reversals. [< NL]

dys•pep•sia (dis PEP shə) *n.* difficult or painful digestion. [< L]

dys•pep•tic (dis PEP tik) *adj.* **1.** relating to or suffering from dyspepsia. **2.** gloomy; peevish. —*n.* a dyspeptic person.

dysp•ne•a (disp NEE ə) *n. Pathol.* labored breathing. [< L *dyspnoea*]

dys•to•pi•a (dis TOH pee ə) *n.* a place of utter wretchedness. [< NL]

E

e, E (ee) *n. pl.* **e's** or **es, E's** or **Es 1.** the fifth letter of the English alphabet. **2.** any sound represented by the letter *e.* —*symbol* **1.** *Music* the third tone in the diatonic scale of C. **2.** *Math.* the base of the system of natural logarithms, approximately 2.718.

each (eech) *adj.* being one of two or more that together form a group; every. —*pron.* every one of any number or group considered individually; each one. —*adv.* for or to each person, article, etc.; apiece: one dollar *each.* [ME *eche*]

each other a compound reciprocal pronoun: They saw *each other.*

ea·ger (EE gər) *adj.* impatiently desirous of something. [ME *egre*]

ca·gle (EE gəl) *n.* **1.** a large bird of prey, esp. the **bald** (or **American) eagle,** dark brown, with the head, neck, and tail white, the national emblem of the U.S. **2.** a former gold coin of the U.S. having a value of $10. **3.** in golf, a score of two under par on any hole. [ME *egle*] —**ea·gle-eyed** (EE gəl ID) *adj.* having keen sight.

ear[1] (eer) *n.* **1.** the organ of hearing in its entirety. ◆ Collateral adjective: *aural.* **2.** the fleshy external part of the organ of hearing. **3.** the ability to perceive the refinements of music, poetry, or the like. **4.** attentive consideration; heed. **5.** something resembling the ear. [ME *ere*]

ear[2] *n.* the fruit-bearing part of a cereal plant, as corn. —*v.i.* form ears, as grain. [ME *ere*]

ear·ache (EER AYK) *n.* pain in the middle or internal ear.

ear·drum (EER DRUM) *n.* the tympanic membrane.

earl (url) *n.* a member of the British nobility next in rank above a viscount and below a marquis. [ME *erl*] —**earl·dom** (URL dəm) *n.*

ear·lobe (EER LOHB) *n.* the fleshy lower part of the external ear.

ear·ly (UR lee) *adj.* **·li·er, ·li·est 1.** coming near the beginning of a period of time or a series: *early* American painting. **2.** belonging to a distant time or stage of development: *early* man. **3.** occurring ahead of the usual or arranged time: an *early* dinner. **4.** occurring in the near future: an *early* truce

is expected. —*adv.* **1.** near the beginning of any specified period or series of things. **2.** far back in time. **3.** before the usual or arranged time. [ME *erlich*]

ear·mark (EER MAHRK) *n.* **1.** a distinctive mark made on an animal's ear to denote ownership. **2.** any mark of identification. —*v.t.* **1.** put an earmark on. **2.** set aside, as money, for a particular purpose.

earn (urn) *v.t.* **1.** receive or deserve as recompense for labor, service, or performance. **2.** produce as profit. [ME *ernien*]

ear·nest[1] (UR nist) *adj.* **1.** intent and direct in purpose; zealous: an *earnest* student. **2.** of a serious or important nature. —**in earnest** with serious intent or determination. [ME *erneste*]

ear·nest[2] *n. Law* money paid in advance to bind a contract. Also **earnest money.** [ME *ernest*]

carn·ings (UR ningz) *n.pl.* wages or profits.

ear·ring (EER RING) *n.* an ornament worn at the ear lobe.

ear·shot (EER SHOT) *n.* the distance at which sounds may be heard.

earth (urth) *n.* **1.** the dry land surface of the globe, as distinguished from the oceans and sky; ground. **2.** soil; dirt. **3.** *Often cap.* the planet on which people live. —**run to earth** hunt down and find, as a fox. [ME *erthe*]

earth·bound (URTH BOWND) *adj.* **1.** having material interests. **2.** confined to the earth.

earth·en (UR thən) *adj.* made of earth or baked clay.

earth·en·ware (UR thən WAIR) *n.* dishes, pots, and the like, made of baked clay.

earth·ling (URTH ling) *n.* an earth dweller.

earth·ly (URTH lee) *adj.* **1. a** of or relating to the earth; terrestrial. **b** of or relating to the material qualities of the earth; worldly; secular. **2.** possible; imaginable: of no *earthly* use. [ME *erthely*]

earth·quake (URTH KWAYK) *n.* a shaking of the earth's crust. ◆ Collateral adjective: *seismic.*

earth science any of a group of sciences concerned with origin, structure, composition, and physical features of the earth, as geology, geography, etc.

earth·shak·ing (URTH shay king) *adj.* of great importance or having great effect; momentous.

earth·ward (URTH wərd) *adv.* toward the earth. Also **earth'wards.** —*adj.* moving toward the earth.

earth·y (UR thee) *adj.* **earth·i·er, earth·i·est 1.** of or like earth. **2.** unrefined; coarse. **3.** natural; robust; lusty. [ME *erthy*] —**earth'i·ness** *n.*

ear·wax (EER waks) *n.* a waxy secretion found in the outer ear: also called *cerumen.*

ease (eez) *n.* **1.** freedom from physical discomfort or mental agitation. **2.** freedom from great effort or difficulty. **3.** naturalness; poise. —*v.* **eased, eas·ing** *v.t.* **1.** relieve or lessen pain or oppression of. **2.** lessen the pressure, weight, tension, etc., of: *ease* an axle. **3.** make easier; facilitate. **4.** put in place slowly and carefully. —*v.i.* **5.** lessen in severity, tension, speed, etc.: often with *up* or *off.* [ME *ese*]

ea·sel (EE zəl) *n.* a folding frame or tripod used to support an artist's canvas, etc. [< Du. *ezel* easel, ass]

case·ment (EEZ mənt) *n.* **1.** anything that gives ease or comfort. **2.** *Law* the right to use another's property.

east (eest) *n.* **1.** the direction of the sun in relation to an observer on earth at sunrise. **2.** one of the four cardinal points of the compass, directly opposite *west.* **3.** *Sometimes cap.* any region east of a specified point. —**the East 1.** Asia and its adjacent islands; the Orient. **2.** the eastern U.S. —*adj.* **1.** to, toward, facing, or in the east. **2.** coming from the east. —*adv.* in or toward the east. [ME *est*]

east·bound (EEST bownd) *adj.* going eastward.

East·er (EE stər) *n.* **1.** a Christian festival commemorating the resurrection of Christ. **2.** the day on which this festival is celebrated, the Sunday immediately after the first full moon that occurs on or after the spring equinox: also **Easter Sunday.** [ME *ester*]

east·er·ly (EE stər lee) *adj.* **1.** in, of, toward, or pertaining to the east. **2.** from the east, as a wind. —*adv.* toward or from the east. —*n. pl.* **·lies** a wind or storm from the east.

east·ern (EE stərn) *adj.* **1.** to, toward, or in the east. **2.** native to or inhabiting the east. **3.** *Sometimes cap.* of or like the east or the East.

east·ern·er (EE stər nər) *n.* **1.** one who is native to or lives in the east. **2.** *Usu. cap.* one who lives in or comes from the eastern U.S.

Eastern Orthodox Church the modern churches derived from the medieval Eastern Church, including the Greek and Russian Orthodox churches: also called *Eastern Church, Orthodox Church.*

east·ward (EEST wərd) *adv.* toward the east. Also **east'wards.** —*adj.* to, toward, facing, or in the east.

eas·y (EE zee) *adj.* **eas·i·er, eas·i·est 1.** requiring little effort; offering few difficulties: *easy* tasks. **2.** free from trouble or anxiety: an *easy* mind. **3.** characterized by rest or comfort: an *easy* life. **4.** informal; relaxed: an *easy* manner. **5.** not strict; indulgent. **6.** not burdensome; moderate: buy on *easy* terms. **7.** well-to-do; affluent: *easy* circumstances. —**be on easy street** be well-to-do; live in comfort. —*adv.* in an easy manner. —**go easy on** *Informal* **1.** use with moderation, as liquor. **2.** be lenient with. —**take it easy 1.** relax. **2.** remain calm. [ME *aisie*] —**eas'i·ly** *adv.*

eas·y·go·ing (EE zee GOH ing) *adj.* not inclined to effort or worry.

eat (eet) *v.* **ate, eat·en, eat·ing** *v.t.* **1.** consume food. **2.** consume or destroy as by eating: usu. with *away* or *up.* **3.** make (a hole etc.) by gnawing or corroding. —*v.i.* **4.** take food; have a meal. [ME *eten*]

eaves (eevz) *n.pl.* the lower projecting edge of a sloping roof. [ME *eves*]

eaves·drop (EEVZ drop) *v.i.* **·dropped, ·drop·ping** listen secretly, as to a private conversation. —**eaves'drop'per** *n.*

ebb (eb) *v.i.* **1.** recede, as the tide: opposed to *flow.* **2.** decline or weaken. —*n.* **1.** the flowing back of tidewater to the ocean: opposed to *flood.* Also **ebb tide. 2.** a condition of decline or decay. [ME *ebbe*]

eb·on·y (EB ə nee) *n. pl.* **·ies** a hard, heavy wood, usu. black; also a tropical hardwood tree yielding this wood. —*adj.* **1.** made of ebony. **2.** like ebony; black.

e·bul·lient (i BUUL yənt) *adj.* **1.** full of enthusiasm; exuberant. **2.** boiling or bubbling up. [< L, boiling up] —**e·bul'lience** *n.*

eb·ul·li·tion (EB ə LISH ən) *n.* **1.** the bubbling of a liquid; boiling. **2.** any sudden or violent agitation, as of emotions. [< L]

ec·cen·tric (ik SEN trik) *adj.* **1.** differing conspicuously in behavior, appearance, or opinions. **2.** not situated in the center, as an axis. **3.** deviating from a perfect circle: said chiefly of an elliptical orbit. **4.** *Math.* not having the same center. —*n.* an odd or erratic person. [< Med.L *eccentricus* out of center] —**ec·cen'tri·cal·ly** *adv.*

ec·cen·tric·i·ty (EK sən TRIS i tee) *n. pl.* **·ties 1.** deviation from what is regular or expected. **2.** a peculiarity. [< Med.L *eccentricitas*]

ec·cle·si·as·tic (i KLEE zee AS tik) *adj.* ecclesiastical. —*n.* a cleric; church person. [< LL *ecclesiasticus*]

ec·cle·si·as·ti·cal (i KLEE zee AS ti kəl) *adj.* of or pertaining to the church, esp. as an organized and governing power.

ech·e·lon (ESH ə LON) *n.* **1.** a stepped formation of troops, ships, or airplanes. **2.** *Mil.* a subdivision of a military force, based on position. **3.** a level in an organization; also, the persons at this level. [< F *échelon*, orig., ladder rung]

ech·o (EK oh) *n. pl.* **·oes 1.** the repetition of a sound caused by reflection; also, the sound so produced. **2.** any similar repetition or reproduction. **3.** one who imitates another or repeats own words. —*v.t.* **1.** repeat or send back (sound) by echo. **2.** repeat the words, opinions, etc. of. **3.** repeat in imitation. —*v.i.* **4.** be repeated or given back. —**e·cho·ic** *adj.* [ME *ecco*]

é·clair (ay KLAIR) *n.* a small oblong pastry shell filled with custard or whipped cream. [< F, lightning]

é·clat (ay KLAH) *n.* **1.** brilliance of action or effect. **2.** acclaim; conspicuous success. [< F, brilliance]

ec·lec·tic (i KLEK tik) *adj.* **1.** selecting what is considered best from different systems or sources. **2.** composed of elements selected from diverse sources. —*n.* one who selects from various schools or methods, as in philosophy or art. [< Gk. *eklektikós* selective] —**ec·lec·ti·cism** (i KLEK tə SIZ əm) *n.*

e·clipse (i KLIPS) *n.* **1.** *Astron.* the dimming or elimination of light from one heavenly body by another. A **lunar eclipse** is caused by the passage of the moon through the earth's shadow; a **solar eclipse** by the passage of the moon between the sun and the observer. **2.** any overshadowing or dimming, as of power or reputation. —*v.t.* **e·clipsed, e·clips·ing 1.** cause an eclipse of; darken. **2.** obscure by overshadowing or surpassing. [ME]

e·clip·tic (i KLIP tik) *n.* *Astron.* the apparent path of the sun among the stars.

e·co·cide (EK ə SID) *n.* **1.** the destruction of an ecosystem. **2.** that which is capable of destroying an ecosystem.

e·col·o·gy (i KOL ə jee) *n.* the division of biology that treats of the relations between organisms and their environment. —**ec·o·log·i·cal** *adj.* —**e·col'o·gist** *n.*

ec·o·nom·ic (EK ə NOM ik) *adj.* **1.** of or pertaining to the development and management of the material wealth of a community. **2.** relating to the science of economics. **3.** of or pertaining to financial matters. **4.** of practical use. [< MF *economique*]

ec·o·nom·i·cal (EK ə NOM i kəl) *adj.* **1.** frugal; thrifty. **2.** done with minimum waste of money, energy, time, etc. —**ec'o·nom'i·cal·ly** *adv.*

ec·o·nom·ics (EK ə NOM iks) *n.* **1.** (*construed as sing.*) the science that treats of the production, distribution, and consumption of wealth. **2.** (*construed as pl.*) economic matters.

e·con·o·mist (i KON ə mist) *n.* a specialist in economics.

e·con·o·mize (i KON ə MĪZ) *v.i.* **·mized, ·miz·ing** manage thriftily.

e·con·o·my (i KON ə mee) *n. pl.* **·mies 1.** frugal management of money, resources, etc.; also, an example of this. **2.** the administration of material resources, as of a country. **3.** the distribution and interplay of resources, materials, etc., in a structure or system: the *economy* of nature. [< MF *economie*]

e·co·sys·tem (EK oh SIS təm) *n.* a community in nature including plants and animals and the environment, both physical and chemical, associated with them.

ec·sta·sy (EK stə see) *n. pl.* **·sies 1.** a state of overpowering emotion. **2.** intense delight; rapture. [ME *extasie* trance] —**ec·stat·ic** (ek STAT ik) *adj.*

-ectomy *combining form* removal of a part by cutting out; surgical removal: *appendectomy.* [< NL *-ectomia*]

ec·u·men·i·cal (EK yuu MEN i kəl) *adj.* worldwide in scope, esp. of the Christian church: an *ecumenical* council. [< LL *oecumenicus* belonging to the world] —**ec·u·men·ism** (EK yuu mə NIZ əm), **ec·u·men·i·cal·ism** *n.*

ec·ze·ma (EG zə mə) *n.* *Pathol.* an inflammatory disease of the skin attended by itching, watery discharge. [< NL]

ed·dy (ED ee) *n. pl.* **·dies** a backward circling current of water or air. [ME] —*v.t. & v.i.* •**died,** •**dying**

e•de•ma (i DEE mə) *n. pl.* •**mas** *Pathol.* an abnormal accumulation of fluid in organs, cavities, or tissues of the body; swelling. [< NL *oedema* swelling] —e•dem•a•tous (i DEM ə təs) *adj.*

E•den (EED n) *n.* 1. in the Bible, the garden that was the first home of Adam and Eve: often called *Paradise.* 2. any delightful place or condition. [< Hebrew *ēden* delight]

edge (ej) *n.* 1. a bounding or dividing line; also, the part along a boundary; border; margin. 2. the cutting side of a blade. 3. sharpness; keenness. 4. advantage; superiority. —**on edge** 1. tense; irritable. 2. eager; impatient. —*v.* edged, edg•ing *v.t.* 1. sharpen. 2. furnish with an edge or border. 3. push sidewise or by degrees. —*v.i.* 4. move sidewise or by degrees. [ME *egge*]

edge•wise (EJ WIZ) *adv.* 1. with the edge forward. 2. on, by, with, or toward the edge. Also **edge′ways′** (-WAYZ).

edg•y (EJ ee) *adj.* edg•i•er, edg•i•est tense, nervous, or irritable. —edg′i•ness *n.*

ed•i•ble (ED ə bəl) *adj.* fit to eat. —*n. Usu. pl.* something fit to eat. [< LL *edibilis*]

e•dict (EE dikt) *n.* an official decree publicly proclaimed. [ME]

ed•i•fice (ED ə fis) *n.* a building or other structure, esp. a large and imposing one. [ME]

ed•i•fy (ED ə fi) *v.t.* •fied, •fy•ing enlighten and benefit, esp. morally or spiritually. [ME *edifien*] —ed′i•fi•ca′tion *n.*

ed•it (ED it) *v.t.* 1. prepare for publication by revising, compiling, etc. 2. prepare (film) for viewing by selecting, cutting, etc. 3. direct the preparation of (a newspaper, magazine, etc.).

e•di•tion (i DISH ən) *n.* 1. the form in which a book is published: a three-volume *edition.* 2. the total number of copies of a publication issued at any one time; also, such a copy. [< MF]

ed•i•tor (ED i tər) *n.* 1. one who edits. 2. a writer of editorials. [< Med.L]

ed•i•to•ri•al (ED i TOR ee əl) *n.* an article in a newspaper, magazine, etc., expressing an opinion of the editors or publishers. —*adj.* of, pertaining to, or written by an editor. ed•i•to•ri•al•ize (ED i TOR ee ə LIZ) *v.t. & v.i.* •ized, •iz•ing 1. express opinions (on a subject) editorially. 2. insert editorial opinions (into a news item, etc.).

ed•u•cate (EJ uu KAYT) *v.t.* •cat•ed, •cat•ing 1. develop or train by instruction or study; teach. 2. form or develop (taste, special ability, etc.). 3. provide schooling for. [< L *educatus* brought up] — ed•u•ca•ble (EJ uu kə bəl) *adj.* —ed′u•ca′tor *n.*

ed•u•cat•ed (EJ uu KAY tid) *adj.* 1. developed by education; instructed; trained. 2. having a cultivated mind, speech, manner, etc.

ed•u•ca•tion (EJ uu KAY shən) *n.* 1. the act of educating; development or training of the mind, capabilities, or character, esp. through formal schooling. 2. acquisition of knowledge or skills. 3. knowledge, skills, or cultivation acquired through instruction or study. 4. the study of teaching methods and the learning process; pedagogy. [< MF]

e•duce (i DOOS) *v.t.* e•duced, e•duc•ing 1. call forth; bring out; elicit. 2. infer or develop from data; deduce. [ME]

ee•rie (EER ee) *adj.* •ri•er, •ri•est inspiring fear; weird; ghostly. [ME *eri* cowardly]

ef•face (i FAYS) *v.t.* •faced, •fac•ing 1. rub out; erase. 2. obliterate. 3. make less prominent or insignificant. [< MF *effacer*]

ef•fect (i FEKT) *n.* 1. something brought about by some cause; result; consequence. 2. capacity to produce some result; efficacy. 3. the condition or fact of being in active force: put a law into *effect.* 4. the state of being actually accomplished or realized. 5. the particular way in which something affects something else. 6. the overall reaction or impression produced by something. 7. a technique used to produce a certain impression. 8. meaning; purport. 9. *pl.* movable goods; belongings. —**in effect** 1. in actual fact. 2. for all practical purposes; virtually. 3. in active force or operation. —*v.t.* bring about; cause; esp., accomplish: effect an escape. [ME]

ef•fec•tive (i FEK tiv) *adj.* 1. producing the desired or proper result. 2. being in force, as a law. 3. producing a striking impression.

ef•fec•tu•al (i FEK choo əl) *adj.* 1. producing an intended effect. 2. legally valid or binding. [ME *effectuel*]

ef•fec•tu•ate (i FEK choo AYT) *v.t.* •at•ed, •at•ing bring about; accomplish; effect. [< Med.L *effectuatus* brought about]

ef•fem•i•nate (i FEM ə nit) *adj.* 1. having womanlike traits; unmanly. 2. characterized by weakness or self-indulgence. [ME] —ef•fem′•i•na•cy *n.*

ef·fer·vesce (EF ər VES) v.i. •vesced,
•vesc·ing 1. give off or rise out in bubbles,
as a gas. 2. be lively or exhilarated. [< L
effervescere heat up] —ef'fer·ves'·cence
n. —ef'fer·ves'cent adj.

ef·fete (i FEET) adj. 1. having lost strength
or virility. 2. weakened; decadent. 3. incapable of further production; barren. [< L
effeta worn out from breeding]

ef·fi·ca·cious (EF i KAY shəs) adj. producing an intended effect. [< L efficere bring
about] —ef·fi·ca·cy (EF i kə see) n.

ef·fi·cien·cy (i FISH ən see) n. pl. •cies 1.
the quality of being efficient. 2. the ratio of
work done or energy expended to the energy supplied in the form of food or fuel. [<
L efficentia]

ef·fi·cient (i FISH ənt) adj. 1. productive of
results with a minimum of wasted effort. 2.
producing an effect. [ME]

ef·fi·gy (EF i jee) n. pl. •gies 1. a likeness or
representation; esp., a sculptured portrait.
2. a crude image of a disliked person. [<
MF]

ef·flu·ent (EF loo ənt) adj. flowing out. —n.
an outflow, as of water from a lake, industrial sewage, etc. [< L effluere flow out] —
ef'flu·ence n.

ef·fort (EF ərt) n. 1. expenditure of physical, mechanical, or mental energy to get
something done. 2. something produced by
exertion. [< MF] —ef'fort·less adj.

ef·front·er·y (i FRUN tə ree) n. pl. •ies
impudence; audacity. [< F effronterie
shamelessness]

ef·ful·gent (i FUL jənt) adj. shining brilliantly; radiant; splendid. [< L effulgere
shine] —ef·ful'gence n.

ef·fuse (i FYOOZ) v.i. •fused, •fus·ing 1.
pour forth. 2. talk without stopping. [ME]
—ef·fu'sion n.

ef·fu·sive (i FYOO siv) adj. 1. overflowing
with sentiment; demonstrative; gushing. 2.
pouring forth; overflowing. —ef·fu'sive·
ness n.

e·gal·i·tar·i·an (i GAL i TAIR ee ən) adj. of,
relating to, or believing in political and social equality. —n. one who believes in political and social equality. [< F égalitaire] —
e·gal'i·tar'i·an·ism n.

egg¹ (eg) n. 1. the round or oval reproductive body of female birds, insects, and most
reptiles and fishes, enclosed in a shell or
membrane, and from which young hatch.
2. Biol. the reproductive cell of female animals; ovum: also **egg cell.** 3. the hen's egg

as a food. 4. something oval like a hen's
egg. 5. Informal person: a good egg. —
lay an egg Informal fail completely.
[ME]

egg² v.t. incite; urge: usu. with on. [ME]

egg·head (EG hed) n. Informal an intellectual; high-brow: often derisive.

egg·nog (EG nog) n. a drink made of
beaten eggs, milk, sugar, nutmeg, and
sometimes liquor.

egg·shell (EG shel) n. the hard, brittle covering of a bird's egg. —adj. 1. thin and
fragile. 2. of pale yellow or ivory color.

e·go (EE goh) n. pl. e·gos 1. the self that is
aware of its distinction from the objects of
its thought and perceptions. 2. Psychoanal.
the conscious aspect of the psyche that develops through contact with the external
world and resolves conflicts between the id
and the superego. 3. self-centeredness;
conceit. [< L, I]

e·go·cen·tric (EE goh SEN trik) adj. excessively concerned with oneself. —n. an ego-
centric person.

e·go·ism (EE goh IZ əm) n. 1. inordinate
concern for oneself. 2. Philos. a doctrine
that regards the self or self-interest as primary. [< F égoisme] —e'go·ist n.

e·go·tism (EE gə TIZ əm) n. excessive concern with or reference to oneself; conceit;
selfishness. —e'go·tist n.

e·gre·gious (i GREE jəs) adj. conspicuously bad; glaring; flagrant. [< L egregius
preeminent]

e·gress (EE gres) n. 1. a going out; emer-
gence; also, the right of going out. 2. a place
of exit. [< L egressus escape]

E·gyp·tol·o·gy (EE jip TOL ə jee) n. the
study of the antiquities of Egypt. —
E'gyp·tol'o·gist n.

ei·ther (EE thər) adj. 1. one or the other of
two: Use either foot. 2. each of two; one and
the other: They sat on either side of her. —
pron. one or the other: Choose either. —
conj. in one of two or more cases, indeter-
minately or indifferently: a disjunctive correlative used with or: Either I or he will. —
adv. any more so: used after the denial of an
alternative, or to emphasize a preceding
negative: He could not speak, and I could
not either. [ME]

e·jac·u·late (i JAK yə LAYT) v. •lat·ed,
•lat·ing v.t. 1. utter suddenly, as a brief
exclamation. 2. discharge suddenly and
quickly, as seminal fluid. —v.i. 3. ejaculate
something. —n. (-yə lit) that which is ejacu-

lated. [< L *ejaculatus* shot out] —
e·jac′u·la′tion n.

e·ject (i JEKT) v.t. **1.** throw out with sudden
force; expel. **2.** *Law* dispossess; evict. [< L
ejectus thrown out] —**e·jec′tion** n.

eke (eek) v.t. **eked, ek·ing 1.** supplement;
extend: with *out*. **2.** make (a living) with
difficulty: with *out*. [ME *eken* increase]

e·lab·o·rate (i LAB ər it) adj. **1.** worked out
with great thoroughness or in minute detail. **2.** ornate and complex. —v. (ee LAB ə
RAYT) **·rat·ed, ·rat·ing** v.t. **1.** work out in
detail; develop carefully. —v.i. **2.** add details or embellishments: with *on* or *upon*.
[< L *elaboratus* worked out] —
e·lab′o·ra′tion n.

é·lan (ay LAHN) n. enthusiasm; dash; vivacity. [< F]

e·lapse (i LAPS) v.i. **e·lapsed, e·laps·ing**
slip by; pass away: said of time. [< L *elapsus*
slipped away]

e·las·tic (i LAS tik) adj. **1.** spontaneously
regaining former size or shape, after compression, extension, or other distortion. **2.**
adjusting readily; flexible or resilient. —n.
1. a stretchable material. **2.** a rubber band.
[< NL *elasticus* expanding]

e·las·tic·i·ty (i la STIS i tee) n. the property
or quality of being elastic; resilience.

e·late (i LAYT) v.t. **e·lat·ed, e·lat·ing** raise
the spirits of; make joyful; excite. [ME *elat*
proud] —**e·la′tion** n.

el·bow (EL boh) n. **1.** the joint at the bend of
the arm; esp., the projecting outer side of
this joint. **2.** the joint corresponding to an
elbow in the shoulder of a quadruped. **3.**
something, as a pipe fitting, bent like an
elbow. —**rub elbows with** associate
closely with (celebrities etc.). —v.t. **1.** push
with or with the elbows. **2.** make (one's way)
by such pushing. —v.i. **3.** push one's way
along. [ME *elbowe*]

el·bow·room (EL boh ROOM) n. enough
room to move or work without hindrance.

eld·er (EL dər) adj. **1.** of earlier birth; older;
senior. **2.** superior or prior in rank, office,
etc. **3.** earlier; former. —n. **1.** *Often pl.* an
older person; also, a forefather or predecessor. **2.** an influential senior member of a
family, community, etc. **3.** *Eccl.* a governing
or counseling officer in certain Christian
churches. **4.** an aged person. [ME] —**eld′**
er·ly adj. quite old.

eld·est (EL dist) adj. alternative superlative
of OLD.

e·lect (i LEKT) v.t. **1.** choose for an office by

vote. **2.** pick out; select. **3.** *Theol.* set aside
by divine will for salvation. —v.i. **4.** make a
choice. —adj. **1.** chosen; selected. **2.** elected to office, but not yet installed: used in
compounds: president-*elect*. —n. an elect
person or group. [ME]

e·lec·tion (i LEK shən) n. **1.** the formal
choice of a person for any position, usu. by
ballot. **2.** a popular vote on any question
officially proposed. **3.** *Theol.* predestination
to salvation. [ME *eleccioun*]

e·lec·tion·eer (i LEK shə NEER) v.i. work
for votes for a candidate or political party.

e·lec·tive (i LEK tiv) adj. **1.** of or pertaining
to a choice by vote. **2.** obtained or settled by
election. **3.** subject to choice; optional. —n.
an optional subject in a school or college
curriculum. [< Med.L *electivus*]

e·lec·tor (i LEK tər) n. **1.** one who elects; a
person qualified to vote. **2.** a member of the
electoral college. —**e·lec′tor·al** adj.

electoral college a body of electors, chosen
by the voters, which formally elects the
president and vice president of the United
States.

e·lec·tor·ate (i LEK tər it) n. **1.** the whole
body of voters. **2.** a district of voters.

e·lec·tric (i LEK trik) adj. **1.** relating to,
produced by, or operated by electricity. **2.**
producing or carrying electricity: *electric
cable*. **3.** thrillingly exciting. [< NL *elec-
tricus* amber] —**e·lec′tri·cal·ly** adv.

e·lec·tri·cian (i lek TRISH ən) n. a techni-
cian who installs, operates, or repairs electrical apparatus.

e·lec·tric·i·ty (i lek TRIS i tee) n. **1.** a fundamental property of matter, associated
with atomic particles whose movements
develop fields of force and generate kinetic
or potential energy. **2.** a current or charge of
energy so generated. **3.** the science that
deals with the laws, theory, and application
of electric energy. **4.** a state of great tension
or excitement.

e·lec·tri·fy (i LEK trə FI) v.t. **·fied, ·fy·ing
1.** charge with or subject to electricity. **2.**
equip or adapt for operation by electric
power. **3.** arouse; thrill.

e·lec·tro·car·di·o·gram (i LEK troh
KAHR dee ə GRAM) n. *Med.* the record
made by an electrocardiograph.

e·lec·tro·car·di·o·graph (i LEK troh
KAHR dee ə GRAF) n. *Med.* an instrument
for recording the electric current produced
by the action of the heart muscle.

e·lec·tro·chem·is·try (i LEK troh KEM ə

stree) n. the study of electricity as active in effecting chemical change. —e·lec'·tro·chem'i·cal adj.

e·lec·tro·cute (i LEK trə KYOOT) v.t. ·cut·ed, ·cut·ing kill by electricity. — e·lec'tro·cu'tion n.

e·lec·tro·en·ceph·a·lo·gram (i LEK troh en SEF ə lə GRAM) n. Med. the record made by an electroencephalograph.

e·lec·tro·en·ceph·a·lo·graph (i LEK troh en SEF ə lə GRAF) n. Med. an instrument for recording the strength and character of electrical impulses in the brain.

e·lec·trol·y·sis (i lek TROL ə sis) n. 1. the application of a direct current to an electrolyte so as to attract its positive ions to the cathode and its negative ions to the anode. 2. the removal of hair by treating the follicle with an electrically charged needle.

e·lec·tro·lyze (i LEK trə LĪZ) v.t. ·lyzed, ·lyz·ing decompose by electric current.

e·lec·tro·mag·net (i LEK troh MAG nit) n. a core of soft iron that temporarily becomes a magnet when an electric current passes through a coil of wire surrounding it.

e·lec·tro·mag·net·ism (i LEK troh MAG ni TIZ əm) n. 1. magnetism developed by electricity. 2. the science that treats of the relations between electricity and magnetism.

e·lec·tron (i LEK tron) n. a negatively charged elementary particle existing outside the nucleus of an atom. [< Gk. ēlektron amber]

e·lec·tron·ic (i lek TRON ik) adj. 1. of or pertaining to electrons or electronics. 2. operating or produced by the movement of free electrons, as in radio and radar.

e·lec·tron·ics (i lek TRON iks) n. (construed as sing.) the study of the properties and behavior of electrons, esp. with reference to technical and industrial applications.

electron microscope a microscope that projects a greatly enlarged image of an object held in the path of a sharply focused electron beam.

e·lec·tro·plate (i LEK trə PLAYT) v.t. ·plat·ed, ·plat·ing coat (an object) with metal by electrolysis. —n. an electroplated article.

e·lec·tro·shock therapy (í LEK trə SHOK) a treatment for mental disorders in which a coma is induced by passing an electric current through the brain.

el·ee·mos·y·nar·y (EL ee MOS ə NER ee)

adj. of, pertaining to, or aided by charity or alms. [< Med.L.eleemosynarius charitable]

el·e·gance (EL i gəns) n. 1. the state or quality of being elegant or refined. 2. something elegant. [< MF]

el·e·gant (ELi gənt) adj. 1. tastefully ornate in dress, furnishings, etc. 2. marked by grace and refinement, as in style, manners, etc. [ME]

el·e·gi·ac (EL i JĬ ək) adj. of, pertaining to, or like an elegy. —n. verse composed in elegiac form. [< MF]

el·e·gy (EL i jee) n. pl. ·gies 1. a poem of mourning and praise for the dead. 2. any meditative poem of lamentation. 3. Music a work of lamentation or mourning. [< MF] —el'e·gize v.t. & v.i ·gized, ·giz·ing

el·e·ment (EL ə mənt) n. 1. a relatively simple constituent that is a basic part of a whole; an essential part. 2. a group or class of people distinguished by belief, behavior, etc.: a rowdy element in a crowd. 3. one of four substances (earth, air, fire, water) anciently viewed as composing the physical universe. 4. the surrounding conditions best suited to some person or thing. 5. pl. atmospheric powers or forces: the fury of the elements. 6. Physics & Chem. a substance, as oxygen, carbon, silver, etc., composed entirely of atoms having the same atomic number, and which may not be decomposed by ordinary chemical means. [ME]

el·e·men·tal (EL ə MEN tl) adj. 1. of or relating to an element or elements. 2. fundamental and relatively simple; basic. 3. of or suggestive of the powerful forces of nature. 4. chemically uncombined.

el·e·men·ta·ry (EL ə MEN tə ree) adj. 1. elemental. 2. fundamental; basic. 3. simple and rudimentary.

elementary school a school giving a course of education of six or eight years: also called grade school, grammar school.

el·e·phant (EL ə fənt) n. a massively built, almost hairless mammal of Asia and Africa, having a flexible trunk and long ivory tusks. [ME]

el·e·phan·ti·a·sis (EL ə fən TĪ ə sis) n. Pathol. a disease caused by a parasitic worm, characterized by a hardening of the skin, and an enormous enlargement of the part affected. [< L]

el·e·phan·tine (EL ə FAN teen) adj. 1. of or pertaining to an elephant. 2. enormous; unwieldy; ponderous. [< L elephantinus]

el•e•vate (EL ə VAYT) *v.t.* **•vat•ed, •vat•ing** **1.** lift up; raise. **2.** raise in rank, status, etc. **3.** raise the spirits of; cheer; elate. **4.** raise the pitch or loudness of. **5.** raise the moral or intellectual level of. [< L *elevatus* raised up]

el•e•vat•ed (EL ə VAY tid) *adj.* **1.** raised up; high. **2.** lofty in character; sublime. —*n.* an overhead railroad.

el•e•va•tion (EL ə VAY shən) *n.* **1.** the act of elevating, or the state of being elevated. **2.** an elevated place. **3.** height above sea level. **4.** loftiness of thought, position, etc. **5.** in dancing, the ability to leap. **6.** in drafting, a side, front, or rear view of a structure.

el•e•va•tor (EL ə VAY tər) *n.* **1.** one who or that which elevates. **2.** a mechanism for hoisting grain. **3.** a granary. **4.** a movable platform or car that carries passengers or freight up and down.

elf (elf) *n. pl.* **elves** (elvz) in folklore, a dwarf-ish sprite with magical powers, usu. mis-chievous. [ME] —**elf'in, elf'ish** *adj.*

e•lic•it (i LIS it) *v.t.* **1.** draw out or forth; evoke: *elicit* a reply. **2.** bring to light: *elicit* the truth. [< L *elicitus* drawn out]

e•lide (i LĪD) *v.t.* **e•lid•ed, e•lid•ing 1.** omit (a vowel or syllable) in pronunciation. **2.** suppress; omit; ignore. [< L *elidere* strike out]

el•i•gi•ble (EL i jə bəl) *adj.* **1.** capable of and qualified for. **2.** fit for or worthy of choice. [< MF] —**el'i•gi•bil'i•ty** *n.*

e•lim•i•nate (i LIM ə NAYT) *v.t.* **•nat•ed, •nat•ing 1.** get rid of. **2.** remove (a contes-tant, team, etc.) from further competition by defeating. **3.** *Physiol.* void; excrete. [< L *eliminatus* sent out the door] — **e•lim'i•na'tion** *n.*

e•li•sion (i LIZH ən) *n.* omission of a vowel or syllable, as in "th'empress." [< L *elidere* strike out]

e•lite (i LEET) *n.* **1.** the choicest part, as of a social group. **2.** a size of typewriter type, having 12 characters to the inch. [ME *elit*] —**e•lite'** *adj.*

e•lit•ism (i LEE tiz əm) *n.* **1.** rule or domina-tion by an elite. **2.** advocacy of elite leader-ship. **3.** pride in belonging to an elite. — **e•lit'ist** *n. & adj.*

e•lix•ir (i LIK sər) *n.* **1.** a sweetened alco-holic medicinal preparation. **2.** in ancient philosophy, a substance sought by alche-mists for changing base metals into gold, or for prolonging life. **3.** a cure-all. [ME]

E•liz•a•be•than (i LIZ ə BEE thən) *adj.* of or

pertaining to Elizabeth I of England, or to her era. —*n.* an English person living dur-ing the reign of Elizabeth I.

el•lipse (i LIPS) *n. Geom.* an oval-shaped curve; a conic section. [< F]

el•lip•sis (i LIP sis) *n. pl.* **•ses** (-seez) **1.** *Gram.* the omission of a word or words nec-essary for the complete grammatical con-struction of a sentence, but not required for the understanding of it. **2.** marks, as (. . .), indicating omission. [< L, an omission]

el•lip•ti•cal (i LIP ti kəl) *adj.* **1.** of, pertain-ing to, or shaped like an ellipse. **2.** *Gram.* characterized by ellipsis; shortened.

el•o•cu•tion (EL ə KYOO shən) *n.* the art of public speaking, including vocal delivery and gesture. [< L *elocutio* a speaking out]

e•lon•gate (i LAWNG gayt) *v.t. & v.i.* **•gat•ed, •gat•ing** increase in length; stretch. —*adj.* drawn out; lengthened. [< LL *elongatus* lengthened] —**e•lon-ga•tion** (i lawng GAY shən) *n.*

e•lope (i LOHP) *v.i.* **e•loped, e•lop•ing** run away with a lover, usu. to get married. [ME] —**e•lope'ment** *n.*

el•o•quence (EL ə kwəns) *n.* fluent, pol-ished, and effective use of language. [ME]

el•o•quent (EL ə kwənt) *adj.* **1.** possessed of or manifesting eloquence. **2.** visibly expres-sive of emotion: *eloquent* sighs. [ME]

else (els) *adv.* **1.** in a different place, time, or way; instead: Where *else?* How *else?* **2.** if the case or facts were different; other-wise: Hurry, or *else* you will be caught. — *adj.* additional; different: somebody *else.* [ME]

else•where (ELS HWAIR) *adv.* in or to an-other place or places; somewhere or any-where else. [ME *elleswher*]

e•lu•ci•date (i LOO si DAYT) *v.t. & v.i.* **•dat•ed, •dat•ing** explain; clarify. [< LL *elucidatus* enlightened] —**e•lu'ci•da'tion** *n.*

e•lude (i LOOD) *v.t.* **e•lud•ed, e•lud•ing 1.** avoid or escape from; evade. **2.** escape the notice or understanding of: The mean-ing *eludes* me. [< L *eludere* deceive]

e•lu•sive (i LOO siv) *adj.* tending to slip away; hard to grasp or perceive: an *elusive* fragrance. —**e•lu'sive•ness** *n.*

elves (elvz) plural of ELF.

e•ma•ci•ate (i MAY shee AYT) *v.t.* **•at•ed, •at•ing** make abnormally lean; cause to lose flesh. [< L *emaciatus* wasted away]

em•a•nate (EM ə NAYT) *v.i.* **•nat•ed, •nat•ing** flow forth from a source; issue. [<

L *emanatus* having flowed out] —
em′a•na′tion n.

e•man•ci•pate (i MAN sə PAYT) v.t.
•pat•ed, •pat•ing release from bondage,
oppression, or authority; set free. [< L
emancipatus freed from bondage] —
e•man′ci•pa′tion n.

e•mas•cu•late (i MAS kyə LAYT) v.t.
•lat•ed, •lat•ing 1. deprive of procreative
power; castrate; geld. **2.** deprive of strength
and vigor; weaken. —adj. (-kyə lit) emascu-
lated; effeminate; weakened. [< L *emascu-
latus*] —**e•mas′cu•la′tion** n.

em•balm (em BAHM) v.t. preserve (a dead
body) from decay by treatment with chemicals, etc. [ME *embalmen*] —**em•balm′er**
n.

em•bank•ment (em BANGK mənt) n. a
mound or bank raised to hold back water,
support a roadway, etc.

em•bar•go (em BAHR goh) n. pl. **•goes 1.**
an order by a government restraining merchant vessels from leaving or entering its
ports. **2.** authoritative stoppage of foreign
commerce or of any special trade. [< Sp.]
—**em•bar′go** v.t. **•goed, •go•ing**

em•bark (em BAHRK) v.t. **1.** put or take
aboard a vessel. —v.i. **2.** go aboard a vessel
for a voyage. **3.** engage in a venture. [< MF
embarquer] —**em•bar•ka′tion** (EM bahr
KAY shən) n.

em•bar•rass (em BAR əs) v.t. **1.** make self-
conscious and uncomfortable; disconcert.
2. involve in financial difficulties. **3.** hamper; impede. [< F *embarrasser*] —
em•bar′rass•ment n.

em•bas•sy (EM bə see) n. pl. **•sies 1.** an
ambassador together with the ambassador's
staff. **2.** the mission, function, or position of
an ambassador. **3.** the official residence or
headquarters of an ambassador. [< MF
ambassee]

em•bat•tle (em BAT l) v.t. **•tled, •tling** prepare or equip for battle. [ME *embatailen*]

em•bed (em BED) v.t. **•bed•ded,
•bed•ding** set firmly in surrounding matter.

em•bel•lish (em BEL ish) v.t. **1.** ornament;
decorate. **2.** heighten the interest of (a narrative) by adding fictitious details. [ME *em-
belisshen* beautify] —**em•bel′lish•ment**
n.

em•ber (EM bər) n. **1.** a live coal or unex-
tinguished piece of wood, as in a fire. **2.** pl. a
dying fire. [ME *eymere*]

em•bez•zle (em BEZ əl) v.t. **•zled, •zling**

appropriate fraudulently to one's own use,
as money entrusted to one's care. [ME *em-
besilen* make away with] —**em•bez′zler** n.

em•bit•ter (em BIT ər) v.t. make bitter or
unhappy. —**em•bit′ter•ment** n.

em•blem (EM bləm) n. an object or pictorial
device that serves as a symbol, as of an idea,
institution, etc. [ME] —**em′blem•at′ic**
adj.

em•bod•i•ment (em BOD ee mənt) n. **1.**
the act of embodying, or the state of being
embodied. **2.** that which embodies, or in
which something is embodied.

em•bod•y (em BOD ee) v.t. **•bod•ied,
•bod•y•ing 1.** put into visible or concrete
form: *embody* ideals in action. **2.** make part
of an organized whole; incorporate. —
em•bod•i•ment n.

em•bo•lism (EM bə LIZ əm) n. *Pathol.* the
clogging of a vein or artery by an embolus.
[ME]

em•bo•lus (EM bə ləs) n. pl. **•li** (-lī) *Pathol.* a
foreign body that forms an obstruction in a
blood vessel, as a blood clot or an air bubble. [< L]

em•boss (em BAWS) v.t. **1.** cover with
raised figures, designs, etc. **2.** raise (designs, figures, etc.) from or upon a surface.
[ME *embosen*]

em•bou•chure (AHM buu SHUUR) n. **1.**
the mouth of a river. **2.** *Music* **a** the mouthpiece of a wind instrument. **b** the position
or application of the lips and tongue in playing a wind instrument. [< F]

em•brace (em BRAYS) v. **•braced,
•brac•ing** v.t. **1.** clasp in the arms; hug. **2.**
accept willingly; adopt, as a religion or doctrine. **3.** surround; encircle. **4.** include; contain. **5.** take in visually or mentally. —v.i. **6.**
hug each other. —n. the act of embracing.
[ME]

em•broi•der (em BROI dər) v.t. & v.i. **1.**
ornament (cloth) with designs in needlework. **2.** execute (a design) in needlework.
3. exaggerate; embellish. [ME *embro-
deren*] —**em•broi′der•y** n.

em•broil (em BROIL) v.t. **1.** involve in dissension or strife. **2.** complicate or confuse.
[< MF *embrouiller*]

em•bry•o (EM bree OH) n. pl. **•os 1.** *Biol.* an
organism in the earliest stages of development; in the human species, the first eight
weeks. **2.** *Bot.* the rudimentary plant within
the seed. **3.** anything in its rudimentary
stage. [< Med.L *embryon* swelling] —
em•bry•on•ic (EM bree ON ik) adj.

em·bry·ol·o·gy (EM bree OL ə jee) *n.* the science that deals with the origin, structure, and development of the embryo. — **em′bry·ol′o·gist** *n.*

e·mend (iMEND) *v.t.* make corrections or changes in (a text). [ME] — **e·men·da·tion** (EE men DAY shən) *n.*

e·merge (i MURJ) *v.i.* **e·merged, e·merg·ing 1.** come forth, as from water, a hiding place, etc. **2.** come to light; become apparent. [< L *emergere* rise out of] —**e·mer′gence** *n.*

e·mer·gen·cy (i MUR jən see) *n. pl.* **·cies** a sudden and unexpected turn of events calling for immediate action.

e·mer·i·tus (i MER i təs) *adj.* retired from active service, usu. because of age, but retained in an honorary position: *professor emeritus.* [< L *emeritus* having fully earned]

e·met·ic (ə MET ik) *adj.* tending to produce vomiting. [< L *emeticus* causing vomiting] —**e·met′·ic** *n.*

em·i·grant (EM i grənt) *adj.* moving from one place or country to settle in another. — *n.* a person who emigrates.

em·i·grate (EM i GRAYT) *v.i.* **·grat·ed, ·grat·ing** move away from one country, or section of a country, to settle in another. [< L *emigratus* moved away] —**em′i·gra′tion** *n.*

em·i·nence (EM ə nəns) *n.* **1.** superiority in rank, power, achievement, etc. **2.** a person having such rank or power. **3.** a high place or elevation, as a hill. [ME]

em·i·nent (EM ə nənt) *adj.* **1.** superior; outstanding; distinguished: *eminent* scholars. **2.** noteworthy; conspicuous: *eminent* valor. **3.** high; lofty. [ME]

eminent domain *Law* the right or power of the state to take or control private property for public use.

e·mir (ə MEER) *n.* **1.** a Muslim prince or commander. **2.** a high Turkish official. [< Arabic *amīr* ruler] —**e·mir′ate** *n.*

em·is·sar·y (EM ə SER ee) *n. pl.* **·sar·ies 1.** a person sent on a mission as an agent or representative of a government. **2.** a secret agent; spy. [< L *emissarius* a person sent out]

e·mit (i MIT) *v.t.* **e·mit·ted, e·mit·ting 1.** send forth or give off (light, heat, sound, etc.); discharge. **2.** give expression to; utter, as an opinion. **3.** put into circulation, as money. [< L *emittere* send forth] — **e·mis·sion** (ə MISH ən) *n.*

e·mol·lient (i MOL yənt) *adj.* softening or soothing, esp. to the skin. —*n. Med.* a softening or soothing medication. [< L *emollire* soften up]

e·mol·u·ment (i MOL yə mənt) *n.* a salary or fee as for a service. [< L *emolumentum* benefit]

e·mote (i MOHT) *v.i.* **e·mot·ed, e·mot·ing** exhibit an exaggerated emotion, as in acting. [< EMOTION]

e·mo·tion (i MOH shən) *n.* a strong surge of feeling, as of love, hate, or fear. [< MF *esmotion*]

e·mo·tion·al (i MOH shə nl) *adj.* **1.** of, pertaining to, or expressive of emotion. **2.** easily or excessively affected by emotion. **3.** arousing the emotions.

e·mo·tive (i MOH tiv) *adj.* characterized by, expressing, or tending to excite emotion.

em·pa·thize (EM pə THIZ) *v.t. & v.i.* **·thized, ·thiz·ing** regard with or feel empathy.

em·pa·thy (EM pə thee) *n.* intellectual or imaginative apprehension of another's condition or state of mind. [< Gk. *empátheia* affection] —**em·pa·thet·ic** (EM pə THET ik) *adj.*

em·per·or (EM pər ər) *n.* the sovereign of an empire. [ME *emperour*]

em·pha·sis (EM fə sis) *n. pl.* **·ses** (-seez) **1.** stress given by voice, gesture, etc., to a particular syllable, word, or phrase. **2.** force or intensity of meaning, action, etc. **3.** special importance or attention assigned to something. [< L] —**em·pha·size** (EM fə SIZ) *v.t.* **·sized, ·siz·ing**

em·phat·ic (em FAT ik) *adj.* **1.** spoken or done with emphasis; forcibly expressive. **2.** characterized by forcefulness or intensity. **3.** striking; decisive. [< Gk. *emphatikós* forceful] —**em·phat′i·cal·ly** *adv.*

em·phy·se·ma (EM fə SEE mə) *n. Pathol.* a lung condition marked by loss of elasticity of the air sacs, causing difficulty in breathing. [< NL]

em·pire (EM pīr) *n.* **1.** a state, or union of states, governed by an emperor; also, the historical period of such government. **2.** a union of dispersed states and unrelated peoples under one rule. **3.** wide and supreme dominion. [ME]

em·pir·i·cal (em PIR i kəl) *adj.* relating to or based on direct experience or observation alone: *empirical* knowledge.

em·pir·i·cism (em PIR ə SIZ əm) *n.* **1.** *Philos.* the doctrine that all knowledge is derived from sensory experience. **2.** reliance on sensory observation and experiment as the bases of knowledge. —**em·pir′i·cist** n.

em·ploy (em PLOI) v.t. **1.** engage the services of; hire. **2.** provide work and livelihood for. **3.** make use of as a means or instrument. —n. the state of being employed; service. [ME employen]

em·pow·er (em POW ər) v.t. **1.** authorize; delegate authority to. **2.** enable; permit.

em·press (EM pris) n. **1.** a woman who rules an empire. **2.** the wife or widow of an emperor. [ME emperesse]

emp·ty (EMP tee) adj. **·ti·er, ·ti·est 1.** containing nothing: an empty room. **2.** without significance; unsubstantial; hollow: empty promises. **3.** destitute or devoid of: with of: empty of compassion. **4.** hungry. —v. **·tied, ·ty·ing** v.t. **1.** remove the contents of. **2.** transfer the contents of (a container): to empty a bucket. **3.** unburden; clear: with of. —v.i. **4.** discharge itself or its contents. —n. pl. **·ties** an empty container, vehicle, etc. [ME] —**emp′ti·ness** n.

emp·ty-hand·ed (EMP tee HAN did) adj. carrying nothing.

em·u·late (EM yə LAYT) v.t. **·lat·ed, ·lat·ing** try to equal or surpass, esp. by imitating. [< L aemulatus rivaled] —**em′u·la′tion** n.

e·mul·si·fy (i MUL sə FI) v.t. **·fied, ·fy·ing** make into an emulsion. —**e·mul′si·fi′er** n.

e·mul·sion (iMUL shən) n. **1.** a liquid mixture in which a fatty or resinous substance is suspended in minute globules, as butterfat in milk. **2.** Photog. a light-sensitive coating for film, plates, etc. [< NL]

en·a·ble (en AY bəl) v.t. **·bled, ·bling 1.** supply with adequate power or opportunity; make able. **2.** make possible or practicable.

en·act (en AKT) v.t. **1.** make into a law; decree. **2.** represent in or as in a play; act the part of. —**en·act′ment** n.

e·nam·el (i NAM əl) n. **1.** a vitreous, usu. opaque material applied by fusion to surfaces of metal, glass, or porcelain as a decoration or a protective covering. **2.** a piece executed in enamel. **3.** a paint that dries to form a hard, glossy surface. **4.** Anat. the hard outer layer of the teeth. —v.t. **en·am·eled, en·am·el·ing 1.** cover or inlay with enamel. **2.** surface with or as with enamel. [ME enamalen]

en·am·or (i NAM ər) v.t. inflame with love;

also, charm; fascinate: chiefly in the passive, followed by of: He is enamored of his cousin. [ME enamouren]

en·cap·su·late (en KAP sə LAYT) v.t. **·lat·ed, ·lat·ing 1.** enclose in or as in a capsule. **2.** summarize or condense. —**en·cap′su·la′tion** n.

en·case (en KAYS) v.t. **·cased, ·cas·ing** enclose in or as in a case. —**en·case′ment** n.

en·ceinte (en SANT) adj. pregnant. [< F]

en·ceph·a·li·tis (en SEF ə LĪ tis) n. Pathol. inflammation of the brain.

en·chant (en CHANT) v.t. **1.** put a spell on; bewitch. **2.** charm completely; delight. [ME] —**en·chant′ment** n.

en·ci·pher (en SĪ fər) v.t. convert (a message, report, etc.) from plain text into code.

en·cir·cle (en SUR kəl) v.t. **·cled, ·cling 1.** form a circle around. **2.** go around.

en·clave (EN klayv) n. **1.** a territory completely or partially enclosed by a foreign territory to which it is not politically subject. **2.** a district, as in a city, inhabited by a minority group. [< F]

en·close (en KLOHZ) v.t. **·closed, ·clos·ing 1.** close in on all sides; surround. **2.** transmit within the cover of a letter. **3.** contain.

en·clo·sure (en KLOH zhər) n. **1.** the act of enclosing, or the state of being enclosed. **2.** an enclosed object or area. **3.** that which encloses, as a wall.

en·code (en KOHD) v.t. **·cod·ed, ·cod·ing** convert (a message, document, etc.) into code.

en·co·mi·um (en KOH mee əm) n. pl. **·mi·ums** or **·mi·a** (-mee ə) a formal expression of praise; eulogy. [< L]

en·com·pass (en KUM pəs) v.t. **1.** form a circle around; surround. **2.** enclose; contain.

en·core (AHNG kor) interj. again! once more! —n. the call by an audience for repetition of a performance or for an additional performance; also, that which is performed in response to this call. —v.t. **·cored, ·cor·ing** call for a repetition of (a performance) or by (a performer). [< F, yet]

en·coun·ter (en KOWN tər) n. **1.** a meeting with a person or thing, esp. when casual or unexpected. **2.** a hostile meeting; contest. —v.t. **1.** meet, esp. by chance. **2.** meet in battle. **3.** be faced with or contend against (opposition, difficulties, etc.). [ME encountren]

encounter group a group of persons seeking to develop self-awareness, sensitivity to others, etc. through uninhibited expression of feelings and physical contact.

en·cour·age (en KUR ij) *v.t.* **·aged, ·ag·ing 1.** inspire with courage, hope, or resolution. **2.** help or foster. [ME *encoragen*] **—en·cour'age·ment** *n.*

en·croach (en KROHCH) *v.i.* intrude stealthily or gradually: with *on* or *upon.* [ME *encrochen*] **—en·croach'·ment** *n.*

en·crust (en KRUST) *v.* see INCRUST.

en·cum·ber (en KUM bər) *v.t.* **1.** hinder in action or motion, as with a burden; impede. **2.** block up; crowd, as with obstacles. **3.** weigh down, as with debts. [ME *encombren*]

en·cyc·li·cal (en SIK li kəl) *adj.* intended for general circulation: said of letters. **—***n.* a letter addressed by the Pope to the bishops of the world. [< LL *encyclicus*]

en·cy·clo·pe·di·a (en sI klə PEE dee ə) *n.* a comprehensive work made up of articles covering the whole range of knowledge or treating of one particular field. [< NL *encyclopaedia*] **—en·cy'clo·pe'dic** *adj.*

en·cy·clo·pe·dist (en sI klə PEE dist) *n.* a writer for or compiler of an encyclopedia.

end (end) *n.* **1.** the terminal point or part of anything that has length: the *end* of a street. **2.** the extreme limit of something; boundary: the *ends* of the earth. **3.** the point in time at which something ceases. **4.** the purpose of an action. **5.** a conclusion; final part. **6.** a natural consequence. **7.** the termination of existence; death. **8.** fragment; remnant: odds and *ends.* **9.** in football, a player positioned at either end of the line. **—make (both) ends meet** live within one's income. **—***v.t.* **1.** bring to a finish or termination. **2.** be the end of. **—***v.i.* **3.** come to an end. [ME]

en·dan·ger (en DAYN jər) *v.t.* expose to danger; imperil.

en·dan·gered (en DAYN jərd) *adj.* in danger of extinction: an *endangered* species.

en·dear (en DEER) *v.t.* make dear or beloved. **—en·dear'ing** *adj.*

en·dear·ment (en DEER mənt) *n.* **1.** The act of endearing, or the state of being endeared. **2.** a loving word, act, etc.

en·deav·or (en DEV ər) *n.* an attempt or effort. **—***v.t.* **1.** make an effort to do or effect; try. **—***v.i.* **2.** strive. [ME *endeveren*]

en·dem·ic (en DEM ik) *adj.* **1.** peculiar to a particular country or people. **2.** *Med.* confined to or characteristic of a given locality: said of a disease. [< NL *endemicus*]

end·ing (EN ding) *n.* **1.** the act of bringing or coming to an end. **2.** the concluding or final part. **3.** one or more concluding letters or syllables added to the base of a word, esp. to indicate an inflection. [ME]

en·dive (EN dīv) *n.* an herb whose leaves are used in salads. [ME]

end·less (END lis) *adj.* **1.** enduring forever; eternal. **2.** having no end in space; infinite. **3.** continually recurring; incessant. **4.** forming a closed loop or circle.

en·do·crine (EN də krin) *Physiol. adj.* **1.** secreting internally. **2.** of or pertaining to an endocrine gland or its secretion. [< *endo-* within + Gk. *krinein* separate]

endocrine gland *Anat.* a ductless gland, as the thyroid etc., whose secretions are released directly into the blood.

en·do·cri·nol·o·gy (EN doh krə NOL ə jee) *n. Med.* a science dealing with the endocrine glands. **—en'do·cri·nol'o·gist** *n.*

en·dorse (en DORS) *v.t.* **·dorsed, ·dors·ing 1.** write on the back of (a paper); esp., transfer ownership or assign payment of (a check, note, etc.). **2.** give sanction or support to. **3.** state one's personal approval of (a product) to promote its sale. [< Med.L *indorsare*]

en·dow (en DOW) *v.t.* **1.** bestow a permanent fund or income upon. **2.** furnish or equip, as with talents: usu. with *with.* [ME *endowen* furnish a dowry] **—en·dow'ment** *n.*

en·dur·ance (en DUUR əns) *n.* the act or capacity of bearing up, as under hardship or prolonged stress.

en·dure (en DUUR) *v.* **·dured, ·dur·ing** *v.t.* **1.** bear up under: *endure* hardships. **2.** put up with; tolerate. **—***v.i.* **3.** continue to be; last. **4.** suffer without yielding. [ME *enduren*] **—en·dur'a·ble** *adj.*

en·dur·ing (en DUUR ing) *adj.* **1.** lasting; permanent. **2.** long-suffering.

end·wise (END wīz) *adv.* **1.** with the end foremost or uppermost. **2.** on end. **3.** lengthwise. Also **end·ways** (END WAYZ).

en·e·ma (EN ə mə) *n. Med.* **1.** a liquid injected into the rectum for cleansing or diagnostic purposes. **2.** the injection of such a liquid. [< LL]

en·e·my (EN ə mee) *n. pl.* **·mies 1.** one who harbors hatred or malicious intent toward another; also, one who or that which opposes a person, cause, etc. **2.** a hostile power or military force; also, a member of a hostile force. —*adj.* of or pertaining to a hostile army or power. [ME *enimi*]

en·er·get·ic (EN ər JET ik) *adj.* having or displaying energy; forceful and efficient. —**en′er·get′i·cal·ly** *adv.*

en·er·gize (EN ər JIZ) *v.t.* ·**gized,** ·**giz·ing** give energy, force, or strength to; activate. —**en′er·giz′er** *n.*

en·er·gy (EN ər jee) *n. pl.* ·**gies 1.** vigor or intensity of action or expression. **2.** capacity or tendency for vigorous action. **3.** *Physics* the capacity for doing work and for overcoming inertia. **Potential energy** is due to the position of one body relative to another, and **kinetic energy** is manifested by bodies in motion. [< LL *energia*]

en·er·vate (EN ər VAYT) *v.t.* ·**vat·ed,** ·**vat·ing** weaken in body or will. [< L *enervatus* weakened] —**en′er·va′tion** *n.*

en·fee·ble (en FEE bəl) *v.t.* ·**bled,** ·**bling** make feeble.

en·fold (en FOHLD) *v.t.* **1.** envelop. **2.** embrace.

en·force (en FORS) *v.t.* ·**forced,** ·**forc·ing 1.** compel observance of (a law, etc.). **2.** impose (obedience, etc.) by force. [ME *enforcen*] —**en·force′a·ble** *adj.*

en·fran·chise (en FRAN chīz) *v.t.* ·**chised,** ·**chis·ing 1.** endow with a franchise, as with the right to vote. **2.** set free, as from bondage or legal liabilities. [< MF *enfranchir* free] —**en·fran·chise·ment** (en FRAN chiz mənt) *n.*

en·gage (en GAYJ) *v.* ·**gaged,** ·**gag·ing** *v.t.* **1.** hire or employ (a person, service, etc.). **2.** reserve the use of, as lodgings. **3.** hold the interest or attention of; engross. **4.** occupy; keep busy. **5.** bind by a pledge, contract, etc. **6.** betroth: usu. in the passive. **7.** enter into conflict with: *engage* the enemy. **8.** *Mech.* mesh or interlock with. —*v.i.* **9.** occupy oneself in an undertaking. **10.** pledge oneself; warrant. **11.** enter into combat. **12.** *Mech.* mesh. [< MF *engager* pledge]

en·gage·ment (en GAYJ mənt) *n.* **1.** the act of engaging, or the state of being engaged. **2.** something that engages or binds, as an obligation. **3.** betrothal. **4.** an appointment; date. **5.** employment, esp. for a limited period. **6.** a hostile encounter; battle.

en·gag·ing (en GAY jing) *adj.* winning; pleasing. —**en·gag′ing·ly** *adv.*

en·gen·der (en JEN dər) *v.t.* cause to exist; produce. [ME, generate]

en·gine (EN jin) *n.* **1.** a machine that converts heat energy into mechanical work. **2.** a

locomotive. **3.** an apparatus or mechanical contrivance for producing some effect. [ME *engin*]

en·gi·neer (EN jə NEER) *n.* **1.** one versed in or practicing any branch of engineering. **2.** one who operates an engine. **3.** *Mil.* a member of a corps of soldiers engaged in engineering projects. —*v.t.* **1.** put through or manage by contrivance: *engineer* a scheme. **2.** plan and superintend as engineer.

en·gi·neer·ing (EN jə NEER ing) *n.* **1.** the art and science of designing, constructing, and operating roads, bridges, buildings, etc. **2.** clever planning or maneuvering.

Eng·lish (ING glish) —*n.* **1.** the people of England collectively: with *the.* **2.** the language of England, the United States, and areas formerly controlled by England. —**Old English** or **Anglo-Saxon** the English language from about A.D. 450 to 1050. —**Middle English** the language of England after the Norman Conquest, from about 1050 to 1475. —**Modern English** the English language since 1475. **3.** in billiards, a twist or spin given to a ball. [ME] —**Eng′lish** *adj.*

en·gorge (en GORJ) *v.t.* ·**gorged,** ·**gorg·ing 1.** fill with blood, as an artery. **2.** devour or swallow greedily. [< MF *engorger*]

en·grave (en GRAYV) *v.t.* ·**graved,** ·**grav·ing 1.** carve or etch figures, letters, etc. into (a surface). **2.** cut (pictures, lettering, etc.) into metal, stone, or wood, for printing. **3.** print from plates so made. [< MF *engraver*] —**en·grav′er** *n.*

en·grav·ing (en GRAY ving) *n.* **1.** the act or art of cutting designs, etc., into a surface. **2.** an engraved design; plate. **3.** an impression printed from an engraved plate; print.

en·gross (en GROHS) *v.t.* **1.** occupy completely; absorb. **2.** copy legibly in a large hand, as a document. [ME *engrossen* gather in large amounts]

en·gross·ing (en GROH sing) *adj.* holding the attention or interest completely; absorbing.

en·gulf (en GULF) *v.t.* flow over, bury, or overwhelm completely.

en·hance (en HANS) *v.t.* ·**hanced,** ·**hanc·ing** heighten or increase, as in reputation, beauty, or quality. [ME *enhauncen*] —**en·hance′ment** *n.*

e·nig·ma (ə NIG mə) *n.* **1.** an obscure or ambiguous saying. **2.** anything that puzzles or baffles. [< L *aenigma* riddle] — **en·ig·mat·ic** (EN ig MAT ik) *adj.*

en·join (en JOIN) *v.t.* **1.** order or command (a person or group). **2.** impose (a condition, course of action, etc.). **3.** forbid or prohibit, esp. by judicial order. [ME *enjoinen* yoke]

en·joy (en JOI) *v.t.* **1.** experience joy or pleasure in. **2.** have the use or benefit of [ME *enjoyen* make joyful]

en·large (en LAHRJ) *v.* **·larged, ·larg·ing** *v.t.* **1.** make larger. —*v.i.* **2.** become larger. **3.** express oneself in greater detail or at greater length: with *on* or *upon.*

en·light·en (en LĪT n) *v.t.* give revealing or broadening knowledge to. [ME *enlight-enen*] —**en·light'·en·ment** *n.*

en·list (en LIST) *v.t.* **1.** engage (someone) for the armed forces. **2.** secure the active aid or participation of (a person, etc.). —*v.i.* **3.** enter military service without being drafted. **4.** join some venture, cause, etc.: with *in.*

en·liv·en (en LĪ vən) *v.t.* make lively, cheerful, or sprightly.

en masse (ahn MAS) in a mass; all together. [< F]

en·mesh (en MESH) *v.t.* ensnare in or as in a net.

en·mi·ty (EN mi tee) *n. pl.* **·ties** deepseated unfriendliness; hostility. [ME *ene-mite*]

en·nui (ahn WEE) *n.* a feeling of listlessness and boredom. [< F]

e·nor·mi·ty (i NOR mə tee) *n. pl.* **·ties 1.** the quality of being outrageous; heinousness. **2.** an outrageous offense; atrocity. [ME *enormite*]

e·nor·mous (i NOR məs) *adj.* far exceeding the usual size, amount, degree, etc. — **e·nor'·mous·ly** *adv.*

e·nough (i NUF) *adj.* adequate for any demand or need; sufficient. —*n.* an ample supply; a sufficiency. —*adv.* **1.** so as to be sufficient. **2.** quite; very. **3.** adequately; fairly; tolerably. [ME *enogh*]

en·quire (en KWĪR) see INQUIRE.

en·rage (en RAYJ) *v.t.* **·raged, ·rag·ing** throw into a rage.

en·rap·ture (en RAP chər) *v.t.* **·tured, ·tur·ing** bring into a state of rapture; delight.

en·rich (en RICH) *v.t.* **1.** make rich or increase the wealth of. **2.** make more productive, as soil. **3.** add attractive or desirable elements to; make better, more interesting, etc., by adding. —**en·rich'ment** *n.*

en·roll (en ROHL) *v.t.* **1.** write or record (a name) in a roll; register; list. **2.** enlist. **3.** place on record; record. —*v.i.* **4.** enlist; register oneself.

en·roll·ment (en ROHL mənt) *n.* **1.** an enrolling or being enrolled. **2.** a record of persons or things enrolled. **3.** the number of persons or things enrolled.

en route (ahn ROOT) on the way. [< F]

en·sconce (en SKONS) *v.t.* **·sconced, ·sconc·ing 1.** fix securely or comfortably in some place. **2.** shelter; hide.

en·sem·ble (ahn SAHM bəl) *n.* **1.** all the parts of a thing viewed as a whole. **2.** an individual's entire costume, including accessories. **3.** the entire cast of a play, ballet, etc. **4.** *Music* a group of players or singers performing together. [< F, together]

en·shrine (en SHRĪN) *v.t.* **·shrined, ·shrin·ing 1.** place in or as in a shrine. **2.** cherish devoutly; hold sacred.

en·shroud (en SHROWD) *v.t.* shroud; conceal.

en·sign (EN sin) *n.* **1.** a flag or banner. **2.** *Naval* a commissioned officer of the lowest grade. **3.** a badge, symbol, or distinguishing mark. [ME *ensigne* insignia]

en·si·lage (EN sə lij) *n.* **1.** the process of preserving green fodder in closed pits or silos. **2.** silage. [< F] —**en·sile** (en SĪL) *v.t.* **·siled, ·sil·ing 1.** preserve fodder in this way. **2.** make into silage.

en·slave (en SLAYV) *v.t.* **·slaved, ·slav·ing 1.** make a slave of. **2.** dominate; control.

en·snare (en SNAIR) *v.t.* **·snared, ·snar·ing** catch in a snare; trick.

en·sue (en SOO) *v.i.* **·sued, ·su·ing 1.** follow subsequently; occur afterward. **2.** follow as a consequence; result. [ME *ensuen*]

en·sure (en SHUUR) *v.t.* **·sured, ·sur·ing 1.** make sure or certain; guarantee. **2.** make safe: with *from* or *against.* [ME *ensuren*]

en·tail (en TAYL) *v.t.* **1.** impose, involve, or result in by necessity. **2.** *Law* restrict or leave the inheritance of (real property) to an unalterable succession of heirs. [ME *en-tailen*]

en·tan·gle (en TANG gəl) *v.t.* **·gled, ·gling 1.** catch in or as in a snare; hamper. **2.** make tangled; snarl. —**en·tan'gle·ment** *n.*

en·tente (ahn TAHNT) *n.* a mutual agreement; also, the parties entering into a mutual agreement. [< F]

en·ter (EN tər) *v.t.* **1.** come or go into. **2.** penetrate; pierce. **3.** set in; insert. **4.** become a member of; join. **5.** start out upon;

embark on. **6.** obtain admission to (a school etc.). **7.** cause to be admitted. **8.** write down, as in a list. **9.** record officially. —*v.i.* **10.** come or go into a particular place. — **enter into 1.** start out; embark on. **2.** engage in. **3.** form a part or constituent of. **4.** consider or discuss. [ME *entren*]

en·ter·prise (EN tər PRĪZ) *n.* **1.** any project, undertaking, or task, especially when difficult or important. **2.** boldness and energy in practical affairs. [ME]

en·ter·pris·ing (EN tər PRĪ zing) *adj.* energetic and venturesome.

en·ter·tain (EN tər TAYN) *v.t.* **1.** amuse; divert. **2.** extend hospitality to; receive as a guest. **3.** take into consideration, as a proposal. **4.** keep or bear in mind. —*v.i.* **5.** receive and care for guests. [ME *entertenen* hold jointly] —**en'ter·tain'er** *n.*

en·ter·tain·ing (EN tər TAY ning) *adj.* amusing; diverting.

en·ter·tain·ment (EN tər TAYN mənt) *n.* **1.** the act of entertaining, or the state of being entertained. **2.** something that entertains, as a play.

en·thrall (en THRAWL) *v.t.* **1.** spellbind; fascinate. **2.** subjugate.

en·thuse (en THOOZ) *v.t. & v.i.* **·thused, ·thus·ing** make or become enthusiastic.

en·thu·si·asm (en THOO zee AZ əm) *n.* **1.** keen, animated interest in and preoccupation with something. **2.** a cause or object of intense, lively interest. [< LL *enthusiasmus* inspiration] —**en·thu·si·ast** (en THOO zee AST) *n.*

en·tice (en TĪS) *v.t.* **·ticed, ·tic·ing** attract by arousing hope of pleasure, profit, etc.; allure. [ME *enticen* incite]

en·tire (en TĪR) *adj.* **1.** having no part missing; whole; complete. **2.** not broken; in one piece; intact. [ME *entere*] —**en·tire·ty** (en TĪR tee) *n. pl.* **·ties 1.** the state or condition of being whole or complete. **2.** that which is entire.

en·ti·tle (en TĪT l) *v.t.* **·tled, ·tling 1.** give the right to receive, demand, or do something. **2.** give a name, title, or designation to.

en·ti·ty (EN ti tee) *n. pl.* **·ties 1.** something existing objectively or in the mind. **2.** existence as opposed to nonexistence. [< Med.L *entitas*]

en·tomb (en TOOM) *v.t.* place in or as in a tomb; bury. [ME *entoumben*] —**en·tomb' ment** *n.*

en·to·mol·o·gy (EN tə MOL ə jee) *n.* the branch of zoology that treats of insects. — **en'to·mol'o·gist** *n.*

en·tou·rage (AHN tuu RAHZH) *n.* a group of followers or attendants; retinue. [< F]

en·tr'acte (AHN trakt) *n.* **1.** the interval between the acts of a play, opera, etc. **2.** music, dance, etc., performed between acts. [< F]

en·trails (EN traylz) *n.pl.* the internal parts of a person or animal; esp., the intestines; bowels; guts. [ME *entrailles*]

en·trance¹ (EN trəns) *n.* **1.** the act of entering. **2.** a place or passage allowing entry. **3.** the right or power of entering; admittance. [ME *entraunce*]

en·trance² (en TRANS) *v.t.* **·tranced, ·tranc·ing** delight; charm.

en·trant (EN trənt) *n.* one who enters; esp., one who enters a contest.

en·trap (en TRAP) *v.t.* **·trapped, ·trap·ping 1.** catch in or as in a trap. **2.** trick into danger or difficulty. —**en·trap' ment** *n.*

en·treat (en TREET) *v.t. & v.i.* **1.** beseech with intensity; implore. **2.** request; petition. [ME *entreten*] —**en·treat'ing·ly** *adv.* — **en·treat·y** (en TREE tee) *n. pl.* **·ies** an earnest request.

en·tre·chat (AHN trə SHAH) *n. French* in ballet, a leap upward in which the dancer repeatedly crosses the feet.

en·trée (AHN tray) *n.* **1.** the act or privilege of entering; admission. **2.** the principal course at a meal. [< F]

en·trench (en TRENCH) *v.t.* **1.** fortify or protect with or as with a trench. **2.** establish firmly: The idea was *entrenched* in his mind. —*v.i.* **3.** encroach: with *on* or *upon*.

en·tre·pre·neur (AHN trə prə NUUR) *n.* one who undertakes to start and conduct an enterprise or business. [< F] —**en'tre· pre·neur'i·al** *adj.*

en·trust (en TRUST) *v.t.* **1.** give over to another for care or performance. **2.** place something in the care or trust of.

en·try (EN tree) *n. pl.* **·tries 1.** the act of coming in; entrance. **2.** a place of entrance. **3.** the act of entering anything in a register, list, etc.; also, the item entered. **4.** a contestant listed for a race, competition, etc. [ME *entre*]

e·nu·mer·ate (i NOO mə RAYT) *v.t.* **·at·ed, ·at·ing 1.** name one by one; list. **2.** ascertain the number of. [< L *enumeratus* counted] —**e·nu'mer·a'tion** *n.*

e·nun·ci·ate (i NUN see AYT) *v.* **·at·ed, ·at·ing** *v.t.* **1.** articulate (speech sounds), esp. clearly. **2.** state with exactness. **3.** announce or proclaim. —*v.i.* **4.** pronounce words, esp. clearly. [< L *enuntiatus* announced] —**e·nun′ci·a′tion** *n.*

en·u·re·sis (EN yə REE sis) *n. Pathol.* involuntary urination; bed-wetting. [< NL]

en·vel·op (en VEL əp) *v.t.* **·oped, ·op·ing 1.** wrap; enclose. **2.** hide; conceal. **3.** surround. [ME *envolupen*] —**en·vel′op·ment** *n.*

en·ve·lope (EN və LOHP) *n.* **1.** a paper case or wrapper for enclosing a letter or the like, usu. having a gummed flap for sealing. **2.** any enveloping cover or wrapper. [< F *enveloppe*]

en·vi·a·ble (EN vee ə bəl) *adj.* so admirable or desirable as to arouse envy.

en·vi·ous (EN vee əs) *adj.* full of, characterized by, or expressing envy. [ME]

en·vi·ron·ment (en VI rən mənt) *n.* **1.** the external circumstances, conditions, and things that affect the existence and development of an individual, organism, or group. **2.** surroundings. —**en·vi′ron·men′tal** *adj.*

en·vi·ron·ment·al·ist (en VI rən MEN tl ist) *n.* **1.** one who advocates preservation of the environment. **2.** one who attaches more importance to environment than to heredity in the development of a person.

en·vi·rons (en VI rənz) *n.pl.* a surrounding, outlying area, as about a city; outskirts. [< F]

en·vis·age (en VIZ ij) *v.t.* **·aged, ·ag·ing** form a mental image of; visualize; conceive of. [< F *envisager*]

en·vi·sion (en VIZH ən) *v.t.* see or foresee in the mind.

en·voy¹ (EN voi) *n.* **1.** a diplomatic representative, ranking next below an ambassador. **2.** a person, as a diplomat, entrusted with a mission. [< F *envoyé* envoy]

en·voy² *n.* the closing lines of a poem or prose work, often in the form of a dedication. Also **envoi.** [ME *envoye* message]

en·vy (EN vee) *n. pl.* **·vies 1.** a feeling of resentment or discontent over another's superior attainments, endowments, or possessions. **2.** any object of envy. —*v.* **·vied, ·vy·ing** *v.t.* **1.** regard with envy; feel envy because of. —*v.i.* **2.** feel or show envy. [ME *envie*]

en·zyme (EN zīm) *n. Biochem.* a complex, mostly protein substance able to initiate or accelerate specific chemical reactions in the metabolism of plants and animals; an organic catalyst. [< Med.Gk. *énzymos* leavened]

e·on (EE ən) *n.* **1.** an incalculable period of time. **2.** *Geol.* a time interval including two or more eras. Also spelled *aeon.* [< L *aeon*]

ep·au·let (EP i LET) *n. Mil.* a shoulder ornament, usu. with a fringe, as on military and naval uniforms. Also **ep′au·lette.** [< F *épaulette*]

é·pée (ay PAY) *n.* a dueling sword with a sharp point and no cutting edge. [F]

e·phem·er·al (i FEM ər əl) *adj.* **1.** lasting but a short time. **2.** living one day only, as certain insects. —*n.* anything lasting for a very short time. [< Gk. *ephēmeros* lasting only a day]

ep·ic (EP ik) *n.* **1.** a long, formal, narrative poem, typically about heroic exploits and achievements. **2.** a novel, drama, etc., that in scale or subject resembles such a poem. —*adj.* **1.** of, pertaining to, or suitable as a theme for an epic. **2.** heroic; grandiose. [< L *epicus*]

ep·i·cene (EP i SEEN) *adj.* **1.** belonging to one sex and having characteristics of the other. **2.** lacking characteristics of either sex; sexless. —*n.* an epicene person. [ME]

ep·i·cen·ter (EP ə SEN tər) *n. Geol.* the point or area on the earth's surface directly above the focus of an earthquake. [< NL *epicentrum*]

ep·i·cure (EP i KYUUR) *n.* one given to luxurious living; a sensualist; esp., a devotee of good food and drink. [ME *Epicures*] —**ep′i·cu·re′an** *adj. & n.*

Ep·i·cu·re·an·ism (EP i kyuu REE ə niz əm) *n.* the doctrines of Epicurus, Greek philosopher, who taught that the chief aim of life is pleasure regulated by temperance, peace of mind, and cultural pursuits.

ep·i·dem·ic (EP i DEM ik) *adj.* breaking out suddenly and spreading rapidly in a particular area: said esp. of contagious diseases. —*n.* **1.** an epidemic disease. **2.** anything temporarily widespread, as a fad. [< F *épidémique*]

ep·i·der·mis (EP i DUR mis) *n.* **1.** *Anat.* the outer layer of the skin: also called *cuticle.* **2.** *Bot.* the outermost covering of a plant when there are several layers of tissue. [< LL]

ep·i·gram (EP i GRAM) *n.* **1.** a brief, clever, pointed, usu. paradoxical remark or observation. **2.** a short, witty, often satirical verse. [ME] —**ep·i·gram·mat·ic** (EP i grə MAT ik) *adj.*

ep·i·graph (EP i GRAF) *n.* **1.** an inscription

on a monument, tomb, etc. **2.** a quotation prefixed to a book. [< Gk. *epigraphé* inscription]

ep·i·lep·sy (EP ə LEP see) *n. Pathol.* a disorder of the nervous system marked by attacks of unconsciousness with or without convulsions. See GRAND MAL, PETIT MAL. [< LL *epilepsia*] —**ep'i·lep'tic** *n. & adj.*

ep·i·logue (EP ə LAWG) *n.* **1.** a short section appended to a novel, poem, etc., by way of commentary. **2.** a short speech appended to a play. Also **ep'i·log.** [ME *epiloge*]

e·piph·a·ny (ə PIF ə nee) *n.* **1.** *cap. Eccl.* a festival, held on January 6, commemorating the visit of the Magi to the infant Christ. **2.** any sudden mental perception. [ME *epiphanie* manifestation]

e·pis·co·pal (i PIS kə pəl) *adj.* of, pertaining to, or governed by bishops. [ME]

Episcopal Church the Protestant Episcopal Church.

E·pis·co·pa·li·an (i PIS kə PAYL yən) *adj.* belonging to the Protestant Episcopal Church.

ep·i·sode (EP ə SOHD) *n.* **1.** a section of a novel, poem, etc., complete in itself. **2.** a part of a serialized story or play; installment. **3.** an event or related series of events. [< Gk. *episodion*]

ep·i·sod·ic (EP ə SOD ik) *adj.* **1.** of, relating to, or resembling an episode. **2.** broken up into episodes; esp., disjointed.

e·pis·te·mol·o·gy (i PIS tə MOL ə jee) *n. pl.* **·gies** the branch of philosophy that investigates the nature of human knowledge. [< Gk. *epistēmē* knowledge]

e·pis·tle (i PIS əl) *n.* **1.** a letter, esp. when long or formal. **2.** *Usu. cap. Eccl.* **a** one of the letters written by an apostle. **b** a selection taken from one of these letters and read as part of a service. [ME] —**e·pis·to·lar·y** (i PIS tl ER ee) *adj.*

ep·i·taph (EP i TAF) *n.* an inscription on a tomb or monument in memory of the dead. [ME *epitaphe*]

ep·i·thet (EP ə THET) *N.* **1.** a descriptive word or phrase characterizing a person or thing. **2.** a disparaging or abusive name. [< L *epitheton*]

e·pit·o·me (i PIT ə mee) *n.* **1.** a typical or extreme example; embodiment. **2.** a concise summary; abridgment. [< L] —**e·pit'o·mize** v.t. **·mized, ·miz·ing**

ep·och (EP ək) *n.* **1.** a point in time marked by the beginning of a new development or

state of things. **2.** an interval of time memorable for extraordinary events, important influences, etc. **3.** *Geol.* a time interval less than a period. [< NL *epocha* fixed point] —**ep'och·al** *adj.*

ep·o·nym (EP ə nim) *n.* a real or legendary personage from whom something derives its name. —**e·pon·y·mous** (ə PON ə məs) *adj.* [< Gk. *epōnymía* surname]

e·pox·y (i POK see) *n. pl.* **·ies** a thermosetting resin, with strong adhesive qualities. Also **epoxy resin.**

ep·si·lon (EP sə LON) *n.* the fifth letter and second vowel in the Greek alphabet (E, ε), corresponding to English short *e.*

eq·ua·ble (EK wə bəl) *adj.* **1.** not varying greatly; even. **2.** not easily upset; tranquil. **3.** evenly proportioned; uniform. [< L *aequabilis* similar]

e·qual (EE kwəl) *adj.* **1.** identical in size, extent, etc. **2.** having the same rights, rank, etc. **3.** having the same abilities, degree of excellence, etc. **4.** evenly proportioned; balanced. **5.** affecting or shared by all alike: *equal* rights. **6.** having the requisite ability, power, etc.: with *to: equal* to the task. —*v.t.* **e·qualed, e·qual·ing 1.** be equal to; match. **2.** do or produce something equal to. —*n.* a person or thing equal to another. [ME] —**e·qual·i·ty** (i KWOL i tee) *n.*

e·qual·ize (EE kwə LIZ) *v.t.* **·ized, ·iz·ing** make equal or uniform. —**e'qual·iz'er** *n.*

e·qua·nim·i·ty (EE kwə NIM i tee) *n.* evenness of mind or temper. [< L *aequanimitas* evenmindedness]

e·quate (i KWAYT) *v.t.* **e·quat·ed, e·quat·ing** consider as equivalent or comparable. [ME]

e·qua·tion (i KWAY zhən) *n.* **1.** the act of making equal, or the state of being equal. **2.** *Math.* a statement expressing the equality of two quantities. **3.** *Chem.* a symbolic representation of a chemical reaction.

e·qua·tor (i KWAY tər) *n.* the great circle of the earth, an imaginary line equally distant from the North and South Poles. [ME] —**e·qua·to·ri·al** (EE kwə TOR ee əl) *adj.*

e·ques·tri·an (i KWES tree ən) *adj.* **1.** pertaining to horses or horsemanship. **2.** on horseback. —*n.* a rider on horseback. [< L *equestris* of a horseman]

e·qui·lat·er·al (EE kwə LAT ər əl) *adj.* having sides of equal length. [< LL *aequilateralis*]

e·qui·lib·ri·um (EE kwə LIB ree əm) *n. pl.* **·ri·ums** or **·ri·a** (-ree ə) a state of balance between two or more opposing forces. [< L *aequilibrium*]

e•quine (EE kwīn) *adj.* of, pertaining to, or like a horse. —*n.* a horse. [< L *equinus*]

e•qui•nox (EE kwə NOKS) *n.* one of two opposite points at which the sun crosses the celestial equator, when the days and nights are equal; also, the time of this crossing (about March 21, the **vernal** or **spring equinox**, and Sept. 21, the **autumnal equinox**). [ME] —e•qui•noc•tial (EE kwə NOK shəl) *adj.*

e•quip (i KWIP) *v.t.* e•quipped, e•quip•ping furnish or fit out with whatever is needed for any purpose or undertaking. [< MF *equiper* fit out]

e•quip•ment (i KWIP mənt) *n.* 1. the act of equipping, or the state of being equipped. 2. material with which a person or organization is provided.

eq•ui•ta•ble (EK wi tə bəl) *adj.* impartially just; fair. —eq'ui•ta•bly *adv.*

eq•ui•ty (EK wi tee) *n. pl.* •ties 1. fairness or impartiality. 2. *Law* a system of jurisprudence based on concepts of fairness, administered by courts of equity, and supplementing common law. 3. in business or property, the value remaining in excess of any liability or mortgage. [ME *equite* fairness]

e•quiv•a•lent (i KWIV ə lənt) *adj.* equal in value, force, meaning, effect, etc. —*n.* that which is equivalent. [ME] —e•quiv'a•lence *n.*

e•quiv•o•cal (i KWIV ə kəl) *adj.* 1. having a doubtful meaning; ambiguous. 2. of uncertain origin, character, value, etc.; dubious. 3. questionable or suspicious. [ME *equivoc* ambiguous] —e•quiv'o•cal•ly *adv.*

e•quiv•o•cate (i KWIV ə KAYT) *v.i.* •cat•ed, •cat•ing use ambiguous language with intent to mislead or deceive. [ME] — e•quiv'o•ca'tion *n.*

e•ra (EER ə) *n.* 1. a period of time measured from some fixed point: the Christian *era*. 2. a period of time characterized by certain events, conditions, etc. 3. the beginning of a particular period; an epoch. 4. *Geol.* a division of geological history. [< LL *aera* fixed date]

e•rad•i•cate (i RAD i KAYT) *v.t.* •cat•ed, •cat•ing 1. pull up by the roots. 2. destroy. [< L *eradicatus* rooted out] — e•rad•i•ca•ble (i RAD i kə bəl) *adj.* — e•rad'i•ca'tor *n.*

e•rase (i RAYS) *v.t.* e•rased, e•ras•ing obliterate, as by rubbing out. [< L *erasus* scraped out] —e•ras'a•ble *adj.* —e•ras'er *n.*

e•ra•sure (i RAY shər) *n.* 1. the act of erasing, or the state of being erased. 2. that which is erased. 3. a mark left on a surface by erasing something.

ere (air) *prep.* prior to; before in time. — *conj.* 1. before. 2. sooner than; rather than. [ME]

e•rect (i REKT) *v.t.* 1. put up (a structure), 2. assemble the parts of; set up. 3. set upright; raise. 4. establish or found. 5. work out or formulate. —*v.i.* 6. *Physiol.* become rigidly upright, as through an influx of blood. —*adj.* marked by a vertical position; upright. [ME] —e•rec'tion *n.*

e•rec•tile (i REK tl) *adj.* capable of becoming erect.

er•e•mite (ER ə MĪT) *n.* a hermit, esp., a religious recluse. [ME]

er•go (ER goh) *conj. & adv. Latin* hence; therefore.

er•got (UR gət) *n.* 1. a fungus attacking rye and other cereal grasses. 2. the disease caused by this fungus. 3. a medicinal preparation, derived from this fungus, used to contract involuntary muscle and to check hemorrhage. [< F, lit., rooster's spur]

er•mine (UR min) *n. pl.* er•mine 1. a weasel of the northern hemisphere, having brown fur that in winter turns white. 2. its white fur. [ME]

e•rode (i ROHD) *v.* e•rod•ed, e•rod•ing *v.t.* 1. wear away gradually by constant friction. 2. eat into; corrode. 3. make (a channel, gully, etc.) by wearing away or eating into. —*v.i.* 4. become eroded. [< L *erodere* gnaw away] —e•ro•sive (i ROH siv) *adj.*

e•rog•e•nous (i ROJ ə nəs) *adj.* 1. sexually sensitive: *erogenous* zones. 2. exciting sexual feelings.

e•ro•sion (i ROH zhən) *n.* 1. the act of eroding, or the state of being eroded. 2. *Geol.* the wearing away of the earth's surface by the action of wind, water, glaciers, etc.

e•rot•ic (i ROT ik) *adj.* 1. of, pertaining to, or concerned with sexual love. 2. designed to arouse sexual desire. [< Gk. *erōtikos* caused by love] —e•rot'i•cal•ly *adv.* — e•rot•i•cism (i ROT ə SIZ əm) *n.*

err (er) *v.i.* erred, err•ing 1. make a mistake. 2. go astray morally. [ME *erren*]

er•rand (ER ənd) *n.* 1. a trip made to perform some task, often for someone else. 2.

the business of such a trip. [ME *erend* message]

er•rant (ER ənt) *adj.* **1.** roving or wandering, esp. in search of adventure. **2.** straying from the proper course or standard. [ME *erraunt*]

er•rat•ic (i RAT ik) *adj.* **1.** not conforming to usual standards; eccentric. **2.** lacking regularity. [ME] —**er•rat′i•cal•ly** *adv.*

er•ra•tum (i RAH təm) *n. pl.* **•ta** (-tə) an error, as in writing or printing. [< L]

er•ro•ne•ous (i ROH nee əs) *adj.* marked by error; incorrect. [ME] —**er•ro′ne•ous•ly** *adv.*

er•ror (ER ər) *n.* **1.** something done, said, or believed incorrectly; a mistake. **2.** the condition of deviating from what is correct or true. **3.** in baseball, a misplay by a member of the team not batting. [ME *errour*]

erst•while (URST hwīl) *adj.* former.

e•ruct (i RUKT) *v.t. & v.i.* belch. [< L *eructare* vomit] —**e•ruc′ta′tion** *n.*

er•u•dite (ER yuu DīT) *adj.* very learned; scholarly. [ME] —**er′u•dite•ly** *adv.* — **er′u•di′tion** (ER yuu DISH ən) *n.*

e•rupt (i RUPT) *v.i.* **1.** cast forth lava, steam, etc., as a volcano or geyser. **2.** become suddenly and violently active. **3.** break out in a rash. —*v.t.* **4.** cast forth (lava, etc.). [< L *eruptus* burst forth] —**e•rup′tion** *n.* — **e•rup′tive** *adj.*

es•ca•late (ES kə LAYT) *v.t. & v.i.* **•lat•ed, •lat•ing** increase or be increased gradually: -*escalate* a war. —**es′ca•la′tion** *n.*

es•ca•la•tor (ES kə LAY tər) *n.* a moving stairway.

es•ca•pade (ES kə PAYD) *n.* a reckless, unconventional prank or adventure; fling; spree. [< F]

es•cape (i SKAYP) *v.* **•caped, •cap•ing** *v.i.* **1.** get free. **2.** avoid some danger or evil. **3.** seep or leak out gradually. —*v.t.* **4.** get away from (prison, captors, etc.). **5.** succeed in avoiding (capture, harm, etc.). **6.** get away from the notice or recollection of: Nothing *escaped* him. **7.** slip out from unintentionally: A cry *escaped* her lips. —*n.* **1.** the act of escaping, or the fact of having escaped. **2.** a means of escaping. —*adj.* **1.** escapist. **2.** that provides a means of escape. [ME *escapen*]

es•cap•ee (i skay PEE) *n.* one who has escaped, as from prison.

es•cap•ism (i SKAY piz əm) *n.* a desire or tendency to escape reality through diversions or daydreaming.

es•cap•ist (i SKAY pist) *adj.* providing a means of indulging in escapism: *escapist* literature. —*n.* one given to escapism.

es•carp•ment (i SKAHRP mənt) *n.* **1.** a precipitous artificial slope in front of a fortification. **2.** a steep slope or cliff. [< F *escarpement*]

es•cha•tol•o•gy (ES kə TOL ə jee) *n.* theology treating of death, judgment, and the future of the soul. [< Gk. *eschatos* last + -LOGY] —**es•cha•to•log•i•cal** (ES kə tl OJ i kəl) *adj.*

es•chew (es CHOO) *v.t.* shun. [ME *eschewen*]

es•cort (ES kort) *n.* **1.** one or more people, cars, planes, etc., accompanying another to give protection, guidance, etc. **2.** a person accompanying another. —*v.t.* (i SKORT) accompany as an escort. [< F]

es•crow (ES kroh) *n. Law* **1.** a written deed, contract, etc., placed in the custody of a third party and effective on fulfillment of a stipulated condition. **2.** the condition of being an escrow. [< AF *escrouwe* scroll]

e•soph•a•gus (i SOF ə gəs) *n. pl.* **•gi** (-jī) *Anat.* the tube from the mouth to the stomach. [< NL *oesophagus*] —**e•so•phag•e•al** (i SOF ə JEE əl) *adj*

es•o•ter•ic (ES ə TER ik) *adj.* **1.** understood by or meant for a chosen few. **2.** confidential; secret. [< Gk. *esōterikós* inner]

ESP extrasensory perception.

es•pal•ier (i SPAL yay) *n.* **1.** a flat framework on which small trees, etc., are trained to grow. **2.** a tree or plant so trained. —*v.t.* furnish with or train on an espalier. [< F]

es•pe•cial (i SPESH əl) *adj.* preeminent; special. [ME]

es•pe•cial•ly (i SPESH ə lee) *adv.* to a special extent or degree; particularly.

Es•pe•ran•to (ES pə RAHN toh) *n.* an artificial language based on the major European languages. [< the pseudonym of the inventor]

es•pi•o•nage (ES pee ə NAZH) *n.* **1.** the practice of spying. **2.** the work of spies. [< F *espionnage*]

es•pla•nade (ES plə NAHD) *n.* a level, open stretch of land, used as a roadway or public walk. [< F]

es•pouse (i SPOWZ) *v.t.* **•poused, •pous•ing 1.** make one's own; support, as a cause or doctrine. **2.** take or give as a spouse; marry. [ME] —**es•pou′sal** *n.*

es•pres•so (e SPRES oh) *n. pl.* **•sos** coffee

brewed from darkly roasted beans by steam pressure. [< Ital.]

es•prit (e SPREE) *n.* spirit; wit. [< F]

esprit de corps (e SPREE də KOR) *French* a spirit of devotion to the common goals of a group.

es•say (ES ay) *n.* **1.** a short composition dealing with a single topic and typically personal in approach. **2.** (e SAY) an attempt; endeavor. —*v.t.* (e SAY) attempt to do or accomplish; try. [< MF *essayer* assay]

es•say•ist (ES ay ist) *n.* a writer of essays.

es•sence (ES əns) *n.* **1.** that in which the real nature of a thing consists; intrinsic or fundamental nature. **2.** the distinctive quality of something. **3.** an extract, as of a plant or food; also, an alcoholic solution of such an extract. **4.** a perfume. [ME *essencia*]

es•sen•tial (i SEN shəl) *adj.* **1.** of, belonging to, or constituting the essence of something. **2.** extremely important; vital; indispensable. **3.** complete, total, or absolute. —*n.* something fundamental or indispensable. —**es•sen′tial•ly** *adv.*

es•tab•lish (i STAB lish) *v.t.* **1.** make secure, stable, or permanent. **2.** set up, found, or institute. **3.** install: *establish* oneself in a new home. **4.** cause to be recognized and accepted: *establish* oneself as a writer. **5.** clear from doubt; demonstrate; prove. [ME *establissen* make stable]

es•tab•lish•ment (i STAB lish mənt) *n.* **1.** the act of establishing, or the state or fact of being established. **2.** something established, as a business, residence, etc. —**the Establishment** those collectively who occupy positions of influence and status in a society.

es•tate (i STAYT) *n.* **1.** a usu. extensive piece of landed property or the residence built on it. **2.** one's entire property and possessions. **3.** a particular condition or state: man's *estate.* **4.** a particular social or political class. [ME *estat*]

es•teem (i STEEM) *v.t.* **1.** have a high opinion of; value greatly. **2.** think of as; rate. —*n.* **1.** high regard or respect. **2.** judgment. [ME *estemen* estimate]

es•thete (ES theet) see AESTHETE.

es•thet•ic (es THET ik) *adj.* see AESTHETIC.

es•thet•ics (es THET iks) see AESTHETICS.

es•ti•ma•ble (ES tə mə bəl) *adj.* worthy of respect or admiration. [ME]

es•ti•mate (ES tə MAYT) *v.* **•mat•ed, •mat•ing** *v.t.* **1.** form an approximate opinion of (size, amount, number, etc.). **2.** form an

opinion about; judge. —*v.i.* **3.** make or submit an estimate. —*n.* (ES tə mit) **1.** a rough calculation. **2.** a statement of the approximate cost for certain work. **3.** a judgment or opinion. [< L *aestimatus* estimated]

es•ti•ma•tion (ES tə MAY shən) *n.* **1.** the act of estimating. **2.** a conclusion arrived at by estimating. **3.** esteem; regard.

es•ti•val (ES tə vəl) *adj.* of or pertaining to summer.

es•ti•vate (ES tə VAYT) *v.i.* **•vat•ed, •vat•ing** pass the summer in a dormant state. [< L *aestivatus* resided during summer]

es•trange (i STRAYNJ) *v.t.* **•tranged, •trang•ing** **1.** make (someone previously friendly or affectionate) indifferent or hostile; alienate. **2.** remove or dissociate (oneself etc.). [< MF] —**es•trange′ment** *n.*

es•tro•gen (ES trə jən) *n.* *Biochem.* any of various substances that influence estrus or produce changes in the sexual characteristics of female mammals. —**es•tro•gen•ic** (ES trə JEN ik) *adj.*

es•trus (ES trəs) *n. Biol.* **a** the entire reproductive cycle of most female mammals. **b** the peak of the sexual cycle, culminating in ovulation; heat. [L *oestrus*]

es•tu•ar•y (ES choo ER ee) *n. pl.* **•ar•ies** a wide mouth of a river where its current meets the sea. [< L *aestuarium* channel]

e•ta (AY tə) *n.* the seventh letter in the Greek alphabet (H, η), corresponding to English long *e.*

et•cet•er•a (et SET ər ə) *n. pl.* **ras** and other things; and the rest; and so forth. Abbr. *etc.* [< L]

etch (ech) *v.t.* **1.** engrave by means of acid or other corrosive fluid, esp. on a plate for printing. **2.** produce (a drawing, design, etc.) by etching. **3.** outline or sketch by scratching lines with a pointed instrument. [< D *etsen*] —**etch•ant** *n.* (ECH ənt)

etch•ing (ECH ing) *n.* **1.** a process of engraving in which lines are scratched on a plate covered with a coating, and the parts exposed are subjected to acid. **2.** a figure or design formed by etching. **3.** an impression from an etched plate.

e•ter•nal (i TUR nl) *adj.* **1.** existing without beginning or end; forever existent. **2.** unending. —**e•ter′nal•ly** *adv.*

e•ter•ni•ty (i TUR ni tee) *n. pl.* **•ties** **1.** existence without beginning or end; endless duration. **2.** the endless time following death. **3.** a very long time. [ME *eternite*]

e·ther (EE thər) *n.* **1.** an inflammable liquid used as an anesthetic. **2.** a substance formerly assumed to pervade all of space. **3.** the clear, upper regions of space. [ME]

e·the·re·al (i THEER ee əl) *adj.* **1.** resembling ether or air; airy. **2.** delicate or spiritual. **3.** of or existing in the upper regions; celestial. [< L *aethereus*]

eth·ic (ETH ik) *n.* a philosophy or system of morals; ethics. [ME]

eth·i·cal (ETH i kəl) *adj.* **1.** pertaining to or treating of ethics and morality. **2.** conforming to right principles of conduct.

eth·ics (ETH iks) *n.* **1.** (construed as sing.) the study and philosophy of human conduct, with emphasis on the determination of right and wrong. **2.** (construed as pl.) the principles of right conduct with reference to a specific profession, mode of life, etc. [ME]

eth·nic (ETH nik) *adj.* of, belonging to, or distinctive of a particular racial, cultural, or language division of mankind. [< ME *ethnik* heathen]

eth·nol·o·gy (eth NOL ə jee) *n. pl.* **·gies** the branch of anthropology concerned with the study of racial and ethnic groups in their origins, distribution, and cultures. — **eth·nol'o·gist** *n.*

e·thol·o·gy (ee THOL ə jee) *n.* the science of animal behavior. [< F *éthologie*] — **e·thol'o·gist** *n.*

e·thos (EE thos) *n.* the character of a particular group or people. [< Gk., custom]

e·ti·ol·o·gy (EE tee OL ə jee) *n. pl.* **·gies 1.** the study of causes or reasons. **2.** *Med.* a theory of the cause of a disease. **3.** the giving of a cause or reason for anything; also, the reason given. [< L *aetiologia* establishing the cause of]

et·i·quette (ET i kit) *n.* the rules conventionally established for behavior in polite society or in official or professional life. [< F]

é·tude (AY tood) *n. Music* an exercise or composition for solo instrument or voice. [< F]

et·y·mol·o·gy (ET ə MOL ə jee) *n. pl.* **·gies 1.** the development of a word, as shown by the histories of its antecedent forms or basic elements; also, a statement of this. **2.** the study of the derivation of words. [ME] — **et'y·mol'o·gist** *n.*

eu- *prefix* good; well; easy; agreeable: *euphony.* [< Gk.]

Eu·char·ist (YOO kə rist) *n.* a Christian sacrament in which bread and wine are conse-

crated and received in commemoration of the Passion and the death of Jesus: also called *Communion.* [ME *eukarist* gratitude]

eu·gen·ics (yoo JEN iks) *n.* (construed as sing.) the science of improving the physical and mental qualities of human beings through control of the factors influencing heredity. — **eu·gen'ic** *adj.* [< Gk. *eugenēs* wellborn]

eu·lo·gize (YOO lə JIZ) *v.t.* **·gized, ·giz·ing** speak or write a eulogy about.

eu·lo·gy (YOO lə jee) *n. pl.* **·gies 1.** a spoken or written piece of high praise, esp. when delivered publicly. **2.** great praise. [< LL *eulogia* speak] — **eu'lo·gist** *n.*

eu·nuch (YOO nək) *n.* a castrated man. [ME *eunuk*]

eu·phe·mism (YOO fə MIZ əm) *n.* **1.** substitution of a mild or roundabout word or expression for another felt to be too blunt or painful. **2.** a word or expression so substituted, as "the departed" for "the dead." [< Gk. *euphēmismós* use of words of good omens]

eu·pho·ni·ous (yoo FOH nee əs) *adj.* agreeable and pleasant in sound.

eu·pho·ri·a (yoo FOR ee ə) *n.* a feeling of well-being, relaxation, and happiness. [< NL] — **eu·phor'ic** *adj.*

eu·re·ka (yuu REE kə) *interj.* I have found (it): an exclamation of triumph or achievement. [< Gk. *heúrēka* I have found]

eu·rhyth·mics (yuu RITH miks) *n.* (construed as sing.) a system for developing grace and rhythm through bodily movements done to music. [< L *eurythmia* rhythmical movement] — **eu·ryth'mic** *adj.*

eu·tha·na·si·a (yoo thə NAY zhə) *n.* **1.** painless, peaceful death. **2.** the deliberate putting to death painlessly of a person suffering from a fatal disease or the like: also called *mercy killing.* [< NL]

e·vac·u·ate (i VAK yoo AYT) *v.* **·at·ed, ·at·ing** *v.t.* **1.** move out or withdraw (troops, inhabitants, etc.) from a threatened area or place. **2.** depart from and leave vacant; vacate. **3.** remove the contents of. **4.** *Physiol.* discharge or eject, as from the bowels. — *v.i.* **5.** withdraw, as from an area. [ME] — **e·vac'u·a'tion** *n.*

e·vade (i VAYD) *v.t. & v.i.* **e·vad·ed, ·vad·ing 1.** get away from (pursuers etc.) by tricks or cleverness. **2.** get out of or avoid (a responsibility, question, etc.). [< L *evadere* pass over]

e·val·u·ate (i VAL yuu AYT) *v.t.* **·at·ed,**

•**at•ing 1.** find the amount, worth, etc., of. **2.** judge the value of. —**e•val′u•a′tion** *n.*

e•va•nesce (EV ə NES) *v.i.* •**nesced,** •**nesc•ing** disappear by degrees; vanish gradually. [< L *evanescere* vanish] —**ev′a•nes′cent** *adj.*

e•van•gel•i•cal (EE van JEL i kəl) *adj.* **1.** of, relating to, or contained in the New Testament. **2.** of, relating to, or maintaining the doctrine that the Bible is the only rule of faith. **3.** evangelistic. —*n.* a member of an evangelical church. [< LL *evangelicus*]

e•van•gel•ism (i VAN jə LIZ əm) *n.* the zealous preaching or spreading of the gospel.

e•van•gel•ist (i VAN jə list) *n.* **1.** *Usu. cap.* one of the four writers of the New Testament Gospels. **2.** an itinerant or missionary preacher. —**e•van′gel•is′tic** *adj.*

e•van•gel•ize (i VAN jə LIZ) *v.* •**ized,** •**iz•ing** *v.t.* **1.** preach the gospel to. —*v.i.* **2.** act as an evangelist; preach. [ME *evangelisen*]

e•vap•o•rate (i VAP ə RAYT) *v.* •**rat•ed,** •**rat•ing** *v.t.* **1.** convert into vapor; vaporize. **2.** remove moisture or liquid from (milk, fruit, etc.) so as to dry or concentrate. —*v.i.* **3.** become vapor. **4.** yield vapor. **5.** vanish; disappear. [ME *evaporaten*] —**e•vap′o•ra′tion** *n.*

evaporated milk unsweetened canned milk thickened by the removal of water.

e•va•sion (i VAY zhən) *n.* **1.** the act of evading. **2.** a means used to evade, as a vague answer. [ME]

e•va•sive (i VAY siv) *adj.* **1.** given to or characterized by evasion; not direct and frank. **2.** elusive.

eve (eev) *n.* **1.** *Often cap.* the evening before a holiday: Christmas *Eve.* **2.** the time immediately preceding some event. **3.** *Poetic* evening. [ME]

e•ven (EE vən) *adj.* **1.** flat and smooth; level. **2.** extending to the same height or depth: a tree *even* with the housetop. **3.** extending along; parallel to. **4.** equally distributed; uniform: an *even* coat of paint. **5.** calm and controlled: an *even* disposition. **6.** equally matched; balanced. **7.** being the same (score) for each side or competitor. **8.** having settled a debt. **9.** identical in quantity, number, measure, etc.: *even* portions. **10.** exactly divisible by 2: an *even* number: opposed to *odd.* —**break even** end up with neither profit nor loss, as in a business deal. —**get even 1.** break even or settle debts. **2.**

have revenge. —*adv.* **1.** to a greater extent or degree; still: an *even* better plan. **2.** during the very same moment: with *as: Even* as they watched, the ship sank. **3.** in exactly the same way: with *as:* Do *even* as I do. **4.** indeed; actually: She feels glad, *even* delighted. **5.** unlikely as it may seem: He was kind *even* to his enemies. **6.** all the way; as far as: faithful *even* to death. **7.** nevertheless; not withstanding: *Even* with that handicap, he won. **8.** not otherwise than; right: It is happening *even* now. —**even if** although; notwithstanding. —*v.t. & v.i.* make or become even: often with *up* or *off.* [ME] —**e′ven•ness** *n.*

e•ven•hand•ed (EE vən HAN did) *adj.* treating all alike; impartial. —**e′ven•hand′ed•ness** *n.*

eve•ning (EEV ning) *n.* **1.** the latter part of day and the first part of night. **2.** an evening's entertainment or activity. **3.** the declining years of life, a career, etc. [ME]

evening star a bright planet visible in the west just after sunset, esp. Venus.

e•vent (i VENT) *n.* **1.** something that takes place; a happening or an incident. **2.** an actual or possible situation or set of circumstances: in the *event* of failure. **3.** final outcome. **4.** one of the items in a program of sports. —**in any event** or **at all events** regardless of what happens. [< L *eventus* outcome]

e•vent•ful (i VENT fəl) *adj.* **1.** marked by important events. **2.** having important consequences: an *eventful* decision.

e•ven•tu•al (i VEN choo əl) *adj.* occurring or resulting in due course of time.

e•ven•tu•al•i•ty (i VEN choo AL i tee) *n. pl.* •**ties** a likely or possible occurrence or outcome.

e•ven•tu•ate (i VEN choo AYT) *v.i.* •**at•ed,** •**at•ing** result ultimately.

ev•er (EV ər) *adv.* **1.** at any time; on any occasion: Did you *ever* see it? **2.** in any possible or conceivable way: Do it as fast as *ever* you can. **3.** at all times; invariably: They remained *ever* on guard. **4.** throughout the entire course of time; always; forever: usu. followed by *since, after,* or *afterward.* —**ever so** to a great extent or degree: It was *ever so* pleasant. [ME]

ev•er•glade (EV ər GLAYD) *n.* a tract of low, swampy land.

ev•er•green (EV ər GREEN) *adj.* having foliage that remains green until the formation of new foliage: distinguished from *de-ciduous.* —*n.* an evergreen tree or plant.

ev·er·last·ing (EV ər LAS ting) *adj.* 1. existing or lasting forever; eternal. 2. continuing for an indefinitely long period; perpetual. 3. incessant; interminable. —*n.* endless duration; eternity. [ME] —**ev′er·last′ing·ly** *adv.*

e·vert (i VURT) *v.t.* turn outward or inside out. [ME] —**e·ver·sion** (i VUR zhən) *n.*

eve·ry (EV ree) *adj.* 1. each without excepting any of a group or set. 2. each (member or unit singled out in some way) of a series: *every* tenth man. 3. the utmost; all possible: Show him *every* consideration. —**every now and then** from time to time; occasionally. —**every other** each alternate (specified thing). [ME]

eve·ry·bod·y (EV ree BOD ee) *pron.* every person.

eve·ry·day (EV ree DAY) *adj.* 1. happening every day; daily. 2. commonplace; ordinary.

eve·ry·one (EV ree WUN) *pron.* everybody.

every one each individual person or thing out of the whole number, excepting none: *Every one* of them is ill.

eve·ry·thing (EV ree THING) *pron.* 1. whatever exists; all things whatsoever. 2. whatever is relevant, needed, or important: I have *everything.*

eve·ry·where (EV ree HWAIR) *adv.* at, in, or to every place.

e·vict (i VIKT) *v.t.* expel (a tenant) by legal process; dispossess; put out. [ME *evicten*] —**e·vic′tion** *n.*

ev·i·dence (EV i dəns) *n.* 1. that which serves to prove or disprove something; support; proof. 2. that which serves as a ground for knowing or believing something; corroboration. 3. an indication; sign. 4. *Law* that which is properly presented before a court as a means of establishing or disproving something alleged or presumed. —**in evidence** readily seen or noticed; present. —**turn state's evidence** testify in court against one's acomplices. —*v.t.* •**denced,** •**denc·ing** show. [ME]

ev·i·dent (EV i dənt) *adj.* easily perceived or recognized; clear; plain. [ME]

ev·i·den·tial (EV i DEN shəl) *adj.* relating to, serving as, or based on evidence. [< L *evidentia* evidence]

ev·i·dent·ly (EV i dənt lee) *adv.* 1. to all appearances; apparently. 2. quite clearly; obviously.

e·vil (EE vəl) *adj.* 1. morally bad; wicked. 2. causing injury or any other undesirable result. 3. marked by or threatening misfortune: an *evil* omen. —*n.* 1. that which is evil; as: **a** that which is morally bad. **b** that which is injurious. **c** that which causes suffering or misfortune. 2. some particular act etc., that is evil. [ME *evel*]

e·vil·do·er (EE vəl DOO ər) *n.* one who does evil.

e·vince (i VINS) *v.t.* **e·vinced, e·vinc·ing** 1. indicate clearly; demonstrate. 2. give an outward sign of having (a quality, feeling, etc.). [< L *evincere* overcome]

e·vis·cer·ate (i VIS ə RAYT) *v.t.* •**at·ed,** •**at·ing** 1. disembowel. 2. remove the vital part of. [< L *evisceratus* torn to pieces]

e·voke (i VOHK) *v.t.* **e·voked, e·vok·ing** 1. call or summon forth. 2. draw forth or produce (a response, reaction, etc.). [< L *evocare* call out] —**ev·o·ca·tion** (EV ə KAY shən) *n.* —**e·voc·a·tive** (i VOK ə tiv) *adj.*

ev·o·lu·tion (EV ə LOO shən) *n.* 1. the process of unfolding, growing or developing, usu. by slow stages. 2. *Biol.* **a** the theory that all forms of life originated by descent from earlier forms. **b** the series of changes, as by natural selection, mutation, etc., through which a given type of organism has acquired its present characteristics. [< L] —**ev′o·lu′tion·ar·y** *adj.*

ev·o·lu·tion·ist (EV ə LOO shə nist) *n.* 1. a proponent of the theory of biological evolution. 2. one who advocates progress through gradual stages, as in political structure. —*adj.* 1. evolutionary. 2. of or relating to evolutionists. —**ev′o·lu′tion·ism** *n.*

e·volve (i VOLV) *v.* **e·volved, e·volv·ing** *v.t.* 1. work out; develop gradually. 2. *Biol.* develop to a more highly organized state: usu. in the passive. 3. unfold or expand. — *v.i.* 4. undergo the process of evolution. [< L *evolvere* unroll]

ewe (yoo) *n.* a female sheep. [ME]

ew·er (YOO ər) *n.* a wide-mouthed jug or pitcher for water. [ME]

ex·ac·er·bate (ig ZAS ər BAYT) *v.t.* •**bat·ed,** •**bat·ing** make more sharp or severe; aggravate. [< L *exacerbatus* made harsh]

ex·act (ig ZAKT) *adj.* 1. clear and complete in every detail; precise. 2. altogether accurate. 3. being precisely (what is specified): the *exact* amount necessary. 4. extremely careful about detail and accuracy: an *exact* editor. 5. rigorously demanding: an *exact* schoolmaster. —*v.t.* **1.** demand rigorously. **2.** obtain by or as if by force. [ME *exacten* drive out] —**ex·act'i·tude** *n.*

ex·act·ing (ig ZAK ting) *adj.* **1.** making rigorous demands; severe. **2.** involving constant hard work, attention, etc.

ex·act·ly (ig ZAKT lee) *adv.* **1.** in an exact manner; accurately. **2.** precisely right; just so.

ex·ag·ger·ate (ig ZAJ ə RAYT) *v.t. & v.i.* **·at·ed, ·at·ing** represent or look upon (something) as greater than is actually the case; overstate. [< L *exaggeratus* heaped up]

ex·alt (ig ZAWLT) *v.t.* **1.** raise in rank, character, honor, etc. **2.** glorify or praise. **3.** fill with delight, pride, etc.; elate. [ME *exalten*] —**ex·al·ta·tion** (EG zawl TAY shən) *n.*

ex·am·i·na·tion (ig ZAM ə NAY shən) *n.* **1.** the act of examining, or the state of being examined. **2.** medical scrutiny and testing. **3.** a formal test of knowledge or skills. [ME *examinacioun*]

ex·am·ine (ig ZAM in) *v.t.* **·ined, ·in·ing 1.** inspect with care; inquire into. **2.** subject to medical scrutiny and testing. **3.** test by questions or exercises as to qualifications, fitness, etc. [ME]

ex·am·ple (ig ZAM pəl) *n.* **1.** a typical or representative specimen. **2.** something deserving imitation; model. **3.** an instance or object of punishment etc., designed to warn or deter others. **4.** a particular problem or exercise. —**for example** by way of illustration. [ME *exaumple*]

ex·as·per·ate (ig ZAS pə RAYT) *v.t.* **·at·ed, ·at·ing 1.** make annoyed or angry; infuriate. **2.** make still worse; aggravate. [< L *exasperatus* provoked] —**ex·as'per·at' ing** *adj.*

ex·ca·vate (EKS kə VAYT) *v.t.* **·vat·ed, ·vat·ing 1.** make a hole or cavity in. **2.** form or make (a hole etc.) by hollowing, digging out, or scooping. **3.** remove by digging or scooping out, as soil. **4.** uncover by digging, as ruins; unearth. [< L *excavatus* hollowed out] —**ex'ca·va'tion** *n.*

ex·ceed (ik SEED) *v.t. & v.i.* **1.** surpass or be superior. **2.** go or be beyond (a limit). [ME *exceden*]

ex·ceed·ing (ik SEE ding) *adj.* greater than usual. —**ex·ceed'ing·ly** *adv.*

ex·cel (ik SEL) *v.t. & v.i.* **·celled, ·cel·ling** surpass; outstrip; be outstanding. [ME *excellen*]

Ex·cel·len·cy (EK sə lən see) *n. pl.* **·cies** an honorary title or form of address: often preceded by *His, Her, Your.*

ex·cel·lent (EK sə lənt) *adj.* being of the best quality; exceptionally good. [ME]

ex·cept (ik SEPT) *prep.* with the exclusion or omission of; aside from. —*conj.* **1.** aside from the fact that: also **except that. 2.** otherwise than. —*v.t.* **1.** exclude from consideration, enumeration, etc.; leave deliberately out of account. —*v.i.* **2.** raise an objection, esp. a formal objection: now usu. with *to.* [ME]

ex·cept·ing (ik SEP ting) *prep.* barring; except.

ex·cep·tion (ik SEP shən) *n.* **1.** the act of excepting, or the state of being excepted. **2.** something excluded from or not conforming to a general class, rule, etc. **3.** *Law* a formal objection to the decision of a court during trial. [ME *excepcioun*] —**take exception 1.** express disagreement. **2.** feel resentful.

ex·cep·tion·a·ble (ik SEP shə nə bəl) *adj.* open to exception or objection.

ex·cep·tion·al (ik SEP shə nl) *adj.* unusual; extraordinary.

ex·cerpt (EK surpt) *n.* an extract from a book, speech, etc. —*v.t.* (ik SURPT) pick out and cite (a passage from a book etc.). [ME]

ex·cess (ik SES) *n.* **1.** the condition or fact of going beyond what is usual, necessary, allowed, proper, etc.; also, the quantity, extent, or degree of this. **2.** an overabundance; superfluity. **3.** overindulgence; intemperance. —*adj.* (EK ses) **1.** being over and above what is expected or usual. **2.** immoderate. [ME]

ex·ces·sive (ik SES iv) *adj.* going beyond what is usual, necessary, proper, etc.; extreme. —**ex·ces'sive·ly** *adv.*

ex·change (iks CHAYNJ) *v.* **·changed, ·chang·ing** *v.t.* **1.** give and receive reciprocally. **2.** give up for something taken as a replacement. **3.** transfer to another in return for the equivalent in goods or money; trade. —*v.i.* **4.** exchange something. —*n.* **1.** the act of giving or receiving one thing as equivalent for another. **2.** a giving and receiving in turn. **3.** the substitution of one thing for another. **4.** a place where brokers meet to buy, sell, or trade commodities or securities: stock *exchange.* **5.** a central telephone system. **6.** a bill of exchange; also, the system of using a bill of exchange; also the fee for it. **7.** the mutual giving and receiving of equal sums of money, as between two countries using different currencies; also, the value of one currency relative to another. [ME *eschaungen* exchange] —**ex‧change′a‧ble** *adj.*

ex‧cise[1] (EK sīz) *n.* **1.** an indirect tax on certain commodities produced, sold, used, or transported within a country. Also **excise tax. 2.** a license fee charged for various sports, trades, etc. —*v.t.* **•cised, •cis‧ing** levy an excise upon. [< MDu. *excijs* tax]

ex‧cise[2] (ik SĪZ) *v.t.* **•cised, •cis‧ing 1.** cut out, as a growth. **2.** delete (a word, passage, etc.). [< L *excisus* cut out]. —**ex‧ci‧sion** (ek SIZH ən) *n.*

ex‧cit‧a‧ble (ik SĪ tə bəl) *adj.* **1.** easily excited; high-strung. **2.** *Physiol.* susceptible to stimuli. —**ex‧cit′a‧bil′i‧ty** *n.*

ex‧cite (ik SĪT) *v.t.* **•cit‧ed, •cit‧ing 1.** arouse (a feeling, reaction, etc.) into being or activity. **2.** arouse strong feeling in; rouse. **3.** bring about; stir up; provoke. [ME]

ex‧cite‧ment (ik SĪT mənt) *n.* **1.** the state of being excited; agitation. **2.** that which excites.

ex‧cit‧ing (ik SĪ ting) *adj.* causing excitement; thrilling.

ex‧claim (ik SKLAYM) *v.t. & v.i.* cry out abruptly; speak vehemently, as in surprise or anger. [< L *exclamare* cry out]

ex‧cla‧ma‧tion (EK sklə MAY shən) *n.* an abrupt or emphatic utterance, outcry, etc. —**ex‧clam‧a‧to‧ry** (ik SKLAM ə TOR ee) *adj.*

exclamation point a mark (!) used in punctuation after an exclamation or interjection. Also **exclamation mark.**

ex‧clude (ik SKLOOD) *v.t.* **•clud‧ed, •clud‧ing 1.** keep from entering; bar. **2.** refuse to notice, consider, or allow for; leave out. **3.** put out; eject. [ME] —**ex‧clu‧sion** (ik SKLOO zhən) *n.*

ex‧clu‧sive (ik SKLOO siv) *adj.* **1.** intended for or possessed by a single individual or group. **2.** belonging to or found in a single source: an *exclusive* news story. **3.** having no duplicate; original: an *exclusive* design. **4.** admitting or catering to only a very select group. **5.** complete and undivided: *exclusive* attention. **6.** inconsistent or incompatible with another: mutually *exclusive* doctrines. **7.** being the only one: the *exclusive* owner. **8.** not including: usu. with *of:* the cost *exclusive* of fees. [ME] —*n.* an exclusive news story. —**ex‧clu‧siv‧i‧ty** (EKS kloo SIV i tee) *n.*

ex‧com‧mu‧ni‧cate (EKS kə MYOO ni KAYT *v.t.* **•cat‧ed, •cat‧ing** cut off by ecclesiastical authority from sharing in the sacraments, worship, etc. of a church. [ME *excommunicaten*] —**ex′com‧mu′ni‧ca′tion** *n.*

ex‧co‧ri‧ate (ik SKOR ee AYT) *v.t.* **•at‧ed, •at‧ing 1.** tear, chafe, or burn away strips of (skin, bark, etc.). **2.** upbraid or denounce scathingly. [ME]

ex‧cre‧ment (EK skrə mənt) *n.* waste matter expelled from the body; esp., feces. [< L *excrementum*]

ex‧cres‧cence (ik SKRES əns) *n.* **1.** an unnatural or disfiguring outgrowth, as a wart. **2.** any outgrowth or addition. [ME]

ex‧cre‧ta (ik SKREE tə) *n.pl.* excretions, as sweat, urine, feces, etc. [< L]

ex‧crete (ik SKREET) *v.t.* **•cret‧ed, •cret‧ing** throw off or eliminate (waste matter). [< L *excretus* sifted out]

ex‧cru‧ci‧ate (ik SKROO shee AYT) *v.t.* **•at‧ed, •at‧ing** inflict extreme pain or agony upon. [< L *excruciatus* tormented]

ex‧cul‧pate (EK skul PAYT) *v.t.* **•pat‧ed, •pat‧ing** free from blame, or prove innocent. [< L *exculpatus* freed from blame] —**ex‧cul‧pa‧to‧ry** (ik SKUL pə TOR ee) *adj.*

ex‧cur‧sion (ik SKUR zhən) *n.* **1.** a short trip, as for relaxation. **2.** a trip on a bus etc. at reduced rates. [< L]

ex‧cuse (ik SKYOOZ) *v.t.* **•cused, •cus‧ing 1.** apologize for. **2.** grant pardon or forgiveness to. **3.** accept or overlook. **4.** free from censure or blame. **5.** release or exempt, as from a duty. **6.** allow to leave. —*n.* (ik SKYOOS) **1.** a reason given as a ground for being excused. **2.** a factor that frees from blame. [ME *excusen*]

ex‧e‧cra‧ble (EK si krə bəl) *adj.* **1.** detestable. **2.** extremely bad. [ME] —**ex′e‧cra‧bly** *adv.*

ex‧e‧crate (EK si KRAYT) *v.t.* **•crat‧ed, •crat‧ing 1.** call down evil upon; curse. **2.** detest; abhor. [< L *execratus* cursed] —**ex′e‧cra′tion** *n.*

ex‧e‧cute (EK si KYOOT) *v.t.* **•cut‧ed, •cut‧ing 1.** carry out fully. **2.** put into force, as a law. **3.** put to death legally. **4.** make (a will, deed, etc.) legal or valid. **5.** perform (something demanding skill). **6.** produce or fashion. [ME *executen* carry out] —**ex′e‧cut′er** *n.*

ex‧e‧cu‧tion (EK si KYOO shən) *n.* **1.** the act of executing, or the fact or condition of being executed. **2.** the way in which something is done. [ME *execucioun*]

ex·e·cu·tion·er (EK si KYOO shə nər) *n.* one who executes a death sentence.

ex·e·cu·tive (ig ZEG yə tiv) *adj.* **1.** relating or adapted to the putting into effect of plans, projects, etc. **2.** relating or adapted to the execution of laws and the administration of judgments, decrees, etc. —*n.* **1.** an individual or a group managing the administrative affairs of a nation, state, etc. **2.** an individual responsible for the management of a business, etc. [ME]

ex·e·cu·tor (ig SEK yə tər) *n.* **1.** *Law* one who is appointed to carry out the terms of a will. **2.** executer. [ME *executour*]

ex·e·ge·sis (EK si JEE sis) *n. pl.* **·ses** (-seez) critical explanation of the meaning of a literary or religious text. [< Gk., explanation] —**ex·e·gete** (EK si JEET) *n.*

ex·em·plar (ig ZEM plər) *n.* **1.** a model, pattern, or original. **2.** a typical example or specimen. [ME]

ex·em·pla·ry (ig ZEM plə ree) *adj.* **1.** serving as a worthy model or example. **2.** serving as a warning. [< L *exemplaris*]

ex·em·pli·fy (ig ZEM plə FI) *v.t.* **·fied, ·fy·ing** show by example; illustrate. [ME *exemplifien* copy] —**ex·em'pli·fi·ca'tion** *n.*

ex·empt (ig ZEMPT) *v.t.* free or excuse from some obligation to which others are subject. —*adj.* free, clear, or excused, as from some duty. [ME] —**ex·emp' tion** *n.*

ex·er·cise (EK sər SIZ) *v.* **·cised, ·cis·ing** *v.t.* **1.** subject to drills etc. so as to train or develop. **2.** make use of; employ. **3.** exert, as authority. **4.** make anxious or fretful. —*v.i.* **5.** perform exercises. —*n.* **1.** a putting into use: an *exercise* of patience. **2.** activity performed for physical conditioning. **3.** a lesson, problem, etc., designed to teach a skill. **4.** *Usu. pl.* a ceremony, etc., as at a graduation. [ME]

ex·ert (ig ZURT) *v.t.* put forth or into action, as force or influence. [< L *exertus* thrust out] —**ex·er'tion** *n.*

ex·e·unt (EK see ənt) they go out: a stage direction. [< L]

ex·hale (eks HAYL) *v.* **·haled, ·hal·ing** *v.i.* **1.** expel air or vapor; breathe out. **2.** pass off as a vapor or emanation. —*v.t.* **3.** breathe forth or give off, as air or an aroma. [ME *exhalen* breathe out] —**ex·ha·la·tion** (EKS hə LAY shən) *n.*

ex·haust (ig ZAWST) *v.t.* **1.** make extremely

tired. **2.** drain of resources, strength, etc. **3.** draw off, as gas, steam, etc., from or as from a container. **4.** empty; drain. **5.** study, treat of, or develop thoroughly. —*n.* **1.** the escape or discharge of waste gases, fluid, etc.; also, the gases etc. that escape. **2.** a pipe or other engine part through which gases, etc., escape. [< L *exhaustus* drained out] —**ex·haust'i·ble** *adj.*

ex·haust·ing (ig ZAW sting) *adj.* extremely tiring.

ex·haus·tion (ig ZAWS chən) *n.* **1.** extreme fatigue. **2.** the condition of being completely used up or drained. [< NL]

ex·haus·tive (ig ZAWS tiv) *adj.* **1.** that exhausts or tends to exhaust; exhausting. **2.** thorough; comprehensive. —**ex·haus' tive·ness** *n.*

ex·hib·it (ig ZIB it) *v.t.* **1.** put on view, esp. publicly. **2.** make evident; reveal. **3.** *Law* submit (evidence etc.) formally. —*v.i.* **4.** put something on display. —*n.* **1.** a putting on view; display. **2.** an object displayed. **3.** *Law* an object or document submitted as evidence. [ME *exhibiten* show]

ex·hi·bi·tion (EK sə BISH ən) *n.* **1.** the act of exhibiting. **2.** that which is exhibited. **3.** a public display, as of art works.

ex·hi·bi·tion·ism (EK sə BISH ə NIZ əm) *n.* **1.** a tendency to attract attention to oneself. **2.** a tendency toward deviant sexual display. —**ex'hi·bi'tion·ist** *n.*

ex·hil·a·rate (ig ZIL ə RAYT) *v.t.* **·rat·ed, ·rat·ing** make happy; elate. [< L *exhilaratus* gladdened] —**ex·hil'a·ra'tion** *n.*

ex·hort (ig ZORT) *v.t. & v.i.* urge by earnest appeal or argument; advise or recommend strongly. [ME *exhorte* greatly encourage] —**ex·hor·ta·tion** (EG zor TAY shən) *n.*

ex·hume (ig ZOOM) *v.t.* **·humed, ·hum·ing** disinter. [ME] —**ex·hu·ma·tion** (EKS hyuu MAY shən) *n.*

ex·i·gen·cy (EK si jən see) *n. pl.* **·cies 1.** urgency. **2.** a situation that requires immediate attention. **3.** *Usu. pl.* a pressing need or necessity. [< Med.L *exigentia*] —**ex' i·gent** *adj.*

ex·ig·u·ous (ig ZIG yoo əs) *adj.* small in amount; scanty. [< L *exiguus*]

ex·ile (EG zīl) *n.* **1.** separation from one's native country, home, etc. **2.** one who is so separated. [ME *exil* banishment] —**ex'ile** *v.t.* **·iled, ·il·ing**

ex·ist (ig ZIST) *v.i.* **1.** have actual being or reality; be. **2.** continue to live or be. **3.** be present; occur. [< L *existere* appear]

ex•is•tence (ig ZIS tɔns) *n.* **1.** the state or fact of being or continuing to be. **2.** animate being; life. **3.** way or mode of living. **4.** presence; occurrence. **5.** anything or all that exists. [ME] —**ex•is•ten•tial** (EG zis TEN shɔl) *adj.*

ex•is•ten•tial•ism (EG zi STEN shɔ LIZ ɔm) *n.* a philosophy that stresses existence, as opposed to essence, and the active role of the will. —**ex'is•ten'tial•ist** *adj. & n.*

ex•it (EG zit) *n.* **1.** a way out; egress. **2.** a departure of an actor from a stage. **3.** any departure. [< L *exitus*] —*v.i.* depart.

ex•o•dus (EK sɔ dɔs) *n.* a going forth. —**the Exodus** the departure of the Israelites from Egypt, described in **Exodus**, the second book of the Old Testament. [< L]

ex of•fi•ci•o (EKS ɔ FISH ee OH) *Latin* by virtue of or because of office or position.

ex•on•er•ate (ig ZON ɔ RAYT) *v.t.* •**at•ed,** •**at•ing 1.** free from accusation or blame. **2.** relieve or free from a responsibility or the like. [ME]

ex•or•bi•tant (ig ZOR bi tɔnt) *adj.* excessive, as in price or demand; extravagant. [ME]

ex•or•cise (EK sor SIZ) *v.t.* •**cised,** •**cis•ing 1.** cast out (an evil spirit) by prayers or incantations. **2.** free of an evil spirit. [ME] — **ex'or•cist** *n.* —**ex'or•cism** *n.*

ex•ot•ic (ig ZOT ik) *adj.* **1.** belonging to another part of the world; not native. **2.** strangely different and fascinating. [< L *exoticus* foreign]

ex•pand (ik SPAND) *v.t.* **1.** increase the range, size, etc., of. **2.** spread out by unfolding; open. **3.** develop more fully the details or form of. —*v.i.* **4.** grow larger, wider, etc. [ME *expanden*] —**ex•pand'a•ble, ex•pan'si•ble** *adj.* —**ex•pan•sion** (ik SPAN shɔn) *n.*

ex•panse (ik SPANS) *n.* **1.** a wide, continuous area or stretch. **2.** expansion. [< NL *expansum*]

ex•pan•sive (ik SPAN siv) *adj.* **1.** capable of expanding or tending to expand. **2.** broad; extensive. **3.** outgoing.

ex•pa•ti•ate (ik SPAY shee AYT) *v.i.* •**at•ed,** •**at•ing** speak or write at length; elaborate: with *on.* [< L *expatiatus* digressed]

ex•pa•tri•ate (eks PAY tree AYT) *v.* •**at•ed,** •**at•ing** *v.t.* **1.** banish. **2.** exile (oneself). — *v.i.* **3.** leave one's country and reside elsewhere. [< Med.L *expatriatus* banished] — **ex•pa•tri•ate** (eks PAY tree it) *n. & adj.*

ex•pect (ik SPEKT) *v.t.* **1.** look forward to as certain or probable. **2.** look for as right, proper, or necessary. **3.** *Informal* presume; suppose. [< L *expectare* look out]

ex•pect•an•cy (ik SPEK tɔn see) *n. pl.* •**cies 1.** the action or state of expecting. **2.** an object of expectation: life *expectancy.*

ex•pect•ant (ik SPEK tɔnt) *adj.* **1.** having expectations. **2.** pregnant; expecting.

ex•pec•ta•tion (EK spek TAY shɔn) *n.* **1.** the action of expecting, or the state of mind of one who expects; anticipation. **2.** the state of being expected: preceded by *in.* **3.** something expected or anticipated. [< L]

ex•pec•to•rate (ik SPEK tɔ RAYT) *v.t. & v.i.* •**rat•ed,** •**rat•ing 1.** expel (phlegm etc.) by spitting. **2.** spit. [< L *expectoratus* expelled from the breast] —**ex•pec'to•ra'tion** *n.*

ex•pe•di•en•cy (ik SPEE dee ɔn see) *n. pl.* •**cies 1.** the state or quality of being expedient. **2.** that which is expedient. **3.** adherence to what is opportune or politic. [< LL *expedientia*]

ex•pe•di•ent (ik SPEE dee ɔnt) *adj.* **1.** serving to promote a desired end. **2.** pertaining to or prompted by utility, interest, or advantage rather than by what is right. —*n.* **1.** something expedient. **2.** a device; makeshift. [ME]

ex•pe•dite (EK spi DIT) *v.t.* •**dit•ed,** •**dit•ing 1.** speed up the process or progress of; facilitate. **2.** do with quick efficiency. [ME]

ex•pe•di•tion (EK spi DISH ɔn) *n.* **1.** a journey or march for a purpose. **2.** a group of persons engaged in such a journey, together with their equipment. [ME] —**ex'pe•di'tion•ar'y** *adj.*

ex•pe•di•tious (EK spi DISH ɔs) *adj.* speedy.

ex•pel (ik SPEL) *v.t.* •**pelled,** •**pel•ling 1.** drive out by force. **2.** force to end attendance at a school, terminate membership, etc.; oust. [ME *expellen* drive out]

ex•pend (ik SPEND) *v.t.* pay out or use up. [ME]

ex•pend•a•ble (ik SPEN dɔ bɔl) *adj.* **1.** available for spending. **2.** considered a thing or person that can be sacrificed.

ex•pen•di•ture (ik SPEN di chɔr) *n.* the act of expending, or the amount expended.

ex•pense (ik SPENS) *n.* **1.** outlay or consumption of money. **2.** the cost of something; money required. **3.** something that involves the spending of money. **4.** *pl.* funds allotted or spent to cover incidental costs.

[ME] —**ex·pen·sive** (ik SPEN siv) *adj.* involving much expense; costly.

ex·pe·ri·ence (ik SPEER ee əns) *n.* **1.** actual participation in or direct contact with something. **2.** knowledge or skill derived from actual participation or training. **3.** the totality of whatever one has engaged in or undergone. —*v.t.* **·enced, ·enc·ing** be personally involved in; undergo. [ME]

ex·pe·ri·en·tial (ik SPEER ee EN shəl) *adj.* pertaining to or acquired by experience; empirical.

ex·per·i·ment (ik SPER ə mənt) *n.* **1.** an act or operation designed to discover, test, or illustrate a truth, principle, or effect. **2.** the conducting of such operations. —*v.i.* (ek SPER ə MENT) make experiments; make a test or trial. [ME] —**ex·per'i·men·ta' tion** *n.*

ex·per·i·men·tal (ik SPER ə MEN tl) *adj.* **1.** pertaining to or resulting from experiment. **2.** based on experience; empirical. **3.** for the purpose of experiment or testing. **4.** provisional; tentative.

ex·pert (EK spurt) *n.* one who has special skill or knowledge; a specialist. —*adj.* **1.** skillful as the result of training or experience. **2.** characteristic of or produced by an expert. [ME] —**ex'·pert·ness** *n.*

ex·per·tise (EK spər TEEZ) *n.* the knowledge, skill, or experience of an expert. [< F]

ex·pi·ate (EK spee AYT) *v.t.* **·at·ed, ·at·ing** atone for; make amends for. [< L *expiatus* atoned for] —**ex·pi·a·ble** (EK spee ə bəl) *adj.*

ex·pire (ik SPĪR) *v.* **·pired, ·pir·ing** *v.i.* **1.** come to an end, as a contract. **2.** exhale. **3.** die. —*v.t.* **4.** breathe out from the lungs. [ME] —**ex·pi·ra·tion** (EK spə RAY shən) *n.*

ex·plain (ik SPLAYN) *v.t.* **1.** make plain or understandable. **2.** give the meaning of; interpret. **3.** give reasons for; account for. — *v.i.* **4.** give an explanation. [ME *explanen*]

ex·pla·na·tion (EK splə NAY shən) *n.* **1.** the act or process of explaining. **2.** a statement that clarifies or accounts for something. **3.** the meaning given to explain something; sense. [ME *explanacioun*] —**ex·plan· a·to·ry** (ik SPLAN ə TOR ee) *adj.*

ex·ple·tive (EK spli tiv) *n.* an exclamation, often profane. [< LL *expletivuus* acting to fill out]

ex·pli·ca·ble (EK spli kə bəl) *adj.* capable of explanation.

ex·pli·cate (EK spli KAYT) *v.t.* **·cat·ed,** **·cat·ing** explain in detail. [< L *explicatus* unfolded] —**ex'pli·ca'tion** *n.* interpretation; explanation.

ex·plic·it (ik SPLIS it) *adj.* **1.** plainly expressed; clear. **2.** frank; straightforward. [< L *explicitus* unfolded] —**ex·plic'it·ness** *n.*

ex·plode (ik SPLOHD) *v.* **·plod·ed,** **·plod·ing** *v.t.* **1.** cause to burst or blow up violently and with noise; detonate. **2.** disprove utterly; refute. **3.** cause to expand violently or pass suddenly from a solid to a gaseous state. —*v.i.* **4.** burst into pieces; blow up. **5.** be exploded, as gunpowder. **6.** break out suddenly or violently into tears, laughter, etc. [< L *explodere* drive off the stage by clapping] —**ex·plo·sion** (ik SPLOH zhən) *n.*

ex·ploit (EK sploit) *n.* a deed or act, esp. a daring one; feat. —*v.t.* (ik SPLOIT) **1.** use for one's own gain or advantage: *exploit* workers. **2.** use for profitable ends: *exploit* water power. [ME] —**ex'ploi·ta'tion** *n.*

ex·plo·ra·tion (EK splə RAY shən) *n.* the act of exploring; esp., the exploring of unfamiliar or unknown regions. —**ex·plor· a·to·ry** (ik SPLOR ə TOR ee) *adj.*

ex·plore (ik SPLOR) *v.t. & v.i.* **·plored, ·plor·ing 1.** search or examine closely; scrutinize. **2.** travel through (unfamiliar territory, etc.). [< L *explorare* examine]

ex·plo·sive (ik SPLOH siv) *adj.* **1.** pertaining to or marked by explosion. **2.** liable to explode or to cause explosion. —*n.* anything that, on impact or by ignition, reacts by a violent expansion of gases and the liberation of heat. —**ex·plo'sive·ness** *n.*

ex·po·nent (EK spoh nənt) *n.* **1.** one who or that which explains or expounds. **2.** one who or that which represents or symbolizes something: an *exponent* of fair play. **3.** *Math.* a number or symbol placed as a superscript to the right of a quantity to indicate a power: 2 is an *exponent* in 3^2. [< L *exponere* set forth]

ex·port (ik SPORT) *v.t.* carry or send, as merchandise or raw materials, to other countries for sale or trade. —*n.* (EK sport) **1.** the act of exporting. **2.** that which is exported. —*adj.* (EK sport) of or pertaining to exports. [< L *exportare* carry away]

ex·pose (ik SPOHZ) *v.t.* **·posed, ·pos·ing 1.** lay open to criticism, ridicule, etc.: *expose* oneself to scorn. **2.** lay open to some force, influence, etc.: *expose* a mixture to heat. **3.** present to view by baring. **4.** reveal, as a crime. **5.** unmask (an evildoer). **6.** *Pho-*

tog. admit light to (a sensitized film or plate). [< ME *exposen*]

ex·po·sé (EK spoh ZAY) *n.* a public revelation of an evil or disgrace. [< F]

ex·po·si·tion (EK spə ZISH ən) *n.* **1.** the act of presenting, explaining, or expounding facts or ideas. **2.** a presentation, commentary, or interpretation. **3.** a large public display or show.

ex·pos·i·to·ry (ik SPOZ i TOR ee) *adj.* of or pertaining to exposition; explanatory.

ex·pos·tu·late (ik SPOS chə LAYT) *v.i.* •lat·ed, •lat·ing reason earnestly, esp. to dissuade; remonstrate: usu. with *with.* [< L *expostulatus* urgently demanded]

ex·po·sure (ik SPOH zhər) *n.* **1.** the act of exposing, or the state of being exposed. **2.** situation in relation to the sun, elements, or points of the compass: southern *exposure.* **3.** *Photog.* **a** the act of subjecting a sensitized plate or film to light rays, X-rays, etc. **b** the time required for this. **c** a single film or plate so acted upon.

ex·pound (ik SPOWND) *v.t.* **1.** set forth in detail; state. **2.** explain; interpret. [ME *expounen*]

ex·press (ik SPRES) *v.t.* **1.** formulate in words; verbalize; state. **2.** give a sign of; reveal: *express* anger. **3.** indicate by means of a symbol, formula, etc. **4.** squeeze out (a liquid); press out. **5.** send (goods etc.), by a system of rapid delivery. —*adj.* **1.** communicated or indicated clearly; explicit. **2.** made or intended for a precise purpose. **3.** designed for or operating at high speed: an *express* train. **4.** of or relating to a system of rapid delivery of goods, etc. **5.** exact; precise. —*adv.* by rapid delivery. —*n.* **1.** a system designed to convey goods, money, etc., rapidly. **2.** any means of rapid conveyance. **3.** a train or other conveyance operating at high speed and making few stops. [ME *expressen*]

ex·pres·sion (ik SPRESH ən) *n.* **1.** communication of thought, opinion, etc. **2.** outward indication of some feeling, condition, etc. **3.** a conventional sign or set of signs used to indicate something; symbolization. **4.** a particular cast of the features that expresses a feeling, meaning, etc. **5.** the particular way in which one expresses oneself. **6.** a word or phrase used in communication.

Ex·pres·sion·ism (ik SPRESH ə NIZ əm) *n.* an early 20th-c. movement in the arts, stressing the artist's subjective interpretation of objects and experiences. — **ex·pres′sion·ist** *n. & adj.*

ex·pres·sive (ik SPRES iv) *adj.* **1.** of or characterized by expression. **2.** serving to express or indicate: a manner *expressive* of contempt. **3.** significant: an *expressive* sigh. [ME] —**ex·pres′sive·ness** *n.*

ex·press·ly (ik SPRES lee) *adv.* **1.** with definitely stated intent or application. **2.** exactly and unmistakably; plainly. [ME]

ex·pro·pri·ate (eks PROH pree AYT) *v.t.* •at·ed, •at·ing take or transfer (property) from the owner, esp. for public use. [< Med.L *expropriatus* separated from one's own property] —**ex·pro′pri·a′tion** *n.*

ex·pul·sion (ik SPUL shən) *n.* the act of expelling, or the state of being expelled. [ME]

ex·punge (ik SPUNJ) *v.t.* •punged, •pung·ing erase or wipe out. [< L *expungere* obliterate]

ex·pur·gate (EK spər GAYT) *v.t.* •gat·ed, •gat·ing **1.** take out obscene or otherwise objectionable material from: *expurgate* a novel. **2.** remove or omit (objectionable matter). [< L *expurgatus* cleansed] — **ex′pur·ga′tion** *n.*

ex·qui·site (ek SKWI zit) *adj.* **1.** marked by rare and delicate beauty, craftsmanship, etc. **2.** superb; excellent; admirable. **3.** highly sensitive; discriminating. **4.** extremely refined; fastidious. **5.** intensely keen or acute, as pleasure or pain. [ME]

ex·tant (EK stənt) *adj.* still existing; not lost or destroyed; surviving. [< L *exstare* stand out]

ex·tem·po·ra·ne·ous (ik STEM pə RAY nee əs) *adj.* uttered, performed, or composed with little or no advance preparation; improvised; spontaneous. [< LL *extemporaneus*]

ex·tend (ik STEND) *v.t.* **1.** open or stretch to full length. **2.** make longer. **3.** prolong; continue. **4.** spread out; expand. **5.** hold out or put forth, as the hand. **6.** give or offer to give: *extend* hospitality. —*v.i.* **7.** be extended; stretch. [ME *extenden* stretch out] —**ex·tend′ed** *adj.*

extended family parents and close relatives living together as a family.

ex·ten·si·ble (ik STEN sə bəl) *adj.* capable of being extended. —**ex·ten′si·bil′i·ty** *n.*

ex·ten·sion (ik STEN shən) *n.* **1.** the act of extending, or the state of being extended. **2.** an extended part; addition. **3.** range; extent. **4.** educational courses and programs offered outside the school proper: *extension* courses.

ex·ten·sive (ik STEN siv) *adj.* **1.** large in area. **2.** having a wide range; farreaching.

ex·tent (ik STENT) *n.* **1.** the dimension, degree, or limit to which anything is extended; size. **2.** size within given limits; scope: the *extent* of one's powers. [ME *extente* evaluation]

ex·ten·u·ate (ik STEN yoo AYT) *v.t.* **·at·ed, ·at·ing** represent (a fault, crime, etc.) as less blameworthy; make excuses for. [ME] —**ex·ten'u·at'ing** *adj.*

ex·te·ri·or (ik STEER ee ər) *adj.* **1.** of, pertaining to, or situated on the outside; external. **2.** coming or acting from without. —*n.* **1.** that which is outside, as an external surface. **2.** outside appearance or demeanor. [< L, more foreign]

ex·ter·mi·nate (ik STUR mə NAYT) *v.t.* **·nat·ed, ·nat·ing** destroy (living things) entirely; annihilate. [< L *exterminatus* driven out] —**ex·ter'mi·na'tion** *n.*

ex·ter·nal (ik STUR nl) *adj.* **1.** of, pertaining to, derived from, or situated on the outside; exterior; extrinsic. **2.** pertaining to the outer self; superficial. **3.** pertaining to foreign countries. **4.** relating to, affecting, or meant for the outside of the body: *external* use. —*n.* **1.** the outside; exterior. **2.** *Usu. pl.* outward or superficial aspects, circumstances, etc. [ME]

ex·tinct (ik STINGKT) *adj.* **1.** extinguished; inactive, as a volcano. **2.** no longer existing: *extinct* animals. [ME] —**ex·tinc'tion** *n.*

ex·tin·guish (ik STING gwish) *v.t.* **1.** put out or quench, as a fire. **2.** make extinct; wipe out. **3.** obscure; eclipse. [< L *extinguere* quench]

ex·tir·pate (EK stər PAYT) *v.t.* **·pat·ed, ·pat·ing** root out or up; destroy wholly. [< L *extirpatus* plucked ·out] —**ex'tir·pa' tion** *n.*

ex·tol (ik STOHL) *v.t.* **·tolled, ·tol·ling** praise highly; exalt. [ME *extollen*]

ex·tort (ik STORT) *v.t.* obtain (money etc.) from a person by threat, oppression, or abuse of authority. [ME] —**ex·tor'tive** *adj.*

ex·tor·tion (ik STOR shən) *n.* **1.** the act or practice of extorting. **2.** the exaction of an exorbitant price. **3.** that which has been extorted. [ME *extorcion*] —**ex·tor'tion·ist** *n.*

ex·tra (EK strə) *adj.* **1.** over and above what is normal, required, expected, etc.; additional. **2.** larger or better than usual. —*n.* **1.** something beyond what is usual or required. **2.** a special edition of a newspaper issued to cover important news. **3.** in mo-

tion pictures, a person hired for a small part. —*adv.* unusually: *extra* good.

extra- *prefix* beyond or outside the scope, area, or limits of—used in such words as *extramarital* and *extramural*.

ex·tract (ik STRAKT) *v.t.* **1.** draw or pull out by force. **2.** derive or deduce. **3.** obtain by pressure, distillation, etc. **4.** select or copy out (a passage, etc.), as for quotation. **5.** *Math.* calculate (the root of a number). —*n.* (EK strakt) something extracted, as: **a** a concentrated form of a food, drug, etc. **b** a passage selected from a book. [ME] —**ex·tract'a·ble** *adj.*

ex·trac·tion (ik STRAK shən) *n.* **1.** the act of extracting, or the state of being extracted. **2.** that which is extracted. **3.** descent: of foreign *extraction*. [ME *extraccioun*]

ex·tra·cur·ric·u·lar (EK strə kə RIK yə lər) *adj.* of or pertaining to organized student activities that are not part of the curriculum.

ex·tra·dite (EK strə DIT) *v.t.* **·dit·ed, ·dit·ing** deliver up (an accused person) to the jurisdiction of some other government. —**ex·tra·di·tion** (EK strə DISH ən) *n.* [< F]

ex·tra·mar·i·tal (EK strə MAR i tl) *adj.* adulterous.

ex·tra·mu·ral (EK strə MYUUR əl) *adj.* **1.** situated outside the walls, as of a fortified city. **2.** relating to activities taking place outside an educational institution.

ex·tra·ne·ous (ik STRAY nee əs) *adj.* **1.** coming from without; foreign. **2.** unrelated to the matter at hand. [< L *extraneus* external]

ex·traor·di·nar·y (ik STROR dn ER ee) *adj.* **1.** being beyond or out of the common order, course, or method. **2.** far exceeding the usual; exceptional; remarkable. **3.** employed on an exceptional occasion; special: envoy *extraordinary*. [ME *extraordinarie*]

ex·trap·o·late (ik STRAP ə LAYT) *v.t. & v.i.* **·lat·ed, ·lat·ing** infer (an unknown value etc.) from facts that are known. —**ex·trap'o·la'tion** *n.*

ex·tra·sen·so·ry (EK strə SEN sə ree) *adj.* beyond the range of normal sensory experience or capability: *extrasensory* perception.

ex·tra·ter·res·tri·al (EK strə tə RES tree əl) *adj.* pertaining to the universe outside the earth.

ex·trav·a·gance (ik STRAV ə gəns) *n.* **1.** wasteful expenditure of money. **2.** extreme lack of moderation in behavior or speech. **3.** an instance of wastefulness or excess. [< F]

ex·trav·a·gant (ik STRAV ə gənt) *adj.* **1.** overly lavish in expenditure; wasteful. **2.** immoderate; unrestrained: *extravagant* praise. **3.** flagrantly high; exorbitant: *extravagant* costs. [ME]

ex·trav·a·gan·za (ik STRAV ə GAN zə) *n.* a lavish, spectacular theatrical production. [< Ital. *estravaganza*]

ex·treme (ik STREEM) *adj.* **1.** exceedingly great or severe: *extreme* danger. **2.** going far beyond the bounds of moderation: an *extreme* reactionary. **3.** very strict or drastic: *extreme* measures. **4.** outermost: the *extreme* border of a country. **5.** last; final. —*n.* **1.** the highest degree; utmost point: the *extreme* of cruelty. **2.** one of the two ends or farthest limits of anything: the *extremes* of joy and sorrow. [ME] —**go to extremes** carry something to excess.

ex·trem·ist (ik STREE mist) *n.* **1.** one who advocates extreme measures or holds extreme views. **2.** one who carries something to excess. —**ex·trem′ism** *n.*

ex·trem·i·ty (ik STREM i tee) *n. pl.* **·ties 1.** the utmost or farthest point. **2.** the greatest degree: the *extremity* of grief. **3.** *pl.* extreme measures: resort tó *extremities.* **4.** a limb or appendage of the body; esp., a hand or foot. [ME]

ex·tri·cate (EK stri kayt) *v.t.* **·cat·ed, ·cat·ing** free from entanglement, hindrance, or difficulties; disentangle. [< L *extricatus*] —**ex·tri·ca·ble** (EK stri kə bəl) *adj.*

ex·trin·sic (ik STRIN sik) *adj.* **1.** being outside the nature of something; not inherent: opposed to *intrinsic.* **2.** External; extraneous. [< LL *extrinsecus* outward]

ex·tro·ver·sion (EK strə VUR zhən) *n. Psychol.* the turning of one's interest toward objects and actions outside the self. —**ex′ tro·vert** (EK strə VURT) *n. & adj.*

ex·trude (ik STROOD) *v.* **·trud·ed, ·trud·ing** *v.t.* **1.** force, thrust, or push out. **2.** shape (plastic, metal, etc.) by forcing through dies under pressure. —*v.i.* **3.** protude. [< L *extrudere* thrust out] —**ex·tru·sion** (ik STROO zhən) *n.*

ex·u·ber·ant (ig ZOO bər ənt) *adj.* **1.** abounding in high spirits and vitality; full of joy and vigor. **2.** overflowing; lavish: *exuberant* praise. **3.** luxuriant: *exuberant* foliage. [ME] —**ex·u′ber·ance** *n.*

ex·ude (ig ZOOD) *v.* **·ud·ed, ·ud·ing** *v.i.* **1.** ooze or trickle forth, as sweat, sap, etc. — *v.t.* **2.** discharge gradually in this manner. **3.** manifest; display: *exude* confidence. [< L *exudare* sweat out] —**ex·u·da·tion** (EKS yuu DAY shən) *n.*

ex·ult (ig ZULT) *v.i.* rejoice greatly, as in triumph; be jubilant. [< L *exultare* leap up] —**ex·ul·ta·tion** (EG zul TAY shən) *n.*

ex·ul·tant (ig ZUL tnt) *adj.* jubilant; triumphant; elated.

eye (ī) *n.* **1.** the organ of vision in man and animals, usu. a nearly spherical mass set in the skull. **2.** the area around the eye. **3.** the iris of the eye, in regard to its color. **4.** a look; gaze. **5.** attentive observation. **6.** sight; view: in the public *eye.* **7.** capacity to see or discern with discrimination. **8.** judgment; opinion. **9.** *Meteorol.* the calm central area of a hurricane or cyclone. **10.** anything resembling the human eye: the *eye* of a needle. —**catch one's eye** get one's attention. —**give (someone) the eye** *Informal* look at (someone) admiringly or invitingly. — **keep an eye out (or peeled)** watch for something; keep alert. —**make eyes at** look at amorously or covetously. —**with an eye** to with a view to; looking to. —*v.t.* **eyed, ey·ing** or **eye·ing** look at carefully. [ME *eie*]

eye·brow (Ī BROW) *n.* the bony ridge over the eyes; also the hair growing there.

eye·ful (Ī fuul) *n.* **1.** an amount of something in the eye. **2.** a good look. **3.** *Informal* a strikingly attractive person.

eye·glass (Ī GLAS) *n.* **1.** *pl.* a pair of corrective glass lenses mounted in a frame: also called *glasses, spectacles.* **2.** any lens used to assist vision. **3.** an eyepiece.

eye·lash (Ī LASH) *n.* one of the stiff, curved hairs growing from the edge of the eyelids.

eye·lid (Ī LID) *n.* either of the movable folds of skin that close over the eyes.

eye·piece (Ī pees) *n.* the lens or lenses nearest the eye in a telescope, microscope, etc.

eye shadow a tinted cosmetic preparation, applied to the eyelids.

eye·sight (Ī SĪT) *n.* **1.** the power or faculty of sight. **2.** extent or range of vision.

eye·sore (Ī SOR) *n.* something ugly.

eye·strain (Ī STRAYN) *n.* weariness of the eyes caused by excessive or improper use.

eye·wash (Ī WOSH) *n.* **1.** a medicinal wash for the eye. **2.** *Informal* nonsense.

eye·wit·ness (Ī WIT nis) *n.* one who has seen something happen and can give testimony about it. —**eye′wit′ness** *adj.*

ey·rie (AIR ee) see AERIE.

F

f, F (ef) *n. pl.* **f's** or **fs, F's** or **Fs 1.** the sixth letter of the English alphabet. **2.** the sound represented by the letter *f*. —*symbol Music* **a** the fourth tone in the diatonic scale of C. **b** forte.

fa (fah) *n. Music* the fourth tone of the diatonic scale in solmization.

fa·ble (FAY bəl) *n.* **1.** a brief tale embodying a moral, sometimes using animals or objects as characters. **2.** a legend or myth. [ME] —**fa′bled** *adj.* —**fab·u·list** (FAB yə list) *n.*

fab·ric (FAB rik) *n.* **1.** a woven, felted, or knitted material, as cloth. **2.** structure or framework: the social *fabric.* [< MF *fabrique*]

fab·ri·cate (FAB ri kayt) *v.t.* **·cat·ed, ·cat·ing 1.** make or manufacture; build. **2.** make up or invent, as a lie or story. [ME] —**fab′ri·ca′tion** *n.*

fab·u·lous (FAB yə ləs) *adj.* **1.** beyond belief; astounding. **2.** mythical. [< L *fabulosus* fictitious]

fa·cade (fə SAHD) *n.* **1.** *Archit.* the front or principal face of a building. **2.** a front or a false appearance: a *facade* of respectability. [< F]

face (fays) *n.* **1.** the front portion of the head; countenance. **2.** the expression of the countenance. **3.** a grimacing expression. **4.** external aspect or appearance; look. **5.** effrontery; audacity. **6.** the front or principal surface of anything: the *face* of a clock. —**in the face of 1.** confronting. **2.** in spite of. —**on the face of it** judging by all appearances; apparently. — **fly in the face of** act in defiance of. — **lose face** lose one's dignity. —**save face** preserve one's dignity. —*v.* **faced, fac·ing** *v.t.* **1.** bear or turn the face toward. **2.** cause to turn in a given direction. **3.** meet face to face; confront. **4.** realize or be aware of. **5.** cover with a layer or surface of another material. —*v.i.* **6.** turn or be turned with the face in a given direction. —**face up to** meet with courage. [< ME] —**face′less** *adj.*

face·lift·ing (FAYS LIFT ing) *n.* **1.** plastic surgery to tighten facial tissues. **2.** a slight renovation; superficial alteration. —**face·lift** (FAYS LIFT) *n. & v.t.*

face-off (FAYS AWF) *n.* **1.** a confrontation. **2.** in ice hockey, the start of play when the puck is dropped between two opposing players.

fac·et (FAS it) *n.* **1.** one of the small plane surfaces cut upon a gem. **2.** a phase or aspect of a topic or person. —*v.t.* **fac·et·ed, fac·et·ing** cut facets upon. [< F *facette* small face]

fa·ce·tious (fə SEE shəs) *adj.* given to or marked by levity or flippant humor.

face value 1. the value stated on a bond, note, etc. **2.** apparent value.

fa·cial (FAY shəl) *adj.* of or for the face. —*n.* a cosmetic treatment for the face.

fac·ile (FAS il) *adj.* **1.** easily achieved or performed; also, superficial. **2.** ready or quick in performance; also, smooth; glib. [< L *facilis* easy to do]

fa·cil·i·tate (fə SIL i TAYT) *v.t.* **·tat·ed, ·tat·ing** make easy or easier. —**fa·cil′i·ta′tor** *n.*

fa·cil·i·ty (fə SIL i tee) *n. pl.* **·ties 1.** ease of performance or action. **2.** ready skill or ability. **3.** *Usu. pl.* something that makes an action or operation easier: research *facilities.* **4.** something built or established for a particular purpose: a first-aid *facility.* [ME *facilite*]

fac·ing (FAY sing) *n.* **1.** a lining or covering of a garment, often sewn on lapels, cuffs, etc. **2.** a fabric used for this. **3.** any ornamental or protective covering. [ME]

fac·sim·i·le (fak SIM ə lee) *n.* **1.** an exact copy. **2.** *Telecom.* a method of transmitting messages, drawings, etc., by means of radio, telephone, etc. [< L *fac simile* make similar]

fact (fakt) *n.* **1.** something that actually exists or has occurred. **2.** something asserted to be true or to have happened. **3.** reality or actuality. **4.** a criminal deed: now only in legal phrases, as **before** (or **after**) **the fact.** [< L *factum* something done] —**as a matter of fact, in fact, in point of fact** in reality; actually.

fac·tion (FAK shən) *n.* **1.** a group of people operating within, and often in opposition to, a larger group. **2.** dissension. [< L] — **fac′tion·al·ism** *n.*

fac·ti·tious (fak TISH əs) *adj.* not spontaneous; affected or artificial. [< L *factitius* artificial]

fac·tor (FAK tər) *n.* **1.** an element or cause that contributes to a result. **2.** *Math.* one or two or more quantities that, when multiplied together, produce a given quantity. **3.** one who transacts business for another on a commission basis. —*v.t. Math.* resolve into factors. [ME *factour* maker]

fac·to·ry (FAK tə ree) *n. pl.* **·ries** an establishment for the manufacture or assembly of goods. [< Med.L *factoria*]

fac·to·tum (fak TOH təm) *n.* any person or a servant having diverse duties. [< Med.L]

fac·tu·al (FAK choo əl) *adj.* pertaining to, containing, or consisting of facts; literal and exact.

fac·ul·ty (FAK əl tee) *n. pl.* **·ties 1.** a natural or acquired power or ability. **2.** the entire teaching staff of an educational institution. **3.** a department of learning at a university: the law *faculty*. [< ME *faculte*]

fad (fad) *n.* a temporary style, amusement, fashion, etc. —**fad′dist** *n.* —**fad′dish** *adj.* —**fad′dish·ness** *n.*

fade (fayd) *v.* **fad·ed, fad·ing** *v.i.* **1.** lose brightness or clearness. **2.** vanish slowly. **3.** lose freshness, vigor, youth, etc. —*v.t.* **4.** cause to fade. —**fade in** or **out** in television, motion pictures, and radio, cause the picture or sound to appear or dissolve gradually. [ME *faden*]

fag (fag) *v.* **fagged, fag·ging** *v.t.* **1.** exhaust by hard work: usu. with *out*. —*v.i.* **2.** weary oneself by working. —*n. Slang* a cigarette. [ME *fagge* loose end]

fag end 1. the frayed end, as of a rope. **2.** a remnant or last part.

fag·ot (FAG ət) *n.* **1.** a bundle of sticks, twigs, or branches. **2.** a bundle of pieces of wrought iron or steel for working into bars etc. —*v.t.* **1.** make a fagot of. **2.** ornament by fagoting. [ME]

Fahr·en·heit scale (FAR ən HIT) a temperature scale in which the freezing point of water is 32° and the boiling point 212° at standard atmospheric pressure. [after G.D. *Fahrenheit*, 1686–1736, German physicist]

fail (fayl) *v.i.* **1.** be deficient or wanting, as in ability. **2.** miss doing or accomplishing something: They *failed* to make themselves clear. **3.** prove inadequate; fall short; give out. **4.** decline in health or strength. **5.** go bankrupt. **6.** receive a grade of failure. —

v.t. **7.** prove of no help to; desert. **8. a** receive a grade of failure in (a course or examination). **b** assign a grade of failure to (a student). —*n.* failure: in the phrase **without fail.** [ME *failen*]

fail·ing (FAY ling) *n.* **1.** a fault; defect. **2.** the act of one who or that which fails. —*prep.* in default of. —*adj.* that fails; indicating failure.

fail·ure (FAYL yər) *n.* **1.** an unsuccessful or disappointing outcome or performance. **2.** a breakdown in health, efficiency, etc. **3.** nonperformance; neglect: *failure* to obey the law. **4.** bankruptcy. **5.** one who or that which fails. **6.** in education, a failing to pass, or the grade indicating this.

faint (faynt) *v.i.* lose consciousness; swoon. —*adj.* **1.** feeble; weak. **2.** lacking in distinctness, brightness, etc. **3.** dizzy; weak. **4.** lacking courage; timid. —*n.* a sudden, temporary loss of consciousness. [ME]

faint·heart·ed (FAYNT HAHR tid) *adj.* cowardly; timid.

fair¹ (fair) *adj.* **1.** light in coloring; not dark or sallow. **2.** pleasing to the eye; beautiful. **3.** free from blemish or imperfection. **4.** sunny; clear. **5.** just; upright. **6.** according to rules, principles, etc.; legitimate: a *fair* win. **7.** properly open to attack: He is *fair* game. **8.** moderately good or large. **9.** likely; promising. **10.** in baseball, within the area bounded by the foul lines; not foul. —*adv.* **1.** in a fair manner. **2.** squarely; directly. [ME] —**fair′ness** *n.*

fair² *n.* **1.** a periodic, usu. competitive exhibit of agricultural products, machinery, etc. **2.** a large exhibition or show of products, etc.: a world's *fair*. [ME *feire*]

fair·ground (FAIR GROWND) *n.* a large, open space where fairs are held.

fair·haired (FAIR HAIRD) *adj.* **1.** having blond hair. **2.** favorite.

fair·ly (FAIR lee) *adv.* **1.** justly; equitably. **2.** moderately; somewhat. **3.** positively; completely: The crowd *fairly* roared. **4.** clearly; distinctly.

fair·mind·ed (FAIR MIN did) *adj.* **1.** just. **2.** unprejudiced. —**fair′mind′ed·ness** *n.*

fair·way (FAIR WAY) *n.* that part of a golf course, between a tee and a putting green, where the grass is kept short.

fair·weath·er (FAIR WETH ər) *adj.* **1.** suitable for fair weather, as a racetrack. **2.** not helpful in adversity.

fair·y (FAIR ee) *n. pl.* **fair·ies** an imaginary

being, usu. small and having magic powers. —*adj.* of or like fairies. [ME *faierie*]

fair•y•land (FAIR ee LAND) *n.* **1.** the abode of fairies. **2.** any delightful place.

fairy tale *n.* **1.** a tale about fairies; also, a lie. **2.** a fantastic story; also, a lie.

faith (fayth) *n.* **1.** confidence in or dependence on a person or thing as trustworthy. **2.** belief without need of certain proof. **3.** belief in God or religious writings. **4.** a system of religious belief. **5.** allegiance. —**bad faith** deceit; dishonesty. —**in good faith** with honorable intentions. —**break faith 1.** betray one's principles or beliefs. **2.** break a promise. —**keep faith 1.** adhere to one's principles or beliefs. **2.** keep a promise. [ME *feith*]

faith•ful (FAYTH fəl) *adj.* **1.** true or trustworthy in the performance of duty, the fulfillment of promises, etc.; loyal. **2.** true in detail or accurate in description: a *faithful* copy. [ME *feithful*] —**the faithful 1.** the followers of a religious faith. **2.** the loyal members of any group.

fake (fayk) *n.* any person or thing not genuine. —*adj.* not genuine; spurious. —*v.* **faked, fak•ing** *v.t.* **1.** make up and attempt to pass off as genuine: *fake* a pedigree. **2.** simulate; feign. —*v.i.* **3.** practice faking. —**fak′er•y** *n.*

fa•kir (fə KEER) *n.* **1.** a Muslim ascetic or religious mendicant. **2.** loosely, any Hindu yogi or religious devotee. [< Arabic *faqir* poor man]

fall (fawl) *v.i.* **fell, fall•en, fall•ing 1.** drop from a higher to a lower place or position. **2.** drop suddenly, striking the ground with some part of the body. **3.** collapse. **4.** become less in number, value, etc.: Prices *fell.* **5.** become less in rank, importance, etc. **6.** drop wounded or slain. **7.** be captured or overthrown. **8.** yield to temptation; sin. **9.** slope downward. **10.** hang down; droop. **11.** come as though descending: Night *fell.* **12.** pass into some specified condition: *fall* asleep. **13.** come or happen by chance or lot: *fall* among thieves. **14.** happen; occur at a specified time or place. **15.** pass by right or inheritance. **16.** be classified or divided: with *into* or *under.* —**fall back** retreat. —**fall back on** (or **upon**) resort to; have recourse to; retreat to. —**fall down** *Informal* perform disappointingly. —**fall for** *Slang* **1.** be deceived by. **2.** fall in love with. —**fall in with** meet and accompany. —**fall off 1.** withdraw. **2.** become less. —**fall through**

come to nothing; fail. —*n.* **1.** the act of falling; a descending. **2.** that which falls. **3.** the amount that falls. **4.** the distance through which anything falls. **5.** a sudden descent from a vertical or erect position. **6.** a hanging down. **7.** a downward direction or slope. **8.** *Usu. pl.* a waterfall; cascade. **9.** a loss or reduction in value, reputation, etc. **10.** a moral lapse. **11.** a surrender or downfall. **12.** autumn. [ME *fallen*]

fal•la•cious (fə LAY shəs) *adj.* **1.** deceptive or misleading. **2.** containing or involving a fallacy. [< L *fallaciosus* deceitful]

fal•la•cy (FAL ə see) *n. pl.* **•cies 1.** a mistaken or misleading notion. **2.** unsoundness or incorrectness, as of judgment. **3.** reasoning contrary to the rules of logic. [< L *fallacia* trick]

fall•en (FAW lən) past participle of FALL. —*adj.* **1.** having come down by falling. **2.** brought down. **3.** overthrown; vanquished. **4.** disgraced; ruined. **5.** slain.

fal•li•ble (FAL ə bəl) *adj.* **1.** liable to err. **2.** liable to be misled or deceived. **3.** liable to be erroneous or false. [ME] —**fal′li•bil′i•ty** *n.*

fal•lo•pi•an tube (fə LOH pee ən) *Anat.* one of a pair of long, slender passages from the ovary to the uterus. [after Gabriello *Fallopio*, 1523–62, Italian anatomist]

fall•out (FAWL owt) *n.* **1.** *Physics* airborne radioactive debris from a nuclear explosion. **2.** any unexpected outcome. **3.** result.

fal•low (FAL oh) *n.* **1.** land left unseeded after plowing. **2.** the process of working land and leaving it unseeded for a time. —*adj.* **1.** unseeded; uncultivated. **2.** unused; idle; dormant. [ME *falwe*]

false (fawls) *adj.* **1.** contrary to truth or fact. **2.** incorrect. **3.** not genuine; artificial. **4.** deceptive or misleading. **5.** given to lying. **6.** wanting in fidelity; faithless. —*adv.* in a false manner. [ME] —**fal′si•ty** *n.*

false•hood (FAWLS huud) *n.* **1.** lack of accord to fact or truth. **2.** an intentional untruth; lie.

fal•set•to (fawl SET oh) *n. pl.* **•tos 1.** the register of a voice, esp. of an adult male, above its normal range. **2.** a man who sings or speaks in this register. [< Ital.] —**fal•set′to** *adj. & adv.*

fal•si•fy (FAWL sə fī) *v.* **•fied, •fy•ing** *v.t.* **1.** tell lies about; misrepresent. **2.** alter or tamper with, esp. in order to deceive. **3.** prove to be false. —*v.i.* **4.** tell lies. [ME *falsifien*] —**fal′si•fi•ca′tion** *n.*

fal·ter (FAWL tər) *v.i.* **1.** be hesitant or uncertain; waver. **2.** move unsteadily. **3.** speak haltingly. —*n.* an uncertainty or hesitation in voice or action. [ME *falteren*] —**fal′ter·ing** *adj.*

fame (faym) *n.* **1.** widespread and illustrious reputation; renown. **2.** public reputation or estimation. [ME] —**famed** *adj.*

fa·mil·ial (fə MIL yəl) *adj.* of, pertaining to, or associated with the family. [< F]

fa·mil·iar (fə MIL yər) *adj.* **1.** having thorough knowledge of something; followed by *with.* **2.** well-known; customary. **3.** intimate; close. **4.** unduly intimate; forward. —*n.* a friend or close associate. [ME]

fa·mil·i·ar·i·ty (fə MIL ee AR i tee) *n. pl.* **·ties 1.** thorough knowledge of something. **2.** friendly closeness; intimacy. **3.** offensively familiar conduct. **4.** *Often pl.* an action warranted only by intimate acquaintance. [ME *familiarite*]

fa·mil·iar·ize (fə MIL yə RĪZ) *v.t.* **·ized,·iz·ing 1.** make (oneself or someone) familiar with something. **2.** cause (something) to be familiar. —**fa·mil′iar·i·za′tion** *n.*

fam·i·ly (FAM ə lee) *n. pl.* **·lies 1.** parents and their children. **2.** the children as distinguished from the parents. **3. a** a group or succession of persons connected by blood, name, etc.; clan. **b** a criminal group operating within a larger criminal organization. **4.** distinguished or ancient lineage or descent. **5.** any class or group of like or related things. **6.** *Biol.* a taxonomic category higher than a genus and below an order. [ME *familie*]

fam·ine (FAM in) *n.* **1.** a widespread scarcity of food. **2.** a great scarcity of anything; dearth. **3.** starvation. [ME]

fam·ish (FAM ish) *v.t. & v.i.* suffer or to cause to suffer from extreme hunger. [ME *famisshe*]

fa·mous (FAY məs) *adj.* **1.** celebrated in history or public report; well-known; renowned. **2.** *Informal* excellent; admirable. [ME]

fan¹ (fan) *n.* **1.** a hand-held device for putting the air into motion; esp. a light, flat implement, often collapsible and opening into a wedgelike shape, a circle, etc. **2.** anything shaped like a fan. **3.** a machine fitted with blades that revolve rapidly about a central hub, for stirring air etc. —*v.* **fanned, fan·ning** *v.t.* **1.** move or stir (air) with or as with a fan. **2.** direct air upon; cool or refresh with or as with a fan. **3.** move or stir to action; excite: *fan* their anger. **4.** spread like a fan. **5.** in baseball, cause (a batter) to strike out. —*v.i.* **6.** spread out like a fan. **7.** in baseball, strike out [ME]

fan² *n.* a devotee of a sport, celebrity, etc. [From FANATIC]

fa·nat·ic (fə NAT ik) *n.* one who is moved by excessive enthusiasm or zeal; esp., a religious zealot. [< L *fanaticus* frantic] —**fa·nat·i·cism** (Fə nat ə SIZ əm) *n.*

fan·cied (FAN seed) *adj.* imaginary.

fan·ci·er (FAN see ər) *n.* **1.** one having a special taste for or interest in something. **2.** a breeder of animals.

fan·ci·ful (FAN si fəl) *adj.* **1.** produced by or existing only in the fancy. **2.** marked by fancy in design. **3.** indulging in fancies.

fan·cy (FAN see) *n. pl.* **·cies 1.** imagination of a capricious or whimsical sort. **2.** an odd or whimsical idea, invention, or image. **3.** a caprice or whim. **4.** a liking or inclination. **5.** taste or judgment in art, style, etc. —*adj.* **·ci·er, ·ci·est 1.** adapted to please the fancy; ornamental. **2.** coming from the fancy; imaginary. **3.** capricious; whimsical. **4.** of higher grade than the average: *fancy* fruits. **5.** exorbitant: *fancy* prices. —*v.t.* **·cied, ·cy·ing 1.** imagine; picture. **2.** take a fancy to. **3.** suppose. —*interj.* an exclamation of surprise. [ME *fansy*]

fan·fare (FAN fair) *n.* **1.** a short, lively passage, as of trumpets. **2.** a noisy or showy display. [< F]

fang (fang) *n.* **1.** a long, pointed tooth or tusk of an animal for tearing at prey. **2.** one of the long teeth with which a venomous serpent injects its poison. [ME]

fan·tail (FAN TAYL) *n.* **1.** a variety of domestic pigeon having fanlike tail feathers. **2.** any fan-shaped end or tail. **3.** the rear deck of a ship.

fan·ta·si·a (fan TAY zhə) *n. Music* **1.** a fanciful, free-form composition. **2.** a medley of various themes. [< Ital., fantasy]

fan·ta·size (FAN tə SĪZ) *v.i.* **·sized, ·siz·ing** create mental fantasies.

fan·tas·tic (fan TAS tik) *adj.* **1.** odd, grotesque, or whimsical. **2.** wildly fanciful or exaggerated. **3.** capricious or impulsive. **4.** *Informal* wonderful; remarkable. [ME *fantastik*] —**fan·tas′ti·cal·ly** *adv.*

fan·ta·sy (FAN tə see) *n. pl.* **·sies 1.** imagination unrestrained by reality; wild fancy. **2.** an odd or unreal mental image. **3.** an odd or whimsical notion. **4.** an ingenious or highly imaginative creation. **5.** a daydream; sequence of imagined events. [ME *fantasie*]

far (fahr) *adv.* **1.** at, to, or from a great distance. **2.** to or at a particular distance, point, or degree. **3.** to a great degree; very much: *far wiser.* **4.** very remotely in time, degree, quality, etc.: *far from pleasant.* **—by far** in a great degree; very much. **—far and away** very much; decidedly. **—so far as** to the extent that. **—adj. far•ther** or **fur•ther, far•thest** or **fur•thest 1.** very remote in space or time. **2.** extending widely or at length. **3.** more distant: the *far* end of the garden. [ME]

far•ad (FAR əd) *n. Electr.* the unit of capacitance; the capacitance of a condenser that retains one coulomb of charge with one volt difference of potential. [after Michael *Faraday*]

far•a•way (FAHR ə WAY) *adj.* **1.** distant. **2.** absent-minded; abstracted: *a faraway* look.

farce (fahrs) *n.* **1.** a comedy employing ludicrous or exaggerated situations. **2.** a ridiculous action or situation. [ME *fars* stuffing] **—far′ci•cal** *adj.*

fare (fair) *v.i.* **fared, far•ing 1.** be in a specified state; get on: He *fares* poorly. **2.** turn out: It *fared* well with him. **3.** eat and drink. **—n. 1.** the fee for conveyance in a vehicle, etc. **2.** a passenger carried for hire. **3.** food and drink; diet. [ME *faren*]

fare•well (FAIR WELL) *n.* **1.** a parting salutation; a good-by. **2.** leave-taking. **—interj.** goodby. **—adj.** parting; closing. [ME *farwel*]

far-fetched (FAHR FECHT) *adj.* neither natural nor obvious; forced; strained.

far-flung (FAHR FLUNG) *adj.* extending over great distances.

fa•ri•na (fə REE nə) *n.* a meal or flour obtained chiefly from grain and used as a breakfast cereal or in puddings. [ME]

farm (fahrm) *n.* **1.** a tract of land forming a single property and devoted to agriculture. **2.** a tract of water used for the cultivation of marine life. **3.** in baseball, a minor-league club used by a major-league club for training its recruits: also **farm club, farm team. —v.t. 1.** cultivate (land). **2.** let at a fixed rental, as the authority to collect taxes, etc.: usu. with *out.* **3.** let out the services of (a person) for hire. **4.** arrange for (work) to be done outside the main organization: with *out.* **—v.i. 5.** practice farming. [ME *ferme*]

farm•ing (FAHR ming) *n.* the business of

operating a farm; agriculture. **—adj.** engaged in, suitable for, or used for agriculture.

far-off (FAHR AWF) *adj.* distant; remote.

far•ra•go (fə RAH goh) *n. pl.* **•goes** a confused mixture; medley. [< L, mixed grains]

far•row (FAR oh) *n.* a litter of pigs. **—v.t. &** *v.i.* give birth to (young): said of swine. [ME *farwen* (of pigs) give birth]

far•see•ing (FAHR SEE ing) *adj.* **1.** having foresight. **2.** able to see distant objects clearly.

far•sight•ed (FAHR SĪ tid) *adj.* **1.** able to see things at a distance more clearly than things at hand. **2.** having foresight.

far•ther (FAHR thər) comparative of FAR. **—adv.** to or at a more advanced point in space or, less often, time. **—adj.** more distant or remote. [ME *ferther*]

far•thest (FAHR thist) superlative of FAR. **—adv.** to or at the greatest distance. **—adj. 1.** most distant or remote. **2.** longest or most extended: the *farthest* way around. [ME *ferthest*]

far•thing (FAHR thing) *n.* a small coin, formerly used in England and worth one-fourth of a penny. [ME *ferthing*]

fas•ci•cle (FAS i kəl) *n.* **1.** a small bundle or cluster, as of leaves. **2.** one of the sections of a book that is published in installments. [< L *fasciculus* small bundle] **—fas•cic•u•lar** (fə SIK yə lər) *adj.*

fas•ci•nate (FAS ə NAYT) *v.* **•nat•ed, •nat•ing** *v.t.* **1.** attract irresistibly, as by charm; captivate. **2.** hold spellbound, as by terror. **—v.i. 3.** be charming, captivating, etc. [< L *fascinatus* bewitched] **—fas′ci•na′tion** *n.*

fas•cism (FASH iz əm) *n.* **1.** a system of government characterized by one-party dictatorship, centralized governmental control of industry and finance, and militant nationalism. **2.** a political philosophy favoring such a system. [< Ital. *fascismo*] **—fas′cist** *n. & adj.* **—fa•scis•tic** (fə SHIS tik) *adj.*

fash•ion (FASH ən) *n.* **1.** the mode of dress, manners, living, etc., prevailing in society. **2.** a current practice or usage. **3.** an object of enthusiasm among fashionable people. **4.** manner; way. **5.** kind; sort. **—after a fashion** to a limited extent. **—v.t. 1.** give shape or form to. **2.** adapt; fit. [ME *facioun* manner]

fash•ion•a•ble (FASH ə nə bəl) *adj.* **1.** conforming to the current fashion. **2.**

associated with, characteristic of, or patronized by persons of fashion. —**fash′ ion·a·bly** adv.

fast¹ (fast) adj. **1.** firm in place; not easily moved. **2.** constant; steadfast: *fast* friends. **3.** not liable to fade or run: said of colors. **4.** acting or moving quickly. **5.** performed quickly: *fast* work. **6.** permitting quick movement: a *fast* track. **7.** in advance of the true time. **8.** dissipated; sexually promiscuous. —**play fast and loose** act in a tricky or untrustworthy fashion. —adv. **1.** firmly; securely. **2.** soundly: *fast* asleep. **3.** quickly. **4.** dissipatedly: live *fast*. [ME]

fast² n. **1.** abstinence from food or from prescribed kinds of food, particularly as a religious duty. **2.** a period prescribed for fasting. —v.i. abstain from eating; eat sparingly. —v.t. put on a fast. [ME *fasten*]

fas·ten (FAS ən) v.t. **1.** attach to something else; connect. **2.** make fast; secure. **3.** direct (the attention, eyes, etc.) steadily. —v.i. **4.** become attached. [ME *fastenen*] —**fas′ ten·er** n.

fas·ten·ing (FAS ə ning) n. **1.** the act of making fast. **2.** that which fastens.

fas·tid·i·ous (fa STID ee əs) adj. exceedingly delicate or refined; overnice; squeamish. [ME] —**fas·tid′i·ous·ness** n.

fat (fat) adj. **fat·ter, fat·test 1.** having superfluous flesh or fat; obese; plump. **2.** containing much fat, oil, etc. **3.** rich or fertile, as land. **4.** abundant; plentiful: a *fat* profit. **5.** thick; broad. —**a fat chance** *Slang* very little chance; no chance at all. —n. **1.** *Biochem.* an oily or greasy, solid or liquid substance widely distributed in plant and animal tissues. **2.** animal tissue containing large quantities of such compounds. **3.** any vegetable or animal fat or oil used in cooking. **4.** plumpness. **5.** the richest or most desirable part of anything. **6.** excess; superfluity. [ME] —**fat′ness** n.

fa·tal (FAYT l) adj. **1.** resulting in or capable of causing death. **2.** ruinous; destructive. **3.** highly significant or decisive; fateful: the *fatal* hour. **4.** destined; inevitable. [ME]

fa·tal·ism (FAYT l ɪz əm) n. **1.** the doctrine that all events are predetermined and thus unalterable. **2.** a disposition to accept every event or condition as inevitable. —**fa′tal· ist** n.

fa·tal·i·ty (fay TAL i tee) n. pl. **·ties 1.** a death brought about through disaster or calamity. **2.** the capability of causing death

or disaster. **3.** a decree of fate. [< L *fatalitas*]

fate (fayt) n. **1.** a force viewed as determining events in advance; destiny. **2.** that which inevitably happens. **3.** final result or outcome. **4.** an evil destiny; esp., death or destruction. [ME]

fat·ed (FAY tid) adj. **1.** controlled by fate; destined. **2.** condemned to ruin; doomed.

fate·ful (FAYT fəl) adj. **1.** determining destiny; momentous. **2.** brought about by or as if by fate. **3.** bringing death or disaster; fatal. **4.** ominously prophetic.

Fates, the in classical mythology, the three goddesses that control human destiny.

fa·ther (FAH thər) n. **1.** a male parent. **2.** any male ancestor; forefather. **3.** a male who founds or establishes something. **4.** any elderly man: a title of respect. **5.** a leader or elder of a council, assembly, etc. **6.** *Eccl. usu. cap.* a priest or other church dignitary. **7.** *cap.* God; esp., the first person of the Trinity. —v.t. **1.** beget. **2.** act as a father toward. **3.** found or make. [ME *fader*]

fa·ther-in-law (FAH thər in law) n. pl. **fa·thers-in-law** the father of one's husband or wife.

fath·om (FATH əm) n. pl. **·oms** or **·om** a measure of length, 6 feet or 1,829 meters, used principally in marine and mining measurements. —v.t. **1.** find the depth of; sound. **2.** understand; interpret. [ME *fathme* the span of two arms outstretched] —**fath′om·a·ble** adj. —**fath′om·less** adj.

fa·tigue (fə TEEG) n. **1.** the condition of being very tired as a result of exertion. **2.** *Mech.* structural weakness in metals etc., produced by excessive strain. **3.** *Mil.* a special work assignment done by soldiers in training: also **fatigue duty. b** pl. strong, durable clothes worn on fatigue duty. —v.t. & v.i. **·tigued, ·ti·guing 1.** tire out; weary. **2.** weaken, as metal. [< F]

fat·ten (FAT n) v.t. **1.** cause to become fat. **2.** enrich (land). **3.** add to (a sum of money, etc.) so as to make larger and more attractive. —v.i. **4.** grow fatter, heavier, etc.

fat·ty (FAT ee) adj. **·ti·er, ·ti·est 1.** containing, possessing, or made of fat. **2.** having the properties of fat; greasy; oily.

fatty acid *Chem.* any of a class of organic acids occurring in plant and animal fats.

fa·tu·i·ty (fə TOO i tee) n. pl. **·ties 1.** smug stupidity. **2.** a stupid action, remark, etc. [< L *fatuitas*]

fat·u·ous (FACH oo əs) *adj*. foolish and silly in a self-satisfied way; inane. [< L *fatuus* foolish]

fau·cet (FAW sit) *n*. a fixture with an adjustable valve that controls the flow of liquids. [ME]

fault (fawlt) *n*. **1.** whatever impairs excellence; a flaw. **2.** a mistake or blunder. **3.** responsibility for some mishap, blunder, etc.; blame. **4.** *Geol.* a break in the continuity of rock strata or veins of ore. **5.** tn tennis, squash, etc., failure to serve the ball into the prescribed area of the opponent's court. —**to a fault** immoderately; excessively. —*v.t.* find fault with; blame. [ME *faute*] —**fault′less** *adj*.

fault-find·ing (FAWLT FĪN ding) *adj*. inclined to find fault; critical; carping. —**fault′find′er** *n*.

fault·y (FAWL tee) *adj*. **fault·i·er, fault·i·est** having faults; defective; imperfect. [ME *faulty*] —**fault′i·ness** *n*.

faun (fawn) *n*. a satyr. [ME]

fau·na (FAW nə) *n. pl.* **·nas** or **·nae** (-nee) the animal life within a given area or environment or during a stated period. [< NL]

faux pas (foh PAH) *pl.* **faux pas** (foh PAHZ) a social blunder. [< F]

fa·vor (FAY vər) *n*. **1.** a helpful or considerate act. **2.** friendliness or approval. **3.** the condition of being looked upon with liking or approval. **4.** unfair partiality: show *favor*. **5.** a small gift. **6.** *pl.* consent to sexual intimacy. —**in favor of 1.** on the side of. **2.** to the furtherance or advantage of. **3.** made out to the benefit of. —*v.t.* **1.** do a favor for; oblige. **2.** look upon with approval or liking. **3.** show special consideration to, often in an unfair way. **4.** increase the chances of success of. **5.** show a resemblance to in features. **6.** be careful of. [ME *favour*]

fa·vor·a·ble (FAY vər ə bəl) *adj*. **1.** granting something requested or hoped for. **2.** boding well; promising; approving. **3.** well-disposed or indulgent; friendly. —**fa′vor·a·bly** *adv*.

fa·vored (FAY vərd) *adj*. **1.** looked upon with favor. **2.** endowed with good qualities. **3.** having an (indicated) aspect or appearance: *an ill-favored* countenance. [ME *favoured*]

fa·vor·ite (FAY vər it) *adj*. regarded with special favor; preferred. —*n*. **1.** a person or thing greatly liked or preferred. **2.** a contestant or candidate considered to have the best chance of winning. [< MF]

favorite son a candidate favored by the political leaders of his or her state at a presidential nominating convention.

fa·vor·it·ism (FAY vər i TIZ əm) *n*. preferential treatment, esp. when unjust.

fawn[1] (fawn) *v.i.* **1.** show cringing fondness, as a dog: often with *on* or *upon*. **2.** show affection or seek favor in such a manner. [ME *fawnen* rejoice]

fawn[2] *n*. **1.** a young deer, esp. in its first year. **2.** the yellowish brown color of a young deer. —*adj*. yellowish brown. [< ME]

fax (faks) *n*. electronic transmission (on a **fax machine**) of graphic material. [< FACSIMILE]

faze (fayz) *v.t.* **fazed, faz·ing** worry; disconcert.

fear (feer) *n*. **1.** an agitated feeling aroused by awareness of danger, trouble, etc. **2.** an uneasy feeling that something may happen contrary to one's desires. **3.** a feeling of deep awe and dread. —*v.t.* **1.** be frightened of. **2.** be uneasy or apprehensive over (an unpleasant possibility). **3.** have a deep awe of. —*v.i.* **4.** feel uneasy. [ME *fere*] —**fear′less** *adj*.

fear·ful (FEER fəl) *adj*. **1.** filled with dread or terror. **2.** filled with uneasiness; apprehensive. **3.** filled with awe. **4.** causing dread or terror; terrifying; frightening. **5.** Showing fear. **6.** extremely bad. [ME *ferful*]

fear·some (FEER səm) *adj*. **1.** causing fear; alarming. **2.** timid; frightened.

fea·si·ble (FEE zə bəl) *adj*. **1.** capable of being put into effect or accomplished; practicable. **2.** capable of being successfully utilized; suitable. **3.** fairly probable; likely. [ME *feseable*] —**fea′si·bil′i·ty** *n*.

feast (feest) *n*. **1.** a sumptuous meal. **2.** something affording great pleasure to the senses or intellect. **3.** a day or days of celebration regularly set aside for a commemorative or religious purpose: also **feast day**. —*v.t.* **1.** give a feast for; entertain lavishly. **2.** delight; gratify. —*v.i.* **3.** partake of a feast; eat heartily. **4.** dwell delightedly, as on a painting. [ME *feste*]

feat (feet) *n*. a notable act, as one displaying skill or daring. [ME *fet*]

feath·er (FETH ər) *n*. **1.** any of the horny, elongated structures that form the plumage of birds and much of the wing surface. **2.** *pl.* plumage. **3.** *pl.* dress; attire. **4.** the hairy fringe on the legs and tails of some dogs. **5.** class or species; kind: birds of a *feather*. —**a feather in one's cap** an achievement to be proud of. —*v.t.* **1.** fit with a feather, as an arrow. **2.** cover, adorn, line, or fringe with feathers. **3.** in rowing, turn (the oar blade) horizontally after each stroke. **4.** *Aeron.* turn off (an engine) while in flight. —*v.i.* **5.** grow feathers or become covered with feathers. [ME *fether*] —**feath′ered** *adj.*

feath·er·bed·ding (FETH ər BED ing) *n.* the practice of requiring the employment of more workers than are needed.

feath·er·weight (FETH ər WAYT) *n.* **1.** a boxer or wrestler weighing up to 126 pounds. **2.** any person or thing relatively light in weight or size. —*adj.* **1.** of or like a featherweight. **2.** insignificant; trivial.

fea·ture (FEE chər) *n.* **1.** a distinctive part of the face, as the eyes, nose, or mouth. **2.** *Usu. pl.* the overall appearance or structure of a face. **3.** a distinguishing mark, part, or quality. **4.** a full-length motion picture: also **feature film. 5.** anything given special prominence, as: **a** a special article, department, etc. in a magazine or newspaper. **b** a special attraction, as on a program etc. —*v.t.* **·tured, ·tur·ing 1.** give special prominence to. **2.** be a distinctive characteristic of. **3.** *Informal* form an idea of; imagine. [ME *feture*]

feb·ri·fuge (FEB rə FYOOJ) *n.* a medicine for reducing or removing fever. [< F]

fe·brile (FEE brəl) *adj.* feverish. [< NL *febrilis*]

Feb·ru·ar·y (FEB roo ER ee) *n. pl.* **·ar·ies** the second month of the year. Abbr. *Feb.* [ME]

fe·ces (FEE seez) *n.pl.* animal excrement; ordure. [ME] —**fe′cal** (FEE kəl) *adj.*

feck·less (FEK lis) *adj.* **1.** devoid of energy or effectiveness; feeble. **2.** careless and irresponsible. [ME] —**feck′·less·ness** *n.*

fe·cund (FEE kund) *adj.* fruitful; prolific. [ME] —**fe·cun·di·ty** (fi KUN di tee) *n.*

fed (fed) past tense and past participle of FEED. —**fed up** bored, tired, or disgusted.

fed·er·al (FED ər əl) *adj.* **1.** of, relating to, or formed by an agreement among two or more states, groups, etc., to merge into a union in which control of common affairs is granted to a central authority, with each member retaining jurisdiction over its own internal affairs. **2.** of or pertaining to a confederacy (def. 1). [< L *foedus* league]

fed·er·al·ism (FED ər ə LIZ əm) *n.* the doctrine, system, or principle of federal union or federal government. —**fed′er·al·ist** *n. & adj.*

fed·er·al·ize (FED ər ə LIZ) *v.t.* **·ized, ·iz·ing 1.** bring under control of a federal union. **2.** federate.

fed·er·ate (FED ə RAYT) *v.t. & v.i.* **·at·ed, ·at·ing** unite in a federal union. —*adj.* (FED ər it) united in a federation. [< L *foederatus* allied]

fed·er·a·tion (FED ə RAY shən) *n.* **1.** the joining together of two or more states, groups, etc., into a federal union or a confederacy. **2.** a league or confederacy. [< LL *foederatio*]

fee (fee) *n.* a charge, compensation, or payment for something; a sum charged. [ME]

fee·ble (FEE bəl) *adj.* **·bler, ·blest 1.** lacking strength; very weak. **2.** lacking energy, direction, or effectiveness: *feeble* efforts. [ME *feble*]

fee·ble-mind·ed (FEE bəl MIN did) *adj.* mentally deficient. —**fee′ble-mind′ed·ness** *n.*

feed (feed) *v.* **fed, feed·ing** *v.t.* **1.** supply with food: *feed* a family. **2.** give (something) as food or nourishment to: *feed* carrots to rabbits. **3.** serve as food or nourishment for; also, produce food for: acreage that will *feed* many. **4.** keep supplied, as with fuel: *feed* a fire; also, keep supplying: *feed* data into a computer. **5.** keep or make more intense or greater: *feed* suspicions. —*v.i.* **6.** eat: said chiefly of animals. —*n.* **1.** food given to animals. **2.** material supplied, as to a machine. **3.** a mechanical part, as of a sewing machine, that keeps supplying material to be worked on etc. **4.** *Informal* a meal. —**off one's feed** *Slang* having little appetite. [ME *feden*]

feed·back (FEED BAK) *n.* **1.** the return of part of the output of a system into the input, esp. to modify or control that output. **2.** a response, or criticism or suggestions, to a proposal, action, process, etc.

feel (feel) *v.* **felt, feel·ing** *v.t.* **1.** examine or explore with the hands, fingers, etc. **2.** be aware of; sense the touch of. **3.** experience consciously (an emotion, pain, etc.). **4.** perceive or be aware of through thought: *feel* the need for reform. **5.** think; suppose; judge. **6.** experience the force or impact of. —*v.i.* **7.** have physical sensation. **8.** produce a sensory impression of being hard, soft, cold, hot, etc. **9.** experience consciously the sensation or condition of being: *feel* joyful. **10.** produce an indicated condition, impression, or reaction: It *feels* good to be home. **11.** experience compassion or pity: with *for*. **12.** have convictions or opinions: *feel* strongly about an issue. **13.** search by touching; grope. **—feel like** *Informal* have a desire or inclination for. **—feel out** try to learn indirectly and cautiously the viewpoint of (a person). —*n*. **1.** perception by touch or contact. **2.** the quality of something as perceived by touch. **3.** a sensation or impression. [ME *felen*]

feel•er (FEE lər) *n*. **1.** any action, hint, proposal, etc., intended to draw out the views or intentions of another. **2.** *Zool.* an organ of touch.

feel•ing (FEE ling) *n*. **1.** the faculty by which one perceives sensations of pain, heat, etc. **2.** any particular sensation of this sort: a *feeling* of warmth. **3.** an emotion. **4.** a sensation or awareness of something. **5.** *pl.* sensibilities; sensitivities: His *feelings* are easily hurt. **6.** sympathy; compassion. **7.** an opinion or sentiment; also, a foreboding. —*adj*. **1.** having sensation; sentient. **2.** having warm emotions; sympathetic: a *feeling* heart. **3.** marked by or indicating emotion. [ME]

feet (feet) plural of FOOT. **—on one's feet** in or into a condition of health or stability: get a business *on its feet*.

feign (fayn) *v.t.* **1.** make a false show of; sham: *feign* madness. **2.** think up (a false story) and give out as true; fabricate. [ME *feignen* invent]

feint (faynt) *n*. a deceptive movement; esp., a pretended blow or attack meant to divert attention. [ME *feint v.t. & v.i.*

fe•lic•i•tate (fə LIS i TAYT) *v.t.* **•tat•ed, •tat•ing** congratulate. [< LL *felicitatus* made happy] **—fe•lic'i•ta'tion** *n*.

fe•lic•i•tous (fə LIS i təs) *adj.* **1.** most appropriate; apt. **2.** agreeably pertinent or effective.

fe•lic•i•ty (fi LIS i tee) *n. pl.* **•ties 1.** happiness; bliss. **2.** a source of happiness. **3.** an agreeably pertinent or effective manner or style. **4.** a pleasantly appropriate remark. [ME *felicite*]

fe•line (FEE līn) *adj.* **1.** of or relating to a cat or the cat family. **2.** catlike; stealthy. —*n*. an animal of the cat family. [< L *felis* cat]

fell¹ (fel) past tense of FALL.

fell² *v.t.* **felled, fell•ing 1.** strike and cause to fall down. **2.** cut down (timber). **3.** in sewing, to finish (a seam) by joining the edges, folding them under, and stitching flat. —*n*. **1.** the timber cut down during one

season. **2.** in sewing, a felled seam. [ME *fellen*]

fell³ *adj.* cruel; vicious; inhuman. [ME *fel*]

fel•lah (FEL ə) *n. pl.* **fel•lahs** or *Arabic* **fel•la•hin** (FEL ə HEEN) in Arabic-speaking countries, a peasant or laborer. [< Arabic *fallāh* peasant]

fel•lat•i•o (fə LAY shee oh) *n.* oral stimulation of the penis. [< NL] **—fel•late** (fə LAYT) *v.t.* **•lat•ed, •lat•ing**

fel•low (FEL oh) *n.* **1.** a man or boy: often in informal address. **2.** a person; anybody; one. **3.** a comrade or companion. **4.** an individual belonging to the same kind, class, or group as oneself. **5.** either one of a pair; mate. **6.** a member of one of several learned societies. **7.** a graduate student of a university or college who is granted financial assistance to pursue further study. —*adj*. joined through some common occupation, interests, objectives, etc.: *fellow* citizens. [ME *felowe* partner]

fel•low•ship (FEL oh SHIP) *n.* **1.** companionship; association. **2.** a body of individuals joined together through similar interests, beliefs, etc. **3.** the status of being a fellow at a university or college; also, the financial grant made to a fellow.

fel•on¹ (FEL ən) *n. Law* one who has committed a felony. [< ME *feloun* wicked]

fel•on² *n. Pathol.* an acute inflammation of a finger or toe in the terminal joint or at the cuticle. [ME *feloun* tumor]

fel•o•ny (FEL ə nee) *n. pl.* **•nies** *Law* a major crime, as murder, arson, or burglary, for which a punishment greater than that for a misdemeanor is provided. [ME *felonie*] **—fe•lo•ni•ous** (fə LOH nee əs) *adj.*

felt¹ (felt) past tense, past participle of FEEL.

felt² *n.* **1.** an unwoven fabric made by matting together fibers of wool, fur, or hair. **2.** something made of felt, as a hat. [ME] — **felt** *adj.*

fe•male (FEE mayl) *adj.* **1.** of or pertaining to the sex that brings forth young or produces ova. **2.** characteristic of this sex; feminine. **3.** *Bot.* designating a plant that is capable of being fertilized and of producing fruit. **4.** *Mech.* denoting or having a bore or slot designed to receive a correlated inserted part, called *male,* as some electric plugs. [ME] **—fe'male** *n.*

fem•i•nine (FEM ə nin) *adj.* **1.** of or pertaining to the female sex; female. **2.** typical of or appropriate to women and girls. **3.** lacking manly qualities; effeminate. **4.** *Gram.*

applicable only or to persons or things classified grammatically as female. —*n. Gram.* 1. the feminine gender. 2. a word or form belonging to the feminine gender. [ME] —**fem′i·nin′i·ty** *n.*

fem·i·nism (FEM ə NIZ əm) *n.* 1. a doctrine advocating social, political, and economic equality for women and men. 2. a movement championing women's rights and interests. —**fem′i·nist** *n. & adj.*

fem·i·nize (FEM ə NIZ) *v.t. & v.i.* •**nized,** •**niz·ing** make or become feminine or effeminate. —**fem′i·ni·za′tion** *n.*

fe·mur (FEE mər) *n. pl.* **fe·murs** or **fem·o·ra** (FEM ər ə) *Anat.* the long bone extending from the pelvis to the knee. [< L, thigh] —**fem·o·ral** (FEM ər əl) *adj.*

fen (fen) *n.* a marsh; bog. [ME]

fence (fens) *n.* 1. a structure of rails, stakes, strung wire, etc., erected as an enclosure, barrier, or boundary. 2. *Informal* a dealer in stolen goods. —*v.* **fenced, fenc·ing** *v.t.* 1. enclose with or as with a fence. 2. cause to be separated by or as by a fence. 3. *Informal* deal in (stolen goods). —*v.i.* 4. practice the art of fencing. 5. avoid giving direct answers. [ME *fens*] —**fenc′er** *n.*

fenc·ing (FEN sing) *n.* 1. the art or practice of using a foil, sword, or similar weapon. 2. the art or practice of making parrying remarks, as in a debate. 3. material used in making fences; also, fences collectively. [ME *fensing* maintenance]

fend (fend) *v.t.* 1. ward off; parry: usu. with *off.* —*v.i.* 2. provide: with *for: fend* for oneself. [ME *fenden*]

fend·er (FEN dər) *n.* 1. one who or that which fends or wards off. 2. a part projecting over each wheel of a car or other vehicle. 3. a metal guard set before an open fire. 4. a part projecting from the front of a locomotive. [ME *fendour* defender]

fe·ral (FER əl) *adj.* 1. not domesticated; wild. 2. of, relating to, or typical of a wild beast; savage. [< Med.L *feralis* bestial]

fer·ment (FUR ment) *n.* 1. any substance or agent producing fermentation. 2. fermentation. 3. excitement or agitation. —*v.* (fər MENT) —*v.t.* 1. produce fermentation in. 2. excite with passion; agitate. —*v.i.* 3. undergo fermentation. 4. be agitated, as with emotion; seethe. [ME]

fer·men·ta·tion (FUR men TAY shən) *n.* 1. *Chem.* the decomposition of organic compounds through the action of bacteria etc. 2. commotion, agitation, or excitement.

fern (furn) *n.* a plant that bears no flowers or seeds, has large, feathery fronds, and reproduces by means of asexual spores. [ME *ferne*]

fern·er·y (FUR nə ree) *n. pl.* •**er·ies** 1. a place in which ferns are grown. 2. a standing growth or bed of ferns.

fe·ro·cious (fə ROH shəs) *adj.* 1. savage, fierce, bloodthirsty, or cruel. 2. very intense. [< L *ferox* savage] —**fe·roc·i·ty** (fə ROS i tee) *n.*

fer·ret (FER it) *n.* a small polecat of Europe, often used in hunting rodents. —*v.t.* 1. search out by careful investigation: with *out.* 2. drive out of hiding or hunt with a ferret. —*v.i.* 3. search. 4. hunt by means of ferrets. [ME]

fer·rule (FER əl) *n.* a metal ring or cap used on or near the end of a cane, tool handle, etc., for protection or reinforcement. —*v.t.* •**ruled,** •**rul·ing** equip with a ferrule. [ME *virole* bracelet]

fer·ry (FER ee) *n. pl.* •**ries** a boat used in conveying people, cars, or merchandise across a river or other body of water. —*v.* •**ried,** •**ry·ing** *v.t.* 1. convey across a river, etc., by boat. 2. cross (a river, etc.) in a boat. 3. deliver (an airplane) under its own motive power. —*v.i.* 4. cross a river, etc., by or as by a ferry. [ME *ferien* carry] —**fer′ry·boat′** *n.*

fer·tile (FUR tl) *adj.* 1. yielding or capable of producing abundant crops or vegetation. 2. reproducing or able to reproduce. 3. inventive or productive: a *fertile* talent. [ME] —**fer·til·i·ty** (fər TIL i tee) *n.*

fer·til·ize (FUR tl IZ) *v.t.* •**ized,** •**iz·ing** 1. make fertile; cause to be productive or fruitful. 2. cause (a female or female reproductive cell), by introduction of the male reproductive cell or cells, to begin development of a new individual. 3. spread manure or other enriching material on (land). —**fer′til·i·za′tion** *n.*

fer·ti·liz·er (FUR tl I zər) *n.* any material used to enrich land.

fer·ule (FER əL) *n.* a flat stick or ruler sometimes used for punishing children. —*v.t.* •**uled,** •**ul·ing** punish with a ferule. [ME *ferula* giant plant of the carrot family]

fer·vent (FUR vənt) *adj.* warm or intense, as in emotion or enthusiasm; ardent. [ME] —**fer·ven·cy** (FUR vən see) *n.*

fer·vid (FUR vid) *adj.* 1. fervent; impassioned. 2. very hot; burning. [< L *fervidus* boiling] —**fer′vid·ness** *n.*

fer·vor (FUR vər) *n.* **1.** great warmth or intensity, as of emotion; ardor. **2.** heat; warmth. [ME *fervour*]

fes·ter (FES tər) *v.i.* **1.** develop pus; ulcerate. **2.** be or become rotten and foul. **3.** be a constant source of irritation; rankle. —*n.* an ulcer. [ME *fister* ulcer]

fes·ti·val (FES tə vəl) *n.* **1.** a particular feast, holiday, or celebration. **2.** any occasion for rejoicing or feasting. **3.** a special series of performances, exhibitions, etc.: a Shakespeare *festival*. [ME]

fes·tive (FES tiv) *adj.* of, relating to, or suitable for a feast or other celebration. [< L *festivus* merry]

fes·tiv·i·ty (fe STIV i tee) *n. pl.* **·ties 1.** a festival. **2.** gladness and rejoicing. **3.** *pl.* festive merrymaking. [ME *festivite*]

fes·toon (fe STOON) *n.* **1.** flowers, colored paper, ribbon, etc., hanging in loops between two points. **2.** an ornamental carving, sculpture, etc., representing this. —*v.t.* decorate, fashion into, or link together by festoons. [< Ital. *festone* decoration]

fe·tal (FEET l) *adj.* of or typical of a fetus.

fetch (fech) *v.t.* **1.** go after and bring back. **2.** draw forth; elicit. **3.** draw in (breath); also, give forth (a sigh, groan, etc.); heave. **4.** cost or sell for. **5.** give or deal (a blow, slap, etc.). —*v.i.* **6.** go after something and bring it back. [ME *fecchen*]

fetch·ing (FECH ing) *adj.* attractive; charming.

fete (fayt) *n.* **1.** a festival. **2.** an outdoor celebration, as a dinner, bazaar, etc. —*v.t.* **fet·ed, fet·ing** honor with festivities. Also **fête.** [< F *fête*]

fet·id (FET id) *adj.* having a foul odor; stinking. [< L *fetidus*]

fet·ish (FET ish) *n.* **1.** an object regarded as having magical powers. **2.** something to which one is devoted excessively or irrationally. **3.** *Psychiatry* some object, not in itself erotic, that is regarded as sexually stimulating. [< Pg. *feitiço* charm] —**fet′ish·ism** *n.*

fet·ter (FET ər) *n.* **1.** a chain or other bond put about the ankles. **2.** *Usu. pl.* anything checking freedom of movement or expression. [ME] —**fet′ter** *v.t.*

fet·tle (FET l) *n.* proper condition of health or spirits: in fine *fettle*. [ME *fetle* prepare]

fe·tus (FEE təs) *n. pl.* **·tus·es** the individual organism after its embryonic stage but before birth. [ME]

feud (fyood) *n.* prolonged hostility between two or more individuals, families, etc. —*v.i.* take part in a feud. [ME *fede*]

feu·dal (FYOOD l) *adj.* of, relating to, or typical of feudalism. [< Med.L *feudalis*]

feu·dal·ism (FYOOD l z əm) *n.* a social, political, and economic system in medieval Europe in which vassals were granted land by their lords in return for military or other services.

fe·ver (FEE vər) *n.* **1.** a disorder marked by unduly high body temperature. **2.** any of several diseases that produce this symptom. **3.** emotional excitement or restless eagerness. ◆ Collateral adjective: *febrile*. —*v.t.* affect with fever. [ME]

fe·ver·ish (FEE vər ish) *adj.* **1.** having a fever, esp. a low fever. **2.** of or resembling a fever. **3.** tending to produce fever. **4.** agitated, uneasy, or restless. [ME *feverisch*]

few (fyoo) *adj.* small in number; not very many. —*pron. & n.* a small number; not very many. —**quite a few** many. [ME *fewe*]

fey (fay) *adj.* **1.** acting as if enchanted. **2.** suggestive of a sprite. [ME]

fez (fez) *n. pl.* **fez·zes** a brimless, tapering, felt cap, usu. red and having a black tassel. [after *Fez*, Morocco]

fi·an·cé (FEE ahn SAY) *n.* a man engaged to be married. [< F]

fi·an·cée (FEE ahn SAY) *n.* a woman engaged to be married. [< F]

fi·as·co (fee AS koh) *n. pl.* **·cos** or **·coes** a complete or humiliating failure. [< Ital., bottle]

fi·at (FEE at) *n.* **1.** a commandment or decree. **2.** authorization. [< L, let it be done]

fib (fib) *n.* a trivial lie. —*v.i.* **fibbed, fib·bing** tell a fib. —**fib′ber** *n.*

fi·ber (FĪ bər) *n.* **1.** a fine, threadlike substance, esp. one capable of being spun or woven. **2.** *Biol.* one of similar threadlike structures that together form animal or plant tissue or parts: a nerve *fiber*. **3.** the particular composition or structure of something. **4.** character: moral *fiber*. [ME *fibre*] —**fi·brous** (FĪ brəs) *adj.*

Fi·ber·glas (FĪ bər GLAS) *n.* a flexible, nonflammable material of glass spun into filaments: a trade name.

fiber optics the science of light carried by thin glass or plastic fibers, to convey images, sound, data signals, etc.

fi·bril (FĪ brəl) *n.* **1.** a minute fiber. **2.** *Bot.* a root hair. [< NL *fibrilla* little fiber]

fi·bril·la·tion (FĪ brə LAY shən) *n.* **1.** the

formation of fibers. **2.** *Pathol.* rapid contraction of muscle fibers of the heart.

fi•broid (FĪ broid) *adj.* made up of or resembling fibrous tissue.

fiche (feesh) *n.* a microfiche.

fick•le (FIK əl) *adj.* inconstant in feeling or purpose; capricious. [ME *fikel* crafty]

fic•tion (FIK shən) *n.* **1.** prose works in narrative form, the characters and incidents of which are wholly or partly imaginary; also, such works collectively. **2.** something imagined or deliberately falsified. [ME] —**fic′tion•al** *adj.*

fic•ti•tious (fik TISH əs) *adj.* **1.** not corresponding to actual fact; artificially invented. **2.** not genuine; false. **3.** fictional. [< L *ficticius*]

fic•tive (FIK tiv) *adj.* **1.** fictitious. **2.** relating to the creation of fiction.

fid•dle (FĪD l) *n.* a violin. —**fit as a fiddle** enjoying perfect health. —*v.* **•dled, •dling** *v.i.* **1.** play a violin. **2.** fidget. —*v.t.* **3.** spend (time) in a careless way: usu. with *away.* [ME] —**fid′dler** *n.*

fid•dle•stick (FID l stik) *n.* **1.** a bow used on a violin, etc. **2.** something trifling. —*interj. pl.* nonsense.

fi•del•i•ty (fi DEL i tee) *n. pl.* **•ties 1.** faithfulness to duties, vows, truth, etc. **2.** exactness of reproductive detail. **3.** the extent to which a tape recorder etc. receives and transmits input signals without distortion. [ME *fidelite*]

fidg•et (FIJ it) *v.i.* make nervous or restless movements. —*n.* **1.** *Usu. pl.* the condition of being restless or nervous. **2.** one who fidgets: also **fidg′et•er.** [< earlier *fidge* fidget]

fi•du•ci•ar•y (fi DOO shee ER ee) *adj.* **1.** of, pertaining to, or acting as a trustee. **2.** held in trust. —*n. pl.* **•ar•ies** one who holds something in trust. [< L *fiduciarius* of a sum held in trust]

field (feeld) *n.* **1.** a piece of land covered primarily with grass, weeds, or similar vegetation. **2.** a piece of land set aside for use as pasture or for crops. **3.** a large expanse, as of open country. **4.** an area in which a natural resource is found: an oil *field.* **5.** an airport. **6.** the whole extent or a particular division of knowledge, research, or study. **7.** in sports and athletics. **a** the bounded area where a game is played or where contests, exhibitions, etc. are held. **b** the members of a team etc. engaged in active play. **c** the competitors

in a contest, esp. in horse racing. **8.** *Mil.* a region of active operations or maneuvers. **9.** in business, the area away from the home office. **10.** an area for active work or direct observation (**field work**), as opposed to library research, analysis of data, etc. **11.** *Physics* an extent of space within which lines of magnetic or electric force are in operation: also **field of force. 12.** *Optics* the area within which objects are seen in a telescope etc. **13.** the part of a painting canvas, flag, etc. used for background. —**take the field** begin a game, military campaign, etc. —*v.t.* **1.** in baseball, cricket, etc., catch or pick up (a ball) and throw to the appropriate player. **2.** organize or put (a team) into competition. **3. a** reply to (questions) adequately. **b** answer (questions) extemporaneously. —*v.i.* **4.** in baseball, cricket, etc., play in a field position. [ME] —**field′er** *n.*

field glass a compact, portable, binocular telescope. Also **field glasses.**

field goal 1. in football, a goal scored by a kick from the field. **2.** in basketball, a goal scored while the ball is in active play.

field•stone (FEELD stohn) *n.* loose stone found near a construction site and used in building. —*adj.* consisting of or having the appearance of fieldstone: a *fieldstone* house.

field test a test to determine how a new product or process will perform with normal use. —**field-test** (FEELD test) *v.t.*

fiend (feend) *n.* **1.** an evil spirit; devil; demon. **2.** an intensely wicked or cruel person. **3.** *Informal* one who is addicted to a substance, game, etc.: a bridge *fiend.* [ME *feend*]

fiend•ish (FEEN dish) *adj.* exceedingly cruel or malicious; diabolical. —**fiend′ish•ness** *n.*

fierce (feers) *adj.* **1.** having a violent, cruel nature. **2.** violent in action or force. **3.** vehement; intense: *fierce* anger. **4.** *Informal* very disagreeable, bad, etc. [ME *feirs* wild]

fier•y (FĪ ə ree) *adj.* **fier•i•er, fier•i•est 1.** like, containing, or composed of fire. **2.** brightly glowing; blazing. **3.** passionate; impetuous. [ME *firy*] —**fier′i•ness** *n.*

fi•es•ta (fee ES tə) *n.* **1.** a religious festival. **2.** any holiday or celebration. [< Sp.]

fife (fif) *n.* a small, shrill-toned flute. —*v.t. & v.i.* **fifed, fif•ing** play on a fife. [< G *Pfeife* pipe] —**fif′er** *n.*

fif•teen (FIF TEEN) *n.* the sum of fourteen

and one: a cardinal number written 15, XV. [ME] **—fif′teenth′** n. & adj.

fifth (fifth) adj. **1.** next after the fourth. **2.** being one of five equal parts. —n. **1.** one of five equal parts. **2.** that which follows the fourth. **3.** Music the interval between a tone and another tone five steps from it. **4.** one fifth of a U.S. gallon, used as a measure of liquors. [ME fifte] —adv.

fifth wheel a superfluous person or thing.

fif•ty (FIF tee) n. pl. •ties the sum of forty and ten: a cardinal number written 50, L. [ME] **—fif′ti•eth** n. & adj.

fight (fit) v. fought, fight•ing v.t. **1.** struggle against in battle or physical combat. **2.** struggle against in any manner. **3.** make (one's way) by struggling. —v.i. **4.** take part in combat. **5.** struggle in any manner. [ME fighten] **—fight it out** fight until a final decision is reached. —n. **1.** strife or struggle; conflict; combat. **2.** power or disposition to fight; pugnacity.

fight•er (FĪ tər) n. **1.** one who fights. **2.** Mil. a fast, highly maneuverable airplane for aerial fighting: also **fighter plane.**

fig•ment (FIG mənt) n. a fantasy or fiction; fabrication. [ME, something made or made up]

fig•ur•a•tive (FIG yər ə tiv) adj. **1.** based on, like, or containing a figure or figures of speech; metaphorical. **2.** representing by means of a form or figure. **3.** pertaining to pictorial or sculptural representation. [ME]

fig•ure (FIG yər) n. **1.** a character or symbol representing a number. **2.** pl. the use of such characters in calculating. **3.** an amount stated in numbers. **4.** the visible form of anything; shape; outline. **5.** the human form or body. **6.** a personage or character, esp. a prominent one. **7.** the impression a person makes. **8.** a representation or likeness, as in painting or sculpture. **9.** a pattern or design, as in a fabric. **10.** a printed illustration. **11.** a movement or series of movements, as in a dance. —v. •ured, •ur•ing v.t. **1.** compute numerically; calculate. **2.** make a representation of; depict. **3.** ornament with a design. **4.** picture mentally; imagine. **5.** express by a figure of speech; symbolize. **6.** Informal believe; predict. —v.i. **7.** appear prominently; be conspicuous. **8.** compute; reckon. **—figure on** (or **upon**) Informal **1.** count on; rely on. **2.** plan on. **—figure out 1.** solve; compute. **2.** make

out; understand. [ME] **—fig′ured** adj.

fig•ure•head (FIG yər HED) n. **1.** a person having nominal leadership but no real power. **2.** a carved or ornamental figure on the prow of a vessel.

figure of speech an expression that deviates from literal meaning so as to create a vivid effect, as a simile, metaphor, etc.

fig•u•rine (FIG yə REEN) n. a small, molded or carved figure; statuette. [< Ital. figurina]

fil•a•ment (FIL ə mənt) n. **1.** a fine thread or threadlike structure. **2.** the slender wire in a light bulb or electron tube. [< NL filamentum thread]

filch (filch) v.t. steal in small amounts; pilfer. [ME filchen] **—filch′er** n.

file¹ (fil) n. **1.** any device in which papers are systematically arranged for quick reference, as a folder, drawer, or cabinet. **2.** a collection of papers thus arranged. **3.** a line of persons, animals, or things placed one behind another. **4.** Computers a collection of data stored in an electronic format. **—on file** in a file. —v. filed, fil•ing v.t. **1.** store (papers etc.) in systematic order. —v.i. **2.** march in file, as soldiers. **3.** put papers, etc., in a file. **4.** make application, as for a job. [ME filen]

file² n. an instrument with sandy or ridged surfaces, used to abrade, smooth, or polish. —v.t. filed, fil•ing **1.** cut, smooth, or sharpen with or as with a file. **2.** remove with a file. [ME]

fi•let (fi LAY) n. **1.** net lace having a square mesh. **2.** fillet (def. 2). —v.t. fi•leted, fi•let•ing fillet. [< F]

fi•let mi•gnon (fi LAY min YON) a small boneless cut of beef from the inside of the loin. [< F]

fil•i•al (FIL ee əl) adj. of, pertaining to, or befitting the relations of children to parents. [ME]

fil•i•bus•ter (FIL ə BUS tər) n. **1.** in a legislative body, the use of delaying tactics, esp. time-consuming speeches; also, an instance of such tactics. **2.** an adventurer who takes part in an unlawful military expedition. [< Sp. filibustero freebooter] **—fil′i•bus′ter** v.t. & v.i.

fil•i•gree (FIL i GREE) n. **1.** delicate ornamental work formed of intertwined gold or silver wire. **2.** anything fanciful and delicate. —adj. resembling, made of, or adorned with filigree; ornate: also **fil′i•greed.** —v.t. •greed, •gree•ing adorn with or work in filigree. Sometimes spelled *filagree*. [< F *filigrane* filigree]

fil·ings (FĪ lingz) *n. pl.* particles scraped off by a file.

fill (fil) *v.t.* **1.** supply (a container, space, etc.) with as much of something as can be contained. **2.** supply fully, as with food. **3.** occupy or pervade the whole of. **4.** stop up; plug: *fill* a tooth. **5.** supply what is indicated in (an order, prescription, etc.). **6.** satisfy or meet (a need, requirements, etc.). **7.** occupy (an office or position). **8.** level out (an embankment, ravine, etc.) by adding stone, gravel, etc. —*v.i.* **9.** become full. —**fill** (someone) **in on** give (someone) additional facts or details about. —**fill out 1.** make or become fuller or more rounded. **2.** make complete, as an application. —**fill the bill** do or be what is wanted or needed. —**fill up** make or become full. —*n.* **1.** that which fills or is sufficient to fill. **2.** an embankment built up by filling in with stone, gravel, etc. [ME *fillen*]

fil·let (FIL it) *n.* **1.** a narrow band or ribbon for binding the hair. **2.** a strip of boneless meat or fish. **3.** any narrow band. —*v.t.* slice into fillets. [ME *filet* thread]

fill·ing (FIL ing) *n.* **1.** that which is used to fill something; esp. the material put into a prepared cavity in a tooth. **2.** the act of becoming full.

fil·lip (FIL əp) *n.* **1.** the snap of a finger that has been pressed down by the thumb and suddenly released. **2.** something that excites or stimulates. —*v.t.* **1.** strike or project by or as by a fillip. **2.** stimulate; arouse. —*v.i.* **3.** make a fillip. [ME *philippe* snap the fingers]

fil·ly (FIL ee) *n. pl.* **·lies** a young mare. [ME *fyly*]

film (film) *n.* **1.** a thin covering or layer. **2.** a thin haze or blur. **3.** *Photog.* a sheet, roll, or strip of transparent material coated with a light-sensitive emulsion and used for making photographs. **4.** a motion picture. —*v.t.* **1.** cover or obscure by or as by a film. **2.** photograph on film. **3.** make a motion picture of. —*v.i.* **4.** become covered or obscured by a film. **5.** make a motion picture. [ME *filme* membrane]

film·strip (FILM STRIP) *n.* a length of processed film containing frames of still pictures that are projected on a screen.

film·y (FIL mee) *adj.* **film·i·er, film·i·est 1.** of or like film; gauzy. **2.** covered with a film.

fil·ter (FIL tər) *n.* **1.** a device, as paper, cloth, or charcoal, used as a strainer for clearing or purifying liquids, air, etc. **2.** a device for screening out electrical oscillations or light waves of certain frequencies. —*v.t.* **1.** pass (liquids, air, etc.) through a filter; strain. **2.** separate or remove (impurities etc.) by or as by a filter. **3.** act as a filter for. —*v.i.* **4.** pass through a filter. **5.** leak out, as news. [ME *filtre*] —**fil'ter·a·ble** or **fil'tra·ble** *adj.*

filth (filth) *n.* **1.** anything foul or dirty. **2.** a foul condition. **3.** moral defilement; obscenity. [ME] —**filth·y** (FIL thee) *adj.* **filth·i·er, filth·i·est 1.** of the nature of or containing filth. **2.** morally foul; obscene. **3.** highly unpleasant.

fil·trate (FIL trayt) *v.t.* **·trat·ed, ·trat·ing** filter. —*n.* the liquid that has been separated by filtering. [< Med.L *filtratus* filtered] —**fil·tra'tion** *n.*

fin (fin) *n.* **1.** a membranous extension from the body of a fish or other aquatic animal, serving to propel, balance, or steer it in the water. **2.** anything finlike or projecting part, appendage, or attachment, as a flipper. [ME]

fi·na·gle (fi NAY gəl) *v.* **·gled, ·gling** *v.t.* **1.** get (something) by trickery or deceit. **2.** cheat or trick (someone). —*v.i.* **3.** use trickery or deceit; be sly. —**fi·na'gler** *n.*

fi·nal (FĪN l) *adj.* **1.** pertaining to or coming at the end; ultimate; last. **2.** precluding further action or controversy; conclusive. **3.** relating to or consisting in the end or purpose aimed at: a *final* cause. —*n.* **1.** something that is terminal or last. **2.** *Often pl.* something decisively final, as the last match in a tournament. **3.** the last examination in a course. [ME] —**fi·nal·i·ty** (ffi NAL i tee) *n. pl.* **·ties** —**fin'nal·ly** *adv.*

fi·na·le (fi NAL ee) *n.* the last part, as the final scene in a play. [< Ital.]

fi·nal·ist (FĪN l ist) *n.* in games, contests, etc., a contestant in the finals.

fi·nal·ize (FĪN l IZ) *v.t.* **·ized, ·iz·ing** put into final or complete form; bring to completion.

fi·nance (fi NANS) *n.* **1.** the science of monetary affairs. **2.** *pl.* monetary matters; funds; revenue; income. —*v.t.* **·nanced, ·nanc·ing 1.** supply the money for. **2.** manage the finances of. [ME *finaunce*] —**fi·nan'cial** (fi NAN shəl) *adj.*

fin·an·cier (FIN ən SEER) *n.* one engaged or skilled in financial operations. [< F]

find (find) *v.* **found, find·ing** *v.t.* **1.** come

upon unexpectedly. **2.** discover after search, experience, or effort. **3.** recover (something lost). **4.** arrive at; reach. **5.** gain, or recover the use of: She *found* her tongue. **6.** determine by legal inquiry and declare. —*v.i.* **7.** express a decision after legal inquiry. —*n.* **1.** the act of finding. **2.** something found or discovered; esp., a valuable discovery. [ME *finden*]

find•er (FĪN dər) *n.* **1.** one who or that which finds. **2.** a small telescope by the side of a large one, used to locate an object. **3.** a camera attachment that shows a scene as it will appear in the photograph.

find•ing (FĪN ding) *n.* **1.** the act of one who finds. **2.** that which is found; a discovery or conclusion.

fine[1] (fin) *adj.* **fin•er, fin•est 1.** superior in quality or ability; excellent. **2.** highly satisfactory; very good. **3.** light or delicate in texture, workmanship, etc. **4.** composed of very small particles: *fine* powder. **5.** very thin: *fine* thread. **6.** keen; sharp: a *fine* edge. **7.** subtle; discriminating. **8.** elegant; polished; also, overelegant; affected. **9.** cloudless; clear. —*adv. Informal* very well: It suits me *fine.* —*v.t. & v.i.* make or become fine or finer. [ME]

fine[2] *n.* a sum of money required as the penalty for an offense. —*v.t.* **fined, fin•ing** punish by fine. [ME *fin*]

fine arts the arts of painting, drawing, sculpture, and architecture, and sometimes including literature, music, drama, and the dance.

fin•er•y (FĪ nə ree) *n. pl.* **•er•ies** fine clothes or decorations. [< MF *finerie*]

fine-spun (FĪN SPUN) *adj.* **1.** drawn or spun out to extreme fineness. **2.** excessively subtle.

fi•nesse (fi NES) *n.* **1.** highly refined skill; adroitness. **2.** smoothness and tact, as in handling a delicate situation; also, artful strategy. [ME] —*v.t. & v.i.* **•nessed, •ness•ing 1.** bring about by finesse. **2.** use finesse.

fin•ger (FING gər) *n.* **1.** one of the terminating members of the hand, usu. excluding the thumb. **2.** that part of a glove made to fit the finger. **3.** anything that resembles or serves as a finger. **4.** a unit of measure based on the width of a finger or on the length of the middle finger. —**have a finger in the pie 1.** take part in some matter. **2.** meddle. —**put one's finger on** identify or indicate correctly. —*v.t.* **1.** touch or handle with the fingers; toy with. **2.** *Music* **a** play (an instrument) with the fingers. **b** mark the fingering of (music). **3.** *Slang* betray, as to the police. —*v.i.* **4.** touch or feel anything with the fingers. [ME] —**fin′ger•er** *n.*

fin•ger•ing (FING gər ring) *n.* **1.** the act of touching or feeling with the fingers. **2.** *Music* **a** the action or technique of using the fingers in playing an instrument. **b** the notation indicating which fingers are to be used.

fin•ger•ling (FING gər ling) *n.* a young, small fish. [ME]

fin•ger•nail (FING gər NAYL) *n.* the horny substance at the end of a finger.

fin•ger•print (FING gər PRINT) *n.* an impression of the skin pattern on the inner surface of a finger tip, used for identification. —*v.t.* take the fingerprints of.

fin•i•al (FIN ee əl) *n. Archit.* an ornament at the apex of a spire, pinnacle, or the like. [ME]

fin•ick•y (FIN i kee) *adj.* **•ick•i•er, •ick•i•est** excessively fastidious or precise; fussy.

fin•is (FIN is) *n.* the end. [< L]

fin•ish (FIN ish) *v.t.* **1.** complete or bring to an end. **2.** use up completely. **3.** perfect (a person) in social graces, education, etc. **4.** give (fabric, wood, etc.) a particular surface quality. **5.** kill, destroy, or defeat. —*v.i.* **6.** reach or come to an end; stop. —*n.* **1.** the conclusion or last stage of anything. **2.** something that finishes, completes, or perfects. **3.** perfection or polish in manners, education, etc. **4.** the surface quality or appearance of textiles, paint, etc. [ME *finisshen*] —**fin′•ished** *adj.* —**fin′ish•er** *n.*

fi•nite (FĪ NIT) *adj.* **1.** having bounds, ends, or limits. **2.** that may be determined, counted, or measured. —*n.* finite things collectively, or that which is finite. [ME] —**fi′nite•ly** *adv.*

fink (fingk) *n. Slang* **1.** a strikebreaker. **2.** an informer. **3.** any untrustworthy or unsavory person.

fiord (fyord) see FJORD.

fire (fir) *n.* **1.** the visible, active phase of combustion, manifested in light and heat. **2.** a burning mass of fuel, as in a fireplace. **3.** a destructive burning, as of a building. **4.** a flash or spark: strike *fire.* **5.** a discharge of firearms. **6.** flashing brightness; brilliance. **7.** intensity of spirit or feeling; passion. **8.** warmth or heat, as of liquor. **9.** an affliction or grievous trial. —**on fire 1.** burning; ablaze. **2.** ardent; zealous. —**catch fire a**

begin to burn. **b** create enthusiasm —**hang fire 1.** fail to fire promptly, as a firearm. **2.** be delayed or undecided. —**open fire 1.** begin to shoot. **2.** commence. —**play with fire** do something rash or dangerous. —**set fire to** or **set on fire 1.** make burn. **2.** inflame or excite. —**under fire 1.** exposed to gunshot or artillery fire. **2.** subjected to severe criticism. —v. **fired, fir•ing** v.t. **1.** set on fire. **2.** tend the fire of. **3.** subject to the heat of fire. **4.** set off, as explosives. **5.** set off explosives within or near: *fire* an oil well. **6.** discharge, as a gun or bullet. **7.** hurl: *fire* questions. **8.** dismiss from employment. **9.** bake, as pottery, in a kiln. **10.** inspire; excite. —v.i. **11.** catch fire; become ignited. **12.** go off, as a gun. **13.** set off firearms, a rocket, etc. **14.** hurl a missile. —**fire away** start off and proceed energetically, esp. in asking questions. [ME]

fire•arm (FĪR AHRM) n. any weapon, usu. small, from which a missile, as a bullet, is hurled by an explosive.

fire•ball (FĪR BAWL) n. **1.** a luminous meteor. **2.** ball-shaped lightning. **3.** a hot, incandescent sphere of air and vaporized debris, formed around the center of a nuclear explosion. **4.** *Informal* a remarkably energetic person or thing.

fire•bomb (FĪR BOM) n. an incendiary bomb. —**fire′bomb′** v.t.

fire•brand (FĪR BRAND) n. **1.** a piece of burning or glowing wood. **2.** one who excites the passions of others; an agitator.

fire•break (FĪR BRAYK) n. a strip of land plowed or cleared to prevent the spread of fire.

fire extinguisher a portable apparatus containing fire-extinguishing chemicals.

fire•fight•er (FĪR FĪ tər) n. a volunteer who fights a fire or a person employed to extinguish fires.

fire•fly (FĪR FLĪ) n. pl. **-flies** a night-flying beetle emitting a phosphorescent light.

fire•house (FĪR HOWS) n. a building housing fire-fighting equipment and personnel.

fire•place (FĪR PLAYS) n. a recess or structure in which a fire is built; esp., the part of a chimney opening into a room.

fire•pow•er (FĪR POW ər) n. *Mil.* **1.** capacity for delivering fire, as from the guns of a ship, battery, etc. **2.** the amount or effectiveness of fire delivered by a given weapon or unit.

fire•proof (FĪR PROOF) adj. resistant to

fire; relatively incombustible. —v.t. make resistant to fire.

fire•side (FĪR SĪD) n. **1.** the hearth or space before the fireplace. **2.** home or home life.

fire•trap (FĪR TRAP) n. a building that is notoriously inflammable or which, if on fire, is likely to trap persons inside.

fire•work (FĪR WURK) n. **1.** *Usu. pl.* a device containing combustibles or explosives that, when ignited, produce brilliant light or a loud noise. **2.** *pl.* a display made by or as by these devices.

firing squad a military detachment assigned to execute, by shooting, a person condemned to death.

firm[1] (furm) adj. **1.** relatively solid, compact, or unyielding to touch or pressure. **2.** difficult to move, loosen, etc. **3.** fixedly settled and established. **4.** constant and steadfast. **5.** full of or indicating strength; steady. —v.t. & v.i. make or become firm. —adv. solidly; resolutely; fixedly. [< L *firmus*] —**firm′ly** adv.

firm[2] n. a partnership or other organization for conducting business. [< Sp. *firma*]

fir•ma•ment (FUR mə mənt) n. the heavens; sky. [ME]

first (furst) adj. **1.** preceding all others in the order of numbering. **2.** prior to all others in time; earliest. **3.** nearest or foremost in place. **4.** highest or foremost in character, rank, etc.; chief. —**in the first place** to begin with. —n. **1.** one who or that which is first in time, rank, order, or position. **2.** the beginning: from *first* to last. **3.** the winning position in a race or contest. **4.** pl. the best grade of certain merchandise, as of sheets. —**at first** at the beginning. —adv. **1.** before all others in order, time, place, rank, etc.: also **firstly. 2.** for the first time. **3.** in preference to something else: He would die *first*. [ME]

first aid treatment given in an emergency before full medical care can be obtained.

first•born (FURST BORN) adj. first brought forth; eldest. —n. the firstborn child.

first-class (FURST KLAS) adj. **1.** of highest rank or best quality. **2.** of a class of sealed mail consisting wholly or partly of written matter. **3.** of the most luxurious accommodations on a ship, plane, etc. —adv. by first-class mail or conveyance.

first•hand (FURST HAND) adj. & adv. direct from the original source.

first mate a ship's officer ranking next below captain.

first person 1. a grammatical form in which the pronoun and verb (such as *I* and *am*) refer to the speaker or writer. **2.** narration using this form.

first-rate (FURST RAYT) *adj.* of the finest class or quality; excellent. —*adv.* very well.

first-string (FURST STRING) *adj.* **1.** being the regular or preferred choice, as of a member of a team. **2.** first-rate.

fis·cal (FIS kəl) *adj.* of or pertaining to the treasury or finances of a government; financial. [< L *fiscalis*]

fiscal year any twelve-month period at the end of which accounts are balanced.

fish (fish) *n. pl.* **fish** or (with reference to different species) **fish·es 1.** a vertebrate, cold-blooded aquatic animal with permanent gills, fins, and usu. scales. ◆ Collateral adjective: *piscine*. **2.** the flesh of fish used as food. —*v.t.* **1.** catch or try to catch fish in (a body of water). **2.** catch or try to catch (fish, eels, etc.). **3.** grope for and bring out: with *out* or *up*: *fish* money out of one's pocket. —*v.i.* **4.** catch or try to catch fish. **5.** try to get something in an artful or indirect manner: with *for*. [ME]

fish·bowl (FISH BOHL) *n.* **1.** a bowl, usu. of glass, serving as a small aquarium for fish. **2.** a condition in which one's actions are in plain view.

fish·er·y (FISH ə ree) *n. pl.* **·er·ies 1.** the operation or business of catching fish or other aquatic animals. **2.** a place for fishing; fishing ground. **3.** a fish hatchery.

fish hatchery a place designed for the artificial propagation and nurture of fish.

fish·hook (FISH HUUK) *n.* a hook, usu. barbed, for fishing.

fishing tackle equipment for fishing.

fish meal *n.* ground dried fish, used as fertilizer and feed for animals.

fish story *Informal* an extravagant or incredible narrative.

fish·wife (FISH WIF) *n. pl.* **·wives** (-WIVZ) **1.** a woman who sells fish. **2.** a coarse, abusive woman.

fish·y (FISH ee) *adj.* **fish·i·er, fish·i·est 1.** of or like fish. **2.** abounding in fish. **3.** *Informal* improbable. —**fish'i·ness** *n.*

fis·sile (FIS əl) *adj.* **1.** capable of being split or separated into layers. **2.** tending to split. [< L *fissilis* separable]

fis·sion (FISH ən) *n.* **1.** the act of splitting or breaking apart. **2.** *Biol.* spontaneous division of a cell or organism into new cells or organisms. **3.** *Physics* the disintegration of the nucleus of an atom, leading to the release of energy. —**fis'sion·a·ble** *adj.*

fis·sure (FISH ər) *n.* **1.** a narrow opening, cleft, or furrow. **2.** the act of cleaving, or the state of being cleft. **3.** *Anat.* any cleft or furrow of the body. —*v.t. & v.i.* **·sured, ·sur·ing** crack; split; cleave. [ME]

fist (fist) *n.* the hand closed tightly, as for striking; also, grip; clutch. —*v.t.* make a fist; strike with the fist. [ME]

fist·ful (FIST fuul) *n. pl.* **·fuls** a handful.

fist·i·cuff (FIS ti KUF) *n.* **1.** *pl.* a fight with the fists. **2.** *pl.* boxing. **3.** a blow with the fist. —*v.t. & v.i.* fight with the fists.

fit[1] (fit) *adj.* **fit·ter, fit·test 1.** adapted to an end, aim, or design; suited. **2.** proper or appropriate; becoming. **3.** qualified; competent. **4.** prepared; ready. **5.** in good physical condition; healthy. —*v.* **fit·ted** or **fit, fit·ting** *v.t.* **1.** be suitable or proper for. **2.** be of the right size and shape for. **3.** prepare or alter to the proper size or purpose. **4.** equip. **5.** put in place carefully or exactly. —*v.i.* **6.** be suitable or proper. **7.** be of the proper size, shape, etc. —**fit out** (or **up**) supply; outfit. —*n.* **1.** condition or manner of fitting. **2.** something that fits. **3.** the act of fitting. [ME *fitten*] —**fit·ness** (FIT nis) *n.*

fit[2] *n.* **1.** a sudden onset of a disorder, often attended by convulsions; spasm. **2.** a sudden surge of emotion. **3.** impulsive and irregular exertion or action. [ME]

fit·ful (FIT fəl) *adj.* characterized by irregular actions or moods; capricious. —**fit'ful·ness** *n.*

fit·ting (FIT ing) *adj.* fit; proper; appropriate. —*n.* **1.** the act of one who fits. **2.** a piece of equipment or an appliance used in an adjustment. **3.** *pl.* furnishings, fixtures, or decorations. —**fit'ting·ly** *adv.*

five (fiv) *n.* the sum of four and one: a cardinal number written 5, V. [ME]

fix (fiks) *v.t.* **1.** make firm or secure; fasten so as to be immovable. **2.** set or place permanently. **3.** render unchangeable: *fix* a color. **4.** turn or direct (the attention, gaze, etc.) steadily. **5.** determine or establish. **6.** place (blame or responsibility) on a person. **7.** adjust. **8.** repair or mend. **9.** prepare. **10.** *Informal* arrange or influence the outcome etc. of (a race, game, etc.) as by bribery. **11.** *Photog.* bathe (a film or plate) in chemicals to remove light-sensitive substances and prevent fading. **12.** *Informal* neuter (a dog, cat, etc.) —v.i. **13.** become firm or stable. —n. **1.** Informal a difficult situation; predicament. **2.** the relative position of a ship or aircraft in transit. **3.** Slang an outcome arranged by bribery or other corrupt means. **4.** Slang an injection of heroin or other narcotic. [ME fixen]

fix·a·tion (fik SAY shən) n. **1.** the act of fixing, or the state of being fixed. **2.** Chem. the conversion of free nitrogen from the air into useful compounds. **3.** Psychoanal. a preoccupation or obsession.

fix·a·tive (FIK sə tiv) n. that which serves to render permanent or fixed.

fixed (fikst) adj. **1.** placed or fastened securely. **2.** steadily or intently directed; set. **3.** stationary or unchanging in relative position. **4.** definite and unalterable. **5.** permanent. **6.** Informal arranged beforehand as to outcome or decision. —**fix·ed·ly** (FIK sid lee) adv.

fix·i·ty (FIK si tee) n. pl. •ties **1.** the state or quality of being fixed; stability; permanence. **2.** that which is fixed. [< NL fixitas]

fix·ture (FIKS chər) n. **1.** anything securely fixed or fastened into position: a lighting fixture. **2.** a person or thing regarded as fixed in a particular place or job. [< LL fixura]

fizz (fiz) v.i. make a hissing or sputtering noise. —n. **1.** a hissing sound. **2.** an effervescent beverage made with soda water, liquor, etc.: gin fizz. —**fizz·y** (FIZ ee) adj. **fizz·i·er, fizz·i·est**

fiz·zle (FIZ əl) v.i. •zled, •zling **1.** make a hissing or sputtering sound. **2.** Informal fail, esp. after a good start. —n. **1.** hissing. **2.** Informal a failure. [Obs. fysel break wind]

fjord (fyord) n. a long, narrow arm of the sea between high, rocky cliffs or banks: also spelled fiord. [< Norw.]

flab·ber·gast (FLAB ər GAST) v.t. astound.

flab·by (FLAB ee) adj. •bi·er, •bi·est **1.** lacking strength or firmness; soft. **2.** lacking vigor or force. —**flab'bi·ness** n.

flac·cid (FLAK sid) adj. lacking firmness or elasticity; limp; flabby. [< L flaccidus flabby] —**flac·cid'i·ty** n.

flag¹ (flag) n. **1.** a piece of cloth or bunting, usu. oblong, bearing devices and colors to designate a nation, state, organization, etc. **2.** something resembling a flag, as the bushy part of the tail of a dog. —v.t. **flagged, flag·ging 1.** mark out or adorn with flags. **2.** signal with or as with a flag.

flag² v.i. **flagged, flag·ging 1.** grow tired or weak. **2.** become limp. —**flag'ing** adj.

flag³ n. a flagstone. —v.i. **flagged, flag·ging** pave with flags. [ME flagge piece of turf]

flag·el·late (FLAJ ə LAYT) v.t. •lat·ed, •lat·ing whip; scourge. —**flag'el·la'tion** n.

flag·ging (FLAG ing) n. **1.** a pavement of flagstones; also, flagstones collectively. **2.** the act of paving with flagstones.

fla·gi·tious (flə JISH əs) adj. flagrantly wicked. [ME flagicious scandalous]

flag·pole (FLAG POHL) n. a pole on which a flag is displayed.

fla·grant (FLAY grənt) adj. openly disgraceful; notorious. [ME] —**fla'grant·ly** adv.

fla·gran·te de·lic·to (flə GRAN tee di LIK toh) in the act of committing an offense. [< L]

flag·ship (FLAG SHIP) n. the ship in a naval formation that carries the commander and displays the commander's flag. —adj. designating the first, largest, most important, etc. of its kind: the network's flagship station.

flag·staff (FLAG STAFF) n. pl. •staffs or •staves a flagpole.

flag·stone (FLAG STOHN) n. a broad, flat stone for pavements.

flail (flayl) n. an implement for threshing grain by hand. —v.t. & v.i. beat as with a flail. [ME fleil whip]

flair (flair) n. **1.** a talent or aptitude. **2.** a sense of fashion. **3.** smartness in style. [ME]

flak (flak) n. **1.** antiaircraft fire. **2.** severe criticism; opposition. [< G Fl(ieger)a(bwehr)k(anone) antiaircraft gun]

flake (flayk) n. **1.** a thin piece peeled or split off from a surface. **2.** a small piece of light substance: a flake of snow. **3.** a stratum or layer. **4.** Slang an eccentric. —v.t. & v.i. **flaked, flak·ing 1.** peel off in flakes. **2.** form into flakes. [ME]

flak·y (FLAY kee) adj. **flak·i·er, flak·i·est 1.** resembling or consisting of flakes. **2.** splitting off or easily separated into flakes. **3.** Slang exhibiting odd behavior. —**flak'i·ness** n.

flam·boy·ant (flam BOI ənt) adj. **1.** extravagantly ornate; showy. **2.** brilliant; resplendent. [< F, flaming] —**flam·boy'ance** n.

flame (flaym) n. **1.** a mass of burning vapor or gas rising from a fire in streams or darting tongues of light. **2.** a single tongue of flame.

3. *Often pl.* a state of bright, intensely active combustion. **4.** something resembling a flame, as in brilliance. **5.** intense passion or emotion; ardor. **6.** *Informal* a sweetheart. **7.** a bright, red-yellow color. —*v.i.* **flamed, flam·ing 1.** give out flame; blaze; burn. **2.** light up or glow as if on fire; flash. **3.** become enraged or excited. [ME *flaume*]

fla·men·co (flah MENG koh) *n.* **1.** a fiery, strongly rhythmic style of singing and dancing practiced esp. by the Gypsies of Andalusia. **2.** a song or dance in this style. [< Sp.]

fla·min·go (flə MING goh) *n. pl.* •**gos** or •**goes** a long-necked wading bird of a pink or red color, having very long legs. [< Pg. *flamengo*]

flam·ma·ble (FLAM ə bəl) *adj.* inflammable. —**flam′ma·bil′i·ty** *n.*

flange (flanj) *n.* **1.** a projecting rim or collar on a wheel, designed to keep it on a fixed track. **2.** a similar projecting part of a beam, pipe, etc. designed to aid attachment or to increase stiffness. —*v.t. & v.i.* **flanged, flang·ing** provide with or take the shape of a flange. [ME *flaunche* curving charge on a shield]

flank (flangk) *n.* **1.** the part between the ribs and the hip at either side of the body of an animal or human being; also, a cut of meat from such a part. **2.** loosely, the outside part of the thigh. **3.** the side of something. **4.** *Mil.* the right or left section of an army, fleet, fortification, etc. —*v.t.* **1.** be at the side of. **2.** *Mil.* defend, launch an attack against, or move around the flank of. —*v.i.* **3.** be located at the side of something. [ME]

flan·nel (FLAN l) *n.* **1.** a woven fabric made of wool, or of wool and cotton. **2.** a soft fabric made chiefly of cotton, with a nap on one or both sides. **3.** *pl.* a garment made of flannel. [ME *flaunneol* woolen garment]

flap (flap) *v.i. & v.t.* **flapped, flap·ping 1.** move (wings, arms, etc.) vigorously up and down. **2.** move or cause to move irregularly, esp. with a noise, as a flag. **3.** slap. —*n.* **1.** something hanging loosely and usu. broad and flat, as a *flap* of an envelope, a tent, etc. **2.** the motion or sound produced by a moving flap. **3.** *Slang* an agitated reaction; a commotion. [ME *flappe*]

flap·per (FLAP ər) *n.* **1.** one who or that which flaps. **2.** a sophisticated young woman of the 1920's.

flare (flair) *v.* **flared, flar·ing** *v.i.* **1.** blaze up or burn with a wavering light, esp. sud-denly; often with *up.* **2.** break out in sudden or violent emotion or action: often with *up* or *out.* **3.** gradually open outward, as the sides of a bell. —*v.t.* **4.** cause to flare. **5.** signal with flares. —*n.* **1.** a bright, flickering light. **2.** an outburst, as of emotion. **3.** a spreading outward; also, that which so flares. **4.** a signal that gives off a bright white or colored light.

flare·up (FLAIR up) *n.* a sudden outburst of flame, anger, etc.

flash (flash) *v.i.* **1.** burst forth suddenly or repeatedly into brilliant light or fire. **2.** gleam brightly; glitter. **3.** move suddenly or with lightning speed. —*v.t.* **4.** cause to shine or glitter brightly. **5.** emit bursts of (light, fire, etc.). **6.** send or communicate with lightning speed. **7.** show suddenly or abruptly; also, make a display of. **8.** provide (a roof etc.) with flashing. —*n.* **1.** a quick blaze of light or fire, lasting an instant. **2.** a sudden, brilliant manifestation, as of wit. **3.** an instant. **4.** a brief news dispatch sent by radio etc. —*adj.* done or occurring very quickly. [ME *flasshen*] —**flash′er** *n.* something or someone that flashes, esp. (*Slang*) a man who briefly exposes his genitals in public.

flash·back (FLASH bak) *n.* a break in the continuity of a novel, drama, motion picture, etc. to give a scene occurring earlier; also, the scene itself.

flash·bulb (FLASH bulb) *n. Photog.* an electrical device emitting an intense light of brief duration.

flash·card (FLASH kahrd *n.* a learning aid consisting of a card having words, math problems, etc., briefly displayed as by a teacher to a class.

flash flood a sudden, rushing flood.

flash-for·ward (FLASH FOR wərd) *n.* a break in a narrative to present a scene set in the future; also the scene itself.

flash·gun (FLASH gun *n. Photog.* a device that ignites a flashbulb.

flash·ing (FLASH ing) *n.* sheet metal used to cover joints or angles, as of a roof.

flash·light (FLASH līt) *n.* a small, portable device that emits a beam of light, usu. powered by dry batteries.

flash point 1. the lowest temperature at which the vapors of combustible liquids will ignite. **2.** a time when someone or something suddenly bursts into action or being.

flash·y (FLASH ee) *adj.* **flash·i·er, flash·**

i•est **1.** brilliant for a moment; sparkling. **2.** showy; cheap. —**flash′i•ness** n.

flask (flask) n. any of various small containers made of glass, metal, etc., with a narrow neck. [ME, cask]

flat¹ (flat) adj. **flat•ter, flat•test 1.** extended horizontally with little or no slope. **2.** smooth and regular. **3.** stretched out level or prostrate. **4.** having the front or back in full contact with an even surface. **5.** shallow: a flat dish. **6.** absolute and unqualified: a flat refusal. **7.** lifeless; insipid; dull. **8.** lacking variety or contrast. **9.** deflated: a flat tire. **10.** Informal having little or no money: also **flat broke. 11.** fixed; uniform: a flat rate. **12.** exact; precise: in one minute flat. **13.** Music a lowered in pitch by a semitone. **b** lower than the correct, true pitch. **14.** Phonet. designating the vowel sound in man, as opposed to the sound in calm. —adv. **1.** in a flat state, position, or manner. **2.** exactly. **3.** in finance, without interest. **4.** Music below the true pitch. —**fall flat** fail to achieve a desired effect. —n. **1.** the flat, plane surface or part of something. **2.** something that has a flat surface, as a piece of stage scenery or a level area of land. **3.** a tire from which the air has escaped. **4.** pl. women's shoes with flat heels. **5.** Music a sign (♭) placed before a note to indicate it is at a semitone lower in pitch. —v.t. & v.i. **flat•ted, flat•ting** make or become flat. [ME]

flat² n. an apartment. [< OE flet floor]

flat•foot (FLAT FUUT) n. **1.** Pathol. a condition caused by a flattened arch. **2.** Slang a policeman.

flat•foot•ed (FLAT FLUUT id) adj. having flat feet. —**catch flatfooted 1.** catch in the act of committing an offense. **2.** surprise, esp. in an unprepared state.

flat•ten (FLAT n) v.t. & v.i. make or become flat or flatter.

flat•ter (FLAT ər) v.t. **1.** praise excessively, esp. without sincerity. **2.** try to gain favor by praising. **3.** play on the hopes or vanity of; please, as by compliments. **4.** show as more attractive. —v.i. **5.** flatter someone or something. [ME flatteren fawn upon] —**flat′ter•er** n.

flat•ter•y (FLAT ə ree) n. pl. **•ter•ies 1.** the act of flattering. **2.** a flattering remark.

flat•u•lence (FLACH ə ləns) n. **1.** gas in the intestines. **2.** windy boastfulness. Also **flat′u•len•cy.** —**flat′u•lent** adj. [< MF]

flat•ware (FLAT WAIR) n. **1.** dishes that are

flat, as plates and saucers. **2.** table utensils, as knives, forks, and spoons.

flaunt (flawnt) v.i. **1.** make a brazen or gaudy display. **2.** wave freely. —v.t. **3.** display. —n. the act of flaunting.

flau•tist (FLOW tist) n. a flutist. [< Ital. flautista small flute]

fla•vor (FLAY vər) n. **1.** taste; esp., a distinctive element in the overall taste of something. **2.** a flavoring. **3.** a special, subtle quality pervading something. —v.t. give flavor to. [ME] —**fla′vor•some** adj.

fla•vor•ing (FLAY vər ing) n. something that heightens flavor or gives a distinctive taste.

flaw (flaw) n. **1.** something missing or faulty; defect. **2.** something questionable. **3.** a crack or fissure. —v.t. **1.** produce a flaw in. —v.i. **2.** become cracked or torn. [ME flawe] —**flaw′less** adj.

flax (flaks) n. **1.** a plant that yields the fiber used in making linen. **2.** the fiber. [ME]

flax•en (FLAK sən) **1.** pertaining to or made of flax. **2.** having a light golden color.

flax•seed (FLAKS SEED) n. the seed of flax, yielding linseed oil.

flay (flay) v.t. **1.** remove the skin or covering of, esp. by lashing. **2.** attack with scathing criticism. [ME flen] —**flay′er** n.

flea (flee) n. a small, wingless insect that sucks the blood of mammals and birds. [ME fle]

flea-bit•ten (FLEE BIT n) adj. **1.** bitten by or covered with fleas. **2.** shabby.

flea market a bazaar, usu. temporary and often outdoors, offering used articles and antiques.

fleck (flek) n. **1.** a tiny streak or spot. **2.** a speck. —v.t. mark with flecks. [ME flekked spotted]

fled (fled) past tense, past participle of FLEE.

fledge (flej) v. **fledged, fledg•ing** v.t. **1.** furnish with feathers. **2.** bring up (a young bird). —v.i. **3.** grow enough feathers for flight. [ME fledge capable of flying]

fledg•ling (FLEJ ling) n. **1.** a fledged bird. **2.** a beginner.

flee (flee) v. **fled, flee•ing** v.i. **1.** run away, as from danger. **2.** move swiftly; leave abruptly. —v.t. **3.** run away from (a person, place, etc.). [ME flen]

fleece (flees) n. **1.** the coat of wool covering a sheep or similar animal. **2.** the amount of wool sheared from a sheep. **3.** anything resembling fleece. **4.** a textile fabric with a soft, silky pile. —v.t. **fleeced, fleec•ing 1.**

flip

shear the fleece from. **2.** swindle; defraud. [ME *flees*] —**fleec′y** *adj.* **fleec·i·er, fleec·i·est** covered with, made of, or resembling fleece.

fleet[1] (fleet) *n.* **1.** all the ships belonging to one government; navy; also, a number of ships under one command. **2.** a group of aircraft, trucks, etc. organized into a unit. [ME *flete*]

fleet[2] *adj.* swift; quick. [ME *fleten* float] —**fleet′ly** *adv.*

fleet·ing (FLEE ting) *adj.* passing quickly. —**fleet′ing·ly** *adv.*

flesh (flesh) *n.* **1.** the soft substance of the body of a human being or animal, esp. muscle. **2.** the edible substance of animals; meat. **3.** the soft, pulpy substance of fruits and vegetables. **4.** the color of the skin of a white person. **5.** plumpness; weight. **6.** the physical nature of humans as opposed to the spiritual. **7.** kindred; kin: also **flesh and blood.** [ME *flesc*]

flesh·ly (FLESH lee) *adj.* **·li·er, ·li·est 1.** pertaining to the body. **2.** sensuous. **3.** worldly.

flesh·pot (FLESH pot) *n.* **1.** luxurious living. **2.** *pl.* places for sensual indulgence.

flesh·y (FLESH ee) *adj.* **flesh·i·er, flesh·i·est 1.** of or resembling flesh. **2.** plump; fat. **3.** firm and pulpy. —**flesh′i·ness** *n.*

fleur-de-lis (FLUR dl EE) *n. pl.* **fleurs-de-lis** (—EEZ) an emblem in the form of three leaves or petals bound near the base, used esp. by the former royal family of France. [< F *fleur-de-lys* lily flower]

flew (floo) past tense of FLY[1].

flex (fleks) *v.t. & v.i.* **1.** bend, as the arm. **2.** contract, as a muscle. [< L *flexus* bent] —**flex·ion** (FLEK shən) *n.* [< L]

flex·i·ble (FLEK sə bəl) *adj.* **1.** capable of being bent, twisted, etc.; pliant. **2.** yielding; tractable. **3.** able to adjust; adaptable. [ME] —**flex′i·bil′i·ty** *n.*

flib·ber·ti·gib·bet (FLIB ər tee JIB it) *n.* an impulsive, flighty, or gossipy person. [ME *flepergebet*]

flick (flik) *n.* a quick, light, snapping movement or blow. —*v.t.* **1.** strike or remove with a quick, light stroke, as with a whip. **2.** cause to move or snap with a quick movement. —*v.i.* **3.** move in a darting manner. **4.** flutter. [ME *flykke*]

flick·er[1] (FLIK ər) *v.i.* **1.** burn or shine with an unsteady or wavering light. **2.** flash up and die away quickly. **3.** flutter or quiver. —*v.t.* **4.** cause to flicker. —*n.* **1.** a wavering or unsteady light. **2.** a quivering or fluttering. **3.** a slight stirring, as of emotion. [ME *flikeren* flutter]

flick·er[2] *n.* a woodpecker of North America.

flied (flīd) past tense and past participle of FLY[1] (def. 7).

fli·er (FLI ər) *n.* **1.** one who or that which flies, as an aviator. **2.** one who or that which moves very fast, as an express train. **3.** *Informal* a leap or jump. **4.** *Informal* a risky financial investment. **5.** a handbill. Also spelled *flyer.*

flight[1] (flīt) *n.* **1.** the act or manner of flying; also, the power of flying. **2.** any swift movement through the air. **3.** the distance traveled or the course followed by an airplane, bird, etc. **4.** a journey by airplane; also, a scheduled trip by airplane. **5.** a group flying through the air together. **6.** a soaring: a *flight* of the imagination. **7.** a continuous series of stairs. [ME]

flight[2] *n.* hasty escape. [ME]

flight·y (FLI tee) *adj.* **flight·i·er, flight·i·est 1.** moving erratically from one idea or topic to another. **2.** impulsive; fickle. —**flight′i·ness** *n.*

flim·flam (FLIM FLAM) *Informal v.t.* **·flammed, ·flam·ming** swindle; trick. —*n.* **1.** nonsense; silly talk. **2.** petty trickery or deception.

flim·sy (FLIM zee) *adj.* **·si·er, ·si·est 1.** not strong or solid in structure. **2.** light, thin, and delicate in texture. **3.** lacking validity or effectiveness: a *flimsy* excuse. —**flim′si·ness** *n.*

flinch (flinch) *v.i.* shrink back or wince. [< MF *flenchir* bend] —**flinch** *n.*

fling (fling) *v.t.* **flung, fling·ing 1.** toss or hurl, esp. with violence. **2.** throw (oneself) into something with energy. **3.** send forth, move, or put suddenly or violently. —*n.* **1.** the act of casting out, down, or away. **2.** a brief period of self-indulgence, unrestraint, etc. **3.** an attempt. [ME]

flint (flint) *n.* **1.** a hard stone that produces a spark when struck with steel. **2.** anything very hard or cruel. [ME]

flint·y (FLIN tee) *adj.* **flint·i·er, flint·i·est 1.** containing or resembling flint. **2.** unmerciless; unyielding.

flip (flip) *v.* **flipped, flip·ping** *v.t.* **1.** throw or move with a jerk; flick. **2.** propel, as a coin, by a fillip, or flick, of a finger. **3.** turn or toss over. —*v.i.* **4.** move with a jerk. **5.** turn over, esp. with a leap. **6.** *Slang* become angry; lose self-control; become excited or enthusiastic. —*n.* **1.** a quick, light snapping movement, as of a lash. **2.** a drink made with liquor, egg, etc. —*adj. Informal* pert; impertinent.

flip·pan·cy (FLIP ən see) *n. pl.* **•cies 1.** impertinence; sauciness. **2.** an impertinent act or remark.

flip·pant (FLIP ənt) *adj.* lacking due respect or seriousness; impertinent; saucy.

flip·per (FLIP ər) *n.* **1.** a broad, flat limb adapted for swimming, as in seals, etc. **2.** a paddlelike shoe used by skin divers and other swimmers.

flirt (flurt) *v.i.* **1.** act in a coquettish manner; play at love. **2.** expose oneself to something carelessly or lightly; *flirt* with danger. **3.** dart; flit. —*v.t.* **4.** move or toss quickly. —*n.* **1.** one who plays at love. **2.** a sudden movement.

flir·ta·tion (flur TAY shən) *n.* **1.** flirting behavior. **2.** a brief, casual love affair. — **flir·ta'tious** *adj.*

flit (flit) *v.i.* **flit·ted, flit·ting 1.** move or fly rapidly and lightly; dart; skim. **2.** pass away quickly. —*n.* a flitting movement. [ME *flitten* move] —**flit'ter** *n.*

flitch (flich) *n.* **1.** a salted and smoked cut of meat from a pig. **2.** a piece of timber cut lengthwise. [ME *flicche*]

flit·ter (FLIT ər) *v.t. & v.i.* flutter.

float (floht) *v.t.* **1.** rest on or at the surface of a liquid. **2.** remain suspended in a liquid or gas, esp. in the atmosphere. **3.** move lightly and effortlessly. **4.** go about from one person or thing to another in a random or unstable way. —*v.t.* **5.** cause to float. **6.** place (a stock, bond, etc.) on the market. **7.** launch (a business venture, scheme, etc.). —*n.* **1.** an object that floats in a liquid, as a piece of cork attached to a fishing line. **2.** an anchored raft. **3.** a display carried on a wheeled platform in parades or pageants. **4.** a soda or milk shake with a ball of ice cream in it. **5.** uncashed checks and notes in process of transfer. [ME *floten*]

floc·cu·late (FLOK yə LAYT) *v.t. & v.i.* **•lat·ed, •lat·ing** form into small, lumpy masses, as clouds. —**floc·cu·lant** (FLOK yə lənt) *n.* a chemical that causes such formation.

floc·cu·lent (FLOK yə lənt) *adj.* **1.** having soft, fluffy wool or hair. **2.** marked by or producing woolly tufts. —**floc'cu·lence** *n.*

flock¹ (flok) *n.* **1.** a group of animals of the same kind, esp. sheep or birds, feeding, living, or kept together. **2.** a group of members

of the same church or congregation. **3.** any group of persons under someone's care or supervision. **4.** a large number or assemblage of persons or things. —*v.i.* come or go in crowds. [ME]

flock² *n.* **1.** refuse wool, rags, etc., used to stuff furniture. **2.** wool, hair, etc. used for this. **3.** tiny fibers applied to fabric, wallpaper, etc. to give a velvetlike appearance: also **flock'ing.** —*v.t.* cover or fill with flock. [ME *flok*]

floe (floh) *n.* a large field of floating ice, or a detached section of this. [< Norw. *flo* flat layer]

flog (flog) *v.t.* **flogged, flog·ging** beat hard with a whip, strap, etc.

flood (flud) *n.* **1.** an unusually large flow or rise of water, esp. over land not usu. covered with water; deluge. **2.** the coming in of the tide; high tide: opposed to *ebb:* also **flood tide. 3.** any copious flow or stream. —*v.t.* **1.** cover or inundate with a flood. **2.** fill or overwhelm as with a flood. —*v.i.* **3.** rise to a flood; overflow. **4.** flow in a flood. [ME *flod*]

flood·light (FLUD LIT) *n.* **1.** a lamp that throws a bright, broad beam of light. **2.** the light of this lamp. —*v.t.* **•light·ed** or **•lit, •light·ing** illuminate with a floodlight.

flood plain a plain, subject to flooding by a river, and often formed by deposits of such flooding. **1. floor** (flor) *n.* **1.** the surface in a room or building on which one stands or walks. **2.** the area between two adjacent levels of a building; story. **3.** the bottom surface of any cavity: ocean *floor.* **4.** a level structure or platform for some special purpose: a threshing *floor.* **5.** the part of a legislative house, stock exchange, etc. where members gather to conduct business. **6.** the right to speak to an assembly: be given the *floor.* **7.** the lowest or minimum price for anything. —*v.t.* **1.** cover or provide with a floor. **2.** knock down, as to the floor. **3.** confound or vanquish completely. [ME *flor*]

floor·ing (FLOR ing) *n.* **1.** material for a floor. **2.** a floor; also, floors collectively.

floor leader a party leader in the U.S. Congress who directs the party's business on the floor.

floor show entertainment presented in a night club or cabaret.

flop (flop) *v.* **flopped, flop·ping** *v.i.* **1.** move, flap, or beat about heavily or clumsily. **2.** fall loosely and heavily. **3.** be completely unsuccessful. —*v.t.* **4.** cause to drop or fall heavily. **5.** flap in a loose, awkward, or noisy way, as wings. —*n.* **1.** the act of flopping. **2.** a flopping noise. **3.** a total failure. —**flop′py** *adj.* **•pi•er, •pi•est**

flop•house (FLOP HOWS) *n.* a cheap, shabby hotel.

flo•ra (FLOR ə) *n. pl.* **flo•ras** or **flo•rae** (-ee) the aggregate of plants growing in and usu. peculiar to a particular region or period. [< NL]

flo•ral (FLOR əl) *adj.* of, like, or pertaining to flowers.

flor•id (FLOR id) *adj.* **1.** having a ruddy color; flushed with redness. **2.** ornate; flowery. [< L *floridus* in bloom]

flo•rist (FLOR ist) *n.* a dealer in flowers.

floss (flaws) *n.* one of several light, silk or silklike substances or fibers, as tassels or corn or the outside fibers on the cocoon of a silkworm. [< OF *flosche* down] —**floss′y** *adj.* **floss•i•er, floss•i•est**

flo•ta•tion (floh TAY shən) *n.* **1.** the act or state of floating. **2.** the act of financing a business undertaking, as by an issue of stocks or bonds.

flo•til•la (floh TIL ə) *n.* a fleet of small vessels; also, a numerically small fleet. [< Sp.]

flot•sam (FLOT səm) *n.* parts of a wrecked ship, or goods from it, found floating in the sea. [< AF *floteson*]

flounce[1] (flowns) *n.* a gathered or pleated strip of material used for trimming skirts etc. —*v.t.* **flounced, flounc•ing** furnish with flounces. [ME *frouncen* curl]

flounce[2] *v.i.* **flounced, flounc•ing 1.** move or go with exaggerated tosses of the body, as in anger or petulance. **2.** plunge or flounder: said of animals. —**flounce** *n.*

floun•der[1] (FLOWN dər) *v.i.* **1.** struggle clumsily, as if mired. **2.** proceed in a stumbling or confused manner. —*n.* a stumbling or struggling motion.

floun•der[2] *n.* any of certain edible flatfish. [ME]

flour (flowr) *n.* **1.** a fine, soft, powder obtained by sifting and grinding the meal of a grain, esp. wheat. **2.** any finely powdered substance. —*v.t.* **1.** sprinkle or cover with flour. **2.** make into flour. [ME]

flour•ish (FLUR ish) *v.i.* **1.** grow; thrive. **2.** be at the peak of success or development. **3.** move with sweeping motions. —*v.t* **4.** wave about or brandish, as a weapon or flag. **5.** display ostentatiously. —*n.* **1.** a brandishing, as of a sword. **2.** a curved or decorative stroke in penmanship. **3.** something done

primarily for display. **4.** ornate language. **5.** *Music* **a** a fanfare. **b** a florid passage. [ME *florisshen*]

flout (flowt) *v.t.* **1.** scoff at; defy with open contempt. —*v.i.* **2.** express contempt. —*n.* a contemptuous act or remark. [Prob. ME *flouten* play the flute] —**flout′er** *n.*

flow (floh) *v.i.* **1.** move along steadily, as a fluid. **2.** well out or pour forth. **3.** move steadily and effortlessly. **4.** have pleasing continuity: The lines of the statue *flow.* **5.** hang in rich profusion, as hair. **6.** overflow; abound. **7.** of the tide, rise: opposed to *ebb.* **8.** arise; derive. —*n.* **1.** the act of flowing. **2.** something that flows, as a current or stream. **3.** a continuous stream or outpouring. **4.** the amount of that which flows. **5.** the manner of flowing. **6.** an overflowing. [ME *flowen*] —**flow′ing** *adj.*

flow•er (FLOW ər) *n.* **1.** a simple or complex cluster of petals, usu. brightly colored, and enclosing the reproductive parts of a seed-bearing plant; blossom. **2.** *Bot.* the reproductive structure of any plant. **3.** the condition in which the reproductive parts of a plant are mature, esp. when marked by open petals. **4.** the stage of fullest growth, development, or vigor; prime: usu. preceded by *in.* **5.** the finest or choicest part of something. —*v.i.* **1.** produce flowers; bloom. **2.** reach fullest development or vigor. [ME *flour* flower]

flow•er•y (FLOW ə ree) *adj.* **•er•i•er, •er•i•est 1.** full of or covered with flowers. **2.** ornate; highly embellished. **3.** having a floral pattern. —**flow′er•i•ness** *n.*

flown (flohn) past participle of FLY[1].

flu (floo) *n.* influenza.

flub (flub) *v.t. & v.i.* **flubbed, flub•bing** make a mess of (an opportunity, performance, etc.). —*n.* a botch or blunder.

fluc•tu•ate (FLUK choo AYT) *v.i.* **•at•ed, •at•ing 1.** change or vary often and in an irregular manner; waver. **2.** undulate. [< L *fluctuatus* flowed] —**fluc′tu•a′tion** *n.*

flue (floo) *n.* **1.** a pipe or tube through which smoke, hot air, steam, etc., is drawn off, as from a furnace or boiler. **2.** in an organ, a flue pipe.

flu•ent (FLOO ənt) *adj.* **1.** capable of speaking or writing with effortless ease. **2.** marked by smoothness, grace, and expressiveness. **3.** running freely, as a stream of water; fluid. [< L *fluere* flow] —**flu′en•cy** *n.*

fluff (fluf) *n.* **1.** a soft, light cluster of loosely gathered fibers of wool, cotton, etc. **2.** a mass of soft, fine feathers; down. **3.** an error, as by an actor, in speaking lines. —*v.t.* **1.** make (pillows, blankets, etc.) soft and light by patting or shaking. **2,** make an error in speaking (lines).

fluff•y (FLUF ee) *adj.* **fluff•i•er, fluff•i•est** of, covered with, or like fluff. —**fluff'i•ness** *n.*

flu•id (FLOO id) *adj.* **1.** capable of flowing; not solid. **2.** consisting of or pertaining to liquids. **3.** readily changing; not fixed. —*n.* a substance capable of flowing; esp., a liquid or gas. [< L *fluidus* flowing] —**flu•id'i•ty** *n.*

fluke[1] (flook) *n.* **1.** one of several parasitic worms having a flattened appearance. **2.** a flatfish or flounder. [ME *floke*]

fluke[2] *n.* **1.** the barb of an arrowhead, harpoon, etc. **2.** the triangular head at the end of either arm of an anchor.

fluke[3] *n.* **1.** a lucky stroke. **2.** anything that happens by chance. —**fluk'y** *adj.* **fluk•i•er, fluk•i•est** —**fluk'ey** *adj.* **fluk•i•er, fluk•i•est**

flume (floom) *n.* **1.** a narrow gap in a mountain through which a torrent passes. **2.** a chute or trough for carrying water. —*v.t.* **flumed, flum•ing** drain away, divert, or transport by means of a flume. [ME *flum* river]

flung (flung) past tense, past participle of FLING.

flunk (flungk) *v.t.* **1.** fail in (an examination, course, etc.). **2.** give a failing grade to. —*v.i.* **3.** fail, as in an examination. —*n.* a failure in an examination.

flun•ky (FLUNG kee) *n. pl.* **•kies 1.** a servile person. **2.** a manservant in livery. Also **flunk'ey.**

fluo•resce (fluu RES) *v.i.* **•resced, •resc•ing** become fluorescent.

fluo•res•cence (fluu RES əns) *n.* **1.** the property of absorbing radiation of a particular wavelength and emitting it as light. **2.** the light so produced. —**fluo•res'cent** *adj.*

fluorescent lamp a tubular lamp in which ultraviolet light is reradiated as visible light after striking a coating of phosphors.

fluor•i•date (FLUUR i DAYT) *v.t.* **•dat•ed, •dat•ing** add sodium fluoride to (drinking water), esp. to prevent tooth decay. —**fluor'i•da'tion** *n.*

fluor•o•scope (FLUUR ə SKOHP) *n.* a device for observing the internal structure of an opaque object by means of a fluorescent

screen and a beam of X-rays or other radiation. —**fluor•o•scop•ic** (FLUUR ə SKOP ik) *adj.*

flur•ry (FLUR ee) *v.* **•ried, •ry•ing** *v.t.* **1.** bewilder or confuse. —*v.i.* **2.** move in a flurry. —*n. pl.* **•ries 1.** a sudden commotion or excitement. **2.** a sudden, light gust of wind. **3.** a light, brief rain or snowfall, accompanied by small gusts. **4.** in the stock exchange, a sudden, brief increase in trading.

flush[1] (flush) *v.i.* **1.** blush. **2.** glow with a reddish brightness. **3.** flow or rush suddenly and copiously. **4.** be cleansed or purified through a quick gush of water etc. —*v.t.* **5.** wash out with a sudden gush of water. **6.** cause to glow red or blush. **7.** excite or elate: usu. in the passive: be *flushed* with success. —*n.* **1.** a heightened, reddish color. **2.** a pervasive feeling of being hot. **3.** a warm feeling of elation, excitement, etc. **4.** glowing bloom or freshness. **5.** a sudden gush or flow of water, etc.

flush[2] *adj.* **1.** even or level with another surface. **2.** of a line of print, even with the margin. **3.** having an even or unbroken surface. **4.** having plenty of money on hand. **5.** marked by prosperity. **6.** having a heightened, reddish color. **7.** of a blow, direct: a *flush* hit. —*adv.* **1.** in an even position with another surface; also, in alignment with a margin. **2.** in a direct manner; squarely.

flush[3] *n.* in poker etc., a hand of cards all of one suit.

flush[4] *v.t.* **1.** drive (an animal or person) from cover. —*v.i.* **2.** rush out or fly from cover. [ME *flusshen*]

flus•ter (FLUS tər) *v.t. & v.i.* make or become confused or agitated. —*n.* confusion or agitation of mind. [ME *flostren* hurry]

flute (floot) *n.* **1.** a tubular, reedless, woodwind instrument, equipped with holes and keys, and producing tones of a high pitch and clear quality. **2.** *Archit.* a rounded groove, as in a column. **3.** a small groove, as in pleated cloth. [ME *floute*] —**flut'ed** *adj.*

flut•ing (FLOO ting) *n.* flutes or grooves collectively.

flut•ist (FLOO tist) *n.* a flute player: also called *flautist.*

flut•ter (FLUT ər) *v.i.* **1.** wave or flap rapidly and irregularly. **2.** flap the wings rapidly in or as in erratic flight. **3.** move or proceed with irregular motion. **4.** dart about; flit. **5.** be excited or nervous. **6.** beat rapidly or unevenly, as the heart. —*v.t.* **7.** cause to

flutter; agitate. **8.** excite or confuse; fluster.
—*n.* **1.** a vibrating or quivering motion. **2.** nervous agitation; commotion. [ME *floteren*]

flu·vi·al (FLOO vee əl) *adj.* pertaining to, found in, or formed by a river. [ME]

flux (fluks) *n.* **1.** a flowing or discharge. **2.** constant movement or change. **3.** the flowing in of the tide. **4.** the act or process of melting. **5.** *Metall.* a substance that promotes the fusing of metals or that serves to purify metals or prevent undue oxidation of metal surfaces. **6.** *Physics* the rate of flow of fluids, heat, electricity, light, etc. —*v.t.* **1.** make fluid; melt. **2.** treat, as metal, with a flux. [ME] —**flux·ion** (FLUK shən) *n.*

fly[1] (flī) *v.* **flew** or (*for def.* 7) **flied, flown** or (*for def.* 7) **flied, fly·ing** *v.i.* **1.** move through the air on wings, as a bird. **2.** move or travel through the air by aircraft. **3.** rush or be propelled through the air, as an arrow. **4.** wave or flutter in the air. **5.** move or go by swiftly. **6.** flee; escape. **7.** in baseball, bat the ball high over the field. —*v.t.* **8.** cause to fly or float in the air. **9.** operate (an aircraft). **10.** transport by aircraft. **11.** flee from. —**fly at** attack suddenly. —**fly in the face of** defy openly. —**fly into** enter suddenly into (an outburst of rage etc.). —**fly off the handle** lose one's temper. —**fly out** in baseball, be retired by batting a ball high over the field and having it caught by an opposing player. —*n. pl.* **flies 1.** a flap of material concealing the zipper or other fastening in a garment, esp. in a pair of trousers. **2.** the flap at the entrance to a tent. **3.** in baseball, a ball batted high over the field: also called **fly ball. 4.** a flywheel. **5.** *pl.* in a theater, the space above the stage and behind the proscenium. [ME *flien*]

fly[2] *n. pl.* **flies 1.** any of various small, usu. two-winged insects; esp., the housefly. **2.** a fishhook to which colored bits of material, feathers, etc. are attached to resemble an insect. —**fly in the ointment** some small thing that detracts from the enjoyment of something. [ME *flie*]

fly·blown (FLĪ BLOHN) *adj.* spoiled or contaminated, as by eggs or larvae of flies.

fly·by (FLĪ BĪ) *n. pl.* **·bys** a flight, usu. at low altitude, by an aircraft or spacecraft past a designated location.

fly-by-night (FLĪ bī NĪT) *adj.* unreliable, esp. in business. —*n.* one who flees to cheat a creditor.

fly·er (FLĪ ər) see FLIER.

flying buttress *Archit.* a bracing structure connected to a wall by an arch to receive the outward thrust of the wall.

flying fish a fish with large pectoral fins that enable it to glide through the air.

flying saucer any of various unidentified flying objects vaguely resembling saucers.

fly·leaf (FLĪ LEEF) *n. pl.* **·leaves** (-LEEVZ) a blank sheet at the beginning or end of a book, pamphlet, etc.

fly·weight (FLĪ WAYT) *n.* a boxer weighing up to 112 pounds.

fly·wheel (FLĪ HWEEL) *n.* a wheel heavy enough to resist sudden changes of speed, used to secure uniform motion in the working parts of a machine.

foal (fohl) *n.* one of the young of an animal of the horse family. —*v.t. & v.i.* give birth to (a foal). [ME *fole*]

foam (fohm) *n.* **1.** a frothy mass of bubbles produced on the surface of a liquid by agitation, fermentation, etc. **2.** any frothy mass. —*v.i.* become foam or become covered with foam. [ME *fom*] —**foam′y** *adj.* **foam·i·er, foam·i·est**

foam rubber a firm, spongy rubber produced by chemical treatment.

fob[1] (fob) *n.* **1.** a small pocket at the front of trousers or a vest, designed to hold a watch. **2.** a short chain or ribbon attached to a watch and worn dangling from such a pocket; also, a small ornament attached to such a chain or ribbon.

fob[2] *v.t.* **fobbed, fob·bing 1.** dispose of by fraud or trickery: with *off*. **2.** put off by lies, evasion, etc. [ME *fobben*]

fo·cal (FOH kəl) *adj.* of or placed at a focus. [< NL *focalis*]

focal length *Optics* the distance from the center of a lens or curved mirror to the point where rays from a distant object converge. Also **focal distance.**

fo′c's′le (FOHK səl) see FORECASTLE.

fo·cus (FOH kəs) *n. pl.* **·cus·es** or **·ci** (-sī) **1.** *Optics* **a** the point at which light rays converge or appear to converge after being reflected or refracted. **b** the point at which such rays appear to diverge and where they would meet if their direction were reversed. **2.** the adjustment of the eye, a camera lens, etc. so that a clear image is produced. **3.** focal length. **4.** any central point, as of importance or interest. **5.** *Physics* the meeting point of any system of rays, beams, or waves. [< L. hearth] —*v.* **·cused, ·cus·ing** *v.t.* **1.** adjust the focus of (the eye, a lens, etc.) to receive a clear image. **2.** fix; concentrate. —*v.i.* **3.** become focused.

fod·der (FOD ər) *n.* coarse feed for horses, cattle, etc., as the stalks and leaves of field corn; raw material. —*v.t.* feed with or as with fodder. [ME]

foe (foh) *n.* an enemy; adversary. [ME *foo*]

fog (fog) *n.* **1.** a cloud formed at the surface of the earth by the condensation of atmospheric vapor and interfering to some extent with visibility. **2.** any hazy condition of the atmosphere. **3.** a state of mental bewilderment or blurred perception. —*v.t. & v.i.* **fogged, fog·ging 1.** become or cause to become foggy; mist. **2.** become or cause to become confused or bewildered. —**fog′gy** *adj.* **·gi·er, ·gi·est.**

fog bank fog seen at a distance, esp. at sea.

fog·bound (FOG BOWND) *adj.* prevented from traveling because of fog.

fog·horn (FOG HORN) *n.* a horn or whistle for sounding a warning during a fog.

fo·gy (FOH gee) *n. pl.* **·gies** a person of old-fashioned or ultraconservative notions: usu. preceded by *old.* Also **fo′gey.**

foi·ble (FOI bəl) *n.* a personal weakness or failing. [< F, obs. form of *faible* weak]

foil¹ (foil) *v.t.* prevent the success of; thwart. [ME *foilen* trample]

foil² *n.* **1.** a metal hammered or rolled into thin, pliant sheets. **2.** a person or thing serving by contrast to enhance the qualities of another. —*v.t.* **1.** apply foil to. **2.** intensify or set off by contrast. [ME, leaf]

foil³ *n.* **1.** a blunted, rapierlike implement used in fencing. **2.** *pl.* the art of fencing with a foil.

foist (foist) *v.t.* **1.** impose (someone or something) slyly or wrongfully; palm off. **2.** insert or introduce fraudulently. [< Du. *vuisten* hold in the hand]

fold¹ (fohld) *v.t.* **1.** turn back or bend over so that one part covers or lies alongside another. **2.** close or collapse: often with *up.* **3.** wrap up; enclose. **4.** place together and interlock: *fold* one's hands; also, bring (wings) close to the body. **5.** embrace; enfold. **6.** wind; coil: with *about, around,* etc. **7.** in cooking, mix into other ingredients by gently turning one part over the other: with *in.* —*v.i.* **8.** become folded. **9.** *Informal* **a** fail financially; close. **b** collapse, as from exhaustion. —*n.* **1.** one part folded over another. **2.** the space between two folded

parts. **3.** the crease made by folding. **4.** the act of folding. [ME *folden*]

fold² *n.* **1.** a pen, as for sheep. **2.** the sheep enclosed in a pen. **3.** a flock of sheep. **4.** a group of people, as the congregation of a church, having a leader, a common purpose, etc. —*v.t.* shut up in a fold, as sheep. [ME]

fold·er (FOHL dər) *n.* **1.** one who or that which folds. **2.** a road map, timetable, etc., designed to be folded. **3.** a binder for loose papers.

fol·de·rol (FOL də ROL) *n.* **1.** nonsense. **2.** a useless ornament; a trifle.

fo·li·age (FOH lee ij) *n.* **1.** the growth of leaves on a tree or other plant; also, leaves collectively. **2.** an ornamental representation of leaves, flowers, and branches. [ME *foilage*]

fo·li·a·tion (FOH lee AY shən) *n.* **1.** *Bot.* **a** the act of bursting into leaf, or the state of being in leaf. **b** the arrangement or formation of leaves in a bud. **2.** the consecutive numbering of the leaves of a book.

fo·li·o (FOH lee OH) *n. pl.* **·li·os 1.** a sheet of paper folded once to form four pages (two leaves) of a book. **2.** a book, manuscript, etc. having oversize pages made from such a sheet; also, the size of such a work. **3.** a leaf of a book, manuscript, etc., only one side of which is numbered. **4.** the number of a page. —*v.t.* **·li·oed, ·li·o·ing** number in order the pages of (a book, manuscript, etc.). [ME]

folk (fohk) *n. pl.* **folk** (*esp. def. 1*) or **folks 1.** a people; nation. **2.** *Usu. pl.* people of a particular group or class: old *folks.* **3.** *pl.* people in general: *folks* will talk. **4.** *pl. Informal* one's family, esp. one's parents: My *folks* always help. —*adj.* originating among or characteristic of the common people. [ME]

folk·lore (FOHK LOR) *n.* **1.** the traditions, beliefs, customs, stories, etc., preserved among the common people. **2.** the study of folk cultures. —**folk′lor′ic** *adj.*

folk song 1. a song, usu. of unknown authorship, originating among the common people and handed down orally. **2.** a song copying the style of such a song. —**folk singer** *n.*

fol·li·cle (FOL i kəl) *n. Anat.* a small cavity or sac in certain parts of the body, having a protective or secretory function. [< L *folliculus* small bag]

fol·low (FOL oh) *v.t.* **1.** go or come after and in the same direction. **2.** succeed in time or order. **3.** pursue. **4.** hold to the course of: *follow* a road. **5.** obey or conform to. **6.** imitate. **7.** watch or observe closely. **8.** have an active interest in: *follow* sports. **9.** understand. **10.** be a consequence of. **11.** be under the leadership or authority of. —*v.i.* **12.** move or come after. **13.** pay attention. **14.** understand. **15.** come as a result or consequence. —**follow suit 1.** in card games, play a card of the suit led. **2.** follow another's example. —**follow through 1.** swing to the full extent of a stroke, as in tennis or golf. **2.** perform fully. —**follow up 1.** bring to full completion. **2.** take further action regarding. —*n.* the act of following. [ME *folwen*]

fol•low•er (FOL oh ər) *n.* one who or that which follows; esp., a disciple.

fol•low•ing (FOL oh ing) *adj.* that comes next in time or sequence. —*n.* a body of attendants or disciples.

fol•low-through (FOL oh THROO) *n.* **1.** in sports, the continuation and full completion of a motion. **2.** any continuing or completion.

fol•low-up (FOL oh UP) *n.* **1.** the act of following up. **2.** something, as an action or letter, used in following up.

fol•ly (FOLee) *n. pl.* **•lies 1.** foolishness. **2.** a foolish idea or action. **3.** a foolish or ruinous undertaking. [ME *folie*]

fo•ment (foh MENT) *v.t.* **1.** stir up or instigate (rebellion, discord, etc.). **2.** treat with warm water or medicated lotions, as in applying a dressing. [ME *fomenten*] —**fo′men•ta′tion** *n.*

fond (fond) *adj.* **1.** having affection (for someone or something specified): with *of*. **2.** loving or deeply affectionate. **3.** doting. **4.** beloved; cherished. [ME, foolish]

fon•dle (FON dl) *v.t.* **•dled, •dling** handle lovingly; caress. —**fon′dler** *n.*

fon•due (fon DOO) *n.* **1.** a saucelike dish of melted cheese into which pieces of bread are dipped. **2.** various other dishes served in a similar manner. [< F]

font[1] (font) *n.* **1.** a basin, often of stone, for the water used in baptism. **2.** a receptacle for holy water. **3.** source; origin. [ME]

font[2] *n. Printing* an assortment of type of a particular face and size. [< MF *fonte* founding]

food (food) *n.* **1.** that which is ingested by an organism for the maintenance of life and the growth and repair of tissues. **2.** nourishment in solid form as opposed to liquid

form. **3.** anything nourishing: *food* for gossip. [ME *fode*]

food chain the sequence in an ecological system in which organisms use lower organisms as food.

food poisoning a gastrointestinal disorder caused by eating food contaminated with bacteria, chemicals, etc.

food•stuff (FOOD stuf) *n.* **1.** any substance suitable for food. **2.** any substance that enters into the composition of food.

fool (fool) *n.* **1.** a person lacking understanding, judgment, or common sense. **2.** a clown formerly kept by noblemen for entertainment; jester. **3.** one who has been duped or imposed upon. —*v.i.* **1.** act like a fool. **2.** act, speak, etc. in a playful or teasing manner. —*v.t.* **3.** make a fool of; deceive. —**fool around 1.** waste time on trifles. **2.** play idly with. **3.** engage in casual love affairs. **4.** experiment: with *with*. —**fool with 1.** meddle with. **2.** play or toy aimlessly with —*adj. Informal* stupid or silly. [ME *fol*]

fool•er•y (FOO lə ree) *n. pl.* **•er•ies** foolish behavior, speech, etc.; also, an instance of this.

fool•har•dy (FOOL HAHR dee) *adj.* **•di•er, •di•est** bold in a reckless way. —**fool′har′di•ness** *n.*

fool•ish (FOO lish) *adj.* **1.** marked by or showing a lack of good sense; silly. **2.** resulting from folly or stupidity. **3.** ridiculous; absurd. —**fool′ish•ness** *n.*

fool•proof (FOOL PROOF) *adj.* **1.** so simple and strong as to be incapable of damage or harm even through misuse. **2.** having no weak points; infallible: a *foolproof* plan.

foot (fuut) *n. pl.* **feet 1.** the terminal section of the limb of a vertebrate animal, upon which it stands or moves. **2.** any part of an animal, plant, or object corresponding in form or position to the foot. **3.** the part of a boot or stocking that covers the wearer's foot. **4.** the lower part of anything; base; esp.: **a** the base of a hill or mountain. **b** the part of a bed, grave, etc. where the feet rest. **c** the bottom of a page, ladder, etc. **5.** the inferior part or section: the *foot* of the class. **6.** a measure of length, equivalent to 12 inches. **7.** in prosody, a group of syllables forming a major unit of poetic rhythm. —**on foot** walking or standing. —**put one's foot down** act firmly. —*v.i.* **1.** walk or dance. —*v.t.* **2.** move on or through by foot. **3.** pay, as a bill. [ME]

foot•age (FUUT ij) *n.* **1.** length expressed in

feet. **2.** a segment of exposed motion-picture film or videotape, usu. containing a scene or relating to a subject.

foot·ball (FUUT nawl) *n.* **1.** a game played between two teams of 11 players (12 in Canada) on a field with goals at each end. **2.** the inflated, leather-covered ball with an ellipsodal shape used in this game. **3.** in Great Britain, soccer.

foot·bridge (FUUT BRIJ) *n.* a bridge for pedestrians.

foot-can·dle (FUUT KAN dl) *n.* the illumination thrown on one square foot of surface at a distance of one foot from a uniform source of light or one candle.

foot·fall (FUUT FAWL) *n.* the sound of a footstep.

foot·hill (FUUT HIL) *n.* a low hill at the base of a mountain.

foot·hold (FUUT HOHLD) *n.* a place on which the foot can rest securely, as in climbing.

foot·ing (FUUT ing) *n.* **1.** a place on which to stand, walk, or climb securely. **2.** a foothold. **3.** social or professional status in relation to others; standing.

foot·lights (FUUT LITS) *n. pl.* in a theater, lights in a row near the front of the stage, nearly level with the performers' feet.

foot·loose (FUUT LOOS) *adj.* free to travel or do as one pleases; unattached.

foot·note (FUUT NOHT) *n.* an explanatory note or reference to the text, usu. at the bottom of a page. —*v.t.* **-not·ed, ·not·ing** furnish with footnotes.

foot·path (FUUT PATH) *n.* a narrow path for persons on foot.

foot·print (FUUT PRINT) *n.* the outline or impression made by a foot on a surface.

foot·rest (FUUT REST) *n.* something on which the feet can be propped or rested.

foot·sore (FUUT SOR) *adj.* having sore or tired feet.

foot·step (FUUT STEP) *n.* **1.** the action of taking a step with the foot. **2.** the distance covered by a step. **3.** the sound made by a foot in stepping. **4.** a footprint. **5.** a step of a stairway etc.

foot·stool (FUUT STOOL) *n.* a low stool used as a footrest.

foot·wear (FUUT WAIR) *n.* articles worn on the feet, as shoes.

foot·work (FUUT WURK) *n.* **1.** use or control of the feet, as in boxing or tennis. **2.** maneuvering.

fop (fop) *n.* a man overly concerned with

fashion; a dandy. [ME *foppe*] —**fop'pish** *adj.*

for (for) *prep.* **1.** to the extent of: flat *for* miles. **2.** through the duration of: *for* weeks. **3.** to the number or amount of: a check *for* six dollars. **4.** at the cost or payment of: *for* a dollar. **5.** on account of. **6.** in honor of: She is named *for* her mother. **7.** appropriate to. **8.** in place of: using a table *for* a desk. **9.** in favor, support, or approval of. **10.** in the interest or behalf of. **11.** directed toward: an eye *for* bargains. **12.** as affecting (in a particular way): good *for* your health. **13.** sent, given, or assigned to. **14.** in proportion to: big *for* his age. **15.** as the equivalent to or requital of: blow *for* blow. **16.** in spite of. **17.** in order to reach or go *toward*. **18.** in order to find or obtain: looking *for* a hat. **19.** at (a particular time or occasion): meet *for* the last time. **20.** as being or seeming: We took him *for* an honest man. **21.** in consideration of the usual characteristics of: She is tall *for* a woman. **22.** with the purpose of. —*conj.* inasmuch as; because. [ME]

for·age (FOR ij) *n.* **1.** food suitable for cattle or other domestic animals; fodder. **2.** a search or raid to find food or supplies. —*v.* **·aged, ·ag·ing** *v.i.* **1.** search about, esp. for food or supplies. **2.** make a raid to get supplies. —*v.t.* **3.** search through for food, supplies, etc. **4.** obtain by a search or raid. **5.** provide with food or supplies. [ME] —**for' ag·er** *n.*

for·ay (FOR ay) *v.t. & v.i.* plunder; raid. —*n.* an expedition or raid, as for plunder. [ME *forraien* plunder]

for·bear¹ (for BAIR) *v.* **·bore, ·borne, ·bear·ing** *v.t.* **1.** refrain or abstain from (some action). **2.** cease or desist from. —*v.i.* **3.** abstain. **4.** be patient. [ME *forberen*] —**for·bear'ance** *n.*

for·bear² (FOR BAIR) see FOREBEAR.

for·bear·ing (for BAIR ing) *adj.* patient.

for·bid (fər BID) *v.t.* **·bade** (-BAD) or **·bad, ·bid·den** or **·bid, ·bid·ding** **1.** command (a person) not to do something; prohibit from doing, having, etc. **2.** prohibit the doing, use, etc. of. **3.** have the effect of preventing; hinder. [ME *forbeden*] —**for·bid·dance** (fər BID ns) *n.*

for·bid·ding (fər BID ing) *adj.* **1.** grim and unfriendly. **2.** threatening; ominous.

for·bore (for BOR) past tense of FORBEAR¹.

for·borne (for BORN) past participle of FORBEAR¹.

force (fors) *n.* **1.** power or energy; strength.

2. power exerted on any resisting person or thing; coercion. **3.** power or influence; ability to produce an effect. **4.** a body of individuals belonging to one of a nation's military divisions: the armed *forces*. **5.** any body of individuals organized for some specific work; police *force*. **6.** *Physics* anything that changes or tends to change the state of rest or motion in a body. —**in force 1.** still operative. **2.** with no one missing. —*v.t.* **forced, forc·ing 1.** compel; coerce. **2.** get or obtain by or as by force. **3.** bring forth or about by or as by effort. **4.** drive or move despite resistance. **5.** assault and capture, as a fortification. **6.** open by force, as a passage or lock. **7.** press or impose upon someone as by force. **8.** stimulate the growth of artificially, as plants in a hothouse. [ME] — **for'ci·ble** *adj.*

forced (forst) *adj.* **1.** done under force; compulsory. **2.** strained; affected: *forced* laughter. **3.** done in an emergency.

force·ful (FORS fəl) *adj.* full of or done with force; vigorous; effective.

force·meat (FORS MEET) *n.* finely chopped, seasoned meat. [< *force* alter. of F *farse* stuffing]

for·ceps (FOR səps) *n. pl.* **·ceps** a pair of pincers used in surgery, dentistry, etc. [< L, tongs]

ford (ford) *n.* a shallow place in a stream, river, etc., that can be crossed by wading. — *v.t.* cross (a river etc.) at a shallow place. [ME] —**ford'a·ble** *adj.*

fore (for) *adj.* situated at or toward the front; anterior. —*n.* the front part of something. —**to the fore 1.** to or at the front part of something. **2.** in or into a prominent or conspicuous position. —*interj.* in golf, a cry made to warn anyone standing in the line of a ball. —*adv. Naut.* at or toward the bow of a ship.

fore- *prefix* **1.** prior in time or place. **2.** situated at or near the front.

fore·arm[1] (FOR AHRM) *n.* the part of the arm between the elbow and the wrist.

fore·arm[2] (for AHRM) *v.t.* arm beforehand.

fore·bear (FOR BAIR) *n.* an ancestor: also spelled *forbear*.

fore·bode (for BOHD) *v.t. & v.i.* **·bod·ed, ·bod·ing 1.** indicate in advance; portend. **2.** have a premonition of (something evil or harmful).

fore·cast (FOR KAST) *v.t.* **·cast** or **·cast·ed, ·cast·ing 1.** calculate beforehand, esp. to predict (weather conditions). **2.** fore-

shadow. —*n.* a prediction. —**fore'cast'er** *n.*

fore·cas·tle (FOHK səl) *n. Naut.* **1.** that part of the upper deck of a ship located forward of the mast nearest the bow. **2.** a section of a merchant ship near the bow, in which the sailors' living quarters are located. Also spelled *fo'c's'le*.

fore·close (for KLOHZ) *v.* **·closed, ·clos·ing** *v.t.* **1.** *Law* **a** deprive (a mortgagor in default) of the right to redeem mortgaged property. **b** take away the power to redeem (a mortgage or pledge). **2.** shut out; exclude. —*v.i.* **3.** foreclose a mortgage. [ME *forclosen* exclude] —**fore·clo'sure** (for KLOH zhər) *n.*

fore·fa·ther (FOR FATH ər) *n.* an ancestor.

fore·front (FOR FRUNT) *n.* **1.** the very front of something. **2.** the position of most importance.

fore·go[1] (for GOH) *v.t. & v.i.* **·went, ·gone, ·go·ing** precede in time, place, etc. [< OE *foregān*]

fore·go[2] see FORGO.

fore·go·ing (for GOH ing) *adj.* previous; preceding; antecedent.

fore·gone (for GAWN) *adj.* already gone, finished, or determined.

fore·ground (FOR GROWND) *n.* **1.** the part of a landscape, picture, etc., nearest or represented as nearest to the spectator. **2.** the position of most prominence.

fore·hand (FOR HAND) *adj.* **1.** of or pertaining to a stroke in tennis etc., in which the palm of the hand faces the direction of the stroke. **2.** first or foremost; leading. — **fore·hand** *n.*

fore·head (FOR id) *n.* the part of the face from the eyebrows to the hair.

for·eign (FOR in) *adj.* **1.** belonging to or located in, characteristic of, or concerned with another country, region, society, etc. **2.** unfamiliar; strange. **3.** occurring in a place or context in which it is not normally found. [ME *forein*] —**for·eign·er** (FOR ə nər) *n.* a native or citizen of a foreign country or region; alien.

fore·judge (for JUJ) *v.t. & v.i.* **·judged, ·judg·ing** judge in advance.

fore·man (FOR mən) *n. pl.* **·men 1.** the overseer of a body of workers. **2.** the chairperson of a jury. —**fore·la·dy** *n.fem. pl.* **·dies.**

fore·most (FOR MOHST) *adj.* first in place, rank, etc.; chief. [ME *formest*] — **fore·most** *adv.*

fore·named (FOR NAYMD) *adj.* previously named or mentioned.

fore·noon (FOR NOON) *n.* the period of daylight preceding midday; morning.

fo·ren·sic (fə REN sik) *adj.* relating to, characteristic of, or used in courts of law or public debate. [< L *forensis* of the forum]

fore·or·dain (FOR or DAYN) *v.t.* 1. decree or appoint in advance. 2. fix the fate of in advance.

fore·run·ner (FOR RUN ər) *n.* 1. one who or that which precedes another; also, an ancestor. 2. one who proclaims the coming of another. 3. an omen. [ME *forrenner*]

fore·see (for SEE) *v.t.* •saw, •seen, •see·ing see or know in advance. [ME] —**fore·see′a·ble** *adj.*

fore·shad·ow (for SHAD oh) *v.t.* give an advance indication of; presage.

fore·short·en (for SHOR tn) *v.t.* in drawing, to shorten parts of (an object) so as to create the illusion of depth and distance.

fore·sight (FOR sīt) *n.* 1. the act or capacity of foreseeing. 2. prudent anticipation of the future. —**fore′sight′ed·ness** *n.*

fore·skin (FOR SKIN) *n. Anat.* the prepuce.

for·est (FOR ist) *n.* a large tract of land covered with trees; also, the trees themselves. —*adj.* of, pertaining to, or inhabiting forests. —*v.t.* plant with trees; make a forest of. [ME]

fore·stall (for STAWL) *v.t.* 1. hinder, prevent, or guard against in advance. 2. deal with or realize beforehand; anticipate. [ME *forstallen* waylay]

for·est·a·tion (for ə STAY shən) *n.* the planting of trees so as to make a forest. —**for·est·er** (FOR ə stər) *n.* one skilled in forestry.

for·est·ry (FOR ə stree) *n.* 1. the science of forest management. 2. forest land.

fore·tell (for TEL) *v.t. & v.i.* •told, •tell·ing tell of or about in advance; predict; prophesy.

fore·thought (FOR thawt) *n.* 1. advance consideration. 2. prudence; foresight.

for·ev·er (for EV ər) *adv.* 1. throughout eternity. 2. incessantly; constantly.

for·ev·er·more (for EV ər MOR) *adv.* forever: an intensive form.

fore·warn (for WORN) *v.t.* warn in advance.

fore·word (FOR WURD) *n.* an introductory statement preceding the text of a book.

for·feit (FOR fit) *n.* the giving up or loss of something as a penalty for an offense, etc.; also, that which is lost. —*v.t.* incur the deprivation of as a penalty. —*adj.* taken away or lost as a penalty. [ME *forfet*]

for·fei·ture (FOR fi chər) *n.* 1. the giving up or loss of something by way of penalty. 2. that which is forfeited.

for·gath·er (for GATH ər) *v.i.* 1. meet or assemble. 2. meet by chance. 3. associate or converse socially.

for·gave (fər GAYV) past tense of FORGIVE.

forge¹ (forj) *n.* 1. an apparatus for heating and softening metal. 2. a place in which such an apparatus is used. 3. a furnace for melting or refining metals. —*v.* forged, forg·ing 1. heat (metal) in a forge and work into shape; also, to produce or form as if by hammering into shape. 2. counterfeit (a signature etc.). —*v.i.* 3. produce a fraudulent imitation of something. 4. work at a forge. [ME *forgen*]

forge² *v.i.* forged, forg·ing advance despite difficulties etc.: *forge* ahead.

for·ger·y (FOR jə ree) *n. pl.* •ger·ies 1. the act of making fraudulent imitations. 2. a fraudulent imitation.

for·get (fər GET) *v.* •got, •got·ten or •got, •get·ting *v.t.* 1. be unable to recall (something). 2. neglect (to do or take something). 3. lose interest in or regard for. —*v.i.* 4. lose remembrance of something. —**forget oneself** 1. be unselfish. 2. lose self-control. 3. be lost in thought. [ME *foryeten*] —**for·get′ta·ble** *adj.*

for·get·ful (fər GET fəl) *adj.* 1. inclined to forget. 2. neglectful; inattentive. —**for·get′ful·ness** *n.*

for·give (fər GIV) *v.* •gave, •giv·en, •giv·ing *v.t.* 1. grant pardon for or remission of (something). 2. cease to blame or feel resentment against. 3. remit, as a debt. —*v.i.* 4. show forgiveness; grant pardon. [ME *foryiven*] —**for·giv′a·ble** *adj.*

for·giv·ing (fər GIV ing) *adj.* disposed to forgive; merciful.

for·go (for GOH) *v.t.* •went, •gone, •go·ing give up or refrain from; go without. Also spelled *forego.* [ME *forgon* pass over]

for·got (fər GOT) past tense, past participle of FORGET.

for·got·ten (fər GOT ən) past participle of FORGET.

fork (fork) *n.* 1. an implement with two or more prongs, as: **a** a utensil used at table. **b** an agricultural tool used for digging, tossing, etc. 2. the division of something into branches; also, the point at which this division begins, or any one of the parts. —v.t. **1.** convey, lift, etc. with a fork. **2.** give the shape of a fork to. —v.i. **3.** divide into branches. [ME *forke*]

forked (forkt) *adj.* having a fork or forking parts.

fork•lift (FORK LIFT) *n.* a powered machine that lifts and moves heavy objects by means of a two-pronged part inserted under the object.

for•lorn (for LORN) *adj.* **1.** left in distress; abandoned. **2.** wretched; desolate. **3.** hopeless. [ME *foreloren* lost]

form (form) *n.* **1.** the shape or contour of something. **2.** the body of a living being. **3.** a mold, frame, etc. **4.** the particular state, character, etc. in which something presents itself. **5.** a specific type or species. **6.** the style or manner of a poem, play, picture, etc. **7.** proper arrangement or order. **8.** the manner in which something is done: diving *form.* **9.** a document having spaces for the insertion of names, dates, etc. **10.** mere outward formality; convention. **11.** a model formula or draft, as of a letter. —v.t. **1.** give shape or form to; mold. **2.** devise, as a plan. **3.** combine or organize into, as a club. **4.** develop or acquire, as a habit. **5.** be an element of. —v.i. **6.** take shape; assume a specific pattern or arrangement. **7.** begin to exist. [ME *forme*] —**form′less** *adj.*

-form combining form like; in the shape of: *cuneiform* [< L *-formis*]

for•mal (FOR məl) *adj.* **1.** based on established methods or conventions. **2.** requiring elaborate detail, ceremony, dress, etc. **3.** appropriate for ceremonial occasions. **4.** binding and valid: *formal* agreement. **5.** pertaining to external appearance or structure, as of a poem. **6.** pertaining to study in regular academic institutions. **7.** of language, more elaborate or stylized than common speech. —n. something formal in character, as an evening gown or a formal dance.

for•mal•de•hyde (for MAL də HID) *n.* *Chem.* a colorless, pungent gas used in solution as an antiseptic, preservative, etc.

for•mal•ism (FOR mə LIZ əm) *n.* scrupulous observance of prescribed forms.

for•mal•i•ty (for MAL i tee) *n. pl.* **•ties 1.** the state, quality, or practice of being formal. **2.** excessive devotion to outward form. **3.** a proper or customary method, practice, or observance. [< L *formalitas*]

for•mal•ize (FOR mə LIZ) *v.* •ized, •iz•ing

v.t. **1.** make formal. **2.** give form to. —v.i. **3.** be formal; act formally.

for•mat (FOR mat) *n.* **1.** the form, size, and general style of a publication. **2.** the general form or arrangement of anything. —v.t. •mat•ted, •mat•ting provide with a format; produce in a specified form. [< F]

for•ma•tion (for MAY shən) *n.* **1.** the act or process of forming, or the state of being formed. **2.** that which is formed. **3.** the manner in which a thing is shaped or formed. **4.** *Mil.* the arrangement of troops, tanks, aircraft, etc. **5.** *Geol.* mineral deposits, or rock masses, having common characteristics. [ME *formacioun*]

form•a•tive (FOR mə tiv) *adj.* **1.** having power to shape or mold: a *formative* influence. **2.** of or pertaining to formation or development: *formative* years.

for•mer (FOR mər) *adj.* **1.** being the first of two persons or things referred to: often preceded by *the.* **2.** previous: my *former* colleague. **3.** earlier: *former* times. [ME]

for•mer•ly (FOR mər lee) *adv.* previously.

for•mi•da•ble (FOR mi də bəl) *adj.* **1.** exciting fear or dread by reason of strength, size, etc. **2.** extremely difficult. [ME]

for•mu•la (FOR myə lə) *n. pl.* **•las** or **•lae** (-LEE) **1.** an exact or prescribed method for doing something. **2.** a fixed order or form of words. **3.** a prescription or recipe; also, the mixture prepared. **4.** a liquid milk substitute fed to babies. **5.** *Math.* a rule or combination expressed in algebraic or symbolic form. **6.** *Chem.* a symbolic representation of a chemical compound. [< L, rule]

for•mu•late (FOR myə LAYT) *v.t.* •lat•ed, •lat•ing **1.** express in a formula. **2.** express in a systematic form. **3.** prepare according to a formula. **4.** devise, as a policy. —**for′•mu•la′tion** *n.*

for•ni•cate (FOR ni KAYT) *v.i.* •cat•ed, •cat•ing commit fornication. [< LL *fornicatus* having patronized prostitutes] —**for′ni•ca′tor** *n.*

for•ni•ca•tion (FOR ni KAY shən) *n.* voluntary sexual intercourse between persons not married to one another.

for•sake (for SAYK) *v.t.* •sook, •sak•en, •sak•ing **1.** renounce or relinquish. **2.** abandon; desert. [ME *forsaken* reject]

for•swear (for SWAIR) *v.* •swore, •sworn, •swear•ing *v.t.* **1.** renounce or abandon emphatically or upon oath. **2.** deny absolutely. —v.i. **3.** swear falsely; commit perjury. [ME *forsweren*]

fort

fort (fort) *n.* **1.** a fortified enclosure or structure for military defense. **2.** a permanent army post. [< MF]

forte[1] (fort) *n.* that which one does with excellence. [< MF]

for•te[2] (FOR tay) *adj. Music* loud; forceful. [< Ital.] **—for′te** *adv.*

forth (forth) *adv.* **1.** forward in place, time, or order. **2.** out, as from seclusion etc. **3.** away or out, as from a place of origin: go *forth.* **—and so forth** and the rest; and so on. [ME]

forth•com•ing (FORTH KUM ing) *adj.* **1.** drawing near in time. **2.** ready or about to appear, arrive, etc. **3.** available or produced when expected or due. **—n.** arrival or appearance of something due or expected.

forth•right (FORTH RĪT) *adj.* **1.** candid; frank. **2.** going forward in a straight line; direct. **—forth′right′ly** *adv.*

forth•with (FORTH WITH) *adv.* immediately.

for•ti•fi•ca•tion (FOR tə fi KAY shən) *n.* **1.** the act, art, or science of fortifying. **2.** that which fortifies, as walls, ditches, etc. **3.** a military place of defense. [ME]

for•ti•fy (FOR tə FĪ) *v.* **•fied, •fy•ing** *v.t.* **1.** strengthen or reinforce, esp. against attack. **2.** give physical or moral strength to. **3.** confirm. **4.** strengthen, as wine, by adding alcohol. **5.** enrich (food) by adding minerals, vitamins, etc. **—v.i. 6.** raise defensive works. [ME *fortifien*]

for•tis•si•mo (for TIS ə MOH) *Music adj.* very loud. **—adv.** very loudly. **—n. pl. •mos** a fortissimo note, chord, or passage. [< Ital., loudest]

for•ti•tude (FOR ti TOOD) *n.* courage and strength of mind in the face of adversity or peril. [ME]

fort•night (FORT NĪT) *n.* two weeks. [ME *fourtenight*, lit., fourteen nights] **—fort′night′ly** *adj. & adv.*

for•tress (FOR tris) *n.* **1.** a fortified place. **2.** any place of security. [ME *forteresse*]

for•tu•i•tous (for TOO i təs) *adj.* occurring by chance rather than by design; accidental. [< L *fortuitus* by chance] **—for•tu′i•tous•ly** *adv.*

for•tu•i•ty (for TOO i tee) *n. pl. •ties* a chance occurrence; also, chance.

for•tu•nate (FOR chə nit) *adj.* **1.** happening by a favorable chance; lucky. **2.** favored with good fortune. **—for′tu•nate•ly** *adv.*

for•tune (FOR chən) *n.* **1.** that which happens or is to happen to one, whether good or bad. **2.** luck or chance, esp. when favorable. **3.** an amount of wealth or possessions. **4.** a particular condition or state of life, usu. prosperous. [ME *fortunat*]

for•tune-tell•er (FOR chən TEL ər) *n.* one who claims to foretell events in a person's future. **—for′tune-tell′ing** *n. & adj.*

for•ty (FOR tee) *n. pl. •ties* the sum of thirty and ten: a cardinal number written 40, XL. [ME *fourti*] **—for•ty** *adj.* **—for′ti•eth** *adj. & n.*

forty winks *Informal* a nap.

fo•rum (FOR əm) *n. pl.* **fo•rums, fo•ra** (FOR ə) **1.** the public marketplace of an ancient Roman city, where legal and political business was transacted. **2.** a tribunal; court. **3.** an assembly for discussion of public affairs. [ME]

for•ward (FOR wərd) *adv.* **1.** toward what is ahead or in front; onward. Also **for′wards.** **2.** at or in the front part, as of a ship. **3.** out into a conspicuous position; to the forefront. **—forward of** in front of. **—adj. 1.** being at or near the front. **2.** moving or directed toward a point lying ahead. **3.** bold or presumptuous. **4.** developing or developed earlier than usual; precocious. **5.** extremely progressive or unconventional, as in political opinions. **6.** made or done in advance. **—n.** in basketball, hockey, etc., a player, usu. offensive, in a forward position. **—v.t. 1.** help onward or ahead. **2.** send onward; esp., send (mail) on to a new address. [ME] **—for′ward•ness** (-nis) *n.*

fos•sil (FOS əl) *n.* **1.** the remains of plants or animals, preserved in the rocks of the earth's crust. **2.** some petrified trace of the existence of an early organism, as a petrified footprint. **3.** one who or that which is out of date. [< L *fossilis* dug up] **—fos′sil** *adj.*

fos•sil•ize (FOS e LĪZ) *v.* **•ized, •iz•ing** *v.t.* **1.** change into a fossil; petrify. **2.** make antiquated or out of date. **—v.i. 3.** become a fossil. **—fos′sil•i•za′tion** *n.*

fos•ter (FAW stər) *v.t.* **1.** bring up (a child); rear. **2.** promote growth or development of: *foster* talent. **3.** keep alive (feelings etc.) within oneself; cherish. [ME]

foster child a child reared by foster parents.

foster parent one bringing up a child not one's own by birth or adoption.

fought (fawt) past tense, past participle of FIGHT.

foul (fowl) *adj.* **1.** offensive or revolting to the senses; disgusting. **2.** full of dirt or impure matter; filthy. **3.** spoiled or rotten, as food. 4. unfavorable; adverse: *foul* weather. 5. obscene; vulgar. 6. morally offensive; wicked. 7. unjust; unfair. 8. impeded or entangled: a *foul* anchor. 9. in baseball etc., designating boundary lines (**foul lines**) in a playing area; also, designating a ball that falls outside these lines. 10. very bad; unsatisfactory. —*n.* 1. an act of fouling, colliding, or becoming entangled. 2. in baseball, a ball batted outside of the foul lines: also **foul ball.** 3. a breach of rule in various sports. —*v.t.* 1. make foul or dirty. 2. dishonor; disgrace. 3. clog or choke, as a drain. 4. entangle or snarl, as a rope. 5. cover or encumber (a ship's bottom) with barnacles, seaweed, etc. 6. collide with. 7. in sports, commit a foul against. 8. in baseball, bat (the ball) outside of the foul lines. —*v.i.* 9. become foul or dirty. 10. become clogged or encumbered. 11. become entangled. 12. collide. 13. in sports, violate a rule. 14. in baseball, bat a foul ball. —**foul up** *Informal* 1. throw into disorder or confusion. 2. blunder. [ME *ful*] —**foul′ly** *adv.*

fou•lard (fə LAHRD) *n.* 1. a lightweight, satiny fabric, usu. with a printed design. 2. a scarf, necktie, or other article made of this fabric. [< F]

foul•mouthed (FOWL MOWTHD) *adj.* using abusive or obscene language.

foul play 1. in games and sports, a violation of rule. 2. any unfair or treacherous action.

foul-up (FOWL UP) *n.* 1. a mix-up; a state of confusion. 2. a mechanical failure.

found¹ (fownd) *v.t.* 1. originate or establish. 2. lay the foundation of. —*v.i.* 3. be established or based: with *on, upon.* [ME *founden*]

found² *v.t.* 1. cast, as iron, by melting and pouring into a mold. 2. make by casting molten metal. [ME *fonden* cast]

found³ past tense, past participle of FIND.

foun•da•tion (fown DAY shən) *n.* 1. the act of founding or establishing. 2. the state of being founded or established. 3. that on which anything is founded; basis. 4. a base on which a structure rests or is built. 5. a fund for the maintenance of an institution; an endowment. 6. an endowed institution. 7. a foundation garment. [ME *foundacioun*]

foundation garment a girdle or corset.

found•er¹ (FOWN dər) *n.* one who establishes. [ME]

found•er² *n.* one who makes metal castings. [ME]

foun•der³ *v.i.* 1. sink after filling with water as a boat. 2. fall or cave in, as land or buildings. 3. fail completely; collapse. 4. stumble and become lame, as a horse. —*v.t.* 5. cause to sink. —*n.* the act of foundering. [ME *foundren* submerge]

found•ling (FOWND ling) *n.* a deserted infant of unknown parentage. [ME *foundeling*]

foun•dry (FOWN dree) *n. pl.* •**dries** an establishment in which metal, etc., is cast. [< F *fonderie*]

fount (fownt) *n.* 1. a fountain. 2. any source.

foun•tain (FOWN tn) *n.* 1. a spring or jet of water issuing from the earth. 2. the origin or source of anything. 3. a jet or spray of water forced upward artificially. 4. a basinlike structure for such a jet to rise and fall in. [ME *fontayne*]

foun•tain•head (FOWN tn HED) *n.* 1. a spring from which a stream takes its source. 2. any source or origin.

four (for) *n.* the sum of three and one: a cardinal number written 4, IV. —**on all fours** 1. on hands and knees. 2. on all four feet. [ME] —*adj.* —**fourth** (forth) *adj. & n.*

four•hand•ed (FOR HAN did) *adj* 1. designed for four players. 2. designed for performance by two persons, as a piano duet.

four-post•er (FOR POH stər) *n.* a bed with tall posts at the corners and typically with a canopy or curtains.

four•some (FOR səm) *n.* 1. a game, esp. of golf, in which four players take part, two on each side; also, the players in such a game. 2. any group of four.

four•square (FOR SKWAIR) *adj.* 1. having four equal sides; square. 2. firm; solid. 3. forthright; direct. —*adv.* squarely; bluntly.

four•teen (FOR TEEN) *n.* the sum of thirteen and one: a cardinal number written 14, XIV. [ME *fourtene*] —**four•teen** *adj.* —**four′•teenth** *adj. & n.*

fourth estate the public press; journalism.

fourth•ly (FORTH lee) *adv.* in the fourth place.

fowl (fowl) *n. pl.* **fowl** or **fowls** 1. the common domestic hen or cock; a chicken. 2. any related bird, as the duck, goose, etc. 3. the flesh of fowl. 4. birds collectively. —*v.i.* catch or hunt wild fowl. [ME *foul*] —**fowl′er** *n.* —**fowl•ing** *n.* the hunting of birds for sport.

fox (foks) *n.* 1. any of several small, wild mammals of the dog family, having long, pointed muzzles, bushy tails. **2.** the fur of the fox. **3.** a sly, crafty person. —*v.t. & v.i.* trick; outwit; act slyly or cunningly. [ME]

fox·hole (FOKS HOHL) *n.* a shallow pit dug as cover against enemy fire.

fox·y (FOK see) *adj.* **fox·i·er, fox·i·est 1.** wily; cunning. **2.** *Slang* sexually attractive: said of a woman. —**fox'i·ness** *n.*

foy·er (FOI ər) *n.* an entrance room; lobby. [< F, lit., hearth]

fra·cas (FRAY kəs) *n.* a noisy disturbance or dispute; brawl. [< F, row]

frac·tion (FRAK shən) *n.* **1.** a disconnected part of anything; small portion; fragment. **2.** *Math.* a quantity less than a whole number, expressed as a decimal (0.25) or with numerator and denominator ($\frac{1}{4}$ or $\frac{1}{3}$). **3.** *Chem.* one of the components separated from a substance by fractionation. —*v.t.* set or separate into fractions. [ME *fraccioun*] —**frac'tion·al** *adj.*

frac·tion·ate (FRAK shə NAYT) *v.t.* **·at·ed, ·at·ing** separate into fractions; divide; break up. —**frac'tion·a'tion** *n.* —**frac'tion·al·ly** *adv.*

frac·tious (FRAK shəs) *adj.* **1.** apt to be unruly or rebellious. **2.** easily annoyed or angered. —**frac'tious·ness** *n.*

frac·ture (FRAK chər) *n.* **1.** the act of breaking, or the state of being broken. **2.** a break; crack; rupture. **3.** *Med.* the breaking or cracking of a bone. —*v.t. & v.i.* **·tured, ·tur·ing** break or be broken; crack. [ME]

frag·ile (FRAJ əl) *adj.* easily broken or damaged; frail; delicate. [< L *fragilis*] —**fra·gil·i·ty** (frə JIL i tee) *n.*

frag·ment (FRAG mənt) *n.* **1.** a part broken off; a small detached portion. **2.** a part or portion of something unfinished: a *fragment* of a novel. —*v.t. & v.i.* break into fragments. [ME] —**frag·men·ta·tion** (FRAG mən TAY shən) *n.*

frag·men·tar·y (FRAG mən TER ee) *adj.* composed of fragments; broken; incomplete.

fra·grant (FRAY grənt) *adj.* having an agreeable aroma. [ME] —**fra'grance** *n.*

frail (frayl) *adj.* **1.** delicately constituted; weak. **2.** fragile. **3.** deficient in moral strength. [ME *fraile*]

frail·ty (FRAYL tee) *n. pl.* **·ties 1.** the state or quality of being frail. **2.** a moral weakness. [ME *frailte*]

frame (fraym) *n.* **1.** a case or border made to enclose something, as a picture. **2.** a supporting structure surrounding something,

as around a window or door. **3.** a framework; skeleton. **4.** the general arrangement, structure, or constitution of a thing. **5.** bodily structure or build, esp. of the human body. **6.** a machine built in the form of or utilizing a framework; a silk *frame.* **7.** in bowling, one of the ten divisions of the game. **8.** one of the individual pictures on a roll of motion-picture film, in a comic strip, or in a series of television images. —**frame of mind** mental state; mood. —*v.t.* **framed, fram·ing 1.** surround with or put into a frame, as a picture. **2.** put together: *frame* a house. **3.** put into words; utter. **4.** conceive or devise (a theory, law, etc.). **5.** *Informal* incriminate falsely. [ME *framen* prepare]

frame-up (FRAYM UP) *n. Informal* a conspiracy to convict a person on a false charge.

frame·work (FRAYM WURK) *n.* **1.** a structure for supporting or enclosing something; also, frames, collectively. **2.** the basic structure of something: the *framework* of society.

franc (frangk) *n.* the standard monetary unit of France and various other countries. [ME *frank*]

fran·chise (FRAN chīz) *n.* **1.** the right to vote; suffrage. **2.** a right or privilege granted by a governing body to an individual or a corporate group. **3.** authorization given by a business to market its products or services. **4.** the territory over which any of these privileges or dispensations extend. —*v.t.* grant a franchise to. [ME]

fran·gi·ble (FRAN jə bəl) *adj.* easily broken; brittle. [ME]

frank[1] (frangk) *adj.* **·er, ·est 1.** completely honest and unreserved; candid. **2.** unconcealed: *frank* hostility. —*v.t.* mark (a letter, package, etc.) in indication that no charge is to be made for delivery; also, send (a letter etc.) marked in this way. —*n.* **1.** the right to send mail without charge. **2.** the mark used to indicate this right. [ME] —**frank'ness** *n.*

frank[2] *n. Informal* frankfurter.

frank·furt·er (FRANGK fər tər) *n.* a cooked smoked sausage made of beef or beef and pork. [< G, sausage of Frankfort]

fran·tic (FRAN tik) *adj.* **1.** nearly driven out of one's mind, as with grief, fear, or rage. **2.** madly excited. [ME *frantik*] —**fran'ti·cal·ly** *adv.*

fra·ter·nal (frə TUR nl) *adj.* **1.** pertaining to or befitting a brother; brotherly. **2.** of or pertaining to a brotherhood or society. **3.** *Genetics* designating either of a pair of twins that develop from separately fertilized ova; distinguished from *identical*. [ME] —**fra·ter′nal·ism** *n.*

fra·ter·ni·ty (frə TUR ni tee) *n. pl.* **·ties 1.** the state of being brothers; also, the spirit of fraternal regard or affection. **2.** in schools, a society of male students. **3.** any brotherhood or similar society. **4.** a body of people sharing the same interests. [ME *fraternite*]

frat·er·nize (FRAT ər NIZ) *v.i.* **·nized, ·niz·ing 1.** associate with someone in a comradely way. **2.** mingle with one's opponents, or with citizens of a conquered country. [< F *fraterniser*] —**frat′er·ni·za′tion** *n.*

frat·ri·cide (FRA tri sID) *n.* **1.** the killing of one's brother. **2.** one who has killed one's brother. [< MF] —**frat′ri·ci′dal** *adj.*

fraud (frawd) *n.* **1.** willful deceit; trickery. **2.** an instance of this. **3.** a deceptive or spurious person or thing. [ME *fraude*]

fraud·u·lent (FRAW jə lənt) *adj.* **1.** practicing or given to fraud; dishonest or deceitful. **2.** proceeding from, obtained by, or characterized by fraud. [ME] —**fraud′u·lence** *n.*

fraught (frawt) *adj.* filled; laden: with *with:* a task *fraught* with danger. [ME]

fray[1] (fray) *n.* conflict; fight; also a noisy uproar or disturbance. [ME *frai*]

fray[2] *v.t.* **1.** cause (cloth, rope, etc.) to become worn by friction. **2.** wear holes in (cloth etc.) by rubbing or chafing. —*v.i.* **3.** become frayed. —*n.* a frayed place, as of a sleeve. [ME *fraien* rub]

fraz·zle (FRAZ əl) *Informal v.t. & v.i.* **·zled, ·zling 1.** fray, or become frayed or tattered. **2.** tire out; weary. —*n.* the state of being frazzled.

freak (freek) *n.* **1.** a deformed human being, animal, or plant; monstrosity. **2.** anything unusual or bizarre. **3.** a sudden whim; caprice. **4.** *Slang* **a** a drug addict. **b** an enthusiast: a *jazz freak.* —*adj.* strange; abnormal. —**freak out** *Slang* **1.** abandon reality, esp. by taking drugs. **2.** experience hallucinations as the result of taking drugs. **3.** become extremely upset. **4.** put into a state of intense excitement: The music *freaked* him out. [? OE *frician* dance] —**freak′ish** *adj.*

freck·le (FREK əl) *n.* a small brownish spot on the skin. —*v.t. & v.i.* **·led, ·ling** mark or become marked with freckles. [ME *frekne*]

free (free) *adj.* **fre·er, fre·est 1.** having personal liberty. **2.** having civil, political, or religious liberty. **3.** not controlled by a foreign power; autonomous. **4.** not bound by impositions, restrictions, regulations: *free* trade. **5.** given or provided without charge. **6.** cleared or devoid of something: with *from, of.* **7.** not controlled or hampered by external agents or influences. **8.** not hindered by burdens, debts, discomforts, etc.: with *from, of.* **9.** not occupied; not busy. **10.** not attached; loose: the *free* end of a rope. **11.** unimpeded. **12.** not adhering to strict form or rule: *free* verse. **13.** not literally following the original: a *free* translation. **14.** informal; unconventional. **15.** frank and honest; candid. **16.** generous in giving; liberal: *free* with advice. **17.** *Chem.* uncombined. —**free and clear** *Law* held without a mortgage or other encumbrance. —**set free** release, as from a prison, slavery, or other restraint. —*adv.* **1.** in a free manner; easily. **2.** without cost; gratuitously. —**make free with 1.** use freely. **2.** treat with undue familiarity. —*v.t.* **freed, free·ing 1.** release from confinement, worry, etc. **2.** clear or rid of obstruction or hindrance. [ME *fre*] —**free′ly** *adv.*

free·boot·er (FREE BOO tər) *n.* a pirate or plunderer. [< Du. *vrijbuiter*]

free·dom (FREE dəm) *n.* **1.** the state or condition of being free; esp., the condition of enjoying civil liberty. **2.** political autonomy, as of a nation or people. **3.** liberty from slavery or imprisonment. **4.** liberty to move, choose, act, etc. without outside interference, coercion, or restriction. **5.** release or immunity from any stated thing or condition: with *from: freedom* from pain. **6.** facility or ease, as in moving or acting. **7.** openness or frankness. **8.** excessive familiarity or candor. [ME *fredom*]

free enterprise private ownership and operation of business with little or no governmental control.

free-for-all (FREE fər AWL) *n.* a generalized brawl.

free·hand (FREE HAND) *adj.* drawn or sketched by hand without drafting instruments etc.

free hand full liberty to act as one sees fit.

free·lance (FREE LANS) *v.i.* **·lanced, ·lanc·ing** work as a free lance. —*adj.* & *adv.* —*n.* a writer etc. whose services are not sold exclusively to any one buyer.

free-spo·ken (FREE SPOH kən) *adj.* unreserved or frank in speech.

free·style (FREE STĪL) *adj.* in swimming, using or permitting any stroke the swimmer desires.

free·think·er (FREE THING kər) *n.* one who forms opinions without regard to established authority.

free trade international commerce largely or wholly free from government regulations and duties.

free verse verse marked by an absence or irregularity of rhyme.

free·way (FREE WAY) *n.* a highway avoiding populated areas and intersections.

free·wheel·ing (FREE HWEE ling) *adj.* unhampered or unrestricted in manner or action.

free will 1. the power of personal self-determination. **2.** the doctrine that the ability to choose is not completely determined by circumstances.

freeze (freez) *v.* **froze, fro·zen, freez·ing** *v.i.* **1.** become ice or a similar hard solid through loss of heat. **2.** become sheeted or filled with ice, as water pipes. **3.** become stiff or hard with cold, as wet clothes. **4.** adhere to something by the formation of ice. **5.** be extremely cold. **6.** be damaged or killed by great cold. **7.** become suddenly motionless, inactive, or rigid, as through shock. **8.** become icily aloof: often with *up.* —*v.t.* **9.** cause to become solid through loss of heat. **10.** cause ice to form on or in. **11.** make stiff or hard by freezing the moisture of. **12.** make adhere by the formation of ice. **13.** make extremely cold. **14.** damage or kill by great cold. **15.** make motionless or rigid, as through fear; paralyze. **16.** alienate. **17.** check abruptly the ardor, enthusiasm, etc. of. **18.** fix or stabilize (prices, wages, etc.) at a particular level. **19.** prohibit the continued making, use, or selling of (a raw material). **20.** prohibit the liquidation, collection, or use of (funds or other assets). —**freeze one's blood** fill one with terror. —**freeze onto** (or **to**) hold tightly to. —*n.* **1.** the act of freezing, or the state of being frozen. **2.** freezing weather. [ME *fresen*]

freight (frayt) *n.* **1.** the service of transporting commodities by land, air, or water. **2.** the commodities so transported. **3.** the price paid for the transportation of commodities. **4.** a railroad train for carrying freight: also **freight train.** [ME *freyght*] —*v.t.* **1.** load with commodities for transportation. **2.** load; burden. **3.** send or transport as or by freight.

freight·er (FRAY tər) *n.* a ship used primarily for transporting cargo.

French (french) *n.* **1.** the people of France collectively: preceded by *the.* **2.** the language of France. —**Old French** the French language from about 850 to 1400. —**Middle French** the French language from about 1400 to 1600. —**Modern French** the language of France after 1600. [ME *Frensh*] —*adj.*

French cuff a cuff of a sleeve turned back and secured with a link.

French doors a pair of doors attached to opposite doorjambs and opening in the middle.

French fries potatoes cut in strips and deep-fried.

French toast bread dipped in a batter of beaten eggs and milk and fried in shallow fat.

fre·net·ic (frə NET ik) *adj.* feverishly excited; frenzied; frantic. [ME] —**fre·net'i·cal·ly** *adv.*

fren·zy (FREN zee) *n. pl.* **·zies** a state of extreme excitement or agitation, bordering on madness. —*v.t.* **·zied, ·zy·ing** make frantic. [ME *frenesie*] —**fren'zied** *adj.*

fre·quen·cy (FREE kwən see) *n. pl.* **·cies** **1.** the state or fact of being frequent; repeated occurrence. **2.** the number of times something occurs during a particular time. **3.** *Stat.* the number of times a given case, value, or event occurs relative to the whole sample; distribution. **4.** *Physics* the number of occurrences of a periodic phenomenon, as oscillation, per unit time.

fre·quent (FREE kwənt) *adj.* **1.** happening again and again: *frequent* relapses. **2.** showing up often; appearing repeatedly: *frequent* visitors. —*v.t.* go to repeatedly; be in or at often: *frequent* clubs. [< ME, ample]

fres·co (FRES koh) *n. pl.* **·coes** or **·cos 1.** the art of painting on plaster that is still moist. **2.** a picture so painted. —*v.t.* **·coed, ·co·ing** paint in fresco. [< Ital.]

fresh[1] (fresh) *adj.* **·er, ·est 1.** newly made, obtained, etc.: *fresh* coffee; *fresh* footprints. **2.** new; novel: a *fresh* approach. **3.** recent; latest: *fresh* news. **4.** additional; further: *fresh* supplies. **5.** not smoked, frozen, or otherwise preserved: *fresh* vegetables. **6.** not spoiled, stale, etc. **7.** retaining original vividness, as colors or memories. **8.** not salt: *fresh* water. **9.** pure and clear: *fresh* air. **10.** appearing healthy or youthful. **11.** not fatigued; energetic. **12.** inexperienced; untrained: *fresh recruits.* [ME]

fresh² *adj. Informal* saucy; impudent; disrespectful.

fresh·en (FRESH ən) *v.t. & v.i.* make or become fresh. —**fresh′en·er** *n.*

fresh·et (FRESH it) *n.* **1.** a sudden rise or overflow of a stream. **2.** a freshwater stream emptying into the sea.

fresh·wa·ter (FRESH WAW tər) *adj.* **1.** pertaining to or living in fresh water. **2.** lacking skill or experience; little known: *a freshwater* college.

fret¹ (fret) *v.* **fret·ted, fret·ting** *v.i.* **1.** be vexed, annoyed, or troubled. **2.** become worn, chafed, or corroded. **3.** eat through something by or as if by corrosion. **4.** rankle; fester. **5.** become rough or agitated, as water. —*v.t.* **6.** vex, annoy, or trouble. **7.** wear away by or as if by chafing, gnawing, or corrosion. **8.** roughen or agitate (the surface of water). —*n.* **1.** vexation. **2.** the act of chafing or gnawing. **3.** a worn spot. [ME *freten* devour]

fret² *n.* one of a series of ridges to guide the fingers in stopping the strings of aguitar, ukulele, etc. —*v.t.* **fret·ted, fret·ting** provide (a guitar etc.) with frets.

fret³ *n.* an ornamental band or border consisting of symmetrically arranged lines. —*v.t.* **fret·ted, fret·ting** adorn with a fret. [ME *frette*]

fret·ful (FRET fəl) *adj.* inclined to fret; peevish or restless. —**fret′ful·ness** *n.*

fret·work (FRET WURK) *n.* **1.** ornamental openwork, usu. composed of frets or interlaced parts. **2.** a pattern, as of light and shade, resembling such openwork.

Freud·i·an (FROI dee ən) *adj.* of, pertaining to, or conforming to the teachings of Sigmund Freud. —*n.* an adherent of the theories of Freud. —**Freu′di·an·ism** *n.*

fri·a·ble (FRĪ ə bəl) *adj.* easily crumbled. [< L *friabilis* crumbly] —**fri′a·bil′i·ty** *n.*

fri·ar (FRĪ ər) *n.* a man who is a member of one of several religious orders, esp. the mendicant orders. [ME *frier* brother]

fric·as·see (FRIK ə SEE) *n.* a dish of meat cut small, stewed, and served with gravy. —*v.t.* **·seed, ·see·ing** make into a fricassee. [< F *fricassé*]

fric·tion (FRIK shən) *n.* **1.** the rubbing of one object against another. **2.** conflict of opinions, differences in temperament, etc. [< L *fricare* rub] —**fric′tion·al** *adj.*

Fri·day¹ (FRĪ day) *n.* the sixth day of the week. [ME]

Fri·day² *n.* a devoted helper: *man Friday; girl Friday.* [after the servant in Defoe's *Robinson Crusoe*]

fried (frīd) past tense, past participle of FRY.

friend (frend) *n.* **1.** a favored companion; intimate. **2.** a valued associate or acquaintance. **3.** one with whom one is united in some purpose, cause, etc. **4.** a patron or supporter. [ME] —**friend′ship** *n.*

Friend *n.* a member of the Society of Friends; Quaker.

friend·ly (FREND lee) *adj.* **·li·er, ·li·est** **1.** of, pertaining to, or typical of a friend. **2.** well-disposed; not antagonistic. **3.** helpful; favorable: *a friendly* wind. [ME *frendly*] —**friend′li·ness** *n.*

fri·er (FRĪ ər) see FRYER.

frieze (freez) *n.* a decorative horizontal strip, as along the top of a wall of a room or building. [< MF *frise*]

fright (frīt) *n.* **1.** sudden, violent alarm or fear. **2.** one who or that which is repellent. [ME]

fright·en (FRĪT n) *v.t.* **1.** make suddenly alarmed, fearful, or terrified; scare. **2.** drive, force, etc. (away, out, into, etc.) by scaring. —*v.i.* **3.** become afraid.

fright·ful (FRĪT fəl) *adj.* **1.** repulsive, shocking, or contemptible. **2.** most distressing; very bad: *a frightful* headache. **3.** *Informal* very large: *a frightful* number of losses. **4.** alarming or terrifying. [ME]

frig·id (FRIJ id) *adj.* **1.** bitterly cold. **2.** lacking warmth of feeling; formal. **3.** habitually lacking sexual feeling or response: said of women. [< L *frigidus* coldness] —**fri·gid·i·ty** (fri JID i tee) *n.* [ME *frigidite*]

frill (fril) *n.* **1.** an ornamental strip of lace etc. gathered together and attached along one edge; ruffle. **2.** any showy or superfluous detail of dress, manner, etc. —*v.t.* **1.** make into a frill. **2.** put frills on. —**frill′y** *adv.* **frill·i·er, frill·i·est**

fringe (frinj) *n.* **1.** an ornamental border of hanging cords, threads, etc. **2.** something resembling such a border: *a fringe* of grass along a sidewalk. **3.** a peripheral area: the *fringes* of a city. —*v.t.* **fringed, fring·ing** **1.** provide with or as with a fringe. **2.** constitute a fringe on or along. —*adj.* outer; marginal: *a fringe* area. [ME *frenge*]

fringe benefit anything of value given an employee in addition to salary or wages.

frisk (frisk) *v.i.* **1.** move or leap about playfully; frolic. —*v.t.* **2.** move with quick jerks: a lamb *frisking* its tail. **3.** search (someone) for a concealed weapon, etc., by quickly feeling the pockets and clothing. [ME, frisky] —*n.* **1.** a playful skipping about. **2.** a search of someone for a weapon, etc.

frisk·y (FRIS kee) *adj.* **frisk·i·er, frisk·i·est** lively or playful. —**frisk'i·ness** *n.*

frit·ter[1] (FRIT ər) *v.t.* waste or squander little by little, as money, time, etc.: usu. with *away.*

frit·ter[2] *n.* a small, fried cake, often containing corn, meat, fruit, etc. [ME *friture*]

friv·o·lous (FRIV ə ləs) *adj.* **1.** lacking importance or significance; petty. **2.** flippant; silly; fickle. [ME, worthless] —**fri·vol·i·ty** (fri VOL i tee) *n.*

fro (froh) *adv.* away from; back: used in the phrase *to and fro.* [ME]

frock (frok) *n.* **1.** a long, loose-fitting robe with wide sleeves worn by monks. **2.** any of several types of garments, as a woman's dress or a worker's smock. —*v.t.* **1.** furnish with or clothe in a frock. **2.** invest with ecclesiastic office. [ME *froke*]

frog (frog) *n.* **1.** one of a genus of small, tailless, web-footed animals with short front legs and large, strong hind legs adapted to leaping. **2.** one of several similar animals, as a tree frog. **3.** a slight throat irritation producing hoarseness. **4.** an ornamental braid or cord, as on a jacket, often looped, so as to permit passage of a button. —*v.i.* **frogged, frog·ging** hunt frogs. [ME *frogge*]

frol·ic (FROL ik) *n.* **1.** merriness. **2.** a joyous occasion or diversion. **3.** a playful prank. —*v.i.* **·icked, ·ick·ing 1.** move about or behave in a frisky way. **2.** be prankish. [< Du. *vrolijk* joyful] —**frol'ick·er** *n.*

frol·ic·some (FROL ik səm) *adj.* happy and lighthearted. —**frol'ic·some·ness** *n.*

from (frum, *unstressed* frəm) *prep.* **1.** starting at (a particular place or time): a plane *from* London. **2.** with (a particular person, place, or thing) as the origin or instrument: a letter *from* her. **3.** out of (a container etc.). **4.** out of the control of: He escaped *from* his captors. **5.** out of the totality of: subtract 3 *from* 8. **6.** at a distance in relation to: far *from* a city. **7.** beyond the possibility of: kept *from* falling. **8.** by reason of; because of. **9.** as being other or another than: He couldn't tell me *from* my brother. [ME]

frond (frond) *n. Bot.* **1.** a leaflike expansion, as in ferns and seaweeds. **2.** a large leaf of

tropical plants and trees, as of the palm tree. [< L *frons* foliage]

front (frunt) *n.* **1.** the part or side of an object or body that faces forward or is viewed as facing forward. **2.** an area or position located directly ahead or before: She stood in *front* of us. **3.** an area or position of most important activity. **4.** *Mil.* **a** the lateral space from flank to flank occupied by a unit. **b** the line of contact of two opposing forces. **5.** the side of a building where the main entrance is. **6.** frontage. **7.** a group or movement of individuals with a common aim. **8.** *Informal* one chosen to head a group to give it prestige, often lacking real authority. **9.** an apparently respectable person, business, etc. used for cloaking objectionable activities. **10.** one's bearing or attitude: put on a bold *front.* **11.** an outward air of pretense of wealth, social importance, etc. **12.** *Meteorol.* the leading part of a mass of warm or cold air; also, the line of separation between masses of warm and cold air. —*adj.* **1.** of, pertaining to, or directed toward the front. **2.** located on, in, or at the front. —*v.t.* **1.** face toward. **2.** meet face to face. **3.** provide with a front. **4.** serve as a front for. —*v.i.* **5.** face toward something: usu. with *on.* [ME *frount* brow]

front·age (FRUN tij) *n.* **1.** the front part of a lot or building; also, the linear extent of this. **2.** the direction in which something faces; exposure. **3.** land adjacent to a street, body of water, etc.

fron·tal (FRUN tl) *adj.* **1.** of or pertaining to the front. **2.** of or pertaining to the forehead or to the bone forming the front part of the skull. —**fron'tal·ly** *adv.*

fron·tier (frun TEER) *n.* **1.** the part of a nation's territory lying along the border of another country. **2.** the part of a settled region lying along the border of an unsettled region. **3.** a new or unexplored area of thought or knowledge. [ME *frounter*] —**fron·tiers·man** (frun TEERZ mən) *n.*

fron·tis·piece (FRUN tis PEES) *n.* a picture or drawing on the page facing the title page of a book. [< F *frontispice*]

front runner *n.* the leading contender in a contest or selection process.

frost (frawst) *n.* **1.** a feathery deposit of ice formed on surfaces by dew or water vapor that has frozen. **2.** temperature cold enough to freeze. **3.** coldness of manner. —*v.t.* **1.** cover with frost. **2.** damage or kill by frost. **3.** produce a frostlike surface or effect

on (glass etc.). **4.** apply frosting to. [ME] —
frost'y adj. **frost•i•er, frost•i•est**

frost•bite (FRAWST BĪT) n. the partial
freezing of some part of the body, sometimes resulting in gangrene. —v.t. **•bit,
•bit•ten, •bit•ing** injure, as a part of the
body, by partial freezing. —**frost•bit•ten**
(FRAWST BIT n) adj.

frost•ing (FRAW sting) n. **1.** a sweet mixture
used to cover cakes. **2.** a frostlike, rough,
dull surface produced on metal, glass, etc.
—**frost'ed** adj.

froth (frawth) n. **1.** a mass of bubbles resulting from fermentation or agitation. **2.** any
foamy excretion or exudation, as of saliva. **3.**
any unsubstantial or trivial thing. —v.t. **1.**
cause to foam. **2.** cover with froth. **3.** give
forth in the form of foam. —v.i. **4.** form or
give off froth. [ME frothe scum] —**froth'y**
adj. **froth•i•er, froth•i•est**

frown (frown) v.i. **1.** contract the brow, as in
displeasure or concentration. **2.** look with
distaste: with on or upon. —v.t. **3.** make
known (one's displeasure, disgust, etc.) by
contracting one's brow. [ME frounen] —
frown n.

frow•zy (FROW zee) adj. **•zi•er, •zi•est**
1. slovenly in appearance; unkempt. **2.**
having a disagreeable smell; musty. Also
frow'sy.

froze (frohz) past tense of FREEZE.

fro•zen (FROH zən) past participle of
FREEZE. —adj. **1.** changed into, covered
with, or clogged with ice, as a river. **2.** killed
or damaged by cold. **3.** preserved by freezing: frozen foods. **4.** extremely cold, as a
climate. **5.** cold and unfeeling in manner. **6.**
made rigid or immobile: frozen with fear. **7.**
Econ. **a** arbitrarily maintained at a given
level: said of prices, wages, etc. **b** not readily
convertible into cash: frozen assets. **8.**
made solid by cold.

fruc•ti•fy (FRUK tə FĪ) v. **•fied, fy•ing** v.t.
1. make fruitful; fertilize. —v.i. **2.** bear
fruit. [ME fructifien] —**fruc'ti•fi•ca'tion**
n.

fru•gal (FROO gəl) adj. **1.** exercising economy; saving. **2.** costing little money: a frugal
meal. [< L frugalis economical] —
fru•gal'•i•ty n.

fruit (froot) n. **1.** Bot. **a** the pulpy, usu. edible
mass covering the seeds of various plants
and trees. **b** in flowering plants, the mature
seed vessel and its contents. **2.** any useful
plant product. **3.** any offspring. **4.** the outcome or result of some action, effort, etc. —

v.i. & v.t. produce or cause to produce fruit.
[ME]

fruit fly 1. any of various flies whose larvae
attack fruit. **2.** a fly whose larvae feed on
fruit and which is used in research in genetics.

fruit•ful (FROOT fəl) adj. **1.** bearing fruit or
offspring abundantly. **2.** producing results:
a fruitful discussion. [ME] —**fruit'ful•
ness** n.

fru•i•tion (froo ISH ən) n. **1.** accomplishment; fulfillment. **2.** the bearing of fruit.
[ME fruicioun]

fruit•less (FROOT lis) adj. **1.** yielding no
fruit; barren. **2.** ineffectual; useless; unproductive. [ME]

fruit•y (FROO tee) adj. **fruit•i•er,
fruit•i•est** suggestive of or having the flavor of fruit.

frump (frump) n. a dowdy woman. —
frump'y adj. **frump•i•er, frump•i•est**

frus•trate (FRUS trayt) v.t. **•trat•ed,
•trat•ing 1.** keep (someone) from doing or
achieving something; thwart. **2.** keep, as
plans or schemes, from being fulfilled.
[ME] —**frus•tra•tion** (frʌ STRAY shən) n.

fry¹ (frī) v.t. & v.i. **fried, fry•ing** cook in hot
fat, usu. over direct heat. —n. pl. **fries 1.** a
dish of anything fried. **2.** a social occasion,
at which foods are fried and eaten. [ME
frien]

fry² n. pl. **fry 1.** very young fish. **2.** the young
of certain animals, as of frogs, when pro-
duced in very large quantities. **3.** young
children: small fry. [ME frie seed]

fry•er (FRĪ ər) n. **1.** one who or that which
fries. **2.** a young chicken suitable for frying.
Also spelled frier.

fuch•sia (FYOO shə) n. **1.** a plant with
drooping, four-petaled flowers. **2.** a bright
bluish red. [after Leonhard Fuchs, 1501–
66, German botanist]

fud•dle (FUD l) v. **•dled, •dling** v.t. **1.** confuse or stupefy. **2.** make drunk. —v.i. **2.**
tipple.

fud•dy-dud•dy (FUD ee DUD ee) n. pl.
-dud•dies 1. an old-fashioned person. **2.** a
faultfinding, fussy person.

fudge (fuj) n. **1.** a soft, cooked confection
made of butter, sugar, chocolate, etc. **2.**
humbug: nonsense. —v. **fudged, fudg•
ing** v.i. **1.** avoid commitment; equivocate.
—v.t. **2.** make, adjust, or fit together in a
clumsy or dishonest manner.

fu•el (FYOO əl) n. **1.** combustible matter
used as a source of heat or power. **2.** any-

thing that sustains or heightens emotion etc. —*v.t. & v.i.* **fu·eled, fu·el·ing** supply with or take in fuel. [ME]

fu·gi·tive (FYOO ji tiv) *adj.* **1.** fleeing or having fled, as from arrest. **2.** transient; fleeting. **3.** wandering about; shifting. —*n.* one who flees, as from pursuit; runaway. [< L *fugitivus* fleeing]

fugue (fyoog) *n. Music* a composition in which a theme is introduced by one part, repeated by other parts, and subjected to complex development. [< F]

ful·crum (FUUL krəm) *n. pl.* **·crums 1.** the support on which a lever rests or about which it turns. **2.** any prop or support. [< LL, support]

ful·fill (fuul FIL) *v.t.* **·filled, ·fill·ing 1.** bring about accomplishment of (something promised, hoped for, anticipated, etc.). **2.** execute or perform (something commanded or requested). **3.** come up to or satisfy (something stipulated). **4.** get through to the end of (a period of time, a task, etc.); finish up. [ME *fulfillen*] — **ful·fill'ment** *n.*

full¹ (fuul) *adj.* **1.** filled up. **2.** containing an abundant or sufficient supply. **3.** complete or entire: a *full* pint. **4.** maximum in size, extent, degree, etc.: a *full* load; *full* speed. **5.** having had ample food or drink. **6.** of the face, figure, etc., well rounded; plump. **7.** having satisfying resonance and volume: *full* tones. **8.** of garments, cut in ample folds; flowing. —**in full cry** in close pursuit: said esp. of dogs. —*n.* the maximum size, degree, etc. —**in full 1.** to the entire amount: paid *in full.* **2.** without abridgment: reprinted *in full.* —*adv.* **1.** to a complete degree or extent: now chiefly in compounds: *full-fledged.* **2.** directly; straight; right: I looked him *full* in the face. [ME] —**full'ness** *n.*

full² *v.t. & v.i.* shrink or thicken (cloth, yarn, etc.), as by moistening and beating or pressing. [ME *fullen*]

full-blood·ed (FULL BLUD id) *adj.* **1.** of unmixed ancestry. **2.** related to another through descent from the same parents.

full-blown (FUUL BLOHN) *adj.* **1.** blooming fully. **2.** fully developed.

full-bod·ied (FUUL BOD eed) *adj.* of beverages, having a satisfying richness and strength.

full·er (FUUL ər) *n.* one who fulls cloth, etc. [ME]

full-fledged (FUUL FLEJD) *adj.* **1.** of full standing. **2.** completely developed or trained.

full-length (FUUL LENGKTH) *adj.* **1.** showing the entire length of an object or figure: a *full-length* portrait. **2.** not abridged; of the usual length.

full moon 1. the moon with its whole face illuminated. **2.** the time of month when this occurs.

full-scale (FUUL SKAYL) *adj.* **1.** scaled to actual size; not reduced. **2.** all-out; unrestrained.

full swing the height of activity: a party in *full swing.*

ful·ly (FUUL ee) *adv.* **1.** to the fullest extent or degree; entirely: *fully* convinced. **2.** adequately; sufficiently: *fully* fed. **3.** at the lowest estimate: *fully* three hundred. [ME]

ful·mi·nate (FUL mə NAYT) *v.* **·nat·ed, ·nat·ing** *v.i.* **1.** make loud or violent denunciations; inveigh. **2.** explode suddenly and violently, as a chemical. —*v.t.* **3.** issue (decrees, censures, etc.) in scathing rebuke or condemnation. **4.** cause, as a chemical, to explode with sudden violence. —*n. Chem.* any explosive compound. [ME *fulminaten* flash with lightning] —**ful'mi·na'tion** *n.*

ful·some (FUUL səm) *adj.* distastefully excessive; insincere. [ME *fulsom*] —**ful'some·ly** *adv.*

fum·ble (FUM bəl) *v.* **·bled, ·bling** *v.i.* **1.** try to locate something by groping blindly or clumsily: with *for, after.* **2.** try awkwardly to do something: with *at.* **3.** in football etc., lose hold of the ball. —*v.t.* **4.** handle awkwardly or ineffectually; botch. **5.** drop awkwardly (a ball in one's grasp). —*n.* the act of fumbling. [Prob. < Scand.]

fume (fyoom) *n.* **1.** a gaseous exhalation or smoke, esp. when otherwise disagreeable. **2.** a sharply penetrating odor. —*v.* **fumed, fum·ing** *v.i.* **1.** give off fumes. **2.** pass off in a mist or vapor. **3.** be filled with or show rage, irritation, etc. —*v.t.* **4.** subject to fumes. [ME]

fu·mi·gate (FYOO mi GAYT) *v.t.* **·gat·ed, ·gat·ing** subject to smoke or fumes, esp. to kill vermin. [< L *fumigatus* smoked out] — **fu'mi·ga'tion** *n.*

fun (fun) *n.* **1.** pleasant diversion or amusement. **2.** lighthearted playfulness: full of *fun.* —**like fun** *Informal* absolutely not; by no means. —**make fun of** ridicule. —*adj. Informal* full of fun: a *fun* game. —*v.i.* **funned, fun·ning** *Informal* behave or speak in jest.

func·tion (FUNGK shən) n. **1.** the specific, natural, or proper action or activity of anything. **2.** the special duties or action required of anyone in an occupation, office, or role. **3.** a formal or elaborate social gathering or ceremony. **4.** any fact, quality, or thing depending upon or varying with another. **5.** *Math.* a quantity whose value depends on the value of some other quantity. —*v.i.* **1.** perform as expected or required. **2.** perform the role of something else. [< L *functio* performance] —**func'tion·less** *adj.* —**func·tion·al** (FUNGK shə nəl) *adj.* **1.** of or pertaining to a function or functions. **2.** designed for or suited to a particular operation or use. **3.** affecting the functions of an organ or part: *functional* disease: distinguished from *organic*. —**func'tion·al·ly** *adv.*

func·tion·al·ism (FUNGK shə nl IZ əm) n. the doctrine that the use of an object should determine its design.

func·tion·ar·y (FUNGK shə NER ee) n. pl. **·ar·ies** one who serves in a specific capacity; esp., an official.

fund (fund) n. **1.** a sum of money, or its equivalent, accumulated or reserved for a specific purpose. **2.** pl. money readily available. **3.** a ready supply: a *fund* of humor. —*v.t.* **1.** in finance: **a** convert into a long-term debt. **b** accumulate or furnish a fund for. **2.** gather up a supply of. [< L *fundus* bottom]

fun·da·ment (FUN də mənt) n. the buttocks; also, the anus. [< L *fundamentum* foundation]

fun·da·men·tal (FUN də MEN tl) *adj.* **1.** pertaining to or constituting a foundation; basic. **2.** *Music* of or pertaining to the basic tone of a chord; root. **3.** *Physics* designating the lowest frequency harmonic component of a complex wave. —n. **1.** anything that serves as the basis of a system, as a truth, law, etc. **2.** *Music* the basic tone of a chord. **3.** *Physics* that frequency on which a harmonic or group of harmonics is based. [ME]

fun·da·men·tal·ism (FUN də MEN tl IZ əm) n. **1.** the belief that all statements in the Bible are to be taken literally. **2.** a movement among Protestants holding such a belief. —**fun'da·men'tal·ist** n. & adj.

fu·ner·al (FYOO nər əl) n. **1.** the final disposal of the body of a dead person, together with accompanying services. **2.** a procession held on this occasion. —adj. of, per-

taining to, or suitable for a funeral. [ME] —**fu·ner·ar·y** (FYOO nə RER ee) adj.

fu·ne·re·al (fyoo NEER ee əl) adj. **1.** depressingly sad or gloomy; doleful. **2.** pertaining to or suitable for a funeral.

fun·gi·cide (FUN jə SID) n. something, as a chemical compound, used in destroying fungi. —**fun'gi·ci'dal** adj.

fun·gi·ble (FUN jə bəl) adj. *Finance* freely exchangeable; interchangeable: *fungible* assets. [< Med.L *fungibilis*]

fun·gus (FUNG gəs) n. pl. **fun·gus·es** or **fun·gi** (FUN jī) any nonflowering plant that has no chlorophyll and grows on dead organic matter or lives parasitically, including mushrooms and molds. [< L, mushroom] —**fun'gal** adj. & n. —**fun'gous** adj.

fu·nic·u·lar (fyoo NIK yə lər) adj. moved by the pull of a cable, as a streetcar in a hilly section. —n. a railway along which cable cars are drawn: also **funicular railway.** [< L *funiculus* small rope]

funk (fungk) n. **1.** a state of fear or panic: esp. in the phrase **be in a funk. 2.** a feeling of despondency. [? Du. *fonck* fear]

funk·y (FUNG kee) adj. **funk·i·er, funk·i·est 1.** earthy and unpolished in style: *funky* blues. **2.** evil-smelling.

fun·nel (FUN l) n. **1.** a utensil with a wide mouth tapering to a narrow tube, through which fluids are poured into bottles etc. having narrow necks. **2.** a smokestack, as of a large ship, locomotive, etc. —v.t. & v.i. **fun·neled, fun·nel·ing** pass through or as through a funnel. [ME *fonel*]

fun·ny (FUN ee) adj. **·ni·er, ·ni·est 1.** causing one to laugh or be amused; comical. **2.** peculiar; strange; odd. —**fun'ni·ness** n.

funny bone 1. the part of the elbow which, when struck, produces an unpleasant, tingling sensation in the arm and hand. **2.** a sense of humor.

fur (fur) n. **1.** the soft, fine, hairy coat covering the skin of many mammals. **2.** an animal skin covered with such a coat, esp. when prepared for use in garments, rugs, etc.; also, such skins collectively. **3.** a layer of foul matter, as on the tongue. —adj. made of, lined with, or trimmed with fur: also **furred.** —v.t. **furred, fur·ring 1.** cover, line, trim, or clothe with fur. **2.** cover, as the tongue, with a layer of foul matter. **3.** apply furring. [ME *furre*] —**fur'ry** adj. **fur· ri·er, fur·ri·est**

fur·bish (FUR bish) v.t. **1.** make bright by

rubbing; burnish. **2.** restore to brightness or beauty; renovate: often with *up*. [ME *furbishen* polish]

fur·cate (FUR kayt) *v.i.* **·cat·ed, ·cat·ing** divide into branches. —*adj.* forked. [< LL *furcatus* forked] —**fur·ca′tion** *n.*

fu·ri·ous (FYUUR ee əs) *adj.* **1.** extremely angry; raging. **2.** extremely violent or intense; fierce. **3.** pushed to the limit: a *furious* pace. [ME]

furl (furl) *v.t.* **1.** roll up (a sail, flag, etc.) and make secure, as to a mast or staff. —*v.i.* **2.** become furled. —*n.* **1.** the act of furling, or the state of being furled. **2.** a rolled-up section of a sail, flag, etc. [< MF *ferler* fasten]

fur·long (FUR lawng) *n.* a measure of length, equal to ⅛ mile. [ME]

fur·lough (FUR loh) *n.* permission to be absent from duty, esp. in the armed services; leave. [< Du. *verlof* leave] —**fur′lough** *v.t.*

fur·nace (FUR nis) *n.* **1.** an enclosed chamber designed to produce intense heat for warming a building, melting metal, etc. **2.** any intensely hot place. [ME *furneis* oven]

fur·nish (FUR nish) *v.t.* **1.** equip, or fit out, as with fittings or furniture. **2.** supply; provide. [ME *furnisshen* provide]

fur·nish·ings (FUR ni shingz) *n.pl.* **1.** articles of clothing, including accessories. **2.** furniture and other fixtures for a home, office, etc.

fur·ni·ture (FUR ni chər) *n.* **1.** the movable articles used in a home, office, etc., as sofas, tables, or mirrors. **2.** any necessary equipment, as for a factory or ship. [< F *fourniture*]

fur·or (FYUUR or) *n.* **1.** a great stir; commotion. **2.** a state of intense excitement or enthusiasm. [< L, a rage]

fur·ri·er (FUR ee ər) *n.* one who deals in, processes, repairs, or stores furs. [ME *furrer*]

fur·ring (FUR ing) *n.* strips of wood, metal, etc., affixed to a wall, floor, etc., so as to make a level surface or create air spaces. [ME]

fur·row (FUR oh) *n.* **1.** a narrow channel made in the ground by or as if by a plow. **2.** any long, narrow, deep depression, as a groove, rut, or deep wrinkle. [ME *forwe*] —**fur′row** *v.t. & v.i.*

fur·ther (FUR thər) comparative of FAR. —*adv.* **1.** at or to a more distant or remote point in time or space. **2.** to a greater degree; more. **3.** in addition; besides; more-

over. —*adj.* **1.** more distant or advanced in time or degree. **2.** farther. **3.** additional. —*v.t.* help forward; promote. [ME] —**fur′·ther·ance** (-əns) *n.*

fur·ther·more (FUR thər MOR) *adv.* in addition; moreover.

fur·ther·most (FUR thər MOHST) *adj.* furthest.

fur·thest (FUR *th*ist) superlative of FAR. —*adv.* **1.** at or to the most remote or distant point in space or time. **2.** to the greatest degree. —*adj.* **1.** most distant, remote, or advanced in time or degree. **2.** most distant in space.

fur·tive (FUR tiv) *adj.* **1.** done in secret; surreptitious; stealthy. **2.** evasive; shifty. [< L *furtivus* thieving] —**fur′tive·ly** *adv.*

fu·ry (FYUUR ee) *n. pl.* **·ries 1.** vehement and uncontrolled anger or rage. **2.** a fit of such anger or rage. **3.** violent action or agitation; fierceness: the storm's *fury.* [ME]

fuse (fyooz) *n.* **1.** a length of combustible material, passing into the charge of an explosive, and igniting the charge when lit. **2.** *Mil.* any device designed to detonate a bomb, projectile, etc. **3.** fuze *Electr.* a small metallic device that melts, breaking a circuit, when the current becomes excessive. —*v.t. & v.i.* **fused, fus·ing 1.** liquefy by heat; melt. **2.** join by or as if by melting together. [< L *fusus* melted]

fu·se·lage (FYOO sə LAHZH) *n.* *Aeron.* the body of an airplane. [< F]

fu·si·ble (FYOO zə bəl) *adj.* capable of being fused. [ME] —**fu′si·bil′i·ty** *n.*

fu·sil·lade (FYOO sə LAYD) *n.* **1.** a simultaneous or quickly repeated discharge of firearms. **2.** anything resembling this: a *fusillade* of insults. —*v.t.* **·lad·ed, ·lad·ing** attack or bring down with a fusillade. [< F]

fu·sion (FYOO zhən) *n.* **1.** a melting or blending together. **2.** something formed by fusing. **3.** in politics, the union of two parties or two factions within a party. **4.** *Physics* a thermonuclear reaction in which the nuclei of a light element are transformed into those of a heavier element, with the release of great energy. [< L *fusio* a melting]

fuss (fus) *n.* nervous activity; commotion. —*v.t. & v.i.* bother or be bothered with trifles.

fuss·budg·et (FUS BUJ it) *n.* one excessively concerned with trifles.

fuss·y (FUS ee) *adj.* **fuss·i·er, fuss·i·est 1.** too much concerned with trifles; finicky. **2.** fidgety; fretful. **3.** requiring meticulous attention; fastidious. —**fuss′i·ness** *n.*

fus·tian (FUS chən) *n.* **1.** a coarse, twilled cotton fabric, as corduroy. **2.** pretentious verbiage; bombast. [ME] —*adj.* bombastic; cheap.

fust·y (FUS tee) *adj.* **fust·i·er, fust·i·est 1.** musty; moldy; rank. **2.** old-fashioned; fogyish. [< ME *fusti* moldy] —**fust'i·ly** *adv.* —**fust'i·ness** *n.*

fu·tile (FYOOT l) *adj.* **1.** being of no avail; useless. **2.** frivolous; idle. [< L *futilis* worthless] —**fu·til·i·ty** (fyoo TIL i tee) *n.*

fu·ture (FYOO chər) *n.* **1.** the time yet to come. **2.** what will be in time to come. **3.** a condition, usu. of success or prosperity, in time to come: someone with a *future.* **4.** *Usu. pl.* any commodity or security sold or bought upon agreement of future delivery. **5.** *Gram.* **a** a verb tense denoting action that will take place at some time to come. **b.** a verb in this tense. —*adj.* **1.** such as will be in time to come. **2.** pertaining to or expressing time to come. [ME *futur*] —**fu'tur·is'tic** *adj.*

fu·tu·ri·ty (fyoo TUUR i tee) *n. pl.* **·ties 1.** the future. **2.** the state or quality of being future. **3.** a future event or possibility. **4.** in horse racing, a race in which the entrants are designated well before the race is run.

fuze (fyooz) see FUSE.

fuzz (fuz) *n.* **1.** fine, loose particles, fibers, or hairs. **2.** a fluffy mass of these. —*v.t. & v.i.* become or cause to become fuzzy.

fuzz·y (FUZ ee) *adj.* **fuzz·i·er, fuzz·i·est 1.** having fuzz. **2.** resembling fuzz. **3.** lacking sharp distinctness or clarity; blurred. —**fuzz'i·ness** *n.*

-fy *suffix of verbs* **1.** cause to be or become: *deify.* **2.** become: *liquefy.* [< OF *-fien* make]

G

g, G (jee) *n. pl.* **g's** or **gs, G's** or **Gs 1.** the seventh letter of the English alphabet. **2.** any sound represented by the letter *g*. **3.** *Usu. cap. Slang* one thousand dollars; a grand. —*symbol* **1.** *Music* the fifth tone in the diatonic scale of C. **2.** *Physics* the acceleration of a body due to the earth's gravity, about 32 feet per second per second; also, a unit of acceleration equal to that of gravity.

gab (gab) *v.i.* **gabbed, gab·bing** talk, esp. glibly or excessively. —**gab** *Informal n.* —**gab′ber** *n.*

gab·ar·dine (GAB ər DEEN) *n.* **1.** a firm, twilled, worsted fabric, used for coats, suits, etc. **2.** a similar, softer fabric of cotton. [< GABERDINE]

gab·ble (GAB əl) *v.i.* **bled, ·bling 1.** talk quickly or incoherently. **2.** utter rapid, cackling sounds, as geese. —*n.* **1.** glib, incoherent, or foolish talk. **2.** cackling sounds, as of geese. —**gab′bler** *n.*

gab·er·dine (GAB ər DEEN *n.* a coarse, long coat worn by men, chiefly by Orthodox Jews. [< MF *gauvardine*]

gab·fest (GAB FEST) *n. Informal* an informal gathering for chatty conversation.

ga·ble (GAY bəl) *n. Archit.* the triangular top of an end wall of a building, formed by the sloping ends of a roof. [ME] —**ga′ble** *v.t. & v.i.*

gad (gad) *v.i.* **gad·ded, gad·ding** roam about restlessly or capriciously; ramble. [ME *gadden*] —**gad′der** *n.*

gad·a·bout (GAD ə BOWT) *n.* one who goes about aimlessly, frivolously, etc.

gad·fly (GAD FLI) *n. pl.* **·flies 1.** one of various large flies that bite cattle, horses, etc. **2.** a bothersome and persistently critical individual.

gadg·et (GAJ it) *n.* any small device or contrivance.

gaff (gaf) *n.* **1.** a sharp iron hook at the end of a pole, for landing a large fish; also, the pole. **2.** *Slang* rough treatment. —**stand the gaff** endure adversity. —*v.t.* strike or land with a gaff. [ME]

gaffe (gaf) *n.* a blunder; faux pas. [< F]

gaf·fer (GAF ər) *n.* an old man. [Contr. of GODFATHER]

gag (gag) *n.* **1.** something, as a wadded cloth, forced into or over the mouth to stifle speech or outcries. **2.** any suppression of free speech, as by censorship. **3.** a device to keep the jaws open, as in dentistry. **4.** *Informal* a joke or hoax. —*v.* **gagged, gag·ging** *v.t.* **1.** stifle speech by means of a gag. **2.** keep from speaking freely, as by force or authority. **3.** cause nausea in; cause to retch. —*v.i.* **4.** heave with nausea; also, choke on something. [ME *gaggen* suffocate]

gage¹ (gayj) see GAUGE.

gage² *n.* **1.** something given as security for an action to be performed; pledge. **2.** *Obs.* anything, as a glove, offered as a challenge. **3.** any challenge. [ME]

gag·gle (GAG əl) *v.i.* **·gled, ·gling** cackle; gabble. —*n.* **1.** a flock of geese. **2.** any group. [ME *gagelen* cackle]

gai·e·ty (GAY i tee) *n. pl.* **·ties 1.** the state of being gay; cheerfulness. **2.** bright colorfulness or showiness, as of dress. **3.** *Often pl.* fun; merrymaking. [< F *gaieté*]

gai·ly (GAY lee) *adv.* in a gay manner. [ME]

gain (gayn) *v.t.* **1.** obtain; acquire. **2.** succeed in winning (a victory etc.). **3.** increase: *gain momentum.* **4.** put on (weight). **5.** earn (a living etc.). **6.** arrive at; reach: *gain home port.* —*v.i.* **7.** grow better: *gain in health.* **8.** draw nearer; also, increase one's lead: usu. with *on* or *upon.* —*n.* **1.** *Often pl.* profits; winnings. **2.** an advantage or lead. **3.** an increase, as in size, amount, etc. **4.** the act of gaining. [ME] —**gain·er** *n.*

gain·ful (GAYN fəl) *adj.* profitable; lucrative. —**gain′ful·ly** *adv.*

gain·say (GAYN SAY) *v.t.* **·said, ·say·ing 1.** deny. **2.** contradict. **3.** act against; oppose. [ME *gainsaien*] —**gain′·say′er** *n.*

gait (gayt) *n.* **1.** one's manner of moving along on foot. **2.** one of the ways in which a horse steps or runs. —*v.t.* train (a horse) to take a gait. [ME]

ga·la (GAY lə) *adj.* appropriate to a festive occasion; festive. —*n.* an occasion marked by joyous festivity. [< F]

Gal·a·had (GAL ə HAD) *n.* a noble or gallant man. [after *Sir Galahad*, in Arthurian legend]

gal·ax·y (GAL ək see) *n. pl.* **·ax·ies 1.** *Astron.* any very large system of stars, nebulae, or other celestial bodies. **2.** *Usu. cap.* the Milky Way. **3.** a brilliant group, as of persons. [ME. *galaxie*] —**ga•lac•tic** (gə LAK tik) *adj.*

gale (gayl) *n.* **1.** a strong wind. **2.** an outburst, as of hilarity.

gall[1] (gawl) *n.* **1.** *Physiol.* the bitter fluid secreted by the liver; bile. **2.** bitter feeling; rancor. **3.** something bitter. **4.** impudence. [ME]

gall[2] *n.* **1.** an abrasion or sore produced by friction. **2.** something that irritates or vexes. **3.** exasperation. —*v.t.* **1.** injure (the skin) by friction; chafe. **2.** vex or irritate. —*v.i.* **3.** become or be chafed. [ME *galle*]

gall[3] *n.* an abnormal plant growth, induced by various causes. [ME *galle*]

gal•lant (GAL ənt) *adj.* **1.** spirited; courageous; brave. **2.** chivalrously attentive to women; also, dashingly amorous. **3.** stately; imposing. —*n.* (gə LANT) **1.** a brave, spirited man. **2.** a man chivalrously attentive to women or amorous in a courtly way. [ME *galaunt*] —**gal′lant•ry** *n.* [< MF *galanterie*]

gall bladder *Anat.* a small pouch serving as a reservoir for bile conducted from the liver through the **gall duct.**

gal•le•on (GAL ee ən) *n.* a large sailing vessel of the 15th to 17th c. [< Sp. *galeón*]

gal•ler•y (GAL ə ree) *n. pl.* **•ler•ies 1.** a roofed promenade, esp. an open-sided one, extending along an inner or outer wall of a building. **2.** *Southern U.S.* a veranda. **3.** the topmost balcony of a theater etc. **4.** a group of spectators, as of those in a grandstand. **5.** a part of the general public viewed as uninformed, undiscriminating, etc. **6.** a room or building in which works of art etc. are displayed. **7.** a room or building in which auctions are held. **8.** an enclosed place, as at a fair, where one shoots at targets for amusement. **9.** a tunnel or underground passage, as in a mine. —**play to the gallery** play or cater to the common crowd. [ME]

gal•ley (GAL ee) *n. pl.* **•leys 1.** a long, low vessel used in ancient times, propelled by oars and sails. **2.** a large rowboat. **3.** the kitchen of a ship, trailer, etc. **4.** *Printing* **a** a long tray for holding composed type. **b** a galley proof. [ME *galei*]

galley proof *Printing* a proof taken from type composed in a galley and used for making corrections.

galley slave 1. a slave or convict condemned to row a galley. **2.** a drudge.

Gal•lic (GAL ik) *adj.* of or pertaining to ancient Gaul or modern France; French. [< L *Gallicus*]

gall•ing (GAW ling) *adj.* exasperating.

gal•li•vant (GAL ə VANT) *v.i.* roam about capriciously; gad.

gal•lon (GAL ən) *n.* a liquid measure that by the U.S. standard contains 4 quarts. [ME *galon*]

gal•lop (GAL əp) *n.* **1.** the fastest gait of a horse, etc. **2.** a ride at a gallop. **3.** any rapid pace. —**gal′lop** *v.i. & v.t.* [ME *galopen*]

gal•lows (GAL ohz) *n. pl.* **•lows•es** or **•lows** an upright framework supporting a beam, used for execution by hanging. [ME *galwes*]

gall•stone (GAWL stohn) *n. Pathol.* a small, stony mass sometimes formed in the gall bladder or bile passages.

gal•op (GAL əp) *n.* **1.** a lively dance. **2.** music for this dance. [< F]

ga•lore (gə LOR) *adv.* in great numbers or abundance. [< Irish *go leōr* enough]

ga•losh (gə LOSH) *n. Usu. pl.* a high overshoe worn in bad weather. [ME]

gal•van•ic (gal VAN ik) *adj.* **1.** of or caused by electricity as produced by chemical action. **2.** stimulating; exciting.

gal•va•nism (GAL və NIZ əm) *n.* electricity as produced by chemical action. [after Luigi *Galvani*, 1737—98, Italian physiologist]

gal•va•nize (GAL və NIZ) *v.t.* **•nized, •niz•ing 1.** stimulate to muscular action by electricity. **2.** excite. **3.** plate steel etc. with a protective coating of zinc.

galvanized iron iron coated with zinc, as for protection against rust.

gam•bit (GAM bit) *n.* **1.** in chess, an opening in which a player risks or sacrifices a piece to gain a favorable position. **2.** any opening move, as one to promote discussion. **3.** a calculated move; a stratagem. [< F]

gam•ble (GAM bəl) *v.* **•bled, •bling** *v.i.* **1.** risk or bet something of value on the outcome of a game of chance etc. **2.** take a risk to obtain a result. —*v.t.* **3.** wager or bet (something of value). **4.** lose by taking risks: usu. with *away.* —*n.* any risky venture. [ME *gamenen* sport, play] —**gam′bler** *n.*

gam•bol (GAM bəl) *v.i.* **•boled, •bol•ing** skip or leap about in play; frolic. [< MF *gambade* leap] —**gam′bol** *n.*

game[1] (gaym) *n.* **1.** a contest governed by set rules. **2.** *pl.* athletic competitions. **3.** a single contest forming part of a fixed series. **4.** a win, as in tennis. **5.** the score during a contest: The *game* was 6–6. **6.** the equipment used in playing games. **7.** playing style or prowess: His *game* of golf is poor. **8.** any form of play. **9.** *Informal* any profession, business, etc.: the publishing *game.* **10.** animals, fish, etc. that are hunted or taken; also, the flesh of such animals etc. **11.** anything hunted; quarry. **12.** a target for ridicule, criticism, etc.: They were fair *game.* —**play the game** act in accordance with what is expected. —*v.i.* **gamed, gam•ing** gamble at cards etc. for money or other stakes. —*adj.* **1.** of hunted animals etc. or their flesh. **2.** having a fighting spirit; plucky. **3.** *Informal* ready; willing. [ME *gamen*] —**game′•ness** *n.*

game² *adj.* lame: a *game* leg.

game•keep•er (GAYM KEE pər) *n.* a person having the care of game, as on an estate.

game plan a strategy designed to achieve some specified objective.

gam•ete (GAM eet) *n. Biol.* a mature reproductive cell. [< NL *gameta*]

game theory a mathematical theory dealing with strategies of maximizing gains and minimizing losses in games, warfare, etc.

gam•in (GAM in) *n.* a homeless boy; street urchin; waif. [< F]

ga•mine (GAM een) *n.* **1.** a homeless girl. **2.** a girl with elfin appeal. [< F]

gam•ma (GAM ə) *n.* the third letter in the Greek alphabet (), corresponding to *g* (as in *go*).

gamma rays *Physics* a type of electromagnetic radiation of great-penetrating power.

gam•ut (GAM ət) *n.* the entire range of anything: the *gamut* of emotions. [ME]

gam•y (GAY mee) *adj.* **gam•i•er, gam•i•est 1.** having the flavor or odor of game, esp. when somewhat tainted. **2.** full of pluck. Also **gam′ey.** —**gam′i•ness** *n.*

gan•der (GAN dər) *n.* **1.** a male goose. **2.** *Slang* a look or glance: take a *gander.* [ME]

gang (gang) *n.* **1.** a group of persons organized or associated together for disreputable or illegal purposes. **2.** a crew of persons who work together. **3.** a group of persons associated together for some purpose. **4.** a set of similar tools or other devices designed to operate as a unit: *gang* of tractors. —*v.t. & v.i.* unite into or form a gang. —**gang up on** combine against or attack as a group. [ME]

gan•gling (GANG gling) *adj.* awkwardly tall and lanky. Also **gan′gly.** [Obs. E *gangrel* gangling person]

gan•gli•on (GANG glee ən) *n. pl.* **•gli•a** (-glee ə) or **•gli•ons 1.** *Physiol.* a bundle of nerve cells, outside of the central nervous system. **2.** any center of energy, activity, or strength. [< LL]

gang•plank (GANG PLANGK) *n.* a movable bridge for passengers between a vessel and a wharf.

gan•grene (GANG green) *n. Pathol.* the rotting of body tissue, caused by a failure in blood circulation, as from infection. [< MF] —**gan′grene** *v.t. & v.i.* **•grened, •gren•ing** —**gan•gre•nous** (GANG grə nəs) *adj.*

gang•ster (GANG stər) *n.* a member of a criminal gang.

gang•way (GANG way) *n.* **1.** a passageway through, into, or out of any enclosure. **2.** *Naut.* **a** a passage on a ship's upper deck. **b** an opening in a ship's side for passengers or freight. **c** a gangplank. —*interj.* get out of the way! [< OE *gangweg*]

gant•let (GANT lit) see GAUNTLET.

gan•try (GAN tree) *n. pl.* **•tries 1.** a bridgelike framework for holding the rails of a traveling crane or for supporting railway signals. **2.** a frame to support a barrel in a horizontal position. [ME *gauntre* frame]

gaol (jayl) *n. Brit.* jail. —**gaol′er** *n.*

gap (gap) *n.* **1.** an opening or wide crack, as in a wall. **2.** a deep notch or ravine in a mountain ridge. **3.** a break in continuity; interruption. **4.** a difference, as in character, opinions, etc. —*v.t.* **gapped, gap•ping** make or adjust a breach or opening in. [ME]

gape (gayp) *v.i.* **gaped, gap•ing 1.** stare with or as with the mouth wide open. **2.** open the mouth wide, as in yawning. **3.** be or become wide open. —*n.* **1.** the act of gaping. **2.** a wide opening. [ME]

ga•rage (gə RAHZH) *n.* a building in which motor vehicles are stored, serviced, or repaired. —*v.t.* **•raged, •rag•ing** put or keep in a garage. [< F]

garage sale a sale of used household goods held in one's garage or on one's premises. Also called *tag sale.*

garb (gahrb) *n.* **1.** clothes; esp., apparel characteristic of some office, rank, etc. **2.** external appearance, form, or expression. —*v.t.* clothe; dress. [< MF *garbe* gracefulness]

gar•bage (GAHR bij) *n.* **1.** kitchen refuse. **2.** anything worthless or useless. **3.** useless or garbled data in a computerized system. [ME, animal entrails]

gar·ble (GAHR bəl) *v.t.* **·bled, ·bling** mix up, confuse, or distort (a story, facts, etc.). —*n.* **1.** the act of garbling. **2.** that which is garbled. [ME *garbelen* sift]

gar·çon (gahr SAWN) *n. pl.* **·çons** (-SAWN) *French* **1.** a boy or youth. **2.** a waiter.

gar·den (GAHR dn) *n.* **1.** a place for the cultivation of flowers, vegetables, or small plants. **2.** any territory remarkable for the beauty of its vegetation. **3.** *Often pl.* an area commonly used as a place of public resort. —*adj.* grown or capable of being grown in a garden. —*v.t.* **1.** cultivate as a garden. — *v.i.* **2.** till or work in a garden. [ME *gardin*] —**gar'den·er** *n.*

garden variety ordinary; run-of-the-mill.

gar·gan·tu·an (gahr GAN choo ən) *adj.* extremely large; enormous; gigantic. [after *Gargantua,* satire (1534) by Rabelais]

gar·gle (GAHR gəl) *v.i.* **·gled, ·gling** rinse the throat with a liquid kept agitated by the slow expulsion of air. —*n.* a liquid used for gargling. [< MF *gargouiller* gargle]

gar·goyle (GAHR goil) *n.* a waterspout, usu. made in the form of a grotesque human or animal figure, projecting from a building. [ME *gargoile*]

gar·ish (GAIR ish) *adj.* vulgarly showy or gaudy. [Obs. *gaurish*] —**gar'ish·ly** *adv.*

gar·land (GAHR lənd) *n.* **1.** a wreath or rope of flowers, leaves, vines, etc. **2.** a collection of poems, bits of prose, etc. —*v.t.* decorate with or make into a garland. [ME *gerlande*]

gar·lic (GAHR lik) *n.* a plant having a compound bulb, the bulbs (or cloves) of which are used in cooking. [ME *garlec*] —**gar'lick·y** *adj.*

gar·ment (GAHR mənt) *n.* **1.** an article of clothing, esp. of outer clothing. **2.** *pl.* clothes. [ME *garnement*]

gar·ner (GAHR nər) *v.t.* gather or store; accumulate. [ME]

gar·nish (GAHR nish) *v.t.* **1.** decorate; embellish. **2.** in cookery, decorate (a dish) with flavorsome or colorful trimmings. [ME *garninshen* furnish] —**gar·ni·ture** (GAHR ni chər) *n.*

gar·nish·ee (GAHR ni SHEE) *Law v.t.* **·nish·eed, ·nish·ee·ing** attach (a debtor's assets) by garnishment. —*n.* a person who has been garnished.

gar·ret (GAR it) *n.* a room or set of rooms in an attic. [ME *garite* watchtower]

gar·ri·son (GAR ə sən) *n.* **1.** the military force stationed in a fort, town, etc. **2.** the place where such a force is stationed. —*v.t.* **1.** place troops in, as a fort or town, for defense. **2.** occupy as a garrison. [ME *garisoun* stronghold]

gar·rote (gə ROHT) *n.* a former Spanish method of execution with a cord or metal collar tightened by a screwlike device; also, the cord or collar used. —*v.t.* **·rot·ed, ·rot·ing 1.** execute with a garrote. **2.** throttle in order to rob, silence, etc. [< Sp.]

gar·ru·lous (GAR ə ləs) *adj.* **1.** talkative; glib. **2.** rambling; wordy. [< L *garrulus* talkative] —**gar·ru·li·ty** (gə ROO li tee) *n.*

gar·ter (GAHR tər) *n.* a band worn around the leg or a tab attached to an undergarment to hold a stocking in place. [ME]

gas (gas) *n. pl.* **gas·es 1.** a form of matter having extreme molecular mobility and capable of diffusing and expanding rapidly in all directions. **2.** any of various gases or mixtures of gases with explosive, combustive, anesthetic, or poisonous properties. **3.** a noxious exhalation given off by improperly digested food in the stomach or intestines. **4.** gasoline. **5.** *Slang* long-winded talking. **6.** *Slang* something very exciting, satisfying, etc. —*v.* **gassed, gas·sing** —*v.t.* **1.** subject to or affect with gas. **2.** fill or supply with gas. —*v.i.* **3.** give off gas. **4.** *Slang* talk excessively. [Coined by J. B. van Helmont, 1577–1644, Belgian chemist] —**gas·e·ous** (GASH əs) *adj.* —**gas'sy** *adj.* **·si·er, ·si·est**

gash (gash) *v.t.* make a long, deep cut in. [ME *garsen* wound] —**gash** *n.*

gas·ket (GAS kit) *n.* a ring or plate of rubber etc., used to make a joint leakproof.

gas mask a protective mask with an air filter worn for protection against noxious gases.

gas·o·hol (GAS ə HAWL) *n.* a mixture of gasoline and alcohol, used as a motor fuel, esp. in automobiles.

gas·o·line (GAS ə LEEN) *n.* a colorless, volatile, flammable liquid hydrocarbon, made by distillation of crude petroleum and used chiefly as a fuel.

gasp (gasp) *v.i.* **1.** take in the breath suddenly and sharply, as from fear. **2.** have great longing or desire: with *for* or *after.* —*v.t.* **3.** say or utter while gasping. [ME *gaspen*] — **gasp** *n.*

gas·tric (GAS trik) *adj.* of or pertaining to the stomach.

gastric juice *Biochem.* a fluid secreted by stomach glands, essential to digestion.

gas·tri·tis (ga STRĪ tis) n. Pathol. inflammation of the stomach lining.

gas·tro·in·tes·ti·nal (GAS troh in TES tə nl) adj. of or pertaining to the stomach and intestines.

gas·tro·nome (GAS trə NOHM) n. a gourmet. [< F]

gas·tro·nom·ic (GAS trə NOM ik) adj. of or pertaining to gastronomes or gastronomy.

gas·tron·o·my (ga STRON ə mee) n. the art of good eating; epicurism. [< F gastronomie]

gate (gayt) n. 1. a movable barrier, commonly swinging on hinges, that closes or opens a passage through a wall, fence, etc. 2. a passage through a wall or fence. 3. anything that gives access: the gate to success. 4. a structure or valvelike device for controlling the supply of water, oil, gas, etc. 5. the total paid attendance at a sports event, stage show, etc.; also, the money collected. [ME gat]

gate-crash·er (GAYT KRASH ər) n. Informal one who enters without paying or being invited.

gate·way (GAYT way) n. 1. an entrance that is or may be closed with a gate. 2. any means of entry or exit.

gath·er (GATH ər) v.t. 1. bring together into one place or group. 2. bring together from various places, sources, etc. 3. harvest or pick, as crops, fruit, etc. 4. accumulate or muster: The storm gathered force. 5. clasp or enfold. 6. wrinkle (the brow). 7. draw into folds, as cloth on a thread. 8. become aware of; infer. —v.i. 9. come together or assemble. 10. increase by accumulation. 11. become wrinkled or creased, as the brow. 12. come to a head, as a boil. —n. Usu. pl. a pleat or fold in cloth, secured by a thread. [ME gaderen] —gath·er·er n.

gath·er·ing (GATH ər ing) n. 1. the action of one who or that which gathers. 2. that which is gathered. 3. an assemblage of people; group. 4. a series of gathers in cloth, etc. 5. an abscess or boil. 6. in bookbinding, a collection of printed sheets in proper order.

gauche (gohsh) adj. awkward; clumsy; boorish. [< F, left, awkward]

gauche·rie (GOH shə REE) n. 1. awkward or tactless behavior. 2. an instance of this. [< F]

gaud·y (GAW dee) adj. gaud·i·er, gaud·i·est tastelessly bright or showy; garish. —gaud'i·ly adv. —gaud'i·ness n.

gauge (gayj) v.t. gauged, gaug·ing 1. determine the dimensions, amount, force, etc. of. 2. determine the contents or capacity of, as a cask. 3. estimate, appraise, or judge. 4. make conform to a standard measurement. —n. 1. a standard measurement. 2. a means of comparing; criterion. 3. an instrument for measuring or recording. 4. thickness, diameter, or fineness of something. 5. the diameter of a bore of a gun. Also spelled gage. [ME]

Gaul (gawl) n. 1. a native of ancient Gaul. 2. that country.

gaunt (gawnt) adj. 1. emaciated, as from hunger, illness, or age; haggard. 2. desolate or gloomy in appearance: a gaunt region. [ME] —gaunt'ness n.

gaunt·let[1] (GAWNT lit) n. 1. in medieval armor, a glove covered with metal plates to protect the hand. 2. any glove with a long, often flaring extension over the wrist. — **take up the gauntlet** accept a challenge. —**throw** (or **fling**) **down the gauntlet** challenge to combat. [ME gantelet mitten]

gaunt·let[2] n. a former military punishment in which the offender ran between two lines of men, who struck the offender with clubs, whips, etc. while passing. —**run the gauntlet** 1. undergo such punishment. 2. suffer a barrage of problems, criticism, etc.

gauss (gows) n. Physics the electromagnetic unit of magnetic induction. [after K. F. Gauss, 1777—1855, German mathematician]

gauze (gawz) n. 1. a lightweight, transparent fabric with an open weave, made of silk, cotton, etc. 2. any thin, open-mesh material. [< F gaze]

gave (gayv) past tense of GIVE.

gav·el (GAV əl) n. a mallet used, as by a presiding officer, to call for order or attention. —v. use a gavel to bring order etc.

gawk (gawk) v.i. 1. stare stupidly; gape. 2. move about or behave awkwardly. — **gawk'i·ness** n. —**gawk'y** adj. **gawk·i·er, gawk·i·est** clumsy; awkward.

gay (gay) adj. 1. happy and carefree; merry. 2. brightly colorful or ornamental. 3. jaunty; sporty. 4. homosexual. [ME gai] — n. a homosexual person, esp. a male.

gaze (gayz) v.i. gazed, gaz·ing look steadily or fixedly at something; stare. [ME gasen] —gaze n.

ga·ze·bo (gə ZAY boh) n. pl. ·bos, ·boes a structure, as a summerhouse, affording a view of the surrounding landscape.

ga·zette (gə ZET) n. **1.** a newspaper or similar periodical. **2.** an official publication, as of a government or society. [< F]

gaz·et·teer (CAZ i TEER) n. **1.** a listing of countries, cities, rivers, etc., together with their location, size, etc. **2.** a writer for or publisher of a gazette.

gear (geer) n. **1.** Mech. **a** a mechanical assembly of interacting parts that serves to transmit motion or to change the rate or direction of motion. **b** a related group of parts that work together for a special purpose: steering gear. **2.** clothing. **3.** movable property. **4.** any equipment used for a special task: fishing gear. —**out of gear 1.** not in good working order. **2.** disengaged; unconnected. —v.t. **1.** Mech. **a** put into gear. **b** equip with gears. **c** connect by means of gears. **2.** regulate so as to match or suit something else: gear production to demand. **3.** get ready; prepare: with up. **4.** put gear on; dress. —v.i. **5.** come into or be in gear; mesh. [ME gere] —**gear'ing** n.

gear·shift (GEER SHIFT) n. Mech. a device for engaging or disengaging the gears in a transmission system.

geck·o (GEK oh) n. pl. •os or •oes any of a family of small lizards having toes with adhesive disks. [< NL gekko]

gee (jee) interj. an exclamation expressing mild surprise, sympathy, etc. Also **gee whiz.**

geese (gees) plural of GOOSE.

Gei·ger counter (GĪ gər) Physics an instrument for detecting radioactive substances or cosmic rays. [after Hans Geiger, 1882–1947, German physicist]

gei·sha (GAY shə) n. pl. •sha or •shas a Japanese woman trained as an entertainer and companion for men. [< Japanese]

gel·a·tin (JEL ə tn) n. **1.** a glutinous protein substance, derived from animals and used in food, drug preparations, photographic film, plastics, etc. **2.** a jelly made from gelatin. [< F gélatine] —**ge·lat·i·nous** (jə LAT n əs) adj.

geld (geld) v.t. **geld·ed** or **gelt, geld·ing** castrate or spay. [ME gelden] —**geld'ing** n. a castrated animal, esp. a horse.

gel·id (JEL id) adj. very cold; icy. [< L gelidus]

gem (jem) n. **1.** a cut and polished precious or semiprecious stone; jewel. **2.** one who or that which is treasured. —v.t. **gemmed, gem·ming** decorate or set with or as with gems. [ME gemme]

gem·stone (JEM STOHN) n. a precious or semiprecious stone, esp. before it is cut and polished.

gen·darme (ZHAHN dahrm) n. pl. •darmes (-dahrmz) one of a corps of armed police, esp. in France. [< MF gens d'armes people-at-arms]

gen·der (JEN dər) n. **1.** Gram. **a** one of two or more categories of words or affixes based on differences of sex or sometimes on other distinctions. **b** such categories collectively, or a system of such categories. **c** the distinctive forms used for such categories. **2.** sex. [ME]

gene (jeen) n. Biol. a complex unit of heredity characters, found along a segment of DNA. [< G Gen]

ge·ne·al·o·gy (JEE nee AL ə jee) n. pl. •gies **1.** a family tree. **2.** descent in a direct line from a progenitor; pedigree. **3.** the study of pedigrees. [ME genealogie] —**ge·ne·a·log·i·cal** (JEE nee ə LOJ i kəl) adj.

gen·e·ra (JEN ə rə) plural of GENUS. [< L]

gen·er·al (JEN ər əl) adj. **1.** pertaining to or of the whole; not particular. **2.** common to or current among the majority: the general opinion. **3.** miscellaneous: a general cargo. **4.** not detailed or precise: a general idea. **5.** not specialized: a general practitioner. **6.** superior in rank: a second element in some titles: attorney general. —n. Mil. **1.** in the U.S. Army and Air Force an officer of the next to highest rank, equivalent to an admiral in the navy. **2.** in the U.S. Marine Corps the highest ranking officer. —**in general 1.** without going into detail. **2.** all things considered. **3.** usually; commonly. [ME]

gen·er·al·i·ty (JEN ə RAL i tee) n. pl. •ties **1.** the state or quality of being general. **2.** something lacking detail or precision, as a statement or idea. **3.** the greater number of a group; mass. [ME generalite]

gen·er·al·ize (JEN ər ə LIZ) v. •ized, •iz·ing v.t. **1.** make general; as: **a** make broad in application. **b** avoid making detailed. **c** cause to be widespread. **2.** derive a broad conclusion, principle, etc. from (particular instances, facts, etc.). —v.i. **3.** write or speak without going into details etc. —**gen'er·al·i·za'tion** n.

gen·er·al·ly (JEN ə rə lee) adv. **1.** for the most part; ordinarily. **2.** without going into specific details: generally speaking. **3.** commonly: generally believed.

general officer *Mil.* any officer ranking above a colonel.

General of the Air Force the highest ranking officer of the U.S. Air Force.

General of the Army the highest rank in the U.S. Army.

general practitioner a physician whose practice is not limited to a medical specialty.

general staff 1. a body of officers who direct the military policy and strategy of a nation. **2.** a group of officers who assist the commander in directing operations.

gen·er·ate (JEN ə RAYT) *v.t.* **·at·ed, ·at·ing 1.** produce or cause to be; originate. **2.** beget; procreate. [ME]

gen·er·a·tion (JEN ə RAY shən) *n.* **1.** the process of begetting offspring. **2.** a successive step or degree in natural descent, or the average period between two such steps. **3.** any group of individuals born at about the same time. **4.** the act or process of generating or being generated. [ME *generacioun*] —**gen·er·a·tive** (JEN ə rə tiv) *adj.*

gen·er·a·tor (JEN ə RAY tər) *n.* **1.** one who or that which generates. **2.** *Chem.* an apparatus designed to generate a gas. **3.** any of a class of machines for the conversion of mechanical energy into electrical energy.

ge·ner·ic (jə NER ik) *adj.* **1.** pertaining to a genus or class of related things. **2.** applicable to every member of a class or genus. **3.** having a wide, general application. Also **ge·ner'i·cal.** —*n.* a generic drug. [< F *générique*]

generic drug a drug not having a trademark.

gen·er·ous (JEN ər əs) *adj.* **1.** marked by or showing great liberality; munificent. **2.** having gracious or noble qualities: a *generous* nature. **3.** abundant and overflowing: a *generous* serving. [< MF *généreux*] —**gen·er·os·i·ty** (JEN ə ROS i tee) *n.* [ME *generosite*]

gen·e·sis (JEN ə sis) *n. pl.* **·ses** (-seez) **1.** the act or mode of originating. **2.** origin. [< Gk. *genēsis*]

Gen·e·sis (JEN ə sis) the first book of the Old Testament.

gene splicing recombinant DNA research.

ge·net·ic (jə NET ik) *adj.* **1.** of, pertaining to, or based on genetics. **2.** of or pertaining to the origin or development of something. —**ge·net'i·cal·ly** *adv.*

genetic code the arrangement of DNA, constituting the biochemical basis of heredity.

ge·net·ics (jə NET iks) *n.* **1.** (*construed as sing.*) the science of heredity. **2.** (*construed as pl.*) the inherited characteristics of an organism. —**ge·net'i·cist** (jə NET ə sist) *n.*

gen·ial (JEEN yəl) *adj.* **1.** kindly, pleasant, or cordial in disposition or manner. **2.** imparting warmth, comfort, or life. [< L *genialis* jovial] —**ge·ni·al·i·ty** (JEE nee AL i tee) *n.*

ge·nie (JEE nee) *n.* see JINNI.

gen·i·tal (JEN ə təl) *adj.* of or pertaining to reproduction or the reproductive organs. [ME]

gen·i·tals (JEN ə təlz) *n.pl.* the external sexual organs. Also **gen·i·ta·li·a** (JEN i TAY lee ə).

gen·i·tive (JEN i tiv) *adj. Gram.* pertaining to a case in Latin, Greek, etc., corresponding in part to the English possessive. —*n. Gram.* **1.** the genitive case. **2.** a word in this case. [ME]

gen·i·to·u·ri·nar·y (JEN i toh YUUR ə NER ee) *adj.* of or pertaining to the genital and urinary organs.

gen·ius (JEEN yəs) *n. pl.* **gen·ius·es 1.** extraordinary intelligence; also, one who possesses such intelligence. **2.** an outstanding gift for a certain activity; also, one so gifted. **3.** the essential spirit or distinguishing characteristics of a particular people, era, etc. **4.** one who exerts a strong influence over another. [ME]

gen·o·cide (JEN ə SID) *n.* the systematic extermination of an entire people or national group. [< Gk. *genos* race, tribe + *-cide* killer]

gen·o·type (JEN ə TIP) *n. Biol.* **1.** the genetic constitution of an organism. **2.** a group of organisms with the same genetic constitution. —**gen·o·typ·i·cal** (JEN ə TIP i kəl) *adj.*

gen·re (ZHAHN rə) *n.* **1.** a particular sort, kind, or category; esp., a category of art or literature. **2.** a class of painting or other art depicting everyday life. [< F] —*adj.* of or pertaining to a genre: *genre* painting.

gen·teel (jen TEEL) *adj.* **1.** well-bred; elegant; polite. **2.** pertaining or appropriate to well-bred persons. **3.** affectedly refined. [< MF *gentil*] —**gen·teel'ness** *n.*

gen·tile (JEN TIL) *adj.* **1.** of or pertaining to a tribe or people. **2.** of or pertaining to Gentiles. [ME]

Gen·tile (JEN TIL) *n.* **1.** among Jews, one not a Jew. **2.** among Christians, a heathen or pagan. **3.** among Mormons, one not a Mormon.

gen•til•i•ty (jen TIL i tee) *n. pl.* **•ties 1.** the quality of being genteel; refinement. **2.** gentle birth; good extraction. **3.** well-born or well-bred persons collectively. [ME]

gen•tle (JEN tl) *adj.* **•tler, •tlest 1.** mild in nature, quality or disposition. **2.** not steep or abrupt; gradual: a *gentle* ascent. **3.** easily managed; docile. **4.** of good family and breeding. **5.** well-behaved; polite. —*v.t.* **•tled, •tling** make easy to control; tame. [ME] **—gen′tle•ness** *n.*

gen•tle•man (JEN tl mən) *n. pl.* **•men 1.** a man of good birth and social position. **2.** a courteous, considerate man. **3.** any man: in the plural, used as a form of address. — **gen′tle•man•ly** *adj.*

gen•tle•wom•an (JEN tl wuum ən) *n. pl.* **•wom•en 1.** a woman of good family or superior social position; lady. **2.** a gracious, well-mannered woman.

gen•try (JEN tree) *n.* people of good family or superior social standing. [ME]

gen•u•flect (JEN yuu FLEKT) *v.i.* bend the knee, as in worship. [< Med.L *genuflectere* bend the knee] **—gen′u•flec′tion** *n.*

gen•u•ine (JEN yoo in) *adj.* **1.** being of the origin, authorship, or character claimed. **2.** not spurious or counterfeit. [< L *genuinus* innate] **—gen′u•ine•ness** *n.*

ge•nus (JEE nəs) *n. pl.* **gen•e•ra** (JEN ər ə) **1.** *Biol.* a grouping or category of plants and animals ranking next above the species and next below the family or subfamily. **2.** *Logic* a class of things divisible into two or more subordinate classes or species. **3.** a particular sort, kind, or class. [< L, race, kind]

ge•o•cen•tric (JEE oh SEN trik) *adj.* **1.** calculated or viewed relative to the earth's center. **2.** assuming that the earth is the center of the universe.

ge•o•chem•is•try (JEE oh KEM ə stree) *n.* a branch of chemistry dealing with the composition of the earth's crust.

ge•ode (JEE ohd) *n. Geol.* a rock, usually globular, having a cavity lined with crystals. [< L *geodes*] **—ge•od•ic** (jee OD ik) *adj.*

ge•o•des•ic (JEE ə DEE sik) *adj.* **1.** of or pertaining to the geometry of geodesic lines or curved surfaces. **2.** geodetic. —*n.* a geodesic line.

geodesic dome *Archit.* a dome made of prefabricated lattice modules and covered with a thin, strong material.

ge•od•e•sy (jee OD ə see) *n.* the science dealing with the determination and representation of the shape, area, and curvature of the earth. Also **ge•o•det•ics** (JEE ə DET iks). [*géodesie*] **—ge•od′e•sist** *n.*

ge•o•det•ic (JEE ə DET IK) *ADJ.* **1.** of or pertaining to geodesy. **2.** geodesic.

ge•og•ra•phy (jee OG rə fee) *n. pl.* **•phies 1.** the science that describes the surface of the earth and its associated physical, biological, economic, political, and demographic characteristics. **2.** the natural aspect, features, etc. of a place or area. **3.** a particular work on or system of geography. [< L *geographia*] **—ge•og′ra•pher** *n.* **—ge•o•graph•i•cal** (JEE ə GRAF i kəl) or **ge′o•graph′ic** *adj.*

ge•ol•o•gy (jee OL ə jee) *n. pl.* **•gies 1.** the science that treats of the origin, structure, and history of the earth, esp. as shown by rocks and rock formations. **2.** the structure of the earth in a given region. **—ge′o•log′ i•cal** *adj.* **—ge•ol′o•gist** *n.*

ge•o•met•ric (JEE ə ME trik) *adj.* **1.** pertaining to or according to the rules and principles of geometry. **2.** forming, consisting of, or characterized by straight lines, bars, crosses, zigzags, etc., as in painting or sculpture. Also **ge′o•met′ri•cal.**

geometric progression *Math.* a numerical sequence whose terms are related by a constant ratio, as 2, 4, 8, 16.

ge•om•e•try (jee OM i tree) *n. pl.* **•tries** the branch of mathematics that treats of space and its relations, esp. as shown in the properties and measurement of points, lines, angles, surfaces, and solids. [ME]

ge•o•phys•ics (JEE oh FIZ iks) *n. (construed as sing.)* the study of the physics of the earth, including its oceans, weather, earthquakes, volcanoes, magnetic fields, and radioactivity. **—ge′o•phys′i•cal** *adj.* **—ge′o•phys′i•cist** *n.*

ge•o•pol•i•tics (JEE oh POL i tiks) *n. (construed as sing.)* **1.** the study of political and economic geography. **2.** a theory that the physical geography of a country determines its political outlook. **—ge•o•po•lit•i•cal** (JEE oh pə LIT i kəl) *adj.*

ge•o•ther•mal (JEE oh THUR məl) *adj.* of the earth's internal heat.

ger•i•at•rics (JER ee A triks) *n. (construed as sing.)* **1.** the branch of medicine that deals with diseases and physiology of old age. **2.** gerontology. **—ger′i•at′ric** *adj.* **—ger′ i•at′rist** *n.*

germ (jurm) *n.* **1.** a microorganism that

causes disease; a microbe. **2.** something in its essential though rudimentary form: the *germ* of an idea. **3.** *Biol.* **a** a reproductive cell. **b** an organism in its embryonic form. [ME]

Ger·man (JUR mən) *n.* **1.** a native or inhabitant of Germany. **2.** the language of the Germans. —**High German** the standard literary and spoken language used in Germany, Austria, and parts of Switzerland and Alsace: also called *New High German.* —**Low German** collectively, the languages of the Low Countries, including Dutch, Flemish, and Frisian, and of the northern lowlands of Germany (*Plattdeutsch*). —**Old High German** the language of southern Germany from about 800 to 1100. —**Middle High German** the High German language from 1100 to 1450. —**Middle Low German** the Low German language from 1100 to 1450. [< L *Germanus*] —**Ger'man** *adj.*

ger·mane (jər MAYN) *adj.* related to what is being discussed or considered; pertinent; relevant.

Ger·man·ic (jər MAN ik) *adj.* **1.** of or pertaining to a group of early Indo-European tribes living in the region bounded by the Rhine, Danube, and Vistula rivers, later including the Germans, English, Dutch, Flemings, Danes, Scandinavians, and German-Swiss. **2.** relating to the language or customs of any of these people. —*n.* a branch of the Indo-European family of languages, divided into **East Germanic,** including Gothic (extinct); **North Germanic** or Scandinavian, including Norwegian, Swedish, Danish, Icelandic, and Faroese; and **West Germanic,** including all the High and Low German languages and dialects.

German measles *Pathol.* a contagious virus disease accompanied by fever, sore throat, and a skin rash: also called *rubella.*

germ cell *Biol.* a cell specialized for reproduction.

ger·mi·nal (JUR mə nl) *adj.* **1.** of, relating to, or constituting a germ or germ cell. **2.** pertaining to the earliest stage of development. [< F]

ger·mi·nate (JUR mə NAYT) *v.* •**nat·ed,** •**nat·ing** *v.i.* **1.** begin to grow or develop; sprout. —*v.t.* **2.** cause to sprout. [< L *germinatus* sprouted] —**ger'mi·na'tion** *n.*

geronto- *combining form* old age; pertaining to old people: *gerontology.* Also, be-

fore vowels, **geront-.** [< Gk. *gerōn* old man]

ger·on·tol·o·gy (JER ən TOL ə jee) *n.* **1.** the scientific study of the processes and problems of aging. **2.** geriatrics. —**ge·ron·to·log·i·cal** *adj.* —**ger'on·tol'o·gist** *n.*

ger·ry·man·der (JER i MAN dər) *v.t.* alter (a voting area) so as to advance unfairly the interest of a political party. —*n.* the act or result of gerrymandering. [after Elbridge *Gerry,* 1744–1814, + (SALA)MANDER: from the shape of a district formed in Massachusetts while he was governor]

ger·und (JER ənd) *n.* *Gram.* a form of a verb used like a noun: in English, the *-ing* form of a verb, as *doing,* or a compound tense made with the *-ing* form of an auxiliary, as *having done.* [< LL *gerundium*]

ge·stalt (gə SHTAHLT) *n.* *pl.* •**stalts** or •**stalt·en** (-SHTAHL tn) a synthesis of separate elements of emotion, experience, etc. that constitutes more than the mechanical sum of the parts. Also **Ge·stalt'.** [< G, form]

Gestalt psychology psychology based on the theory of the gestalt. Also **gestalt psychology.**

Ge·sta·po (gə STAH poh) *n.* the German secret police under the Nazi regime, noted for their brutality. [< G *Ge(heime) Sta(ats)po(lizei)*]

ges·tate (JES tayt) *v.t.* •**tat·ed,** •**tat·ing** carry in the uterus during pregnancy. [< L *gestatus* carried in the womb] —**ges·ta'tion** *n.*

ges·tic·u·late (je STIK yə LAYT) *v.* •**lat·ed,** •**lat·ing** *v.i.* **1.** make emphatic or expressive gestures, as in speaking. —*v.t.* **2.** express by gestures. [< L *gesticulatus* gestured] —**ges·tic'u·la'tion** *n.*

ges·ture (JES chər) *n.* **1.** a meaningful bodily motion, as of the hands in speaking. **2.** such motions collectively. **3.** something said or done as a mere formality, or for effect. [ME] —**ges'ture** *v.t. & v.i.* •**tured,** •**tur·ing**

get (get) *v.* **got, got** or **got·ten, get·ting** *v.t.* **1.** come into possession of; obtain. **2.** go for and bring back. **3.** capture; seize. **4.** cause to come, go, etc. **5.** prepare: *get* lunch. **6.** bring to a state or condition: *get* the work done. **7.** persuade: *Get* her to sign the paper. **8.** find out or obtain by calculation, experiment, etc. **9.** give or receive (reward or punishment). **10.** become sick with. **11.**

establish contact with: I'll get him on the phone. **12.** catch, as a train; board. **13.** beget: now said chiefly of animals. **14.** *Informal* come to an understanding of. **15.** *Informal* possess: with *have* or *has*: He has *got* quite a temper. **16.** *Informal* be obliged or forced (to do something specified): with *have* or *has*. **17.** hit: The shrapnel *got* him in the arm. **18.** *Informal* puzzle or baffle. **19.** *Informal* please, irritate, etc.: That music *gets* me. —*v.i.* **20.** arrive: When does the train *get* there? **21.** come, go, or move: *Get* in here. **22.** board; enter: with *on, in*, etc. **23.** become. —**get across** be successful, as in projecting one's personality or conveying one's meaning. —**get ahead** attain success. —**get along 1.** leave; go: *Get along* with you! **2.** be successful, as in business. **3.** be friendly or compatible. **4.** grow old or older. —**get around 1.** become known, as gossip. **2.** move about. **3.** attend social or public functions etc. **4.** dodge; circumvent. —**get around to** give attention to after some delay. —**get at 1.** arrive at; reach. **2.** intend; mean: I don't see what you're *getting at*. **3.** apply oneself to: *get at* a problem. **4.** *Informal* prevail upon; influence. —**get away 1.** escape. **2.** leave; go. **3.** start, as a race horse. —**get away with** do (something) without discovery, criticism, or punishment. —**get back at** revenge oneself on. —**get by 1.** pass: This *got by* the censor. **2.** manage to survive. —**get down to** (business, facts, etc.) begin to act on, investigate, or consider. —**get in 1.** arrive or enter. **2.** slip in (a remark etc.). **3.** become involved or familiar with. **4.** be elected. —**get it** *Informal* **1.** understand. **2.** be punished in some way. —**get off 1.** descend from; dismount. **2.** depart. **3.** be relieved or freed, as of a duty or penalty. **4.** utter: *get off* a joke. **5.** *Slang* enjoy: with *on*. —**get on 1.** mount (a horse, vehicle, etc.). **2.** get along. —**get out 1.** depart. **2.** escape. **3.** become known, as a secret. **4.** publish. **5.** express or utter. —**get out of 1.** obtain from. **2.** escape or evade. **3.** depart from. —**get over 1.** recover from (illness, surprise, anger, etc.). **2.** get across. —**get through (to) 1.** establish communication (with). **2.** make clear (to). —**get to 1.** begin. **2.** be able to (do something). **3.** get through to. —**get together 1.** assemble. **2.** come to an agreement. —**get up 1.**

arise. **2.** climb. **3.** devise. **4.** acquire, develop, or work up. **5.** dress up. [ME *geten*] —**get'ter** *n.*

get·a·way (GET ə WAY) *n.* **1.** an escape, as of a criminal. **2.** the start, as of an automobile, race horse, etc. **3.** any departure.

get-to·geth·er (GET tə GETH ər) *n.* a gathering.

get·up (GET UP) *n. Informal* costume.

get-up-and-go (GET UP ən GOH) *n.* vigorous initiative.

gew·gaw (GYOO gaw) *n.* some little ornamental article of small value. [ME *giugeaue*]

gey·ser (GĪ zər) *n.* a natural hot spring from which intermittent jets of steam, hot water, or mud are ejected in a fountainlike column. [< Icel. *geysir* gusher]

ghast·ly (GAST lee) *adj.* **·li·er, ·li·est 1.** horrible; terrifying. **2.** deathlike in appearance; very pale. **3.** very bad or unpleasant. [ME *gastly*] —**ghast'li·ness** *n.*

ghee (gee) *n.* in India, a kind of clarified butter, usu. made from buffalo milk. [< Hind. *ghi*]

gher·kin (GUR kin) *n.* **1.** a very small cucumber pickled as a relish. **2.** the plant producing it. **3.** any small, immature cucumber used for pickling. [< Du. *gurken*]

ghet·to (GET oh) *n. pl.* **·tos, -toes 1.** an often run-down section of a city inhabited chiefly by a minority group. **2.** a section in certain European cities in which Jews were required to live. [< Ital.]

ghost (gohst) *n.* **1.** a disembodied spirit; a wraith, specter, or phantom. **2.** a haunting recollection of something: *ghosts* from the past. **3.** a mere suggestion of something: a *ghost* of a smile. **4.** *Informal* a ghostwriter. **5.** *Optics & Telecom.* an unwanted false or secondary image. —**give up the ghost 1.** die. **2.** cease to function. —*v.t.* ghostwrite. [ME *goost*] —**ghost'ly** *adj.* **·li·er, ·li·est**
ghost town a deserted town.

ghost·write (GOHST RIT) *v.t. & v.i.* **·wrote, ·writ·ten, ·writ·ing** write (a speech etc.) for someone else who receives credit as author. —**ghost' writ'er** *n.*

ghoul (gool) *n.* **1.** one who robs graves. **2.** one who takes pleasure in revolting things. **3.** in Muslim legend, an evil spirit who preys on corpses. [< Arabic *ghūl*] —**ghoul'ish** *adj.*

gi·ant (JĪ ənt) *n.* **1.** in legend, a person of supernatural size and strength. **2.** any person or thing of great size, capability, etc.

[ME *geant*] — **gi'ant** *adj.* —**gi'ant·ess** *n. fem.*

gib·ber (JIB ər) *v.i. & v.t.* talk rapidly and incoherently; jabber. —*n.* gibberish.

gib·ber·ish (JIB ər ish) *n.* **1.** rapid or unintelligible talk; gabble. **2.** needlessly difficult or obscure language.

gib·bet (JIB it) *n.* a gallows. —*v.t.* **gib·bet·ed, gib·bet·ing 1.** execute by hanging. **2.** hold up to public contempt. [ME]

gib·bous (GIB əs) *adj.* **1.** irregularly rounded or convex, as the moon when more than half full and less than full. **2.** hunchbacked. [ME] —**gib·bos·i·ty** (gi BOS i tee) *n.* [ME]

gibe (jīb) *v.* gibed, gib·ing *v.i.* **1.** utter jeers or derisive remarks. —*v.t.* **2.** taunt. —*n.* a jeer. Also *jibe.* —**gib'er** *n.*

gib·let (JIB lit) *n. Usu. pl.* the edible heart, liver, gizzard, etc., of a fowl. [ME]

gid·dy (GID ee) *adj.* **·di·er, ·di·est 1.** affected by a reeling or whirling sensation; dizzy. **2.** tending to cause such a sensation. **3.** frivolous; heedless. —*v.t. & v.i.* **·died, ·dy·ing** make or become dizzy. [ME *gidy* insane] —**gid'di·ness** *n.*

gift (gift) *n.* **1.** something that is given; present. **2.** the act or right of giving. **3.** a natural aptitude; talent. [ME]

gift·ed (GIF tid) *adj.* endowed with talent.

gig[1] (gig) *n.* **1.** a light, two-wheeled vehicle drawn by one horse. **2.** *Naut.* a long ship's boat, usu. for the captain. [ME *gigge* flighty girl]

gig[2] *n.* an arrangement of fishhooks. —*v.t. & v.i.* **gigged, gig·ging** catch (fish) with a gig. [< earlier *fishgig* harpoon]

gig[3] *n.* a demerit, as in the army, school, etc. —*v.t.* **gigged, gig·ging 1.** give a demerit to. **2.** punish.

gig[4] *n. Slang* a job; esp., a musician's engagement.

giga- *combining form* a billion (10^9) times (a specified unit).

gi·gan·tic (jī GAN tik) *adj.* **1.** of, like, or suited to a giant. **2.** tremendous; huge.

gi·gan·tism (jī GAN tiz əm) *n.* abnormal size; esp. when due to pituitary malfunction.

gig·gle (GIG əl) *v.i.* **·gled, ·gling** laugh in a high-pitched, silly, or nervous manner. —*n.* a titter. —**gig'gler** *n.* —**gig·gly** *adj.* **·gli·er, ·gli·est**

gig·o·lo (JIG ə LOH) *n. pl.* **·los 1.** a woman's paid male escort. **2.** a man supported by a

woman not his wife. [< F < *gigolette* prostitute]

Gi·la monster (HEE lə) an orange and black lizard of the North American desert. [after the *Gila* River, Arizona]

gild (gild) *v.t.* **gild·ed** or **gilt, gild·ing 1.** coat with a thin layer of gold. **2.** brighten or adorn. **3.** gloss over. [ME *gilden*] —**gild'er** *n.*

gill[1] (gil) *n. Zool.* the breathing organ of fishes, amphibians, and other aquatic vertebrates. —**green around the gills** sickly in appearance. [ME *gile*]

gill[2] (jil) *n.* a liquid measure equal to $\frac{1}{4}$ pint. [ME *gille*]

gilt (gilt) alternative past tense, past participle of GILD. —*adj.* gold-colored; gilded. —*n.* a material for gilding.

gilt-edged (GILT EJD) *adj.* **1.** having the edges gilded. **2.** of the best quality: *gilt-edged* securities. Also **gilt'-edge'.**

gim·bals (GIM bəlz) *n.* (*construed as sing.*) a set of three metal rings so arranged as to maintain an object supported by it, as a ship's compass, on a horizontal plane.

gim·crack (JIM KRAK) *n.* a useless, gaudy object. —*adj.* cheap and showy. —**gim'·crack'er·y** *n.*

gim·let (GIM lit) *n.* a small, sharp tool with a pointed, spiral tip for boring holes. [ME] —**gim'let** *v.t.*

gimlet eyes sharp eyes. —**gim'let-eyed'** *adj.*

gim·mick (GIM ik) *n.* **1.** a novel or clever scheme or detail. **2.** a hidden or deceptive device, as one used by a magician. —**gim'mick·ry** *n.* —**gim'mick·y** *adj.*

gin[1] (jin) *n.* an aromatic alcoholic liquor, usu. flavored with juniper berries. [< Du. *jenever* juniper]

gin[2] *n.* **1.** a cotton gin. **2.** a machine for hoisting. **3.** a snare or trap. —*v.t.* **ginned, gin·ning 1.** remove the seeds from (cotton) in a gin. **2.** trap or snare. [ME *gyn* engine]

gin·ger (JIN jər) *n.* **1.** the pungent rhizome of a tropical plant, used in medicine and cookery. **2.** the plant itself. **3.** a tawny, reddish brown color. **4.** *Informal* pep. [ME] —**gin'ger·y** *adj.*

gin·ger·bread (JIN jər BRED) *n.* **1.** a dark, ginger-flavored cake or cookie. **2.** elaborate decoration or trim, as on the exterior of a house. —*adj.* ornate, gaudy, or superfluous.

gin·ger·ly (JIN jər lee) *adv.* in a cautious manner. —*adj.* careful. [< MF *gensor* pretty]

ging·ham (GING əm) *n.* a cotton fabric, woven in solid colors, checks, etc. [< Du. *gingang* striped]

gin·gi·vi·tis (JIN jə VĪ tis) *n. Pathol.* inflammation of the gums. [< NL]

gink·go (GING koh) *n. pl.* **·goes** a large tree native to China, with edible fruits and nuts. Also **ging′ko.** [< NL]

gin·seng (JIN seng) *n.* **1.** an herb native to China and North America. **2.** the root of this herb, used in a medicinal preparation. [< Chinese *jen shen*]

gi·raffe (jə RAF) *n.* an African ruminant, the tallest of all mammals, having a very long neck and long slender legs. [< F *girafe*]

gird (gurd) *v.t.* **gird·ed** or **girt, gird·ing 1.** surround or make fast with a belt or girdle. **2.** encircle; surround. **3.** prepare (oneself) for action. **4.** clothe, equip, or endow, as with some quality or attribute. [ME *girden*]

gird·er (GUR dər) *n.* a long heavy beam that supports the joists of a floor etc.

gir·dle (GUR dl) *n.* **1.** a belt or cord worn around the waist; sash. **2.** anything that encircles like a belt. **3.** a flexible undergarment worn to give support and shape. **4.** an encircling cut made through the bark of a tree trunk or branch. —*v.t.* **·dled, ·dling 1.** fasten a girdle or belt around. **2.** encircle; encompass. **3.** make an encircling cut through the bark of (a branch or tree). [ME]

girl (gurl) *n.* **1.** a female infant or child. **2.** a young, unmarried woman. **3.** formerly, a female servant or employee. **4.** a sweetheart. **5.** *Informal* any woman of any age. [ME *gurle*] —**girl′ish** *adj.*

girth (gurth) *n.* **1.** the circumference of anything. **2.** a band passed under the belly of a horse or other animal to fasten a saddle etc. **3.** a girdle or band. —*v.t.* **1.** bind with a girth. **2.** encircle; girdle. —*v.i.* **3.** measure in girth. [ME]

gist (jist) *n.* the main idea, as of an argument, question, etc. [< AF, it lies]

give (giv) *v.* **gave, giv·en, giv·ing** *v.t.* **1.** transfer freely (what is one's own) to the permanent possession of another without asking anything in return. **2.** make available to another for temporary use; let have. **3.** put into the grasp of another: *Give* me your hand. **4.** be a source of. **5.** grant or concede, as permission. **6.** administer (a dose of medicine, a treatment, etc.). **7.** assign or allot. **8.** transmit or communicate (a disease etc.). **9.** perform or do: *give* a play. **10.** de-

vote, as oneself, to a cause etc. —*v.i.* **11.** make donations; make free gifts. **12.** move, yield, collapse, etc., as under pressure: The door *gave.* **13.** be springy, flexible, etc.: The bed *gives* comfortably. **14.** furnish a view or passage; open: with *on* or *onto.* —**give away 1.** bestow as a gift. **2.** present (the bride) to the bridegroom. **3.** make known, as a secret; reveal. —**give birth to 1.** bear (offspring). **2.** create or originate, as an idea. **3.** result in. —**give in 1.** yield, as to something demanded. **2.** deliver or hand in (a report, resignation, etc.). —**give off** send forth, as odors; emit. —**give out 1.** send forth; emit. **2.** hand out or distribute. **3.** make known; publish. **4.** become completely used up or exhausted. —**give up 1.** surrender. **2.** stop; cease. **3.** desist from as hopeless. **4.** lose all hope for, as a sick person. **5.** devote wholly: *give* oneself *up* to art. —**give way 1.** collapse, bend, fail, etc., as under pressure or force. **2.** draw back. **3.** concede or yield. **4.** abandon oneself, as to despair. —*n.* **1.** resilience; elasticity. **2.** the act or process of bending or yielding. [ME] —**giv′er** *n.*

give-and-take (GIV ən TAYK) *n.* the making of mutual concessions, exchanges, etc.

give·a·way (GIV ə WAY) *n.* **1.** a disclosure or betrayal, generally unintentional. **2.** something given free or at a greatly reduced price. —*adj.* offering prizes.

giv·en (GIV ən) *adj.* **1.** presented; bestowed. **2.** habitually inclined; addicted: with *to.* **3.** specified; stated: a *given* date. **4.** admitted as a fact. —**given name** the name bestowed on a person at birth, or shortly thereafter.

giz·zard (GIZ ərd) *n.* **1.** a second stomach in birds, in which partly digested food is finely ground. **2.** the human stomach. [ME *giser* entrails]

gla·brous (GLAY brəs) *adj. Biol.* **1.** devoid of hair or down. **2.** smooth. [< L *glaber* smooth]

gla·cé (gla SAY) *adj.* **1.** sugared or candied, as preserved fruits. **2.** having a glossy surface, as certain leathers. **3.** iced; frozen. —*v.t.* **·céed, ·cé·ing 1.** cover with icing. **2.** make smooth and glossy. [< F]

gla·cial (GLAY shəl) *adj.* **1.** pertaining to, caused by, or marked by the presence of glaciers. **2.** freezingly cold. **3.** indifferent. [< L *glacialis* icy] —**gla′cial·ly** *adv.*

gla·ci·ate (GLAY shee AYT) *v.t.* **·at·ed,**

•**at•ing** cover with or subject to the action of glaciers. —**gla′ci•a′tion** n.

gla•cier (GLAY shər) n. a slow-moving ice field, formed in regions of perennial frost from compacted snow. [< L *glacies* ice]

glad (glad) adj. **glad•der, glad•dest** 1. having a feeling of joy, pleasure, or content; gratified: often with *of* or *at*. 2. showing joy; brightly cheerful. 3. giving reason to rejoice; bringing joy. 4. very willing: He'd be *glad* to help. [ME] —**glad′ly** adv.

glad•den (GLAD n) v.t. make glad.

glade (glayd) n. a clearing in a wood. [akin to *glad* in obs. sense "bright"]

glad•i•a•tor (GLAD ee AY tər) n. 1. in ancient Rome, a slave, captive, or paid freeman who fought other men or animals as public entertainment. 2. any combatant. [< L, sword wielder]

glam•or•ize (GLAM ə RĪZ) v.t. •**ized,** •**iz•ing** make glamorous.

glam•or•ous (GLAM ər əs) adj. full of glamour; alluring.

glam•our (GLAM ər) n. alluring charm or fascination. Also **glam′or.**

glance (glans) v.i. **glanced, glanc•ing** 1. take a quick look. 2. touch briefly on some matter. 3. be deflected at an angle after striking obliquely. —n. 1. a quick look. 2. a flash; glint. 3. oblique impact and deflection. [ME *glancen*]

gland (gland) n. Anat. any of various bodily organs that secrete a substance for use or discharge. [< L *glans* acorn] —**glan•du•lar** (GLAN jə lər) adj.

glare (glair) v. **glared, glar•ing** v.i. 1. shine with a steady and dazzling intensity. 2. gaze or stare fiercely or in hostility. 3. be conspicuous or showy. —v.t. 4. express or send forth with a glare. —n. 1. a dazzling, steady light or reflection. 2. an intense, piercing look or gaze, usually hostile. [ME *glaren*] —**glar′ing** adj.

glass (glas) n. 1. a hard, brittle, usu. transparent substance made by fusing one or more substances, followed by rapid cooling to prevent crystallization. ♦ Collateral adjective: *vitreous.* 2. any substance made of or resembling glass. 3. an article made wholly or partly of glass; as: **a** a windowpane, lens, mirror, etc. **b** pl. a pair of eyeglasses; also, binoculars. 4. the contents of a drinking glass; glassful. —v.t. 1. put in a glass container. 2. enclose in or cover with glass. —adj. 1. of, pertaining to, or consisting of

glass. 2. fitted with glass: a *glass* frame. [ME *glas*]

glass•ful (GLAS fuul) n. pl. •**fuls** the amount contained in a drinking glass. [ME]

glass•ware (GLAS WAIR) n. glass articles.

glass•y (GLAS ee) adj. **glass•i•er, glass•i•est** 1. resembling glass. 2. fixed, blank, and uncomprehending: a *glassy* stare.

glau•co•ma (glow KOH mə) n. Pathol. a disease of the eye characterized by pressure of fluids within the eyeball, with gradual loss of vision. [< Gk. *glaukōma* opacity of the eye]

glaze (glayz) v. **glazed, glaz•ing** v.t. 1. fit, as a window, with glass panes; also, provide (a building etc.) with windows. 2. cover or coat with a thin film; as: **a** coat (pottery) with a glasslike surface applied by fusing. **b** cover (foods) with a thin coating of eggs, syrup, etc. **c** cover (paintings) with a thin, transparent coating to modify the tone. —v.i. 3. become covered with a thin coating or film. —n. 1. a thin, glossy coating; also, the substance used to make such a coating. 2. a filmy haze. [ME *glasen*]

gla•zier (GLAY zhər) n. one who fits windows etc. with panes of glass.

gleam (gleem) n. 1. an intermittent or momentary ray or beam of light. 2. a soft radiance; glow; also, reflected light. 3. a brief manifestation, as of humor; a faint trace, as of hope. —v.i. 1. shine softly; emit gleams. 2. appear briefly as in a small burst of light. [ME *gleme*]

glean (gleen) v.t. & v.i. 1. collect (facts etc.) by patient effort. 2. gather (the leavings) from a field after the crop has been reaped. [ME *glenen*] —**glean′er** n.

glean•ing (GLEE ning) n. Usu. pl. that which is gleaned.

glee (glee) n. 1. lively, exuberant joy. 2. a musical composition for male voices, without accompaniment. [ME]

glee club a group of singers organized to sing choral songs.

glee•ful (GLEE fəl) adj. feeling or exhibiting glee; mirthful.

glen (glen) n. a small, secluded valley. [< Scot. Gaelic *gleann*]

glib (glib) adj. **glib•ber, glib•best** 1. speaking fluently; smooth in manner. 2. more facile than sincere. [< obs. *glibbery* slippery] —**glib′ly** adv.

glide (glīd) v. **glid•ed, glid•ing** v.i. 1. move, slip, or flow smoothly or effortlessly. 2. pass unnoticed or imperceptibly, as time: often with *by*. **3.** *Aeron.* descend along an oblique line gradually without motor power; also, fly a glider. —*v.t.* **4.** cause to glide. —*n.* the act of gliding. [ME *gliden*]

glid•er (GLI dər) *n.* **1.** one who or that which glides. **2.** *Aeron.* an engineless airplane, constructed to soar on air currents. **3.** a swing gliding in a metal frame.

glim•mer (GLIM ər) *v.i.* **1.** gleam unsteadily; flicker. **2.** appear fitfully or faintly. —*n.* **1.** a faint, unsteady light. **2.** a trace; inkling. [ME *glimeren* gleam] —**glim′mer•ing** *n. & adj.*

glimpse (glimps) *n.* **1.** a momentary view or look. **2.** an inkling. —*v.* **glimpsed, glimps•ing** *v.t.* **1.** see for an instant; catch a glimpse of. —*v.i.* **2.** look for an instant: with *at.* [ME *glimsen* glow]

glint (glint) *v.i.* **1.** gleam; glitter. **2.** dart. —*n.* **1.** a gleam. **2.** a luster, as of metal. [ME]

glis•ten (GLIS ən) *v.i.* shine, as reflected light. —*n.* brightness; sparkle. [ME *glistnen* glitter]

glit•ter (GLIT ər) *v.i.* **1.** sparkle brightly or brilliantly. **2.** display striking magnificence; be brilliantly shown. [ME] — **glit′ter** *n.*

gloam•ing (GLOH ming) *n.* the dusk of early evening; twilight. [ME *gloming*]

gloat (gloht) *v.i.* take or express malicious delight: usu. with *over.* [? ON *glotta* grin]

glob (glob) *n.* **1.** a small drop or ball of something. **2.** a large, rounded mass of something. —**glob•al** (GLOH bəl) *adj.* **1.** involving the whole world. **2.** spherical. — **glob′al•ly** *adv.*

globe (glohb) *n.* **1.** a perfectly round body; a sphere, or anything like one. **2.** the earth. **3.** a spherical model of the earth or heavens. —*v.t. & v.i.* **globed, glob•ing** form into a globe. [ME]

glob•u•lar (GLOB yə lər) *adj.* **1.** spherical. **2.** formed of globules.

glob•ule (GLOB yuul) *n.* a tiny sphere or drop. [< L *globulus* little ball]

glob•u•lin (GLOB yə lin) *n. Biochem.* any of various simple plant and animal proteins, soluble in dilute salt solutions.

gloom (gloom) *n.* **1.** partial or total darkness; heavy shadow. **2.** darkness or depression of the mind or spirits. [ME *gloumben* frown]

gloom•y (GLOOM ee) *adj.* **gloom•i•er, gloom•i•est 1.** dark; dismal. **2.** melancholy; morose. **3.** producing gloom or melancholy. —**gloom′•i•ly** *adv.* —**gloom′i•ness** *n.*

glop (glop) *n. Informal* **1.** something soft and

messy looking. **2.** banal sentimentality: He wrote *glop.*

glo•ri•fy (GLOR ə FI) *v.t.* •**fied,** •**fy•ing 1.** make glorious. **2.** honor; worship. **3.** give great praise to; laud. **4.** make seem more splendid than is so. [ME] —**glo′ri•fi•ca′ tion** *n.*

glo•ri•ous (GLOR ee əs) *adj.* **1.** full of glory; illustrious. **2.** bringing glory or honor. **3.** resplendent. **4.** delightful. [ME]

glo•ry (GLOR ee) *n. pl.* •**ries 1.** distinguished honor or praise; exalted reputation. **2.** something bringing praise. **3.** worshipful adoration: give *glory* to God. **4.** magnificence; splendor: the *glory* that was Rome. **5.** heavenly bliss. **6.** a state of extreme well-being: in one's *glory.* —*v.i.* •**ried,** •**ry•ing** take pride: with *in.* [ME]

gloss¹ (glos) *n.* **1.** the luster or sheen of a polished surface. **2.** a deceptive or superficial appearance. —*v.t.* **1.** make lustrous, as by polishing. **2.** hide (errors, etc.) by falsehood: usu. with *over.* [< Du. *gloos* shining]

gloss² *n.* **1.** an explanatory note, esp. marginal or interlinear; a commentary or translation. **2.** an artful or deceptive explanation to cover up a fault, etc. —*v.t.* **1.** write glosses for (a text, etc.); annotate. **2.** excuse by false explanations. [ME *glose*, lit., language]

glos•sa•ry (GLOS ə ree) *n. pl.* •**ries** a lexicon of the words of a work or field. [ME *glossarye*]

gloss•y (GLOS ee) *adj.* **gloss•i•er, gloss•i•est 1.** having a bright sheen; lustrous. **2.** made superficially attractive. —**gloss′i•ly** *adv.* —**gloss′i•ness** *n.*

glove (gluv) *n.* **1.** a covering for the hand, having a separate sheath for each finger. **2.** in baseball, a large leather mitt for catching the ball. **3.** a boxing glove. —**handle with kid gloves** use great care in dealing with. —*v.t.* **gloved, glov•ing 1.** put gloves on. **2.** furnish with gloves. [ME]

glov•er (GLUV ər) *n.* one who makes or sells gloves. [ME]

glow (gloh) *v.i.* **1.** give off light, esp. without flame. **2.** be red, as from heat; flush. **3.** be animated, as with emotion etc. —*n.* **1.** the incandescence given off by a heated substance. **2.** ruddiness, as from health. **3.** strong emotion; ardor. [ME *glowen*] — **glow′ing** *adj.* —**glow′ing•ly** *adv.*

glow•er (GLOU ər) *v.i.* stare with an angry frown; scowl sullenly. [ME *glowren*]

glu•cose (GLOO kohs) *n.* **1.** *Chem.* a sugar

found in plants and animals. **2.** a syrup used in confectionery, baking, etc. [< F]

glue (gloo) *n.* **1.** an adhesive made from animal substances, as skin, bones, etc. **2.** an adhesive or cement made of casein or other synthetics. —*v.t.* **glued, glu·ing** stick or fasten with or as with glue. [ME *glu*] — **glue·y** (GLOO ee) *adj.* **glu·i·er, glu·i·est** [ME]

glum (glum) *adj.* **glum·mer, glum·mest** moody and silent; sullen. [ME] —**glum′ly** *adv.*

glut (glut) *v.t.* **glut·ted, glut·ting 1.** feed or supply to excess; satiate. **2.** supply (the market) with an excess of goods so that the price falls. —*n.* **1.** an excessive supply. **2.** the act of glutting or being glutted. [ME *gluten glutton*]

glu·te·us (GLOO tee əs) *n. pl.* **·te·i** (-tee I) *Anat.* any of three muscles of the buttocks. [< NL] —**glu·te′al** *adj.*

glu·ti·nous (GLOOT n əs) *adj.* resembling glue; sticky.

glut·ton (GLUT n) *n.* **1.** one who eats to excess. **2.** one who has a great appetite or capacity for something. [ME *glutun*] — **glut′ton·y** *n.*

glyc·er·in (GLIS ər in) *n.* glycerol. Also **glyc′er·ine.**

glyc·er·ol (GLIS ə RAWL) *n. Chem.* a sweet, oily, colorless alcohol formed by decomposition of natural fats, used in medicine, industry, and the arts.

gnarl (nahrl) *n.* a protuberance on a tree; a tough knot. —*v.t.* make knotty and twisted like an old tree. —**gnarled, gnarl′y** *adj.*

gnash (nash) *v.t.* grind or snap (the teeth) together, as in rage. [ME *gnasten*] —*n.*

gnat (nat) *n.* any of various small stinging or biting flies. [ME]

gnaw (naw) *v.* **gnawed, gnawed** or **gnawn, gnaw·ing** *v.t.* **1.** eat away gradually with or as with the teeth; also, bite on repeatedly. **2.** torment or oppress with fear, pain, etc. — *v.i.* **3.** bite, chew, or corrode persistently. **4.** cause constant worry, etc. [ME *gnawen*]

gnaw·ing (NAW ing) *n.* a dull, persistent sensation of discomfort or distress.

gnome (nohm) *n.* **1.** in folklore, one of a group of dwarfish old men, living in caves and guarding buried treasure, etc. **2.** an international banker: the *gnomes* of Zurich. [< NL *gnomus*] —**gnom′ish** *adj.*

gno·mic (NOH mik) *adj.* consisting of or resembling maxims; aphoristic. [< Gk. *gnōmikós* aphoristic]

gnos·tic (NOS tik) *adj.* of or possessing knowledge or insight. Also **gnos′ti·cal.**

gnu (noo) *n. pl.* **gnus** or **gnu** a South African antelope having an oxlike head with curved horns, a mane, and a long tail: also called *wildebeest.*

go[1] (goh) *v.* **went, gone, go·ing** *v.i.* **1.** proceed or pass along; move. **2.** move from a place; leave; depart: often used as a command or signal, as in a race: *Go!* **3.** be in operation; also, work or function properly. **4.** extend or reach: *This pipe goes to the roof.* **5.** emit a specified sound or act in a certain way: *The chain goes "clank."* **6.** fail, give way, or collapse; also, to disappear. **7.** have a specific place; belong: *The plates go on the shelf.* **8.** be awarded or given. **9.** pass from one person to another. **10.** pass into a condition; become: *go insane.* **11.** be, continue, or appear in a specified state: *go unpunished.* **12.** happen or end in a specific manner: *The election went badly.* **13.** be considered or ranked: *good as lunches go.* **14.** be suitable; harmonize; fit. **15.** have a certain form: *How does the tune go?* **16.** have recourse; resort: *go to court.* **17.** die. **18.** pass: said of time. **19.** be abolished or given up: *These expenses must go.* **20.** be sold or bid for: with *at* or *for.* **21.** subject oneself; put oneself: *He went to great pains.* **22.** be about to: used in the progressive form and followed by the present infinitive: *They are going to protest.* —*v.t.* **23.** furnish or provide (bail). **24.** *Informal* risk or bet; wager. —**go about 1.** be occupied or busy with. **2.** circulate. **3.** *Naut.* tack; turn. —**go after 1.** try to catch; chase. **2.** follow in sequence. —**go around** be enough for all to have some. —**go at** attack; work at. —**go back on 1.** be disloyal to; forsake. **2.** fail to fulfill. —**go by 1.** pass. **2.** conform to or be guided by. **3.** be known by. —**go for 1.** try to get. **2.** advocate. **3.** attack. **4.** be attracted by. —**go in for 1.** strive for; advocate. **2.** like or participate in. —**go into 1.** investigate. **2.** take up, as a study or profession. — **go off 1.** explode or be discharged, as a gun. **2.** depart; leave. **3.** occur. —**go on 1.** happen: *What's going on here?* **2.** persevere; endure. **3.** in the theater, make an entrance. —**go (someone) better** surpass (someone). —**go out 1.** go to social gatherings etc. **2.** be extinguished, as a light. **3.** become outdated, as fashions. **4.** go on strike. —**go over 1.** repeat; also, rehearse. **2.** examine carefully. **3.** succeed. **4.** change sides or allegiance. —**go through with** perform to the finish; complete. —**go under 1.** be overwhelmed. **2.** fail, as a business. —**go with 1.** harmonize with. **2.** accompany. **3.** be sweethearts. —**let go 1.** release one's hold; set free. **2.** abandon. —**let oneself go** be uninhibited. —n. **1.** the act of going. **2.** the capacity for action; He has plenty of go. **3.** an attempt: have a go at something. **4.** a success: He made a go of it. **5.** Informal an agreement; bargain: It's a go. —**no go** Informal useless; hopeless; a failure. —**on the go** in constant motion; very busy. —adj. functioning and ready: All systems are go. [ME gon]

go² n. a Japanese board game.

goad (gohd) n. **1.** a stick for urging on oxen etc. **2.** something that drives. —v.t. drive; incite. [ME gode]

go·a·head (GOH ə HED) n. a signal or permission to move ahead or proceed.

goal (gohl) n. **1.** something toward which effort or movement is directed; an end or objective. **2.** the terminal point of a journey or race. **3.** in some games, the point to which the players try to bring the ball, puck, etc. to score; also, the score itself. [ME gol]

goal·ie (GOH lee) n. in hockey, soccer, etc., a player whose function is to prevent the ball or puck from passing over the goal for a score. Also **goal·keep·er, goal·tend·er.**

goat (goht) n. **1.** a cud-chewing mammal related to the sheep and having hollow horns. **2.** a lecherous man. **3.** one who is the butt of a joke; scapegoat. —**get one's goat** Informal move one to anger or annoyance. [ME got] —**goat'ish** adj.

goat·ee (goh TEE) n. a short, pointed beard.

gob¹ (gob) n. **1.** a piece or lump, as of a soft substance. **2.** pl. Informal a great quantity. [ME gobbe mouthful]

gob² n. Slang a sailor of the U.S. Navy.

gob·ble¹ (GOB əl) v. **·bled, ·bling** v.t. **1.** swallow (food) greedily. **2.** seize in a grasping manner. —v.i. **3.** eat greedily. —**gob'bler** n.

gob·ble² v.i. **·bled, ·bling** make the throaty sound of a male turkey. —**gob'ble** n.

gob·ble·de·gook (GOB əl dee GUUK) n. unintelligible, pompous jargon. Also **gob·ble·dy·gook.**

gob·bler (GOB lər) n. a male turkey.

go·be·tween (GOH bi TWEEN) n. an agent or mediator.

gob·let (GOB lit) n. **1.** a drinking vessel, typically with a base and stem. **2.** a large, festive shallow drinking cup. [ME gobelet]

gob·lin (GOB lin) n. in folklore, an ugly elf regarded as evil or mischievous. [ME gobelin]

god (god) n. **1.** one of various beings, usu. male, conceived of in polytheistic religions or mythologies as having supernatural aspects or powers. **2.** any person or thing much loved. [ME] —**god'like** adj.

God (god) n. in monotheism, the creator and ruler of life and the universe.

god·child (GOD CHILD) n. pl. **·chil·dren** a child whom a person sponsors at baptism, circumcision, etc.

god·damned (GOD DAMD) adj. Informal utterly detestable or outrageous. —adv. Informal to an extreme degree; very.

god·daugh·ter (GOD DAW tər) n. a female godchild.

god·dess (GOD əs) **1.** a female god. **2.** a woman adored for her beauty or charm.

god·fa·ther (GOD FAH thər) n. a male godparent.

god·fear·ing (GOD FEER ing) adj. **1.** having reverence for God. **2.** pious; devout.

god·for·sak·en (GOD fər SAY kən) adj. **1.** abandoned by God. **2.** wretched; desolate.

god·less (GOD lis) adj. **1.** having or believing in no god. **2.** wicked. —**god'less·ness** n.

god·ly (GOD lee) adj. **·li·er, ·li·est** filled with love for God. —**god'li·ness** n.

god·moth·er (GOD MUTH ər) n. a female godparent.

god·par·ent (GOD PAIR ənt) n. the sponsor of a child at baptism, circumcision, etc.

god·send (GOD SEND) n. something that unexpectedly fulfills one's needs or wants.

god·son (GOD SUN) n. a male godchild.

go·get·ter (GOH GET ər) n. Informal a hustling, energetic, aggressive person.

gog·gle (GOG əl) n. pl. spectacles designed to protect the eyes against dust, wind, etc. —v. **·gled, ·gling** v.i. **1.** roll the eyes erratically. **2.** of the eyes, move erratically, bulge, or be fixed in a stare. —v.t. **3.** cause (the eyes) to goggle. [ME gogelen look aside] —**gog'gle-eyed'** (-ID) adj.

go-go (GOG GOH) adj. **1.** of or describing discothèques, the dances performed there, or the women dancers. **2.** lively; energetic. **3.** modern; up-to-date. **4.** speculative, as stocks. [< F à gogo galore]

go·ing (GOH ing) n. **1.** the act of departing or moving; leaving. **2.** the condition of ground or roads as affecting walking, riding, racing, etc. **—goings on** actions or behavior: used chiefly to express disapproval. **—adj. 1.** that goes, moves, or works. **2.** continuing to function; moving ahead: a *going* concern. **3.** prevailing: the *going* rate.

goi·ter (GOI tər) *n. Pathol.* any abnormal enlargement of the thyroid gland. [< F *goitre*]

gold (gohld) *n.* **1.** a precious, yellow, metallic element (symbol Au) that is highly ductile and resistant to oxidation. **2.** coin made of this metal. **3.** wealth; riches. **4.** a bright yellow color. [ME] *—adj.*

gold·en (GOHL dən) *adj.* **1.** made of, containing, or resembling gold. **2.** bright yellow. **3.** happy, prosperous, etc.

golden age 1. in Greek and Roman legend, an early period marked by perfect innocence, peace, and happiness. **2.** any period of prosperity or excellence. **3.** the later years of life, esp. over age 65.

golden anniversary a fiftieth anniversary.

golden mean moderation; avoidance of extremes.

golden rule the principle of treating others as one wants to be treated.

golden wedding the fiftieth anniversary of a marriage.

gold-filled (GOHLD FILD) *adj.* filled with a base metal and covered with a layer of gold.

gold foil thin sheets of gold.

gold leaf sheets of gold hammered to extreme thinness, used in gilding etc.

gold mine 1. a mine producing gold ore. **2.** any source of great profit, riches, etc.

gold plate vessels and utensils of gold, collectively.

gold·smith (GOHLD SMITH) *n.* one who makes or deals in articles of gold.

golf (golf) *n.* an outdoor game played on a large course (**golf course**) with a small ball and a set of clubs (**golf clubs**). *—v.i.* play golf. [ME] *—golf′er n.*

Gol·go·tha (GOL gə thə) *n.* a place near Jerusalem where Jesus was crucified; Calvary. [< LL]

Go·li·ath (gə LĪ əth) a giant. [after the Philistine *Goliath*, slain by David]

go·nad (GOH nad) *n. Anat.* a male or female sex gland, in which the reproductive cells develop; an ovary or testis. [< NL]

gon·do·la (GON dl ə) *n.* **1.** a long, narrow, flat-bottomed Venetian boat. **2.** a large, flat-bottomed, river boat; also, a gondola car. **3.** *Aeron.* the car attached below a dirigible. [< Ital.]

gondola car a long, shallow, open freight car.

gon·do·lier (GON dl EER) *n.* the boatman of a gondola. [< Ital. *gondoliere*]

gone (gawn) past participle of GO. *—adj.* **1.** moved away; left. **2.** beyond hope; ruined; lost. **3.** dead; departed. **4.** ended; past. **5.** consumed; spent.

gong (gong) *n.* **1.** a heavy metal disk giving a deep, resonant tone when struck. **2.** a flat, saucerlike bell struck with a small mechanical hammer. [< Malay]

gon·or·rhe·a (gon ə REE ə) *n. Pathol.* a contagious venereal infection of the genitourinary tract. [< LL]

goo·ber (GOO bər) *n. Southern U.S.* a peanut. Also **goober pea.** [< Bantu *nguba*]

good (guud) *adj. bet·ter, best* **1.** morally excellent; virtuous. **2.** honorable; worthy: a *good* reputation. **3.** generous; loving; kind. **4.** well-behaved; tractable. **5.** proper; desirable: *good* manners. **6.** favorable: a *good* opinion. **7.** having beneficial effects; helpful: *good* advice. **8.** reliable; safe: a *good* investment. **9.** skillful; expert: She is *good* at sports. **10.** genuine; valid: a *good* excuse. **11.** backed by sufficient funds: a *good* check. **12.** excellent in quality or degree: *good* literature. **13.** orthodox; conforming. **14.** unspoiled; fresh: *good* meat. **15.** healthy: *good* lungs. **16.** attractive or striking: He looks *good* in that hat. **17.** great in amount; also, maximum; full. **—good and** *Informal* completely; very: *good and* hot. **—good for 1.** capable of lasting for. **2.** able to pay, give, or produce. **—n. 1.** that which is fitting etc. **2.** benefit: for the *good* of mankind. **3.** that which is morally or ethically desirable. **—make good 1.** be successful. **2.** compensate for. **3.** fulfill. **4.** prove; substantiate. *—interj.* an exclamation of satisfaction. *—adv. Informal* Well. [ME] **—good′ness** *n.*

good-bye (GUUD BĪ) *adj., n. & interj. pl.* **-byes** farewell. Also **good′by′.** [Contraction of *God be with ye*]

good-for-noth·ing (GUUD fər NUTH ing) *n.* a worthless person. *—adj.* of no use or value.

good·heart·ed (GUUD HAHR tid) *adj.* kind; charitable; generous. **—good′heart′ed·ly** *adv.*

good-hu·mored (GUUD HYOO mərd) *adj.* having a cheerful temper or mood.

good-look·ing (GUUD LUUK ing) *adj.* handsome.

good·ly (GUUD lee) *adj.* **·li·er, ·li·est 1.** having a pleasing appearance. **2.** of fine quality. **3.** large. [ME]

good-na·tured (GUUD NAY chərd) *adj.* having a pleasant disposition; not easily provoked.

goods (guudz) *n.pl.* **1.** merchandise; wares. **2.** fabric; material. **3.** property, esp. when personal and movable.

good·will (GUUD WIL) *n.* **1.** a desire for the well-being of others; benevolence. **2.** cheerful, ready consent or willingness. **3.** intangible assets in terms of prestige and friendly relations. [ME]

good·y (GUUD ee) *n. pl.* **good·ies** *Informal Usu. pl.* something tasty. —*interj.* a childish exclamation of pleasure.

goof (goof) *Slang n.* **1.** a dull-witted person; dope. **2.** a mistake; blunder. —*v.t.* **2.** make a mess of: usu. with *up.* —**goof off** *Slang* loaf. [< MF *goffe* awkward]

goon (goon) *n.* **1.** *Informal* a thug or hoodlum. **2.** *Slang* an oaf. [after a character created by E.C. Segar, 1894–1938, U.S. cartoonist]

goose (goos) *n. pl.* **geese 1.** a web-footed bird larger than ducks. **2.** the female: distinguished from *gander.* **3.** the flesh as food. **4.** a fool. —**cook one's goose** *Informal* spoil one's chances. —*v.t.* **goosed, goos·ing 1.** *Slang* poke between the buttocks to startle or annoy. **2.** *Informal* stimulate to activity: The ad *goosed* sales. [ME *gose*]

goose flesh a taut, prickling sensation in the skin. Also **goose bumps, goose pimples.**

goose-step (GOOS STEP) *v.i.* **-stepped, -step·ping** march along or mark time kicking stiffly and sharply. —**goose step** *n.*

Gor·di·an knot (GOR dee ən) any difficulty solved only by drastic measures. [after a legendary knot cut by Alexander the Great]

gore[1] (gor) *n.* blood that has been shed, esp. in copious amounts. [ME] —**gor'y** *adj.*

gore[2] *v.t.* **gored, gor·ing** pierce with the horns or tusks. [ME *goren*]

gore[3] *n.* a triangular or tapering section set into a garment for greater fullness. —*v.t.* **gored, gor·ing 1.** cut into gore-shaped pieces. **2.** furnish with gores. [ME]

gorge (gorj) *n.* **1.** a narrow, deep ravine, esp. with a stream flowing through. **2.** the throat. **3.** deep or violent disgust. **4.** a mass obstructing a passage. —*v.* **gorged, gorg·ing** *v.t.* **1.** stuff with food. **2.** swallow gluttonously. —*v.i.* **3.** stuff oneself with food. [ME] —**gorg'er** *n.*

gor·geous (GOR jəs) *adj.* **1.** dazzlingly colorful; brilliant. **2.** extremely beautiful, etc. [< OF *gorgias* elegant]

gor·gon (GOR gən) *n.* a terrifyingly ugly woman. [ME]

gos·ling (GOZ ling) *n.* a young goose. [ME *goselyng*]

gos·pel (GOS pəl) *n.* **1.** the teachings of the Christian church as originally preached by Jesus Christ and the apostles. **2.** any information accepted as unquestionably true. [ME]

gos·sa·mer (GOS ə mər) *n.* **1.** fine strands of spider's silk, esp. when floating in the air. **2.** any flimsy, delicate substance, as filmy, gauzelike fabric. —*adj.* resembling gossamer; flimsy; unsubstantial. [ME *gossomer* < *gos somer*, goose summer]

gos·sip (GOS əp) *n.* **1.** idle, sometimes malicious talk, esp. about others. **2.** informal talk or writing, as of personages. **3.** a person who indulges in idle talk. —*v.i.* **gos·siped, gos·sip·ing** talk idly or maliciously about others. [ME *gossib* kinsman]

gos·sip·y (GOS ə pee) *adj.* **1.** indulging in gossip. **2.** chatty.

got (got) past tense, past participle of GET.

Goth (goth) *n.* a member of a Germanic people that invaded the Roman Empire in the third to fifth centuries: including the Ostrogoths (**East Goths**) and Visigoths (**West Goths**). [ME *Gothe*]

Goth·ic (GOTH ik) *adj.* **1.** of or pertaining to the Goths or to their language. **2.** of a style of European architecture, from about 1200 to 1500, characterized by pointed arches, ribbed vaulting, flying buttresses, etc. **3.** *Often not cap.* denoting a literature characterized by isolated settings and mysterious events. —*n.* **1.** the extinct East Germanic language of the Goths. **2.** Gothic architecture or art. **3.** *Often not cap.* a gothic novel.

got·ten (GOT n) a past participle of GET.

gouache (gwahsh) *n.* **1.** a method of painting using opaque colors mixed with water and gum. **2.** the opaque pigment so used. **3.** a painting done in this medium. [< F]

gouge (gowj) *n.* a chisel having a scoop-shaped blade, used for wood carving. —*v.t.* **gouged, goug·ing 1.** cut or carve as with a gouge. **2.** scoop, force, or tear out. **3.** cheat; esp., charge exorbitant prices. [ME] —**goug'er** *n.*

gou·lash (GOO lahsh) *n.* a stew of meat and vegetables, seasoned with paprika, etc. [< Hung. *gulyás* shepherd's stew]

gourd (guurd) *n.* **1.** the fruit of any of various plants, having hard, durable shells. **2.** the fruit of the calabash tree. **3.** a utensil, as a ladle, made from the dried shell. [ME *gourde*]

gour·mand (guur MAHND) *n.* one who takes hearty pleasure in eating. [< F]

gour·met (guur MAY) *n.* a devotee and connoisseur of good food and drink. [< F]

gout (gowt) *n. Pathol.* a metabolic disease characterized by painful inflammation of the joints. [ME *goute*] —**gout'y** *adj.* **gout·i·er, gout·i·est**

gov·ern (GUV ərn) *v.t.* **1.** rule or direct by right or authority. **2.** guide or control the action of; influence. **3.** serve as a rule or deciding factor for. **4.** keep in check. —*v.i.* **5.** exercise authority; rule. [ME] —**gov'ern·a·ble** *adj.*

gov·ern·ance (GUV ər nəns) *n.* exercise of authority.

gov·ern·ess (GUV ər nis) *n.* a woman employed in a private household to take charge of and instruct children.

gov·ern·ment (GUV ərn mənt) *n.* **1.** the authoritative administration of the affairs of a nation, state, etc.; the jurisdiction exercised over the people; rule. **2.** the official governing body of a nation, community, etc. **3.** the system or established form by which a nation etc. is controlled: democratic *government.* —**gov·ern·men·tal** (GUV ərn MEN tl) *adj.*

gov·er·nor (GUV ər nər) *n.* **1.** one who governs; as: **a** the elected chief executive of any state in the U.S. **b** an official appointed to administer a province, territory, etc. **2.** *Mech.* a device for controlling speed, as of a motor.

gown (gown) *n.* **1.** a woman's dress, esp. one for formal occasions. **2.** any long, loose garment. **3.** a long, loose outer robe worn by certain officials, scholars, etc. [ME *goune*] —*v.t. & v.i.* dress in a gown.

grab (grab) *v.* **grabbed, grab·bing** *v.t.* **1.** grasp or seize suddenly. **2.** take possession of by force or by dishonest means. **3.** *Slang* impress powerfully; affect: The idea *grabs* me. —*v.i.* **4.** make a sudden grasp. —*n.* **1.** the act of grabbing. **2.** a dishonest acquisition. [< MDu. *grabben* grip] —**grab'ber** *n.* —**grab'by** *adj.* **·bi·er, ·bi·est**

grab bag 1. a bag or other receptacle filled with unidentified articles, from which items are picked at random. **2.** anything resembling a grab bag in providing an assortment of items.

grace (grays) *n.* **1.** beauty or harmony of motion, form, or manner. **2.** any attractive quality. **3.** service freely rendered; good will. **4.** the act of showing favor. **5.** clemency; mercy. **6.** an extension of time granted after a set date, as for paying a debt. **7.** a short prayer at a meal. **8.** *Theol.* **a** the love of God toward man. **b** the divine influence operating in man. —**be in the good graces of** be regarded with favor by. —**with good grace** in a willing manner. —*v.t.* **graced, grac·ing 1.** add grace and beauty to; adorn. **2.** dignify; honor. [ME]

grace·ful (GRAYS fəl) *adj.* characterized by grace, elegance, or beauty. —**grace'ful·ly** *adv.*

grace·less (GRAYS lis) *adj.* **1.** lacking grace, charm, or elegance; clumsy. **2.** having no sense of what is right or decent. —**grace'·less·ly** *adv.*

grace note *Music* a note played or sung as an embellishment.

gra·cious (GRAY shəs) *adj.* **1.** having or showing kindness, affability, etc. **2.** full of compassion; merciful. —*interj.* an exclamation of mild surprise. [ME]

gra·da·tion (gray DAY shən) *n.* **1.** an orderly and gradual progression or arrangement according to size, quality, rank, etc. **2.** a step, degree, or relative position in such a progression. **3.** the act of arranging in grades. —**gra'date** *v.t. & v.i.* **·dat·ed, ·dat·ing** form or arrange in a gradation.

grade (grayd) *n.* **1.** a degree or step in any scale, as of quality, merit, rank, etc. **2.** a stage or degree in an orderly progression, classification, or process. **3.** a group or category. **4.** in education: **a** a level of progress in school, usu. a year's work. **b** the pupils in such a division. **5.** a rating or mark indicating the quality of school work done. **6.** in the armed forces, rank or rating. **7.** the degree of inclination of a road, track, or other surface. —**make the grade** succeed in an undertaking. —*v.t.* **grad·ed, grad·ing 1.** arrange or classify by grades or degrees; sort according to size, quality, type, etc. **2.** level or reduce (a road, ground, etc.) to a desirable gradient. **3.** gradate. [< F]

grad·er (GRAY dər) *n.* **1.** one who or that which grades. **2.** a pupil in a specified school grade: a third *grader.*

gra·di·ent (GRAY dee ənt) n. 1. the degree of inclination, as in a slope; grade. 2. an incline; ramp. 3. *Physics* a rate of change, as of pressure, temperature, etc. —adj. rising or descending gradually or by uniform degrees. [< L *gradiens* walking]

grad·u·al (GRAJ oo əl) adj. 1. moving, changing, etc., slowly and by degrees. 2. having a slight degree of inclination; not abrupt or steep, as a slope. [ME] —grad'u·al·ly adv. —grad'u·al·ness n.

grad·u·ate (GRAJ oo AYT) v. •at·ed, •at·ing v.i. 1. receive a diploma or degree on completion of a course of study. 2. change gradually or by degrees. —v.t. 3. grant an academic diploma or degree to (someone). 4. arrange or sort according to size, degree, etc. 5. mark (a thermometer, scale, etc.) in units or degrees; calibrate. —n. (GRAJ oo it) 1. one who has been granted a diploma or degree by an educational institution. 2. a beaker or similar vessel marked in units or degrees. —adj. (GRAJ oo it) 1. of a student working toward a degree beyond the bachelor's degree. 2. holding a bachelor's degree or diploma. [ME] —grad'u·a'tion n.

graduate student a college graduate working toward an advanced degree.

graf·fi·ti (grə FEE tee) n. 1. any designs or scribbles drawn on a wall or other surface. 2. *Archeol.* a pictograph scratched on a surface. —graf·fi·to (-toh) n.sing. [< Ital.]

graft[1] (graft) n. 1. a shoot (the scion) inserted into a prepared slit in a tree or plant (the stock) so as to become a living part of it. 2. *Surg.* a piece of viable tissue transplanted to another part of the body or to the body of another individual. —v.t. 1. insert (a scion) into a tree or plant. 2. *Surg.* transplant (a piece of viable tissue) as a graft. 3. attach or incorporate, as by grafting: *graft* new ideas on outworn concepts. [ME *graften*]

graft[2] n. 1. the act of getting personal advantage or profit by dishonest or unfair means, esp. through one's political connections. 2. anything thus gained. —v.i. practice graft. —graft'er n.

Grail (grayl) n. 1. in medieval legend, the cup or dish used at the Last Supper by Jesus. 2. *Usu. not cap. Informal* an ultimate reward. [ME *graal* bowl]

grain (grayn) n. 1. a hard seed or kernel; esp., that of any of the cereal plants, as wheat, oats, etc. 2. the harvested seeds of these plants. 3. these plants collectively. 4.

any very small, hard mass. 5. the smallest unit of weight used in several systems in the U.S. 6. the direction or arrangement of the fibers or fibrous particles in wood, meat, etc. 7. the side of a piece of leather from which the hair has been removed; also, the characteristic texture or patterned markings of this side. 8. the comparative size or texture of the particles composing a substance, surface, or pattern: marble of fine *grain*. —against the grain contrary to one's temperament or inclinations. —v.t. 1. form into grains; granulate. 2. paint or stain in imitation of the grain of wood, marble, etc. 3. give a roughened or granular appearance or texture to. [ME] —grain'y adj. grain·i·er, grain·i·est

grain elevator a building designed to store grain.

gram (gram) n. the unit of mass or weight in the metric system, equivalent to 15.432 grains, or one thousandth of a kilogram. [< F *gramme*]

gram·mar (GRAM ər) n. 1. the scientific study and description of the morphology and syntax of a language or dialect. 2. a system of rules for regulation of a given language. 3. a treatise or book dealing with grammatical matters. 4. speech or writing considered with regard to current standards of correctness. [ME *gramere*]

gram·mar·i·an (grə MAIR ee ən) n. a specialist in grammar.

grammar school an elementary school.

gram·mat·i·cal (grə MAT i kəl) adj. 1. of or pertaining to grammar. 2. conforming to the usage of standard speech or writing.

gra·na·ry (GRAY nə ree) n. pl. •ries a storehouse for threshed grain. [< L *granarium*]

grand (grand) adj. 1. impressive in size, extent, or splendor. 2. in literature and the arts, lofty or sublime in subject or treatment. 3. worthy of respect because of age, experience, or dignity. 4. of high or highest rank or official position: a *grand* duke. 5. principal; main: *grand* ballroom. 6. characterized by pomp or luxury. 7. having a family relationship one degree more distant than: used in combination: *grandson*. 8. highly satisfactory; excellent. —n. 1. a grand piano. 2. *Informal* a thousand dollars. [ME *graund*] —grand'ly adv.

grand·child (GRAN CHILD) n. pl. •chil·dren a child of one's son or daughter.

grand·daugh·ter (GRAN DAW tər) n. a daughter of one's son or daughter.

grande dame (GRAN DAM) an elderly woman of commanding presence or prestige. [< F]

gran·deur (GRAN jər) n. 1. the quality or condition of being grand; magnificence. 2. greatness of character. [< F]

grand·fa·ther (GRAN FAH thər) n. 1. the father of one's father or mother. 2. a male ancestor.

grandfather's clock a clock having a pendulum and enclosed in a tall cabinet. Also **grandfather clock.**

gran·dil·o·quent (gran DIL ə kwənt) adj. pompous; bombastic. [< L grandiloquus using lofty language] —**gran·dil·o·quence** n.

gran·di·ose (GRAN dee OHS) adj. 1. producing an effect of grandeur; imposing. 2. pretentiously grand; pompous; bombastic. [< F] —**gran·di·os·i·ty** (GRAN dee OS i tee) n.

grand jury a body of persons charged with determining whether evidence of criminal misconduct warrants an indictment.

grand mal (GRAN MAHL) Pathol. a type of epilepsy characterized by severe convulsions and loss of consciousness: distinguished from petit mal. [< F, lit., great sickness]

grand·moth·er (GRAN MUTH ər) n. 1. the mother of one's father or mother. 2. a female ancestor.

grand opera a form of opera, usu. having a serious plot, in which the entire text is set to music.

grand·par·ent (GRAN PAIR ənt) n. a grandmother or grandfather.

grand piano a large piano having strings arranged horizontally in a curved, wooden case.

grand slam 1. in bridge, the winning by the declarer of all thirteen tricks in a deal. 2. in baseball, a home run with the bases filled. 3. any great success.

grand·son (GRAN SUN) n. a son of one's child.

grand·stand (GRAN STAND) n. a raised series of seats for spectators at a racetrack, stadium, etc. —v.i. act in a way so as to impress others or win applause.

grange (graynj) n. 1. a farm, with its outbuildings. 2. cap. an association of U.S. farmers. [ME graunge barn]

gran·ite (GRAN it) n. 1. a hard, coarsegrained rock, much used as a building material etc. 2. great hardness, firmness, endurance, etc. [< Ital. granito grainy] —**gra·nit·ic** (grə NIT ik) adj.

gra·niv·o·rous (grə NIV ə rəs) adj. feeding on grain.

gran·ny (GRAN ee) n. pl. •nies 1. grandmother: used familiarly. 2. an old woman. 3. a fussy, interfering person.

gra·no·la (grə NOH lə) n. any of various cereal foods containing whole grain products, unrefined sugars, and dried fruits.

grant (grant) v.t. 1. confer or bestow, as a privilege, charter, etc. 2. allow (someone) to have; give, as permission. 3. admit as true, as for the sake of argument. —n. 1. the act of granting. 2. that which is granted, as a piece of property, a sum of money, or a special privilege. [ME graunten]

gran·tee (gran TEE) n. the grant recipient.

grant·or (GRAN tər) n. the grant maker.

gran·u·lar (GRAN yə lər) adj. 1. composed of, like, or containing grains or granules. 2. having a granulated surface. —**gran·u·lar·i·ty** (GRAN yə LAR ə tee) n.

gran·u·late (GRAN yə LAYT) v.t. & v.i. •lat·ed, •lat·ing make or become granular; form into grains or granules. —**gran·u·la·tion** n.

gran·ule (GRAN yuul) n. a small grain or particle; tiny pellet.

grape (grayp) n. 1. one of the smoothskinned, juicy, edible berries borne in clusters by various climbing vines or small shrubs, cultivated in many species as a fruit and for making wine. 2. any of the vines bearing these berries. 3. a dark, purplish blue color. 4. grapeshot. —**the grape** wine. [ME]

grape·fruit (GRAYP FROOT) n. 1. a large citrus fruit with a yellow rind and tart, juicy pulp. 2. the tree bearing this fruit.

grape·shot (GRAYP SHOT) n. a cluster of shot consisting of iron balls, fired from cannons.

grape·vine (GRAYP VIN) n. 1. a vine that bears grapes. 2. an informal means of relaying information, usu. from person to person.

graph (graf) n. a diagram representing the relationship between data using bars, lines, etc. —v.t. express or represent in the form of a graph.

-graph combining form 1. that which writes or records: seismograph. 2. a writing or record: autograph. [< Gk. graphein write]

-grapher combining form forming nouns of

agency corresponding to words in -*graph* or -*graphy*: *photographer.*

graph•ic (GRAF ik) *adj.* **1.** describing in full detail; vivid. **2.** of, pertaining to, or illustrated by graphs or diagrams. **3.** pertaining to, consisting of, or expressed by writing. **4.** of, pertaining to, or characteristic of the graphic arts. Also **graph′i•cal.** [< L *graphicus* of drawing] —**graph′i•cal•ly** *adv.*

graphic arts 1. those visual arts involving the use of lines or strokes on a flat surface, as painting, drawing, engraving, etc. **2.** those arts that involve impressions or reproductions taken from blocks, plates, type, or the like.

graph•ite (GRAF īt) *n.* a soft, black variety of carbon having a metallic luster and a slippery texture, used as a lubricant and in making pencils etc. [< G *Graphit*]

graph•ol•o•gy (gra FOL ə jee) *n.* the study of handwriting, esp. as a method of estimating the writer's character. —**graph•ol′o•gist** (-jist) *n.*

grap•nel (GRAP nl) *n.* **1.** a small anchor with several flukes at the end of the shank. **2.** any of various devices consisting of a hook or arrangement of hooked parts, used to seize and hold objects. [ME *grapenel* small hook]

grap•ple (GRAP əl) *v.* •**pled,** •**pling** *v.t.* **1.** seize or take hold of with or as with a grapnel. —*v.i.* **2.** struggle in close combat, as in wrestling. **3.** struggle or contend: with *with.* **4.** use a grapnel. —*n.* **1.** a grapnel. **2.** the act of grappling. —**grap′pler** *n.*

grappling iron a grapnel.

grasp (grasp) *v.t.* **1.** seize firmly with or as with the hand; grip. **2.** grab. **3.** comprehend. —*v.i.* **4.** make the motion of grasping or clutching. —*n.* **1.** the act of grasping; also, a grip of the hand. **2.** the power or ability to seize. reach. **3.** intellectual comprehension or mastery. [ME *graspen* seize]

grasp•ing (GRASP ing) *adj.* **1.** greedy. **2.** that grasps.

grass (gras) *n.* **1.** any plant of a large family having rounded, hollow jointed stems and narrow, sheathing leaves. **2.** herbage generally; esp., the herbaceous plants eaten by grazing animals. **3.** ground on which grass is growing. **4.** grazing ground; pasture. **5.** *Slang* marijuana. [ME *gras*] —**grass′y** *adj.* **grass•i•er, grass•i•est**

grass•hop•per (GRAS hop ər) *n.* any of several insects with powerful hind legs adapted for leaping.

grass•land (GRAS LAND) *n.* **1.** land reserved for pasturage or mowing. **2.** land in which grasses are the predominant vegetation.

grass roots the common people, esp. the electorate of a locality. —**grass-roots** (GRAS ROOTS) *adj.* **1.** coming from, pertaining to, or directed toward the common people. **2.** basic or fundamental.

grate[1] (grayt) *v.* **grat•ed, grat•ing** *v.t.* **1.** reduce to fine pieces or powder by rubbing against a rough or sharp surface. **2.** rub or grind to produce a harsh sound. —*v.i.* **3.** produce a harsh sound or have an irritating effect. [ME *graten*] —**grat′er** *n.*

grate[2] *n.* **1.** a framework of crossed or parallel bars placed over a window, drain, etc. **2.** a metal framework to hold burning fuel in a furnace, etc. [< ME, lattice]

grate•ful (GRAYT fəl) *adj.* **1.** thankful for benefits or kindnesses; appreciative; also, expressing gratitude. **2.** giving pleasure; welcome; agreeable. [< L *gratus* pleasing] —**grate′ful•ness** *n.*

grat•i•fy (GRAT ə FI) *v.t.* •**fied,** •**fy•ing 1.** give pleasure or satisfaction to. **2.** satisfy, humor, or indulge. [ME *gratifien*] —**grat•i•fi•ca•tion** (GRAT ə fi KAY shən) *n.*

grat•ing[1] (GRAY ting) *n.* an arrangement of bars or slats used as a cover or screen.

grat•ing[2] *adj.* **1.** garsh or disagreeable in sound; rasping. **2.** irritating; annoying. —**grat′ing•ly** *adv.*

grat•is (GRAT is) *adj. & adv.* free of charge. [< L, out of kindness]

grat•i•tude (GRAT i TOOD) *n.* appreciation for favors, kindness, etc. [ME]

gra•tu•i•tous (grə TOO i təs) *adj.* **1.** given or obtained without payment or return; free. **2.** lacking cause or justification; uncalled-for. [< L *gratuitus* freely given] —**gra•tu′i•tous•ly** *adv.*

gra•tu•i•ty (grə TOO i tee) *n. pl.* -**ties** a gift, usu. of money, given in return for services rendered; tip. [< MF *gratuité*]

gra•va•men (grə VAY mən) *n. pl.* •**vam•i•na** (VAM ə nə) *Law* **1.** the burden or gist of a charge. **2.** a grievance. [< LL, burden]

grave[1] (grayv) *adj.* **grav•er, grav•est 1.** of great importance; weighty: *grave* responsibility. **2.** filled with danger; critical: *grave* situation. **3.** solemn and dignified; sober. **4.** somber, as colors. **5.** *Music* slow and solemn. —*n.* (grahv) a mark used in French to indicate open *e*, (è) or to make a distinction,

as in *ou, où*: also **grave accent.** [< MF] —
grave′ly *adv.*

grave[2] *n.* **1.** a burial place for a dead body,
usu. a hole in the earth. **2.** a tomb. **3.** death.
[ME]

grave[3] *v.t.* **graved, grav•en, grav•ing 1.**
carve or sculpt. **2.** engrave or incise. **3.** impress firmly, as on the memory. [ME
graven] —**grav′er** *n.*

grave•dig•ger (GRAYV DIG ər) *n.* one who
digs graves.

grav•el (GRAV əl) *n.* a mixture of small,
rounded pebbles or fragments of stone, often with sand. —*v.t.* **grav•eled, grav•el•**
ing cover or pave with gravel. [ME] —
grav′el•ly *adj.*

grave•stone (GRAYV STOHN) *n.* a stone
marking a grave.

grave•yard (GRAYV YAHRD) *n.* a cemetery.

graveyard shift 1. a work shift during the
night, usu. beginning at midnight. **2.** the
workers on this shift.

grav•i•tate (GRAV i TAYT) *v.i.* **•tat•ed,**
•tat•ing 1. move or tend to move as a result
of the force of gravity. **2.** move as though
from a force or natural impulse. **3.** sink or
settle to a lower level. [< NL *gravitatus*
made heavy]

grav•i•ta•tion (GRAV i TAY shən) *n.* **1.**
Physics the force whereby any two bodies
attract each other. **2.** the act or process of
gravitating. —**grav′i•ta′tion•al** *adj.*

grav•i•ty (GRAV i tee) *n. pl.* **•ties 1.** *Physics*
gravitation as manifested by the tendency
of material bodies to fall toward the center
of the earth. **2.** weight; heaviness. **3.** great
importance; seriousness. **4.** solemnity; dignified reserve. [< MF *gravité*]

gra•vy (GRAY vee) *n. pl.* **•vies 1.** the juice
exuded by cooking meat; also, a sauce made
from it. **2.** *Slang* money or profit easily acquired. [ME *gravey*]

gray (gray) *adj.* **1.** of a color produced by a
mixture of black and white. **2.** dark or dull,
as from insufficient light; dismal. **3.** having
gray hair. **4.** characteristic of old age; old. —
n. **1.** a color consisting of a mixture of black
and white. **2.** the state of being unbleached
or undyed: said of fabrics. —*v.t. & v.i.* make
or become gray. Also, *Brit.*, **grey.** [ME] —
gray′ness *n.*

gray•beard (GRAY BEERD) *n.* an old man.

gray matter 1. *Anat.* the nerve tissue of the
brain and spinal cord. **2.** *Informal* brains;
intelligence.

graze[1] (grayz) *v.* **grazed, graz•ing** *v.i.* **1.**

feed upon growing grass or herbage. —*v.t.*
2. put (livestock) to feed on pasturage. [ME
grasen] —**graz′er** *n.*

graze[2] *v.t.* **grazed, graz•ing 1.** brush
against lightly in passing. **2.** scrape or
abrade slightly: The bullet *grazed* her arm.
—*n.* **1.** a grazing. **2.** a scrape made by grazing.

graz•ing (GRAY zing) *n.* pasturage. [ME]

grease (grees) *n.* **1.** animal fat in a soft state,
as after melting or rendering. **2.** any thick
fatty or oily substance, as a lubricant. —*v.t.*
greased, greas•ing smear or lubricate
with grease or fat. [ME *grese*]

grease paint theatrical makeup.

greas•y (GREE see) *adj.* **greas•i•er,**
greas•i•est 1. smeared or spotted with
grease. **2.** containing grease or fat; oily. **3.**
appearing or feeling like grease; smooth. —
greas′i•ness *n.*

great (grayt) *adj.* **•er, •est 1.** very large in
bulk, volume, expanse, etc.; immense; big.
2. large in amount or number. **3.** prolonged
in duration or extent. **4.** of unusual importance; momentous; also, renowned. **5.**
marked by nobility of thought, action, etc.
6. unusual in ability or achievement; highly
gifted. **7.** impressive; remarkable. **8.** of a
relationship, being more remote by a single
generation: used in combination: *great-
uncle.* —*n.* **1.** those who are eminent, powerful, etc.: preceded by *the.* **2.** *Often pl.* an
outstanding person: one of baseball's
greats. —*adv. Informal* very well; splen-
didly. [ME *greet*] —**great′ness** *n.*

great-aunt (GRAYT ANT) *n.* an aunt of either of one's parents.

great•er (GRAY tər) comparative of GREAT.
—*adj. Usu. cap.* comprising a (specified)
city and suburbs: *Greater* Chicago.

great-grand•child (GRAYT GRAN CHILD)
n. a child of a grandchild.

great-grand•fa•ther (GRAYT GRAN FAH
thər) *n.* the father of a grandparent.

great-grand•moth•er (GRAYT GRAN
MUTH ər) *n.* the mother of a grandparent.

great-grand•par•ent (GRAYT GRAN PAIR
ənt) *n.* the father or mother of a grandparent.

great-heart•ed (GRAYT HAHR tid) *adj.* **1.**
noble or generous in spirit; magnanimous.
2. high-spirited; courageous.

great•ly (GRAYT lee) *adv.* **1.** to a great degree; very much. **2.** in a way characteristic
of or befitting greatness.

great-un•cle (GRAYT UNG kəl) *n.* an uncle of either of one's parents.

Gre•cian (GREE shən) *adj.* Greek. —*n.* a Greek.

greed (greed) *n.* selfish and grasping desire for possession, esp. of wealth; avarice; covetousness. [< GREEDY]

greed•y (GREE dee) *adj.* **greed•i•er**, **greed•i•est 1.** excessively eager for acquisition or gain; covetous; grasping. **2.** having an excessive appetite for food and drink; voracious; gluttonous. [ME *gredy*] — **greed'i•ly** *adv.*

Greek (greek) *n.* **1.** one of the people of ancient or modern Greece. **2.** the Indo-European language of ancient or modern Greece. **3.** *Informal* anything that is unintelligible: It's *Greek* to me. [ME] —**Greek** *adj.*

Greek Orthodox Church the established church of Greece, a branch of the Eastern Orthodox Church.

green (green) *adj.* **1.** of the color between blue and yellow in the spectrum, as in the foliage of growing plants. **2.** covered with or abounding in grass, growing plants, etc. **3.** consisting of edible green leaves or plant parts: a *green* salad. **4.** not fully developed; immature. **5.** not cured or ready for use. **6.** pale or sickly. —*n.* **1.** the color between blue and yellow in the spectrum, characteristic of the foliage of growing plants. **2.** a green pigment, dye, or substance. **3.** a smooth grassy area or plot: the village *green*. **4.** in golf, the area of clipped grass surrounding the hole. **5.** *pl.* freshly cut leaves, branches, vines, etc. **6.** *pl.* the edible leaves and stems of certain plants, as spinach, beets, etc. —*v.t. & v.i.* make or become green. [ME *grene*]

green•back (GREEN BAK) *n.* one of a class of U.S. notes used as legal tender.

green•belt (GREEN BELT) *n.* an area of parks or undeveloped land surrounding or within a planned community.

green•er•y (GREE nə ree) *n. pl.* **•er•ies 1.** green plants; verdure. **2.** a place where plants are grown or kept.

green-eyed (GREEN ID) *adj.* **1.** having green eyes. **2.** jealous; envious.

green•horn (GREEN HORN) *n.* **1.** an inexperienced person; beginner. **2.** a dupe.

green•house (GREEN HOWS) *n.* a heated shed or building, usu. constructed chiefly of glass, in which tender or exotic plants are grown or sheltered: also called *hothouse*.

green light 1. a green signal indicating that vehicles, pedestrians, etc., may proceed. **2.** approval; authorization.

green party any political party focusing on environmental issues. —**green** *n.* a supporter or candidate of such a party.

green•room (GREEN ROOM) *n.* the waiting room in a theater, TV studio, etc., used by performers when offstage.

green•sward (GREEN SWORD) *n.* grassy turf.

green thumb a knack for raising plants.

Green•wich Time (GREN ich) time as reckoned from the meridian at Greenwich, England.

greet (greet) *v.t.* **1.** express friendly recognition or courteous respect to, as on meeting. **2.** present itself to; be evident to: The warmth of a fire *greeted* us. [ME *greten*] — **greet'er** *n.*

greet•ing (GREE ting) *n.* **1.** the act of one who greets; salutation; welcome. **2.** a friendly or complimentary message.

gre•gar•i•ous (gri GAIR ee əs) *adj.* **1.** habitually associating or found with others, as in flocks, herds, or groups. **2.** enjoying or seeking others; sociable. [< L *gregarius* belonging to a flock] —**gre•gar'i•ous•ness** *n.*

grem•lin (GREM lin) *n.* a mischievous, imaginary creature jokingly said to cause mechanical trouble.

gre•nade (gri NAYD) *n.* a small explosive device, designed to be thrown by hand or projected from a rifle. [< F]

grew (groo) past tense of GROW.

grey (gray) see GRAY.

grey•hound (GRAY HOWND) *n.* one of a breed of slender, smooth-coated dogs noted for their speed. [ME *greihund*]

grid (grid) *n.* **1.** an arrangement of regularly spaced parallel or intersecting bars, wires, etc.; grating; gridiron. **2.** a system of intersecting parallel lines dividing a map, chart, etc. into squares. **3.** a network of high-tension wires transmitting electric power over a wide area. **4.** *Electr.* a perforated or grooved metal plate in a storage cell or battery. **5.** *Electronics* an electrode that controls the flow of electrons in an electron tube. [Back formation < GRIDIRON]

grid•dle (GRID l) *n.* a flat pan used for cooking pancakes, etc. —*v.t.* **•dled**, **•dling** cook on a griddle. [ME *gridel*]

grid•dle•cake (GRID l KAYK) *n.* a pancake baked on a griddle.

grid•i•ron (GRID l ərn) *n.* **1.** a football field.

2. a metal grating set in a frame, used for broiling meat, fish, etc. [ME *gridirne* griddle]

grid·lock (GRID LOK *n.* **1.** a seemingly hopeless stoppage of traffic flow. **2.** any apparently hopeless blockage: The peace negotiations ended in *gridlock.*

grief (greef) *n.* **1.** deep sorrow or mental distress caused by loss, remorse, affliction, etc. **2.** a cause of such sorrow. [ME *gref*]

griev·ance (GREE vəns) *n.* **1.** a real or imaginary wrong regarded as cause for complaint or resentment. **2.** a feeling of resentment arising from a sense of having been wronged. [ME *grevaunce*]

grieve (greev) *v.* **grieved, griev·ing** *v.t.* **1.** cause to feel sorrow or grief. —*v.i.* **2.** feel sorrow or grief. [ME *greven* heavy] — **griev'er** *n.*

griev·ous (GREE vəs) *adj.* **1.** causing grief, sorrow, or misfortune. **2.** meriting severe punishment or censure: *grievous* sin. — **griev'ous·ness** *n.*

grif·fin (GRIF in) *n.* in Greek mythology, a creature with the head and wings of an eagle and the body of a lion. Also **grif'fon.** [ME *griffoun*]

grift·er (GRIF tər) *n. Slang* a petty swindler, esp. one who operates a dishonest game of chance at a carnival or circus.

grill (gril) *v.t.* **1.** cook on a gridiron or similar utensil. question or cross-examine persistently and searchingly. —*v.i.* **3.** undergo grilling. —*n.* **1.** a gridiron or similar cooking utensil. **2.** a meal or portion of grilled food. **3.** a grillroom. **4.** a grille. [< F *gril* gridiron] —**grill'er** *n.*

grille (gril) *n.* a grating, often of decorative, open metalwork, used as a screen, divider, etc.: also spelled *grill.* [< F]

grill·room (GRIL ROOM) *n.* a restaurant serving grilled foods.

grim (grim) *adj.* **grim·mer, grim·mest 1.** stern or forbidding in appearance or character. **2.** unyielding; relentless. **3.** sinisterly ironic; ghastly: a *grim* joke. **4.** savagely destructive; fierce. [ME] —**grim'ness** *n.*

grim·ace (GRIM əs) *n.* a distorted facial expression, usu. indicative of pain, annoyance, disgust, etc. —*v.i.* •**maced,** •**mac·ing** distort the features; make faces. [< F]

gri·mal·kin (gri MAL kin) *n.* **1.** a cat, particularly an old female cat. **2.** a shrewish old woman.

grime (grīm) *n.* dirt, esp. soot, rubbed into or coating a surface. —*v.t.* **grimed, grim·ing** make dirty. [ME *grim*] —**grim'y** *adj.* **grim·i·er, grim·i·est**

grin (grin) *v.* **grinned, grin·ning** *v.i.* **1.** smile broadly. **2.** draw back the lips so as to show the teeth. —*v.t.* **3.** express by grinning. [ME *grinnen*] —**grin** *n.*

grind (grīnd) *v.* **ground, grind·ing** *v.t.* **1.** reduce to fine particles, as by crushing; pulverize. **2.** sharpen, polish, or wear down by friction or abrasion. **3.** rub together or press down with a scraping or turning motion: *grind* the teeth. **4.** oppress; crush. **5.** produce by or as by grinding. **6.** produce mechanically or laboriously: followed by *out.* —*v.i.* **7.** perform the operation or action of grinding. **8.** undergo grinding. **9.** *Informal* study or work steadily and laboriously: followed by *away.* —*n.* **1.** the act of grinding. **2.** the sound made by grinding. **3.** a specified state of pulverization, as of coffee. **4.** prolonged and laborious work or study. **5.** *Informal* a student who studies constantly. [ME *grinden*]

grind·er (GRIN dər) *n.* **1.** one who grinds; esp., one who sharpens tools, etc. **2.** a device used for grinding, as a coffee mill, etc. **3.** a molar. **4.** hero (def.5).

grind·stone (GRIND STOHN) *n.* **1.** a flat, circular stone rotated on an axle, used for sharpening tools, polishing, etc. **2.** a millstone. —**keep** (or **put**) **one's nose to the grindstone** work hard and continuously.

grip (grip) *n.* **1.** the act of seizing and holding firmly. **2.** the ability to seize or maintain a hold; grasping power. **3.** control; domination. **4.** mental or intellectual grasp. **5.** the manner of grasping or holding something, as a tool or implement. **6.** a distinctive handclasp used in greeting. **7.** the handle of an object. **8.** a device or mechanical part that seizes or holds something. **9.** the strength of the hand in grasping. **10.** a suitcase or valise. **11.** a stagehand. —**come to grips with** confront; deal decisively or energetically, as with a problem. —*v.t.* **gripped, grip·ping 1.** seize; grasp firmly. **2.** capture, as the mind or imagination; attract and hold the interest of. **3.** join or attach securely with a grip or similar device. [ME]

gripe (grīp) *v.* **griped, grip·ing** *v.t.* **1.** *Informal* annoy; anger. **2.** cause sharp pain or cramps in the bowels of. —*v.i.* **3.** *Informal* complain; grumble. —n. **1.** *Informal* a grievance. **2.** *Usu. pl.* spasmodic pain in the bowels. [ME *gripen*]

gris·ly (GRIZ lee) *adj.* **·li·er, ·li·est** inspiring horror; gruesome. [ME] **—gris′li·ness** n.

grist (grist) n. **1.** grain that is to be ground; also, a batch of such grain. **2.** ground grain. **—grist for one's mill** something that can be used to one's advantage. [ME]

gris·tle (GRIS əl) n. cartilage, esp. in meat. [ME] **—gris′tly** *adj.* **·tli·er, ·tli·est**

grist·mill (GRIST MIL.) n. a mill for grinding grain.

grit (grit) n. **1.** small, rough, hard particles, as of sand, stone, etc. **2.** resolute spirit; pluck. —*v.t.* **grit·ted, grit·ting** grind or press together, as the teeth. [ME *gret*] **—grit′ty** *adj.* **·ti·er, ·ti·est**

grits (grits) *n.pl.* **1.** coarse meal. **2.** coarsely ground hominy: also called *hominy grits.* [ME *gryttes*]

griz·zle (GRIZ əl) *v.t. & v.i.* **·zled, ·zling** become or cause to become gray. —n. **1.** the color gray, esp. when produced by intermixed specks of black and white. **2.** gray or graying hair. —*adj.* gray. [ME *grisel*] **—griz′zled** *adj.*

griz·zly (GRIZ lee) *adj.* **·zli·er, ·zli·est** grayish; grizzled. —n. pl. **·zlies** a grizzly bear.

grizzly bear a bear of North America.

groan (grohn) *v.i.* **1.** utter a low, prolonged sound of or as of pain, disapproval, etc. **2.** make a noise resembling such a sound; creak harshly. **3.** suffer, as from cruel or unfair treatment: usu. with *under* or *beneath.* **4.** be overburdened. —*v.t.* **5.** utter or express with or as with a groan. [ME *gronen*] **—groan·n.**

groats (grohts) n. (*used with sing. or pl. verb*) hulled, usu. coarsely crushed grain, as barley, oats, or wheat. [ME *grotes*]

gro·cer (GROH sər) n. one who deals in foodstuffs and various household supplies. [ME]

gro·cer·y (GROH sə ree) n. pl. **·cer·ies 1.** a store in which foodstuffs and household supplies are sold. **2.** pl. the merchandise sold by a grocer. [ME *grocerie*]

grog·gy (GROG ee) *adj.* **·gi·er, ·gi·est** dazed or not fully conscious, as from a blow or exhaustion. **—grog′gi·ness** n.

groin (groin) n. **1.** *Anat.* the fold or crease formed at the juncture of either of the thighs with the abdomen. **2.** *Archit.* the curve formed by the intersection of two vaults. [ME *grinde*]

grom·met (GROM it) n. **1.** a reinforcing eyelet of metal or other material, through which a rope, cord, or fastening may be passed. **2.** *Naut.* a ring of rope or metal used to secure the edge of a sail.

groom (groom) n. **1.** one employed to tend horses. **2.** a bridegroom. —*v.t.* **1.** attend to the neatness or appearance of. **2.** take care of (an animal) by cleaning, combing, etc. **3.** prepare by giving special training or attention to, as for a political office. [ME *grom*]

groove (groov) n. **1.** a long, narrow indentation or furrow cut into a surface, esp. by a tool. **2.** any narrow depression, channel, or rut. **3.** a fixed, settled routine or habit. —*v.* **grooved, groov·ing** *v.t.* **1.** cut a groove in. —*v.i. Slang* **2.** enjoy: often with *on.* **3.** relate successfully. [ME *grofe* mine shaft]

groov·y (GROO vee) *adj.* **groov·i·er, groov·i·est** *Slang* satisfying; delightful.

grope (grohp) *v.* **groped, grop·ing** *v.i.* **1.** feel about with or as with the hands; feel one's way. **2.** search bewilderedly or uncertainly. —*v.t.* **3.** seek out or find by or as by groping. **4.** fondle for sexual pleasure. [ME *gropien*] **—grope·n. —grop′er** n.

gross (grohs) *adj.* **1.** undiminished by deductions; total: distinguished from *net: gross income.* **2.** conspicuously bad or wrong: *gross errors.* **3.** excessively fat or large. **4.** coarse in composition, structure, or texture. **5.** coarse or obscene in character. —n. pl. **gross** for def. 1, **gross·es** for def. 2 **1.** a unit of quantity comprising twelve dozen. **2.** the entire amount; bulk. —*v.t.* earn or produce as total income or profit, before deductions for expenses etc. [ME] **—gross′ly** *adv.*

gross weight total weight.

gro·tesque (groh TESK) *adj.* **1.** distorted, incongruous, or fantastically ugly in appearance or style; outlandish. **2.** characterized by fantastic combinations of human and animal figures with conventional design forms. —n. one who or that which is grotesque. [< F] **—gro·tesque′ness** n.

grot·to (GROT oh) n. pl. **·toes** or **·tos 1.** a cave. **2.** a cavelike structure, as for a shrine. [< Ital., crypt]

grouch (growch) n. **1.** a discontented, grumbling person. **2.** a grumbling, sulky mood. **—grouch** *v.t.* **—grouch′y** *adj.* **grouch·i·er, grouch·i·est**

ground¹ (grownd) n. **1.** the layer of solid substances constituting the surface of the earth; land. **2.** soil, sand, etc., at or near the earth's surface. **3.** *Sometimes pl.* an area or tract of land; esp., one reserved or used for a specific purpose: burial *ground.* **4.** *pl.* private land, as the surrounding premises of a dwelling etc. **5.** *Usu. pl.* the fundamental cause, reason, or motive for an action, belief, etc.: *grounds* for suspicion. **6.** *pl.* sediment; dregs; esp., the particles remaining after coffee has been brewed. **7.** in various arts and crafts, the background against which colors and designs are placed. **8.** *Electr.* the connection of an electrical current or circuit with the earth through a conductor. **—gain ground 1.** advance; make headway. **2.** increase in favor, influence, etc. **—hold (or stand) one's ground** refuse to yield or retreat. **—lose ground 1.** fail to maintain an advantage or gain. **2.** decline in favor, influence, etc. **—adj. 1.** being on, near, or at a level with the ground. **2.** living, growing, or active on or in the ground. **—v.t. 1.** place on the ground. **2.** base on or as on a foundation; establish; found. **3.** teach fundamentals to. **4.** *Aeron.* restrict (an aircraft, pilot, etc.) to the ground. **5.** *Electr.* place in connection with the earth or a ground, as a circuit. **6.** *Naut.* run (a vessel) aground. **—v.i. 7.** come or fall to the ground. [ME *grownd*]

ground² past tense, past participle of GRIND.

ground ball in baseball, a batted ball that rolls or bounces along the ground. Also **ground•er** (GROWN dər).

ground crew *Aeron.* those responsible for servicing aircraft on the ground.

ground floor in a building, the floor that is level or almost level with the ground. **—get in on the ground floor** *Informal* enter upon a project at its beginning.

ground•less (GROWND lis) *adj.* having no reason or cause; baseless.

ground plan 1. a plan of any floor of a building. **2.** any preliminary plan or basic outline.

ground•swell (GROWND SWEL) *n.* **1.** a billowing of the ocean in deep waves caused by a prolonged storm, earthquake, etc. **2.** a rapid, spontaneous growth, as of public opinion.

ground water underground water, accumulating by seepage.

ground•work (GROWND WURK) *n.* a foundation; basis.

ground zero the point on the ground directly beneath or above the point of detonation of a nuclear bomb.

group (groop) *n.* **1.** a collection or assemblage of persons or things, considered as a unit. **2.** a number of persons or things having in common certain characteristics, interests, etc. **3.** *Biol.* a number of plants or animals considered to be related because of common characteristics. [< F *groupe*] **— group** *v.i. & v.t.*

group•ie (GROO pee) *n. Informal* **1.** a young fan, esp. female, of a rock star or group. **2.** an ardent fan of any celebrity.

group therapy a form of therapy in which several persons discuss and analyze their problems with the aid of a person qualified to direct the discussion.

grouse¹ (grows) *n. pl.* **grouse** any of a family of game birds characterized by rounded bodies and mottled plumage.

grouse² *Informal v.i.* **groused, grous•ing** grumble. **—n.** a complaint.

grove (grohv) *n.* a small wood or group of trees, esp. when cleared of underbrush. [ME]

grov•el (GRUV əl) *v.i.* **•eled, •el•ing 1.** lie prostrate or crawl face downward, as in abjection, fear, etc. **2.** act with abject humility. **3.** take pleasure in what is base or sensual. [Back formation < obs. *groveling* face down] **—grov′el•er** *n.*

grow (groh) *v.* **grew, grown, grow•ing** *v.i.* **1.** increase in size by the assimilation of nutriment; progress toward maturity. **2.** germinate and develop to maturity, as from a seed or spore. **3.** flourish; thrive. **4.** become: She *grew* angry. **—v.t. 5.** cause to grow; cultivate. **6.** produce by a natural process: *grow* hair. **7.** cover with a growth: used in the passive. **—grow out of 1.** outgrow. **2.** result from. [ME *growen*]

growl (growl) *v.i.* **1.** utter a deep, guttural sound, as that made by a hostile or agitated animal. **2.** speak gruffly and angrily. **3.** rumble, as distant thunder. **—v.t. 4.** utter or express by growling. [ME *groule* rumble] **—n.**

grown (grohn) past participle of GROW. **— adj.** arrived at full growth or stature; mature.

grown-up (GROHN UP) *adj.* **1.** physically or mentally mature; adult. **2.** characteristic of or appropriate to an adult. **—grown′up′** *n.*

growth (grohth) *n.* **1.** the act or process of growing. **2.** a gradual increase in size, influence, etc. **3.** something grown or in the process of growing: a *growth* of timber. **4.** *Pathol.* an abnormal formation of tissue.

grub (grub) *v.* **grubbed, grub·bing** *v.i.* **1.** dig in the ground. **2.** lead a dreary or miserable existence; drudge. **3.** make careful or plodding search; rummage. —*v.t.* **4.** dig from the ground; root out: often with *up* or *out.* **5.** *Slang* scrounge. —*n.* **1.** the wormlike larva of certain insects. **2.** *Slang* food. [ME *grubben*] —**grub'ber** *n.*

grub·by (GRUB ee) *adj.* **·bi·er, ·bi·est 1.** dirty; sloppy. **2.** infested with grubs. —**grub'bi·ness** *n.*

grub·stake (GRUB stayk) *n.* **1.** money, supplies, or equipment provided a prospector on condition of sharing finds with the donor. **2.** money or assistance furnished to advance any venture. —*v.t.* **·staked, ·stak·ing** supply with a grubstake.

grudge (gruj) *n.* a feeling of ill will, rancor, or enmity, harbored for a remembered wrong etc. —*v.t.* **grudged, grudg·ing 1.** be displeased or resentful because of the possessions, good fortune, etc. of (another). **2.** give or allow unwillingly and resentfully. [ME *grudgen*] —**grudg'ing·ly** *adv.*

gru·el (GROO əl) *n.* a cereal made by boiling meal in water or milk. [ME]

gru·el·ing (GROO ə ling) *adj.* causing strain or exhaustion.

grue·some (GROO səm) *adj.* inspiring repugnance; frightful. [< Scot. *grue* shudder + -SOME¹] —**grue'some·ness** *n.*

gruff (gruf) *adj.* **1.** brusque and rough in manner or speech. **2.** hoarse and guttural; harsh. [< MDu. *grof* rough] —**gruff'ness** *n.*

grum·ble (GRUM bəl) *v.* **·bled, ·bling** *v.i.* **1.** complain in a surly manner. **2.** utter low, throaty sounds; growl. **3.** rumble. —*v.t.* **4.** utter or express by grumbling. [? < Du. *grommelen* growl] —*n.* —**grum'bler** *n.*

grump·y (GRUM pee) *adj.* **grump·i·er, grump·i·est** ill-tempered; cranky; surly. —**grump'i·ness** *n.*

grunt (grunt) *v.i.* **1.** make the deep, guttural sound of a hog. **2.** make a similar sound, as in annoyance, assent, effort, etc. —*v.t.* **3.** utter or express by grunting. —*n.* a short, deep, guttural sound, as of a hog. [ME *grunten*]

G-string (JEE STRING) *n.* **1.** a narrow loincloth supported by a waistband. **2.** a similar garment worn by stripteasers. **3.** on musical instruments, a string tuned to G.

gua·no (GWAH noh) *n. pl.* **·nos 1.** the excrement of sea birds, found on the Peruvian coast, and used as a fertilizer. **2.** any similar fertilizer. [< Quechua *huanu* dung]

guar·an·tee (GAR ən TEE) *n.* **1.** a pledge or formal promise that something will meet stated specifications or that a specified act will be performed or continued: also called *warranty.* **2.** a guaranty (def. 2). —*v.t.* **·teed, ·tee·ing 1.** certify; vouch for: We *guarantee* our work. **2.** accept responsibility for. **3.** give security to (a person or thing), as against loss, damage, injury, etc. [Var. of GUARANTY]

guar·an·tor (GAR ən TOR) *n.* one who gives a guaranty.

guar·an·ty (GAR ən TEE) *n. pl.* **·ties 1.** a pledge or promise to be responsible for the contract, debt, or duty of another person in case of his default or miscarriage. **2.** something given or taken as security. —*v.t.* **·tied, ·ty·ing** guarantee. [< OF *guarantie*]

guard (gahrd) *v.t.* **1.** watch over or care for; protect. **2.** watch over so as to prevent escape etc. **3.** maintain cautious control over. **4.** furnish (something) with a protective device or shield. —*v.i.* **5.** take precautions: followed by *against.* **6.** serve as a guard. —*n.* **1.** one who guards; as: **a** a security officer; keeper. **b** one who has control over a point of entry, exit, etc. **2.** a group of persons serving as a ceremonial escort. **3.** the act of guarding. **4.** a defensive posture or stance, as in boxing or fencing. **5.** in football, one of the two linemen whose position is usu. between a tackle and center. **6.** in basketball, one of two players who are stationed in the backcourt. —**off guard** unprepared. —**on guard** watchful; cautious. —**stand guard** maintain a protective watch, as a sentry. [ME *garde* guardianship]

guard·ed (GAHR did) *adj.* **1.** cautious; reserved: *guarded* criticism. **2.** closely defended or kept under surveillance by a guard. **3.** needing close care: a patient in *guarded* condition. —**guard'ed·ly** *adv.*

guard·house (GAHRD HOWS) *n.* **1.** the quarters and headquarters for military guards. **2.** a jail confining military personnel convicted of minor offenses etc.

guard·i·an (GAHR dee ən) *n.* **1.** one who guards or watches over something. **2.** one who is legally assigned care of the person, property, etc., esp. of an infant or minor. [ME *gardein*] —*adj.* keeping guard; protecting. —**guard'i·an·ship** *n.*

guard•room (GAHRD room) *n.* a room for the use and accommodation of military or other guards.

gu•ber•na•to•ri•al (GOO bər nə TOR ee əl) *adj.* of or pertaining to a governor. [< L *gubernator* governor]

guer•ril•la (gə RIL ə) *n.* one of an irregular combat unit whose tactic is to neutralize the numerical superiority of the enemy through stealth and surprise. —*adj.* of guerrillas or their warfare. Also **gue•ril'la** [< Sp.]

guess (ges) *v.t.* 1. form a judgment or opinion of (some quantity, fact, etc.) on uncertain or incomplete knowledge. 2. conjecture correctly. 3. suppose: I *guess* we'll be late. —*v.i.* 4. form a judgment or opinion on uncertain or incomplete knowledge: often with *at*. 5. conjecture correctly: How did you *guess?* [ME *gessen*] —**guess** *n.*

guess•work (GES wurk) *n.* 1. the process of guessing. 2. something based on a guess or guesses, as an opinion.

guest (gest) *n.* 1. one who is received and entertained by another or others, as at a party or meal, or for a visit. 2. one who pays for lodging etc., as at a hotel. —*adj.* 1. intended for guests. 2. acting on invitation. [ME *gest*]

guff (guf) *n. Informal* empty talk; nonsense.

guf•faw (gə FAW) *n.* a loud burst of boisterous laughter. —*v.i.* utter such a laugh.

guid•ance (GID ns) *n.* 1. the act, process, or result of guiding. 2. something that guides.

guide (gīd) *v.* **guid•ed, guid•ing** *v.t.* 1. lead or direct, as to a destination. 2. direct the motion or physical progress of, as a vehicle, tool, animal, etc. 3. lead or direct the affairs, standards, opinions, etc. of. —*v.i.* 4. act as a guide. —*n.* 1. a person who guides; esp., one who conducts others on trips, through museums, etc. 2. one who or that which is taken as a model. 3. a book that guides or explains; esp., a guidebook. 4. *Mech.* any device that regulates or controls the operation of a part. [ME *giden*]

guide•book (GID buuk) *n.* a handbook containing information for tourists, visitors, etc.

guided missile *Mil.* an unmanned missile whose course can be altered during flight.

guide•line (GID līn) *n.* 1. a line, as a rope, for guiding. 2. any suggestion, rule, etc., intended as a guide.

guide•post (GID pohst) *n.* 1. a post on which directions for travelers are given. 2. a guideline (def. 2).

guild (gild) *n.* 1. in medieval times, an association of artisans or merchants. 2. any similar association or fellowship. [ME *gild*]

guile (gīl) *n.* treacherous cunning or craft; deceit. [ME] —**guile'ful** *adj.* —**guile' less** *adj.*

guil•lo•tine (GIL ə TEEN) *n.* 1. the instrument of capital punishment in France, consisting of a weighted blade that slides down between two vertical guides and beheads the victim. 2. a similar machine for cutting paper etc. —**•tined, •tin•ing** behead with the guillotine. [< F, after J.I. *Guillotin*, 1738—1814, French physician]

guilt (gilt) *n.* 1. the fact or condition of having committed a legal or moral offense. 2. a feeling of remorse arising from a real or imagined commission of an offense. 3. guilty conduct. [ME *gilt*] —**guilt'less** *adj.*

guilt•y (GIL tee) *adj.* **guilt•i•er, guilt•i•est** 1. deserving of blame for some offense. 2. convicted of some offense. 3. involving, pertaining to, or showing guilt. [ME] — **guilt'i•ly** *adv.*

guinea pig 1. a small rodent widely used in biological and medical experiments. 2. *Informal* any person used in experimentation.

guise (gīz) *n.* 1. external appearance or aspect; semblance. 2. assumed or false appearance; pretense. [ME *gise*]

gulch (gulch) *n.* a deep, narrow ravine cut out by a rushing stream. [ME *gulchen* gush]

gulf (gulf) *n.* 1. a large area of ocean or sea partially enclosed by an extended sweep of land. 2. an abyss; chasm; gorge. 3. a wide or impassable separation, as in social position, education, etc. [ME *goulf*]

gull[1] (gul) *n.* a long-winged sea bird, usu. white and gray. [ME *gulle*]

gull[2] *n.* a person easily tricked. —*v.t.* deceive; swindle; cheat.

Gul•lah (GUL ə) *n.* 1. one of a group of inhabitants of a narrow coastal strip of South Carolina, Georgia, and NE Florida. 2. the mixed (English and African) language of these people.

gul•let (GUL it) *n.* 1. the passage from the mouth to the stomach; esophagus. 2. the throat; pharynx; also, anything resembling a throat. [ME *golet*]

gul•li•ble (GUL ə bəl) *adj.* easily cheated or fooled; credulous. —**gul'li•bil'i•ty** *n.*

gul•ly (GUL ee) *n. pl.* **•lies** a channel, ravine, or ditch; esp., a ravine cut in the earth by running water. —*v.t.* •**lied**, •**ly•ing** cut or wear a gully in.

gulp (gulp) *v.t.* **1.** swallow greedily or in large amounts. **2.** choke back or stifle. —*v.i.* **3.** swallow convulsively as a sign of surprise, etc. —*n.* **1.** the act of gulping. **2.** the amount swallowed in gulping. [ME *gulpen*]

gum¹ (gum) *n.* **1.** a sticky substance exuded from various trees and plants, soluble in water and hardening on exposure to air. **2.** any similar substance, as resin. **3.** a preparation made from gum and used in art, industry, etc. **4.** chewing gum. **5.** glue. **6.** the gum tree. **7.** rubber. —*v.* **gummed, gum•ming** *v.t.* **1.** smear, stiffen, or clog with gum. **2.** glue or stick together with gum. —*v.i.* **3.** become sticky or clogged with gum. — **gum up** *Slang* spoil. [ME *gomme*] —**gum′my** *adj.* •**mi•er**, •**mi•est**

gum² *n. Often pl.* the fleshy tissue that covers the arches of the jaws and surrounds the necks of the teeth. —*v.t. & v.i.* **gummed, gum•ming** chew without teeth. [ME *goma*]

gum•bo (GUM boh) *n. pl.* •**bos** **1.** the okra or its edible, slippery pods. **2.** a thick soup or stew containing okra pods. **3.** a patois of French spoken in Louisiana. [< Louisiana F *gombo*]

gum•drop (GUM DROP) *n.* a small, round piece of jellylike candy, usu. sugar-coated.

gump•tion (GUM shən) *n. Informal* **1.** bold, energetic initiative. **2.** courage.

gun (gun) *n.* **1.** a weapon or projectile de-vice from which a missile is thrown by the force of an explosive, by compressed air, by a spring, etc. **2.** *Mil.* **a** any of various cannons with a flat trajectory, high muzzle velocity, and a barrel of over .25 caliber: anti-tank *gun.* **b** any of various automatic weapons, as a machine gun. **3.** any device resembling a gun: grease *gun.* **4.** *Slang* a gunman. —**big gun** *Slang* a person of influence. —**give it the gun** *Slang* **1.** in-crease sharply the speed of a motor. **2.** give added speed, efficiency, etc. to some action. —**go great guns** *Informal* work or perform with great skill, speed, etc. — **stick to one's guns** continue in one's plans, opinions, etc. despite opposition. —*v.* **gunned, gun•ning** *v.i.* **1.** go shooting or hunting with a gun. —*v.t.* **2.** open the throttle of (an engine). **3.** shoot (a person) with a gun. —**gun for 1.** seek with intent to injure or kill. **2.** seek out in order to win favor, etc. [ME *gunne*]

gun•fight (GUN FIT) *n.* a fight between per-sons using guns. —**gun′fight′er** *n.*

gun•fire (GUN FIR) *n.* **1.** the firing of a gun or guns. **2.** *Mil.* the use of artillery or small arms in warfare.

gung ho (GUNG HOH) eager; enthusiastic: *gung ho* about army life. [< Chinese]

gun•man (GUN mən) *n. pl.* •**men** **1.** a man armed with a gun; esp., an armed criminal. **2.** a gunsmith.

gun•met•al (GUN MET l) *adj.* of a dark bluish gray color.

gun•nel (GUN l) see GUNWALE.

gun•ner (GUN ər) *n.* **1.** one who operates a gun. **2.** a Marine Corps warrant officer aboard a navy vessel who has charge of ord-nance. **3.** a soldier, airman, etc. who fires or assists in firing a gun.

gun•ner•y (GUN ə ree) *n.* the art of con-structing and operating guns.

gun•ny (GUN ee) *n. pl.* •**nies** **1.** a coarse, heavy material made of jute or hemp. **2.** a bag or sack made from this material: also **gunny sack.** [< Hind. *goni* gunny sack]

gun•pow•der (GUN POW dər) *n.* an explo-sive mixture of charcoal, sulfur, etc. used in blasting and fireworks, and still occasionally as a propellant in guns.

gun•run•ning (GUN RUN ing) *n.* the smug-gling of guns and ammunition into a coun-try. —**gun′run′ner** *n.*

gun•shot (GUN SHOT) *n.* **1.** the range or reach of a gun. **2.** the shooting of a gun; also, the noise or the shot. —*adj.* caused by a gunshot.

gun•shy (GUN SHI) *adj.* afraid of guns or their sound.

gun•smith (GUN SMITH) *n.* one who makes or repairs guns.

gun•stock (GUN STOK) *n.* the wooden stock of a gun.

gun•wale (GUN l) *n. Naut.* the upper edge of the side of a boat: also spelled *gunnel.* [ME]

gup•py (GUP ee) *n. pl.* •**pies** a small, tropi-cal, freshwater fish. [after R.J.L. *Guppy,* 1836—1916, Trinidadian scientist]

gur•gle (GUR gəl) *v.* •**gled**, •**gling** *v.i.* **1.** flow irregularly, with a bubbling sound. **2.** make such a sound. —*v.t.* **3.** utter with a gurgling sound. —**gur′gle** *n.*

gu•ru (GUUR oo) *n.* **1.** in Hinduism, a spiri-tual teacher or guide. **2.** anyone claiming to impart special knowledge, power, etc. [< Hind., venerable]

gush (gush) *v.i.* **1.** pour out in volume and

with sudden force. **2.** emit a sudden flow, as of blood, tears, etc. **3.** be overly enthusiastic. —*v.t.* **4.** pour forth (blood, tears, words, etc.). —*n.* a sudden flow or outburst. [ME] —**gush′ing·ly** *adv.*

gush·er (GUSH ər) *n.* **1.** one who gushes. **2.** an oil well that spurts oil naturally.

gush·y (GUSH ee) *adj.* **gush·i·er, gush·i·est** overly enthusiastic. —**gush′i·ness** *n.*

gus·set (GUS it) *n.* a triangular piece inserted into a garment, glove, shoe, etc. for added strength or roomier fit. —*v.t.* furnish with a gusset. [ME]

gus·sy (GUS ee) *v.t. & v.i.* **·sied, ·sy·ing** *Informal* **1.** dress up. **2.** embellish. Also **gussy up.**

gust (gust) *n.* **1.** a sudden, violent rush of wind or air. **2.** a sudden burst or outpouring, as of emotion. —**gust′i·ness** *n.* —**gust′y** *adj.* **gust·i·er, gust·i·est** [< ON *gustr*]

gus·ta·to·ry (GUS tə TOR ee) *adj.* of or pertaining to the sense of taste or to tasting. [< L *gustare* taste]

gus·to (GUS toh) *n. pl.* **·toes** keen enjoyment or enthusiasm; relish. [< Ital.]

gut (gut) *n.* **1.** the alimentary canal or any part of it; esp., the stomach or intestine. **2.** *pl.* bowels; entrails. **3.** the specially prepared intestines of certain animals, used as strings for musical instruments, surgical sutures, etc. **4.** *pl. Informal* **a** courage; stamina; grit. **b** effrontery. —*v.t.* **gut·ted, gut·ting 1.** take out the intestines of. **2.** destroy the contents of. —*adj.* **1.** basic and fundamental: a *gut* issue. **2.** involving one's emotions; not reasoned; instinctive: a *gut* reaction. **3.** not difficult: a *gut* course. [ME]

guts·y (GUT see) *adj. Informal* **guts·i·er, guts·i·est** forceful; courageous.

gut·ta-per·cha (GUT ə PUR chə) *n.* a coagulated, rubberlike material, used in electrical insulation, in making golf balls, etc. [< Malay *getah* sap + *perca* rag]

gut·ter (GUT ər) *n.* **1.** a channel or ditch at the side of a street, for carrying off surface water. **2.** a trough fixed below or along the eaves of a house, for carrying off rain water from the roof. **3.** a state or condition of life, marked by poverty, filth, etc. **4.** any groove or channel. —*v.i.* melt rapidly: said of lighted candles. [ME]

gut·ter·snipe (GUT ər SNIP) *n.* a street urchin.

gut·tur·al (GUT ər əl) *adj.* **1.** pertaining to the throat. **2.** having a harsh, or muffled,

grating quality. **3.** *Phonet.* produced or sounded in the throat. [< NL *gutturalis* of the throat]

guy¹ (gī) *n. Informal* a man or boy; fellow. [after *Guy* Fawkes, 1570–1606, conspirator in the Gunpowder Plot of 1605 in England]

guy² *n.* a rope, cable, wire, etc., used to steady, guide, or secure something. —*v.t.* steady, etc., with a guy. [ME *gye* guide]

guz·zle (GUZ əl) *v.t. & v.i.* **·zled, ·zling** drink greedily or to excess. —**guz′zler** *n.*

gym (jim) *n.* **1.** a gymnasium. **2.** *Informal* a course in physical training.

gym·na·si·um (jim NAY zee əm) *n. pl.* **·si·ums, ·si·a** (-zee ə) a building or room equipped for certain athletic activities. [< L]

Gym·na·si·um (gim NAH zee əm) *n.* in Europe, esp. Germany, a secondary school to prepare students for the universities.

gym·nast (JIM nast) *n.* one skilled in gymnastics.

gym·nas·tics (jim NAS tiks) *n.* **1.** (construed *as pl.*) physical exercises designed to improve strength, agility, etc. **2.** (construed *as sing.*) the art or practice of such exercises. —**gym·nas′tic** *adj.* —**gym·nas′ti·cal·ly** *adv.*

gy·ne·col·o·gy (GI ni KOL ə jee) *n.* that branch of medicine dealing with the functions and diseases peculiar to women. —**gy′ne·col′o·gist** *n.*

gyp (jip) *v.t. & v.i.* **gypped, gyp·ping** cheat, swindle, or defraud. —*n.* a swindle. [< GYPSY]

Gyp·sy (JIP see) *n. pl.* **·sies 1.** a wandering Caucasian people believed to have migrated to Europe from India, and known as fortunetellers, musicians, etc. **2.** *Usu. not cap.* anyone who looks like or leads a life like that of a Gypsy. **3.** *Not cap.* a gypsy cab. —*v.i.* **·sied, ·sy·ing** live or wander like a Gypsy. [Var. of *Egyptian*] —**Gyp′sy, gyp′sy** *adj.*

gypsy cab a taxicab licensed only to pick up passengers who call on the telephone for service.

gypsy moth a moth having larvae destructive to foliage.

gy·rate (JĪ RAYT) *v.i.* **·rat·ed, ·rat·ing 1.** rotate or revolve, usu. around a fixed point or axis. **2.** turn in a spiral motion. —*adj.* winding or coiled about; convolute. [< L *gyratus* turned around] —**gy·ra′tion** *n.*

gy·ro (JĪ roh) *n.* a gyroscope or gyrocompass.

gy•ro (JEER oh) *n.* in Greek cookery, meat roasted on a spit, usu. served as a sandwich of pita bread.

gy•ro•com•pass (JĪ roh KUM pəs) *n.* a compass that employs a gyroscope rotor, so mounted that its axis of rotation maintains a constant position with reference to the true or geographic north.

gy•ro•scope (JĪ roh SKOHP) *n.* any of a class of devices consisting essentially of a heavy wheel, so mounted that when set to rotate at high speeds it resists forces tending to change the angular position of its axis of rotation. [< F] —**gy•ro•scop•ic** (JĪ rə SKOP ik) *adj.*

H

h, H (aych) n. pl. **h's** or **hs, H's** or **Hs 1.** the eighth letter of the English alphabet. **2.** the sound represented by the letter h. **3.** Slang heroin. —symbol **1.** Chem. hydrogen. **2.** Physics strength or intensity of magnetic field (symbol H). **3.** Electr. henry (symbol H).

ha (hah) n. & interj. an exclamation or sound expressing surprise, discovery, triumph, laughter, etc. Also spelled hah.

ha·be·as cor·pus (HAY bee əs KOR pəs) Law a writ commanding a detained person to be produced before a court, esp. to determine the lawfulness of the detention. [< L, lit., you have the body]

hab·er·dash·er (HAB ər DASH ər) n. a shopkeeper who deals in men's furnishings, as shirts, hats, etc. [ME haberdasshere]

hab·er·dash·er·y (HAB ər DASH ə ree) n. pl. **·er·ies 1.** the goods sold by haberdashers. **2.** a haberdasher's shop. [ME haberdashrye]

ha·bil·i·tate (hə BIL i TAYT) v.t. **·tat·ed, ·tat·ing 1.** provide with clothing, equipment, or the like. **2.** train; educate. [< LL habilitatus equipped] —**ha·bil'i·ta'tion** n.

hab·it (HAB it) n. **1.** an act or practice so frequently repeated as to become almost automatic. **2.** a tendency or disposition. **3.** an addiction. **4.** the clothing associated with a particular profession, etc.: nun's habit. **5.** a characteristic action, aspect, or mode of growth of a plant or animal. [ME]

hab·it·a·ble (HAB i tə bəl) adj. suitable for habitation. [ME habitabilis] —**hab'it·a·bil'i·ty** n.

hab·i·tant (HAB i tənt) n. an inhabitant. [< L habitare inhabit]

hab·i·tat (HAB i TAT) n. the region or environment where a plant or animal is normally found. [< L, it inhabits]

hab·i·ta·tion (HAB i TAY shən) n. **1.** a place of abode; residence. **2.** the act of dwelling or inhabiting. [ME habitacioun]

hab·it-form·ing (HAB it FOR ming) adj. producing a habitual practice or addiction.

ha·bit·u·al (hə BICH oo əl) adj. **1.** practiced or recurring by habit; customary. **2.** expected from habit or usage. [< Med.L habitualis] —**ha·bit'u·al·ly** adv.

ha·bit·u·ate (hə BICH oo AYT) v.t. **·at·ed, ·at·ing** accustom to a condition by repetition. [< LL habituatus conditioned] —**ha·bit'u·a'tion** n.

ha·bit·u·é (hə BICH oo AY) n. one who frequents a specific restaurant, club, etc. [< F]

ha·ci·en·da (HAH see EN də) n. in Spanish America, a landed estate; a country house. [< Sp.]

hack¹ (hak) v.t. **1.** cut or chop crudely or irregularly, as with an ax. —v.i. **2.** cut, strike, or thrash with heavy, crude blows. **3.** emit short, dry coughs. —**hack it** perform competently. —n. **1.** a gash, cut, or nick made by or as by a sharp instrument. **2.** a tool for hacking. **3.** a short, dry cough. [ME hacken] —**hack'er** n.

hack² n. **1.** a horse for hire, as a saddle horse. **2.** a worn-out horse; jade. **3.** a person hired to do routine work, esp. literary work. **4.** a hackney carriage. **5.** Informal a taxicab. **6.** Informal a hackie. —v.i. Informal drive a taxicab. —**hack around** pass time idly. —adj. **1.** hired as a hack: hack writer. **2.** of a mercenary or hackneyed nature. [< HACKNEY]

hack·ie (HAK ee) n. Informal the driver of a taxicab.

hack·le (HAK əl) n. **1.** one of the long, narrow feathers on the neck of a rooster, pigeon, etc.; also, such feathers collectively. **2.** pl. the hairs on the neck and back of a dog, which rise in anger. —**raise (someone's) hackles** infuriate. [ME hakell]

hack·ney (HAK nee) n. pl. **·neys 1.** a horse of medium size used for ordinary driving and riding. **2.** a carriage for hire. [< ME hakeney < the name of an English town]

hack·neyed (HAK need) adj. made commonplace by frequent use; trite.

hack·saw (HAK saw) n. a saw with a fine-toothed, narrow blade set in a frame, used for cutting metal.

had (had) past tense, past participle of HAVE.

Ha·des (HAY deez) in Greek mythology, the abode of the dead.

hadj (haj) n. the pilgrimage to Mecca required of every Muslim. Also spelled hajj. [< Arabic hājj pilgrimage]

hadj·i (HAJ ee) *n.* a Muslim who has made the hadj. Also spelled *hajji*.

hadst (hadst) archaic second person singular past indicative of HAVE.

haft (haft) *n.* a handle of a knife, sword, etc. [ME]

hag (hag) *n.* **1.** a repulsive old woman. **2.** a witch [ME *hagge* witch] —**hag′gish** *adj.*

hag·gard (HAG ərd) *adj.* having a worn, gaunt look. —**hag′gard·ly** *adv.*

hag·gis (HAG is) *n.* a Scottish dish made of calf's or sheep's heart, lungs, or liver, mixed with suet, oatmeal, and onions. [ME *hageys*]

hag·gle (HAG əl) *v.i.* ·gled, ·gling bargain or argue in a petty, mean way. —**hag′gler** *n.*

hagio- *combining form* sacred.

hag·i·og·ra·phy (HAG ee OG rə fee) *n. pl.* ·phies **1.** the study of the lives of saints. **2.** a book of such studies. —**hag′i·og′ra·pher** *n.*

hag·i·ol·o·gy (HAG ee OL ə jee) *n. pl.* ·gies **1.** that part of literature dealing with the lives of the saints. **2.** a book on saints' lives. **3.** a list of saints. —**hag′i·ol′o·gist** *n.*

hah (hah) see HA.

hai·ku (HĪ koo) *n. pl.* ·ku a Japanese verse form of 17 syllables arranged in three lines. [< Japanese]

hail[1] (hayl) *n.* **1.** small lumps of ice that fall from the sky during a storm; hailstones. **2.** a rapid or heavy showering: a *hail* of blows. —*v.i.* **1.** the pour down hail. **2.** fall like hail. —*v.t.* **3.** hurl or pour like hail. [ME]

hail[2] *v.t.* **1.** call loudly to, as in greeting. **2.** acclaim or approve. —**hail from** come from, as a birthplace or home. —*n.* **1.** the act of hailing. **2.** a shout, as of greeting. **3.** the distance a shout can be heard; earshot. [ME *haile*]

hail-fel·low (HAYL FEL oh) *n.* a pleasant companion. Also **hail-fellow well met.**

Hail Mary see AVE MARIA.

HAIL·STONE (HAYL STOHN) *n.* a piece of hail.

hair (hair) *n.* **1.** one of the fine, threadlike structures that grow from the skin of most mammals. **2.** such structures collectively. **3.** *Bot.* a hairlike outgrowth of the outer cells in plants. **4.** any exceedingly minute measure etc. —**get in one's hair** *Informal* annoy one. —**not turn a hair** show no reaction. —**let one's hair down** *Informal* discard one's reserve. —**make one's hair stand on end** horrify one. —**split hairs** make trivial distinctions. —*adj.* **1.** like, or made of, hair. **2.** for the hair. [ME *heer*] —**hair′less** *adj.*

hair·ball (HAIR bAWL) *n.* a rounded mass of hair often found in stomachs of animals that groom themselves by licking.

hair·breadth (HAIR BREDTH) *n.* an extremely small space or margin. —*adj.* very narrow or close.

hair·cloth (HAIR KLAWTH) *n.* a stiff fabric of horsehair.

hair·cut (HAIR KUT) *n.* the act of cutting the hair or the style in which it is cut.

hair·do (HAIR DOO) *n. pl.* ·dos **1.** the style of arranging a woman's hair. **2.** the hair so arranged.

hair·dress·er (HAIR DRES ər) *n.* one who cuts or arranges the hair, esp. women's hair.

hair·line (HAIR LĪN) *n.* **1.** the edge of the growth of hair on the head. **2.** a very thin line. **3.** a tiny crack.

hair·piece (HAIR PEES) *n.* a toupee or wig.

hair·pin (HAIR PIN) *n.* a thin, U-shaped piece of metal etc., used by women to hold the hair or a headdress in place. —*adj.* bending sharply in a U: a *hairpin* curve.

hair-rais·er (HAIR RAY zər) *n.* something that causes excitement or fear. —**hair′-rais′ing** *adj.*

hair shirt a garment made of haircloth, worn next to the skin by religious ascetics as a penance or mortification.

hair·split·ting (HAIR SPLIT ing) *n.* insistence upon minute or trival distinctions. —**hair′·split′ter** *n.*

hair·spring (HAIR SPRING) *n.* the spring that regulates the balance wheel in a watch or clock.

hair trigger a trigger on a firearm responding to slight pressure.

hair-trig·ger (HAIR TRIG ər) *adj.* responsive to the slightest provocation.

hair·y (HAIR ee) *adj.* hair·i·er, hair·i·est **1.** covered with or having much hair. **2.** *Informal* causing anxiety. [ME *heeri*] —**hair′i·ness** *n.*

hajj (haj) see HADJ.

ha·kim (hah KEEM) *n.* in Muslim countries: **1.** a judge or governor. **2.** a physician. [< Arabic, wise]

hal·cy·on (HAL see ən) *n.* a legendary bird supposed to calm the sea so as to be able to breed on the water. —*adj.* calm; peaceful. [< L]

hale[1] (hayl) *v.t.* haled, hal·ing compel to go: *hale* into court. [ME *halen* pull]

hale² *adj.* healthy; vigorous; robust. [ME]

half (haf) *n. pl.* **halves** (havz) **1.** either of two equal parts into which a thing may be divided. **2.** in basketball, football, etc., either of two periods into which a game is divided, between which play is suspended. — **better half** *Informal* one's spouse. —*adj.* **1.** being either of two equal parts of a thing, amount, value, etc. **2.** not complete; partial; imperfect. —*adv.* **1.** to the extent of half or approximately half. **2.** to a considerable extent; very nearly. **3.** to any extent; at all: used with *not:* not *half* bad. [ME]

half-and-half (HAF ən HAF) *n.* a mixture of half one thing and half another, as of porter and ale. —*adj.* half of one thing and half of another. —*adv.* in equal parts.

half-back (HAF BAK) *n.* **1.** in football, either of two offensive players positioned behind the quarterback. **2.** in soccer, field hockey, etc., a player behind the forward line.

half-baked (HAF BAYKT) *adj.* **1.** incompletely baked. **2.** stupid or immature; not fully developed.

half-caste (HAF KAST) *n.* a person having parents of different races, esp. a Eurasian.

half cock in a firearm, the position of the hammer when raised halfway and so locked. —**go off half-cocked** act or speak too hastily.

half-heart·ed (HAF HAHR tid) *adj.* possessing or showing little interest, enthusiasm, etc.

half-hour (HAF OWR) *n.* **1.** thirty minutes. **2.** thirty minutes past the beginning of an hour. —*adj.* **1.** lasting for a half-hour. **2.** occurring at the half-hour. —**half′-hour′ly** *adj. & adv.*

half life *Physics* the period of time during which half the atoms of a radioactive substance will disintegrate.

half-mast (HAF MAST) *n.* the position of a flag flown about halfway up the staff, used in public mourning. Also *half-staff.*

half-moon (HAF MOON) *n.* the moon when only half its disk is brightly illuminated.

half note *Music* a note having half the time value of a whole note.

half-staff (HAF STAF) *n.* half-mast.

half·tone (HAF TOHN) *n.* in photoengraving, an image whose lights and shadows are composed of dots obtained by photographing the original through a fine screen.

half tone *Music* a semitone.

half-track (HAF TRAK) *n.* a vehicle propelled by caterpillar treads in the rear and wheels in front.

half·way (HAF WAY) *adv.* **1.** at or to half the distance. **2.** incompletely; partially. —*adj.* **1.** midway between two points. **2.** partial; inadequate.

halfway house a facility for helping persons readjust to normal life after being released from prisons, hospitals, etc.

half-wit (HAF WIT) *n.* a feeble-minded, stupid, or foolish person. —**half′-wit′ted** *adj.*

hal·ite (HAL īt) *n.* rock salt.

hal·i·to·sis (HAL i TOH sis) *n.* foul-smelling breath. [< NL]

hall (hawl) *n.* **1.** a passage or corridor in a building. **2.** a vestibule; lobby. **3.** a large building or room used for public business or entertainment. **4.** in a university or college, a building used for various purposes, as for dormitories, classrooms, etc. **5.** in medieval times, the main room of a castle. [ME]

hal·le·lu·jah (HAL ə LOO yə) *interj.* Praise ye the Lord! —*n.* a musical composition of praise. [< Hebrew *halalūyāh* praise ye Yahweh]

hall·mark (HAWL MAHRK) *n.* **1.** an official mark stamped on gold and silver articles in England to guarantee their purity. **2.** any proof of excellence. [< Goldsmiths' *Hall,* London + MARK]

hal·low (HAL oh) *v.t.* **1.** make holy; consecrate. **2.** revere; reverence. [ME *halowen*]

hal·lowed (HAL ohd) *adj.* **1.** made holy. **2.** honored as holy. [ME *halwed*]

Hal·low·een (HAL ə WEEN) *n.* the evening of Oct. 31, vigil of All Saints' Day, celebrated by children with masquerading.

hal·lu·ci·nate (hə LOO sə NAYT) *v.* ·**nat·ed,** ·**nat·ing** *v.t.* **1.** experience as an hallucination. —*v.i.* **1.** have hallucinations. [< L *hallucinatus* dreamt] — **hal·lu·ci·na·to·ry** (hə LOO sə nə TOR ee) *adj.*

hal·lu·ci·na·tion (hə LOO sə NAY shən) *n. Psychol.* an auditory, visual, or tactile perception that has no corresponding external cause or stimulus. [< L]

hal·lu·ci·no·gen (hə LOO sə nə jən) *n.* any drug or chemical capable of inducing hallucinations. —**hal·lu·ci·no·gen·ic** (hə LOO sə nə JEN ik) *adj.*

hall·way (HAWL way) *n.* **1.** a hall or corridor. **2.** a passage or room leading into the main part of a building.

ha·lo (HAY loh) *n. pl.* ·**los** or ·**loes 1.** in art, a disk or ring of light surrounding the head of a deity or holy person; nimbus. **2.** *Meteorol.* a luminous circle around the sun or moon. —*v.t.* **·loed, ·lo·ing** enclose with a halo. [< L *halos*]

halt[1] (hawlt) *n.* a complete but temporary stop in any activity or movement. —*v.t. & v.i.* bring or come to a halt. [< G]

halt[2] *v.i.* **1.** *Archaic* be imperfect. **2.** be in doubt; waver. —**the halt** lame or crippled persons. [ME, lame]

hal·ter (HAWL tər) *n.* **1.** a strap or rope to lead or secure a horse, cow, etc. **2.** a woman's upper garment designed to leave the arms and back bare, and held up by a band around the neck. **3.** a rope with a noose for hanging a person. —*v.t.* catch or secure with a halter. [ME]

halve (hav) *v.t.* **halved, halv·ing 1.** divide into two equal parts; share equally. **2.** lessen by half; take away half of. [ME *halven*]

halves (havz) *n.* plural of HALF. —**by halves 1.** imperfectly. **2.** half-heartedly.

hal·yard (HAL yərd) *n.* a rope for hoisting or lowering a sail, yard, or flag. [ME *halier* rope]

ham (ham) *n.* **1.** the thigh of an animal, as of the hog. **2.** the meat of a hog's thigh, used for food. **3.** *pl.* the back of the thigh together with the buttocks. **4.** an actor who overacts. **5.** an amateur radio operator. —*v.t. & v.i.* **hammed, ham·ming** act in an exaggerated manner. [ME *hamme*] —**ham'my** *adj.*

ham·burg·er (HAM BUR gər) *n.* **1.** ground or chopped beef. Also **hamburger steak. 2.** a sandwich consisting of such meat cooked, and placed between the halves of a round roll.

ham·let (HAM lit) *n.* a little village. [ME *hamelet*]

ham·mer (HAM ər) *n.* **1.** a tool usu. consisting of a handle with a metal head set crosswise at one end, used for driving nails etc. **2.** any object or machine resembling this or used this way. **3.** a mechanical part that operates by striking; as: **a** the part of a gun that strikes the primer or firing pin. **b** one of the levers that strike the strings of a piano. **4.** a metal ball attached to a flexible handle, thrown for distance in athletic contests. — **under the hammer** for sale at an auction. —*v.t.* **1.** strike, beat, or drive with or as with a hammer. **2.** produce, shape, join, etc. with or as with hammer blows. —*v.i.* **3.** strike

blows with or as with a hammer. **4.** work persistently: *hammer* away. [ME *hamer*]

ham·mer·head (HAM ər HED) *n.* a shark of warm seas, having a transversely elongated head with the eyes at each end.

ham·mer·lock (HAM ər LOK) *n.* a wrestling hold in which an opponent's arm is twisted behind the back and upward.

ham·mock (HAM ək) *n.* a hanging bed or couch of sturdy cloth or netting, suspended from a support at each end. [< Sp. *hamaca*]

ham·per[1] (HAM pər) *v.t.* interfere with the movements of; impede. [ME *hampren*]

ham·per[2] *n.* a large, usu. covered basket or basketlike container. [ME *hampere*]

ham·string (HAM STRING) *n.* **1.** one of the tendons at the back of the human knee. **2.** the large tendon at the back of the hock of a quadruped. —*v.t.* **·strung, ·string·ing 1.** cripple by cutting the hamstring of. **2.** render powerless; thwart.

hand (hand) *n.* **1.** in humans and in other primates, the end of the forearm beyond the wrist, comprising the palm, fingers, and thumb. **2.** in other organisms, a part that serves a similar function. **3.** the use of the hand or hands: launder by *hand*. **4.** a characteristic mark, or kind of work: the *hand* of an expert. **5.** a part or role: We all had a *hand* in it. **6.** assistance: gave him a *hand*. **7.** *Usu. pl.* custody or control: I was in her *hands*. **8.** a pledge or promise, often of marriage. **9.** a position to the side: on the right *hand*. **10.** a source, as of information. **11.** a person, considered as producing something. **12.** a manual laborer. **13.** style of handwriting. **14.** a show of approval by clapping. **15.** something that resembles a hand in function, as the pointer of a clock. **16.** a unit of measurement four inches long, used to state the height of horses. **17.** in card games: **a** the cards held by a player in one deal. **b** the player. **c** the complete playing of all the cards given out at one deal. — **at hand 1.** near by; readily available. **2.** about to occur. —**at the hand** (or **hands**) **of** by the action of. —**clean hands** freedom from guilt. —**from hand to mouth** on an income so meager it is used up immediately. —**hand and glove** in close alliance or connection. —**hands down** with ease; effortlessly. —**in hand 1.** in one's immediate possession. **2.** under control. —**off one's hands** out of one's care or responsibility. —**on hand 1.** in one's possession; available **2.** present. —**on one's hands** in

one's care or responsibility. **—out of hand**
1. unruly; uncontrollable. **2.** finished and
done with. **3.** immediately; without discussion or delay. **—to hand 1.** within reach;
readily accessible. **2.** in one's possession. **—**
have one's hands full have a great amount
of work. **—keep one's hand in** practice or
keep up with an activity or interest. **—show**
one's hand disclose one's involvement or
intentions. **—turn** (or **put**) **one's hand to**
engage in; undertake. **—throw up one's**
hands give up in despair. **—wash one's**
hands of refuse further responsibility for.
—upper hand the controlling advantage.
—with a heavy hand 1. in a clumsy manner. **2.** in an overbearing manner. **—with a**
high hand in an arrogant, tyrannical manner. *—v.t.* give, offer, assist, or transmit
with the hand or hands. **—hand down 1.**
transmit to one's heirs. **2.** deliver the decision of a court. **—hand in** submit; give. **—**
hand it to *Informal* give praise or recognition to. **—hand out** distribute. **—hand**
over give up possession of. *—adj.* of or
pertaining to the hand or hands; as: **a** suitable for carrying in the hand. **b** operated by
hand. **c** executed by hand. [ME]

hand•bag (HAND BAG) *n.* **1.** a woman's
purse or a similar bag. **2.** a small suitcase.

hand•ball (HAND BAWL) *n.* a game in
which the players hit a ball with their hands
against the wall or walls of a court.

hand•bill (HAND BIL) *n.* a printed advertisement or notice.

hand•book (HAND BUUK) *n.* a small guidebook or book or instructions.

hand•clasp (HAND KLASP) *n.* the act of
clasping a person's hand, as in greeting.

hand•craft (HAND KRAFT) *v.t.* make or
fashion by hand. *—n.* (HAND KRAFT)
handicraft.

hand•cuff (HAND KUF) *n.* one of a pair of
sturdy rings joined by a chain, designed to
lock around the wrist or wrists; a manacle.
—v.t. **1.** apply handcuffs to. **2.** restrain;
thwart.

hand•ed (HAN did) *adj.* **1.** characterized by
or designed for the use of a (specified)
hand: a *left-handed* batter. **2.** having or
characterized by a (specified kind of) hand
or (a specified number of) hands: *four-*
handed; empty-handed.

hand•ful (HAND fuul) *n. pl.* **•fuls 1.** as
much or as many as a hand can hold at once.
2. a small number or quantity. **3.** *Informal*
something or someone difficult to control.

hand•gun (HAND GUN) *n.* a pistol or revolver held and fired in one hand.

hand•i•cap (HAN də KAP) *n.* **1.** a race or
contest in which disadvantages or advantages are imposed on contestants, so that
each may have an equal chance of winning.
2. one of the conditions stipulated. **3.** any
disadvantage or disability. *—v.t.* **•capped,**
•cap•ping 1. serve as a hindrance or disadvantage to. **2.** assign handicaps in a race. **—**
hand′i•cap′per *n.*

hand•i•craft (HAN də KRAFT) *n.* **1.** skill in
working with the hands. **2.** an occupation
requiring such skill. Also *handcraft.* [ME
handi-crafte]

hand•i•ly (HAN di lee) *adv.* **1.** easily. **2.** conveniently.

hand•i•work (HAN dee WURK) *n.* **1.** work
done by the hands; any article or articles
made by hand. **2.** the result or product of
working or action. [ME *handiwerk*]

hand•ker•chief (HANG kər chif) *n.* a piece
of cloth used for wiping the nose or face.

han•dle (HAN dl) *v.* **•dled, •dling** *v.t.* **1.**
touch, hold, work, or move with the hand or
hands. **2.** control; manage. **3.** dispose of;
deal with. **4.** treat of or discuss. **5.** act or
behave toward. **6.** trade or deal in. *—v.i.* **7.**
respond to manipulation or control. *—n.* **1.**
that part of an object designed to be
grasped in the hand. **2.** something that resembles or serves as a handle. **3.** a means to
achieve a desired end. **4.** *Slang* a name or
alias. **—fly off the handle** become angry.
[ME *handel*] **—han•dler** (HAND lər) *n.*

han•dle•bar (HAN dl BAHR) *n.* **1.** *Usu. pl.*
the curved steering bar of a bicycle, etc. **2.** a
mustache resembling handlebars: also
handlebar mustache.

hand-me-down (HAND mee DOWN) *n.* a
used garment given to another person.

hand•out (HAND OWT) *n.* **1.** any free ration
of food, money, apparel, etc. **2.** a prepared,
distributed statement.

hand•pick (HAND PIK) *v.t.* **1.** gather by
hand. **2.** choose with care.

hand•rail (HAND RAYL) *n.* a railing for
grasping in the hand, on a staircase etc.

hand•shake (HAND SHAYK) *n.* the act of
clasping and shaking a person's hand, as in
greeting etc.

hand•some (HAN səm) *adj.* **1.** pleasing or
well-proportioned in appearance. **2.** considerable; ample. **3.** generous; gracious.
[ME *handsom* easy to handle] **—hand′**
•some•ly *adv.*

hand·spring (HAND SPRING) n. an acrobatic feat in which the body is supported by one or both hands while the feet are quickly passed in an arc over the head.

hand-to-hand (HAND tə HAND) adj. at close quarters.

hand·work (HAND WURK) n. work done by hand.

hand·writ·ing (HAND RĪ ting) n. 1. writing done by hand, as with a pen; calligraphy. 2. a characteristic style or form of writing. —**see the handwriting on the wall** be aware beforehand of impending misfortune.

hand·y (HAN dee) adj. **hand·i·er, hand·i·est** 1. available; nearby. 2. skillful. 3. useful. —**hand'i·ness** n.

hang (hang) v. **hung** or (esp. for defs. 3, 11) **hanged, hang·ing** v.t. 1. fasten, attach, or support from above only. 2. attach, fasten, or support off the ground, with a hinge, wire, hook, etc. 3. kill by suspending by the neck. 4. bend or drop downward. 5. decorate with things suspended. 6. fasten (wallpaper) to a wall. 7. cause (a jury etc.) to be unable to reach a decision. —v.i. 8. be suspended; dangle. 9. be attached so as to swing easily. 10. fall or drape. 11. be put to death or die by hanging. 12. bend or project downward; droop. 13. keep one's hold; cling: with on or onto. 14. hover; float in the air. 15. be imminent; threaten: with over. 16. depend; be contingent: with on or upon. 17. be undecided. —**be hung up** be halted or delayed. —**be hung up on** have an emotional problem regarding. —**hang around** Informal loiter or spend one's time. —**hang back** be reluctant. —**hang in** persevere. —**hang in the balance** be subject to a decision. —**hang loose** Slang keep calm. —**hang on** be tenacious. —**hang out** Informal spend one's time. —**hang together** be coherent or consistent. —**hang up** 1. end a telephone conversation by replacing the receiver. 2. delay or suspend the progress of. —**let it all hang out** Slang hide nothing. —n. 1. the way in which a thing hangs. 2. the least bit: I don't give a hang. —**get the hang of** Informal learn to do or understand. [ME]

hang·ar (HANG ər) n. a shelter, esp. one for aircraft. [< F]

hang·dog (HANG DAWG) adj. furtive or guilty.

hang·er (HANG ər) n. 1. a device on or from which something may be hung, esp. garments. 2. one who hangs something.

hang·er-on (HANG ər ON) n. pl. **hang·ers-on** a self-seeking follower.

hang·fire (HANG FĪR) n. a delay in the explosion of a propelling charge, igniter, etc.

hang glider a kitelike glider from which a rider hangs while gliding down from a high place. —**hang' glid'ing** n.

hang·ing (HANG ing) n. 1. execution by being hanged from the neck. 2. something hung on a wall, window, etc. — **hang'ing** adj.

hang·man (HANG mən) n. a public executioner who hangs condemned persons.

hang·nail (HANG NAYL) n. skin partially torn loose at the side or root of a fingernail. [ME angenayle corn]

hang·out (HANG OWT) n. Informal a habitual loitering or dwelling place.

hang·o·ver (HANG OH vər) n. 1. the discomfort following overindulgence in alcoholic liquor. 2. something or someone remaining from a past time.

hang-up (HANG UP) n. Slang 1. an emotional problem that can prevent action or affect judgment. 2. any block or obstacle.

hank (hangk) n. 1. a skein of yarn or thread. 2. a measure of yarn or thread. 3. a loop or curl, as of hair. [ME]

han·ker (HANG kər) v.i. yearn; have desire: with after, for, or to. [< Du. hunkeren hang] —**hank'er·ing** n.

han·ky-pan·ky (HANG kee PANG kee) n. Informal deceitful or mischievous behavior.

han·som (HAN səm) n. a low, two-wheeled, one-horse carriage, with the driver seated behind and above the cab: also **hansom cab.** [after J.A. Hansom, 1803—82, English inventor]

Ha·nuk·kah (HAH nə kə) n. a Jewish festival, lasting eight days, in memory of the rededication of the temple at Jerusalem in 164 B.C.: also Chanukah. [< Hebrew hanukkah dedication]

hap·haz·ard (hap HAZ ərd) adj. accidental; random; chance. —adv. by chance; at random. —**hap·haz'ard·ly** adv.

hap·less (HAP lis) adj. unfortunate; unlucky. —**hap'less·ly** adv. —**hap'less·ness** n.

hap·pen (HAP ən) v.i. 1. take place or occur; come to pass. 2. occur by chance. 3. chance: We happened to hear him sing. —

happen to 1. befall. **2.** become of. [ME *happenen*]

hap·pen·ing (HAP ə ning) *n.* **1.** an event. **2.** a staged event, usu. partly improvised.

hap·pen·stance (HAP ən STANS) *n.* a chance occurrence; accident.

hap·py (HAP ee) *adj.* **·pi·er, ·pi·est 1.** enjoying, showing, or characterized by pleasure; joyous; contented. **2.** fortunate; lucky. **3.** produced or uttered with skill and aptness; felicitous. [ME] —**hap'pi·ly** *adv.* —**hap'pi·ness** *n.*

hap·py-go-luck·y (HAP ee goh LUK ee) *adj.* cheerful; unconcerned; easygoing.

ha·ra-ki·ri (HAH rə KEER ee) *n.* suicide by disembowelment, traditionally practiced by the Japanese samurai when disgraced. [< Japanese *hara* belly + *kiri* cut]

ha·rangue (hə RANG) *n.* a lengthy, loud, and vehement speech; tirade. —*v.t. & v.i.* **·rangued, ·rangu·ing** address in or deliver a harangue. [< MF *harangue*]

ha·rass (hə RAS) *v.t.* **1.** trouble or pursue relentlessly; torment. **2.** *Mil.* worry by raids and small attacks. [< F *harasser*] —**ha·rass'er** *n.* —**ha·rass'ment** *n.*

har·bin·ger (HAHR bin jər) *n.* one who or that which goes before and announce the coming of something; herald. —*v.t.* presage; herald. [ME *herbegere* host]

har·bor (HAHR bər) *n.* **1.** a sheltered place on the coast of a sea, lake, etc. used to provide protection and anchorage for ships; port. **2.** any place of refuge or rest. —*v.t.* **1.** give refuge to; shelter. **2.** entertain in the mind; cherish. —*v.i.* **3.** take shelter in or as in a harbor. [ME *herberge*]

hard (hahrd) *adj.* **1.** resisting indentation or compression; solid; firm; unyielding. **2.** requiring vigorous mental or physical effort; difficult. **3.** energetic and steady; industrious. **4.** showing little mercy or feeling; stern. **5.** strict or exacting. **6.** having force or intensity; severe; violent. **7.** involving or inflicting sorrow, discomfort, poverty, etc. **8.** verified and specific: said of information etc. **9.** cruel or disreputable; tough. **10.** containing certain mineral salts that interfere with the cleansing action of soap: said of water. **11.** containing more than 22.5 percent alcohol: *hard* liquor. —**hard and fast** fixed and unalterable. —**hard of hearing** deaf or partially deaf. —**hard up** *Informal* **1.** poor; broke. **2.** in need of (something): with *for.* —**be hard on** be severe, cruel, or damaging to. —*adv.* **1.** with great energy or force; vigorously. **2.** intently; earnestly. **3.** with effort or difficulty: breathe *hard.* **4.** with resistance; reluctantly: die *hard.* **5.** securely; tightly. **6.** so as to become firm or solid. **7.** in close proximity; near: with *after, by,* or *upon.* —**be hard put** have great difficulty. —**go hard with** be very painful and harsh for. [ME] —**hard'ness** *n.*

hard-bit·ten (HAHRD BIT n) *adj.* stubborn; tough.

hard-boiled (HAHRD BOILD) *adj.* **1.** boiled until cooked through: said of an egg. **2.** *Informal* callous; tough.

hard cider cider that has fermented.

hard coal anthracite.

hard-core (HAHRD KOR) *adj.* **1.** irreducible. **2.** of or relating to the chronically unemployed. **3.** being explicit and graphic: *hard-core* pornography. **4.** unlikely to change; inflexible.

hard·en (HAHR dn) *v.t. & v.i.* make or become hard. —**hard'en·er** *n.*

hard-hat (HAHRD HAT) *n. Informal* **1.** a construction worker. **2.** a working-class conservative or reactionary. —**hard-hat** *adj.*

hard·head (HAHRD HED) *n.* **1.** a shrewd and practical person. **2.** an obstinate person.

hard·head·ed (HAHRD HED id) *adj.* **1.** shrewd and practical. **2.** stubborn; obstinate. —**hard'head'ed·ness** *n.*

hard·heart·ed (HAHRD HAHR tid) *adj.* lacking pity; unfeeling. —**hard'heart' ed·ly** *adv.* —**hard'heart'ed·ness** *n.*

hard labor compulsory physical labor imposed on convicts.

hard-line (HAHRD LIN) *adj.* consistently firm in attitude or policy; undeviating. —**hard'-lin'er** *n.*

hard·ly (HAHRD lee) *adv.* **1.** scarcely; barely. **2.** not quite; not: *hardly* enough.

hard-nosed (HAHRD NOHZD) *adj. Informal* hard-bitten; unyielding.

hard·pan (HAHRD PAN) *n.* **1.** a layer of very hard, often claylike matter under soft soil. **2.** solid, unbroken ground. **3.** the firm foundation of anything.

hard-shell (HAHRD SHEL) *adj.* **1.** having a hard shell. **2.** rigidly orthodox.

hard·ship (HAHRD ship) *n.* a difficult, painful condition, as from privation, suffering, etc. [ME]

hard·tack (HAHRD TAK) *n.* hard, crackerlike biscuit.

hard·top (HAHRD TOP) *n.* an automobile

with the body design of a convertible, but with a rigid top.

hard·ware (HAHRD WAIR) *n.* **1.** manufactured articles of metal, as utensils or tools. **2.** weapons: military *hardware*. **3.** any of the machinery that makes up a digital computer installation: distinguished from *software*.

hard·wood (HAHRD WUUD) *n.* **1.** wood from deciduous trees, as distinguished from wood of coniferous trees. **2.** any hard, compact, heavy wood. **3.** a tree yielding such wood.

har·dy (HAHR dee) *adj.* **·di·er, ·di·est 1.** able to endure hardship; robust; tough. **2.** courageous. **3.** able to survive the winter outdoors: said of plants. [ME *hardi*] —**har′di·ness** *n.*

hare (hair) *n. pl.* **hares** or **hare 1.** a mammal allied to but larger than the rabbit. **2.** the common American rabbit. [ME]

hare·brained (HAIR BRAYND)) *adj.* foolish; flighty.

hare·lip (HAIR LIP) *n.* a congenital fissure of the upper lip, resembling the cleft lip of a hare. —**hare′lipped′** *adj.*

har·em (HAIR əm) *n.* **1.** the apartments of a Muslim household reserved for females. **2.** the women occupying the harem. [< Arabic *harim*]

hark (hahrk) *v.i.* listen; hearken: usu. in the imperative. —**hark back** return to some previous point; revert. —*n.* a cry used to urge on or guide hounds. [ME *herken*]

hark·en (HAHR kən) see HEARKEN.

har·le·quin (HAHR lə kwin) *n.* a buffoon. —*adj.* like a harlequin or his costume. [< F]

har·le·quin (HAHR lə kwin) *Often cap.* a traditional, mischievous character in comedy and pantomine, usu. dressed in particolored tights, with masked face, and bearing a wooden sword.

har·lot (HAHR lət) *n.* a prostitute. [ME] —**har′lot·ry** *n.*

harm (HAHRM) *n.* **1.** injury; damage; hurt. **2.** wrong; evil. —*v.t.* do harm to; damage; hurt. [ME]

harm·ful (HAHRM fəl) *adj.* having power to injure or do harm. —**harm′ful·ly** *adv.*

harm·less (HAHRM lis) *adj.* inflicting no injury; not harmful; innocuous. —**harm′·less·ly** *adv.*

har·mon·ic (hahr MON ik) *adj.* **1.** producing, characterized by, or pertaining to harmony; consonant; harmonious. **2.** *Music* pertaining to the formation and progression of chords in musical composition. —*n. Music* an overtone, having a vibration rate that is an integral multiple of a given primary tone. [< L *harmonicus* musical]

har·mon·i·ca (hahr MON i kə) *n.* a wind instrument consisting of metal reeds fixed in slots in a small oblong frame: also called *mouth organ.*

har·mon·ics (hahr MON iks) *n.* **1.** (construed as sing.) the branch of acoustics dealing with musical sounds. **2.** (construed as pl.) *Music* the overtones of a fundamental.

har·mo·ni·ous (hahr MOH nee əs) *adj.* **1.** made up of sounds, colors, or other elements that combine agreeably. **2.** manifesting agreement and concord. **3.** pleasing to the ear. [< Gk. *harmónios* melodious] —**har·mo′ni·ous·ly** *adv.*

har·mo·nize (HAHR mə NĪZ) *v.t. & v.i.* **·nized, ·niz·ing 1.** make or become harmonious, suitable, or agreeable. **2.** arrange or sing in musical harmony.

har·mo·ny (HAHR mə nee) *n. pl.* **·nies 1.** accord or agreement. **2.** a state of order, agreement, or aesthetically pleasing relationships among the elements of a whole. **3.** pleasing sounds; music. **4.** *Music* **a** a simultaneous combination of tones, esp. a pleasing one. **b** musical structure in terms of the relations between successive harmonies. **c** the science or study of this structure. [ME *armonye*]

har·ness (HAHR nis) *n.* **1.** the gear of a draft animal, used to attach it to a wheeled vehicle or plow. **2.** any similar arrangement of straps, cords, etc., esp. one used for attaching something, as a parachute, to the body. —**in harness** working at one's job. —*v.t.* **1.** put harness on. **2.** make use of the power or potential of. [ME *harneis*]

harp (hahrp) *n.* a musical instrument, consisting of a frame with strings set in it, played by plucking the strings with the fingers. —*v.i.* play a harp. —**harp on** (or **upon**) talk or write about persistently and vexatiously. [ME *harpe*] —**harp′ist** *n.*

har·poon (hahr POON) *n.* a barbed spear, carrying a long cord, for striking whales or large fish. —*v.t.* strike, take, or kill with or as with a harpoon. [< OF *harpon* clasp] —**har·poon′er** *n.*

harp·si·chord (HAHRP si KORD) *n.* a keyboard instrument, esp. of the 18th c., having the strings plucked by quills or leather points instead of struck. [< NL *harpichor-dium*]

har·py (HAHR pee) *n. pl.* **·pies 1.** a rapacious, predatory person, esp. a woman. **2.** a shrewish woman. [< L *Harpyia*, a mythical monster]

har·ri·dan (HAR i dn) *n.* a hateful old woman; vicious hag. [< F *haridelle* nag]

har·ri·er (HAR ee ər) *n.* **1.** a small hound used for hunting hares. **2.** a cross-country runner.

har·row (HAR oh) *n.* a farm implement set with spikes or disks, for leveling plowed ground, breaking clods, etc. —*v.t.* **1.** draw a harrow over. **2.** disturb painfully; distress. [ME *harwe*]

har·row·ing (HAR oh ing) *adj.* lacerating to the feelings. —**har′row·ing·ly** *adv.*

har·ry (HAR ee) *v.t.* **·ried, ·ry·ing 1.** lay waste, as in war or invasion; pillage. **2.** harass in any way. [ME *herien*]

harsh (hahrsh) *adj.* **1.** grating, rough, or unpleasant to any of the senses. **2.** ungraceful; crude. **3.** severe; cruel. [ME *harsk*]

harte·beest (HAHR tə BEEST) *n.* a large, grayish brown antelope of Africa. [< Afrikaans]

har·um-scar·um (HAIR əm SKAIR əm) *adj.* reckless and wild; harebrained. —*adv.* in a wild, unrestrained manner.

har·vest (HAHR vist) *n.* **1.** the act of gathering or collecting a ripened crop. **2.** the yield of such a crop; also, the crop itself. **3.** the time of year when crops are gathered. **4.** the products of any effort. —*v.t. & v.i.* gather in (a crop). [ME]

har·vest·er (HAHR və stər) *n.* **1.** one who harvests. **2.** a reaping machine.

harvest moon the full moon that occurs near the autumnal equinox.

has (haz) present indicative, third person singular of HAVE.

has-been (HAZ BIN) *n.* one who or that which is no longer popular or effective.

hash¹ (hash) *n.* **1.** chopped meat and potatoes or other vegetables, mixed and browned. **2.** a mess; jumble; mishmash. —**make a hash of** bungle; spoil. —**settle one's hash** *Informal* deal with punitively; subdue. —*v.t.* **1.** cut into small pieces; mince. **2.** discuss at length: often with *over.* [< F *hacher* chop up]

hash² *n. Slang* hashish.

hash·ish (HASH eesh) *n.* the tops of hemp, used as a narcotic and intoxicant. Also

hash′eesh. [< Arabic *hashīsh*, lit., dry vegetation]

has·n't (HAZ ənt) contr. of has not.

hasp (hasp) *n.* a hinged fastening for a door, lid, etc., esp. one that passes over a staple and is secured by a padlock. [ME]

has·sle (HAS əl) *n. Informal* an argument; squabble; fight. —*v.t.* **·sled, ·sling** harass; antagonize.

has·sock (HAS ək) *n.* **1.** an upholstered stool or cushion, used for kneeling or as a footstool. **2.** a tuft of coarse grass. [ME]

hast (hast) archaic second person singular, present tense of HAVE: used with *thou.*

haste (hayst) *n.* **1.** swiftness of motion; rapidity. **2.** undue or reckless hurry. **3.** the need to act quickly; urgency. —**make haste** hurry. [ME]

has·ten (HAY sən) *v.t. & v.i.* hurry.

hast·y (HAY stee) *adj.* **hast·i·er, hast·i·est 1.** speedy; quick; rapid. **2.** excessively quick; rash. **3.** manifesting anger: *hasty* words. [ME] —**hast′i·ly** *adv.*

hat (hat) *n.* a covering for the head, esp. one with a crown and brim. —**pass the hat** collect contributions of money. —**talk through one's hat** talk nonsense; also, bluff. —**throw (toss) one's hat into the ring** enter a contest, esp. for political office. —**under one's hat** secret; private. [ME]

hatch¹ (hach) *n.* **1.** an opening in a floor, deck, etc., giving access to spaces beneath: also **hatch′way′. 2.** a cover over such an opening: also **hatch cover. 3.** a small opening: an escape *hatch.* [ME *hacche*]

hatch² *v.t.* **1.** bring forth (young) from (the egg) by incubation. **2.** devise, as a plan. —*v.i.* **3.** emerge from the egg. —*n.* **1.** the act of hatching. **2.** the brood hatched. [ME *hacchen*]

hatch³ *v.t.* mark with close parallel or crossed lines. —*n.* any of these lines. [< MF *hacher* chop up]

hatch·back (HACH BAK) *n.* an automobile having a sloping back that contains a rear window and that opens upward. —**hatch′back′** *adj.*

hatch·er·y (HACH ə ree) *n. pl.* **·er·ies** a place for hatching eggs, esp. of poultry or fish.

hatch·et (HACH it) *n.* a small, short-handled ax, for use with one hand. —**bury the hatchet** make peace. [ME]

hatchet job a malicious attack on someone's actions or character.

hatchet man 1. a professional killer. **2.** one

who uses unethical or illegal means to persuade, attack, or affect adversely.

hate (hayt) v. **hat·ed, hat·ing** v.t. 1. regard with extreme aversion; detest. 2. dislike. — v.i. 3. feel hatred. —n. 1. an extreme feeling of dislike or animosity; hatred. 2. a person or thing detested. [ME *hatien*] —**hate·ful** (HAYT fəl) adj. —**hate'ful·ly** adv.

hath (hath) archaic or poetic third person singular, present tense of HAVE.

ha·tred (HAY trid) n. intense dislike or aversion; animosity; enmity. [ME]

hat·ter (HAT ər) n. one who makes or sells hats.

haugh·ty (HAW tee) adj. **·ti·er, ·ti·est** exhibiting disdain; supercilious. [ME *haute*] —**haugh'ti·ness** n.

haul (hawl) v.t. & v.i. 1. pull or draw strongly; drag; tug. 2. transport or carry a load in a truck, car, etc. 3. pull or drag; tug. —**haul off** draw back the arm so as to punch. — **haul up** 1. compel to go: I was *hauled up* before the court. 2. come to a stop. —n. 1. a strong pull; tug. 2. that which is caught, won, etc. at one time. 3. the distance over which something is hauled. 4. that which is hauled. —**haul'er** n.

haunch (hawnch) n. 1. in people and animals, the upper thigh, including the hip and buttock. 2. the leg and loin of an animal, considered as meat. [ME *haunche*]

haunt (hawnt) v.t. 1. visit (a person or place) repeatedly; esp., do so as a ghost or spirit. 2. recur persistently to the mind or memory of. 3. linger about; pervade. —n. a place often visited. [ME *haunten*]

haunt·ed (HAWN tid) adj. 1. supposedly visited by ghosts. 2. preoccupied.

haunt·ing (HAWN ting) adj. recurring to the mind; hard to forget: a *haunting* refrain.

haute cou·ture (OHT koo TUUR) 1. the designers of women's clothes, and their establishments, whose creations are advanced in style, exclusive, of expensive fabrics, etc. 2. the clothes so created. [< F]

haute cui·sine (OHT kwi ZEEN) the elaborate preparation of fine food; also the food so prepared. [< F]

hau·teur (hoh TUR) n. haughtiness. [< F]

have (hav) v.t. present indicative: I, you, we, they **have** (Archaic **thou hast**) he, she, it **has** (Archaic **hath**); past indicative **had** (Archaic **thou hadst**); present subjunctive **have**; past subjunctive **had**; pp. **had**; ppr. **hav·ing** 1. possess as property; own. 2. be

connected with; be possessed of: *have* a good government. 3. bear or possess as an attribute, quality, etc. 4. hold in the mind or among the feelings; entertain. 5. receive, take, or acquire. 6. suffer from. 7. engage in: *have* a quarrel. 8. undergo or experience. 9. plan and carry out: *have* a party. 10. give birth to. 11. manifest or exercise: *have* patience. 12. cause to, or cause to be: *Have* it cleaned. 13. allow; tolerate. 14. maintain; declare: So rumor *has* it. 15. catch (someone) at a disadvantage in a game etc. 16. as an auxiliary, *have* is used: **a** with past participles to form perfect tenses expressing completed action: I *have* gone. **b** with the infinitive to express obligation or compulsion: I *have* to go. —**have at** attack. — **have done** stop; desist. —**have it in for** hold a grudge against. —**have it out** continue a fight or discussion to a final settlement. —**have on** be dressed in. —**let someone have it** attack or assault someone. —n. a relatively wealthy person or country: the *haves* and the have-nots. [ME *haven*]

ha·ven (HAY vən) n. 1. a harbor; port. 2. a refuge; shelter. [ME]

have-not (HAV NOT) n. a person or country relatively lacking in wealth.

have·n't (HAV ənt) contr. of have not.

hav·er·sack (HAV ər SAK) n. a bag for carrying rations, etc., on a march or hike. [< F *havresac*]

hav·oc (HAV ək) n. general carnage or destruction; ruin. [ME *havok*]

haw (haw) v.i. hesitate in speaking: hem and *haw*. —n. & interj. a hesitating sound made by a speaker.

hawk¹ (hawk) n. 1. any of a large family of birds of prey, having broad, rounded wings, a long tail, and powerful talons. 2. one who urges forceful action in a dispute; an advocate of war: opposed to *dove*. —v.i. hunt game with hawks. [ME *hauke*]

hawk² (hawk) v.t. & v.i. cry (goods) for sale in the streets; peddle. —**hawk'er** n.

hawk³ (hawk) v.t. & v.i. cough up (phlegm) with a rasping sound. [Imit.]

hawk-eyed (HAWK ID) adj. having keen eyesight.

haw·ser (HAW zər) n. Naut. a rope or cable used for mooring, towing, etc. [ME *haucer*]

hay (hay) n. grass, clover, or the like, cut and dried for fodder. —**hit the hay** Informal go to bed. —**make hay while the sun shines** take full advantage of an opportunity. —*v.i.* **1.** mow, cure, gather, and store hay. [ME]

hay fever *Pathol.* an allergic reaction to pollen of certain plants, characterized by sneezing, runny nose, etc.

hay·loft (HAY LAWFT) *n.* an open upper section of a barn or stable, used for storing hay.

hay·seed (HAY SEED) *n.* **1.** the chaff, seeds, etc., that fall from hay. **2.** a yokel; a country bumpkin.

hay·wire (HAY WIR) *adj. Informal* **1.** broken; broken down. **2.** crazy; nutty.

haz·ard (HAZ ərd) *n.* **1.** danger of loss, injury, etc.; peril. **2.** chance; accident. **3.** an obstacle or trap on a golf course. —*v.t.* **1.** put in danger; risk. **2.** venture (a statement, effort, etc.). **3.** gamble or gamble on. [ME *hasard*]

haz·ard·ous (HAZ ər dəs) *adj.* **1.** risky; dangerous. **2.** dependent on chance.

haze¹ (hayz) *n.* **1.** a light suspension of water vapor, smoke, dust, etc., in the air. **2.** mental confusion.

haze² *v.t.* **hazed, haz·ing** subject (newcomers or initiates) to pranks and humiliating horseplay. [< MF *haser* irritate] — **haz'er** *n.* —**haz'ing** *n.*

ha·zel (HAY zəl) *n.* **1.** a bushy shrub or small tree of the birch family; also, the wood of this tree. **2.** the hazelnut. **3.** a medium yellowish brown. [ME *hasel*] —*adj.*

ha·zel·nut (HAY zəl NUT) *n.* the edible nut of the hazel; the filbert.

ha·zy (HAY zee) *adj.* ·**zi·er**, ·**zi·est** **1.** misty. **2.** lacking clarity; vague. [ME *haswy*] — **haz'i·ly** *adv.* —**haz'i·ness** *n.*

H-bomb (AYCH BOM) *n.* a hydrogen bomb.

he (hee) *pron., possessive* **his,** *objective* **him;** *pl. nominative* **they,** *possessive* **their** or **theirs,** *objective* **them** **1.** the nominative singular pronoun of the third person, used of the male person or animal previously mentioned. **2.** that person; anyone; one. — *n. pl.* **hes** a male person or animal. —*adj.* male: a *he-tiger.* [ME]

head (hed) *n. pl.* **heads** or *for def. 12* **head** **1.** the part of a vertebrate animal situated at the top or front of the spinal column, containing the brain, eyes, ears, nose, and mouth. **2.** the analogous part of other animals and organisms. **3.** a part like a head: *head* of a pin. **4.** a representation of the head. **5.** a leader or chief person. **6.** the position or rank of a leader. **7.** the front or beginning part of something. **8.** the highest part of something. **9.** the source, as of a

river. **10.** mind; intelligence. **11.** a person: two dollars a *head.* **12.** of certain animals, a single specimen. **13.** a newspaper headline. **14.** the side of a coin on which a face is struck. **15.** a climax, culmination, or crisis. **16.** the foam on the surface of beer or ale. **17.** an amount of stored-up pressure. **18.** the taut, sounding membrane of a drum, tambourine, etc. **19.** the part of a tape recorder that imparts magnetic patterns to the tape or removes them from it. **20.** *Naut.* a toilet. **21.** *Slang* one who habitually uses a drug that distorts perception. —**head over heels 1.** end over end. **2.** rashly; impetuously. **3.** entirely; totally. —**heads up!** *Informal* watch out! —**out of one's head 1.** crazy. **2.** *Informal* delirious. —**over one's head 1.** too hard to understand. **2.** beyond one's power to manage. **3.** to a higher authority. —**come to a head 1.** of boils etc., form a core or tip of pus. **2.** reach a crisis. — **give someone his** (or **her**) **head** give someone freedom of action. —**go to someone's head 1.** intoxicate someone. **2.** make someone conceited. —**make head or tail of** comprehend: usu. used in the negative. —**turn someone's head** make someone vain by praising. —*v.t.* **1.** be first or most prominent on: *head* the list. **2.** command; preside over. **3.** direct the course of. **4.** cut off the head or top of. —*v.i.* **5.** move in a specified direction or toward a specified point. **6.** come to or form a head. **7.** originate: said of streams. —**head off** intercept the course of. —*adj.* **1.** principal; chief. **2.** situated at the front. **3.** bearing against the front: a *head* tide. [ME *heed*]

head·ache (HED AYK) *n.* **1.** a pain in the head. **2.** a difficulty or vexation. — **head·ach·y** (HED AY kee) *adj.*

head·board (HED BORD) *n.* a board at the head end of a bed etc.

head·cheese (HED CHEEZ) *n.* a cooked and jellied meat loaf made of the head, feet, etc. of a hog or calf.

head·dress (HED DRES) *n.* **1.** a covering or ornament for the head. **2.** the style in which the hair is arranged; coiffure.

head·ed (HED id) *adj.* **1.** having a course: *headed* for home. **2.** having or characterized by a (specified kind of) head or (a specified number of) heads: used in combination: *clear-headed; two-headed.*

head·er (HED ər) *n.* **1.** one who or that which makes or puts on heads, as of nails or rivets. **2.** *Agric.* a harvesting machine that cuts off the ripe ends of the grain. **3.** *Informal* a fall or plunge: now only in **take a header.**

head·first (HED FURST) *adv.* **1.** with the head first. **2.** rashly.

head·gear (HED GEER) *n.* a hat, headdress, etc.

head·hunt·er (HED HUN tər) *n.* **1.** one of a tribe that keeps heads of enemies as trophies. **2.** an individual or agency that recruits people for jobs and positions.

head·hunt·ing (HED HUN ting) *n.* among certain peoples, the practice of decapitating slain enemies and preserving the heads as trophies.

head·ing (HED ing) *n.* **1.** a caption or title. **2.** the front or top part of anything. **3.** *Naut. & Aeron.* direction; course.

head·land (HED lənd) *n.* **1.** a cliff projecting into the water. **2.** a strip of unplowed land.

head·line (HED LIN) *n.* **1.** a summarizing word or words set in bold type, as in a newspaper. **2.** a line at the top of a page, containing title, page number, etc. —*v.t.* **·lined, ·lin·ing 1.** provide with a headline, as a news story. **2.** be a headliner in (a show, etc.).

head·lin·er (HED LI nər) *n.* a performer billed as the main attraction or star.

head·long (HED LAWNG) *adv.* **1.** headfirst. **2.** recklessly; rashly. **3.** with unbridled speed or force. —*adj.* **1.** made with the head foremost. **2.** rash. [ME *hedlong*]

head·mas·ter (HED MAS tər) *n.* the principal of a school, esp. a private school.

head·mis·tress (HED MIS tris) *n.* the female principal of a school.

head·most (HED MOHST) *adj.* most advanced; foremost.

head·on (HED ON) *adj. & adv.* front end to front end.

head·quar·ters (HED KWOR tərz) *n. (construed as sing. or pl.)* **1.** the place from which a chief or leader directs the operations of a military unit, police force, etc. **2.** any center of operations; also, the persons working there.

head start an early start; also, an advantage.

head·stone (HED STOHN) *n.* the memorial stone at the head of a grave.

head·strong (HED STRAWNG) *adj.* **1.** stubborn; determined. **2.** proceeding from willfulness or obstinacy. [ME *heed-stronge*]

head·wait·er (HED WAY tər) *n.* a restau-

rant employee who supervises waiters, seats guests, takes reservations, etc.

head·wa·ters (HED WAW tərz) *n.pl.* the tributaries or other waters that form the source of a river.

head·way (HED WAY) *n.* **1.** forward motion; progress. **2.** rate of clearance.

head·wind (HED WIND) *n.* a wind blowing directly opposite to one's course.

head·y (HED ee) *adj.* **head·i·er, head·i·est 1.** tending to affect the senses; intoxicating; a *heady* fragrance. **2.** clever: *heady* behavior. [ME *hevedy*] —**head'i·ness** *n.*

heal (heel) *v.t.* **1.** restore to health or soundness. **2.** bring about the remedy or cure of. —*v.i.* **3.** become well. **4.** mend. [ME *helen*] —**heal'er** *n.*

health (helth) *n.* **1.** freedom from defect or disease. **2.** general condition of body or mind. **3.** a toast wishing health or happiness. —*adj.* of, pertaining to, connected with, or conducive to health. [ME *helthe*] —**health·ful** (HELTH fəl) *adj.* promoting health; salubrious.

health·y (HEL thee) *adj.* **health·i·er, health·i·est 1.** having good health. **2.** conducive to health. **3.** indicative of sound condition. —**health'i·ness** *n.*

heap (heep) *n.* **1.** a collection of things piled up; a pile; mound. **2.** *Informal* a large number; a lot. —*v.t.* **1.** assemble into a heap. **2.** fill (a container) full or more than full. **3.** bestow in great quantities. —*v.i.* **4.** form or rise in a heap or pile. [ME *heep*]

hear (heer) *v.* **heard** (hurd), **hear·ing** *v.t.* **1.** perceive by means of the ear. **2.** listen to; give ear to. **3.** be informed of. **4.** listen officially or judicially: *hear* a case. —*v.i.* **5.** perceive sound. **6.** be informed or made aware. —**hear of** approve of: usu. in the negative: He won't *hear of* it. [ME *heren*] —**hear'er** *n.*

hear·ing (HEER ing) *n.* **1.** the capacity to hear. **2.** the act of perceiving sound. **3.** reach or range within which sound may be heard. **4.** an opportunity to be heard, as in a court. **5.** an official examination, usu. public, of an issue or person.

heark·en (HAHR kən) *v. Poetic* listen; heed. [ME *hercnen*]

hear·say (HEER SAY) *n.* report; rumor.

hearse (hurs) *n.* a vehicle for conveying a dead person to the place of burial. [ME *herse*]

heart (hahrt) *n.* **1.** *Anat.* the primary organ of the circulatory system of animals, a hollow muscular structure that maintains the circulation of the blood by regular contractions. ◆ Collateral adjective: *cardiac.* **2.** the seat of emotion. **3.** tenderness; love. **4.** courage. **5.** enthusiasm; energy. **6.** state of mind; mood. **7.** the central or inner part of anything. **8.** the vital or essential part. **9.** anything represented as or shaped like a heart. **10.** a playing card bearing red, heart-shaped spots. —**after one's own heart** suiting one's taste. —**at heart** in one's deepest thoughts or feelings. —**by heart** by memory. —**from the heart, from the bottom of one's heart** with all sincerity. —**heart and soul** with complete sincerity. —**break the heart of** cause deep disappointment and sorrow to. —**eat one's heart out 1.** endure great remorse or grief. **2.** have a great longing. —**have a heart** be sympathetic and generous. —**have a change of heart** change one's opinions, attitudes, etc. —**have the heart** be callous or cruel enough: usu. in the negative. —**lose heart** become discouraged. —**set one's heart on** long for. —**take to heart 1.** consider seriously. **2.** be concerned or anxious about. —**with all one's heart 1.** willingly; fully. **2.** sincerely. [ME *herte*]

heart·ache (HAHRT AYK) *n.* mental anguish; grief; sorrow.

heart·beat (HAHRT BEET) *n. Physiol.* a pulsation of the heart consisting of one full systole and diastole.

heart·break (HAHRT BRAYK) *n.* deep grief; overwhelming sorrow. —**heart'break'er** *n.*

heart·bro·ken (HART BROH kən) *adj.* overwhelmingly grieved.

heart·en (HAHR tn) *v.t.* give heart or courage to.

heart·felt (HAHRT FELT) *adj.* deeply felt; most sincere.

hearth (hahrth) *n.* **1.** the floor of a fireplace, furnace, or the like. **2.** the fireside; home. [ME *herthe*]

hearth·stone (HAHRTH STOHN) *n.* **1.** a stone forming a hearth. **2.** the fireside; home.

heart·i·ly (HAHR tl ee) *adv.* **1.** with sincerity or cordiality. **2.** abundantly and with good appetite. **3.** completely; thoroughly. [ME *hertili*]

heart·land (HAHRT LAND) *n.* in geopolitics, any central, strategically important area.

heart·less (HAHRT lis) *adj.* **1.** having no sympathy or kindness; pitiless. **2.** having little courage or enthusiasm; dispirited. [ME *herteles*]

heart·rend·ing (HAHRT REN ding) *adj.* causing great distress or emotional anguish; grievous.

heart·sick (HAHRT SIK) *adj.* deeply disappointed or despondent. Also **heart·sore** (HAHRT SOR).

heart·strings (HAHRT STRINGZ) *n.pl.* the strongest feelings or affections.

heart-to-heart (HAHRT tə HAHRT) *adj.* marked by frankness, intimacy, and sincerity.

heart·warm·ing (HAHRT WOR ming) *adj.* causing pleasant and sympathetic feelings.

heart·y (HAHR tee) *adj.* **heart·i·er, heart·i·est 1.** full of affectionate warmth or cordiality. **2.** strongly felt. **3.** healthy and strong. **4.** supplying abundant nourishment. [ME *herti*] —**heart'i·ness** *n.*

heat (heet) *n.* **1.** the state or quality of being hot; hotness; also, degree of hotness. **2.** *Physics* a form of energy associated with and proportional to the molecular motions of a substance or body. ◆ Collateral adjective: *thermal.* **3.** the sensation produced by hotness. **4.** hot weather or climate. **5.** warmth supplied for a building, room, etc. **6.** a single effort or trial, esp. in a race. **7.** great intensity of feeling. **8.** the highest point of excitement or fury. **9.** *Zool.* the period of sexual excitement. **10.** *Slang* **a** coercive pressure; also, intensive police action. **b** the police. —*v.t. & v.i.* **1.** make or become hot or warm. **2.** excite or become excited. [ME *hete*] —**heat'·ed** *adj.*

heat·er (HEE tər) *n.* an apparatus for producing heat.

heat exhaustion mild heat stroke.

heath (heeth) *n.* **1.** any of a large genus of hardy evergreen shrubs. **2.** the common heather. **3.** an area of open land overgrown with coarse herbage. [ME]

hea·then (HEE thən) *n. pl.* **·thens** or **·then 1.** one who has not adopted Christianity, Judaism, or Islam. **2.** any irreligious or uncultivated person. —*adj.* **1.** unbelieving; irreligious. **2.** of or pertaining to heathen peoples. [ME *hethen*] —**hea'then·ism** *n.*

heath·er (HETH ər) *n.* **1.** a hardy evergreen shrub related to the heath and having pinkish flowers. **2.** a purplish pink color. [ME *hather*]

heat prostration heat exhaustion.

heat·stroke (HEET STROHK *n.* a state of

collapse, accompanied by fever, caused by excessive heat.

heat wave a period of very hot weather.

heave (heev) v. **heaved** or (*esp. Naut.*) **hove, heav•ing** v.t. **1.** throw or hurl, esp. with great effort. **2.** raise with effort. **3.** cause to rise or bulge. **4.** *Naut.* **a** pull or haul on (a rope etc.). **b** cause (a ship) to move in a specified direction. —v.i. **5.** rise or swell up; bulge. **6.** rise and fall repeatedly. **7.** vomit; retch. **8.** *Naut.* **a** move or proceed: said of ships. **b** haul or pull, as on a rope. — **heave, ho!** *Naut.* pull (or push) hard together! **—heave to 1.** bring (a ship) to a standstill by heading into the wind with the sails hauled in or shortened. **2.** lie to. —n. the act of heaving. [ME *heven* lift]

heav•en (HEV ən) n. **1.** *Theol.* the abode of God, the angels, and virtuous souls. **2.** *Usu. pl.* the regions around and above the earth; sky. **3.** any condition of great happiness. **4.** any place resembling heaven. [ME *heven* heaven] **—heav′en•ly** adj.

heav•en•ward (HEV ən wərd) adv. toward heaven. Also **heav′en•wards.** —adj. directed toward heaven.

heav•i•er-than-air (HEV ee ər *thən* AIR) adj. having a weight greater than that of the air it displaces: said of airplanes etc.

heav•y (HEV ee) adj. **heav•i•er, heav•i•est 1.** having great weight; hard to move. **2.** having relatively great weight in relation to size: *heavy* metals. **3.** having more than usual quantity etc.: a *heavy* snowfall. **4.** practicing or indulging on a large scale: a *heavy* smoker. **5.** having force and severity. **6.** having great importance; grave; serious. **7.** hard to do or accomplish: *heavy* labor. **8.** hard to endure or bear; oppressive: *heavy* taxes. **9.** of food, not easily digested. **10.** giving an impression of weight; thick: *heavy* lines. **11.** despondent: a *heavy*. heart. **12.** lacking animation and grace; tedious. **13.** lacking precision and delicacy: a *heavy* hand. **14.** producing massive or basic goods: *heavy* industry. **15.** pregnant: *heavy* with child. **16.** *Mil.* designating the more massive types of weapons. —adv. in a heavy manner. **—hang heavy** drag by tediously, as time. [ME *hevi*]

heav•y (HEV ee) n. pl. **ies 1.** in the theater, the role of a villainous or tragic personage; also, the actor portraying him. **2.** *Slang* an important person: a conference of government *heavies*.

heav•y-du•ty (HEV ee DOO tee) adj. strongly constructed for hard use.

heav•y-hand•ed (HEV ee HAN did) adj. **1.** bungling; clumsy. **2.** oppressive; cruel. — **heav′y-hand′ed•ness** n.

heav•y-heart•ed (HEV ee HAHR tid) adj. melancholy; sad. **—heav′y-heart′ed•ly** adv.

heav•y-lad•en (HEV ee LAYD n) adj. **1.** bearing a heavy burden. **2.** troubled; oppressed.

heav•y•weight (HEV ee WAYT) n. **1.** a person or animal of much more than average weight. **2.** a boxer or wrestler weighing over 175 pounds. **3.** a person or group of great influence. **—heav′y-weight′** adj.

He•bra•ic (hə BRAY ik,) adj. relating to or characteristic of the Hebrew people and their culture and language. [ME]

He•brew (HEE broo) n. **1.** a member of that group of Semitic peoples claiming descent from the house of Abraham; Israelite; Jew. **2.** the ancient Semitic language of the Israelites. **3.** the modern Hebrew language. [ME *Hebreu*]

heck•le (HEK əl) v.t. **-led, •ling** try to annoy with taunts, questions, etc. [ME. *hekelen*] **—heck′ler** n.

hec•tare (HEK tair) n. in the metric system, a unit of area equal to 2.47 acres.

hec•tic (HEK tik) adj. characterized by great excitement, turmoil, haste, etc.: a *hectic* trip. [ME] **—hec′ti•cal•ly** adv.

hecto- *combining form* in the metric system and in technical usage, a hundred times (a specified unit). Also spelled *hekto-*. [< F]

hec•to•gram (HEK tə GRAM) n. in the metric system, a measure of weight equal to 3.5 ounces.

hec•to•li•ter (HEK tə LEE tər) n. in the metric system, a measure of capacity equal to 26.4 gallons.

hec•to•me•ter (HEK tə MEE tər) n. in the metric system, a measure of length equal to 109.36 yards.

hec•tor (HEK tər) v.t. & v.i. **1.** bluster; rant. **2.** tease; torment. [< L < Gk. *Hektor* Trojan hero of the *Iliad*]

he′d (heed) contr. of **1.** he had. **2.** he would.

hedge (hej) n. **1.** a fence or barrier formed of privet or other bushes; also, any boundary or barrier. **2.** the act of hedging a bet, risk, etc.; also, that which is used to hedge. —v. **hedged, hedg•ing** v.t. **1.** border or separate with a hedge. **2.** set barriers and restrictions to; hem: often with *in* or *about*. **3.**

guard against undue loss from (a bet, investment, etc.) by making compensatory bets etc. —*v.i.* **4.** make compensatory bets etc. **5.** avoid forthright statement or action. [ME *hegge*] —**hedg′er** *n.*

hedge·hog (HEJ HOG) *n.* **1.** a small, nocturnal mammal of Europe, having stout spines on the back and sides. **2.** the porcupine.

hedge·hop (HEJ HOP) *v.i.* **-hopped, -hop·ping** fly close to the ground in an airplane.

hedge·row (HEJ ROH) *n.* a dense row of bushes, trees, etc., planted as a hedge. [ME]

he·don·ism (HEED n IZ əm) *n.* **1.** the doctrine that pleasure is the only proper goal of moral endeavor. **2.** the pursuit of pleasure. [< Gk. *hēdonē* pleasure] —**he′don·ist** *n.*

heed (heed) *v.t.* **1.** pay attention to. —*v.i.* **2.** pay attention; listen. —*n.* careful attention. [ME *heden*]

heed·ful (HEED fəl) *adj.* attentive; mindful.

heed·less (HEED lis) *adj.* inattentive; reckless.

heel[1] (heel) *n.* **1.** in humans, the rounded posterior part of the foot in back of the ankle; also, the rounded part of the palm of the hand nearest the wrist. **2.** that part of a stocking etc. covering the heel. **3.** in a shoe or boot, the built-up portion on which the rear of the foot rests. **4.** something analogous to the human heel, as the rounded end of a loaf of bread. **5.** a dishonorable person. —**at one's heels** close behind. —**down at the heels** shabby; run-down. —**on** (or **upon**) **the heels of** right behind; quickly following. —**cool one's heels** be kept waiting. —**to heel 1.** to an attendant position close behind one. **2.** to submission; under control. —**kick up one's heels 1.** have a good time. **2.** let oneself go. —**take to one's heels** run away; flee. —*v.t.* **1.** supply with a heel, as a shoe. **2.** pursue closely. —*v.i.* **3.** follow at one's heels. [ME]

heel[2] *v.t. & v.i. Naut.* lean or cause to lean to one side; cant, as a ship. [ME *helden*] —*n.*

heeled (heeld) *adj.* **1.** having a certain type of heel: *high-heeled.* **2.** provided with money: *well-heeled.* **3.** *Slang* supplied with a gun.

heft (heft) *v.t.* **1.** weigh by lifting. **2.** lift. —*n.* weight.

heft·y (HEF tee) *adj.* **heft·i·er, heft·i·est 1.** heavy; weighty. **2.** big and powerful; muscular.

he·gem·o·ny (hi JEM ə nee) *n. pl.* **-nies** domination or leadership, esp. of one state over others. [< Gk. *hēgemonia* supremacy] —**heg·e·mon·ic** (HEJ ə MON ik) *adj.*

he·gi·ra (hə JĪ rə) *n.* **1.** *Often cap.* the flight of Muhammad from Mecca in 622. **2.** any flight to a safer place. Also spelled *hejira.* [< Med.L]

heif·er (HEF ər) *n.* a young cow that has not produced a calf. [ME *hayfre*]

height (hīt) *n.* **1.** the state or quality of being high or relatively high. **2.** the distance from the base to the top; altitude. **3.** the distance above a given level, as the sea or horizon. **4.** *Often pl.* a lofty or high place; eminence. **5.** the highest part of anything; summit. **6.** the highest degree. [ME]

height·en (HĪT n) *v.t. & v.i.* **1.** make or become high or higher; raise or lift. **2.** make or become more in degree, amount, size, etc.; intensify.

hei·nous (HAY nəs) *adj.* extremely wicked; atrocious; odious. [ME *heynous*]

heir (air) *n.* **1.** anyone inheriting or likely to inherit rank or property. **2.** one who succeeds or is the beneficiary of some forerunner. [ME *eir*] —**heir′ess** *n.fem.*

heir apparent *pl.* **heirs apparent 1.** *Law* one who must by course of law become the heir if he or she survives the ancestor. **2.** anyone whose succession to a position seems ensured.

heir·loom (AIR LOOM) *n.* **1.** anything that has been handed down in a family for generations. **2.** *Law* those chattels and articles that descend to an heir along with the estate. [ME *heirlome*]

heir presumptive *pl.* **heirs presumptive** *Law* an heir whose claim to an estate may become void by the birth of a nearer relative.

heist (hīst) *Slang v.t.* steal. —*n.* a robbery.

he·ji·ra (hə JĪ rə) see HEGIRA.

held (held) past tense, past participle of HOLD.

hel·i·cal (HEL i kəl) *adj.* pertaining to or shaped like a helix.

hel·i·cop·ter (HEL i KOP tər) *n. Aeron.* a type of aircraft lifted by airfoil blades rotating around a vertical axis, and capable of rising and descending vertically. [< F *hélicoptère*]

he·li·o·cen·tric (HEE lee oh SEN trik) *adj.* having or regarding the sun as the center.

hel·i·port (HEL ə PORT) *n.* an airport for helicopters.

he·li·um (HEE lee əm) *n.* an inert, odorless, nonflammable, gaseous element, used to inflate balloons, dirigibles, etc. [< NL]

he·lix (HEE liks) *n. pl.* **he·lix·es** or **hel·i·ces** (HEL ə SEEZ) **1.** a line, thread, wire, or the like, curved as if wound in a single layer round a cylinder; a form like a screw thread. **2.** any spiral. [< L]

hell (hel) *n.* **1.** *Sometimes cap.* in various religions, the abode of the dead or the place of punishment for the wicked after death. **2.** any condition or cause of great suffering. **—be hell on** *Slang* be unpleasant or damaging to. **—catch** (or **get**) **hell** *Slang* be scolded or punished. **—give someone hell** *Informal* scold or punish (someone) severely. **—raise hell** *Slang* create a disturbance. **—interj.** an exclamation used as an expression of anger or impatience. [ME]

he'll (heel) contr. of he will.

hell·bent (HEL BENT) *adj.* determined to have or do; recklessly eager.

Hel·len·ic (he LEN ik) *adj.* Greek; Grecian. **—n.** a group of Indo-European languages, including Greek.

Hel·len·ism (HEL ə NIZ əm) *n.* **1.** ancient Greek character, ideals, or civilization. **2.** an idiom or turn of phrase peculiar to Greek.

Hel·le·nis·tic (HEL ə NIS tik) *adj.* **1.** pertaining to or characteristic of Hellenism. **2.** of or pertaining to the period that began with the conquests of Alexander the Great and ended about 300 years later, characterized by the spread of Greek language and culture throughout the Near East.

Hel·le·nize (HEL ə NIZ) *v.t. & v.i.* **·nized, ·niz·ing** make or become Greek.

hell·fire (HEL FIR) *n.* the flames or the punishment of hell.

hel·lion (HEL yən) *n. Informal* a wild, mischievous person.

hell·ish (HEL ish) *adj.* **1.** of, like, or pertaining to hell. **2.** fiendish; horrible.

hel·lo (he LOH) *interj.* an exclamation of greeting or surprise, or one used to gain attention. **—n. pl. ·loes** the saying or calling of "hello." **—v.t. & v.i. ·loed, ·lo·ing** call or say "hello" to.

helm (helm) *n.* **1.** *Naut.* the steering apparatus of a vessel, esp. the tiller or wheel. **2.** any place of control or responsibility. [ME *helme* handle]

hel·met (HEL mit) *n.* a protective covering for the head, made out of metal, plastic, etc., and worn by workers, soldiers, etc. [ME] **—hel'met·ed** *adj.*

helms·man (HELMZ mən) *n. pl.* **·men** one who steers a ship.

hel·ot (HEL ət) *n.* a slave; serf. [< L *helotes*, slaves] **—hel'ot·ry** *n.*

help (help) *v.t.* **1.** assist (someone or something). **2.** provide relief to; remedy. **3.** refrain from: I *couldn't help* laughing. **4.** serve; wait on, as a salesclerk. **—v.i. 5.** give assistance. **—cannot help but** cannot avoid; be obliged to. **—help oneself** take without requesting or being offered. **—n. 1.** the act of helping. **2.** remedy; relief. **3.** one who or that which gives assistance. **4.** any hired worker or helper. [ME *helpen*]

help·ful (HELP fəl) *adj.* affording help; beneficial. **—help'ful·ly** *adv.*

help·ing (HEL ping) *n.* a single portion of food served at table.

help·less (HELP lis) *adj.* **1.** unable to help oneself; powerless. **2.** without recourse to help; defenseless. **—help'less·ly** *adv.*

help·mate (HELP mayt) *n.* **1.** a helper; partner. **2.** a spouse. Also **help·meet** (HELP meet).

hel·ter-skel·ter (HEL tər SKEL tər) *adv. & adj.* in or displaying a hurried and confused manner.

helve (helv) *n.* the handle, as of an ax or hatchet. **—v.t.** **helved, helv·ing** furnish with a helve. [ME]

hem[1] (hem) *n.* **1.** a finished edge made on a piece of fabric or a garment by turning the raw edge under and sewing it down. **2.** any similar border or edging. **—v.t.** **hemmed, hem·ming 1.** provide with a hem. **2.** shut in; enclose; restrict: usu. with *in.* [ME]

hem[2] *interj.* a sound made as in clearing the throat to attract attention, cover embarrassment, etc. **—v.i.** **hemmed, hem·ming** make the sound "hem." **—hem and haw** hesitate in speaking so as to keep from being explicit. [Imit.]

he·ma·tol·o·gy (HEE mə TOL ə jee) *n.* the branch of biology that treats of the blood and its diseases. **—he'ma·tol'o·gist** *n.*

he·ma·to·ma (HEE mə TOH mə) *n. pl.* **·mas, ·ma·ta** (mə tə) *Pathol.* a tumor or swelling formed by the effusion of blood.

hem·i·ple·gi·a (HEM i PLEE jee ə) *n. Pathol.* paralysis of one side of the body. [< NL] **—hem'i·ple'·gic** (-jik) *adj. & n.*

hem·i·sphere (HEM i SFEER) *n.* **1.** half of a sphere, formed by a plane passing through the center of the sphere. **2.** a half of the terrestrial or celestial globe, or a map or projection of one. The world is usu. divided either at the equator into the **Northern** and **Southern Hemispheres,** or at some meridian between Europe and America into the **Eastern** and **Western Hemispheres.** [< L *hemisphaerium*] — **hem·i·spher·ic** (HEE i SFER ik) or **·i·cal** *adj.*

hem·line (HEM LIN) *n.* the line formed by the lower edge of a garment, as a dress.

hem·lock (HEM LOK) *n.* **1.** one of several evergreen trees of the pine family, having coarse, nonresinous wood used for paper pulp. **2.** a biennial herb of the parsley family, yielding a poison: also **poison hemlock.** [ME *hemlok*]

he·mo·glo·bin (HEE mə GLOH bin) *n. Biochem.* the respiratory pigment in red blood corpuscles, serving as a carrier of oxygen from the lungs to body cells.

he·mo·phil·i·a (HEE mə FIL ee ə) *n. Pathol.* a disorder characterized by immoderate bleeding even from slight injuries. [< NL] —**he'mo·phil'i·ac** (-ee AK) *adj. & n.*

hem·or·rhage (HEM ər ij) *n.* copious discharge of blood from a ruptured blood vessel. —*v.i.* **·rhaged, ·rhag·ing** bleed copiously. [< L *haemorrhagia*] — **hem·or·rhag·ic** (HEM ə RAJ ik) *adj.*

hem·or·rhoid (HEM ə ROID) *n. Pathol.* a tumor or dilation of a vein in the anal region: also, in the plural, **piles.** [ME *emoroides*] —**hem'or·rhoi'dal** [-dəl] *adj.*

he·mo·stat (HEE mə STAT) *n. Med.* a device or drug for checking the flow of blood from a ruptured vessel.

hemp (hemp) *n.* **1.** a tall herb of the mulberry family, with small green flowers and a tough bark: also called *bhang, cannabis, Indian hemp, marijuana.* **2.** a narcotic prepared from this plant. **3.** the tough, strong fiber from this plant, used for cloth and cordage. [ME] —**hemp·en** (HEM pən) *adj.*

hem·stitch (HEM STICH) *n.* the ornamental finishing of a hem, made by pulling out several threads and drawing the cross threads together in groups. —*v.t.* embroider with a hemstitch.

hen (hen) *n.* **1.** the mature female of the domestic fowl and related birds. **2.** the female of the lobster. [ME]

hence (hens) *adv.* **1.** as a consequence; therefore. **2.** from this time or date: a week *hence.* **3.** away from this place. [ME *hens*]

hence·forth (HENS FORTH) *adv.* from this time on. Also **hence'for'ward.**

hench·man (HENCH mən) *n. pl.* **·men 1.** a faithful follower. **2.** an unscrupulous subordinate, usu. criminal. **3.** a political supporter who works chiefly for personal gain. [ME]

hen·pecked (HEN PEKT) *adj.* dominated by one's wife.

hen·ry (HEN ree) *n. pl.* **·ries** or **·rys** *Electr.* the unit equal to the inductance of a circuit in which the variation of a current at the rate of one ampere per second induces an electromotive force of one volt. [after Joseph *Henry*, 1797—1878, U.S. physicist]

he·pat·ic (hi PAT ik) *adj.* of or like the liver. [ME *epatik*]

hep·a·ti·tis (HEP ə TI tis) *n. Pathol.* inflammation of the liver. [< Gk.]

hep·tam·e·ter (hep TAM i tər) *n.* in prosody, a line of verse consisting of seven metrical feet. [< Med.L *heptametrum*]

her (hur) *pron.* the objective case of the pronoun *she.* —*adj.* the possessive case of *she.* [ME *here*]

her·ald (HER əld) *n.* **1.** any bearer of important news; messenger. **2.** one who or that which shows what is to follow; harbinger. — *v.t.* announce or proclaim publicly. [ME *herauld*]

her·ald·ry (HER əl dree) *n. pl.* **·ries** the art or science that treats of coats of arms, genealogies, etc. [ME]

herb (urb) *n.* **1.** a plant without woody tissue, which withers and dies after flowering. **2.** any such plant as a medicine, seasoning, scent, etc. [ME *herbe*] —**herb·al** (UR bəl) *adj. & n.*

her·ba·ceous (hur BAY shəs) *adj.* **1.** like herbs. **2.** having the semblance, color, or structure of a leaf. [< L *herbaceus* grassy]

herb·age (UR bij) *n.* **1.** herbs collectively, esp. pasturage. **2.** the succulent parts of herbaceous plants. [ME]

herb·al·ist (HUR bə list) *n.* a dealer in herbs; a collector of herbs.

her·bar·i·um (hur BAIR ee əm) *n. pl.* **·bar·i·ums** or **·bar·i·a** (-BAIR ee ə) **1.** a collection of dried plants scientifically arranged. **2.** a room or building containing such a collection. [< LL]

her·bi·cide (HUR bi SID) *n.* an agent, as a chemical, that destroys plants, esp. weeds.

her·biv·o·rous (hur BIV ər əs) *adj.* **1.** feeding on vegetable matter; plant-eating. **2.** belonging to a group of mammals that feed mainly on herbage, as cows, horses, camels, etc. [< NL *herbivorus*]

her·cu·le·an (HUR kyə LEE ən) *adj.* **1.** having great strength. **2.** requiring great strength. [< L *Herculeus* of Hercules]

Her·cu·les (HUR kyə LEEZ) *n.* any man of great strength. [< *Hercules*, in Greek mythology]

herd (hurd) *n.* **1.** a number of cattle or other animals feeding, moving about, or kept together. **2.** a large crowd of people: a contemptuous term. —*v.t. & v.i.* bring together or move in a herd. [ME]

herds·man (HURDZ mən) *n. pl.* •**men** one who owns or tends a herd. [ME *hird-man*]

here (heer) *adv.* **1.** in, at, or about this place: opposed to *there.* Also used to indicate or emphasize: George *here* is a good swimmer. **2.** to this place; hither. **3.** at this time, in an action etc.: *Here* are my reasons. **4.** in the present life: distinguished from *hereafter.* —*interj.* an exclamation used to answer a roll call, attract attention, etc. —**neither here nor there** beside the point; irrelevant. —*n.* **1.** this place. **2.** this time; this life: the *here* and now. [ME]

here·a·bout (HEER ə BOWT) *adv.* about this place; in this vicinity. Also **here′·a·bouts′.**

here·af·ter (heer AF tər) *adv.* **1.** at some future time. **2.** from this time forth. —*n.* a future state or existence, esp. after death. [ME]

here·by (heer BĪ) *adv.* by means or by virtue of this.

he·red·i·tar·y (hə RED i TER ee) *adj.* **1.** derived from ancestors; inherited. **2.** *Biol.* transmitted or transmissible genetically from an animal or plant to its offspring: distinguished from *congenital.* **3.** *Law* **a** passing by inheritance to an heir. **b** holding possession or title through inheritance. [ME]

he·red·i·ty (hə RED i tee) *n. pl.* •**ties** *Biol.* **1.** genetic transmission of characteristics from parents to offspring. **2.** the sum total of an individual's inherited characteristics. [< MF *heredite* inheritance]

here·in (heer IN) *adv.* **1.** in or into this place. **2.** in this case, circumstance, etc. [ME]

here·in·af·ter (HEER in AF tər) *adv.* in a subsequent part of this document, contract, etc.

here·of (heer UV) *adv.* **1.** of this. **2.** in regard to this. [ME *her of*]

here·on (heer ON) *adv.* on this; hereupon. [ME *her on*]

her·e·sy (HER ə see) *n. pl.* •**sies 1.** a belief contrary to the established doctrines of a church or religious system. **2.** any belief contrary to established doctrine. **3.** the holding of such a belief or opinion. [ME *heresie*] —**he·ret·i·cal** (hə RET i kəl) *adj.*

her·e·tic (HER i tik) *n.* **1.** one who holds beliefs or opinions contrary to established religious doctrines. **2.** one who maintains unorthodox opinions on any subject. [ME *heretik*]

here·to (heer TOO) *adv.* to this thing, matter, etc. [ME *herto*]

here·to·fore (HEER tə FOR) *adv.* before now. [ME *heretoforn*]

here·up·on (HEER ə PON) *adv.* immediately resulting from or following this. [ME *herupon*]

here·with (heer WITH) *adv.* **1.** along with this. **2.** by means of or through this. [ME *herwith*]

her·i·ta·ble (HER i tə bəl) *adj.* that can be inherited. [ME] —**her′i·ta·bil′i·ty** *n.*

her·i·tage (HER i tij) *n.* **1.** that which is inherited. **2.** a cultural tradition, body of knowledge, etc., handed down from past times. [ME]

her·maph·ro·dite (hur MAF rə DĪT) *n.* an individual, often a plant, having both male and female reproductive organs. [ME *hermofrodite*] —**her·maph′ro·dite,** **her·maph′ro·dit′ic** (hur MAF rə DIT ik) *adj.*

her·met·ic (hur MET ik) *adj.* **1.** airtight. **2.** of or relating to alchemy; magical; hard to understand. [< Med.L *hermeticus,* pertaining to Hermes] —**her·met′i·cal·ly** *adv.*

her·mit (HUR mit) *n.* one who lives in seclusion, often for religious reasons. [ME *ermite*]

her·mit·age (HUR mi tij) *n.* **1.** the dwelling of a hermit. **2.** any secluded dwelling place. [ME]

hermit crab any of various soft-bodied crustaceans that live in the empty shells of sandsnails etc.

her·ni·a (HUR nee ə) *n. pl.* •**ni·as** or •**ni·ae** (-nee ə) *Pathol.* the protrusion of a bodily part, as of the intestine, through an opening in the wall surrounding it; rupture. [ME]

he·ro (HEER oh) *n. pl.* •**roes 1.** a person distinguished for exceptional courage, fortitude, or bold enterprise. **2.** a person idealized for superior qualities or deeds of any kind. **3.** the principal male character in a drama, fictional work, etc. **4.** in classical mythology and legend, a man of great nobility or physical prowess. **5.** *pl.* **heros** a sandwich made with a long roll cut lengthwise, and usu. filled with cold cuts, cheese, etc.: also called *grinder, hoagy, submarine.* [ME *heroes* heroes]

he·ro·ic (hə ROH ik) *adj.* **1.** characteristic of, befitting, or resembling a hero. **2.** showing great daring or boldness; extreme in action or effect: a *heroic* attempt. **3.** grandiose in style or language. [< L *heroicus*] —*n.* **1.** *Often pl.* heroic verse. **2.** *pl.* melodramatic or extravagant behavior. —**he·ro'i·cal·ly** *adv.*

heroic couplet a verse form consisting of two rhyming lines of iambic pentameter.

heroic verse one of several verse forms used especially in epic and dramatic poetry, as the iambic pentameter of the heroic couplet and blank verse.

her·o·in (HER oh in) *n.* an addictive, narcotic drug derived from morphine. [< G *Heroin*]

her·o·ine (HER oh in) *n.fem.* **1.** a woman of heroic character; also **hero.** **2.** the principal female character of a drama, fictional work, etc. [< L]

her·o·ism (HER oh IZ əm) *n.* **1.** the qualities of a he o or heroine. **2.** heroic behavior. [< F *héroïsme*]

hero worship enthusiastic or extravagant admiration for heroes or other persons. — **hero worshiper**

her·pes (HUR peez) *n. Pathol.* a virus infection of the skin and mucous membranes, characterized by the eruption of blisters. [ME]

herpes zos·ter (ZOS tər) *Pathol.* shingles. [< NL, lit., belt herpes]

her·pe·tol·o·gy (HUR pə TOL ə jee) *n.* the branch of zoology that treats of reptiles and amphibians. [< Gk. *herpetón* reptile + -LOGY] —**her'pe·tol'o·gist** *n.*

her·ring (HER ing) *n. pl.* **·rings** or **·ring 1.** a small food fish of the North Atlantic. **2.** any of various fish related to the herring, as the sardine. [ME *hering*]

her·ring·bone (HER ing BOHN) *n.* **1.** a pattern using a design, resembling the spinal structure of a herring, in which the ribs form slanting parallel lines on either side of the spine. **2.** something made in or consisting of such a pattern. —*adj.* resembling herringbone.

hers (hurz) *pron.* **1.** the possessive case of the pronoun *she,* used predicatively: That

book is *hers.* **2.** the one or ones belonging to or relating to her. [ME *hirs*]

her·self (hər SELF) *pron.* a form of the third person singular feminine pronoun, used: **1.** as a reflexive: She excused *herself.* **2.** as an intensive form of *she:* She *herself* called the police. **3.** as a designation of a usual state: After her illness, she was *herself* again. [ME *hire-selfe*]

hertz (hurts) *n.* a unit of frequency equal to one cycle per second. Abbr. *Hz.* [after H.R. *Hertz,* 1857–94, German physicist]

he's (heez) *contr.* of **1.** he is. **2.** he has.

hes·i·tant (HEZ i tənt) *adj.* lacking certainty or decisiveness; hesitating. —**hes'i·tan·cy** *n.*

hes·i·tate (HEZ i TAYT) *v.i.* **·tat·ed, ·tat·ing 1.** be slow or doubtful in acting, making a decision, etc.; waver. **2.** be reluctant. **3.** pause. **4.** falter in speech. [< L *haesitatus* stuck fast] —**hes'i·ta'tion** *n.*

het·er·o·dox (HET ər ə DOKS) *adj.* **1.** at variance with accepted doctrines or beliefs. **2.** holding unorthodox opinions. [< Gk. *heteródoxos* holding another opinion] — **het'er·o·dox'y** *n.*

het·er·o·ge·ne·ous (HET ər ə JEE nee əs) *adj.* **1.** consisting of dissimilar parts or elements; not homogeneous. **2.** differing in nature or kind; unlike. [< Med.L *heterogeneus*] —**het'er·o·ge·ne'i·ty** (-NEE i tee) *n.*

het·er·o·sex·u·al (HET ər ə SEK shoo əl) *adj.* **1.** of or having sexual desire for those of the opposite sex. **2.** *Biol.* of or pertaining to the opposite sex or to both sexes. —*n.* a heterosexual person. —**het'er·o·sex'u·al'i·ty** (-AL i tee) *n.*

heu·ris·tic (hyuu RIS tik) *adj.* **1.** aiding or guiding in discovery. **2.** designating an educational method by which a pupil is stimulated to make his or her own investigations and discoveries. [< NL *heuristicus* found out]

hew (hyoo) *v.* **hewed, hewn** or **hewed, hew·ing** *v.t.* **1.** make or shape with or as with blows of an ax. **2.** fell with or as with ax blows. —*v.i.* **3.** make cutting and repeated blows, as with an ax or sword. **4.** conform, as to a principle. [ME *hewen*] —**hew'er** *n.*

hex (heks) *n.* **1.** spell. **2.** a witch. —*v.t.* bewitch. [< G *Hexe* witch]

hex·a·gon (HEK sə GON) *n. Geom.* a polygon having six sides and six angles. [< Gk. *hexágonon*] —**hex·ag·o·nal** (hek SAG ə nl) *adj.*

hex•a•gram (HEK sə GRAM) *n.* a six-pointed
star made by or as by completing the equi-
lateral triangles based on the sides of a regular hexagon.

hex•am•e•ter (hek SAM i tər) *n.* **1.** in prosody, a line of verse consisting of six metrical
feet. **2.** the dactylic verse of Greek and
Latin epic poetry. [< L]

hey•day (HAY DAY) *n.* a period of greatest
vigor; height, as of power or prosperity.

hi•a•tus (hī AY təs) *n. pl.* **•tus•es 1.** a gap or
space from which something is missing. **2.**
any break or interruption. [< L, opening]

hi•ba•chi (hi BAH chee) *n. pl.* **•chis** a charcoal stove, used for cooking. [< Japanese]

hi•ber•nate (HĪ bər NAYT) *v.i.* **•nat•ed,**
•nat•ing 1. pass the winter in a dormant
state, as certain animals. **2.** remain inactive
or secluded. [< L *hibernatus* passed the
winter] —**hi′ber•na′tion** *n.*

hic•cup (HIK up) *n.* **1.** an involuntary contraction of the diaphragm, causing a sudden, audible inspiration of breath checked
by a spasmodic closure in the larynx. **2.** *pl.* a
condition characterized by repetition of
such spasms. Also **hic•cough** (HIK up). —
hic′cup *v.i.* **•cuped, •cup•ing**

hick (hik) *n.* one having the clumsy, unsophisticated manners, etc., supposedly typical of rural areas. [after *Hick,* nickname for
Richard] —**hick** *adj.*

hick•ey (HIK ee) *n. pl.* **•eys** *Slang* **1.** any
gadget or contrivance. **2.** a pimple or blemish.

hid (hid) past tense, alternative past participle of HIDE¹.

hid•den (HID n) past participle of HIDE¹.
—*adj.* not seen or known; concealed; obscure.

hide¹ (hīd) *v.* **hid, hid•den** or **hid, hid•ing**
v.t. **1.** put or keep out of sight; conceal. **2.**
keep secret; withhold from knowledge. **3.**
block or obstruct the sight of. —*v.i.* **4.** keep
oneself out of sight; be concealed. —**hide
out** remain in concealment, esp. as a fugitive. [ME *hiden* conceal]

hide² *n.* **1.** the skin of an animal, esp. when
stripped from the carcass or made into
leather. **2.** *Informal* the human skin. [ME]

hide•a•way (HĪD ə WAY) *n.* a place of concealment; hideout.

hide•bound (HĪD BOWND) *adj.* **1.** obstinately fixed in opinion; narrow-minded;
bigoted. **2.** having the skin too tightly adhering to the back and ribs: said of cattle
etc.

hid•e•ous (HID ee əs) *adj.* **1.** extremely
ugly: *a hideous sight.* **2.** morally odious or
detestable; shocking. [ME *hidous*] —**hid′**
e•ous•ness *n.*

hide•out (HĪD OWT) *n.* a place of concealment or refuge.

hid•ing¹ (HĪ ding) *n.* **1.** the act of one who or
that which hides. **2.** a state or place of concealment.

hid•ing² *n. Informal* a flogging; whipping.

hie (hī) *v.t. & v.i.* **hied, hie•ing** or **hy•ing**
hasten; hurry: often reflexive: I *hied* myself
home. [ME *hien*]

hi•er•ar•chy (HĪ ə RAHR kee) *n. pl.* **•chies**
1. any group of persons or things arranged
in successive orders or classes. **2.** a body of
ecclesiastics so arranged. **3.** government or
rule by such a body of ecclesiastics. [<
Med.L *hierarchia*] —**hi•er•ar•chi•cal** (HĪ
ə RAHR ki kəl) *adj.*

hi•er•o•glyph•ic (HĪ ər ə GLIF ik) *n.* **1.** *Usu.*
pl. a picture or symbol representing an object, idea, or sound, as in the writing system
of the ancient Egyptians. **2.** *pl.* a system of
writing using such pictures or symbols. **3.**
any symbol or character having a hidden
meaning. Also **hi′er•o•glyph′.** [< LL *hi-*
eroglyphicus sacred writing]

hi-fi (HĪ FĪ) *n.* **1.** high fidelity. **2.** radio, phonograph, or recording equipment capable
of reproducing sound with high fidelity. —
hi-fi *adj.*

hig•gle•dy-pig•gle•dy (HIG əl dee PIG əl
dee) *adj.* disordered or confused; jumbled.
—*adv.* in chaotic confusion or disorder.

high (hī) *adj.* **1.** reaching upward to some
great distance; lofty; tall. **2.** having a specified elevation: ten feet *high.* **3.** produced or
extending to or from a height: the *high*
jump. **4.** greater or more than is usual or
normal in degree, amount, etc.: *high* fever;
high speed. **5.** superior or exalted in quality,
rank, kind, etc.: a *high* official. **6.** most important; main. **7.** having serious consequences: *high* crimes. **8.** elated; joyful: *high*
spirits. **9.** *Informal* feeling the effects of
liquor, drugs, etc.; intoxicated. **10.** expensive; costly. **11.** luxurious or fashionable:
high living. **12.** advanced to the fullest extent or degree: *high* tide. **13.** complex; advanced: usu. in the comparative degree:
higher mathematics. **14.** slightly decomposed: said of meat. **15.** of sounds, having
relatively short wavelengths; shrill. —**high
and dry 1.** completely above water level. **2.**
stranded; helpless. —**high and mighty**

overbearing; haughty. —*adv.* **1.** to or at a high level, position, degree, price, rank, etc. **2.** in a high manner. —**high and low** everywhere. —*n.* **1.** a high level, position, etc. **2.** *Meteorol.* **a** an area of high barometric pressure. **b** the highest temperature, as for a day. [ME *heigh*] —**high′ly** *adv.*

high·ball (HĪ BAWL) *n.* a drink of whiskey or other liquor mixed with soda etc.

high·born (HĪ BORN) *adj.* of noble birth. [ME]

high·boy (HĪ BOI) *n.* a tall chest of drawers, on legs.

high·brow (HĪ BROW) *n.* one who has or claims to have intellectually superior tastes. —*adj.*

high·chair (HĪ CHAIR) *n.* a baby's chair standing on tall legs.

high-class (HĪ KLAS) *adj.* high or superior in quality, condition, status, etc.

high·er-up (HĪ ər UP) *n. Informal* a person of superior rank or position.

high·fa·lu·tin (HĪ fə LOOT n) *adj. Informal* extravagant, pompous, or high-flown in manner, speech, etc. Also **high′fa·lu′ting** (-LOO ting).

high fashion 1. clothes that are new in style or design. **2.** haute couture.

high fidelity *Electronics* the reproduction of sound with a minimum of distortion, esp. by phonographic or tape-recording equipment: also called *hi-fi.*

high-flown (HĪ FLOHN) *adj.* **1.** bombastic in style, language, etc. **2.** pretentious.

High German see under GERMAN.

high-grade (HĪ GRAYD) *adj.* of superior quality.

high-hand·ed (HĪ HAN did) *adj.* arbitrary and overbearing. —**high′-hand′ed·ness** *n.*

high-hat (HĪ HAT) *v.t. Informal* -**hat·ted,** -**hat·ting** snub. —*adj.* snobbish. —**high-hat·ter** *n.* a snob.

high·jack (HĪ JAK) see HIJACK.

high jump in track, a jump for height.

high·land (HĪ lənd) *n.* **1.** elevated land, as a plateau or promontory. **2.** *Usu. pl.* a hilly or mountainous region. —**high′land** *adj.* [ME]

High·land·er (HĪ lən dər) *n.* a native or inhabitant of the Highlands.

High·lands (HĪ ləndz) the mountainous parts of northern and western Scotland.

high·light (HĪ LĪT) *n.* **1.** an area, as in a painting, that is brightly lighted. **2.** an event, detail, etc. of special importance. —

v.t. **1.** give special emphasis to; feature. **2.** provide or emphasize with a highlight or highlights.

high-mind·ed (HĪ MĪN did) *adj.* possessing or manifesting noble thoughts or sentiments. —**high′-mind′ed·ness** *n.*

high·ness (HĪ nis) *n.* **1.** the state or quality of being high. **2.** *cap.* a title or form of address for persons of royal rank: often preceded by *His, Her, Your,* etc.

high-pitched (HĪ PICHT) *adj.* **1.** high in pitch; shrill. **2.** of a roof, having a steep slope.

high-pres·sure (HĪ PRESH ər) *adj.* **1.** using or sustaining high steam pressure, as an engine. **2.** having or showing high barometric pressure. **3.** exerting vigorously persuasive methods or tactics. —*v.t.* **·sured, ·sur·ing** employ aggressive or insistent methods of persuasion.

high-rise (HĪ RĪZ) *n.* a building having many stories and requiring elevators. —*adj.*

high·road (HĪ ROHD) *n.* an easy or sure course: the *highroad* to fame.

high school a school following elementary school or junior high school.

high seas the open waters of an ocean or sea, beyond the territorial jurisdiction of any nation.

high-sound·ing (HĪ SOWN ding) *adj.* pretentious or imposing: *high-sounding* praise.

high-spir·it·ed (HĪ SPIR i tid) *adj.* having a courageous or fiery spirit.

high-strung (HĪ STRUNG) *adj.* very sensitive or nervous; excitable.

high-ten·sion (HĪ TEN shən) *adj. Electr.* having or operating under very high voltage.

high-test (HĪ TEST) *adj.* denoting a grade of gasoline with a low boiling point.

high tide 1. the maximum level reached by the incoming tide. **2.** a culminating point.

high time 1. so late as to be almost past the proper time. **2.** an enjoyable time.

high-toned (HĪ TOHND) *adj.* **1.** stylish; modish. **2.** lofty in character.

high treason treason against the sovereign or state.

high-wa·ter mark (HĪ WAW tər) **1.** the highest point reached by a body of water, as during high tide, a flood, etc. **2.** a point of highest achievement or development.

high·way (HĪ way) *n.* a large public road.

high·way·man (HĪ WAY mən) *n. pl.* **·men** formerly, a robber who waylaid travelers on public roads.

hi·jack (HĪ JAK) *v.t.* **1.** seize illegally while in transit, as cargo, vehicles, etc. **2.** hold up and rob (a truck etc.). Also spelled *highjack.* —**hi′jack′er** *n.*

hike (hīk) *v.* **hiked, hik·ing** *v.i.* **1.** walk for a considerable distance. **2.** rise or be uneven, as part of a garment: often with *up.* —*v.t.* **3.** increase (prices etc.): usu. with *up.* —*n.* **1.** a long walk. **2.** an increase. —**hik′er** *n.*

hi·lar·i·ous (hi LAIR ee əs) *adj.* boisterously cheerful. [< L *hilarus* cheerful] —**hi·lar′i·ous·ness** *n.*

hi·lar·i·ty (hi LAR i tee) *n. pl.* **·ties** noisy gaiety.

hill (hil) *n.* **1.** an elevation of the earth's surface, not as high as a mountain. **2.** a heap or pile: often used in combination: a *molehill.* **3.** a small mound of earth. —*v.t.* surround or cover with small mounds of earth, as potatoes. [ME]

hill·bil·ly (HIL BIL ee) *n. pl.* **·lies** *Offensive* a person coming from or living in the mountains or a backwoods area, esp. in the southern U.S.

hill·ock (HIL ək) *n.* a small hill. [ME *hilloc*]

hill·y (HIL ee) *adj.* **hill·i·er, hill·i·est** **1.** having many hills. **2.** steep. —**hill′i·ness** *n.*

hilt (hilt) *n.* the handle of a sword, dagger, etc. —**to the hilt** thoroughly; fully. [ME]

him (him) *pron.* the objective case of *he.*

him·self (him SELF) *pron.* a form of *he,* used: **1.** as a reflexive: he cut *himself.* **2.** as an intensive: He *himself* will do it. **3.** as a designation of a usual state: He is not *himself.* [ME *him selven*]

hind¹ (hīnd) *adj.* at or toward the rear part; posterior. [ME *hinde*]

hind² *n.* the female of the deer, esp. when fully grown. [ME]

hind·er (HIN dər) *v.t.* **1.** interfere with the progress of; impede; obstruct. **2.** prevent from acting or occurring; deter; thwart. [ME *hindren* hold back]

Hin·di (HIN dee) *n.* **1.** the principal language of northern India, a branch of the Indo-Iranian languages. **2.** a form of literary Hindustani used by Hindus.

hind·most (HĪND MOHST) *adj.* farthest behind. [ME]

hind·quar·ter (HĪND KWOR tər) *n.* **1.** one of the two back quarters of a carcass of beef, lamb, etc. **2.** *pl.* the rump.

hin·drance (HIN drəns) *n.* **1.** the act of hindering. **2.** one who or that which hinders. [ME *hinderaunce*]

hind·sight (HĪND SĪT) *n.* **1.** the understanding of an event after it has happened. **2.** the rear sight of a gun, rifle, etc.

Hin·du (HIN doo) *n.* **1.** a native of India who speaks one of the Indic languages. **2.** one whose religion is Hinduism. —*adj.* of, pertaining to, or characteristic of the Hindus or Hinduism.

Hin·du·ism (HIN doo IZ əm) *n.* the religion of the Hindus of India.

hinge (hinj) *n.* **1.** a device consisting of two parts that form a movable joint on which a door, gate, etc. swings or turns. **2.** a natural movable joint connecting two parts, as the shells of a clam. —*v.* **hinged, hing·ing** *v.t.* **1.** attach by or equip with a hinge. —*v.i.* **2.** depend or be contingent: with *on.* [ME *henge*]

hint (hint) *n.* **1.** an indirect suggestion or implication. **2.** a slight indication or trace. —*v.t.* **1.** suggest indirectly; imply. —*v.i.* **2.** give a slight indication or suggestion: with *at.* [ME *henten*]

hin·ter·land (HIN tər LAND) *n.* **1.** a region adjacent to a coast. **2.** a region remote from urban areas. [< G, lit., land behind]

hip¹ (hip) *n.* **1.** the part of the human body projecting below the waist on either side, formed by the edge of the pelvis and the upper part of the femur. **2.** an analogous part in animals. [ME *hipe*]

hip² *n.* the ripened fruit of a rose. [ME *hepe*]

hip³ *adj. Slang* aware; informed.

hip·pie (HIP ee) *n.* one of a group of chiefly young people whose unconventional dress and behavior and use of drugs expressed withdrawal from middle-class life and indifference to its values.

hip·po·drome (HIP ə DROHM) *n.* **1.** an arena or similar structure for horse shows, circuses, etc. **2.** in ancient Greece and Rome, a course for horse races and chariot races. [< L *hippodromos*]

hip·po·pot·a·mus (HIP ə POT ə məs) *n. pl.* **·mus·es** or **·mi** (-MĪ) a large, chiefly aquatic mammal, native to Africa, having short legs, a massive, thick-skinned body, and a very broad muzzle. [< L]

hire (hīr) *v.t.* **hired, hir·ing** **1.** obtain the services of (a person) for payment. **2.** acquire the use of (a thing) for a fee; rent. **3.** grant the use or services of (someone or something) in return for payment: often with *out.* —**hire out** provide one's services in return for payment. —*n.* **1.** payment for labor, services, etc. **2.** the act of hiring, or the condition of being hired. [ME *hiren*]

hire•ling (HĪR ling) *n.* one who works only for pay. [ME *hirlyng*]

hir•sute (hur SOOT) *adj.* covered with hair. [< L *hirsutus* shaggy] —**hir′•sute•ness** *n.*

his (hiz) *pron.* **1.** the possessive case of *he;* used predicatively: This room is *his.* **2.** the one or ones belonging or pertaining to him: Her book is better than *his.* —*pronominal adj.* used *attributively: his* book. [ME]

His•pan•ic (hi SPAN ik) *adj.* pertaining to the people, language, or culture of Spain or Latin America.

hiss (his) *v.i.* **1.** produce a sibilant sound. **2.** utter such a sound as an expression of disapproval or derision. —*v.t.* **3.** utter with a hiss. **4.** express disapproval of by hissing. [ME *hissen*] —**hiss** *n.*

his•ta•mine (HIS tə MEEN) *n.* Biochem. a white, crystalline substance, found in plant and animal tissues and released in allergic reactions.

his•to•ri•an (hi STOR ee ən) *n.* a writer of or authority on history.

his•tor•ic (hi STOR ik) *adj.* **1.** important or famous in history: *historic* dates. **2.** memorable; significant: a *historic* occasion. **3.** historical. [< L *historicus*]

his•tor•i•cal (hi STOR i kəl) *adj.* **1.** belonging to history: a *historical* event. **2.** concerned with or treating the events of history: a *historical* account. **3.** based on known facts as distinct from legendary or fictitious accounts. —**his•tor′i•cal•ly** *adv.*

his•to•ri•og•ra•pher (hi STOR ee OG rə fər) *n.* a historian, esp. an official one. —**his•to′ri•og′ra•phy** *n.* the techniques of historical research.

his•to•ry (HIS tə ree) *n. pl.* **•ries 1.** that branch of knowledge concerned with past events. **2.** a record or account, usu. written and in chronological order, of past events. **3.** past events in general. **4.** An unusual or noteworthy past. **5.** a narrative or story. [ME *historie*]

his•tri•on•ic (HIS tree ON ik) *adj.* **1.** of or pertaining to actors or acting. **2.** overly dramatic. [< LL *histrionicus* of actors]

his•tri•on•ics (HIS tree ON iks) *n.* (*construed as sing. or pl.*) **1.** theatrical art or performances. **2.** feigned emotional display.

hit (hit) *v.* **hit, hit•ting** *v.t.* **1.** give a blow to; strike. **2.** reach with a missile, hurled or falling object, etc. **3.** collide with. **4.** cause to make forcible contact; bump. **5.** set in motion or propel by striking. **6.** arrive at,

achieve, or discover. **7.** affect adversely; cause to suffer. **8.** in baseball, succeed in making (a specified kind of base hit). **9.** *Informal* begin to journey on: *hit* the road. **10.** arrive at or reach (a place). —*v.i.* **11.** deliver a blow; strike. **12.** make forcible contact; bump. **13.** come or light; happen: followed by *on* or *upon: hit* on the right answer. —**hit it off** be friendly; get along well. —*n.* **1.** a blow, stroke, shot, etc. that reaches its target. **2.** a forceful impact; collision. **3.** a success. **4.** in baseball, a base hit. **5.** *Slang* a murder ordered by a criminal gang. **6.** *Slang* a dose of a narcotic drug. [ME *hitten*] —**hit′ter** *n.*

hit-and-run (HIT n RUN) *adj.* designating or caused by the driver of a vehicle who illegally keeps driving after hitting a pedestrian or another vehicle.

hitch (hich) *v.t.* **1.** fasten or tie, esp. temporarily. **2.** harness to a vehicle: sometimes with *up.* **3.** move, pull, raise, etc. with a jerk: often with *up.* **4.** obtain (a ride) by hitchhiking. —*v.i.* **5.** move with a jerk: *hitch* forward. **6.** become fastened, caught, or entangled. —*n.* **1.** an obstacle; halt; delay. **2.** a sudden, jerking movement; tug. **3.** a fastening or device used to fasten. **4.** *Slang* a period of enlistment in military service. **5.** *Slang* in hitchhiking, a ride. [ME *hytchen*]

hitch•hike (HICH HIK) *v.i.* •**hiked,** •**hik•ing** travel by securing rides in passing vehicles.

hith•er (HITH ər) *adv.* to or toward this place: Come *hither.* —*adj.* situated toward this side; nearer. [ME]

hith•er•to (HITH ər TOO) *adv.* until this time. [ME *hiderto*]

hit-or-miss (HIT ər MIS) *adj.* haphazard; careless.

hive (hīv) *n.* **1.** an artificial structure serving as a habitation for bees; beehive. **2.** a colony of bees inhabiting a hive; swarm. **3.** a place swarming with activity. —*v.t.* **hived, hiv•ing** induce (bees) to enter into or collect in a hive. [ME]

hives (hīvz) *n.* (*construed as sing. or pl.*) any of various skin disorders characterized by eruptions, itching, etc.

hoa•gy (HOH gee) *n.* hero (def. 5). Also **hoa′gie.**

hoard (hord) *n.* an accumulation of something stored away for safekeeping or future use. —*v.t. & v.i.* amass and store or hide (money, valuables, etc.). [ME *horde* treasure]

hoar·frost (HOR frawst) *n.* frost whitening the surface on which it is formed. [ME *hor-frost*]

hoarse (hors) *adj.* **hoars·er, hoars·est 1.** deep, harsh, and grating in sound. **2.** having a husky, gruff, or croaking voice. [ME *hors*] —**hoarse'ness** *n.*

hoar·y (HOR ee) *adj.* **hoar·i·er, hoar·i·est 1.** ancient; aged. **2.** gray or white with age. **3.** white or whitish in color. —**hoar'i·ness** *n.*

hoax (hohks) *n.* a trick or deception, usu. on the public. —*v.t.* deceive by a hoax.

hob (hob) *n.* a hobgoblin or elf. —**play** (or **raise**) **hob** cause mischief or confusion. [ME]

hob·ble (HOB əl) *v.* **·bled, ·bling** *v.i.* **1.** move clumsily or with a limp. —*v.t.* **2.** hamper the free movement of, as a horse, by fettering the legs. [ME *hobelen*] —*n.* **1.** a clumsy or limping gait. **2.** a rope etc., used to hobble the legs of an animal. —**hob'bler** *n.*

hob·by (HOB ee) *n. pl.* **·bies** an activity or pursuit undertaken for pleasure during one's leisure; a vocation. [ME *hobyn*]

hob·by·horse (HOB ee HORS) *n.* **1.** a rocking horse. **2.** a toy consisting of a stick surmounted by a horse's head.

hob·gob·lin (HOB GOB lin) *n.* **1.** an imaginary cause of terror or dread. **2.** a mischievous imp.

hob·nail (HOB NAYL) *n.* a nail used to stud the soles of heavy shoes against wear or slipping.

hob·nob (HOB NOB) *v.i.* **·nobbed, ·nob·bing** associate in a friendly manner; be on intimate terms. [< OE *habban* have + *nabban* have not]

ho·bo (HOH boh) *n. pl.* **·bos** or **·boes 1.** a tramp. **2.** an itinerant, usu. unskilled worker.

hock[1] (hok) *n.* the joint of the hind leg in the horse, ox, etc., corresponding to the ankle in man. [ME *hogh* heel]

hock[2] *n.* a type of white wine. [< G *hochheimer*]

hock[3] *v.t.* pawn. —**in hock 1.** in pawn. **2.** in debt. [< Du. *hok* prison]

hock·ey (HOK ee) *n.* **1.** a game played on ice (**ice hockey**), in which players, wearing skates and wielding sticks, try to drive a disk (**puck**) into the opponent's goal. **2.** a similar game played on a field (**field hockey**), in which a small ball is used instead of a puck.

hock·shop (HOK SHOP) *n.* a pawnshop.

ho·cus-po·cus (HOH kəs POH kəs) *n.* **1.** a verbal formula used in conjuring or sleight of hand. **2.** any trickery or deception. —*v.t. & v.i.* **-po·cused, -po·cus·ing** trick; cheat. [a sham Latin phrase]

hod (hod) *n.* **1.** a trough rested on the shoulder, to carry bricks, etc. **2.** a coal scuttle. [ME *hot* basket]

hodge·podge (HOJ POJ) *n.* a jumbled mixture or collection.

hoe (hoh) *n.* an implement for weeding etc., having a flat blade attached to a long handle. —*v.t. & v.i.* **hoed, hoe·ing** dig with a hoe. [ME *howe*]

hoe·down (HOH DOWN) *n.* a lively country dance or square dance; also, its music.

hog (hawg) *n.* **1.** a pig, esp. one weighing more than 120 pounds and raised for the market. **2. a** a gluttonous or filthy person. **b** a selfish or greedy person. —*v.t.* **hogged, hog·ging** take more than one's share of; grab selfishly. [ME] —**hog'gish** *adj.*

ho·gan (HOH gawn) *n.* a Navajo Indian dwelling, made of timbers covered with earth. [< Navajo *hooghan* home]

hogs·head (HAWGZ HED) *n.* **1.** a large cask, esp. one with a capacity of 63 to 140 gallons. **2.** a liquid measure, esp. one equal to 63 gallons, or 8.42 cubic feet.

hog·tie (HAWG TĪ) *v.t.* **-tied, -ty·ing 1.** tie together four feet, or the hands and feet of. **2.** render (a person) ineffective or helpless.

hog·wash (HAWG WOSH) *n.* **1.** kitchen refuse etc., fed to hogs. **2.** any nonsense; insincere talk.

hog-wild (HAWG WĪLD) *adj.* lacking in restraint.

hoi pol·loi (HOI pə LOI) the common people; the masses. [< Gk., the many]

hoist (hoist) *v.t.* raise or lift, esp. by mechanical means. —*n.* **1.** any machine for raising large objects. **2.** the act of hoisting. —**hoist by one's own petard** destroyed by a plot intended for another.

ho·kum (HOH kəm) *n.* nonsense; bunk.

hold[1] (hohld) *v.* **held, held, hold·ing** *v.t.* **1.** take and keep in the hand, arms, etc.; clasp. **2.** sustain, as in position; support: *hold* one's head high. **3.** contain or enclose: The barrel *holds* ten gallons. **4.** keep under control; restrain; also, retain possession of. **5.** keep in reserve. **6.** have the benefit or responsibilities of: *hold* office. **7.** regard in a specified manner: *hold* someone dear. **8.** bind by contract or duty: *Hold* him to his agreement. **9.** *Law* **a** adjudge; decide. **b** have title to. **10.** maintain in the mind; harbor: *hold* a grudge. **11.** engage in; carry on: *hold* a conference. —*v.i.* **12.** maintain a grip or grasp. **13.** withstand strain or remain unbroken: The rope *holds*. **14.** remain in effect. **15.** adhere, as to a principle or purpose; cling. —**hold back 1.** keep in check; restrain. **2.** refrain. **3.** retain. —**hold down 1.** suppress; keep under control. **2.** be employed at (a job). —**hold forth** preach or speak at great length. —**hold out 1.** stretch forth; offer. **2.** last; endure: Our supplies *held out*. **3.** continue resistance. —**hold over 1.** put off to a later time. **2.** remain or retain beyond the expected limit, as in office. —**hold up 1.** support; prop. **2.** exhibit to view. **3.** delay; stop. **4.** endure; remain firm. **5.** stop so as to rob. **6.** charge too high a price. —**hold water** be believable or sound, as an argument. —*n.* **1.** the act or method of grasping, as with the hands. **2.** a controlling force or influence. [ME *halden*]

hold² *n. Naut.* the space below the decks of a vessel, where cargo is stowed. [< Du. *hol*]

hold·er (HOHL dər) *n.* **1.** one who or that which holds. **2.** an owner; possessor: chiefly in compounds: *householder*.

hold·ing (HOHL ding) *n.* **1.** the act of one who or that which holds. **2.** a piece of land rented. **3.** *Often pl.* property held by legal right, esp. stocks or bonds.

holding company a company that invests in the stocks of one or more other corporations, which it may thus control.

holding pattern a course flown by an aircraft over or near an airport while waiting to land.

hold·o·ver (HOHLD OH vər) *n.* an incumbent continuing in office after his or her term has expired.

hold·up (HOHLD UP) *n.* **1.** stoppage or delay. **2.** a waylaying and robbing.

hole (hohl) *n.* **1.** a cavity in a solid mass or body; pit. **2.** an opening in anything; aperture. **3.** an animal's burrow or enclosed hiding place. **4.** any small, crowded, squalid place. **5.** a defect; fault. **6.** an awkward situation. **7.** in golf: **a** a small cavity into which the ball is played. **b** a division of the course, usu. one of nine or eighteen. —**hole in one** in golf, the sinking of the ball into a hole with one drive from the tee. —**in the hole** in debt. —*v.t. & v.i.* **holed, hol·ing** make a hole in. —**hole up** hide away; isolate oneself. [ME]

hol·i·day (HOL i DAY) *n.* **1.** a day appointed

by law for suspension of business in commemoration of some event. **2.** any day of rest. **3.** a day for special religious observance. —*v.i.* spend a holiday or vacation. [ME]

ho·li·ness (HOH lee nis) *n.* **1.** the state or quality of being holy. **2.** *cap.* a title or form of address for the Pope: preceded by *His* or *Your*. [ME *holynesse*]

ho·lism (HOH liz əm) *n.* **1.** the theory that the whole, esp. a living organism, is more than the sum of its parts. **2.** *Med.* care of a patient in all respects. —**ho·lis'tic** *adj.*

hol·low (HOL oh) *adj.* **·low·er, ·low·est 1.** having a cavity within; enclosing an empty space. **2.** having a deep opening; concave. **3.** sunken; fallen: *hollow* cheeks. **4.** deep or muffled in tone. **5.** not genuine; meaningless; empty. —*n.* **1.** a cavity or empty space in anything; depression; hole. **2.** a valley. —*v.t. & v.i.* make or become hollow: usu. with *out*. [ME *holwe*] —**hol'low·ness** *n.*

hol·o·caust (HOL ə KAWST) *n.* a wholesale destruction and loss of life, esp. by fire. —**the Holocaust** the genocidal destruction of Jews by Nazi Germany and its allies. [ME]

hol·o·gram (HOL ə GRAM) *n.* a picture made by holography.

hol·o·graph (HOL ə GRAF) *adj.* denoting a document, as a will, in the handwriting of the person whose signature it bears. —*n.* a document so written.

hol·o·graph·ic (HOL ə GRAF ik) *adj.* **1.** pertaining to holographs. **2.** pertaining to holograms.

ho·log·ra·phy (hə LOG rə fee) *n.* a technique of producing a three-dimensional picture on photographic film using laser beams and without the aid of a camera.

hol·ster (HOHL stər) *n.* a case for a pistol, generally worn on a belt or attached to a saddle. [< Du.]

ho·ly (HOH lee) *adj.* **·li·er, ·li·est 1.** having a divine origin; associated with God; sacred. **2.** having spiritual and moral worth. **3.** designated for religious worship; consecrated: *holy* days. **4.** evoking or meriting reverence or awe: a *holy* man. [ME *holi*]

holy orders *Eccl.* the rite of admission to the priesthood or ministry; ordination.

hom·age (HOM ij) *n.* **1.** respect or honor given or shown. **2.** a payment, etc., indicating allegiance. [ME *omage*]

home (hohm) *n.* **1.** a house or other dwelling where one lives. **2.** a family or other group dwelling together: a happy *home.* **3.** the country, region, city, etc. where one lives. **4.** a peaceful or restful place; haven. **5.** the natural environment of an animal. **6.** the place in which something originates or is found: the *home* of jazz. **7.** a shelter for care of the aged, orphaned, needy, etc. **8.** in some games, esp. baseball, the goal or base that must be reached in order to win or score. —*adj.* **1.** of or pertaining to one's home, country, etc.; domestic. **2.** being at the base of operations or place of origin: the *home* office. —*adv.* **1.** to or at one's home. **2.** to the place or point intended; to the mark. **3.** deeply and intimately; to the heart. —*v.* **homed, hom·ing** *v.t.* **1.** cause (an aircraft or guided missile) to proceed toward a target by means of radio waves, radar, etc. —*v.i.* **2.** go home; return home. **3.** be directed toward a target by automatic devices: said of guided missiles: usu. with *in* or *in on.* [ME *hom*] —**home′less** *adj.*

home·land (HOHM LAND) *n.* the country of one's birth or allegiance.

home·ly (HOHM lee) *adj.* **·li·er, ·li·est 1.** having a familiar, everyday character. **2.** having plain or ugly features. **3.** lacking in refinement. [ME *homly*] —**home′li·ness** *n.*

home·made (HOHM MAYD) *adj.* **1.** made at home. **2.** simply or crudely fashioned.

home·mak·er (HOHM MAY kər) *n.* one in charge of managing one's own home.

ho·me·op·a·thy (HOH mee OP ə thee) *n.* a system of therapy using minute doses of medicines that produce the symptoms of the disease treated. —**ho·me·o·path·ic** (HOH mee ə PATH ik) *adj.*

home plate in baseball, the marker at which a batter stands, and to which he or she returns in scoring a run.

hom·er (HOH mər) *n.* in baseball, a home run.

home rule self-government in local affairs by a state etc.

home run in baseball, a hit that enables the batter to touch all the bases and score a run.

home·sick (HOHM SIK) *adj.* unhappy or ill through longing for home; nostalgic. —**home′sick′ness** *n.*

home·spun (HOHM SPUN) *adj.* **1.** spun at home. **2.** plain and simple; unsophisticated. **3.** made of homespun. —*n.* **1.** fabric woven at home or by hand. **2.** a rough, loosely woven fabric similar to this.

home·stead (HOHM STED) *n.* **1.** a house and its land etc. **2.** a tract of public land acquired and occupied under U.S. law. [< OE *hamstede*] —*v.t. & v.i.* settle on (land) under provisions described in U.S. law. —**home′stead·er** *n.*

home·stretch (HOHM STRECH) *n.* **1.** the straight portion of a racetrack forming the final approach to the finish. **2.** the last stage of any journey or endeavor.

home·ward (HOHM wərd) *adv.* toward home. Also **home′wards.** —*adj.* directed toward home.

home·work (HOHM WURK) *n.* work done at home, esp. school work.

hom·ey (HOH mee) *adj.* **hom·i·er, hom·i·est** suggesting the comforts of home. Also **homy.** —**hom′ey·ness, hom′i·ness** *n.*

hom·i·cide (HOM ə SID) *n.* **1.** the killing of any human being by another. **2.** a person who has killed another. [ME] —**hom·i·cid·al** (HOM ə SID l) *adj.*

hom·i·ly (HOM ə lee) *n. pl.* **·lies 1.** a sermon. **2.** a solemn speech on morals or conduct. [ME *omelie*] —**hom·i·let·ic** (HOM ə LET ik) *adj.*

hom·ing (HOH ming) *adj.* **1.** returning home. **2.** helping or causing an aircraft, missile, etc. to home.

homing pigeon a pigeon capable of making its way home from great distances: also called *carrier pigeon.*

hom·i·ny (HOM ə nee) *n.* kernels of dried, hulled white corn, prepared as a food by boiling. [< Algonquian *uskatahomen,* lit., something beaten]

hominy grits grits (def. 2).

homo- *combining form* same; like. [< Gk.]

ho·mo·ge·ne·ous (HOH mə JEE nee əs) *adj.* **1.** having the same composition, structure, or character throughout; uniform. **2.** similar or identical in nature or form; like. [< Med.L *homogeneus* of the same kind] —**ho·mo·ge·ne·i·ty** (HOH mə jə NEE i tee) *n.*

ho·mog·en·ize (hə MOJ ə NIZ) *v.t.* **·ized, ·iz·ing 1.** make homogeneous. **2.** process, as milk, so as to break up fat globules and disperse them uniformly.

hom·o·graph (HOHM ə GRAF) *n.* a word identical with another in spelling, but differing from it in origin, meaning, or pronunciation, as *wind,* an air current, and *wind,* coil. [< Gk. *homos* same + *graphein* write]

ho·mol·o·gous (hə MOL ə gəs) *adj.* **1.** similar or related in structure, position, value,

homonym

etc. **2.** *Biol.* corresponding in structure or origin: *The foreleg of a horse and the wing of a bird are homologous.* [< Med.L *homologus*]

hom•o•nym (HOM ə nim) *n.* **1.** a word identical with another in pronunciation but differing from it in origin, spelling, and meaning, as *fair* and *fare, read* and *reed:* also called *homophone.* **2.** a word identical with another in spelling and pronunciation, but differing from it in origin and meaning, as *butter,* the food, and *butter,* one who butts. [< L *homonymum*]

hom•o•phone (HOM ə fohn) *n.* a homonym (def. 1).

Ho•mo sa•pi•ens (HOH moh SAY pee ənz) the scientific name for a modern human. [< NL, rational man]

ho•mo•sex•u•al (HOH mə SEK shoo əl) *adj.* of or having sexual desire for persons of the same sex. —*n.* a homosexual individual. —**ho′mo•sex′u•al′i•ty** (-AL i tee) *n.*

ho•mun•cu•lus (hə MUNG kyə ləs) *n. pl.* **-li** (-LI) a little man; dwarf. [< L]

hon•cho (HON choh) *n. Slang* one in charge; a boss. [< Jap. *hanchō* group leader]

hone (hohn) *n.* a fine, compact stone used for sharpening edged tools, razors, etc. [ME] —*v.t.* **honed, hon•ing** sharpen, as a razor, on a hone.

hon•est (ON ist) *adj.* **1.** truthful, forthright, and just; full of integrity. **2.** not false or misleading: *an honest statement.* **3.** having full worth or value; genuine. **4.** performed or earned in a conscientious manner. **5.** sincere; frank. [ME *honeste*] —**hon•es•ty** (ON ə stee) *n.*

hon•est•ly (ON ist lee) *adv.* **1.** in an honest manner. **2.** really; truly; indeed: *Honestly,* I'll go. [ME]

hon•ey (HUN ee) *n. pl.* **hon•eys 1.** a sweet, viscous substance made by bees from nectar gathered from flowers. **2.** sweetness. **3.** *Informal* darling; a term of endearment. **4.** *Informal* something regarded as a superior example of its kind: *a honey of a car.* —*v.t.* **hon•eyed** or **hon•ied, hon•ey•ing 1.** sweeten with or as with honey. **2.** talk in a loving or flattering manner to. —*adj.* of or like honey. [ME *hony*]

hon•ey•bee (HUN ee BEE) *n.* a bee that produces honey.

hon•ey•comb (HUN ee KOHM) *n.* **1.** a structure consisting of series of wax cells, made by bees for the storage of honey, pollen, or their eggs. **2.** any similar structure. —*v.t.* fill with small holes or cavities; riddle.

hon•ey•dew (HUN ee DOO) *n.* a sweetish substance secreted by some insects.

honeydew melon a melon having a smooth, white skin and sweet, greenish pulp.

hon•eyed (HUN eed) *adj.* **1.** full of, consisting of, or resembling honey. **2.** sweet, soothing, or flattering.

hon•ey•moon (HUN ee MOON) *n.* **1.** a vacation spent by a newly married couple. **2.** the first, happy period of a marriage. **3.** the early, happy period of any relationship. —*v.i.* spend one's honeymoon.

honk•y•tonk (HONG kee TONGK) *n.* a noisy, squalid bar or dance hall.

hon•or (ON ər) *n.* **1.** high regard, respect, or esteem. **2.** glory; fame; credit. **3.** *Usu. pl.* an outward token, sign, act, etc. of regard or esteem. **4.** a reputation for high standards of conduct. **5.** a cause or source of esteem or pride. **6.** a privilege or pleasure. **7.** in bridge, one of the five highest cards of a suit. **8.** *cap.* a title or form of address for a judge, mayor, etc.: preceded by *Your, His,* or *Her.* —**do the honors 1.** act as host or hostess. **2.** perform any of various social courtesies, as proposing toasts. —*v.t.* **1.** regard with honor or respect. **2.** treat with courtesy. **3.** confer an honor upon; dignify. **4.** accept or pay, as a check. [ME *honour*]

hon•or•a•ble (ON ər ə bəl) *adj.* **1.** worthy of honor or respect. **2.** conferring honor or credit. **3.** having eminence or high rank. **4.** morally correct; upright. **5.** *cap.* a formal title of courtesy for certain important officials, as cabinet members, justices of the Supreme Court, etc.: preceded by *The.* [ME *honourable*] —**hon′or•a•bly** *adv.*

hon•o•rar•i•um (ON ə RAIR ee əm) *n. pl.* **•rar•i•ums** or **•rar•i•a** (-RAIR ee ə) a payment given, as to a professional person, for services rendered when law or propriety forbids a set fee. [< L, fee]

hon•or•ar•y (ON ə RER ee) *adj.* **1.** designating an office, title, etc. bestowed as an honor, without the customary powers, duties, etc. **2.** bringing, conferred in, or denoting honor. [< L *honorarius*]

hon•or•if•ic (ON ə RIF ik) *adj.* conferring or implying honor or respect.

hood[1] (huud) *n.* **1.** a covering for the head and back of the neck, sometimes forming part of a garment. **2.** anything resembling a hood in form or use; as: **a** the movable cover protecting the engine of an automobile. **b** a projecting cover for a ventilator etc. **3.** *Zool.* in certain animals, as the cobra, the folds of skin near the head, capable of expansion. — *v.t.* cover or furnish with or as with a hood. [ME *hode*] —**hood′ed** *adj.*

hood² *n. Slang* a hoodlum.

-hood *suffix of nouns* **1.** condition or quality of; state of being: *babyhood, falsehood.* **2.** class or totality of those having a certain character: *priesthood.* [ME *-hode*]

hood•lum (HOOD ləm) *n.* **1.** a young street rowdy or tough. **2.** a thug or ruffian.

hoo•doo (HOO doo) *n.* **1.** voodoo. **2.** a jinx. —*v.t.* **•dooed, •doo•ing** bring bad luck to.

hood•wink (HUUD wingk) *v.t.* trick or deceive; cheat.

hoof (huuf) *n. pl.* **hoofs** or **hooves 1.** the horny sheath encasing the foot in various mammals, as horses. **2.** the entire foot of such an animal. —**on the hoof** alive; not butchered: said of cattle. —*v.t. & v.i.* **1.** trample with the hoofs. **2.** *Informal* walk or dance: usually with *it.* [ME] —**hoofed** (huuft) *adj.*

hoof•er (HUUF ər) *Slang* a professional dancer.

hook (huuk) *n.* **1.** a curved or bent implement used to catch hold of something. **2.** something resembling a hook. **3.** in baseball, a curve. **4.** in boxing, a short, swinging blow, with the elbow bent. **5.** in golf, a stroke that sends the ball curving to the left. —**by hook or by crook** by any means. —**off the hook** free from a troublesome situation, obligation, etc. —**on one's own hook** *Informal* by one's own efforts. —*v.t.* **1.** fasten or take hold of with or as with a hook. **2.** make (a rug, mat, etc.) by looping yarn through a backing of canvas or burlap. **3.** in baseball, pitch (the ball) in a curve. **4.** in boxing, strike with a short, swinging blow. **5.** in golf, drive (the ball) so that it hooks. **6.** *Slang* entrap into a bad habit. **7.** *Informal* steal. —*v.i.* **8.** curve like a hook; bend. **9.** be fastened with or as with a hook or hooks. — **hook up** put together or connect. [ME *hoke*]

hook•ah (HUUK ə) *n.* an Oriental tobacco pipe having a long, flexible tube that passes through a vessel of water, thus cooling the smoke. [< Arabic *huqqah*]

hook•er (HUUK ər) *n.* **1.** *Slang* a prostitute. **2.** a drink of usu. undiluted liquor.

hook•y (HUUK ee) *n.* absence from school without permission. —**play hooky** be a truant.

hoo•li•gan (HOO li gən) *n.* a hoodlum; ruffian.

hoop (hoop) *n.* **1.** a circular band of metal, wood, etc.; esp., such a band used to confine the staves of a barrel. **2.** one of the rings of flexible metal etc. used to make a woman's skirt stand out. —*v.t.* surround or fasten with a hoop or hoops. [ME *hope*]

hoop•la (HOOP lah) *n. Informal* noise and excitement.

hoose•gow (HOOS gow) *n. Slang* a jail. [< Sp. *juzgado* jail]

hoot (hoot) *n.* **1.** the cry of an owl. **2.** a sound similar to this, as of a train whistle. **3.** a loud, derisive outcry. —*v.i.* **1.** make such a sound. —*v.t.* **2.** jeer at or mock with derisive cries. [ME *hoten*]

hoot•en•an•ny (HOOT n an ee) *n. pl.* **•nies** a gathering of folk singers, especially for a public performance.

hooves (huuvz) alternative plural of HOOF.

hop¹ (hop) *v.* **hopped, hop•ping** *v.i.* **1.** move by making short leaps on one foot. **2.** move in short leaps on both feet or on all four feet. **3.** *Informal* make a short trip. — *v.t.* **4.** jump over, as a fence. **5.** *Informal* board a vehicle: *hop a freight car.* —*n.* **1.** the act of hopping. **2.** *Informal* a dance or dancing party. **3.** a short trip, esp. by airplane. [ME *hoppen*]

hop² *n.* **1.** a perennial climbing herb with scaly fruit. **2.** *pl.* the dried cones, used medicinally and as a flavoring in beer. —**hop up** *Slang* **1.** increase the power of, as an engine. **2.** stimulate, as with drugs. [ME *hoppe*]

hope (hohp) *v.* **hoped, hop•ing** *v.t.* **1.** desire with expectation of fulfillment. **2.** wish; want. —*v.i.* **3.** have desire or expectation: usually with *for.* —*n.* **1.** desire accompanied by expectation of fulfillment. **2.** that which is desired. **3.** one who or that which is a cause of hopeful expectation. [ME]

hope•ful (HOHP fəl) *adj.* **1.** full of or showing hope. **2.** affording grounds for hope; promising. —*n.* a young person who seems likely to succeed. —**hope′ful•ness** *n.*

hope•ful•ly (HOHP fə lee) *adv.* **1.** in a hopeful manner. **2.** it is hoped: We worked *hopefully.*

hope•less (HOHP lis) *adj.* **1.** without hope; despairing. **2.** affording no ground for hope. —**hope′less•ly** *adv.* —**hope′less•ness** *n.*

hop•per (HOP ər) *n.* **1.** one who or that which hops. **2.** a funnel-shaped receptacle for storing coal, grain, etc. that is emptied through the bottom. **3.** a container in which bills to be considered by a legislative body are placed. [ME]

hop·scotch (HOP SKOCH) *n.* a children's game in which the player hops on one foot over the lines of a diagram, so as to recover a block or pebble.

horde (hord) *n.* a multitude, pack, or swarm, as of people, animals, etc. —*v.i.* **hord·ed, hord·ing** gather in or live in a horde. [< Polish *horda*]

ho·ri·zon (hə RĪ zən) *n.* **1.** the line of the apparent meeting of the sky with the earth or sea. **2.** the bounds or limits of one's observation, knowledge, or experience. [< L]

hor·i·zon·tal (HOR ə ZON tl) *adj.* **1.** of, pertaining to, or close to the horizon. **2.** parallel to the horizon; level: opposed to *vertical.* **3.** consisting of individuals of similar status: *horizontal* trade unionism. —*n.* a line, plane, etc., assumed to be parallel with the horizon. —**hor′i·zon′tal·ly** *adv.*

hor·mone (HOR mohn) *n.* **1.** *Physiol.* an internal secretion produced by one of the endocrine glands and carried by body fluids to other parts of the body, where it has a specific effect. **2.** *Bot.* a similar substance in plants. [< Gk. *hormon* exciting] —**hor·mo′nal** *adj.*

horn (horn) *n.* **1.** a hard, permanent growth of epidermal tissue projecting from the head of various hoofed animals. **2.** the substance of which animal horn is made. **3.** something made from horn: powder *horn.* **4.** something shaped like a horn or the point of a horn: a saddle *horn.* **5.** a device for sounding warning signals: an auto *horn.* **6.** *Music* any of the various brass instruments. **7.** *Geog.* **a** one of the branches forming the delta of a stream or river. **b** a cape or peninsula. —**blow one's own horn** brag. —*adj.* made of horn. —**horn in** *Informal* intrude. [ME]

horned (hornd) *adj.* **1.** having a horn or horns. **2.** having a projection or projections resembling a horn, as a **horned** owl.

hor·net (HOR nit) *n.* any of various wasps capable of inflicting a severe sting. [ME *harnete*]

horn of plenty cornucopia.

horn·y (HOR nee) *adj.* **horn·i·er, horn·i·est 1.** made of horn. **2.** having horns. **3.** hard as horn; tough. **4.** *Vulgar slang* sexually excited. —**horn′i·ness** *n.*

ho·rol·o·gy (haw ROL ə jee) *n.* the science

of the measurement of time or of the construction of timepieces. [< Gk. *hōra* time + -LOGY] —**ho·rol′o·gist** (-jist) *n.*

hor·o·scope (HOR ə SKOHP) *n.* **1.** in astrology, the aspect of the heavens, with special reference to the positions of the planets at any specific instant, esp. at a person's birth. **2.** the diagram of the twelve divisions, or houses, of the heavens. [ME *horoscopus*]

hor·ren·dous (haw REN dəs) *adj.* horrible; frightful. [< L *horrendus*] —**hor·ren′dous·ly** *adv.*

hor·ri·ble (HOR ə bəl) *adj.* **1.** exciting or tending to excite horror; shocking. **2.** inordinate; excessive: a *horrible* liar. **3.** unpleasant; ugly. [ME] —**hor′ri·bly** *adj.*

hor·rid (HOR id) *adj.* **1.** causing great aversion or horror; dreadful. **2.** very objectionable; offensive. [< L *horridus*]

hor·ri·fy (HOR ə FI) *v.t.* **·fied, ·fy·ing 1.** affect or fill with horror. **2.** shock or surprise painfully; startle. [< L *horrificare* induce horror]

hor·ror (HOR ər) *n.* **1.** a painful, strong emotion caused by extreme fear, dread, repugnance, etc. **2.** one who or that which excites such an emotion. **3.** *Informal* something disagreeable, ugly, etc. [< L]

hors d'oeuvre (or DURV) *Usu. pl.* an appetizer, as olives, celery, etc. [< F, lit., outside of work]

horse (hors) *n. pl.* **hors·es 1.** a large, strong, herbivorous mammal with solid hoofs and a long mane and tail, domesticated as a draft or pack animal or for riding. **2.** the full-grown male horse as contrasted with the mare; a gelding or stallion. **3.** mounted soldiers; cavalry. **4.** something likened to a horse, as a workhorse. —**hold one's horses** *Informal* restrain one's impetuosity or impatience. —*v.* **horsed, hors·ing** *v.t.* **1.** furnish with a horse or horses. **2.** put on horseback. —*v.i.* **3.** mount or ride on a horse. **4.** *Slang* engage in horseplay: often with *around.* [ME]

horse·back (HORS BAK) *n.* a horse's back. —**horse′back** *adv.*

horse·car (HORS KAHR) **1.** a streetcar drawn by horses. **2.** a car for transporting horses.

horse·flesh (HORS FLESH) *n.* horses collectively.

horse fly a large fly, the female of which sucks the blood of horses, cattle, etc.

horse·hair (HORS HAIR) *n.* **1.** the hair of horses, esp. that of their manes and tails. **2.**

a fabric made of such hair; haircloth. —**horse′hair′** adj.

horse•hide (HORS HĪD) n. leather made from a horse's hide.

horse latitudes Naut. a belt at about 35° north or south latitude, characterized by calms and light variable winds.

horse•laugh (HORS LAF) n. a loud, scornful laugh.

horse•man (HORS mən) n. pl. **•men** a person skilled in riding a horse. —**horse′•man•ship** n.

horse•play (HORS PLAY) n. rough, boisterous play or fun.

horse•pow•er (HORS POW ər) n. Mech. a unit of the rate of work, equal to 550 pounds lifted one foot in one second.

horse sense common sense.

horse•shoe (HORS SHOO) n. **1.** a U-shaped piece of metal that is nailed to a horse's hoof as a protective device. **2.** something resembling a horseshoe in shape. **3.** pl. a game in which horseshoes are thrown over or near a stake. —v.t. **•shoed, •shoe•ing** furnish with horseshoes.

horseshoe crab a large marine animal having a horseshoe-shaped shell: also called king crab.

horse•whip (HORS HWIP) n. a whip for managing horses. —v.t. **•whipped, •whip•ping** flog with a horsewhip.

horse•wom•an (HORS WUUM ən) n. pl. **•wom•en** a woman skilled in riding a horse.

hors•y (HOR see) adj. **hors•i•er, hors•i•est 1.** resembling, suggesting, or having to do with a horse or horses. **2.** associated with or devoted to horses, horseracing, etc. —**hors′i•ness** n.

hor•ta•to•ry (HOR tə TOR ee) adj. characterized by or giving advice or encouragement. [< LL hortatorius encouraging]

hor•ti•cul•ture (HOR ti KUL chər) n. **1.** the cultivation of a garden. **2.** the art or science of growing garden vegetables, fruits, flowers, etc. [< L hortus garden + E culture cultivation] —**hor′ti•cul′tur•al** adj. —**hor′ti•cul′tur•ist** n.

ho•san•na (hoh ZAN ə) interj. praised be the Lord. —n. **1.** a cry of "hosanna." **2.** any exultant praise. [ME osanna]

hose (hohz) n. pl. **hose** for def. 1; **hos•es** for def. 2 **1.** pl. stockings or socks. **2.** a flexible tube of rubber, plastic, etc., for conveying water and other fluids. [ME] —v.t. **hosed, hos•ing** water, drench, or douse with a hose.

ho•sier•y (HOH zhə ree) n. stockings and socks of all types.

hos•pice (HOS pis) n. **1.** a place of rest or shelter, usu. maintained by a religious order. **2.** Med. a facility for those who are terminally ill. [< F]

hos•pi•ta•ble (HOS pi tə bəl) adj. **1.** kind and generous. **2.** affording or expressing welcome and generosity. **3.** receptive in mind. [< L hospitare entertain]

hos•pi•tal (HOS pi tl) n. an institution that provides medical, surgical, or psychiatric treatment and nursing care. [ME hospitale]

hos•pi•tal•i•ty (HOS pi TAL i tee) n. pl. **•ties** the spirit, practice, or act of being hospitable.

hos•pi•tal•ize (HOS pi tl ĪZ) v.t. **•ized, •iz•ing** put in a hospital for treatment and care. —**hos′pi•tal•i•za′tion** n.

host[1] (hohst) n. **1.** a person who extends hospitality to others, usu. to guests in the person's home. **2.** Biol. any living organism from which a parasite obtains nourishment and protection. [ME hoste]

host[2] n. **1.** a large number; a multitude. **2.** an army. [ME hoste enemy]

Host[3] n. Eccl. the Eucharistic bread or wafer. [ME hoste wafer]

hos•tage (HOS tij) n. a person given or held as a pledge until specified conditions are met, as in war. [ME]

hos•tel (HOS tl) n. a supervised lodging house for young travelers. Also called youth hostel. [ME, hospice]

hos•tel•ry (HOS tl ree) n. pl. **•ries** a lodging place; inn. [ME hostelrye] —**hos•tel•er** (HOS tl ər) n. a person who operates a hostel.

host•ess (HOH stis) n. **1.** a woman who performs the duties of a host. **2.** a woman employed in a restaurant etc. to greet and seat guests. [ME hostesse]

hos•tile (HOS tl) adj. having or expressing enmity or opposition; unfriendly. [< L hostilis] —**hos′tile•ly** adv.

hos•til•i•ty (ho STIL i tee) n. pl. **•ties 1.** the state of being hostile. **2.** a hostile act. **3.** pl. war or acts of war. [ME hostilite]

hot (hot) adj. **hot•ter, hot•test 1.** having or giving off great heat; having a high temperature. **2.** feeling abnormal bodily warmth. **3.** giving the sensation of heat or burning: hot pepper. **4.** carrying an electric current, esp. one of high voltage. **5.** dangerously radioactive. **6.** not far behind: in hot pursuit. **7.** showing strong or violent emotion: *hot* words. **8.** marked by intense activity; raging; violent: a *hot* battle. **9.** *Slang* lustful; sexually aroused. **10.** controversial: a *hot* issue. **11.** *Informal* in demand: a *hot* item. **12.** *Informal* excellent, skillful, etc.: often in the negative: not too *hot* an actor. **13.** *Slang* recently stolen. **14.** recent; fresh: *hot* news. [ME] —**hot′ly** *adv.*

hot air *Informal* empty or pretentious talk; exaggeration.

hot•bed (HOT BED) *n.* **1.** a bed of rich earth, protected by glass and used to promote the growth of plants. **2.** a place or condition favoring rapid growth or great activity.

hot-blood•ed (HOT BLUD id) *adj.* easily moved or excited.

hot dog a frankfurter.

hot-dog (HOT DAWG) *v.i.* •**dogged,** •**dog•ging** *Informal* perform showy maneuvers in skiing or surfing.

hos•tel (hoh TEL) *n.* an establishment or building providing lodging, food, etc. to travelers and permanent residents. [< OF *hôtel*]

hot•head (HOT HED) *n.* a hotheaded person.

hot-head•ed (HOT HED id) *adj.* **1.** quick-tempered. **2.** impetuous. —**hot′head′ed•ness** *n.*

hot•house (HOT HOWS) *n.* a greenhouse.

hot line a direct means of communication, esp. a telephone line for emergency use between Washington and Moscow.

hot plate a small portable gas or electric stove.

hot rod *Slang* an automobile modified for high speeds.

hou•dah (HOW də) see HOWDAH.

hound (hownd) *n.* **1.** a dog kept for hunting, esp. one that hunts by scent and in a pack. **2.** a dog of any breed. —*v.t.* **1.** hunt or pursue with or as with hounds. **2.** *Informal* nag; pester. [ME]

hour (owr) *n.* **1.** a space of time equal to 1/24 of a day; sixty minutes. **2.** a time of day. **3.** an indefinite period of time: My happiest *hour.* **4.** *pl.* a set period of time for work or other pursuits: school *hours.* [ME *houre*]

hour•glass (OWR GLAS) *n.* a timing device having two glass vessels connected by a narrow neck through which a quantity of sand or mercury runs in a stated interval of time, usu. an hour.

hou•ri (HUUR ee) *n. pl.* •**ris** in Muslim belief, one of the beautiful virgins allotted to those who attain Paradise. [< F]

hour•ly (OWR lee) *adj.* **1.** happening or done every hour. **2.** happening or done within an hour. **3.** frequent. —*adv.* **1.** at intervals of an hour. **2.** hour by hour. **3.** frequently; continually.

house (hows) *n. pl.* **hous•es** (HOW ziz) **1.** a building used as a dwelling for human beings. **2.** a household; family. **3.** a communal dwelling, as a dormitory. **4.** a building used for any of various purposes: a *house* of correction. **5.** a theater or other place of entertainment. **6.** the audience in such a place of entertainment. **7.** a legislative or deliberative body: *House* of Representatives. **8.** a business firm or establishment: a publishing *house.* **9.** in astrology: **a** one of the twelve divisions of the heavens. **b** a sign of the zodiac considered as the seat of greatest influence of a particular planet. [ME *hous*] —*v.* (howz) **housed, hous•ing** *v.t.* **1.** take or put into a house; lodge. **2.** store in a house or building. **3.** encase or enclose. —*v.i.* **4.** take shelter or lodgings; dwell. —**house′ful** (HOWS fuul) *n. pl.* •**fuls.**

house•boat (HOWS BOHT) *n.* a barge or flat-bottomed boat fitted out as a dwelling and used in quiet waters.

house•break•ing (HOWS BRAY king) *n.* the act of breaking into and entering another's home with intent to commit theft or some other felony. —**house′break′er** *n.*

house•bro•ken (HOWS BROH kən) *adj.* trained to urinate and defecate outdoors or in a specific place, as a dog. •

house•coat (HOWS KOHT) *n.* a woman's garment, usu. long, for informal wear within the house.

house•fly (HOWS FLI) *n. pl.* •**flies** the common fly.

house•hold (HOWS HOHLD) *n.* **1.** a group of persons sharing a dwelling. **2.** a home or the affairs of a home. [ME *household*] —**house′hold** *adj.*

house•hold•er (HOWS HOHL dər) *n.* **1.** one who owns or occupies a house. **2.** the head of a family.

household word a widely familiar name.

house•keep•er (HOWS KEE pər) *n.* **1.** one who performs the tasks of maintaining a home. **2.** a hotel employee who supervises the cleaning staff. —**house′•keep′ing** *n.*

house•maid (HOWS MAYD) *n.* a female servant employed to do housework.

House of Commons 1. the lower house of the British Parliament. **2.** the lower house of the Canadian Parliament.

House of Lords the upper, nonelective house of the British Parliament, made up of peers and the highest ranking clergy.

House of Representatives 1. the lower branch of the United States Congress, and of many state legislatures, whose members are elected on the basis of population. **2.** a similar legislative body, as in Australia, Mexico, etc.

house organ a publication issued by a business organization for its employees and clients.

house party an entertainment of guests for several days.

house·top (HOWS TOP) n. the roof of a house.

house·wares (HOWS WAIRZ) n.pl. kitchen utensils, dishes, etc. used in the home.

house·warm·ing (HOWS WOR ming) n. a party held to celebrate a move into a new home.

house·wife (HOWS WĪF) n. pl. ·wives (-WIVZ) a married woman who manages her own household. [ME huswif]

house·work (HOWS WURK) n. the chores involved in keeping house.

hous·ing (HOW zing) n. **1.** the act of providing shelter or lodging; also, the shelter or lodging so provided. **2.** houses or dwelling collectively. **3.** a structure that covers or protects.

hove (hohv) a past tense of HEAVE.

hov·el (HUV əl) n. **1.** a small, wretched dwelling. **2.** a shed for sheltering cattle, tools, etc. [ME hovell] —v.t. **hov·eled, hov·el·ing** shelter or lodge in a hovel.

hov·er (HUV ər) v.i. **1.** remain suspended in or near one place in the air. **2.** linger or remain nearby, as if watching: with around, near, etc. **3.** remain in an uncertain or irresolute state: with between. —n. the act or state of hovering. [ME hoveren]

how (how) adv. **1.** in what way or manner. **2.** to what degree, extent, or amount. **3.** in what state, or condition. **4.** for what reason or purpose. **5.** by what name or designation. **6.** what: How about having lunch? —n. a manner or means of doing. [ME]

how·dah (HOW də) n. a seat for riders on an elephant or camel, often fitted with a canopy. [< Hind. haudah]

how-do-you-do (HOW də yə DOO) n. pl. -dos Informal an embarrassing or difficult situation: usu. preceded by fine, pretty, etc.

how·ev·er (how EV ər) adv. **1.** in whatever manner. **2.** to whatever degree or extent. —conj. nevertheless; in spite of; still; yet.

how·it·zer (HOW it sər) n. a cannon of medium length operating at a high angle of fire. [< Du. houvietser]

howl (howl) v.i. **1.** utter the loud wail of a dog, wolf, or other animal. —v.t. **2.** utter or express with howling. [ME hulen] —howl n.

howl·er (HOW lər) n. **1.** one who or that which howls. **2.** an absurd blunder.

howl·ing (HOW ling) adj. **1.** producing, characterized by, or filled with howls: a howling mob. **3.** Informal very great: a howling success.

how·so·ev·er (HOW soh EV ər) adv. **1.** in whatever manner. **2.** to whatever degree or extent. [ME]

hoy·den (HOID n) n. a boisterous or ill-mannered girl. —adj. boisterous. —hoy'den·ish adj.

hua·ra·che (wə RAH chee) n. a flat sandal having a top of woven leather strips. [< Mexican Sp.]

hub (hub) n. **1.** the center part of a wheel into which the axle is inserted. **2.** any center of great activity or interest.

hub·bub (HUB ub) n. a loud, confused noise, as of many voices shouting or talking.

hub·cap (HUB KAP) n. a detachable cover for the hub of a wheel.

hu·bris (HYOO bris) n. arrogant pride. [< Gk. hybris]

hud·dle (HUD l) v. ·dled, ·dling v.i. **1.** crowd or nestle together closely. **2.** draw or hunch oneself together. **3.** in football, gather in a huddle. —v.t. **4.** bring or crowd together closely. —n. **1.** a number of persons or things crowded together. **2.** in football, the grouping of a team before play. **3.** any small conference.

hue¹ (hyoo) n. **1.** the attribute of a color that determines its position in the spectrum. **2.** color: autumnal hues. **3.** a particular tint or shade of color. [ME hewe] —hued adj.

hue² n. an outcry; shouting. —hue and cry any great public stir. [ME hu]

huff (huf) n. a fit of sudden anger or irritation. —v.i. puff; blow. —huff'ish adj.

huf·fy (HUF ee) adj. **huff·i·er, huff·i·est 1.** touchy. **2.** petulant; sulky. —huff'i·ness n.

hug (hug) v.t. **hugged, hug·ging 1.** hold against the body, as in affection. **2.** cherish or cling to, as a belief. **3.** keep close to. —hug n.

huge (hyooj) *adj.* very great in size, quantity, extent, etc. [ME]

hulk (hulk) *n.* **1.** the body of an old or wrecked ship. **2.** any bulky, unwieldy object or person. —*v.i.* appear or move as if a hulk. [ME *hulke*]

hulk·ing (HUL king) *adj.* big and unwieldy.

hull (hul) *n.* **1.** the outer covering of certain fruits or seeds. **2.** any outer covering. **3.** *Naut.* the body of a ship, exclusive of the masts, etc. —*v.t.* remove the hull of. [ME]

hul·la·ba·loo (HUL ə bə LOO) *n.* a loud, confused noise; uproar.

hum (hum) *v.* **hummed, hum·ming** *v.i.* **1.** make a low, murmuring or droning sound. **2.** sing with the lips closed. **3.** be very busy or active: *The office hummed.* —*v.t.* **4.** sing with closed lips without words. **5.** affect by humming: *hum an infant to sleep.* [ME] —**hum** *n.* —**hum′mer** *n.*

hu·man (HYOO mən) *adj.* of, characteristic of, or having the nature or attributes of a human being. [ME] —**hu′man** *n.* —**hu′man·ness** *n.*

human being a person.

hu·mane (hyoo MAYN) *adj.* **1.** having kindness, sympathy, etc.; benevolent. **2.** tending to refine or civilize: *humane studies.*

hu·man·ism (HYOO mə NIZ əm) *n.* **1.** the character or quality of being human. **2.** a system or attitude in thought, religion, etc. in which human ideals are made central. **3.** *Often cap.* the intellectual and literary movement of the Renaissance, characterized by the study of Greek and Roman classics. **4.** the study of the humanities. —**hu′man·ist** *n.* —**hu′man·is′tic** *adj.*

hu·man·i·tar·i·an (hyoo MAN i TAIR ee ən) *n.* one who seeks to promote the welfare of mankind; philanthropist. —**hu·man′i·tar′i·an** *adj.* —**hu·man′i·tar′i·an·ism** *n.*

hu·man·i·ty (hyoo MAN i tee) *n. pl.* **·ties 1.** the human race; humankind. **2.** the state of being human; human nature. **3.** the state of being humane; benevolence. —**the humanities 1.** the study of classical Greek and Latin literature. **2.** literature, philosophy, the fine arts, etc., as distinguished from the sciences. [ME *humanite*]

hu·man·ize (HYOO mə NIZ) *v.t.* **·ized, ·iz·ing 1.** make human; give human characteristics to. **2.** make gentle, kindly, etc.

hu·man·kind (HYOO mən KIND) *n.* people; humanity.

hu·man·ly (HYOO mən lee) *adv.* **1.** in a human manner. **2.** within human power or ability: *humanly possible.* **3.** in accordance with people's experience or knowledge.

hu·man·oid (HYOO mə NOID) *adj.* almost human in characteristics and form. —*n.* an almost human creature, as: **a** an early ancestor of modern man. **b** a creature of science fiction.

hum·ble (HUM bəl) *adj.* **·bler, ·blest 1.** free from pride or vanity; modest. **2.** lowly in station, condition, etc.; unpretentious. **3.** respectful. —*v.t.* **·bled, ·bling 1.** reduce the pride of. **2.** lower in rank or dignity. [ME] —**hum′bly** *adv.*

hum·bug (HUM BUG) *n.* **1.** anything intended or used to delude; fraud. **2.** one who seeks to deceive others. —*v.t.* **·bugged, ·bug·ging** delude; trick.

hum·ding·er (HUM DING ər) *n. Informal* anyone or anything remarkable or extraordinary.

hum·drum (HUM DRUM) *adj.* lacking interest, variety, or excitement; dull.

hu·mer·us (HYOO mər əs) *n. pl.* **·mer·i** (-mə RI) *Anat.* the bone of the upper part of the arm, from shoulder to elbow. [ME] —**hu′mer·al** (-əl) *adj.*

hu·mid (HYOO mid) *adj.* moist; damp. [ME]

hu·mid·i·fy (hyoo MID ə FI) *v.t.* **·fied, ·fy·ing** make moist. —**hu·mid′i·fi′er** *n.*

hu·mid·i·ty (hyoo MID i tee) *n.* moisture; dampness, esp. of the atmosphere. [ME *humydite*]

hu·mi·dor (HYOO mi DOR) *n.* a container in which moisture is retained, used for cigars or other tobacco products.

hu·mil·i·ate (hyoo MIL ee AYT) *v.t.* **·at·ed, ·at·ing** lower the pride or self-esteem of; mortify. [< LL *humiliatus* humbled] —**hu·mil′i·a′tion** *n.*

hu·mil·i·ty (hyoo MIL i tee) *n.* the state or quality of being humble. [ME *humilite*]

hum·mock (HUM ək) *n.* a low mound of earth or rock; hillock.

hu·mon·gous (hyoo MUNG gəs) *adj. Slang* extraordinarily large.

hu·mor (HYOO mər) *n.* **1.** the quality of anything that is funny or appeals to the comic sense. **2.** the ability to appreciate or express what is amusing, comic, etc. **3.** speech, writing, or actions that are amusing or comic. **4.** temperament; disposition. **5.** *Med. physiol.* a liquid or semiliquid substance of the body, as blood, bile, lymph, etc. —*v.t.* comply with the moods of; indulge. [ME *humour* moisture] —**hu′mor·less** *adj.* —**hu′mor·ous** *adj.*

hu·mor·ist (HYOO mər ist) *n.* **1.** one who exercises a sense of humor; joker; wit. **2.** a professional writer, entertainer, etc. specializing in humor or jokes.

hump (hump) *n.* **1.** a rounded protuberance, esp. on the back, as in the camel, or the deformity produced in a person by a curvature of the spine. **2.** a low mound; hummock. —**over the hump** beyond the most critical point.

hump·back (HUMP BAK) *n.* **1.** a hunchback. **2.** a large whale. —**hump′backed′** *adj.*

hu·mus (HYOO məs) *n.* the black or brown substance of the soil, formed by the decay of animal and vegetable matter, and providing nutrition for plant life. [< L, soil]

hunch (hunch) *n.* a premonition of some coming event. —*v.t. & v.i.* bend or draw up so as to form a hump.

hunch·back (HUNCH BAK) *n.* **1.** a deformed back with a hump. **2.** a person so deformed. —**hunch′backed′** *adj.*

hun·dred (HUN drid) *n.* the sum of ninety and ten, written as 100 or C: a cardinal number. [ME] —**hun′dred** *adj.* —**hun·dredth** (HUN dridth) *adj. & n.*

hung (hung) past tense, past participle of HANG.

hun·ger (HUNG gər) *n.* **1.** the state of discomfort or weakness caused by lack of food. **2.** a desire or need for food. **3.** any strong desire or craving. —*v.i.* **1.** be hungry. **2.** have a desire or craving: with *for* or *after.* [ME]

hunger strike a fast undertaken as a means of protest.

hun·gry (HUNG gree) *adj.* **·gri·er, ·gri·est 1.** desiring or in need of food. **2.** eagerly craving: *hungry* for applause. **3.** indicating hunger: a *hungry* look. [ME] —**hun′·gri·ly** *adv.*

hunk (hungk) *n.* a large piece or lump; chunk. [< Du. *hunke*]

hun·ky-do·ry (HUNG kee DOR ee) *adj. Slang* fully satisfactory; all right.

hunt (hunt) *v.t.* **1.** pursue (game) for the purpose of killing or catching. **2.** range over (an area) in search of game. **3.** pursue with hostility, violence, etc. **4.** search for eagerly; seek: *hunt* the truth. —*v.i.* **5.** seek or pursue game. **6.** search or seek: often with *for* or *after.* —**hunt down 1.** pursue until caught or killed. **2.** search for until found.

—*n.* **1.** the act of hunting game; chase. **2.** a group of huntsmen. **3.** a search; pursuit. [ME *hunten*] —**hunt′ing** *n. & adj.*

hunt·er (HUN tər) *n.* **1.** one who hunts. **2.** an animal used in hunting, as a dog or horse.

hunts·man (HUNTS mən) *n. pl.* **·men 1.** one who hunts game; hunter. **2.** one who directs a hunt, hounds, etc.

hur·dle (HUR dl) *n.* **1.** a light, portable barrier. **2.** *pl.* a race in which such barriers are used: often with *the.* **3.** an obstacle or difficulty to be surmounted. —*v.t.* **·dled, ·dling 1.** leap over (a barrier) in a race. **2.** surmount or overcome (a difficulty etc.). [ME *hirdel*] —**hur′dler** *n.*

hur·dy-gur·dy (HUR dee GUR dee) *n. pl.* **·dies** a musical instrument played by turning a crank.

hurl (hurl) *v.t.* **1.** throw, fling, pitch, or send with force. **2.** utter with vehemence. —*n.* the act of hurling. [ME *hurlen*] —**hurl′er** *n.*

hurl·ing (HUR ling) *n.* an Irish game resembling field hockey. [ME]

hur·ly-bur·ly (HUR lee BUR lee) *n.* tumult; confusion; turmoil. [< earlier *hurling and burling*]

hur·rah (hə RAH) *n. & interj.* an exclamation expressing triumph, joy, encouragement, etc. [< G *hurra*] —**hur·rah′** *v.i.*

hur·ri·cane (HUR ə KAYN) *n.* a severe tropical cyclone, esp. one originating in the Caribbean, having a wind velocity exceeding 75 miles per hour. [< Sp. *huracán*]

hur·ried (HUR eed) *adj.* **1.** urged or forced to move, act, etc. in haste. **2.** done or carried on in great or too great haste: a *hurried* decision. —**hur′ried·ly** *adv.*

hur·ry (HUR ee) *v.* **·ried, ·ry·ing** *v.i.* **1.** act or move rapidly or in haste; hasten. —*v.t.* **2.** cause or urge to act or move more rapidly. **3.** hasten the progress etc. of, often unduly. —*n.* **1.** the act of hurrying; haste. **2.** eagerness to move, act, etc. [? ME *horyed* rushed]

hurt (hurt) *v.* **hurt, hurt·ing** *v.t.* **1.** cause physical harm or pain to; injure. **2.** impair in some way: *hurt* one's reputation. **3.** grieve or distress. —*v.i.* **4.** cause discomfort, suffering, or damage. [ME *hurten* damage] —**hurt** *n.* —**hurt′ful** (-fəl) *adj.*

hur·tle (HUR tl) *n.* **·tled, ·tling** *v.i.* **1.** rush headlong or impetuously. —*v.t.* **2.** throw or drive violently. [ME]

hus·band (HUZ bənd) *n.* a married man. —

v.t. use or spend wisely; conserve: *husband* one's savings. [ME *husbonde*]

hus·band·ry (HUZ bən dree) *n.* **1.** the occupation or business of farming. **2.** thrift. [ME *husbondrie*]

hush (hush) *v.t.* **1.** make silent; cause to be quiet. **2.** keep hidden or secret: usu. with *up.* **3.** soothe or allay, as fears. —*n.* deep silence; quiet. —*interj.* be quiet!

hush-hush (HUSH HUSH) *adj.* secret.

hush puppy *Southern U.S.* a small fried ball of cornmeal.

husk (husk) *n.* **1.** the outer coating of certain fruits or seeds, esp. of an ear of corn. **2.** any outer covering, esp. when comparatively worthless. —*v.t.* remove the husk or outer covering of. [ME *huske*]

husk·y¹ (HUS kee) *adj.* **husk·i·er, husk·i·est** rough or coarse in vocal quality. —**husk'i·ness** *n.*

husk·y² *adj.* **husk·i·er, husk·i·est** physically strong; burly. —*n. pl.* **husk·ies 1.** a strong or powerful person. **2.** a heavy-coated working dog of the Arctic.

hus·sar (huu ZAHR) *n.* a member of a cavalry regiment found in some European armies and usu. distinguished by brilliant dress uniforms. ◄< Hungarian *huszár*]

hus·sy (HUS ee) *n. pl.* **·sies 1.** an immoral woman. **2.** a pert or forward girl; minx.

hust·ings (HUS tingz) *n.* (*usu. construed as sing.*) **1.** the election campaign trail. **2.** any place where political speeches are made. [ME]

hus·tle (HUS əl) *v.* **·tled, ·tling** *v.t.* **1.** push about or crowd roughly; jostle. **2.** force, push, or thrust hurriedly. **3.** cause to proceed rapidly or too rapidly; hurry. **4.** *Slang* sell or solicit (something) in an aggressive or unethical manner. —*v.i.* **5.** push or shove; elbow. **6.** move or work with great energy. **7.** *Slang* make money by clever or unscrupulous means. **8.** *Slang* solicit clients: said of a prostitute. —*n.* **1.** the act of hustling. **2.** energetic activity; drive; push. **3.** *Slang* a scheme for making money. [< Du. *husselen* shake, toss]

hus·tler (HUS lər) *n.* **1.** an energetic, enterprising person. **2.** *Slang* one who engages in petty frauds and thievery. **3.** *Informal* a professional gambler. **4.** *Slang* a prostitute.

hut (hut) *n.* a small, rude house or cabin; hovel. [< F *hutte*]

hutch (huch) *n.* **1.** a coop or pen for small animals. **2.** a chest, locker, or bin in which to store things; also, a cupboard for dishes. **3.** a small cottage or cabin. [ME *hucche*]

hutz·pah (KHUUT spə) see CHUTZPAH.

huz·zah (hə ZAH) *n. & interj.* an exclamation of joy, triumph, etc. —**huz·zah'** *v.i. & v.t.*

hy·brid (HĪ brid) *n.* **1.** an animal or plant produced by a male and female of different species, varieties, or breeds. **2.** anything of mixed origin. [< L *hybrida* crossbred animal] —**hy'brid** *adj.* —**hy·brid·ism** (HĪ bri DIZ əm) *n.*

hy·brid·ize (HĪ bri DĪZ) *v.t. & v.i.* **ized, ·iz·ing** produce or cause to produce hybrids. —**hy'brid·iz'er** *n.*

hy·dra (HĪ drə) *n. pl.* **·dras** or **·drae** (-dree) any of various freshwater polyps, having a long, slender body and tentacles. [< L]

hy·drant (HĪ drənt) *n.* a large, upright pipe connected to a water main, used for firefighting.

hy·drau·lic (hī DRAW lik) *adj.* **1.** of or pertaining to hydraulics. **2.** operated by water or other liquid under pressure. **3.** hardening under water: *hydraulic* cement. [< L *hydraulicus* hydraulic organ] —**hy·drau'li·cal·ly** *adv.*

hy·drau·lics (hī DRAW liks) *n.* (*construed as sing.*) the science of the laws governing the motion of water and other liquids and of their practical applications in engineering.

hydro- *combining form* water; of, related to, or resembling water. [< Gk., combing form of *hydōr* water]

hy·dro·car·bon (HĪ drə KAHR bən) *n. Chem.* one of a large and important group of organic compounds that contain hydrogen and carbon only.

hy·dro·ceph·a·lus (HĪ drə SEF ə ləs) *n. Pathol.* an accumulation of fluid within the brain, causing abnormal enlargement of the head. Also **hy'dro·ceph'a·ly.** [< LL *hydrocephalus* water-headed] —**hy·dro·ce·phal·ic** (HĪ droh sə FAL ik) *adj.*

hy·dro·dy·nam·ics (HĪ droh dī NAM iks) *n.* (*construed as sing.*) the branch of dynamics dealing with the motions and forces of liquids, esp. water. —**hy'dro·dy·nam'ic** *adj.*

hy·dro·e·lec·tric (HĪ droh i LEK trik) *adj.* of or pertaining to electricity generated by the energy of running water.

hy·dro·foil (HĪ drə FOIL) *n.* **1.** a structure designed to lift and support the hull of a boat moving at high speed in water. **2.** such a boat.

hy·dro·gen (HĪ drə jən) *n.* the lightest of the elements (symbol H), an odorless, colorless, flammable gas, occurring chiefly in combination. —**hy·drog·e·nous** (HĪ DROJ ə nəs) *adj.*

hy·dro·gen·ate (HĪ drə jə NAYT) *v.t.* •**at·ed, •at·ing** *Chem.* combine with, treat with, or expose to the chemical action of hydrogen.

hydrogen bomb a thermonuclear weapon releasing energy by the fusion, under extremely high temperatures, of light elements: also called *H-bomb.*

hydrogen peroxide *Chem.* an unstable, colorless liquid, used for bleaching etc.

hy·drog·ra·phy (hī DROG rə fee) *n.* the science of surveying, describing, and mapping seas, rivers, etc. —**hy·drog′ra·pher** *n.* —**hy·dro·graph·ic** (HĪ drə GRAF ik) *adj.*

hy·drol·o·gy (hī DROL ə jee) *n.* the branch of physical geography that deals with the waters of the earth and their distribution, characteristics, and effects in relation to human activities. —**hy·drol′o·gist** *n.*

hy·drom·e·ter (hī DROM i tər) *n.* an instrument for determining the specific gravity of a liquid.

hy·dro·pho·bi·a (HĪ drə FOH bee ə) *n.* **1.** rabies. **2.** a morbid fear of water. — **hy′dro·pho′bic** *adj.*

hy·dro·plane (HĪ drə PLAYN) *n.* **1.** a seaplane. **2.** a type of motorboat designed so that its hull is raised partially out of the water when driven at high speeds. **3.** a hydrofoil (def. 2). —*v.i.* •**planed, •plan·ing** move at great speed on the water.

hy·dro·pon·ics (HĪ drə PON iks) *n.* (*construed as sing.*) the science of growing plants with their roots in nutrient solutions rather than in soil. —**hy′dro·pon′ic** *adj.*

hy·dro·sphere (HĪ drə SFEER) *n.* **1.** the total water on the surface of the earth. **2.** the moisture in the earth's atmosphere.

hy·dro·stat·ics (HĪ drə STAT iks) *n.* (*construed as sing.*) the science that deals with the pressure and equilibrium of fluids. — **hy′dro·stat′ic** *adj.*

hy·dro·ther·a·py (HĪ drə THER ə pee) *n.* the scientific use of water to treat various diseases.

hy·e·na (hī EE nə) *n.* any of a group of wolflike mammals of Africa and Asia, with short hind legs, a bristly mane, and strong teeth. [ME *hiena* hog]

hy·giene (HĪ jeen) *n.* the science of health. [< F *hygiène*]

hy·gi·en·ic (HĪ jee EN ik) *adj.* **1.** of or pertaining to hygiene. **2.** sanitary. — **hy·gien·ist** (hī JEE nist) *n.*

hygro- *combining form* wet; moist. [< Gk., combining form of *hygrós* water]

hy·grom·e·ter (hī GROM i tər) *n.* an instrument for measuring humidity or moisture in air.

hy·gro·scop·ic (HĪ grə SKOP ik) *adj.* absorbing moisture from the air.

hy·men (HĪ mən) *n. Anat.* a thin mucous membrane partially covering the vaginal orifice. [< LL]

hy·me·ne·al (HĪ mə NEE əl) *adj.* nuptial. —*n.* a wedding song or poem. [after *Hymen,* Greek god of marriage]

hymn (him) *n.* a song of praise, adoration, thanksgiving, etc., esp. one sung at a religious service. [< L *hymnus*] —**hymn** *v.t. & v.i.* —**hym′nist** *n.*

hym·nal (HĪM nl) *n.* a book of hymns. Also **hymn′book′.** —*adj.* of or relating to a hymn or hymns.

hype (hīp) *v.t.* **hyped, hyp·ing** *Informal* **1.** increase artificially: *hype* the profit figure. **2.** stimulate: often with *up.* **3.** deceive. **4.** publicize extravagantly. —*n.* **1.** a narcotics addict, esp. one using a hypodermic needle. **2.** a deception. **3.** one who or that which is promoted by hype.

hyper- *prefix* **1.** over; above; excessive: *hyperaggressive, hypercautious.* **2.** *Med.* denoting an abnormal state of excess: *hyperglycemia.* [< Gk. *hyper* above]

hy·per·a·cid·i·ty (HĪ pər ə SID i tee) *n. Med.* an excess of acidity, as of the gastric juice.

hy·per·ac·tive (HĪ pər AK tiv) *adj.* abnormally active. —**hy′per·ac·tiv′i·ty** *n.*

hy·per·bar·ic (HĪ pər BAR ik) *adj.* relating to the use of oxygen under pressure: *hyperbaric* chamber.

hy·per·bo·la (hī PUR bə lə) *n. Math.* the curve produced by the intersection of a plane through the surface of a cone. [< NL]

hy·per·bo·le (hī PUR bə lee) *n.* an exaggeration or overstatement not intended to be taken literally, as: *I slept forever.* [< Gk. *hyperbolē* exaggeration]

hy·per·bol·ic (HĪ pər BOL ik) *adj.* **1.** of, pertaining to, or using hyperbole. **2.** *Math.* of or pertaining to the hyperbola.

hy·per·crit·i·cal (HĪ pər KRIT i kəl) *adj.* excessively critical or carping; faultfinding.

hy·per·gly·ce·mi·a (HĪ pər glī SEE mee ə) *n.* an abnormally high level of sugar in the blood. [< NL] —**hy'per·gly·ce'mic** *adj.*

hy·per·sen·si·tive (HĪ pər SEN si tiv) *adj.* **1.** excessively sensitive. **2.** allergic. —**hy'per·sen'si·tiv'i·ty** *n.*

hy·per·son·ic (HĪ pər SON ik) *adj.* of, pertaining to, or characterized by supersonic speeds of mach 5 or greater.

hy·per·ten·sion (HĪ pər TEN shən) *n. Pathol.* high blood pressure. —**hy'per·ten'sive** (-siv) *adj.*

hy·per·text (HĪ pər TEKST) *n. Computers* a sophisticated system of cross-links, analogous to cross-references in a printed text, that alerts computer users to the availability of related information and enables them to gain immediate access to it.

hy·per·thy·roid·ism (HĪ pər THĪ roi DIZ əm) *n. Pathol.* **1.** excessive activity of the thyroid gland. **2.** any disorder caused by this. —**hy'per·thy'roid** *adj. & n.*

hy·per·tro·phy (hī PUR trə fee) *n. pl.* **·phies** *Pathol.* **1.** the excessive development of an organ or part. **2.** the enlargement resulting from such a condition. —*v.i. & v.t.* **·phied, ·phy·ing** grow or cause to grow excessively. —**hy·per·troph·ic** (hī pər TROF ik) *adj.*

hy·phen (HĪ fən) *n.* a mark (-) used to connect the elements of certain compound words or to show division of a word at the end of a line. —*v.t.* hyphenate. [< LL]

hy·phen·ate (HĪ fə NAYT) *v.t.* **·at·ed, ·at·ing 1.** connect by a hyphen. **2.** write with a hyphen. —**hy'phen·a'tion** *n.*

hypno- *combining form* sleep. [< Gk. *hypnos* sleep]

hyp·no·sis (hip NOH sis) *n. pl.* **·ses** (-seez) a trancelike condition that can be artificially induced, characterized by an increased responsiveness to suggestion.

hyp·not·ic (hip NOT ik) *adj.* **1.** pertaining to hypnosis or hypnotism. **2.** readily hypnotized. **3.** tending to produce sleep. —*n.* **1.** a drug or other agent producing sleep. **2.** a hypnotized person, or one susceptible to hypnosis. **3.** a sedative. —**hyp·not'i·cal·ly** *adv.*

hyp·no·tism (HIP nə TIZ əm) *n.* the act, practice, or study of hypnosis. —**hyp'no·tist** *n.*

hyp·no·tize (HIP nə TĪZ) *v.t.* **·tized, ·tiz·ing 1.** produce hypnosis in. **2.** fascinate; charm.

hy·po¹ (HĪ poh) *n. Photog.* sodium thiosulfate, used as a fixing agent.

hy·po² *n. pl.* **·pos** *Informal* a hypodermic injection.

hypo- *prefix* **1.** under; beneath. **2.** less than. **3.** *Med.* denoting a lack of or deficiency in. [< Gk. *hypo* under]

hy·po·chon·dri·a (HĪ pə KON dree ə) *n.* a persistent anxiety about one's health, often with imagined symptoms of illness. [< LL] —**hy'po·chon'dri·ac'** *adj. & n.*

hy·poc·ri·sy (hi POK rə see) *n. pl.* **·sies** the pretense of having feelings or characteristics one does not possess; esp., the deceitful assumption of virtue. [ME *ipocrisie*]

hyp·o·crite (HIP ə krit) *n.* one who practices hypocrisy. —**hyp'o·crit'i·cal** *adj.* [ME *ipocrite*]

hy·po·der·mic (HĪ pə DUR mik) *adj.* **1.** of or pertaining to the area under the skin. **2.** injected under the skin. —*n.* a hypodermic injection or syringe.

hypodermic syringe a syringe having a hollow needle for injection of substances beneath the skin.

hy·po·gly·ce·mi·a (HĪ POH GLĪ SEE MEE ə) *N.* an abnormally low level of sugar in the blood. —**hy'po·gly·ce'mic** *adj.*

hy·pot·e·nuse (hī POT n OOS) *n. Geom.* the side of a right triangle opposite the right angle. [< L *hypotenusa*]

hy·poth·e·cate (hī POTH i KAYT) *v.t.* **·cat·ed, ·cat·ing** *Law* pledge (personal property) as security for debt without transfer of possession. [< Med.L *hypothecatus* pledged] —**hy·poth'e·ca'tion** *n.*

hy·poth·e·sis (hī POTH ə sis) *n. pl.* **·ses** (-seez) **1.** an unproved scientific conclusion drawn from known facts. **2.** an assumption or set of assumptions provisionally accepted, esp. as a basis for further investigation. [< Gk., supposition]

hy·poth·e·size (hī POTH ə SĪZ) *v.* **·sized, ·siz·ing** *v.t.* **1.** offer or assume as a hypothesis. —*v.i.* **2.** make a hypothesis; theorize.

hy·po·thet·i·cal (hī pə THET i kəl) *adj.* based on hypothesis; theoretical; supposed. —*n.* a hypothetical example.

hy·po·thy·roid·ism (HĪ pə THĪ roi DIZ əm) *n. Pathol.* **1.** deficient functioning of the thyroid gland. **2.** a disorder resulting from this, as goiter. —**hy'po·thy'roid** *adj. & n.*

hys·ter·ec·to·my (HIS tə REK tə mee) *n. pl.* **·mies** *Surg.* removal of the uterus.

hys•te•ri•a (hi STER ee ə) *n.* **1.** abnormal excitement; wild emotionalism; frenzy. **2.** *Psychiatry* a psychoneurotic condition characterized by emotional outbursts and sensory disturbances. **—hys•ter'ic** *n. & adj.*

hys•ter•i•cal (hi STER i kəl) *adj.* **1.** resembling hysteria; uncontrolled; violent. **2.** characterized or caused by hysteria. **3.** inclined to hysteria. **4.** extremely funny. [< L *hystericus*] **—hys•ter'i•cal•ly** *adv.*

I

i, I (ī) *n. pl.* **i's** or **is, i's** or **is 1.** the ninth letter of the english alphabet. **2.** any sound represented by the letter *i*. —*symbol* **1.** the Roman numeral for 1. **2.** *Chem.* iodine (symbol I).

I (ī) *pron.* **mine,** *objective* **me;** *pl. nominative* **we,** *possessive* **ours,** *objective* **us** the nominative singular pronoun of the first person, used by a speaker or writer in referring to himself. [*see my*] —*n. pl.* **I's 1.** the pronoun *I* used as a noun. **2.** *Philos.* the ego. [ME *ik*]

i·amb (ī am) *n.* **1.** in prosody, a metrical foot consisting of an unaccented syllable followed by an accented one. **2.** a line of verse made up of such feet. Also **i·am·bus** (ī AM bəs). —**i·am′bic** (ī AM bik) *n. & adj.* [< L *iambicus*]

-iatrics *combining form* medical treatment: *pediatrics*. [< Gk. *iatrikos* pertaining to the art of healing]

i·at·ro·gen·ic (ī A trə JEN ik) *adj.* resulting from or aggravated by medical treatment.

-iatry *combining form* medical or curative treatment: *psychiatry*. [< Gk. *iatreia* healing]

I·be·ri·an (ī BEER ee ən) *adj.* of, pertaining to, or characteristic of the land, people, or culture of Spain or Portugal.

i·bi·dem (IB i dəm) *adv. Latin* in the same place; in the work, chapter, etc. just mentioned. Abbr. *ibid.*

-ic *suffix* **1.** forming adjectives with the meanings: **a** of, pertaining to, or connected with: *volcanic*. **b** of the nature of; resembling: *angelic*. **c** produced by or in the manner of: *Homeric*. **d** consisting of; containing: *alcoholic*. **e** *Chem.* having a higher valence than that indicated by *-ous*: said of elements in compounds: *sulfuric* acid. **2.** forming nouns by the substantive use of adjectives in *-ic*: *classic, lunatic*. [ME]

ice (īs) *n.* **1.** frozen water; also a sheet, cube, etc., of this. ♦ Collateral adjective: *glacial.* **2.** a frozen dessert made without cream. **3.** *Slang* **a** a diamond or diamonds. **b** protection money. —**break the ice 1.** dispel reserve or formality, esp. at a social gathering. **2.** make a start. —**cut no ice** *Informal* have no influence. —**on ice** *Informal* set aside; in reserve. —*v.* **iced, ic·ing** *v.t.* **1.** cause to turn to ice; freeze. **2.** chill with ice. **3.** decorate with icing. —*v.i.* **4.** turn to ice. [ME *is*] —**iced** *adj.*

ice bag a flexible container designed to hold ice, applied to parts of the body.

ice·berg (ĪS burg) *n.* a large mass of glacial ice floating in the ocean. [< Dan. *ijsberg* ice mountain]

ice·boat (ĪS BOHT) *n.* **1.** a framework with skatelike runners and sails for sailing over ice. **2.** an icebreaker (def. 1).

ice·bound (ĪS BOWND) *adj.* surrounded or obstructed by ice.

ice·break·er (ĪS BRAY kər) *n.* **1.** a vessel used to break up ice in waterways and harbors. **2.** a structure for deflecting floating ice from the base of a bridge, a pier, etc. **3.** an opening action, remark, etc. intended to relieve formality.

ice·cap (ĪS KAP) *n.* a covering of ice and snow permanently overlying a tract of land.

ice cream a frozen mixture of milk or cream, butterfat, flavoring, and sweetening.

ice field 1. an icecap. **2.** a large expanse of floating sea ice.

ice floe (floh) **1.** an ice field. **2.** an ice cap.

ice hockey see under HOCKEY.

ice·house (ĪS HOWS) *n.* a building for storing ice.

Ice·land·ic (īs LAN dik) *adj.* of or pertaining to Iceland, its inhabitants, or their language. —*n.* the North Germanic language of Iceland. —**Old Icelandic** the language of Iceland before the 16th c.: sometimes called *Old Norse.*

ice·man (ĪS MAN) *n. pl.* **·men** one who sells or delivers ice.

ice pack 1. a large expanse of ice frozen into a single mass. **2.** an ice bag.

ice pick a pointed tool for chipping ice.

ichthyo- *combining form* fish. [< Gk. *ichthys*]

ich·thy·ol·o·gy (IK thee OL ə jee) *n.* the branch of zoology that treats of fishes. —**ich′thy·ol′o·gist** (-jist) *n.*

i·ci·cle (Ī si kəl) *n.* a hanging rod of ice formed by dripping water. [ME *isikel*]

ic·ing (Ī sing) *n.* **1.** a coating made of sugar, usu. mixed with egg whites or cream, used to cover cakes, pastry, etc. **2.** the formation of ice on the surface of an aircraft.

i·con (Ī kon) *n.* **1.** in the Eastern Orthodox

Church, a pictorial representation of Jesus Christ or some other sacred figure. **2.** an image; likeness. Also spelled *eikon* and *ikon*. [< L]

i·con·o·clast (ī KON ə KLAST) *n.* **1.** one who attacks cherished beliefs and institutions. **2.** one who opposes the use of religious images. [< Med.L *iconclastes*] —**i·con'o·clas'tic** *adj.*

i·cy (ī see) *adj.* **i·ci·er, i·ci·est** **1.** consisting of or covered with ice. **2.** like ice: *icy* blue. **3.** extremely cold. **4.** forbiddingly aloof: *icy* stare. [ME *isy*] —**i'ci·ly** *adv.* —**i'ci·ness** *n.*

id (id) *n. Psychoanal.* the unconscious part of the psyche, considered the source of fundamental impulses toward fulfilling instinctual needs. [< L *id* it]

ID (ī DEE) a card, document, etc. by which identity can be established.

I'd (īd) **1.** I would. **2.** I should. **3.** I had.

i·de·a (ī DEE ə) *n.* **1.** that which is conceived in the mind; a thought. **2.** an impression or notion. **3.** a conviction; belief. **4.** an intention; plan. **5.** significance; meaning: Do you get the *idea*? [< LL]

i·de·al (ī DEE əl) *n.* **1.** a concept of perfection. **2.** a person or thing taken as a standard of perfection. **3.** a high principle; lofty aim. **4.** that which exists only as a concept of the mind. —*adj.* **1.** perfect; supremely excellent. **2.** completely satisfactory. **3.** capable of existing as a mental concept only; utopian; imaginary. **4.** pertaining to or existing in the form of an idea or ideas. [< LL *idealis*]

i·de·al·ism (ī DEE ə LIZ əm) *n.* **1.** the envisioning of things as they should be or are wished to be rather than as they are; also, action based on such idealizing. **2.** pursuit of an ideal. **3.** in literature and art, the idealization of subject matter. **4.** *Philos.* any of several theories holding that there is no reality apart from mind or consciousness. —**i·de'al·ist** *n.* —**i'de·al·is'tic** *adj.*

i·de·al·ize (ī DEE ə LĪZ) *v.* **·ized, ·iz·ing** *v.t.* **1.** consider to be ideal; hold in high esteem. **2.** glorify. —*v.i.* **3.** form an ideal or ideals. **4.** consider or represent things in their ideal form. —**i·de'al·i·za'tion** *n.*

i·de·al·ly (ī DEE ə lee) *adv.* **1.** in conformance with an ideal; perfectly. **2.** as conceived in the mind.

i·de·ate (ī dee AYT) *v.t. & v.i.* **·at·ed, ·at·ing** form an idea or ideas of something; think. —**i'de·a'tion** *n.*

i·dem (ī dem) *pron. & adj. Latin* the same: used as a reference to what has been previously mentioned.

i·den·ti·cal (ī DEN ti kəl) *adj.* **1.** one and the same; the very same. **2.** alike in every respect. **3.** *Genetics* designating human twins that develop from a single fertilized ovum: distinguished from *fraternal.* [< Med.L *identicus*] —**i·den'ti·cal·ly** *adv.*

i·den·ti·fi·ca·tion (ī DEN tə fi KAY shən) *n.* **1.** the act of identifying, or the state of being identified. **2.** anything by which identity can be established.

i·den·ti·fy (ī DEN tə FĪ) *v.t.* **·fied, ·fy·ing** **1.** establish as being a particular person or thing; recognize. **2.** regard as the same. **3.** serve as a means of recognizing; be characteristic of. **4.** associate closely. **5.** consider (oneself) as like or one with another person. [< Med.L *identificare*] —**i·den'ti·fi'a·ble** *adj.*

i·den·ti·ty (ī DEN ti tee) *n. pl.* **·ties** **1.** the state of being identical. **2.** the state of being a specific person or thing and no other. **3.** the distinctive character belonging to an individual. [< LL *identitas*]

id·e·o·gram (ID ee ə GRAM) *n.* **1.** a pictorial symbol of an object or idea. **2.** a graphic symbol, as +, 4, $. Also **id·e·o·graph** (ID ee ə GRAF).

i·de·ol·o·gy (ID ee OL ə jee) *n. pl.* **·gies** **1.** the ideas and objectives that influence a community, political party, or national culture, shaping its social and political procedure. **2.** the science that treats of the origin, evolution, and expression of human ideas. **3.** fanciful or visionary speculation. —**i·de·o·log·i·cal** (ID ee ə LOJ ə kəl) *adj.*

ides (īdz) *n.pl.* in the ancient Roman calendar, the 15th of March, May, July, and October, and the 13th of the other months. [ME]

idio- *combining form* one's own; individual: *idiosyncrasy.* [< Gk. *idios* one's own]

id·i·o·cy (ID ee ə see) *n. pl.* **·cies** **1.** the condition of being an idiot. **2.** extreme stupidity or foolishness.

id·i·om (ID ee əm) *n.* **1.** an expression peculiar to a language, not readily understandable from the meaning of its parts, as *put up with* (tolerate, endure). **2.** the language or dialect of a region or people. **3.** the special terminology of a class, occupational group, etc. **4.** the distinctive character of a specific language. **5.** typical style, form, or character, as in art, literature, or music. [< L *idioma*]

id·i·o·mat·ic (ID ee ə MAT ik) *adj.* **1.** characteristic of a specific language. **2.** of the nature of an idiom. **3.** employing many idioms. —**id'i·o·mat'i·cal·ly** *adv.*

id·i·o·syn·cra·sy (ID ee ə SING krə see) *n. pl.* **·sies** a habit, expression, etc., peculiar to an individual; oddity. [< Gk. *idiosynkrasia*] —**id·i·o·syn·crat·ic** (ID ee oh sin KRAT ik) *adj.* —**id'i·o·syn·crat'i·cal·ly** *adv.*

id·i·ot (ID ee ət) *n.* **1.** a person exhibiting mental deficiency in its most severe form. **2.** an extremely foolish or stupid person. [ME] —**id·i·ot·ic** (ID ee OT ik) *adj.* —**id'i·ot'i·cal·ly** *adv.*

i·dle (ID l) *adj.* **idler, i·dlest** **1.** not engaged in work. **2.** not being used; not operating. **3.** unwilling to work; lazy. **4.** spent in inactivity; reserved for leisure. **5.** having no basis or effectiveness: *idle* threats. **6.** frivolous; trifling. —*v.* **i·dled, i·dling** *v.i.* **1.** be engaged in trivial activities; loaf. **2.** move or progress lazily or aimlessly; linger. **3.** *Mech.* operate without transmitting power: said of motors or machines. —*v.t.* **4.** spend (time) wastefully; fritter: often with *away*. **5.** cause to be idle. **6.** cause to idle, as a motor. [ME *idel* empty] —**i'dler** *n.* —**i'dly** *adv.*

i·dol (ID l) *n.* **1.** an image representing a god, and worshiped as divine. **2.** in the Christian and Jewish religions, a false god; object of heathen worship. **3.** one who is loved or admired to an excessive degree. **4.** a false or misleading idea. [ME]

i·dol·a·ter (ī DOL ə tər) *n.* **1.** one who worships an idol or idols. **2.** a blindly devoted admirer.

i·dol·a·try (ī DOL ə tree) *n. pl.* **·tries** **1.** the worship of idols. **2.** excessive admiration; blind infatuation. [ME *idolatrie*] —**i·dol'a·trous** (-trəs) *adj.*

i·dol·ize (ID l īz) *v.* **·ized, ·iz·ing** *v.t.* **1.** love or admire to excess; adore. **2.** worship as an idol. —*v.i.* **3.** worship idols.

i·dyll (ID l) *n.* **1.** a poem or prose piece depicting simple scenes of pastoral, domestic, or country life. **2.** an event, scene, etc. suitable for an idyll. Also **i'dyl.** [< L *idyllium* pastoral poem]

i·dyl·lic (ī DIL ik) *adj.* **1.** of or having the qualities of an idyl. **2.** charmingly simple or picturesque.

i.e. that is. [< L *id est*]

if (if) *conj.* **1.** in the event that; in case. **2.** on condition that; provided that. **3.** allowing the possibility that; granting that: *If* I am wrong, I apologize. **4.** whether: See *if* the mail has come. **5.** even though; although: Her clothes are neat, *if* not stylish. —*n.* a possibility or condition. [ME *yif*]

if·fy (IF ee) *adj.* **·fi·er, ·fi·est** *Informal* dependent on many uncertain factors; questionable.

ig·loo (IG loo) *n. pl.* **·loos** a dome-shaped hut used by Eskimos, usu. built of blocks of snow. [< Eskimo *iglu* house]

ig·ne·ous (IG nee əs) *adj.* **1.** *Geol.* formed by the action of great heat within the earth, as rocks consolidated from a molten state. **2.** of or like fire. [< L *igneus* of fire]

ig·nis fat·u·us (IG nis FACH oo əs) *pl.* **ig·nes fat·u·i** (IG neez FACH oo ī) **1.** a flickering, phosphorescent light sometimes seen over marshes, thought to be caused by the spontaneous combustion of marsh gas. **2.** a deceptive hope or goal. Also called *will-o'-the-wisp.* [< Med.L, lit., foolish fire]

ig·nite (ig NĪT) *v.* **·nit·ed, ·nit·ing** *v.t.* **1.** set on fire; make burn. **2.** enkindle; arouse. **3.** *Chem.* cause to glow with intense heat; bring to combustion. —*v.i.* **4.** begin burning. [< L *ignitus* set afire] —**ig·nit'a·ble** *adj.* —**ig·nit'er** *n.*

ig·ni·tion (ig NISH ən) *n.* **1.** the act of igniting, or the state of being ignited. **2.** the process of igniting the explosive mixture of fuel and air in a cylinder of an internal-combustion engine. **3.** the device or system that fires this mixture.

ig·no·ble (ig NOH bəl) *adj.* **1.** dishonorable; base. **2.** not of noble rank. **3.** of low quality; inferior. [ME] —**ig·no'bly** *adv.*

ig·no·min·i·ous (IG nə MIN ee əs) *adj.* **1.** marked by or involving dishonor or disgrace; shameful. **2.** meriting disgrace; despicable. **3.** humiliating.[ME] —**ig'no·min'i·ous·ly** *adv.*

ig·no·min·y (IG nə MIN ee) *n. pl.* **·min·ies** **1.** disgrace; dishonor. **2.** that which causes disgrace; dishonorable conduct. [< L *ignominia*]

ig·no·ra·mus (IG nə RAY məs) *n.* an ignorant person. [< L, we ignore]

ig·no·rant (IG nər ənt) *adj.* **1.** having no learning or education. **2.** lacking awareness: with *of: ignorant* of the facts. **3.** uninformed; inexperienced: with *in*. [ME *ignoraunt*] —**ig'no·rance** (-rəns) *n.*

ig·nore (ig NOR) *v.t.* **·nored, ·nor·ing** refuse to notice or recognize; disregard. [< L *ignorare* disregard]

i·gua·na (i GWAH nə) *n.* any of several very large tropical American lizards. [< Sp.]

i·kon (Ī kon) see ICON.

il·e·um (IL ee əm) n. Anat. the lowest of the three divisions of the small intestine. [< NL] —**il·e·i·tis** (IL ee Ī tis) n. inflammation of the ileum.

Il·i·ad (IL ee əd) n. an ancient Greek epic poem ascribed to Homer, describing the siege of Troy. [< L Ilias Troy]

il·i·um (IL ee əm) n. pl. **il·i·a** Anat. the large upper portion of bones of the pelvis. [< NL]

ilk (ilk) n. breed; sort. [ME ilke the same]

ill (il) adj. **worse, worst** 1. not in good health; sick. 2. destructive; harmful. 3. hostile or malevolent. 4. portending danger or disaster; unfavorable. 5. morally bad; evil. 6. not meeting accepted standards. —n. 1. evil; wrong. 2. injury; harm. 3. a cause of unhappiness, misfortune, etc. 4. disaster; trouble. 5. a malady; sickness. —adv. 1. not well; badly. 2. with difficulty; hardly. 3. unsuitably; poorly. [ME] **Ill,** used in combination, has the meaning badly or insufficiently, as: **ill-conceived, ill-considered, ill-equipped.**

I'll (īl) 1. I will. 2. I shall.

ill-ad·vised (IL əd VĪZD) adj. not wise; rash.

ill-bred (IL BRED) adj. impolite; rude.

ill-con·sid·ered (IL kən SID ərd) adj. done with insufficient deliberation; unwise.

ill-dis·posed (IL di SPOHZD) adj. 1. unpleasant; unfriendly. 2. disinclined; averse.

il·le·gal (i LEE gəl) adj. 1. not legal; contrary to law. 2. violating official rules. —**il·le·gal·i·ty** (IL ee GAL i tee) n.

il·leg·i·ble (i LEJ ə bəl) adj. not legible; incapable of being read. —**il·leg'i·bil'i·ty** n.

il·le·git·i·mate (IL i JIT ə mit) adj. 1. born out of wedlock. 2. not according to law; unlawful. 3. contrary to good usage; incorrect. 4. contrary to logic; unsound. —**il'le·git'i·ma·cy** (-mə see) n.

ill-fat·ed (IL FAY tid) adj. 1. having an unhappy fate; doomed. 2. characterized by misfortune; unlucky.

ill-fa·vored (IL FAY vərd) adj. 1. homely; ugly. 2. objectionable; disagreeable.

ill-found·ed (IL FOWN did) adj. based on weak or incorrect evidence or premises; unsupported.

ill-got·ten (IL GOT n) adj. obtained illegally or evilly.

il·lib·er·al (i LIB ər əl) adj. 1. not generous; stingy. 2. narrowminded; intolerant. —**il·lib'er·al'i·ty** (-AL ə tee) n.

il·lic·it (i LIS it) adj. not permitted; unlawful.[< L illicitus] —**il·lic'it·ly** adv. —**il·lic'it·ness** n.

il·lim·it·a·ble (i LIM i tə bəl) adj. incapable of being limited; boundless. —**il·lim'it·a·bly** adv.

il·lit·er·ate (i LIT ər it) adj. 1. lacking education; esp., unable to read and write. 2. of language, characteristic of the uneducated. —n. an illiterate person. —**il·lit'er·a·cy** (-ər ə see) n.

ill-man·nered (IL MAN ərd) adj. rude.

ill nature unpleasant disposition; surliness. —**ill-na·tured** (IL NAY chərd) adj. —**ill'-na'·tured·ly** adv.

ill·ness (IL nis) n. 1. the state of being in poor health; sickness. 2. an ailment.

il·log·i·cal (i LOJ i kəl) adj. not logical; neglectful of reason. —**il·log'i·cal'i·ty** (-KAL i tee) n. —**il·log'i·cal·ly** adv.

ill repute evil reputation. —**house of ill repute** brothel.

ill-spent (IL SPENT) adj. wasted; misspent.

ill-starred (IL STAHRD) adj. unlucky.

ill temper crossness; irritability. —**ill-tem·pered** (IL TEM pərd) adj.

ill-timed (IL TĪMD) adj. occurring at an unsuitable time.

ill-treat (IL TREET) v.t. act cruelly toward; abuse.

il·lu·mi·nant (i LOO mə nənt) n. something that gives light.

il·lu·mi·nate (i LOO mə NAYT) v. **-nat·ed, -nat·ing** v.t. 1. give light to; light up. 2. clarify; explain. 3. enlighten. 4. decorate, as a manuscript, with ornamental borders, figures, etc., often of gold. —v.i. 5. shed light; become lighted. [ME] —**il·lu'mi·na'tion** n. —**il·lu'mi·na'tor** n.

il·lu·mine (i LOO min) v.t. & v.i. **-mined, -min·ing** illuminate or be illuminated. [ME illuminen]

ill-use (IL YOOZ) v.t. **-used, -us·ing** treat cruelly or unjustly; abuse. —n. (IL YOOS) bad or unjust treatment.

il·lu·sion (i LOO zhən) n. 1. a false, misleading, or overly optimistic idea. 2. an impression not consistent with fact. [ME]

il·lu·sive (i LOO siv) adj. unreal; illusory.

il·lu·so·ry (i LOO sə ree) adj. of the nature of illusion; deceptive. —**il·lu'so·ri·ness** n.

il·lus·trate (IL ə STRAYT) v.t. **-trat·ed, -trat·ing** 1. explain or make clear by means of examples, comparisons, etc. 2. supply or

illustration 374

accompany (a book etc.) with pictures, as for instruction or decoration. [< L *illustratus* clarified] —**il′lus·tra′tor** *n.*

il·lus·tra·tion (IL ə STRAY shən) *n.* 1. an example, comparison, anecdote, etc., by which a statement is explained. 2. a print, drawing, or picture in a text. 3. the act or art of illustrating. [ME]

il·lus·tra·tive (i LUS trə tiv) *adj.* serving to illustrate. —**il·lus′tra·tive·ly** *adv.*

il·lus·tri·ous (i LUS tree əs) *adj.* 1. greatly distinguished; renowned. 2. conferring greatness or glory. [< L *illustris* famous] —**il·lus′tri·ous·ness** *n.*

ill will hostile feeling; malevolence.

I′m (īm) I am.

im·age (IM ij) *n.* 1. a representation or likeness of a real or imaginary person, creature, or object. 2. a mental picture. 3. the way in which a person or thing is popularly perceived or regarded: a politician's *image.* 4. a person or thing that closely resembles another. 5. a representative example; embodiment. 6. a literary device that evokes a mental picture, as a figure of speech. 7. *Optics* the counterpart of an object produced by reflection, refraction, or the passage of rays through a small aperture. —*v.t.* •**aged,** •**ag·ing** 1. form a mental picture of. 2. make a visible representation of; portray. 3. mirror; reflect. 4. describe effectively or vividly. 5. symbolize. [ME]

im·age·ry (IM ij ree) *n. pl.* •**ries** 1. mental images collectively. 2. the act or process of forming mental images. 3. the use of vivid descriptions or figures of speech. 4. images used in art or decoration. [ME *imagerie*]

im·ag·i·nar·y (i MAJ ə NER ee) *adj.* existing in the imagination only; unreal. [ME]

im·ag·i·na·tion (i MAJ ə NAY shən) *n.* 1. the process of forming mental images of the objects of perception or thought in the absence of the corresponding external stimuli. 2. the mental ability to create original and striking images and concepts. 3. creativity or originality of any sort. 4. a creation of the mind; mental image. 5. an absurd fancy. [ME]

im·ag·i·na·tive (i MAJ ə nə tiv) *adj.* 1. endowed with imagination. 2. given to flights of fancy. 3. of or characterized by the creative imagination. —**im·ag′i·na·tive·ly** *adv.*

im·ag·ine (i MAJ in) *v.t. & v.i.* •**ined,** •**in·ing** 1. form a mental picture or idea of

(anything). 2. suppose; guess. [ME *imaginen*] —**im·ag′i·na·ble** *adj.*

Im·a·gism (IM ə JIZ əm) *n.* an early 20th c. movement in poetry characterized by precise images and freedom in form.

i·ma·go (i MAY goh) *n. pl.* •**goes** or •**gi·nes** (-gə NEEZ) *Entomol.* an insect in its adult, sexually mature stage. [< NL]

i·mam (i MAHM) *n.* 1. the leader of prayer in a mosque. 2. *cap.* the title of a Muslim leader; esp., a successor of Muhammad. [< Arabic *imām*]

im·bal·ance (im BAL əns) *n.* the state of being out of balance or not coordinated.

im·be·cile (IM bə səl) *n.* 1. a person exhibiting a degree of mental deficiency between that of the idiot and the moron. 2. a foolish or stupid person. —*adj.* 1. mentally deficient. 2. stupid; senseless. [< L *imbecillus* weak] —**im′be·cil′ic** (-SIL ik) *adj.* —**im′be·cil′i·ty** *n.*

im·bibe (im BĪB) *v.* •**bibed,** •**bib·ing** *v.t.* 1. drink. 2. suck up; absorb. 3. take in mentally. —*v.i.* 4. drink. [< L *imbibere* drink in] —**im·bib′er** *n.*

im·bri·cate (IM bri kit) *adj.* 1. arranged with overlapping edges, as shingles on a roof. 2. covered or decorated with a design resembling overlapping scales, leaves, etc. —*v.t. & v.i.* (IM bri KAYT) •**cat·ed,** •**cat·ing** overlap in a regular arrangement. [< LL *imbricatus* covered with tiles] —**im′bri·ca′tion** *n.*

im·bro·glio (im BROHL yoh) *n. pl.* •**glios** 1. a confused state of affairs. 2. a confused heap or tangle. [< Ital.]

im·brue (im BROO) *v.t.* •**brued,** •**bru·ing** stain or drench, esp. with blood. [ME *enbrewen*]

im·bue (im BYOO) *v.t.* •**bued,** •**bu·ing** 1. pervade or permeate. 2. wet thoroughly or saturate, as with color. [< L *imbuere* soak]

im·i·tate (IM i TAYT) *v.t.* •**tat·ed,** •**tat·ing** 1. behave or attempt to behave in the same way as; follow the example of. 2. mimic or impersonate. 3. make a copy or reproduction of. 4. have or take on the appearance of. [< L *imitatus* copied] —**im′i·ta·ble** (-tə bəl) *adj.* —**im′i·ta′tor** *n.*

im·i·ta·tion (IM i TAY shən) *n.* 1. the act of imitating. 2. that which is done by or results from imitating; copy. —*adj.* resembling or made to resemble something superior; not genuine. [ME]

im·i·ta·tive (IM i TAY tiv) *adj.* 1. tending to imitate; characterized by imitation. 2. pat-

immunology

terned after or reproducing the characteristics of an original. **3.** not genuine; spurious.

im·mac·u·late (i MAK yə lit) *adj.* **1.** without spot or stain; unsullied. **2.** without sin; pure. **3.** without error or blemish; flawless. [ME] —**im·mac'u·late·ly** *adv.* —**im·mac'u·late·ness** *n.*

im·ma·te·ri·al (IM ə TEER ee əl) *adj.* **1.** of little or no importance; inconsequential. **2.** not consisting of material substance. [ME]

im·ma·ture (IM ə CHUUR) *adj.* not mature, ripe, or developed. [< L *immaturus* unripe] —**im'ma·tur'i·ty** *n.*

im·meas·ur·a·ble (i MEZH ər ə bəl) *adj.* not capable of being measured; without limit; immense. —**im·meas'ur·a·bly** *adv.*

im·me·di·ate (i MEE dee it) *adj.* **1.** done or occurring without delay; instant. **2.** pertaining to the present moment: no *immediate* vacancies. **3.** nery near or close. **4.** occurring or acting without an intervening agency or cause. [< Med.L *immediatus*] —**im·me'di·a·cy** *n.*

im·me·mo·ri·al (IM ə MOR ee əl) *adj.* reaching back beyond memory; ancient. [< Med.L *immemorialis*]

im·mense (i MENS) *adj.* **1.** of great size, degree, or extent; huge. **2.** having no limits; infinite. **3.** *Informal* excellent. [ME] —**im·men'si·ty** *n.*

im·merse (i MURS) *v.t.* **·mersed, ·mers·ing 1.** plunge or dip into water or other fluid so as to cover completely. **2.** involve deeply; engross. **3.** baptize by plunging the entire body under water. [< L *immersus* dipped] —**im·mer·sion** (i MUR zhən) *n.*

im·mi·grant (IM i grənt) *n.* a person who immigrates. —*adj.* of or pertaining to immigration or immigrants.

im·mi·grate (IM i GRAYT) *v.i.* **·grat·ed, ·grat·ing** come into a country or region of which one is not a native in order to settle there. [< L *immigratus* moved into]

im·mi·gra·tion (IM i GRAY shən) *n.* **1.** the act of immigrating. **2.** the total number of immigrants entering a country during a stated period.

im·mi·nent (IM ə nənt) *adj.* about to happen; impending: said esp. of danger or catastrophe. [< L *imminere* overhang] —**im'mi·nence** *n.* —**im'mi·nent·ly** *adv.*

im·mis·ci·ble (i MIS ə bəl) *adj.* not capable of being mixed, as oil and water. —**im·mis'ci·bly** *adv.*

im·mo·bile (i MOH bəl) *adj.* **1.** incapable of being moved. **2.** not moving; motionless. [ME] —**im'mo·bil'i·ty** *n.*

im·mo·bi·lize (i MOH bə LIZ) *v.t.* **·lized, ·liz·ing 1.** make immovable; fix in place. **2.** make unable to move or mobilize, as a body of troops. —**im·mo'bi·li·za'tion** *n.*

im·mod·er·ate (i MOD ər it) *adj.* not moderate; excessive. —**im·mod'er·ate·ly** *adv.* —**im·mod'er·a'tion** *n.*

im·mod·est (i MOD ist) *adj.* **1.** without sense of decency; improper. **2.** lacking humility; bold. [< L *immodestus*] —**im·mod'es·ty** *n.*

im·mo·late (IM ə LAYT) *v.t.* **·lat·ed, ·lat·ing 1.** sacrifice; esp., kill as a sacrificial victim. **2.** destroy by fire. [< L *immolatus* sacrificed] —**im'mo·la'tion** *n.* —**im'mo·la'tor** *n.*

im·mor·al (i MOR əl) *adj.* **1.** contrary to conscience or public morality. **2.** licentious.

im·mo·ral·i·ty (IM ə RAL i tee) *n. pl.* **·ties 1.** the state or quality of being immoral; wickedness; dissoluteness. **2.** sexual misconduct. **3.** an immoral act.

im·mor·tal (i MOR tl) *adj.* **1.** not subject to death; living forever. **2.** having unending existence; eternal. **3.** pertaining to immortality or to beings or concepts that are immortal. **4.** of enduring fame.[ME] —*n.* **1.** an immortal being. **2.** *pl.* the gods of classical mythology. **3.** a person who has gained enduring fame. —**im·mor'tal·ly** *adv.*

im·mor·tal·i·ty (IM or TAL i tee) *n.* **1.** unending existence. **2.** eternal fame. [ME *immortalite*]

im·mor·tal·ize (i MOR tl IZ) *v.t.* **·ized, ·iz·ing** make immortal; endow with perpetual fame.

im·mov·a·ble (i MOO və bəl) *adj.* **1.** incapable of being moved. **2.** unable to move; stationary. **3.** firm; unyielding. **4.** not easily aroused; impassive. [ME] —**im·mov'a·bly** *adv.*

im·mune (i MYOON) *adj.* **1.** protected against a disease, poison, or the like, as by inoculation. **2.** not subject to obligation, penalty, harm, etc. [ME *immunite*] —**im·mu'ni·ty** *n.* [ME *immunite*]

im·mu·nize (IM yə NIZ) *v.t.* **·nized, ·niz·ing** make immune. —**im'mu·ni·za'tion** *n.*

im·mu·nol·o·gy (IM yə NOL ə jee) *n.* the branch of medical science dealing with immunity to disease. —**im·mu·no·log·i·cal**

(IM yə nl OJ ik əl) *adj.* —**im'mu·nol'o·gist** *n.*

im·mure (i MYUUR) *v.t.* **·mured, ·mur·ing 1.** enclose within walls; imprison. **2.** entomb within a wall. [< Med.L *immurare* wall in] —**im·mure'ment** *n.*

im·mu·ta·ble (i MYOO tə bəl) *adj.* not mutable; unchanging; unalterable. [ME] —**im·mu'ta·bil'i·ty** *n.* —**im·mu'ta·bly** *adv.*

imp (imp) *n.* **1.** a small demon. **2.** a mischievous child. [ME *impe* plant shoot]

im·pact (IM pakt) *n.* **1.** a striking together; collision. **2.** the force of such a contact; shock. **3.** strong influence; powerful effect. —*v.t.* (im PAKT) press or drive firmly into something.

im·pact·ed (im PAK tid) *adj.* **1.** pressed firmly together; wedged. **2.** *Dent.* denoting a tooth unable to emerge through the gum. [< L *impactus* fastened] —**im·pac·tion** (im PAK shən) *n.*

im·pair (im PAIR) *v.t.* cause to become less in quality, power, or value; make worse. [ME *empairen* worsen] —**im·pair'ment** *n.*

im·pale (im PAYL) *v.t.* **·paled, ·pal·ing 1.** fix upon a pale or a sharp stake. **2.** make helpless as if by fixing upon a stake. [< Med.L *impalare*] —**im·pale'ment** *n.*

im·pal·pa·ble (im PAL pə bəl) *adj.* **1.** not capable of being perceived by the sense of touch. **2.** not capable of being distinguished by the mind. —**im·pal'pa·bly** *adv.*

im·pan·el (im PAN l) *v.t.* **im·pan·eled, im·pan·el·ing 1.** enroll in a panel or list, as for jury duty. **2.** choose (members of a jury, etc.) from such a list. Also spelled *empanel.* [ME *empanellen*] —**im·pan'el·ment** *n.*

im·part (im PAHRT) *v.t.* **1.** make known; disclose. **2.** bestow a measure or quantity of. [ME] —**im·part'a·ble** *adj.*

im·par·tial (im PAHR shəl) *adj.* free from bias; fair. —**im·par·ti·al·i·ty** (im PAHR shee AL i tee) *n.* —**im·par'tial·ly** *adv.*

im·pass·a·ble (im PAS ə bəl) *adj.* that cannot be traveled over or through: an *impassable* road. —**im·pass'a·bly** *adv.*

im·passe (IM pas) *n.* **1.** a situation in which no further progress is possible; deadlock. **2.** a dead end. [< F]

im·pas·si·ble (im PAS ə bəl) *adj.* **1.** incapable of emotion; unfeeling. **2.** incapable of suffering pain. **3.** impassive. [ME] —**im·pas'si·bly** *adv.*

im·pas·sioned (im PASH ənd) *adj.* filled with passion or strong feeling; fervent. —**im·pas'sioned·ly** *adv.*

im·pas·sive (im PAS iv) *adj.* not feeling or tending to feel emotion; unmoved; calm. —**im·pas·siv·i·ty** (IM pa SIV i tee) *n.*

im·pas·to (im PAS toh) *n.* **1.** painting in which the paint is applied in heavy strokes. **2.** paint so applied./[< Ital.]

im·pa·ti·ens (im PAY shənz) *n.* a plant with stems enlarged at the joints and irregular flowers. [< NL < L, impatient]

im·pa·tient (im PAY shənt) *adj.* **1.** lacking patience; restless; irritable. **2.** unwilling to tolerate: with *of.* **3.** restlessly eager. **4.** exhibiting lack of patience. [ME *impacient*] —**im·pa'tience** *n.*

im·peach (im PEECH) *v.t.* **1.** charge (a public official) before a legally constituted tribunal with crime or misdemeanor in office. **2.** challenge or bring discredit upon the honesty or validity of. [ME *empechen* hinder] —**im·peach'·a·ble** *adj.* —**im·peach'ment** *n.*

im·pec·ca·ble (im PEK ə bəl) *adj.* free from error, fault, or flaw. [< L *impeccabilis* sinless] —**im·pec'ca·bil'i·ty** *n.* —**im·pec'ca·bly** *adv.*

im·pe·cu·ni·ous (IM pi KYOO nee əs) *adj.* having no money; penniless. [< *im-* without + *obs. pecunious* wealthy] —**im·pe·cu·ni·os·i·ty** (IM pi KYOO nee OS i tee) *n.*

im·ped·ance (im PEED əns) *n. Electr.* the total opposition to an alternating current presented by a circuit.

im·pede (im PEED) *v.t.* **·ped·ed, ·ped·ing** retard or hinder; obstruct. [< L *impedire* entangle]

im·ped·i·ment (im PED ə mənt) *n.* **1.** that which hinders or obstructs; an obstacle. **2.** a physical handicap, esp. a speech defect. [ME]

im·pel (im PEL) *v.t.* **·pelled, ·pel·ling 1.** force or drive to an action; push; urge on. **2.** drive or push forward. [ME *impellen*] —**im·pel'ler** *n.*

im·pend (im PEND) *v.i.* **1.** be about to occur; be imminent. **2.** be suspended: with *over.* [< L *impendere* threaten]

im·pend·ing (im PEN ding) *adj.* **1.** about to occur; imminent. **2.** overhanging.

im·pen·e·tra·ble (im PEN i trə bəl) *adj.* **1.** incapable of being penetrated; that cannot be pierced, entered, seen through, etc. **2.** incapable of being understood. [ME *impenetrabel*] —**im·pen'e·tra·bil'i·ty** *n.* —**im·pen'e·tra·bly** *adv.*

im·pen·i·tent (im PEN i tənt) *adj.* not penitent; obdurate. —**im·pen'i·tent·ly** *adv.*

im·per·a·tive (im PER ə tiv) *adj.* **1.** urgently necessary; obligatory. **2.** having the nature of or expressing a command. **3.** *Gram.* designating the mood used to express commands, requests, exhortations, etc. —*n.* **1.** that which is imperative. **2.** *Gram.* the imperative mood. [< LL *imperativus* imposed] —**im·per'a·tive·ly** *adv.*

im·per·cep·ti·ble (IM pər SEP tə bəl) *adj.* **1.** that can barely be perceived, as by reason of smallness, subtlety, etc. **2.** not discernible. —**im'per·cep'ti·bil'i·ty** *n.* —**im' per·cep'ti·bly** *adv.*

im·per·cep·tive (IM pər SEP tiv) *adj.* not perceptive; lacking the power of perception.

im·per·fect (im PUR fikt) *adj.* **1.** falling short of perfection; faulty. **2.** wanting in completeness; deficient. **3.** *Gram.* denoting a tense that indicates uncompleted or continuing past action. —*n. Gram.* the imperfect tense. —**im·per'fect·ly** *adv.*

im·per·fec·tion (IM pər FEK shən) *n.* **1.** the state or quality of being imperfect. **2.** a defect; flaw. [ME *imperfeccioun*]

im·per·fo·rate (im PUR fər it) *adj.* **1.** without perforations. **2.** not separated by lines of perforations: said of stamps. Also **im· per'fo·rat'ed.** —*n.* an imperforated stamp.

im·pe·ri·al (im PEER ee əl) *adj.* **1.** of or pertaining to an empire or to the ruler of an empire. **2.** designating a nation having sovereign power over colonies or dependencies. **3.** imperious; overbearing. **4.** possessing commanding power or dignity; majestic. [ME]

im·pe·ri·al·ism (im PEER ee ə LIZ əm) *n.* **1.** the creation, maintenance, or extension of an empire, comprising many nations and areas, all controlled by a central government. **2.** a system of imperial government. **3.** imperial character, authority, or spirit. —**im·pe'ri·al·ist** *n. & adj.*

im·per·il (im PER əl) *v.t.* **·iled, ·il·ing** place in peril; endanger.

im·pe·ri·ous (im PEER ee əs) *adj.* **1.** commanding; domineering. **2.** urgent; imperative. [< L *imperiosus* commanding] —**im·pe'ri·ous·ness** *n.*

im·per·ish·a·ble (im PER i shə bəl) *adj.* not perishable; enduring. —**im·per'ish·a·bly** *adv.*

im·per·ma·nent (im PUR mə nənt) *adj.* not

permanent; fleeting. —**im·per'ma· nence** *n.*

im·per·me·a·ble (im PUR mee ə bəl) *adj.* **1.** not permitting passage or penetration. **2.** impervious to moisture. —**im·per' me·a·bil'i·ty** *n.*

im·per·mis·si·ble (IM pər MIS ə bəl) *adj.* not to be permitted. —**im'per·mis'si·bly** *adv.*

im·per·son·al (im PUR sə nl) *adj.* **1.** not personal; objective. **2.** not having the characteristics of a person: an *impersonal* deity. **3.** *Gram.* of a verb, having no specific subject: in English the word *it* is usu. used with such verbs. —*n. Gram.* an impersonal verb. —**im·per'son·al·ly** *adv.*

im·per·son·ate (im PUR sə NAYT) *v.t.* **·at·ed, ·at·ing** act the part of or pretend to be (another person), esp. for purposes of entertainment or fraud. —**im·per'son·a' tion** *n.* —**im·per'son·a'tor** *n.*

im·per·ti·nent (im PUR tn ənt) *adj.* **1.** deliberately disrespectful or unmannerly; impudent. **2.** not pertinent; irrelevant. **3.** not suitable; inappropriate. [ME] —**im·per' ti·nence** *n.*

im·per·turb·a·ble (IM pər TUR bə bəl) *adj.* incapable of being agitated; calm. — **im'per·turb'a·bil'i·ty** *n.*

im·per·vi·ous (im PUR vee əs) *adj.* **1.** incapable of being passed through; impermeable. **2.** not open; unreceptive. [< L *impervius*] —**im·per'vi·ous·ness** *n.*

im·pe·ti·go (IM pi TĪ goh) *n. Pathol.* a contagious skin disease marked by pustules. [ME]

im·pet·u·ous (im PECH oo əs) *adj.* **1.** tending to act on sudden impulse. **2.** resulting from sudden impulse; hasty. **3.** moving with violent force. [ME] —**im·pet'u·os'i·ty** (-OS i tee), **im·pet'u·ous·ness** *n.*

im·pe·tus (IM pi təs) *n.* **1.** the force that sets a body in motion; also, the energy with which a body moves or is driven. **2.** any motivating force; stimulus; incentive. [< L, attack]

im·pi·e·ty (im PĪ ə tee) *n. pl.* **·ties 1.** lack of reverence for God; ungodliness. **2.** lack of respect for those to whom respect is due. **3.** an impious act. [ME *impietie*]

im·pinge (im PINJ) *v.i.* **·pinged, ·ping·ing 1.** strike; fall: with *on, upon,* or *against.* **2.** encroach; infringe: with *on* or *upon.* [< Med.L *impingere* strike against] — **im·pinge'·ment** *n.*

im·pi·ous (IM pee əs) *adj.* **1.** lacking in reverence for God; blasphemous. **2.** lacking in due respect. [< L *impius*]

imp·ish (IM pish) *adj.* characteristic of or resembling an imp; mischievous. —**imp′ish·ly** *adv.* —**imp′ish·ness** *n.*

im·pla·ca·ble (im PLAK ə bəl) *adj.* that cannot be appeased or pacified. [ME] —**im·pla′ca·bly** *adv.*

im·plant (im PLANT) *v.t.* **1.** fix firmly, as in the ground; embed. **2.** instill in the mind; inculcate. **3.** *Med.* insert or embed in (living tissue). —*n.* (IM PLANT) *Med.* a tissue or device implanted in the body. —**im′plan·ta′tion** *n.*

im·plau·si·ble (im PLAW zə bəl) *adj.* not plausible; lacking the appearance of truth or trustworthiness. —**im·plau′si·bil′i·ty** *n.*

im·ple·ment (IM plə mənt) *n.* **1.** a piece of equipment used in some form of work or activity; tool; utensil. **2.** any means or agent for the accomplishment of a purpose. —*v.t.* (IM plə MENT **1.** carry out; accomplish; fulfill. **2.** furnish with implements. [ME] —**im′ple·men·ta′tion** *n.*

im·pli·cate (IM pli KAYT) *v.t.* •**cat·ed,** •**cat·ing 1.** show to be involved, as in a plot or crime. **2.** imply. [< L *implicatus* interwoven] —**im·pli·ca·to·ry** (IM pli kə TOR ee) *adj.*

im·pli·ca·tion (IM pli KAY shən) *n.* **1.** the act of involving, or the state of being involved. **2.** the act of implying, or the state of being implied. **3.** that which is implied. [ME *implicacioun*]

im·plic·it (im PLIS it) *adj.* **1.** unreserved; absolute. **2.** implied or understood, but not specifically expressed: *implicit* agreement. **3.** essentially contained, but not apparent; inherent: with *in.* [< L *implicitus* involved] —**im·plic′it·ly** *adv.*

im·plied (im PLĪD) *adj.* understood, suggested, or included without being specifically expressed.

im·plode (im PLOHD) *v.t. & v.i.* •**plod·ed,** •**plod·ing** burst inward. —**im·plo·sion** (im PLOH *zh*ən) *n.*

im·plore (im PLOR) *v.t. & v.i.* •**plored,** •**plor·ing** beg humbly or urgently; beseech. [< L *implorare* cry out] —**im·plor′ing·ly** *adv.*

im·ply (im PLĪ) *v.t.* •**plied, ·ply·ing 1.** involve necessarily as a circumstance, condition, effect, etc. **2.** indicate or suggest without stating. **3.** signify. [ME *implien*]

im·po·lite (IM pə LĪT) *adj.* lacking in polite-

ness; discourteous; rude. —**im′po·lite′ly** *adv.* —**im′po·lite′ness** *n.*

im·pol·i·tic (im POL i tik) *adj.* not prudent; injudicious. —**im·pol′i·tic·ly** *adv.*

im·pon·der·a·ble (im PON dər ə bəl) *adj.* incapable of being estimated, calculated, or valued. —*n.* an imponderable factor. —**im·pon′der·a·bil′i·ty** *n.*

im·port[1] (im PORT) *v.t.* **1.** bring into a country from abroad for commercial purposes, as merchandise. **2.** bring in from an outside source; introduce. **3.** have as its meaning; signify. [ME *importen*] —*n.* (IM port) **1.** an imported commodity. **2.** the act of importing. **3.** that which is implied; meaning. —**im·port′er** *n.*

im·port[2] (IM port) *n.* importance. —*v.i.* (im PORT) be of consequence; matter.

im·por·tance (im POR tns) *n.* **1.** the quality of being important; consequence; significance. **2.** worthiness of esteem; standing. **3.** pretentiousness. [< L *importantia*]

im·por·tant (im POR tnt) *adj.* **1.** having much significance, value, or influence. **2.** deserving of special notice or attention; noteworthy. **3.** having special relevance; mattering greatly: with *to.* **4.** pompous. —**im·por′tant·ly** *adv.*

im·por·ta·tion (IM por TAY shən) *n.* **1.** the act of importing. **2.** that which is imported.

im·por·tu·nate (im POR chə nit) *adj.* **1.** persistent in demand; insistent. **2.** of a demand or request, repeatedly made; pressing. —**im·por′tu·nate·ly** *adv.*

im·por·tune (IM por TOON) *v.* •**tuned,** •**tun·ing** *v.t.* **1.** harass with persistent demands or requests. **2.** ask for persistently. —*v.i.* make persistent requests or demands. —*adj.* importunate. [ME] —**im′por·tu′ni·ty** *n.*

im·pose (im POHZ) *v.t.* •**posed, ·pos·ing 1.** establish by authority as an obligation, penalty, etc.: *impose* a fine. **2.** force (oneself, one's will, etc.) upon others. [ME] —**impose on** (or **upon**) take advantage of. —**im·po·si·tion** (IM pə ZISH ən) *n.*

im·pos·ing (im POH zing) *adj.* impressive; grand; stately. —**im·pos′ing·ly** *adv.*

im·pos·si·bil·i·ty (im POS ə BIL i tee) *n. pl.* •**ties 1.** the quality of being impossible. **2.** something impossible. [ME *impossibilite*]

im·pos·si·ble (im POS E bəl) *adj.* **1.** incapable of existing or taking place. **2.** incapable of being done or put into practice. **3.** contrary to fact or reality; inconceivable. **4.** not acceptable; intolerable. [ME] **—im·pos'si·bly** adv.

im·post (IM pohst) n. a tax or customs duty. **—**v.t. classify (imported goods) for the purpose of determining customs duties. [< Med.L impostus tax]

im·pos·tor (im POS tər) n. one who deceives; esp., one who assumes the name of another. [< LL]

im·pos·ture (im POS chər) n. deception by means of false pretenses; esp., the act of posing under a false name. [< LL impostura]

im·po·tent (IM pə tənt) adj. **1.** powerless to act or to accomplish anything. **2.** physically weak. **3.** incapable of sexual intercourse: said of males. [ME] **—im'po·tence, im'po·ten·cy** n.

im·pound (im POWND) v.t. **1.** shut up in a pound, as a stray dog. **2.** place in legal custody. **3.** collect (water) for irrigation. **—im·pound'ment** n.

im·pov·er·ish (im POV ər ish) v.t. **1.** reduce to poverty. **2.** exhaust the fertility of, as soil. [ME empoverishen] **—im·pov'er·ish·ment** n.

im·prac·ti·ca·ble (im PRAK ti kə bəl) adj. **1.** incapable of being carried out or put into effect; not feasible. **2.** incapable of being used for an intended purpose. **—im·prac'ti·ca·bil'i·ty** n.

im·prac·ti·cal (im PRAK ti kəl) adj. not practical. **—im·prac·ti·cal·i·ty** (im PRAK ti KAL i tee) n.

im·pre·cate (IM prə KAYT) v.t. **·cat·ed, ·cat·ing** invoke or call down (some curse or calamity). [< L imprecatus invoked] **—im'pre·ca'tion** n.

im·preg·na·ble (im PREG nə bəl) adj. **1.** incapable of being taken by force. **2.** incapable of being overcome. [ME] **—im·preg'na·bil'i·ty** n. **—im·preg'na·bly** adv.

im·preg·nate (im PREG nayt) v.t. **·nat·ed, ·nat·ing 1.** make pregnant. **2.** fertilize, as an ovum. **3.** saturate or permeate. **4.** fill or imbue, as with ideas. **—**adj. (im PREG nit) made pregnant. [< LL impraegnatus fertilized] **—im'preg·na'tion** n.

im·pre·sa·ri·o (IM prə SAHR ee OH) n. pl. **·ri·os** one who manages or sponsors performers or performances for entertainment. [< Ital.]

im·press¹ (im PRES) v.t. **1.** produce a marked effect upon the mind or feelings of; influence. **2.** establish firmly in the mind. **3.** form or make (a mark) by pressure; stamp. **4.** form or make an imprint or mark upon. **—**n. (IM pres) **1.** the act or process of impressing. **2.** a mark produced by pressure. **3.** distinctive character or mark; stamp. [ME]

im·press² v.t. **1.** force to enter public service, esp. naval service. **2.** seize (property) for public use. **—**n. (IM pres) the act of impressing. **—im·press'ment** n.

im·press·i·ble (im PRES ə bəl) adj. capable of being impressed or of receiving an impression; susceptible.

im·pres·sion (im PRESH ən) n. **1.** an effect produced on the mind, the senses, or the feelings. **2.** a vague remembrance or uncertain belief. **3.** a mark made by pressure. **4.** the act or process of impressing. **5.** an imitation of a person done for entertainment. [ME impressioun]

im·pres·sion·a·ble (im PRESH ə nə bəl) adj. highly receptive to impressions; readily influenced; sensitive. [< F impressionnable]

im·pres·sion·ism (im PRESH ə NIZ əm) n. **1.** cap. in painting, a style, developed in the 19th c., that attempts to reproduce the impressions made by the actual reflection of light in pure colors. **2.** in literature and music, a style that attempts to create impressions or moods. **—im·pres'sion·ist** n. & adj.

im·pres·sive (im PRES iv) adj. producing or tending to produce an impression; exciting emotion or admiration. **—im·pres'sive·ness** n.

im·pri·ma·tur (IM pri MAH tər) n. **1.** official license or approval for publication of a literary work. **2.** authorization in general. [< L, let it be printed]

im·print (im PRINT) v.t. **1.** produce (a mark) by pressure. **2.** mark or produce a mark on, as with a stamp or seal. **3.** fix firmly in the heart, mind, etc. **—**n. (IM print) **1.** a mark or indentation made by printing, stamping, or pressing. **2.** characteristic effect; impression; stamp. **3.** the name of the publisher, place of publication, date of issue, etc., printed in a book, usu. on the title page. [ME empreynten]

im·pris·on (im PRIZ ən) v.t. **1.** put into a prison; hold in confinement. **2.** confine or restrain. [ME enprisonen] **—im·pris'on·ment** n.

im·prob·a·bil·i·ty (im PROB ə BIL i tee) n. pl. **·ties 1.** the quality of being improbable;

unlikelihood. **2.** an unlikely circumstance, event, or result.

im·prob·a·ble (im PROB ə bəl) *adj.* not probable; unlikely. —**im·prob'a·bly** *adv.*

im·promp·tu (im PROMP too) *adj.* made, done, or uttered on the spur of the moment. —*adv.* without preparation. [< F]

im·prop·er (im PROP ər) *adj.* **1.** deviating from fact, truth, or established usage. **2.** deviating from accepted standards of conduct or taste. **3.** unsuitable. —**im·prop' er·ly** *adv.*

improper fraction *Math.* a fraction whose numerator is greater than the denominator.

im·pro·pri·e·ty (IM prə PRĪ ə tee) *n. pl.* **·ties 1.** the quality of being improper. **2.** an improper action. **3.** an improper usage in speech or writing. [< LL *improprietas*]

im·prove (im PROOV) *v.* **·proved, ·prov·ing** *v.t.* **1.** raise to a higher or more desirable quality, value, or condition; make better. **2.** increase the value or profit of. **3.** use to good advantage; utilize. —*v.i.* **4.** become better. —**improve on** (or **upon**) do or produce something better than. [ME *im-prouen* profit from]

im·prove·ment (im PROOV mənt) *n.* **1.** the act of making better, or the state of becoming better. **2.** a modification or addition that improves something. **3.** a person, thing, or process that constitutes an advance in excellence.

im·prov·i·dent (im PROV i dənt) *adj.* lacking foresight; incautious; thriftless. —**im·prov'i·dence** *n.* —**im·prov'i·dent·ly** *adv.*

im·pro·vise (IM prə vīz) *v.* **·vised, ·vis·ing** *v.t.* **1.** produce (music, drama, etc.) without previous thought or preparation. **2.** contrive or construct from whatever comes to hand. —*v.i.* **3.** produce anything extemporaneously. [< F *improviser*] —**im·pro·vi·sa·tion** (IM PROV ə ZAY shən) *n.* —**im'pro·vis'er** *n.*

im·pru·dent (im PROOD nt) *adj.* not prudent; lacking discretion; unwise. [ME] —**im·pru'dence** *n.*

im·pu·dent (IM pyə dənt) *adj.* offensively bold; insolently assured; saucy. [ME] —**im'pu·dence** *n.*

im·pugn (im PYOON) *v.t.* attack (a statement, motives, etc.) with criticism or arguments; dispute the truth of. [ME *impugnen* attack] —**im·pugn'ment** *n.* —**im·pugn' er** *n.*

im·pulse (IM puls) *n.* **1.** a brief exertion or

communication of force tending to produce motion. **2.** the motion produced. **3.** a sudden, unreasoned inclination to action. **4.** *Physiol.* the transference of a stimulus through a nerve fiber. [< L *impulsus* impulse]

im·pul·sion (im PUL shən) *n.* **1.** the act of impelling or the state of being impelled. **2.** an impelling force.

im·pul·sive (im PUL siv) *adj.* **1.** actuated by impulse; spontaneous. **2.** having the power of inciting to action. —**im·pul'sive·ness** *n.*

im·pu·ni·ty (im PYOO ni tee) *n.* freedom or exemption from punishment, harm, or unpleasant consequence. [< L *impunitas*]

im·pure (im PYUUR) *adj.* **1.** containing something offensive or contaminating. **2.** mixed with an inferior or worthless substance; adultered. **3.** contrary to moral purity; sinful. **4.** having the characteristics of more than one style, period, color, language, etc.; mixed. —**im·pure'ly** *adv.*

im·pu·ri·ty (im PYUUR i tee) *n. pl.* **·ties 1.** the state or quality of being impure. **2.** that which is impure. [ME *impurite*]

im·put·a·ble (im PYOOT ə bəl) *adj.* capable of being imputed; chargeable. —**im·put'a·bly** *adv.*

im·pute (im PYOOT) *v.t.* **·put·ed, ·put·ing 1.** attribute (a fault, crime, etc.) to a person; charge. **2.** consider as the cause or source of; ascribe; with *to.* [ME *inputen*] —**im·pu·ta·tion** (IM pyuu TAY shən) *n.*

in (in) *prep.* **1.** held by or within the confines of; enclosed by: apples *in* a bag. **2.** surrounded by; amidst: buried *in* mud. **3.** within the limits, area, or range of. **4.** within the category, class, or number of; belonging to: twelve inches *in* a foot. **5.** existing as a part or characteristic of: *in* the works of Shaw. **6.** affected by; under the influence of: to shout *in* rage. **7.** wearing. **8.** made of a specified color, style, or material. **9.** arranged so as to form: trees *in* a row. **10.** engaged at; occupied by: *in* business. **11.** for the purpose of: run *in* pursuit. **12.** by means of: speaking *in* whispers. **13.** according to: *in* my opinion. **14.** with regard or respect to: Students vary *in* talent. **15.** during. —**in that** for the reason that; because; since. —*adv.* **1.** to or toward the inside from the outside. **2.** indoors. **3.** in or into some activity; join *in.* **4.** into some place, condition, or position: Tuck the baby *in.* **5.** into some understood substance, object, etc.: Blend *in* the oil. —**be in for** be certain to experience (usu. something unpleasant). —**have it in for** hold a grudge against. —*adj.* **1.** that is in or remains within. **2.** that has gained power or control: the *in* group. **3.** reflecting the latest trends; fashionable: an *in* resort. —*n.* **1.** a member of the group in power or at an advantage. **2.** a means of entrance or access; also, a position of favor or influence: have an *in*. —**ins and outs** the full complexities or particulars: the *ins* and *outs* of business. [ME]

in-[1] *prefix* not; without; un-; non-. Also: *i-* before *gn*, as in *ignore*; *il-* before *l*, as in *illiterate*; *im-* before *b, m, p*, as in *imbalance, immiscible, impecunious*; *ir-* before *r*, as in *irresistible*. [< L] Some self-explanatory words beginning with *in-*[1]:

inadvisability	inedible
inadvisable	ineducable
indemonstrable	insobriety
indiscoverable	insusceptible

in-[2] *prefix* in; into; on; within; toward: *include, incur, invade*: also used intensively, as in *inflame*. Also *il-* before *l*, as in *illuminate*; *im-* before *b, m, p*, as in *imbibe, immigrate, impress*; *ir-* before *r*, as in *irradiate*. [< OE]

in·a·bil·i·ty (IN ə BIL i tee) *n.* the state or quality of being unable; lack of the necessary power or means.

in ab·sen·ti·a (in ab SEN shə) *Latin* in absence (of the person concerned).

in·ac·ces·si·ble (IN ak SES ə bəl) *adj.* not accessible; incapable of being reached or closely approached. —**in′ac·ces′si·bil′i·ty** *n.*

in·ac·cu·rate (in AK yər it) *adj.* inexact; incorrect. —**in·ac′cu·ra·cy** *n.*

in·ac·tion (in AK shən) *n.* absence of action; idleness.

in·ac·ti·vate (in AK tə vayt) *v.t.* **·vat·ed, ·vat·ing** make inactive. —**in·ac′ti·va′tion** *n.*

in·ac·tive (in AK tiv) *adj.* **1.** characterized by inaction; idle; inert. **2.** slow or indolent. **3.** *Mil.* not mobilized. —**in′ac·tiv′i·ty** *n.*

in·ad·e·quate (in AD i kwit) *adj.* not adequate; not equal to that which is required; insufficient. —**in·ad′e·qua·cy** (-kwi see) *n.*

in·ad·mis·si·ble (IN əd MIS ə bəl) *adj.* not admissible; not to be considered, approved, or allowed. —**in′ad·mis′si·bil′i·ty** *n.*

in·ad·ver·tent (IN əd VUR tnt) *adj.* **1.** not exercising due care or consideration; negligent. **2.** resulting from inattention or oversight; unintentional. —**in′ad·ver′tence, in′ad·ver′ten·cy** *n.*

in·al·ien·a·ble (in AYL yə nə bəl) *adj.* not transferable; that cannot be rightfully taken away. —**in·al′ien·a·bly** *adv.*

in·ane (i NAYN) *adj.* **1.** lacking in sense; silly. **2.** empty of meaning; pointless. [< L *inanis*] —**in·ane′ly** *adv.*

in·an·i·mate (in AN ə mit) *adj.* **1.** not living or animate. **2.** lacking animation; torpid; spiritless.

in·an·i·ty (i NAN i tee) *n.* **1.** lack of sense or meaning; silliness; foolishness. **2.** *pl.* **·ties** a foolish remark, action, etc. **3.** emptiness. [< L *inanitas*]

in·ap·pli·ca·ble (in AP li kə bəl) *adj.* not applicable; irrelevant; unsuitable. —**in·ap′·pli·ca·bil′i·ty** *n.*

in·ap·pre·ci·a·ble (IN ə PREE shee ə bəl) *adj.* imperceptible; unnoticeable. —**in′ap·pre′ci·a·bly** *adv.*

in·ap·pro·pri·ate (IN ə PROH pree it) *adj.* not appropriate; unsuitable; unfitting. —**in′ap·pro′pri·ate·ness** *n.*

in·ar·tic·u·late (IN ahr TIK yə lit) *adj.* **1.** uttered without the distinct sounds of spoken language: *inarticulate* cries. **2.** incapable of speech; dumb. **3.** unable to speak coherently. **4.** unspoken; unexpressed. —**in′ar·tic′u·late·ness** *n.*

in·as·much as (IN əz MUCH əz) **1.** considering the fact that; seeing that; because. **2.** insofar as; according as. [ME *in as muche as*]

in·at·ten·tion (IN ə TEN shən) *n.* lack of attention. —**in′at·ten′tive** *adj.*

in·au·di·ble (in AW də bəl) *adj.* incapable of being heard. —**in·au′di·bil′i·ty** *n.*

in·au·gu·ral (in AW gyər əl) *adj.* of or pertaining to an inauguration. —*n.* a speech made at an inauguration.

in·au·gu·rate (in AW gyə RAYT) *v.t.* **·rat·ed, ·rat·ing 1.** begin formally; initiate. **2.** induct into office with formal ceremony. **3.** celebrate the public opening of. [< L *inauguratus* consecrated by augury] —**in·au′gu·ra′tion** *n.*

in·aus·pi·cious (IN aw SPISH əs) *adj.* not auspicious; ill-omened; unfavorable. —**in′·aus·pi′cious·ly** *adv.*

in·board (IN bord) *adj. & adv.* **1.** *Naut.* **a** inside the hull. **b** toward the center line of a vessel. **2.** *Aeron.* inward from the tip of an airfoil; close to the fuselage.

in·born (IN BORN) *adj.* existing from birth; natural; inherent. [ME]

in·bound (IN BOWND) *adj.* inward bound.

in·bred (IN BRED) *adj.* **1.** inborn; innate. **2.** produced by inbreeding.

in·breed (IN BREED) *v.t.* **·bred**, **·breed·ing** breed by continual mating of closely related stock.

in·cal·cu·la·ble (in KAL kyə lə bəl) *adj.* **1.** unable to be calculated. **2.** unpredictable. —**in·cal′cu·la·bil′i·ty** *n.*

in camera in closed or secret session; privately. [< L, in a room]

in·can·desce (IN kən DES) *v.t. & v.i.* **·desced**, **·desc·ing** be or become, or cause to become, luminous with heat.

in·can·des·cent (IN kən DES ənt) *adj.* **1.** luminous or glowing with intense heat. **2.** shining with intense brilliance. [< L *incandescere* glow] —**in′can·des′cence** *n.*

in·can·ta·tion (IN kan TAY shən) *n.* **1.** the uttering or intoning of words or syllables supposed to produce magical results. **2.** the magic words or formula so uttered. [ME]

in·ca·pac·i·tate (IN kə PAS i TAYT) *v.t.* **·tat·ed**, **·tat·ing** **1.** deprive of ability, power, or fitness; disable. **2.** *Law* deprive of legal capacity; disqualify. —**in′ca·pac′i·ty** *n.*

in·car·cer·ate (in KAHR sə RAYT) *v.t.* **·at·ed**, **·at·ing** **1.** put in prison; imprison. **2.** confine; enclose. —*adj.* (in KAHR sər it) imprisoned. [< Med.L *incarceratus* imprisoned] —**in·car′cer·a′tion** *n.*

in·car·nate (in KAHR nit) *adj.* **1.** embodied in flesh, esp. in human form. **2.** personified; exemplified. —*v.t.* (in KAHR nayt) **·nat·ed**, **·nat·ing** **1.** give bodily form to. **2.** invest with concrete form. [ME]

in·car·na·tion (IN kahr NAY shən) *n.* **1.** the assumption of bodily form, esp. human form. **2.** a person, animal, or thing in which some ideal or quality is embodied. —**the Incarnation** *Theol.* the assumption by Jesus Christ of the human form and condition. [ME *incarnacion*]

in·cen·di·ar·y (in SEN dee ER ee) *adj.* **1.** of or pertaining to the malicious burning of property. **2.** inciting to riot, rebellion, etc.; inflammatory. **3.** capable of generating intense heat. —*n. pl.* **·ar·ies** **1.** one who maliciously sets fire to property. **2.** one who stirs up mob violence, etc. [< L *incendiarius* kindled]

in·cense[1] (in SENS) *v.t.* **·censed**, **·cens·ing** inflame with anger; enrage. [ME *incensen*]

in·cense[2] (IN sens) *n.* **1.** an aromatic substance that gives off an agreeable odor when burned. **2.** the odor or smoke produced in burning such a substance. **3.** any pleasant fragrance. —*v.t.* **·censed**, **·cens·ing** perfume with incense. [ME]

in·cen·tive (in SEN tiv) *n.* that which incites, or tends to incite, to action; motivating force. —*adj.* serving to incite to action. [ME]

in·cep·tion (in SEP shən) *n.* beginning; start. [ME *incepcion*]

in·cep·tive (in SEP tiv) *adj.* beginning; incipient; initial.

in·cer·ti·tude (in SUR ti TOOD) *n.* **1.** uncertainty; doubtfulness. **2.** insecurity. [< LL *incertitudo*]

in·ces·sant (in SES ənt) *adj.* continuing without interruption; never ceasing. [ME *incessaunte*] —**in·ces′san·cy** *n.*

in·cest (IN sest) *n.* sexual intercourse between persons so closely related that marriage between them is forbidden by law or taboo. [ME] —**in·ces·tu·ous** (in SES choo əs) *adj.*

inch (inch) *n.* a measure of length equal to $1/12$ of a foot: symbol ". —**every inch** in every way; completely. —*v.t. & v.i.* move or advance by small degrees. [ME]

in·cho·ate (in KOH it) *adj.* **1.** in an early or rudimentary stage. **2.** lacking order, form, coherence, etc. [< L *inchoatus* begun] —**in·cho′ate·ness** *n.*

in·ci·dence (IN si dəns) *n.* the degree of occurrence or effect: the *incidence* of illiteracy. [ME]

in·ci·dent (IN si dənt) *n.* **1.** a distinct event or piece of action. **2.** a minor episode or event. —*adj.* **1.** naturally or usually attending: with *to*: dangers *incident* to travel. **2.** falling or striking: *incident* rays of light. [ME]

in·ci·den·tal (IN si DEN tl) *adj.* **1.** occurring in the course of something. **2.** naturally or usually attending. **3.** minor; secondary. —*n.* **1.** an incidental circumstance or event. **2.** *pl.* minor expenses.

in·ci·den·tal·ly (IN si DEN tl ee) *adv.* **1.** as a subordinate or chance occurrence along with something else. **2.** by the way.

in·cin·er·ate (in SIN ə RAYT) *v.t.* **·at·ed**, **·at·ing** consume with fire; cremate. [< Med.L *incineratus* burned to ashes] —**in·cin′er·a′tion** *n.*

in·cin·er·a·tor (in SIN ə RAY tər) *n.* an apparatus for burning refuse.

in·cip·i·ent (in SIP ee ənt) *adj.* coming into existence; just beginning to appear. [< L *incipere* begin] —**in·cip′i·en·cy** *n.*

in·cise (in SĪZ) *v.t.* •cised, •cis·ing 1. cut into, or cut marks upon, with a sharp instrument. 2. engrave; carve. [< L *incisus* carved] —**in·cised′** *adj.*

in·ci·sion (in SIZH ən) *n.* 1. the act of incising. 2. a cut; gash. 3. *Surg.* a cut made in soft tissue. 4. incisiveness. [ME]

in·ci·sive (in SĪ siv) *adj.* 1. sharp; keen. 2. cutting; sarcastic. [< Med.L *incisivus*] —**in·ci′sive·ly** *adv.* —**in·ci′sive·ness** *n.*

in·ci·sor (in SĪ zər) *n.* a front tooth adapted for cutting; in people, one of eight such teeth, four in each jaw. [< NL, lit., cutter]

in·cite (in SĪT) *v.t.* •cit·ed, •cit·ing spur to action; urge on; instigate. [< L *incitare* rouse] —**in·cite′·ment** *n.* —**in·cit′er** *n.*

in·clem·ent (in KLEM ənt) *adj.* 1. of the weather, severe; stormy. 2. without mercy; harsh. —**in·clem′en·cy** *n.*

in·cli·na·tion (in klə NAY shən) *n.* 1. a personal preference or tendency; bent; liking. 2. a tendency toward a condition; trend. 3. the act of inclining, or the state of being inclined. 4. deviation or degree of deviation from the vertical or horizontal. 5. a sloping surface. [ME *inclinacioun*]

in·cline (in KLĪN) *v.* •clined, •clin·ing *v.i.* 1. diverge from the horizontal or vertical; slant. 2. have a bent or preference; be disposed. 3. tend in some quality or degree: orange *inclining* toward red. —*v.t.* 4. cause to bend, lean, or slope. 5. impart a tendency or leaning to (a person); influence. 6. bow or nod, as the head. —*n.* (IN klīn) a gradient; slope. [ME *inclinen* lean] —**in·clined′** *adj.*

in·clude (in KLOOD) *v.t.* •clud·ed, •clud·ing 1. have as a component part or parts; comprise; contain. 2. place in a general category, group, etc.; consider in a reckoning. 3. have or involve as a subordinate part, quality, etc.; imply. [ME] —**in·clud′a·ble, in·clud′i·ble** *adj.* —**in·clu′sion** (-zhən) *n.*

in·clu·sive (in KLOO siv) *adj.* 1. including: with *of.* 2. including the limits specified: from 1959 to 1964 *inclusive.* 3. comprehensive: an *inclusive* report. [ME] —**in·clu′sive·ly** *adv.* —**in·clu′·sive·ness** *n.*

in·cog·ni·to (IN kog NEE toh) *adj. & adv.*

under an assumed name or identity; in disguise. [< Ital.]

in·co·her·ent (IN koh HEER ənt) *adj.* 1. lacking in logical connection; confused. 2. unable to think clearly or express oneself logically. 3. consisting of parts or ingredients that do not stick together. 4. lacking in agreement or harmony; disorganized. —**in′co·her′ence** *n.* —**in′co·her′ent·ly** *adv.*

in·com·bus·ti·ble (IN kəm BUS tə bəl) *adj.* incapable of being burned; fireproof. [ME] —*n.* an incombustible substance or material. —**in′com·bus′ti·bil′i·ty** *n.*

in·come (IN kum) *n.* money, or sometimes its equivalent, received periodically by an individual, a corporation, etc., in return for labor or services rendered, or from property etc.

income tax a tax levied on annual income over a specified amount.

in·com·ing (IN KUM ing) *adj.* coming in or about to come in. —*n.* arrival.

in·com·men·su·ra·ble (IN kə MEN sər ə bəl) *adj.* 1. lacking a common measure or standard of comparison. 2. greatly out of proportion; not in accordance.

in·com·men·su·rate (IN kə MEN sər it) *adj.* inadequate; disproportionate.

in·com·mode (IN kə MOHD) *v.t.* •mod·ed, •mod·ing inconvenience; disturb. [< L *incommodus* inconvenient]

in·com·mo·di·ous (IN kə MOH dee əs) *adj.* 1. uncomfortably small; cramped. 2. causing discomfort; inconvenient. —**in′com·mo′di·ous·ly** *adv.*

in·com·mu·ni·ca·do (IN kə MYOO ni KAH doh) *adj. & adv.* onfined without means of communication. [< Sp.]

in·com·mu·ni·ca·tive (IN kə MYOO ni kə tiv) *adj.* not communicative; taciturn; reserved.

in·com·pa·ra·ble (IN KOM pər ə bəl) *adj.* 1. incapable of being equaled or surpassed; matchless. 2. lacking in qualities or characteristics that can be compared. —**in·com′pa·ra·bly** *adv.*

in·com·pat·i·ble (IN kəm PAT ə bəl) *adj.* 1. incapable of coexisting harmoniously. 2. disagreeing in nature; conflicting. 3. *Med.* having a harmful or undesirable effect when combined or used together. [< Med.L *incompatibilis*] —*n.pl.* incompatible persons, drugs, etc. —**in′com·pat′i·bil′i·ty** *n.*

in·com·pe·tent (in KOM pi tənt) *adj.* 1.

lacking in ability or skill; inadequate to the task; unfit. **2.** reflecting a lack of skill. **3.** not legally qualified. —*n.* one who is incompetent. —**in·com'pe·tence, in·com'pe·ten·cy** *n.* —**in·com'pe·tent·ly** *adv.*

in·com·plete (IN kəm PLEET) *adj.* **1.** not having all essential elements or parts; unfinished. **2.** not fully developed; imperfect: *incomplete* growth. —**in'com·plete'ly** *adv.* —**in'com·plete'ness** *n.*

in·com·pre·hen·si·ble (IN kom pri HEN sə bəl) *adj.* incapable of being understood; unintelligible. [ME] —**in'com·pre·hen' si·bil'i·ty** *n.* —**in'com·pre·hen'si·bly** *adv.*

in·com·pre·hen·sion (IN kom pri HEN shən) *n.* lack of understanding.

in·con·ceiv·a·ble (IN kən SEE və bəl) *adj.* incapable of being conceived by the mind; unbelievable. —**in'con·ceiv'a·bil'i·ty** *n.* —**in'con·ceiv'a·bly** *adv.*

in·con·clu·sive (IN kən KLOO siv) *adj.* **1.** not leading to an ultimate conclusion; indeterminate; not decisive. **2.** not achieving a definite result; ineffective.

in·con·gru·ous (in KONG groo əs) *adj.* **1.** not suitable; inappropriate. **2.** not corresponding or conforming; at odds: with *with* or *to.* **3.** consisting of elements or qualities not properly belonging together. [< L *incongruus* inconsistent] —**in·con·gru·i·ty** (IN kən GROO i tee) *n.* —**in·con' gru·ous·ly** *adv.*

in·con·se·quen·tial (IN kon si KWEN shəl) *adj.* having little or no consequence; unimportant; trivial. —**in·con·se·quen· ti·al·i·ty** (IN kon si KWEN shee AL i tee) *n.* —**in'con·se·quen'tial·ly** *adv.*

in·con·sid·er·a·ble (IN kən SID ər ə bəl) *adj.* **1.** small in quantity, size or value. **2.** not worth considering; trivial. —**in'con·sid' er·a·bly** *adv.*

in·con·sid·er·ate (IN kən SID ər it) *adj.* **1.** lacking in concern for others; thoughtless. **2.** not carefully considered or thought out. [ME] —**in'con·sid'er·ate·ness** *n.*

in·con·sis·ten·cy (IN kən SIS tən see) *n. pl. ·cies* **1.** the quality of being inconsistent. **2.** something that is inconsistent.

in·con·sis·tent (IN kən SIS tənt) *adj.* **1.** lacking in agreement or compatibility; at variance. **2.** containing contradictory elements or parts. **3.** lacking uniformity in behavior or thought; erratic; changeable.

in·con·sol·a·ble (IN kən SOH lə bəl) *adj.* not to be consoled; disconsolate; dejected.

[< L *inconsolabilis*] —**in'con·sol'a·bil' i·ty** *n.* —**in'con·sol'a·bly** *adv.*

in·con·spic·u·ous (IN kən SPIK yoo əs) *adj.* not conspicuous; not attracting attention. [< L *inconspicuus*] —**in'con·spic'u·ous· ness** *n.*

in·con·stant (in KON stənt) *adj.* not constant; variable; fickle. [ME *inconstaunt*] — **in·con'stan·cy** *n.*

in·con·test·a·ble (IN kən TES tə bəl) *adj.* not admitting of question; unassailable: *incontestable* evidence. —**in'con· test'a·bil'·i·ty** *n.* —**in'con·test'a·bly** *adv.*

in·con·ti·nent (in KON tn ənt) *adj.* **1.** exercising little control or restraint, esp. in sexual desires. **2.** incapable of controlling the elimination of urine or feces. **3.** unrestrained; unchecked. [ME] —**in·con'ti· nence** *n.*

in·con·trol·la·ble (IN kən TROH lə bəl) *adj.* incapable of being controlled; uncontrollable. —**in'con·trol'la·bly** *adv.*

in·con·tro·vert·i·ble (IN kən trə VUR tə bəl) *adj.* not admitting of controversy; undeniable. —**in'con·tro·vert'i·bil'i·ty** *n.* —**in'con·tro·vert'i·bly** *adv.*

in·con·ven·ience (IN kən VEEN yəns) *n.* **1.** the state or quality of being inconvenient. **2.** something that is inconvenient. [ME] — *v.t.* **·ienced, ·ienc·ing** cause inconvenience to.

in·con·ven·ient (IN kən VEEN yənt) *adj.* causing or lending itself to discomfort and difficulty; troublesome; awkward. [ME]

in·cor·po·rate (in KOR pə RAYT) *v.* **·rat·ed, ·rat·ing** *v.i.* **1.** form a legal corporation or a similar association. **2.** become combined or merged as one body or whole. —*v.t.* **3.** take in, put in, or include as part of a whole. **4.** form (persons, groups, etc.) into a legal corporation or a similar association. **5.** combine or merge into a whole. [ME] — *adj.* (in KOR pər it) **1.** combined into a single unit or whole. **2.** legally incorporated. —**in·cor'po·ra'tion** *n.* —**in·cor' po·ra·ta'tor** *n.*

in·cor·po·rat·ed (in KOR pə RAY tid) *adj.* **1.** forming one body or whole; combined. **2.** organized into a legal corporation: abbr. *inc., Inc.*

in·cor·po·re·al (IN kor POR ee əl) *adj.* **1.** not consisting of matter. **2.** of or pertaining to nonmaterial things; spiritual. — **in'cor·po're·al·ly** *adv.*

in·cor·rect (IN kə REKT) *adj.* **1.** inaccurate

or untrue as to fact or usage; wrong. **2.** improper; unsuitable. [ME] —**in'cor•rect'ness** *n.*

in•cor•ri•gi•ble (in KOR i jə bəl) *adj.* incapable of being reformed or corrected. [ME] —*n.* one who is incorrigible. —**in•cor'ri•gi•bly** *adv.*

in•cor•rupt (IN kə RUPT) *adj.* **1.** not morally corrupt; honest; good. **2.** not spoiled or decayed; untainted; fresh. **3.** free from errors or alterations, as a literary text. Also **in'cor•rupt'ed.** [ME]

in•cor•rupt•i•ble (IN kə RUP tə bəl) *adj.* **1.** not accessible to bribery; honest. **2.** incapable of corruption; not subject to decay or spoilage. [ME] —**in'cor•rupt'i•bil'i•ty** *n.*

in•crease (in KREES) *v.* •**creased,** •**creas•ing** *v.i.* **1.** become greater, as in amount, size, degree, etc.; grow. **2.** grow in number; multiply; reproduce. —*v.t.* **3.** make greater, as in amount, size, degree, etc.; enlarge. [ME *incresen* grow] —*n.* (IN krees) **1.** a growing or becoming greater. **2.** the amount of growth; increment. —**in•creas'ing•ly** *adv.*

in•cred•i•ble (in KRED ə bəl) *adj.* not credible; unbelievable. **2.** amazing; wonderful. —**in•cred'i•bly** *adv.*

in•cred•u•lous (in KREJ ə ləs) *adj.* **1.** not willing or not disposed to believe; skeptical. **2.** characterized by or showing disbelief. [< L *incredulus*] —**in•cre•du•li•ty** (IN kri DOO li tee) *n.*

in•cre•ment (IN krə mənt) *n.* **1.** a quantity added to another quantity. **2.** the act of increasing; enlargement. [ME] —**in'cre•men'tal** (IN krə MEN tl) *adj.*

in•crim•i•nate (in KRIM ə NAYT) *v.t.* •**nat•ed, •nat•ing 1.** imply the wrongdoing or guilt of (a person, etc.). **2.** charge with a crime or fault. [< LL *incriminatus* accused] —**in•crim'i•na'tion** *n.* —**in•crim'i•na•to'ry** (-nə TOR ee) *adj.*

in•crust (in KRUST) *v.t. & v.i.* furnish with or form a crust. Also spelled *encrust.*

in•cu•bate (IN kyə BAYT) *v.* •**bat•ed,** •**bat•ing** *v.t.* **1.** sit on (eggs) in order to hatch them; brood. **2.** hatch (eggs) in this manner or by artificial heat. **3.** maintain under conditions favoring optimum growth or development, as bacterial cultures. —*v.i.* **4.** undergo incubation. [< L *incubatus* sat on] —**in'cu•ba'tive** *adj.*

in•cu•ba•tion (IN kyə BAY shən) *n.* **1.** the act of incubating, or the state of being incubated. **2.** *Med.* the period between the time

of exposure to an infectious disease and the appearance of the symptoms.

in•cu•ba•tor (IN kyə BAY tər) *n.* **1.** an apparatus kept at a uniform warmth for artificial hatching of eggs. **2.** *Bacteriol.* a device for the artificial development of microorganisms. **3.** an apparatus for keeping warm a prematurely born baby.

in•cu•bus (IN kyə bəs) *n.* *pl.* •**bi** (-BI) or •**bus•es 1.** anything that tends to oppress or discourage. **2.** a nightmare. **3.** in folklore, a male demon that has sexual intercourse with sleeping women. [ME]

in•cul•cate (in KUL kayt) *v.t.* •**cat•ed,** •**cat•ing** impress upon the mind by frequent repetition or forceful admonition; instill. [< L *inculcatus* trampled] —**in'•cul•ca'tion** *n.* —**in'cul'ca'tor** *n.*

in•cul•pate (in KUL payt) *v.t.* •**pat•ed,** •**pat•ing** involve in an accusation; incriminate. [< L *inculpatus* blamed] —**in'cul•pa'tion** *n.*

in•cum•ben•cy (in KUM bən see) *n.* **1.** the state of being incumbent. **2.** *pl.* •**cies** that which is incumbent; the holding of an office or the period in which it is held.

in•cum•bent (in KUM bənt) *adj.* **1.** resting upon one as a moral obligation, or as necessary; obligatory. **2.** resting, leaning, or weighing upon something. —*n.* one who holds an office. [ME] —**in•cum'bent•ly** *adv.*

in•cu•nab•u•la (IN kyuu NAB yə lə) *n. sing.* •**u•lum 1.** specimens of early European printing; esp., books printed before A.D. 1500. **2.** the earliest stages of development; beginnings. [< L, cradle]

in•cur (in KUR) *v.t.* •**curred, •cur•ring** become subject to (unpleasant consequences); bring on oneself. [ME] —**in•cur'rence** *n.*

in•cur•a•ble (in KYUUR ə bəl) *adj.* not curable or remediable. [ME] —*n.* one suffering from an incurable disease. —**in•cur'a•bly** *adv.*

in•cur•sion (in KUR zhən) *n.* **1.** a hostile, often sudden entrance into a territory; raid. **2.** a running in or against; encroachment. [ME] —**in•cur'sive** (-siv) *adj.*

in•cus (ING kəs) *n. pl.* **in•cu•des** (in KYOO deez) *Anat.* the anvil-shaped central bone of the group of three bones in the middle ear: also called *anvil.* [< NL]

in•debt•ed (in DET id) *adj.* **1.** legally obligated to pay for value received; in debt. **2.** morally obligated to acknowledge benefits or favors. [ME *endetted*] —**in•debt'ed•ness** *n.*

in•de•cen•cy (in DEE sən see) *n.* **1.** the quality or condition of being indecent. **2.** *pl.* **•cies** an indecent act, speech, etc. [< L *indecentia*]

in•de•cent (in DEE sənt) *adj.* **1.** offensive to one's sense of modesty or morality. **2.** contrary to propriety or good taste; vulgar.

in•de•ci•pher•a•ble (in di SĪ fər ə bəl) *adj.* not decipherable; unreadable.

in•de•ci•sion (in di SIZH ən) *n.* inability to make decisions.

in•de•ci•sive (in di SĪ siv) *adj.* **1.** not bringing about a definite conclusion, solution, etc. **2.** unable or unwilling to make decisions. —**in'de•ci'sive•ly** *adv.* —**in'de•ci'sive•ness** *n.*

in•de•cor•um (in di KOR əm) *n.* lack of propriety. [< L] —**in•dec•o•rous** (in DEK ər əs) *adj.*

in•deed (in DEED) *adv.* in fact; in truth. — *interj.* Is that true?

in•de•fat•i•ga•ble (in di FAT i gə bəl) *adj.* not yielding readily to fatigue; tireless; unflagging. [< L *indefatigabilis* untiring] — **in'de•fat'i•ga•bly** *adv.*

in•de•fen•si•ble (in di FEN sə bəl) *adj.* **1.** incapable of being justified. **2.** incapable of being defended. —**in'de•fen'si•bil'i•ty** *n.*

in•de•fin•a•ble (in di FĪ nə bəl) *adj.* incapable of being defined or described; vague; ineffable. —**in'de•fin'a•bly** *adv.*

in•def•i•nite (in DEF ə nit) *adj.* **1.** not definite or precise; vague. **2.** Without a fixed number; indeterminate. **3.** *Gram.* not definite or determining. —**in•def'i•nite•ly** *adv.*

indefinite article see under ARTICLE.

indefinite pronoun *Gram.* a pronoun that represents an object or person indefinitely or generally, as *each, none, another.*

in•del•i•ble (in DEL ə bəl) *adj.* **1.** incapable of being blotted out or effaced. **2.** leaving a mark or stain not easily erased. [< Med.L *indelibilis* indestructible] —**in•del'i•bly** *adv.*

in•del•i•ca•cy (in DEL i kə see) *n.* **1.** the quality of being indelicate; coarseness. **2.** *pl.* **•cies** an indelicate thing, act, etc.

in•del•i•cate (in DEL i kit) *adj.* **1.** lacking or offending a sense of delicacy or good taste; crude. **2.** tactless. —**in•del'i•cate•ly** *adv.*

in•dem•ni•fy (in DEM ni fī) *v.t.* **•fied, •fy•ing 1.** compensate (a person, etc.) for

loss or damage sustained. **2.** make good (a loss). **3.** give security against future loss or punishment. [< L *indemnis* unharmed] — **in•dem'ni•fi•ca'tion** *n.*

in•dem•ni•ty (in DEM ni tee) *n.* *pl.* **•ties 1.** that which is given as compensation for a loss or for damage. **2.** an agreement to remunerate another for loss or protect him against liability. **3.** exemption from penalties or liabilities. [ME *indemnite*]

in•dent¹ (in DENT) *v.t.* **1.** set in from the margin, as the first line of a paragraph. **2.** cut or mark the edge of with toothlike notches; serrate. —*v.i.* **3.** be notched or cut. **4.** set a line, paragraph, etc. in from the margin. —*n.* (IN dent) **1.** a cut or notch on the edge of a thing. **2.** an indention (def. 1). [ME]

in•dent² *v.t.* push in so as to form a dent or depression. —*n.* (IN dent) a dent or depression.

in•den•ta•tion (in den TAY shən) *n.* **1.** a notch or series of notches in an edge or border. **2.** the act of notching, or the condition of being notched. **3.** a dent. **4.** an indention.

in•den•tion (in DEN shən) *n.* **1.** the setting in of a line of type, writing, etc, at the left side; also, the space thus left. **2.** a dent.

in•den•ture (in DEN chər) *n.* **1.** a deed or contract made between two or more parties. **2.** *pl.* such a contract between master and apprentice. [ME] —*v.t.* **•tured, •tur•ing** bind by indenture.

in•de•pen•dence (in di PEN dəns) *n.* the quality or condition of being independent.

in•de•pen•dent (in di PEN dənt) *adj.* **1.** not subject to the authority of another; autonomous. **2.** not dependent on or part of some larger group, system, etc. **3.** not an adherent of a party or faction. **4.** not readily influenced or guided by others; self-reliant. **5.** self-supporting. **6.** having sufficient financial means to live comfortably. —*n.* one who or that which is independent; esp., one not an adherent of a party or faction.

in•de•scrib•a•ble (in di SKRĪ bə bəl) *adj.* incapable of being described; esp., too complex, extreme, etc., to be described. — **in'de•scrib'a•bly** *adv.*

in•de•struc•ti•ble (in di STRUK tə bəl) *adj.* incapable of being destroyed; very tough and durable. —**in'de•struc'ti•bil'i•ty** *n.*

in•de•ter•mi•na•ble (in di TUR mə nə bəl) *adj.* **1.** incapable of being ascertained. **2.**

incapable of being decided. —**in′de·ter′mi·na·bly** adv.

in·de·ter·mi·nate (IN di TUR mə nit) adj. **1.** not definite or precise; vague. **2.** not decided; unsettled. **3.** not fixed; inconclusive. —**in′de·ter′mi·na·cy** n. —**in′de·ter′mi·na′tion** n. **1.** lack of determination. **2.** the condition of being indeterminate.

in·dex (IN deks) n. pl. **·dex·es** or **·di·ces** (-də SEEZ) **1.** an alphabetical list, as at the end of a book, of topics, names, etc., and the numbers of the pages where they occur. **2.** a descriptive list, as of items in a collection. **3.** anything that serves as an indicator, as a needle on a dial. **4.** anything that indicates or gives evidence of; sign: Alertness is an *index* of intelligence. **5.** a numerical expression of the ratio between one dimension or magnitude and another. **6.** *Math.* a subscript or superscript. —v.t. **1.** provide with an index, as a book. **2.** enter in an index, as a subject. **3.** indicate. [ME] —**in′dex·er** n.

In·dex n. formerly, a list of books that the Roman Catholic Church forbade its members to read except with special permission.

index finger the finger next to the thumb: also called *forefinger*.

Indian giver *Informal* one who gives a present and then wants it back.

Indian summer a period of mild, warm weather occurring in late autumn.

India paper a thin printing paper, used chiefly in taking the finest proofs from engraved plates.

in·di·cate (IN di KAYT) v.t. **·cat·ed, ·cat·ing 1.** be or give a sign of; signify. **2.** direct attention to; point out. **3.** make known. [< L *indicatus* made known]

in·di·ca·tion (IN di KAY shən) n. **1.** the act of indicating. **2.** that which indicates; sign. **3.** a degree or quantity shown on a measuring instrument.

in·dic·a·tive (in DIK ə tiv) adj. **1.** suggestive of; pointing out. **2.** *Gram.* denoting a mood in which an act or condition is stated or questioned as a fact. —n. *Gram.* **a** the indicative mood. **b** a verb in this mood. —**in·dic′a·tive·ly** adv.

in·di·ca·tor (IN di KAY tər) n. **1.** one who or that which indicates or points out. **2.** an instrument that measures or shows position; also, its pointer or needle.

in·di·ces (IN di SEEZ) a plural of INDEX.

in·dict (in DĪT) v.t. **1.** *Law* prefer an indict-

ment against. **2.** charge with a crime or offense. —**in·dict′a·ble** adj.

in·dict·ment (in DĪT mənt) n. **1.** the act of indicting, or the state of being indicted. **2.** *Law* a formal written charge of crime, presented by a grand jury. [ME *enditement*]

in·dif·fer·ent (in DIF rənt) adj. **1.** having no interest or feeling; unconcerned. **2.** lacking in distinction; mediocre. **3.** only average in size, amount, etc. **4.** having little importance or significance. **5.** showing no preference; unbiased. [ME] —**in·dif′fer·ence** n. —**in·dif′fer·ent·ly** adv.

in·dig·e·nous (in DIJ ə nəs) adj. **1.** originating or occurring naturally in the place specified; native. **2.** innate; inherent. [< LL *indigenus* native]

in·di·gent (IN di jənt) adj. lacking means of subsistence; poor. [ME] —**in′di·gence, in′di·gen·cy** n.

in·di·gest·i·ble (IN di JES tə bəl) adj. difficult to digest; not digestible. —**in′di·gest′i·bil′i·ty** n. —**in′di·gest′i·bly** adv.

in·di·ges·tion (IN di JES chən) n. difficulty in digesting food. [ME]

in·dig·nant (in DIG nənt) adj. feeling or showing indignation. —**in·dig′nant·ly** adv.

in·dig·na·tion (IN dig NAY shən) n. anger aroused by injustice or baseness. [ME *indignacioun*]

in·dig·ni·ty (in DIG ni tee) n. pl. **·ties** an act that humiliates or injures self-respect. [< L *indignitas* unworthiness]

in·di·go (IN di GOH) n. pl. **·gos** or **·goes 1.** a blue coloring substance obtained from certain plants or made synthetically. **2.** a deep violet blue. Also **indigo blue.** —**in·di·go** adj. [< Sp.]

in·di·rect (IN də REKT) adj. **1.** not following a direct line, course, or procedure. **2.** not straightforward or open; underhand. **3.** not coming as an immediate result: *indirect* benefits. **4.** not expressed in the exact words of the source: an *indirect* quotation. —**in′di·rec′tion** n. —**in′di·rect′ly** adv.

indirect object see under OBJECT.

indirect tax a tax whose burden is ultimately passed on to another.

in·dis·cern·i·ble (IN di SUR nə bəl) adj. incapable of being discerned; imperceptible. —**in′dis·cern′i·bly** adv.

in·dis·creet (IN di SKREET) adj. lacking discretion; imprudent. —**in′dis·creet′ly** adv.

in·dis·crete (IN di SKREET) *adj.* not discrete; not separated into parts.

in·dis·cre·tion (IN di SKRESH ən) *n.* 1. the state or quality of being indiscreet. 2. an indiscreet act, speech, etc. [ME]

in·dis·crim·i·nate (IN di SKRIM ə nit) *adj.* 1. showing no discrimination; not perceiving differences. 2. confused; chaotic. —**in'dis·crim'i·nate·ly** *adv.* —**in'dis·crim'i·na'tive** *adj.*

in·dis·pen·sa·ble (IN di SPEN sə bəl) *adj.* not to be dispensed with; essential. [< Med.L *indispensabilis*] —**in'dis·pen'sa·bil'i·ty** *n.* —**in'dis·pen'sa·bly** *adv.*

in·dis·pose (IN di SPOHZ) *v.t.* ·posed, ·pos·ing 1. render unwilling; disincline. 2. render unfit. 3. make slightly ill or ailing. —**in·dis·po·si·tion** (IN dis pə ZISH ən) *n.*

in·dis·posed (IN di SPOHZD) *adj.* 1. mildly ill; unwell. 2. disinclined; not willing.

in·dis·put·a·ble (IN di SPYOO tə bəl) *adj.* incapable of being disputed. —**in'dis·put'a·bil'i·ty** *n.* —**in'dis·put·a·bly** *adv.*

in·dis·sol·u·ble (IN di SOL yə bəl) *adj.* 1. incapable of being dissolved, separated into its elements, or destroyed. 2. binding; extremely durable. [< L *indissolubilis*] —**in'dis·sol'u·bly** *adv.*

in·dis·tinct (IN di STINGKT) *adj.* 1. not clearly defined or outlined; blurred. 2. not readily distinguishable; confused. —**in'dis·tinct'ly** *adv.* —**in'dis·tinct'ness** *n.*

in·dis·tin·guish·a·ble (IN di STING gwi shə bəl) *adj.* Incapable of being perceived or distinguished. —**in'dis·tin'guish·a·bly** *adv.*

in·di·vid·u·al (IN də VIJ oo əl) *adj.* 1. existing as a unit; single. 2. separate, as distinguished from others of the same kind. 3. pertaining to or meant for a single person, animal, etc. 4. differentiated from others by distinctive characteristics. —*n.* 1. a single human being as distinct from others. 2. a person. [ME] —**in'di·vid'u·al·ly** *adv.*

in·di·vid·u·al·ism (IN də VIJ oo ə LIZ əm) *n.* 1. personal independence in action, thought, etc. 2. the state of being individual. 3. a theory or doctrine that emphasizes the importance of the individual. —**in'di·vid'u·al·ist** *n.* —**in'di·vid'u·al·is'tic** *adj.*

in·di·vid·u·al·i·ty (IN də VIJ oo AL i tee) *n.* *pl.* ·ties 1. a quality or trait that distinguishes one person or thing from others. 2. strikingly distinctive character or personality. 3. the state of having separate, independent existence.

in·di·vid·u·al·ize (IN də VIJ oo ə LIZ) *v.t.* ·ized, ·iz·ing 1. make individual; distinguish. 2. treat, mention, or consider individually. 3. adapt to the needs of an individual. —**in'di·vid'u·al·i·za'tion** *n.*

in·di·vis·i·ble (IN də VIZ ə bəl) *adj.* not divisible; incapable of being divided. [ME] —*n.* something indivisible. —**in'di·vis'i·bil'i·ty** *n.* —**in'di·vis'i·bly** *adv.*

in·doc·tri·nate (in DOK trə NAYT) *v.t.* ·nat·ed, ·nat·ing instruct in doctrines; esp., to teach (someone) partisan or sectarian dogmas. [< Med.L *indoctrinatus* taught] —**in·doc'tri·na'tion** *n.*

In·do-Eu·ro·pe·an (IN doh YUUR ə PEE ən) *adj.* designating the largest family of languages in the world, comprising most of the languages of Europe and many languages of India and SW Asia. —**In'do-Eu'ro·pe'an** *n.*

in·do·lent (IN dl ənt) *adj.* averse to exertion or work; lazy. [< LL *indolere* feel pain] —**in'do·lence** *n.* —**in'do·lent·ly** *adv.*

in·dom·i·ta·ble (in DOM i tə bəl) *adj.* not easily defeated or subdued. [< LL *indomitabilis* untamed] —**in·dom'i·ta·bly** *adv.*

In·do·ne·sian (IN də NEE zhən) *n.* 1. an inhabitant of Indonesia. 2. the languages, collectively, spoken by the peoples native to Indonesia: also called *Malayan.* —**In'do·ne'sian** *adj.*

in·door (IN DOR) *adj.* 1. pertaining to or meant for the interior of a house or building. 2. located or performed indoors.

in·doors (in DORZ) *adv.* inside or toward the inside of a building.

in·du·bi·ta·ble (in DOO bi tə bəl) *adj.* not to be doubted. [< L *indubitabilis*] —**in·du'bi·ta·bly** *adv.*

in·duce (in DOOS) *v.t.* ·duced, ·duc·ing 1. cause to act, speak, etc.; influence; persuade. 2. bring on; cause. 3. infer by inductive reasoning. [ME] —**in·duc'i·ble** *adj.*

in·duce·ment (in DOOS mənt) *n.* 1. that which induces; incentive. 2. the act of inducing.

in·duct (in DUKT) *v.t.* 1. bring (a draftee) into military service. 2. install formally in an office, etc. 3. initiate in knowledge, experience, etc. 4. *Physics* produce by induction. [ME]

in·duct·ance (in DUK təns) n. *Electr.* the ability of a circuit to produce induction.

in·duc·tee (IN duk TEE) n. one inducted or being inducted.

in·duc·tion (in DUK shən) n. **1.** the act of inducting, or state of being inducted. **2.** the act of inducing or causing. **3.** a process of reasoning whereby a general statement is inferred from particular instances; also, the general statement itself. **4.** *Electr.* the production of magnetization or electrification in a body by the mere proximity of a magnetic field or electric charge, or of an electric current in a conductor by the variation of the magnetic field in its vicinity. [ME *induccioun*]

induction coil *Electr.* a device that changes a low steady voltage into a high intermittent alternating voltage by electromagnetic induction.

in·duc·tive (in DUK tiv) adj. **1.** pertaining to or resulting from induction. **2.** *Electr.* produced by or causing induction or inductance. [< LL *inductivus*] —**in·duc´tive·ly** adv.

in·dulge (in DULJ) v. **·dulged, ·dulg·ing** v.t. **1.** yield to or gratify, as desires or whims. **2.** yield to or gratify (another); humor. — v.i. **3.** yield to one's own desire: with *in*. [< L *indulgere* be kind to] —**in·dulg´er** n.

in·dul·gence (in DUL jəns) n. **1.** the act of indulging, or state of being indulgent. **2.** that which is indulged in. **3.** something granted as a favor. **4.** in business, permission to defer paying a bill etc. **5.** in the Roman Catholic Church, remission of temporal punishment due for a sin after it has been forgiven through sacramental absolution. [ME]

in·dul·gent (in DUL jənt) adj. prone to indulge; lenient. —**in·dul´gent·ly** adv.

in·du·rate (in DUU RAYT) v.t. & v.i. **·rat·ed, ·rat·ing 1.** make or become hard or unfeeling. **2.** make or become hardy. —adj. (IN duu rit) hard; unfeeling: also **in´du·rat´ed**. [ME *indurat* harden] —**in´du·ra´tion** n. —**in´du·ra´tive** adj.

in·dus·tri·al (in DUS tree əl) adj. **1.** of, characteristic of, used in, or resulting from industry. **2.** having many industries: an *industrial* park. **3.** relating to workers in industry. —n.pl. stocks or securities of industrial enterprises. —**in·dus´tri·al·ly** adv.

industrial arts the technical skills used in industry, esp. as subjects of study in schools.

in·dus·tri·al·ism (in DUS tree ə liz əm) n. an economic system based chiefly on large-scale industries and production of goods.

in·dus·tri·al·ist (in DUS tree ə list) n. an owner or manager in industry.

in·dus·tri·a·lize (in DUS tree ə LĪZ) v.t. **·ized, ·iz·ing 1.** establish large-scale industries in. **2.** make or form into an industry. —**in·dus´tri·al·i·za´tion** n.

in·dus·tri·ous (in DUS tree əs) adj. hardworking. —**in·dus´·tri·ous·ness** n.

in·dus·try (IN də stree) n. pl. **·tries 1.** any specific branch of production or manufacture. **2.** manufacturing and productive interests collectively. **3.** diligent and regular application to work or tasks. [< L *industria* diligence]

in·e·bri·ate (in EE bree AYT) v.t. **·at·ed, ·at·ing** make drunk; intoxicate. —n. (in EE bree it) habitual drunkard. —adj. (in EE bree it) intoxicated. [ME] —**in·e´bri·a´ted** adj. —**in·e´bri·a´tion** n.

in·ef·fa·ble (in EF ə bəl) adj. **1.** too overpowering to be expressed in words; indescribable. **2.** too sacred to be uttered. [ME] —**in·ef´fa·bly** adv.

in·ef·fec·tive (IN i FEK tiv) adj. **1.** not effective. **2.** incompetent. —**in´ef·fec´tive·ly** adv. —**in´ef·fec´tive·ness** n.

in·ef·fec·tu·al (IN i FEK choo əl) adj. **1.** not effectual. **2.** unsuccessful; fruitless. —**in´ef·fec´tu·al·ly** adv.

in·ef·fi·ca·cious (IN ef i KAY shəs) adj. not producing the effect desired or intended, as a medicine. —**in·ef·fi·ca·cy** (in EF i kə see) n. [< LL *inefficacia*]

in·ef·fi·cient (IN i FISH ənt) adj. **1.** not efficient; not performing a function economically; wasteful. **2.** incompetent. —**in´ef·fi´cien·cy** n. —**in´ef·fi´cient·ly** adv.

in·el·e·gant (in EL i gənt) adj. **1.** not elegant. **2.** coarse; crude. —**in·el´e·gance, in·el´e·gan·cy** n. —**in·el´e·gant·ly** adv.

in·e·luc·ta·ble (IN i LUK tə bəl) adj. not to be escaped from or avoided; inevitable. [< L *ineluctabilis* insurmountable] —**in´e·luc´ta·bly** adv.

in·ept (in EPT) adj. **1.** not suitable or appropriate. **2.** clumsy; awkward. [< L *ineptus* unfit] —**in·ep´ti·tude, in·ept´ness** n.

in·e·qual·i·ty (IN i KWOL i tee) n. pl. **·ties 1.** the state of being unequal. **2.** an instance of this. **3.** lack of evenness of proportion; variableness. **4.** disparity of social position, opportunity, justice, etc. [ME]

in·eq·ui·ta·ble (in EK wi tə bəl) *adj.*
not equitable; unfair. **—in·eq'ui·ta·bly**
adv.

in·eq·ui·ty (in EK wi tee) *n.* **1.** ack of equity;
injustice. **2.** *pl.* **·ties** an unfair act or course
of action.

in·e·rad·i·ca·ble (IN i RAD i kə bəl) *adj.*
not eradicable; impossible to remove or
root out. **—in'e·rad'i·ca·bly** *adv.*

in·ert (in URT) *adj.* **1.** lacking independent
power to move or to resist applied force. **2.**
disinclined to move or act; sluggish. **3.**
Chem. devoid or almost devoid of active
properties. [< L, unskillful] **—in·ert'ly**
adv.

in·er·tia (in UR shə) *n.* **1.** the state of being
inert; inactivity. **2.** *Physics* the tendency of
any physical body to persist in its state of
rest or of uniform motion until acted upon
by some external force. [< L, laziness] **—**
in·er'tial *adj.*

in·es·cap·a·ble (IN ə SKAY pə bəl) *adj.* impossible to escape; unavoidable. **—in'**
es·cap'a·bly *adv.*

in·es·ti·ma·ble (IN ES tə mə bəl) *adj.* **1.** not
to be estimated or evaluated. **2.** having
great value. **—in·est'ti·ma·bly** *adv.*

in·ev·i·ta·ble (in EV i tə bəl) *adj.* that cannot be avoided or prevented from happening. [ME] **—in·ev'i·ta·bil'i·ty** *n.* **—**
in·ev'i·ta·bly *adv.*

in·ex·act (IN ig ZAKT) *adj.* not exact; not
completely accurate or true. **—in'ex·act'**
ness, in'ex·act'i·tude *n.*

in·ex·cus·a·ble (IN ik SKYOO zə bəl) *adj.*
not excusable; impossible to excuse or justify. **—in'ex·cus'a·bly** *adv.*

in·ex·haust·i·ble (IN ig ZAWS tə bəl) *adj.* **1.**
incapable of being exhausted or used up. **2.**
incapable of fatigue; tireless. **—in'**
ex·haust'i·bil'i·ty *n.* **—in'ex·haust'**
i·bly *adv.*

in·ex·o·ra·ble (in EK sər ə bəl) *adj.* **1.** not to
be moved by entreaty or persuasion; unyielding. **2.** unalterable; relentless. [< L
inexorabilis] **—in·ex'o·ra·bly** *adv.*

in·ex·pe·di·ent (IN ik SPEE dee ənt) *adj.*
not expedient; inadvisable. **—in'ex·pe'di·**
ence, in'ex·pe'di·en·cy *n.* **—in'ex·pe'**
di·ent·ly *adv.*

in·ex·pert (in EKS purt) *adj.* not expert;
unskilled; inept. **—in·ex'pert·ly** *adv.*

in·ex·pi·a·ble (in EKS pee ə bəl) *adj.* incapable of being expiated; unpardonable. [<
inexpiabilis]

in·ex·pli·ca·ble (in EK spli kə bəl) *adj.* not

explicable; impossible to explain. [ME] **—**
in·ex'pli·ca·bly *adv.*

in·ex·press·i·ble (IN ik SPRES ə bəl) *adj.*
incapable of being expressed or put into
words. **—in'ex·press'i·bly** *adv.*

in ex·tre·mis (IN ik STREE mis) *Latin* at
the point of death.

in·ex·tri·ca·ble (in EK stri kə bəl) *adj.* **1.**
impossible to extricate oneself from. **2.** impossible to disentangle or undo. **3.** too intricate to be solved. [ME] **—in·ex'tri·ca·bly**
adv.

in·fal·li·ble (in FAL ə bəl) *adj.* **1.** exempt
from fallacy or error of judgment. **2.** not
liable to fail; sure. **3.** in Roman Catholic
doctrine, incapable of error in matters of
faith and morals. [ME] **—in·fal'li·bil'i·ty**
n. **—in·fal'li·bly** *adv.*

in·fa·mous (IN fə məs) *adj.* **1.** having a vile
reputation. **2.** deserving or producing infamy; odious. [ME] **—in'fa·mous·ly** *adv.*

in·fa·my (IN fə mee) *n.* **1.** dishonor; disgrace. the state of being infamous. **3.** *pl.*
·mies an infamous act. [ME *infamye*]

in·fan·cy (IN fən see) *n. pl.* **·cies** **1.** the state
or period of being an infant; babyhood. **2.**
the beginnings of anything. **3.** *Law* the
years before attaining the age of legal majority. [< L *infantia*]

in·fant (IN fənt) *n.* **1.** a child in the earliest
stages of life; baby. **2.** *Law* one who has not
attained the age of legal majority; a minor.
—adj. **1.** of, for, or typical of infancy or
infants. **2.** beginning to exist or develop. [<
L *infans* child]

in·fan·ti·cide (in FAN ti sīD) *n.* **1.** the killing of an infant, esp. at birth. **2.** one who has
killed an infant. [< LL *infanticidium*]

in·fan·tile (in fən TIL) *adj.* **1.** of infancy or
infants. **2.** characteristic of infancy or infants; babyish.

infantile paralysis poliomyelitis.

in·fan·try (IN fən tree) *n. pl.* **·tries** soldiers,
units, or a branch of an army trained and
equipped to fight on foot. [< Ital. *infan-
teria*] **—in'fan·try·man** (-mən) *n.*

in·farct (IN FAHRKT) *n. Med.* an area of tissue that is dying because its supply of blood
is obstructed: also **in·farc'tion.** [< NL *in-
farctus* stuffed]

in·fat·u·ate (in FACH oo AYT) *v.t.* **·at·ed,**
·at·ing inspire with a foolish and unreasoning love or passion. [ME] **—in·fat'u·at'ed**
adj. **—in·fat'u·a'tion** *n.*

in·fect (in FEKT) *v.t.* **1.** affect with disease-
producing organisms, as a wound. **2.** cause

(a person, etc.) to contract a communicable disease. **3.** affect or inspire, as with attitudes or beliefs, esp. harmfully. [ME *infecten*]

in·fec·tion (in FEK shən) *n.* **1.** an invasion of body tissue by disease-producing organisms. **2.** a disease resulting from such an invasion. **3.** the transference of a disease, idea, mood, etc.

in·fec·tious (in FEK shəs) *adj.* **1.** liable to produce infection. **2.** denoting diseases communicable by infection. **3.** tending to excite similar reactions: *infectious* laughter. —**in·fec′tious·ness** *n.*

in·fec·tive (in FEK tiv) *adj.* infectious.

in·fe·lic·i·tous (IN fə LIS i təs) *adj.* not suitable. —**in′fe·lic′i·tous·ly** *adv.*

in·fe·lic·i·ty (IN fə LIS i tee) *n.* **1.** the state of being infelicitous. **2.** *pl.* **·ties** that which is infelicitous, as an inappropriate remark. [ME *infelicite*]

in·fer (in FUR) *v.* **·ferred, ·fer·ring** *v.t.* **1.** derive by reasoning; conclude from evidence or premises. **2.** involve as a conclusion: said of facts, statements, etc. —*v.i.* **3.** draw an inference. [< L *inferre* carry into] —**in·fer′a·ble** *adj.* —**in·fer′a·bly** *adv.*

in·fer·ence (IN fər əns) *n.* **1.** a conclusion. **2.** the act or process of inferring. — **in·fer·en·tial** (IN fə REN shəl) *adj.*

in·fe·ri·or (in FEER ee ər) *adj.* **1.** lower in quality, worth, or adequacy. **2.** lower in rank or importance. **3.** lower in position; situated below. —*n.* a person inferior in rank or in attainments. [< L, lower] —**in·fe·ri·or·i·ty** (in FEER ee OR i tee) *n.*

in·fer·nal (in FUR nl) *adj.* **1.** of or pertaining to the mythological world of the dead, or to hell. **2.** diabolical; hellish. **3.** damnable; hateful. [ME]

in·fer·no (in FUR noh) *n. pl.* **·nos 1.** hell. **2.** any place comparable to hell. [< Ital.]

in·fest (in FEST) *v.t.* **1.** overrun or occupy in large numbers so as to be annoying or dangerous. **2.** be a parasite on or in. [ME] — **in′fes·ta′tion** *n.*

in·fi·del (IN fi dl) *n.* **1.** one who rejects all religious belief; unbeliever. **2.** one who rejects a particular religion, esp. Christianity or Islam. —*adj.* **1.** being an infidel. **2.** of or relating to infidels or unbelief. [ME]

in·fi·del·i·ty (IN fi DEL i tee) *n. pl.* **·ties 1.** lack of fidelity. **2.** a disloyal act. **3.** adultery. **4.** lack of belief in a particular religion, esp. Christianity or Islam. [ME]

in·field (IN FEELD) *n.* in baseball: **a** the playing space within or adjacent to the base lines of the field. **b** the infielders collectively.

in·field·er (IN FEEL dər) *n.* in baseball, the first baseman, second baseman, shortstop, or third baseman.

in·fil·trate (in FIL TRAYT) *v.* **·trat·ed, ·trat·ing** *v.t.* **1.** enter (an organization etc.) secretly or stealthily in order to spy, gain control, etc. **2.** cause (a liquid or gas) to pass into or through pores. **3.** filter or move through or into. —*v.i.* **4.** pass into or through a substance. —*n.* that which infiltrates. —**in′fil·tra′tion** *n.*

in·fi·nite (IN fə nit) *adj.* **1.** having no boundaries or limits; extending without end. **2.** very numerous or great; vast. **3.** all-embracing; perfect. **4.** *Math.* of or designating a quantity conceived as always exceeding any other quantity in value. —*n. Math.* an infinite quantity. [ME] —**in′fi·nite·ly** *adv.*

in·fin·i·tes·i·mal (IN fin i TES ə məl) *adj.* **1.** infinitely small. **2.** so small as to be incalculable. —*n.* an infinitesimal quantity. [< NL *infinitesimus*] —**in′fin·i·tes′i·mal·ly** *adv.*

in·fin·i·tive (in FIN i tiv) *Gram. adj.* **1.** without limitation of person or number. **2.** of or pertaining to the infinitive. —*n.* a verb form generally used either as the principal verb of a verb phrase, most often without *to*, or as a noun, most often with *to*. [ME]

in·fin·i·ty (in FIN i tee) *n. pl.* **·ties 1.** the state of being infinite. **2.** something considered infinite, as space or time. **3.** a very large amount or number. [ME *infinite*]

in·firm (in FURM) *adj.* **1.** feeble or weak, as from old age. **2.** lacking firmness of purpose. [ME *infirme*]

in·fir·ma·ry (in FUR mə ree) *n. pl.* **·ries** a place for the treatment of the sick, esp. in a school etc. [ME]

in·fir·mi·ty (in FUR mi tee) *n. pl.* **·ties 1.** the state of being infirm. **2.** a physical or mental defect. [ME *infirmite*]

in·fix (in FIKS) *v.t.* **1.** set firmly or insert in. **2.** implant in the mind. **3.** *Gram.* insert (an infix) within a word. —*n.* (IN FIKS *Gram.* a modifying addition inserted in the body of a word. [< L *infixus* fastened in]

in·flame (in FLAYM) *v.t. & v.i.* **·flamed, ·flam·ing 1.** ignite; kindle. **2.** excite or become excited, esp. with rage, hate, passion, etc. **3.** increase or intensify, as a violent emotion. **4.** produce or suffer inflammation. [ME *enflamen*]

in·flam·ma·ble (in FLAM ə bEl) *adj.* **1.** combustible. **2.** aasily excited or aroused. —*n.* an inflammable thing or substance. [< Med.L *inflammabilis*] —**in·flam′ma·bil′i·ty** *n.*

in·flam·ma·tion (IN flə MAY shən) *n.* **1.** the state of being inflamed. **2.** *Pathol.* a diseased condition characterized by redness, swelling, and pain.

in·flam·ma·to·ry (in FLAM ə TOR ee) *adj.* **1.** tending to arouse excitement, anger, etc. **2.** *Med.* characterized by or causing inflammation. [< L *inflammatus*]

in·flate (in FLAYT) *v.* **·flat·ed, ·flat·ing** *v.t.* **1.** cause to expand by filling with or as with gas or air. **2.** enlarge excessively; puff up. **3.** *Econ.* increase (prices, credit, etc.) in excess of usual or prior levels. —*v.i.* **4.** become inflated. [< L *inflatus* puffed out] —**in·flat′a·ble** *adj.*

in·fla·tion (in FLAY shən) *n.* **1.** the act of inflating, or the state of being inflated. **2.** *Econ.* an unstable rise in price levels. —**in·fla′tion·ar′y** *adj.*

in·flect (in FLEKT) *v.t.* **1.** vary the tone or pitch of (the voice); modulate. **2.** bend. **3.** *Gram.* give the inflections of (a word). [ME *inflecten* bend into]

in·flec·tion (in FLEK shən) *n.* **1.** the act of inflecting, or the state of being inflected. **2.** an angle or bend. **3.** modulation of the voice. **4.** *Gram.* **a** a change in form undergone by words to express grammatical and syntactical relations, as of case, number, tense, etc. **b** an inflected form. —**in·flec′ ·tion·al** *adj.*

in·flex·i·ble (in FLEK sə bəl) *adj.* **1.** incapable of being bent; rigid. **2.** unyielding; stubborn. **3.** that cannot be altered; fixed. [ME] —**in·flex′i·bil′i·ty** *n.* —**in·flex′i·bly** *adv.*

in·flict (in FLIKT) *v.t.* **1.** deal; lay on: *inflict* a blow. **2.** impose. [< L *inflictus* dashed against]

in·flic·tion (in FLIK shən) *n.* **1.** the act of inflicting. **2.** that which is inflicted, as pain, punishment, etc.

in·flow (IN FLOH) *n.* **1.** the act of flowing in. **2.** that which flows in.

in·flu·ence (IN floo əns) *n.* **1.** the power of persons or things to produce effects on others, esp. by indirect means. **2.** power resulting from social position, wealth, etc. **3.** one who or that which possesses the power to affect others. —*v.t.* **·enced, ·enc·ing** **1.** produce an effect on the actions or thought of. **2.** have an effect on.

[ME] —**in·flu·en·tial** (IN floo EN shəl) *adj.*

in·flu·en·za (IN FLOO EN zə) *n.* *Pathol.* a contagious, infectious viral disease characterized by respiratory inflammation and fever: also called *flu.* [< Ital., lit., influence]

in·flux (IN FLUKS) *n.* **1.** a flowing in, as of a fluid. **2.** a continuous coming, as of people. **3.** the mouth of a river. [< LL *influxus* flowed in]

in·form (in FORM) *v.t.* **1.** notify. **2.** give character to: with *with* or *by.* —*v.i.* **3.** disclose information. **4.** act as an informer. [ME *informen*]

in·for·mal (in FOR məl) *adj.* **1.** not in the usual or prescribed form; unofficial. **2.** without formality; casual. **3.** not requiring formal attire. **4.** characteristic of or suitable to the language of ordinary conversation or familiar writing. —**in′for·mal′i·ty** (IN for MAL i tee) *n.*

in·form·ant (in FOR mənt) *n.* one who gives information; informer.

in·for·ma·tion (IN fər MAY shən) *n.* **1.** knowledge acquired or derived; facts. **2.** timely knowledge; news. **3.** the act of informing, or the state of being informed. [ME]

in·form·a·tive (in FOR mə tiv) *adj.* affording information; instructive.

in·formed (in FORMD) *adj.* having a high degree of information or education.

in·form·er (in FOR mər) *n.* **1.** one who secretly informs authorities of criminal or disapproved acts of others; stool pigeon. **2.** an informant. [ME]

infra- *prefix* below; beneath; on the lower part. [< L]

in·frac·tion (in FRAK shən) *n.* the act of breaking or violating (a pledge, law, etc.); infringement. [< L *infractio*]

in·fra·red (IN frə RED) *adj.* *Physics* having a wavelength greater than that of visible red light, and radiating heat. —*n.* this part of the spectrum.

in·fra·struc·ture (IN frə STRUK chər) *n.* **1.** the basic framework of a system or organization. **2.** basic technological installations, such as roads, communication systems, etc.

in·fre·quent (in FREE kwənt) *adj.* present or occurring at widely separated intervals; uncommon. —**in·fre′quent·ly** *adv.*

in·fringe (in FRINJ) *v.t.* **·fringed, ·fring·ing** break or disregard the terms of, as a law; violate. —**infringe on** (or **upon**) transgress or trespass on rights or privi-

leges. [< L *infringere* weaken] —
in·fringe′·ment *n.*

in·fu·ri·ate (in FYUUR ee AYT) *v.t.* ·at·ed,
·at·ing make furious; enrage. [< Med.L
infuriatus maddened] —in·fu′ri·at′
ing·ly *adv.*

in·fuse (in FYOOZ) *v.t.* ·fused, ·fus·ing 1.
instill or inculcate, as principles. 2. inspire;
imbue: with *with* 3. pour in. [ME] —
in·fus′i·ble *adj.*

in·fu·sion (in FYOO zhən) *n.* 1. the act of
infusing. 2. that which is infused. 3. a liquid
extract obtained by soaking a substance in
water.

in·gen·ious (in JEEN yəs) *adj.* inventive;
clever. [< MF *ingenieux*] —in·gen′
ious·ly *adv.*

in·ge·nue (AN zhə NOO) *n.* the role of a
young girl in a play, film, etc.; also, an actress who plays such roles. [< F *ingénue*]

in·ge·nu·i·ty (IN jə NOO i tee) *n.* 1. inven-
tiveness. 2. originality of design or execution. [< L *ingenuitas* virtue]

in·gen·u·ous (in JEN yoo əs) *adj.* 1. candid;
frank. 2. innocent and simple; naive. [< L
ingenuus virtuous] —in·gen′u·ous·ness
n.

in·gest (in JEST) *v.t.* take or put (food, etc.)
into the body by swallowing or absorbing.
[< L *ingestus* poured into] —in·ges′tion
n.

in·gle·nook (ING gəl NUUK) *n.* 1. a corner
by a fireplace. 2. a bench for this corner.

in·glo·ri·ous (in GLOR ee əs) *adj.* not reflecting honor or courage; disgraceful. [< L
inglorius] —in·glo′ri·ous·ly *adv.*

in·got (ING gət) *n.* a mass of cast metal from
the crucible or mold. [ME]

in·grain (in GRAYN) *v.t.* impress firmly on
the mind.

in·grained (in GRAYND) *adj.* 1. worked
into the inmost texture; deep-rooted. 2.
thorough; inveterate.

in·grate (IN grayt) *n.* an ungrateful person.
[ME *ingrat*]

in·gra·ti·ate (in GRAY shee AYT) *v.t.*
·at·ed, ·at·ing bring (oneself) deliberately
into the favor or confidence of others. —
in·gra′ti·at′ing·ly *adv.* —in·gra′ti·a′
tion *n.*

in·grat·i·tude (in GRAT i TOOD) *n.* lack of
gratitude; insensibility to kindness;
thanklessness. [ME]

in·gre·di·ent (in GREE dee ənt) *n.* 1. anything that enters into the composition of a
mixture. 2. a component of anything. [ME]

in·gress (IN gres) *n.* 1. a going in, as into a
building. 2. a place of entrance. [ME]

in-group (IN GROOP) *n.* any group with
strong feelings of cohesiveness, shared
identity, and exclusivity.

in·grown (IN GROHN) *adj.* 1. grown into the
flesh, as a toenail. 2. grown within; innate:
ingrown vice. —in′grow′ing (-GROH ing)
adj.

in·gui·nal (ING gwə nl) *adj.* Anat. of, pertaining to, or located in the groin. [< L
inguinalis of the groin]

in·hab·it (in HAB it) *v.t.* live in; occupy as a
home. [ME *enhabiten* dwell in] —in·hab′
it·a·ble *adj.* —in·hab′i·tant (-i tənt) *n.*

in·ha·la·tor (IN hə LAY tər) *n.* a device for
enabling one to inhale air, medicinal vapors, etc.

in·hale (in HAYL) *v.t. & v.i.* ·haled,
·hal·ing draw (a substance) into the lungs;
breathe in. —in·ha·la·tion (IN hə LAY
shən) *n.*

in·hal·er (in HAY lər) *n.* 1. one who inhales.
2. *Med.* an inhalator.

in·har·mo·ni·ous (IN hahr MOH nee əs)
adj. lacking harmony; discordant. —
in′har·mo′ni·ous·ly *adv.*

in·here (in HEER) *v.i.* ·hered, ·her·ing be
a permanent or essential part: with *in*. [< L
inhaerere stick in] —in·her′ence *n.*

in·her·ent (in HEER ənt) *adj.* forming an
essential element or quality of something.
—in·her′ent·ly *adv.*

in·her·it (in HER it) *v.t.* 1. receive (property, title, etc.) by legal succession or will. 2.
derive (traits, qualities, etc.) from one's parents or ancestors. 3. recieve from one's pre-
decessors. —*v.i.* 4. take possession of an
inheritance. [ME *enheriten* appoint an
heir] —in·her′i·tor *n.*

in·her·it·a·ble (in HER i tə bəl) *adj.* 1. capable of being inherited. 2. entitled to inherit. [ME] —in·her′it·a·bly *adv.*

in·her·i·tance (in HER i təns) *n.* 1. the act
of inheriting. 2. that which is legally transmissible to an heir; legacy. 3. derivation of
qualities from one's forebears; also, the
qualities so derived.

in·hib·it (in HIB it) *v.t.* restrain; check; repress. [ME *inhibiten* restrain] —in·hib′
i·tor *n.* —in·hib′i·tive, in·hib′i·to′ry
adj.

in·hi·bi·tion (IN i BISH ən) *n.* 1. restraint or
prohibition. 2. *Psychol.* the blocking of an
impulse or thought.

in·hos·pi·ta·ble (in HOS pi tə bəl) *adj.* 1.

not hospitable. **2.** not affording shelter, comfort, etc. —**in·hos'pi·ta·bly** adv.

in·house (IN HOWS) adj. occurring or originating within an organization, business, group, etc. —**in-house** (IN HOWS) adv.

in·hu·man (in HYOO mən) adj. **1.** not befitting human nature; bestial. **2.** not human. [ME inhumain]

in·hu·mane (IN hyoo MAYN) adj. not humane; cruel.

in·hu·man·i·ty (IN hyoo MAN i tee) n. pl. **·ties 1.** lack of human or humane qualities. **2.** a cruel act, word, etc.

in·im·i·cal (i NIM i kəl) adj. **1.** characterized by harmful opposition; antagonistic. **2.** behaving as an enemy; hostile. [< L inimicus unfriendly] —**in·im'i·cal·ly** adv.

in·im·i·ta·ble (i NIM i tə bəl) adj. matchless; unique. [< L inimitabilis] —**in·im' i·ta·bly** adv.

in·iq·ui·ty (i NIK wi tee) n. pl. **·ties 1.** grievous violation of right or justice; wickedness. **2.** a wrongful act; sin. [ME] —**in·iq'ui·tous** (-təs) adj.

in·i·tial (i NISH əl) adj. **1.** standing at the beginning. **2.** of or pertaining to the beginning; first. —n. **1.** pl. the first letters of one's proper name. **2.** the first letter of a word, name, etc. —v.t. **·tialed, ·tial·ing** mark or sign with initials. [< L initialis beginning] —**in·i'tial·ly** adv.

in·i·ti·ate (i NISH ee AYT) v.t. **·at·ed, ·at·ing 1.** begin; commence; originate. **2.** admit to membership in an organization, cult, etc. **3.** instruct in fundamentals. —adj. (i NISH ee it) initiated. —n. (i NISH ee it) one who has been ritually admitted to an organization, cult, etc. [< L initiatus inducted] —**in·i'ti·a'tion** n. —**in·i'ti·a'tor** n.

in·i·ti·a·tive (i NISH ə tiv) n. **1.** the power or right to take the first step or the next step in some action. **2.** the action of commencing or originating. **3.** the spirit needed to originate action. **4.** in government: **a** the right or power to propose legislative measures. **b** the process by which the electorate acts to originate legislation. —adj. **1.** of or pertaining to initiation. **2.** serving to initiate.

in·ject (in JEKT) v.t. **1.** drive (a fluid, drug, etc.) into a bodily cavity, blood vessel, etc. by means of a syringe, needle, etc. **2.** introduce or interject: with into. [< L injectus thrown in] —**in·jec'tion** n.

in·ju·di·cious (IN juu DISH əs) adj. unwise; imprudent. —**in'ju·di'cious·ly** adv.

in·junc·tion (in JUNGK shən) n. **1.** the act of enjoining. **2.** an authoritative order. **3.** Law a judicial order requiring the party to do or refrain from some specified action. [< MF injonction] —**in·junc'tive** adj.

in·jure (IN jər) v.t. **·jured, ·jur·ing 1.** harm, damage, or impair, esp. physically; hurt. **2.** wrong or offend. —**in'jur·er** n.

in·ju·ry (IN jə ree) n. pl. **·ries 1.** harm, damage, or distress inflicted or suffered. **2.** a particular instance of such harm. [ME injurie] —**in·ju·ri·ous** (in JUUR ee əs) adj.

in·jus·tice (in JUS tis) n. **1.** the fact or quality of being unjust. **2.** an unjust act; wrong.

ink (ingk) n. **1.** any of various colored liquids used for writing, drawing, and printing. **2.** the dark fluid ejected by an octopus etc. — v.t. stain, color, or depict with ink. [ME inke] —**ink'er** n.

ink·blot test (INGK BLOT) Rorschach test.

ink·ling (INGK ling) n. **1.** a slight suggestion or hint. **2.** a vague idea or notion. [ME inklen hint]

ink·y (ING kee) adj. **ink·i·er, ink·i·est 1.** resembling ink in color; dark; black. **2.** of, pertaining to, or containing ink. **3.** smeared or stained with ink. —**ink'i·ness** n.

in·laid (IN LAYD) adj. **1.** decorated with material embedded flush with the surface. **2.** inserted as an inlay.

in·land (IN lənd) adj. **1.** remote from the sea or the border. **2.** pertaining to or located in the interior of a country. —n. (IN LAND) the interior of a country. —adv. (IN LAND) in or toward the interior of a land.

in-law (IN LAW) n. a close relative by marriage.

in·lay (IN LAY) v.t. **·laid, ·lay·ing 1.** set or embed (ivory, gold, etc.) flush into a surface so as to form a pattern. **2.** decorate by inserting such designs. —n. **1.** that which is inlaid. **2.** a design so produced. **3.** Dent. a type of filling for a tooth.

in·let (IN let) n. **1.** a relatively narrow channel of water, as a stream or bay leading into land. **2.** an opening.

in lo·co pa·ren·tis (in LOH koh pə REN tis) Latin in the role of a parent.

in·mate (IN MAYT) n. one who is confined with another or others, esp. in a prison, asylum, etc.

in me·mo·ri·am (in mə MOR ee əm) Latin in memory (of); as a memorial (to).

in·most (IN MOHST) *adj.* **1.** located farthest from the outside. **2.** most private or intimate. [ME]

inn (in) *n.* a hotel, etc., where travelers may obtain meals or lodging. [ME, house]

in·nards (IN ərdz) *n.pl.* the internal organs or parts of the body, a machine, etc.; insides. [var. of *inwards*]

in·nate (i NAYT) *adj.* inherent in one's nature; inborn; not acquired. [ME] — **in·nate′ly** *adv.*

in·ner (IN ər) *adj.* **1.** located or occurring farther inside or toward the center; internal; interior. **2.** pertaining to the mind or spirit; subjective. **3.** more obscure; hidden; esoteric. [ME]

inner city a central part of a large city, usu. characterized by poverty.

inner ear the essential organ of hearing and equilibrium, located in the temporal bone and supplied by the auditory nerve.

in·ner·most (IN ər MOHST) *adj.* inmost; farthest within.

in·ning (IN ing) *n.* in baseball, a division of the game during which each team has a turn to bat.

inn·keep·er (IN KEE pər) *n.* the proprietor or host of an inn.

in·no·cent (IN ə sənt) *adj.* **1.** not tainted with sin, evil, or moral wrong; pure. **2.** free from blame or guilt, esp. legally. **3.** not tending or intended to harm or injure. **4.** lacking in worldly knowledge; naive. **5.** devoid of; entirely lacking in: with *of.* —*n.* **1.** one who is free from evil or sin. **2.** a simple or unsuspecting person. [ME] —**in′no·cence** *n.* —**in′no·cent·ly** *adv.*

in·noc·u·ous (i NOK yoo əs) *adj.* having no harmful qualities or effects; harmless. [< L *innocuus*] —**in·noc′u·ous·ly** *adv.*

in·no·vate (IN ə VAYT) *v.t. & v.i.* **·vat·ed,** **·vat·ing** introduce or bring in (something new). [< L *innovatus* renewed] —**in′no·va′tive** *adj.* —**in′no·va′tor** *n.*

in·no·va·tion (IN ə VAY shən) *n.* **1.** something newly introduced, as an idea, method, etc. **2.** the act of introducing something new.

in·nu·en·do (IN yoo EN doh) *n. pl.* **·dos,** **·does** an indirect comment, hint, or suggestion, usu. derogatory. [< L, by hinting]

in·nu·mer·a·ble (i NOO mər ə bəl) *adj.* too numerous to be counted; numberless. — **in·nu′mer·a·bly** *adv.*

in·oc·u·late (i NOK yə LAYT) *v.t.* **·lat·ed,** **·lat·ing** inject (serum, a vaccine, etc.) into, esp. so as to produce immunity. [ME *inoculaten* insert a bud in a plant] — **in·oc′u·la′tion** *n.*

in·of·fen·sive (IN ə FEN siv) *adj.* giving no offense; innocuous. —**in′of·fen′sive·ly** *adv.*

in·op·er·a·ble (in OP ər ə bəl) *adj.* **1.** incapable of being cured or improved by surgical operation. **2.** not practicable; unworkable. —**in·op′er·a·bil′i·ty** *n.* — **in·op′er·a·bly** *adv.*

in·op·er·a·tive (in OP ər ə tiv) *adj.* **1.** not functioning. **2.** not effectual or in effect.

in·op·por·tune (in OP ər TOON) *adj.* untimely or inappropriate; unsuitable. [< L *inopportunus*]

in·or·di·nate (in OR dn it) *adj.* immoderate; excessive; unrestrained. [ME *inordinat*] —**in·or′di·nate·ly** *adv.*

in·or·gan·ic (IN or GAN ik) *adj.* **1.** not having the organized structure of living things; not living; inanimate. **2.** not characterized by life processes. **3.** *Chem.* designating compounds that are not hydrocarbons.

in·pa·tient (IN PAY shənt) *n.* a patient who is lodged in a hospital.

in·put (IN PUUT) *n.* **1.** energy or power delivered to a machine, circuit, etc. **2.** information put into a computer. **3.** suggestions or data to be applied in making a decision, preparing a report, etc. —*v.t.* **·put·ted,** **·put·ting**

in·quest (IN kwest) *n.* a legal investigation into a special matter; esp., one undertaken before a jury or by a coroner. [ME]

in·qui·e·tude (in KWĪ i TOOD) *n.* **1.** a state of restlessness; uneasiness. **2.** *pl.* anxieties; disquieting thoughts. [ME]

in·quire (in KWĪR) *v.* **·quired,** **·quir·ing** *v.i.* **1.** seek information by asking questions; ask. **2.** make an investigation: with *into.* — *v.t.* **3.** ask information about. Also spelled *enquire.* [ME] —**in·quir′ing·ly** *adv.*

in·quir·y (in KWĪR ee) *n. pl.* **·quir·ies 1.** the act of inquiring or seeking. **2.** investigation; research. **3.** a question; query. Also spelled *enquiry.* [ME *enquery*]

in·qui·si·tion (IN kwə ZISH ən) *n.* **1.** an investigation of the beliefs and activities of individuals or political groups for the ultimate purpose of enforcing orthodoxy. **2.** *cap.* a former judicial system of the Roman Catholic Church for discovery, examination, and punishment of heretics. **3.** the act of inquiring or searching out. **4.** an official

inquiry. [ME *inquisicioun*] —
in·quis'i·tor (in KWIZ i tər) *n.*

in·quis·i·tive (in KWIZ i tiv) *adj.* 1. curious;
prying. 2. eager for knowledge. —**in·quis'
i·tive·ness** *n.*

in·quis·i·to·ri·al (in KWIZ i TOR ee əl) *adj.*
of, pertaining to, or resembling an inquisi-
tor or inquisition; offensively curious.

in re (in RAY) *Latin* in the matter (of); concerning.

in·road (IN ROHD) *n.* 1. a serious encroachment; harmful trespass: with *on* or *upon.* 2.
a hostile raid.

in·rush (IN RUSH) *n.* a sudden rushing in.

in·sane (in SAYN) *adj.* 1. not sane; mentally
deranged or unsound. 2. characteristic of
one who is not sane. 3. extremely foolish.
[< L *insanus*] —**in·sane'ly** *adv.* —
in·san·i·ty (in SAN i tee) *n.* [< L *insan-
itas*]

in·sa·tia·ble (in SAY shə bəl) *adj.* incapable
of being sated or satisfied; extremely
greedy. —**in·sa'tia·bil'i·ty** *n.* —**in·sa'
ti·a·bly** *adv.*

in·scribe (in SKRĪB) *v.t.* •**scribed,**
•**scrib·ing** 1. write, mark, or engrave
(words etc.). 2. mark (a document etc.) with
writing or engraving. 3. enter (a name) on a
formal or official list. 4. sign or dedicate (a
book etc.) for presentation. 5. *Geom.* draw
(one figure) in another so that the latter
circumscribes the former. [< L *inscribere*
write in] —**in·scrib'er** *n.*

in·scrip·tion (in SKRIP shən) *n.* 1. that
which is inscribed; the act of inscribing. 2. a
durable marking or engraving on a solid
object. 3. an informal written dedication.
[ME *inscripcioun*]

in·scru·ta·ble (in SKROO tə bəl) *adj.* that
cannot be searched into or understood; in-
comprehensible. [ME] —**in·scru'ta·bil'
i·ty** *n.*

in·sect (IN sekt) *n.* 1. *Zool.* any of a large
class of small to minute air-breathing invertebrate animals, having six legs, a body divided into a head, thorax, and abdomen,
and usu. two pairs of wings. 2. loosely, any
small invertebrate resembling an insect, as
a spider, tick, etc. [< L *insectum*].

in·sec·ti·cide (in SEK tə SĪD) *n.* a substance
used for killing insects.

in·sec·tiv·o·rous (IN sek TIV ər əs) *adj.*
feeding or subsisting upon insects.

in·se·cure (IN si KYUUR) *adj.* 1. liable to
break, fail, collapse, etc.; unsafe. 2. troubled by anxiety and apprehensiveness;

threatened. [< Med.L *insecurus*] —
in'se·cu'ri·ty *n.*

in·sem·i·nate (in SEM ə NAYT) *v.t.*
•**nat·ed, ·nat·ing** 1. make pregnant; inject
semen into the vagina of. 2. sow or implant.
[< L *inseminatus* impregnated] —
in·sem'i·na'tion *n.*

in·sen·sate (in SEN sayt) *adj.* 1. showing a
lack of humane feeling; brutish. 2. stupid;
foolish. 3. lacking physical sensation; inanimate. [< LL *insensatus* irrational]

in·sen·si·ble (in SEN sə bəl) *adj.* 1. deprived of consciousness; unconscious. 2. incapable of feeling or perceiving. 3. so slight
or gradual as to escape notice; imperceptible. —**in·sen'si·bil'i·ty** *n.*

in·sen·si·tive (in SEN si tiv) *adj.* 1. not
keenly responsive; crude; dull. 2. without
physical feeling or sensation. 3. not affected
by or aware of: with *to.* —**in·sen'si·tiv'i·ty**
n.

in·sen·ti·ent (in SEN shee ənt) *adj.* lacking
senses or consciousness; inanimate. —
in·sen'ti·ence *n.*

in·sep·a·ra·ble (in SEP rə bəl) *adj.* incapable of being separated or parted. —**in·sep'
a·ra·bly** *adv.*

in·sert (in SURT) *v.t.* 1. put in; place; set. 2.
introduce into written matter. —*n.* (IN
surt) 1. that which is inserted. 2. in bookbinding, illustrations, maps, etc., not part of
the printed text, bound into the finished
book. 3. a circular, pamphlet, etc. set within
a newspaper, magazine, or book. [< L *in-
sertus* inserted]

in·ser·tion (in SUR shən) *n.* 1. the act of
inserting. 2. that which is inserted; as: **a** a
word, sentence, etc. **b** a strip of lace or
embroidery sewn into plain cloth.

in·set (in SET) *v.t.* •**set, ·set·ting** set in;
insert; implant. —*n.* (IN set) 1. something
inserted. 2. a small diagram, map, etc. inserted in the border of a larger one. 3. a
piece of material let or set into a garment.

in·shore (IN SHOR) *adj.* near or coming
toward the shore. —*adv.* toward the shore.

in·side (IN SĪD) *n.* 1. the part, surface,
space, etc., that lies within; interior. 2. the
internal nature or workings that are concealed. 3. *pl. Informal* the inner parts of the
body or a machine; innards. —**inside out**
reversed so that the inside is exposed. —
adj. (IN SĪD 1. situated within; internal;
interior. 2. restricted to a few; confidential.
3. suitable for, used, or working indoors;
indoor. —*adv.* (IN SĪD 1. in or into the

interior; within. **2.** indoors. —*prep.* (IN
SĪD in or into the interior of. [ME] —
inside of *Informal.* **1.** within; enclosed by.
2. within the time or distance specified:
inside of a year.

in·sid·er (IN SĪ dər) *n.* **1.** a member of a
given group, club, etc. **2.** one close to a
source, as of knowledge or influence.

in·sid·i·ous (in SID ee əs) *adj.* **1.** subtly
cunning or deceitful; treacherous; wily. **2.**
progressing imperceptibly but harmfully:
insidious disease. [< L *insidiosus* deceitful]
—**in·sid′i·ous·ly** *adv.*

in·sight (IN SĪT) *n.* perception into the inner
nature or real character of a thing. —
in·sight′ful *adj.*

in·sig·ni·a (in SIG nee ə) *n. pl. of* **in·sig·ne**
(in SIG nee) *(but construed usu. as sing.,
with pl.* **in·sig·ni·as**) **1.** badges, emblems,
etc., used as marks of membership, office,
or honor. **2.** marks or signs of anything. [<
L]

in·sig·nif·i·cant (IN sig NIF i kənt) *adj.* **1.**
unimportant; trifling. **2.** meaningless. **3.**
lacking size or quantity. **4.** of persons, lacking distinction, character, etc. —**in′
sig·nif′i·cance** *n.*

in·sin·cere (IN sin SEER) *adj.* not sincere;
hypocritical. —**in·sin·cer·i·ty** (IN sin SER
i tee) *n.*

in·sin·u·ate (in SIN yoo AYT) *v.* **·at·ed,
·at·ing** *v.t.* **1.** suggest by innuendo; hint. **2.**
introduce subtly and gradually. —*v.i.* **3.**
give sly and indirect intimations. [< L *in-
sinuatus* instilled] —**in·sin′u·at′ing·ly**
adv. —**in·sin′u·a′tor** *n.*

in·sin·u·a·tion (in SIN yoo AY shən) *n.* **1.**
that which is insinuated; a sly hint. **2.** the act
of insinuating.

in·sip·id (in SIP id) *adj.* **1.** lacking spirit and
vivacity; vapid; dull. **2.** tasteless; bland. [<
L *insipidus* unsavory] —**in·si·pid·i·ty** (IN
si PID i tee), **in·sip′id·ness** *n.*

in·sist (in SIST) *v.i.* **1.** demand or assert
firmly and forcefully: with *on* or *upon.* **2.**
dwell on or repeatedly emphasize: with *on*
or *upon.* —*v.t.* **3.** demand or maintain
forcefully: He *insisted* that I stay away. [< L
insistere persist in] —**in·sis′tence** *n.*

in·sis·tent (in SIS tənt) *adj.* insisting; persistent; urgent. —**in·sis′tent·ly** *adv.*

in·so·far (IN sə FAHR) *adv.* to such an extent; in such measure: followed by *as.*

in·sole (IN SOHL) *n.* **1.** the inside sole of a
shoe. **2.** a removable sole added for
warmth, comfort, etc.

in·so·lent (IN sə lənt) *adj.* overbearing or
offensively impertinent; insulting; disrespectful. [ME] —**in′so·lence** *n.* —**in′so·
lent·ly** *adv.*

in·sol·u·ble (in SOL yə bəl) *adj.* **1.** incapable of being dissolved. **2.** not solvable: also
in·solv′a·ble. —**in·sol′u·bly** *adv.*

in·sol·vent (in SOL vənt) *adj.* **1.** unable to
meet the claims of creditors; bankrupt. **2.** of
or pertaining to bankrupt persons or bankruptcy. —*n.* an insolvent person. —**in·sol′
ven·cy** *n.*

in·som·ni·a (in SOM nee ə) *n.* chronic inability to sleep. [< L] —**in·som′ni·ac**
(-nee ak) *n.*

in·so·much (IN sə MUCH) *adv.* **1.** to such a
degree: with *that* or *as.* **2.** inasmuch: with
as.

in·sou·ci·ant (in SOO see ənt) *adj.* lighthearted; carefree; unconcerned. [< F] —
in·sou′ci·ance *n.*

in·spect (in SPEKT) *v.t.* **1.** look at or examine carefully, esp. for faults or defects. **2.**
examine or review officially, as troops. [< L
inspectus looked into] —**in·spec′tion** *n.*

in·spec·tor (in SPEK tər) *n.* **1.** one who
inspects. **2.** an official examiner or checker.
3. a high-ranking officer of police, firemen,
etc. [< L] —**in·spec′tor·ate** (-tə rit) *n.*

in·spi·ra·tion (IN spə RAY shən) *n.* **1.** a creative feeling or impulse. **2.** the state or quality of being inspired. **3.** one who or that
which acts as an inspiring influence. **4.**
something that results from being inspired,
as an idea. **5.** the act of drawing in the
breath; inhalation. [ME *inspiracioun*] —
in′spi·ra′tion·al *adj.*

in·spire (in SPĪR) *v.t.* **·spired, ·spir·ing** *v.t.*
1. stir or move (a person) to creative activity
or vigorous action; fill with a motivating
emotion. **2.** arouse or create (a feeling, idea,
etc.); generate: *inspire* fear. **3.** direct or
guide, as by special divine influence. **4.**
breathe in; inhale. —*v.i.* **5.** inhale. **6.** give or
provide inspiration. [ME *inspiren*]

in·spir·it (in SPIR it) *v.t.* fill with renewed
spirit or life; animate. —**in·spir′it·ing·ly**
adv.

in·sta·bil·i·ty (IN stə BIL i tee) *n. pl.* **·ties 1.**
lack of stability. **2.** unsteadiness of character; unreliability.

in·stall (in STAWL) *v.t.* **1.** fix in position and
adjust for service or use. **2.** place in any
office, rank, etc. **3.** establish in a place or
position; settle. [ME] —**in·stall′er** *n.*

in·stal·la·tion (IN stə LAY shən) *n.* **1.** any

device or system, esp. mechanical, set in place and readied for use. **2.** the act of installing, or the state of being installed. **3.** *Mil.* any large, fixed base or facility of an armed service.

in·stall·ment[1] (in STAWL mənt) *n.* **1.** a portion of a debt or sum of money made payable in specified amounts at specified intervals. **2.** one of several parts, as of a serial in a newspaper or magazine.

in·stall·ment[2] *n.* installation.

in·stance (IN stəns) *n.* **1.** a case or example. **2.** a step in proceedings: in the first *instance.* **—for instance** for example. **—v.t.** **·stanced, ·stanc·ing** cite as an example. [ME]

in·stant (IN stənt) *n.* **1.** a very short time; moment. **2.** a specific point in time. **—adj. 1.** instantaneous; immediate. **2.** pressing; urgent. **3.** prepared quickly by the addition of water, milk, etc.: *instant* coffee. [ME]

in·stan·ta·ne·ous (IN stən TAY nee əs) *adj.* happening or done with no delay; immediate. **—in'stan·ta'ne·ous·ly** *adv.*

in·stant·ly (IN stənt lee) *adv.* without delay; at once.

in·stead (in STED) *adv.* **1.** in place or lieu; rather than: with *of.* **2.** in the place of that just mentioned: look for silver and find gold *instead.* [ME]

in·step (IN STEP) *n.* **1.** the arched upper part of the human foot, extending from the toes to the ankle. **2.** the part of a shoe or stocking covering this.

in·sti·gate (IN sti GAYT) *v.t.* **·gat·ed, ·gat·ing 1.** spur on or goad; incite. **2.** foment; provoke: *instigate* treason. [< L *instigatus* impelled] **—in'sti·ga'tion** *n.* **— in'sti·ga'tor** *n.*

in·still (in STIL) *v.t.* **1.** introduce (a quality, feeling, idea, etc.) gradually or by degrees: *instill* courage. **2.** pour in gradually by drops. [< L *instillare* drip into] **— in·stil·la·tion** (IN stə LAY shən) *n.* **— in·still'ment** *n.*

in·stinct (IN stingkt) *n.* **1.** an innate tendency or response of a species to act in ways essential to its preservation. **2.** a natural aptitude; knack. [ME] **—in·stinc'tive, in· ·stinc·tu·al** (in STINGK choo əl) *adj.*

in·sti·tute (IN sti TOOT) *v.t.* **·tut·ed, ·tut·ing 1.** set up or establish; found. **2.** set in operation; initiate; start. **3.** *Eccl.* place (a minister) in spiritual charge of a parish: with *in* or *into.* **—n. 1.** a group or society devoted to promotion of some field of

knowledge or art; also, the building or buildings housing such a society. **2.** in education: **a** a school for specialized instruction, often technical. **b** a center for postgraduate study and research. **3.** something instituted, as an established principle, rule, or order. [ME]

in·sti·tu·tion (IN sti TOO shən) *n.* **1.** a principle, custom, etc. that forms part of a society or civilization. **2.** a corporate body organized to perform a particular function, often in education, charity, etc.; also, the building or buildings housing such a body. **3.** a mental hospital, prison, or other place of confinement. **4.** a familiar and characteristic object, custom, or person. **5.** the act of establishing or setting in operation. [ME] **—in'sti·tu'tion·al** *adj.*

in·sti·tu·tion·al·ize (IN sti TOO shə nl IZ) *v.t.* **·ized, ·iz·ing 1.** turn into or regard as an institution. **2.** put (someone) in an institution, as for treatment. **—in'sti·tu' tion·al·i·za'tion** *n.*

in·struct (in STRUKT) *v.t.* **1.** impart knowledge or skill to, esp. by systematic method; teach. **2.** give specific orders or directions to; order. [ME]

in·struc·tion (in STRUK shən) *n.* **1.** the act of instructing or teaching. **2.** knowledge imparted; also, an item of such knowledge, as a rule, precept, or lesson. **3.** *pl.* directions; orders. **4.** an order or command. [ME *instruccioun*] **—in·struc'tion·al** *adj.*

in·struc·tive (in STRUK tiv) *adj.* serving to instruct; informative. **—in·struc'tive·ly** *adv.*

in·struc·tor (in STRUK tər) *n.* **1.** one who instructs; teacher. **2.** a college teacher below professorial rank. [ME]

in·stru·ment (IN strə mənt) *n.* **1.** a tool or implement, esp. one used for exacting work. **2.** a device for producing musical sounds. **3.** an apparatus for measuring, recording, etc. **4.** anything serving to accomplish a purpose; means; agency. **5.** a formal legal document, as a contract, deed, etc. [ME]

in·stru·men·tal (IN strə MEN tl) *adj.* **1.** serving as a means or instrument; useful; helpful. **2.** of or pertaining to an instrument. **3.** of, pertaining to, composed for, or performed on musical instruments.

in·stru·men·tal·ist (IN strə MEN tl ist) *n.* one who plays a musical instrument.

in·stru·men·tal·i·ty (IN strə men TAL i tee) *n. pl.* **·ties 1.** anything serving to ac-

complish a purpose; means; agency. **2.** the
condition of being instrumental.

in·stru·men·ta·tion (IN strə men TAY
shən) n. **1.** the use of instruments; work
performed with instruments. **2.** *Music* **a** the
study of the characteristics and groupings
of instruments. **b** loosely, orchestration. **3.**
instrumentality.

in·sub·or·di·nate (IN sə BOR dn it) adj. not
obedient; rebellious. —**in'sub·or'di·na'
tion** n.

in·sub·stan·tial (IN səb STAN shəl) adj. **1.**
not real; imaginary; illusive. **2.** not substantial or firm; flimsy. —**in'sub·stan'ti·al'
i·ty** n.

in·suf·fer·a·ble (in SUF ər ə bəl) adj. not to
be endured; intolerable. —**in·suf'fer·a·
bly** adv.

in·suf·fi·cient (IN sə FISH ənt) adj. not
enough; inadequate; deficient. [ME] —
in'suf·fi'cien·cy n.

in·su·lar (IN sə lər) adj. **1.** of or like an
island. **2.** narrow or limited in customs,
opinions, etc.; provincial. [< LL *insularis*]
—**in'su·lar'i·ty** n.

in·su·late (IN se LAYT) v.t. **·lat·ed, ·lat·ing**
1. surround or separate with nonconducting material in order to prevent or lessen
the leakage of electricity, heat, etc. **2.** isolate. [< L *insulatus* made into an island] —
in'su·la'tor n.

in·su·la·tion (IN sə LAY shən) n. **1.** material
used for insulating. **2.** the act of insulating,
or the state of being insulated.

in·su·lin (IN sə lin) n. *Biochem.* **1.** a hormone secreted by the pancreas, essential in
regulating the metabolism of sugar. **2.** a
preparation of this hormone, used in treating diabetes. [< NL]

in·sult (in SULT) v.t. treat with insolence or
contempt; disparage; affront. —n. (IN sult)
an act, remark, etc. that offends or affronts.
[< L *insultare* jump on] —**in·sult'er** n. —
in·sult'ing adj. —**in·sult'ing·ly** adv.

in·su·per·a·ble (in SOO pər ə bəl) adj. incapable of being overcome. [ME] —**in·su'
per·a·bly** adv.

in·sup·port·a·ble (IN sə POR tə bəl) adj. **1.**
not bearable; insufferable. **2.** unjustifiable.
—**in'sup·port'a·bly** adv.

in·sur·ance (in SHUUR əns) n. **1.** financial
protection against risk, guaranteed in return for the payment of premiums; also, the
business providing this protection. **2.** a contract guaranteeing such protection: also **insurance policy. 3.** the payment made by

the insured party. **4.** the amount for which
anything is insured. **5.** any safeguard
against risk or harm.

in·sure (in SHUUR) v.t. **·sured, ·sur·ing**
1. provide insurance for or on. **2.** ensure.
[ME] —**in·sur'a·ble** adj.

in·sur·er (in SHUUR ər) n. a person or
company that insures against specified loss.

in·sur·gent (in SUR jənt) adj. rising in revolt against established authority; rebellious. —n. an insurgent person. [< L
insurgere rise up] —**in·sur'gen·cy** n.

in·sur·mount·a·ble (IN sər MOWN tə bəl)
adj. incapable of being surmounted or overcome. —**in'sur·mount'a·bly** adv.

in·sur·rec·tion (IN sə REK shən) n. an
organized resistance to established government. [ME] —**in'sur·rec'tion·ar'y** adj.
& n. —**in'sur·rec'tion·ist** n.

in·tact (in TAKT) adj. remaining whole and
undamaged. [ME]

in·ta·glio (in TAL yoh) n. pl. **·glios 1.** incised carving; a sunken design. **2.** the art of
making such designs. **3.** a work, esp. a gem,
with incised carving. **4.** *Printing* the process
of printing from sunken or incised plates.
[< Ital.]

in·take (IN TAYK) n. **1.** the act of taking in or
absorbing. **2.** that which is taken in. **3.** the
amount of quantity taken in. **4.** the place
where water etc. is drawn into a pipe or
conduit.

in·tan·gi·ble (in TAN jə bəl) adj. **1.** incapable of being perceived by touch; impalpa-
ble. **2.** indefinite or vague to the mind. —n.
that which is intangible; esp., any incorporeal asset, as good will. [< Med.L *intan-
gibilis*] —**in·tan'gi·bly** adv.

in·te·ger (IN ti jər) n. **1.** any of the numbers
1, 2, 3, etc., as distinguished from a fraction
or mixed number: also called *whole number.* **2.** a whole entity. [< L, undivided]

in·te·gral (in TEG rəl) adj. **1.** being an indispensable part of a whole; essential; constituent. **2.** formed of parts that together
constitute a unity: an *integral* whole. **3.**
whole; entire; complete. **4.** *Math.* (IN ti
grəl) **a** pertaining to an integer. **b** produced
by integration. —n. **1.** an entire thing; a
whole. **2.** *Math.* the result of integration. [<
Med.L *integralis*] —**in'te·gral·ly** adv.

in·te·grate (IN tə GRAYT) v. **·grat·ed,
·grat·ing** v.t. **1.** bring together into a
whole; unify. **2.** make the use or occupancy
of (a school etc.) available to persons of all
races. **3.** make whole or complete by the

addition of necessary parts. —*v.i.* **4.** become integrated. [< L *integratus* renewed] —**in'te·gra'tion** *n.*

integrated circuit a circuit of electronic components formed in or on a tiny slice of material.

in·teg·ri·ty (in TEG ri tee) *n. pl.* **·ties 1.** uprightness of character; honesty. **2.** the condition or quality of being unimpaired or sound. **3.** the state of being complete or undivided. [ME *integrite*]

in·tel·lect (IN tl EKT) *n.* **1.** the power of the mind to grasp ideas and relations, and to exercise rational judgment; reason. **2.** a mind or intelligence, esp. a brilliant one. **3.** an intelligent person. [ME]

in·tel·lec·tu·al (IN tl EK choo əl) *adj.* **1.** of or pertaining to the intellect; mental. **2.** requiring use of the intellect. **3.** possessing or showing intellect, esp. of a high order. —*n.* one who pursues matters of the intellect. — **in'tel·lec'tu·al·ly** *adv.*

in·tel·li·gence (in TEL i jəns) *n.* **1.** the faculty of perceiving and comprehending meaning; understanding. **2.** the ability to adapt to new situations. **3.** the collection of secret information, as by the military. **4.** information thus collected; also, the persons so occupied. [ME]

intelligence quotient *Psychol.* a number indicating the level of a person's mental development, obtained by multiplying mental age by 100, and dividing by chronological age. Abbr. *IQ.*

in·tel·li·gent (in TEL i jənt) *adj.* **1.** having an active, able mind; acute. **2.** marked by or characterized by intelligence. **3.** endowed with intellect or understanding; reasoning. [< L *intelligens* understanding] —**in·tel'li·gent·ly** *adv.*

in·tel·li·gent·si·a (in TEL i JENT see ə) *n. pl.* intellectuals collectively. [< Russ.]

in·tel·li·gi·ble (in TEL i jə bəl) *adj.* capable of being understood. [ME] —**in·tel'li·gi·bil'i·ty** *n.*

in·tem·per·ate (in TEM pər it) *adj.* **1.** lacking moderation; unrestrained. **2.** given to excessive use of alcoholic drinks. **3.** excessive or extreme, as climate. —**in·tem'per·ance** *n.*

in·tend (in TEND) *v.t.* **1.** have as a specific aim or purpose; plan. **2.** make, design, or destine for a purpose. **3.** mean or signify; indicate. [ME *entenden* intend]

in·tend·ed (in TEN did) *adj.* **1.** planned;

proposed. **2.** prospective: *my intended wife.* —*n.* *Informal* prospective spouse.

in·tense (in TENS) *adj.* **1.** having great force; overpowering: *intense* feelings. **2.** performed strenuously and steadily: *intense* study. **3.** expressing or characterized by strong and earnest feelings. **4.** having its quality strongly concentrated. [ME] — **in·tense'ly** *adv.*

in·ten·si·fy (in TEN sə FI) *v.t. & v.i.* **·fied, ·fy·ing 1.** make or become more intense or acute. **2.** make or become intense. — **in·ten'si·fi·ca'tion** *n.* —**in·ten'si·fi'er** *n.*

in·ten·si·ty (in TEN si tee) *n. pl.* **·ties 1.** the state or quality of being intense. **2.** the strength or degree of some action, quality, feeling, etc.: pain of low *intensity.* **3.** power and vehemence of thought or feeling; also, extreme effort and concentration.

in·ten·sive (in TEN siv) *adj.* **1.** of, pertaining to, or marked by intensity. **2.** intensifying. **3.** *Gram.* adding emphasis or force. — *n.* **1.** that which gives intensity or emphasis. **2.** *Gram.* an intensive particle, word, or phrase. [ME] —**in·ten'sive·ly** *adv.*

in·tent (in TENT) *n.* **1.** purpose; aim; design. **2.** the act of intending. **3.** *Law* the state of mind in which or the purpose with which one does an act; also, the character that the law imputes to an act. —*adj.* **1.** firmly directed or fixed: an *intent* stare. **2.** directing one's mind or efforts steadfastly: with *on* or *upon.* [ME] —**in·tent'ly** *adv.*

in·ten·tion (in TEN shən) *n.* **1.** purpose; aim; goal. **2.** the act of intending. **3.** *pl.* attitude with regard to marriage. [ME *intencioun*]

in·ten·tion·al (in TEN shə nəl) *adj.* deliberate; intended. —**in·ten'tion·al·ly** *adv.*

in·ten·tioned (in TEN shənd) *adj.* having or characterized by (a specified kind of) intention: used in combination: *well-intentioned.*

in·ter (in TUR) *v.t.* **·terred, ·ter·ring** place in a grave; bury. [ME *enterren*]

inter- *prefix* **1.** with each other; together: *intertwine.* **2.** mutual; mutually: *intercommunicate.* **3.** between or among (the units signified): *intercollegiate.* **4.** occurring or situated between: *interlinear.* [< L]

in·ter·act (in tər AKT) *v.i.* act on each other. —**in'ter·ac'tion** *n.* —**in'ter·ac'tive** *adj.*

in·ter·breed (IN tər BREED) *v.* **·bred, ·breed·ing** *v.t.* **1.** crossbreed. **2.** produce (offspring) by crossbreeding. —*v.i.* **3.**

breed genetically dissimilar stocks or individuals.

in·ter·cede (IN tər SEED) *v.i.* **·ced·ed, ·ced·ing** **1.** plead or petition in behalf of another or others. **2.** come between parties in a dispute; mediate. [< L *intercedere*]

in·ter·cel·lu·lar (IN tər SEL yə lər) *adj.* *Biol.* situated between or among cells.

in·ter·cept (IN tər SEPT) *v.t.* **1.** stop or obstruct on the way; interrupt the course of. **2.** meet, as a moving person, ship, etc. **3.** *Math.* mark off or bound a line, plane, surface, or solid. —*n.* (IN tər SEPT) *Math.* an intercepted part, or a point of interception. [< L *interceptus* seized between] — **in'ter·cep'ter, in'ter·cep'tor** *n.*

in·ter·ces·sion (IN tər SESH ən) *n.* the act of interceding; entreaty or prayer in behalf of others. [ME]

in·ter·change (IN tər CHAYNJ) *v.* **·changed, ·chang·ing** *v.t.* **1.** put each of (two things) in the place of the other. **2.** cause to alternate. **3.** give and receive in return, as gifts. —*v.i.* **4.** change places one with the other. —*n.* (IN tər CHAYNJ) **1.** a reciprocal giving in exchange. **2.** an exchanging of places. **3.** alternation. **4.** an intersection of a superhighway with another highway, so designed that vehicles may enter or turn off without obstructing traffic. [ME *entrechaungen*] —**in'ter·change'a·ble** *adj.* —**in'ter·change'a·bly** *adv.*

in·ter·col·le·giate (IN tər kə LEE jit) *adj.* pertaining to or involving two or more colleges.

in·ter·con·nect (IN tər kə NEKT) *v.t. & v.i.* connect or be connected.

in·ter·con·ti·nen·tal (IN tər KON tn EN tl) *adj.* reaching from one continent to another; also, involving two or more continents.

in·ter·course (IN tər KORS) *n.* **1.** mutual exchange; communication; commerce. **2.** sexual connection; coitus. [ME *intercurse*]

in·ter·de·pen·dent (IN tər di PEN dənt) *adj.* dependent one on another; reciprocally dependent. —**in'ter·de·pen'den·cy** *n.*

in·ter·dict (IN tər DIKT) *v.t.* **1.** prohibit or ban officially. **2.** restrain (someone) from doing, or forbid use of (something). **3.** *Eccl.* exclude from participation in rites and services. —*n.* (IN tər DIKT an official prohibition; ban. [< L *interdictum* prohibition] — **in'ter·dic'tion** *n.* —**in'ter·dic'tive** *adj.*

in·ter·est (IN tər ist) *n.* **1.** a feeling of curiosity or attentiveness. **2.** the power to arouse curiosity or attentiveness; also, something that has such power. **3.** that which is of advantage; benefit. **4.** involvement, or concern in something; also, selfish concern. **5.** payment for the use of money or credit, usu. expressed as a percentage of the amount owed or used. **6.** legal or financial claim or share, as in a business. **7.** *Usu. pl.* a group of persons involved in a particular business, cause, etc.: the dairy *interests*. —**in the interest** (or **interests**) **of** in behalf of. —*v.t.* **1.** excite or hold the curiosity or attention of. **2.** cause to be concerned in; involve: with *in*. [ME]

in·ter·est·ed (IN tər stid) *adj.* **1.** having or displaying curiosity or attention. **2.** having a concern or wish for something. **3.** having a right or share in. **4.** seeking personal advantage; biased.

in·ter·est·ing (IN trə sting) *adj.* exciting interest; attractive; noteworthy. —**in'ter·est·ing·ly** *adv.*

in·ter·face (IN tər FAYS) *n.* **1.** a surface forming the common boundary between adjacent solids, spaces, etc. **2.** the meeting of two systems that interact: *interface* of language and computer. —*v.i. & v.t.* **·faced, fac·ing** come together at an interface.

in·ter·fere (IN tər FEER) *v.i.* **·fered, ·fer·ing** **1.** get in the way; impede: often with *with*. **2.** intervene and take part in the affairs of others, esp. without invitation; meddle. **3.** in sports, obstruct the play of an opponent illegally. —**in'ter·fer'er** *n.*

in·ter·fer·ence (IN tər FEER əns) *n.* **1.** the act of interfering. **2.** in football, clearing the way for the ball carrier by blocking opponents. **3.** *Physics* the effect produced by two or more sets of waves, as of light or sound, that on meeting tend to neutralize or augment each other. **4.** *Telecom.* a disturbance in the reception of radio, etc. due to conflict with undesired signals.

in·ter·im (IN tər əm) *n.* a time between periods or events. —*adj.* for an intervening period of time; temporary. [< L, in the meantime]

in·te·ri·or (in TEER ee ər) *adj.* **1.** of or situated on the inside; inner. **2.** remote from the coast or border; inland. **3.** pertaining to the internal affairs of a country. **4.** not exposed to view; private. —*n.* **1.** the internal part; the inside. **2.** the inland region of a country, continent, etc. **3.** the domestic affairs of a country. **4.** a representation of the inside of a building or room. [< L, farther inward]

interior design the design, decoration, and furnishing of interiors, as homes, offices, etc.; also, this occupation. Also **interior decoration. —interior designer** *n.*

in·ter·ject (IN tər JEKT) *v.t.* throw or introduce in between other things: *interject* a comment. [< L *interjectus* thrown between]

in·ter·jec·tion (IN tər JEK shən) *n.* **1.** the act of interjecting. **2.** that which is interjected. **3.** *Gram.* an exclamation.

in·ter·lace (IN tər LAYS) *v.t. & v.i.* •**laced,** •**lac·ing** join by or as by weaving together; intertwine; interlock.

in·ter·lard (IN tər LAHRD) *v.t.* **1.** vary by interjecting something different. **2.** be intermixed in. [< MF *entrelarder*]

in·ter·leave (IN tər LEEV) *v.t.* •**leaved,** •**leav·ing** insert extra leaves into (a book).

in·ter·line[1] (IN tər LĪN) *v.t.* •**lined,** •**lin·ing 1.** insert (words, phrases, etc.) between written or printed lines. **2.** annotate between the lines.

in·ter·line[2] (IN tər LĪN) *v.t.* •**lined,** •**lin·ing** put a lining between the usual lining and the outer fabric of (a garment). —**in'ter·lin'ing** *n.*

in·ter·lin·e·ar (IN tər LIN ee ər) *adj.* **1.** situated or written between the lines. **2.** having lines inserted between the lines. Also **in'ter·lin'e·al.**

in·ter·lock (IN tər LOK) *v.t. & v.i.* join firmly.

in·ter·loc·u·tor (IN tər LOK yə tər) *n.* **1.** one who takes part in a conversation; also, an interrogator. **2.** the man between the other two performers in a minstrel show.

in·ter·lope (IN tər LOHP) *v.i.* intrude in the affairs of others; meddle. —**in'ter·lop'er** *n.*

in·ter·lude (IN tər LOOD) *n.* **1.** a period that occurs in and divides some longer process. **2.** in drama, a separate episode performed between the acts. **3.** a short passage of instrumental music played between the stanzas of a hymn etc. [ME]

in·ter·me·di·ar·y (IN tər MEE dee ER ee) *adj.* **1.** intermediate. **2.** acting as a mediator. —*n. pl.* •**ar·ies 1.** one who acts as a mediator. **2.** an intermediate form, stage, or product.

in·ter·me·di·ate[1] (IN tər MEE dee it) *adj.* situated or occurring between two points,

places, levels, etc. —*n.* something intermediate. [< Med.L *intermediatus*]

in·ter·me·di·ate[2] (IN tər MEE dee AYT) *v.i.* •**at·ed,** •**at·ing** act as an intermediary; mediate. —**in'ter·me'di·a'tion** *n.*

in·ter·ment (in TUR mənt) *n.* the act of interring; burial. [ME *enterement*]

in·ter·mez·zo (in tər MET soh) *n. pl.* •**zos** or •**zi** (-see) **1.** a short musical offering given between the acts of a play or opera. **2.** *Music* a short movement connecting the main divisions of a large musical composition. [< Ital.]

in·ter·mi·na·ble (in TUR mə nə bəl) *adj.* having no apparent end or limit; endless. —**in·ter'mi·na·bly** *adv.*

in·ter·min·gle (in tər MING gəl) *v.t. & v.i.* •**gled,** •**gling** mingle together; mix.

in·ter·mis·sion (in tər MISH ən) *n.* **1.** an interval of time between events or activities; recess. **2.** the act of intermitting, or the state of being intermitted. **3.** the time between acts of a play, opera, etc: [ME]

in·ter·mit (in tər MIT) *v.t. & v.i.* •**mit·ted,** •**mit·ting** stop temporarily or at intervals. [< L *intermittere* send between]

in·ter·mit·tent (in tər MIT nt) *adj.* ceasing from time to time; coming at intervals. —**in'ter·mit'tent·ly** *adv.*

in·tern (IN turn) *n.* **1.** a medical graduate serving in and living at a hospital for clinical training before being licensed to practice medicine. **2.** one who is interned; internee. —*v.t.* (in TURN) **1.** confine or detain during wartime. —*v.i.* **2.** serve as an intern. [< F *interne*] —**in·tern'ment** *n.* the act or state of being confined, esp. in wartime.

in·ter·nal (in TUR nl) *adj.* **1.** of or situated on the inside; inner. **2.** belonging to or derived from the inside: *internal* evidence. **3.** pertaining to the inner self or the mind. **4.** pertaining to the domestic affairs of a country. **5.** intended to be taken or applied inwardly, as medication. [< Med.L *internalis*] —**in·ter'nal·ly** *adv.*

in·ter·nal-com·bus·tion (in TUR nl kəm BUS chən) *adj.* designating an engine in which fuel burns inside the engine itself, most often in a cylinder.

internal medicine the branch of medicine concerned with the diseases of the internal organs.

in·ter·na·tion·al (IN tər NASH ə nl) *adj.* **1.** existing or conducted among nations. **2.** of or affecting various nations and their peoples. —*n.* an organization or person having ties with more than one nation. — **in·ter·na'tion·al·ly** *adv.*

in·ter·na·tion·al·ize (IN tər NASH ə nl IZ) *v.t.* **·ized, ·iz·ing** place under international control; make international.

in·ter·ne·cine (IN tər NEE seen) *adj.* **1.** pertaining to conflict within a group. **2.** destructive to both sides. **3.** involving great slaughter. [< L *internecinus* murderous]

in·tern·ee (IN tur NEE) *n.* an interned person.

in·ter·nist (in TUR nist) *n.* a specialist in internal medicine.

in·ter·plan·e·tar·y (IN tər PLAN i TER ee) *adj.* between or among planets.

in·ter·play (IN tər PLAY) *n.* reciprocal action, movement, or influence. —*v.i.* (IN tər PLAY) interact.

in·ter·po·late (in TUR pə LAYT) *v.* **·lat·ed, ·lat·ing** *v.t.* **1.** introduce (additions, comments, etc.) into a discourse, process, or series. **2.** interrupt with additions. **3.** *Math.* **a** compute intermediate values in (a series). **b** insert (intermediate values) into a series. —*v.i.* **4.** make additions, insertions, interruptions, etc. [< L *interpolatus* refurbished] —**in·ter'po·la'tion** *n.*

in·ter·pose (IN tər POHZ) *v.* **·posed, ·pos·ing** *v.t.* **1.** put between other things, esp. as a separation or barrier. **2.** put in or inject (a comment etc.) in the course of speech or argument. **3.** exercise (authority, action, etc.) in order to intervene. —*v.i.* **4.** come between; intervene. **5.** put in a remark. —**in'ter·po·si'tion** (-pə ZISH ən) *n.*

in·ter·pret (in TUR prit) *v.* **·pret·ed, ·pret·ing** *v.t.* **1.** give the meaning of; explain. **2.** judge (persons, events, etc.) in a personal way. **3.** convey the meaning of (an experience, a play, etc.) by artistic representation or performance. —*v.i.* **4.** explain or construe. **5.** restate orally in one language what is said in another. [ME *interpreten*] —**in·ter'pret·er** *n.*

in·ter·pre·ta·tion (in TUR pri TAY shən) *n.* **1.** the process of interpreting. **2.** the meaning assigned to actions, intentions, works of art, etc.

in·ter·pre·tive (in TUR pri tiv) *adj.* **1.** of or pertaining to interpretation. **2.** providing an interpretation; explanatory. —**in'ter' pre·tive·ly** *adv.*

in·ter·ra·cial (IN tər RAY shəl) *adj.* **1.** of or for members of different races. **2.** between,

among, or affecting different races, or persons of different races.

in·ter·reg·num (IN tər REG nəm) *n.* **1.** an interval between the reigns of sovereigns. **2.** any suspension of the ruling powers of a state. **3.** any break in continuity. [< L]

in·ter·re·late (IN tər ri LAYT) *v.t. & v.i.* **·lat·ed, ·lat·ing** have, discover, or bring about a mutual or reciprocal relation. — **in'ter·re·la'tion** *n.*

in·ter·ro·gate (in TER ə GAYT) *v.t. & v.i.* **·gat·ed, ·gat·ing** examine formally by questioning; question. [< L *interrogatus* examined] —**in·ter'ro·ga'tion** *n.* — **in·ter'ro·ga'tor** *n.*

in·ter·rog·a·tive (IN tə ROG ə tiv) *adj.* **1.** asking or having the nature of a question. **2.** *Gram.* used to ask or indicate a question. — *n. Gram.* an interrogative word, phrase, etc.

in·ter·rog·a·to·ry (IN tə ROG ə TOR ee) *adj.* of, expressing, or implying a question. —*n. pl.* **·tor·ies** a question.

in·ter·rupt (IN tə RUPT) *v.t.* **1.** break the continuity or regularity of. **2.** hinder or stop (someone talking etc.) by intervening. — *v.i.* **3.** intervene abruptly. [ME *interrupten*] —**in'ter·rup'tion** *n.* —**in'ter·rup'tive** *adj.*

in·ter·sect (IN tər SEKT) *v.t.* **1.** divide by cutting or passing across. —*v.i.* **2.** cross each other. [< L *intersectus* severed]

in·ter·sec·tion (IN tər SEK shən) *n.* **1.** a place of crossing; esp., where streets or roads cross. **2.** the act of intersecting, or the state of being intersected.

in·ter·sperse (IN tər SPURS) *v.t.* **·spersed, ·spers·ing 1.** scatter among other things. **2.** diversify with other things; interlard. [< L *interspersus* scattered]

in·ter·stel·lar (IN tər STEL ər) *adj.* occurring or situated among the stars.

in·ter·stice (in TUR stis) *n. pl.* **·sti·ces** (-stə SEEZ) a narrow opening or crack. [< L *interstitium*] —**in·ter·sti·tial** (IN tər STISH əl) *adj.*

in·ter·twine (IN tər TWĪN) *v.t. & v.i.* **·twined, ·twin·ing** unite by twisting together or interlacing; intertwist.

in·ter·ur·ban (IN tər UR bən) *adj.* between or among cities.

in·ter·val (IN tər vəl) *n.* **1.** the time coming between two events, points in time, etc. **2.** a space between two objects or distance between two points. **3.** a break in the continuity or course of something. **4.** *Music* the difference in pitch between two tones. [ME *intervalle*]

in·ter·vene (IN tər VEEN) *v.i.* **•vened, •ven·ing 1.** interfere or take a decisive role, esp. to correct or settle something. **2.** occur so as to modify an action, expectation, etc. **3.** be located between. **4.** occur between other events or times. [< L *intervenire* come between]

in·ter·ven·tion (IN tər VEN shən) *n.* the act of intervening, esp. in the affairs of foreign governments. **—in'ter·ven'tion·ist** *adj. & n.*

in·ter·view (IN tər VYOO) *n.* **1.** a conversation conducted, as by a reporter, with a person from whom information is sought; also, the record of such a conversation. **2.** a meeting with a person applying for a job. [< MF *entrevue*] **—***v.t.* have an interview with.

in·ter·weave (IN tər WEEV) *v.t. & v.i.* **•wove** or **•weaved, •wo·ven** or **wove** or **weaved, •weav·ing** weave together; blend.

in·tes·tate (in TES tayt) *adj.* **1.** not having made a valid will before death. **2.** not legally disposed of by will. **—***n.* one who dies intestate. [ME] **—in·tes'ta·cy** (-tə see) *n.*

in·tes·tine (in TES tin) *n. Anat. Often pl.* the section of the alimentary canal extending from the stomach to the anus, consisting of the long, narrow **small intestine** and the **large intestine.** [< L *intestinum*] **—in·tes'ti·nal** *adj.*

in·ti·mate[1] (IN tə mit) *adj.* **1.** characterized by pronounced closeness of friendship or association. **2.** deeply personal; private. **3.** having illicit sexual relations: with *with.* **4.** resulting from close study. **—***n.* a close or confidential friend. [< L *intimus* close friend] **—in'ti·ma·cy** (-mə see) *n.* **—in'ti·mate·ly** *adv.*

in·ti·mate[2] (IN tə MAYT) *v.t.* **•mat·ed, •mat·ing** make known without direct statement; hint. [< LL *intimatus* impressed upon] **—in'ti·ma'tion** *n.*

in·tim·i·date (in TIM i DAYT) *v.t.* **•dat·ed, •dat·ing 1.** make timid; scare. **2.** discourage from acting by threats or violence. [< L *intimidatus* made afraid] **—in·tim'i·da'·tion** *n.*

in·to (IN too) *prep.* **1.** to or toward the inside of from outside: to go *into* the forest. **2.** to a time in the midst of: far *into* the night. **3.** to the form or condition of: change water *into* steam. **4.** dividing: Two *into* six is three. **5.**

Informal keenly interested in; involved with: She's *into* modern art. [ME]

in·tol·er·a·ble (in TOL ər ə bəl) *adj.* not tolerable; that cannot be borne; insufferable. [ME] **—in·tol'er·a·bly** *adv.*

in·tol·er·ant (in TOL ər ənt) *adj.* **1.** not tolerant; bigoted. **2.** unable or unwilling to bear or endure. **—in·tol'er·ance** *n.*

in·to·na·tion (in toh NAY shən) *n.* **1.** way of speaking a language or utterance; esp., the meaning and melody given to speech by changing levels of pitch. **2.** the act of intoning. **3.** *Music* **a** the production of tones of accurate pitch. **b** pitch or the accuracy of pitch.

in·tone (in TOHN) *v.t.* **•toned, •ton·ing 1.** utter or recite in a musical monotone; chant. **2.** give particular tones or intonation to. [< Med.L *intonare* intone]

in to·to (in TOH toh) *Latin* in the whole; altogether; entirely.

in·tox·i·cant (in TOK si kənt) *n.* that which intoxicates. **—***adj.* intoxicating.

in·tox·i·cate (in TOK si KAYT) *v.t.* **•cat·ed, •cat·ing 1.** make drunk. **2.** elate or excite to a degree of frenzy. [ME] **—in·tox'i·ca'tion** *n.*

intra- *prefix* situated or occurring within: **intracollegiate, intracontinental, intramolecular.** [< LL *intra-* within]

in·trac·ta·ble (in TRAK tə bəl) *adj.* **1.** not tractable; unruly. **2.** difficult to manipulate, treat, or work. [< L *intractabilis*] **—in·trac'ta·bil'i·ty** *n.*

in·tra·mu·ral (in trə MYUUR əl) *adj.* **1.** taking place within a school, college, etc.: *intramural* football. **2.** situated or occurring within the walls or limits of a city, building, organization, etc. **—in'tra·mu'ral·ly** *adv.*

in·tra·mus·cu·lar (in trə MUS kyə lər) *adj.* situated in or affecting the inside of a muscle.

in·tran·si·gent (in TRAN si jənt) *adj.* refusing to compromise or come to terms; unbending. **—***n.* one who is intransigent. [< Sp. *intransigente*] **—in·tran'si·gence, in·tran'si·gen·cy** *n.*

in·tran·si·tive (in TRAN si tiv) *Gram. adj.* of or pertaining to intransitive verbs. **—***n.* an intransitive verb. **—in·tran'si·tive·ly** *adv.*

intransitive verb *Gram.* a verb that has or needs no direct object to complete its meaning and does not form a passive.

in·tra·u·ter·ine device (IN trə YOO tər in)

an object inserted into and retained in the uterus to prevent conception. Abbr. *IUD.*

in·tra·ve·nous (IN trə VEE nəs) *adj.* situated in or affecting the inside of a vein.

in·trep·id (in TREP id) *adj.* unshaken by fear; bold. [< L *intrepidus*] —**in'tre·pid'i·ty** *n.*

in·tri·cate (IN tri kit) *adj.* **1.** perplexingly entangled, complicated, or involved. **2.** difficult to follow or understand; puzzling. [ME] —**in'tri·ca·cy** *n. pl.* **·cies**

in·trigue (in TREEG) *v.* **·trigued, ·tri·guing** *v.t.* **1.** arouse the interest or curiosity of; fascinate; beguile. —*v.i.* **2.** plot; conspire. **3.** carry on a secret or illicit love affair. —*n.* **1.** the act of plotting or scheming. **2.** a plot or scheme. **3.** a secret or illicit love affair. **4.** the quality or power of arousing interest. [< F *intriguer* entangle] — **in·tri'guer** *n.*

in·trin·sic (in TRIN sik) *adj.* belonging to or arising from the true or fundamental nature of a thing; inherent; opposed to *extrinsic.* [< Med.L *intrinsecus*] —**in·trin'si·cal·ly** *adv.*

intro- *prefix* in; within: *introvert.* [< L *intro-* inwardly]

in·tro·duce (IN trə DOOS) *v.t.* **·duced, ·duc·ing 1.** make (a person or persons) acquainted face to face with another or others, usu. in a formal manner: often with *to.* **2.** bring into use or notice first; launch: *introduce* a new technique. **3.** broach or propose. **4.** add or insert. **5.** present (a person, product, etc.) to a specific group or to the public. **6.** bring to first knowledge of something: with *to.* **7.** begin; open. [ME]

in·tro·duc·tion (IN trə DUK shən) *n.* **1.** the act of introducing. **2.** first knowledge or acquaintance; initiation. **3.** something that introduces or leads up to what follows, as the first part of a book, or an elementary text.

in·tro·duc·to·ry (IN trə DUK tə ree) *adj.* serving as an introduction; preliminary.

in·tro·spect (IN trə SPEKT) *v.i.* practice introspection.

in·tro·spec·tion (IN trə SPEK shən) *n.* the observation and analysis of one's own mental processes and emotional states. [< L *introspectus* looked within] —**in'tro·spec'tive** *adj.*

in·tro·vert (IN trə VURT) *n.* **1.** *Psychol.* a person whose interest is directed primarily toward the self. **2.** one who is sober, reserved, and withdrawn. —*v.t.* (IN trə

VURT) **1.** turn inward; cause to bend in an inward direction. **2.** turn (the mind or thoughts) toward the self. —*adj.* characterized by or tending to introversion: also **in'tro·vert'ed.** —**in·tro·ver·sion** (IN trə VUR *zh*ən) *n.*

in·trude (in TROOD) *v.* **·trud·ed, ·trud·ing** *v.t.* **1.** thrust or force in. —*v.i.* **2.** come in without leave or invitation: often with *upon.* [< L *intrudere* thrust in]

in·tru·sion (in TROO *zh*ən) *n.* **1.** the act or condition of intruding; encroachment. **2.** that which intrudes. —**in·tru'sive** (-siv) *adj.*

in·tu·it (in TOO it) *v.t. & v.i.* **·tu·it·ed, ·tu·it·ing** know or discover by intuition. [From INTUITION]

in·tu·i·tion (IN too ISH ən) *n.* **1.** a direct knowledge or awareness of something without conscious attention or reasoning. **2.** anything thus perceived. **3.** the ability or quality of perceiving without conscious attention or reasoning. [ME] — **in·tu·i·tive** (in TOO i tiv) *adj.* —**in·tu'i·tive·ness** *n.*

in·tu·mesce (IN tuu MES) *v.i.* **·mesced, ·mesc·ing** swell; enlarge. [< L *intumescere* swell up] —**in'tu·mes'cence** *n.* —**in'tu·mes'cent** *adj.*

in·un·date (IN ən DAYT) *v.t.* **·dat·ed, ·dat·ing 1.** cover by overflowing; flood. **2.** overwhelm with abundance or excess. [< L *inundatus* flooded] —**in'un·da'tion** *n.*

in·ure (in YUUR) *v.t.* **·ured, ·ur·ing** cause to accept or tolerate by use or exercise; habituate. [ME *enuren*]

in·vade (in VAYD) *v.* **·vad·ed, ·vad·ing** *v.t.* **1.** enter by force with the intent of conquering or plundering. **2.** rush or swarm into. **3.** intrude upon. **4.** penetrate and spread through injuriously. —*v.i.* **5.** make an invasion. [< L *invadere* go into]

in·va·lid[1] (IN və lid) *n.* a sick, disabled, or bedridden person. —*adj.* **1.** enfeebled by ill health. **2.** of or pertaining to disabled persons. —*v.t.* **1.** cause to become an invalid; disable. **2.** release or classify (a soldier, sailor, etc.) as unfit for duty because of ill health. [< F *invalide*] —**in'va·lid·ism** *n.*

in·va·lid[2] (in VAL id) *adj.* not valid; having no force or cogency; null; void. [< Med.L *invalidus* weak] —**in·val·i·di·ty** (IN və LID i tee) *n.* —**in·val'id·ly** *adv.*

in·val·i·date (in VAL i DAYT) *v.t.* **·dat·ed, ·dat·ing** weaken or destroy the validity of;

render invalid; annul. —**in·val'i·da'tion** *n.*

in·val·u·a·ble (in VAL yoo ə bəl) *adj.* having a value beyond estimation; priceless. —**in·val'u·a·bly** *adv.*

in·var·i·a·ble (in VAIR ee ə bəl) *adj.* not variable; not changeable; constant. —**in·var'i·a·bil'i·ty** *n.* —**in·var'i·a·bly** *adv.*

in·var·i·ant (in VAIR ee ənt) *adj.* not subject to change or variation; constant. —*n. Math.* an invariant quantity; constant.

in·va·sion (in VAY zhən) *n.* **1.** the act of invading with hostile armed forces. **2.** any attack or onset of something injurious. **3.** encroachment by intrusion or trespass. **4.** entrance as though to overrun. [ME] —**in·va·sive** (in VAY siv) *adj.*

in·vec·tive (in VEK tiv) *n.* violent accusation or denunciation; abuse. [ME] —**in·vec'tive** *adj.* —**in·vec'tive·ness** *n.*

in·veigh (in VAY) *v.i.* utter vehement censure or invective: with *against*. [< L *invehi* attack in words]

in·vei·gle (in VAY gəl) *v.t.* **·gled, ·gling** entice or induce by guile or flattery; draw; cajole: often with *into*. [< MF *aveugler* hoodwink] —**in·vei'gle·ment** *n.* —**in·vei'gler** *n.*

in·vent (in VENT) *v.t.* **1.** devise or create (a device, contrivance, process, etc.) by original effort. **2.** make up, as something untrue or contrary to fact. [ME *invented* discovered] —**in·ven'tor** *n.*

in·ven·tion (in VEN shən) *n.* **1.** the act or process of inventing. **2.** a device, contrivance, etc. conceived or made by original effort. **3.** the skill or ingenuity needed for inventing or contriving. **4.** a fabrication of the mind. [ME *invencioun*]

in·ven·tive (in VEN tiv) *adj.* **1.** skillful at invention or contrivance; ingenious. **2.** characterized by or created by invention. [ME *inventif*] —**in·ven'tive·ly** *adv.* —**in·ven'tive·ness** *n.*

in·ven·to·ry (IN vən TOR ee) *n. pl.* **·ries 1.** a list of articles, materials, property, etc.; esp., a list of goods in stock. **2.** the process of making such a list. **3.** the goods or stock of a business; also, their value. [ME *inventorie*] —*v.t.* **·ried, ·ry·ing 1.** make an inventory of. **2.** insert in an inventory.

in·verse (in VURS) *adj.* **1.** reversed or opposite in order, effect, etc. **2.** turned upside down; inverted. —*n.* that which is in direct contrast or opposition; the reverse; opposite. —**in·verse'ly** *adv.*

in·ver·sion (in VUR zhən) *n.* **1.** the act of inverting, or the state of being inverted. **2.** that which is inverted. **3.** in grammar and rhetoric, a reversing of the usual word order in a phrase, clause, or sentence.

in·vert (in VURT) *v.t.* **1.** turn upside down; turn completely over. **2.** reverse the order, effect, or operation of. —*v.i.* **3.** undergo inversion. [< L *invertere* turn upside down] —**in·vert'i·ble** *adj.*

in·ver·te·brate (in VUR tə brit) *adj. Zool.* lacking a backbone or spinal column. —*n.* an invertebrate animal.

in·vest (in VEST) *v.t.* **1.** commit or use (money) for the purchase of property, a business, etc. with the expectation of profit. **2.** spend or use (money, time, effort, etc.) for: often with *in*. **3.** place in office formally; install. **4.** give power, authority, or rank to. **5.** array or cover with or as with a garment. —*v.i.* **6.** make an investment or investments. [< Med.L *investire* invest] —**in·ves'tor** *n.*

in·ves·ti·gate (in VES ti GAYT) *v.* **·gat·ed, ·gat·ing** *v.t.* **1.** search or inquire into; make a formal or official examination of. —*v.i.* **2.** conduct a search or inquiry. [< L *investigatus* searched out] —**in·ves'ti·ga'tor** *n.* —**in·ves'ti·ga'tion** *n.* —**in·ves'ti·ga'tive** *adj.* —**in·ves'ti·ga·to'ry** *adj.*

in·ves·ti·ture (in VES ti chər) *n.* the act or ceremony of investing with an office, authority, or right. [ME]

in·vest·ment (in VEST mənt) *n.* **1.** money or capital invested to gain profit. **2.** the form of property in which one invests. **3.** the act of investing, or the state of being invested. **4.** investiture.

in·vet·er·ate (in VET ər it) *adj.* **1.** firmly established by long continuance; deep-rooted. **2.** confirmed or hardened: an *inveterate* habit. [ME]

in·vid·i·ous (in VID ee əs) *adj.* **1.** exciting or creating ill will or dislike; offensive. **2.** provoking anger or resentment by unjust discrimination. [< L *invidiosus* hateful] —**in·vid'i·ous·ness** *n.*

in·vig·or·ate (in VIG ə RAYT) *v.t.* **·at·ed, ·at·ing** give vigor and energy to; animate. —**in·vig'or·a'tion** *n.* —**in·vig'or·a'tive** *adj.*

in·vin·ci·ble (in VIN sə bəl) *adj.* not to be overcome; unconquerable. —**in·vin'ci·bil'i·ty** *n.* —**in·vin'ci·bly** *adv.*

in·vi·o·la·ble (in VĪ ə lə bəl) *adj.* **1.** not to be profaned, defiled, etc.; sacrosanct. **2.** not to be violated or broken. —**in·vi·o·la·bil'i·ty** n.

in·vi·o·late (in VĪ ə lit) adj. 1. not violated; not profaned or broken; intact. 2. inviolable. —**in·vi'o·la·cy** n.

in·vis·i·ble (in VIZ ə bəl) adj. 1. not visible; not capable of being seen. 2. not in sight; concealed. 3. not publicly or openly acknowledged. [ME] —**in·vis'i·bil'i·ty** n.

in·vi·ta·tion (IN vi TAY shən) n. 1. the act of inviting. 2. the means or words by which one invites. 3. the act of alluring; enticement. —**in'vi·ta'tion·al** adj.

in·vite (in VĪT) v.t. ·**vit·ed, ·vit·ing** 1. ask (someone) courteously to be present in some place or to perform some action. 2. make formal or polite request for: invite suggestions. 3. present opportunity or inducement for: her opinions invite criticism. 4. tempt; entice. [< L invitare] —n. Informal an invitation.

in·vit·ing (in VĪ ting) adj. that invites or allures; attractive. —**in·vit'ing·ly** adv.

in·vo·ca·tion (IN və KAY shən) n. 1. the act of invoking. 2. a prayer, as at the opening of a ceremony. [ME invocacioun]

in·voice (IN vois) n. 1. a descriptive list of merchandise sent or services rendered to a purchaser, including quantities, costs, etc. 2. the merchandise or services so itemized. —v.t. **voiced, ·voic·ing** list on an invoice.

in·voke (in VOHK) v.t. ·**voked, ·vok·ing** 1. appeal to (a deity or other agent) for aid, protection, etc. 2. declare relevant and operative, as a law, power, right, etc. 3. appeal to for confirmation; quote as an authority. 4. summon or conjure by incantation. 5. call or petition for. [< L invocare call upon] —**in·vok'er** n.

in·vol·un·tar·y (in VOL ən TER ee) adj. 1. done or occurring without one's consent or choice; unintentional. 2. Physiol. functioning without conscious control. —**in·vol'un·tar'i·ly** adv.

in·vo·lute (IN və LOOT) adj. 1. having complications and intricacies. 2. Bot. having the edges rolled inward, as a leaf. 3. Zool. having whorls concealing the axis, as a shell. Also **in'vo·lut'ed.** [< L involutus rolled up] —n. (IN və LOO shən) n. —**in'vo·lu'tion·al** adj.

in·volve (in VOLV) v.t. ·**volved, ·volv·ing** 1. include as a relevant or necessary aspect. 2. have effect on; affect by drawing in or spreading. 3. implicate; associate significantly: usu. with in or with. 4. absorb or engross: usu. with in. 5. make intricate or tangled. [ME involven] —**in·volve'ment** n.

in·volved (in VOLVD) adj. complicated; intricate.

in·vul·ner·a·ble (in VUL nər ə bəl) adj. 1. not capable of being wounded or injured. 2. unconquerable. —**in·vul'ner·a·bil'i·ty** n. —**in·vul'ner·a·bly** adv.

in·ward (IN wərd) adv. 1. toward the inside, center, or interior. 2. in or into the mind or thoughts. Also **in'wards.** —adj. 1. situated within; internal. 2. pertaining to the mind or spirit. 3. proceeding toward the inside: an inward thrust. [ME]

in·ward·ly (IN wərd lee) adv. 1. within the mind or heart; secretly. 2. on the inside; within. 3. toward the center or interior. 4. essentially; intrinsically. —**in'ward·ness** (-nis) n.

i·o·dine (Ī ə DĪN) n. a grayish black nonmetallic element (symbol I), used as an antiseptic. [< F iode]

i·o·dize (Ī ə DĪZ) v.t. ·**dized, ·diz·ing** treat or combine with iodine. —**i'o·diz'er** n.

i·on (Ī ən) n. Physics an electrically charged atom, radical, or molecule. [< Gk. ión going] —**i·on·ic** (ī ON ik) adj.

I·o·ni·an (ī OH nee ən) adj. of or pertaining to Ionia, the ancient coastal region of western Asia Minor, colonized by the Greeks in the 11th c. B.C. —n. a native of Ionia. —**I·on'ic** adj. [< Gk. Iōnikos]

i·on·ize (Ī ə NĪZ) v.t. & v.i. ·**ized, ·iz·ing** convert or become converted, totally or in part, into ions. —**i'on·i·za'tion** n.

i·on·o·sphere (ī ON ə SFEER) n. the outermost region of the earth's atmosphere, consisting of several layers subject to ionization.

i·o·ta (ī OH tə) n. 1. the ninth letter in the Greek alphabet (I, ι), corresponding to English i. 2. a very small or insignificant amount. [< Gk. iōta]

IOU a written acknowledgment of indebtedness having on it these letters (meaning I owe you). Also **I.O.U.**

ip·so fac·to (IP soh FAK toh) Latin by the fact itself; by that very fact or act.

IQ intelligence quotient.

I·ra·qi (i RAK ee) adj. of or pertaining to Iraq, its people, or their language. —n. a native or inhabitant of Iraq.

i·ras·ci·ble (i RAS ə bəl) adj. easily angered; quick-tempered. [ME irascibel] —**i·ras'ci·bil'i·ty** n. —**i·ras'ci·bly** adv.

i·rate (ī RAYT) *adj.* angry; enraged. [< L *iratus* angered] —**i·rate′ly** *adv.*

ire (īr) *n.* wrath; anger. [ME]

i·ren·ic (ī REN ik) *adj.* peaceful in purpose; conciliatory. [< Gk. *eirēnikós* peaceful]

ir·i·des·cent (IR i DES ənt) *adj.* displaying the colors of the rainbow in shifting hues and patterns, as soap bubbles, mother-of-pearl, etc. —**ir′i·des′·cence** *adj.*

i·ris (Ī ris) *n. pl.* **·ris·es** or **ir·i·des** (IR i DEEZ) **1.** *Anat.* the colored, circular, contractile membrane between the cornea and the lens of the eye, having the pupil as its central aperture. **2.** *Bot.* a plant with sword-shaped leaves and large flowers, as the crocus, gladiolus, etc. [ME]

I·rish (Ī rish) *n.* **1.** the people of Ireland or of Irish ancestry: preceded by *the.* **2.** the ancient or modern Celtic language of Ireland: also called **Irish Gaelic.** [ME *Irisch*] —**I′rish** *adj.*

Irish coffee hot coffee with sugar, Irish whiskey, and whipped cream.

I·rish·man (Ī rish mən) *n. pl.* **·men** a man of Irish birth or ancestry. —**I·rish·wom·an** (Ī rish WUUM ən) *n. pl.* **·wom·en** a woman of Irish birth or ancestry.

irk (urk) *v.t.* annoy or weary; vex. [ME *irken*] —**irk·some** (URK səm) *adj.*

i·ron (Ī ərn) *n.* **1.** a tough, abundant, malleable, and strongly magnetic metallic element (symbol Fe). **2.** that which is firm, harsh, or indestructible. **3.** an implement or tool made of iron. **4.** a metal appliance having a smooth, flat undersurface and a handle, and used, when heated, to press cloth etc. **5.** *pl.* chains used to confine a prisoner; shackles. **6.** a golf club having a metal head with an angled face. —**have irons in the fire** be engaged in various enterprises. —**strike while the iron is hot** act at the right moment. —*adj.* **1.** made of or consisting of iron. **2.** resembling iron. **3.** inexorable; unyielding; firm. **4.** grim; pitiless. —*v.t. & v.i.* smooth or press (clothes etc.) with a heated iron. —**iron out** remove, as difficulties. [ME]

i·ron·clad (Ī ərn KLAD) *adj.* **1.** covered by or in armor. **2.** strict; unbreakable, as a rule, contract, etc.

iron curtain a barrier of censorship and secrecy; esp., that imposed by the former Soviet Union between its sphere of influence and the rest of the world.

i·ron·hand·ed (Ī ərn HAN did) *adj.* exerting severe discipline; despotic.

i·ron·ic (ī RON ik) *adj.* **1.** of the nature of or characterized by irony. **2.** given to the use of irony. Also **i·ron′i·cal.** [< LL *ironicus* insincere] —**i·ron′i·cal·ly** *adv.*

i·ron·stone (Ī ərn STOHN) *n.* **1.** glazed, usu. white pottery. **2.** rock that is rich in iron.

i·ron·work (Ī ərn WURK) *n.* **1.** parts or objects made of iron, as parts of a building. **2.** the act of working in iron.

i·ro·ny (Ī rə nee) *n. pl.* **·nies 1.** a sarcastic or humorous manner of discourse in which what is said is meant to express its opposite. **2.** a result, ending, etc., the reverse of what was expected. [< L *ironia* sarcasm]

ir·ra·di·ant (i RAY dee ənt) *adj.* sending forth light; shining. —**ir·ra′di·ance** *n.*

ir·ra·di·ate (i RAY dee AYT) *v.* **·at·ed, ·at·ing** *v.t.* **1.** light up; illuminate. **2.** make clear or understandable. **3.** send forth in or as in rays of light. **4.** subject to X-rays, ultraviolet light, or similar rays. —*v.i.* **5.** be radiant; shine. [< L *irradiatus* shone upon] —**ir·ra′di·a′tion** *n.*

ir·ra·tion·al (i RASH ə nl) *adj.* **1.** incapable of exercising the power of reason. **2.** absurd. **3.** *Math.* denoting a number that cannot be expressed as an integer or a quotient of integers. [ME] —**ir·ra′tion·al·ism** *n.* —**ir·ra′·tion·al′i·ty** (i RASH ə NAL i tee) *n.*

ir·re·claim·a·ble (IR i KLAY mə bəl) *adj.* incapable of being reclaimed. —**ir′re·claim′a·bly** *adv.*

ir·rec·on·cil·a·ble (i REK ən SI lə bəl) *adj.* not able or willing to be reconciled or brought into accord. —**ir·rec′on·cil′a·bly** *adv.*

ir·re·cov·er·a·ble (IR i KUV ər ə bəl) *adj.* **1.** incapable of being recovered. **2.** incapable of being remedied. —**ir′re·cov′er·a·bly** *adv.*

ir·re·deem·a·ble (IR i DEE mə bəl) *adj.* **1.** incapable of being recovered, bought back, or paid off. **2.** not to be converted into coin: said of some types of paper money. **3.** beyond redemption or change; incorrigible. —**ir′re·deem′a·bly** *adv.*

ir·re·duc·i·ble (IR i DOO sə bəl) *adj.* **1.** incapable of being decreased or diminished. **2.** incapable of being converted to a simpler or more basic form. —**ir′re·duc′i·bly** *adv.*

ir·ref·ra·ga·ble (i REF rə gə bəl) *adj.* that cannot be refuted or disproved. [< LL *irrefragabilis* unopposable] —**ir·ref′ra·ga·bly** *adv.*

ir•ref•u•ta•ble (i REF yə tə bəl) *adj.* incapable of being disproved. —**ir'ref'u•ta•bly** *adv.*

ir•reg•u•lar (i REG yə lər) *adj.* **1.** lacking symmetry or uniformity. **2.** occurring at unequal intervals. **3.** not according to established rules, standards, or procedure. **4.** *Gram.* not conforming to the usual pattern of inflection or conjugation. **5.** *Mil.* of troops, not belonging to a regularly organized military force. —*n.* one who or that which is irregular. [ME *irreguler*] —**ir•reg•u•lar'i•ty** *n.* —**ir•reg'u•lar•ly** *adv.*

ir•rel•e•vant (i REL ə vənt) *adj.* not relevant; not pertinent; inapplicable. —**ir•rel'e•vance, ir•rel'e•van•cy** *n.*

ir•re•lig•ious (IR i LIJ əs) *adj.* **1.** lacking in religious faith or piety. **2.** profane.

ir•re•me•di•a•ble (IR i MEE dee ə bəl) *adj.* incapable of being remedied; incurable; irreparable. —**ir're•me'di•a•bly** *adv.*

ir•rep•a•ra•ble (i REP ər ə bəl) *adj.* incapable of being repaired, rectified, or made good. —**ir•rep'a•ra•bil'i•ty** *n.*

ir•re•place•a•ble (IR ə PLAY sə bəl) *adj.* not replaceable.

ir•re•pres•si•ble (IR i PRES ə bəl) *adj.* not repressible; incapable of being controlled or restrained. —**ir're•pres'si•bly** *adv.*

ir•re•proach•a•ble (IR i PROH chə bəl) *adj.* not meriting reproach; blameless.

ir•re•sis•ti•ble (IR i ZIS tə bəl) *adj.* not resistible, esp. fascinating or enchanting. —**ir're•sis'ti•bil'i•ty** *n.* —**ir're•sis'ti•bly** *adv.*

ir•res•o•lute (i REZ ə LOOT) *adj.* not resolute or resolved; wavering; hesitating. —**ir•res'o•lute'ly** *adv.* —**ir•res'o•lu'tion** *n.*

ir•re•spec•tive (IR i SPEK tiv) *adj.* without regard to: *irrespective* of what you say.

ir•re•spon•si•ble (IR i SPON sə bəl) *adj.* **1.** lacking in responsibility; unreliable. **2.** free from or incapable of responsibility. —**ir're•spon'si•bil'i•ty** *n.* —**ir're•spon'si•bly** *adv.*

ir•re•spon•sive (IR i SPON siv) *adj.* not responsive. —**ir're•spon'sive•ness** *n.*

ir•re•triev•a•ble (IR i TREE və bəl) *adj.* not retrievable; irrecoverable; irreparable. —**ir're•triev'a•bil'i•ty** *n.* —**ir're•triev'a•bly** *adv.*

ir•rev•er•ence (i REV ər əns) *n.* **1.** lack of awe, veneration, or respect. **2.** behavior indicative of this. —**ir•rev'er•ent** *adj.*

ir•re•vers•i•ble (IR i VUR sə bəl) *adj.* **1.** incapable of being turned in the opposite direction. **2.** incapable of being annulled, repealed, or undone. —**ir're•vers'i•bil'i•ty** *n.*

ir•rev•o•ca•ble (i REV ə kə bəl) *adj.* **1.** incapable of being revoked. **2.** incapable of being brought back. —**ir•rev'o•ca•bil'i•ty** *n.*

ir•ri•gate (IR i GAYT) *v.t.* **•gat•ed, •gat•ing** **1.** supply (land) with water, as by means of ditches. **2.** *Med.* moisten or wash out with water. [< L *irrigatus* wetted] —**ir'ri•ga•ble** (-gə bəl) *adj.* —**ir'ri•ga'tion** *n.*

ir•ri•ta•ble (IR i tə bəl) *adj.* **1.** easily annoyed or angered. **2.** *Biol.* responding to stimuli. **3.** *Pathol.* influenced abnormally by the action of stimulants. [< L *irritabilis*] —**ir'ri•ta•bil'i•ty** *n.*

ir•ri•tant (IR i tnt) *n.* that which irritates or causes irritation. —*adj.* causing irritation. —**ir'ri•tan•cy** *n.*

ir•ri•tate (IR i TAYT) *v.t.* **•tat•ed, •tat•ing** **1.** excite annoyance, impatience, or ill temper in; vex. **2.** make sore or inflamed. **3.** *Biol.* stimulate (a cell, tissue, or organ) to a characteristic function or action. [< L *irritare*] —**ir'ri•ta'ting** *adj.*

ir•ri•ta•tion (IR i TAY shən) *n.* **1.** the act of irritating, or the state of being irritated; annoyance. **2.** that which irritates. **3.** *Pathol.* a condition of abnormal excitability or sensitivity in an organ or part.

is (iz) present indicative, third person singular of BE. [ME]

Is•lam (is LAHM) *n.* **1.** the religion of the Muslims, which maintains that there is but one God, Allah, and that Muhammad is his prophet. **2.** Muslims collectively. **3.** the areas of the world where Islam is the main religion. [< Arabic *islām* submission to God] —**Is•lam'ic** *adj.*

is•land (Ī lənd) *n.* **1.** a tract of land smaller than a continent entirely surrounded by water. **2.** something resembling an island and set apart from its surroundings. [ME *iland*]

is•land•er (Ī lən dər) *n.* a native or inhabitant of an island.

isle (īl) *n.* a small island. Also **is•let** (Ī lit). [< MF *islette*]

isn't (IZ ənt) is not.

iso- *combining form* equal; the same; identical. [< Gk. *isos* equal]

i•so•bar (Ī sə BAHR) *n.* **1.** *Meteorol.* a line drawn on a weather map connecting all points having the same barometric pressure for a given time or period. **2.** *Physics* any of two or more atoms having the same mass number but different atomic numbers. [< Gk. *isobares* of equal weight] —**i·so·bar·ic** (I sə BAR ik) *adj.*

i·so·late (I sə LAYT) *v.t.* **·lat·ed, ·lat·ing 1.** set apart; cause to be alone. **2.** *Chem.* obtain (an element or substance) in a free or uncombined state. —**i·so·la·ble** (I sə lə bəl) *adj.* —**i'so·la'tion** *n.*

i·so·la·tion·ism (I sə LAY shə NIZ əm) *n.* a national policy of avoiding international alliances. —**i'so·la'tion·ist** *adj. & n.*

i·so·mer (I sə mər) *n.* **1.** *Chem.* one of two or more compounds identical in composition, but having different structural arrangements and different properties. **2.** *Physics* one of two or more nuclides having the same mass and atomic number but differing in energy characteristics. —**i·so·mer·ic** (I sə MER ik) *adj.*

i·so·met·ric (I sə ME trik) *adj.* **1.** pertaining to or characterized by equality in dimensions or measurements. **2.** relating to isometrics.

i·so·met·rics (I sə ME triks) *n. (construed as sing. or pl.)* exercises that strengthen muscles by tensing them against opposing muscles or an immovable resistance.

i·so·mor·phism (I sə MOR fiz əm) *n.* a similarity in form shown by substances of different composition, or by organisms belonging to different groups. —**i'so·morph'** *n.* —**i'so·mor'phic** *adj.*

i·sos·ce·les (ī SOS ə LEEZ) *adj. Geom.* of a triangle, having two sides of equal length. [< LL]

i·so·therm (I sə THURM) *n. Meteorol.* a line drawn on a weather map connecting all points having the same mean temperature.

i·so·tope (I sə TOHP) *n. Chem.* any of two or more forms of an element having the same atomic number and similar chemical properties but differing in mass number and radioactive behavior. [< ISO- + Gk. *topos* place] —**i·so·top·ic** (I sə TOP ik) *adj.*

Is·sei (EES SAY) *n. pl.* **·sei** a Japanese immigrant to the U.S. [< Japanese, lit., first generation]

is·sue (ISH oo) *n.* **1.** the act of giving out or publishing, esp. from an official source. **2.** an item or set of items, as stamps, magazines, etc., published at a single time. **3.** a result; consequence; outcome. **4.** a matter of importance to be resolved. **5.** an outflow;

discharge. **6.** offspring; progeny. —**at issue** in question; in controversy. —**take issue** disagree. —*v.* **·sued, ·su·ing** *v.i.* **1.** come forth; flow out; emerge. **2.** be derived or descended; originate. **3.** come as a consequence; result. **4.** terminate: often followed by *in.* **5.** be circulated or published; appear. **6.** be produced as profit. —*v.t.* **7.** publish; announce. **8.** give out; distribute, as supplies. [ME] —**is'su·a·ble** *adj.* —**is'su·ance** *n.*

isth·mus (IS məs) *n. pl.* **·mus·es** a narrow piece of land connecting two larger land masses. [< L]

it (it) *pron., possessive* **its;** *pl. nominative* **they,** *possessive* **their** or **theirs,** *objective* **them** the nominative and objective singular neuter pronoun of the third person, used: **1.** as a substitute for a specific noun. **2.** to represent some implied idea, condition, action, or situation: How was *it?* **3.** as the subject or predicate nominative of a verb whose logical subject is anticipated: Who is *it?* **4.** as the subject of an impersonal verb: *It* rained yesterday. **5.** as the indefinite subject of a verb introducing a clause or a phrase: *It* seems he knew. **6.** as the indefinite object after certain verbs in idiomatic expressions: brazen *it* out. —*n.* in certain children's games, the player required to perform some specified act. [ME]

I·tal·ian (i TAL yən) *n.* **1.** a native or naturalized inhabitant of Italy. **2.** the Romance language of Italy. —**I·tal'ian** *adj.*

i·tal·ic (i TAL ik) *n. Usu. pl.* a style of type in which the letters slant, often used to denote emphasis: *These words are printed in italics.* —**i·tal'ic** *adj.*

i·tal·i·cize (i TAL ə stz) *v.t. & v.i.* **·cized, ·ciz·ing** print in italics.

itch (ich) *v.i.* **1.** experience or feel an irritation that causes a desire to scratch or rub the affected area. **2.** have a restless desire to do something; hanker. —*n.* **1.** an itching sensation. **2.** any of various skin diseases accompanied by itching. **3.** a restless desire or yearning. [ME *icchen*]

itch·y (ICH ee) *adj.* **itch·i·er, itch·i·est** having or producing an itching sensation. —**itch'i·ness** *n.*

-ite *suffix of nouns* **1.** a native or inhabitant of: *suburbanite.* **2.** a follower of or sympathizer with: *Pre-Raphaelite.* **3.** a descendant of: *Israelite.* **4.** resembling or related to: *dynamite.* **5.** *Mineral.* a rock or mineral: *graphite.* [ME]

i•tem (Ī′təm) *n.* **1.** a single unit of a category, series, or enumeration. **2.** an entry in an account. **3.** a brief article of news, etc. as in a newspaper. —*adv.* likewise; also. [ME, likewise]

i•tem•ize (Ī′tə MĪZ′) *v.t.* •**ized,** •**iz•ing** set down or specify by items. —**i′tem•i•za′ tion** *n.*

it•er•ate (IT′ə RAYT′) *v.t.* •**at•ed,** •**at•ing** state or utter again or repeatedly. [< L *iteratus* repeated] —**it′er•a′tion** *n.* —**it′ er•a′tive** *adj.*

i•tin•er•ant (ī TIN′ər ənt) *adj.* going from place to place; wandering. —*n.* one who travels from place to place. [< LL] —**i•tin′ er•an•cy, i•tin′er•a•cy** *n.*

i•tin•er•ar•y (ī TIN′ə RER ee) *n. pl.* •**ar•ies 1.** a route followed in traveling. **2.** a plan for a journey. **3.** a record of a journey. [ME]

-itis *suffix Pathol.* inflammation of: *tonsillitis.* [< NL]

it'll (IT l) **1.** it will. **2.** it shall.

its (its) *pronominal adjective* the possessive case of the pronoun *it,* used attributively: *its* leaves.

it's (its) **1.** it is. **2.** it has.

it•self (it SELF) *pron.* a form of the third person singular neuter pronoun, used: **a** as a reflexive or as object of a preposition in a reflexive sense: The motor started by *itself.* **b** as an intensifier or to give emphasis: simplicity *itself.* **c** as a designation for a normal or usual state: The house isn't *itself* with the children gone. [ME]

IUD intrauterine device.

IV (Ī VEE′) *n. pl.* **IVs, IV's** an intravenous device for delivering fluids; an intravenous injection.

I've (īv) I have.

i•vied (Ī′ veed) *adj.* covered or overgrown with ivy.

i•vo•ry (Ī′və ree) *n. pl.* •**ries 1.** a hard, white, smooth-textured dentine, the chief substance of the tusks of elephants, walruses, etc. **2.** the yellowish white color of ivory. **3.** *Usu. pl.* articles made of ivory. **4.** *pl. Slang* **a** the keys of a piano. **b** dice. —*adj.* **1.** made of or resembling ivory. **2.** of the color ivory. [ME]

ivory tower a condition or attitude of withdrawal from the world and reality.

i•vy (Ī′ vee) *n. pl.* **i•vies** a climbing plant, having glossy, evergreen leaves: also **English ivy.** [ME *ivi*]

-ize *suffix of verbs* **1.** cause to become or resemble: *Christianize.* **2.** subject to the action of: *oxidize.* **3.** change into: *mineralize.* **4.** act in the manner of: *sympathize.* [< Gk. *-izein*]

J

j, J (jay) *n. pl.* **j's** or **js, J's** or **Js 1.** the tenth letter of the English alphabet. **2.** the sound represented by the letter *j*.

jab (jab) *v.t. & v.i.* **jabbed, jab·bing 1.** poke or thrust sharply. **2.** punch or strike with a quick, sharp blow. —*n.* a sharp thrust or punch.

jab·ber (JAB ər) *v.t. & v.i.* speak rapidly or without making sense. —*n.* rapid or unintelligible talk; chatter. —**jab′ber·er** *n.*

jack (jak) *n.* **1.** a man or boy, esp.: **a** a laborer: usu. in combination: *jack-of-all-trades; lumberjack.* **b** a sailor. **2.** any of various devices used for raising heavy weights through short distances, usu. by means of a lever. **3. a** a male of certain animals: sometimes used in combination: *jackass.* **b** any of various kinds of animals: often in combination: *jack rabbit.* **4.** a playing card showing the picture of a young man; the knave. **5.** a flag, flown at the bow of a ship. **6.** *Slang* money. **7.** a six-pronged metal piece used in a children's game (**jacks**) in which the pieces are tossed and picked up. **8.** *Electr.* a metallic connecting device with clips to which the wires of a circuit may be attached. —*v.t.* **1.** raise with or as with a jack: usu. with *up.* **2.** *Informal* increase, as a price: with *up.*

jack·al (JAK əl) *n.* **1.** any of various African or Asian doglike carnivorous mammals. **2.** an accomplice in base activities. [< Persian *shaghal*]

jack·ass (JAK AS) *n.* **1.** a male ass. **2.** a stupid person.

jack·et (JAK it) *n.* **1.** a short coat, usu. not extending below the hips. **2.** an outer covering or case, as a paper cover for a book. —*v.t.* cover or clothe with or as with a jacket. [ME *jaket*]

jack·ham·mer (JAK HAM ər) *n.* a pneumatic tool for drilling rock etc.

jack-in-the-box (JAK in thə BOKS) *n.* a toy consisting of a box containing a grotesque figure that springs up when the lid is unfastened.

jack·knife (JAK NIF) *n. pl.* **knives 1.** a large pocketknife. **2.** a dive in which the body is doubled forward, with the hands touching the ankles, and then straightened. —*v.t. &*

v.i. **·knifed, ·knif·ing** double up in the manner of a jackknife.

jack-of-all-trades (JAK əv AWL TRAYDZ) *n.* one who is able to do many kinds of work.

jack-o'-lan·tern (JAK ə LAN tərn) *n.* **1.** a lantern made of a pumpkin hollowed and carved into a face. **2.** ignis fatuus.

jack·pot (JAK POT) *n.* **1.** in poker, a pot that accumulates until a player is dealt a pair of jacks or better, with which the player may open the betting. **2.** any similar pot, pool, or prize. —**hit the jackpot** *Informal* **1.** win the biggest possible prize. **2.** achieve a major success.

jack rabbit a large American hare.

jacks (jaks) see JACK (def. 7).

jade¹ (jayd) *n.* **1.** a hard, translucent mineral, usu. green, used as a gemstone. **2.** a green color characteristic of jade. [< F]

jade² *n.* **1.** an old or worthless horse. **2.** a disreputable or ill-tempered woman; hussy. [ME] —*v.t. & v.i.* **jad·ed, jad·ing** weary through hard work or overuse; tire.

jad·ed (JAY did) *adj.* **1.** worn-out; exhausted. **2.** dulled or apathetic, as from over-indulgence. —**jad′ed·ly** *adv.* —**jad′ed·ness** *n.*

jag¹ (jag) *n.* a sharp, projecting point; notch; tooth. —*v.t.* **jagged, jag·ging 1.** cut notches or jags in. **2.** cut unevenly; slash. [ME *jagge*]

jag² *n.* **1.** a period of unrestrained activity. **2.** a drunken spree.

jag·ged (JAG id) *adj.* having jags or notches. [ME] —**jag′ged·ly** *adv.* —**jag′ged·ness** *n.*

jai a·lai (HĪ LĪ) a game popular in Latin America, similar to handball but played with a long, curved wicker basket strapped to the arm. [< Sp.]

jail (jayl) *n.* **1.** a place of confinement for those guilty of minor offenses or those awaiting trial. **2.** loosely, any prison. —*v.t.* put or hold in jail; imprison. [ME *gaiole*]

jail·bird (JAYL BURD) *n.* a prisoner or ex-prisoner.

jail·er (JAY lər) *n.* the officer in charge of a jail.

ja·lop·y (jə LOP ee) *n. pl.* **·lop·ies** an old, rundown automobile.

jal·ou·sie (JAL ə SEE) *n.* a window blind or

shutter of overlapping horizontal slats or strips that may be tilted. [< F]

jam¹ (jam) v. **jammed, jam·ming** v.t. **1.** force or ram into or against something. **2.** pack and block up by crowding. **3.** cause to become wedged or stuck. **4.** interfere electronically with (a radio broadcast etc.). — v.i. **5.** become wedged; stick. **6.** cease operation, as a machine, because parts have stuck or wedged together. **7.** take part in a jam session. —n. **1.** a crowding together, as of people, cars, etc. **2.** the act of jamming. **3.** *Informal* an embarrassing or dangerous predicament.

jam² n. a pulpy, sweet preserve of whole fruit boiled with sugar.

jamb (jam) n. a side post or side of a doorway, window, etc. [ME *jambe*, lit., leg]

jam·bo·ree (JAM bə REE) n. **1.** a boisterous frolic. **2.** a large, esp. international, assembly of Boy Scouts.

jam session a gathering of jazz musicians performing improvisations.

jan·gle (JANG gəl) v. **·gled, ·gling** v.i. **1.** make harsh sounds. **2.** wrangle; bicker. — v.t. **3.** cause to sound discordantly. **4.** annoy or irritate; unsettle. —n. **1.** a discordant sound. **2.** a quarrel; wrangling. [ME *janglen* haggle]

jan·i·tor (JAN i tər) n. one who is employed to care for a building etc. [< L, doorkeeper] —**jan′i·to′ri·al** (JAN i TOR ee əl) adj.

Jan·u·ar·y (JAN yoo ER ee) n. pl. **·ar·ies** the first month of the year, containing 31 days. [< L *Januarius*]

Ja·nus-faced (JAY nəs FAYSD) adj. two-faced; deceitful. [after *Janus*, Roman god usu. depicted as having two faces]

Jap·a·nese (JAP ə NEEZ) n. pl. **·nese 1.** a native of Japan, or a person of Japanese ancestry. **2.** the language of Japan. — adj.

jape (jayp) v.i. **japed, jap·ing** joke or play tricks. —n. a jest or trick. [ME *japen*] —**jap′er·y** n.

jar¹ (jahr) n. **1.** a wide-mouthed vessel of glass or earthenware, usu. deep and cylindrical. **2.** the quantity a jar contains: also **jar′ful**. [< MF *jarre*]

jar² v. **jarred, jar·ring** v.t. **1.** strike against or bump so as to move or shake; jolt. **2.** disturb or shock. —v.i. **3.** have an unpleasant or painful effect: with *on* or *upon*. **4.** disagree or conflict; clash. **5.** bump or jolt: with *against*. **6.** make or have a disagreeable sound. —n. **1.** a shaking, shock, or jolt. **2.** a disagreeable sound or jumble of sounds. **3.** a shock to the feelings.

jar·di·niere (JAHR dn EER) n. an ornamental pot or stand for flowers or plants. [< F *jardinière* a female gardener]

jar·gon (JAHR gən) n. **1.** confused, unintelligible speech; gibberish. **2.** the technical or specialized vocabulary or phraseology used by the members of a particular profession, sect, etc.: legal *jargon*. **3.** a mixture of two or more languages, often serving as a lingua franca; pidgin. [ME *jargoun*]

jaun·dice (JAWN dis) n. **1.** *Pathol.* a diseased condition of the liver characterized by yellowness of the skin and eyeballs. **2.** an embittered state of mind. —v.t. **·diced, ·dic·ing 1.** affect with jaundice. **2.** make bitter or biased. [ME *jaundis*]

jaunt (jawnt) n. a short journey, esp. for pleasure. —v.i. make such a journey.

jaun·ty (JAWN tee) adj. **jaunt·i·er, jaunt·i·est 1.** lively and self-confident. **2.** trim; dashing. [< F *gentil* gentle] —**jaunt′i·ly** adv. —**jaunt′i·ness** n.

jave·lin (JAV lin) n. **1.** a light spear thrown as a weapon. **2.** a long spear thrown for distance in an athletic contest. [< MF *javeline*]

jaw (jaw) n. **1.** *Anat.* either of the two bony structures forming the framework of the mouth and holding the teeth. **2.** one of a pair of gripping parts capable of opening and closing, as of a tool. **3.** anything suggesting the action of the jaws. —v.i. *Slang* talk. [ME *jawe*]

jaw·bone (JAW BOHN) n. one of the bones of the jaw, esp. that of the lower jaw. —v.i. & v.t. **·boned, ·bon·ing** *Informal* use the power of persuasive talk to convince.

jay·walk (JAY WAWK) v.i. cross a street recklessly, violating traffic regulations or signals. —**jay′walk′er** n.

jazz (jaz) n. **1.** a kind of music that originated among black musicians in the southern U.S., characterized by melodic, harmonic, and rhythmic variation, and a melody played against various chord patterns. **2.** *Slang* jive talk. —adj. of or pertaining to jazz. —v.t. **1.** *Informal* **a** quicken; speed up. **b** jive. **2.** play or arrange (music) as jazz. — **jazz up** *Informal* make more exciting. — **jazz′y** adj. **jazz·i·er, jazz·i·est**

jeal·ous (JEL əs) adj. **1.** fearful or suspicious of being displaced by a rival in affection or favors. **2.** vindictive toward another because of rivalry. **3.** vigilant in guarding:

jealous of a privilege. **4.** resulting or arising from jealousy. [ME *jealous*]

jeal·ou·sy (JEL ə see) *n. pl.* **·ou·sies** the attitude, feeling, or condition of being jealous. [ME *gelusie*]

jean (jeen) *n.* **1.** a sturdy, twilled cotton cloth. **2.** *pl.* trousers made of this or a similar material.

jeer (jeer) *v.t. & v.i.* speak or shout at in a derisive, mocking manner. —*n.* a derisive word or remark. —**jeer′ing·ly** *adv.*

je·june (ji JOON) *adj.* **1.** lacking in substance or interest; dry; barren; dull. **2.** callow; childish. [< L *jejunus* empty]

jell (jel) *v.t. & v.i.* **1.** congeal. **2.** assume or cause to assume definite form.

jel·lied (JEL eed) *adj.* **1.** made gelatinous. **2.** covered with or prepared in jelly.

jel·ly (JEL ee) *n. pl.* **·lies 1.** a food made with gelatin or pectin, and having a semi-solid consistency such that it quivers when shaken; esp., such a food made of boiled and sweetened fruit juice. **2.** any gelatinous substance. —*v.* **·lied, ·ly·ing** *v.t.* **1.** make into a jelly. **2.** cover or fill with jelly. —*v.i.* **3.** become jelly. [ME *gely*]

jel·ly·fish (JEL ee FISH) *n. pl.* **·fish** or **·fish·es 1.** any of a number of marine animals jellylike substance, often having umbrella-shaped bodies with trailing tentacles. **2.** *Informal* a person lacking determination or stamina; weakling.

jen·ny (JEN ee) *n. pl.* **·nies 1.** a spinning jenny. **2.** the female of the ass. **3.** a female wren: a *jenny* wren.

jeop·ard·ize (JEP ər DĪZ) *v.t.* **·ized, ·iz·ing** put in jeopardy; imperil.

jeop·ard·y (JEP ər dee) *n.* **1.** danger of death, loss, or injury; peril. **2.** *Law* the peril in which a defendant is put when placed on trial for a crime. [ME *jeuparti*]

jer·e·mi·ad (JER ə MĪ əd) *n.* a lamentation or tale of woe. [< *Jeremiah*]

Jer·e·mi·ah (JER ə MĪ ə) *n.* the 7th c. B.C. Hebrew prophet Jeremiah.

jerk¹ (jurk) *v.t.* **1.** give a sharp, sudden pull or twist to. **2.** move or do with a sharp, suddenly arrested motion. **3.** make and serve (ice cream sodas etc.). —*v.i.* **4.** give or move with a jerk or jerks. —*n.* **1.** a sudden, sharp pull, twitch, twist, or thrust. **2.** *Slang* a stupid, inept person. [< OE *gearcian*]

jerk² *v.t.* cure (meat) by cutting into strips and drying. —*n.* jerked meat. [< Sp. *charqui* dried beef]

jer·kin (JUR kin) *n.* a close-fitting jacket or vest, usu. sleeveless; esp., such a garment, often of leather, worn in the 16th and 17th c.

jerk·wa·ter (JURK WAW tər) *Informal adj.* **1.** not on a main railroad line: a *jerkwater* town. **2.** insignificant; small.

jerk·y¹ (JUR kee) *adj.* **1.** characterized by or moving in jerks. **2.** *Slang* stupid or inept.

jerk·y² *n.* meat cured by cutting into strips and dried.

jer·o·bo·am (JER ə BOH əm) *n.* a wine bottle holding about ⅕ gallon. [after *Jeroboam* I, a Hebrew king]

jer·ry-build (JER ee BILD) *v.t.* **·built, ·build·ing** build flimsily and with inferior materials. —**jerry-built** *adj.*

jer·sey (JUR zee) *n. pl.* **·seys 1.** a ribbed, knitted fabric used for clothing. **2.** a sweater.

jest (jest) *n.* **1.** something said or done to provoke laughter; joke. **2.** playfulness; fun. **3.** an object of laughter; laughingstock. —*v.i.* **1.** make amusing remarks; quip. **2.** speak or act playfully. [ME] —**jest′ing** *n. & adj.*

jest·er (JES tər) *n.* one who jests; esp., a court fool.

Jes·u·it (JEZH oo it) *n.* a member of the Society of Jesus, a Roman Catholic religious order. —**Jes′u·it′ic** or **·i·cal** *adj.*

Je·sus (JEE zəs) founder of Christianity. Also **Jesus Christ, Jesus of Nazareth.**

jet¹ (jet) *n.* **1.** a hard, black coal, taking a high polish, used for jewelry, buttons, etc. **2.** a deep, glossy black. —*adj.* **1.** made of or resembling jet. **2.** jet-black. [ME]

jet² *n.* **1.** a sudden spurt or gush of liquid or gas emitted from a narrow orifice. **2.** a spout or nozzle. **3.** an aircraft propelled by a jet engine. —*v.t. & v.i.* **jet·ted, jet·ting** spurt forth or emit in a stream. [< MF *jeter* throw]

jet-black (JET BLAK) *adj.* deep black, like jet.

jet engine a reaction and heat engine that takes in outside air to oxidize fuel that it converts into the energy of a powerful jet of heated gas expelled to the rear under high pressure.

jet lag fatigue, confusion, etc. due to long jet flights across time zones.

jet·sam (JET səm) *n.* **1.** goods thrown into the sea to lighten an imperiled vessel. **2.** such goods washed ashore. [Earlier *jetson*, short for JETTISON]

jet set an international group of wealthy and fashionable persons. —**jet′-set′ter** n.

jet stream 1. the strong flow of gas or other fluid expelled from a jet engine, rocket motor, etc. **2.** *Meteorol.* a high-velocity wind circulating, usu. from west to east, near the base of the stratosphere.

jet·ti·son (JET ə sən) *v.t.* **1.** throw overboard (goods or cargo). **2.** discard (something that hampers). —n. **1.** the act of jettisoning. **2.** jetsam. [ME *jetteson* throwing]

jet·ty (JET ee) n. pl. **·ties 1.** a structure of piling, rocks, etc., extending out into a body of water to protect a harbor, etc. **2.** a wharf or pier. [ME *gettey* projection]

Jew (joo) n. **1.** a member or descendant of the Hebrew people. **2.** any person professing Judaism. [ME *jewe*] —**Jew′ish** adj.

jew·el (JOO əl) n. **1.** a precious stone; gem. **2.** an article of jewelry. **3.** a person or thing of rare excellence or value. —v.t. **jew·eled, jew·el·ing** adorn with jewels. [ME *jouel*] —**jew′el·er** n.

jew·el·ry (JOO əl ree) n. **1.** jewels, collectively. **2.** articles of personal adornment collectively, as rings, bracelets, necklaces, etc. [ME *juelrie*]

Jew·ry (JOO ree) n. the Jewish people. [ME *jewerie*]

jew's harp n. a small, lyre-shaped musical instrument held between the teeth and played by plucking a flexible steel tongue with the finger.

jibe¹ (jīb) *v.i.* **jibed, jib·ing 1.** *Naut.* swing from one side of a vessel to the other, as a sail or its boom. **2.** change course so that the sails shift in this manner. Also **jib.** [< Du. *gijben*]

jibe² *v.i.* **jibed, jib·ing** agree; be in accordance.

jif·fy (JIF ee) n. pl. **·fies** *Informal* a moment.

jig (jig) n. **1.** a fast, lively dance; also, the music for such a dance. **2.** *Mech.* **a** a device for holding the material being worked or for guiding a tool. **b** any of various devices operated by jiggling or jolting, as a sieve for cleaning coal in water. **3.** in fishing, any of various lures that are jiggled. —**the jig is up** *Slang* all hope of success is gone. —*v.t.* & *v.i.* **jigged, jig·ging 1.** dance or play (a jig). **2.** jiggle. **3.** make with or use a jig. [? MF *giguer* frolic]

jig·ger (JIG ər) n. **1.** a small glass or cup for measuring liquor, holding about one and one half ounces; also, the amount of liquor so measured. **2.** a jig used in catching fish. **3.** *Mech.* a jig. —*v.t.* **1.** interfere with. **2.** manipulate, esp., accomplish something illegally: *jigger* the books.

jig·gle (JIG əl) *v.t.* & *v.i.* **·gled, ·gling** move back and forth or up and down with quick jerks. —**jig′gle** n.

jig·saw (JIG saw) n. a saw having a slim blade set vertically in a frame, used for cutting curved or irregular lines.

jilt (jilt) *v.t.* cast off (a sweetheart). [Earlier *jilt*, harlot]

Jim Crow in the U.S., racial segregation. —**Jim-Crow** adj. —**Jim′ Crow′ism**

jim·my (JIM ee) n. pl. **·mies** a burglar's crowbar. —*v.t.* **·mied, ·my·ing** break or pry open with or as with a jimmy.

jin·gle (JING gəl) *v.t.* & *v.i.* **·gled, ·gling** make or cause to make light ringing or tinkling sounds. —n. **1.** a tinkling, clinking, or rapidly ringing sound. **2.** a catchy, short song or poem, esp. one used for advertising. **3.** rapid repetition in rhyme, rhythm, alliteration, etc. [ME *gynglen*] —**jin′gly** adj.

jin·go (JING goh) n. pl. **·goes** a boastful patriot who favors an aggressive foreign policy: also **jin′go·ist.** [Originally a magician's nonsense word] —**jin′go·ism** n. —**jin′go·is′tic** adj.

jinn (jin) n. pl. **jinns** in Islamic mythology, one of the supernatural beings able to assume human or animal form and often at the service of men. Also **jin·ni** (ji NEE). [< Arabic *jinnī*]

jin·rik·i·sha (jin RIK shaw) n. a small oriental two-wheeled carriage drawn by one or two men: also called *ricksha, rickshaw.* Also **jin·rick′sha.** [< Japanese *jinrikisha* person-power vehicle]

jinx (jingks) n. a person or thing supposed to bring bad luck. —*v.t.* bring bad luck to.

jit·ney (JIT nee) n. a motor vehicle that carries passengers for a small fare.

jit·ter (JIT ər) *v.i.* be nervous. —**the jitters** intense nervousness. —**jit′ter·y** adj. **·ter·i·er, ·ter·i·est**

jit·ter·bug (JIT ər BUG) n. **1.** an energetic, free-moving dance for couples, done to jazz or similar popular music. **2.** one who dances a jitterbug. —*v.i.* **·bugged, ·bug·ging** dance a jitterbug.

jiu·jit·su (joo JIT soo) n. Also **jiu·jut·su.** see JUJITSU.

jive (jīv) n. **1.** the jargon of swing music and musicians. **2.** swing music. **3.** *Slang* empty or deceptive talk. —*v.* **jived, jiv·ing** *v.t.*

Slang **1.** deceive with insincere talk. **2.** tease. —*v.i.* **3.** dance to swing music.

job (job) *n.* **1.** anything that is to be done; esp., a definite single piece of work done for a set fee; also, the thing worked on. **2.** a position or situation of employment. **3.** *Slang* a robbery or other criminal act. —**lie** (or **lay**) **down on the job** *Informal* evade work or responsibility. —*v.* **jobbed, job-bing** *v.i.* **1.** work by the job or piece. **2.** be a jobber or middleman. —*v.t.* **3.** buy and resell (goods) as a jobber. **4.** assign (work) among separate contractors. —**job′less** (-lis) *adj.* —**job′less·ness** *n.*

Job (johb) *n.* a book of the Old Testament concerning the sufferings of Job, a man whose faith was tested by God.

job action a disruptive action by workers short of strike, such as a slowdown, the deliberate enforcement of all rules, etc.

job·ber (JOB ər) *n.* **1.** one who buys goods in bulk from the manufacturer or importer and sells to the retailer; wholesaler. **2.** one who works by the job or on small jobs; pieceworker.

job·hold·er (JOB HOHL dər) *n.* one who has a steady job.

jock (jok) *n. Slang* an athlete; esp., one noted for physical skills rather than intellect. [< *jockstrap*]

jock·ey (JOK ee) *n. pl.* **·eys** one employed to ride horses in races. —*v.t. & v.i.* **·eyed, ·ey·ing 1.** maneuver for an advantageous position. **2.** ride (a horse) in a race.

jock·strap (JOK STRAP *n.* a protector for the genitals, worn by men participating in sports; an athletic supporter.

jo·cose (joh KOHS) *adj.* humorous; playful; joking. [< L *jocosus* joking] —**jo·cose′ly** *adv.* —**jo·cos·i·ty** (joh KOS i tee) *n.*

joc·u·lar (JOK yə lər) *adj.* given to joking; also, like a joke. [< L *jocularis*] —**joc·u·lar·i·ty** (JOK yə LAR i tee) *n.*

joc·und (JOK ənd) *adj.* cheerful; gay; jovial. [ME *jocound*] —**jo·cun·di·ty** (joh KUN di tee) *n.*

jodh·purs (JOD pərz) *n.pl.* wide riding breeches, close-fitting from knee to ankle. [after *Jodhpur*, India]

jog (jog) *v.* **jogged, jog·ging** *v.i.* **1.** run, ride, or proceed at a moderate pace; trot. —*v.t.* **2.** push or touch lightly; nudge. —*n.* **2.** the act of jogging. **2.** a nudge. **3.** a slow, jolting motion or pace. **4.** an angle or projection in a surface; jag. **5.** a sudden temporary turn-

ing or veering. [ME *shoggen* shake] —**jog′ ger** *n.*

jog·gle (JOG əl) *v.t. & v.i.* **·gled, ·gling** shake slightly; jog; jiggle. —**jog′gle** *n.*

John Bull 1. England. **2.** a typical English-man.

John Doe a name to designate a fictitious or real personage in any legal transaction or proceeding.

joie de vi·vre (zhwahd VEE vrə) *French* delight in being alive; lit., joy of living.

join (join) *v.t.* **1.** become a member of, as a club, party, etc. **2.** come to as a companion or participant. **3.** unite in act or purpose. **4.** come to a junction with. **5.** connect. —*v.i.* **6.** enter into association or agreement: often with *with.* **7.** take part: with *in.* **8.** come together; connect; unite. [ME *joinen*] —**join battle** engage in a battle or conflict. —*n.* a joint or seam.

join·er (JOI nər) *n.* **1.** one who or that which joins. **2.** one who joins many clubs etc. [ME *joinour*]

joint (joint) *n.* **1.** a place or point at which two or more parts of the same thing are joined together. **2.** *Anat.* a place of union between two separate bones, usu. permitting movement; articulation. **3.** a large cut of meat from a shoulder or leg containing the bone, used for roasting. **4.** *Slang* **a** a place of low repute, as for drinking, gambling, etc. **b** a marijuana cigarette. [ME] —**out of joint 1.** dislocated. **2.** disordered; disorganized. —*adj.* **1.** belonging to or used by two or more. **2.** produced by combined action. —*v.t.* **1.** fasten by means of a joint or joints. **2.** cut at the joints, as meat. —**joint′ed** *adj.*

joint·ly (JOINT lee) *adv.* unitedly. [ME]

joist (joist) *n.* any of the parallel beams placed horizontally from wall to wall, to which the boards of a floor or the laths of a ceiling are fastened. [ME *giste*] —**joist** *v.t.*

joke (johk) *n.* **1.** something said or done to amuse; esp., a funny story. **2.** something said or done in fun rather than in earnest. **3.** one who or that which excites mirth. —*v.i.* **joked, jok·ing** tell or make jokes; jest. [< L *jocus* jest] —**jok′ing·ly** *adv.*

jok·er (JOH kər) *n.* **1.** one who jokes. **2.** in a deck of cards, an extra card used in certain games. **3.** an unobtrusive clause in a legislative bill, undermining or nullifying its original purpose.

jol·ly (JOL ee) *adj.* **·li·er, ·li·est 1.** full of good humor and high spirits. **2.** festive;

merry. —*v.t.* •**lied,** •**ly•ing** *Informal* attempt to put or keep in good humor: often with *along* or *up.* [ME *joli*] —**jol′li•ty** *n.*

jolt (johlt) *v.t.* **1.** strike or knock against; jar; jostle. **2.** shake with a blow or bump. —*v.i.* **3.** move with a series of irregular bumps or jars, as over a rough road. —*n.* **1.** a sudden bump or jar. **2.** an unexpected surprise or emotional shock. [from *jot* bump + *joll* bump]

Jo•nah (JOH nə) *n.* **1.** the 8th or 9th c. B.C. Hebrew prophet who survived being swallowed by a great fish. **2.** any person regarded as bringing bad luck.

josh (josh) *v.t. & v.i.* tease; banter. —*n.* a good-natured joke. —**josh′er** *n.*

joss (jos) *n.* a Chinese god. [< Chinese Pidgin English]

joss stick a stick of perfumed paste burned as incense.

jos•tle (JOS əl) *v.t. & v.i.* •**tled,** •**tling** push roughly so as to shake up; elbow; shove. [ME *justle*] —**jos′tler** *n.*

jot (jot) *v.t.* **jot•ted, jot•ting** make a hasty and brief note of: usu. with *down.* —*n.* the least bit; iota. [< L *iota*]

jot•ting (JOT ing) *n.* that which is jotted down; short note.

jounce (jowns) *v.t. & v.i.* **jounced, jounc•ing** bounce; jolt. —*n.* a shake; a bounce. [ME]

jour•nal (JUR nl) *n.* **1.** a diary or record of daily occurrences, as a ship's log, a bookkeeper's daybook, etc. **2.** a newspaper, esp. one published daily. **3.** any periodical or magazine. [ME]

jour•nal•ese (JUR nl EEZ) *n.* the style of writing regarded as characteristic of newspapers, magazines, etc.: a derogatory term.

jour•nal•ism (JUR nl IZ əm) *n.* the occupation, practice, and academic field concerned with writing, editing, and publishing or broadcasting news. —**jour′nal•ist** *n.*

jour•ney (JUR nee) *n.* **1.** travel from one place to another. **2.** the distance traveled. —*v.i.* make a trip; travel. [ME *journee* day]

jour•ney•man (JUR nee mən) *n. pl.* •**men** a worker who has completed apprenticeship in a skilled trade.

joust (jowst) *n.* a combat between two mounted knights armed with lances, esp. as part of a tournament. —*v.i.* **1.** engage in a joust. **2.** contend. [ME *justen*] —**joust′er** *n.*

jo•vi•al (JOH vee əl) *adj.* good-natured; convivial; jolly. [< Med.L *jovialis* of the planet Jupiter (exerting a happy influence)] —**jo′vi•al′i•ty** (JOH vee AL i tee) *n.*

jowl[1] (jowl) *n.* the fleshy part under the lower jaw, esp. when hanging. [ME *cholle* throat]

jowl[2] *n.* **1.** the jaw; esp., the lower jaw. **2.** the cheek. [ME *chawl* jaw]

joy (joi) *n.* **1.** a strong feeling of happiness; gladness; delight. **2.** anything that causes delight or gladness. [ME *joye*] —**joy′less** *adj.*

joy•ful (JOI fəl) *adj.* **1.** full of joy. **2.** showing or causing joy. —**joy′ful•ly** *adv.*

joy•ous (JOI əs) *adj.* joyful. [ME]

joy•ride (JOI RID) **1.** a ride taken for pleasure. **2.** a reckless ride in a stolen vehicle. —*v.i.* go on a joyride.

ju•bi•lant (JOO bə lənt) *adj.* joyful or triumphant. [< L *jubilare* shout] —**ju′bi•lance** *n.*

ju•bi•la•tion (joo bə LAY shən) *n.* rejoicing; exultation. [ME *jubilacioun*] —**ju′bi•late** *v.t. & v.i.* •**lat•ed,** •**lat•ing**

ju•bi•lee (JOO bə LEE) *n.* **1.** a special anniversary, esp. the 25th or 50th, of an event. **2.** any time of rejoicing. [ME]

Ju•da•ic (joo DAY ik) *adj.* of or pertaining to the Jews or Judaism. [< L *judaicus*]

Ju•da•ism (JOO dee IZ əm) *n.* the religious beliefs or practices of the Jews. [< LL *judaismus*]

Ju•das (JOO dəs) *n.* one who betrays another under the guise of friendship. [< *Judas,* betrayer of Jesus]

judge (juj) *n.* **1.** a public officer invested with the power to administer justice by hearing cases in a court of law. **2.** one appointed to make decisions. **3.** one who makes critical evaluations. **4.** one appointed to rate contestants or entries, as in a horse show, essay contest, etc. —*v.* **judged, judg•ing** *v.t.* **1.** hear and decide the merits of (a case) or the guilt of (a person). **2.** decide authoritatively, as a contest. **3.** hold as judgment or opinion. **4.** form an opinion or judgment concerning. —*v.i.* **5.** act as a judge. [ME *jugen*]

judg•ment (JUJ mənt) *n.* **1.** the act of judging. **2.** the decision or opinion reached through judging. **3.** the ability to judge wisely. **4.** *Law* **a** a sentence or decision. **b** a debt resulting from such a decision. [ME *juggement*]

ju•di•cial (joo DISH əl) *adj.* **1.** of or pertaining to the administering of justice, to courts of law, or to judges. **2.** decreed or enforced by a court of law. **3.** of or befitting a judge. [ME]

ju·di·ci·ar·y (joo DISH ee ER ee) *adj.* of or pertaining to courts, judges, or judgments. —*n. pl.* **·ar·ies 1.** the department of government that administers the law. **2.** the system of courts set up to carry out this function. **3.** judges collectively.

ju·di·cious (joo DISH əs) *adj.* having, showing, or exercising good judgment; prudent. [< L *judicium* judgment] —**ju·di'·cious·ly** *adv.* —**ju·di'·cious·ness** *n.*

ju·do (JOO doh) *n.* a Japanese system of physical conditioning, based on jujitsu. [< Japanese, lit., gentle way of life]

jug (jug) *n.* **1.** a pitcher or similar vessel for holding liquids. **2.** *Slang* a prison or jail. —*v.t.* **jugged, jug·ging 1.** put into a jug. **2.** *Slang* imprison.

jug·ger·naut (JUG ər NAWT) *n.* any massive and irresistible destructive force. [< Skt. *jagannātha* lord of the universe]

jug·gle (JUG əl) *v.* **·gled, ·gling** *v.t.* **1.** keep (two or more objects) continuously moving from the hand into the air. **2.** manipulate dishonestly. —*v.i.* **3.** perform as a juggler. —*n.* an act of juggling. [ME *jogelen* jest] —**jug'gler** *n.*

jug·u·lar (JUG yə lər) *adj. Anat.* of or pertaining to the throat or the jugular vein. —*n. Anat.* a jugular vein. [< LL *jugularis* pertaining to the throat]

jugular vein *Anat.* one of the large veins on either side of the neck that returns blood from the brain, face, and neck.

juice (joos) *n.* **1.** the liquid part of a vegetable, fruit, or animal. **2.** the natural fluids of the body. **3.** *Slang* **a** electricity. **b** gasoline. **c** alcoholic liquor. **d** strength. [ME *juis* juice]

juic·er (JOO sər) *n.* a device for extracting juice.

juic·y (JOO see) *adj.* **juic·i·er, juic·i·est 1.** abounding with juice; moist. **2.** full of interest; spicy. —**juic'i·ness** *n.*

ju·jit·su (joo JIT soo) *n.* a Japanese system of hand-to-hand defense in which surprise and a knowledge of anatomy and leverage are used: also spelled *jiujitsu, jiujutsu, jujutsu.* [< Japanese, lit., soft technique]

ju·jube (JOO joob) *n.* a gelatinous candy lozenge. [ME]

juke·box (JOOK BOKS) *n.* a large automatic phonograph, usu. coin-operated and permitting selection of the records to be played.

ju·lep (JOO lip) *n.* **1.** a mint julep. **2.** a sweetened, syrupy drink. [ME]

ju·li·enne (joo lee EN) *adj.* cut into thin strips. [< F]

Ju·ly (juu LI) *n. pl.* **·lies** the seventh month of the calendar year, having 31 days. [ME *Julie* < *Julius* Caesar]

jum·ble (JUM bəl) *v.* **·bled, ·bling** *v.t.* **1.** mix in a confused mass; put or throw together without order. —*v.i.* **2.** meet or unite confusedly. —*n.* a confused mixture or collection; hodgepodge.

jum·bo (JUM boh) *n. pl.* **·bos** a very large person, animal, or thing. —*adj.* very large. [after *Jumbo,* an unusually large elephant exhibited by P.T. Barnum in 1882]

jump (jump) *v.i.* **1.** spring from the ground, floor, etc. by using the foot and leg muscles; leap; bound. **2.** rise or move abruptly. **3.** pass suddenly, as if by leaping: *jump* to a conclusion. **4.** start in astonishment. **5.** spring down from or out of a window, ladder, airplane, etc. **6.** skip or leap over something. —*v.t.* **7.** leap over or across. **8.** cause to leap over or across: *jump* a horse. **9.** increase (prices, demands, etc.). **10.** pass over; skip; omit. **11.** attack suddenly or by surprise. —**jump at** accept hastily. —**jump bail** forfeit a bail bond by failing to appear when legally summoned. —**jump off** *Mil.* begin an attack. —**jump on** (or **all over**) assail with abuse; scold. —**jump the gun 1.** begin before the starting signal is given. **2.** begin prematurely. —**jump the track** of a train, leave the rails. —*n.* **1.** the act of jumping; a leap; spring; bound. **2.** an abrupt movement upward or outward; a jerk. **3.** a sudden rise or transition. **4.** something that is jumped over or across, as a hurdle. **5.** a leap by parachute from an airplane. **6.** in sports, a competition in jumping: broad *jump.* —**get** (or **have**) **the jump on** get or have a head start on or an advantage over. [< Scand. *gumpe* jump]

jump·er¹ (JUM pər) *n.* **1.** one who or that which jumps. **2.** *Electr.* a wire used to bypass or join parts of a circuit.

jum·per² (JUM pər) *n.* **1.** a sleeveless dress, usu. worn over a blouse or sweater. **2.** a loose jacket or smock worn over other clothes.

jump·y (JUM pee) *adj.* **jump·i·er, jump·i·est** given to startled movements; nervous. —**jump'i·ness** *n.*

junc·tion (JUNGK shən) *n.* **1.** the act of joining, or the state of being joined. **2.** the place where lines or routes, as roads, railways, streams, etc., come together or cross.

junc·ture (JUNGK chər) n. **1.** the act of joining, or the state of being joined; junction. **2.** a point or line of junction; a joint or seam. **3.** a point in time; esp., a critical time. [ME]

June (joon) n. the sixth month of the calendar year, having 30 days. [< L *Junius,* after the name of a Roman family]

jun·gle (JUNG gəl) n. **1.** a dense tropical thicket of high grass, reeds, vines, brush, or trees, usu. inhabited by wild animals. **2.** any similar tangled growth. **3.** a place of ruthless competition. [< Hind. *jangal* a rough place]

jun·ior (JOON yər) adj. **1.** younger in years or lower in rank. **2.** denoting the younger of two. **3.** belonging to youth or earlier life. **4.** later in effect or tenure. **5.** pertaining to the third year of a school course of four years. —n. **1.** the younger of two. **2.** one later or lower in service or standing. **3.** a student in the junior year. Abbr. *jr., Jr.* [< L, younger]

junk[1] (jungk) n. **1.** castoff material, as scrap iron, old bottles, or paper. **2.** rubbish; trash. **3.** *Slang* narcotics, esp. heroin. —v.t. discard as trash; scrap. [ME *jonke*]

junk[2] n. a large Chinese sailing vessel of traditional design. [< Pg. *junco* a ship]

jun·ket (JUNG kit) n. **1.** a feast or pleasure trip. **2.** a trip taken by a public official with all expenses paid from public funds. **3.** a custardlike dessert made of sweetened milk and rennet. —v.i. go on a trip, esp. at public expense. —v.t. entertain. [ME *jonket*]

junk·ie (JUNG kee) n. *Informal* a drug addict. Also **junk'y.**

junk·man (JUNGK MAN) n. pl. **-men** one who purchases, collects, and sells junk.

Ju·no·esque (JOO noh ESK) adj. stately and beautiful. [after *Juno,* in Roman mythology, queen of the gods]

jun·ta (HUUN tə) n. **1.** in Spain or Latin America, a legislative council. **2.** a group engaged in political intrigue; esp. military officers who take over a government. [< Sp., a meeting]

Ju·pi·ter (JOO pi tər) n. the largest planet of the solar system, fifth in order from the sun. [after the Roman god *Jupiter,* ruler of all gods]

ju·rid·i·cal (juu RID i kəl) adj. pertaining to the law and to the administration of justice. Also **ju·rid'ic.** [< L *juridicus*]

ju·ris·dic·tion (JUUR is DIK shən) n. **1.** the

lawful right to exercise authority. **2.** the scope or things over which such authority may be exercised. [ME]

ju·ris·pru·dence (JUUR is PROOD ns) n. **1.** the philosophy or science of law. **2.** a system of laws. [< L *juris* law + *prudentia* knowledge] —**ju·ris·pru·den·tial** (JUUR is proo DEN shəl) adj.

ju·ris·pru·dent (JUUR is PROOD nt) adj. skilled in the law.

ju·rist (JUUR ist) n. one versed in the law.

ju·ror (JUUR ər) n. one who serves on a jury. [ME *jurour*]

ju·ry[1] (JUUR ee) n. pl. **-ries 1.** a body of persons summoned to serve on a judicial tribunal and give a verdict. **2.** a committee of award in a competition. [ME *jurie*]

ju·ry[2] adj. *Naut.* makeshift. [ME *iuwere* help]

ju·ry-rig (JUUR ee RIG v. **-rigged, -rig·ging** assemble for temporary use.

just (just) adj. **1.** fair and impartial. **2.** upright; honest. **3.** legally valid; legitimate. **4.** merited; deserved. **5.** true; correct; accurate. **6.** fitting; proper. —adv. **1.** to the exact point; precisely: *just* right. **2.** precisely now: They are *just* leaving. **3.** a moment ago: He *just* left. **4.** by very little; barely. **5.** only; merely. **6.** really; very: It's *just* lovely. [ME] —**just'ly** adv. —**just'ness** n.

jus·tice (JUS tis) n. **1.** the quality of being just. **2.** the rendering of what is due or merited; also, that which is due or merited. **3.** conformity to the law. **4.** the administration of law. **5.** a judge. **6.** the abstract principle by which right and wrong are defined. [ME] —**bring to justice** arrest and try (a wrongdoer). —**do justice to** show appreciation of.

jus·ti·fi·a·ble (JUS tə FI ə bəl) adj. capable of being justified; defensible. [< MF]

jus·ti·fi·ca·tion (JUS tə fi KAY shən) n. **1.** the act of justifying, or the state of being justified. **2.** that which justifies or is thought to justify.

jus·ti·fy (JUS tə FI) v. **-fied, -fy·ing** v.t. **1.** show to be just, right, or reasonable; vindicate. **2.** absolve. **3.** provide adequate grounds for; warrant. **4.** *Printing* adjust (lines) to the proper length by spacing. —v.i. **5.** *Printing* be properly spaced; fit. [ME *justifien*] —**jus'ti·fi'er** n.

jut (jut) v.i. **jut·ted, jut·ting** extend beyond the main portion; protrude: often with *out.* —n. anything that juts; a projection.

jute (joot) n. **1.** a tall annual Asian herb. **2.**

the tough fiber obtained from this plant, used for cordage etc. [< Skt. *jūta* braid of hair]

ju·ve·nes·cent (JOO və NES ənt) *adj.* **1.** becoming young or becoming young again. **2.** making young; rejuvenating. [< L *juvenescere* grow youthful] —**ju′ve·nes′ cence** *n.*

ju·ve·nile (JOO və NIL) *adj.* **1.** young; youthful; also, immature. **2.** designed for young persons. —*n.* **1.** a young person. **2.** an actor of youthful roles. [< L *juvenilis* youthful]

juvenile delinquent one who is guilty of antisocial behavior or of violations of the law but is too young to be punished as an adult criminal. —**juvenile delinquency**

ju·ve·nil·i·a (JOO və NIL ee ə) *n.pl.* works produced in youth, esp. writings or paintings. [< L]

jux·ta·pose (JUK stə POHZ) *v.t.* •**posed,** •**pos·ing** place together; put side by side. —**jux·ta·po·si·tion** (JUK stə pə ZISH ən) *n.*

K

k, K (kay) *n. pl.* **k's** or **ks, K's** or **Ks 1.** the eleventh letter of the English alphabet. **2.** the sound represented by the letter *k.* — *symbol Chem.* potassium (K).

ka·bu·ki (kə BOO kee) *n.* a form of Japanese play on popular or comic themes, employing elaborate costume, stylized gesture, music, and dancing. [< Japanese]

Kad·dish (KAH dish) *n.* in Judaism, a prayer recited by mourners and as part of the daily service. [< Aramaic *qaddish* holy]

kai·ser (KĪ zər) *n.* a German emperor. [< G < L *Caesar*]

ka·lei·do·scope (kə LĪ də SKOHP) *n.* **1.** a tube-shaped optical toy that shows constantly changing symmetrical patterns as loose bits of colored glass are moved about under a set of mirrors. **2.** a swiftly changing scene, pattern, etc. [< Gk. *kalós* beautiful + *eídos* form + -SCOPE] —**ka·lei·do·scop'ic** (kə LĪ də SKOP ik) *adj.*

kan·ga·roo (KANG gə ROO) *n. pl.* **·roos** a herbivorous marsupial of Australia and Tasmania, having short forelimbs, stout tail, and powerful hind limbs adapted for leaping. [< Austral.]

kangaroo court an unauthorized court in which the law is disregarded or willfully misinterpreted.

kap·pa (KAP ə) *n.* the tenth letter in the Greek alphabet (K κ) corresponding to the English *k.*

ka·put (kah PUUT) *adj. Slang* ruined; done for. [< G]

kar·at (KAR ət) *n.* **1.** the twenty-fourth part by weight of gold in an article: 18-*karat* gold has ¹⁸⁄₂₄ or ³⁄₄ gold by weight. **2.** loosely, a carat. [Var. of CARAT]

ka·ra·te (kə RAH tee) *n.* an Oriental method of hand-to-hand defense utilizing a variety of sudden, forceful blows. [< Japanese, lit., empty hand]

kar·ma (KAHR mə) *n.* **1.** *Hinduism & Buddhism* the spiritual force generated by one's actions, which determines one's reincarnated situation. **2.** loosely, fate. **3.** vibration (def.3). [< Skt.]

ka·ty·did (KAY tee did) *n.* a green, arboreal insect allied to the grasshoppers and crickets. [From sound produced by the males]

kay·ak (KĪ ak) *n.* the hunting canoe of arctic America, made of seal skins stretched over a frame, with a hole amidships where the user sits. [< Eskimo *qajaq*]

ka·zoo (kə ZOO) *n.* a toy instrument, an open tube with a top hole fitted with a membrane that vibrates when one hums into the tube.

keel (keel) *n.* **1.** *Naut.* the main structural member of a vessel, running lengthwise along the bottom, to which all the crosswise members are solidly fixed; the backbone of a ship. **2.** any part or object resembling a keel in shape or function. —**on an even keel** in equilibrium; steady. [ME *kele*] —**keel over 1.** turn bottom up; capsize. **2.** fall over, as in a faint or from an injury.

keel·haul (KEEL hawl) *v.t.* **1.** *Naut.* haul (a person) under the keel of a ship as punishment. **2.** reprove severely; castigate. [< Du. *kielhalen*]

keen¹ (keen) *adj.* **·er, ·est 1.** able to cut or penetrate readily; very sharp. **2.** acute or refined, as in intelligence or perception. **3.** eager; enthusiastic. **4.** of senses or sense organs, acute; sensitive. **5.** having a piercing, intense quality or impact. **6.** fond of: with *about, for,* or on. **7.** *Slang* fine; excellent. [ME *kene*]

keen² *n.* a wailing lamentation for the dead. —*v.i.* wail loudly over the dead. [< Irish *caoine* lament] —**keen'er** *n.* —**keen'ing** *n.*

keep (keep) *v.* **kept, keep·ing** *v.t.* **1.** retain possession or control of; avoid releasing or giving away: *keep* one's earnings. **2.** hold or continue to hold in some specified state, relation, place, etc.: *Keep* the car in good repair. **3.** store, hold, or confine in a regular place. **4.** maintain. **5.** be faithful to or abide by (a promise, vow, etc.). **6.** care for; tend. **7.** detain. **8.** prevent: with *from.* **9.** observe, as with rites or ceremony: *keep* the Sabbath. **10.** write down and preserve in good order: *keep* a diary. **11.** maintain for use or employ for service. —*v.i.* **12.** persist in; continue: often with *on.* **13.** remain; stay: *Keep* away. **14.** stay in good condition. **15.** remain fresh for a later time: The news will *keep.* —**keep back 1.** restrain. **2.** withhold. —**keep to oneself 1.** remain solitary. **2.** avoid revealing. —**keep track of** (or **tabs on**) continue to be informed about. —**keep up 1.** hold the pace. **2.** maintain in good condition. **3.** continue. **4.** cause to stay awake or out of bed. —**keep up with** stay abreast of. —*n.* **1.** means of subsistence: earn one's *keep.* **2.** guard or custody. **3.** the strongest building of a castle; also, a castle or fortress. —**for keeps 1.** very seriously. **2.** permanently. [ME *kepen* observe]

keep·er (KEE pər) *n.* **1.** one who keeps or guards. **2.** one in charge of (a specified place, thing, etc.): used in combination: *gatekeeper.*

keep·ing (KEE ping) *n.* **1.** the act of one who keeps. **2.** custody, charge, or possession. **3.** maintenance; support. —**in keeping (with)** in accordance with.

keep·sake (KEEP sayk) *n.* anything kept, or given to be kept, for the sake of the giver; a memento.

keg (keg) *n.* a small, strong barrel. [ME *cag*]

kelp (kelp) *n.* **1.** any of various large, coarse, brown algae. **2.** the ashes of such algae, a source of iodine. [ME *culp*]

Kel·vin scale (KEL vin) *Physics* the absolute scale of temperature, in which zero is equal to $-273°$ 0 Celsius or $-459.4°$ f Fahrenheit. [after Lord *Kelvin*, 1824–1907, English physicist]

ken (ken) *n.* range of sight or knowledge. [ME *kennen*]

ken·nel (KEN l) *n.* **1.** a house for a dog or for a pack of hounds. **2.** *Often pl.* an establishment where dogs are bred, sold, trained, etc. —*v.t.* **ken·neled, ken·nel·ing** keep or confine in or as in a kennel. [ME *kenel*]

kep·i (KAY pee) *n. pl.* **kep·is** a flat-topped military cap with a visor. [< F]

kept (kept) past tense, past participle of KEEP.

ker·chief (KUR chif) *n.* a square of fabric used to cover the head or neck, or as a handkerchief. [ME *kerchef*]

ker·nel (KUR nl) *n.* **1.** the entire contents of a seed or grain within its coating. **2.** the edible part of a nut. **3.** the central part of anything. [ME *kirnel* corn seed]

ker·o·sene (KER ə seen) *n.* a mixture of hydrocarbons distilled from crude petroleum and used in lamps, stoves, and some engines.

ketch (kech) *n.* a two-masted vessel similar to a yawl. [ME *cache*]

ketch·up (KECH əp) *n.* a spicy sauce or condiment, usu. made of tomatoes: also spelled *catsup.* [< Malay *kēchap* fish sauce]

ket·tle (KET l) *n.* **1.** a metallic vessel for boiling or stewing. **2.** a teakettle. [ME *ketel*]

ket·tle·drum (KET l DRUM) *n.* a large drum having a brass hemispherical shell and a parchment head that can be tuned through a small range of definite pitches.

key[1] (kee) *n. pl.* **keys 1.** an instrument for moving the bolt or tumblers of a lock in order to lock or unlock. **2.** an instrument for holding and turning a screw, valve, or the like. **3.** anything serving to disclose, open, or solve something. **4.** a gloss, table, or group of notes interpreting certain symbols, problems, etc. **5.** any one of the finger levers in typewriters, computers, etc. **6.** *Telecom.* a circuit breaker or opener operated by the fingers, as in a telegraph apparatus. **7.** *Music* **a** in musical instruments, a lever to be pressed by the finger or thumb. **b** a system of tones in which all the tones bear a definite relationship to some specific tone (the keynote or tonic): the *key* of C. **8.** the tone or pitch of the voice. **9.** level of intensity of expression or emotion. **10.** *Mech.* a wedge, cotter pin, etc., used to secure various parts. —*v.t.* **keyed, key·ing 1.** fasten with or as with a key. **2.** provide with a key or keys. **3.** provide with a cross-reference or a system of cross-references. **4.** *Music* regulate the pitch or tone of. **5.** regulate for a particular audience or in accord with a particular idea. —**key up** cause excitement, expectancy, etc. in. —*adj.* of chief and decisive importance. [ME *keye*]

key[2] *n. pl.* **keys** a low island, esp., one of coral, along a coast; cay. [< Sp. *cayo*]

key·board (KEE bord) *n.* **1.** a row of keys, as in a piano. **2.** a group of keys for operating a machine, as a typewriter, a computer, etc. —*v.t.* feed (data) into a computer by use of a keyboard. —**key'board'er** *n.*

key·hole (KEE hohl) *n.* **1.** a hole for a key. **2.** a shape resembling a key.

key·note (KEE noht) *n.* **1.** the basic idea or principle of a political platform, speech, etc. **2.** *Music* the tonic of a key, from which it is named. —*v.t.* **·not·ed, ·not·ing 1.** sound the keynote of. **2.** deliver the keynote address of.

keynote address an opening address, esp. at a political convention, presenting basic issues and partisan principles. Also **keynote speech.**

key·punch (KEE punch) *n.* a keyboard machine for punching holes in cards used in electronic data processing. —**key'punch'** *v.t.* —**key'punch'er** *n.*

key•stone (KEE STOHN) *n.* **1.** *Archit.* the uppermost and last-set stone of an arch. **2.** a fundamental element, as of a plan.

khak•i (KAK ee) *n. pl.* **khak•is 1.** a color ranging from light sand to medium brown. **2.** a stout cotton cloth of this color. **3.** *pl.* trousers or a uniform made of khaki. —*adj.* of the color khaki. [< Hindi *khākī* dust-colored]

khan (kahn) *n.* **1.** the title of the imperial successors to the Mongol conqueror Genghis Khan. **2.** a title for rulers, officials, or dignitaries in Central Asia, Iran, etc. [ME *caan*]

kib•butz (ki BUUTS) *n. pl.* **•but•zim** (-buut SEEM) a cooperative or collective farm in Israel. [< Hebrew, gathering]

kib•itz (KIB its) *v.i. Informal* act as a kibitzer. [< Yiddish *kibitsen*]

kib•itz•er (KIB it sər) *n. Informal* one who meddles in the affairs of others; esp., a spectator who gives gratuitous advice to card players. [< Yiddish]

kick (kik) *v.i.* **1.** strike out with the foot or feet. **2.** of firearms, recoil. **3.** in football, kick the ball. **4.** *Informal* object or complain. —*v.t.* **5.** strike with the foot. **6.** drive or impel by striking with the foot. **7.** in football, score (a point or field goal) by kicking the ball. —**kick around** *Informal* **1.** abuse; neglect. **2.** roam from place to place. **3.** give thought to; discuss. —**kick back** *Informal* pay back (part of a salary, fee, etc.) to someone, usu. as a bribe. —**kick in** contribute or participate by contributing. — **kick off 1.** in football, put the ball in play by kicking it toward the opposing team. **2.** *Slang* die. —**kick out** *Informal* eject suddenly, as with a kick. —**kick the bucket** *Slang* die. —**kick up** make or stir up (trouble, confusion, etc.). —*n.* **1.** a blow or thrust with the foot. **2.** *Informal* an objection or complaint. **3.** power; force. **4.** *Informal* a thrill. **5.** the recoil of a firearm. **6.** in football, a kicking of the ball. [ME *kiken*]

kick•back (KIK BAK) *n.* **1.** a recoil; repercussion. **2.** a paying back of part of a fee etc.; also, the money so paid.

kick•off (KIK AWF) *n.* **1.** in football, the kick with which play is begun. **2.** any beginning.

kid (kid) *n.* **1.** a young goat. **2.** kidskin. **3.** the meat of a young goat. **4.** *Informal* a child; youngster. —*adj.* **1.** made of kid. **2.** *Infor-*

mal younger: *kid* brother. —*v.t. & v.i.* **kid•ded, kid•ding** *Informal* **1.** make fun of (someone); tease. **2.** deceive or try to deceive (someone); fool. [ME *kide*] —**kid'der** *n.*

kid•dy (KID ee) *n. pl.* **•dies** *Informal* a small child. Also **kid'die.**

kid•nap (KID nap) *v.t.* **•napped, •nap•ping** seize and carry off (someone) by force or fraud, usu. so as to demand a ransom. — **kid'nap•per** *n.*

kid•ney (KID nee) *n. pl.* **•neys 1.** *Anat.* either of two glandular organs situated at the back of the abdominal cavity, serving to separate waste products from the blood and to excrete them as urine. ♦ Collateral adjective: *renal.* **2.** the meat of the kidney of certain animals, used as food. **3.** temperament, nature, or type. [ME *kidenei*]

kidney bean 1. a kidney-shaped bean. **2.** the bean of the scarlet runner.

kidney stone *Pathol.* an abnormal stone formed in the kidney.

kid•skin (KIS SKIN) *n.* **1.** leather tanned from the skin of a young goat, used for gloves, shoes, etc. **2.** *pl.* gloves etc. made of kidskin.

kiel•ba•sa (kil BAH sə) *n. pl.* **•sas** or **•sy** (-see) smoked sausage. [< Polish]

kill[1] (kil) *v.t.* **1.** cause the death of. **2.** bring to an end; destroy. **3.** *Informal* overwhelm, as with laughter, exhaustion, etc. **4.** destroy the active qualities of; neutralize. **5.** cancel by contrast, as a color. **6.** cancel or delete. **7.** turn off or stop, as a motor. **8.** pass (time) aimlessly. **9.** veto or quash (legislation). — *v.i.* **10.** cause death. **11.** murder; slay. —*n.* **1.** the act of killing, esp. in hunting. **2.** an animal or animals killed as prey. [ME *cullen*]

kill[2] *n.* a creek, stream, or channel: an element in geographical names. [< Du. *kil* channel]

kill•ing (KIL ing) *n.* **1.** homicide. **2.** the act of one who or that which kills. —**make a killing** earn or win a large amount of money. —*adj.* **1.** used to kill. **2.** likely to kill. **3.** resulting in death; fatal. **4.** *Informal* **a** extremely funny; hilarious. **b** exhausting; destructive.

kill-joy (KIL JOI) *n.* one who spoils pleasure for others.

kiln (kil) *n.* an oven or furnace for baking or drying bricks etc. [ME *kilne*]

ki•lo (KEE loh) *n. pl.* **•os 1.** a kilogram. **2.** a kilometer.

kilo- *prefix* in the metric system, a thousand times (a specified unit): *kilogram.* [< F]

kil·o·cy·cle (KIL ə I kəl) *n.* kilohertz: 1000 cycles per second.

kil·o·gram (KIL ə GRAM) *n.* in the metric system, a thousand grams.

kil·o·hertz (KIL ə HURTS) *n. pl.* **·hertz** a unit of frequency equal to one thousand hertz: 1000 cycles per second.

kil·o·li·ter (KIL ə LEE tər) *n.* in the metric system, a thousand liters.

ki·lo·me·ter (ki LOM i tər) *n.* in the metric system, a thousand meters. —**kil·o·met·ric** (KIL ə ME trik) *adj.*

kil·o·watt (KIL ə WOT) *n. Electr.* a unit of power equal to 1000 watts.

kil·o·watt-hour (KIL ə WOT OWR) *n.* the work done or the energy resulting from one kilowatt acting for one hour.

kilt (kilt) *n.* a short pleated skirt, as worn in Scotland. [ME *kylte*]

kil·ter (KIL tər) *n.* proper or working condition. —**out of kilter** in poor operating condition; inoperative.

ki·mo·no (kə MOH nə) *n. pl.* **·nos** 1. a loose robe fastened with a wide sash, worn in Japan as an outer garment. 2. any similar robe. [< Japanese]

kin (kin) *n.* one's relatives collectively. — **next of kin** in law, one's nearest relative or relatives. —*adj.* 1. related by blood. 2. similar; kindred. [ME]

kind¹ (kīnd) *adj.* **·er,** **·est** gentle and considerate; goodhearted. [ME *kinde* natural]

kind² *n.* 1. a class or grouping; type. 2. the distinguishing character of something. — **in kind** 1. with a thing of the same sort. 2. in produce instead of money. —**kind of** *Informal* somewhat. —**of a kind** of the same class, nature, etc. [ME *kinde* nature]

kin·der·gar·ten (KIN dər GAHR tn) *n.* a school or class for young children, usu. from the ages of four to six. [< G, lit., children's garden]

kind·heart·ed (KĪND HAHR tid) *adj.* having or showing a kind nature. —**kind' heart'ed·ness** *n.*

kin·dle (KIN dl) *v.* **·dled,** **·dling** *v.t.* 1. cause to burn; ignite. 2. excite, as the feelings. —*v.i.* 3. take fire. 4. become excited or inflamed. [ME *kindlen*]

kin·dling (KIND ling) *n.* sticks, wood chips, etc. with which a fire is started.

kind·ly (KĪND lee) *adj.* **·li·er,** **·li·est** 1. having or showing kindness; sympathetic. 2. having a favorable effect. —*adv.* in a kind

manner; good-naturedly. [ME *kyndly*] — **take kindly to** like. —**kind'li·ness** *n.*

kind·ness (KĪND nis) *n.* 1. the quality of being kind. 2. a kind act or service; a favor.

kin·dred (KIN drid) *adj.* 1. related by blood; akin. 2. alike; similar. —*n.* one's relatives. [ME]

kin·e·scope (KIN ə SKOHP) *n.* 1. the cathode-ray tube of a television set, which reproduces the image recorded by the television camera: also called *picture tube.* 2. a film of a television program made from a kinescope.

ki·net·ic (ki NET ik) *adj.* 1. of or pertaining to motion. 2. producing or caused by motion: *kinetic* energy. [< Gk. *kinetikós* moving]

ki·ne·tics (ki NET iks) *n. (construed as sing.)* the branch of physics dealing with the effect of forces in the production or modification of motion in bodies.

king (king) *n.* 1. the sovereign male ruler of a kingdom; monarch. ♦ Collateral adjective: *regal.* 2. one who is preeminent: a cattle *king.* 3. a playing card bearing the likeness of a king. 4. in chess, the principal piece, whose defense is essential. 5. in checkers, a piece that, having reached the opponent's last rank of squares, may move in any direction. [ME]

king·dom (KING dəm) *n.* 1. the territory or people ruled by a king or a queen; monarchy. 2. any area thought of as a sovereign domain. 3. any of the three primary divisions of natural objects, the **animal, vegetable,** and **mineral kingdoms.** [ME]

king·fish·er (KING FISH ər) *n.* any of several large, crested birds that feed on fish.

King James Bible an English translation of the Bible from Hebrew and Greek, proposed by James I of England and completed in 1611.

king·ly (KING lee) *adj.* **·li·er,** **·li·est** of or worthy of a king; regal. —*adv.* in a kingly way. —**king'li·ness** *n.*

king·pin (KING PIN) *n.* 1. in bowling, the foremost pin. 2. in ninepins, the center pin. 3. *Informal* a person of central importance.

king-size (KING IZ) *adj.* greater in size than is usual. Also **king'sized'.**

kink (kingk) *n.* 1. an abrupt bend, curl, or tangle in a line, wire, hair, etc. 2. a mental quirk. 3. a bizarre practice or preference, esp. sexual. 4. a painful muscular spasm; crick. —*v.i. & v.t.* form or cause to form a kink. [< Du., a twist]

kink·y (KING kee) *adj.* **kink·i·er, kink·i·est 1.** kinked; frizzy. **2.** *Slang* bizarre; eccentric. —**kink′i·ness** *n.*

kin·ship (KIN ship) *n.* relationship, esp. by blood.

ki·osk (KEE osk) *n.* a small, roofed structure, used as a booth, newsstand, etc. [< Persian *kūshk* portico]

kip·per (KIP ər) *n.* a herring cured by kippering. —*v.t.* cure (fish) by splitting, salting, and drying or smoking. [ME *kypra* spawning salmon]

kirk (kurk) *n. Scot.* a church.

kis·met (KIZ mit) *n.* appointed lot; fate. [< Arabic *qismah* portion]

kiss (kis) *v.t. & v.i.* **1.** touch with the lips as a sign of greeting, love, etc. **2.** meet or touch lightly. [ME *kissen*] —**kiss** *n.*

kiss·er (KIS ər) *n.* **1.** one who kisses. **2.** *Slang* the mouth or the face.

kit (kit) *n.* **1.** a collection of articles, tools, etc. for a special purpose. **2.** a set of parts etc. from which something is to be made. **3.** one's effects or outfit, esp. for traveling. **4.** a bag, knapsack, etc. [ME]

kitch·en (KICH ən) *n.* a room equipped for cooking. [ME *kichene*]

kitch·en·ette (KICH ən NET) *n.* a small, compactly arranged kitchen.

kitch·en·ware (KICH ən WAIR) *n.* kitchen utensils.

kite (kīt) *n.* **1.** a light frame, covered with paper, fabric, etc., to be flown in the wind at the end of a string. **2.** a long-winged bird of the hawk family. **3.** in commerce, any negotiable paper not representing a genuine transaction, employed to obtain money, credit, etc. —*v.t. & v.i.* **kit·ed, kit·ing 1.** fly, as a kite. **2.** in commerce, issue or pass (a kite). [ME]

kith (kith) *n.* one's friends, acquaintances, or associates: now only in **kith and kin.** [ME]

kitsch (kich) *n.* art or literary works etc. having broad popular appeal and little aesthetic merit. [< G, something thrown together, as a work of art]

kit·ten (KIT n) *n.* a young cat. [ME *kitoun*]

kit·ten·ish (KIT n ish) *adj.* playfully coy. —**kit′ten·ish·ness** *n.*

kit·ty[1] (KIT ee) *n. pl.* **·ties 1.** money pooled, as by associates, for any specific purpose. **2.** in card games, a hand or part of a hand left over after a deal.

kit·ty[2] *n. pl.* **·ties** a kitten or cat.

klep·to·ma·ni·a (KLEP tə MAY nee ə) *n.* an obsessive impulse to steal. [< Gk. *kléptēs*

thief + -MANIA] —**klep′to·ma′ni·ac′** (-nee AK) *n.*

klutz (kluts) *n.* **1.** an awkward, clumsy person. **2.** a stupid person. [< Yiddish *klots*, lit., a wooden beam] —**klutz′y** *adj.* **klutz·i·er, klutz·i·est**

knack (nak) *n.* the ability to do something readily and well; adroitness. [ME]

knap·sack (NAP sak) *n.* a case or bag worn strapped across the shoulders, for carrying equipment or supplies; rucksack. [< LG]

knave (nayv) *n.* **1.** a dishonest person; rogue. **2.** a playing card, the jack. [ME] —**knav′ish** *adj.*

knav·er·y (NAY və ree) *n. pl.* **·er·ies 1.** deceitfulness; rascality. **2.** an act of deceit.

knead (need) *v.t.* **1.** mix and work (dough, clay, etc.), usu. by pressing and pulling with the hands. **2.** work on by squeezes of the hands; massage. **3.** make by kneading. [ME *kneden*]

knee (nee) *n.* **1.** *Anat.* the joint in the middle part of the human leg. **2.** *Zool.* a part corresponding to the human knee. **3.** something like a bent knee, as a bent piece of metal used in construction. —*v.t.* **kneed, knee·ing** touch or strike with the knee. [ME *cneo*]

knee·cap (NEE KAP) *n.* the patella.

knee-deep (NEE DEEP) *adj.* **1.** rising or sunk to the knee. **2.** enmeshed, as in scandal.

knee·hole (NEE hohl) *n.* a space for the knees, as in a desk.

kneel (neel) *v.i.* **knelt** or **kneeled, kneel·ing** fall or rest on the bent knee or knees. [ME *knelen*]

knell (nel) *n.* **1.** the tolling of a bell, esp. one announcing a death. **2.** any sad or doleful sound. —*v.i.* **1.** sound a knell. —*v.t.* **2.** proclaim by or as by a knell. [ME *knellen* knock]

knelt (nelt) past tense, past participle of KNEEL.

knew (noo) past tense of KNOW.

knick·knack (NIK NAK) *n.* a trifling article; trinket; trifle.

knife (nīf) *n. pl.* **knives** (nīvz) **1.** an instrument or weapon for cutting, piercing, or spreading, with one or more sharp-edged, often pointed blades, commonly set in a handle. **2.** a blade for cutting. —*v.* **knifed, knif·ing** *v.t.* **1.** stab or cut with a knife. **2.** discredit or betray behind one's back. —*v.i.* **3.** move straight and swiftly. [ME *knif*]

knight (nīt) *n.* **1.** in medieval times: **a** a feudal tenant serving his superior as a mounted soldier. **b** a gentleman trained for mounted combat and raised to the order of chivalry. **2.** in Great Britain, the holder of a non-hereditary dignity, conferred by the sovereign. **3.** in chess, a piece usu. bearing a horse's head. —*v.t.* make (a man) a knight. [ME] —**knight′hood** (-huud) *n.*

knish (knish) *n.* dough filled with potatoes, meat, etc., and baked or fried. [< Yiddish]

knit (nit) *v.t. & v.i.* **knit** or **knit·ted, knit·ting 1.** form (a fabric or garment) by interlocking loops of yarn or thread by means of needles. **2.** unite or grow together, as broken bones. **3.** draw (the brows) together into wrinkles. —*n.* the fabric made by knitting. [ME *knitte*]

knit·ting (NIT ing) *n.* **1.** the act of one who or that which knits. **2.** the fabric produced by knitting.

knives (nīvz) plural of KNIFE.

knob (nob) *n.* **1.** a rounded protuberance, bunch, or lump. **2.** a rounded handle, as of a door. **3.** a rounded mountain; knoll. [ME *knobbe*] —**knobbed** *adj.* —**knob′by** *adj.* **·bi·er, ·bi·est**

knock (nok) *v.t.* **1.** deal a blow to; hit, esp. with a thumping or rapping noise. **2.** strike together. **3.** make by striking or pounding. **4.** strike or push so as to make fall: with *down, over, off,* etc. **5.** *Slang* find fault with; disparage. —*v.i.* **6.** strike a blow or blows; rap. **7.** make a pounding or clanking noise, as an engine. —**knock around** (or **about**) *Informal* **1.** wander from place to place. **2.** treat roughly; abuse. —**knock down 1.** take apart for shipping or storing. **2.** at auctions, sell. **3.** *Slang* earn. **4.** reduce (a price, estimate, etc.). —**knock off 1.** *Informal* stop or leave off (an activity). **2.** deduct. **3.** *Informal* do or make quickly or easily. **4.** *Slang* kill; also, overwhelm or defeat. **5.** *Informal* make a copy of; plagiarize. —**knock out 1.** make a great effort. **2.** become exhausted. **3.** make quickly or easily **4.** in boxing, defeat by knocking to the canvas for a count of ten. **5.** make unconscious. **6.** overwhelm or amaze. —**knock together** make hurriedly. —*n.* **1.** a sharp blow; rap. **2.** a noise made by knocking. **3.** a misfortune or reversal. **4.** *Informal* hostile criticism; disparagement. [ME *knoken*]

knock·er (NOK ər) *n.* **1.** one who or that which knocks; esp., a hinged device on a door, used for knocking. **2.** a persistently pessimistic critic.

knock-knee (NOK NEE) *n.* **1.** inward curvature of the legs that causes the knees to knock or rub together in walking. **2.** *pl.* legs so curved. —**knock′-kneed′** *adj.*

knock·out (NOK OWT) *n.* **1.** a knocking unconscious or out of action. **2.** in boxing, a flooring of one fighter for a count of ten: abbr. KO. **3.** *Informal* an impressive person or thing. —**knock′out′** *adj.*

knoll (nohl) *n.* a small round hill; a mound. [ME *cnol*]

knot (not) *n.* **1.** an intertwining of rope, string, etc., as by passing one free end through a loop and drawing it tight; also, the lump thus made. **2.** an ornamental bow of silk, braid, etc. **3.** a hard portion of the trunk of a tree, or the round mark on lumber left by this. **4.** a cluster or tight group. **5.** an enlargement in a muscle, of a gland, etc. resembling a knot. **6.** *Naut.* **a** a speed of one nautical mile in an hour, equivalent to 1.1516 statute miles per hour. **b** a nautical mile. —*v.* **knot·ted, knot·ting** *v.t.* **1.** tie in a knot. **2.** fasten by a knot. —*v.i.* **3.** become knotted or tangled. [ME *knotte*]

knot·ty (NOT ee) *adj.* **·ti·er, ·ti·est 1.** full of or tied in knots. **2.** difficult or intricate; puzzling. —**knot′ti·ness** *n.*

knout (nowt) *n.* a whip formerly used for flogging. [< F] —*v.t.* flog with a knout.

know (noh) *v.* **knew, known, know·ing** *v.t.* **1.** be cognizant of; have a concept of in the mind. **2.** be certain of. **3.** be acquainted or familiar with. **4.** be able: with *how.* **5.** recognize; distinguish. **6.** understand; have skill in. —*v.i.* **7.** have awareness; apprehend. **9.** have understanding or certainty; be sure. —**know better** be aware of something truer or more correct than what one says or does. —**in the know** having inside or special information. [ME *knowen*] —**know′a·ble** *adj.*

know-how (NOH HOW) *n.* mastery of a complicated operation; technical skill.

know·ing (NOH ing) *adj.* **1.** perceptive; astute; also, hinting at having secret knowledge. **2.** conscious; intentional. **3.** having knowledge or information. —**know′ing·ly** *adv.*

knowl·edge (NOL ij) *n.* **1.** a result or product of knowing; information or understanding acquired through experience; practical ability or skill. **2.** learning; erudition. **3.** the cumulative culture of the human race. **4.** the act, process, or state of knowing; cognition. **5.** any object of knowing or mental

apprehension; that which is or may be
known. [ME *knowlege*] **—knowl•
edge•a•ble** (NOL i jə bəl) *adj.* well-
informed.

known (nohn) past participle of KNOW. —
adj. recognized by all as the truth; understood; axiomatic: *known* facts.

knuck•le (NUK əl) *n.* **1.** one of the joints of
the fingers, or the region about it; esp., one
of the joints connecting the fingers to the
hand. **2.** the knee or hock joint of the pig,
calf, etc., the flesh of which is used as food.
—knuckle down apply oneself seriously.
—knuckle under give in. [ME *knokel*]

knurl (nurl) *n.* **1.** a protuberance; lump. **2.**
one of a series of small ridges on the edge of
a metal object, as a coin. —*v.t.* ridge or mill,
as the edge of a coin.

KO (KAY OH) *n. pl.* **KO's** in boxing, a knockout.

kook (kook) *n. Slang* **1.** an eccentric or unbalanced person. **2.** a spy.

ko•peck (KOH pek) *n.* a Russian coin, the
hundredth part of a ruble. Also **ko′pek.** [<
Russ. *kopeika*]

Ko•ran (kə RAN) *n.* the sacred book of the
Muslims, recording the revelations of Allah
to Muhammad. [< Arabic *Qur′ān* book]

ko•sher (KOH shər) *adj.* **1.** permitted by or
conforming to Jewish (ceremonial) law. **2.**
Informal legitimate; proper. [< Hebrew
kāshēr fit, proper]

kow•tow (KOW TOW) *v.i.* **1.** behave in an
obsequious, servile manner. **2.** touch the
forehead to the ground as a sign of reverence etc. —*n.* the act of kowtowing. [<
Chinese *kòutóu* knock the head] **—kow′
tow′er** *n.*

kraal (krahl) *n.* **1.** in South Africa, a village or
group of native huts, usu. surrounded by a
stockade. **2.** a fenced enclosure for domestic animals in southern Africa. [< Afri-
kaans]

Krem•lin (KREM lin) **1.** the walled citadel
of Moscow containing government offices.
2. the government of Russia. [< Russ.
kreml′ citadel]

krill (kril) *n. pl.* **kril** tiny marine crustaceans,
the main food of certain whales. [< Norw.
kril very young fish]

ku•dos (KOO dohz) *n.* (*construed as sing.*)
glory; credit; acclaim. [< Gk. *kydos*]

kud•zu (KUUD zoo) *n.* a rapidly growing, perennial vine, used for forage or erosion control. Also **kudzu vine.** [< Jap.
kuzu]

Ku Klux Klan (KOO KLUKS KLAN) **1.** a
secret society formed in the South after the
Civil War with the purpose of suppressing
the rights of former slaves. **2.** any of similarly named groups, devoted to white Protestant supremacy. **—Ku′ Klux′er, Ku′
Klux′ism** *n.*

küm•mel (KIM əl) *n.* a liqueur flavored with
aniseed, cumin, or caraway. [< G *Kümmel*,
lit., caraway seed]

kung fu (KUUNG FOO) a Chinese art of
self-defense, similar to karate. [< Chinese,
lit. boxing principles]

kvetch (kvech) *Slang v.i.* complain habitually. [< Yiddish] **—kvetch** *n.* **—kvetch′er**
n.

kwash•i•or•kor (KWAH shee OR kor) *n. Pathol.* a disease of children, producing
stunted growth, swollen belly, etc., caused
by deficient diet.

L

l, L (el) *n. pl.* **l's** or **ls, L's** or **Ls 1.** the twelfth
letter of the English alphabet. **2.** the sound
represented by the letter *l.* **3.** anything
shaped like the letter L. —*symbol* the Roman numeral 50.

la (lah) *n. Music* the sixth tone of the diatonic
scale in solmization.

la·bel (LAY bəl) *n.* **1.** a slip of paper, printed
legend, etc. on a container or article showing its nature, producer, destination, etc. **2.**
a term or phrase used to classify or describe. **3.** a brand; make. —*v.t.* **·beled,**
·bel·ing 1. mark with a label. **2.** classify.
[ME] —**la'bel·er** *n.*

la·bi·a (LAY bee ə) plural of LABIUM.

la·bi·al (LAY bee əl) *adj.* **1.** of or pertaining
to a labium or the lips. **2.** *Phonet.* articulated or modified by the lips, as are (p), (b),
(m), (w), or the rounded vowels (ō) and
(oo). [< Med.L *labialis*] —*n.* a labial sound.

la·bi·um (LAY bee əm) *n. pl.* **·bi·a** (-bee ə)
Anat. **1.** a lip or liplike part. **2.** one of four
folds of the vulva, the outer two of skin
(**labia majora**) and the inner two of mucous membrane (**labia minora**). [< L, lip]

la·bor (LAY bər) *n.* **1.** physical or manual
work done for hire. **2.** arduous physical or
mental exertion. **3.** the working class collectively, esp. as organized into labor unions. **4.**
a task. **5.** *Med.* the process of childbirth. —
v.i. **1.** work hard physically or mentally. **2.**
progress with great effort or painful exertion. **3.** be oppressed or hampered. —*v.t.*
dwell on excessively: *labor* the point. [ME
labour]

lab·o·ra·to·ry (LAB rə TOR ee) *n. pl.* **·ries** a
building or room equipped for conducting
scientific experiments, analyses, etc. [<
Med.L *laboratorium* workshop]

la·bored (LAY bərd) *adj.* **1.** performed with
difficulty: *labored* breathing. **2.** lacking
grace or spontaneity: *labored* prose.

la·bor·er (LAY bər ər) *n.* one who performs
physical or manual labor, esp. unskilled labor.

la·bo·ri·ous (lə BOR ee əs) *adj.* **1.** requiring
much labor; toilsome. **2.** diligent; industrious. —**la·bo'ri·ous·ly** *adv.*

la·bor·sav·ing (LAY bər SAY ving) *adj.* removing or reducing the need for manual
work.

labor union an association of workers organized to improve and advance mutual interests: also called *trade union.*

lab·y·rinth (LAB ə rinth) *n.* **1.** a system of
intricate, confusing passages or paths;
maze. **2.** any intricate or perplexing set of
difficulties. [< L *labyrinthus*] —
lab·y·rin·thine (LAB ə RIN thin) *adj.*

lace (lays) *n.* **1.** a cord or string passed
through eyelets or over hooks for fastening
together the edges of a shoe, garment, etc.
2. a delicate openwork fabric, usu. figured.
3. an ornamental braid used to decorate
uniforms, hats, etc. —*v.* **laced, lac·ing** *v.t.*
1. fasten or draw together by tying the lace
or laces of. **2.** trim with or as with lace. **3.**
compress the waist of (a person) by tighten-
ing laces of a corset. **4.** intertwine or interlace. **5.** give added zest or flavor to: *lace*
coffee with whiskey. —*v.i.* **6.** be fastened by
means of laces. —**lace into 1.** strike or
attack. **2.** scold; berate. [ME *las*]

lac·er·ate (LAS ə RAYT) *v.t.* **·at·ed, ·at·ing**
1. tear raggedly; esp., wound (the flesh) by
tearing. **2.** injure: *lacerate* one's feelings. [<
L *laceratus* torn up] —**lac'er·a'tion** *n.*

lach·ry·mal (LAK rə məl) *adj.* of, pertaining
to, or producing tears: **lachrymal** glands.
Also **lac'ri·mal.** [< Med.L *lachrymalis*]

lach·ry·mose (LAK rə MOHS) *adj.* **1.** tearful. **2.** provoking tears; sad. [< L *lac-
rimosus*]

lac·ing (LAY sing) *n.* **1.** a cord or string for
holding together opposite parts of a shoe
etc. **2.** a fastening made with lacing. **3.** a
thrashing; beating. **4.** an additional flavoring; dash or zest.

lack (lak) *n.* **1.** deficiency or complete absence of something. **2.** that which is absent
or deficient; need. —*v.t.* **1.** be without. **2.**
be short by. —*v.i.* **3.** be wanting or deficient. [ME *lak*]

lack·a·dai·si·cal (LAK ə DAY zi kəl) *adj.*
showing lack of interest; not lively; listless.

lack·ey (LAK ee) *n. pl.* **·eys 1.** a male servant of low status, usu. in livery. **2.** any servile follower. [< MF *laquais*]

lack·lus·ter (LAK LUS tər) *adj.* **1.** lacking
brightness; dull. **2.** lacking spirit; mediocre:
lackluster singing.

la·con·ic (lə KON ik) *adj.* brief and concise

in expression. [< L *laconicus* Spartan] — **la·con'i·cal·ly** *adv.*

lac·quer (LAK ər) *n.* a transparent coating, made from resins, shellac, etc. dissolved in a volatile solvent, which dries to give a glossy finish. —*v.t.* coat with or as with lacquer. [< Pg. *lacré* sealing wax]

la·crosse (lə KRAWS) *n.* a ball game played with long, racketlike sticks by two teams of ten players each. [< Canadian F, the stick used in the sport]

lac·tate (LAK tayt) *v.i.* **·tat·ed, ·tat·ing** form or secrete milk. [< L *lactare* secrete milk] —**lac·ta'tion** *n.*

lac·te·al (LAK tee əl) *adj.* of, pertaining to, or resembling milk; milky. [< L *lacteus* of milk]

lac·tic (LAK tik) *adj.* of, pertaining to, or derived from milk.

lactic acid *Chem.* a syrupy acid with a bitter taste, present in sour milk.

lac·tose (LAK tohs) *n. Biochem.* an odorless, crystalline sugar, present in milk.

la·cu·na (lə KYOO nə) *n. pl.* **·nae** (-nee) or **·nas** a space from which something is missing or has been omitted, esp. in a manuscript; hiatus. [< L, cap]

lac·y (LAY see) *adj.* **lac·i·er, lac·i·est** made of or resembling lace. —**lac'i·ness** *n.*

lad (lad) *n.* **1.** a boy or youth. **2.** *Informal* an affectionate term for a man. [ME *ladde*]

lad·der (LAD ər) *n.* a device of wood, metal, rope, etc. for climbing and descending, usu. consisting of two parallel side pieces connected by a series of rungs placed at regular intervals to serve as footholds. [ME]

lade (layd) *v.t.* **lad·ed, lad·en** or **lad·ed, lad·ing** load with a cargo or burden; also, load as a cargo. [ME *laden* load]

lad·en (LAYD n) *adj.* **1.** burdened; oppressed. **2.** weighed down; loaded. —*v.t.* & *v.i.* **lad·ened, lad·en·ing** lade.

lad·ing (LAY ding) *n.* a load or cargo, as in a bill of *lading*.

la·dle (LAYD l) *n.* a cup-shaped vessel with a long handle, for dipping liquids. —*v.t.* **·dled, ·dling** dip up or carry in a ladle. [ME *ladel*]

la·dy (LAY dee) *n. pl.* **·dies 1.** a woman showing refinement, gentility, and tact. **2.** a woman of superior position in society. **3.** a term of reference or address for any woman. **4.** a woman at the head of a household, also **lady of the house. 5.** a wife. [ME *ladie*]

la·dy-kill·er (LAY dee KIL ər) *n. Informal* a man supposed to be unusually fascinating to women.

la·dy·like (LAY dee LĪK) *adj.* like or suitable to a lady.

lag (lag) *v.i.* **lagged, lag·ging** move slowly; stay or fall behind; straggle: sometimes followed by *behind*. —*n.* **1.** the condition or act of retardation or falling behind. **2.** the amount or period of retardation. [< Scand.]

la·ger (LAH gər) *n.* a beer stored for aging before use. Also **lager beer.** [< G *Lagerbier*]

lag·gard (LAG ərd) *n.* one who lags; straggler. —*adj.* falling behind; loitering; slow.

la·gniappe (lan YAP) *n.* **1.** a small present given to the purchaser of an article by a storekeeper. **2.** anything given beyond strict obligation; a gratuity. [< Louisiana F]

la·goon (lə GOON) *n.* a body of shallow water, as a bay or inlet, usu. connecting with a river, lake, or the sea; esp., the water within a coral atoll. [< Ital. *Laguna*]

laid (layd) past tense, past participle of LAY[1].

laid·back (LAYD BAK) *adj. Slang* relaxed; easygoing.

lain (layn) past participle of LIE[1].

lair (lair) *n.* a resting place or den, esp. that of a wild animal. [ME]

lais·sez faire (LES ay FAIR) **1.** the theory that the state should exercise minimal control in trade and industrial affairs. **2.** noninterference or indifference. [< F, lit., allow to act]

la·i·ty (LAY i tee) *n. pl.* **·ties 1.** the people collectively; laypersons. **2.** all of those outside a specific profession or occupation.

lake (layk) *n.* **1.** a sizable inland body of water. **2.** a large pool of any liquid. [ME *lak*]

lam (lam) *Slang n.* sudden flight or escape. —**on the lam** in flight; fleeing.

la·ma (LAH mə) *n.* a Buddhist priest or monk of Tibet or Mongolia. [< Tibetan]

La·ma·ism (LAH mə IZ əm) *n.* the form of Buddhism practiced in Tibet and Mongolia. —**La'ma·ist** *n.*

la·ma·ser·y (LAH mə SER ee) *n. pl.* **·ser·ies** a Buddhist monastery for lamas. [< F *lamaserie*]

lamb (lam) *n.* **1.** a young sheep. **2.** the meat of a lamb used as food. **3.** any gentle or innocent person. —**the Lamb** Christ. — *v.i.* give birth: said of a ewe. [ME]

lam·baste (lam BAYST) *v.t.* **·bast·ed, ·bast·ing** *Informal* **1.** beat or thrash. **2.** scold; castigate.

lamb·da (LAM də) n. the eleventh letter in the Greek alphabet (Λ λ), corresponding to the English l.

lam·bent (LAM bənt) adj. 1. flickering; licking: a lambent flame. 2. softly radiant. 3. lightly and playfully brilliant: lambent wit. [< L lambere lick] —**lam'ben·cy** n.

lamb·skin (LAM SKIN) n. 1. the dressed hide and wool of a lamb. 2. dressed leather made from a lamb's hide.

lame (laym) adj. **lam·er, lam·est** 1. crippled or disabled, esp. in the legs or feet. 2. sore; painful: a lame back. 3. weak; ineffective: a lame effort. —v.t. **lamed, lam·ing** make lame. [ME] —**lame'ness** n.

lame duck 1. an officeholder whose term continues for a time after defeat for reelection. 2. an ineffectual or disabled person.

la·ment (lə MENT) v.t. feel remorse or regret over. —v.i. feel or express sorrow, grief, or regret. —n. 1. an expression of grief; lamentation. 2. an elegiac melody or writing. [< L lamentum lament] —**lam·en·ta·tion** (LAM ən TAY shən) n.

lam·en·ta·ble (LAM ən tə bəl) adj. that warrants lamenting; deplorable: a lamentable failure. —**lam'en·ta·bly** adv.

lam·ent·ed (lə MEN tid) adj. grieved over.

lam·i·na (LAM ə nə) n. pl. **·nae** (-nee) or **·nas** 1. a thin scale or sheet. 2. a layer or coat lying over another, as in bone, minerals, etc. [< L]

lam·i·nate (LAM ə NAYT) v. **·nat·ed, ·nat·ing** v.t. 1. beat, roll, or press (metal) into thin sheets. 2. unite layers by heat and pressure. —v.i. 3. separate into sheets. [< NL laminatus leaved] —**lam'i·na'tion** n.

lam·i·nat·ed (LAM ə NAY tid) adj. made up of or arranged in thin sheets.

lamp (lamp) n. 1. a device for holding one or more electric light bulbs; also, an electric light bulb. 2. any of various devices for producing light by combustion, incandescence, etc. 3. any of several devices for producing therapeutic heat or rays: sun lamp. [ME lampe]

lam·poon (lam POON) n. a satirical attack in prose or verse directed against a person. —v.t. satirize in a lampoon. [< F lampon] —**lam·poon'ist** n.

lance (lans) n. 1. a spearlike weapon used by mounted soldiers or knights. 2. a lancet. —v.t. **lanced, lanc·ing** 1. pierce with a lance. 2. cut or open with a lancet. [ME launce spear]

lan·cet (LAN sit) n. a small, two-edged, usu.

pointed surgical knife, used to open abscesses etc. [ME lancette]

land (land) n. 1. the solid, exposed surface of the earth as distinguished from the seas. 2. a country or region, esp. considered as a place of human habitation. 3. ground considered with reference to its uses, character, etc.: cleared land. 4. Law any tract that may be owned as property together with all its resources, buildings, etc. —v.t. 1. put ashore. 2. bring (something in flight) down to rest. 3. bring to some point or state: Her words landed her in trouble. 4. pull (a fish) out of the water; catch. 5. deliver (a blow). —v.i. 6. go or come ashore from a ship or boat. 7. descend and come to rest after a flight or jump. 8. come to some place or state; end up: land in jail. [ME]

land·ed (LAN did) adj. 1. having an estate in land: landed gentry. 2. consisting in land: landed property.

land·fall (LAND FAWL) n. a sighting of or coming to land; also, the land so sighted or reached.

land·fill (LAND FIL) n. 1. garbage or trash buried in the ground. 2. the area, usu. of low or wet ground, where landfill is buried.

land·ing (LAN ding) n. 1. the act of going ashore from a craft or vessel. 2. the place where a vessel lands; pier. 3. the act of descending and settling on the ground after a flight, leap, etc. 4. the platform or floor at the top of a flight of stairs.

landing gear the understructure with wheels etc. that supports an aircraft on land or water.

land·la·dy (LAND LAY dee) n. pl. **·dies** a woman who owns and rents out real estate.

land·locked (LAND LOKT) adj. surrounded by land; having no seacoast.

land·lord (LAND LORD) n. a man who owns and rents out real estate. [ME]

land·lub·ber (LAND LUB ər) n. an awkward or inexperienced person on board a ship.

land·mark (LAND MAHRK) n. 1. a fixed object serving as a boundary mark to a tract of land, as a guide to travelers etc. 2. a prominent object in the landscape. 3. a distinguishing fact, event, etc. [ME]

land mine Mil. a bomb placed in the ground.

land·own·er (LAND OH nər) n. one who owns real estate.

land·scape (LAND SKAYP) n. 1. a stretch of inland natural scenery as seen from a single point. 2. a picture representing such scenery. —*v.t.* •scaped, •scap•ing improve or change the features or appearance of a park, garden, etc. [< Du. *landschap*] — **land′scap•er** *n.*

land•slide (LAND SLID) *n.* **1.** the slipping down of a mass of soil, rock, and debris on a mountain side or other steep slope. **2.** the mass of soil, rock, etc. slipping down. **3.** an overwhelming plurality of votes for one political party or candidate in an election.

land•ward (LAND wərd) *adj. & adv.* facing or going toward the land.

lane (layn) *n.* **1.** a narrow rural path or way, confined between fences, hedges, or similar boundaries; also, a narrow city street. **2.** a prescribed route for shipping or for aircraft. **3.** a marked division of a highway or road for traffic moving in the same direction. **4.** any of a set of parallel courses for contestants in races. [ME]

lan•guage (LANG gwij) *n.* **1.** communication between human beings by means of speech and hearing. **2.** the words used in communication among members of a single nation or group at a given period. **3.** the vocabulary used in a specific activity. **4.** one's characteristic use of speech. **5. a** any of several sets of codes and rules for programming computers. **b** machine language. [ME]

lan•guid (LANG gwid) *adj.* **1.** indisposed toward physical exertion; lacking energy. **2.** feeling little interest in anything; listless. **3.** lacking in activity or quickness of movement. [< L *languidus* faint] —**lan′guid•ly** *adv.*

lan•guish (LANG gwish) *v.i.* **1.** become weak or feeble; grow listless. **2.** droop gradually from restless longing; pine. **3.** pass through a period of external discomfort and mental anguish: *languish* in prison. [ME]

lan•guish•ing (LANG gwish ing) *adj.* **1.** lacking alertness or force. **2.** melancholy. **3.** becoming weak or listless.

lan•guor (LANG gər) *n.* **1.** lassitude of body; weakness; fatigue. **2.** a lack of energy or enthusiasm. **3.** a mood of tenderness or sentimental dreaminess. [ME *langour* woe]

lan•guor•ous (LANG gər əs) *adj.* **1.** languid. **2.** producing languor.

lank (langk) *adj.* •er, •est **1.** lean; shrunken. **2.** long, flat, and straight; *lank* hair. [ME *lanc*] —**lank′ness** *n.*

lank•y (LANG kee) *adj.* lank•i•er, lank•i•est ungracefully tall and thin; bony. —**lank′i•ness** *n.*

lan•tern (LAN tərn) *n.* **1.** a protective, usu. portable, case with transparent or translucent sides for enclosing a light. **2.** a lighthouse, esp. the top that protects the light. **3.** a slide projector. [ME *lanterne*]

lan•yard (LAN yərd) *n.* **1.** *Naut.* a small, usu. four-stranded hemp rope used on a ship for fastening riggings etc. **2.** a cord worn around the neck, used by sailors for attaching a knife. [ME *lanyer*]

lap¹ (lap) *n.* **1.** the shape formed by the lower torso and thighs of a person seated. **2.** a place of nurture or fostering: fortune's *lap.* **3.** control, care, or custody: in the *lap* of the gods. [ME *lappe*]

lap² *n.* **1.** the state of overlapping. **2.** a rotating disk used for grinding and polishing gems etc. **3.** one circuit of a race course. **4.** the part of one thing that lies over another. —*v.* lapped, lap•ping *v.t.* **1.** enfold; wrap. **2.** lay (one thing) partly over or beyond another. **3.** overlap. —*v.i.* **4.** project beyond or into something else. [ME *lappen* wrap]

lap³ *v.t. & v.i.* lapped, lap•ping **1.** drink (a liquid) by taking it up with the tongue, as an animal does. **2.** wash against (the shore etc.). —**lap up 1.** drink by lapping. **2.** eat or drink gluttonously. **3.** *Informal* listen to eagerly.

lap dog a pet dog small enough to be held on the lap.

la•pel (lə PEL) *n.* the front of a coat, jacket, etc., that is folded back to form an extension of the collar.

lap•i•dar•y (LAP i DER ee) *n. pl.* •dar•ies **1.** one whose work is to cut, engrave, or polish precious stones: also **lap′i•dist. 2.** the art of such a worker. **3.** an expert in precious stones. Also **la•pid•ar•ist** (lə PID ər ist). [ME *lapidarie*] —**lap′i•dar′y, lap′i•dar′i•an** *adj.*

lap•is laz•u•li (LAP is LAZ yuu lee) **1.** a bluish violet gemstone. **2.** a bluish violet color. [ME]

lapse (laps) *n.* **1.** a gradual passing away, as of time. **2.** a pronounced fall into ruin, decay, or disuse. **3.** a slip or mistake, usu. trivial. —*v.i.* lapsed, laps•ing **1.** sink slowly; slip: *lapse* into a coma. **2.** fall into ruin or a state of neglect. **3.** deviate from one's principles or beliefs. **4.** become void, usually by failure to meet obligations. **5.** pass away, as time. [< L *lapsus* error]

lar·board (LAHR bərd) *Naut. n.* the port side of a ship. [ME *ladeborde*]

lar·ce·ny (LAHR sə nee) *n. pl.* **·nies** *Law* the unlawful removal of the personal goods of another with intent to defraud the owner; theft. [ME] —**lar'cen·ist** *n.* —**lar'ce·nous** *adj.*

lard (lahrd) *n.* the semisolid fat of a hog after rendering. —*v.t.* **1.** cover or smear with lard. **2.** prepare (lean meat or poultry) by inserting strips of fat before cooking. **3.** embellish (speech or writing) with quotations, etc. [ME] —**lard'y** *adj.* **lard·i·er, lard·i·est**

lar·der (LAHR dər) *n.* a room or cupboard where articles of food are stored. [ME]

large (lahrj) *adj.* **larg·er, larg·est 1.** having considerable size, quantity, capacity, extent, etc.; big. **2.** bigger than another. **3.** sympathetic and broad in scope: take a *large* view. —*adv.* in a size greater than usual: Print *large.* —**at large 1.** free; at liberty. **2.** in general: the people *at large.* **3.** not representing a specific district: delegate-*at-large.* [ME]

large·ly (LAHRJ lee) *adv.* **1.** to a great extent; mainly; chiefly. **2.** on a big scale; extensively.

large-scale (LAHRJ SKAYL) *adj.* of large size or scope.

lar·gess (lahr JES) *n.* liberal giving; also, something liberally given. Also **lar·gesse'.** [< F *largesse*]

lar·go (LAHR goh) *Music adj.* slow; broad. —*adv.* in a slow tempo. —*n. pl.* **·gos** a slow movement or passage. [< Ital.]

lar·i·at (LAR ee ət) *n.* **1.** a rope for tethering animals. **2.** a lasso. [< Sp. *la reata* the lasso]

lark[1] (lahrk) *n.* any of numerous small singing birds, as the skylark. [ME]

lark[2] *n.* **1.** a hilarious time. **2.** a prank. —*v.i.* **1.** frolic or sport. **2.** play pranks. —**lark'er** *n.*

lar·va (LAHR və) *n. pl.* **·vae** (-vee) **1.** *Entomol.* the first stage of an insect after leaving the egg, as the maggot. **2.** *Zool.* the immature form of any animal that must undergo metamorphosis. [< NL] —**lar'val** *adj.*

lar·yn·gi·tis (LAR ən JĪ tis) *n. Pathol.* inflammation of the larynx.

lar·ynx (LAR ingks) *n. pl.* **la·ryn·ges** (lə RIN jeez) or **lar·ynx·es** *Anat.* an organ of the respiratory tract situated at the upper part of the trachea, and consisting of a cartilaginous box containing the vocal cords. [< NL]

la·sa·gna (lə ZAHN yə) *n.* broad, flat noodles, often served baked in a meat and tomato sauce. [< Ital.]

las·civ·i·ous (lə SIV ee əs) *adj.* having, manifesting, or arousing sensual desires; lustful. [ME] —**las·civ'i·ous·ly** *adv.* —**las·civ'i·ous·ness** *n.*

la·ser (LAY zər) *n. Physics* a device that amplifies light waves to produce an intense narrow beam: also called *optical maser.* [< *l*ight *a*mplification by *s*timulated *e*mission of *r*adiation]

lash[1] (lash) *n.* **1.** a whip or scourge. **2.** a single whip stroke. **3.** anything that wounds the feelings. **4.** an eyelash. —*v.t.* **1.** strike, punish, or command with or as with a whip; flog. **2.** switch spasmodically: The lion *lashes* its tail. **3.** assail sharply in speech or writing. —**lash out 1.** hit out suddenly and violently. **2.** break into angry verbal abuse. [ME *lashe*]

lash[2] *v.t.* bind or tie with rope or cord. [ME]

lass (las) *n.* **1.** a young woman; girl. **2.** a sweetheart. [ME]

las·si·tude (LAS i TOOD) *n.* a state of weariness or fatigue; languor. [< L *lassitudo* weariness]

las·so (LAS oh) *n. pl.* **·sos** or **·soes** a long rope with a running noose, used for catching horses etc. —*v.t.* catch with a lasso. [< Sp. *lazo*] —**las'so·er** *n.*

last[1] (last) *adj.* **1.** coming after all others; final. **2.** most recent: *last* year. **3.** least probable or suitable: the *last* person for the job. **4.** conclusive; final: the *last* word. —*adv.* **1.** after all others in time or order. **2.** at a time next preceding the present: He was *last* seen at his desk. **3.** in conclusion; finally. — *n.* **1.** the end; final part or portion. **2.** the final appearance, experience, or mention: We'll never hear the *last* of this. —**at last** finally. [ME]

last[2] *v.i.* **1.** remain in existence; endure. **2.** continue unimpaired or unaltered. **3.** hold out: Will our supplies *last?* [ME *lasten* follow]

last[3] *n.* a shaped form, usu. of wood, on which to make a shoe or boot. [ME *leste*]

last·ing (LAS ting) *adj.* continuing; durable; permanent. —*n.* endurance; continuance. —**last'ing·ly** *adv.*

Last Judgment *Theol.* **a** the final judgment by God of all manking. **b** the time of this.

last·ly (LAST lee) *adv.* in the last place; in conclusion.

last rites *Eccl.* sacraments administered to persons in peril of death.

Last Supper the last meal of Jesus Christ and the disciples before the Crucifixion.

last word 1. the final and most authoritative utterance. **2.** the most fashionable thing.

latch (lach) *n.* a fastening for a door or gate, usu. a movable bar that falls or slides into a notch. —*v.t. & v.i.* fasten by means of a latch; close. —**latch onto** *Informal* obtain, esp. something desirable. [ME *lachen* seize]

latch·key (LACH KEE) *n.* a key for releasing a latch or lock. —**latchkey child** a child returning from school who must spend part of the day without supervision, as when the parents are at work.

latch·string (LACH STRING) *n.* a string on the outside of a door, used for lifting the latch.

late (layt) *adj.* **lat·er** or **lat·ter, lat·est** or **last 1.** appearing or coming after the expected time; tardy. **2.** occurring at an unusually advanced time: a *late* hour. **3.** recent or comparatively recent: the *late* war. **4.** deceased: the *late* president. —*adv.* **1.** after the expected time; tardily. **2.** at or until an advanced time of the day, month, year, etc. —**of late** recently. [ME] —**late'ness** *n.*

la·tent (LAYT nt) *adj.* not visible or apparent, but capable of developing or being expressed; dormant. [< L *latere* lie hidden] —**la'ten·cy** *n.*

lat·er·al (LAT ər əl) *adj.* pertaining to the side or sides; situated at, occurring, or coming from the side. —*n.* a lateral part. [< L *lateralis* of the side] —**lat'er·al·ly** *adv.*

la·tex (LAY teks) *n. pl.* **lat·i·ces** (LAT tə seez) or **la·tex·es 1.** the sticky emulsion secreted by certain plants that forms the basis of natural rubber. **2.** a synthetic emulsion, used mainly as a base for paints. [< NL]

lath (lath) *n.* a thin strip of wood etc., nailed to studs or joists to support a coat of plaster, or to rafters to support shingles or slates. —*v.t.* cover or line with laths. [ME *lathe*] —**lath·er** (LATH ər) *n.*

lathe (layth) *n.* a machine that holds and spins pieces of wood, metal, plastic, etc., so that they are cut and shaped when the operator holds cutting tools against them. —*v.t.* **lathed, lath·ing** form on a lathe. [ME, frame]

lath·er (LATH ər) *n.* **1.** the suds or foam formed by soap or detergents and water. **2.** the foam of profuse sweating, as of a horse. —**in a lather** in a state of intense excitement or agitation. —*v.t. & v.i.* cover with or form lather. [ME]

lath·ing (LATH ing) *n.* laths collectively.

Lat·in (LAT n) *adj.* **1.** pertaining to ancient Rome, its inhabitants, culture, or language. **2.** pertaining to or denoting the peoples or countries with languages derived from Latin. **3.** of or belonging to the Roman Catholic Church. —*n.* **1.** the language of the Roman Empire. **2.** a member of one of the modern Latin peoples. —**Old Latin** the language before the first century B.C. —**Classical Latin** the literary and rhetorical language of the period 80 B.C. to A.D. 200. —**Late Latin** the language from 200–600. —**Low Latin** the language of any period after the classical, such as Medieval Latin. —**Medieval Latin** the language used by the writers of the Middle Ages, from 600–1500, also called **Middle Latin.** —**New Latin** a form of the language based on Latin and Greek elements, now used chiefly for scientific and taxonomic terms. —**Vulgar Latin** the popular speech of the Romans from about A.D. 200 through the medieval period. [ME]

Latin America the countries of the western hemisphere south of the Rio Grande, in which the official languages are derived from Latin. —**Lat·in·A·mer·i·can** *adj.* —**Latin American** *n.*

Lat·in·ism (LAT n IZ əm) *n.* an idiom in another language taken from or imitating Latin.

Latin Quarter a section of Paris known for centuries for its many artists and students.

lat·i·tude (LAT i TOOD) *n.* **1.** *Geog.* the angular distance on the earth's surface northward or southward of the equator, measured in degrees along a meridian. **2.** *Often pl.* a region or place considered with reference to its distance from the equator. **3.** freedom from narrow restrictions. [ME] —**lat'i·tu'di·nal** *adj.* —**lat'i·tu'di·nal·ly** *adv.*

la·trine (lə TREEN) *n.* a toilet, as in a barracks. [< F]

lat·ter (LAT ər) *adj.* **1.** being the second of two persons or things referred to: often preceded by *the*: The *latter* statement is more nearly true than the former. **2.** later or nearer to the end: His *latter* years were happy. [ME *lattere* later]

lat·tice (LAT is) *n.* **1.** a structure consisting

of strips of metal, wood, etc. crossed or interlaced to form regularly spaced openings. **2.** a window, screen, etc. having a lattice construction. —*v.t.* **•ticed, •tic•ing** furnish or enclose with a lattice. [ME *latis*]

lat•tice•work (LAT is wurk) *n.* openwork made from or resembling a lattice.

laud (lawd) *v.t.* praise highly; extol. [ME *lauden*]

laud•a•ble (LAW də bəl) *adj.* deserving approbation. —**laud′a•bil′i•ty** *n.* —**laud′a•bly** *adv.*

lau•da•num (LAWD n əm) *n.* tincture of opium. [< NL]

laud•a•to•ry (LAW də TOR ee) *adj.* expressing or containing praise; complimentary. [< LL *laudatorius*]

laugh (laf) *v.i.* **1.** produce the characteristic sounds and physical expressions of merriment, elation, etc. **2.** express or experience amusement, satisfaction, etc. —*v.t.* **3.** induce, persuade, or bring about by or as by laughing: I *laughed* myself sick. —**laugh at 1.** express amusement at **2.** ridicule; mock. **3.** make light of. —**laugh away** dispel or minimize with laughter. —**laugh off** rid oneself of or dismiss laughingly. —**laugh up one's sleeve** be covertly amused or exultant. —*n.* **1.** an act or sound of laughing. **2.** *Informal* a cause for or provocation to laughter. —**have the last laugh** triumph or succeed after seeming at a disadvantage. [ME *laughen*] —**laugh′ing•ly** *adv.*

laugh•a•ble (LAF ə bəl) *adj.* provoking laughter; amusing. —**laugh′a•bly** *adv.*

laughing gas nitrous oxide.

laugh•ing•stock (LAF ing STOK) *n.* one who or that which provokes ridicule; a butt.

laugh•ter (LAF tər) *n.* the sound, expression, or action of laughing.

launch[1] (lawnch) *v.t.* **1.** move (a vessel etc.) into the water, esp. for the first time. **2.** set in flight or motion, as a rocket, missile, etc. **3.** start (a person etc.) on a career or course of action. **4.** initiate; open: *launch* a campaign. **5.** hurl; fling. —*n.* the action of launching a vessel, spacecraft, etc. [ME *launche*]

launch[2] *n.* an open or half-decked motor boat. [< Sp. *lancha*]

launch pad *Aerospace* the platform from which a rocket or guided missile is fired. Also **launch′ing pad.**

laun•der (LAWN dər) *v.t.* **1.** wash (clothing, linens, etc.). **2.** *Informal* pass (funds) through various accounts in order to con-

ceal their source. —*v.i.* **3.** undergo washing. [ME] —**laun′der•er** *n.*

laun•dress (LAWN dris) *n.* a woman paid or employed to do laundry.

laun•dro•mat (LAWN drə MAT) *n.* an establishment where laundry is washed and dried in coin-operated machines. [< *Laundromat*, a trade name]

laun•dry (LAWN dree) *n. pl.* **•dries 1.** a room, commercial establishment, etc. where laundering is done. **2.** articles to be laundered.

laun•dry•man (LAWN dree mən) *n. pl.* **•men** a man who operates or is employed by a laundry.

lau•re•ate (LOR ee it) *adj.* **1.** singled out for special honor. **2.** crowned or decked with laurel as a mark of honor. —*n.* a person honored with a prize or award: Nobel *laureate.* [ME]

lau•rel (LOR əl) *n.* **1.** an evergreen tree or shrub. **2.** *Often pl.* a crown or wreath of laurel leaves, conferred as a symbol of honor, achievement, etc. **3.** *pl.* honor or distinction gained by outstanding achievement. —**look to one's laurels** be on guard against losing a position of eminence, honor, etc. —**rest on one's laurels** be content with what one has already achieved. [ME *laurer* a type of tree]

la•va (LAH və) *n.* **1.** molten rock that issues from an active volcano or through a volcano vent. **2.** rock formed by the solidifying of this substance. [< Ital., avalanche]

lav•a•to•ry (LAV ə TOR ee) *n. pl.* **•ries 1.** a room equipped with washing and usu. toilet facilities. **2.** a basin, sink, etc., used for washing. [ME *lavatorie*]

lav•en•der (LAV ən dər) *n.* **1.** a plant of the mint family, having spikes of fragrant, pale violet flowers. **2.** the dried flowers and foliage of this plant, used to scent linen, clothing, etc. **3.** a pale, reddish violet color. —*adj.* pale reddish violet. [ME *lavendre*]

lav•ish (LAV ish) *adj.* **1.** generous and unrestrained in giving, spending, etc.; prodigal. **2.** provided or expended in great abundance. —*v.t.* give or bestow generously. [ME *lavas* profusion]

law (law) *n.* **1.** a rule of conduct, recognized by custom or decreed by formal enactment, considered as binding on the members of a community, nation, etc. **2.** a system or body of such rules. **3.** the body of rules relating to a specified subject or activity: criminal *law.* **4.** remedial justice as administered by legal authorities: resort to the *law.* **5.** the branch of knowledge concerned with jurisprudence. **6.** the legal profession. **7.** *Often cap.* divine will, command, or precept; also, a body of rules having such divine origin. **8.** any generally accepted rule, procedure, or principle governing a specified area of conduct, body of knowledge, etc. **9.** in science and philosophy, a formal statement of regularities found in natural phenomena. **—go to law** engage in litigation. **—lay down the law** utter one's wishes, instructions, etc. in an authoritative manner. [ME]

law·a·bid·ing (LAW ə BĪ ding) *adj.* obedient to the law.

law·break·er (LAW BRAY kər) *n.* one who violates the law. **—law'break'ing** *n. & adj.*

law·ful (LAW fəl) *adj.* **1.** permitted by or according to law. **2.** recognized by the law: *lawful* debts. **—law'ful·ness** *n.*

law·giv·er (LAW GIV ər) *n.* one who originates or institutes a law or system of laws.

law·less (LAW lis) *adj.* **1.** not controlled by law, authority, discipline, etc. **2.** contrary to law. **—law'less·ness** *n.*

law·mak·er (LAW MAY kər) *n.* one who enacts or helps to enact laws; a legislator.

lawn[1] (lawn) *n.* an area of mown grass near a house, in a park, etc. [ME *launde* glade]

lawn[2] *n.* a fine, thin linen or cotton fabric. [ME *lawnd*]

law·suit (LAW SOOT) *n.* a case, action, or proceeding brought to a court of law for settlement. **—law·yer** (LAW yər) *n.* a member of the legal profession.

lax (laks) *adj.* **·er, ·est 1.** lacking strictness or discipline. **2.** lacking precision; vague. **3.** lacking firmness or rigidity. [ME] **—lax'i·ty, lax'ness** *n.*

lax·a·tive (LAK sə tiv) *n.* a medicine taken to produce evacuation of the bowels. **—***adj.* loosening or producing evacuation of the bowels. [ME *laxatif*]

lay[1] (lay) *v.* **laid, lay·ing** *v.t.* **1.** place in a horizontal, reclining, or low position. **2.** put or place. **3.** establish as a basis or support: *lay* the groundwork. **4.** place or arrange in proper position: *lay* bricks. **5.** produce internally and deposit (an egg or eggs). **6.** think out; devise: *lay* plans. **7.** attribute or ascribe: *lay* the blame. **8.** set forth; present: *lay* one's claim before a court. **9.** bury, as in a grave; inter. **10.** set or prepare (a trap etc.). **11.** twist strands so as to produce (rope, cable, etc.). **—***v.i.* **12.** produce and deposit eggs. **—lay away 1.** store up; save.

2. bury in or as in a grave. **—lay into** attack vigorously. **—lay it on** exaggerate, esp. in praise or flattery. **—lay low** strike down; prostrate. **—lay off** dismiss from a job, usu. temporarily. **—lay out 1.** arrange or display for use, inspection, etc. **2.** arrange according to a plan; map. **3.** spend or supply (a sum of money). **4.** prepare (a corpse) for burial. **—lay over** stop for a time in the course of a journey. **—lay up 1.** make a store of. **2.** incapacitate or confine, as by illness, injury, etc. **—***n.* the manner in which something lies or is placed: *lay* of the land. [ME *layen*]

lay[2] *adj.* **1.** of or belonging to the laity; secular. **2.** not belonging to or endorsed by a learned profession: a *lay* opinion. [ME]

lay[3] past tense of LIE[1].

lay[4] *n.* **1.** a song, ballad, or narrative poem. **2.** a melody. [ME *lai*]

lay·a·way (LAY ə WAY) *n.* merchandise kept by the seller until paid for in full.

lay·er (LAY ər) *n.* **1.** a single thickness, coating, covering, etc. **2.** one who or that which lays; esp., a hen considered as an egg producer. **—***v.t. & v.i.* form a layer. [ME *leyer*]

layer cake a cake, usu. frosted, made in layers having a sweetened filling between them.

lay·ette (lay ET) *n.* clothing, bedding, etc., for a newborn infant. [< F]

lay·off (LAY AWF) *n.* **1.** the temporary dismissal of employees. **2.** a period of enforced unemployment.

lay·out (LAY OWT) *n.* **1.** a planned arrangement, as: **a** the relative positions of streets, rooms, etc. **b** written matter, illustrations, etc., arranged for printing. **2.** that which is laid out or provided; as equipment.

lay·o·ver (LAY OH vər) *n.* a break in a journey.

lay·per·son (LAY PUR sən) *n.* **1.** one without training or skill in a profession or branch of knowledge; also **layman** and **laywoman**. **2.** one belonging to the laity, as distinguished from the clergy.

laz·ar (LAZ ər) *n.* a beggar or pauper afflicted with disease; esp., a leper. [ME]

laze (layz) *v.t. & v.i.* **lazed, laz·ing** loaf or idle.

la·zy (LAY zee) *adj.* **·zi·er, ·zi·est 1.** unwilling to work or engage in energetic activity; slothful. **2.** moving or acting slowly or heavily. **3.** characterized by idleness or languor. [Prob. < MLG *lasich* feeble] **—la'zi·ly** *adv.* **—la'zi·ness** *n.*

lazy Susan a revolving tray, often divided into compartments, used to hold condiments, etc. Also **lazy susan.**

lea (lee) *n.* a grassy field. [ME *lege*]

leach (leech) *v.t.* **1.** subject to the filtering action of a liquid. **2.** remove or dissolve by or as by filtering. —*v.i.* **3.** be removed or dissolved by percolation or filtration. —*n.* the process of leaching. [ME *leche* infusion]

lead[1] (leed) *v.* **led, lead•ing** *v.t.* **1.** go with or ahead of so as to show the way; guide. **2.** cause to progress by or as by pulling or holding: *lead* by the hand. **3.** serve as or indicate a route for: The path *led* home. **4.** control the actions or affairs of; direct. **5.** influence the ideas, conduct, or actions of. **6.** be first among. **7.** experience or live; also, cause to experience or go through: *lead* a merry life: They *led* him a merry chase. **8.** in card games, begin a round by playing (a specified card). —*v.i.* **9.** act as guide; conduct. **10.** afford a way or passage: The road *leads* through a swamp. **11.** be conducive; tend: followed by *to:* Delinquency *leads* to crime. **12.** have control or command. — **lead off 1.** make a start; begin. **2.** in baseball, be the first batter in a line-up or inning. —**lead on 1.** entice or tempt, esp. to wrongdoing. **2.** go first or in advance. —*n.* **1.** position in advance or at the head. **2.** the distance or interval by which someone or something leads. **3.** guidance; example: Follow her *lead.* **4.** indication; clue: Give me a *lead.* **5.** in dramatic presentations: **a** a starring role. **b** a performer having such a role. **6.** in journalism, the introductory portion or paragraph of a news story. **7.** in card games: **a** the right to play first in a game or round. **b** the card, suit, etc. thus played. **8.** *Electr.* a short wire or conductor, used as a connection to a source of current. **9.** a cord, leash, etc. for leading an animal. [ME *leden*]

lead[2] (led) *n.* **1.** a soft, heavy, malleable metallic element (symbol Pb). **2.** any of various objects made of lead or similar metal; esp., a weight used in sounding etc. **3.** graphite, esp. in the form of thin rods, used as the writing material in pencils. **4.** bullets, shot, etc. **5.** *Printing* a thin strip of type metal used to provide space between printed lines. —*v.t.* cover, weight, fasten, treat, or fill with lead. [ME *lede*]

lead•en (LED n) *adj.* **1.** dull gray, as lead. **2.** made of lead. **3.** weighty; inert: a *leaden*

mass. **4.** heavy or labored in movement etc.; sluggish. —**lead′en•ness** *n.*

lead•er (LEE dər) *n.* **1.** one who or that which goes ahead or in advance. **2.** one who acts as a guiding force, commander, etc. **3.** a pipe for draining a liquid, as rainwater.

lead•er•ship (LEE dər SHIP) *n.* **1.** the office, position, or capacity of a leader; guidance. **2.** ability to lead, exert authority, etc. **3.** a group of leaders.

lead•ing[1] (LEE ding) *adj.* **1.** having the capacity or effect of controlling, influencing, guiding, etc. **2.** most important; chief. **3.** situated or going at the head; first. —*n.* the act of one who or that which leads; guidance.

lead•ing[2] (LED ing) *n.* **1.** the act or process of filling, covering, or separating with lead. **2.** *Printing* spacing between lines.

lead•off (LEED AWF) *n.* **1.** a beginning action, move, etc., as the opening play in a competitive game. **2.** a player or participant who begins the action in a game or competition. —**lead′off** *adj.*

lead poisoning (led) *Pathol.* poisoning caused by the absorption of lead by the tissues.

leaf (leef) *n. pl.* **leaves** (leevz) **1.** one of the outgrowths from the stem of a plant, commonly flat, thin, and green in color, and functioning as the principal area of photosynthesis. **2.** foliage collectively; leafage. **3.** a product, as tobacco, tea, etc., in the form of gathered leaves. **4.** one of the sheets of paper in a book etc. **5.** a flat piece, hinged or otherwise movable, constituting part of a table, gate, etc. **6.** metal in a very thin sheet or plate: gold *leaf.* —**turn over a new leaf** begin anew, esp. with the intention of improving one's ways. —*v.i.* put forth or produce leaves. [ME *leef*] —**leaf′less** *adj.*

leaf•age (LEE fij) *n.* leaves collectively; foliage.

leaf•let (LEEF lit) *n.* **1.** one of the divisions of a compound leaf. **2.** a small printed sheet or circular, often folded. **3.** a little leaf or leaflike part.

leaf•y (LEE fee) *adj.* **leaf•i•er, leaf•i•est 1.** bearing, covered with, or characterized by a profusion of leaves. **2.** consisting of or resembling leaves. —**leaf′i•ness** *n.*

league[1] (leeg) *n.* a measure of distance usu. reckoned as approximately 3 miles. [ME *lege*]

league[2] *n.* **1.** an association or confederation of persons, organizations, or states. **2.** a

compact or covenant binding such a union.
3. an association of athletic teams. **—in league** in close alliance. **—v.t. & v.i.** **leagued, lea·guing** unite in a league. [ME *ligg*]

leak (leek) *n.* **1.** an opening, as a crack, permitting an undesirable escape or entrance of fluid, light, etc. **2.** any condition or agency by which something is disclosed or escapes: a *leak* in the security system. **3.** an act or instance of leaking; leakage. **—v.i.** **1.** pass, flow, or escape through a hole, crack, etc. **2.** be divulged despite secrecy: The plans *leaked* out. **—v.t.** **3.** let (a liquid etc.) escape. **4.** disclose (information etc.) without authorization. [ME *leken*]

leak·age (LEE kij) *n.* **1.** the act or circumstance of leaking. **2.** that which escapes by leaking.

leak·y (LEE kee) *adj.* **leak·i·er, leak·i·est** having a leak; permitting leakage.

lean¹ (leen) *v.i.* **1.** rest or incline for support: usu. with *against* or *on.* **2.** bend or slant from an erect position. **3.** have a tendency, preference, etc. **4.** depend for support etc.; rely. **—v.t.** **5.** cause to incline. **—n.** the act or condition of leaning; slant. [ME *lenen*]

lean² *adj.* **1.** not fat or plump; thin; spare. **2.** not containing fat: *lean* meat. **3.** not rich, plentiful, or satisfying; meager; *lean* times. **—n.** meat or flesh having little or no fat. [ME *lene*] **—lean'ness** *n.*

lean·ing (LEE ning) *n.* n inclination; tendency.

lean-to (LEEN too) *n. pl.* **-tos 1.** a crude hut of branches, etc. sloping to the ground from a raised support. **2.** a shed or extension of a building having a sloping roof and supported by an adjoining wall or structure.

leap (leep) *v.* **leaped** or **leapt** (lept), **leap·ing** *v.i.* **1.** rise or project oneself by a sudden thrust from the ground; jump; spring. **2.** move, react, etc., suddenly or impulsively. **3.** make an abrupt transition. **—v.t.** **4.** traverse by a jump. **—n.** **1.** the act of leaping. **2.** the space traversed by leaping. **3.** an abrupt transition. [ME *lepen*]

leap·frog (LEEP FROG) *n.* a game in which each player leaps over another, who is bending over. **—v.t. & v.i.** **·frogged, ·frog·ging** jump or cause to move as if in leapfrog: Prices may *leapfrog* once demand picks up.

leap year a year of 366 days, in which a 29th day is added to February. [ME *lepe yere*]

learn (lurn) *v.* **learned** (lurnd) or **learnt,**

learn·ing *v.t.* **1.** acquire knowledge of or skill in by study, practice, etc. **2.** find out; become aware of. **3.** commit to memory; memorize. **4.** acquire by experience or example. **—v.i.** **5.** gain knowledge or acquire skill. [ME *lernen*]

learn·ed (LUR nid) *adj.* **1.** having profound or extensive knowledge. **2.** characterized by or devoted to scholarship.

learn·ing (LUR ning) *n.* **1.** knowledge obtained by study; erudition. **2.** the act of acquiring knowledge or skill.

lease (lees) *n.* **1.** a contract for the temporary occupation or use of premises, property, etc. in exchange for payment of rent. **2.** the period of such occupation or use. **—v.t.** **leased, leas·ing 1.** grant use of under a lease. **2.** hold under a lease. [ME *les*] **—leas'a·ble** *adj.*

leash (leesh) *n.* a strap etc. by which a dog or other animal is led or restrained. **—v.t.** hold or secure by a leash. [ME *lesh*]

least (leest) alternative superlative of LIT- TLE. **—adj.** smallest in degree, value, size, etc.; slightest. **—n.** that which is smallest, slightest, or most insignificant. **—at least 1.** by the lowest possible estimate. **2.** at any rate. **—adv.** in the lowest or smallest degree. [ME *leest*]

leath·er (LETH ər) *n.* animal skin, usu. with the hair removed, prepared for use by tanning. **—v.t.** cover or equip with leather. [ME *lether*]

leath·ern (LETH ərn) *adj.* **1.** made of leather. **2.** resembling leather; leathery.

leath·er·neck (LETH ər NEK) *n. Slang* a U.S. marine.

leath·er·y (LETH ə ree) *adj.* resembling leather in texture or appearance; tough.

leave¹ (leev) *v.* **left, leav·ing** *v.t.* **1.** go or depart from. **2.** allow to remain behind or in a specified place, condition, etc. **3.** have or cause as an aftermath: Oil may *leave* stains. **4.** commit for action etc.; entrust: *Leave* it to me. **5.** terminate one's connection or association with. **6.** abandon; forsake. **7.** transmit as a legacy; bequeath. **—v.i.** **8.** go away; set out. **—leave off** stop; cease. **—leave out 1.** omit. **2.** exclude. [ME *leven*]

leave² *n.* **1.** permission to do something. **2.** permission to be absent; esp., **a** official permission to be absent from duty. **b** the period covered by such permission: also **leave of absence. 3.** formal farewell: usu. in the phrase **take (one's) leave. —on leave** absent from work or duty with permission. [ME *leven*]

leav·en (LEV ən) *n.* **1.** an agent of fermentation, as yeast, added to dough or batter to produce a light texture. **2.** any pervasive influence that produces a significant change. Also **leav'en·ing.** —*v.t.* **1.** cause fermentation in. **2.** affect in character; temper. [ME *levain* raise]

leave-tak·ing (LEEV TAY king) *n.* a farewell; departure.

leav·ings (LEE vingz) *n.pl.* leftovers; remnants.

lech·er·y (LECH ə ree) *n.* unconstrained sexual indulgence. [ME *lecherie*] —**lech'er** *n.* —**lech'er·ous** *adj.*

lec·tern (LEK tərn) *n.* **1.** a stand on which a speaker, instructor, etc., may place books or papers. **2.** in some churches, a reading desk from which certain parts of the service are read. [ME *lectryn*]

lec·ture (LEK chər) *n.* **1.** a discourse on a specific subject, delivered to an audience for instruction or information. **2.** a formal reproof or lengthy reprimand. —*v.* **·tured, ·tur·ing** *v.i.* **1.** deliver a lecture or lectures. —*v.t.* **2.** deliver a lecture to. **3.** rebuke sternly or at length. [ME] —**lec'tur·er** *n.*

led (led) past tense, past participle of LEAD[1]

ledge (lej) *n.* **1.** a narrow, shelflike projection along the side of a rocky formation. **2.** a shelf or sill projecting from or forming the top of a wall etc. **3.** an underwater or coastal ridge. [ME *legge*]

ledg·er (LEJ ər) *n.* an account book in which all final entries of business transactions are recorded.

lee (lee) *n.* **1.** shelter or protection, esp. from the wind. **2.** *Chiefly Naut.* the side sheltered from the wind. [ME] —*adj.*

leech (leech) *n.* **1.** any of a class of carnivorous or bloodsucking, chiefly aquatic worms; esp. the **medicinal leech,** formerly used for bloodletting. **2.** one who clings to another for gain; a parasite. —*v.t. Archaic* treat with leeches. —*v.i.* hang on to another in the manner of a leech. [ME *leche*]

leek (leek) *n.* an herb of the lily family, closely allied to the onion but having a narrow bulb and broader leaves. [ME]

leer (leer) *n.* a sly look or sidewise glance expressing salacious desire, malicious intent, etc. [ME *leor*] —**leer** *v.i.*

leer·y (LEER ee) *adj.* **leer·i·er, leer·i·est** suspicious; wary.

lees (leez) *n.pl.* sediment, esp. in wine or liquor; dregs. [ME *lies*]

lee·ward (LOO ərd) *adj.* being on or toward the side sheltered from the wind. —*n.* the side or direction toward which the wind is blowing. —*adv.* toward the lee. Opposed to *windward.*

lee·way (LEE way) *n.* **1.** additional space, time, range, etc., providing greater freedom of action. **2.** *Naut.* the lateral drift of a vessel or an aircraft in motion.

left[1] (left) past tense, past participle of LEAVE[1].

left[2] *adj.* **1.** pertaining to, designating, or being on the side of the body that is toward the north when one faces east. **2.** nearest to or tending in the direction of the left side. **3.** worn on a left hand, foot, etc. **4.** *Sometimes cap.* designating a person, party, faction, etc. having liberal, socialistic, or laborite views and policies. —*n.* **1.** any part, area, etc. on or toward the left side. **2.** *Often cap.* a group, party, etc. whose views and policies are left (*adj.* def. 4). **3.** in boxing, a blow with the left hand. [ME, weak] —**left** *adv.*: *went left.*

left-hand (LEFT HAND) *adj.* **1.** of, for, pertaining to, or situated on the left side or the left hand. **2.** turning, opening, or swinging to the left.

left-hand·ed (LEFT HAN did) *adj.* **1.** using the left hand habitually and more easily than the right. **2.** adapted or intended for use by the left hand. **3.** turning or moving from right to left. **4.** ironical or insincere in intent or effect: *a left-handed* compliment. —*adv.* with the left hand. —**left'hand'ed·ness** *n.*

left·ist (LEF tist) *n.* one whose views and policies are left (*adj.* def. 4). —*adj.* left (*adj.* def. 4). —**left'ism** *n.*

left·o·ver (LEFT OH vər) *n.* *Usu. pl.* an unused part, esp. of prepared food. —*adj.*: *leftover* food.

left wing a party, group, faction, etc., having leftist policies. —**left'-wing'** *adj.* —**left'-wing'er** *n.*

leg (leg) *n.* **1.** one of the limbs or appendages serving as a means of support and locomotion in animals and man. **2.** *Anat.* **a** a lower limb of an animal or human body, extending from the hip to the ankle. **b** the part of the lower limb between the knee and the ankle. **3.** a support resembling a leg in shape, position, or function. **4.** the portion of an article of clothing, as trousers, that covers a leg. **5.**

a division or section of a course or journey. —**on one's last legs** on the verge of collapse or death. —**pull one's leg** make fun of; fool. —**shake a leg** *Informal* hurry. [ME] —**leg′less** *adj.*

leg·a·cy (LEG ə see) *n. pl.* **·cies 1.** personal property, money, etc. bequeathed by will; bequest. **2.** anything received from or passed on by an ancestor, predecessor, or earlier era. [ME *legacie* the district of a legate]

le·gal (LEE gəl) *adj.* **1.** of or concerned with law: *legal* documents. **2.** established, authorized, or permitted by law. **3.** characteristic of or appropriate to those who practice law. [< L *legalis* of the law] —**le′gal·ly** *adv.*

le·gal·ism (LEE gə LIZ əm) *n.* **1.** strict and literal conformity to law, rather than to its spirit. **2.** an example of this. —**le′gal·is′tic** *adj.*

le·gal·i·ty (lee GAL i tee) *n. pl.* **·ties 1.** the condition or quality of being legal; lawfulness. **2.** adherence to law.

le·gal·ize (LEE gə LĪZ) *v.t.* **·ized, ·iz·ing** make legal. —**le′gal·i·za′tion** *n.*

legal tender money that may be legally offered in payment of a debt and that a creditor must accept.

leg·ate (LEG it) *n.* **1.** an ecclesiastic appointed as an official representative of the Pope. **2.** an official envoy, usu. acting as a diplomatic representative of a government. [ME *legat*]

leg·a·tee (LEG ə TEE) *n.* one to whom a legacy is bequeathed.

le·ga·tion (li GAY shən) *n.* **1.** the official residence or business premises of a diplomatic minister or envoy of lower rank than an ambassador. **2.** the official staff of a foreign envoy or diplomatic mission.

leg·end (LEJ ənd) *n.* **1.** an unauthenticated story from earlier times, preserved by tradition and popularly thought to be historical. **2.** an inscription, as on a coin, banner, etc. **3.** a caption or explanatory description accompanying an illustration, chart, etc. [ME *legende*]

leg·en·dar·y (LEJ ən DER ee) *adj.* **1.** of, presented in, or of the nature of a legend. **2.** famous; celebrated.

leg·er·de·main (LEJ ər də MAYN) *n.* **1.** sleight of hand. **2.** any artful trickery or deception. [< MF, lit., light of hand]

leg·ged (LEG id, legd) *adj.* having or characterized by (a specified kind or number of) legs: *two-legged* animal.

leg·ging (LEG ing) *n.* a covering for the leg, usu. extending from the knee to the instep.

leg·gy (LEG ee) *adj.* **·gi·er, ·gi·est 1.** having disproportionately long legs. **2.** having or displaying attractive, shapely legs. —**leg′gi·ness** *n.*

leg·i·ble (LEJ ə bəl) *adj.* capable of being read or deciphered; easy to read. [ME] —**leg′i·bil′i·ty** *n.* —**leg′i·bly** *adv.*

le·gion (LEE jən) *n.* **1.** in ancient Rome, a major military unit, comprising up to 6000 men. **2.** a great number; multitude. **3.** any of various military or honorary organizations, usu. national in character. [ME *legioun*]

le·gion·naire (LEE jə NAIR) *n. Often cap.* a member of a legion (def. 3). [< F]

legionnaires' disease a disease, resembling pneumonia, caused by a bacterium. [from an outbreak after an American Legion Convention in Philadelphia in 1976]

leg·is·late (LEJ is LAYT) *v.* **·lat·ed, ·lat·ing** *v.i.* **1.** make a law or laws. —*v.t.* **2.** effect by legislation: often with *into* or *out of.*

leg·is·la·tion (LEJ is LAY shən) *n.* **1.** the act or procedures of enacting laws. **2.** an officially enacted law or laws.

leg·is·la·tive (LEJ is LAY tiv) *adj.* **1.** of, pertaining to, or involved in legislation. **2.** having the power to legislate: the *legislative* branch. **3.** of or pertaining to a legislature.

leg·is·la·tor (LEJ is LAY tər) *n.* a lawmaker; member of a legislature. [< L *legis lator* proposer of a law]

leg·is·la·ture (LEJ is LAY chər) *n.* a body of persons officially constituted and empowered to make and enact the laws of a nation or state; esp., in the U.S., the law-making body of a state, territory, etc., as distinguished from Congress.

le·git·i·mate (li JIT ə mit) *adj.* **1.** in accordance with law; lawful. **2.** authentic; valid. **3.** born in wedlock. **4.** according to or based on strict hereditary right. **5.** in the theater, denoting drama performed by living actors before an audience. —*v.t.* (li JIT ə MAYT) **·mat·ed, ·mat·ing 1.** make or establish as legitimate. **2.** show reason or authorization for. [< Med.L *legitimatus* made lawful] —**le·git′i·ma·cy** (li JIT ə mə see) *n.* —**le·git′i·mate·ly** *adv.*

le·git·i·mize (li JIT ə MĪZ) *v.t.* **·mized, ·miz·ing** legitimate. Also **le·git′i·ma·tize** (li JIT ə mə TĪZ).

leg·man (LEG MAN) *n. pl.* **·men 1.** a reporter who covers news events in person. **2.**

one who runs errands or collects information.

leg•ume (LEG yoom) *n.* **1.** the fruit or seed of any leguminous plant, esp. when used as food or fodder. **2.** any leguminous plant. [< F *légume* vegetable]

le•gu•mi•nous (li GYOO mə nəs) *adj.* of or belonging to a large family of plants producing seed-filled pods, including peas, beans, etc.

leg•work (LEG wurk) *n.* work, as the gathering of information, requiring physical activity.

lei (lay) *n. pl.* **leis** a garland of flowers, leaves, etc. [< Hawaiian]

lei•sure (LEE zhər) *n.* **1.** freedom from the demands of work or duty. **2.** time available for recreation or relaxation. **—at leisure 1.** free from pressing obligation. **2.** unemployed. **3.** when one has time or opportunity: also **at one's leisure.** *—adj.* **1.** not spent in work or necessary activity: *leisure* time. **2.** having considerable leisure: the *leisure* classes. [ME *leisir*]

lei•sure•ly (LEE zhər lee) *adj.* done without exertion or pressure; relaxed. Also **lei'sured. —lei•sure•ly** *adv.*

leit•mo•tif (LĪT moh TEEF) *n. Music* a theme used for a certain person, event, or idea throughout an opera etc. [< G, leading motive]

lem•on (LEM ən) *n.* **1.** a citrus fruit having juicy, acid pulp and a yellow rind. **2.** the tree bearing this fruit. **3.** a bright, clear yellow. **4.** *Informal* something or someone unsatisfactory. *—adj.* bright, clear yellow. [ME *lymon*]

lem•on•ade (LEM ə NAYD) *n.* a drink made of lemon juice, water, and sugar.

lend (lend) *v.* **lent, lend•ing** *v.t.* **1.** grant for temporary use or possession. **2.** grant the use of (money) at a stipulated rate of interest. **3.** impart, as an abstract quality. **4.** make available, as for aid or support. *—v.i.* **5.** make a loan or loans. **—lend itself (or oneself) to** adapt or accommodate for a specific purpose. [ME *lenden*]

length (lengkth) *n.* **1.** linear extent from end to end; usu., the longest dimension of a thing, as distinguished from its width and thickness. **2.** extent from beginning to end, as of a period of time, series, book, etc. **3.** duration or continuance, esp. in respect to time. **4.** the measurement along, extent of, or distance equivalent to something specified: arm's *length*. **5.** *Often pl.* the limit of

one's efforts, ability, etc.: go to great *lengths*. **6.** in racing, the extent from front to back of a competing horse, boat, etc., used as a unit of estimating position. **—at length 1.** finally. **2.** in full. [ME *lengthe*]

length•en (LENGK thən) *v.t. & v.i.* make or become longer.

length•wise (LENGKTH wīz) *adv.* in the direction or dimension of length. Also **length'ways'** (-wayz). *—adj.* according to length.

length•y (LENGK thee) *adj.* **length•i•er, length•i•est** unusually or unduly long. **—length'i•ness** *n.*

le•ni•ent (LEEN yənt) *adj.* gentle or merciful in disposition, effect, etc.; mild. [< L *lenire* soften] **—le'ni•en•cy, le'ni•ence** *n.*

len•i•tive (LEN i tiv) *adj.* having the power or tendency to allay pain or distress; soothing. *—n.* a lenitive medicine; laxative. [< Med.L *lenitivus* softened]

len•i•ty (LEN i tee) *n. pl.* **•ties** the state or quality of being lenient; a lenient act. [< L *lenitas*]

lens (lenz) *n.* **1.** *Optics* a piece of glass or other transparent substance by which rays of light are made to converge or diverge. **2.** two or more such pieces in combination. **3.** any device that concentrates or disperses radiation etc., other than light, by action similar to that of an optical lens. **4.** *Anat.* a transparent body situated behind the iris of the eye and serving to focus an image on the retina. [< L, lentil (from its form)]

lent (lent) past tense, past participle of LEND.

Lent (lent) *n. Eccl.* the period of forty days, excluding Sundays, from Ash Wednesday to Easter, observed as a Christian season of fasting, penitence, and self-denial. [ME *lente* springtime] **—Lent•en** (LEN tn) *adj.*

len•til (LEN til) *n.* **1.** a leguminous plant, having broad pods containing flattish, edible seeds. **2.** the seed of this plant. [ME]

le•o•nine (LEE ə NĪN) *adj.* resembling, or characteristic of a lion. [ME *leonyn*]

le•o•tard (LEE ə TAHRD) *n.* a skintight garment worn by dancers, acrobats, etc. [after Jules *Léotard*, 19th-c. French aerialist]

lep•er (LEP ər) *n.* one afflicted with leprosy. [ME *lepre* leprosy]

lep•re•chaun (LEP rə KAWN) *n.* in Irish folklore, a tiny elf supposed to own hidden treasure. [< Irish *leipreachán*]

lep•ro•sy (LEP rə see) *n. Pathol.* a chronic, communicable disease characterized by skin lesions, nerve paralysis, and physical mutilation: also called *Hansen's disease.* [< Med.L *leprosia*] —**lep·rous** (LEP rəs) *adj.*

les·bi·an (LEZ bee ən) *n.* a homosexual woman. [< L *Lesbius*, alluding to the poet Sappho of Lesbos, who wrote of her relations with other women] —**les·bi·an** *adj.* —**les'bi·an·ism** *n.*

lese majesty (leez) an offense against sovereign authority or a sovereign; treason. [< F *lèse-majesté*]

le·sion (LEE zhən) *n.* **1.** *Pathol.* any abnormal or harmful change in the structure of an organ or tissue. **2.** an injury; damage. [ME]

less (les) alternative comparative of LITTLE. —*adj.* **1.** not as great in quantity or degree; not as much. **2.** inferior in degree; smaller; lower: with *than.* —*adv.* to a smaller degree or extent. —*n.* a smaller amount or part. —*prep.* with the subtraction of; minus. [ME]

-less *suffix of adjectives* **1.** devoid of; without: *blameless, harmless.* **2.** deprived of; lacking: *motherless, stemless.* **3.** unable to (do something): *restless.* [ME *-les* free from]

les·see (le SEE) *n.* one to whom a lease is granted.

less·en (LES ən) *v.t.* **1.** decrease. **2.** make little of; disparage. —*v.i.* **3.** become less.

less·er (LES ər) *adj.* not as large or important; minor.

les·son (LES ən) *n.* **1.** an instance or experience from which useful knowledge may be gained. **2.** an assignment to be studied or learned, as by a student. **3.** a reprimand; reproof. **4.** a portion of the Bible read or designated to be read at a religious service. [ME]

les·sor (LES or) *n.* one who grants a lease; a landlord letting property under a lease.

lest (lest) *conj.* **1.** in order to prevent the chance that (something might happen); for fear that. **2.** that: after expressions denoting anxiety: We worried *lest* the money dry up. [ME *leste*]

let[1] (let) *v.* **let, let·ting** *v.t.* **1.** allow; permit. **2.** grant or assign, as a contract for work to be performed. **3.** an auxiliary verb; usu. in the imperative, signifying: **a** an exhortation or command: *Let's* go! **b** acquiescence; inability to prevent the inevitable: *Let* it rain. **c** an assumption or suggestion: *Let* x equal the sum of two numbers. **4.** rent (an apartment etc.) to a tenant. **5.** cause to flow, as blood. —*v.i.* **6.** admit of being rented: rooms to *let.* —**let down 1.** cause to fall or

descend; loosen, as hair. **2.** disappoint. —**let loose** set free; release. —**let off 1.** emit; release, as from pressure or tension. **2.** discharge, dismiss, or excuse, as from work or obligation. —**let up 1.** grow less; abate. **2.** reduce tension. —**let up on** cease to subject to force or severe treatment. [ME *leten*]

let[2] *n.* in tennis or similar games, a service, point, etc., that must be repeated. [ME *letten* make late]

let·down (LET DOWN) *n.* **1.** a decrease; slackening, as of speed, force, or energy. **2.** disappointment.

le·thal (LEE thəl) *adj.* **1.** causing death; deadly; fatal. **2.** pertaining to or characteristic of death. [< L *letalis* deadly]

leth·ar·gy (LETH ər jee) *n. pl.* **·gies 1.** a state of indifference; apathy. **2.** *Pathol.* excessive drowsiness or abnormally deep sleep. [< LL *léthargia*] —**le·thar·gic** (lə THAHR jik) *adj.*

let·ter (LET ər) *n.* **1.** a standardized character used in writing or printing to represent a speech sound. **2.** a written or printed message directed to a specified person or group. **3.** an official document granting certain rights or privileges to a specified person: *letter* of credit. **4.** literal meaning: the *letter* of the law. **5.** *pl.* literature in general; literary profession: a man of *letters.* **6.** an emblem in the form of the initial letter of a college etc., awarded for outstanding performance in athletics. —*v.t.* **1.** inscribe letters on; mark with letters. —*v.i.* **2.** form letters, as by hand. [ME] —**let'ter·er** *n.*

let·tered (LET ərd) *adj.* **1.** versed in letters; educated. **2.** inscribed or marked with letters.

let·ter·head (LET ər HED) *n.* a printed heading, as a name and address, on a sheet of writing paper; also, a sheet of paper bearing this.

let·ter·ing (LET ər ing) *n.* **1.** the act or art of forming letters; process of marking or stamping with letters. **2.** the letters in an inscription etc.

let·ter-per·fect (LET ər PUR fikt) *adj.* correct in all details.

let·tuce (LET is) *n.* **1.** a cultivated herb having crisp, edible leaves; also, the leaves. **2.** *Slang* paper money. [ME *letuse*]

let-up (LET UP) *n. Informal* **1.** a lessening, as of intensity; lull. **2.** a respite; pause.

leu·ke·mi·a (loo KEE mee ə) *n. Pathol.* a cancer of the bone marrow, preventing

manufacture of white and red blood cells.
[< NL]

lev·ee¹ (LEV ee) *n.* **1.** an embankment along the shore of a river, built for protection against floods. **2.** a landing place; wharf. [< F *levée* embankment]

lev·ee² *n.* a reception, usu. held early in the day by a person of rank or distinction. [< F *levé* an arising]

lev·el (LEV əl) *n.* **1.** relative place, degree, or stage: a high *level* of development. **2.** position on a vertical scale; height: the *level* of the lower branches. **3.** a horizontal line or surface: sea *level*. **4.** a flat expanse, as of land. **5.** any of various devices used to find the conformity of a line or surface with the horizontal plane. —**on the level** *Informal* fair, honest. —*adj.* **1.** having a surface with no irregularities in height; even; flat. **2.** conforming to a horizontal plane. **3.** being at the same height as something else. **4.** measured so as to have a surface even with the edge of the container. **5.** equal to something or someone else, as in importance, development, etc. —**a level head** a calm and sensible mind. —**one's level best** the best one can possibly do. —*v.* **·eled, ·el·ing** *v.t.* **1.** give an even or horizontal surface to. **2.** destroy by or as by smashing to the ground. **3.** knock down. **4.** bring to a common state or condition. **5.** aim or point as a weapon. **6.** aim or direct (something) with force of emphasis: *level* an accusation. —*v.i.* **7.** bring persons or things to a common state or condition. **8.** speak truthfully. —*adv.* in an even line or plane. [ME] —**lev′el·er** *n.* —**lev′el·ness** *n.*

lev·el·head·ed (LEV əl HED id) *adj.* characterized by common sense and cool judgment. —**lev′el·head′ed·ness** *n.*

lev·er (LEV ər) *n.* **1.** *Mech.* a device, as a straight bar, pivoting on a fixed support (the fulcrum), and serving to impart pressure or motion from a force or effort applied at one point to a resisting force at another point. **2.** any of various tools, devices, or parts operating on the same principle, as a crowbar. **3.** any means of exerting effective power. —*v.t.* move or pry with or as with a lever. [ME]

lev·er·age (LEV ər ij) *n.* **1.** the action or mechanical effect of a lever. **2.** speculation, esp. with the use of borrowed money, to gain a high return. **3.** the power to effect or accomplish something. —*v.t.* **·aged,**

·ag·ing speculate or cause to speculate on borrowed money.

le·vi·a·than (li VĪ ə thən) *n.* **1.** a gigantic water beast mentioned in the Bible. **2.** any enormous creature or thing. [ME]

Le·vi's (LEE vīz) *n.pl.* close-fitting, heavy denim trousers having rivets to reinforce points of greatest strain: a registered trademark.

lev·i·tate (LEV i TAYT) *v.* **·tat·ed, ·tat·ing** *v.i.* **1.** rise and float in the air, as through buoyancy or supposed supernatural power. —*v.t.* **2.** cause to rise and float in the air. [ME] —**lev′i·ta′tion** *n.*

lev·i·ty (LEV i tee) *n. pl.* **·ties** lack of seriousness; inappropriate gaiety; frivolity. [< L *levitas* lightness]

lev·y (LEV ee) *v.* **lev·ied, lev·y·ing** *v.t.* **1.** impose and collect by authority or force, as a tax, fine, etc. **2.** enlist or call up (troops etc.) for military service. **3.** prepare for, begin, or wage (war). —*v.i.* **4.** *Law* seize property in order to fulfill a judgment: usu. with *on.* —*n. pl.* **lev·ies 1.** the act of levying. **2.** that which is levied, as money or troops. [ME *levee* raise]

lewd (lood) *adj.* **1.** characterized by or inciting to lust or debauchery. **2.** obscene; ribald; bawdy. [ME *leud* unlearned]

lex·i·cog·ra·phy (LEK si KOG rə fee) *n.* the art or profession of compiling dictionaries. —**lex′i·cog′ra·pher** *n.*

lex·i·con (LEK si KON) *n.* **1.** a dictionary; esp., a dictionary of Latin, Greek, or Hebrew. **2.** the vocabulary of a language, a particular subject, occupation, etc. [< Med.L]

li·a·bil·i·ty (LĪ ə BIL i tee) *n. pl.* **·ties 1.** the state or condition of being liable. **2.** that for which one is liable, as a debt. **3.** *pl.* the debts or obligations of a business: opposed to *assets.* **4.** any obstacle or hindrance.

li·a·ble (LĪ ə bəl) *adj.* **1.** justly or legally responsible, as for damages; answerable. **2.** subject or susceptible, as to injury, illness, etc. **3.** likely, apt.

li·ai·son (LEE ə ZON) *n.* **1.** communication or unity, as between parts of an armed force. **2.** an illicit love affair. [< F]

li·ar (LĪ ər) *n.* one who lies or utters falsehoods. [ME *lier*]

lib (lib) *n. Informal* liberation: women's *lib.*

li·ba·tion (lī BAY shən) *n.* **1.** a liquid ceremonially poured out, as in honor of a deity; also, the act of pouring such a liquid. **2.** humorously, a drink. [ME *libacioun*]

li·bel (LĪ bəl) n. **1.** *Law* **a** a written statement or graphic representation, esp. in published form, that damages a person's reputation. **b** the act or crime of publishing such a statement. **2.** any defamatory or grossly unflattering statement. —v.t. **•beled, •bel·ing** publish or perpetrate a libel against. [ME] —**li′bel·er** n.

li·bel·ous (LĪ bə ləs) adj. constituting, containing, or like a libel.

lib·er·al (LIB ər əl) adj. **1.** favoring progress or reform, as in politics or religion. **2.** not intolerant or prejudiced. **3.** generous; lavish in giving. **4.** given freely or in large quantity; ample. **5.** not literal or strict. —n. one having liberal opinions or convictions, esp. in politics or religion. [ME] —**lib′er·al·ly** adv.

liberal arts a group of college courses including literature, languages, and history, distinguished from scientific, technical, or purely practical subjects.

lib·er·al·ism (LIB ə LIZ əm) n. liberal beliefs or policies, esp. in regard to politics, social changes, etc.

lib·er·al·i·ty (LIB ə RAL i tee) n. **1.** generosity. **2.** broad-mindedness.

lib·er·al·ize (LIB ər ə LĪZ) v.t. & v.i. **•ized, •iz·ing** make or become liberal. —**lib′er·al·i·za′tion** n.

lib·er·ate (LIB ə RAYT) v.t. **•at·ed, •at·ing 1.** set free, as from slavery or confinement. **2.** release from chemical combination, as a gas. **3.** bring about equal rights or status (for). [< L liberatus freed] —**lib′er·a′tion** n. —**lib′er·a′tor** n.

lib·er·tar·i·an (LIB ər TAIR ee ən) n. one who advocates liberty of thought or conduct. —**lib·er·tar′i·an** adj. —**lib′er·tar′i·an·ism** n.

lib·er·tine (LIB ər TEEN) n. one lacking moral restraint; a profligate. [ME *libertyn*] —adj. —**lib′er·tin·ism** (LIB ər tee NIZ əm) n.

lib·er·ty (LIB ər tee) n. pl. **•ties 1.** freedom from oppression, tyranny, or harsh domination. **2.** freedom from confinement or slavery. **3.** freedom of thought or action, or exemption from forms of compulsion or indignity, regarded as a human right. **4.** an overly free, familiar, or disrespectful act or manner. **5.** in the U.S. Navy, official permission to be absent from one's ship or place of duty, usu. for a short time. —**at liberty 1.** free; authorized or permitted (to do something). **2.** not engaged in an activity or occupation; unemployed. **3.** able to move about freely. [ME *liberte*]

li·bid·i·nous (li BID i nəs) adj. characterized by or inclining toward excesses of sexual desire; lustful. [ME] —**li·bid′i·nous·ness** n.

li·bi·do (li BEE doh) n. **1.** sexual desire or impulse. **2.** *Psychoanal.* the instinctual craving or drive behind all human activities. [< L, lust] —**li·bid′i·nal** (li BID n əl) adj.

li·brar·i·an (lī BRAIR ee ən) n. **1.** one who has charge of a library. **2.** a person qualified by training for library service.

li·brar·y (LĪ BRER ee) n. pl. **•brar·ies 1.** a collection of books, pamphlets, etc.; esp., such a collection arranged to facilitate reference. **2.** a building, room, etc. housing such a collection. **3.** a commercial establishment that rents books. [ME *libraire*]

li·bret·tist (li BRET ist) n. the writer of a libretto.

li·bret·to (li BRET oh) n. pl. **•bret·tos** or **•bret·ti** (-BRET ee) **1.** the verbal text of an opera or other large-scale vocal work. **2.** a book containing such a text. [< Ital., little book]

lice (līs) plural of LOUSE.

li·cense (LĪ səns) n. **1.** an official document giving permission to engage in a specified activity, perform a specified act, etc. **2.** abuse of freedom or privilege. **3.** deviation from established rules or standards, esp. for artistic effect: poetic *license.* —v.t. **•censed, •cens·ing** grant a license to or for; authorize. [ME *licence*] —**li′cen·ser** or *Law* **li′cen·sor** n.

li·cen·see (LĪ sən SEE) n. one to whom a license has been granted.

li·cen·tious (lī SEN shəs) adj. lacking in moral restraint; lewd. [< L *licentiosus* unrestrained] —**li·cen′tious·ly** adv. —**li·cen′tious·ness** n.

li·chee (LEE chee) n. see LITCHI.

li·chen (LĪ kən) n. any of various flowerless plants composed of fungi and algae, commonly growing in flat patches on rocks, trees, etc. [< L]

lic·it (LIS it) adj. lawful. [< L *licitus* permitted] —**lic′it·ly** adv.

lick (lik) v.t. **1.** pass the tongue over the surface of. **2.** remove or consume by taking with the tongue: often followed by *up, off,* etc. **3.** move or pass lightly over or about: The flames *licked* the coals. **4.** *Informal* **a** defeat. **b** thrash; beat. —**lick one's chops** show pleased anticipation. —n. **1.** a stroke of the tongue in licking. **2.** a small amount. **3.** a salt lick. **4.** *Informal* **a** a blow; whack. **b** stroke; spell, as of work. —**lick and a promise** a hasty washing or cleaning. [ME *licken*]

lick·e·ty-split (LIK i tee SPLIT) *adv. Informal* at full speed.

lick·ing (LIK ing) *n. Informal* a whipping; defeat.

lic·o·rice (LIK ər ish) *n.* **1.** a perennial herb of Europe. **2.** the dried root of this plant, or an extract made from it, used in medicine and confections. **3.** a confection flavored with this extract. [ME *lycorys*]

lid (lid) *n.* **1.** a hinged or removable cover placed at the top of a receptacle or over an opening. **2.** an eyelid. [ME] —**lid'ded** *adj.* —**lid'less** *adj.*

lie[1] (lī) *v.i.* **lay, lain, ly·ing 1.** be in a recumbent or prostrate position. **2.** place oneself in a recumbent position; rest at full length: often with *down.* **3.** be placed on or rest against a surface, esp. in a horizontal position. **4.** be or remain in a specified condition or state: *lie* dormant. **5.** occupy a location; be situated. —**lie low** remain in concealment; conceal one's intentions. —*n.* the position, manner, or situation in which something lies; aspect. [ME *lien*]

lie[2] *n.* **1.** an untrue statement made with the intent of deceiving; a falsehood. **2.** that which creates or is intended to produce a false impression. —**give the lie (to)** expose as false. —**white lie** a false statement made with the intent of being polite or kind. —*v.i.* **lied, ly·ing 1.** make an untrue statement or statements, esp. with intent to deceive. **2.** give an erroneous or misleading impression: Figures don't *lie.* [ME]

lied (leed) *n. pl.* **lied·er** (LEE dər) a German song; esp., a ballad or lyric poem set to music. [< G]

lie detector a polygraph used to establish the truth or falsity of an accused person's statements.

lief (leef) *adv.* willingly; readily: used chiefly in the phrase **would as lief.** [ME *leef*]

lien (leen) *n.* a legal right to claim or dispose of property in payment of or as security for a debt or charge. [< AF]

lieu (loo) *n.* place; stead: now only in the phrase **in lieu of.** [< MF]

lieu·ten·ant (loo TEN ənt) *n.* **1.** *Mil.* a commissioned officer holding either of two ranks, **first** or **second lieutenant,** the former ranking next below a captain. **2.** *Naval*

a commissioned officer holding either of two ranks, **lieutenant** or **lieutenant (junior grade),** the former ranking next below a lieutenant commander and the latter next above an ensign. **3.** one deputized to perform the duties of a superior. [ME] —**lieu·ten'an·cy** *n.*

lieutenant colonel *Mil.* an officer ranking next above a major and next below a colonel.

lieutenant commander *Naval* an officer ranking next above a lieutenant and next below a commander.

lieutenant general *Mil.* an officer ranking next above a major general.

lieutenant governor an elected official who performs the duties of the governor of a state when the governor is absent or disabled or when the governor resigns or dies.

life (līf) *n. pl.* **lives** (līvz) **1.** the form of existence that distinguishes animals and plants from inorganic substances and dead organisms, characterized by metabolism, growth, reproduction, etc. **2.** existence regarded as a desirable condition: *life,* liberty, and the pursuit of happiness. **3.** living organisms collectively. **4.** a living being; person: save a *life.* **5.** the period of an individual's existence between birth and death; also, a specified portion of this period. **6.** a biography. **7.** the period during which something continues to be effective, useful, etc.: the *life* of an engine. **8.** manner of existence; characteristic activities, as of a specified group, locality, etc.: city *life.* **9.** energetic force; animation: full of *life.* —**bring to life. 1.** make vital; animate. **2.** recall vividly to the mind or senses. —**come to life 1.** regain consciousness. **2.** become animated. **3.** seem to be real or alive. —**take life** kill. [ME *lif*] —**life'less** *adj.*

life belt a life preserver in the form of a belt.

life·blood (LĪF BLUD) *n.* **1.** the blood necessary to life. **2.** anything indispensable to existence; vital force.

life·boat (LĪF BOHT) *n.* a boat, usu. carried on board a larger vessel, for saving lives at sea.

life buoy a life preserver, often in the form of a ring.

life·guard (LĪF GAHRD) *n.* an expert swimmer employed at a beach, etc., to protect the safety of bathers.

life jacket a life preserver in the form of a jacket or vest.

life·like (LĪF LIK) *adj.* **1.** resembling actual

life. **2.** accurately representing a person or thing.

life•line (LĪF LIN) *n.* **1.** a rope affording support to those in precarious situations. **2.** any route used for transporting vital supplies.

life•long (LĪF LAWNG) *adj.* lasting through life.

life preserver a buoyant device, either inflatable or filled with cork, kapok, etc., used to keep afloat those in danger of drowning.

life raft a raftlike structure used as a rescue craft; esp., an inflatable rubber boat.

life•sav•er (LĪF SAY vər) *n.* **1.** one who saves, or is trained to save, another's life. **2.** one who or that which provides aid, relief, etc. in time of need. **—life′sav′ing** *n. & adj.*

life-size (LĪF SĪZ) *adj.* having the same size as the thing or person portrayed. Also **life′ -sized′.**

life span the extreme length of life regarded as biologically possible in an organism or the group to which it belongs.

life•time (LĪF TĪM) *n.* **1.** the period of animate existence. **2.** the period of effective functioning: the *lifetime* of the car.

lift (lift) *v.t.* **1.** take hold of and raise to a higher place or position; hoist. **2.** move, direct, or cause to rise to a higher position or level. **3.** hold up. **4.** bring to a higher or more desirable degree or condition; exalt. **5.** perform surgery on (the face) to remove signs of age. **6.** *Informal* take surreptitiously; steal; also, plagiarize. **—v.i. 7.** exert effort in attempting to raise something. **8.** become dispersed or move away by or as by rising: the fog *lifted.* **—n. 1.** the act of lifting or raising. **2.** the ability to lift or impart upward motion. **3.** the distance or degree to which something is raised. **4.** a ride given to a traveler by a motorist. **5.** a feeling of exaltation, exhilaration, or well-being. **6.** a machine or device used in lifting or hoisting. **7.** any of the layers of leather etc. constituting the heel of a shoe. **8.** *Aeron.* the component of aerodynamic forces acting on an aircraft, exerted perpendicular to the relative wind and generally opposing the pull of gravity. [ME *liften*]

lift•off (LIFT AWF) *n. Aerospace* the initial vertical ascent of a rocket or spacecraft from its launch pad.

lig•a•ment (LIG ə mənt) *n. Anat.* a band of firm, fibrous tissue forming a connection between bones, or supporting an organ. [ME]

li•gate (LĪ gayt) *v.t.* **•gat•ed, •gat•ing** bind or constrict with a ligature. [< L *ligatus* tied] **—li•ga′tion** *n.*

lig•a•ture (LIG ə chər) *n.* **1.** the act of tying up or constricting by binding. **2.** a band, strip, etc., used to tie, bind, or constrict. **3.** in printing, a character consisting of two or more connected letters, as œ. [ME]

light[1] (līt) *n.* **1.** *Physics* **a** the form of radiant energy that makes vision possible. **b** a form of radiant energy not stimulating human vision; ultraviolet or infrared light. **2.** the condition or medium that makes vision possible; illumination. **3.** any source of brightness, as a lamp, the sun, etc. **4.** an emission of brightness, esp. from a particular source or direction. **5.** daylight; also, the period of daylight. **6.** a mental or spiritual understanding or insight. **7.** a way of being regarded; aspect: see things in a new *light.* **8.** *pl.* ability and understanding: live according to one's own *lights.* **9.** an instance of kindling; ignition. **10.** an opening admitting illumination, as a window. **11.** a person of authority or eminence; luminary: a lesser *light.* **—in (the) light of** in view of; considering. **—see the light 1.** come into being. **2.** be presented to public notice. **3.** become enlightened. **—adj. 1.** full of light; bright. **2.** diluted or combined with white, as a color; pale. **—v. light•ed** or **lit, light•ing** *v.t.* **1.** ignite; kindle. **2.** illuminate or cause to illuminate. **3.** make bright, cheerful, animated, etc. **4.** guide or conduct with light. **—v.i. 5.** become ignited. **6.** become luminous, radiant, or bright: often with *up.* [ME] **—light′ness** *n.*

light[2] *adj.* **•er, •est 1.** having little weight; not heavy. **2.** having little weight in proportion to bulk or size. **3.** having less than standard or correct weight. **4.** not burdensome or oppressive. **5.** not difficult or arduous. **6.** having comparatively little effect; not intense, severe, etc. **7.** not great in degree or concentration; thin: *light* fog. **8.** exerting little force or pressure; gentle: a *light* tap. **9.** not clumsy, coarse, or massive in form or appearance; delicate. **10.** intended or enjoyed as entertainment: *light* verse. **11.** slight in importance or consequence. **12.** morally unrestrained; wanton. **13.** slightly faint or delirious; giddy. **14.** easily eaten or digested. **15.** comparatively low in alcoholic content: *light* wines. **16.** *Mil.* designating the less massive types of weapons or equipment. **—make light of** treat or consider as trifling. **—v.i. light•ed** or **lit, light•**

ing 1. descend and settle down after flight, as a bird. **2.** happen or come, as by chance: with *on* or *upon*. —**light into** *Informal* attack; assail. —**light out** *Slang* depart in haste. —*adv.* **1.** lightly. **2.** without encumbrance or excess equipment. [ME] — **light′ness** *n.*

light·en[1] (LĪT n) *v.t.* **1.** make light or bright; illuminate. —*v.i.* **2.** become light; grow brighter. **3.** emit or display lightning. [ME *lighten*]

light·en[2] *v.t.* **1.** reduce the weight or load of; make less heavy. **2.** make less oppressive, troublesome, etc.; diminish the severity of. **3.** relieve, as of distress, uneasiness, etc. — *v.i.* **4.** become less heavy. [ME *lighten*]

light·er[1] (LĪ tər) *n.* one who or that which lights; esp., a device used to light cigarettes, cigars, etc.

light·er[2] *n. Naut.* a bargelike vessel used in loading or unloading ships, or in transporting loads for short distances.

light·face (LĪT FAYS) *n. Printing* type having characters formed of light thin lines.

light-fin·gered (LĪT FING ərd) *adj.* expert at picking pockets etc.

light-foot·ed (LĪT FUUT id) *adj.* **1.** stepping with buoyancy and grace. **2.** running lightly and swiftly.

light-head·ed (LĪT HED id) *adj.* **1.** frivolous; giddy. **2.** dizzy.

light-heart·ed (LĪT HAHR tid) *adj.* free from care; blithe; gay. —**light′heart′ed·ly** *adv.*

light·house (LĪT HOWS) *n.* a tower or similar structure equipped with a powerful beacon, erected at or near a dangerous place to serve as a warning or guide for ships.

light·ing (LĪ ting) *n.* **1.** the providing of light or the state of being lighted. **2.** a system or apparatus supplying illumination, as in a public building, theater, etc. **3.** the arrangement or effect of lighted areas in a painting etc.

light·ly (LĪT lee) *adv.* **1.** with little weight or pressure; gently. **2.** to a slight degree; moderately. **3.** with a swift, buoyant step or motion. **4.** in a carefree manner or spirit. **5.** with insufficient seriousness or concern; frivolously: often with the negative.

light·ning (LĪT ning) *n.* a sudden flash of light caused by the discharge of atmospheric electricity between electrified regions of cloud, or between a cloud and the earth. [ME]

lightning rod a metal rod that protects

buildings from lightning by grounding it harmlessly through a cable.

lights (līts) *n.pl.* the lungs, esp. of animals used as food. [ME *lihtes*]

light·ship (LĪT SHIP) *n.* a vessel equipped with warning lights, signals, etc., and moored in dangerous waters as a guide to ships.

light·weight (LĪT WAYT) *n.* **1.** a person or animal of much less than average weight. **2.** a boxer or wrestler weighing between 126 and 135 pounds. **3.** *Informal* an unimportant, incompetent, or inadequate person. —*adj.* of less than average or required weight.

light-year (LĪT YEER) *n. Astron.* a unit of interstellar space measurement equal to the distance traversed by light in one year, approximately six trillion miles.

lig·nite (LIG nīt) *n.* a soft coal, often retaining a wood-like structure.

lik·a·ble (LĪ kə bəl) *adj.* of a nature to be liked; attractive; pleasing. Also **like′a·ble.**

like[1] (līk) *v.* **liked, lik·ing** *v.t.* **1.** take pleasure in; enjoy. **2.** feel affectionately toward; be fond of. **3.** desire; prefer: I *like* that one. —*v.i.* **4.** feel disposed; choose: Do as you *like*. —*n. Usu. pl.* preference; inclination. [ME *lic*]

like[2] *prep.* **1.** having a close resemblance to; similar to. **2.** with the characteristics or qualities of: smell *like* a rose. **3.** characteristic or typical of: How *like* him to behave that way! **4.** indicative of; likely to result in: It looks *like* rain. **5.** such as: a city *like* London. **6.** in the manner of: He used the board *like* a hammer. —*adj.* **1.** having the same or similar characteristics; related. **2.** equal or nearly equal; equivalent. **3.** similar to what is portrayed or represented, as a portrait. — *n.* **1.** anything similar or in the same category: preceded by *the:* physics, chemistry, and the *like*. **2.** one of equal value, standing, etc.: We will not see his *like* again. —*conj.* **1.** just as: It turned out *like* you said it would. **2.** as if: It looks *like* it's going to rain.

like·li·hood (LĪK lee HUUD) *n.* **1.** the state or quality of being probable; probability. **2.** something probable.

like·ly (LĪK lee) *adj.* **·li·er, ·li·est 1.** having or showing an apparent tendency or possibility: He is *likely* to go. **2.** seemingly about to happen; imminent; probable. **3.** apparently true; plausible; believable. **4.** suitable; appropriate: a *likely* spot. —*adv.* probably.

lik·en (LĪ kən) *v.t.* represent as similar; compare.

like·ness (LĪK nis) *n.* **1.** the state or quality of being like; resemblance. **2.** a pictorial representation; portrait; image. **3.** imitative form; guise.

like·wise (LĪK wīz) *adv.* **1.** moreover; also; too. **2.** in like manner; similarly.

lik·ing (LĪ king) *n.* **1.** feeling of attraction or affection; fondness. **2.** preference; taste.

Lil·li·pu·tian (LIL i PYOO shən) *adj.* extremely small; miniature or minute. [< *Lilliput*, in Swift's *Gulliver's Travels*]

lilt (lilt) *n.* **1.** a lively quality of speech, voice, song, etc. with pronounced variations of pitch. **2.** a light, buoyant motion or manner. —*v.i. & v.t.* speak, sing, move, etc. in a cheerful rhythmic manner. [ME *lulte*]

limb (lim) *n.* **1.** a part of the animal or human body attached to but distinct from the torso, as an arm, leg, or wing. **2.** one of the major divisions of a tree trunk; a large branch. **3.** an extended or branching part, division, etc. —**out on a limb** in a risky, vulnerable, or questionable position. [ME *lim*] —**limb′less** *adj.*

limbed (limd) *adj.* **1.** having limbs. **2.** having or characterized by a (specified kind of) limb or (a specified number of) limbs: used in combination: *strong-limbed; short-limbed.*

lim·ber (LIM bər) *adj.* **1.** pliant; flexible. **2.** able to bend or move easily; lithe. —*v.t.* **1.** make pliant. —*v.i.* **2.** exercise so as to become limber: with *up.*

lim·bo[1] (LIM boh) *n. pl.* **·bos 1.** *Theol.* a place for the souls of the righteous who died before the coming of Christ, and those of infants who die before baptism. **2.** a place or condition for unwanted or forgotten persons, things, etc. **3.** a vague state or condition. [ME]

lim·bo[2] *n. pl.* **·bos** a West Indian acrobatic dance in which the dancer passes face up under a bar placed at successively lower levels.

lime[1] (līm) *n.* a white, earthy substance, used in mortars and cements. —*v.t.* **limed, lim·ing** treat, mix, or spread with lime. [ME *līm*]

lime[2] *n.* **1.** a small, green, lemonlike citrus fruit whose juice is used for flavoring, in beverages, etc. **2.** the tree yielding this fruit. [< Sp. *lima*]

lime·light (LĪM līt) *n.* **1.** public attention or notice. **2.** a bright light used to illuminate a performer, stage area, etc., and originally produced by heating lime to incandescence.

lim·er·ick (LIM ər ik) *n.* a humorous verse of five lines. [after *Limerick*, Ireland]

lime·stone (LĪM stohn) *n.* a sedimentary rock used extensively in building, and yielding lime when burned.

lim·it (LIM it) *n.* **1.** the furthest extent, range, degree, etc. beyond which an activity, power, or function cannot or may not proceed: one's *limit* of endurance. **2.** *Usu. pl.* the boundaries or extent of a specified area. **3.** the greatest permissible amount. —**off limits** forbidden to a specified group, as soldiers, students, etc. —**the limit** *Informal* **1.** one who or that which tries one's patience, credulity, etc. to the utmost. **2.** to the utmost extent: usu. with *go.* —*v.t.* set bounds to; confine; restrict. [ME *lymyt*] —**lim′i·ta′tion** *n.* —**lim′it·less** *adj.*

lim·it·ed (LIM i tid) *adj.* **1.** confined within or defined by a limit or limits; restricted. **2.** falling short of fullness or impressiveness: a *limited* success. **3.** having powers restricted by constitutional law or authority, as a government. **4.** of a train, bus, etc., making few stops.

lim·ou·sine (LIM ə ZEEN) *n.* **1.** a large automobile or small bus, used esp. to convey passengers to and from an airport. **2.** any large, luxurious automobile, esp. one driven by a chauffeur. [< F]

limp[1] (limp) *v.i.* **1.** walk with a halting or irregular step, as with an injured leg or foot. **2.** progress in an irregular or labored manner. —*n.* the manner of walking of one who is lame. [OE *lemphealt* limping]

limp[2] *adj.* **·er, ·est 1.** lacking stiffness or firmness; flabby. **2.** lacking force or vigor; weak. —**limp′ly** *adv.* —**limp′ness** *n.*

lim·pid (LIM pid) *adj.* **1.** characterized by crystalline clearness; transparent. **2.** characterized by clarity, lucidity, or purity, as of style. [< L *limpidus* clear]

linch·pin (LINCH pin) *n.* **1.** a pin placed through the end of an axle in order to keep a wheel from sliding off. **2.** something that holds together the elements of a complex organization etc. Also **lynchpin.** [ME *lynspin*]

line[1] (līn) *n.* **1.** a continuous mark or indentation, as made with a pen, pencil, or pointed tool. **2.** any narrow band or strip resembling such a mark. **3.** a wrinkle or crease in the skin. **4.** a division or boundary between adjoining areas; border. **5.** a demarcation or limit separating contrasting concepts, kinds of behavior, etc. **6.** a row of persons or things. **7.** a chronological succession of persons: the royal *line*. **8.** a row of written or printed words. **9.** a single row of words forming a verse, as of a stanza. **10.** course of movement or progress; route: *line* of march. **11.** course of action, thought, or performance: a *line* of thought. **12.** *Often pl.* general plan or concept, as of form, content, etc.: a work on heroic *lines*. **13.** alignment; agreement; accord; bring into *line*. **14.** scope or field of activity, ability, etc. **15.** kind of work; occupation. **16.** merchandise of a particular sort. **17.** *pl.* the words of an actor's or performer's part. **18.** *Informal* a glib manner of speech intended to ingratiate or persuade. **19.** a pipe, conduit, or system of channels to convey liquids, gas, etc. **20.** in telephonic communication, etc.: **a** a wire or cable carrying power signals. **b** a connection or channel of communication: keep a *line* open. **21.** any system of public transportation over an established route or routes. **22.** the roadbed, track, or system of tracks of a railroad. **23.** a rope, string, cord, or the like, as used in fishing, measuring, etc. **24.** *Math.* the theoretical trace or course of a moving point, conceived of as having length, but no other dimension. **25.** *Mil.* a system of fortifications presenting an extended front. **26.** in football, the players positioned at the line of scrimmage. **—in line for** next in order for. **—out of line. 1.** not in conformity with accepted standards or practices. **2.** insubordinate; unruly. **—get a line on** *Informal* acquire information about. — **hold the line 1.** maintain a defense or opposition. **2.** wait while maintaining an open telephone connection. **3.** in football, prevent the opposing team from gaining ground. **—***v.* **lined, lin•ing** *v.t.* **1.** mark with lines. **2.** place in a line. **3.** form a row or line along; border. **—***v.i.* **4.** form a line; assume positions in a line: usually with *up.* **—line up 1.** form a line. **2.** bring into alignment. **3.** gather; marshal. [ME *ligne* cord]

line² *v.t.* **lined, lin•ing 1.** put a covering or facing on the inner surface of. **2.** constitute a covering or surface for: Tapestries *lined* the room. **3.** fill or stuff, as with money, food, etc. [ME *lynen*]

lin•e•age (LIN ee ij) *n.* **1.** line of descent from a progenitor. **2.** ancestry; family; stock. [ME *linage*]

lin•e•al (LIN ee əl) *adj.* **1.** being or occurring in the direct line of descent. **2.** pertaining to or based upon direct descent. **3.** consisting of lines; linear. [ME] **—lin′ e•al•ly** *adv.*

lin•e•a•ment (LIN ee ə mənt) *n. Often pl.* **1.** a facial contour or feature. **2.** a distinguishing characteristic.

lin•e•ar (LIN ee ər) *adj.* **1.** of or pertaining to a line or lines. **2.** involving or pertaining to length: *linear* measure. **3.** composed of lines. **4.** resembling a line. **—lin′e•ar•ly** *adv.*

line drive in baseball, a batted ball that travels in an approximately horizontal trajectory: also called *liner.*

line•man (LĪN mən) *n. pl.* **•men 1.** a person who installs or repairs telephone or electric power lines: also *linesman.* **2.** in football, any of the players normally positioned at the line of scrimmage.

lin•en (LIN ən) *n.* **1.** a fabric woven from the fibers of flax. **2.** articles or garments made of linen, cotton, etc.: bed *linen.* [ME] — **lin′en** *adj.*

line of scrimmage in football, the imaginary line on which the ball rests and along which the opposing linemen take position at the start of play.

lin•er¹ (LĪN ər) *n.* **1.** a ship or airplane operated by a transportation line. **2.** in baseball, a line drive.

lin•er² *n.* **1.** one who makes or fits linings. **2.** something used as a lining.

lines•man (LĪNZ mən) *n. pl.* **•men 1.** in certain games, as tennis, an official making decisions on play at the lines of the court. **2.** in football, the official marking the distances gained or lost in each play. **3.** a lineman (def. 1).

line•up (LĪN up) *n.* **1.** an arrangement of persons or things in a line. **2.** in sports, a list of the team members playing at the start of a game. **3.** in police work, a row of possible criminal suspects.

lin•ger (LING gər) *v.i.* **1.** stay on as if reluctant to leave. **2.** proceed in a slow manner; dawdle. **3.** pause or dwell with interest, pleasure, etc.: usu. with *over.* [ME *lengeren* delay]

lin•ge•rie (LAHN zhə RAY) *n.* women's light undergarments, nightgowns, etc. [< F]

lin•gua fran•ca (LING gwə FRANG kə) **1.**

any jargon or pidgin used as a commercial or trade language, as Pidgin English. **2.** a mixture of French, Spanish, Italian, Greek, and Arabic, spoken in Mediterranean ports. [< Ital., lit., language of the Franks]

lin·gual (LING gwəl) *adj.* of or pertaining to the tongue or a tonguelike part. [ME]

lin·guist (LING gwist) *n.* **1.** one who is fluent in several languages. **2.** a student of or specialist in linguistics.

lin·guis·tics (ling GWIS tiks) *n. (construed as sing.)* the scientific study of language. —**lin·guis'tic** *adj.* —**lin·guis'ti·cal·ly** *adv.*

lin·i·ment (LIN ə mənt) *n.* a liquid rubbed on the skin to relieve pain and stiffness. [ME]

lin·ing (LĪ ning) *n.* an inner surface or facing inserted in a garment, container, etc., as for protection, reinforcement, etc.; also, the material used.

link (lingk) *n.* **1.** one of the loops, rings, or interlocking parts constituting a chain. **2.** a single element in a series, sequence, or set: a weak *link* in his argument. **3.** that which joins or connects separate parts, concepts, etc. **4.** a single sausage. —*v.t. & v.i.* join or connect by or as by links; interlock; couple; unite. [ME *linke*]

link·age (LING kij) *n.* **1.** the act of linking, or the state of being linked. **2.** a system of links.

links (lingks) *n. (construed as pl.)* a golf course. [ME *lynkys* slopes]

link·up (LINGK UP) *n.* a joining together, as of machines, groups, interests.

lin·seed (LIN SEED) *n.* flaxseed. [ME *linsed*]

linseed oil a yellowish oil made from flaxseed and used as a drying agent in the preparation of oil paints etc.

lint (lint) *n.* **1.** bits of thread, fluff, etc. **2.** a downy substance used as a surgical dressing. [ME]

lin·tel (LIN tl) *n.* a horizontal part above the opening of a door or window, supporting the structure above it. [ME *lyntel* limit]

li·on (LĪ ən) *n.* **1.** a large, tawny or brownish gray carnivorous mammal of the cat family. ◆ Collateral adjective: *leonine.* **2.** one of noble courage, great strength, etc. **3.** a celebrity. —**the lion's share** the largest portion; an unduly large part. [ME] —**li'on·ess** (LĪ ə nis) *n.fem.*

li·on·heart·ed (LĪ ən HAHRT tid) *adj.* exceptionally brave.

li·on·ize (LĪ ə NĪZ) *v.t.* •**ized,** •**iz·ing** treat or regard as a celebrity. —**li'on·iz'er** *n.*

lip (lip) *n.* **1.** one of the two folds of flesh that bound the mouth and serve as organs of speech. **2.** a marginal part or structure resembling this. **3.** the flared edge of a pitcher, bell, etc. **4.** *Slang* brash and impudent talk. —**keep a stiff upper lip** maintain one's fortitude. —**smack one's lips** express anticipatory or remembered gusto; gloat. —*v.t.* **lipped, lip·ping** touch with the lips; apply the lips to. —*adj.* **1.** of, pertaining to, or applied to the lips. **2.** made or formed by the lips or a lip; labial. [ME *lippe*] —**lipped** (lipt) *adj.*

lip reading the interpretation of speech by watching the movement of the lips, as by the deaf. —**lip·read** (LIP REED) *v.t. & v.i.* •**read** (-RED), read·ing —**lip reader** *n.*

lip service insincere expression of assent, loyalty, etc.

liq·ue·fac·tion (LIK wə FAK shən) *n.* the process of liquefying, or the state of being liquid.

liq·ue·fy (LIK wə FĪ) *v.t. & v.i.* •**fied,** •**fy·ing** convert into or become liquid. [ME *lyquefyen*]

li·queur (li KUR) *n.* an alcoholic beverage usu. made by adding sugar syrup and flavoring to brandy: also called *cordial.* [< F]

liq·uid (LIK wid) *adj.* **1.** capable of flowing or of being poured. **2.** clear and flowing, as sounds. **3.** free and facile, as movement; fluent. **4.** consisting of or readily converted into cash. **5.** *Physics* not gaseous or solid. —*n.* a substance in that state in which the molecules move freely among themselves but remain in one mass; a fluid that is not a gas. [ME *liquyd*] —**li·quid·i·ty** (li KWID i tee) *n.*

liq·ui·date (LIK wi DAYT) *v.* •**dat·ed,** •**dat·ing** *v.t.* **1.** pay off or settle, as an obligation or debt. **2.** wind up the affairs of (a business firm, etc.) by using the assets to settle debts. **3.** convert into cash, as securities. **4.** kill or murder. —*v.i.* **5.** settle one's debts. [< LL *liquidatus* melted] —**liq'ui·da'tion** *n.*

liquid oxygen oxygen liquefied by a reduction of temperature and an increase of pressure, used as an oxidizer in rocket fuels: also called *lox.*

liq·uor (LIK ər) *n.* **1.** any alcoholic beverage; esp., distilled spirits, as whiskey, brandy, etc. **2.** a liquid such as broth, juice, etc. —*v.t. Informal* ply with alcoholic drink: usu. with *up*. [ME *licour*]

lisp (lisp) *n.* a speech defect or affectation in which the sibilants (s) and (z) are articulated like (th) in *thank* and (th) in *this*. —*v.t. & v.i.* **1.** pronounce with a lisp. **2.** speak in a childlike manner. [ME *wlispen*] —**lisp′er** *n.*

lis•some (LIS əm) *adj.* **1.** flexible; pliant. **2.** agile; lithe. Also **lis′som.**

list[1] (list) *n.* **1.** an itemized series of names, words, etc., usu. recorded in a set order. **2.** a classification of persons or things belonging in the same category. —*v.t.* **1.** place on or in a list. **2.** include in a register, catalog, etc. [< Ital. *lista* list of names]

list[2] *v.t. & v.i. Naut.* of a vessel, lean or tilt to one side. —*n.* a leaning to one side.

list[3] *Archaic v.t.* **1.** listen to; hear. —*v.i.* **2.** listen. [ME *listen*]

lis•ten (LIS ən) *v.i.* **1.** make conscious use of the sense of hearing; be attentive in order to hear. **2.** pay attention; give heed. **3.** be influenced or persuaded. [ME *listnen*] —**lis′ten•er** *n.*

list•ing (LIS ting) *n.* **1.** the act of one who or that which lists. **2.** an entry in a list. **3.** a list.

list•less (LIST lis) *adj.* languidly indifferent; apathetic. —**list′less•ness** *n.*

lit (lit) alternative past tense, past participle of LIGHT[1] and LIGHT[2].

lit•a•ny (LIT n ee) *n. pl.* **•nies 1.** *Eccl.* a liturgical form of prayer consisting of a series of supplications said by the clergy, with fixed responses by the congregation. **2.** any tiresome story, complaint, etc. that is frequently repeated. [< LL *litania*]

li•tchi (LEE chee) *n.* **1.** the edible fruit of a tree native to China, having a hard seed and sweet pulp within a thin, brittle shell: also **litchi nut. 2.** the tree itself. Also spelled *lichee.* [< Chinese *lizhi*]

li•ter (LEE tər) *n.* in the metric system, a measure of capacity equal to the volume of one kilogram of water at 4° C. and normal atmospheric pressure, or to 1.0567 liquid quarts. [< F *litre*]

lit•er•al (LIT ər əl) *adj.* **1.** restricted to the exact, stated meaning; not figurative: the *literal* sense of the Scriptures. **2.** following the exact words and order of an original: a *literal* translation. **3.** tending to recognize or accept stated meanings only; matter-of-fact. [ME] —**lit′er•al•ness** *n.*

lit•er•al•ly (LIT ər ə lee) *adv.* **1.** in a literal

manner; in the strictest sense. **2.** actually; really. **3.** in effect; virtually.

lit•er•ar•y (LIT ə RER ee) *adj.* **1.** of, pertaining to, or treating of literature. **2.** characteristic of or appropriate to literature. **3.** versed in or devoted to literature.

lit•er•ate (LIT ər it) *adj.* **1.** able to read and write. **2.** educated; cultured. **3.** literary. [ME] —**lit′er•a•cy** *n.*

lit•e•ra•ti (LIT ə RAH tee) *n.pl.* **1.** scholars. **2.** literate or educated persons collectively. [< L]

lit•er•a•ture (LIT ər ə chər) *n.* **1.** written works collectively, esp. those of enduring importance, exhibiting creative imagination and artistic skill. **2.** poetry, fiction, essays, etc., as distinguished from factual writing. **3.** the writings pertaining to a particular subject. [ME *litterature*]

-lith *combining form* stone; rock. [< Gk. *lithos*]

lithe (lĭth) *adj.* bending easily or gracefully; supple. [ME *lith*] —**lithe′ness** *n.*

-lith•ic *combining form* pertaining to a (specified) anthropological stage in the use of stone implements: *Neolithic.*

lith•o•graph (LITH ə GRAF) *n.* a print produced by the process of lithography. —*v.t.* produce or reproduce by lithography. —**li•thog′ra•pher** (li THOG rə fər) *n.* —**lith′o•graph′ic** *adj.*

li•thog•ra•phy (li THOG rə fee) *n.* a process of printing from a flat stone or metal plate where the area to remain blank is treated with an ink-repellant material.

lith•o•sphere (LITH ə SFEER) *n.* the solid crust of the earth.

lit•i•gant (LIT ə gənt) *n.* a participant in a lawsuit.

lit•i•gate (LIT i GAYT) *v.* **•gat•ed, •gat•ing** *v.t.* **1.** bring (a dispute, claim, etc.) before a court of law for decision; contest at law. —*v.i.* **2.** engage in a lawsuit. —**lit′i•ga′tion** *n.* —**lit′i•ga′tor** *n.*

li•tig•ious (li TIJ əs) *adj.* **1.** inclined to litigation; quarrelsome. **2.** subject to litigation. **3.** of or pertaining to litigation. —**li•tig′ious•ly** *adv.* —**li•tig′ious•ness** *n.*

lit•mus (LIT məs) *n.* a blue dye that is turned red by acids and remains blue when treated with an alkali. [< ON *litmosi* a type of moss]

litmus paper paper dyed with litmus, used to test acidity.

lit•ter (LIT ər) *n.* **1.** waste materials, objects, etc., carelessly strewn about. **2.** untidy or chaotic condition; mess. **3.** the young brought forth at one birth by any mammal normally having several offspring at one time. **4.** a stretcher for carrying sick or wounded persons. **5.** a couch carried between shafts. **6.** straw, hay, etc., spread in animal pens, or over plants as protection. —*v.t.* **1.** make untidy or unsightly by carelessly discarding trash, etc. **2.** drop or scatter carelessly. —*v.i.* **3.** give birth to a litter of young. **4.** drop or scatter refuse. [ME *litere*]

lit•ter•bug (LIT ər BUG) *n.* one who litters public places with trash.

lit•tle (LIT l) *adj.* **lit•tler** or (for defs. 2 and 3) **less, lit•tlest** or (for defs. 2 and 3) **least 1.** small, or smaller compared to others, in physical size: a *little* house. **2.** not long; short; brief: a *little* time; a *little* distance away. **3.** small or relatively small in quantity or degree: *little* wealth; *little* probability. **4.** narrow or limited in viewpoint; petty: *little* minds. —*adv.* **less, least 1.** only slightly; not much: He sleeps *little*. **2.** not at all: used before a verb: She *little* suspects. —*n.* **1.** a small amount: Give me a *little*. **2.** an insignificant amount: *Little* can be done about it. —**little by little** by small degrees; gradually. [ME]

lit•to•ral (LIT ər əl) *adj.* of a shore or coastal region. —*n.* a shore and its adjacent areas. [< L *littoralis*]

lit•ur•gy (LIT ər jee) *n. pl.* **•gies** in various religions, the prescribed form for public worship; religious ritual. [< LL *liturgia* public worship] —**li•tur•gi•cal** (li TUR ji kəl) *adj.* —**lit'ur•gist** (LIT ər jist) *n.*

liv•a•ble (LIV ə bəl) *adj.* **1.** suitable or agreeable for living in. **2.** worth living; tolerable. **3.** agreeable, as for companionship. Also **live'a•ble.**

live¹ (liv) *v.* **lived, liv•ing** *v.i.* **1.** function as an animate organism; be alive. **2.** remain alive: as long as you *live*. **3.** remain or persist, as in the mind. **4.** remain valid or operative; endure. **5.** have as one's home; reside: with *in* or *at*. **6.** maintain or support oneself: with *on* or *by*: *live on* one's income. **7.** pass life in a specified manner: *live* in peace. **8.** enjoy a varied or satisfying life. —*v.t.* **9.** spend or pass (life, time, etc.). **10.** put into practice: *live* one's religion. —**live down** live or behave so as to expiate the memory of (an error, crime, etc.). —**live through** survive or withstand (an experience). —**live up to 1.** satisfy (an ideal, expectations,

etc.). **2.** fulfill (a bargain, obligation, etc.). [ME *liven*]

live² (līv) *adj.* **liv•er, liv•est 1.** functioning as an animate organism; alive. **2.** pertaining to, characteristic of, or abounding in life. **3.** of present interest and importance: a *live* issue. **4.** forceful and energetic; dynamic. **5.** burning or glowing: *live* coals. **6.** charged with electricity: a *live* wire. **7.** capable of being detonated, as a bomb. **8.** in television, radio, etc., performed by persons present at the time of transmission. **9.** in sports, being in play, as a ball.

lived (līvd) *adj.* having a (specified kind of) life or life span: used in combination: *long-lived*.

live-in (LIV IN) *adj.* residing at one's place of employment: *live-in* help.

live•li•hood (LĪV lee HUUD) *n.* a means of supporting or maintaining one's existence. [ME *livelod*]

live•long (LIV LAWNG) *adj.* long or seemingly long in passing; entire: the *livelong* day. [ME *lefe longe*]

live•ly (LĪV lee) *adj.* **•li•er, •li•est 1.** full of vigor or motion; energetic. **2.** arousing activity or excitement: a *lively* tune. **3.** striking and forceful to the mind: a *lively* impression. **4.** invigorating; brisk: a *lively* breeze. —*adv.* in a lively manner; briskly: now usu. in the expression **step lively**, hurry up. [ME] —**live'li•ness** *n.*

liv•en (LĪV ən) *v.t. & v.i.* make or become lively or cheerful: often with *up*.

liv•er¹ (LIV ər) *n.* **1.** *Anat.* the glandular organ of vertebrates, secreting bile and active in metabolism. **2.** a similar digestive gland in invertebrates. **3.** food consisting of or prepared from the liver of certain animals. [ME]

liv•er² *n.* **1.** one who lives in a specified manner: a high *liver*. **2.** a dweller.

liv•er•ied (LIV ə reed) *adj.* dressed in livery (def.1).

liv•er•wurst (LIV ər WURST) *n.* a sausage made primarily of liver. [< G *Leberwurst*]

liv•er•y (LIV ə ree) *n. pl.* **•er•ies 1.** the distinctive clothing or uniform worn by male household servants. **2.** the stabling and care of horses for pay. **3.** a livery stable. [ME *livere*]

livery stable a stable where horses and vehicles are cared for or kept for hire.

lives (līvz) plural of LIFE.

live•stock (LĪV STOK) *n.* domestic farm animals, as cattle, esp. when raised for profit.

live wire *Informal* an energetic, enterprising person; a go-getter.

liv·id (LIV id) *adj.* **1.** having the skin abnormally discolored, as: **a** flushed, purplish, etc., as from intense emotion. **b** black-and-blue, as from contusion. **2.** having a leaden pallor; bluish gray. **3.** furious; enraged. [< F *livide*]

liv·ing (LIV ing) *adj.* **1.** alive; animate; not dead. **2.** of or characteristic of everyday life: *living* conditions. **3.** used or intended for maintaining existence: a *living* wage. **4.** having contemporary value, force, or application: *living* languages. —*n.* **1.** the state of one who or that which lives. **2.** manner or conduct of life: clean *living*. **3.** means of supporting existence; livelihood.

living room a room designed for the general use, social activities, etc. of a household.

liz·ard (LIZ ərd) *n.* **1.** any of various reptiles typically having long, scaly bodies, long tails, and four legs. **2.** leather made from the skin of a lizard. [ME *liserd*]

lla·ma (LAH mə) *n.* a ruminant of South America, having thick, woolly hair. [< Sp.]

lo (loh) *interj.* look! observe! [ME]

load (lohd) *n.* **1.** the weight or quantity placed on and sustained by a vehicle, bearer, surface, etc. **2.** a quantity borne or conveyed: often used in combination: *carload*. **3.** a cause of physical or mental strain; burden. **4.** *pl. Informal* an ample amount; lots: *loads* of time. **5.** *Electr.* the power delivered by a generating system. —**get a load of** *Slang* listen to or look at. —*v.t.* **1.** place a large quantity, burden, cargo, etc. upon. **2.** place or take (cargo, people, etc.) as on a conveyance. **3.** burden or oppress: often with *down*. **4.** charge (a firearm etc.) with explosive or ammunition. **5.** put film or a photographic plate into (a camera). **6.** make prejudicial: *load* the evidence. —*v.i.* **7.** put on or receive a load or cargo. **8.** charge a firearm, cartridge, etc. with ammunition. [ME *lode*]

load·ed (LOH did) *adj. Slang* **1.** wealthy. **2.** intoxicated.

load·stone (LOHD stohn) see LODE-STONE.

loaf[1] (lohf) *v.i.* **1.** loiter lazily or aimlessly. **2.** shirk or dawdle over one's work. —*v.t.* **3.** spend (time) idly: with *away*.

loaf[2] *n. pl.* **loaves** (lohvz) **1.** a rounded or elongated mass of bread baked in a single piece. **2.** any shaped mass of food, as of ground meat. [ME *lof* bread]

loaf·er (LOH fər) *n.* **1.** one who loafs; an idler or slacker. **2.** a casual shoe resembling a moccasin.

loam (lohm) *n.* loose-textured soil consisting of a mixture of sand, clay, and organic matter. [ME *lome*] —**loam′y** *adj.*

loan (lohn) *n.* **1.** something lent; esp., a sum of money lent at interest. **2.** the act of lending: the *loan* of a car. —*v.t. & v.i.* make a loan. [ME *lone*]

loath (lohth) *adj.* strongly disinclined; reluctant; unwilling: often followed by *to*. Also spelled *loth*. [ME *loth*]

loathe (lohth) *v.t.* **loathed, loath·ing** feel great hatred or disgust for; abhor; detest. [ME *lothien*]

loath·ing (LOH thing) *n.* extreme dislike; abhorrence. —**loath′ing·ly** *adv.*

loath·some (LOHTH səm) *adj.* causing revulsion; repulsive. —**loath′some·ness** *n.*

loaves (lohvz) plural of LOAF.

lob (lob) *v.t.* **lobbed, lob·bing** pitch or strike (a ball etc.) in a high, arching curve. —*n.* in tennis, a stroke that sends the ball high into the air. [ME]

lo·bar (LOH bahr) *adj.* of or pertaining to a lobe, as of the lungs. [< NL *lobaris*]

lob·by (LOB ee) *n. pl.* **·bies 1.** an entrance hall, vestibule, or public lounge in an apartment house, theater, etc. **2.** a group representing persons or organizations with a common interest that attempts to influence the votes of legislators. —*v.i.* **·bied, ·by·ing** attempt to influence legislators in favor of some interest. [< Med.L *lobia* a covered way] —**lob′by·ist** *n.*

lobe (lohb) *n.* **1.** a rounded division, protuberance, or part, as of a leaf. **2.** the soft lower part of the human ear. **3.** *Anat.* any of several well-defined portions of an organ or part of the body, as of the brain. [< Med.L *lobus*] —**lobed** *adj.*

lo·bot·o·my (lə BOT ə mee) *n. pl.* **·mies** *Surg.* the cutting into a lobe of the brain, esp. to relieve a mental disorder.

lo·cal (LOH kəl) *adj.* **1.** pertaining to, characteristic of, or confined to a relatively small area. **2.** of or pertaining to a particular place or position in space: *local* time. **3.** stopping at all stations along its run, as a train. **4.** *Med.* relating to or affecting a specific part of the body. —*n.* **1.** a branch or chapter of an organization, as a trade union. **2.** a bus, train, etc. that stops at all stations. [ME] —**lo′cal·ly** *adv.*

lo·cale (loh KAL) *n.* **1.** a place or locality,

esp. with reference to some event or circumstance. **2.** the setting of a literary, dramatic, or artistic work; scene. [< F]

lo·cal·ism (LOH kə LIZ əm) *n.* a word, meaning of a word, pronunciation, etc. peculiar to a locality.

lo·cal·i·ty (loh KAL i tee) *n. pl.* **·ties 1.** a place, region, etc. **2.** position, esp. in relation to surroundings. [< LL *localitas*]

lo·cal·ize (LOH kə LIZ) *v.t.* **·ized, ·iz·ing 1.** make local; confine or assign to a specific area. **2.** determine the place of origin of.

lo·cate (loh KAYT) *v.* **·cat·ed, ·cat·ing** *v.t.* **1.** discover the position of; find. **2.** establish or place at a particular site: The store is *located* on the corner. **3.** place hypothetically as to setting etc. —*v.i.* **4.** settle. [< L *locatus* placed] —**lo·cat'a·ble** *adj.*

lo·ca·tion (loh KAY shən) *n.* **1.** the act of locating, or the state of being located. **2.** a site or situation, esp. considered in regard to its surroundings. **3.** exact position or place occupied. **4.** a motion picture or television locale away from the studio: usu. in **be on location.**

loch (lok) *n. Scot.* a lake; arm of the sea.

lo·ci (LOH sī) plural of LOCUS.

lock¹ (lok) *n.* **1.** a mechanical fastening device having a bolt secured or released by a key, dial, etc., and used to prevent unauthorized entry, access, or operation. **2.** a section of a canal enclosed, etc. bounded by gates, within which the water depth may be raised or lowered. **3.** the mechanism that explodes the charge of a gun. **4.** an interlocking, fastening, or jamming together of parts. **5.** a wrestling grip or hold. —*v.t.* **1.** fasten or secure by means of a lock. **2.** keep, confine, etc. in or as in a locked enclosure: with *in, up,* or *away.* **3.** fit together securely; interlock. **4.** clasp or grip in or as in a firm hold. —*v.i.* **5.** become locked. **6.** become firmly joined or interlocked. —**lock out 1.** prevent (employees) from working by closing a factory, shop, etc. **2.** keep out by locking. [ME]

lock² *n.* **1.** strands of hair forming a curl. **2.** *pl.* the hair of the head. [ME *locke*]

lock·er (LOK ər) *n.* **1.** a closet, cabinet, storage space, etc., fastened with a lock, as: **a** one of a series of metal cabinets, as in a gymnasium, in which clothes, equipment, etc. are kept. **b** a cabinet in which frozen foods are kept. **2.** a chest etc., as on a ship, in which equipment or personal belongings are kept.

lock·et (LOK it) *n.* a small ornamental case for enclosing a picture or keepsake, usu. worn on a chain, ribbon, etc. around the neck. [ME *lokat* latch]

lock·out (LOK OWT) *n.* the closing of a place of business by an employer in order to influence striking employees.

lock·smith (LOK SMITH) *n.* a maker or repairer of locks.

lo·co·mo·tion (LOH kə MOH shən) *n.* the act or power of moving from one place to another.

lo·co·mo·tive (LOH kə MOH tiv) *n.* an engine that moves by its own power, used to pull trains on a railroad. —*adj.* of, pertaining to, or used in locomotion.

lo·cus (LOH kəs) *n. pl.* **·ci** (-sī) **1.** a place; locality; area. **2.** *Math.* a surface or curve regarded as traced by a line or point moving under specified conditions. [< L]

lo·cust¹ (LOH kəst) *n.* **1.** any of a family of winged insects resembling grasshoppers, including those of migratory habits that destroy vegetation. **2.** a cicada. [ME]

lo·cust² *n.* **1.** a tree of North America, having compound leaves and clusters of fragrant white flowers. **2.** the wood of this tree. [ME]

lo·cu·tion (loh KYOO shən) *n.* **1.** a verbal expression or phrase. **2.** manner of speech or expression. [ME]

lode (lohd) *n. Mining* **1.** a deposit of metallic ore filling fissures in native rock. **2.** any deposit of ore located between definite boundaries of associated rock; vein. [ME]

lode·stone (LOHD STOHN) *n.* **1.** magnetite that possesses polarity. **2.** something that attracts by or as by magnetism. Also spelled *loadstone.*

lodge (loj) *n.* **1.** a local branch of a fraternal society; also, the meeting place of such a society. **2.** a small hut, cabin, etc., esp. one used as a base for outdoor activity. **3.** an inn, motel, etc. **4.** a small house on the grounds of an estate etc. **5.** the characteristic den of certain animals, as beavers. —*v.* **lodged, lodg·ing** *v.t.* **1.** furnish with temporary quarters; house. **2.** serve as a shelter or dwelling for. **3.** place or implant firmly, as by thrusting or inserting. **4.** deposit for safekeeping or storage. **5.** submit or enter (a complaint etc.) formally. **6.** confer or invest (power etc.): usu. with *in* or *with.* —*v.i.* **7.** take temporary quarters. **8.** become fixed or embedded. [ME *logge*] —**lodg'er** *n.*

lodg·ing (LOJ ing) *n.* **1.** a temporary dwelling place. **2.** *pl.* living quarters in another's house.

loft (lawft) *n.* **1.** a floored space directly under a roof; attic. **2.** a large, open workroom or storeroom on an upper story of a commercial building. **3.** a hayloft. **4.** an upper section or gallery, as in a church: the choir *loft.* —*v.t. & v.i.* strike (a ball) so that it travels in a high arc. [ME *lofte*]

loft·y (LAWF tee) *adj.* **loft·i·er, loft·i·est** **1.** having great or imposing height. **2.** elevated in character, quality, etc.; noble. **3.** arrogant; haughty. —**loft′i·ness** *n.*

log[1] (lawg) *n.* **1.** a section of a felled tree trunk, limb, etc. stripped of branches. **2.** *Naut.* **a** a record of the daily progress of a vessel and of the events of a voyage. **b** any of various devices for measuring the speed and mileage of a vessel. **3.** a record of operation or progress, as of an aircraft in flight. —*v.* **logged, log·ging** *v.t.* **1.** *Naut. & Aeron.* **a** enter in a logbook. **b** travel (a specified distance etc.). —*v.i.* **2.** engage in the operation of felling and transporting timber. [ME *logge*]

log[2] logarithm.

log·a·rithm (LAW gə RITH əm) *n.* *Math.* the power to which a fixed number, called the base, must be raised in order to produce a given number. [< NL *logarithmus*] —**log′a·rith′mic** *adj.*

log·book (LAWG buuk) *n.* the book in which the official record of a ship, aircraft, etc. is entered.

loge (lohzh) *n.* a box or a section in a theater. [< F]

log·ger (LAW gər) *n.* **1.** a person engaged in logging; lumberjack. **2.** a machine for hauling and loading logs.

log·ger·head (LAW gər HED) *n.* a blockhead. —**at loggerheads** engaged in a quarrel; unable to agree.

log·ging (LAW ging) *n.* the occupation of felling and transporting timber to a mill.

log·ic (LOJ ik) *n.* **1.** the science concerned with the principles of valid reasoning and correct inference. **2.** correct or sound reasoning. **3.** the apparently inevitable chain of events involved in an outcome etc. **4.** the principles governing the interconnection of electronic circuits for certain computer operations; also the circuits themselves. [ME *logik*] —**log′i·cal** *adj.* —**log′i·cal·ly** *adv.* —**lo·gi·cian** (loh JISH ən) *n.* one versed in logic.

lo·gis·tics (loh JIS tiks) *n.* (construed as

sing.) the branch of military science dealing with supplying, equipping, and moving troops. [< F *logistique* art of computing] —**lo·gis′tic** or **·ti·cal** *adj.*

log·roll (LAWG ROHL) *v.t.* obtain passage of (a bill) by logrolling. —*v.i.* engage in logrolling.

log·roll·ing (LAWG ROH ling) *n.* the trading of votes and influence between politicians; also, any such trading of help or approval for one's own benefit.

lo·gy (LOH gee) *adj.* **·gi·er, ·gi·est** dull; lethargic.

-logy *combining form* **1.** the science or study of. **2.** speech; discourse. [ME *-logie*]

loin (loin) *n.* **1.** *Usu. pl.* the part of the back and flanks between the lower ribs and the hipbone. **2.** *pl.* the lower back, thighs, and groin. **3.** a cut of meat from the hindquarters of beef, lamb, etc. —**gird (up) one's loins** prepare for action. [ME *loyne*]

loin·cloth (LOIN KLAWTH) *n.* a strip of cloth worn about the loins and hips.

loi·ter (LOI tər) *v.i.* **1.** linger idly or aimlessly; loaf. **2.** dawdle. —*v.t.* **3.** pass (time) idly: with *away.* [ME *loteren*] —**loi′ter·er** *n.*

loll (lol) *v.i.* **1.** lie or lean in a relaxed or languid manner; lounge. **2.** hang loosely; droop. —*v.t.* **3.** permit to droop or hang, as the tongue. —*n.* a person who lolls. [ME *lollen*] —**loll′er** *n.*

lol·li·pop (LOL ee POP) *n.* a lump of candy on the end of a stick: also spelled **lol·ly·pop.**

lone (lohn) *adj.* **1.** being without companions; solitary. **2.** isolated. **3.** only; sole. [ME]

lone·ly (LOHN lee) *adj.* **·li·er, ·li·est** **1.** unfrequented by human beings; deserted; desolate. **2.** sad from lack of companionship or sympathy; lonesome. **3.** characterized by or inducing loneliness. —**lone′li·ness** *n.*

lon·er (LOH nər) *n.* one who prefers to work, live, etc. alone. Also **lone wolf.**

lone·some (LOHN səm) *adj.* **1.** depressed or uneasy because of being alone; lonely; forlorn. **2.** inducing a feeling of loneliness. **3.** unfrequented; secluded: a *lonesome* retreat.

long[1] (lawng) *adj.* **1.** being great in proportion to width; not short. **2.** having relatively great duration in time; prolonged. **3.** being extended: a *long* tunnel. **4.** being of a specified measurement in extent or duration: ten miles *long;* three hours *long.* **5.** having more than the usual: a *long* ton, a *long* play. **6.**

slow; tedious. **7.** well supplied: *long on excuses.* **8.** in gambling, denoting odds indicating little likelihood of winning. **9.** *Phonet.* denoting the vowel sounds of *Dane, dean, dine, dome, dune* as contrasted with the short vowels of *Dan, den, din, don, duck.* **10.** in prosody, stressed, as in English verse. —*adv.* **1.** for an extensive period of time: *Will he stay long?* **2.** for a time or period (to be specified): *How long will he stay?* **3.** for the entire duration (of a specified period): *all day long.* **4.** at a considerably distant time: *long after midnight.* —**as** (or **so**) **long as 1.** for or during the time that. **2.** inasmuch as; since. —*n.* a long syllable or sound, as in phonetics, prosody, etc. —**before long** soon. [ME *longe*] **Long,** meaning "for a long time," is a combining form, as in: **long-accustomed, long-lived, long-delayed.**

long[2] *v.i.* have a strong or eager desire; wish earnestly; yearn. [ME *longen*]

long·bow (LAWNG BOH) *n.* a large bow drawn by hand and projecting long, feathered arrows.

long distance telephone service that handles calls outside the immediate locality.

long·dis·tance (LAWNG DIS təns) *adj.* connecting or covering relatively long distances or places. —*adv.* **1.** by long-distance telephone. **2.** at or to a distance.

long division arithmetical division, usu. with large numbers in which all the steps of the process are shown.

long-drawn-out (LAWNG DRAWN OWT) *adj.* prolonged; protracted. Also **drawn'-out'.**

lon·gev·i·ty (lon JEV i tee) *n.* **1.** great age or length of life. **2.** the tendency to live long. [< L *longaevitas*]

long·ing (LAWNG ing) *n.* a strong, earnest, persistent craving; desire. —**long'ing** *adj.* —**long'ing·ly** *adv.*

lon·gi·tude (LON ji TOOD) *n. Geog.* distance east or west on the earth's surface, usu. measured by the angle that the meridian through a particular place makes with the prime meridian, which runs through Greenwich, England. [ME] —**lon·gi·tu·di·nal** (LON ji TOOD n l) *adj.* —**lon'gi·tu'di·nal·ly** *adv.*

long-lived (LAWNG LIVD) *adj.* having a long life or period of existence.

long-play·ing (LAWNG PLAY ing) *adj.* see **LP.**

long-range (LAWNG RAYNJ) *adj.* **1.** designed to shoot or move over distances. **2.** taking account of, or extending over, a long span of future time: *long-range* plans.

long·shore·man (LAWNG SHOR mən) *n. pl.* **·men** a laborer employed on the waterfront to load and unload cargo.

long shot in betting, a gambling choice backed at great odds and having little chance of winning. —**not by a long shot** decidedly not.

long·stand·ing (LAWNG STAN ding) *adj.* having existed over a long period: a *longstanding* debt.

long-suf·fer·ing (LAWNG SUF ər ing) *adj.* patiently enduring injuries, misfortune, etc. for a long time.

long-term (LAWNG TURM) *adj.* involving or extending over a relatively long period of time: a *long-term* contract.

long-time (LAWNG TIM) *adj.* being such for a considerable period of time: a *long-time* friend.

long ton see under TON.

long-wind·ed (LAWNG WIN did) *adj.* tiresomely long in speaking or writing: a *long-winded* lecturer. —**long'-wind'ed·ness** *n.*

look (luuk) *v.i.* **1.** use one's sense of sight. **2.** turn the eyes in a specified direction. **3.** gaze so as to convey a specific feeling or meaning. **4.** use one's eyes in order to examine, repair, etc.: *Let's look* at the engine. **5.** seem: *He looks* reliable. **6.** face in a specified direction. —**look after** take care of. —**look alive** be alert or attentive. —**look down on** (or **upon**) regard with condescension or contempt: also **look down one's nose on** (or **upon**). —**look in** (or **in on**) make a short visit to. —**look into 1.** examine closely. **2.** make inquiries about. —**look out for 1.** protect. **2.** be on guard against. —**look the other way** ignore or avoid an unpleasant or unfavorable situation, sight, etc. —**look to 1.** attend to **2.** turn to, as for help, advice, etc. —**look up 1.** search for and find, as in a file, book, etc. **2.** discover the whereabouts of. **3.** improve; become better. —**look up to** have respect for. —*n.* **1.** the act of looking. **2.** a search, examination, etc. by or as by means of one's eyes. **3.** aspect or expression: a saintly *look.* **4.** *pl.* general appearance: I like the *looks* of this place. **5.** *pl.* personal appearance or attractiveness. —*interj.* **1.** see! **2.** listen! [ME *lōkien*] —**look'er** *n.*

look·ing glass a glass mirror.

look·out (LUUK owt) n. 1. the act of watching for someone or something. 2. a place where such a watch is kept. 3. the person or persons watching.

loom¹ (loom) v.i. 1. appear or come into view indistinctly, as through a mist. 2. appear to the mind as large or threatening.

loom² n. a machine on which thread or yarn is woven into fabric. [ME *lome* tool]

loon¹ (loon) n. a diving, fish-eating waterfowl, having a weird cry.

loon² n. a stupid or crazy person. [ME *lowen*]

loon·y (LOO nee) *Informal adj.* **loon·i·er, loon·i·est** 1. lunatic or demented. 2. foolish; erratic; silly. —n. pl. **·ies** an insane person. [< LUNATIC]

loop (loop) n. 1. a folding or doubling over of one end of a piece of thread, rope, wire, etc. so as to form an oval opening. 2. a ring or bent piece of metal, wood, thread, etc., serving as a fastener, staple, or the like. 3. something having or suggesting the shape of a loop. 4. *Aeron.* a complete circular turn made by an aircraft flying in a vertical plane. —v.t. 1. form a loop in or of. 2. fasten or encircle by means of a loop. 3. *Aeron.* fly (an aircraft) in a loop or loops. —v.i. 4. make a loop or loops. —**loop the loop** make a vertical circular turn in the air, esp. in an aircraft. [ME *loupe*]

loop·hole (LOOP hohl) n. 1. a narrow slit in a wall, esp. one in a fortification. 2. an opportunity for escaping or evading something, as a law.

loose (loos) adj. **loos·er, loos·est** 1. not fastened; unattached. 2. not taut: a *loose* rein. 3. freed from restraint. 4. not firmly fitted or embedded. 5. not closely fitted, as clothing. 6. not bound or fastened together. 7. not compact, firm, or dense: *loose* soil. 8. not constricted; open: said of the bowels or a cough. 9. dissolute; unchaste. 10. lacking in exactness or precision: a *loose* translation. —**on the loose** 1. not confined; at large. 2. behaving in a free, uninhibited, and usu. dissolute manner. —adv. 1. in a loose manner; loosely. 2. so as to be or become loose: break *loose*. —**cut loose** behave in a free, uninhibited manner. —v.t. **loosed, loos·ing** 1. set free, as from bondage, penalty, etc. 2. untie or undo. 3. let fly; shoot, as an arrow. [ME *los*] —**loose′ly** adv. —**loose′ness** n.

loose end something left undecided or undone, as a task or decision. —**at loose ends**

1. in an unsettled state. 2. without a job, plans, etc.

loose-joint·ed (LOOS JOIN tid) adj. 1. having joints not tightly articulated. 2. limber or flexible in movement.

loose-leaf (LOOS LEEF) adj. having pages that are easily inserted or removed, as a notebook.

loos·en (LOO sən) v.t. 1. untie or undo, as bonds. 2. set free; release. 3. make less tight, firm, or compact. —v.i. 4. become loose or looser. [ME *loosnen*] —**loosen up** 1. relax. 2. talk with ease; talk freely. 3. give more generously, as money.

loot (loot) n. 1. goods taken as booty by a victorious army from a sacked city, enemy forces, etc. 2. anything unlawfully taken. 3. *Slang* money. —v.t. 1. plunder; pillage. —v.i. 2. engage in plundering. [< Hindi *lūt*] —**loot′er** n.

lop¹ (lop) v.t. **lopped, lop·ping** 1. cut or trim the branches, twigs, etc., from 2. cut off. —n. a part lopped off. [ME *loppe*] —**lop′per** n.

lop² v. **lopped, lop·ping** v.i. 1. droop or hang down loosely. 2. move about in an awkward manner. —v.t. 3. allow to droop or hang down loosely.

lope (lohp) v.t. & v.i. **loped, lop·ing** run or cause to run with a steady, swinging stride or gallop. —n. a slow, easy stride or gallop. [ME]

lop·sid·ed (LOP SĪ did) adj. heavier or sagging on one side. —**lop′sid·ed·ness** n.

lo·qua·cious (loh KWAY shəs) adj. characterized by continuous talking. —**lo·qua′cious·ly** adv.

lo·quac·i·ty (loh KWAS i tee) n. talkativeness. [< L *loquacitas*]

lord (lord) n. 1. one possessing great power and authority. 2. in Great Britain: **a** any one of the noblemen or peers having the title of marquis, earl, viscount, or baron. **b** any of the higher churchmen. 3. in feudal law, the owner of a manor. —**lord it (over)** act in a domineering or arrogant manner (toward). [ME]

Lord n. 1. God: preceded by *the* except in direct address. 2. Jesus Christ. 3. in Great Britain, a title of honor or nobility.

lord·ly (LORD lee) adj. **·li·er, ·li·est** 1. befitting the rank and position of a lord. 2. noble; dignified. 3. arrogant; haughty. —adv. in a lordly manner. —**lord′li·ness** n. —**lord′ship** n.

lore (lor) n. 1. the body of traditional, popular, often anecdotal knowledge about a particular subject: the *lore* of the woods. **2.** learning or erudition. [ME]

lor·gnette (lorn YET) *n.* **1.** a pair of eyeglasses with an ornamental handle. **2.** an opera glass with a long handle. [< F]

lose (looz) *v.* **lost, los·ing** *v.t.* **1.** be unable to find; mislay. **2.** fail to keep, control, or maintain: *lose* one's footing. **3.** be deprived of; suffer the loss of: *lose* a leg. **4.** fail to win. **5.** fail to take advantage of; miss. **6.** fail to keep in sight, memory, etc. **7.** occupy or absorb wholly; engross. **8.** squander; waste. **9.** cause (someone or something) to be or become lost. **10.** outdistance or elude. **11.** cause the loss of: His rashness *lost* the election. **12.** bring to destruction or death; ruin. —*v.i.* **13.** suffer loss. **14.** be defeated, as in battle or a contest. —**lose oneself** become engrossed or absorbed. —**lose out** fail or be defeated. —**lose out on** fail to secure; miss. [ME *losen*] —**los′er** *n.*

los·ing (LOO zing) *adj.* **1.** incurring loss: a *losing* business. **2.** not winning.

loss (laws) *n.* **1.** the act of losing or the state of being lost. **2.** one who or that which is lost. **3.** the harm, inconvenience, etc. caused by losing something or someone. **4.** *pl. Mil.* casualties. **5.** the amount by which cost exceeds selling price. —**at a loss** perplexed. [ME]

lost (lawst) *adj.* **1.** not to be found or recovered. **2.** no longer possessed, seen, or known: *lost* friends. **3.** not won, gained, or secured. **4.** having gone astray. **5.** bewildered; perplexed. **6.** not used or taken advantage of; wasted. **7.** destroyed; ruined. **8.** no longer known or practiced: a *lost* art. —**be lost in** be absorbed or engrossed in. —**be lost upon** (or **on**) have no effect upon.

lot (lot) *n.* **1.** that which is used in determining something by chance, as objects drawn at random from a container. **2.** the share or portion that comes to one as a result of drawing lots. **3.** one's portion in life as ascribed to chance, fate, custom, etc. **4.** a number of things or persons considered as a single group. **5.** a job lot. **6.** a plot or quantity of land: a parking *lot*. **7.** a type of person: He's a bad *lot*. **8.** *Often pl.* a great deal: *lots* of trouble. —**a lot** (or **lots**) very much: He is a *lot* better; *lots* better. —**the lot** the whole of a certain number or quantity: He bought *the lot*. —**cast** (or **draw**) **lots** come to a decision or solution by the use of lots. —**cast** (or **throw**) **in one's lot**

with join with and share the fortunes of. [ME]

loth (lohth) see LOATH.

lo·tion (LOH shən) *n.* a liquid preparation used for external cleansing of the skin, eyes, etc. [ME *locion* a washing]

lot·ter·y (LOT ə ree) *n. pl.* **·ter·ies** a drawing for prizes for which numbered tickets are sold, the winning tickets being selected by lot. [< MDu. *loterie*]

lo·tus (LOH təs) *n.* **1.** in Greek legend, a fruit inducing indolence and forgetfulness. **2.** any of various water plants having large floating leaves and showy flowers. [< L]

lo·tus-eat·er (LOH təs EE tər) *n.* anyone considered to be living an indolent, irresponsible existence.

loud (lowd) *adj.* **1.** having great volume or intensity of sound: *loud* thunder. **2.** emphatic or urgent; insistent: *loud* demands. **3.** crude; vulgar, as manners, persons, etc. **4.** excessively showy: a *loud* shirt. —*adv.* in a loud manner. [ME] —**loud′ly** *adv.* —**loud′ness** *n.*

loud-mouthed (LOWD mowTHd) *adj.* offensively clamorous or talkative. —**loud′mouth′** (-MOWTH) *n.*

loud·speak·er (LOWD SPEE kər) *n.* any of various devices for converting an electric current into sound, as in a radio.

lounge (lownj) *v.i.* **lounged, loung·ing 1.** recline, walk, etc. in a relaxed, lazy manner. **2.** pass time in doing nothing. —*n.* **1.** a couch or sofa. **2.** a room in a hotel, club, etc. suitable for lounging and often having facilities for drinking. **3.** the act of lounging; also, a period of lounging.

louse (lows) *n. pl.* **lice** (līs) **1.** a small, wingless insect living as an external parasite on some animals. **2.** any of various other parasitic insects. **3.** *Slang* a contemptible person. —*v.t. & v.i.* **loused, lous·ing** *Slang* ruin; bungle: with *up*. [ME *lous*]

lous·y (LOW zee) *adj.* **lous·i·er, lous·i·est 1.** infested with lice. **2.** *Informal* contemptible; mean; worthless; inferior. **3.** *Slang* having plenty (of): with *with: lousy* with money.

lou·ver (LOO vər) *n.* a narrow opening serving as an outlet for heated air. [ME *lover*] —**lou′·vered** *adj.*

lov·a·ble (LUV ə bəl) *adj.* worthy of love; amiable; also, evoking love. Also **love′a·ble.** —**lov′·a·bly** *adv.*

love (luv) *n.* **1.** a deep devotion or affection for another person or persons: *love* for one's children. **2.** a strong sexual passion for another person. **3.** sexual passion in general or the gratification of it. **4.** one who is beloved. **5.** a very great interest in, or enjoyment of, something; also, the thing so enjoyed. **6.** in tennis, a score of zero. —**in love** experiencing love for someone or something. —**make love 1.** kiss, embrace, etc. **2.** have sexual intercourse. —*v.* **loved, lov•ing** *v.t.* **1.** feel love or affection for. **2.** take pleasure or delight in: *love* good food. —*v.i.* **3.** be in love. [ME]

love•less (LUV lis) *adj.* having or receiving no love. —**love′less•ness** *n.*

love•lorn (LUV LORN) *adj.* pining for one's lover.

love•ly (LUV lee) *adj.* **•li•er, •li•est 1.** possessing qualities that inspire admiration or love. **2.** beautiful: a *lovely* rose. **3.** delightful; pleasing. [ME *luvelich*] —**love′li•ness** *n.*

love•mak•ing (LUV MAY king) *n.* the act of making love; also, wooing; courtship.

lov•er (LUV ər) *n.* **1.** one who loves: a *lover* of humanity. **2.** one in love with or making love to another. **3.** one who especially enjoys diversion, pursuit, etc.: a *lover* of golf. [ME]

lov•ing (LUV ing) *adj.* **1.** affectionate; devoted; kind. **2.** indicative of love.

loving cup an ornamental cup given as a trophy.

low[1] (loh) *adj.* **•er, •est 1.** having relatively little upward extension; not high or tall. **2.** located or placed below the normal or usual level: a *low* marsh. **3.** near the horizon: a *low* moon. **4.** pertaining to latitudes nearest the equator. **5.** relatively small in depth, height, amount, degree, etc. **6.** of or producing sounds of relatively long wavelengths: *low* pitch. **7.** not loud; faint: a *low* rustle. **8.** melancholy or sad; depressed: *low* spirits. **9.** lacking vigor; feeble. **10.** not adequately provided with; short of: be *low* on groceries. **11.** having little or no ready money. **12.** poor, unfavorable, or disparaging: have a *low* estimate of one's abilities. **13.** humble or inferior, as in origin, rank, position, etc. **14.** inferior in quality: a *low* grade of tobacco. **15.** vulgar or morally base. **16.** relatively simple in structure, function, or organization: a *low* form of animal life. **17.** opposed to ritualism: *low* church. —*adv.* **1.** in or to a low level, position, degree, etc. **2.** in a low manner. **3.** softly; quietly. **4.** with a low pitch. **5.** in or to

a humble, poor, or degraded condition. —*n.* **1.** a low level, position, degree, etc. **2.** *Meteorol.* an area of low barometric pressure. **3.** *Mech.* an arrangement of gears that yields a slow or the slowest output speed. [ME *lowe*]

low[2] *v.i.* **1.** make the low, bellowing sound of cattle; moo. —*v.t.* **2.** utter by lowing. —*n.* the vocal sound made by cattle: also **low′ing.** [ME *lowen*]

low•brow (LOH BROW) *n.* a person of uncultivated or vulgar tastes. —*adj.* (LOH BROW) of or suitable for such a person.

low•er[1] (LOW ər) *v.i.* **1.** look sullen; scowl. **2.** appear dark and threatening, as the weather. [ME *lour* frown] —**low′er•ing** *adj.*

low•er[2] (LOH ər) comparative of LOW. —*adj.* **1.** inferior in rank, value, etc. **2.** situated below something else. —*n.* that which is beneath something else; esp., a lower berth. —*v.t.* **1.** bring to a lower position or level; let down, as a window. **2.** reduce in degree, quality, amount, etc. **3.** undermine or weaken. **4.** bring down in estimation, rank, etc. **5.** change (a sound) to a lower pitch or volume. —*v.i.* **6.** become less; decrease; sink. [ME]

low frequency *Telecom.* radio waves having a frequency of from 30 to 300 kilohertz.

Low German see under GERMAN.

low-key (LOH KEE) *adj.* being low in intensity; understated. Also **low′-keyed′.**

low•land (LOH lənd) *n. Usu. pl.* land lying lower than the adjacent country. —**low′land** *adj.*

Low Latin see under LATIN.

low•ly (LOH lee) *adj.* **•li•er, •li•est 1.** humble or low in rank, origin, nature, etc. **2.** full of humility; meek. **3.** situated or lying low. [ME]

low-mind•ed (LOH MĪN did) *adj.* having low, vulgar, or mean thoughts, sentiments, or motives. —**low′-mind′ed•ness** *n.*

low-pitched (LOH PICHT) *adj.* **1.** low in tone or range of tone. **2.** having little slope, as a roof.

low-pres•sure (LOH PRESH ər) *adj.* **1.** having or operating under a low degree of pressure. **2.** *Meteorol.* designating atmospheric pressure below that normal at sea level.

low profile a low-keyed or inconspicuous attitude or style.

low tide 1. the ebb tide at its lowest stage. **2.** the time this lowest stage occurs.

lox[1] (loks) *n.* a salty, brine-cured salmon. [< Yiddish *laks*]

lox[2] *n.* liquid oxygen.

loy·al (LOI əl) *adj.* **1.** bearing true allegiance to a constituted authority, as to one's government. **2.** constant and faithful in any relation or obligation. **3.** indicating or professing loyalty. [< MF *loial*]

loy·al·ist (LOI ə list) *n.* one who supports and defends his or her government, esp. in times of crisis.

loy·al·ty (LOI əl tee) *n. pl.* **·ties** the state, quality, or fact of being loyal; allegiance. [ME *loialte*]

loz·enge (LOZ inj) *n.* a small sweetened tablet or candy, now usu. medicated. [ME *losenge*]

LP (EL PEE) *adj.* designating a phonograph record pressed with microgrooves and played at a speed of 33⅓ revolutions per minute: also *long-playing.* —*n.* an LP record.

LSD (EL ES DEE) *n.* a drug that produces states similar to those of schizophrenia: *ly*sergic acid *d*iethylamide.

lu·au (loo OW) *n.* a Hawaiian feast. [< Hawaiian]

lu·bri·cant (LOO bri kənt) *n.* a substance, as oil, grease, graphite, etc., used to coat moving parts in order to reduce friction and wear. —*adj.* lubricating.

lu·bri·cate (LOO bri KAYT) *v.t.* **·cat·ed, ·cat·ing** **1.** apply a lubricant to. **2.** make slippery or smooth. [< L *lubricatus* made slippery] —**lu′bri·ca′tion** *n.*

lu·bric·i·ty (loo BRIS i tee) *n. pl.* **·ties** **1.** lewdness; lasciviousness. **2.** slipperiness. [< Med.L *lubricitas* lechery]

lu·cent (LOO sənt) *adj.* **1.** showing or giving off radiance. **2.** transparent or semi-transparent. [< L *lucere* shine]

lu·cid (LOO sid) *adj.* **1.** easily understood; clear: a *lucid* explanation. **2.** mentally sound, clear, or rational: a *lucid* interval. **3.** shining; bright. [< L *lucidus* shiny] —**lu·cid′i·ty, lu′cid·ness** *n.* —**lu′cid·ly** *adv.*

Lu·ci·fer (LOO sə fər) *n.* the archangel who led the revolt of the angels and fell from Heaven: identified with *Satan.* [ME]

luck (luk) *n.* **1.** that which happens by chance; fortune; lot. **2.** good fortune; success. **3.** any object regarded as bringing good fortune. —**try one's luck** attempt to do something without any certainty of success. [ME *luk*] —**luck′·less** *adj.*

luck·y (LUK ee) *adj.* **luck·i·er, luck·i·est** **1.** accompanied by or having good fortune. **2.** bringing or resulting in good fortune. **3.** believed to bring good fortune. —**luck′i·ly** *adv.*

lu·cra·tive (LOO krə tiv) *adj.* producing or yielding gain, profit, or wealth; profitable. [ME *lucratif*] —**lu′cra·tive·ness** *n.*

lu·cre (LOO kər) *n.* money or riches: now chiefly in the humorous phrase: **filthy lucre.** [ME]

lu·cu·bra·tion (LOO kyuu BRAY shən) *n.* **1.** earnest and labored study. **2.** the product of such study; esp., a pedantic literary composition. [< L *lucubrare* work by candlelight]

lu·di·crous (LOO di krəs) *adj.* exciting laughter or ridicule; ridiculous; absurd. [< L *ludicrus* playful] —**lu′di·crous·ness** *n.*

lug·gage (LUG ij) *n.* suitcases, trunks; baggage.

lu·gu·bri·ous (luu GOO bree əs) *adj.* very sad or mournful, esp. in a ludicrous manner. [< L *lugribus* sad] —**lu·gu′bri·ous·ness** *n.*

luke·warm (LOOK WORM) *adj.* **1.** moderately warm; tepid. **2.** lacking in enthusiasm or conviction; indifferent. [ME *lukewarme*]

lull (lul) *v.t.* **1.** quiet or put to sleep by soothing sounds or motions. **2.** calm or allay, esp. by deception: *lull* someone's suspicions. [ME *lullen*] —*n.* **1.** a brief interval of calm or quiet during noise or confusion. **2.** a period of diminished activity, prosperity, etc.: a *lull* in business.

lull·a·by (LUL ə BI) *n. pl.* **·bies** **1.** a song to lull a child to sleep; a cradlesong. **2.** a piece of instrumental music in the manner of a lullaby.

lum·bar (LUM bər) *adj.* pertaining to or situated near the loins. [< NL *lumbaris*]

lum·ber[1] (LUM bər) *n.* **1.** timber sawed into boards, planks, etc., of specified lengths. —*adj.* made of, pertaining to, or dealing in lumber. —*v.t.* **1.** fell (timber); also, fell the timber of (an area). —*v.i.* **2.** fell or saw timber for marketing. —**lum′ber·ing** *n.*

lum·ber[2] *v.i.* **1.** move or proceed in a heavy or awkward manner. **2.** make a rumbling noise. [ME *lomeren*]

lum·ber·jack (LUM bər JAK) *n.* a person who fells or transports timber; a logger.

lum·ber·yard (LUM bər YAHRD) *n.* a yard for storage or sale of lumber.

lu·mi·nar·y (LOO mə NER ee) *n. pl.* **·nar·ies** **1.** any body that gives light, esp.

the sun or the moon. **2.** one who has achieved great eminence. [ME *luminarye*]

lu·mi·nes·cence (LOO mə NES əns) *n.* an emission of light, such as phosphorescence, not directly attributable to the heat that produces incandescence. —**lu'mi·nes'cent** *adj.*

lu·mi·nous (LOO me nəs) *adj.* **1.** full of light. **2.** giving off light; shining. **3.** easily understood; clear. [ME] —**lu·mi·nos·i·ty** (LOO mə NOS i tee) *n.*

lump¹ (lump) *n.* **1.** a shapeless, usu. small mass. **2.** a swelling. **3.** a mass of things thrown together; aggregate. —*adj.* formed in a lump or lumps: *lump* sugar. —*v.t.* **1.** put together in one mass, group, etc. **2.** make lumps in or on. [ME] —**lump'i·ness** *n.* —**lump'y** *adj.* **lump·i·er, lump·i·est**

lump² *v.t. Informal* put up with; endure: Like it or *lump* it.

lu·na·cy (LOO nə see) *n. pl.* •**cies 1.** irresponsible or senseless conduct. **2.** *Law* insanity.

lu·nar (LOO nər) *adj.* **1.** of the moon. **2.** round or crescent-shaped like the moon. **3.** measured by the revolutions of the moon: a *lunar* month. [< L *lunaris*]

lunar month see under MONTH.

lunar year a period of twelve lunar months, one month being added at intervals to make the mean length of the astronomical year, as in the Hebrew calendar.

lu·na·tic (LOO nə tik) *adj.* **1.** insane. **2.** wildly foolish or irrational. **3.** of or for the insane. —*n.* an insane person. [ME *lunatik*]

lunatic fringe extreme or fanatical followers or devotees of a movement, idea, etc.

lunch (lunch) *n.* **1.** a light meal, esp. the noonday meal. **2.** food for a lunch. —*v.i.* eat lunch.

lunch·eon (LUN chən) *n.* a noonday meal, esp. a formal one.

lunch·eon·ette (LUN chə NET) *n.* a restaurant where light meals may be obtained.

lung (lung) *n. Anat.* **1.** either of two organs of respiration in the thorax of air-breathing vertebrates. ◆ Collateral adjective: *pulmonary.* **2.** an analogous organ in certain invertebrates. [ME *lungen*]

lunge (lunj) *n.* **1.** a sudden pass or thrust, as with a sword, etc. **2.** a quick movement or plunge forward. —*v.* **lunged, lung·ing** —*v.i.* **1.** make a lunge; thrust. **2.** move with a

lunge. —*v.t.* **3.** cause to lunge. [< F *allonger* lengthen]

lurch¹ (lurch) *v.i.* **1.** roll suddenly to one side. **2.** stagger. —*n.* **1.** a sudden swaying. **2.** a reeling.

lurch² *n.* an embarrassing or difficult position; predicament: now only in the phrase **leave in the lurch.** [< MF *lourche* deceived]

lure (luur) *n.* **1.** anything that attracts or entices. **2.** in angling, an artificial bait. —*v.t.* **lured, lur·ing** attract or entice; allure. [ME]

lu·rid (LUUR id) *adj.* **1.** shocking or sensational. **2.** pale and sickly in color; livid. **3.** lighted up with a yellowish red glare or with, esp. in smoke or darkness. [< L *luridus* sallow] —**lu'rid·ly** *adv.* —**lu'rid·ness** *n.*

lurk (lurk) *v.i.* **1.** lie hidden, as in ambush. **2.** move secretly or furtively; slink. [ME *lurken*] —**lurk'er** *n.*

lus·cious (LUSH əs) *adj.* **1.** very pleasurable to the sense of taste or smell. **2.** pleasing to any sense. [ME *lucius*]

lush¹ (lush) *adj.* •**er, •est 1.** abounding in vigorous growth. **2.** elaborate in effects, etc. [< L *lusch* loose] —**lush'ness** *n.*

lush² *n. Slang* a heavy drinker; drunkard.

lust (lust) *n.* **1.** sexual appetite. **2.** excessive sexual appetite, esp. that seeking immediate or ruthless satisfaction. **3.** an overwhelming desire: a *lust* for power. —*v.i.* have passionate or inordinate desire. [ME *luste* desire] —**lust'ful** *adj.*

lus·ter (LUS tər) *n.* **1.** sheen; gloss. **2.** brilliance of light; radiance. **3.** splendor, glory, or distinction. **4.** any of various substances used to give a polish to a surface. [< MF *lustre*] —**lus'·trous** *adj.*

lust·y (LUS tee) *adj.* **lust·i·er, lust·i·est 1.** full of vigor; robust. **2.** powerful. —**lust'i·ly** *adv.*

lute (loot) *n.* an old musical instrument having strings that are plucked by the fingers, a large body shaped like half of a pear, and a long, fretted neck. [ME] —**lu'te·nist** *n.*

lux·u·ri·ant (lug ZHUUR ee ənt) *adj.* **1.** growing lushly and profusely, as vegetation. **2.** abundant, exuberant, or ornate, as in design, etc.

lux·u·ri·ate (lug ZHUUR ee AYT) *v.i.* •**at·ed, •at·ing 1.** take great pleasure; indulge oneself fully: with *in.* **2.** live sumptuously. **3.** grow profusely. [< L *luxuriare* live immoderately]

lux·u·ri·ous (lug ZHUUR ee əs) *adj.* **1.** characterized by or conducive to luxury or extreme comfort; opulent; sumptuous. **2.** indulging in or given to luxury.

lux·u·ry (LUG zhə ree) *n. pl.* **·ries 1.** anything, usu. expensive or rare, that gives comfort or pleasure but is not a necessity to life, health, etc. **2.** free indulgence in that which is expensive, rare, or extremely gratifying. [ME *luxurie* extravagance]

ly·cée (lee SAY) *n. French* in France, a secondary school financed by the government.

ly·ce·um (lī SEE əm) *n.* **1.** an organization providing popular instruction by lectures, concerts, etc.; also, its building. **2.** a hall for presenting lectures, concerts, etc. [< L]

lye (lī) *n.* a solution leached from ashes or derived from a substance containing alkali, used in making soap. [ME *lie*]

ly·ing[1] (LĪ ing) *n.* the act of telling lies; untruthfulness. —*adj.* deceitful or false.

ly·ing[2] present participle of LIE[1].

lymph (limf) *n. Physiol.* a yellowish alkaline fluid derived from the body tissues, containing white blood cells and a plasma similar to that of blood. [< L *lympha* water] — **lym·phat·ic** (lim FAT ik) *adj.* pertaining to lymph or the lymph nodes.

lymph node *Anat.* any of numerous glandlike bodies found in the course of the lymphatic vessels and producing cells that become lymphocytes. Also **lymph gland.**

lym·pho·cyte (LIM fə sīt) *n. Physiol.* a variety of white blood cells formed in the tissue of the lymph nodes. Also **lymph cell.**

lynch (linch) *v.t.* kill (a person accused of a crime) by mob action, as by hanging, without due process of law. —**lynch law** the punishment of presumed crime without due process of law. [after William *Lynch*, 1742—1820, Virginia justice of the peace] —**lynch'ing** *n.*

lyre (līr) *n.* an ancient harplike stringed instrument, used by the Greeks to accompany poetry and song. [ME *lire*]

lyr·ic (LIR ik) *adj.* **1.** of poetry, expressing the poet's inner feelings; also, pertaining to the method, personality, etc., of a writer of such verse. **2.** meant to be sung. **3.** *Music* having a singing voice of a light, flexible quality: a *lyric* soprano. Also **lyr'i·cal.** —*n.* **1.** *Usu. pl.* the words of a song. **2.** a lyric poem. [< L *lyricus*]

lyr·i·cism (LIR ə siz əm) *n.* the quality of emotional self-expression in the arts.

lyr·i·cist (LIR ə sist) *n.* **1.** one who writes the words of a song or the lyrics for a musical play. **2.** a lyric poet.

ly·ser·gic acid di·eth·yl·am·ide (lī SUR jik AS id dī ETH ə LAM īd) see LSD.

ly·sis (LĪ sis) *n.* **1.** *Med.* the gradual disappearing of the symptoms of a disease. **2.** *Biochem.* the process of disintegration or destruction of cells, bacteria, etc. [< NL] —**ly·tic** (LIT ik) *adj.*

-lysis *combining form* a loosing, dissolving, etc.: *hydrolysis, paralysis.* [< Gk.]

-lyte *combining form* a substance decomposed by a (specified) process: *electrolyte.*

-lyt·ic *combining form* loosing; dissolving: used in adjectives corresponding to nouns in *-lysis: hydrolytic, paralytic.*

-lyze *combining form of verbs* perform, cause, or undergo: formed from nouns in *-lysis: electrolyze, paralyze.*

M

m, M (em) *n. pl.* **m's** or **ms, M's** or **Ms** **1.** the thirteenth letter of the English alphabet. **2.** the sound represented by the letter *m*. — *symbol* the Roman numeral 1000.

ma'am (mam) *n.* a term of respectful address used to women; madam.

ma·ca·bre (mə KAHB) *adj.* suggesting death and decay; gruesome; ghastly. [< F]

mac·ad·am (mə KAD əm) *n.* **1.** a pavement or road of small stones usu. held together with tar or asphalt. **2.** broken stone used in this type of road. [after John L. *McAdam*, 1756—1836, Scottish engineer who invented it] —**mac·ad'am·ize** *v.t.* •ized, •iz·ing

mac·a·ro·ni (MAK ə ROH nee) *n.* a dried paste of wheat flour made into short tubes and prepared as a food by boiling. [< Ital. *maccheroni*]

mac·a·roon (MAK ə ROON) *n.* a small cookie made of ground almonds or sometimes coconut, egg, and sugar. [< F *macaron*]

ma·caw (mə KAW) *n.* any of various large tropical American parrots with a harsh voice and brilliant plumage. [< Pg. *macao*]

mace¹ (mays) *n.* **1.** a heavy medieval war club, usu. with a spiked metal head. **2.** a club-shaped staff symbolic of office or authority. [ME]

mace² *n.* a spice ground from the covering between the husk and the seed of the nutmeg. [ME]

Mace (mays) *n.* a chemical solution similar to tear gas that temporarily blinds or incapacitates one when sprayed in the face, used as a weapon: a trade name.

mac·er·ate (MAS ə RAYT) *v.* •at·ed, •at·ing *v.t.* **1.** reduce (a solid substance) to a soft mass by soaking in liquid. **2.** break down the structure of (food) in digestion. —*v.i.* **3.** become macerated. [< L *maceratus* softened] —**mac'er·a'tion** *n.*

mach (mahk) *n.* see MACH NUMBER.

ma·chet·e (mə SHET ee) *n.* a heavy knife used as an implement and a weapon in tropical America. [< Sp.]

Mach·i·a·vel·li·an (MAK ee ə VEL yən) *adj.* achieving and maintaining power, esp. political power, by unprincipled means. —*n.* one who follows or subscribes to such prin-

ciples. [after Niccolà *Machiavelli*, 16th c. Florentine statesman]

mach·i·nate (MAK ə NAYT) *v.t. & v.i.* •nat·ed, •nat·ing scheme or contrive. [< L *machinatus* invented]

mach·i·na·tion (MAK ə NAY shən) *n. Usu. pl.* a concealed working and scheming for some devious purpose.

ma·chine (mə SHEEN) *n.* **1.** any combination of interrelated parts for using or applying energy to do work. **2.** a controlling political group. **3.** the organization and operating principles of a complex structure: the human *machine*. **4.** a motorized vehicle, esp. an automobile. —*adj.* **1.** of machines. **2.** produced by machine. —*v.t.* •chined, •chin·ing shape, mill, make, etc., by machine. [< F]

machine gun a rapid-firing automatic gun, usu. mounted. —**machine gunner**

ma·chine-gun (mə SHEEN GUN) *v.t.* -gunned, -gun·ning fire at or shoot with a machine gun.

machine language codes used directly by a computer.

ma·chin·er·y (mə SHEE nə ree) *n.* **1.** a collection of machines or machine parts. **2.** the operating parts and principles of a complex structure: the *machinery* of the law.

machine tool a power-driven tool, partly or wholly automatic in action, for cutting, shaping, boring, milling, etc.

ma·chin·ist (mə SHEE nist) *n.* one who operates or repairs machines or machine tools.

ma·chis·mo (mah CHEEZ moh) *n.* an exaggerated sense of masculinity. [< Sp.]

mach number (mahk) a number representing the ratio between the speed of an object moving through a fluid medium, as air, and the speed of sound in the same medium. *Mach 2* denotes a speed twice that of sound. Also **Mach number.** [after Ernst *Mach*, 1833—1916, Austrian physicist]

ma·cho (MAH choh) *adj.* exaggeratedly masculine. [< Sp., male]

mac·ra·mé (MAK rə MAY) *n.* **1.** decoratively knotted string or cord, formed into belts, handbags, wall hangings, etc. **2.** the craft of producing macramé. [< F]

macro- *combining form* large or over-developed: **macromolecule, macro-scale.** [< Gk. *makros* long]

mac·ro·bi·ot·ic (MAK roh bī OT ik) *adj.* designating a usu. meatless diet, believed to promote good health and prolong life. —**mac′ro·bi·ot′ics** *n.* (construed as sing.)

mac·ro·cosm (MAK rə KOZ əm) *n.* the whole universe, esp. when regarded in contrast to man. [< F *macrocosme*]

ma·cron (MAY kron) *n.* a straight line over a vowel letter to show that it represents a long sound, as ā in *made*. [< Gk. *makrón* long]

mad (mad) *adj.* **mad·der, mad·dest 1.** suffering from or manifesting severe mental disorder; insane; psychotic. **2.** angry. **3.** wildly foolish; rash: a *mad* project. **4.** of animals, rabid. **5.** showing a passionate infatuation with or desire for: with *about, for,* or *over.* **6.** flamboyant; daring. —**like mad** *Informal* frantically. —*n.* a show of temper: now only in the phrase **have a mad on,** be angry. [ME] —**mad′ly** *adv.* —**mad′ness** *n.*

mad·am (MAD əm) *n. pl.* **mes·dames** (may DAHM) *for def. 1;* **mad·ams** *for def. 2.* **1.** my lady; mistress: a title of courtesy. **2.** a woman who manages a brothel. [ME *madame*]

mad·ame (MAD əm) *n. pl.* **mes·dames** (may DAHM) the French title of courtesy for a married woman, equivalent to the English *Mrs.* [< F]

mad·cap (MAD KAP) *adj.* wild; rattlebrained. —*n.* one who acts wildly or rashly.

mad·den (MAD n) *v.t. & v.i.* make or become mad or insane; inflame; infuriate. —**mad′den·ing** *adj.* —**mad′den·ing·ly** *adv.*

mad·ding (MAD ing) *adj.* being or growing mad; delirious; raging. [ME] —**mad′ding·ly** *adv.*

made (mayd) past tense, past participle of MAKE. —*adj.* produced by fabrication, invention, or skill; not occurring naturally. —**have it made** *Informal* be sure of success.

mad·e·moi·selle (MAD ə mə ZEL) *n. pl.* **mad·e·moi·selles** (-zelz), *Fr.* **mes·de·moi·selles** (MAY də mwah ZEL) the French title of courtesy for unmarried women, equivalent to *Miss.* [< F]

made-up (MAYD UP) *adj.* **1.** invented; fictitious. **2.** adorned or altered by cosmetics. **3.** complete; finished: a *made-up* sample. **4.** compensated for: said of work, money, etc.

mad·house (MAD HOWS) *n.* **1.** a hospital for the mentally ill; insane asylum. **2.** a place of confusion or uproar; bedlam.

mad·man (MAD MAN) *n. pl.* **·men** an insane man; lunatic.

Ma·don·na (mə DON ə) *n.* the Virgin Mary. [< Ital., my lady]

mad·ras (MAD rəs) *n.* **1.** a cotton cloth usu. striped, corded, or checked. **2.** a silk cloth, usu. striped. [after *Madras,* India]

mad·ri·gal (MAD ri gəl) *n.* **1.** *Music* an unaccompanied part song, often in counterpoint, popular during the 16th and 17th c. **2.** a short lyric poem. [< Ital. *madrigale*]

mad·wom·an (MAD WUUM ən) *n. pl.* **·wom·en** an insane woman; lunatic.

mael·strom (MAYL strəm) *n.* **1.** any dangerous and irresistible force, or a place where it prevails. **2.** a whirlpool. [< Du. *maelstroom* whirling stream]

maes·tro (MI stroh) *n. pl.* **·tros** a master in any art; esp., an eminent conductor. [< Ital., master]

Ma·fi·a (MAH fee ə) *n.* **1.** a secret criminal organization believed to exist in many countries, including the U.S. **2.** *Often not cap.* a dominating and often ruthless ingroup. [< Ital.]

ma·fi·o·so (MAH fee OH soh) *n. pl.* **·si** (-see) a member of the Mafia. [< Ital.]

mag·a·zine (MAG ə ZEEN) *n.* **1.** a periodical publication, containing articles, stories, etc., by various writers. **2.** a warehouse or depot, esp. for explosives and ammunition. **3.** a supply chamber in a gun, battery, camera, etc. [< Arabic *makhāzin* storehouses]

mag·da·lene (MAG də LEEN) *n.* a reformed prostitute. Also **Mag′da·lene.** [after Mary *Magdalene*]

ma·gen·ta (mə JEN tə) *n.* a purplish red color. [after *Magenta,* Italy]

mag·got (MAG ət) *n.* the legless larva of an insect, esp. one found in decaying matter. [ME *magot*] —**mag′got·y** *adj.*

Ma·gi (MAY jī) *n. pl. of* **Ma·gus** (-gəs) the three wise men from the east who came to Bethlehem to pay homage to the infant Jesus. [< L]

mag·ic (MAJ ik) *n.* **1.** seeming control over or foresight of natural events, forces, etc. through supernatural agencies. **2.** an overpowering influence: the *magic* of his voice. **3.** sleight of hand. —*adj.* **1.** of or used in magic. **2.** mysteriously impressive; beautiful. [ME *magike*] —**mag′i·cal** *adj.*

ma·gi·cian (mə JISH ən) *n.* one who performs magic; esp., an entertainer who uses illusion and sleight of hand.

mag·is·te··ri·al (MAJ ə STEER ee əl) *adj.* **1.** of or like a master; authoritative. **2.** of or pertaining to a magistrate. [ly Med.L *magisterialis* of authority]

mag·is·tra·cy (MAJ ə strə see) *n. pl.* **·cies** the office, function, or term of a magistrate.

mag·is·trate (MAJ ə STRAYT) *n.* **1.** a public official with the power to enforce the law. **2.** a minor judicial officer, as a justice of the peace. [ME *magistrat*]

mag·ma (MAG mə) *n. Geol.* the mass of molten rock from which igneous rocks are formed. [ME]

mag·nan·i·mous (mag NAN ə məs) *adj.* manifesting generosity in forgiving insults or injuries. [< L *magnanimus* having great spirit] **—mag·na·nim·i·ty** (MAG nə NIM i tee) *n.* **—mag·nan′i·mous·ly** *adv.*

mag·nate (MAG nayt) *n.* one notable or powerful, esp. in industry: a railroad *magnate*. [ME *magnates* important people]

mag·net (MAG nit) *n.* **1.** a body that has a magnetic field and therefore attracts iron and other magnetic material. **2.** a lodestone. **3.** one who or that which exercises a strong attraction. [ME *magnete*]

mag·net·ic (mag NET ik) *adj.* **1.** pertaining to magnetism or a magnet. **2.** capable of setting up a magnetic field. **3.** possessing personal magnetism. **—mag·net′i·cal·ly** *adv.*

magnetic field the region in the neighborhood of a magnet or current-carrying body in which magnetic forces are observable.

magnetic north the direction, usu. differing from true north, toward which the needle of a compass points.

magnetic pole 1. either of the poles of a magnet. **2.** either of two points (**north magnetic pole** and **south magnetic pole**) on the surface of the earth where the lines of magnetic force converge.

magnetic tape *Electronics* a thin ribbon, coated with magnetic particles, for recording sound, television programs, etc.

mag·net·ism (MAG ni TIZ əm) *n.* **1.** the specific properties of a magnet. **2.** the science treating of the laws and conditions of magnetic phenomena. **3.** the amount of magnetic force in a magnetized body. **4.** a personal quality that attracts.

mag·net·ite (MAG nə TĪT) *n.* a black iron oxide that that is an iron ore: called *lode-*

stone when magnetic. **—mag·net·it·ic** (MAG nə TIT ik) *adj.*

mag·net·ize (MAG ni TĪZ) *v.t.* **·ized,** **·iz·ing 1.** communicate magnetic properties to. **2.** attract by personal influence. **— mag′·net·i·za′tion** *n.*

mag·ne·to (mag NEE toh) *n. pl.* **·tos** any of various devices using a permanent magnet to generate an electric current, used esp. to produce the ignition spark in some internal-combustion engines.

mag·ne·to·sphere (mag NEE tə SFEER) *n. Physics* a region of the upper atmosphere forming a continuous band of ionized particles trapped by the earth's magnetic field.

mag·nif·i·cent (mag NIF ə sənt) *adj.* **1.** presenting an extraordinarily imposing appearance; splendid; beautiful. **2.** exceptionally pleasing; superb. **3.** exalted or sublime in expression or concept. **—mag·nif′i·cence** *n.*

mag·ni·fy (MAG nə FĪ) *v.* **·fied, ·fy·ing** *v.t.* **1.** increase the perceived size of, as by a lens. **2.** increase the size of; enlarge. **3.** cause to seem greater or more important; exaggerate. *—v.i.* **5.** increase or have the power to increase the apparent size of an object, as a lens. [ME *magnifien*] **—mag′ni·fi′er** *n.*

mag·nil·o·quent (mag NIL ə kwənt) *adj.* speaking or spoken in a grandiose style; grandiloquent. [< L *magniloquentia* lofty language] **—mag·nil′o·quence** *n.*

mag·ni·tude (MAG ni TOOD) *n.* **1.** size or extent. **2.** greatness or importance: the *magnitude* of the achievement. **3.** *Astron.* the relative brightness of a star, ranging from a rating of one for the brightest to six for those just visible to the naked eye. [ME]

mag·num (MAG nəm) *n.* a wine bottle holding about ⅖ of a gallon; also, such a quantity. [< L, large]

magnum o·pus (OH pəs) a great work; masterpiece; esp., the greatest single work of a writer, artist, etc. [< L]

Ma·gus (MAY gəs) singular of MAGI.

ma·ha·ra·jah (MAH hə RAH jə) *n.* a title of certain princes of India, particularly one ruling an Indian state. [< Hindi *maharājā* great king]

ma·hat·ma (mə HAHT mə) *n. Sometimes cap.* in some Asian religions, a title of respect for a holy man. [< Skt. *mahātman*]

mah-jongg (MAH JONG) *n.* a game of Chinese origin, usu. played with 144 pieces or tiles. [< Chinese *ma ch'iao* house sparrow; from the design on one of the tiles]

ma·hog·a·ny (mə HOG ə nee) *n. pl.* **·nies** **1.** any of various tropical trees yielding fine-grained reddish hardwood much used for furniture and cabinet work. **2.** the wood itself. **3.** a brownish red. —*adj.* brownish red.

ma·hout (mə HOWT) *n.* in India and the East Indies, the keeper and driver of an elephant. [< Hindi *mahāut*]

maid (mayd) *n.* **1.** a young unmarried woman or girl; maiden. **2.** a female servant. [ME]

maid·en (MAYD n) *n.* **1.** an unmarried woman, esp. if young. **2.** a virgin. —*adj.* **1.** of, pertaining to, or befitting a maiden. **2.** unmarried: said of women. **3.** of or pertaining to the first use, trial, or experience: *maiden* race. [ME] —**maid'en·hood'** (-HUUD) *n.*

maid·en·head (MAYD n HED) *n.* the hymen.

maiden name a woman's surname before marriage.

mail¹ (mayl) *n.* **1.** letters, parcels, etc. sent or received through a postal system. **2.** the postal system itself. **3.** postal matter collected or delivered at a specified time: the morning *mail.* —*adj.* —*v.t.* send by mail, as letters; post. [ME *male*] —**mail'er** *n.*

mail² *n.* **1.** flexible armor made of interlinked rings or overlapping scales. **2.** loosely, any defensive armor. [ME *maille*]

mail·box (MAYL BOKS) *n.* **1.** a box in which letters etc. are deposited for collection. **2.** a box into which private mail is delivered.

mail·man (MAYL MAN) *n. pl.* **·men** one who carries and delivers letters: also called **mail carrier.** Also **postman.**

maim (maym) *v.t.* **1.** deprive of the use of a bodily part; mutilate; cripple or disable. **2.** render imperfect; make defective. [ME *mayme*]

main (mayn) *adj.* **1.** first or chief in size, importance, etc.; leading: *main* event. **2.** fully exerted; sheer: by *main* force. —*n.* **1.** a principal conduit or pipe in a system conveying gas, water, etc. **2.** utmost effort; force: now chiefly in the phrase **with might and main. 3.** the chief or most important point or part. [ME *meyn*]

main·land (MAYN lənd) *n.* the main part of a continent, as distinguished from an island or peninsula.

main·line (MAYN LIN) *v.t. & v.i.* **·lined,**

·lin·ing *Slang* inject (a narcotic drug) into a large vein. —**main'lin'er** *n.*

main line the principal line of a railroad or highway.

main·ly (MAYN lee) *adv.* chiefly; principally.

main·spring (MAYN SPRING) *n.* **1.** the principal spring of a mechanism, as of a watch. **2.** the principal or most compelling cause or agency.

main·stay (MAYN STAY) *n.* a chief support: the *mainstay* of my old age.

main·stream (MAYN STREEM) *n.* the main or middle course.

main·tain (mayn TAYN) *v.t.* **1.** carry on or continue; keep in existence. **2.** preserve or keep. **3.** keep in proper condition. **4.** supply with a livelihood; support. **5.** claim to be true; uphold. [ME *mantenen*]

main·te·nance (MAYN tə nəns) *n.* **1.** the act of maintaining, or the state of being maintained. **2.** means of support or subsistence; livelihood. **3.** the work of keeping roads, buildings, etc., in good condition. [ME *maintenaunce*]

maî·tre d'hô·tel (MAY tər doh TEL) **1.** a headwaiter or steward. Also *Informal* **maî·tre d'** (MAY tər DEE). **2.** the proprietor or manager of a hotel. [< F]

maize (mayz) *n.* **1.** corn (def. 1). **2.** a deep yellow color. [< Sp. *maíz*]

ma·jes·tic (mə JES tik) *adj.* stately; royal. —**ma·jes'ti·cal·ly** *adv.*

maj·es·ty (MAJ ə stee) *n. pl.* **·ties 1.** exalted dignity; stateliness; grandeur. **2.** sovereign authority: the *majesty* of the law. **3.** *Cap.* a title or form of address for a sovereign: preceded by *His, Her, Your,* etc. [ME *majeste*]

ma·jor (MAY jər) *adj.* **1.** greater in quantity, number, or extent. **2.** having primary or greater importance, excellence, rank, etc.: *major* writers. **3.** of, relating to, or making up a majority. **4.** *Music* **a** denoting the larger of two similarly named intervals: *major* third. **b** denoting a triad in which the third above the fundamental is major. **c** denoting a type of diatonic scale, or a key based on this scale. **5.** in education, pertaining to the principal area of specialized study of a degree candidate in a college or university. —*n.* **1.** *Mil.* an officer ranking next above a captain and next below a lieutenant colonel. **2.** the principal area of specialized study of a degree candidate in a college or university. **3.** *pl.* in baseball, the major leagues.

—*v.i.* in education, study as a major: with *in.* [< L, greater]

major general *Mil.* an officer ranking next above a brigadier general.

ma·jor·i·ty (mə JOR i tee) *n. pl.* **•ties 1.** more than half of a given number or group; the greater part. **2.** the number of votes cast for a particular candidate, bill, etc., over and above the total number of remaining votes. Distinguished from *plurality.* **3.** the party or group having the most power. **4.** the age when full civil and personal rights may be legally exercised. **5.** the rank, commission, or office of a major. [< Med.L *majoritas*]

major league in baseball, either of the two main groups of professional teams in the U.S., the **National League** or the **American League.**

make (mayk) *v.* **made, mak·ing** *v.t.* **1.** produce, construct, or fashion. **2.** cause: Don't *make* trouble. **3.** bring to some state: The wind *makes* him cold. **4.** put into a specified rank or position: They *made* her president. **5.** form or create in the mind, as a plan, conclusion, or judgment. **6.** compose (a poem). **7.** utter or express, as an announcement. **8.** put forward: *make* friendly overtures. **9.** engage in: *make* war. **10.** earn or acquire: *make* a fortune. **11.** amount to; add up to. **12.** draw up, enact, or frame, as laws, treaties, etc. **13.** estimate to be; reckon. **14.** prepare or arrange for use: *make* a bed. **15.** induce or force; compel. **16.** afford or provide: Venison *makes* good eating. **17.** become through development: He will *make* a good soldier. **18.** cause the success of: Her last book *made* her. **19.** perform (a specific physical movement). **20.** cover (distance) by traveling. **21.** travel at the rate of. **22.** arrive at; reach: *make* Boston. **23.** arrive in time for. **24.** win a place or position, as on a team; also, achieve the rank or status of: *make* colonel. —*v.i.* **25.** cause something to assume a specified condition: *make* sure. **26.** act or behave in a certain manner: *make* merry. —**make away with 1.** carry off; steal. **2.** get rid of; destroy. —**make believe** pretend; feign. —**make do** get along with what is available, esp. with an inferior substitute. —**make for 1.** go toward, esp. rapidly. **2.** rush at in order to attack. —**make it** *Informal* succeed; succeed in doing something. —**make off** leave suddenly; run away. —**make off with** steal. —**make or break** bring about the success or failure of. —**make out 1.** see; discern. **2.** comprehend. **3.** fill out or draw up, as a document. **4.** succeed. **5.** do well enough; get by. **6.** *Slang* a kiss and caress amorously. **b** engage in sexual intercourse. —**make over 1.** renovate; refashion. **2.** transfer title or possession of. —**make up 1.** compose; compound, as a prescription. **2.** be the parts of; constitute. **3.** settle differences and become friendly again. **4.** supply what is lacking in. **5.** compensate; atone. **6.** settle; decide: *make up* one's mind. **7.** *Printing* arrange lines of type, illustrations, etc. for (a book etc.). **8.** put cosmetics on (the face). **9.** in education: **a** repeat (an examination or course one has failed). **b** take (an examination one has missed). —*n.* **1.** style or type: a good *make* of car. **2.** the manner in which something is made. —**on the make** *Informal* **1.** greedy for profit or advancement. **2.** eager for amorous conquest. [ME *maken*] —**mak'er** *n.*

make-be·lieve (MAYK bi LEEV) *n.* **1.** pretense; sham. **2.** a pretending to believe; imagination. —*adj.* pretended; unreal.

make·shift (MAYK SHIFT) *n.* a temporary means devised for an emergency; stopgap. —*adj.* having the nature of or used as a temporary substitute.

make·up (MAYK UP) *n.* **1.** the arrangement or combination of parts or qualities of which anything is composed. **2.** the cosmetics etc. used by an actor in a specific role. **3.** cosmetics used by women. **4.** physical or mental constitution. **5.** *Printing* the arranging of composed type and cuts into pages, columns, or forms.

make·work (MAYK WURK) *n.* work assigned to keep one occupied.

mak·ings (MAY kingz) *n.pl.* **1.** the materials or qualities from which something can be made. **2.** paper and tobacco for cigarettes.

mal·ad·just·ed (MAL ə JUS tid) *adj.* **1.** poorly adjusted. **2.** *Psychol.* poorly adapted to one's environment. —**mal'ad·just' ment** *n.*

mal·a·droit (MAL ə DROIT) *adj.* lacking skill; clumsy; blundering. [< F] —**mal'a·droit'ness** *n.*

mal·a·dy (MAL ə dee) *n. pl.* **•dies 1.** a disease, esp. when chronic or deep-seated. **2.** any disordered or disturbed condition. [ME *maladie*]

mal·aise (ma LAYZ) *n.* a feeling of vague discomfort or lassitude, sometimes indicating the beginning of an illness. [< F]

mal·a·prop·ism (MAL ə prop ĭz əm) *n.* **1.** the absurd misuse of words. **2.** an instance of this. [after Mrs. *Malaprop*, in Sheridan's play *The Rivals*]

mal·ap·ro·pos (MAL ap rə POH) *adj.* not appropriate. —*adv.* inappropriately. [< F *mal à propos* not to the point]

ma·lar·i·a (mə LAIR ee ə) *n. Pathol.* any of several forms of a disease caused by certain parasites carried by the anopheles mosquito and characterized by periodic attacks of chills, fever, and profuse sweating. [< Ital. *mala aria* bad air] —**ma·lar′i·al** *adj.*

mal·con·tent (MAL kən TENT) *adj.* discontented or dissatisfied, esp. with a government or economic system. —*n.* one who is malcontent.

male (mayl) *adj.* **1.** of or belonging to the sex that begets young or produces sperm. **2.** of, characteristic of, or suitable for members of this sex; masculine. **3.** made up of men or boys. **4.** *Bot.* designating a plant having stamens but no pistil. **5.** *Mech.* denoting a part, as in some electric plugs etc., designed to be inserted into a correlated slot or bore known as *female.* —*n.* **1.** a male person or animal. **2.** *Bot.* a male plant. [ME] —**male′ness** *n.*

mal·e·dic·tion (MAL i DIK shən) *n.* **1.** the pronouncing of a curse against someone. **2.** slander; calumny. [ME *malediccion*]

mal·e·fac·tor (MAL ə FAK tər) *n.* **1.** one who commits a crime; criminal. **2.** an evildoer. [ME *malefactour*] —**mal·e·fac·tress** (MAL ə FAK tris) *n. fem.*

ma·lef·i·cent (mə LEF ə sənt) *adj.* causing or doing evil or mischief. —**ma·lef′i·cence** *n.*

ma·lev·o·lent (mə LEV ə lənt) *adj.* wishing evil toward others; malicious. [< L *malevolens* spiteful] —**ma·lev′o·lence** *n.*

mal·fea·sance (mal FEE zəns) *n. Law* the performance of some act that is wrongful or that one has specifically contracted not to perform: said usu. of official misconduct. —**mal·fea′·sant** *adj. & n.*

mal·for·ma·tion (MAL for MAY shən) *n.* defective structure, esp. in an organism. —**mal·formed′** (mal FORMD) *adj.*

mal·func·tion (mal FUNGK shən) *n.* **1.** failure to function. **2.** defective functioning. —*v.i.* **1.** fail to function. **2.** function improperly.

mal·ice (MAL is) *n.* **1.** an intention or desire to injure another; spite. **2.** *Law* a willfully formed design to do another an injury: also,

malice aforethought. [ME] —**ma·li·cious** (mə LISH əs) *adj.*

ma·lign (mə LĪN) *v.t.* speak slander of; defame. —*adj.* **1.** having an evil disposition toward others; malevolent. **2.** tending to injure; pernicious. [ME *maligne*] —**ma·lign′er** *n.*

ma·lig·nant (mə LIG nənt) *adj.* **1.** *Pathol.* **a** of tumors, rapidly growing and liable to metastasize: opposed to *benign.* **b** becoming progressively worse; virulent. **2.** having an evil disposition toward others; malign. —**ma·lig′nan·cy** *n.*

ma·lin·ger (mə LING gər) *v.i.* pretend sickness so as to avoid work or duty. [< F *malingre* sickly] —**ma·lin′ger·er** *n.*

mall (mawl) *n.* **1.** a promenade or walk, usu. public and often shaded. **2.** a shopping center.

mal·le·a·ble (MAL ee ə bəl) *adj.* **1.** capable of being hammered or rolled out without breaking: said esp. of metals. **2.** capable of adapting; flexible; pliable. [ME *malliable*] —**mal′le·a·bil′i·ty** *n.*

mal·let (MAL it) *n.* **1.** a hammer having a head of wood, rubber, etc. **2.** a long-handled hammer used in croquet, polo, etc. [ME *maillet*]

mal·le·us (MAL ee əs) *n. pl.* **mal·le·i** (MAL ee ī) *Anat.* the club-shaped bone of the middle ear, articulating with the incus: also called *hammer.* [< L, hammer]

mal·nu·tri·tion (MAL noo TRISH ən) *n.* faulty or inadequate nutrition; undernourishment. —**mal·nour·ished** (mal NUR isht) *adj.*

mal·o·dor·ous (mal OH dər əs) *adj.* having a disagreeable smell. —**mal·o′dor·ous·ly** *adv.*

mal·prac·tice (mal PRAK tis) *n.* **1.** in medicine, the improper, injurious, or negligent treatment of a patient. **2.** improper or immoral professional conduct.

malt (mawlt) *n.* **1.** grain, usu. barley, germinated by soaking and then kiln-dried. **2.** liquor made with malt, as beer, ale, etc. [ME] —**malt′y** *adj.* **malt′i·er, malt′i·est**

malted milk (MAWL tid) **1.** a beverage made of milk, a powder of malted cereals and dried milk, and usu. ice cream: also **malt′ed.** **2.** the powder used in this beverage.

Mal·thu·si·an (mal THOO zhən) *adj.* of or pertaining to the theory that population tends to outrun its means of support, and will be checked by disaster unless births are restricted. —*n.* a believer in this theory. [after Thomas *Malthus*, 1766—1834, English economist]

mal·treat (mal TREET) *v.t.* treat badly, roughly, or unkindly; abuse. [< F *maltraiter*]

mam·mal (MAM əl) *n.* any of a class of vertebrates whose females have mammary glands to nourish their young. [< NL *Mammalia*] —**mam·ma·li·an** (mə MAYL yən) *adj. & n.*

mam·ma·ry gland (MAM ə ree) in mammals, the organ that secretes milk.

mam·mo·gram (MAM ə GRAM) *n.* an X-ray of the breast.

mam·mog·ra·phy (ma MOG rə fee) *n.* the X-ray examination of the breasts to detect tumors.

mam·mon (MAM ən) *n. Often cap.* the personification of riches, avarice, and worldly gain. [ME]

mam·moth (MAM əth) *n. Paleontol.* a large, now extinct elephant having a thick hairy coat and long curved tusks. —*adj.* huge; gigantic. [< Russian *mammot*]

man (man) *n. pl.* **men** **1.** an adult male human being. **2.** human beings collectively; mankind; humankind. **3.** a person or individual. **4.** one having pronounced masculine traits and virtues. **5.** an adult male subordinate or employee; as: **a** a worker in a factory, office, etc. **b** a servant, esp. a valet. **6.** a husband. **7.** a piece or counter used in certain games, as chess, checkers, etc. — **the Man** *Slang* **1.** the white establishment, esp. as viewed by African Americans. **2.** the police. —**to a man** unanimously. —**be one's own man** be independent. —*interj. Slang* an exclamation of surprise, pleasure, etc. —*v.t.* **manned, man·ning 1.** supply with men, as for work, defense, etc.: *man* the barricades. **2.** take stations on, at, or in, for work, defense, etc.: *Man* the pumps! [ME]

man·a·cle (MAN ə kəl) *n.* **1.** *Usu. pl.* a device for restraining the hands; shackle; handcuff. **2.** anything that constrains. —*v.t.* **·cled, ·cling 1.** put manacles on. **2.** constrain or hamper. [ME *manicle* handcuff]

man·age (MAN ij) *v.* **·aged, ·ag·ing** *v.t.* **1.** direct or control the affairs or interests of. **2.** arrange; contrive: He *managed* to stay. **3.** cause to do one's bidding: *manage* a crowd. **4.** handle or wield; use, as a weapon etc.— *v.i.* **5.** direct or control business, affairs, etc. **6.** be able to continue or thrive. [< Ital.

maneggiare] —**man'age·a·bil'i·ty** *n.* —**man'age·a·ble** *adj.*

man·age·ment (MAN ij mənt) *n.* **1.** the act, art, or practice of managing. **2.** the person or persons who manage a business etc. **3.** managers collectively, esp. in their relations with labor unions. **4.** the skillful use of means.

man·ag·er (MAN i jər) *n.* **1.** one who manages; esp., one who directs an enterprise, business, etc. **b** one skilled in managing, esp. business affairs. —**man·a·ge·ri·al** (MAN i JEER ee əl) *adj.*

ma·ña·na (mah NYAH nə) *n. & adv. Spanish* tomorrow; some other time.

man·da·mus (man DAY məs) *n. Law* a writ issued by a higher court to a subordinate court, officer, corporation, etc., commanding that some specified thing be done. [< L, lit., we command]

man·da·rin (MAN də rin) *n.* **1.** an official of the Chinese Empire. **2.** a powerful person; esp., an intellectual arbiter. [< Skt. *mantra* councilor]

Man·da·rin (MAN də rin) *n.* the Chinese language of north and west China, including the Peking dialect on which the official language of the country is based.

man·date (MAN dayt) *n.* **1.** in politics, an instruction from an electorate to its representative, expressed by the result of an election. **2.** formerly, a charge to a nation from the League of Nations authorizing the administration of a territory, colony, etc.; also, the territory given in charge. **3.** an authoritative command; order. —*v.t.* **·dat·ed, ·dat·ing** assign (a territory, etc.) to a specific nation under a mandate. [< L *mandatum* commissioned]

man·da·to·ry (MAN də TOR ee) *adj.* **1.** required by or as if by mandate or command; obligatory. **2.** of or pertaining to a mandate. **3.** holding a mandate. [< LL *mandatorius*]

man·di·ble (MAN də bəl) *n. Biol.* **1.** the lower jaw bone. **2.** either part of the beak of a bird. [ME] —**man·dib·u·lar** (man DIB yə lər) *adj.*

man·do·lin (MAN dl in) *n.* a musical instrument with a fretted neck, a pear-shaped body, and eight metal strings. [< Ital. *mandolino*]

man·drel (MAN drəl) *n. Mech.* **1.** a shaft or spindle on which material may be fixed for working on a machine. **2.** a metal bar used as a core about which wire, glass, metal, etc. may be bent, forged, or shaped.

mane (mayn) *n.* the long hair growing on and about the neck of some animals, as the horse, lion, etc. [ME]

ma·nège (ma NEZH) *n.* the art of training and riding horses; also, a school for horsemanship. [< F]

ma·neu·ver (mə NOO vər) *n.* **1.** *Mil.* **a** a planned movement or shift, as of troops, warships, etc. **b** *pl.* large-scale tactical exercises simulating war. **2.** any skillful move or stroke. —*v.t.* **1.** manage or conduct skillfully. **2.** put (troops, vessels, etc.) through a maneuver or maneuvers. —*v.i.* **3.** perform a maneuver or maneuvers. **4.** use artful moves or strokes. [< F *manoeuvre*] —**ma·neu′ver·a·ble** *adj.*

man Friday a person devoted or subservient to another; a factotum. [after *Friday*, a devoted servant in Daniel Defoe's *Robinson Crusoe*]

mange (maynj) *n. Vet.* an itching skin disease of dogs and other domestic animals, caused by parasitic mites. [ME *manjewe*]

man·ger (MAYN jər) *n.* a trough or box for feeding horses or cattle. [ME]

man·gle[1] (MANG gəl) *v.t.* **·gled, ·gling 1.** disfigure or mutilate by cutting, bruising, crushing, etc. **2.** mar or ruin; spoil. [ME] —**man′gler** *n.*

man·gle[2] *n.* a machine for smoothing and pressing fabrics by passing them between rollers. [< Du. *mangel*]

man·gy (MAYN jee) *adj.* **·gi·er, ·gi·est 1.** affected with or resembling mange. **2.** squalid; shabby. —**man′gi·ness** *n.*

man·han·dle (MAN HAN dl) *v.t.* **·dled, ·dling** handle roughly.

man·hole (MAN HOHL) *n.* a usu. covered opening by which a person may enter a sewer etc.

man·hood (MAN huud) *n.* **1.** the state of being an adult male human being. **2.** masculine qualities collectively. **3.** men collectively.

man·hour (MAN OWR) *n.* the amount of work a person can do in an hour.

ma·ni·a (MAY nee ə) *n.* **1.** an extraordinary enthusiasm, craving, etc. **2.** *Psychiatry* an exaggerated sense of well-being with excessive mental and physical activity. [ME]

-mania *combining form* an exaggerated or irrational craving for or interest in, for example: **acromania** (high places), **agoramania** (open places), **heliomania** (exposure to sun).

ma·ni·ac (MAY nee AK) *n.* a violently insane person; madman. —*adj.* insane; mad. —**ma·ni·a·cal** (mə NĪ ə kəl) *adj.*

-maniac *combining form* used to form nouns and adjectives from nouns ending in *-mania: kleptomaniac.*

man·ic (MAN ik) *adj.* of or affected by mania.

man·ic-de·pres·sive (MAN ik di PRES iv) *adj. Psychiatry* denoting or characteristic of a mental disorder in which periods of depression alternate with periods of excitement. —*n.* one who suffers from this disorder.

man·i·cure (MAN ə KYUUR) *n.* the care of the hands and fingernails. —*v.t. & v.i.* **·cured, ·cur·ing** treat (the nails, etc.). [< F] —**man′i·cur′ist** *n.*

man·i·fest (MAN ə FEST) *adj.* plainly apparent; obvious. —*v.t.* **1.** reveal; show; display. **2.** prove; be evidence of. —*n.* in transportation, an itemized account or list, as of passengers or cargo. [ME *manifesten*] —**man′i·fest′ly** *adv.*

man·i·fes·ta·tion (MAN ə fə STAY shən) *n.* **1.** the act of manifesting, or the state of being manifested. **2.** a sign; indication.

man·i·fes·to (MAN ə FES toh) *n. pl.* **·toes** a public and formal declaration or explanation of principles, intentions, etc., usu. by a political faction or similar group. [< Ital.]

man·i·fold (MAN ə FOHLD) *adj.* **1.** having many and varied forms, types, instances, etc.: *manifold* sorrows. **2.** having an assortment of features etc. —*n.* **1.** *Mech.* a pipe or chest having several or many openings, as for exhaust gas. **2.** a copy made by manifolding. —*v.t.* **1.** make more than one copy of. **2.** multiply. [ME]

man·i·kin (MAN i kin) *n.* **1.** a little man; dwarf. **2.** mannequin. [< Du. *manneken* little man]

ma·nip·u·late (mə NIP yə LAYT) *v.t.* **·lat·ed, ·lat·ing 1.** manage or control (persons, figures, stocks, etc.) shrewdly and deviously for one's own profit or purposes. **2.** control, move, treat, etc. with or as with the hands; esp., handle skillfully. —**ma·nip′u·la′tion** *n.* —**ma·nip′u·la′tor** *n.*

man·kind *n.* **1.** (MAN KĪND) the whole human species; humankind; humanity. **2.** (MAN KĪND) men collectively, as distinguished from women.

man·ly (MAN lee) *adj.* **·li·er, ·li·est 1.** pertaining to or appropriate for a man; virile: *manly* charm. **2.** having the qualities and virtues of a man, as courage, determination, strength, etc. —**the manly art** boxing. — **man'li·ness** n.

man·na (MAN ə) n. **1.** the food miraculously given to the Israelites in the wilderness as they fled from Egypt. **2.** any nourishment, help, etc. received as by divine bounty. [ME]

man·ne·quin (MAN i kin) n. **1.** a full-sized model of a human figure used for cutting, fitting, or displaying garments. **2.** a woman who models clothing. [< F]

man·ner (MAN ər) n. **1.** a way of doing or a way in which something happens or is done. **2.** a style of speech and action: a grave *manner*. **3.** pl. social conduct; etiquette; esp., polite and civil social behavior. **4.** pl. the modes of social behavior prevailing in a group, nation, period, etc. **5.** a characteristic style in literature, music, art, etc. —**in a manner of speaking** approximately. [ME *manere*]

man·nered (MAN ərd) adj. **1.** having (a specific kind of) manner or manners: used in combination: *mild-mannered*. **2.** having mannerisms in writing, speaking, etc.

man·ner·ism (MAN ə RIZ əm) n. **1.** marked use of a distinctive style, as in writing or painting. **2.** a distinctive trait; idiosyncrasy.

man·ner·ly (MAN ər lee) adj. well-behaved; polite.

ma·nom·e·ter (mə NOM i tər) n. any of various instruments used to measure pressure, as of gases, liquids, or vapors. [< F *manomètre*]

man·or (MAN ər) n. **1.** in England: **a** formerly, a feudal domain. **b** a landed estate. **2.** a mansion. **3.** in colonial America, a landed estate with hereditary feudal rights. [ME *maner*]

man·pow·er (MAN POW ər) n. **1.** the force of human physical strength. **2.** the number of people whose strength and skill are available to a nation, army, project, etc.; personnel.

man·ser·vant (MAN SUR vənt) n. an adult male servant.

man·sion (MAN shən) n. a large and impressive house. [ME]

man·slaugh·ter (MAN SLAW tər) n. *Law* the unlawful killing of a human being without malice. [ME]

man·tel (MAN tl) n. **1.** the shelf above a fireplace. **2.** a facing of wood, brick, etc., around a fireplace.

man·til·la (man TEE yə) n. a light scarf, often of black lace, worn over the head and shoulders of women in Spain and Spanish America. [< Sp.]

man·tle (MAN tl) n. **1.** anything that clothes, envelops, or conceals. **2.** the earth's layer beneath the crust and above the core. —v.t. **·tled, ·tling** cover with or as with a mantle; conceal. [ME *mantel*]

man·tra (MAN trə) n. an incantation or chant, as in Hinduism. [< Skt.]

man·u·al (MAN yoo əl) adj. involving, used, or operated by the hands. —n. **1.** a small book of instructions. **2.** an organ keyboard. **3.** a prescribed drill in manipulating a rifle, flag, etc. [< L *manualis*] —**man'u·al·ly** adv.

man·u·fac·ture (MAN yə FAK chər) v.t. **·tured, ·tur·ing 1.** make or process a product, esp. on a large scale and with machinery. **2.** invent (a lie, alibi, etc.). —n. **1.** the act or process of manufacturing. **2.** something that is manufactured. — **man'u·fac'tur·er** n.

man·u·mit (MAN yə MIT) v.t. **·mit·ted, ·mit·ting** free from bondage, as a slave. [ME] —**man'u·mis'sion** (-MISH ən) n.

ma·nure (mə NYUUR) n. dung, compost, etc., used to fertilize soil. —v.t. **·nured, ·nur·ing** apply manure or other fertilizer to, as soil. [ME *manouren* cultivate]

man·u·script (MAN yə SKRIPT) n. **1.** the text of a book, article, document, etc., prepared or submitted for publication. **2.** something written by hand. [< Med.L *manuscriptus* written by hand]

man·y (MEN ee) adj. **more, most** adding up to a large number; numerous. —n. **1.** a large number. **2.** the masses: with *the*. — **many a** (or **an** or **another**) many: with singular noun. —pron. a large number of persons or things. [ME *mani*]

Mao·ism (MOW iz əm) n. the communist doctrines or practices of Mao Tse-tung. [after *Mao Zedong*, 1893—1976, former chairman of the People's Republic of China] —**Mao'ist** n. & adj.

Ma·o·ri (MAH oh ree) n. **1.** one of an aboriginal people of New Zealand, chiefly Polynesian mixed with Melanesian. **2.** the Polynesian language of these people. — **Ma'o·ri** adj.

map (map) n. **1.** a representation on a plane surface of any region, as of the earth's surface; a chart. **2.** anything resembling a map. —v.t. **mapped, map·ping 1.** make a map

of. **2.** plan in detail: often with *out.* —
map•ping n. [ME *mappe*]

ma•ple (MAY pəl) n. **1.** any of numerous
deciduous trees of the north temperate
zone, with opposite leaves and a double-
winged fruit, as the sugar maple. **2.** the
wood of these trees. **3.** the flavor of the sap
of the sugar maple. [ME *mapel*]

maple sugar sugar made from the sap of the
sugar maple.

maple syrup the refined sap of the sugar
maple.

ma•quis (ma KEE) n. a zone of shrubby,
mostly evergreen plants in the Mediterranean region, known as cover for game, ban-
dits, etc. [< F, thicket]

mar (mahr) v.t. **marred, mar•ring 1.** damage. **2.** injure so as to deface. —n. a disfiguring mark; blemish. [ME *merren*]

ma•ra•ca (mə RAH kə) n. a percussion
instrument made of a gourd or gourd-
shaped rattle with beans or beads inside it.
[< Pg.]

mar•a•schi•no (MAR ə SKEE noh) n. a cordial distilled from the fermented juice of a
small wild cherry. [< Ital.]

mar•a•thon (MAR ə THON) n. **1.** a footrace
of 26 miles, 385 yards. **2.** any endurance
contest. [from a messenger's run from Marathon, Greece, to Athens to announce the
victory of the Athenians over the Persians at
Marathon in 490 B.C.]

ma•raud (mə RAWD) v.i. **1.** rove in search
of plunder. —v.t. **2.** invade for plunder. [<
F *marauder*] —**ma•raud′er** n.

mar•ble (MAHR bəl) n. **1.** a compact, granular limestone occurring in many colors,
used for building, sculpture, etc. **2.** a small
ball of this stone, or of glass, porcelain, etc.
3. pl. a children's game played with balls of
glass etc. —v.t. •**bled,** •**bling** color or vein
in imitation of marble, as book edges. [ME
marbel] —**mar′ble** adj.

mar•bling (MAHR bling) n. the streaked
appearance of lean meat, caused by the intermingling of fat.

march (mahrch) v.i. **1.** walk or proceed with
measured, regular steps, as a soldier or
body of troops. **2.** walk in a solemn or dignified manner. **3.** advance steadily. —v.t. **4.**
cause to march. —n. **1.** the act of marching.
2. a regular, measured step, as of a body of
troops. **3.** the distance passed over in
marching: a full day's *march.* **4.** onward
progress. **5.** a musical composition for
marching. [ME *marchen*] —**mar′•cher** n.

March (mahrch) the third month of the year,
containing 31 days. [ME *Marche*]

mar•chion•ess (MAHR shə nis) n. the wife
or widow of a marquis.

Mar•di Gras (MAHR dee GRAH) the last
Tuesday before Lent, often a carnival. [< F,
lit., fat Tuesday]

mare[1] (mair) n. the mature female of the
horse or other equine animal. [ME]

ma•re[2] (MAHR ay) n. pl. **mar•i•a** (-ee ə) any
of a number of dark, seemingly flat areas of
the moon's surface. [< L, sea]

mar•ga•rine (MAHR jər in) n. a substitute
for butter, made from vegetable oils and
sometimes milk: also called *oleomargarine.*

mar•gin (MAHR jin) n. **1.** the part of a page
around the body of printed or written text.
2. a bounding line or surface; border. **3.** an
extra amount of something, as space, time,
money, etc. **4.** in commerce, the difference
between the cost and selling price of a commodity. **5.** security deposited with a stockbroker as protection against loss in trading.
[ME]

mar•gi•nal (MAHR jn əl) adj. **1.** situated or
written at or on a margin. **2.** *Econ.* barely
profitable. **3.** not essential; peripheral.

mar•gi•na•li•a (MAHR jə NAY lee ə) n.pl.
marginal notes.

mar•i•jua•na (MAR ə WAH nə) n. **1.** the
hemp plant. **2.** the dried leaves and flower
tops of this plant, used as a narcotic. Also
ma′ri•hua′na. [< Am. Sp. *marihuana*]

ma•ri•na (mə REE nə) n. a docking area or
basin for small vessels. [< Ital.]

mar•i•nade (MAR ə NAYD) n. **1.** a sauce
sometimes flavored with wine, oil, spices,
etc., in which meat or fish is soaked before
cooking. **2.** meat or fish treated this way. —
v.t. •**nad•ed,** •**nad•ing** (MAR ə NAYD [<
F]

mar•i•nate (MAR ə NAYT) v.t. •**nat•ed,**
•**nat•ing** steep (food) in marinade. [? <
Ital. *marinato* pickled]

ma•rine (mə REEN) adj. **1.** of, pertaining
to, existing in, or formed by the sea. **2.**
pertaining to the navigation or handling of
ships at sea; nautical. **3.** relating to the
navy; naval. **4.** used or intended for use at
sea or in navigation. —n. **1.** a soldier
trained for service at sea and on land; a
member of the Marine Corps. **2.** shipping
vessels, shipping, or the navy collectively.
[ME *maryne*]

Marine Corps a branch of the U.S. armed
forces within the Department of the Navy.

officially the **United States Marine Corps.**

mar·i·ner (MAR ə nər) *n.* one who navigates a ship; sailor; seaman. [ME]

mar·i·on·ette (MAR ee ə NET) *n.* a small jointed figure of wood, cloth, etc., animated by manipulation of strings. [< F *marionnette*]

mar·i·tal (MAR ə tl) *adj.* of or pertaining to marriage. [< L *maritalis*]

mar·i·time (MAR ə TIM) *adj.* 1. situated on or near the sea. 2. of or pertaining to the sea or its navigation, commerce, etc. [< L *maritimus* pertaining to the sea]

mark¹ (mahrk) *n.* 1. a visible trace, impression, or figure on something, as a line, spot, etc. 2. an identifying symbol; trademark. 3. a cross or other sign made by one who cannot write. 4. a letter or number used to rate a student's work; grade. 5. an object, point, sign, etc. serving to indicate, guide, or direct. 6. a visible indication of some quality, trait, position, etc. 7. that which is aimed at, or toward which effort is directed. 8. a standard or criterion of quality, performance, etc. 9. *Slang* a person easily duped or victimized. 10. in track, the starting line of the contest. 11. *Naut.* a knot, twist, etc. on a lead line indicating fathoms of depth. —**make one's mark** succeed. —**wide of the mark** 1. striking far from the point aimed at. 2. irrelevant. —*v.t.* 1. make a mark on. 2. trace the boundaries of: often with *out.* 3. indicate or show by a mark or sign. 4. characterize; distinguish: a year *marked* by great events. 5. designate, appoint, or select, as if by marking: be *marked* for death. 6. pay attention to; notice; heed. 7. evaluate by giving marks to. 8. keep (record or score) in various games. 9. produce by drawing, writing, etc. —*v.i.* 10. take notice; pay attention; consider. —**mark down** 1. note down by writing. 2. put a lower price on, as for sale. —**mark time** 1. keep time by moving the feet but not advancing. 2. pause in action or progress temporarily. —**mark up** 1. make marks on; scar. 2. increase the price of. [ME]

mark² *n.* the standard monetary unit of Germany, also called the *Deutsche mark.*

marked (mahrkt) *adj.* 1. clearly evident; noticeable. 2. having a mark or marks. —**a marked man** one singled out for vengeance, punishment, etc. —**mark·ed·ly** (MAHR kid lee) *adv.*

mar·ket (MAHR kit) *n.* 1. trade and commerce in a specific service or commodity: the boat *market;* also, trade and commerce generally: with *the.* 2. a region where one can buy or sell; also, a category of potential buyers: the college *market.* 3. a place where something is offered for sale. 4. a public gathering, often weekly, for buying and selling. —**in the market** seeking to buy. —**on the market** up for sale. —*v.t.* 1. sell. —*v.i.* 2. deal in a market. [ME]

mar·ket·a·ble (MAHR ki tə bəl) *adj.* suitable for sale; in demand. —**mar'ket·a·bil'i·ty** *n.*

mar·ket·place (MAHR kit PLAYS) *n.* 1. a market (def. 3). 2. the imagined place where ideas, opinions, etc., are tested and traded.

mark·ing (MAHR king) *n.* 1. a mark or an arrangement of marks. 2. *Often pl.* the color pattern on a bird, animal, etc.

marks·man (MAHRKS mən) *n. pl.* **·men** one skilled in hitting the mark, as with a rifle or other weapon. Also **marks'wom'an** *n.* —**marks'man·ship** *n.*

mark·up (MAHRK up) *n.* 1. a raising of price. 2. the amount of price increase.

mar·ma·lade (MAHR mə LAYD) *n.* a preserve made by boiling with sugar the pulp and rind of fruits, usu. citrus fruits. [< Pg. *marmelada* quince jam]

mar·mo·re·al (mahr MOR ee əl) *adj.* pertaining to, made of, or resembling marble. [< L *marmoreus* made of marble]

ma·roon¹ (mə ROON) *v.t.* 1. put ashore and abandon on a desolate island or coast. 2. abandon; leave helpless. [< F *marron*]

ma·roon² *n.* a dark red color. —*adj.* [< F *marron,* lit., chestnut]

mar·quee (mahr KEE) *n.* 1. a canopy used as a shelter over the sidewalk in front of a theater, hotel, etc. 2. a large field tent, as one used at outdoor parties.

mar·quis (MAHR kwis) *n. pl.* **·quis·es, ·quis** (-MEEZ) the title of a nobleman next in rank below a duke. [ME *markis*]

mar·quise (mahr KEEZ) *n. pl.* **·quis·es** the wife or widow of a French marquis.

mar·riage (MAR ij) *n.* 1. the state of being married; a legal contract, entered into by a man and a woman, to live together as husband and wife; wedlock. 2. the act of marrying; also, the accompanying rites or festivities; wedding; nuptials. 3. any close union. [ME *mariage*] —**mar'riage·a·ble** *adj.*

mar·ried (MAR eed) *adj.* 1. united in matrimony; having a spouse. **2.** of or pertaining to marriage or to persons united in marriage. **3.** closely related or joined.

mar·row (MAR oh) *n.* **1.** a soft, vascular tissue found in the central cavities of bones. **2.** the essence of anything; pith. **3.** vitality. [ME *marowe*]

mar·row·bone (MAR oh BOHN) *n.* a bone, as the shinbone, containing edible marrow.

mar·ry (MAR ee) *v.* **·ried, ·ry·ing** *v.t.* **1.** accept as husband or wife; take in marriage. **2.** join as husband and wife in marriage. **3.** unite closely. —*v.t.* **4.** take a spouse. **5.** join or unite closely. [ME *marien*]

Mars (mahrz) *n.* the seventh largest planet of the solar system and fourth from the sun. [after L *Mars*, god of war]

marsh (mahrsh) *n.* a tract of low, wetland; swamp. [ME *mershe*] —**marsh'y** *adj.* **marsh'i·er, marsh'i·est**

mar·shal (MAHR shəl) *n.* **1.** in various countries, a military officer of high rank, usu. just below the commander in chief: a field *marshal.* **2.** *U.S.* **a** an officer of the federal courts, assigned to a judicial district and having duties similar to those of a sheriff. **b** in some cities, the chief of the police or fire department. **3.** an officer authorized to organize or preside at processions, ceremonies, etc. —*v.t.* **·shaled, ·shal·ing 1.** arrange or dispose in order, as facts. **2.** array or draw up, as troops for battle. **3.** lead; usher. [ME]

marsh gas methane.

marsh·mal·low (MAHRSH MEL oh) *n.* a confection made of starch, sugar, corn syrup, and gelatin.

mar·su·pi·al (mahr SOO pee əl) *n.* any member of an order of mammals, as the kangaroos, whose females carry their undeveloped young in an abdominal pouch. [< NL *marsupialis* pertaining to a bag] —*adj.*

mar·tial (MAHR shəl) *adj.* **1.** of, pertaining to, or concerned with war or the military life. **2.** suggestive of or suitable for war or military operations. **3.** of or characteristic of a warrior. [ME]

martial law temporary rule by military forces over the citizens of an area where civil law no longer is effective.

Mar·tian (MAHR shən) *adj. Astron.* of or pertaining to the planet of Mars. —*n.* one of the supposed inhabitants of Mars. [ME *marcien*]

mar·ti·net (MAHR tn ET) *n.* one who demands rigid adherence to rules etc. [after

General Jean *Martinet,* 17th c. French drillmaster]

mar·ti·ni (mahr TEE nee) *n. pl.* **·nis** a cocktail made of gin, or vodka, and dry vermouth.

mar·tyr (MAHR tər) *n.* **1.** one who suffers death rather than renounce his or her religion. **2.** one who dies, suffers, or sacrifices everything for a principle, cause, etc. **3.** one who suffers much, as from ill health or misfortune. —*v.t.* also **martyrize 1.** make a martyr of. **2.** torture or persecute. [ME *marter*] —**mar'tyr·dom** (-dəm) *n.*

mar·vel (MAHR vəl) *v.i.* **·veled, ·vel·ing** be filled with wonder, surprise, etc. —*n.* that which excites wonder; a prodigy. [ME *mervel*]

mar·vel·ous (MAHR və ləs) *adj.* **1.** causing astonishment and wonder; amazing; extraordinary. **2.** very good; excellent; admirable. [ME *merveillous*] —**mar'vel·ous·ly** *adv.*

Marx·ism (MAHRK siz əm) *n.* the body of socialist doctrines formulated by Karl Marx and Friedrich Engels. —**Marx'ist, Marx'i·an** *n. & adj.*

mar·zi·pan (MAHR zə PAN) *n.* a confection of grated almonds, sugar, and egg whites, usu. made into a paste and molded into various shapes. [< Ital. *marzapane*]

mas·car·a (ma SKAR ə) *n.* a cosmetic preparation used to color the eyelashes and eyebrows. [< Sp., *máscara* mask]

mas·cot (MAS kot) *n.* a person, animal, or object thought to bring good luck by its presence. [< F *mascotte*]

mas·cu·line (MAS kyə lin) *adj.* **1.** of or pertaining to the male sex; male. **2.** of, or pertaining to, typical of, or appropriate for men or boys: *masculine* attitudes. **3.** applicable only to persons or things grammatically classified as male. —*n. Gram.* the masculine gender. [ME *masculin*] —**mas'cu·lin'i·ty** *n.*

ma·ser (MAY zər) *n. Physics* a device that generates or amplifies electromagnetic waves of precise frequency without loss of frequency and phase. [*m*icrowave *a*mplification by *s*timulated *e*mission of *r*adiation]

mash (mash) *n.* **1.** a soft, pulpy mixture or mass. **2.** a mixture of meal, bran, etc. and water, fed warm to horses and cattle. **3.** crushed or ground grain or malt, steeped in hot water to produce wort for making beer. —*v.t.* **1.** crush into a mash or pulp. **2.** steep (malt, grain meal, etc.) in hot water to produce wort. [ME]

mask (mask) *n.* **1.** a covering used to conceal all or part of the face as a disguise or for protection. **2.** a cast of a face, usu. made of plaster. **3.** that which conceals something from the sight or mind: under the *mask* of piety. **4.** a masquerade. **5.** see MASQUE. —*v.t.* **1.** cover (the face, head, etc.) with a mask. **2.** disguise. —*v.i.* **3.** put on a mask; assume a disguise. [< MF *masque*] —**masked** *adj.*

mas·och·ism (MAS ə kɪz əm) *n.* **1.** *Psychol.* a condition in which sexual gratification depends largely on undergoing physical pain or humiliation. **2.** a tendency to derive pleasure from one's own suffering. [after Leopold von Sacher-*Masoch*, 1835—95, Austrian novelist who described this condition] —**mas'o·chist** *n.* —**mas'o·chis'tic** *adj.*

ma·son (MAY sən) *n.* **1.** one skilled in building with stone, brick, concrete, etc. **2.** a stonecutter. **3.** *cap.* a Freemason, a member of the secret or fraternal order called *Free and Accepted Masons.* [ME] — **ma·son·ic** (mə SON ik) *adj.* —**ma·son·ry** (MAY sən ree) *n.*

masque (mask) *n.* **1.** an elaborately staged dramatic performance, popular esp. during the 17th c. in England; also, something written for this. **2.** a masquerade. Also spelled *mask.*

mas·quer·ade (MAS kə RAYD) *n.* **1.** a social gathering in which the guests are masked and dressed in fancy costumes. **2.** the costumes worn at such a gathering. **3.** a false show, disguise, or pretense. —*v.i.* •**ad·ed,** •**ad·ing 1.** take part in a masquerade. **2.** disguise one's true character. [< MF]

mass (mas) *n.* **1.** a body of matter having no definite shape but relatively large size. **2.** an assemblage of individual parts or objects that collectively make up a single body. **3.** a great amount or number of anything. **4.** the greater part of anything; majority. **5.** the volume or magnitude of a solid body; bulk; size. **6.** *Physics* the measure of the inertia of a body, expressed as the quotient of the weight of the body divided by the acceleration due to gravity. —**the masses** the great body or majority of ordinary people. —*adj.* **1.** attended by, designed for, characteristic of, or affecting a large mass of people. **2.** produced in large amounts. **3.** total: the

mass effect. —*v.t.* & *v.i.* form into a mass; assemble. [ME *masse*]

Mass (mas) *n. Eccl.* **1.** in the Roman Catholic and some Anglican churches, the liturgy, regarded as a commemoration or repetition of Christ's sacrifice on the Cross. **2.** a celebration of this liturgy. **3.** a musical setting for some of the fixed portions of this liturgy. [ME *masse*]

mas·sa·cre (MAS ə kər) *n.* **1.** a savage and indiscriminate killing of human beings. **2.** *Informal* a crushing defeat, as in sports. — *v.t.* •**cred,** •**cring 1.** kill indiscriminately or in great numbers. **2.** *Informal* defeat decisively, as in sports. [< MF] —**mas'sa·crer** (-krər) *n.*

mas·sage (mə SAHZH) *n.* a manipulation of parts of the body, as by rubbing, kneading, or slapping, used to promote circulation, relax muscles, etc. —*v.t.* •**saged,** •**sag·ing** treat by massage. [< F]

mas·seur (mə SUR) *n.* a man who practices or gives massage. [< F] —**mas·seuse** (mə SOOS) *n.fem.*

mas·sive (MAS iv) *adj.* **1.** forming or constituting a large mass; having great bulk and weight. **2.** imposing or impressive in scale, scope, degree, etc. **3.** *Pathol.* extending over or affecting a large area: a *massive* swelling. [ME *massif*]

mass media the various means of disseminating information to a wide public audience, as newspapers, radio, etc.

mass meeting a large public gathering for the discussion or promotion of some topic or cause, usu. political.

mass·pro·duce (MAS prə DOOS) *v.t.* •**duced,** •**duc·ing** manufacture or produce (goods or articles) in great quantities, usu. by machine. —**mass production**

mast (mast) *n.* **1.** *Naut.* a pole or spar set upright in a sailing vessel to sustain the sails etc. **2.** any large, upright pole, as of a derrick, crane, etc. —**before the mast** serving as a common sailor. [ME]

mas·tec·to·my (ma STEK tə mee) *n. pl.* •**mies** the surgical removal of a breast.

mas·ter (MAS tər) *n.* **1.** one who has control, direction, or authority over someone or something, as over a household, an animal, etc. **2.** one exceptionally gifted or skilled in an art, science, etc.: a *master* of oratory. **3.** a craftsman or worker qualified to practice alone and to train apprentices. **4.** a teacher or leader in philosophy, religion, etc. who has followers or disciples. **5.** a male teacher.

6. one who has received a college degree beyond the bachelor's but less than the doctor's. **7.** something, as a matrix, stencil, etc., from which copies or impressions are made. **8.** *Usu. cap.* a youth or boy; also a title prefixed to a boy's name. **9.** a victor or conqueror. **10.** *Law* an officer of the court who assists the judge. —*v.t.* **1.** bring under control; defeat. **2.** become expert in: *master* Greek. **3.** control or govern as a master. —*adj.* **1.** of, pertaining to, or characteristic of a master. **2.** having or exercising control. **3.** principal; main: the *master* plan. [ME *maistre*]

mas·ter·ful (MAS tər fəl) *adj.* **1.** vigorously bold or authoritative in conduct, manner, etc. **2.** having or displaying the skill of a master. —**mas′ter·ful·ly** *adv.*

mas·ter·ly (MAS tər lee) *adj.* characteristic of or befitting a master.

mas·ter·mind (MAS tər MIND) *n.* a person of great executive ability; esp., one who plans and directs at the highest levels of policy and strategy. —*v.t.* plan and direct (a project etc.) at the highest strategic level.

master of ceremonies a person presiding over an entertainment or dinner and introducing the performers or speakers.

mas·ter·piece (MAS tər PEES) *n.* **1.** something of notable excellence; an unusually brilliant achievement. **2.** something considered the greatest achievement of its creator. Also **mas′ter·work′** (-WURK).

master sergeant *Mil.* **1.** a noncommissioned officer in the U.S. Army and U.S. Marines ranking below a sergeant major. **2.** in the U.S. Air Force a noncommissioned officer ranking below a chief master sergeant.

mas·ter·stroke (MAS tər STROHK) *n.* a masterly or decisive action or achievement.

mas·ter·y (MAS tə ree) *n. pl.* **·ter·ies 1.** superior knowledge or skill. **2.** victory or superiority, as in a contest. **3.** the act of mastering a craft, technique, etc.

mast·head (MAST HED) *n.* **1.** *Naut.* the top of a mast. **2.** the part of a periodical that gives the names of the editors etc.

mas·ti·cate (MAS ti KAYT) *v.t.* **·cat·ed, ·cat·ing 1.** chew. **2.** reduce, as rubber, to a pulp by crushing or kneading. [< LL *masticatus* chewed]

mas·tiff (MAS tif) *n.* a large hunting dog, having a thickset, heavy body, drooping ears, and pendulous lips. [ME *mastif*]

mas·to·don (MAS tə DON) *n. Paleontol.* any of various large, extinct mammals resembling the elephant. [< NL]

mas·toid (MAS toid) *adj. Anat.* designating a nipple-shaped process of the bone located behind the ear. [< NL *mastoides*] —**mas′toid** *n.*

mas·tur·ba·tion (MAS tər BAY shən) *n.* stimulation of the sexual organs, usu. by oneself. —**mas′tur·bate** *v.i.* **·bat·ed, ·bat·ing**

mat¹ (mat) *n.* **1.** a flat piece of material made of fiber, rubber, etc., used to cover floors. **2.** a thickly padded piece of material placed on the floor for protection in various gymnastic sports. **3.** a small, flat piece of material, as lace, straw, or plastic, used as a table protection, ornament, etc. **4.** any dense, twisted, or tangled mass, as of hair. —*v.* **mat·ted, mat·ting** *v.t.* **1.** cover with or as with a mat or mats. —*v.i.* **2.** become entangled together. [ME *matte*]

mat² *n.* **1.** a border of cardboard or other material, serving as the frame or part of the frame of a picture. **2.** a lusterless, dull finish, as on metal or glass; also **matte.** —*v.t.* **mat·ted, mat·ting 1.** produce a dull surface on, as on metal or glass. **2.** furnish (a picture) with a mat. —*adj.* having a lusterless surface; also **matte.**

mat·a·dor (MAT ə DOR) *n.* in bullfighting, the person who kills the bull after completing various maneuvers with a cape in order to tire the animal. [< Sp.]

match¹ (mach) *n.* **1.** one who or that which is similar to another in some quality or characteristic. **2.** one who or that which is exactly equal to another. **3.** one who or that which is able to cope with or oppose another as an equal. **4.** either of two things that harmonize or correspond with each other. **5.** a game or contest. **6.** a marriage or mating; also, an agreement to marry or mate. —*v.t.* **1.** be similar to or in accord with in quality, degree, etc. **2.** make, provide, or select as equals or as suitable for one another: *match* pearls. **3.** compare so as to decide superiority; test. **4.** set (equal opponents) in opposition. **5.** equal; oppose successfully. **6.** place together as mates; marry. —*v.i.* **7.** be equal or similar. [ME *macche* mate] —**match′er** *n.*

match² *n.* a splinter of soft wood or a piece of cardboard tipped with a combustible composition that ignites by friction. [ME *macche* wick]

match·less (MACH lis) *adj.* having no

match or equal; peerless. **—match'less•ly** *adv.*

match•mak•er (MACH MAY kər) *n.* **1.** one who arranges a marriage. **2.** one who arranges an athletic match. **3.** one who makes matches for lighting.

mate[1] (mayt) *n.* **1.** something matched, paired, or joined with another. **2.** a husband or wife. **3.** either of two animals paired for propagation. **4.** a companion. **5.** an officer of a merchant vessel, ranking next below the captain. **—v.t. & v.i. mat•ed, mat•ing 1.** join together; pair. **2.** join in marriage. **3.** unite for breeding, as animals. [ME]

mate[2] *v.t.* **mat•ed, mat•ing** in chess, checkmate. **—n.** a checkmate.

ma•te•ri•al (mə TEER ee əl) *n.* **1.** that of which anything is composed, created, or developed. **2.** *pl.* the tools, instruments, etc. for doing something. **3.** cloth or fabric. **—adj. 1.** of, pertaining to, or composed of matter; physical. **2.** of, related to, or affecting the body: *material* comforts. **3.** concerned with or devoted to things primarily worldly rather than spiritual or intellectual. **4.** substantial; important. [ME]

ma•te•ri•al•ism (mə TEER ee ə LIZ əm) *n.* **1.** *Philos.* the doctrine that everything in the universe is reducible to matter and can be explained in terms of physical laws. **2.** undue regard for the material aspects of life. **—ma•te'ri•al•ist** *n.* **—ma•te'ri•al•is'tic** *adj.*

ma•te•ri•al•ize (mə TEER ee ə LIZ) *v.* **•ized, •iz•ing** *v.t.* **1.** give material or actual form to. **2.** in spiritualism, cause (a spirit etc.) to appear in visible form. **—v.t. 3.** assume material or visible form; appear. **4.** take form or shape; be realized.

ma•te•ri•al•ly (mə TEER ee ə lee) *adv.* **1.** in an important manner or to a considerable degree. **2.** physically.

ma•té•ri•el (mə TEER ee EL) *n.* **1.** the equipment and supplies of a military force. **2.** the equipment of any organization. Also **ma•te'ri•el.** [< F]

ma•ter•nal (mə TUR nl) *adj.* **1.** of, pertaining to, or characteristic of a mother; motherly. **2.** derived from, related through, or connected with one's mother. [< Med.L *maternalis*] **—ma•ter'nal•ly** *adv.*

ma•ter•ni•ty (mə TUR ni tee) *n.* **1.** the state of being a mother. **2.** the qualities of a mother. **—adj. 1.** fashioned for pregnant women: *maternity* clothes. **2.** designed to accommodate women and babies during

and after childbirth: *maternity* ward. [< Med.L *maternitas*]

math•e•ma•ti•cian (MATH ə mə TISH ən) *n.* one who specializes or is expert in mathematics.

math•e•mat•ics (MATH ə MAT iks) *n.* *(construed as sing.)* the study of quantity, form, arrangement, and magnitude; esp., the methods and processes for disclosing the properties and relations of quantities and magnitudes. **—math'e•mat'i•cal** *adj.*

mat•i•née (MAT n AY) *n.* a performance or entertainment, as a play, concert, etc., held in the daytime, usu. in the afternoon. Also **mat'i•nee'.** [< F, morning]

ma•tri•arch (MAY tree AHRK) *n.* a woman holding the position corresponding to that of a patriarch in her family or tribe. **—ma'tri•ar'chal** *adj.*

ma•tri•ar•chy (MAY tree AHR kee) *n.* *pl.* **•chies** a social organization having the mother as the head of the family, in which descent is traced through the mother.

mat•ri•cide (MA tri SID) *n.* **1.** the killing of one's mother. **2.** one who kills his or her mother. [< L *matricidium*] **—mat'ri•ci'dal** *adj.*

ma•tric•u•late (mə TRIK yə LAYT) *v.t. & v.i.* **•lat•ed, •lat•ing** register or enroll in a college or university as a candidate for a degree. [< Med.L *matriculatus* enrolled] **—ma•tric'u•la'tion** *n.*

mat•ri•mo•ny (MA trə MOH nee) *n.* *1.* the state or condition of being married. **2.** *pl.* **•nies** the act, ceremony, or sacrament of marriage. [ME] **—mat'ri•mo'ni•al** *adj.*

ma•trix (MAY triks) *n.* *pl.* **ma•tri•ces** (MAY tri SEEZ) or **ma•trix•es 1.** that in which anything originates, develops, takes shape, or is contained. **2.** a mold in or from which anything is cast or shaped. [< L, womb]

ma•tron (MAY trən) *n.* **1.** a married woman, esp. one who is mature in age or manner. **2.** a female attendant or guard, as in a woman's prison, rest room, etc. **3.** a female superintendent of an institution, etc. [ME *matrone*] **—ma'tron•ly** *adj. & adv.*

matron of honor a married woman acting as chief attendant to a bride at a wedding.

mat•ter (MAT ər) *n.* **1.** that which makes up the substance of anything; constituent material. **2.** that which is material and physical, occupies space, and is perceived by the senses. **3.** a specific kind of substance: organic *matter.* **4.** an object of discussion, concern, etc.: a *matter* of faith. **5.** something of importance or consequence. **6.** a usu. unpleasant condition or circumstance: with *the*: What's the *matter* with you? **7.** the content or meaning of a book etc., as distinguished from the style or form. **8.** pus. **9.** that which is written, printed, etc.: reading *matter*. **10.** anything sent by mail: third-class *matter*. —*v.i.* be of concern: It *matters* little. [ME *materc*]

mat·ter-of-fact (MAT ər əv FAKT) *adj.* **1.** closely adhering to facts; literal. **2.** straightforward; blunt. —**mat′ter-of-fact′ly** *adv.*

mat·ting[1] (MAT ing) *n.* **1.** a woven fabric of fiber, straw, or other material, used as a floor covering, for packing, etc. **2.** mats collectively.

mat·ting[2] *n.* **1.** a mat for framing a picture. **2.** a dull, lusterless surface, as on metal or glass.

mat·tress (MA tris) *n.* a large pad made of a strong fabric and filled with a resilient material, as cotton, rubber, feathers, etc., used on or as a bed. [ME *materas*]

mat·u·rate (MACH ə RAYT) *v.i.* ·rat·ed, ·rat·ing **1.** form pus. **2.** ripen or mature. [< L *maturatus* ripened] —**mat′u·ra′tion** *n.*

ma·ture (mə CHUUR) *adj.* **1.** completely developed; fully ripe, as plants, fruits, or animals. **2.** highly developed in intellect, outlook, etc.: a *mature* thinker. **3.** thoroughly developed, perfected, etc.: a *mature* scheme. **4.** due and payable: a *mature* bond. —*v.* ·tured, ·tur·ing *v.t.* **1.** cause to ripen; bring to full development. —*v.i.* **2.** come to full development. **3.** become due, as a note. [ME] —**ma·tur′i·ty** *n.*

mat·zo (MAHT sə) *n. pl.* ·zos or ·zot (-soht) a large, flat piece of unleavened bread, traditionally eaten during Passover. Also **mat′zoh.** [< Hebrew]

maud·lin (MAWD lin) *adj.* **1.** excessively emotional or sentimental. **2.** overly sentimental or emotional from too much liquor. [ME *Maudelen*, (Mary) Magdalene, a penitent sinner, often depicted weeping]

maul (mawl) *n.* a heavy mallet for driving wedges, piles, etc. —*v.t.* **1.** beat and bruise. **2.** handle roughly; manhandle; abuse. [ME *malle* hammer] —**maul′er** *n.*

maun·der (MAWN dər) *v.i.* **1.** talk in an incoherent manner; drivel. **2.** move dreamily or idly. —**maun′der·er** *n.*

mau·so·le·um (MAW sə LEE əm) *n. pl.* ·le·ums or ·le·a (-LEE ə) a large, stately tomb. [ME]

mauve (mohv) *n.* any of various purplish rose shades. [< F]

ma·ven (MAY vən) *n.* an expert; connoisseur. [< Yiddish]

mav·er·ick (MAV ər ik) *n.* **1.** an unbranded or orphaned animal, as a calf. **2.** one who is independent in ideas, attitudes, etc. [after Samuel A. *Maverick*, 1803—70, Texas pioneer who did not brand his cattle]

maw (maw) *n.* **1.** the jaws, mouth, or gullet of a voracious mammal or fish. **2.** the craw of a bird. **3.** the stomach. [ME *mawe*]

mawk·ish (MAW kish) *adj.* **1.** characterized by false or childish sentimentality. **2.** sickening or insipid. [ME] —**mawk′ish·ness** *n.*

max·im (MAK sim) *n.* a brief statement of a general principle, truth, or rule of conduct. [ME *maxime*]

max·i·mal (MAK sə məl) *adj.* of or being a maximum; greatest or highest possible.

max·i·mize (MAK sə MIZ) *v.t.* ·mized, ·miz·ing make as great as possible.

max·i·mum (MAK sə məm) *n. pl.* ·mums or ·ma (-mə) **1.** the greatest possible quantity, amount, or degree. **2.** the greatest quantity, degree, etc., reached or recorded. —*adj.* [< L, greatest]

may (may) *v.* past: **might** a defective verb now used only in the present and past tenses as an auxiliary to express: **1.** permission or allowance: *May* I go? **2.** desire, prayer, or wish: *May* your tribe increase! **3.** contingency, esp. in clauses of result, concession, purpose, etc.: He died that we *might* live. **4.** possibility: You *may* be right. [ME *mai*]

May (may) *n.* **1.** the fifth month of the year, containing 31 days. **2.** the prime of life; youth. [ME]

Ma·ya (MAH yə) *n. pl.* **Ma·ya** or ·**yas 1.** one of a tribe of Central American Indians, having an early advanced civilization and still living in Yucatán and parts of northern Central America. **2.** the language of the Mayas. —**Ma′yan** *adj. & n.*

may·be (MAY bee) *adv.* perhaps; possibly.

May Day the first day of May, traditionally celebrated as a spring festival and, in recent times, celebrated in some countries by demonstrations honoring labor.

may·hem (MAY hem) *n.* **1.** *Law* the offense of inflicting injury so that the victim is less capable of self-defense. **2.** any situation characterized by violence, confusion, noise, etc. [ME *maheym*]

may·on·naise (MAY ə NAYZ) n. a dressing, as for salads, made by beating together raw egg yolk, oil, lemon juice or vinegar, and condiments. [< F]

may·or (MAY ər) n. the chief executive of a city, borough, etc. [< Med. L major greater] —**may′or·al** adj.

may·or·al·ty (MAY ər əl tee) n. pl. •ties the office or term of service of a mayor.

maze (mayz) n. **1.** an intricate network of paths or passages; a labyrinth. **2.** a state of bewilderment, uncertainty, or perplexity. [ME mase]

me (mee) pron. the objective case of the pronoun I.

mead·ow (MED oh) n. a tract of grassland, usu. used for grazing or for growing hay. Also **mead′ow·land′**. [ME medwe]

mea·ger (MEE gər) adj. **1.** deficient in quantity or quality; scanty; inadequate. **2.** lacking in fertility, strength, or richness: meager soil. **3.** thin; emaciated. [ME megre lean] —**mea′ger·ly** adv.

meal¹ (meel) n. **1.** the edible seeds of any grain, coarsely ground and unsifted. **2.** any material having a similar texture. [ME mele]

meal² n. **1.** the food served or eaten regularly at certain times during the day. **2.** the time or occasion of taking such food. [ME]

meal ticket 1. a ticket or card bought for a specified price and redeemable at a restaurant for food. **2.** Informal one who or that which provides a livelihood for another.

meal·y (MEE lee) adj. **meal·i·er, meal·i·est 1.** resembling meal; dry; powdery. **2.** containing meal. —**meal′i·ness** n.

meal·y-mouthed (MEE lee MOWTHd) adj. unwilling to express facts or opinions plainly and frankly.

mean¹ (meen) v. **meant** (ment), **mean·ing** v.t. **1.** have in mind as a purpose or intent. **2.** intend or design for some purpose, destination, etc.: Was that remark meant for me? **3.** have as the particular sense or significance. —v.i. **4.** be of specified importance: Her work means everything to her. —**mean well** have good intentions. [ME menen]

mean² adj. **1.** poor or inferior in grade or quality. **2.** having little worth or consequence. **3.** ignoble in mind or character. **4.** miserly; stingy. **5.** poor in appearance; shabby. **6.** humble in birth, rank, or station. **7.** disagreeable; nasty; vicious. **8.** difficult; troublesome. **9.** Slang excellent; expert. [ME mene ordinary] —**mean′ness** n.

mean³ n. **1.** pl. the medium, method, or instrument by which some end is or may be accomplished. **2.** pl. money; wealth. **3.** the middle point or state between two extremes. **4.** an average. —**by all means** without hesitation; certainly. —**by any means** in any manner possible; at all; somehow. —**by means of** with the help of; through using. —**by no means** most certainly not. —adj. **1.** intermediate or average in size, degree, quality, etc.; medium. **2.** halfway between extremes; average. [ME mene]

me·an·der (mee AN dər) v.i. **1.** wind and turn in course. **2.** wander aimlessly. —n. **1.** Often pl. a tortuous or winding course. **2.** aimless wandering. [< L maeander]

mean·ing (MEE ning) n. **1.** that which is intended; aim; purpose. **2.** that which is signified; sense; interpretation. **3.** importance or significance.

mean·ing·ful (MEE ning fəl) adj. full of meaning.

mean·ing·less (MEE ning lis) adj. having no meaning, significance, or importance.

meant (ment) past tense, past participle of MEAN¹.

mean·time (MEEN TĪM) n. intervening time. —adv. **1.** in or during the intervening time. **2.** at the same time. [ME]

mean·while (MEEN HWĪL) n. & adv. meantime. [ME]

mea·sles (MEE zəlz) n. (construed as sing. or pl.) **1.** an acute, highly contagious virus disease affecting children and sometimes adults, characterized by an eruption of small red spots: also called rubeola. **2.** any similar disease, as German measles: also called rubella. [ME mesels]

mea·sly (MEE zlee) adj. **sli·er, •sli·est** Informal contemptibly stingy, scanty, or petty.

meas·ur·a·ble (MEZH ər ə bəl) adj. **1.** capable of being measured or compared. **2.** notable; significant. [ME mesurable] —**meas′ur·a·bly** adv.

meas·ure (MEZH ər) n. **1.** the extent, dimensions, capacity, etc. of anything. **2.** a standard or unit of measurement. **3.** any standard of criticism or judgment. **4.** a system of measurements: liquid measure. **5.** an instrument for taking measurements. **6.** the act of measuring. **7.** a fixed or suitable limit or bound: talkative beyond all measure. **8.** a certain amount, extent, or degree of anything: a measure of freedom. **9.** Often pl. a specific action, step, or procedure. **10.**

a legislative bill. **11.** rhythmic movement or beat. **12.** *Music* the portion of music contained between two bar lines; bar. —**for good measure** as something extra. —*v.* **•ured, •ur•ing** *v.t.* **1.** take or ascertain the dimensions, quantity, capacity, etc. of. **2.** set apart, mark off, allot, etc. by or as by measuring: often with *off* or *out.* **3.** estimate; judge; weigh. **4.** serve as the measure of. **5.** bring into competition or comparison. —*v.i.* **6.** make or take measurements. **7.** yield a specified measurement. —**measure up to,** fulfill or meet, as expectations. [ME *mesure*]

meas•ured (MEZH ərd) *adj.* **1.** determined by some standard. **2.** slow and stately; rhythmical. **3.** carefully considered or weighed; deliberate.

meas•ure•less (MEZH ər lis) *adj.* incapable of being measured; very great; immense.

meas•ure•ment (MEZH ər mənt) *n.* **1.** the act or process of measuring anything. **2.** the amount, capacity, or extent determined by measuring. **3.** a system of measures.

meat (meet) *n.* **1.** the flesh of animals used as food, esp. the flesh of mammals as opposed to fish or fowl. **2.** the edible part of anything. **3.** the essence, gist, or main idea of something. [ME]

meat•y (MEE tee) *adj.* **meat•i•er, meat•i•est 1.** of, pertaining to, or like meat. **2.** full of meat. **3.** full of substance; significant. — **meat′i•ness** *n.*

mec•ca (MEK ə) *n.* **1.** a place or attraction visited by many people. **2.** the goal of one's aspirations. [after the city of *Mecca*, to which Muslims make pilgrimages]

me•chan•ic (mə KAN ik) *n.* one who builds, operates, or repairs tools or machinery. [ME]

me•chan•i•cal (mə KAN i kəl) *adj.* **1.** of, involving, or having to do with machinery or tools. **2.** operated or produced by a machine. **3.** of the science of mechanics. **4.** done without spontaneity or by force of habit; automatic. —**me•chan′i•cal•ly** *adv.*

me•chan•ics (mə KAN iks) *n.* (*construed as sing. in defs. 1 and 2*) **1.** the branch of physics that treats of motion and of the action of forces on material bodies. **2.** the body of knowledge dealing with the design, operation, and maintenance of machinery. **3.** (*construed as pl.*) the technical aspects of anything.

mech•a•nism (MEK ə NIZ əm) *n.* **1.** the parts of arrangement of parts of a machine.

2. something similar to a machine. **3.** the process or technique by which something works. —**mech′a•nis′tic** (-NIS tik) *adj.*

mech•a•nize (MEK ə NIZ) *v.t.* **•nized, •niz•ing 1.** make mechanical. **2.** convert (an industry etc.) to machine production. **3.** *Mil.* equip with tanks, trucks, etc. — **mech′a•ni•za′tion** *n.*

med•al (MED l) *n.* a small piece of metal bearing an image, inscription, etc., and often given as an award for some outstanding act or service. [< MF *medaille*]

med•al•ist (MED l ist) *n.* **1.** a collector or maker of medals. **2.** the recipient of a medal awarded for services or merit.

me•dal•lion (mə DAL yən) *n.* **1.** a large medal. **2.** something resembling a large medal, as a beef *medallion.* [< F *médaillon*]

med•dle (MED l) *v.i.* **•dled, •dling 1.** participate or interfere officiously: often with *in* or *with.* **2.** tamper. [ME *medlen*] — **med′dle•some** (-səm) *adj.*

me•di•a (MEE dee ə) alternative plural of MEDIUM. —*n.* the various forms of mass communication, considered collectively: often with *the.*

me•di•ae•val (mid EE vəl) see MEDIEVAL.

me•di•an (MEE dee ən) *adj.* **1.** pertaining to or situated in the middle. —*n.* **1.** a median point, line, or number. **2.** *Stat.* designating the middle point in a series of values: 8 is the *median* of 2, 5, 8, 10, 13. [< L *medianus* in the middle]

median strip a strip of land, raised pavement, etc. that divides traffic lanes.

me•di•ate (MEE dee AYT) *v.* **•at•ed, •at•ing** *v.t.* **1.** settle or reconcile (differences) by intervening as a peacemaker. — *v.i.* **2.** act between disputing parties to bring about a settlement, etc. —*adj.* (-it) **1.** acting as an intervening agency. **2.** being in an intermediate position. [ME] —**me′di•a′tion** *n.* —**me′di•a′tor** *n.*

med•i•ca•ble (MED i kə bəl) *adj.* capable of being relieved by medical treatment; curable. [< L *medicabilis* curative]

Med•i•caid (MED i KAYD) *n.* a state and federal program providing monetary aid for medical care to those who cannot afford to pay for it.

med•i•cal (MED i kəl) *adj.* **1.** of or pertaining to medicine. **2.** having curative properties.

med•i•ca•ment (mə DIK ə mənt) *n.* any substance for the cure of disease or the alleviation of pain. [< L *medicamentum*]

Med·i·care (MED i KAIR) *n.* a federal program that funds medical care for the aged and certain social security beneficiaries.

med·i·cate (MED i KAYT) *v.t.* •cat·ed, •cat·ing 1. treat medicinally. 2. impregnate with medicine. [< L *medicatus* medicated] —**med′i·ca′tion** *n.* —**med′i·ca′tive** *adj.*

me·dic·i·nal (mə DIS ə nəl) *adj.* pertaining to or having the properties of medicine; healing, curative, or alleviating.

med·i·cine (MED ə sin) *n.* 1. any substance used in the treatment of disease or in the relief of pain. 2. the science of the preservation and restoration of health and of treating disease, esp. as distinguished from surgery. 3. the profession of medicine. [ME *medicin*]

me·di·e·val (mid EE vəl) *adj.* of, like, or characteristic of the Middle Ages: also spelled *mediaeval.*

me·di·e·val·ism (mid EE və LIZ əm) *n.* 1. the spirit, beliefs, customs, and practices of the Middle Ages. 2. devotion to the Middle Ages. 3. any custom, idea, etc. surviving from the Middle Ages. Also spelled *mediaevalism.*

me·di·e·val·ist (mid EE və list) *n.* 1. a scholar or specialist in medieval history, literature, or art. 2. one devoted to the Middle Ages. Also spelled *mediaevalist.*

Medieval Latin see under LATIN.

me·di·o·cre (MEE dee OH kər) *adj.* of only average quality; ordinary. [< MF]

me·di·oc·ri·ty (MEE dee OK ri tee) *n. pl.* •ties 1. the condition or quality of being mediocre. 2. mediocre ability or performance. 3. a mediocre person.

med·i·tate (MED i TAYT) *v.* •tat·ed, •tat·ing *v.i.* 1. engage in continuous and contemplative thought. —*v.t.* 2. think about doing; plan. [< L *meditatus* contemplated] —**med′i·ta′tive** *adj.* —**med′i·ta′tion** *n.*

Med·i·ter·ra·ne·an (MED i tə RAY nee ən) *adj.* of or pertaining to the Mediterranean Sea or its shores. —*n.* one who lives in a Mediterranean country. [< L *mediterraneus* inland]

me·di·um (MEE dee əm) *n. pl.* •di·ums (*for def.* 5) or •di·a (-dee ə) 1. an intermediate degree or condition; mean. 2. the surrounding or enveloping element; environment. 3. an intervening substance in which something may act or an effect be produced. 4. a means or agency; instru-

ment: an advertising *medium.* 5. one through whom the spirits of the dead are believed to communicate with the material world. 6. an area or form of artistic expression, or the materials used. —*adj.* intermediate in quantity, quality, size, etc. [< L, the middle]

med·ley (MED lee) *n.* 1. a mingled and confused mass of elements; jumble. 2. a musical composition made up of different airs or parts of songs. [ME *medlee*]

me·du·sa (mə DOO sə) *n. pl.* •sas or •sae (-see) a jellyfish. [< L *Medusa*, a Gorgon who could turn her beholder to stone by a glance]

meek (meek) *adj.* •er, •est 1. having a patient, gentle disposition. 2. submissive. [ME *meke*]

meet¹ (meet) *v.* **met, meet·ing** *v.t.* 1. come upon; encounter. 2. be at or go to the place of arrival of: *meet* them at the station. 3. make the acquaintance of. 4. come into contact or conjunction with. 5. keep an appointment with. 6. come into the perception or recognition of (the eye, ear, etc.). 7. oppose in battle. 8. deal or cope with; handle. 9. fulfill (an obligation, need, requirement, etc.). —*v.i.* 10. come together; come face to face. 11. assemble. 12. make acquaintance or be introduced. 13. come together in conflict or opposition; contend. —**meet with** 1. come upon; encounter. 2. deal or confer with. 3. experience. —*n.* an assembling for a sport or an athletic contest. [ME *meten*]

meet² *adj.* suitable; proper. [ME *mete*]

meet·ing (MEE ting) *n.* 1. a coming together. 2. an assembly or gathering of persons; also, the persons present. 3. a joining or conjunction of things.

mega- *combining form* 1. great; large: **megastructure.** 2. one million times a specified unit: **megavolt, megohm.** Before vowels, **meg-.** [< Gk. *mégas* large]

meg·a·byte (MEG ə BIT) *n.* a million bytes.

meg·a·cy·cle (MEG əsI kəl) *n.* megahertz.

meg·a·hertz (MEG ə HURTS) *n. pl.* •hertz a unit of frequency equal to one million hertz.

meg·a·lo·ma·ni·a (MEG ə loh MAY nee ə) *n. Psychiatry* a symptom of mental illness characterized by delusions of great wealth or position. —**meg′a·lo·ma′ni·ac** *adj. & n.*

meg·a·ton (MEG ə TUN) *n.* 1. one million

tons. 2. a unit equal to the explosive power of one million tons of TNT.

me·gil·lah (mə GIL ə) n. *Slang* a long, complicated account. [< Yiddish, lit. scroll, esp., the Book of Esther]

mel·an·cho·li·a (MEL ən KOH lee ə) n. *Psychiatry* deep depression of spirits without apparent or sufficient cause. [< LL]

mel·an·chol·y (MEL ən KOL ee) adj. 1. excessively gloomy; sad. 2. suggesting or promoting sadness: a *melancholy* day. —n. pl. **·chol·ies** low spirits; depression. [ME *melancholie* condition of having black bile] — **mel'an·chol'ic** adj.

mé·lange (may LAHNZH) n. *French* a medley.

mel·a·nin (MEL ə nin) n. *Biochem.* a brownish black pigment contained in animal tissues, as the skin and hair.

meld (meld) v.t. & v.i. in pinochle and other card games, announce or declare (a combination of cards) for inclusion in one's total score. —n. a group of cards to be declared, or the act of declaring them. [< G *melden* announce]

me·lee (MAY lay) n. a confused, general hand-to-hand fight; affray. [< F *mêlée*]

mel·io·rate (MEEL yə RAYT) v.t. & v.i. **·rat·ed, ·rat·ing** improve, as in quality or condition; ameliorate. [< L *melioratus* improved] —**mel'io·ra'tive** adj.

mel·lif·er·ous (mə LIF ər əs) adj. producing or bearing honey. [< L *mellifer* honeybearing]

mel·lif·lu·ous (mə LIF loo əs) adj. sweetly or smoothly flowing: *mellifluous* speech. [ME] —**mel·lif'lu·ous·ly** adv. —**mel·lif'lu·ous·ness** n.

mel·low (MEL oh) adj. 1. soft, sweet, and full-flavored by reason of ripeness, as fruit. 2. well-matured, as wines. 3. rich and soft in quality, as colors or sounds. 4. made gentle and sympathetic by maturity or experience. —v.t. & v.i. make or become mellow; soften. [ME *melowe*]

me·lo·di·ous (mə LOH dee əs) adj. 1. producing or characterized by melody; tuneful. 2. pleasant to hear.

mel·o·dra·ma (MEL ə DRAH mə) n. 1. a drama in which the emotions displayed are violent or extravagantly sentimental, and the plot is made up of sensational, incidents. 2. sensational and highly emotional behavior or language. [< F *mélodrame*] — **mel·o·dra·mat·ic** (MEL ə drə MAT ik) adj.

mel·o·dra·mat·ics (MEL ə drə MAT iks) n.pl. melodramatic writing or behavior.

mel·o·dy (MEL ə dee) n. pl. **·dies** 1. pleasing sounds, or an agreeable succession of such sounds. 2. *Music* an organized succession of tones, usu. in the same voice or instrument; a tune or air. [ME *melodie*] — **me·lod·ic** (mə LOD ik) adj.

mel·on (MEL ən) n. 1. the large fruit of any of various plants of the gourd family, as the watermelon. 2. any of these plants. [ME]

melt (melt) v.t. & v.i. **melt·ed, melt·ed** or **mol·ten, melt·ing** 1. change from a solid to a liquid state by heat. 2. disappear or cause to disappear: often with *away.* 3. blend by imperceptible degrees: often with *into.* 4. make or become softened in feeling or attitude. —n. 1. something melted. 2. a single operation of fusing. [ME *melten*]

melting point the temperature at which a specified solid substance melts or fuses.

mem·ber (MEM bər) n. 1. one who belongs to a society, club, party, etc. 2. in government, one who belongs to a legislative body. 3. a part or organ of an animal body, esp. a limb. 4. a part or element of a whole. [ME *membre*]

mem·ber·ship (MEM bər SHIP) n. 1. the state or fact of being a member. 2. the members of an organization, etc., collectively; also, the total number of members.

mem·brane (MEM brayn) n. a thin, pliable layer of animal or vegetable tissue serving to cover or line an organ or part, separate adjoining cavities, or connect adjoining structures. [ME] —**mem'bra·nous** (-brə nəs) adj.

me·men·to (mə MEN toh) n. pl. **·tos** or **·toes** anything that serves as a hint or reminder of the past; souvenir. [ME]

mem·oir (MEM wahr) n. 1. pl. a personal reminiscence or record; esp., a narrative of events based on the writer's personal observations and experiences. 2. pl. an account of the proceedings of a learned society. [< F *mémoire*]

mem·o·ra·bil·i·a (MEM ər ə BIL ee ə) n.pl. things or events worthy of remembrance and record. [< L]

mem·o·ra·ble (MEM ər ə bəl) adj. worthy to be remembered; noteworthy.

mem·o·ran·dum (MEM ə RAN dəm) n. pl. **·dums** or **·da** (-də) 1. a brief note of something to be remembered. 2. a record of transactions. 3. an informal letter, usu. sent between departments in an office. 4. *Law* a brief written outline of the terms of a transaction or contract. [ME]

me·mo·ri·al (mə MOR ee əl) *adj.* **1.** serving to keep in memory a deceased person or an event; commemorative. **2.** of or pertaining to memory. —*n.* **1.** something serving to keep in remembrance a person, event, etc. **2.** a written summary or presentation of facts, often in the form of a petition. [ME]

me·mo·ri·al·ize (mə MOR ee ə LIZ) *v.t.* **·ized, ·iz·ing 1.** commemorate. **2.** present a memorial to; petition.

mem·o·rize (MEM ə RIZ) *v.t.* **·rized, ·riz·ing** commit to memory. — **mem′o·ri·za′tion** *n.*

mem·o·ry (MEM ə ree) *n. pl.* **·ries 1.** the mental capacity of recalling or recognizing previously learned behavior or past experience. **2.** the total of what is remembered. **3.** one who or that which is remembered. **4.** the period of time covered by one's ability to remember. **5.** remembrance or commemoration. **6.** computer components that store data; also the capacity for such storage. [ME *memorie*]

men (men) plural of MAN.

men·ace (MEN is) *v.* **·aced, ·ac·ing** *v.t.* **1.** threaten with evil or harm. —*v.i.* **2.** make threats; appear threatening. —*n.* **1.** a threat. **2.** a troublesome person; pest. [ME] —**men′ac·er** *n.* —**men′ac·ing·ly** *adv.*

mé·nage (may NAHZH) *n.* **1.** the persons of a household, collectively. **2.** housekeeping. —**ménage à trois** (ah TRWAH) an arrangement in which three persons live together having sexual relationships with one another. [< F]

me·nag·er·ie (mə NAJ ə ree) *n.* a collection of wild animals kept for exhibition. [< F]

mend (mend) *v.t.* **1.** make sound or serviceable again by repairing. **2.** correct errors or faults in: *Mend* your ways. —*v.i.* **3.** become better, as in health. —*n.* **1.** a repairing. **2.** a mended place, as on a garment. —**on the mend** recovering health.

men·da·cious (men DAY shəs) *adj.* **1.** lying; deceitful. **2.** untrue; false. —**men·da′cious·ly** *adv.* —**men·dac·i·ty** (men DAS i tee) *n.* **1.** lying. **2.** a lie. [< L *mendax* a lie]

men·di·cant (MEN di kənt) *adj.* **1.** begging; depending on alms for a living. **2.** pertaining to or like a beggar. —*n.* **1.** a beggar. **2.** a begging friar. [ME] —**men′di·can·cy** *n.*

me·ni·al (MEE nee əl) *adj.* **1.** pertaining to or appropriate to servants. **2.** servile; abject.

—*n.* **1.** a domestic servant. **2.** one who has a servile nature. [ME *menyal*]

me·nin·ges (mə NIN jeez) *n. pl.* of **meninx** (MEE ningks) *Anat.* the three membranes enveloping the brain and spinal cord. [< NL] —**me·nin′ge·al** (mə NIN jee əl) *adj.*

men·in·gi·tis (MEN in JĪ tis) *n. Pathol.* inflammation of the meninges, esp. through infection. [< NL]

me·nis·cus (mi NIS kəs) *n. pl.* **·nis·cus·es** or **·nis·ci** (-NIS ī) **1.** a crescent or crescent-shaped body. **2.** *Optics* a lens concave on one side and convex on the other. **3.** *Physics* the curved upper surface of a liquid column. [< NL]

men·o·pause (MEN ə PAWZ) *n. Physiol.* the final cessation of menstruation, occurring usually between the ages of 45 and 55. [< F *ménopause*]

men·ses (MEN seez) *n.* (*considered sing. or pl.*) *Physiol.* menstruation. [< L, months]

men·stru·a·tion (MEN stroo AY shən) *n. Physiol.* the periodic flow of bloody fluid from the uterus, usually occurring monthly. —**men′stru·al** *adj.* —**men′·stru·ate** *v.i.* **·at·ed, ·at·ing**

men·su·ra·ble (MEN shər ə bəl) *adj.* measurable. [< LL *mensurabilis*]

men·tal (MEN tl) *adj.* **1.** of or pertaining to the mind or intellect. **2.** taking place in the mind: *mental* calculations. **3.** affected by mental illness: *mental* patients. **4.** for the care of the mentally ill: *mental* hospitals. [ME] —**men′tal·ly** *adv.*

men·tal·i·ty (men TAL i tee) *n. pl.* **·ties 1.** mental capacity. **2.** the cast or habit of mind.

men·tion (MEN shən) *v.t.* refer to incidentally or briefly. —*n.* **1.** the act of one who mentions. **2.** slight reference; casual allusion. [ME *mencioun*]

men·tor (MEN tər) *n.* a wise and trusted teacher or guide. [after *Méntor,* a loyal adviser in the *Odyssey*]

men·u (MEN yoo) *n.* **1.** a list of dishes available or served at a meal. **2.** the dishes included in it. [< F]

me·phit·ic (mə FIT ik) *adj.* **1.** poisonous; foul. **2.** offensive to the sense of smell. [< LL *mephiticus*]

mer·can·tile (MUR kən TEEL) *adj.* of, pertaining to, or characteristic of merchants or commerce. [< F]

mer·ce·nar·y (MUR sə NER ee) *adj.* **1.** influenced by a desire for gain or reward. **2.**

serving for pay: said of soldiers hired by a
foreign state. —*n. pl.* •**nar•ies** a hireling;
esp., a hired soldier in foreign service. [ME
mercenarie]

mer•chan•dise (MUR chən DĪZ) *n.* anything bought and sold for profit; goods;
wares. [ME *marchandise*] —*v.t.* & *v.i.*
•**dised,** •**dis•ing 1.** buy and sell; trade. **2.**
promote the sale of (goods) through advertising, etc. —**mer'•chan•dis'er** *n.*

mer•chant (MUR chənt) *n.* **1.** one who buys
and sells commodities for profit. **2.** a storekeeper. —*adj.* **1.** of or pertaining to merchants or trade. **2.** of or pertaining to the
merchant marine. [ME *marchant*]

merchant marine the trading vessels of a
nation, collectively. **2.** the officers and men
employed on these vessels.

mer•ci•ful (MUR si fəl) *adj.* full of or characterized by mercy. —**mer'ci•ful•ly** *adv.*

mer•ci•less (MUR si lis) *adj.* without mercy;
pitiless. —**mer'ci•less•ly** *adv.*

mer•cu•ri•al (mər KYUUR ee əl) *adj.* **1.**
lively; volatile; clever: like a *mercurial* wit. **2.** of,
containing, or caused by the action of mercury. [ME] —**mer•cu'ri•al•ly** *adv.*

mer•cu•ry (MUR kyə ree) *n. pl.* •**ries 1.** a
heavy, silver-white metallic element (symbol Hg), liquid at ordinary temperatures:
also called *quicksilver.* **2.** this element as
used in a thermometer or barometer to indicate temperature, etc.

Mer•cu•ry (MUR kyə ree) *n.* the smallest
planet of the solar system, and that nearest
the sun. [< *Mercury*, messenger of the Roman gods]

mer•cy (MUR see) *n.* **1.** *pl.* •**cies** kind or
compassionate treatment of an adversary,
prisoner, etc. in one's power. **2.** a disposition
to be kind, forgiving, or helpful. **3.** the
power to show mercy or compassion. **4.** *pl.*
•**cies** a thing to be thankful for. —**at the
mercy of** wholly in the power of. [ME
merci]

mercy killing euthanasia.

mere (meer) *adj.* being nothing more or less
than: a *mere* trifle. [ME] —**mere'ly** *adv.*

mer•e•tri•cious (MER i TRISH əs) *adj.* artificially and vulgarly attractive. [< L *meretricius* pertaining to prostitutes] —
mer'e•tri'cious•ness *n.*

merge (murj) *v.t.* & *v.i.* **merged, merg•
ing** combine or be combined so as to lose
separate identity; blend. [< L *mergere*
dip]

merg•er (MUR jər) *n.* **1.** the combining of

two or more commercial interests into one.
2. the act of merging.

me•rid•i•an (mə RID ee ən) *n.* **1.** *Geog.* a
great circle drawn from any point on the
earth's surface and passing through both
poles. **2.** *Astron.* an analogous great circle
on the celestial sphere. **3.** a highest or culminating point; zenith. —*adj.* **1.** of or pertaining to a meridian. **2.** of or pertaining to
midday. [ME]

me•ringue (mə RANG) *n.* baked beaten egg
whites and sugar, used as a topping for pies,
or made into a small cake or tart shell. [< F
méringue]

mer•it (MER it) *n.* **1.** worth or excellence;
high quality. **2.** that which deserves esteem,
praise, or reward. **3.** *Sometimes pl.* the
quality or fact of being entitled to reward,
praise, etc. **4.** *pl.* the actual rights or wrongs
of a matter, esp. a legal matter. —*v.t.* earn
as a reward or punishment; deserve. [ME]

mer•i•to•ri•ous (MER i TOR ee əs) *adj.* deserving of reward or praise. —**mer'i•to'
ri•ous•ly** *adv.*

mer•maid (MUR MAYD) *n.* a legendary marine creature having the head and upper
body of a woman and the tail of a fish. [ME
mermayde]

mer•ri•ment (MER i mənt) *n.* laughter; fun.

mer•ry (MER ee) *adj.* •**ri•er,** •**ri•est 1.** full
of mirth and laughter; joyous; gay. **2.** characterized by or conducive to mirth, cheerfulness, etc. [ME *merie*] —**mer'ri•ly** *adv.*

mer•ry-go-round (MER ee goh ROWND) *n.*
1. a revolving platform fitted with wooden
horses, seats, etc. on which people, esp.
children, ride for amusement; carousel. **2.** a
whirl, as of business or pleasure.

mer•ry-mak•ing (MER ee MAY king) *n.* the
act of having fun and making merry. —*adj.*
festive. —**mer'ry-mak'er** *n.*

me•sa (MAY sə) *n.* a high, flat tableland descending sharply to the surrounding plain,
common in the SW U.S. [< Sp., table]

mes•cal (me SKAL) *n.* **1.** a spineless cactus,
native to the SW U.S. and northern Mexico,
whose dried tops, **mescal buttons,** are
chewed for their narcotic effect: also called
peyote. **2.** an intoxicating liquor distilled
from certain desert plants. [< Mexican Sp.]

mes•ca•line (MES kə LEEN) *n.* a hallucinogen extracted from mescal buttons.

mes•dames (may DAHM) plural of MA-
DAME.

mes•de•moi•selles (MAY də mə ZEL) plural
of MADEMOISELLE.

mesh (mesh) *n.* **1.** one of the open spaces between the cords of a net or the wires of a screen. **2.** *pl.* the cords or wires bounding such a space or spaces. **3.** a net or network. **4.** *Mech.* the engagement of gear teeth. —*v.t. & v.i.* **1.** make or become entangled, as in a net. **2.** make or become engaged, as gear teeth. [ME *mesch*]

mes·mer·ize (MEZ mə RĪZ) *v.t.* ·ized, ·iz·ing hypnotize. —**mes·mer·ism** (MEZ mə RĪZ əm) *n.* hypnotism Also called *animal magnetism*. [after Franz Anton *Mesmer*, 1733–1815, German physician]

meso- *combining form* **1.** situated in the middle. **2.** intermediate in size or degree. Also, before vowels, *mes-*. [< Gk. *mésos* middle]

mes·o·derm (MEZ ə DURM) *n.* the middle layer in the embryo of animals, developing into the skeletal and muscular systems.

mes·o·mor·phic (MEZ ə MOR fik) *adj.* of human body types, characterized by a sturdy, muscular body structure. —**mes′o·morph** *n.*

mes·quite (me SKEET) *n.* a spiny shrub of the SW U.S. and Mexico that yields sweet pods used for cattle fodder. [< Mexican Sp. *mezquite*]

mess (mes) *n.* **1.** a state of disorder; esp., a condition of dirty or untidy confusion. **2.** a confusing, difficult, or embarrassing situation or condition; muddle. **3.** an unpleasant or confused mixture or collection; hodgepodge. **4.** a quantity of food sufficient for a meal or dish. **5.** a number of persons who regularly take their meals together, as in the military; also, a meal taken by them. —*v.i.* **1.** busy oneself; dabble: often with *around* or *about*. **2.** make a mess; bungle: often with *up*. **3.** eat as a member of a mess. —*v.t.* **4.** make a mess of; botch: often with *up*. **5.** make dirty: often with *up*. [ME *mes*]

mes·sage (MES ij) *n.* **1.** a communication sent by any of various means. **2.** a communication embodying important principles or counsel. [ME]

mes·sen·ger (MES n jər) *n.* **1.** one sent with a message or on an errand; esp., one whose work is running errands. **2.** a courier. **3.** *Archaic* a harbinger. [ME *messager*]

Mes·si·ah (mə SĪ ə) *n.* **1.** in Judaism, a deliverer of Israel promised by God and expected by the Jews. **2.** in Christianity, Jesus regarded as this deliverer. **3.** any expected liberator of a country, people, etc. [< LL] —**Mes·si·an·ic** (MES ee AN ik) *adj.*

mes·sieurs (MES ərz) *n.pl.* of Fr. MONSIEUR sirs; gentlemen: in English in the contracted form *Messrs.*, used as plural of *Mr.*

mess·y (MES ee) *adj.* **mes·si·er, mes·si·est** being in or causing a condition of dirt or confusion; untidy. —**mess′·i·ness** *n.*

mes·ti·zo (me STEE zoh) *n. pl.* ·zos or ·zoes a person of mixed ancestry, esp., a person of Spanish and Indian ancestry. [< Sp.] —**mes·ti′za** (-zə) *n.fem.*

met (met) past tense, past participle of MEET[1].

meta- *prefix* **1.** changed in place or form; reversed; altered: *metamorphosis*. **2.** *Anat. & Zool.* behind; after; on the farther side of; beyond: *metacarpus*. **3.** over; transcending: *metaphysics*. **4.** *Chem.* **a** a modification of. **b** a derivative of. [< Gk.]

me·tab·o·lism (mə TAB ə LIZ əm) *n. Biol. & Physiol.* the aggregate of all chemical processes constantly taking place in a living organism, including those that use energy to convert nutritive materials into protoplasm and those that release energy for vital processes in breaking down protoplasm into simpler substances. [< Gk. *metaballein* change] —**met·a·bol·ic** (MET ə BOL ik) *adj.* —**me·tab′o·lize** (mə TAB ə LIZ) *v.t. & v.i.* ·lized, ·liz·ing

met·a·car·pus (MET ə KAHR pəs) *n. Anat.* the part of the hand between the wrist and the bones of the fingers. [< NL] —**met′a·car′pal** *adj. & n.*

met·al (MET l) *n.* **1.** any of a class of elements characterized by a distinctive luster, malleability, ductility, and conductivity. **2.** a composition of such metallic elements; alloy. **3.** the constituent material of anything. [ME] —**me·tal·lic** (mə TAL ik) *adj.*

met·al·lur·gy (MET l UR jee) *n.* **1.** the science of extracting metal from ores. **2.** the science of metals and alloys. [< NL *metallurgia* metal working] —**met′al·lur′gist** *n.*

met·a·mor·phism (MET ə MOR fiz əm) *n.* **1.** *Geol.* the changes in the composition and texture of rocks caused by force, heat, pressure, moisture, etc. **2.** metamorphosis. —**met′a·mor′phic** *adj.*

met·a·mor·phose (MET ə MOR fohz) *v.t.* ·phosed, ·phos·ing **1.** change the form of. —*v.i.* **2.** undergo metamorphosis.

met·a·mor·pho·sis (MET ə MOR fə sis) *n. pl.* ·pho·ses (-fə seez) **1.** change from one form, shape, or substance into another by any means. **2.** complete transformation of character, purpose, circumstances, etc. **3.** one who or that which is metamorphosed. **4.** *Biol.* any marked change in the form and structure of an animal in its development from embryo to adult, as from tadpole to frog. [< NL]

met·a·phor (MET ə FOR) *n.* a figure of speech in which one object is likened to another by speaking of it as if it were that other, as *He was a lion in battle:* distinguished from *simile.* [< L *metaphora*] — **met'a·phor'i·cal** or **met'a·phor'ic** *adj.*

met·a·phys·i·cal (MET ə FIZ i kəl) *adj.* **1.** of, pertaining to, or of the nature of metaphysics. **2.** highly abstruse; obscure.

met·a·phys·ics (MET ə FIZ iks) *n. (construed as sing.)* **1.** the branch of philosophy that investigates ultimate principles of reality, esp. those principles not subject to empirical confirmation. **2.** all speculative philosophy. [< Med.L *metaphysica*]

me·tas·ta·sis (mə TAS tə sis) *n. pl.* **·ses** (-seez) *Pathol.* **1.** the transfer of a disease from one part of the body to another, as in certain types of cancer. **2.** a site to which such a transfer has been made. [< Gk. *metástasis* a changing] —**met·a·stat·ic** (MET ə STAT ik) *adj.*

me·tas·ta·size (mə TAS ti SĪZ) *v.i.* **·sized, ·siz·ing** *Pathol.* shift or spread from one part of the body to another, as a malignant growth.

me·tath·e·sis (mə TATH ə sis) *n. pl.* **·ses** (-seez) the transposition of letters, syllables, or sounds in a word: Old English *bridd* became *bird* by *metathesis.* [< LL]

mete (meet) *v.t.* **met·ed, met·ing** allot or distribute by or as by measure: usu. followed by *out.* [ME]

me·te·or (MEE tee ər) *n.* **1.** *Astron.* a meteoroid that on entering the earth's atmosphere at great speed is heated to luminosity and is visible as a streak of light: also called *shooting star.* **2.** loosely, a meteorite or meteoroid. [< NL *meteorum*]

me·te·or·ic (MEE tee OR ik) *adj.* **1.** of, pertaining to, or consisting of meteors. **2.** resembling a meteor; brilliant, rapid, and dazzling: a *meteoric* career.

me·te·or·ite (MEE tee ə RĪT) *n.* a portion of a meteor that has fallen to earth.

me·te·or·oid (MEE tee ə ROID) *n. Astron.* one of the pieces of matter moving through outer space, that upon entering the earth's atmosphere form meteors.

me·te·or·ol·o·gy (MEE tee ə ROL ə jee) *n.* the science treating of atmospheric phenomena, esp. those relating to weather. [< Gk. *meteōrología* discussion of celestial phenomena]   —**me'te·or·ol'o·gist** *n.*

me·ter[1] (MEE tər) *n.* an instrument or device used to measure or indicate variation in amount. —*v.t.* measure or test by means of a meter. [< F *mètre*]

me·ter[2] *n.* **1.** a measured rhythm constituting one of the chief characteristics of verse. **2.** *Music* the combining of rhythmic pulses into successive groups having like arrangement and duration. [ME *metir*]

me·ter[3] *n.* the basic unit of length in the metric system, equivalent to 39.37 inches. [< F *mètre*]

-meter *combining form* **1.** a device for measuring (a specified quality, thing, etc.). **2.** division into (a specified number of) prosodic feet: *pentameter.* **3.** a (specified kind of) unit in the metric system: *kilometer*.

meth·a·done (METH ə DOHN) *n.* a synthetic narcotic drug used as a substitute in the treatment of heroin addiction. Also spelled *methadon.*

meth·ane (METH ayn) *n. Chem.* a colorless, odorless, flammable gas that is the chief constituent of marsh gas and is obtained commercially from natural gas.

meth·a·nol (METH ə NAWL) *n. Chem.* a colorless, flammable, highly toxic alcohol obtained by the destructive distillation of wood and widely used in industry and the arts. Also called *methyl alcohol, wood alcohol.*

meth·od (METH əd) *n.* **1.** a manner of proceeding; esp., a regular, systematic, or orderly way of doing anything. **2.** system, order, or regularity in action or thought. **3.** the techniques used in a particular field of knowledge, thought, practice, etc.: the scientific *method.* [ME]

me·thod·i·cal (mə THOD i kəl) *adj.* **1.** arranged in or performed in systematic order. **2.** orderly or systematic in habits, behavior, etc.: a *methodical* person.

Meth·od·ist (METH ə dist) *n.* a member of any of the Protestant denominations having their origin in a religious movement begun in England in the 18th c. by John Wesley. — **Meth'od·ism** *n.*

meth·od·ol·o·gy (METH ə DOL ə jee) *n. pl.* **·gies** **1.** the principles, practices, etc. of orderly thought or procedure applied to a particular branch of learning. **2.** the branch

of logic dealing with such procedures. —
meth·od·o·log·i·cal (METH ə dl OJ i kəl)
adj.

meth·yl alcohol (METH əl) *Chem.* methanol.

me·tic·u·lous (mə TIK yə ləs) *adj.* extremely precise about details, esp. in minor or trivial matters. [< L *meticulosus* fearful] **—me·tic'u·lous·ly** *adv.* **—me·tic'u·lous·ness** *n.*

mé·tier (MAY tyay) *n.* **1.** one's occupation, trade, or profession. **2.** work or activity for which one is especially well suited. [< F]

met·ric (ME trik) *adj.* of, pertaining to, or using the meter as a unit of measurement. [< F *métrique*]

met·ri·cal (ME tri kəl) *adj.* **1.** of, pertaining to, or characterized by meter; rhythmic. **2.** composed in or constituting a unit of poetic meter. **3.** of, pertaining, to, or involving measurement. Also **met'ric.**

met·ri·cize (ME trə sīz) *v.t.* **·cized, ·ciz·ing** convert into the metric system.

metric system a decimal system of weights and measures having as fundamental units the gram, the meter, and the liter.

metric ton a unit of weight equal to 1000 kilograms, or 2204.62 pounds avoirdupois.

metro- *combining form* measure. [< Gk. *métron*]

met·ro·nome (ME trə NOHM) *n.* an instrument for indicating exact tempo in music, usu. producing audible clicks controlled by a reversed pendulum whose motion is regulated by a sliding weight. [< METRO- + Gk. *nomos* law]

me·trop·o·lis (mi TROP ə lis) *n. pl.* **·lis·es 1.** the capital or the largest or most important city of a country, state, or area. **2.** an urban center of activity, culture, trade, etc. [ME] **—met·ro·pol·i·tan** (ME trə POL i tn) *adj. & n.*

met·tle (MET l) *n.* **1.** character or temperament. **2.** courage; pluck. **—on one's mettle** aroused to one's best efforts. **—met·tle·some** (-səm) *adj.*

mews (myooz) *n.* (*construed as sing.*) *Chiefly Brit.* a narrow street or alley, often with dwellings converted from stables.

mewl (myool) *v.i.* whimper or cry feebly, as an infant.

Mex·i·can (MEK si kən) *n.* **1.** a native or inhabitant of Mexico. **2.** a language indigenous to Mexico, as Nahuatl. **—Mex·i·can** *adj.*

mez·za·nine (MEZ ə NEEN) *n.* **1.** an intermediate story, usu. not of full width, between two main floors. **2.** in a theater, the first balcony, or the front rows of the balcony. [< F]

mez·zo·so·pran·o (MET soh sə PRAN oh) *n. pl.* **·pran·os 1.** a female voice intermediate between a soprano and a contralto. **2.** a person having such a voice. **—adj.** of or pertaining to such a voice. [< Ital.]

mi (mee) *n.* *Music* the third tone of the diatonic scale in solmization.

mi·as·ma (mī AZ mə) *n. pl.* **·mas** or **·ma·ta** (-mə tə) **1.** noxious or unwholesome influence, etc. **2.** the poisonous emanation once supposed to rise from swamps, etc. [< NL] **—mi·as'mic** *adj.*

mi·ca (MĪ kə) *n.* any of a class of minerals cleaving into thin, often transparent and flexible, layers: formerly called *isinglass.* [< L, morsel]

mice (mīs) plural of MOUSE.

micro- *combining form* **1.** very small; minute; **microparticle, micrometeorite. 2.** of a science involving a microscope: **microbiology, microsurgery. 3.** one millionth of a specified unit: **microfarad.** [< Gk. *mikrós* small]

mi·crobe (MĪ krohb) *n.* a microscopic organism; esp., one of the bacteria that cause disease. [< F]

mi·cro·cosm (MĪ krə KOZ əm) *n.* **1.** a little world; the universe in miniature. **2.** man regarded as epitomizing the universe. [ME *microcosme*]

mi·cro·e·lec·tron·ics (MI kroh i lek TRON iks) *n.* the technology dealing with miniaturized electronic circuits. **—mi'cro·e·lec·tron'ic** *adj.*

mi·cro·fiche (MĪ krə FEESH) *n. pl.* **·fiche** or **·fich·es** a sheet of microfilm containing tiny copies of printed matter etc. Also *fiche.* [< MICRO- + F *fiche* card]

mi·cro·film (MĪ krə FILM) *n.* a photographic reproduction on film of a printed page, document, etc., highly reduced for ease in transmission and storage. **—mi'cro·film** *v.t. & v.i.*

mi·cro·gram (MĪ krə GRAM) *n.* one millionth of a gram.

mi·crom·e·ter (mī KROM i tər) *n.* an instrument used for measuring very small distances or dimensions. **—mi·crom·e·try** (-tree) *n.*

mi·cron (MĪ kron) *n. pl.* **·crons** or **·cra** (-krə) a unit of measurement equal to one thousandth of a millimeter.

mi·cro·or·gan·ism (MĪ kroh OR gə NIZ əm)
n. any organism, as a bacterium or protozoan, too small to be seen without magnifi-
cation.

mi·cro·phone (MĪ krə FOHN) *n.* a device
for converting sound waves into electric
currents, forming the principal element of
a telephone transmitter or of any sound-
reproducing system, as in broadcasting. —
mi·cro·phon·ic (MĪ krə FON ik) *adj.*

mi·cro·pho·to·graph (MĪ krə FOH tə
GRAF) *n.* **1.** a very small or microscopic photograph, as on microfilm. **2.** loosely, a pho-
tomicrograph. —**mi·cro·pho·tog·ra·**
phy (MĪ kroh fə TOG rə fee) *n.*

mi·cro·scope (MĪ krə SKOHP) *n.* an optical
instrument used for magnifying objects too
small to be seen or clearly observed by ordinary vision. [< NL *microscopium*]

mi·cro·scop·ic (MĪ krə SKOP ik) *adj.* **1.** so
minute as to be visible only under a microscope. **2.** exceedingly small. **3.** of, pertaining to, or of the nature of a microscope
or microscopy. —**mi'cro·scop'i·cal·ly**
adv.

mi·cros·co·py (mī KROS kə pee) *n.* **1.** the
process or technique of using the microscope. **2.** investigation by means of the microscope.

mi·cro·tome (MĪ krə TOHM) *n.* an instrument for cutting very thin sections of organic tissue etc. for microscopic observations.

mi·cro·wave (MĪ krə WAYV) *n.* **1.** an electromagnetic wave, esp. one between about
100 centimeters and 1 centimeter in wavelength. **2. a microwave oven,** one in which
food is cooked by the heat produced as a
result of microwave penetration.

mic·tu·rate (MIK chə RAYT) *v.i.* •**rat·ed,**
•**rat·ing** urinate. [< L *micturire* desire to
urinate] —**mic·tu·ri·tion** (MIK chə RISH
ən) *n.*

mid¹ (mid) *adj.* being approximately in the
middle; central. [ME]

mid² *prep.* amid.

mid- *combining form* middle or middle part
of: **midafternoon, mid-Atlantic.**

mid·air (mid AIR) *n.* a point or region seemingly in the middle or midst of the air.

mid·day (MID DAY) *n.* the middle of the
day; noon. —**mid·day** *adj.* (MID DAY)

mid·dle (MID l) *adj.* **1.** equally distant from
the extremes, periphery, etc.; central. **2.** intermediate in position, status, etc. **3.** intervening between the earlier part and the

latter part of a sequence, period of time,
etc. **4.** *Usu. cap.* designating a language in a
stage between an earlier and a recent form:
Middle English. —*n.* **1.** the area or point
equally distant from the extremes, etc. **2.**
the intermediate section of anything. **3.** the
middle part of the body; the waist. [ME
middel]

middle age the time of life between youth
and old age, usu. thought of as the years
approximately between 45 and 65. —
mid·dle-aged (MID l AYJD) *adj.*

Middle Ages the period in European history
between classical antiquity and the Renaissance, usu. regarded as extending from
about 500 to about 1450.

Middle America the conservative American middle class.

middle class the part of a society occupying
a social or economic position between the
laboring class and the very wealthy or the
nobility. —**mid'dle-class'** *adj.*

Middle East the region including Egypt and
the countries of SW Asia west of Pakistan.

Middle English see under ENGLISH.

Middle French see under FRENCH.

Middle Latin see under LATIN.

mid·dle·man (MID l MAN) *n. pl.* •**men 1.**
one who acts as an agent; go-between. **2.**
one who buys in bulk from producers and
sells to retailers or consumers.

middle of the road a moderate position or
course. —**middle-of-the-road** (MID l əv
thə ROHD) *adj.* —**mid'dle-of-the-road'**
er *n.*

mid·dle·weight (MID l WAYT) *n.* **1.** a person or animal of average weight. **2.** a boxer
or wrestler weighing between 147 and 160
pounds.

mid·dling (MID ling) *adj.* **1.** of middle
size, quality, or condition. **2.** commonplace; mediocre. [ME] —*adv.* fairly; moderately.

midge (mij) *n.* **1.** a gnat or small fly. **2.** an
extremely small person or creature. [ME
mygge]

midg·et (MIJ it) *n.* **1.** a person of abnormally
small size but of normal physical proportions. **2.** anything very small of its kind. —
adj. very small; diminutive.

mid·land (MID lənd) *n.* the central or interior part of a country or region. —
mid·land *adj.*

mid·night (MID NĪT) *n.* twelve o'clock at
night. —*adj.* **1.** of or occurring at midnight.
2. resembling midnight; very dark. [ME]

—**burn the midnight oil** work or study late into the night.

midnight sun the sun visible at midnight during summer at latitudes greater than 70° north or south of the equator.

mid·riff (MID rif) *n.* the part of the body between the chest and the abdomen, in the region of the diaphragm; also, the diaphragm itself. [ME *mydryf*]

mid·ship·man (MID SHIP mən) *n. pl.* •**men** in the U.S. Navy, a student training to be commissioned as an officer.

midst (midst) *n.* **1.** the condition of being surrounded, as by people or things, or beset, as by troubles: used chiefly in the phrase **in the midst of. 2.** the central part; middle. —**in our (your, their) midst** among us (you, them). —*prep.* amid. [ME]

mid·sum·mer (MID SUM ər) *n.* the middle of summer.

mid·way (MID WAY) *adv.* in the middle of the way or distance. —*adj.* being in the middle of the way or distance. —*n.* (MID WAY) at a fair, exposition, etc., the area where amusements, sideshows, or exhibitions are situated. [ME *midwei*]

mid·week (MID WEEK) *n.* the middle of the week.

mid·wife (MID WIF) *n. pl.* •**wives** (-WIVZ) a trained person who assists women in childbirth. [ME *midwif*] —**mid'wife'ry** (mid WIF ree) *n.*

mid·win·ter (MID WIN tər) *n.* the middle of winter.

mien (meen) *n.* manner, expression, etc.

miff (mif) *v.t.* offend; annoy.

might[1] (mīt) past tense of MAY.

might[2] *n.* **1.** power to dominate; force; strength. **2.** physical strength. —**with might and main** with all strength or ability. [ME *myght*]

might·y (MĪ tee) *adj.* **might·i·er, might·i·est 1.** possessed of might; powerful. **2.** of great size, importance, etc. —*adv. Informal* very; exceedingly. [ME] —**might'i·ly** (MĪT I ee) *adv.*

mi·graine (MĪ grayn) *n.* a type of severe, recurrent headache, usu. in one side of the head. [ME]

mi·grant (MĪ grənt) *adj.* migrating. —*n.* one who or that which migrates, as a bird or animal, an itinerant worker, etc.

mi·grate (MĪ grayt) *v.i.* •**grat·ed,** •**grat·ing 1.** move from one country, region, etc., to settle in another. **2.** move seasonally from one region or climate to another, as birds or fish. [< L *migratus* changed]

mi·gra·tion (mī GRAY shən) *n.* **1.** an act or instance of migrating. **2.** those participating in a single instance of migrating. —**mi·gra·to·ry** (MĪ grə TOR ee) *adj.*

mi·ka·do (mi KAH doh) *n. pl.* •**dos** an emperor of Japan. [< Japanese *mi* august + *kado* door]

mil (mil) *n.* **1.** a unit of length equal to one thousandth of an inch or .0254 millimeter. **2.** *Mil.* **a** a unit of angular measure equal to ¹⁄₆₄₀₀ of a circumference. **b** a unit of angular measure equal to 0.001 radian. [< L *mille* thousand]

milch (milch) *adj.* giving milk, as a cow. [ME *milche*]

mild (mīld) *adj.* **1.** kind or amiable in disposition or manners. **2.** gentle or moderate: *mild* words; *mild* weather. **3.** not intense or strong: a *mild* flavor. [ME *milde*] —**mild'ly** *adv.* —**mild'ness** *n.*

mil·dew (MIL DOO) *n.* **1.** a disease of plants usu. caused by a parasitic fungus that deposits a whitish or discolored coating. **2.** any similar coating. **3.** any of the fungi causing such a disease. —*v.t. & v.i.* affect or be affected with mildew. [ME]

mile (mīl) *n.* a measure of distance used in the U.S. and other English-speaking countries, equal to 5280 feet or 1.609 kilometers: also called *statute mile.* —**geographical, nautical,** or **air mile** one sixtieth of a degree of the earth's equator; 6080.2 feet or 1853.24 meters. [ME]

mile·age (MĪ lij) *n.* **1.** total length or distance expressed in miles. **2.** number of miles a vehicle can travel for each gallon of fuel used. **3.** period or extent of usefulness. **4.** a travel allowance estimated at a fixed amount per mile. Also **mil'age.**

mile·post (MĪL POHST) *n.* **1.** a post or similar marker indicating distance in miles, as along a highway. **2.** a milestone.

mile·stone (MĪL STOHN) *n.* **1.** a milepost. **2.** an important event or turning point.

mi·lieu (mil YUU) *n.* environment; surroundings. [< F]

mil·i·tant (MIL i tənt) *adj.* **1.** combative or warlike; aggressive. **2.** engaged in conflict; fighting. —*n.* one who is militant. [ME] —**mil'i·tan·cy** *n.*

mil·i·ta·rism (MIL i tə RIZ əm) *n.* **1.** the ideals characteristic of a military class; emphasis on martial qualities. **2.** a national policy that promotes a powerful military position. —**mil′i·ta·rist** *n.* —**mil′i·ta·ris′tic** *adj.*

mil·i·ta·rize (MIL i tə RĪZ) *v.t.* •**rized, •riz·ing** **1.** convert to a military system or adapt for military purposes. **2.** prepare for warfare.

mil·i·tar·y (MIL i TER ee) *adj.* **1.** of or pertaining to the armed forces. **2.** of or characteristic of warfare. **3.** characteristic of or befitting a soldier. —*n.* soldiers collectively; armed forces: preceded by *the.* [< L *militaris*]

mil·i·tate (MIL i TĀYT) *v.i.* •**tat·ed, ·tat·ing** have influence or effect: usu. with *against.*

mi·li·tia (mi LISH ə) *n.* a body of citizens enrolled and drilled in military organizations other than the regular military forces, and called out only in emergencies. [< L, military service]

milk (milk) *n.* **1.** the whitish liquid secreted by the mammary glands of female mammals for the nourishment of their young. **2.** any of various liquids resembling this, as the sap of certain plants or the liquid contained in a coconut. —*v.t.* **1.** draw or express milk from the mammary glands of. **2.** draw or extract something from: *milk* him for information. **3.** exploit; take advantage of: *milk* a client. —*v.i.* **4.** milk a cow, cows, etc. [ME] —**milk′i·ness** *n.* —**milk′y** *adj.* **milk·i·er, milk·i·est**

Milky Way a luminous band visible across the night sky, composed of distant stars and nebulae not separately distinguishable to the naked eye: also called the *Galaxy.*

mill¹ (mil) *n.* **1.** a machine that grinds, crushes, shapes, cuts, etc. **2.** a machine or building in which grain is ground. **3.** any of various machines that process materials: used in combination: *sawmill; windmill.* **4.** a manufacturing or industrial establishment; factory. **5.** a trying experience; ordeal: used chiefly in the phrase **through the mill.** —*v.t.* **1.** grind, roll, shape, polish, etc. in or with a mill. **2.** raise, indent, or ridge the edge of (a coin etc.). —*v.i.* **3.** move with a circular or surging motion, as cattle. [ME *milne*]

mill² *n.* a tenth of a cent. [< L *millesimus* thousandth]

mil·len·ni·um (mi LEN ee əm) *n. pl.* •**ni·a** (-nee ə) or •**ni·ums** **1.** a period of a thousand years. **2.** *Theol.* the thousand years during which Christ is to rule on earth. **3.** any period of happiness, prosperity, etc. [< NL] —**mil·len′ni·al** *adj.*

mill·er (MIL ər) *n.* **1.** one who operates or tends a mill. **2.** a milling machine. **3.** any of various moths having pale, dusty wings.

mil·let (MIL it) *n.* **1.** a grass cultivated for forage and for its small, edible seeds. **2.** the seed of these grasses. [ME *milet*]

milli- *combining form* one thousandth of a specified unit: **milliampere, millivolt.**

mil·li·gram (MIL i GRAM) *n.* a unit of weight equal to one thousandth of a gram.

mil·li·li·ter (MIL ə LEE tər) *n.* a unit of capacity equal to one thousandth of a liter.

mil·li·me·ter (MIL ə MEE tər) *n.* a unit of length equal to one thousandth of a meter.

mil·li·ner (MIL ə nər) *n.* one who makes or sells women's hats. [< *Milaner*, a dealer in clothing imported from Milan, Italy]

mil·li·ner·y (MIL ə NER ee) *n.* **1.** the articles made or sold by milliners. **2.** the business of a milliner.

mil·lion (MIL yən) *n.* **1.** a thousand thousands, written as 1,000,000: a cardinal number. **2.** an indefinitely great number. [< Ital. *millione*] —**mil·lion** *adj.* —**mil′lionth** *n. & adj.*

mil·lion·aire (MIL yə NAIR) *n.* one whose wealth is valued at a million or more, as of dollars, pounds, etc. [< F *millionnaire*]

mil·li·pede (MIL ə PEED) *n.* any of various wormlike animals having a rounded body divided into numerous segments, each bearing two pairs of legs. [< L *milipeda*]

mill·pond (MIL POND) *n.* a body of water dammed up to supply power for running a mill.

mill·race (MIL RAYS) *n.* **1.** the current of water that operates a mill wheel. **2.** the channel in which it runs.

mill·stone (MIL STOHN) *n.* **1.** one of a pair of thick, heavy, stone disks used for grinding grain, etc. **2.** a heavy or burdensome weight.

mill·stream (MIL STREEM) *n.* **1.** a stream whose current is used to operate a mill. **2.** the water in a millrace.

mill·work (MIL WURK) *n.* objects or material finished or processed in a mill; esp., woodwork ready for use.

mill·wright (MIL RĪT) *n.* one who plans, builds, or repairs mills or mill machinery.

milque·toast (MILK TOHST) *n.* a timid, meek, or very apologetic person. [after Caspar *Milquetoast*, a character created by H.T. Webster, 1858–1952, U.S. cartoonist]

milt (milt) *n.* **1.** fish sperm. **2.** the reproductive organs of a male fish when filled with seminal fluid. [ME *milte*]

mime (mīm) n. **1.** a performer who specializes in pantomime. **2.** a performance by a mime or mimes. —*v.* **mimed, mim·ing** *v.i.* **1.** play a part with gestures and usu. without words. —*v.t.* **2.** portray by pantomime. [< L *mimus*]

mim·e·o·graph (MIM ee ə GRAF) n. a duplicating device that reproduces copies of written matter etc., by means of a stencil wrapped around a drum. —*v.t. & v.i.* reproduce by mimeograph. [< *Mimeograph*, formerly a trade name]

mim·ic (MIM ik) *v.t.* **·icked, ·ick·ing 1.** imitate the speech or actions of. **2.** copy closely; ape. —*n.* one who mimics or imitates. [< L *mimicus*] —**mim′ick·er** n.

mim·ic·ry (MIM ik ree) n. pl. **·ries 1.** the act, practice, or art of mimicking. **2.** *Biol.* a resemblance of an organism to another or to its environment, for purposes of concealment etc.

min·a·ret (MIN ə RET) n. a high, slender tower attached to a Muslim mosque and surrounded by balconies, from which a muezzin calls the summons to prayer. [< F]

min·a·to·ry (MIN ə TOR ee) *adj.* conveying or expressing a threat. [< LL *minatorius*]

mince (mins) v. **minced, minc·ing** *v.t.* **1.** cut or chop into small bits, as food. **2.** moderate the force or strength of (language, ideas, etc.): She didn't *mince* words with me. —*v.i.* **3.** walk with short steps or affected daintiness. [ME *mincen*] —**minc′er** n.

mince·meat (MINS MEET) n. a mixture of chopped apples, raisins, spices, and often meat, used as a pie filling.

mince pie a pie filled with mincemeat.

minc·ing (MIN sing) *adj.* affectedly precise, refined, or dainty, as in manner, gait, etc.

mind (mīnd) n. **1.** the aggregate of processes originating in or associated with the brain, involving thought, interpretation of perceptions, imagination, etc. **2.** memory: within the *mind* of man. **3.** opinion; sentiment: change one's *mind*. **4.** desire; inclination: have a *mind* to leave. **5.** way or state of thinking or feeling: a logical *mind*. **6.** intellectual power or capacity: She has the *mind* for such work. **7.** attention: keep one's *mind* on a subject. —**out of one's mind 1.** insane; mad. **2.** distracted; frantic. —**be of one mind** be in accord; agree. —**blow one's mind** *Slang* **1.** experience drug-induced hallucinations. **2.** excite or stimulate. —**have a good mind** feel strongly disposed (to do something). —**make up one's mind** decide; be determined. —*v.t.* **1.** pay attention to. **2.** be careful concerning: *Mind* your step. **3.** obey: *Mind* your leaders. **4.** look after; tend. **5.** object to: Do you *mind* the noise? —*v.i.* **6.** pay attention; heed: *Mind* you now, not a word. **7.** be obedient. **8.** be concerned; care; object; I don't *mind*. [ME *mynde*]

mind·blowing (MĪND BLOH ing) *adj. Slang* **1.** hallucinogenic. **2.** exciting and stimulating.

mind·bog·gling (MĪND BOG ling) *adj. Slang* amazing or overwhelming.

mind·ed (MĪN did) *adj.* **1.** having or characterized by a (specified kind of) mind: used in combination: *evil-minded*. **2.** having an inclination; disposed: often with *to*.

mind·ful (MĪND fəl) *adj.* keeping in mind; aware. [ME *mindeful*] —**mind′ful·ly** *adv.*

mind·less (MĪND lis) *adj.* **1.** devoid of intelligence; senseless. **2.** not giving heed or attention; careless. [ME *myndles*] —**mind′less·ly** *adv.*

mind-set (MĪND SET) n. prevailing attitudes or opinions; intellectual climate.

mine[1] (mīn) n. **1.** an excavation in the earth dug to obtain coal, precious stones, etc. **2.** the site of such an excavation, together with its buildings, equipment, etc. **3.** any deposit of ore, coal, etc. **4.** any source or abundant store of something: a *mine* of talent. **5.** *Mil.* an explosive charge placed in the earth or water and designed to be actuated by contact, a time fuse, or remote control. —*v.* **mined, min·ing** *v.t.* **1.** dig (coal, ores, etc.) from the earth. **2.** dig into (the earth etc.) for coal, ores, etc. **3.** obtain useful material or information from. **4.** place an explosive mine in or under. —*v.i.* **5.** dig in a mine for coal, ores, etc. **6.** place explosive mines. [ME *minen*] —**min′er** n.

mine[2] *pron.* **1.** the possessive case of the pronoun *I*, used as a predicate adjective: That book is *mine*. **2.** the one relating to me: His work is better than *mine*. —**of mine** belonging or relating to me; my. —*Archaic* my: formerly used before a vowel or *h*: *mine* eyes. [ME]

mine·field (MĪN FEELD) n. an area in which explosive mines have been placed.

mine·lay·er (MĪN LAY ər) n. a vessel provided with special equipment for laying explosive mines.

min·er·al (MIN ər əl) n. **1.** a naturally occurring crystalline element or compound. **2.** inorganic material, esp. as distinguished from animal or vegetable matter. **3.** ore. [ME] —**min·er·al** adj.

mineral kingdom minerals collectively.

min·er·al·o·gy (MIN ə RAL ə jee) n. pl. **·gies 1.** the science of minerals, embracing their origin, structure, characteristics, properties, and classification. **2.** a treatise on minerals. —**min'er·al'o·gist** n.

mineral water any water impregnated with mineral salts or gases.

min·e·stro·ne (MIN ə STROH nee) n. a thick vegetable soup having a meat stock. [< Ital.]

min·gle (MING gəl) v. **·gled, ·gling** v.t. **1.** mix together; blend. —v.i. **2.** be or become mixed, or closely joined. **3.** mix or associate, as with a crowd. [ME menglen]

mini- combining form small: **minibus, minicomputer.**

min·i·a·ture (MIN ee ə chər) n. **1.** a representation of anything on a small scale. **2.** reduced dimensions, form, or extent. **3.** a painting done on a very small scale. —adj. being on a very small or reduced scale. [< Ital. miniatura miniature painting]

min·i·a·tur·ize (MIN ee ə chə RIZ) v.t. **·ized, ·iz·ing** reduce the size of. —**min'i·a·tur'i·za'tion** n.

min·im (MIN əm) n. **1.** a liquid measure, ¹/₆₀ of a fluid dram, or about one drop. **2.** Music a half note. **3.** one who or that which is very small or insignificant. [ME]

min·i·mal (MIN ə məl) adj. of a minimum amount, degree, etc.; least possible. —**min'i·mal·ly** adv.

min·i·mize (MIN ə MIZ) v.t. **·mized, ·miz·ing 1.** reduce to the smallest amount or degree. **2.** regard or represent as of the least possible importance, size, etc.

min·i·mum (MIN ə məm) n. pl. **·mums** or **·ma** (-mə) **1.** the least possible quantity, amount, or degree. **2.** the lowest quantity, degree, number, etc., reached or recorded. [< L, smallest] —**min·i·mum** adj.

minimum wage the smallest wage, fixed by law or by agreement, that an employer may offer an employee.

min·ing (MI ning) n. the act, process, or business of extracting coal etc. from mines.

min·ion (MIN yən) n. a servile favorite or follower. [< MF mignon darling]

min·is·ter (MIN ə stər) n. **1.** one who is authorized to preach, administer the sacraments, etc. in a church; clergyman; pastor. **2.** one appointed to head an administrative department of a government. **3.** a diplomat ranking next below an ambassador. **4.** one who or that which acts as the agent of another. — v.i. **1.** provide for the wants or needs of someone. **2.** be helpful or useful. —v.t. **3.** administer or apply (a sacrament, medicine, etc.). [ME ministre] —**min·is·te·ri·al** (MIN ə STEER ee əl) adj.

min·is·tra·tion (MIN ə STRAY shən) n. **1.** the act of serving. **2.** Often pl. help or aid. [ME ministracioun]

min·is·try (MIN ə stree) n. pl. **·tries 1.** the profession, duties, length of service, etc., of a minister of religion. **2.** the clergy. **3.** Govt. **a** an executive or administrative department presided over by a minister; also, its building. **b** a body of ministers collectively. **4.** the act of ministering. [ME]

min·now (MIN oh) n. **1.** a small European fish of the carp family. **2.** any small fish. [ME minwe]

Mi·no·an (mi NOH ən) adj. of an advanced civilization that flourished in Crete from about 3000 to 1100 B.C.

mi·nor (MI nər) adj. **1.** less in quantity, number, or extent. **2.** of secondary or lesser importance: minor poets. **3.** under legal age. **4.** Music **a** denoting an interval smaller by a half step than the corresponding major interval. **b** denoting a triad in which the third above the fundamental is minor. **c** denoting a type of diatonic scale or a key based on this scale. **5.** in education, of or pertaining to an area of specialized study usu. requiring fewer class hours than a major field of study. —n. **1.** one who is below full legal age. **2.** in education, a minor subject or area of study. —v.i. in education, study as a minor subject: with in. [ME]

mi·nor·i·ty (mi NOR i tee) n. pl. **·ties 1.** the smaller in number of two parts or groups. **2.** a racial, religious, political, or national group smaller than and usu. different in some ways from the larger group. **3.** the state or period of being under legal age. [< Med.L minoritas]

minor league any professional sports league not having the standing of a major league. —**mi·nor-league** (MI nər LEEG) adj.

min·strel (MIN strəl) n. **1.** in the Middle Ages, a wandering musician who earned a living by singing and reciting poetry. **2.** a performer in a minstrel show. **3.** a poet, musician, etc. [ME ministrel]

minstrel show a comic variety show of songs, dances, jokes, etc. given by a company of performers in blackface.

mint¹ (mint) *n.* **1.** a place where the coin of a country is lawfully manufactured. **2.** an abundant supply, esp. of money. —*v.t.* **1.** make (money) by stamping; coin. **2.** invent or fabricate (a word, etc.). —*adj.* in original condition; unused. [ME *mynt*] —**mint′•age** *n.*

mint² *n.* **1.** any of several aromatic herbs; esp. spearmint and peppermint, used as a flavoring, garnish, etc. **2.** a mint-flavored candy. [ME]

mint julep a drink made of bourbon, crushed ice, sugar, and sprigs of fresh mint.

min•u•end (MIN yoo END) *n. Math.* the number from which another is to be subtracted. [< L *minuendus*]

min•u•et (MIN yoo ET) *n.* **1.** a stately dance for couples, introduced in France in the 17th c. **2.** music for or in the manner of this dance. [< F *menuet*]

mi•nus (MĪ′nəs) *prep.* **1.** lessened or reduced by; less. **2.** lacking; deprived of. —*adj.* **1.** of or denoting subtraction. **2.** negative: *minus* values. —*n.* **1.** the minus sign. **2.** a minus quantity. **3.** a deficit or loss. [ME]

mi•nus•cule (MIN ə SKYOOL) *n.* any small or lower-case letter. —*adj.* **1.** of, pertaining to, like, or composed of minuscules. **2.** very small; miniature or minimal. [< L *minusculus* smallish]

min•ute¹ (MIN it) *n.* **1.** the sixtieth part of an hour; 60 seconds. **2.** any very brief period of time; moment. **3.** a specific instant of time. **4.** a unit of angular measure equal to the sixtieth part of a degree, indicated by the minute sign (∥): also called **minute of arc.** **5.** *pl.* an official record of the business discussed and transacted at a meeting, conference, etc. —*v.t.* •**ut•ed,** •**ut•ing 1.** make a brief note of; record. **2.** time to the minute. [ME]

mi•nute² (mī NOOT) *adj.* **1.** exceedingly small; tiny. **2.** having little importance or value. **3.** demonstrating or characterized by careful, precise attention to small details. [ME] —**mi•nute′ly** *adv.*

Min•ute•man (MIN it MAN) *n. pl.* •**men** in the American Revolution, one of the armed citizens who volunteered to be ready for combat at a minute's notice.

mi•nu•ti•ae (mi NOO shee EE) *n. pl. of*

mi•nu•ti•a (mi NOO shee ə) small or unimportant details; trifles. [< L]

minx (mingks) *n.* a saucy, bold, or flirtatious girl.

mir•a•cle (MIR ə kəl) *n.* **1.** an event that is not explained by any known natural law and is attributed to a supernatural source. **2.** any wonderful or amazing thing, fact, or event. [ME] —**mi•rac•u•lous** (mi RAK yə ləs) *adj.* —**mi•rac′u•lous′ly** *adv.*

mi•rage (mi RAHZH) *n.* **1.** an optical illusion caused by reflection of light through the atmosphere. **2.** anything that appears to be real but is not. [< F]

mire (mīr) *n.* **1.** an area of wet, yielding earth; swampy ground. **2.** deep mud or slush. —*v.* mired, mir•ing *v.t.* **1.** cause to sink or become stuck in mire. **2.** soil with mud; defile. **3.** entangle or entrap. —*v.i.* **4.** sink in mire; bog down. [ME] —**mir′y** *adj.* **mir•i•er, mir•i•est**

mir•ror (MIR ər) *n.* **1.** any smooth reflecting surface, as of glass backed with a coating of silver, aluminum, etc. **2.** whatever reflects or depicts truly. —*v.t.* reflect or show an image of. [ME *mirour*]

mirth (murth) *n.* spirited gaiety; social merriment. [ME *mirthe*] —**mirth′ful** (-fəl) *adj.*

mis- *prefix* bad; badly; wrong; wrongly; unfavorably: *miscopy, misfile, mistranslate.* [ME *mis-* wrong]

mis•ad•ven•ture (MIS əd VEN chər) *n.* a mishap.

mis•an•thrope (MIS ən THROHP) *n.* a hater of humankind. [< Gk. *misánthrōpos* misanthropic] —**mis•an•throp•ic** (MIS ən THROP ik) *adj.*

mis•ap•pro•pri•ate (MIS ə PROH pree AYT) *v.t.* •**at•ed,** •**at•ing** use or take improperly or dishonestly. —**mis′ap•pro′pri•a′•tion** *n.*

mis•be•have (MIS bi HAYV) *v.i.* •**haved,** •**hav•ing** behave badly. —**mis′be•hav′ior** (-yər) *n.*

mis•cal•cu•late (mis KAL kyə LAYT) *v.t. & v.i.* •**lat•ed,** •**lat•ing** calculate wrongly. — **mis′cal•cu•la′tion** *n.*

mis•car•ry (mis KAR ee) *v.i.* •**ried,** •**ry•ing 1.** fail; go wrong. **2.** bring forth a nonviable fetus prematurely. —**mis•car•riage** (mis KAR ij) *n.*

mis•ce•ge•na•tion (mi SEJ ə NAY shən) *n.* a mixture of races, esp. marriage or cohabitation between a black person and a white person.

mis·cel·la·ne·ous (MIS ə LAY nee əs) *adj.* **1.** composed of various and diverse things or elements; mixed. **2.** possessing diverse qualities or capabilities. [< L *miscellaneus* mixed]

mis·cel·la·ny (MIS ə LAY nee) *n. pl.* **·nies** a miscellaneous collection, esp. of literary works.

mis·chief (MIS chif) *n.* **1.** action, often playful, that causes some irritation or trouble. **2.** the disposition to annoy or disturb. **3.** harm or injury: *High winds can cause great mischief.* **4.** a cause of damage, evil, etc. [ME *meschef*]

mis·chie·vous (MIS chə vəs) *adj.* **1.** inclined to mischief. **2.** troubling, harmful, or annoying. **3.** having a playful, teasing nature. [ME *mischevous*] —**mis′chie·vous·ly** *adv.*

mis·ci·ble (MIS ə bəl) *adj.* capable of being mixed. [< L *miscere* mix] —**mis′ci·bil′i·ty** *n.*

mis·con·ceive (MIS kən SEEV) *v.t. & v.i.* **·ceived, ·ceiv·ing** conceive wrongly; misunderstand. —**mis′con·cep′tion** (-SEP shən) *n.*

mis·con·duct (mis KON dukt) *n.* **1.** improper or immoral behavior. **2.** unlawful conduct.

mis·con·strue (MIS kən STROO) *v.t.* **·strued, ·stru·ing 1.** interpret wrongly; misunderstand. **2.** *Gram.* construe incorrectly. [ME]

mis·cre·ant (MIS kree ənt) *n.* an unscrupulous wretch; evildoer. —*adj.* villainous; vile. [ME]

mis·deed (mis DEED) *n.* a wrong or immoral act.

mis·de·mean·or (MIS də MEE nər) *n. Law* any offense less serious than a felony, or for which the punishment is less severe.

mi·ser (MĪ zər) *n.* one who saves or hoards avariciously, often sacrificing comfort. [< L, wretched] —**mi′ser·li·ness** *n.*

mis·er·a·ble (MIZ ər ə bəl) *adj.* **1.** being in a state of misery, poverty, or wretched unhappiness. **2.** causing extreme discomfort: a *miserable* headache. **3.** proceeding from or exhibiting misery: a *miserable* life. **4.** meager, skimpy, or worthless. **5.** disreputable; shameful: a *miserable* scoundrel. [ME] —**mis′er·a·bly** *adv.*

mis·er·y (MIZ ə ree) *n. pl.* **·er·ies 1.** a condition of great wretchedness or suffering, as caused by poverty, pain, etc. **2.** intense mental or emotional anguish; extreme un-

happiness. **3.** a cause or source of suffering or unhappiness. [ME *miserie*]

mis·fea·sance (mis FEE zəns) *n. Law* the performance of a lawful act in an unlawful or culpable manner. [< AF *mesfesance*]

mis·fire (mis FĪR) *v.i.* **·fired, ·fir·ing 1.** fail to fire, ignite, or explode at the desired time, as a firearm, internal-combustion engine, etc. **2.** fail in achieving the proper or desired effect. —**mis′fire** *n.*

mis·fit (MIS FIT) *n.* **1.** something that fits badly. **2.** one who is not well adjusted to his or her environment. **3.** the act or condition of fitting badly.

mis·for·tune (mis FOR chən) *n.* **1.** adverse or ill fortune; bad luck. **2.** a calamity; mishap.

mis·giv·ing (mis GIV ing) *n.* a feeling of doubt, distrust, or apprehension.

mis·guide (mis GĪD) *v.t.* **·guid·ed, ·guid·ing** guide wrongly; mislead. —**mis·guid′ance** *n.*

mis·guid·ed (mis GĪD id) *adj.* guided or directed wrongly in thought or action. —**mis·guid′ed·ly** *adv.*

mis·hap (MIS hap) *n.* an unfortunate accident. [ME]

mish·mash (MISH MASH) *n.* a confused mess; hodgepodge.

mis·in·form (MIS in FORM) *v.t.* give false or erroneous information to. —**mis′in·for·ma′tion** (-fər MAY shən) *n.*

mis·in·ter·pret (MIS in TUR prit) *v.t.* interpret or understand incorrectly. —**mis′·in·ter′pre·ta′tion** *n.*

mis·judge (mis JUJ) *v.t. & v.i.* **·judged, ·judg·ing** judge wrongly or unfairly. —**mis·judg′ment** *n.*

mis·lead (mis LEED) *v.t.* **·led** (-LED) **·lead·ing 1.** guide or lead in the wrong direction. **2.** lead into error, as of judgment or conduct. —**mis·lead′ing** *adj.*

mis·match (mis MACH) *v.t.* match badly or inappropriately, as in marriage. —**mis′·match** *n.*

mis·no·mer (mis NOH mər) *n.* **1.** a name wrongly applied to someone or something. **2.** an error in naming, esp. in a legal document. [ME]

miso- *combining form* hating; hatred. [< Gk. *misein* hate]

mi·sog·a·my (mi SOG ə mee) *n.* hatred of marriage. —**mis·og′a·mist** *n.*

mi·sog·y·ny (mi SOJ ə nee) *n.* hatred of women. [< NL *misogynia*] —**mi·sog′y·nist** *n.*

mis·place (mis PLAYS) *v.t.* **·placed,
·placing 1.** put in a wrong place. **2.** put
(confidence, faith, trust, etc.) in an unworthy or unsuitable person, thing, or idea. **3.**
mislay.

mis·print (mis PRINT) *v.t.* print incorrectly.
—**mis′print** *n.*

mis·quote (mis KWOHT) *v.t. & v.i.*
·quot·ed, ·quot·ing quote incorrectly. —
mis′quo·ta′tion *n.*

mis·read (mis REED) *v.t.* **·read** (-RED),
·read·ing read incorrectly; misinterpret.

mis·rep·re·sent (MIS rep ri ZENT) *v.t.* give
an incorrect or false representation of. —
mis′rep·re·sen·ta′tion *n.*

mis·rule (mis ROOL) *v.t.* **·ruled, ·rul·ing**
rule unwisely or unjustly; misgovern. —*n.*
1. bad or unjust rule or government. **2.**
disorder or confusion, as from lawlessness.

miss¹ (mis) *v.t.* **1.** fail to hit, reach, or land
upon (a specified object). **2.** fail to meet or
catch, as a train. **3.** fail to obtain, accomplish, or achieve: *miss* the presidency by
few votes. **4.** fail to see, hear, perceive, etc.
5. fail to attend, keep, perform, etc. **6.** discover the absence of, usu. belatedly: *miss*
one's wallet. **7.** feel the loss or absence of.
—*v.i.* **8.** fail to hit; strike wide of the mark.
9. be unsuccessful; fail. —*n.* a failure to hit,
find, succeed, etc. [ME *missen*]

miss² *n.* **1.** *cap.* a title used in speaking to a
woman or girl: used without name. **2.** a
young girl. **3.** *cap.* a title of address used
before the name of a girl or unmarried
woman.

mis·sal (MIS əl) *n.* **1.** a book containing the
prayers, responses, etc., for celebrating
Mass throughout the year. **2.** loosely, any
prayer book. [ME]

mis·shape (mis SHAYP) *v.t.* **·shaped,
·shaped** or **·shap·en, ·shap·ing** shape
badly; deform. —**mis·shap′en** *adj.*

mis·sile (MIS əl) *n.* **1.** an object, esp. a
weapon, intended to be thrown or discharged, as a bullet, arrow, etc. **2.** a guided
missile.

miss·ing (MIS ing) *adj.* **1.** not present; absent; lacking. **2.** *Mil.* absent: said of one
whose whereabouts or fate in battle has not
been determined: also **missing in action.**

mis·sion (MISH ən) *n.* **1.** any body of persons sent to perform a specific work or service; esp., such a body sent to a foreign
country to conduct business, negotiations,
etc. on behalf of its own country. **2.** the
specific task a person or body of persons is

assigned to do. **3.** a group of missionaries. **4.**
the place or establishment where missionaries carry on their work. **5.** the permanent
foreign office of an ambassador or envoy;
embassy. **6.** the particular work or goal one
is or feels destined to do or accomplish; a
calling. [< NL]

mis·sion·ar·y (MISH ə NER ee) *n. pl.*
·ar·ies 1. a person sent to an area to propagate religion or to do educational or charitable work. **2.** one who advocates or spreads
any new system or doctrine. —**mis·
sion·ar·y** *adj.*

mis·sive (MIS iv) *n.* a letter, esp. one of an
official nature. [ME]

mis·state (mis STAYT) *v.t.* **·stat·ed,
·stat·ing** state wrongly or falsely. —
mis·state′ment *n.*

mis·step (mis STEP) *n.* **1.** a stumble. **2.** an
error or blunder, as in conduct.

mist (mist) *n.* **1.** an aggregation of fine drops
of water suspended in the atmosphere at or
near the earth's surface. **2.** *Meteorol.* a very
thin fog with a horizontal visibility arbitrarily set at not more than two kilometers.
3. a film or haze before the eyes that blurs
one's vision. —*v.i.* **1.** be or become dim or
misty; blur. **2.** rain in very fine drops. —*v.t.*
3. make dim or misty. [ME]

mis·take (mi STAYK) *n.* an error or fault in
action, judgment, perception, understanding, etc. —*v.t.* **·took, ·tak·en, ·tak·ing 1.**
understand wrongly; acquire a wrong conception of. **2.** take (a person or thing) to be
another. [ME *mistaken*] —**mis·tak′a·ble**
adj.

mis·tak·en (mi STAY kən) *adj.* **1.** based on
or arising from error, as of judgment, perception, etc. **2.** wrong in opinion, action,
etc. —**mis·tak′en·ly** *adv.*

mis·ter (MIS tər) *n.* **1.** *Informal* sir: used
without the name. **2.** *cap.* master: a title of
address prefixed to the name and to some
official titles of a man: commonly written
Mr.

mis·time (mis TĪM) *v.t.* **·timed, ·tim·ing 1.**
time wrongly or inappropriately. **2.** mis-
judge the time of. [ME *mistimen*]

mis·tle·toe (MIS əl TOH) *n.* a parasitic shrub
having yellowish green leaves and white
berries, used as a Christmas decoration.
[ME *mistelto*]

mis·took (mi STUUK) past tense of MIS-
TAKE.

mis·treat (mis TREET) *v.t.* treat badly or
improperly. —**mis·treat′ment** *n.*

mis·tress (MIS tris) *n.* **1.** a woman in a position of authority or control; as: **a** the head of a household, institution, or estate. **b** the head of a staff of servants. **2.** a woman who has a continuing sexual relationship with a man to whom she is not married. **3.** a woman who has mastered a skill, craft, or branch of learning. **4.** *cap.* formerly, a title of address applied to women. [ME *maistresse*]

mis·tri·al (mis TRĪL) *n.* *Law* **1.** a trial made void because of legal errors or defects. **2.** a trial terminated by the jury's inability to agree on a verdict.

mis·trust (mis TRUST) *v.t.* regard (someone or something) with suspicion or doubt; be skeptical of. —*n.* lack of trust or confidence.

mis·trust·ful (mis TRUST fəl) *adj.* suspicious.

mist·y (MIS tee) *adj.* **mist·i·er, mist·i·est** **1.** consisting of, characterized by, or like mist. **2.** dimmed or obscured. **3.** lacking clarity; vague. —**mist′i·ness** *n.*

mis·un·der·stand (MIS un dər STAND) *v.t. & v.i.* **·stood, ·stand·ing** understand wrongly; misinterpret.

mis·un·der·stand·ing (MIS un dər STAN ding) *n.* **1.** a failure to understand the meaning, motive, etc., of someone or something. **2.** a disagreement or quarrel.

mis·un·der·stood (MIS un dər STUUD) *adj.* **1.** wrongly understood. **2.** not valued or appreciated.

mis·use (mis YOOS) *n.* erroneous or improper use. —*v.t.* (mis YOOZ) **·used, ·us·ing** **1.** use or apply wrongly or improperly. **2.** treat badly; abuse. [ME] —**mis·us·age** (mis YOO sij) *n.*

mite¹ (mīt) *n.* any of various small arachnids, many of which are parasitic on men, animals, and plants. [ME *myte* midge]

mite² *n.* **1.** a very small particle, object, or creature. **2.** any very small coin or sum of money. [ME *myte* small coin]

mi·ter (MĪ tər) *n.* **1.** a tall ornamental headdress, rising in peaks at the front and back, worn by popes, bishops, and abbots. **2.** in carpentry, a miter joint. —*v.t.* **1.** confer a miter upon; raise to the rank of bishop. **2.** make or join with a miter joint. [ME *mitre*]

miter joint a joint made of two pieces of material whose joined ends have been beveled at equal angles, as at the corner of a picture frame.

mit·i·gate (MIT i GAYT) *v.t. & v.i.* **·gat·ed,**

·gat·ing make or become milder or less severe. [< L *mitigatus* soothed] —**mit′i·ga′tion** *n.*

mi·to·sis (mī TOH sis) *n.* *Biol.* a process of cell division in which the nucleus divides, producing two cells, each having the same number of chromosomes as the original cell. [< NL] —**mi·tot·ic** (mī TOT ik) *adj.*

mitt (mit) *n.* **1.** in baseball, a large glove, used to protect the hand catching the ball. **2.** a mitten. **3.** *Slang* a hand.

mit·ten (MIT n) *n.* a covering for the hand, encasing the four fingers together and the thumb separately. [ME *miteyn*]

mix (miks) *v.* **mixed, mix·ing** *v.t.* **1.** combine or put together in one mass or compound. **2.** make by combining ingredients: *mix* cake batter. **3.** put or add, as an ingredient. **4.** bring into contact with; cause to mingle. —*v.i.* **5.** become mixed or have the capacity to become mixed; mingle. **6.** associate; get along: He does not *mix* well with others. —**mix up 1.** mix or blend together. **2.** confuse. **3.** implicate or involve. —*n.* **1.** the act or product of mixing. **2.** a mixture of ingredients, often prepared and sold commercially: a cake *mix.*

mixed (mikst) *adj.* **1.** mingled or blended together in a single mass or compound. **2.** composed of different, dissimilar, or incongruous elements, qualities, classes, races, etc.: *mixed* motives. **3.** made up of or involving persons of both sexes. [ME *mixt*]

mixed marriage marriage between persons of different religions or races.

mixed number a number, as 3Ô, that is the sum of an integer and a fraction.

mixed-up (MIKST UP) *adj.* **1.** confused; bewildered. **2.** emotionally unstable.

mix·er (MIK sər) *n.* **1.** one who or that which mixes. **2.** a person with ability to mix socially or get along well in groups. **3.** a dance or gathering for the purpose of getting acquainted. **4.** a beverage, as water, soda, etc., used with alcoholic beverages in a drink.

mix·ture (MIKS chər) *n.* **1.** something formed by or resulting from mixing. **2.** anything composed of unlike or various elements, as a blend of different kinds or qualities of tea, tobacco, etc. **3.** the act of mixing, or the state of being mixed. [ME]

mix-up (MIKS UP) *n.* **1.** a state of confusion; also, an instance of this. **2.** a fight.

mne·mon·ics (ni MON iks) *n.* *(construed as sing.)* a system of principles and formulas designed to assist or improve the memory.

[< Gk. *mnemonikós* related to remembering] —**mne·mon'ic** *adj.*

moan (mohn) *n.* **1.** a low, sustained, mournful sound, as from grief or pain. **2.** any similar sound. —*v.t. & v.i.* **1.** utter moans or with moans. **2.** complain or lament. [ME *mone*]

moat (moht) *n.* a deep, wide, and usu. water-filled trench around a castle, fortress, or town, designed to discourage attempts at invasion. —*v.t.* surround with or as with a moat. [ME *mote* embankment]

mob (mob) *n.* **1.** a disorderly or lawless crowd or throng; a rabble. **2.** any large assemblage of individuals. **3.** the lower class or classes of people; the masses. **4.** a criminal gang, esp. the Mafia. —*v.t.* **mobbed, mob·bing 1.** attack in a mob. **2.** crowd around and jostle or molest, as from adulation or curiosity. **3.** attend or crowd into (a hall, theater, etc.). [< L *mobile vulgus* vacillating crowd]

mo·bile (MOH bəl) *adj.* **1.** characterized by freedom of movement. **2.** moving easily from one thing, mood, etc. to another. **3.** capable of being easily and quickly moved. **4.** capable of moving with relative ease from one social group or status to another. **5.** of, pertaining to, or like a mobile. —*n.* (MOH beel) a form of freely moving sculpture consisting of parts that are suspended from rods, wires, etc. [< MF] —**mo·bil·i·ty** (moh BIL i tee) *n.*

mo·bi·lize (MOH bə LIZ) *v.* **·lized, ·liz·ing** *v.t.* **1.** make ready for war, as an army. **2.** put into circulation or use. —*v.i.* **3.** become ready or organized, as for war. —**mo'bi·li·za'tion** *n.*

moc·ca·sin (MOK ə sin) *n.* **1.** a heelless foot covering made of soft leather, formerly worn by North American Indians. **2.** a shoe or slipper resembling a moccasin. [< Algonquian *mokkussin*]

mo·cha (MOH kə) *n.* **1.** a choice, pungent coffee, originally brought from Mocha, South Yemen. **2.** a flavoring made of coffee or of coffee and chocolate.

mock (mok) *v.t.* **1.** treat or address scornfully or derisively. **2.** mimic, as in sport, derision, or contempt. **3.** deceive or disappoint; delude. **4.** defy. —*v.i.* **5.** express or show ridicule or contempt; scoff. —*adj.* merely imitating or resembling the reality; sham. [ME *mokken*] —**mock'·er·y** *n.* —**mock'ing·ly** *adv.*

mock·up (MOK UP) *n.* a model, usu. full-

scale, of a proposed structure, machine, etc.

mode (mohd) *n.* **1.** manner or form of being, doing, etc.; way. **2.** prevailing or current style or fashion, as in dress. **3.** *Gram.* mood. **4.** *Music* any of the arrangements of tones within a diatonic scale. **5.** *Stat.* the value, magnitude, or score that occurs the greatest number of times in a given series of observations: also called *norm.* [ME *moede* manner] —**mo'dal** *adj.*

mod·el (MOD l) *n.* **1.** an object, usu. in miniature and often built according to scale, that represents something to be made or something already existing. **2.** a pattern, example, or standard that is or may be used for imitation or comparison. **3.** one who poses for an artist, sculptor, etc. **4.** one who is employed to display or advertise merchandise; esp. one who displays articles of clothing by wearing them. **5.** a representative style, plan, or design. **6.** in merchandise, a particular style or design. —*v.* **·eled, ·el·ing** *v.t.* **1.** plan or fashion after a model or pattern. **2.** shape or fashion. **3.** display by wearing. —*v.i.* **4.** pose or serve as a model. —*adj.* **1.** serving or used as a model. **2.** worthy of emulation: a *model* student. [< MF *modelle*]

mod·el·ing (MOD l ing) *n.* **1.** the act or art of making a model, esp. a sculptor's clay or wax model. **2.** in painting, drawing, etc., the representation of depth or three-dimensional solidity. **3.** the act or occupation of being a model (defs. 3 & 4).

mod·er·ate (MOD ər it) *adj.* **1.** keeping or kept within reasonable limits; temperate. **2.** holding or characterized by ideas or convictions that are not extreme or radical. **3.** of medium or average quality, quantity, scope, extent, etc. —*n.* one having moderate views or practices, esp. in politics or religion. —*v.* (MOD ə RAYT) **·at·ed, ·at·ing** *v.t.* **1.** reduce the violence, severity, etc. of. **2.** preside over. —*v.i.* **3.** become less intense or violent. [ME] —**mod'er·a'tion** *n.*

mod·er·a·tor (MOD ə RAY tər) *n.* **1.** one who or that which moderates. **2.** one who presides over a meeting, forum, or debate. **3.** the arbitrator of a dispute.

mod·ern (MOD ərn) *adj.* **1.** of or pertaining to the present or recent time. **2.** characteristic of or serving to express the current times; up-to-date. —*n.* **1.** one who lives in modern times. **2.** one who has opinions, habits, prejudices, etc. characteristic of modern times. [< MF *moderne*] —**mo·der·ni·ty** (mo DUR ni tee) n.

mod·ern·ism (MOD ər NIZ əm) n. 1. the character or quality of thought, action, etc. that is peculiar to modern times. 2. something characteristic of modern times, as an act, practice, idiom, attitude, etc. —**mod'·ern·ist** n. —**mod'ern·is'tic** adj.

mod·ern·ize (MOD ər NIZ) v. -ized, -iz·ing v.t. 1. make modern in method, style, character, etc.; bring up to date. —v.i. 2. accept or adopt modern ways, ideas, idioms, etc. —**mod'ern·i·za'tion** n.

mod·est (MOD ist) adj. 1. having or displaying a moderate or unexaggerated regard for oneself or one's abilities, accomplishments, etc. 2. not showy or ostentatious. 3. not excessive or extreme; moderate. 4. reserved in speech, manner, dress, etc. [< L *modestus* restrained] —**mod'es·ty** n.

mod·i·cum (MOD i kəm) n. a moderate or small amount. [ME]

mod·i·fi·er (MOD ə FI ər) n. 1. one who or that which modifies. 2. *Gram.* a word, phrase, or clause that restricts or qualifies the meaning of another word or group of words.

mod·i·fy (MOD ə FI) v. -fied, -fy·ing v.t. 1. make somewhat different in form, character, etc. 2. revise by making less extreme, severe, or uncompromising. 3. *Gram.* qualify the meaning of; limit. —v.i. 4. be or become modified. [ME *modifien* regulate]—**mod'·i·fi·ca'tion** n.

mod·ish (MOH dish) adj. conforming to the current mode or fashion; stylish.

mod·u·late (MOJ ə LAYT) v. -lat·ed, -lat·ing v.t. 1. vary the tone, inflection, pitch, or volume of. 2. regulate or adjust; modify. 3. *Telecom.* alter some characteristic of (a radio carrier wave). —v.i. 4. *Music* change from one key to another. [< L *modulatus* regulated] —**mod'u·la'tion** n.

mod·ule (MOJ ool) n. 1. a standard or unit of measurement. 2. a standard structural component repeatedly used, as in a building computer, etc. 3. a self-contained component or subassembly: a housing *module*. [< L *modulus* small measure] —**mod'u·lar** adj.

mo·dus op·er·an·di (MOH dəs OP ə RAN dee) *Latin pl.* **mo·di** (MOH dī) **op·er·an·di** a manner of operating or proceeding.

modus vi·ven·di (vi VEN dee) *Latin pl.*

mo·di (MOH dī) **vi·ven·di** a manner of living.

mo·gul (MOH gəl) n. a very important, wealthy, or influential person. [after the *Moguls*, 16th-c. Mongol conquerors of India]

Mo·ham·me·dan (muu HAM i dn) n. & adj. a follower of the prophet Mohammad or a Muslim. —**Mo·ham'me·dan·ism'** n.

moi·e·ty (MOI i tee) n. pl. **·ties** 1. a half. 2. any portion, part, or share. 3. *Anthropol.* either of two basic groups that together constitute a tribe. [ME *moite* half]

moist (moist) adj. 1. slightly wet or damp. 2. saturated with or characterized by moisture or liquid. [ME *moiste*]

mois·ten (MOI sən) v.t. & v.i. make or become moist. —**mois'ten·er** n.

mois·ture (MOIS chər) n. water or other liquid causing dampness or wetness. [ME]

mo·lar (MOH lər) n. a grinding tooth, of which there are 12 in humans, situated behind the bicuspids and having a broad, flattened crown. [< L *molaris* grinder] —adj.

mo·las·ses (mə LAS iz) n. any of various thick, dark-colored syrups obtained from sugar, sorghum, etc., during the refining process. [< Pg. *melaço*]

mold¹ (mohld) n. 1. a form or matrix that gives a particular shape to anything in a fluid or plastic condition. 2. that which is shaped or made in or on a mold. 3. general shape, form, or pattern. 4. distinctive nature, character, or type. 5. *Archit.* a molding or set of moldings. —v.t. 1. work into a particular shape or form. 2. shape or form in or as in a mold. 3. influence, determine, or direct: *mold* public sentiment. —v.i. 4. assume or come to a particular shape or pattern. —**mold'er** n. [ME *molde*]

mold² (mohld) n. 1. any of a variety of tiny fungi commonly found on the surfaces of decaying food or in warm, moist places, and usu. having a woolly or furry texture. 2. a fungus producing one of these growths. —v.i. become moldy. [ME *mowlde*]

mold³ n. soft, loose earth that is rich in decaying organic matter. [ME *molde*]

mold·er (MOHL dər) v.i. 1. decay gradually and turn to dust; crumble. 2. atrophy from lack of use. —v.t. 3. cause to crumble.

mold·ing (MOHL ding) n. 1. the act or process of one who or that which molds. 2. that which is molded. 3. *Archit.* a cornice or other depressed or projecting member, used to decorate the surface or angle of a building, room, etc. **4.** a strip of decoratively shaped wood or other material, used to decorate or finish walls, doors, etc.

mold•y (MOHL dee) *adj.* **mold•i•er, mold•i•est 1.** covered with or containing mold. **2.** musty, as from age, lack of use, etc. — **mold′i•ness** *n.*

mole[1] (mohl) *n.* a small, congenital spot on the human skin, slightly protuberant and often dark and hairy. [ME]

mole[2] *n.* any of a number of small insectivorous mammals that live mainly underground and have soft fur, small eyes, and broad forefeet adapted for digging and burrowing. [ME *molle*]

mol•e•cule (MOL ə KYOOL) *n. Chem.* one or more atoms constituting the smallest part of an element or compound that can exist separately without losing the characteristics of the substance. [< NL] —**mo•lec•u•lar** (mə LEK yə lər) *adj.*

mole•hill (MOHL HIL) *n.* a small heap or mound of earth raised by a burrowing mole.

mo•lest (mə LEST) *v.t.* **1.** disturb or annoy by unwarranted, excessive, or malicious interference. **2.** interfere with improperly or illicitly, esp. with a sexual motive. [ME *molesten*] —**mo•les•ta•tion** (MOH le STAY shən) *n.* —**mo•lest′er** *n.*

mol•li•fy (MOL ə FI) *v.t.* **•fied, •fy•ing 1.** make less angry, violent, or agitated; soothe. **2.** reduce the harshness, severity, or intensity of. [ME]

mol•lusk (MOL əsk) *n.* one of a large group of unsegmented, soft-bodied invertebrates, usu. protected by a shell of one or more pieces, and including snails, oysters, clams, etc. Also **mol′lusc.** [< F *mollusque*]

mol•ly•cod•dle (MOL ee KOD l) *n.* any overprotected or pampered person; also, an effeminate man or boy. —*v.t.* **•dled, •dling** pamper; coddle. [< *Molly*, a name + CODDLE] —**mol′ly•cod′dler** *n.*

molt (mohlt) *v.t. & v.i.* cast off or shed (feathers, horns, skin, etc.) in preparation for periodic replacement by new growth. —*n.* **1.** the act or process of molting. **2.** that which is molted. [ME *mouten* change]

mol•ten (MOHL tn) a past participle of MELT. —*adj.* **1.** made fluid by heat; melted: *molten* metal. **2.** made by melting and casting in a mold: *molten* images. [ME]

mo•ment (MOH mənt) *n.* **1.** a very short or relatively short period of time. **2.** a particular point in time, usu. the present time. **3.** a particular period or stage in a series of events: a great *moment* in history. **4.** importance; consequence: matters of great *moment.* [ME]

mo•men•tar•i•ly (MOH mən TER ə lee) *adv.* **1.** for a moment: *momentarily* at a loss. **2.** in a moment; at any moment.

mo•men•tar•y (MOH mən TER ee) *adj.* **1.** lasting no more than a moment; fleeting. **2.** occurring or operating at every moment.

mo•men•tous (moh MEN təs) *adj.* of great importance or consequence.

mo•men•tum (moh MEN təm) *n.* **1.** *Physics* the quantity of motion in a body as measured by the product of its mass and velocity. **2.** impetus, as of a body in motion. [< L]

mon•arch (MON ərk) *n.* **1.** a hereditary constitutional ruler, as a king, queen, etc. **2.** formerly, a sole ruler of a state. **3.** one who or that which surpasses others of the same kind. **4.** *Entomol.* a large, orange and brown butterfly. [ME] —**mo•nar•chi•cal** (mə NAR ki kəl) *adj.*

mon•arch•ist (MON ər kist) *n.* one who favors monarchical government. —**mon′arch•ist** *adj.*

mon•ar•chy (MON ər kee) *n. pl.* **•chies 1.** government by a monarch; sovereign control. **2.** a government or territory ruled by a monarch. —**absolute monarchy** a government in which the will of the monarch is positive law. —**constitutional or limited monarchy** a monarchy in which the power and prerogatives of the sovereign are limited by constitutional provisions. [ME *monarchie*] —**mon′arch•ism** *n.*

mon•as•ter•y (MON ə STER ee) *n. pl.* **•ter•ies 1.** a dwelling place occupied by monks living under religious vows and in seclusion. **2.** the monks living in such a place. [ME]

mo•nas•tic (mə NAS tik) *adj.* **1.** of, pertaining to, or characteristic of monasteries or their inhabitants; ascetic. **2.** characteristic of a life of religious seclusion. —*n.* a monk or other religious recluse. [ME *monastik*] —**mon•as′ti•cal•ly** *adv.*

mo•nas•ti•cism (mə NAS tə SIZ əm) *n.* the monastic life or system.

mon•au•ral (mon OR əl) *adj. Electronics* designating a system of sound reproduction in which the sound is perceived as coming from one direction only.

Mon•day (MUN day) *n.* the second day of the week. [ME *Moneday* day of the moon]

mon•e•ta•rism (MON i tə RIZ əm) *n.* a theory that the economy can be controlled by regulating the flow of money. —**mon′e•ta•rist** n. & adj.

mon•e•tar•y (MON i TER ee) adj. **1.** of or pertaining to currency or coinage. **2.** pertaining to or concerned with money. [< LL *monetarius* of a mint] —**mon′e•tar′i•ly** adv.

mon•ey (MUN ee) n. pl. **mon•eys** or **mon•ies 1.** officially issued coins and paper currency that serve as a medium of exchange and may be used as payment for goods and services and for settlement of debts. **2.** property of any type having monetary value. **3.** money of account. [ME *moneie*]

mon•eyed (MUN eed) adj. **1.** possessed of money; wealthy. **2.** consisting of, arising from, or representing money or wealth: *moneyed* interests. Also spelled *monied*.

mon•ey•lend•er (MUN ee LEN dər) n. one whose business is the lending of money at interest.

mon•ey•mak•ing (MUN ee MAY king) adj. likely to bring in money; profitable. —n. the acquisition of money or wealth. — **mon′ey•mak′er** n.

mon•ger (MUNG gər) n. one who engages in discreditable matters: chiefly in compounds: a *scandalmonger*. [ME, trader]

Mon•gol (MONG gəl) n. **1.** a member of any of the native tribes of Mongolia. **2.** any of the Mongolian languages. **3.** a member of the Mongoloid ethnic division. —adj. Mongolian.

Mon•go•li•an (mong GOH lee ən) adj. of or pertaining to Mongolia, its people, or their languages. —n. **1.** a native of Mongolia. **2.** A subfamily of languages, including the languages of the Mongols.

Mon•go•loid (MONG gə LOID) adj. **1.** Anthropol. of, pertaining to, or belonging to a major ethnic division of the human species, characterized by yellowish skin, high cheek bones, etc. **2.** resembling, related to, or characteristic of Mongols or Mongolians.

mon•grel (MUNG grəl) n. **1.** the progeny produced by crossing different breeds or varieties of plants or animals; esp., a dog of mixed breed. **2.** any incongruous mixture. —adj. of mixed breed, origin, nature, etc.: often a contemptuous term: a *mongrel* language. [ME]

mon•ied (MUN eed) see MONEYED.

mon•ism (MON iz əm) n. *Philos.* the doctrine that there is but one principle of being or ultimate substance, as mind or matter.

[< G *Monismus*] —**mo•nis′tic** or **•ti•cal** adj.

mo•ni•tion (mə NISH ən) n. **1.** a warning or admonition, as of impending danger. **2.** an official, legal, or formal notice. [ME *monicioun* warning]

mon•i•tor (MON i tər) n. **1.** in some schools, a student who helps to keep records, maintain order, etc. **2.** one who or that which examines, as to maintain quality. **3.** *Telecom.* a receiver or other apparatus used to check radio or television broadcasts for quality of transmission, frequency, compliance with laws, etc. —v.t. & v.i. **1.** *Telecom.* listen to or watch (a broadcast) with a monitor. **2.** regulate or keep track of (a performance, heartbeat, etc.). [< L, adviser]

mon•i•to•ry (MON i TOR ee) adj. conveying a warning; admonitory. [ME]

monk (mungk) n. one who has taken the religious vows of poverty, chastity, and obedience, usu. a member of a monastic order. [ME]

mon•key (MUNG kee) n. **1.** any of the primates, excluding humans and the anthropoid apes, having elongate limbs, and hands and feet adapted for grasping. **2.** one who acts in a way suggestive of a monkey, as a mischievous child. —v.i. *Informal* play or trifle; meddle; fool: often with *with* or *around*.

monkey wrench a wrench having an adjustable jaw for grasping nuts, bolts, etc., of various sizes. —**throw a monkey wrench into** disrupt.

mono- *combining form* single; one: *monologue.* [< Gk. *mónos* single]

mon•o•chro•mat•ic (MON ə kroh MAT ik) adj. **1.** having only one color. **2.** consisting of one wavelength.

mon•o•chrome (MON ə KROHM) n. a painting or drawing in a single color or in various shades of the same color. [< Med.L *monochroma*]

mon•o•cle (MON ə kəl) n. an eyeglass for one eye. [< F] —**mon′o•cled** adj.

mo•nog•a•my (mə NOG ə mee) n. the condition or practice of having only one spouse at a time. [< LL *monogamia*] —**mo•nog′a•mous** (-məs) adj.

mon•o•gram (MON ə GRAM) n. two or more letters combined into a design; esp., the initials of one's name. —v.t. **mon•o•grammed, mon•o•gram•ming** mark with a monogram. [< LL *monogramma*]

mon•o•graph (MON ə GRAF) n. a book,

pamphlet, or treatise on one subject or on a single aspect of a subject.

mon·o·lith (MON ə lith) n. **1.** a single block of stone, usu. very large, used in architecture and sculpture. **2.** anything of an inflexible nature. [< L *monolithus*]

mon·o·lith·ic (MON ə LITH ik) adj. **1.** of or resembling a monolith. **2.** having a massive, uniform structure that does not permit individual variations: a *monolithic* state.

mon·o·logue (MON ə LAWG) n. **1.** a lengthy speech by one person. **2.** a play or dramatic composition for one actor only. **3.** a soliloquy. Also **mon'o·log.** [< F] **—mon'o·logu'ist, mo·nol·o·gist** (mə NOL ə jist) n.

mo·no·mi·al (moh NOH mee əl) adj. consisting of a single word or term. **—mo·no'mi·al** n.

mon·o·nu·cle·o·sis (MON ə NOO klee OH sis) n. *Pathol.* an acute infectious disease marked by fever, swelling of the lymph nodes, and an increase of lymphocytes in the blood. Also *Informal* **mon'o.**

mo·nop·o·lize (mə NOP ə LIZ) v.t. **·lized, ·liz·ing 1.** obtain a monopoly of. **2.** assume exclusive possession or control of.

mo·nop·o·ly (mə NOP ə lee) n. pl. **·lies 1.** the exclusive control of a commodity, service, or means of production in a particular market, with the resulting power to fix prices. **2.** a company having a monopoly. **3.** exclusive possession or control of anything. [< L *monopolium* exclusive right to trade] **—mo·nop'o·lis'tic** adj.

mon·o·rail (MON ə RAYL) n. **1.** a single rail serving as a track for cars either suspended from it or balanced upon it. **2.** a railway using such a track.

mon·o·so·di·um glu·ta·mate (MON ə SOH dee əm GLOO tə MAYT) a crystalline salt used to flavor food. Abbr. *MSG.*

mon·o·syl·la·bic (MON ə si LAB ik) adj. **1.** having only one syllable. **2.** using or speaking in monosyllables.

mon·o·syl·la·ble (MON ə SIL ə bəl) n. a word of one syllable, as *no.*

mon·o·the·ism (MON ə thee IZ əm) n. the doctrine or belief that there is but one God. **—mon'o·the·is'tic** adj.

mon·o·tone (MON ə TOHN) n. **1.** the utterance of a succession of words, etc., in a single tone. **2.** sameness in expression, style, color, etc. **3.** a single musical tone unvaried in pitch.

mo·not·o·nous (mə NOT n əs) adj. **1.** un-

varied in tone. **2.** tiresomely uniform or repetitive. [< LGk. *monótonos*] **—mo·not'o·ny** n.

mon·ox·ide (mon OK sīd) n. *Chem.* an oxide containing a single atom of oxygen in each molecule.

mon·sieur (məs YUR) n. pl. **mes·sieurs** (MES ərz) the French title of courtesy for men, equivalent to *Mr.* and *sir.*

Mon·si·gnor (mon SEE nyər) n. in the Roman Catholic Church, a title of honor of certain prelates. [< Ital.]

mon·soon (mon SOON) n. *Meterol.* **1.** a seasonal wind of the Indian Ocean and southern Asia, blowing in winter from the northeast and in summer from the southwest. **2.** the summer monsoon, characterized by heavy rains. [< Obs. Du. *monssoen*]

mon·ster (MON stər) n. **1.** one who or that which is abnormal, unnatural, or hideous in form. **2.** one who or that which inspires hate or horror because of cruelty, wickedness, etc. **3.** a huge person or thing. **—adj.** huge. [ME *monstre*] **—mon'strous** (-strəs) adj.

mon·stros·i·ty (mon STROS i tee) n. pl. **·ties 1.** one who or that which is monstrous. **2.** the condition or character of being monstrous.

mon·tage (mon TAZH) n. **1.** a picture made by superimposing or arranging a number of different pictorial elements; also, the art or process of making such a picture. **2.** in motion pictures or television, a rapid sequence of images used to illustrate a group of associated ideas. **3.** similar techniques in radio and writing. [< F]

month (munth) n. **1.** one of the twelve parts (**calendar month**) into which the calendar year is divided. **2.** a period of thirty days or four weeks. **3.** the twelfth part (**solar month**) of the solar year. **4.** the period (**lunar month**), equivalent to 29.53 days, during which the moon makes a complete revolution. [ME]

month·ly (MUNTH lee) adj. **1.** happening, done, appearing, etc., every month. **2.** of or pertaining to a month. **—adv.** once a month. **—n.** pl. **·lies 1.** a periodical published once a month. **2.** *Informal* a menstrual period.

mon·u·ment (MON yə mənt) n. **1.** a statue, plaque, etc., erected to perpetuate the memory of a person, event, or historical period. **2.** a tombstone. **3.** any conspicuous or fine structure surviving from the past. **4.**

a work of art, scholarship, etc., regarded as having enduring value. [ME]

mon·u·men·tal (MON yə MEN tl) *adj.* **1.** of, pertaining to, or serving as a monument. **2.** enduring; imposing; massive. **3.** having great significance: a *monumental* study. **4.** very large; huge: a *monumental* bore.

mooch (mooch) *v.t. Slang* **1.** obtain without paying; beg; cadge. **2.** steal. [ME, skulk] — **mooch'er** *n.*

mood[1] (mood) *n.* **1.** a specific state of mind or feeling, esp. a temporary one. **2.** an inclination or attitude; disposition. —**in the mood** disposed; inclined. [ME]

mood[2] *n. Gram.* the set of distinctive forms of a verb showing the attitude and understanding of the speaker regarding the action or condition expressed: also *mode*.

mood·y (MOO dee) *adj.* **mood·i·er, mood·i·est** **1.** given to sudden moods of moroseness. **2.** expressive of such moods. [ME *mody*] —**mood'i·ness** *n.*

Moog synthesizer (moog) an electronic musical instrument with a keyboard. [after R.A. *Moog*, 1934— , U.S. engineer, its inventor]

moon (moon) *n.* **1.** a celestial body revolving around the earth from west to east every 29.53 days, and accompanying the earth in its yearly revolution about the sun. **2.** any satellite revolving about a planet. **3.** a month; esp., a lunar month. —*v.i.* stare or wander about abstractedly. [ME *mone*]

moon·light (MOON LIT) *n.* the light of the moon. —*adj.* —**moon'lit'** (-LIT) *adj.*

moon·light·ing (MOON LI ting) *n.* the act of one who holds a job in addition to the regular day's work. —**moon'light'** *v.i.* —**moon'light'er** *n.*

moon·shine (MOON SHIN) *n.* **1.** moonlight. **2.** nonsense. **3.** *Informal* smuggled or illicitly distilled whiskey etc. —**moon'·shin'er** *n.*

moon·struck (MOON STRUK) *adj.* **1.** lunatic; deranged. **2.** romantically obsessed. Also **moon'strick'en** (STRIK ən).

moor[1] (muur) *n.* a tract of wasteland sometimes covered with heath, often elevated, marshy, and abounding in peat; a heath. [ME *more*]

moor[2] *v.t. & v.i.* secure (a ship, etc.) in place by means of cables attached to shore, anchors, etc. —**moor·age** (MUUR ij) *n.*

Moor (muur) *n.* **1.** a Muslim of Berber and Arab ancestry; esp., one of the invaders of

Spain in the 8th c. **2.** a native of Morocco. [ME *More*] —**Moor'ish** *adj.*

moor·ing (MUUR ing) *n.* **1.** a place where ships, etc., can be moored. **2.** *pl.* that which secures an object, as a cable. **3.** *pl.* a person's stability: lost his *moorings*.

moot (moot) *adj.* **1.** open to discussion: debatable. **2.** hypothetical; academic: a *moot* court. —*v.t.* bring up for discussion or debate. [ME *mot* assembly]

mop (mop) *n.* **1.** a device for cleaning floors, consisting of a sponge, a bunch of heavy cotton yarn, etc., attached to a handle. **2.** any loosely tangled bunch, esp. of hair. —*v.t.* **mopped, mop·ping** rub or wipe with or as with a mop. —**mop up** *Informal* finish. [ME *mappe*]

mope (mohp) *v.i.* **moped, mop·ing** be gloomy, listless, or dispirited. —*n.* a person who mopes. —**mop'er** *n.*

mo·ped (MOH PED) *n.* a motorized bicycle. [< G]

mop·pet (MOP it) *n.* a child.

mo·raine (mə RAYN) *n. Geol.* debris that has been carried by a glacier. [< F]

mor·al (MOR əl) *adj.* **1.** of or related to conduct or character from the point of view of right and wrong: *moral* goodness. **2.** of good character; right or proper in behavior. **3.** sexually virtuous. **4.** arising from a sense of duty and right conduct: a *moral* obligation. **5.** acting not by physical force but by appeal to character, etc.: *moral* support. —*n.* **1.** the teaching contained in or implied by a fable, poem, etc. **2.** *pl.* conduct or behavior with regard to right and wrong, esp. in sexual matters. **3.** a maxim. [ME] —**mor'al·ly** *adv.*

mo·rale (mə RAL) *n.* state of mind with reference to confidence, courage, hope, zeal, etc. [< F]

mor·al·ist (MOR ə list) *n.* **1.** a teacher of morals. **2.** one who practices morality.

mo·ral·i·ty (mə RAL i tee) *n.* **1.** the quality of being morally right; virtue. **2.** virtuous conduct; esp., sexual virtue. **3.** *pl.* **·ties** a system of the principles of right and wrong conduct; ethics. [ME *moralite*]

mor·al·ize (MOR ə LIZ) *v.i.* **·ized, ·iz·ing** make moral reflections; talk about morality. [ME *moralisen*]

mo·rass (mə RAS) *n.* **1.** a tract of low-lying, soft, wet ground; marsh. **2.** anything that impedes, perplexes, or traps. [< Du. *moeras* marsh]

mor·a·to·ri·um (MOR ə TOR ee əm) *n. pl.*

•ri•a (-ree ə), •ri•ums 1. a legal authorization to a debtor to suspend payments for a given period. 2. any authorized suspension or deferment of action. [< NL]

mor•bid (MOR bid) adj. 1. taking or showing an excessive interest in matters of a gruesome or unwholesome nature. 2. grisly; gruesome: a morbid fantasy. 3. pertaining to, arising from, or affected by disease. [< L morbidus sickly] —**mor′bid•ly** adv.

mor•dant (MOR dnt) adj. 1. biting; cutting; sarcastic: a mordant wit. 2. incisive. [ME] —**mor′dant•ly** adv.

more (mor) adj. superlative **most** 1. greater in amount, extent, degree, or number: comparative of much and many. 2. additional: More coffee, please. —n. 1. a greater or additional quantity, amount, etc.: Will you have more? 2. that which exceeds or excels something else. —adv. 1. in or to a greater extent or degree: used to form the comparative of many adjectives and adverbs: more beautiful. 2. in addition; further. —**more or less** 1. in some undetermined degree. 2. approximately. [ME]

more•o•ver (mor OH vər) adv. beyond what has been said; further; besides. [ME more over]

mo•res (MOR ayz) n.pl. Sociol. 1. the established customs regarded by a social group as essential to its preservation. 2. the accepted conventions of a group. [< L, customs]

morgue (morg) n. 1. a place where the bodies of dead persons are kept for identification. 2. a newspaper's files of reference material, biographical material, etc. [< F]

mor•i•bund (MOR ə BUND) adj. at the point of death; dying. [< L moribundus dying]

Mor•mon (MOR mən) n. a member of the Mormon Church; a Latter-day Saint. —**Mor′mon** adj. —**Mor′mon•ism** n.

Mormon Church the Church of Jesus Christ of Latter-day Saints, founded by Joseph Smith in 1830.

morn (morn) n. Poetic morning.

morn•ing (MOR ning) n. 1. the early part of the day; the time from midnight to noon, or from sunrise to noon. 2. the early part or stage of anything. —adj. pertaining to or occurring in the morning. [ME]

morning star a planet, esp. Venus, when rising in the east shortly before the sun.

mo•roc•co (mə ROK oh) n. a fine flexible leather, made from goatskin. Also **morocco leather**. [after Morocco, Africa]

mo•ron (MOR on) n. 1. a person exhibiting the mildest degree of mental deficiency, permitting adequacy in simple activities. 2. loosely, a very stupid person. [< Gk. mōrón foolish] —**mo•ron•ic** (mə RON ik) adj.

mo•rose (mə ROHS) adj. ill-humored; sullen; gloomy, as a person, mood, etc. [< L morosus peevish] —**mo•rose′ly** adv.

mor•pheme (MOR feem) n. Ling. the smallest meaningful unit of a language or dialect, whether a word, base, or affix. [< F morphème]

mor•phine (MOR feen) n. Chem. a bitter, white compound made from opium, used as a painkiller and narcotic. [< F < Morpheus, god of dreams]

mor•phol•o•gy (mor FOL ə jee) n. pl. •gies 1. Biol. the study of the form and structure of plants and animals considered apart from function. 2. Ling. the arrangement and interrelationship of morphemes in words. —**mor•pho•log•i•cal** adj. (MOR fə LOJ i kəl) —**mor•phol′o•gist** n.

Morse code a system of telegraphic signals composed of dots and dashes representing the letters of the alphabet, numerals, etc. [after Samuel F.B. Morse, 1791—1872, U.S. inventor]

mor•sel (MOR səl) n. 1. a small fragment or bite of food. 2. a tidbit. 3. a small piece or bit of something. [ME]

mor•tal (MOR tl) adj. 1. subject to death. 2. of or relating to this life or world. 3. causing or liable to cause death. 4. grievous; dire: mortal terror. 5. likely to remain so until death; implacable: a mortal enemy. 6. Theol. incurring spiritual death unless repented of and forgiven: distinguished from venial: mortal sin. —n. one who is mortal; a human being. [ME] —**mor•tal•ly** (MOR tl ee) adv. 1. fatally. 2. after the manner of a mortal. 3. extremely: mortally offended.

mor•tal•i•ty (mor TAL i tee) n. pl. •ties 1. the condition of being mortal or subject to death. 2. the frequency of death; death rate. [ME mortalite]

mor•tar[1] (MOR tər) n. a bowl-shaped vessel in which substances are crushed with a pestle. [ME]

mor•tar[2] n. a mixture of lime, cement, etc., with sand and water, used in bricklaying etc. [ME morter]

mor•tar[3] n. Mil. a smooth-bored or rifled muzzleloading weapon, firing a relatively heavy shell, having a shorter range and higher trajectory than a howitzer. [< F *mortier*]

mort·gage (MOR gij) *n. Law* **1.** a transfer of property pledged as security for the repayment of a loan. **2.** the contract specifying such a pledge. —*v.t.* **•gaged, •gag·ing** make over or pledge (property) by mortgage. [ME]

mort·ga·gee (MOR gə JEE) *n.* the holder of a mortgage.

mort·ga·gor (MOR gə jər) *n.* one who mortgages property to another as security for a loan. Also **mort'gag·er.**

mor·ti·cian (mor TISH ən) *n.* an undertaker.

mor·ti·fy (MOR tə FI) *v.* **•fied, •fy·ing** *v.t.* **1.** humiliate. **2.** discipline (the body, appetites, etc.) by fasting or other ascetic practices. —*v.i.* **3.** practice ascetic self-discipline. [ME *mortifien*] —**mor'ti·fi·ca'tion** *n.*

mor·tise (MOR tis) *n.* a space hollowed out in a piece of timber, stone, etc., and shaped to fit a tenon to which it is to be joined. —*v.t.* **•tised, •tis·ing 1.** cut or make a mortise in. **2.** join by a tenon and mortise. Also **mor'tice.** [ME *morteys*]

mor·tu·ar·y (MOR choo ER ee) *n. pl.* **•ar·ies** a place for the temporary reception of the dead before burial. [ME *mortuarie*]

mo·sa·ic (moh ZAY ik) *n.* **1.** inlaid work composed of bits of stone, glass, etc., forming a pattern or picture. **2.** a design, arrangement, etc., resembling such work. [ME] —**mo·sa'ic** *adj.*

Mos·lem (MOZ ləm) *n. & adj.* see MUSLIM.

mosque (mosk) *n.* a Muslim temple of worship. [< MF]

mos·qui·to (mə SKEE toh) *n. pl.* **•toes** or **•tos** any of various winged insects, having in the female a long proboscis for sucking the blood of animals. [< Sp.]

moss (maws) *n.* **1.** a delicate plant with a stem and distinct leaves, which grows in tufts or clusters on the ground, decaying wood, rocks, etc. **2.** any of several similar plants, as certain lichens. [ME *mos*]

moss·back (MAWS BAK) *n.* **1.** an old fish or turtle on whose back is a growth of algae or the like. **2.** *Informal* a very conservative or old-fashioned person; fogy.

most (mohst) *adj.* **1.** consisting of the greatest number: superlative of *many.* **2.** consisting of the greatest amount or degree: superlative of *much.* **3.** in the greatest num-

ber of instances: *Most* people are honest. — **for the most part** generally; mostly. —*n.* **1.** (construed as *pl.*) the greatest number; the largest part. **2.** the greatest amount, quantity, or degree. —*adv.* **1.** in or to the greatest or highest degree, quantity, extent, etc.: used with adjectives and adverbs to form the superlative degree. **2.** very. [ME]

-most *suffix* most: added to adjectives and adverbs to form superlatives: *innermost.*

most·ly (MOHST lee) *adv.* for the most part; principally.

mot (moh) *n.* a witty or pithy remark. [< F, *word*]

mote (moht) *n.* a minute particle or speck, esp., of dust. [ME *mot*]

mo·tel (moh TEL) *n.* a hotel for motorists, usu. having rooms directly accessible to parking facilities. [*motor + hotel*]

mo·tet (moh TET) *n. Music* a polyphonic vocal composition of a sacred nature, usu. unaccompanied. [ME]

moth (mawth) *n. pl.* **moths** (mawthz) any of a large group of insects, usu. nocturnal, distinguished from the butterflies by smaller wings, stouter bodies, and duller coloring. [ME *motthe*]

moth-eat·en (MAWTH EET n) *adj.* **1.** eaten or damaged by moths. **2.** worn out. **3.** out of fashion.

moth·er (MUTH ər) *n.* **1.** a female who has borne offspring. **2.** a female who adopts a child, or who otherwise holds a maternal relationship toward another. **3.** anything that creates, nurtures, or protects something else. **4.** *Usu. cap.* a title given to a nun having authority. —*adj.* **1.** native: *mother* tongue. **2.** relating to or characteristic of a mother: *mother* love. **3.** holding a maternal relation: the *mother* church. —*v.t.* **1.** bring forth as a mother; produce; create. **2.** care for or protect as a mother. [ME] —**moth'er·hood** (-huud) *n.*

mother-in-law (MUTH ər in LAW) *n. pl.* **moth·ers-in-law** the mother of one's spouse.

moth·er·land (MUTH ər LAND) *n.* **1.** the land of one's birth; native land. **2.** the land of one's ancestors.

moth·er·ly (MUTH ər lee) *adj.* resembling, characteristic of, or like a mother.—*adv.* in the manner of a mother. —**moth'er·li·ness** *n.*

moth·er-of-pearl (MUTH ər əv PURL) *n.* the pearly, iridescent internal layer of certain shells, used in ornamental work, for buttons, etc.: also called *nacre*.

mother tongue one's native language.

mo·tif (moh TEEF) *n.* the underlying theme or main element in a literary or artistic work. [< F]

mo·tile (MOHT l) *adj. Zool.* having the power of motion, as certain minute organisms. —**mo·til'i·ty** *n.*

mo·tion (MOH shən) *n.* 1. the act or process of changing position; movement: also, an instance of this. 2. a formal proposal or suggestion in an assembly or meeting. 3. an impulse; inclination. —**in motion** moving; in operation. —*v.i.* 1. make a gesture of direction or intent, as with the hand. —*v.t.* 2. direct or guide by a gesture. [ME *mocioun*]

motion picture 1. a sequence of pictures of moving objects photographed on a strip of film, that, when projected on a screen, gives the illusion of continuous movement. 2. a specific drama, story, etc. made by means of such photographs: also called *film, movie, moving picture.*

motion sickness nausea, dizziness, etc. caused by the effects of motion, as in travel.

mo·ti·vate (MOH tə VAYT) *v.t.* **·vat·ed, ·vat·ing** provide with a motive. —**mo'ti·va'tion** *n.* —**mo'ti·va'tion·al** *adj.*

mo·tive (MOH tiv) *n.* 1. a conscious or unconscious need, drive, etc., that incites a person to some action or behavior; incentive; goal. 2. a motif. —*adj.* 1. causing or having the power to cause motion. 2. relating to or acting as a motive. [ME]

mot·ley (MOT lee) *adj.* 1. made up of diverse elements; heterogeneous. 2. variegated in color. —*n.* 1. a heterogeneous mixture or collection. 2. a garment of various colors such as formerly worn by court jesters. [ME]

mo·tor (MOH tər) *n.* 1. an engine; esp., an internal-combustion engine propelling an automobile. 2. something that imparts or produces motion. —*adj.* 1. causing, producing, or imparting motion. 2. equipped with or driven by a motor. 3. *Physiol.* transmitting impulses from nerve centers to the muscles. —*v.i.* travel or ride in an automobile. [< L, *mover*]

mo·tor·boat MOH tər BOHT() *n.* a boat propelled by a motor.

mo·tor·cade (MOH tər KAYD) *n.* a procession of automobiles.

mo·tor·cy·cle (MOH tər SI kəl) *n.* a two-wheeled vehicle, larger and heavier than a bicycle, propelled by an internal-combustion engine. —*v.i.* **·cled, ·cling** travel or ride on a motorcycle. —**mo'tor·cy'clist** *n.*

mo·tor·ist (MOH tər ist) *n.* one who drives or travels by automobile.

mo·tor·ize (MOH tə RIZ) *v.t.* **·ized, ·iz·ing** 1. equip with a motor. 2. equip with motor-propelled vehicles.

mo·tor·man (MOH tər mən) *n. pl.* **·men** one who operates a streetcar or subway train.

motor vehicle a wheeled vehicle with a motor, as a bus or car, for use on streets or roads.

mot·tle (MOT l) *v.t.* **·tled, ·tling** mark with spots or streaks of different colors or shades; blotch. —*n.* a spotted, blotched, or variegated appearance, as of skin or marble. —**mot'tled** *adj.*

mot·to (MOT oh) *n. pl.* **·toes** or **·tos** 1. a word or phrase expressing a rule of conduct, principle, etc.; a maxim. 2. an appropriate or indicative phrase inscribed on something, prefixed to a literary work, etc. [< Ital.]

moue (moo) *n.* a pouting grimace. [< F]

mound (mownd) *n.* 1. a heap or pile of earth, debris, etc., either natural or artificial. 2. a small natural elevation; a hillock. 3. in baseball, the slightly raised ground from which the pitcher pitches. —*v.t.* heap up in a mound.

mount¹ (mownt) *v.t.* 1. ascend or climb (a slope, stairs, etc.). 2. get up on; climb upon. 3. put or set on horseback. 4. furnish with a horse. 5. set, fix, or secure in or on a support, frame, etc., as for exhibition or use: *mount* a specimen on a slide. 6. furnish with scenery, costumes, etc.: *mount* a play. 7. *Mil.* **a** set or raise into position, as a gun. **b** prepare and begin: *mount* an offensive. —*v.i.* 8. rise or ascend; go or come up. 9. increase in amount, number, or degree. —*n.* 1. anything on or in which an object is placed for use, preparation, display, etc., as a setting for a jewel etc. 2. a horse or other animal used for riding. [ME *mounten*] —**mount'ed** *adj.*

mount² *n.* a mountain: used poetically or as part of a placename. [ME]

moun·tain (MOWN tn) *n.* 1. a natural elevation of the earth's surface, typically having steep sides and a narrow summit, and rising higher than a hill. 2. anything of great size: a *mountain* of a man. —*adj.* 1. of or like a mountain. 2. living, growing, or situated on mountains. [ME *mountaine*] — **moun·tain·ous** (MOWN tn əs) *adj.*

moun·tain·eer (MOWN tn EER) *n.* 1. an inhabitant of a mountainous district. 2. one who climbs mountains. —*v.i.* climb mountains for sport.

moun·te·bank (MOWN tə BANGK) *n.* 1. one who sells quack medicines at fairs. 2. any charlatan. [< Ital. *montimbanco*]

mourn (morn) *v.i.* 1. feel or express grief or sorrow, esp. for the dead; grieve. —*v.t.* 2. lament or sorrow for (someone dead). 3. grieve over or bemoan (misfortune, failure, etc.). [ME *mournen*] —**mourn'er** *n.*

mourn·ful (MORN fəl) *adj.* 1. indicating, expressing, or exciting grief. 2. doleful; melancholy; sad. —**mourn'ful·ly** *adv.*

mourn·ing (MOR ning) *n.* 1. the act of one who mourns. 2. the manifestations of grief, as the wearing of black dress, etc. 3. the period during which one mourns. —*adj.* of or expressive of mourning.

mouse (mows) *n. pl.* **mice** (mīs) 1. one of various small rodents frequenting human habitations throughout the world. 2. a timid person. 3. *Informal* a black eye. —*v.i.* **moused, mous·ing** hunt or catch mice. [ME *mous*] —**mous·er** (MOW zər) *n.*

mousse (moos) *n.* 1. any of various light desserts made with whipped cream, egg white, etc., and sugar and flavoring. 2. a hair dressing to help hold hair in place. [< F, froth]

mous·tache (MUS tash) see MUSTACHE.

mous·y (MOW see) *adj.* **mous·i·er, mous·i·est** 1. of or resembling a mouse. 2. characterized by timidity, shyness, drabness, etc. Also **mous'ey.** —**mous'i·ness** *n.*

mouth (mowth) *n. pl.* **mouths** (mowthz) 1. the opening at which food is taken into the body; also, the cavity between the lips and throat. ◆ Collateral adjective: *oral.* 2. one who needs food: so many *mouths* to feed. 3. the organ or instrument of speech: shut one's *mouth.* 4. something resembling a mouth; as: **a** the part of a stream where its waters are discharged into another body of water. **b** the entrance or opening of something, as a cave, mine, or jar. —**down in** (or **at**) **the mouth** *Informal* disconsolate; dejected. —*v.t.* (mowth) 1. speak in a forced or affected manner. 2. form (words etc.) silently with the lips and tongue. [ME] — **mouth·er** (MOW thər) *n.*

mouthed (mowthd) *adj.* 1. having a mouth or mouths. 2. having a (specified kind of) mouth or (a specified number of) mouths: used in combination: *evil-mouthed.*

mouth·ful (MOWTH fuul) *n. pl.* **·fuls** 1. as much as can be held in the mouth. 2. a long word or group of words difficult to say. 3. *Informal* an important or perceptive remark: chiefly in the phrase **say a mouthful.**

mouth organ harmonica.

mouth·piece (MOWTH pees) *n.* 1. that part of a musical instrument, telephone, etc. that is used in or near the mouth. 2. one who acts as spokesman for an individual, group, belief, etc. 3. *Slang* a lawyer who frequently represents criminals.

mouth·wash (MOWTH wosh) *n.* an antiseptic and scented solution used for cleaning the mouth.

mov·a·ble (MOO və bəl) *adj.* 1. capable of being moved. 2. *Eccl.* varying in date from year to year: *movable* feast. —*n. Usu. pl.* anything that can be moved; esp., an article of furniture. Also **move'a·ble.**

move (moov) *v.* **moved, mov·ing** *v.i.* 1. change place or position; go to or from a place. 2. change one's residence. 3. make progress; advance. 4. live or carry on one's life: *move* in cultivated circles. 5. operate, work, revolve, etc., as a machine. 6. take or begin to take action; act. 7. be disposed of by sale. 8. make an application or proposal: *move* for adjournment. 9. evacuate: said of the bowels. —*v.t.* 10. change the place or position of, as by carrying, pushing, pulling, etc. 11. set or keep in motion. 12. dislodge or force from a set position: *move* him from his purpose. 13. affect or arouse the emotions, sympathies, etc. of; touch. 14. propose for action, deliberation, etc. 15. cause (the bowels) to evacuate. —*n.* 1. an act of moving; movement. 2. an action for some purpose or design; step; maneuver. 3. a change in residence. 4. in checkers, chess, etc., the transfer of a piece. [ME *moven*]

move·ment (MOOV mənt) *n.* 1. the act of moving; any change of place or position. 2. a specific instance or manner of moving: a dance *movement.* 3. the actions by individuals or organizations toward some end: the peace *movement.* 4. *Music* one of the sections of a work, as of a symphony, string quartet, etc. 5. an emptying of the bowels. [ME]

mov·ie (MOO vee) *n.* 1. a motion picture. 2. *pl.* the showing of a motion picture. 3. *pl.* the motion-picture industry.

mov·ing (MOO ving) *adj.* **1.** going or capable of going from place to place, position to position, etc. **2.** affecting, arousing, or touching the feelings or passions.

moving picture a motion picture.

mow (moh) *v.t. & v.i.* **mowed, mowed** or **mown, mow·ing 1.** cut down (grain, grass, etc.) with a scythe or machine. **2.** cut the grain or grass of (a field, lawn, etc.). —**mow down** cut down or kill rapidly or indiscriminately. [ME *mowen*] — **mow′er** *n.*

moz·za·rel·la (MOT sə REL lə) *n.* a soft, mild curd cheese. [< Ital.]

Mr. (MIS tər) *n.* MISTER.

Mrs. (MIS iz) *n.* a title prefixed to the name of a married woman: abbreviation of *Mistress.*

Ms. (miz) *n. pl.* **Mses** a title prefixed to the name of a woman that disregards marital status.

mu (myoo) *n.* **1.** the twelfth letter in the Greek alphabet (M, μ), corresponding to the English *m.* **2.** micron (symbol μ).

much (much) *adj.* **more, most** great in quantity, amount, extent, etc.: *much* noise. —*n.* **1.** a considerable quantity or amount; a great deal. **2.** a remarkable or important thing: It isn't *much.* —**make much of 1.** treat as very important. **2.** treat with great courtesy, regard, etc. —*adv.* **more, most 1.** greatly: *much* obliged. **2.** for the most part; almost. [ME *muche*]

mu·ci·lage (MYOO sə lij) *n.* **1.** an aqueous solution of vegetable gum or the like, used as an adhesive. **2.** any of various gummy or gelatinous substances found in some plants. [ME *muscilage*] —**mu·ci·lag·i·nous** (MYOO sə LAJ ə nəs) *adj.*

muck (muk) *n.* **1.** any wet and clinging material that soils; esp., viscid mud. **2.** moist dung mixed with decomposed vegetable matter, used as a soil fertilizer; manure. **3.** a dark, rich soil consisting largely of decomposing vegetable materials. **4.** a confusing or uncertain state or condition; mess. —*v.t.* **1.** fertilize with manure. **2.** *Informal* bungle; make dirty; pollute. [ME *muk*] — **muck′y** *adj.* **muck′i·er, muck′i·est**

muck·rake (MUK RAYK) *v.i.* **·raked, ·rak·ing** search for or expose real or alleged corruption on the part of political officials, businessmen, etc. —**muck′rak′er** *n.* —**muck′rak′ing** *n.*

mu·cous (MYOO kəs) *adj.* **1.** secreting mucus. **2.** pertaining to, consisting of, or resembling mucus. —**mu·cos·i·ty** (myoo KOS i tee) *n.*

mucous membrane *Anat.* a lubricating membrane that lines various body passages.

mu·cus (MYOO kəs) *n. Biol.* a viscid substance secreted by the mucous membranes. [< L, snot]

mud (mud) *n.* **1.** soft and sticky wet earth. **2.** *Informal* the most degrading information or situation: drag one into the *mud.* —*v.t.* **mud·ded, mud·ding** soil or cover with or as with mud. [ME *mudde*]

mud·dle (MUD l) *v.* **·dled, ·dling** *v.t.* **1.** confuse or confound (the mind, speech, etc.). **2.** mess up or mismanage; bungle. **3.** make muddy or turbid. —*v.i.* **4.** act or think in a confused manner. —**muddle through** achieve one's object despite confusion or mistakes. —*n.* a state or condition of confusion, disorder, or uncertainty.

mud·dle·head·ed (MUD l HED id) *adj.* mentally confused; stupid.

mud·dy (MUD ee) *adj.* **·di·er, ·di·est 1.** covered, spattered, or filled with mud. **2.** not clear, bright, or distinct, as color, liquid, etc. **3.** confused or obscure in thought, expression, meaning, etc. —*v.t. & v.i.* **·died, ·dy·ing** make or become muddy. —**mud′di·ness** *n.*

mud·sling·er (MUD SLING ər) *n.* one who casts malicious slurs, esp. at a political opponent. —**mud′sling′ing** *n.*

mu·ez·zin (myoo EZ in) *n.* in Islam, a crier who calls the faithful to prayer. [< Turkish *müezzin*]

muff¹ (muf) *v.t. & v.i.* perform (some act) clumsily; esp., fail to catch (a ball). —*n.* an awkward action.

muff² *n.* a pillowlike or tubular case of fur or cloth, open at the ends, used for warming the hands.

muf·fin (MUF in) *n.* a small, cup-shaped quick bread.

muf·fle (MUF əl) *v.t.* **·fled, ·fling 1.** wrap up in a blanket, scarf, etc., as for warmth or concealment: often with *up.* **2.** deaden the sound of by or as by wrapping. **3.** deaden (a sound). [ME *mufeln* wrap up]

muf·fler (MUF lər) *n.* **1.** a device to reduce noise, as from the exhaust of an engine. **2.** a heavy scarf worn about the neck for warmth.

mug¹ (mug) *n.* a large drinking cup.

mug² *n. Slang* **1.** the face. **2.** a photograph of the face: also **mug shot.** —*v.* **mugged, mug·ging** *v.t.* **1.** assault viciously and rob.

—*v.i.* **2.** make funny faces; overact to win an audience. —**mug′ger** *n.*

mug•gy (MUG ee) *adj.* •**gi•er,** •**gi•est** warm, humid, and close; sultry. [< dial. E *mug* drizzle] —**mug′gi•ness** *n.*

mug•wump (MUG WUMP) *n.* one who asserts his or her independence, esp. in politics. [< Algonquian *mugwomp* captain]

Mu•ham•ma•dan (muu HAM ə dən) *n.* see MOHAMMEDAN.

mu•lat•to (mə LAT oh) *n. pl.* •**toes 1.** a person having one white and one black parent; not in scientific use. **2.** anyone having mixed white and black ancestry. —*adj.* having the light brown color of a mulatto. [< Sp. *mulato* young mule]

mul•ber•ry (MULBER ee) *n. pl.* •**ries 1.** any of various trees having a berrylike fruit and whose leaves are valued for silkworm culture. **2.** a purplish red color. [ME *mulberie*]

mulch (mulch) *n.* any loose material, as straw, leaves, etc., placed about the stalks of plants to protect their roots. —*v.t.* cover with mulch.

mulct (mulkt) *v.t.* **1.** defraud or cheat (someone). **2.** punish with a fine. —*n.* a fine or similar penalty. [< L *mulcta* a fine]

mule[1] (myool) *n.* **1.** a hybrid between the ass and horse; esp., a hybrid between a jackass and mare. **2.** *Informal* a stubborn person. [ME] —**mul′ish** *adj.*

mule[2] *n.* a backless lounging slipper. [< MF]

mull[1] (mul) *v.t.* heat and spice, as wine or ale.

mull[2] *v.t.* ponder: usu. with *over*. [ME *mullen* pulverize]

mul•li•ga•taw•ny (MUL i gə TAW nee) *n.* a strongly flavored soup of the East Indies, made of meat and curry. [< Tamil *milakutanni* peppery soup]

mul•lion (MUL yən) *n. Archit.* a vertical dividing piece in a window. —*v.t.* divide by means of mullions.

multi- *combining form* **1.** many; consisting of many: **multicolor, multipurpose. 2.** having more than two (or more than one): **multispeed. 3.** many times over: **multimillionaire.** [< L *multi-* much, many]

mul•ti•col•ored (MUL ti KUL ərd) *adj.* having many colors.

mul•ti•far•i•ous (MUL tə FAIR ee əs) *adj.* having great diversity or variety. [< LL *multifarius* many-sided] —**mul′ti•far′i•ous•ly** *adv.*

mul•ti•lat•er•al (MUL ti LAT ər əl) *adj.* **1.** having many sides. **2.** *Govt.* involving more

than two nations: also *multipartite.* —**mul′•ti•lat′er•al•ly** *adv.*

mul•ti•lin•gual (MUL tee LING gwəl) *n. & adj.* polyglot.

mul•ti•me•di•a (MUL ti MEE dee ə) *adj.* involving simultaneous use of several communications media.

mul•ti•na•tion•al (MUL tee NASH ə nl) *adj.* involving more than two nations. —*n.* a corporation with significant operations in more than two nations.

mul•ti•par•tite (MUL ti PAHR tīt) *adj.* **1.** divided into many parts. **2.** *Govt.* multilateral (def. 2).

mul•ti•ple (MUL tə pəl) *adj.* **1.** having, consisting of, or relating to more than one part, aspect, individual, etc.; manifold. **2.** happening more than once; repeated. —*n. Math.* any of the products of a given number and some other number: 8 and 12 are *multiples* of 4.

multiple sclerosis a degenerative disease of the nervous system, usu. affecting young people.

mul•ti•plex (MUL tə PLEKS) *adj.* **1.** multiple; manifold. **2.** *Telecom.* designating a system for the simultaneous transmission of two or more signals over the same wire or radio frequency channel.

mul•ti•pli•ca•tion (MUL tə pli KAY shən) *n.* **1.** the act of multiplying, or the state of being multiplied. **2.** *Math.* the process of finding the sum of a number repeated a given number of times.

mul•ti•plic•i•ty (MUL tə PLIS i tee) *n. pl.* •**ties 1.** the condition or quality of being manifold or various. **2.** a large number.

mul•ti•ply (MUL tə PLI) *v.t. & v.i.* •**plied,** •**ply•ing 1.** increase in number, amount, or degree. **2.** *Math.* determine the product of (two numbers) by multiplication. [ME *multiplien*]

mul•ti•tude (MUL ti TOOD) *n.* a great number. —**the multitude** the common people. [ME] —**mul′ti•tu′di•nous** *adj.*

mum[1] (mum) *adj.* silent; saying nothing. —*interj.* hush! —**mum's the word** keep silent; be secretive.

mum[2] *n.* chrysanthemum.

mum•ble (MUM bəl) *v.t. & v.i.* •**bled,** •**bling** speak low and indistinctly; mutter. —*n.* a low, indistinct speech or sound; mutter. [ME *momelen*] —**mum′bler** *n.*

mum•bo jum•bo (MUM boh JUM boh) meaningless, complicated, or obscure ritual, observance, incantation, etc.

mum·mer (MUM ər) *n.* **1.** one who acts or makes sport in a mask or disguise. **2.** an actor. —**mum′mer·y** *n.*

mum·mi·fy (MUM ə FĪ) *v.* •**fied**, •**fy·ing** *v.t.* **1.** make a mummy of; preserve by embalming, drying, etc. **2.** make dry and lifeless, as an idea, institution, etc. —*v.i.* **3.** dry up; shrivel. —**mum′mi·fi·ca′tion** *n.*

mum·my (MUM ee) *n. pl.* •**mies** a human or animal body embalmed in the ancient Egyptian manner. [ME *mummie*]

mumps (mumps) *n.* *(construed as sing.) Pathol.* a contagious viral disease characterized by fever and swelling of the salivary glands.

munch (munch) *v.t. & v.i.* chew steadily with a crunching noise. [ME *monchen*]

mun·dane (mun DAYN) *adj.* **1.** pertaining to or characterized by that which is practical, routine, or ordinary: *mundane* concerns. **2.** of or relating to the world; earthly. [< L *mundanus*]

mu·nic·i·pal (myoo NIS ə pəl) *adj.* **1.** of or pertaining to a town or city or its local government. **2.** having local self-government. [< L *municipalis*]

mu·nic·i·pal·i·ty (myoo NIS ə PAL i tee) *n. pl.* •**ties** an incorporated district, as a town. [< F *municipalité*]

mu·nif·i·cent (myoo NIF ə sənt) *adj.* extraordinarily generous or bountiful; liberal. [< L *munificentia* generosity] —**mu·nif′i·cence** *n.*

mu·ni·tion (myoo NISH ən) *n. Usu. pl.* ammunition and all other necessary war matériel. [< L *munire* fortify]

mu·ral (MYUUR əl) *n.* a painting or decoration applied to a wall or ceiling. —*adj.* **1.** placed or executed on a wall: a *mural* painting. **2.** of, pertaining to, or resembling a wall. [ME] —**mu′ral·ist** *n.*

mur·der (MUR dər) *n.* **1.** the unlawful, malicious, and intentional killing of one human being by another. **2.** *Slang* something exceedingly difficult, painful, or hazardous. —*v.t.* **1.** kill (a human being) unlawfully and with deliberate malice. **2.** spoil or mar by a bad performance, improper pronunciation, etc. —*v.i.* **3.** commit murder. [ME *mourdre*]

mur·der·ous (MUR dər əs) *adj.* **1.** of, pertaining to, or involving murder. **2.** capable of or given to murder. **3.** brutal; deadly. —**mur′der·ous·ly** *adv.*

murk (murk) *n.* darkness; gloom. [ME *mirke*]

murk·y (MUR kee) *adj.* **mur·ki·er, mur·ki·est** **1.** dark, gloomy, or obscure: the *murky* depths. **2.** hazy, thick, or misty, as atmosphere, color, etc. **3.** unclear; confused; abstruse.[ME *mirky*] —**murk′i·ness** *n.*

mur·mur (MUR mər) *n.* **1.** a low, indistinct, continuously repeated sound, as of many voices. **2.** a mumbled complaint; grumbling. **3.** *Med.* a soft, low sound originating in certain organs; esp., an abnormal, rasping sound produced within the heart. —*v.i.* **1.** make a low, indistinct sound. **2.** complain in low, muttered tones. —*v.t.* **3.** mutter. [ME *murmuren*] —**mur′mur·ous** *adj.*

mus·cle (MUS əl) *n.* **1.** *Anat.* a tissue composed of bundles of elongated fibers that produce bodily movements by expanding or contracting. **2.** an organ or structure consisting of such tissue. **3.** muscular strength; brawn. —*v.t.* •**cled**, •**cling** *Informal* force one's way by or as by sheer brawn: often with *in*. [< L *musculus*, lit., little mouse] —**mus′cled** *adj.*

mus·cu·lar (MUS kyə lər) *adj.* **1.** pertaining to or composed of muscle. **2.** having strong muscles; brawny. —**mus′cu·lar′i·ty** *n.*

muscular dys·tro·phy (DIS trə fee) *Pathol.* one of various diseases characterized by a progressive degeneration of muscle tissue.

mus·cu·la·ture (MUS kyə lə chər) *n.* **1.** the arrangement of muscles in a part or organ. **2.** the muscle system as a whole.

muse[1] (myooz) *n.* **1.** a spirit or power regarded as inspiring artists, poets, etc. **2.** *cap.* one of nine Greek goddesses presiding over the arts and sciences. [ME *Muse*]

muse[2] *v.t. & v.i.* **mused, mus·ing** consider thoughtfully or at length; ponder; meditate. [ME *musen* mutter]

mu·se·um (myoo ZEE əm) *n.* a place or building for preserving and exhibiting works of art, scientific objects, curiosities, etc. [< L, shrine of the Muses]

mush[1] (mush) *n.* **1.** a thick porridge made with corn meal boiled in water or milk. **2.** anything soft and pulpy. **3.** mawkish sentimentality. —**mush′i·ness** *n.* —**mush′y** *adj.* **mush·i·er, mush·i·est**

mush[2] *v.i.* in arctic regions, travel over snow with a dog sled. —*interj.* get along!: a command to a dog team. [< F Canadian *marchons*! let's go!]

mush·room (MUSH room) *n.* **1.** any of various fleshy, rapidly growing, umbrella-shaped fungi, esp. the common edible **field**

mushroom and certain poisonous varieties loosely called *toadstools*. **2.** anything resembling a mushroom in shape or rapid growth. —*v.i.* grow or spread rapidly. [ME *muscheron*]

mu·sic (MYOO zik) *n.* **1.** the art of producing arrangements of sounds, usu. with reference to rhythm, pitch, and tone color. **2.** such compositions or arrangements. **3.** a succession or combination of sounds, esp. if pleasing to the ear. —**face the music** accept the consequences of one's acts. [ME *musike*]

mu·si·cal (MYOO zi kəl) *adj.* **1.** of, pertaining to, or capable of creating music. **2.** having the nature or characteristics of music; melodious; harmonious. **3.** fond of or versed in music. **4.** set to music. —*n.* a musical comedy. —**mu′si·cal′i·ty** *n.*

musical comedy a show with music, songs, dances, jokes, colorful staging.

mu·si·cale (MYOO zi KAL) *n.* a private concert or recital, as in a home. [< F *soirée musicale* musical evening]

mu·si·cian (myoo ZISH ən) *n.* **1.** a professional performer or composer of music. **2.** one skilled in performing or composing music. [ME *musicien*]

mu·si·col·o·gy (MYOO zi KOL ə jee) *n. pl.* **·gies** the scientific and historical study of the forms, theory, methods, etc. of music. —**mu′si·col′o·gist** *n.*

musk (musk) *n.* a soft, powdery secretion with a penetrating odor, obtained from the sac (**musk bag**) of certain deer, and used in making perfumes and in medicine. [ME *muske*] —**musk′y** *adj.* **musk·i·er, musk·i·est**

mus·ket (MUS kit) *n.* an archaic firearm designed to be fired from the shoulder. [< MF *mouscet*] —**mus′ket·ry** *n.*

mus·ket·eer (MUS ki TEER) *n.* formerly, a soldier armed with a musket. [< F *mousquetaire*]

Mus·lim (MUZ lim) *n. pl.* **·lims** a believer in Islam. —*adj.* of or pertaining to Islam. Also called *Moslem.* [< Arabic, one who surrenders to God]

mus·lin (MUZ lin) *n.* any of several plain-weave cotton fabrics of varying fineness. [< F *mousseline*]

muss (mus) *n.* a state of disorder or untidiness; mess. —*v.t.* make messy or untidy; rumple: often with *up.*

must¹ (must) *v.* a defective verb now used only as an auxiliary followed by the infini-

tive, with *to* (the sign of the infinitive) understood, to express: **a** compulsion: *Must you go?* **b** requirement: *You must* be healthy to be accepted. **c** probability or supposition: *You must* be tired. **d** conviction or certainty: *War must* follow. —*n.* anything that is required or vital: *Safety is a must.* [ME *moste*]

must² *n.* mustiness; mold. [< MUSTY]

must³ *n.* the expressed unfermented juice of the grape or other fruit. [ME]

mus·tache (MUS tash) *n.* **1.** the growth of hair on the upper lip. **2.** the hair or bristles growing near the mouth of an animal. Also, *moustache.* [< MF *moustache*]

mus·tang (MUS tang) *n.* a wild horse of the American plains. [< Sp. *mestengo* stray animal]

mus·tard (MUS tərd) *n.* **1.** a pungent condiment prepared as a paste or powder from the seed of the mustard plant. **2.** any of several plants of a large family that includes broccoli, cabbage, etc. **3.** the yellowish or brownish color of ground mustard. [ME]

mustard gas *Chem.* an oily liquid, having an odor of mustard or garlic, and used in warfare because of its powerful blistering effect.

mus·ter (MUS tər) *v.t.* **1.** summon or assemble (troops etc.). **2.** collect, gather, or summon: often with *up.* —*v.i.* **3.** gather or assemble, as troops. —*n.* **1.** an assembling or gathering, as of troops. **2.** an official list of officers and men in a military unit or ship's crew. —**pass muster** measure up to a standard. [ME *mostren* muster]

must·y (MUS tee) *adj.* **must·i·er, must·i·est 1.** having a moldy odor or flavor, as a close room. **2.** dull or stale with age. **3.** apathetic; lifeless. —**must′i·ness** *n.*

mu·ta·ble (MYOO tə bEl) *adj.* **1.** capable of or subject to change. **2.** liable to frequent change. [ME] —**mu′ta·bil′i·ty** *n.*

mu·tant (MYOOT nt) *n.* a plant or animal organism differing from its parents as a result of mutation. —**mu′tant** *adj.*

mu·tate (MYOO tayt) *v.t. & v.i.* **·tat·ed, ·tat·ing** undergo or subject to change or mutation. [< L *mutatus* changed]

mu·ta·tion (myoo TAY shən) *n.* **1.** the act or process of changing. **2.** a change or modification in form, structure, function, etc. **3.** *Biol.* **a** a sudden, transmissible variation in a plant or animal. **b** an individual, species, etc. resulting from such a variation.

mute (myoot) *adj.* **mut·er, mut·est 1.** not

producing speech or sound; silent. **2.** lacking the power of speech; dumb. **3.** *Phonet.* not pronounced; silent, as the *e* in *gone*. —*n.* **1.** one who is unable to speak; esp. a deafmute. **2.** *Music* a device used to muffle the tone of an instrument. —*v.t.* **mut·ed, mut·ing 1.** deaden the sound of (a musical instrument etc.). **2.** in art, soften (a color, a shade, etc.). [< L *mutus* dumb]

mu·ti·late (MYOOT l ayt) *v.t.* **·lat·ed, ·lat·ing 1.** deprive (a person, animal, etc.) of a limb or essential part; maim. **2.** damage or make imperfect: *mutilate* a speech. [< L *mutilatus* maimed] —**mu'ti·la'tion** *n.*

mu·ti·ny (MYOOT n ee) *n. pl.* **·nies** rebellion against constituted authority; insubordination; esp., a revolt of soldiers or sailors against their commanders. —*v.i.* **·nied, ·ny·ing** take part in a mutiny. [< MF *mutiner* rebel] —**mu'ti·neer'** (MYOOT n EER) *n.* —**mu'ti·nous** *adj.*

mut·ter (MUT ər) *v.i.* **1.** speak in a low, indistinct tone, as in complaining. **2.** complain; grumble. **3.** make a low, rumbling sound. —*v.t.* **4.** say in a low, indistinct tone. —*n.* a low, indistinct utterance or tone. [ME *muteren*] —**mut'ter·er** *n.*

mut·ton (MUT n) *n.* the flesh of sheep, esp. mature sheep, used as food. [ME *moton* sheep] —**mut'ton·y** *adv.*

mut·ton·chops (MUT n CHOPS) *n.pl.* side whiskers narrow at the temples and broad at the lower cheeks.

mu·tu·al (MYOO choo əl) *adj.* **1.** felt, expressed, or performed for or toward each other; reciprocal: *mutual* dislike. **2.** having the same attitude toward or relationship with each other: *mutual* friends. **3.** possessed in common. [< MF *mutuel*] —**mu'tu·al'i·ty** (-AL i tee) *n.*

mutual fund an investment company that manages the pooled capital of its investors.

muz·zle (MUZ əl) *n.* **1.** the projecting part of an animal's head, including the jaws, mouth, and snout. **2.** a guard or covering for the snout. **3.** the front end of the barrel of a firearm. —*v.t.* **·zled, ·zling 1.** put a muzzle on (an animal etc.). **2.** restrain from speaking, expressing opinions, etc.; gag. [ME *musel*]

my (mī) *pronominal adj.* the possessive case of the pronoun *I*, used attributively: also used in certain forms of address: *my* lord; *my* good man. —*interj.* an exclamation of surprise, dismay, etc.: Oh, *my!* [ME *mī*]

my·as·the·ni·a (MĪ əs THEE nee ə) *n. Pa-*

thol. muscular weakness, often, as in **my·asthenia gravis** (GRAV əs), accompanied by progressive exhaustion. [< NL]

my·col·o·gy (mī KOL ə jee) *n.* the branch of botany dealing with fungi. —**my·col'o·gist** *n.*

my·e·li·tis (MĪ ə LĪ tis) *n. Pathol.* inflammation of the spinal cord or of the bone marrow.

my·o·car·di·um (MĪ ə KAHR dee əm) *n. Anat.* the muscular tissue of the heart. —**my'o·car'di·al** *adj.*

my·o·pi·a (mī OH pee ə) *n.* **1.** *Pathol.* a visual defect in which objects are seen clearly only when close to the eye; nearsightedness. **2.** lack of insight or discernment; obtuseness. [< NL] —**my·op'ic** (mī OP ik) *adj.*

myr·i·ad (MIR ee əd) *adj.* countless; innumerable. —*n.* a vast indefinite number. [< Gk. *myriás* ten thousand]

myr·mi·don (MUR mi DON) *n.* a faithful, unquestioning follower. [ME]

myrrh (mur) *n.* an aromatic gum resin that exudes from certain small trees of Arabia and eastern Africa, used as incense, perfume, and in medicine. [ME]

my·self (mī SELF) *pron.* a form of the first person singular pronoun, used: **1.** as a reflexive or as the object of a preposition in a reflexive sense: I saw *myself* in the mirror. **2.** as an emphatic or intensive form of *I*: I *myself* invented the yo-yo. **3.** as a designation of a normal, proper, or usual state: Once out of uniform, I was *myself* again in no time. [ME *meself*]

mys·te·ri·ous (mi STEER ee əs) *adj.* **1.** implying or characterized by mystery. **2.** unexplained; puzzling. —**mys·te'ri·ous·ly** *adv.*

mys·ter·y (MIS tə ree) *n. pl.* **·ter·ies 1.** something that is not or cannot be known, understood, or explained. **2.** any action, affair, or thing that arouses curiosity or suspense because it is not fully revealed. **3.** a story, play, movie, etc. narrating or dramatizing such an affair. **4.** *Theol.* a truth that can be known only through divine revelation. [ME *mysterie*]

mys·tic (MIS tik) *adj.* **1.** of the nature of or pertaining to mysteries. **2.** of or pertaining to mystics or mysticism. **3.** baffling or enigmatic. —*n.* one who believes in mysticism, or professes to have had mystical experiences. [ME *mystik*]

mys·ti·cal (MIS ti kəl) *adj.* **1.** of the nature

of a direct, intuitive, or subjective perception beyond the ordinary range of human experience, esp. one of a religious character. **2.** having a spiritual character or reality beyond human reason. **3.** mystic (defs. 1 & 2). —**mys′ti·cal·ly** *adv.*

mys·ti·cism (MIS tə siz əm) *n.* the belief that through contemplation and love man can achieve a direct knowledge of God or of divine truth, etc., without the use of reason or of the senses.

mys·ti·fy (MIS tə fī) *v.t.* •**fied,** •**fy·ing 1.** confuse or perplex, esp. deliberately. **2.** make obscure or mysterious. [< F *mystifier*] —**mys′ti·fi·ca′tion** *n.*

mys·tique (mi STEEK) *n.* a body of attitudes, opinions, or ideas that become associated with a person, thing, institution, etc., and give it a mythic status: the *mystique* of bullfighting. [< F]

myth (mith) *n.* **1.** a traditional story, usu. focusing on the deeds of gods or heroes, often in explanation of some natural phenomenon. **2.** an imaginary or fictitious person, thing, event, or story. [< LL *mythos*] —**myth′i·cal** or **myth′ic** *adj.*

my·thol·o·gy (mi THOL ə jee) *n. pl.* •**gies** the collective myths and legends of a particular people, institution, etc.; the study of myths. [ME *mythologie*] —**myth·o·log·i·cal** (MITH ə LOJ i kəl) *adj.* —**my·thol′o·gist** *n.*

N

n, N (en) *n. pl.* **n's** or **ns, N's** or **Ns 1.** the fourteenth letter of the English alphabet. **2.** the sound represented by the letter *n.* — *symbol* **1.** *Chem.* nitrogen. **2.** *Math.* an indefinite number.

nab (nab) *v.t.* **nabbed, nab·bing** *Informal* **1.** catch or arrest. **2.** take or seize suddenly; snatch.

na·bob (NAY bob) *n.* **1.** a person, esp. a European, who has become rich in India. **2.** any very rich or powerful man. [< Hind. *nawāb* viceroy]

na·celle (nə SEL) *n. Aeron.* an enclosure on an aircraft, esp. one for an engine. [< F, small boat]

na·cre (NAY kər) *n.* mother-of-pearl. [< MF] —**na·cre·ous** (NAY kree əs) *adj.*

na·dir (NAY dər) *n.* **1.** the point of the celestial sphere opposite the zenith. **2.** the lowest point. [ME]

nag[1] (nag) *v.* **nagged, nag·ging** *v.t.* **1.** annoy by repeatedly urging, scolding, carping, etc. —*v.i.* **2.** urge, scold, carp, etc. continually. **3.** be bothered by. —*n.* one who nags. [< Scand.] —**nag'ging** *adj.* —**nag'·ging·ly** *adv.*

nag[2] *n.* a horse, esp. one that is old or decrepit. [ME *nagge*]

Na·hua·tl (NAH waht l) *n.* **1.** the Uto-Aztecan language of the Aztecs, spoken mostly in Mexico. **2.** a person whose native language is Nahuatl. —**Na'hua·tl** *adj.*

nai·ad (NAY ad) *n. pl.* **·ads** or **·a·des** (-ə DEEZ) **1.** in classical mythology, one of the water nymphs believed to dwell in fountains, springs, rivers, lakes, and wells. **2.** *Entomol.* the aquatic young of certain insects. [< Gk. *Naias* water nymph]

nail (nayl) *n.* **1.** a slender piece of metal, used esp. to hold or fasten wood etc. **2.** a thin, horny plate growing on the end of each of the fingers and toes of man and other primates. —**hit the nail on the head** do or say something exactly to the point. —*v.t.* **1.** hold or fasten in place with a nail or nails. **2.** make certain or definite: often with *down.* **3.** *Informal* catch or arrest. **4.** *Slang* hit (someone). [ME]

na·ive (nah EEV) *adj.* **1.** having a simple nature that lacks worldly experience; artless. **2.** uncritical: *naive* ideas. Also **na·ïve.**

[< F *naïve*] —**na·if** (nah EEF) *n.* a naive person. —**na·if'** *adj.*

na·ive·té (nah eev TAY) *n.* **1.** the state or quality of being naive. **2.** a naive incident, remark, etc. [< F]

na·ked (NAY kid) *adj.* **1.** having no clothes on; nude. **2.** having no covering. **3.** without addition, adornment, or qualification; stark: a *naked* lie. **4.** unaided by an optical instrument: the *naked* eye. **5.** open or exposed to view: a *naked* sword. [ME] —**na'ked·ly** *adv.* —**na'ked·ness** *n.*

name (naym) *n.* **1.** a word or words by which a person, thing, animal, class, or concept is known or referred to. **2.** a usu. derogatory word or phrase: call someone *names.* **3.** popular or general reputation. —**in name only** being such in appearance only. —**in the name of 1.** for the sake of. **2.** by the authority of. —**to one's name** of one's own: He hasn't a friend *to his name.* —*v.t.* **named, nam·ing 1.** give a name to; call. **2.** identify. **3.** fix or determine: *name* the day. **4.** nominate; appoint. —*adj.* famous. [ME]

name·less (NAYM lis) *adj.* **1.** undistinguished or obscure: a *nameless* multitude. **2.** that cannot be named; indescribable: *nameless* terror. **3.** having no name; esp., having no legal name; illegitimate.

name·ly (NAYM lee) *adv.* that is to say.

name·sake (NAYM sayk) *n.* one who is named after or has the same name as another.

nan·ny (NAN ee) *n. pl.* **·nies** a child's nursemaid.

nano- *combining form* very small; in technical uses, one billionth of (a specified unit): *nanosecond.* [< Gk. *nânos* dwarf]

nap[1] (nap) *n.* a short sleep; doze. —*v.i.* **napped, nap·ping 1.** take a nap; doze. **2.** be unprepared. [ME *nappen*]

nap[2] *n.* the short fibers forming a downy or fuzzy surface on certain fabrics. [ME *noppe*] —**nap'less** *adj.* —**nap'py** *adj.* **·pi·er, ·pi·est**

na·palm (NAY pahm) *n.* a jellylike mixture that is combined with gasoline to form an incendiary fuel, as in bombs.

nape (nayp) *n.* the back of the neck. [ME]

naph·tha (NAF thə) *n.* a volatile, colorless

petroleum distillate, used as a solvent, cleaning fluid, fuel, etc. [< L]

nap·kin (NAP kin) n. 1. a small, usu. square cloth or paper, used at meals for wiping the hands and mouth or protecting the clothes. 2. a small piece of toweling. [ME]

na·po·le·on (nə POH lee ən) n. a rich pastry composed of thin layers of dough filled with cream, custard, etc. [< F napoléon]

nar·cis·sism (NAHR sə SIZ əm) n. 1. excessive admiration for or fascination with oneself. 2. Psychoanal. erotic interest in one's own body. Also **nar·cism** (NAHR siz əm). [< G Narzissismus, after Narcissus, the youth of Greek mythology who fell in love with his own image.] —**nar'cis·sist** n. —**nar'cis·sis'tic** adj.

nar·co·sis (nahr KOH sis) n. deep stupor produced by a drug. [< NL]

nar·cot·ic (nahr KOT ik) n. a drug, as opium or morphine, that relieves pain and induces sleep, but may be habit-forming. [ME narcotik] —**nar·cot'ic** adj.

nar·co·tize (NAHR kə TIZ) v.t. ·tized, ·tiz·ing bring under the influence of a narcotic; stupefy.

nar·rate (NAR ayt) v. ·rat·ed, ·rat·ing v.t. 1. tell, as a story. 2. speak in accompaniment and explanation of (a motion picture, television program, etc.). —v.i. 3. tell a story, etc. [< L narratus related] —**nar·ra·tor** (NAR ay tər) n.

nar·ra·tion (na RAY shən) n. 1. the act of narrating. 2. a narrative. 3. an account that narrates, as in fiction.

nar·ra·tive (NAR ə tiv) n. 1. something narrated. 2. the act, art, or process of narrating.

nar·row (NAR oh) adj. ·er, ·est 1. having little width. 2. limited or small, as in extent or scope. 3. narrow-minded. 4. nearly unsuccessful or disastrous: a narrow escape. —v.t. & v.i. make or become narrow or narrower, as in width or scope. —n. Usu. pl. a narrow passage; esp., the narrowest part of a strait, isthmus, etc. [ME] —**nar'row·ness** n.

nar·row·ly (NAR oh lee) adv. 1. barely; hardly. 2. so as to be narrow. 3. in a narrow manner.

nar·row-mind·ed (NAR oh MĪN did) adj. having or characterized by narrow views or sentiments; illiberal; bigoted. —**nar'row-mind'ed·ness** n.

na·sal (NAY zəl) adj. 1. of or pertaining to the nose. 2. produced with the voice passing through the nose. —n. a nasal sound.

[ME] —**na·sal·i·ty** (nay ZAL i tee) n. —**na'sal·ly** adv.

nas·cent (NAY sənt) adj. beginning to exist or develop; newly conceived. [< L nasci be born]

nas·ty (NAS tee) adj. ·ti·er, ·ti·est 1. offensive; disgusting. 2. indecent; obscene: nasty language. 3. disagreeable; unpleasant: nasty weather. 4. mean; spiteful: nasty remarks. 5. serious or painful: nasty cuts. [ME] —**nas'ti·ly** adv. —**nas'ti·ness** n.

na·tal (NAYT l) adj. of or pertaining to one's birth. [ME]

na·tion (NAY shən) n. 1. a body of persons associated with a particular territory and organized under a government. 2. a body of persons having a common origin and language and a distinctive cultural and social way of life. 3. a tribe or federation, esp. of American Indians. [ME]

na·tion·al (NASH ə nl) adj. 1. of, belonging to, or representative of a nation as a whole. 2. characteristic of or peculiar to a nation. —n. a subject or citizen of a nation. [< F]

National Guard a militia of a state, a territory, or the District of Columbia, maintained in part by the U.S. government and subject to federal service in national emergencies.

na·tion·al·ism (NASH ə nl IZ əm) n. 1. devotion to one's own nation. 2. a desire or movement for national independence. —**na'·tion·al·ist** adj. & n. —**na'tion·al·is'tic** adj.

na·tion·al·i·ty (NASH ə NAL i tee) n. pl. ·ties 1. a body of people having the same traditions, language, or ethnic origin, and forming a nation. 2. the state or fact of being related to a particular nation, as by birth or citizenship. 3. national character or quality. 4. the fact or quality of existing as a nation.

na·tion·al·ize (NASH ə nl IZ) v.t. ·ized, ·iz·ing 1. place (industries, resources, etc.) under governmental control. 2. make national, as in character or scope. 3. accept as a national; naturalize. —**na'tion·al·i·za'tion** n.

Nation of Islam see under BLACK MUSLIM.

na·tion·wide (NAY shən WĪD) adj. extending throughout the nation.

na·tive (NAY tiv) adj. 1. born in a particular place or region. 2. linked to a person by birth: native language. 3. produced or grown in a particular region or country; indigenous. 4. of, pertaining to, or characteristic of any particular area or its inhabitants. **5.** natural rather than acquired; inborn. **6.** occurring in nature in a pure state: *native* copper. —*n.* **1.** a lifelong resident of a country or region. **2.** a person or thing native to a specified country or place. [< L *nativus* natural]

Native American a member or descendant of any of the tribes inhabiting North America north of Mexico.

na·tive-born (NAY tiv BORN) *adj.* born in the region or country specified.

na·tiv·i·ty (nə TIV i tee) *n. pl.* **·ties** birth, esp. with regard to the time, place, or circumstances surrounding it. —**the Nativity** **1.** the birth of Christ. **2.** Christmas. [ME *nativite*]

NATO (NAY toh) North Atlantic Treaty Organization.

nat·ty (NAT ee) *adj.* **·ti·er, ·ti·est** neat and smart looking. —**nat'ti·ly** *adv.*

nat·u·ral (NACH ər əl) *adj.* **1.** produced by or existing in nature; not artificial. **2.** resulting from one's nature; innate: *natural* talent. **3.** free from affectation or awkwardness: *natural* manner. **4.** *Music* neither sharp nor flat. **5.** related by blood rather than through adoption: *natural* mother. **6.** born out of wedlock. —*n.* **1.** *Music* a note that is neither sharp nor flat. **2.** one who or that which is naturally gifted. [ME]

natural gas a gas consisting chiefly of methane, generated naturally in underground oil deposits and used as a fuel.

natural history the observation and study of the material universe, esp. the biological and earth sciences.

nat·u·ral·ism (NACH ər ə LIZ əm) *n.* **1.** closeness to nature or human life, as in literature, painting, etc. **2.** *Philos.* the doctrine that everything is derived from natural causes and can be explained by scientific laws. **3.** action or thought resulting only from natural desires and instincts. —**nat'u·ral·is'tic** *adj.*

nat·u·ral·ist (NACH ər ə list) *n.* **1.** one who is versed in natural history, as a zoologist or botanist. **2.** an adherent of the doctrine of naturalism.

nat·u·ral·ize (NACH ər ə LIZ) *v.* **·ized, ·iz·ing** *v.t.* **1.** confer the rights and privileges of citizenship upon. **2.** adapt (a foreign plant, animal, etc.) to the environment of a country or area. —*v.i.* **3.** become as if native; adapt. —**nat'u·ral·i·za'tion** *n.*

nat·u·ral·ly (NACH ər ə lee) *adv.* **1.** in a natural manner. **2.** by inherent nature. **3.** of course; certainly.

natural resource *Usu. pl.* a source of wealth provided by nature, as forests, minerals, and water supply.

natural science 1. the sciences collectively that deal with the physical universe. **2.** any one of these sciences, as biology or physics.

natural selection *Biol.* the process by which traits advantageous to an organism in a certain environment tend to be passed on to later generations; survival of the fittest forms.

na·ture (NAY chər) *n.* **1.** the essential character of something: the *nature* of democracy. **2.** the entire material universe and its phenomena. **3.** the basic character or disposition of a person or animal. **4.** sort; kind; variety: nothing of that *nature*. **5.** a wild or uncivilized condition. **6.** that which is within the accepted or legal limits of morality: an act against *nature*. —**by nature** by birth or disposition. [ME *natur*]

naught (nawt) *n.* **1.** nothing. **2.** a cipher; zero; the character O. Also spelled *nought*. [ME]

naugh·ty (NAW tee) *adj.* **·ti·er, ·ti·est 1.** mischievous; disobedient. **2.** indecent or improper. [ME] —**naugh'ti·ly** *adv.* —**naugh'ti·ness** *n.*

nau·se·a (NAW zee ə) *n.* **1.** a sick feeling in the stomach accompanied by an impulse to vomit. **2.** strong disgust. [< L, seasickness] —**nau·seous** (NAW shəs) *adj.*

nau·se·ate (NAW zee AYT) *v.t. & v.i.* **·at·ed, ·at·ing** affect with or feel nausea or disgust.

nau·ti·cal (NAW ti kəl) *adj.* pertaining to or involving ships, seamen, or navigation. [< L *nauticus*]

nautical mile see under MILE.

Nav·a·jo (NAV ə HOH) *n. pl.* **·jos, ·joes, ·jo** (*collectively*) one of a tribe of Native Americans.

na·val (NAY vəl) *adj.* **1.** of, involving, or having a navy. **2.** of or pertaining to ships. [< L *navalis*]

nave (nayv) *n. Archit.* the main body of a church, situated between the side aisles. [< Med.L *navis*]

na·vel (NAY vəl) *n.* the depression on the abdomen where the umbilical cord was attached. [ME]

navel orange a seedless orange having a depression at its apex that contains a small, secondary fruit.

nav·i·ga·ble (NAV i gə bəl) *adj.* **1.** broad or deep enough to admit of passage by boat. **2.** capable of being steered. [< L *navigabilis*] —**nav′i·ga·bil′i·ty** *n.*

nav·i·gate (NAV i GAYT) *v.* •**gat·ed,** •**gat·ing** *v.t.* **1.** travel on or through, as by ship or aircraft. **2.** plot the course of (a ship, aircraft, etc.). —*v.i.* **3.** guide or steer a ship, aircraft, etc. [< L *navigatus* sailed] —**nav′i·ga′tion** *n.* —**nav′i·ga′tor** *n.*

na·vy (NAY vee) *n. pl.* •**vies 1.** the entire military sea force of a country. **2.** the warships of a nation, taken collectively. **3.** navy blue. [ME *navie*]

navy blue a very dark blue: also *navy.*

nay (nay) *adv.* not exactly that, but rather. — *n.* a negative vote or voter. [ME *nai*]

Na·zi (NAHT see) *n. pl.* •**zis** a member of the fascist National Socialist German Workers' Party, the ruling party in Germany from 1933 to 1945 under the dictatorship of Adolf Hitler. [< G, short for *Nazionalsozialist* National Socialist] —**Na′zi** *adj.* —**Na′zism** or **Na′zi·ism** *n.*

Ne·an·der·thal man (nee AN dər THAWL) *Anthropol.* an extinct species of man of the Stone Age. [< G *Neanderthal* a valley in Germany, where remains of this species were found]

near (neer) *adv.* •**er,** •**est 1.** at, to, or within a little distance; not remote. **2.** nearly; almost. **3.** in a close relation; intimately. **4.** stingily. —*adj.* •**er,** •**est 1.** not distant in place, time, or degree. **2.** closely approximating; almost achieved: a *near* success. **3.** narrow; close. **4.** closely related, as by blood. **5.** intimate. **6.** stingy; miserly. — *prep.* close by or to. —*v.t. & v.i.* come or draw near (to); approach. [ME *nere*] — **near′ness** *n.*

near·by (NEER BĪ) *adj. & adv.* close by; near; adjacent.

Near East the countries lying east of the Mediterranean, mostly in SW Asia.

near·ly (NEER lee) *adv.* **1.** almost; practically. **2.** closely.

near·sight·ed (NEER SĪ tid) *adj.* able to see clearly at short distances only; myopic. — **near′sight′ed·ness** *n.*

neat (neet) *adj.* •**er,** •**est 1.** orderly, tidy, and clean. **2.** precise. **3.** clever: a *neat* trick. **4.** undiluted, as liquor; straight. [ME *net*] — **neat′ly** *adv.* —**neat′ness** *n.*

neb·u·la (NEB yə lə) *n. pl.* •**lae** (-LEE) or •**las** *Astron.* any interstellar mass of vast

extent, composed of gaseous matter. [< L, mist] —**neb′u·lar** *adj.*

neb·u·lous (NEB yə ləs) *adj.* **1.** vague or confused; hazy. **2.** of, pertaining to, or like a nebula. Also **neb′u·lose.** [ME] —**neb′u·lous·ly** *adv.*

nec·es·sar·i·ly (NES ə SER ə lee) *adv.* **1.** as a necessary consequence. **2.** of necessity.

nec·es·sar·y (NES ə SER ee) *adj.* **1.** absolutely needed; indispensable; essential. **2.** that must exist or occur; inevitable. **3.** caused by or acting under compulsion. —*n. pl.* •**sar·ies** *Often pl.* that which is indispensable. [ME *necessarie*]

ne·ces·si·tate (nə SES i TAYT) *v.t.* •**tat·ed,** •**tat·ing 1.** make necessary. **2.** compel or oblige.

ne·ces·si·tous (nə SES i təs) *adj.* **1.** extremely needy; destitute. **2.** urgent; compelling.

ne·ces·si·ty (nə SES i tee) *n. pl.* •**ties 1.** *Often pl.* that which is indispensable. **2.** the quality, condition, or fact of being necessary. **3.** the conditions that make compulsory a particular course of action. **4.** urgent or desperate need. [ME *necessite*] —**of necessity** by necessity; inevitably.

neck (nek) *n.* **1.** *Anat.* **a** the part of an animal that connects the head with the trunk. **b** any similarly constricted part of an organ, bone, etc. **2.** the narrowed part of an object: the *neck* of a bottle. **3.** something likened to a neck, as a narrow strip of land. **4.** the part of a garment close to or covering the neck. — **neck and neck** abreast of one another, as horses in a race. —*v.i.* **1.** *Slang* kiss and caress in lovemaking. —*v.t.* **2.** *Slang* make love to (someone) in such a manner. [ME *nekke*]

necked (nekt) *adj.* **1.** having a neck or necks. **2.** having or characterized by (a specified kind of) neck: used in combination: *long-necked.* [ME]

neck·ing (NEK ing) *n. Informal* kissing and caressing in lovemaking.

neck·lace (NEK lis) *n.* an ornament worn around the neck.

neck·tie (NEK TĪ) *n.* a strip of material worn around the neck and knotted under the chin.

ne·crol·o·gy (nə KROL ə jee) *n. pl.* •**gies 1.** a list of persons who have died. **2.** an obituary notice. —**ne·crol′o·gist** *n.*

nec·ro·man·cy (NEK rə MAN see) *n.* **1.** the art of divining the future through alleged communication with the dead. **2.** black magic; sorcery. [ME *nigromancie*] —**nec′ ro•man′cer** *n.*

ne•crop•o•lis (nə KROP ə lis) *n.* a cemetery. [< Gk. *nekrópolis*]

ne•cro•sis (nə KROH sis) *n. Pathol.* death of tissue in a living animal, resulting from infection or burns; gangrene. [< NL] — **ne•crot′ic** (nə KROT ik) *adj.*

nec•tar (NEK tər) *n.* **1.** in Greek mythology, the drink of the gods. **2.** any delicious drink. **3.** *Bot.* the sweet secretion of plants, collected by bees to make honey. [< L]

nee (nay) *adj.* born with the name of: used chiefly to note the maiden name of a married woman: Mrs. Mary Lincoln, *nee* Todd. Also **née.** [< F]

need (need) *v.t.* **1.** have an urgent use for; want; require. —*v.i.* **2.** be in want. **3.** be obliged or compelled; have to: He *need* not go. —*n.* **1.** the lack of something necessary or desirable. **2.** obligation; necessity: no *need* to be afraid. **3.** something wanted or required: modest *needs.* **4.** poverty. [ME *nede*]

nee•dle (NEED l) *n.* **1.** a slender, pointed instrument, usu. of steel, for carrying thread through fabric in sewing. **2.** a hypodermic needle. **3.** a pointer, as in a compass. **4.** a pointed instrument of steel, diamond, etc. that transmits sound vibrations from the grooves of a phonograph record; stylus. **5.** a slender rod of steel, bone, etc., used in knitting or crocheting. **6.** a needle-shaped leaf, as that of a pine tree. —*v.* **•dled, •dling** *v.t.* **1.** sew or pierce with a needle. **2.** *Informal* tease or heckle repeatedly. —*v.i.* **3.** sew or work with a needle. [ME *nedle*]

nee•dle•point (NEED l POINT) *n.* embroidery on canvas.

need•less (NEED lis) *adj.* not needed or necessary. —**need′less•ly** *adv.*

nee•dle•work (NEED l WURK) *n.* work done with a needle.

needs (needz) *adv.* of necessity: often with *must:* He *needs* must go. [ME *nedis*]

need•y (NEE dee) *adj.* **need•i•er, need•i•est** being in need, want, or poverty. [ME *nedi*] —**need′i•ness** *n.*

ne′er-do-well (NAIR doo WEL) *n.* a worthless, unreliable person. —**ne′er′-do-well′** *adj.*

ne•far•i•ous (ni FAIR ee əs) *adj.* extremely wicked; vile. [< L *nefarius*]

ne•gate (ni GAYT) *v.t.* **•gat•ed, •gat•ing 1.** render ineffective or void; nullify. **2.** deny or contradict. [< L *negatus* denied]

ne•ga•tion (ni GAY shən) *n.* **1.** the absence or opposite of something. **2.** the act of denying or contradicting. **3.** something negative.

neg•a•tive (NEG ə tiv) *adj.* **1.** characterized by or expressing negation, denial, or refusal. **2.** not positive or affirmative: a *negative* attitude. **3.** *Math.* less than zero; minus: usu. denoted by the minus sign (−). **4.** characterized by an excess of electrons. **5.** *Med.* not indicating the presence of a particular disease, organism, etc.: a *negative* blood test. **6.** *Photog.* having the lights and darks reversed from what they were in the original scene. —*n.* **1.** *Photog.* a negative image; also, the film or plate on which it appears. **2.** an expression of denial or refusal. **3.** the side that denies or contradicts what the other side affirms, as in a debate. **4.** *Math.* a negative symbol or quantity. **5.** *Electr.* a negative pole, plate, terminal, etc. **6.** *Gram.* a negative particle, as *not.* —*v.t.* **•tived, •tiv•ing 1.** reject; veto. **2.** deny; contradict. **3.** prove to be false. [< L *negativus*]

neg•a•tiv•ism (NEG ə ti VIZ əm) *n.* an attitude characterized by the questioning of traditional beliefs; skepticism. —**neg′a• tiv•ist** *n. & adj.*

ne•glect (ni GLEKT) *v.t.* **1.** fail to heed or take note of; disregard. **2.** fail to give proper attention to. **3.** fail to do or perform; leave undone. —*n.* **1.** habitual want of attention or care. **2.** the act of neglecting, or the state of being neglected. [< L *neglectus* ignored] —**ne•glect′ful** (-fəl) *adj.*

neg•li•gee (NEG li ZHAY) *n.* **1.** a loose, flowing, usu. decorative dressing gown worn by women. **2.** any informal attire. [< F *négligé* undress]

neg•li•gent (NEG li jənt) *adj.* **1.** neglecting to do what ought to be done. **2.** lazily careless. [ME] —**neg′li•gence** *n.*

neg•li•gi•ble (NEG li jə bəl) *adj.* not worth considering. —**neg′li•gi•bly** *adv.*

ne•go•ti•a•ble (ni GOH shee ə bəl) *adj.* **1.** capable of being negotiated. **2.** open to discussion. **3.** that can be legally transferred to another party. —**ne•go′ti•a•bil′i•ty** *n.*

ne•go•ti•ate (ni GOH shee AYT) *v.* **•at•ed, •at•ing** *v.i.* **1.** discuss or confer with another party in order to reach an agreement. —*v.t.* **2.** arrange or conclude by discussion. **3.** transfer (a note, bond, etc.) to another for a value received. **4.** manage to accomplish or cope with (something difficult): *negotiate* a steep hill. [< L *negotiatus* traded] — **ne•go′ti•a′tion** *n.* —**ne•go′ti•a′tor** *n.*

Neg·ri·tude (NEG ri TOOD) *n.* awareness of and pride in one's black African heritage.

Ne·gro (NEE groh) *n. pl.* **•groes** a member of the black division of mankind: no longer in scientific use. [< Sp.] **—Ne′gro** *adj.*

Ne·groid (NEE groid) *adj. Anthropol.* of, pertaining to, or belonging to a major ethnic division of mankind characterized by skin color ranging from brown to almost black. —*n.* a Negroid person.

neigh (nay) *v.i.* utter the cry of a horse; whinny. [ME *neyen*] **—neigh** *n.*

neigh·bor (NAY bər) *n.* **1.** one who lives near another. **2.** one who or that which is near another. —*adj.* living nearby. —*v.t. & v.i.* live or be near to next to. [ME] — **neigh′bor·ing** *adj.*

neigh·bor·hood (NAY bər HUUD) *n.* **1.** a small area or region that has some specific quality or character. **2.** the people who live near one another.

neigh·bor·ly (NAY bər lee) *adj.* like a good neighbor; friendly. **—neigh′bor·li·ness** *n.*

nei·ther (NEE thər) *adj.* not the one nor the other; not either. —*pron.* not the one nor the other: *Neither* of them is here. —*conj.* **1.** not either (usu. with *nor*): *Neither Carol nor her assistant is at work.* **2.** nor yet: *Neither can he.* [ME]

nem·e·sis (NEM ə sis) *n. pl.* **•ses** (-SEEZ) **1.** a strong and stubborn opponent. **2.** an instrument of vengeance. [< L]

neo- *combining form* new; recent. Also, before vowels, usu. **ne-.** [< Gk. *néos*]

ne·o·clas·sic (NEE oh KLAS ik) *adj.* of, pertaining to, or denoting a revival of classical style, as in literature or art. **—ne·o· clas·si·cism** (NEE oh KLAS ə SIZ əm) *n.*

ne·o·co·lo·ni·al·ism (NEE oh kə LOH nee ə LIZ əm) *n.* the use of economic and political control by a powerful nation over developing countries, former colonies, etc. — **ne′o·co·lo′ni·al·ist** *n. & adj.*

ne·ol·o·gism (nee OL ə JIZ əm) *n.* a new word or phrase. Also **ne·ol′o·gy.** [< F *néologisme*]

ne·on (NEE on) *n.* a gaseous element (symbol Ne) occurring in the atmosphere in very small amounts. —*adj.* **1.** of or pertaining to neon. **2.** composed of or using neon. [< NL]

ne·o·phyte (NEE ə FIT) *n.* **1.** a recent convert, esp. in the early Christian church. **2.** any beginner. [< LL *neophytus* newly planted]

ne·pen·the (ni PEN thee) *n.* **1.** a drug or potion supposed by the ancient Greeks to banish pain and sorrow. **2.** anything causing oblivion. [< L *nepenthes* an herb for soothing]

neph·ew (NEF yoo) *n.* the son of a brother or brother-in-law or of a sister or sister-in-law. [ME *neveu*]

ne·phrit·ic (nə FRIT ik) *adj.* **1.** of or pertaining to the kidney or kidneys; renal. **2.** of, pertaining to, or suffering from nephritis.

ne·phri·tis (nə FRĪ tis) *n. Pathol.* inflammation of the kidneys. [< LL]

nep·o·tism (NEP ə TIZ əm) *n.* favoritism; esp. governmental patronage to relatives. [< Ital. *nepotismo*]

Nep·tune (NEP toon) *n.* the fourth largest planet and eighth in order from the sun.

nerve (nurv) *n.* **1.** *Physiol.* any of the fibers that convey impulses between the brain or spinal cord and other parts or organs. **2.** courage or boldness; daring. **3.** impudence; brashness. **4.** *Usu. pl.* unsteadiness of mind; nervous condition; anxiety. —*v.t.* **nerved, nerv·ing** provide with nerve or nerves. — **nerve oneself** summon up one's courage. [ME]

nerve-rack·ing (NURV RAK ing) *adj.* extremely irritating; harrowing. Also **nerve′ -rack′ing.**

nerv·ous (NUR vəs) *adj.* **1.** characterized by or exhibiting restlessness, anxiety, tension, etc.; high-strung; excitable. **2.** neural. **3.** caused by or acting on the nerves or nervous system. [ME] **—ner′vous·ness** *n.*

nervous breakdown popularly, any severe emotional disturbance, usu. requiring hospitalization.

nervous system *Physiol.* a system in animals that includes the brain and spinal cord, and that controls and regulates various organic activities by receiving and transmitting stimuli.

nest (nest) *n.* **1.** the dwelling place prepared or selected by a bird for the hatching of eggs and the rearing of young. **2.** a place used by fishes, turtles, etc. for laying eggs. **3.** a cozy or snug place. **4.** a haunt or den. **5.** a series or set of similar things designed to fit into one another, as bowls, boxes, etc. —*v.t.* **1.** place in or as in a nest. **2.** pack or place one inside another. —*v.i.* **3.** build or occupy a nest. [ME]

nest egg 1. a sum of money set aside for emergencies, etc. **2.** an artificial egg kept in a nest to induce a hen to lay eggs.

nes·tle (NES əl) v. **·tled, ·tling** v.i. **1.** lie or press closely; cuddle; snuggle. —v.t. **2.** place or press snugly or lovingly. **3.** place or shelter in or as in a nest. [ME *nestlen*]

nest·ling (NEST ling) n. **1.** a bird too young to leave the nest. **2.** a young child. [ME]

net[1] (net) n. **1.** a fabric of thread, rope, etc. woven to form a meshwork and used to catch fish, birds, etc. **2.** anything that traps or entangles; a snare. **3.** something constructed with meshes: cargo *net;* tennis *net.* —v.t. **net·ted, net·ting 1.** catch in or as in a net; ensnare. **2.** cover, enclose, or shelter with a net. [ME]

net[2] adj. **1.** obtained after deducting all expenses, losses, taxes, etc.: distinguished from *gross.* **2.** free from anything extraneous; fundamental; basic: *net* results. —n. a net profit, amount, weight, etc. —v.t. **net·ted, net·ting** earn or yield as clear profit. [ME]

neth·er (NETH ər) adj. situated beneath or below. [ME *nethere*]

nether world 1. the world of the dead. **2.** the world of punishment after death; hell.

net·ting (NET ing) n. **1.** a net; network. **2.** the act or operation of making net. **3.** the use of fishing nets.

net·tle (NET l) n. **1.** an herb having minute stinging hairs. **2.** any of various plants considered to resemble this herb. —v.t. **·tled, ·tling** annoy or irritate; provoke. [ME]

net·tle·some (NET l səm) adj. vexing or irritating.

net·work (NET wurk) n. **1.** a system of interlacing lines, tracks, or channels. **2.** a meshwork fabric; netting. **3.** *Telecom.* a chain of broadcasting stations. **4.** any interconnected system: a spy *network.*

neu·ral (NUUR əl) adj. of or pertaining to the nerves or nervous system.

neu·ral·gi·a (nuu RAL jə) n. *Pathol.* acute pain along the course of a nerve.

neu·ras·the·ni·a (NUUR əs THEE nee ə) n. a condition marked by debility, depression, and bodily disturbances. —**neu·ras·then·ic** (-THEN ik) adj. & n.

neu·ri·tis (nuu RĪ tis) n. *Pathol.* inflammation of a nerve.

neu·rol·o·gy (nuu ROL ə jee) n. the branch of medicine that deals with the nervous system and its disorders. [< NL *neurologia*] —**neu·ro·log·i·cal** (NUUR ə LOJ i kəl) adj. —**neu·rol'o·gist** n.

neu·ron (NUUR on) n. *Physiol.* the cellular unit of the nervous system: also called *nerve cell.* [< Gk. *neûron*]

neu·ro·sis (nuu ROH sis) n. pl. **·ses** (-seez) *Psychiatry* any of various emotional disturbances, usu. involving anxiety and depression: also called *psychoneurosis.* [< NL]

neu·rot·ic (nuu ROT ik) adj. pertaining to or suffering from neurosis. —n. a neurotic person.

neu·ter (NOO tər) adj. **1.** *Gram.* neither masculine nor feminine in gender. **2.** *Biol.* having nonfunctioning or imperfectly developed sex organs, as a worker bee. —n. **1.** *Biol.* a neuter plant or animal. **2.** a castrated animal. —v.t. make neuter; castrate. [ME *neutre*]

neu·tral (NOO trəl) adj. **1.** not taking the part of either side in a dispute or war. **2.** of or belonging to neither side in a dispute or war. **3.** having no decided color; grayish. **4.** *Biol.* neuter; esp., without stamens or pistils. **5.** *Chem.* neither acid nor alkaline. **6.** *Electr.* neither positive nor negative. —n. **1.** one who or that which is neutral. **2.** *Mech.* the state in which transmission gears are disengaged. —**neu'tral·ly** adv.

neu·tral·ism (NOO trə liz əm) n. in foreign affairs, the policy of not aligning a nation with any side of a power conflict. —**neu'tral·ist** adj. & n.

neu·tral·i·ty (noo TRAL i tee) n. neutral condition, status, attitude, policy, etc., as of a nation during a war. [ME]

neu·tral·ize (NOO trə LĪZ) v.t. **·ized, ·iz·ing 1.** counteract or destroy the force, influence, or effect of. **2.** declare neutral during a war. **3.** make electrically or chemically neutral. [< F *neutraliser*]

neu·tron (NOO tron) n. *Physics* an electrically neutral particle of the atomic nucleus having a mass approximately equal to that of the proton.

neutron bomb a nuclear weapon producing great radiation but causing limited property damage.

nev·er (NEV ər) adv. **1.** not at any time; not ever. **2.** not at all. [ME]

nev·er·the·less (NEV ər thə LES) adv. nonetheless; however; yet. [ME]

new (noo) adj. **·er, ·est 1.** having recently been made, developed, or discovered. **2.** having never existed or occurred before. **3.** unfamiliar; strange. **4.** not accustomed or experienced: *new* at the job. **5.** fresh; unspoiled. **6.** repeated; renewed: a *new* plea. **7.** additional; increased: a *new* supply. **8.**

rejuvenated; refreshed: a *new* man. **9.** modern; current; fashionable. **10.** *cap.* designating the most recent form or period: *New* Latin. —*adv.* newly; freshly; recently. [ME *newe*] —**new′•ness** *n.*

new•born (NOO BORN) *adj.* **1.** just lately born. **2.** reborn. —*n.* a newborn infant or animal.

new•com•er (NOO KUM ər) *n.* one who has recently arrived.

New Deal the political, economic, and social policies and principles of the administration under Franklin D. Roosevelt. —**New Dealer** *n.*

new•el (NOO əl) *n. Archit.* **1.** the post at the end of a staircase. **2.** the central pillar or upright of a spiral staircase. Also **newel post.** [ME *nowel*]

new•fan•gled (NOO FANG gəld) *adj.* lately come into fashion; novel. [ME]

New Latin see under LATIN.

new•ly (NOO lee) *adv.* **1.** very recently; lately. **2.** once more; anew. **3.** in a new or different way. [ME]

new•ly•wed (NOO lee WED) *n.* a person recently married.

new moon the phase of the moon when its disk is invisible. [ME]

news (nooz) *n. (construed as sing.)* **1.** information of a recent event, as reported in a newspaper or on a newscast. **2.** any new or unfamiliar information. [ME *newis* new things]

news•cast (NOOZ KAST) *n.* a radio or television broadcast of news. —**news′cast′er** *n.*

news•let•ter (NOOZ LET ər) *n.* a specialized news report sent by mail.

news•mag•a•zine (NOOZ MAG ə ZEEN) *n.* a periodical reporting the news.

news•pa•per (NOOZ PAY pər) *n.* a printed publication usu. issued daily or weekly, containing news, editorials, special features, and advertisements.

news•print (NOOZ PRINT) *n.* the low-grade paper on which newspapers are printed.

news•reel (NOOZ REEL) *n.* a short motion picture showing current events.

news•stand (NOOZ STAND) *n.* a stall where newspapers and periodicals are sold.

news•worth•y (NOOZ WUR *thee*) *adj.* important enough to be reported in a newspaper or newscast.

New Testament that portion of the Bible containing the life and teachings of Christ and his followers.

New World the Western Hemisphere.

New Year the first day of the year; January 1. Also **New Year's Day.**

New Year's Eve the night of December 31.

next (nekst) *adj.* **1.** coming directly after in time, order, or position. **2.** nearest or closest in space. **3.** adjacent or adjoining. —*adv.* **1.** immediately afterward. **2.** on the first succeeding occasion: when *next* we meet. —*prep.* nearest to: *next* his heart. —**next door 1.** the adjacent house, building, or apartment. **2.** in, at, or to the adjacent house, etc. [ME *nexte*]

nex•us (NEK səs) *n. pl.* **nexus 1.** a bond or tie between the several members of a group or series; link. **2.** a connected series. [< L, a binding]

nib (nib) *n.* **1.** the point of a pen. **2.** the projecting, pointed part of anything; tip.

nib•ble (NIB əl) *v.* **•bled, •bling** *v.t.* **1.** eat with small, quick bites. **2.** bite gently: *nibble* an ear. —*v.i* **3.** eat or bite, esp. with small, gentle bites: often with *at.* —*n.* A little bit or morsel. [ME *nebbilen* peck at] —**nib′bler** *n.*

nice (nīs) *adj.* **nic•er, nic•est 1.** agreeable; pleasing; suitable. **2.** friendly; kind. **3.** having or showing good breeding; respectable. **4.** having or showing discrimination; delicate or subtle. **5.** precise or accurate, as an instrument. [ME, foolish] —**nice′ly** *adv.*

ni•ce•ty (NĪ si tee) *n. pl.* **•ties 1.** *Usu. pl.* a minute or subtle point, detail, or distinction. **2.** *Usu. pl.* a delicacy or refinement: *niceties* of living. **3.** precision or accuracy: exactness. [ME]

niche (nich) *n.* **1.** a recessed space in a wall. **2.** any position or purpose that is best suited: find one's *niche.* [< F]

nick (nik) *n.* a slight cut or notch on a surface or edge. —**in the nick of time** at the exact or crucial moment. —**nick** *v.t.*

nick•el (NIK əl) *n.* **1.** a hard, silver-white metallic element (symbol Ni). **2.** a five-cent coin of the U.S., made of an alloy of nickel and copper. —*v.t.* **•eled, •el•ing** plate with nickel. [< G *Kupfernickel*, lit., copper demon]

nick•el•o•de•on (NIK ə LOH dee ən) *n.* **1.** formerly, a motion-picture theater charging five cents for admission. **2.** a jukebox or other automatic music machine.

nick•name (NIK NAYM) *n.* **1.** a familiar form of a proper name, as *Tom* for *Thomas.* **2.** a descriptive name, as *Honest Abe.* —*v.t.* **•named, •nam•ing** give a nickname to or call by a nickname. [ME *nekename* surname; the phrase *an ekename* was mis-construed as *a nekename*]

nic·o·tine (NIK ə TEEN) *n.* an acrid, poi-sonous, oily compound contained in the leaves of tobacco. [< F, after Jean *Nicot*, 1530—1600, French courtier who intro-duced tobacco into France] —**nic′o·tin′ic** (NIK ə TIN ik) *adj.*

niece (nees) *n.* the daughter of a brother or sister. [ME *nece*]

nif·ty (NIF tee) *adj.* •ti·er, •ti·est *Informal* stylish; pleasing.

nig·gard (NIG ərd) *n.* a stingy person. —*adj.* niggardly. [ME *nyggard*]

nig·gard·ly (NIG ərd lee) *adj.* 1. stingy. 2. scanty. —*adv.* in the manner of a niggard. —**nig′gard·li·ness** *n.*

nig·gle (NIG əl) *v.i.* •gled, •gling occupy oneself with trifles. [< Scand.]

nig·gling (NIG ling) *adj.* 1. fussy; over-precise. 2. mean; petty. 3. annoying; nag-ging.

nigh (nī) *adj.* **nigh·er, nigh·est** close; near. —*adv.* 1. near in time or place. 2. almost: often with *on* or *onto*: *nigh* on a year. —*prep.* near. [ME *nighe*]

night (nīt) *n.* 1. the period from sunset sun-rise, esp. the part that is dark. ◆ Collateral adjective: *nocturnal.* 2. the period of eve-ning. 3. darkness; the dark. 4. a period of gloom, unhappiness, etc. [ME] —**night** *adj.*

night blindness vision that is abnormally poor in dim light but normal in daylight.

night·cap (NĪT KAP) *n.* 1. a cap worn in bed. 2. *Informal* a drink of liquor taken just be-fore going to bed.

night·clothes (Nklohz) *n.pl.* clothes worn in bed.

night·fall (NĪT FAWL) *n.* the close of day.

night·gown (NĪT GOWN) *n.* a loose gown worn in bed.

night·life (NĪT LIF) *n.* entertainment, as theaters and nightclubs, open at night.

night·ly (NĪT lee) *adj.* 1. of, pertaining to, or occurring each night. 2. pertaining to or occurring at night. —*adv.* each night: take place *nightly.*

night·mare (NĪT MAIR) *n.* 1. a horrible and frightening dream. 2. any experience or condition resembling a nightmare. [ME] —**night′mar·ish** *adj.*

night·shirt (NĪT SHURT) *n.* a long, loose garment worn in bed.

night·time (NĪT TIM) *n.* the time from sun-set to sunrise, or from dark to dawn.

ni·hil·ism (NĪ ə LIZ əm) *n.* 1. *Philos.* a doc-trine that denies all traditional principles, beliefs, and institutions. 2. in politics, a doc-trine advocating the destruction of all polit-ical, economic, and social institutions. —**ni′hil·ist** *n.* —**ni′hil·is′tic** *adj.*

nil (nil) *n.* nothing. [< L]

nim·ble (NIM bəl) *adj.* •bler, •blest 1. light and quick in movement; lively. 2. charac-terized by a quick and ready intellect. [ME *nymel*] —**nim′bly** *adv.*

nim·bus (NIM bəs) *n. pl.* •bi (-bī) or •bus·es a light believed to surround a deity or holy person. [< L, rainstorm]

nine (nīn) *n.* 1. the sun of eight and one: a cardinal number written 9, IX. 2. anything consisting of nine units, as a baseball team etc. [ME] —**nine** *adj.* —**ninth** *adj. & n.*

nine·teen (NĪN TEEN) *n.* the sum of eigh-teen and one: a cardinal number written 19, XIX. [ME *nintene*] —**nine′teen′** *adj.* —**nine′·teenth′** *adj. & n.*

nine·ty (NĪN tee) *n. pl.* •ties the sum of eighty and ten: a cardinal number written 90, XC. [ME *ninti*] —**nine′ty** *adj.* —**nine′ti·eth** *adj. & n.*

nip¹ (nip) *v.* **nipped, nip·ping** *v.t.* 1. pinch between two surfaces; bite. 2. sever or re-move by pinching, biting, or clipping: usu-ally with *off.* 3. check, arrest, or destroy the growth or development of. 4. affect pain-fully or injuriously, as by cold. 5. *Informal* steal. —*v.i.* 6. *Slang* move nimbly or rap-idly; flee. —*n.* 1. the act of one who or that which nips. 2. any small portion: a *nip* of tea. 3. severe cold or frost. 4. a sharp, pun-gent flavor. —**nip and tuck** very close or even; uncertain. [ME *nyppe* pinch]

nip² *n.* a small quantity of liquor. —*v.t. & v.i.* **nipped, nip·ping** sip (liquor). [< Du. *nip-pen* sip]

nip·per (NIP ər) *n.* 1. one who or that which nips. 2. *pl.* an implement used for nipping, as pliers etc. 3. the large claw of a crab or lobster. 4. *Informal* a small boy; lad.

nip·ple (NIP əl) *n.* 1. the protuberance on a breast of higher mammals, esp. that of the female; teat. 2. the rubber mouthpiece of a nursing bottle.

nip·py (NIP ee) *adj.* •pi·er, •pi·est biting or sharp, as cold weather.

nir·va·na (nir VAH nə) *n.* 1. in Buddhism, the state of absolute bliss attained through the annihilation of the self. 2. freedom from care and pain; bliss. [< Skt. *nirvāna* extinc-tion]

Ni·sei (NEE SAY) *n. pl.* **·sei** a native American of immigrant Japanese parentage. [< Jap., lit., second generation]

ni·si (NĪ SĪ) *adj. Law* unless: used after *order, rule, decree,* etc., signifying that it shall become effective at a certain time, unless modified or avoided. [< L]

nit (nit) *n.* **1.** the egg of a louse or other parasitic insect. **2.** an immature louse. [ME *nite*] —**nit'ty** *adj.* **·ti·er, ·ti·est**

nit·pick (NIT PIK) *v.t.* **1.** fuss over or find fault with. —*v.i.* **2.** engage in nitpicking. —**nit'pick'er** *n.*

nit·pick·ing (NIT PIK ing) *n.* a fussing over trivial details, esp. to find fault.

ni·tro·gen (NĪ trə jən) *n.* an odorless, colorless gaseous element (symbol N) forming about four-fifths of the atmosphere by volume and playing a decisive role in the formation of compounds essential to life. [< F *nitrogène*] —**ni·trog·e·nous** (nī TROJ ə nəs) *adj.*

ni·tro·glyc·er·in (NĪ trə GLIS ər ən) *n. Chem.* an oily liquid, colorless to pale yellow, used as an explosive, propellant, etc.

nitrous oxide (NĪ trəs) a gas used as an anesthetic in dental surgery: also called *laughing gas.*

nit·ty-grit·ty (NIT ee GRIT ee) *n. Slang* the basic questions or details; essence. —*adj.* basic.

nit·wit (NIT WIT) *n.* a silly or stupid person.

nix (niks) *n. Slang* **1.** nothing. **2.** no. —*adv.* no. —*v.t.* forbid or disagree with. [< G *nichts* nothing]

no[1] (noh) *adv.* **1.** not so. **2.** not at all; not in any way: *no* better than the other. **3.** not: used to express an alternative after *or:* whether or *no.* —*n. pl.* **noes 1.** a negative reply; a denial. **2.** a negative vote or voter. [ME]

no[2] *adj.* not any; not one. [ME]

No[3] (noh) *n.* the classical drama of Japan, tragic or noble in theme, having music and dancing: also spelled *noh.* [< Jap.]

nob[1] (nob) *n. Slang* the head.

nob[2] *n. Chiefly Brit. Slang* one who is rich, influential, etc.

no·bil·i·ty (noh BIL i tee) *n. pl.* **·ties 1.** a class in society composed of persons having hereditary title, rank, and privileges. **2.** in Great Britain, the peerage. **3.** the state or quality of being noble. [ME *nobilite*]

no·ble (NOH bəl) *adj.* **·bler, ·blest 1.** having excellence or dignity. **2.** magnificent and imposing in appearance; grand; stately.

3. of or pertaining to the nobility; aristocratic. —*n.* **1.** a nobleman. **2.** in Great Britain, a peer. [ME] —**no'ble·ness** *n.* —**no'bly** *adv.*

no·ble·man (NOH bəl mən) *n. pl.* **·men** a man of noble rank; in Great Britain, a peer.

no·blesse o·blige (noh BLES oh BLEEZH) the obligation of those of high birth, wealth, or social position to behave generously or nobly toward others. [< F, lit., nobility obligates]

no·ble·wom·an (NOH bəl WUUM ən) *n. pl.* **·wom·en 1.** a woman of noble rank. **2.** in Great Britain, a peeress.

no·bod·y (NOH BOD ee) *pron.* not anybody. —*n. pl.* **·bod·ies** a person of no importance or influence.

noc·tur·nal (nok TUR nl) *adj.* **1.** of, pertaining to, or occurring at night. **2.** *Biol.* active by night. [< LL *nocturnalis*]

noc·turne (NOK turn) *n. Music* a composition of a pensive or romantic nature.

nod (nod) *v.* **nod·ded, nod·ding** *v.i.* **1.** lower the head forward briefly, as in agreement. **2.** let the head fall forward slightly, as when drowsy. **3.** be inattentive or careless. **4.** sway or bend, as trees. —*v.t.* **5.** lower (the head) by nodding. **6.** express or signify (assent etc.) by nodding the head. [ME *nodde*] —**nod** *n.*

node (nohd) *n.* **1.** a knot, knob, or swelling. **2.** *Bot.* a joint or knob of a stem. **3.** *Astron.* either of two points at which the orbit of a celestial object intersects the ecliptic. [< L *nodus* knot] —**nod'al** *adj.*

nod·ule (NOJ ool) *n.* **1.** a little knot or node. **2.** *Bot.* a tubercle. —**nod'u·lar** (NOJ ə lər) *adj.*

No·el (noh EL) *n.* Christmas. [< F *Noël*]

no-fault (NOH FAWLT) *adj.* designating a system whereby claims may be settled without assigning blame to one party. —*n.* no-fault insurance.

no-frills (NOH FRILZ) *adj.* without additional features of extras: *no-frills* plane flight.

nog·gin (NOG ən) *n.* **1.** *Informal* a person's head. **2.** a small mug or cup. **3.** a measure of liquor equal to about ¼ pint.

no-good (NOH GUUD) *adj.* worthless; contemptible. —*n.* a contemptible person.

noh (noh) see NO[3]

no-hit·ter (NOH HIT ər) in baseball, a game in which the pitcher allows no base hits.

noise (noiz) *n.* **1.** loud, confused, or disturbing sound. **2.** any random electronic disturbance. —*v.t.* **noised, nois•ing** spread, report, or rumor: often with *about* or *abroad.* [ME]

noise•less (NOIZ lis) *adj.* causing or making little or no noise; quiet; silent.

noise•mak•er (NOIZ MAY kər) *n.* a horn, bell, etc. for making noise at celebrations.

noise pollution loud or annoying noise considered harmful to people.

noi•some (NOI səm) *adj.* **1.** offensive or disgusting, esp. in smell. **2.** injurious; noxious. [ME < *noy* annoyance]

nois•y (NOI zee) *adj.* **nois•i•er, nois•i•est 1.** making a loud noise. **2.** characterized by or full of noise. —**nois'i•ly** *adv.* —**nois' i•ness** *n.*

nol•le pros•e•qui (NOL ee PROS i KWEE) *Law* an entry in the record of a civil or criminal case signifying that the plaintiff or prosecutor will not press it. [< L, be unwilling to pursue]

no-load (NOH LOHD) *adj.* offered for sale without a sales commission added: said of mutual funds.

no•lo con•ten•de•re (NOH loh kən TEN də rə) *Law* a plea by a defendant in a criminal action that has the same legal effect as an admission of guilt but does not debar the defendant from denying the truth of the charges in any other proceedings. [< L, I do not wish to contend]

no•mad (NOH mad) *n.* **1.** one of a group of people that moves from place to place to find food, etc. **2.** one who constantly moves about, usu. without purpose. [< L] —**no•mad'ic** *adj.* —**no'mad•ism** *n.*

no man's land 1. a tract of wasteland. **2.** in war, the land between opposing armies.

no•men•cla•ture (NOH mən KLAY chər) *n.* **1.** the system of names used in science, art, etc.; terminology. **2.** the specific names for the parts or stages of a device, process, etc.[< L *nomenclatura* list of names]

nom•i•nal (NOM ə nəl) *adj.* **1.** existing in name only; not actual. **2.** slight; trifling. [ME *nominalle*] —**nom'i•nal•ly** *adv.*

nom•i•nate (NOM ə NAYT) *v.t.* **•nat•ed, •nat•ing** propose as a candidate for elective office or honor. [< L *nominatus* named] —**nom'i•na'tion** *n.*

nom•i•na•tive (NOM ə nə tiv) *adj. Gram.* designating the case of the subject of a verb. —*n. Gram.* **1.** the nominative case. **2.** a word in this case.

nom•i•nee (NOM ə NEE) *n.* one who receives a nomination.

non- *prefix* not. [< L *non*] The list found below contains self-explanatory words beginning with *non-*.

non•age (NON ij) *n.* **1.** the period of legal minority. **2.** a period of immaturity. [ME]

non•a•ge•nar•i•an (NON ə jə NAIR ee ən) *n.* a person between 90 and 100 years of age. [< L *nonagenarius* of ninety] — **non'a•ge•nar'i•an** *adj.*

non•a•ligned (NON ə LĪND) *adj.* not allied with any powerful world political bloc.

nonce word (nons) a word coined for a single occasion. [ME *nones*; the phrase *for then onse,* for once, was misconstrued as *for the nones*]

non•cha•lant (NON shə LAHNT) *adj.* marked by or exhibiting a lack of interest or excitement; casually indifferent. [< F] — **non'cha•lance'** *n.*

non•com (NON KOM) *n. Informal* a non-commissioned officer.

non•com•bat•ant (NON kəm BAT nt) *n.* **1.** one whose duties as a member of a military force do not entail fighting, as a chaplain. **2.** a civilian in wartime.

non•com•mis•sioned officer (NON kə MISH ənd) *Mil.* an enlisted person appointed to any grade from corporal to sergeant major in the U.S. Army.

non•com•mit•tal (NON kə MIT l) *adj.* not involving or revealing a commitment to any particular attitude, opinion, etc. — **non'•com•mit'tal•ly** *adv.*

non•con•duc•tor (NON kən DUK tər) *n.* a substance that offers resistance to the passage of some form of energy, as of heat or electricity. —**non'con•duct'ing** *adj.*

non•con•form•ist (NON kən FOR mist) *n.* **1.** one who does not conform to an approved manner of behaving or thinking; dissenter. **2.** *Often cap.* an English Protestant who refuses to conform to the Church of England. —**non'con•for'mi•ty** *n.*

non•de•script (NON di SKRIPT) *adj.* not distinctive enough to be described; lacking individual character.

none (nun) *pron.* (construed as *sing.* or *pl.*) **1.** not one; no one. **2.** no or not one (specified person or thing); not any (of a class of things). **3.** no part or portion; not any: It is *none* of my business. —*adv.* by no means; not at all: He is *none* too bright. [ME *non*]

nonabrasive
nonabsorbent
nonacceptance
nonacid
nonaction
nonactive
nonaddictive
nonadministrative
nonaffiliated
nonaggression
nonagreement
nonalcoholic
nonallergic
nonappearance
nonaquatic
nonassignable
nonathletic
nonattendance
nonattributive

nonautomatic
nonbeliever
nonbelieving
nonbelligerent
nonblending
nonbreakable
nonbureaucratic
noncancerous
noncandidate
noncapitalistic
nonchargeable
noncitizen
noncivilized
nonclassifiable
nonclinical
nonclotting
noncoagulating
noncognitive
noncohesive

non•en•ti•ty (non EN ti tee) *n. pl.* **•ties 1.** one who or that which is of little or no account; a nothing. **2.** that which does not exist, or exists solely in the imagination.

nones (nohnz) *n. Eccl.* the fifth of the seven canonical hours. [ME]

none•the•less (NUN *th*ə LES) *adv.* in spite of everything; nevertheless.

non•fat (NON FAT) *adj.* having fat removed: *nonfat* milk.

non•fea•sance (non FEE zəns) *n. Law* the nonperformance of some act that one is legally bound to perform.

non•fer•rous (non FER əs) *adj.* not containing iron; esp., pertaining to metals other than iron, as copper, tin, etc.

non•fic•tion (non FIK shən) *n.* prose literature other than fiction, as historical works, biographies, etc. —**non•fic′tion•al** *adj.*

non•in•ter•ven•tion (NON in tər VEN shən) *n.* the refusal or failure to intervene; esp., the policy or practice of a nation of not intervening in the affairs of other nations. —**non′in•ter•ven′tion•ist** *adj. & n.*

no-no (NOH NOH) *n. pl.* **-nos, -no's** *Informal* something forbidden or to be avoided.

non•ob•jec•tive (NON əb JEK tiv) *adj.* not objective; esp., denoting a style of nonrepresentational art.

noncollapsible
noncollectable
noncombat
noncombining
noncombustible
noncommercial
noncommunicable
non-Communist

nonconsular
noncontagious
noncontiguous
noncontinuous
noncontributing
noncontributory
noncontroversial
nonconventional

noncompensating
noncompetitive
noncompliance
noncomplying
noncompression
nonconcurrent
nonconfidential
nonconflicting
nonconforming
noncongealing
noncongestion
nonconsecutive
nonconsenting
nonconstructive

nonconvergent
nonconversant
nonconvertible
noncorrective
noncorroborative
noncorrosive
noncreative
noncriminal
noncritical
noncrystalline
nonculpable
noncumulative
nondecaying
nondeferrable

non•pa•reil (NON pə REL) *adj.* having no equal; unrivaled. —*n.* **1.** one who or that which has no equal; a paragon. **2.** a chocolate candy disk covered with sweet pellets. [ME *nonparaille*]

non•par•ti•san (non PAHR tə zən) *adj.* not partisan; esp., not controlled by, associated with, or in support of the interests of any one political party.

non•per•son (non PUR sən) *n.* a person having no social or legal status, or no official recognition.

non•plus (non PLUS) *v.t.* **•plussed,** **•plus•sing** cause to be at a loss; baffle; perplex. [< L *non plus*, lit., no more]

non•prof•it (non PROF it) *adj.* not organized or maintained for the making of a profit: *nonprofit* enterprises.

non•rep•re•sen•ta•tion•al (NON rep ri zen TAY shə nl) *adj.* denoting a style of art that does not seek to represent objects as they appear in nature.

non•res•i•dent (non REZ i dənt) *adj.* not resident; esp., not residing permanently in the locality where one works, owns property, attends school, etc. —*n.* one who is nonresident.

non•re•sis•tant (NON ri ZIS tənt) *adj.* **1.** not resistant; esp., incapable of resistance, as to infection. **2.** characteristic of a nonresistant. —*n.* one who is passive in the face of violence. —**non′re•sis′tance** *n.*

non•re•stric•tive (NON ri STRIK tiv) *adj.* **1.** not restrictive. **2.** *Gram.* denoting a word or word, group, esp. an adjective clause, that describes its antecedent but may be omitted without loss of essential meaning, as *which is for sale* in *Our house, which is for sale, needs repairs.*

non•sec•tar•i•an (NON sek TAIR ee ən) *adj.* not restricted to or associated with any one religion.

non·sense (NON sens) *n*. **1.** words or actions that are meaningless or absurd. **2.** things of no importance or use; trifles. **3.** foolish or frivolous conduct. **—non·sen′ si·cal** *adj*.

nondelivery
nondemocratic
nondepartmental
nondepletion
nondepreciating
nonderivable
nonderivative
nondestructive
nondetachable
nondetonating
nondevelopment
nondiplomatic
nondirectional
nondiscountable
nondiscrimination
nondiscriminatory
nondisposal
nondistinctive
nondivergent
nondivisible
nondomesticated
nondramatic
nondrying

nonearning
nonecclesiastical
noneconomic
nonedible
noneducable
noneducational
nonelastic
nonelective
nonelectric
nonelementary
nonemotional
nonempirical
nonenforceable
nonentry
nonepicurean
nonequation
nonequatorial
nonequilibrium
nonequivalent
nonequivocating
nonerotic
nonerudite
nonessential

non se·qui·tur (non SEK wi tər) **1.** *Logic* an inference that does not follow from the premises. **2.** any comment not relevant to what has preceded it. [< L, it does not follow]

non·stan·dard (NON STAN dərd) *adj*. **1.** varying or deviating from the standard. **2.** *Ling.* designating those usages or varieties of a language that differ from the standard.

non·sup·port (NON sə PORT) *n*. failure to provide for the support of a legal dependent.

non·un·ion (non YOON yən) *adj*. **1.** not belonging to or associated with a labor union. **2.** not recognizing, contracting with, or employing the members of any union: *nonunion* shop.

noo·dle[1] (NOOD l) *n*. **1.** a simpleton. Also **noo′dle·head′** (-HED). **2.** *Slang* the head.

noo·dle[2] *n*. a thin strip of dried dough, usu. containing egg, used in soup, etc. [< G *Nudel*]

nook (nuuk) *n*. **1.** an interior corner or angle, as in a room. **2.** any narrow place, as a recess. [ME *nok*]

noon (noon) *n*. **1.** the middle of the day; twelve o'clock in the daytime. **2.** the highest or culminating point; zenith. —*adj.* of, per-

taining to, or occurring at or about noon. [ME *none*]

noon·day (NOON DAY) *n*. noon. —*adj.* of or at noon.

no one not any person; nobody.

noon·time (NOON TĪM) *n*. **1.** midday. **2.** the culminating point or period. Also **noon′ tide′**. [ME *none tyme*]

noose (noos) *n*. **1.** a loop furnished with a running knot, as in a hangman's halter or a snare. **2.** anything that entraps, restrains, or binds. —*v.t.* **noosed, noos·ing** capture or secure with a noose. [ME *nose*]

nonethereal
nonevangelical
nonevolutionary
nonexchangeable
nonexclusive
nonexecution
nonexemplary
nonexempt
nonexistence
nonexistent
nonexpansive
nonexpendable
nonexperimental
nonexpert
nonexplosive
nonexportable
nonextended
nonextension
nonextinction
nonextradition
nonfactual
nonfading

nonfatal
nonfattening
nonfederal
nonfederated
nonfertility
nonfinancial
nonfinite
nonfiscal
nonfissionable
nonflammable
nonflowering
nonflowing
nonfluctuating
nonflying
nonfocal
nonformal
nonfulfillment
nonfunctional
nongaseous
nongelatinous
nongovernmental
nongraded

nor (nor) *conj.* and not; likewise not. [ME]

nor′·east·er (NOR EE stər) see NORTH-EASTER.

norm (norm) *n*. **1.** a pattern, model, or standard regarded as typical of a specified group. **2.** *Psychol.* the standard of performance in a given function or test, usu. the average achievement for the group concerned. [< L *norma*, lit., carpenter's square]

nor·mal (NOR məl) *adj*. **1.** conforming to or consisting of a pattern, process, or standard regarded as usual or typical; natural. **2.** *Psychol.* **a** well adjusted; without marked or persistent mental aberrations. **b** of average skill, intelligence, etc. —*n.* **1.** the common or natural condition, form, degree, etc. **2.** the usual or accepted rule or process. [< L *normalis*, see NORM] —**nor·mal·i·ty** (nor MAL i tee) *n*.

nor·mal·ize (NOR mə LĪZ) *v.t.* **·ized,**

•iz•ing bring into accord with a norm or standard form; make normal. — **nor′mal•i•za′tion** n.

nor•mal•ly (NOR mə lee) adv. **1.** as a rule; usually. **2.** in a normal manner.

nor•ma•tive (NOR mə tiv) adj. **1.** of, pertaining to, or based upon a norm, esp. one regarded as a standard or rule of usage. **2.** implying, supporting, or establishing a norm.

nonhabitable	noninflected
nonhabitual	noninformative
nonhazardous	noninheritable
nonhereditary	noninjurious
nonheritable	noninstrumental
nonheroic	nonintellectual
nonhistoric	noninterference
nonhuman	noninternational
nonhumorous	noninterrupted
nonidentical	nonintersecting
nonimitative	nonintoxicating
nonimperative	nonintuitive
nonimperial	nonionized
nonimportation	nonirritant
nonimprovement	nonjudicial
noninclusive	nonjuristic
nonindependent	nonlegal
nonindictable	nonlethal
nonindividual	nonlicensed
nonindustrial	nonlimiting
noninfallible	nonliquefying
noninfectious	nonliterary
noninflammatory	nonliturgical

Norse (nors) adj. **1.** Scandinavian. **2.** of or pertaining to Norway, Iceland, and the Faroe Islands; West Scandinavian. —n. **1.** the Scandinavians or West Scandinavians collectively: used with the. **2.** the Scandinavian or North Germanic group of the Germanic languages; esp., Norwegian. **3.** the West Scandinavian languages. —**Old Norse 1.** the ancestor of the North Germanic languages. [? < MDu. nordsch northern]

north (north) n. **1.** the direction to one's left when facing the sun at sunrise. **2.** one of the four cardinal points of the compass, directly opposite south. **3.** Sometimes cap. any region north of a specified point. — **the North** in the U.S.: **a** the population or territory of the northern or northeastern states. **b** the states opposed to the Confederacy in the Civil War. —adj. **1.** to, toward, facing, or in the north. **2.** coming from the north. —adv. in or toward the north. [ME]

north•bound (NORTH BOWND) adj. going northward.

north•east (NORTH EEST) n. **1.** the direction midway between north and east. **2.** any region lying in or toward this direction. — adj. **1.** to, toward, facing, or in the northeast. **2.** coming from the northeast. —adv. in or toward the northeast. —**north′•east′ ern** adj.

north•east•er (NORTH EE stər) n. **1.** a gale or storm from the northeast. **2.** a sailor's hat with a sloping brim worn in stormy weather. Also spelled nor′easter.

north•east•er•ly (NORTH EE stər lee) adj. **1.** in, of, or toward the northeast. **2.** from the northeast, as a wind. —adv. toward or from the northeast.

north•er (NOR thər) n. **1.** a gale or storm from the north. **2.** a violent, cold north wind blowing over the plains of the SW states.

nonliving	nonmobile
nonlocal	nonmunicipal
nonloving	nonmuscular
nonlustrous	nonmystical
nonmagnetic	nonnaval
nonmalignant	nonnavigable
nonmalleable	nonnegotiable
nonmarital	nonneutral
nonmarketable	nonnuclear
nonmarrying	nonnutrient
nonmartial	nonnutritive
nonmaterial	nonobligatory
nonmaterialistic	nonobservance
nonmathematical	nonobservant
nonmechanical	nonoccupational
nonmechanistic	nonoccurrence
nonmedical	nonofficial
nonmember	nonoily
nonmercantile	nonoperative
nonmigratory	nonoptional
nonmilitant	nonorthodox
nonmilitary	nonowner
nonmineral	nonoxidizing

north•er•ly (NOR thər lee) adj. **1.** in, of, toward, or pertaining to the north. **2.** from the north, as a wind. —adv. toward or from the north. —n. a wind or storm from the north.

north•ern (NOR thərn) adj. **1.** to, toward, or in the north. **2.** native to or inhabiting the north. **3.** Sometimes cap. of, pertaining to, or characteristic of the north or the north. **4.** from the north, as a wind.

north•ern•er (NOR thər nər) n. **1.** one who is native to or lives in the north. **2.** Usu. cap. one who lives in or comes from the North.

Northern Hemisphere see under HEMI-SPHERE.

northern lights the aurora borealis.

North Pole the northern extremity of the earth's axis.

North Star Polaris.

north·ward (NORTH wərd) adv. toward the north. Also **north'wards.** —adj. to, toward, facing, or in the north.

north·ward·ly (NORTH wərd lee) adj. & adv. toward or from the north.

north·west (NORTH WEST) n. **1.** the direction midway between north and west. **2.** any region lying in or toward this direction. —adj. **1.** to, facing, or in the northwest. **2.** coming from the northwest. —adv. in or toward the northwest. —**north'·west'ern** adj.

north·west·er (NORTH WES tər) n. a gale or storm from the northwest: also **nor'·west'er.**

north·west·er·ly (NORTH WES tər lee) adj. **1.** in, of, or toward the northwest. **2.** from the northwest, as a wind. —adv. toward or from the northwest.

Nor·we·gian (nor WEE jən) n. **1.** a native or inhabitant of Norway. **2.** the North Germanic language of Norway. —**Nor·we'gian** adj.

nose (nohz) n. **1.** the part of the face in people or the forward end of an animal that contains the nostrils and the organ of smell, and that in man encloses cavities used in the respiratory process. **2.** the sense of smell or the power of smelling. **3.** the ability to perceive or discover by or as if by the sense of smell: a nose for scandal. **4.** something resembling a nose, as the forward part of an aircraft. —**on the nose** Informal **a** exactly; precisely. **b** in betting, to win only. —**pay through the nose** pay an excessively high price. —v. **nosed, nos·ing** v.t. **1.** nuzzle. **2.** make (one's) way carefully with the front end foremost. **3.** perceive or discover by or as if by smell; scent. —v.i. **4.** pry or interfere; snoop: with around or about. **5.** move forward, esp. carefully. —**nose out** defeat by a narrow margin. [ME]

nonoxygenated
nonpalatal
nonparallel
nonparasitic
nonparental
nonparliamentary
nonparochial
nonparticipant

nonplastic
nonpoetic
nonpoisonous
nonpolitical
nonporous
nonpredictable
nonpreferential
nonprejudicial

nonpartisanship
nonpaying
nonpayment
nonperforated
nonperformance
nonperishable
nonpermanent
nonpermeable
nonpermissible
nonperseverance
nonpersistence
nonphilanthropic
nonphysical
nonphysiological
nonpigmented

nonprescriptive
nonpreservative
nonpresidential
nonprevalent
nonproducer
nonproductive
nonprofessional
nonprofessorial
nonprogressive
nonprohibitive
nonprolific
nonproprietary
nonprotection
nonprotective
nonpublication

nose cone Aerospace the cone-shaped forward section of a rocket or missile.

nose·dive (NOHZ DIV) **1.** a steep, downward plunge of an aircraft, nose end foremost. **2.** any steep, sudden drop. —**nose'·dive'** v.i. -**dived, -div·ing** [< L, ours]

nose·gay (NOHZ GAY) n. a small bunch of flowers; bouquet. [ME]

nosh (nosh) v.t. & v.i. Informal nibble or snack. —n. a snack. [< Yiddish nashn]

nos·tal·gi·a (no STAL jə) n. **1.** a longing for familiar or beloved circumstances that are now remote or irrecoverable. **2.** any longing for something far away or long ago. [< NL] —**nos·tal'gic** adj.

nos·tril (NOS trəl) n. one of the external openings of the nose. [ME nostrill]

nos·trum (NOS trəm) n. **1.** a medicine of one's own preparation; also, a quack medicine. **2.** a panacea. [< L, ours]

nos·y (NOH zee) adj. **nos·i·er, nos·i·est** prying; snooping; inquisitive: also spelled **nos'ey** (NOH zee) **nos·i·er, nos·i·est.**

not (not) adv. in no way, or to no extent or degree: used to note the absence, reverse, or opposite of something or to express negation, prohibition, or refusal. [ME]

nonpuncturable
nonracial
nonradical
nonrational
nonreactive
nonreality
nonreciprocal
nonrecoverable
nonrecurrent
nonrecurring
nonredeemable
nonrefillable
nonregenerating
nonregenerative

nonrepetitive
nonrepresentative
nonreproductive
nonresidential
nonresinous
nonresisting
nonresonant
nonrestricted
nonretention
nonretiring
nonretractile
nonreturnable
nonreversible
nonrevolving

nonregimented   nonrhetorical
nonregistered   nonrhythmic
nonreigning   nonrival
nonreligious   nonromantic
nonremovable   nonrotating
nonremunerative   nonrural
nonrenewable   nonrusting
nonrepentant   nonsacred
nonrepetition   nonsacrificial

no•ta•ble (NOH tə bəl) *adj.* worthy of note; remarkable; distinguished. —*n.* one who is distinguished, famous, etc. [ME *notabile*]

no•ta•rize (NOH tə-RĪZ) *v.t.* •rized, •riz•ing attest to or authenticate as a notary public.

no•ta•ry public (NOH tə ree) *pl.* **notary publics** one who is legally authorized to administer oaths, certify contracts, etc. Also **notary** *pl.* **notaries.**

no•ta•tion (noh TAY shən) *n.* **1.** a system of signs, figures, or abbreviations used for convenience in recording a quantity, relation, process, etc.: musical *notation*. **2.** a note or comment. [< L *notatus* noted]

notch (noch) *n.* **1.** a V-shaped cut in a surface. **2.** a nick cut into a stick etc., as for keeping count. **3.** a narrow passage between mountains; a defile. **4.** *Informal* a step; level: She is a *notch* above him. —*v.t.* make a notch or notches in. [< earlier *an otch* < OF *oche* notch]

note (noht) *n.* **1.** *Often pl.* a brief record or summary of facts set down for future study or reference: take *notes*. **2.** a brief account or jotting to aid the memory. **3.** *Music* **a** a symbol representing a tone or sound of a given duration and pitch. **b** a tone or sound of a definite pitch. **c** a key of the keyboard. **4.** a mark or sign: a *note* of sadness. **5.** a piece of paper currency issued by a government or authorized bank and negotiable as money: a bank *note*. **6.** a promissory note. **7.** a formal, written communication of an official or diplomatic nature. **8.** a brief letter, esp. of an informal character. **9.** distinction; importance; reputation: a gentleman of *note*. **10.** notice; attention: worthy of *note*. —*v.t.* **not•ed, not•ing 1.** become aware of; observe. **2.** pay attention to; h_ed carefully. **3.** set down for remembering; make a note of. [ME]

nonsalaried   nonsolvent
nonscheduled   nonsparing
nonscholastic   nonsparkling
nonscientific   nonspecialized
nonseasonal   nonspecific

nonsecular   nonspectral
nonsegmented   nonspeculative
nonsegregated   nonspiritual
nonselective   nonsporting
nonsensitive   nonstandardized
nonsensitized   nonstarting
nonsensuous   nonstatistical
nonseparable   nonstatutory
nonsexual   nonstrategic
nonshattering   nonstretchable
nonshatterproof   nonstriker
nonshrinkable   nonstriking
nonsinkable   nonstructural
nonsmoker   nonsubscriber
nonsmoking   nonsupporter
nonsocial   nonsupporting
nonsocialistic   nonsustaining
nonsolid   nonsymbolic

not•ed (NOH tid) *adj.* well known by reputation; famous.

note•wor•thy (NOHT WUR thee) *adj.* remarkable; significant. —**note′wor′thi•ness** *n.*

noth•ing (NUTH ing) *n.* **1.** not anything; naught. **2.** no part or element: He knew *nothing* of it. **3.** one who or that which is of little or no importance. **4.** insignificance or unimportance: rise from *nothing*. **5.** zero. **6.** a state of nonexistence; also, that which is nonexistent. [ME]

noth•ing•ness (NUTH ing nis) *n.* **1.** the condition, quality, or fact of being nothing; nonexistence. **2.** utter worthlessness or insignificance. **3.** unconsciousness.

no•tice (NOH tis) *v.t.* •ticed, •tic•ing **1.** pay attention to or become aware of. **2.** refer to or comment on. —*n.* **1.** the act of noticing or observing. **2.** announcement; information; warning. **3.** a formal announcement: give *notice*. **4.** a short advertisement or review. [ME]

no•tice•a•ble (NOH ti sə bəl) *adj.* **1.** that can be noticed; perceptible. **2.** worthy of notice.

no•ti•fy (NOH tə FĪ) *v.t.* •fied, •fy•ing give notice to; inform. [ME *notifien*] —**no′ti•fi•ca′tion** *n.*

no•tion (NOH shən) *n.* **1.** a general idea or impression; a vague conception. **2.** an opinion, belief, or idea. **3.** intention; inclination. **4.** *pl.* small miscellaneous articles for sale. [< L *notio* idea]

no•tion•al (NOH shə nl) *adj.* **1.** pertaining to, expressing, or consisting of notions or concepts. **2.** existing in imagination only. **3.** impulsive or capricious.

no·to·ri·e·ty (NOH tə RĪ ə tee) *n. pl.* **•ties** the state or character of being notorious. [< Med.L *notorietas*]

no·to·ri·ous (noh TOR ee əs) *adj.* 1. widely known and generally disapproved of or deplored. 2. generally known; acknowledged. [< Med.L *notorius* evdient]

not·with·stand·ing (NOT with STAN ding) *prep.* in spite of: He left *notwithstanding* your orders. —*adv.* all the same; nevertheless: Though closely guarded, she escaped *notwithstanding*. —*conj.* in spite of the fact that; although.

nonsymmetrical	nonuser
nonsympathizer	nonutilitarian
nonsymptomatic	nonutilization
nontarnishable	nonvascular
nontaxable	nonvegetative
nonteaching	nonvenomous
nontechnical	nonvenous
nontemporal	nonverbal
nontenured	nonviable
nonterrestrial	nonvibratory
nonterritorial	nonviolence
nontheatrical	nonvirulent
nontheological	nonviscous
nontherapeutic	nonvitreous
nonthinking	nonvocal
nontoxic	nonvocational
nontraditional	nonvolatile
nontransferable	nonvolition
nontransparent	nonvoluntary
nontropical	nonvoter
nontypical	nonvoting
nonuniform	nonworking
nonuniversal	nonyielding

nou·gat (NOO gət) *n.* a confection of nuts and fruits in a honey or sugar paste. [< F]

nought (nawt) see NAUGHT.

noun (nown) *n. Gram.* a word used as the name of a thing, quality, or action. [ME *nowne* name]

nour·ish (NUR ish) *v.t.* 1. furnish food or other material to sustain the life and promote the growth of (a living plant or animal). 2. support; maintain; foster. [ME *norisshe*] —**nour'ish·ing** *adj.*

nour·ish·ment (NUR ish mənt) *n.* 1. that which nourishes; nutriment. 2. the act of nourishing, or the state of being nourished.

nou·veau riche (NOO voh REESH) *French pl.* **nou·veaux riches** (NOO voh REESH) one who has recently become rich.

no·va (NOH və) *n. pl.* **•vae** (-vee) or **•vas** *Astron.* a star that suddenly brightens and then dims after a period of a few months or years. [< NL, new]

nov·el (NOV əl) *adj.* new, strange, or unusual. —*n.* a fictional prose narrative of considerable length, usu. having an overall pattern or plot. [< Ital. *novella* new kind of (story)]

nov·el·ette (NOV ə LET) *n.* a short novel: also *novella*.

nov·el·ist (NOV ə list) *n.* a writer of novels.

nov·el·ize (NOV ə LIZ) *v.t.* **·ized, ·iz·ing** put into the form of a novel. — **nov'el·i·za'tion** *n.*

no·vel·la (noh VEL ə) *n.* 1. a short tale or narrative, usu. with a moral. 2. a novelette. [< Ital.]

nov·el·ty (NOV əl tee) *n. pl.* **·ties** 1. something novel or unusual. 2. the quality of being novel or new. 3. *Usu. pl.* asmall manufactured article. [ME *novelte*]

No·vem·ber (noh VEM bər) the eleventh month of the year, containing 30 days. [ME]

no·ve·na (noh VEE nə) *n.* in the Roman Catholic Church, devotions made on nine successive days, for some special religious purpose. [< Med.L]

nov·ice (NOV is) *n.* 1. a beginner in any occupation; an inexperienced person. 2. *Eccl.* one who enters a religious order or community on probation. [ME *novyce*]

now (now) *adv.* 1. at once. 2. at or during the present time. 3. nowadays. 4. at this point in the proceedings, narrative, etc.: The war was *now* virtually over. —*n.* the present time, moment, or occasion. —**now and then** from time to time; occasionally: also **now and again.** —**now that** seeing that; since. [ME]

now·a·days (NOW ə DAYZ) *adv.* in the present time or age.

no·way (NOH WAY) *adv.* in no way, manner, or degree. Also **no'ways'.**

no·where (NOH HWAIR) *adv.* in no place; not anywhere. —*n.* a nonexistent place.

no·wise (NOH WĪZ) *adv.* in no manner or degree.

nox·ious (NOK shəs) *adj.* causing or tending to cause injury to health or morals; hurtful. [< L *noxius* harmful] —**nox'·ious·ness** *n.*

noz·zle (NOZ əl) *n.* 1. a projecting spout or pipe serving as an outlet, as of a teapot or hose. 2. *Slang* the nose.

nth (enth) *adj.* 1. *Math.* representing an ordinal equivalent to *n.* 2. infinitely or indefinitely large (or small); most extreme: to the *nth* degree.

nu·ance (NOO ahns) *n. pl.* **·anc·es** a fine or subtle variation, as in color, tone, or meaning; gradation. [< F, shade]

nub (nub) *n.* **1.** a knob or protuberance. **2.** a small piece, as of a pencil. **3.** the core; gist. [Var. of KNOB]

nu·bile (NOO bíl) *adj.* ready or suitable for marriage: said of young women. [< L *nubilis* marriageable] —**nu·bil'i·ty** (noo BIL i tee) *n.*

nu·cle·ar (NOO klee ər) *adj.* **1.** of, pertaining to, or resembling a nucleus or nuclei. **2.** of or using atomic energy: *nuclear* reactor.

nuclear family a family consisting of parents and child or children considered as a discrete group.

nuclear physics the branch of physics that investigates the structure and properties of the atomic nucleus.

nu·cle·ic acid (noo KLEE ik) *Biochem.* any of a group of complex organic acids, as DNA, found esp. in cell nuclei.

nu·cle·on (NOO klee ON) *n. Physics* a proton or a neutron. —**nu'cle·on'ic** *adj.*

nu·cle·o·tide (NOO klee ə TID) *n. Biochem.* a compound, containing a sugar, a nitrogen base, and a phosphate group, and that is the basic unit of DNA and RNA.

nu·cle·us (NOO klee əs) *n. pl.* **·cle·i** (-klee I) **1.** a central point or part around which other things are gathered; core. **2.** a center of growth or development. **3.** *Biol.* a complex body surrounded by a thin membrane and embedded in the protoplasm of most plant and animal cells, essential to the process of heredity and to other vital activities of the cell. **4.** *Physics* the positively charged central core of an atom, containing nucleons that provide its effective mass. [< L, kernel]

nu·clide (NOO klīd) *n. Physics* a specific, relatively stable atom as defined by the composition and properties of its nucleus.

nude (nood) *adj.* **nud·er, nud·est** without clothing or covering; naked. —*n.* **1.** a nude figure, esp. in painting, sculpture, etc. **2.** the state of being nude. [< L *nudus* naked] —**nu'di·ty** *n.*

nudge (nuj) *v.t.* **nudged, nudg·ing** touch or push gently, as with the elbow, in order to attract attention, etc. —**nudge** *n.*

nud·ism (NOO diz əm) *n.* the doctrine or practice of living in the state of nudity. —**nud'ist** *adj. & n.*

nug·get (NUG it) *n.* a lump; esp., a lump of gold found in its native state.

nui·sance (NOO səns) *n.* anything that annoys, bothers, or irritates. [ME *nuisaunce*]

nuisance tax a tax on various consumer goods and services, etc., regarded as more of a bother than a burden.

null (nul) *adj.* **1.** of no legal force or effect; void; invalid. **2.** of no value; negative. **3.** of no avail; useless. —**null and void** without legal force or effect. [< L *nullus* not any] —**nul'li·ty** *n.*

nul·li·fy (NUL ə FI) *v.t.* **·fied, ·fy·ing 1.** make useless or ineffective; undo. **2.** deprive of legal force or effect. [< LL *nullificare* despise] —**nul'li·fi·ca'tion** *n.*

numb (num) *adj.* **·er, ·est 1.** having no sensation; without feeling. **2.** unable to move. —*v.t.* make numb. [ME *nome*, lit., taken]

num·ber (NUM bər) *n.* **1.** a specific quantity or place in a sequence. **2.** one of a series of symbols or words used to designate number; a numeral **3.** *Often pl.* a sizable collection or grouping: *numbers* of people. **4.** an indefinite quantity or collection: a *number* of facts. **5.** a specific sum or total count. **6.** one of a series of things to which numbers are assigned: the March *number* of the magazine. **7.** a part of a program of music or entertainment. **8.** quantity, as composed of units. **9.** *Gram.* the representation in a language of singleness or plurality. **10.** *Informal* an item or article, as of merchandise. —**any number of** a good many; rather a lot. —**without number** too numerous to be counted. —**the numbers** an illegal lottery in which bets are made on the appearance of some 3-digit number: also **numbers game,** *policy, policy game.* —*v.t.* **1.** determine the total number of; reckon. **2.** assign a number to. **3.** include as one of a collection or group. **4.** amount to; total. **5.** set or limit the number of. —*v.i.* **6.** make a count; total. [ME]

num·ber·less (NUM bər lis) *adj.* **1.** very numerous; countless. **2.** having no number.

numb·skull (NUM SKULL) *see* NUMSKULL.

nu·mer·a·ble (NOO mər ə bəl) *adj.* that can be numbered. [< L *numerabilis* countable]

nu·mer·al (NOO mər əl) *n.* a symbol, letter, or word that is used alone or in combination with others to express a number. —*adj.* used in expressing or representing a number. [< LL *numeralis*]

nu·mer·ate (NOO mə RAYT) *v.t.* **·at·ed, ·at·ing 1.** enumerate; count. **2.** read, as a numerical expression. [ME] —**nu′mer•a′ tion** n.

nu•mer•a•tor (NOO mə RAY tər) n. **1.** Math. the term above the line in a fraction indicating how many of the parts of a unit are to be taken. **2.** one who or that which numbers.

nu•mer•i•cal (noo MER i kəl) adj. **1.** of or denoting number. **2.** numerable. **3.** represented by or consisting of numbers or figures rather than letters. [< L numerus number] —**nu•mer′i•cal•ly** adv.

nu•mer•ous (NOO mər əs) adj. consisting of a great number of units; being many.

nu•mis•mat•ics (NOO miz MAT iks) n. (construed as sing.) the study of coins, medals, and related objects. [< NL numismaticus currency] —**nu′mis•mat′ic** adj. — **nu•mis•ma•tist** (noo MIZ mə tist) n.

num•skull (NUM skul) n. a blockhead; dunce: also spelled numbskull.

nun (nun) n. a woman belonging to a religious order and usu. living in a convent under vows of poverty, chastity, and obedience. [ME]

nun•ci•o (NUN shee OH) n. pl. •ci•os a diplomatic envoy of the Pope to a foreign government. [< Ital.]

nun•ner•y (NUN ə ree) n. pl. •ner•ies a convent. [ME nonnerie]

nup•tial (NUP shəl) adj. of or pertaining to marriage or the marriage ceremony. —n. Usu. pl. a marriage or wedding. [< L nuptialis]

nurse (nurs) n. **1.** a person who cares for the sick, injured, or infirm; esp., one who is trained to do such work. **2.** one who is a graduate of a school of nursing. —v. **nursed, nurs•ing** v.t. **1.** take care of (the sick, injured, or infirm). **2.** feed (an infant) at the breast; suckle. **3.** promote the growth and development of; foster; cherish. **4.** take steps to cure. **5.** preserve or prolong deliberately. —v.i. **6.** act or serve as a nurse. **7.** take nourishment from the breast. **8.** suckle an infant. [ME]

nurse•maid (NURS MAYD) n. a woman employed to care for children.

nurs•er•y (NUR sə ree) n. pl. •er•ies **1.** a place where trees, shrubs, etc., are raised, as for sale. **2.** a room or area set apart for the use of children. **3.** anything that fosters, breeds, or develops.

nursery school a place where children of preschool age regularly meet for training and supervised play.

nursing home a residence for those unable to care for themselves, as the aged or infirm.

nurs•ling (NURS ling) n. **1.** an infant or animal in the stage of being nursed. **2.** anything that is carefully tended or supervised. Also **nurse′ling.**

nur•ture (NUR chəe) n. **1.** that which nourishes; food; sustenance. **2.** training; breeding; education. —v.t. •**tured, •tur•ing 1.** feed or support; nourish. **2.** bring up or train; educate. [ME norture nourish]

nut (nut) n. **1.** a dry fruit consisting of a kernel or seed enclosed in a woody shell, as a walnut, pecan, etc. **2.** a small block of metal having an internal screw thread so that it may be fitted upon a bolt, screw, or the like. **3.** Slang a crazy, irresponsible, or eccentric person. —v.i. **nut•ted, nut•ting** gather nuts. [ME nute]

nut•crack•er (NUT KRAK ər) n. a device for cracking the hard shells of nuts.

nut•meg (NUT meg) n. the aromatic kernel of the fruit of various tropical trees that is ground and used as a spice. [ME notemuge]

nu•tri•ent (NOO tree ənt) n. something that nourishes; food. [< L nutrire nourish] — **nu•tri•ent** adj.

nu•tri•ment (NOO trə mənt) n. **1.** that which nourishes; food. **2.** anything that promotes development. [ME]

nu•tri•tion (noo TRISH ən) n. **1.** the processes by which food is converted into tissue in living organisms. **2.** that which nourishes. —**nu•tri′tion•ist** n.

nu•tri•tious (noo TRISH əs) adj. promoting growth; nourishing. Also **nu•tri•tive** (NOO tri tiv)

nuts (nuts) adj. Slang **1.** crazy; demented; eccentric. **2.** extremely enthusiastic or in love: with about. —interj. an exclamation of contempt, disappointment, etc.

nut•shell (NUT SHEL) n. the shell of a nut. —**in a nutshell** in brief and concise statement or form.

nut•ty (NUT ee) adj. •ti•er, •ti•est **1.** having the flavor of nuts. **2.** Slang crazy. —**nut′ ti•ness** n.

nuz•zle (NUZ əl) v. •zled, •zling v.i. **1.** rub, press, or dig with or as with the nose. **2.** nestle or snuggle; lie close. —v.t. **3.** push or rub the nose, etc., into or against. [ME noselen grovel]

ny•lon (NI lon) n. **1.** a synthetic material of strong fibers; esp., cloth made from these fibers. **2.** pl. stockings made of nylon.

nymph (nimf) *n.* **1.** in Greek and Roman mythology, any of a class of minor female divinities living in forests, fountains, etc. **2.** a young woman or girl. **3.** *Entomol.* the young of an insect undergoing incomplete metamorphosis, at which stage the wing pads are first evident. [ME *nimphe*]

nym·pho·ma·ni·a (NIM fə MAY nee ə) *n.* extreme and ungovernable sexual desire in women. —**nym′pho·ma′ni·ac** *adj. & n.*

O

o, O (oh) *n. pl.* **o's** or **os, O's** or **Os, oes 1.** the fifteenth letter of the English alphabet. **2.** any sound represented by the letter *o.* — *symbol Chem.* oxygen.

o' (ə, oh) *prep.* of: one *o'*clock, man-*o'*-war, jack-*o'*-lantern.

O (oh) *interj.* unsed in direct address, as in prayer or invocation: *O* Lord!

oaf (ohf) *n. pl.* **oafs** a stupid, bungling person. [ME *alfe*] — **oaf'ish** *adj.* — **oaf'ish•ness** *n.*

oak (ohk) *n.* **1.** an acorn-bearing tree or shrub of the beech family, valued for its timber. **2.** the wood of the oak. [ME *ook*] — **oak'en** *adj.*

oar (or) *n.* an implement for propelling or steering a boat, consisting of a long shaft with a blade at one end. [ME *ore*]

o•a•sis (OH ə sis) *n. pl.* **•ses** (-seez) an area in a desert made fertile by groundwater or by irrigation. [< LL]

oat (oht) *n.* **1.** *Usu. pl.* a cereal grass widely cultivated for its edible grain. **2.** *Usu. pl.* the grain itself. **3.** any similar grass. [ME *ote*] — **oat'en** *adj.*

oath (ohth) *n. pl.* **oaths** (oh*th*z) **1.** a formal declaration in support of a pledge or promise, usu. based on an appeal to God. **2.** a profane or vulgar utterance. [ME *ooth*]

oat•meal (OHT MEEL) *n.* a cereal food made from the cooked meal of oats; also, the meal itself.

ob- *prefix* **1.** toward; to; facing: *obverse.* **2.** against; in opposition to: *object, obstruct.* **3.** over; upon: *obliterate.* **4.** completely: *obdurate.* [ME]

ob•bli•ga•to (OB li GAH toh) *n. Music* a part or accompaniment, esp. a solo instrumental accompaniment, essential to the performance of a composition. Also **ob'li•ga'to.** [< Ital.]

ob•du•rate (OB duu rit) *adj.* **1.** unmoved by feelings or moral influence; hardhearted. **2.** difficult to manage; stubborn or unruly. [ME *obdurat* hardened] — **ob'du•rate•ly** *adv.* — **ob'du•ra•cy** *n.*

o•be•di•ent (oh BEE dee ənt) *adj.* **1.** complying with a command, restraint, etc. **2.** yielding to laws or to those in authority. — **o•be'di•ence** *n.*

o•bei•sance (oh BAY səns) *n.* courtesy, reverence, or homage; also, an act or gesture expressing this. [ME *obeisaunce*] — **o•bei'sant** *adj.*

ob•e•lisk (OB ə lisk) *n.* a four-sided shaft of stone, usu. tapering, with a pyramidal top. [< L *obeliscus*]

o•bese (oh BEES) *adj.* very fat. [< L *obesus* eaten up] — **o•bes'i•ty** *n.*

o•bey (oh BAY) *v.t.* **1.** comply with the command etc. of. **2.** comply with (a command etc.). **3.** be guided by. —*v.i.* **4.** be obedient; comply. [ME *obeien*]

ob•fus•cate (OB fə SKAYT) *v.t.* **•cat•ed, •cat•ing 1.** confuse or perplex; bewilder. **2.** darken or obscure. [< LL *obfuscatus* darkened] — **ob'fus•ca'tion** *n.*

o•bi (OH bee) *n.* a broad sash tied with a bow in the back, worn with a kimono. [< Jap., girdle]

o•bit•u•ar•y (oh BICH oo ER ee) *n. pl.* **•ar•ies** a published notice of a person's death. —*adj.* of or recording a death. [< Med.L *obituarius*]

ob•ject[1] (əb JEKT) *v.i.* **1.** feel or state opposition or disapproval. —*v.t.* **2.** offer in opposition. [ME *objecten*] — **ob•jec'tion** *n.*

ob•ject[2] (OB jikt) *n.* **1.** anything that can be apprehended by the senses. **2.** the purpose or end of an action. **3.** one who or that which is the focus or center of thought, action, etc. **4.** *Gram.* **a** a substantive that receives or is affected by the action of the verb, called the **direct object** when it receives the **direct action**, as *pie* in *She gave him the pie,* and the **indirect object** when it receives the secondary action, as *him* in the same sentence. **b** a substantive following a preposition. [ME]

ob•jec•ti•fy (əb JEK tə FI) *v.t.* **•fied, •fy•ing** make objective. — **ob•jec'ti•fi•ca'tion** *n.*

ob•jec•tion•a•ble (əb JEK shə nə bəl) *adj.* deserving of disapproval; offensive.

ob•jec•tive (əb JEK tiv) *adj.* **1.** free from personal feelings, prejudice, etc.; unbiased. **2.** pertaining to what is independent of the mind; real. **3.** treating of or stressing actual phenomena, as distinct from inner or imaginary feelings and thoughts. **4.** *Gram.* denoting the case of the object of a transitive verb or preposition. —*n.* **1.** a goal; end. **2.** *Gram.* **a** the objective case. **b** a word in this case. **3.** a lens or set of lenses, as in a telescope, that is nearest to the object being viewed: also called **object glass.** —**ob·jec'tive·ly** adv. —**ob·jec·tiv·i·ty** (OB jik TIV i tee), **ob·jec'tive·ness** n.

object lesson an example of a principle or moral in a striking instance or occurrence.

ob·jur·gate (OB jər GAYT) v.t. •gat·ed, •gat·ing rebuke severely. [< L objurgatus scolded] —**ob'jur·ga'tion** n.

ob·late (OB layt) adj. flattened at the poles. [< NL oblatus lengthened]

ob·la·tion (o BLAY shən) n. any religious or solemn offering. [ME oblacion]

ob·li·gate (OB li GAYT) v.t. •gat·ed, •gat·ing bind or compel, as by contract, conscience, promise, etc. —adj. (OB li git) bound or restricted.

ob·li·ga·tion (OB li GAY shən) n. **1.** a duty, promise, contract, etc. by which one is bound. **2.** any duty or requirement. **3.** the constraining or binding power of a law, promise, conscience, etc. **4.** what one owes in return for a service, favor, etc. [ME obligacioun] —**o·blig·a·to·ry** (ə BLIG ə TOR ee) adj.

o·blige (ə BLĪJ) v.t. •bliged, •blig·ing **1.** place (one) under obligation, as for a service, favor, etc.: with to. **2.** compel, bind, or constrain. **3.** do a favor or service for. [ME obligen bind]

o·blig·ing (ə BLĪ jing) adj. disposed to do favors. —**o·blig'ing·ly** adv.

o·blique (ə BLEEK) adj. **1.** deviating from the perpendicular or horizontal; slanting. **2.** not direct or straightforward in meaning, expression, etc. —n. an oblique thing, as a line. —v.i. •liqued, •li·quing deviate from the perpendicular or horizontal; slant. [ME oblike] —**o·bliq·ui·ty** (ə BLIK wi tee), **ob·lique'ness** n.

oblique angle Geom. an angle not a right angle; an acute or obtuse angle.

ob·lit·er·ate (ə BLIT ə RAYT) v.t. •at·ed, •at·ing **1.** destroy utterly. **2.** blot or wipe out, as writing. [< L oblitteratus effaced] —**ob·lit'er·a'tion** n.

ob·liv·i·on (ə BLIV ee ən) n. **1.** the state or fact of being completely forgotten. **2.** the state of forgetting completely. [ME]

ob·liv·i·ous (ə BLIV ee əs) adj. **1.** not conscious or aware; with of or to. **2.** forgetful. [ME] —**ob·liv'i·ous·ness** n.

ob·long (OB LAWNG) adj. longer in one dimension than in another; rectangular. —n.

an oblong figure, object, etc. [ME oblonge somewhat long]

ob·lo·quy (OB lə kwee) n. pl. •quies **1.** abusive and defamatory language; vilification. **2.** disgrace resulting from such abuse. [ME]

ob·nox·ious (əb NOK shəs) adj. highly disagreeable; offensive. [< L obnoxiosus harmful]

o·boe (OH boh) n. a double-reed woodwind instrument with a conical bore, having a high, penetrating tone. [< Ital.] —**o'bo·ist** n.

ob·scene (əb SEEN) adj. **1.** offensive to prevailing concepts of morality or decency; indecent; lewd. **2.** disgusting; loathsome; foul. [< L obscenus] —**ob·scen·i·ty** (əb SEN i tee) n.

ob·scure (əb SKYUUR) adj. •scur·er, •scur·est **1.** not clear or plain to the mind; hard to understand. **2.** not readily discovered; hidden; remote. **3.** without distinction or fame; inconspicuous. **4.** having little or no light; dark. —v.t. •scured, •scur·ing **1.** conceal; hide. **2.** cover or darken so as to make dim, indistinct, etc. [ME] —**ob·scu'ri·ty** n.

ob·se·quies (OB si kweez) n. pl. funeral rites. [ME obseques]

ob·se·qui·ous (əb SEE kwee əs) adj. excessively obedient or submissive; sycophantic; servile. [ME] —**ob·se'qui·ous·ness** n.

ob·ser·vance (əb ZUR vəns) n. **1.** the act of observing a command, law, etc. **2.** the act of celebrating a holiday, ceremony, etc. **3.** a customary rite, ceremony, etc. **4.** notice; attention. **5.** Eccl. the rule or constitution of a religious order.

ob·ser·vant (əb ZUR vənt) adj. **1.** perceptive; heedful; alert. **2.** strict or careful in obeying or keeping a custom, law, etc.

ob·ser·va·tion (OB zur VAY shən) n. **1.** the act of observing, or the fact of being observed. **2.** close examination for the purpose of scientific study. **3.** an opinion or judgment.

ob·ser·va·to·ry (əb ZUR və TOR ee) n. pl. •ries a building equipped for the observation of astronomical or other natural phenomena.

ob·serve (əb ZURV) v. •served, •serv·ing v.t. **1.** see or notice; perceive. **2.** make careful observation of, esp. for scientific purposes. **3.** comment; remark. **4.** comply with (a law, custom, etc.); abide by. **5.** celebrate as a holiday. —v.i. **6.** look on or attend without taking part, as at a meeting. [ME *obserpen*] —**ob•serv′a•ble** *adj.*

ob•sess (əb SES) *v.t.* occupy or trouble the mind of; preoccupy. [< L *obsessus* occupied] —**ob•ses′sive** *adj.*

ob•ses•sion (əb SESH ən) *n.* **1.** that which obsesses, as a persistent idea or feeling. **2.** the state of being obsessed.

ob•so•les•cent (OB sə LES ənt) *adj.* going out of use or fashion. —**ob′so•les′cence** *n.*

ob•so•lete (OB sə LEET) *adj.* **1.** gone out of fashion; out-of-date. **2.** no longer used or practiced. [< L *obsoletus* become disused]

ob•sta•cle (OB stə kəl) *n.* a hindrance or obstruction. [ME]

ob•stet•ri•cian (OB sti TRISH ən) *n.* a physician specializing in obstetrics.

ob•stet•rics (əb STE triks) *n. (construed as sing.)* the branch of medicine dealing with pregnancy and childbirth. [< L *obstetrix* midwife] —**ob•stet′ric, ob•stet′ri•cal** *adj.*

ob•sti•nate (OB stə nit) *adj.* unreasonably fixed in one's purpose or opinion; stubborn. [ME] —**ob′sti•na•cy** (-nə see) *n.* —**ob′ sti•nate•ly** *adv.*

ob•strep•er•ous (əb STREP ər əs) *adj.* unruly or noisy, esp. in resistance to control, advice, etc. [< L *obstreperus* noisy]

ob•struct (əb STRUKT) *v.t.* **1.** stop movement through (a way or passage) by obstacles. **2.** block or retard the progress or way of; impede. **3.** be in front of so as to prevent a clear view. [< L *obstructus* piled up] —**ob•struc′tive** *adj.*

ob•struc•tion (əb STRUK shən) *n.* **1.** that which obstructs. **2.** the act of obstructing, or the state of being obstructed.

ob•struc•tion•ist (əb STRUK shə nist) *n.* one who makes a practice of obstructing; esp., one who obstructs debate, legislation, etc. —**ob•struc′tion•ism** *n.*

ob•tain (əb TAYN) *v.t.* **1.** gain possession of, esp. by effort. —*v.i.* **2.** be prevalent or in effect. [ME *obteinen*] —**ob•tain′a•ble** *adj.*

ob•trude (əb TROOD) *v.* **•trud•ed, •trud•ing** *v.t.* **1.** thrust or force (oneself, an opinion, etc.) upon another without request or warrant. **2.** push forward or out; eject. —*v.i.* **3.** intrude oneself. [< L *obtrudere* thrust] —**ob•tru•sive** (əb TROO siv) *adj.* —**ob•tru′sive•ness** *n.*

ob•tuse (əb TOOS) *adj.* **1.** lacking in sharpness of intellect; not quick-witted. **2.** not

sharp; blunt or rounded. [< L *obtusus* dulled] —**ob•tuse′•ness** *n.*

obtuse angle *Geom.* an angle greater than 90° and less than 180°.

ob•verse (ob VURS) *adj.* **1.** turned toward or facing one. **2.** narrower at the base than at the apex. **3.** constituting a counterpart. —*n.* (OB vurs) **1.** the front or principal side of anything; esp., the side of a coin bearing the main design. **2.** a counterpart. [< L *obversus* turned against]

ob•vi•ate (OB vee AYT) *v.t.* **•at•ed, •at•ing** take care of ahead of time; make unnecessary. [< L *obviatus* withstood]

ob•vi•ous (OB vee əs) *adj.* immediately evident. [< L *obvius* in the path] —**ob′vi•ous•ness** *n.*

oc•a•ri•na (OK ə REE nə) *n.* a small musical instrument in the shape of a sweet potato, with a mouthpiece and finger holes. [< Ital., dim. of *oca* goose]

oc•ca•sion (ə KAY zhən) *n.* **1.** the particular time of an event or occurrence; also, the event or occurrence itself. **2.** an important or extraordinary event. **3.** a favorable time or condition; opportunity. **4.** the immediate cause of some action or state. —**on occasion** now and then. —*v.t.* cause, esp. in an accidental or incidental manner. [ME *occasioun*]

oc•ca•sion•al (ə KAY zhə nl) *adj.* **1.** occurring, appearing, etc., now and then. **2.** made, intended, or suitable for a particular occasion: *occasional* verse. —**oc•ca′sion•al•ly** *adv.*

Oc•ci•dent (OK si dənt) *n.* **1.** the countries west of Asia; esp., Europe. **2.** the western hemisphere. [ME]

oc•ci•den•tal (OK si DEN tl) *adj. usu. cap.* of or belonging to the west, or to the countries constituting the Occident. —*n. cap.* one born or living in a western country.

oc•clude (ə KLOOD) *v.* **•clud•ed, •clud•ing** *v.t.* **1.** shut up or close, as pores or openings. **2.** shut in, out, or off. —*v.i.* **3.** meet so that the corresponding cusps fit closely together: said of the teeth. [< L *occludere* close up] —**oc•clu•sion** (ə KLOO zhən) *n.* —**oc•clu′sive** *adj.*

oc•cult (ə KULT) *adj.* **1.** of or pertaining to various magical arts and practices. **2.** beyond human understanding; mysterious. **3.** not divulged or disclosed; secret. —*n.* occult arts or practices. [< L *occultus* hidden] —**oc•cult′ism** *n.*

oc•cul•ta•tion (OK ul TAY shən) *n. Astron.*

concealment of one celestial body by another interposed in the line of vision.

oc·cu·pan·cy (OK yə pən see) *n. pl.* **·cies** the act of occupying, or the state of being occupied.

oc·cu·pant (OK yə pənt) *n.* **1.** one who occupies a place, position, etc. **2.** a tenant.

oc·cu·pa·tion (OK yə PAY shən) *n.* **1.** one's regular, principal, or immediate business or job. **2.** the act of occupying; the state of being occupied. **3.** the taking and holding of land by a military force. —**oc·cu·pa'tion·al** *adj.*

occupational therapy *Med.* the treatment of disabilities by means of work designed to promote recovery or readjustment.

oc·cu·py (OK yə PI) *v.t.* **·pied, ·py·ing 1.** take and hold possession of, as by conquest. **2.** fill or take up (space or time). **3.** inhabit; dwell in. **4.** hold; fill, as an office or position. **5.** busy or engage; employ. [ME *occupien*] —**oc'cu·pi'er** *n.*

oc·cur (ə KUR) *v.i.* **·curred, ·cur·ring 1.** happen or take place; come about. **2.** be found or met with; appear. **3.** suggest itself; come to mind. [< L *occurrere* arrive]

oc·cur·rence (ə KUR əns) *n.* **1.** the act or fact of occurring. **2.** that which occurs; an event.

o·cean (OH shən) *n.* **1.** the body of salt water that covers about 70 percent of the earth's surface. **2.** *Often cap.* any of the five divisions of this body of water, the Atlantic, Pacific, Indian, Arctic, and Antarctic. **3.** a very large expanse or quantity. [ME *oceane*] —**o·ce·an·ic** (OH shee AN ik) *adj.*

o·cea·nog·ra·phy (OH shə NOG rə fee) *n.* the branch of physical geography that treats of oceanic life and phenomena. —**o'cean·og'ra·pher** *n.* —**o'cean·o·graph'ic** *adj.*

o·cher (OH kər) *n.* **1.** an iron oxide mixed with various earthy materials and varying from light yellow to deep red, largely used as a pigment. **2.** a dark yellow color derived from or resembling ocher. Also **o'chre.** [ME *oker*]

o'clock (ə KLOK) of or according to the clock.

oc·ta·gon (OK tə GON) *n. Geom.* a polygon having eight sides and eight angles. [< L *octagonon*] —**oc·tag·o·nal** (ok TAG ə nl) *adj.*

oc·tave (OK tiv) *n.* **1.** *Music* **a** the interval between a tone and another having twice as many or half as many vibrations per second.

b a tone at this interval above or below any other, considered in relation to that other. **2.** any group or series of eight. —*adj. Music* producing tones an octave higher. [ME]

oc·tet (ok TET) *n.* **1.** a musical composition for eight singers or instrumentalists. **2.** a group of eight singers or instrumentalists. **3.** any group of eight. Also **oc·tette'.**

Oc·to·ber (ok TOH bər) the tenth month of the year, containing 31 days. [ME]

oc·to·ge·nar·i·an (OK tə jə NAIR ee ən) *n.* a person between 80 and 90 years of age. —*adj.* [< L *octogenarius* containing eighty]

oc·to·pus (OK tə pəs) *n. pl.* **·pus·es** or **·pi** (-pī) **1.** an eight-armed marine mollusk having a large oval head and rows of suckers along the arms. **2.** any organized power regarded as far-reaching and potentially destructive; esp., a powerful business organization. [< NL]

oc·to·roon (OK tə ROON) *n.* a person of one-eighth black ancestry.

oc·u·lar (OK yə lər) *adj.* of, like, or related to the eye or sight. —*n.* an eyepiece of an optical instrument. [< L *ocularis*]

oc·u·list (OK yə list) *n.* **1.** ophthalmologist. **2.** optometrist.

OD (OH DEE) *v.i.* **OD'd** or **ODed, OD'ing, OD·ing** become ill or die from an overdose of a narcotic. —*n.* **1.** an overdose of a narcotic. **2.** one who takes such an overdose. [< O(VER)D(OSE)]

o·da·lisque (OHD l isk) *n.* a female slave or concubine in an Oriental harem. Also **o'da·lisk.** [< F]

odd (od) *adj.* **·er, ·est 1.** strange or unusual in appearance or behavior; peculiar. **2.** not part of what is regular, usual, or required: *odd jobs.* **3.** being the remainder of an incomplete pair: an *odd* slipper. **4.** leaving a remainder when divided by two: opposed to *even.* **5.** additional to a stated number: seventy-*odd* dollars. [ME *odde*] —**odd'ly** *adv.* —**odd'ness** *n.*

odd·ball (OD BAWL) *n. Informal* an eccentric person. —**odd'ball'** *adj.*

odd·i·ty (OD i tee) *n. pl.* **·ties 1.** one who or that which is odd. **2.** an odd or peculiar quality or trait; an eccentricity. **3.** the state of being odd; strangeness.

odds (odz) *n.pl. (construed as pl.)* **1.** an equalizing allowance or advantage given to a weaker opponent. **2.** a difference to the advantage of one side. —**at odds** at variance; disagreeing.

odds and ends miscellaneous things; scraps.

odds-on (ODZ ON) *adj.* having a better than even chance to win.

ode (ohd) *n.* a lyric poem often in the form of an elaborate address and usually characterized by loftiness of tone, feeling, and style. [< LL *oda*]

o·di·ous (OH dee əs) *adj.* exciting hate or disgust; offensive. [ME] —**o'di·ous·ly** *adv.* —**o'di·ous·ness** *n.*

o·di·um (OH dee əm) *n.* **1.** the state of being odious. **2.** extreme dislike or aversion; hatred. **3.** the reproach or disgrace associated with something hateful. [< L, hatred]

o·dom·e·ter (oh DOM i tər) *n.* a device for measuring distance traveled by a vehicle.

o·dor (OH dər) *n.* **1.** that quality of a substance that renders it perceptible to the sense of smell; scent. **2.** regard or estimation. [< L] —**o'dor·less** *adj.* —**o'dor·ous** *adj.*

o·dor·if·er·ous (OH də RIF ər əs) *adj.* having or giving off an odor, especially a pleasant odor. [ME] —**o'dor·if'er·ous·ness** *n.*

od·ys·sey (OD ə see) *n.* a long, wandering journey. [after the *Odyssey*, an epic poem attributed to Homer]

Oed·i·pus complex (ED ə pəs) *Psychoanal.* a strong attachment of a child to the parent of the opposite sex, esp. of a son to his mother, with antagonism toward the other parent. [after *Oedipus*, legendary Greek ruler who unwittingly killed his father and married his mother] —**Oed'i·pal** (ED ə pəl) *adj.*

of (əv, uv) *prep.* **1.** coming from: Anne *of* Cleves. **2.** included among: Are they *of* our party? **3.** located at: the Leaning Tower of Pisa. **4.** away or at a distance from: within six miles *of* home. **5.** named; specified as: a fall *of* ten feet. **6.** characterized by: men *of* strength. **7.** with reference to: quick *of* wit. **8.** about; concerning: Good is said *of* her. **9.** because of: dying *of* cancer. **10.** possessing. **11.** belonging to: the lid *of* a box. **12.** pertaining to: the majesty *of* the law. **13.** composed of: a ship *of* steel. **14.** containing: a glass *of* water. **15.** from the number or class of: six *of* the seven conspirators. **16.** so as to be without: relieved *of* anxiety. **17.** produced by: the plays *of* Shakespeare. **18.** directed toward: love *of* country. **19.** during, on, or at a specified time: *of* recent years. **20.** set aside for or devoted to: a program *of* music. **21.** before; until: used in telling time: ten minutes *of* ten. [ME]

of course 1. as expected. **2.** certainly.

off (awf) *adj.* **1.** farther or more distant; remote: an *off* chance. **2.** in a (specified) circumstance or situation: well *off*. **3.** incorrect. **4.** not up to standard: an *off* season for roses. **5.** no longer in effect: The deal is *off*. **6.** not on duty: *off* hours. —*adv.* **1.** to a distance; away: My horse ran *off*. **2.** to or at a (specified) future time: put it *off* for a week. **3.** so as to be no longer in place: Take *off* your hat. **4.** so as to be no longer living, continuing, or in operation: kill *off* one's enemies: break *off* talks. **5.** so as to be away from one's work or duties: take the day *off*. **6.** so as to be below standard: His game dropped *off*. —**off and on** now and then; intermittently. —**be off** leave; depart. —*prep.* **1.** so as to be distant from (a position, source, etc): twenty miles *off* course. **2.** not engaged in or occupied with: *off* duty. **3.** extending away or out from; no longer on: *off* Broadway. **4.** so as to be below standard: be *off* one's game. **5.** on or from: living *off* nuts and berries. [ME]

of·fal (AW fəl) *n.* **1.** the waste parts of a butchered animal. **2.** rubbish or refuse of any kind. [ME]

off·beat (AWF BEET) *n. Music* any secondary or weak beat in a measure. —*adj.* (AWF BEET) out of the ordinary; unconventional.

off-col·or (AWF KUL ər) *adj.* **1.** unsatisfactory in color. **2.** indecent; risqué.

of·fend (ə FEND) *v.t.* **1.** give displeasure or offense to; anger. **2.** be disagreeable to (the sense of smell, sight, etc.). —*v.i.* **3.** give displeasure or offense; be offensive. **4.** commit an offense. [ME *offenden* displease]

of·fense (ə FENS) *n.* **1.** a breach of a law; crime or sin. **2.** the act of offending. **3.** that which offends. **4.** the act of attacking or assaulting. **5.** (AW fens) in football, hockey, etc., the team possessing the ball or puck. [ME *offence*] —**give offense** offend. —**take offense** be offended.

of·fen·sive (ə FEN siv) *adj.* **1.** unpleasant or disagreeable. **2.** giving displeasure or offense; causing anger. **3.** of, pertaining to, or characterized by attack. **4.** in sports, of or relating to a team or player in possession of the ball or puck. [< Med.L *offensivus*] —*n.* the movement, attitude, or position of offense or attack. —**of·fen'sive·ly** *adv.* —**of·fen'sive·ness** *n.*

of·fer (AW fər) *v.t.* **1.** present for acceptance or rejection. **2.** suggest for consideration or action; propose. **3.** propose or threaten: *offer* battle. **4.** attempt to do or inflict; also, do or inflict. **5.** suggest as payment: bid. **6.** present for sale. —*v.i.* **7.** present itself; appear. —*n.* **1.** the act of offering. **2.** that which is offered. [ME *offren* present]

of·fer·ing (AW fər ing) *n.* **1.** the act of making an offer. **2.** that which is offered, as a sacrifice or contribution.

of·fer·to·ry (AW fər TOR ee) *n.* *pl.* **·ries** *Eccl.* **1.** *Usu. cap.* a section of the mass during which the bread and wine to be consecrated are offered. **2.** any collection taken during a religious service. **3.** a hymn or anthem sung during this service. [ME *offertorie*]

off·hand (AW HAND) *adv.* without preparation. Also **off'hand'ed·ly.** —*adj.* **1.** done, said, or made offhand. **2.** casual; informal; curt. Also **off'hand'ed.**

of·fice (AW fis) *n.* **1.** a place in which business is carried out; also, those working in such a place. **2.** any post or position of authority. **3.** a duty, charge, or trust. **4.** any act done or intended to be done for another; favor: through his kind *offices*. **5.** a prescribed religious or devotional service; also, any ceremony or rite. [ME]

of·fi·cer (AW fə sər) *n.* **1.** in the armed forces, one holds a position of command or authority. **2.** one holding a position of authority or trust. **3.** on a merchant or passenger ship, the captain or any of the mates. **4.** one who enforces the law, as a police officer. [ME]

of·fi·cial (ə FISH əl) *adj.* **1.** of or relating to an office or position of authority. **2.** supported by or derived from authority. **3.** authorized to carry out some special duty. **4.** formal: *official* banquets. —*n.* one holding an office. [ME] —**of·fi'cial·ly** *adv.*

of·fi·cial·dom (ə FISH əl dəm) *n.* **1.** officials collectively or as a class. **2.** rigid adherence to official forms or routines.

of·fi·ci·ate (ə FISH ee AYT) *v.i.* **·at·ed,** **·at·ing** **1.** act or serve as a priest or minister. **2.** perform the duties or functions of any office.

of·fi·cious (ə FISH əs) *adj.* unduly forward in offering one's services or advice. [< L *officiosus* obliging]

off·ing (AW fing) *n.* that part of the sea visible at some distance from the shore. —**in the offing** soon to happen.

off-put·ting (AWF PUUT ing) *adj.* disagreeable.

off·set (AWF SET) *n.* **1.** that which balances or compensates for something else. **2.** offset printing; also, an impression made by offset printing. **3.** a bend or curve made in a pipe, rod, etc. to enable it to pass an obstacle. —*v.t.* **·set, ·set·ting** **1.** balance or compensate for. **2.** reproduce by offset printing.

offset printing a method of printing in which the inked impression from a plate is transferred to a cylinder, and then onto the paper.

off·shoot (AWF SHOOT) *n.* **1.** *Bot.* a branch from the main stem of a plant. **2.** anything that branches off from a main source.

off·shore (AWF SHOR) *adj.* **1.** situated away from shore: *offshore* structures. **2.** situated beyond the boundaries or control of a government. —*adv.* off or away from shore: The wind blew *offshore*.

off·spring (AWF SPRING) *n.* *pl.* **·spring** or **·springs** the progeny of a person, animal, or plant; descendant.

off-the-shelf (AWF *th*ə SHELF) *adj.* designating a standard part, component, etc. ready for use.

oft·en (AW fən) *adv.* frequently or repeatedly. [ME *oftin*]

o·gle (OH gəl) *v.t. & v.i.* **o·gled, o·gling** look at (someone) or stare in an amorous or coquettish manner. —*n.* an amorous or coquettish look. —**o'gler** *n.*

o·gre (OH gər) *n.* **1.** in fairy tales, a man-eating giant or monster. **2.** one who is brutal, hideous, or feared. [< F]

oh (oh) *interj.* an exclamation expressing surprise, sudden emotion, etc. —*n.* the interjection *oh.*

ohm (ohm) *n.* the unit of electrical resistance. [after George S. *Ohm,* 1787—1854, German physicist]

ohm·me·ter (OHM MEE tər) *n.* a galvanometer for measuring resistance.

oil (oil) *n.* **1.** a greasy, sometimes combustible liquid of vegetable, animal, or mineral origin, used as food, for lubricating, illuminating, and fuel, and in the manufacture of many substances. **2.** petroleum. **3.** an oil color; also, an oil painting. **4.** anything of an oily consistency. —*v.t.* smear, lubricate, or supply with oil. —*adj.* **1.** of or resembling oil. **2.** using, obtained from, or yielding oil. [ME *olie*]

oil color a color or paint made of pigment ground in oil, used chiefly by artists.

oil painting **1.** a painting done in pigments

mixed in oil. 2. the art of painting in oil colors.

oil·y (OI lee) *adj.* **oil·i·er, oil·i·est** 1. of, pertaining to, or containing oil. 2. coated, smeared, or soaked with oil; greasy. 3. smooth or suave in behavior, speech, etc.; unctuous. —**oil′i·ness** *n.*

oint·ment (OINT mənt) *n.* a fatty or oily preparation applied to the skin as a medicine or cosmetic; unguent. [ME *oignement*]

OK (OH KAY) *interj., adj., & adv.* all correct; all right: used to express approval, agreement, etc. —*v.t.* approve, endorse, or agree to; especially, sign with an *OK*. —*n.* approval; agreement; endorsement. Also **O.K.**

o·kra (OH krə) *n.* 1. a tall annual herb. 2. its green pods, used in soups and stews, or as a vegetable. 3. gumbo. [? < West African]

old (ohld) *adj.* **old·er** or **eld·er, old·est** or **eld·est** 1. existing for a long time. 2. showing the characteristics of advanced life, age, or repeated use. 3. having a specified age: a child two months *old*. 4. familiar through long acquaintance or use: an *old* friend. 5. belonging to a remote period in history; ancient. 6. *Usu. cap.* denoting the earlier or earliest of two or more things, periods, developments, etc.: *Old* English; the *Old* Testament. —*n.* past time: days of *old*. [ME] —**old′ish** *adj.*

Old English 1. *Printing* a style of black letter. 2. see under ENGLISH.

old fashioned a cocktail of whisky, sugar, fruit, etc.

old-fash·ioned (OHLD FASH ənd) *adj.* characteristic of or favoring former times, and old customs, beliefs, and ways.

old fo·gy (FOH gee) one who is extremely conservative or old-fashioned. Also **old fo′gey.**

Old French see under FRENCH.

Old Glory the flag of the United States.

old guard the conservative element in a community, political party, etc.

old hat out of style; obsolete.

Old High German see under GERMAN.

Old Icelandic see under ICELANDIC.

Old Latin see under LATIN.

old-line (OHLD LĪN) *adj.* 1. traditional in action or thought. 2. long-established.

old master any of the famous painters who lived between the 13th and 16th centuries; also, any of their paintings.

Old Norse see under NORSE.

Old Testament the first of the two main divisions of the Bible, divided principally into the Pentateuch and the Prophets.

old-time (OHLD TĪM) *adj.* 1. of or characteristic of a former time. 2. of long standing; long-established.

old-tim·er (OHLD TĪM ər) *n. Informal* 1. one who has been a member, resident, etc., for a long time. 2. an old-fashioned person.

old-world (OHLD WURLD) *adj.* 1. of or pertaining to the Old World or Eastern Hemisphere. 2. ancient; antique.

Old World the Eastern Hemisphere, including Europe, Asia and Africa; esp., Europe.

o·le·o (OH lee OH) short for OLEOMARGARINE.

o·le·o·mar·ga·rine (OH lee oh MAHR jə rin) *n.* margarine. Also **o′le·o·mar′ga·rin.**

ol·fac·to·ry (ol FAK tə ree) *adj.* of or pertaining to the sense of smell. —*n. pl.* **·ries** *Usu. pl.* the organ of smell. [< L *olfactorius* smelled at]

ol·i·garch (OL i GAHRK) *n.* a ruler in an oligarchy.

ol·i·gar·chy (OL i GAHR kee) *n. pl.* **·chies** 1. a form of government in which power is restricted to a few; also, a state so governed. 2. the ruling oligarchs. [< Med.L *oligarchia*] —**ol′i·gar′chic, ol′i·gar′chi·cal** *adj.*

ol·ive (OL iv) *n.* 1. a small, oily fruit native to southern Europe and the Middle East. 2. the evergreen tree yielding this fruit. 3. the dull, yellowish green color of the unripe olive: also **olive green.** [ME] —**ol′ive** *adj.*

olive branch 1. a branch of the olive tree as an emblem of peace. 2. any peace offering.

olive drab 1. greenish brown. 2. a woolen or cotton material of this color. 3. a uniform or a pair of trousers made of this cloth.

olive oil oil pressed from olives.

O·lym·pi·ad (ə LIM pee AD) *n.* 1. the interval of four years between two successive celebrations of the Olympic games. 2. the modern Olympic games.

O·lym·pic games (ə LIM pik) 1. in ancient Greece, athletic games held every four years at the plain of Olympia. 2. a modern international revival of the ancient athletic games, held every four years. Also **O·lym′pics.**

om·buds·man (OM bədz mən) *n. pl.* **·men** an official (often a government official) appointed to investigate employees' grievances against their organization, or citizens' grievances against their government. [< Sw.]

o•me•ga (oh MAY gə) *n.* **1.** the twenty-fourth and last letter in the Greek alphabet (Ω, ω), corresponding to English long *o*. **2.** the end; the last. [< Gk. *ō mega* great *o*]

om•e•let (OM lit) *n.* eggs beaten together with milk and cooked slowly over low heat. Also **om′e•lette**. [< F *omelette*]

o•men (OH mən) *n.* a phenomenon or incident regarded as a prophetic sign. [< L]

om•i•cron (OM i KRON) *n.* the fifteenth letter of the Greek alphabet (O, o), corresponding to English short *o*. [< Gk. *o mikron* small *o*]

om•i•nous (OM ə nəs) *adj.* of the nature of or foreshadowed by an evil omen; threatening. [< L *ominosus*] **—om′i•nous•ly** *adv.*

o•mit (oh MIT) *v.t.* **o•mit•ted, o•mit•ting** **1.** leave out; fail to include. **2.** fail to do, make, etc.; neglect. [ME *omitten*] **—o•mis•si•ble** (oh MIS ə bəl) *adj.* **—o•mis•sion** (oh MISH ən) *n.* [ME]

omni- *combining form* all; totally: *omnipotent.* [< L]

om•ni•bus (OM nə BєS) *n.* **1.** a bus. **2.** a printed anthology. **—adj.** providing for many things at the same time: an *omnibus* bill. [< L, for all]

om•nip•o•tent (om NIP ə tənt) *adj.* almighty; not limited in authority or power. **—the Omnipotent** God. [ME] **—om•nip′o•tence** *n.* **—om•nip′o•tent•ly** *adv.*

om•ni•pres•ence (OM nə PREZ əns) *n.* the quality of being everywhere present at the same time. **—om′ni•pres′ent** *adj.* [< Med.L *omnipraesens*]

om•nis•cient (om NISH ənt) *adj.* knowing all things. [< NL *omnisciens*] **—om•nis′ cience** *n.*

om•niv•o•rous (om NIV ər əs) *adj.* **1.** eating both animal and vegetable food. **2.** eager and indiscriminate: an *omnivorous* eater, an *omnivorous* taste for literature. [< L *omnivorus*] **—om•niv′o•rous•ly** *adv.*

on (on) *prep.* **1.** above and supported by. **2.** in contact with any surface or outer part of: a blow *on* the head. **3.** attached to or suspended from: *on* a string. **4.** directed or moving along the course of. **5.** near: the cottage *on* the lake. **6.** within the duration of. **7.** at the occasion of: *On* seeing her, I left. **8.** at the moment or point of: *on* the hour. **9.** in a state or condition of: *on* fire; *on* record. **10.** by means of: *on* wheels. **11.**

using as a means of sustenance, activity, etc.: living *on* fruit. **12.** following after: disease *on* the heels of famine. **13.** sustained or confirmed by: *on* good authority. **14.** with reference to: bet *on* a horse. **15.** concerning; about: a book *on* economics. **16.** engaged in: *on* a journey; *on* duty. **17.** as a result of: making a profit *on* tips. **18.** directed, tending, or moving toward or against: making war *on* the enemy. **19.** *Informal* with: Do you have five dollars *on* you? **20.** *Informal* at the expense of: The joke is *on* them. **—have something on** *Informal* have knowledge, possess evidence, etc., against. **—adv.** **1.** in or into a position or condition of contact, covering, etc.: He put his hat *on*. **2.** in the direction of an activity, performance, etc.: He looked *on* while they played. **3.** ahead, in space or time: later *on*. **4.** in continuous course or succession: The music went *on*. **5.** in or into operation, performance, or existence. **—and so on** and like what has gone before; et cetera. **—on and on** continuously. **—on to** aware of, informed about, or alert to. **—adj.** **1.** being in operation, progress, or application. **2.** near. [ME]

once (wuns) *adv.* **1.** one time; without repetition. **2.** at or during some past time. **3.** at any time; ever. **—once and for all** finally. **—once in a while** occasionally. **—adj.** former. **—conj.** as soon as; whenever. **—n.** one time. **—all at once 1.** all at the same time. **2.** all of a sudden. **—at once 1.** simultaneously. **2.** immediately. [ME *ones*]

once-o•ver (WUNS OH vər) *n. Informal* a quick glance or survey.

on•com•ing (ON KUM ing) *adj.* approaching. **—n.** an approach.

one (wun) *adj.* **1.** being a single person or thing: *one* dollar, in *one* hour. **2.** being or designating an unspecified person or thing: go to Europe *one* day. **3.** being or designating a specified person or thing: *one* friend after another. **4.** closely united or alike; the same: *one* people. **—n.** **1.** a single unit, the first and lowest integer in the numerical series: a cardinal number written 1, I. **2.** a single person or thing. **—pron.** **1.** someone or something; anyone or anything. **2.** an individual or unit among persons or things already mentioned. **—at one** in harmony or accord. **—one another** each other. **— one by one** singly and in succession. [ME *oon*]

one-horse (WUN HORS) *adj.* small; unimportant: *a one-horse town.*

one·ness (WUN nis) *n.* **1.** singleness; unity; sameness. **2.** agreement; concord. **3.** quality of being unique.

on·er·ous (ON ər əs) *adj.* burdensome or oppressive. [ME] **—on'er·ous·ly** *adv.*

one·self (wun SELF) *pron.* a form of the indefinite pronoun *one,* used as a reflexive or as object of a preposition. Also **one's self.**

one-sid·ed (WUN SĪ did) *adj.* **1.** having only one side. **2.** biased; unfair. **3.** unequal or unbalanced: *a one-sided* contest. **—one' -sid'ed·ly** *adv.* **—one'-sid'ed·ness** *n.*

one-time (WUN TĪM) *adj.* former: *a one-time* winner.

one-track (WUN TRAK) *adj.* limited to a single idea or pursuit: *a one-track* mind.

one-up (WUN UP) *adj.* **1.** ahead by one point, as in a game. **2.** in a position of advantage. **—***v.t.* **-upped, -up·ping** gain an advantage over; best.

one-up·man·ship (WUN UP mən SHIP) *n.* the process of gaining or maintaining an advantage.

one-way (WUN WAY) *adj.* moving, or permitting movement, in one direction only.

on·ion (UN yən) *n.* the edible bulb of an herb of the lily family, having a pungent odor and taste. [ME *onyon*]

on-line (ON LĪN) *adj.* being in direct communication with a computer. **—on-line** *adv.*

on·look·er (ON LUUK ər) *n.* one who looks on; a spectator.

on·ly (OHN lee) *adv.* **1.** in one manner or for one purpose alone. **2.** solely; exclusively. **3.** merely; just. **—***adj.* **1.** alone in its class; sole. **2.** standing alone by reason of superior excellence. **—***conj.* except that; but. [ME]

on·o·mat·o·poe·ia (ON ə MAT ə PEE ə) *n.* **1.** the formation of words in imitation of natural sounds, as *crack* or *bow-wow.* **2.** an imitative word. **3.** the use of such words. [< LL] **—on'o·mat'o·poe'ic, on'o·mat'o· po·et'ic** (-poh ET ik) *adj.*

on·rush (ON RUSH) *n.* an onward rush or flow.

on·set (ON SET) *n.* **1.** an attack; assault. **2.** an initial stage, as of illness. **3.** outset; start.

on·shore (ON SHOR) *adv. & adj.* to, toward, or on the shore.

on·slaught (ON SLAWT) *n.* a violent assault. [< Du. *aanslag* attack]

on-the-job (ON thə JOB) *adj.* pertaining to skills acquired while actually doing the job: *on-the-job* training.

on·to (ON too) *prep.* **1.** upon the top of; to and upon. **2.** *Informal* aware of: I'm *onto* (or *on* to) your tricks.

on·tog·e·ny (on TOJ ə nee) *n. Biol.* the history of the development of the individual organism. **—on·to·ge·net·ic** (ON tə jə NET ik) *adj.*

o·nus (OH nəs) *n.* a burden or responsibility. [< L, burden]

on·ward (ON wərd) *adv.* forward in space or time; ahead. Also **on'wards. —***adj.* moving or tending to be forward. [ME]

ooze[1] (ooz) *v.* **oozed, ooz·ing** *v.i.* **1.** flow or leak out slowly or gradually. **2.** exude moisture. **3.** escape or disappear little by little. **—***v.t.* **4.** give off or exude in or as in droplets or a trickle. **—***n.* **1.** a slow, gradual leak. **2.** that which oozes. [ME *wose* moisture]

ooze[2] *n.* **1.** slimy mud or moist, spongy matter, esp. that deposited on the ocean bottom. **2.** muddy or marshy ground; bog.

o·pal (OH pəl) *n.* an amorphous, variously colored mineral, including some varieties esteemed as gemstones. [ME]

o·paque (oh PAYK) *adj.* **1.** impervious to light or other forms of radiation. **2.** impervious to reason; unintelligent. **3.** having no luster; dull. **4.** unintelligible; obscure. [ME *opake* dark] **—o·pac·i·ty** (oh PAS i tee) *n.*

OPEC (OH pek) Organization of Petroleum Exporting Countries.

o·pen (OH pən) *adj.* **1.** affording approach, view, or passage: an *open* door. **2.** public; accessible to all. **3.** not secret or hidden. **4.** expanded; unfolded: an *open* flower. **5.** not enclosed or covered: an *open* car. **6.** ready for business, appointment, etc. **7.** not settled or decided; pending: an *open* question. **8.** available: The job is still *open.* **9.** unbiased; receptive: an *open* mind; *open* to conviction. **10.** generous; liberal: an *open* hand. **11.** having openings or perforations, as needlework. **12.** not deceptive: an *open* face. **13.** without restraints or controls: *open* season. **14.** not restricted by rigid classes, control, etc.: an *open* society. **—***v.t.* **1.** set open or ajar, as a door; unclose; unfasten. **2.** make passable; free from obstacles. **3.** remove the covering, lid, etc. of. **4.** bring into view; unroll; unfold. **5.** make an opening or openings into. **6.** make or declare ready for commerce, use, etc. **7.** give access. **8.** make more receptive to ideas or sentiments: *open* the mind. **9.** reveal: *open* one's heart. **10.** begin; start. —*v.i.* **11.** become open. **12.** come apart or break open; rupture. **13.** come into view; unroll. **14.** afford access or view: The door *opened* on a courtyard. **15.** begin, as a season, theatrical production, etc. —*n.* any wide space not enclosed, obstructed, or covered: usu. with *the:* in the *open.* [ME] —**o'pen·er** *n.* —**o'pen·ly** *adv.* —**o'pen·ness** *n.*

o·pen-air (OH pən AIR) *adj.* occurring, done, etc., out of doors: an *open-air* concert.

o·pen-and-shut (OH pən ən SHUT) *adj.* obvious; easily determined.

open door the policy of giving to all nations the same commercial privileges. —**o·pen-door** (OH pən DOR) *adj.*

o·pen-eyed (OH pən ĪD) *adj.* **1.** having the eyes open; aware; watchful. **2.** amazed: in *open-eyed* wonder.

o·pen-faced (OH pən FAYST) *adj.* **1.** having an honest face. **2.** having a face or side uncovered: an *open-faced* sandwich.

o·pen-hand·ed (OH pən HAN did) *adj.* giving freely.

o·pen-heart·ed (OH pən HAHR tid) *adj.* frank; candid.

o·pen-heart surgery (OH pən HAHRT) surgery during which the heart is open and its circulatory function is performed mechanically.

open house 1. a house or a social event in which hospitality is extended to all who wish to come. **2.** an occasion when a school, factory, institution, etc. is open to visitors.

o·pen·ing (OH pə ning) *n.* **1.** the act of becoming open or of causing to be open. **2.** an open space. **3.** the first part or stage. **4.** a first time or beginning: the play's *opening.* **5.** in chess, checkers, etc., a specific series of early moves. **6.** an opportunity: a job *opening.*

open market a market accessible to all buyers and sellers.

o·pen-mind·ed (OH pən MĪN did) *adj.* free from prejudiced conclusions; receptive. —**o'pen·mind'ed·ness** *n.*

open shop 1. an establishment employing both union and nonunion labor. **2.** an establishment whose policy is to hire only nonunion labor.

op·er·a (OP ər ə) plural of OPUS. —*n.* **1.** a form of drama set to music in which all parts are sung. **2.** an opera house. [< Ital.] —**op·er·at·ic** (OP ə RAT ik) *adj.* —**op'er·at'i·cal·ly** *adv.*

op·er·a·ble (OP ər ə bəl) *adj.* **1.** capable of treatment by surgical operation. **2.** practicable. —**op'er·a·bil'i·ty** *n.*

opera glass small binoculars suitable for use at the theater. Also **opera glasses.**

opera house a theater adapted for performance of operas.

op·er·ate (OP ə RAYT) *v.* **·at·ed, ·at·ing** *v.i.* **1.** act or function; work. **2.** bring about the proper or intended effect. **3.** *Surg.* perform an operation. **4.** carry on a military or naval operation: usu. with *against.* —*v.t.* **5.** control the working of, as a machine. **6.** manage or conduct the affairs of. **7.** bring about or cause; effect. [< LL *operatus* worked]

op·er·a·tion (OP ə RAY shən) *n.* **1.** the act or process of operating. **2.** a method of operating; mode of action. **3.** a transaction, esp. in the stock market. **4.** a course or series of acts to effect a certain purpose; process. **5.** the state of being in action. **6.** *Surg.* the removal or repair of diseased or injured parts of the body by means of surgery. **7.** *Math.* any procedure, as multiplication, addition, etc., that results in a change in the value or form of a quantity. **8.** a military or naval campaign.

op·er·a·tion·al (OP ə RAY shə nl) *adj.* **1.** pertaining to an operation. **2.** checked and serviced for ready operation.

op·er·a·tive (OP ər ə tiv) *adj.* **1.** exerting force or influence. **2.** moving or working efficiently; effective. **3.** being in operation or in force. **4.** connected with surgical operations. **5.** concerned with practical work, mechanical or manual. —*n.* **1.** a skilled worker, as in a mill or factory. **2.** a detective.

op·er·a·tor (OP ə RAY tər) *n.* **1.** one who operates a machine or mechanism; esp., one who operates a telephone switchboard. **2.** one who runs a commercial or industrial establishment.

op·e·ret·ta (OP ə RET ə) *n.* a type of short, humorous opera with dialogue: also called *light opera.* [< Ital.]

oph·thal·mi·a (of THAL mee ə) *n. Pathol.* inflammation of the eye, its membranes, or its lids. [< LL]

oph·thal·mic (of THAL mik) *adj.* of or pertaining to the eye.

oph·thal·mol·o·gy (of thəl MOL ə jee) *n.* the science dealing with the structure, functions, and diseases of the eye. —**oph'thal·mol'o·gist** *n.*

oph·thal·mo·scope (of THAL mə SKOHP)

n. an optical instrument for viewing the center of the eye.

o·pi·ate (OH pee it) *n.* **1.** medicine containing opium or one of its derivatives. **2.** something inducing relaxation or sleep. —*v.t.* (OH pee AYT •at•ed, •at•ing **1.** treat with opium or an opiate. **2.** deaden; dull. —**o' pi·ate** (-it) *adj.*

o·pine (oh PIN) *v.t. & v.i.* **o·pined, o·pin·ing** hold or express as an opinion. [< L *opinari* think]

o·pin·ion (ə PIN yən) *n.* **1.** a conclusion or judgment held with confidence, but falling short of positive knowledge. **2.** an expert judgment given formally. **3.** an evaluation. **4.** a prevailing sentiment: public *opinion.* [ME]

o·pin·ion·at·ed (ə PIN yə NAY tid) *adj.* obstinately attached to one's own opinion.

o·pi·um (OH pee əm) *n.* a narcotic drug obtained from the unripe capsules of the **opium poppy,** containing a mixture of alkaloids, including morphine. [ME]

o·pos·sum (ə POS əm) *n.* a tree-dwelling American marsupial, having a tail and feet adapted for grasping. [< Algonquian]

op·po·nent (ə POH nənt) *n.* one who opposes another, as in battle; antagonist. [< L *opponens* placing against]

op·por·tune (OP ər TOON) *adj.* timely; suitable. [< L *opportunus* favorable] — **op'·por·tune'ly** *adv.* —**op'·por·tune' ness** *n.*

op·por·tu·nist (OP ər TOO nist) *n.* one who uses every opportunity to contribute to achievement of an end, with little concern for principles or sentiment. —**op'·por· tu·nis'tic** *adj.* —**op'·por·tu'nism** *n.*

op·por·tu·ni·ty (OP ər TOO ni tee) *n. pl.* **·ties 1.** a fit or convenient time. **2.** favorable circumstance. **3.** a chance for advancement in business. [ME *opportunite*]

op·pos·a·ble (ə POH zə bəl) *adj.* **1.** capable of being placed opposite something else: said esp. of the thumb. **2.** that can be opposed.

op·pose (ə POHZ) *v.* **·posed, ·pos·ing** *v.t.* **1.** act or be in opposition to; resist. **2.** set in opposition or contrast. **3.** place before or in front. —*v.i.* **4.** act or be in opposition.- [ME]

op·po·site (OP ə zit) *adj.* **1.** situated or placed on the other side, or on each side. **2.** facing or moving the other way: *opposite* directions. **3.** contrary in tendency or character: *opposite* opinions. —*n.* something or

someone that is opposite. —*adv.* in an opposite or complementary direction or position. —*prep.* **1.** across from; facing. **2.** complementary to, as in theatrical roles: He played *opposite* her. [ME]

op·po·si·tion (OP ə ZISH ən) *n.* **1.** the act of opposing or resisting. **2.** the state of being opposite or opposed; antithesis. **3.** a position confronting another or a placing in contrast. **4.** that which is or furnishes an obstacle to some result. [ME *opposicioun*]

op·press (ə PRES) *v.t.* **1.** burden or keep down by harsh and unjust use of force or authority. **2.** lie heavily upon physically or mentally. [ME *oppressen*] —**op·pres'sor** *n.*

op·pres·sion (ə PRESH ən) *n.* **1.** the act of oppressing, or the state of being oppressed. **2.** mental depression. **3.** that which oppresses. [ME *oppressioun*]

op·pres·sive (ə PRES iv) *adj.* **1.** burdensome; tyrannical; harsh. **2.** producing a state of oppression. [< Med.L *oppresivus*] —**op·pres'sive·ness** *n.*

op·pro·bri·ous (ə PROH bree əs) *adj.* **1.** contemptuously abusive. **2.** shameful; disgraceful. [ME] —**op·pro'bri·ous·ness** *n.*

op·pro·bri·um (ə PROH bree əm) *n.* **1.** the state of being scornfully reproached. **2.** reproach mingled with disdain. **3.** a cause of disgrace or reproach. [< L, reproach]

opt (opt) *v.i.* choose; decide. [< F *opter* choose]

op·tic (OP tik) *adj.* pertaining to the eye or vision. [< Med.L *opticus*]

op·ti·cal (OP ti kəl) *adj.* **1.** pertaining to optics. **2.** of or pertaining to eyesight. **3.** designed to assist or improve vision.

op·ti·cian (op TISH ən) *n.* one who makes or deals in optical goods and instruments. [< F *opticien*]

op·tics (OP tiks) *n. (construed as sing.)* the science that deals with light, vision, and sight.

op·ti·mal (OP tə məl) *adj.* most favorable; best.

op·ti·mism (OP tə MIZ əm) *n.* **1.** a disposition to look on the bright side of things. **2.** the doctrine that everything is constantly tending toward a better state. [< F *optimisme*] —**op'ti·mist** (-mist) *n.* —**op'ti·mis'tic** *adj.* —**op'ti·mis'ti·cal·ly** *adv.*

op·ti·mum (OP tə məm) *n. pl.* **·ma** (-mə), **·mums** the condition or degree producing the best result. —*adj.* producing the best results. [< L, best]

op·tion (OP shən) *n.* **1.** the right or power of choosing; discretion. **2.** the act of choosing. **3.** the purchased privilege of either buying or selling something at a specified price within a specified time. **4.** a thing that is or can be chosen. [< F]

op·tion·al (OP shə nl) *adj.* not required.

op·tom·e·try (op TOM i tree) *n.* the profession of measuring vision and prescribing corrective lenses to compensate for visual defects. —**op·tom′e·trist** *n.*

op·u·lent (OP yə lənt) *adj.* **1.** possessing great wealth. **2.** plentiful; abundant; profuse. [< L *opulentus* wealthy] —**op′u·lence** *n.*

o·pus (OH pəs) *n. pl.* **op·er·a** (OH pər ə), **o·pus·es** a literary or musical work or composition. [< L, work]

or (or, ər) *conj.* introducing an alternative: stop *or* go: Will you take milk *or* coffee? [ME]

or·a·cle (OR ə kəl) *n.* **1.** in ancient Greece, a priest who gave out prophecies inspired by a deity. **2.** a person of unquestioned wisdom or knowledge. **3.** any saying perceived as wise. [ME]

o·rac·u·lar (aw RAK yə lər) *adj.* **1.** of or pertaining to an oracle. **2.** obscure; enigmatic. **3.** prophetic; farseeing. [< L *oraculum* oracle] —**o·rac′u·lar′i·ty** (aw RAK yə LAR i tee) *n.*

o·ral (OR əl) *adj.* **1.** uttered through the mouth; spoken. **2.** of or pertaining to the mouth; also, situated at or near the mouth. **3.** taken by mouth. —*n. Usu. pl.* an academic examination in which the student speaks answers aloud. —**o′ral·ly** *adv.*

or·ange (OR inj) *n.* **1.** a round, juicy fruit with a reddish yellow rind and a sweetish pulp. **2.** any of the trees yielding this fruit. **3.** a reddish yellow color. [ME] —**or′ange** *adj.*

o·rate (aw RAYT) *v.i.* **·rat·ed, ·rat·ing** speak in an overly elaborate or pompous manner.

o·ra·tion (ə RAY shən) *n.* an elaborate public speech, esp. one given at a formal occasion. [ME *oracion*]

or·a·tor (OR ə tər) *n.* one who delivers an oration; an eloquent public speaker. [< L]

or·a·to·ri·o (OR ə TOR ee OH) *n. pl.* **·os** a large musical composition for solo voices, chorus, and orchestra, usu. based on a sacred story. [< Ital., small chapel]

or·a·to·ry (OR ə TOR ee) *n.* **1.** the art of public speaking; eloquence. **2.** eloquent language. [< L *oratoria*] —**or′a·tor′i·cal** *adj.*

orb (orb) *n.* **1.** a rounded mass; a sphere. **2.** the eyeball. [< MF *orbe*]

or·bit (OR bit) *n.* **1.** the path in space along which a heavenly body or artificial satellite moves about its center of attraction. **2.** a range of influence or action. —*v.t. & v.i.* move or cause to move in an orbit, as an artificial satellite. [ME] —**or′bi·tal** *adj.*

or·bit·er (OR bi tər) *n.* one who or that which orbits; esp., an artificial satellite.

or·chard (OR chərd) *n.* an area containing trees grown for their products, as fruit, nuts, etc.; also, the trees. [ME *orchiard*]

or·ches·tra (OR kə strə) *n.* **1.** a comparatively large group of musicians playing together. **2.** in a theater, the area in front of the stage, occupied by the musicians: also **orchestra pit. 3.** the main floor of a theater. [< L] —**or·ches·tral** (or KES trəl) *adj.*

or·ches·trate (OR kə STRAYT) *v.t.* **·trat·ed, ·trat·ing 1.** compose or arrange (music) for an orchestra. **2.** organize or direct (diverse elements or aspects) to produce a desired continuity: *orchestrate* a political campaign. —**or′ches·tra′tion** *n.*

or·chid (OR kid) *n.* **1.** any of a family of herbs of temperate and tropical regions, having bulbous roots and often showy flowers. **2.** a pale purple color. [< L *orchis*]

or·dain (or DAYN) *v.t.* **1.** order or decree. **2.** predestine: said of God, fate, etc. **3.** invest with ministerial or priestly functions. [ME *ordeinen* arrange]

or·deal (or DEEL) *n.* a severe test of character or endurance. [ME *ordal*]

or·der (OR dər) *n.* **1.** a methodical, proper, or harmonious arrangement of things. **2.** established method, procedure, or condition. **3.** a command, direction, or regulation. **4.** a style of classical architecture; also, the architectural column representing the style. **5.** a commission or instruction to supply, purchase, or sell something; also, that which is supplied or purchased. **6.** a body of persons united by some common bond: the *Order* of Odd Fellows. **7.** *Eccl.* **a** any of the various grades or degrees of the Christian ministry. **b** the rite or sacrament of ordination. **8.** *Biol.* a taxonomic category ranking next below the class and above the family. —**in order 1.** in accordance with rule or proper procedure. **2.** neat; tidy. —**in order**

that so that; to the end that. **—in order to** for the purpose of. **—in short order** quickly. **—on order** ordered but not yet delivered. **—on the order of** similar to. **—out of order 1.** not in working condition. **2.** not in proper arrangement or sequence. **3.** not according to a rule. **4.** not suitable or appropriate. **—to order** according to the buyer's specifications. *—v.t.* **1.** give a command or direction to. **2.** give an order that (something be done). **3.** put in an orderly arrangement. *—v.i.* **4.** give an order or orders. [ME *ordre*]

or•der•ly (OR dər lee) *adj.* **1.** having regard for arrangement, method, or system. **2.** peaceful. **3.** characterized by neatness and order. **4.** pertaining to orders. *—n. pl.* **•lies 1.** a hospital attendant. **2.** a soldier detailed to perform chores. *—adv.* methodically; regularly. **—or′der•li•ness** *n.*

ordinal number (OR dn əl) *Math.* a number that shows the order of a unit in a given series, as first, second, third, etc.: distinguished from *cardinal number.*

or•di•nance (OR dn əns) *n.* **1.** an order, decree, or law of a municipal body. **2.** a religious rite or ceremony. [ME *ordinaunce* arrangement]

or•di•nar•i•ly (OR dn ER ə lee) *adv.* **1.** in ordinary cases; usually. **2.** in the usual manner. **3.** to the usual extent; normally.

or•di•nar•y (OR dn ER ee) *adj.* **1.** of common or everyday occurrence; usual. **2.** according to an established order; normal. **3.** common in rank or degree; average; commonplace. *—n. pl.* **•nar•ies** that which is usual or common. **—out of the ordinary** not common or usual; extraordinary. [ME *ordinarie* regular] **—or′di•nar′i•ness** *n.*

or•di•nate (OR dn IT) *n. Math.* **1.** the distance of any point from the X-axis, measured on a line parallel to the Y-axis in a coordinate system. **2.** the line or number indicating such distance.

or•di•na•tion (OR dn AY shən) *n.* **1.** *Eccl.* the rite of consecration to the ministry. **2.** the state of being ordained, regulated, or settled.

ord•nance (ORD nəns) *n.* **1.** military weapons, ammunition, and other materiel. **2.** cannon or artillery. [see ORDINANCE]

or•dure (OR jər) *n.* excrement; feces. [ME]

ore (or) *n.* a natural substance, as a rock, containing a valuable metal or nonmetallic mineral. [ME]

or•gan (OR gən) *n.* **1.** a musical instrument

with pipes and reeds made to sound by means of compressed air controlled by keyboards and knobs. **2.** any musical instrument resembling this. **3.** any part of a plant or animal performing some definite function. **4.** a newspaper or periodical published in the interest of a special group. [ME, musical instrument]

or•gan•ic (or GAN ik) *adj.* **1.** of, pertaining to, or of the nature of animals and plants. **2.** affecting or altering the structure of an organ or part: *organic* disease: distinguished from *functional.* **3.** *Chem.* of or pertaining to compounds containing carbon. **4.** inherent in or pertaining to the fundamental structure of something. **5.** grown without artificial fertilizers, pesticides, etc. [ME] **—or•gan′i•cal•ly** *adv.*

organic chemistry the branch of chemistry dealing with compounds containing carbon.

or•gan•ism (OR gə NIZ əm) *n.* **1.** a living animal or plant. **2.** anything seen as similar to a living thing: the social *organism.*

or•gan•ist (OR gə nist) *n.* one who plays the organ.

or•gan•i•za•tion (OR gə nə ZAY shən) *n.* **1.** the act of organizing, or the state of being organized; also, that which is organized. **2.** a number of individuals systematically united for some end or work.

or•gan•ize (OR gə NIZ) *v.* **•ized, •iz•ing** *v.t.* **1.** bring together or form as a whole or combination, as for a common objective. **2.** arrange systematically; order. **3.** furnish with organic structure. **4.** enlist (workers) in a trade union. **5.** unionize the workers of (a factory, etc.). *—v.i.* **6.** form or join an organization.

or•gasm (OR gaz əm) *n. Physiol.* the peak of excitement at the culmination of a sexual act. [< NL *orgasmus*] **—or•gas′mic** *adj.*

or•gy (OR jee) *n. pl.* **•gies 1.** wild or wanton revelry. **2.** a party characterized by promiscuous sexual behavior. **3.** any excessive indulgence. [< MF *orgie*] **—or•gi•as•tic** (OR jee AS tik) *adj.*

o•ri•ent (OR ee ənt) *n.* the east. *—v.t.* (OR ee ENT) **1.** cause to face or turn to the east. **2.** place or adjust, as a map, in exact relation to the points of the compass. **3.** adjust in relation to a situation, institution, etc. [ME] **—o•ri•en•tal** (OR ee EN tl) *adj.*

O•ri•ent (OR ee ənt) *n.* **1.** the countries east of Europe; esp., eastern Asia. **2.** the eastern hemisphere. **—O•ri•en•tal** (OR ee EN tl) *adj.* —**Oriental** *n.* an Asiatic: considered objectionable by many. [ME]

o·ri·en·ta·tion (OR ee en TAY shən) *n.* **1.** the act of orienting, or the state of being oriented. **2.** a meeting or series of meetings designed to acquaint newcomers with the rules, programs, etc., of a school, business, etc.

or·i·fice (OR ə fis) *n.* an opening into a cavity; aperture. [< MF]

or·i·ga·mi (OR i GAH mee) *n.* the ancient Japanese art of folding single sheets of paper into the forms of animals, flowers, etc. [< Jap.]

or·i·gin (OR i jin) *n.* **1.** the beginning of the existence of anything. **2.** a primary source; cause. **3.** parentage; ancestry. [ME]

o·rig·i·nal (ə RIJ ə nl) *adj.* **1.** of or belonging to the beginning, origin, or first stage of existence of a thing. **2.** produced by one's own mind; not copied or imitative. **3.** able to produce new works without imitating others; creative; inventive. —*n.* **1.** the first form of anything. **2.** an original work, as distinct from a reproduction or copy. **3.** a person of unique character or genius. [ME] —**o·rig'i·nal'i·ty** (ə RIJ ə NAL i tee) *n.* — **o·rig'i·nal·ly** *adv.*

o·rig·i·nate (ə RIJ ə NAYT) *v.* **·nat·ed, ·nat·ing** *v.t.* **1.** bring into existence; create; initiate. —*v.i.* **2.** come into existence; arise. —**o·rig'i·na'tor** *n.*

or·na·ment (OR nə mənt) *n.* **1.** something that adorns or beautifies; a decoration. **2.** ornaments, collectively. **3.** *Music* a tone or group of tones used to embellish a melody without materially affecting its harmonic content. —*v.t.* (OR nə MENT **1.** furnish with ornaments; decorate. **2.** be an ornament to. [ME] —**or'na·men·ta'tion** *n.*

or·na·men·tal (OR nə MEN tl) *adj.* of the nature of or serving as an ornament. —*n.* an ornamental object; esp., a plant used as decoration. —**or'na·men'tal·ly** *adv.*

or·nate (or NAYT) *adj.* **1.** elaborately or excessively ornamented; overdecorative. **2.** showy, as a style of writing. [ME]

or·ner·y (OR nə ree) *adj. Dial.* **1.** contrary or stubborn. **2.** mean; ugly. **3.** ordinary; common. [Alter. of ORDINARY] —**or'ner·i·ness** *n.*

or·ni·thol·o·gy (OR nə THOL ə jee) *n.* the branch of zoology that treats of birds. [< NL *ornithologia*] —**or'ni·tho·log'i·cal** *adj.* —**or'ni·thol'o·gist** *n.*

o·ro·tund (OR ə TUND) *adj.* **1.** full, clear, rounded, and resonant: said of the voice. **2.** pompous; inflated, as a manner of speech. [< L *ore rotundo* with round mouth] — **o'ro·tun'di·ty** *n.*

or·phan (OR fən) *n.* a child whose parents are dead; also, less commonly, a child with one surviving parent. —*adj.* **1.** that is an orphan. **2.** of or for orphans. [ME] —*v.t.* make an orphan of.

or·phan·age (OR fə nij) *n.* an institution for care of orphans or other abandoned children.

ort (ort) *n. Usu. pl.* a scrap or bit of food left after a meal. [ME]

or·thi·con (OR thi KON) *n.* a sensitive television camera tube using low-velocity electrons in scanning.

ortho- *combining form* **1.** straight; in line. **2.** at right angles; perpendicular. **3.** correct; proper; right: *orthography.* **4.** *Med.* the correction of irregularities or deformities of: *orthopedics.* [< Gk. *orthós* straight]

or·tho·don·tics (OR thə DON tiks) *n.* the branch of dentistry concerned with the prevention and correction of irregularities of the teeth. Also **or'tho·don'tia** (-shə). — **or'tho·don'tist** *n.*

or·tho·dox (OR thə DOKS) *adj.* holding the commonly accepted or established views or beliefs, esp. in religion; correct or sound in doctrine. [< LL *orthodoxus*] —**or' tho·dox'y** *n.*

Or·tho·dox *adj.* **1.** of, belonging to, or characteristic of the Eastern Orthodox Church. **2.** designating any of the bodies in this Church.

Orthodox Church the Eastern Orthodox Church.

Orthodox Judaism the branch of Judaism that accepts the Mosaic laws and their authoritative rabbinical interpretations in the Talmud and elsewhere as binding for today.

or·thog·ra·phy (or THOG rə fee) *n. pl.* **·phies 1.** a mode or system of spelling, esp. of spelling correctly. **2.** the study dealing with letters and spelling. [ME *ortografye*] —**or·thog'ra·pher, or·thog'ra·phist** *n.* —**or·tho·graph·ic** (OR thə GRAF ik) *adj.*

or·tho·pe·dics (OR thə PEE diks) *n. (construed as sing.)* the branch of medicine concerned with the correction of deformities of the skeletal system. —**or'tho·pe'dic** *adj.* —**or'tho·pe'dist** *n.*

os·cil·late (OS ə LAYT) *v.i.* **·lat·ed, ·lat·ing 1.** swing back and forth, as a pendulum. **2.** fluctuate; hesitate; waver. [< L *oscillatus* swung] **—os'cil·la'tion** n. **—os·cil·la·to·ry** (OS ə lə TOR ee) adj.

os·cil·lo·graph (ə SIL ə GRAF) n. a device for recording and measuring any oscillating system convertible into wave forms, as sound, light, heartbeats, etc.

os·cil·lo·scope (ə SIL ə SKOHP) n. any of various electronic instruments displaying electromagnetic waves on a fluorescent screen.

os·cu·late (OS kyə LAYT) v.t. & v.i. **·lat·ed, ·lat·ing 1.** kiss: used humorously. **2.** come into close contact or union. [< L osculatus kissed] **—os'cu·la'tion** n.

-ose[1] suffix of adjectives **1.** full of or abounding in (the main element): verbose. **2.** like; resembling (the main element): grandiose. [< L -osus]

-ose[2] suffix Chem. indicating a sugar or other carbohydrate: lactose, fructose.

-osis suffix of nouns **1.** the condition, process, or state of: metamorphosis. **2.** Med. **a** a diseased or abnormal condition of: neurosis. **b** a formation of: sclerosis. [< Gk.]

os·mo·sis (oz MOH sis) n. Chem. **1.** the diffusion of a fluid through a semipermeable membrane, resulting in equalization of concentrations on each side. **2.** the tendency of a fluid to act in such a manner. [< NL] **—os'mose** (OZ mohs) v.i. **·mosed, ·mos·ing —os·mot·ic** (oz MOT ik) adj.

os·si·fy (OS i FI) v.t. & v.i. **·fied, ·fy·ing 1.** convert or be converted into bone. **2.** make or become rigid or inflexible in habits, beliefs, etc.; harden. **—os'si·fi·ca'tion** n.

os·ten·si·ble (o STEN sə bəl) adj. offered as real or genuine; apparent. [< F] **—os·ten'si·bly** adv.

os·ten·sive (o STEN siv) adj. manifest; apparent; ostensible. **—os·ten'sive·ly** adv.

os·ten·ta·tion (OS tən TAY shən) n. **1.** the act of displaying vainly or pretentiously. **2.** excessive exhibition; showiness. [ME ostentacioun] **—os'ten·ta'tious** adj. **—os'ten·ta'tious·ness** n.

osteo- combining form bone; pertaining to bone or bones. [< Gk. ostéon bone]

os·te·op·a·thy (os tee OP ə thee) n. a system of healing based on the theory that many diseases are the result of structural abnormalities of the body and may be cured by manipulation of the affected parts. [< OSTEO- + -PATHY] **—os·te·o·path** (OS tee ə PATH) n. **—os·te·o·path·ic** (OS tee ə PATH ik) adj.

os·tra·cize (OS trə SIZ) v.t. **·cized, ·ciz·ing 1.** shut out or exclude, as from society or from a particular group; banish. **2.** exile by ostracism. [< Gk. ostrakízein banish] **—os·tra·cism** (OS trə SIZ əm) n.

os·trich (OS trich) n. **1.** a flightless bird of Africa and Arabia, the largest of existing birds. **2.** anyone who tries to ignore unpleasant situations. [ME ostriche]

oth·er (UTH ər) adj. **1.** different, esp. from the one or ones specified or implied. **2.** noting the remaining one of two persons or things: the other eye. **3.** additional; more. **4.** alternate; second: every other day. **5.** former: in other times. **—pron. 1.** another or different person or thing. **2.** the other person or thing: this hand, not the other. **—adv.** differently; otherwise: with than. [ME] **—oth'er·ness** n.

oth·er·wise (UTH ər WIZ) adv. **1.** in a different manner; by other means. **2.** in other circumstances or conditions. **3.** in all other respects: an otherwise sensible person. **—adj.** other than supposed; different.

oth·er·world·ly (UTH ər WURLD lee) adj. concerned with matters of the spirit or intellect, esp. to the neglect of material things. **—oth'er·world'li·ness** n.

o·ti·ose (OH shee OHS) adj. **1.** being at rest; indolent; lazy. **2.** having no use or effect; futile. [< L otiosus idle]

ou·bli·ette (OO blee ET) n. a secret dungeon with an entrance only through the top. [< F]

ouch (owch) interj. an exclamation of sudden pain.

ought (awt) v. present 3rd person sing. an auxiliary followed by the infinitive, with to expressed or understood, meaning: **1.** have a moral duty: People ought to keep their promises. **2.** be advisable: You ought to be careful. **3.** be expected as something probable, natural, or logical: The engine ought to run. [ME]

Oui·ja (WEE jə) n. a board inscribed with the alphabet and other characters and over which is moved a small board resting on three legs, which is considered to spell out communications: a trade name. Also **Ouija board.**

ounce (owns) n. **1.** a unit of weight; $\frac{1}{16}$ pound avoirdupois or 28.349 grams; $\frac{1}{12}$ pound troy or 31.1 grams. **2.** a fluid ounce. **3.** a small quantity. [ME unce]

our (OW ər) pronominal adj. the possessive case of the pronoun we, used attributively: our child. [ME oure]

ours (OW ərz) *pron.* **1.** a form of the possessive case of *we*, used predicatively: That dog is *ours*. *Ours* is better. **2.** the one or ones belonging or relating to us: their country and *ours*.

our•selves (ahr SELVZ) *pron.pl.* (**ourself**, the singular, is used by monarchs etc.) a form of *we*, used: **1.** as a reflexive: We helped *ourselves*. **2.** as an emphatic or intensive: We *ourselves* want to know. **3.** as a designation of a normal, proper, or usual state: We weren't *ourselves* then.

oust (owst) *v.t.* force out or remove, as from a place or position. [ME]

oust•er (OW stər) *n.* **1.** the act or condition of ousting. **2.** one who ousts. [< AF]

out (owt) *adv.* **1.** away from the inside or center. **2.** in or into the open air. **3.** away from a specified or usual place: *out* to lunch. **4.** from a container or source: pour *out* wine. **5.** from among others: pick *out*. **6.** so as to remove, deplete, or exhaust: sweep *out*. **7.** thoroughly: tired *out*. **8.** into extinction or inactivity: The excitement died *out*. **9.** to a conclusion; to the end: Hear me *out*. **10.** into being or activity, or into a perceptible form: The sun came *out*. **11.** in or into circulation: bring *out* a new edition. **12.** aloud and boldly: speak *out*. **13.** so as to be extended or projecting: lean *out*. **14.** into the care or control of another or others: deal *out* cards. **15.** into a state of tension, irritation, etc.: be put *out* over trifles. **16.** in or into a condition of disuse or obsolescence. **17.** in baseball, so as to be or count as an out. **18.** into unconsciousness: pass *out*. —**out and away** by far; incomparably. —**out of 1.** from the inside of; from among. **2.** beyond the limits, scope, or usual position of: *out of* sight; *out of* joint. **3.** from (a material etc.): made *out of* tin. **4.** inspired or caused by: *out of* pity. **5.** without (any): *out of* breath. —**out to** with the intention of. —*adj.* **1.** external; exterior. **2.** irregular: an *out* size. **3.** not in working order. **4.** at a financial loss: *out* five dollars. **5.** not to be considered: That approach is *out*. **6.** distant; outlying. **7.** not in office or in power. **8.** no longer in use; out-of-date. —*prep.* from within; forth from: *out* the door. —*n.* **1.** one who or that which is out. **2.** a way of dodging responsibility or involvement: look for an *out*. **3.** in baseball, the retirement of a batter or base runner. —**on the outs** *Informal* involved

in a disagreement; at odds. —*v.i.* come out; be revealed: Murder will *out*. —*interj.* Get out! Away! [ME]

out- *combining form* **1.** living or situated outside; away from the center; detached: *outlying, outpatient.* **2.** going forth; outward: *outbound, outstretch.* **3.** to a greater extent; more; better.

Out- (def. 3) is used to form compounds, as in the list below.

outact	outbeg
outargue	outbellow
outbargain	outbluff
outblush	outplay
outbluster	outpopulate
outboast	outpreach
outbox	outprice
outbrag	outproduce
outbrazen	outquote
outbuild	outrank
outbully	outrival
outcharm	outrun
outclimb	outsatisfy
outcook	outscold
outcurse	outscream
outdazzle	outshout
outdress	outshriek
outdrink	outsleep
outeat	outsparkle
outfight	outstare
outflatter	outstay
outgallop	outstretch
outgamble	outstrive
outglitter	outswagger
outguess	outswindle
outhear	outtalk
outjump	outtrick
outlast	outvalue
outlearn	outvote
outmaneuver	outwrestle
outperform	outyield

out•age (OW tij) *n.* an accidental break in operation, as of electrical power.

out-and-out (OWT n OWT) *adj.* unqualified; outright.

out•bid (OWT BID) *v.t.* **•bid, •bid•den** or **•bid, •bid•ding** offer a higher bid than.

out•board (OWT BORD) *adj. & adv.* *Naut.* **1.** outside the hull. **2.** away from the center line of a vessel.

outboard motor a portable motor for attachment to the stern of a small boat.

out•bound (OWT BOWND) *adj.* outward bound.

out•break (OWT BRAYK) *n.* a sudden bursting forth, as of a disease; an eruption.

out·build·ing (OWT BIL ding) n. a building separate from and subordinate to a main building, as a woodshed or barn.

out·burst (OWT BURST) n. a bursting out; esp., a sudden and violent display, as of anger.

out·cast (OWT KAST) n. 1. one who is cast out or excluded. 2. a homeless person or vagabond. 3. anything cast out, as refuse. —adj. rejected; discarded; forlorn.

out·class (OWT KLAS) v.t. surpass decisively.

out·come (OWT KUM) n. consequence or result.

out·crop (OWT KROP) n. Geol. 1. the exposure at or above the surface of the ground of any rock stratum, vein, etc. 2. the rock so exposed. —v.i. (OWT KROP) •cropped, •crop·ping crop out above the ground, as rocks.

out·cry (OWT KRĪ) n. pl. •cries 1. a loud cry or clamor. 2. a vehement outburst of alarm, indignation, etc. —v.t. (OWT KRĪ) •cried, •cry·ing surpass in noise or crying.

out·date (OWT DAYT) v.t. •dat·ed, •dat·ing make obsolete or out-of-date.

out·dat·ed (OWT DAY tid) adj. out-of-date; old-fashioned.

out·dis·tance (OWT DIS təns) v.t. •tanced, •tanc·ing 1. outrun, as in a race; outstrip. 2. surpass completely.

out·do (OWT DOO) v.t. •did, •done, •do·ing exceed in performance; surpass.

out·door (OWT DOR) adj. 1. being or done in the open air. 2. intended for the outdoors.

out·doors (OWT DORZ) adv. outside of the house; in the open air. —n. the world beyond the house; the open air.

out·er (OW tər) adj. 1. being on the exterior side. 2. farther from a center or the inside. [ME]

out·er·most (OW tər MOHST) adj. most remote from the inside or inner part; farthest out. [ME]

outer space the space beyond the outer limits of the earth's atmosphere.

out·face (OWT FAYS) v.t. •faced, •fac·ing 1. face or stare down. 2. defy or confront fearlessly or impudently.

out·field (OWT FEELD) n. in baseball: a the space beyond the infield. b the outfielders collectively.

out·field·er (OWT FEEL dər) n. in baseball, any of three players whose positions are in the outfield.

out·fit (OWT FIT) n. 1. the tools or equipment needed for any particular purpose, as a trade etc. 2. a group of persons regarded as a unit; esp., a military unit. 3. a set of clothing. —v.t. & v.i. •fit·ted, •fit·ting provide with or acquire an outfit.

out·flank (OWT FLANGK) v.t. 1. get around the flank of; flank. 2. outmaneuver.

out·flow (OWT FLOH) n. 1. that which flows out. 2. the act or process of flowing out.

out·fox (OWT FOKS) v.t. outwit.

out·go·ing (OWT GOH ing) adj. 1. going out; leaving. 2. friendly; expansive. —n. the act of going out.

out·group (OWT GROOP) n. Sociol. those not in an in-group.

out·grow (OWT GROH) v.t. •grew, •grown, •grow·ing 1. grow too large for. 2. lose or get rid of in the course of time or growth: outgrow a habit. 3. surpass in growth.

out·growth (OWT GROHTH) n. 1. that which grows out of something else; an excrescence. 2. a natural result or development. 3. the process of growing out.

out·house (OWT HOWS) n. an outdoor toilet.

out·ing (OW ting) n. 1. a short pleasure trip; an excursion. 2. the act of going out; an airing.

out·land·ish (owt LAN dish) adj. 1. strange or unfamiliar. 2. freakish; crazy. 3. far-off; remote. [ME] —**out·land'ish·ly** adv. —**out·land'ish·ness** n.

out·law (OWT LAW) n. 1. one who habitually breaks or defies the law; a criminal. 2. one deprived of the protection or benefit of the law. —v.t. 1. prohibit; ban. 2. deprive of legal force or protection, as a contract. 3. declare (a person) an outlaw. [ME outlawe] —**out'law'ry** n.

out·lay (OWT LAY) n. 1. the act of disbursing or spending. 2. the amount spent; expenditure. —v.t. (OWT LAY) •laid, •lay·ing expend (money etc.).

out·let (OWT let) n. 1. a passage or vent for escape or discharge. 2. a channel of expression or escape. 3. in commerce, a market for any commodity; also, a store handling the goods of a particular manufacturer. 4. Electr. the point in a wiring system at which the current is taken to supply electrical apparatus.

out·line (OWT LĪN) n. 1. Sometimes pl. a sketch of the principal features of a thing; general plan. 2. a systematic statement of the structure or content of an essay etc. 3. the bordering line that defines a figure. 4. a sketch made of such lines. —v.t. •lined, •lin•ing 1. make an outline of. 2. draw the outline of.

out•live (OWT LIV) v.t. •lived, •liv•ing 1. live longer than. 2. live through; survive. [ME outliven]

out•look (OWT LUUK) n. 1. a point of view. 2. the prospects of a thing. 3. a place where something is viewed. 4. the expanse in view.

out•mo•ded (OWT MOH did) adj. out of fashion.

out-of-date (OWT əv DAYT) adj. old-fashioned; archaic.

out-of-doors (OWT əv DORZ) adv. & n. outdoors.

out-of-the-way (OWT əv thə WAY) adj. 1. remote; difficult to reach; secluded. 2. out of the common range; odd.

out•pa•tient (OWT PAY shənt) n. a patient treated at but not formally admitted to a hospital.

out•post (OWT POHST) n. 1. a detachment of troops stationed at a distance from the main body as a guard against surprise attack. 2. the station occupied by such troops. 3. any outlying settlement, as at a frontier.

out•pour (OWT POR) v.t. & v.i. pour out. —n. (OWT POR a free outflow. —out'•pour'ing n.

out•put (OWT PUUT) n. 1. the amount of anything produced in a given time. 2. the effective work done by a machine. 3. Electr. the electrical energy delivered by a generator, circuit, amplifier, etc.

out•rage (OWT rayj) n. 1. an act of shocking violence, cruelty, immorality, or indecency. 2. a profound insult or injury. 3. a state of anger over an outrageous act. —v.t. •raged, •rag•ing 1. commit an outrage upon. 2. provoke to anger by an outrage. 3. rape. [ME]

out•ra•geous (owt RAY jəs) adj. 1. of the nature of an outrage; awful; atrocious. 2. heedless of authority or decency. —out•ra'geous•ly adv. —out•ra'geous•ness n.

ou•tré (oo TRAY) adj. French strikingly odd; exaggerated.

out•reach (OWT REECH) v.t. 1. reach or go beyond; surpass. 2. extend (something). —v.i. 3. reach out. —n. (OWT REECH the act or extent of reaching out.

out•rig•ger (OWT RIG ər) n. 1. a part that projects beyond a natural outline, as of a vessel or machine, esp. the projection terminating in a float, braced to the side of a canoe to prevent capsizing. 2. a boat equipped with an outrigger.

out•right (OWT RIT) adj. 1. free from reserve or restraint; downright. 2. complete; entire. —adv. (OWT RIT 1. without reservation or limitation; openly. 2. entirely; utterly. 3. without delay.

out•set (OWT SET) n. a beginning; start.

out•shine (OWT SHIN) v.t. •shone, •shin•ing 1. shine brighter than. 2. surpass.

out•side (OWT SID) n. 1. the outer or exterior surface or side. 2. the space beyond a bounding line or surface. 3. the part that is seen; outward appearance. 4. mere outward display. —at the outside at the utmost limit. —adj. (OWT SID) 1. pertaining to, located on, or restricted to the outside. 2. originating, caused by, or situated beyond designated limits or boundaries. 3. reaching the limit; extreme: an outside estimate. 4. slight; slim: an outside possibility. —adv. (OWT SID) 1. on or to the outside; externally. 2. beyond the outside limits of. 3. outdoors. —prep. (OWT SID) 1. on or to the exterior of. 2. beyond the limits of. —outside of excepting; other than.

out•size (OWT SIZ) n. an irregular size, as of clothing; esp., an uncommonly large size. —out'size', out'sized' adj.

out•skirts (OWT SKURTS) n.pl. a place remote from the main area.

out•spo•ken (OWT SPOH kən) adj. bold in speech; frank. —out'•spo'ken•ness n.

out•spread (OWT SPRED) v.t. & v.i. •spread, •spread•ing spread out; extend. [ME outspredden] —out•spread adj. (OWT SPRED)

out•stand•ing (OWT STAN ding) adj. 1. prominent; excellent. 2. still standing or unsettled, as a debt. 3. projecting; abutting.

out•strip (OWT STRIP) v.t. •stripped, •strip•ping 1. leave behind; outrun. 2. excel; surpass.

out•ward (OWT wərd) adj. 1. of, pertaining to, or leading to the outside; external. 2. superficially evident or readily apparent: no outward sign of trouble. —adv. toward the outside: also out'wards. [ME] —out'ward•ly adv. —out'ward•ness n.

out•weigh (OWT WAY) v.t. 1. weigh more than. 2. exceed in importance, value, etc.

out•wit (OWT WIT) v.t. •wit•ted, •wit•ting trick or baffle by superior cunning.

out·work (OWT WURK) *v.t.* **·worked** or **·wrought, ·work·ing** work faster or better than. —*n. Mil.* (OWT WURK) any outer defense, as beyond the ditch of a fort. [ME]

o·va (OH və) plural of OVUM.

o·val (OH vəl) *adj.* **1.** having the shape of an egg. **2.** resembling an ellipse. —*n.* an oval shape or figure. [< NL *ovalis*]

o·va·ry (OH və ree) *n. pl.* **·ries 1.** *Zool.* the genital gland of female animals in which the ova are produced. **2.** *Bot.* in plants, that organ in which the ovules are contained. [< NL *ovarium*] —**o·var·i·an** (oh VAIR ee ən) *adj.*

o·va·tion (oh VAY shən) *n.* a spontaneous acclamation of popularity; enthusiastic applause. [< L *ovatio*]

ov·en (UV ən) *n.* an enclosed chamber for baking, heating, or drying. [ME]

o·ver (OH vər) *prep.* **1.** in or to a place or position above; higher than. **2.** so as to pass or extend across: walking *over* a bridge. **3.** on the other side of: *over* the ocean. **4.** upon the surface or exterior of. **5.** here and there upon or within: traveling *over* land and sea. **6.** at or up to a level higher than: water *over* one's head. **7.** so as to close or cover. **8.** during or beyond: stay *over* Christmas. **9.** more than; in excess of. **10.** in preference to. **11.** in a position to guide or control. **12.** with regard to: time wasted *over* trifles. —**over and above** in addition to; besides. — *adv.* **1.** above; overhead. **2.** to another or opposite side, or to a specified place; across: Try to leap *over.* Bring your friend *over.* **3.** at or on the other side; at a distance in a specified direction or place: *over* in France. **4.** from one side, opinion, or attitude to another. **5.** from one person, condition, or custody to another. **6.** so as to close, cover, or be covered: The pond froze *over.* **7.** from beginning to end: I'll think the matter *over.* **8.** so as to bring the underside upward. **9.** from an upright position. **10.** once more; again. **11.** so as to constitute a surplus: have some left *over.* **12.** beyond or until a stated time. —**over and over** time and again; repeatedly. —*adj.* **1.** finished; done; past. **2.** on the other side; having got across. **3.** outer; superior; upper. **4.** in excess or addition; extra. [ME]

over- *combining form* **1.** above; superior: *overlord.* **2.** passing above; going beyond the top or limit of: *overflow.* **3.** excessively; excessive.

Over- (def. 3) is widely used to form compounds, as in the list beginning below.

overabundance	overbusy
overabundant	overbuy
overaccentuate	overcapable
overactive	overcareful
overambitious	overcaring
overambitiously	overcautious
overanalyze	overcautiously
overanxious	overcharitable
overapprehensive	overcivilized
overassertive	overclean
overassess	overcompensate
overassessment	overcompetitive
overattached	overcomplacent
overattentive	overcompliant
overattentively	overconcern
overbake	overconfidence
overbid	overconfident
overbold	overconscientious
overboldly	overconservative
overborrow	overconsiderate
overbred	overconsumption
overbreed	overcook
overbuild	overcount

o·ver·age¹ (OH vər ij) *n.* in commerce, an amount of money or goods in excess of that which is listed as being on hand.

o·ver·age² (OH vər AYJ) *adj.* **1.** over a specified age. **2.** too old to be of use.

o·ver·all (OH vər AWL) *adj.* including or covering everything.

o·ver·alls (OH vər AWLZ) *n.pl.* loose, coarse trousers, often with suspenders and a piece extending over the breast.

o·ver·awe (OH vər AW) *v.t.* **awed, ·aw·ing** subdue or restrain by awe.

o·ver·bear·ing (OH vər BAIR ing) *adj.* **1.** arrogant; domineering. **2.** overwhelming.

o·ver·blown (OH vər BLOHN) *adj.* **1.** blown up or swollen, as with conceit; bombastic. **2.** past full bloom, as a flower.

o·ver·board (OH vər BORD) *adv.* over the side of or out of a boat or ship. —**go over-board** go to extremes, esp. in approval or disapproval of someone or something.

overcourteous	overestimate
overcritical	overexcitable
overcrowd	overexcite
overcurious	overexercise
overdecorate	overexert
overdelicate	overexertion
overdelicately	overexpand
overdevelop	overexuberant
overdevoted	overexuberant
overdiligent	overfamiliar

overhead

overdiscipline
overdiversify
overdramatic
overdress
overdrink
overeager
overeat
overeducated
overembellish
overemotional
overemphasis
overemphasize
overenthusiastic

overfastidious
overfed
overfeed
overfill
overfond
overfull
overfulness
overfurnish
overgeneralize
overgenerous
overgraze
overhastily
overhasty

o·ver·bur·den (OH vər BUR dn) *v.t.* load with too much weight, care, etc.

o·ver·cast (OH vər KAST) *adj.* covered or obscured, as with clouds. —*n.* (OH vər KAST) **1.** a covering or mantle, as of clouds. **2.** *Meteorol.* a cloud or clouds covering more than nine-tenths of the sky. —*v.t. & v.i.* (OH vər KAST) **·cast, ·cast·ing** make or become overcast. [ME]

o·ver·charge (OH vər CHARJ) *v.t.* **·charged, ·charg·ing 1.** charge too high a price. **2.** overburden. —*n.* (OH vər CHARJ) an excessive charge.

o·ver·come (OH vər KUM) *v.* **·came, ·come, ·com·ing** *v.t.* **1.** get the better of in a conflict; conquer. **2.** prevail over or surmount, as difficulties. **3.** render (someone) helpless, as by emotion, sickness, etc. —*v.i.* **4.** gain mastery; win. [ME]

o·ver·do (OH vər DOO) *v.t.* **·did, ·done, ·do·ing 1.** do excessively; exaggerate. **2.** overtax the strength of; exhaust. **3.** cook too much, as meat. [ME *overdon*]

o·ver·dose (OH vər DOHS) *v.t.* **·dosed, ·dos·ing** dose to excess. —*n.* an excessive dose.

o·ver·draft (OH vər DRAFT) *n.* **1.** the act of overdrawing an account, as at a bank. **2.** the amount by which an account is overdrawn.

o·ver·draw (OH vər DRAW) *v.t.* **·drew, ·drawn, ·draw·ing 1.** draw against (an account) beyond one's credit. **2.** draw or strain excessively, as a bow. **3.** exaggerate. [ME]

o·ver·drive (OH vər DRĪV) *v.t.* **·drove, ·driv·en, ·driv·ing** drive too hard or too far. —*n.* (OH vər DRĪV) *Mech.* a gearing device that turns a drive shaft at a speed greater than that of the engine, thus decreasing power output.

overheat
overholy
overidealistic

overneat
overnice
overoptimistic

overimaginative
overimpress
overindulge
overindulgence
overindulgent
overindustrialize
overinflate
overinsure
overinvest
overkind
overlarge
overliberal
overlofty
overlong
overloud
overluxuriant
overluxurious
overmild
overmix
overmodest

overpatriotic
overpay
overpessimistic
overplump
overpopulate
overpopulated
overpraise
overpriced
overproduce
overproduction
overproductive
overprotect
overprovide
overpublicize
overpunish
overqualified
overrank
overreact
overreadiness
overrefine

o·ver·due (OH vər DOO) *adj.* past due; that should have arrived, been paid, etc. earlier.

o·ver·flow (OH vər FLOH) *v.* **·flowed, ·flow·ing** *v.i.* **1.** flow or run over the brim or bank, as water, rivers, etc. **2.** be filled beyond capacity. —*v.t.* **3.** flow over the brim or bank of. **4.** flow or spread over; cover; flood. **5.** cause to overflow. —*n.* (OH vər FLOH) **1.** the act or process of overflowing. **2.** that which flows over. **3.** the amount by which a capacity is exceeded; surplus. **4.** an outlet for liquid. [ME *overflowen*]

o·ver·grow (OH vər GROH) *v.* **·grew, ·grown, ·grow·ing** *v.t.* **1.** grow over; cover with growth. **2.** grow too big for; outgrow. —*v.i.* **3.** increase excessively; grow too large. [ME *overgrowen*]

o·ver·hang (OH vər HANG) *v.* **·hung, ·hang·ing** *v.t.* **1.** hang or project over; jut over. **2.** threaten; menace. —*v.i.* **3.** hang or jut over something. —*n.* (OH vər HANG) an overhanging portion of a structure; also, the amount of such projection.

o·ver·haul (OH vər HAWL) *v.t.* **1.** examine for needed repairs. **2.** repair; renovate. **3.** catch up with; gain on. —*n.* (OH vər HAWL) a thorough inspection and repair.

o·ver·head (OH vər HED) *adj.* **1.** situated or working above the level of one's head. **2.** of or relating to the overhead of a business. —*n.* the operating expenses of a business, as rent, light, heat, taxes, etc. —*adv.* (OH vər HED) over or above the head. [ME]

overrefined
overrefinement
overreligious

overstress
overstrict
overstrong

overripe
oversalty
overscrupulous
overseason
overseasoned
oversensitive
overseverely
oversimplification
oversimplify
overslow
oversmall
oversolicitous
oversophistication
overspecialization
overspend
oversqueamish
overstimulate
overstimulation
overstock
overstrain

overstudious
oversubscribe
oversubtle
oversubtlety
oversusceptible
oversuspicious
oversuspiciously
oversweet
overtax
overtechnical
overtire
overtrain
overtrustful
overuse
overvalue
overvehement
overweight
overwide
overwilling
overzealous

o·ver·hear (OH vər HEER) *v.t.* **·heard, ·hear·ing** hear (something said or someone speaking) without the knowledge or intention of the speaker.

o·ver·joy (OH vər JOI) *v.t.* delight or please greatly.

o·ver·kill (OH vər KIL) *n.* **1.** the military capacity for destruction far beyond the resources and population of an enemy. **2.** excess of any sort.

o·ver·land (OH vər LAND) *adj. & adv.* across, over, or via land.

o·ver·lap (OH vər LAP) *v.t. & v.i.* **·lapped, ·lap·ping 1.** lie or extend partly over or upon (another or each other). **2.** cover and project beyond (something). —*n.* (OH vər LAP) **1.** the state or extent of overlapping. **2.** the part that overlaps.

o·ver·lay (OH vər LAY) *v.t.* **·laid, ·lay·ing 1.** cover, as with a decorative pattern or layer. **2.** lay or place over or upon something else. —*n.* (OH vər LAY) anything that covers or partly covers something. [ME]

o·ver·leaf (OH vər LEEF) *adv.* on the other side of a page.

o·ver·lie (OH vər LĪ) *v.t.* **·lay, ·lain, ·ly·ing** lie over or upon.

o·ver·load (OH vər LOHD) *v.t.* load excessively; overburden. —*n.* (OH vər LOHD) **1.** an excessive burden. **2.** *Electr.* an amperage in excess of that which can be safely carried.

o·ver·look (OH vər LUUK) *v.t.* **1.** fail to notice; miss. **2.** disregard purposely or indulgently; ignore. **3.** look over or see from a higher place. **4.** afford a view of: The castle *overlooks* the harbor. **5.** supervise. **6.** in-

spect. —*n.* (OH vər LUUK) an elevated place affording a view. [ME]

o·ver·ly (OH vər lee) *adv.* to an excessive degree; too much; too. [ME]

o·ver·mas·ter (OH vər MAS tər) *v.t.* overcome; overpower.

o·ver·night (OH vər NĪT) *adj.* **1.** done, happening, etc. during the night, esp. the previous night. **2.** done, happening, etc. in or as in one night: an *overnight* success. **3.** used for short trips: an *overnight* bag. —*adv.* (OH vər NĪT) during, in, or through the night or one night. [ME]

o·ver·pass (OH vər PAS) *n.* an elevated section of road crossing other lines of travel.

o·ver·play (OH vər PLAY) *v.t.* **1.** play or act (a part or role) to excess. **2.** rely too much on the strength or value of.

o·ver·pow·er (OH vər POW ər) *v.t.* gain supremacy over; subdue; overcome. — **o·ver·pow·er·ing** *adj.* —**o·ver·pow'er·ing·ly** *adv.*

o·ver·rate (OH vər RAYT) *v.t.* **·rat·ed, ·rat·ing** rate or value too highly; overestimate.

o·ver·reach (OH vər REECH) *v.t.* **1.** reach over or beyond. **2.** defeat (oneself), as by attempting something beyond one's capability. **3.** miss by stretching or reaching too far. —*v.i.* **4.** reach too far. [ME]

o·ver·ride (OH vər RĪD) *v.t.* **·rode, ·rid·den, ·rid·ing 1.** disregard summarily; supersede. **2.** ride over. **3.** trample down; suppress. [ME *overridden*]

o·ver·rule (OH vər ROOL) *v.t.* **·ruled, ·rul·ing 1.** decide against or nullify; invalidate. **2.** disallow the arguments of (someone). **3.** prevail over.

o·ver·run (OH vər RUN) *v.* **·ran, ·run, ·run·ning** *v.t.* **1.** spread or swarm over, as vermin or invaders. **2.** overflow. **3.** pass the limit of. —*v.i.* **4.** run over; overflow. —*n.* (OH vər RUN) **1.** an instance of overrunning. **2.** the amount of overrunning; esp., the cost of something in excess of the original estimate. [ME *overrinnen*]

o·ver·seas (OH vər SEEZ) *adv.* beyond the sea; abroad. —*adj.* (OH vər SEEZ) situated, coming from, or for use beyond the sea; foreign.

o·ver·see (OH vər SEE) *v.t.* **·saw, ·seen, ·see·ing 1.** direct; superintend. **2.** survey; watch. [ME *overseen*]

o·ver·seer (OH vər SEER) *n.* one who supervises workers. [ME]

o·ver·sell (OH vər SEL) *v.t.* **·sold, ·sell·ing**

1. sell with excessive enthusiasm or exaggerated claims. **2.** sell more of (a stock etc.) than one can provide.

o•ver•sexed (OH vər SEKST) *adj.* having or characterized by excessive sexual desire or interest.

o•ver•shad•ow (OH vər SHAD oh) *v.t.* **1.** render unimportant or insignificant by comparison; dominate. **2.** throw a shadow over; obscure.

o•ver•shoe (OH vər SHOO) *n.* a shoe worn over another for protection against water, mud, etc.

o•ver•shoot (OH vər SHOOT) *v.* •shot, •shoot•ing *v.t.* **1.** shoot or go over or beyond (the mark, target, etc.). **2.** exceed, as a limit. **3.** drive or force (something) beyond the proper limit. —*v.i.* **4.** shoot or go over or beyond the mark. **5.** go too far. [ME]

o•ver•shot (OH vər SHOT) *adj.* **1.** projecting, as the upper jaw beyond the lower jaw. **2.** driven by water flowing over from above: an *overshot* wheel.

o•ver•sight (OH vər SĪT) *n.* **1.** an inadvertent mistake or omission. **2.** watchful supervision. [ME]

o•ver•spread (OH vər SPRED) *v.t.* •spread, •spread•ing extend over; cover completely. [ME *overspreden*]

o•ver•state (OH vər STAYT) *v.t.* •stat•ed, •stat•ing state in too strong terms; exaggerate. —**o'ver•state'ment** *n.*

o•ver•stay (OH vər STAY) *v.t.* stay beyond the limits or duration of.

o•ver•step (OH vər STEP) *v.t.* •stepped, •step•ping exceed (a limit).

o•ver•sup•ply (OH vər sə PLĪ) *n. pl.* •plies an excessive supply. —**o•ver•sup•ply** *v.t.* (OH vər sə PLĪ) •plied, •ply•ing

o•vert (oh VURT) *adj.* **1.** open to view; observable. **2.** *Law* done with criminal intent. [ME] —**o•vert'ly** *adv.*

o•ver•take (OH vər TAYK) *v.t.* •took, •tak•en, •tak•ing **1.** catch up with. **2.** come upon suddenly.

o•ver•throw (OH vər THROH) *v.t.* •threw, •thrown, •throw•ing **1.** bring down or remove from power by force; defeat; ruin. **2.** throw over or down; upset. —*n.* (OH vər THROH) **1.** the act of overthrowing; demolition. **2.** in baseball etc., a throwing of the ball over and beyond the player or base aimed at.

o•ver•time (OH vər TĪM) *n.* time used in working beyond the specified hours. —**o'ver•time'** *adj. & adv.*

o•ver•tone (OH vər TOHN) *n.* **1.** *Music* a partial tone heard with and above a fundamental tone. **2.** a connotation, implication, etc. of language, thoughts, etc.

o•ver•ture (OH vər chər) *n.* **1.** *Music* **a** an instrumental prelude to an opera or other large work. **b** any of various orchestral pieces, often having programmatic content. **2.** an act or proposal intended to initiate a relationship, negotiations, etc. [ME]

o•ver•turn (OH vər TURN) *v.t.* **1.** turn or throw over; upset. **2.** overthrow; defeat; ruin. —*v.i.* **3.** turn over; capsize.

o•ver•view (OH vər VYOO) *n.* a broad survey or review of a subject, activity, etc.

o•ver•ween•ing (OH vər WEE ning) *adj.* **1.** presumptuously proud or conceited. **2.** excessively; exaggerated. [ME *overwening*] —**o'ver•ween'ing•ly** *adv.*

o•ver•weigh (OH vər WAY) *v.t.* **1.** outweigh; overbalance. **2.** overburden; oppress. [ME *overweien*]

o•ver•whelm (OH vər HWELM) *v.t.* **1.** bury or submerge completely. **2.** defeat; crush. **3.** overcome; overpower. [ME]

o•ver•work (OH vər WURK) *v.t.* **1.** cause to work too hard. **2.** work on or elaborate excessively. —*v.i.* **3.** work too hard. —*n.* (OH vər WURK) excessive work. [OE *oferwyrcan*]

o•ver•write (OH vər RĪT) *v.t. & v.i.* •wrote, •writ•ten, •writ•ing **1.** write in too elaborate or labored a style. **2.** write too much about (a subject) or at too great length.

o•ver•wrought (OH vər RAWT) *adj.* **1.** worked up or excited excessively. **2.** too elaborate.

o•vi•duct (OH vi DUKT) *n. Anat.* a fallopian tube. [< NL *oviductus*]

o•vip•a•rous (oh VIP ər əs) *adj. Zool.* producing eggs or ova that mature and are hatched outside the body, as birds and most fishes and reptiles. [< L *oviparus*]

o•void (OH void) *adj.* egg-shaped. —*n.* an egg-shaped body. [< F *ovoïde*]

o•vo•vi•vip•a•rous (OH voh vī VIP ər əs) *adj. Zool.* producing eggs that are hatched within the parent's body, but without formation of a placenta, as some reptiles and fishes.

o•vu•late (OV yə LAYT) *v.i.* •lat•ed, •lat•ing produce ova; discharge ova from an ovary. —**o•vu•la'tion** *n.*

o•vule (OV yool) *n.* **1.** *Bot.* the body within the ovary that upon fertilization becomes the seed. **2.** *Zool.* an immature ovum. [< L *ovulum* little egg] **—o•vu•lar** (OV yə lər) *adj.*

o•vum (OH vəm) *n. pl.* **o•va** (OH və) *Biol.* the female reproductive cell of animals, produced in the ovary. [< L]

owe (oh) *v.* **owed, ow•ing** *v.t.* **1.** be indebted to the amount of. **2.** be obligated to render or offer. **3.** have by virtue of some condition or cause: with *to.* **—v.i. 4.** be in debt. [ME *owen* possess]

ow•ing (OH ing) *adj.* due; yet to be paid. [ME] **—owing to** attributable to; on account of.

owl (owl) *n.* **1.** a predatory nocturnal bird, having large eyes and head, a short, sharply hooked bill, and long powerful claws. **2.** a person with nocturnal habits. [ME *oule*] **—owl'ish** *adj.* **—owl'ish•ly** *adv.*

own (ohn) *adj.* **1.** belonging or relating to oneself: following the possessive as an intensive or to indicate the exclusion of others: my *own* horse. **2.** identifying the subject rather than indicating ownership: her *own* doctor. **—come into one's own 1.** obtain possession of one's property. **2.** achieve maturity or success. **3.** receive one's reward. **—hold one's own 1.** maintain one's place or position. **2.** keep up with one's work. **3.** remain undefeated. **—on one's own** entirely dependent on oneself for support or success. **—v.t. 1.** have or hold as one's own; possess. **2.** admit or acknowledge. **—v.i. 3.** confess: with *to.* **—own up** confess fully. [ME *owen* possess]

own•er (OH nər) *n.* one who has the legal right to or has possession of a thing. [ME] **—own'er•less** *adj.* **—own'er•ship** *n.*

ox (oks) *n. pl.* **ox•en** (OK sən) **1.** an adult castrated male bovine, esp. of the domesticated species. **2.** any bovine quadruped, as a buffalo, bison, or yak. [ME *oxe*]

ox•blood (OKS BLUD) *n.* a reddish brown color.

ox•bow (OKS BOH) *n.* **1.** a bent piece of wood in an ox yoke, that forms a collar for the ox. **2.** a bend in a river shaped like this. [ME]

ox•ford (OKS fərd) *n.* **1.** a low shoe laced at the instep. **2.** a cotton cloth of basket weave, used for shirts. [after *Oxford,* England]

ox•i•da•tion (ok si DAY shən) *n. Chem.* **1.** the process or state of undergoing combination with oxygen. **2.** the process by which atoms lose electrons, thus increasing their valence.

ox•ide (OK sīd) *n. Chem.* a compound of oxygen with another element. [< F]

ox•i•dize (OK si DĪZ) *v.* **•dized, •diz•ing** *Chem. v.t.* **1.** convert (an element) into its oxide; combine with oxygen. **2.** increase the valence of an atom or group of atoms by the loss of electrons. **—v.i. 3.** become oxidized. Also **ox•i•date** (OK si DAYT).

ox•tail (OKS TAYL) *n.* the tail of an ox, esp. when skinned for use in soup.

ox•y•gen (OK si jən) *n.* a colorless, odorless gaseous element (symbol O), occurring free in the atmosphere, of which it forms about one-fifth by volume and is essential for combustion and respiration. [< F *oxygène*]

ox•y•gen•ate (OK si jə NAYT) *v.t.* **•at•ed, •at•ing** treat, combine, or impregnate with oxygen. **—ox'y•gen•a'tion** *n.*

oxygen mask a device worn over the nose and mouth, used for inhaling oxygen.

oxygen tent a tentlike canopy placed over a patient's head and shoulders, within which pure oxygen may be circulated.

ox•y•mo•ron (OK si MOR on) *n. pl.* **•mo•ra** (-MOR ə) a figure of speech in which contradictory terms are brought together, as in *"O heavy lightness, serious vanity!"* [< LL *oxymorum*]

o•yez (OH yes) *interj.* hear! an introductory word to call to attention, as by a court officer. [ME]

oys•ter (OI stər) *n.* a bivalve mollusk, found in shallow water. **—v.i.** gather or farm oysters. [ME *oistre*]

oyster bed a place where oysters breed or are grown.

o•zone (OH zohn) *n.* **1.** an unstable form of oxygen with a pungent odor, formed variously, as by the passage of electricity through the air. **2.** fresh air. [< G *Ozon*]

ozone layer a narrow layer in the stratosphere, containing a high concentration of ozone, and serving to screen out ultraviolet rays from the sun. Also **o•zon•o•sphere** (oh ZOH nə SFEER).

P

p, P (pee) *n. pl.* **p's** or **ps, P's** or **Ps** **1.** the sixteenth letter of the English alphabet. **2.** the sound represented by the letter *p*. —*symbol Chem.* phosphorus (symbol P). —**mind one's P's and Q's** be careful of one's behavior.

pab·lum (PAB ləm) *n.* naive or simplistic writings or ideas.

pab·u·lum (PAB yə ləm) *n.* **1.** any substance giving nourishment; food. **2.** nourishment for the mind; food for thought. **3.** pablum. [< L, food]

pace (pays) *n.* **1.** a step in walking; also, the distance covered in one such movement, usu. considered to be three feet. **2.** the manner or speed of movement in going on the legs; carriage and action, esp. of a horse. **3.** rate of speed, as in movement, work, etc. **4.** a gait of a horse etc. in which both feet on the same side are lifted and moved forward at once. —**put through one's paces** test the abilities, speed, etc. of. —*v.* **paced, pac·ing** *v.t.* **1.** walk back and forth across. **2.** measure by paces. **3.** set or make the pace for. —*v.i.* **4.** walk with regular steps or back and forth. **5.** go at a pace: said of a horse. [ME *pase*]

pace·mak·er (PAYS MAY kər) *n.* **1.** one who makes or sets the pace for another in a race. **2.** a mass of tissue in the heart that normally regulates the heartbeat. **3.** an electronic device implanted beneath the skin for regulating the heartbeat.

pa·chin·ko (pə CHING koh) *n.* a vertical pinball game played in Japan. [< Jap., little click]

pach·y·derm (PAK i DURM) *n.* any of certain thick-skinned, nonruminant hoofed animals, esp. an elephant. [< NL *Pachyderma*]

pa·cif·ic (pə SIF ik) *adj.* **1.** tending or leading to peace or conciliation. **2.** peaceful. [< L *pacificus*]

pac·i·fi·er (PAS ə FĪ ər) *n.* one who or that which pacifies. **2.** a rubber or plastic device for babies to suck or bite on.

pac·i·fist (PAS ə fist) *n.* one who opposes war, usu. under all circumstances. —**pac'i·fism** *n.*

pac·i·fy (PAS ə FĪ) *v.t.* **·fied, ·fy·ing** **1.**

bring peace to (an area). **2.** calm; quiet; soothe. [ME] —**pac'i·fi·ca'tion** *n.*

pack¹ (pak) *n.* **1.** a bundle or large package, esp. one to be carried on the back. **2.** a collection of anything; heap. **3.** a full set of like or associated things, as cards. **4.** a group of dogs, wolves, etc. that hunt together. **5.** any gang or band. **6.** any of various substances or materials applied as a compress, dressing, wrapping, etc.: an ice *pack*. —*v.t.* **1.** make a bundle of. **2.** place compactly in a trunk, box, etc. for storing or carrying. **3.** fill compactly. **4.** compress tightly; crowd together. **5.** fill to overflowing; cram. **6.** cover, fill, or surround so as to prevent leakage, damage, etc.: *pack* a joint. **7.** prepare and place (food) in containers for storage or sale. **8.** carry or wear habitually: *pack* a gun. **9.** send or dispatch summarily: with *off* or *away*. **10.** *Informal* be able to inflict: That drink *packs* a wallop. —*v.i.* **11.** place one's clothes and belongings in trunks etc. for storing or carrying. **12.** be capable of being stowed or packed. **13.** crowd together. **14.** settle in a hard, firm mass. —**send packing** send away or dismiss summarily. [ME *pak*] —**pack'er** *n.*

pack² *v.t.* arrange to one's own advantage: *pack* a jury.

pack·age (PAK ij) *n.* **1.** something packed, as for transportation. **2.** a box etc., used for packing. **3.** a combination of items considered as a unit: a legislative *package*. —*v.t.* **·aged, ·ag·ing** arrange or tie into a package.

package store a liquor store.

pack animal an animal used to carry burdens.

pack·et (PAK it) *n.* **1.** a small package. **2.** a steamship for conveying mail, passengers, and freight at stated times: also **packet boat**. [< MF *pacquet*]

pack·ing (PAK ing) *n.* **1.** the act or operation of one who or that which packs. **2.** any material used in packing, closing a joint, stopping a wound, etc.

packing plant a factory where meat, vegetables, or fruit is processed and packed. Also **packing house**.

pack rat 1. a North American rat that carries

off and hides small articles in its nest. **2.** one who saves often unneeded items.

pact (pakt) *n.* an agreement; compact. [ME *pacte*]

pad[1] (pad) *n.* **1.** a cushion; also, any stuffed, cushionlike thing. **2.** a number of sheets of paper gummed together at one edge. **3.** a large floating leaf of an aquatic plant: a lily *pad.* **4.** a soft cushionlike enlargement of skin on the undersurface of the toes of many animals. **5.** the foot of a fox, otter, etc. **6.** the footprint of an animal. **7.** a launch pad. **8.** *Slang* living quarters. —*v.t.* **pad·ded, pad·ding 1.** stuff, line, or protect with pads or padding. **2.** insert unnecessary matter into (a report, speech, etc.). **3.** add to (an expense account, voting register, etc.) for fraudulent purposes.

pad[2] *v.i.* **pad·ded, pad·ding** walk, esp. with soft footsteps. —*n.* a dull, padded sound, as of a footstep. [< MDu. *pad* path]

pad·ding (PAD ing) *n.* **1.** the act of one who or that which pads. **2.** material used to pad.

pad·dle (PAD l) *n.* **1.** a flat-bladed implement resembling a short oar, used without a rowlock in propelling a canoe or small boat. **2.** a flat board for inflicting bodily punishment. **3.** a small, rounded, flat piece of wood with a handle, used in table tennis. —*v.* **·dled, ·dling** *v.i.* **1.** move a canoe etc. by means of a paddle. **2.** swim or dabble in water with short, downward strokes. —*v.t.* **3.** convey or propel by means of a paddle or paddles. **4.** beat with a paddle; spank. — **paddle one's own canoe** be independent. [ME *padell*] —**pad'dler** *n.*

pad·dock (PAD ək) *n.* **1.** a pasture or enclosure for exercising horses, adjoining a stable. **2.** a grassy enclosure at a racecourse where horses are walked and saddled. [ME *parrok*]

pad·dy (PAD ee) *n. pl.* **·dies 1.** rice in the husk, whether gathered or growing. **2.** a rice field. [< Malay *padi*]

paddy wagon *Informal* a patrol wagon.

pad·lock (PAD lok) *n.* a detachable lock, having a pivoted hasp to be passed through a staple or ring and then locked. —*v.t.* fasten with or as with a padlock. [ME *padlok*]

pa·dre (PAH dray) *n.* **1.** father: a title used in Italy, Spain, and Spanish America in addressing or speaking of priests. **2.** a chaplain. [< Sp., father]

pae·an (PEE ən) *n.* a song of joy or exultation. [< L, hymn]

pa·gan (PAY gən) *n.* **1.** one who is neither a

Christian, a Jew, nor a Muslim; a heathen. **2.** an irreligious person. [ME] —**pa'gan** *adj.* —**pa'gan·ism** *n.*

page[1] (payj) *n.* **1.** a male attendant; esp., a youth in training for knighthood or attending a royal personage. **2.** one employed to perform chores for legislators while the legislature is in session. **3.** one employed in a hotel etc. to perform light duties. —*v.t.* **paged, pag·ing** seek or summon (a person) by calling out the name. [ME]

page[2] *n.* **1.** one side of a leaf of a book, letter, etc. **2.** an entire leaf. **3.** a single sheet of writing paper. —*v.* **paged, pag·ing** *v.t.* **1.** mark the pages of with numbers. —*v.i.* **2.** turn pages: usu. with *through.* [< MF]

pag·eant (PAJ ənt) *n.* **1.** an exhibition or spectacular parade devised for a public celebration. **2.** a theatrical spectacle, often with historical themes. [ME *pagyn*]

pag·eant·ry (PAJ ən tree) *n. pl.* **·ries 1.** pageants collectively. **2.** ceremonial splendor or display. **3.** empty or showy display.

pag·i·nate (PAJ ə NAYT) *v.t.* **·nat·ed, ·nat·ing** number the pages of (a book) consecutively.

pag·i·na·tion (PAJ ə NAY shən) *n.* **1.** the numbering of the pages, as of a book. **2.** the system of figures and marks used in paging. **3.** the arrangement and number of pages.

pa·go·da (pə GOH də) *n.* in the Far East, a sacred tower or temple, usu. pyramidal. [< Pg. *pagode* temple]

paid (payd) past tense, past participle of PAY.

pail (payl) *n.* **1.** a cylindrical vessel with a handle, for carrying liquids etc. **2.** the amount carried in this vessel. [ME *payle*] —**pail'ful** (-FUUL)

pain (payn) *n.* **1.** the unpleasant sensation or feeling resulting from or accompanying a physical injury, overstrain, or disorder. **2.** any distressing or afflicting emotion. **3.** *pl.* care, effort, etc. expended on anything: with great *pains.* —**on** (or upon or **under**) **pain of** with the penalty of (some specified punishment). —*v.t. & v.i.* cause pain; hurt. [ME *peine*] —**pain'less** *adj.*

pained (paynd) *adj.* **1.** hurt or distressed. **2.** showing pain.

pain·ful (PAYN fəl) *adj.* **1.** causing or affected with pain. **2.** laborious; arduous. — **pain'ful·ly** *adv.* —**pain'ful·ness** *n.*

pain·kill·er (PAYN kil ər) *n.* a drug that alleviates pain.

pains·tak·ing (PAYNZ TAY king) *adj.* careful; assiduous. —*n.* diligent care. —**pains′ tak′ing·ly** *adv.*

paint (paynt) *n.* **1.** a color or pigment, either dry or mixed with oil, water, etc. **2.** a cosmetic, as rouge or greasepaint. **3.** a coat of pigment applied to the surface of an object. —*v.t.* **1.** in art: **a** make a representation of in paints or colors. **b** make (a picture) with paints or colors. **2.** describe vividly, as in words. **3.** cover, coat, or decorate with or as with paint. —*v.i.* **4.** practice the art of painting; paint pictures. **5.** apply cosmetics to the face etc. [ME *peinten*]

paint·er[1] (PAYN tər) *n.* one who paints.

paint·er[2] *n. Naut.* a rope with which to fasten a boat by its bow. [ME *peyntour*]

paint·ing (PAYN ting) *n.* **1.** the act of applying paint. **2.** the art of creating meaningful effects on a surface by the use of pigments. **3.** a picture made with pigments.

pair (pair) *v.t. & v.i.* **1.** bring or come together as a pair. **2.** mate. —**pair off 1.** separate into couples. **2.** arrange by pairs. —*n.* **1.** two persons or things of a kind, that are joined, related, or associated. **2.** a single thing having two correspondent parts dependent on each other: a *pair* of scissors. [ME *paire*]

pa·ja·mas (pə JAH məz) *n.* (construed as *pl.*) **1.** a garment consisting of loose trousers and jacket, used for sleeping. **2.** in the Orient, similar trousers worn by both men and women. [< Hindi *pājāma*]

pal·ace (PAL is) *n.* **1.** a royal residence, or the official residence of some high dignitary, as of a bishop. **2.** any splendid residence or stately building. [ME]

pal·a·din (PAL ə dən) *n.* a knight, esp. a heroic one. [< F]

pal·an·quin (PAL ən KEEN) *n.* a type of covered litter used as a means of conveyance in the Orient, borne by poles on the shoulders of two or more men. [< Pg. *palanquim*]

pal·at·a·ble (PAL ə tə bəl) *adj.* **1.** agreeable to the taste; savory. **2.** acceptable.

pal·a·tal (PAL ə tl) *adj.* **1.** pertaining to the palate. **2.** *Phonet.* **a** produced by placing the front (not the tip) of the tongue near or against the hard palate, as *y* in English *yoke*. **b** produced with the blade of the tongue near the hard palate, as *ch* in *child*.

pal·a·tal·ize (PAL ə tl IZ) *v.t. & v.i.* **·ized, ·iz·ing** *Phonet.* change (a nonpalatal sound) to a palatal one.

pal·ate (PAL it) *n.* **1.** *Anat.* the roof of the mouth, consisting of the anterior **hard palate,** having a bony skeleton, and the posterior **soft palate,** composed of muscular tissue. **2.** the sense of taste. [ME]

pa·la·tial (pə LAY shəl) *adj.* of, like, or befitting a palace; magnificent.

pa·lat·i·nate (pə LAT n AYT) *n.* a political division ruled over by a count or earl possessing certain prerogatives of royalty within his own domain.

pal·a·tine (PAL ə TIN) *adj.* **1.** of or pertaining to a royal palace or its officials. **2.** possessing royal prerogatives: a count *palatine*. —*n.* the ruler of a palatinate. [< L *palatium* palace]

pa·lav·er (pə LAV ər) *n.* **1.** talk intended to flatter or deceive. **2.** idle, lengthy talk. [< Pg. *palavra* word] —**pa·lav′er** *v.t. & v.i.* talk or cajole.

pale[1] (payl) *n.* **1.** a pointed stick or stake. **2.** a fence enclosing a piece of ground. **3.** any boundary or limit. **4.** that which is enclosed within bounds. [ME, stake]

pale[2] *adj.* **1.** of a whitish or ashen appearance. **2.** lacking in brightness or intensity of color. **3.** feeble or weak. —*v.t. & v.i.* **paled, pal·ing** make or turn pale; blanch. —**pale·ness** *n.* [ME]

paleo- *combining form* **1.** ancient; old. **2.** primitive. [< Gk. *palaiós* old]

pa·le·og·ra·phy (PAY lee OG rə fee) *n.* the study of describing or deciphering ancient writings. [< PALEO- + *-graphy* writing] —**pa′le·og′ra·pher** *n.*

pa·le·ol·o·gy (PAY lee OL ə jee) *n.* the study of antiquity or antiquities; archeology. [< PALEO- + -LOGY] —**pa′le·ol′o·gist** *n.*

pa·le·on·tol·o·gy (PAY lee ən TOL ə jee) *n.* the science that treats of ancient forms of life or of fossil organisms. [< F *paléontologie*] —**pa′le·on·tol′o·gist** *n.*

Pal·es·tin·i·an (PAL ə STIN ee ən) *adj.* **1.** of or relating to ancient Palestine or to the former modern country Palestine. **2.** of or relating to the inhabitants of ancient Palestine. —**Pal′es·tin′i·an** *n.*

pal·ette (PAL it) *n.* **1.** a thin board or tablet with a hole for the thumb, upon which artists lay and mix their colors. **2.** the range of colors characteristic of a particular artist, painting, etc. Also **pallete**. [< F]

pal·imp·sest (PAL imp SEST) *n.* a parchment, manuscript, etc., written upon two or three times, the earlier writing having been wholly or partially erased. [< L *palimpsestus*]

pal•in•drome (PAL in DROHM) *n.* a word, sentence, verse, etc., that is the same read forward or backward, as "Madam, I'm Adam." [< Gk. *palíndromos* running back again]

pal•ing (PAY ling) *n.* **1.** one of a series of upright pales forming a fence. **2.** pales or pickets collectively. **3.** a fence or enclosure made of pales or pickets.

pal•i•sade (PAL ə SAYD) *n.* **1.** a barrier or fortification made of strong timbers set in the ground. **2.** one of the stakes forming such a barrier. **3.** *pl.* an extended cliff or rocky precipice. —*v.t.* **•sad•ed, •sad•ing** enclose or fortify with a palisade. [< F *palissade*]

pall[1] (pawl) *n.* **1.** a covering, usu. of black cloth, thrown over a coffin or tomb. **2.** a dark, heavy covering, cloud, etc. **3.** a gloomy or oppressive atmosphere, effect, etc. —*v.t.* cover with or as with a pall. [ME]

pall[2] *v.i.* **1.** become insipid or uninteresting. **2.** have a dulling or displeasing effect: followed by *on.* —*v.t.* **3.** satiate; cloy. [ME *pallen*]

pall•bear•er (PAWL BAIR ər) *n.* one who forms part of an escort for a coffin at a funeral.

pal•let[1] (PAL it) *n.* **1.** any of various flat-bladed tools. **2.** a skid (def. 2). [< MF *palette* small spade]

pal•let[2] *n.* **1.** a small straw bed or mattress. **2.** a small, hard bed. [ME *pailet* straw]

pal•li•ate (PAL ee AYT) *v.t.* **•at•ed, •at•ing** **1.** cause (a crime, fault, etc.) to appear less serious or offensive. **2.** relieve the symptoms or effects of (a disease, etc.) without curing. [< LL *palliatus* cloaked] —**pal′li•a•tive** *adj. & n.* [< F *palliatif*]

pal•lid (PAL id) *adj.* pale or wan; lacking in color. [< L *pallidus*] —**pal′lid•ness** *n.*

pal•lor (PAL ər) *n.* the state of being pale or pallid; paleness. [< L]

palm[1] (pahm) *n.* the inner surface of the hand between the wrist and the base of the fingers. —*v.t.* hide (something) in the hand, as in sleight of hand. —**palm off** pass off or impose fraudulently. [ME *paume*]

palm[2] *n.* **1.** any of a large and varied group of tropical evergreen trees or shrubs, usu. having an unbranched trunk topped by a crown of large palmate or pinnate leaves. **2.** A leaf or branch of the palm, used as a symbol of victory or joy. **3.** Triumph; victory. [ME]

pal•mate (PAL mayt) *adj.* **1.** resembling an open hand. **2.** broad and flat, with fingerlike projections, as antlers. Also **pal′mat•ed.** [< L *palmatus* shaped like a palm]

pal•met•to (pal MET oh) *n. pl.* **•tos** or **•toes** any of various palms having fanlike foliage. [< Sp.]

palm•is•try (PAH mə stree) *n.* the practice of supposedly discovering a person's past or future from the lines and marks in the palm of the hand. [ME *pawmestry*] —**palm′ist** *n.*

Palm Sunday the Sunday before Easter, in commemoration of Christ's triumphal entry into Jerusalem. [ME]

palm•y (PAH mee) *adj.* **palm•i•er, palm•i•est** **1.** prosperous; flourishing. **2.** abounding in palms.

pal•o•mi•no (PAL ə MEE noh) *n. pl.* **•nos** a tan or golden brown horse with a cream-colored mane and tail. [< Am.Sp.]

pal•pa•ble (PAL pə bəl) *adj.* **1.** capable of being touched or felt. **2.** readily perceived; obvious. **3.** perceptible by touching. [ME] —**pal′pa•bil′i•ty** *n.* —**pal′pa•bly** *adv.*

pal•pate (PAL PAYT) *v.t.* **•pat•ed, •pat•ing** feel or examine by touch, esp. for medical diagnosis. [< L *palpare* touch]

pal•pi•tate (PAL pi TAYT) *v.i.* **•tat•ed, •tat•ing** **1.** quiver; tremble. **2.** beat more rapidly than normal; flutter: said esp. of the heart. [< L *palpitare* tremble]. —**pal′pi•ta′tion** *n.*

pal•sy (PAWL zee) *n. pl.* **•sies** **1.** paralysis. **2.** any impairment or loss of ability to control movement. —*v.t.* **•sied, •sy•ing** **1.** paralyze. **2.** cause to tremble. [ME *palsie*] —**pal′sied** *adj.*

pal•ter (PAWL tər) *v.i.* **1.** speak or act insincerely; equivocate. **2.** trifle. **3.** haggle or quibble. —**pal′ter•er** *n.*

pal•try (PAWL tree) *adj.* **•tri•er, •tri•est** **1.** having little or no worth or value; trifling; trivial. **2.** contemptible; petty. [< LG *paltrig* ragged] —**pal′tri•ness** *n.*

pam•pas (PAM pəz) *n.pl.* the great treeless plains south of the Amazon river. [< Quechua *pampa* plain]

pam•per (PAM pər) *v.t.* treat very indulgently; coddle. [ME *pamperen*]

pam•phlet (PAM flit) *n.* a printed work stitched or pasted, but not permanently bound; esp., a brief treatise or essay on a subject of current interest published in this form. [ME *pamflet*]

pam•phlet•eer (PAM fli TEER) *n.* one who

writes pamphlets. —*v.i.* write and issue pamphlets.

pan[1] (pan) *n.* **1.** a wide, shallow vessel, usu. of metal, used for holding liquids or in cooking. **2.** any similar receptacle or vessel. —*v.* **panned, pan·ning** *v.t.* **1.** separate (gold) by washing (gold-bearing earth) in a pan. **2.** *Informal* criticize severely. —*v.i.* **3.** search for gold by washing earth, gravel, etc. in a pan. [ME *panne*] —**pan out** *Informal* turn out, esp. successfully.

pan[2] *v.t.* **panned, pan·ning** move (a motion-picture or television camera) so as to photograph an entire scene, follow a particular character, etc. [< PANORAMA]

pan- *combining form* **1.** all; every; the whole: *panchromatic.* **2.** comprising, including, or applying to all: usu. capitalized when preceding proper nouns or adjectives, as in *Pan-American.* [< Gk. *pan-* all]

pan·a·ce·a (PAN ə SEE ə) *n.* a remedy for all diseases or ills; cure-all. [< L]

pa·nache (pə NASH) *n.* **1.** a plume, esp. on a helmet. **2.** dash; verve. [< MF]

Pan-A·mer·i·can (PAN ə MER i kən) *adj.* including or pertaining to both North and South America, or to all Americans.

pan·a·tel·a (PAN əTEL ə) *n.* a long slender cigar: also spelled *panetella.* [< Sp.]

pan·cake (PAN KAYK) *n.* **1.** a flat cake made from batter, fried in a pan or on a griddle. **2.** a cosmetic resembling face powder: also **pancake makeup.**

pan·chro·mat·ic (PAN kroh MAT ik) *adj.* *Photog.* sensitive to light of all colors of the spectrum, as film.

pan·cre·as (PANG kree əs) *n.* *Anat.* a large gland situated behind the lower part of the stomach, secreting digestive enzymes and producing insulin. [< NL] —**pan·cre·at·ic** (PANG kree AT ik) *adj.*

pan·da (PAN də) *n.* **1.** a small, raccoonlike carnivore of the SE Himalayas, with long, reddish brown fur and ringed tail. **2.** a large, bearlike mammal, the **giant panda,** of Tibet and China, with black-and-white coat and rings around the eyes. [< F < Nepalese]

pan·dem·ic (pan DEM ik) *adj.* **1.** *Med.* widely epidemic. **2.** universal; general. —*n.* a pandemic disease. [< LL *pandemus* of all people]

pan·de·mo·ni·um (PAN də MOH nee əm) *n.* **1.** the abode of all demons. **2.** a place marked by disorder and uproar. **3.** riotous uproar. [< NL]

pan·der (PAN dər) *n.* **1.** a go-between in sexual intrigues; pimp. **2.** one who ministers to the passions or base desires of others. Also **pan'der·er** —*v.t. & v.i.* act as a pander for (another or others). [ME *Pandare* < L *Pandarus,* in legend, a pander]

pane (payn) *n.* **1.** one of the sections of a window, door, etc. filled with a sheet of glass. **2.** a sheet of glass for such a section. **3.** a panel in a door, ceiling, etc. [ME *pan*]

pan·e·gyr·ic (PAN i JIR ik) *n.* **1.** a formal public eulogy. **2.** elaborate praise. [< L *panegyricus* assembly] —**pan'e·gyr'ist** *n.*

pan·e·gy·rize (PAN ə jə RIZ) *v.t. & v.i.* **·rized, ·riz·ing** deliver or write a panegyric upon (someone); eulogize.

pan·el (PAN l) *n.* **1.** a rectangular or square piece forming part of a ceiling, door, etc. **2.** one or more pieces of fabric inserted lengthwise in a woman's skirt. **3.** *Law* **a** the official list of persons summoned for jury duty. **b** the body of persons composing a jury. **4.** a small group of persons selected to hold a discussion, judge a contest, etc. **5.** an instrument panel. —*v.t.* **·eled, ·el·ing 1.** fit, furnish, or adorn with panels. **2.** divide into panels. [ME]

panel discussion a discussion before an audience of a specific topic by a group of selected speakers.

pan·el·ing (PAN l ing) *n.* **1.** wood or other materials used in making panels. **2.** panels collectively.

pan·el·ist (PAN l ist) *n.* a person serving on a panel.

pang (pang) *n.* **1.** a sudden sharp pain. **2.** a spasm of mental anguish.

pan·han·dle[1] (PAN HAN dl) *n.* **1.** the handle of a pan. **2.** a narrow strip of land shaped like the handle of a pan: the Texas *panhandle.*

pan·han·dle[2] *v.i.* **·dled, ·dling** *Informal* beg, esp. on the street. [< PAN[1] (for alms) + HANDLE, *v.*] —**pan'han'dler** *n.*

pan·ic (PAN ik) *n.* **1.** a sudden, unreasonable, overpowering fear, esp. when affecting a large number simultaneously. **2.** an instance of such fear. [< F *panique*] —*v.t. & v.i.* **·icked, ·ick·ing** affect or become affected with panic. —**pan'ick·y** *adj.*

pan·ic-strick·en (PAN ik STRIK ən) *adj.* overcome by panic.

pan·jan·drum (pan JAN drəm) *n.* a self-important or pretentious official. [Coined by Samuel Foote, 1720—77, English dramatist]

pan·o·ply (PAN ə plee) n. pl. **·plies 1.** the complete equipment of a warrior. **2.** any complete covering that protects. [< Gk. *panoplía* full armor] —**pan'o·plied** adj.

pan·o·ram·a (PAN ə RAM ə) n. **1.** a series of pictures representing a continuous scene, arranged to pass before the spectator. **2.** a comprehensive view. [< PAN- + Gk. *hórama* sight] —**pan'o·ram'ic** adj.

pan·sy (PAN zee) n. pl. **·sies 1.** a garden violet having blossoms of a variety of colors. **2.** *Offensive slang* an effeminate or homosexual man. [< MF *pensée*, lit., thóught]

pant (pant) v.i. **1.** breathe rapidly or spasmodically; gasp for breath. **2.** gasp with desire; yearn: with *for* or *after.* —v.t. **3.** breathe out or utter gaspingly. —n. **1.** the act of panting. **2.** a gasp. [ME *panten*]

pan·ta·loons (PAN tl OONZ) n.pl. formerly, a tight-fitting garment for the hips and legs; trousers. [< MF *Pantalon*, old nickname for a Venetian]

pan·the·ism (PAN thee IZ əm) n. the doctrine that the whole universe is God, or that every part of the universe is a manifestation of God. [< F *panthéisme*] —**pan'the·ist** n. —**pan'the·is'tic** adj.

pan·the·on (PAN thee ON) n. **1.** all the gods of a people collectively. **2.** a temple commemorating the great of a nation. **3.** a temple dedicated to the gods of a nation. [ME *panteon*]

pant·ies (PAN teez) n.pl. a woman's or child's underpants.

pan·to·mime (PAN tə MIM) n. **1.** any play in which the actors express meaning by action without dialogue. **2.** gestures without speech. —v.t. & v.i. **·mimed, ·mim·ing** act or express in pantomime. [< L] —**pan'to·mi'mist** n.

pan·try (PAN tree) n. pl. **·tries** a room or closet for provisions, dishes, table linen, etc. [ME *panetrie*]

pants (pants) n.pl. **1.** trousers. **2.** underpants. [Short for PANTALOONS]

pan·ty·hose (PAN tee HOHZ) n. *(construed as pl.)* a one-piece garment combining panties and stockings.

pap (pap) n. **1.** any soft food for babies. **2.** anything lacking value or substance. [ME]

pa·pa (PAH pə) n. father: used familiarly. [< F]

pa·pa·cy (PAY pə see) n. pl. **·cies 1.** the dignity, office, or jurisdiction of the pope. **2.** the succession of popes. **3.** the period during which a pope is in office. **4.** *cap.* the system of government of the Roman Catholic Church. [ME *papacie*]

pa·pal (PAY pəl) adj. **1.** of, pertaining to, or ordered by the pope. **2.** of or pertaining to the papacy. [ME]

pa·pa·ya (pə PAH yə) n. **1.** the yellow, melonlike fruit of a tropical American evergreen tree. **2.** the tree. Also **paw·paw** (PAW paw). [< Sp.]

pa·per (PAY pər) n. **1.** a substance made from pulp obtained from rags, wood, etc., usu. formed into thin sheets for writing, printing, wrapping, etc. **2.** a sheet of this material. **3.** wallpaper. **4.** a printed or written document, discourse, or treatise. **5.** a newspaper. **6.** in schools and colleges, a piece of written work, as an assignment, a report, etc. **7.** pl. personal documents or identification; credentials. **8.** in business, negotiable written or printed pledges to pay. —**on paper 1.** in written or printed form. **2.** on theory, as distinguished from fact. —v.t. **1.** cover with wallpaper. **2.** *Slang* issue free tickets of admission to (a place of amusement). —adj. **1.** made of paper. **2.** existing only in writing. [ME *papire*] —**pa'per·y** adj.

pa·per·back (PAY pər BAK) adj. of books, having a flexible paper cover or binding. —n. a book so bound.

pa·per·weight (PAY pər WAYT) n. a small, heavy object, placed on loose papers to secure them.

pap·er·work (PAY pər WURK) n. work involving the preparation or handling of reports, forms, etc.

pa·pier-mâ·ché (PAY pər mə SHAY) n. a material consisting of paper pulp mixed with size, paste, etc., that can be molded when wet and that becomes hard when dry. [< F, lit., chewed paper]

pa·pri·ka (pa PREE kə) n. a condiment made from the ripe fruit of a mild variety of red pepper. [< Hung.]

Pap test (pap) a method of early detection of cervical cancer. Also **Pap smear.** [after George *Papanicolaou*, 1883–1962, U.S. scientist]

pa·py·rus (pə PĪ rəs) n. pl. **·ri** (-rī), **·py·rus·es 1.** a tall, rushlike aquatic plant, formerly common in Egypt. **2.** a type of writing paper made by the ancient Egyptians from this plant. **3.** a manuscript written on this material. [ME *papirus*]

par (pahr) n. **1.** an accepted standard or level used for comparison: *His work is on a par* with that of most students. **2.** the average in amount, quality, or degree: *My health is below par.* **3.** in commerce, equality between the face value and the market value of shares of stock, bonds, etc. **4.** in golf, the number of strokes allotted to a hole or round when played well. —*adj.* **1.** normal; average. **2.** in commerce, having the face value normal. [< L, equal]

para-¹ *prefix* **1.** beside; along with: *paramilitary.* **2.** beyond; aside from; amiss: *paradox.* [< Gk. *para-* beside]

para-² *combining form* shelter or protection against: *parasol.* [< F]

par·a·ble (PAR ə bəl) *n.* a short narrative making a moral or religious point by comparison with natural or homely things. [ME *parabil*]

pa·rab·o·la (pə RAB ə lə) *n. Math.* the curve formed by the edges of a plane when cutting through a right circular cone at an angle parallel to one of its sides. [< NL] — **par·a·bol·ic** (PAR ə BOL ik) *adj.*

par·a·chute (PAR ə SHOOT) *n.* a large, umbrella-shaped apparatus for retarding the speed of a body descending through the air, esp. from an airplane. —*v.t. & v.i.* **·chut·ed, ·chut·ing** drop, descend, or convey by parachute. [< F] —**par'a·chut' ist** *n.*

pa·rade (pə RAYD) *n.* **1.** a procession or march for ceremony, display, or inspection. **2.** a ground where military reviews are held. **3.** a promenade or public walk; also, the persons promenading. —**on parade** on display. —*v.* **·rad·ed, ·rad·ing** *v.t.* **1.** walk or march through or about. **2.** display ostentatiously; flaunt. **3.** cause to assemble for military parade. —*v.t.* **4.** march formally. **5.** walk in public for the purpose of showing oneself. [< F]

par·a·digm (PAR əDIM) *n. Gram.* **1.** a list of all the inflected forms of a word showing declension, conjugation, etc. **2.** any pattern or example. [< LL *paradigma*] — **par·a·dig·mat·ic** (PAR ə dig MAT ik) *adj.*

par·a·dise (PAR ə DĪS) *n.* **1.** heaven. **2.** *Often cap.* Eden. **3.** a place or state of great beauty or delight. [ME *paradis*] — **par·a·di·sa·i·cal** (PAR ə di SAY i kəl) *adj.*

par·a·dox (PAR ə DOKS) *n.* **1.** a statement seemingly absurd or contradictory, yet in fact true. **2.** a statement essentially self-contradictory, false, or absurd. [< L *paradoxum*] —**par'a·dox'i·cal** *adj.* — **par'a·dox'i·cal·ly** *adv.*

par·a·gon (PAR ə GON) *n.* a model or pattern of excellence. [< MF]

par·a·graph (PAR ə GRAF) *n.* **1.** a distinct section of a written discourse, begun on a new line and generally containing a unified statement of a particular point. **2.** a short article, item, or comment, as in a newspaper. **3.** a mark () used to indicate where a paragraph is to be begun. —*v.t.* arrange in or into paragraphs. [< Gk. *paragraphé* marked passage]

par·a·keet (PAR ə KEET) *n.* any of certain small parrots with long, wedge-shaped tails. [< MF *paroquet*]

par·a·le·gal (PAR ə LEE gəl) *n.* an attorney's trained assistant. —*adj.* of or pertaining to a paralegal or the duties of a paralegal.

par·al·lax (PAR ə LAKS) *n.* the apparent displacement of an object, esp. of a heavenly body, when it is viewed successively from two points not in the same line of sight. [< Gk. *parállaxis* change]

par·al·lel (PAR ə LEL) *adj.* **1.** being a uniform distance away or apart throughout a certain area or extent. **2.** *Geom.* not meeting, however far extended: said of straight lines and of planes. **3.** having a close resemblance. **4.** *Electr.* connecting like terminals, as a group of cells, condensers, etc. —*n.* **1.** an object or surface equidistant from another. **2.** *Geom.* a parallel line or plane. **3.** a counterpart; match. **4.** comparison: draw a *parallel* between two things. **5.** *Geog.* any of the circles imagined as drawn parallel to the earth's equator, each of which marks a latitude. **6.** *Electr.* connection between like terminals: usu. in the phrase **in parallel.** —*v.t.* **·leled, ·lel·ing 1.** make, be, go, or extend parallel to. **2.** correspond to. **3.** compare; liken. [< L *parallelus*] — **par·al·lel·ism** (PAR ə le LIZ əm) *n.*

par·al·lel·e·pi·ped (PAR ə LEL ə PĪ pid) *n.* a prism with six faces, each of which is a parallelogram. [< Gk. *parallēlepípedon*]

par·al·lel·o·gram (PAR ə LEL ə GRAM) *n.* **1.** *Geom.* a four-sided plane figure whose opposite sides are parallel and equal. **2.** any area or object having such form. [< LL *parallelogrammum*]

pa·ral·y·sis (pə RAL ə sis) *n. pl.* **·ses** (-SEEZ) **1.** *Pathol.* partial or complete loss of motor function. **2.** cessation or crippling of normal activities. [< L] —**par·a·lyt·ic** (PAR ə LIT ik) *adj. & n.*

par·a·lyze (PAR ə līz) *v.t.* **·lyzed, ·lyz·ing 1.** bring about paralysis in; make paralytic.

2. render powerless, ineffective, or inactive.

par·a·me·ci·um (PAR ə MEE see əm) *n. pl.* **·ci·a** (-see ə) any of various oval-shaped protozoa having cilia. [< NL]

par·a·med·ic (PAR ə MED ik) *n.* one trained to assist a physician. — **par'a·med'i·cal** *adj.*

pa·ram·e·ter (pə RAM i tər) *n.* **1.** *Math.* a constant or variable term that determines the operation or characteristics of a system. **2.** loosely, a fixed limit or guideline. [< NL *parametrum*]

par·a·mil·i·tar·y (PAR ə MIL i TER ee) *adj.* having a military structure; capable of becoming or supplementing a military force. [< PARA-¹ + MILITARY]

par·a·mount (PAR ə MOWNT) *adj.* superior to all others; chief in importance or authority. [< AF *paramont*]

par·a·mour (PAR ə MUUR) *n.* a lover, esp. one who unlawfully takes the place of a spouse. [ME]

par·a·noi·a (PAR ə NOI ə) *n. Psychiatry* a form of mental disorder characterized by delusions of persecution or of grandeur. [< NL] —**par'a·noid'** *adj. & n.*

par·a·nor·mal (PAR ə NOR məl) *adj.* not explainable scientifically.

par·a·pet (PAR ə pit) *n.* a low wall about the edge of a roof, terrace, bridge, etc. [< Ital. *parapetto*] —**par'a·pet'ed** *adj.*

par·a·pher·na·li·a (PAR ə fər NAYL yə) *n. pl.* (construed sometimes as sing.) **1.** personal effects. **2.** a group of articles, esp. as used in some activity; equipment. [< Med.L]

par·a·phrase (PAR ə FRAYZ) *n.* a restatement of the meaning of a passage, work, etc., as for clarity. —*v.t. & v.i.* **·phrased, ·phras·ing** express in or make a paraphrase. [< MF] —**par'a·phras'er** *n.* — **par'a·phras'a·ble** *adj.*

par·a·ple·gi·a (PAR ə PLEE jee ə) *n. Pathol.* paralysis of the lower half of the body, due to disease or injury of the spinal cord. [< NL] —**par·a·ple'gic** *adj. & n.*

par·a·pro·fes·sion·al (PAR ə prə FESH ə nl) *n.* one trained to assist professionals, as teachers.

par·a·psy·chol·o·gy (PAR ə sī KOL ə jee) *n.* the study of alleged psychic phenomena. — **par'a·psy·chol'o·gist** *n.*

par·a·site (PAR ə SĪT) *n.* **1.** *Biol.* an animal or plant that lives in or on another organism, the host, and from whom it obtains

nourishment. **2.** one who lives at another's expense without making proper return. [< MF] —**par·a·sit·ic** (PAR ə SIT ik) or **·i·cal** *adj.* —**par'a·sit'ism** *n.*

par·a·sol (PAR ə SAWL) *n.* a small umbrella used as protection against the sun. [< F]

par·a·sym·pa·thet·ic (PAR ə SIM pə THET ik) *adj. Anat.* denoting a part of the nervous system having among its functions the constriction of the pupil, the slowing of the heart, and the dilation of the blood vessels.

par·a·thy·roid (PAR ə THĪ roid) *Anat. adj.* **1.** lying near the thyroid gland. **2.** of or pertaining to any of the small glands found near or on the thyroid gland and serving to control the amount of calcium in the blood. —*n.* one of the parathyroid glands.

par·boil (PAHR BOIL) *v.t.* boil partially. [ME *parboylen*]

par·cel (PAHR səl) *n.* **1.** something that is wrapped up; package. **2.** a quantity of some commodity put up for sale; lot. **3.** an indefinite number of persons or things. **4.** a distinct portion of land. —*v.t.* **par·celed, par·cel·ing** divide or distribute in parts or shares: usu. with *out.* —*adj. & adv.* part; partly. [ME]

parcel post a postal service for delivering relatively small parcels.

parch (pahrch) *v.t.* **1.** make extremely dry. **2.** make very thirsty. **3.** dry (corn, peas, etc.) by exposing to great heat. **4.** dry up or shrivel by exposing to cold. —*v.i.* **5.** become dry. **6.** become dry with thirst. [ME *perchen*]

parch·ment (PAHRCH mənt) *n.* **1.** the prepared skin of sheep, goats, and other animals, used for writing or painting upon. **2.** a writing on this material. **3.** paper made in imitation of parchment. [ME *parchemin*]

par·don (PAHR dn) *v.t.* **1.** remit the penalty of (an offense, insult, etc.). **2.** forgive (a person) for an offense. **3.** grant courteous allowance for or to. —*n.* **1.** the act of pardoning; forgiveness. **2.** an official warrant declaring such a remission. [ME] —**par' don·a·ble** *adj.* —**par'don·a·bly** *adv.*

pare (pair) *v.t.* **pared, par·ing 1.** cut off the covering layer or part of. **2.** cut off or trim away (a covering layer or part): often with *off* or *away.* **3.** diminish gradually. [ME *paren*] —**par'er** *n.*

par·e·gor·ic (PAR i GOR ik) *n. Med.* a tincture of opium, used primarily to treat diarrhea. [< LL *paregoricus* soothing]

par·ent (PAR ənt) *n.* **1.** a father or mother. **2.** one exercising the functions of a father or mother. **3.** a progenitor; forefather. **4.** any organism that generates another. [ME] —**pa·ren·tal** (pə REN tl) *adj.*

par·ent·age (PAR ən tij) *n.* descent or derivation from parents; lineage; origin. [< MF]

pa·ren·the·sis (pə REN thə sis) *n. pl.* •ses (-seez) **1.** either of the upright curved lines ( ) used to enclose an interjected, explanatory, or qualifying remark, mathematical quantities, etc. **2.** *Gram.* a word, phrase, or clause inserted in a sentence that is grammatically complete without it. [< LL] —**par·en·thet·i·cal** (PAR ən THET i kəl) *or* **par'en·thet'ic** *adj.* —**par'en·thet'i·cal·ly** *adv.*

pa·re·sis (pə REE sis) *n. Pathol.* **1.** partial paralysis affecting muscular motion but not sensation. **2.** a late manifestation of syphilis: **general paresis,** characterized by chronic paralysis. [< NL]

par·fait (pahr FAY) *n.* a frozen dessert made with eggs, sugar, whipped cream, and fruit or other flavoring. [< F, lit., perfect]

pa·ri·ah (pə RĪ ə) *n.* **1.** a member of an extensive low caste of southern India and Burma. **2.** a social outcast. [< Tamil *paraiyar*]

par·i·mu·tu·el (PAR i MYOO choo əl) *n.* **1.** a system of betting at races in which those who have bet on the winners share in the total amount wagered. **2.** a parimutuel machine. [< F]

parimutuel machine a machine for recording pari-mutuel bets: also called *totalizator, totalizer.*

par·ing (PAIR ing) *n.* **1.** the act of one who pares. **2.** *Often pl.* the part pared off.

par·ish (PAR ish) *n.* **1.** *Eccl.* in the Anglican, Roman Catholic, and some other churches, a district with its own church. **2.** in Louisiana, a civil district corresponding to a county. **3.** the people of a parish; esp., those who worship at the same church. ◆ Collateral adjective: *parochial.* [ME]

pa·rish·ion·er (pə RISH ə nər) *n.* a member of a parish.

par·i·ty (PAR i tee) *n.* **1.** equality, as of condition, rank, value, etc.; also, a like state or degree. **2.** equality between the currency or prices of commodities of two countries or cities. **3.** perfect analogy; close resemblance. **4.** a level for farm prices that gives to farmers the same purchasing power that they averaged during each year of a chosen base period. [< LL *paritas*]

park (pahrk) *n.* **1.** a tract of land for public recreation in or near a city. **2.** land preserved by a government because of its historical, scientific, or scenic interest. **3.** a large tract of land surrounding a country estate. [ME] —*v.t. & v.i.* place or leave (an automobile etc.) standing for a time, as on a street.

par·ka (PAHR kə) *n.* **1.** hooded outer garment of undressed skins worn in regions of extreme cold. **2.** any similar garment. [< Aleut]

par·kin·son·ism (PAHR kin sə NIZ əm) *Pathol.* a form of paralysis characterized by muscular rigidity, tremor, and weakness. Also **Park'·in·son's disease.** [after James *Parkinson,* 1755—1824, English physician who first described it]

Parkinson's Law the jocular observation that the amount of work done is in inverse proportion to the number of people employed to accomplish it. [< a book (1957) by C. Northcote *Parkinson,* English historian]

park·land (PAHRK LAND) *n. Often pl.* **1.** land used or designated as a park. **2.** grassland with trees.

park·way (PAHRK WAY) *n.* a wide thoroughfare planted with turf and trees.

par·lance (PAHR ləns) *n.* manner of speech; language. [< AF]

par·lay (PAHR lay) *v.t. & v.i.* place (an original bet and its winnings) on a later race, contest, etc. —*n.* such a bet. [< F]

par·ley (PAHR lee) *n.* a conference, as with an enemy. [ME *parlai*] —**par'ley** *v.i.* confer; talk.

par·lia·ment (PAHR lə mənt) *n.* **1.** an assembly for consultation and deliberation. **2.** a national legislature. **3.** *cap.* the supreme legislature of any of several countries, esp. of Great Britain and Northern Ireland. [ME]

par·lia·men·tar·i·an (PAHR lə men TAIR ee ən) *n.* one versed in parliamentary procedure or debate.

par·lia·men·ta·ry (PAHR lə MEN tə ree) *adj.* **1.** of, pertaining to, or enacted by a parliament. **2.** according to the rules of a parliament.

parliamentary procedure the rules by which meetings of deliberative assemblies etc. are formally conducted. Also **parliamentary law.**

par·lor (PAHR lər) *n.* **1.** formerly, a room for reception of callers or entertainment of guests. **2.** a business establishment: ice-cream *parlor*. [ME *parlour*]

parlor car a railway car fitted with comfortable chairs.

pa·ro·chi·al (pə ROH kee əl) *adj.* **1.** pertaining to, supported by, or confined to a parish. **2.** narrow; provincial. —**pa·ro'chi·al·ism** *n.*

parochial school a school supported and directed by the parish of a church.

par·o·dy (PAR ə dee) *n. pl.* **·dies** a humorous or burlesque imitation of a literary or musical work or style. [< L *parodia*] —**pa·rod·ic** (pə ROD ik) or **·i·cal** *adj.* —**par'o·dist** *n.* —**par'o·dy** *v.t.* **·died, ·dy·ing**

pa·role (pə ROHL) *n.* **1.** the conditional release of a prisoner before the entire sentence has been served. **2.** the duration of such conditional freedom. —**on parole** freed from prison under conditions of parole. —*v.t.* **·roled, ·rol·ing** release (a prisoner) on parole. [< MF *parole d'honneur* word of honor] —**pa·rol'ee** *n.*

par·ox·ysm (PAR ək SIZ əm) *n.* **1.** a sudden and violent outburst, as of emotion or action. **2.** *Pathol.* a sudden intensification of the symptoms of a disease, usu. occurring at intervals. [< Gk. *paroxysmós* irritation] —**par'ox·ys'mal** *adj.*

par·quet (pahr KAY) *n.* **1.** flooring of parquetry. **2.** the main floor of a theater, esp. from the orchestra pit to the parquet circle: also called *orchestra.* —*v.t.* **·quet·ed** (-KAYD), **·quet·ing** (-KAY ing) make (a floor etc.) of parquetry. [< F]

parquet circle the section of theater seats at the rear of the parquet and under the balcony: also called *parterre.*

par·quet·ry (PAHR ki tree) *n. pl.* **·ries** inlaid mosaic of wood, used esp. for floors.

par·ri·cide (PAR ə SID) *n.* **1.** the killing of a parent. **2.** one who has killed a parent. [< L *parricidum* killing of a relative]

par·rot (PAR ət) *n.* any of certain birds native in warm regions, having a hooked bill and often brilliant plumage, some of which imitate human speech and laughter. —*v.t.* repeat or imitate by rote.

par·ry (PAR ee) *v.t. & v.i.* **·ried, ·ry·ing** ward off or evade (a thrust in fencing, a hostile question, etc.). —*n. pl.* **·ries** a defensive stroke or diversion in or as in fencing. [< F *parer* ward off]

parse (pahrs) *v.t.* **parsed, pars·ing** analyze (a sentence) grammatically by giving the form and syntactic function of each of its words. [< L *pars* part]

par·sec (PAHR SEK) *n. Astron.* a unit of distance used in expressing stellar distances, equivalent to 3.26 light-years.

par·si·mo·ny (PAHR sə MOH nee) *n.* undue sparingness in the expenditure of money; stinginess. [ME *parcimony*] —**par'si·mo'ni·ous** *adj.* —**par'si·mo'ni·ous·ly** *adv.*

pars·ley (PAHR slee) *n.* a cultivated herb with aromatic leaves, widely used to garnish and flavor foods. [ME *persely*]

par·son (PAHR sən) *n.* **1.** a clergyman; minister. **2.** in some churches, a clergyman in charge of a parish. [ME *persone*]

par·son·age (PAHR sə nij) *n.* a clergyman's dwelling, esp. one provided by the parish.

part (pahrt) *n.* **1.** a portion of a whole; segment. **2.** a distinct piece or portion that fulfills a specific function in the working of the whole, as of a machine, animal body, etc. **3.** *Usu. pl.* a region; territory: in foreign *parts.* **4.** one's proper share, as of obligation or performance: do one's *part.* **5.** a role in a play. **6.** one side in a dispute. **7.** participation in something. **8.** *Usu. pl.* an endowment of mind or character: a person of *parts.* **9.** the melody intended for a single voice or instrument in a concerted piece; also, the written music for this. **10.** the dividing line on the scalp made by combing sections of the hair in opposite directions. —**for one's part** as far as one is concerned. —**for the most part** to the greatest extent; in general. —**in part** partly. —**part and parcel** an essential part. —**take part** participate; share or cooperate: usu. with *in.* —**take someone's part** support someone in a contest or disagreement. —*v.t.* **1.** divide or break (something) into parts. **2.** separate; keep or move apart. **3.** comb (the hair) so as to leave a dividing line on the scalp. —*v.i.* **4.** become divided or broken into parts. **5.** go away from each other; cease associating. **6.** depart. —**part from** separate from; leave. —**part with 1.** give up; relinquish. **2.** part from. —*adv.* to some extent; partly. [ME]

par·take (pahr TAYK) *v.i.* **·took, ·tak·en, ·tak·ing 1.** take part or have a share: with *in.* **2.** receive or take a portion or share: with *of.* **3.** have something of the quality or character: with *of.* [ME *part taking*] —**par·tak'er** *n.*

par·terre (pahr TAIR) *n.* **1.** a flower garden having beds arranged in a pattern. **2.** the parquet circle in a theater. [< F *par terre* on the ground]

par•the•no•gen•e•sis (PAHR thə noh JEN ə sis) *n. Biol.* reproduction by means of unfertilized eggs, seeds, or spores. [< NL] — **par'the•no•ge•net'ic** (-jə NET ik) *adj.*

par•tial (PAHR shəl) *adj.* **1.** pertaining to, constituting, or involving a part only. **2.** favoring one side; biased. **3.** having a special liking: usu. with *to*. [ME *parcial* particular] —**par•ti•al•i•ty** (PAHR shee AL i tee) *n.* — **par'tial•ly** *adv.*

par•tic•i•pant (pahr TIS ə pənt) *adj.* sharing; taking part in. —*n.* one who participates.

par•tic•i•pate (pahr TIS ə PAYT) *v.i.* **•pat•ed, •pat•ing** take part or have a share in common with others: with *in*. [< L *participatus* shared] —**par•tic'i•pa'tion** *n.* —**par•tic•i•pa•to•ry** (pahr TIS i pə TOR ee) *adj.*

par•ti•cip•i•al (PAHR tə SIP ee əl) *adj. Gram.* **1.** having the nature, form, or use of a participle. **2.** characterized by, consisting of, or based on a participle. —*n.* a participle. [< L *participialis*]

par•ti•ci•ple (PAHR tə SIP ee əl) *n. Gram.* a verb form that can also function as an adjective. The **present participle** ends in *-ing* and the **past participle** commonly in *-d*, *-ed*, *-en*, *-n*, or *-t*. [ME]

par•ti•cle (PAHR ti kəl) *n.* **1.** a minute part, piece, or portion, as of matter. **2.** a very small amount or slight degree. **3.** *Physics* one of the elementary components of an atom, as an electron etc. **4.** *Gram.* a short, uninflected part of speech, as an article, preposition, etc. [ME]

particle board a hard board made of bonded wood chips.

par•tic•u•lar (pər TIK yə lər) *adj.* **1.** peculiar or pertaining to an individual person, object, or instance; not universal; specific. **2.** referring to one as distinguished from others. **3.** especially noteworthy. **4.** requiring or giving minute attention to details; fastidious. —*n.* **1.** *Usu. pl.* an item; detail. **2.** an individual instance; a single or separate case. —**in particular** particularly. [ME *particuler*]

par•tic•u•lar•i•ty (pər TIK yə LAR i tee) *n. pl.* **•ties 1.** the state or quality of being particular. **2.** that which is particular, as a circumstance, detail, or peculiarity.

par•tic•u•lar•ize (pər TIK yə lə RĪZ) *v.* **•ized, •iz•ing** *v.t.* **1.** speak of or treat indi-

vidually or in detail. —*v.i.* **2.** give particular details; be specific.

par•tic•u•lar•ly (pər TIK yə lər lee) *adv.* **1.** with specific reference; distinctly. **2.** in an unusually great degree; especially. **3.** part by part; in detail.

part•ing (PAHR ting) *adj.* **1.** given or done at parting: a *parting* glance. **2.** departing; declining. **3.** separating; dividing. —*n.* **1.** the act of separating, or the state of being separated. **2.** a leave-taking; esp., a final separation. **3.** a place of separation.

par•ti•san (PAHR tə zən) *n.* **1.** one who supports or upholds a party, cause, etc.; esp., an overly zealous adherent. **2.** *Mil.* a member of a body of detached or irregular troops; a guerrilla. —*adj.* **1.** of, relating to, or characteristic of a partisan. **2.** advocated by or composed of members of one party. **3.** *Mil.* of or carried on by partisans. [< MF] — **par'ti•san•ship** *n.*

par•tite (PAHR tīt) *adj.* divided into or composed of parts: used in combination: *bipartite, tripartite.* [< L *partitus* divided]

par•ti•tion (pahr TISH ən) *n.* **1.** the act of dividing, separating, or distributing; also, the state of being divided, etc. **2.** something that divides or separates, as a light interior wall dividing a room. **3.** one of the parts, sections, compartments, etc., into which a thing is divided. —*v.t.* **1.** divide into parts, sections, segments, etc. **2.** separate by a partition: often with *off*. [ME]

par•ti•tive (PAHR ti tiv) *adj.* **1.** separating into integral parts or distinct divisions. **2.** *Gram.* denoting a part as distinct from the whole. —**par'ti•tive•ly** *adv.*

part•ly (PAHRT lee) *adv.* in part; partially.

part•ner (PAHRT nər) *n.* one who is united or associated with another or others in some action, enterprise, etc.; as: **a** one of the joint owners of a business. **b** a spouse. **c** one of a couple who dance together. **d** one of two or more players on the same side in a game. **e** a colleague or associate. [ME] — **part'ner•ship** *n.*

part of speech *Gram.* one of the eight traditional classes of words in English: noun, pronoun, verb, adverb, adjective, conjunction, preposition, and interjection.

par•took (pahr TUUK) past tense of PAR-TAKE.

part song a song of three or more parts; esp., a choral piece without accompaniment.

part-time (PAHRT TĪM) *adj.* for, during, or by part of the time: a *part-time* student. —

parturition

adv. (PAHRT-TĪM): She worked *part-time*.

par·tu·ri·tion (pahr TUU RISH ən) *n.* childbirth. [< LL] —**par·tu·ri·ent** (pahr TUUR ee ənt) *adj.*

par·ty (PAHR tee) *n. pl.* **·ties 1.** a social gathering for pleasure or entertainment. **2.** a group of persons associated or gathered together for some common purpose; as: **a** a political group organized to gain control of government through the election of its candidates to public office. **b** a small body of persons selected for some special mission or assignment: a demolition *party.* **c** a group formed for a sport or other diversion. **3.** *Law* either of the persons or groups involved in legal proceedings. **4.** one who takes part or participates in an action, plan, etc.: a *party* to his crime. **5.** a person. [ME *partie*]

party line 1. a telephone line or circuit serving two or more subscribers: also **party wire. 2.** the essential beliefs or policies of a political party.

party politics policies and acts aimed at furthering the interests of one political party.

par·ve·nu (PAHR və NOO) *n.* one who has risen above his class through the sudden attainment of wealth or position; an upstart. [< F]

pas (pah) *n.* a dance step or series of steps. [< F]

pas·chal (PAS kəl) *adj.* pertaining to Passover or to Easter. [ME]

pa·sha (PAH shə) *n.* formerly, a Turkish honorary title placed after the name of generals, governors of provinces, etc. [< Turkish *pasa*]

pass (pas) *v.t.* **1.** go by or move past. **2.** succeed in meeting the requirements of (a test, trial, etc.). **3.** go beyond or surpass. **4.** spend (a specified period of time). **5.** cause or allow to move, go past, proceed, etc. **6.** approve or sanction; enact: *pass* a bill. **7.** be approved or sanctioned by. **8.** cause or allow to get through (a test, trial, etc.). **9.** convey or transfer from one to another; transmit. **10.** in football, hockey, etc., transfer (the ball etc.) to another player on the same team. **11.** utter or pronounce, esp. judicially: *pass* sentence. **12.** discharge or excrete (waste). —*v.i.* **13.** go or move; proceed; advance. **14.** go by or move past. **15.** obtain or force a way: *pass* through a crowd. **16.** lead or extend; run: The river *passes* under a bridge. **17.**

go by or elapse. **18.** come to an end; terminate. **19.** change or move from one condition, place, form, etc., to another. **20.** take place; occur. **21.** be allowed or permitted without challenge, censure, etc. **22.** undergo a test etc. successfully. **23.** be approved, sanctioned, ratified, etc. **24.** be excreted or voided. **25.** *Law* give or pronounce sentence, judgment, etc.: with *on* or *upon.* **26.** in football, hockey etc., transfer the ball etc. to a teammate. **27.** in card games, decline to make a play, bid, etc. — **pass away 1.** come to an end. **2.** die. **3.** allow (time) to elapse. —**pass for** be accepted or regarded as, usu. erroneously. —**pass off 1.** give out or circulate as genuine; palm off. **2.** be emitted, as vapor. —**pass out 1.** distribute or circulate. **2.** *Informal* faint. —**pass over** fail to notice or consider. —**pass up 1.** reject or fail to take advantage of, as an offer or opportunity. **2.** pass over. —*n.* **1.** a way or opening through which one can pass; esp., a narrow passage between mountains. **2.** a permit, order, or license giving the bearer authority to enter, move about, depart, etc. without the usual restrictions; as: **a** *Mil.* permission to be absent from duty; also, the period of absence covered by it. **b** a free ticket for a theater, movie, train, etc. **3.** in magic, hypnotism, etc., a movement of the hand, a wand, etc. over a person or thing. **4.** a state of affairs; situation: bring events to a critical *pass.* **5.** the act of passing. —**bring to pass** cause to be fulfilled or accomplished. —**come to pass** happen. —**make a pass at 1.** attempt to hit. **2.** *Informal* attempt to become sexually intimate with; proposition. [ME *passen*]

pass·a·ble (PAS ə bəl) *adj.* **1.** capable of being passed, penetrated, crossed, etc.: *passable* rivers. **2.** fairly good or acceptable; tolerable. —**pass'a·bly** *adv.*

pas·sage (PAS ij) *n.* **1.** a portion of a writing, speech, or musical composition, usu. of small or moderate length. **2.** a way, channel, duct, etc. by which a person or thing may pass. **3.** a hall, corridor, etc. between apartments in a building. **4.** the act of passing, changing, etc.; esp., the transition from one state or period to another. **5.** a journey, esp. by sea. **6.** the right, power, or freedom to pass. **7.** the passing or enactment of a legislative measure. [ME]

pas·sage·way (PAS ij WAY) *n.* a way affording passage; esp., a hall or corridor.

pas•sé (pa SAY) *adj.* **1.** past the prime; faded. **2.** out-of-date; old-fashioned. [< F]

pas•sel (PAS əl) *n.* a large number; a group.

pas•sen•ger (PAS ən jər) *n.* one who travels in a conveyance. [ME *passager*]

pas•ser•by (PAS ər BĪ) *n. pl.* **pas•sers•by** one who passes by, usu. casually.

pass•ing (PAS ing) *adj.* **1.** going by or away. **2.** transitory; fleeting. **3.** happening or occurring; current. **4.** done, said, etc. in a cursory or casual manner. **5.** that serves to pass: a *passing* grade. —*n.* **1.** the act of one who or that which passes. **2.** death. —**in passing** incidentally. —*adv.* in a surpassing degree or manner.

pas•sion (PASH ən) *n.* **1.** any intense, extreme, or overpowering emotion or feeling, as love, anger, etc. **2.** intense sexual desire or lust. **3.** an outburst of strong feeling, esp. of violence or anger. **4.** a strong desire or affection for some object, cause, etc. **5.** the object of such a desire or affection. [ME] —**pas'sion•less** *adj.* cold, unemotional; calm

Pas•sion (PASH ən) *n.* the sufferings of Christ, esp. after the Last Supper and on the Cross.

pas•sion•ate (PASH ə nit) *adj.* **1.** capable of or inclined to strong passion; excitable. **2.** expressing or characterized by passion or strong emotion; ardent. **3.** strong or vehement, as a feeling or emotion. —**pas'sion•ate•ly** *adv.*

passion play a religious drama representing the Passion of Christ.

pas•sive (PAS iv) *adj.* **1.** not acting, working, or operating; inactive; inert. **2.** acted upon, affected, or influenced by something external. **3.** receiving or receptive to an external force, etc. **4.** submitting or yielding without resistance or opposition; submissive. **5.** *Gram.* designating a voice of the verb that indicates that the subject is receiving the action. —*n. Gram.* **1.** the passive voice. **2.** a verb or construction in this voice. [ME] —**pas•siv•i•ty** (pa SIV i tee) *n.*

Pass•o•ver (PAS OH vər) *n.* a Jewish feast commemorating the deliverance of the ancient Israelites from slavery in Egypt. [Referring to the night when God, smiting the first-born of the Egyptians, passed over the houses of the children of Israel]

pass•port (PAS port) *n.* an official warrant certifying the citizenship of the bearer and affording protection to him when traveling abroad. [< MF *passeport*]

pass•word (PAS WURD) *n.* **1.** a secret word

or phrase enabling the speaker to pass a guard or sentry. **2.** anything that gains entrance or access for one.

past (past) *adj.* **1.** ended or finished; done with. **2.** having existed in or belonging to a former time: *past* civilizations. **3.** just passed or gone by: the *past* few days. —*n.* **1.** past or antecedent time, conditions, or events: usu. with *the*. **2.** something, as a former life or career, that is kept secret. **3.** *Gram.* **a** a verb tense denoting a past action or condition. **b** a verb in this tense. —*adv.* in such a manner as to go by: run *past*. —*prep.* beyond, as in time, position, amount, or influence. [ME]

pas•ta (PAH stə) *n.* a noodlelike paste or dough, as spaghetti etc. [< Ital.]

paste (payst) *n.* **1.** a mixture used as an adhesive. **2.** any of various soft, moist, smooth preparations used as foods, in cooking, etc. **3.** a vitreous composition used in making imitation gems; also, a gem made of this composition. —*v.t.* **past•ed, past•ing 1.** stick or fasten with or as with paste. **2.** cover by applying pasted material. [ME]

pas•tel (pa STEL) *n.* **1.** a picture drawn with colored crayons. **2.** a paste made of ground pigment in a gum solution; also, a hard crayon made of this paste. **3.** a delicate, soft, or slightly grayish tint. —**pas•tel'** *adj.*

pas•teur•ize (PAS chə RĪZ) *v.t.* •**ized, •iz•ing** slow down fermentation and destroy disease-causing bacteria (in milk, beer, etc.) by heating. [after Louis *Pasteur*, 1822–95, French chemist] —**pas'teur•i•za'tion** *n.*

pas•tiche (pa STEESH) *n.* a work of art, music, or literature made up of fragments from other sources. [< F]

pas•time (PAS TĪM) *n.* something that serves to make time pass agreeably. [< MF *passetemps*]

pas•tor (PAS tər) *n.* a Christian clergyman who has a church or congregation under his or her charge. [< L, shepherd]

pas•tor•al (PAS tər əl) *adj.* **1.** of or pertaining to shepherds, rustics, or rural life. **2.** having the characteristics usu. associated with rural life, as innocence, simplicity, etc. **3.** pertaining to a clergyman or to his duties. —*n.* **1.** a literary work, esp. a poem, dealing with rural life, scenes, etc. **2.** a picture illustrating rural scenes. [ME]

pas•tor•ate (PAS tər it) *n.* **1.** the office or jurisdiction of a pastor. **2.** the duration of a pastoral charge.

past participle see under PARTICIPLE.

past perfect *Gram.* the verb tense indicating an action completed prior to the occurrence of some other past action, as *had finished* in *He had finished before the bell rang.* Also called *pluperfect.*

pas·tra·mi (pə STRAH mee) *n.* heavily seasoned, smoked beef, usu. cut from the shoulder. [< Yiddish < Rumanian, cured meat]

pas·try (PAY stree) *n. pl.* **·tries** sweet, baked food, usu. made with a crust of dough, as pies, tarts, etc.

pas·tur·age (PAS chər ij) *n.* **1.** grass and herbage for cattle. **2.** ground used or suitable for grazing.

pas·ture (PAS chər) *n.* **1.** ground for the grazing of domestic animals. **2.** grass or herbage that grazing animals eat. — *v.t.* **·tured, ·tur·ing** put in a pasture to graze. [ME]

pas·ty¹ (PAY stee) *adj.* **past·i·er, past·i·est** like paste. — **past'ies** (PAY steez) *n.* small round coverings for a woman's nipples, esp. worn by a stripteaser.

past·y² (PAS tee) *n. Brit. pl.* **pasties** a pie; esp., a meat pie. [ME *pastee*]

pat (pat) *v.t.* **pat·ted, pat·ting** **1.** touch or tap lightly with something flat, esp. with the hand. **2.** shape or mold by a pat. —*n.* **1.** a light, caressing stroke; a gentle tap. **2.** the sound of patting or pattering. **3.** a small, molded mass, as of butter. —*adj.* **1.** exactly suitable; apt. **2.** glib; facile. —*adv.* firm; steadfast: stand *pat.* [ME *patte*] —**pat'ness** *n.*

patch (pach) *n.* **1.** a small piece of material used to repair a garment etc. **2.** a piece of adhesive tape or the like, applied to the skin. **3.** a piece of material worn over an injured eye. **4.** any small part of a surface not sharing the general character of the whole. —*v.t.* **1.** put a patch on. **2.** repair or put together, esp. hurriedly or crudely: often with *up* or *together.* **3.** make of patches, as a quilt. [ME *pacche*] —**patch'a·ble** *adj.*

patch·work (PACH wurk) *n.* **1.** a fabric made of patches of cloth, as for quilts etc. **2.** work done hastily or carelessly.

patch·y (PACH ee) *adj.* **patch·i·er, patch·i·est** **1.** made up of patches. **2.** careless; jumbled. —**patch'i·ness** *n.*

pate (payt) *n.* the head or top of the head; also, the brains or intellect: usu. humorous or derogatory. [ME]

pâ·té (pah TAY) a seasoned paste of cooked meats or poultry. [< F]

pa·tel·la (pə TEL ə) *n. pl.* **·tas, ·tel·lae** (-TEL ee) *Anat.* the flat, movable, oval bone in front of the knee joint; kneecap. [< L] —**pa·tel'lar** *adj.*

pat·en (PAT n) *n.* **1.** a plate; esp., a plate for the eucharistic bread. **2.** a thin, metallic plate or disk. [ME *pateyne*]

pat·ent (PAT nt) *n.* **1.** a government protection to an inventor, securing for a specific time the exclusive right of manufacturing and selling an invention. **2.** any official document securing a right. **3.** that which is protected by a patent or its distinctive marks or features. —*v.t.* obtain a patent on (an invention). —*adj.* **1.** manifest or apparent to everybody. **2.** open for general inspection or use. [ME] —**pat'·ent·a·ble** *adj.*

pat·en·tee (PAT n TEE) *n.* holder of a patent.

pa·tent·ly (PAT nt lee) *adv.* manifestly; clearly.

pa·ter·nal (pə TUR nl) *adj.* **1.** of, pertaining to, or characteristic of a father; fatherly. **2.** derived from, related through, or connected with one's father. [ME] —**pa·ter'nal·ly** *adv.*

pa·ter·nal·ism (pə TUR nl iz əm) *n.* the care or control of a country, community, group of employees, etc., in a manner suggestive of a father looking after his children. —**pa·ter'nal·is'tic** *adj.*

pa·ter·ni·ty (pə TUR ni tee) *n.* **1.** the condition of being a father. **2.** parentage on the male side. **3.** origin in general. [ME *paternite*]

path (path) *n. pl.* **paths** (pathz) **1.** a walk or way used by people or animals on foot. **2.** a track or course. **3.** a course of life or action. [ME] —**path'less** *adj.*

pa·thet·ic (pə THET ik) *adj.* of the nature of, expressing, or arousing sadness, pity, tenderness, etc. [< LL *patheticus*] —**pa·thet'i·cal·ly** *adv.*

path·find·er (PATH fīn dər) *n.* one skilled in leading or finding a way, esp. in unknown regions.

patho- *combining form* suffering; disease. [< Gk. *páthos* suffering]

path·o·gen (PATH ə jən) *n.* any disease-producing bacterium or microorganism. —**path'o·gen'ic** (PATH ə JEN ik) *adj.*

path·o·log·i·cal (PATH ə LOJ i kəl) *adj.* **1.** of pathology. **2.** related to or caused by disease. —**path'o·log'i·cal·ly** *adv.*

pattern

pa•thol•o•gy (pə THOL ə jee) n. pl. •gies 1. the branch of medical science that treats of the origin, nature, causes, and development of disease. 2. the sum of the conditions, processes, and effects in the course of a disease. —**pa•thol′o•gist** n.

pa•thos (PAY thos) n. the quality, esp. in literature or art, that arouses feelings of pity, sorrow, compassion, etc. [< Gk. páthos suffering]

-pathy combining form 1. suffering; affection. 2. Med. disease, or the treatment of disease: psychopathy. [< Gk. páthos suffering]

pa•tience (PAY shəns) n. the state, quality, or fact of being patient; also, the ability to be patient.

pa•tient (PAY shənt) adj. 1. possessing or demonstrating quiet, uncomplaining endurance under distress or annoyance. 2. tolerant, tender, and forbearing. 3. persevering; diligent. —n. a person undergoing treatment for disease or injury. [ME pacient] —**pa′tient•ly** adv.

pat•i•na (pə TEE nə) n. a green rust that covers ancient copper coins etc. [< Ital.]

pat•i•o (PAT ee OH) n. pl. •i•os 1. an open inner court. 2. a paved area adjoining a house, used for parties, barbecues, etc. [< Sp.]

pat•ois (PA twah) n. pl. **pat•ois** (PA twahz) a type of local dialect, esp. one that is rustic or illiterate. [< F]

pa•tri•arch (PAY tree AHRK) n. 1. the leader of a family or tribe who rules by paternal right. 2. a venerable man; esp., the founder of a religion, order, etc. 3. Eccl. in the Greek Orthodox Church, any of the bishops of Constantinople, Alexandria, Antioch, or Jerusalem. [ME patriarke] —**pa′tri•ar′chal** adj.

pa•tri•ar•chy (PAY tree AHR kee) n. pl. •chies a system of government in which the father or the male heir of his choice rules.

pa•tri•cian (pə TRISH ən) adj. 1. of or pertaining to the aristocracy. 2. noble or aristocratic. —n. 1. an aristocrat. 2. any one of the upper classes. [< L patricius patrician]

pat•ri•cide (PA trə SID) n. 1. the killing of one's father. 2. one who has done this. [< L patricida] —**pat′ri•ci′dal** adj.

pat•ri•lin•e•al (PA trə LIN ee əl) adj. derived from or descending through the male line.

pat•ri•mo•ny (PA trə MOH nee) n. pl. •nies an inheritance from a father or an ancestor; also, anything inherited. [ME patrimonie] —**pat′ri•mo′ni•al** adj.

pa•tri•ot (PAY tree ət) n. one who loves his or her country and zealously guards its welfare. [ME patriote] —**pa•tri•ot•ic** (PAY tree OT ik) adj. —**pa•tri•ot•ism** (PAY tree ə TIZ əm) n.

pa•tris•tic (pə TRIS tik) adj. of or pertaining to the fathers of the Christian church or to their writings.

pa•trol (pə TROHL) v.t. & v.i. •trolled, •trol•ling walk or go through or around (an area, town, etc.) for the purpose of guarding or inspecting. —n. 1. one or more soldiers, policemen, etc., patrolling a district. 2. a military reconnaissance or combat group. 3. the act of patrolling. [< F patrouille]

pa•tron (PAY trən) n. 1. one who protects, fosters, or supports some person or enterprise. 2. a regular customer. [ME] —**pa′tron•ess** n.fem.

pa•tron•age (PAY trə nij) n. 1. the protection or support of a patron. 2. in the public service, the power or right to distribute offices, esp. political offices. 3. the financial support given by customers to a commercial establishment.

pa•tron•ize (PAY trə NIZ) v.t. •ized, •iz•ing 1. act as a patron toward; give support to. 2. treat in a condescending manner. 3. trade with as a regular customer; frequent. —**pa′tron•iz′ing•ly** adv.

pat•ro•nym•ic (PA trə NIM ik) n. 1. a name derived from the name of one's father or paternal ancestor. 2. a name formed by adding a prefix or suffix to a proper name, as Johnson, son of John. [< LL patronymicus] —adj.

pat•ter¹ (PAT ər) v.i. 1. make a succession of light, sharp sounds. 2. move with light, quick steps. —**pat′ter** n.

pat•ter² v.t. & v.i. speak or say glibly or rapidly; chatter. —n. 1. glib and rapid talk, as used by comedians, etc. 2. any professional jargon.

pat•tern (PAT ərn) n. 1. an original or model proposed for or worthy of imitation. 2. anything shaped or designed to serve as a model or guide in making something else. 3. any decorative design or figure. 4. the stylistic composition or design of a work of art. 5. a complex of integrated parts functioning as a whole: the behavior pattern of a five-year-old. 6. a representative example, sample, or instance. —v.t. make after a model or pattern: with *on*, *upon*, or *after*. [ME *patron*]

pat·ty (PAT ee) *n. pl.* **·ties 1.** a small, flat piece of chopped meat, fish, etc. **2.** a small pie. [< PATÉ]

pau·ci·ty (PAW si tee) *n.* **1.** smallness of number or quantity. **2.** scarcity; insufficiency. [ME *paucite*]

paunch (pawnch) *n.* the abdomen or the belly, esp. if protruding. [ME *paunche*]

pau·per (PAW pər) *n.* **1.** one who receives, or is entitled to receive, public charity. **2.** any very poor person. [< L, poor] —**pau'per·ize** *v.t.* **·ized, ·iz·ing** make a pauper of

pause (pawz) *v.i.* **paused, paus·ing 1.** cease action or utterance temporarily; hesitate. **2.** dwell or linger: with *on* or *upon*. —*n.* **1.** a temporary ceasing of action; rest. **2.** a holding back because of doubt or irresolution; hesitation. **3.** a momentary cessation in speaking or music for the sake of meaning or expression. [ME]

pav·ane (pə VAHN) *n.* a slow, stately dance of the 16th and 17th c. [< MF]

pave (payv) *v.t.* **paved, pav·ing** cover with asphalt, concrete, etc., as a road. —**pave the way (for)** make preparation (for); lead up (to). [ME *paven*]

pave·ment (PAYV mənt) *n.* **1.** a paved road or footway. **2.** the material with which a surface is paved.

pa·vil·ion (pə VIL yən) *n.* **1.** a movable or open structure, as a large tent or small building. **2.** a related or connected part of a principal building, as for hospital patients. **3.** a canopy. —*v.t.* provide or shelter with a pavilion. [ME *pavilon*]

paw (paw) *n.* the foot of an animal having nails or claws. —*v.t. & v.i.* **1.** strike or scrape with the feet or paws: *paw* the air. **2.** *Informal* handle or caress rudely or clumsily; maul. [ME *pawe*]

pawn[1] (pawn) *n.* **1.** a chess piece of lowest rank. **2.** any insignificant person used at another's will. [ME *poun*]

pawn[2] *n.* **1.** something pledged as security for a loan. **2.** the condition of being held as a pledge for money loaned. —*v.t.* give as security for a loan. [< MF *pan*]

pawn·brok·er (PAWN BROH kər) *n.* one engaged in the business of lending money at interest on pledged personal property.

pawn·shop (PAWN SHOP) *n.* the shop of a pawnbroker.

pay (pay) *v.* **paid** or (*Obs.* except for def. 2 of *pay out*) **payed, pay·ing** *v.t.* **1.** give (some-

one) what is due for a debt, purchase, etc.; remunerate. **2.** give (money etc.) for a purchase, service rendered, etc. **3.** provide or hand over the amount of, as a debt, bill, etc. **4.** yield as return or recompense. **5.** afford profit or benefit to. **6.** render or give, as a compliment, attention, etc. **7.** make, as a call or visit. —*v.i.* **8.** make recompense or payment. **9.** be worthwhile: It *pays* to be honest. —**pay back** repay. —**pay off 1.** pay the entire amount of (a debt, mortgage, etc.). **2.** pay the wages of and discharge. **3.** make a full return. **4.** *Informal* bribe. —**pay out 1.** disburse or expend. **2.** *Naut.* let out by slackening, as a rope or cable. —**pay up** make full payment (of). —*n.* **1.** that which is given as a recompense; wages. **2.** paid employment: in the *pay* of our enemies. **3.** requital; reward; also, retribution. —*adj.* **1.** of or pertaining to payments, to persons who pay, or services paid for: *pay* day. **2.** requiring payment on use: *pay* phone. [ME *payen*] —**pay·ee'** *n.* —**pay'er** *n.*

pay·check (PAY CHEK) *n.* **1.** a check in payment of wages or salary. **2.** wages or salary.

pay dirt 1. soil containing enough metal to be profitable to mine. **2.** anything profitable.

pay·load (PAY LOHD) *n.* **1.** that part of a cargo producing revenue. **2.** the warhead of a guided missile. **3.** the persons, instruments, etc. carried in a spacecraft that are directly related to the objective of the flight.

pay·ment (PAY mənt) *n.* **1.** the act of paying, or that which is paid. **2.** punishment.

pay·off (PAY AWF) *n.* **1.** any settlement, reward, or punishment. **2.** *Informal* the climax or outcome of an incident or narrative. **3.** *Informal* a bribe.

pay·roll (PAY ROHL) *n.* a list of those entitled to receive pay, with the amounts due them; also, the total sum of money needed to make the payments.

PCP phencyclidine.

peace (pees) *n.* **1.** a state of mental or physical quiet or tranquillity; calm. **2.** the absence or cessation of war. **3.** public order and tranquillity. **4.** a state of reconciliation after strife or enmity. —**at peace 1.** in a quiet state; tranquil. **2.** in a state or condition of order and harmony. —**hold (or keep) one's peace** be silent. —*v.i. Obs. except as* be or become quiet. [ME *pes*] —**peace'ful** *adj.* —**peace'ful·ly** *adv.*

Peace Corps a U.S. government organization that sends trained volunteers to live in and aid developing countries by teaching, farming, etc.

peace·a·ble (PEE sə bəl) *adj.* **1.** inclined to peace. **2.** peaceful; tranquil. **—peace′a·bly** *adv.*

peace·mak·er (PEES MAY kər) *n.* one who effects a reconciliation between unfriendly parties.

peace pipe calumet.

peace·time (PEES TIM) *n.* a time of peace. **—adj.** of, characterized by, or used in peace.

peach (peech) *n.* **1.** the edible fruit of a tree of the rose family, widely cultivated in many varieties. **2.** the tree itself. **3.** a yellowish pink color. **4.** *Informal* an especially attractive person or thing. [ME *peche*]

pea·cock (PEE KOK) *n.* **1.** a male peafowl, having erectile, brilliantly iridescent tail feathers marked with eyelike spots. **2.** a vain person. [ME *pecok*]

pea·fowl (PEE FOWL) *n.* a large pheasant of Asia.

pea·hen (PEE HEN) *n.* a female peafowl.

peak (peek) *n.* **1.** a projecting point or edge; any end terminating in a point. **2.** a conspicuous or precipitous mountain; also, the summit of such a mountain. **3.** the maximum development, strength, value, etc. of something. **—v.t. 1.** make into a peak or point. **—v.i. 2.** assume the form of a peak. **3.** reach or attain a peak. **—peaked** (peekt) *adj.*

peak·ed (PEE kid) *adj.* having a thin or sickly appearance.

peal (peel) *n.* **1.** a prolonged, sonorous sound, as of a bell or thunder. **2.** a set of large bells. **3.** a change rung on a set of bells. **—v.t. & v.i.** sound with a peal or peals. [ME *pele*]

pea·nut (PEE NUT) *n.* **1.** the nutlike seed or seed pod of an annual vine ripening underground from the flowers that bury themselves after fertilization. **2.** the plant bearing this nut.

pear (pair) *n.* **1.** the juicy, edible, fleshy fruit of a tree of the rose family. **2.** the tree. [ME *pere*]

pearl (purl) *n.* **1.** a smooth, rounded body formed in the shells of various mollusks and largely used as a gem. **2.** something like such a jewel in form, luster, value, etc. **3.** mother-of-pearl. **4.** a very pale bluish gray: also **pearl blue, pearl gray. —adj.** pertaining to, consisting of, set with, or made of

pearl. **—v.i. 1.** seek or fish for pearls. **—v.t. 2.** adorn or set with or as with pearls. [ME *perle*] **—pearl′y** *adj.* **pearl′i·er, pearl′i·est**

peas·ant (PEZ ənt) *n.* **1.** in Europe, a farmer, farm laborer, or rustic workman. **2.** a boorish or simple-minded person. [ME *paissaunt*]

peas·ant·ry (PEZ ən tree) *n.* **1.** the peasant class; a body of peasants. **2.** rusticity.

peat (peet) *n.* **1.** a substance consisting of partially carbonized vegetable material, found usu. in bogs. **2.** a block of this substance, pressed and dried for fuel: also called *turf.* [ME *pete*] **—peat′y** *adj.* **peat′i·er, peat′i·est**

peat bog a marsh containing peat.

peat moss a moss from which peat may form.

peb·ble (PEB əl) *n.* a small, rounded fragment of rock, shaped by the action of water, ice, etc. **—v.t. ·bled, ·bling 1.** impart a rough grain to (leather). **2.** cover or pelt with pebbles. [ME *pobble*] **—peb·bly** (PEB lee) *adj.*

pec·ca·dil·lo (PEK ə DIL oh) *n. pl.* **·loes** or **·los** a slight or trifling sin. [< Sp.]

pec·cant (PEK ənt) *adj.* guilty of sin; sinful. [< L *peccare* sin]

pec·ca·ry (PEK ə ree) *n. pl.* **·ries** a hoglike animal of Central and South America. [< Carib]

pec·ca·vi (pe KAH vee) *n. pl.* **·vis** *Latin* a confession of guilt; lit., I have sinned.

peck[1] (pek) *v.t.* **1.** strike with the beak, as a bird does, or with something pointed. **2.** make by striking thus: *peck* a hole in a wall. **3.** pick up, as food, with the beak. **—v.i. 4.** make strokes with the beak or with something pointed. **5.** eat in small amounts or without appetite: with *at.* **—n. 1.** a quick, sharp blow, as with a beak. **2.** a quick kiss. [ME *pecke*] **—peck′er** *n.*

peck[2] *n.* **1.** a measure of capacity equal to ¼ bushel. **2.** a great quantity. [ME *pek*]

pec·tin (PEK tin) *n. Biochem.* any of a class of carbohydrates found in apples, lemons, etc. and used as a gel in fruit jellies.

pec·to·ral (PEK tə rəl) *adj.* of or pertaining to the breast or chest. **—n.** a pectoral organ, fin, or muscle. [ME]

pectoral fin *Zool.* one of the anterior paired fins of fishes, corresponding to the anterior limb of higher vertebrates.

pec·u·late (PEK yə LAYT) *v.t. & v.i.* **·lat·ed, ·lat·ing** steal or appropriate (funds) wrongfully; embezzle. [< L *peculatus* embezzled] —**pec'u·la'tion** n.

pe·cul·iar (pi KYOOL yər) *adj.* **1.** having a character exclusively its own; specific. **2.** singular; strange or eccentric. **3.** belonging particularly or exclusively to one. [ME] —**pe·cul'iar·ly** *adv.*

pe·cu·li·ar·i·ty (pi KYOO lee AR i tee) *n. pl.* **·ties 1.** a characteristic. **2.** the quality of being peculiar.

pe·cu·ni·ar·y (pi KYOO nee ER ee) *adj.* consisting of or relating to money. [< L *pecuniarius* propertied]

ped·a·gog·ic (PED ə GOJ ik) *adj.* **1.** of or pertaining to the art of teaching. **2.** of or belonging to a pedagogue; affected with a conceit of learning.

ped·a·gogue (PED ə GOG) *n.* **1.** a schoolmaster; educator. **2.** a pedantic, narrow-minded teacher. Also **ped'a·gog.** [ME *pedagoge* tutor]

ped·a·go·gy (PED ə GOH jee) *n.* the art or profession of teaching.

ped·al (PEED l) *adj.* **1.** of or pertaining to a foot, feet, or a footlike part. **2.** Of or pertaining to a pedal. —*n.* (PED l) *Mech.* a lever operated by the foot and having various functions: a bicycle *pedal*, a piano *pedal*. —*v.t. & v.i.* **ped·aled, ped·al·ing** (PED əl ing) move or operate by working pedals. [< F *pédale*]

ped·ant (PED nt) *n.* one who makes needless display of learning, or who insists upon the importance of trifling points of scholarship. [< Ital. *pedante* teacher] —**pe·dan·tic** (pə DAN tik) *adj.* —**ped'ant·ry** (PED n tree) *n.*

ped·dle (PED l) *v.t. & v.i.* **·died, ·dling 1.** travel about selling small wares. **2.** sell or dispense in small quantities. —**ped'dler** *n.*

ped·er·as·ty (PED ə RAS tee) *n.* sexual relations between men and boys [< NL *pederastia*] —**ped'er·ast** *n.*

ped·es·tal (PED ə stl) *n.* **1.** a base or support for a column, statue, or vase. **2.** any foundation or support. —**put on a pedestal** hold in high estimation; put in the position of an idol or hero. [< MF *piedestal*]

pe·des·tri·an (pə DES tree ən) *adj.* **1.** moving on foot; walking. **2.** pertaining to common people; plebeian. **3.** commonplace, prosaic, or dull. —*n.* one who journeys or moves from place to place on foot; a walker. [< L *pedester* going on foot]

pe·di·at·rics (PEE dee A triks) *n. (construed as sing.)* the branch of medicine dealing with the disease and hygienic care of children. —**pe·di·a·tri·cian** (PEE dee ə TRISH ən) *n.*

pe·dic·u·lo·sis (pə DIK yə LOH sis) *n. Pathol.* the condition of being infested with lice. [< L *pediculus* louse] —**pe·dic'u·lous** *adj.*

ped·i·cure (PED i KYUUR) *n.* the cosmetic treatment of the feet and toenails. [< F *pédicure*]

ped·i·gree (PED i GREE) *n.* **1.** a line of ancestors; lineage. **2.** a list or table of descent and relationship, esp. of an animal of pure breed. [ME *pedegru*] —**ped'i·greed** *adj.*

ped·i·ment (PED ə mənt) *n. Archit.* **1.** a broad triangular part above a portico or door. **2.** any similar piece surmounting a door, bookcase, etc.

pe·dom·e·ter (pə DOM i tər) *n.* an instrument that records the number of steps taken by the person who carries it. [< F *pédomètre*]

peek (peek) *v.i.* look furtively, slyly, or quickly; peep. —*n.* a peep, glance. [ME *piken*]

peel (peel) *n.* the natural coating of certain kinds of fruit, as oranges and lemons; skin; rind. —*v.t.* **1.** strip off the bark, skin, etc., of. **2.** strip off; remove. —*v.i.* **3.** lose bark, skin, etc. **4.** come off: said of bark, skin, etc. **5.** *Informal* undress. —**keep one's eye peeled** *Informal* keep watch; be alert. [ME *pelen*]

peel·ing (PEE ling) *n.* something peeled off, as rind, skin, etc.

peen (peen) *n.* the end of a hammer head opposite the flat, striking face, usu. shaped like a wedge. —*v.t.* beat, bend, or shape with the peen. [< Scand.]

peep¹ (peep) *v.i.* **1.** utter the small, sharp cry of a young bird or chick; chirp; cheep. **2.** speak in a weak, small voice. —*n.* **1.** the cry of a chick or a small bird, or of a young frog; chirp. **2.** a small sandpiper. [ME *pepen*]

peep² *v.i.* **1.** look through a small hole, from concealment etc. **2.** look furtively or quickly. **3.** begin to appear; be just visible. —*n.* **1.** a furtive look; a glimpse or glance. **2.** the earliest appearance: the *peep* of day. [ME *pepe*] —**peep'er** *n.*

peep·er (PEE pər) *n.* an animal that peeps, as a chick or any of several tree frogs.

peep·hole (PEEP HOHL) *n.* an aperture, as a hole or crack, through which one may peep; also, a small window in a door.

Peep'ing Tom one who peeps in at windows. [after the legendary tailor who peeped at Lady Godiva as she rode naked through town]

peep show n. an exhibition of pictures etc. viewed through a small orifice fitted with a magnifying lens.

peer¹ (peer) v.i. **1.** look narrowly or searchingly, as in an effort to see clearly. **2.** come partially into view.

peer² n. **1.** an equal, as in natural gifts or in social rank. **2.** an equal before the law. **3.** a noble, esp. a British duke, marquis, earl, viscount, or baron. [ME *per* equal] — **peer·ess** n.fem.

peer·age (PEER ij) n. **1.** the office or rank of a peer or nobleman. **2.** peers collectively.

peer·less (PEER lis) adj. of unequaled excellence. —**peer'less·ness** n.

peeve (peev) v.t. **peeved, peev·ing** make peevish. —n. a complaint, annoyance, or grievance. [< PEEVISH]

pee·vish (PEE vish) adj. **1.** irritable or querulous; cross. **2.** showing discontent and vexation. [ME *pevysh*] —**pee'vish·ly** adv. — **pee'vish·ness** n.

pee·wee (PEE wee) n. anything or anyone small or diminutive. —adj. Informal tiny.

peg (peg) n. **1.** a pin, usu. of wood or metal, used to fasten articles together, to stop a hole, etc. **2.** a projecting pin upon which something may be hung, or which may serve to keep a score etc. **3.** a reason or excuse. **4.** a degree or step, as in rank or estimation. —**take (one) down a peg** lower the self-esteem of (a person). —v. **pegged, peg·ging** v.t. **1.** drive or force a peg into; fasten with pegs. **2.** mark with pegs. **3.** strike or pierce with a peg or sharp instrument. **4.** Informal throw. —v.i. **5.** work or strive hard and perseveringly: usu. with *away*. **6.** Informal throw a ball. [ME *pegge*]

Peg·a·sus (PEG ə səs) n. a constellation, the Winged Horse.

peg·board (PEG bord) n. any perforated board into which pegs may be inserted for holding things, keeping score, etc.

peign·oir (payn WAHR) n. a loose dressing gown or negligee worn by women. [< F]

pe·jo·ra·tive (pi JOR ə tiv) adj. having or giving a derogatory or disparaging meaning or sense: a *pejorative* statement. [< LL *pejorare* worsen] —**pe·jo'ra·tive** n. — **pe·jo'ra·tive·ly** adv.

pe·koe (PEE koh) n. a black tea of India,

Ceylon, and Java, made from the young buds of the tea plant. [< dial. Chinese *pek* white + *hóu* empress]

pe·lag·ic (pə LAJ ik) adj. of, pertaining to, or inhabiting the sea or ocean far from land. [< L *pelagicus*]

pelf (pelf) n. money; wealth, esp. if dishonestly acquired. [ME, booty]

pel·i·can (PEL i kən) n. a large, web-footed bird of warm regions, having a pouch on the lower jaw for the temporary storage of fish. [ME *pellican*]

pel·let (PEL it) n. **1.** a small round ball, as of medicine or paper. **2.** a small bullet. —v.t. strike or hit with pellets; form into pellets. [ME *pelet* ball]

pell-mell (PEL MEL) adv. **1.** in a confused or disordered way. **2.** in wild haste. —adj. devoid of order; confused. Also **pell mell.** [< MF *pelemele*]

pel·lu·cid (pə LOO sid) adj. **1.** permitting to a certain extent the passage of light. **2.** transparently clear and simple: a *pellucid* style. [< L *pellucidus*]

pelt¹ (pelt) n. the skin of an animal, usu. with the fur left on. [ME]

pelt² v.t. **1.** strike repeatedly with or as with blows. —v.i. **2.** deliver repeated blows. **3.** move rapidly; hurry. —n. **1.** a blow. **2.** a swift pace.

pel·vis (PEL vis) n. pl. **·vis·es, ·ves** (-veez) **1.** Anat. the part of the skeleton that forms a bony girdle joining the lower or hind limbs to the body. **2.** a basinlike structure. [< NL] —**pel'vic** adj.

pen¹ (pen) n. **1.** an instrument for writing with fluid ink, usu. a metal point split in the middle and fitted to a holder. **2.** any of various writing instruments requiring an ink supply. **3.** the quality of one's penmanship. —v.t. **penned, pen·ning** write with or as with a pen. [ME *penne*]

pen² n. **1.** a small enclosure, as for pigs; also, the animals contained in a pen. **2.** Slang a penitentiary. —v.t. **penned, pen·ning** enclose in or as in a pen; confine. [ME *penne*]

pe·nal (PEEN l) adj. **1.** of or pertaining to punishment. **2.** liable, or rendering liable, to punishment. **3.** enacting or prescribing punishment: a *penal* code. [ME]

pe·nal·ize (PEEN l tz) v.t. **·ized, ·iz·ing 1.** subject to a penalty, as for a violation. **2.** declare (an action) subject to a penalty.

pen·al·ty (PEN l tee) n. pl. **·ties 1.** the legal punishment for having violated a law. **2.** a sum of money to be forfeited as punishment; fine. **3.** the loss of suffering incurred by some act: the *penalty* of sin. **4.** in sports and games, any handicap imposed for a violation of rules. [< Med.L *poenalitas*]

pen·ance (PEN əns) *n.* **1.** *Eccl.* a sacramental rite involving contrition, confession of sins to a priest, the acceptance of penalties, and absolution. **2.** any voluntary act of atonement for sin. [ME *penaunce*]

pence (pens) *Brit.* a plural of PENNY: used to refer to a sum of money, not to a coin; often used in combination: *twopence.*

pen·chant (PEN chənt) *n.* a strong liking or inclination for something. [< F]

pen·cil (PEN səl) *n.* **1.** a writing, drawing, or marking implement, usu. containing graphite. **2.** a small stick of some substance: a styptic *pencil.* —*v.t.* •**ciled,** •**cil·ing** mark, write, draw, or color with or as with a pencil. [ME *pencel*] —**pen'cil·er** *n.*

pend (pend) *v.i.* **1.** await adjustment or settlement. **2.** hang; depend. [< L *pendere* hang]

pend·ant (PEN dənt) *n.* an ornament that hangs from something else. —*adj.* pendent. [ME *pendaunt*]

pend·ent (PEN dənt) *adj.* **1.** hanging downward; suspended. **2.** projecting; overhanging. **3.** undetermined; pending. Also spelled *pendant.* —*n.* pendant. [< L *pendere* hang]

pend·ing (PEN ding) *adj.* **1.** remaining unfinished or undecided. **2.** imminent; impending. —*prep.* **1.** during the process or continuance of. **2.** while awaiting; until.

pen·du·lous (PEN jə ləs) *adj.* **1.** hanging, esp. so as to swing. **2.** undecided; wavering. [< L *pendulus*]

pen·du·lum (PEN jə ləm) *n.* **1.** a suspended body free to oscillate between two extremes. **2.** such a device serving to regulate the movement of a clock. [< NL]

pen·e·trate (PEN i TRAYT) *v.* •**trat·ed,** •**trat·ing** *v.t.* **1.** force a way into or through; pierce; enter. **2.** spread or diffuse itself throughout. **3.** perceive the meaning of; understand. —*v.i.* **4.** enter or pass through something. [< L *penetratus* put within] —**pen'e·tra·ble** (-trə bəl) *adj.* —**pen'e·tra·bil'i·ty** *n.*

pen·e·trat·ing (PEN i TRAY ting) *adj.* **1.** tending or having power to penetrate. **2.** acute; discerning: a *penetrating* mind. Also **pen'e·tra'tive.**

pen·e·tra·tion (PEN i TRAY shən) *n.* **1.** the act or power of penetrating physically. **2.** ability to penetrate mentally; acuteness; discernment. **3.** the depth to which something penetrates.

pen·guin (PENG gwin) *n.* a web-footed flightless aquatic bird of the southern hemisphere, with flipperlike wings and short legs. [< Welsh *pen gwyn* white head]

pen·i·cil·lin (PEN ə SIL in) *n.* an antibiotic found in a mold fungus, used to treat bacterial infections.

pe·nin·su·la (pə NIN sə lə) *n.* a piece of land almost surrounded by water, and connected with the mainland by an isthmus. [< L *paeninsula*] —**pe·nin'su·lar** *adj.*

pe·nis (PEE nis) *n. pl.* •**nis·es** or •**nes** (-neez) the male organ of copulation. [< L, orig., tail] —**pe'nile** (PEEN l) *adj.*

pen·i·tent (PEN i tənt) *adj.* affected by a sense of one's own guilt, and resolved on reform. —*n.* one who is penitent. [ME] —**pen'i·tence** *n.*

pen·i·ten·tial (PEN i TEN shəl) *adj.* of or expressing penitence or penance.

pen·i·ten·tia·ry (PEN i TEN shə ree) *n. pl.* •**ries** a prison, esp. one operated by a state or federal government for those convicted of serious crimes. —*adj.* **1.** of or pertaining to penance. **2.** relating to or used for the punishment of criminals.

pen·knife (PEN NIF) *n. pl.* •**knives** a small pocket knife.

pen·man·ship (PEN mən SHIP) *n.* **1.** the art of writing. **2.** the style or quality of handwriting.

pen name an author's pseudonym; nom de plume.

pen·nant (PEN ənt) *n.* **1.** a long, narrow flag, usu. triangular, used as a school emblem, etc. **2.** a similar flag awarded to sports winners. [< PENNON]

pen·ni·less (PEN i lis) *adj.* poverty-stricken.

pen·non (PEN ən) *n.* **1.** a small, pointed flag, borne by medieval knights on their lances. **2.** a wing. [ME *penon*]

pen·ny (PEN ee) *n. pl.* **pen·nies** or *Brit.* **pence** (pens) **1.** in the U.S. and Canada, a cent. **2.** in the United Kingdom, a coin equal in value to $1/100$ pound. —**a pretty penny** *Informal* a large amount of money. [ME *peni*]

penny pincher a stingy person. —**pen'ny-pinch'ing** *adj. & n.*

penny-wise and pound-foolish economical in small matters, but wasteful in large ones.

pe·nol·o·gy (pee NOL ə jee) *n.* the study of crime and of the management of prisons. —**pe·nol'o·gist** *n.*

pen·sion (PEN shən) *n.* a periodic allowance to a person when certain conditions, as age, length of service, etc., have been fulfilled. —*v.t.* **1.** grant a pension to. **2.** dismiss with a pension: with *off.* [ME] —**pen'sion·a·ble** *adj.*

pen·sion·er (PEN shə nər) *n.* one who receives a pension or is dependent on the bounty of another.

pen·sive (PEN siv) *adj.* **1.** engaged in or given to serious, quiet reflection. **2.** expressive of, suggesting, or causing a melancholy thoughtfulness. [< F] —**pen'sive·ly** *adv.* —**pen'sive·ness** *n.*

pent (pent) *adj.* closely confined.

penta- *combining form* five: *pentagon.* [< Gk. *pénte*]

pen·ta·gon (PEN tə GON) *n. Geom.* a polygon having five sides and five angles. [< LL *pentagonum*] —**pen·tag·o·nal** (pen TAG ə nl) *adj.*

pen·tam·e·ter (pen TAM ə tər) *n.* **1.** a line of verse consisting of five metrical feet. **2.** verse composed of pentameters. —*adj.* having five metrical feet. [< L *pentametrus*]

Pen·ta·teuch (PEN tə TOOK) *n.* the first five books of the Old Testament: Genesis, Exodus, Leviticus, Numbers, and Deuteronomy. [< LL *Pentateuchus*]

pen·tath·lon (pen TATH lən) *n.* an athletic contest consisting of five separate events, in all of which each contestant must participate. [< Gk. *péntathlon*]

Pen·te·cost (PEN ti KAWST) *n.* a Christian festival, the seventh Sunday after Easter, commemorating the descent of the Holy Ghost upon the Apostles. [ME *pentecoste*] —**Pen'te·cos'tal** *adj.*

pent·house (PENT HOWS) *n.* an apartment on the roof or upper floor of a building.

pent-up (PENT UP) *adj.* repressed: *pent-up anger.*

pe·nult (PEE nult) *n.* the syllable next to the last in a word. [< L *paenultima* almost the last]

pe·nul·ti·mate (pi NUL tə mit) *adj.* **1.** next to the last. **2.** of or belonging to the penult. —*n.* a penultimate part.

pe·num·bra (pi NUM brə) *n. pl.* **·brae** (-bree) or **·bras 1.** a partially lit area around a shadow, as in an eclipse. **2.** the dark fringe around the central part of a sunspot. [< NL] —**pe·num'·bral** *adj.*

pe·nu·ri·ous (pə NUUR ee əs) *adj.* **1.** excessively sparing in the use of money; stingy. **2.** extremely poor. [< Med.L *penuriosus*]

pen·u·ry (PEN yə ree) *n.* extreme poverty or want. [ME]

pe·on (PEE ən) *n.* **1.** in Latin America, a laborer; servant. **2.** formerly, a debtor kept in servitude to work off debt. [< Sp., peasant] —**pe'on·age** (PEE ə nij) *n.*

peo·ple (PEE pəl) *n. pl.* **peo·ple;** *for def. 1,* also **peo·ples 1.** the entire body of human beings living in the same country, under the same government, and speaking the same language: the *peoples* of Europe. **2.** in a state or nation, the body of persons invested with political rights. **3.** a group of persons having the same interests, profession, condition of life, etc.: poor *people.* **4.** persons considered collectively: *people* say. **5.** ordinary persons; the populace: usu. with *the.* **6.** one's family or relatives. —*v.t.* **·pled,** **·pling** fill with inhabitants; populate. [ME *peple*]

pep (pep) *n. Informal* energy and high spirits; vigorous activity. —*v.t.* **pepped,** **pep·ping** fill or inspire with energy or pep: usu. with *up.* [< PEPPER]

pep·per (PEP ər) *n.* **1.** a pungent condiment consisting of the dried immature berries of a plant native to India. When ground entire it is **black pepper,** but when the outer coating of the seeds is removed, the product is **white pepper. 2.** the plant producing these berries. **3.** red pepper. **4.** green pepper. —*v.t.* **1.** season with pepper. **2.** sprinkle freely. **3.** shower, as with missiles; spatter; pelt. [ME *peper*]

pep·per-and-salt (PEP ər ən SAWLT) *adj.* consisting of a mixture of white and black, so as to present a grayish appearance. —*n.* a pepper-and-salt cloth.

pep·per·mint (PEP ər MINT) *n.* **1.** a pungent herb used in medicine and confectionery. **2.** an oil made from this herb. **3.** a confection flavored with peppermint.

pep·per·o·ni (PEP ə ROH nee) *n.* a highly seasoned, hard sausage. [< Ital.]

pep·per·y (PEP ə ree) *adj.* **1.** pertaining to or like pepper; pungent. **2.** quick-tempered; hasty. —**pep'per·i·ness** *n.*

pep·py (PEP ee) *adj.* **·pi·er, ·pi·est** *Informal* full of energy; lively. —**pep'pi·ness** *n.*

pep talk a brief, vigorous talk meant to inspire confidence or enthusiasm.

per (pər) *prep.* **1.** by; by means of; through: used in commercial and business English: *per* bearer. **2.** to or for each: ten cents *per* yard. **3.** by the; every: esp. in Latin phrases: *per diem.* [< L]

per·am·bu·late (pər AM byə LAYT) *v.* **·lat·ed, ·lat·ing** *v.t.* **1.** walk through or over. **2.** walk through or around so as to inspect, etc. —*v.i.* **3.** stroll. [< L *perambulatus* walked through] —**per·am'bu·la'tion** *n.*

per an·num (pər AN əm) *Latin* by the year.

per·cale (pər KAYL) *n.* a closely woven cotton fabric without gloss. [< F]

per cap·i·ta (pər KAP i tə) *Latin* for each person; lit., by heads.

per·ceive (pər SEEV) *v.t. & v.i.* **·ceived, ·ceiv·ing 1.** become aware of (something) through the senses; see, hear, feel, taste, or smell. **2.** come to understand. [ME *perceiven*] —**per·ceiv'a·ble** *adj.* —**per·ceiv'a·bly** *adv.*

per·cent (pər SENT) *n.* the number of units in proportion to one hundred: symbol, %. Also **per cent.** —*adj. & adv.* in every hundred. [Short for Med.L *per centum* by the hundred]

per·cent·age (pər SEN tij) *n.* **1.** a proportion or part considered in its quantitative relation to the whole. **2.** advantage; profit.

per·cen·tile (pər SEN til) *n. Stat.* any of 100 points spaced at equal intervals, each point denoting that percentage of the total cases lying below it in the series.

per·cep·ti·ble (pər SEP tə bəl) *adj.* that can be perceived; appreciable. —**per·cep'ti·bly** *adv.*

per·cep·tion (pər SEP shən) *n.* **1.** the act or process of perceiving. **2.** the result or effect of perceiving. **3.** any insight, knowledge, etc., arrived at by or as by perceiving. **4.** the capacity for perceiving. —**per·cep'tu·al** (-choo əl) *adj.*

per·cep·tive (pər SEP tiv) *adj.* **1.** having a quick capacity for perceiving. **2.** of or pertaining to perception. —**per·cep'tive·ly** *adv.* —**per·cep'tive·ness** *n.*

perch[1] (purch) *n.* **1.** a horizontal pole used as a roost for poultry. **2.** any place on which birds alight or rest. **3.** any place for sitting or standing, esp. if elevated. —*v.t. & v.i.* alight or sit on or as on a perch. [ME *perche*]

perch[2] *n. pl.* **perch** or **perches 1.** a small,

spiny-finned fresh-water food fish. **2.** any of various related fishes. [ME *perche*]

per·cip·i·ent (pər SIP ee ənt) *adj.* **1.** having the power of perception. **2.** perceiving rapidly or keenly. [< L *percipere* take in] —**per·cip'i·ence** *n.*

per·co·late (PUR kə LAYT) *v.t. & v.i.* **·lat·ed, ·lat·ing** of a liquid, pass or cause to pass through a porous substance; filter. —*n.* (PUR kə lit) that which has percolated. [< L *percolatus* filtered] —**per'co·la'tion** *n.*

per·co·la·tor (PUR kə LAY tər) *n.* a type of coffeepot in which boiling water rises to the top in a tube and then filters down through finely ground coffee to a container below.

per·cus·sion (pər KUSH ən) *n.* **1.** the sharp striking of one body against another. **2.** the shock, vibration, or sound produced by a striking of one body against another. —*adj.* of, pertaining to, or operating by percussion. [< L *percussio* a beating]

percussion cap a small cap of thin metal, containing a detonating compound, used in ammunition to explode the propelling charge.

percussion instrument a musical instrument whose tone is produced by striking, as the drums, cymbals, piano, etc.

per di·em (pər DEE əm) **1.** by the day. **2.** an allowance for expenses each day. [< L]

per·di·tion (pər DISH ən) *n.* **1.** eternal damnation; the utter loss of a soul. **2.** the place of eternal damnation; hell. [< L]

per·e·gri·nate (PER i grə NAYT) *v.* **·nat·ed, ·nat·ing** *v.i.* **1.** travel from place to place. —*v.t.* **2.** travel through or along. [< L *peregrinatus* traveled abroad]

per·emp·to·ry (pə REMP tə ree) *adj.* **1.** not admitting of appeal; decisive; absolute. **2.** positive in opinion, etc.; imperious. [< L *peremptorius* decisive] —**per·emp'to·ri·ness** *n.*

per·en·ni·al (pə REN ee əl) *adj.* **1.** continuing or enduring through the year or through many years. **2.** perpetual; everlasting; unceasing. **3.** *Bot.* lasting more than two years. —*n.* a plant that grows for three or more years, usu. blooming annually. [< L *perennis* lasting an entire year] —**per·en'ni·al·ly** *adv.*

per·fect (PUR fikt) *adj.* **1.** having all the elements or qualities requisite to its nature or kind; complete. **2.** without defect; flawless. **3.** accurately corresponding to a type or original; exact: *a perfect replica.* **4.** thorough; utter: He made a *perfect* nuisance of himself. **5.** very great: a *perfect* horror of spiders. **6.** *Gram.* denoting the tense of a verb expressing action completed in the past. **7.** *Music* denoting the three intervals whose accuracy of intonation the human ear can recognize: the **perfect octave,** the **perfect fifth,** and the **perfect fourth.** — *n. Gram.* the perfect tense; also, a verb in this tense. —*v.t.* (pər FEKT) **1.** bring to perfection; complete. **2.** make thoroughly skilled or accomplished: *perfect* oneself in an art. [< L *perfectus* finished] — **per·fect′i·bil′i·ty** *n.* —**per·fect′i·ble** *adj.*

per·fec·tion (pər FEK shən) *n.* **1.** the state or quality of being perfect. **2.** the embodiment of something that is perfect: As a host, he is *perfection.* **3.** the highest degree of something.

per·fec·tion·ist (pər FEK shə nist) *n.* one who demands of himself, herself, or others a high degree of excellence.

per·fer·vid (pər FUR vid) *adj.* excessively fervid; ardent; zealous. [< NL *perfervidus*]

per·fi·dy (PUR fi dee) *n. pl.* **·dies** the act of violating faith, trust, or allegiance; treachery. [< L *perfidia*] —**per·fid·i·ous** (pər FID ee əs) *adj.*

per·fo·rate (PUR fə RAYT) *v.t.* **·rat·ed, ·rat·ing 1.** make a hole or holes through, by or as by stamping or drilling. **2.** pierce with holes in rows or patterns. —*adj.* (PER fə rit) perforated. [< L *perforatus* bored through] —**per′fo·ra·ble** *adj.* —**per′fo·ra′tion** *n.*

per·fo·rat·ed (PUR fə RAY tid) *adj.* pierced with a hole or holes; esp., pierced with lines of holes, as sheets of stamps.

per·form (pər FORM) *v.t.* **1.** carry out in action; execute; do. **2.** fulfill; discharge, as a duty or command. **3.** act (a part) or give a performance of (a play, piece of music, etc.). —*v.i.* **4.** carry through to completion an action, undertaking, etc. **5.** give an exhibition or performance. [ME *performen*]

per·form·ance (pər FOR məns) *n.* **1.** an entertainment of some kind before an audience or spectators. **2.** a public presentation: The music had its first *performance* here. **3.** the act of manner of performing. **4.** any act, deed, or accomplishment.

per·fume (PUR fyoom) *n.* **1.** a fragrant substance, usu. a volatile liquid, prepared to emit a pleasant odor; scent. **2.** a pleasant odor, as from flowers; fragrance. —*v.t.* (pər

FYOOM) **·fumed, ·fum·ing** fill or scent with a fragrant odor. [< MF *parfum* perfume] —**per·fum·er** (pər FYOO mər) *n.*

per·fum·er·y (pər FYOO mə ree) *n. pl.* **·er·ies 1.** the art or business or preparing perfumes. **2.** perfumes in general. **3.** a place where perfumes are made.

per·func·to·ry (pər FUNGK tə ree) *adj.* done mechanically or superficially; careless; cursory. [< LL *perfunctorius* careless] —**per·func′to·ri·ly** *adv.*

per·go·la (PUR gə lə) *n.* an arbor or covered walk made of trelliswork. [< Ital.]

per·haps (pər HAPS) *adv.* maybe; possibly.

peri- *prefix* **1.** around; encircling: *periphery.* **2.** situated near; adjoining: *perihelion.* [< Gk. *peri* around]

per·i·car·di·um (PER i KAHR dee əm) *n. pl.* **·di·a** (-dee ə) *Anat.* a membranous bag that surrounds and protects the heart. [< NL] —**per′i·car′di·al** *adj.*

per·i·gee (PER i jee) *n. Astron.* the point in the orbit of the moon or of an artificial satellite at which it is nearest the earth: opposed to *apogee.* [< F *perigée*]

per·i·he·li·on (PER i HEE lee ən) *n. pl.* **·li·a** (-lee ə) *Astron.* the point in the orbit of a planet or comet where it is nearest the sun: opposed to *aphelion.* [< PERI- + Gk. *hélios* sun]

per·il (PER əl) *n.* exposure to the chance of injury; danger; risk. —*v.t.* **·iled, ·il·ing** expose to danger; imperil. [ME]

per·il·ous (PER ə ləs) *adj.* involving or attended with peril; hazardous; risky.

pe·rim·e·ter (pə RIM i tər) *n.* **1.** the boundary line of any figure of two dimensions. **2.** the length of this boundary. [< F *périmètre*]

pe·ri·od (PEER ee əd) *n.* **1.** a portion of time marked or defined by certain conditions, events, etc.: rest *periods.* **2.** a portion or lapse of time, as in a process or development; stage. **3.** a portion of time into which something is divided: The school day has seven *periods.* **4.** *Geol.* one of the divisions of geologic time. **5.** *Physics* the time that elapses between any two successive similar phases of an oscillation or other regularly repeated cyclical motion. **6.** a dot (.) placed on the line, used as a mark of punctuation after every complete declarative sentence, after most abbreviations, etc.: also called *point.* **7.** an occurrence of menstruation. [ME *periode*]

pe·ri·od·ic (PEER ee OD ik) *adj.* **1.** of, pertaining to, or like a period. **2.** recurring at regular intervals. **3.** intermittent. — **pe•ri•o•dic•i•ty** (PEER ee ə DIS i tee) *n.*

pe•ri•od•i•cal (PEER ee OD i kəl) *adj.* **1.** of publications published at regular intervals. **2.** periodic. —*n.* a periodical publication.

periodic sentence a sentence so constructed as to suspend completion of both sense and structure until the close.

per•i•o•don•tics (PER ee ə DON tiks) *n.* the branch of dentistry dealing with diseases of the gums and the bones around the teeth. Also **per′i•o•don′tia** (-shə). [< NL *periodontia*] —**per′i•o•don′tist** *n.*

per•i•pa•tet•ic (PER ə pə TET ik) *adj.* walking about from place to place. —*n.* one given to walking about. [ME]

pe•riph•er•al (pə RIF ər əl) *adj.* **1.** of or concerning a periphery. **2.** not central; marginal: *of peripheral importance.*

pe•riph•er•y (pə RIF ə ree) *n. pl.* **•er•ies 1.** the outer part, surface, or boundary of something. **2.** a surrounding region, area, or country. [< LL *peripheria*]

pe•riph•ra•sis (pə RIF rə sis) *n. pl.* **•ses** (-SEEZ) a roundabout expression of something; circumlocution. [< L] — **per•i•phras•tic** (PER ə FRAS tik) *adj.*

per•i•scope (PER ə SKOHP) *n.* an optical instrument consisting of prisms or mirrors so arranged as to allow an observer to see around or over an obstacle. —**per•i•scop•ic** (PER ə SKOP ik) *adj.* [< Gk. *periskopein* look about]

per•ish (PER ish) *v.i.* **1.** suffer a violent or untimely death. **2.** pass from existence. [ME *perissen*]

per•ish•a•ble (PER i shə bəl) *adj.* **1.** liable to perish. **2.** liable to speedy decay, as fruit in transportation. —*n.* something liable to decay, as food. —**per′ish•a•bil′i•ty** *n.*

per•i•stal•sis (PER ə STAWL sis) *n. pl.* **•ses** (-seez) *Physiol.* a contractile muscular movement of any hollow organ, as of the intestines, forcing the contents onward. [< NL] —**per′i•stal′tic** *adj.*

per•i•to•ne•um (PER i tn EE əm) *n. pl.* **•ne•ums, •ne•a** (-EE ə) *Anat.* a membrane lining the abdominal cavity and serving as a covering for the viscera. [< LL]

per•i•to•ni•tis (PER i tn Ī tis) *n. Pathol.* inflammation of the peritoneum.

per•jured (PUR jərd) *adj.* guilty of or constituting perjury.

per•ju•ry (PUR jə ree) *n. pl.* **•ries** *Law* the willful giving of false testimony or the withholding of material facts or evidence while under oath in a judicial proceeding. [ME *perjurie*] —**per′jure** *v.t.* **•jured, •jur•ing** —**per′jur•er** *n.*

perk¹ (purk) *v.i.* **1.** recover one's spirits or vigor: with *up.* **2.** carry oneself or lift one's head jauntily. —*v.t.* **3.** raise quickly or smartly, as the ears: often with *up.* [ME *perken*]

perk² *v.i. Informal* percolate.

perk•y (PUR kee) *adj.* **perk•i•er, perk•i•est 1.** jaunty; sprightly; pert. **2.** spirited and self-assured. —**perk′i•ly** *adv.* — **perk′i•ness** *n.*

per•ma•frost (PUR mə FRAWST) *n.* the part of the earth's surface in arctic regions that is permanently frozen.

per•ma•nent (PUR mə nənt) *adj.* continuing in the same state or without essential change; enduring; durable; fixed. —*n.* a permanent wave. [ME] —**per′ma•nence, per′ma•nen•cy** *n.*

permanent wave an artificial wave mechanically or chemically set in the hair and lasting several months.

per•me•a•ble (PUR mee ə bəl) *adj.* allowing passage, esp. of fluids. [ME] — **per′me•a•bil′i•ty** *n.*

per•me•ate (PUR mee AYT) *v.* **•at•ed, •at•ing** *v.t.* **1.** spread thoroughly through; pervade. **2.** pass through the pores or interstices of. —*v.i.* **3.** spread itself. [< L *permeatus* passed through]

per•mis•si•ble (pər MIS ə bəl) *adj.* that can be permitted; allowable.

per•mis•sion (pər MISH ən) *n.* **1.** the act of permitting or allowing. **2.** formal authorization or consent. [ME]

per•mis•sive (pər MIS iv) *adj.* **1.** permitting; granting permission. **2.** not strict in discipline. [ME] —**per•mis′sive•ness** *n.*

per•mit (pər MIT) *v.* **•mit•ted, •mit•ting** *v.t.* **1.** allow the doing of; consent to. **2.** give (someone) leave or consent; authorize. **3.** afford opportunity for. —*v.i.* **4.** afford possibility or opportunity. —*n.* (PUR mit) **1.** permission to do something. **2.** an official document or certificate authorizing performance of a specified activity; license. [ME]

per•mu•ta•tion (PUR myuu TAY shən) *n.* **1.** the act of rearranging; transformation. **2.** *Math.* change in the order of sequence of elements or objects in a series. [ME *permutacioun*]

per•mute (pər MYOOT) *v.t.* **•mut•ed, •mut•ing** subject to permutation; esp., change the order of. [ME] —**per·mut′ a·ble** *adj.*

per·ni·cious (pər NISH əs) *adj.* **1.** having the power of destroying or injuring; deadly. **2.** malicious; wicked. [< L *perniciosus* ruinous] —**per·ni′cious·ly** *adj.*

per·nick·e·ty (pər NIK i tee) *adj.* persnickety.

per·o·rate (PER ə RAYT) *v.i.* **·rat·ed, ·rat·ing 1.** speak at length; harangue. **2.** sum up or conclude a speech. [< L *peroratus* declaimed]

per·o·ra·tion (PER ə RAY shən) *n.* the concluding portion of an oration, or the summing up of an argument. [< L]

per·pen·dic·u·lar (PUR pən DIK yə lər) *adj.* **1.** being at right angles to the plane of the horizon; upright or vertical. **2.** *Math.* meeting a given line or plane at right angles. —*n.* a perpendicular line or plane. [< L *perpendicularis* vertical]

per·pe·trate (PUR pi TRAYT) *v.t.* **·trat·ed, ·trat·ing** do, perform, or commit (a crime etc.). [< L *perpetratus* carried out] —**per′ pe·tra′tor** *n.*

per·pet·u·al (pər PECH oo əl) *adj.* **1.** continuing or lasting forever or for an unlimited time. **2.** incessant. [ME *perpetuall*] —**per·pet′u·al·ly** *adv.*

per·pet·u·ate (pər PECH oo AYT) *v.t.* **·at·ed, ·at·ing 1.** make perpetual or enduring. **2.** cause to remain known, current, etc. —**per·pet′u·a′tion** *n.* [< L *perpetuatus* uninterrupted]

per·pe·tu·i·ty (PUR pi TOO i tee) *n. pl.* **·ties 1.** the quality or state of being perpetual. **2.** something perpetual, as a perpetual annuity. **3.** unending or unlimited time. [ME *perpetuite*]

per·plex (pər PLEKS) *v.t.* cause to hesitate or become confused, as from doubt, difficulties encountered, etc.; puzzle. —**per·plex′i·ty** *n.* —**per·plex′ing** *adj.* —**per·plex′ing·ly** *adv.*

per·plexed (pər PLEKST) *adj.* **1.** confused; puzzled; bewildered. **2.** of a complicated character; involved. [ME *perplex* confused]

per·qui·site (PUR kwə zit) *n.* **1.** any incidental profit, payment, etc., beyond what is earned as salary or wages. **2.** any privilege or benefit owed or claimed as one's due. [ME]

per se (pər SAY) *Latin* by itself; intrinsically.

per·se·cute (PUR si KYOOT) *v.t.* **·cut·ed, ·cut·ing 1.** annoy or harass persistently. **2.** maltreat or oppress because of race, religion, or beliefs. [ME] —**per′se·cu′tion** *n.* —**per′se·cu′tor** *n.*

per·se·vere (PUR sə VEER) *v.i.* **·vered, ·ver·ing** persist in any purpose or enterprise; strive in spite of difficulties, etc. [ME *perseveren*] —**per′se·ver′·ance** *n.* —**per′se·ver′ing·ly** *adv.*

per·si·flage (PUR sə FLAHZH) *n.* a light, flippant style of conversation or writing. [< F, banter]

per·sist (pər SIST) *v.i.* **1.** continue firmly in some course, state, etc., esp. despite opposition or difficulties. **2.** continue to exist; endure. [< L *persistere* stand firm] —**per·sis′tence, per·sis′ten·cy** *n.*

per·sis·tent (pər SIS tənt) *adj.* **1.** persevering or stubborn in a course or resolve. **2.** enduring; permanent. **3.** constantly repeated. —**per·sis′tent·ly** *adv.*

per·snick·e·ty (pər SNIK i tee) *adj. Informal* **1.** unduly fastidious; fussy. **2.** demanding minute care or pains. Also *pernickety.* —**per·snick′et·i·ness** *n.*

per·son (PUR sən) *n.* **1.** any human being considered as a distinct entity or personality; an individual. **2.** one's characteristic appearance or physical condition. **3.** *Law* any human being, corporation, or body politic having legal rights and duties. **4.** *Gram.* a modification of the pronoun and verb that distinguishes the speaker (**first person**), the person or thing spoken to (**second person**), and the person or thing spoken of (**third person**). —**in person 1.** physically present. **2.** acting for oneself. [ME *persone*]

per·so·na (pər SOH nə) *n. pl.* (*for def. 1*) **·nae** (-nee) or (*for def. 2*) **·nas 1.** *Usu. pl.* a character in a drama, novel, etc. **2.** one's personality as seen by others. [< L]

per·son·a·ble (PUR sə nə bəl) *adj.* attractive or pleasing in personal appearance.

per·son·age (PUR sə nij) *n.* **1.** a man or woman of importance or rank. **2.** a character in fiction, drama, history, etc.

per·son·al (PUR sə nl) *adj.* **1.** pertaining to or concerning a particular person; not general or public. **2.** done in person: a *personal* service. **3.** of or pertaining to the body or appearance: *personal* beauty. **4.** directly referring to an individual, esp. in a disparaging manner: *personal* remarks. **5.** *Law* pertaining to property regarded as movable or temporary. **6.** *Gram.* denoting or indicating person: *personal* pronouns. —*n.* **1.** *Often pl. Law* a movable article or property;

chattel. 2. a paragraph or advertisement of personal reference or application. [ME] —**per'son·al·ly** *adv.*

per·son·al·i·ty (PUR sə NAL i tee) *n. pl.* **·ties** 1. distinctive qualities or characteristics of a person. 2. a person of outstanding or distinctive qualities. 3. *Often pl.* a remark or reference, often disparaging, of a personal nature.

per·son·al·ize (PUR sə nl IZ) *v.t.* **·ized,** **·iz·ing** 1. make personal. 2. mark with one's name, initials, etc., as stationery or handkerchiefs.

personal pronoun *Gram.* a pronoun that varies in form according to person, gender, case, and number, as *we, they, him.*

per·so·na non gra·ta (pər SOH nə non GRAH tə) *Latin* a person who is not welcome or acceptable.

per·son·ate (PUR sə NAYT) *v.t.* **·at·ed,** **·at·ing** *Law* impersonate with intent to deceive. —**per'son·a'tion** *n.* —**per'son·a' tor** *n.*

per·son·i·fy (pər SON ə FI) *v.t.* **·fied,** **·fy·ing** 1. think of or represent as having life or human qualities. 2. represent (an abstraction or inanimate object) as a person. 3. be the embodiment of; typify. [< F *personnifier*] —**per·son'i·fi·ca'tion** *n.*

per·son·nel (PUR sə NEL) *n.* the persons employed in a business, in military service, etc. [< F]

per·spec·tive (pər SPEK tiv) *n.* 1. the art or theory of representing solid objects on a flat surface in such a way as to convey the impression of depth and distance. 2. the relative importance of facts or matters from any special point of view. 3. judgment of facts, circumstances, etc. with regard to their importance. [ME]

per·spi·ca·cious (PUR spi KAY shəs) *adj.* keenly discerning or understanding. [< L *perspicere* see through] —**per'spi·cac' i·ty** (-KAS i tee) *n.*

per·spic·u·ous (pər SPIK yoo əs) *adj.* having clarity of expression or style; lucid. —**per·spi·cu·i·ty** (PUR spi KYOO i tee) *n.* [< L *perspicuitas*]

per·spi·ra·tion (PUR spə RAY shən) *n.* 1. the act or process of perspiring. 2. the fluid excreted; sweat. 3. arduous physical effort. [< NL]

per·spire (pər SPIR) *v.i.* **·spired, ·spir·ing** give off a saline fluid through the pores of the skin; sweat. [< L *perspirare* breathe through]

per·suade (pər SWAYD) *v.t.* **·suad·ed,** **·suad·ing** 1. induce (someone) to do something. 2. induce to a belief; convince. [< L *persuadere*]

per·sua·sion (pər SWAY zhən) *n.* 1. the act of persuading or of using persuasive methods. 2. ability to persuade. 3. settled opinion; conviction. 4. an accepted creed or belief.

per·sua·sive (pər SWAY siv) *adj.* having power or tendency to persuade. —*n.* that which persuades or tends to persuade. —**per·sua'sive·ly** *adv.* —**per·sua'sive· ness** *n.*

pert (purt) *adj.* **·er, ·est** 1. impertinent; saucy. 2. energetic; lively. [ME] —**pert'ly** *adv.* —**pert'ness** *n.*

per·tain (pər TAYN) *v.i.* 1. have reference; relate. 2. belong as an adjunct, function, quality, etc. —**pertaining to** having to do with; belonging or relating to. [ME *pertenen*]

per·ti·na·cious (PUR tn AY shəs) *adj.* 1. tenacious of purpose; adhering fixedly to a pursuit or opinion. 2. stubbornly or doggedly persistent. —**per'ti·na'cious·ly** *adv.* —**per'ti·nac'i·ty** (-tn AS i tee) *n.*

per·ti·nent (PUR tn ənt) *adj.* related to or properly bearing upon the matter in hand; relevant. [ME] —**per'ti·nence** *n.*

per·turb (pər TURB) *v.t.* 1. disquiet or disturb greatly; alarm; agitate. 2. throw into disorder; cause confusion in. [ME *perturben*] —**per·tur·ba·tion** (PUR tər BAY shən) *n.*

pe·ruse (pə ROOZ) *v.t.* **·rused, ·rus·ing** 1. read carefully or attentively. 2. read. 3. examine; scrutinize. —**pe·rus'a·ble** *adj.* —**pe·rus'al** *n.*

per·vade (pər VAYD) *v.t.* **·vad·ed,** **·vad·ing** spread through every part of; be diffused throughout; permeate. [< L *pervadere* pass through] —**per·va'sive** (-VAY siv) *adj.* —**per·va'sive·ly** *adv.*

per·verse (pər VURS) *adj.* 1. willfully deviating from acceptable or conventional behavior, opinion, etc. 2. refractory; capricious. 3. petulant; cranky. [ME] —**per·verse'ly** *adv.* —**per·verse'·ness** *n.*

per·ver·sion (pər VUR zhən) *n.* 1. the act of perverting, or the state of being perverted. 2. a perverted form, act, use, etc. 3. deviation from the normal in sexual behavior. [ME]

per·vert (pər VURT) *v.t.* 1. turn to an improper use or purpose; misapply. 2. turn from approved opinions or conduct; lead astray. **3.** deprave; debase; corrupt. — *n.* (PUR vərt) one characterized by or practicing sexual perversion. [ME *perverten*]

per·vert·ed (pər VUR tid) *adj.* **1.** deviating widely from what is right or acceptable; distorted. **2.** characterized by viciousness, sexual perversion, etc. —**per·vert'ed·ly** *adv.*

pes·ky (PES kee) *adj.* **·ki·er, ·ki·est** *Informal* annoying; troublesome. —**pes'ki·ness** *n.*

pes·si·mism (PES ə MIZ əm) *n.* **1.** a disposition to take a gloomy or cynical view of affairs. **2.** the doctrine that the world and life are essentially evil. [< F *pessimisme*] —**pes'si·mist** *n.* —**pes'si·mis'tic** *adj.*

pest (pest) *n.* **1.** an annoying person or thing. **2.** a destructive or injurious insect, plant, etc. **3.** a virulent epidemic, esp. of plague. [< ME *peste*]

pes·ter (PES tər) *v.t.* harass with petty and persistent annoyances; bother; plague. [< MF *empestrer* hobble]

pes·ti·cide (PES tə SID) *n.* a chemical or other substance used to destroy plant and animal pests.

pes·tif·er·ous (pe STIF ər əs) *adj.* **1.** *Informal* annoying; bothersome. **2.** carrying or spreading infectious disease. [ME] —**pes·tif'er·ous·ness** *n.*

pes·ti·lence (PES tl əns) *n.* any widespread, often fatal infectious or contagious disease, as cholera or the bubonic plague.

pes·ti·lent (PES tl ənt) *adj.* **1.** tending to produce pestilence. **2.** having a malign influence or effect. **3.** making trouble; vexatious. [ME]

pes·tle (PES əl) *n.* an implement used for crushing, pulverizing, or mixing substances in or as in a mortar. —*v.t. & v.i.* **·tled, ·tling** pound, grind, or mix with or as with a pestle. [ME *pestel*]

pet[1] (pet) *n.* **1.** a tame animal treated lovingly or kept as a companion or playmate. **2.** a favorite; teacher's *pet.* —*adj.* **1.** tamed or kept as a pet. **2.** favorite; cherished. —*v.* **pet·ted, pet·ting** *v.t.* **1.** stroke or caress. **2.** treat indulgently; coddle. —*v.i.* **3.** *Informal* make love by kissing and caressing.

pet[2] *n.* a fit of pique or ill temper.

pet·al (PET l) *n. Bot.* one of the divisions or leaflike parts of a corolla. [< NL *petalum*] —**pet'aled** *adj.*

pe·tard (pi TAHRD) *n.* **1.** an explosive device used to break through walls, gates, etc.

2. a small firecracker exploding with a loud report. [< MF *peter* break wind]

pet·cock (PET kok) *n. Mech.* a small valve or faucet, used for draining, releasing pressure, etc.

pe·ter (PEE tər) *v.i.* diminish gradually and then cease or disappear: with *out.*

Peter Principle the observation that persons in an organization are promoted beyond the level of their competence. [Title of a book by L.J. *Peter*, 1919– , Canadian educator]

pet·it (PET ee) *adj. Law* small; lesser; minor: *petit* larceny. [ME]

pe·tite (pə TEET) *adj.* diminutive; little. [< F]

pet·it four (PET ee FOR) *pl.* **pet·its fours** (PET ee FORZ) a small, decoratively iced cake. [< F, lit., little oven]

pe·ti·tion (pə TISH ən) *n.* **1.** a formal request addressed to a person or group in authority and asking for some benefit, the redress of a grievance, etc. **2.** something formally requested or entreated. —*v.t.* **1.** make a petition to. **2.** ask for. —*v.i.* **3.** make a petition. [ME *peticioun*] —**pe·ti'·tion·er** *n.*

pe·tit mal (PET ee MAHL) *Pathol.* a mild form of epilepsy characterized by a momentary loss of consciousness: distinguished from *grand mal.* [< F, lit., small sickness]

pet·it point (PET ee) **1.** a fine tapestry stitch used in decorative needlework. **2.** needlework done in this stitch.

pet·rel (PE trəl) *n.* any of various small sea birds, usu. found far from shore.

pet·ri·fy (PE trə FI) *v.* **·fied, ·fy·ing** *v.t.* **1.** convert (organic material) into a substance of stony character. **2.** make fixed and unyielding. **3.** daze or paralyze with fear, surprise, etc. —*v.i.* **4.** become stone or like stone. [< MF *petrifier*] —**pet'ri·fac'tion** (PE trə FAK shən) *n.*

petro- *combining form* rock; stone. [< Gk. *pétra* rock, *pétros* stone]

pet·ro·chem·i·cal (PE troh KEM i kəl) *n.* a chemical derived from petroleum or natural gas. —**pet'ro·chem'i·cal** *adj.*

pet·ro·chem·is·try (PE troh KEM ə stree) *n.* the chemistry of petroleum and its derivatives.

pe·tro·le·um (pə TROH lee əm) *n.* an oily, liquid mixture of numerous hydrocarbons, found in subterranean deposits, used in its natural state for heat and light, and as the source of gasoline, kerosene, etc. [< Med.L, lit., rock oil]

pe·trol·o·gy (pi TROL ə jee) n. the science of the origin, structure, constitution, and characteristics of rocks. —**pe·trol'o·gist** n.

pet·ti·coat (PET ee KOHT) n. 1. a skirt or skirtlike undergarment hanging from the waist. 2. something resembling a petticoat. 3. *Informal* a woman: a humorous or disparaging term. —*adj.* of or influenced by women: *petticoat* politics.

pet·ti·fog·ger (PET ee FOG ər) n. 1. an inferior lawyer, esp. one dealing with insignificant cases or resorting to tricks. 2. one who quibbles or fusses over trivialities. —**pet'ti·fog** v.i. ·**fogged**, ·**fog·ging** 1. quibble; bicker. 2. practice trickery. 3. engage in a shifty law practice. —**pet'ti·fog'ger·y** n.

pet·tish (PET ish) adj. capriciously ill-tempered; petulant; peevish.

pet·ty (PET ee) adj. ·**ti·er**, ·**ti·est** 1. having little worth or importance; trifling; insignificant. 2. having little scope or generosity; narrow-minded. 3. mean; spiteful. 4. having a comparatively low rank or position; minor. 5. *Law* petit. [ME *peti* minor] —**pet'ti·ness** n.

petty cash a supply of money kept for minor expenses, as in a business office.

petty officer *Naval* any of a class of noncommissioned officers.

pet·u·lant (PECH ə lənt) adj. displaying or characterized by capricious fretfulness; peevish. [< L *petulans* impudence] —**pet'u·lant·ly** adv. —**pet'u·lance** n.

pew (pyoo) n. a bench for seating people in church, frequently with a kneeling rack attached. [ME *puwe*]

pew·ter (PYOO tər) n. 1. an alloy, usu. of tin and lead, formerly much used for tableware. 2. a dull gray color. [ME *pewtre*] —adj. made of pewter.

pe·yo·te (pay OH tee) n. mescal. [< Mexican Sp.]

-phage *combining form* one who or that which eats or consumes: *bacteriophage*. [< Gk. *phágein* eat]

-phagous *combining form* consuming; tending to eat. [< Gk. *phágein* eat]

pha·lanx (FAY langks) n. pl. **pha·lan·ges** (fə LAN jeez); *also for defs. 1 and 2* **pha·lanx·es** 1. in ancient Greece, a marching order of heavy infantry with close ranks and files. 2. any massed or compact body or corps. 3. *Anat.* one of the bones articu-

lating with the joints of the fingers or toes. [< L]

phal·lus (FAL əs) n. pl. ·**li** (FAL ī), **phal·lus·es** 1. a representation of the male generative organ, often used as a symbol of the generative power of nature. 2. *Anat.* the penis; the clitoris. [< L] —**phal'lic** adj.

phan·tasm (FAN taz əm) n. 1. an imaginary appearance; phantom. 2. a mental image; fancy. [< L *phantasma*] —**phan·tas'mal** adj.

phan·tas·ma·go·ri·a (fan TAZ mə GOR ee ə) n. 1. a changing, incoherent series of apparitions or phantasms, as in a dream. 2. an apparition. [< F *fantasmagorie*] —**phan·tas'ma·gor'ic** adj.

phan·tom (FAN təm) n. 1. something that exists only in appearance. 2. an apparition; specter. 3. the visible representative of an abstract state or incorporeal person. —adj. illusive; ghostlike. [ME *fantosme*]

-phany *combining form* appearance; manifestation: *epiphany*. [< Gk. *phaínesthai* appear]

Phar·aoh (FAR oh) n. any one of the monarchs of ancient Egypt. [ME *Pharao*] —**Phar·a·on·ic** (FAR ay ON ik) adj.

Phar·i·see (FAR ə SEE) n. 1. a member of an ancient Jewish sect that emphasized strict observance of ritual. 2. **pharisee** a formal, sanctimonious, hypocritical person. [ME *Pharise*] —**Phar·i·sa·ic** (FAR ə SAY ik) or **pharisaic** or ·**i·cal** adj.

phar·ma·ceu·ti·cal (FAHR mə SOO ti kəl) adj. pertaining to, using, or relating to pharmacy or the pharmacopoeia: also **phar'ma·ceu'tic**. —n. a pharmaceutical product. [< LL *pharmaceuticus* druggist]

phar·ma·cist (FAHR mə sist) n. a qualified druggist.

phar·ma·col·o·gy (FAHR mə KOL ə jee) n. the science of the nature, preparation, administration, and effects of drugs. —**phar'ma·co·log'i·cal** adj.

phar·ma·co·poe·ia (FAHR mə kə PEE ə) n. 1. a book, usu. published by an authority, containing standard formulas and methods for the preparation of medicines, drugs, and other remedial substances. 2. a collection of drugs. [< NL]

phar·ma·cy (FAHR mə see) n. pl. ·**cies** 1. the art or business of compounding and identifying drugs, and of compounding and dispensing medicines. 2. a drugstore. [< Med.L]

phar·ynx (FAR ingks) n. pl. **pha·ryn·ges**

(fə RIN jeez) or **phar·ynx·es** *Anat.* the part of the alimentary canal between the palate and the esophagus, serving as a passage for air and food. [< NL] — **pha·ryn·ge·al** (fə RIN jee əl) *adj.*

phase (fayz) *n.* **1.** the view that anything presents to the eye; any one of varying distinctive manifestations of an object. **2.** *Astron.* one of the appearances or forms presented periodically by the moon and planets. **3.** *Physics* any particular stage in the complete cycle of a periodic system. **4.** *Biol.* any characteristic or decisive stage in the growth, development, or life pattern of an organism. —**in phase** reaching corresponding phases simultaneously, as two waves. —**phase out** (or **in**) plan and execute the orderly and gradual completion (or initiation) of an enterprise.

phen·cy·cli·dine (fen SĪ kli DEEN) *n.* a nitrogen compound used as a tranquilizer for animals and in a powdered form as a hallucinogenic drug by people. Also *PCP.*

phe·no·bar·bi·tal (FEE noh BAHR bi TAWL) *n.* *Chem.* a white, odorless, slightly bitter, crystalline powder, used as a sedative.

phe·nom·e·nal (fi NOM ə nl) *adj.* **1.** pertaining to phenomena. **2.** extraordinary or marvelous. **3.** *Philos.* perceptible through the senses. —**phe·nom'e·nal·ly** *adv.*

phe·nom·e·non (fi NOM ə NON) *n. pl.* **phe·nom·e·na** (-nə); *for defs. 2 & 3, often* **phe·nom·e·nons 1.** something visible or directly observable, as an appearance, action, change, etc. **2.** any unusual occurrence; marvel. **3.** a person having some remarkable talent, power, or ability; prodigy. [< LL *phaenomenon* appearance]

phe·no·type (FEE nə TIP) *n.* *Biol.* the aggregate of genetic characteristics visibly manifested by an organism. [< G *Phänotypus*]

pher·o·mone (FER ə MOHN) *n.* an animal secretion that stimulates a specific response in animals of the same species. [< Gk. *pheréin* carry + (HOR)MONE]

phi (fi) *n.* the twenty-first letter in the Greek alphabet (Φ, φ), corresponding to English *ph* and *f.*

phi·lan·der (fi LAN dər) *v.i.* make love without serious intentions: said of a man. —*n.* a male flirt: also **phi·lan'der·er.** [< Gk. *philandros* one who loves]

phi·lan·thro·py (fi LAN thrə pee) *n. pl.* **·pies 1.** the effort to promote the happi-

ness or social elevation of mankind, as by making donations, etc. **2.** love or benevolence toward mankind in general. [< Gk. *philanthropía* love for humanity] —**phil·an·throp·ic** (FIL ən THROP ik) or **·i·cal** *adj.* —**phi·lan'thro·pist** (-thrə pist) *n.*

phi·lat·e·ly (fi LAT l ee) *n.* the study and collection of postage stamps, stamped envelopes, etc.; stamp collecting. [< F *philatélie*] —**phi·lat'e·list** *n.*

-phile *combining form* one who supports or is fond of; one devoted to: *bibliophile.* [< Gk. *-philos* dear]

phil·har·mon·ic (FIL hahr MON ik) *adj.* *Sometimes cap.* fond of music: often used in the names of musical societies. —*n.* **1.** *Sometimes cap.* a group that sponsors or supports a symphony orchestra. **2.** a symphony orchestra. [< F *philharmonique*]

-philia *combining form* **1.** a tendency toward: *hemophilia.* **2.** an excessive affection or fondness for: *necrophilia.* [< Gk. *philía* friendship]

phi·lip·pic (fə LIP ik) *n.* an impassioned speech characterized by invective; tirade. [< MF *philippique*]

phi·lis·tine (FIL ə STEEN) *n.* an ignorant, narrow-minded person, devoid of culture and indifferent to art. Also **Philistine.** [after the *Philistines,* an ancient warlike people] —**phi'lis·tin·ism** *n.*

philo- *combining form* loving; fond of. [< Gk. *phílos* loving]

phi·lol·o·gy (fi LOL ə jee) *n.* **1.** the study of written records, chiefly literary works, to set up accurate texts and determine their meaning. **2.** linguistics, esp. comparative and historical. [< Gk. *philología* love of learning] —**phil·o·log·i·cal** (FIL ə LOJ i kəl) *adj.* —**phi·lol'o·gist** *n.*

phi·los·o·pher (fi LOS ə fər) *n.* **1.** a student of or specialist in philosophy. **2.** one who lives, makes judgments, etc. according to a philosophy. **3.** one who is calm and patient, esp. under difficult circumstances.

phil·o·soph·i·cal (FIL ə SOF i kəl) *adj.* **1.** of or founded on the principles of philosophy. **2.** proper to or characteristic of a philosopher. **3.** self-restrained; rational; thoughtful. Also **phil'o·soph'ic.**

phi·los·o·phize (fi LOS ə FIZ) *v.i.* **·phized, ·phiz·ing** speculate like a philosopher; theorize.

phi·los·o·phy (fi LOS ə fee) *n. pl.* **·phies 1.** the inquiry into the most comprehensive principles of reality in general, or of some sector of it, as human knowledge or human values. **2.** the love of wisdom, and the search for it. **3.** a philosophical system; also, a treatise on such a system. **4.** a theory governing any field of endeavor: the *philosophy* of banking. **5.** practical wisdom; fortitude. [ME]

phle•bi•tis (flə BĪ tis) *n. Pathol.* inflammation of the inner membrane of a vein. [< NL] —**phle•bit′ic** (-BIT ik) *adj.*

phle•bot•o•my (flə BOT ə mee) *n. pl.* •**mies** *Surg.* the practice of opening a vein for letting blood as a remedial measure; bloodletting. [< Gk. *phlebotomía*] —**phle•bot′o•mist** *n.*

phlegm (flem) *n.* **1.** *Physiol.* a viscid mucus secreted in the air passages, esp. such mucus discharged through the mouth. **2.** Cold, undemonstrative temper. [ME *fleem*]

phleg•mat•ic (fleg MAT ik) *adj.* not easily moved or excited. —**phleg•mat′i•cal•ly** *adv.*

phlo•em (FLOH em) *n. Bot.* the complex tissue serving for the conduction of the sap in plants. [< Gk. *phlóos* bark]

pho•bi•a (FOH bee ə) *n.* **1.** a compulsive and persistent fear of any specified type of object, stimulus, or situation. **2.** any strong aversion or dislike. —**pho′bic** *adj.*

-phobia *combining form* an exaggerated dread of or aversion to: **acrophobia** (high places), **agoraphobia** (open spaces), **ailurophobia** (cats), **androphobia** (men), **claustrophobia** (enclosed places), **gephyrophobia** (crossing a bridge), **gynophobia** (women), **hemophobia** (blood), **hydrophobia** (water), **musophobia** (mice), **nyctophobia** (darkness), **ophidiophobia** (reptiles), **pyrophobia** (fire), **thanatophobia** (death), **triskaidekaphobia** (13). [< Gk. *phobos* fear]

phoe•nix (FEE niks) *n.* in Egyptian mythology, a bird of great beauty, said to live for 500 or 600 years and then consume itself by fire, rising from its ashes to live through another cycle. [< Gk. *phoînix*]

phone (fohn) *n.* a telephone. —*v.t. & v.i.* **phoned, phon•ing** telephone.

-phone *combining form* voice; sound: *microphone.* [< Gk. *phōnē* voice]

pho•neme (FOH neem) *n. Ling.* the smallest element of speech sounds, which functions to distinguish one utterance from another, as /t/ and /p/ in the words *tin* and *pin.* [< Gk. *phōnēma* utterance] —**pho•ne′mic** (fə NEE mik) *adj.*

pho•ne•ti•cian (FOH ni TISH ən) *n.* a specialist in phonetics.

pho•net•ics (fə NET iks) *n. (construed as sing.)* the branch of linguistics dealing with the analysis, description, and classification of the sounds of speech. [< Gk. *phōnētikós* vocal] —**pho•net′ic** *adj.* —**pho•net′i•cal•ly** *adv.*

phon•ic (FON ik) *adj.* pertaining to or of the nature of sound, esp. speech sounds. —**phon′i•cal•ly** *adv.*

phon•ics (FON iks) *n. (construed as sing.)* **1.** the phonetic rudiments used in teaching reading and pronunciation. **2.** the science of sound; acoustics.

phono- *combining form* sound; speech; voice. [< Gk. *phōnē* sound]

pho•no•graph (FOH nə GRAF) *n.* a record player. —**pho′no•graph′ic** *adj.*

phonograph record a grooved disk that reproduces sounds on a record player.

pho•ny (FOH nee) *adj.* •**ni•er,** •**ni•est** fake; false; spurious; counterfeit. —*n. pl.* •**nies** **1.** something fake or not genuine. **2.** one who tries to be something he or she is not.

-phony *combining form* a (specified) type of sound or sounds: *cacophony.* [< Gk. *phōnē* voice]

phos•phate (FOS fayt) *n.* **1.** *Chem.* an organic compound of phosphoric acid. **2.** *Agric.* any fertilizer valued for its phosphoric acid. **3.** a flavored carbonated beverage. [< F]

phos•phor (FOS fər) *n.* any of a class of substances that will emit light under the action of certain chemicals or radiations. [< F *phosphore*]

phos•phor•es•cence (FOS fə RES əns) *n.* **1.** the emission of light without perceptible heat; also, the light so emitted. **2.** the property of continuing to shine in the dark after exposure to light, shown by many mineral substances. —**phos′phor•esce′** *v.i.* •**esced,** •**esc•ing** —**phos′phor•es′cent** *adj.*

phos•phor•ic (fos FOR ik) *adj. Chem.* derived from phosphorus, esp. in its highest valence.

phosphoric acid *Chem.* one of three acids of phosphorus, used as a reagent and in beverages.

phos•pho•rous (FOS fər əs) *adj. Chem.* derived from phosphorus, esp. in its lower valence.

phos·pho·rus (FOS fər əs) *n.* a soft, non-metallic element (symbol P), found only in combination. [< NL *phōsphorus*]

pho·tic (FOH tik) *adj.* **1.** of or relating to light or to the production of light. **2.** designating underwater regions penetrated by sunlight.

pho·to (FOH toh) *n. pl.* **·tos** photograph.

photo- *combining form* **1.** light; of, pertaining to, or produced by light. **2.** photograph; photographic: *photoengrave*. [< Gk. *phōs* light]

pho·to·cell (FOH toh SEL) *n.* an electron tube, one of whose electrodes is sensitive to variations in the intensity of light, incorporated in electrical circuits as a controlling, testing, and counting device.

pho·to·com·po·si·tion (FOH toh KOM pə ZISH ən) *n.* the composing of printed matter by photographic means. —**pho′to·com·pose′** *v.t.* **·posed, ·pos·ing.**

pho·to·cop·y (FOH tə KOP ee) *n. pl.* **·cop·ies** a photographic reproduction of printed or other graphic material. —*v.* **·cop·ied, ·cop·y·ing** *v.t.* **1.** make a photocopy of. —*v.i.* **2.** make a photocopy. — **pho′to·cop′i·er** *n.*

pho·to·e·lec·tric (FOH toh i LEK trik) *adj.* of or pertaining to the electrical or electronic effects due to the action of light. Also **pho′to·e·lec′tri·cal.** —**pho′to·e·lec′tri·cal·ly** *adv.*

photoelectric cell photocell.

pho·to·e·lec·tron (FOH toh i LEK tron) *n.* an electron emitted from a metal surface when exposed to suitable radiation.

pho·to·e·mis·sion (FOH toh i MISH ən) the ejection of photoelectrons.

pho·to·en·grav·ing (FOH toh en GRAY ving) *n.* **1.** the process of producing by the aid of photography a relief block or plate for printing. **2.** a plate or picture so produced. —**pho′to·en·grave′** *v.t.* **·graved, ·grav·ing** —**pho′to·en·grav′er** *n.*

photo finish 1. a race so closely contested that only a photograph of the finish can determine the winner. **2.** any close contest.

pho·to·gen·ic (FOH tə JEN ik) *adj.* **1.** being a good subject for a photograph, esp. for esthetic reasons. **2.** *Biol.* producing phosphorescence. —**pho′to·gen′i·cal·ly** *adv.*

pho·to·graph (FOH tə GRAF) *n.* a picture taken by photography. —*v.t.* **1.** take a photograph of —*v.t.* **2.** practice photography. **3.** be depicted in photographs: They *photo-*

graph beautifully. —**pho·tog·ra·pher** (fə TOG rə fər) *n.*

pho·tog·ra·phy (fə TOG rə fee) *n.* **1.** the process of forming and fixing an image of an object by the chemical action of light and other forms of radiant energy on photosensitive surfaces. **2.** the art or business of producing and printing photographs. —**pho·to·graph·ic** (FOH tə GRAF ik) *adj.* —**pho′to·graph′i·cal·ly** *adv.*

pho·to·gra·vure (FOH tə grə VYUUR) *n.* **1.** the process of making an intaglio plate from a photograph for use in printing. **2.** a picture so produced. [< F]

pho·tom·e·ter (foh TOM i tər) *n.* any instrument for measuring or comparing the intensity of light. —**pho·to·met·ric** (FOH tə ME trik) *adj.* —**pho·tom′e·try** *n.*

pho·to·mi·cro·graph (FOH tə MĪ krə GRAF) *n.* a photograph taken through a microscope. —**pho·to·mi·crog·ra·phy** (FOH tə mī KROG rə fee) *n.*

pho·to·mon·tage (FOH tə mon TAHZH) *n.* montage produced by photography.

pho·ton (FOH ton) *n. Physics* a quantum of radiant energy, moving with the velocity of light.

pho·to·off·set (FOH toh AWF SET) *n.* offset printing from a metal surface on which the text or design has been imprinted by photography.

pho·to·sen·si·tive (FOH tə SEN si tiv) *adj.* sensitive to light. —**pho′to·sen′si·tiv′i·ty** *n.*

pho·to·sphere (FOH tə SFEER) *n. Astron.* the visible shining surface of the sun.

Pho·to·stat (FOH tə STAT) *n.* a camera designed to reproduce facsimiles of documents, drawings, etc. directly as positives: a trade name. —*v.t. & v.i.* **·stat·ed, ·stat·ing** make a reproduction (of) with a Photostat. —*n.* the reproduction so produced. — **pho′to·stat′ic** *adj.*

pho·to·syn·the·sis (FOH tə SIN thə sis) *n. Biochem.* the process by which plants form carbohydrates from carbon dioxide, inorganic salts, and water through the agency of sunlight acting upon chlorophyll. — **pho·to·syn·thet·ic** (FOH tə sin THET ik) *adj.*

pho·to·trop·ic (FOH tə TROP ik) *adj. Biol.* turning in a particular direction under the influence of light. —**pho·tot·ro·pism** (foh TO trə PIZ əm) *n.*

phrase (frayz) *n.* **1.** *Gram.* a group of two or

more associated words, not containing a subject and predicate. **2.** a word or group of words spoken in one breath. **3.** a concise, catchy statement. **4.** *Music* a brief statement, usu. comprising several measures. — *v.t. & v.i.* **•phrased, •phras•ing 1.** express in words or phrases. **2.** divide (a sentence etc.) into phrases when speaking. **3.** *Music* divide (a melody) into phrases. [< L *phrasis* diction] —**phras'al** *adj.* —**phras' ing** *n.*

phra•se•ol•o•gy (FRAY zee OL ə jee) *n.* the choice and arrangement of words and phrases in expressing ideas.

phre•nol•o•gy (fri NOL ə jee) *n.* the belief that the conformation of the human skull indicates the degree of development of various mental faculties and characteristics. — **phre•nol'o•gist** *n.*

phy•lac•ter•y (fi LAK tə ree) *n. pl.* **•ter•ies** in Judaism, one of two small leather cases containing strips inscribed with Scriptural passages, and bound on the forehead or around the left arm by men during morning prayer. [ME *philaterie*]

phy•log•e•ny (fi LOJ ə nee) *n. Biol.* the history of the evolution of a species or group. [< Gk. *phylon* race + *-geneia* origin]

phy•lum (FĪ ləm) *n. pl.* **•la** (-lə) *Biol.* a major division of animals or plants whose members are believed to have a common evolutionary ancestor. [< NL]

phys•ic (FIZ ik) *n.* a cathartic; a purge. —*v.t.* **•icked, •ick•ing 1.** treat with medicine, esp. with a cathartic. **2.** cure or relieve. [ME *phisik*]

phys•i•cal (FIZ i kəl) *adj.* **1.** of or relating to the human body, as distinguished from the mind or spirit. **2.** of the nature of or pertaining to matter or material things. **3.** of or relating to the material universe or to the sciences that treat of it. **4.** of or pertaining to physics: a *physical* law. —*n.* a medical examination of one's body: also **physical examination.** —**phys'i•cal•ly** *adv.*

physical education athletic training and development of the human body; also, education in hygiene.

physical geography geography dealing with the natural features of the earth, as vegetation, land forms, drainage, ocean currents, climate, etc.: also called *physiography.*

physical science any of the sciences that treat of inanimate matter or energy, as physics, astronomy, chemistry, or geology.

physical therapy the treatment of disability, injury, and disease by external physical means, as by electricity, heat, massage, etc.: also called *physiotherapy.* —**physical therapist**

phy•si•cian (fi ZISH ən) *n.* one who is legally authorized to practice medicine; a doctor.

phys•i•cist (FIZ ə sist) *n.* a specialist in physics.

phys•ics (FIZ iks) *n.* (*construed as sing.*) the science that treats of motion, matter, and energy, and of their interactions.

phys•i•og•no•my (FIZ ee OG nə mee) *n. pl.* **•mies 1.** the face or features considered as revealing character or disposition. **2.** the outward look of a thing. [ME *phisonomie*]

phys•i•og•ra•phy (FIZ ee OG rə fee) *n.* **1.** a description of nature. **2.** physical geography.

phys•i•ol•o•gy (FIZ ee OL ə jee) *n.* **1.** the science that treats of the processes and mechanisms by which living animals and plants function under varied conditions. **2.** the aggregate of vital processes: the *physiology* of the frog. [< Gk. *physiologia*] — **phys'i•o•log'i•cal** (FIZ ee ə LOJ i kəl) *adj* —**phys'i•ol'o•gist** *n.*

phys•i•o•ther•a•py (FIZ ee oh THER ə pee) *n.* physical therapy.

phy•sique (fi ZEEK) *n.* the structure or appearance of the body. [< F]

pi (pī) *n. pl.* **pis** (pīz) **1.** the sixteenth letter in the Greek alphabet (Π, π), corresponding to English *p.* **2.** *Math.* **a** this letter used to designate the ratio of the circumference of a circle to its diameter. **b** the ratio itself (3.14159...).

pi•a•nis•si•mo (PEE ə NIS ə MOH) *adj. & adv. Music* very soft or very softly. —*n. pl.* **•mos** a passage so played. [< Ital.]

pi•an•ist (pee AN ist) *n.* one who plays the piano; esp., a professional performer on the piano. [< F *pianiste*]

pi•an•o¹ (pee AN oh) *n. pl.* **•an•os** a musical instrument having felt-covered hammers operated from a manual keyboard that strike upon steel wires to produce musical tones. [Short for PIANOFORTE]

pi•a•no² *adj. & adv. Music* soft or softly: a direction to the performer. [< Ital.]

pi•an•o•for•te (pee AN ə FORT) *n.* a piano. [< Ital. *piano e forte* soft and loud]

pi•az•za (pee AZ ə) *n.* **1.** an open area or public square in a city or town, esp. in Italy. **2.** a covered outer walk or gallery. [< Ital., courtyard]

pi·ca (PĪ kə) *n.* **1.** a size of type; 12-point; about ⅙ inch. **2.** a size of typewriter type equivalent to 12-point, with 10 characters to the inch.

pic·a·resque (PIK ə RESK) *adj.* **1.** of or involving rogues or vagabonds. **2.** denoting a form of fiction involving rogues and vagabonds. [< Sp. *picaresco* roguish]

pic·a·yune (PIK ə YOON) *ADJ.* **1. of small value; paltry; contemptible. 2.** petty; niggling; mean. Also **pic′a·yun′ish.** —*n. Informal* anything of trifling value. [< Pg. *picaioun* small coin]

pic·ca·lil·li (PIK ə LIL ee) *n.* a relish of chopped vegetables.

pic·co·lo (PIK ə LOH) *n. pl.* **·los** a small flute pitched an octave higher than the ordinary flute. [< Ital., lit., small]

pick[1] (pik) *v.t.* **1.** choose; select, as from a group or number. **2.** detach or pluck, as with the fingers. **3.** clear (a field, tree, etc.) in such a manner. **4.** remove extraneous matter from (the teeth etc.), as with the fingers or with a pointed instrument. **5.** touch, irritate, or remove with a fingernail etc. **6.** nibble at or peck. **7.** break up, penetrate, or indent with or as with a pointed instrument. **8.** pull apart, as rags. **9.** seek or point out critically: *pick* flaws. **10.** remove the contents of by stealth: *pick* a pocket. **11.** open (a lock) by means other than the key. **12.** provoke: *pick* a fight. —*v.i.* **13.** work with a pick. **14.** eat without appetite; nibble. **15.** select carefully. —**pick at 1.** eat without appetite. **2.** nag. —**pick off 1.** remove by picking. **2.** hit, as with a bullet. **3.** in baseball, put out (a base runner) caught off base. —**pick on** *Informal* tease or annoy. —**pick out 1.** select. **2.** distinguish (something) from its surroundings. **3.** produce the notes of (a tune) singly or slowly, as by ear. —**pick over** examine carefully or one by one. —**pick up 1.** take up, as with the hand. **2.** take up or receive into a group, vehicle, etc. **3.** acquire casually or by chance. **4.** gain speed; accelerate. **5.** be able to receive, as radio transmission. **6.** recover spirits, health, etc.; improve. **7.** *Informal* make the acquaintance of (a stranger, esp. of the opposite sex) under casual circumstances. —*n.* **1.** right of selection; choice. **2.** that which is selected, esp. the choicest part. **3.** the quantity of certain crops picked by hand. **4.** the act of picking. [ME *pyken*]

pick[2] *n.* **1.** a double-headed, pointed metal tool mounted on a wooden handle, used for

breaking ground etc. **2.** any of various implements for picking. **3.** a small implement for striking the strings of a guitar, etc.: also called *plectrum.* [ME *pikke*]

pick·ax (PIK AKS) *n.* a pick with one end of the head edged like a chisel and the other pointed; also, a pick with both ends pointed. Also **pick′axe′.**

pick·et (PIK it) *n.* **1.** a pointed stick or post, used as a fence paling, tent peg, etc.; stake. **2.** a person stationed at the outside of a place affected by a strike, for the purpose of publicizing alleged grievances, etc. **3.** a person engaged in public protest. **4.** *Mil.* a soldier or detachment of soldiers posted to guard a camp, army, etc. —*v.t.* **1.** be a picket or station pickets outside of: *picket* a factory. **2.** fence or fortify with pickets. **3.** tie to a picket, as a horse. **4.** *Mil.* guard by means of a picket. —*v.i.* **5.** act as a picket (defs. 2 & 3). [< F *piquet*]

pick·ing (PIK ing) *n.* **1.** that which is or may be picked. **2.** *pl.* that which is left: scanty *pickings.* **3.** *Usu. pl.* that which is taken by questionable means; spoils.

pick·le (PIK əl) *n.* **1.** a cucumber that has been preserved and flavored in brine or vinegar. **2.** any article of food so preserved or flavored. **3.** a liquid preservative, as brine or vinegar, sometimes spiced, for meat, fish, etc. **4.** *Informal* an embarrassing condition or position. —*v.t.* **·led, ·ling** preserve or flavor in a pickle solution. [ME *pikkyl*]

pick·pock·et (PIK POK it) *n.* one who steals from pockets.

pick·up (PIK UP) *n.* **1.** acceleration, as in the speed of an automobile, engine, etc. **2.** *Electronics* a device that converts the oscillations of a needle in a record groove into electrical impulses. **3.** a small, usu. open truck for light loads: also **pickup truck. 4.** *Telecom.* in television: **a** the scanning of an image by the electron beam. **b** the scanning apparatus. **5.** renewed or increased activity: a *pickup* in business. **6.** *Informal* a stranger with whom a casual acquaintance is made.

pic·nic (PIK nik) *n.* **1.** an outdoor social outing for which food is usu. provided by the people participating. **2.** *Informal* an easy or pleasant time or experience. —*v.i.* **·nicked, ·nick·ing** have or attend a picnic. [< F *pique-nique*] —**pic′nick·er** *n.*

pico- *combining form* one trillionth (10⁻¹²) of a specified quantity or dimension: *pico- second.*

pic·to·graph (PIK tə GRAF) *n.* **1.** a picture

representing an idea, as a hieroglyph. 2. a record of such pictures. Also **pic′to•gram** (-GRAM). [< L*pictus* painted + -GRAPH] — **pic•tog•ra•phy** (pik TOG rə fee) n. picture writing.

pic•to•ri•al (pik TOR ee əl) *adj.* 1. pertaining to, composed of, or concerned with pictures. 2. graphic; vivid. —*n.* a periodical that devotes considerable space to pictures.

pic•ture (PIK chər) n. 1. a visual representation of an object or scene upon a flat surface, as a painting, drawing, engraving, or photograph. 2. a vivid or graphic verbal description. 3. a mental image or impression of the nature of a situation, event, etc. 4. an overall situation. 5. one who or that which resembles or embodies another person or thing: She is the *picture* of despair. —*v.t.* •**tured, •tur•ing** 1. form a mental image of. 2. describe graphically; depict verbally. 3. make a picture of. [ME]

pic•tur•esque (pik chə RESK) *adj.* 1. having a striking beauty, quaintness, or charm. 2. abounding in striking or original expression or imagery. 3. like or suitable for a picture. [< F] —**pic′tur•esque′ness** n.

picture tube kinescope.

pid•dle (PID l) v. •**dled, •dling** *v.t.* 1. trifle; dawdle: usu. with *away.* —*v.i.* 2. trifle; dawdle.

pid•dling (PID ling) *adj.* unimportant; trivial; trifling.

pidg•in (PIJ ən) n. a mixed language combining the vocabulary and grammar of dissimilar languages.

pidgin English a jargon composed of English and elements of local non-English dialects, used as the language of commerce esp. in the Orient. Also called **Pidgin English.**

pie (pī) n. a baked food consisting of one or two layers or crusts of pastry with a filling of fruit, custard, meat, etc. [ME]

pie•bald (PĪ bawld) *adj.* having spots, esp. of white and black. —*n.* a spotted or mottled animal, esp. a horse.

piece (pees) n. 1. a portion or quantity existing as an individual entity or mass: a *piece* of paper. 2. a small portion considered as forming a distinct part of a whole. 3. a coin: a fifty-cent *piece.* 4. an instance; example: a *piece* of luck. 5. one of a class or group: a *piece* of furniture. 6. a work of esthetic interest, as a literary or musical composition, a play, etc. 7. one of the disks or counters used in checkers, backgammon, etc. 8. a

quantity or length in which an article is manufactured or sold. —**a piece of one's mind** criticism or censure frankly expressed. —**go to pieces** 1. fall apart. 2. lose emotional self-control. —**have a piece of** *Slang* have a financial interest in. —*v.t.* **pieced, piec•ing** 1. add or attach a piece or pieces to, as for enlargement. 2. unite or reunite the pieces of, as in mending. 3. unite (parts) into a whole. [ME *pece*]

pièce de ré•sis•tance (pee ES də ri zee STAHNS) *pl.* **pièces de résistance** (pee ES də ri zee STAHNS) *French* 1. a principal or most important item. 2. the chief dish of a dinner.

piece•meal (PEES MEEL) *adv. & adj.* piece by piece; gradually. [ME *pecemele*]

piece•work (PEES WURK) n. work done or paid for by the piece or quantity. —**piece′ •work′er** n.

pied (pīd) *adj.* spotted; piebald; mottled.

pied-à-terre (pee AYD ə TAIR) n. *pl.* **pieds-à-terre** (pee AYD ə TAIR) a temporary or secondary lodging. [< F, lit., foot on the ground]

pier (peer) n. 1. a structure extending over the water, secured by piles and serving as a landing place for vessels; wharf. 2. a plain, detached mass of masonry, usu. serving as a support: the *pier* of a bridge. 3. an upright projecting portion of a wall; a buttress. [ME *pere*]

pierce (peers) v. **pierced, pierc•ing** *v.t.* 1. pass into or through, with or as if with a pointed instrument; puncture; stab. 2. force a way into or through: *pierce* the wilderness. 3. make an opening or hole in, into, or through. 4. cut through as if stabbing; cleave. 5. solve; understand: *pierce* a mystery. —*v.i.* 6. enter; penetrate. [ME *percen*] —**pierc′ing•ly** *adv.*

pi•e•ty (PĪ i tee) n. *pl.* •**ties** 1. reverence toward God or the gods. 2. honor and obedience due to parents, etc. 3. a pious act, wish, etc. [ME *piete*]

pi•e•zo•e•lec•tric•i•ty (pī EE zoh i lek TRIS i tee) n. electricity or electric phenomena resulting from pressure upon certain bodies, esp. crystals. —**pi•e′zo•e•lec′tric** *adj.*

pif•fle (PIF əl) *Informal* *v.i.* •**fled, •fling** talk nonsensically; babble. —*n.* nonsense; babble.

pig (pig) n. 1. a cloven-hoofed mammal having a long, mobile snout, esp. a small, young one: also called *swine.* ◆ Collateral adjective: *porcine*. **2.** the flesh of a pig; pork. **3.** an oblong mass of metal, esp. iron or lead, just run from the smelter and cast in a rough mold. **4.** a person who is filthy, gluttonous, or coarse. —*v.i.* **pigged, pig·ging** bring forth pigs. [ME *pigge*]

pig·eon (PIJ ən) *n.* **1.** a bird having short legs, a small head, and a sturdy body. **2.** *Slang* one who is easily swindled. [ME *pejon*, young dove]

pig·eon·hole (PIJ ən HOHL) *n.* **1.** a hole for pigeons to nest in. **2.** a small compartment, as in a desk, for filing papers. —*v.t.* **·holed, ·hol·ing** **1.** place in a pigeonhole; file. **2.** file away and ignore. **3.** place in categories.

pig·eon·toed (PIJ ən TOHD) *adj.* having the toes or feet turned inward.

pig·gish (PIG ish) *adj.* like a pig; greedy; dirty; selfish. —**pig'gish·ness** *n.*

pig·gy·back (PIG ee BAK) *adv.* **1.** on the back or shoulders: ride *piggyback*. **2.** on a railway flat car: ship trailers *piggyback*. —**pig'gy·bak'** *adj.* —**pig'gy·back'ing** *n.*

pig·head·ed (PIG HED id) *adj.* stupidly obstinate. —**pig'·head'ed·ness** *n.*

pig iron crude iron poured from a blast furnace into variously shaped molds of sand or the like.

pig·ment (PIG mənt) *n.* **1.** finely powdered coloring matter suitable for making paints, enamels, etc. **2.** any substance that imparts color to animal or vegetable tissues, as melanin and chlorophyll. [ME]

pig·men·ta·tion (PIG mən TAY shən) *n.* **1.** coloration resulting from pigment. **2.** *Biol.* deposition of pigment by cells. —**pig'·ment'ed** *adj.*

Pig·my (PIG mee) see PYGMY.

pig·pen (PIG PEN *n.* **1.** a pen for keeping pigs. **2.** any untidy or filthy place.

pig·skin (PIG SKIN) *n.* **1.** the skin of a pig. **2.** something made of this skin, as a saddle. **3.** *Informal* a football.

pig·sty (PIG STĪ) *n. pl.* **·sties** pigpen

pig·tail (PIG TAYL) *n.* a braid or plait of hair extending down from the back of the head.

pike¹ (pīk) *n.* a long pole having a metal spearhead. —*v.t.* **piked, pik·ing** run through or kill with a pike. [< MF *pique*]

pike² *n.* **1.** a widely distributed freshwater food fish having a slender body and a long snout. **2.** any of several other fishes resembling the pike.

pike³ *n.* a turnpike.

pike⁴ *n.* a spike or sharp point, as the end of a spear.

pik·er (PĪ kər) *n.* *Informal* **1.** one who bets or speculates in a small, niggardly way. **2.** one who acts in a petty or niggling way. [ME]

pi·laf (PEE lahf) *n.* a Middle Eastern dish of rice, raisins, spice, and a meat or fowl sauce. Also **pi·lau** and **pi·law**. [< Persian and Turkish *pilău*]

pile¹ (pīl) *n.* **1.** a quantity of anything gathered or thrown together in one place; a heap. **2.** a funeral pyre. **3.** a massive building or group of buildings. **4.** *Informal* a large accumulation, quantity, or number of something. **5.** *Informal* a large amount of money. —*v.* **piled, pil·ing** *v.t.* **1.** make a heap or pile of: often with *up*. **2.** cover or burden with a pile or piles: *pile* a plate with food. —*v.i.* **3.** form a heap or pile. **4.** proceed or go in a confused mass: with *in, on, off, out,* etc. —**pile up** accumulate. [ME]

pile² *n.* a column, as of wood or steel, forced into the earth to support a building, pier, etc. —*v.t.* **piled, pil·ing** **1.** drive piles into. **2.** furnish or strengthen with piles. [ME, shaft]

pile³ *n.* **1.** the cut or uncut loops that form the surface of certain fabrics, as velvets, plushes, and corduroys. **2.** soft, fine hair; down. [ME *piles* hair] —**piled** *adj.*

pi·le·at·ed (PIL ee AY tid) *adj.* *Ornithol.* having the feathers on the top of the head elongated or conspicuous; crested. Also **pi'le·ate** (PIL ee it). [< L *pileatus* capped]

piles (pīlz) *n.pl.* hemorrhoids. [ME]

pil·fer (PIL fər) *v.t. & v.i.* steal in small quantities. [ME *pllfre* booty] —**pil'·fer·age** *n.* —**pil'fer·er** *n.*

pil·grim (PIL grəm) *n.* **1.** one who journeys to some sacred place from religious motives. **2.** any wanderer or wayfarer. **3.** *cap.* one of the English Puritans who founded Plymouth Colony in 1620. [ME *pilegrim*]

pil·grim·age (PIL grə mij) *n.* **1.** a journey made to a shrine or sacred place. **2.** any long or arduous journey.

pil·ing (PĪ ling) *n.* a structure formed of piles.

pill (pil) *n.* **1.** a pellet or globule containing medicine, convenient for swallowing whole. **2.** *Slang* a person difficult to bear with; a bore. —**the pill** or **the Pill** any of various oral contraceptive drugs in tablet form, taken by women. —*v.t.* **1.** form into pills. **2.** dose with pills. [ME *pille* ball]

pil·lage (PIL ij) *n.* **1.** the act of taking money or property by open violence; looting. **2.**

spoil; booty. —v. •laged, •lag·ing v.t. 1. plunder. 2. take as loot. —v.i. 3. take plunder. [ME *pilage* plunder] —pil′lag·er *n.*

pil·lar (PIL ər) *n.* 1. a vertical support, usu. slender in relation to its height; column. 2. a structure of similar form used as a decoration or monument. 3. one who strongly supports a work or cause. —v.t. support or adorn with pillars. [ME *pillare*]

pill·box (PIL BOKS) *n.* 1. a small box for pills. 2. a small, round, concrete emplacement for a machine gun, antitank gun, etc.

pil·lo·ry (PIL ə ree) *n. pl.* •ries a framework in which an offender was fastened by the neck and wrists and exposed to public scorn. —v.t. •ried, •ry·ing 1. set in the pillory. 2. hold up to public scorn. [ME *pyllory*]

pil·low (PIL oh) *n.* 1. a case, usu. of cloth, filled with a soft or yielding material, as feathers or foam rubber, used to cushion the head, as during sleep. 2. a small, usu. decorative cushion. —v.t. 1. rest on or as on a pillow. 2. act as a pillow for. —v.i. 3. recline on or as on a pillow. [ME *pilwe*]

pil·low·case (PIL oh KAYS) *n.* a covering drawn over a pillow. Also **pillow slip.**

pi·lot (PĪ lət) *n.* 1. one who operates or guides an aircraft or spacecraft during flight. 2. one who is licensed to conduct ships in and out of port or through certain waters difficult to navigate. 3. the helmsman of a ship. 4. any guide. 5. a television program offered as typical of a projected series. —v.t. 1. act as the pilot of; steer. 2. guide or conduct, as through difficult circumstances. 3. serve as a pilot on, over, or in. —adj. 1. serving as a guide or control. 2. serving as a trial situation. [< Ital. *pilota*]

pilot light a small flame kept burning for igniting the main burner when desired: also **pilot burner.**

pil·sner (PILZ nər) *n. Often cap.* 1. a light beer. 2. a tall, tapered glass for beer.

pi·men·to (pi MEN toh) *n. pl.* •tos 1. the dried, unripe, aromatic berry of a West Indian tree of the myrtle family. 2. pimiento. [Alter. of Sp. *pimiento*]

pi·mien·to (pi MYEN toh) *n. pl.* •tos a sweet pepper or its ripe fruit, used as a relish and as a stuffing in olives: also called *pimento.* [< Sp., pepper plant]

pimp (pimp) *n.* one who solicits for a prostitute in exchange for a share of the earnings. —v.i. act as a pimp. —v.t. act as a pimp for.

pim·ple (PIM pəl) *n.* a small swelling or elevation of the skin, with an inflamed base. [ME] —pim′pled, pim′ply *adj.*

pin (pin) *n.* 1. a short, stiff piece of wire with a sharp point and a round head, used for fastening together parts of clothing, sheets of paper, etc. 2. an ornament mounted on a pin or having a pin with a clasp. 3. anything resembling a pin in form or use, as a hairpin. 4. a peg or bar, as of metal or wood, used in fastening or supporting, as the bolt of a door etc. 5. in bowling and similar games, one of the rounded clubs that are set up as the target. 6. in golf, a pole with a small flag attached to mark the position of a hole. 7. *pl. Informal* the legs. —**on pins and needles** uneasy or anxious; nervous. —v.t. **pinned, pin·ning** 1. fasten with or as with a pin or pins. 2. seize and hold firmly; make unable to move. 3. transfix with a pin, spear, etc. 4. force (someone) to make a decision, follow a definite course of action, etc.: usu. with *down.* —**pin something on someone** *Informal* hold responsible for (a wrongdoing etc.); accuse of. [ME *pinne* peg]

pin·a·fore (PIN ə FOR) *n.* a sleeveless apronlike garment for a child or woman.

pin·ball (PIN bawl) *n.* a game in which a ball is propelled by a spring to the top of an inclined board, and in its descent touches any of various numbered pins, holes, etc., the contacts so made determining the player's score.

pince-nez (PANS NAY) *n. pl.* pince-nez (PANS NAYZ) eyeglasses held upon the nose by a spring. [< F, LIT., PINCH-NOSE]

pin·cer (PIN sər) *n.* 1. *Usu. pl.* an instrument having two handles and a pair of jaws working on a pivot, used for holding objects. 2. *Zool.* a grasping organ, as the claw of a lobster. [ME *pinser*, pincher]

pinch (pinch) *v.t.* 1. squeeze between two hard edges or surfaces, as a finger and thumb, etc. 2. bend or compress painfully. 3. contract or make thin, as from cold or hunger. 4. reduce in means; distress, as for lack of money. 5. *Slang* capture or arrest. 6. *Slang* steal. —v.i. 7. squeeze; hurt. 8. be stingy. —**pinch pennies** be economical or stingy. —n. 1. the act of pinching, or the state of being pinched. 2. as much of a substance as can be taken between the finger and thumb; a small amount. 3. an emergency. 4. *Slang* an arrest or raid. [ME *pinchen*]

pinch-hit (PINCH HIT) *v.i.* **-hit, -hit·ting** **1.** in baseball, go to bat in place of a regular player. **2.** *Informal* substitute for another in an emergency. —**pinch hitter**.

pin·cush·ion (PIN KUUSH ən) *n.* a small cushion into which pins are stuck when they are not in use.

pine¹ (pīn) *n.* **1.** any of various cone-bearing trees having needle-shaped evergreen leaves growing in clusters. **2.** the wood of a pine tree. [ME]

pine² *v.i.* **pined, pin·ing 1.** grow thin or weak with longing, grief, etc. **2.** have great longing: usu. with *for*. [ME *pinen* torment]

pine·ap·ple (PĪ NAP əl) *n.* **1.** a tropical plant having spiny leaves and a cone-shaped fruit tipped with a rosette of spiked leaves. **2.** its edible fruit.

pin·feath·er (PIN FETII ər) *n. Ornithol.* a rudimentary feather, esp. one just beginning to grow through the skin.

pin·head (PIN HED) *n.* **1.** the head of a pin. **2.** any small or insignificant object. **3.** *Slang* a stupid person.

pin·hole (PIN HOIL) *n.* a minute puncture made by or as by a pin.

pin·ion¹ (PIN yən) *n.* **1.** the wing of a bird. **2.** the outer segment of a bird's wing, bearing the flight feathers. —*v.t.* **1.** cut off one pinion or bind the wings of (a bird) so as to prevent flight. **2.** shackle; confine. [ME *pynyon* feather]

pin·ion² *n. Mech.* a gear driving or driven by a larger gear. [< F *pignon* cogwheel]

pink¹ (pingk) *n.* **1.** a pale red color. **2.** any of several garden plants with narrow, grasslike leaves and fragrant flowers. **3.** the flower of any of these plants. **4.** *Slang* a person who holds somewhat radical economic or political views. —**in the pink (of condition)** in excellent health. —*adj.* **1.** being pink in color. **2.** *Slang* moderately radical. —**pink′ish** *adj.*

pink² *v.t.* **1.** prick or stab with a pointed weapon. **2.** decorate, as cloth or leather, with a pattern of holes. **3.** cut the edges of (cloth) with a notched pattern. [ME *pynken* prick]

pin money an allowance of money for minor incidental expenses.

pin·na·cle (PIN ə kəl) *n.* **1.** a small turret or tall ornament, as on a parapet. **2.** anything resembling a pinnacle, as a mountain peak. **3.** the highest point or place; apex; summit. —*v.t.* **·cled, ·cling 1.** place on or as on a pinnacle. **2.** furnish with a pinnacle; crown. [ME *pinacle* gable]

pi·noch·le (PEE nok əl) *n.* a card game played with a deck of 48 cards.

pin·point (PIN POINT) *n.* **1.** the point of a pin. **2.** something extremely small: a *pinpoint* of light. —*v.t.* locate or define precisely.

pin·stripe (PIN STRIP) *n.* a very narrow stripe, as in a fabric. —**pin′striped′** *adj.*

pint (pīnt) *n.* **1.** a dry and liquid measure of capacity equal to Ó quart: the liquid pint is equal to .473 liter and the dry pint to .55 liter. **2.** a container having such a capacity. [ME *pynte*]

pin·to (PIN toh) *adj.* spotted; mottled, as an animal. —*n. pl.* **·tos 1.** a pinto horse or pony. **2.** a kind of spotted bean of the SW U.S.: also **pinto bean.** [< Am.Sp.]

pin·up (PIN UP) *n.* a picture of an attractive person, suitable for hanging on a wall. —*adj.* **1.** capable of being attached to a wall, as a lamp. **2.** having the qualities of or suitable for a pinup: a *pinup* girl.

pin·wheel (PIN HWEEL) *n.* **1.** a firework that revolves when ignited, forming a wheel of fire. **2.** a child's toy resembling a windmill, revolving on a pin attached to a stick.

pin·worm (PIN WURM) *n.* a small worm parasitic in the lower intestine of a person.

pin·y (PĪ nee) *adj.* **pin·i·er, pin·i·est** pertaining to, suggestive of, or covered with pines.

pin·yin (PIN YIN) *n. Sometimes cap.* a system for transliterating Chinese into the English alphabet. [< Chinese, lit., phonetic spelling]

pi·o·neer (PĪ ə NEER) *n.* **1.** one of the first explorers or settlers of a new country or region. **2.** one of the first investigators or developers in a new field of research, enterprise, etc. —*v.t.* **1.** be a pioneer of. —*v.i.* **2.** act as a pioneer. [< MF *pionier*]

pi·ous (PĪ əs) *adj.* **1.** actuated by reverence for a supreme being; religious; godly. **2.** marked by a reverential spirit. **3.** Affectedly devout or virtuous. [< L*pius* dutiful] —**pi′ous·ly** *adv.* —**pi′ous·ness** *n.*

pip¹ (pip) *n.* the seed of an apple, orange, etc.

pip² *n.* a spot, as on a playing card, domino, or die.

pip³ *n.* **1.** *Vet.* a contagious disease of birds. **2.** any mild human ailment, used facetiously. [ME *pippe*]

pipe (pīp) *n.* **1.** a small bowl with a hollow stem, for smoking tobacco etc. **2.** a long conducting passage of wood, metal, tiling, etc. for conveying a fluid. **3.** *Music* **a** a tubular flute or woodwind instrument. **b** one of the tubes of a pipe organ. **c** *pl.* the bagpipe. —*v.* **piped, pip·ing** *v.i.* **1.** play on a pipe. **2.** make a shrill sound. —*v.t.* **3.** convey by or as by means of pipes. **4.** play, as a tune, on a pipe. **5.** utter shrilly or in a high key. — **pipe down** *Slang* become silent; stop talking or making noise. [ME]

pipe dream a groundless hope or wish.

pipe fitting *n.* **1.** a piece of pipe used to connect two or more pipes together. **2.** the work of joining pipes together. —**pipe fitter** a person who installs and repairs piping.

pipe·line (PĪP LIN) *n.* **1.** a line of pipe, as for the transmission of water, oil, etc. **2.** a channel for the transmission of information, usu. private or secret. —*v.t.* **·lined, ·lin·ing** convey by pipeline.

pipe organ an organ having pipes, as distinguished from an electric organ etc.

pip·er (PĪ pər) *n.* one who plays upon a pipe, esp. a bagpipe. —**pay the piper** suffer the unfavorable consequence of one's actions.

pi·pette (pī PET) *n.* a small tube for removing or transferring measured quantities of a liquid. Also **pi·pet′.** — *v.t.* **·pet·ted, ·pet·ting** measure or transfer liquid in this way. [< F]

pip·ing (PĪ ping) *adj.* **1.** hissing or sizzling; very hot. **2.** having a shrill sound. —*n.* **1.** the act of one who pipes. **2.** music of or suggesting that of pipes; a wailing or whistling sound. **3.** a system of pipes, as for drainage. **4.** a narrow strip of cloth folded on the bias, used for trimming edges or seams.

pip·pin (PIP in) *n.* **1.** an apple of many varieties. **2.** a seed; pip. [ME *pipin* seed]

pip·squeak (PIP SKWEEK) *n. Informal* a small, insignificant person.

pi·quant (PEE kənt) *adj.* **1.** having an agreeably pungent or tart taste. **2.** lively and interesting. [< F, pricking] —**pi′quan·cy** *n.*

pique (peek) *n.* a feeling of irritation or resentment. —*v.t.* **piqued, pi·quing** **1.** excite resentment in. **2.** stimulate or arouse; provoke. [< MF]

pi·qué (pī KAY) *n.* a fabric of cotton, rayon, or silk, with raised cord running lengthwise. [< F, pricked]

pi·ra·cy (PĪ rə see) *n. pl.* **·cies** **1.** robbery of craft on the high seas or in the air. **2.** the unauthorized use of another's invention, idea, or literary creation. [< Med.L *piratia*]

pi·ra·nha (pi RAHN yə) *n.* a small fish of tropical South America with massive jaws and sharp teeth, known to attack man and larger animals. [< Tupi, toothed fish]

pi·rate (PĪ rət) *n.* one engaged in piracy; esp., a roving robber at sea. —*v.t. & v.i.* **·rat·ed, ·rat·ing** **1.** practice or commit piracy (upon). **2.** plagiarize. [ME] — **pi·rat·i·cal** (pī RAT i kəl) *adj.*

pir·ou·ette (PIR oo ET) *n.* a rapid whirling upon the toes in dancing. [< F] —*v.i.* **·et·ted, ·et·ting** perform a pirouette.

pis·ca·to·ri·al (PIS kə TOR ee əl) *adj.* **1.** pertaining to fishes or fishing. **2.** engaged in fishing. Also **pis′ca·to′ry.** [< L *piscatorius*]

pis·cine (PĪ seen) *adj.* of, pertaining to, or resembling a fish or fishes. [< L *piscinus*]

pis·mire (PIS MĪR) *n.* an ant. [ME *pissemyre*]

pis·ta·chi·o (pi STASH ee OH) *n. pl.* **·chi·os** a small tree bearing edible greenish nuts; also, the nut. [< Ital. *pistacchio*]

pis·til (PIS tl) *n. Bot.* the seed-bearing organ of flowering plants. [< L *pistillum* pestle] —**pis·til·late** (-tl it) *adj.*

pis·tol (PIS tl) *n.* a small firearm having a short barrel, and fired from one hand. [< MF *pistole*]

pis·ton (PIS tən) *n.* **1.** *Mech.* a rigid disk fitted to slide in a cylinder, and connected with a rod for receiving the pressure of or exerting pressure on a fluid in the cylinder. **2.** a valve in a wind instrument for altering the pitch of tones. [< F]

pit[1] (pit) *n.* **1.** cavity in the ground, esp. when wide and deep. **2.** a pitfall for snaring animals; snare. **3.** the usu. sunken area in front of the stage of a theater, housing the orchestra. **4.** an enclosed space in which fighting cocks etc. are pitted against each other. **5.** any natural cavity or depression in the body: the *pit* of the stomach. **6.** any slight depression in the skin, as a pockmark. **7.** a mining excavation, or the shaft of a mine. —**the pits** *Slang* a profoundly unpleasant event, situation, experience, etc. —*v.* **pit·ted, pit·ting** *v.t.* **1.** mark with dents, pits, or hollows. **2.** match as antagonists. —*v.i.* **3.** become marked with pits. [ME]

pit[2] *n.* the kernel of certain fruits, as the plum. —*v.t.* **pit·ted, pit·ting** remove pits from, as fruits. [< MDu. *pitte* kernel]

pi·ta bread (PEE tə) a flat bread originating in Greece and the Middle East. Also **pi′ta.** [< Gk. *pitta* bread]

pit·a·pat (PIT ə PAT) *v.i.* **·pat·ted, ·pat·ting** remove or sound with light, quick steps or pulsations. —*n.* a tapping, or a succession of taps, steps, or similar sounds. —*adv.* with a pitapat; flutteringly.

pitch¹ (pich) *n.* **1.** a dark, viscous substance obtained by boiling down tar, used in coating seams. **2.** the resinous sap of pines. —*v.t.* smear, cover, or treat with or as with pitch. [ME *pich*]

pitch² *v.t.* **1.** throw or hurl; fling. **2.** erect or set up (a tent, camp, etc.). **3.** set the level, angle, degree, etc. of. **4.** in baseball, deliver (the ball) to the batter. —*v.i.* **5.** fall or plunge forward or headlong. **6.** lurch; stagger. **7.** rise and fall alternately at the bow and stern, as a ship. **8.** incline downward; slope. **9.** in baseball, deliver the ball to the batter; act as pitcher. —**pitch in** *Informal* **1.** work together; cooperate. **2.** start vigorously. —**pitch into** *Informal* attack; assail. —*n.* **1.** an act or manner of pitching. **2.** the degree of descent or slope. **3.** the frequency of a sound wave perceived by the ear; the highness or lowness of a sound. **4.** a throw. **5.** in baseball, the delivery of the ball by the pitcher. **6.** the act of dipping or plunging downward, as a ship. **7.** *Informal* a practiced talk or appeal intended to influence or persuade. **8.** a level or intensity of some quality or action: activity at a high *pitch*. [ME *picchen* thrust]

pitch-black (PICH BLAK) *adj.* intensely black, as pitch.

pitch-dark (PICH DAHRK) *adj.* very dark; as black as pitch.

pitch·er¹ (PICH ər) *n.* one who pitches; esp., in baseball, the player who delivers the ball to the batter.

pitch·er² *n.* a container with a spout and a handle, used for holding liquids to be poured out. [ME *picher*]

pitch·fork (PICH FORK) *n.* a large fork with which to handle hay, straw, etc. —*v.t.* lift and throw with or as with a pitchfork. [ME]

pitch·man (PICH mən) *n. pl.* **·men** one who sells small articles from a temporary stand, as at a fair, etc.; a sidewalk vendor.

pitch pipe *Music* a small pipe or group of pipes that sound a particular tone when blown, used to adjust the pitch of a voice or instrument.

pitch·y (PICH ee) *adj.* **pitch·i·er, pitch·i·est 1.** resembling pitch; intensely dark. **2.** full of or daubed with pitch. —**pitch'i·ness** *n.*

pit·e·ous (PIT ee əs) *adj.* exciting pity, sorrow, or sympathy. [ME]

pit·fall (PIT FAWL) *n.* **1.** a hidden danger or unexpected difficulty. **2.** a pit for entrapping wild beast or men. [ME *pitte-falle*]

pith (pith) *n.* **1.** *Bot.* the cylinder of soft, spongy tissue in the center of the stems and branches of certain plants. **2.** the marrow of bones or of the spinal cord. **3.** the essential part; gist. [ME]

pith·y (PITH ee) *adj.* **pith·i·er, pith·i·est 1.** of or like pith. **2.** terse and forceful. —**pith'i·ly** *adv.* —**pith'i·ness** *n.*

pit·i·a·ble (PIT ee ə bəl) *adj.* **1.** arousing or meriting pity or compassion. **2.** insignificant; contemptible. —**pit'i·a·bly** *adv.*

pit·i·ful (PIT i fəl) *adj.* **1.** calling forth pity or compassion; wretched. **2.** evoking contempt. —**pit'i·ful·ly** *adv.*

pit·i·less (PIT i lis) *adj.* having no pity; ruthless. —**pit'i·less·ly** *adv.*

pit·tance (PIT ns) *n.* a small allowance of money. [ME *pitaunce* monk's food allotment]

pit·ter-pat·ter (PIT ər PAT ər) *n.* a rapid series of light sounds or taps. [ME, babbled prayer]

pi·tu·i·tar·y gland (pi TOO i TER ee) *Anat.* a small, rounded body at the base of the brain that secretes hormones affecting growth, metabolism, and other functions of the body. [< L *pituitarius* secreting phlegm]

pit·y (PIT ee) *n. pl.* **pit·ies 1.** grief or pain awakened by the misfortunes of others; compassion. **2.** that which arouses compassion; misfortune. —*v.t. & v.i.* **pit·ied, pit·y·ing** feel pity (for). [ME *pite*] —**pit'i·er** *n.* —**pit'y·ing·ly** *adv.*

piv·ot (PIV ət) *n.* **1.** *Mech.* something upon which a related part turns, oscillates, or rotates. **2.** a person or thing upon which an important matter hinges or turns. —*v.t.* **1.** place on, attach by, or provide with a pivot. —*v.i.* **2.** turn on or as on a pivot; swing. [< F] —**piv'ot·al** (PIV ə tl) *adj.*

pix·ie (PIK see) *n. pl.* **pix·ies** a fairy or elf. Also **pix'y.**

pi·zazz (pə ZAZ) *n. Informal* **1.** exuberance; pep. **2.** dashing style. Also **piz·zazz'.**

piz·za (PEET sə) *n.* an Italian food usu. consisting of a doughy crust spread with a mixture of cheese, tomatoes, spices, etc., and baked. [< Ital.]

piz·ze·ri·a (PEET sə REE ə) *n.* a place

where pizzas are prepared, sold, and eaten. [< Ital.]

piz·zi·ca·to (PIT si KAH toh) *Music adj.* plucked with the fingers. —*adv.* in a pizzicato manner. —*n.* a tone or passage played in a pizzicato manner. [< Ital., plucked]

plac·ard (PLAK ərd) *n.* **1.** a paper publicly displayed, as a poster. **2.** a tag or plate bearing the owner's name. —*v.t.* **1.** announce by means of placards. **2.** post placards on or in. [< MF]

pla·cate (PLAY kayt) *v.t.* **·cat·ed, ·cat·ing** appease the anger of; pacify. [< L *placatus* calmed] —**pla'ca·ble** (PLAK ə bəl) *adj.* — **pla·cat·er** (PLAY kay tər) *n.*

pla·ca·to·ry (PLAY kə TOR ee) *adj.* tending or intended to placate. Also **pla'ca·tive.**

place (plays) *n.* **1.** a particular point or portion of space; a definite locality or location. **2.** an abode or quarters; **3.** an open space or square in a city; also, a court or street. **4.** position in a sequence or series. **5.** station in life; rank. **6.** one's employment; position. **7.** room; way: One thing gives *place* to another. **8.** a particular passage or page in a book etc. **9.** the second position among the first three finishers in a race, as in a horse race. —**in place 1.** in a natural or suitable position. **2.** in its original site. —**in place of** instead of. —**take place** happen; occur. — *v.* **placed, plac·ing** *v.t.* **1.** put in a particular place or position. **2.** find a place, situation, home, etc. for. **3.** identify; classify. **4.** bestow or entrust. —*v.i.* **5.** in racing: **a** finish second. **b** finish among the first three finishers. [ME]

pla·ce·bo (plə SEE boh) *n. pl.* **·bos** or **·boes** *Med.* any harmless substance given to humor a patient or as a test in controlled experiments. [< L, lit., I shall please]

place kick in football, a kick for a goal in which the ball is placed on the ground for kicking. —**place-kick** (PLAYS KIK) *v.t. & v.i.* make or score with a place kick. — **place'-kick'er** *n.*

place mat a mat on which a table setting is placed.

place·ment (PLAYS mənt) *n.* **1.** the act of placing, or the state of being placed. **2.** relative position; arrangement. **3.** the business of placing persons in jobs.

pla·cen·ta (plə SEN tə) *n. pl.* **·tas** or **·tae** (-tee) *Anat.* in higher mammals, the spongy organ of interlocking fetal and uterine structures by which the fetus is nourished

in the uterus. [< NL, flat object] — **pla·cen'tal** *adj.*

plac·er¹ (PLAY sər) *n.* one who or that which places.

plac·er² *n. Mining* **1.** an alluvial or glacial deposit of sand, gravel, etc., containing gold in particles large enough to be obtained by washing. **2.** any place where deposits are washed for valuable minerals. [Var. of Sp., sandbank]

plac·id (PLAS id) *adj.* having a smooth surface or nature; unruffled; calm. [< L *placidus* calm] —**pla·cid·i·ty** (plə SID i tee) *n.*

pla·gia·rize (PLAY jə RĪZ) *v.t. & v.i.* **·rized, ·riz·ing** appropriate and pass off as one's own (the writings, ideas, etc. of another). [< L *plagiarius* plunderer] —**pla'gia·rism** (PLAY jə əm) *n.* —**pla'gia·rist** *n.*

plague (playg) *n.* **1.** *Pathol.* any of various forms of a virulent, highly contagious, and often pandemic disease; esp., the bubonic plague. **2.** a nuisance; bother. —*v.t.* **plagued, pla·guing 1.** vex; annoy. **2.** afflict with plague or disaster. [ME *plage*]

plaid (plad) *n.* **1.** a rectangular woolen scarf of tartan or checkered pattern; any fabric of this pattern. **2.** a checkered pattern of vertical and horizontal stripes of varying widths. [< Scot. Gaelic *plaide* blanket] —**plaid** *adj.*

plain (playn) *adj.* **·er, ·est 1.** open and unobstructed: *plain* view. **2.** clear; understandable. **3.** straightforward; guileless. **4.** lowly in condition or station. **5.** unadorned; without ornamentation. **6.** homely. **7.** not rich; simple: *plain* food. —*n.* an expanse of level land; a prairie. [ME] —**plain'ly** *adv.* — **plain'ness** *n.*

plain·song (PLAYN SAWNG) *n.* the old ecclesiastical chant, having simple melody, not governed by strict rules of meter but by accentuation of the words. [Trans. of Med.L *cantus planus*]

plain·spo·ken (PAYN SPOH kən) *adj.* candid; frank.

plain·tiff (PLAYN tif) *n. Law* the party that begins an action at law; the complaining party in an action. [ME *plaintif* complaining person]

plain·tive (PLAYN tiv) *adj.* expressing a subdued sadness; mournful. —**plain'tive·ly** *adv.* —**plain'tive·ness** *n.*

plait (playt) *v.t.* **1.** braid (hair etc.). **2.** pleat. —*n.* **1.** a braid, esp. of hair. **2.** a pleat. [ME *pleyt* fold]

plan (plan) *n.* **1.** a scheme, method, or design for the attainment of some object. **2.** a drawing showing the proportion and relation of parts, as of a building. —*v.* **planned, plan•ning** *v.t.* **1.** form a scheme or method for doing, achieving, etc. **2.** make a plan of, as a building; design. —*v.i.* **3.** make plans. [< F] —**plan′ner** *n.*

plane[1] (playn) *n.* **1.** *Geom.* a surface such that a straight line joining any two of its points lies wholly within the surface. **2.** any flat surface. **3.** a grade of development; level: a *plane* of thought. **4.** *Aeron.* a supporting surface of an airplane. **5.** an airplane. —*adj.* **1.** level; flat. **2.** dealing only with flat surfaces: *plane* geometry. [< L *planus* level] —**pla•nar** (PLAY nər) *adj.*

plane[2] *n.* a tool used for smoothing boards or other surfaces of wood. —*v.* **planed, plan•ing** *v.t.* **1.** make smooth or even with a plane. **2.** remove with a plane. —*v.i.* **3.** use a plane. [< L *planare* level] —**plan•er** (PLAY nər) *n.*

plane[3] *v.i.* **planed, plan•ing 1.** rise partly out of the water, as a power boat when driven at high speed. **2.** glide; soar. **3.** travel by airplane. [< F *planer*]

plan•et (PLAN it) *n. Astron.* one of the celestial bodies revolving around the sun and shining only by reflected light: Mercury, Venus, Earth, Mars, Jupiter, Saturn, Uranus, Neptune, and Pluto. [ME *planete*] —**plan•e•tar•y** (PLAN i TER ee) *adj.*

plan•e•tar•i•um (PLAN i TAIR ee əm) *n. pl.* **•i•ums** or **•i•a** (-ee ə) **1.** an apparatus for exhibiting the features of the heavens, consisting of slide projectors or other optical equipment installed in a room having a circular dome. **2.** a room or building having such an apparatus. **3.** an apparatus or model representing the planetary system.

plan•gent (PLAN jənt) *adj.* **1.** dashing noisily; resounding; as the sound of bells. **2.** loud and mournful-sounding. [< L *plangere* lament, strike] —**plan′•gen•cy** *n.* —**plan′gent•ly** *adv.*

plank (plangk) *n.* **1.** a broad piece of sawn timber, thicker than a board. **2.** one of the principles of a political platform. —**walk the plank** walk off a plank projecting from the side of a ship, a method once used by pirates for executing prisoners. —*v.t.* **1.** cover, furnish, or lay with planks. **2.** broil or bake and serve on a plank, as fish. **3.** put down forcibly. [ME *planke*]

plank•ing (PLANG king) *n.* **1.** the act of laying planks. **2.** anything made of planks. **3.** planks collectively.

plank•ton (PLANGK tən) *n. Biol.* the marine animal and plant organisms that drift with currents, waves, etc., unable to influence their own course and ranging in size from microorganisms to jellyfish. [< G] —**plank•ton•ic** (plangk TON ik) *adj.*

plant (plant) *n.* **1.** a living organism of the vegetable kingdom, characterized by growth chiefly from the synthesis of simple, usu. inorganic food materials from soil, water, and air. **2.** one of the smaller forms of vegetable life, as distinct from shrubs and trees. **3.** a set of machines, buildings, apparatus, etc., necessary to conduct a business or other enterprise. **4.** a slip or cutting from a tree or bush; sapling. —*v.t.* **1.** set in the ground for growing. **2.** furnish with plants or seed. **3.** set or place firmly; put in position. **4.** introduce into the mind. **5.** stock, as a river. **6.** place or station for purposes of deception, observation, etc.: *plant* evidence. [ME *plaunte* a sprout]

plan•tar (PLAN tər) *adj.* pertaining to the sole of the foot. [< L *plantaris*]

plan•ta•tion (plan TAY shən) *n.* **1.** a farm or estate of many acres, planted with crops and worked by resident laborers. **2.** a grove cultivated for its wood. [ME *plantacioune*]

plant•er (PLAN tər) *n.* **1.** one who or that which plants. **2.** an early settler or colonizer. **3.** an owner of a plantation. **4.** a decorative container in which shrubs and flowers are planted. [ME *plaunter*]

plaque (plak) *n.* **1.** a plate, disk, or slab of metal, porcelain, ivory, etc., artistically ornamented, as for wall decoration. **2.** a whitish film, containing bacteria, that forms on teeth. [< F]

plas•ma (PLAZ mə) *n.* **1.** the liquid portion of nutritive animal fluids, as blood, lymph, or intercellular fluid. **2.** the clear, fluid portion of blood, freed from blood cells and used for transfusions. **3.** *Physics* a gas composed of ionized particles. Also **plasm** (PLAZ əm). [< LL] —**plas•mat•ic** (plaz MAT ik) *adj.*

plas•ter (PLAS tər) *n.* **1.** a composition of lime, sand, and water that hardens when dry, used for coating walls and partitions. **2.** a viscid substance spread on cloth and applied to some part of the body, used for healing. **3.** an adhesive dressing or protective bandage. —*v.t.* **1.** cover or overlay with or as with plaster. **2.** apply a plaster to, as a part of the body. **3.** apply like plaster or a plaster: *plaster* posters on a wall. [ME] — **plas′ter•er** n.

plas•tic (PLAS tik) *adj.* **1.** giving form or fashion to matter. **2.** capable of being molded; pliable. **3.** pertaining to modeling or molding. **4.** made of plastic. **5.** artificial; synthetic. —*n.* **1.** any substance or material that may be molded. **2.** *Chem.* one of a large class of synthetic organic compounds capable of being molded, extruded, cast, or drawn into filaments. [< L *plasticus* moldable]

plas•tic•i•ty (pla STIS i tee) *n.* **1.** the quality or state of being plastic. **2.** capacity for being shaped or molded.

plastic surgery the branch of surgery that deals with the restoration or healing of lost, wounded, or deformed parts of the body. — **plastic surgeon**

plat (plat) *n.* **1.** a plot of land. **2.** a map or plan, as one showing building lots. —*v.t.* **plat•ted, plat•ting** make a map or plan of. [ME]

plate (playt) *n.* **1.** a flat, extended, rigid body of metal or any material of slight thickness. **2.** a shallow vessel made of crockery, wood, etc., for serving or eating food. **3.** household articles, as trays, coated with a precious metal. **4.** a portion of food served at table. **5.** a piece of metal, plastic, etc. bearing a design or inscription or intended for reproduction. **6.** an impression from an engraving, woodcut, etc., as reproduced in a book. **7.** *Dent.* a piece of plastic or other material fitted to the mouth and holding one or more artificial teeth. **8.** a thin part of the brisket of beef. **9.** *Photog.* a sensitized sheet, as of glass, for taking photographs. **10.** in baseball, home plate. **11.** a dish used in taking up collections, as in churches; also, a collection. —*v.t.* **plat•ed, plat•ing 1.** coat with a thin layer of gold, silver, etc. **2.** cover or sheathe with metal plates for protection. [ME] —**plat′er** n.

pla•teau (pla TOH) *n. pl.* **•teaus** or **•teaux** (-TOHZ) **1.** an extensive stretch of elevated and comparatively level land; mesa. **2.** a stage or period of leveling off in the development of something. [< F]

plate•ful (PLAYT fuul) *n. pl.* **•fuls** the quantity that fills a plate.

plate glass glass in clear, thick sheets, suitable for mirrors, store windows, etc.

plat•en (PLAT n) *n. Mech.* **1.** the part of a printing press, typewriter, or the like, on which the paper is supported to receive the impression. **2.** in a machine tool, the adjustable table that carries the work. [ME *plateyne* chalice cover]

plate tectonics the theory that the earth's crust consists of a few huge plates and that their drifting and colliding determine land masses and earthquakes.

plat•form (PLAT form) *n.* **1.** any floor or flat surface raised above the adjacent level, as a stage or a walk upon which railroad passengers alight. **2.** a formal scheme of principles; esp., the document stating the principles of a political party. [< MF, lit., flat form]

plat•ing (PLAY ting) *n.* **1.** a layer or coating of metal. **2.** a sheathing of metal plates, as armor. **3.** the act or process of sheathing or coating something with plates or metal.

plat•i•num (PLAT n əm) *n.* **1.** a heavy, steel gray, malleable and ductile metallic element (symbol Pt) that is resistant to most acids and has a high electrical resistance. **2.** a color resembling that of platinum. [< NL]

platinum blonde 1. a very light, almost white blond. **2.** one having platinum blond hair.

plat•i•tude (PLAT i TOOD) *n.* a flat, dull, or commonplace statement; an obvious truism. [< F, lit., flatness] —**plat′i•tu′di•nous** *adj.*

pla•ton•ic (plə TON ik) *adj. Often cap.* purely spiritual, or devoid of sensual feeling. [after *Plato*, 4th c. B.C. Gk. philosopher]

pla•toon (plə TOON) *n.* **1.** a subdivision of a company, troop, or other military unit, commanded by a lieutenant. **2.** a company of people; esp., in football, a defensive or offensive unit. —*v.t.* in football, use as or in a platoon. [< F *peloton* small detachment]

platoon sergeant in the U.S. Army, a non-commissioned officer ranking below a first sergeant.

plat•ter (PLAT ər) *n.* **1.** a large shallow dish for serving meat, etc. **2.** *Slang* a phonograph record. [ME *plater*]

plat•y•pus (PLAT i pəs) *n.* a burrowing, egg-laying, aquatic mammal of Australia, having a ducklike bill: also called *duckbilled platypus.* [< NL]

plau•dit (PLAW dit) *n.* an expression of applause; praise. [< L *plaudere* applaud]

plau•si•ble (PLAW zə bəl) *adj.* seeming to be likely, trustworthy, believable, etc. [< L *plausibilis* deserving applause] — **plau′si•bil′i•ty** *n.* —**plau′si•bly** *adv.*

play (play) *v.i.* **1.** engage in sport or diversion; amuse oneself. **2.** take part in a game of skill or chance. **3.** act in a way that is not to be taken seriously. **4.** act or behave in a specified manner: *play* false. **5.** behave lightly or insincerely; with *with.* **6.** move quickly or irregularly as if frolicking: lights *playing* along a wall. **7.** perform on a musical instrument. **8.** give forth musical sounds. **9.** be performed or exhibited. **10.** act on or as on a stage; perform. —*v.t.* **11.** engage in (a game etc.). **12.** perform sportively: *play* a trick. **13.** oppose in a game or contest. **14.** move or employ in a game. **15.** cause: *play* havoc. **16.** perform upon (a musical instrument). **17.** perform or produce, as a piece of music, a play, etc. **18.** act the part of on or as on the stage. **19.** in angling, let (a hooked fish) tire itself by maintaining pressure on the line. **20.** bet or bet on. —**play at** pretend to be doing; do halfheartedly. —**play down** minimize. —**play into the hands of** act to the advantage of (a rival or opponent). —**play off 1.** oppose against one another. **2.** decide (a tie) by playing one more game. —**play on 1.** take unscrupulous advantage of (another's hopes, emotions, etc.). **2.** continue. —**play out 1.** come to an end; be exhausted. **2.** continue to the end. —**play the game** behave in a fair manner. —**play up** emphasize. —**play up to** *Informal* flatter. —*n.* **1.** a dramatic composition; drama. **2.** exercise or action for recreation or diversion. **3.** a maneuver or turn in a game. **4.** manner of playing, dealing, acting, etc.: rough *play.* **5.** in sports, a state of being actively and legitimately in use or motion: in *play.* **6.** the act of playing a game, esp. gambling. **7.** fun; joking. **8.** action or operation that is light, free, and unencumbered. **9.** light, quick, fitful movement. —**make a play for** *Informal* **1.** attempt to gain. **2.** attempt to seduce. [ME *pleye*] —**play′a•ble** *adj.*

play•back (PLAY BAK) *n.* **1.** the act of reproducing a sound recording. **2.** a method or machine for reproducing sound recordings.

play•bill (PLAY BIL) *n.* **1.** a bill or poster advertising a play. **2.** a program of a play.

play•boy (PLAY BOI) *n.* a wealthy, frivolous man who constantly seeks pleasure.

play-by-play (PLAY bī PLAY) *adj.* dealing with each play or event as it happens.

play•er (PLAY ər) *n.* **1.** one who takes part or specializes in a game. **2.** an actor. **3.** a performer on a musical instrument.

play•ful (PLAY fəl) *adj.* **1.** lightly humorous; joking. **2.** high-spirited; frolicsome. — **play′•ful•ly** *adv.* —**play′ful•ness** *n.*

play•go•er (PLAY GOH ər) *n.* one who goes often to the theater.

play•ground (PLAY GROWND) *n.* an outdoor area for playing, usu. used by children.

playing card one of a pack of cards used in playing various games, the pack usu. consisting of four suits (spades, hearts, diamonds, clubs) of 13 cards each.

play•mate (PLAY MAYT) *n.* a companion in sports or in play.

play•off (PLAY AWF) *n.* in sports, a decisive game or series of games to decide a championship.

play•pen (PLAY PEN) *n.* a small, usu. collapsible enclosure for a baby or small child.

play•thing (PLAY THING) *n.* a thing to play with; a toy.

play•wright (PLAY RĪT) *n.* a writer of plays.

pla•za (PLAH zə) *n.* an open square or marketplace in a town or city. [< Sp.]

plea (plee) *n.* **1.** an appeal or entreaty. **2.** an excuse, pretext, or justification. **3.** *Law* **a** an allegation made by either party in a cause. **b** a statement made by or for a defendant concerning the charge against him. [ME *ple*]

plead (pleed) *v.* **plead•ed** or **pled, plead•ing** *v.i.* **1.** make earnest entreaty; beg. **2.** *Law* present a case or plea. —*v.t.* **3.** allege as an excuse or defense. **4.** *Law.* argue (a case). [ME *plaiden*] —**plead′er** *n.*

plead•ing (PLEE ding) *n.* **1.** the act of making a plea. **2.** *Law* **a** the art or system of preparing pleas. **b** *Usu. pl.* any one of such pleas. —**plead′ing•ly** *adv.*

pleas•ant (PLEZ ənt) *adj.* **1.** pleasing; enjoyable. **2.** agreeable in manner, appearance, etc. [ME *plesaunt*]

pleas•an•try (PLEZ ən tree) *n. pl.* **•tries** an amusing or good-natured remark. [< F *plaisanterie*]

please (pleez) *v.* **pleased, pleas•ing** *v.t.* **1.** give pleasure to; be agreeable to. **2.** be the wish or will of. **3.** be so kind as to; be willing to: usu. in the imperative: *Please* pass the bread. —*v.i.* **4.** give satisfaction or pleasure. **5.** have the will or preference; wish: Go when you *please.* [ME *plesen*]

pleas•ing (PLEE zing) *adj.* affording pleasure. —**pleas′ing•ly** *adv.* —**pleas′ing•ness** *n.*

pleas·ur·a·ble (PLEZH ər ə bəl) *adj.* gratifying; pleasant. **—pleas′ur·a·bly** *adv.*

pleas·ure (PLEZH ər) *n.* **1.** an agreeable or delightful sensation or emotion; enjoyment. **2.** something that gives such a feeling. **3.** amusement or diversion. **4.** one's preference; choice. [ME]

pleat (pleet) *n.* a fold of cloth doubled on itself and pressed or sewn in place. *—v.t.* make a pleat in. Also *plait.* [ME]

plebe (pleeb) *n.* a member of the first year class in a military or naval academy. [Short for PLEBEIAN]

ple·be·ian (pli BEE ən) *adj.* **1.** of or pertaining to the common people. **2.** common or vulgar. *—n.* **1.** one of the common people, esp. of ancient Rome. **2.** anyone who is coarse or vulgar. [< L *plebeius* of the common people, *plebes*]

pleb·i·scite (PLEB ə SIT) *n.* an expression of the popular will by means of a vote by the whole people. [< F]

plec·trum (PLEK trəm) *n. pl.* **·trums** or **·tra** (-trə) a pick for a musical instrument. [< L]

pled (pled) alternative past tense and past participle of PLEAD.

pledge (plej) *v.t.* **pledged, pledg·ing 1.** give or deposit as security for a loan etc. **2.** bind by or as by a pledge. **3.** promise solemnly. **4.** offer (one's word, life, etc.) as a guaranty or forfeit. **5.** drink a toast to. *—n.* **1.** a promise or agreement to perform or fulfill some act, contract, or duty. **2.** the drinking of a toast to one's health etc. **3.** a person or thing given as security for a debt or obligation. **4.** the state of being given or held as security: put property in *pledge.* [ME *plege*]

pledg·ee (plej EE) *n.* **1.** one to whom something is pledged. **2.** one with whom a pledge is deposited.

pledg·or (PLEJ ər) *n. Law* one who gives a pledge.

ple·na·ry (PLEE nə ree) *adj.* **1.** full in all respects or requisites; complete. **2.** fully or completely attended, as an assembly. [< LL *plenarius*]

plen·i·po·ten·ti·ar·y (PLEN ə pə TEN shee ER ee) *adj.* possessing or conferring full powers. *—n. pl.* **·ar·ies** a person fully empowered to represent a government. [< Med.L *plenipotentiarius* fully empowered]

plen·i·tude (PLEN i TOOD) *n.* the state of being full, complete, or abounding.

plen·te·ous (PLEN tee əs) *adj.* **1.** amply sufficient. **2.** yielding an abundance. **—plen′te·ous·ly** *adv.* **—plen′te·ous·ness** *n.*

plen·ti·ful (PLEN ti fəl) *adj.* **1.** existing in great quantity; abundant. **2.** yielding or containing plenty; affording ample supply. **—plen′ti·ful·ly** *adv.*

plen·ty (PLEN tee) *n.* **1.** the state of being sufficient and in abundance. **2.** as much as can be required; an abundance or sufficiency: I have *plenty.* *—adj.* existing in abundance; plentiful. *—adv. Informal* in a sufficient degree: *plenty* large enough. [ME *plente*]

ple·num (PLE nəm) *n. pl.* **·nums** or **·na** (-nə) **1.** space fully occupied by matter: opposed to *vacuum.* **2.** a meeting attended by all members, as of a legislature. [< L, full]

ple·o·nasm (PLEE ə NAZ əm) *n.* **1.** the use of needless words; redundancy; also, an instance of it. **2.** a redundant word or phrase. **3.** superabundance. [< LL *pleonasmus* surplus] **—ple′o·nas′tic** *adj.*

pleth·o·ra (PLETH ər ə) *n.* a state of excessive fullness; superfluity. [< LL] **—ple·thor·ic** (plə THOR ik) *adj.*

Plex·i·glas (PLEK si GLAS) *n.* a lightweight, transparent thermoplastic acrylic resin: a trade name.

plex·us (PLEK səs) *n. pl.* **plex·us·es** or **plex·us 1.** a network or complicated interlacing of parts. **2.** *Anat.* a network of cordlike structures, as blood vessels or nerves. [< NL]

pli·a·ble (PLĪ ə bəl) *adj.* **1.** easily bent or twisted; flexible. **2.** easily persuaded or controlled; tractable. [ME] **—pli′a·bil′i·ty** *n.*

pli·ant (PLĪ ənt) *adj.* **1.** capable of being bent or twisted with ease. **2.** easily yielding to influence; compliant. [ME] **—pli′an·cy** *n.*

pli·er (PLĪ ər) *n.* **1.** *pl.* small pincers for bending, holding, or cutting. **2.** one who or that which plies.

plight[1] (plīt) *n.* a condition, state, or circumstance, usu. of a dangerous or complicated nature. [ME *plit* condition]

plight[2] *v.t.* pledge or promise. **—plight one's troth 1.** pledge one's solemn word. **2.** promise oneself in marriage. [ME]

plod (plod) *v.* **plod·ded, plod·ding** *v.i.* **1.** walk heavily or laboriously. **2.** work in a steady, laborious manner. *—v.t.* **3.** walk heavily over or along. *—n.* **1.** the act of plodding. **2.** the sound of a heavy step. **—plod′der** *n.* **—plod′ding·ly** *adv.*

plop (plop) *v.t. & v.i.* **plopped, plop·ping** drop with a sound like that of something striking water heavily. —*adv.* suddenly with a plopping sound. —**plop** *n.*

plo·sion (PLOH *zh*ən) *n. Phonet.* the sudden release of breath after closure of the oral passage in the articulation of a stop consonant, as after the *p* in *pat.* [< EXPLOSION]

plo·sive (PLOH siv) *adj. Phonet.* designating a sound produced by plosion. —*n.* [< EXPLOSIVE]

plot (plot) *n.* **1.** a piece or patch of ground, usu. used for some special purpose. **2.** a chart or diagram, as of a building; also, a surveyor's map. **3.** a secret plan; conspiracy. **4.** the scheme or pattern of the events and situations of a story, play, etc. —*v.* **plot·ted, plot·ting** *v.t.* **1.** make a map, chart, or plan of. **2.** plan for secretly. **3.** arrange the plot of (a novel, movie, etc.). **4.** *Math.* represent graphically the position of. —*v.i.* **5.** form a plot; scheme. [ME] —**plot'ter** *n.*

plow (plow) *n.* **1.** a farm implement for cutting, turning over, or breaking up the soil. **2.** any implement that operates like a plow: often in combination: a *snowplow.* —*v.t.* **1.** turn up the surface of (land) with a plow. **2.** make or form (a furrow, one's way, etc.) by or as by means of a plow. **3.** dig out or remove with a plow: with *up* or *out.* **4.** move or cut through (water). —*v.i.* **5.** turn up soil with a plow **6.** move or proceed as a plow does: usu. with *through* or *into.* **7.** advance laboriously; plod. —**plow into 1.** hit hard. **2.** undertake vigorously to accomplish, finish, or solve (a meal, problem, etc.). Also **plough.** [ME *plouh*] —**plow'er** *n.*

plow·man (PLOW mən) *n. pl.* **·men 1.** one who plows land. **2.** a farm laborer; rustic.

plow·share (PLOW SHAIR) *n.* the blade of a plow.

ploy (ploi) *n.* a maneuver or stratagem, as in a game or conversation. [< MF *ployer* fold]

pluck (pluk) *v.t.* **1.** pull out or off; pick. **2.** pull out the feathers, hair, etc. of. **3.** give a twitch or pull to, as a sleeve. **4.** cause the strings of (a musical instrument) to sound by quickly pulling or picking them. —*v.i.* **5.** give a sudden pull; tug: with *at.* —**pluck up** rouse (one's courage). —*n.* **1.** courage; nerve. **2.** a sudden pull; twitch. —**pluck'er** *n.* [ME *plukken*]

pluck·y (PLUK ee) *adj.* **pluck·i·er, pluck·i·est** brave and spirited; coura-

geous. —**pluck'i·ly** *adv.* —**pluck'i·ness** *n.*

plug (plug) *n.* **1.** anything, as a piece of wood or a cork, used to stop a hole. **2.** *Electr.* a pronged device attached to the end of a wire or cable and inserted in a socket or jack to make a connection. **3.** a spark plug. **4.** a fireplug. **5.** a flat cake or piece of tobacco. **6.** *Slang* an old, worn-out horse. **7.** *Informal* a favorable piece of publicity for someone or something. —*v.* **plugged, plug·ging** *v.t.* **1.** stop or close, as a hole, by inserting a plug: often with *up.* **2.** *Slang* shoot a bullet into. **3.** *Slang* hit or punch. **4.** *Informal* advertise frequently or insistently. —*v.i.* **5.** work doggedly. **6.** *Slang* hit or shoot. **7.** *Informal* favor or work for a cause, person, etc.: usu. with *for.* —**plug in** insert the plug of (a lamp, etc.) in an electrical outlet. [< MDu. *plugge*]

plum (plum) *n.* **1.** the edible fruit of any of various trees of the rose family; also the tree itself. **2.** the plumlike fruit of any of various other trees; also, a tree bearing such fruit. **3.** a raisin, esp. as used in cooking. **4.** a dark, reddish purple. **5.** something desirable, as a post or appointment. [ME]

plum·age (PLOO mij) *n.* the feathers of a bird. [ME]

plumb (plum) *n.* a lead weight (**plumb bob**) on the end of a line (**plumb line**) used to find the exact perpendicular, to sound the depth of water, etc. —**off** (or **out of**) **plumb** not in alignment. —*adj.* **1.** conforming to a true vertical or perpendicular. **2.** *Informal* sheer; absolute. —*adv.* **1.** in a vertical line; vertically **2.** *Informal* utterly; completely. —*v.t.* **1.** test the perpendicularity of with a plumb. **2.** test the depth of; sound. **3.** reach the lowest level or extent of. [ME *plumbe*]

plumb·er (PLUM ər) *n.* one whose occupation is the installing or repairing of plumbing.

plumb·ing (PLUM ing) *n.* **1.** the art or trade of putting into buildings the tanks, pipes, etc. for water, gas, sewage, etc. **2.** the pipe system of a building.

plume (ploom) *n.* **1.** a feather, esp. when long and ornamental. **2.** *Biol.* a featherlike form or part. **3.** anything resembling a plume. **4.** a decoration of honor. —*v.t.* **plumed, plum·ing 1.** furnish with or as with plumes. **2.** smooth (itself or its feathers); preen. **3.** congratulate or pride (oneself): with *on* or *upon.* [ME]

plum•met (PLUM it) n. **1.** a plumb bob. **2.** something that oppresses or weighs down. —v.i. drop straight down; plunge. [ME *plommet*]

plump¹ (plump) adj. **•er, •est 1.** somewhat fat; chubby. **2.** well filled or rounded out. —v.t. & v.i. make or become plump: often with *up* or *out*. [ME] —**plump′ness** n.

plump² v.i. **1.** fall suddenly or heavily; drop. **2.** give one's complete support: with *for*. —v.t. **3.** drop or throw down heavily or all at once. —n. **1.** the act of plumping or falling. **2.** the sound made by this. —adj. blunt; downright. —adv. **1.** with a sudden impact or fall. **2.** straightforwardly; bluntly. **3.** straight down. [ME *plumpen*]

plum•y (PLOO mee) adj. **plum•i•er, plum•i•est 1.** made of, covered with, or adorned with feathers. **2.** like a plume or feather.

plun•der (PLUN dər) v.t. **1.** rob of goods or property by open violence, as in war; pillage. **2.** despoil by robbery or fraud. —v.i. **3.** take plunder. —n. **1.** that which is taken by plundering; booty. **2.** the act of plundering or robbing. [< Du. *plunderen*] —**plun′der•er** n.

plunge (plunj) v. **plunged, plung•ing** v.t. **1.** thrust or force suddenly into a fluid, penetrable substance, hole, etc. **2.** force into some condition or state: *plunge* a nation into debt. —v.i. **3.** dive, jump, or fall into a body of water, chasm, etc. **4.** move suddenly or violently forward or downward. **5.** descend abruptly or steeply, as a road or cliff. **6.** gamble or speculate heavily. —n. **1.** the act of plunging; a leap; dive. **2.** a swim. **3.** a heavy or extravagant bet, expenditure, or speculation. [ME]

plung•er (PLUN jər) n. **1.** one who or that which plunges. **2.** a cuplike device made of rubber and attached to a stick, used to clean out clogged drains etc.: also called **plumber's friend. 3.** *Mech.* any appliance having a plunging motion, as a piston.

plunk (plungk) v.t. **1.** pluck; strum. **2.** place or throw heavily: with *down*. —v.i. **3.** emit a twanging sound. **4.** fall heavily. —n. a twang or thump. —adv. *Informal* directly; exactly.

plu•per•fect (ploo PUR fikt) n. *Gram.* the past perfect. [< LL *plusquamperfectus*, lit., more than perfect]

plu•ral (PLUUR əl) adj. **1.** containing, consisting of, or designating more than one. **2.** *Gram.* of or designating a linguistic form

that denotes more than one. [ME] —**plu′ral** n. —**plu′ral•ly** adv.

plu•ral•ism (PLUUR ə LIZ əm) n. **1.** the condition of being plural. **2.** a social condition in which disparate religious, ethnic, and racial groups are part of a common community. **3.** *Philos.* the doctrine that there are several ultimate substances. —**plu′ral•ist** n. —**plu′ral•is′tic** adj.

plu•ral•i•ty (pluu RAL i tee) n. pl. **•ties 1.** in U.S. politics: **a** the number of votes cast for a candidate over and above the number cast for the nearest opponent. **b** in a contest having more than two candidates, the greatest number of votes cast for any one candidate but not more than half the total number of votes cast (distinguished from *majority*). **2.** the larger or greater portion of anything. **3.** the state or condition of being plural or numerous. [ME *pluralite*]

plu•ral•ize (PLUUR ə LIZ) v.t. **•ized, •iz•ing 1.** make plural. **2.** express in the plural. —**plu′ral•i•za′tion** n.

plus (plus) prep. **1.** added to: three *plus* two. **2.** increased by. —adj. **1.** of, pertaining to, or involving addition. **2.** extra; supplemental. **3.** positive: a *plus* quantity. **4.** more of something specified: She has personality *plus*. —n. pl. **plus•es, plus•ses 1.** the plus sign. **2.** an addition or an extra quantity. **3.** a positive quantity. [< L, more]

plush (plush) n. a pile fabric having a deeper pile than velvet. —adj. **•er, •est 1.** of plush. **2.** luxurious. [< MF *peluche*]

plush•y (PLUSH ee) adj. **plush•i•er, plush•i•est 1.** of or resembling plush. **2.** *Informal* luxurious. —**plush′i•ness** n.

plus sign a sign (+) denoting addition or a positive quantity.

plu•toc•ra•cy (ploo TOK rə see) n. pl. **•cies 1.** government by the wealthy. **2.** a wealthy class that controls the government. [< Gk. *ploutokratía*]

plu•to•crat (PLOO tə KRAT) n. **1.** a member of a plutocracy. **2.** *Informal* any wealthy person. —**plu′to•crat′ic** adj.

plu•to•ni•um (ploo TOH nee əm) n. a radioactive element (symbol Pu), formed by the decay of neptunium. [< NL]

plu•vi•al (PLOO vee əl) adj. **1.** of or pertaining to rain. **2.** caused by the action of rain. [< L *pluvialis* rainy]

ply¹ (pli) n. pl. **plies 1.** a layer, fold, or thickness, as of cloth, plywood, etc. **2.** one of the folds, twists, or strands of which rope, yarn, etc. is composed. [ME *plien* fold]

ply² *v.* **plied, ply•ing** *v.t.* **1.** use in working, fighting, etc.; wield; employ. **2.** work at; be engaged in. **3.** supply with or offer repeatedly: *ply* a person with drink. **4.** address or assail repeatedly. **5.** traverse regularly. —*v.i.* **6.** make regular trips; sail: usu. with *between.* **7.** work steadily. [ME *plien* apply]

ply•wood (PLĪ WUUD) *n.* a structural material consisting of layers of wood glued together.

pneu•mat•ic (nuu MAT ik) *adj.* **1.** pertaining to pneumatics. **2.** operated by compressed air. **3.** pertaining to or containing air or gas. [< L *pneumaticus* pertaining to wind] —*n.* a tire inflated with compressed air. —**pneu•mat'i•cal•ly** *adv.*

pneu•mat•ics (nuu MAT iks) *n.* (*construed as sing.*) the branch of physics that treats of the mechanical properties of air and other gases.

pneu•mo•coc•cus (NOO mə KOK əs) *n. pl.* **•coc•ci** (-KOK sī) any of a group of bacteria that inhabit the respiratory tract. —**pneu'•mo•coc'cal** (-KOK əl), **pneu'mo•coc'cic** (-KOK sik) *adj.*

pneu•mo•co•ni•o•sis (NOO mə KOH nee OH sis) *n.* a disease of the lungs caused by inhalation of irritants such as asbestos, also called *black lung.*

pneu•mo•nia (nuu MOHN yə) *n. Pathol.* inflammation of the lungs, a disease of bacterial or viral origin occurring in many forms, as **bronchial pneumonia** or **lobar pneumonia.** [< NL]

poach¹ (pohch) *v.t.* cook (eggs, fish, etc.) in boiling water or other liquid. [ME *pochen*]

poach² *v.t. & v.i.* **1.** trespass (on another's property etc.), esp. for the purpose of taking game or fish. **2.** take (game or fish) unlawfully. [< MF *pocher* gouge] —**poach'er** *n.*

pock (pok) *n.* **1.** a pustule in an eruptive disease, as in smallpox. **2.** a pockmark. [ME *pokke*]

pock•et (POK it) *n.* **1.** a small pouch inserted in a garment, for carrying money etc. **2.** any opening, receptacle, or container. **3.** money, means, or financial interests. **4.** an air pocket. **5.** a region or area, usu. small and differentiated in some way from the surrounding area. —**in one's pocket** under one's influence or control. —*adj.* **1.** that can be put in a pocket; diminutive. **2.** pertaining to, for, or carried in a pocket. —*v.t.* **1.** put into or confine in a pocket. **2.** appropriate as one's own, esp. dishonestly. **3.** con-

ceal or suppress: *Pocket* your pride. [ME *poket*] —**pock'et•a•ble** *adj.*

pock•et•book (POK it BUUK) *n.* **1.** a purse or handbag. **2.** a book, usu. paperbound and smaller than standard size: also **pocket book.** **3.** money or financial resources.

pock•et•ful (POK it FUUL) *n. pl.* **•fuls** as much as a pocket will hold.

pock•et•knife (POK it NIF) *n. pl.* **•knives** a knife having one or more blades that fold into the handle.

pocket money money for small expenses.

pocket veto in the U.S., an act whereby the President, on being presented a bill by Congress for signature of approval, retains it unsigned until the session has adjourned, thus causing it to fail without a direct veto.

pock•mark (POK MAHRK) *n.* a pit or scar left on the skin by smallpox or a similar disease. —**pock'-marked'** *adj.*

pod¹ (pod) *n.* **1.** a seed vessel or capsule, esp. of a leguminous plant. **2.** *Aeron.* a separate enclosure on an aircraft, esp. one beneath the wing for a jet engine. —*v.i.* **pod•ded, pod•ding** produce pods.

pod² *n.* a group of animals, esp. of seals, whales, or walruses.

po•di•a•try (pə DĪ ə tree) *n.* chiropody. —**po•di'a•trist** *n.*

po•di•um (POH dee əm) *n. pl.* **•di•ums** or **•di•a** (-dee ə) **1.** a small platform or dais for the conductor of an orchestra, a speaker, etc. **2.** *Zool.* a foot, or any footlike structure. [< L, raised place]

po•em (POH əm) *n.* a composition in verse, characterized by the imaginative treatment of experience and a condensed use of language. [< MF *poeme*]

po•e•sy (POH ə zee) *n. pl.* **•sies 1.** *Archaic* poetry taken collectively. **2.** the art of writing poetry. [ME *poesie*]

po•et (POH it) *n.* **1.** one who writes poems. **2.** one who is highly skilled and creative. [ME *poete*] —**po'et•ess** (POH i tis) *n.fem.*

po•et•as•ter (POH it AS tər) *n.* an inferior poet. [< NL]

po•et•ic (poh ET ik) *adj.* **1.** of or pertaining to a poet or poetry. **2.** having the nature or quality of or expressed in poetry. Also **po•et'i•cal.**

poetic justice the ideal distribution of rewards to the good and punishment to the evil.

poetic license the departure from fact or rigid rule for the sake of an artistic effect.

poet laureate *pl.* **poets laureate 1.** in

Great Britain, the official poet of the realm, charged with writing verses for particular occasions. 2. someone honored for achievement in the art of poetry.

po·et·ry (POH i tree) *n.* 1. the art or craft of writing poems. 2. poems collectively. 3. the quality, effect, or spirit of a poem. [ME *poetrie*]

po·go stick (POH goh) a toy consisting of a pole with a spring at the base and two projections for the feet, on which a person may stand and hop.

po·grom (pǝ GRUM) *n.* an organized and often officially instigated local massacre, esp. one directed against the Jews. [< Yiddish < Russ. *pogróm*, lit., destruction]

poi (poi) *n.* a native Hawaiian food made from the root of the taro. [< Hawaiian]

poign·ant (POIN yǝnt) *adj.* 1. painful and afflicting to the feelings; profoundly moving. 2. sharp; penetrating: *poignant wit.* [ME *poinaunt* pricking] —**poign'an·cy** *n.* —**poign'ant·ly** *adv.*

poin·set·ti·a (poin SET ee ǝ) *n.* any of various American plants having large, showy red bracts. [after J.R. *Poinsett*, U.S. statesman, discoverer of the plant in 1828]

point (point) *n.* 1. the sharp, tapering end of a thing. 2. something sharp or tapering, as a needle or dagger. 3. in printing or writing, a dot or similar mark, esp. a period. 4. that which is conceived to have position, but not parts, dimension, or extent. 5. a spot, place, or locality. 6. a tapering tract of land extending into water. 7. a fixed place from which position and distance are reckoned. 8. a particular degree, state, or limit reached or determined: the boiling *point.* 9. one of the 32 equal divisions that indicate direction on a mariner's compass card. 10. a particular moment of time. 11. the important or main idea or purpose. 12. an important, striking, or effective fact, idea, etc.: good *points* in an argument. 13. any single item or particular; detail. 14. a prominent or distinguishing feature. 15. *pl.* the extremities of an animal, as a horse. 16. a spike or prong on the antler of a deer. 17. a unit, as in measuring, evaluating, rating, scoring, etc.: A touchdown equals six *points.* 18. *Printing* a unit of type size, about 1/72 of an inch. 19. in commerce, one dollar: used in quoting prices of bonds etc. 20. *Electr.* a contact or conducting part for making or breaking a circuit, as in a distributor, relay, etc. 21. the act of pointing. —**at** (or **on, upon**) **the point of** on the

verge of. —**beside the point** irrelevant. —**in point** pertinent: a case *in point.* —**in point of** in the matter of; as regards. —**make a point of** treat as vital or essential. —**see the point** understand the purpose or meaning of something. —**stretch a point** interpret a rule, definition, etc. broadly, so as to make an exception. —**to the point** relevant; apt. —*v.t.* 1. direct or aim, as a finger or weapon. 2. indicate; direct attention to: often with *out.* 3. give force to; emphasize: often with *up.* 4. shape or sharpen to a point. 5. punctuate, as writing. 6. mark or separate with points, as decimal fractions: with *off.* 7. in hunting, indicate the presence of (game) by standing rigid and directing the muzzle toward it: said of dogs. 8. in masonry, fill and finish the joints of (brickwork) with mortar. —*v.i.* 9. call attention or indicate direction by or as by extending the finger: usually with *at* or *to.* 10. be directed; tend; face: with *to* or *toward.* 11. point game: said of hunting dogs. [ME]

point-blank (POINT BLANGK) *adj.* 1. aimed directly at the mark; in gunnery, fired horizontally. 2. close enough to aim directly at the mark: *point-blank* range. 3. direct; plain: a *point-blank* question. —*adv.* 1. in a straight line; from close range. 2. directly; bluntly.

point·ed (POIN tid) *adj.* 1. having a point. 2. sharply precise and cutting, as an epigram. 3. directed or aimed, as at a particular person. —**point'ed·ly** *adv.* —**point' ed·ness** *n.*

point·er (POIN tǝr) *n.* 1. one who or that which points. 2. an arrow or other indicator, as on a scale. 3. a long, tapering rod used to point out things. 4. one of a breed of smooth-haired dogs trained to scent and point out game. 5. a piece of advice.

poin·til·lism (PWAN tl iz ǝm) *n.* in painting, a method of producing effects of light by placing small spots of varying hues close together on a surface. [< F *pointillisme*]

point·less (POINT lis) *adj.* 1. having no point; blunt. 2. having no relevance or meaning. 3. having no points scored.

point of honor something that vitally affects one's honor.

point of no return 1. that stage in any enterprise, action, etc., beyond which there can be no return to the starting point. 2. the point in the flight of an aircraft over an ocean, for example, at which the remaining fuel is insufficent for a return to the starting point, so the aircraft must proceed.

point of order a question as to whether correct parliamentary procedure is being observed.

point of view 1. the place or position from which one views an object, situation, etc. **2.** an attitude or viewpoint.

poise (poiz) v. **poised, pois·ing** v.t. **1.** bring into or hold in balance; maintain in equilibrium. **2.** hold; support, as in readiness. — v.i. **3.** be balanced or suspended; hover. — n. **1.** the state or quality of being balanced; equilibrium. **2.** repose and dignity of manner; self-possession. **3.** physical ease or balance. [ME *poyse* weight]

poi·son (POI zən) n. **1.** any substance that acts chemically upon the tissues of an organism in such a way as to harm or destroy them. **2.** anything that tends to harm, destroy, or corrupt. —v.t. **1.** administer poison to; kill or injure with poison. **2.** put poison into or on. **3.** corrupt; pervert. [ME] —**poi'son·er** n. —**poi'son·ous** adj.

poison ivy a climbing shrub related to sumac, having glossy, variously notched leaves and that may cause a skin rash in one who touches its leaves.

poison oak 1. any of various shrubs related to poison ivy or poison sumac. **2.** a species of poison ivy common in the western U.S.

poison sumac a shrub or small tree growing in swamps, having smooth leaflets and that may cause a skin rash in one who touches its leaves.

poke[1] (pohk) v. **poked, pok·ing** v.t. **1.** push or prod, as with the end of a stick; jab. **2.** make by or as by thrusting. **3.** thrust or push in, out, through, from, etc.: *poke* one's head from a window. —v.i. **4.** make thrusts, as with a stick: often with *at*. **5.** intrude or meddle; pry. **6.** proceed slowly; dawdle: often with *along*. —**poke one's nose into** meddle in. —**poke fun at** ridicule. —n. **1.** a push; prod. **2.** a slowpoke; dawdler. **3.** a jab or punch. [ME *poken*]

poke[2] n. a pocket or small bag. [ME]

pok·er[1] (POH kər) n. **1.** one who or that which pokes. **2.** a metal rod for poking a fire.

pok·er[2] n. any of several games of cards in which the players bet on the value of the cards dealt to them. [< MLG *poken* play]

poker face a face that reveals nothing, as the face of a skillful poker player.

pok·y (POH kee) adj. **pok·i·er, pok·i·est**

Informal **1.** dull; slow. **2.** shabby or dowdy. **3.** cramped; stuffy. Also **pok·e'y pok·i·er, pok·i·est**.

po·lar (POH lər) adj. **1.** of the poles of a sphere, magnet, etc. **2.** of, from, or near the North or South Pole. **3.** directly opposite in character, etc. [< Med.L *polaris*]

polar bear a large, white bear of arctic regions.

po·lar·i·ty (pə LAR i tee) n. pl. **·ties 1.** the quality or condition of having poles. **2.** *Physics* the possession by a body of opposite magnetic poles. **3.** the quality or condition of being attracted to one pole and repelled from the other. **4.** the possession of two contrary qualities, tendencies, etc.

po·lar·i·za·tion (POH lər ə ZAY shən) n. **1.** the act of polarizing, or the state of being polarized. **2.** *Physics* a condition of electromagnetic waves, most noticeable in light, in which one component of its oscillation is limited to a certain plane.

po·lar·ize (POH lə RĪZ) v. **·ized, ·iz·ing** v.t. **1.** develop polarization in. —v.i. **2.** acquire polarity. **3.** separate into or concentrate around two opposing viewpoints, groups, etc. —**po'lar·iz'a·ble** adj. —**po'lar·iz'er** n.

pole[1] (pohl) n. **1.** either of the two extremities of the axis of a sphere or any spheroidal body. **2.** one of the two points where the earth's axis of rotation meets the surface, called the North Pole and the South Pole. **3.** *Physics* one of the two points at which opposite qualities or forces are concentrated, as in a magnet. **4.** either of two diametrically opposite forces, tendencies, etc. —**be poles apart** differ greatly. [ME]

pole[2] n. **1.** a long, comparatively slender piece of wood or metal. **2.** a unit of linear measure, usu. equal to 16.5 feet. —v.t. & v.i. **poled, pol·ing** propel or push (a boat, raft, etc.) with a pole. [ME]

pole·cat (POHL KAT) n. **1.** a European mammal, allied to the weasel, noted for its offensive odor. **2.** a skunk. [ME *polcat*]

po·lem·ic (pə LEM ik) adj. of or pertaining to controversy; disputation. Also **po·lem'i·cal**. —n. **1.** an argument or controversy. **2.** one who engages in argument or controversy. [< Gk. *polemikós* of war]

po·lem·ics (pə LEM iks) n. *(construed as sing.)* the art or practice of disputation. —**po·lem'i·cist** (ə sist), **po·lem'ist** n.

pole vault an athletic event in which a vault or leap over a high, horizontal bar is made

with the help of a long pole. —pole-vault
(POHL VAWLT) v.i. —pole′-vault′er n.

po•lice (pə LEES) n. 1. an official civil force
organized to maintain order, prevent and
detect crime, and enforce law. 2. (construed as pl.) the members of such a force.
3. in the U.S. Army: a the cleaning of a
camp or garrison. b a group of soldiers assigned to some specific duty: kitchen police.
—v.t. •liced, •lic•ing 1. protect, regulate,
etc. with or as with police. 2. make clean or
orderly. [< MF, government]

police officer n. a member of a police force:
also po•lice•man & po•lice′wom′an.

police state a country whose citizens are
rigidly supervised by a secret police force.

pol•i•cy¹ (POL ə see) n. pl. •cies 1. any plan
of action, esp. in governmental or business
administration. 2. prudence, wisdom, or
shrewdness, as in the management of one's
affairs. [ME policie government]

pol•i•cy² n. pl. •cies 1. a written contract of
insurance. 2. the numbers (see under NUM-
BER). [< MF police certificate]

policy game the numbers (see under NUM-
BER).

po•li•o (POH lee OH) n. poliomyelitis.

po•li•o•my•e•li•tis (POH lee oh MI ə LĪ tis)
n. Pathol. an acute virus disease, occurring
esp. in children, and characterized by inflammation of the gray matter of the spinal
cord, followed by paralysis: also called infantile paralysis. [< NL, lit., inflammation
of gray matter]

pol•ish (POL ish) n. 1. smoothness or glossi-
ness of surface. 2. a substance used to produce a smooth or glossy surface. 3.
refinement or elegance. 4. the act of polishing. —v.t. 1. make smooth or lustrous, as by
rubbing. 2. perfect or refine. —v.i. 3. take a
gloss. —polish off 1. do or finish completely. 2. dispose of. —polish up improve. [ME polishen] —pol′•ished adj. —
pol′ish•er n.

Po•lish (POH lish) adj. of or pertaining to
Poland, its inhabitants, or their language.
—n. the West Slavic language of the Poles.

po•lite (pə LĪT) adj. •lit•er, •lit•est 1. courteous; mannerly. 2. refined; cultured. [ME]
—po•lite′ly adv. —po•lite′ness n.

pol•i•tic (POL i tik) adj. 1. skillful, ingenious, or shrewd. 2. wise, prudent, or expedient. [ME politik civic]

po•lit•i•cal (pə LIT i kəl) adj. 1. of or concerned with government. 2. of, relating to,
or involved in politics. 3. having an orga-

nized system of government. [< L politicus
civic] —po•lit′i•cal•ly adv.

political science the study of the form, principles, and conduct of civil government. —
political scientist.

pol•i•ti•cian (POL i TISH ən) n. one who is
engaged in politics, esp. professionally.

pol•i•tics (POL i tiks) n. (construed as sing.
or pl.) 1. the art of government. 2. the activities or policies of those controlling or seeking to control a government; also, the
profession or area of activity of such persons. 3. the acts or practices of those who
seek any position of power or advantage.

pol•i•ty (POL i tee) n. pl. •ties 1. the form or
method of government of a nation, state,
church, etc. 2. any community living under
some definite form of government. [< L
politia citizenship]

pol•ka (POHL kə) n. 1. a lively dance consisting of three quick steps and a hop. 2. music
for this dance. —v.i. 1. dance the polka. 2.
dance the polka. [< Czech, lit., a Polish woman]

pol•ka dot (POH kə) 1. one of a series of
round dots decorating a textile fabric. 2.
a pattern or fabric made up of such
dots.

poll (pohl) n. 1. the voting at an election. 2.
the total number of votes cast. 3. pl. the
place where votes are cast and counted. 4. a
survey of public opinion on a given subject.
5. a list of persons. 6. the head; esp., the top
or back of the head where hair grows. —v.t.
1. receive (a specified number of votes). 2.
enroll, as for voting; register. 3. cast (a vote).
4. canvass in a poll. 5. cut off or trim, as hair,
horns, etc. 6. cut off or trim the hair, horns,
top, etc., of: poll cattle. [ME polle head, hair
of the head] —poll′er n.

pol•len (POL ən) n. the male or fertilizing
element in a seed plant, consisting of fine
yellowish powder. [< NL]

pollen count a measure of the relative concentration of pollen grains in the atmosphere.

pol•li•nate (POL ə NAYT) v.t. •nat•ed,
•nat•ing Bot. supply or convey pollen to.
—pol′li•na′tion n.

pol•li•wog (POL ee WOG) n. a tadpole. Also
pol′ly•wog. [ME polwygle]

poll•ster (POHL stər) n. one who takes
polls.

poll tax a tax on a person, esp. as a prerequisite for voting.

pol•lute (pə LOOT) v.t. •lut•ed, •lut•ing
make unclean or impure; contaminate.

[ME *polluten*] —**pol•lut′er** *n.* —**pol•lu′tion** *n.*

Pol•ly•an•na (POL ee AN ə) *n.* one who persistently finds good in everything. [after a character in stories by Eleanor H. Porter, 1868–1920, American writer]

po•lo (POH loh) *n.* **1.** a game played on horseback with a ball and mallets. **2.** a similar game played in water: **water polo**. [< Tibetan]

pol•o•naise (POL ə NAYZ) *n.* **1.** a stately, marchlike Polish dance. **2.** music for this dance. [< F *(danse) polonaise* Polish (dance)]

pol•ter•geist (POHL tər GIST) *n.* a rambunctious ghost. [< G, lit., noisy ghost]

pol•troon (pol TROON) *n.* a mean-spirited coward; dastard. [< Ital. *poltrone* idler]

poly- *combining form* **1.** many; several; much: *polygamy*. **2.** excessive; abnormal. [< Gk. *polys* much, many]

pol•y•an•dry (POL ee AN dree) *n.* the condition or practice of having more than one husband at the same time. [< Gk. *polyandría*] —**pol′y•an′drous** (-drəs) *adj.*

pol•y•clin•ic (POL ee KLIN ik) *n.* a hospital or clinic in which all forms of diseases are treated.

pol•y•es•ter (POL ee ES tər) *n.* a polymer used in making fibers and plastics.

pol•y•eth•y•lene (POL ee ETH ə LEEN) *n.* a plastic resin used in making moisture-proof plastics for packaging.

po•lyg•a•my (pə LIG ə mee) *n.* **1.** the condition or practice of having more than one spouse at the same time. **2.** *Zool.* the state of having more than one mate at the same time. [< Gk. *polygamía*] —**po•lyg′a•mist** *n.* —**po•lyg′a•mous** *adj.*

pol•y•glot (POL ee GLOT) *adj.* expressed in or speaking several languages; multilingual. —*n.* **1.** a polyglot book or person. **2.** a mixture of several languages.

pol•y•gon (POL ee GON) *n. Geom.* a closed plane figure bounded by straight lines. [< LL *polygonum*] —**po•lyg•o•nal** (pə LIG ə nl) *adj.*

pol•y•graph (POL i GRAF) *n.* an electrical device for simultaneously recording variations in heartbeat, blood pressure, etc., sometimes used as a lie detector. —**po•ly•graph•ic** (POL i GRAF ik) *adj.*

po•lyg•y•ny (pə LIJ ə nee) *n.* the condition or practice of having more than one wife at a time. —**po•lyg′y•nous** *adj.*

pol•y•math (POL ee MATH) *n.* a person of extensive and diversified learning. [< Gk. *polymathēs* very learned]

pol•y•mer (POL ə mər) *n.* a compound of high molecular weight formed by the chemical combination of two or more molecules of the same kind. —**po•lym•er•i•za•tion** (pə LIM ər ə ZAY shən) *n.* —**po•lym•er•ize** (pə LIM ə RIZ) *v.t. & v.i.* **•ized, •iz•ing**

pol•y•no•mi•al (POL ə NOH mee əl) *adj.* of or consisting of many names or terms. —*n. Math.* an expression, as in algebra, containing two or more terms.

pol•yp (POL ip) *n.* **1.** *Pathol.* a smooth growth found in mucous membrane. **2.** *Zool.* a hydra. [< MF *polype* nasal growth, octopus]

pol•y•phon•ic (POL i FON ik) *adj.* **1.** consisting of many sounds or voices. **2.** *Music* designating or involving the simultaneous combination of two or more independent melodic parts.

po•lyph•o•ny (pə LIF ə nee) *n. pl.* **•nies 1.** multiplicity of sounds. **2.** polyphonic music. [< Gk. *polyphonía* multi-toned]

pol•y•sty•rene (POL ee STĪ reen) *n.* a clear plastic, used esp. in foams and in molded and sheet forms.

pol•y•syl•lab•ic (POL ee si LAB ik) *adj.* **1.** having or pertaining to several syllables, esp. to more than three. **2.** characterized by words of more than three syllables. [< Med.L *polysyllabus*]

pol•y•syl•la•ble (POL ee SIL ə bəl) *n.* a polysyllabic word.

pol•y•tech•nic (POL ee TEK nik) *adj.* embracing many arts. —*n.* a school of applied science and the industrial arts. [< F *polytechnique*]

pol•y•the•ism (POL ee thee IZ əm) *n.* the belief in more gods than one. [< F *polythéisme*] —**pol′y•the•is′tic** *adj.*

pol•y•un•sat•u•rate (POL ee un SACH ər it) *n.* an unsaturated fat or oil. —**pol•y•un•sat•u•rat•ed** (POL ee un SACH ə RAY tid) *adj.*

po•made (po MAYD) *n.* a perfumed dressing for the hair or scalp. —*v.t.* **•mad•ed, •mad•ing** apply pomade. [< Ital. *pomata* salve]

pome•gran•ate (POM i GRAN it) *n.* **1.** the fruit of a tropical Asian and African tree, about the size of an orange and having many seeds. **2.** the tree itself. [ME *poumgarnet*]

pom•mel (PUM əl) *n.* **1.** a knob, as on the

hilt of a sword. **2.** a knob at the front and top of a saddle. —*v.t.* **•meled, •mel•ing** beat with or as with the fists or a pommel. Also spelled *pummel*. [ME *pomel*]

po•mol•o•gy (poh MOL ə jee) *n.* the science that deals with fruits and fruit culture. [< NL *pomologia*] **—po•mol′o•gist** *n.*

pomp (pomp) *n.* **1.** magnificent display; splendor. **2.** ostentatious display. [ME]

pom•pa•dour (POM pə DOR) *n.* a style of arranging hair by puffing it over the forehead. [after Madame *Pompadour*, 1721–64, mistress of Louis XV of France]

pomp•ous (POM pəs) *adj.* **1.** marked by exaggerated dignity or self-importance. **2.** bombastic and florid, as speech. [ME] **—pom•pos•i•ty** (pom POS i tee) *n.*

pon•cho (PON choh) *n. pl.* **•chos 1.** a cloak like a blanket with a hole in the middle for the head. **2.** a similar waterproofed garment. [< Sp.]

pond (pond) *n.* a body of still water, smaller than a lake. [ME *ponde*]

pon•der (PON dər) *v.t. & v.i.* weigh (a matter) in the mind; consider carefully. [ME *pondren*]

pon•der•a•ble (PON dər ə bəl) *adj.* capable of being considered carefully; having appreciable weight. **—pon′der•a•bil′i•ty** *n.*

pon•der•ous (PON dər əs) *adj.* **1.** having great weight; also, huge. **2.** dull; lumbering. [ME] **—pon′der•ous•ness** *n.* **—pon′der•ous•ly** *adv.*

pon•tiff (PON tif) *n.* in the Roman Catholic Church: **a** the Pope. **b** any bishop. [< F *pontif*]

pon•tif•i•cal (pon TIF i kəl) *adj.* **1.** of, pertaining to, or suitable for a pope or bishop. **2.** haughty; pompous; dogmatic.

pon•tif•i•cate (pon TIF i KAYT) *v.i.* **•cat•ed, •cat•ing 1.** act or speak pompously or dogmatically. **2.** perform the office of a pontiff. —*n.* (pon TIF i kit) the office or term of a pontiff.

pon•toon (pon TOON) *n.* **1.** *Mil.* a flat-bottomed boat, metal cylinder, or the like, used in the construction of temporary floating bridges. **2.** either of the floats on the landing gear of a seaplane. [< F *ponton* floating bridge]

pontoon bridge a bridge supported on pontoons.

po•ny (POH nee) *n. pl.* **•nies 1.** one of a breed of very small horses, esp. not over 14 hands high. **2.** any small horse. **3.** *Slang* a literal translation used to prepare foreign language lessons: also called *trot.* **4.** a very small glass for liquor, or its contents. —*v.t. & v.i.* **•nied, •ny•ing** *Informal* pay (money) that is due: with *up.*

pony express a former postal system by which mail was relayed by horseback riders.

po•ny•tail (POH nee TAYL) *n.* **1.** a style of arranging long hair by gathering it tightly at the back of the head and letting it hang down like a pony's tail. **2.** hair so worn.

pooch (pooch) *n. Informal* a dog.

Pooh Bah (POO BAH) *n.* a pompous official. [after a character in Gilbert and Sullivan's *The Mikado*]

pooh-pooh (POO POO) *v.t.* reject or speak of disdainfully.

pool[1] (pool) *n.* **1.** a small body of fresh water, as a spring. **2.** a deep place in a stream. **3.** any small, isolated body of liquid: a *pool* of blood. **4.** a swimming pool. [ME]

pool[2] *n.* **1.** in certain gambling games, a collective stake. **2.** in business or finance, any combination formed for mutual advantage, as for price fixing or a speculative operation. **3.** any combining of efforts or resources: a secretarial *pool.* **4.** any of various games played on a six-pocket billiard table: also *pocket billiards.* —*v.t. & v.i.* combine in a mutual fund or pool. [< F *poule,* lit., hen]

pool•room (POOL ROOM) *n.* a commercial establishment or room equipped for the playing of pool, billiards, etc.

pool table a six-pocket billiard table for playing pool.

poop[1] (poop) *n. Naut.* **1.** the stern of a ship. **2.** a short deck built over the main deck at the stern of a ship: also **poop deck.** [< MF *poupe*]

poop[2] *v.t. Slang* tire: usu. in the passive.

poop[3] *n. Slang* information. —*adj.* supplying information: *poop* sheet.

poor (puur) *adj.* **•er, •est 1.** lacking means of comfortable subsistence; needy. **2.** characterized by poverty. **3.** not abundant; scanty; meager. **4.** lacking in fertility; sterile: *poor* soil. **5.** inferior in quality. **6.** feeble; frail: *poor* health. **7.** lacking proper ability; unsatisfactory. **8.** deserving of pity. [ME *povre*] **—poor′ly** *adv. & adj.*

poor•house (PUUR HOWS) *n. pl.* **•hous•es** (-HOW ziz) a public establishment maintained as a dwelling for paupers.

poor-mouth (PUUR MOWTH) *v.* **-mouthed** (mowthd), **-mouth•ing** *Informal v.t.* **1.** disparage; belittle. —*v.i.* **2.** complain of or claim poverty.

poor-spir·it·ed (PUUR SPIR i tid) *adj*. having little spirit or courage.

pop[1] (pop) *v*. **popped, pop·ping** *v.i.* **1.** make a sharp, explosive sound. **2.** burst open or explode with such a sound. **3.** move or go suddenly or quickly: with *in, out*, etc. **4.** bulge: His eyes *popped*. —*v.t.* **5.** cause to burst or explode, as kernels of corn. **6.** thrust or put suddenly: with *in, out*, etc. **7.** *Informal* swallow (drugs): *pop* pills. —**pop the question** *Informal* make a proposal of marriage. —*n.* **1.** a sharp, explosive noise. **2.** a shot. **3.** soda (def. 2). —*adv.* **1.** like or with the sound of a pop. **2.** suddenly. [ME *poppe*]

pop[2] *n. Informal* father.

pop[3] *adj*. **1.** featuring popular or light classical music: a *pop* concert. **2.** of or relating to mass culture: *pop* styles. [Short for POPULAR]

pop art a style of art of the 1950's and 1960's influenced by commercial art.

pope (pohp) *n. Often cap.* in the Roman Catholic Church, the bishop of Rome and the head of the Church. [ME] —**pope'dom** (-dəm) *n.*

pop·er·y (POH pə ree) *n.* the practices, doctrines, etc. of the Roman Catholic Church: an offensive term.

pop·eyed (POP ID) *adj*. having bulging eyes.

pop·in·jay (POP in JAY) *n.* a vain, conceited person. [ME *papejay*]

pop·ish (POH pish) *adj*. pertaining to popes or popery: a usu. offensive term. —**pop'ish·ly** *adv*. —**pop'ish·ness** *n.*

pop·lin (POP lin) *n.* a durable silk, cotton, or rayon fabric with a ribbed surface. [< F *popeline*]

pop·o·ver (POP OH vər) *n.* a very light egg muffin.

pop·per (POP ər) *n.* **1.** one who or that which pops. **2.** a device for popping corn.

pop·py (POP ee) *n. pl.* **·pies 1.** any of various plants having showy flowers, as the **opium poppy**. **2.** the bright scarlet color of certain poppy blossoms: also **poppy red.** [ME]

pop·py·cock (POP ee KOK) *n.* pretentious talk; humbug; nonsense.

poppy seed the black seed of the poppy plant, used to flavor and top rolls etc.

pop·u·lace (POP yə ləs) *n.* the common people; the masses. [< F]

pop·u·lar (POP yə lər) *adj*. **1.** approved of, admired, or liked by most people. **2.** having

many friends. **3.** of or pertaining to the people at large. **4.** suited to ordinary people. [ME *populer*] —**pop·u·lar·i·ty** (POP yə LAR i tee) *n.* —**pop'u·lar·ly** *adv*.

pop·u·lar·ize (POP yə lə RIZ) *v.t.* **·ized, ·iz·ing** make popular. —**pop'u·lar·i·za'tion** *n.* —**pop'u·lar·iz'er** *n.*

pop·u·late (POP yə LAYT) *v.t.* **·lat·ed, ·lat·ing 1.** furnish with inhabitants; people. **2.** inhabit. [< Med.L *populatus* peopled]

pop·u·la·tion (POP yə LAY shən) *n.* **1.** the total number of persons living in a specified area. **2.** the total number of persons of a particular group, class, etc., residing in a place. **3.** *Stat.* a group of items or individuals.

pop·u·list (POP yə list) *n.* one who supports broad-based social and political reforms similar to those advocated by the Populists. —**pop'u·lism** *n.*

Pop·u·list (POP yə list) *n.* a member of the Populist or People's Party, formed in the U.S. in 1891 and advocating public control of railways, an income tax, and limitation of ownership of land.

pop·u·lous (POP yə ləs) *adj*. containing many inhabitants; thickly settled.

por·ce·lain (POR sə lin) *n.* a white, hard, translucent ceramic ware, usu. glazed; chinaware. [< F *porcelaine*]

porch (porch) *n.* a covered structure or recessed space at a side of a building; veranda. [ME *porche*]

por·cine (POR sīn) *adj*. of, pertaining to, or characteristic of swine. [< L *porcinus*]

por·cu·pine (POR kyə PIN) *n.* any of various large rodents covered with erectile spines or quills: also called *hedgehog*. [ME *porcupyne*]

pore[1] (por) *v.i.* **pored, por·ing 1.** gaze steadily or intently. **2.** study or read with care: with *over*. [ME *pouren*]

pore[2] *n.* **1.** a minute orifice or opening, as in the skin or a leaf, serving as an outlet for perspiration or as a means of absorption. **2.** any similar opening, as in rock. [ME *poore*]

pork (pork) *n.* the flesh of swine used as food. [ME *porc*]

pork barrel *Informal* a government appropriation for some local enterprise that will favorably impress a representative's constituents.

pork·er (POR kər) *n.* a pig or hog.

pork·pie (PORK PI) *n.* **1.** a pie filled with pork. **2.** a man's hat with a low, flat crown.

pork·y (POR kee) *adj.* **pork·i·er, pork·i·est 1.** of or like pork. **2.** obese; fat.

porn (porn) *adj. Informal* pornographic. —*n.* pornography. Also **por·no** (POR noh).

por·nog·ra·phy (por NOG rǝ fee) *n.* obscene books, movies, etc. [< Gk. *pornographos* writing about prostitutes] —**por·nog′ra·pher** *n.* —**por·no·graph·ic** (POR nǝ GRAF ik) *adj.*

po·rous (POR ǝs) *adj.* **1.** having pores. **2.** permeable by fluids or light. [ME] —**po·ros·i·ty** (pǝ ROS i tee) *n.* —**po′rous·ly** *adv.*

por·poise (POR pǝs) *n. pl.* **·pois·es** or **·poise** a dolphinlike whale with a blunt, rounded snout. [ME *porpoys*]

por·ridge (POR ij) *n.* oatmeal or other meal cooked in water or milk.

por·rin·ger (POR in jǝr) *n.* a small, relatively shallow bowl for porridge or soup. [ME *potinger*]

port[1] (port) *n.* **1.** a city or place of customary entry and exit of ships, esp. for commerce. **2.** a harbor or haven. [ME]

port[2] *n. Naut.* the left side of a vessel as one faces the front or bow: opposed to *starboard.* —*v.t. & v.i.* put or turn to the port side. —*adj.* left.

port[3] *n.* **1.** *Naut.* **a** a porthole. **b** a covering for a porthole. **2.** *Mech.* an orifice for the passage of air, gas, etc. [ME]

port[4] *n.* a sweet wine, usu. dark red.

port[5] *v.t. Mil.* carry (a rifle, saber, etc.) diagonally across the body and sloping to the left shoulder. —*n.* this position of the weapon. [ME]

port·a·ble (POR tǝ bǝl) *adj.* that can be readily carried or moved. —*n.* something portable, as a word processor or radio. [ME] —**port′a·bil′i·ty** *n.*

port·age (POR tij) *n.* **1.** the act of transporting (canoes, boats, etc.) from one navigable water to another; also, that which is transported. **2.** the route over which such transportation is made. **3.** the charge for transportation. —*v.t. & v.i.* **·taged, ·tag·ing** carry (boats etc.) over a portage. [ME]

por·tal (POR tl) *n.* an entrance, door, or gate, esp. one that is grand and imposing. [ME]

port·cul·lis (port KUL is) *n.* a grating that can be let down to close the gateway of a fortified place. [ME *portcolys*]

porte-co·chère (PORT kǝ SHAIR) *n.* **1.** a large covered gateway leading into a courtyard. **2.** a porch over a driveway at the entrance of a building. [< F, coach gate]

por·tend (por TEND) *v.t.* warn of as an omen; forebode. [ME]

por·tent (POR tent) *n.* **1.** a sign of what is to happen, esp. of something momentous; omen. **2.** ominous significance. [< L *portentum*] —**por·ten′tous** *adj.*

por·ter[1] (POR tǝr) *n.* **1.** one who carries travelers luggage, etc., for hire. **2.** an attendant in a railroad car. [ME *portour*]

por·ter[2] *n.* a doorkeeper. [ME]

por·ter[3] *n.* a dark brown, heavy ale.

por·ter·house (POR tǝr hows) *n.* a choice cut of beefsteak including a part of the tenderloin, usu. next to the sirloin: also **porterhouse steak.**

port·fo·li·o (port FOH lee oh) *n. pl.* **·li·os 1.** a portable case for holding drawings, papers, etc. **2.** the office of a minister of state or a cabinet member. **3.** the total investments, securities, etc., of a bank or investor. [< Ital. *portafoglio*]

port·hole (PORT hohl) *n.* **1.** a small, usu. round opening in a ship's side. **2.** any similar opening, as in an aircraft.

por·ti·co (POR ti koh) *n. pl.* **·coes** or **·cos** an open space with a roof upheld by columns; a porch. [< Ital.] —**por′ti·coed** *adj.*

por·tiere (por TYAIR) *n.* a curtain for a doorway, used instead of a door. Also **por·tière′.** [< F]

por·tion (POR shǝn) *n.* **1.** a part of a whole. **2.** an allotment or share. **3.** the quantity of food usu. served to one person. —*v.t.* **1.** divide into shares for distribution; parcel: usu. with *out.* **2.** assign; allot. [ME]

port·ly (PORT lee) *adj.* **port·li·er, port·li·est 1.** corpulent; stout. **2.** stately; impressive. —**port′li·ness** *n.*

port·man·teau (port MAN toh) *n. pl.* **·teaus** or **·teaux** (-tohz) a large suitcase. [< MF *portemanteau*]

portmanteau word a word formed from parts of two related words, as *brunch* from *breakfast* and *lunch.*

port of call a port where vessels put in for supplies, repairs, taking on of cargo, etc.

port of entry *Law* a place, whether on the coast or inland, designated as a point at which persons or merchandise may enter or leave a country: also called *port.*

por·trait (POR trit) *n.* **1.** a likeness of a person, esp. of the face, by an artist or photographer. **2.** a vivid word description, esp. of a person. [< MF] —**por′trait·ist** *n.*

por·trai·ture (POR tri chər) *n.* **1.** the art or practice of making portraits. **2.** portraits collectively. [ME]

por·tray (por TRAY) *v.t.* **1.** represent by drawing, painting, etc. **2.** describe or depict in words. **3.** represent, as in a play; act. [ME *portrayen*] —**por·tray'al** *n.*

Por·tu·guese (POR chə GEEZ) *n.* **1.** a native or inhabitant of Portugal. **2.** the Romance language of Portugal and Brazil. — **Por'tu·guese'** *adj.*

Portuguese man-of-war any of several large marine animals, having long, stinging tentacles hanging down from a bladderlike float.

pose¹ (pohz) *n.* **1.** the position of the whole or part of the body, esp. such a position assumed for or represented by an artist or photographer. **2.** a mode of behavior, role, attitude, etc., adopted for effect. —*v.* **posed, pos·ing** *v.i.* **1.** assume or hold a pose, as for a portrait. **2.** affect an attitude, role, etc.: *pose* as an expert. —*v.t.* **3.** cause to assume a pose, as an artist's model. **4.** state or propound; put forward as a question, etc. [ME *posen*]

pose² *v.t.* **posed, pos·ing** puzzle or confuse by asking a difficult question.

pos·er¹ (POH zər) *n.* one who poses.

pos·er² *n.* a baffling question.

po·seur (poh ZUR) *n.* one who affects an attitude, mode of behavior, etc., to make an impression on others. [< F]

posh (posh) *adj.* luxurious; fashionable.

pos·it (POZ it) *v.t.* **1.** put; place. **2.** assume as a fact or basis of argument; postulate. [< L *positus* placed]

po·si·tion (pə ZISH ən) *n.* **1.** the manner in which a thing is placed. **2.** disposition of the body or parts of the body. **3.** the locality or place occupied by a person or thing. **4.** the proper or appropriate place: in *position*. **5.** an attitude or point of view; stand. **6.** relative social standing; status; also, high social standing. **7.** employment; job. **8.** in sports, the assignment of an area covered by a particular player. —**be in a position to** have the means or opportunity. —*v.t.* place in a particular or appropriate position. [ME *posicioun*]

pos·i·tive (POZ i tiv) *adj.* **1.** that is or may be directly affirmed; actual. **2.** characterized by or expressing affirmation: a *positive* attitude. **3.** openly and plainly expressed: a *positive* denial. **4.** not admitting of doubt or denial. **5.** *Math.* greater than zero; plus: said

of quantities and usu. denoted by the sign (+). **6.** *Med.* denoting the presence of a specific condition or organism. **7.** *Photog.* having the lights and darks in their original relation, as in a print made from a negative. **8.** *Electr.* characterized by a deficiency of electrons. —*n.* **1.** that which is positive or capable of being directly or certainly affirmed. **2.** *Math.* a positive symbol or quantity. **3.** *Electr.* a positive pole, terminal, etc. **4.** *Photog.* a positive picture or print. **5.** *Gram.* the uncompared degree of an adjective or adverb; also, a word in this degree. [ME *positif*] —**pos'i·tive·ly** *adv.* —**pos'i·tive·ness** *n.*

pos·i·tiv·ism (POZ i tə VIZ əm) *n.* a way of thinking that regards nothing as ascertained or ascertainable beyond the facts of physical science or of sense. —**pos'i·tiv·ist** *n.*

pos·i·tron (POZ i TRON) *n. Physics* the positive counterpart of an electron.

pos·se (POS ee) *n.* a force armed with temporary legal authority. [< Med.L *posse comitatus* authority of the county]

pos·sess (pə ZES) *v.t.* **1.** have as property; own. **2.** have as a quality, attribute, skill, etc. **3.** enter and exert control over; dominate: often used passively: *possessed* by the idea. [ME *possesen*]

pos·sessed (pə ZEST) *adj.* **1.** having; owning. **2.** controlled by or as if by evil spirits; frenzied.

pos·ses·sion (pə ZESH ən) *n.* **1.** the act or fact of possessing. **2.** the state of being possessed. **3.** that which is possessed or owned. **4.** *pl.* property; wealth. **5.** self-possession.

pos·ses·sive (pə ZES iv) *adj.* **1.** of or pertaining to possession or ownership. **2.** having a strong desire to dominate another person. **3.** *Gram.* designating a case of the noun or pronoun that denotes possession, origin, or the like. —*n. Gram.* **1.** the possessive case. **2.** a possessive form or construction. [< L *possessivus*] —**pos·ses'sive·ness** *n.*

pos·si·bil·i·ty (POS ə BIL i tee) *n. pl.* **·ties 1.** the fact or state of being possible. **2.** that which is possible.

pos·si·ble (POS ə bəl) *adj.* **1.** capable of happening or proving true. **2.** capable of being done or of coming about; feasible. **3.** that may or may not happen. [ME] —**pos'si·bly** *adv.*

pos·sum (POS əm) *n.* opposum. —**play possum** feign death, sleep. [< OPOSSUM]

post[1] (pohst) *n.* an upright piece of timber or other material; as: **a** a support for a sign. **b** a bearing or framing member in a building. **c** an indicator of the starting or finishing point of a racecourse, etc. —*v.t.* **1.** put up (a poster etc.) in some public place. **2.** fasten posters upon. **3.** announce by or as by a poster: *post* a reward. **4.** publish the name of on a list. [ME]

post[2] *n.* **1.** a position of employment; esp., a public office. **2.** *Mil.* **a** a place occupied by a detachment of troops. **b.** the buildings and grounds of such a place. **3.** an assigned beat, position, or station, as of a sentry, policeman, etc. **4.** a trading post or settlement. —*v.t.* assign to a particular post; station, as a sentry. [< F *poste*]

post[3] *n.* **1.** *Chiefly Brit.* a single delivery of mail to a home, office, etc.; also, the mail itself. **2.** *Chiefly Brit.* an established, usu. government, system for transporting the mails; also, a local post office. —*v.t.* **1.** *Chiefly Brit.* mail. **2.** inform. **3.** in bookkeeping, transfer (items or accounts) to the ledger. —*v.i.* **4.** travel with speed; hasten. **5.** ride to a horse's trot by raising and lowering oneself in rhythm with the gait. —*adv.* speedily; rapidly. [< F *poste*]

post- *prefix* after in time, order, or position; following: *postdate, postwar.* [< L *post* behind, after]

post·age (POH stij) *n.* **1.** the charge levied on mail. **2.** stamps, etc., representing payment of this charge.

postage stamp a small, printed label issued and sold by a government to be used in payment of postage.

pos·tal (POHS tl) *adj.* pertaining to the mails or to mail service.

post·bel·lum (pohst BEL əm) *adj.* occurring after a war, esp. after the Civil War. [< L *post bellum* after the war]

post·card (POHST KAHRD) *n.* **1.** a card, issued officially, for carrying a message through the mails. **2.** any similar, unofficial card, usu. having a picture on one side.

post·date (pohst DAYT) *v.t.* **·dat·ed, ·dat·ing 1.** assign or fix a date later than the actual date to (a check, document, etc.). **2.** follow in time.

post·er (POH stər) *n.* a placard or bill used for advertising, public information, etc. to be posted on a wall or other surface.

pos·te·ri·or (po STEER ee ər) *adj.* **1.** situated behind or toward the hinder part. **2.** subsequent in time; later. —*n.* the buttocks. [< L, coming after]

pos·ter·i·ty (po STER i tee) *n.* **1.** future generations taken collectively. **2.** all of one's descendants. [ME *posterite*]

post exchange *Mil.* an establishment for the sale of merchandise and services to military personnel. Abbr. **PX.**

post·grad·u·ate (pohst GRAJ oo it) *adj.* of or pertaining to studies pursued beyond the bachelor's degree. —*n.* one who pursues such studies.

post·haste (POHST HAYST) *n. Archaic* great haste. —*adv.* with utmost speed.

post·hu·mous (POS chə məs) *adj.* **1.** denoting a child born after the father's death. **2.** published after the author's death, as a book. **3.** arising or continuing after one's death. [< L *postumus* late-born] —**post'·hu·mous·ly** *adv.*

Post·Im·pres·sion·ism (POHST im PRESH ə NIZ əm) *n.* the theories and practice of a group of painters of the late 19th c. who stressed structure, space, or expressionism. —**Post'-Im·pres'sion·ist** *n. & adj.* —**Post'-Im·pres'sion·is'tic** *adj.*

post·mark (POHST MAHRK) *n.* any official mark stamped on mail to cancel stamps. —*v.t.* stamp with a postmark.

post·mas·ter (POHST MAS tər) *n.* an official having charge of a post office. —**post'mis'·tress** (-MIS tris) *n.fem.*

postmaster general *pl.* **postmasters general** the executive head of the postal service of a government.

post·me·rid·i·an (POHST mə RID ee ən) *adj.* pertaining to or occurring in the afternoon.

post me·rid·i·em (POHST mə RID ee əm) after noon. Abbr. *p.m., P.M.* [< L]

post·mor·tem (pohst MOR təm) *adj.* **1.** happening or performed after death. **2.** of or pertaining to a post-mortem examination. —*n.* **1.** a post-mortem examination. **2.** an analysis or discussion of an accomplished fact. [< L *post mortem* after death]

post-mortem examination *Med.* a thorough examination of a human body after death: also called *autopsy.*

post·na·tal (pohst NAY tl) *adj.* occurring after birth.

post office 1. the branch of a government charged with delivering the mails. **2.** any local office that delivers mail, sells stamps, etc.

post·op·er·a·tive (pohst OP ər ə tiv) *adj.* occurring or done after surgery.

post·par·tum (pohst PAHR təm) *adj. Med.* after childbirth. [< NL *post partum* after childbirth]

post·pone (pohst POHN) *v.t.* **·poned,** **·pon·ing** put off to a future time; defer; delay. [< L *postponere* put after] — **post·pon'a·ble** *adj.* —**post·pone'ment** *n.*

post·pran·di·al (pohst PRAN dee əl) *adj.* after a meal.

post·script (POHST SKRIPT) *n.* a sentence or other addition at the end of a letter or other document. Abbr. *p.s., P.S.* [< NL *postscriptum*]

pos·tu·lant (POS chə lənt) *n. Eccl.* an applicant for admission into a religious order. [< F] —**pos'tu·lan·cy** *n.*

pos·tu·late (POS chə LAYT) *v.t.* **·lat·ed,** **·lat·ing** assume the truth or reality of. —*n.* (POS chə lit) a principle assumed to be true and used as the basis for further reasoning.

pos·ture (POS chər) *n.* **1.** the position or carriage of the body or parts of the body. **2.** a mental attitude; frame of mind. **3.** a situation or condition, esp. if a consequence of policy: national defense *posture.* —*v.i.* **·tured, ·tur·ing** assume or adopt a bodily pose or a character not natural to one. [< F] —**pos'tur·er** *n.*

post·war (POHST WOR) *adj.* being or happening after a war.

pot (pot) *n.* **1.** a round, fairly deep vessel of metal, earthenware, or glass, generally having a handle, used for cooking and other domestic purposes. **2.** the amount a pot will hold. **3.** in card games, esp. poker, the amount of stakes wagered or played for. **4.** *Slang* marijuana. —**go to pot** deteriorate. —*v.* **pot·ted, pot·ting** *v.t.* **1.** put into a pot or pots: *pot* plants. **2.** preserve (meat, etc.) in pots or jars. **3.** shoot or kill with a pot shot. —*v.i.* **4.** take a pot shot; shoot. [ME *pott*]

po·ta·ble (POH tə bəl) *adj.* suitable for drinking: said of water. —*n. Often pl.* something drinkable; beverage. [< LL *potabilis* drinkable]

po·tage (poh TAHZH) *n. French* any thick soup.

po·ta·tion (poh TAY shən) *n.* the act of drinking; also, a drink, esp. of an alcoholic beverage. [ME *potacion*]

po·ta·to (pə TAY toh) *n. pl.* **·toes 1.** an edible tuber of a plant of a family that includes tobacco, the pepper, and the tomato. **2.** the plant. **3.** the sweet potato. [< Sp. *patata*]

pot·bel·ly (POT BEL ee) *n. pl.* **·lies 1.** a protuberant belly. **2.** an upright wood- or coal-burning stove with bulging sides: **potbelly stove;** also **potbellied stove.** — **pot'bel'lied** *adj.*

pot·boil·er (POT BOI lər) *n.* an inferior literary or artistic work produced merely for money.

po·tent (POHT nt) *adj.* **1.** physically powerful. **2.** having great authority. **3.** exerting great influence on mind or morals; very convincing: a *potent* argument. **4.** of a drug, liquor, etc., strong in its physical and chemical effects. **5.** sexually competent: said of the male. [ME] —**po·ten·cy** (POHT n see) *n.*

po·ten·tate (POHT n TAYT) *n.* one having great power or sway; a sovereign. [ME]

po·ten·tial (pə TEN shəl) *adj.* **1.** possible but not actual. **2.** having capacity for existence, but not yet existing; latent. —*n.* **1.** a possible development; potentiality. **2.** *Electr.* the charge on a body as referred to another body or to a given standard, as the earth, considered as having zero potential. [ME *potencial*] —**po·ten'tial·ly** *adv.*

potential energy see under ENERGY.

po·ten·ti·al·i·ty (pə TEN shee AL i tee) *n. pl.* **·ties 1.** inherent capacity for development or accomplishment. **2.** that which is potential or capable of being realized.

pot·hole (POT HOHL) *n.* a deep hole, as in a road.

pot·hook (POT HUUK) *n.* **1.** a curved or hooked piece of iron for lifting or hanging pots. **2.** an S-shaped stroke made in writing.

po·tion (POH shən) *n.* a draft, as a large dose of liquid medicine: often used of a magic or poisonous draft. [ME *pocion*]

pot·luck (POT LUK) *n.* whatever food may have been prepared: usu. in the phrase **take potluck.**

pot·pie (POT PI) *n.* **1.** a meat pie baked in a deep dish. **2.** meat stewed with dumplings.

pot·pour·ri (POH puu REE) *n.* **1.** a mixture of dried flower petals kept in a jar and used to perfume a room. **2.** a musical medley or literary miscellany. [< F, lit., rotten pot]

pot·sherd (POT SHURD) *n.* a bit of broken earthenware.

pot·shot (POT SHOT *n.* **1.** a shot fired to kill, without regard to the rules of sports. **2.** a shot fired, as from ambush, at a person or animal within easy range.

pot·tage (POT ij) n. a thick broth or stew of vegetables with or without meat. [ME *potage*]

pot·ted (POT id) adj. **1.** placed or kept in a pot. **2.** cooked or preserved in a pot. **3.** *Slang* drunk.

pot·ter[1] (POT ər) v.t. & v.i. *Chiefly Brit.* putter. [ME *poten*] —**pot'·ter·er** n.

pot·ter[2] n. one who makes pottery. [ME]

potter's field a burial ground for the destitute and the unknown.

pot·ter·y (POT ə ree) n. pl. **·ter·ies 1.** ware molded from clay and hardened by intense heat. **2.** the art of making earthenware or porcelain. **3.** a place where pottery is made.

pouch (powch) n. **1.** a small bag, sack, or other container, used for carrying money, pipe tobacco, ammunition, etc. **2.** *Zool.* a saclike structure of certain animals, as the kangaroo, for carrying and nurturing young. **3.** a mailbag. —v.t. **1.** put in a pouch. —v.i. **2.** form a pouchlike cavity. [ME *pouche*]

poul·tice (POHL tis) n. a hot, soft mass applied to a sore part of the body. —v.t. **·ticed, ·tic·ing** cover with a poultice. [< Med.L *pultes* pap]

poul·try (POHL tree) n. domestic fowls, generally or collectively, as hens. [ME *pultrie*]

pounce (powns) v.i. **pounced, pounc·ing** swoop or spring in or as in seizing prey: with *on, upon,* or *at.* [ME] —n. a swoop.

pound[1] (pownd) n. **1.** a unit of weight varying in different countries and at different periods. **2.** in Great Britain and the U.S., either of two legally fixed units, the avoirdupois pound and the troy pound. **3.** the standard monetary unit of the United Kingdom: also **pound sterling.** Symbol £. **4.** a standard monetary unit of various other countries. [ME]

pound[2] n. **1.** a place, enclosed by authority, in which stray animals, seized property, etc. are left until claimed or redeemed. **2.** a place of confinement for lawbreakers. —v.t. confine in a pound; impound. [ME *poond*]

pound[3] v.t. **1.** strike heavily and repeatedly; beat. **2.** reduce to a pulp or powder by beating. —v.i. **3.** strike heavy, repeated blows: with *on, at,* etc. **4.** move or proceed heavily. **5.** throb heavily or resoundingly. —n. **1.** a heavy blow. **2.** the act of pounding. [ME *pounen*]

pound cake a rich cake originally made with ingredients equal in weight, as a pound each of flour, butter, and sugar, with eggs added.

pound-fool·ish (POWND FOO lish) adj. extravagant with large sums, but watching small sums closely: penny-wise and *pound-foolish.*

pour (por) v.t. **1.** cause to flow in a continuous stream, as water, sand, etc. **2.** emit or utter profusely or continuously. —v.i. **3.** flow in a continuous stream; gush. **4.** rain heavily. **5.** move in great numbers; swarm. —n. a pouring, flow, or downfall. [ME *pouren*] —**pour'er** n.

pout (powt) v.i. **1.** thrust out the lips, esp. in ill humor. **2.** be sullen; sulk. —v.t. **3.** thrust out (the lips etc.). **4.** utter with a pout. [ME *pouten*] —n. the act or expresion of pouting.

pout·er (POW tər) n. **1.** one who pouts. **2.** a breed of pigeon having the habit of puffing out the crop.

pov·er·ty (POV ər tee) n. **1.** the condition or quality of being poor. **2.** scantiness of essential elements: a *poverty* of imagination. [ME *poverte*]

pov·er·ty-strick·en (POV ər tee STRIK ən) adj. suffering from poverty; destitute.

pow·der (POW dər) n. **1.** a finely ground or pulverized mass of loose particles formed from a solid substance in the dry state. **2.** any of various substances prepared in this form, as a cosmetic, medicine, or explosive. —v.t. **1.** reduce to powder; pulverize. **2.** sprinkle or cover with or as with powder. —v.i. **3.** be reduced to powder. [ME *poudre*] —**pow'der·y** adj.

pow·er (POW ər) n. **1.** ability to act; capability. **2.** potential capacity. **3.** strength or force actually put forth. **4.** the right, ability, or capacity to exercise control; legal authority. **5.** an important and influential sovereign nation. **6.** *Often pl.* a mental or physical faculty. **7.** any form of energy available for doing work, esp. electrical energy. **8.** *Physics* the time rate at which energy is transferred, or converted into work. **9.** *Math.* the number of times a number is to be multiplied by itself, expressed as an exponent. **10.** *Optics* magnifying capacity, as of a lens. —v.t. supply with power; esp., provide with means of propulsion. [ME *pouere*]

pow·er·ful (POW ər fəl) adj. **1.** possessing great force or energy; strong. **2.** exercising great authority, or manifesting high quali-

ties. **3.** having great effect on the mind. —
adv. Dial. very. —**pow′er·ful·ly** *adv.*

pow·er·house (POW ər HOWS) *n.* **1.** *Electr.*
a station where electricity is generated: also
power plant. 2. a forceful, powerful, or
energetic person.

pow·er·less (POW ər lis) *adj.* **1.** destitute of
power; unable to accomplish an effect; impotent. **2.** without authority. —**pow′**
er·less·ness *n.*

power of attorney *Law* **1.** the authority or
power to act conferred upon an agent. **2.**
the document conferring such authority.

pow·wow (POW wow) *n.* **1.** *Informal* any
meeting or conference. **2.** a Native American ceremony to cure the sick, effect success in war, etc. **3.** a conference with or of
Native Americans. —*v.i.* hold a powwow.
[< Algonquian *pauwaw*, lit., he who
dreams]

pox (poks) *n.* **1.** any disease characterized by
purulent eruptions: *chickenpox.* **2.** syphilis.

prac·ti·ca·ble (PRAK ti kə bəl) *adj.* **1.** that
can be put into practice; feasible. **2.** that can
be used; usable. —**prac′ti·ca·bil′i·ty** *n.*

prac·ti·cal (PRAK ti kəl) *adj.* **1.** pertaining
to actual use and experience, as contrasted
with speculation. **2.** trained by or derived
from practice or experience. **3.** applicable
to use. **4.** manifested in practice. **5.** being
such to all intents and purposes; virtual.
[ME] —**prac′ti·cal′i·ty** *n.*

practical joke a trick having a victim or victims.

prac·ti·cal·ly (PRAK tik lee) *adv.* **1.** in a
practical manner. **2.** in effect; virtually.

practical nurse one who has training in
nursing but who is not a registered nurse.

prac·tice (PRAK tis) *v.* **·ticed, ·tic·ing** *v.t.*
1. make use of habitually or often: *practice
economy.* **2.** apply in action; make a practice of. **3.** work at as a profession. **4.** do or
perform repeatedly in order to acquire skill
or training; rehearse. —*v.i.* **5.** repeat or
rehearse something in order to acquire skill
or proficiency. **6.** work at a profession. [ME
practisen] —*n.* **1.** any customary action or
proceeding; habit. **2.** an established custom
or usage. **3.** the act of doing or performing,
as distinguished from theory. **4.** the regular
prosecution of a profession. **5.** frequent and
repeated exercise in any matter. **6.** *pl.* strat-
agems or schemes for bad purposes; tricks.

prac·ticed (PRAK tist) *adj.* **1.** expert
through practice; experienced. **2.** acquired
by practice.

prac·ti·tion·er (prak TISH ə nər) *n.* one
who practices an art or profession.

prag·mat·ic (prag MAT ik) *adj.* **1.** pertaining to or concerned with events or everyday
occurrences; practical. **2.** *Philos.* pertaining
to pragmatism. Also **prag·mat′i·cal.** [< L
pragmaticus skilled in law] —**prag·mat′**
i·cal·ly *adv.*

prag·ma·tism (PRAG mə TIZ əm) *n. Philos.*
the doctrine that ideas have value only in
terms of their practical consequences. —
prag′ma·tist *n.*

prai·rie (PRAIR ee) *n.* a tract of grassland;
esp., the broad, grassy plain of central
North America. [< F, meadow]

prairie schooner a covered wagon used for
travel by pioneers.

praise (prayz) *n.* **1.** an expression of approval
or commendation. **2.** the glorifying and
honoring of a god, ruler, hero, etc. —*v.t.*
praised, prais·ing 1. express approval and
commendation of; applaud. **2.** express adoration of; glorify, esp. in song. [ME *preisen*
value]

praise·wor·thy (PRAYZ WUR *thee*) *adj.*
worthy of praise. —**praise′·wor′thi·ness**
n.

prance (prans) *v.* **pranced, pranc·ing** *v.i.*
1. move proudly with high steps, as a spirited horse; spring from the hind legs; also,
ride a horse moving thus. **2.** move in an
arrogant or elated manner; swagger. —*v.t.*
3. cause to prance. —*n.* the act of prancing;
caper. [ME *praunce*] —**pranc′er** *n.*

pran·di·al (PRAN dee əl) *adj.* of or pertaining to a meal. [< L *prandium* meal]

prank (prangk) *n.* a mischievous act; trick.
—*v.i.* play pranks or tricks. —**prank′ish**
adj. —**prank′ster** *n.*

prate (prayt) *v.t. & v.i.* **prat·ed, prat·ing**
talk or utter idly and at length; chatter. —*n.*
idle talk; prattle. [ME *praten*]

prat·fall (PRAT FAWL) *n.* **1.** a fall on the
buttocks. **2.** a defeat.

prat·tle (PRAT l) *v.t. & v.i.* **·tled, ·tling** talk
or utter in a foolish or childish way. —*n.*
childish or foolish talk.

prawn (prawn) *n.* any of various shrimplike
crustaceans of tropical and temperate waters, used as food. —*v.i.* fish for prawns.
[ME *prane*]

pray (pray) *v.i.* **1.** address prayers to a deity,
idol, etc. **2.** make earnest request or entreaty; beg. —*v.t.* **3.** say prayers to. [ME
preien]

prayer[1] (prair) *n.* **1.** a devout request or petition to a deity. **2.** the act of praying, esp. to God. **3.** *Often pl.* a religious service. **4.** something prayed for. **5.** any earnest request. [ME *preiere*]

pray·er² (PRAY ər) *n.* one who prays.

prayer book (prair) a book of prayers for worship.

prayer·ful (PRAIR fəl) *adj.* inclined or given to prayer; devotional.

pre- *prefix*
1. before in time; preceding:

pre-Christian	premarital
predawn	prerevolutionary
preglacial	preschooler
preinaugural	preteen
prekindergarten	prewar

2. before in position: **precardiac, pre-cerebral, prevertebral**

3. preliminary to; preparing for: **pre-college, predoctorate**

4. beforehand; in advance:

prearrange	prechill
prearm	precool
preexamine	preplan
preheat	presell
prepackage	preset

[< L *prae* before]

preach (preech) *v.t.* **1.** advocate or recommend urgently. **2.** proclaim or expound upon: *preach* the gospel. **3.** deliver (a sermon, etc.). —*v.i.* **4.** deliver a sermon. **5.** give advice, esp. in an officious or moralizing manner. [ME *prechen*]

preach·er (PREE chər) *n.* one who preaches; esp., a clergyman.

preach·ment (PREECH mənt) *n.* a sermon or moral lecture, esp. a tedious one.

preach·y (PREE chee) *adj.* **preach·i·er, preach·i·est** given to preaching; sanctimonious. —**preach′i·ness** *n.*

pre·am·ble (PREE AM bəl) *n.* **1.** an introductory statement or preface. **2.** an introductory act, event, fact, etc. [ME]

pre·am·pli·fi·er (pree AM plə FI ər) *n.* in a sound reproduction system, an auxiliary amplifier used to reinforce weak signals before sending them into the main amplifier. Also **pre′amp.**

preb·end (PREB ənd) *n.* **1.** a stipend allotted from the revenues of a cathedral or collegiate church to a member of the clergy. **2.** the land or tithe yielding the stipend. [ME *prebende*]

preb·en·dar·y (PREB ən DER ee) *n. pl.* **·dar·ies** a person who holds a prebend.

pre·car·i·ous (pri KAIR ee əs) *adj.* **1.** sub-

ject to continued risk; uncertain. **2.** subject or exposed to danger; hazardous. [< L *precarius* obtained by prayer]

pre·cau·tion (pri KAW shən) *n.* **1.** a step or preparation taken to avoid a possible danger, evil, etc. **2.** preparation for a possible emergency. [< F *précaution*] —**pre·cau′tion·ar′y** *adj.*

pre·cede (pri SEED) *v.* **·ced·ed, ·ced·ing** *v.t.* **1.** go or be before in place, rank, time, etc. **2.** preface; introduce. —*v.i.* **3.** go or be before; take precedence. [< L *praecedere*]

prec·e·dence (PRES i dəns) *n.* the act, right, or state of preceding in place, time, or rank.

prec·e·dent (PRES i dənt) *n.* an act or instance capable of being used as a guide or standard in evaluating future actions. —*adj.* (pri SEED nt) former; preceding.

pre·ced·ing (pri SEE ding) *adj.* going before, as in time, place, or rank; earlier; foregoing.

pre·cept (PREE sept) *n.* a rule for guiding conduct or action; a maxim. [ME] —**pre·cep·tive** (pri SEP tive) *adj.*

pre·cep·tor (pri SEP tər) *n.* a teacher [< L *praeceptor*] —**pre·cep·to·rial** (PREE sep TOR ee əl) *adj.*

pre·ces·sion (pree SESH ən) *n.* the act of preceding. —**pre·ces′sion·al** *adj.*

pre·cinct (PREE singkt) *n.* **1.** an election district of a town, township, county, etc. **2.** a subdivision of a city or town under the jurisdiction of a police unit. **3.** a place marked off by fixed limits; also, the boundary of such a place. **4.** *pl.* neighborhood; environs. [ME]

pre·ci·os·i·ty (PRESH ee OS i tee) *n. pl.* **·ties** extreme fastidiousness or affected refinement, as in speech or style.

pre·cious (PRESH əs) *adj.* **1.** highly priced or prized; valuable: a *precious* stone. **2.** greatly esteemed or cherished. **3.** affectedly delicate or sensitive, as a style of writing. —*n.* precious one; sweetheart. —*adv.* extremely; very. [ME *preciose*] —**pre′cious·ness** *n.*

precious stone a valuable, rare gem, as the diamond, ruby, sapphire, or emerald.

prec·i·pice (PRES ə pis) *n.* a high vertical or overhanging face of rock; the brink of a cliff. [< MF]

pre·cip·i·tate (pri SIP i TAYT) *v.* **·tat·ed, ·tat·ing** *v.t.* **1.** hasten the occurrence of. **2.** hurl from or as from a height. **3.** *Meteorol.*

cause (vapor, etc.) to condense and fall as dew, rain, etc. **4.** *Chem.* separate (a substance) in solid form, as from a solution. — *v.i.* **5.** *Meteorol.* fall as condensed vapor, etc. **6.** *Chem.* separate and settle, as a substance held in solution. —*adj.* (pri SIP i tit) **1.** moving speedily or hurriedly; rushing headlong. **2.** lacking due deliberation; hasty; rash. —*n.* (pri SIP i tit) *Chem.* a deposit of solid matter formed by precipitation. [< L *praecipitatus* cast down] — **pre·cip′i·tate·ly** *adv.* —**pre·cip′i·tate·ness** *n.*

pre·cip·i·ta·tion (pri SIP i TAY shən) *n.* **1.** *Meteorol.* **a** the depositing of moisture from the atmosphere upon the surface of the earth. **b** the amount of rain, snow, etc., deposited. **2.** *Chem.* the process of separating in the form of a solid any of the constituents of a solution. **3.** rash haste or hurry.

pre·cip·i·tous (pri SIP i təs) *adj.* **1.** like a precipice; very steep. **2.** having many precipices. —**pre·cip′i·tous·ly** *adv.* — **pre·cip′i·tous·ness** *n.*

pré·cis (pray SEE) *n. pl.* **pré·cis** (-SEEZ) a concise summary of a book, article, or document; abstract. [< F]

pre·cise (pri SIS) *adj.* **1.** sharply and clearly determined or defined. **2.** no more and no less than; exact in amount. **3.** scrupulously observant of rule. [ME] —**pre·cise′ly** *adv.* —**pre·cise′ness** *n.*

pre·ci·sion (pri SIZH ən) *n.* the state or quality of being precise; accuracy. —*adj.* designed for extremely accurate measurement: *precision* instruments.

pre·clude (pri KLOOD) *v.t.* **·clud·ed, ·clud·ing 1.** make impossible or ineffectual by prior action. **2.** shut out; exclude. [< L *praeclaudere* close off] —**pre·clu·sion** (pri KLOO *zh*ən) *n.* —**pre·clu·sive** (pri KLOO siv) *adj.*

pre·co·cious (pri KOH shəs) *adj.* unusually developed or advanced for one's age. — **pre·co′cious·ly** *adv.* **pre·co′cious·ness, pre·coc′i·ty** (pri KOS i tee) *n.*

pre·con·ceive (PREE kən SEEV) *v.t.* **·ceived, ·ceiv·ing** conceive in advance; form an idea or opinion or beforehand. — **pre′con·cep′tion** (-SEP shən) *n.*

pre·con·di·tion (PREE kən DISH ən) *n.* a condition that must be met before a certain result is attained; prerequisite.

pre·cur·sor (pri KUR sər) *n.* one who or that which precedes and suggests the course of future events. [< L *praecursor*]

pre·da·cious (pri DAY shəs) *adj.* living by preying upon others, as a beast or bird; raptorial: also *predatory.* Also **pre·da′ceous.**

pre·date (PREE DAYT) *v.t.* **·dat·ed, ·dat·ing 1.** date before the actual time. **2.** precede in time.

pred·a·to·ry (PRED ə TOR ee) *adj.* **1.** of, relating to, or characterized by plundering. **2.** predacious. [< L *praedatorius* plundering] —**pred′a·tor** (-tər) *n.*

pre·de·cease (PREE di SEES) *v.t.* **·ceased, ·ceas·ing** die before (someone else).

pred·e·ces·sor (PRED ə SES ər) *n.* **1.** one who goes or has gone before another in time. **2.** a thing succeeded by something else. **3.** an ancestor. [ME *predecessour*]

pre·des·ti·na·tion (pri DES tə NAY shən) *n.* *Theol.* the foreordination of all things by God, including the salvation or damnation of men. [ME *predestinacioun*] —**pre·des′ti·nate** *v.t.* **·nat·ed, ·nat·ing**

pre·des·tine (pri DES tin) *v.t.* **·tined, ·tin·ing** destine or decree beforehand; foreordain.

pre·de·ter·mine (PREE di TUR min) *v.t.* **·mined, ·min·ing** determine beforehand; foreordain.

pred·i·ca·ble (PRED i kə bəl) *adj.* capable of being predicated or affirmed. [< L *praedicabilis*]

pre·dic·a·ment (pri DIK ə mənt) *n.* a trying or embarrassing situation; plight. [ME]

pred·i·cate (PRED i KAYT) *v.* **·cat·ed, ·cat·ing** *v.t.* **1.** found or base (an argument, proposition, etc.): with *on* or *upon.* **2.** affirm as a quality or attribute of something. —*v.i.* **3.** make a statement or affirmation. —*n.* (-kit) *Gram.* the verb in a sentence or clause together with its complements and modifiers. [ME] —**pred·i·ca′tion** *n.*

pre·dict (pri DIKT) *v.t.* **1.** make known beforehand; prophesy. **2.** assert on the basis of data, theory, or experience but in advance of proof. —*v.i.* **3.** make a prediction. [< L *praedictus* foretold] —**pre·dict′a·ble** *adj.* —**pre·dict′a·bly** *adv.*

pre·dic·tion (pri DIK shən) *n.* **1.** the act of predicting. **2.** something predicted. — **pre·dic′tive** *adj.* —**pre·dic′tive·ly** *adv.*

pre·di·lec·tion (PREE l EK shən) *n.* a preference or bias in favor of something; a partiality: with *for.* [< F *prédilection*]

pre·dis·pose (PREE di SPOHZ) *v.t.* **·posed, ·pos·ing** give a tendency or inclination to; make susceptible.

pre·dom·i·nant (pri DOM ə nənt) *adj.* superior in power, influence, effectiveness, number, or degree. —**pre·dom′i·nance** n. —**pre·dom′i·nant·ly** adv.

pre·dom·i·nate (pri DOM ə NAYT) v.i. **·nat·ed, ·nat·ing 1.** have governing influence or control; be in control: often with over. **2.** be superior to all others. **3.** prevail.

pre·em·i·nent (pree EM ə nənt) adj. distinguished above all others; outstanding. [ME] —**pre·em′i·nence** n. —**pre·em′ i·nent·ly** adv.

pre·empt (pree EMPT) v.t. **1.** acquire or appropriate beforehand. **2.** occupy (public land) so as to acquire by preemption. **3.** take the place of; replace.

pre·emp·tion (pree EMP shən) n. **1.** the right to purchase something before others; also, the act of so purchasing. **2.** public land obtained by exercising this right. [< L prae-ēmptus bought beforehand] —**pre·emp′ tive** adj.

preen (preen) v.t. **1.** trim and dress (feathers etc.) with the beak, as a bird. **2.** dress or adorn (oneself) carefully. **3.** pride or congratulate (oneself): with on. —v.i. **4.** primp. [ME prene]

pre·ex·ist (PREE ig ZIST) v.t. & v.i. exist before. —**pre′ex·is′tent** adj.

pre·fab·ri·cate (pree FAB ri KAYT) v.t. **·cat·ed, ·cat·ing** manufacture in standard sections that can be rapidly assembled.

pref·ace (PREF is) n. **1.** a statement or brief essay, included in the front matter of a book, etc., and dealing primarily with the purpose and scope of the work. **2.** any introductory speech, writing, etc. —v.t. **·aced, ·ac·ing 1.** furnish with a preface. **2.** serve as a preface for. [ME] —**pref·a·to·ry** (PREF ə TOR ee) adj.

pre·fect (PREE fekt) n. **1.** in ancient Rome, any of various civil and military officials. **2.** any magistrate, chief official, etc. [ME] —**pre·fec·ture** (PREE fek chər) n.

pre·fer (pri FUR) v.t. **·ferred, ·fer·ring 1.** hold in higher regard or esteem; value more. **2.** choose (something or someone) over another or others; like better. **3.** give priority to, as certain securities over others. [ME preferre]

pref·er·a·ble (PREF ər ə bəl) adj. that is preferred; more desirable. —**pref· er·a·bly** adv. [< F préférable]

pref·er·ence (PREF ər əns) n. **1.** the choosing of one person or thing over another or others; also, the privilege of so choosing. **2.** one who or that which is preferred. **3.** the

granting of special advantage to one over others.

pref·er·en·tial (PREF ə REN shəl) adj. **1.** showing or arising from preference or partiality. **2.** giving preference. —**pref′er·en′ tial·ly** adv.

pre·fer·ment (pri FUR mənt) n. **1.** the act of promoting to higher office; advancement. **2.** a position, rank, or office of social prestige or profit. **3.** the act of preferring. [ME]

preferred stock stock on which dividends must be paid before dividends can be paid on common stocks, usu. also receiving preference in the distribution of assets on liquidation.

pre·fig·ure (pree FIG yər) v.t. **·ured, ·ur·ing 1.** serve as an indication or suggestion of; foreshadow. **2.** imagine or picture to oneself beforehand. [ME]

pre·fix (PREE fiks) n. Gram. an addition at the beginning of a word, altering or modifying its meaning, as re- in renew. —v.t. put or attach before or at the beginning; add as a prefix. [ME prefixen]

preg·na·ble (PREG nə bəl) adj. **1.** capable of being captured, as a fort. **2.** open to attack; vulnerable; assailable. [ME prenable]

preg·nan·cy (PREG nən see) n. pl. **·cies 1.** the state of being pregnant. **2.** an instance of being pregnant.

preg·nant (PREG nənt) adj. **1.** carrying a growing fetus in the uterus. **2.** having considerable weight or significance; full of meaning. [ME]

pre·hen·sile (pri HEN sil) adj. adapted for grasping or holding, as the tail of a monkey. [< F préhensile]

pre·hen·sion (pri HEN shən) n. the act of grasping, physically or mentally. [< L prehendere seize]

pre·his·tor·ic (PREE hi STOR ik) adj. of or belonging to the period before written history.

pre·his·to·ry (pree HIS tə ree) n. pl. **·ries** the history of mankind in the period preceding written records.

pre·judge (pree JUJ) v.t. **·judged, ·judg·ing** judge beforehand or without proper inquiry. [< F préjuger] —**pre·judg′ment** n.

prej·u·dice (PREJ ə dis) n. **1.** a judgment or opinion formed before the facts are known; esp., an unfavorable, irrational opinion. **2.** hatred of or dislike for a particular group, race, religion, etc. **3.** injury or damage to a person arising from a hasty and unfair judgment by others. —*v.t.* •diced, •dic•ing 1. cause to have a prejudice; bias; influence. 2. damage or impair by some act, judgment, etc. [ME]

prej•u•di•cal (PREJ ə DISH əl) *adj.* tending to prejudice or injure; detrimental.

prel•ate (PREL it) *n.* an ecclesiastic of high rank, as a bishop, archbishop, etc. [ME *prelat*] —**prel'a•cy** *n.*

pre•lim•i•nar•y (pri LIM ə NAR ee) *adj.* before or introductory to the main event, proceeding, or business. —*n. pl.* •nar•ies 1. a preparatory step or act. 2. a preliminary examination. 3. in sports, a minor, introductory event, as a boxing match. [< F *préliminaire*] —**pre•lim'i•nar'i•ly** *adv.*

prel•ude (PREL yood) *n.* 1. *Music* **a** an instrumental composition of a moderate length, in a free style. **b** an opening section or movement of a musical composition. 2. any introductory or opening performance or event. [< Med.L *praeludium*] —*v.t.* •ud•ed, •ud•ing 1. introduce with a prelude. 2. serve as a prelude to.

pre•ma•ture (PREE mə CHUUR) *adj.* existing, happening, or developed before the natural or proper period; untimely. [< L *praematurus* ripened early] —**pre'ma•ture'ly** *adv.*

pre•med•i•tate (pri MED i TAYT) *v.t. & v.i.* •tat•ed, •tat•ing plan or consider beforehand. [< L *praemeditatus* pondered beforehand] —**pre•med'i•ta'tion** *n.*

pre•mier (pri MEER) *adj.* 1. first in rank or position; principal. 2. first in order or occurrence; senior. —*n.* a prime minister. [ME *primer*] —**pre•mi•er'ship** *n.*

pre•miere (pri MEER) *n.* the first performance of a play, movie, etc. —*v.t. & v.i.* •miered, •mier•ing give the first performance of (a play, movie, etc.). Also **pre•mière'**. [< F *première* first]

prem•ise (PREM is) *n.* 1. a proposition that serves as a ground for argument or for a conclusion. 2. *pl.* a definite portion of real estate; land with its appurtenances; also, a building or part of a building. —*v.* •mised, •mis•ing *v.t.* 1. state or assume as a premise or basis of argument. —*v.i.* 2. make a premise. [ME *premiss*]

pre•mi•um (PREE mee əm) *n.* 1. an object or service offered free as an inducement to buy, rent, or contract for another object or service. 2. the amount paid or payable for insurance, usu. in periodical installments.

3. an extra amount or bonus paid in addition to a fixed price, wage, etc. 4. high regard or value. 5. a reward or prize awarded in a competition. —**at a premium** 1. valuable and in demand. 2. above par. [< L *praemium* reward]

pre•mo•ni•tion (PREE mə NISH ən) *n.* 1. a presentiment of the future not based on information received; an instinctive foreboding. 2. a warning of something yet to occur. [ME *premunicioun*] —**pre•mon•i•to•ry** (pri MON i TOR ee) *adj.*

pre•na•tal (pree NAYT l) *adj.* prior to birth: *prenatal* care. —**pre•na'tal•ly** *adv.*

pre•oc•cu•pied (pree OK yə PĪD) *adj.* 1. engrossed in thought or in some action. 2. previously occupied.

pre•oc•cu•py (pree OK yə PĪ) *v.t.* •pied, •py•ing 1. engage fully; engross the mind. 2. occupy or take possession of first. —**pre•oc'cu•pa'tion** *n.*

pre•or•dain (PREE or DAYN) *v.t.* ordain beforehand; foreordain. —**pre•or•di•na•tion** (PREE or dn AY shən) *n.*

prep (prep) *adj.* preparatory: a *prep* school. —*v.t.* prepped, prep•ping prepare for an examination, for surgery, etc.

prep•a•ra•tion (PREP ə RAY shən) *n.* 1. the act or process of preparing. 2. an act or proceeding undertaken in advance of some event; provision. 3. the fact or state of being prepared. 4. something made or prepared, as a medicine. [ME *preparacion*]

preparatory school (pri PAR ə TOR ee) a private school that prepares students for college admission: also **prep school.**

pre•pare (pri PAIR) *v.* •pared, •par•ing *v.t.* 1. make ready, fit, or qualified; put in readiness. 2. provide with what is needed; equip: *prepare* an expedition. 3. bring to a state of completeness: *prepare* a meal. —*v.i.* 4. make preparations; get ready. [< L *praeparare* ready beforehand] —**pre•par•a•to•ry** (pri PAR ə TOR ee) *adj.*

pre•par•ed•ness (pri PAIR id nis) *n.* readiness; esp., military readiness for war.

pre•pay (pree PAY) *v.t.* •paid, •pay•ing pay or pay for in advance. —**pre•pay'ment** *n.*

pre•pon•der•ant (pri PON dər ənt) *adj.* having superior force, weight, importance, quantity, etc. —**pre•pon'der•ance** *n.*

pre•pon•der•ate (pri PON də RAYT) *v.i.* •at•ed, •at•ing be of greater power, importance, quantity, etc.; predominate; prevail. [< L *praeponderatus* outweighed] —**pre•pon'der•a'tion** *n.*

prep·o·si·tion (PREP ə ZISH ən) *n. Gram.* in some languages, a word, as *by, for, from,* that combines with a noun to form an adjectival or adverbial modifier. [ME *preposicioun*] —**prep′o·si′tion·al** *adj.*

pre·pos·sess (PREE pə ZES) *v.t.* **1.** preoccupy to the exclusion of other ideas, beliefs, etc. **2.** impress or influence beforehand or at once, esp. favorably. —**pre′pos·ses′sion** *n.*

pre·pos·sess·ing (PREE pə ZES ing) *adj.* inspiring a favorable opinion; pleasing. —**pre′·pos·sess′ing·ly** *adv.*

pre·pos·ter·ous (pri POS tər əs) *adj.* contrary to nature or common sense; utterly absurd. [< L *praeposterus* with rear end first] —**pre·pos′ter·ous·ness** *n.*

pre·puce (PREE pyoos) *n. Anat.* the fold of skin covering the glans of the penis or clitoris: also called *foreskin.* [ME]

Pre-Raph·a·el·ite (pree RAF ee ə LIT) *n.* any of a group of painters formed in 1848 to restore the practices characteristic of Italian art before the time of Raphael.

pre·req·ui·site (pri REK wə zit) *adj.* required for something that follows. —*n.* something prerequisite.

pre·rog·a·tive (pri ROG ə tiv) *n.* an exclusive and unquestionable right belonging to a person or body of persons; esp., a hereditary or official right. [ME]

pres·age (PRES ij) *n.* **1.** an indication of something to come; omen. **2.** a presentiment; foreboding. —*v.* •**saged,** •**sag·ing** *v.t.* **1.** give a presage or portent of; foreshadow. **2.** predict; foretell. —*v.i.* **3.** make a prediction. [ME]

pres·by·ter (PREZ bi tər) *n. Eccl.* **1.** in various hierarchical churches, a priest. **2.** in a Presbyterian church: **a** an ordained clergyman. **b** a layperson who is a member of the governing body of a congregation. [< LL, elder]

pres·by·te·ri·an (PREZ bi TEER ee ən) *adj.* pertaining to any of various Protestant churches that have church government by presbyters. —**Pres′by·te′ri·an** *n.* — **Pres′by·te′ri·an·ism** *n.*

pres·by·ter·y (PREZ bi TER ee) *n. pl.* •**ter·ies** **1.** in a Presbyterian church, a court composed of the ministers and one or two presbyters of each church in a district. **2.** that part of a church set apart for the clergy. [< LL *presbyterium* assembly of elders]

pre·science (PRESH əns) *n.* knowledge of events before they take place; foreknowledge. [ME] —**pre′scient** *adj.*

pre·scribe (pri SKRIB) *v.* •**scribed,** •**scrib·ing** *v.t.* **1.** set down as a direction or rule to be followed. **2.** *Med.* order the use of (a medicine, treatment, etc.). —*v.i.* **3.** lay down laws or rules; give directions. [ME] —**pre·scrip′tive** (pri SKRIP tiv) *adj.*

pre·scrip·tion (pri SKRIP shən) *n.* **1.** *Med.* **a** a physician's order for a medicine, including directions for its use. **b** the remedy so prescribed. **2.** the act of prescribing. **3.** that which is prescribed. [ME]

pres·ence (PREZ əns) *n.* **1.** the state or fact of being present. **2.** the area immediately surrounding a person, esp. one of superior rank, as a sovereign; also, the person or personality of a sovereign, ruler, etc. **3.** personal appearance; esp., a pleasing or dignified bearing. **4.** an invisible spirit or influence felt to be near.

pres·ent[1] (PREZ ənt) *adj.* **1.** now going on; not past or future. **2.** of or pertaining to time now occurring; current. **3.** being in the place or company referred to. **4.** being actually considered, written, discussed, etc.: *present* issues. **5.** *Gram.* denoting a tense or verb form that expresses a current or habitual action or state. —*n.* **1.** present time; the time being; now. **2.** *Gram.* the present tense. —**at present** now. [ME]

pre·sent[2] (pri ZENT) *v.t.* **1.** bring into the presence or acquaintance of another; introduce, esp. to one of higher rank. **2.** exhibit to view or notice. **3.** suggest to the mind: This *presents* a problem. **4.** put forward for consideration or action; submit, as a petition. **5.** make a gift or presentation of or to, usu. formally. —**present arms** *Mil.* salute by holding a gun vertically in front of one's body with the muzzle up and the trigger facing forward. —*n.* (PREZ ənt) something presented or given; a gift. [ME] —**pre·sent′er** *n.*

pre·sent·a·ble (pri ZEN tə bəl) *adj.* **1.** fit to be presented; in suitable condition or attire for company. **2.** capable of being offered, exhibited, or bestowed. —**pre·sent′a·bly** *adv.*

pres·en·ta·tion (PREZ ən TAY shən) *n.* **1.** the act of presenting or proffering for acceptance, approval, etc., or the state of being presented. **2.** an exhibition or representation, as of a play. [ME]

pres·ent-day (PREZ ənt DAY) *adj.* modern; current.

pre·sen·ti·ment (pri ZEN tə mənt) *n.* a prophetic sense of something to come; a foreboding. [< F *pressentiment*]

pres·ent·ly (PREZ ənt lee) *adv.* **1.** after a little time; shortly. **2.** at the present time; now. [ME]

pre·sent·ment (pri ZENT mənt) *n.* the act of presenting; also, the state or manner of being presented or exhibited. [ME *presentement*]

present participle see under PARTICIPLE.

pre·ser·va·tive (pri ZUR və tiv) *adj.* serving or tending to preserve. —*n.* a preservative agent; esp., a chemical substance added to food to retard spoilage. [ME]

pre·serve (pri ZURV) *v.* •**served**, •**serv·ing** *v.t.* **1.** keep in safety; guard: *May the gods preserve you.* **2.** keep intact or unimpaired; maintain. **3.** prepare (food) for future consumption, as by boiling with sugar or by salting. **4.** keep from decomposition or change, as by chemical treatment. **5.** make preserves, as of fruit. —*n.* **1.** *Usu. pl.* fruit that has been cooked, usu. with sugar, to prevent its fermenting. **2.** an area set apart for the protection of wildlife, forests, etc. [ME *preserven* guard] —**pres·er·va·tion** (PREZ ər VAY shən) *n.*

pre·side (pri ZĪD) *v.i.* •**sid·ed**, •**sid·ing 1.** sit in authority, as over a meeting; act as chairperson or president. **2.** exercise direction or control. [< L *praesidere* preside over]

pres·i·den·cy (PREZ i dən see) *n. pl.* •**cies** the office, function, or term of office of a president.

pres·i·dent (PREZ i dənt) *n.* **1.** one who is chosen to preside over an organized body. **2.** *Often cap.* the chief executive of a republic. **3.** the chief executive officer of a department, corporation, society, or similar body. [ME] —**pres·i·den·tial** (PREZ i DEN shəl) *adj.*

pre·sid·i·o (pri SID ee OH) *n. pl.* •**sid·i·os** a garrisoned post; fortified settlement. [< Sp.]

pre·sid·i·um (pri SID ee əm) *n. pl.* •**i·a** (-ee ə), •**i·ums** *Often cap.* an executive committee in a country that acts for a larger governmental body. [< L *praesidium*]

press¹ (pres) *v.t.* **1.** act upon by weight or pressure: *press* a button. **2.** compress so as to extract the juice: *press* grapes. **3.** exert pressure upon so as to smooth, shape, make compact, etc. **4.** smooth or shape by heat and pressure, as clothes; iron. **5.** embrace closely; hug. **6.** distress or harass; place in difficulty. **7.** urge persistently; entreat: *They pressed me for an answer.* **8.** put forward insistently: *press* a claim. **9.** produce (a phonograph record) from a matrix. —*v.i.* **10.** exert pressure; bear heavily. **11.** advance forcibly or with speed. **12.** crowd; cram. **13.** be urgent or importunate. —*n.* **1.** newspapers or periodicals collectively, or the persons concerned with such publications, as editors, reporters, etc. **2.** criticism, news, etc. in newspapers and periodicals. **3.** the place of business where printing is carried on. **4.** a printing press. **5.** an apparatus by which pressure is applied, as for crushing grapes. **6.** the act of crowding together. **7.** hurry or pressures of affairs. **8.** the proper creases in a pressed garment. [ME *presse* crowd]

press² *v.t.* force into military or naval service.

press agent a person employed to advance the interests of another by means of publicity.

press conference an interview granted by a celebrity, official, etc. to a number of journalists at the same time.

press·ing (PRES ing) *adj.* urgent; demanding immediate attention.

press·man (PRES mən) *n. pl.* •**men** one in charge of a press, as a printing press.

press release a bulletin prepared by a public relations department etc., announcing an event, decision, etc.

pres·sure (PRESH ər) *n.* **1.** the act of pressing, or the state of being pressed. **2.** any force that acts against an opposing force. **3.** urgent demands on one's time or strength. **4.** the oppressive influence or depressing effect of something hard to bear; weight. **5.** *Physics* the force acting upon a surface per unit of area. —*v.t.* •**sured**, •**sur·ing** compel, as by forceful persuasion. [ME].

pressure cooker 1. a strong, airtight pot for cooking food at high temperature under pressure. **2.** any situation inducing intense pressure on a person or persons.

pressure group a group that seeks to influence legislators and public opinion in behalf of its own special interests.

pres·sur·ize (PRESH ə RĪZ) *v.t.* •**ized**, •**iz·ing 1.** subject to high pressure. **2.** establish normal atmospheric pressure (in an aircraft etc.) when at high altitudes. —**pres′sur·i·za′tion** *n.*

pres·ti·dig·i·ta·tion (PRES ti DIJ i TAY

shэn] *n.* the practice of sleight of hand. [<
F] —**pres′ti·dig′i·ta′tor** *n.*

pres·tige (pre STEEZH) *n.* authority or importance based on past achievements, reputation, power, etc. [< F]

pres·tig·ious (pre STIJ эs) *adj.* having prestige; honored or well-known; illustrious.

pres·to (PRES toh) *adj. Music* quick; faster
than allegro. —*adv.* **1.** *Music* in a presto
manner. **2.** at once; speedily. —*n. Music* a
presto movement or passage. [< Ital.]

pre·stressed concrete (pree STREST)
concrete containing steel cables under tension to increase its strength and counteract
external stresses.

pre·sum·a·ble (pri ZOO mэ bэl) *adj.* that
may be assumed; reasonable. —**pre·sum′**
a·bly *adv.*

pre·sume (pri ZOOM) *v.* •**sumed,**
•**sum·ing** *v.t.* **1.** assume to be true until
disproved. **2.** take upon oneself without
permission; venture: usu. with *to.* **3.** indicate the probability of: *A concealed weapon
presumes the intent to commit a crime.* —
v.i. **4.** act presumptuously or overconfi-
dently. [ME *presumen*] —**pre·sum′**
•**ed·ly** *adv.*

pre·sump·tion (pri ZUMP shэn) *n.* **1.** offensively forward or arrogant conduct or
speech; insolence. **2.** the act of presuming;
also, something presumed. **3.** that which
may be logically assumed true until disproved. **4.** *Law* the inference of a fact from
circumstances that usually or necessarily
attend such a fact. [ME]

pre·sump·tive (pri ZUMP tiv) *adj.* **1.** creating or affording reasonable grounds for belief. **2.** based on presumption: *an heir
presumptive.* —**pre·sump′tive·ly** *adv.*

pre·sump·tu·ous (pri ZUMP choo эs) *adj.*
unduly confident or bold; audacious; arrogant. —**pre·sump′tu·ous·ness** *n.*

pre·sup·pose (PREE sэ POHZ) *v.t.* •**posed,**
•**pos·ing 1.** assume beforehand. **2.** imply
as a necessary antecedent condition. —
pre·sup·po·si·tion (PREE sup э ZISH эn)
n.

pre·tend (pri TEND) *v.t.* **1.** assume or display a false appearance of; feign. **2.** claim or
assert falsely. **3.** feign in play; make believe.
—*v.i.* **4.** make believe, as in play or deception. **5.** put forward a claim: with *to.* [ME
pretenden]

pre·tend·er (pri TEN dэr) *n.* **1.** one who
advances a claim or title; a claimant to a
throne. **2.** one who pretends.

pre·tense (pri TENS) *n.* **1.** a pretended
claim; pretext. **2.** a false assumption of a
character or condition. **3.** the act or state of
pretending. —**pre·ten′sion** (-shэn) *n.*

pre·ten·tious (pri TEN shэs) *adj.* **1.** making
an ambitious outward show; ostentatious.
2. making claims, esp. when exaggerated or
false. —**pre·ten′tious·ness** *n.*

pre·ter·nat·u·ral (PREE tэr NACH эr эl)
adj. **1.** diverging from or exceeding the
common order of nature; unusual or abnormal. **2.** outside the natural order. [< Med.L
praeteraturalis]

pre·text (PREE tekst) *n.* **1.** a fictitious reason or motive advanced to conceal a real
one. **2.** a specious excuse or explanation. [<
L *praetextum*]

pret·ti·fy (PRIT э FI) *v.t.* •**fied,** •**fy·ing**
make pretty; embellish overmuch.

pret·ty (PRIT ee) *adj.* •**ti·er,** •**ti·est 1.** characterized by delicacy, gracefulness, or proportion rather than by striking beauty. **2.**
pleasant; attractive: *a pretty melody.* **3.** *Informal* rather large in size or degree; considerable. —*adv.* to a fair extent; rather: He
looked *pretty* well. —**sitting pretty** *Informal* in good circumstances. —*n. pl.* •**ties** a
pretty person or thing. [ME *pratie* cun-
ning] —**pret′ti·ly** *adv.* —**pret′ti·ness** *n.*

pret·zel (PRET sэl) *n.* a glazed, salted biscuit, usu. baked in the form of a loose knot.
[< G *Bretzel*]

pre·vail (pri VAYL) *v.i.* **1.** gain mastery; triumph. **2.** be effective or efficacious. **3.** use
persuasion or influence successfully: with
on, upon, or *with.* **4.** be or become a predominant feature or quality; be prevalent.
[ME *prevayllen* grow strong]

pre·vail·ing (pri VAY ling) *adj.* **1.** current;
prevalent. **2.** having effective power or influence; efficacious.

prev·a·lent (PREV э lэnt) *adj.* **1.** of wide
extent or frequent occurrence; common. **2.**
predominant; superior. —**prev′a·lence** *n.*

pre·var·i·cate (pri VAR i KAYT) *v.i.* •**cat·ed,**
•**cat·ing** speak or act in a deceptive or evasive manner; lie. [< L *praevaricatus* bent
outward] —**pre·var′i·ca′tion** *n.* —
pre·var′i·ca′tor *n.*

pre·vent (pri VENT) *v.t.* **1.** keep from happening, as by previous preparations; pre-
clude; thwart. **2.** keep from doing
something; forestall; hinder. [ME] —
pre·vent′a·ble or **pre·vent′i·ble** *adj.* —
pre·ven′tion *n.*

pre·ven·tive (pri VEN tiv) *adj.* intended or

serving to ward off harm, disease, etc.: *preventive* medicine. —*n.* that which prevents or hinders.

pre·view (PREE vyoo) *n.* **1.** an advanced showing, as of a motion picture, esp. before public viewing. **2.** a showing of scenes from a motion picture, television show, etc., as advertising: also **pre′vue. 3.** a preliminary view; foretaste. —*v.t.* view in advance.

pre·vi·ous (PREE vee əs) *adj.* **1.** existing or taking place before something else in time or order. **2.** *Informal* acting or occurring too soon; premature. —**previous to** antecedent to; before. [< L *praevius* going before] —**pre′vi·ous·ly** *adv.*

pre·vi·sion (pri VIZH ən) *n.* **1.** the act or power of foreseeing; prescience; foresight. **2.** an anticipatory vision.

prey (pray) *n.* **1.** any animal seized by another for food. **2.** a victim of a harmful or hostile person or influence.—*v.i.* **1.** seek or take prey for food. **2.** make someone a victim, as by cheating. **3.** exert a wearing or harmful influence; usu. with *on* or *upon.* [ME *preye*] —**prey′er** *n.*

price (prīs) *n.* **1.** the amount of money, goods, etc. for which something is bought or sold. **2.** the cost at which something is obtained. **3.** value; worth. **4.** a reward for the capture or death of someone. —*v.t.* **priced, pric·ing 1.** set a price on; establish a price for. **2.** ask the price of. [ME *prise*]

price fixing 1. the establishment and maintenance of a scale of prices by specified groups of producers or distributors. **2.** the establishing by law of maximum or minimum or fixed prices for certain goods and services.

price·less (PRĪS lis) *adj.* **1.** beyond price or valuation; invaluable. **2.** wonderfully amusing or absurd.

prick (prik) *v.t.* **1.** pierce slightly, as with a sharp point; puncture. **2.** affect with a sharp mental sting; spur. **3.** outline or indicate by punctures. **4.** urge on with or as with a spur; goad. —*v.i.* **5.** have or cause a stinging or piercing sensation. —**prick up one's (or its) ears 1.** raise the ears erect. **2.** listen attentively. —*n.* **1.** the act of pricking; also, the sensation of being pricked. **2.** a mental sting or spur. **3.** a slender, sharp-pointed thing, as a thorn or weapon. [ME *prike*] — **prick′er** *n.*

prick·le (PRIK əl) *n.* **1.** a small, sharp point, as on a plant. **2.** a tingling or stinging sensation. —*v.* **·led, ·ling** *v.t.* **1.** prick; pierce. **2.**

cause a tingling or stinging sensation in. — *v.i.* **3.** have a stinging sensation; tingle. [ME *prykel*]

prick·ly (PRIK lee) *adj.* **·li·er, ·li·est 1.** furnished with prickles. **2.** stinging, as if from a prick or sting.

prickly heat a rash characterized by redness, itching, and small eruptions.

pride (prīd) *n.* **1.** an undue sense of one's own superiority; arrogance; conceit. **2.** a proper sense of personal dignity and worth. **3.** that of which one is justly proud. **4.** the best time or the flowering of something: the *pride* of summer. **5.** a group or company: said of lions. —*v.t.* **prid·ed, prid·ing** take pride in (oneself) for something: with *on* or *upon.* [ME]

pride·ful (PRĪD fəl) *adj.* full of pride; haughty; disdainful.

priest (preest) *n.* **1.** one consecrated to the service of a divinity, and serving as mediator between the divinity and worshipers. **2.** in hierarchical churches, a member of the clergy ranking next below a bishop, and having authority to administer the sacraments. [ME *preste*] —**priest′ess** *n.fem.* **priest′ly** *adj.*

priest·hood (PREEST huud) *n.* **1.** the priestly office or character. **2.** priests collectively.

prig (prig) *n.* a narrow-minded person who assumes superior virtue and wisdom. — **prig′gish** *adj.* —**prig′gish·ness** *n.*

prim (prim) *adj.* **prim·mer, prim·mest** minutely or affectedly precise and formal; stiffly proper and neat. —*v.t.* **primmed, prim·ming** fix (the face, mouth, etc.) in a precise or prim expression.—**prim′ly** *adv.* —**prim′ness** *n.*

pri·ma·cy (PRĪ mə see) *n.* **1.** the state of being first, as in rank or excellence. **2.** *pl.* **·cies** the office or province of a primate; archbishopric. **3.** *pl.* **·cies** in the Roman Catholic Church, the office of the Pope. [ME *primacie*]

pri·ma don·na (PREE mə DON ə) *pl.* **pri·ma don·nas 1.** a leading female singer, as in an opera company. **2.** a temperamental or vain person. [< Ital., lit., first lady]

pri·ma fa·ci·e (PRĪ mə FAY shə) *Latin* at first view; so far as it first appears.

prima facie evidence evidence that, if unexplained or uncontradicted, would establish the fact alleged.

pri·mal (PRĪ məl) *adj.* **1.** being at the beginning or foundation; first; original. **2.** most important; chief. [< Med.L *primalis*]

pri•ma•ri•ly (prī MER ə lee) *adv.* in the first place; originally; essentially.

pri•ma•ry (PRĪ mer ee) *adj.* **1.** first in time or origin; primitive. **2.** first in a series or sequence. **3.** first in rank or importance; chief. **4.** constituting the fundamental or original elements of which a whole is composed; basic; elemental. **5.** of the first stage of development; elementary; lowest: *primary* school. —*n. pl.* **•ries 1.** that which is first in rank, dignity, or importance. **2.** *Usu. pl.* a direct primary election. **3.** one of the primary colors. [ME]

primary accent see under ACCENT.

primary cell *Electr.* any of several devices consisting of two electrodes immersed in an electrolyte and capable of generating a current by chemical action when the electrodes are in contact through a conducting wire. Also called *voltaic cell.*

primary colors any set of colors considered basic to all other colors, as red, yellow, and blue or red, green, and blue.

primary election a meeting or election by local voters to choose their candidates for office or to select delegates to a nominating convention.

primary school a school for very young pupils; elementary school.

pri•mate (PRĪ mayt) *n.* **1.** the prelate highest in rank in a nation or province. [ME *primat* religious leader] **2.** any of an order of mammals including the monkeys, apes, and man. [< NL]

prime (prīm) *adj.* **1.** first in rank or importance. **2.** first in value or quality. **3.** first in time or order; original; primitive. **4.** *Math.* divisible by no whole number except itself and 1. —*n.* **1.** the period of full vigor, beauty, and power succeeding youth and preceding middle age. **2.** the period of full perfection in anything; dawn. **4.** the best of anything. **5.** *Math.* a number that cannot be divided except by itself or by 1. **6.** a mark or accent (′) written above and to the right of a letter or figure; also, an inch, a minute, etc., as indicated by that sign. —*v.* **primed, prim•ing** *v.t.* **1.** prepare; make ready. **2.** put a primer into (a gun etc.) preparatory to firing. **3.** pour water into (a pump) so as to displace air and promote suction. **4.** cover (a surface) with sizing, a first coat of paint, etc. **5.** supply beforehand with information; brief.

—*v.i.* **6.** make something ready, as for firing, pumping, etc. [ME]

prime meridian a meridian from which longitude is reckoned, now, generally, the one that passes through Greenwich, England.

prime minister the chief minister and head of a cabinet, and often the chief executive of a government.

prim•er[1] (PRIM ər) *n.* **1.** an elementary textbook; esp., a beginning reading book. **2.** an introductory book on any subject. [ME]

prim•er[2] (PRĪ mər) *n.* **1.** any device, as a cap, tube, etc., used to detonate the main charge of a gun, mine, etc. **2.** any substance used in priming, as the first layer of paint applied to a surface.

pri•me•val (prī MEE vəl) *adj.* belonging to the first ages; primitive. [< L *primaevus* young] —**pri•me′val•ly** *adv.*

prim•i•tive (PRIM i tiv) *adj.* **1.** pertaining to the beginning or origin; earliest; primary. **2.** eesembling the manners or style of early times; simple; crude. **3.** *Anthropol.* of or pertaining to the earliest anthropological forms or civilizations. **4.** *Biol.* being or occurring at an early stage of development or growth; rudimentary. —*n.* **1.** an artist, or a work of art, belonging to an early period; also, a work resembling such art, or an artist producing it. **2.** one who or that which is primitive. [ME] —**prim′i•tive•ness** *n.*

pri•mo•gen•i•tor (PRĪ mə JEN i tər) *n.* an earliest ancestor; a forefather. [< LL, ancestor]

pri•mo•gen•i•ture (PRĪ mə JEN i chər) *n.* **1.** the state of being the first-born child. **2.** the exclusive right of the eldest son to inherit the property, title, etc., of a parent. [< Med.L *primogenitura* first birth]

pri•mor•di•al (prī MOR dee əl) *adj.* **1.** first in time; original; elemental. **2.** *Biol.* first in order or appearance in the growth or development of an organism. [ME] —**pri•mor′di•al•ly** *adv.*

primp (primp) *v.t. & v.i.* dress up, esp. with superfluous attention to detail.

prince (prins) *n.* **1.** a nonreigning male member of a royal family; esp., the son of a sovereign. **2.** a male monarch or sovereign. **3.** one of the highest rank of any class: merchant *prince.* [ME]

prince consort the husband of a reigning female sovereign.

prince•ly (PRINS lee) *adj.* **•li•er, •li•est 1.** liberal; generous. **2.** like or suitable for a prince. **3.** having the rank of a prince. —

adv. in a princely manner. **—prince′ li•ness** *n.*

prin•cess (PRIN sis) *n.* **1.** a nonreigning female member of a royal family; esp., the daughter of a sovereign. **2.** the consort of a prince.

prin•ci•pal (PRIN sə pəl) *adj.* first in rank, character, or importance. **—n. 1.** one who takes a leading part in some action. **2.** *Law* **a** the perpetrator of a crime, or one present aiding and abetting. **b** the employer of one who acts as an agent. **c** one primarily liable for whom another has become surety. **3.** the head teacher or officer of a school. **4.** property or capital, as opposed to interest or income. [ME] **—prin′ci•pal•ly** *adv.*

prin•ci•pal•i•ty (PRIN sə PAL i tee) *n. pl.* **•ties** the territory of a reigning prince. [ME *principalite*]

principal parts the inflected forms of a verb.

prin•ci•ple (PRIN sə pəl) *n.* **1.** a general truth or law, basic to other truths. **2.** a rule of personal conduct. **3.** moral standards collectively: a person of *principle*. **4.** a primary source or fundamental cause. **5.** an established mode of action or operation in natural phenomena: the *principle* of relativity. [ME]

prin•ci•pled (PRIN sə pəld) *adj.* having or characterized by ethical principles: often in combination: *high-principled.*

print (print) *n.* **1.** an impression with ink from type, plates, etc.; printed characters collectively; also, any printed matter. **2.** anything printed from an engraved plate or lithographic stone. **3.** a mark made by pressure; imprint. **4.** any fabric stamped with a design. **5.** *Photog.* a positive picture made from a negative. [ME *prente*] **—in print** printed; also, for sale in printed form. **— out of print** no longer on sale, the edition being exhausted: said of books etc. **—v.t. 1.** mark, as with inked type, a stamp, die, etc. **2.** fix as if by impressing: The scene is *printed* on my memory. **3.** produce (a book, newspaper, etc.) by the application of inked type, plates, etc. to paper or similar material. **4.** cause to be put in print; publish. **5.** write in letters similar to those used in print. **6.** *Photog.* produce (a positive picture) by transmitting light through a negative onto a sensitized surface. **—v.i. 7.** take or give an impression in printing. **8.** form letters similar to printed ones. **—print′ a•ble** *adj.*

print•ing (PRIN ting) *n.* **1.** the making and issuing of printed matter. **2.** the act of reproducing a design upon a surface. **3.** the number of copies of anything printed at one time. **4.** writing that resembles printed matter.

printing press a mechanism for printing from an inked surface, operating by pressure.

print•out (PRINT owt) *n.* material printed automatically, as by a computer.

pri•or[1] (PRĪ ər) *adj.* preceding in time, order, or importance. **—prior to** before. [< L, superior]

pri•or[2] *n.* in a monastery, an officer next in rank below an abbot. [< L] **—pri′or•ate** (-it) *n.*

pri•or•ess (PRĪ ər is) *n.* a woman holding a position corresponding to that of a prior; a nun next below an abbess.

pri•or•i•ty (PRĪ OR i tee) *n. pl.* **•ties 1.** antecedence; precedence. **2.** a first right established on emergency or need. [ME]

pri•o•ry (PRĪ ə ree) *n. pl.* **•or•ies** a monastic house presided over by a prior or prioress. [ME *priorie*]

prism (PRIZ əm) *n.* **1.** *Geom.* a solid whose ends are equal and parallel plane figures, and whose lateral faces are parallelograms. **2.** *Optics* a transparent prism, usu. having triangular ends, used to produce a spectrum or to refract light beams. [< LL *prisma*] **—pris•mat′ic** (priz MAT ik) *adj.*

pris•on (PRIZ ən) *n.* **1.** a public building for the safekeeping of persons in legal custody; a penitentiary. **2.** a place or state of confinement. [ME]

pris•on•er (PRIZ ə nər) *n.* one who is confined in a prison or whose liberty is forcibly restrained.

pris•sy (PRIS ee) *adj.* **•si•er, •si•est** effeminate; overprecise; prim. [Blend of PRIM + SISSY]

pris•tine (PRIS teen) *adj.* **1.** of or pertaining to the earliest state or time; primitive. **2.** extremely pure; untouched; unspoiled. [< L *pristinus* early]

pri•va•cy (PRĪ və see) *n. pl.* **•cies 1.** the condition of being private; seclusion. **2.** the state of being secret; secrecy.

pri•vate (PRĪ vit) *adj.* **1.** removed from public view; secluded. **2.** not for public or common use. **3.** having no official rank, character, office, etc.: a *private* citizen. **4.** not generally known; secret. **5.** individual; personal: my *private* opinion. **—n. 1.** *Mil.* a soldier ranking below a corporal. **2.** *pl.* the genitals; also **private parts.** **—in private** in secret. [ME] **—pri′vate·ly** *adv.*

private detective a detective employed by a private citizen, business enterprise, etc., rather than by a city or state.

pri·va·teer (PRĪ və TEER) *n.* **1.** a vessel owned and commanded by private persons, but carrying on maritime war under government authorization. **2.** the commander or one of the crew of a privateer. **—***v.i.* cruise in or as a privateer.

private eye *Slang* a private detective.

private first class a soldier ranking next above a private and below a corporal.

pri·va·tion (prī VAY shən) *n.* the state of lacking something necessary or desirable; esp., want of the common comforts of life. [ME *privacion*] **—priv·a·tive** (PRIV ə tiv) *adj.*

priv·i·lege (PRIV ə lij) *n.* **1.** a special or peculiar benefit, favor, or advantage. **2.** an exemption or immunity by virtue of one's office or station. **3.** a fundamental civil, legal, or political right: the *privilege* of voting. **—***v.t.* **·leged, ·leg·ing** grant a privilege to. [ME]

priv·i·leged (PRIV ə lijd) *adj.* having or enjoying a privilege.

priv·y (PRIV ee) *adj.* knowing about a secret transaction: with *to.* **—***n. pl.* **priv·ies 1.** *Law* one who is concerned with another in a matter affecting the interests of both. **2.** a small toilet or outhouse. [ME *prive*]

prix fixe (PREE FEEKS) a meal served at a fixed price. [< F]

prize¹ (prīz) *n.* **1.** that which is offered or won as a reward, as in a contest or lottery. **2.** anything to be striven for. **—***adj.* **1.** offered or awarded as a prize: a *prize* horse. **2.** highly valued or esteemed. **—***v.t.* **prized, priz·ing 1.** value highly. **2.** estimate the value of; appraise. [ME *pris*]

prize² *n.* property, as a vessel and cargo, captured by a belligerent at sea. **—***v.t.* **prized, priz·ing 1.** seize as a prize, as a ship. **2.** raise or force with a lever; pry. [ME *prise*]

prize·fight (PRĪZ FĪT) *n.* a professional boxing match. **—prize′fight′er** *n.* **—prize′fight′ing** *n.*

pro¹ (proh) *n. pl.* **pros 1.** an argument or vote in favor of something. **2.** *Usu. pl.* one who votes for or favors a proposal. **—***adv.* in behalf of; in favor of; for. [< L, for]

pro² *n. pl.* **pros** *Informal* **1.** a professional

athlete. **2.** an expert in any field. [Short for PROFESSIONAL]

pro-¹ *prefix* **1.** forward; toward the front from a position behind: *project.* **2.** forward in time or direction: *proceed.* **3.** in behalf of: *prolocutor.* **4.** in place of; substituted for: *proconsul.* **5.** in favor of: *pro-Russian.* [< L *pro* before]

pro-² *prefix* **1.** prior; occurring earlier in time: *prognosis.* **2.** situated in front; forward; before: *prognathous.* [ME]

prob·a·bil·i·ty (PROB ə BIL i tee) *n. pl.* **·ties 1.** the state or quality of being probable; likelihood. **2.** a probable event, statement, condition, etc.

prob·a·ble (PROB ə bəl) *adj.* **1.** likely to be true or to happen, but leaving room for doubt. **2.** that renders something worthy of belief, but falls short of demonstration: *probable* evidence. [ME]

prob·a·bly (PROB ə blee) *adv.* in all probability.

pro·bate (PROH bayt) *adj.* **1.** of or pertaining to a probate court. **2.** pertaining to making proof. **—***v.t.* **·bat·ed, ·bat·ing** establish legal proof of, as a will. [ME *probat*]

probate court a court having jurisdiction of the proof of wills, of guardianships, and of the settlement of estates.

pro·ba·tion (proh BAY shən) *n.* **1.** *Law* a method of allowing a convicted person to go at large but usu. under supervision. **2.** a proceeding or period designed to test character, qualifications, etc., as of a new employee. **—pro·ba′tion·ar′y** *adj.*

pro·ba·tive (PROH bə tiv) *adj.* **1.** serving to prove or test. **2.** pertaining to probation; proving.

probe (prohb) *v.* **probed, prob·ing** *v.t.* **1.** explore with a probe. **2.** investigate or examine thoroughly. **—***v.i.* **3.** penetrate; search. **—***n.* **1.** *Surg.* an instrument for exploring cavities, wounds, etc. **2.** a searching investigation or inquiry, esp. into crime. [< Med.L *proba* examination] **—prob′er** *n.*

pro·bi·ty (PROH bi tee) *n.* integrity; honesty. [< MF *probité*]

prob·lem (PROB ləm) *n.* **1.** a perplexing question or situation, esp. when difficult or uncertain of solution. **2.** any puzzling or difficult circumstance or person. [ME *probleme*] **—***adj.*

prob·lem·at·ic (PROB lə MAT ik) *adj.* constituting or involving a problem; questionable; contingent. Also **prob′lem·at′i·cal.**

pro•bos•cis (prə BOS is) *n. pl.* **•bos•cis•es** or **•bos•ci•des** (-BOS i deez) *Zool.* **a** a long, flexible snout. **b** the trunk of an elephant. **c** *Humorous* the human nose. [< L]

pro•ce•dure (prə SEE jər) *n.* **1.** a manner of proceeding or acting in any course of action. **2.** the methods or forms of conducting a business, parliamentary affairs, etc. [< F *procédure*] —**pro•ce'du•ral** (-jər əl) *adj.*

pro•ceed (prə SEED) *v.i.* **1.** go on or forward, esp. after a stop. **2.** begin and carry on an action or process. **3.** issue or come, as from some source: with *form*. [ME *proceden*]

pro•ceed•ing (prə SEE ding) *n.* **1.** an act or course of action; also, a particular act or course of action. **2.** the act of one who or that which proceeds. **3.** *pl.* the records or minutes of the meetings of a society, etc. **4.** *Law* any action instituted in a court.

pro•ceeds (PROH seedz) *n.pl.* the amount derived from the disposal of goods, work, or the use of capital; return; yield.

pro•cess (PROS es) *n.* **1.** a course or method of operations in the production of something. **2.** a series of continuous actions that bring about a particular result: the *process* of growth. **3.** a forward movement; advance; course. **4.** *Law* **a** any judicial writ, esp. an order to bring a defendant into court. **b** the whole course of proceedings in a cause. **5.** *Biol.* an outgrowth of an organism. —*adj.* produced by a special method: *process* cheese. —*v.t.* **1.** subject to a routine procedure: *process* an application. **2.** treat or prepare by a special method. [ME *proces*] —**proc'es•sor** *n.*

pro•ces•sion (prə SESH ən) *n.* an array, as of persons or vehicles, arranged in succession and moving in a formal manner; a parade; also, any continuous course: the *procession* of the stars. [ME]

pro•ces•sion•al (prə SESH ə nl) *adj.* of, pertaining to, or moving in a procession. —*n.* **1.** a hymn sung at the opening of a church service, during the entrance of the choir, etc. **2.** the music played or sung during a procession.

pro•claim (proh KLAYM) *v.t.* **1.** announce or make known publicly or officially; declare. **2.** make plain; manifest. [ME] —**proc•la•ma•tion** (PROK lə MAY shən) *n.*

pro•cliv•i•ty (proh KLIV i tee) *n. pl.* **•ties** natural tendency. [< L *proclivitas*]

pro•cras•ti•nate (proh KRAS tə NAYT) *v.* **•nat•ed, •nat•ing** *v.i.* **1.** put off taking ac-

tion until a future time; be dilatory. —*v.t.* **2.** defer or postpone. [< L *procrastinatus* put off] —**pro•cras'ti•na'tion** *n.* —**pro•cras'ti•na'tor** *n.*

pro•cre•ate (PROH kree AYT) *v.t. & v.i.* **•at•ed, •at•ing** engender or beget (offspring). [< L *procreatus* bred] —**pro'cre•a'tive** *adj.* —**pro'cre•a'tion** *n.*

Pro•crus•te•an (proh KRUS tee ən) *adj.* ruthlessly or violently bringing about conformity. [< L *Procrustes*, giant of Greek mythology, who stretched or maimed captives to fit his iron bed]

procto- *combining form Med.* related to or affecting the rectum. [< Gk. *proktós* anus]

proc•tol•o•gy (prok TOL ə jee) *n.* the branch of medicine that treats of the diseases of the rectum. —**proc•tol'o•gist** *n.*

proc•tor (PROK tər) *n.* one charged with maintaining order, supervising examinations, etc. —*v.t. & v.i.* supervise (an examination). [ME]

pro•cure (proh KYUUR) *v.* **•cured, •cur•ing** *v.t.* **1.** obtain by some effort or means; acquire. **2.** bring about; cause. **3.** obtain (women) for the sexual gratification of others. —*v.i.* **4.** be a procurer. [ME *procuren*] —**pro•cur'a•ble** *adj.* —**pro•cure'ment** *n.*

pro•cur•er (proh KYUUR ər) *n.* one who procures for another, as to gratify lust; a pimp.

prod (prod) *v.t.* **prod•ded, prod•ding 1.** punch or poke with or as with a pointed instrument. **2.** arouse mentally; goad. —*n.* **1.** any pointed instrument used for prodding; a goad. **2.** a thrust or poke. **3.** a reminder. —**prod'der** *n.*

prod•i•gal (PROD i gəl) *adj.* **1.** addicted to wasteful expenditure, as of money, time, or strength; extravagant. **2.** yielding in profusion; bountiful. —*n.* one who is wasteful or profligate; a spendthrift. [< L *prodigus* wasteful] —**prod•i•gal•i•ty** (PROD i GAL i tee) *n.* —**prod•i•gal•ly** (PROD i gə lee) *adv.*

pro•di•gious (prə DIJ əs) *adj.* **1.** enormous or extraordinary in size, quantity, or degree; vast. **2.** marvelous; amazing. [< L *prodigiosus* marvelous] —**pro•dig'ious•ly** *adv.* —**pro•dig'ious•ness** *n.*

prod•i•gy (PROD i jee) *n. pl.* **•gies 1.** a person having remarkable qualities or powers: a violin *prodigy*. **2.** something extraordinary. [< L *prodigium* omen]

pro•duce (prə DOOS) *v.* **•duced, •duc•ing**

v.t. **1.** bring forth or bear; yield, as young or a natural product. **2.** bring forth by mental effort; compose, write, etc. **3.** bring about: His words *produced* a violent reaction. **4.** bring to view; exhibit: *produce* evidence. **5.** manufacture; make. **6.** bring to performance before the public, as a play. —*v.i.* **7.** yield or generate an appropriate product or result. —*n.* (PROD oos) that which is produced; a product; esp., farm products collectively. [ME *producen* extend] — **pro·duc′er** *n.* —**pro·duc′i·ble** *adj.*

prod·uct (PROD əkt) *n.* **1.** anything produced or obtained as by generation, growth, labor, study, or skill. **2.** *Math.* the result obtained by multiplication. [ME]

pro·duc·tion (prə DUK shən) *n.* **1.** the act or process of producing. **2.** any tangible result of industrial, artistic, or literary effort. [ME]

pro·duc·tive (prə DUK tiv) *adj.* **1.** producing; creative, as of artistic things. **2.** producing profits or increase in quantity, quality, or value. **3.** causing; resulting in: with *of.* — **pro·duc·tiv·i·ty** (PROH duk TIV ə tee), **pro·duc′tive·ness** *n.*

pro·em (PROH em) *n.* an introductory statement; preface. [ME *proheme*]

pro·fane (proh FAYN) *v.t.* **-faned, -fan·ing 1.** treat (something sacred) with irreverence or abuse; desecrate; pollute. **2.** put to an unworthy or degrading use; debase. — *adj.* **1.** manifesting irreverence or disrespect toward God or sacred things. **2.** not religious or concerned with religious things; secular. **3.** vulgar; common; coarse. [ME *prophane*] —**prof·a·na·tion** (PROF ə NAY shən) *n.*

pro·fan·i·ty (prə FAN i tee) *n. pl.* **-ties 1.** the state of being profane. **2.** profane speech or action.

pro·fess (prə FES) *v.t.* **1.** declare openly; avow; affirm. **2.** assert, usu. insincerely: *profess* remorse. **3.** declare or affirm faith in. **4.** have as one's profession: *profess* the law. —*v.i.* **5.** make open declaration; avow. [ME]

pro·fess·ed·ly (prə FES id lee) *adv.* **1.** by open profession; avowedly. **2.** pretendedly.

pro·fes·sion (prə FESH ən) *n.* **1.** an occupation that properly involves a liberal, scientific, or artistic education. **2.** the collective body of those following such occupations. **3.** the act of professing or declaring; declaration. **4.** that which is avowed or professed; a declaration. [ME]

pro·fes·sion·al (prə FESH ə nl) *adj.* **1.** connected with, preparing for, engaged in, appropriate to, or conforming to a profession. **2.** of or pertaining to an occupation pursued for gain: *professional* athlete. —*n.* **1.** one who pursues as a business some vocation or occupation. **2.** one who engages for money to compete in sports. —**pro·fes′ ·sion·al·ism** *n.* —**pro·fes′sion·al·ly** *adv.*

pro·fes·sor (prə FES ər) *n.* a teacher of the highest rank in a university or college. [ME] —**pro·fes·so·ri·al** (PROH fə SOR ee əl) *adj.* —**pro·fes′sor·ship** *n.*

prof·fer (PROF ər) *v.t.* offer for acceptance. [ME *profren*] —*n.* an offer; suggestion.

pro·fi·cient (prə FISH ənt) *adj.* thoroughly versed, as in an art or science. —*n.* an expert. [< L *proficere* accomplish] —**pro·fi′ cien·cy** *n.* —**pro·fi′cient·ly** *adv.*

pro·file (PROH fil) *n.* **1.** the outline of a human face or figure as seen from the side; also, a drawing of this outline. **2.** any outline or contour. **3.** a short biographical sketch. —*v.t.* **-filed, -fil·ing 1.** draw a profile of. **2.** write or make a profile of. [< Ital. *profilo*]

prof·it (PROF it) *n.* **1.** any advantage or gain; benefit. **2.** *Often pl.* excess of returns over outlay or expenditure. **3.** the return from the employment of capital after deducting the amount paid for raw material and for wages, rent, interest, etc. —**gross profit** the excess of receipts from sales over expenditures for production or purchase. —**net profit** the surplus remaining after all necessary deductions, as for interest, bad debts, etc. —*v.i.* **1.** be of advantage or benefit. **2.** derive gain or benefit. —*v.t.* **3.** be of profit or advantage to. [ME] —**prof′it·less** *adj.*

prof·it·a·ble (PROF i tə bəl) *adj.* bringing profit or gain; advantageous. —**prof′ it·a·bil′i·ty** *n.* —**prof′it·a·bly** *adv.*

prof·i·teer (PROF i TEER) *v.i.* seek or obtain excessive profits. —*n.* one who is given to making excessive profits, esp. to the detriment of others. —**prof′i·teer′ing** *n.*

prof·li·ga·cy (PROF li gə see) *n.* the state or quality, or an instance of being profligate.

prof·li·gate (PROF li git) *adj.* **1.** lost or insensible to principle, virtue, or decency. **2.** recklessly extravagant; in great profusion. —*n.* **1.** a depraved or dissolute person. **2.** a reckless spendthrift. [< L *profligatus* struck down] —**prof′li·gate·ly** *adv.*

pro·found (prə FOWND) *adj.* **1.** intellectually deep or penetrating. **2.** reaching to, arising from, or affecting the depth of one's nature: *profound* respect. **3.** situated far below the surface; unfathomable. **4.** thorough; exhaustive: *profound* changes. [ME] —**pro·found'ly** *adv.*

pro·fun·di·ty (prə FUN di tee) *n.* **1.** the state or quality of being profound. **2.** *Usu. pl.* •**ties** a profound or abstruse statement, theory, etc. [ME *profundite*]

pro·fuse (prə FYOOS) *adj.* **1.** giving or given forth lavishly; liberal; extravagant. **2.** copious; overflowing; abundant: *profuse* vegetation. [ME] —**pro·fuse'ly** *adv.* — **pro·fuse'ness** *n.*

pro·fu·sion (prə FYOO zhən) *n.* **1.** a lavish supply or condition: a *profusion* of ornaments. **2.** the act of pouring forth or supplying in great abundance; prodigality.

pro·gen·i·tor (proh JEN i tər) *n.* a forefather or parent. [ME]

prog·e·ny (PROJ ə nee) *n. pl.* •**ny,** •**nies** offspring. [ME *progenie*]

prog·no·sis (prog NOH sis) *n. pl.* •**ses** (-seez) **1.** *Med.* a prediction or conclusion regarding the course of a disease and the probability of recovery. **2.** any prediction or forecast. [< LL]

prog·nos·tic (prog NOS tik) *adj.* **1.** of, pertaining to, or serving as a prognosis. **2.** predicting or foretelling. —*n.* a sign of some future occurrence; forecast.

prog·nos·ti·cate (prog NOS ti KAYT) *v.t.* •**cat·ed,** •**cat·ing** foretell (future events, etc.) by present indications. —**prog·nos'ti·ca'tion** *n.* —**prog·nos'ti·ca'tor** *n.*

pro·gram (PROH gram) *n.* **1.** a performance or show, esp. one given at a scheduled time on television or radio. **2.** a printed announcement or schedule of events, esp. one for a theatrical performance. **3.** any prearranged, proposed, or desired plan or course of proceedings. **4.** coded instructions for the sequence of operations to be performed by a computer. —*v.t.* **pro·grammed** or **gramed, pro·gram·ming** or **gram·ing 1.** arrange or include in a program. **2.** make up a program for (a radio station, a computer, etc.). [< F *programme* public notice]

pro·gram·mat·ic (PROH grə MAT ik) *adj.* **1.** of or pertaining to a program or programs. **2.** of or pertaining to program music or its references.

pro·gram·mer (PROH gram ər) *n.* one who makes up a computer program.

program music music intended to suggest a story, an event, or an idea.

prog·ress (PROG rəs) *n.* **1.** movement forward nearer a goal. **2.** advancement toward maturity or completion; improvement. — *v.i.* (prə GRES) **1.** move forward or onward. **2.** advance toward completion or fuller development. [ME *progresse*]

pro·gres·sion (prə GRESH ən) *n.* **1.** the act of progressing; advancement. **2.** any sequence or succession of numbers, musical chords, etc.

pro·gres·sive (prə GRES iv) *adj.* **1.** moving forward; advancing. **2.** proceeding gradually or step by step. **3.** aiming at or characterized by progress. **4.** spreading from one part to others; increasing: said of a disease: *progressive* paralysis. **5.** striving for or favoring progress or reform, esp. social, political, educational, or religious. —*n.* one who believes in progress or in progressive methods; esp., one who favors or promotes reforms, as in politics or religion. — **pro·gres'sive·ly** *adv.* —**pro·gres'siv·ism** *n.*

pro·hib·it (proh HIB it) *v.t.* **1.** forbid, esp. by authority or law; interdict. **2.** prevent or hinder. [ME *prohibiten*]

pro·hi·bi·tion (proh ə BISH ən) *n.* **1.** the act of prohibiting, preventing, or stopping; also, a decree or order forbidding anything. **2.** the forbidding of the manufacture, transportation, and sale of alcoholic liquors as beverages; esp. *cap.* the period in the U.S. when this act was in force.

pro·hib·i·tive (proh HIB i tiv) *adj.* **1.** prohibiting or tending to prohibit. **2.** preventing the sale, purchase, etc., of something: *prohibitive* costs. Also **pro·hib'i·to'ry.**

proj·ect (PROJ ekt) *n.* **1.** something proposed; a plan. **2.** an organized or assigned undertaking. —*v.* (prə JEKT) *v.t.* **1.** cause to extend forward or out. **2.** throw forth or forward, as missiles. **3.** cause (an image, shadow, etc.) to fall on a surface. **4.** propose or plan. **5.** use or produce (one's voice, words, etc.) so as to be heard clearly and at a distance. —*v.i.* **6.** protrude. **7.** *Psychol.* attribute one's own ideas, impulses, etc., to others. [ME *projecte* plan] —**pro·jec·tion** (prə JEK shən) *n.*

pro·jec·tile (prə JEK til) *adj.* **1.** projecting, or impelling forward. **2.** capable of being or intended to be projected or shot forth. —*n.* **1.** a body projected or thrown forth by force. **2.** *Mil.* a missile for discharge from a gun or cannon. [< NL]

pro•jec•tion•ist (prə JEK shə nist) *n.* one who operates a motion-picture or slide projector.

pro•jec•tor (prə JEK tər) *n.* an apparatus for throwing illuminated images or motion pictures upon a screen.

pro•le•tar•i•an (PROH li TAIR ee ən) *adj.* of or pertaining to the proletariat. —*n.* a member of the proletariat. [< L *proletarius*, belonging to the lowest class of the Roman state] —**pro′le•tar′i•an•ism** *n.*

pro•le•tar•i•at (PROH li TAIR ee ət) *n.* the working class: a term used esp. in Marxism.

pro•lif•er•ate (prə LIF ə RAYT) *v.t. & v.i.* **•at•ed, •at•ing** produce, reproduce, or grow, esp. with rapidity, as cells in tissue formation. —**pro•lif′er•a′tion** *n.*

pro•lif•ic (prə LIF ik) *adj.* **1.** producing abundantly, as offspring or fruit; fertile. **2.** producing results abundantly: a *prolific* writer. [< F *prolifique*] —**pro•lif′i•ca•cy** *n.* —**pro•lif′i•cal•ly** *adv.*

pro•lix (proh LIKS) *adj.* unduly long and verbose. [ME] —**pro•lix′i•ty** *n.*

pro•logue (PROH lawg) *n.* **1.** a prefatory statement to a poem, discourse, or performance; esp., an introduction spoken or sung before a play or opera. **2.** any anticipatory act or event. —*v.t.* **•logued, •loguing** introduce with a prologue or preface. Also **pro′log.** [ME *prolog*]

pro•long (prə LAWNG) *v.t.* extend in time or space; continue; lengthen. [ME *prolongen*] —**pro•lon•ga•tion** (PROH lawng GAY shən) *n.*

prom (prom) *n.* a formal college or school dance. [Short for PROMENADE]

prom•e•nade (PROM ə NAYD) *n.* **1.** a walk for amusement or exercise, or as part of a formal or social entertainment. **2.** a place for promenading. **3.** a concert or ball opened with a formal march; also, the march. —*v.* **•nad•ed, •nad•ing** *v.i.* **1.** take a promenade. —*v.t.* **2.** take a promenade through or along. [< F]

prom•i•nence (PROM ə nəns) *n.* **1.** the state of being prominent. **2.** That which is prominent. **2.** *Astron.* one of the great flames shooting out from the sun's surface, seen during total eclipses.

prom•i•nent (PROM ə nənt) *adj.* **1.** jutting out; projecting. **2.** conspicuous in position, character, or importance. **3.** well-known; eminent. [< L *prominere* jut forward]

pro•mis•cu•ous (prə MIS kyoo əs) *adj.* **1.** composed of individuals or things confusedly or indiscriminately mingled. **2.** indiscriminate, esp. in sexual relations. **3.** lacking plan or purpose; casual; random. [< L *promiscuus* mixed up] —**pro•mis•cu•i•ty** (PROM i SKYOO i tee) *n.* —**pro•mis′cu•ous•ly** *adv.* —**pro•mis′cu•ous•ness** *n.*

prom•ise (PROM is) *n.* **1.** an assurance given by one person to another that a specified act will or will not be performed. **2.** reasonable ground for hope or expectation, esp. of future excellence or satisfaction. **3.** something promised. —*v.* **•ised, •is•ing** *v.t.* **1.** engage or pledge by a promise: used with the infinitive or a clause. **2.** make a promise of (something) to someone. **3.** give reason for expecting. **4.** assure (someone). —*v.i.* **5.** make a promise. [ME *promisse*]

prom•is•ing (PROM ə sing) *adj.* giving promise of good results: *promising* signs.

prom•is•so•ry (PROM ə SOR ee) *adj.* containing or of the nature of a promise.

promissory note a written promise to pay a sum of money at a specified time or on demand.

prom•on•to•ry (PROM ən TOR ee) *n. pl.* **•ries** a high point of land extending into the sea; headland. [< L *promonturium*]

pro•mote (prə MOHT) *v.t.* **•mot•ed, •mot•ing 1.** contribute to the progress, development, or growth of; further; encourage. **2.** advance to a higher position, grade, or honor. **3.** work in behalf of; advocate actively. **4.** seek to make (a commercial product, business venture, etc.) popular or successful, as by securing capital or by advertising. [ME *promoten* move forward] —**pro•mot′er** *n.* —**pro•mo′tion** *n.* —**pro•mo′tion•al** *adj.*

prompt (prompt) *v.t.* **1.** incite to action; instigate. **2.** suggest or inspire (an act, thought, etc.). **3.** remind; give a cue to. —*adj.* **1.** acting or ready to act at the moment; punctual. **2.** done readily; taking place at the appointed time. —*n.* an act of prompting. [ME] —**prompt′er** *n.* —**prompt′ly** *adv.* —**prompt′•ness** *n.*

prom•ul•gate (PROM əl GAYT) *v.t.* **•gat•ed, •gat•ing** make known or announce formally; put into effect by public proclamation, as a law or dogma. [< L *promulgatus* promulgated] —**pro′mul•ga′tion** *n.*

prone (prohn) *adj.* **1.** lying flat, esp. with the

face, front, or palm downward; prostrate. **2.** mentally inclined or predisposed: with *to.* [ME] —**prone′ness** *n.*

prong (prong) *n.* **1.** a pointed end of an instrument, as the time of a fork. **2.** any pointed, projecting part, as the end of an antler. —*v.t.* prick or stab with or as with a prong. [ME *pronge*]

pronominal adjective the possessive case of a personal pronoun used attributively, as *my, your, his, her,* etc.

pro·noun (PROH nown) *n. Gram.* a word that may be used instead of a noun, as *who, which, he,* or *that.* [ME *pronom*] —**pro·nom·i·nal** (proh NOM ə nl) *adj.*

pro·nounce (prə NOWNS) *v.* •**nounced,** •**nounc·ing** *v.t.* **1.** utter or deliver officially or solemnly; proclaim: *pronounce* judgment. **2.** assert; declare, esp., as one's judgment. **3.** utter the constituent sounds of (a word or phrase) in a particular sequence or with a particular accent. **4.** utter (the sound of a letter). —*v.i.* **5.** make a judgment or pronouncement. [ME *pronouncen*] —**pro·nounce′a·ble** *adj.*

pro·nounced (prə NOWNST) *adj.* of marked or clearly indicated character.

pro·nounce·ment (prə NOWNS mənt) *n.* **1.** the act of pronouncing. **2.** a formal declaration or announcement.

pron·to (PRON toh) *adv. Informal* quickly; promptly; instantly. [< Sp.]

pro·nun·ci·a·men·to (prə NUN see ə MEN toh) *n. pl.* •**tos** a public announcement; proclamation; manifesto. [< Sp. *pronunciamiento*]

pro·nun·ci·a·tion (prə NUN see AY shən) *n.* the act or manner of uttering words. [ME *pronunciacion*]

proof (proof) *n.* **1.** the act or process of proving; esp., the establishment of a fact by evidence or a truth by other truths. **2.** a trial of strength, truth, excellence, etc. **3.** evidence and argument sufficient to induce belief. **4.** *Law* anything that serves to determine a verdict. **5.** the standard of strength of alcoholic liquors. **6.** *Printing* a trial sheet printed from type or a plate. **7.** *Photog.* a trial print from a negative. **8.** *Math.* a process to check a computation by using its result; also, a demonstration. —*adj.* **1.** capable of resisting successfully: with *against.* **2.** of standard alcoholic strength, as liquors. [ME]

-proof *combining form* **1.** impervious to;

able to withstand: *bombproof.* **2.** protected against: *mothproof.*

proof·read (PROOF REED) *v.t. & v.i.* •**read** (-RED), •**read·ing** read and correct (printers' proofs etc.). —**proof′read′er** *n.* —**proof′read′ing** *n.*

prop¹ (prop) *n.* a rigid object, as a beam or pole, that bolsters or sustains weight. —*v.t.* **propped, prop·ping 1.** support or keep from falling with or as with a prop. **2.** lean or place: usu. with *against.* [ME *proppe*]

prop² *n.* a stage property.

prop·a·gan·da (PROP ə GAN də) *n.* **1.** a systematic effort to persuade a body of people to support or adopt a particular opinion, attitude, or course of action. **2.** any selection of facts, ideas, or allegations forming the basis of such an effort. [< NL, from *Congregatio de propaganda fide* Congregation for propagating the faith] —**prop′a·gan′dist** *n. & adj.* —**prop′a·gan′dize** (-GAN dīz) *v.t. & v.i.* •**dized,** •**diz·ing**

prop·a·gate (PROP ə GAYT) *v.* •**gat·ed,** •**gat·ing** *v.t.* **1.** cause (animals, plants, etc.) to multiply by natural reproduction. **2.** spread from person to person, as a doctrine or belief; disseminate. **3.** transmit through a medium: *propagate* heat. —*v.i.* **4.** have offspring; breed. [< L *propagatus* propagated] —**prop′a·ga′tion** *n.*

pro·pel (prə PEL) *v.t.* •**pelled,** •**pel·ling** cause to move forward or ahead; drive or urge forward. [ME *propellen*]

pro·pel·lant (prə PEL ənt) *n.* one who or that which propels, as an explosive, a rocket fuel, etc. Also **pro·pel′lent.** —**pro·pel′lant** or **pro·pel′lent** *adj.*

pro·pel·ler (prə PEL ər) *n.* any device for propelling a craft through water or air, esp. one having blades mounted on a shaft that produce a thrust by their rotary action: also *screw propeller.*

pro·pen·si·ty (prə PEN si tee) *n. pl.* •**ties** a natural disposition or tendency; bent.

prop·er (PROP ər) *adj.* **1.** specially suited or adapted for some end; appropriate. **2.** conforming to a prevalent standard of conduct or manners; fitting. **3.** understood in a strict or literal sense: usu. following the noun modified: part of the book *proper.* **4.** naturally belonging to a particular person, thing, or class. **5.** modest; decent. **6.** *Esp. Brit. Informal* thorough; unmitigated: a *proper* bore. [ME *propre*] —**prop′er·ly** *adv.*

proper noun *Gram.* a noun that names a

particular person, place, or thing, and is always capitalized, as *Paul, Venice, U.S.S. Nautilus.*

prop·er·tied (PROP ər teed) *adj.* owning property.

prop·er·ty (PROP ər tee) *n. pl.* **·ties 1.** any object of value that a person may lawfully acquire and hold; that which may be owned, as stocks, land, etc. **2.** the legal right to the possession, use, enjoyment, and disposal of a thing. **3.** a parcel of land. **4.** any of the qualities or characteristics that together make up the nature or basic structure of a thing. **5.** in the theater, any portable article used in a performance other than scenery and costumes: also called *prop.* [ME *proprete* possession] —**prop'er·ty·less** *adj.*

proph·e·cy (PROF ə see) *n. pl.* **·cies 1.** a prediction made under divine influence and direction. **2.** any prediction. [ME *prophecie*]

proph·e·sy (PROF ə SI) *v.* **·sied, ·sy·ing** *v.t.* **1.** utter or foretell with or as with divine inspiration. **2.** predict (a future event). — *v.i.* **3.** speak by divine influence, or as a medium between God and man. **4.** foretell the future. [ME *prophesien*]

proph·et (PROF it) *n.* **1.** one who delivers divine messages or interprets the divine will. **2.** one who foretells the future; esp., an inspired predictor. **3.** a religious leader. — **the Prophet** according to Islam, Muhammad. [ME *prophete*]

pro·phet·ic (prə FET ik) *adj.* **1.** of or pertaining to a prophet or prophecy. **2.** pertaining to or involving prediction or presentiment; predictive. Also **pro·phet'i·cal.**

pro·phy·lac·tic (PROH fə LAK tik) *adj.* tending to protect against or ward off something, esp. disease; preventive. —*n.* a prophylactic medicine or appliance. [< Gk. *prophylaktikós* of guarding]

pro·phy·lax·is (PROH fə LAK sis) *n.* preventive treatment for disease. [< NL]

pro·pin·qui·ty (proh PING kwi tee) *n.* **1.** nearness in place or time. **2.** kinship. [ME *propinquite*]

pro·pi·ti·ate (prə PISH ee AYT) *v.t.* **·at·ed, ·at·ing** cause to be favorably disposed; conciliate. [< L *propitiatus* conciliated] — **pro·pi'ti·a'tion** *n.* —**pro·pi'ti·a'tive** *adj.* —**pro·pi'ti·a'tor** *n.*

pro·pi·tious (prə PISH əs) *adj.* **1.** attended by favorable circumstances; auspicious. **2.** kindly disposed; gracious. [ME *propicius*]

—**pro·pi'tious·ly** *adv.* —**pro·pi'tious·ness** *n.*

pro·po·nent (prə POH nənt) *n.* one who advocates or supports a cause or doctrine. [< L *proponere* put forth]

pro·por·tion (prə POR shən) *n.* **1.** relative magnitude, number, or degree, as existing between parts, a part and a whole, etc. **2.** fitness and harmony; symmetry. **3.** a proportionate or proper share. **4.** an equality or identity between ratios. **5.** *pl.* size; dimensions. [ME *proporcion*] —*v.t.* adjust; make proportional. —**pro·por'tion·ment** *n.*

pro·por·tion·al (prə POR shə nl) *adj.* of or being in proportion. —**pro·por'tion·al·ly** *adv.* —**pro·por'tion·al'i·ty** *n.*

pro·por·tion·ate (prə POR shə nit) *adj.* being in due proportion; proportional. — *v.t.* (prə POR shə NAYT) **·at·ed, ·at·ing** make proportionate. —**pro·por'tion·ate·ly** *adv.* —**pro·por'tion·ate·ness** *n.*

pro·pose (prə POHZ) *v.* **·posed, ·pos·ing** *v.t.* **1.** put forward for acceptance or consideration. **2.** intend; aim. **3.** suggest the drinking of (a toast). —*v.i.* **4.** form or announce a plan or design. **5.** make an offer, as of marriage. [ME] —**pro·pos'al** *n.*

prop·o·si·tion (PROP ə ZISH ən) *n.* **1.** a scheme or proposal offered for consideration or acceptance. **2.** any matter to be dealt with. **3.** a subject or statement presented for discussion or proof. [ME *proposicioun*] —**prop'o·si'tion** *v.t.* make a proposal to; esp., suggest sexual intercourse.

pro·pound (prə POWND) *v.t.* put forward for consideration, solution, etc.; submit. [ME *proponen*] —**pro·pound'er** *n.*

pro·pri·e·tar·y (prə PRĪ i TER ee) *adj.* **1.** of or belonging to a proprietor. **2.** designating an article, as a medicine, protected by copyright, patent, etc. —*n. pl.* **·tar·ies** a proprietor or proprietors collectively. [ME]

pro·pri·e·tor (prə PRĪ i tər) *n.* a person having the exclusive title to anything. — **pro·pri'e·tor·ship'** *n.*

pro·pri·e·ty (prə PRĪ i tee) *n. pl.* **·ties** the character or quality of being proper; esp., accordance with recognized usage or principles. —**the proprieties** the standards of good society. [ME *propriete*]

pro·pul·sion (prə PUL shən) *n.* **1.** the act or operation of propelling. **2.** a propelling force. —**pro·pul'sive** (-siv) *adj.*

pro ra·ta (proh RAH tə) in proportion. [< L]

pro·rate (proh RAYT) *v.t. & v.i.* **·rat·ed,**

•rat•ing distribute or divide proportionately. [< PRO RATA]

pro•rogue (proh ROHG) v.t. •rogued, •ro•guing 1. discontinue a session of (an assembly). 2. discontinue. [ME prorogen] —pro•ro•ga•tion (PROH rǝ GAY shǝn) n.

pro•sa•ic (proh ZAY ik) adj. 1. commonplace; dull. 2. of or like prose. Also pro•sa'i•cal. [< LL prosaicus] —pro•sa'i•cal•ly adv.

pro•sce•ni•um (proh SEE nee ǝm) n. pl. •ni•a (-nee ǝ) the part of a theater stage in front of the curtain. [< L]

proscenium arch the arch framing a stage.

pro•scribe (proh SKRĪB) v.t. •scribed, •scrib•ing 1. denounce or condemn; prohibit. 2. outlaw or banish. [< L proscribere] —pro•scrip'tion (-SKRIP shǝn) n. — pro•scrip'tive (-tiv) adj.

prose (prohz) n. speech or writing without metrical structure: distinguished from verse. —v.t. & v.i. prosed, pros•ing write or speak in prose. [ME] —adj. of, relating to, or written in prose.

pros•e•cute (PROS i KYOOT) v. •cut•ed, •cut•ing v.t. 1. go on with so as to complete. 2. Law a bring suit against. b. seek to enforce, as a claim, by legal process. —v.i. 3. begin and carry on a legal proceeding. [ME prosecuten] —pros'e•cu'tor n.

prosecuting attorney the attorney acting in behalf of the state, county, or national government in prosecuting for penal offenses.

pros•e•cu•tion (PROS i KYOO shǝn) n. 1. the act or process of prosecuting. 2. Law the instituting and carrying forward of a judicial or criminal proceeding; also, the party instituting and conducting it.

pros•e•lyte (PROS ǝ LĪT) n. one who has been brought over to any opinion, belief, sect, or party, esp. from one religious belief to another. [ME proselite] —v.t. & v.i. •lyt•ed, •lyt•ing proselytize. —pros•e•lyt•ism (-li TIZ ǝm) n.

pros•e•lyt•ize (PROS ǝ li TĪZ) v.t. & v.i. •ized, •iz•ing try to convert (someone) to another opinion, religion, etc. —pros'e•lyt•iz'er n.

pros•o•dy (PROS ǝ dee) n. the study of poetical forms, including accent of syllables, meter, and versification. [ME] —pro•sod•ic (prǝ SOD ik) or •i•cal adj. —pros'o•dist n.

pros•pect (PROS pekt) n. 1. Often pl. a future probability; the chance for future success. 2. an extended view. 3. an exposure;

outlook. 4. a prospective buyer. [ME prospecte] —v.t. & v.i. explore (a region) for gold, oil, etc. —pros'pec•tor n.

pro•spec•tive (prǝ SPEK tiv) adj. 1. anticipated. 2. looking toward the future. — pro•spec'tive•ly adv.

pro•spec•tus (prǝ SPEK tǝs) n. pl. •tus•es 1. a paper containing information of a proposed undertaking. 2. a summary; outline. [< L, view]

pros•per (PROS pǝr) v.e. be prosperous; thrive; flourish. [ME prosperen]

pros•per•i•ty (pro SPER i tee) n. the state of being prosperous; material well-being.

pros•per•ous (PROS pǝr ǝs) adj. 1. successful; flourishing. 2. auspicious or favorable. [< L prosperus]

pros•tate (PROS tayt) n. Anat. a partly muscular gland at the base of the bladder and surrounding the urethra in male mammals, providing some of the chemicals necessary to maintain the sperm for reproduction. Also prostate gland. [< NL prostata prostate gland]

pros•the•sis (pros THEE sis) n. pl. •ses (-seez) an artificial part fitted to the body, as an artificial limb, false tooth, etc. [< LL] — pros•thet•ic (-THET ik) adj.

pros•thet•ics (pros THET iks) n. (construed as sing.) the branch of surgery or dentistry that specializes in artificial parts. — pros•the•tist (PROS thi tist) n.

pros•ti•tute (PROS ti TOOT) n. 1. a person offering sexual intercourse for money. 2. a person performing services for unworthy purposes, usu. to obtain money. —v.t. •tut•ed, •tut•ing 1. apply (talent, etc.) to unworthy purposes. 2. offer (oneself or another) for sexual relations, esp. for money. [< L prostitutus offered for sale] — pros'ti•tu'tion n.

pros•trate (PROS trayt) adj. 1. lying prone, or with the face to the ground, as in adoration or subjection. 2. brought low in mind or spirit. 3. Bot. trailing along the ground. —v.t. •trat•ed, •trat•ing 1. bow or cast (oneself) down, as in adoration or pleading. 2. throw flat; lay on the ground. 3. overcome; make helpless. [ME prostrat] — pros•tra'tion n.

pros•y (PROH zee) adj. pros•i•er, pros•i•est 1. like prose; prosaic. 2. dull; tedious. —pros'i•ly adv. —pros'i•ness n.

pro•tag•o•nist (proh TAG ǝ nist) n. 1. the actor who played the chief part in a Greek drama. **2.** any leading character, contender, etc. [< Gk. *prōtagōnistēs*]

pro•te•an (PROH tee ən) *adj.* readily assuming different forms or various aspects; changeable. [< *Proteus*, sea god of Greek mythology who assumed many forms]

pro•tect (proh TEKT) *v.t.* shield or defend from attack, harm, or injury. [< L *protectus* covered] —**pro•tect′ing•ly** *adv.*

pro•tec•tion (prə TEK shən) *n.* **1.** the act of protecting, or the state of being protected. **2.** *Econ.* a system aiming to protect the industries of a country by imposing duties.

pro•tec•tion•ism (prə TEK shə NIZ əm) *n.* the economic doctrine or system of protection. —**pro•tec′tion•ist** *n.*

protective tariff a tariff that protects domestic industries against foreign competition.

pro•tec•tor•ate (prə TEK tər it) *n.* **1.** a relation of protection and partial control by a strong nation over a weaker power. **2.** a country or region under the protection of another. **3.** the office, or period of office, of a protector of a kingdom.

pro•té•gé (PROH tə zhay) *n.* one specially cared for by another who is older or more powerful. [< F] —**pro•té•gée** *n.fem.*

pro•tein (PROH teen) *n. Biochem.* any of a class of highly complex amino acids essential in animal metabolism. [< F *protéine*]

pro tem•po•re (PROH TEM pə REE) *Latin* for the time being; temporarily; temporary.

pro•test (PROH test) *n.* **1.** a solemn or formal objection or declaration. **2.** a public expression of dissent. —*adj.* of or relating to public protest: *protest* demonstrations. —*v.* (prə TEST) *v.t.* **1.** assert earnestly or positively. **2.** make a protest against; object to. —*v.i.* **3.** make solemn affirmation. **4.** make a protest; object. [ME] —**pro•test′er, pro•test′or** *n.*

Prot•es•tant (PROT ə stənt) *n.* one who belongs to a Christian church or sect other than the Roman Catholic and Eastern Orthodox Churches. [< MF] —*adj.* of or relating to Protestants, their religion, or their churches. —**Prot•es•tant•ism** (PROT ə stən TIZ əm) *n.*

Protestant Episcopal Church a religious body in the U.S. that is descended from the Church of England: also called *Episcopal Church in America.*

prot•es•ta•tion (PROT ə STAY shən) *n.* **1.** the act of protesting; also, that which is pro-

tested. **2.** a formal declaration of dissent. **3.** any solemn or urgent avowal.

pro•to•col (PROH tə KAWL) *n.* **1.** the rules of diplomatic and state etiquette and ceremony. **2.** the preliminary draft of diplomatic negotiation or of an official document. [< MF *prothocole*]

pro•ton (PROH ton) *n. Physics* one of the elementary particles in the nucleus of an atom, having a positive electrical charge. [< Gk. *prōton* first]

pro•to•plasm (PROH tə PLAZ əm) *n. Biol.* a complex substance that forms the essential living matter of plant and animal cells. [< NL *prōtoplasma*] —**pro′to•plas′mic** *adj.*

pro•to•type (PROH tə TIP) *n.* **1.** *Biol.* a primitive or ancestral organism; an archetype. **2.** an original model on which subsequent forms are to be based. [< F] —**pro′to•typ′i•cal** *adj.*

pro•to•zo•an (PROH tə ZOH ən) *n. pl.* **•zo•ans, •zo•a** (-ZOH ə) any of a phylum of microscopic single-celled organisms, largely aquatic and including many parasites. [< NL *Protozoa*] —*adj.* pertaining to the protozoans.

pro•tract (proh TRAKT) *v.t.* **1.** extend in time; prolong. **2.** *Anat.* protrude or extend. [< L *protractus* prolonged] —**pro•trac′tion** *n.*

pro•trac•tor (proh TRAK tər) *n.* **1.** an instrument for measuring and laying off angles. **2.** *Anat.* a muscle that extends a limb or moves it forward.

pro•trude (proh TROOD) *v.t. & v.i.* **•trud•ed, •trud•ing** push or thrust out; project outward. [< L *protrudere*] —**pro•tru′sion** (proh TROO zhən) *n.*

pro•tru•sive (proh TROO siv) *adj.* **1.** tending to protrude; protruding. **2.** pushing or driving forward. —**pro•tru′sive•ly** *adv.* —**pro•tru′sive•ness** *n.*

pro•tu•ber•ance (proh TOO bər əns) *n.* **1.** something that protrudes; a knob; prominence. **2.** the state of being protuberant. [< L *protuberare* bulge out] —**pro•tu′ber•ant** *adj.*

proud (prowd) *adj.* **•er, •est 1.** actuated by, possessing, or manifesting pride; arrogant; also, self-respecting. **2.** sensible of honor and personal elation: generally followed by *of* or by a verb in the infinitive. **3.** high-spirited, as a horse. **4.** being a cause of honorable pride, as a distinction. [ME] —**proud′ly** *adv.*

prove (proov) *v.* **proved, proved** or

prov•en, prov•ing *v.t.* **1.** show to be true or genuine, as by evidence or argument. **2.** determine the quality or genuineness of; test: *prove* a gun. **3.** *Math.* verify the accuracy of (a calculation etc.). —*v.i.* **4.** be shown to be by the result or outcome; turn out to be. [ME *proven* test] **—prov′a•ble** *adj.*

prov•e•nance (PROV ə nəns) *n.* origin or source. [< F]

Pro•ven•çal (PROH vən SAHL) *n.* **1.** a native or resident of Provence, France. **2.** the Romance language of Provence, used esp. in the 12th and 13th c. in the lyric literature of the troubadours. —*adj.*

prov•en•der (PROV ən dər) *n.* **1.** food for cattle, esp. dry food, as hay. **2.** provisions generally. —*v.t.* provide with food, as cattle. [ME *provendre*]

pro•ve•ni•ence (proh VEEN yəns) *n.* provenance; origin or source. [Alter. of PROVENANCE]

prov•erb (PROV ərb) *n.* a pithy saying, esp. one condensing the wisdom of experience; adage; saw; maxim. [ME *proverbe*] —**pro•ver•bi•al** (prə VUR bee əl) *adj.* —**pro•ver′bi•al•ly** *adv.*

pro•vide (prə VĪD) *v.* **•vid•ed, •vid•ing** *v.t.* **1.** supply or furnish. **2.** afford; yield. **3.** prepare, make ready, or procure beforehand. —*v.i.* **4.** take measures in advance: with *for* or *against*. **5.** furnish means of subsistence: usu. with *for*. **6.** make a stipulation. [ME *providen* foresee] —**pro•vid′er** *n.*

pro•vid•ed (prə VĪ did) *conj.* on condition; if: He will get the loan *provided* he offers good security. Also **pro•vid′ing.**

prov•i•dence (PROV i dəns) *n.* **1.** the care exercised by God over the universe. **2.** the exercise of foresight and care for the future. **3.** *cap.* God. [ME]

prov•i•dent (PROV i dənt) *adj.* anticipating and making ready for future wants.

prov•i•den•tial (PROV i DEN shəl) *adj.* **1.** resulting from or involving God's providence. **2.** lucky; opportune.

prov•ince (PROV ins) *n.* **1.** any large administrative division of a country. **2.** *pl.* regions lying at a distance from the capital or most populous part of a country. **3.** a sphere of knowledge, activity, or endeavor. [< F]

pro•vin•cial (prə VIN shəl) *adj.* **1.** of or pertaining to a province. **2.** confined to a province; rustic. **3.** narrow; uncultured. —*n.* a narrow person. —**pro•vin′cial•ly** *adv.*

pro•vin•cial•ism (prə VIN shə LIZ əm) *n.* **1.**

the quality of being provincial. **2.** a provincial custom, esp. of speech.

pro•vi•sion (prə VIZH ən) *n.* **1.** the act of providing, or the state of being provided. **2.** measures taken or means made ready in advance. **3.** *pl.* food or a supply of food. **4.** the part of an agreement, instrument, etc., referring to one specific thing; a stipulation. —*v.t.* provide with food or provisions. [ME] —**pro•vi′sion•er** *n.*

pro•vi•sion•al (prə VIZH ə nl) *adj.* provided for a present service or temporary necessity; adopted tentatively. —**pro•vi′sion•al•ly** *adv.*

pro•vi•so (prə VĪ zoh) *n.* *pl.* **•sos, •soes** a stipulation or clause, as in a contract, limiting, modifying, or rendering conditional its operation. [ME]

prov•o•ca•tion (PROV ə KAY shən) *n.* **1.** the act of provoking. **2.** an incitement to action.

pro•voc•a•tive (prə VOK ə tiv) *adj.* serving to provoke; stimulating. —*n.* that which provokes or tends to provoke. —**pro•voc′a•tive•ly** *adv.* —**pro•voc′a•tive•ness** *n.*

pro•voke (prə VOHK) *v.t.* **•voked, •vok•ing 1.** stir to anger or resentment; vex. **2.** arouse or stimulate to some action. **3.** stir up or bring about: *provoke* a quarrel. [ME]

pro•vost (PROH vohst) *n.* **1.** a high-ranking official or authority. **2.** in some English and American colleges, the head of the faculty. [ME]

pro•vost marshal (PROH voh) a military or naval officer exercising police functions.

prow (prow) *n.* the fore part of the hull of a vessel; the bow. [ME *proue*]

prow•ess (PROW is) *n.* **1.** strength, skill, and courage, esp. in battle. **2.** exceptional ability. [ME]

prowl (prowl) *v.t. & v.i.* roam about stealthily, as in search of prey or plunder. —*n.* the act of prowling. [ME *prollen*] —**prowl′er** *n.*

prowl car a police patrol car.

prox•i•mate (PROK sə mit) *adj.* being in immediate relation with something else; next. [< LL *proximatus* nearest] —**prox′i•mate•ly** *adv.*

prox•im•i•ty (prok SIM i tee) *n.* the state or fact of being near or next; nearness. [< MF *proximité*]

proximity fuze an electronic device in a projectile that detonates by proximity to the target.

prox•y (PROK see) *n. pl.* **prox•ies 1.** a person empowered by another to act for him. **2.** the office or right to so act, or the instrument conferring it. [ME *prokesye*]

prude (prood) *n.* a person who makes an affected display of modesty and propriety, esp. in matters relating to sex. [< F] —**prud′er·y, prud′ish·ness** *n.* —**prud′ish** *adj.* —**prud′ish·ly** *adv.*

pru·dent (PROOD nt) *adj.* **1.** cautious; discreet. **2.** exercising sound judgment. **3.** not extravagant. [ME] —**pru′dence** *n.* —**pru·den·tial** (proo DEN shəl) *adj.* —**pru′dent·ly** *adv.*

prune¹ (proon) *n.* the dried fruit of the plum. [ME]

prune² *v.t. & v.i.* **pruned, prun·ing** trim or cut branches or parts from (trees etc.) so as to improve growth, appearance, etc. [ME *prouynen*] —**prun′er** *n.*

pru·ri·ent (PRUUR ee ənt) *adj.* **1.** having lustful cravings or desires. **2.** lewd. [< L *prurire* itch] —**pru′ri·ence** *n.* —**pru′ri·ent·ly** *adv.*

Prus·sian (PRUSH ən) *adj.* **1.** of or pertaining to Prussia, its inhabitants, or their language. **2.** militaristic; overbearing. —*n.* a native or inhabitant of Prussia.

pry¹ (prī) *v.i.* **pried, pry·ing** look or peer carefully, curiously, or slyly; snoop. —*n. pl.* **pries 1.** a sly and searching inspection. **2.** one who pries; an inquisitive, prying person. [ME *pryen*] —**pry′ing·ly** *adv.*

pry² *v.t.* **pried, pry·ing 1.** raise, move, or open by means of a lever; prize. **2.** obtain by effort. —*n.* a lever, as a bar, stick, or beam; also, leverage. [< PRIZE²]

psalm (sahm) *n.* **1.** *Often cap.* a sacred song or lyric contained in the Old Testament Book of Psalms. **2.** any sacred song. —*v.t.* celebrate or praise in psalms. [ME] —**psalm′ist** *n.*

Psalms (sahmz) a book of the Old Testament, containing 150 hymns. Also **Book of Psalms.**

psal·ter·y (SAWL tə ree) *n. pl.* **·ter·ies** an ancient stringed instrument played by plucking with a pick. [ME *psalterie*]

pseu·do (SOO doh) *adj.* pretended; sham.

pseudo- *combining form* false; pretended. [< Gk. *pseudēs* false]

pseu·do·nym (SOOD n im) *n.* a fictitious name; pen name. [< Gk. *pseudónymon* false name] —**pseu·don·y·mous** (soo DON ə məs) *adj.*

pshaw (shaw) *interj.* an exclamation of annoyance, disapproval, disgust, or impa-

tience. —*v.t. & v.i.* exclaim *pshaw* at (a person or thing).

psi (sī) *n.* the twenty-third letter in the Greek alphabet (Ψ, ψ).

pso·ri·a·sis (sə RĪ ə sis) *n. Pathol.* a noncontagious, inflammatory skin disease, characterized by reddish patches and white scales. [< NL]

psych (sīk) *v.t. & v.i. Informal* **1.** become or cause to become emotionally aroused or prepared: also **psych up. 2.** lose or cause to lose courage, resolve, etc.: also **psych out.** —**psych out** figure out psychologically; unsettle.

psy·che (SĪ kee) *n.* **1.** the human soul. **2.** *Psychoanal.* the mind, often regarded as an entity functioning apart from or independently of the body. [< Gk. *psychē* soul]

psych·e·del·ic (sī kə DEL ik) *adj.* **1.** causing or having to do with an abnormal stimulation of consciousness or perception. **2.** resembling the effects of taking psychedelic drugs: *psychedelic* art. [< Gk. *psychē* soul + *dēloun* show]

psy·chi·a·try (si KĪ ə tree) *n.* the branch of medicine dealing with the diagnosis and treatment of mental disorders. —**psy·chi·at·ric** (sī kee A trik) *adj.* —**psy·chi′a·trist** *n.*

psy·chic (SĪ kik) *adj.* **1.** pertaining to the mind. **2.** pertaining to mental phenomena that appear to be independent of normal sensory stimuli, as clairvoyance, telepathy, and extrasensory perception. **3.** sensitive to mental or occult phenomena. Also **psy′chi·cal.** —*n.* one sensitive to extrasensory phenomena. [See PSYCHE.] —**psy′chi·cal·ly** *adv.*

psy·cho (SĪ koh) *n. pl.* **·chos** *Slang* one who is mentally disturbed.

psycho- *combining form* mind; soul; spirit: *psychosomatic.* [< Gk. *psychē*]

psy·cho·a·nal·y·sis (sī koh ə NAL ə sis) *n.* a system of psychotherapy that seeks to alleviate neuroses and other mental disorders by the analysis of unconscious factors as revealed in dreams, free association, etc. —**psy′cho·an′a·lyst** (-AN ə list) *n.* —**psy′cho·an′a·lyt′ic** (-AN ə LIT ik) or **·i·cal** *adj.*

psy·cho·an·a·lyze (sī koh AN ·i Íz) *v.t.* **·lyzed, ·lyz·ing** treat by psychoanalysis.

psy·cho·gen·ic (sī kə JEN ik) *adj.* having mental origin, or being affected by mental conflicts and states.

pys·cho·his·to·ry (sī koh HIS tə ree) *n.* history of great persons or events from a psychological point of view. —**psy•cho•his•to'ri•an** (-TOR ee ən) n.

psy•chol•o•gize (sī KOL ə jīz) v. •**gized,** •**giz•ing** —v.t. **1.** interpret by means of psychology. —v.i. **2.** theorize on psychology.

psy•chol•o•gy (sī KOL ə jee) n. pl. •**gies 1.** the study of the human mind in any of its aspects, operations, powers, or functions. **2.** the behavior patterns regarded as characteristic of an individual, type, group, etc. [< NL psychologia] —**psy•cho•log•i•cal** (sī kə LOJ i kəl) adj. —**psy•chol•o'gist** n.

psy•cho•neu•ro•sis (sī koh nuu ROH sis) n. pl. •**ses** (-seez) Psychiatry neurosis. —**psy'cho•neu•rot'ic** (-ROT ik) adj. & n.

psy•cho•path (SĪ kə PATH) n. one who is mentally unstable, esp. in a criminal or antisocial manner.

psy•chop•a•thy (sī KOP ə thee) n. mental disorder. —**psy•cho•path•ic** (sī kə PATH ik) adj.

psy•cho•sis (sī KOH sis) n. pl. •**ses** (-seez) Psychiatry a severe mental disorder, often involving disorganization of the total personality. [< NL]

psy•cho•so•mat•ic (sī koh sə MAT ik) adj. of or pertaining to the effect of emotional states upon the body, with special reference to certain disorders.

psy•cho•ther•a•py (sī koh THER ə pee) n. pl. •**pies** the treatment of mental disorders by psychological methods, as hypnosis, reeducation, psychoanalysis, etc. —**psy'cho•ther'a•pist** n.

psy•chot•ic (sī KOT ik) n. one suffering from a psychosis. —adj. of or characterized by a psychosis.

pter•o•dac•tyl (TER ə DAK til) n. Paleontol. any of a genus of extinct flying reptiles. [< NL Pterodactylus]

pub (pub) n. a bar or tavern.

pu•ber•ty (PYOO bər tee) n. the period during which an individual becomes physiologically capable of reproduction [ME puberte]

pu•bes•cent (pyoo BES ənt) adj. **1.** arriving or having arrived at puberty. **2.** having a growth of soft, fine hairs, as certain plants. [< L pubescere attain puberty] —**pu•bes'cence** n.

pu•bic (PYOO bik) adj. of or pertaining to the region in the lower part of the abdomen.

pub•lic (PUB lik) adj. **1.** of, pertaining to, or

affecting the people at large or the community. **2.** maintained by or for the public: public parks. **3.** participated in by the people: a public demonstration. **4.** well-known; open; notorious: a public scandal. **5.** acting before or for the community: a public official. —n. **1.** people as a whole; the community. **2.** an audience; esp., the admirers of an actor or other celebrity. [ME publique] —**pub'lic•ly** adv.

pub•li•ca•tion (PUB li KAY shən) n. **1.** the act of publishing. **2.** any printed work placed on sale or otherwise distributed or offered for distribution. [ME publicacioun]

public domain lands owned by a government; public lands. —**in the public domain** available for unrestricted use: said of material on which copyright or patent right has expired.

public enemy a person, esp. a criminal, regarded as a menace to the public.

pub•li•cist (PUB lə sist) n. one engaged in public relations work; a publicity agent.

pub•lic•i•ty (pə BLIS i tee) n. **1.** information or personal news intended to promote the interests of individuals, institutions, etc. **2.** the attention or interest of the public gained by any method.

pub•li•cize (PUB lə sīz) v.t. •**cized,** •**ciz•ing** advertise.

public opinion the prevailing ideas, beliefs, and aims of the people, collectively.

public relations the activities and techniques used by organizations and individuals to establish favorable attitudes and responses in their behalf; also, the occupation of establishing such attitudes and responses.

public school 1. U.S. a school maintained by public funds for the free education of the children of the community, usu. covering elementary and secondary grades. **2.** Brit. a private or endowed school, esp. one that prepares students for the universities.

public utility a business organization or industry that supplies water, electricity, gas, etc. to the public and is subject to governmental regulation.

public works works or improvements built with public money, as parks, roads, etc.

pub•lish (PUB lish) v.t. **1.** print and issue (a book, magazine, map, etc.) to the public. **2.** make known or announce publicly; promulgate; proclaim. [ME publisshen] —**pub'•lish•er** n.

puck[1] (puk) n. an evil sprite or hobgoblin. [ME *pouke*]

puck[2] n. the hard, black rubber disk used in playing ice hockey.

puck·er (PUK ər) v.t. & v.i. gather or draw up into small folds or wrinkles. —n. a wrinkle or group of wrinkles.

puck·ish (PUK ish) adj. mischievous; impish.

pud·ding (PUUD ing) n. 1. a sweetened and flavored dessert of soft food, usu. made of boiled milk, flavoring, a thickening agent, etc. 2. a sausage of seasoned minced meat usu. boiled or broiled. [ME *poding* sausage]

pud·dle (PUD l) n. 1. a small pool of water, esp. dirty water. 2. a small pool of any liquid. —v.t. •dled, •dling Metall. convert (molten pig iron) into wrought iron by melting and stirring in the presence of oxidizing substances. [ME *podel*]

pud·dling (PUD ling) n. Metall. the operation or business of making wrought iron from pig iron.

pudg·y (PUJ ee) adj. pudg·i·er, pudg·i·est short and fat; dumpy; chubby. —pudg'i·ness n.

pueb·lo (PWEB loh) n. pl. •los 1. a communal adobe or stone building or group of buildings of the Indians of the SW U.S. 2. a town or village of Indians or Spanish Americans, as in Mexico. [< Sp., village]

pu·er·ile (PYOO ər il) adj. 1. pertaining to or characteristic of childhood; juvenile. 2. immature; weak; silly: a *puerile* suggestion. [< L *puerilis* boyish]

pu·er·per·al (pyoo UR pər əl) adj. Med. of or connected with childbirth. [< NL *puerperalis*]

puff (puf) n. 1. a breath emitted suddenly and with force; also, a sudden emission, as of air, smoke, or steam. 2. a light, air-filled piece of pastry. 3. a light ball or pad for dusting powder on the hair or skin. 4. excessive praise, as in a newspaper or advertisement. —v.i. 1. blow in puffs, as the wind. 2. breathe hard, as after violent exertion. 3. smoke a cigar etc., with puffs. 4. move, act, or exert oneself while emitting puffs: with *away*, *up*, etc. 5. swell or distend: with *up* or *out*. —v.t. 6. send forth or emit with short puffs or breaths. 7. smoke, as a pipe or cigar, with puffs. 8. swell or distend. [ME *puf*] —puff'er·y n. pl. •er·ies flattering publicity; excessive commendation.

puff·y (PUF ee) adj. puff·i·er, puff·i·est 1.

swollen with or as with air, etc. 2. inflated in manner; bombastic. 3. blowing in puffs. —puff'i·ly adv. —puff'i·ness n.

pug[1] (pug) n. clay worked with water, for molding pottery or bricks. —v.t. pugged, pug·ging knead or work (clay) with water, as in brickmaking.

pug[2] n. 1. a breed of dog characterized by a short, square body, upturned nose, curled tail, and short, smooth coat. 2. a pug nose.

pu·gi·lism (PYOO jə LIZ əm) n. the art or practice of boxing or fighting with the fists. [< L *pugil* boxer] —pu'gi·list n. —pu'gi·lis'tic adj.

pug·na·cious (pug NAY shəs) adj. disposed or inclined to fight; quarrelsome. [< L *pugnacitas* combativeness] —pug·na'cious·ly adv. —pug·nac'i·ty (pug NAS i tee) n.

pug nose a short nose tilted upward at the end. —pug-nosed (PUG NOHZD) adj.

pu·is·sant (PYOO ə sənt) adj. powerful; mighty. [ME] —pu'is·sance n.

puke (pyook) v.t. & v.i. puked, puk·ing vomit or cause to vomit. —n. vomit.

pul·chri·tude (PUL kri TOOD) n. beauty; grace; physical charm. [ME] —pul'chri·tu'di·nous adj.

pull (puul) v.t. 1. apply force so as to cause motion toward; drag; tug. 2. draw or remove from a fixed place. 3. give a pull or tug to. 4. pluck, as a fowl. 5. rip; tear; rend. 6. strain so as to cause injury. 7. draw out so as to use. 8. *Printing* make or obtain by impression from type: *pull* a proof. 9. in boxing, deliver (a punch etc.) with less than one's full strength. —v.i. 10. use force in hauling, dragging, moving, etc. 11. move: with *out*, *in*, *away*, *ahead*, etc. 12. drink or inhale deeply. 13. propel a boat with oars; row. —pull for 1. strive in behalf of. 2. declare one's allegiance to. —pull off *Informal* perform successfully; accomplish. —pull oneself together regain one's composure. —pull out withdraw, as from an established position. —pull over direct a car to the side of a car. —pull through manage to succeed, recover, etc. —n. 1. the act or result of pulling. 2. something that is pulled, as the handle of a drawer. 3. an impression made by pulling the lever of a hand press. 4. a long swallow; a deep puff. 5. any steady, continuous effort. 6. *Informal* a means of influencing those in power; influence. 7. the amount of resistance met in drawing a bowstring, pulling a trigger, etc., usu. measured in pounds. [ME *pullen*]

pull·back (PUUL BAK) *n.* a retreat, esp. a withdrawal of military forces.

pul·let (PUUL it) *n.* a young hen, or one not fully grown. [< ME *polet*]

pul·ley (PUUL ee) *n. pl.* **·leys 1.** a wheel grooved to receive a rope, and usu. mounted in a block, used to increase the mechanical advantage of an applied force. **2.** a block with its pulleys or tackle. **3.** a wheel driving, carrying, or being driven by a belt. [ME *poley* pivot]

pull·out (PUUL OWT) *n.* **1.** a withdrawal, as of troops. **2.** *Aeron.* the maneuver of an airplane in passing from a dive to horizontal flight.

pull·o·ver (PUUL OH vər) *n.* a garment put on by being drawn over the head, as a sweater.

pul·mo·nar·y (PUUL mə NER ee) *adj.* **1.** of, pertaining to, or affecting the lungs. **2.** having lunglike organs. [< L *pulmonarius* of the lungs]

pulp (pulp) *n.* **1.** a moist, soft, slightly cohering mass of matter, as the succulent part of fruit. **2.** the moist mixture of ground wood fibers or rags that forms the substance of paper. **3.** a magazine printed on rough, unglazed paper, and usu. having contents of a cheap, sensational nature. **4.** *Dent.* the soft tissue of vessels and nerves that fills the central cavity of a tooth. [< L *pulpa* pulp of fruit] —*v.t. & v.i.* remove or become pulp. —**pulp′y** *adj.* **·i·er, ·i·est**

pul·pit (PUUL pit) *n.* an elevated stand or desk for a preacher in a church. [ME]

pulp·wood (PULP WUUD) *n.* the wood of certain trees, as the spruce, used in the manufacture of paper.

pul·sar (PUL sahr) *n.* a rotating, collapsed neutron star, a source of regularly pulsing radio waves. [< PULSATING STAR]

pul·sate (PUL sayt) *v.i.* **·sat·ed, ·sat·ing 1.** move or throb with rhythmical impulses, as the pulse or heart. **2.** vibrate; quiver. [< L *pulsatus* struck] —**pul·sa′tion** *n.*

pulse (puls) *n.* **1.** *Physiol.* the rhythmical beating of the arteries resulting from the successive contractions of the heart. **2.** *Telecom.* a brief surge of electrical or electromagnetic energy, usu. transmitted as a signal in communication. —*v.i.* **pulsed, puls·ing** pulsate; throb. [< L *pulsus* a beat]

pul·ver·ize (PUL və RĪZ) *v.* **·ized, ·iz·ing** *v.t.* **1.** reduce to powder or dust, as by

crushing. **2.** demolish; annihilate. —*v.i.* **3.** become reduced to powder or gas. [< MF *pulveriser*] —**pul′ver·iz′er** *n.*

pum·ice (PUM is) *n.* spongy volcanic lava, used as an abrasive and polishing material, esp. when powdered. Also **pumice stone.** —*v.t.* **·iced, ·ic·ing** smooth, polish, or clean with pumice. [ME *pomise*]

pum·mel (PUM əl) *v.t.* beat with or as with the fists. Also spelled *pommel.*

pump[1] (pump) *n.* a mechanical device for raising, circulating, exhausting, or compressing a liquid or gas. —*v.t.* **1.** raise with a pump, as water. **2.** remove the water etc. from. **3.** inflate with air by means of a pump. **4.** force from or as if from a pump. **5.** obtain information from persistently or subtly: *pump* a witness. —*v.i.* **6.** work a pump; raise water or other liquid with a pump. **7.** move up and down like a pump handle. [ME *pumpe*]

pump[2] *n.* a low-cut shoe without a fastening.

pum·per·nick·el (PUM pər NIK əl) *n.* a coarse, dark, sour bread made from unsifted rye. [< G *Pumpernickel*]

pump·kin (PUMP kin) *n.* a large, round, edible, yellow-orange fruit borne by a coarse trailing vine with heart-shaped leaves. [< MF *popon* melon]

pun (pun) *n.* the humorous use of a word having two different, more or less incongruous meanings. —*v.i.* **punned, punning** make a pun. —**pun′ning·ly** *adv.*

punch[1] (punch) *n.* a tool for perforating, stamping, shaping, or indenting. —*v.t.* perforate, shape, indent, etc., with a punch. [Short for PUNCHEON]

punch[2] *v.t.* **1.** strike sharply, esp. with the fist. **2.** operate; work; use: *punch* a time clock. **3.** In the West, drive (cattle). —*n.* **1.** a swift blow with the fist. **2.** vitality; force: an editorial with *punch.* [ME *punchen*]

punch[3] *n.* a beverage having wine or spirits, milk, tea, or fruit juices as a basic ingredient, sweetened, and sometimes spiced.

punch card in data processing, a card with punched holes that convey information by their position on the card. Also **punch′ card.**

punch-drunk (PUNCH DRUNGK) *adj.* **1.** groggy; slow in movement, speech, etc., from repeated blows to the head: said of prizefighters. **2.** confused; dazed.

pun·cheon (PUN chən) *n.* a liquor cask of variable capacity, usu. 80 gallons. [ME *ponchoun*]

punching bag 1. an inflated or stuffed ball, usu. suspended, that is punched with the fists for exercise. **2.** *Informal* a scapegoat.

punc·til·i·ous (pungk TIL ee əs) *adj.* very careful in the observance of forms of etiquette, behavior, etc. —**punc·til′i·ous·ly** *adv.* —**punc·til′i·ous·ness** *n.*

punc·tu·al (PUNGK choo əl) *adj.* **1.** acting or arriving promptly. **2.** done or made precisely at an appointed time. [ME] —**punc′tu·al′i·ty** (PUNGK choo AL i tee) *n.* —**punc′tu·al·ly** *adv.*

punc·tu·ate (PUNGK choo AYT) *v.* •**at·ed,** •**at·ing** *v.t.* **1.** divide or mark with punctuation. **2.** interrupt at intervals. **3.** emphasize; stress. —*v.i.* **4.** use punctuation. [< Med.L *punctatus* pointed] —**punc′tu·a′tor** *n.*

punc·tu·a·tion (PUNGK choo AY shən) *n.* the use of marks in written or printed matter to indicate the separation of the words into sentences, clauses, and phrases, and to aid in the better comprehension of the meaning; also, the marks so used (**punctuation marks**). The chief punctuation marks are:

period (point)	.	braces	‖
colon	:	dash (em-dash)	—
semicolon	;	(en-dash)	–
comma	,	hyphen	-
question mark	?	quotation marks	" "
exclamation point	!	single quotation marks	' '
apostrophe	'		
parentheses	( )	ellipsis	...
brackets	[ ]	slash (solidus)	/

punc·ture (PUNGK chər) *v.t. & v.i.* •**tured,** •**tur·ing** pierce or be pierced, as with a sharp point. —*n.* **1.** a small hole made by piercing with a sharp point. **2.** the act of puncturing. [ME]

pun·dit (PUN dit) *n.* **1.** a learned person; esp., in India, one versed in laws and religion of the Hindus. **2.** an authority. [< Skt. *pandita*]

pun·gent (PUN jənt) *adj.* **1.** sharp or acrid to taste or smell; keen; penetrating: *pungent* odors. **2.** caustic; biting: *pungent* sarcasm. [< L *pungere* prick] —**pun′gen·cy** *n.* —**pun′gent·ly** *adv.*

pun·ish (PUN ish) *v.t.* **1.** subject (a person) to pain, confinement, or other penalty for a crime or fault. **2.** impose a penalty on. **3.** use roughly; injure. [ME *punisshen*] —**pun′ish·a·ble** *adj.*

pun·ish·ment (PUN ish mənt) *n.* **1.** a penalty imposed, as for transgression of law. **2.** any ill suffered in consequence of wrongdoing. **3.** the act of punishing. **4.** rough handling, as in a prizefight.

pu·ni·tive (PYOO ni tiv) *adj.* pertaining to or inflicting punishment: *punitive* measures.

punk¹ (pungk) *n.* **1.** wood decayed through the action of a fungus, useful as tinder. **2.** an artificial preparation that will smolder without flame.

punk² *Slang n.* **1.** a petty hoodlum. **2.** a young, inexperienced person: a contemptuous term. —*adj. Informal* **1.** worthless. **2.** unwell.

pun·ster (PUN stər) *n.* one who puns. Also **pun′ner.**

punt¹ (punt) *n.* a flat-bottomed, square-ended boat, often propelled by a pole, used in shallow waters. —*v.t.* **1.** propel (a boat) by pushing with a pole against the bottom of a shallow stream, lake, etc. —*v.i.* **2.** go or hunt in a punt. [OE] —**punt′er** *n.*

punt² *n.* in football, a kick made by dropping the ball from the hands and kicking it before it strikes the ground. —**punt** *v.t. & v.i.* —**punt′er** *n.*

pu·ny (PYOO nee) *adj.* •**ni·er,** •**ni·est** of small and feeble development or importance; weak and insignificant. [< MF *puisné* younger] —**pu′ni·ness** *n.*

pup (pup) *n.* **1.** a puppy. **2.** the young of the seal, the shark, and certain other animals. —*v.i.* **pupped, pup·ping** bring forth pups. [Short for PUPPY]

pu·pa (PYOO pə) *n. pl.* •**pae** (-pee), **-pas** *Entomol.* the quiescent stage in the development of an insect, following the larval and preceding the adult stage. [< NL] —**pu·pal** (PYOO pəl) *adj.*

pu·pil¹ (PYOO pəl) *n.* a person of any age under the care of a teacher; learner. [ME *pupille*]

pu·pil² *n. Anat.* the opening in the iris of the eye, through which light reaches the retina. [< MF *pupille*]

pup·pet (PUP it) *n.* **1.** a small figure of a person, animal, etc., animated by the hand. **2.** a marionette. **3.** one slavishly subject to the will of another. —*adj.* **1.** of or pertaining to puppets. **2.** not autonomous: a *puppet* state. [ME *popet* doll]

pup·pet·eer (PUP i TEER) *n.* one who manipulates puppets.

pup·py (PUP ee) *n. pl.* •**pies 1.** a young dog: also called *pup.* **2.** any of the young of cer-

tain fishes and animals (see PUP, def. 2). —
pup'py•ish adj.

puppy love sentimental, adolescent love or
infatuation.

pup tent a small wedge-shaped portable
tent.

pur•chase (PUR chəs) v.t. •chased,
•chas•ing 1. acquire by paying money or its
equivalent; buy. 2. obtain by exertion, sacrifice, flattery, etc. [ME *purchasen* procure]
—n. 1. something purchased. 2. the act of
purchasing. 3. a firm grasp or hold on something so as to prevent slipping, etc. 4. a
device that gives a mechanical advantage,
as a tackle or lever; also, leverage. —pur'
chas•a•ble adj. —pur'chas•er n.

pur•dah (PUR də) n. *Anglo-Indian* 1. a curtain or screen used to seclude women. 2.
the state or system of such seclusion. [<
Persian *pardah* curtain]

pure (pyuur) adj. pur•er, pur•est 1. free
from anything that weakens, impairs, or
pollutes. 2. free from adulteration; clear;
clean. 3. free from moral defilement; innocent; chaste. 4. abstract; nonobjective: *pure*
form. 5. concerned with fundamental research, as distinguished from practical application; theoretical: said of sciences. 6.
nothing but; sheer: *pure* luck. [ME *pur*] —
pure'ness n.

pure•bred (PYUUR BRED) adj. *Biol.* bred
from stock having had no admixture for
many generations: said esp. of livestock. —
n. a purebred animal.

pu•rée (pyuu RAY) n. a thick pulp, usu. of
vegetables, boiled and strained. [< F]

pure•ly (PYUUR lee) adv. 1. so as to be free
from admixture, taint, or any harmful substance. 2. completely; totally. 3. merely;
simply.

pur•ga•tive (PUR gə tiv) adj. tending to
purge; esp., precipitating a bowel movement. —n. a purgative agent. [ME *pur-
gatif*]

pur•ga•to•ry (PUR gə TOR ee) n. pl. •ries
1. in Roman Catholic theology, a state or
place where the souls of those who have
died penitent are made fit for paradise. 2.
any place or state of temporary banishment, suffering, or punishment. [ME *pur-
gatorie*]

purge (purj) v. purged, purg•ing v.t. 1.
cleanse of what is impure or extraneous;
purify. 2. rid (a group, nation, etc.) of elements regarded as undesirable or inimical,
esp. by killing. 3. cleanse or rid of sin, fault,

or defilement. 4. *Med.* cause evacuation of
(the bowels etc.). —v.i. 5. become clean or
pure.—n. 1. the act or process of purging:
also **pur•ga•tion** (pur GAY shən). 2. that
which purges, esp. a cathartic. [ME *purgen*
cleanse]

pu•ri•fy (PYUUR i FI) v. •fied, •fy•ing v.t.
1. make pure or clean. 2. free from sin. —
v.i. 3. become pure or clean. [ME *purifien*]
—**pu'ri•fi•ca'•tion** n. —**pu'ri•fi'er** n.

pur•ist (PYUUR ist) n. one who believes in
or practices exact or meticulous usage, as of
a language, style, etc. —**pur'ism** n. —
pu•ris'tic adj.

Pu•ri•tan (PYUUR i tn) n. one of a group of
English Protestants who in the 16th and
17th c. advocated simpler forms of creed
and ritual in the Church of England. [< LL
puritas purity] —**Pu'i•tan** adj. —**Pu'ri•
tan•ism** n.

pu•ri•tan (PYUUR i tn) n. one who is scrupulously strict or exacting in religious observance or moral life: often used disparagingly. —adj. puritanical.

pu•ri•tan•i•cal (PYUUR i TAN i kəl) adj. 1.
rigidly scrupulous or exacting in religious
observance or morals; strict. 2. *Often cap.*
of or characteristic of the Puritans. —
pu'ri•tan'i•cal•ly adv. —**pu'ri•tan'i•
cal•ness** n.

pu•ri•ty (PYUUR i tee) n. 1. the quality or
state of being pure. 2. saturation: said of a
color. [ME *purete*]

purl[1] (purl) v.i. 1. whirl; turn. 2. flow with a
bubbling sound. 3. move in eddies. —n. a
circling movement of water; an eddy. [Cf.
Norw. *purla* bubble]

purl[2] n. in knitting, the inversion of the knit
stitch, giving a horizontal rib effect. [Earlier
pirl twist] —**purl** v.t. & v.i.

pur•loin (pər LOIN) v.t. & v.i. steal; filch.
[ME *purloinen*] —**pur•loin'er** n.

pur•ple (PUR pəl) n. 1. a bluish red color. 2.
royal power or dignity: usu. in the phrase
born to the purple. —v.t. & v.i. •pled,
•pling make or become purple. —adj. 1. of
the color of purple. 2. imperial; regal. 3.
ornate; flowery: a *purple* passage of prose.
[ME *purpel*]

pur•port (pər PORT) v.t. 1. have as its
meaning; signify; imply. 2. claim or profess
(to be), esp. falsely. —n. (PUR port) 1. that
which is suggested as the meaning or intention; import. 2. the substance of a statement etc.; gist. [ME *purporten* carry] —
pur•port'•ed•ly adv.

pur·pose (PUR pəs) *n.* **1.** an idea or ideal kept before the mind as an end of effort or action; design; aim. **2.** practical advantage or result; use: *words to little purpose.* **3.** settled resolution; determination. **—on purpose** intentionally. *—v.t. & v.i.* **·posed, ·pos·ing** have the intention of doing or accomplishing (something); intend; aim. [ME *purpos* propose] **—pur'pose·ful** *adj.* **—pur'pose·ful·ness** *n.* **—pur'pose·less** *adj.*

pur·pose·ly (PUR pəs lee) *adv.* for a purpose; intentionally.

pur·po·sive (PUR pə siv) *adj.* pertaining to, having, or indicating purpose.

purr (pur) *n.* a murmuring sound, such as a cat makes when pleased. *—v.i.* **1.** make such a sound. *—v.t.* **2.** express by or as by purring.

purse (purs) *n.* **1.** a small bag or pouch, esp. one for carrying money. **2.** available resources or means; treasury: *the public purse.* **3.** a sum of money offered as a prize. *—v.t.* **pursed, purs·ing** contract into wrinkles or folds: *purse the lips.* [ME *purs* bag]

purs·er (PUR sər) *n.* an officer having charge of the accounts etc. of a vessel.

pur·su·ance (pər SOO əns) *n.* the act of pursuing; a following up; prosecution: usu. in the phrase **in pursuance of.**

pur·su·ant (pər SOO ənt) *adj.* done in accordance with or by reason of something. *—adv.* in accordance: usu. with *to.* [ME]

pur·sue (pər SOO) *v.* **·sued, ·su·ing** *v.t.* **1.** follow in an attempt to overtake or capture; chase. **2.** seek or attain. **3.** advance along the course of. **4.** apply one's energies to or have as one's chief interest: *pursue one's studies.* *—v.i.* **5.** follow; chase. [ME *pursuen*] **—pur·su'er** *n.*

pur·suit (pər SOOT) *n.* **1.** the act of pursuing; a chase. **2.** that which is followed as a continued employment, pastime, etc.

pu·ru·lent (PYUUR ə lənt) *adj.* consisting of or secreting pus. [< L. *purulentus*] **—pu'ru·lence** *n.* **—pu'ru·lent·ly** *adv.*

pur·vey (pər VAY) *v.t. & v.i.* furnish (provisions, etc.). [ME *purveien*] **—pur·vey'or** *n.*

pur·view (PUR vyoo) *n.* **1.** extent, sphere, or scope of anything, as of official authority. **2.** range of view, experience, or understanding; outlook. [ME *purveu*]

pus (pus) *n.* a yellowish secretion from inflamed tissues. [< L]

push (puush) *v.t.* **1.** exert force upon or against (an object) for the purpose of moving. **2.** force (one's way), as through a crowd, jungle, etc. **3.** urge, advocate, or promote vigorously and persistently: *push* a new product. **4.** bear hard upon; harass: I am *pushed* for time. **5.** *Slang* sell (illegal narcotics). *—v.i.* **6.** exert steady pressure against something so as to move it. *—n.* **1.** the act of pushing; a shove. **2.** determined activity; energy. [ME *pushen*]

push button a button or knob that on being pushed opens or closes a circuit in an electric system. **—push·but·ton** (PUUSH BUT n) *adj.*

push·cart (PUUSH KAHRT) *n.* a cart pushed by hand, used by vendors, peddlers, etc.

push·er (PUUSH ər) *n.* **1.** one who or that which pushes; esp., an active, energetic person. **2.** *Slang* one who illegally sells narcotics to users.

push·ing (PUUSH ing) *adj.* **1.** possessing enterprise and energy. **2.** aggressive; impertinent.

push·o·ver (PUUSH OH vər) *n. Informal* **1.** one who is easily defeated, taken advantage of, etc. **2.** anything that can be done with little or no effort.

push-pull (PUUSH PUUL) *adj. Electronics* designating a circuit or system that uses two similar components operating in opposite phase.

push-up (PUUSH UP) *n.* an exercise in which a prone person alternately pushes the body up from the floor with the arms and lowers it.

push·y (PUUSH ee) *adj.* **·i·er, ·i·est** *Informal* offensively aggressive; bossy. **—push'i·ness** *n.*

pu·sil·lan·i·mous (PYOO sə LAN ə məs) *adj.* lacking courage or spirit; cowardly. [< LL *pusillanimis* very small] **—pu'sil·la·nim'i·ty** (-lə NIM i tee) *n.* **—pu'sil·lan'i·mous·ness** *n.*

puss¹ (puus) *n.* a cat.

puss² *n. Slang* the mouth; face. [< Irish *pus* mouth]

pus·sy¹ (PUS ee) *adj.* **·si·er, ·si·est** filled with or discharging pus.

puss·y² (PUUS ee) *n. pl.* **·sies** a cat. Also **puss'y·cat'.**

puss·y·foot (PUUS ee FUUT) *v.i.* **1.** move softly and stealthily, as a cat does. **2.** act or proceed without committing oneself or revealing one's intentions.

puss·y willow (PUUS ee) a small American willow with silky catkins in early spring.

pus·tu·late (PUS chə LAYT) v.t. & v.i. **·lat·ed, ·lat·ing** form into or become pustules. —adj. (PUS chə lit) covered with pustules. [< LL pustulatus] —**pus′tu·la′ tion** n.

pus·tule (PUS chuul) n. Pathol. a small elevation of the skin with an inflamed base containing pus; pimple. [ME] — **pus·tu·lar** (PUS chə lər) adj.

put (puut) v. **put, put·ting** v.t. **1.** bring into or set in place or position; lay. **2.** bring into a specified state: put a prisoner to death. **3.** bring to bear; apply: Put your back into it. **4.** impose. **5.** ascribe or attribute, as the wrong interpretation on a remark. **6.** place according to one's estimation: I put the time at five o'clock. **7.** throw with a pushing motion of the arm: put the shot. **8.** bring forward for debate, answer, consideration, etc. **9.** subject. **10.** express in words: That's putting it mildly. —v.i. **11.** go; proceed: put to sea. — **put aside** (or **away** or **by**) **1.** place in reserve; save. **2.** thrust aside; discard. —**put down 1.** repress; crush. **2.** write down; record. **3.** Informal disparage. —**put forth. 1.** extend, as the arm or hand. **2.** grow, as shoots or buds. **3.** exert. —**put forward** advance; urge, as a claim. —**put in 1.** interpolate; interpose. **2.** devote; expend, as time. **3.** advance (a claim etc.). —**put off 1.** delay; postpone. **2.** evade. —**put on. 1.** clothe oneself. **2.** simulate; pretend. **3.** give a representation of; stage. **4.** Informal deceive; mock. —**put out. 1.** extinguish. **2.** expel; eject. **3.** inconvenience. **4.** in baseball, retire (a base runner). —**put over 1.** place in command or charge. **2.** accomplish successfully. —**put something over on** take advantage of; deceive. —**put through 1.** bring to successful completion. **2.** cause to undergo. —**put up 1.** erect; build. **2.** preserve or can. **3.** wager; bet. **4.** provide (money, capital, etc.). **5.** sheathe, as a weapon. **6.** shelter; house. —**put upon** take advantage of. —**put up with** endure. —n. a throw or cast. —adj. Informal fixed; settled: My hat won't stay put. [ME putten]

pu·ta·tive (PYOO tə tiv) adj. supposed; reputed. [ME] —**pu′ta·tive·ly** adv.

put-on (PUUT ON) n. Informal a hoax or deception.

put·out (PUUT OWT) n. in baseball, the act of causing an out, as of a batter or base runner.

pu·tre·fy (PYOO trə FI) v.t. & v.i. **·fied, ·fy·ing 1.** decay or cause to decay with a fetid odor; rot. **2.** make or become gangrenous. [ME putrefien] —**pu′tre·fac′ tion** (PYOO trə FAK shən) n.

pu·tres·cent (pyoo TRES ənt) adj. **1.** becoming putrid. **2.** pertaining to putrefaction. —**pu·tres′cence** n.

pu·trid (PYOO trid) adj. **1.** being in a state of putrefaction; rotten. **2.** indicating or produced by putrefaction: a putrid smell. **3.** rotten; corrupt. [ME] —**pu′trid·ness** n.

putsch (puuch) n. an outbreak or rebellion; an attempted coup d'etat. [< G Putsch]

putt (put) n. in golf, a light stroke made to place the ball in or near the hole. [Var. of PUT] —**putt** v.t. & v.i.

put·tee (pu TEE) n. a strip of cloth wound spirally about the leg from knee to ankle. [< Hindi patti bandage]

put·ter[1] (PUT ər) n. **1.** in golf, one who putts. **2.** the club used in putting.

put·ter[2] v.i. **1.** act or work in a dawdling manner. —v.t. **2.** waste (time etc.) in dawdling. Also potter.

put·ty (PUT ee) n. whiting mixed with linseed oil to the consistency of dough, used for filling cracks in surfaces, securing panes of glass in the sash, etc. —v.t. **·tied, ·ty·ing** fill, stop, fasten, etc. with putty. [< F potée] —**put′ti·er** n.

put-up (PUUT UP) adj. Informal planned or contrived in an artful manner: a put-up job.

puz·zle (PUZ əl) v. **·zled, ·zling** v.t. **1.** confuse or perplex. **2.** solve by investigation and study, as something perplexing: with out. —v.i. **3.** be perplexed or confused. — **puzzle over** attempt to understand or solve. —n. **1.** something that puzzles; enigma. **2.** a toy, word game, etc. designed to test one's ingenuity or patience. —**puz′ zler** n. —**puz′zle·ment** n.

pyg·my (PIG mee) adj. **1.** diminutive; dwarfish. **2.** trivial; unimportant. —n. pl. **·mies** a small person or thing regarded as insignificant. Also spelled pigmy. [ME pigme]

Pyg·my (PIG mee) n. pl. **·mies** a member of a people of equatorial Africa, ranging in height from four to five feet. Also Pigmy.

py·lon (PĪ lon) n. **1.** Archit. an entrance to an Egyptian temple, consisting of a central gateway flanked on each side by a truncated pyramidal tower. **2.** a tower or post at an airport for guiding aviators or for marking the turning point in an air race. **3.** one of the steel towers supporting a high-tension electric power line. [< Gk. *pylōn* gateway]

py·or·rhe·a (pī ə REE ə) *n. Pathol.* an inflammation of the gums, usu. with a discharge of pus. [< NL]

pyr·a·mid (PIR ə mid) *n.* **1.** *Archit.* a large structure of masonry, typically having a square base and triangular sides meeting at the top, used as tombs or temples in ancient Egypt. **2.** *Geom.* a solid in this form. —*v.t. & v.i.* **1.** arrange or form in the shape of a pyramid. **2.** buy or sell (stock) with paper profits, and continue so buying or selling. [ME *pyramis*] —**py·ram·i·dal** (pi RAM i dl) *adj.*

pyre (pīr) *n.* a heap of combustibles arranged esp. for burning a dead body. [< L *pyra*]

py·rite (PĪ rīt) *n. pl.* **py·ri·tes** (pī RĪ teez) a metallic, pale yellow mineral: also called *fool's gold, iron pyrites*. [< L *pyritēs*]

pyro- *combining form* fire; heat. [< Gk. *pyr* fire]

py·rol·y·sis (pī ROL ə sis) *n. Chem.* decomposition of compounds by the action of heat. —**py·ro·lit·ic** (pī rə LIT ik) *adj.*

py·ro·ma·ni·a (pī rə MAY nee ə) *n.* a compulsion to set things on fire. —**py′ro·ma′ ni·ac** (-nee ak) *adj. & n.*

py·rom·e·ter (pī ROM i tər) *n.* an instrument for measuring high degrees of heat. —**py·rom′e·try** *n.*

py·ro·tech·nics (pī) *n.* (*construed as sing. or pl.*) **1.** the art of making or using fireworks. **2.** a display, as of oratory. — **py′ro·tech′nist** *n.*

Pyr·rhic victory (PIR ik) a victory gained at a ruinous loss. [after the victory of *Pyrrhus*, king of Epirus, over the Romans in 279 B.C.]

Py·thag·o·re·an theorem (pi THAG ə REE ən) *Geom.* the theorem of Pythagoras that the sum of the squares of the legs of a right triangle is equal to the square of the hypotenuse.

py·thon (PĪ thon) *n.* **1.** a large, nonvenomous serpent that crushes its prey. **2.** any nonvenomous constrictor. [< NL]

pyx (pix) *n. Eccl.* a vessel or casket, usu. of precious metal, in which the Host is preserved. [ME *pyxe*]

Q

q, Q (kyoo) *n. pl.* **q's** or **qs, Q's** or **Qs 1.** the seventeenth letter of the English alphabet. **2.** the sound represented by the letter *q*.

qua (kway, kwah) *adv.* in the capacity of; insofar as. [< L]

quack¹ (kwak) *v.i.* utter a harsh, croaking cry, as a duck. —**quack** *n.*

quack² *n.* **1.** a pretender to medical knowledge or skill. **2.** one who falsely poses as an expert. —*v.i.* play the quack. [Short for QUACKSALVER] —*adj.* —**quack′er•y** *n.*

quack•sal•ver (KWAK SAL vər) *n.* a medical quack. [< Du. *kwakzalver*]

quad¹ (kwod) *n. Informal* a quadrangle, as on a college campus.

quad² *n. Printing* a piece of type metal of less height than the letters, used for spacing.

quad•ran•gle (KWOD RANG gəl) *n.* **1.** *Geom.* a plane figure having four sides and four angles. **2.** a court, either square or oblong; also, the buildings that surround such a court. [< LL *quadrangulum*] —**quad•ran•gu•lar** (kwo DRANG gyə lər) *adj.*

quad•rant (KOWD rənt) *n.* **1.** a quarter section of a circle, subtending an arc of 90°; also, the arc subtended. **2.** an instrument used in navigation, surveying, and astronomy for measuring altitudes. [ME]

quad•ra•phon•ic (KWOD rə FON ik) *adj.* relating to a system of recording and reproducing sound through four tracks.

quad•rat•ic (kwo DRAT ik) *adj.* **1.** of or like a square. **2.** *Math.* pertaining to an equation, curve, surface, etc., involving quantities raised to no higher power than a square. —*n. Math.* a quadratic equation, curve, etc. —**quad•rat′ics** *n. (construed as sing.)* the branch of algebra dealing with quadratic equations.

quad•ren•ni•al (kwo DREN ee əl) *adj.* **1.** occurring once in four years. **2.** lasting four years. [< L *quadriennium*] —**quad•ren′ni•al•ly** *adv.*

quad•ri•lat•er•al (KWOD rə LAT ər əl) *adj.* formed or bounded by four lines; four-sided. —*n. Geom.* a plane figure having four sides and four angles. [< L *quadrilaterus* four-sided]

quad•rille (kwo DRIL) *n.* a square dance for four couples, having five figures. [< F]

quad•ril•lion (kwo DRIL yən) *n.* **1.** a thousand trillions, written as 1 followed by 15 zeros: a cardinal number. **2.** *Brit.* a million trillions (def. 2), written as 1 followed by 24 zeros: a cardinal number. —**quad•ril′lion** *adj.* —**quad•ril′lionth** *adj. & n.*

quad•roon (kwo DROON) *n.* a person of one-quarter black ancestry. [< Sp. *cuarterón*]

quad•ru•ped (KWOD ruu PED) *n.* an animal having four feet; esp., a four-footed mammal. [< L] —*adj.*

quad•ru•ple (kwo DROO pəl) *v.t. & v.i.* •**pled, •pling** multiply by four; make or become four times larger. —*adj.* consisting of or multiplied by four. —*n.* a number four times as great as another. [< L *quadruplus*]

quad•ru•plet (kwo DRUP lit) *n.* **1.** a group of four things or objects, usu. of the same kind. **2.** one of four offspring born at one birth.

quad•ru•pli•cate (kwo DROO pli kit) *adj.* quadruple; fourfold. —*n.* one of four like things. —*v.t. & v.i.* (-pli KAYT •**cat•ed, •cat•ing** make or become quadruple. [< L *quadruplicatus*]

quaff (kwof) *v.t. & v.i.* drink, esp. copiously or with relish. —*n.* a drink; swallow. —**quaff′er** *n.*

quag•mire (KWAG MĪR) *n.* **1.** marshy ground that gives way under the foot. **2.** a difficult situation. —**quag′mired′** *adj.*

qua•hog (KWAW hawg) *n.* an edible, hard-shelled American clam. Also **qua′haug.** [< Algonquian *poquauhock*]

quail¹ (kwayl) *n.* any of various small American game birds related to the patridge; esp., the bobwhite. [ME *quaille*]

quail² *v.i.* shrink with fear; lose heart or courage. [ME]

quaint (kwaynt) *adj.* •**er, •est** pleasingly odd or old-fashioned. [ME *queinte*] —**quaint′ness** *n.*

quake (kwayk) *v.i.* **quaked, quak•ing 1.** shake, as with violent emotion or cold. **2.** tremble, as ground during an earthquake. —*n.* **1.** the act of quaking. **2.** an earthquake. [ME] —**quak′y** *adj.* **quak•i•er, quak•i•est**

Quak•er (KWAY kər) *n.* a popular name for a member of the Society of Friends. [<

QUAKE, ref. to the founder's admonition to tremble at the word of the Lord] **—Quak′er·ism** n. **—Quak′er·ly** adj. & adv.

qual·i·fi·ca·tion (KWOL ə fi KAY shən) n. **1.** the act of qualifying, or the state of being qualified. **2.** any ability, training, etc. that fits a person for a specific office, role, position, etc. **3.** a restriction or modification.

qual·i·fied (KWOL ə FID) adj. **1.** competent or fit. **2.** restricted or modified.

qual·i·fy (KWOL ə FI) v. **-fied, -fy·ing** v.t. **1.** make fit or capable, as for an office, occupation, or privilege. **2.** make legally capable. **3.** limit or restrict. **4.** make less strong or extreme. **5.** Gram. modify. —v.i. **6.** meet the requirements, as for entering a race. [< Med.L qualificare] **—qual′i·fi′er** n.

qual·i·ta·tive (KWOL i TAY tiv) adj. of or pertaining to quality: distinguished from quantitative. [< LL qualitativus] **—qual′i·ta′tive·ly** adv.

qual·i·ty (KWOL i tee) n. pl. **-ties 1.** a distinguishing element or characteristic. **2.** the basic or essential character, nature, etc. of something. **3.** excellence. **4.** the degree of excellence. [ME qualite]

qualm (kwahm) n. **1.** a feeling of sickness. **2.** a twinge of conscience; moral scruple. **3.** a sensation of fear or misgiving. **—qualm′ish** adj. **—qualm′ish·ly** adv. **—qualm′ish·ness** n.

quan·da·ry (KWON də ree) n. pl. **-da·ries** a state of hesitation or perplexity.

quan·ta (KWON tə) n. plural of QUANTUM.

quan·ti·ta·tive (KWON ti TAY tiv) adj. of or pertaining to quantity: distinguished from qualitative. **—quan′ti·ta′tive·ly** adv.

quan·ti·ty (KWON ti tee) n. pl. **-ties 1.** an amount, number, weight, etc. **2.** Often pl. a large amount: abundance. [ME quantite]

quan·tize (KWON tīz) v.t. **-tized, -tiz·ing** Physics **1.** restrict the possible values of (an observable quantity or magnitude). **2.** express as multiples of a given quantity or quantum. **—quan′ti·za′tion** n.

quan·tum (KWON təm) n. pl. **-ta** (-tə) Physics a fundamental unit of energy. [< L, how much]

quantum theory Physics the theory that energy is not a smoothly flowing continuum but is manifested by the emission from radiating bodies of discrete particles, or quanta.

quar·an·tine (KWOR ən TEEN) n. **1.** the enforced isolation in port for a fixed period of time of ships suspected of carrying a con-

tagious disease. **2.** a place designated for the enforcement of such interdiction. **3.** the enforced isolation of any person or place infected with contagious disease. **4.** any enforced isolation. —v.t. **-tined, -tin·ing** isolate by or as by quarantine. [< Ital. quarantina, originally a period of forty days]

quark (kwahrk) n. Physics a hypothetical elementary particle. [after "Three quarks for Muster Mark" in James Joyce's Finnegan's Wake]

quar·rel (KWOR əl) n. **1.** an unfriendly, angry, or violent dispute. **2.** the cause for dispute. —v.i. **-reled, -rel·ing** engage in a quarrel. [ME querele] **—quar′rel·er** n.

quar·rel·some (KWOR əl səm) adj. inclined to quarrel. **—quar′rel·some·ness** n.

quar·ry¹ (KWOR ee) n. pl. **-ries 1.** a beast or bird hunted or killed, as in the chase. **2.** anything hunted, slaughtered, or pursued. [ME querre entrails]

quar·ry² n. pl. **-ries** an excavation from which stone is cut, blasted, etc. —v.t. **-ried, -ry·ing** cut, dig, or take from or as from a quarry. [ME quarey] **—quar′ri·er** n.

quart (kwort) n. **1.** a measure of capacity equal to Ā gallon, or two pints. In the U.S., the dry quart is equal to 1.10 liters, and the liquid quart is equal to 0.946 liter. **2.** a container having such a capacity. [ME]

quar·ter (KWOR tər) n. **1.** one of four equal parts into which anything is or may be divided. **2.** a coin having the value of 25 cents. **3.** fifteen minutes or a fourth of an hour. **4.** three months or a fourth of a year. **5.** Astron. a fourth part of the moon's revolution about the earth. **6.** a particular district or locality, as of a city: the native quarter. **7.** Usu. pl. proper or assigned station, as of officers and crew on a warship. **8.** pl. a place of lodging or residence. **9.** mercy shown to a vanquished enemy. **—at close quarters** close by; at close range. —adj. **1.** being one of four equal parts. **2.** having one fourth of a standard value. —v.t. **1.** divide into four equal parts. **2.** divide into a number of parts or pieces. **3.** furnish with quarters or shelter; lodge. —v.i. **2.** be stationed or lodged. [ME]

quar·ter·back (KWOR tər BAK) n. in football, the back who directs offensive play.

quar·ter·deck (KWOR tər DEK) n. Naut. the rear part of a ship's upper deck, reserved for officers.

quarter horse a strong horse developed for short-distance races.

quar•ter•ly (KWOR tər lee) *adj.* **1.** containing or being a fourth part. **2.** occurring at intervals of three months. —*n. pl.* **•lies** a publication issued once every three months. —*adv.* **1.** once in a quarter of a year. **2.** in or by quarters. [ME]

quar•ter•mas•ter (KWOR tər MAS tər) *n.* **1.** an officer responsible for the supply of food, fuel, clothing, etc. **2.** on shipboard, a petty officer responsible for steering and related functions. [ME *quarter maister*]

quarter note *Music* a note having one fourth the time value of a whole note.

quar•tet (kwor TET) *n.* **1.** a composition for four voices or instruments; also the four persons performing it. **2.** any group or set of four things of a kind. Also **quar•tette'.** [< Ital. *quartetto*]

quar•to (KWOR toh) *adj.* having four leaves or eight pages to the sheet: a *quarto* book. —*n. pl.* **•tos** a book or pamphlet having pages the size of a fourth of a sheet. [< NL *in quarto* in fourth]

quartz (kworts) *n.* a hard, vitreous mineral, usu. transparent and colorless. [< G *Quarz*]

qua•sar (KWAY zahr) *n.* a galaxy-like formation in remote space that emits radio waves and vast energy. [< QUAS(I-STELL.)AR (RADIO SOURCE)]

quash (kwosh) *v.t.* **1.** *Law* make void or set aside, as an indictment; annul. **2.** put down or suppress forcibly or summarily: *quash* a rebellion. [ME *quashen* smash]

qua•si (KWAY zī) *adj.* resembling but not exactly of the same kind.

quasi- *combining form* resembling; nearly; in some degree: *quasi-official.*

quat•rain (KWO trayn) *n.* a stanza or poem of four lines. [< F]

quat•re•foil (KAT ər FOIL) *n.* **1.** a leaf etc. having four leaflets. **2.** *Archit.* an ornament with four lobes. [ME]

quat•tro•cen•to (KWAH troh CHEN toh) *n.* the 15th c. as connected with the revival of art and literature, esp. in Italy. [< Ital.]

qua•ver (KWAY vər) *v.i.* **1.** tremble or shake: said usu. of the voice. **2.** produce trills or quavers in singing or in playing a musical instrument. —*v.t.* **3.** utter or sing in a tremulous voice. —*n.* **1.** a quivering or tremulous motion. **2.** a trill. [ME *quaveren* tremble] —**qua'•ver•y** *adj.*

quay (kee) *n.* a wharf where vessels may load or unload. [< OF *cay*]

quea•sy (KWEE zee) *adj.* **•si•er, •si•est 1.** sick at the stomach. **2.** easily nauseated. [ME *qweysy*] —**quea'si•ness** *n.*

queen (kween) *n.* **1.** the wife of a king. **2.** a female sovereign or monarch. **3.** a woman preeminent in a given sphere. **4.** in chess, the most powerful piece, capable of moving any number of squares in a straight or diagonal line. **5.** a playing card bearing a picture of a queen. **6.** *Entomol.* the single fully developed female in a colony of bees, ants, etc. —*v.t.* **1.** make a queen of. **2.** in chess, make a queen of (a pawn) by moving it to the eighth row. —*v.i.* **3.** reign as or play the part of a queen. [ME *quene*]

queen dowager the widow of a king.

queen mother a queen dowager who is mother of a reigning sovereign.

queer (kweer) *adj.* **•er, •est 1.** unusual; strange. **2.** eccentric. **3.** *Slang* counterfeit. **4.** *Offensive slang* homosexual. —*n. Slang* **1.** counterfeit money. **2.** *Offensive* a homosexual person. —*v.t.* jeopardize or spoil.

quell (kwel) *v.t.* **1.** put down or suppress by force; extinguish. **2.** quiet; allay, as pain. [ME *quellen* kill]

quench (kwench) *v.t.* **1.** put out or extinguish, as a fire. **2.** put an end to; subdue. **3.** slake or satisfy (thirst). **4.** cool, as heated iron or steel, by thrusting into water or other liquid. [ME *quenchen*] —**quench'a•ble** *adj.*

quer•u•lous (KWER ə ləs) *adj.* **1.** disposed to complain or be fretful. **2.** of a complaining or whining manner. [< LL *querulus* complaining] —**quer'u•lous•ly** *adv.* —**quer'u•lous•ness** *n.*

que•ry (KWEER ee) *v.t. & v.i.* **•ried, •ry•ing** question. —*n. pl.* **•ries** an inquiry or question. [< L *quaere* ask]

quest (kwest) *n.* **1.** the act of looking for something; a search. **2.** an adventure or expedition. [ME *queste*] —*v.t. & v.i.* go on a quest or to search for (something). —**quest'er** *n.*

ques•tion (KWES chən) *n.* **1.** an interrogative sentence calling for an answer; an inquiry. **2.** a subject of inquiry or debate; a matter to be decided; problem. **3.** possibility of disagreement or dispute; doubt: no *question* about it. —**out of the question** not to be thought of; impossible. —*v.t.* **1.** put a question to; interrogate. **2.** be uncertain of; doubt. **3.** make objection to; challenge; dispute. —*v.i.* **4.** ask a question. [ME *questioun*] —**ques'tion•er** *n.*

ques·tion·a·ble (KWES chə nə bəl) *adj.* **1.** characterized by doubtful integrity, honesty, respectability, etc. **2.** liable to be called in question; debatable. —**ques′tion·a·bil′i·ty, ques′tion·a·ble·ness** *n.* —**ques′·tion·a·bly** *adv.*

question mark a mark of punctuation (?) indicating that the sentence it closes is a direct question: also called *interrogation point.*

ques·tion·naire (KWES chə NAIR) *n.* a written or printed series of questions submitted to a number of persons to obtain information. [< F]

queue (kyoo) *n.* **1.** a pigtail. **2.** a line of persons or vehicles. —*v.i.* **queued, queu·ing** form a line: usu. with *up.* [< MF]

quib·ble (KWIB əl) *n.* **1.** an evasion of a point or question. **2.** a trivial distinction or objection; cavil. —*v.i.* **·bled, ·bling** raise trivial objections. —**quib′bler** *n.*

quick (kwik) *adj.* **·er, ·est 1.** done or occurring in a short time; rapid; swift. **2.** responding readily to impressions or instruction: a *quick* mind. **3.** easily aroused or excited; hasty: a *quick* temper. **4.** nimble: *quick* fingers. —*n.* **1.** those who are alive: the *quick* and the dead. **2.** the living flesh, esp. the tender flesh under a fingernail. **3.** the feelings: cut to the *quick.* —*adv.* rapidly. [ME *quik* swift] —**quick′ly** *adv.* —**quick′ness** *n.*

quick·en (KWIK ən) *v.t.* **1.** cause to move or act more rapidly. **2.** give or restore life to. **3.** excite or arouse; stimulate. —*v.i.* **4.** move or act more rapidly. **5.** come or return to life; revive. **6.** begin to manifest signs of life: said of the fetus. —**quick′en·er** *n.*

quick·sand (KWIK SAND) *n.* a bed of water-soaked sand that engulfs anything on it.

quick·sil·ver (KWIK SIL vər) *n.* mercury in its liquid form. [ME *qwyksilver*]

quick·step (KWIK STEP) *n.* a march or dance written in a rapid tempo; a lively step used in marching.

quick-tem·pered (KWIK TEM pərd) *adj.* easily angered.

quick time a marching step of 120 paces a minute, each pace of 30 inches.

quick-wit·ted (KWIK WIT id) *adj.* having a ready wit or quick discernment; keen; alert. —**quick′-wit′ted·ness** *n.*

quid (kwid) *n.* **1.** a small portion of chewing tobacco. **2.** a cud, as of a cow. [Var. of CUD.]

quid pro quo (KWID proh KWOH) *Latin* something for something; an equivalent in return.

qui·es·cent (kwee ES ənt) *adj.* being in a state of repose or inaction; quiet; still. [< L *quiescere* be quiet] —**qui·es′cence** *n.* —**qui·es′cent·ly** *adv.*

qui·et (KWĪ it) *adj.* **·er, ·est 1.** making little or no noise. **2.** having little or no motion; still; calm. **3.** characterized by silence; also, retired or secluded: a *quiet* spot. **4.** free from excessive activity, turmoil, or vexation: a *quiet* day. **5.** gentle; mild: a *quiet* temperament. **6.** not showy or pretentious; modest. **7.** in commerce, not busy or active. —*n.* the quality or condition of being quiet; peace, tranquillity. —*v.t. & v.i.* make or become quiet: often with *down.* —*adv.* in a quiet or peaceful manner. [ME] —**qui′et·ly** *adv.* —**qui′et·ness** *n.*

qui·e·tude (KWĪ i TOOD) *n.* a condition of calm or tranquility; repose; rest.

qui·e·tus (kwī EE təs) *n. pl.* **·tus·es 1.** anything that kills, as a blow; also, death itself. **2.** a final discharge, as of a debt. [< Med.L, quit]

quill (kwil) *n.* **1.** *Ornithol.* one of the large, strong flight feathers or tail feathers of a bird. **2.** something made from a quill, as a pen. **3.** *Zool.* one of the large, sharp spines of a porcupine or hedgehog. [ME *quil*]

quilt (kwilt) *n.* **1.** a bedcover made by stitching together firmly two layers of cloth or patchwork with some soft and warm substance (as wool or cotton) between them. **2.** any bedcover, esp. if thick. —*v.t.* **1.** stitch together (two pieces of material) with a soft substance between. **2.** pad or line with something soft. —*v.i.* **3.** make a quilt or quilted work. [ME *quilte*]

qui·nine (KWĪnīn) *n. Chem.* a white, very bitter substance, the salts of which are used in medicine, esp. in the treatment of malaria. [< Sp. *quina*]

quinine water a carbonated beverage flavored with quinine: also called *tonic.*

quin·sy (KWIN zee) *n. Pathol.* an inflammation of the tonsils. [ME *quinesie*]

quin·tes·sence (kwin TES əns) *n.* **1.** an extract from anything, containing in concentrated form its most essential principle. **2.** the purest example of something. [< Med.L *quinta essentia* fifth essence] —**quin·tes·sen·tial** (KWIN tə SEN shəl) *adj.*

quin·tet (kwin TET) *n.* **1.** a musical composition for five voices or instruments; also, the five persons performing it. **2.** any group of five persons or things. Also **quin·tette′.** [< Ital. *quintetto*]

quin·tu·ple (kwin TOO pəl) *v.t. & v.i.* **·pled, ·pling** multiply by five; make or become five times larger. —*adj.* consisting of or multiplied by five. —*n.* a number five times as great as another. [< MF]

quin·tu·plet (kwin TUP lit) *n.* **1.** five things of a kind used or occurring together. **2.** one of five born at one birth.

quin·tu·pli·cate (kwin TOO pli kit) *adj.* **1.** fivefold. **2.** raised to the fifth power. —*v.t. & v.i.* (-pli KAYT) **·cat·ed, ·cat·ing** multiply by five; quintuple. —*n.* (-pli kit) one of five identical things.

quip (kwip) *n.* a sarcastic or witty jest or retort. —*v.i.* **quipped, quip·ping** make a witty remark; jest. —**quip'ster** *n.*

quire (kwīr) *n.* the twentieth part of a ream of paper; 24 sheets. —*v.t.* **quired, quir·ing** fold or separate into quires. [ME *quayer*]

quirk (kwurk) *n.* **1.** a personal peculiarity, mannerism, or caprice. **2.** a sharp turn or twist. —**quirk'i·ness** *n.* —**quirk'y** *adj.*

quis·ling (KWIZ ling) *n.* a traitor who collaborates with the invaders of the traitor's country by serving in a puppet government. [after Vidkum *Quisling*, 1887—1945, Norwegian Nazi party leader and traitor]

quit (kwit) *v.* **quit or quit·ted, quit·ting** *v.t.* **1.** cease or desist from; discontinue. **2.** give up; renounce. **3.** go away from; leave. —*v.i.* **4.** stop; cease; discontinue. **5.** resign from a position etc. —*adj.* released, relieved, or absolved from something; clear; free; rid. —*n.* the act of quitting. —**be quits** be even (with another). —**call it quits 1.** stop working. **2.** end a friendship or other association. [ME *quitte*]

quite (kwīt) *adv.* **1.** to the fullest extent; totally: *quite* dead. **2.** really; truly. **3.** to a great or considerable extent; noticeably; very: *quite* ill. [ME]

quit·ter (KWIT ər) *n.* one who gives up or quits easily.

quiv·er¹ (KWIV ər) *v.i.* shake with a slight, tremulous motion; vibrate; tremble. —*n.* the act or fact of quivering; a trembling or shaking.

quiv·er² *n.* a portable case for arrows; also, its contents. [ME]

quix·ot·ic (kwik SOT ik) *adj.* ridiculously chivalrous or romantic; having high but impractical sentiments, aims, etc. [after *Don Quixote*, protagonist of a Cervantes novel] —**quix·ot'·i·cal·ly** *adv.* —**quix·ot·ism** (KWIK sə TIZ əm) *n.*

quiz (kwiz) *n.* **1.** the act of questioning; esp., an informal oral or written examination. **2.** an eccentric person or thing. **3.** a hoax; practical joke. —*v.t.* **quizzed, quiz·zing** examine by asking questions. —**quiz'·zer** *n.*

quiz·zi·cal (KWIZ i kəl) *adj.* **1.** given to chaffing or bantering. **2.** queer; odd. **3.** questioning; puzzled: a *quizzical* smile. — **quiz'zi·cal·ly** *adv.*

quoin (koin) *n.* **1.** an external angle or corner of a building. **2.** a stone or stones forming such an angle. —*v.t.* provide, secure, or support with a quoin or quoins. [Var. of COIN]

quoit (kwoit) *n.* **1.** a ring of metal, rope, etc., thrown in a game at a short stake, either encircling it or coming as close to it as possible. **2. quoits** *(construed as sing.)* the game so played. [ME *coyte*]

quon·dam (KWON dəm) *adj.* having been formerly; former. [< L]

quo·rum (KWOR əm) *n.* the number of members of any deliberative or corporate body as is necessary for the legal transaction of business. [< L, of whom]

quo·ta (KWOH tə) *n.* the proportional share required for making up a certain quantity. [< Med.L]

quot·a·ble (KWOH tə bəl) *adj.* suitable for quotation. —**quot'a·bil'i·ty** *n.*

quo·ta·tion (kwoh TAY shən) *n.* **1.** the act of quoting. **2.** the words quoted or cited. **3.** a price quoted or current, as of securities etc. [< Med.L]

quotation mark either of a pair of punctuation marks (" or ' and " or ') used to enclose a quotation, the single marks being used to set off a quotation within a quotation.

quote (kwoht) *v.t.* **quot·ed, quot·ing 1.** reproduce the words of. **2.** repeat or cite (a rule, author, etc.), as for authority or illustration. **3.** in commerce: **a** state (a price). **b** give the current or market price of. —*n.* loosely, a quotation. **2.** a quotation mark. [ME *coten*] —**quot'er** *n.* —**quote'wor'thy** (KWOHT wur thee) *adj.*

quo·tid·i·an (kwoh TID ee ən) *adj.* **1.** recurring or occurring every day. **2.** commonplace. [< L *quotidianus* daily]

quo·tient (KWOH shənt) *n. Math.* the result obtained by division; a number indicating how many times one quantity is contained in another. [< L *quotiens* how often]

R

r, R (ahr) *n. pl.* **R's** or **Rs, r's** or **rs** **1.** the eighteenth letter of the English alphabet. **2.** the sound represented by the letter *r.* — **the three R's** reading, writing, and arithmetic regarded as the essential elements of a primary education.

Ra (rah) *n.* the supreme Egyptian deity, the sun god.

rab·bet (RAB it) *n.* a groove in or near the edge of one piece of wood etc., cut so as to receive the edge of another piece. —*v.* **·bet·ed, ·bet·ing** *v.t.* **1.** cut a rabbet in. **2.** unite in a rabbet. —*v.i.* **3.** be jointed by a rabbet. [ME *rabet*]

rab·bi (RAB ī) *n. pl.* **·bis** in Judaism: **a** the spiritual head of a Jewish community, authorized to perform religious duties. **b** master; teacher: a title for one learned in the Law. [ME *rabi*] —**rab·bin′i·cal** *adj.*

rab·bin·ate (RAB ə nit) *n.* **1.** the office or term of office of a rabbi. **2.** rabbis collectively.

rab·bit (RAB it) *n.* **1.** any of a family of various small, long-eared mammals. **2.** the pelt of a rabbit or hare. —*v.i.* hunt rabbits. [ME *rabet*] —**rabbit fever** tularemia.

rabbit punch a short chopping blow at the base of the skull or back of the neck.

rab·ble (RAB əl) *n.* a disorderly crowd or mob. —**the rabble** the populace or lower classes: a contemptuous term. [ME *rabel*]

rab·ble-rous·er (RAB əl ROW zər) *n.* one who incites mobs by arousing passions.

Rab·e·lai·si·an (RAB ə LAY zhən) *adj.* bawdy and boisterous. [after François *Rabelais*, 1494?—1553, French satirist]

rab·id (RAB id) *adj.* **1.** affected with rabies. **2.** fanatical; violent. **3.** furious; raging. [< L *rabidus* mad] —**rab′·id·ly** *adv.* —**rab′id·ness** *n.*

ra·bies (RAY beez) *n.* an acute, infectious, usu. fatal disease of certain animals, esp. of dogs, readily transmissible to man by the bite of an affected animal: also called *hydrophobia.* [< L, madness]

rac·coon (ra KOON) *n.* **1.** a North American nocturnal carnivore, grayish brown with a black-and-white-ringed bushy tail. **2.** the fur of this animal. [< Algonquian *aroughcun*]

race¹ (rays) *n.* **1.** one of the major subdivi-

sions of mankind, regarded as having a common origin and exhibiting a relatively constant set of physical traits. **2.** loosely, a nation, tribe, or ethnic group. **3.** a genealogical or family stock; clan. **4.** pedigree; lineage. **5.** *Biol.* a variety or species. [< F]

race² *n.* **1.** a contest to determine the relative speed of the contestants. **2.** any contest. **3.** duration of life; course; career. **4.** a swift current of water or its channel. **5.** a sluice or channel by which to conduct water to or from a water wheel or around a dam. —*v.* **raced, rac·ing** *v.i.* **1.** take part in a contest of speed. **2.** move at great or top speed. **3.** move at an accelerated or too great speed: said of machinery. —*v.t.* **4.** contend against in a race. **5.** cause to race. [ME *ras*]

race·horse (RAYS HORS) *n.* a horse bred and trained for contests of speed.

race·track (RAYS TRAK) *n.* a track or course over which a horse race, dog race, etc. is run.

race·way (RAYS WAY) *n.* **1.** a channel for conducting water. **2.** a racetrack for trotting horses.

ra·cial (RAY shəl) *adj.* of, pertaining to, or characteristic of a race or descent. —**ra′cial·ly** *adv.*

rac·ism (RAY siz əm) *n.* **1.** an irrational belief in the superiority of a given people or nation, usu. one's own. **2.** action or policy based upon such a belief. —**ra′cist** *n. & adj.*

rack¹ (rak) *n.* **1.** an open grating, framework, or the like in or on which articles may be placed. **2.** *Mech.* a bar or the like having teeth that engage with those of a gearwheel etc. **3.** an instrument of torture that stretches the limbs of victims. —*v.t.* **1.** place or arrange in or on a rack. **2.** torture on or as on the rack. **3.** strain, as with the effort of thinking: *rack* one's brains. —**rack up** achieve: *rack up* a perfect score. [ME *rakke*]

rack² *n.* see WRACK.

rack·et¹ (RAK it) *n.* **1.** a light hoop, usu. strung with nylon, and having a handle, used in striking a tennis ball etc. **2.** **rackets** *(construed as sing.)* a game played with a ball and rackets in a court with four walls. Also **rac′quet.** [< MF *raquette*]

rack•et² n. **1.** a clattering or confused noise. **2.** a scheme or business for getting money by illegitimate means. **3.** *Slang* any business or occupation. —*v.i.* make a loud, clattering noise.

rack•et•eer (RAK i TEER) n. one engaged in an organized, illegal enterprise; gangster. —**rack′et•eer′ing** n.

rack•et•y (RAK i tee) adj. noisy.

rac•on•teur (RAK ən TUR) n. a skilled storyteller. [< F]

rac•y (RAY see) adj. **rac•i•er, rac•i•est 1.** having a spirited or pungent interest; spicy. **2.** having a characteristic flavor assumed to be indicative of origin, as wine. **3.** suggestive; slightly immodest: a *racy* story. —**rac′i•ly** adv. —**rac′i•ness** n.

ra•dar (RAY dahr) n. *Telecom.* an electronic device that locates objects by beaming radio-frequency impulses that are reflected back from the object. [< *radio detection and ranging*]

ra•di•al (RAY dee əl) adj. **1.** of, pertaining to, or resembling a ray or radius. **2.** *Anat.* denoting the radius. —n. a radiating part. —**ra′di•al•ly** adv.

radial tire an automotive tire having cords perpendicular to the wheel rim. Also called **radial**.

ra•di•an (RAY dee ən) n. *Math.* **1.** an arc equal in length to the radius of the circle of which it is a part. **2.** the angle subtended by such an arc.

ra•di•ance (RAY dee əns) n. the quality or state of being radiant; brightness. Also **ra′di•an•cy.**

ra•di•ant (RAY dee ənt) adj. **1.** emitting rays of light or heat. **2.** beaming with light or brightness, kindness, or love. **3.** resembling rays. **4.** consisting of or transmitted by radiation. —n. that which radiates. [ME] —**ra′di•ant•ly** adv.

radiant energy *Physics* the energy transmitted in the form of waves, esp. electromagnetic waves, as heat, light, X-rays, etc.

ra•di•ate (RAY dee AYT) v. •**at•ed,** •**at•ing** v.i. **1.** emit rays or radiation; be radiant. **2.** issue forth in rays, as light from the sun. **3.** spread out from a center, as the spokes of a wheel. —v.t. **4.** send out or emit in or as in rays. —**ra′di•a′tive** adj.

ra•di•a•tion (RAY dee AY shən) n. **1.** the act of radiating, or the state of being radiated. **2.** *Physics* the emission and propagation of radiant energy, esp. by radioactive substances capable of affecting living tissue.

radiation sickness *Pathol.* a condition due to absorption of excess radiation and marked by fatigue, vomiting, internal hemorrhage, and progressive tissue breakdown.

ra•di•a•tor (RAY dee AY tər) n. **1.** a chamber, coil, etc., through which is passed steam or hot water for warming a space. **2.** in engines, a nest of tubes for cooling water flowing through them. **3.** *Physics* a source of radiation or radioactivity.

rad•i•cal (RAD i kəl) adj. **1.** of, proceeding from, or pertaining to the root or foundation; fundamental. **2.** thoroughgoing; extreme. **3.** *Math.* pertaining to the root or roots of a number. **4.** of or pertaining to political radicals. —n. **1.** one who advocates widespread changes and reforms in government, social institutions, etc. at the earliest opportunity. **2.** *Math.* **a** quantity that is the root of another quantity. **b** the radical sign. **3.** *Chem.* a group of atoms that acts as a unit in a compound and may pass unchanged through a series of reactions. [< LL *radicalis* having roots] —**rad′i•cal•ly** adv.

rad•i•cal•ism (RAD i kə LIZ əm) n. **1.** the state of being radical. **2.** advocacy of radical measures.

radical sign *Math.* the symbol ✓ placed before a quantity to indicate that a designated root is to be taken.

ra•di•i (RAY dee ī) plural of RADIUS.

ra•di•o (RAY dee OH) n. pl. •**di•os 1.** the science and technique of communicating by means of electromagnetic waves that have been modulated to carry information in the form either of sound or of a code. **2.** a receiver, transmitter, or other radio apparatus. **3.** the radio business and industry. —v.t. & v.i. •**di•oed,** •**di•o•ing 1.** transmit (a message etc.) by radio. **2.** communicate with (someone) by radio. [< *radiotelegraphy*] —adj.

ra•di•o•ac•tiv•i•ty (RAY dee oh ak TIV i tee) n. *Physics* the spontaneous nuclear disintegration of certain elements, with the emission of radiation in the form of particles or rays. —**ra′di•o•ac′tive** adj.

radio astronomy the branch of astronomy and astrophysics that studies celestial objects by the analysis of radio waves received.

ra•di•o•car•bon (RAY dee oh KAHR bən) n. *Physics* the radioactive isotope of carbon of mass 14 with a half life of about 5570 years, used in the dating of fossils, artifacts, etc.: also called *carbon 14*.

radio frequency any frequency lying between the audio sound waves and infrared light portion of the frequency spectrum, used in radio and television transmission.

ra·di·ol·o·gy (RAY dee OL ə jee) *n.* the branch of science that relates to radiant energy and its applications, esp. in the diagnosis and treatment of disease. —**ra'di·ol'o·gist** *n.*

ra·di·om·e·ter (RAY dee OM i tər) *n.* an instrument for detecting and measuring radiant energy by converting it into mechanical energy. —**ra'di·om'e·try** *n.*

ra·di·os·co·py (RAY dee OS kə pee) *n.* the examination of opaque bodies with the aid of X-rays or some other form of radiant energy. —**ra'di·o·scop'ic** *adj.*

ra·di·o·sonde (RAY dee oh SOND) *n. Meteorol.* an airborne device, usu. attached to a balloon, that transmits meteorological data to the ground. [< F]

radio telescope *Astron.* a radio receiver designed to receive radio waves from outer space.

ra·di·o·ther·a·py (RAY dee oh THER ə pee) *n. Med.* the treatment of disease by X-rays and other forms of radioactivity.

radio wave any electromagnetic wave having a radio frequency.

ra·di·um (RAY dee əm) *n.* a powerfully radioactive metallic element (symbol Ra). [< NL]

radium therapy the treatment of diseases, esp. of cancer, by means of radium.

ra·di·us (RAY dee əs) *n. pl.* **·di·i** (-dee I) 1. a straight line from the center of a circle or sphere to the circumference or surface. 2. *Anat.* the outer bone of the two long bones of the forearm, located on the same side as the thumb. 3. a circular area or boundary measured by the length of its radius. 4. sphere, scope, or limit, as of activity. [< L, rod]

ra·dome (RAY DOHM) *n.* a protective housing for the antenna of a radar assembly. [< RA(DAR) + DOME]

ra·don (RAY don) *n.* a gaseous, radioactive element (symbol Rn), formed by the disintegration of radium.

raf·fi·a (RAF ee ə) *n.* 1. a cultivated palm of Madagascar, the leafstalks of which furnish fiber for making hats, mats, baskets, etc. 2. its fiber. [< earlier *rafia*]

raff·ish (RAF ish) *adj.* 1. tawdry; gaudy; flashy. 2. disreputable.

raf·fle (RAF əl) *n.* a form of lottery in which one buys a chance on a prize. —*v.t.* **·fled, ·fling** dispose of by a raffle: often with *off*. [ME *rafle* a game of dice]

raft[1] (raft) *n.* 1. a float of logs, planks, etc., fastened together for transportation by water. 2. any similar float, as one anchored for use by swimmers. 3. a life raft. —*v.t.* 1. transport on a raft. —*v.i.* 2. travel by raft. [ME *rafte*]

raft[2] *n. Informal* a large number or collection of any kind. [ME]

raft·er (RAFT ər) *n.* a beam giving form, slope, and support to a roof. [ME]

rag[1] (rag) *v.t.* **ragged, rag·ging** *Informal* 1. tease or annoy. 2. scold.

rag[2] *n.* 1. a torn or discarded piece of cloth. 2. a small cloth used for washing, cleaning, etc. 3. *pl.* cotton or linen textile remnants used in the making of rag paper. 4. *pl.* tattered or shabby clothing. —**glad rags** *Slang* one's best clothes. [ME *ragge*]

rag·a·muf·fin (RAG ə MUF in) *n.* anyone, esp. a child, wearing ragged clothes. [after *Ragamoffyn*, demon in William Langland's *Piers Plowman* (1393)]

rage (rayj) *n.* 1. violent anger; wrath; fury. 2. any great violence or intensity. 3. extreme eagerness or emotion; great enthusiasm. 4. something popular or in demand; a fad. —*v.i.* **raged, rag·ing** 1. speak or act with great anger. 2. act or proceed with violence or intensity. [ME] —**rag'ing·ly** *adv.*

rag·ged (RAG id) *adj.* 1. torn or worn into rags; frayed. 2. wearing worn, frayed, or shabby garments. 3. of rough or uneven character or aspect. [ME *ragget*]

ra·gout (ra GOO) *n.* a highly seasoned dish of stewed meat and vegetables. [< F *ragoût*]

rag·time (RAG TIM) *n.* 1. a kind of American dance music, developed from about 1890 to 1920, characterized by highly syncopated rhythm in fast time. 2. the rhythm of this music.

raid (rayd) *n.* 1. a hostile or predatory incursion by a rapidly moving body of troops or an armed vessel; a foray. 2. an air raid. 3. any sudden invasion, capture, or seizure. —*v.t.* 1. make a raid on. —*v.i.* 2. participate in a raid. [ME *raide* expedition] —**raid'er** *n.*

rail[1] (rayl) *n.* 1. a bar of wood, metal, etc., resting on supports, as in a fence, at the side of a stairway, etc.; a railing. 2. one of a series of parallel bars of iron or steel resting upon crossties and forming a support and guide for wheels, as of a railroad. **3.** a railroad considered as a means of transportation: ship by *rail.* —*v.t.* furnish or shut in with rails; fence. [ME *raile* beam]

rail² *n.* any of numerous marsh birds having long legs and a short, turned-up tail. [ME *rale*]

rail³ *v.i.* use abusive language; scold: with *at* or *against.* [ME *railen*]

rail·ing (RAY ling) *n.* **1.** a series of rails; a balustrade. **2.** rails, or material from which rails are made.

rail·ler·y (RAY lə ree) *n. pl.* **·ler·ies** merry jesting or teasing; banter. [< F *raillerie*]

rail·road (RAYL ROHD) *n.* **1.** a graded road having metal rails supported by ties, for the passage of trains or rolling stock drawn by locomotives. **2.** the system of tracks, stations, etc., used in transportation by rail. **3.** the corporation or persons owning or operating such a system. —*v.t.* **1.** transport by railroad. **2.** *Informal* rush or force with great speed or without deliberation. **3.** *Informal* cause to be imprisoned on false charges or without fair trial. —*v.i.* **4.** work on a railroad.

rail·way (RAYL WAY) *n.* **1.** a railroad. **2.** any track or set of rails similar to those of a railroad.

rai·ment (RAY mənt) *n.* wearing apparel; clothing; garb. [ME *rayment*]

rain (rayn) *n.* **1.** the condensed water vapor of the atmosphere falling in drops. **2.** the fall of such drops. **3.** a fall or shower of anything. **4.** a rainstorm. **5.** *pl.* the rainy season, as in a tropical country. —*v.i.* **1.** fall from the clouds in drops of water: usu. with *it* as the subject. **2.** fall like rain, as tears. —*v.t.* **3.** send down like rain; shower. —**rain out** cause (an outdoor event) to be canceled or postponed because of rain. [ME *rein*] —**rain'y** *adj.* **rain·i·er, rain·i·est**

rain·bow (RAYN BOH) *n.* an arch of prismatic colors formed in the sky opposite the sun and caused by refraction, reflection, and dispersion of light in raindrops falling through the air. [ME *reinbowe*]

rain check 1. the stub of a ticket to an outdoor event, as a baseball game, entitling the holder to admission at a future date if the event is called off. **2.** a postponed invitation.

rain·coat (RAYN KOHT) *n.* a coat, often waterproof, intended to be worn in rainy weather.

rain·fall (RAYN FAWL) *n.* **1.** a fall of rain. **2.** *Meteorol.* the amount of water, measured in inches, precipitated in a given region over a stated time, as rain, hail, snow, or the like.

rain forest a dense tropical forest on which 100 inches or more of rain falls each year.

rain gauge an instrument for measuring the amount of rainfall at a given place or time.

rain·mak·ing (RAYN MAY king) *n.* production of rain, or an attempt to produce it, esp. by seeding clouds. —**rain'mak'er** *n.*

raise (rayz) *v.* **raised, rais·ing** *v.t.* **1.** cause to move upward or to a higher level; elevate. **2.** place erect; set up. **3.** construct or build. **4.** make greater in amount, size, or value: *raise* prices. **5.** advance or elevate in rank, estimation, etc. **6.** increase the strength, intensity, or degree of. **7.** breed; grow. **8.** rear (children, a family, etc.). **9.** cause; occasion. **10.** stir to action or emotion; animate. **11.** gather together; obtain or collect. **12.** bring up for consideration, as a question. **13.** cause to swell or become lighter; leaven. **14.** put an end to, as a siege. **15.** in poker, bet more than. —*v.i.* **16.** in poker, make a raise. —**raise the devil** (or **the dickens, hell, the roof, a rumpus,** etc.) *Informal* make a great disturbance; stir up confusion. —*n.* **1.** the act of raising. **2.** an increase, as of wages or a bet. [ME *reisen*]

rai·sin (RAY zin) *n.* a grape dried for eating. [ME]

rai·son d'ê·tre (RAY zohn DE trə) *French* reason or excuse for existing; literally, reason for being.

ra·jah (RAH jə) *n.* a Hindu prince or chief of a tribal state in India; also, a Malay or Javanese ruler: often used as a courtesy title. Also **ra'ja.** [< Skt. *rājan* king]

rake¹ (rayk) *n.* a toothed implement for drawing together loose material, loosening the surface of the soil, etc. —*v.* **raked, rak·ing** *v.t.* **1.** scrape or gather together with or as with a rake. **2.** smooth, clean, or prepare with a rake. **3.** direct heavy gunfire along the length of, as a ship or column of troops. —*v.i.* **4.** use a rake. [ME]

rake² *n.* a dissolute, lewd man; a roué. [Earlier *rakehell*]

rak·ish¹ (RAY kish) *adj.* dashing; jaunty; smart. —**rak'ish·ly** *adv.* —**rak'ish·ness** *n.*

rak·ish² *adj.* characteristic of a rake; dissolute; profligate. —**rak'ish·ness** *n.*

rale (ral) *n. Pathol.* a sound additional to that

rally   652

of normal respiration, indicative of disease. [< F *râle*]

ral·ly[1] (RAL ee) *n. pl.* **·lies 1.** a meeting of persons for a common purpose. **2.** a rapid recovery, as after exhaustion. **3.** a return, as of scattered troops, to order or action. **4.** in tennis etc., the interchange of several strokes. **5.** a driving competition or procession, as for sports cars, antique automobiles, etc. —*v.* **·lied, ·ly·ing** *v.t.* **1.** bring together and restore to normal order, as troops. **2.** summon up or revive. **3.** bring together for common action. —*v.i.* **4.** return to discipline or action. **5.** unite for common action. **6.** make a return to a normal condition; improve. **7.** in tennis etc., engage in a rally. [< F *reallier* rejoin]

ral·ly[2] *v.t. & v.i.* **·lied, ·ly·ing** mock or tease with raillery; banter. [< F *railler* mock]

ram (ram) *n.* **1.** a male sheep. **2.** a device for driving, forcing, or crushing by heavy blows or thrusts. [ME] —*v.t.* **rammed, ram·ming 1.** strike with or as with a ram; dash against. **2.** drive or force down or into something.

ram·ble (RAM bəl) *v.i.* **·bled, ·bling 1.** walk about freely and aimlessly; roam. **2.** write or talk aimlessly. **3.** proceed with turns and twists; meander. —*n.* **1.** an aimless stroll. **2.** a meandering path.

ram·bler (RAM blər) *n.* **1.** one who or that which rambles. **2.** a climbing rose.

ram·bunc·tious (ram BUNGK shəs) *adj.* boisterous; rough.

ram·e·kin (RAM i kin) *n.* **1.** a small dish for baking eggs, macaroni, etc. **2.** a serving of eggs etc. baked in such a dish. Also **ram'e·quin.** [< F *ramequin*]

ram·i·fi·ca·tion (RAM ə fi KAY shən) *n.* **1.** the act or process of ramifying. **2.** a result, consequence, etc., stemming from a main source.

ram·i·fy (RAM ə FI) *v.t. & v.i.* **·fied, ·fy·ing** divide or spread out into or as into branches; branch out. [< MF *ramifier*]

ramp (ramp) *n.* **1.** an inclined passageway, roadway, or runway. **2.** a movable stairway by which passengers enter or leave an airplane. [ME *rampen* climb]

ram·page (RAM payj) *n.* violent action or excitement. —*v.i.* (ram PAYJ) **·paged, ·pag·ing 1.** rush or act violently. **2.** storm; rage. —**ram'pag·er** *n.*

ram·pant (RAM pənt) *adj.* **1.** exceeding all bounds; wild; widespread. **2.** standing on the hind legs; rearing. [ME, climbing] —**ram'pan·cy** *n.*

ram·part (RAM pahrt) *n.* **1.** the embankment surrounding a fort, on which the parapet is raised. **2.** a bulwark or defense. —*v.t.* supply with or as with ramparts; fortify. [< MF *remparer* fortify]

ram·rod (RAM ROD) *n.* **1.** a rod used to drive home the charge of a muzzleloading gun or pistol. **2.** a similar rod used for cleaning the barrel of a rifle etc.

ram·shack·le (RAM SHAK əl) *adj.* likely to go to pieces, as from age or neglect.

ran (ran) past tense of RUN.

ranch (ranch) *n.* **1.** an establishment for raising or grazing cattle, horses, etc., in large herds. **2.** the buildings, personnel, and lands connected with it. **3.** a large farm. —*v.i.* manage or work on a ranch. [< Sp. *rancho*] —**ranch'er** *n.*

ranch house 1. the main building of a ranch. **2.** a one-story house, usu. having a low roof with a wide overhang.

ran·cid (RAN sid) *adj.* **1.** having an unpleasant taste or smell; rank. **2.** spoiled, as food. [< L *rancidus*]

ran·cor (RANG kər) *n.* bitter enmity; spitefulness. [ME *rancour*] —**ran'cor·ous** *adj.* —**ran'cor·ous·ly** *adv.*

ran·dom (RAN dəm) *n.* lack of definite aim or intention: now chiefly in the phrase **at random**, without definite purpose or aim; haphazardly. —*adj.* done at random. [ME *raundon*] —**ran'dom·ly** *adv.*

rang (rang) past tense of RING[2].

range (raynj) *n.* **1.** the area over which anything moves, operates, or is distributed. **2.** an extensive tract of land over which animals roam and graze. **3.** extent or scope. **4.** the extent of variation of anything: the temperature *range*. **5.** a line, row, or series, as of mountains. **6.** a place for shooting at a mark: a rifle *range*. **7.** a cooking stove. —*adj.* of or pertaining to a range. —*v.* **ranged, rang·ing** *v.t.* **1.** arrange in definite order, as in rows. **2.** assign to a class, division, or category. **3.** move about or over (a region etc.). —*v.i.* **4.** move over an area in a thorough, systematic manner, **5.** rove; roam. **6.** extend or proceed. **7.** exhibit variation within specified limits. [ME]

rang·er (RAYN jər) *n.* **1.** one who or that which ranges; a rover. **2.** one of an armed band designed to protect large tracts of country. **3.** a warden employed in patrolling forest tracts. **4.** *Often cap.* one of a select group of U.S. soldiers trained for raiding action on enemy territory.

rang•y (RAYN jee) *adj.* **rang•i•er, rang•i•est** having long, slender limbs, as a person. —**rang′i•ness** *n.*

rank[1] (rangk) *n.* **1.** a series of objects ranged in a line or row; a range. **2.** relative standing or position, as in the armed forces; status; grade. **3.** a line of soldiers drawn up side by side in close order. **4.** *pl.* an army; also, the mass of soldiery. **5.** high degree or position: persons of *rank.* —*v.t.* **1.** arrange in a rank or ranks. **2.** place in a class, order, etc. —*v.i.* **3.** hold a specified place or rank. **4.** have the highest rank or grade. [< MF *renc*]

rank[2] *adj.* •**er,** •**est 1.** flourishing in growth, as vegetation. **2.** strong and disagreeable to the taste or smell. **3.** utter; complete: *rank injustice.* [ME] —**rank′ly** *adv.* —**rank′ •ness** *n.*

rank and file 1. the common soldiers of an army. **2.** the ordinary members of any group.

rank•ing (RANG king) *adj.* superior in rank; taking precedence over others.

ran•kle (RANG kəl) *v.* •**kled,** •**kling** *v.i.* **1.** cause continued resentment, irritation, etc.; fester. —*v.t.* **2.** irritate; embitter. [ME *ranclen* fester]

ran•sack (RAN sak) *v.t.* search through every part of for or as if for plunder; pillage. [ME *ransaken*]

ran•som (RAN səm) *v.t.* secure the release of (a person, property, etc.) for a required price, as from captivity. —*n.* the payment for such a release. [ME *ransoun*]

rant (rant) *v.i.* **1.** speak in loud, violent, or extravagant language; rave. —*v.t.* **2.** utter in a ranting manner. —*n.* bombastic talk. [< MDu. *ranten* rave] —**rant′er** *n.*

rap[1] (rap) *v.* **rapped, rap•ping** *v.t.* **1.** strike sharply and quickly; hit. **2.** utter in a sharp manner: with *out.* **3.** *Slang* criticize severely. —*v.i.* **4.** strike sharp, quick blows. **5.** *Slang* have a frank discussion; talk. —*n.* **1.** a sharp blow. **2.** a knocking or tapping sound. **3.** *Slang* a charge of wrongdoing; blame. **4.** *Slang* a talk; discussion. [ME *rappen*] — **rap′per** *n.*

rap[2] *n.* the least bit: I don't give a *rap.*

ra•pa•cious (rə PAY shəs) *adj.* **1.** given to plunder or rapine. **2.** grasping; greedy. **3.** subsisting on prey seized alive, as hawks, etc. [< L *rapax* greedy] —**ra•pa′cious•ly** *adv.* —**ra•pa′cious•ness** *n.* —**ra•pac• i•ty** (rə PAS i tee) *n.*

rape (rayp) *v.* **raped, rap•ing** *v.t.* commit rape upon; ravish. —*n.* **1.** illegal, esp. forcible, sexual intercourse with a woman or girl. **2.** forcible sexual relations, whether with a female or male. [ME *rapen* seize] — **rap′ist** *n.*

rap•id (RAP id) *adj.* having, moving, or done with great speed; swift. —*n. Usu. pl.* a swift-running descent in a river. [< L *rapidus* swift] —**ra•pid•i•ty** (rə PID i tee), **rap′ id•ness** *n.* —**rap′id•ly** *adv.*

rapid eye movement rapid movement of the closed eyes during sleep, associated with dreaming and a characteristic pattern of electrical activity of the brain. Also called *REM.*

rap•id-fire (RAP id FĪR) *adj.* **1.** firing or designed for firing shots in rapid succession. **2.** characterized by speed.

ra•pi•er (RAY pee ər) *n.* **1.** a long, straight, two-edged sword, used chiefly for thrusting. **2.** a shorter straight sword without cutting edge, used for thrusting only. [< MF *rapière*]

rap•ine (RAP in) *n.* the taking of property by force, as in war; pillage. [ME]

rap music a style of popular music, beginning in the 1970's in the U.S., in which a persistent beat provides the background for rapid, rhyming patter. Also called **rap.**

rap•port (ra POR) *n.* harmony or sympathy of relation; agreement; accord. [< F]

rap•proche•ment (RAP rohsh MAHN) *n. French* a state of harmony or reconciliation.

rapt (rapt) *adj.* **1.** carried away with lofty emotion; enraptured; transported. **2.** engrossed; intent. [ME]

rap•to•ri•al (rap TOR ee əl) *adj.* **1.** seizing prey; predatory. **2.** having talons adapted for seizing prey, as hawks, vultures, eagles, etc. [< L *raptor* plunderer]

rap•ture (RAP chər) *n.* **1.** the state of being rapt or transported; ecstatic joy; ecstasy. **2.** *Often pl.* an act or expression of excessive delight. —*v.t.* •**tured,** •**tur•ing** enrapture. [< RAPT] —**rap′tur•ous** *adj.*

rare[1] (rair) *adj.* **rar•er, rar•est 1.** infrequent in occurrence, distribution, etc. **2.** highly esteemed; exceptional. **3.** rarefied. [ME]

rare[2] *adj.* **rar•er, rar•est** partially cooked, as broiled meat, so as to retain its redness and juices. [ME *rere*]

rare•bit (RAIR bit) *n.* Welsh rabbit.

rar•e•fy (RAIR ə FĪ) *v.t. & v.i.* •**fied,** •**fy•ing** make or become thin, less solid, or less dense. [ME *rarefien*] **—rar′e•fac′tion** (RAIR ə FAK shən) *n.*

rare•ly (RAIR lee) *adv.* **1.** not often; infrequently. **2.** exceptionally.

rar•i•ty (RAIR i tee) *n. pl.* **•ties 1.** that which is exceptionally valued because of scarceness. **2.** the state of being rare. [< L *raritas*]

ras•cal (RAS kəl) *n.* a rogue; knave: sometimes used playfully. [ME *rascaile* rabble] **—ras•cal′i•ty** (ras KAL i tee) *n.* **—ras′ •cal•ly** *adj. & adv.*

rash[1] (rash) *adj.* **•er, •est** acting or done without due caution; reckless. [ME] **— rash′ness** *n.*

rash[2] *n.* **1.** a superficial eruption of the skin, often localized. **2.** a great number of instances within a short period. [< F *rache*]

rash•er (RASH ər) *n.* **1.** a thin slice of meat, esp. bacon. **2.** a portion of bacon.

rasp (rasp) *n.* **1.** a file having coarse projections for abrasion. **2.** the act or sound of rasping. *—v.t.* **1.** scrape or rub with or as with a rasp. **2.** utter in a rough voice. *—v.i.* **3.** grate; scrape. **4.** make a rough, harsh sound. [ME *raspen* scrape] **—rasp′er** *n.* **—rasp′y** *adj.* **rasp•i•er, rasp•i•est.**

rasp•ber•ry (RAZ BER ee) *n. pl.* **•ries 1.** the round fruit of certain brambles of the rose family. **2.** any plant yielding this fruit. **3.** *Slang* a noisy fluttering of the lips to show contempt or derision, also called a **Bronx cheer.**

rat (rat) *n.* **1.** a destructive and injurious rodent of worldwide distribution, larger and more aggressive than the mouse. **2.** *Slang* a person who deserts or betrays his associates. **3.** a pad over which a woman's hair is combed. **—smell a rat** suspect that something is wrong. *—v.i.* **rat•ted, rat•ting 1.** hunt rats. **2.** *Slang* inform; betray: with *on.* [ME *ratte*]

ratch•et (RACH it) *n.* **1.** a mechanism consisting of a notched wheel, the teeth of which engage with a corresponding mechanism, the **pawl,** permitting motion of the wheel in one direction only. **2.** the pawl or wheel thus used. Also **ratchet wheel.** [< F *rochet* bobbin]

rate[1] (rayt) *n.* **1.** the measure of a variable in relation to some fixed unit. **2.** degree of value; price; also, the unit cost of a commodity or service. **3.** comparative rank or class. **4.** a fixed allowance, amount, or ratio. **—at any rate** in any case; anyhow. *—v.* **rat•ed, rat•ing** *v.t.* **1.** estimate the value or worth of; appraise. **2.** place in a certain rank or grade. **3.** consider; regard. **4.** deserve. *— v.i.* **5.** have rank, rating, or value. [ME] **— rat′a•ble, rate′a•ble** *adj.*

rate[2] *v.t. & v.i.* **rat•ed, rat•ing** reprove with vehemence; rail at. [ME *raten*]

rath•er (RATH ər) *adv.* **1.** more willingly. **2.** with more reason, wisdom, etc. **3.** more precisely, strictly, or accurately. **4.** somewhat: *rather* cold. **5.** on the contrary. *— interj.* (RAHTH UR) *Brit.* emphatically yes. [ME]

rat•i•fy (RAT ə FĪ) *v.t.* **•fied, •fy•ing** give sanction to, esp. official sanction; confirm. [ME *ratifien* fix] **—rat′i•fi•ca′tion** *n.*

rat•ing (RAY ting) *n.* **1.** classification according to a standard; grade; rank. **2.** an evaluation, as of the financial standing of a business. **3.** a numerical index of the size of the audience of a television or radio broadcast, estimated from a sample poll.

ra•tio (RAY shoh) *n. pl.* **•tios 1.** the relation of degree, number, etc.; proportion; rate. **2.** the relation of two quantities, esp. the quotient of the first divided by the second. [< L, a reckoning]

ra•tion (RASH ən) *n.* **1.** a portion; share. **2.** *Often pl.* a fixed allowance or portion of food etc., allotted in time of scarcity. **3.** *Mil.* food for one person for one day. *—v.t.* **1.** issue rations to. **2.** give out or allot in rations. [< F] **—ra′•tion•ing** *n.*

ra•tion•al (RASH ə nl) *adj.* **1.** possessing the faculty of reasoning. **2.** not delirious, mad, etc.; sane. **3.** reasonable; judicious; sensible. **4.** attained by reasoning. **5.** *Math.* denoting an algebraic expression containing no variables within irreducible radicals. [ME *racional*] **—ra•tion•al•i•ty** (RASH ə NAL i tee) *n.* **—ra′tion•al•ly** *adv.*

ra•tion•ale (RASH ə NAL) *n.* **1.** the rational or logical basis of something. **2.** a rational explanation of principles. [< L]

ra•tion•al•ism (RASH ə nl IZ əm) *n.* **1.** the formation of opinions by reason alone. **2.** *Philos.* the theory that truth and knowledge are attainable through reason rather than by empirical means. **—ra′tion•al•ist** *n.*

ra•tion•al•ize (RASH ə nl Īz) *v.* **•ized, •iz•ing** *v.t.* **1.** *Psychol.* explain or base (one's behavior) on grounds ostensibly rational but not in accord with the actual or unconscious motives. **2.** explain or treat from a rationalistic point of view. **3.** make rational or reasonable. *—v.i.* **4.** *Psychol.* devise ostensibly rational grounds for one's behavior. **5.** think in a rational or rationalistic manner. —**ra′tion·al·i·za′tion** n. — **ra′tion·al·iz′er** n.

rat race Informal any fruitless struggle.

rat's nest Informal a cluttered and messy place.

rat·tan (ra TAN) n. **1.** the long, tough, flexible stem of various tropical palms, used in making light furniture etc. **2.** the palm itself. [< Malay rotan]

rat·tle (RAT l) v. **·tled, ·tling** v.i. **1.** make a series of sharp noises in rapid succession, as of hard objects striking one another. **2.** move or act with such noises. **3.** talk rapidly and foolishly; chatter. —v.t. **4.** cause to rattle. **5.** utter or perform rapidly or noisily. **6.** confuse; disconcert. —n. **1.** a series of short, sharp sounds in rapid succession. **2.** a toy, implement, etc. made to produce a rattling noise. **3.** any of the jointed horny rings in the tail of a rattlesnake. [ME ratelen]

rat·tle·brain (RAT l BRAYN) n. a talkative, flighty person; foolish chatterer. —**rat′tle·brained′** adj.

rat·tle·snake (RAT l SNAYK) n. any of several venomous American snakes with a tail ending in a series of horny, loosely connected, modified joints that make a rattling noise when the tail is vibrated. Also **rat′tler.**

rat·tle·trap (RAT l TRAP) n. a vehicle etc. that is rickety or worn out.

rat·trap (RAT TRAP) n. **1.** a trap for catching rats. **2.** a rundown building. **3.** any hopeless or involved predicament.

rat·ty (RAT ee) adj. **·ti·er, ·ti·est 1.** ratlike. **2.** abounding in rats. **3.** disreputable; shabby.

rau·cous (RAW kəs) adj. **1.** strident; harsh. **2.** boisterous; unruly. [< L raucus hoarse] —**rau′cous·ly** adv. —**rau′cous·ness** n.

raun·chy (RAWN chee) adj. **·chi·er, ·chi·est** Informal **1.** dirty; sloppy. **2.** risqué; obscene. **3.** lustful; lecherous.

rav·age (RAV ij) v. **·aged, ·ag·ing** v.t. **1.** lay waste, as by pillaging; despoil. —v.i. **2.** wreak havoc; be destructive. —n. destructive action, or its result; ruin. [< F]

rave (rayv) v.i. **raved, rav·ing 1.** speak wildly or incoherently. **2.** praise extravagantly. —n. **1.** the act or state of raving; a frenzy. **2.** enthusiastic praise. —adj. extravagantly enthusiastic. [ME raven be delirious]

rav·el (RAV əl) v.t. & v.i. **rav·eled, rav·el·ing** separate into parts; unravel; fray. —n.

1. a broken or loose thread. **2.** a tangle. [< MDu. rafelen tangle] —**rav′el·er** n.

ra·ven[1] (RAY vən) n. a large bird, related to the crow, having lustrous black plumage. —adj. black and shining, like a raven. [ME]

rav·en[2] (RAV ən) v.t. **1.** devour hungrily or greedily. —v.i. **2.** search for prey or plunder. **3.** eat voraciously. —n. the act of plundering; pillage. [ME]

rav·en·ing (RAV ə ning) adj. **1.** seeking prey; rapacious. **2.** devouring; voracious.

rav·en·ous (RAV ə nəs) adj. violently voracious or hungry. [ME]

ra·vine (rə VEEN) n. a deep gorge or gully, esp. one worn by a flow of water. [ME]

rav·ing (RAY ving) adj. **1.** delirious; frenzied. **2.** Informal outstanding. —adv. extremely; wildly. —n. furious or irrational utterance.

ra·vi·o·li (RAV ee OH lee) n. (construed as s. and pl.) little envelope of dough filled with meat or cheese. [< Ital., pl. of raviolo little turnip]

rav·ish (RAV ish) v.t. **1.** fill with strong emotion, esp. delight; enrapture. **2.** commit a rape upon. [ME ravishen seize] —**rav′ish·er** n.

rav·ish·ing (RAV i shing) adj. filling with delight; enchanting. —**rav′ish·ing·ly** adv.

raw (raw) adj. **·er, ·est 1.** not changed or prepared by cooking; uncooked. **2.** having the skin irritated or abraded. **3.** bleak; chilling: a raw wind. **4.** in a natural state; crude. **5.** inexperienced; undisciplined. **6.** obscene; coarse. **7.** harshly unfair; ruthless. —n. a sore or abraded spot: with the. —**in the raw 1.** in a raw or unrefined state. **2.** Informal naked; nude. [ME]

raw·boned (RAW BOHND) adj. bony; gaunt.

raw·hide (RAW HID) n. **1.** a hide dressed without tanning. **2.** a whip made of such hide.

ray[1] (ray) n. **1.** a narrow beam of light. **2.** anything representing or suggesting this. **3.** a slight manifestation; glimmer; hint. **4.** Zool. a radiating part, as of a starfish. **5.** Physics **a** a line of propagation of any form of radiant energy. **b** a stream of particles spontaneously emitted by a radioactive substance. —v.i. **1.** emit rays; shine. **2.** issue forth as rays; radiate. —v.t. **3.** send forth as rays. [ME raie rod]

ray[2] n. any of various fishes having a flattened body with expanded pectoral fins and gill openings on the lower surface. [ME *raye*]

ray•on (RAY on) *n.* **1.** a synthetic fiber produced from cellulose. **2.** a fabric made from such fibers.

raze (rayz) *v.t.* **razed, raz•ing 1.** demolish, as a building. **2.** scrape or shave off. [ME *rasen* scrape]

ra•zor (RAY zər) *n.* a sharp cutting implement used for shaving off the beard or hair, etc. [ME *rasour*]

razz (raz) *Slang n.* a raspberry, a **Bronx cheer.** —*v.t.* heckle; deride. [< RASP-BERRY]

raz•zle-daz•zle (RAZ əl DAZ əl) *n. Informal* bewildering, exciting, or dazzling activity or performance.

re¹ (ray) *n. Music* the second tone of the diatonic scale in solmization.

re² *prep.* concerning; about: used in business letters, law, etc. [< L, in the matter of]

re- *prefix* **1.** back: *rebound, remit.* **2.** again; anew; again and again. [< L]

The list starting below contains self-explanatory words beginning with *re-* (def. 2).

reabsorb	reannex
reabsorption	reannexation
reaccept	reanoint
reaccommodate	reappear
reacquire	reappearance
readapt	reapplication
readdress	reapply
readjourn	reappoint
readjournment	reappointment
readjust	reapportion
readjustment	reapportionment
readmission	reappraisal
readmit	reappraise
readmittance	reargue
readopt	rearrest
readoption	reascend
readorn	reascension
reaffirm	reascent
reaffirmation	reassail
realign	reassemble
realignment	reassembly
reallocate	reassert
reallocation	reassertion
reanalysis	reassess
reanalyze	reassessment

reach (reech) *v.t.* **1.** stretch out or forth, as the hand; extend. **2.** be able to touch or grasp: Can you *reach* the top shelf? **3.** arrive at or come to by motion or progress. **4.** achieve communication with; gain access to. —*v.i.* **5.** stretch the hand, foot, etc. out or forth. **6.** attempt to touch or grasp something. **7.** have extent in space, time, etc. — *n.* **1.** the act or power of reaching. **2.** the distance one is able to reach, as with the hand, an instrument, etc. **3.** extent of thought, influence, etc.; scope. **4.** an unbroken stretch; a vista or expanse. [ME *rechen*]

re•act (ree AKT) *v.i.* **1.** act in response, as to a stimulus. **2.** act in a manner contrary to some preceding act. **3.** *Physics* exert an opposite and equal force on an acting or impinging body. **4.** *Chem.* undergo a reaction.

re•ac•tance (ree AK təns) *n. Electr.* in a circuit, the opposition to an alternating current caused by inductance and capacitance.

re•ac•tion (ree AK shən) *n.* **1.** a responsive action, attitude, etc. **2.** a tendency toward a former state of things; esp., a trend toward an earlier social, political, or economic policy or condition. **3.** the action of a muscle, nerve, etc. in response to a stimulus; reflex action. **4.** *Physics* **a** the equal and opposite force exerted on an agent by the body acted upon. **b** a nuclear reaction. **5.** *Chem.* the interaction of substances, resulting in a chemical change. **6.** *Med.* the response, esp. adverse, to a drug, serum, etc.

re•ac•tion•ar•y (ree AK shə NER ee) *adj.* pertaining to, favoring, or characterized by reaction (def. 2). —*n. pl.* •**ar•ies** one who favors political or social reaction.

re•ac•ti•vate (ree AK tə VAYT) *v.t.* •**vat•ed,** •**vat•ing** make active or effective again. — **re•ac'ti•va'tion** *n.*

reassign	recapitalize
reassimilate	rechallenge
reassimilation	rechange
reassort	rechannel
reassume	recharge
reassumption	recharter
reattach	recheck
reattack	rechristen
reattempt	recircle
reauthorize	recirculate
reavow	reclasp
reawake	reclean
reawaken	reclothe
rebaptism	recoat
rebaptize	recoin
rebid	recoinage
rebind	recolonization
rebloom	recolonize
reblossom	recolor
reboil	recomb
reborn	recombination

rebuild
rebuilt
rebury
recalculate

recombine
recommence
recommission
recompose

re·ac·tive (ree AK tiv) *adj.* reacting or tending to react. —**re'ac·tiv'i·ty** *n.*

re·ac·tor (ree AK tər) *n.* **1.** one who or that which reacts. **2.** *Electr.* a device for introducing reactance into a circuit, as for starting motors, controlling current, etc. **3.** *Physics* any of various assemblies for generation and control of a chain reaction with nuclear materials.

read (reed) *v.* **read** (red), **read·ing** (REE ding) *v.t.* **1.** apprehend the meaning of (a book, writing, etc.) by perceiving the form and relation of the printed or written characters. **2.** utter aloud (something printed or written). **3.** understand the significance, intent, etc. of as if by reading. **4.** discover the true nature of (a person, character, etc.) by observation or scrutiny. **5.** interpret (something read) in a specified manner. **6.** take as the meaning of something read. **7.** have as its wording: The passage *reads* "principal," not "principle." **8.** indicate or register, as an instrument. **9.** bring into a specified condition by reading: I *read* her to sleep. —*v.i.* **10.** apprehend written or printed characters, as of words, music, etc. **11.** utter aloud the words or contents of a book etc. **12.** gain information by reading: with *of* or *about.* **13.** have a specified wording: How does the contract *read?* **14.** admit of being read in a specified manner; also, have the quality of a specified style of writing: His work *reads* well. It *reads* like poetry. **15.** give a public reading or recital. —**read between the lines** perceive what is not expressed or obvious. —**read up** (or **up on**) learn by reading. —*adj.* informed by reading: well *read.* [ME *reden*]

read·a·ble (REE də bəl) *adj.* **1.** legible. **2.** interesting or enjoyable to read. —**read'a·bil'i·ty** *n.*

read·er (REE dər) *n.* **1.** one who reads. **2.** a textbook containing exercises in reading. **3.** an anthology of writings on a particular subject.

recompute
reconcentrate
recondensation
recondense
reconduct
reconfine
reconfirm

rededication
redefine
redemand
redemonstrate
redeploy
redeployment
redeposit

reconfirmation
reconnect
reconquer
reconquest
reconsecrate
reconsolidate
recontaminate
recontamination
reconvene
recook
recopy
recouple
recrown
recrystallize
recultivate
recultivation
recut
rededicate

redesign
redetermine
redip
rediscover
rediscovery
redissolve
redistill
redistribute
redistribution
redivide
redivision
redo
redrive
redye
reedit
reelect
reelection
reembark

read·er·ship (REE dər SHIP) *n.* the readers, collectively, of a publication or type of publication.

read·ing (REE ding) *n.* **1.** the act or practice of one who reads. **2.** a public or formal recital of something written. **3.** matter that is read or is designed to be read. **4.** the indication of a meter, dial, etc. **5.** the form in which any passage or word appears in any copy of a work. **6.** a specific interpretation. —*adj.* **1.** pertaining to or suitable for reading. **2.** of or pertaining to a reader or readers.

read·out (REED owt) *n.* **1.** data or information from a computer in a readable form, usu. as a printed sheet or as a display on a screen. **2.** the process of producing information in such a form.

read·y (RED ee) *adj.* **read·i·er, read·i·est** **1.** prepared for use or action. **2.** prepared in mind; willing. **3.** likely or liable: with *to: ready* to criticize. **4.** quick to act, follow, occur, or appear; prompt. **5.** immediately available or at hand; convenient; handy. —*n.* the position in which a rifle is held before aiming. —*v.t.* **read·ied, read·y·ing** make ready; prepare. [ME *redy*] —**read'i·ly** *adv.*

read·y-made (RED ee MAYD) *adj.* **1.** not made to order; prepared or kept on hand for general demand: said esp. of clothing. **2.** prepared beforehand.

ready money money on hand; cash.

read·y-to-wear (RED ee tə WAIR) *adj.* ready-made: said of clothing.

re·a·gent (ree AY jənt) *n. Chem.* any substance that takes part in a chemical reaction.

real (REE əl) *adj.* **1.** having existence or actuality as a thing or state; not imaginary: a *real* event. **2.** not artificial or counterfeit; genuine. **3.** unaffected; unpretentious: *real* people. **4.** *Law* pertaining to property regarded as immovable or permanent, as land or buildings. —*adv. Informal* very; extremely. [ME]

reembodiment	reexamine
reembody	reexchange
reembrace	reexhibit
reemerge	reexpel
reemergence	reexperience
reemphasis	reexport
reemphasize	reexpulsion
reemploy	reface
reemployment	refashion
reenact	refasten
reenactment	refertilize
reencouragement	refigure
reendow	refilm
reengage	refinance
reengagement	refinish
reenlist	refire
reenlistment	reflower
reenslave	refocus
reenter	refold
reentrance	reforge
reequip	reformulate
reerect	refortification
reestablish	refortify
reestablishment	reframe
reexamination	refreeze

real estate land, including whatever is made part of or attached to it by people or nature, as trees, houses, etc. —**real'-es·tate'** *adj.*

re·al·ism (REE ə LIZ əm) *n.* **1.** the tendency to be concerned with and act in accordance with facts rather than ideals, feelings, etc. **2.** in literature and art, the treatment of subject matter in conformance with nature or real life. —**re'al·ist** *n.*

re·al·i·ty (ree AL i tee) *n. pl.* **·ties 1.** the fact, state, or quality of being real or genuine. **2.** that which is real; an actual thing, situation, or event. **3.** the sum or totality of real things. [< Med.L *realitas*]

re·al·ize (REE ə LIZ) *v.* **·ized, ·iz·ing** *v.t.* **1.** understand or appreciate fully. **2.** make real or concrete. **3.** cause to appear real. **4.** obtain as a profit or return. —*v.i.* **5.** sell property for cash. —**re'al·i·za'tion** *n.*

re·al-life (REE əl LIF) *adj.* actual; true.

re·al·ly (REE ə lee) *adv.* **1.** in reality; as a matter of fact; actually; indeed. **2.** honestly; truly: used for emphasis.

re·al·ly (REE ə LĪ) *v.t. & v.i.* **·al·lied, ·al·ly·ing** ally again.

realm (relm) *n.* **1.** a kingdom or domain. **2.** the scope or range of any power or influence. [ME *realme*]

re·al·po·li·tik (ray AHL POH li TEEK) *n.* practical or realistic politics; ruthless pursuit of national or party interests, without regard for ethical principles. [< G]

real time the actual time during which a physical process occurs. —**real'-time'** *adj.*

refuel	reinaugurate
refurnish	reincorporate
regather	reincur
regear	reinduce
regild	reinfect
reglaze	reinfection
reglue	reinflame
regrade	reinfuse
regraft	reinoculate
regrant	reinoculation
regroup	reinscribe
rehandle	reinsert
rehear	reinsertion
rehearing	reinspect
reheat	reinspection
reheel	reinstall
rehire	reinstruct
reignite	reintegrate
reimplant	reintegration
reimpose	reinter
reimposition	reinterment
reimpress	reinterpret
reimprint	reinterpretation
reimprison	reintroduce
reimprisonment	reintroduction

Re·al·tor (REE əl tər) *n.* a realty broker who is a member of the National Association of Real Estate Boards: a trade name. Also **re'al·tor.**

re·al·ty (REE əl tee) *n.* real estate or real property in any form.

ream¹ (reem) *n.* **1.** a unit of quantity of paper consisting of 480 sheets (**short ream**), 500 sheets (**long ream**), or 516 sheets (**printer's** or **perfect ream**). **2.** *pl.* a prodigious amount. [ME *reme* bundle]

ream² *v.t.* **1.** increase the size of (a hole). **2.** enlarge or taper (a hole) with a rotating cutter or reamer.

ream·er (REE mər) *n.* **1.** a finishing tool with a rotating cutting edge for reaming: a pipe *reamer.* **2.** a device with a ridged cone for extracting juice from citrus fruits.

re·an·i·mate (REE AN ə MAYT) *v.t.* **·mat·ed, ·mat·ing 1.** bring back to life;

resuscitate. **2.** give renewed strength or vigor to; revive.

reap (reep) *v.t.* **1.** harvest or gather (a crop) with a scythe, reaper, etc. **2.** obtain as the result of action or effort; receive as a return or result. —*v.i.* **3.** harvest grain, etc. **4.** receive a return or result. [ME *repen*]

reap·er (REE pər) *n.* **1.** one who reaps. **2.** a machine for harvesting grain.

rear[1] (reer) *n.* **1.** the back or hind part. **2.** a place or position behind any person or thing. **3.** the portion of a military force that is farthest from the front. —*adj.* being in the rear.

rear[2] *v.t.* **1.** place upright; raise. **2.** build; erect. **3.** care for and bring to maturity. **4.** breed or grow. —*v.i.* **5.** rise on the hind legs, as a horse. **6.** rise high; tower, as a mountain. [ME *reren* raise]

rear admiral *Naval* a commissioned officer ranking next below a vice admiral.

reinvent	rematch
reinvest	remeasure
reinvestigate	remelt
reinvestigation	remigrate
reinvestment	remigration
reinvigorate	remilitarization
reinvigoration	remilitarize
reinvolve	remix
rejudge	remodification
rekindle	remodify
reknit	remold
relabel	rename
relace	renavigate
relaunch	renegotiate
relaunder	renegotiation
relearn	renominate
relight	renomination
reline	renumber
relive	reoccupation
reload	reoccupy
reloan	reoccur
remade	reoccurrence
remake	reopen
remarriage	reoppose
remarry	reordination

rear guard a body of troops to protect the rear of an army.

re·arm (ree AHRM) *v.t. & v.i.* **1.** arm again. **2.** arm with more modern weapons. — **re·ar·ma·ment** (ree AHR mə mənt) *n.*

re·ar·range (ree ə RAYNJ) *v.t. & v.i.* **·ranged, ·rang·ing** arrange again or in some new way. —**re'ar·range'ment** *n.*

rear·ward (REER wərd) *adj.* coming last or toward the rear; hindward. —*adv.* toward

or at the rear; backward: also **rear'wards.** —*n.* the rear; end.

rea·son (REE zən) *n.* **1.** a motive or cause for an action, belief, thought, etc. **2.** an explanation for or defense of an action, belief, etc.; justification. **3.** the faculty of thinking logically. **4.** good judgment; common sense. **5.** a normal state of mind; sanity. —**by reason of** because of. —**it stands to reason** is logical or reasonable. —**with reason** justifiably; properly. —*v.i.* **1.** think logically; obtain inferences or conclusions from known or presumed facts. **2.** talk or argue logically. —*v.t.* **3.** think out carefully and logically; analyze: with *out.* [ME *resoun*]

rea·son·a·ble (REE zə nə bəl) *adj.* **1.** conformable to reason; sensible. **2.** rational. **3.** governed by reason. **4.** moderate, as in price; fair. —**rea'son·a·ble·ness** *n.* — **rea'son·a·bly** *adv.*

rea·son·ing (REE zə ning) *n.* the process of drawing conclusions from known or presumed facts.

re·as·sure (REE ə SHUUR) *v.t.* **·sured, ·sur·ing 1.** restore to courage or confidence. **2.** assure again. —**re'as·sur'ance** *n.*

re·bate (REE bayt) *v.t.* **·bat·ed, ·bat·ing 1.** allow as a deduction. **2.** make a deduction from. —*n.* a deduction from a gross amount; discount. [ME *rebaten*]

reorient	resaddle
repacify	resail
repack	reseal
repackage	reseat
repaint	reseed
repaper	resegregate
repass	reseize
repave	reseizure
rephotograph	resell
replant	resend
replay	resettle
repledge	resettlement
repolish	resew
repopulate	reshape
repopulation	resharpen
repour	reship
reprocess	reshipment
republication	reshuffle
republish	resift
repurchase	resilver
repurify	resolder
reread	resow
rerecord	respell
reroll	respread
reroute	restack

re·bel (ri BEL) *v.i.* **·belled, ·bel·ling** 1. rise in armed resistance, esp. against a government or ruler. 2. resist any authority or established usage. 3. react with violent aversion: usu. with *at.* —*n.* (REB əl) one who rebels. —*adj.* (REB əl) rebellious; refractory. [ME *rebellen*]

re·bel·lion (ri BEL yən) *n.* 1. the act of rebelling. 2. organized resistance to a lawful government or authority. [ME *rebellioun*]

re·bel·lious (ri BEL yəs) *adj.* 1. being in a state of rebellion; insubordinate. 2. of or pertaining to a rebel or rebellion. [ME]

re·birth (ree BURTH) *n.* 1. a second birth. 2. a revival or renaissance.

re·bound (ri BOWND) *v.t. & v.i.* bound back or cause to bound back; recoil. —*n.* (REE BOWND 1. the act or state of rebounding; recoil. 2. something that rebounds or resounds. [ME]

re·buff (ri BUF) *v.t.* 1. reject or refuse abruptly or rudely. 2. drive or beat back; repel. —*n.* 1. a sudden repulse; curt denial. 2. a sudden check; defeat. 3. a check to action. [< MF *rebuffer* reprimand]

re·buke (ri BYOOK) *v.t.* **·buked, ·buk·ing** reprove sharply; reprimand. —*n.* a strong expression of disapproval. [ME *rebuken*]

re·bus (REE bəs) *n. pl.* **·bus·es** a puzzle representing a word, phrase, sentence, etc., by letters, numerals, pictures, etc. [< L, by things]

re·but (ri BUT) *v.t.* **·but·ted, ·but·ting** refute by contrary evidence or proof; disprove. [ME *rebouten*] —**re·but'tal** (ri BUT l) *n.*

restaff	retransmit
restock	retraverse
restraighten	retrim
restrengthen	retype
restrike	reunification
restring	reunify
restructure	revaluate
restudy	revaluation
restuff	revalue
resubject	revarnish
resubjection	reverification
resubmit	reverify
resummon	revindicate
resummons	revindication
resupply	revisit
resurvey	revitalize
resynthesize	rewarm
reteach	rewash
retell	rewater

retest	reweave
rethink	rewed
retie	reweigh
retool	rewind
retrain	rework
retranslate	rezone

re·cal·ci·trant (ri KAL si trənt) *adj.* not complying; obstinate; rebellious. —*n.* one who is recalcitrant. [< L *recalcitrare* kick back] —**re·cal'ci·trance, re·cal'ci·tran·cy** *n.*

re·call (ri KAWL) *v.t.* 1. call back; order or summon to return. 2. recollect; remember. 3. take back; revoke. —*n.* 1. a summons to come back. 2. the ability to remember. 3. revocation. 4. a system whereby officials may be removed from office by popular vote. 5. a request by a manufacturer for the return of a possibly defective product. 6. the ability of a computer to retrieve stored data.

re·cant (ri KANT) *v.t. & v.i.* withdraw formally one's belief in (something previously believed or maintained). [< L *recantare* sing again] —**re·can·ta·tion** (REE kan TAY shən) *n.* —**re·cant'er** *n.*

re·cap (REE KAP) *v.t.* **·capped, ·cap·ping** recondition the tread of (an automobile tire) with new rubber. —*n.* a tire that has been recapped.

re·ca·pit·u·late (REE kə PICH ə LAYT) *v.t. & v.i.* **·lat·ed, ·lat·ing** review briefly (a discussion, report, etc.); sum up. [< LL *recapitulare*] —**re'ca·pit'u·la'tion** *n.*

re·cap·ture (ree KAP chər) *v.t.* **·tured, ·tur·ing** 1. capture again. 2. recall; remember. —*n.* 1. the act of retaking. 2. anything recaptured.

re·cast (ree KAST) *v.t.* **·cast, ·cast·ing** 1. form anew; cast again. 2. calculate anew. —*n.* (REE KAST) something that has been recast.

re·cede (ri SEED) *v.i.* **·ced·ed, ·ced·ing** 1. move back, as flood waters. 2. slope backward. 3. become more distant. [< L *recedere* fall back]

re·ceipt (ri SEET) *n.* 1. the act or state of receiving anything. 2. *Usu. pl.* that which is received: cash *receipts.* 3. a written acknowledgment of payment, delivery, etc. 4. a recipe. —*v.t.* give a receipt for the payment of. [ME *receite*]

re·ceiv·a·ble (ri SEE və bəl) *adj.* 1. capable of being received; fit to be received, as legal tender. 2. maturing for payment: said of a bill. —*n.pl.* outstanding accounts listed among the assets of a business.

re•ceive (ri SEEV) *v.* **•ceived, •ceiv•ing** *v.t.* **1.** take into one's hand or possession; acquire. **2.** gain knowledge of: *receive* good news. **3.** bear; support. **4.** experience; undergo. **5.** contain; hold. **6.** allow entrance to; admit; greet. —*v.i.* **7.** welcome visitors. **8.** *Telecom.* convert radio waves into sounds or images. [ME *receven*]

re•ceiv•er (ri SEE vər) *n.* **1.** one who receives; a recipient. **2.** *Law* a person appointed by a court to have charge of the property or funds of another pending judicial action. **3.** something that receives; a receptacle. **4.** *Telecom.* **a** an instrument serving to receive and reproduce signals transmitted from another part of a circuit: a telephone *receiver.* **b** any of various electronic devices that convert radio waves into sounds or images. **5.** in football, an offensive player designated to receive a forward pass.

re•ceiv•er•ship (ri SEE vər SHIP) *n.* **1.** the office and functions pertaining to a receiver under appointment of a court. **2.** the state of being in the hands of a receiver.

re•cent (REE sənt) *adj.* pertaining to, or formed, developed, or created in time not long past; modern. [ME] —**re'cent•ly** *adv.* —**re'cen•cy** *n.*

re•cep•ta•cle (ri SEP tə kəl) *n.* anything that serves to contain or hold something else. [ME]

re•cep•tion (ri SEP shən) *n.* **1.** the act of receiving, or the state of being received. **2.** a formal social entertainment of guests. **3.** the manner of receiving: a cold *reception.* **4.** *Telecom.* the act or process of receiving, or the quality of reproduction achieved. [ME *recepcion*]

re•cep•tion•ist (ri SEP shə nist) *n.* one employed to receive callers at the entrance to an office.

re•cep•tive (ri SEP tiv) *adj.* **1.** able or inclined to receive, as truths or impressions. **2.** able to take in or hold. —**re•cep•tiv•i•ty** (REE sep TIV i tee) *n.*

re•cep•tor (ri SEP tər) *n. Anat.* a nerve ending that receives stimuli and transmits them to the spinal cord and brain.

re•cess (ri SES) *n.* **1.** a depression or indentation in any surface, esp. in a wall; niche. **2.** a time of cessation from employment or occupation. **3.** *Usu pl.* a secluded spot; withdrawn or inner place. —*v.t.* **1.** place in

or as in a recess. **2.** make a recess in. **3.** adjourn for a recess. —*v.i.* **4.** take a recess. [< L *recessus* withdrawal]

re•ces•sion (ri SESH ən) *n.* **1.** the act of receding; a withdrawal. **2.** the procession of the clergy, choir, etc. after a church service. **3.** an economic setback in commercial and industrial activity.

re•ces•sion•al (ri SESH ə nl) *adj.* af or pertaining to recession. —*n.* a hymn sung as the choir or clergy leaves the service.

re•ces•sive (ri SES iv) *adj.* **1.** having a tendency to recede or go back; receding. **2.** *Genetics* designating one of a pair of hereditary characters that, appearing in an offspring, is masked by a contrasting character: opposed to *dominant.* —**re•ces'sive•ness** *n.*

re•cher•ché (rə SHAIR shay) *adj. French* **1.** rare and exquisite; choice. **2.** elegant and refined; also, overrefined.

re•cid•i•vism (ri SID ə VIZ əm) *n.* repetition of criminal acts by an offender, or the tendency to do so. [< L *recidivus* relapsing] —**re•cid'i•vist** *n.* —**re•cid'i•vis'tic** *adj.*

rec•i•pe (RES ə pee) *n.* **1.** a formula or list of ingredients of a mixture, giving proper directions for compounding, cooking, etc. **2.** a method prescribed for attaining a desired result. [ME]

re•cip•i•ent (ri SIP ee ənt) *adj.* receiving or ready to receive; receptive. —*n.* one who or that which receives. [< L *recipere* receive]

re•cip•ro•cal (ri SIP rə kəl) *adj.* **1.** done or given by each of two to the other; mutual. **2.** corresponding; matching. **3.** alternating; moving to and fro. **4.** *Gram.* expressive of mutual relationship or action. **5.** *Math.* of or pertaining to various types of mutual relations between two quantities. —*n.* **1.** that which is reciprocal. **2.** *Math.* the quotient obtained by dividing 1 by a number or expression, as $1/x$ is the *reciprocal* of x. [< L *reciprocus*] —**re•cip'ro•cal•ly** *adv.*

re•cip•ro•cate (ri SIP rə KAYT) *v.t. & v.i.* **•cat•ed, •cat•ing** **1.** move backward and forward alternately. **2.** give and receive mutually; interchange. **3.** make a return (of an emotion, response, etc.) in kind. —**re•cip'ro•ca'tion** *n.*

rec•i•proc•i•ty (RES ə PROS i tee) *n.* reciprocal obligation, action, or relation.

re•ci•sion (ri ZIZH ən) *n.* a cancellation; annulment. [< MF]

re•cit•al (ri SĪTl) *n.* **1.** a telling over in detail, or that which is thus told. **2.** a public delivery of something previously memorized. **3.** a musical program performed usu. by one person or several appearing as soloists.

rec•i•ta•tion (RES i TAY shən) n. **1.** the act of repeating from memory. **2.** the reciting of a lesson, or the meeting of a class for that purpose. [< L]

re•cite (ri SĪT) v. **•cit•ed, •cit•ing** v.t. **1.** declaim or say from memory, esp. formally, as a lesson in class. **2.** tell in detail; relate. — v.i. **3.** declaim from memory. **4.** repeat a lesson in class. [ME *reciten*]

reck•less (REK lis) adj. foolishly heedless of danger; rash; careless. [ME *rekles*] — **reck′less•ly** adv. —**reck′less•ness** n.

reck•on (REK ən) v.t. **1.** count; compute; calculate. **2.** look upon as being; regard. — v.i. **3.** make computation; count up. **4.** think; figure. **5.** rely or depend: with *on* or *upon*. —**reckon with 1.** settle accounts with. **2.** take into consideration. [ME *rekenen* compute]

reck•on•ing (REK ə ning) n. **1.** the act of counting; computation; a settlement of accounts. **2.** account; score; bill.

re•claim (ri KLAYM) v.t. **1.** bring (swamp, desert, etc.) into arable condition, as by draining or irrigating. **2.** obtain (a substance) from used or waste products. **3.** cause to return from sinful ways. —n. the act of reclaiming, or state of being reclaimed. [ME *reclamen* cry out against] — **re•claim′ant** n. —**rec•la•ma•tion** (REK lə MAY shən) n.

re•cline (ri KLĪN) v.t. & v.i. **•clined, •clin•ing** assume or cause to assume a recumbent position; lie or lay down or back. [ME *reclinen*] —**re•clin′er** n.

re•cluse (REK loos) n. one who lives in retirement or seclusion. —adj. (ri KLOOS) secluded or retired from the world. [ME] —**re•clu′sive** adj.

rec•og•ni•tion (REK əg NISH ən) n. **1.** the act of recognizing, or the state of being recognized. **2.** acknowledgment of a fact or claim. [ME *recognicion*]

re•cog•ni•zance (ri KOG nə zəns) n. Law an obligation of record, with condition to do some particular act, as to appear and answer. [ME]

rec•og•nize (REK əg NĪZ) v.t. **•nized, •niz•ing 1.** perceive or be aware of as known previously. **2.** identify, as by previous experience: I *recognize* honesty when I see it. **3.** perceive as true; realize. **4.** acknowledge the independence and validity

of, as a government. **5.** indicate appreciation of. **6.** regard as valid or genuine. **7.** give (someone) permission to speak, as in a legislative body. [ME *recognisen*] — **rec′og•niz′a•ble** adj. —**rec′og•niz′a•bly** adv.

re•coil (ri KOIL) v.i. **1.** start back, as in fear or loathing; shrink. **2.** spring back, as from force of discharge or impact. **3.** rebound; react: with *on* or *upon*. —n. REE (KOIL) a backward movement, as of a gun at the moment of firing; also, a shrinking. [ME *recoilen*]

rec•ol•lect (REK ə LEKT) v.t. & v.i. call (something) back to the mind; remember. [< Med.L *recollectus* remembered]

re•col•lect (REE kə LEKT) v.t. **1.** collect again, as things scattered. **2.** collect or compose (one's thoughts or nerves); recover (oneself).

rec•ol•lec•tion (REK ə LEK shən) n. **1.** the act or power of remembering. **2.** something remembered.

recombinant DNA research work that involves introduction of new characteristics into an organism by recombining or splicing together genetic material: also called *gene splicing*.

re•com•bi•na•tion (REE kom bə NAY shən) n. Genetics an interchange of genetic material that produces an organism having characteristics different from those of the parent organism. —**re•com′bi•nant** adj.

rec•om•mend (REK ə MEND) v.t. **1.** commend with favorable representations. **2.** make attractive or acceptable. **3.** advise; urge. **4.** give in charge; commend. [ME *recommenden*]

rec•om•men•da•tion (REK ə men DAY shən) n. **1.** the act of recommending. **2.** something recommended. **3.** a letter, statement, etc. recommending a person.

re•com•mit (REE kə MIT) v.t. **•mit•ted, •mit•ting 1.** commit again. **2.** refer back to a committee, as a bill. —**re′com•mit′tal** n.

rec•om•pense (REK əm PENS) v.t. **•pensed, •pens•ing 1.** give compensation to; pay or repay; reward. **2.** compensate for, as a loss. —n. an equivalent for anything given or done; payment; compensation. [ME]

rec•on•cil•a•ble (REK ən sī lə bəl) adj. capable of being reconciled, adjusted, or harmonized. —**rec′on•cil′a•bil′i•ty** n.

rec•on•cile (REK ən SĪL) v.t. **•ciled, •cil•ing 1.** bring back to friendship after estrangement. **2.** settle or adjust, as a quarrel. **3.** bring to acquiescence, acceptance, or submission. **4.** make or show to be consistent or congruous; harmonize: often with *to* or *with*. [ME *reconcilen*] — **rec•on•cil•i•a•tion** (REK ən SIL ee AY shən) *n.*

rec•on•dite (REK ən DĪT) *adj.* **1.** remote from ordinary or easy perception; abstruse; secret. **2.** hidden [< L *reconditus* hidden] —**rec′on•dite′ly** *adv.*

re•con•di•tion (REE kən DISH ən) *v.t.* put into good or working condition, as by making repairs; overhaul.

re•con•nais•sance (ri KON ə səns) *n.* **1.** a preliminary survey, as of the territory and resources of a country. **2.** *Mil.* the act of obtaining information, esp. regarding the position, strength, and movement of enemy forces. [< F]

re•con•noi•ter (REE kə NOI tər) *v.t.* examine or survey. —*v.i.* make a reconnaissance. [< F *Obs. reconnoître* recognize]

re•con•sid•er (REE kən SID ər) *v.t. & v.i.* consider again, esp. with a view to a reversal of previous action. —**re′con•sid′er•a′tion** *n.*

re•con•sti•tute (ree KON sti TOOT) *v.t.* •**tut•ed,** •**tut•ing** constitute again; make over. —**re•con′sti•tu′tion** *n.*

re•con•struct (REE kən STRUKT) *v.t.* build again; rebuild.

re•con•struc•tion (REE kən STRUK shən) *n.* **1.** the act of reconstructing, or the state of being reconstructed. **2.** *cap.* the restoration of the seceded states as members of the Union following the Civil War; also, the period of and following this restoration: also called **Reconstruction period.** — **re′con•struc′tive** *adj.*

re•cord (REK ərd) *n.* **1.** an account in written or other permanent form serving as a memorial or evidence of a fact or event. **2.** information preserved and handed down: the heaviest rainfall on *record.* **3.** the known career or performance of a person, organization, etc. **4.** the best listed achievement, as in a competitive sport. **5.** a phonograph record. —**off the record 1.** unofficially or unofficial. **2.** not for quotation or publication. —**on the record 1.** official or officially. **2.** for quotation or publication. —*adj.* surpassing any previously recorded achievement, amount, etc. —*v.* (ri KORD) *v.t.* **1.** write down or otherwise inscribe or preserve as a record. **2.** indicate;

register. **3.** make a tape, compact disk, or phonograph record of. —*v.i.* **4.** record something. [ME *recorden* remember]

re•cord•er (ri KOR dər) *n.* **1.** one who or that which records. **2.** any of a group of flutes having eight finger holes. **3.** a tape or wire recorder.

re•cord•ing (ri KOR ding) *n.* **1.** *Telecom.* the registration of a physical record of sounds or other communicable signals. **2.** a phonograph record or compact disk.

record player a motor-driven turntable with a pickup attachment and auxiliary equipment for the playing of phonograph records: also called *phonograph.*

re•count (ri KOWNT) *v.t.* narrate in detail; relate. [ME *recounten*]

re•count (ree KOWNT) *v.t.* count again. — *n.* (REE KOWNT) a repetition of a count; esp., a second count of votes cast.

re•coup (ri KOOP) *v.t.* **1.** recover or make up, as a loss. **2.** reimburse for a loss; indemnify. —*n.* the act or process of recouping. [ME] —**re•coup′a•ble** *adj.*

re•course (REE kors) *n.* **1.** resort to or application for help or security. **2.** one who or that which is resorted to for help or supply. [ME]

re•cov•er (ri KUV ər) *v.t.* **1.** regain after losing; retrieve. **2.** reclaim, as land. **3.** *Law* gain or regain in legal proceedings. —*v.i.* **4.** regain health, composure, etc. [ME *recoveren*] —**re•cov′er•a•ble** *adj.*

re•cov•er (ree KUV ər) *v.t.* cover again.

re•cov•er•y (ri KUV ə ree) *n. pl.* •**er•ies 1.** the act or process of recovering. **2.** restoration from sickness, misfortune, etc. **3.** the retrieval of a space vehicle etc. after it has fallen to earth.

rec•re•ant (REK ree ənt) *adj.* **1.** unfaithful to a cause or pledge; false. **2.** craven; cowardly. —*n.* a coward; also, a deserter. [ME]

rec•re•ate (REK ree AYT) *v.* •**at•ed,** •**at•ing** *v.t.* **1.** impart fresh vigor to; refresh. —*v.i.* **2.** take recreation. [ME *recreaten* revive] —**rec′re•a′tive** *adj.*

re•cre•ate (REE kree AYT) *v.t.* •**at•ed,** •**at•ing** create anew.

rec•re•a•tion (REK ree AY shən) *n.* refreshment of body or mind; diversion; amusement. —**rec′re•a′tion•al** *adj.*

re•crim•i•nate (ri KRIM ə NAYT) *v.t. & v.i.* •**nat•ed,** •**nat•ing** accuse (someone) in return. [< Med.L *recriminatus*] —**re•crim′i•na′tion** *n.* —**re•crim′i•na•to•ry** (ri KRIM ə nə TOR ee) *adj.*

re·cru·desce (REE kroo DES) *v.i.* **•desced,** **•desc·ing** break out afresh. [< L *re- crudescere* become raw again] — **re'cru·des'cence** *n.* —**re'cru·des'cent** *adj.*

re·cruit (ri KROOT) *v.t. & v.i.* **1.** enlist (personnel) for military service; also to raise (an army) by enlistment. **2.** seek or hire (new members, employees, etc.). —*n.* a newly enlisted member of an organization, esp. of the armed forces. [< F *recrue*] —**re·cruit' er** *n.* —**re·cruit'ment** *n.*

rec·tal (REK tl) *adj. Anat.* of, for, or in the rectum.

rec·tan·gle (REK TANG gəl) *n.* a parallelogram with all its angles right angles. [< Med.L *rectangulum*] —**rec·tan·gu·lar** (rek TANG gyə lər) *adj.*

rec·ti·fi·er (REK tə FI ər) *n.* **1.** one who or that which rectifies. **2.** *Electr.* a device used to convert an alternating current into a direct current.

rec·ti·fy (REK tə FI) *v.t.* **•fied, •fy·ing 1.** correct; amend. **2.** *Electr.* change (an alternating current) into a direct current. [ME *rectifien* straighten] —**rec'ti·fi·ca'tion** *n.*

rec·ti·tude (REK ti TOOD) *n.* **1.** uprightness in principles and conduct. **2.** correctness, as of judgment. [ME]

rec·to (REK toh) *n. pl.* **•tos** a right-hand page, as of a book: opposed to *verso.* [< L *recto (folio)* on the right-hand (page)]

rec·tor (REK tər) *n.* **1.** a clergyman in charge of a church, congregation, or parish. **2.** the head of a seminary or university. [ME *rectour* ruler]

rec·to·ry (REK tə ree) *n. pl.* **•ries** a rector's dwelling.

rec·tum (REK təm) *n. pl.* **•tums, •ta** (-tə) *Anat.* the terminal portion of the large intestine, connecting the colon with the anus. [< NL *rectum (intestinum)* straight (intestine)]

re·cum·bent (ri KUM bənt) *adj.* **1.** lying down, wholly or partly. **2.** *Biol.* tending to rest on or extend from a surface. [< L *recumbere* lie back]

re·cu·per·ate (ri KOO pə RAYT) *v.* **•at·ed, •at·ing** *v.i.* **1.** regain health or strength. **2.** recover from loss, as of money. —*v.t.* **3.** obtain again after loss; recover. [< L *recuperatus* recovered] —**re·cu'per·a'tion** *n.* —**re·cu'per·a'tive** *adj.*

re·cur (ri KUR) *v.i.* **•curred, •cur·ring 1.** happen again or repeatedly, esp., at regular intervals. **2.** come back or return; esp., return to the mind. [ME *recurren*] — **re·cur'rence** *n.* —**re·cur'rent** *adj.* — **re·cur'rent·ly** *adv.*

re·cy·cle (ree SI kəl) *v.t.* **•cy·cled, •cy· cling** reclaim (waste materials, as newsprint) by using in the manufacture of new products. —**re·cy'cla·ble** *adj.*

red (red) *adj.* **red·der, red·dest 1.** being of or having a bright color resembling that of blood. **2.** radically left. —*n.* **1.** one of the primary colors, occurring at the opposite end of the spectrum from violet; the color of blood. **2.** *Often cap.* an ultraradical in political views, esp. a communist. —**in the red** operating at a loss; owing money. — **see red** *Informal* be very angry. [ME] — **red'ness** *n.*

red-blood·ed (RED BLUD id) *adj.* having vitality and vigor.

red·den (RED n) *v.t.* **1.** make red. —*v.i.* **2.** grow red; flush; blush.

re·deem (ri DEEM) *v.t.* **1.** regain possession of, as mortgaged property, by paying a price. **2.** pay off; receive back and satisfy, as a promissory note. **3.** turn in and receive a specified value for (a coupon, etc.). **4.** *Theol.* rescue from sin and its penalties. **5.** fulfill, as an oath or promise. **6.** compensate for; atone for. **7.** save; restore, as to favor. [ME *redemen*] —**re·deem'a·ble** *adj.*

re·deem·ing (ri DEE ming) *adj.* compensating for faults, lacks, poor quality, etc.

re·demp·tion (ri DEMP shən) *n.* **1.** the act of redeeming, or the state of being redeemed. **2.** that which redeems. — **re·demp'tive, re·demp'to·ry** *adj.*

Red Ensign the Canadian flag, bearing both the Union Jack and the arms of Canada.

re·de·vel·op (REE di VEL əp) *v.t.* **1.** develop (something) again. **2.** *Photog.* intensify with chemicals and put through a second developing process. —*v.i.* **3.** develop again. —**re'de·vel'op·ment** *n.* — **re'de·vel'op·er** *n.*

red-hand·ed (RED HAN did) *adj. & adv.* in the act of committing, or having just committed, a crime or misdeed.

red herring 1. herring dried and smoked to a reddish color. **2.** something that diverts attention from the main subject, question, etc.

re·di·rect (REE di REKT) *v.t.* direct again or anew: *redirect* a letter. —*adj. Law* designating the examination of a witness, after cross-examination, by the party who first examined the witness.

red·let·ter day (RED LET ər) a memorable occasion.

red-light district (RED LIT) a part of a city or town in which brothels are numerous.

red·lin·ing (RED LI ning) n. the practice by banks of refusing to grant mortgages in deteriorating neighborhoods. [from the supposed red lines on maps that define such areas] —**red'line'** v.t. & v.i. •**lined,** •**lin·ing**

red·o·lent (RED l ənt) adj. **1.** pleasantly fragrant. **2.** reminiscent; suggestive. [ME] —**red'o·lence** n. —**red'o·lent·ly** adv.

re·dou·ble (ree DUB əl) v.t. & v.i. •**led,** •**ling 1.** make or become double. **2.** increase greatly. **3.** in bridge, double (an opponent's double). —n. in bridge, the doubling of an opponent's double.

re·doubt (ri DOWT) n. an enclosed fortification, esp. a temporary one of any form. [< F redoute]

re·doubt·a·ble (ri DOW tə bəl) adj. **1.** inspiring fear; formidable. **2.** deserving respect or deference. [ME redoutable]

re·dound (ri DOWND) v.i. have an effect, as by reaction, on the original agent; accrue. [ME redounden overflow]

re·draft (REE DRAFT) n. a second draft or copy. —**re·draft** (ree DRAFT) v.t. & v.i.

re·dress (ri DRES) v.t. **1.** set right, as a wrong, by compensation or by punishment of the wrong doer; make reparation for. **2.** make reparation to; compensate. **3.** remedy; correct. **4.** adjust, as balances. —n. (REE dres) **1.** satisfaction for wrong done; reparation; amends. **2.** a restoration; correction. [ME redressen]

red tape rigid official procedure involving delay or inaction. [from the tying of public documents with red tape]

re·duce (ri DOOS) v. •**duced,** •**duc·ing** v.t. **1.** make less in size, amount, number, intensity, etc.; diminish. **2.** bring to a lower condition; degrade. **3.** bring to submission; conquer. **4.** bring to a specified condition or state: with to. **5.** thin (paint etc.) with oil or turpentine. **6.** Math. change (an expression) to a more elementary form. **7.** Surg. restore (displaced parts) to normal position. —v.i. **8.** become less in any way. **9.** decrease one's weight, as by dieting. [ME reducen] —**re·duc'i·ble** adj. —**re·duc'i·bly** adv.

re·duc·tion (ri DUK shən) n. **1.** the act or process of reducing. **2.** something made by reducing. **3.** the amount by which something is reduced. [< MF] —**re·duc'tive** adj.

re·dun·dan·cy (ri DUN dən see) n. pl. •**cies 1.** something that is redundant. **2.** the condition or quality of being redundant.

re·dun·dant (ri DUN dənt) adj. **1.** being more than is required; constituting an excess. **2.** ynnecessarily verbose; tautological. [< L redundare overflow]

re·du·pli·cate (ri DOO pli KAYT) v. •**cat·ed,** •**cat·ing** v.t. **1.** repeat again and again; redouble; iterate. **2.** Ling. affix a reduplication to. —v.i. **3.** undergo reduplication. —adj. (-pli kit) repeated again and again; duplicated. [< LL reduplicatus] —**re·du'·pli·ca'tive** adj.

re·du·pli·ca·tion (ri DOO pli KAY shən) n. **1.** the act of reduplicating, or the state of being reduplicated; a redoubling. **2.** Ling. a the repetition of an initial element in a word. b the doubling of all or part of a word, often with vowel or consonant change, as in razzle-dazzle.

re·ech·o (ree EK oh) v.t. & v.i. •**ech·oed,** •**ech·o·ing** echo back or again.

reed (reed) n. **1.** the slender, frequently jointed stem of certain tall grasses growing in wet places, or the grasses themselves. **2.** a thin, elastic plate of reed, wood, or metal nearly closing an opening, used in instruments to produce a musical tone. **3.** a musical pipe made of the hollow stem of a plant. —v.t. **1.** fashion into or decorate with reeds. **2.** thatch with reeds. [ME]

re·ed·u·cate (ree EJ uu KAYT) v.t. •**cat·ed,** •**cat·ing 1.** educate again. **2.** rehabilitate, as a criminal, by education. —**re'ed·u·ca'tion** n.

reed·y (REE dee) adj. **reed·i·er, reed·i·est 1.** full of reeds. **2.** like a reed. **3.** having a thin, sharp tone, like a reed instrument. —**reed'i·ness** n.

reef¹ (reef) n. a ridge of sand or rocks, or esp. of coral, at or near the surface of the water. [< Du. rif]

reef² Naut. n. the part of a sail that is taken in or let out in regulating its size on the mast. —v.t. **1.** reduce (a sail) by folding a part and fastening it to a yard or boom. **2.** shorten or lower, as a topmast by taking part of it in. [ME refe]

reef·er¹ (REE fər) n. **1.** one who reefs. **2.** a close-fitting jacket of heavy material.

reef·er² n. Slang a marijuana cigarette.

reek (reek) v.i. **1.** give off a strong, offensive smell. **2.** be pervaded with anything offensive. —*v.t.* **3.** give off or emit (fumes, an odor, etc.) [ME *reke*] —**reek'er** *n.* —**reek'y** *adj.*

reel¹ (reel) *n.* **1.** a rotary device or frame for winding rope, film, etc. **2.** motion picture film wound on one reel, used as a unit of length. **3.** a wooden spool for wire, thread, etc. —*v.t.* **1.** wind on a reel or bobbin, as a line. **2.** pull by reeling a line: with *in.* **3.** say, do, etc., easily and fluently: with *off.* [ME *rele*]

reel² *v.i.* **1.** stagger, sway, or lurch, as when giddy or drunk. **2.** whirl round and round. **3.** have a sensation of giddiness or whirling. **4.** waver or fall back, as attacking troops. [ME *relen*] —*n.* a staggering motion; giddiness.

reel³ *n.* a lively dance, chiefly Scottish or Irish; also, the music for this dance.

re·en·force (REE ən FORS) see REIN-FORCE.

re·en·try (ree EN tree) *n. pl.* **·tries 1.** the act of entering again. **2.** *Aerospace* the return of a rocket or other object to the atmosphere of the earth.

re·e·val·u·ate (REE ə VAL yoo AYT) *v.t.* **·at·ed, ·at·ing** consider anew. —**re'e·val'u·a'tion** *n.*

re·fec·tion (ri FEK shən) *n.* **1.** refreshment with food and drink. **2.** a light meal. [ME *refeccioun*]

re·fec·to·ry (ri FEK tə ree) *n. pl.* **·ries** a dining hall, esp. in a religious house. [< LL *refectorium*]

re·fer (ri FER) *v.* **·ferred, ·fer·ring** *v.t.* **1.** direct or send for information, assistance, etc. **2.** submit for consideration, settlement, etc. **3.** assign to a source, class, period, etc. —*v.i.* **4.** make reference; allude. **5.** turn, as for information, help, or authority. [ME *referren*] —**ref·er·a·ble** (REF ər ə bəl) *adj.* —**re·fer'ral** *n.* —**re·fer'·rer** *n.*

ref·e·ree (REF ə REE) *n.* **1.** a person to whom something is referred for arbitration. **2.** in certain sports, a supervisory official.— *v.t. & v.i.* **·reed, ·ree·ing** judge as a referee.

ref·er·ence (REF ər əns) *n.* **1.** the act of referring. **2.** an allusion or direction of the attention: *reference* to a recent event. **3.** a note or other indication in a book, referring to some other book or passage. **4.** one who or that which is or may be referred to. **5.** the state of being referred or related: used in the phrase **with** (or **in**) **reference to. 6.** a

person to whom one seeking employment may refer for recommendation.

ref·er·en·dum (REF ə REN dəm) *n. pl.* **·dums** or **·da** (-də) **1.** the submission of a proposed law to a vote of the people for ratification or rejection. **2.** the vote in such a procedure. [< NL]

ref·er·ent (REF ər ənt) *n.* the object, concept, etc. to which reference is made. [< L]

re·fill (ree FIL) *v.t.* fill again. —*n.* (REE FIL) any commodity packaged to fit and fill a container originally containing that commodity.

re·fine (ri FĪN) *v.* **·fined, ·fin·ing** *v.t.* **1.** free from impurities or extraneous matter. **2.** make polished or cultured. **3.** improve or change by subtle or precise alterations. — *v.i.* **4.** become fine or pure. —**re·fin'er** *n.*

re·fined (ri FĪND) *adj.* **1.** characterized by refinement; cultivated; polished. **2.** free from impurity. **3.** exceedingly precise.

re·fine·ment (ri FĪN mənt) *n.* **1.** fineness of thought, taste, language, etc.; culture. **2.** the act, effect, or process of refining. **3.** a nice distinction; subtlety. **4.** fastidiousness.

re·fin·er·y (ri FĪ nə ree) *n. pl.* **·er·ies** a place where crude material, as sugar or petroleum, is purified.

re·fit (ree FIT) *n. & v.i.* **·fit·ted, ·fit·ting** make or be made fit or ready again, as by repairs, replacement of equipment, etc. — *n.* the repair of damages or wear, esp. of a ship.

re·flect (ri FLEKT) *v.t.* **1.** turn or throw back, as waves of light, heat, or sound. **2.** give back an image of; mirror. **3.** manifest as a result of influence, imitation, etc. —*v.i.* **4.** send back rays, as of light or heat. **5.** give back an image. **6.** think carefully; ponder. **7.** bring blame, discredit, etc.: with *on* or *upon.* [ME *reflecten*] —**re·flec'tion** *n.* —**re·flec'tive** *adj.* —**re·flec'tive·ly** *adv.* —**re·flec'tive·ness** *n.* —**re'flec·tiv'i·ty** *n.*

re·flec·tor (ri FLEK tər) *n.* **1.** that which reflects. **2.** a polished surface for reflecting light, heat, sound, etc. **3.** a telescope that transmits an image from a reflecting surface.

re·flex (REE fleks) *adj.* **1.** *Physiol.* of, pertaining to, or produced by involuntary response to a stimulus. **2.** turned or directed backward or in the opposite direction. **3.** bent back; reflexed. —*n. Physiol.* an involuntary movement or response to a stimulus, as in sneezing, shivering, etc.: also **reflex action.** [< L REFLEXUS *bent back*]

re·flex·ive (ri FLEK siv) *adj. Gram.* **a** of verbs, having an object that is identical with the subject as "dresses" in "He dresses himself." **b** of pronouns in the objective case, being identical with the subject, as "herself" in "She hurt herself." —*n. Gram.* a reflexive verb or pronoun. —**re·flex′·ive·ly** *adv.* —**re·flex′ive·ness** *n.*

re·flux (REE FLUKS) *n.* a flowing back; ebb. [ME]

re·for·est (ree FOR ist) *v.t. & v.i.* replant (an area) with trees. —**re′for·es·ta′tion** *n.*

re·form (ri FORM) *v.t.* **1.** make better by removing abuses, altering, etc. **2.** improve morally; persuade or educate to a better life. —*v.i.* **3.** give up sin or error; become better. —*n.* an act or result of reformation; change for the better. [ME *reformen*] —**re·form′er, re·form′ist** *n.*

re-form (ree FORM) *v.t. & v.i.* form again. [ME]

ref·or·ma·tion (REF ər MAY shən) *n.* **1.** the act of reforming, or the state of being reformed; esp., moral improvement. **2.** *cap.* the 16th c. religious movement that established Protestantism.

re·for·ma·to·ry (ri FOR mə TOR ee) *n. pl.* **·ries** an institution for the reformation and instruction of juvenile offenders. —*adj.* tending to reform.

re·formed (ri FORMD) *adj.* **1.** restored to a better state. **2.** improved in conduct, habits, etc.

Reform Judaism the branch of Judaism that interprets traditional law and ritual in relation to modern times.

re·fract (ri FRAKT) *v.t.* **1.** deflect (a ray) by refraction. **2.** *Optics* determine the degree of refraction of (an eye or lens). [< L *refractus* forced back]

re·frac·tion (ri FRAK shən) *n. Physics* the change of direction of a ray, as of light or heat, in passage from one medium to another of different density. —**re·frac′tive** *adj.* —**re·frac·tiv·i·ty** (REE frak TIV i tee) *n.*

re·frac·tor (ri FRAK tər) *n.* **1.** that which refracts. **2.** a telescope focused primarily by means of a lens: also **refracting telescope.**

re·frac·to·ry (ri FRAK tə ree) *adj.* **1.** not amenable to control; unmanageable; obstinate. **2.** resisting heat or ordinary methods of reduction, as an ore. —*n. pl.* **·ries** any of various materials highly resistant to the action of great heat. [< L *refractarius* stubborn] —**re·frac′to·ri·ness** *n.*

re·frain¹ (ri FRAYN) *v.i.* keep oneself back; abstain from action. [ME *refreinen*]

re·frain² *n.* a phrase or strain in a poem or song repeated at the end of each stanza. [ME *refreyne*]

re·fresh (ri FRESH) *v.t.* **1.** make fresh or vigorous again, as by food or rest; reinvigorate; revive. **2.** make fresh, clean, cool, etc. **3.** stimulate, as the memory. —*v.i.* **4.** become fresh again; revive. **5.** take refreshment. [ME *refresshen*]

re·fresh·er (ri FRESH ər) *adj.* reviewing material previously studied: a *refresher* course. —*n.* one who or that which refreshes.

re·fresh·ing (ri FRESH ing) *adj.* **1.** serving to refresh. **2.** enjoyably novel or unusual.

re·fresh·ment (ri FRESH mənt) *n.* **1.** the act of refreshing, or the state of being refreshed. **2.** that which refreshes. **3.** *pl.* food, or food and drink. [ME *refresshement*]

re·frig·er·ate (ri FRIJ ə RAYT) *v.t.* **·at·ed, ·at·ing 1.** keep or make cold. **2.** freeze or chill (foodstuffs etc.) for preservation. [< L *refrigeratus* cooled] —**re·frig′er·ant** (-ər ənt) *n. & adj.* —**re·frig′er·a′tion** *n.*

re·frig·er·a·tor (ri FRIJ ə RAY tər) *n.* a box, cabinet, room, etc. equipped with a cooling apparatus for preserving perishable foods etc.

ref·uge (REF yooj) *n.* **1.** shelter or protection as from danger or distress. **2.** one who or that which shelters or protects. **3.** a safe place; asylum. [ME]

ref·u·gee (REF yuu JEE) *n.* one who flees to another country to escape from invasion, persecution, or political danger.

re·ful·gent (ri FUL jənt) *adj.* shining brilliantly; radiant. [< L *refulgere* shine] —**re·ful′gence** *n.*

re·fund (ri FUND) *v.t. & v.i.* give or pay back (money etc.); repay. —*n.* (REE fund) a repayment; also, the amount repaid. [ME *refunden*]

re·fur·bish (ree FUR bish) *v.t.* renovate or freshen; polish up; brighten.

re·fuse¹ (ri FYOOZ) *v.* **·fused, ·fus·ing** *v.t.* **1.** decline to do, permit, take, or yield. **2.** decline to jump over: said of a horse at a ditch, hedge, etc. —*v.i.* **3.** decline to do, permit, take, or yield something. [ME *refusen*] —**re·fus′al** *n.*

ref·use² (REF yoos) *n.* anything worthless; rubbish. —*adj.* rejected as worthless. [ME]

re·fute (ri FYOOT) v.t. **-fut·ed, -fut·ing 1.** prove the incorrectness of falsity of (a statement). **2.** prove (a person) to be in error; confute. [< L *refutare* suppress] **—re·fut′a·ble** adj. **—ref·u·ta·tion** (REF yuu TAY shən) n.

re·gain (ree GAYN) v.t. **1.** get possession of again, as something lost; recover. **2.** get back to: He *regained* the street.

re·gal (REE gəl) adj. **1.** of a king; royal. **2.** stately. [ME] **—re·gal·i·ty** (ri GAL i tee) n.

re·gale (ri GAYL) v. **-galed, -gal·ing** v.t. **1.** give unusual pleasure to; delight. **2.** entertain sumptuously; feast. **—**v.i. **3.** feast. [< F *régaler*]

re·ga·li·a (ri GAYL yə) n.pl. **1.** the insignia and emblems of royalty, as the crown, scepter, etc. **2.** the distinctive symbols, insignia, etc. of any society, order, or rank. **3.** fine clothes; fancy trappings. [< Med.L, things pertaining to a king]

re·gard (ri GAHRD) v.t. **1.** look at or observe closely. **2.** think of in a certain manner: I *regard* him as a friend. **3.** take into account; consider. **4.** have relation or pertinence to; concern. **—**v.i. **5.** pay attention. **—**n. **1.** careful attention or notice; heed; consideration. **2.** esteem; respect. **3.** *Usu. pl.* good wishes; affection. [ME]

re·gard·ing (ri GAHR ding) prep. in reference to; concerning.

re·gard·less (ri GAHRD lis) adj. having no regard or consideration; heedless; negligent: often with *of*. **—**adv. in spite of everything.

re·gat·ta (ri GAT ə) n. a boat race, or a series of such races. [< Ital.]

re·gen·cy (REE jən see) n. pl. **-cies 1.** the government or office of a regent or body of regents. **2.** the period during which a regent governs. **3.** a body of regents. [ME]

re·gen·er·ate (ri JEN ə RAYT) v. **-at·ed, -at·ing** v.t. **1.** cause complete moral and spiritual reformation in. **2.** produce or form anew; recreate; reproduce. **3.** *Biol.* grow or form (new tissue). **—**v.i. **4.** form anew; be reproduced. **5.** become spiritually regenerate. **—**adj. (ri JEN ər it) **1.** having new life; restored. **2.** spiritually renewed. **— re·gen′er·a′tion** n. **—re·gen·er·a·tive** (ri JEN ər ə tiv) adj.

re·gent (REE jənt) n. **1.** one who rules in the name and place of a sovereign. **2.** one of various educational officers, as of a state. **—**

adj. exercising authority in another's place. [ME]

reg·gae (REG ay) n. a type of Jamaican popular music, usu. with accents on the second and fourth beats.

reg·i·cide (REJ ə SID) n. **1.** the killing of a king or sovereign. **2.** one who has killed a king or sovereign.

re·gime (rə ZHEEM) n. **1.** system of government or administration. **2.** a social system. **3.** regimen. Also **ré·gime′** [< F *régime*]

reg·i·men (REJ ə mən) n. a systematized course of living, as to food, clothing, etc.: also *regime*. [ME]

reg·i·ment (REJ ə mənt) n. **1.** *Mil.* an administrative and tactical unit of infantry, artillery, etc. comprising several battalions. **2.** any large body of persons. **—**v.t. (REJ ə MENT) **1.** form into a regiment or regiments; organize. **2.** systematize or make uniform. [ME] **—reg′i·men′tal** adj. **— reg′i·men·ta′tion** n.

re·gion (REE jən) n. **1.** an indefinite portion of territory or space, usu. of considerable extent. **2.** a particular area or place: the delta *region* of the Nile. [ME]

re·gion·al (REE jə nl) adj. **1.** of or pertaining to a particular region; sectional; local: *regional* planning. **2.** of or pertaining to an entire region or section. **—re′gion·al·ly** adv.

reg·is·ter (REJ ə stər) n. **1.** a formal or official record or account, as of names or transactions; also, a book containing such a record. **2.** any of various devices for counting or recording: a cash *register*. **3.** a device by which heated or cooled air is admitted to a room. **4.** the act of recording or registering; registry. [ME *registre*] **—**v.t. **1.** enter in or as in a register; record officially or exactly. **2.** indicate, as on a scale. **3.** express; show: His face *registered* shock. **4.** cause (mail) to be recorded, on payment of a fee, when deposited with the postal system, so as to insure delivery. **—**v.i. **5.** enter one's name in a register. **6.** cause one's name to be included on a list of eligible voters. **7.** have an effect; make an impression. **—reg′is·tered** adj. **—reg′is·trant** n.

registered nurse a graduate nurse licensed to practice by the appropriate state authority.

reg·is·trar (REJ ə STRAHR) n. an authorized keeper of a register or of records; esp., a college or university officer who records the enrollment of students, their grades, etc.

reg·is·tra·tion (REJ ə STRAY shən) *n.* **1.** the act of entering in a registry; also, such an entry. **2.** the registering of voters; also, the number of voters registered. **3.** enrollment in a school, college, or university. [< MF]

reg·is·try (REJ ə stree) *n. pl.* **·tries 1.** the act of registering; registration. **2.** a register, or the place where it is kept.

re·gress (REE gres) *n.* **1.** passage back; return. **2.** the power or right of passing back. **3.** withdrawal; retrogression. —*v.i.* (ri GRES) go back; move backward; return. [ME *regresse* return] —**re·gres'·sive** *adj.*

re·gres·sion (ri GRESH ən) *n.* **1.** the act of regressing. **2.** *Psychoanal.* a retreat to earlier and less mature forms of behavior.

re·gret (ri GRET) *v.* **·gret·ted, ·gret·ting** —*v.t.* **1.** look back upon with a feeling of distress or loss. —*v.i.* **2.** feel sorrow or grief. [ME *regretten* —*n.* **1.** distress of mind over loss or circumstances beyond one's control. **2.** remorseful sorrow; compunction. **3.** *pl.* a polite refusal in response to an invitation.] —**re·gret'ful** *adj.* —**re·gret'ta·ble** *adj.* —**re·gret'ta·bly** *adv.*

reg·u·lar (REG yə lər) *adj.* **1.** made according to rule; symmetrical; normal. **2.** acting according to rule; methodical; orderly: *regular* habits. **3.** constituted, appointed, or conducted in the proper manner; duly authorized: a *regular* meeting. **4.** *Gram.* undergoing the inflection that is normal or most common. **5.** *Mil.* pertaining or belonging to the permanent military services. **6.** in politics, adhering loyally to a party organization or platform. **7.** *Informal* thorough; unmitigated; absolute. —*n.* **1.** a regular soldier. **2.** one regularly employed or engaged; also, a habitual customer. **3.** a person loyal to a certain political party. [ME *reguler*] —**reg'u·lar'i·ty** (REG yə LAR i tee) *n.*

reg·u·lar·ize (REG yə lə RIZ) *v.t.* **·ized, ·iz·ing** make regular.

reg·u·late (REG yə LAYT) *v.t.* **·lat·ed, ·lat·ing 1.** direct or control according to certain rules, principles, etc. **2.** adjust according to a standard, degree, etc.: *regulate* currency. **3.** adjust to accurate operation. **4.** put in order. [< LL *regulatus* ruled] —**reg'u·la·to'ry** (-lə TOR ee) *adj.* —**reg'u·la'tor** *n.*

reg·u·la·tion (REG yə LAY shən) *n.* **1.** the act of regulating, or the state of being regulated. **2.** a rule of conduct.

re·gur·gi·tate (ri GUR ji TAYT) *v.* **·tat·ed, ·tat·ing** *v.i.* **1.** rush, pour, or surge back. —*v.t.* **2.** cause to surge back, as partially digested food; vomit. [< Med.L *regurgitatus*] —**re·gur'gi·ta'tion** *n.*

re·ha·bil·i·tate (REE hə BIL i TAYT) *v.t.* **·tat·ed, ·tat·ing 1.** restore to a former state, capacity, privilege, rank, etc.; reinstate. **2.** restore to a state of health, useful activity, etc. through training, therapy, or guidance. **3.** put back into good condition. [< Med.L *rehabilitatus* restored] —**re'ha·bil'i·ta'tion** *n.*

re·hash (ree HASH) *v.t.* work into a new form; go over again. —*n.* (REE hash) something rehashed.

re·hearse (ri HURS) *v.* **·hearsed, ·hears·ing** *v.t.* **1.** perform privately in preparation for public performance, as a play or song. **2.** instruct by rehearsal. **3.** say over again; repeat aloud; recite. —*v.i.* **4.** rehearse a play, song, etc. [ME *rehersen*] —**re·hears'al** *n.*

reign (rayn) *n.* **1.** the possession or exercise of supreme power, esp. royal power; sovereignty. **2.** the time or duration of a sovereign's rule. —*v.i.* **1.** hold and exercise sovereign power. **2.** prevail: *Peace reigns.* [ME *reine*]

re·im·burse (REE im BURS) *v.t.* **·bursed, ·burs·ing** pay back. —**re'im·burs'a·ble** *adj.* —**re'im·burse'ment** *n.*

rein (rayn) *n.* **1.** *Usu. pl.* a strap attached to the bit to control a horse or other draft animal. **2.** any means of restraint or control; a check. —*v.t.* **1.** guide, check, or halt with or as with reins. —*v.i.* **2.** check or halt a horse by mean of reins. [ME *rene* hold back]

re·in·car·na·tion (REE in kahr NAY shən) *n.* a rebirth of the soul in successive bodies; also, the belief in such rebirth. —**re'in·car'nate** *v.t.* **·nat·ed, ·nat·ing**

rein·deer (RAYN DEER) *n. pl.* **·deer** a deer of northern regions, having branched antlers in both sexes and used as a pack animal. [ME *rayndere*]

re·in·force (REE in FORS) *v.t.* **·forced, ·forc·ing 1.** give new force or strength to. **2.** *Mil.* strengthen with additional personnel or equipment. **3.** add some strengthening part or material to.

reinforced concrete concrete containing

metal rods or netting to increase its tensile strength and durability.

re·in·force·ment (REE in FORS mənt) *n.*
1. the act of reinforcing. 2. *Often pl. Mil.* a fresh body of troops or additional vessels.

re·in·state (REE in STAYT) *v.t.* •stat·ed, •stat·ing restore to a former state, position, etc.

re·it·er·ate (ree IT ə RAYT) *v.t.* •at·ed, •at·ing say or do again and again. [< L *reiteratus* repeated] —**re·it´er·a´tion** *n.*

re·ject (ri JEKT) *v.t.* 1. refuse to accept, recognize, believe, etc. 2. refuse to grant; deny, as a petition. 3. cast away as worthless; discard. —*n.* (REE jekt) one who or that which has been rejected. [< L *rejectus* thrown back] —**re·jec´tion** *n.*

re·joice (ri JOIS) *v.* •joiced, •joic·ing *v.i.* 1. feel joyful; be glad. —*v.t.* 2. fill with joy; gladden. [ME *rejoicen*] —**re·joic´ing** *n. & adj.*

re·join[1] (ri JOIN) *v.t.* 1. say in reply; answer. —*v.i.* 2. answer. [ME *rejoinen*]

re·join[2] (ree JOIN) *v.t.* 1. come again into company with. 2. join together again: reunite. —*v.i.* 3. come together again.

re·join·der (ri JOIN dər) *n.* an answer to a reply; also, any reply or retort. [< MF *rejoindre*]

re·ju·ve·nate (ri JOO və NAYT) *v.t.* •nat·ed, •nat·ing give new vigor or youthfulness to. —**re·ju´ve·na´tion** *n.*

re·lapse (ri LAPS) *v.i.* •lapsed, •laps·ing 1. lapse back, as into a disease. 2. return to bad habits or ways; backslide. —*n.* the act or condition of relapsing. [ME]

re·late (ri LAYT) *v.* •lat·ed, •lat·ing *v.t.* 1. tell the particulars of; narrate. 2. bring into connection or relation. —*v.i.* 3. have relation: with *to*. 4. have reference: with *to*. [< L *relatus* carried back]

re·lat·ed (ri LAY tid) *adj.* 1. standing in relation; connected. 2. connected by blood or marriage. 3. narrated; told. —**re·lat´ed·ness** *n.*

re·la·tion (ri LAY shən) *n.* 1. the fact or condition of being related or connected in some way. 2. connected by blood or marriage; kinship. 3. a person connected by blood or marriage. 4. reference; regard; allusion: in *relation* to that matter. 5. *pl.* conditions or connections between or among individuals; also, any conditions or connections by which one country may come into contact with another politically and commercially. 6. the act of narrating; also, that

which is narrated. [ME *relacion*] —**re·la·tion·ship** *n.*

rel·a·tive (REL ə tiv) *adj.* 1. having connection; pertinent: an inquiry *relative* to one's health. 2. resulting from or depending upon relation; comparative. 3. intelligible only in relationship. 4. referring to an antecedent term: a *relative* pronoun. —*n.* one who is related. —**rel´a·tive·ly** *adv.*

rel·a·tiv·i·ty (REL ə TIV i tee) *n.* 1. the quality or condition of being relative. 2. *Physics* the principle of the interdependence of matter, energy, space, and time, as formulated by Albert Einstein.

re·lax (ri LAKS) *v.t.* 1. make lax or loose; make less tight or firm. 2. make less stringent or severe, as discipline. 3. abate; slacken, as efforts. 4. relieve from strain or effort. —*v.i.* 5. become lax or loose; loosen. 6. become less stringent or severe. 7. rest; repose. [ME *relaxen*] —**re·lax·a·tion** (REE lak SAY shən) *n.*

re·lay (REE lay) *n.* 1. a fresh set, as of people, horses, or dogs, to replace or relieve a tired set. 2. a relay race; one of its laps or legs. 3. *Electr.* a device that utilizes variations in the condition of a current in a circuit to effect the operation of similar devices in the same or another circuit. —*v.t.* (ri LAY) 1. send onward by or as by relays. 2. *Electr.* operate or retransmit by means of a relay. [ME *relaien* unleash]

re·lay (ree LAY) *v.t.* -laid, -lay·ing lay again.

relay race a race between teams, each member of which races a set part of the course and is relieved by a teammate.

re·lease (ri LEES) *v.t.* •leased, •leas·ing 1. set free; liberate. 2. deliver from worry, pain, obligation, etc. 3. free from something that holds, binds, etc. 4. permit the circulation, sale, performance, etc. of, as a phonograph record or news item. —*n.* 1. the act of releasing or the state of being released. 2. a discharge from responsibility or penalty, as from a debt. 3. *Law* a document by which one relinquishes all claim to something. 4. anything formally released to the public, as news, a motion picture, etc. [ME *relesen*]

rel·e·gate (REL i GAYT) *v.t.* •gat·ed, •gat·ing 1. send off or consign, as to an obscure position or place. 2. assign, as to a particular class or sphere. 3. refer (a matter) to someone for decision. 4. banish; exile. [ME] —**rel´e·ga´tion** *n.*

re·lent (ri LENT) *v.i.* soften in temper; become less severe. [ME]

re·lent·less (ri LENT lis) *adj.* **1.** unremitting; continuous. **2.** indifferent to the pain of others; pitiless. **—re·lent′less·ly** *adv.*

rel·e·vant (REL ə vənt) *adj.* pertinent; applicable: usu. with *to.* [< Med.L. *relevare* raise up] **—rel′e·vance, rel′e·van·cy** *n.*

re·li·a·ble (ri LĪ ə bəl) *adj.* that may be relied upon; worthy of confidence; trustworthy. **—re·li′a·bil′i·ty** *n.* **—re·li′a·bly** *adv.*

re·li·ance (ri LĪ əns) *n.* **1.** the act of relying, or the condition of being reliant. **2.** something or someone relied upon. **—re·li′ant** *adj.*

rel·ic (REL ik) *n.* **1.** some remaining portion or fragment of that which has vanished or been destroyed. **2.** a keepsake or memento. **3.** the body or part of the body of a saint; also, any sacred memento. [ME]

re·lief (ri LEEF) *n.* **1.** the act of relieving, or the state of being relieved. **2.** that which relieves. **3.** charitable aid, as food or money. **4.** the release, as from one's post or duty, and the substitution of someone else; also, the one so substituted. **5.** in architecture and sculpture, the projection of a figure, ornament, etc. from a surface. **6.** *Geog.* the elevations and unevenness of land surface. [ME *relef*]

re·lieve (ri LEEV) *v.t.* **·lieved, ·liev·ing 1.** free from pain, embarrassment, etc. **2.** lessen or alleviate, as pain or anxiety. **3.** release from duty, as a sentinel, by providing or serving as a substitute. **4.** make less monotonous, harsh, or unpleasant; vary. **5.** bring into relief or prominence. [ME *releven*] **—re·liev′a·ble** *adj.*

re·lig·ion (ri LIJ ən) *n.* the beliefs, attitudes, emotions, behavior, etc. constituting a person's relationship with the powers and principles of the universe, esp. with a deity or deities. [ME *religioun*]

re·li·gi·os·i·ty (ri LIJ ee OS i tee) *n.* devoutness; also, pious sentimentality. [ME *religiosite*]

re·lig·ious (ri LIJ əs) *adj.* **1.** feeling and manifesting religion; devout; pious. **2.** of or pertaining to religion: a *religious* teacher. **3.** strict in performance; conscientious: a *religious* loyalty. **—n.** *pl.* **·ious** a monk or nun. [ME]

re·lin·quish (ri LING kwish) *v.t.* **1.** give up; abandon. **2.** renounce: *relinquish* a claim.

3. let go (a hold, etc.). [ME *relinquisshen*] **—re·lin′quish·ment** *n.*

rel·i·quar·y (REL i KWER ee) *n. pl.* **·quar·ies** a repository for religious relics. [ME *reliquaire*]

rel·ish (REL ish) *n.* **1.** appetite; appreciation; liking. **2.** the flavor, esp. when agreeable, in food and drink. **3.** the quality in anything that lends spice or zest: *Danger* gives *relish* to adventure. **4.** something taken with food to lend it flavor, as chopped pickles. **—v.t. 1.** like the savor of; enjoy. **—v.i. 2.** have an agreeable flavor; afford gratification. [ME *reles* taste]

re·luc·tance (ri LUK təns) *n.* **1.** the state of being reluctant. **2.** *Electr.* capacity for opposing magnetic induction.

re·luc·tant (ri LUK tənt) *adj.* marked by unwillingness, or performed unwillingly. [< L *reluctari* fight against] **—re·luc′tant·ly** *adv.*

re·ly (ri LĪ) *v.i.* **·lied, ·ly·ing** place trust or confidence: with *on* or *upon.* [ME *relien*] **—re·li′er** *n.*

REM (rem) *n.* rapid eye movement.

re·main (ri MAYN) *v.i.* **1.** stay or be left behind after the removal of other persons or things. **2.** continue in one place, condition, or character: He *remained* in office. **3.** be left as something to be done, dealt with, etc.: It *remains* to be proved. **4.** endure or last; abide. [ME *remainen*]

re·main·der (ri MAYN dər) *n.* **1.** that which remains after a subtraction, expenditure, or passing over of a part. **2.** *Math.* the quantity left after subtraction or division. **3.** a copy of a book sold at reduced price by a publisher after sales have slowed. **—adj.** leftover; remaining. **—v.t.** sell (books etc.) as a remainder.

re·mains (ri MAYNZ) *n.pl.* **1.** that which is left after a part has been removed or destroyed. **2.** the body of a deceased person.

re·mand (ri MAND) *v.t.* **1.** order or send back. **2.** *Law* recommit to custody, as an accused person after a preliminary examination. [ME *remaunden*] **—n.** a remanding, or being remanded.

re·mark (ri MAHRK) *n.* **1.** an oral or written comment or saying; a casual observation. **2.** the act of observing or noticing; observation; notice. **—v.t. 1.** say or write by way of comment. **2.** take particular notice of. **—v.i. 3.** make remarks: with *on* or *upon.* [< F *remarquer*]

re·mark·a·ble (ri MAHR kə bəl) *adj.* **1.**

worthy of notice. **2.** extraordinary; unusual; conspicuous; distinguished. [< F *remarquable*] **—re·mark'a·ble·ness** *n.* **—re·mark'a·bly** *adv.*

re·me·di·a·ble (ri MEE dee ə bəl) *adj.* capable of being cured or remedied. [< MF]

re·me·di·al (ri MEE dee əl) *adj.* of the nature of or adapted to be used as a remedy: *remedial* help in spelling.

rem·e·dy (REM i dee) *n. pl.* **·dies 1.** that which cures or affords relief to bodily disease or ailment; a medicine; also, remedial treatment. **2.** a means of counteracting or removing an error, evil, etc. **—v.t.** **·died, ·dy·ing** serve as a remedy for. [ME *remedie*]

re·mem·ber (ri MEM bər) *v.t.* **1.** bring back or recall again to the mind or memory. **2.** keep in mind carefully, as for a purpose. **3.** bear in mind as worthy of a reward, gift, etc. **—v.i. 4.** have or use one's memory. **— remember (one) to** inform a person of the regard of: *Remember* me *to* your husband. [ME *remembren*]

re·mem·brance (ri MEM brəns) *n.* **1.** the act or power of remembering, or the state of being remembered. **2.** that which is remembered. **3.** *Often pl.* a memento; keepsake. **4.** mindful regard. [ME]

re·mind (ri MĪND) *v.t.* bring to (someone's) mind; cause to remember. **—re·mind'ful** *adj.*

rem·i·nis·cence (REM ə NIS əns) *n.* **1.** the recalling to mind of past incidents and events. **2.** the narration of past experiences. [< MF] **—rem'i·nisce'** *v.i.* **·nisced, ·nisc·ing —rem'i·nis'cent** *adj.*

re·miss (ri MIS) *adj.* slack or careless in matters requiring attention; negligent. [ME] **—re·miss'·ness** *n.*

re·mis·sion (ri MISH ən) *n.* **1.** the act of remitting, or the state of being remitted. **2.** deliverance from penalty, debt, or obligation. **3.** *Med.* temporary abatement of a disease or pain. Also **re·mit·tal** (ri MIT l).

re·mit (ri MIT) *v.* **·mit·ted, ·mit·ting** *v.t.* **1.** send, as money in payment for goods; transmit. **2.** refrain from exacting or inflicting, as a penalty. **3.** pardon; forgive, as a sin or crime. **4.** abate; relax, as vigilance. **5.** refer or submit for judgment, settlement, etc. **—v.i. 6.** send money, as in payment. **7.** diminish; abate. [ME *remitten*]

re·mit·tance (ri MIT ns) *n.* the act of sending money or credit; also, the money or credit so sent.

rem·nant (REM nənt) *n.* **1.** that which remains. **2.** the piece of cloth, etc. left over after the last cutting. [ME]

re·mon·strance (ri MON strəns) *n.* the act of remonstrating; protest; expostulation.

re·mon·strant (ri MON strənt) *adj.* having the character of a remonstrance; expostulatory. **—n.** one who remonstrates.

re·mon·strate (ri MON strayt) *v.* **·strat·ed, ·strat·ing** *v.t.* say or plead in protest. **—v.i. 2.** urge strong reasons against any course or action; protest; object. [< Med.L *remonstratus* exhibited] **—re·mon'stra·tive** (-strə tiv) *adj.* **—re·mon·stra·tor** (ri MON stray tər) *n.*

re·morse (ri MORS) *n.* the keen or hopeless anguish caused by a sense of guilt; distressing self-reproach. [ME] **—re·morse'ful** *adj.* **—re·morse'ful·ness** *n.* **—re·morse'less** *adj.* **—re·morse'less·ness** *n.*

re·mote (ri MOHT) *adj.* **·mot·er, ·mot·est 1.** located far from a specified place. **2.** distant in time. **3.** having slight relation or connection: a *remote* cousin. **4.** not obvious; slight. **5.** distant in manner; aloof. [ME] **—re·mote'ness** *n.*

re·move (ri MOOV) *v.* **·moved, ·mov·ing** *v.t.* **1.** take or move away, as from one place to another. **2.** take off; doff, as a hat. **3.** get rid of; do away with: *remove* abuses. **4.** displace or dismiss, as from office. **5.** take out; extract: with *from.* **—v.i. 6.** change one's place of residence or business. [ME *removen*] **—n. 1.** the act of removing, as one's business or belongings. **2.** the space moved over in changing an object from one position to another. **—re·mov'a·ble** *adj.* **—re·mov'al** *n.*

re·moved (ri MOOVD) *adj.* separated, as by intervening space, time, or relationship, or by difference in kind: a cousin twice *removed.*

re·mu·ner·ate (ri MYOO nə RAYT) *v.t.* **·at·ed, ·at·ing** make just or adequate return to or for; pay or pay for. [< L *remuneratus* repaid] **—re·mu'ner·a'tion** *n.* **—re·mu'ner·a·tive** (ri MYOO nər ə tiv) *adj.*

re·nais·sance (REN ə SAHNS) *n.* **1.** a new birth; resurrection; renascence. **2.** *cap.* the revival of letters and art in Europe, marking the transition from medieval to modern history, roughly from the 14th through 16th c.: also *Renascence.* **—adj. cap.** of or characteristic of the Renaissance. [< F]

re·nal (REEN l) *adj.* of, pertaining to, affecting, or near the kidneys. [< LL *renalis*]

re·nas·cence (ri NAY sǝns) *n.* 1. a rebirth; revival. 2. *cap.* the Renaissance. —**re·nas'cent** *adj.*

rend (rend) *v.* **rent, rend·ing** *v.t.* 1. tear apart forcibly. 2. pull or remove forcibly: with *away, from, off,* etc. 3. pass through (the air) violently and noisily. 4. distress (the heart etc.). —*v.i.* 5. split; part. [ME *renden*]

ren·der (REN dǝr) *v.t.* 1. present for action, approval, payment, etc. 2. provide; give: *render* aid to the poor. 3. give as due: *render* obedience. 4. perform: *render* great service. 5. represent or depict, as in painting. 6. cause to be: *render* a ship seaworthy. 7. translate. 8. melt and clarify, as lard. [ME *rendren*] —**ren'der·a·ble** *adj.*

ren·dez·vous (RAHN dǝ VOO) *n. pl.* **·vous** (-VOOZ) 1. an appointed place of meeting. 2. a meeting or an appointment to meet. —*v.t. & v.i.* **·voused** (-VOOD), **·vous·ing** (-VOO ing) assemble at a certain place or time. [< MF *rendez-vous* present yourselves]

ren·di·tion (ren DISH ǝn) *n.* 1. the interpretation of a text; a translation. 2. artistic, dramatic, or musical interpretation. 3. the act of rendering; also, that which is rendered. [< MF]

ren·e·gade (REN i GAYD) *n.* 1. one who forsakes faith etc. 2. a traitor; deserter. [< Sp. *renegado*] —*adj.* traitorous; of or like a renegade.

re·nege (ri NIG) *v.i.* **·neged, ·neg·ing** 1. in card games, fail to follow suit when able and required by the rules to do so; revoke. 2. fail to fulfill a promise. [< Med.L *renegare*] —**re·neg'er** *n.*

re·new (ri NOO) *v.t.* 1. make new or as if new again; restore to a former or sound condition. 2. begin again; resume. 3. repeat: *renew* an oath. 4. cause to continue in effect; extend. 5. replenish or replace, as provisions. —*v.i.* 6. become new again. [ME *renewen*] —**re·new'a·ble** *adj.* —**re·new'al** *n.*

ren·net (REN it) *n.* 1. the mucous membrane lining the stomach of a suckling calf or sheep. 2. *Biochem.* a substance that yields rennin, obtained from the stomach of such an animal. [ME]

ren·nin (REN in) *n. Biochem.* a milk-curdling enzyme present in rennet.

re·nounce (ri NOWNS) *v.t.* **·nounced, ·nounc·ing** 1. give up, esp. by formal statement. 2. disown; repudiate. [ME *renouncen*]

ren·o·vate (REN ǝ VAYT) *v.t.* **·vat·ed, ·vat·ing** 1. make as good as new; repair. 2. renew; refresh. [< L *renovatus* made new] —**ren'o·va'tion** *n.*

re·nown (ri NOWN) *n.* exalted reputation; celebrity; fame. [ME *renoun*] —**re·nowned'** *adj.*

rent[1] (rent) *n.* 1. compensation paid to a landlord or owner for the use of land, buildings, etc. 2. similar payment for the use of any property, movable or fixed. 3. *Econ.* income derived by the owner from the use or cultivation of land or property. —*v.t.* 1. obtain temporary possession and use of for a rent. 2. grant such temporary possession and use. —*v.i.* 3. be let for rent. [ME *rente*]

rent[2] past tense, past participle of REND. —*n.* 1. a hole or slit made by rending or tearing. 2. a violent separation; schism. [ME]

rent·al (REN tl) *n.* 1. the revenue from rented property; also the property rented. 2. the act of renting. —*adj.* of or for rent. [ME]

re·nun·ci·a·tion (ri NUN see AY shǝn) *n.* the act of renouncing or disclaiming; a repudiation. [ME]

re·or·gan·ize (ree OR gǝ NIZ) *v.t. & v.i.* **·ized, ·iz·ing** organize anew. —**re'or·gan·i·za'tion** *n.*

re·pair[1] (ri PAIR) *v.t.* 1. restore to sound or good condition after damage, injury, etc. 2. make up, as a loss; compensate for. [ME *repairen*] —*n.* 1. the act or process of repairing. 2. condition after use or after repairing: in good *repair.*

re·pair[2] *v.i.* betake oneself; go: *repair* to the garden. [ME *repairen* return]

rep·a·ra·ble (REP ǝr ǝ bǝl) *adj.* capable of being repaired. Also **re·pair'a·ble.**

rep·a·ra·tion (REP ǝ RAY shǝn) *n.* 1. the act of making amends; atonement. 2. *pl.* indemnities paid by defeated countries for acts of war. [ME *reparacion*]

rep·ar·tee (REP ǝr TEE) *n.* 1. conversation marked by quick and witty replies. 2. a witty or quick reply; a sharp rejoinder. [< F *repartie* reply]

re·past (ri PAST) *n.* 1. food taken at a meal. 2. a meal. [ME]

re·pa·tri·ate (ri PAY tree AYT) *v.t.* **·at·ed, ·at·ing** return to one's own country or to the place of one's citizenship. —*n.* (ree PAY tree it) one who has been repatriated. [<

LL *repatriatus* returned to one's native land] —**re·pa'tri·a'tion** *n*.

re·pay (ri PAY) *v.* **·paid, ·pay·ing** *v.t.* **1.** pay back; refund. **2.** pay back or refund something to. **3.** give a reward or inflict a penalty for. —*v.i.* **4.** make repayment or requital. —**re·pay'ment** *n*.

re·peal (ri PEEL) *v.t.* rescind, as a law; revoke. [ME *repelen*] —*n*. the act of repealing; revocation.

re·peat (ri PEET) *v.t.* **1.** say again; iterate. **2.** recite from memory. **3.** do, make, or experience again. —*v.i.* **4.** say or do something again. [ME *repeten*] —*n*. **1.** the act of repeating; a repetition. **2.** anything repeated.

re·peat·ed (ri PEE tid) *adj.* occurring or spoken again and again; reiterated. —**re·peat'ed·ly** *adv.*

re·peat·er (ri PEE tər) *n*. **1.** one who or that which repeats. **2.** a firearm that can shoot several bullets without reloading. **3.** one who has been repeatedly imprisoned.

re·pel (ri PEL) *v.* **·pelled, ·pel·ling** *v.t.* **1.** force or drive back; repulse. **2.** reject; refuse, as a suggestion. **3.** cause to feel distaste or aversion. **4.** push or keep away; resist. —*v.i.* **5.** act so as to drive something back or away. [ME *repellen*]

re·pel·lent (ri PEL ənt) *adj.* **1.** serving, tending, or having power to repel. **2.** repugnant; repulsive. —*n*. something that repels. Also **re·pel'lant**.

re·pent (ri PENT) *v.t. & v.i.* feel remorse or regret for (an action etc.). [ME *repenten*] —**re·pen'tance** *n*. —**re·pen'tant** *adj.*

re·per·cus·sion (REE pər KUSH ən) *n*. **1.** a stroke or blow given in return; also, the recoil after impact. **2.** the indirect result of something; aftereffect. [ME]

rep·er·toire (REP ər TWAHR) *n*. the songs, plays, operas, or the like, that a person or company is prepared to perform. [< F *répertoire*]

rep·er·to·ry (REP ər TOR ee) *n. pl.* **·ries 1.** loosely, repertoire. **2.** the presentation of several plays, often alternately, by a theatrical company in one season. [< LL *repertorium* inventory]

rep·e·ti·tion (REP i TISH ən) *n*. **1.** the doing, making, or saying of something again. **2.** that which is repeated. —**re·pet·i·tive** (ri PET i tiv) *adj.* —**re·pet'i·tive·ly** *adv.*

rep·e·ti·tious (REP i TISH əs) *adj.* characterized by or containing repetition, esp. useless or tedious repetition. —**rep'e·ti'tious·ly** *adv.* —**rep'e·ti'tious·ness** *n*.

re·place (ri PLAYS) *v.t.* **·placed, ·plac·ing 1.** put back in place. **2.** take or fill the place of; supersede. **3.** refund; repay. —**re·place'a·ble** *adj.* —**re·place'ment** *n*.

re·plen·ish (ri PLEN ish) *v.t.* **1.** fill again, as something wholly or partially emptied. **2.** supply again; restock. [ME *replenisshen*] —**re·plen'ish·ment** *n*.

re·plete (ri PLEET) *adj.* **1.** full or supplied to the utmost. **2.** gorged with food or drink; sated. [ME *repleet*]

rep·li·ca (REP li kə) *n*. any close copy or reproduction, esp. of a work of art. [< Ital., repetition]

rep·li·cate (REP li KAYT) *v.t.* **·cat·ed, ·cat·ing 1.** make a replica of; reproduce. **2.** fold over. [< LL *replicatus* folded back] —**rep·li·ca·tion** (REP li KAY shən) *n*. [ME *replicacioun*] —**rep'li·ca'tive** *adj.*

re·ply (ri PLĪ) *v.* **·plied, ·ply·ing** *v.i.* **1.** give an answer orally or in writing. **2.** respond by some act, gesture, etc. —*v.t.* **3.** say in answer: often with a clause as object. [ME *replien*] —*n. pl.* **·plies** something said, written, or done by way of answer.

re·port (ri PORT) *v.t.* **1.** make or give an account of, often formally. **2.** relate, as information obtained by investigation. **3.** complain about, esp. to a superior. —*v.i.* **4.** make a report. **5.** act as a reporter. **6.** present oneself, as for duty. [ME *reporten*] —*n*. **1.** that which is reported. **2.** a statement or record of an investigation, transaction, etc. **3.** common talk; rumor. **4.** an explosive sound.

re·port·ed·ly (ri POR tid lee) *adv.* according to report.

re·port·er (ri POR tər) *n*. **1.** one who reports; esp., one who reports news for a newspaper, magazine, etc. **2.** one who reports cases in court for official publication. —**rep·or·to·ri·al** (REP ər TOR ee əl) *adj.*

re·pose[1] (ri POHZ) *n*. **1.** the act of taking rest, or the state of being at rest. **2.** calm; peace. **3.** ease of manner; graceful and dignified calmness. —*v.* **·posed, ·pos·ing** *v.t.* **1.** lay or place in a position of rest. —*v.i.* **2.** lie at rest. [ME *reposen*]

re·pose[2] *v.t.* **·posed, ·pos·ing** place, as confidence or hope: with in. [ME *reposen*]

re·pos·i·to·ry (ri POZ i TOR ee) *n. pl.* **·ries 1.** a place in which goods are or may be stored. **2.** a person to whom a secret is entrusted. **3.** a receptacle for relics. [< L *repositorium*]

re·pos·sess (REE pə ZES) *v.t.* have posses-

sion of again; regain possession of, esp. in default of payment. —**re′pos·ses′sion** n.

rep·re·hend (REP ri HEND) v.t. criticize sharply; blame or censure. [ME *reprehenden*] —**rep′re·hen′sion** n. —**rep′re·hen′sive** adj.

rep·re·hen·si·ble (REP ri HEN sə bəl) adj. deserving blame or censure. —**rep′re·hen′si·bil′i·ty** n. —**rep′re·hen′si·bly** adv.

rep·re·sent (REP ri ZENT) v.t. **1.** serve as the symbol, expression, or designation of; symbolize. **2.** depict; portray, as in painting or sculpture. **3.** act the part of; impersonate. **4.** serve as or be the delegate, agent, etc. of. **5.** describe: They *represented* her as a genius. **6.** serve as an example, specimen, type, etc. of. [ME *representen*]

rep·re·sen·ta·tion (REP ri zen TAY shən) n. **1.** the act of representing or the state of being represented. **2.** anything that represents, as a picture, a statue, etc. **3.** a dramatic performance. **4.** the right of acting authoritatively for others, esp. in a legislative body. **5.** representatives collectively. **6.** a formal statement setting forth a proposal, objection, etc. [ME *representacion*] —**rep′re·sen·ta′·tion·al** adj.

rep·re·sen·ta·tive (REP ri ZEN tə tiv) adj. **1.** typifying or typical of a group of class. **2.** acting as a qualified agent. **3.** made up of representatives. **4.** based on or pertaining to the political principle of representation. —n. **1.** one who or that which is fit to stand as a type; a typical instance. **2.** one who is a qualified agent of any kind. **3.** a member of a legislative body, esp. of the lower house. —**rep′re·sen′ta·tive·ness** n.

re·press (ri PRES) v.t. **1.** keep under restraint or control. **2.** put down; quell, as a rebellion. **3.** *Psychoanal.* cause the repression of, as fears, impulses, etc. [ME *repressen*] —**re·pres′sive** adj. —**re·pres′sive·ness** n.

re·pres·sion (ri PRESH ən) n. **1.** the act of repressing or the condition of being repressed. **2.** *Psychoanal.* the exclusion from consciousness of painful or unacceptable memories etc.

re·prieve (ri PREEV) v.t. **·prieved, ·priev·ing 1.** suspend temporarily the execution of a sentence upon. **2.** relieve for a time from suffering, danger, or trouble. —n. **1.** the temporary suspension of a sentence, or the document ordering it. **2.** the temporary relief of pain or ill. **3.** the act of reprieving, or the state of being reprieved.

rep·ri·mand (REP rə MAND) v.t. reprove sharply or formally. —n. severe reproof or censure. [< F *réprimande*]

re·pri·sal (ri PRI zəl) n. **1.** a retaliatory act by one nation against another; also, an instance of such an act. **2.** any act of retaliation. [ME *reprisail*]

re·proach (ri PROHCH) v.t. **1.** charge with or blame for something wrong; rebuke; censure. **2.** bring discredit or disgrace upon. —n. **1.** the act of reproaching; censure; rebuke. **2.** a cause of blame or disgrace. **3.** disgrace; discredit. [ME *reproche*] —**re·proach′a·ble** adj. —**re·proach′ful** adj. —**re·proach′ful·ness** n.

rep·ro·bate (REP rə BAYT) adj. having lost all sense of duty; depraved. —n. a depraved or profligate person. [ME *reprobaten*] —**rep′ro·ba′tion** n.

re·pro·duce (REE prə DOOS) v. **·duced, ·duc·ing** v.t. **1.** make a copy, image, or reproduction of. **2.** *Biol.* produce (offspring) by sexual or asexual generation. **3.** produce again. —v.i. **4.** produce offspring. **5.** undergo copying, reproduction, etc. —**re′pro·duc′i·ble** adj.

re·pro·duc·tion (REE prə DUK shən) n. **1.** the act or power of reproducing. **2.** *Biol.* the process by which an animal or plant generates another of its kind. **3.** that which is reproduced, as a copy of a picture. —**re′pro·duc′tive** adj.

re·proof (ri PROOF) n. **1.** the act of reproving. **2.** a rebuke; blame; censure. Also **re·prov·al** (ri PROO vəl).

re·prove (ri PROOV) v.t. **·proved, ·prov·ing 1.** censure, as for a fault; rebuke. **2.** express disapproval of (an act). [ME *reproven*] —**re·prov′ing·ly** adv.

rep·tile (REP til) n. any of a class of cold-blooded, air-breathing vertebrates, including the snakes, lizards, and turtles. [ME *reptil*] —adj. of or resembling a reptile. —**rep·til′i·an** (rep TIL yən) adj. & n.

re·pub·lic (ri PUB lik) n. a state in which the sovereignty resides in the people, and the legislative and administrative powers are lodged in officers elected by them. [< F *république*]

re·pub·li·can (ri PUB li kən) adj. **1.** of, like, or suitable for a republic. **2.** supporting republican government. **3.** *cap.* pertaining to or belonging to the Republican Party. —n. **1.** one who advocates a republican form of government. **2.** *cap.* a member of the Republican Party.

Republican Party one of the two major political parties of the U.S., founded in 1854 in opposition to the extension of slavery.

re•pu•di•ate (ri PYOO dee AYT) *v.t.* •**at•ed,** •**at•ing 1.** refuse to accept as valid or binding; reject. **2.** cast off; disown, as a son. [< L *repudiatus* rejected] —**re•pu′di•a′tion** *n.*

re•pug•nant (ri PUG nənt) *adj.* offensive to taste or feeling; exciting aversion or repulsion. [ME *repugnaunt*] —**re•pug′nance** *n.*

re•pulse (ri PULS) *v.t.* •**pulsed,** •**puls•ing 1.** drive back; repel, as an attacking force. **2.** repel by coldness, discourtesy, etc.; reject; rebuff. —*n.* **1.** the act of repulsing or the state of being repulsed. **2.** rejection; refusal. [< L *repulsus* repelled]

re•pul•sion (ri PUL shən) *n.* **1.** the act of repelling, or the state of being repelled. **2.** aversion; repugnance. **3.** *Physics* the mutual action of two bodies that tends to drive them apart.

re•pul•sive (ri PUL siv) *adj.* **1.** exciting feelings of dislike, disgust, or horror; grossly offensive. **2.** such as to forbid approach or familiarity; forbidding. **3.** acting to repel or force back: *repulsive* forces. —**re•pul′ sive•ness** *n.*

rep•u•ta•ble (REP yə tə bəl) *adj.* having a good reputation; estimable; honorable. —**rep′u•ta•bly** *adv.*

rep•u•ta•tion (REP yə TAY shən) *n.* **1.** the general estimation in which a person or thing is held by others. **2.** the state of being in high regard or esteem. [ME *reputacioun*]

re•pute (ri PYOOT) *v.t.* •**put•ed,** •**put•ing** consider to be as specified; esteem: They are *reputed* to be intelligent. [ME *reputen*] —*n.* **1.** reputation or regard. **2.** public opinion; general report.

re•put•ed (ri PYOO tid) *adj.* generally reported: a *reputed* criminal. —**re•put′ ed•ly** *adv.*

re•quest (ri KWEST) *v.t.* **1.** express a desire for. **2.** ask (a person) to do a favor, answer an inquiry, etc. —*n.* **1.** the act of requesting; petition. **2.** that which is requested. —*adj.* having been asked for: a *request* program. [ME *requeste*]

re•qui•em (REK wee əm) *n.* **1.** any musical composition or service for the dead. **2.** *cap.* in the Roman Catholic Church, a solemn mass sung for the dead: also **Requiem**

mass. **3.** *cap.* a musical setting for such a mass. [ME]

re•quire (ri KWIR) *v.* •**quired,** •**quir•ing** *v.t.* **1.** have need of; find necessary. **2.** demand authoritatively; insist upon. —*v.i.* **3.** make demand or request. [ME *requiren*] —**re•quire′ment** *n.*

req•ui•site (REK wə zit) *adj.* required by the nature of things or by circumstances; indispensable. [ME] —*n.* a necessary thing, quality, etc.

req•ui•si•tion (REK wə ZISH ən) *n.* **1.** a formal request or demand, as for supplies. **2.** the state of being required. —*v.t.* demand or take on requisition. [ME]

re•quite (ri KWIT) *v.t.* •**quit•ed,** •**quit•ing 1.** make equivalent return for, as kindness, service, or injury; make up for. **2.** avenge; retaliate. —**re•quit′al** *n.*

re•scind (ri SIND) *v.t.* make void, as an act; abrogate; repeal. [< L *rescindere* cut away again] —**re•scind′a•ble** *adj.* —**re•scis•sion** (ri SIZH ən) *n.*

res•cue (RES kyoo) *v.t.* •**cued,** •**cu•ing** save or free from danger, captivity, evil, etc.; deliver. [ME *rescuen*] —*n.* the act of rescuing; deliverance. —**res′cu•er** *n.*

re•search (ri SURCH) *n.* **1.** diligent, protracted investigation; studious inquiry. **2.** a systematic investigation of some phenomenon. —*v.t. & v.i.* undertake research (on). [< MF *recercher* seek] —**re•search′er** *n.*

re•sem•blance (ri ZEM bləns) *n.* the quality of similarity in nature, form, etc.; likeness.

re•sem•ble (ri ZEM bəl) *v.t.* •**bled,** •**bling** be similar to in appearance, quality, or character. [ME *resemblen*]

re•sent (ri ZENT) *v.t.* feel or show resentment at; be indignant at. [< F *ressentir* feel emotional about] —**re•sent′ful** *adj.*

re•sent•ment (ri ZENT mənt) *n.* anger and ill will in view of real or fancied wrong or injury.

res•er•va•tion (REZ ər VAY shən) *n.* **1.** the act of reserving. **2.** that which is reserved, kept back, or withheld. **3.** a qualification or condition, as to an opinion or commitment. **4.** an arrangement to reserve a seat in a restaurant, hotel room, etc. in advance. **5.** a tract of government land reserved for a special purpose, as for the use and occupancy of a Native American tribe. [ME *reservacioun*]

re•serve (ri ZURV) *v.t.* •**served,** •**serv•ing 1.** hold back or set aside for special or future use. **2.** keep as one's own; retain. **3.** arrange for ahead of time; have set aside for one's use. [ME *reserven*] —*n.* **1.** something stored up for future use or set apart for a particular purpose. **2.** a reservation of land. **3.** in banking, the amount of funds reserved in order to meet anticipated demands. **4.** the act of reserving. **5.** silence or reticence as to one's feelings, opinions, or affairs. **6.** *Usu. pl.* a fighting force held back from action to meet possible emergencies. **7.** a branch of the armed forces composed of persons subject to call in emergencies. —*adj.* held in reserve; constituting a reserve.

re•served (ri ZURVD) *adj.* **1.** characterized by reserve of manner; distant; undemonstrative. **2.** retained; kept back. —**re•serv•ed•ly** (ri ZUR vid lee) *adv.*

re•serv•ist (ri ZUR vist) *n.* a member of a military reserve.

res•er•voir (REZ ər vwAHR) *n.* a lake, either natural or artificial, for collecting and containing a supply of water, as for use in a city. [< F *réservoir*]

re•side (ri ZĪD) *v.i.* **•sid•ed, •sid•ing 1.** dwell for a considerable time; make one's home; live. **2.** exist as an attribute or quality: with *in.* **3.** be vested: with *in.* [ME *residen*]

res•i•dence (REZ i dəns) *n.* **1.** The place or the house where one resides. **2.** the act of residing. **3.** the length of time one resides in a place. Also *residency.* [ME]

res•i•den•cy (REZ i dən see) *n. pl.* **•cies 1.** residence. **2.** an official abode of the representative of a government. **3.** *Med.* the period of advanced clinical training served by a physician.

res•i•dent (REZ i dənt) *n.* **1.** one who resides or dwells in a place. **2.** a diplomatic representative residing at a foreign seat of government. **3.** *Med.* one serving a residency. —*adj.* **1.** having a residence. **2.** abiding in a place in connection with one's official work: a *resident* physician.

res•i•den•tial (REZ i DEN shəl) *adj.* **1.** of, pertaining to, or restricted to residences. **2.** consisting of or suitable for residences or living quarters.

re•sid•u•al (ri ZIJ oo əl) *adj.* **1.** having the nature of a remainder. **2.** left over as a residue. —*n.* **1.** something that remains. **2.** a payment to a writer, actor, etc. for each additional showing of a television commercial or program.

res•i•due (REZ i DOO) *n.* **1.** a remainder or surplus after a part has been separated or otherwise treated. **2.** *Chem.* insoluble mat-

ter left after filtration or separation from a liquid. **3.** *Law* the portion of an estate that remains after all charges, debts, and particular bequests have been satisfied: also **re•sid•u•um** (ri ZIJ oo əm). [ME]

re•sign (ri ZĪN) *v.t.* **1.** give up, as a position, office, or trust. **2.** give over (oneself, one's mind, etc.), as to fate or domination. —*v.i.* **3.** resign a position etc. [ME *resignen*]

res•ig•na•tion (REZ ig NAY shən) *n.* **1.** the act of resigning, as a position or office. **2.** a written declaration of such intent. **3.** the quality of being submissive or acquiescent. [ME]

re•signed (ri ZĪND) *adj.* characterized by resignation; submissive. —**re•sign•ed•ly** (ri ZĪ nid lee) *adv.*

re•sil•ient (ri ZIL yənt) *adj.* springing back to a former shape, position, or state. [< L *resilire* spring back] —**re•sil'ience, re•sil'ien•cy** *n.*

res•in (REZ in) *n.* **1.** a yellowish substance exuded from certain plants and trees. **2.** any similar synthetic substance, esp. one used in the making of plastics. —*v.t.* apply resin to. [ME] —**res'i•nous** *adj.*

re•sist (ri ZIST) *v.t.* **1.** strive against; act counter to. **2.** be proof against; withstand. —*v.i.* **3.** offer opposition. [ME *resisten*] —**re•sist'er** *n.* —**re•sist'i•ble** *adj.*

re•sis•tance (ri ZIS təns) *n.* **1.** the act of resisting. **2.** any force tending to hinder motion. **3.** *Electr.* the opposition that a conductor offers to the passage of a current, resulting from the conversion of energy into heat, light, etc. **4.** a guerrilla movement opposing an occupying power. [ME] —**re•sis'tant** *adj. & n.*

re•sis•tive (ri ZIS tiv) *adj.* having or exercising the power of resistance.

re•sis•tiv•i•ty (REE zis TIV i tee) *n.* the capacity or power to resist.

re•sis•tor (ri ZIS tər) *n. Electr.* a device, as a coil of wire, for introducing resistance into an electrical circuit.

res•o•lute (REZ ə LOOT) *adj.* **1.** having a fixed purpose; determined. **2.** bold; unflinching. [ME] —**res'o•lute•ness** *n.*

res•o•lu•tion (REZ ə LOO shən) *n.* **1.** the act of resolving. **2.** the state of being resolute; active fortitude. **3.** the purpose or course resolved upon. **4.** the separation of anything into component parts. **5.** a proposition offered to or adopted by an assembly. [ME]

re•solve (ri ZOLV) *v.* **•solved, •solv•ing** *v.t.*

1. decide or determine (to do something). **2.** cause to decide or determine. **3.** separate or break down into constituent parts. **4.** make clear; explain or solve, as a problem. **5.** explain away; remove (doubts etc.). **6.** state or decide by vote, as in a legislative assembly. **7.** *Optics* make distinguishable the structure or parts of (an image), as in a microscope or telescope. —*v.i.* **8.** make up one's mind; arrive at a decision: with *on* or *upon*. [ME *resolven*] —*n.* **1.** fixity of purpose; resolution. **2.** a fixed determination; a resolution. —**re·solv′a·ble** *adj.*

re·solved (ri ZOLVD) *adj.* fixed or set in purpose; determined.

res·o·nant (REZ ə nənt) *adj.* **1.** sending back or prolonging sound. **2.** resounding. **3.** intensifying sound. [< L *resonare* sound again] —**res′o·nance** *n.* —**res′o·nant·ly** *adv.*

res·o·nate (REZ ə NAYT) *v.i.* **·nat·ed, ·nat·ing 1.** exhibit enhanced or intensified sound. **2.** manifest sympathetic vibration, as a resonator. [< L *resonatus* sounded again]

res·o·na·tor (REZ ə NAY tər) *n.* any device that resounds or increases sounds by resonance.

re·sort (ri ZORT) *v.i.* **1.** go frequently or habitually; repair. **2.** have recourse; apply or betake oneself for relief or aid: with *to.* [ME *resorten*] —*n.* **1.** a place frequented for recreation or rest. **2.** the use of something as a means; a recourse.

re·sound (ri ZOWND) *v.i.* **1.** be filled with sound; echo; reverberate. **2.** make a loud, prolonged, or echoing sound. **3.** be extolled. —*v.t.* **4.** give back (a sound etc.). [ME *resounen*]

re·sound·ing (ri ZOWN ding) *adj.* **1.** reverberating. **2.** emphatic; unmistakable: a *resounding* success.

re·source (ri ZORS) *n.* **1.** that which is resorted to for aid or support; resort. **2.** *pl.* available means or property; any natural advantages or products. **3.** skill or ingenuity in meeting any situation; resourcefulness. [< F *ressource*]

re·source·ful (ri ZORS fəl) *adj.* capable of dealing with problems. —**re·source′ful·ly** *adv.* —**re·source′ful·ness** *n.*

re·spect (ri SPEKT) *v.t.* **1.** have deferential regard for; esteem. **2.** regard as inviolable; avoid intruding upon. **3.** have relation or reference to; concern. —*n.* **1.** regard for and appreciation of worth; honor and es-

teem. **2.** *pl.* expressions of consideration or esteem; compliments: pay one's *respects.* **3.** conformity to duty or obligation: *respect* for the law. **4.** the condition of being honored or respected. **5.** reference or relation: usu. with *to:* with *respect* to profits. [ME] —**re·spect′ful** *adj.* —**re·spect′ful·ly** *adv.*

re·spect·a·ble (ri SPEK tə bəl) *adj.* **1.** deserving of respect; also, respected. **2.** being of moderate size or excellence; average. **3.** having a good appearance; presentable. **4.** conventionally correct or socially acceptable in conduct. —**re·spect′a·bil′i·ty** *n.*

re·spect·ing (ri SPEK ting) *prep.* concerning; regarding.

re·spec·tive (ri SPEK tiv) *adj.* individual; separate or particular: our *respective* careers.

re·spec·tive·ly (ri SPEK tiv lee) *adv.* in the order designated: The first three prizes went to John, Jane, and Robert *respectively.*

res·pi·ra·tion (RES pə RAY shən) *n.* **1.** the act of inhaling and exhaling; breathing. **2.** the process by which an organism takes in oxygen and gives off carbon dioxide and other products of oxidation. [ME *respiracioun*] —**res·pir·a·to·ry** (RES pə ə TOR ee) *adj.* —**re·spire** (ri SPĪR) *v.i. & v.t.* **·spired, ·spir·ing** breathe.

res·pi·ra·tor (RES pə RAY tər) *n.* **1.** a screen, as of fine gauze, worn over the mouth or nose as a protection against dust etc. **2.** a device worn over the nose and mouth for the inhalation of oxygen etc. **3.** an apparatus for artificial respiration.

res·pite (RES pit) *n.* **1.** postponement; delay. **2.** an interval of rest. [ME *respit*] —*v.t.* **·pit·ed, ·pit·ing 1.** relieve by a pause or rest. **2.** grant delay in the execution of (a penalty, sentence, etc.).

re·splen·dent (ri SPLEN dənt) *adj.* shining with brilliant luster; splendid; gorgeous. [ME] —**re·splen′dence, re·splen′den·cy** *n.*

re·spond (ri SPOND) *v.i.* **1.** give an answer; reply. **2.** act in reply or return; react. —*v.t.* **3.** say in answer; reply. [ME]

re·spond·ent (ri SPON dənt) *adj.* answering; responsive. —*n.* **1.** one who responds or answers. **2.** *Law* a defendant.

re·sponse (ri SPONS) *n.* **1.** the act of responding, or that which is responded; reply; reaction. **2.** *Eccl.* a portion of a liturgy or church service said or sung by the congregation or choir in reply to the officiating minister. **3.** *Biol.* the behavior of an organism resulting from a stimulus or influence; a reaction.

re·spon·si·bil·i·ty (ri SPON sə BIL i tee) *n.* *pl.* **·ties 1.** the state of being responsible or accountable. **2.** that for which one is answerable; a duty or trust.

re·spon·si·ble (ri SPON sə bəl) *adj.* **1.** answerable legally or morally for the discharge of a duty, trust, or debt. **2.** having capacity to distinguish between right and wrong. **3.** having sufficient property or means for the payment of debts. **4.** involving accountability or obligation. — **re·spon′si·bly** *adv.*

re·spon·sive (ri SPON siv) *adj.* **1.** inclined or ready to respond. **2.** constituting, or of the nature of, response or reply. **3.** characterized by or containing responses. — **re·spon′sive·ly** *adv.* —**re·spon′sive·ness** *n.*

rest¹ (rest) *v.i.* **1.** cease working, exerting oneself, etc. so as to refresh oneself. **2.** obtain ease or refreshment by lying down, sleeping, etc. **3.** be at peace; be tranquil. **4.** remain unchanged. **5.** be supported; stand, lean, lie, or sit: with *against, on,* or *upon.* **6.** be founded or based: with *on* or *upon.* **7.** be placed as a burden or responsibility: with *on* or *upon.* **8.** be or lie in a specified place. **9.** *Law* cease presenting evidence in a case. — *v.t.* **10.** give rest to; refresh by rest. **11.** put, lay, lean, etc., as for support or rest. **12.** direct (the gaze). **13.** *Law* cease presenting evidence in (a case). —*n.* **1.** the act or state of resting; repose. **2.** freedom from disturbance or disquiet; tranquillity. **3.** sleep. **4.** that on which anything rests; a support. **5.** a place of repose or quiet; a stopping place; abode. **6.** *Music* a pause or interval of silence that corresponds to the time value of a note. [ME]

rest² *n.* **1.** that which remains or is left over; a remainder. **2.** (*construed as pl.*) those remaining or not enumerated; the others. — *v.i.* be and remain; stay: *Rest* content. [ME *resten*]

res·tau·rant (RES tər ənt) *n.* a place where refreshments or meals are bought; a public dining room. [< F]

res·tau·ra·teur (RES tər ə TUR) *n.* the owner or operator of a restaurant. [< F]

rest·ful (REST fəl) *adj.* **1.** full of or giving rest; affording freedom from disturbance, work, or trouble. **2.** being at rest or in repose; quiet. [ME] —**rest′ful·ness** *n.*

res·ti·tu·tion (RES ti TOO shən) *n.* **1.** the act of restoring something that has been taken away or lost. **2.** the act of making good or rendering an equivalent for injury or loss. [ME *restitucioun*]

res·tive (RES tiv) *adj.* **1.** impatient of control; unruly. **2.** restless; fidgety. [ME *restif*] —**res′tive·ness** *n.*

rest·less (REST lis) *adj.* **1.** having no rest; never quiet. **2.** unable or disinclined to rest. **3.** constantly seeking change; discontented. —**rest′less·ness** *n.*

res·to·ra·tion (RES tə RAY shən) *n.* **1.** the act of restoring a person or thing to a former place or condition. **2.** the reconstruction or repair of something so as to restore it to its original or former state; also, an object that has been so restored. —**the Restoration** the return of Charles II to the English throne in 1660; also, the following period until 1685. [ME]

re·stor·a·tive (ri STOR ə tiv) *n.* that which restores; esp., something to restore good health or consciousness. —*adj.* serving to restore.

re·store (ri STOR) *v.t.* **·stored, ·stor·ing 1.** bring into existence or effect again. **2.** bring back to a former or original condition, appearance, etc., as a painting. **3.** bring back to health and vigor. **4.** give back (something lost or taken away). [ME *restoren*]

re·strain (ri STRAYN) *v.t.* **1.** hold back from acting, proceeding, or advancing; repress. **2.** deprive of freedom or liberty, as by placing in a prison. **3.** restrict or limit. [ME *restreynen*] —**re·strain′·ed·ly** *adv.* —**re·strain′er** *n.*

re·straint (ri STRAYNT) *n.* **1.** the act of restraining. **2.** the state of being restrained; confinement. **3.** that which restrains; a restriction. **4.** self-repression; constraint. [ME *restreinte*]

re·strict (ri STRIKT) *v.t.* hold or keep within limits or bounds. [< L *restrictus* drawn back] —**re·stric′tive** *adj.*

re·strict·ed (ri STRIK tid) *adj.* **1.** limited, confined. **2.** not available to the general public; limited to a specific group: *restricted* information. —**re·strict′ed·ly** *adv.*

re·stric·tion (ri STRIK shən) *n.* **1.** the act of restricting, or the state of being restricted. **2.** that which restricts.

re·sult (ri ZULT) *n.* **1.** the outcome of an action, course, process, or agency; consequence; effect; conclusion. **2.** *Math.* a quantity or value ascertained by calculation. —*v.i.* be a result or outcome; be a physical or logical consequent; follow: with *from*. [ME *resulten*]

re•sult•ant (ri ZULT tənt) *adj.* arising or following as a result. —*n.* that which results; a consequence.

re•sume (ri ZOOM) *v.* •sumed, •sum•ing *v.t.* 1. take up again after cessation or interruption; begin again. 2. take or occupy again. —*v.i.* 3. continue after cessation or interruption. [ME *resumen*] — **re•sump•tion** (ri ZUMP shən) *n.*

ré•su•mé (REZ uu MAY) *n.* a summary, as of one's employment record. Also **re'su•me'**. [< F]

re•surge (ri SURJ) *v.i.* •surged, •surg•ing 1. rise again into life or activity. 2. surge or sweep back again, as the tide. [< L *resurgere* rise again] —**re•sur'gence** *n.* — **re•sur'gent** *adj.*

res•ur•rec•tion (REZ ə REK shən) *n.* 1. a rising again from the dead. 2. any revival or renewal, as of a practice or custom, after disuse, decay, etc.; restoration. —**the Resurrection** the rising of Christ from the dead. [ME] —**res'ur•rect'** *v.t. & v.i.*

re•sus•ci•tate (ri SUS i TAYT) *v.t. & v.i.* •tat•ed, •tat•ing bring or come back to life; revive from unconsciousness. [< L *resuscitatus* reawakened] —**re•sus'ci•ta'tion** *n.* —**re•sus'ci•ta'tor** *n.*

ret (ret) *v.t.* **ret•ted, ret•ting** steep or soak, as flax, to separate the fibers. [ME *reten*]

re•tail (REE tayl) *n.* the selling of goods in small quantities, esp. to the ultimate consumer: distinguished from *wholesale*. — *adj.* involving or engaged in the sale of goods at retail. —*v.t.* 1. sell at retail. 2. (ri TAYL) repeat, as gossip. —*v.i.* 3. be sold at retail. [ME] —**re'tail•er** *n.*

re•tain (ri TAYN) *v.t.* 1. keep or continue to keep in one's possession; hold. 2. keep in a fixed condition or place. 3. hire; also, engage (an attorney or other representative) by paying a retainer. [ME *reteinen*]

re•tain•er[1] (ri TAY nər) *n.* 1. a servant. 2. one who retains or keeps.

re•tain•er[2] *n.* a fee paid to a lawyer to secure services. [ME *reteinir*]

re•take (ree TAYK) *v.t.* •took, •tak•en, •tak•ing 1. take back; receive again. 2. recapture. 3. photograph again. —*n.* (REE TAYK) a motion-picture or television scene, part of a musical or other recording done again.

re•tal•i•ate (ri TAL ee AYT) *v.* •at•ed, •at•ing *v.i.* 1. return like for like; esp., repay evil with evil. —*v.t.* 2. repay (an injury, wrong, etc.) in kind; revenge. [< LL *retaliatus* punished in kind] —**re•tal'i•a'tion** *n.* —**re•tal•i•a•to•ry** (ri TAL ee ə TOR ee) *adj.*

re•tard (ri TAHRD) *v.t.* 1. cause to move or proceed slowly; delay. —*v.i.* 2. be delayed. —*n.* the act of retarding; delay. [< L *retardare* delay] —**re•tard'ant** (ri TAHR dnt) *n. & adj.* —**re•tar•da•tion** (REE tahr DAY shən) *n.* —**re•tard•a•tive** (ri TAHR də tiv) *adj.*

re•tard•ed (ri TAHR did) *adj.* slowed down or backward in mental development.

retch (rech) *v.i.* make an effort to vomit; strain; heave. [OE *hroecan* spit]

re•ten•tion (ri TEN shən) *n.* 1. the act of retaining, or the state of being retained. 2. the ability to remember. 3. the capacity or ability to retain.

re•ten•tive (ri TEN tiv) *adj.* having the power or tendency to retain. —**re•ten'tive•ness** *n.*

ret•i•cent (RET ə sənt) *adj.* habitually silent or reserved in utterance. [< L *reticere* be silent] —**ret'i•cence** *n.*

ret•i•na (RET n ə) *n. pl.* •nas or •nae (-NEE) *Anat.* the light-sensitive inner membrane at the back of the eyeball that receives the image. [ME] —**ret'i•nal** *adj.*

ret•i•nue (RET n YOO) *n.* the body of followers attending a person of rank; entourage. [ME]

re•tire (ri TĪR) *v.* •tired, •tir•ing *v.i.* 1. go away or withdraw, as for privacy, shelter, or rest. 2. go to bed. 3. withdraw oneself from business, public life, or active service. 4. fall back; retreat, as troops under attack. —*v.t.* 5. remove from active service. 6. in baseball etc., put out (a batter or side). [< MF *retirer* withdraw] —**re•tire'ment** *n.* — **re•tired** *adj.*

re•tir•ing (ri TĪR ing) *adj.* shy; modest; reserved.

re•tort[1] (ri TORT) *v.t.* 1. direct (a word or deed) back upon the originator. 2. reply to, as an accusation or argument, by a similar accusation, etc. —*v.i.* 3. make answer, esp. sharply. —*n.* 1. a keen rejoinder or retaliatory speech; caustic repartee. 2. the act of retorting. [< L *retortus* bent back]

re•tort[2] *n. Chem.* a vessel with a bent tube for the heating of substances or for distillation. [< MF *retorte*]

re·touch (ree TUCH) *v.t.* **1.** modify; revise. **2.** *Photog.* change or improve, as a print. [< MF *retoucher*] —*n.* (REE TUCH) an additional touch, as to a picture, model, or other work of art. —**re·touch′er** *n.*

re·trace (ri TRAYS) *v.t.* **·traced, ·trac·ing 1.** go back over; follow backward, as a path. **2.** trace the whole story of, from the beginning. [< F *retracer*] —**re·trace′a·ble** *adj.*

re-trace (ree TRAYS) *v.t.* **-traced, -trac·ing** trace again.

re·tract (ri TRAKT) *v.t. & v.i.* **1.** take back or disavow (an assertion, admission, etc.); recant. **2.** draw back or in, as the claws of a cat. [ME *retracten*] —**re·trac′tion** *n.*

re·trac·tor (ri TRAK tər) *n.* **1.** one who or that which retracts. **2.** *Surg.* an instrument used to draw back the edges of an incision.

re·treat (ri TREET) *v.i.* **1.** go back or backward; withdraw; retire. **2.** curve or slope backward. [ME *retreten*] —*n.* **1.** the act of retreating. **2.** the retirement of a military force from a position of danger or from an enemy. **3.** *Mil* a signal, as by bugle, for the lowering of the flag at sunset. **4.** retirement; seclusion; solitude. **5.** a place of retirement, quiet, or security; a refuge; haunt. —**beat a retreat 1.** give a signal for retreat, as by the beat of drums. **2.** turn back; flee.

re·trench (ri TRENCH) *v.t.* **1.** cut down or reduce; curtail (expenditures). —*v.i.* **2.** reduce expenses; economize. [< F *retrencher*] —**re·trench′·ment** *n.*

ret·ri·bu·tion (RE trə BYOO shən) *n.* **1.** the act of requiting; esp., impartial infliction of punishment. **2.** that which is done or given in requital as a reward or punishment. [ME *retribucioun*] —**re·trib·u·tive** (ri TRIB yə tiv) *adj.*

re·trieve (ri TREEV) *v.* **·trieved, ·triev·ing** *v.t.* **1.** get back; regain. **2.** restore; revive, as flagging spirits. **3.** find and bring in (wounded or dead game): said of dogs. **4.** *Electronics* obtain or extract (specific information) from the storage unit of an electronic computer. —*v.i.* **5.** retrieve game. [ME *retreven*] —*n.* the act of retrieving; recovery. —**re·triev′a·ble** *adj.* —·re·triev′al *n.*

re·triev·er (ri TREE vər) *n.* **1.** a sporting dog specially trained to retrieve game. **2.** one who retrieves.

ret·ro·ac·tive (RE troh AK tiv) *adj.* taking effect at a (usu. specified) time prior to its enactment, ratification, etc., as a provision in a law or contract.

ret·ro·fire (RE troh FIR) *v.t. Aerospace* **·fired, ·fir·ing** ignite (a retrorocket).

ret·ro·grade (RE trə GRAYD) *adj.* **1.** going or tending backward; reversed. **2.** declining to or toward a worse state or character. **3.** reversed; inverted. [ME] —*v.* **·grad·ed, ·grad·ing** *v.i.* **1.** move or appear to move backward. **2.** degenerate. —*v.t.* **3.** cause to move backward; reverse.

ret·ro·gress (RE trə GRES) *v.i.* go back to an earlier or worse state. [< L *retrogressus* gone backward]

ret·ro·gres·sion (RE trə GRESH ən) *n.* **1.** the act or process of retrogressing. **2.** *Biol.* return to or toward an earlier form or structure. —**ret′ro·gres′sive** (-GRES iv) *adj.*

ret·ro·spect (RE trə SPEKT) *n.* a view or contemplation of something past. —**ret′ro·spec′tion** *n.*

ret·ro·spec·tive (RE trə SPEK tiv) *adj.* **1.** looking back on the past. **2.** applying retroactively, as legislation. —*n.* an exhibition of past work, as of an artist.

re·turn (ri TURN) *v.i.* **1.** come or go back, as to or toward a former place or condition. **2.** revert to a former owner. **3.** answer; respond. —*v.t.* **4.** bring, carry, send, or put back; replace. **5.** repay or requite, esp. with an equivalent: *return* a compliment. **6.** yield or produce, as a profit or interest. **7.** send back; reflect, as light or sound. **8.** report or announce officially. [ME *retornen*] —*n.* **1.** the act, process, state, or result of coming back or returning. **2.** that which is returned. **3.** that which accrues, as from investments, labor, or use; profit. **4.** a report, list, etc.; esp., a formal or official report. **5.** *pl.* a set of tabulated statistics: election *returns*. —*adj.* **1.** of, pertaining to, or for a return: a *return* ticket. **2.** given, taken, or done in return: a *return* visit. **3.** reversing direction; doubling back, as a U-shaped bend.

re·un·ion (ree YOON yən) *n.* **1.** the act of reuniting. **2.** a gathering of persons who have been separated.

re·u·nite (REE yoo NIT) *v.t. & v.i.* **·nit·ed, ·nit·ing** unite, cohere, or combine again after separation.

re·vamp (ree VAMP) *v.t.* patch up; make over; renovate.

re·veal (ri VEEL) *v.t.* **1.** make known; disclose; divulge. **2.** make visible; expose to view; show. [ME *revelen*]

rev·eil·le (REV ə lee) *n.* **1.** a morning signal by drum or bugle, notifying military personnel to rise. **2.** the hour at which this signal is sounded. [< F *réveillez* wake up!]

rev·el (REV əl) *v.i.* **·eled, ·el·ing 1.** take delight: with *in*: She *revels* in her freedom. **2.** engage in boisterous festivities; make merry. [ME *revelen*] —*n.* **1.** merrymaking; carousing. **2.** *Often pl.* an occasion of boisterous festivity; a celebration. —**rev′el·er** *n.* —**rev·el·ry** *n.*

rev·e·la·tion (REV ə LAY shən) *n.* **1.** the act or process of revealing. **2.** that which is or has been revealed. **3.** *Theol.* the act of revealing or communicating divine truth, esp. by divine agency. —**re·ve·la·to·ry** (ri VEL ə TOR ee) *adj.*

re·venge (ri VENJ) *v.t.* **·venged, ·veng·ing 1.** inflict punishment, injury, or loss in return for. **2.** take or seek vengeance in behalf of. [ME *revengen*] —*n.* **1.** the act of revenging. **2.** a means of avenging oneself or others. **3.** a desire for vengeance.

rev·e·nue (REV ə NYOO) *n.* **1.** total current income of a government, except duties on imports: also called *internal revenue.* **2.** income from any form of property. [ME]

re·ver·ber·ate (ri VUR bə RAYT) *v.t. & v.i.* **·at·ed, ·at·ing 1.** resound; reecho, as a sound. **2.** reflect or be reflected. [< L *reverberatus* lashed back] —**re·ver′ber·a′tion** *n.*

re·vere (ri VEER) *v.t.* **·vered, ·ver·ing** regard with reverence; venerate. [< L *revereri* feel respect]

rev·er·ence (REV ər əns) *n.* **1.** a feeling of profound respect often mingled with awe and affection; veneration. **2.** an act of respect; an obeisance. **3.** *cap.* a title or form of address for members of the clergy: usu. preceded by *His, Your,* etc. —*v.t.* **·enced, ·enc·ing** regard with reverence.

rev·er·end (REV ər ənd) *adj.* **1.** worthy of reverence. **2.** *cap.* a title of respect often used with the name of a member of the clergy. —*n. Informal* a member of the clergy; minister.

rev·er·ent (REV ər ənt) *adj.* **1.** feeling reverence. **2.** expressing reverence: also **rev·er·en·tial** (REV ər EN shəl). —**rev′er·ent·ly, rev′er·en′tial·ly** *adv.*

rev·er·ie (REV ə ree) *n. pl.* **·er·ies 1.** abstracted musing; dreaming. **2.** a product of such musing. [ME]

re·verse (ri VURS) *adj.* **1.** having a contrary or opposite direction, character, order, etc.; turned backward. **2.** causing backward motion: the *reverse* gear of an automobile. —

n. **1.** that which is directly opposite or contrary. **2.** the back or secondary side of anything. **3.** a change for the worse; a check or partial defeat. [ME *revers*] **4.** *Mech.* a reversing gear or movement. —*v.* **·versed, ·vers·ing** *v.t.* **1.** turn upside down or inside out. **2.** turn in an opposite direction. **3.** set aside; annul: *reverse* a decree. **4.** *Mech.* cause to have an opposite motion or effect. —*v.i.* **5.** move or turn in the opposite direction. **6.** reverse its action, as an engine. —**re·ver′sal** *n.*

re·vers·i·ble (ri VUR sə bəl) *adj.* **1.** capable of being reversed in direction or position. **2.** capable of going either forward or backward, as a chemical reaction or physiological process. **3.** capable of being used or worn inside out or backward, as a coat. —*n.* a reversible coat.

re·ver·sion (ri VUR ZHən) *n.* **1.** a return to or toward some former state, condition, practice, or belief. **2.** *Biol.* the reappearance in an individual of characteristics that had not been evident for two or more generations. **3.** *Law* the right of succession to an estate.

re·vert (ri VURT) *v.i.* **1.** go or turn back to a former place, condition, attitude, etc. **2.** *Biol.* return to or show characteristics of an earlier type. **3.** *Law* return to the former owner or the heirs. [ME *reverten*]

re·view (ri VYOO) *v.t.* **1.** go over or examine again; look at or study again. **2.** look back upon; think of retrospectively. **3.** make an inspection of, esp. formally. **4.** write or make a critical review of, as a new book. **5.** *Law* reexamine (something done or decided by a lower court). —*v.i.* **6.** write reviews, as for a magazine. —*n.* **1.** a new view or study of something; a retrospective survey. **2.** a lesson studied or recited again. **3.** critical study or examination. **4.** an article containing a critical discussion of some work. **5.** a periodical devoted to essays in criticism and on general subjects. **6.** a formal inspection, as of troops. **7.** *Law* a judicial consideration by a superior court of the order or decree of a subordinate court. [< MF *revue*] —**re·view′er** *n.*

re·vile (ri VĪL) *v.t.* **·viled, ·vil·ing** assail with abusive or contemptuous language; vilify; abuse. [ME *revilen*] —**re·vile′ment** *n.* —**re·vil′er** *n.*

re·vise (ri VĪZ) *v.t.* **·vised, ·vis·ing 1.** read over so as to correct errors, make changes, etc. **2.** change; alter. [< F *reviser*] —*n.* the act or result of revising; a revision.

re•vi•sion (ri VIZH ən) *n.* **1.** the act or process of revising. **2.** something revised, as a new version of a book. —**revi'sion•ar'y** *adj.*

re•viv•al (ri VĪ vəl) *n.* **1.** the act of reviving, or the state of being revived. **2.** a restoration, as after neglect or obscurity. **3.** a series of evangelical meetings to reawaken faith.

re•viv•al•ist (ri VĪ və list) *n.* a preacher or leader in a religious revival movement. —**re•viv•al•ism** (ri VĪ və LIZ əm) *n.*

re•vive (ri VĪV) *v.* •**vived,** •**viv•ing** *v.t.* **1.** bring back to life or to consciousness. **2.** give new health etc. to. **3.** bring back into use. **4.** produce again, as an old play. —*v.i.* **5.** come back to life again. **6.** assume new vigor, health, etc. **7.** come back into use. [ME *reviven*]

rev•o•ca•ble (REV ə kə bəl) *adj.* capable of being revoked. —**rev•o•ca•tion** (REV ə KAY shən) *n.*

re•voke (ri VOHK) *v.* •**voked,** •**vok•ing** *v.t.* **1.** annul or make void by recalling; cancel; rescind. —*v.i.* **2.** in card games, fail to follow suit. [ME *revoken*] —*n.* in card games, a renege. —**re•vok'er** *n.*

re•volt (ri VOHLT) *n.* **1.** an uprising against authority; rebellion. **2.** an act of protest, refusal, or disgust. **3.** the state of a person or persons who revolt: be in *revolt.* —*v.i.* **1.** rise in rebellion against constituted authority; mutiny. **2.** turn away in disgust: with *against, at,* or *from.* —*v.t.* **3.** cause to feel disgust; repel. [< MF *revolter*]

re•volt•ing (ri VOHL ting) *adj.* abhorrent; loathsome; nauseating. —**re•volt'ing•ly** *adv.*

rev•o•lu•tion (REV ə LOO shən) *n.* **1.** a motion in a closed curve around a center, or a complete circuit made by a body in such a course. **2.** *Mech.* rotation about an axis. **3.** *Astron.* the movement of a planet around the sun or of any celestial body around a center of attraction. **4.** a cycle of successive events or changes. **5.** the overthrow and replacement of a government or political system by those governed. **6.** a drastic change in a condition, method, idea, etc. [ME *revolucion*]

rev•o•lu•tion•ar•y (REV ə LOO shə NER ee) *adj.* **1.** pertaining to, causing, or of the nature of revolution, esp. political. **2.** rotating; revolving. —*n. pl.* •**ar•ies** one who advo-

cates or participates in a political revolution.

rev•o•lu•tion•ize (REV ə LOO shə NIZ) *v.t.* •**ized,** •**iz•ing** effect a radical change in the character, operation, etc. of.

re•volve (ri VOLV) *v.* •**volved,** •**volv•ing** *v.i.* **1.** move in an orbit about a center. **2.** spin around on an axis; rotate. **3.** recur periodically. —*v.t.* **4.** cause to move in a circle or orbit. **5.** turn over mentally; consider. [ME *revolven*]

re•volv•er (ri VOL vər) *n.* a pistol having a revolving cylinder designed to hold several cartridges that may be fired in succession without reloading.

re•vue (ri VYOO) *n.* a show consisting of songs, dances, and skits that satirize contemporary people and events. [< F]

re•vul•sion (ri VUL shən) *n.* **1.** a sudden change of or strong reaction in feeling. **2.** a feeling of disgust. [< L *revulsio*]

re•ward (ri WORD) *n.* **1.** something given or done in return; esp., a gift, prize, etc. for merit, service, or achievement. **2.** money offered for information, for the return of lost goods etc. —*v.t.* **1.** give a reward to or for. **2.** be a reward for. [ME *rewarden*]

re•word (ree WURD) *v.t.* say again in other words; express differently.

re•write (ree RĪT) *v.t.* •**wrote,** •**writ•ten,** •**writ•ing** **1.** write over again. **2.** in journalism, put into publishable form (a story submitted by a reporter). —*n.* (REE RĪT) a news item written in this manner.

rhap•so•dize (RAP sə DIZ) *v.t. & v.i.* •**dized,** •**diz•ing** express or exclaim rhapsodically. —**rhap'so•dist** *n.*

rhap•so•dy (RAP sə dee) *n. pl.* •**dies** **1.** a series of disconnected and often extravagant utterances composed under excitement. **2.** *Music* an instrumental composition of irregular form, often suggestive of improvisation. [< L *rhapsodia*] —**rhap•sod•ic** (rap SOD ik) or •**i•cal** *adj.* —**rhap•sod'i•cal•ly** *adv.*

rhe•o•stat (REE ə STAT) *n. Electr.* a variable resistor used to control current and voltage strength in a circuit.

rhe•sus (REE səs) *n.* a monkey widely used in biological and medical research. [< NL]

rhet•o•ric (RET ər ik) *n.* **1.** the art of discourse, both written and spoken. **2.** affected and exaggerated display in the use of language. [< L *rhetorica*]

rhe•tor•i•cal (ri TOR i kəl) *adj.* **1.** pertaining to rhetoric; oratorical. **2.** designed for showy oratorical effect. —**rhe·tor′i·cal·ly** *adv.*

rhetorical question a question put only for oratorical or literary effect, the answer being implied in the question: Who cares?

rheumatic fever *Pathol.* an infectious disease chiefly affecting children, characterized by painful inflammation around the joints, fever, and inflammation of the heart valves.

rheu·ma·tism (ROO mə TIZ əm) *n. Pathol.* **1.** a painful inflammation and stiffness of the muscles, joints, etc. **2.** rheumatoid arthritis. [< L *rheumatismus*] —**rheu·mat′ic** (ruu MAT ik) *adj. & n.* —**rheu′ma·toid** (ROO mə-TOID) *adj.*

rheumatoid arthritis *Pathol.* a persisting inflammatory disease of the joints, marked by atrophy, weakening of the bones, and deformities.

Rh factor (AHR AYCH) *Biochem.* a property present in the blood of most persons (who are said to be **Rh positive**) and that may cause antigenic reactions under certain conditions, as during pregnancy or following transfusions with persons lacking this factor (who are said to be **Rh negative**). [< RH(ESUS)]

rhi·noc·e·ros (rī NOS ər əs) *n. pl.* **·ros·es** or **·ros** a large, herbivorous mammal of Africa and Asia, having one or two horns on the snout and a very thick hide. [ME *rinoceros*]

rhi·zome (RĪ zohm) *n. Bot.* a subterranean rootlike stem, producing roots from its lower surface and leaves or shoots from its upper surface. [< NL *rhizoma* root]

rho (roh) *n.* the seventeenth letter in the Greek alphabet (P ρ), corresponding to the English *r*. [ME]

rho·do·den·dron (ROH də DEN drən) *n.* any of a genus of evergreen shrubs or small trees, with clusters of white, pink, or purple flowers. [< L]

rhu·barb (ROO bahrb) *n.* **1.** a stout perennial herb having large leaves and small clusters of flowers on tall stalks, esp. one whose leafstalks are used in cooking. **2.** *Slang* an argument or quarrel. [ME *rubarb*]

rhyme (rīm) *n.* **1.** a correspondence of sounds in two or more words, esp. at the ends of lines of poetry. **2.** poetry; verse. —*v.* **rhymed, rhym·ing** *v.i.* **1.** make rhymes or verses. **2.** correspond in sound or in terminal sounds. —*v.t.* **3.** put or write in rhyme or verse. [ME *rime*]

rhyme·ster (RĪM stər) *n.* a writer of jingles.

rhythm (RITH əm) *n.* **1.** the recurrence or repetition of stress, beat, sound, accent, motion, etc., usu. occurring in a regular or harmonious pattern or manner. **2.** *Music* the relative duration and accent of musical sounds. **3.** in painting, sculpture, etc., a regular or harmonious recurrence of lines, forms, colors, etc. [< L *rhythmus*] —**rhyth·mic** (-mik), **rhyth·mi·cal** (-mi kəl) *adj.*

rhythm method birth control by sexual abstinence during the woman's period of fertility.

rib (rib) *n.* **1.** *Anat.* one of the series of bony rods attached to the spine of most vertebrates, and nearly encircling the thorax. **2.** something resembling a rib: the *rib* of an umbrella. **3.** a curved side timber bending away from the keel in a boat or ship. **4.** a raised wale or stripe in cloth or knit goods. —*v.t.* **ribbed, rib·bing 1.** make with ridges: *rib* a piece of knitting. **2.** make fun of; tease. [ME]

rib·ald (RIB əld) *adj.* pertaining to or indulging in coarse language or vulgar jokes. —*n.* one who uses coarse or abusive language. [ME] —**rib′ald·ry** *n.*

rib·bon (RIB ən) *n.* **1.** a narrow strip of fine fabric, having finished edges and used as trimming. **2.** *Often pl.* a narrow strip; shred: torn to *ribbons.* **3.** an inked strip of cloth for giving the impression in a computer printer or similar device. **4.** a colored strip of cloth worn as a military badge etc. —*v.t.* ornament with ribbons; also, form or tear into ribbons. [ME *riband*]

ri·bo·nu·cle·ic acid (RĪ boh noo KLEE ik) *Biochem.* a complex nucleic acid associated with DNA in the synthesis of cell proteins. Abbr. *RNA.*

ri·bose (RĪ bohs) *n. Chem.* a sugar occurring in certain nucleic acids. [< G *Ribose*]

rice (rīs) *n.* **1.** the edible seeds of an annual cereal grass, rich in carbohydrates. **2.** the grass itself. [ME *ris*]

rich (rich) *adj.* **·er, ·est 1.** having great possessions, as of money, goods, or lands; wealthy; opulent. **2.** composed of rare or precious materials; costly: *rich* fabrics. **3.** luscious to the taste, often implying an excess of fats, flavoring, etc. **4.** full, satisfying, and pleasing, as a tone, voice, color, etc. **5.** luxuriant; abundant: *rich* hair; *rich* crops. **6.** abundantly supplied: often with *in* or *with*. [ME] —**rich′ly** *adv.* —**rich′ness** *n.*

rich·es (RICH iz) *n.pl.* **1.** abundant possessions; wealth. **2.** abundance of whatever is precious.

Rich·ter scale (RIK tər) a scale for measuring the magnitude of earthquakes. [after C.F. *Richter*, 1900–85, U.S. seismologist]

rick·et·y (RIK i tee) *adj.* **·et·i·er, ·et·i·est 1.** ready to fall; tottering. **2.** feeble; infirm; unsteady. **—rick'et·i·ness** *n.*

rick·sha (RIK shaw) *n.* jinriksha. Also **rick'shaw.**

ric·o·chet (RIK ə SHAY) *v.i.* **·cheted** (-SHAYD), **·chet·ing** (-SHAY ing) glance from a surface, as a stone thrown over the water; make a series of skips or bounds. — *n.* a bounding, as of a projectile over or off a surface. [< F]

rid (rid) *v.t.* **rid** or **rid·ded, rid·ding** free, as from a burden or annoyance: usu. with *of.* —*adj.* free; clear; quit: with *of*: We are well *rid* of him. [ME *ridden*] **—rid·dance** (RID ns) *n.*

rid·den (RID n) past participle of RIDE.

rid·dle¹ (RID l) *v.t.* **·dled, ·dling 1.** perforate in numerous places, as with shot. **2.** sift through a coarse sieve. —*n.* a coarse sieve. [ME *riddil*] **—rid'dler** *n.*

rid·dle² *n.* **1.** a puzzling question stated as a problem to be solved by clever ingenuity; a conundrum. **2.** any puzzling object or person. [ME *redel*] —*v.* **·dled, ·dling** *v.t.* **1.** solve; explain. —*v.i.* **2.** utter or solve riddles.

ride (rīd) *v.* **rode, rid·den, rid·ing** *v.i.* **1.** sit on and be borne along by a horse or other animal. **2.** travel or be carried on or in a vehicle or other conveyance. **3.** be supported in moving: The wheel *rides* on the shaft. **4.** carry a rider in a specified manner: This car *rides* easily. **5.** *Naut.* lie at anchor, as a ship. **6.** work or move upward out of place: with *up.* **7.** *Informal* continue unchanged: Let it *ride.* —*v.t.* **8.** sit on and control the motion of (a horse, bicycle, etc.). **9.** overlap or overlie. **10.** travel or traverse (an area etc.) on horseback, in an automobile etc. **11.** control imperiously or oppressively. **12.** accomplish by riding: *ride* a race. **13.** tease or harass by ridicule or petty criticisms; tyrannize. [ME *riden*] — **ride out** survive; endure successfully. —*n.* **1.** an excursion by any means of conveyance, as on horseback, by car, etc. **2.** a road intended for riding. **—rid'a·ble** *adj.*

rid·er (RĪ dər) *n.* **1.** one who or that which rides. **2.** one who breaks in horses. **3.** any

device that rides upon or weighs down something else. **4.** a separate piece of writing or print added to a document, record, or the like.

ridge (rij) *n.* **1.** a long, relatively narrow elevation of land. **2.** that part of a roof at the top where the rafters meet. **3.** any raised strip, as on fabric, etc. [ME *rigge*] —*v.t. & v.i.* **ridged, ridg·ing** form into or mark with ridges.

rid·i·cule (RID i KYOOL) *n.* language or actions calculated to make a person or thing the object of contemptuous or humorous derision or mockery. [< L *ridiculum* joke] —*v.t.* **·culed, ·cul·ing** make fun of; deride.

ri·dic·u·lous (ri DIK yə ləs) *adj.* exciting ridicule; absurd and unworthy of consideration. **—ri·dic'u·lous·ly** *adv.*

rid·ing (RĪ ding) *n.* the act of one who rides; a ride. —*adj.* suitable for riding.

rife (rīf) *adj.* **1.** great in number or amount; abundant. **2.** prevalent; current. [ME]

riff (rif) *n.* in jazz music, a melodic phrase or motif played repeatedly as background or used as the main theme.

rif·fle (RIF əl) *n.* **1.** a shoal or rocky obstruction lying beneath the surface of a river or other stream. **2.** a stretch of shallow, choppy water caused by such a shoal. —*v.t. & v.i.* **·fled, ·fling 1.** cause or form a rapid. **2.** shuffle (cards). **3.** thumb through (pages of a book).

riff·raff (RIF RAF) *n.* **1.** the populace; rabble. **2.** miscellaneous rubbish. [ME *rif and raf* one and all]

ri·fle¹ (RĪ fəl) *n.* **1.** a firearm having a spirally grooved bore, fired from the shoulder. **2.** an artillery piece having a spirally grooved bore. **3.** *pl.* a body of soldiers equipped with rifles. —*v.t.* **·fled, ·fling** cut a spirally grooved bore in (a firearm etc.). [< LG *rifeln* groove]

ri·fle² *v.t.* **·fled, ·fling** search through and rob, as a safe. [ME *rifel* plunder] **—ri'fler** *n.*

ri·fle·man (RĪ fəl mən) *n. pl.* **·men** one armed or skilled with the rifle.

ri·fling (RĪ fling) *n.* **1.** the operation of forming the grooves in a rifle. **2.** the grooves of a rifle collectively.

rift (rift) *n.* **1.** an opening made by riving or splitting; a cleft; fissure. **2.** any disagreement or lack of harmony, as between friends, nations, etc. —*v.t. & v.i.* burst open; split. [ME]

rig¹ (rig) *v.t.* **rigged, rig·ging 1.** fit out; equip. **2.** *Naut.* fit, as a ship, with rigging. **3.** dress; clothe, esp. in finery. **4.** make or construct hurriedly: often with *up.* —*n.* **1.** *Naut.* the arrangement of sails, rigging, spars, etc. on a vessel. **2.** *Informal* a style of dress; costume. **3.** a horse or horses and vehicle. **4.** any apparatus, gear, or tackle: an oil *rig.* [< Scand.]

rig² *v.t.* **rigged, rig·ging** control fraudulently; manipulate: *rig* an election.

rig·ger (RIG ər) *n.* **1.** one who rigs. **2.** a ship having a specified rig: used in combination: a *square-rigger.*

rig·ging (RIG ing) *n.* *Naut.* the entire cordage system of a vessel.

right (rīt) *adj.* **·er, ·est 1.** done in accordance with moral law; equitable; just; righteous. **2.** conformable to truth or fact. **3.** conformable to a standard of propriety; proper. **4.** most desirable or preferable; also, fortunate. **5.** pertaining to, designating, or situated on the side of the body that is toward the south when one faces east. **6.** properly placed, disposed, or adjusted; well-regulated; orderly. **7.** sound in mind or body; healthy; well. **8.** designed to be worn outward or when in use placed toward an observer. **9.** *Often cap.* designating a person, party, faction, etc. having conservative or reactionary views and policies. —**to rights** in a proper or orderly condition: put a room *to rights.* —*adv.* **1.** in accordance with justice or moral principle. **2.** according to the fact or truth; correctly. **3.** in a straight line; directly. **4.** very: used in some titles: *Right* Reverend. **5.** suitably; properly. **6.** precisely; just; also, immediately. **7.** toward the right. **8.** completely. The house burned *right* to the ground. —**right on** an exclamation of agreement, encouragement, etc. —*n.* **1.** that which is right; moral rightness; also, justice. **2.** *Often pl.* a just and proper claim or title. **3.** the right hand, side, or direction. **4.** *Often cap.* a group, party, etc. whose views and policies are predominantly conservative. **5.** in boxing, a blow delivered with the right hand. —*v.t.* **1.** restore to an upright or normal position. **2.** put in order; set right. **3.** make correct or in accord with facts. **4.** make reparation for. —*v.i.* **5.** regain an upright or normal position. [ME] —**right'ness** *n.*

right angle *Geom.* an angle whose sides are perpendicular to each other; an angle of 90° 0. —**right'-an·gled** *adj.*

right·eous (RĪ chəs) *adj.* **1.** conforming to a standard of right and justice; virtuous. **2.** morally right; equitable: a *righteous* act. [ME] —**right'eous·ly** *adv.* —**right'eous·ness** *n.*

right·ful (RĪT fəl) *adj.* **1.** characterized by or conforming to a right or just claim: *rightful* heritage. **2.** consonant with moral right or with justice and truth. **3.** proper; fitting. **4.** Upright; just. [ME] —**right'ful·ly** *adv.*

right-hand (RĪT HAND) *adj.* **1.** of, for, pertaining to, or situated on the right side or right hand. **2.** chiefly depended on: *right-hand* man. **3.** toward the right.

right-hand·ed (RĪT HAN did) *adj.* **1.** using the right hand more easily than the left. **2.** done with or adapted for the right hand. **3.** moving from left to right, as the hands of a clock. —**right'-hand'ed·ness** *n.*

right·ist (RĪ tist) *n.* one whose views and policies are conservative. —*adj.* conservative or reactionary.

right·ly (RĪT lee) *adv.* **1.** correctly. **2.** honestly; uprightly. **3.** properly; aptly.

right-mind·ed (RĪT MĪN did) *adj.* having correct or proper feelings or opinions.

right of way *pl.* **rights of way, right of ways 1.** *Law* the right of a person to pass over the land of another; also, the piece of land used. **2.** the strip of land over which a railroad lays its tracks, on which a public highway is built, or above which a high-tension power line is built. **3.** the legal or customary precedence that allows one vehicle or vessel to cross in front of another.

right triangle a triangle containing a right angle.

right wing a party, group, faction, etc. having rightist policies. —**right'-wing'** *adj.* —**right'-wing'er** *n.*

rig·id (RIJ id) *adj.* **1.** resisting change of form; stiff. **2.** rigorous; inflexible; severe. **3.** not moving; fixed. **4.** strict; exact, as reasoning. [< L *rigidus*] —**rig'·id·ly** *adv.* —**ri·gid'i·ty, rig'id·ness** *n.*

rig·ma·role (RIG mə ROHL) *n.* **1.** incoherent talk or writing; nonsense. **2.** any complicated procedure. Also **rig'a·ma·role'.**

rig·or (RIG ər) *n.* **1.** the condition of being stiff or rigid. **2.** stiffness of opinion or temper; harshness. **3.** exactness without allowance or indulgence; inflexibility; strictness. **4.** inclemency, as of the weather; hardship. [ME *rigour* stiffness] —**rig'or·ous** *adj.* —**rig'or·ous·ly** *adv.*

rig·or mor·tis (RIG ər MOR tis) the muscular rigidity that ensues after death. [< L,
stiffness of death]

rile (rīl) v.t. **riled, ril·ing 1.** vex; irritate. **2.**
make (a liquid) muddy.

rill (ril) n. a small stream; brook. [< Du.]

rim (rim) n. **1.** the edge of a usu. circular
object. **2.** the peripheral part of a wheel,
connected to the hub by spokes. **3.** the
frame of eyeglasses, surrounding the
lenses. —v.t. **rimmed, rim·ming 1.** provide with a rim; border. **2.** in sports, roll
around the edge of (the basket, cup, etc.)
without falling in. [ME]

rime (rīm) n. **1.** a milky white, granular deposit of ice formed on objects by fog or
water vapor that has frozen. **2.** frost. [ME
rim] —v.t. & v.i. **rimed, rim·ing** cover
with or congeal into rime.

rind (rīnd) n. the skin or outer coat that may
be peeled or taken off, as of bacon, fruit,
cheese, etc. [ME]

ring[1] (ring) n. **1.** any circular object, line,
arrangement, etc. **2.** a circular band, usu. of
precious metal, worn on a finger. **3.** any
metal or wooden band used for holding or
carrying something. **4.** a group of persons,
as in a conspiracy. **5.** one of a series of concentric layers of wood in the trunk of a tree,
formed by annual growth. **6.** an area or
arena, as that used for circuses or boxing
matches. **7.** political competition or rivalry:
She tossed her hat into the ring. —**the ring**
prizefighting in general. —**run rings
around** be superior to in some way. —v.t.
ringed, ring·ing 1. surround with a ring;
encircle. **2.** form into a ring or rings. **3.** in
certain games, cast a ring over (a peg or
pin). [ME] —**ringed** adj.

ring[2] v. **rang, rung, ring·ing** v.i. **1.** give
forth a resonant, sonorous sound, as a bell
when struck. **2.** reverberate or resound. **3.**
cause a bell or bells to sound. **4.** have or
suggest a specified quality: His story rings
true. **5.** have a continuing sensation of ringing or buzzing: My ears ring. —v.t. **6.** cause
(a bell etc.) to ring. **7.** produce, as a sound,
by or as by ringing. **8.** announce or proclaim
by ringing: ring the hour. **9.** summon, escort, usher, etc. in this manner: with in or
out: ring out the old year. **10.** call on the
telephone: often with up. [ME ringen] —
ring up 1. total, esp. on a cash register. **2.**
score. —n. **1.** the sound produced by a bell
or other vibrating, sonorous object. **2.** the
act of sounding a bell. **3.** a telephone call. **4.**

characteristic sound or impression: the ring
of truth.

ring·er[1] (RING ər) n. **1.** one who or that
which rings (a bell or chime). **2.** Slang an
athlete, horse, etc. illegally entered in a
contest by concealing disqualifying facts, as
age, professional status, etc. **3.** Slang a person who bears a marked resemblance to
another: You are a dead ringer for Jones.

ring·er[2] n. **1.** one who or that which encircles. **2.** a horseshoe that falls around one of
the posts.

ring·lead·er (RING LEE dər) n. a leader or
organizer of any undertaking, esp. of an
unlawful one, as a riot.

ring·let (RING lit) n. a spiral lock of hair; a
curl.

ring·worm (RING wurm) n. Pathol. any
of several contagious skin diseases caused
by certain fungi and marked by the appearance of scaly patches on the skin.
[ME]

rink (ringk) n. **1.** a smooth, artificial surface
of ice, used for ice-skating or hockey. **2.** a
smooth floor used for roller-skating. **3.** a
building containing a surface for skating.
[ME renk area for battle]

rinse (rins) v.t. **rinsed, rins·ing 1.** remove
soap from by putting through clear water. **2.**
wash lightly, as by dipping in water or by
running water over or into. [ME ryncen] —
n. **1.** the act of rinsing, or the solution in
which something is rinsed. **2.** a hair coloring agent.

ri·ot (RĪ ət) n. **1.** a disturbance consisting of
wild and turbulent conduct of a large number of persons, as a mob. **2.** a brilliant or
sometimes confusing display: a riot of color.
3. boisterous festivity; revelry. **4.** an up-
roariously amusing person, thing, or performance. —**run riot 1.** act or move wildly
and without restraint. **2.** grow profusely or
luxuriantly, as vines. —v.i. take part in a riot
or public disorder. [ME] —**ri'ot·ous** adj.
—**ri'ot·ous·ly** adv.

riot act any forceful warning or reprimand.
—**read the riot act to** reprimand bluntly
and severely.

rip[1] (rip) v. **ripped, rip·ping** v.t. **1.** tear or
cut apart roughly or violently; slash. **2.** tear
or cut from something else in a rough or
violent manner: with off, away, out, etc. **3.**
saw or split (wood) in the direction of the
grain. —v.i. **4.** be torn or cut apart; split. **5.**
Informal rush headlong. —**rip off** Slang **1.**
steal or steal from. **2.** swindle. —n. a place

rip

torn or ripped open; a tear. [< MDu. *rip-pen*]

rip[2] *n.* a ripple; a rapid in a river.

ri•par•i•an (ri PAIR ee ən) *adj.* of or growing on a bank of a river or stream. [< L *ripa* bank of a river]

ripe (rīp) *adj.* •er, •est **1.** grown to maturity and fit for food, as fruit or grain. **2.** brought to a condition for use, as cheese. **3.** in full readiness to do or try; prepared; ready. [ME] —**ripe′ness** *n.*

rip•en (RĪ pən) *v.t. & v.i.* make or become ripe; mature.

rip-off (RIP AWF) *n. Slang* **1.** an act of stealing or cheating. **2.** anything dishonest, illegal, or exploitative.

rip•ple (RIP əl) *v.* **•pled, •pling** *v.i.* **1.** become slightly agitated on the surface, as water blown on by a light breeze. **2.** make a sound like that of water flowing in small waves. —*v.t.* **3.** cause to form ripples. —*n.* **1.** one of the wavelets on the surface of water. **2.** any sound like that made by rippling. —**rip′ply** *adj.*

rip•saw (RIP SAW) *n.* a saw used for cutting wood in the direction of the grain.

rip•tide (RIP TĪD) *n.* water agitated and made dangerous for swimmers by conflicting tides or currents.

rise (rīz) *v.i.* **rose, ris•en, ris•ing** **1.** move upward; go from a lower to a higher position. **2.** slope gradually upward. **3.** gain elevation in rank, status, etc. **4.** swell up: Dough *rises.* **5.** become greater in force, intensity, height, etc.; also, become higher in pitch, as the voice. **6.** become greater in amount, value, etc. **7.** stand up. **8.** get out of bed. **9.** revolt; rebel. **10.** appear above the horizon: said of the sun, moon, etc. **11.** have origin; begin. —**rise above** prove superior to; show oneself indifferent to. —*n.* **1.** the act of rising; ascent. **2.** degree of ascent; elevation; also, an ascending course. **3.** a beginning; an origin. **4.** an elevated place; a small hill. **5.** increase or advance, as in price or value. **6.** advance or elevation, as in rank, prosperity, or importance. **7.** the height of a stair step. **8.** *Informal* an emotional reaction; a response or retort. [ME *risen*]

ris•en (RIZ ən) past participle of RISE.

ris•er (RĪZ ər) *n.* **1.** one who rises or gets up, as from bed: She is an early *riser.* **2.** the vertical part of a step or stair.

ris•i•ble (RIZ ə bəl) *adj.* **1.** having the power of laughing. **2.** exciting laughter; funny. **3.** pertaining to laughter. [< LL *risibilis*] —**ris′i•bly** *adv.* —**ris′i•bil′i•ty** *n.*

ris•ing (RĪ zing) *adj.* **1.** increasing in wealth, power, or distinction. **2.** ascending; also, sloping upward: a *rising* hill. **3.** advancing to adult years; growing: the *rising* generation. —*n.* **1.** that which rises above the surrounding surface. **2.** an insurrection or revolt. [ME]

risk (risk) *n.* **1.** a chance of encountering harm or loss; hazard. **2.** in insurance: **a** the hazard or chance of loss. **b** an insurance applicant who is considered a hazard to the insurer. —*v.t.* **1.** expose to a chance of injury or loss. **2.** incur the risk of. [< F *risque*]

risk•y (RIS kee) *adj.* **risk•i•er, risk•i•est** attended with risk; hazardous, dangerous. —**risk′i•ness** *n.*

ris•qué (ri SKAY) *adj.* bordering on or suggestive of impropriety; bold; off-color: a *risqué* story. [< F]

rite (rīt) *n.* **1.** a solemn or religious ceremony performed in an established or prescribed manner; also, the words or acts constituting or accompanying it. **2.** any formal practice or custom. [ME]

rit•u•al (RICH oo əl) *n.* a prescribed form or method for the performance of a religious or solemn ceremony; any body of rites or ceremonies. [< L *ritualis*] —*adj.* practiced as a rite. —**rit′u•al•ly** *adv.*

rit•u•al•ism (RICH oo ə LIZ əm) *n.* **1.** adherence to ritual. **2.** excessive concern with ritual. —**rit′u•al•ist** *n.* —**rit′u•al•is′tic** *adj.*

ri•val (RĪ vəl) *n.* **1.** one who competes in pursuit of the same object as another; a competitor. **2.** one equaling or nearly equaling another in any respect. [< MF] —*v.t.* **ri•valed, ri•val•ing 1.** strive to equal or excel; compete with. **2.** be the equal of or a match for. —*adj.* competing as a rival. —**ri′val•ry** *n.*

riv•er (RIV ər) *n.* **1.** a large, natural stream of water, usu. fed by converging tributaries along its course and discharging into a larger body of water. **2.** a large stream of any kind. [ME]

riv•et (RIV it) *n.* a short, soft metal bolt, having a head on one end, used to join objects, as metal plates, by passing the shank through holes and flattening out the headless end. —*v.t.* **1.** fasten with or as with a rivet. **2.** batter the headless end of (a bolt etc.) so as to make fast. **3.** engross or attract (the eyes, attention, etc.). [ME *revette*] — **riv'•et•er** *n.*

riv•u•let (RIV yə lit) *n.* a small stream or brook; streamlet. [< Ital. *rivoletto*]

RNA ribonucleic *a*cid.

roach (rohch) *n.* **1.** a cockroach. **2.** *Slang* the butt of a marijuana cigarette.

road (rohd) *n.* **1.** an open way for public passage; esp., a narrow one. **2.** any way of advancing or progressing: the *road* to fame. —**on the road 1.** on tour: said of theatrical companies etc. **2.** traveling, as a salesperson. **3.** living the life of a hobo. [ME *rode*]

road•bed (ROHD BED) *n.* **1.** the graded foundation of gravel etc. on which the ties, rails, etc. of a railroad are laid. **2.** the graded foundation or surface of a road.

road•block (ROHD BLOK) *n.* **1.** an obstruction in a road, esp. one for blocking passage of enemy troops etc. **2.** any obstacle to progress.

road•side (ROHD SID) *n.* the area along the side of a road. —*adj.* situated on the side of a road.

roam (rohm) *v.t. & v.i.* move or wander about (an area, place, etc.); rove; range. [ME *romen*] —*n.* the act of roaming.

roan (rohn) *adj.* of a horse, having a color consisting of bay, sorrel, or chestnut, thickly interspersed with gray or white. —*n.* **1.** a roan color. **2.** an animal of a roan color. [< MF]

roar (ror) *v.i.* **1.** utter a deep, prolonged cry, as of rage or distress. **2.** make a loud noise, as the sea or a cannon. **3.** laugh loudly. — *v.t.* **4.** utter or express by roaring. [ME *roren* bellow] —*n.* **1.** a full, deep, resonant cry, as of a lion or an enraged person. **2.** any loud, prolonged sound.

roast (rohst) *v.t.* **1.** cook (meat etc.) by subjecting to the action of heat, as in an oven. **2.** cook before an open fire or on embers etc. **3.** *Informal* criticize or ridicule severely. — *v.i.* **4.** roast food in an oven etc. **5.** be cooked by this method. **6.** be uncomfortably hot. [ME *rosten*] —*n.* **1.** something roasted; esp., a piece of roasted meat. **2.** a piece of meat adapted or prepared for roasting. **3.** the act of roasting. **4.** a gathering at which a person is ridiculed in a spirit of fun. —*adj.* roasted.

roast•er (ROH stər) *n.* **1.** one who or that which roasts. **2.** a pan or contrivance for roasting something. **3.** something suitable for roasting, esp. a chicken.

rob (rob) *v.* **robbed, rob•bing** *v.t.* **1.** seize and carry off the property of by unlawful violence or threat of violence. **2.** deprive of something belonging or due. **3.** steal from. —*v.i.* **4.** commit robbery. [ME *robben*] — **rob'ber•y** *n.*

robe (rohb) *n.* **1.** a long, loose garment, worn over other dress; a gown. **2.** *pl.* such a garment worn as a badge of office or rank. **3.** a bathrobe. **4.** a blanket or covering, as for use in an automobile: lap *robe.* —*v.t. & v.i.* **robed, rob•ing** dress in a robe. [ME]

ro•bot (ROH bot) *n.* **1.** a manlike machine. **2.** one who works mechanically; automaton. **3.** any mechanism that operates automatically or is remotely controlled. [< Czechoslovakian < *robota* forced labor]

ro•bust (roh BUST) *adj.* strong and healthy; rugged. [< L *robustus* oaken] —**ro•bust'ly** *adv.* —**ro•bust'ness** *n.*

roc (rok) *n.* in Arabian and Persian legend, an enormous and powerful bird of prey. [< Persian *rukh*]

rock[1] (rok) *n.* **1.** a large mass of stone or stony material. **2.** a fragment of rock; stone. **3.** *Geol.* the material forming the essential part of the earth's crust. **4.** something resembling or suggesting a rock, as a firm support, source of strength, etc. **5.** *Slang* a gemstone, esp., a large diamond. —**on the rocks** *Informal* **1.** ruined; also, destitute or bankrupt. **2.** served with ice cubes but without soda or water. [ME *rokke*]

rock[2] *v.t. & v.i.* **1.** move backward and forward or from side to side; sway. **2.** reel or stagger; shake. —*n.* **1.** the act of rocking; a rocking motion. **2.** rock-and-roll. [ME *rocken*]

rock-and-roll (ROK ən ROHL) *adj.* denoting a form of popular music characterized by repetitious melody and insistent rhythms. —*n.* rock-and-roll music: also *rock 'n' roll.*

rock bottom the lowest possible level: Prices hit *rock bottom.* —**rock'-bot'tom** *adj.*

rock-bound (ROK BOWND) *adj.* encircled by or bordered with rocks.

rock•er (ROK ər) *n.* **1.** one who or that which rocks. **2.** one of the curved pieces on which a rocking chair etc. rocks. **3.** a rocking chair. —**off one's rocker** *Slang* mentally unbalanced.

rock•et (ROK it) *n.* **1.** a firework, projectile, missile, or other device, usu. cylindrical in form, that is propelled by the reaction of escaping gases produced during flight. **2.** a type of vehicle operated by rocket propulsion and designed for space travel. —*v.i.* **1.** move like a rocket. —*v.t.* **2.** propel by means of a rocket. [< Ital. *rocchetta*]

rock•e•teer (ROK i TEER) *n.* one who designs or launches rockets.

rocket engine a reaction engine fueled by a liquid or solid propellant containing its own oxidizing agent.

rock•et•ry (ROK i tree) *n.* the science, art, and technology of rocket flight, design, construction, etc.

rocking chair a chair with legs set on rockers.

rock 'n' roll see ROCK-AND-ROLL.

rock•ribbed (ROK RIBD) *adj.* **1.** having rocky ridges. **2.** unyielding; inflexible.

rock salt common salt occurring in large beds; also called *halite*.

rock•y¹ (ROK ee) *adj.* **rock•i•er, rock•i•est 1.** consisting of, abounding in, or resembling rocks. **2.** tough; unfeeling; hard.

rock•y² *adj.* **rock•i•er, rock•i•est 1.** inclined to rock or shake; unsteady. **2.** dizzy or weak. —**rock′i•ness** *n.*

ro•co•co (rə KOH koh) *n.* **1.** an ornate style of art and architecture that developed in France in the 18th c. **2.** florid, fantastic, or odd style. —*adj.* **1.** in the rococo style. **2.** overly elaborate; florid. [< F]

rod (rod) *n.* **1.** a straight, slim piece of wood, metal, or other material. **2.** a stick or several sticks together, used as an instrument of punishment. **3.** discipline; correction: with *the.* **4.** a scepter or badge of office; wand. **5.** a bar, typically of metal, forming part of a machine: a connecting *rod.* **6.** a measure of length equal to 5.5 yards; also, a square rod. **7.** one of the rodlike bodies of the retina sensitive to faint light. **8.** a rod-shaped bacterium. **9.** *Slang* a pistol. [ME *rodd*]

rode (rohd) past tense of RIDE.

ro•dent (ROHD nt) *n.* any of a large order of gnawing mammals, having in each jaw two (rarely four) prominent incisors, as a squirrel, beaver, or rat. —*adj.* **1.** gnawing; corroding. **2.** of or pertaining to a rodent or rodents. [< NL *Rodentia*]

ro•de•o (ROH dee OH) *n. pl.* **•os 1.** the driving of cattle together to be branded, inspected, etc.; roundup. **2.** a public spectacle featuring the riding of broncos, lariat throwing, etc. [< Sp., cattle ring]

roe¹ (roh) *n.* the spawn or eggs of female fish. [ME *rowe*]

roe² *n.* a small deer of Europe and western Asia. Also **roe deer.** [ME *roo*]

roent•gen (RENT gən) *n.* a measure of the intensity of gamma or X-rays. [after Wilhelm Konrad *Roentgen*, 1845–1923, German physicist]

rog•er (ROJ ər) *interj.* **1.** message received: used in radio communication. **2.** *Informal* O.K. [after *Roger*, name representing *r* in telecommunication]

rogue (rohg) *n.* **1.** a dishonest and unprincipled person; rascal. **2.** one who is innocently mischievous. **3.** a fierce and dangerous animal, as an elephant, separated from the herd. —*v.t.* **rogued, ro•gu•ing** practice roguery upon; defraud. — **ro•guer•y** (ROH gə ree) *n.* —**ro•guish** (ROH gish) *adj.* —**ro′guish•ly** *adv.* —**ro′ •guish•ness** *n.*

rogues' gallery a collection of photographs of criminals.

roil (roil) *v.t.* **1.** make muddy or turbid, as by stirring up sediment. **2.** vex; irritate; rile.

roist•er (ROI stər) *v.i.* **1.** bluster; swagger. **2.** engage in tumultuous merrymaking; revel. [< MF *ruistre* boor] —**roist′er•er** *n.*

role (rohl) *n.* **1.** a part or character taken by an actor. **2.** any assumed character or function. Also **rôle.** [< F *rôle*]

roll (rohl) *v.i.* **1.** move forward on a surface by turning round and round, as a ball or wheel. **2.** move or be moved on wheels or rollers. **3.** move or appear to move in undulations or swells, as waves. **4.** assume the shape of a ball or cylinder by turning over and over, as a ball of yarn, or by curling up, as an animal: often with *up.* **5.** pass; elapse: with *on* or *by.* **6.** make a prolonged sound, as thunder. **7.** rotate wholly or partially. **8.** sway or move from side to side, as a ship. **9.** walk with a swaying motion. **10.** move ahead; progress. —*v.t.* **11.** cause to move along a surface by turning round and round, as a ball, log, etc. **12.** move, push forward, etc. on wheels or rollers. **13.** wrap round and round upon itself or on an axis: often with *up.* **14.** spread or make flat by pressing with a roller or rollers, as dough. **15.** wrap or envelop in or as in a covering. **16.** rotate, as the eyes. **17.** utter, emit, etc. with a trilling or rumbling sound: *roll one's r's.* **18.** cast (dice). **19.** *Slang* rob (a person who is asleep). —**roll back 1.** force back; push or pull back. **2.** in commerce, cause (prices, wages, etc.) to return to a previous, lower level, as by government direction. —**roll in**

Informal **1.** arrive, esp. in numbers or large amounts. **2.** wallow; luxuriate: *roll in money.* —*n.* **1.** anything rolled up in cylindrical form. **2.** a register or list of names. **3.** any food rolled up in preparation for use; also, a small, individually shaped portion of bread. **4.** a rolling gait or movement, as of a ship. **5.** a reverberating, rumbling, or trilling sound. **6.** a swell or undulation of a surface, as of land or water. **7.** *Informal* a wad of paper money. **8.** the act of rolling, or the state of being rolled. **9.** *Aeron.* a complete rotation of an airplane about its longitudinal axis without change in the direction of flight. [ME]

roll bar an overhead metal bar to protect passengers when a vehicle overturns.

roll call the act of calling a roll or list of the names of a number of persons, as soldiers, to determine which are present.

roll•er (ROH lər) *n.* **1.** one who or that which rolls. **2.** any of various cylindrical devices that roll or rotate. **3.** the wheel of a caster or roller skate. **4.** a heavy cylinder for rolling, smoothing, or crushing something: a steam *roller.* **5.** one of a series of long, swelling waves that break on a coast, esp. after a storm.

roller coaster a railway with small, open cars run over a route of steep inclines and sharp turns, common at amusement parks.

roller derby a contest between two teams of roller skaters on a banked oval track.

roller skate a skate having wheels instead of a runner. —**roll•er-skate** (ROH lər SKAYT) *v.i.* -**skat•ed,** -**skat•ing**

rol•lick (ROL ik) *v.i.* move or behave in a careless, frolicsome manner. [Blend of ROMP and FROLIC] —**rol′lick•ing** *adj.*

roll•ing (ROH ling) *adj.* **1.** turning round and round, esp. so as to move forward on a surface. **2.** having a succession of sloping elevations and depressions: *rolling* hills. **3.** turning on or as if on wheels; rotating. **4.** of sounds, trilling, rumbling, or reverberating; resounding. **5.** recurring; elapsing. —*n.* the act of one who or that which rolls or is rolled.

ro•ly•po•ly (ROH lee POH lee) *adj.* short and fat; pudgy; dumpy. —*n. pl.* -**po•lies** a roly-poly person or thing.

ro•man (ROH mən) *Sometimes cap. n.* a common style of type or lettering characterized by vertical rather than slanted strokes: This line is set in *roman.* —*adj.*

pertaining to, designating, or printed in roman. [< ROMAN]

Ro•man (ROH mən) *adj.* **1.** of, pertaining to, or characteristic of modern or ancient Rome or its people. **2.** of or pertaining to the Latin language. —*n.* **1.** a native or citizen of ancient or modern Rome. **2.** the language of ancient Rome; Latin. [< L *Romanus*]

Roman candle a firework consisting of a tube that discharges colored sparks of fire.

Roman Catholic a member of the Roman Catholic Church. —**Roman Catholicism.**

Roman Catholic Church the Christian church that recognizes the Pope as its supreme head.

Ro•mance (roh MANS) *adj.* pertaining or belonging to one or more, or all, of the languages that have developed from Latin, including French, Italian, and Spanish.

ro•mance (roh MANS) *n.* **1.** a love affair. **2.** a kind of love between the sexes, characterized by high ideals of devotion, strong ardor, etc. **3.** adventurous, heroic, or exotic nature: the *romance* of faraway places. **4.** a narrative, sometimes in verse, presenting chivalrous ideals and heroes. **5.** any fictional narrative about adventure and love. [ME *romaunce*] —*v.* -**manced,** -**manc•ing** *v.i.* **1.** tell or write romances. **2.** think or act in a romantic manner. **3.** *Informal* make love. —*v.t.* **4.** *Informal* woo. —**ro•manc′er** *n.*

Roman Empire the empire of ancient Rome, established in 27 B.C. and continuing until A.D. 395.

Ro•man•esque (ROH mə NESK) *adj.* of, pertaining to, or designating a style of Western architecture that prevailed from the 5th to the 12th c., characterized by round arches and general massiveness. —*n.* the Romanesque style of architecture.

Roman holiday **1.** a time of debauchery; also, enjoyment or profit derived from the suffering of others. **2.** a day of gladiatorial and other contests in ancient Rome.

Ro•man•ic (roh MAN ik) *adj.* **1.** Roman. **2.** Romance.

Roman numerals the numerals used by the ancient Romans as symbols in arithmetical notation. The basic numerals are I (1), V (5), X (10), L (50), C (100), D (500), and M (1000).

ro•man•tic (roh MAN tik) *adj.* **1.** of, characterized by, or of the nature of romance. **2.** characterized by or given to feelings of romance. **3.** suitable for or conducive to love or amorousness. **4.** visionary; impractical. **5.** of or pertaining to romanticism. —*n.* one who is romantic. [< F *romantique*] — **ro•man'ti•cal•ly** *adv.*

ro•man•ti•cism (roh MAN tə SIZ əm) *n.* **1.** *Usu. cap.* a movement in art, music, and literature originating in Europe in the late 18th c., characterized by a revolt against neoclassic rules, forms, and traditions and by an exalting of the feelings and individualism: distinguished from *classicism.* **2.** romantic quality. —**ro•man'ti•cist** *n.*

Ro•me•o (ROH mee OH) **1.** a man who is an ardent lover. **2.** a philanderer. [after the hero of Shakespeare's *Romeo and Juliet*]

romp (romp) *v.i.* **1.** play boisterously. **2.** win easily. —*n.* **1.** one who romps. **2.** a lively frolic or play. **3.** an easy win.

romp•er (ROM pər) *n.* **1.** one who romps. **2.** *pl.* a garment combining a waist and bloomers, worn by young children.

ron•do (RON doh) *n. Music* a composition or movement having a main theme and several contrasting episodes, the main theme being repeated after each subordinate them. [< Ital.]

rood (rood) *n.* **1.** a cross or crucifix. **2.** a land measure equivalent to ¼ acre, or 40 square rods; also **square rood.** [ME]

roof (roof) *n.* **1.** the exterior upper covering of a building; also **roof'top. 2.** any top covering, as of a car. **3.** the most elevated part of anything. —*v.t.* cover with or as with a roof. [ME]

roof•er (ROO fər) *n.* one who constructs or repairs roofs.

roof•ing (ROO fing) *n.* **1.** material for roofs. **2.** a roof; covering.

rook¹ (ruuk) *n.* **1.** an Old World crow. **2.** a trickster or cheat. —*v.t. & v.i.* cheat; defraud. [ME *roke*]

rook² *n.* a castle-shaped chess piece that can move any number of unoccupied squares horizontally or vertically: also called *castle.* [< Persian *rukh*]

rook•er•y (RUUK ə ree) *n. pl.* **•er•ies 1.** a colony or breeding place of rooks. **2.** a breeding place of sea birds, seals, etc.

rook•ie (RUUK ee) *n.* a recruit or novice.

room (room) *n.* **1.** an extent of space used for some implied or specified purpose. **2.** a space for occupancy or use enclosed on all sides, as in a building. **3.** *pl.* lodgings. —*v.i.* occupy a room; lodge. [ME *roume*]

room•ful (ROOM fuul) *n. pl.* **•fuls 1.** as

many or as much as a room will hold. **2.** a number of persons present in a room.

room•mate (ROOM MAYT) *n.* one who shares lodgings with another or others.

room•y (ROO mee) *adj.* **room•i•er, room•i•est** having abundant room; spacious. — **room'i•ness** *n.*

roost (roost) *n.* **1.** a perch or place where birds rest at night. **2.** any temporary resting place. —*v.i.* **1.** perch upon a roost. **2.** come to rest; settle. [ME]

roost•er (ROO stər) *n.* a male chicken.

root¹ (root) *n.* **1.** the underground portion of a plant, which absorbs moisture, obtains or stores nourishment, and provides support. **2.** any underground growth, as a tuber or bulb. **3.** that from which anything derives origin, growth, or support. **4.** a rootlike part of an organ or structure, as of a tooth. **5.** *Ling.* a base to which affixes may be added to form words. **6.** *Math.* a quantity that, multiplied by itself a specified number of times, will yield a given quantity: 3 is the square *root* of 9. **7.** *Music* the fundamental tone of a chord. —*v.i.* **1.** put forth roots. **2.** be or become firmly fixed. —*v.t.* **3.** fix by or as by roots. **4.** pull, dig, or tear up by or as by the roots: with *up* or *out.* [ME] —**root'•less** *adj.*

root² *v.t.* **1.** dig up with the snout, as swine do. —*v.i.* **2.** turn up the earth with the snout. **3.** search; rummage. [OE *wrōtan*] — **root'er** *n.*

root³ *v.i.* cheer for or encourage a contestant, team, etc.: with *for.* —**root'er** *n.*

root beer a carbonated beverage made with yeast and root extracts.

root•let (ROOT lit) *n.* a small root.

rope (rohp) *n.* **1.** a construction of twisted fibers, as of hemp, so intertwined in strands as to form a thick cord. **2.** a collection of things united in a line. **3.** a slimy or glutinous filament or thread. **4.** a cord or halter used in hanging. **5.** a lasso. —**give (one) plenty of rope** allow (a person) to pursue unchecked a course that will end in disaster. —**know the ropes** *Informal* be familiar with all the conditions in any sphere of activity. —*v.t.* **roped, rop•ing 1.** tie or fasten with or as with rope. **2.** enclose or divide with a rope: usu. with *off.* **3.** catch with a lasso. [ME]

Ror•schach test (ROR shahk) *Psychol.* a test of personality characteristics based on analysis of the subject's interpretation of standard patterns formed by inkblots. [after

Hermann *Rorschach*, 1884–1922, Swiss psychiatrist]

ro•sa•ry (ROH zə ree) *n. pl.* **•ries** *Eccl.* **1.** a series of prayers. **2.** a string of beads for keeping count of these prayers. [ME *rosarie*]

rose[1] (rohz) *n.* **1.** any of a large genus of erect or climbing shrubs, with rodlike, prickly stems. **2.** the flower of such a shrub, usu. white, yellow, pink, or red. **3.** any of various similar plants or flowers. **4.** a light pinkish red. —**bed of roses** a peaceful or carefree time, place, or condition. —*v.t.* **rosed, ros•ing** redden. [ME]

rose[2] past tense of RISE.

ro•sé (roh ZAY) *n.* a pink wine. [F, lit., pink]

ro•se•ate (ROH zee it) *adj.* **1.** rosy; rose-colored. **2.** cheerful; optimistic. [< L *roseus*]

rose-col•ored (ROHZ KUL ərd) *adj.* pink or crimson, as a rose. —**see through rose-colored glasses** see things in an unduly favorable light.

Ro•set•ta stone (roh ZET ə) **1.** a tablet inscribed with Egyptian hieroglyphics and Greek translations, found near Rosetta, Egypt, in 1799. **2.** the key to solving a problem or puzzle.

ro•sette (roh ZET) *n.* a circular ornament or badge having some resemblance to a rose. [< F, little rose]

rose window a circular window filled with tracery, often radiating from the center.

Rosh Ha•sha•na (ROHSH hah SHAH nə) the Jewish New Year, celebrated in September or October. [< Hebrew, the head of the year]

ros•in (ROZ in) *n.* the hard, amber-colored resin forming the residue after the distillation of oil from crude turpentine. —*v.t.* apply rosin to. [ME]

ros•ter (ROS tər) *n.* **1.** a list of personnel in a military unit. **2.** any list of names. [< Du. *rooster* list]

ros•trum (ROS trəm) *n. pl.* **•trums** or **•tra** (-trə) *for def. 1,* **•tra** *for def. 2* **1.** a pulpit or platform. **2.** in ancient Rome: **a** a beaklike part on the prow of a ship. **b** the orators' platform in the Roman forum, embellished with such parts. [< L, beak]

ros•y (ROH zee) *adj.* **ros•i•er, ros•i•est 1.** like a rose; rose red; blushing. **2.** bright, pleasing, or flattering. **3.** auguring success; optimistic. —**ros′i•ly** *adv.* —**ros′i•ness** *n.*

rot (rot) *v.* **rot•ted, rot•ting** *v.i.* **1.** undergo decomposition; decay. **2.** become morally

rotten. —*v.t.* **3.** cause to decompose. —*n.* **1.** the process of rotting or the state of being rotten. **2.** that which is rotten. **3.** any of various diseases involving decay in humans, plants, and animals. **4.** nonsense. —*interj.* nonsense! [ME *rotten*]

ro•ta•ry (ROH tə ree) *adj.* **1.** turning or designed to turn around its axis, like a wheel. **2.** having some part that turns on its axis. —*n. pl.* **•ries** a rotary device or part. [< Med.L *rotarius*]

rotary engine *Mech.* **1.** an engine in which rotary motion is directly produced, as in a turbine. **2.** a radial engine revolving about a fixed crankshaft.

rotary press a printing press using curved type plates that revolve against the paper.

ro•tate (ROH tayt) *v.t. & v.i.* **•tat•ed, •tat•ing 1.** turn or cause to turn on or as on its axis. **2.** alternate in a definite order or succession. [< L *rotatus* caused to spin] —**ro′tat•a•ble** *adj.* —**ro•ta′tion** *n.*

ro•ta•to•ry (ROH tə TOR ee) *adj.* **1.** having, pertaining to, or producing rotation. **2.** following in succession. **3.** alternating or recurring.

rote (roht) *n.* mechanical routine, as the repetition of words, with slight attention to the sense. —**by rote** mechanically; without intelligent attention. [ME]

ro•tis•se•rie (roh TIS ə ree) *n.* **1.** a restaurant or shop specializing in roasted meat, **2.** a rotating device for roasting meat etc. [< F, roasting place]

ro•to•gra•vure (ROH tə grə VYUUR) *n.* **1.** the process of printing from cylinders etched from photographic plates and run through a rotary press. **2.** a picture printed by this process. **3.** the section of a newspaper containing such pictures.

ro•tor (ROH tər) *n.* **1.** the rotating section of a motor, turbine, etc. **2.** *Aeron.* the horizontally rotating unit of a helicopter or autogiro, consisting of the airfoils and hub.

rot•ten (ROT n) *adj.* **1.** decomposed by natural process; putrid. **2.** untrustworthy; treacherous. **3.** corrupt; venal. **4.** liable to break; unsound. **5.** worthless. [ME *roten*] —**rot′ten•ness** *n.*

ro•tund (roh TUND) *adj.* **1.** rounded out; plump. **2.** full-toned; sonorous. [< L *rotundus* round] —**ro•tun′di•ty** *n.*

ro•tun•da (roh TUN də) *n.* a circular building or an interior hall, surmounted with a dome. [< Ital.]

rou·é (roo AY) *n.* a licentious man; sensualist. [< F]

rouge (roozh) *n.* **1.** any cosmetic used for coloring the cheeks or lips pink or red. **2.** a reddish powder used in polishing metals and glass. —*v.t. & v.i.* **rouged, roug·ing** use rouge on (cheeks, lips, etc.). [< F, red]

rough (ruf) *adj.* •**er,** •**est 1.** having an uneven surface; not smooth or polished. **2.** coarse in texture. **3.** disordered or ragged; shaggy. **4.** harsh; rude; violent. **5.** boisterous or tempestuous; stormy. **6.** not refined or cultured; crude. **7.** done or made hastily and without attention to details, as a drawing. —*n.* **1.** a crude, incomplete, or unpolished object, material, or condition. **2.** any part of a golf course on which tall grass, bushes, etc. grow. —**in the rough** in a crude or unpolished state. —*v.t.* **1.** make rough; roughen. **2.** treat roughly. **3.** make, cut, or sketch roughly: with *in* or *out*. —**rough it** live, camp, or travel under rough or harsh conditions. —*adv.* in a rude manner; roughly. [ME] —**rough·ly** *adv.* —**rough·ness** *n.*

rough·age (RUF ij) *n.* **1.** coarse or tough substance. **2.** any food matter containing a high percentage of indigestible constituents; fiber.

rough-and-read·y (RUF ən RED ee) *adj.* crude but competent or effective.

rough-and-tum·ble (RUF ən TUM bəl) *adj.* marked by the disregard of rules; scrambling; disorderly. —*n.* a rough-and-tumble fight.

rough·en (RUF ən) *v.t. & v.i.* make or become rough.

rough-hew (RUF HYOO) *v.t.* •**hewed,** •**hewed** or •**hewn,** •**hew·ing 1.** hew or shape roughly or irregularly. **2.** make crudely.

rough·house (RUF HOWS) *n.* a boisterous or violent game; rough play. —*v.* •**housed,** •**hous·ing** *v.i.* **1.** engage in horseplay or violence. —*v.t.* **2.** treat roughly.

rough·neck (RUF NEK) *n.* a rowdy.

rough·shod (RUF SHOD) *adj.* shod with rough shoes to prevent slipping, as a horse. —**ride roughshod over** act overbearingly.

rou·lette (roo LET) *n.* **1.** a game of chance, played at a table having a rotating disk (**roulette wheel**) on which a ball is rolled until it drops into a numbered space. **2.** an engraver's disk of tempered steel, as for tracing points on a copperplate; also, a

draftsman's wheel for making dotted lines. —*v.t.* •**let·ted,** •**let·ting** perforate or mark with a roulette. [< F]

round (rownd) *adj.* •**er,** •**est 1.** having a contour that is circular or approximately so; spherical, ring-shaped, or cylindrical. **2.** having a curved contour or surface; not angular or flat. **3.** liberal; ample; large. **4.** easy and free, as in motion; brisk. **5.** of full cadence; full-toned. **6.** made without reserve; outspoken. **7.** open; just. **8.** formed or moving in rotation or a circle. **9.** returning to the point of departure. **10.** of a number, increased or decreased by a relatively small amount for the sake of simplicity. **11.** *Phonet.* formed or spoken with the lips rounded. —*n.* **1.** something round, as a portion of the thigh of a beef. **2.** *Often pl.* a circular course; circuit; beat. **3.** a single revolution; also, revolving motion. **4.** a series of recurrent movements; routine: the daily *round* of life. **5.** one of a series of concerted actions performed in succession: a *round* of applause. **6.** one of the divisions of a boxing match. **7.** in golf, a number of holes or an interval of play in a match. **8.** *Music* a short canon in which each voice enters in turn and returns to the beginning upon reaching the end. **9.** a single shot or complete unit of ammunition. —**go the rounds** pass from person to person of a certain group. —**make the rounds** take a usual walk or tour, as of inspection. —*v.t.* **1.** make round or full. **2.** bring to completion; perfect: usu. with *off* or *out*. **3.** *Phonet.* utter (a vowel) with the lips in a rounded position. **4.** travel or go around. —*v.i.* **5.** become round or plump. **6.** come to completeness or perfection. **7.** turn around. —**round off 1.** make round. **2.** make into a round number. —**round up 1.** collect (cattle etc.) in a herd, as for driving to market. **2.** assemble; gather. —*adv.* **1.** on all sides. **2.** with a circular or rotating motion. **3.** through a circle or circuit, as from point to point. **4.** in circumference. **5.** from one view or position to another; to and fro. —*prep.* **1.** enclosing; encircling. **2.** on every side of, or from every side toward; surrounding. **3.** toward every side from; about. [ME *rond*] —**round'ed** *adj.* —**round'ness** *n.*

round·a·bout (ROWND ə BOWT) *adj.* **1.** circuitous; indirect. **2.** encircling. —*n.* (ROWND ə BOWT) **1.** a circuitous route. **2.** a traffic circle.

round·ly (ROWND lee) *adv.* **1.** in a round

manner or form; circularly; spherically. **2.** severely; thoroughly. **3.** frankly; bluntly.

round number a number expressed to the nearest ten, hundred, thousand, etc.

round-shoul·dered (ROWND SHOHL dərd) *adj.* having the upper back rounded or the shoulders stooping.

round table 1. a meeting place for conference. **2.** any discussion group. —**round·ta·ble** (ROWND TAY bəl) *adj.*

round-the-clock (ROWND *thə* KLOK) *adj.* through all 24 hours of the day.

round trip a trip to a place and back again; a two-way trip. —**round'-trip'** *adj.*

round·up (ROWND UP) *n.* **1.** the bringing together of cattle etc. scattered over a range. **2.** the team employed in this work. **3.** the bringing together of persons or things. **4.** a summary of information etc.

rouse (rowz) *v.t. & v.i.* **roused, rous·ing 1.** awaken. **2.** excite or become excited. **3.** flush or start from cover: said of game. —*n.* the act of rousing.

rous·ing (ROW zing) *adj.* **1.** able to rouse or excite. **2.** lively; vigorous.

roust (rowst) *v.t. & v.i.* arouse and drive (a person or thing); stir up: usu. with *out.*

roust·a·bout (ROWST ə BOWT) *n.* a casual or unskilled laborer for heavy work, as on the waterfront, on a cattle ranch, or in a circus.

rout¹ (rowt) *n.* **1.** a disorderly and overwhelming defeat or flight. **2.** a mob. —*v.t.* defeat disastrously; put to flight. [ME]

rout² *v.i.* **1.** root, as swine. **2.** search; rummage. —*v.t.* **3.** turn up with the snout. **4.** dig up; discover; disclose: with *out.* **5.** hollow or scrape, as with a scoop. **6.** drive or force out.

route (root) *n.* **1.** a course, road, or way taken in traveling. **2.** the specific course followed, as in delivering mail. [ME] —*v.t.* **rout·ed, rout·ing** dispatch or send by a certain way, as passengers, goods, etc.

rou·tine (roo TEEN) *n.* **1.** a detailed method of procedure, regularly followed. **2.** habitual methods or actions. —*adj.* **1.** customary; adhering to procedure. **2.** commonplace. [< F] —**rou·tine'ly** *adv.*

roux (roo) *n. French* butter and flour mixed and cooked together as a thickening agent.

rove (rohv) *v.* **roved, rov·ing** *v.i.* **1.** wander from place to place. —*v.t.* **2.** roam over, through, or about. —*n.* an act of roving; a ramble. —**ro'ver** *n.* wanderer; pirate. [ME *roven* shoot at rovers] —**rov'er** *n.*

row¹ (roh) *n.* **1.** an arrangement or series of persons or things in a continued line; a rank; file. **2.** a line of seats, as in a theater. —**a long row to hoe** a difficult undertaking. —*v.t.* arrange in a row: with *up.* [ME *rowe*]

row² *v.i.* **1.** use oars in propelling a boat. —*v.t.* **2.** propel or transport by rowing. —*n.* **1.** the act of rowing. **2.** a trip in a rowboat. [ME *rowen*]

row³ (row) *n.* **1.** a noisy disturbance or quarrel; a brawl. **2.** any dispute or disturbance. —*v.t. & v.i.* engage in a row or brawl.

row·boat (ROH вонт) *n.* a boat propelled by oars.

row·dy (ROW dee) *n. pl.* **·dies** a rough, disorderly person. —*adj.* **·di·er, ·di·est** rough and loud; disorderly. —**row'di·ness, row'dy·ism** *n.*

roy·al (ROI əl) *adj.* **1.** pertaining to a monarch. **2.** connected with or under the authority of a monarch. **3.** like or befitting a monarch; regal. [ME] —**roy'al·ly** *adv.*

royal blue a brilliant blue, often with reddish overtones.

Royal Canadian Mounted Police the federal police force of Canada.

Roy·al·ist (ROI ə list) *n.* **1.** in English history, an adherent of King Charles I. **2.** in French history, a supporter of various claimants to the throne since 1793. **3.** in the American Revolution, a Tory.

roy·al·ist (ROI ə list) *n.* a supporter of a royal dynasty. —*adj.* of or pertaining to royalists.

roy·al·ty (ROI əl tee) *n. pl.* **·ties 1.** the rank, birth, or lineage of a king or queen. **2.** a royal personage; also, royal persons collectively. **3.** a share of proceeds paid to a proprietor, author, or inventor. [ME *roialte*]

rub (rub) *v.* **rubbed, rub·bing** *v.t.* **1.** move or pass over the surface of with pressure and friction. **2.** cause (something) to move in this way. **3.** cause to become worn or sore from friction. **4.** clean, shine, etc. by means of pressure and friction. **5.** apply or spread by this means. **6.** remove or erase by friction: with *off* or *out.* —*v.i.* **7.** move along a surface with friction; scrape. **8.** exert pressure and friction. **9.** become worn or sore from friction; chafe. **10.** undergo removal by rubbing: with *off, out,* etc. —**rub it in** *Informal* harp on someone's errors, faults, etc. —**rub out** *Slang* kill. —**rub the wrong way** irritate; annoy. —*n.* **1.** a rubbing. **2.** a hindrance, doubt, etc. [ME *rubben*]

rub·ber[1] (RUB ər) *n.* **1.** an elastic material obtained from certain tropical plants, and also made synthetically. **2.** anything used for rubbing, erasing, etc. **3.** an article made of rubber, as an overshoe. **4.** one who or that which rubs. —*adj.* made of rubber. —**rub′ber·y** *adj.*

rub·ber[2] *n.* in some card games, a series of two or three games terminated when one side has won two games; also, the odd game that breaks a tie.

rub·ber-stamp (RUB ər STAMP) *v.t.* **1.** mark or approve with a rubber stamping device. **2.** approve as a matter of routine.

rub·bish (RUB ish) *n.* **1.** waste material; trash. **2.** nonsense; rot. [ME *rubbes*]

rub·ble (RUB əl) *n.* **1.** rough pieces of broken stone. **2.** the debris to which buildings, walls, etc. are reduced by earthquakes, bombings, etc. **3.** rough pieces of stone for use in construction; also, masonry composed of such pieces. [ME *rubel*]

rub·down (RUB DOWN) *n.* a massage.

ru·bel·la (roo BEL ə) *n.* German measles. [< NL]

ru·be·o·la (ROO bee OH lə) *n.* measles. [< NL]

ru·bi·cund (ROO bi KUND) *adj.* red; rosy. [< L *rubicundus*]

ru·bric (ROO brik) *n.* **1.** a part of an early book that appears in red, as an initial letter. **2.** *Eccl.* a direction in a religious service. **3.** a heading or title. **4.** any direction or rule of conduct. —*adj.* **1.** red. **2.** written in red. [< L *rubrica* red earth]

ru·bri·cate (ROO bri KAYT) *v.t.* **·cat·ed, ·cat·ing** mark or illuminate with red, as a book. [< L *rubricatus* colored red]

ru·by (ROO bee) *n. pl.* **·bies 1.** a translucent, deep red gemstone. **2.** a red color. [ME *rubi*] —*adj.* ruby-colored.

ruck[1] (ruk) *n.* **1.** a mass of ordinary things; heap. **2.** the ordinary run of people or things. **3.** trash; rubbish. [ME *ruke*]

ruck[2] *v.t. & v.i.* wrinkle; rumple. —*n.* a wrinkle; crease. [< ON *hrukka* wrinkle]

ruck·sack (RUUK SAK) *n.* a type of knapsack. [< G, lit., back sack]

ruck·us (RUK əs) *n.* an uproar; commotion.

ruc·tion (RUK shən) *n.* a disturbance; quarrel.

rud·der (RUD ər) *n.* a broad, flat, movable device at the rear of a vessel or aircraft for steering. [ME *rodder*]

rud·dy (RUD ee) *adj.* **·di·er, ·di·est 1.** tinged with red. **2.** having a healthy glow; rosy. [ME *rudi*] —**rud′di·ness** *n.*

rude (rood) *adj.* **rud·er, rud·est 1.** offensively blunt or uncivil; impudent. **2.** lacking refinement; uncouth. **3.** crudely made or done; rough. **4.** startling; sudden: *rude awakening.* [ME] —**rude′ly** *adv.* —**rude′ ness** *n.*

ru·di·ment (ROO də mənt) *n.* **1.** a first principle, step, stage, or condition. **2.** something undeveloped or only partially developed. [< L *rudimentum* early training] —**ru·di·men·ta·ry** (ROO də MEN tə ree) *adj.*

rue[1] (roo) *v.t. & v.i.* **rued, ru·ing** feel sorrow or remorse for (something). —*n.* sorrowful remembrance; regret. [ME *ruen*] —**rue·ful** (ROO fəl) *adj.* —**rue′·ful·ly** *adv.* —**rue′ful·ness** *n.*

rue[2] *n.* a small herb with bitter, acrid leaves, formerly much used in medicine. [ME]

ruff[1] (ruf) *n.* **1.** a pleated, round, heavily starched collar popular in the 16th c. **2.** ruffle[1] (def. 1). **3.** a natural collar of projecting feathers or hair around the neck of a bird or mammal. [? Short for RUFFLE[1]] —**ruffed** *adj.*

ruff[2] *v.t. & v.i.* trump (a card). [< MF *roffle*] —*n.* the act of trumping.

ruf·fi·an (RUF ee ən) *n.* a lawless, brutal man; a tough. —*adj.* brutal or cruel. [< MF] —**ruf′fi·an·ism** *n.*

ruf·fle[1] (RUF əl) *n.* **1.** a pleated strip or frill of fabric, lace, etc.: also *ruff.* **2.** a slight disturbance, as a ripple. —*v.* **·fled, ·fling** *v.t.* **1.** disturb the smoothness of; wrinkle or rumple. **2.** draw into ruffles; gather. **3.** erect (the feathers) in a ruff. **4.** irritate; upset. —*v.i.* **5.** be or become rumpled or disordered. **6.** become disturbed or irritated. [ME *ruffelen* rumple]

ruf·fle[2] *n.* a low, continuous beat of a drum. —*v.t.* **·fled, ·fling** beat a drum in this way.

ru·fous (ROO fəs) *adj.* dull red; brownish red. [< L *rufus* red]

rug (rug) *n.* **1.** a heavy piece of fabric to cover a portion of a floor. **2.** *Slang* a toupee. [< Scand.]

rug·by (RUG bee) *n.* a type of football played by teams of 15 members in which the ball is propelled toward the opponents' goal by kicking or carrying; also called *rugby football.*

rug·ged (RUG id) *adj.* **1.** having a surface broken into irregular points or crags; uneven. **2.** shaggy; unkempt. **3.** harsh; rough;

severe. **4.** having strongly marked features. **5.** lacking refinement; rude. **6.** robust; sturdy; hale. [ME] **—rug′ged·ness** n.

ru·gose (ROO gohs) adj. wrinkled, as some leaves. **—ru·gos·i·ty** (roo GOS i tee) n. [< L rugosus wrinkled]

ru·in (ROO in) n. **1.** total destruction of value or usefulness. **2.** loss of honor, wealth, etc. **3.** Often pl. the remains of something demolished or decayed. **4.** a condition of desolation or destruction; also, the cause of this. —v.t. & v.i. bring to or fall into ruin. [ME ruine] **—ru·in·a·tion** (ROO ə NAY shən) n.

ru·in·ous (ROO ə nəs) adj. **1.** causing or tending to ruin. **2.** falling to ruin; decayed. **—ru′in·ous·ly** adv.

rule (rool) n. **1.** controlling power, or its possession and exercise; dominion; authority. **2.** a prescribed method or procedure: the rules of a game. **3.** regulations laid down by or for a religious order. **4.** an established form or method, as for grammatical usage. **5.** something belonging to the ordinary course of events or condition of things. **6.** Law a judicial decision on some motion or special application. **7.** ruler (def. 2). [ME riule] **—as a rule** ordinarily; usually. —v.t. & v.i. **ruled, rul·ing 1.** control or govern; have authority over. **2.** decide or determine a matter judicially or authoritatively. **3.** mark (a paper etc.) with straight, parallel lines.

rule of thumb a rough, practical measure, rather than a scientific one.

rul·er (ROO lər) n. **1.** one who rules or governs. **2.** a straight-edged instrument for use in measuring or in drawing lines.

rul·ing (ROO ling) adj. controlling; predominant. —n. a decision, as by a judge.

rum[1] (rum) n. **1.** an alcoholic liquor distilled from fermented molasses or cane juice. **2.** any alcoholic liquor.

rum[2] adj. Chiefly Brit. queer; strange; peculiar.

Ru·ma·ni·an (ruu MAYN yən) n. **1.** a native or inhabitant of Rumania. **2.** the Romance language of the Rumanians. —adj. of or pertaining to Rumania, Rumanians, or Rumanian.

rum·ba (RUUM bə) n. **1.** a dance of Cuban origin. **2.** music for or in the manner of such a dance. Also spelled rhumba. [< Am.Sp.]

rum·ble (RUM bəl) v. **·bled, ·bling** v.i. **1.** make a low, heavy, rolling sound, as thunder. **2.** move or proceed with such a sound. —v.t. **3.** cause to make a low, heavy, rolling sound. **4.** utter with such a sound. [ME romblen] —n. **1.** a rumbling sound. **2.** a seat or baggage compartment in the rear of a carriage. **3.** a folding seat recessed into the back of some old automobiles; also **rumble seat. 4.** Slang a street fight between rival gangs.

ru·men (ROO min) n. pl. **ru·mi·na** (-mə nə) the first stomach of a ruminant. [< L. throat]

ru·mi·nant (ROO mə nənt) n. one of a division of cud-chewing mammals, as the deer, cow, etc., having a stomach with four cavities. —adj. **1.** chewing the cud. **2.** of or pertaining to a ruminant. **3.** meditative. [< L ruminari chew over]

ru·mi·nate (ROO mə NAYT) v.t. & v.i. **·NAT·ED, ·NAT·ING 1.** chew the cud. **2.** meditate or reflect upon (an issue etc.); ponder. **—ru′mi·na′tion** n. **—ru′mi·na′tive** adj.

rum·mage (RUM ij) v.t. & v.i. **·maged, ·mag·ing** search through (a place, box, etc.) by disarranging the contents; ransack. —n. odds and ends. **—rum′mag·er** n.

rummage sale a sale of old or unwanted objects, as to obtain money for charity.

rum·my[1] (RUM ee) n. a card game in which the object is to obtain sets of three or four cards of the same denomination, or sequences of three or more cards of the same suit.

rum·my[2] n. pl. **·mies** Slang a drunkard. —adj. of or resembling rum.

ru·mor (ROO mər) n. **1.** an unverified or unfounded report circulating from person to person. **2.** common gossip; hearsay. —v.t. tell or spread as a rumor. [ME rumour]

rump (rump) n. **1.** the rounded or fleshy upper part of the hindquarters of an animal. **2.** the analogous region in man; the buttocks. **3.** a cut of beef between the loin and the round. **4.** a last, often undesirable remnant. [ME rumpe]

rum·ple (RUM pəl) v.t. & v.i. **·pled, ·pling** crease; wrinkle; ruffle. —n. an untidy wrinkling or creasing. [< MDu. rompelen]

rum·pus (RUM pəs) n. a row; wrangle; a controversy.

rumpus room a room for games, informal gatherings, etc.

run (run) v. **ran, run, run·ning** v.i. **1.** move by rapid steps, faster than walking, in such a manner that both feet are off the ground for a portion of each step. **2.** move rapidly; go swiftly. **3.** flee; take flight. **4.** make a brief or rapid journey. **5.** make regular trips. **6.** be a candidate or contestant. **7.** finish a race in a specified position. **8.** move or pass easily; flow. **9.** elapse; pass. **10.** proceed in direction or extent: This road *runs* north. **11.** move in or as in a stream; flow. **12.** become liquid and flow, as wax; also, spread, as colors when wet. **13.** move or pass into a specified condition: *run* into trouble. **14.** climb or grow in long shoots, as vines. **15.** become torn by unraveling. **16.** suppurate. **17.** leak. **18.** continue or proceed: The dispute *ran* on. **19.** be in operation; work. **20.** continue in existence, effect, action, etc.; extend in time. **21.** proceed; go: The story *runs* as follows. **22.** migrate, as salmon from the sea. **23.** incline; tend. —*v.t.* **24.** lay, build, draw, etc., in or as in a particular course: *run* a road through a wilderness. **25.** go along by running, as a route, course, or path. **26.** make one's way over, through, or past: *run* rapids. **27.** perform or accomplish by or as by running: *run* an errand. **28.** enter (a horse, candidate, etc.) in a race. **29.** drive or force: with *out of, off, into, through,* etc. **30.** move (the eye, hand, etc.) quickly or lightly. **31.** cause to move, slide, etc., as into a specified position. **32.** transport or convey. **33.** smuggle. **34.** cause to flow. **35.** give forth a flow of; emit: Her eyes *ran* tears. **36.** operate, as a machine, vehicle, etc. **37.** direct; oversee. **38.** become liable to; incur: *run* a risk. **39.** publish in a magazine or newspaper: *run* an ad. **40.** suffer from (a fever etc.). —**run across** meet by chance. — **run down 1.** pursue and overtake, as a fugitive. **2.** strike down while moving. **3.** speak of disparagingly; decry. **4.** find the source of; search out. **5.** cease to operate, as a watch. —**run in 1.** insert; include. **2.** *Printing* print without a paragraph or break. **3.** *Slang* arrest and place in confinement. —**run into 1.** meet by chance. **2.** collide with. —**run off 1.** make copies, as with a duplicator, printing press, etc. **2.** decide (a tied race, game, etc.) by the outcome of another, subsequent race, game, etc. **3.** flee or escape; elope. —**run out** come to an end; be exhausted, as supplies. —**run out of** exhaust one's supply of. — **run over 1.** ride or drive over; run down. **2.** overflow. **3.** go over or examine hastily or quickly; rehearse. —**run through 1.** spend wastefully; squander. **2.** stab or pierce. **3.** run over (def.3). —**run up 1.**

allow to continue or mount up, as a bill. **2.** produce; make hurriedly, as on a sewing machine. —*n.* **1.** an act or instance of running or going rapidly. **2.** the movement or gait of running: break into a *run*. **3.** a distance covered by running. **4.** a habitual course or route. **5.** a rapid, brief journey. **6.** an inclined course, as for skiing. **7.** a swift stream or current. **8.** the privilege of free use or access: have the *run* of the place. **9.** a series, succession, or sequence, as of playing cards in consecutive order. **10.** a continuous spell of a specified condition: a *run* of luck. **11.** a continuous period of performances, action, effect, etc. **12.** an unusually great or sustained demand, as for a commodity. **13.** a broadly inclusive category: the general *run* of readers. **14.** a period of continuous operation, as of a machine or factory. **15.** the output during such a period. **16.** a continuous length or extent of something: a *run* of pipe. **17.** a lengthwise rip in knitted fabric. **18.** a mass migration or movement of animals, esp. of fish to spawn. **19.** an enclosure for animals or poultry. **20.** *Music* a rapid succession of tones. **21.** in baseball, the scoring of a point by a player's making a complete circuit of the bases; also, a point so scored. **22.** *Mining* a vein of ore or rock. —**a run for one's money 1.** an instance of demanding competition. **2.** profit or enjoyment for one's efforts. —**in the long run** as the ultimate outcome. — *adj.* **1.** liquefied; melted: *run* butter. **2.** made by a process of melting and casting or molding: *run* metal. [ME *rinnan*]

run·a·round (RUN ə ROWND) *n.* artful deception; evasion.

run·a·way (RUN ə WAY) *adj.* **1.** escaping or escaped; fugitive. **2.** brought about by running away. **3.** easily won, as a horse race. **4.** characterized by a rapid rise, as of prices. — *n.* **1.** one who or that which runs away. **2.** a horse that has broken away from the control of its driver. **3.** an easily won victory, as in a race.

run·down (RUN DOWN) *n.* a summary.

run-down (RUN DOWN) *adj.* **1.** debilitated; tired out. **2.** dilapidated. **3.** stopped because not wound: said of a clock etc.

rung¹ (rung) *n.* **1.** a step of a ladder. **2.** a piece used in chairs to support the legs or back. **3.** a spoke of a wheel. [ME]

rung² past participle of RING².

run-in (RUN IN) *n.* **1.** a quarrel. **2.** *Printing* inserted matter. —*adj. Printing* inserted.

run•nel (RUN l) *n.* a small stream.

run•ner (RUN ər) *n.* **1.** one who or that which runs. **2.** that part on which an object slides: the *runner* of a skate. **3.** *Mech.* a device to assist sliding motion. **4.** any of various fishes of warm and temperate seas. **5.** *Bot.* **a** a slender, trailing stem rooting at the end and nodes, as in the strawberry plant. **b** any of various twining plants. **6.** a long, narrow rug. **7.** a narrow strip of cloth, used on tables etc.

run•ner-up (RUN ər UP) *n. pl.* **•ners-up** a contestant or team finishing in second place.

run•ning (RUN ing) *adj.* **1.** moving or going rapidly. **2.** creeping or clinging, as a plant. **3.** flowing or oozing. **4.** slipping, moving, pulling, etc. easily and freely. **5.** being or able to be in operation: a *running* engine. **6.** liquid or fluid. **7.** in a straight line: three feet *running*. **8.** current, as an account. **9.** continuous; repeated. **10.** accomplished or performed with a run. **11.** of or pertaining to a trip or run. —*adv.* without intermission; in succession. —*n.* **1.** the act of one who or that which runs. **2.** that which runs or flows. **3.** the amount or quantity that runs. **4.** competition or race: He is out of (or in) the *running*.

running knot a knot made so as to slip along a rope etc. and tighten when pulled upon: also called *slipknot*.

running light one of the lights displayed at night by a ship or aircraft.

running mate the candidate for the lesser of two related offices; esp., a vice-presidential candidate.

run•ny (RUN ee) *adj.* **•ni•er, •ni•est 1.** flowing; liquid: *runny* custard. **2.** of the nose, discharging mucus.

run•off (RUN AWF) *n.* **1.** the part of the rainfall that is drained off in streams. **2.** a special contest held to break a tie.

run-of-the-mill (RUN əv thə MIL) *adj.* average; ordinary. Also **run-of-the-mine.**

runt (runt) *n.* **1.** a small or stunted animal or plant. **2.** a small person: often a contemptuous term. —**runt'y** *adj.* **runt•i•er, runt•i•est**

run•way (RUN WAY) *n.* **1.** a way or path over or through which something runs. **2.** a pathway extending from a stage into the audience. **3.** a channel, track, etc. along or in which something runs. **4.** *Aeron.* a road-like surface used for the takeoff and landing of aircraft.

rup•ture (RUP chər) *n.* **1.** the act of breaking apart, or the state of being broken apart. **2.** *Pathol.* abdominal hernia. **3.** breach of friendship or concord. —*v.t. & v.i.* **•tured, •tur•ing 1.** break apart; separate into parts. **2.** cause or suffer a rupture. [< Med.L. *ruptura*]

ru•ral (RUUR əl) *adj.* **1.** of or pertaining to the country; rustic. **2.** of or pertaining to farming or agriculture. [ME]

rural free delivery a government service of house-to-house free mail delivery in rural districts. Abbr. *RFD, R.F.D.*

ruse (rooz) *n.* an action intended to mislead or deceive. [ME]

rush¹ (rush) *v.i.* **1.** move or go swiftly or with violence. **2.** make an attack; charge: with *on* or *upon.* **3.** proceed recklessly or rashly; plunge: with *in* or *into.* **4.** come, surge, flow, etc. suddenly. —*v.t.* **5.** drive or push with haste or violence; hurry. **6.** do or perform hurriedly. **7.** make a sudden assault upon; also, capture by such an assault. **8.** consider for membership in a fraternity or sorority. [ME *ruschen*] —*n.* **1.** the act of rushing. **2.** a state of impatient activity; hurry. **3.** a sudden surge, flow, or outpouring. **4.** a sudden pressing demand. **5.** a sudden or urgent flow or press of traffic, business, etc. **6.** *pl.* in motion pictures, the first film prints of a scene or series of scenes. **7. a** *Slang* the sudden pleasurable feeling experienced after taking a drug. **b** any sudden feeling. —*adj.* **1.** requiring urgency or haste: a *rush* order. **2.** characterized by much traffic, business, etc.

rush² *n.* any one of various grasslike herbs, growing in marshy ground and having pliant, leafless stems, often used for making mats, etc. [ME *rusch*] —**rush'y** *adj.* **rush•i•er, rush•i•est**

rush hour a time of day when traffic is at its height. —**rush'-hour'** *adj.*

rus•set (RUS it) *n.* **1.** a reddish or yellowish brown. **2.** coarse homespun cloth or clothing of this color. **3.** a winter apple of greenish color, mottled with brown. —*adj.* **1.** of the color russet. **2.** made of russet cloth; also, coarse; homespun. [ME]

Rus•sian (RUSH ən) *n.* **1.** a native or citizen of the former Soviet Union or Russian Empire. **2.** the East Slavic language of the Russian people. —**Rus'sian** *adj.*

Russian Orthodox Church an autonomous branch of the Eastern Orthodox Church, under the patriarch of Moscow.

Russian roulette a dangerous game in which a participant spins the cylinder of a revolver containing only one cartridge, aims at the head, and pulls the trigger.

rust (rust) *n.* **1.** the reddish or yellow coating formed on iron and steel by exposure to air and moisture. **2.** any film formed on the surface of a metal by oxidation. **3.** a disease of plants, caused by fungi and characterized by orange or reddish brown spots. **4.** any coating or accretion formed by a corrosive or degenerative process. **5.** any of several shades of reddish brown. —*v.t. & v.i.* **1.** become or cause to become rusty. **2.** contract or cause to contract rust. **3.** become or cause to become weakened or impaired because of inactivity or disuse. **4.** make or become rust-colored. [ME]

rus•tic (RUS tik) *adj.* **1.** typical of or appropriate to simple country life. **2.** plain; simple; homely. **3.** uncultured; rude. **4.** unaffected; artless. —*n.* **1.** one who lives in the country. **2.** a country person of simple manners or character; also, a coarse or clownish person. [ME] —**rus•tic•i•ty** (ru STIS i tee) *n.*

rus•ti•cate (RUS ti KAYT) *v.* **•cat•ed, •cat•ing** *v.i.* **1.** go to the country. **2.** stay or live in the country. —*v.t.* **3.** send or banish to the country. **4.** make rustic. —**rus′ti•ca′ tion** *n.*

rus•tle¹ (RUS əl) *v.t. & v.i.* **•tled, •tling** fall, move, or cause to move with a quick succession of small, light sounds, as dry leaves. [ME *rustlen*] —*n.* a rustling sound. —**rus•tler** (RUS lər) *n.*

rus•tle² *v.t. & v.i.* **•tled, •tling 1.** act with or obtain by energetic or vigorous action. **2.** steal (cattle etc.). —**rus•tler** (RUS lər) *n.*

rust•y (RUS tee) *adj.* **rust•i•er, rust•i•est 1.** covered or affected with rust. **2.** having the color of rust. **3.** impaired by inaction or want of exercise; also, stiff. **4.** ineffective or weakened through neglect; also, having lost skill for want of practice. —**rust′i•ness** *n.*

rut¹ (rut) *n.* **1.** a sunken track worn by a wheel, as in a road; also, a groove forming a path for anything. **2.** a settled habit or course of procedure; routine. —*v.t.* **rut• ted, rut•ting** wear or make a rut or ruts in.

rut² *n.* **1.** the sexual excitement of various animals, esp. of deer and other ruminants; estrus. **2.** the period during which this excitement lasts. —*v.i.* **rut•ted, rut•ting** be in rut. [ME *rutte*]

ruth•less (ROOTH lis) *adj.* having no compassion; merciless. [ME] —**ruth′less•ly** *adv.* —**ruth′less•ness** *n.*

rut•tish (RUT ish) *adj.* disposed to rut; lustful; libidinous.

rye (rī) *n.* **1.** the grain or seeds of a cereal grass closely allied to wheat. **2.** the grass. **3.** whiskey distilled from rye or partly from rye. [ME]

S

s, S (es) *n. pl.* **s's** or **ss, S's** or **Ss 1.** the nineteenth letter of the English alphabet. **2.** the sound represented by the letter *s*, usu. a voiceless sibilant, but often voiced between vowel sounds, as in *easy*. —*symbol* **1.** anything shaped like an S. **2.** *Chem.* sulfur (symbol S).

Sab•bath (SAB əth) *n.* **1.** the seventh day of the week (Saturday), a day of rest observed by Jews and some Christians. **2.** Sunday, the day of rest and worship observed by most Christians. **3.** the institution or observance of a day of rest. [< Hebrew *shabbāth* rest]

sab•bat•i•cal (sə BAT i kəl) *adj.* offering rest. —*n.* a release from normal teaching duties granted in some American educational institutions and intended for study or travel, usu. given every seven years: also **sabbatical year.**

sa•ber (SAY bər) *n.* **1.** a heavy one-edged cavalry sword with a thick-backed blade, often curved. **2.** in fencing, a light swordlike instrument, used for both thrusting and slashing. —*v.t.* strike, wound, or kill with a saber. [< F *sabre*]

sa•ble (SAY bəl) *n. pl.* **•bles 1.** a carnivore of northern Asia and Europe, prized for its valuable fur. **2.** the dressed fur of a sable. **3.** *pl.* a garment made wholly or partly of this fur. **4.** the color black; also, mourning or a mourning garment. —*adj.* **1.** black, esp. as the color of mourning. **2.** made of or having the color of sable fur; dark brown. [ME]

sab•o•tage (SAB ə TAHZH) *n.* **1.** deliberate destruction, as of installations, railways, etc., by enemy agents during a war, or of an employer's property by workers on strike. **2.** any act performed to hamper or obstruct. —*v.* **•taged, •tag•ing** *v.i.* **1.** engage in sabotage. —*v.t.* **2.** damage or destroy by sabotage. [< F]

sab•o•teur (SAB ə TUR) *n.* one who engages in sabotage. [< F]

sa•bra (SAH brə) *n.* a native-born Israeli. [< Modern Hebrew *sabre* cactus]

sac (sak) *n. Biol.* a pouch or receptacle in an animal or plant, as for containing a liquid: the ink *sac* of a squid. [< L *saccus*]

sac•cha•rin (SAK ər in) *n. Chem.* a white crystalline compound, used as a sweetening agent.

sac•cha•rine (SAK ər in) *adj.* cloyingly sweet: a *saccharine* manner.

sac•er•do•tal (SAS ər DOHT l) *adj.* **1.** pertaining to a priest or priesthood; priestly. **2.** believing in the divine authority of the priesthood. [ME]

sa•chem (SAY chəm) *n.* a Native American hereditary chief. [< Algonquian]

sa•chet (sa SHAY) *n.* a small ornamental bag for perfumed powder. [< MF]

sack¹ (sak) *n.* **1.** a bag for holding bulky articles. **2.** a loose jacketlike garment, worn by women and babies: also **sacque. 3.** *Slang* dismissal: esp. in the phrases **get the sack** and **give (someone) the sack. 4.** *Slang* bed. [ME *sak*] —**hit the sack** *Slang* go to bed. —**sack out** *Slang* go to bed. —*v.t.* **1.** put into a sack or sacks. **2.** dismiss.

sack² *v.t.* plunder or pillage (a town or city) after capturing. —*n.* **1.** the pillaging of a captured town or city. **2.** loot or booty obtained by pillage. [< Ital. *sacco* loot]

sack•cloth (SAK KLAWTH) *n.* **1.** a coarse cloth used for making sacks. **2.** coarse cloth worn in penance.

sack•ful (SAK fuul) *n. pl.* **•fuls** enough to fill a sack.

sack•ing (SAK ing) *n.* a coarse cloth made of hemp or flax and used for sacks.

sa•cral¹ (SAY krəl) *adj.* of, pertaining to, or situated near the sacrum. —*n.* a sacral vertebra or nerve.

sa•cral² *adj.* pertaining to sacred rites. [< L *sacrum* sacred thing]

sac•ra•ment (SAK rə mənt) *n.* **1.** *Eccl.* any of certain rites ordained by Christ or by the church, as baptism or the Eucharist. **2.** *Often cap. Eccl.* the Eucharist. [ME] —**sac′ra•men′tal** *adj.*

sa•cred (SAY krid) *adj.* **1.** set apart or dedicated to religious use; hallowed. **2.** pertaining or related to a deity or religion. **3.** consecrated or dedicated to a person or purpose. **4.** entitled to reverence or respect. [ME] —**sa′cred•ness** *n.*

sacred cow something or someone regarded as above criticism or reproach.

sac•ri•fice (SAK rə FIS) *n.* **1.** the act of making an offering to a deity, in worship or atonement; also, that which is so offered. **2.** a giving up of something valued for the sake of something else; also, that which is so given up. **3.** in baseball, a sacrifice hit. —*v.* **•ficed, •fic•ing** *v.t.* **1.** make an offering or sacrifice of, as to a god or deity. **2.** give up (something valued) for the sake of something else. —*v.i.* **3.** make a sacrifice. **4.** make a sacrifice hit. [ME] —**sac•ri•fi•cial** (SAK rə FISH əl) *adj.*

sacrifice fly in baseball, a fly ball that enables a runner on third base to score after the catch.

sacrifice hit in baseball, a bunt that enables a runner or runners to advance a base while the batter is being retired.

sac•ri•lege (SAK rə lij) *n.* the act of violating or profaning anything sacred. [ME] —**sac•ri•le•gious** (SAK rə LEEJ əs) *adj.*

sac•ris•ty (SAK ri stee) *n. pl.* **•ties** a room in a religious house for the sacred vessels and vestments; vestry. [ME]

sac•ro•il•i•ac (SAK roh IL ee AK) *adj. Anat.* pertaining to the sacrum and the ilium and to the joints or ligaments connecting them.

sac•ro•sanct (SAK rə SANGKT) *adj.* extremely sacred; inviolable. [< L *sacro-sanctus*]

sa•crum (SAK rəm) *n. pl.* **sa•cra** (SAK rə) *Anat.* a composite bone formed by the union of five vertebrae, constituting the dorsal part of the pelvis. [< NL]

sad (sad) *adj.* **sad•der, sad•dest 1.** sorrowful or depressed. **2.** causing sorrow or pity; unfortunate. **3.** dark-hued; somber. [ME] —**sad′ly** *adv.*—**sad′ness** *n.*

sad•den (SAD n) *v.t. & v.i.* make or become sad.

sad•dle (SAD l) *n.* **1.** a seat or pad, usu. of leather, for a rider, as on the back of a horse. **2.** the two hindquarters of a carcass, as of mutton or venison. —**in the saddle 1.** in control. **2.** at work. —*v.t.* **•dled, •dling 1.** put a saddle on. **2.** load, as with a burden. [ME *sadel*]

saddle soap a softening and preserving soap for leather.

sa•dism (SAY diz əm) *n.* a sexual perversion in which gratification is obtained by inflicting physical or mental pain on others. [< F *sadisme*] —**sa′dist** *n. & adj.* —**sa•dis•tic** (sə DIS tik) *adj.*

sa•fa•ri (sə FAHR ee) *n. pl.* **•ris** an expedition or journey, esp. for hunting. [< Arabic *safariy* of travel]

safe (sayf) *adj.* **saf•er, saf•est 1.** free from danger or evil. **2.** having escaped injury or damage; unharmed. **3.** not involving risk or

loss. **4.** conferring safety; also, not likely to cause or do harm or injury. **5.** in baseball, having reached base without being retired. [ME *saf*] —*n.* a strong metal receptacle for protecting valuables. —**safe′ly** *adv.* —**safe′ness** *n.*

safe-con•duct (SAYF KON dukt) *n.* an official document intended to ensure protection on a journey or voyage, as in time of war; a passport.

safe•guard (SAYF GAHRD) *n.* one who or that which guards or protects against accident or injury. —*v.t.* defend; protect; guard.

safe•keep•ing (SAYF KEE ping) *n.* the act or state of keeping or being kept in safety; protection.

safe•ty (SAYF tee) *n. pl.* **•ties 1.** freedom from danger or injury. **2.** a device or catch designed as a safeguard, as in a firearm. **3.** in football: **a** a defensive player positioned deep in the backfield. **b** a play in which the ball is grounded by the offense behind its own goal line, the opponent scoring two points. **4.** *Slang* a condom. [ME *sauvete*]

safety belt 1. a strap or strong belt encircling the user and fastened to a fixed object, worn as a safeguard against falling. **2.** a seat belt.

safety glass two sheets of glass having a film of transparent, adhesive plastic tightly pressed between them.

safety valve 1. *Mech.* a valve in a steam boiler etc. for automatically relieving excessive pressure. **2.** any outlet for pent-up energy or emotion.

sag (sag) *v.* **sagged, sag•ging** *v.i.* **1.** bend or sink downward, esp. in the middle. **2.** hang unevenly. **3.** weaken, as from exhaustion or depression: *His spirits sagged.* —*v.t.* **4.** cause to sag. [ME *saggen*]—*n.* **1.** a sagging. **2.** a sagging or sunken place or part.

sa•ga (SAH gə) *n.* **1.** a medieval Icelandic story dealing with legendary or historical Scandinavian heroes and their exploits. **2.** a long story, often telling the history of a family. [< ON]

sa•ga•cious (sə GAY shəs) *adj.* characterized by discernment, shrewdness, and wisdom.] —**sa•ga′cious•ly** *adv.* —**sa•gac′i•ty** (sə GAS i tee) *n.* [< L *sagacitas* wisdom]

sage[1] (sayj) *n.* a person of wisdom and prudence. —*adj.* **sag•er, sag•est** wise; prudent. [ME] —**sage′ly** *adv.*

sage[2] *n.* **1.** a plant of the mint family, having gray-green leaves used for flavoring meats.

2. the leaves of this plant. **3.** the sagebrush. [ME *sauge*]

sage·brush (SAYJ BRUSH) *n.* a small, aromatic shrub, widely distributed on the plains of the western U.S.

sa·gua·ro (sə WAHR oh) *n. pl.* **·ros** a large desert cactus with an erect, columnar trunk and strong spines. [< Mexican Sp.]

sa·hib (SAH ib) *n.* master; sir: used in India and Pakistan for people of rank and, esp. formerly, for Europeans. [< Urdu]

said (sed) past tense, past participle of SAY.

sail (sayl) *n. pl.* **sails;** *for def. 2, often* sail **1.** *Naut.* a piece of strong material attached to a vessel's mast for propulsion by catching the wind. **2.** a sailing vessel or craft. **3.** a trip in any watercraft. **4.** anything resembling a sail. —*v.i.* **1.** move across the water by the action of wind or mechanical power. **2.** travel over water in a ship or boat. **3.** manage a sailing craft. **4.** glide or float in the air. —*v.t.* **5.** move or travel across the surface of (a body of water) in a ship or boat. **6.** navigate (a ship etc.). [ME] —**sail'a·ble** *adj.*

sail·boat (SAYL BOHT) *n.* a small boat propelled by a sail or sails.

sail·cloth (SAYL KLAWTH) *n.* a very strong cotton canvas suitable for sails.

sail·or (SAY lər) *n.* a seaman; mariner.

saint (saynt) *n.* **1.** a holy or godly person. **2.** in certain churches, such a person who has died and been canonized. **3.** any one of the blessed in heaven. **4.** a patient, unselfish person. [ME] —**saint'ed** *adj.* —**saint' hood** (SAYNT huud) *n.*

Saint For entries not found under *Saint,* see under ST.

Saint Bernard a working dog of great size and strength, used formerly to rescue travelers.

saint·ly (SAYNT lee) *adj.* **·li·er, ·li·est** like, concerned with, or suitable for a saint. —**saint'li·ness** *n.*

Saint Patrick's Day March 17, a day celebrated by the Irish in honor of their patron saint.

Saint Valentine's Day February 14, the anniversary of the martyrdom of St. Valentine, and a day when valentines are exchanged.

sake[1] (sayk) *n.* **1.** purpose; aim; intent. **2.** interest; account; advantage: for your own *sake.* [ME]

sa·ke[2] (SAH kee) *n.* a fermented liquor made in Japan from rice. [< Jap.]

sa·laam (sə LAHM) *n.* **1.** an oriental greeting made with a low bow, the palm of the

right hand being held to the forehead. **2.** a respectful or ceremonious greeting. —*v.t. & v.i.* greet with or make a salaam. [< Arabic *salām* peace]

sal·a·ble (SAY lə bəl) *adj.* such as can be sold; marketable; also spelled *saleable.* —**sal'a·bil'i·ty** *n.*

sa·la·cious (sə LAY shəs) *adj.* **1.** lustful; lewd. **2.** obscene: a *salacious* joke. [< L *salax* lustful] —**sa·la'cious·ly** *adv.* —**sa·la'cious·ness** *n.*

sal·ad (SAL əd) *n.* **1.** green herbs or vegetables, served with a dressing. **2.** cold meat or fish, eggs, etc. served with a dressing. **3.** a similar dish made with fruit. [ME *salade*]

sal·a·man·der (SAL ə MAN dər) *n.* a lizardlike amphibian having a smooth, moist skin. [ME *salamandre*]

sa·la·mi (sə LAH mee) *n.* a salted, spiced sausage, originally Italian. [< Ital.]

sal·a·ry (SAL ə ree) *n. pl.* **·ries** a periodic, fixed payment for services or work. [ME *salarie*] —*v.t.* **·ried, ·ry·ing** pay a salary to. —**sal'a·ried** *adj.*

sale (sayl) *n.* **1.** the exchange or transfer of property for money. **2.** an auction. **3.** the selling of something at bargain prices. **4.** opportunity of selling; market. [ME]

sale·a·ble (SAY lə bəl) see SALABLE.

sales·girl (SAYLS GURL) see SALESWOMAN.

sales·man (SAYLS mən) *n. pl.* **·men** a man hired to sell goods, services, etc.

sales·man·ship (SAYLZ mən SHIP) *n.* ability or skill in selling.

sales·peo·ple (SAYLZ PEE pəl) *n.pl.* salespersons.

sales·per·son (SAYLZ PUR sən) *n.* a person hired to sell merchandise in a store.

sales·room (SAYLZ ROOM) *n.* a room where merchandise is displayed for sale.

sales·wom·an (SAYLZ WUUM ən) *n. pl.* **·wom·en** a woman or girl hired to sell merchandise in a store. Also **sales'la'dy.**

sa·li·ent (SAYL yənt) *adj.* **1.** standing out prominently; conspicuous. **2.** protruding; projecting. —*n.* the part of a fortification or line of defense that protrudes most toward the enemy. [< L *salire* leap] —**sa'li·ence** *n.* —**sa'li·ent·ly** *adv.*

sa·line (SAY leen) *adj.* made of, characteristic of, or containing salt; salty. —*n.* **1.** a metallic salt. **2.** a salt solution. [ME] —**sa·lin·i·ty** (sə LIN i tee) *n.*

sa·li·va (sə LĪ və) *n. Physiol.* the fluid, secreted by the glands of the mouth, that promotes digestion. [< L] —**sal·i·var·y** (SAL ə VER ee) *adj.*

sal·i·vate (SAL ə VAYT) *v.* **·vat·ed, ·vat·ing** *v.i.* secrete saliva. —*v.t.* produce an abnormally increased flow of saliva in. — **sal′i·va′tion** *n.*

sal·low (SAL oh) *adj.* of an unhealthy yellowish color. [ME *salowe*] —**sal′low·ness** *n.*

sal·ly (SAL ee) *v.i.* **·lied, ·ly·ing 1.** rush out suddenly. **2.** set out energetically. —*n. pl.* **·lies 1.** a rushing forth, as of troops against besiegers; sortie. **2.** a bantering remark or witticism. **3.** a walk or other short excursion. [< MF *saillie* attack]

sal·ma·gun·di (SAL mə GUN dee) *n.* **1.** a saladlike dish of chopped meat, anchovies, oil, etc. **2.** any medley or mixture. [< MF *salmingondin*]

salm·on (SAM ən) *n.* **1.** any of various food fishes with pinkish flesh. **2.** a reddish or pinkish orange color: also **salmon pink.** — *adj.* having a salmon color. [ME *salmoun*]

sa·lon (sə LAHN) *n.* **1.** a room in which guests are received; a drawing room. **2.** a gathering of noted persons. **3.** an establishment devoted to some specific purpose: a *beauty salon.* [< F]

sa·loon (sə LOON) *n.* **1.** a place where alcoholic drinks are sold; a bar. **2.** a room for assemblies etc. [< F *salon*]

salt (sawlt) *n.* **1.** a crystalline compound used as a seasoning and preservative; sodium chloride. ◆ Collateral adjective: *saline.* **2.** *Chem.* any compound consisting of the positive ion of a base and the negative ion of an acid. **3.** *pl.* a salt used as a laxative or cathartic; also, *smelling salts.* **4.** *Informal* a sailor: an old *salt.* —**take with a grain of salt** have doubts about. —*adj.* **1.** flavored with salt; briny. **2.** cured or preserved with salt. —*v.t.* **1.** season, preserve, or cure with salt. **2.** furnish with salt: *salt cattle.* —**salt away** store up; save. [ME] —**salt′ed** *adj.* —**salt′i·ness** *n.* —**salt′y** *adj.* **·i·er, ·i·est**

salt·cel·lar (SAWLT SEL ər) *n.* a small receptacle for salt. [ME]

salt lick 1. a place, as a salt spring or dried salt pond, to which animals go to lick salt. **2.** a block of salt provided for cattle, deer, etc.

salt·wa·ter (SAWLT WAW tər) *adj.* of composed of, or living in salty water.

sa·lu·bri·ous (sə LOO bree əs) *adj.* conducive to health. [< L *salubris* promoting health] —**sa·lu′bri·ous·ly** *adv.* —**sa·lu′ bri·ous·ness** *n.*

sal·u·tar·y (SAL yə TER ee) *adj.* **1.** beneficial. **2.** salubrious. [< L *salutaris*]

sal·u·ta·tion (SAL yə TAY shən) *n.* **1.** the act of saluting. **2.** any form of greeting. **3.** the opening words of a letter, as *Dear Sir.*

sa·lute (sə LOOT) *n.* **1.** a greeting by display of military or other official honors. **2.** the act of or attitude assumed in giving a military salute. **3.** a gesture of greeting. —*v.* **·lut·ed, ·lut·ing** *v.t.* **1.** greet with a sign of welcome, respect, etc. **2.** honor in some prescribed way, as by raising the hand to the cap. —*v.i.* **3.** make a salute. [ME *saluten* greet]

sal·vage (SAL vij) *v.t.* **·vaged, ·vag·ing** save from loss or destruction. —*n.* **1.** the saving of a ship, cargo, etc. from loss. **2.** any act of saving property. **3.** compensation to persons who save a vessel, its cargo, or the lives of those belonging to it. **4.** that which is saved, as from a fire. [< F] —**sal′ vage·a·ble** *adj.*

sal·va·tion (sal VAY shən) *n.* **1.** the process or state of being saved. **2.** *Theol.* deliverance from sin and its penalty. **3.** that which saves. [ME *salvatioun*]

salve (sav) *n.* an ointment for local ailments. —*v.t.* **salved, salv·ing 1.** dress with ointment. **2.** soothe; appease. [ME]

sal·vo (SAL voh) *n. pl.* **·vos, ·voes** a simultaneous or successive firing of artillery. [< Ital.]

same (saym) *adj.* **1.** having specific identity as the very one; identical: with *the.* **2.** similar in kind, quality, or quantity; equivalent. —*pron.* the same person, thing, etc. —*adj.* in like manner; equally: with *the.* [ME] — **same′ness** *n.*

sam·o·var (SAM ə VAHR) *n.* a metal urn for heating water, as for making tea. [< Russ., lit., self-boiler]

sam·pan (SAM pan) *n.* a small flat-bottomed boat used along rivers and coasts of the Far East. [< Chinese *sanban* three-board (boat)]

sam·ple (SAM pəl) *n.* a portion, part, or piece shown as a representative of the whole. —*v.t.* **·pled, ·pling** test or examine by means of a sample. [ME]

sam·pler[1] (SAM plər) *n.* one who tests by sampling.

sam·pler[2] *n.* a piece of needlework, originally designed to show a beginner's skill. [ME *samplere*]

sam·pling (SAM pling) *n.* a small part of

something selected for analysis in order to estimate the nature of the whole.

sam·u·rai (SAM uu RĪ) *n. pl.* **·rai** under the Japanese feudal system, a member of the soldier class of the lower nobility; also, the class itself. [< Jap.]

san·a·to·ri·um (SAN ə TOR ee əm) *n. pl.* **·ri·ums** or **·ri·a** (-ree ə) **1.** an institution for the treatment and care of invalids and convalescents. **2.** sanitarium. [< NL]

sanc·ti·fy (SANGK tə FĪ) *v.t.* **·fied, ·fy·ing 1.** set apart as holy; consecrate. **2.** purify or make holy. [< LL *sanctificare*] — **sanc'ti·fi·ca'tion** *n.*

sanc·ti·mo·ni·ous (SANGK tə MOH nee əs) *adj.* making a display of devoutness. — **sanc'ti·mo'ni·ous·ly** *adv.* — **sanc'ti·mo'ni·ous·ness** *n.*

sanc·ti·mo·ny (SANGK tə MOH nee) *n. a* display of holiness or devoutness. [< L *sanctimonia* holiness]

sanc·tion (SANGK shən) *v.t.* **1.** approve; confirm. **2.** countenance; allow. —*n.* **1.** approval; confirmation. **2.** a measure adopted to force a nation that is violating international law to desist. [< L *sanctus* made holy]

sanc·ti·ty (SANGK ti tee) *n. pl.* **·ties 1.** the state of being sanctified; holiness. **2.** sacredness. [ME *sauntite*]

sanc·tu·ar·y (SANGK choo ER ee) *n. pl.* **·ar·ies 1.** a holy or sacred place. **2.** the most sacred place in a sacred structure. **3.** a place of refuge; also, immunity. [ME]

sanc·tum (SANGK təm) *n. pl.* **·tums, ·ta** (tə) a private room where one is not to be disturbed. [< L, holy]

sand (sand) *n.* **1.** a hard, granular rock material. **2.** *pl.* stretches of sandy beach, desert, etc. **3.** *pl.* sandy grains in an hourglass. — *v.t.* **1.** sprinkle or cover with sand. **2.** smooth or polish with sandpaper or other abrasive. [ME] —**sand'y** *adj.* **sand·i·er, sand·i·est**

san·dal (SAN dl) *n.* **1.** a foot covering, consisting of a sole held to the foot by thongs. **2.** a light slipper. [< F *sandale*] —**san'daled** *adj.*

sand bar a ridge of sand in rivers, along beaches, etc., formed by the action of currents or tides.

sand·blast (SAND BLAST) *n.* a fine jet of sand, propelled under pressure and used to clean, grind, or decorate hard surfaces. — *v.t.* clean or engrave by means of a sandblast.

sand-cast (SAND KAST) *v.t.* **-cast, -cast·ing** make (a casting) by pouring metal into a mold of sand.

sand·hog (SAND HOG) *n.* one who works in a caisson to build underwater tunnels.

sand·pa·per (SAND PAY pər) *n.* heavy paper coated with sand for smoothing or polishing. —*v.t.* rub or polish with sandpaper.

sand·stone (SAND STOHN) *n.* a rock consisting chiefly of quartz sand cemented with silica, feldspar, lime, or clay.

sand·storm (SAND STORM) *n.* a high wind that propels masses of sand or dust.

sand·wich (SAND wich) *n.* **1.** two slices of bread with meat, cheese, etc. between them. **2.** any combination of dissimilar things pressed together. —*v.t.* place between two layers or objects. [after the fourth Earl of *Sandwich*]

sane (sayn) *adj.* **san·er, san·est 1.** mentally sound; not deranged. **2.** proceeding from a sound mind. [< L *sanus* healthy] —**sane'ly** *adv.*

sang (sang) past tense of SING.

sang-froid (sahn FRWAH) *n.* calmness amid trying circumstances; coolness; composure. [< F, lit., cold blood]

san·gri·a (sang GREE ə) *n.* red wine flavored with fruit juices. [< Sp. *sangría*]

san·gui·nar·y (SANG gwə NER ee) *adj.* **1.** involving bloodshed. **2.** bloodthirsty.

san·guine (SANG gwin) *adj.* **1.** full of hope and cheer. **2.** ruddy; robust. [< L *sanguineus* bloody] —**san'guine·ly** *adv.* — **san'guine·ness** *n.*

san·i·tar·i·um (SAN i TAIR ee əm) *n. pl.* **·tar·i·ums** or **·tar·i·a** (-TAIR ee ə) sanatorium. [< NL]

san·i·tar·y (SAN i TER ee) *adj.* **1.** having to do with health. **2.** favorable to health; clean. [< F *sanitaire*]

sanitary napkin an absorbent pad worn by women during menstruation.

san·i·ta·tion (SAN i TAY shən) *n.* the use of sanitary measures favorable to health.

san·i·tize (SAN i TĪZ) *v.t.* **·tized, ·tiz·ing** make sanitary.

san·i·ty (SAN i tee) *n.* the state of being sane; soundness of mind. [ME *sanite*]

sank (sangk) a past tense of SINK.

sans (sanz) *prep.* without. [< F]

San·sei (SAHN say) *n.* an American of Japanese descent whose grandparents settled in the U.S. [< Jap., third generation]

San·skrit (SAN skrit) *n.* the ancient and classical language of the Hindus of India, belonging to the Indic branch of the Indo-Iranian subfamily of Indo-European languages. [< Skt. *samskrta* perfected]

sans ser·if (san SER əf) *Printing* a type face without serifs: also called *gothic*.

sap¹ (sap) *n.* **1.** in plants, the juices that contain and transport the materials necessary to growth. **2.** any vital fluid. **3.** *Slang* a foolish or gullible person. [ME] —**sap′less** *adj.*

sap² *v.t.* **sapped, sap·ping 1.** weaken or destroy gradually; exhaust. **2.** undermine (an enemy fortification) by digging a trench or tunnel. [< Ital. *zappa* spade] —**sap′ per** *n.*

sa·pi·ent (SAY pee ənt) *adj.* wise; sagacious. [ME *sapyent*] —**sa′pi·ence** *n.*

sap·ling (SAP ling) *n.* **1.** a young tree. **2.** a youth. [ME]

sap·o·na·ceous (sap ə NAY shəs) *adj.* soapy. [< NL *saponaceus*]

sa·pon·i·fy (sə PON i FĪ) *v.t.* **·fied, ·fy·ing** *Chem.* convert (a fat or oil) into soap by the action of an alkali. [< F *saponifier*] —**sa·pon′i·fi·ca′tion** *n.*

sap·phire (SAF īr) *n.* **1.** a deep blue gem. **2.** deep, pure blue. [ME *safir*]

sap·wood (SAP wuud) *n. Bot.* the new wood next to the bark of a tree.

Sar·a·cen (SAR ə sən) *n.* **1.** originally, a nomad Arab of the Syrian-Arabian desert. **2.** a Muslim, esp. during the Crusades. [ME]

sar·casm (SAHR kaz əm) *n.* an ironical or scornful utterance; contemptuous and taunting language. [< F *sarcasme*] —**sar·cas·tic** (sahr KAS tik) *adj.* —**sar·cas′ ti·cal·ly** *adv.*

sar·co·ma (sahr KOH mə) *n. pl.* **·mas, ·ma·ta** (-mə tə) *Pathol.* a malignant tumor, made up of cells resembling those of embryonic connective tissue. [< NL] —**sar·co·ma·tous** (sahr KOH mə təs) *adj.*

sar·coph·a·gus (sahr KOG ə gəs) *n. pl.* **·gi** (-jī) a stone coffin, often large and ornamental. [< L]

sar·dine (sahr DEEN) *n.* a small, herringlike fish commonly preserved in oil as a food. [ME *sardeine*]

sar·don·ic (sahr DON ik) *adj.* scornful or derisive; mocking. [< F *sardonique*] —**sar·don′i·cal·ly** *adv.*

sar·gas·so (sahr GAS oh) *n. pl.* **·sos** an olive-brown seaweed having small air bladders on its stalks, native in tropical American waters. Also **sar·gas′sum** (-əm) [< Pg.]

sa·ri (SAHR ee) *n. pl.* **·ris** the principal garment of Hindu women, made of a long piece of cloth and worn round the body from the head or shoulder to the feet. [< Hind. *sarī*]

sa·rong (sə RONG) *n.* a skirtlike garment of colored silk or cotton cloth worn by both sexes in the Malay Archipelago, etc. [< Malay *sārung*]

sar·sa·pa·ril·la (SAS pə RIL ə) *n.* **1.** the dried roots of certain tropical American climbing plants. **2.** a medicinal preparation or a beverage made from such roots. [< Sp. *zarzaparilla*]

sar·to·ri·al (sahr TOR ee əl) *adj.* **1.** pertaining to a tailor or tailoring. **2.** pertaining to men's clothes. [< LL *sartor* tailor]

sash¹ (sash) *n.* an ornamental band or scarf worn around the waist or over the shoulder. [< Arabic *shāsh* turban]

sash² *n.* a frame, as of a window, in which glass is set. —*v.t.* furnish with a sash.

sa·shi·mi (SAHSH ə mee) *n.* a dish of sliced raw fish. [< Jap.]

sas·sa·fras (SAS ə FRAS) *n.* **1.** a tree of the laurel family. **2.** the root bark of this tree, used for flavoring and yielding a volatile oil. [< Sp. *sasafrás*]

sas·sy (SAS ee) *adj.* **·si·er, ·si·est** *Informal* saucy; impertinent.

sat (sat) past tense of SIT.

Sa·tan (SAYT n) in the Bible, the great adversary of God and tempter of mankind; the Devil. [< Hebrew *sātān* enemy]

sa·tan·ic (sə TAN ik) *adj.* devilish; infernal; wicked. Also **sa·tan′i·cal.**

satch·el (SACH əl) *n.* a small handbag or suitcase. [ME *sachel* sack]

sate (sayt) *v.t.* **sat·ed, sat·ing** satisfy the appetite of; satiate. [< OE *sadian*]

sat·el·lite (SAT l īt) *n.* **1.** *Astron.* a smaller body revolving round a larger one; a moon. **2.** any obsequious attendant. **3.** a small nation that is dependent on a great power. **4.** any manufactured object revolving around the earth. [< MF]

sa·ti·a·ble (SAY shə bəl) *adj.* capable of being satiated. —**sa′ti·a·bil′i·ty** *n.*

sa·ti·ate (SAY shee AYT) *v.t.* **·at·ed, ·at·ing 1.** satisfy the appetite or desire of; gratify. **2.** fill or gratify beyond natural desire; glut. —*adj.* (SAY shee it) filled to satiety; satiated. [< L *satiatus* satisfied] —**sa′ti·a′tion** *n.*

sa·ti·e·ty (se TĪ ə tee) *n.* the state of being satiated. [< MF *societé*]

sat·in (SAT n) *n.* a fabric of silk, rayon, etc. of thick texture, with glossy face and dull back.

—*adj.* of or resembling satin; glossy; smooth. [ME *satyne*] —**sat′in•y** *adj.*

sat•ire (SAT īr) *n.* **1.** sarcasm, irony, or wit used to ridicule or expose abuses or follies. **2.** a written composition in which satire is used. [< MF] —**sa•tir•ic** (sə TIR ik) or **•i•cal** *adj.* —**sa•tir′i•cal•ly** *adv.* —**sat′i•r•ist** (SAT ər ist) *n.* —**sat′i•rize** (SAT ə RĪZ) *v.t.*

sat•is•fac•tion (SAT is FAK shən) *n.* **1.** the act of satisfying, or the state of being satisfied; gratification. **2.** the making of amends, reparation, or payment. **3.** that which satisfies.

sat•is•fac•to•ry (SAT is FAK tə ree) *adj.* giving satisfaction; answering all requirements. —**sat′is•fac′to•ri•ly** *adv.*

sat•is•fy (SAT is FĪ) *v.* **•fied, •fy•ing** *v.t.* **1.** supply fully with what is desired, expected, or needed; gratify. **2.** free from doubt or anxiety; convince. **3.** give what is due to. **4.** pay or discharge (a debt, obligation, etc.). **5.** answer sufficiently or convincingly, as a question or objection. **6.** fulfill the conditions or requirements of. —*v.i.* **7.** give satisfaction. [ME *satisfien*] —**sat′is•fy′ing•ly** *adv.*

sa•trap (SAY trap) *n.* **1.** a governor of a province in ancient Persia. **2.** a subordinate, often despotic, ruler or governor. [ME] —**sa•trap•y** (SAY trə pee) *n. pl.* **•trap•ies**

sat•u•rate (SACH ə RAYT) *v.t.* **•rat•ed, •rat•ing** **1.** soak thoroughly. **2.** fill or charge (something) to capacity. [< L *saturatus* filled] —**sat•u•ra•ble** (SACH ər ə bəl) *adj.* —**sat′u•ra′tion** *n.*

Sat•ur•day (SAT ər DAY) *n.* the seventh day of the week; the Sabbath day as observed by Jews and certain Christians. [ME *Saturdai*]

Sat•urn (SAT ərn) *n.* the second largest planet of the solar system and sixth in order from the sun. [after *Saturnus,* Roman god of agriculture] —**Sa•tur•ni•an** (sə TUR nee ən) *adj.* **1.** pertaining to Saturn. **2.** prosperous; happy.

sat•ur•na•li•a (SAT ər NAY lee ə) *n.* (*Usu. construed as sing.*) any season or period of license or revelry. [< L *Saturnalia*] —**sat′ur•na′li•an** *adj.*

sat•ur•nine (SAT ər nīn) *adj.* having a grave, gloomy, or morose disposition or character. [ME]

sa•tyr (SAY tər) *n.* **1.** in classical mythology, a lecherous woodland deity in human form, having pointed ears, goat's legs, and budding horns. **2.** a lascivious man. [ME] —**sa•tyr•ic** (sə TIR ik) or **•i•cal** *adj.*

sauce (saws) *n.* **1.** a dressing or liquid relish for food. **2.** a dish of fruit pulp stewed and sweetened. **3.** *Informal* pertness, impudence. **4.** *Slang* whiskey: on the *sauce.* —*v.t.* **sauced, sauc•ing 1.** flavor with sauce; season. **2.** give zest to. **3.** *Informal* be saucy to. [ME]

sauce•pan (SAWS PAN) *n.* a pan with projecting handle, for cooking food.

sau•cer (SAW sər) *n.* a small dish for holding a cup. [ME]

sau•cy (SAW see) *adj.* **•ci•er, •ci•est 1.** disrespectful to superiors; impudent. **2.** piquant; sprightly; amusing. —**sau′ci•ly** *adv.* —**sau′ci•ness** *n.*

sau•er•bra•ten (SOW ər BRAHT n) *n.* beef marinated in vinegar before cooking. [< G]

sau•er•kraut (SOW ər KROWT) *n.* shredded and salted cabbage fermented in its own juice. [< G]

sau•na (SAW nə) *n.* **1.** a room or house for taking steam baths in steam produced by throwing water on hot stones; also, such a steam bath. **2.** a dry heat bath; also, the room for such baths. [< Finnish]

saun•ter (SAWN tər) *v.i.* walk in a leisurely way; stroll. —*n.* **1.** a slow, aimless manner of walking. **2.** an idle stroll.

sau•sage (SAW sij) *n.* chopped and highly seasoned meat, commonly stuffed into casings. [ME *sausige*]

sau•té (soh TAY) *v.t.* **•téed, •té•ing** fry quickly in a little fat. [< F] —*n.* a sautéed dish.

sav•age (SAV ij) *adj.* **1.** having a wild nature; not domesticated. **2.** ferocious; fierce. **3.** primitive or uncivilized: *savage* tribes. **4.** vicious; cruel. —*n.* **1.** a primitive or uncivilized human being. **2.** a brutal, fierce, and cruel person. —*v.t.* **•aged, •ag•ing** attack savagely. [ME *sauvage*] —**sav′age•ly** *adv.* —**sav′age•ness** *n.* —**sav′age•ry** *n.*

sa•van•na (sə VAN ə) *n.* tropical or subtropical grassland, with trees and spiny shrubs. Also **sa•van′nah.** [Earlier *zavana* < Sp.]

sa•vant (sa VAHNT) *n.* a person of exceptional learning. [< F, scholar]

save[1] (sayv) *v.* **saved, sav•ing** *v.t.* **1.** preserve or rescue from danger, harm, wear, etc. **2.** keep from being spent or lost. **3.** set aside for future use; accumulate. **4.** *Theol.* rescue from sin and its penalties; redeem. —*v.i.* **5.** avoid waste; be economical. [ME *saven*]

save² *prep. & conj.* except; but. [ME]

sav·ing (SAY ving) *adj.* that saves. —*n.* **1.** preservation from loss or danger. **2.** avoidance of waste; economy. **3.** the extent of something saved. **4.** *pl.* sums of money not spent. —*prep.* with the exception of; save. —*conj.* except; but.

sav·ior (SAYV yər) *n.* one who saves. Also **sav'iour.** [ME *saveour*]

Sav·ior (SAYV yər) *n.* Jesus Christ.

sa·voir-faire (SAV wahr FAIR) *French* knowledge of what to say and what to do; tact.

sa·vor (SAY vər) *n.* **1.** flavor or aroma. **2.** specific quality. **3.** relish; zest. —*v.i.* **1.** have a specified flavor, aroma, or quality: with *of.* —*v.t.* **2.** give flavor to; season. **3.** taste or enjoy with pleasure; relish. [ME *savour*] —**sa'vor·er** *n.* —**sa'vor·less** *adj.* tasteless; insipid.

sa·vor·y¹ (SAY və ree) *adj.* **1.** of an agreeable flavor and odor; appetizing. **2.** piquant to the taste. **3.** in good repute; respectable. —*n. Brit.* a small, hot serving of food eaten at the end or beginning of a dinner. [ME *savori*] —**sa'vor·i·ness** *n.*

sa·vor·y² *n.* a hardy aromatic herb used for seasoning. Also **summer savory.** [ME *saverey*]

sav·vy (SAV ee) *Informal v.i.* **·vied, ·vy·ing** understand. —*n.* understanding; good sense. [< Sp. *sabe* know]

saw¹ (saw) *n.* a cutting instrument having pointed teeth along the blade, used to cut wood etc. —*v.* **sawed, sawed** or **sawn, saw·ing** *v.t.* **1.** cut, shape, or fashion with a saw. —*v.i.* **2.** use a saw. **3.** be cut with a saw: This wood *saws* easily. [ME *sawe*]

saw² *n.* a proverbial or familiar saying; old maxim. [ME]

saw³ past tense of SEE¹.

saw·dust (SAW DUST) *n.* small particles of wood produced by sawing.

saw·horse (SAW HORS) *n.* a frame on which to rest wood for sawing.

saw·mill (SAW MIL.) *n.* an establishment for sawing logs with power-driven machinery.

sawn (sawn) alternative past participle of SAW¹.

saw-toothed (SAW TOOTHT) *adj.* toothed or notched like a saw; serrate.

saw·yer (SAW yər) *n.* one whose occupation is the sawing of wood. [ME *sawier*]

Sax·on (SAK sən) *n.* **1.** a member of a Germanic tribe that formerly inhabited northwestern Germany and invaded England in the fifth and sixth centuries A.D. **2.** an Anglo-Saxon. —*adj.* **1.** of or pertaining to the Saxons or their language. **2.** Anglo-Saxon; English. [ME]

sax·o·phone (SAK sə FOHN) *n.* a metal wind instrument having a single reed. [after A.J. *Sax,* 1814–94, Belgian instrument maker] —**sax'o·phon'ist** *n.*

say (say) *v.t.* **said, say·ing 1.** pronounce or utter; speak. **2.** declare or express in words. **3.** state positively or as an opinion: *Say* which you prefer. **4.** report; allege. **5.** assume; suppose. —**that is to say** in other words. —*n.* **1.** right or turn to speak: have one's *say.* **2.** authority: have the final *say* in the matter. —*interj.* an exclamation to command attention, show surprise, etc. [ME *seyen*]

say·ing (SAY ing) *n.* **1.** a maxim; adage. **2.** something said.

says (sez) third person singular, present indicative of SAY.

say-so (SAY soh) *n.* **1.** an assertion or decision. **2.** right or power to make decisions.

scab (skab) *n.* **1.** a crust formed on the surface of a wound or sore. **2.** *Vet.* scabies. **3.** a plant disease characterized by a roughened or warty appearance. **4.** a worker who will not join or act with a labor union; strikebreaker. —*v.i.* **scabbed, scab·bing 1.** form or become covered with a scab. **2.** take the job of a striker. [ME]

scab·bard (SKAB ərd) *n.* a sheath for a weapon, as for a bayonet or a sword. [ME *scalburde*]

scab·by (SKAB ee) *adj.* **·bi·er, ·bi·est 1.** having, consisting of, or resembling a scab or scabs. **2.** having scab. **3.** *Informal* contemptible. —**scab'bi·ness** *n.*

sca·bies (SKAY beez) *n.* **1.** a skin disease caused by a mite; itch. **2.** *Vet.* a similar skin disease of cattle and sheep: also called *scab.* [ME]

scab·rous (SKAB rəs) *adj.* **1.** roughened with minute points; scurfy. **2.** off-color; risqué. [< L *scaber* rough] —**sca'brous·ness** *n.*

scads (skadz) *n.pl. Informal* a large amount or quantity.

scaf·fold (SKAF əld) *n.* **1.** a structure for the support of workers, materials, etc., as in building. **2.** a platform for the execution of criminals. —*v.t.* furnish or support with a scaffold. [ME *scaffot*]

scaf·fold·ing (SKAF əl ding) *n.* a scaffold or

system of scaffolds, or the materials for constructing them.

scal·a·wag (SKAL ə WAG) *n.* a worthless person; scamp.

scald (skawld) *v.t.* **1.** burn with or as with hot liquid or steam. **2.** cleanse or treat with boiling water. **3.** heat (a liquid) to a point just short of boiling. —*v.i.* **4.** be or become scalded. —*n.* **1.** a burn to the skin by a hot liquid. **2.** a destructive parasitic disease of plants. [ME *scalden*]

scale[1] (skayl) *n.* **1.** one of the thin, horny, membranous or bony outgrowths of the skin of various animals, as most fishes. **2.** any similar thin formation, piece, or part. **3.** *Metall.* the coating of oxide that forms on heated iron etc. —*v.* **scaled, scal·ing** *v.t.* **1.** strip or clear of scales. —*v.i.* **2.** come off in scales; peel. [ME]

scale[2] *n.* **1.** an instrument bearing accurately spaced lines or gradations for use in measurement. **2.** any system of designating units of measurement: the Celsius *scale.* **3.** a fixed proportion used in determining measurements or dimensions: a *scale* of one inch to the mile. **4.** *Music* an arrangement of tones in ascending or descending order through the interval of an octave. —*v.* **scaled, scal·ing** *v.t.* **1.** climb to the top of. **2.** make according to a scale. **3.** regulate or adjust according to a scale or ratio. —*v.i.* **4.** climb; ascend. **5.** rise in steps or stages. [ME] —**scal'a·ble** *adj.*

scale[3] *n.* **1.** any weighing machine. **2.** a pan, platform, etc. that holds something to be weighed in a balance. **3.** *Usu. pl.* a balance (defs. 1 & 2). —**turn the scales** determine; decide. —*v.t. & v.i.* **scaled, scal·ing** weigh or be weighed in scales. [ME]

scale insect one of many small insects that feed on plants and as adults have a scalelike, protective shield.

scal·lop (SKOL əp) *n.* **1.** a bivalve mollusk having a rounded, ridged shell whose valves are snapped together in swimming. **2.** an edible muscle of certain species of this mollusk. **3.** one of a series of semicircular curves along an edge, as for ornament. —*v.t.* **1.** shape the edge of with scallops. **2.** bake (food) in a casserole. [ME *scalop*]

scalp (skalp) *n.* the skin of the top and back of the human skull, usu. covered with hair. —*v.t.* **1.** cut or tear the scalp from. **2.** *Informal* buy and resell (tickets) at prices above the established rate. —*v.i.* **3.** *Informal* scalp tickets etc. [ME] —**scalp'er** *n.*

scal·pel (SKAL pəl) *n.* a small pointed knife with a very sharp, thin blade, used in dissection and in surgery. [< L *scalpellus* small chisel]

scal·y (SKAY lee) *adj.* **scal·i·er, scal·i·est** having or resembling scales. —**scal'i·ness** *n.*

scamp (skamp) *n.* a rogue; good-for-nothing. —**scamp'ish** *adj.*

scamp·er (SKAM pər) *v.i.* run quickly or hastily. —*n.* a hurried run. —**scamp'per·er** *n.*

scam·pi (SKAM pee) *n.pl.* large shrimp or similar shellfish, usu. broiled and served with a garlic sauce. [< Ital.]

scan (skan) *v.* **scanned, scan·ning** *v.t.* **1.** examine in detail. **2.** pass the eyes over quickly; glance at. **3.** separate (verse) into metrical feet. **4.** *Telecom.* pass a beam of light or electrons rapidly over. —*v.i.* **5.** conform to metrical rules: said of verse. [ME *scannen*] —**scan'na·ble** *adj.* —**scan'ner** *n.*

scan·dal (SKAN dl) *n.* **1.** heedless or malicious gossip. **2.** disgrace caused by shameful or dishonorable conduct; ignominy. [< LL *scandalum* offense]

scan·dal·ize (SKAN dl IZ) *v.t.* **·ized, ·iz·ing** shock the moral feelings of.

scan·dal·mong·er (SKAN dl MUNG gər) *n.* one who spreads scandal.

scan·dal·ous (SKAN dl əs) *adj.* **1.** causing or tending to cause scandal; disgraceful. **2.** consisting of or spreading scandal. —**scan'dal·ous·ly** *adv.*

Scan·di·na·vi·an (SKAN də NAY vee ən) *adj.* of or pertaining to Scandinavia, its people, or their languages. —*n.* **1.** a native or inhabitant of Scandinavia. **2.** the North Germanic group of languages: see under GERMANIC. —**Old Scandinavian** Old Norse. See under NORSE.

scant (skant) *adj.* **·er, ·est** **1.** scarcely enough; meager. **2.** being just short of the measure specified: a *scant* five yards. —*v.t.* limit or restrict; stint. [ME] —**scant'ly** *adv.* —**scant'ness** *n.*

scant·y (SKAN tee) *adj.* **scant·i·er, scant·i·est** limited or restricted; meager. — **scant'i·ly** *adv.* —**scant'i·ness** *n.*

scape·goat (SKAYP GOHT) *n.* a person or group that bears the blame for others.

scape·grace (SKAYP GRAYS) *n.* an unmitigated rogue.

scar (skahr) *n.* **1.** the mark left on the skin after the healing of a wound or sore. **2.** any mark, damage, or lasting effect resulting from past injury, stress, etc. —*v.t. & v.i.* **scarred, scar·ring** mark or become marked with or as if with a scar. [ME]

scar·ab (SKAR əb) *n.* **1.** a large, black beetle held sacred by the ancient Egyptians. **2.** a gem or ornament representing this beetle. [< MF *scarabee*]

scarce (skairs) *adj.* **scarc·er, scarc·est 1.** rarely seen or found. **2.** not plentiful. [ME *scars*] —**make oneself scarce** *Informal* go away or stay away. —**scarce′ness** *n.* — **scar·ci·ty** (SKAIR si tee) *n.*

scarce·ly (SKAIRS lee) *adv.* **1.** only just; barely. **2.** not quite; hardly.

scare (skair) *v.* **scared, scar·ing** *v.t.* **1.** strike with sudden fear; frighten. **2.** drive or force by frightening: with *off* or *away.* —*v.i.* **3.** become scared. [ME *skerren* frighten] —*n.* **1.** a sudden fright. **2.** a time of worry. — **scar′ing·ly** *adv.*

scare·crow (SKAIR KROH) *n.* **1.** any crude figure of a person set up to scare crows and other birds away from growing crops. **2.** a person of ragged or disreputable appearance.

scarf (skahrf) *n. pl.* **scarfs** or **scarves 1.** a band or square of cloth worn about the head, neck, etc. **2.** a necktie, cravat, etc. — *v.t.* cover or decorate with or as with a scarf.

scar·i·fy (SKAR i FIɪ) *v.t.* **-fied, -fy·ing 1.** scratch or make slight incisions in, as the skin in surgery. **2.** criticize severely. [ME *scarifie* scratch] —**scar′i·fi·ca′tion** *n.*

scar·let (SKAHR lit) *n.* a brilliant red. [ME] —*adj.* **1.** of the color scarlet. **2.** glaringly offensive.

scarlet fever *Pathol.* an acute infectious disease characterized by a scarlet rash.

scarp (skahrp) *n.* **1.** a steep slope. **2.** an embankment or wall at the outer part of a fortification. [< Ital. *scarpa*]

scarves (skahrvz) a plural of SCARF.

scar·y (SKAIR ee) *adj.* **scar·i·er, scar·i·est 1.** easily scared; timid. **2.** causing fear or alarm; frightening.

scat (skat) *v.i.* **scat·ted, scat·ting 1.** go away: usu. in the imperative. **2.** move fast.

scathe (skayth) *v.t.* **scathed, scath·ing 1.** criticize severely. **2.** injure severely. —*n.* harm; injury. [ME *scath* harm]

scath·ing (SKAY thing) *adj.* mercilessly severe: a *scathing* rebuke. —**scath′ing·ly** *adv.*

sca·tol·o·gy (skə TOL ə jee) *n.* **1.** the study of, or a preoccupation with, excrement. **2.**

interest in obscene matters, esp. in literature. —**scat·o·log·i·cal** (SKAT l OJ i kəl *adj.*

scat·ter (SKAT ər) *v.t.* **1.** throw about; sprinkle. **2.** separate and drive away; disperse. — *v.i.* **3.** separate and go in different directions. [ME *scatere*] —**scat′ter·er** *n.*

scat·ter·brain (SKAT ər BRAYN) *n.* a flighty or forgetful person. —**scat′ter·brained′** *adj.*

scav·enge (SKAV inj) *v.* **·enged, ·eng·ing** *v.t.* **1.** remove filth, rubbish, and refuse from. —*v.i.* **2.** act as a scavenger. **3.** search or rummage, as for food. [Back formation < SCAVENGER]

scav·en·ger (SKAV in jər) *n.* **1.** an animal that feeds on carrion, as the buzzard. **2.** one who searches refuse, garbage, etc., for usable material. [ME *skawager* toll collector]

sce·nar·i·o (si NAIR ee OH) *n. pl.* **·nar·i·os 1.** the written plot and arrangement of incidents of a motion picture. **2.** a plan of a projected series of actions or events. [< Ital.]

scene (seen) *n.* **1.** a locality as presented to view. **2.** the place in which the action of a drama is supposed to occur; setting. **3.** the place and surroundings of any event. **4.** a division of an act of a play. **5.** an event, situation, or continuous related action in a motion picture, play, etc. **6.** scenery (def. 2). **7.** a display of excited feeling. **8.** *Slang* a place or realm of a currently popular activity: the pop music *scene.* —**behind the scenes 1.** out of sight of a theater audience. **2.** privately; in secret. [< MF, stage]

scen·er·y (SEE nə ree) *n. pl.* **·er·ies 1.** the appearance of a landscape, locality, etc. **2.** the settings, backdrops, etc. of a theatrical production.

sce·nic (SEE nik) *adj.* **1.** of or pertaining to natural scenery; picturesque. **2.** relating to stage scenery. Also **sce′ni·cal.**

scent (sent) *n.* **1.** an odor, esp. a pleasant one. **2.** an animal's odor, by which it can be tracked. **3.** a trail, trace, or clue. **4.** a perfume. **5.** the sense of smell. **6.** a suggestion; hint. —*v.t.* **1.** smell. **2.** get a hint of. **3.** make fragrant; perfume. [ME *senten* sense]

scep·ter (SEP tər) *n.* a staff carried by a ruler as a symbol of authority. [ME *sceptre*]

sched·ule (SKEJ uul) *n.* **1.** a list of details or items: a *schedule* of postal rates. **2.** a timetable. **3.** a detailed and timed plan; program: a production *schedule.* —**behind schedule** not on time; late. —**on schedule** ac-

cording to plan; on time. —*v.t.* •**uled,**
•**ul•ing 1.** place on a schedule. **2.** plan for a
specified time. [ME *cedule*]

sche•ma (SKEE mə) *n. pl.* •**ma•ta** (-mə tə) a
plan or diagram of a process, etc. Also **sche-**
•**mat•ic** (ski MAT ik). [< Gk. *schêma*] —
sche•mat'ic or •**i•cal** *adj.* —**sche•mat'**
i•cal•ly *adv.*

sche•ma•tize (SKEE mə TĪZ) *v.t.* •**tized,**
•**tiz•ing 1.** form into or arrange according
to a plan or design. **2.** depict in a diagram.

scheme (skeem) *n.* **1.** a plan for doing something. **2.** a systematic arrangement or design. **3.** a secret or underhand plot. **4.** an
outline or sketch; diagram. —*v.t. & v.i.*
schemed, schem•ing plan or plot, esp. in
an underhand manner. [< L *schema* ar-
rangement] —**schem'er** *n.*

scher•zo (SKERT soh) *n. pl.* •**zos** or •**zi**
(-see) *Music* a playful movement, as in a
symphony. [< Ital., jest]

schism (SIZ əm) *n.* **1.** a division or split, esp.
in a religious group. **2.** the offense of causing such division. **3.** discord within a group;
dissension. [ME *scisme*] —**schis•mat•ic**
(siz MAT ik) or •**i•cal** *adj.*

schist (shist) *n. Geol.* a rock that readily splits
into parallel layers. [< F *schiste*]

schiz•o•phre•ni•a (SKIT sə FREE nee ə) *n.
Psychiatry* any of a group of psychotic disorders characterized by delusions, withdrawal, conflicting emotions, and
deterioration of the personality. [< NL] —
schiz•o•phren•ic (SKIT sə FREN ik) *adj.*
& n.

schle•miel (shlə MEEL) *n. Slang* an inept,
easily duped person; bungler; dolt. Also
shlemiel. [< Yiddish]

schlep (shlep) *Slang v.* **schlepped, schlep-**
•**ping** *v.t.* **1.** drag awkwardly; lug. —*v.i.* **2.**
proceed wearily or heavily. —*n.* **1.** a difficult journey. **2.** a stupid, awkward person.
Also *shlep.* [< Yiddish, drag] —**schlep'**
per *n.*

schlock (shlok) *Slang n.* shoddy, inferior
merchandise. —*adj.* of inferior quality.
Also *shlock.* [< Yiddish, nuisance] —
schlock'y *adj.*

schmaltz (shmahlts) *n.* **1.** *Informal* sentimental music, literature, etc. **2.** fat or
grease. [< Yiddish, rendered fat] —
schmaltz'y *adj.* **schmaltz•i•er, schma-**
ltz•i•est

schnapps (shnahps) *n.* any strong liquor,
esp. a type of gin. Also **schnaps.** [< LG]

schol•ar (SKOL ər) *n.* **1.** a learned or erudite

person. **2.** one considered an authority in a
specific field, esp. in the humanities. **3.** a
student or pupil. [ME *scoler*] —**schol'**
ar•ly *adj. & adv.*

schol•ar•ship (SKOL ər SHIP) *n.* **1.** knowledge and qualities of a scholar; learning;
erudition. **2.** scholarly inquiry or research.
3. a sum of money awarded to a student to
help pay for his or her education; stipend.

scho•las•tic (skə LAS tik) *adj.* **1.** of or characteristic of scholars, education, or schools.
2. *Often cap.* of or characteristic of medieval scholasticism. —*n. Often cap.* an advocate of scholasticism. [< Med.L
scholasticus] —**scho•las'ti•cal•ly** *adv.*

scho•las•ti•cism (skə LAS tə SIZ əm) *n. Often cap.* the systematized logic, philosophy,
and theology of medieval Christian
scholars.

school[1] (skool) *n.* **1.** an institution for instructing students in certain skills, a particular field, etc.; also, the classrooms and
buildings of such an institution. **2.** the students and teachers of an educational institution. **3.** a subdivision of a university: the
school of medicine. **4.** a group following
the same system, methods, or style; also,
the system etc. of such a group. —*v.t.* **1.**
instruct in or as in a school; train; educate.
2. subject to rule or discipline. [ME *scole*]

school[2] *n.* a large number of fish, whales,
etc., of the same kind swimming together;
shoal. —*v.i.* swim together in a school. [ME
schole]

school•ing (SKOO ling) *n.* instruction given
at school.

school•man (SKOOL mən) *n. pl.* •**men** one
of the theologians of the Middle Ages; a
scholastic.

school•mas•ter (SKOOL MAS tər) *n.* a man
who teaches in or directs a school.

schoon•er (SKOO nər) *n.* **1.** a fore-and-aft
rigged vessel having two or more masts. **2.** a
large beer glass.

schuss (shuus) *n.* in skiing, a straight, fast
downhill run; also, a straight, steep downhill course. —*v.i.* execute a schuss. [< G]

schuss•boom•er (SHUUS BOO mər) *n.* one
who skis at great speed.

schwa (shwah) *n. Phonet.* a weak, neutral
sound occurring in most unstressed syllables in English, as the *a* in *alone* or the *u*
in *circus:* written ə. [< G < Hebrew
shewa]

sci•at•i•ca (sī AT i kə) *n. Pathol.* **1.** pain and
tenderness affecting the sciatic nerve. **2.**

any painful affection of the hip or thighs. [< Med.L]

sciatic nerve a long nerve extending down the back of the thigh and leg.

sci•ence (SĪ əns) n. **1.** any branch of knowledge, such as biology or chemistry, characterized by close observation, experimentation, classification of data, and the establishment of verifiable principles. **2.** the body of systematized knowledge based on such methods. **3.** skill, esp. a group of techniques using a systematic approach: the *science* of cooking. [ME]

science fiction fiction in which scientific facts or theories are imaginatively employed.

sci•en•tif•ic (sī ən TIF ik) adj. **1.** of, discovered by, derived from, or used in science. **2.** agreeing with or using the principles or methods of science; systematic; exact. [< Med.L *scientificus*]

scientific method the method used in the sciences for obtaining knowledge, in which hypotheses are tested by experimentation and observation.

sci•en•tist (SĪ ən tist) n. a person engaged in biology, chemistry, or other science as a profession.

scim•i•tar (SIM i tər) n. a curved Oriental sword or saber. [< Ital. *scimitarra*]

scin•til•la (sin TIL ə) n. a spark; trace; iota: a *scintilla* of truth. [< L]

scin•til•late (SIN tl AYT) v.i. •lat•ed, •lat•ing **1.** give off sparks. **2.** be brilliant, exciting, or witty; sparkle. **3.** twinkle, as a star. [< L *scintillatus* flashed] — **scin'•til•la'tion** n.

sci•o•lism (SĪ ə LIZ əm) n. superficial knowledge. —**sci'o•list** n. —**sci'o•lis'tic** adj. [< LL *sciolus* smatterer]

sci•on (SĪ ən) n. **1.** descendant; heir. **2.** a twig or shoot cut from a plant or tree, esp. for grafting. Also spelled *cion*. [ME, twig]

scis•sor (SIZ ər) v.t. & v.i. cut with scissors.

scis•sors (SIZ ərz) n. (construed as sing. or pl.) **1.** a cutting implement with a pair of blades pivoted face to face so that the opposed edges may be brought together. Also **pair of scissors. 2.** in wrestling, a hold secured by clasping the legs about the body or head of the opponent. [ME *cisoures*]

scle•ro•sis (skli ROH sis) n. pl. •ses (-seez) *Pathol.* the thickening and hardening of body tissue. [ME] —**scle•rot•ic** (skli ROT ik) adj.

scoff (skof) v.i. speak with contempt or deri-

sion; jeer: often with *at*. —n. an expression of contempt or derision. [ME *scof*] — **scoff'er** n. —**scoff'ing•ly** adv.

scoff•law (SKOF LAW) n. a habitual violator of traffic laws.

scold (skohld) v.t. & v.i. find fault with (someone) harshly; chide. —n. one who scolds, esp. a shrewish woman. [ME]

sconce (skons) n. an ornamental wall bracket for holding a candle or other light. [ME]

scone (skohn) n. a round tea cake or biscuit. [< MDu. *schoonbrot* fine bread]

scoop (skoop) n. **1.** a small shovellike implement for taking up flour, sugar, etc. **2.** an implement for dispensing portions of ice cream etc. **3.** the large, deep bucket of a steam shovel or dredge. **4.** a scoopful. **5.** a long, sweeping movement. **6.** in journalism, a news story published ahead of rival papers. [ME *scope*] —v.t. **1.** take out with or as with a scoop. **2.** hollow out. **3.** form with or as with a scoop. **4.** gather up with a low, sweeping motion. **5.** publish a news story before (a rival). —**scoop'er** n.

scope (skohp) n. **1.** the range, area, or sphere in which an activity takes place. **2.** the range of one's views or abilities. **3.** opportunity for development, expression, etc. [< Ital. *scopo* goal]

-scope combining form an instrument for viewing: *telescope*. [< NL -*scopium* watch]

-scopy combining form observation; viewing: *microscopy*. [See -SCOPE.]

scorch (skorch) v.t. **1.** burn or char the surface of. **2.** wither or shivel by heat. **3.** criticize severely. —v.i. **4.** become scorched. — n. a superficial burn. [ME *scorchen* shrivel] —**scorch'ing** adj. —**scorch'ing•ly** adv.

scorched-earth policy (SKORCHT URTH) the military strategy of destroying all crops, industrial equipment, etc. so as to leave nothing useful for the enemy.

score (skor) n. **1.** the number of points made in a game or contest; also, the act of making such points. **2.** a grade or rating in a test. **3.** a debt. **4.** an account of grievances. **5.** a notch or groove cut in something. **6.** a set of twenty. **7.** pl. an indefinitely large number. **8.** *Music* the notation for a composition, showing the various instrumental or vocal parts. **9.** music for a motion picture or theatrical production. [ME] —**know the score** *Informal* be aware of the facts of a situation. —v. **scored, scor•ing** v.t. **1.** mark with notches, cuts, or lines. **2.** make or gain (points, runs, etc.) in a game or contest;

also, record such points, runs, etc. **3.** grade (a test); also, make a grade of: *She scored 100.* **4.** achieve (a victory, success, etc.). **5.** *Music* compose or arrange (music) for an orchestra or for an instrument. —*v.i.* **6.** make points, runs, etc., as in a game. **7.** keep score in a game. **8.** win an advantage or success. —**score′less** *adj.* —**scor′er** *n.*

sco·ri·a (SKOR ee ə) *n. pl.* **·ri·ae** (SKOR ee ee) **1.** refuse remaining after metal has been smelted; slag. **2.** loose lava. [ME, refuse]

scorn (skorn) *n.* a feeling of contempt or loathing; disdain. —*v.t.* **1.** treat with contempt; despise. **2.** reject with contempt; spurn. [ME] —**scorn′ful** *adj.* —**scorn′ful·ness** *n.*

scor·pi·on (SKOR pee ən) *n.* an arachnid with a long, segmented tail ending in a poisonous sting. [ME]

Scot (skot) *n.* **1.** a native of Scotland. **2.** one of a Gaelic people who migrated in the 6th c. to Scotland from Ireland. [ME]

scotch (skoch) *v.t.* **1.** maim or cripple. **2.** crush or suppress. —**Scots′wom′an** *n.fem.*

Scotch (skoch) *adj.* **1.** of Scottish origin. **2.** of or pertaining to Scotland, its people, or their language. —*n.* a smoky-flavored liquor made in Scotland from malted barley: also **Scotch whisky.**

scot-free (SKOT FREE) *adj.* without injury, punishment, or loss; unharmed. [ME]

Scots·man (SKOTS mən) *n. pl.* **·men** a person, esp. a man, who is a native or inhabitant of Scotland. —**Scots′wom′an** *n.fem.*

Scot·tish (SKOT ish) *n.* the people of Scotland. —*adj.* of or pertaining to Scotland, its people, or their language. [ME]

Scottish Gaelic the language of the Scottish Highlands: also called *Erse.*

scoun·drel (SKOWN drəl) *n.* a mean, unprincipled rascal; rogue. —**scound′drel·ly** *adj.*

scour[1] (SKOW ər) *v.t. & v.i.* **1.** clean or brighten by thorough washing and rubbing. **2.** clear by means of a strong current of water; flush. [ME *scouren*]

scour[2] *v.t.* go over thoroughly, as in making a search. —**scour′er** *n.*

scourge (skurj) *n.* **1.** a whip for inflicting punishment. **2.** any means of inflicting punishment or suffering. **3.** a cause of suffering or trouble. [ME, whip] —*v.t.* **scourged, scourg·ing 1.** whip severely; flog. **2.** punish severely; afflict.

scout (skowt) *n.* **1.** a soldier sent out to gather

information about enemy troop movements, terrain, etc. **2.** a talent scout. **3.** a Boy or Girl Scout. —*v.t.* **1.** survey in order to gain information: *scout the area.* —*v.i.* **2.** go or act as a scout. —**scout around** go in search. [ME *skowten* listen]

scow (skow) *n.* a large, flat-bottomed boat with square ends, used for carrying loads and often towed. [< Du. *schouw* ferryboat]

scowl (skowl) *n.* a lowering of the brows, as in anger, disapproval, or sullenness. —*v.i.* **1.** express anger, etc., with such a look. —*v.t.* **2.** express by scowling. [ME *skoulen*]

scrab·ble (SKRAB əl) *v.i.* **·bled, ·bling 1.** scratch, scrape, or paw, as with the hands. **2.** clamber; scramble. **3.** struggle or strive. [< Du. *schrabbelen* scratch]

scrag·gly (SKRAG lee) *adj.* **·gli·er, ·gli·est** unkempt; shaggy.

scram·ble (SKRAM bəl) *v.* **·bled, ·bling** *v.i.* **1.** climb or crawl quickly; clamber. **2.** move hurriedly; rush. **3.** struggle or compete in a disorderly way. —*v.t.* **4.** mix together haphazardly. **5.** fry (eggs) with the yolks and whites stirred together. **6.** *Telecom.* alter or garble (a signal) so that it is unintelligible in transit. —*n.* **1.** a disorderly struggle. **2.** a difficult climb or trek. —**scram′bler** *n.*

scrap[1] (skrap) *n.* **1.** a small piece; bit; fragment. **2.** *pl.* discarded or leftover bits of food. **3.** used or discarded material; esp., metal that can be reclaimed. —*v.t.* **scrapped, scrap·ping 1.** break up into scrap. **2.** discard. [ME *scrappe* scrap]

scrap[2] *v.i.* **scrapped, scrap·ping** *Informal* fight; quarrel. —*n.* a quarrel or fight. —**scrap′per** *n. Informal*

scrap·book (SKRAP buuk) *n.* a blank book in which pictures, clippings, etc. are pasted as mementos.

scrape (skrayp) *v.* **scraped, scrap·ing** *v.t.* **1.** clean or make smooth by rubbing with something sharp or rough. **2.** remove thus: with *off, away,* etc. **3.** rub (a rough or sharp object) across a surface. **4.** rub roughly across or against (a surface). **5.** form by scratching or digging. **6.** gather with effort or difficulty: usu. with *up* or *together.* —*v.i.* **7.** scrape something. **8.** manage or get along with difficulty. [ME *scrapen* scratch] —*n.* **1.** a mark or harsh sound made by scraping. **2.** a difficult situation; predicament. —**scrap′er** *n.*

scrap heap a pile of used or discarded things.

scrap iron iron suitable for reworking.

scrap·ple (SKRAP əl) *n.* a boiled mixture of pork scraps, meal, and seasonings, which is allowed to set and then fried.

scrap·py[1] (SKRAP ee) *adj.* •pi·er, •pi·est not connected; fragmentary.

scrap·py[2] *adj. Informal* •pi·er, •pi·est eager to fight; pugnacious. —**scrap'pi·ness** *n.*

scratch (skrach) *v.t.* **1.** tear or mark the surface of with something sharp or rough. **2.** scrape lightly to relieve itching. **3.** rub with a grating sound; scrape. **4.** write or draw awkwardly or hurriedly. **5.** erase or cancel. **6.** withdraw (an entry) from a race, game, etc. —*v.i.* **7.** use the nails or claws, as in fighting or digging. **8.** scrape the skin so as to relieve itching. **9.** make a harsh, grating noise. **10.** manage or get along with difficulty. —*n.* **1.** a mark or cut made by scratching. **2.** a slight flesh wound. **3.** a harsh, grating sound. —**from scratch** from the beginning; from nothing. —**up to scratch** up to standard. —*adj.* **1.** done by chance; haphazard: a *scratch* hit. **2.** used for quick notes, etc.: a *scratch* pad. [ME *scracche*]

scratch·y (SKRACH ee) *adj.* **scratch·i·er, scratch·i·est 1.** making a grating noise. **2.** uneven; shaggy; rough. **3.** that scratches or irritates. —**scratch'i·ly** *adv.* —**scratch' i·ness** *n.*

scrawl (skrawl) *v.t. & v.i.* write hastily or illegibly. —*n.* irregular or careless writing. —**scrawl'y** *adj.* **scrawl·i·er, scrawl·i·est**

scrawn·y (SKRAW nee) *adj.* **scrawn·i·er, scrawn·i·est** skinny; thin. —**scraw' ni·ness** *n.*

scream (skreem) *v.i.* **1.** utter a loud, piercing cry, as of pain or terror. **2.** make a prolonged, piercing sound. **3.** laugh loudly and wildly. **4.** speak loudly; shout. **5.** make a frantic demand. —*v.t.* **6.** utter with a scream. [ME *screamen*] —*n.* **1.** a loud, shrill cry or sound. **2.** *Informal* a very funny person or situation.

screech (skreech) *n.* a shrill, harsh cry or sound; shriek. —*v.t. & v.i.* utter with or make such a sound. [Var. of obs. *scritch*] — **screech'y** *adj.* **screech·i·er, screech· h·i·est**

screen (skreen) *n.* **1.** a partition, curtain, etc., used to conceal, separate, or protect. **2.** anything having a similar purpose: a smoke *screen*. **3.** a wire mesh or netting forming a partition or panel in a window, door, etc. **4.** a sieve for sifting. **5.** a surface on which motion pictures etc. may be shown. **6.** in television sets, radar apparatus, etc., the surface on which the image is displayed. **7.** the motion-picture industry. —*v.t.* **1.** shield, protect, etc. with or as with a screen. **2.** sift through a screen. **3.** show or exhibit on a screen, as a motion picture. **4.** determine the competence or eligibility of (an individual) for a specified task. [ME *screne*]

screen·ing (SKREE ning) *n.* **1.** the showing of a motion picture. **2.** mesh for window screens etc.

screen·play (SKREEN PLAY) *n.* a motion-picture script.

screw (skroo) *n.* **1.** a naillike fastening device with a spiraling thread. **2.** a similar device of cylindrical form, for insertion into a corresponding grooved part. **3.** anything having the form of a screw. [ME] —**have a screw loose** *Slang* be mentally deranged, eccentric, etc. —**put the screws on** (or **to**) exert pressure or force upon. —*v.t.* **1.** tighten, attach, etc. by or as by a screw. **2.** turn or twist. **3.** twist out of shape; contort. **4.** *Slang* cheat or harm. —*v.i.* **5.** twist or turn as a screw. **6.** be attached or become detached by means of screws: with *on, off,* etc. — **screw up** *Slang* make a mess of; botch.

screw·ball (SKROO BAWL) *n. Slang* **1.** an odd or erratic person. **2.** in baseball, a pitch that curves in a direction opposite to that of a curve ball.

screw·driv·er (SKROO DRĪ vər) *n.* **1.** a tool for turning screws. **2.** a cocktail consisting of vodka and orange juice.

screw·y (SKROO ee) *adj.* **screw·i·er, screw·i·est** *Slang* weird; eccentric; crazy.

scrib·ble (SKRIB əl) *v.t. & v.i.* •bled, •bling **1.** write hastily and carelessly. **2.** make or cover with illegible or meaningless marks. [ME *scribblen*] —*n.* scribbled writing; scrawl. —**scrib'bler** *n.*

scribe (skrīb) *n.* **1.** one who copies manuscripts and other documents. **2.** among the ancient Hebrews, a teacher or interpreter of the Mosaic law. **3.** a writer; journalist. [ME]

scrim (skrim) *n.* a light, loosely woven cloth, used esp. in the theater as a stage backdrop or semitransparent curtain.

scrim·mage (SKRIM ij) *n.* **1.** a rough-and-tumble contest; fracas. **2.** in football: **a** the entire play from the pass from the center to the downing of the ball. **b** a practice session.

[ME] —*v.i.* •maged, •mag•ing engage in a scrimmage.

scrimp (skrimp) *v.i.* spend little money; be frugal; economize. [< Scand.] —scrimp′y *adj.* scrimp•i•er, scrimp•i•est

scrim•shaw (SKRIM SHAW) *n.* carved or engraved articles made of bone, ivory, etc., esp. those made by American whalers.

scrip (skrip) *n.* 1. a provisional document certifying that the holder is entitled to receive something else, as shares of stock or land. 2. any money substitute that can be exchanged for goods or services. 3. paper money for an amount less than a dollar.

script (skript) *n.* 1. handwriting. 2. printing resembling handwriting. 3. the text of a play, motion picture, broadcast, etc. —*v.t.* prepare a script for (a motion picture etc.). [ME]

Scrip•ture (SKRIP chər) *n.* 1. *Often pl.* the books of the Old and New Testaments, including often the Apocrypha. 2. any sacred writings. —scrip′tur•al *adj.*

scroll (skrohl) *n.* 1. a roll of parchment, paper, etc., esp. one containing or intended for writing. 2. an ornament or design resembling a parchment roll. [ME *scrowle*]

scro•tum (SKROH təm) *n. pl.* •ta (-tə), •tums *Anat.* the pouch of skin that contains the testicles in most mammals. [< L]

scrounge (skrownj) *v.t. & v.i.* scrounged, scroung•ing 1. hunt about in order to take (something); pilfer. 2. mooch; sponge; beg. —*n.* one who scrounges: also scroung′er.

scrub¹ (skrub) *v.* scrubbed, scrub•bing *v.t.* 1. rub vigorously in washing. 2. remove (dirt etc.) by such action. 3. cancel; call off. —*v.i.* 4. rub something vigorously, as in washing. [ME *scrobben*] —*n.* the act of scrubbing. —scrub′ber *n.*

scrub² *n.* 1. a thicket of stunted trees or shrubs. 2. a poor, insignificant person. 3. in sports, a player not on the varsity team. [ME] —*adj.* 1. undersized or stunted. 2. made up or played by players not on the varsity or regular team: a *scrub* game.

scrub•by (SKRUB ee) *adj.* •bi•er, •bi•est 1. of stunted growth. 2. covered with scrub or underbrush. —scrub′bi•ness *n.*

scruff (skruf) *n.* the nape of the neck.

scrump•tious (SKRUMP shəs) *adj.* delightful, esp. to one's taste; delectable.

scrunch (skrunch) *v.t.* 1. crush; crunch. 2. crumble. —*v.i.* 3. crouch. 4. make a crunching sound. —*n.* 1. a crunching sound. 2. a crouch.

scru•ple (SKROO pəl) *n.* 1. doubt or uncertainty regarding a question of moral right or duty. 2. an apothecaries' weight of 20 grains. 3. a minute quantity. [< F *scrupule*] —*v.i.* •pled, •pling hesitate over scruples.

scru•pu•lous (SKROO pyə ləs) *adj.* 1. morally strict; conscientious; honest. 2. careful of small details; painstaking; precise. —scru′•pu•lous•ly *adv.* —scru′pu•lous•ness *n.*

scru•ti•nize (SKROOT n īz) *v.t.* •nized, •niz•ing examine in detail; inspect closely.

scru•ti•ny (SKROOT n ee) *n. pl.* •nies close and careful examination. [ME]

scu•ba (SKOO bə) *n.* an underwater breathing apparatus consisting of compressed-air tanks connected by hoses to the swimmer's mouthpiece. [< self-contained underwater breathing apparatus]

scud (skud) *v.i.* scud•ded, scud•ding 1. move, run, or fly swiftly. 2. *Naut.* run rapidly before the wind. [< MLG *schudden* shake] —*n.* light clouds driven rapidly before the wind.

scuff (skuf) *v.i.* 1. walk with a dragging movement; shuffle. 2. become scratched or marred by scraping or wear. —*v.t.* 3. scratch or mar the surface of by scraping or wear. [< MLG *schūven* shove] —*n.* 1. a mark or sound made by scuffing. 2. a flat slipper having no covering for the heel.

scuf•fle (SKUF əl) *v.i.* •fled, •fling 1. struggle roughly or confusedly. 2. drag one's feet; shuffle. —*n.* 1. a disorderly struggle. 2. the sound of shuffling feet.

scull (skul) *n.* 1. a long oar worked from side to side over the stern of a boat. 2. a light, short-handled oar, used in pairs by one person. 3. a light racing boat or shell propelled by sculls. —*v.t. & v.i.* propel (a boat) by a scull or sculls. [ME *sculle*] —scull′er *n.*

scul•ler•y (SKUL ə ree) *n. pl.* •ler•ies a room where kitchen utensils are kept and cleaned, vegetables washed, etc. [ME]

scul•lion (SKUL yən) *n.* 1. a servant who does messy kitchen chores. 2. a base, contemptible person. [ME *sculion*]

sculpt (skulpt) *v.* carve; scultpure. [< F *sculpter*]

sculp•tor (SKULP tər) *n.* one who creates sculpture.

sculp•ture (SKULP chər) *n.* 1. the art of creating three-dimensional figures and designs, as by carving or molding. 2. a figure or design created this way; also, such figures and designs collectively. —*v.t.* •tured,

•tur•ing **1.** create (a statue, bust, or other work of sculpture). **2.** represent or portray in sculpture. **3.** embellish with sculpture. **4.** change, as a canyon, by erosion and deposition. [ME] —**sculp′tur•al** *adj.*

scum (skum) *n.* **1.** a thin layer of impurities, vegetation, etc. on the surface of a liquid. **2.** a vile, despicable person; also, a group of such persons. —*v.* **scummed, scum•ming** *v.t.* **1.** take scum from; skim. —*v.i.* **2.** become covered with or form scum. [ME] —**scum′•my** *adj.* •**mi•er,** •**mi•est**

scup•per (SKUP ər) *n. Naut.* a hole along the side of a ship's deck intended to let water run off.

scurf (skurf) *n.* **1.** dry, scaly skin, as dandruff. **2.** any scaly matter. [ME] —**scurf′y** *adj.* **scurf•i•er scurf•i•est**

scur•ri•lous (SKUR ə ləs) *adj.* grossly and offensively abusive; coarse. —**scur•ril•i•ty** (skə RIL li tee) *n.* —**scur′ri•lous•ly** *adv.* —**scur′ri•lous•ness** *n.*

scur•ry (SKUR ee) *v.i.* •**ried,** •**ry•ing** move or go hurriedly; scamper. —*n. pl.* •**ries** the act or sound of scurrying.

scur•vy (SKUR vee) *adj.* •**vi•er,** •**vi•est** low or contemptible; base. —*n. Pathol.* a disease caused by lack of vitamin C in the diet, characterized by bleeding gums, weakness, etc.

scut•tle[1] (SKUT l) *n.* **1.** a small opening with a cover, esp. on the deck of a ship. **2.** the lid closing such an opening. —*v.t.* •**tled,** •**tling** sink (a ship) by making holes in the bottom.

scut•tle[2] *n.* a metal vessel or hod for coal. [ME]

scut•tle[3] *v.i.* •**tled,** •**tling** run in haste; scurry. —*n.* a hurried run or departure.

scut•tle•butt (SKUT l BUT) *n.* **1.** a drinking fountain aboard ship. **2.** *Informal* rumor; gossip.

scythe (sīth) *n.* an implement used for mowing, reaping, etc., consisting of a long, curved blade fixed at an angle to a long bent handle. [ME *sith*] —*v.t.* **scythed, scyth•ing** cut or mow with or as with a scythe.

sea (see) *n.* **1.** the great body of salt water covering the larger portion of the earth's surface; the ocean. **2.** a large body of salt water partly enclosed by land. **3.** a large inland body of water, salt or fresh. **4.** the swell or surface of the ocean: a calm *sea.* **5.** anything that suggests the sea, as something vast. —**at sea 1.** on the ocean. **2.** at a

loss; bewildered. —**follow the sea** become a sailor. —**go to sea 1.** become a sailor. **2.** take an ocean voyage. —**put to sea** start on an ocean voyage. [ME *see*]

sea•board (SEE BORD) *n.* the land near the sea; seashore or seacoast. —*adj.* bordering on the sea. [ME *seebord* on the seaward side]

sea•coast (SEE KOHST) *n.* the seashore; seaboard.

sea dog 1. the sea lion. **2.** an old or experienced sailor.

sea•far•er (SEE FAIR ər) *n.* a seaman; mariner.

sea•far•ing (SEE FAIR ing) *n.* **1.** travel by sea. **2.** the profession of a seaman. —*adj.* **1.** traveling by sea. **2.** following the sea.

sea•food (SEE FOOD) *n.* edible marine fish or shellfish.

sea•go•ing (SEE GOH ing) *adj.* **1.** adapted for use on the ocean. **2.** of or related to the sea.

sea horse a marine fish, having a prehensile tail and a head like that of a horse.

seal[1] (seel) *n.* **1.** a device for making an impression on wax or other soft substance; also, the impression made. **2.** such an impression affixed to a document as a proof of authenticity. **3.** anything used to fasten, secure, or close a letter, door, etc. **4.** anything that confirms or ratifies; pledge. **5.** an ornamental stamp for packages etc. [ME *seel*] —*v.t.* **1.** affix a seal to in order to attest to weight, quality, authenticity, etc. **2.** fasten or close with or as with a seal. **3.** establish or settle finally; determine. **4.** secure, set, or fill up, as with plaster. —**seal′a•ble** *adj.*

seal[2] *n.* **1.** any of a group of carnivorous sea mammals mostly of northern latitudes. **2.** sealskin. [ME *sele*] —*v.i.* hunt seals.

seal•ant (SEE lənt) *n.* a substance that seals a surface, seam, etc.

sea legs the ability to walk aboard ship, esp. in rough seas, without losing one's balance.

sea level the assumed mean level of the ocean surface, esp. as used in determining elevation on maps etc.

sea lion any of various large seals of the Pacific Ocean, esp., the **California sea lion:** also called *sea dog.*

seal•skin (SEEL SKIN) *n.* **1.** the fur of a seal. **2.** a coat etc. made of this fur.

seam (seem) *n.* **1.** a line of junction between parts, esp. the edges of two pieces of cloth sewn together. **2.** a mark like this, as a crack, fissure, or scar. **3.** a thin stratum of rock.

[ME *seme*] —*v.t.* **1.** unite by means of a seam. **2.** mark with a cut, furrow, wrinkle, etc. —**seam′less** *adj.*

sea·man (SEE mən) *n. pl.* •**men 1.** a sailor. **2.** *Naval* an enlisted person of any of the lowest grades.

sea·man·ship (SEE mən SHIP) *n.* the skill and ability of a seaman.

seam·stress (SEEM stris) *n.* a woman whose occupation is sewing.

seam·y (SEE mee) *adj.* **seam·i·er, seam·i·est** degraded; squalid; sordid. —**seam′i·ness** *n.*

sé·ance (SAY ahns) *n.* a meeting of persons seeking contact with the spirits of the dead. [< F, session]

sea·port (SEE PORT) *n.* **1.** a harbor or port for seagoing ships. **2.** a town on such a harbor.

sear (seer) *v.t.* **1.** wither; dry up. **2.** burn the surface of; scorch. **3.** burn, as with a hot iron; brand. [ME *sere*] —*adj.* sére[1].

search (surch) *v.t.* **1.** look through or explore carefully in order to find something. **2.** examine (a person), as for concealed weapons. **3.** examine closely; probe. **4.** learn by investigation: with *out.* —*v.i.* **5.** make a search. [ME *serchen*] —*n.* the act of searching.

search·ing (SUR ching) *adj.* **1.** investigating minutely. **2.** keenly penetrating: a *searching* gaze. —**search′ing·ly** *adv.*

search·light (SURCH LIT) *n.* an apparatus for throwing a strong beam of light; also, the beam of light.

search warrant a warrant authorizing the search of a house etc. for things alleged to be unlawfully concealed there.

sea·scape (SEE SKAYP) *n.* **1.** an ocean view. **2.** a picture presenting a marine view.

sea·shell (SEE SHEL) *n.* the shell of any marine mollusk.

sea·shore (SEE SHOR) *n.* land bordering on the ocean.

sea·sick·ness (SEE SIK nis) *n.* nausea, dizziness, etc., caused by the motion of a vessel at sea. —**sea′sick′** *adj.*

sea·side (SEE SID) *n.* the seashore, esp. as a vacation place.

sea·son (SEE zən) *n.* **1.** one of the four divisions of the year: spring, summer, autumn, or winter. **2.** a special period: the hunting *season.* **3.** a fit or suitable time. [ME *sesoun*] —**in season 1.** in condition and obtainable for use. **3.** of an animal, in heat. **2.** legally permitted to be killed or taken, as game. —

v.t. **1.** increase the flavor of (food), as by adding spices. **2.** add zest to. **3.** render more suitable for use. **4.** make accustomed or inured; harden. —*v.i.* **5.** become seasoned. —**sea′son·er** *n.*

sea·son·a·ble (SEE zə nə bəl) *adj.* **1.** in keeping with the season. **2.** done at the proper time; timely. —**sea′son·a·bly** *adv.*

sea·son·al (SEE zə nl) *adj.* characteristic of, affected by, or occurring at a certain season. —**sea′son·al·ly** *adv.*

sea·son·ing (SEE zən ing) *n.* **1.** the process by which something, as lumber, is rendered fit for use. **2.** a spice, herb, etc., added to food to give relish; esp., a condiment. **3.** anything that adds enjoyment, zest, etc.

season ticket a ticket or pass for a series of sporting events, concerts, etc.

seat (seet) *n.* **1.** a chair, bench, or other thing to sit on. **2.** the part of a chair, garment, etc. on which one sits; also, the buttocks. **3.** the place where anything is situated or established. **4.** the right of membership in a legislative body etc. [ME *sete*] —*v.t.* **1.** cause to sit down. **2.** have seats for. **3.** locate, settle, or center.

seat belt an anchored strap in a vehicle designed to protect the passenger against sudden stops, accidents, etc.

seat·ing (SEE ting) *n.* **1.** fabric for upholstering seats. **2.** the arrangement of seats in an auditorium etc.

sea wall a wall or embankment to prevent erosion of the shore.

sea·ward (SEE wərd) *adj.* **1.** going toward the sea. **2.** blowing, as wind, from the sea. —*adv.* in the direction of the sea.

sea·way (SEE WAY) *n.* an inland waterway that receives ocean shipping.

sea·weed (SEE WEED) *n.* any of various sea plants, including the kelps etc.

sea·wor·thy (SEE WUR thee) *adj.* in fit condition for a voyage: said of a vessel. —**sea′wor′thi·ness** *n.*

se·ba·ceous (si BAY shəs) *adj. Physiol.* **1.** of or like fat; oily. **2.** designating any of the glands in the skin that secrete **sebum**, a fatty matter. [< NL *sebaceus*]

se·cant (SEE kant) *n.* **1.** *Geom.* a straight line intersecting a given curve. **2.** *Trig.* a function of an acute angle, equal to the ratio of the hypotenuse to the side adjacent to the angle when the angle is included in a right triangle. [< NL *secans*]

se·cede (si SEED) *v.i.* •**ced·ed, ·ced·ing**

withdraw formally, esp. from a political or religious organization. [< L *secedere*]

se•ces•sion (si SESH ən) *n.* **1.** the act of seceding. **2.** *Usu. cap.* the withdrawal of the Southern States from the Union in 1860–61. —**se•ces'sion•ist** *adj. & n.*

se•clude (si KLOOD) *v.t.* •**clud•ed,** •**clud•ing 1.** remove and keep apart from others; isolate. **2.** screen or shut off, as from view. [ME] —**se•clud'ed** *adj.*

se•clu•sion (si KLOO zhən) *n.* a secluding or the state of being secluded; solitude. —**se•clu'sive** (si KLOO siv) *adj.*

sec•ond[1] (SEK ənd) *n.* **1.** a unit of time, $\frac{1}{60}$ of a minute. **2.** a very short amount of time; instant. **3.** *Geom.* a unit of angular measure, $\frac{1}{60}$ of a minute of arc. [ME *seconde*]

sec•ond[2] *adj.* **1.** next in order, responsibility, etc. after the first: the ordinal of *two.* **2.** ranking below the first or best; secondary; subordinate. **3.** like another or preceding one; another. [< L *secundus*] —*n.* **1.** the one next after the first in position, rank, etc. **2.** an attendant who supports or aids another, as in a duel. **3.** *pl.* imperfect or inferior merchandise. **4.** in a car, bus, etc., the forward gear next after the first or low gear. **5.** formal endorsement of an initial proposal or motion. —*v.t.* **1.** give aid or encouragement to. **2.** support formally, as a motion. —*adv.* in the second order, place, or rank.

sec•on•dar•y (SEK ən DER ee) *adj.* **1.** of second rank, grade, or influence; subordinate; auxiliary. **2.** depending on what is primary or original: *secondary* sources. —*n. pl.* •**dar•ies** one who helps or supports; an assistant. —**sec'on•dar'i•ly** *adv.*

secondary accent see under ACCENT.

secondary school a high school or preparatory school intermediate between the elementary school and college.

second best *n.* the next to the best.

second childhood senility; dotage.

sec•ond-class (SEK ənd KLAS) *adj.* **1.** less than the best; inferior. **2.** of or pertaining to travel accommodations below first class. **3.** of or pertaining to a class of mail including printed periodicals. —*adv.* by second-class ticket, mail, etc.

second fiddle any secondary or inferior status, esp. in the phrase **be** (or **play**) **second fiddle.**

sec•ond-guess (SEK ənd GES) *v.t. & v.i.* conjecture about (something) after it has occurred.

second hand the hand that marks the seconds on a clock or a watch.

sec•ond•hand (SEK ənd HAND) *adj.* **1.** previously owned, worn, or used by another; not new. **2.** received from another: *secondhand* information. **3.** dealing in merchandise that is not new. —*adv.* in a secondhand manner.

second lieutenant see under LIEUTENANT.

second nature an acquired trait that is deeply fixed in one's personality.

sec•ond-rate (SEK ənd RAYT) *adj.* of inferior quality, size, etc.; second-class. —**sec' ond-rat'er** *n.*

second sight the alleged power of seeing events occurring at distant places, in the future, etc.; clairvoyance.

second string in sports, the team of players that substitute for the starting team. —**sec' ond-string'** *adj.*

second wind 1. a return of easy breathing while one is running, exercising, etc., and after one has been winded. **2.** any similar restoration of energy.

se•cre•cy (SEE krə see) *n.* **1.** the condition or quality of being secret. **2.** the characteristic of being secretive.

se•cret (SEE krit) *adj.* **1.** kept separate or hidden from view or knowledge; concealed. **2.** beyond normal comprehension; obscure. **3.** known or revealed only to the initiated: *secret* rites. [ME *secrette*] —*n.* **1.** something not to be told. **2.** a thing undiscovered or unknown. **3.** an underlying reason; key. —**in secret** in private. —**se' cret•ly** *adv.*

sec•re•tar•i•at (SEK ri TAIR ee ət) *n.* **1.** the administrative department of an organization, as of the United Nations. **2.** a secretarial department. Also **sec're•tar'i•ate.**

sec•re•tar•y (SEK ri TER ee) *n. pl.* •**tar•ies 1.** a person employed to deal with correspondence and handle clerical business for an organization or person. **2.** one who heads a department of government. **3.** a writing desk. [ME *secretarie* confidant] —**sec're•tar'i•al** (SEK ri TAIR ee əl) *adj.*

sec•re•tar•y-gen•er•al (SEK ri TER ee JEN ər əl) *n. pl.* **secretaries-general** a chief administrative officer.

se•crete (si KREET) *v.t.* •**cret•ed,** •**cret•ing 1.** conceal; hide. **2.** *Physiol.* produce (a secretion).

se•cre•tion (si KREE shən) *n. Physiol.* **1.** the process, generally glandular, by which milk, hormones, etc., are produced in the body. **2.** the substance secreted. [< F *sécrétion*] —**se•cre'to•ry** (si KREE tə ree) *adj.*

se•cre•tive (si KREE tiv) *adj.* **1.** inclined to secrecy; reticent. **2.** *Physiol.* producing or causing secretion. —**se•cre'tive•ly** *adv.* —**se•cre'tive•ness** *n.*

Secret Service a section of the Department of the Treasury concerned with counterfeiting, the protection of the President of the United States, etc.

secret service the secret or espionage work of various government agencies, esp. in time of war.

sect (sekt) *n.* **1.** a body of persons distinguished by peculiarities of faith and practice, esp., the adherents of a particular religious creed. **2.** any number of persons united in opinion or beliefs. [ME *secte*]

sec•tar•i•an (sek TAIR ee ən) *adj.* **1.** pertaining to or belonging to a particular sect. **2.** adhering or confined to a specific group, party, etc.; partisan. —*n.* a member of a sect, esp. if bigoted. —**sec•tar'i•an•ism** *n.*

sec•tion (SEK shən) *n.* **1.** a separate part or division, as a portion of a book or a chapter. **2.** a distinct part of a country, community, etc. **3.** a picture of a building, geological formation, etc., as if cut by an intersecting plane; cross section. **4.** the act of cutting; division by cutting. —*v.t.* cut or divide into sections. [< L]

sec•tion•al (SEK shə nl) *adj.* **1.** pertaining to a section, as of a country; local: a *sectional* dialect. **2.** dividing or alienating one section from another. **3.** made up of sections. —*n.* a sofa having several separate units.

sec•tion•al•ism (SEK shə nl IZ əm) *n.* undue concern for a particular section of the country. —**sec'tion•al•ist** *n.*

sec•tor (SEK tər) *n.* **1.** *Geom.* a part of a circle or ellipse bounded by two radii and the arc subtended by them. **2.** a part or portion. **3.** *Mil.* a defined area for which a unit is responsible. —*v.t.* divide into sectors. [< LL]

sec•u•lar (SEK yə lər) *adj.* **1.** of this world or the present life; temporal; worldly. **2.** not under the control of the church; civil. **3.** not concerned with religion. **4.** not bound by monastic vows. [< Med.L *secularis* worldly] —*n.* **1.** one in holy orders who is not bound by monastic vows. **2.** a layperson.

sec•u•lar•ism (SEK yə lə RIZ əm) *n.* **1.** adherence to nonreligious values, as in morality. **2.** the view that religion should not be introduced into public education or civil affairs. —**sec'u•lar•ist** *n.*

sec•u•lar•ize (SEK yə lə RIZ) *v.t.* **•ized, •iz•ing 1.** convert from sacred to secular uses. **2.** make worldly. —**sec'u•lar•i•za' tion** *n.*

se•cure (si KYUUR) *adj.* **•cur•er, •cur•est 1.** guarded against or not likely to be exposed to danger; safe. **2.** free from fear, worry, etc. **3.** fixed firmly in place. **4.** so strong or well-made as to render loss, escape, or failure impossible. **5.** assured; certain. [< L *securus*] —*v.* **•cured, •cur•ing** *v.t.* **1.** make secure; protect. **2.** make firm or tight; fasten. **3.** make certain; ensure. **4.** obtain; get. —*v.i.* **5.** be or become secure: with *against*, etc. —**se•cure'ly** *adv.*

se•cu•ri•ty (si KYUUR i tee) *n. pl.* **•ties 1.** the state of being secure. **2.** one who or that which secures or guarantees. **3.** something deposited or pledged as a guarantee for payment. **4.** *pl.* stocks, bonds, notes, etc. **5.** protection of secrecy, as in wartime.

Security Council a permanent organ of the United Nations charged with maintaining international peace.

se•dan (si DAN) *n.* a closed automobile having two or four doors and a front and back seat.

sedan chair a portable, enclosed chair, usu. for one passenger, carried by means of poles at the front and back.

se•date (si DAYT) *adj.* **1.** composed; unhurried; calm. **2.** sober and decorous. [< L *sedatus* quieted] —**se•date'ness** *n.*

se•da•tion (si DAY shən) *n.* the act of administering sedatives; also their effect.

sed•a•tive (SED ə tiv) *adj.* allaying irritation; assuaging pain. —*n.* any means, as a medicine, of soothing distress or allaying pain. [ME]

sed•en•tar•y (SED n TER ee) *adj.* **1.** characterized by or requiring much sitting. **2.** settled in one place. [< MF *sedentaire*] —**sed'en•tar'i•ness** *n.*

Se•der (SAY dər) *n.* in Judaism, the Passover feast commemorating the departure of the Israelites from Egypt. [< Hebrew *sedher* order]

sed•i•ment (SED ə mənt) *n.* **1.** matter that settles to the bottom of a liquid; dregs. **2.** *Geol.* fragmentary material deposited by water or air. [< MF]

se•di•tion (si DISH ən) *n.* **1.** language or conduct directed against public order and the safety of the state. **2.** the clandestine incitement of such disorder. **3.** dissension; revolt. [ME *sedicioun*] —**se•di′tious** (si DISH əs) *adj.*

se•duce (si DOOS) *v.t.* •**duced,** •**duc•ing 1.** lead astray; entice into wrong. **2.** induce to engage in illicit sexual intercourse. [< LL *seducere* lead away] —**se•duc′er** *n.* —**se•duc•tion** (si DUK·shən) *n.* —**se•duc′tive** *adj.* —**se•duc′tive•ness** *n.*

sed•u•lous (SEJ ə ləs) *adj.* diligent; assiduous. [< L *sedulus* careful] —**se•du•li•ty** (si DOO li tee), **sed′u•lous•ness** *n.*

see[1] (see) *v.* **saw, seen, see•ing** *v.t.* **1.** perceive with the eyes. **2.** perceive with the mind; understand. **3.** find out or ascertain. **4.** have experience of. **5.** encounter; chance to meet. **6.** visit or receive as a guest, patient, etc. **7.** attend as a spectator; view. **8.** accompany; escort. **9.** take care; be sure: *See* that you do it. —*v.i.* **10.** have or exercise the power of sight. **11.** find out; inquire. **12.** understand. **13.** consider. —**see about 1.** inquire into. **2.** take care of; attend to. —**see (someone) off** accompany to a point of departure, as for a journey. —**see (someone) through** aid or protect, as throughout a period of difficulty or danger. —**see through** penetrate, as a disguise or deception. —**see to** be responsible for; give one's attention to. [ME *seen*]

see[2] *n.* the local seat from which a bishop, archbishop, or pope exercises jurisdiction; also such jurisdiction, authority, rank, or office. —**Holy See** the Pope's jurisdiction or office. [< L *sedes* seat]

seed (seed) *n.* **1.** the fertilized ovule from which a plant may be reproduced. **2.** origin; source. **3.** offspring; children. **4.** the male fertilizing element; semen; sperm. **5.** seeds collectively. —**go to seed 1.** develop and shed seed. **2.** deteriorate. —*v.t.* **1.** sow with seed. **2.** remove the seeds from. **3.** in sports, arrange the matches of (players) in a tournament, so that the more skilled meet only in the later matches. **4.** intersperse (clouds) with silver iodide or other particles in order to produce rainfall. —*v.i.* **5.** sow seed. **6.** grow to maturity and produce or shed seed. [ME *sede*] —**seed′less** *adj.*

seed•ling (SEED ling) *n.* **1.** *Bot.* a plant grown from seed. **2.** a very young tree or plant.

seed pearl a small pearl.

seed•y (SEE dee) *adj.* **seed•i•er, seed•i•est 1.** full of seeds. **2.** gone to seed. **3.** poor; shabby. **4.** feeling or looking wretched. —**seed′i•ness** *n.*

see•ing (SEE ing) *n.* the act of seeing; vision; sight. —*conj.* since; in view of the fact.

seek (seek) *v.* **sought, seek•ing** *v.t.* **1.** go in search of; look for. **2.** strive for; try to obtain. **3.** endeavor or try. **4.** ask for; request. —*v.i.* **5.** make a search or inquiry. [ME *seken*] —**seek′er** *n.*

seem (seem) *v.i.* **1.** give the impression of being; appear. **2.** appear to oneself: I *seem* to hear voices. **3.** be evident or apparent: It *seems* to be raining. [ME *semen*]

seem•ing (SEE ming) *adj.* apparent but not necessarily actual. —*n.* appearance; semblance; esp., false show. —**seem′ing•ly** *adv.*

seem•ly (SEEM lee) *adj.* •**li•er,** •**li•est** proper; decorous. —*adv.* becomingly; decently; appropriately. [ME *semely* honorable] —**seem′li•ness** *n.*

seen (seen) past participle of SEE.

seep (seep) *v.i.* soak through pores or cracks; percolate; ooze. —*n.* a small spring or a place out of which water, oil, etc., oozes. [< OE *sypian*] —**seep•age** (SEE pij) *n.*

seer (SEE ər) *n.* **1.** one who sees. **2.** (*pr.* seer) a prophet. [ME]

seer•suck•er (SEER SUK ər) *n.* a thin fabric, usu. striped in a color, with a crinkled surface. [< Persian *shīr o shakkar*, lit., milk and sugar]

see•saw (SEE saw) *n.* **1.** a balanced board made to move alternately up and down by persons at opposite ends: also called *teeter.* **2.** any up-and-down movement or change. —*v.t. & v.i.* move or cause to move on or as if on a seesaw. —*adj.* moving to and fro; vacillating.

seethe (see*th*) *v.* **seethed, seeth•ing** *v.i.* **1.** boil. **2.** foam or bubble as if boiling. **3.** be agitated, as by rage. —*v.t.* **4.** soak in liquid; steep. —*n.* the act or condition of seething; turmoil. [ME]

seg•ment (SEG mənt) *n.* **1.** a part cut off or divided from the other parts; a section. **2.** *Geom.* **a** a part of a figure, esp., of a circle, cut off by a line or plane. **b** a finite part of a line. —*v.t. & v.i.* (seg MENT) divide into segments. [< L *segmentum*] —**seg•men′tal** *adj.* —**seg′men•ta′tion** *n.*

seg•re•gate (SEG ri GAYT) *v.t.* •**gat•ed,** •**gat•ing 1.** place (a person or thing) apart from others or the rest; isolate. **2.** subject to segregation. —*adj.* (-ri git) set apart from others. [ME *segregat*]

seg·re·ga·tion (SEG ri GAY shən) *n.* **1.** the act or process of segregating. **2.** the practice of requiring separate facilities, for use by different racial groups. **—seg're·ga'tion·ist** *n.*

seine (sayn) *n.* a long fishing net hanging vertically in the water and having floats at the top edge and weights at the bottom. — *v.t. & v.i.* **seined, sein·ing** fish or catch with a seine. [ME *seyne*]

seis·mic (SĪZ mik) *adj.* of, characteristic of, or produced by earthquakes. Also **seis'mal, seis'mi·cal.**

seismic sea wave tsunami.

seis·mo·gram (SĪZ mə GRAM) *n.* the record made by a seismograph.

seis·mo·graph (SĪZ mə GRAF) *n.* an instrument for recording automatically the intensity, direction, and duration of an earthquake shock. **—seis'mo·graph'ic** *adj.* **—seis·mog·ra·pher** (sīz MOG rə fər) *n.*

seis·mog·ra·phy (sīz MOG rə fee) *n.* the study and recording of earthquake phenomena.

seis·mol·o·gy (sīz MOL ə jee) *n.* the science of earthquake phenomena. **—seis'mo·log'i·cal** *adj.* **—seis·mol'o·gist** *n.*

seize (seez) *v.* **seized, seiz·ing** *v.t.* **1.** take hold of suddenly and forcibly. **2.** take possession of by authority or right. **3.** take possession by force. **4.** take prisoner; arrest. **5.** act upon with sudden and powerful effect: Terror *seized* us. —*v.i.* **6.** take a sudden or forcible hold. [ME *saisen*] **—seiz'a·ble** *adj.*

sei·zure (SEE zhər) *n.* **1.** the act of seizing. **2.** a sudden or violent attack, as of epilepsy; fit.

sel·dom (SEL dəm) *adv.* at widely separated intervals; infrequently. [ME]

se·lect (si LEKT) *v.t.* **1.** take in preference to another or others. —*v.i.* **2.** make a choice. —*adj.* **1.** chosen in preference to others; choice. **2.** exclusive. **3.** very particular in selecting. [< L *selectus*] **—se·lect'ness** *n.*

se·lect·ee (si lek TEE) *n.* one selected; esp., one drafted for military or naval service.

se·lec·tion (si LEK shən) *n.* **1.** the act of selecting; choice. **2.** anything selected. **3.** a thing or collection of things chosen with care. **4.** *Biol.* natural selection.

se·lec·tive (si LEK tiv) *adj.* pertaining to selection; tending to select. **—se·lec'tiv'i·ty** *n.*

selective service compulsory military service according to specified conditions of age, fitness, etc.

self (self) *n. pl.* **selves 1.** an individual known or considered as the subject of his own consciousness. **2.** personal interest or advantage. **3.** any thing, class, or attribute that, abstractly considered, maintains a distinct and characteristic individuality or identity. —*adj.* **1.** being of the same color, substance, etc. throughout; uniform. **2.** of a part, accessory, etc., made of the same material as that with which it is used. [ME] *Self* as a combining form has the meanings: **1.** of the self (the object of the root word), as in:

self-abasement	self-guidance
self-abhorrence	self-harming
self-accusation	self-humbling
self-admiration	self-humiliation
self-adornment	self-hypnosis
self-adulation	self-idolatry
self-advancement	self-idolizing
self-advertisement	self-ignorant
self-advertising	self-image
self-affliction	self-immolation
self-aggrandizement	self-impairment
self-analysis	self-improvement
self-annihilation	self-incriminating
self-appreciation	self-indignation
self-approval	self-indulging
self-asserting	self-inspection
self-awareness	self-instruction
self-betrayal	self-insurer
self-blame	self-justification
self-condemnation	self-justifying
self-condemning	self-knowledge
self-confinement	self-laudatory
self-conserving	self-limitation
self-consideration	self-limiting
self-consuming	self-maintenance
self-contempt	self-martyrdom
self-contradicting	self-mastery
self-correction	self-mutilation
self-corruption	self-neglect
self-criticism	self-opinion
self-cure	self-perceptive
self-deceiving	self-perfection
self-defeating	self-perpetuating
self-degradation	self-perpetuation
self-delusion	self-persuasion
self-deprecating	self-pleasing
self-depreciation	self-praise
self-destroying	self-preparation

self-destruction
self-destructive
self-direction
self-disclosure
self-discovery
self-doubt
self-enriching
self-examination
self-expansion
self-exploiting
self-exposure
self-flattery
self-folding
self-forgetful
self-giving
self-glorification
self-gratification
self-tolerant
self-torment
self-torture
self-trust

self-presentation
self-preserving
self-protecting
self-protection
self-punishment
self-realization
self-regulation
self-representation
self-repressing
self-reproach
self-restriction
self-revealing
self-revelation
self-scrutinizing
self-searching
self-soothing
self-study
self-trusting
self-valuing
self-vindication
self-worship

2. by or from oneself or itself, as in:

self-administered
self-apparent
self-approved
self-arising
self-authorized
self-blinded
self-caused
self-complete
self-condemned
self-conducted
self-confessed
self-constituted
self-declared
self-defining
self-deluded
self-deprived
self-derived
self-determined
self-devised
self-doomed
self-elected
self-employed
self-explained
self-explanatory
self-exposed
self-forbidden
self-fulfilling
self-furnished
self-generated
self-healing
self-imposed
self-inclusive
self-incurred

self-induced
self-inflicted
self-initiated
self-instructed
self-invited
self-issuing
self-judged
self-justified
self-limited
self-moving
self-named
self-ordained
self-originating
self-paid
self-perpetuated
self-posed
self-proclaimed
self-professed
self-punished
self-refuting
self-reliance
self-reliant
self-renewing
self-repressed
self-restoring
self-restrained
self-restraint
self-revealed
self-rewarding
self-schooled
self-stimulated
self-sustained
self-sustaining

3. to, toward, in, for, or with oneself, as in:

self-absorbed
self-addressed
self-aid
self-amusement
self-assumed
self-assuming
self-benefit
self-care
self-complacency
self-conflict
self-consistency
self-consistent
self-content
self-contented
self-deception
self-delight
self-dependence
self-dependent
self-directed
self-disgust

self-enclosed
self-gain
self-help
self-injurious
self-injury
self-liking
self-loathing
self-love
self-occupied
self-preference
self-prescribed
self-pride
self-produced
self-purifying
self-relying
self-repellent
self-reproof
self-resentment
self-resigned
self-respectful

4. independent, as in:

self-agency
self-authority
self-credit
self-entity

self-existence
self-ownership
self-rule
self-sovereignty

5. in technology, automatic or automatically, as in:

self-acting
self-adapting
self-adjustable
self-adjusting
self-aligning
self-burning
self-defrosting
self-emptying
self-feeding
self-filling
self-focusing
self-inking
self-lighting
self-locking
self-lubricating

self-charging
self-checking
self-cleaning
self-closing
self-cocking
self-cooled
self-moving
self-oiling
self-priming
self-recording
self-registering
self-regulated
self-regulating
self-righting
self-winding

self·ab·ne·ga·tion (SELF AB ni GAY shən) *n.* the complete putting aside of oneself and one's own claims for the sake of others.

self·ab·sorp·tion (SELF ab ZORP shən) *n.* absorption in or concentration on one's own affairs, work, interests, etc.

self·ap·point·ed (SELF ə POIN tid) *adj.* appointed by oneself rather than by others: a *self-appointed* boss.

self·as·ser·tion (SELF ə SUR shən) *n.* the asserting or putting forward of oneself, one's opinions, claims, or rights. **—self'·as· ser'tive** *adj.*

self·as·sured (SELF ə SHUURD) *adj.* con-

fident in one's own abilities; self-reliant. —
self′-as•sur′ance n.

self-cen•tered (SELF SEN tərd) adj. concerned chiefly with one's own affairs and interests, often with a lack of consideration for others. —**self′-cen′tered•ness** n.

self-con•ceit (SELF kən SEET) n. an unduly high opinion of oneself; vanity.

self-con•fi•dence (SELF KON fi dəns) n. confidence in oneself, one's judgment, etc. —**self′con′fi•dent** adj.

self-con•scious (SELF KON shəs) adj. 1. unduly conscious that one is observed by others; ill at ease. 2. manifesting embarrassment. —**self′-con′scious•ness** n.

self-con•tained (SELF kən TAYND) adj. 1. keeping one's thoughts and feelings to oneself. 2. exercising self-control 3. complete and independent. 4. having all parts needed for working order.

self-con•tra•dic•tion (SELF KON trə DIK shən) n. 1. the act or state of contradicting oneself or itself. 2. that which contradicts itself. —**self′-con′tra•dic′to•ry** adj.

self-con•trol (SELF kən TROHL) n. the act, power, or habit of keeping one's faculties or energies under control of the will.

self-de•fense (SELF di FENS) n. defense of oneself, one's property, or one's reputation.

self-de•ni•al (SELF di NĪ əl) n. the act or power of denying oneself gratification. —**self′de•ny′ing** adj.

self-de•struct (SELF di STRUKT) v.i. destroy itself: The rocket is designed to self-destruct.

self-de•ter•mi•na•tion (SELF di TUR mə NAY shən) n. 1. the principle of free will; decision by oneself. 2. decision by the people of a country or section as to its future political status.

self-dis•ci•pline (SELF DIS ə plin) n. discipline or training of oneself.

self-ef•face•ment (SELF i FAYS mənt) n. the keeping of oneself in the background. —**self′-ef•fac′ing** adj.

self-es•teem (SELF i STEEM) n. a good opinion of oneself.

self-ev•i•dent (SELF EV i dənt) adj. requiring no proof or explanation. —**self′-ev′i•dent•ly** adv.

self-ex•pres•sion (SELF ik SPRESH ən) n. expression of one's own temperament or emotions.

self-gov•ern•ment (SELF GUV ərn mənt)

n. government of a state or region by its own people. —**self′-gov′erned** adj.

self-im•por•tance (SELF im POR təns) n. pompous self-conceit. —**self′-im•por′tant** (-tnt) adj.

self-in•dul•gence (SELF in DUL jəns) n. the indulgence or gratification of one's own desires, weaknesses, etc. —**self′-in•dul′gent** adj.

self-in•ter•est (SELF IN tər ist) n. personal interest or advantage, or the pursuit of it; selfishness. —**self′-in′ter•est•ed** adj.

self•ish (SEL fish) adj. 1. caring chiefly for oneself or one's own interests or comfort, esp. to the point of disregarding the welfare or wishes of others. 2. proceeding from or characterized by undue love of self. —**self′ish•ness** n.

self•less (SELF lis) adj. regardless of self; unselfish. —**self′less•ly** adv. —**self′less•ness** n.

self-made (SELF MAYD) adj. 1. having attained honor, wealth, etc., by one's own efforts. 2. made by oneself.

self-pos•ses•sion (SELF pə ZESH ən) n. 1. control of one's powers or faculties. 2. presence of mind; self-command. —**self′-pos•sessed** (-ZEST) adj.

self-pres•er•va•tion (SELF PREZ ər VAY shən) n. protection of oneself from destruction.

self-pro•pelled (SELF prə PELD) adj. 1. able to propel itself. 2. having the means of propulsion contained within itself, as an automobile.

self-re•gard (SELF ri GAHRD) n. 1. regard or consideration for oneself or one's own interests. 2. estimation of self.

self-re•spect (SELF ri SPEKT) n. proper respect for oneself and one's own character. —**self′-re•spect′ing** adj.

self-right•eous (SELF RĪ chəs) adj. righteous in one's own estimation. —**self′-right′eous•ness** n.

self-sac•ri•fice (SELF SAK rə FIS) n. the sacrifice of one's self or one's personal welfare or wishes for the sake of duty or for the good of others. —**self′-sac′ri•fic′ing** (-FIS ing) adj.

self•same (SELF saym) adj. exactly the same; identical.

self-sat•is•fac•tion (SELF SAT is FAK shən) n. satisfaction with one's own actions and characteristics; conceit; complacency. —**self′-sat′is•fied** adj. —**self′-sat′is•fy′ing** adj.

self-seek•ing (SELF SEE king) *adj.* selfish. —*n.* the actions, motives, etc., characteristic of a self-seeking person.

self-serv•ing (SELF SUR ving) *adj.* tending to advance one's own interests.

self-styled (SELF STĪLD) *adj.* characterized (as such) by oneself: a *self-styled* gentleman.

self-suf•fi•cient (SELF sə FISH ənt) *adj.* able to maintain oneself without aid from others. —**self'-suf•fi'cien•cy** n.

self-taught (SELF TAWT) *adj.* taught by oneself or through one's own efforts.

self-will (SELF WIL) *n.* strong or tenacious adherence to one's own will or wish; obstinacy. —**self -willed'** *adj.*

sell (sel) *v.* **sold, sell•ing** *v.t.* **1.** transfer (property) to another for money or for some other consideration. **2.** deal in; offer for sale. **3.** deliver, surrender, or betray for a price or reward. **4.** promote the sale of. **5.** cause to accept or approve something: with *on: They sold* him on the scheme. **6.** cause the acceptance or approval of. —*v.i.* **7.** transfer ownership for money etc.; engage in selling. **8.** be on sale; be sold. **9.** attract buyers. **10.** gain acceptance or approval. —**sell off** get rid of by selling. —**sell out 1.** sell all one's merchandise, possessions, etc. **2.** betray. [ME *sellen*]

sell•out (SEL OWT) *n.* **1.** a performance for which all seats have been sold. **2.** a betrayal.

selt•zer (SELT sər) *n.* an effervescing mineral water. Also **seltzer water.** [< G *Selterser*, from *Selters,* a village in Prussia]

sel•vage (SEL vij) *n.* the edge of a woven fabric so finished that it will not ravel. Also **sel'vedge.** [ME]

selves (selvz) plural of SELF.

se•man•tic (si MAN tik) *adj.* **1.** of or pertaining to meaning. **2.** of or relating to semantics. —**se•man'ti•cal•ly** *adv.*

se•man•ti•cist (si MAN tə sist) *n.* a specialist in semantics.

se•man•tics (si MAN tiks) *n. (construed as sing.)* **1.** *Ling.* the study of meaning. **2.** *Logic* the relation between signs or symbols and what they signify or denote. [< Gk. *sēmainein* signify]

sem•a•phore (SEM ə FOR) *n.* an apparatus for making signals, as with movable arms. [< Gk. *sēma* + *-phore* sign bearer]

sem•blance (SEM bləns) *n.* **1.** a mere show without reality; pretense. **2.** outward appearance. **3.** a likeness or resemblance. [ME]

se•men (SEE mən) *n.* the impregnating fluid of male humans and animals that contains spermatozoa; seed. [ME]

se•mes•ter (si MES tər) *n.* in colleges etc., a period of instruction, usu. lasting 13 to 18 weeks. [< L *semestris* of six months]

semi- *prefix* **1.** not fully; partially; partly: *semiautomatic.* **2.** exactly half: *semicircle.* **3.** occurring twice (in the periods specified): *semiweekly.* [< L]

Semi- (def. 1) appears as a prefix in many words, as in the list below.

semiagricultural	semideaf
semialcoholic	semidelirious
semianimated	semidependent
semiarid	semideveloped
semiattached	semidigested
semiautonomous	semidomesticated
semibald	semidry
semibarbaric	semienclosed
semibarren	semifailure
semiblind	semifeudalism
semicivilized	semifictional
semicoagulated	semiflexed
semicollapsible	semifluid
semiconfident	semiformal
semiconfinement	semigloss
semiconscious	semi-Gothic
semiconservative	semihard
semicooperative	semihistorical
semidangerous	semihumorous
semidarkness	semi-idle
semi-independent	semireactionary
semi-intoxicated	semireligious
semi-invalid	semirespectable
semiliberal	semiretired
semiliquid	semiretirement
semiliterate	semirustic
semimilitary	semisacred
semimobile	semisatirical
semimodern	semiscientific
semimute	semiserious
semiofficial	semiskilled
semiorganized	semisoft
semiparalysis	semisolid
semipastoral	semisuccessful
semiperishable	semisweet
semipermanent	semitechnical
semiplastic	semitrained
semipolitical	semitransparent
semipublic	semivoluntary
semiradical	semiwild

sem•i•an•nu•al (SEM ee AN yoo əl) *adj.* issued or occurring twice a year; half-yearly. —*n.* a publication issued twice a year. —**sem'i•an'nu•al•ly** *adv.*

sem·i·au·to·mat·ic (SEM ee AW tə MAT ik) *adj.* **1.** partly automatic. **2.** of firearms, self-loading but firing once at each pull on the trigger.

sem·i·co·lon (SEM i KOH lən) *n.* a mark (;) of punctuation, indicating a greater degree of separation than the comma.

sem·i·con·duc·tor (SEM ee kən DUK tər) *n. Physics* one of a class of substances whose electrical conductivity at ordinary temperatures is between that of a metal and an insulator. **—sem′i·con·duct′ing** *adj.*

sem·i·de·tached (SEM ee di TACHT) *adj.* joined to another on one side only; esp., designating a house having one wall in common with another house.

sem·i·fi·nal (SEM ee FĪN əl) *n.* in sports, a competition that precedes the final event. **—adj.** next before the final. **—sem′i·fi′nal·ist** *n.*

sem·i·month·ly (SEM ee MUNTH lee) *adj.* taking place twice a month. **—n. pl. ·lies** a publication issued twice a month. **—adv.** at half-monthly intervals.

sem·i·nal (SEM ə nl) *adj.* **1.** of, pertaining to, or containing seeds or semen. **2.** having productive power; germinal. **3.** not developed; rudimentary. [ME] **—sem′i·nal·ly** *adv.*

sem·i·nar (SEM ə NAHR) *n.* **1.** a group of advanced students meeting regularly with a professor for discussion of research problems. **2.** the course thus conducted. **3.** any meeting for holding discussions.

sem·i·nar·y (SEM ə NER ee) *n. pl. ·nar·ies* a special school, as one for training the clergy or a private school for girls. [ME, nursery]

sem·i·na·tion (SEM ə NAY shən) *n.* **1.** the act of sowing or spreading. **2.** propagation; reproduction. [< L *seminatus* sown]

sem·i·per·me·a·ble (SEM ee PUR mee ə bəl) *adj.* partially permeable, as a membrane that allows some but not all molecules to pass through it.

sem·i·pre·cious (SEM ee PRESH əs) *adj.* designating gemstones that are somewhat less rare or valuable than precious stones.

sem·i·pro·fes·sion·al (SEM ee prə FRESH ə nl) *adj.* engaged in a sport for profit, but not as a full-time occupation. **—n.** a semiprofessional athlete. **—sem′i·pro·fes′sion·al·ly** *adv.*

Sem·ite (SEM it) *n.* one of a people of Caucasian stock, now represented by the Jews and Arabs, but originally including the ancient Babylonians, Assyrians, Phoenicians, etc. [< NL *semita*]

Se·mit·ic (sə MIT ik) *adj.* of or pertaining to the Semites, or to any of their languages. **—n.** the Semitic subfamily of languages.

sem·i·tone (SEM ee TOHN) *n. Music* the smallest interval of the chromatic scale; a tone at an interval a half step from another: also called *half step, half tone.* **sem·i·week·ly** (SEM ee WEEK lee) *adj.* issued or occurring twice a week. **—n. pl. ·lies** a publication issued twice a week. **—adv.** at half-weekly intervals.

sem·i·year·ly (SEM ee YEER lee) *adj.* issued or occurring twice a year. **—n. pl. ·lies** a semiyearly occurrence. **—adv.** at half-yearly intervals.

sem·per fi·de·lis (SEM pər fi DAY lis) *Latin* always faithful: motto of the U.S. Marine Corps.

sem·per pa·ra·tus (SEM pər pə RAY təs) *Latin* always prepared: motto of the U.S. Coast Guard.

sen·ate (SEN it) *n.* **1.** the governing body of some universities and institutions of learning. **2.** a council or legislative body. **3.** *cap.* the upper branch of national or state legislative bodies of the U.S., Canada, France, and other governments. [ME *senat*]

sen·a·tor (SEN ə tər) *n. Often cap.* a member of a senate.

sen·a·to·ri·al (SEN ə TOR ee əl) *adj.* of, pertaining to, or befitting a senator or senate.

send (send) *v.* **sent, send·ing** *v.t.* **1.** cause or direct (a person) to go; dispatch. **2.** cause to be taken or directed to another place; transmit: sometimes with *off.* **3.** cause to issue; emit or discharge, as heat, light, etc. **4.** throw or drive by force; impel. **5.** *Slang* make rapturous with joy. **—v.i.** **6.** dispatch an agent, messenger, or message. **—send for** summon. **—send packing** dismiss quickly and forcefully. **—send up** *Informal* sentence to prison. [ME *senden*]

send-off (SEND awf) *n.* a celebration or demonstration for the beginning of a trip or a new venture.

se·nes·cent (si NES ənt) *adj.* **1.** growing old. **2.** characteristic of old age. [< L *senescere* grow old] **—se·nes′cence** *n.*

se·nile (SEE nīl) *adj.* **1.** pertaining to, proceeding from, or characteristic of old age. **2.** infirm; weak; doting. [< L *senilis* old] **—se·nil·i·ty** (si NIL i tee) *n.*

sen·ior (SEEN yər) *adj.* **1.** older in years or

higher in rank. **2.** denoting the older of two. **3.** belonging to maturity or later life. **4.** pertaining to the last year of a four-year high school or college course. —*n.* **1.** the older of two. **2.** one longer in service or higher in standing. **3.** a student in the senior year of a high school, college, or university. [ME]

senior citizen an elderly person, esp. one of or over the age of retirement.

senior high school a high school, in the U.S. typically comprising grades 10 through 12.

sen·ior·i·ty (seen YOR i tee) *n.* **1.** the state of being senior; priority of age or rank. **2.** *pl.* **·ties** precedence or priority due to length of service.

sen·sate (SEN sayt) *adj.* perceived by the senses. [< LL *sensatus* sensed]

sen·sa·tion (sen SAY shən) *n.* **1.** the consciousness of external stimulation, in the form of hearing, taste, touch, smell, or sight. **2.** *Physiol.* the capacity to respond to such stimulation. **3.** that which produces great interest or excitement. **4.** an excited condition: cause a *sensation.*

sen·sa·tion·al (sen SAY shə nl) *adj.* **1.** pertaining to physical sensation or emotional excitement. **2.** causing excitement; startling.

sen·sa·tion·al·ism (sen SAY shə nə nl IZ əm) *n.* the use of sensational or melodramatic methods, words, etc. —**sen·sa·tion·al·ist** *n.*

sense (sens) *n.* **1.** the faculty of sensation; sense perception. **2.** any of certain agencies by or through which an individual receives impressions of the external world, as taste, touch, hearing, smell, or sight. **3.** rational perception accompanied by feeling: a *sense* of wrong. **4.** *Often pl.* normal power of mind or understanding; sound judgment: She is coming to her *senses.* **5.** signification; import; meaning. **6.** sound reason or judgment; wisdom. **7.** capacity to perceive or appreciate: a *sense* of color. —*v.t.* sensed, sens·ing **1.** become aware of through the senses. **2.** comprehend; understand. [ME]

sense·less (SENS lis) *adj.* **1.** devoid of sense; making no sense; irrational. **2.** unconscious. **3.** incapable of feeling or perception.

sen·si·bil·i·ty (sen sə BIL i tee) *n. pl.* **·ties** **1.** the capability of sensation; power to perceive or feel. **2.** the capacity of sensation and rational emotion, as distinguished from intellect and will. **3.** *Often pl.* susceptibility or sensitiveness to outside influences or

mental impressions. **4.** discerning judgment.

sen·si·ble (SEN sə bəl) *adj.* **1.** possessed of good practical judgment; exhibiting sound sense and understanding. **2.** capable of physical sensation. **3.** emotionally or mentally sensitive. **4.** great enough to be perceived. [ME] —**sen'si·bly** *adv.*

sen·si·tive (SEN si tiv) *adj.* **1.** easily affected by outside influences; excitable or impressionable; touchy. **2.** reacting readily to external agents or forces: paper *sensitive* to light. **3.** closing or moving when touched or irritated, as certain plants. **4.** capable of indicating minute changes or differences; delicate. **5.** of, relating to, or dealing with secret or delicate matters: a *sensitive* federal job. —**sen'si·tive·ly** *adv.*

sen·si·tiv·i·ty (SEN si TIV i tee) *n. pl.* **·ties** the state or degree of being sensitive.

sen·si·tize (SEN si TĪZ) *v.t.* **·tized,** **·tiz·ing** **1.** render sensitive. **2.** *Photog.* make sensitive to light, as a plate or film.

sen·sor (SEN sər) *n.* that which receives and responds to a stimulus or signal; esp., an instrument or device designed to detect and respond to some force, change, or radiation.

sen·so·ry (SEN sə ree) *adj.* **1.** of or pertaining to sensation. **2.** conveying or producing sense impulses. Also **sen·so·ri·al** (sen SOR ee əl).

sen·su·al (SEN shoo əl) *adj.* **1.** unduly indulging the physical appetites as for sex, food, etc. **2.** pertaining to the body or to the physical senses. [ME] —**sen·su·al·i·ty** (SEN shoo AL i tee) *n.* —**sen'su·al·ist** *n.* —**sen'su·al·ly** *adv.*

sen·su·ous (SEN shoo əs) *adj.* **1.** pertaining or appealing to or derived from the senses. **2.** keenly appreciative of and aroused by beauty, refinement, or luxury. —**sen'su·ous·ly** *adv.* —**sen'su·ous·ness** *n.*

sent (sent) past tense, past participle of SEND.

sen·tence (SEN tns) *n.* **1.** *Gram.* a group of words containing a subject and a predicate, as declarative, interrogative, imperative, and exclamatory sentences, or a single word in the case of the simple imperative. **2.** *Law* a penalty pronounced upon a person convicted. —*v.t.* **·tenced,** **·tenc·ing** pass sentence upon. [ME] —**sen·ten·tial** (sen TEN shəl) *adj.*

sen·ten·tious (sen TEN shəs) *adj.* **1.** abounding in or using terse, laconic, or aphoristic language. **2.** pompously formal; moralizing. [ME] **—sen·ten'tious·ness** n.

sen·ti·ent (SEN shənt) adj. possessing powers of sense or sense perception; having sensation or feeling. **—**n. a sentient person or thing. [< L sentiens feeling] **—sen'ti·ence** n. **—sen'ti·ent·ly** adv.

sen·ti·ment (SEN tə mənt) n. **1.** noble, tender, or artistic feeling; sensibility. **2.** a mental attitude or response to a person, object, or idea, based on feeling instead of reason. **3.** Often pl. an opinion or judgment. [< F]

sen·ti·men·tal (SEN tə MEN tl) adj. **1.** characterized by sentiment or emotion. **2.** experiencing, displaying, or given to sentiment, often in an extravagant or mawkish manner: a sentimental novel.

sen·ti·men·tal·i·ty (SEN tə men TAL i tee) n. pl. **·ties 1.** the state or quality of being mawkishly sentimental. **2.** any expression of sentiment. Also **sen'ti·men'tal·ism** (-tl IZ əm). **—sen'ti·men'tal·ist** (-tl ist) n.

sen·ti·men·tal·ize (SEN tə MEN tl Iz) v. **·tized, ·iz·ing** v.t. **1.** make sentimental. **2.** cherish sentimentally. **—**v.i. **3.** behave sentimentally.

sen·ti·nel (SEN tn l) n. **1.** a sentry. **2.** any watcher or guard. **—**v.t. **·neled, ·nel·ing** watch over as a sentinel. [< MF sentinelle]

sen·try (SEN tree) n. pl. **·tries 1.** a soldier stationed on guard duty to prevent passage of unauthorized persons and to warn of danger. **2.** the watch or guard kept by a sentry.

sep·a·ra·ble (SEP ər ə bəl) adj. capable of being separated. **—sep'a·ra·bil'i·ty** n. **— sep'a·ra·bly** adv.

sep·a·rate (SEP ə RAYT) v. **·rat·ed, ·rat·ing** v.t. **1.** disunite or disjoin; sever. **2.** occupy a position between; serve to keep apart. **3.** divide into components, parts, etc. **—**v.i. **4.** become divided or disconnected; draw apart. **5.** part company; withdraw from association or combination. **—**adj. (SEP ər it) **1.** existing or considered apart from others; individual. **2.** disunited from the body; disembodied. **3.** separated; disjoined. [ME] **—sep'a·rate·ly** adv. **—sep' a·rate·ness** n. **—sep'a·ra'tor** n.

sep·a·ra·tion (SEP ə RAY shən) n. **1.** the act or process of separating; division. **2.** the state of being disconnected or apart. **3.** something that separates. **4.** Law relinquishment of cohabitation between husband and wife by mutual consent.

sep·a·ra·tist (SEP ər ə tist) n. one who advocates or upholds separation, esp. one who secedes. **—sep'a·ra·tism** n.

sep·sis (SEP sis) n. Pathol. infection by pathogenic microorganisms. [< NL]

sep·ta (SEP tə) plural of SEPTUM.

Sep·tem·ber (sep TEM bər) n. the ninth month of the year, containing 30 days. [ME Septembre]

sep·tet (sep TET) n. **1.** a group of seven persons, things, etc. **2.** Music a composition for seven singers or instrumentalists. Also **sep·tette'.** [< G]

sep·tic (SEP tik) adj. **1.** of, pertaining to, or caused by sepsis. **2.** producing sepsis; infective. [< L septicus] **—sep·tic·i·ty** (sep TIS i tee) n.

sep·ti·ce·mi·a (SEP tə SEE mee ə) n. Pathol. an infection of the blood by pathogenic microorganisms; blood poisoning. [< NL] **—sep'ti·ce'mic** adj.

septic tank a tank in which sewage is kept until purified by bacterial action.

sep·til·lion (sep TIL yən) n. in the U.S., a cardinal number written as 1 followed by 24 zeros. **—sep·til'lionth** n. & adj.

sep·tu·a·ge·nar·i·an (SEP choo ə jə NAIR ee ən) n. a person between 70 and 80 years of age. [< L septuaginarius]

Sep·tu·a·gint (SEP too ə JINT) n. an old Greek version of the Old Testament Scriptures. [< L septuaginta seventy]

sep·tum (SEP təm) n. pl. **·ta** (-tə) Biol. a dividing wall between two cavities: the nasal septum. [< L]

sep·ul·cher (SEP əl kər) n. **1.** a burial place; tomb; vault. **2.** a receptacle for relics, esp. in an altar slab. **—**v.t. place in a sepulcher; bury. Also **sep'ul·chre.** [ME sepulcre]

se·pul·chral (sə PUL krəl) adj. **1.** pertaining to a sepulcher. **2.** suggestive of the grave; dismal. **3.** unnaturally low and hollow in tone, as a voice. **—se·pul'chral·ly** adv.

sep·ul·ture (SEP əl chər) n. **1.** the act of entombing; burial. **2.** a sepulcher. [ME]

se·quel (SEE kwəl) n. **1.** something that follows and serves as a continuation; a development from what went before. **2.** a narrative discourse that, though complete in itself, develops from a preceding one. **3.** a consequence; upshot; result. [ME sequele]

se·quence (SEE kwəns) n. **1.** the process or fact of following in space, time, or thought; succession or order. **2.** order of succession; arrangement. **3.** a number of things following one another, considered collectively; series. **4.** an effect or consequence. **5.** a section of motion-picture film presenting a single episode, without time lapses or interruptions. [ME] —**se·quen·tial** (si KWEN shəl) adj. —**se·quen'tial·ly** adv.

se·quent (SEE kwənt) adj. **1.** following in the order of time; succeeding. **2.** consequent; resultant. [< L *sequens* following]

se·ques·ter (si KWES tər) v.t. **1.** place apart; separate. **2.** seclude; withdraw: often used reflexively. [ME *sequestren*] —**se·ques'tered** adj.

se·ques·trate (si KWES trayt) v.t. **·trat·ed, ·trat·ing 1.** seize, esp. for the use of the government; confiscate. **2.** seclude; sequester. —**se·ques·tra·tion** (SEE kwes TRAY shən) n.

se·quin (SEE kwin) n. a small coinlike ornament sewn on clothing. [< F]

se·quoi·a (si KWOI ə) n. one of two gigantic evergreen trees of the western U.S. [after *Sequoyah*, a Cherokee Indian who devised the Cherokee alphabet]

se·ra (SEER ə) n. a plural of SERUM.

se·ra·glio (si RAL yoh) n. the portion of a Muslim house reserved for the wives and concubines; a harem. [< Ital. *serraglio*]

se·ra·pe (sə RAH pee) n. a blanketlike outer garment worn in Latin America. [< Am.Sp. *sarape*]

ser·aph (SER əf) n. pl. **·aphs** or **·a·phim** (-ə fim) an angel having three pairs of wings. [Back formation < *seraphim*] —**se·raph·ic** (si RAF ik) adj.

ser·a·phim (SER ə fim) n. a plural of ser·aph. [< Hebrew]

sere[1] (seer) adj. dried up; withered. Also spelled *sear*. [ME *seere*]

sere[2] n. Ecol. the stages found in a given plant formation from the initial to the ultimate stage. [Back formation < SERIES]

ser·e·nade (SER ə NAYD) n. an evening song, usu. that of a lover beneath his beloved's window. —v.t. & v.i. **·nad·ed, ·nad·ing** entertain with a serenade. [< F *sérénade*]

ser·en·dip·i·ty (SER ən DIP i tee) n. the faculty of happening upon fortunate discoveries when not in search of them. [Coined by Horace Walpole (1754), in *The Three Princes of Serendip*] —**ser'en·dip' i·tous** adj.

se·rene (sə REEN) adj. **1.** clear; calm: a *serene* sky. **2.** marked by peaceful repose; tranquil; placid: a *serene* spirit. **3.** of exalted rank, chiefly in titles: Her *Serene* Highness. [< L *serenus*] —**se·rene'ly** adv.

se·ren·i·ty (sə REN i tee) n. **1.** the state or quality of being serene; peacefulness; repose; clearness. **2.** pl. **·ties** Usu. cap. a title of honor given to certain members of royal families: preceded by *His, Your*, etc.

serf (surf) n. **1.** in feudal times, a person bound in servitude on an estate. **2.** a slave. [< F] —**serf'dom, serf'hood** n.

serge (surj) n. a strong twilled fabric, characterized by a diagonal rib on both sides of the cloth. [< F]

ser·geant (SAHR jənt) n. **1.** Mil. any of several noncommissioned officer grades. **2.** a police officer ranking next below a captain or lieutenant. [ME]

sergeant at arms an executive officer in a legislative body who enforces order.

se·ri·al (SEER ee əl) adj. **1.** of the nature of a series. **2.** published in a series at regular intervals. **3.** Music relating to or composed by serialism. [< NL *serialis*] —n. a novel or other story presented in successive installments, as in a magazine, on television, etc. —**se'ri·al·ize'** v.t. **·ized, ·iz·ing** se'ri·al·i·za'tion n. —**se'ri·al·ly** adv.

se·ri·al·ism (SEER ee ə LIZ əm) n. Music the theory and practice of composition that uses all the tones of the twelve-tone scale in various sequences.

serial killer a murderer who strikes repeatedly, choosing similar victims and killing them in more or less the same way.

se·ries (SEER eez) n. pl. **·ries 1.** an arrangement of one thing after another; a connected succession of persons, things, data, etc. on the basis of like relationships. **2.** Electr. an arrangement of sources or utilizers of electricity in which the positive electrode of one is connected with the negative electrode of another. [< L]

ser·if (SER if) n. Printing a light line or stroke crossing or projecting from the end of a main line or stroke in a letter.

se·ri·ous (SEER ee əs) adj. **1.** grave and earnest in quality, feeling, or disposition; sober. **2.** said, planned, or done with full practical intent; being or done in earnest. **3.** of grave importance: a *serious* problem. **4.** attended with considerable danger or loss: a *serious* accident. [ME] —**se'ri·ous· ness** n.

ser·mon (SUR mən) n. **1.** a discourse based on a passage or text of the Bible, delivered as part of a church service. **2.** any speech of a serious or solemn kind, as a formal exhortation. [ME]

ser•mon•ize (SUR mə NĪZ) *v.t. & v.i.* **•ized, •iz•ing 1.** compose or deliver a sermon (to). **2.** address at length in a moralizing manner.

se•rous (SEER əs) *adj.* pertaining to, containing or resembling serum. [< MF *sereux*]

ser•pent (SUR pənt) *n.* **1.** a snake. **2.** anything of serpentine form or appearance. [ME]

ser•pen•tine (SUR pən TEEN) *adj.* **1.** pertaining to or like a serpent; sinuous. **2.** sly; cunning.

ser•rate (SER ayt) *adj.* **1.** toothed or notched like a saw. **2.** *Bot.* having notched edges, as certain leaves. Also **ser•rat•ed** (SER ay tid). [< L *serratus* sawn] — **ser•ra•tion** (sə RAY shən) *n.*

se•rum (SEER əm) *n. pl.* **se•rums** or **se•ra** (SEER ə) the clear, slightly yellow portion of an animal liquid, as blood, after separation from its solid constituents. [< L, whey]

ser•vant (SUR vənt) *n.* **1.** a person hired to work for another, esp. in the home. **2.** a person working in government: a public *servant*. [ME]

serve (surv) *v.* **served, serv•ing** *v.t.* **1.** work for, esp. as a servant; be in the service of. **2.** promote the interests of; aid. **3.** obey and give homage to: *serve* God. **4.** satisfy the requirements of. **5.** perform the duties connected with, as a public office. **6.** go through (a period of enlistment etc.). **7.** furnish or provide, as with a regular supply. **8.** offer or bring food or drink to (a guest etc.). **9.** in tennis etc., put (the ball) in play by hitting it to one's opponent. **10.** *Law* a deliver (a summons or writ) to a person. **b** deliver a summons or writ to. —*v.i.* **11.** work as or perform the functions of a servant. **12.** wait at table; distribute food or drink. **13.** go through a term of service, as in the army or navy. **14.** be suitable or usable, as for a purpose. —*n.* **1.** in tennis etc., the delivering of the ball by striking it toward an opponent. **2.** the turn of the server. [ME *serven*]

serv•ice (SUR vis) *n.* **1.** assistance or benefit afforded another. **2.** the manner in which one is waited upon or served: The *service* in this restaurant is poor. **3.** a system of labor and material aids for the public or a portion of it: telephone *service*. **4.** a division of public employment devoted to a particular function: the diplomatic *service*. **5.** a public duty or function: jury *service*. **6.** any branch of the armed forces. **7.** military duty or as-

signment. **8.** a formal and public exercise of worship. **9.** a ritual prescribed for a particular ministration or observance: a marriage *service*. **10.** the music for a liturgical office or rite. **11.** the state or position of a servant, esp. a domestic servant. **12.** a set of tableware for a specific purpose. **13.** installation, maintenance, and repair of an article provided a buyer by a seller. **14.** in tennis etc., the act or manner of serving a ball. —*adj.* **1.** pertaining to or for service. **2.** for the use of servants or tradespeople: a *service* entrance. **3.** of, pertaining to, or belonging to a military service. —*v.t.* **•viced, •vic•ing 1.** maintain or repair. **2.** supply service to. [ME]

serv•ice•a•ble (SUR və sə bəl) *adj.* **1.** that can be made of service; beneficial; usable. **2.** capable of rendering long service; durable. —**ser′vice•a•bil′i•ty** *n.* —**ser′vice•a•bly** *adv.*

serv•ice•man (SUR vis MAN) *n. pl.* **•men 1.** a member of one of the armed forces. **2.** a man who performs services of maintenance, supply, repair, etc. —**ser′vice•wom′an** *n.fem. pl.* **•wom•en**

service station a place for supplying automobiles, trucks, etc., with gasoline, oil, water, etc. Also called *filling station, gas station*.

ser•vile (SUR vil) *adj.* **1.** having the spirit of a slave; abject: a *servile* flatterer. **2.** being in a condition of servitude. [ME] —**ser′vile•ly** *adv.* —**ser•vil′i•ty** *n.*

serv•ing (SUR ving) *n.* a portion of food for one person. —*adj.* used for serving food at table: a *serving* cart.

ser•vi•tude (SUR vi TOOD) *n.* **1.** the condition of a slave; bondage. **2.** enforced service as a punishment for crime: penal *servitude*. [ME]

ser•vo (SUR voh) *n. pl.* **•vos** any of various relay devices used in the automatic control of a complex machine, instrument, operation, or process. Also **ser•vo•mech•a•nism** (SUR voh MEK ə NIZ əm)

ses•a•me (SES ə mee) *n.* **1.** an East Indian plant. **2.** the seeds of this plant, used as food and as a source of **sesame oil**, an emollient: also **sesame seeds**. [< L *sesamum*]

sesqui- *prefix* one and a half; one and a half times: *sesquicentennial*.

ses•qui•cen•ten•ni•al (SES kwi sen TEN ee əl) *n.* a 150th anniversary or its celebration. —*adj.* of this anniversary or celebration.

ses•sion (SESH ən) *n.* **1.** a meeting or series

of meetings of a group of persons, convened for a specific purpose or activity. **2.** a division of a school year; term. **3.** a part of a day during which classes meet in a school. [ME]

set[1] (set) v. **set, set•ting** v.t. **1.** put in a certain place or position; place. **2.** put into a fixed or immovable position or state: *set one's jaw*. **3.** bring to a specified state: *set a boat adrift*. **4.** restore to proper position for healing, as a broken bone. **5.** place in readiness for operation or use: *set a trap*. **6.** adjust (an instrument, dial, clock, etc.) to a particular calibration or position. **7.** place knives, forks, etc. on (a table) in preparing for a meal. **8.** appoint or establish: *set a date*. **9.** assign to some specific duty or function; station: *set a guard*. **10.** cause to sit. **11.** present or perform so as to be copied or emulated: *set a bad example*. **12.** direct: *He set his course for home*. **13.** place in a mounting or frame, as a gem. **14.** arrange (hair) in waves, curls, etc. while moist. **15.** place (a hen) on eggs to hatch them. **16.** place (a price or value): with *by* or *on*. **17.** *Printing* arrange (type) for printing; compose. **18.** *Music* arrange an accompaniment for (words or music). **19.** describe (a scene) as taking place: *set the scene in Texas*. **20.** in some games, as bridge, defeat. —v.i. **21.** go or pass below the horizon, as the sun. **22.** wane; decline. **23.** sit on eggs, as fowl. **24.** become hard or firm; congeal. **25.** begin a journey; start: with *forth, out, off,* etc. **26.** *Bot.* begin development or growth, as a rudimentary fruit. —**set about** start doing; begin. —**set aside 1.** place apart or to one side. **2.** reject; dismiss. —**set back** reverse; hinder. —**set down 1.** place on a surface. **2.** write or print; record. **3.** judge or consider. —**set forth** state or declare; express. —**set in 1.** begin to occur: *Rigor mortis has set in.* **2.** blow or flow toward shore, as wind or tide. —**set off 1.** serve as a contrast or foil for. **2.** cause to explode. —**set out 1.** present to view; exhibit. **2.** plant. **3.** start a journey, enterprise, etc. —**set up 1.** place in an upright position. **2.** place in power, authority, etc. **3.** construct or build; assemble. **4.** provide with the means to start a new business. **5.** *Informal* pay for the drinks etc. of; treat. [ME *setten*] —*adj.* **1.** established by authority or agreement; appointed: *a set time; a set method.* **2.** customary; conventional: *a set phrase.* **3.** fixed and motionless; rigid. **4.** fixed in opinion or disposition. **5.**

formed; made: with a qualifying adverb: *deep-set eyes.* **6.** ready; prepared: *get set.* —*n.* **1.** the act or condition of setting. **2.** permanent change of form, as by chemical action, cooling, pressure, etc. **3.** the arrangement, tilt, or hang of a garment, sail, etc. **4.** carriage or bearing: *the set of her shoulders.* **5.** the direction of a current or wind. **6.** a young plant for setting out; a cutting, slip, or seedling. **7.** a group of games constituting a division of a tennis match.

set[2] *n.* **1.** a number of persons regarded as associated through status, common interests, special characteristics, etc. **2.** a number of things belonging together and customarily used together: *a set of dishes.* **3.** a group of volumes issued together. **4.** in motion pictures, television, etc., the properties, structures, etc. required in a scene. **5.** radio or television receiving equipment assembled for use. **6.** *Math.* an array of objects, quantities, magnitudes, etc.: *the set of integers.* [ME *sette* group]

set•back (SET BAK) *n.* **1.** an unexpected reverse or relapse. **2.** *Archit.* in tall buildings, the stepping of upper sections so that they progressively recede from the street line.

set•screw (SET SKROO) *n.* a screw used as a clamp, esp. one used to screw through one part and slightly into another to bind the parts tightly.

set•tee (se TEE) *n.* **1.** a long wooden seat with a high back. **2.** a sofa suitable for two or three people.

set•ting (SET ing) *n.* **1.** that in which something is set; a frame or mounting. **2.** the music adapted to a song or poem. **3.** the scene or background of a play or narrative. **4.** the apparent sinking of the sun etc. below the horizon. **5.** the tableware set out for one person.

set•tle (SET l) v. **•tled, •tling** v.t **1.** put in order; set to rights. **2.** put firmly in place: *She settled herself on the couch.* **3.** free of agitation or disturbance; quiet: *settle one's nerves.* **4.** make clear or transparent, as by causing sediment to sink. **5.** make quiet or orderly: *One blow settled him.* **6.** decide or determine finally, as an argument. **7.** pay, as a debt; satisfy, as a claim. **8.** establish residents or residence in (a country, town, etc.). **9.** establish in a permanent occupation, home, etc. **10.** decide (a suit at law) by agreement between the litigants. **11.** *Law* make over or assign (property) by legal act:

with *on* or *upon.* —*v.i* **12.** come to rest, as after moving about or flying. **13.** sink or come to rest, as dust or sediment. **14.** become more firm or compact. **15.** become clear or transparent, as by the sinking of sediment. **16.** take up residence. **17.** come to a decision; resolve; with *on, upon,* or *with.* **18.** pay a bill etc. —**settle down** start living a regular, orderly life, esp. after a period of wandering or irresponsibility. [ME *settlen*] —*n.* a long seat or bench, generally of wood, with a high back.

set·tle·ment (SET l mənt) *n.* **1.** the act of settling, or the state of being settled; esp., an adjustment of affairs by public authority. **2.** the settling of a new region; colonization. **3.** an area of country newly occupied by those who intend to live and labor there; a colony. **4.** an accounting; adjustment; liquidation in regard to amounts. **5.** the conveyance of property in such form as to provide for financial support, etc.; also, the property so settled. **6.** a welfare institution established in a city, that conducts educational and recreational activities for the community: also **settlement house.**

set·tler (SET lər) *n.* one who settles; esp., a colonist.

set-to (SET TOO) *n. pl.* **-tos** a brief, bitter fight or dispute.

set·up (SET UP) *n.* **1.** the overall scheme or pattern of organization or construction; circumstances. **2.** *Informal* a contest or match arranged to result in an easy victory. **3.** ice, soda water, etc. provided for use in alcoholic drinks.

sev·en (SEV ən) *n.* the sum of six and one: a cardinal number written 7, VII. [ME *seoven*] —*adj.* amIunting to seven.

sev·en·teen (SEV ən TEEN) *n.* the sum of sixteen and one: a cardinal number written 17, XVII. [ME *seventene*] —*adj.* amounting to seventeen. —**sev′en·teenth′** *adj. & n.*

sev·enth (SEV ənth) *adj.* **1.** next after the sixth: the ordinal of *seven.* **2.** being one of seven equal parts. —*n.* **1.** one of seven equal parts. **2.** that which follows the sixth. **3.** *Music* the interval between any tone and the seventh tone above it in the diatonic scale.

Seventh-Day Adventist see under ADVENTIST.

sev·en·ty (SEV ən tee) *n. pl.* **-ties** the sum of sixty and ten: a cardinal number written 70,

LXX. [ME] —*adj.* amounting to seventy. —**sev′en·ti·eth** *adj. & n.*

sev·er (SEV ər) *v.t. & v.i.* divide; separate; break off. [ME *severen*]

sev·er·al (SEV ər əl) *adj.* **1.** more than two, yet not many. **2.** considered individually; single; separate. **3.** individually different; various or diverse. —*n.* several persons or things. [ME] —**sev′er·al·ly** *adv.*

sev·er·ance (SEV ər əns) *n.* **1.** the act of severing, or the condition of being severed. **2.** separation; partition. **3.** money given an employee leaving employment: also **severance pay.** [ME *severaunce*]

se·vere (sə VEER) *adj.* **·ver·er, ·ver·est 1.** rigorous in the treatment of others; unsparing. **2.** serious and austere in disposition or manner. **3.** causing extreme anguish or hardship: a *severe* pain; a *severe* storm. [< L *severus*] —**se·vere′ly** *adv.*

se·ver·i·ty (sə VER i tee) *n. pl.* **·ties 1.** the quality of being severe. **2.** harshness or cruelty of disposition or treatment. **3.** seriousness; austerity. **4.** strict conformity to truth or law.

sew (soh) *v.* **sewed, sewn** or **sewed, sewing** *v.t.* **1.** make, mend, or fasten with needle and thread. —*v.i.* **2.** work with needle and thread. —**sew up** *Informal* **1.** control exclusively. **2.** conclude (a deal etc.). [ME *sewen*] —**sew′er** *n.*

sew·age (SOO ij) *n.* the waste matter from domestic, commercial, and industrial establishments carried off in sewers.

sew·er (SOO ər) *n.* **1.** a conduit, usu. laid underground, to carry off drainage and wastes. **2.** any large public drain. [ME *suere* channel]

sew·er·age (SOO ər ij) *n.* **1.** a system of sewers. **2.** systematic draining by sewers. **3.** sewage.

sew·ing (SOH ing) *n.* **1.** the act or occupation of one who sews. **2.** that which is sewed.

sewn (sohn) a past participle of SEW.

sex (seks) *n.* **1.** either of two divisions, male and female, by which organisms are distinguished with reference to the reproductive functions. **2.** the character of being male or female. **3.** sexual intercourse. [ME] —**sex′less** *adj.* —**sex′less·ness** *n.*

sex·a·ge·nar·i·an (SEK sə jə NAIR ee ən) *n.* a person between 60 and 70 years of age. [< L *sexaginarius*] —*adj.* of such a person.

sex chromosome *Genetics* a chromosome whose presence in the reproductive cells of certain plants and animals is associated with the determination of the sex of offspring.

sex·ism (SEK siz əm) *n.* prejudice against either sex, esp. against women. —**sex'ist** *n. & adj.*

sex·tant (SEK stənt) *n..* an instrument for measuring angular distance between two objects, as a heavenly body and the horizon, used esp. in determining latitude and longitude at sea. [< L *sextans* sixth part]

sex·tet (seks TET) *n.* **1.** *Music* a group of six singers or players; also, a musical composition for six performers. **2.** any collection of six persons or things. Also **sex·tette'.**

sex·til·lion (seks TIL yən) *n.* in the U.S., a cardinal number written as 1 followed by 21 zeros. —**sex·til'lion** *adj.* — **sex·til'lionth** *adj. & n.*

sex·ton (SEK stən) *n.* one having charge of the maintenance of church or synagogue property. [ME *sexteyn*]

sex·tu·ple (seks TOO pəl) *v.t. & v.i.* **·pled, ·pling** multiply by six; make or become six times larger. —*adj.* **1.** consisting of or multiplied by six. **2.** *Music* having six beats to the measure.

sex·tu·plet (seks TUP lit) *n.* one of six offspring produced at a single birth.

sex·u·al (SEK shoo əl) *adj.* **1.** of, pertaining to, or characteristic of sex, the sexes, or the organs or functions of sex. **2.** *Biol.* designating a type of reproduction involving both sexes. [< LL *sexualis*] —**sex·u·al·i·ty** (SEK shoo AL i tee) *n.* —**sex'u·al·ly** *adv.*

sexual intercourse sexual connection, esp. of humans; copulation.

sex·y (SEK see) *adj.* **sex·i·er, sex·i·est** provocative of sexual desire; erotic. —**sex'i·ness** *n.*

shab·by (SHAB ee) *adj.* **·bi·er, ·bi·est 1.** threadbare; ragged. **2.** wearing worn or seedy garments. **3.** mean; paltry. [ME] — **shab'bi·ly** *adv.* —**shab'bi·ness** *n.*

shack (shak) *n.* a rough cabin, as of logs.

shack·le (SHAK əl) *n.* **1.** a fastener for securing a limb. **2.** an impediment or restraint. **3.** one of various forms of fastenings. —*v.t.* **·led, ·ling** restrain or confine with or as with shackles. [ME *schakle*]

shade (shayd) *v.* **shad·ed, shad·ing** *v.t.* **1.** screen from light by intercepting its rays. **2.** make dim; darken. **3.** screen or protect with or as with a shade. **4.** cause to change by gradations. **5.** in graphic arts: **a** represent (degrees of shade, colors, etc.) by gradations of light or dark lines or shading. **b** represent varying shades, colors, etc. in (a picture etc.) thus. —*v.i.* **6.** change or vary by degrees. —*n.* **1.** relative obscurity due to interception of the rays of light. **2.** a shady place; secluded retreat. **3.** a screen that shuts off light, heat, dust, etc. **4.** a gradation of color; also, slight degree; minute difference. **5.** a disembodied spirit; ghost. **6.** *pl. Slang* sunglasses. [ME]

shad·ing (SHAY ding) *n.* the lines, dots, etc., by which degrees of darkness, color, or depth are represented in a picture.

shad·ow (SHAD oh) *n.* **1.** a comparative darkness within an illuminated area, esp. that caused by the interception of light by a body. **2.** the dark image thus produced, representing the approximate shape of the intercepting body. **3.** the shaded portion of a picture. **4.** a delusive image or semblance. **5.** a phantom; ghost; shade. **6.** a remnant; vestige. **7.** gloom; a saddening influence. **8.** an inseparable companion. —*v.t.* **1.** cast a shadow upon. **2.** darken; make gloomy. **3.** follow closely or secretly. **4.** shade in painting etc. [ME *shadwe*]

shad·ow·y (SHAD oh ee) *adj.* **·ow·i·er, ·ow·i·est 1.** full of or providing shadow. **2.** vague; dim. **3.** unsubstantial or illusory.

shad·y (SHAY dee) *adj.* **shad·i·er, shad·i·est 1.** full of shade; casting a shade. **2.** shaded, sheltered, or hidden. **3.** questionable as to honesty or legality; dubious. —**on the shady side of** older than; past the age of.

shaft (shaft) *n.* **1.** the long narrow rod of an arrow, spear, etc. **2.** an arrow. **3.** anything resembling a missile in appearance or effect: *shafts* of ridicule. **4.** a beam of light. **5.** a long handle, as of a hammer etc. **6.** *Mech.* a long bar, esp. if rotating and transmitting motive power. **7.** *Archit.* the portion of a column between capital and base. **8.** an obelisk or memorial column. **9.** a narrow, vertical or inclined, excavation connected with a mine. **10.** an opening through the floors of a building, as for an elevator. [ME]

shag·gy (SHAG ee) *adj.* **·gi·er, ·gi·est 1.** having, consisting of, or resembling rough hair or wool; rugged; rough. **2.** covered with any rough, tangled growth; fuzzy; scrubby. **3.** unkempt. —**shag'gi·ness** *n.*

shake (shayk) *v.* **shook, shak·en, shak·ing** *v.t.* **1.** cause to move to and fro or up and down with short, rapid movements. **2.** affect in a specified manner by or as by vigorous action: with *off, out, from,* etc. **3.** cause to tremble or quiver; vibrate. **4.** weaken or disturb: I could not *shake* her determination. **5.** agitate or rouse: often with *up.* **6.** get rid of or away from. —*v.i.* **7.** move to and fro or up and down in short, rapid movements. **8.** be affected in a specified way by vigorous action: with *off, out, from,* etc. **9.** tremble or quiver, as from cold or fear. [ME *shaken*] —**shake down 1.** cause to fall by shaking; bring down. **2.** cause to settle. **3.** *Informal* extort money from. —**shake off** rid oneself of by or as by shaking. —**shake up 1.** shake, mix, or stir. **2.** shock or jar mentally or physically. —*n.* **1.** a shaking; agitation; jolt. **2.** the state of being shaken. **3.** *pl. Informal* trembling, as with a chill or fever. **4.** *Informal* treatment: a fair *shake.* —**no great shakes** *Informal* of no great importance; mediocre. —**shak'a·ble, shake'a·ble** *adj.*

shake·down (SHAYK DOWN) *n.* **1.** a swindle; extortion. **2.** a flight or cruise made for final adjustment of mechanical parts or training the crew. Also **shakedown flight** or **shakedown cruise.**

shak·er (SHAY kər) *n.* **1.** one who or that which shakes. **2.** a container for shaking or pouring something: cocktail *shaker.* **3.** *cap.* one of a sect practicing celibacy and communal living: so called from their characteristic bodily movements during religious meetings.

Shake·spear·e·an (shayk SPEER ee ən) *adj.* of, pertaining to, or characteristic of Shakespeare, his work, or his style. —*n.* a specialist on Shakespeare or his writings.

shake-up (SHAYK UP) *n.* a radical change of personnel or organization, as in a business office etc.

shak·y (SHAY kee) *adj.* **shak·i·er, shak·i·est 1.** habitually shaking or tremulous; tottering; weak; unsound. **2.** wavering; unreliable. —**shak'i·ly** *adv.* —**shak'i·ness** *n.*

shale (shayl) *n.* a claylike rock resembling slate.

shall (shal) *v.* present **shall;** past **should** a defective verb having a past tense that is now used only as an auxiliary to express simple futurity, determination, command, etc.

shal·lot (SHAL ət) *n.* an onionlike vegetable, allied to garlic but having milder bulbs that are used in seasoning. [< F *échalote*]

shal·low (SHAL oh) *adj.* •**er,** •**est 1.** having the bottom not far below the surface; lacking depth. **2.** lacking intellectual depth; not wise; superficial. [ME *schalowe*] —*n.* a shallow place in a body of water; shoal. —*v.t. & v.i.* make or become shallow. —**shal'low·ness** *n.*

shalt (shalt) *archaic* second person singular, present tense of SHALL: used with *thou.*

sham (sham) *v.* **shammed, sham·ming** *v.t.* **1.** assume or present the appearance of; counterfeit; feign. **2.** represent oneself as; pretend to be. —*v.i.* **3.** make false pretenses. —*adj.* false; counterfeit. —*n.* **1.** a pretense; imposture; deception. **2.** one who simulates a certain character; a pretender: also **sham'mer. 3.** a deceptive imitation.

sha·man (SHAH mən) *n.* a Native American medicine man. [< G *Schamane*]

sham·ble (SHAM bəl) *v.i.* •**bled,** •**bling** walk with shuffling or unsteady gait. —*n.* a shambling walk.

sham·bles (SHAM bəlz) *n. (construed as sing. or pl.)* **1.** a place where butchers kill animals; slaughterhouse. **2.** a place marked by great destruction or disorder.

shame (shaym) *n.* **1.** a painful sense of guilt or degradation caused by consciousness of guilt or of anything degrading, unworthy, or immodest. **2.** a state of dishonor or disgrace. —**put to shame 1.** disgrace; make ashamed. **2.** surpass or eclipse. —*v.t.* **shamed, sham·ing 1.** make ashamed; cause to feel shame. **2.** bring shame upon; disgrace. [ME] —**shame'ful** *adj.* —**shame'ful·ly** *adv.* —**shame'ful·ness** *n.*

shame·faced (SHAYM FAYST) *adj.* easily abashed; showing shame or bashfulness in one's face; modest; bashful. —**shame·face·ed·ly** (SHAYM FAY sid lee) *adv.* —**shame'fac'ed·ness** *n.*

shame·less (SHAYM lis) *adj.* **1.** impudent; brazen; immodest. **2.** done without shame; indicating a want of pride or decency. —**shame'less·ly** *adv.* —**shame'less·ness** *n.*

sham·poo (sham POO) *n.* **1.** a liquid preparation of soap, detergent, etc., used to cleanse the hair and scalp. **2.** the act or process of shampooing. —*v.t.* cleanse the hair and scalp) with a shampoo. [< Hind. *chāmpnā* press] —**sham·poo'er** *n.*

sham·rock (SHAM rok) *n.* a plant with three leaflets, accepted as the national emblem of Ireland. [< Irish *seamróg*]

shang·hai (SHANG hī) *v.t.* •**haied,**

•hai•ing 1. drug or render unconscious and kidnap for service aboard a ship. **2.** cause to do something by force or deception. [after *Shanghai,* China]

Shan•gri-la (SHANG grə LAH) *n.* any imaginary hidden utopia or paradise. [after the locale of James Hilton's novel *Lost Horizon*]

shank (shangk) *n.* **1.** the part of the leg between the knee and the ankle. **2.** a cut of meat from the leg of an animal; the shin. **3.** the part of a tool connecting the handle with the working part. **4.** the chief or best part: the *shank* of the evening. [ME]

shan't (shant) shall not.

shan•ty (SHAN tee) *n. pl.* **•ties** a hastily built shack or cabin; a ramshackle dwelling. [< Canadian F *chantier*]

shape (shayp) *n.* **1.** outward appearance or construction. **2.** a developed expression or definite formulation; cast: put an idea into *shape.* **3.** a phantom. **4.** a pattern or mold; in millinery, a stiff frame. **5.** the lines of a person's body; figure. **6.** condition: Everything is in good *shape.* —**take shape** have or assume a definite form. —*v.* **shaped, shap•ing** *v.t.* **1.** give shape to; mold. **2.** adjust or adapt; modify. **3.** devise; prepare. **4.** give direction or character to. —*v.i.* **5.** take shape; develop; form: often with *up* or *into.* —**shape up 1.** proceed satisfactorily or favorably. **2.** improve one's behavior, work, etc. [ME] —**shaped** *adj.* —**shap′er** *n.*

shape•less (SHAYP lis) *adj.* having no definite shape; lacking symmetry. —**shape′less•ness** *n.*

shape•ly (SHAYP lee) *adj.* **•li•er, •li•est** having a pleasing shape; well-formed; graceful. —**shape′li•ness** *n.*

shard (shahrd) *n.* a broken piece of a brittle substance, as of an earthen vessel; a potsherd; a fragment. [ME]

share (shair) *n.* **1.** a portion; allotted or equitable part. **2.** one of the equal parts into which the capital stock of a company or corporation is divided. —*v.* **shared, shar•ing** *v.t.* **1.** divide and give out in shares or portions; apportion. **2.** enjoy or endure in common; participate in. —*v.i.* **3.** have a part; participate: with *in.* [ME]

share•crop•per (SHAIR KROP ər) *n.* a tenant farmer who pays a share of the crop as rent for the land.

share•hold•er (SHAIR HOHL dər) *n.* one who owns stock in a company.

shark[1] (shahrk) *n.* one of a group of generally large marine fishes.

shark[2] *n.* a greedy and dishonest person: a loan *shark.* [< G *Schurke* scoundrel]

sharp (shahrp) *adj.* **•er, •est 1.** having a keen edge or an acute point. **2.** keen of perception or discernment; also, shrewd and artful. **3.** affecting the mind or senses, as if by cutting or piercing; poignant; acrimonious. **4.** shrill. **5.** pinching; cutting, as cold. **6.** having an acrid or pungent taste. **7.** distinct, as an outline. **8.** *Music* raised in pitch by a semitone. **b** above the right, true pitch. —*adv.* **1.** in a sharp manner; sharply. **2.** promptly; exactly: at 4 o'clock *sharp.* **3.** *Music* above the proper pitch. —*n.* **1.** *Music* a sign (#) placed before a note to indicate that the note is to be sharped. **2.** a sharper. —*v.t. Music* raise in pitch, as by a half step. [ME]

sharp•en (SHAHR pən) *v.t. & v.i.* make or become sharp. —**sharp′en•er** *n.*

sharp•er (SHAHR pər) *n.* a swindler; cheat.

sharp•ie (SHAHR pee) *n.* **1.** a sharper. **2.** an alert, intelligent person: also **sharp′y.** [< SHARP]

sharp•shoot•er (SHAHRP SHOO tər) *n.* a skilled marksman, esp. in the use of the rifle.

shat•ter (SHAT ər) *v.t.* **1.** break into pieces suddenly, as by a blow. **2.** break the health or tone of, as the body or mind. —*v.i.* **3.** break into pieces; burst. [ME *schateren*]

shave (shayv) *v.* **shaved, shaved** or **shav•en, shav•ing** *v.i.* **1.** cut hair, esp. the beard, close to the skin with a razor. —*v.t.* **2.** remove hair from (the face, head, etc.) with a razor. **3.** cut thin slices from, as in preparing the surface; pare; plane. **4.** cut into thin slices. **5.** touch or scrape in passing; graze; come close to. —*n.* **1.** the act or operation of cutting off the beard with a razor. **2.** a knife or blade, mounted between two handles, as for shaving wood. —**a close shave** a narrow escape. [ME *schaven* plane]

shave•ling (SHAYV ling) *n.* a youth.

shav•en (SHAY vən) alternative past participle of SHAVE. —*adj.* **1.** shaved; also, tonsured. **2.** trimmed closely.

shav•ing (SHAY ving) *n.* **1.** the act of one who or that which shaves. **2.** a thin paring shaved from anything, as a board.

shawl (shawl) *n.* a wrap, as a square cloth, or large scarf, worn over the upper part of the body. [< Persian *shāl*]

she (shee) *pron., possessive* **hers,** *objective*

her; *pl. nominative* **they,** *possessive* **theirs,** *objective* **them** the nominative singular pronoun of the third person, used of the female person or animal previously mentioned, or of any things conventionally regarded as feminine. —*n. pl.* **shes** a female person or animal. [ME]

sheaf (sheef) *n. pl.* **sheaves 1.** a quantity of the stalks of cut grain or the like, bound together. **2.** any collection of things, as papers, tied together. **3.** a quiverful of arrows. [ME *shefe*] —*v.t.* bind in a sheaf.

shear (sheer) *n.* **1.** *Physics* a deformation of a solid body, equivalent to a sliding over each other of adjacent layers: also **shearing stress. 2.** the act or result of shearing. —*v.* **sheared, sheared** or **shorn, shear·ing** *v.t.* **1.** cut the hair, fleece, etc. from. **2.** deprive; strip, as of wealth. **3.** cut or clip with or as with shears. —*v.i.* **4.** use shears. **5.** proceed by or as by cutting a way: with *through*. [ME *sheren*] —**shear'er** *n.*

shears (sheerz) *n.* (*usu. construed as pl.*) **1.** any large cutting or clipping instrument worked by the crossing of cutting edges. Also **pair of shears. 2.** the ways or guides, as of a lathe.

sheath (sheeth) *n. pl.* **sheaths** (shee*th*z) **1.** an envelope or case, as for a sword; scabbard. **2.** a close-fitting dress having straight, unbroken lines. —*v.t.* sheathe. [ME *scheth*]

sheathe (shee*th*) *v.t.* **sheathed, sheath·ing 1.** put into a sheath. **2.** encase or protect with a covering. [ME *shethen*]

sheath·ing (SHEE *th*ing) *n.* **1.** a protective covering, as of a ship's hull. **2.** the covering or waterproof material on outside walls or roofs.

sheave¹ (sheev) *v.t.* **sheaved, sheav·ing** gather into sheaves; collect.

sheave² (shiv) *n.* a grooved pulley wheel; also, a pulley wheel and its block. [ME *sheve*]

sheaves (sheevz) plural of SHEAF.

shed¹ (shed) *v.* **shed, shed·ding** *v.t.* **1.** pour forth in drops; emit, as tears. **2.** cause to pour forth. **3.** send forth; radiate. **4.** throw off without allowing to penetrate, as rain; repel. **5.** cast off by natural process, as hair, skin, etc. **6.** rid oneself of. —*v.i.* **7.** cast off or lose skin etc. by natural process. —**shed blood** kill. —*n.* that which sheds, as a sloping surface or watershed. [ME *shedden* divide]

shed² *n.* a small low building, often with front or sides open; also, a lean-to: a wagon *shed.*

she'd (sheed) **1.** she had. **2.** she would.

sheen (sheen) *n.* a glistening brightness, as if from reflection. —*v.i.* shine; glisten. [ME *shene* beautiful]

sheep (sheep) *n. pl.* **sheep 1.** a medium-sized, domesticated ruminant, bred for its flesh, wool, and skin. **2.** a meek, bashful, or timid person. [ME]

sheep·ish (SHEE pish) *adj.* foolish, as a sheep; awkwardly diffident; abashed. —**sheep'ish·ly** *adv.* —**sheep'ish·ness** *n.*

sheep·skin (SHEEP SKIN) *n.* **1.** the skin of a sheep, tanned or untanned, or anything made from it. **2.** a document written on parchment, as an academic diploma.

sheer¹ (sheer) *v.i.* **1.** swerve from a course; turn aside. —*v.t.* **2.** cause to swerve. —*n.* a swerving course.

sheer² *adj.* **·er, ·est 1.** having no modifying conditions; pure, absolute: *sheer* folly. **2.** exceedingly thin and fine: said of fabrics. **3.** perpendicular; steep. [ME *schere*] —*n.* any very thin fabric used for clothes. —*adv.* steeply; perpendicularly. —**sheer'ness** *n.* —**sheer'ly** *adv.*

sheet (sheet) *n.* **1.** a very thin and broad piece of any substance; as: **a** a large rectangular piece of bed linen. **b** a newspaper. **c** a piece of metal or other substance hammered, rolled, or cut very thin. **2.** a broad, flat surface; superficial expanse: a *sheet* of water. **3.** *Naut.* **a** a rope or chain from a lower corner of a sail to extend it or move it. **b** *pl.* in an open boat, the space at the bow and stern not occupied by the thwarts. **c** a sail. —**three sheets in** (or **to**) **the wind** *Slang* drunk. —*v.t.* cover with a sheet. [ME *shete*]

sheet·ing (SHEE ting) *n.* cotton, muslin, etc., used for making sheets for beds.

sheet metal metal rolled and pressed into sheets.

sheet music music printed on unbound sheets of paper.

sheik (sheek) *n.* **1.** a Muslim high priest or a venerable man; also, the chief or head of an Arab tribe or family. **2.** *Slang* a man who considers himself to be irresistibly fascinating to women. [< Arabic *shaykh* old man]

sheik·dom (SHEEK dəm) *n.* the land ruled by a sheik.

shelf (shelf) *n. pl.* **shelves** (shelvz) **1.** a board or slab set horizontally against a wall, in a bookcase, etc. to support articles, as books.

2. contents of a shelf. 3. any flat projecting ledge, as of rock. 4. a reef; shoal. **—on the shelf** no longer in use. [ME]

shell (shel) *n.* 1. any of various hard structures encasing an animal, as a mollusk. 2. the relatively hard covering of a fruit, nut, egg, etc. 3. a hollow structure or vessel, generally thin and weak; also, a case or mold for holding something: pie *shell*. 4. a very light, long, and narrow racing rowboat. 5. a hollow metallic projectile filled with an explosive, chemical, etc. 6. a shape or outline that merely simulates a reality; hollow form; external semblance. [ME] *—v.t.* 1. divest of or remove from a shell. 2. separate from the cob, as corn. 3. bombard with shells, as a fort. *—v.i.* 4. shed the shell or pod. **—shell out** *Informal* hand over, as money.

she'll (sheel) she will.

shel·lac (shə LAK) *n.* 1. a purified resinous substance in the form of thin flakes, extensively used in varnish, sealing wax, insulators, etc. 2. a varnishlike solution of flake shellac, used for coating floors, woodwork, etc. *—v.t.* **·lacked, ·lack·ing** 1. cover or varnish with shellac. 2. *Slang* defeat utterly. Also **shel·lack'.**

shel·lack·ing (shə LAK ing) *n. Slang* 1. a beating; assault. 2. a thorough defeat.

shell·fish (SHEL FISH) *n. pl.* **·fish** or **·fish·es** any aquatic animal having a shell, as a clam.

shell game 1. a swindling game in which the victim bets on the location of a pea covered by one of three nutshells. 2. any fraud or swindle.

shel·ter (SHEL tər) *n.* that which covers or shields from exposure or danger; a place of safety. *—v.t.* 1. provide protection or shelter for; shield, as from danger or inclement weather. *—v.i.* 2. take shelter. **—shel'ter·less** *adj.*

shelve (shelv) *v.t.* **shelved, shelv·ing** 1. place on a shelf. 2. postpone indefinitely; put aside. 3. retire. 4. provide or fit with shelves.

shelves (shelvz) plural of SHELF.

shelv·ing (SHEL ving) *n.* 1. shelves collectively. 2. material for shelves.

she·nan·i·gan (shə NAN i gən) *n. Usu. pl.* 1. trickery. 2. questionable behavior. 3. mischief; nonsense.

shep·herd (SHEP ərd) *n.* 1. a keeper or herder of sheep. 2. a pastor, leader, or guide. *—v.t.* watch and tend as a shepherd.

[ME *shepherde*] **—shep'herd·ess** (SHEP ər dis) *n.fem.*

sher·bet (SHUR bit) *n.* a frozen dessert, usu. fruit-flavored, and sometimes containing milk. [< Turkish]

sher·iff (SHER if) *n.* the law-enforcement officer of a county etc. who executes the mandates of courts, enforces order, etc. [ME *sherref*]

Sher·pa (SHUR pə) *n. pl.* **·pas** or **·pa** one of a Tibetan tribe living on the southern slopes of the Himalayas in Nepal.

she's (sheez) 1. she is. 2. she has.

shib·bo·leth (SHIB ə lith) *n.* 1. a pet phrase; watchword; slogan. 2. a custom or use of language regarded as distinctive of a particular social class, profession, etc. [< Hebrew, stream: used as a password]

shied (shīd) past tense, past participle of SHY.

shield (sheeld) *n.* 1. a broad piece of defensive armor, commonly carried on the left arm. 2. something that protects or defends. *—v.t.* 1. protect from danger as with a shield; defend; guard. *—v.i.* 2. act as a shield or safeguard. [ME *shelde*]

shi·er[1] (SHĪ ər) *adj.* a comparative of SHY.
SHI·ER[2] *n. a horse in the habit of shying. Also spelled shyer.*

shift (shift) *v.t.* 1. change or move from one position, place, etc. to another. 2. change for another or others of the same class. 3. change (gears) from one arrangement to another. *—v.i.* 4. change position, opinion, etc. **—shift for oneself** do the best one can to provide for one's needs. [ME *shiften* arrange] *—n.* 1. the act of shifting. 2. a dodge; artifice; trick. 3. a woman's slip or chemise. 4. a straight, loosely hanging woman's dress. 5. a change of position, place, direction, or form: a *shift* in the wind. 6. a relay of workers; also, the working time of each group.

shift·less (SHIFT lis) *adj.* 1. unable or unwilling to shift for oneself; inefficient or lazy. 2. showing lack of energy or resource. **—shift'less·ness** *n.*

shift·y (SHIF tee) *adj.* **shift·i·er, shift·i·est** artful; tricky; crafty or devious. **—shift'i·ness** *n.*

shill (shil) *n. Slang* the assistant of a sidewalk peddler or gambler, who makes a purchase or bet to encourage onlookers to buy or bet.

shil·le·lagh (shə LAY lee) *n.* in Ireland, a stout cudgel made of oak etc. Also **shil·le'lah.** [after *Shillelagh*, Ireland]

shil·ly-shal·ly (SHIL ee SHAL ee) *v.i.* **·lied,**

•ly•ing act with indecision; be irresolute; vacillate. —*adj.* weak; hesitating. —*n.* weak or foolish vacillation; irresolution. —*adv.* in an irresolute manner. [Reduplication of *shall I?*] —**shil′ly-shal′li•er** *n.*

shim (shim) *n.* a piece of metal or other material used to fill out space, for leveling etc. —*v.t.* **shimmed, shim•ming** fill out by inserting a shim.

shim•mer (SHIM ər) *v.i.* shine faintly; glimmer. —*n.* a tremulous shining or gleaming; glimmer. [ME *schimeren*] —**shim′•mer•y** *adj.*

shim•my (SHIM ee) *n. pl.* •**mies** 1. a chemise. 2. unusual vibration, as in automobile wheels. —*v.i.* •**mied,** •**my•ing** vibrate or wobble.

shin (shin) *n.* 1. the front part of the leg below the knee; also, the shinbone. 2. the lower foreleg: a *shin* of beef. —*v.t. & v.i.* **shinned, shin•ning** climb (a pole, tree, etc.) by gripping with the hands or arms and the shins or legs. [ME *shine*]

shin•bone (SHIN BOHN) *n.* the tibia.

shin•dig (SHIN DIG) *n. Informal* a dance or noisy party.

shine (shīn) *v.i.* **shone** or (*esp. for def.* 5) **shined, shin•ing** 1. emit light; beam; glow. 2. gleam, as by reflected light. 3. excel or be conspicuous in splendor, beauty, etc. —*v.t.* 4. cause to shine. 5. brighten by rubbing or polishing. [ME *schinen*] —**shine up to** *Informal* try to impress (a person). —*n.* 1. the state or quality of being bright or shining; radiance; luster. 2. fair weather; sunshine. 3. a shoeshine. —**take a shine to** *Informal* become fond of.

shin•er (SHĪ nər) *n.* 1. one who or that which shines. 2. *Slang* a black eye (def. 2).

shin•gle¹ (SHING gəl) *n.* 1. a tapering, oblong piece of wood or other material, used in rows to cover roofs. 2. a small sign placed outside the office of a doctor, lawyer, etc. —*v.t.* •**gled,** •**gling** cover (a roof, building, etc.) with or as with shingles. [ME *scincle*] —**shin′gler** *n.*

shin•gle² *n.* rounded, waterworn gravel, found on the seashore. [< Norw. *singel* coarse gravel]

shin•gles (SHING gəlz) *n.* (*construed as sing. or pl.*) *Pathol.* an acute, painful, inflammatory virus disease characterized by blisters along the course of the affected nerves: also called *herpes zoster.* [ME *schingles*]

shin•ing (SHĪ ning) *adj.* 1. emitting or reflecting a continuous light; gleaming; luminous. 2. of unusual brilliance or excellence; conspicuous.

shin•ny (SHIN ee) *v.i.* •**nied,** •**ny•ing** climb using one's shins: usu. with *up.*

Shin•to (SHIN toh) *n.* a religion of Japan, consisting chiefly in ancestor worship, nature worship, and, formerly, a belief in the divinity of the Emperor. Also **Shin′to•ism.** [< Japanese, way of the gods] —**Shin′to•ist** *n.*

shin•y (SHĪ nee) *adj.* **shin•i•er, shin•i•est** 1. glistening; glossy; polished. 2. bright; clear. —**shin′i•ness** *n.*

ship (ship) *n.* 1. any vessel suitable for deep-water navigation; also, its personnel. 2. an airship, airplane, or spacecraft. —*v.* **shipped, ship•ping** *v.t.* 1. transport by ship or other mode of conveyance. 2. send away. 3. set or fit in a prepared place on a boat or vessel, as a mast, or a rudder. —*v.i.* 4. go on board ship; embark. 5. undergo shipment: Raspberries do not *ship* well. 6. enlist as a seaman: usu. with *out.* [ME] —**ship′per** *n.*

ship•board (SHIP BORD) *n.* the side or deck of a ship. —**on shipboard** aboard a seagoing vessel.

ship•load (SHIP LOHD) *n.* the amount a ship carries or can carry; cargo.

ship•mate (SHIP MAYT) *n.* one who serves with another aboard the same vessel.

ship•ment (SHIP mənt) *n.* 1. the act of shipping. 2. that which is shipped.

ship•shape (SHIP SHAYP) *adj.* well arranged, orderly, and neat. —*adv.* in a shipshape manner.

ship•wreck (SHIP REK) *n.* 1. the partial or total destruction of a ship at sea. 2. utter or practical destruction; ruin. —*v.t.* 1. wreck, as a vessel. 2. bring to disaster; ruin.

ship•yard (SHIP YAHRD) *n.* a place where ships are built or repaired.

shirk (shurk) *v.t. & v.i.* avoid doing (something that should be done). —*n.* shirker.

shirk•er (SHUR kər) *n.* one who shirks.

shirr (shur) *v.t.* 1. draw (fabric) into parallel rows of gathers. 2. bake in a buttered dish, as eggs.

shirr•ing (SHUR ing) *n.* the gathering of fabric into parallel rows using short stitches or elastic thread.

shirt (shurt) *n.* 1. a garment for the upper part of the body, usu. having collar and cuffs and a front closing. 2. a closely fitting undergarment. —**lose one's shirt** *Informal* lose everything. [ME *shirte*]

shish ke·bab (SHISH kə BOB) meat roasted or broiled in small pieces on skewers. [< Turkish *siskebabi* roast meat]

shiv·er[1] (SHIV ər) *v.i.* **1.** tremble; shake; quiver. **2.** *Naut.* flutter in the wind, as a sail. —*n.* the act of shivering; a tremble. [ME *shiveren*]

shiv·er[2] *v.t. & v.i.* break suddenly into fragments; shatter. —*n.* a splinter; sliver. [ME, fragment]

shoal[1] (shohl) *n.* **1.** a shallow place in any body of water. **2.** a sandbank or bar, esp. one seen at low water. —*v.i.* **1.** become shallow. —*v.t.* **2.** sail into a lesser depth of (water): said of a ship. —*adj.* shallow. [ME *shold* shallow]

shoal[2] *n.* **1.** an assemblage or multitude; throng. **2.** a school of fish. —*v.i.* throng in multitudes.

shock[1] (shok) *n.* **1.** a violent collision or concussion; impact; blow. **2.** a sudden and severe agitation of the mind or emotions, as in horror or great sorrow. **3.** *Pathol.* prostration of bodily functions, as from sudden injury. **4.** the physical reactions produced by the passage of a strong electric current through the body. —*v.t.* **1.** shake by sudden collision; jar. **2.** disturb the emotions or mind of; horrify; disgust. **3.** give an electric shock to. [< MF *choc*] —**shock'er** *n.*

shock[2] *n.* a number of sheaves of grain, stalks of corn, etc., stacked for drying upright in a field. —*v.t. & v.i.* gather (grain) into a shock. [ME]

shock[3] *adj.* shaggy; bushy. —*n.* a coarse, tangled mass, as of hair.

shock absorber *Mech.* a device designed to absorb the force of shocks, as the springs of an automobile.

shock·ing (SHOK ing) *adj.* **1.** causing a mental or emotional shocks, as with horror or disgust. **2.** terrible; awful.

shock therapy *Psychiatry* the treatment of certain psychotic disorders by the use of drugs or electrical shocks, both methods inducing convulsions or unconsciousness.

shod (shod) past tense and alternative past participle of SHOE.

shod·dy (SHOD ee) *n. pl.* **·dies 1.** wool obtained from used woolens; also, cloth made of such wool. **2.** any inferior goods. —*adj.* **shod·di·er, shod·di·est 1.** poorly made or inferior. **2.** sham. —**shod'di·ly** *adv.* —**shod'di·ness** *n.*

shoe (shoo) *n. pl.* **shoes 1.** an outer covering, usu. of leather, for the human foot. **2.** a rim or plate of iron to protect the hoof of an animal. **3.** the part of the brake that presses upon a wheel or drum. **4.** the tread or outer covering of a pneumatic tire, as for an automobile. [ME *scho*] —*v.t.* **shod** or **shoed, shod** or **shoed** or **shod·den, shoe·ing 1.** furnish with shoes or the like. **2.** furnish with a guard of metal, wood, etc. for protection, as against wear. —**sho'er** *n.*

shoe·lace (SHOO LAYS) *n.* a lace or cord for fastening shoes.

shoe·mak·er (SHOO MAY kər) *n.* one who makes or repairs shoes, boots, etc.

shoe·shine (SHOO SHIN) *n.* the waxing and polishing of a pair of shoes.

shoe·string (SHOO STRING) *n.* a shoelace. —**on a shoestring** with a small sum of money with which to begin a business etc.

sho·far (SHOH far) *n.* a ram's horn used as a trumpet by the ancient Hebrews on solemn occasions and in war, now sounded in the synagogue on Rosh Hashana and Yom Kippur. [< Hebrew *shōphār*]

sho·gun (SHOH gən) *n.* any of the hereditary military dictators who ruled Japan until the 19th century. [< Jap.]

shone (shohn) past tense, past participle of SHINE.

shoo-in (SHOO IN) *n. Informal* a contestant, candidate, etc. who is certain to win.

shook (shuuk) past tense of SHAKE.

shoot (shoot) *v.* **shot, shoot·ing** *v.t.* **1.** hit, wound, or kill with a missile discharged from a weapon. **2.** discharge (a weapon): often with *off*: *shoot* a cannon. **3.** send forth as if from a weapon, as questions, glances, etc. **4.** pass over or through swiftly: *shoot* rapids. **5.** emit, as rays of light. **6.** photograph; film. **7.** cause to stick out or protrude; extend. **8.** send forth (buds, leaves, etc.). **9.** push into or out of the fastening, as the bolt of a door. **10.** propel, discharge, or dump, as down a chute or from a container. **11.** in games: **a** score (a goal, point, etc.) by kicking or otherwise forcing the ball etc. to the objective. **b** play (golf, craps, pool, marbles, etc.). **c** cast (the dice). **12.** *Slang* inject (an addictive drug). —*v.i.* **13.** discharge a missile from a bow, firearm, etc. **14.** go off; discharge. **15.** move swiftly; dart. **16.** jut out; extend or project. **17.** put forth buds, leaves, etc.; germinate; sprout. **18.** take a photograph. **19.** in games, make a play by propelling the ball, puck, etc. in a certain manner. —**shoot at** (or **for**) strive for; attempt to attain or obtain. [ME *shoten*] —*n.* **1.** a young branch or sucker of a plant; offshoot. **2.** an inclined passage down which something may be shot; chute. **3.** the act of shooting; a shot. **4.** a shooting match, hunting party, etc.

shoot•out (SHOOT OWT) *n.* a gunfight that must end in defeat for one side or the other.

shop (shop) *n.* **1.** a place for the sale of goods at retail: also, quaintly, **shoppe. 2.** a place for making or repairing any article. —**talk shop** talk about one's work, often with others involved in similar work. [ME *shoppe* booth] —*v.i.* **shopped, shop•ping** visit shops or stores to purchase or look at goods. —**shop′per** *n.* —**shop′ping** *n.*

shop•keep•er (SHOP KEE pər) *n.* one who runs a shop or store.

shop•lift•er (SHOP LIF tər) *n.* one who steals goods displayed in a shop. —**shop′ lift** *v.t. & v.i.* —**shop′lift′ing** *n.*

shopping mall a group of retail stores, restaurants, etc., including an ample parking area, usu. built as a unit.

shop•talk (SHOP TAWK) *n.* conversation limited to one's job or profession.

shop•worn (SHOP WORN) *adj.* **1.** soiled or otherwise deteriorated from handling in a store. **2.** worn out, as from overuse; stale.

shore[1] (shor) *n.* **1.** the coast or land adjacent to an ocean, sea, lake, or large river. **2.** land: be on *shore*. —**in shore** near or toward the shore. [ME]

shore[2] *v.t.* **shored, shor•ing** prop or brace: usu. with *up*. —*n.* a beam set endwise as a prop or temporary support. [ME *shoren*]

shore•line (SHOR LIN) *n.* the contour of a shore.

shor•ing (SHOR ing) *n.* the operation of supporting or propping.

shorn (shorn) alternative past participle of SHEAR.

short (short) *adj.* •**er,** •**est 1.** having little linear extension; not long; of no great distance. **2.** being below the average stature; not tall. **3.** having little extension in time; of limited duration; brief. **4.** abrupt in manner or spirit; cross. **5.** not reaching or attaining a requirement, result, or mark; inadequate: often with *of.* **6.** having little scope or breadth: a *short* view. **7.** of or pertaining to stocks or commodities not in possession of the seller: *short* sales. **8.** not comprehensive or retentive; in error: a *short* memory. **9.** breaking easily; crumbly. **10.** *Phonet.* de-

noting the vowel sounds of *Dan, den, din, don, duck,* as contrasted with those of *Dane, dean, dine, dome, dune.* **11.** concise; compressed. [ME] —*n.* **1.** anything that is short. **2.** a deficiency, as in a payment. **3.** a short contract or sale. **4.** *pl.* trousers with legs extending part way to the knees. **5.** *pl.* a man's undergarment covering the loins and often a portion of the legs. **6.** in baseball slang, shortstop. **7.** *Electr.* a short circuit. —**for short** by way of abbreviation: Edward was called Ed *for short.* —**in short** in a word; briefly. —*adv.* **1.** abruptly: stop *short.* **2.** curtly; crossly. **3.** so as not to reach or extend to a certain point, condition, etc.: fall *short.* —*v.t. & v.i.* short-circuit. —**short′ness** *n.*

short•age (SHOR tij) *n.* the amount by which anything is short; deficiency.

short•cake (SHORT KAYK) *n.* **1.** a cake made with butter or other shortening. **2.** cake or biscuit served with fruit: strawberry *shortcake.*

short•change (SHORT CHAYNJ) *v.t.* •**changed,** •**chang•ing** give less change than is due to; also, cheat or swindle.

short circuit *Electr.* **1.** a path of low resistance established between any two points in an electric circuit. **2.** any defect in an electric circuit or apparatus that may result in a leakage of current. —**short cir• cuit** (SHORT SUR kit) *v.t. & v.i.*

short•com•ing (SHORT KUM ing) *n.* a failure or deficiency in character, action, etc.

short•cut (SHORT KUT) *n.* **1.** a way between two places that is shorter than the regular way. **2.** anything that saves distance or time. —**short-cut** *v.t. & v.i.* -**cut, -cut• ting** use or create a shortcut.

short•en (SHOR tn) *v.t. & v.i.* make or become shorter. —**short′en•er** *n.*

short•en•ing (SHORT ning) *n.* **1.** a fat, such as lard or butter, used to make pastry crisp. **2.** an abbreviation.

short•hand (SHORT HAND) *n.* any system of rapid writing, usu. employing symbols other than letters, words, etc. —*adj.* written in shorthand.

short-hand•ed (SHORT HAN did) *adj.* not having a sufficient or the usual number of assistants, workers, etc.

short-lived (SHORT LĪVD) *adj.* living or lasting but a short time.

short•ly (SHORT lee) *adv.* **1.** soon. **2.** briefly; abruptly.

short order a serving of food requiring little

time to prepare. **—in short order** without any delay; quickly; abruptly.

short shrift 1. a brief time in which to confess before dying. **2.** little consideration, as in dealing with a person. **—make short shrift of** dispose of quickly.

short-sight•ed (SHORT SĪ tid) *adj.* **1.** unable to see clearly at a distance; near-sighted. **2.** lacking foresight. **3.** resulting from or characterized by lack of foresight. **—short'-sight'ed•ly** *adv.* **—short' -sight'ed•ness** *n.*

short•stop (SHORT STOP) *n.* in baseball, an infielder stationed between second and third bases; also, this position.

short story a narrative prose story far shorter than a novel. **—short-story** *adj.*

short-tem•pered (SHORT TEM pərd) *adj.* easily angered.

short-term (SHORT TURM) *adj.* **1.** in finance, due or payable within a short time, usu. one year: said of loans etc. **2.** applying to a short period of time.

short ton see under TON.

short wave an electromagnetic wave that is 60 meters or less in length. **—short-wave** (SHORT WAYV) *adj.*

short-wind•ed (SHORT WIN did) *adj.* becoming easily out of breath.

shot[1] (shot) *n. pl.* **shots;** *for def. 1* **shot 1.** a solid missile, as a ball of iron or a bullet or pellet of lead, to be discharged from a firearm; also, such pellets collectively. **2.** the act of shooting; any stroke, hit, or blow. **3.** one who shoots; marksman. **4.** the firing of a rocket etc. that is directed toward a specific target: a moon *shot.* **5.** a stroke, esp. in certain games, as in billiards. **6.** an attempted performance. **7.** in shot put, a heavy metal ball a competitor casts. **8.** a hypodermic injection of a drug etc. **9.** a drink of liquor. **10.** a single action or scene recorded on motion-picture or television film or tape. **11.** a photograph or snapshot. **—v.t. shot• ted, shot•ting** load or weight with shot. [ME]

shot[2] past tense, past participle of SHOOT. **—** *adj.* **1.** streaked or spread with color: a sky *shot* with pink. **2.** completely done for; ruined or worn out.

shot•gun (SHOT GUN) *n.* a light, smooth-bore gun, either single or double barreled, adapted for the discharge of shot at short range. **—adj.** coerced with, or as with, a shotgun: a *shotgun* wedding.

shot put *n.* an athletic contest in which a shot is cast for distance. **—shot'-put'ter** *n.* **— shot'-put'ting** *n.*

should (shuud) past tense of SHALL, expressing a wide range of feelings and attitudes: **1.** obligation: You *should* write that letter; *Should* we tell him the truth about his condition? **2.** condition: a simple contingency: If I *should* go, he would go too. **b** assumption: *Should* the space platform prove practicable, as now seems uncertain, a trip to the moon would still not be easy. **3.** surprise: When I reached the station, whom *should* I run into but the detective. **4.** expectation: I *should* be at home by noon. **5.** irony: He'll be fined heavily, but with all his money he *should* not worry. [ME sholde]

shoul•der (SHOHL dər) *n.* **1.** the part of the trunk between the neck and the free portion of the arm or forelimb; also, the joint connecting the arm or forelimb with the body. **2.** anything that supports, bears up, or projects like a shoulder. **3.** the forequarter of various animals. **4.** either edge of a road or highway. **—shoulder to shoulder 1.** side by side and close together. **2.** with united effort; in cooperation. [ME sholder] **—straight from the shoulder** candidly; straightforwardly. **—cry on** (one's) **shoulder** seek sympathy and understanding from (one). **—give the cold shoulder to** treat with scorn, contempt, or coldness. **— put** (one's) **shoulder to the wheel** work with great vigor and purpose. **—v.t. 1.** assume as something to be borne; sustain; bear. **2.** push with or as with the shoulders. **—v.i. 3.** push with the shoulders. **— shoulder arms** rest a rifle against the shoulder, holding the butt with the hand.

shoulder blade *Anat.* the scapula.

should•n't (SHUUD nt) should not.

shout (showt) *n.* a sudden and loud outcry, often expressing joy, anger, etc., or used as a call or command. **—v.t. 1.** utter with a shout; say or express loudly. **—v.i. 2.** utter a shout. [ME *shoute* scold]

shove (shuv) *v.t. & v.i.* **shoved, shov•ing 1.** push, as along a surface. **2.** press forcibly (against); jostle. **—shove off 1.** push along or away, as a boat. **2.** *Informal* depart. **—n.** the act of pushing or shoving. [ME *shoven*]

shov•el (SHUV əl) *n.* a somewhat flattened scoop with a handle, as for digging or lifting earth, snow, etc. **—v. •eled, •el•ing** *v.t.* **1.** take up and move with a shovel. **2.** toss hastily or in large quantities as if with a shovel. **3.** clear with a shovel, as a path. **—**

v.i. **4.** work with a shovel. [ME] —
shov·el·er (SHUV ə lər) *n.*

show (shoh) *v.* **showed, shown** or, sometimes, **showed, show·ing** *v.t.* **1.** cause or
permit to be seen; exhibit, display. **2.** give in
a marked or open manner; bestow: *show
favor.* **3.** cause or allow (something) to be
understood or known; reveal. **4.** cause
(someone) to understand or see; teach. **5.**
make evident; demonstrate. **6.** guide; introduce, as into a room or building: with *in* or
up. **7.** indicate: The thermometer *shows*
the temperature. **8.** enter in a show or exhibition. —*v.i.* **9.** become visible or known.
10. make one's or its appearance; be present. **11.** in racing, finish third. [ME
showen] —**show off 1.** exhibit proudly or
ostentatiously. **2.** make an ostentatious display of oneself or of one's accomplishments.
—**show up 1.** expose or be exposed, as
faults. **2.** be evident or prominent. **3.** make
an appearance. **4.** outdo. —*n.* **1.** an entertainment or performance. **2.** anything
shown or manifested. **3.** an elaborate display: a *show* of wealth. **4.** a pretense or
semblance: a *show* of piety. **5.** any public
exhibition, contest, etc.: an art *show.* **6.** the
third position among the first three winners
of a race.

show·boat (SHOH boht) *n.* **1.** a boat on
which a traveling troupe gives a theatrical
performance. **2.** a person who performs in a
way designed to attract attention, esp. an
athlete.

show·case (SHOH KAYS) *n.* a glass case for
exhibiting and protecting articles for sale.
—*v.t.* **·cased, ·cas·ing** put on display.

show·down (SHOH DOWN) *n.* any action
or disclosure that brings an issue to a
head.

show·er (SHOW ər) *n.* **1.** a fall of rain, hail,
or sleet. **2.** a copious fall, as of tears, sparks,
etc. **3.** a bath in which water is sprayed from
an overhead nozzle: also **shower bath. 4.**
an abundance or profusion of something. **5.**
a party for the bestowal of gifts, as to a
bride; also, the gifts. [ME *shour*] —*v.t.* **1.**
sprinkle or wet with water. **2.** discharge in a
shower; pour out. **3.** bestow liberally. —*v.i.*
4. fall as in a shower. **5.** bathe under a
shower. —**show'er·y** *adj.*

show·ing (SHOH ing) *n.* **1.** a show or display, as of a quality. **2.** a presentation or
statement, as of a subject.

show·man (SHOH mən) *n. pl.* **·men 1.** a
person who exhibits or owns a show. **2.** a

person skilled in presenting something. —
show'man·ship *n.*

shown (shohn) a past participle of SHOW.

show-off (SHOH AWF) *n.* **1.** an ostentatious
display. **2.** one given to such display.

show·piece (SHOH PEES) *n.* **1.** a prized
object considered worthy of special exhibit.
2. an object on display.

show·y (SHOH ee) *adj.* **show·i·er, show·
i·est 1.** making a great or brilliant display.
2. conspicuous; ostentatious. —**show'i·
ness** *n.*

shrank (shrank) a past tense of SHRINK.

shrap·nel (SHRAP nl) *n. Mil.* **1.** a field artillery projectile for use against personnel,
containing metal balls that are expelled by
an explosion in mid-air. **2.** shell fragments.
[after Henry *Shrapnel*, 1761–1842, British
artillery officer]

shred (shred) *n.* **1.** a small irregular strip
torn or cut off. **2.** a bit; fragment. [ME
shrede] —*v.t.* **shred·ded** or **shred,
shred·ding** tear or cut into shreds. —
shred'der *n.*

shrew (shroo) *n.* **1.** a small chiefly insectivorous mammal, having a long pointed
snout and soft fur. **2.** a scolding or nagging
woman. [ME]

shrewd (shrood) *adj.* **·er, ·est 1.** sharp or
wise; sagacious. **2.** artful; sly. [ME *shrewed*]
—**shrewd'ly** *adv.* —**shrew'·ness** *n.*

shrew·ish (SHROO ish) *adj.* ill-tempered;
nagging. —**shrew'·ish·ness** *n.*

shriek (shreek) *v.t. & v.i.* utter (a shrill outcry). [ME] —*n.* a shrill cry. —**shriek'er** *n.*

shrill (shril) *adj.* **·er, ·est 1.** having a high-
pitched and piercing tone quality. **2.** emitting a sharp, piercing sound. —*v.t.* **1.** cause
to utter a shrill sound. —*v.i.* **2.** make a shrill
sound. [ME *shrillen*] —**shrill'ness** *n.*

shrimp (shrimp) *n. pl.* **shrimp** or **shrimps**
for def. 1, **shrimps** *for def. 2* **1.** any of numerous small, long-tailed, principally marine animals, some species of which are
used as food. **2.** *Informal* a small or unimportant person. [ME *shrimpe*]

shrine (shrīn) *n.* **1.** a receptacle for sacred
relics. **2.** a place, as a tomb or a chapel,
sacred to some holy personage. —*v.t.*
shrined, shrin·ing enshrine. [ME]

shrink (shringk) *v.* **shrank** or **shrunk,
shrunk** or **shrunk·en, shrink·ing** *v.i.* **1.**
draw together; contract. **2.** diminish. **3.**
draw back, as from disgust, horror, or timidity; recoil: with *from.* —*v.t.* **4.** cause to
shrink, contract, or draw together. [ME

shrinken] —*n.* **1.** the act of shrinking. **2.** *Slang* a psychotherapist.

shrink·age (SHRING kij) *n.* **1.** the act or fact of shrinking; contraction. **2.** the amount lost by such shrinking. **3.** decrease in value; depreciation.

shrive (shrīv) *v.* **shrove** or **shrived, shriv·en** or **shrived, shriv·ing** *v.t.* **1.** receive the confession of and give absolution to. —*v.i.* **2.** make confession. [ME *shriven*]

shriv·el (SHRIV əl) *v.t. & v.i.* **shriv·eled, shriv·el·ing 1.** contract into wrinkles; shrink and wrinkle: often with *up.* **2.** make or become impotent; wither.

shroud[1] (shrowd) *n.* **1.** a dress or garment for the dead. **2.** something that envelops or conceals like a garment: the *shroud* of night. —*v.t.* envelope, as with a garment. [ME]

shroud[2] *n. Naut.* one of a set of ropes, often of wire, stretched from a masthead to the sides of a ship, serving as means of ascent and as a support for the masts.

shrub (shrub) *n.* a woody perennial plant of low stature, having stems and branches springing from the base. [ME *shrubbe*] — **shrub′by** *adj.* **·bi·er, ·bi·est**

shrub·ber·y (SHRUB ə ree) *n. pl.* **·ber·ies 1.** shrubs collectively. **2.** a collection of shrubs, as in a garden.

shrug (shrug) *v.t. & v.i.* **shrugged, shrug· ging** draw up (the shoulders), as in displeasure, doubt, surprise, etc. —**shrug off** dismiss casually from one's attention. [ME *shruggen*] —*n.* the act of shrugging the shoulders.

shrunk (shrungk) alternative past tense and past participle of SHRINK.

shrunk·en (SHRUNG kən) alternative past participle of SHRINK. —*adj.* contracted and atrophied.

shuck (shuk) *n.* **1.** a husk, shell, or pod. **2.** a shell of an oyster or a clam. —*v.t.* **1.** remove the husk or shell from (corn, oysters, etc.). **2.** take off or cast off, as clothes.

shud·der (SHUD ər) *v.i.* tremble or shake, as from fright or cold; shiver; quake. [ME *shoddren*] —*n.* the act of shuddering.

shuf·fle (SHUF əl) *v.t. & v.i.* **·fled, ·fling 1.** mix or change the order of (playing cards). **2.** move (the feet) along the ground with a dragging gait. **3.** change from one place to another. **4.** dance by pushing one's foot along the floor at each step. [< LG *schuf-feln* walk clumsily] — **shuf·fle** n. —**shuf′ fler** n.

shun (shun) *v.t.* **shunned, shun·ning** keep clear of; avoid; refrain from; ostracize. [ME *shunnen*] —**shun′ner** n.

shunt (shunt) *n.* **1.** the act of shunting. **2.** a railroad switch. **3.** *Electr.* a conductor serving to divert part of the current to an auxiliary circuit; also called *bypass.* —*v.t.* **1.** turn aside. **2.** switch, as a train or car, from one track to another. **3.** *Electr.* distribute by means of shunts. **4.** evade by turning away from; put off on someone else, as a task. —*v.i.* **5.** move to one side; be diverted. [ME *shunten*]

shut (shut) *v.* **shut, shut·ting** *v.t.* **1.** bring into such position as to close an opening or aperture; close, as a door, lid, or valve. **2.** close and fasten securely, as with a latch or lock. **3.** forbid entrance into or exit from. **4.** keep from entering or leaving: with *in, out, from,* etc. **5.** close, fold, or bring together, as extended, expanded, or unfolded parts: *shut* an umbrella. —*v.i.* **6.** be or become closed or in a closed position. [ME *shutten*] —**shut down** cease from operating, as a factory or mine. —**shut one's eyes to** ignore. —**shut out 1.** in sports, keep (an opponent) from scoring during the course of a game. **2.** exclude. —**shut up 1.** stop talking or cause to stop talking. **2.** imprison; confine. —*adj.* made fast or closed. —*n.* the act of shutting.

shut·down (SHUT DOWN) *n.* the stopping of work, as in a factory.

shut-in (SHUT IN) *n.* an invalid who is unable to go out. —*adj.* obliged to stay at home.

shut·out (SHUT OWT) *n.* in sports, a game in which one side is prevented from scoring.

shut·ter (SHUT ər) *n.* **1.** that which shuts out or excludes; esp., a cover or screen, usu. hinged, for closing a window. **2.** *Photog.* any of various mechanisms for momentarily admitting light through a camera lens to the film or plate. —*v.t.* furnish, close, or divide off with shutters.

shut·tle (SHUT l) *n.* **1.** a device used in weaving to carry the weft to and fro between the warp threads. **2.** a similar rotating or other device, as in a sewing machine. **3.** a transport system operating between two nearby points. **4.** space shuttle. [ME *shittle*] —*v.t. & v.i.* **·tled, ·tling** move to and fro, like a shuttle.

shut·tle·cock (SHUT l KOK) *n.* a rounded piece of plastic or cork, with a crown of feathers, as used in badminton. —*v.t.* send or knock back and forth like a shuttlecock.

shy[1] (shī) *adj. v.i.* **shied, shy•ing 1.** start suddenly aside, as in fear: said of a horse. **2.** draw back, as from doubt or caution: with *off* or *away.* —*adj.* **shy•er** or **shi•er, shy•est** or **shi•est 1.** easily frightened or startled; timorous. **2.** bashful; coy. **3.** circumspect, as from motives of caution; wary: with *of.* **4.** short; lacking. [ME *schey*] —*n. pl.* **shies** a starting aside, as in fear. —**shy′ness** *n.*

shy[2] *v.t. & v.i.* **shied, shy•ing** throw with a swift sidelong motion. —*n. pl.* **shies** a careless throw or fling.

Shy•lock (SHĪ lok) *n.* any relentless creditor; moneylender. [after **Shylock,** character in Shakespeare's *Merchant of Venice*]

shy•ly (SHĪ lee) *adv.* in a shy manner.

shy•ster (SHĪ stər) *n. Informal* anyone, esp. a lawyer, who conducts business in an unscrupulous manner.

sib•i•lant (SIB ə lənt) *adj.* **1.** hissing. **2.** *Phonet.* denoting those consonants produced by the frictional passage of breath through a narrow opening in the front part of the mouth, as (s), (z), (sh), and (zh). —*n. Phonet.* a sibilant consonant. [< L *sibilare* hiss] —**sib′i•lance** *n.* —**sib′i•lant•ly** *adv.*

sib•ling (SIB ling) *n.* a brother or sister. [ME]

sib•yl (SIB əl) *n.* a prophet; sorceress. [ME *sibile*] —**sib′yl•line** (SIB ə LEEN) *adj.*

sic (sik) *adv.* so; thus; inserted in brackets after a quotation to indicate that it is accurately reproduced even though it may seem questionable or incorrect. [< L]

sick (sik) *adj.* •**er,** •**est 1.** affected with disease; ill. **2.** of or used by ill persons: often used in combination: *sickbed.* **3.** affected by nausea. **4.** expressive of or experiencing disgust or unpleasant emotion. **5.** impaired or unsound from any cause. **6.** mentally unsound. **7.** pallid; wan. **8.** disinclined by reason of satiety or disgust; surfeited: with *of.* **9.** sadistic or macabre; morbid: *sick* jokes. [ME *sik*] —*n.* sick people collectively: with *the.* —**sick′ness** *n.*

sick bay the part of a ship or of a naval base set aside for the care of the sick.

sick•bed (SIK BED) *n.* the bed a sick person lies on.

sick•en (SIK ən) *v.t. & v.i.* make or become sick or disgusted.

sick•en•ing (SIK ə ning) *adj.* disgusting; revolting; nauseating. —**sick′en•ing•ly** *adv.*

sick•le (SIK əl) *n.* an implement with a curved blade mounted on a short handle, used for cutting tall grass, grains, etc. —*v.t.* •**led,** •**ling** cut with a sickle, as grass. [ME *sikel*]

sickle cell a crescent-shaped red blood corpuscle containing a genetically transmitted type of hemoglobin in which the oxygen concentration is below normal, and causing an anemia (**sickle cell anemia**) occurring chiefly among African Americans.

sick•ly (SIK lee) *adj.* •**li•er,** •**li•est 1.** habitually indisposed; ailing; unhealthy. **2.** nauseating; disgusting. **3.** pertaining to or characteristic of sickness: a *sickly* appearance. **4.** weak; faint. [ME *siklich*] —*adv.* in a sick manner; poorly. —*v.t.* •**lied,** •**ly•ing** make sickly in color. —**sick′li•ness** *n.*

side (sīd) *n.* **1.** any one of the bounding lines of a surface or of the bounding surfaces of a solid object; also, a particular line or surface other than top or bottom: the *side* of a mountain. **2.** either of the two surfaces of a piece of paper, cloth, etc.; also, a specific surface: the rough *side* of sandpaper. **3.** one of two or more contrasted directions, parts, or places: the east *side* of town. **4.** a distinct party or body of competitors or partisans. **5.** an opinion, aspect, or point of view: my *side* of the question. **6.** family connection, esp. by descent through one parent. **7.** either half of the human body. **8.** the space beside someone. **9.** in sports, a team. —**side by side** beside or next to each other. —**take sides** support a particular opinion, point of view, etc. —*adj.* **1.** situated on one side: a *side* window. **2.** being from one side: a *side* glance. **3.** directed toward one side: a *side* blow. **4.** not primary; subordinate: a *side* issue. —*v.t.* **sid•ed, sid•ing** provide with sides, as a building. —**side with** support or take the part of. [ME]

side•arm (SĪD AHRM) *adj.* executed with the hand level with the elbow, as a pitch. —*adv.* in a sidearm manner.

side arm a weapon worn at the side, as pistols etc.

side•board (SĪD BORD) *n.* a piece of diningroom furniture for holding tableware.

side•burns (SĪD BURNZ) *n.pl.* the hair growing on the sides of a man's face below the hairline, esp. when worn as whiskers. [Alter. of *burnsides*, side whiskers]

side effect a secondary, usu. injurious effect, as of a drug.

side·kick (SĪD KIK) n. a close friend; assistant.

side·light (SĪD LĪT) n. an incidental fact or piece of information.

side·line (SĪD LĪN) n. 1. an auxiliary line of goods sold by a store or a commercial traveler. 2. any secondary work differing from one's main job. 3. one of the lines bounding the two sides of a football field, tennis court, etc. —v.t. **·lined, ·lin·ing** prevent or remove (someone) from active participation.

side·long (SĪD LAWNG) adj. 1. inclining, tending, or directed to one side. 2. indirect; sly. —adv. in a lateral or oblique direction.

si·de·re·al (sī DEER ee əl) adj. 1. of or pertaining to stars. 2. measured by means of the stars: sidereal year. [< L sidereus of the stars] —**si·de're·al·ly** adv.

sidereal year the period of 365 days, 6 hours, 9 minutes, and 9 seconds in which the sun apparently returns to the same position among the stars.

side·show (SĪD SHOH) 1. a small show incidental to but connected with a larger or more important one: a circus sideshow. 2. any subordinate issue or attraction.

side·slip (SĪD SLIP) v.i. **·slipped, ·slip·ping** slip or skid sideways. —n. 1. a lateral skid. 2. Aeron. a downward, sideways slipping of an airplane along the lateral axis.

side·step (SĪD STEP) v. **·stepped, ·step·ping** v.i. 1. step to one side. —v.t. 2. avoid, as an issue, or postpone, as a decision; evade.

side·track (SĪD TRAK) v.t. & v.i. 1. move to a siding, as a railroad train. 2. divert or distract from the main issue or subject. —n. a railroad track auxiliary to the main track.

side·walk (SĪD WAWK) n. a path or pavement at the side of the street, for the use of pedestrians.

side·ways (SĪD WAYZ) adv. 1. from the side. 2. so as to incline toward the side, or with the side forward: Hold it sideways. 3. toward one side; obliquely. —adj. moving to or from one side. Also **side'way', side'·wise'**.

sid·ing (SĪ ding) n. 1. a railway track by the side of the main track, opening at both ends to that track. 2. the boarding that covers the side of a house etc.

si·dle (SĪD l) v.i. **·dled, ·dling** move sideways, esp. in a cautious or stealthy manner.

siege (seej) n. 1. the act of surrounding any fortified area with the intention of capturing it. 2. the time during which one under-

goes a protracted illness or difficulty. [ME sege] —**lay siege to** attempt to capture or gain; besiege. —v.t. **sieged, sieg·ing** lay siege to; besiege.

si·er·ra (see ER ə) n. a mountain range having a jagged outline. [< Sp., lit., saw]

si·es·ta (see ES tə) n. a midday or afternoon nap. [< Sp.]

sieve (siv) n. a utensil for straining or sifting, consisting of a frame with a bottom of wire mesh etc. [ME sive] —v.t. & v.i. **sieved, siev·ing** pass through a sieve.

sift (sift) v.t. 1. pass through a sieve. 2. scatter as by a sieve. 3. examine carefully. 4. separate; distinguish: sift fact from fiction. —v.i. 5. use a sieve. [ME siften]

sigh (sī) v.i. 1. draw in and exhale a deep, audible breath, as in expressing sorrow, weariness, etc. 2. make a sound suggestive of a sigh, as the wind. 3. yearn; long: with for. —v.t. 4. express with a sigh. [ME sighen] —n. the act or sound of sighing.

sight (sīt) n. 1. the act or fact of seeing. 2. that which is seen; a view. 3. pl. things worth seeing: the sights of town. 4. the faculty of seeing; vision. 5. the range or scope of vision. 6. a device to assist aim, as on a gun, etc. 7. Informal something unusual or ugly to look at: He was a sight. —**at** (or **on**) **sight** as soon as seen. —**sight unseen** without ever having seen the object in question. —v.t. 1. perceive with the eyes; observe. 2. take a sight of. —v.i. 3. take aim. [ME]

sight·less (SĪT lis) adj. 1. lacking sight; blind. 2. invisible. —**sight'less·ness** n.

sight·ly (SĪT lee) adj. **·li·er, ·li·est** 1. pleasant to the view; comely. 2. affording a fine view.

sight·see·ing (SĪT SEE ing) n. the act of visiting places of interest. —**sight'se'er** n.

sig·ma (SIG mə) n. the eighteenth letter in the Greek alphabet (Σ, σ), corresponding to English s in so.

sign (sīn) n. 1. a motion or action indicating a thought, desire, command, etc. 2. a board, placard, etc., generally bearing an inscription conveying information of some kind: a street sign. 3. any mark, symbol, or token: a sign of mourning. 4. any indication or evidence: signs of poverty. 5. any omen or miraculous occurrence. 6. one of the twelve equal divisions of the zodiac. [ME signe] —v.t. 1. write one's signature or initials on. 2. mark with a sign. 3. engage by obtaining the signature of to a contract; also, hire (oneself) out for work: often with on. 4. dispose

of or transfer title to by signature: with *off*, *over*, or *away*. —*v.i.* **5.** make signs or signals. **6.** write one's signature or initials. —
sign off *Telecom.* cease broadcasting. —
sign up enlist, as in a military service. —
sign′er *n.*

sig·nal (SIG nəl) *n.* **1.** a sign or means of communication agreed upon or understood, used to convey information, a command, etc. **2.** *Telecom.* an electromagnetic impulse that transmits, information, whether direct or in code. —*adj.* **1.** notable; conspicuous. **2.** used to signal. —*v.t. & v.i.* **sig·naled, sig·nal·ing 1.** make signals (to). **2.** communicate by signals. [ME] —
sig′nal·er *n.*

sig·nal·ize (SIG nl Iz) *v.t.* **·ized, ·iz·ing 1.** render noteworthy. **2.** point out with care.

sig·nal·ly (SIG nl ee) *adv.* in a signal manner; eminently.

sig·na·to·ry (SIG nə TOR ee) *adj.* bound by the terms of a signed document; having signed: *signatory* powers. —*n. pl.* **·ries** one who has signed or is bound by a document; esp., a nation so bound. [< L *signatorius* of sealing]

sig·na·ture (SIG nə chər) *n.* **1.** the name of a person written by himself; also, the act of signing one's name. **2.** a distinctive mark, characteristic, etc. **3.** *Printing* a large printed sheet that, when folded, forms four, or a multiple of four, pages of a book. **4.** *Music* a symbol or group of symbols at the beginning of a staff, indicating meter or key. [< Med.L *signatura*]

sig·net (SIG nit) *n.* a seal, esp. one used to authenticate documents, etc. [ME]

sig·nif·i·cance (sig NIF i kəns) *n.* **1.** the character or state of being significant. **2.** meaning. **3.** importance; consequence. Also **sig·nif′i·can·cy.**

sig·nif·i·cant (sig NIF i kənt) *adj.* **1.** having or expressing a meaning. **2.** conveying or having some covert meaning: a *significant* look. **3.** important; weighty; momentous. [< L *significare* signify]

sig·ni·fy (SIG nə FI) *v.* **·fied, ·fy·ing** *v.t.* **1.** make known by signs or words; express. **2.** betoken in any way; import. **3.** amount to; mean. —*v.i.* **4.** have some meaning or importance; matter. [ME *signifien*]

sign language a system of communication by means of signs, largely manual.

sign·post (SĪN POHST) *n.* **1.** a post bearing a sign. **2.** any sign, clue, or indication.

si·lage (SĪ lij) *n.* fodder, grain, etc., stored in

a silo and allowed to ferment, used as feed for livestock.

si·lence (SĪ ləns) *n.* **1.** the state or quality of being silent. **2.** absence of sound or noise; stillness. **3.** a failure to mention something; secrecy. —*v.t.* **·lenced, ·lenc·ing 1.** make silent. **2.** force (guns etc.) to cease firing, as by bombing etc.

si·lenc·er (SĪ lən sər) *n.* a device attached to the muzzle of a firearm to reduce the sound of the report.

si·lent (SĪ lənt) *adj.* **1.** not making any sound or noise; noiseless; still; mute. **2.** not given to speech; taciturn. **3.** unspoken or unuttered: *silent* grief. [< L *silere* be quiet] —
si′lent·ly *adv.*

sil·hou·ette (SIL oo ET) *n.* **1.** a profile drawing or portrait having its outline filled in with uniform color, commonly black. **2.** the outline of a solid figure. —*v.t.* **·et·ted, ·et·ting** cause to appear in silhouette. [< F, after Etienne de *Silhouette*, 1709–67, French minister of finance]

sil·i·ca (SIL i kə) *n.* a hard silicon compound, the principal constituent of quartz and sand. [< NL]

sil·i·cate (SIL i kit) *n. Chem.* a compound of silica.

sil·i·con (SIL i kən) *n.* a widely distributed nonmetallic element (symbol Si).

sil·i·cone (SIL i KOHN) *n. Chem.* an organic silicon compound, used in lubricants, waterproofing materials, etc.

sil·i·co·sis (SIL i KOH sis) *n. Pathol.* a lung disease caused by inhalation of finely powdered silica or quartz.

silk (silk) *n.* **1.** the fine natural fiber produced by silkworms. **2.** a similar threadlike material spun by other insects. **3.** cloth, thread, or garments made of silk. **4.** anything resembling silk. —*adj.* **1.** consisting of silk. **2.** resembling silk. [ME]

silk·en (SIL kən) *adj.* **1.** made of silk. **2.** like silk; glossy; delicate; smooth. **3.** luxurious.

silk·worm (SILK wurm) *n.* the larva of certain moths that spin a dense silken cocoon, esp. the **common silkworm,** yielding commercial silk.

silk·y (SIL kee) *adj.* **silk·i·er, silk·i·est 1.** made of or resembling silk; soft; lustrous. **2.** gentle or insinuating in manner. —**silk′i·ness** *n.*

sill (sil) *n.* a horizontal, lower member of something, as the bottom of a door or window casing. [ME *sille*]

sil·ly (SIL ee) *adj.* **·li·er, ·li·est 1.** lacking

ordinary good sense; foolish. **2.** stupid; absurd. [ME *sely*] —*n. pl.* **-lies** *Informal* a silly person. —**sil'li·ness** *n.*

si·lo (SĪ loh) *n. pl.* **-los 1.** a pit or tower in which fodder, grain, or other food is stored green to be fermented and used as feed for cattle etc. **2.** a similar structure, built underground, for the housing or launching of missiles, esp. nuclear missiles. —*v.t.* **-loed, -lo·ing** put or preserve in a silo; turn into silage. [< Sp.]

silt (silt) *n.* an earthy sediment consisting of fine particles of rock and soil suspended in and carried by water. [ME *cylte*] —*v.i.* **1.** become filled or choked with silt: usu. with *up.* **2.** ooze; drift. —*v.i.* **3.** fill or choke with silt or mud: usu. with *up.* —**silt'y** *adj*

sil·ver (SIL vər) *n.* **1.** a white ductile metallic element (symbol Ag) of high electric conductivity, used in medicine, industry, and the arts. **2.** silver regarded as a commodity or as a standard of currency. **3.** silver coin; cash or change; money in general. **4.** silver plate; silverware. **5.** a pale gray color resembling that of silver. —*adj.* **1.** made of or coated with silver. **2.** of, containing or producing silver. **3.** having a silvery luster. **4.** having the soft, clear tones of a silver bell. **5.** persuasive; eloquent. **6.** white or gray, as the hair. [ME *silvere*] —*v.t.* **1.** coat or plate with silver or with a silverlike substance. —*v.i.* **2.** become silver or white. —**sil'ver·er** *n.*

silver anniversary a 25th anniversary.

silver plate articles, as table utensils, made of silver or metal plated with silver.

sil·ver·ware (SIL vər WAIR) *n.* articles, esp. for table use, made of silver.

sil·ver·y (SIL və ree) *adj.* **1.** containing or adorned with silver. **2.** resembling silver, as in luster or hue. **3.** soft and clear in sound. —**sil'ver·i·ness** *n.*

sim·i·an (SIM ee ən) *adj.* pertaining to, resembling, or characteristic of apes and monkeys. —*n.* an ape or monkey. [< L *simia* ape]

sim·i·lar (SIM ə lər) *adj.* **1.** bearing resemblance to one another or to something else; like, but not identical. **2.** of like characteristics, nature, or degree; of the same scope, order, or purpose. [< F *similaire*] —**sim'i·lar·ly** *adv.*

sim·i·lar·i·ty (SIM ə LAR i tee) *n. pl.* **-ties 1.** the quality or state of being similar. **2.** the point in which the objects compared are similar.

sim·i·le (SIM ə lee) *n.* a figure of speech expressing comparison or likeness by the use of such terms as *like, as, so,* etc.: distinguished from *metaphor.* [ME]

sim·mer (SIM ər) *v.i.* **1.** boil gently; be or stay at or just below the boiling point. **2.** be on the point of breaking forth, as with rage. —*v.t.* **3.** keep at or just below the boiling point. —**simmer down** subside from a state of anger or excitement. —*n.* the state or process of simmering.

sim·per (SIM pər) *v.i.* **1.** smile in a silly, self-conscious manner; smirk. —*v.t.* **2.** say with a simper. —*n.* a silly, self-conscious smile. [< Scand.] —**sim'per·ing·ly** *adv.*

sim·ple (SIM pəl) *adj.* **-pler, -plest 1.** consisting of one thing; single; uncombined. **2.** not complex or complicated; easy. **3.** without embellishment; plain; unadorned. **4.** free from affectation; artless. **5.** of humble rank; lowly. **6.** silly; lacking good sense. **7.** lacking luxury; frugal. **8.** having nothing added; mere. **9.** *Bot.* not divided; entire. —*n.* **1.** that which is simple; an uncomplex, or natural thing. **2.** an ignorant person. [ME]

sim·ple-mind·ed (SIM pəl MIN did) *adj.* **1.** artless or unsophisticated. **2.** mentally defective. **3.** stupid; foolish. —**sim'ple-mind'ed·ly** *adv.* —**sim'ple-mind'ed·ness** *n.*

sim·ple·ton (SIM pəl tən) *n.* an ignorant or silly person.

sim·plic·i·ty (sim PLIS i tee) *n. pl.* **-ties 1.** the state of being simple; freedom from complexity or complication. **2.** sincerity; unaffectedness. **3.** lack of intelligence or good sense. [ME *simplicite*]

sim·pli·fy (SIM plə FĪ) *v.t.* **-fied, -fy·ing** make more simple or less complex. [< F *simplifier*] —**sim'pli·fi·ca'tion** *n.*

sim·plis·tic (sim PLIS tik) *adj.* tending to ignore complications or details; oversimplified. —**sim'plism** *n.*

sim·ply (SIM plee) *adv.* **1.** in a simple manner; intelligibly. **2.** without ostentation or extravagance. **3.** merely; only. **4.** really; absolutely: *simply* charming.

sim·u·late (SIM yə LAYT) *v.t.* **-lat·ed, -lat·ing 1.** have the appearance or form of, without the reality; counterfeit; imitate. **2.** make a pretense of. [< L *simulatus* copied] —**sim'u·lat'ed** *adj.*

sim·u·la·tion (SIM yə LAY shən) *n.* **1.** the act of simulating; counterfeit; sham. **2.** the taking on of a particular aspect or form.

si·mul·cast (SĪ məl KAST) *v.t.* **-cast** or

•cast•ed, •cast•ing broadcast by radio and television simultaneously. [< SIMUL(TANEOUS) + (BROAD)CAST] —n. a simultaneous radio and television broadcast.

si•mul•ta•ne•ous (sī məl TAY nee əs) adj. occurring, done, or existing at the same time. —si'mul•ta'ne•ous•ly adv. — si'mul•ta'ne•ous•ness, si•mul•ta•ne•i•ty (sī məl tə NEE i tee) n.

sin (sin) n. 1. a transgression, esp., when deliberate, of a religious law. 2. any offense against a standard: a literary sin. —v.i. sinned, sin•ning 1. commit sin; transgress the divine law. 2. violate any requirement of right, duty, etc.; do wrong. [ME]

since (sins) adv. 1. from a past time, mentioned or referred to, up to the present. 2. at some time between a certain past time or event and the present. 3. in time before the present; ago; before now. —prep. 1. during or within the time after: since you left. 2. continuously throughout the time after: since noon. —conj. 1. continuously·from the time when. 2. because of or following upon the fact that; inasmuch as. [ME sins]

sin•cere (sin SEER) adj. 1. being in reality as it is in appearance; genuine. 2. free from hypocrisy; honest. [< MF] —sin•cere'ly adv. —sin•cer•i•ty (sin SER i tee) n.

sine (sīn) n. Trig. in a right triangle, a function of an acute angle, equal to the ratio of the side opposite the angle to the hypotenuse. [< NL]

si•ne•cure (SĪ ni KYUUR) n. an office or position for which pay is received, but involving few or no duties. [< Med.L sine cura without care]

si•ne qua non (SIN i kwah NON) Latin that which is indispensable; an essential; literally, without which not.

sin•ew (SIN yoo) n. 1. a tendon or similar fibrous cord. 2. strength, or that which supplies strength. —v.t. strengthen or knit together. [ME]

sin•ew•y (SIN yoo ee) adj. 1. strong; brawny. 2. forceful; vigorous: a sinewy style.

sin•ful (SIN fəl) adj. characterized by, suggestive of, or tainted with sin; wicked; immoral. [ME] —sin'ful•ly adv.

sing (sing) v. sang, sung, sing•ing v.i. 1. produce word sounds that differ from speech in that vowels are lengthened and pitches are clearly defined. 2. use the voice in this manner for musical rendition or performance. 3. produce melodious sounds, as

a bird. 4. make a melodious sound suggestive of singing, as a teakettle. 5. Slang confess; squeal. —v.t. 6. render (a song etc.) by singing. 7. chant, intone, or utter in a song-like manner. 8. bring to a specified condition by singing: Sing me to sleep. 9. relate in or as in song; acclaim: they sing her fame. —sing out Informal call out loudly; shout. [ME singen] —n. a gathering for general participation in singing.

singe (sinj) v.t. singed, singe•ing 1. burn slightly or superficially; scorch. 2. remove bristles or feathers from by passing through flame. 3. burn the ends of (hair etc.). [ME sengen] —n. 1. the act of singeing, esp. as performed by a barber. 2. a superficial burn; scorch.

sing•er (SING ər) n. one who sings, esp. as a profession.

sin•gle (SING gəl) adj. 1. consisting of one only; individual. 2. without another; alone. 3. unmarried. 4. consisting of only one part. 5. designed for use by only one person: a single bed. —n. 1. one person or thing. 2. in baseball, a base hit that enables the batter to reach first base. 3. a hotel room for one person. 4. pl. in tennis etc., a game having one player on each side. 5. Informal a one-dollar bill. 6. an unmarried person: a resort for singles. —v. •gled, •gling v.t. 1. select from others: usu. with out. —v.i. 2. in baseball, make a one-base hit. [ME]

single file a line of persons or things one behind the other.

sin•gle-hand•ed (SING gəl HAN did) adj. 1. without help; unaided. 2. having or using but one hand. —sin'gle-hand'ed, sin' gle-hand'ed•ly adv. —sin'gle-hand'ed• ness n.

sin•gle-mind•ed (SING gəl MĪN did) adj. having but one purpose or aim. —sin'gle-mind'ed•ly adv. —sin'gle-mind'ed• ness n.

sin•gle•ton (SING gəl tən) n. a single card of a suit in a card player's hand.

sin•gly (SING glee) adv. 1. without help; unaided. 2. one by one; separately.

sing•song (SING SAWNG) n. monotonous cadence in speaking or reading. —adj. monotonous; droning.

sin•gu•lar (SING gyə lər) adj. 1. extraordinary; remarkable. 2. odd; peculiar. 3. being the only one of its type; unique. 4. Gram. of or designating a word form that denotes one person or thing. —n. Gram. the singular number or form of a word. [ME] —

sin·gu·lar·i·ty (SING gyə LAR i tee) n. — **sin'gu·lar·ly** adv.

sin·is·ter (SIN ə stər) adj. **1.** malevolent; evil; wicked. **2.** threatening or tending toward disaster; ominous. [< L, left]

sin·is·tral (SIN ə strəl) adj. **1.** on the left side. **2.** left-handed. —**sin'is·tral·ly** adv.

sink (singk) v. **sank, sunk** or **sunk·en, sink·ing** v.i. **1.** go beneath the surface of water or other liquid. **2.** descend or appear to descend to a lower level. **3.** fail, as from ill health; approach death. **4.** become less in force, volume, or degree: His voice *sank* to a whisper. **5.** become less in value, price, etc. **6.** decline in moral level, prestige, wealth, etc. **7.** permeate: The oil *sank* into the wood. **8.** become hollow; cave in, as the cheeks. **9.** be impressed or fixed, as in the mind: with *in*. —v.t. **10.** cause to go beneath the surface or to the bottom. **11.** cause to fall or drop; lower. **12.** force or drive into place: *sink* a fence post. **13.** make (a mine shaft, well, etc.) by digging or excavating. **14.** reduce in force, volume, or degree. **15.** invest and subsequently lose. [ME *sinken*] —n. **1.** a box-shaped or basinlike receptacle with a drainpipe and usu. with a water supply. **2.** a cesspool or sewer. **3.** a basin or other depression in the earth's surface where water collects.

sink·er (SING kər) n. a weight for sinking a fishing line.

sink·hole (SINGK hohl) n. a natural cavity, esp. a hole worn by water.

sin·less (SIN lis) adj. having no sin; guiltless; innocent. —**sin'less·ness** n.

sin·ner (SIN ər) n. one who has sinned.

sin·u·ous (SIN yoo əs) adj. characterized by bends, curves, or folds; winding; undulating. [< L *sinuosus* bent] —**sin·u·os·i·ty** (SIN yoo OS i tee) n. —**sin'u·ous·ly** adv.

si·nus (SĪ nəs) n. **1.** an opening or cavity. **2.** Anat. any of the air-filled cavities in the cranial bones, connected to the nostrils. [< L]

si·nu·si·tis (SĪ nə SĪ tis) n. Pathol. inflammation of a sinus or sinuses.

sip (sip) v.t. & v.i. **sipped, sip·ping** drink (a liquid) a little at a time. [ME *sippen*] —n. a small amount sipped.

si·phon (SĪ fən) n. **1.** a bent or flexible tube through which liquids may be passed from a higher to a lower level by making use of atmospheric pressure. **2.** a siphon bottle; also, *syphon*. —v.t. draw off through a siphon. [< F]

siphon bottle a bottle containing carbonated water that can be expelled by pressure.

sir (sur) n. **1.** the term of respectful address to men, not followed by a proper name. **2.** *cap.* a title of respect, used before the name. [ME]

sire (sīr) n. **1.** a father; begetter. **2.** the male parent of a mammal. **3.** a form of address used in speaking to a king. —v.t. **sired, sir·ing** beget. [ME]

si·ren (SĪ rən) n. **1.** a fascinating, dangerous woman. **2.** a device that emits a loud, wailing sound, used chiefly as a warning signal. [ME]

sir·loin (SUR loin) n. a loin of beef, esp. the upper portion. [< MF *surlonge*]

si·roc·co (sə ROK oh) n. pl. **·cos** a hot, dry, dusty wind blowing from northern Africa to southern Europe. [< Ital. *scirocco*]

sis·sy (SIS ee) n. pl. **·sies** **1.** an effeminate man or boy. **2.** a coward or weakling. —**sis'sy·ish** adj.

sis·ter (SIS tər) n. **1.** a female having the same parents as another. **2.** a member of a club, sorority, etc. for women or girls. **3.** a nun. **4.** *Brit.* a head nurse in a hospital ward. —adj. bearing the relationship of a sister or one suggestive of sisterhood. [ME] —**sis'ter·ly** adv.

sis·ter·hood (SIS tər HUUD) n. **1.** the relationship between sisters. **2.** a body of women united by some common interest.

sis·ter-in-law (SIS tər in LAW) n. pl. **sis·ters-in-law** **1.** a sister of a husband or wife. **2.** a brother's wife. **3.** the wife of a spouse's brother.

sit (sit) v. **sat, sit·ting** v.i. **1.** rest with the buttocks on a supporting surface. **2.** perch or roost, as a bird; also, cover eggs for hatching. **3.** remain passive or inactive. **4.** pose, as for a portrait. **5.** meet in assembly; hold a session. **6.** occupy a seat in a deliberative body. **7.** fit or be adjusted; suit: That plan *sits* well. **8.** be located: The wind *sits* in the east. **9.** baby-sit; serve as company for a child, someone ill, etc. —v.t. **10.** ride (a horse). **11.** seat. —**sit in** join or take part. —**sit out 1.** remain till the end of. **2.** sit aside during: They *sat out* a dance. —**sit tight** wait for the next move. [ME *sitten*] —**sit'ter** n.

si·tar (si TAHR) n. an East Indian stringed instrument resembling a guitar. [< Hind. *sitār*]

site (sīt) *n.* a location or position; scene. [ME]

sit-in (SIT IN) *n.* a demonstration of protest, in which participants enter and remain seated in a public place, commercial establishment, etc.

sit·ting (SIT ing) *adj.* **1.** being in a seated position. **2.** used for sitting: *sitting* room. **3.** occupying a legislative or judicial seat; being in office: a *sitting* chief justice. —*n.* **1.** a single period of remaining seated for a specific purpose. **2.** a session or term. **3.** the time allotted for serving a meal, as in a restaurant or ship.

sitting duck any easy target.

sitting room a small living room.

sit·u·ate (SICH oo AYT) *v.t.* **·at·ed, ·at·ing** place in a certain position or place; locate. [< Med.L. *situatus* placed]

sit·u·at·ed (SICH oo AY tid) *adj.* **1.** having a fixed place or location; placed. **2.** placed in (specified) circumstances, esp. with regard to financial circumstances: He is *well* situated.

sit·u·a·tion (SICH oo AY shən) *n.* **1.** condition; state of affairs; status. **2.** a location or position; place. **3.** one's job.

sit-up (SIT UP) *n.* an exercise in which one rises from a supine to a sitting position.

six (siks) *n.* the sum of five and one: a cardinal number written 6, VI. —**at sixes and sevens 1.** in disorder. **2.** in dispute. [ME] —**six** *adj.*

six·teen (SIKS TEEN) *n.* the sum of fifteen and one: a cardinal number written 16, XVI. [ME] —**six·teen** *adj.* —**six'·teenth'** *adj. & n.*

sixteenth note *Music* a note having one sixteenth the time value of a whole note.

sixth (siksth) *adj.* **1.** next after the fifth: the ordinal of *six*. **2.** being one of six equal parts. —*n.* **1.** one of six equal parts. **2.** that which follows the fifth. **3.** *Music* the interval between any tone and another tone five steps from it in a diatonic scale. —*adv.* in the sixth order, place, etc.

sixth sense intuitive perception; intuition.

six·ty (SIKS tee) *n. pl.* **·ties** the sum of fifty and ten: a cardinal number written 60, LX. [ME] —**six·ty** *adj.* —**six'ti·eth** *adj. & n.*

siz·a·ble (SĪ zə bəl) *adj.* quite large. Also **size'a·ble.** —**siz'a·ble·ness** *n.* —**siz'a·bly** *adv.*

size[1] (sīz) *n.* **1.** measurement or extent of a thing as compared with some standard. **2.** comparative magnitude or bulk. **3.** one of a series of graded measures, as of hats, shoes, etc. **4.** a standard of measurement; specified quantity. **5.** state of affairs; true situation: That's the size of it. —*v.t.* **sized, siz·ing** distribute or classify according to size. —**size up** *Informal* **1.** form an estimate or opinion of. **2.** meet a standard. [ME *syse* control]

size[2] *n.* a pasty substance used to glaze paper, coat walls, etc.: also called *sizing.* —*v.t.* **sized, siz·ing** treat with size. [ME *sise*]

siz·ing (SĪ zing) *n.* **1.** size[2]. **2.** the process of adding or applying size to a fabric, surface, etc.

siz·zle (SIZ əl) *v.i.* **·zled, ·zling 1.** burn, fry, etc. with a hissing sound. **2.** be extremely hot. —*n.* a sizzling sound.

skate[1] (skayt) *n.* **1.** a metal runner attached to the sole of a shoe, used for gliding over ice. **2.** an ice skate or roller skate. —*v.i.* **skat·ed, skat·ing** move over a surface on skates. [< Du. *schaats* stilt] —**skat'er** *n.*

skate[2] *n.* any of various ray fishes having large pectoral fins. [ME *scate*]

skate·board (SKAYT BORD) *n.* a narrow platform on roller-skate wheels. —*v.i.* ride or perform on a skateboard. —**skate'board·er** *n.* —**skate'board·ing** *n.*

ske·dad·dle (ski DAD l) *v.i.* **·dled, ·dling** *Informal* flee in haste.

skeet (skeet) *n.* a type of trapshooting in which targets are fired at from various angles.

skein (skayn) *n.* **1.** a length of yarn, thread, etc., in a loose coil. **2.** a succession of similar things: a *skein* of shutouts. [ME *skeyne*]

skel·e·ton (SKEL i tn) *n.* **1.** the supporting or protective framework of a human or animal body, consisting of the bones and connective cartilage (**endoskeleton**) in man and the vertebrates, or of a hard outer structure (**exoskeleton**), as in crustaceans, insects, etc. **2.** an outline, as of a play; sketch. **3.** a very thin or emaciated person or animal. —**skeleton in the closet** a hidden source of shame or discredit. —*adj.* **1.** of or like a skeleton. **2.** consisting merely of a few workers, a crude outline, etc.: a *skeleton* crew. [< NL] —**skel'e·tal** *adj.*

skeleton key a key modified to open various locks.

skep·tic (SKEP tik) *n.* **1.** one who doubts, disbelieves, or disagrees with generally accepted ideas. **2.** one who questions the doctrines of a religion. [< L *scepticus* thoughtful]

skep·ti·cal (SKEP ti kəl) *adj.* doubting; questioning; disbelieving. **—skep'ti·cal·ly** *adv.*

skep·ti·cism (SKEP ti siz əm) *n.* 1. a doubting or disbelieving attitude. 2. *Philos.* the doctrine that absolute knowledge is unattainable.

sketch (skech) *n.* 1. a rough or rapid drawing or outline. 2. a short or light story, comedy act, etc. —*v.t. & v.i.* make a rough drawing or outline (of). [< Du. *schets*]

sketch·book (SKECH BUUK) *n.* 1. a pad used for sketching. 2. a set or collection of literary sketches.

sketch·y (SKECH ee) *adj.* **sketch·i·er, sketch·i·est** 1. roughly suggested without detail. 2. incomplete. **—sketch'i·ly** *adv.* **—sketch'i·ness** *n.*

skew (skyoo) *v.i.* 1. take an oblique direction; swerve. —*v.t.* 2. give an oblique direction or form to; slant. 3. twist the meaning of; distort. [ME *skewen*] *—adj.* placed or turned obliquely; twisted. *—n.* a deviation from symmetry or straightness; slant.

skew·er (SKYOO ər) *n.* a pin thrust into meat to hold it together while cooking. —*v.t.* run through or fasten with or as with a skewer.

ski (skee) *n. pl.* **skis** one of a pair of wooden, plastic, or metal runners attached to the feet and used in sliding over snow. —*v.i.* **skied, ski·ing** glide on skis, esp. as a sport. [< Norw.] **—ski'er** *n.*

skid (skid) *n.* 1. the act of skidding or slipping. 2. a platform for moving or storing loads: also called *pallet*. 3. a log, rail, etc., used as a track in sliding heavy articles about. 4. *Aeron.* a runner in an airplane's landing gear enabling the aircraft to slide during landing. —*v.i.* **skid·ded, skid·ding** slide or slip, as a car on ice. [? < ON *skith* piece of wood]

skid row (roh) an urban section inhabited by alcoholics and derelicts.

skiff (skif) *n.* a light rowboat or small, open sailing vessel. [< MF *esquif*]

ski·ing (SKEE ing) *n.* the act or sport of skiers.

ski jump a slide or chute that enables skiers to make high jumps.

ski lift a motor-driven conveyor for transporting skiers to the top of a slope. Also called *ski tow*.

skill (skil) *n.* 1. proficiency or ability in any task. 2. a developed art, trade, or technique.

[ME] **—skilled** *adj.* **—skill'ful** *adj.* **—skill'ful·ly** *adv.*

skil·let (SKIL it) *n.* a frying pan. [ME]

skim (skim) *v.* **skimmed, skim·ming** *v.t.* 1. remove floating matter from the surface of: *skim* milk. 2. remove thus: *skim* cream. 3. move lightly and quickly over. 4. read hastily or superficially. —*v.i.* 5. move quickly and lightly over a surface; glide. 6. do something hastily or superficially: with *over* or *through*. [ME *skimmen*]

skimp (skimp) *v.t. & v.i.* scrimp. *—adj.* scanty; skimpy.

skimp·y (SKIM pee) *adj.* **skimp·i·er, skimp·i·est** hardly enough; scanty; meager. **—skimp'i·ly** *adv.* **—skimp'i·ness** *n.*

skin (skin) *n.* 1. the tissue covering the body of an animal. 2. the pelt of an animal. 3. an outside layer, as the rind of a fruit. 4. one's life: save one's *skin*. **—by the skin of one's teeth** very closely or narrowly; barely. **— get under one's skin** be provoking or irritating. —*v.t.* **skinned, skin·ning** remove the skin of; flay; peel. [ME]

skin-deep (SKIN DEEP) *adj.* superficial.

skin-dive (SKIN DIV) *v.i.* **-dived** or **-dove, -div·ing** engage in skin diving.

skin diving underwater swimming with goggles, foot fins, and scuba or snorkel. **—skin diver**

skin·flint (SKIN FLINT) *n.* a miser.

skin game a crooked gambling game; also, any swindle.

skin·ner (SKIN ər) *n.* 1. one who deals in pelts and hides. 2. a mule driver.

skin·ny (SIN ee) *adj.* **·ni·er, ·ni·est** very thin; emaciated. **—skin'ni·ness** *n.*

skin·ny-dip (SKIN ee DIP) *v.i.* **-dipped, -dip·ping** *Informal* swim in the nude.

skin·tight (SKIN TĪT) *adj.* fitting tightly.

skip (skip) *v.* **skipped, skip·ping** *v.i.* 1. move with light springing steps; caper. 2. bounce or ricochet. 3. leave hurriedly; flee. 4. be advanced in school beyond the next grade in order. —*v.t.* 5. leap lightly over. 6. cause to bounce or ricochet. 7. pass over or by; omit. 8. *Informal* leave (a place) hurriedly. *—n.* 1. a light bound or hop. 2. a passing over without notice. [ME *skippen*]

ski pants close-fitting pants worn for skiing.

skip·per (SKIP ər) *n.* the captain of a ship. [< Du. *schip* ship] **—skip'per** *v.t.* act as skipper of. [ME]

skir·mish (SKUR mish) *n.* 1. a brief, minor battle in a war. 2. any minor conflict or argument. —*v.i.* engage in a skirmish. [ME *skyrmissh*] —**skir′•mish•er** *n.*

skirt (skurt) *n.* a garment or part of a garment that hangs below the waist. —*v.t.* **1.** lie along or form the edge of; border. **2.** bypass. **3.** evade or avoid (a subject, issue, etc.). — *v.i.* **4.** pass or be near the edge or border of something. [ME]

ski run a course or slope for skiing.

skit (skit) *n.* a humorous dramatic sketch.

ski tow (toh) a ski lift.

skit•ter (SKIT ər) *v.i.* glide or skim along.

skit•tish (SKIT ish) *adj.* **1.** easily frightened, as a horse. **2.** capricious; uncertain; unreliable. [ME] —**skit′tish•ly** *adv.* —**skit′ tish•ness** *n.*

skit•tle (SKIT l) *n.* **1.** *pl.* a game of ninepins, in which a flattened ball or thick rounded disk is thrown to knock down the pins. **2.** a pin used in this game. —**beer and skittles** carefree existence; drink and play. [? < Dan. *skyttel* a child's earthen ball]

skoal (skohl) *interj.* to your good health: a toast. [< Scand.]

skul•dug•ger•y (skul DUG ə ree) *n.* trickery; underhandedness.

skulk (skulk) *v.i.* move about furtively; slink. [< Scand.] —**skulk′er** *n.*

skull (skul) *n.* **1.** the bony framework of the head of a vertebrate animal; cranium. **2.** the head considered as the seat of the mind. [ME *skulle*]

skull and crossbones a representation of the human skull over two crossed bones, used as a symbol of death or as a warning label on poison.

skull•cap (SKUL KAP) *n.* a small, snug, brimless cap.

skunk (skunk) *n.* **1.** a carnivorous mammal of North America, usu. black with a white stripe and a bushy tail, and ejecting at will a malodorous liquid. **2.** *Informal* a contemptible person. —*v.t. Slang* defeat utterly in a game or contest.

sky (skī) *n. pl.* **skies 1.** the region of the upper air; firmament. **2.** *Often pl.* atmospheric condition: cloudy *skies.* **3.** heaven. —*v.t.* **skied, sky•ing** *Informal* bat or throw (a ball etc.) high into the air. [ME]

sky•cap (SKĪ KAP) *n.* a porter at an airline terminal.

sky•div•ing (SKĪ DI ving) *n.* the sport of jumping from an airplane and performing various maneuvers before opening the parachute. —**sky diver**

sky-high (SKĪ HĪ) *adj. & adv.* very high.

sky•lark (SKĪ LAHRK) *n.* a lark of the Old World that sings as it rises in flight. —*v.i.* frolic boisterously. —**sky′lark′er** *n.*

sky•light (SKĪ LĪT) *n.* a window in a roof or ceiling.

sky•line (SKĪ LĪN) *n.* **1.** the horizon. **2.** the outline of buildings etc. seen against the sky.

sky•scrap•er (SKĪ SKRAY pər) *n.* a very high building.

sky•ward (SKĪ wərd) *adv.* toward the sky. Also **sky′wards.** —*adj.* moving or directed toward the sky.

sky•writ•ing (SKĪ RĪ ting) *n.* **1.** the forming of words in the air by the release of vapor from an airplane. **2.** the words or letters thus formed. —**sky′writ′er** *n.*

slab (slab) *n.* a flat, thick piece or slice. —*v.t.* **slabbed, slab•bing** make or form into slabs. [ME *slabbe*]

slack[1] (slak) *adj.* •**er,** •**est 1.** hanging or extended loosely. **2.** careless; remiss; slovenly. **3.** slow; sluggish. **4.** lacking activity; not busy: a *slack* season. —*v.t.* **1.** slacken. **2.** slake, as lime. —*v.i.* **3.** be or become slack. —**slack off** slow down; be less diligent. — *n.* **1.** a part of a rope, sail, etc. that is slack or loose. **2.** slack condition; looseness. **3.** a period of inactivity. —*adv.* in a slack manner. [ME *slak*] —**slack′ness** *n.*

slack[2] *n.* small pieces of coal left after screening. [ME *sleck*]

slack•en (SLAK ən) *v.i.* **1.** become less active, productive, etc. **2.** become less tense or tight. —*v.t.* **3.** become slow, negligent, or remiss in: *slacken* one's efforts. **4.** loosen.

slack•er (SLAK ər) *n.* one who shirks duties or avoids military service in wartime; shirker.

slacks (slaks) *n. pl.* trousers for informal wear.

slag (slag) *n.* **1.** *Metall.* the waste left after a metal is separated from its ore in smelting. **2.** volcanic lava in small, cinderlike pieces. —*v.t. & v.i.* **slagged, slag•ging** form into slag. [< MLG *slagge*]

slain (slayn) past participle of SLAY.

slake (slayk) *v.* **slaked, slak•ing** *v.t.* **1.** quench or satisfy, as thirst. **2.** cause (lime) to heat and crumble by mixing it with water. —*v.i.* **3.** of lime, crumble. [ME *slaken*]

sla•lom (SLAH ləm) *n.* in skiing, a downhill race over a zigzag course. —*v.i.* ski in such a course. [< Norw.]

slam[1] (slam) *v.* **slammed, slam•ming** *v.t.* **1.** shut, hit, throw, etc. forcefully and noisily.

2. *Informal* criticize harshly. —*v.i.* **3.** close, swing, etc. with force and noise. —*n.* **1.** the act or noise of slamming. **2.** *Informal* harsh criticism; abuse. [? < Scand.]

slam² *n.* in bridge, the winning of all (**grand slam**) or all but one (**little** or **small slam**) of the tricks in a round of play; also, a bid to do so.

slan·der (SLAN dər) *n.* a false statement, particularly when spoken, that damages another's reputation. —*v.t.* **1.** make such a statement against. —*v.i.* **2.** utter slander. [ME *sclaundre*] —**slan'der·er** *n.* —**slan'der·ous** *adj.*

slang (slang) *n.* language of a vigorous, colorful, or taboo nature, invented for specific occasions or uses or derived from the unconventional use of the standard vocabulary.

slang·y (SLANG ee) *adj.* **slang·i·er, slang·i·est** containing or using slang.

slant (slant) *v.t.* **1.** give an oblique or sloping direction to; incline. **2.** write or utter so as to express a special attitude, bias, or opinion. —*v.i.* **3.** have or take an oblique direction; slope. —*adj.* lying at an angle; sloping. [ME *slenten*] —*n.* **1.** a slanting direction, course, or plane; slope. **2.** a bent, bias, or leaning. **3.** a point of view; attitude.

slant·wise (SLANT wīz) *adj.* slanting; oblique. —*adv.* at a slant or slope; obliquely.

slap (slap) *n.* **1.** a blow delivered with the open hand or something flat. **2.** a sharp rebuke; insult; slur. —*v.* **slapped, slap·ping** *v.t.* **1.** hit or strike with the open hand or something flat. —*v.i.* **2.** strike or beat as if with slaps. [< LG *slapp*]

slap·dash (SLAP DASH) *adj.* done or acting in a reckless way; impetuous; careless. — *adv.* in a haphazard manner.

slap·stick (SLAP STIK) *n.* boisterous, loud comedy. —*adj.* using or like slapstick.

slash (slash) *v.t.* **1.** cut violently with sweeping strokes. **2.** make gashes or slits in. **3.** reduce sharply, as prices. —*v.i.* **4.** make sweeping strokes with or as with a knife. — *n.* **1.** a slit or gash. **2.** a slanting line (/) used to indicate two alternatives (and/or), to express *per* (feet/sec.), to form fractions (⅜), etc.: also called *solidus, virgule.* [ME *slaschen*]

slat (slat) *n.* a thin, narrow strip, as in a window blind. —*v.t.* **slat·ted, slat·ting** provide or make with slats. [ME, slate]

slate (slāt) *n.* **1.** a fine-grained rock that splits readily into thin layers. **2.** a piece of slate used for roofing, writing upon, etc. **3.** a list of candidates for election. **4.** a dull bluish gray color. —**a clean slate** a record free of misdeeds, past performances, etc. —*adj.* **1.** made of slate. **2.** having the color of slate. —*v.t.* **slat·ed, slat·ing 1.** roof with slate. **2.** designate for candidacy, appointment, action, etc. [ME] —**slat'er** *n.*

slath·er (SLATH ər) *Informal v.t.* daub thickly or use profusely.

slat·tern (SLAT ərn) *n.* **1.** an untidy or slovenly woman. **2.** a slut. —**slat'tern·li·ness** *n.* —**slat'tern·ly** *adj. & adv.*

slaugh·ter (SLAW tər) *n.* **1.** the butchering of cattle and other animals for market. **2.** wanton or savage killing of human beings; massacre; carnage. —*v.t.* **1.** kill for the market; butcher. **2.** kill wantonly or savagely. [ME] —**slaugh'ter·er** *n.*

slaugh·ter·house (SLAW tər HOWS) *n.* a place where animals are butchered.

Slav (slahv) *n.* a member of any of the Slavic-speaking peoples of northern or eastern Europe.

slave (slāv) *n.* **1.** a person who is the property of another; bondman; serf. **2.** a person who is dominated by a habit, vice, etc.: a *slave* to drink. **3.** a drudge. —*v.i.* **slaved, slav·ing** work like a slave. [ME *sclave*]

slave driver 1. a person who oversees slaves at work. **2.** any severe or demanding employer.

slave·hold·er (SLAYV HOHL dər) *n.* an owner of slaves. —**slave'hold'ing** *adj. &*

slav·er¹ (SLAV ər) *v.i.* dribble saliva; drool. —*n.* saliva dribbling from the mouth. [ME]

slav·er² (SLAY vər) *n.* a person or vessel engaged in the slave trade.

slav·er·y (SLAY və ree) *n.* **1.** the holding of human beings as property; also, the condition of a slave. **2.** drudgery; toil.

slave trade the business of dealing in slaves. —**slave trader**

Slav·ic (SLAH vik) *adj.* of or pertaining to the Slavs or their languages. —*n.* a branch of the Balto-Slavic subfamily of the Indo-European language family, including Russian, Czech, Polish, and Bulgarian.

slav·ish (SLAY vish) *adj.* **1.** of or like a slave; servile; base. **2.** dependent; imitative.

slay (slā) *v.t.* **slew, slain, slay·ing** kill violently. [ME *slen*] —**slay'er** *n.*

slea·zy (SLEE zee) *adj.* ·**zi·er, ·zi·est** of

poor quality; cheap; shoddy. —**slea′zi•ness** n.

sled (sled) n. a vehicle on runners moving over snow and ice; sledge. —v.t. & v.i. **sled•ded, sled•ding** ride or convey on a sled. [ME *sledde*]

sledge¹ (slej) n. a sled. —v.t. & v.i. **sledged, sledg•ing** travel or convey on a sledge. [< Du. *sleeds*]

sledge² n. a heavy hammer wielded with both hands, for breaking stone etc. Also **sledge hammer.** —v.t. **sledged, sledg•ing** strike with a sledge. [ME *segge*]

sleek (sleek) adj. •**er,** •**est 1.** smooth and glossy; slick. **2.** looking prosperous and well-fed. —v.t. make smooth or glossy. —**sleek′ness** n.

sleep (sleep) n. **1.** a period of rest, accompanied by a complete or partial unconsciousness. **2.** any state like sleep, such as a trance or coma. —v. **slept, sleep•ing** v.i. **1.** be or fall asleep; slumber. **2.** be in a state, such as death, that resembles sleep. **3.** be dormant. —v.t. **4.** provide sleeping quarters for: a cabin that *sleeps* four. —**sleep away** (or **off** or **out**) pass or get rid of by or as by sleep: *sleep off* a hangover. —**sleep on** postpone a decision upon. —**sleep with** have sexual relations with. [ME] —**sleep′less** adj. —**sleep′less•ness** n.

sleep•er (SLEE pər) n. **1.** one who sleeps. **2.** a passenger railroad car with accommodations for sleeping: also **sleeping car. 3.** *Informal* a play, book, etc. that achieves unexpected success.

sleep•walk•ing (SLEEP waw king) n. the act of one who walks while asleep. —**sleep′walk′er** n.

sleep•y (SLEE pee) adj. **sleep•i•er, sleep•i•est 1.** inclined to sleep; drowsy. **2.** inactive or sluggish. —**sleep′i•ly** adv. —**sleep′i•ness** n.

sleet (sleet) n. **1.** a mixture of snow and rain. **2.** partly frozen rain. [ME *slete*] —**sleet** v.i.

sleeve (sleev) n. **1.** the part of a garment that covers the arms. **2.** *Mech.* a tube surrounding a shaft etc., for protection or connection. —**up one′s sleeve** hidden but ready for use. [ME *sleve*]

sleigh (slay) n. a vehicle, usu. horse-drawn, with runners for use on snow and ice. —v.i. travel in a sleigh. [< Du. *slee*] —**sleigh′ing** n.

sleight (slīt) n. **1.** skillful manipulation; dexterity. **2.** craft; cunning. [ME]

sleight of hand 1. skill and dexterity in jug-

gling or conjuring. **2.** a trick, as in magic, requiring skillful manipulation: also called *legerdemain.*

slen•der (SLEN dər) adj. •**er,** •**est 1.** long and thin; slim. **2.** small or inadequate; meager. [ME *slendre*] —**slen′der•ness** n.

slen•der•ize (SLEN də RĪZ) v.t. & v.i. •**ized,** •**iz•ing** make or become slender.

slept (slept) past tense, past participle of SLEEP.

sleuth (slooth) n. a detective. —v.t. **1.** follow; track. —v.i. **2.** play the detective.

slew¹ (sloo) past tense of SLAY.

slew² see SLOUGH¹ (def. 2).

slew³ n. *Informal* a large number or amount: also spelled *slue.* [< Irish *sluagh* crowd]

slew⁴ see SLUE¹.

slice (slīs) n. **1.** a thin, broad piece cut off from something. **2.** a part or share. **3.** in golf, a flight of a ball that veers in the direction of the dominant hand of the player hitting it. —v. **sliced, slic•ing** v.t. **1.** cut from a larger piece: often with *off.* **2.** cut into broad, thin pieces. **3.** hit (a golf ball) so that it results in a slice. —v.i. **4.** in golf, slice a ball. [ME] —**slic′er** n.

slick (slik) adj. •**er,** •**est 1.** smooth; slippery; sleek. **2.** crafty; wily: a *slick* operator. **3.** smart and clever, but often of little depth. [ME *slike*] —n. **1.** a smooth area on a surface of water, as from oil. **2.** *Informal* a magazine printed on glossy paper. —v.t. make smooth, glossy, or oily.

slide (slīd) v. **slid** (slid), **slid•ing** v.i. **1.** slip along on ice or other smooth surface. **2.** move easily or smoothly; glide. **3.** slip or fall. **4.** in baseball, throw oneself along the ground toward a base. —v.t. **5.** cause to slide, as over a surface. **6.** move, put, enter, etc. with quietness or dexterity: with *in* or *into.* [ME *sliden*] —n. **1.** an act of sliding. **2.** the fall of a mass of earth, snow, etc.; avalanche. **3.** an inclined plane for children to slide upon. **4.** a small glass plate on which a specimen is mounted and examined through a microscope. **5.** a small plate bearing an image for projection on a screen.

slide projector an optical device for projecting images from transparent slides onto a screen.

slid•er (SLĪ dər) n. **1.** one who or that which slides. **2.** in baseball, a curve ball that breaks slightly and sharply away from the side from which it was thrown.

sliding scale a schedule of prices, wages, etc, that varies under certain conditions.

slight (slīt) *adj.* •**er**, •**est 1.** of small importance; trifling. **2.** small in quantity, intensity, etc.; meager. **3.** slender; frail; flimsy. [ME] —*v.t.* **1.** treat with disrespect; ignore discourteously. **2.** perform carelessly. **3.** treat as trivial or insignificant. —*n.* an act of disrespect; affront. —**slight′ing** *adj.* — **slight′ing·ly** *adv.*

sli·ly (SLĪ lee) see SLYLY.

slim (slim) *adj.* **slim·mer**, **slim·mest 1.** slender; slight; thin. **2.** insufficient; meager: a *slim* attendance. [< Du., inferior] —*v.t. & v.i.* **slimmed**, **slim·ming** make or become thin. —**slim′ness** *n.*

slime (slīm) *n.* any moist, soft, sticky substance. —*v.t.* **slimed**, **slim·ing** smear or cover with slime. [ME]

slim·y (SLĪ mee) *adj.* **slim·i·er**, **slim·i·est 1.** covered with slime. **2.** offensive; foul. — **slim′i·ness** *n.*

sling (sling) *n.* **1.** a strap with strings attached for hurling a stone or other missile. **2.** a strap or rope, as for supporting an injured limb, carrying a rifle, etc. —*v.t.* **slung**, **sling·ing 1.** throw with force; hurl. **2.** place or hang in a sling. [ME]

sling·shot (SLING shot) *n.* a forked stick with an elastic strip for hurling stones etc.

slink (slingk) *v.i.* **slunk**, **slink·ing** creep or steal along furtively or stealthily, as in fear. [ME *slinken*]

slink·y (SLING kee) *adj.* **slink·i·er**, **slink·i·est 1.** sneaking; stealthy. **2.** sinuous or catlike in movement or form. —**slink′i·ness** *n.*

slip¹ (slip) *v.* **slipped** or **slipt**, **slip·ping** *v.t.* **1.** cause to glide or slide. **2.** put on or off easily, as a loose garment. **3.** convey slyly or secretly. **4.** get away from; elude. **5.** escape or pass unobserved: It *slipped* my mind. — *v.i.* **6.** lose one's footing. **7.** fail to hold: It *slipped* out of my hand. **8.** make a mistake; err. **9.** move smoothly and easily. **10.** go or come stealthily or unnoticed: often with *off*, *away*, or *from*. **11.** fall below one's usual level of performance. —**let slip** say without intending to. —**slip one over on** cheat; hoodwink. [ME *slippen*] —*n.* **1.** a loss of one's footing. **2.** a lapse or error; slight mistake. **3.** a space between two wharves; berth. **4.** a woman's undergarment, usu. the length of a dress. —**give (someone) the slip** elude (someone).

slip² *n.* **1.** a cutting from a plant for planting or grafting; scion. **2.** a small piece of paper, esp. one used for a record: a sales *slip*. [ME

slippe] —*v.t.* **slipped**, **slip·ping** cut off for planting.

slip·case (SLIP kays) *n.* a box for a book or a set of books, having one open end.

slip·cov·er (SLIP kuv ər) *n.* a removable fitted cover for a chair, sofa, etc.

slip·knot (SLIP not) *n.* a knot that slips along the line around which it is tied. Also a *running knot.*

slip·o·ver (SLIP oh vər) *n.* a sweater that is donned by drawing it over the head.

slip·per (SLIP ər) *n.* a low, light shoe that is easily slipped on or off the foot. —**slip′·pered** *adj.*

slip·per·y (SLIP ə ree) *adj.* •**per·i·er**, •**per·i·est 1.** having a surface so smooth that objects easily slip or slide on it. **2.** unreliable; elusive; tricky. —**slip′per·i·ness** *n.*

slip·shod (SLIP shod) *adj.* carelessly done; sloppy; slovenly.

slip·stream (SLIP streem) *n.* *Aeron.* the stream of air driven backward by an aircraft propeller.

slip-up (SLIP up) *n.* a mistake; error.

slit (slit) *n.* a long, narrow cut or opening; slash. —*v.t.* **slit**, **slit·ting 1.** make a slit in; slash. **2.** cut into strips. [ME *slitten*]

slith·er (SLITH ər) *v.i.* glide, as a snake. [ME *slitheren*] —**slith′er·y** *adj.*

sliv·er (SLIV ər) *n.* a slender piece cut or torn off; splinter. [ME *slivere*] —*v.t. & v.i.* cut or split into slivers.

slob (slob) *n.* a stupid, careless, or unclean person. [< Irish *slab* mud]

slob·ber (SLOB ər) *v.i.* dribble saliva from the mouth; drivel; slaver. [ME *sloberen*] — *n.* **1.** drivel; slaver. **2.** gushing, sentimental talk. —**slob′ber·er** *n.* —**slob′ber·y** *adj.*

slog (slog) *v.t. & v.i.* **slogged**, **slog·ging** plod (one's way), as through deep mud. — **slog′ger** *n.*

slo·gan (SLOH gən) *n.* a catchword or motto adopted by a group, as a political party. [< Scot. Gaelic *sluagh-ghairm* army cry]

sloop (sloop) *n.* *Naut.* a single-masted sailing vessel. [< Du. *sloep*]

slop (slop) *v.* **slopped**, **slop·ping** *v.i.* **1.** splash or spill. —*v.t.* **2.** cause (a liquid) to spill or splash. **3.** feed (hogs) with slops. — **slop over** overflow and splash. —*n.* **1.** slush; watery mud. **2.** *pl.* unappetizing liquid or watery food. **3.** *Usu. pl.* liquid refuse. **4.** *pl.* waste food or swill, used to feed pigs etc. [ME *sloppe*]

slope (slohp) *v.* **sloped**, **slop·ing** *v.i.* **1.** be inclined; slant. —*v.t.* **2.** cause to slope. —*n.* any slanting surface or line; also, the degree of inclination.

slop•py (SLOP ee) *adj.* **•pi•er, •pi•est 1.** slushy; splashy; wet. **2.** messy; slovenly; untidy. **3.** slipshod; careless. —**slop′pi•ly** *adv.* —**slop′pi•ness** *n.*

slosh (slosh) *v.t.* **1.** throw about, as a liquid. —*v.i.* **2.** splash; flounder: *slosh through a pool.*

slot (slot) *n.* **1.** a long narrow groove or opening; slit: *the slot of a mailbox.* **2.** a job opening. **3.** a place in a sequence. [ME, the hollow between the breasts] —*v.t.* **slot•ted, slot•ting 1.** cut a slot in; groove. **2.** place in a schedule or series.

sloth (slawth) *n.* **1.** indolence; laziness. **2.** (slôth) a slow-moving tree-dwelling mammal of tropical America. [ME *slouthe*]

sloth•ful (SLAWTH fəl) *adj.* sluggish; lazy; indolent. —**sloth′ful•ness** *n.*

slouch (slouch) *v.i.* **1.** have a downcast or drooping gait, look, or posture; slump. **2.** walk with a drooping gait. —*n.* **1.** a drooping gait or posture. **2.** an awkward or incompetent person: usu. in the negative: *He's no slouch at baseball.* —**slouch′y** *adj.*

slough¹ (slow) *n.* **1.** a place of deep mud or mire; bog. **2.** (*also* sloo) a stagnant swamp or backwater: also spelled *slew, slue.* **3.** a state of despair. [ME]

slough² (sluf) *n.* any layer or covering, as a snakeskin, that has been shed or cast off. [ME *slughe*] —*v.t.* cast off; discard; shed: with *off.* Also spelled *sluff.* —**slough′y** *adj.*

slov•en•ly (SLUV ən lee) *adj.* **•li•er, •li•est** of or like a sloven; sloppy; untidy; careless. —*adv.* in a careless manner. —**slov′en•li•ness** *n.*

slow (sloh) *adj.* **1.** having relatively small velocity; not quick in motion, performance, or occurrence. **2.** behind the correct time: said of a timepiece. **3.** not precipitate or hasty: *slow* to anger. **4.** dull or stupid; mentally sluggish. **5.** dull or tedious in character. **6.** inactive: *Business is slow today.* [ME] —*v.t. & v.i.* make, go, or become slow or slower: often with *up* or *down.* —*adv.* in a slow or cautious manner or speed. —**slow′ly** *adv.* —**slow′•ness** *n.*

slow-mo•tion (SLOH MOH shən) *adj.* pertaining to or designating a motion picture filmed at greater than standard speed so that the action appears slow in normal projection.

slow•poke (SLOH POHK) *n. Informal* a person who works or moves slowly; a laggard.

sludge (sluj) *n.* **1.** soft mud; mire. **2.** muddy or pasty refuse, as that produced by sewerage purification. [ME *slitch*] —**sludg′y** *adj.* **sludg•i•er, sludg•i•est**

slue¹ (sloo) *v.t. & v.i.* **slued, slu•ing** move or cause to move sideways, as if some portion were pivoted. —*n.* the act of sluing around sideways. Also spelled *slew.*

slue² see SLEW³.

slue³ see SLOUGH¹ (def. 2).

sluff (sluf) *n. & v.* see SLOUGH².

slug¹ (slug) *n.* **1.** a bullet or shot of irregular or oblong shape. **2.** *Printing* a strip of type metal for spacing matter etc. **3.** any small chunk of metal; esp., one used as a counterfeit coin.

slug² *n.* any of various elongated mollusks related to the snail and having a rudimentary shell. [ME *slugge* sluggard]

slug³ *Informal n.* **1.** a heavy blow, as with the fist. **2.** a drink of undiluted liquor. —*v.i.* **slugged, slug•ging** strike heavily; hit hard. —**slug′ger** *n.*

slug•gard (SLUG ərd) *n.* a person habitually lazy or idle; drone. —*adj.* lazy. —**slug•gard•ly** *adj.*

slug•gish (SLUG ish) *adj.* **1.** slow; inactive; torpid. **2.** idle and lazy. [ME *slugissh*] —**slug′gish•ly** *adv.* —**slug′gish•ness** *n.*

sluice (sloos) *n.* **1.** an artificial channel for conducting water, equipped with a valve or gate (**sluice gate**) to regulate the flow. **2.** any artificial channel. **3.** a trough through which water is run to separate gold ore, float logs, etc. [ME *scluse*] —*v.* **sluiced, sluic•ing** *v.t.* **1.** wet, water, or wash by or as by means of a sluice. **2.** draw out or conduct by or through a sluice. —*v.i.* **3.** flow out or issue from a sluice.

slum (slum) *n. Often pl.* a squalid section of a city, marked by poverty and poor living conditions. —*v.i.* **slummed, slum•ming** visit slums, disreputable establishments, etc. for amusement: *Let's go slumming.*

slum•ber (SLUM bər) *v.i.* **1.** sleep, esp. lightly or quietly. **2.** be inactive; stagnate. —*v.t.* **3.** spend or pass in sleeping. [ME *slumberen*] —*n.* **1.** sleep. **2.** a state of inactivity or quiescence. —**slum′ber•er** *n.*

slum•lord (SLUM LORD) *n.* a landlord of a slum tenement, esp. one who profits by neglecting maintenance.

slump (slump) *v.i.* **1.** fall down or collapse suddenly. **2.** decrease suddenly, as in value or quality. **3.** stand or walk with a stooping posture. —*n.* the act of slumping; a fall, failure, or decline.

slung (slung) past tense, past participle of SLING.

slunk (slungk) past tense, past participle of SLINK.

slur (slur) *v.t.* **slurred, slur·ring 1.** slight; disparage. **2.** pass over lightly or hurriedly. **3.** weaken and elide (speech sounds) by hurried articulation. **4.** *Music* sing or play as indicated by the slur. —*n.* **1.** a disparaging remark. **2.** *Music* a curved line (or) indicating that tones so tied are to be sung to the same syllable or performed without a break between them. **3.** a slurred articulation.

slush (slush) *n.* **1.** soft, sloppy material, as melting snow. **2.** overly sentimental talk or writing; drivel. —**slush′y** *adj.* **slush·i·er, slush·i·est**

slush fund money collected or spent for corrupt purposes, as for bribery.

slut (slut) *n.* **1.** a slatternly woman. **2.** a woman of loose character; hussy. [ME *slutte*] —**slut′tish** *adj.*

sly (slī) *adj.* **sly·er** or **sli·er, sly·est** or **sli·est 1.** artful in doing things secretly; cunning. **2.** mischievous. **3.** done with or marked by cunning and secrecy. —**on the sly** secretly. [ME] —**sly′ness** *n.* —**sly′ly, sli′ly** *adv.* in a sly manner.

smack¹ (smak) *n.* **1.** a quick, sharp sound, as of the lips when separated rapidly. **2.** a sounding blow or slap. **3.** a kiss. —*v.t. & v.i.* give or make a smack.

smack² *v.i.* have a taste or flavor: usu. with *of.* [ME *smacke* taste] —*n.* a taste or flavor.

smack³ *n.* a small vessel used chiefly for fishing. [< Du. *smak*]

smack·ing (SMAK ing) *adj.* brisk; lively; strong.

small (smawl) *adj.* **·er, ·est 1.** comparatively less in size, quantity, extent, etc.; diminutive. **2.** being of slight importance. **3.** narrow; ignoble; mean; paltry. **4.** transacting business in a limited way. **5.** lacking in power or strength. —*n.* a small or slender part: the *small* of the back. —*adv.* **·er, ·est** in a small manner. [ME *smale*] —**small′ness** *n.*

small arms firearms of small caliber, as pistols, rifles, and machine guns.

small change coins of small denomination.

small fry 1. small, young fish. **2.** children.

small hours the early hours of the morning.

small-mind·ed (SMAWL MĬN did) *adj.*

petty; intolerant. —**small′-mind′ed·ness** *n.*

small·pox (SMAWL POKS) *n. Pathol.* an acute, highly contagious virus disease, characterized by fever and pustules.

small talk unimportant or trivial conversation.

small-time (SMAWL TĬM) *adj.* petty; unimportant: a *smalltime* hoodlum.

smart (smahrt) *v.i.* **1.** experience a stinging sensation, generally superficial, either bodily or mental. **2.** cause a stinging sensation. —*v.t.* **3.** cause to smart. —*adj.* **·er, ·est 1.** quick in thought or action; bright; clever. **2.** impertinently witty: often used contemptuously. **3.** vigorous; emphatic; severe; brisk. **4.** sharp, as at trade; shrewd. **5.** stylish; fashionable. [ME *smerten*] —*n.* **1.** an acute stinging sensation, as from a scratch or an irritant. **2.** any distress. —**smart′ly** *adv.* —**smart′·ness** *n.*

smart al·eck (AL ik) a cocky, offensively conceited person. Also **smart al′ec.** —**smart-al·eck·y** (SMAHRT AL ik ee) *adj.*

smart bomb a bomb that is guided to a target by electronic means.

smart·en (SMAHR tn) *v.t. & v.i.* make or become smart: often with *up.*

smash (smash) *v.t.* **1.** break in many pieces suddenly, as by a blow, pressure, or collision. **2.** flatten; crush; destroy. **3.** dash or fling violently so as to crush or break. **4.** strike with a sudden, forceful blow. —*v.i.* **5.** come into violent contact so as to crush or be crushed; collide. —*n.* **1.** an act or instance of smashing, or the state of being smashed. **2.** in tennis etc., a strong overhand shot. **3.** *Informal* something striking or acclaimed: The play was a *smash.*

smash·ing (SMASH ing) *adj.* extremely impressive; overwhelmingly good.

smat·ter·ing (SMAT ə ring) *n.* a superficial knowledge of something. Also **smat′ter.**

smear (smeer) *v.t.* **1.** spread, rub, or cover with grease, paint, dirt, etc. **2.** apply in a thick layer or coating. **3.** defame; slander. **4.** *Slang* defeat utterly. —*v.i.* **5.** be or become smeared. —*n.* **1.** a spoiled spot; stain. **2.** a small quantity of material, as blood, sputum, etc., placed on a microscope slide for analysis. **3.** a slanderous attack; defamation. [ME *smere*] —**smear′y** *adj.* **smear·i·er, smear·i·est**

smell (smel) *v.* **smelled** or **smelt, smell·ing** *v.t.* **1.** perceive by means of the nose and its olfactory nerves; scent. **2.** discover or detect as if by smelling: often with *out*. —*v.i.* 3. emit an odor or perfume: frequently with *of*; also, give indications of, as if by odor: *smell* of treason. 4. be malodorous. 5. use the sense of smell. —*n.* 1. the special sense by means of which odors are perceived. 2. that which is directly perceived by this sense; an odor. 3. a hint; trace. [ME]

smelling salts pungent or aromatic salts, used as a stimulant usu. to relieve faintness.

smel·ly (SMEL ee) *adj.* **·li·er, ·li·est** emitting an unpleasant smell; malodorous. —**smel'li·ness** *n.*

smelt[1] (smelt) *v.t. Metall.* 1. reduce (ores) by fusion in a furnace. 2. obtain (a metal) from the ore by a process including fusion. —*v.i.* 3. melt or fuse, as a metal. [< MDu. *smelten*]

smelt[2] *n. pl.* **smelts** or **smelt** any of various small silvery food fishes of north Atlantic and Pacific waters. [ME]

smelt[3] alternative past tense and past participle of SMELL.

smidg·en (SMIJ ən) *n.* a tiny bit or part.

smile (smīl) *n.* a pleased or amused expression of the face, characterized by a raising up of the corners of the mouth. —*v.* **smiled, smil·ing** *v.i.* 1. give a smile; wear a cheerful aspect. 2. show approval or favor: often with *upon*. —*v.t.* 3. express by means of a smile. [ME *smilen*] —**smil'ing·ly** *adv.*

smirch (smurch) *v.t.* 1. soil, as with grime; smear. 2. defame; degrade. —*n.* a smear or dirty mark.

smirk (smurk) *v.i.* smile in a silly, self-complacent, or affected manner. —*n.* an affected or artificial smile. [ME *smirken*] —**smirk'er** *n.*

smite (smīt) *v.* **smote, smit·ten** or **smit, smit·ing** *v.t.* 1. strike (something). 2. strike with disaster; afflict. 3. affect powerfully with sudden feeling. 4. affect as if by a blow; strike. 5. kill by a sudden blow. —*v.i.* 6. come with sudden force; also, knock against something. [ME *smiten*] —**smit'er** *n.*

smith (smith) *n.* 1. a worker in metal: *goldsmith, tinsmith.* 2. a blacksmith. [ME]

smith·er·eens (SMITH ə REENZ) *n.pl.* fragments. [< Irish Gaelic *smidirin*]

smith·y (SMITH ee) *n. pl.* **smith·ies** a blacksmith's shop; a forge. [ME *smithi*]

smit·ten (SMIT n) alternative past participle of SMITE. —*adj.* 1. struck with sudden force; gravely afflicted. 2. in love.

smock (smok) *n.* a loose outer garment of light material worn to protect one's clothes.

[ME] —*v.t.* 1. clothe in a smock. 2. decorate with smocking.

smock·ing (SMOK ing) *n.* needlework in which the material is stitched into very small pleats or gathers.

smog (smog) *n.* combined smoke and fog. [Blend of SM(OKE) and (F)OG]

smoke (smohk) *n.* 1. the volatilized products of burning substances, as coal, wood, etc. 2. the act of smoking a pipe, cigar, etc. 3. a cigarette, cigar, or pipeful of tobacco. —*v.* **smoked, smok·ing** *v.i.* 1. emit or give out smoke. 2. inhale and exhale the smoke from a pipe, cigarette, etc. —*v.t.* 3. inhale and exhale the smoke of (tobacco etc.); also, use (a pipe etc.) for this purpose. 4. cure (meat, fish, etc.) by treating with smoke. 5. force into the open with or as with smoke: with *out*. [ME] —**smoke'·less** *adj.*

smok·er (SMOH kər) *n.* 1. one who or that which smokes. 2. a place where one may smoke, as a railroad car. 3. an informal gathering.

smoke screen 1. a dense cloud of smoke used to prevent enemy observation of a place, force, or operation. 2. something designed to obscure or mislead.

smoke·stack (SMOHK STAK) *n.* an upright pipe or funnel through which combustion gases from a furnace are discharged into the air.

smok·y (SMOH kee) *adj.* **smok·i·er, smok·i·est** 1. giving forth smoke. 2. mixed with smoke: *smoky* air. 3. discolored with smoke. 4. smoke-colored; dark gray.— **smok'i·ly** *adv.* —**smok'i·ness** *n.*

smol·der (SMOHL dər) *v.i.* 1. burn with little smoke and no flame. 2. exist in a latent or suppressed state. —*n.* dense smoke. Also spelled *smoulder.* [ME]

smooch (smooch) *Informal n.* a kiss. —*v.i.* kiss or neck.

smooth (smooth) *adj.* **·er, ·est** 1. having a surface without irregularities; not rough; continuously even. 2. having no impediments or obstructions; easy; free from shocks or jolts. 3. calm; bland; mild. 4. suave, as in speech: often implying deceit. 5. free from hair; beardless. 6. without lumps. [ME *smothe*] —*adv.* calmly; evenly. —*v.t.* 1. make smooth or even. 2. make easy or less difficult. 3. free from or remove obstructions. 4. render less harsh; soften; palliate: often with *over.* 5. make calm; mollify. —*v.i.* 5. become smooth.— **smooth one's ruffled feathers** mollify.

—*n.* the smooth portion or surface of anything.

smooth•bore (SMOOTH bor) *n.* a firearm with a smooth bore. **—smooth′bored′** *adj.*

smooth•en (SMOOTH ən) *v.t. & v.i.* make or become smooth.

smor•gas•bord (SMOR gəs BORD) *n.* **1.** a variety of hors d'oeuvres such as meats, cheeses, fish, etc. **2.** a buffet meal containing many dishes. **3.** any mixture; mélange. [< Sw.]

smote (smoht) past tense of SMITE.

smoth•er (SMUTH ər) *v.t.* **1.** prevent the respiration of; suffocate; stifle. **2.** cover or coat. **3.** hide or suppress. —*v.i.* **4.** suffocate, as from lack of air, etc. [ME] —*n.* **1.** stifling vapor or dust. **2.** a confused profusion of things.

smoul•der (SMOHL dər) see SMOLDER.

smudge (smuj) *v.* **smudged, smudg•ing** *v.t.* **1.** smear; soil. —*v.i.* **2.** form a smudge. **3.** become smudged. [ME *smogen*] —*n.* **1.** a soiling, as of soot; smear; stain. **2.** a smoky fire or its smoke for driving away insects, preventing frost, etc.

smudg•y (SMUJ ee) *adj.* **smudg•i•er, smudg•i•est** full of or causing smudges.

smug (smug) *adj.* **smug•ger, smug•gest** self-satisfied; complacent. [? < LG *smuck* neat] —**smug′ly** *adv.* **—smug′ness** *n.*

smug•gle (SMUG əl) *v.* **•gled, •gling** *v.t.* **1.** take (goods) into or out of a country without payment of lawful duties. **2.** bring in illicitly. —*v.i.* **3.** practice smuggling. [< LG *smuggeln*] —**smug′gler** *n.* **—smug′•gling** *n.*

smut (smut) *n.* **1.** the blackening made by soot, smoke, etc. **2.** obscenity; obscene language. **3.** a disease of plants in which the affected part changes into a dusty black powder. [< OE *smitte* dirt] —*v.* **smut•ted, smut•ting** *v.t.* **1.** blacken or stain, as with soot or smoke. **2.** affect with smut, as growing grain. —*v.i.* **3.** give off smut. **4.** be or become stained.

smut•ty (SMUT ee) *adj.* **•ti•er, •ti•est 1.** soiled with smut. **2.** affected with smut: *smutty* corn. **3.** obscene. **—smut′•ti•ness** *n.*

snack (snak) *n.* a light, hurried meal. —*v.i.* eat a light meal; also, eat between meals. [ME *snaken* bite]

snag (snag) *n.* **1.** a jagged protuberance; esp., the stumpy base of a branch. **2.** a tear or pulled-out loop in fabric. **3.** the trunk of a tree fixed in the bottom of a river etc. **4.** any

obstacle or difficulty. —*v.t.* **snagged, snag•ging** injure, destroy, or impede by or as by a snag. [< Scand.] —**snag′gy** *adj.* **•gi•er, •gi•est**

snail (snayl) *n.* **1.** any of a large class of slow-moving mollusks of aquatic and terrestrial habits, having a spiral shell. **2.** a slow or lazy person. [ME]

snail's pace a very slow gait or forward movement. **—snail-paced** (SNAYL PAYST) *adj.*

snake (snayk) *n.* **1.** any of a large order of scaly, legless reptiles with long, slim bodies and tapering tails. **2.** a flexible, resilient wire used to clean clogged drains. **3.** a treacherous person. [ME] —*v.* **snaked, snak•ing** *v.t.* **1.** drag by pulling from one end. **2.** pull with jerks. —*v.i.* **3.** move like a snake. **—snak′y** *adj.* **•i•er, •i•est**

snake•bite (SNAYK BIT) *n.* the bite of a snake; also the poisoning it causes.

snap (snap) *v.* **snapped, snap•ping** *v.i.* **1.** make a sharp, quick sound. **2.** break suddenly with a cracking noise. **3.** give way quickly, as when tension is suddenly relaxed. **4.** make the jaws come suddenly together in an effort to bite: often with *up* or *at.* **5.** seize or snatch suddenly: often with *up* or *at.* **6.** speak sharply, harshly, or irritably: often with *at.* **7.** close, fasten, etc. with a click. —*v.t.* **8.** seize suddenly or eagerly, with or as with the teeth: often with *up.* **9.** sever with a snapping sound. **10.** utter harshly, abruptly, or irritably. **11.** close, fasten, etc. with a snapping sound. **12.** cause to move suddenly, neatly, etc. **13.** photograph with a camera. **—snap out of it** recover quickly, as from a state of depression. —*n.* **1.** the act of snapping, or a sharp, quick sound produced by it. **2.** a sudden breaking, or the sound so produced. **3.** a fastener or other similar device. **4.** a sudden seizing or effort to seize with or as with the teeth. **5.** a small, thin, crisp cake or cooky. **6.** *Informal* brisk energy; vigor. **7.** a brief spell; a sudden turn: said chiefly of cold weather. **8.** *Informal* any task easy to perform. **9.** a snapshot. —*adj.* **1.** made or done suddenly and without consideration; offhand. **2.** fastening with a snap. **3.** easy; requiring little work. [< Du. *snappen* seize]

snap•pish (SNAP ish) *adj.* **1.** apt to speak crossly or tartly. **2.** disposed to snap, as a dog. **—snap′pish•ly** *adv.*

snap•py (SNAP ee) *adj.* **•pi•er, •pi•est 1.** *Informal* brisk; energetic. **2.** *Informal* smart; stylish. **3.** snappish. **—make it snappy** *Slang* hurry; speed up. **—snap′pi·ly** *adv.*

snap·shot (SNAP shot) *n.* a photograph taken quickly with a small camera.

snare¹ (snair) *n.* **1.** a device, as a noose, for catching birds or other animals; a trap. **2.** anything that entangles or entraps. **—***v.t.* **snared, snar·ing 1.** catch with a snare. **2.** capture by trickery; entice. [ME]

snare² *n.* **1.** one of the cords or wires stretched across one of the heads of a snare drum to increase resonance. **2.** a snare drum. [< MDu. *snaer* string]

snare drum a small drum having snares on one head.

snarl¹ (snahrl) *n.* a sharp, harsh, angry growl or utterance. **—***v.i.* **1.** growl harshly, as a dog. **2.** speak angrily. **—***v.t.* **3.** utter or express with a snarl. [Freq. of obs. *snar* snarl] **—snarl′er** *n.* **—snarl′·ing·ly** *adv.*

snarl² *n.* **1.** a tangle, as of hair or yarn. **2.** any complication or entanglement. **—***v.t. & v.i.* put or get into a snarl or tangle. [ME *snarle*] **—snarl′er** *n.* **—snarl′ly** *adj.* **snarl·i·er, snarl·i·est**

snatch (snach) *v.t.* **1.** seize suddenly, hastily, or eagerly. **2.** take or remove suddenly. **3.** take or obtain as the opportunity arises. **4.** *Slang* kidnap. **—***v.i.* **5.** attempt to seize swiftly and suddenly: with *at.* [ME *snacchen*]**—***n.* **1.** an act of snatching. **2.** a brief period. **3.** a small amount. **4.** *Slang* a kidnapping. **—snatch′er** *n.*

sneak (sneek) *v.* **sneaked, sneak·ing** *v.i.* **1.** move or go in a stealthy manner. **2.** act with cowardice or servility. **—***v.t.* **3.** put, give, move, etc., secretly or stealthily. [ME *sniken*]**—***n.* **1.** one who sneaks. **2.** an act of sneaking. **—***adj.* stealthy; covert. **—sneak′i·ly** *adv.* **—sneak′i·ness** *n.* **—sneak′y** *adj.* **sneak·i·er, sneak·i·est**

sneak·er (SNEE kər) *n.* a canvas shoe with a rubber or synthetic sole, used esp. for sports.

sneak·ing (SNEE king) *adj.* **1.** acting in an underhand way. **2.** secret: a *sneaking* suspicion. **—sneak′ing·ly** *adv.*

sneak preview the unannounced public showing of a new motion picture before its date of release.

sneer (sneer) *n.* a grimace of contempt or derision made by slightly raising the upper lip. **—***v.i.* **1.** make a sneer. **2.** express derision. **—sneer′ing·ly** *adv.*

sneeze (sneez) *v.i.* **sneezed, sneez·ing** drive air forcibly and audibly out of the mouth and nose by a spasmodic involuntary action. **—not to be sneezed at** *Informal* worthy of consideration. [ME *snesen*] **—***n.* a sound or act of sneezing. **—sneez′er** *n.*

snick·er (SNIK ər) *n.* a half-suppressed laugh, often of derision. **—***v.i.* utter a snicker.

snide (snīd) *adj.* malicious or derogatory; nasty: *snide* comments.

sniff (snif) *v.i.* **1.** breathe through the nose in short, quick, audible inhalations. **2.** express contempt etc. by or as by sniffing: often with *at.* **—***v.t.* **3.** breathe in through the nose; inhale. **4.** smell with sniffs. **—***n.* **1.** an act or the sound of sniffing. **2.** that which is inhaled by sniffing. [ME]

snif·fle (SNIF əl) *v.i.* **-fled, -fling 1.** breathe through the nose noisily. **2.** snivel or whimper. **—the sniffles** a head cold or the sniffling that results. **—***n.* the sound or act of sniffling. **—snif′fler** *n.*

snif·ter (SNIF tər) *n.* a pear-shaped liquor glass.

snig·ger (SNIG ər) *n.* a snicker. **—***v.t. & v.i.* snicker.

snip (snip) *v.t. & v.i.* **snipped, snip·ping** clip or cut with a light stroke of shears: often with *off.* **—***n.* **1.** an act of snipping. **2.** a small piece snipped off. **3.** *Informal* a small or insignificant or presumptuous person.

snipe (snīp) *n. pl.* **snipe** or **snipes** any of several long-billed shore or marsh birds. [ME] **—***v.i.* **sniped, snip·ing 1.** hunt or shoot snipe. **2.** shoot at a person or persons from hiding. **3.** attack a person or a person's actions with petty remarks.

snip·er (SNI pər) *n.* one who shoots a person or persons from hiding.

snip·pet (SNIP it) *n.* **1.** a small piece snipped off. **2.** a small portion or share.

snip·py (SNIP ee) *adj.* **-pi·er, -pi·est 1.** impertinent. **2.** fragmentary; scrappy. Also **snip·pe·ty** (SNIP i tee).

snitch (snich) *Informal v.t.* **1.** grab quickly; steal; swipe. **—***v.i.* **2.** turn informer: with *on.*

sniv·el (SNIV əl) *v.i.* **-eled, -el·ing 1.** cry in a snuffling manner. **2.** whine. **3.** run at the nose. [ME *snivelen*] **—sniv′el·er** *n.*

snob (snob) *n.* one who delights in feeling superior to others. **—snob′ber·y** *n.* **—snob′bish** *adj.* **—snob′bish·ly** *adv.* **—snob′bish·ness** *n.*

snoop (snoop) *Informal v.i.* look or pry into things with which one has no business. [<

Du. *snoepen* obtain or eat food on the sly]
—**snoop, snoop′er** n. —**snoop′i•ness** n.
—**snoop′y** adj. **•i•er, •i•est**

snoot•y (SNOO tee) adj. **snoot•i•er, snoot•i•est** Informal snobbish.

snooze (snooz) v.i. **snoozed, snooz•ing** sleep; doze. —n. a nap.

snore (snor) v.i. **snored, snor•ing** breathe in sleep with a hoarse, rough noise. [ME *snoren*] —n. an act or the noise of snoring. —**snor′er** n.

snor•kel (SNOR kəl) n. **1.** a mouth tube permitting a skin diver to breathe while swimming on the surface with face under water. **2.** a tubelike apparatus for ventilation of a submerged submarine. —v.i. swim with a snorkel. [< G *Schnorchel* air intake] —**snor′•kel•er** n. —**snor′kel•ing** n.

snort (snort) v.i. **1.** force air violently and noisily through the nostrils, as a horse. **2.** express indignation, ridicule, etc. by a snort. **3.** Slang take a drug by inhaling. [ME *snorten*] —n. **1.** the act or sound of snorting. **2.** Slang a small drink; an act of taking a drug by inhaling. —**snort′er** n.

snot (snot) n. **1.** mucus from or in the nose: a vulgar term. **2.** Informal an obnoxious, impudent person. [ME]

snot•ty (SNOT ee) adj. **•ti•er, •ti•est 1.** dirtied with snot: a vulgar term. **2.** Informal impudent; obnoxious. —**snot′ti•ness** n.

snout (snowt) n. **1.** the forward projecting part of an animal's head, as the nose and mouth of a hog. **2.** a person's nose. [ME *snute*]

snow (snoh) n. **1.** water vapor in the air precipitated in the form of small flakes in freezing temperatures. **2.** a fall of snow; snowstorm. **3.** Slang heroin or cocaine. —v.i. **1.** fall as snow. —v.t. **2.** scatter or cause to fall as or like snow. **3.** cover, enclose, or obstruct with or as with snow. **4.** Slang subject to a snow job. —**snow in** force to remain in place because of a heavy snowfall. [ME]

snow•ball (SNOH BAWL) n. a ball of snow, shaped by the hands. —v.i. gain in size, importance, etc., as a snowball that rolls over snow.

snow•bank (SNOH BANGK) n. a large mound of snow.

snow•bound (SNOH BOWND) adj. hemmed in by snow; snowed in.

snow•drift (SNOH DRIFT) n. a snowbank made by the wind.

snow•fall (SNOH FAWL) n. **1.** a fall of snow.

2. the amount of snow that falls in a given period.

snow•flake (SNOH FLAYK) n. one of the small, feathery masses in which snow falls.

snow job Slang an attempt to impress or persuade by use of flattery or deception.

snow•mo•bile (SNOH mə BEEL) n. a vehicle for traveling over snow, ice, etc., often equipped with caterpillar treads on the rear and runners on the front. —v.i. **•biled, •bil•ing** use a snowmobile. —**snow′mo•bil′er** n. —**snow′mo•bil′ing** n.

snow•plow (SNOH PLOW) n. any plowlike device for removing snow from surfaces.

snow•shoe (SNOH SHOO) n. a device, usu. a network of thongs in a wooden frame, fastened on the foot and worn in walking over snow. —**snow′shoe′** v.i. **•shoed, •shoe•ing**

snow•storm (SNOH STORM) n. a storm with a heavy fall of snow.

snub (snub) v.t. **snubbed, snub•bing 1.** treat with contempt or disdain, esp. by ignoring; slight. **2.** stop or check, as a rope in running out, by taking a turn about a post etc. [ME *snubben*] —adj. short; pug: said of the nose. —n. **1.** a deliberate slight. **2.** a sudden checking, as of a running rope.

snuff[1] (snuf) v.t. & v.i. **1.** draw in (air etc.) through the nose. **2.** smell; sniff. [< Du. *snuffen*]

snuff[2] n. the charred portion of a wick. —v.t. **1.** extinguish: with *out*. **2.** crop the snuff from (a wick). [ME *snoffe*]

snuff[3] n. pulverized tobacco to be inhaled into the nostrils. —**up to snuff** Informal meeting the usual standard. [< Du. *snuf*]

snuff•box (SNUF BOKS) n. a box for snuff.

snuf•fle (SNUF əl) v.i. **•fled, •fling 1.** sniffle. **2.** breathe noisily, as a dog following a scent. [< Du. *snuffelen*] —n. the act or sound of snuffling. —**snuf′fler** n.

snug (snug) adj. **snug•ger, snug•gest 1.** closely and comfortably sheltered, covered, or situated. **2.** close or compact; trim. **3.** fitting closely but comfortably. —v. **snugged, snug•ging** v.t. **1.** make snug. —v.i. **2.** snuggle; move close. —**snug, snug′ly** adv. —**snug′ness** n.

snug•gle (SNUG əl) v.t. & v.i. **•gled, •gling** lie or draw close; cuddle: often with *up* or *together*.

so[1] (soh) adv. **1.** to this or that or such a degree; to this or that extent. **2.** in this, that, or such a manner; in the same way. **3.** just as said, directed, suggested or implied. **4.** ac-

cording to fact: That is not *so*. **5.** *Informal*
very or extremely. **6.** about as many or as
much stated: I shall stay a day or *so*. **7.** to
such an extent: used elliptically for *so much:*
I love her *so*. **8.** consequently; thus; therefore. —*conj.* **1.** with the purpose that: usu.
with *that:* Hurry *so* that you won't be late. **2.**
as a consequence of which: He fell asleep,
so they left. [ME]

so² *n. Music* sol.

soak (sohk) *v.t.* **1.** place in liquid until saturated; steep. **2.** wet thoroughly; drench. **3.**
absorb: with *in* or *up*. **4.** take in eagerly or
readily: with *up*. **5.** *Slang* overcharge. —*v.i.*
6. remain or be placed in liquid till saturated. **7.** penetrate; pass: with *in* or *into*.
[ME *soken*] —*n.* **1.** the act of soaking, or
the state of being soaked. **2.** liquid in which
something is soaked. **3.** *Slang* a heavy
drinker.

soap (sohp) *n.* a cleansing agent made by
decomposing fats and oils. —**no soap** *Informal* no; not a chance. —*v.t.* rub or treat
with soap. [ME *sope*] —**soap'y** *adj.* **soap•
i•er, soap•i•est**

soap•box (SOHP BOKS) *n.* an improvised
platform used by street orators.

soap opera a television or radio serial drama
usu. dealing with highly emotional domestic themes.

soar (sor) *v.i.* **1.** rise high into the air. **2.** sail
through the air without perceptibly moving
the wings, as a hawk or vulture. **3.** rise
sharply above the usual level: Prices *soared*.
[ME *soren*] —*n.* **1.** an act or or instance of
soaring. **2.** the height or distance reached in
soaring. —**soar'ing** *n.*

sob (sob) *v.* **sobbed, sob•bing** *v.i.* **1.** weep
with audible, convulsive catches of the
breath. **2.** make a sound like a sob. —*v.t.* **3.**
utter with sobs. [ME *sobben*] —*n.* the act
or sound of sobbing. —**sob'•bing•ly** *adv.*

so•ber (SOH bər) *adj.* **•er, •est 1.** self-
controlled; well-balanced. **2.** grave; sedate.
3. not drunk. **4.** moderate or abstinent. **5.**
subdued or modest in color, manner of
dress, etc. —*v.t. & v.i.* make or become
sober, usu. with *up*. [ME *sobre*] —**so'
ber•ly** *adv.* —**so•bri•e•ty** (sə BRĪ ə tee),
so'ber•ness *n.*

so•bri•quet (SOH brə KAY) *n.* a nickname.
[< F]

so-called (SOH KAWLD) *adj.* called as
stated: often implying a doubtful or incorrect designation.

soc•cer (SOK ər) *n.* a form of football in

which the ball is propelled by kicking or by
striking with the body or head.

so•cia•ble (SOH shə bəl) *adj.* **1.** inclined to
seek company; social. **2.** genial. **3.** characterized by or affording occasion for agreeable, friendly conversation. [< L *sociabilis*]
—**so'cia•bil'i•ty** *n.*

so•cial (SOH shəl) *adj.* **1.** of or pertaining to
society or its organization. **2.** friendly; sociable; also, promoting friendly intercourse: a *social* club. **3.** of or pertaining to
public welfare. **4.** of, pertaining to, or characteristic of persons considered aristocratic, fashionable, etc. **5.** of animals or
insects, living in communities. [< L *so-
cialis*] —*n.* an informal social gathering.

so•cial•ism (SOH shə LIZ əm) *n.* a system of
public collective ownership or control of
the means of production, distribution, and
exchange, with the aim of ensuring each
person an equitable share of goods, services, etc. —**so'cial•ist** *n. & adj.* —
so'cial•is'tic *adj.*

so•cial•ite (SOH shə LIT) *n.* a socially prominent person.

so•cial•ize (SOH shə LIZ) *v.* **•ized, •iz•ing**
v.t. **1.** place under the control of the community, the government, etc. **2.** make cooperative or sociable. **3.** convert or adapt to
the needs of a social group. —*v.i.* **4.** take
part in social activities. —**so•cial•i•za•tion**
(SOH shə lə ZAY shən) *n.*

socialized medicine a system supplying the
public with medical care at reasonable cost,
by means of regulatory laws and public
funding.

social register a directory of persons prominent in fashionable society.

social science 1. sociology. **2.** any field of
knowledge dealing with human society, as
economics, history, etc.

Social Security a program of assistance to
the aged, unemployed, disabled, dependent, etc.

social service organized activity carried on
by trained personnel to advance human
welfare. —**so'cial-serv'ice** *adj.*

social studies in elementary and secondary
schools, a course or unit of study based on
the social sciences.

social work any clinical, social, or recreational service for improving community
welfare, as through health clinics, aid to the
poor, etc.

so•ci•e•ty (sə SĪ i tee) *n. pl.* **•ties 1.** the
system of community life in which individ-

uals form a continuing regulatory association for their mutual benefit and protection. **2.** the body of persons composing such a community. **3.** a number of persons regarded as having certain common interests, similar status, etc. **4.** an organized group having common interests. **5.** the fashionable or aristocratic portion of a community. **6.** association based on friendship or intimacy; companionship. [< MF *societe*] — **so•ci•e•tal** (sə SĪ i tl) *adj.*

Society of Friends a Christian sect founded in England about 1650, characterized by opposition to ritual and violence: commonly known as *Quakers.*

so•ci•o•ec•o•nom•ic (SOH see oh EK ə NOM ik) *adj.* of relating to, or involving a combination of social and economic factors: an upper *socioeconomic* group.

so•ci•ol•o•gy (SOH see OL ə jee) *n.* the study of the origin and evolution of human society and social phenomena. —**so'ci•o•log'i•cal** *adj.* —**so'ci•ol'o•gist** *n.*

sock[1] (sok) *n. pl.* **socks** or **sox** a short stocking reaching above the ankle or just below the knee. [ME *socke*]

sock[2] *Slang v.t.* strike or hit, esp. with the fist; punch. —*n.* a hard blow.

sock•et (SOK it) *n.* a cavity or an opening adapted to receive and hold something. [ME *soket*]

sod (sod) *n.* grassy surface soil held together by the matted roots of grass and weeds; turf. —*v.t.* **sod•ded, sod•ding** cover with sod. [ME]

so•da (SOH də) *n.* **1.** any of several alkaline compounds widely used in medicine, industry, and the arts. **2.** a soft drink containing soda water and flavoring: also **soda pop. 3.** a drink made from soda water, ice cream, and sometimes flavoring. [< Ital.]

soda fountain 1. an apparatus from which soda water is drawn. **2.** a counter at which soft drinks etc. are dispensed.

soda water water charged under pressure with carbon dioxide gas.

sod•den (SOD n) *adj.* **1.** soaked with moisture. **2.** doughy; soggy, as bread. **3.** flabby and pale, esp. from dissipation. **4.** dull; dreary. [ME *soden*]

so•di•um (SOH dee əm) *n.* a silver-white, highly reactive, alkaline metallic element (symbol Na). [< NL]

sodium bicarbonate *Chem.* a white crystalline compound of alkaline taste, used in medicine and cookery: also called *baking soda, bicarbonate of soda.*

sodium chloride salt (def. 1).

sodium hydroxide *Chem.* a strongly basic compound used for bleaching, etc.: also called *caustic soda.*

sodium nitrate *Chem.* a white compound used as a fertilizer and in explosives.

sodium thiosulfate *Chem.* a crystalline salt used in photography as a fixing agent: also called *hypo.* Also **sodium hyposulfite.**

sod•om•y (SOD ə mee) *n.* unnatural sexual relations, esp. between male persons or between a human being and an animal. [ME *sodomie* < Sodom, the Biblical city] — **sod'om•ite** *n.*

so•fa (SOH fə) *n.* a wide upholstered seat, having a back and raised ends. [< Arabic *suffah* long bench]

soft (sawft) *adj.* **•er, •est 1.** being or composed of a substance whose shape is changed easily by pressure; pliable; malleable. **2.** smooth and delicate to the touch. **3.** gentle in its effect upon the ear; not loud or harsh. **4.** mild; gentle. **5.** of subdued coloring or delicate shading. **6.** easily touched in feeling; tender. **7.** of yielding character; weak. **8.** *Informal* involving little effort; easy: a *soft* job. **9.** free from mineral salts that prevent the detergent action of soap: said of water. **10.** bituminous, as opposed to anthracite: said of coal. —*n.* that which is soft; a soft part or material. —*adv.* quietly; gently. [ME] —**soft'ly** *adv. & interj.* — **soft'ness** *n.*

soft coal bituminous coal.

soft drink a nonalcoholic drink, usu. carbonated.

soft•en (SAW fən) *v.t. & v.i.* make or become soft or softer. —**sof'ten•er** *n.*

soft•heart•ed (SAWFT HAHR tid) *adj.* tender-hearted; merciful. —**soft'heart'ed•ness** *n.*

soft pedal a pedal of a piano that mutes the tone.

soft-ped•al (SAWFT PED l) *v.t.* **•aled, •al•ing 1.** mute the tone of (a piano, etc.) by depressing the soft pedal. **2.** *Informal* render less emphatic; moderate.

soft-shell (SAWFT SHEL) *adj.* having a soft shell, as certain clams, crabs, etc., esp. after shedding its hard shell: also **soft'-shelled'.** —*n.* a soft-shelled crab.

soft-shelled crab a crab of North America after it has molted.

soft soap 1. fluid or semifluid soap. **2.** *Informal* flattery.

soft-soap (SAWFT SOHP) *v.t. Informal* flatter; cajole.

soft-spo·ken (SAWFT SPOH kən) *adj.* speaking with a low voice and quiet manner.

soft·ware (SAWFT WAIR) *n.* any of the programs used in operating a digital computer, as input and output programs: distinguished from *hardware*.

soft·wood (SAWFT WUUD) *n.* a coniferous tree or its wood.

soft·y (SAWF tee) *n. pl.* **soft·ies** *Informal* a sentimental, tender-hearted person.

sog·gy (SOG ee) *adj.* **·gi·er, ·gi·est 1.** saturated with moisture; soaked; sodden. **2.** soft; boggy: said of land. **—sog′gi·ness** *n.*

soil[1] (soil) *n.* **1.** finely divided rock mixed with vegetable or animal matter, constituting that portion of the surface of the earth in which plants grow. **2.** land; country: native *soil.* **3.** a particular kind of earth. [ME]

soil[2] *v.t.* **1.** make dirty; smudge. **2.** disgrace; defile. **—***v.i.* **3.** become dirty. [ME *soilen*] **—***n.* **1.** a spot or stain. **2.** filth; sewage; manure.

soi·ree (swah RAY) *n.* a party or reception given in the evening. Also **soi·rée′.** [< F]

so·journ (SOH jurn) *v.i.* stay or dwell temporarily; abide for a time. **—***n.* a temporary stay. [ME *sojournen* rest] **—so′journ·er** *n.*

sol (sohl) *n. Music* the fifth tone of the diatonic scale in solmization: also *so.*

Sol (sohl) *n.* the sun. [< L, the Roman god of the sun]

sol·ace (SOL is) *n.* comfort in grief or trouble; also, that which supplies such comfort. [ME *solas*] **—***v.t.* **·aced, ·ac·ing** comfort or cheer in trouble or grief.

so·lar (SOH lər) *adj.* **1.** pertaining to, proceeding from, or connected with the sun. **2.** affected, determined, or measured by the sun. **3.** operated by the action of the sun's rays: a *solar* engine. [ME]

solar battery a device for direct conversion of solar energy into electricity.

so·lar·i·um (sə LAIR ee əm) *n. pl.* **·i·a** (-ee ə) or **·i·ums** a room or enclosed porch exposed to the sun's rays. [< L, balcony]

solar plexus 1. *Anat.* the large network of nerves found behind the stomach, serving the abdomen. **2.** the pit of the stomach.

solar system the sun together with the planets, moons, etc. that revolve about it.

sold (sohld) past tense, past participle of SELL.

sol·der (SOD ər) *n.* a fusible metal or alloy used for joining metallic surfaces or margins, applied in a melted state. [ME *soudour*] **—***v.t. & v.i.* unite or be united with solder. **—sol′der·er** *n.*

sol·dier (SOHL jər) *n.* **1.** a person serving in an army; esp., an enlisted man or woman. **2.** one who serves loyally in any cause. [ME *soudier*] **—***v.i.* **1.** be a soldier. **2.** pretend to be working while loafing.

soldier of fortune an adventurous, restless person ready to serve anywhere for pay or adventure.

sole[1] (sohl) *n.* **1.** the bottom surface of the foot. **2.** the bottom surface of a shoe, boot, etc. **3.** something resembling a sole; bottom part. [ME] **—***v.t.* **soled, sol·ing** furnish with a sole.

sole[2] *n.* any of a family of flat fishes, many of which are highly esteemed as food. [ME]

sole[3] *adj.* being alone or the only one; only; individual. [< L *solus* alone]

so·le·cism (SOL ə SIZ əm) *n.* **1.** a violation of accepted grammar. **2.** any impropriety or incongruity. [< L *soloecismus*] **—sol′e·cist** *n.* **—sol′e·cis′tic** *adj.*

sole·ly (SOHL lee) *adv.* **1.** by oneself or itself alone; singly. **2.** completely; entirely. **3.** without exception; exclusively.

sol·emn (SOL əm) *adj.* **1.** characterized by mystery or power; awe-inspiring. **2.** grave; serious. **3.** characterized by ceremonial observances; sacred. [ME *solemne*] **—sol′emn·ly** *adv.*

so·lem·ni·ty (sə LEM ni tee) *n. pl.* **·ties 1.** the state or quality of being solemn. **2.** a rite expressive of religious reverence; also, any ceremonious observance.

sol·em·nize (SOL əm NIZ) *v.t.* **·nized, ·niz·ing 1.** perform as a ceremony or solemn rite. **2.** treat or dignify with solemnity. **—sol′em·ni·za′tion** *n.* **—sol′em·niz′er** (-NIZ ər) *n.*

so·le·noid (SOL ə NOID) *n. Electr.* a coiled conducting wire capable of setting up a magnetic field by the passage through it of an electric current. [< F *solénoïde*]

so·lic·it (sə LIS it) *v.t.* **1.** ask for earnestly; seek to obtain by persuasion or entreaty. **2.** entreat (a person). **3.** entice to an unlawful or immoral act. **—***v.i.* **4.** make petition or solicitation. [ME *soliciten* disturb] **—so·lic′i·ta′tion** *n.*

so·lic·i·tor (sə LIS i tər) *n.* **1.** a person who

solicits; esp., one who solicits donations or subscriptions. **2.** a lawyer, esp. a legal adviser in government service. **3.** in England, a lawyer who may advise clients or prepare cases, but who may appear as an advocate in the lower courts only.

so•lic•i•tous (sə LIS i təs) *adj.* **1.** full of concern: *solicitous* about her health. **2.** eager; anxious; careful. —**so•lic′i•tous•ly** *adv.* —**so•lic′i•tude** *n.*

sol•id (SOL id) *adj.* **1.** having definite shape and volume; not fluid. **2.** substantial; firm and stable. **3.** filling the whole of; not hollow. **4.** having no opening or interruption; unbroken. **5.** strong and firm; sound. **6.** satisfactory. **7.** financially sound or safe. **8.** having or relating to the three dimensions of length, breadth, and thickness. **9.** written without a hyphen: said of a compound word. **10.** unadulterated; unalloyed: *solid* gold. **11.** serious; reliable: a *solid* citizen. —*n.* **1.** a state of matter characterized by definite shape and volume. **2.** a geometrical figure that has length, breadth, and thickness, as a cone, cube, sphere, etc. [ME] —**sol′id•ly** *adv.* —**sol′id•ness** *n.*

sol•i•dar•i•ty (SOL i DAR i tee) *n.* unity in nature, relations, or interests, as of a class.

solid fuel *Aerospace* a rocket fuel in solid form. Also **solid propellant.**

solid geometry the geometry that includes all three dimensions of space.

so•lid•i•fy (sə LID ə FI) *v.t. & v.i.* **-fied, -fy•ing 1.** make or become solid, hard, firm, or compact. **2.** bring or come together in unity. —**so•lid′i•fi•ca′tion** *n.*

so•lid•i•ty (sə LID i tee) *n.* **1.** the quality or state of being solid; extension in the three dimensions of space. **2.** mental, moral, or financial soundness; stability.

sol•id-state (SOL id STAYT) *adj.* **1.** *Physics* pertaining to the study of solids at the molecular or atomic level. **2.** *Electronics* pertaining to or composed of solid components, as transistors, as distinct from vacuum tubes.

sol•i•dus (SOL i dəs) *n. pl.* **-di** (-dī) the slash mark (/). [ME]

so•lil•o•quize (sə LIL ə KWIZ) *v.i.* **-quized, -quiz•ing** talk to oneself; utter a soliloquy.

so•lil•o•quy (sə LIL ə kwee) *n. pl.* **-quies** a talking or discourse to oneself, as in a drama; a monologue. [< LL *soliloquium*]

sol•ip•sism (SOL ip SIZ əm) *n.* **1.** *Philos.* the theory that the self is the only thing really existent. **2.** egotistic self-absorption. [< L *solus* alone + *ipse* self] —**sol′ip•sist** *n.*

sol•i•taire (SOL i TAIR) *n.* **1.** a diamond or other gem set alone. **2.** one of many games, esp. of cards, played by one person; also called *patience*. [ME]

sol•i•tar•y (SOL i TER ee) *adj.* **1.** living, being, or going alone. **2.** made, done, or passed alone. **3.** unfrequented by human beings; secluded. **4.** lonesome; lonely. **5.** single; sole. —*n. Informal* solitary confinement. [ME]

sol•i•tude (SOL i TOOD) *n.* **1.** the state of being solitary; seclusion. **2.** a deserted or lonely place.

sol•mi•za•tion (SOL mə ZAY shən) *n. Music* the use of syllables, most commonly *do, re, mi, fa, sol, la, ti,* as names for the tones of a musical scale. [< F *solmisation*]

so•lo (SOH loh) *n. pl.* **-los 1.** a musical composition or passage for a single voice or instrument. **2.** any performance accomplished alone or without assistance. —*adj.* **1.** composed or written for, or executed by, a single voice or instrument. **2.** done by one person. alone: a *solo* flight. —*v.i.* **-loed, -lo•ing** fly an airplane alone, esp. for the first time. [< Ital.] —**so′lo•ist** *n.*

sol•stice (SOL stis) *n. Astron.* **1.** the time of year when the sun is at its greatest distance from the celestial equator; either the **summer solstice,** in the northern hemisphere about June 21, or the **winter solstice,** about Dec. 22. **2.** either of the two points on the ecliptic marking these distances. [ME] —**sol•sti•tial** (sol STISH əl) *adj.*

sol•u•ble (SOL yə bəl) *adj.* **1.** that can be dissolved in a liquid. **2.** that can be solved or explained. [ME] —**sol′u•bil′i•ty** *n.* —**sol′u•bly** *adv.*

sol•ute (SOL yoot) *n.* the substance dissolved in a solution.

so•lu•tion (sə LOO shən) *n.* **1.** a homogeneous mixture formed by dissolving one or more substances, whether solid, liquid, or gaseous, in another substance. **2.** the act or process by which such a mixture is made. **3.** the act, process, or method of solving a problem. **4.** the answer to a problem; explanation. [ME]

solve (solv) *v.t.* **solved, solv•ing** find the answer to; resolve. [ME *solven* loosen] —**solv′er** *n.*

sol•vent (SOL vənt) *adj.* **1.** able to pay all debts. **2.** having the power of dissolving. [< L *solvere* dissolve] —*n.* a substance, generally a liquid, capable of dissolving other substances. —**sol'·ven·cy** n.

so·mat·ic (soh MAT ik) adj. of or relating to the body; physical; corporeal. [< Gk. *sōmatikós* pertaining to the body]

som·ber (SOM bər) adj. 1. dark and gloomy; dusky; murky. 2. melancholy; sad; depressing. [< F *sombre*]

som·bre·ro (som BRAIR oh) n. pl. ·**ros** a broad-brimmed, tall-crowned hat worn in Mexico, SW U.S., etc. [< Sp.]

some (sum) adj. 1. (səm) of an unspecified quantity, number, or amount: Take *some* cherries. 2. certain but not specified or known: *Some* people wrote to him. 3. *Informal* impressive; remarkable: That was *some* cake. —*pron.* 1. a certain undetermined quantity or part. 2. certain ones not known or specified: *Some* did not attend. —*adv.* approximately; about: *Some* eighty persons arrived. [ME]

-some[1] *suffix of adjectives* characterized by or tending to be (what is indicated by the main element): *blithesome, burdensome.* [ME]

-some[2] *suffix of nouns* a body: *chromosome.* [< Gk. *sōma* body]

-some[3] *suffix of nouns* a group consisting of (a specified number): *twosome, foursome.*

some·bod·y (SUM BOD ee) pron. a person unknown or unnamed; someone. —*n. pl.* ·**bod·ies** a person of consequence.

some·day (SUM DAY) adv. at some future time.

some·how (SUM HOW) adv. in some manner not explained.

some·one (SUM wən) pron. somebody.

some·place (SUM PLAYS) adv. somewhere.

som·er·sault (SUM ər SAWLT) n. an acrobatic leap or roll in which the body rolls end over end, making a full revolution of the body. —*v.i.* perform a somersault. [< MF *sombresaut*]

some·thing (SUM THING) n. a thing not specified or known. —**make something of** 1. treat as special or important. 2. fight or argue because of. —*adv.* somewhat: now only in the phrase **something like**: His house is *something like* mine.

some·time (SUM TĪM) adv. at some future time not precisely stated; eventually. —*adj.* former: a *sometime* student.

some·times (SUM TĪMZ) adv. at times; occasionally.

some·what (SUM HWUT) n. an uncertain

quantity or degree; something. —*adv.* in some degree; rather.

some·where (SUM HWAIR) adv. in, at, or to some place unspecified or unknown. —*n.* an unspecified or unknown place.

som·nam·bu·lism (som NAM byə LIZ əm) n. sleepwalking. —**som·nam'bu·list** n.

som·no·lence (SOM nə ləns) n. sleepiness; drowsiness.

som·no·lent (SOM nə lənt) adj. 1. sleepy; drowsy. 2. tending to induce drowsiness. [ME *sompnolent*] —**som'no·lent·ly** adv.

son (sun) n. 1. a male child considered with reference to one or both parents. 2. any male descendant. 3. a person regarded as a native of a particular country or place. —**the Son** Jesus Christ, the second person of the Trinity. [ME *sone*]

so·nar (SOH nahr) n. a device using underwater sound waves for navigation, range finding, detection of submarines, etc. [< *so*und *na*vigation *r*anging]

so·na·ta (sə NAH tə) n. *Music* a composition for one or two instruments, having three or four movements related in key. [< Ital.]

song (sawng) n. 1. a musical composition for one or more voices. 2. any melodious utterance, as of a bird. 3. a lyric or ballad. 4. poetry; verse. —**for a song** at a very low price. [ME]

song·bird (SAWNG BURD) n. a bird that utters a musical call.

song·ster (SAWNG stər) n. 1. a singer. 2. a songbird. 3. a poet. —**song'stress** n.fem.

song·writ·er (SAWNG RĪ tər) n. one who writes music or lyrics, or both, for songs, esp. popular songs.

son·ic (SON ik) adj. of or relating to sound or the speed of sound: *sonic* waves. [< L *sonus* sound]

sonic barrier *Aeron.* sound barrier.

son-in-law (SUN in LAW) n. pl. **sons-in-law** the husband of one's daughter.

son·net (SON it) n. a poem of fourteen lines, properly expressing two successive phases of a single thought or idea. [< Ital. *sonnetto*]

son·net·eer (SON i TEER) n. a composer of sonnets.

so·nor·i·ty (sə NOR i tee) n. pl. ·**ties** sonorous quality or state; resonance.

so·no·rous (SON ər əs) adj. 1. producing sound. 2. loud and full-sounding; resonant. [< L *sonorus* noisy] —**so·no'rous·ly** adv. —**so·no'rous·ness** n.

soon (soon) adv. ·**er**, ·**est** 1. in the near future; shortly. **2.** without delay; quickly. **3.** willingly; readily. **4.** ahead of time; early. [ME]

soot (suut) *n.* a black substance composed chiefly of carbon particles, produced during the burning of coal, wood, etc. [ME] — **soot'y** *adj.* **soot·i·er, soot·i·est**

soothe (sooth) *v.* **soothed, sooth·ing** *v.t.* **1.** make quiet or calm; comfort. **2.** relieve, as pain or grief; alleviate. —*v.i.* **3.** have a calming or relieving effect. [ME *sothen* verify] —**sooth'·ing** *adj.* —**sooth'ing·ly** *adv.*

sooth·say·er (SOOTH SAY ər) *n.* one professes to foretell events. —**sooth'·say' ing** *n.*

sop (sop) *v.* **sopped, sop·ping** *v.t.* **1.** dip or soak in a liquid. **2.** drench. **3.** take up by absorption: often with *up.* —*v.i.* **4.** be absorbed; soak in. —*n.* **1.** anything softened in liquid, as bread. **2.** anything given to pacify, as a bribe. [ME]

soph·ism (SOF iz əm) *n.* a false argument having the appearance of truth, esp. one used to deceive.

soph·ist (SOF ist) *n.* one who argues cleverly but overprecisely and sometimes deceptively. [< L *sophista*]

so·phis·tic (sə FIS tik) *adj.* **1.** pertaining to sophists or sophistry. **2.** fallacious. Also **so·phis'ti·cal** (-ti kəl).

so·phis·ti·cate (sə FIS ti KAYT) *v.t.* **·cat·ed, ·cat·ing 1.** make less simple or ingenuous; make worldly-wise. **2.** increase the complexity of. [ME *sophisticaten*] —*n.* (sə FIS ti kit) a sophisticated person. — **so·phis'ti·ca'tion** *n.*

so·phis·ti·cat·ed (sə FIS ti KAY tid) *adj.* **1.** having refined tastes; wordly-wise; cultured. **2.** appealing to the intellect: a *sophisticated* novel. **3.** very complicated in design, capabilities, etc.

soph·is·try (SOF ə stree) *n. pl.* **·tries** subtly fallacious reasoning or disputation.

soph·o·more (SOF ə MOR) *n.* in American high schools and colleges, a second-year student.

soph·o·mor·ic (SOF ə MOR ik) *adj.* **1.** of or like a sophomore. **2.** marked by shallow perceptions and attitudes; immature; callow.

-sophy *combining form* knowledge pertaining to a (specified) field: *theosophy.* [< Gk. *-sophia* wisdom]

sop·o·rif·ic (SOP ə RIF ik) *adj.* **1.** causing sleep. **2.** drowsy; sleepy. —*n.* a medicine that produces sleep. [? < F *soporifique*]

sop·ping (SOP ing) *adj.* wet through; drenched; soaking.

so·pran·o (sə PRAN oh) *n. pl.* **so·pran·os 1.** a voice of the highest range. **2.** a singer with such a voice. **3.** the music intended for such a voice. —*adj.* of or pertaining to a soprano voice, part, etc. [< Ital.]

sor·cer·er (SOR sər ər) *n.* one who practices sorcery. —**sor'cer·ess** *n.fem.*

sor·cer·y (SOR sə ree) *n. pl.* **·cer·ies** the alleged use of evil, supernatural powers over people; witchcraft. [ME *sorcerie*]

sor·did (SOR did) *adj.* **1.** filthy; dirty. **2.** mercenary. **3.** of degraded character; vile; base. [< L *sordidus*] —**sor'did·ly** *adv.* —**sor' did·ness** *n.*

sore (sor) *adj.* **sor·er, sor·est 1.** painful or tender to the touch: a *sore* muscle. **2.** arousing painful feelings; irritating: a *sore* point. **3.** extreme or severe: *sore* need. **4.** *Informal* offended; aggrieved. —*n.* an area of the body where the skin is bruised, broken, or inflamed. —*adv. Archaic* sorely. [ME] — **sore'ness** *n.*

sore·head (SOR HED) *n. Informal* a disgruntled person. —**sore'head'ed** *adj.*

sore·ly (SOR lee) *adv.* **1.** grievously; distressingly. **2.** greatly; extremely: His aid was *sorely* needed.

sor·ghum (SOR gəm) *n.* **1.** a cereal grass grown for grain, fodder, syrup, etc. **2.** the syrup made from the sweet juices of the plant. [< Ital. *sorgo*]

so·ror·i·ty (sə ROR i tee) *n. pl.* **·ties** a women's association, esp. at a college or university. [< Med.L *sororitas*]

sor·rel¹ (SOR əl) *n.* any of several herbs with sour leaves used in salads. [ME *sorel*]

sor·rel² *n.* **1.** reddish or yellowish brown color. **2.** a horse of this color. [ME *sorelle*]

sor·row (SAHR oh) *n.* **1.** suffering or distress due to loss, injury, or misfortune. **2.** the cause of such suffering. **3.** the expression of grief. —*v.i.* feel sorrow; grieve. [ME]

sor·row·ful (SAHR ə fəl) *adj.* sad; unhappy; mournful. —**sor'row·ful·ly** *adv.*

sor·ry (SAHR ee) *adj.* **·ri·er, ·ri·est 1.** affected by sorrow. **2.** causing sorrow; dismal. **3.** pitiable or worthless. [ME]

sort (sort) *n.* **1.** a group of related persons or things; class; kind; set. **2.** nature; quality; type: remarks of that *sort.* —**of sorts** of a poor or unsatisfactory kind: an actor *of sorts.* —**out of sorts 1.** in an ill humor; irritable. **2.** slightly ill. —**sort of** *Informal* somewhat. —*v.t.* arrange or separate into grades, kinds, or sizes. [ME] —**sort′er** *n.*

sor•tie (SOR tee) *n. Mil.* 1. a movement of troops from a besieged place to attack the besiegers. 2. a single trip of an aircraft on a combat mission. [< F]

SOS (ES OH ES) 1. the code signal of distress used by airplanes, ships, etc. 2. any call for assistance.

so-so (SOH SOH) *adj.* passable; mediocre. —*adv.* tolerably.

sot (sot) *n.* a habitual drunkard. [ME, fool] —**sot′tish** *adj.* —**sot′tish•ness** *n.*

sou•brette (soo BRET) *n.* 1. in light opera or comedy, the role of a pert, intriguing lady's maid. 2. an actress playing such a role. [< F, lady's maid]

souf•flé (soo FLAY) *n.* a light, baked dish made fluffy with beaten egg whites. —*adj.* made light and frothy: also **souf•fléed′**. [< F, puffed]

sought (sawt) past tense, past participle of SEEK.

soul (sohl) *n.* 1. the emotional part of human nature, regarded as a separate entity from the body. 2. *Theol.* a a divine principle of life in mankind. b the moral or spiritual part of a person as related to God. 3. fervor; heartiness; vitality. 4. an essential or vital element: Justice is the *soul* of law. 5. a person considered as the embodiment of a quality or attribute: She is the *soul* of generosity. 6. a person. 7. shared pride and awareness of heritage among African Americans. —*adj.* of, pertaining to, designed for, or characteristic of African Americans: *soul* food, *soul* music. [ME] —**soul′ful** (SOHL fəl) *adj.* full of deep feeling: a *soulful* gaze. —**soul′ful•ly** *adv.* —**soul′ful•ness** *n.*

soul•less (SOHL lis) *adj.* 1. heartless; unemotional. 2. having no soul.

sound¹ (sownd) *n.* 1. any of a class of waves caused by mechanical vibrations, esp. in air. 2. the auditory stimulation produced by waves of this type. 3. something that is heard: the *sound* of laughter. 4. significance; implication: The story has a sinister *sound*. 5. sounding or hearing distance; earshot. —*v.i.* 1. make a sound. 2. give a specified impression; seem: The story *sounds* true. —*v.t.* 3. cause to give forth sound. 4. signal, order, announce, etc.: *sound* retreat. 5. utter audibly; pronounce. 6. test or examine by sound. [ME *soun*] —**sound′less** *adj.* —**sound′less•ly** *adv.*

sound² *adj.* •er, •est 1. free from injury or disease; healthy. 2. free from flaw, decay, etc.: *sound* timber. 3. founded in truth; valid; legal. 4. deep, as sleep; unbroken. 5. complete and effectual; thorough. 6. solid; stable; safe; also, trustworthy. 7. based on good judgment. —*adv.* deeply: *sound* asleep. [ME] —**sound′ly** *adv.* —**sound′ness** *n.*

sound³ *n.* 1. a long, narrow body of water connecting larger bodies. 2. in bony fishes, an air-filled sac that contributes to buoyancy. [ME]

sound⁴ *v.t.* 1. measure the depth of (water), esp. by means of a weighted line. 2. try to discover the views of (a person). —*v.i.* 3. sound depth. 4. investigate; inquire. [ME *sounden*] —*n. Surg.* an instrument for exploring a cavity.

sound barrier *Aeron.* the high resistance of air encountered by aircraft moving at speeds close to that of sound. Also *sonic barrier.*

sound effects in motion pictures, radio, etc., the artificially produced sounds of rain, explosions, etc.

sound•ing¹ (SOWN ding) *adj.* 1. giving forth a full sound; sonorous or resounding. 2. having an imposing sound.

sound•ing² *n.* 1. the act of measuring the depth of water by sounding. 2. *pl.* the depth of water so measured.

sound•proof (SOWND PROOF) *adj.* resistant to the passage of sound. —*v.t.* make soundproof.

sound•track (SOWND TRAK *n.* the portion along the edge of a motion-picture film that carries the sound record.

soup (soop) *n.* 1. a liquid food made by simmering or boiling meat, vegetables, etc. in water. 2. *Slang* a thick overcast or fog. —**in the soup** *Informal* in difficulties. —**soup up** *Slang* modify (an automobile) for high speed. [< F *soupe*]

soup•çon (soop SAWN) *n. French* a slight trace.

sour (sowr) *adj.* 1. sharp to the taste; acid; tart. 2. having a rancid taste; spoiled. 3. having a foul odor: *sour* breath. 4. bad-tempered; cross; morose. 5. acid: said of soil. [ME] —*v.t. & v.i.* become or make sour. —*n.* a sour or acid beverage: a whisky *sour*. —**sour′ly** *adv.* —**sour′ness** *n.*

source (sors) *n.* 1. the cause or origin of something; beginning. 2. a lake or other body of water that gives rise to a river. 3. a person, book, etc., that provides information. [ME *sours*]

sour•dough (SOWR DOH) *n.* fermented dough for use as leaven in making bread. [ME]

sour grapes an attitude of scorn toward something one cannot do or have. [After a fable of Aesop in which a fox describes unreachable grapes as sour]

souse (sows) *v.t. & v.i.* **soused, sous•ing 1.** dip or steep in a liquid. **2.** pickle. —*n.* **1.** the act of sousing. **2.** pickled food, esp. the feet and ears of a pig. **3.** a liquid used in pickling; brine. **4.** *Slang* a drunkard. [ME *sows* pickled]

south (sowth) *n.* **1.** the direction to one's right when facing the sun at sunrise. **2.** one of the four cardinal points of the compass, directly opposite *north*. **3.** *Sometimes cap.* any region south of a specified point. —**the South** in the U.S.: **a** the southern or southeastern states. **b** the Confederacy. —*adj.* **1.** to, toward, or in the south; southern. **2.** coming from the south: the *south* wind. —*adv.* in or toward the south; southward. [ME]

south•bound (SOWTH BOWND) *adj.* going southward.

south•east (SOWTH EEST) *n.* **1.** the direction midway between south and east. **2.** any region lying in or toward this direction. —*adj.* **1.** to, toward, or in the southeast. **2.** coming from the southeast. —*adv.* in or toward the southeast. —**south'•east'ern** *adj.*

south•east•er (SOWTH EE stər) *n.* a gale or storm from the southeast.

south•east•er•ly (SOWTH EE stər lee) *adj.* **1.** in, of, or toward the southeast. **2.** from the southeast, as a wind. —*adv.* toward or from the southeast.

south•er•ly (SUTH ər lee) *adj.* **1.** in, of, toward, or pertaining to the south. **2.** from the south, as a wind. —*adv.* toward or from the south.

south•ern (SUTH ərn) *adj.* **1.** to, toward, or in the south. **2.** native to or inhabiting the south. **3.** *Sometimes cap.* of, pertaining to, or characteristic of the south or South. **4.** from the south, as a wind. [ME]

Southern Cross a southern constellation having four bright stars in the form of a cross.

south•ern•er (SUTH ər nər) *n.* **1.** one who is native to or lives in the south. **2.** *Usu. cap.* one who lives in or comes from the South.

Southern Hemisphere see under HEMI-SPHERE.

southern lights aurora australis.

south•ern•most (SUTH ərn MOHST) *adj.* farthest south.

south•land (SOWTH LAND) *n. Sometimes cap.* a land or region in the south or South.

south•paw (SOWTH PAW) *n. Informal* **1.** in baseball, a left-handed pitcher. **2.** any left-handed person. —*adj.* left-handed.

South Pole the southern extremity of the earth's axis.

south•ward (SOWTH wərd) *adv.* toward the south. Also **south'wards.** —*adj.* to, toward, facing, or in the south.

south•ward•ly (SOWTH wərd lee) *adj. & adv.* toward or from the south.

south•west (SOWTH WEST) *n.* **1.** the direction midway between south and west. **2.** any region lying in or toward this direction. —*adj.* **1.** to, toward, or in the southwest. **2.** coming from the southwest: a *southwest* wind. —*adv.* in or toward the southwest. —**south'west'ern** *adj.*

south•west•er (SOWTH WES tər) *n.* **1.** a gale or storm from the southwest. **2.** a waterproof hat with a broad brim over the neck. Also **sou'•west'er** (SOW WES tər).

south•west•er•ly (SOWTH WES tər lee) *adj.* **1.** in, of, or toward the southwest. **2.** from the southwest, as a wind. —*adv.* toward or from the southwest.

sou•ve•nir (SOO və NEER) *n.* a token of remembrance; memento. [< F]

sov•er•eign (SOV rin) *n.* **1.** the ruler of a monarchy; monarch; also, any supreme ruler of a state. **2.** formerly, an English gold coin equivalent to one pound sterling. —*adj.* **1.** having supreme authority. **2.** independent of all external authority or influence: a *sovereign* state. **3.** of supreme excellence; highest. [ME *soverain*]

sov•er•eign•ty (SOV rin tee) *n. pl.* **-ties 1.** supreme authority. **2.** the supreme and independent political authority.

so•vi•et (SOH vee ET) *n.* in the former Soviet Union, any of the legislative bodies existing at various governmental levels. —*adj.* [< Russ. *sovét* council]

sow[1] (soh) *v.* **sowed, sown** or **sowed, sow•ing** *v.t.* **1.** scatter (seed) over land for growth. **2.** scatter seed over (land). **3.** spread abroad; disseminate: *sow* the seeds of distrust. —*v.i.* **4.** scatter seed. [ME *sowen*]

sow[2] (sow) *n.* a female hog. [ME *sowe*]

soy (soi) *n.* **1.** the soybean. **2.** a salty, dark-brown sauce made from soybeans fermented in brine: also **soy sauce.** [< Japanese *shōyū*]

soy•bean (SOI BEEN) *n.* **1.** a leguminous herb native to China and India, cultivated for forage. **2.** its bean, a source of oil, flour, etc. Also called *soy.*

spa (spah) *n.* **1.** a resort, esp. one frequented for its mineral springs. **2.** a mineral spring. [From the Belgian town *Spa*]

space (spays) *n.* **1.** the infinite expanse within which all things exist. **2.** an interval or area between or within things. **3.** area for some purpose: parking *space.* **4.** outer space. **5.** an interval of time; period. **6.** *Printing* a piece of type metal used for separating words. **7.** an area or time available for advertising in a periodical or in broadcasting. —*v.t.* **spaced, spac•ing 1.** separate by spaces. **2.** divide into spaces. [ME] —**space′less** *adj.* —**spac′er** *n.*

space•craft (SPAYS KRAFT) *n.* any vehicle designed for travel in outer space. Also **space′ship′.**

spaced out *Slang* dazed, disoriented, etc., from or as from use of a narcotic drug.

space•flight (SPAYS FLIT) *n.* flight in outer space.

space shuttle *Often cap.* a manned U.S. spacecraft controllable like an airplane, designed for flights to and from space.

space station an artificial satellite designed as a base for research or for launching or refueling spacecraft. Also **space platform.**

space•suit (SPAYS SOOT) *n.* a pressurized garment designed to allow the wearer to work in outer space.

space•walk (SPAYS WAWK) *n.* a task or mission performed by an astronaut in space outside a spacecraft. —*v.i.* conduct such a task or mission. —**space′walk′er** *n.*

spa•cious (SPAY shəs) *adj.* **1.** of indefinite or vast extent. **2.** affording ample room; roomy. —**spa′cious•ly** *adv.* —**spa′cious•ness** *n.*

spade[1] (spayd) *n.* a heavy shovel with a flat blade. —**call a spade a spade** speak frankly and truly. —*v.t.* **spad•ed, spad•ing** dig or cut with a spade. [ME]

spade[2] *n.* a playing card bearing a black figure resembling an inverted heart with a short handle at the bottom. [< Ital. *spada*]

spade•work (SPAYD WURK) *n.* the preliminary work necessary to get a project under way.

spa•ghet•ti (spə GET ee) *n.* a food consisting of cordlike strands of flour paste. [< Ital.]

span (span) *v.t.* **spanned, span•ning 1.** measure, esp. by the hand with thumb and little finger extended. **2.** stretch across: This road *spans* the continent. —*n.* **1.** the distance between the tips of the thumb and little finger when the hand is spread out, usu. considered as nine inches. **2.** distance or extent between any two extremities. **3.** that which spans, as a bridge. [ME *spanne*]

span•gle (SPANG gəl) *n.* a small bit of sparkling metal or plastic, used for decoration in dress. —*v.* **•gled, •gling** *v.t.* **1.** adorn with or as with spangles; cause to glitter. —*v.i.* **2.** sparkle; glitter. [ME *spangel*]

Span•ish (SPAN ish) *adj.* of or pertaining to Spain, its people, or their language. —*n.* **1.** the language of Spain and Spanish America. **2.** the inhabitants of Spain collectively: with *the.*

Span•ish-A•mer•i•can (SPAN ish ə MER i kən) *adj.* **1.** of or pertaining to Spanish America. **2.** designating or pertaining to the war between the U.S. and Spain, 1898. —*n.* one of Spanish origin living in Central or South America; also, a citizen of the U.S. having Spanish or Spanish-American ancestry.

spank (spangk) *v.t.* slap or strike, esp. on the buttocks with the open hand. —*n.* a smack on the buttocks.

spank•ing (SPANG king) *adj.* moving rapidly; swift. —*n.* the act of spanking as punishment. —*adv. Informal* very: *spanking* clean.

spar[1] (spahr) *n. Naut.* a mast, boom, etc. for extending a sail. —*v.t.* **sparred, spar•ring** furnish with spars. [ME *sparre*]

spar[2] *v.i.* **sparred, spar•ring 1.** box, esp. as a training exercise. **2.** bandy words; wrangle. [ME]

spare (spair) *v.t.* **spared, spar•ing 1.** refrain from injuring, killing, etc. **2.** free or relieve a person from (pain, expense, etc.). **3.** use frugally. **4.** part with; do without: Can you *spare* a dime? [ME *sparen*] —*adj.* **spar•er, spar•est 1.** that can be used at will or held in reserve; extra. **2.** free: a *spare* moment. **3.** having little flesh; lean. **4.** not lavish or abundant; scanty. —*n.* **1.** something extra or held in reserve. **2.** in bowling, the knocking down of all the pins with the two bowls in any frame; also, the score so made. —**spare′ly** *adv.* —**spare′•ness** *n.*

spare•ribs (SPAIR RIBZ) *n.* a cut of pork consisting of closely trimmed ribs.

spar•ing (SPAIR ing) *adj.* frugal or thrifty; economical. —**spar'ing•ly** *adv.*

spark (spahrk) *n.* **1.** an incandescent particle thrown off from a fire, a match, etc. **2.** anything like a spark; flash; sparkle. **3.** anything that kindles or animates. **4.** *Electr.* the luminous effect of a disruptive electric discharge; also, the discharge itself. **5.** a small trace or indication; hint. —*v.i.* **1.** give off sparks. —*v.t.* **2.** activate or stir up; incite: *spark* a revolution. [ME] —**spark'er** *n.*

spar•kle (SPAHR kəl) *v.i.* •**kled,** •**kling 1.** give off flashes of light; glitter. **2.** emit sparks. **3.** bubble; effervesce. **4.** be brilliant or vivacious. —*n.* **1.** a glittering; flash; gleam. **2.** liveliness; brilliance; vivacity. [ME]

spar•kler (SPAHR klər) *n.* **1.** a sparkling gem. **2.** a thin, rodlike firework that emits sparks.

spar•kling (SPAHR kling) *adj.* **1.** giving off sparks or flashes; glittering. **2.** brilliant; vivacious.

spark•plug (SPAHRK PLUG) *n.* a device for igniting the gases in the cylinder of an engine by means of a spark.

sparse (spahrs) *adj.* **spars•er, spars•est** thinly spread; scattered widely; not dense. [< L *sparsus*] —**sparse'ly** *adv.* —**sparse' ness, spar'si•ty** *n.*

Spar•tan (SPAHR tn) *adj.* like the ancient Spartans; brave, austere, stoical, etc. —*n.* a person of Spartan character. [ME] —**Spar'tan•ism** *n.*

spasm (SPAZ əm) *n.* **1.** any sudden, transient burst of energy or activity. **2.** *Pathol.* any involuntary, convulsive muscular contraction. [ME *spasme*]

spas•mod•ic (spaz MOD ik) *adj.* of or like a spasm; violent; fitful; sudden. —**spas• mod'i•cal•ly** *adv.*

spas•tic (SPAS tik) *adj.* of, like, or suffering from spasms. —*n.* a person afflicted with a spastic condition. —**spas'ti•cal•ly** *adv.*

spat[1] (spat) a past tense and past participle of SPIT[1].

spat[2] *n.* a petty dispute. —*v.i.* **spat•ted, spat•ting** engage in a petty quarrel.

spat[3] *n.* *Usu. pl.* a short gaiter worn over a shoe and fastened beneath with a strap.

spate (spayt) *n.* a sudden or vigorous outpouring, as of words. [ME]

spa•tial (SPAY shəl) *adj.* of or involving space. [< L *spatium* space] —**spa'tial•ly** *adv.*

spat•ter (SPAT ər) *v.t.* **1.** scatter in drops or splashes, as mud or paint. **2.** splash with such drops. —*v.i.* **3.** throw off drops or splashes. **4.** fall in a shower, as raindrops. [? < Du. *spatten* splash] —*n.* **1.** the act of spattering, or the matter spattered. **2.** a spattering noise.

spat•u•la (SPACH ə lə) *n.* a knifelike instrument with a flat, flexible blade, used to spread plaster, cake icing, etc. [< LL, spoon] —**spat•u•late** (SPACH ə lit) *adj.*

spawn (spawn) *n.* **1.** *Zool.* the mass of eggs of fishes, amphibians, mollusks, etc. **2.** numerous offspring. **3.** outcome or results; yield. —*v.i.* **1.** produce spawn; deposit eggs or roe. —*v.t.* **2.** produce (spawn). **3.** give rise to. [ME *spawnen*]

spay (spay) *v.t.* remove the ovaries from (a female animal). [ME *spayen*]

speak (speek) *v.* **spoke, spo•ken, speak• ing** *v.i.* **1.** utter words; talk. **2.** make a speech. **3.** talk together; converse. —*v.t.* **4.** utter; say. **5.** make known; reveal. **6.** use (a language) in speaking. —**speak for** speak in behalf of; represent. [ME *speken*] —**speak'a•ble** *adj.*

speak•eas•y (SPEEK EE zee) *n. pl.* •**eas•ies** a saloon or nightclub where liquor was sold illegally during Prohibition.

speak•er (SPEE kər) *n.* **1.** one who speaks. **2.** the presiding officer of a legislative body. **3.** a loudspeaker.

spear (speer) *n.* **1.** a weapon consisting of a pointed head on a long shaft. **2.** a barbed and usu. forked instrument for spearing fish. **3.** a leaf or slender stalk, as of grass. —*v.t.* pierce with a spear. [ME]

spear•head (SPEER HED) *n.* **1.** the point of a spear. **2.** a person or group that leads or strongly influences an action. —*v.t.* be in the lead of.

spear•mint (SPEER MINT) *n.* an aromatic herb similar to peppermint.

spe•cial (SPESH əl) *adj.* **1.** having some peculiar or distinguishing characteristic; distinctive. **2.** designed for a specific purpose. **3.** out of the ordinary; unique; exceptional. **4.** valued highly; favored. [ME] —*n.* **1.** something made for a specific service or occasion. **2.** a product offered for sale at reduced prices. —**spe'cial•ly** *adv.*

spe•cial•ist (SPESH ə list) *n.* **1.** a person devoted to one line of study, occupation, etc.; esp., a physician who practices one branch of medicine. **2.** in the U.S. Army, an enlisted person in a technical or administrative position, corresponding in rank to the grades of corporal through sergeant first class.

spe·cial·ize (SPESH ə LIZ) v.i. **·ized, ·izing 1.** concentrate on one particular activity or subject. **2.** *Biol.* take on a special form; adapt. —**spe'·cial·i·za'tion** n.

spe·cial·ty (SPESH əl tee) n. pl. **·ties 1.** a special occupation, craft, or study. **2.** the state of being special or of having peculiar characteristics. **3.** a unique product or service offered by a business.

spe·cie (SPEE shee) n. coined money; coin. [< L *in specie* in kind]

spe·cies (SPEE sheez) n. pl. **·cies 1.** *Biol.* in plant or animal classification, a group of organisms having a number of traits in common, esp. the ability to breed with one another. **2.** a kind, sort, or variety. [< L, appearance]

spe·cif·ic (spi SIF ik) adj. **1.** distinctly and plainly set forth; definite. **2.** peculiar or special, as characteristics, qualities, etc. **3.** *Med.* effective in treating a specific disease: said of a remedy. [< Med.L *specificus*] —n. **1.** anything specific or adapted to effect a specific result. **2.** *Usu. pl.* a particular; item; instance; remedy. —**spe·cif'i·cal·ly** adv. —**spec·i·fic·i·ty** (SPES ə FIS i tee) n.

spec·i·fi·ca·tion (SPES ə fi KAY shən) n. **1.** the act of specifying. **2.** something specified, as in a contract, plans, etc. **3.** *Usu. pl.* a detailed description of the materials, dimensions, etc. of a projected work.

specific gravity *Physics* the ratio of the mass of a body to that of an equal volume of some standard substance, water in the case of solids and liquids, and air or hydrogen in the case of gases; a measure of density.

spec·i·fy (SPES ə FI) v.t. **·fied, ·fying 1.** mention specifically; describe in detail. **2.** list in a specification. [ME *specifien*] —**spec'i·fi'a·ble** adj.

spec·i·men (SPES ə mən) n. **1.** a person or thing regarded as representative of its class or group; example; sample. **2.** *Med.* a sample of tissue etc.; for analysis and diagnosis. [< L]

spe·cious (SPEE shəs) adj. apparently good or right, but actually not so; deceptively plausible: *specious* reasoning. [ME] —**spe'cious·ly** adv. —**spe'cious·ness** n.

speck (spek) n. **1.** a small spot, stain, or discoloration. **2.** a very small piece; bit; parti-

cle. [ME *specke*] —v.t. mark with specks; speckle.

speck·le (SPEK əl) v.t. **·led, ·ling** mark with specks. —n. a small spot; speck. [ME] —**speck'led** adj.

spec·ta·cle (SPEK tə kəl) n. **1.** a large, public show or exhibition, esp. on a grand scale. **2.** a remarkable or unusual sight or event. **3.** an unwelcome or deplorable exhibition. **4.** pl. eyeglasses. [ME]

spec·ta·cled (SPEK tə kəld) adj. **1.** wearing spectacles. **2.** *Biol.* having markings resembling spectacles.

spec·tac·u·lar (spek TAK yə lər) adj. **1.** very unusual, exciting, etc.; extraordinary: a *spectacular* rescue. **2.** of or like a spectacle. —n. a lavish dramatic or musical production. [< L *spectaculum*] —**spec·tac'u·lar·ly** adv.

spec·ta·tor (SPEK tay tər) n. **1.** one who beholds; eyewitness; onlooker. **2.** one who watches a show, game, etc. [< L]

spec·ter (SPEK tər) n. **1.** a ghost or apparition. **2.** anything of a fearful or horrible nature. Also **spec'tre.** [< F *spectre*]

spec·tra (SPEK trə) n. a plural of SPECTRUM.

spec·tral (SPEK trəl) adj. **1.** of or like a specter; ghostly. **2.** pertaining to a spectrum. —**spec·tral'i·ty** n. —**spec'tral·ly** adv.

spec·tro·gram (SPEK trə GRAM) n. a photograph of the spectrum.

spec·tro·graph (SPEK trə GRAF) n. an apparatus for photographing the spectrum.

spec·trom·e·ter (spek TROM i tər) n. **1.** an instrument for determining the angular deviation or wavelength of a light ray. **2.** a spectroscope fitted with such an instrument.

spec·tro·scope (SPEK trə SKOHP) n. an optical instrument for forming and analyzing the spectrum. —**spec'tro·scop'ic** (-SKOP ik) adj.

spec·tros·co·py (spek TROS kə pee) n. the study of spectra observed with a spectroscope. —**spec·tros'co·pist** n.

spec·trum (SPEK trəm) n. pl. **·tra** (-trə), **·trums 1.** *Physics* **a** the band of color observed when a beam of white light is passed through a prism that separates each component of the light according to wavelengths, ranging from long for red to short for violet. **b** an image formed by radiant energy directed through a spectroscope and forming part of a progressive series. **2.** a range or extent; scope: a wide *spectrum* of political views. [< L, appearance]

spec·u·late (SPEK yə LAYT) *v.i.* **·lat·ed, ·lat·ing 1.** think carefully; reflect; conjecture. **2.** make an investment involving a risk, but with hope of gain. [< L *speculatus* explored] —**spec'u·la'tor** *n.*

spec·u·la·tion (SPEK yə LAY shən) *n.* **1.** serious thinking or conjecturing; also, a conclusion reached by or based upon conjecture. **2.** the act of engaging in risky business transactions that offer a possibility of large profit. —**spec·u·la·tive** (SPEK yə lə tiv) *adj.*

sped (sped) a past tense and past participle of SPEED.

speech (speech) *n.* **1.** the faculty of expressing thought and emotion by spoken words. **2.** the act of speaking. **3.** a public address or talk. **4.** a characteristic manner of speaking. **5.** a particular language, idiom, or dialect: American *speech*. **6.** the study of oral communication. [ME *speche*]

speech·less (SPEECH lis) *adj.* **1.** temporarily unable to speak because of strong emotion, etc. **2.** mute; dumb. **3.** unable to be expressed in words: *speechless* joy. —**speech'less·ness** *n.*

speed (speed) *n.* **1.** the act of moving swiftly; rapidity of motion. **2.** rate of motion; velocity. **3.** rate of performance, as shown by the ratio of work done to time spent. **4.** *Mech.* a transmission gear in a motor vehicle. **5.** *Slang* an amphetamine or related drug used as a stimulant. —*v.* **sped** or **speed·ed, speed·ing** *v.i.* **1.** move rapidly; rush. **2.** exceed a speed limit. —*v.t.* **3.** cause to move rapidly. **4.** further the progress of: *speed* a letter on its way. [ME *spede*] —**speed'er** *n.*

speed·om·e·ter (spee DOM i tər) *n.* a device for indicating the speed of a vehicle.

speed-up (SPEED UP) *n.* an acceleration in work, output, movement, etc.

speed·way (SPEED WAY) *n.* a track for auto or motorcycle races.

speed·y (SPEE dee) *adj.* **speed·i·er, speed·i·est 1.** very fast; rapid. **2.** without delay; prompt. —**speed'i·ly** *adv.* —**speed'i·ness** *n.*

spe·le·ol·o·gy (SPEE lee OL ə jee) *n.* the exploration and study of caves. —**spe'·le·ol'o·gist** *n.*

spell[1] (spel) *v.* **spelled** or **spelt, spell·ing** *v.t.* **1.** name or write the letters of (a word); esp., do so correctly. **2.** form or be the let-

ters of: C-a-t *spells* cat. **3.** signify; mean. —*v.i.* **4.** form words out of letters, esp. correctly. —**spell out** make clear and explicit. [ME *spellen*]

spell[2] *n.* **1.** a word formula used as a charm. **2.** an irresistible fascination or attraction. [ME]

spell[3] *n.* **1.** a brief period of time. **2.** a period of weather of a specific kind: a hot *spell*. **3.** a period of illness, debility, etc. **4.** a turn of duty in relief of another. **5.** a period of work. —*v.t.* relieve temporarily from some work or duty.

spell·bind (SPEL BIND) *v.t.* **·bound, ·bind·ing** make spellbound; enchant. —**spell'·bind'er** *n.*

spell·bound (SPEL BOWND) *adj.* fascinated; enchanted.

spell·er (SPEL ər) *n.* **1.** one who spells. **2.** a spelling book.

spell·ing (SPEL ing) *n.* **1.** the act of one who spells. **2.** the way in which a word is spelled.

spelling bee a competition that is won by the person or team spelling the most words correctly.

spelt (spelt) a past tense and past participle of SPELL.

spe·lunk·er (spi LUNG kər) *n.* an explorer of caves, esp. as a hobby. [< L *spelunca* cave] —**spe·lunk'ing** *n.*

spend (spend) *v.* **spent, spend·ing** *v.t.* **1.** pay out (money). **2.** expend; exhaust; use up. **3.** apply or devote, as thought or effort. **4.** pass: *spend* one's life in jail. —*v.i.* **5.** pay out money. [ME *spenden*] —**spend'er** *n.*

spend·thrift (SPEND THRIFT) *n.* one who spends money lavishly or wastefully. —*adj.* lavish; wasteful.

spent (spent) past tense and past participle of SPEND. —*adj.* tired, exhausted.

sperm[1] (spurm) *n.* **1.** the male fertilizing fluid; semen. **2.** a male reproductive cell; spermatozoon. [ME] —**sper·mat·ic** (spur MAT ik) *adj.*

sperm[2] *n.* **1.** a sperm whale. **2.** spermaceti. [Short for SPERMACETI]

sper·ma·ce·ti (SPUR mə SEE tee) *n.* a white, waxy substance derived from the oil of the sperm whale, used for making candles, ointments, etc. [ME *sperma cete* whale sperm]

sper·ma·to·zo·on (SPUR mə tə ZOH ən) *n. pl.* **·zo·a** (-ZOH ə) *Biol.* the male reproductive or germ cell of an animal; male gamete. [< NL]

sperm whale a large whale of warm seas, having a huge truncate head.

spew (spyoo) *v.t. & v.i.* **1.** vomit; throw up. **2.** send forth with vigor or in large amounts: *spew nonsense.* —*n.* vomit. [ME *spewen*]

sphag·num (SFAG nəm) *n.* any of a genus of whitish gray mosses found in damp places; the bog or peat mosses. [< NL]

sphe·noid bone (SFEE noid) *Anat.* an irregular, compound bone situated at the base of the skull.

sphere (sfeer) *n.* **1.** a solid figure having a surface every point of which is equidistant from the center; globe; ball. **2.** a range or field of interest, activity, etc.; scope. [< LL *sphera*]

-sphere *combining form* **1.** denoting an enveloping spherical mass: *atmosphere.* **2.** denoting a spherical form: *planisphere.*

spher·i·cal (SFER i kəl) *adj.* **1.** shaped like a sphere; globular. **2.** pertaining to a sphere. —**spher′i·cal·ly** *adv.*

sphe·ric·i·ty (sfi RIS i tee) *n.* spherical form; roundness.

sphe·roid (SFEER oid) *n. Geom.* a body having nearly the form of a sphere. —**sphe·roi′dal** *adj.*

sphinc·ter (SFINGK tər) *n. Anat.* a band of muscle that surrounds an opening or tube in the body and serves to close it. [< LL]

sphinx (sfingks) *n. pl.* **sphinx·es** or **sphin·ges** (SFIN jeez) **1.** in Egyptian mythology, a wingless monster with a lion's body and the head of a man, ram, or hawk. **2.** in Greek mythology, a monster, usu. represented as having a woman's head and breasts and a lion's body, that destroyed those unable to guess its riddle. **3.** a mysterious or enigmatical person. —**the Sphinx** the huge stone figure at Giza, Egypt. [ME]

sphyg·mo·ma·nom·e·ter (SFIG moh mə NOM i tər) *n.* an instrument for measuring blood pressure. [< Gk. *sphygmos* pulse + MANOMETER]

spice (spīs) *n.* **1.** an aromatic, pungent vegetable substance, used to flavor food. **2.** such substances collectively. **3.** that which adds zest or interest. —*v.t.* **spiced, spic·ing 1.** season with spice. **2.** add zest to. [ME]

spick-and-span (SPIK ən SPAN) *adj.* neat and clean; fresh.

spic·y (SPĪ see) *adj.* **spic·i·er, spic·i·est 1.** seasoned with spice. **2.** containing much spice; sharp; hot. **3.** having zest or piquancy. **4.** somewhat improper; risqué. —**spic′i·ly** *adv.* —**spic′i·ness** *n.*

spi·der (SPĪ dər) *n.* **1.** any of a large number of eight-legged, wingless arachnids that spin webs. **2.** a long-handled iron frying pan, often having legs. [ME] —**spi′der·y** *adj.*

spied (spīd) past tense, past participle of SPY.

spiel (speel) *Informal n.* a talk; esp., noisy, high-pressure sales talk. —*v.i.* make such a talk. [< G *spielen* play]

spif·fy (SPIF ee) *adj.* **spif·fi·er, spif·fi·est** *Informal* smartly dressed; spruce. —**spif′fi·ness** *n.*

spig·ot (SPIG ət) *n.* **1.** a faucet. **2.** a plug for the bunghole of a cask. [ME]

spike¹ (spīk) *n.* **1.** a long, thick metal nail. **2.** a projecting, pointed piece of metal, as in the soles of shoes to prevent slipping. —*v.t.* **spiked, spik·ing 1.** fasten with spikes. **2.** block; put a stop to. **3.** *Informal* add alcoholic liquor to. [ME]

spike² *n.* **1.** an ear of corn, wheat, or other grain. **2.** *Bot.* a flower cluster having numerous flowers arranged closely on an elongated common axis. [ME]

spill (spil) *v.* **spilled** or **spilt, spill·ing** *v.t.* **1.** allow or cause to flow out of or run over a container. **2.** shed, as blood. **3.** *Informal* make known, as a secret. **4.** unseat (a rider); throw. —*v.i.* **5.** flow or run out. [ME *spillen*] —*n.* **1.** a fall, as from a horse; tumble. **2.** the act of spilling.

spill·way (SPIL way) *n.* a passageway, as in a dam, to release the water in a reservoir.

spilt (spilt) a past tense, past participle of SPILL.

spin (spin) *v.* **spun, spin·ning** *v.t.* **1.** draw out and twist (fibers) into threads. **2.** twist fiber into (threads, yarn, etc.). **3.** form (a web etc.): said of spiders, silkworms, etc. **4.** tell, as a story or yarn. **5.** protract; prolong: with *out.* **6.** cause to whirl rapidly: *spin* a top. —*v.i.* **7.** make thread or yarn. **8.** make a web or thread: said of spiders etc. **9.** whirl rapidly; rotate. **10.** seem to be whirling, as from dizziness. **11.** move rapidly. [ME *spinnen*] —*n.* **1.** an act or instance of spinning; a rapid whirling. **2.** a ride or drive. **3.** *Aeron.* the descent of an airplane in a spiral curve about a vertical axis, with its nose steeply inclined. —**spin′ner** *n.*

spin·ach (SPIN ich) *n.* a plant, the fleshy leaves of which are used as a vegetable. [< MF *espinache*]

spi·nal (SPĪN l) *adj.* of or pertaining to the backbone; vertebral. —*n.* an injection for spinal anesthesia.

spinal column *Anat.* the series of articulated vertebrae that enclose and protect the spinal cord and provide dorsal support for the ribs; backbone.

spinal cord *Anat.* the portion of the central nervous system enclosed by the spinal column.

spin•dle (SPIN dl) *n.* **1.** the slender rod in a spinning wheel, containing a spool or bobbin on which the thread is twisted and wound. **2.** *Mech.* a rotating rod, axis, or shaft. **3.** a needlelike rod used for impaling bills, checks, etc.: also **spindle file.** [ME *spindel*] —*v.t.* **•dled, •dling** impale (bills etc.) on a spindle.

spin•dle-leg•ged (SPIN dl LEG id) *adj.* having long, slender legs.

spin•dle•legs (SPIN dl LEGZ) *n.* (*construed as sing. in def.* 2) **1.** long, slender legs. **2.** *Informal* a person having long, slender legs.

spin•dly (SPIND lee) *adj.* **•dli•er, •dli•est** tall and slender; lanky. —**spin'•dli•ness** *n.*

spine (spīn) *n.* **1.** the spinal column of a vertebrate; backbone. **2.** *Zool.* any of various hard, pointed outgrowths on the bodies of certain animals, as the fin ray of a fish. **3.** *Bot.* a stiff, pointed woody process on the stems of certain plants; thorn. **4.** the back of a bound book. [ME]

spine•less (SPĪN lis) *adj.* **1.** having no backbone; invertebrate. **2.** lacking pointed projections. **3.** lacking courage or will power; cowardly. —**spine'less•ness** *n.*

spin•et (SPIN it) *n.* **1.** a small musical keyboard instrument of the harpsichord class. **2.** a small upright piano. [< F]

spin•na•ker (SPIN ə kər) *n.* *Naut.* a large, bellying sail sometimes carried on the mainmast of a racing vessel opposite the mainsail, used when sailing before the wind.

spin•ner•et (SPIN ə RET) *n.* an organ by which spiders or silkworms produce the filament for webs, cocoons, etc.

spinning jenny a framed mechanism for spinning more than one strand of yarn at a time.

spinning wheel a device used for spinning yarn or thread, consisting of a rotating spindle operated by a treadle and flywheel.

spin-off (SPIN AWF) *n.* a new application or incidental result of an activity or process.

spin•ster (SPIN stər) *n.* **1.** a woman whose occupation is to spin. **2.** a woman unmarried well beyond the usual age of marrying.

—**spin'ster•hood** (-huud) *n.* —**spin'ster•ish** *adj.*

spin•y (SPĪ nee) *adj.* **spin•i•er, spin•i•est 1.** having spines; thorny. **2.** difficult; perplexing. —**spin'i•ness** *n.*

spi•ral (SPĪ rəl) *n.* **1.** *Geom.* any plane curve formed by a point that moves around a fixed center and continually increases or decreases its distance from it. **2.** a curve winding like a screw thread; helix. —*adj.* pertaining to or resembling a spiral; winding. [< Med.L *spiralis*] —*v.* **•raled, •ral•ing** *v.t.* **1.** cause to take a spiral form or course. —*v.i.* **2.** take a spiral form or course. **3.** rise sharply, as prices, costs, etc.

spire[1] (spīr) *n.* **1.** the tapering or pyramidal roof or top of a tower. **2.** any similar high, pointed formation; a pinnacle. **3.** a slender stalk or blade. —*v.i.* **spired, spir•ing** shoot or point up in or as in a spire. [ME]

spire[2] *n.* a spiral or a single turn of one; whorl; twist.

spir•it (SPIR it) *n.* **1.** the vital essence or animating force in living organisms, esp. humans, often considered divine in origin. **2.** the part of a human being characterized by intelligence, personality, self-consciousness, and will; the mind. **3.** *Often cap.* in the Bible, the creative, animating power of God. **4.** a supernatural or immaterial being, as an angel, ghost, specter, etc. **5.** a person: a leading *spirit* in the community. **6.** *Usu. pl.* a state of mind; mood; temper. **7.** vivacity or energy; ardor. **8.** true intent or meaning: the *spirit* of the law. **9.** characteristic temper or disposition: the *spirit* of the Reformation. **10.** *pl.* strong alcoholic liquor. **11.** *Usu. pl. Chem.* the essence or distilled extract of a substance. **12.** *Often pl.* in pharmacy, a solution of a volatile principle in alcohol: *spirits* of ammonia. —*v.t.* carry off secretly: with *away, off,* etc. —*adj.* **1.** of or pertaining to ghosts; spiritualistic. **2.** operated by the burning of alcohol: a *spirit* lamp. [ME]

spir•it•ed (SPIR i tid) *adj.* **1.** full of spirit; animated. **2.** having (a specified kind of) spirit or nature: *high-spirited.* —**spir'it•ed•ly** *adv.* —**spir'it•ed•ness** *n.*

spirit gum a quick-drying solution of a gum in ether.

spir•it•less (SPIR it lis) *adj.* lacking enthusiasm, energy, etc.; listless. —**spir'it•less•ly** *adv.* —**spir'it•less•ness** *n.*

spir•i•tu•al (SPIR i choo əl) *adj.* **1.** of, pertaining to, like, or consisting of spirit, as distinguished from matter; incorporeal. **2.** of or pertaining to God; holy. **3.** sacred or religious; not lay or temporal. —*n.* a spiritual or religious folk song. —**spir′i·tu·al·ly** *adv.* —**spir·i·tu·al·i·ty** (SPIR i choo AL i tee) *n.*

spir·i·tu·al·ism (SPIR i choo ə LIZ əm) *n.* the belief that the spirits of the dead communicate with and manifest their presence to the living. —**spir′i·tu·al·ist** *n.*

spir·i·tu·ous (SPIR i choo əs) *adj.* containing alcohol, as distilled liquors; intoxicating.

spi·ro·chete (SPĪ rə KEET) *n.* any of various bacteria having a corkscrew form, including those that cause syphilis. [< NL *spirochaeta*]

spit[1] (spit) *v.* **spit** or **spat, spit·ting** *v.t.* **1.** eject (saliva etc.) from the mouth. **2.** eject or utter with violence. —*v.i.* **3.** eject saliva etc. from the mouth. **4.** make a hissing or sputtering noise. [ME *spitten*] —*n.* **1.** spittle; saliva. **2.** an act of spitting or expectorating. —**spit and image** exact likeness; counterpart: also **spitting image** and **spit 'n' image.**

spit[2] *n.* **1.** a pointed rod on which meat is roasted. **2.** a point of low land extending into the water. —*v.t.* **spit·ted, spit·ting** impale with or as with a spit. [ME]

spit·ball (SPIT BAWL) *n.* **1.** a ball of chewed paper, for use as a missile. **2.** in baseball, an illegal pitched ball that is moistened with saliva and deviates deceptively in its course.

spite (spīt) *n.* malicious bitterness or hatred; grudge. —**in spite of** notwithstanding. —*v.t.* **spit·ed, spit·ing** treat with spite. [ME]

spite·ful (SPĪT fəl) *adj.* **1.** filled with spite. **2.** prompted by spite. —**spite′ful·ly** *adv.* —**spite′ful·ness** *n.*

spit·fire (SPIT FĪR) *n.* a quick-tempered person.

spit·tle (SPIT l) *n.* the fluid secreted by the mouth; saliva; spit. [ME *spetil*]

splash (splash) *v.t.* **1.** dash or spatter (a liquid etc.) about. **2.** spatter, wet, etc., with a liquid. **3.** make (one's way) with splashes. —*v.i.* **4.** make a splash or splashes. —*n.* **1.** the act or noise of splashing. **2.** a striking impression: make a *splash.*

splash·down (SPLASH DOWN) *n.* the setting down of a spacecraft or a part of it in the seas following its flight.

splash·y (SPLASH ee) *adj.* **splash·i·er, splash·i·est 1.** slushy; wet. **2.** marked by splashes; blotchy. **3.** sensational; showy.

splat·ter (SPLAT ər) *v.t. & v.i.* spatter or splash. —*n.* a spatter; splash.

splay (splay) *adj.* **1.** spread out; broad. **2.** clumsily formed; awkward. —*n.* a slanted surface or beveled edge, as the sides of a doorway. —*v.t. & v.i.* **1.** slant; bevel. **2.** spread out; expand. [ME]

splay·foot (SPLAY FUUT) *n. pl.* **·feet 1.** abnormal flatness and turning outward of the feet. **2.** a foot so deformed. —*adj.* Also **splay′·foot′ed** *adj.*

spleen (spleen) *n. Anat.* **1.** a highly vascular ductless organ located on the upper left side of the abdominal cavity, and effecting certain modifications in the blood. **2.** ill temper; spitefulness. [ME]

splen·did (SPLEN did) *adj.* **1.** magnificent; glorious; illustrious. **2.** brilliant with light; shining. **3.** very good; excellent. [< L *splendidus* brilliant] —**splen′did·ly** *adv.* —**splen′did·ness** *n.*

splen·dif·er·ous (splen DIF ər əs) *adj.* splendid. [ME]

splen·dor (SPLEN dər) *n.* **1.** brilliance from emitted or reflected light. **2.** magnificence; greatness. [ME *splendure*]

sple·net·ic (spli NET ik) *adj.* **1.** pertaining to the spleen. **2.** fretfully spiteful; peevish. Also **sple·net′i·cal.** —*n.* a peevish person.

splice (splīs) *v.t.* **spliced, splic·ing 1.** unite, as by twisting or intertwining the ends of rope, wires, etc. **2.** connect, as timbers, by beveling or overlapping at the ends. **3.** *Informal* join in marriage. —*n.* **1.** a union made by splicing. **2.** the place at which two parts are spliced.

splint (splint) *n.* **1.** a thin, flexible strip of split wood used for basketmaking, chair bottoms, etc. **2.** *Surg.* an appliance, as a strip of wood or metal, used for keeping a fractured limb or other injured part in proper position. —*v.t.* support with a splint. [ME]

splin·ter (SPLIN tər) *n.* a thin, sharp piece of wood, glass, etc. —*v.t. & v.i.* break into splinters; a sliver. —*v.t. & v.i.* break into splinters. [ME] —**splint′er·y** *adj.*

split (split) *v.* **split, split·ting** *v.t.* **1.** separate into parts by force, esp. into two approximately equal parts. **2.** break or divide lengthwise, or along the grain; separate into layers. **3.** disrupt, as a political party; divide. **4.** divide and distribute by portions or shares. **5.** *Slang* leave; quit. —*v.i.* **6.** break apart; become divided; separate. —**split hairs** make unnecessarily fine distinctions.

—**split off** break off by splitting. —**split the difference** divide equally a sum in dispute. —**split up 1.** separate into parts and distribute. **2.** cease association; separate. —*n.* **1.** the act of splitting; also, the result of splitting, as a cleft or rent. **2.** separation into factions; schism. **3.** a share or portion, as of booty. **4.** a confection made of a split banana, ice cream, syrup, etc. **5.** an acrobatic trick in which the legs are extended upon the floor in a straight line at right angles to the body: also **splits.** —*adj.* **1.** cleft, esp. longitudinally; fissured. **2.** divided: a *split* ticket. [< Du. *splitten*]

split infinitive *Gram.* an infinitive in which the sign *to* is separated from the verb, as in "to really believe."

split-level house a dwelling in which the floors of the several levels are less than a story above or below the adjoining one. Also **split'-lev'el.**

split ticket 1. a ballot on which the voter has distributed the vote among candidates of different parties. **2.** a ballot containing names of candidates of more than one party or party faction.

split·ting (SPLIT ing) *adj.* acute or extreme.

splotch (sploch) *n.* a discolored spot, as of ink; a daub; splash; spot. —**splotch** *v.t.* —**splotch'y** *adj.*

splurge (splurj) *n.* an extravagant display or expenditure. —*v.i.* **splurged, splurg·ing** spend money lavishly or wastefully.

splut·ter (SPLUT ər) *v.i.* **1.** make a series of slight, explosive sounds, or throw off small particles, as meat frying. **2.** speak hastily or confusedly. —*v.t.* **3.** utter excitedly or confusedly; sputter. —*n.* a noise as of spluttering. [Blend of SPLASH and SPUTTER] —**splut'ter·er** *n.*

spoil (spoil) *v.* **spoiled** or **spoilt, spoil·ing** *v.t.* **1.** impair or destroy the value, usefulness, or beauty of. **2.** impair the character of, esp. by overindulgence. —*v.i.* **3.** become tainted or decayed, as food. —**be spoiling for** *Informal* be eager for: She was *spoiling* for a fight. —*n. Often pl.* plunder seized by violence; loot. [ME *spoilen* rob] —**spoil'er** *n.*

spoke¹ (spohk) *n.* **1.** one of the rods or bars that serve to support the rim of a wheel by connecting it to the hub. **2.** a stick or bar for insertion in a wheel to prevent its turning. **3.** a rung of a ladder. —*v.t.* **spoked, spok·ing 1.** provide with spokes. **2.** stop with or as with a spoke. [ME]

spoke² past tense of SPEAK.

spo·ken (SPOH kən) past participle of SPEAK. —*adj.* **1.** uttered orally, as opposed to written. **2.** speaking or having (a specified kind of) speech: *smooth-spoken.*

spokes·man (SPOHKS mən) *n. pl.* **·men** one who speaks in the name and behalf of another or others. Also **spokes'per'son** *n.* and **spokes'wom'an** *n.fem.*

spo·li·a·tion (SPOH lee AY shən) *n.* the act of despoiling; esp., the authorized seizure of neutral ships by a belligerent. [ME] —**spo'li·a'tor** *n.*

spon·dee (SPON dee) *n.* a metrical foot consisting of two long syllables or accented syllables. [ME *sponde*] —**spon·da·ic** (spon DAY ik) *adj.*

sponge (spunj) *n.* **1.** any of a varied group of aquatic organisms, characterized by a highly porous body without specialized internal organs and incapable of free movement. **2.** the skeleton or network of elastic fibers of such an organism, used as an absorbent for bathing etc. **3.** any spongelike substance used as an absorbent. **4.** a sponge bath. **5.** one who lives at the expense of another or others; parasite. —**throw in the sponge** *Informal* give up; abandon the struggle. —*v.* **sponged, spong·ing** *v.t.* **1.** wipe, wet, or clean with a sponge. —*v.i.* **2.** live or get something at the expense of others. [ME] —**spong'er** *n.* —**spong'y** *adj.* **·i·er, ·i·est**

sponge bath a bath taken by washing oneself with a cloth or sponge rather than in a bathtub or shower.

sponge cake a cake made with several eggs and containing no shortening.

spon·son (SPON sən) *n.* **1.** a curved projection from the hull of a vessel or seaplane, to give greater stability or increase the surface area. **2.** a similar protuberance on a ship or tank, for storage purposes or for directing a gun.

spon·sor (SPON sər) *n.* **1.** one who assumes responsibility for the debt, duty, etc. of another. **2.** a godparent. **3.** a business enterprise that finances all or part of a broadcast program that advertises its product or service. —*v.t.* act as sponsor for. [< L, guarantor] —**spon'sor·ship** *n.*

spon·ta·ne·ous (spon TAY nee əs) *adj.* **1.** done or resulting from one's own impulse or desire; not premeditated. **2.** arising from inherent qualities; self-generated. [< LL *spontaneus* willingly] —**spon·ta·ne·i·ty**

(SPON tə NEE i tee) n. —spon•ta'ne•ous•ly adv.

spontaneous combustion the burning of a substance through the generation of sufficient internal heat to ignite it.

spoof (spoof) v.t. & v.i. deceive or hoax; joke; parody. —n. deception; parody; hoax. [after a game invented by Arthur Roberts, 1852–1933, British comedian]

spook (spook) n. Informal a ghost; specter. —v.t. haunt. [< Du.] —spook'•i•ly adv. —spook'i•ness n. —spook'y adj. spook•·i•er, spook•i•est

spool (spool) n. 1. a cylinder upon which thread or yarn is wound. 2. the thread or amount of thread held by a spool. 3. anything resembling a spool in shape or purpose. —v.t. wind on a spool. [ME spole]

spoon (spoon) n. 1. a utensil having a shallow bowl and a handle, used in cooking and eating. 2. something resembling a spoon or its bowl. 3. a metallic fishing lure: also spoon bait. 4. a golf club with a wooden head and sloping face. —v.t. 1. lift up or out with a spoon. —v.i. 2. Informal show love, as by caressing or kissing. [ME]

spoon•er•ism (SPOO nə RIZ əm) n. the unintentional transposition of sounds or of parts of words in speaking, as in "half-warmed fish" for "half-formed wish." [after William A. Spooner, 1844–1930, English clergyman known for such transpositions]

spoon-feed (SPOON FEED) v.t. 1. feed with or as with a spoon. 2. pamper. 3. present (ideas etc.) in their easiest, most persuasive form.

spoon•ful (SPOON fuul) n. pl. •fuls as much as a spoon will hold.

spoor (spuur) n. a track or other trace of a wild animal. —v.t. & v.i. track by or follow a spoor. [< Du.]

spo•rad•ic (spə RAD ik) adj. 1. occurring here and there; occasional. 2. separate; isolated. [< Med.L sporadicus scattered] —spo•rad'i•cal•ly adv.

spore (spor) n. Bot. the reproductive body in ferns, fungi, etc., analogous to the seeds of flowering plants, but able to develop asexually into an independent organism or individual. —v.i. spored, spor•ing develop spores: said of plants. [< NL spora seed]

sport (sport) n. 1. that which amuses in general; diversion; pastime. 2. a particular game or play pursued for diversion; esp., an outdoor or athletic game, as baseball,

tennis, etc. 3. a spirit of jesting. 4. mockery; an object of derision; a laughing-stock. 5. Biol. an animal or plant that exhibits sudden and spontaneous variation from the normal type; mutation. 6. Informal one who lives a fast, carefree, or flashy life. 7. a person characterized by his or her manners in games, teasing play, etc.: a good sport. —v.i. 1. amuse oneself; play; jest. —v.t. 2. Informal display or wear ostentatiously; show off. —adj. of, pertaining to, or fitted for sports; also, appropriate for informal wear: also sports. [ME]

sport•ing (SPOR ting) adj. 1. of, engaged in, or connected with sports. 2. fair; conforming to standards of sportsmanship. 3. associated with sports for gambling: a sporting man.

spor•tive (SPOR tiv) adj. playful; frolicsome.

sports car a low automobile, usu. seating two persons, and built for high speed and maneuverability.

sports•cast•er (SPORTS KAST ər) n. one who broadcasts sports news.

sports•man (SPORTS mən) n. pl. •men 1. one who pursues field sports, esp. hunting and fishing. 2. one who abides by a code of fair play in games or in daily practice. —sports'man•like adj. —sports'man•ship n.

sports•wear (SPORTS WAIR) n. clothes made for informal or outdoor activities.

sports•wom•an (SPORTS WUUM ən) n. pl. •wom•en (-WIM in) a woman who participates in sports.

sport•y (SPOR tee) adj. sport•i•er, sport•i•est 1. relating to or characteristic of a sport. 2. flashy, loud, or dissipated. —sport'i•ness n.

spot (spot) n. 1. a particular place of small extent; a definite locality. 2. any small portion of a surface differing, as in color, from the rest; blot. 3. a blemish or fault. 4. Slang a currency note having a specified value: a ten spot. 5. Informal a spotlight. —in a spot in trouble. —hit the spot Informal gratify an appetite or need. —touch a sore spot mention a topic that is painful. —on the spot 1. at once; immediately. 2. at the very place. 3. in danger of death or of being held accountable for some action. —v. spot•ted, spot•ting v.t. 1. mark or soil with spots. 2. decorate with spots; dot. 3. place; locate; station. 4. recognize or detect; see. 5. Sports grant as a handicap in a game. —

v.i. 6. become marked or soiled with spots.
—adj. 1. being on the place or spot. 2.
made at random: a *spot* check. [ME] —
spot′less adj.

spot-check (SPOT CHEK) v.t. inspect at random points. —**spot check** a random sampling.

spot·light (SPOT LIT) n. 1. a circle of powerful light directed at a performer in a theater, night club, etc. 2. the apparatus that produces such a light. 3. notoriety; publicity.

spot·ted (SPOT id) adj. 1. discolored in spots; stained; soiled. 2. characterized or marked by spots.

spot·ter (SPOT ər) n. one who spots or looks out for something, as for enemy aircraft.

spot·ty (SPOT ee) adj. •ti·er, •ti·est 1. having many spots. 2. lacking uniformity. —**spot′·ti·ly** adv. —**spot′ti·ness** n.

spous·al (SPOW zəl) adj. pertaining to marriage. —n. Often pl. the marriage ceremony; nuptials.

spouse (spowz) n. one's husband or wife. [ME]

spout (spowt) v.i. 1. pour out copiously and forcibly, as a liquid under pressure. 2. discharge a fluid either continuously or in jets. 3. *Informal* speak pompously. —v.t. 4. cause to pour or shoot forth. 5. *Informal* utter pompously. [ME *spouten*] —n. 1. a tube, trough, etc. for discharge of a liquid. 2. a continuous stream of fluid. —**spout′er** n.

sprain (sprayn) n. 1. a violent straining or twisting of the ligaments surrounding a joint. 2. the condition due to such strain. —v.t. cause a sprain in.

sprang (sprang) a past tense of SPRING.

sprawl (sprawl) v.i. 1. sit or lie with the limbs stretched out ungracefully. 2. spread out in a straggling manner, as handwriting, vines, etc. —v.t. 3. cause to spread or extend awkwardly or irregularly. [ME *spraulen*] —n. the act or position of sprawling. —**sprawl′er** n.

spray[1] (spray) n. 1. liquid dispersed in fine particles. 2. an instrument for discharging such particles. —v.t. 1. disperse (a liquid) in fine particles. 2. apply spray to. —v.i. 3. send forth spray. 4. go forth as spray. [< MDu. *sprayen*] —**spray′er** n.

spray[2] n. a twig or small branch bearing smaller branches or flowers. [ME]

spread (spred) v. spread, spread•ing v.t. 1. open or unfold to full width or extent, as wings, sails, etc. 2. distribute over a surface;

scatter or smear. 3. cover with a layer of something. 4. force apart or farther apart. 5. extend over a period of time. 6. make more widely known, active, etc. 7. set (a table etc.), as for a meal. —v.i. 8. be extended or expanded. 9. be distributed. 10. become more widely known, active, etc. 11. be forced farther apart. [ME *spreden*] —n. 1. the act of spreading. 2. an open extent or expanse. 3. the limit of expansion of an object. 4. a cloth or covering for a bed, table, etc. 5. *Informal* an informal feast. 6. a food used to spread on bread or crackers. 7. two facing pages of a magazine or newspaper, containing related material. 8. a ranch. —adj. expanded; outstretched.

spread-ea·gle (SPRED EE gəl) adj. resembling the figure of an eagle with extended wings and legs. —v.t. & v.i. -ea·gled, -ea·gling take or cause to take a spread-eagle position.

spree (spree) n. 1. a drinking spell. 2. a gay frolic. 3. excessive indulgence in an activity.

sprig (sprig) n. a shoot or sprout of a tree or plant. [ME *sprigge*]

spright·ly (SPRIT lee) adj. •li·er, •li·est full of animation; lively. —adv. spiritedly; briskly; gaily. —**spright′li·ness** n.

spring (spring) v. **sprang** or **sprung**, **sprung**, **spring·ing** v.i. 1. move or rise suddenly and rapidly; leap; dart. 2. move suddenly as by elastic reaction. 3. move or come as if with a leap. 4. work or snap out of place, as a mechanical part. 5. become warped, bent, loose, etc. 6. rise above surrounding objects. 7. come into being. 8. originate; proceed. 9. develop; grow. —v.t. 10. cause to spring or leap. 11. cause to act, close, open, etc. suddenly, as by elastic reaction: *spring* a trap. 12. cause to happen, become known, or appear suddenly. 13. leap over; vault. 14. cause to warp, sag or split. 15. cause to snap or work out of place. 16. undergo (a leak). 17. *Slang* effect the release or escape of (a person) from prison. [ME *springen*] —n. 1. *Mech.* an elastic body or contrivance, as a coiled steel wire, that yields under stress and returns to its normal form when the stress is removed. 2. elastic quality or energy. 3. the act of flying back from a position of tension. 4. a cause of action. 5. a leap; jump. 6. the season in which vegetation starts anew, occurring between winter and summer. ♦ Collateral adjective: *vernal*. 7. a flow, as of water. 8. any source or origin. —adj. 1. pertaining to the season of spring. **2.** acting like or having a spring.

spring·board (SPRING bord) *n.* **1.** a flexible, resilient board used in leaping, tumbling, or diving. **2.** anything that provides an advantageous start toward a goal.

spring fever the listlessness and restlessness said to overtake many people in spring.

spring·lock (SPRING LOK) *n.* a lock that fastens automatically by a spring.

spring tide the tide occurring at or shortly after the new or full moon, when the rise and fall are greatest.

spring·time (SPRING TĪM) *n.* the season of spring.

sprin·kle (SPRING kəl) *v.* **·kled, ·kling** *v.t.* **1.** scatter in drops or small particles. **2.** scatter on or over. —*v.i.* **3.** fall or rain in scattered drops. [ME *sprenklen*] —*n.* **1.** a falling in drops or particles, or that which so falls; a sprinkling. **2.** a small quantity. — **sprin'kler** *n.*

sprin·kling (SPRING kling) *n.* **1.** that which is sprinkled. **2.** a small number or quantity. **3.** the act of sprinkling.

sprint (sprint) *n.* a short race run at top speed. —*v.i.* run fast, as in a sprint. — **sprint'er** *n.*

sprit (sprit) *n. Naut.* a spar reaching diagonally from a mast to the peak of a sail. [ME *spret*]

sprite (sprīt) *n.* a fairy, elf, or goblin. [ME *sprit*]

spritz (sprits) *Informal n.* a spray or squirt. —*v.t. & v.i.* squirt. [< G *spritzen* squirt]

spritz·er (SPRIT sər) *n.* a drink made of white wine and soda water. [< G *Spritzer*]

sprock·et (SPROK it) *n. Mech.* **1.** a projection, as on the rim of a wheel, for engaging with the links of a chain. **2.** a wheel bearing such projections: also **sprocket wheel.**

sprout (sprowt) *v.i.* **1.** put forth shoots; begin to grow; germinate. **2.** develop or grow rapidly. —*v.t.* **3.** cause to sprout. [ME *sprouten*] —*n.* **1.** a new shoot or bud on a plant. **2.** something like or suggestive of a sprout.

spruce[1] (sproos) *n.* **1.** any of a genus of evergreen trees of the pine family, having a pyramidal crown, needle-shaped leaves, and pendulous cones. **2.** the wood of these trees. [ME]

spruce[2] *adj.* smart and trim; neat. —*v.* **spruced, spruc·ing** *v.t.* **1.** make spruce: often with *up.* —*v.i.* **2.** make oneself

spruce: usu. with *up.* —**spruce'ly** *adv.* — **spruce'ness** *n.*

sprung (sprung) past participle, alternative past tense of SPRING.

spry (sprī) *adj.* **spry·er** or **spri·er, spry·est** or **spri·est** quick and active; agile. —**spry' ly** *adv.* —**spry'ness** *n.*

spud (spud) *n.* **1.** a spadelike tool for removing the roots of weeds. **2.** *Informal* a potato. [ME *spudde* knife] —*v.t.* **spud·ded, spud·ding** remove with a spud.

spume (spyoom) *n.* froth; foam. [ME] — **spume** *v.i.* **spumed, spum·ing**

spu·mo·ne (spə MOH nee) *n.* a dessert of ice cream containing fruit, nuts, etc. Also **spu·mo'ni.** [< Ital.]

spun (spun) past tense, past participle of SPIN.

spunk (spungk) *n.* **1.** punk; tinder. **2.** mettle; pluck.

spunk·y (SPUNG kee) *adj.* **spunk·i·er, spunk·i·est** spirited; courageous. — **spunk'i·ness** *n.*

spur (spur) *n.* **1.** a pricking or goading instrument worn on an equestrian's heel. **2.** anything that incites or urges; incentive. **3.** a part projecting like a spur, as a crag. **4.** a stiff, sharp spine, as on the legs of some insects and birds. **5.** *Bot.* a tubular extension of some part of a flower. **6.** a short side track of a railroad: also **spur track.** —**on the spur of the moment** hastily; impulsively. —*v.* **spurred, spur·ring** *v.t.* **1.** prick or urge with or as with spurs. —*v.i.* **2.** spur one's horse. [ME *spure*] —**spurred** *adj.*

spu·ri·ous (SPYUUR ee əs) *adj.* **1.** not genuine; false. **2.** illegitimate. [< LL *spurius* false] —**spu'ri·ous·ly** *adv.* —**spu'ri·ous· ness** *n.*

spurn (spurn) *v.t.* **1.** reject with disdain; scorn. **2.** kick. [ME *spurnen*] —*n.* the act of spurning. —**spurn'er** *n.*

spurt (spurt) *n.* **1.** a sudden gush of liquid. **2.** any sudden outbreak, effort, etc., usu. of brief duration. —*v.i.* **1.** come out in a jet; gush forth. **2.** make a sudden effort. —*v.t.* **3.** force out in a jet; squirt.

sput·nik (SPUUT nik) *n.* any of a series of Soviet artificial earth satellites. [< Russ. *spútnik* travel companion]

sput·ter (SPUT ər) *v.i.* **1.** throw off solid or fluid particles in a series of slight explosions. **2.** emit particles of saliva from the mouth, as when speaking excitedly. **3.** speak rapidly or confusedly. —*v.t.* **4.** emit in small particles. **5.** utter in a confused or excited manner. —*n.* the act or sound of sputtering; esp., excited talk. —**sput′ter•er** *n.*

spu•tum (SPYOO təm) *n. pl.* **•ta** (-tə) expectorated matter; mucus and saliva. [< L, spit]

spy (spī) *n. pl.* **spies 1.** one who covertly gathers information, esp. about a military enemy. **2.** one who watches others secretly. —*v.* **spied, spy•ing** *v.i.* **1.** act as a spy. —*v.t.* **2.** observe stealthily and with hostile intent: usu. with *out.* **3.** catch sight of; see. [ME *spien*]

spy•glass (SPĪ GLAS) *n.* a small telescope.

squab (skwob) *n.* a young pigeon, esp. when an unfledged nestling.

squab•ble (SKWOB əl) *v.i.* **•bled, •bling** engage in a petty wrangle or scuffle; quarrel. —*n.* a petty wrangle. —**squab′bler** *n.*

squad (skwod) *n.* **1.** a small group of persons organized for the performance of a specific function. **2.** a small detachment of troops or police; esp., the smallest tactical unit in the infantry of the U.S. Army. **3.** a team. [< MF *esquade*]

squad•ron (SKWOD rən) *n.* **1.** *Mil.* a unit of aircraft, naval vessels, or cavalry. **2.** any regularly arranged or organized body. [< Ital. *squadrone*]

squal•id (SKWOL id) *adj.* dirty and wretched. [< L *squalidus*] —**squal′id•ly** *adv.* —**squal′id•ness** *n.*

squall[1] (skwawl) *n.* a loud screaming. —*v.i.* cry loudly; scream. —**squall′er** *n.*

squall[2] *n.* **1.** a sudden, violent burst of wind, often accompanied by rain or snow. **2.** a commotion. —*v.i.* blow a squall. —**squall′ly** *adj.* **squall•li•er, squall•li•est**

squal•or (SKWOL ər) *n.* the state of being squalid; filth and wretched poverty. [< L]

squan•der (SKWON dər) *v.t.* spend (money, time, etc.) wastefully. —*n.* wasteful expenditure. —**squan′der•er** *n.*

square (skwair) *n.* **1.** a parallelogram having four equal sides and four right angles. **2.** any object, part, or surface that has this form, or nearly so. **3.** an instrument having an L- or T-shape by which to measure or lay out right angles. **4.** an open area in a city or town formed by the intersection of several streets, often planted with trees, flowers, etc. **5.** *Math.* the product of a number multiplied by itself. **6.** *Slang* one not conversant with the latest trends or fads. —**on the square 1.** at right angles. **2.** *Informal* in a fair and honest manner. —**out of square**

1. not at right angles. **2.** incorrectly; askew. —*adj.* **squar•er, squar•est 1.** having four equal sides and four right angles; also, resembling a square in form. **2.** formed with or characterized by a right angle. **3.** adapted to forming squares or computing in squares. **4.** direct; fair; honest. **5.** having debit and credit balanced. **6.** absolute; complete. **7.** stocky; sturdy. —**square meal** a satisfying meal. —**square peg in a round hole** a misfit. —*v.* **squared, squar•ing** *v.t.* **1.** make or form like a square. **2.** shape or adjust so as to form a right angle. **3.** test for the purpose of adjusting to a straight line, right angle, or plane surface. **4.** make satisfactory settlement or adjustment of: *square* accounts. **5.** cause to conform; adapt; reconcile. **6.** *Math.* **a** multiply (a number) by itself. **b** determine the area of. —*v.i.* **7.** be at right angles. **8.** conform; agree; harmonize. —**square off** prepare to fight or argue. —*adv.* **squar•er, squar•est 1.** so as to be square, or at right angles. **2.** honestly; fairly. **3.** directly; firmly. [ME] —**square′ness** *n.*

square dance any dance in which the couples form sets in squares.

square-dance (SKWAIR DANS) *v.i.* **-danced, -danc•ing** perform a square dance. —**square′-danc′er** *n.* —**square′-danc′ing** *n.*

square knot a common knot, formed of two overhand knots.

square•ly (SKWAIR lee) *adv.* **1.** in a direct manner. **2.** honestly; fairly. **3.** plainly; unequivocally. **4.** at right angles (to a line or plane).

square measure a unit or system of units for measuring areas.

square-rigged (SKWAIR RIGD) *adj. Naut.* fitted with square sails as the principal sails. —**square′-rig′ger** *n.*

square root *Math.* a number that, multiplied by itself, produces the given number: 4 is the *square root* of 16.

squash[1] (skwosh) *v.t.* **1.** beat or press into a pulp or soft mass; crush. **2.** quell or suppress. —*v.i.* **3.** be smashed or squashed. —*n.* **1.** a soft or overripe object; also, something squashed. **2.** the act of squashing; also, the sound made by squashing. **3.** either of two games played on an indoor court with rackets and a ball. **4.** a beverage of which one ingredient is a fruit juice. [< MF *esquasser* crush] —*adv.* with a squelching, oozy sound.

stabilize

squash² n. **1.** the edible fruit of various trailing annuals of the gourd family. **2.** the plant that bears it. [< Algonquian]

squat (skwot) v. **squat·ted** or **squat, squat·ting** v.i. **1.** sit in a crouching position with the legs drawn up to the body. **2.** crouch down or cower. **3.** settle on a piece of land without title or payment. **4.** settle on government land in accordance with regulations that will eventually give title. —v.t. **5.** cause (oneself) to squat. [ME *squatten* compress] —*adj.* short and thick; squatty. —*n.* **1.** a squatting position. **2.** the act of squatting. —**squat'ter** n.

squat·ty (SKWOT ee) adj. **·ti·er, ·ti·est** disproportionately short and thick.

squaw (skwaw) n. **1.** *Offensive* a Native American woman or wife. **2.** *Slang* a wife. [< Algonquian, woman]

squawk (skwawk) v.i. **1.** utter a shrill, harsh cry, as a parrot. **2.** *Informal* utter loud complaints. —*n.* **1.** the harsh cry of certain birds; also, the act of squawking. **2.** *Informal* a vehement complaint. —**squawk'er** n.

squeak (skweek) n. **1.** a thin, sharp, penetrating sound. **2.** a narrow escape. —*v.t. & v.i.* **1.** utter with or make a squeak. **2.** *squeak by* barely survive; win by a narrow margin. [ME *squeken*] —**squeak'er** n. —**squeak'i·ly** adv. —**squeak'i·ness** n. —**squeak'y** adj. **squeak·i·er, squeak·i·est**

squeal (skweel) v.i. **1.** utter a sharp, shrill, somewhat prolonged cry. **2.** *Slang* turn informer. —*v.t.* **3.** utter with a squeal. [ME *squelen*] —**squeal** n. —**squeal'er** n.

squeam·ish (SKWEE mish) adj. **1.** easily disgusted or shocked; prudish. **2.** easily nauseated. [ME *squemish*] —**squeam'ish·ly** adv. —**squeam'·ish·ness** n.

squeeze (skweez) v. **squeezed, squeez·ing** v.t. **1.** press hard upon; compress. **2.** draw forth by pressure; express: *squeeze juice.* **3.** force or push; cram. **4.** pressure or oppress. **5.** apply pressure. **6.** force one's way; push: with *in, through,* etc. **7.** be pressed; yield to pressure. —*n.* **1.** the act or process of squeezing; pressure. **2.** a firm grasp; also, an embrace; hug. **3.** something, as juice, extracted or expressed. **4.** any pressure exerted for the extortion of money or favors; also, financial pressure.

squelch (skwelch) v.t. **1.** crush; squash. **2.** silence, as with a crushing reply. —*v.i.* **3.** make a splashing or sucking noise, as when walking in deep mud. —*n.* **1.** a

squelching sound. **2.** a crushing reply. —**squelch'er** n.

squib (skwib) n. **1.** a firework to be thrown or rolled swiftly, finally exploding like a rocket. **2.** a short speech or writing in a satirical vein. —*v.* **squibbed, squib·bing** v.i. **1.** write or use squibs; lampoon. —*v.t.* **2.** attack with squibs; lampoon.

squid (skwid) n. any of various ten-armed mollusks having a slender, conical body.

squig·gle (SKWIG əl) n. a meaningless scrawl. —*v.i.* **·gled, ·gling** wriggle. [Blend of SQUIRM and WRIGGLE]

squig·gly (SKWIG lee) adj. **·gli·er, ·gli·est** twisty; crooked.

squint (skwint) v.i. **1.** look with half closed eyes, as into bright light. **2.** look with a side glance. **3.** be cross-eyed. —*v.t.* **4.** hold (the eyes) half shut. —*adj.* **1.** cross-eyed. **2.** looking obliquely or askance; indirect. —*n.* **1.** *Pathol.* strabismus. **2.** the act or habit of squinting. [ME] —**squint'er** n.

squire (skwīr) n. **1.** a title often used in rural areas for justices of the peace, judges, etc. **2.** a young aspirant to knighthood serving as an attendant. **3.** a man who escorts a woman in public. **4.** in England, a landed proprietor or country gentleman. [ME *squier*] —*v.t. & v.i.* **squired, squir·ing** attend or serve (someone) as a squire or escort.

squirm (skwurm) v.i. **1.** bend and twist the body; wriggle; writhe. **2.** show signs of pain or distress. —*n.* a squirming motion; a wriggle. —**squirm'er** n. —**squirm'y** adj. **squirm·i·er, squirm·i·est**

squir·rel (SKWUR əl) n. **1.** any of various rodents having a long bushy tail and feeding chiefly on nuts. **2.** the fur of a squirrel. [ME *squirel*]

squirt (skwurt) v.i. **1.** come forth in a thin stream or jet; spurt. **2.** eject water etc., thus. —*v.t.* **3.** eject (a liquid) forcibly and in a jet. **4.** wet with a squirt or squirts. [ME *squirten*] —*n.* **1.** the act of squirting; also, a jet of liquid squirted forth. **2.** *Informal* a small, impudent person.

stab (stab) v. **stabbed, stab·bing** v.t. **1.** pierce with or as with a pointed weapon; wound. **2.** penetrate; pierce. —*v.i.* **3.** thrust or lunge with a knife, sword, etc. **4.** inflict a wound thus. [ME *stabben*] —*n.* a thrust made with any pointed weapon. —**have (or make) a stab at** make an attempt at. —**stab'ber** n.

sta·bi·lize (STAY bə LIZ) v.t. **·lized, ·liz·ing** make firm or stable; keep steady. —**sta′bi•li•za′tion** n. —**sta′bi•liz′er** (-LĪZ ər) n.

sta•ble[1] (STAY bəl) adj. **1.** standing firmly in place; not easily moved, shaken, or overthrown; fixed. **2.** steadfast. **3.** durable or permanent; abiding. **4.** Chem. not easily decomposed: said of compounds. [ME] — **sta•bil•i•ty** (stə BIL i tee) n. —**sta′bly** adv.

sta•ble[2] n. **1.** a building set apart for horses or cattle; also, the animals. **2.** the racehorses belonging to a particular owner; also, the owner and personnel collectively. —v.t. & v.i. •**bled,** •**bling** put or lodge in a stable. [ME]

stac•ca•to (stə KAH toh) adj. **1.** Music having short breaks between notes. **2.** marked by abrupt, sharp emphasis. —n. pl. •**tos 1.** Music a staccato style or passage. **2.** an abrupt, emphatic manner or sound. [< Ital.] —**stac•ca′to** adv.

stack (stak) n. **1.** an orderly pile of unthreshed grain, hay, or straw. **2.** any systematic pile or heap. **3.** a case composed of several rows of bookshelves one above another. **4.** pl. that part of a library where most of the books are shelved. **5.** a chimney; smokestack. **6.** Informal a great amount; plenty. [ME stak] —v.t. pile up in a stack. —**stack the deck 1.** arrange cards secretly in the pack in a manner favorable to the dealer. **2.** have an advantage secured beforehand. —**stack′er** n.

sta•di•um (STAY dee əm) n. pl. •**di•ums,** •**di•a** (-dee ə) **1.** in ancient Greece, a course for foot races, with banked seats for spectators. **2.** a similar modern structure in which athletic games are played. [ME]

staff (staf) n. pl. **staffs;** for defs. 1, 2, 3, & 6, also **staves** (stayvz) **1.** a stick of wood carried for some special purpose. **2.** a shaft or pole that forms a support or handle. **3.** a stick used in measuring or testing. **4.** Mil. a body of officers not having command but assigned in an executive or advisory capacity. **5.** a body of persons associated in carrying out some special enterprise. **6.** Music the five horizontal lines and four spaces used in writing music: also called stave. [ME staf] —v.t. provide (an office etc.) with a staff.

staff officer 1. an officer on the staff of a military commander. **2.** in the U.S. Navy, an officer without command or operational functions, as a doctor, dentist, chaplain, etc.

stag (stag) n. **1.** the male of the deer. **2.** the male of some other large animals. **3.** a man who attends a social function unaccompanied by a woman. [ME stagge] —adj. of or for men only. —v.i. **stagged, stag•ging** Informal attend a social affair unaccompanied by a woman.

stage (stayj) n. **1.** a raised platform on which the performance in a theater, hall, etc., takes place. **2.** the theater: write for the stage. **3.** the field of action of some event: set the stage for war. **4.** a definite portion of a journey. **5.** a step in some development, progress, or process. **6.** Aerospace one of the separate propulsion units of a rocket vehicle. **7.** a stagecoach; also, a stop on the route of a stagecoach. —**by easy stages** traveling or working without hurry and with frequent stops. —v.t. **staged, stag•ing 1.** put or exhibit on the stage. **2.** conduct; carry on. [ME]

stage•coach (STAYJ KOHCH) n. a large, horse-drawn, four-wheeled vehicle having a regular route from town to town.

stage•craft (STAYJ KRAFT) n. skill in writing or staging plays.

stage door a door to a theater used by actors etc. that leads behind the scenes.

stage fright a sudden panic that sometimes attacks those appearing before an audience.

stage•hand (STAYJ HAND) n. a person in a theater who handles scenery, props, etc.

stage•struck (STAYJ STRUK) adj. enamored of theatrical life.

stage whisper any loud whisper intended to be overheard.

stag•fla•tion (stag FLAY shən) n. an economic condition in which inflation is combined with slow buying and high unemployment. [< stagnation + inflation]

stag•ger (STAG ər) v.i. **1.** walk or run unsteadily; reel. **2.** waver; hesitate. —v.t. **3.** cause to stagger. **4.** affect strongly; overwhelm, as with grief. **5.** alternate or vary, esp. to prevent congestion, inconvenience, etc.: stagger lunch hours. [ME stakeren] — n. the act of staggering, or the condition of being staggered.

stag•ing (STAY jing) n. **1.** a scaffolding or temporary platform. **2.** the process of putting a play on the stage.

stag•nant (STAG nənt) adj. **1.** standing still; not flowing: said of water or air. **2.** foul from standing, as water. **3.** dull; sluggish. — **stag′nan•cy** n. —**stag′nant•ly** adv.

stag•nate (STAG nayt) v.i. •**nat•ed,**

stamp

•nat•ing be or become stagnant. [< L *stag-
natus* fouled] —**stag′na′tion** n.

stag•y (STAY jee) adj. **stag•i•er, stag•i•est**
theatrical; artificial. —**stag′i•ness** n.

staid (stayd) adj. steady and sober. —**staid′
ly** adv. —**staid′ness** n.

stain (stayn) n. 1. a spot; smirch; blot. 2. a
dye or thin pigment used in staining. 3. a
moral taint. —v.t. 1. make a stain upon;
discolor; soil; tarnish. 2. color by the use of a
dye or stain. —v.i. 3. take or impart a stain.
[ME *steynen* paint] —**stain′less** adj. —
stain′less•ly adv.

stained glass colored glass used in church
windows etc. —**stained′-glass′** adj.

stainless steel a steel alloy made resistant to
corrosion, rust, and staining by the addition
of certain ingredients.

stair (stair) n. 1. a step, or one of a series of
steps, for mounting or descending from one
level to another. 2. Usu. pl. a flight of steps.
[ME *steir*]

stair•case (STAIR kays) n. a flight or series
of flights of stairs. Also **stair•way.**

stake (stayk) n. 1. a stick or post sharpened at
one end for driving into the ground, used as
a marker, for a fence, etc. 2. a post to which
a person is bound, to be executed by burning; also, execution in this manner. 3. something wagered or risked. 4. *Often pl.* a prize
in a contest. 5. an interest in an enterprise.
6. a grubstake. —**at stake** in hazard or
jeopardy; in question. —**pull up stakes**
move from a place. —v.t. **staked, stak•ing**
1. fasten or support by means of a stake. 2.
mark the boundaries of with stakes: often
with *off* or *out.* 3. wager; risk. 4. finance.

sta•lac•tite (stə LAK tīt) n. a tapering formation hanging from the roof of a cavern, produced by the dripping of water containing
certain minerals. [< NL *stalactites* drip-
pings] —**stal•ac•tit•ic** (STAL ək TIT ik) adj.

sta•lag•mite (stə LAG mīt) n. an incrustation, usu. cylindrical or conical, formed on
the floor of a cavern by dripping from
above. [< NL *stalagmites* drops] —
stal•ag•mit•ic (STAL əg MIT ik) adj.

stale (stayl) adj. **stal•er, stal•est** 1. having
lost freshness; slightly changed or deteriorated, as beer, bread, etc. 2. dull, as from
overused; trite. 3. sluggish; uninspired, as
after a period of overactivity. —v.i. **staled,
stal•ing** become stale or trite. [ME] —
stale′ness n.

stale•mate (STAYL mayt) n. 1. in chess, a
draw resulting when a player can move only

the king and thus place it in check. 2. any
deadlock. —v.t. v.i. •**mat•ed, •mat•ing**
cause or be in a condition of stalemate. [ME
stale stalemate]

stalk¹ (stawk) n. 1. the stem or axis of a plant.
2. any supporting or connecting part resembling a stem. [ME *stalon*]

stalk² v.i. 1. approach game etc. stealthily. 2.
walk in a stiff, dignified manner. —v.t. 3.
approach (game etc.) stealthily. —n. 1. the
act of stalking game. 2. a stately step or
walk. [ME *stalken* move stealthily] —
stalk′er n.

stalk•ing-horse (STAW king HORS) n. in
politics, a candidate put forth to divide the
opposition or to hide another candidacy.

stall (stawl) n. 1. a compartment in which a
horse, cow, etc. is confined and fed. 2. a
small sales booth in a street, market, etc. 3.
a pew. 4. a stop or standstill, esp. one resulting from a fault in the working of an
engine. 5. an evasion. —v.t. 1. place or
keep in a stall. 2. bring to a standstill; stop,
esp. unintentionally. —v.i. 3. come to a
standstill; stop. 4. make delays; be evasive.
[ME]

stal•lion (STAL yən) n. an uncastrated male
horse. [ME *stalon*]

stal•wart (STAWL wərt) adj. 1. strong; robust. 2. resolute; determined. 3. brave;
courageous. —n. a stalwart person. [ME]
—**stal′wart•ly** adv. —**stal′wart•ness** n.

sta•men (STAY mən) n. pl. **sta•mens,
stam•i•na** (STAM ə nə) *Bot.* the pollen-
bearing organ of a flower. [< L, thread]

stam•i•na (STAM ə nə) n. 1. capacity to
withstand hardship; vitality. 2. see STAMEN.
[< L, pl. of *stamen*]

stam•i•nate (STAM ə nit) adj. *Bot.* 1. having
stamens. 2. having stamens but no pistils.

stam•mer (STAM ər) v.t. & v.i. speak haltingly, with involuntary repetitions or pro-
longations of a sound or syllable. —n. the
act or condition of stammering. [ME *stam-
meren*] —**stam′mer•er** n.

stamp (stamp) v.t. 1. strike heavily with the
sole of the foot. 2. bring down (the foot)
heavily and noisily. 3. strike or crush, as
with the foot. 4. mark by means of a die,
stamp, etc. 5. imprint or impress with a die,
stamp, etc. 6. fix or imprint permanently. 7.
affix an official seal, stamp, etc. to. —v.i. 8.
strike the foot heavily on the ground. 9.
walk with heavy, resounding steps. —n. 1. a
die or block having a pattern or design for
impressing upon a surface. 2. the impres-

sion so made. **3.** any characteristic mark, as a label or imprint; a brand. **4.** a printed device prepared and sold by a government, for attachment to a letter, commodity, etc. as proof that the tax or fee has been paid. [ME *stampen* pound]

stam•pede (stam PEED) *n.* **1.** a sudden starting and rushing off through panic, as of a herd of cattle, horses, etc. **2.** any sudden, tumultuous running movement of a crowd or mob. [< Am.Sp. *estampida*] —*v.t. & v.i.* **•ped•ed, •ped•ing** rush or cause to rush in a stampede. —**stam•ped′er** *n.*

stamp•ing ground a favorite or habitual gathering place.

stance (stans) *n.* a mode of standing; posture. [< OF *estance* standing position]

stanch (stawnch) *v.t.* stop or check the flow of (blood etc.). Also spelled *staunch.* [ME *stanchen* stop] —*adj.* **•er, •est** staunch. —**stanch′ly** *adv.* —**stanch′ness** *n.*

stan•chion (STAN shən) *n.* an upright bar forming a support or barrier. [ME *stanchon*] —*v.t.* provide or confine with stanchions.

stand (stand) *v.* **stood, stand•ing** *v.i.* **1.** assume or maintain an erect position on one's feet. **2.** be in a vertical position; be erect. **3.** measure a specified height when standing. **4.** assume a specified position: *stand* aside. **5.** assume or have a definite opinion, position, or attitude. **6.** be situated; have position or location; lie. **7.** remain unchanged or valid. **8.** have or be in a specified state, condition, or relation: He *stood* in fear of his life. **9.** be of a specified rank or class: She *stands* third. **10.** be or remain firm or resolute. **11.** collect and remain; also, be stagnant, as water. **12.** stop or pause; halt. **13.** be a candidate for election. —*v.t.* **14.** place upright; set in an erect position. **15.** put up with; endure. **16.** be subjected to; undergo: He must *stand* trial. **17.** pay for: *stand* a treat. —**stand a chance** have a chance, as of success. —**stand by 1.** be ready to help or act. **2.** help; support. **3.** abide by; make good. **4.** remain passive and watch, as when help is needed. —**stand clear** remain at a safe distance. —**stand for 1.** represent; symbolize. **2.** put up with; tolerate. —**stand in for** act as a substitute for. —**stand on 1.** be based on; rest. **2.** insist on or demand observance of: *stand* on ceremony. —**stand on one's own (two) feet** manage one's own affairs. —**stand out 1.** project or protrude. **2.** be prominent; appear in relief

or contrast. —**stand pat 1.** in poker, play one's hand as dealt, without drawing new cards. **2.** hold firm to one's decision or or beliefs. —**stand to reason** conform to reason. —**stand up 1.** withstand wear, criticism, analysis, etc. **2.** *Slang* fail to keep an appointment with. —**stand up for** side with; take the part of. —**stand up to** confront courageously; face. [ME *standen*] — *n.* **1.** the act of standing, esp. of standing firmly: make a *stand* against the enemy. **2.** an opinion, attitude, or position, as in a controversy. **3.** a structure or platform upon which persons or things may sit or stand, or on which articles may be kept or displayed. **4.** a rack or other piece of furniture on which hats, canes, etc. may be hung or placed. **5.** in the theater, a performance or performances made while on tour: a onenight *stand*. **6.** the growing trees in a forest. —**take a stand** have or reveal an opinion or attitude, as on a controversial issue.

stand•ard (STAN dərd) *n.* **1.** a flag or banner, used as an emblem of a government, military unit, etc. **2.** any established measure of extent, quantity, quality, or value. **3.** any model for comparison; a criterion of excellence: a *standard* of conduct. **4.** an upright post, esp. as a support. —*adj.* **1.** serving as a gauge or model. **2.** of recognized excellence or authority: a *standard* book. **3.** *Ling.* designating or belonging to those usages of a language that have gained literary, cultural, and social acceptance: *Standard* English. [ME]

stan•dard-bear•er (STAN dərd BAIR ər) *n.* **1.** the member of a military unit who carries the flag. **2.** a leader; a candidate for a leading position, as for a presidency.

Stan•dard•bred (STAN dərd BRED) *n.* a breed of horse notable for its trotters and pacers. —**standard-bred** *adj.* bred so as to be of a required strain, quality, or pedigree, as poultry, horses, etc.

Standard English *Ling.* the usages in English that have gained literary, cultural, and social acceptance.

stand•ard•ize (STAN dər DĪZ) *v.t.* **•ized, •iz•ing** make to or regulate by a standard. —**stan′dard•i•za′tion** *n.*

standard of living the average quantity and quality of goods and services that a person or group uses in daily living.

standard time time as reckoned from a meridian officially established as standard over a large area.

stand·by (STAND BĪ) n. pl. **·bys** a person or thing on call for emergencies.

stand·ee (stan DEE) n. a person who must stand for lack of chairs or seats.

stand-in (STAND IN) n. **1.** a person who takes the place of an actor, as while lights are adjusted. **2.** a substitute or replacement.

stand·ing (STAN ding) adj. **1.** remaining erect. **2.** established; permanent: a *standing* army. **3.** stagnant; not flowing. **4.** begun while standing: a *standing* high jump. —n. **1.** high rank or reputation. **2.** time in which something goes on; duration. **3.** the act of one who stands.

stand·off (STAND AWF) n. a draw or tie, as in a game.

stand·off·ish (STAND AW fish) adj. aloof; coolly reserved. —**stand'off'ish·ness** n.

stand·pat (STAND PAT) adj. opposed to change; conservative. —**stand'pat, stand'pat'ter** n.

stand·point (STAND POINT) n. a position from which things are judged; point of view.

stand·still (STAND STIL) n. a cessation; halt.

stand-up (STAND UP) adj. **1.** having an erect position: a *standup* collar. **2.** done, consumed, etc. while standing.

stank (stangk) a past tense of STINK.

stan·za (STAN zə) n. a number of lines of verse that make up a metrical division of a poem. [< Ital. *station*]

sta·pes (STAY peez) n. pl. **sta·pes** or **sta·pe·des** (stə PEE deez) *Anat.* the innermost bone of the middle ear of mammals: also called *stirrup*. [< NL, stirrup]

staph (staf) n. *Informal* staphylococcus; also, an infection caused by staphylococci.

staph·y·lo·coc·cus (STAF ə lə KOK əs) n. pl. **·coc·ci** (-KOK sī) any of a genus of bacteria, often occurring in clusters; esp., an infective agent in boils and suppurating wounds. [< NL] —**staph·y·lo·coc·cic** (STAF ə lə KOK sik) adj.

sta·ple[1] (STAY pəl) n. **1.** *Usu. pl.* a basic food or other ordinary item of household use. **2.** a principal commodity of a country or region. **3.** a main constituent of something. **4.** the carded or combed fiber of cotton, wool, or flax. **5.** raw material. —adj. **1.** regularly and continually produced, used, or sold. **2.** main; chief. —v.t. **·pled, ·pling** sort or classify according to length, as wool fiber. [ME]

sta·ple[2] n. **1.** a U-shaped piece of metal with

pointed ends, driven into a surface to secure a bolt, hook, hasp, etc. **2.** a thin piece of wire usu. shaped like a bracket ([), driven into paper, fabrics, etc., to serve as a fastening. [ME *stapel* post] —**sta'ple** v.t. **·pled, ·pling** —**sta'pler** n.

star (stahr) n. **1.** any of the heavenly bodies visible from earth as apparently fixed points of light. **2.** *Astron.* one of a class of self-luminous celestial bodies, exclusive of comets, meteors, and nebulae, but including the sun. ◆ Collateral adjectives: *astral, stellar.* **3.** a conventional figure usu. having five or more radiating points, used as an emblem or device, as to indicate the rank of general. **4.** an actor or actress who plays the leading part. **5.** anyone who shines prominently in a calling or profession. **6.** an asterisk. **7.** *Often pl.* fortune; destiny. —**see stars** see bright spots before the eyes, as from a sharp jolt to the head. [ME *sterre*] —v. **starred, star·ring** v.t. **1.** set or adorn with spangles or stars. **2.** mark with an asterisk. **3.** present as a star in a play or motion picture. —v.i. **4.** play the leading part; be the star. —adj. **1.** of or pertaining to a star or stars. **2.** prominent; brilliant. —**star' less** adj. —**star'like'** adj.

star·board (STAHR bərd) *Naut.* n. the right-hand side of a vessel as one faces the front or bow: opposed to *port.* [ME *sterbord* steering side] —**star·board** adj.

starch (stahrch) n. **1.** *Biochem.* a white, odorless, tasteless, granular carbohydrate found in most plants. **2.** a preparation of this substance, used esp. for stiffening fabric. **3.** stiffness or formality. **4.** *Informal* energy; vigor. —v.t. apply starch to; stiffen with or as with starch. [ME *sterchen*]

starch·y (STAHR chee) adj. **starch·i·er, starch·i·est 1.** stiffened with starch; stiff. Also **starched. 2.** prim; formal; precise. **3.** formed of or combined with starch. —**starch'i·ly** adv. —**starch'i·ness** n.

star·dom (STAHR dəm) n. the status of a star (noun defs. 4 & 5).

stare (stair) v. **stared, star·ing** v.i. **1.** gaze fixedly. **2.** be conspicuously or unduly apparent; glare. —v.t. **3.** stare at. [ME *staren*] —n. the act of staring; an intense gaze.

star·fish (STAHR FISH) n. pl. **·fish** or **·fish·es** any of various radially symmetrical marine animals, commonly with a star-shaped body having five or more arms.

star·gaze (STAHR GAYZ) v.i. **·gazed, ·gaz·ing 1.** gaze at or study the stars. **2.**

daydream. —**star′gaz′er** n. —**star′gaz•ing** n. & adj.

stark (stahrk) adj. **1.** bare; plain. **2.** complete; utter: stark misery. **3.** stiff or rigid, as in death. **4.** strict or grim. —adv. **1.** in a stark manner. **2.** completely; utterly: stark mad. [ME, stiff] —**stark′ly** adv.

star•let (STAHR lit) n. a young movie or television actress represented as a future star.

star•light (STAHR LIT) n. the light given by stars. —**star′lit** (-lit) adj.

starred (stahrd) adj. **1.** spangled with stars. **2.** presented or advertised as the star of a play, motion picture, etc. **3.** marked with an asterisk. **4.** affected by astral influence: chiefly in combination: ill-starred.

star•ry (STAHR ee) adj. •ri•er, •ri•est **1.** abounding in stars. **2.** lighted by the stars. **3.** shining as or like the stars. **4.** of or pertaining to the stars. —**star′ri•ness** n.

star•ry-eyed (STAHR ee ID) adj. given to fanciful wishes or yearnings.

start (stahrt) v.i. **1.** make a beginning or start; set out. **2.** begin; commence. **3.** make an involuntary, startled movement, as from fear or surprise. **4.** move suddenly, as with a leap; jump. **5.** seem to bulge or protrude. —v.t. **6.** set in motion or circulation: start an engine. **7.** begin; commence. **8.** set up; establish. **9.** rouse from cover; flush, as game. —**start in** begin; undertake. —**start off** begin a journey; set out. —**start out** make a beginning or start. —**start up 1.** rise or appear suddenly. **2.** begin or cause to begin operation, as an engine. [ME sterten leap] —n. **1.** a setting out or going forth; beginning; also, the place where one begins. **2.** a quick, startled movement. **3.** an advantage or distance in advance at the outset; lead.

start•er (STAHR tər) n. **1.** one who or that which starts. **2.** a mechanism for starting an internal combustion engine without manual cranking.

star•tle (STAHR tl) v. •tled, •tling v.t. **1.** arouse or excite suddenly; cause to start involuntarily; alarm. —v.i. **2.** be thus aroused. [ME stertlen rush]

star•tling (STAHR tling) adj. rousing sudden surprise, alarm, etc. —**star′tling•ly** adv.

starve (stahrv) v. starved, starv•ing v.i. **1.** perish from lack of food. **2.** suffer from extreme hunger. **3.** suffer from lack or need: starve for friendship. —v.t. **4.** cause to suffer from or die of hunger; deprive of food. [ME sterven die] —**star•va′tion** n.

starve•ling (STAHRV ling) n. a person, animal, or plant that is starving, starved, or emaciated. —adj. starving; emaciated.

stash (stash) v.t. hide or conceal (money, valuables, etc.) for storage and safekeeping. —n. a concealed supply or store; cache. [Blend of STOW + CACHE]

sta•sis (STAY sis) n. pl. •ses (STAY seez) **1.** Pathol. stoppage in the circulation of any of the body fluids or retarded movement of the intestinal contents. **2.** retarded movement; stagnation. [< Gk. stásis standing]

-stat combining form a element that stops or makes constant: thermostat, rheostat. [< Gk. -statēs causing to stand]

state (stayt) n. **1.** the mode of existence as determined by circumstances; condition; situation. **2.** a frame of mind; mood. **3.** a mode or style of living; station. **4.** ceremonious style; pomp; formality. **5.** a sovereign political community organized under a distinct government having jurisdiction over a given territory; a nation. **6.** Sometimes cap. one of a number of political communities united to form one sovereign state; esp., one of the United States. **7.** the territorial, political, and governmental entity constituting a state or nation; authority of government. —**lie in state** be placed on public view, with ceremony, before burial. [ME stat] —adj. **1.** of or pertaining to the state, nation, or government. **2.** intended for use on occasions of ceremony. —v.t. **stat•ed, stat•ing 1.** set forth explicitly in speech or writing; assert; declare. **2.** fix; determine; settle.

state•craft (STAYT KRAFT) n. the art or practice of conducting affairs of state.

stat•ed (STAY tid) adj. **1.** announced; specified. **2.** established; regular; fixed.

state•hood (STAYT HUUD) n. the status of being a state.

state•house (STAYT HOWS n. a building used for sessions of a state legislature and for other public purposes; state capitol.

state•less (STAYT lis) adj. without nationality. —**state′less•ness** n.

state•ly (STAYT lee) adj. •li•er, •li•est dignified; lofty. —adv. dignifiedly. —**state′li•ness** n.

state•ment (STAYT mənt) n. **1.** the act of stating. **2.** that which is stated. **3.** a summary of financial assets and liabilities, or of deposits and withdrawals by a customer of a bank. **4.** a bill.

state•room (STAYT ROOM) *n.* a private room on a passenger ship or railroad car.

state's evidence evidence produced by the prosecution in criminal proceedings. — **turn state's evidence** become a witness for the prosecution and inculpate one's accomplices.

state•side (STAYT SID) *adj.* of or in the continental U.S. —*adv.* in or to the continental U.S.

states•man (STAYTS mən) *n. pl.* •**men** one who is skilled in government; a distinguished political leader or public servant. —**states'man•like'**, **states'man•ly** *adj.* —**states'man•ship** *n.*

states' rights 1. the rights and powers not delegated to the U.S. by the Constitution nor prohibited by it to the respective states. **2.** an interpretation of the Constitution that makes these rights and powers as large as possible.

state•wide (STAYT WID) *adj.* throughout a state.

stat•ic (STAT ik) *adj.* **1.** at rest; dormant; not active, moving, or changing. **2.** pertaining to bodies at rest or forces in equilibrium: opposed to *dynamic.* **3.** *Electr.* pertaining to electricity at rest, or to stationary electric charges. [< NL *staticus*] —*n. Telecom.* **1.** a disturbance of a carrier wave; also, the noise caused by this. **2.** *Informal* trouble. —**stat'i•cal•ly** *adv.*

stat•ics (STAT iks) *n. (construed as sing.)* the branch of mechanics dealing with bodies at rest and with the interaction of forces in equilibrium.

sta•tion (STAY shən) *n.* **1.** the headquarters of some official person or group. **2.** an established building or place serving as a starting point or stopping place; terminal; depot. **3.** a place where a person usu. stands or is; an assigned location. **4.** social condition; rank. **5.** *Mil.* the place to which an individual, unit, or ship is assigned for duty; post. **6.** the offices, studios, and technical installations of a radio or television broadcasting unit. [< L] —*v.t.* assign to a station; place in a post or position.

sta•tion•ar•y (STAY shə NER ee) *adj.* **1.** remaining in one place; fixed. **2.** not portable. **3.** exhibiting no change of character or condition.

sta•tion•er (STAY shə nər) *n.* a dealer in stationery and related articles. [ME *staciouner*]

sta•tion•er•y (STAY shə NER ee) *n.* **1.** writing paper and envelopes. **2.** writing materials, as pencils, notebooks, etc.

sta•tis•tic (stə TIS tik) *n.* any fact or datum entering into a statistical statement or array.

sta•tis•ti•cal (stə TIS ti kəl) *adj.* of, pertaining to, consisting of, or derived from statistics. —**sta•tis'ti•cal•ly** *adv.*

sta•tis•tics (stə TIS tiks) *n. (construed as pl. in def. 1)* **1.** quantitative data, pertaining to any subject or group, esp. when systematically gathered and collated. **2.** the science that deals with collection, tabulation, and systematic classification of quantitative data, esp. as a basis for inference and induction. [< G *statistik*] —**stat•is•ti•cian** (STAT i STISH ən) *n.*

stat•u•ar•y (STACH oo ER ee) *n. pl.* •**ar•ies** statues collectively. —*adj.* of or suitable for statues.

stat•ue (STACH oo) *n.* a representation of a person or animal in marble, bronze, etc. [ME]

stat•u•esque (STACH oo ESK) *adj.* resembling a statue, as in grace, pose, or dignity. —**stat'u•esque'ness** *n.*

stat•u•ette (STACH oo ET) *n.* a small statue. [< F]

stat•ure (STACH ər) *n.* **1.** natural height, esp. of a human body. **2.** development; growth; moral *stature.* [ME]

sta•tus (STAY təs) *n.* **1.** state, condition, or relation. **2.** relative position or rank. [< L]

status quo (kwoh) the condition or state in which (a person or thing is or has been). Also **status in quo.** [< L]

stat•ute (STACH oot) *n.* **1.** a legislative enactment; act of Parliament, Congress, etc. **2.** any authoritatively declared rule, ordinance, decree, or law. [ME *statut*]

statute of limitations a statute that limits the time within which legal action can be instituted.

stat•u•to•ry (STACH uu TOR ee) *adj.* **1.** pertaining to a statute. **2.** created by or dependent upon legislation.

statutory rape the crime of having sexual relations with a girl who is under the legal age of consent.

staunch (stawnch) *adj.* **1.** firm and dependable; loyal. **2.** having firm constitution or construction. **3.** strong and vigorous. Also spelled *stanch.* —*v.t.* stanch. [ME] — **staunch'ly** *adv.* —**staunch'ness** *n.*

stave (stayv) *n.* **1.** a curved strip of wood, forming a part of the sides of a barrel, tub, etc. **2.** any narrow strip of material used for a like purpose. **3.** *Music* a staff. **4.** a stanza; verse. **5.** a rod or staff. **6.** a rung of a rack or ladder. —*v.* **staved** or **stove, stav·ing** *v.t.* **1.** break in the staves of. **2.** crush; smash. **3.** ward off, as with a staff: usu. with *off.* —*v.i.* **4.** be broken in, as a vessel's hull. [ME]

staves (stayvz) **1.** alternative plural of STAFF. **2.** plural of STAVE.

stay¹ (stay) *v.* **stayed** or **staid, stay·ing** *v.i.* **1.** cease motion; stop; halt. **2.** continue in a specified place, condition, or state: *stay* healthy. **3.** remain temporarily as a guest, resident, etc. **4.** pause; wait. **5.** have endurance; last. **6.** in poker, remain in a round by meeting an ante, bet, or raise. —*v.t.* **7.** bring to a stop; halt; check. **8.** hinder; delay. **9.** postpone. **10.** remain for the duration of: I will *stay* the night. —**stay put** remain or hold in spite of everything. [ME *staien*] —*n.* **1.** the act or time of staying; sojourn; visit. **2.** that which checks or stops; esp., a suspension of judicial proceedings.

stay² *v.t.* **stayed, stay·ing** be a support to; prop or hold up. —*n.* **1.** anything that props or supports. **2.** a strip of plastic or metal, used to stiffen corsets, girdles, etc.

stay³ *Naut. n.* **1.** a strong rope, often of wire, used to support, steady, or fasten a mast or spar. **2.** any rope supporting a mast or funnel. [ME *steye*] —*v.t.* **1.** support with a stay or stays, as a mast. —*v.i.* **2.** tack: said of vessels.

stay·ing power ability to endure; stamina.

stead (sted) *n.* **1.** the place of another person or thing: preceded by *in.* **2.** a place or attitude of support; service: chiefly in the phrase **stand (one) in good stead.** [ME]

stead·fast (STED FAST) *adj.* **1.** faithful; loyal; constant. **2.** fixed; unwavering; steady. [ME *stedefast*] —**stead'fast'ly** *adv.* —**stead'fast'ness** *n.*

stead·y (STED ee) *adj.* **stead·i·er, stead·i·est** **1.** stable in position; firmly supported; fixed. **2.** moving or acting with uniform regularity; unfaltering. **3.** not readily disturbed or upset. **4.** reliable; sober; temperate. **5.** constant; steadfast. **6.** regular; reliable: a *steady* customer. **7.** uninterrupted; continuous. —*v.t. & v.i.* **stead·ied, stead·y·ing** make or become steady. —*interj.* not so fast; keep calm. —*n. Informal* one's regular sweetheart. —**go**

steady *Informal* date only one boyfriend or girlfriend. —**stead'i·ly** *adv.* —**stead'i·ness** *n.*

steady state theory *Astron.* the theory that the universe is continually expanding, but maintains a constant overall density as new matter is created.

steak (stayk) *n.* a slice of fish or meat, esp. beef, usu. broiled. [ME *steike*]

steal (steel) *v.* **stole, sto·len, steal·ing** *v.t.* **1.** take from another without authority or permission, and usu. in a secret manner. **2.** take or obtain in a surreptitious, artful, or subtle manner. **3.** move, place, or convey stealthily: with *away, from, in, into,* etc. **4.** in baseball, reach (a base) without the aid of a hit or walk. —*v.i.* **5.** commit theft. **6.** move secretly or furtively. [ME *stelen*] —*n.* **1.** the act of stealing. **2.** that which is stolen. **3.** *Informal* a bargain.

stealth (stelth) *n.* the quality or habit of acting secretly; a surreptitious manner of acting. [ME *stelthe*] —**stealth'i·ly** *adv.* —**stealth'i·ness** *n.* —**stealth'y** *adj.* **stealth·i·er, stealth·i·est**

steam (steem) *n.* **1.** water in the form of vapor. **2.** water vapor when used under pressure as a source of energy. **3.** the visible mist into which aqueous vapor is condensed by cooling. **4.** *Informal* vigor; force; speed. —**let** (or **blow**) **off steam** *Informal* give expression to repressed emotions or opinions. [ME *steme*] —*v.i.* **1.** give off or emit steam or vapor. **2.** become covered with condensed water vapor: often with *up.* **3.** move or travel by or as by the agency of steam. —*v.t.* **4.** treat with steam, as in cooking, cleaning, etc. —*adj.* of, driven by, or operated by steam.

steam·boat (STEEM BOHT) *n.* a steamship, esp. a small one.

steam engine an engine that derives its motive force from the action of steam.

steam·er (STEE mər) *n.* **1.** a ship propelled by steam. **2.** a vessel for cooking by steaming. **3.** a clam cooked by steaming.

steam fitter one who installs or repairs steam pipes. —**steam'fit'ting** *n.*

steam·roll·er (STEEM ROH lər) *n.* **1.** a steam-driven machine used in road paving etc. **2.** any force that ruthlessly overcomes opposition. —*v.t.* **1.** work (a road etc.) with a steamroller. **2.** suppress; crush. —*v.i.* **3.** work with or as with a steamroller. —*adj.* resembling the action of a steamroller; aggressive.

steam·ship (STEEM SHIP) n. a large ship propelled by steam; a steamer.

steam shovel a machine for digging and excavation, operated by steam power.

steam·y (STEE mee) adj. **steam·i·er, steam·i·est 1.** consisting of, like, or full of steam. **2.** passionate; erotic: a steamy relationship. **—steam'·i·ly** adv. **—steam' i·ness** n.

steed (steed) n. a horse; esp., a spirited horse. [ME stede]

steel (steel) n. **1.** a tough alloy of iron containing carbon in variable amounts. **2.** something made of steel, as a sword. **3.** hardness of character. [ME stele] **—adj. 1.** made or composed of steel. **2.** resembling steel, as in hardness. **3.** adamant; unyielding. **—v.t. 1.** cover with steel; plate, edge, point, or face with steel. **2.** make hard or strong. **3.** make unfeeling; harden.

steel band a type of percussion band originated in Trinidad that uses oil drums cut in size to provide various pitches when struck.

steel engraving 1. the art and process of engraving on a steel plate. **2.** the impression made from such a plate.

steel·work (STEEL WURK) n. **1.** any article or construction of steel. **2. steelworks** (construed as sing. or pl.) a mill or factory where steel is made. Also steel mill.

steel·work·er (STEEL WUR kər) n. a worker in a steel mill.

steel·y (STEE lee) adj. **steel·i·er, steel·i·est** made of, containing, resembling, or suggesting steel: a steely gaze. **—steel'i· ness** n.

steel·yard (STEEL YAHRD) n. a weighing device consisting of a scaled beam, counterpoise, and hooks.

steep¹ (steep) adj. **·er, ·est 1.** making a large angle with the plane of the horizon; precipitous. **2.** exorbitant; excessive; high, as a price. [ME stepe] **—n.** a precipitous place, as a cliff or hill. **—steep'en** v.t. & v.i. **— steep'ly** adv. **—steep'ness** n.

steep² v.t. **1.** soak in a liquid, as for softening, cleansing, etc. **2.** saturate: a career steeped in intrigue. **—v.i. 3.** undergo soaking in a liquid. [ME stepen] **—n. 1.** the process of steeping, or the state of being steeped. **2.** a liquid for steeping something. **—steep'er** n.

stee·ple (STEE pəl) n. a tall, usu. tapering structure rising above a church tower. [ME stepel]

stee·ple·chase (STEE pəl CHAYS) n. **1.** a race on horseback across country, in which obstacles are to be leaped. **2.** a cross-country run. **—stee'ple·chas'er** n.

stee·ple·jack (STEE pəl JAK) n. a person whose occupation is to climb steeples and other tall structures to inspect or make repairs. [< STEEPLE + obs. jack workman]

steer¹ (steer) v.t. & v.i. **1.** direct the course of (a vessel or vehicle) by means of a rudder, steering wheel, etc. **2.** follow (a course). **3.** guide or be guided. **—steer clear of** avoid. [ME steren] **—n.** Informal a piece of advice: a bum steer. **—steer'a·ble** adj.

steer² n. a castrated bovine animal. [ME]

steer·age (STEER ij) n. **1.** the act of steering. **2.** formerly, the part of an ocean passenger vessel in the forward lower decks.

steering committee a committee, as of a legislature, that arranges the business to be considered.

stein (stīn) n. a beer mug, esp. of earthenware. [< G Stein]

stel·lar (STEL ər) adj. **1.** of or pertaining to the stars; astral. **2.** of, pertaining to, or befitting an outstanding performer in any field. [< LL. stellaris]

stem¹ (stem) n. **1.** the main body or stalk of a plant. **2.** the relatively slender growth supporting the fruit, flower, or leaf of a plant. **3.** the long, slender, usu. cylindrical portion of an instrument, drinking vessel, etc. **4.** in a watch, the small, projecting, knobbed rod used for winding the mainspring. **5.** Ling. a root plus a vowel, as the Latin stem luci- ("light") in lucifer ("light-bearer"), composed of the root luc- plus -i- plus fer. **—v. stemmed, stem·ming** v.t. **1.** remove the stems of or from. **—v.i. 2.** grow out of; develop or arise: usually with from. [ME]

stem² Naut. n. **1.** a nearly upright timber or metal piece uniting the two sides of a vessel at the bow. **2.** the bow or prow of a vessel. **— from stem to stern** from end to end; thoroughly. **—v.t. stemmed, stem·ming 1.** resist or make progress against: stem the tide of conservatism. **2.** stop, hold back, or dam up, as a current. **2.** make tight, as a joint; plug. [ME stemmen dam]

stem·ware (STEM WAIR) n. drinking vessels with stems, as goblets, taken collectively.

stench (stench) n. a foul odor; stink. [ME]

sten·cil (STEN səl) n. **1.** a sheet of paper etc. in which a pattern is cut by means of spaces or dots, through which applied paint or ink penetrates to a surface beneath. **2.** a decoration etc. produced by stenciling. —v.t. **sten·ciled, sten·cil·ing** mark or make with a stencil. [ME *stanselen* ornament] — **sten'cil·er** n.

ste·nog·ra·phy (stə NOG rə fee) n. the art of writing in shorthand. —**ste·nog'ra·pher** n. —**sten·o·graph·ic** (STEN ə GRAF ik) adj.

sten·to·ri·an (sten TOR ee ən) adj. extremely loud. [< *Stentor,* a loud-voiced herald in the *Iliad*]

step (step) n. **1.** an act of progressive motion that requires one foot to be thrust in the direction of the movement and to reassume support of the body; a pace. **2.** the distance passed over in making such a motion. **3.** any short distance. **4.** that which the foot rests upon in ascending or descending, as a stair or ladder rung. **5.** a single action or proceeding regarded as leading to something. **6.** the manner of stepping; gait. **7.** the sound of a footstep. **8.** a footprint; track. **9.** a patterned combination of foot movements in dancing: the tango *step.* **10.** *Music* an interval corresponding to one degree of a scale or staff. —**in step 1.** walking, marching, etc. in accord with the proper rhythm or cadence, or in conformity with others. **2.** in agreement or conformity. —**take steps** adopt measures, as to attain a goal. —v. **stepped, step·ping** v.i. **1.** move by taking a step or steps. **2.** walk a short distance: *step* across the street. **3.** move or act quickly or briskly. **4.** pass into a situation, circumstance, etc. as if in a single step: He *stepped* into a fortune. —v.t. **5.** take (a pace, stride, etc.). **6.** measure by taking steps: often with *off.* —**step down 1.** decrease gradually. **2.** resign from an office or position. —**step in** begin to take part; intervene. —**step on** (or **upon**) reprove or subdue. —**step on it** *Informal* hurry; hasten. —**step out 1.** go outside, esp. for a short while. **2.** go out for fun or entertainment. —**step up** increase; accelerate. [ME *steppen*]

step·broth·er (STEP BRUTH ər) n. the son of one's stepparent by a previous marriage.

step·child (STEP CHILD) n. the child of one's spouse by a previous marriage.

step·daugh·ter (STEP DAW tər) n. a female stepchild.

step-down (STEP DOWN) adj. *Electr.* converting a high voltage into a low voltage, as a transformer.

step·fa·ther (STEP FAH thər) n. the husband of one's mother, other than one's own father.

step·lad·der (STEP LAD ər) n. a set of portable steps, usu. having a hinged frame that may be extended to support the steps in an upright position.

step·moth·er (STEP MUTH ər) n. the wife of one's father, other than one's own mother.

step·par·ent (STEP PAIR ənt) n. a stepfather or stepmother.

steppe (step) n. an extensive plain devoid of forest, esp. in Russia and Siberia. [< Russian *step'*]

step·ping-stone (STEP ing STOHN) n. **1.** a stone affording a footrest, as for crossing a stream. **2.** a step toward a goal.

step·sis·ter (STEP SIS tər) n. the daughter of one's stepparent by a previous marriage.

step·son (STEP SUN) n. a male stepchild.

step-up (STEP UP) adj. **1.** increasing by stages. **2.** *Electr.* converting a low voltage into a high voltage, as a transformer.

-ster *suffix of nouns* **1.** one who makes or is occupied with: often pejorative: *songster, prankster.* **2.** one who belongs or is related to: *gangster.* **3.** one who is: *youngster.* [ME]

ster·e·o (STEER ee OH) n. a stereophonic system. —adj. stereophonic.

ster·e·o·phon·ic (STER ee ə FON ik) adj. **1.** pertaining to the perception of sound by both ears. **2.** *Electronics* designating a system of sound reproduction in which two or more receivers or loudspeakers are placed so that the sound is heard from more than one direction. —**ster'e·o·phon'i·cal·ly** adv.

ster·e·o·scope (STER ee ə SKOHP) n. an instrument for blending into one image two pictures of an object from slightly different points of view, so as to produce a three-dimensional effect. —**ster'e·o·scop'ic** (STER ee ə SKOP ik) adj. —**ster'e·o·scop' i·cal·ly** adv.

ster·e·o·type (STER ee ə TIP) n. **1.** a plate cast in type metal from a matrix and reproducing on its surface the composed type or other material impressed upon the matrix. **2.** a conventional expression, mental image, etc.; esp., a biased, generalized image of the characteristics of an ethnic or social group. —v.t. **·typed, ·typ·ing 1.** make a stereotype of. **2.** fix firmly or unalterably. —**ster' e·o·typed'** adj.

ster·ile (STER il) adj. **1.** having no reproductive power; barren. **2.** containing no bacteria or other microorganisms. **3.** lacking in vigor or imagination: *sterile* language. [< L *sterilis* barren] —**ste•ril•i•ty** (stə RIL i tee) *n.*

ster•il•ize (STER ə LIZ) *v.t.* **•ized, •iz•ing** **1.** free from infective or disease-causing microorganisms. **2.** make powerless. **3.** make barren. —**ster'il•i•za'tion** *n.* —**ster'il•iz'er** *n.*

ster•ling (STUR ling) *n.* **1.** the official standard of fineness for British coins. **2.** British money. **3.** sterling silver (silver of a specified degree of fineness), as used in manufacturing articles; also, articles made of it. [ME, silver penny] —*adj.* **1.** made of or payable in sterling. **2.** valuable; esteemed.

stern[1] (sturn) *adj.* **•er, •est 1.** severe; harsh; unyielding. **2.** resolute; stout: *stern* resolve. [ME] —**stern'ly** *adv.* —**stern'ness** *n.*

stern[2] *n. Naut.* the rear, or aft, part of a ship, boat, etc. [ME *sterne*]

stern•most (STURN mohst) *adj.* farthest to the rear or stern.

ster•num (STUR nəm) *n. pl.* **•na** (-nə) or **•nums** *Anat.* the breastbone that forms the ventral support of the ribs in vertebrates. [< NL]

stern•ward (STURN wərd) *adj. & adv.* toward the stern.

stern-wheel•er (STURN HWEE lər) *n.* a steamboat propelled by a paddle wheel at the stern.

ster•oid (STEER oid) *n. Biochem.* any of a large group of fat-soluble organic compounds, including the sex hormones.

ster•tor•ous (STUR tər əs) *adj.* characterized by snoring or accompanied by a snoring sound. [< L *stertere* snore]

stet (stet) let it stand: a direction used in editing to indicate that a word, letter, etc. marked for deletion or correction is to remain as it originally was. —*v.t.* **stet•ted, stet•ting** cancel a correction or deletion by marking with "stet." [< L, let it stand]

steth•o•scope (STETH ə SKOHP) *n. Med.* an apparatus for listening to a patient's breathing, heartbeat, etc. [< F *stéthoscope*]

ste•ve•dore (STEE vi DOR) *n.* a person or company engaged in stowing or unloading ships. —*v.t. & v.i.* **•dored, •dor•ing** load or unload (a ship). [< Sp. *estibador*]

stew (stoo) *v.t. & v.i.* **1.** boil slowly and gently; seethe; simmer. **2.** *Informal* worry. [ME *stewen*] —*n.* **1.** stewed food, esp. meat or fish and vegetables. **2.** *Informal* mental agitation; worry.

stew•ard (STOO ərd) *n.* **1.** one who is entrusted with the management of property, finances, or affairs of other. **2.** one who buys provisions, manages servants, etc. in a club etc. **3.** on an airplane, ship, or bus, one who waits on the passengers. [ME] —**stew'ard•ess** *n.fem.* —**stew'ard•ship** *n.*

stewed (stood) *adj.* **1.** cooked by stewing. **2.** *Slang* drunk.

stick (stik) *n.* **1.** a slender piece of wood, as a branch cut from a tree or bush; a baton, wand, etc. **2.** a cane; also **walking stick. 3.** anything resembling a stick in form: a *stick* of candy. **4.** a piece of wood of any size, cut for fuel, lumber, or timber. **5.** *Aeron.* the lever of an airplane by which one controls movement. **6.** a poke, stab, or thrust with a pointed instrument. **7.** the control lever of a gearshift, esp. when set vertically. **8.** *Informal* a stiff, inert, or dull person. —**the sticks** *Informal* an obscure rural district; the backwoods or country. —*v.* **stuck, stick•ing** *v.t.* **1.** pierce, stab, or penetrate with a pointed object. **2.** thrust or force, as a sword or pin, into or through something else. **3.** fasten in place with or as with pins, nails, etc. **4.** impale; transfix. **5.** put or thrust: He *stuck* his hand into his pocket. **6.** fasten to a surface by or as by an adhesive substance. **7.** bring to a standstill; obstruct; halt: usu. in the passive: We were *stuck* in Duluth. **8.** baffle; puzzle. **9.** *Informal* force expense, an unpleasant task, etc. upon. —*v.i.* **10.** be or become fixed in place by being thrust in. **11.** become or remain attached to something by or as by adhesion; adhere; cling. **12.** come to a standstill; become blocked or obstructed. **13.** be baffled or disconcerted. **14.** hesitate; scruple: with *at* or *to.* **15.** persist; persevere: with *at* or *to.* **16.** remain firm or resolute; be faithful. **17.** be extended; protrude: with *from, out, through, up,* etc. —**stick around** *Informal* remain near or near at hand. —**stick by** remain faithful to; be loyal to. —**stick it out** persevere to the end. —**stick up** *Informal* rob with a gun. —**stick up for** take the part of; defend. [ME *stikke* n., *stiken* v.]

stick•le (STIK əl) *v.i.* **•led, •ling 1.** argue about trifles. **2.** insist or hesitate for petty reasons. [ME *stightlen*]

stick•ler (STIK lər) *n.* one who stickles, usu. with *for:* a *stickler* for details.

stick shift an automobile gearshift lever mounted on the floor.

stick·up (STIK UP) n. Informal a robbery done with a gun.

stick·y (STIK ee) adj. **stick·i·er, stick·i·est** **1.** adhering to a surface; adhesive. **2.** covered with something adhesive. **3.** warm and humid. —**stick′i·ness** n.

stiff (stif) adj. **·er, ·est 1.** resisting the action of a bending force; rigid. **2.** not easily moved; also, moving or functioning painfully or without suppleness: a stiff neck. **3.** not natural, graceful, or easy; constrained and awkward; formal. **4.** not liquid or fluid; thick; viscous. **5.** having a strong, steady movement: a stiff breeze. **6.** firm in resistance; stubborn. **7.** harsh; severe. **8.** high; dear: a stiff price. **9.** strong or potent, as in alcoholic content. **10.** difficult; arduous. [ME] —n. Slang **1.** a corpse. **2.** a dull or formal person; a bore. **3.** a man; fellow: a working stiff. —**stiff′ly** adv. —**stiff′ness** n.

stiff·en (STIF ən) v.t. & v.i. make or become stiff or stiffer.

stiff·necked (STIF NEKT) adj. **1.** haughty. **2.** not yielding; stubborn.

sti·fle (STĪ fəl) v. **·fled, ·fling** v.t. **1.** keep back; suppress or repress; check. **2.** suffocate; choke. —v.t. **3.** die of suffocation. **4.** experience difficulty in breathing. [ME] —**sti′fling** adj.

stig·ma (STIG mə) n. pl. **stig·ma·ta** (stig MAH tə) or **stig·mas 1.** a mark of infamy, or token of disgrace. **2.** Bot. the part of a pistil that receives the pollen. **3.** stigmata marks resembling the wounds of the crucified body of Christ. **4.** formerly, a brand made on the skins of slaves and criminals. [< L]

stig·ma·tize (STIG mə TĪZ) v.t. **·tized, ·tiz·ing 1.** characterize or brand as ignominious. **2.** mark with a stigma. —**stig′ma·ti·za′tion** n.

sti·let·to (sti LET oh) n. pl. **·tos** or **·toes** a small dagger with a slender blade. —v.t. **·toed, ·to·ing** pierce with a stiletto; stab. [< Ital.]

still¹ (stil) adj. **·er, ·est 1.** making no sound; silent. **2.** peaceful; tranquil. **3.** Without movement; motionless. **4.** subdued; soft. **5.** dead; inanimate. **6.** having no effervescence: said of wines. —n. **1.** stillness. **2.** Photog. a single photograph, as contrasted with a motion picture. —adv. **1.** now as previously; up to this or that time: He is still

here. **2.** all the same: nevertheless. **3.** even; yet: still more food. —conj. nevertheless; and yet. —v.t. **1.** cause to be still or calm. **2.** quiet or allay, as fears. —v.i. **3.** become still. [ME stille] —**still′ness** n.

still² n. **1.** an apparatus for the distillation of liquids, esp. alcoholic liquors. **2.** a distillery. —v.t. & v.i. distill. [ME stillen]

still·born (STIL BORN) adj. dead at birth. —**still·birth** (STIL BURTH) n.

still life pl. **still lifes 1.** in painting, the representation of objects, as tables, flowers, fruit, etc. **2.** a picture of such a subject.

stil·ly (STIL lee) adv. silently; quietly.

stilt (stilt) n. **1.** one of a pair of long, slender poles made with a projection to support the foot some distance above the ground in walking. **2.** a tall post or pillar used as a support, as for a dock. [ME stilte]

stilt·ed (STIL tid) adj. artificially formal; pompous. —**stilt′ed·ly** adv. —**stilt′ed·ness** n.

stim·u·lant (STIM yə lənt) n. anything that quickens or promotes the activity of some physiological process, as a drug. —adj. stimulating.

stim·u·late (STIM yə LAYT) v. **·lat·ed, ·lat·ing** v.t. **1.** rouse; excite; spur. **2.** Physiol. excite (an organ or tissue) by applying some form of stimulus. —v.i. **3.** act as a stimulant. [< L stimulatus goaded] —**stim′u·la′tion** n. —**stim′u·la′tive** adj. & n.

stim·u·lus (STIM yə ləs) n. pl. **·li** (-lī) **1.** anything that rouses the mind or spirits; an incentive. **2.** Physiol. any agent or form of excitation that influences the activity of an organism as a whole or in any of its parts. [< L, goad]

sting (sting) v. **stung, sting·ing** v.t. **1.** pierce or prick painfully, as with a sharp, sometimes venomous organ. **2.** cause to suffer sharp, smarting pain from or as from a sting. **3.** cause to suffer mentally; pain. **4.** Slang get the better of; cheat. —v.i. **5.** have or use a sting, as a bee. **6.** suffer or cause a sharp, smarting pain. **7.** suffer or cause mental pain. [ME stingen] —n. **1.** Zool. a sharp, pointed, sometimes venomous organ, as of a bee, able to inflict a wound. **2.** the act of stinging; also, the wound or the pain thus caused. **3.** any sharp, smarting sensation. —**sting′er** n. —**sting′ing·ly** adv.

stin·gy (STIN jee) adj. **·gi·er, ·gi·est 1.** unwilling to spend or give; miserly. **2.** scanty;

inadequate; meager. —**stin'gi·ly** adv. —
stin'gi·ness n.

stink (stink) n. a strong, foul odor; stench. —
v.i. **stank** or **stunk, stink·ing 1.** give forth
a foul odor. **2.** Informal be of bad quality. —
make (or **raise**) **a stink** Informal protest
vehemently. —**stink out** drive out by a foul
odor. [ME stinken]

stint (stint) v.t. **1.** limit, as in amount or
share; be stingy with. —v.i. **2.** be frugal or
sparing. —n. **1.** a fixed amount, as of work
to be performed within a specified time. **2.**
a limitation. [ME stinten make blunt] —
stint'er n.

sti·pend (STĪ pend) n. an allowance, salary,
or pension. [ME stipendie soldier's pay]

stip·ple (STIP əl) v.t. •**pled,** •**pling** draw,
paint, or engrave with dots or flecks. [< Du.
stippelen] —**stip'pler** n.

stip·u·late (STIP yə LAYT) v. •**lat·ed,**
•**lat·ing** v.t. **1.** specify as the terms of or
condition for an agreement, contract, etc.
2. promise; guarantee. —v.i. **3.** demand
something as a requirement: with for. [< L
stipulatus demanded an agreement] —
stip'u·la'tor n.

stip·u·la·tion (STIP yə LAY shən) n. **1.** the
act of stipulating, or the state of being stipulated. **2.** that which is stipulated; a condition. —**stip·u·la·to·ry** (STIP yə lə TOR ee)
adj.

stir[1] (stur) v. **stirred, stir·ring** v.t. **1.** agitate; mix, as coffee with a spoon. **2.** cause to
move, esp. slightly. **3.** move; bestir. **4.** rouse,
as from inactivity. **5.** incite; provoke: often
with up. **6.** affect strongly; move with emotion. —v.i. **7.** move, esp. slightly. **8.** be active; move about. **9.** happen. **10.** undergo
stirring. [ME stiren] —n. **1.** the act of stirring, or state of being stirred; activity. **2.**
general interest or excitement; agitation.

stir[2] n. Slang prison: in stir.

stir-fry (STUR FRĪ) v.t. **-fried, -fry·ing**
cook quickly by stirring in hot oil.

stir·ring (STUR ing) adj. **1.** stimulating; inspiring. **2.** active; lively. —**stir'ring·ly** adv.

stir·rup (STIR əp) n. **1.** an inverted-
U-shaped support for a rider's foot, hung
from either side of a saddle. **2.** any similarly
shaped support, as for a beam. [ME]

stirrup bone Anat. the stapes.

stitch (stich) n. **1.** a single passage of a
threaded needle through a material and
back again, as in sewing. **2.** a single turn of
thread or yarn around a needle, as in knitting; also, the loop resulting from such a

turn. **3.** any particular arrangement of a
thread: a chain stitch. **4.** a sharp, sudden
pain, esp. in the back or side. **5.** the smallest
bit: not a stitch of work. —v.t. **1.** join together or ornament with stitches. —v.i. **2.**
make stitches; sew. [ME stiche a prick]

sto·chas·tic (stə KAS tik) adj. Statistics depending on chance; involving the law of
probability. [< Gk. stochastikós aimed at]

stock (stok) n. **1.** a quantity of something
acquired or kept for future use. **2.** the total
merchandise or goods that a business has
on hand. **3.** livestock. **4.** in finance: **a** the
capital or fund raised by a corporation
through the sale of shares. **b** the proportional part of this capital credited to an individual stockholder. **c** a certificate showing
ownership of shares. **5.** the trunk or main
stem of a tree or other plant. **6.** a line of
familial descent. **7.** a related group or family, as of languages, people, plants, or animals; also, a type of animal or plant from
which others are derived. **8.** the broth from
boiled meat, vegetables, or fish. **9.** raw material. **10.** pl. a timber frame with holes for
confining the ankles, formerly used in punishing petty offenders. **11.** in firearms: **a** the
rear wooden portion of a rifle etc. to which
the barrel and mechanisms are secured. **b**
the arm on rapid-fire guns, connecting the
shoulder piece to the slide. **c** the handle of a
pistol. **12.** Often pl. a wooden support or
frame for securing an animal. **13.** the handle of certain instruments, as of a whip or
fishing rod. **14.** a theatrical stock company.
—**in stock** on hand and available for sale or
use. —**take stock 1.** take an inventory. **2.**
estimate or appraise. —v.t. **1.** furnish with
livestock or with merchandise. **2.** keep for
sale. **3.** put aside for further use. —v.i. **4.**
lay in supplies or stock: often with up. —
adj. **1.** kept on hand: a stock size. **2.** banal;
commonplace: a stock phrase. **3.** employed
in handling or caring for the stock. —adv.
motionlessly: used in combination: stock-
still [ME]

stock·ade (sto KAYD) n. **1.** a line of posts,
stakes, etc., set upright to form a barrier;
also, the area thus enclosed, used as a
prison etc. **2.** any similar area. —v.t.
•**ad·ed,** •**ad·ing** surround or fortify with a
stockade. [< MF estocade]

stock·breed·er (STOK BREED ər) n. one
who breeds and raises livestock. —**stock'
breed'·ing** n.

stock·bro·ker (STOK BROH kər) n. one

who buys and sells stocks or securities for others. —**stock′bro′ker·age** (-kər ij) n.

stock car an automobile, often a sedan, modified for racing.

stock exchange 1. a place where stocks and bonds are bought and sold. 2. an association of stockbrokers.

stock·hold·er (STOK HOHL dər) n. one who holds certificates of ownership in a company or corporation. —**stock′hold′ ing** adj. & n.

stock·ing (STOK ing) n. 1. a close-fitting woven or knitted covering for the foot and leg. 2. something resembling such a covering. —**in stocking feet** wearing stockings or socks, but no shoes. —**stock′inged** adj.

stock market 1. a stock exchange. 2. the business transacted in such a place.

stock·pile (STOK PIL) n. a storage pile of materials or supplies. —v.t. & v.i. •piled, •pil·ing accumulate a supply or stockpile (of).

stock·room (STOK ROOM) n. a room where reserve stocks of goods are stored.

stock-still (STOK STIL) adj. motionless.

stock·y (STOK ee) adj. **stock·i·er, stock· i·est** solidly built, thickest, and usu. short. —**stock′i·ly** adv. —**stock′i·ness** n.

stock·yard (STOK YAHRD) n. an enclosure where cattle, sheep, etc. are kept ready for shipping or slaughter.

stodg·y (STOJ ee) adj. **stodg·i·er, stodg·i·est** dull, stupid, and commonplace. —**stodg′i·ness** n.

sto·ic (STOH ik) n. a person apparently unaffected by pleasure or pain. —adj. indifferent to pleasure or pain; impassive: also **sto′i·cal.** [ME] —**sto′i·cal·ly** adv. — **sto·i·cism** (STOH ə SIZ əm) n.

stoke (stohk) v.t. & v.i. **stoked, stok·ing** supply (a furnace) with fuel; stir up or tend (a fire or furnace). [< Du. stoken]

stok·er (STOH kər) n. 1. one who supplies fuel to a furnace. 2. a device for feeding coal to a furnace.

stole[1] (stohl) n. 1. Eccl. a long, narrow band of decorated cloth worn about the shoulders. 2. a long scarf worn about the shoulders by women. [ME]

stole[2] past tense of STEAL.

sto·len (STOHL ən) past participle of STEAL.

stol·id (STOL id) adj. having or showing little feeling or perception; impassive; dull. [< L. stolidus dull] —**sto·lid·i·ty** (stə LID i tee), **stol′id·ness** n. —**stol′id·ly** adv.

stom·ach (STUM ək) n. 1. the pouchlike enlargement of the alimentary canal, situated in vertebrates between the esophagus and the small intestine. ◆ Collateral adjective: gastric. 2. any digestive cavity. 3. loosely, the abdomen or belly. 4. desire for food; appetite. 5. any desire or inclination. —v.t. put up with; endure. [ME stomak]

stone (stohn) n. 1. the hard mineral or earthy matter of which rock is composed. 2. a small piece of rock, as a pebble. 3. a precious stone; gem. 4. anything resembling a stone in shape or hardness: a hailstone. 5. a gravestone. 6. a grindstone or millstone. 7. Pathol. a stony mass in the bladder, or a disease characterized by such masses. 8. Bot. the hard covering of the kernel in a fruit. 9. (pl. stone) a unit of weight in England, 14 pounds. —adj. 1. made of stone. 2. made of coarse, hard earthenware. —v.t. **stoned, ston·ing** 1. hurl stones at; pelt or kill with stones. 2. remove the stones or pits from. [ME ston]

stone-broke (STOHN BROHK) adj. having no money.

stoned (stohnd) adj. Slang 1. drunk. 2. dazed from drugs.

stone-deaf (STOHN DEF) adj. completely deaf.

stone·ma·son (STOHN MAY sən) n. one who prepares and lays stones in building.

stone's throw a short distance.

stone·wall (STOHN WAWL) v.i. obstruct, resist, evade, or delay an action.

stone·ware (STOHN WAIR) n. a type of hard ceramic ware.

stone·work (STOHN WURK) n. 1. work concerned with cutting or setting stone; also, something made of stone. 2. pl. a place where stone is prepared for masonry.

ston·y (STOH nee) adj. **ston·i·er, ston·i·est** 1. abounding in stone. 2. made or consisting of stone. 3. hard as stone. 4. unfeeling or inflexible. 5. converting into stone; petrifying. —**ston′i·ly** adv. —**ston′ i·ness** n.

stood (stuud) past tense, past participle of STAND.

stooge (stooj) n. 1. a performer who feeds lines to a comedian, acts as a foil for jokes, etc. 2. anyone who is the tool or dupe of another. —v.i. **stooged, stoog·ing** act as a stooge: usually with for.

stool (stool) n. 1. a backless and armless seat for one person. 2. a low bench or support for the feet or for the knees in kneeling. 3.

the fecal matter evacuated from the bowels at each movement. —*v.i. Slang* serve as a stool pigeon. [ME]

stool pigeon 1. a living or artificial pigeon attached to a perch to decoy others. **2.** *Slang* an informer or spy, esp. for the police.

stoop[1] (stoop) *v.i.* **1.** bend or lean the body forward and down; bow; crouch. **2.** stand or walk with the upper part of the body habitually bent forward; slouch. **3.** lower or degrade oneself: *stoop* to cheating. —*v.t.* **4.** bend (one's head, shoulders, etc.) forward. —*n.* **1.** an act of stooping. **2.** a habitual forward inclination of the head and shoulders. **3.** a decline from dignity or superiority. [ME *stoupen*]

stoop[2] *n.* a small porch or raised platform at the entrance to a house. [< Du. *stoep*]

stop (stop) *v.* **stopped, stop·ping** *v.t.* **1.** bring (something in motion) to a halt; arrest the progress of. **2.** prevent the doing or completion of. **3.** prevent (a person, animal, etc.) from doing something; restrain. **4.** keep back, withhold, block, or cut off. **5.** cease doing; desist from. **6.** block up, obstruct, close, or clog (a passage, hole, etc.): often with *up.* **7.** close with a cork, plug, or other stopper. —*v.i.* **8.** come to a halt; cease progress or motion. **9.** cease doing something; pause or desist. **10.** come to an end. —**stop off** halt temporarily before reaching one's destination. —**stop over 1.** stay at a place temporarily. **2.** interrupt a journey; make a stopover. [ME *stoppen*] —*n.* **1.** the act of stopping, or the state of being stopped; a halt; pause; end. **2.** that which stops or limits the range or time of a movement: a camera *stop.* **3.** an obstruction or obstacle. **4.** in an organ or harpsichord, a knob controlling a register of pipes or strings; also the register so controlled. **5.** a punctuation mark, esp. a period.

stop·gap (STOP GAP) *n.* something improvised to fill a need temporarily; an expedient.

stop·light (STOP LIT) *n.* **1.** the red light on a traffic light; also, the traffic light itself. **2.** a red light on the rear of a motor vehicle that shines when the brakes are applied.

stop·o·ver (STOP OH vər) *n.* a brief visit in a place, esp. while traveling.

stop·page (STOP ij) *n.* **1.** the act of stopping, or the state of being stopped. **2.** an obstruction of some kind; block.

stop payment an order to a bank to refuse payment on a certain check.

stop·per (STOP ər) *n.* **1.** something that stops up or closes, as a plug or cork. **2.** one who or that which stops or checks a movement, action, etc. —*v.t.* close with a stopper.

stop·watch (STOP WOCH) *n.* a watch that has a hand indicating fractions of a second and that may be instantaneously started or stopped, used for timing races etc.

stor·age (STOR ij) *n.* **1.** the depositing of articles in a warehouse for safekeeping. **2.** space for storing goods. **3.** a charge for storing. **4.** memory (def. 6).

storage battery a series of cells that converts chemical energy into electric energy, is a single source of direct current, and is capable of being recharged on reversal of the current.

store (stor) *v.t.* **stored, stor·ing 1.** put away for future use; accumulate. **2.** place in a warehouse or other place of deposit for safekeeping. [ME *storen* restore] —*n.* **1.** a place where merchandise of any kind is kept for sale. **2.** that which is stored or laid up against future need. **3.** *pl.* supplies, as of arms or clothing. **4.** a place where commodities are stored; warehouse. —**in store** forthcoming; impending. —**set store by** value or esteem; regard.

store·house (STOR HOWS) *n.* **1.** a warehouse. **2.** a large fund; reservoir: a *storehouse* of ideas.

store·keep·er (STOR KEE pər) *n.* a person who keeps a retail store; shopkeeper.

store·room (STOR ROOM) *n.* a room in which things are stored, as supplies.

sto·rey (STOR ee) see STORY[2].

sto·ried[1] (STOR eed) *adj.* having or consisting of stories, as a building: usu. in compounds: a six-*storied* house.

sto·ried[2] *adj.* **1.** having a notable history. **2.** related in a story.

stork (stork) *n.* any of a family of large wading birds with long necks and long legs. [ME]

storm (storm) *n.* **1.** rain, snow, etc., usu. accompanied by strong wind. **2.** *Meteorol.* a wind force of 64–72 miles per hour. **3.** a violent outburst, as of passion or excitement. **4.** *Mil.* a violent and rapid assault on a fortified place. **5.** a violent commotion. **6.** a furious flight or shower of objects, esp. of missiles. —*v.i.* **1.** blow with violence; rain, snow, hail, etc. heavily: used impersonally: It *stormed* all day. **2.** be very angry; rage. **3.** move or rush with violence or rage. —*v.t.* **4.**

Mil. take or try to take by rapid assault. [ME]

storm·bound (STORM BOWND) *adj.* delayed, confined, or isolated because of a storm.

storm center *Meteorol.* the center or area of lowest pressure and comparative calm in a cyclonic storm.

storm door an extra outer door for added protection during storms or for greater insulation.

storm window an extra window outside the ordinary one as a protection against storms or for greater insulation.

storm·y (STOR mee) *adj.* **storm·i·er, storm·i·est 1.** characterized by or subject to storms. **2.** tempestuous; violent. —**storm'i·ness** *n.*

sto·ry[1] (STOR ee) *n. pl.* **·ries 1.** a narrative or recital of an event or series of events, whether real or fictitious. **2.** a narrative, usu. of fictitious events, intended to entertain. **3.** a short story. **4.** a report. **5.** a news article; also, the material for such an article. **6.** an anecdote. **7.** a lie. **8.** the plot of a novel, play, etc. [ME *storie*] —*v.t.* **·ried, ·ry·ing** relate as a story.

sto·ry[2] *n. pl.* **·ries** a horizontal division in a building comprising the space between two successive floors. Also, **storey.** [ME *storie*]

story line the plot of a film, novel, etc.

sto·ry·tell·er (STOR ee TEL ər) *n.* **1.** one who relates stories. **2.** a person who tells trivial lies. —**sto'ry·tell'ing** *n.*

stoup (stoop) *n. Eccl.* a basin for holy water at the entrance of a church. [ME *stowp*]

stout (stowt) *adj.* **·er, ·est 1.** strong; sound; tough. **2.** determined; resolute. **3.** fat. **4.** substantial; solid. **5.** muscular; robust. [ME, bold] —*n.* a very dark porter or ale. —**stout'ly** *adv.* —**stout'ness** *n.*

stout·heart·ed (STOWT HAHR tid) *adj.* brave; courageous. —**stout'heart'ed·ness** *n.*

stove[1] (stohv) *n.* an apparatus for heating or cooking. [ME]

stove[2] a past tense and past participle of STAVE.

stove·pipe (STOHV PIP) *n.* **1.** a pipe, usu. of thin sheet iron, for conducting smoke and gases from a stove to a chimney flue. **2.** a tall silk hat: also **stovepipe hat.**

stow (stoh) *v.t.* **1.** place or arrange compactly; pack. **2.** put away; store. —**stow away 1.** put in a place of safekeeping, hiding, etc. **2.** be a stowaway. [ME *stowen*]

stow·age (STOH ij) *n.* **1.** the act or manner of stowing, or the state of being stowed. **2.** space for stowing goods; also, the goods stowed. **3.** a charge for stowing goods.

stow·a·way (STOH ə WAY) *n.* a person who hides aboard a plane or ship to obtain free passage or evade officials.

stra·bis·mus (strə BIZ məs) *n. Pathol.* a condition in which the eyes cannot be focused simultaneously on the same spot. [< NL] —**stra·bis'mic** *adj.*

strad·dle (STRAD l) *v.* **·dled, ·dling** *v.i.* **1.** stand, walk, or sit with the legs spread apart. —*v.t.* **2.** stand, walk, or sit with the legs on either side of. **3.** spread (the legs) wide apart. **4.** favor or appear to favor both sides of (an issue). —**strad'dle** *n.* —**strad'·dler** *n.*

strafe (strayf) *v.t.* **strafed, straf·ing** attack with machine-gun fire from a low-flying airplane. [< G *strafen*] —**straf'er** *n.*

strag·gle (STRAG əl) *v.i.* **·gled, ·gling 1.** stray from or lag behind the main body. **2.** wander about. **3.** occur at irregular intervals. **4.** hang messily or in wisps: said of hair. —**strag'gler** *n.*

strag·gly (STRAG lee) *adj.* **·gli·er, ·gli·est** rambling; straggling.

straight (strayt) *adj.* **·er, ·est 1.** extending uniformly in one direction without curve or bend. **2.** free from kinks; not curly. **3.** not stooped or inclined; erect, as in posture. **4.** fair; honest. **5.** clear; frank; direct. **6.** free from obstruction; uninterrupted; unbroken. **7.** correctly kept, ordered, or arranged. **8.** having nothing added; undiluted. **9.** *Slang* conforming to normal or conventional standards. **10.** *Slang* heterosexual. —*n.* **1.** a straight part, line, or sequence. **2.** the part of a racetrack between the last turn and the finish line; straightaway. **3.** in poker, a numerical sequence of five cards, or a hand containing this. **4.** *Slang* a conventional person. **5.** *Slang* a heterosexual. —*adv.* **1.** in a straight line or a direct course. **2.** closely in line; correspondingly. **3.** at once; straightway. —**go straight** reform after a criminal career. [ME] —**straight'ly** *adv.* —**straight'ness** *n.*

straight angle *Geom.* an angle of 180°.

straight arrow *Informal* an honest and proper person. —**straight'-ar'row** *adj.*

straight·a·way (STRAYT ə WAY) *adj.* having no curve or turn. —*n.* a straight course or track. —*adv.* at once.

straight·en (STRAYT n) v.t. **1.** make straight or tidy. —v.i. **2.** become straight. —**straighten out** restore order to; set right; rectify. —**straighten up 1.** make neat. **2.** stand in erect posture.

straight face a face that betrays no emotion. —**straight'-faced'** adj.

straight·for·ward (STRAYT FOR wərd) adj. **1.** proceeding in a straight course. **2.** honest; frank. —adv. in a straight course or direct manner. —**straight'for'ward·ness** n.

straight man an entertainer who acts as a foil for a comedian.

straight-out (STRAYT OWT) adj. Informal **1.** frank; unreserved. **2.** real; genuine. **3.** uncompromising; all-out.

strain¹ (strayn) v.t. **1.** exert to the utmost. **2.** injure by overexertion; sprain. **3.** pull or draw tight; stretch. **4.** stretch excessively or beyond the proper limit. **5.** pass through a filtering agent or strainer. **6.** remove by filtration. —v.i. **7.** make violent efforts; strive. **8.** be or become wrenched or twisted. **9.** filter, trickle, or percolate. —**strain at 1.** push or pull with violent efforts. **2.** strive for. [ME *streinen*] —n. **1.** an act of straining, or the state of being strained. **2.** the injury resulting from excessive tension or effort. **3.** severe mental or emotional tension. **4.** Often pl. a passage of music. **5.** tone, style, or manner; mood.

strain² n. **1.** a line of descent, or the individuals, collectively, in that line; race; stock. **2.** inborn or hereditary tendency. **3.** Biol. a special line of animals or plants bred from a certain species or variety. [ME *strene*]

strain·er (STRAY nər) n. a utensil or device, containing meshes or porous parts, through which liquids are strained.

strait (strayt) n. Often pl. **1.** a narrow passage of water connecting two larger bodies of water. **2.** a position of perplexity or distress. —adj. Archaic **1.** narrow. **2.** righteous; strict. **3.** difficult. [ME *streit*]

strait·en (STRAYT n) v.t. **1.** make strait or narrow. **2.** embarrass or distress. —**strait'ened** adj. **1.** contracted; narrowed. **2.** suffering privation or hardship, as from lack of money.

strait·jack·et (STRAYT JAK it) n. a garment of strong canvas for restraining a violent patient. —v.t. confine in or as if in a straitjacket.

strait-laced (STRAYT LAYST) adj. strict in morality or conduct.

strand¹ (strand) n. a shore or beach, esp. the portion between high and low tides. —v.t. & v.i. **1.** run aground. **2.** leave or be left in straits or difficulties. [ME]

strand² n. **1.** one of the principal members of a rope, wire, etc. **2.** a fiber, hair, or the like. **3.** a string of beads or pearls. —v.t. make by twisting strands.

strange (straynj) adj. **strang·er, strang·est 1.** previously unknown, unseen, or unheard of; unfamiliar. **2.** not ordinary; remarkable; unusual. **3.** of a different class, character, or kind. **4.** foreign; alien. **5.** reserved; shy. **6.** inexperienced; unaccustomed. —adv. in a strange manner. [ME] —**strange'ly** adv. —**strange'ness** n.

stran·ger (STRAYN jər) n. **1.** one who is not an acquaintance. **2.** an unfamiliar visitor. **3.** one unfamiliar with something specified: with *to*. [ME]

stran·gle (STRANG gəl) v.t. & v.i. **·gled, ·gling** choke to death; throttle; suffocate. [ME *strangelen*] —**stran'gler** n.

strangle hold 1. in wrestling, a usu. illegal hold that chokes one's opponent. **2.** any influence or power that chokes freedom or progress.

stran·gu·late (STRANG gyə LAYT) v.t. **·lat·ed, ·lat·ing 1.** strangle. **2.** Pathol. compress, contract, or obstruct, esp. so as to cut off flow of a fluid. [< L *strangulatus*] —**stran'gu·la'tion** n.

strap (strap) n. **1.** a long, narrow, and flexible strip of leather, canvas, etc., usu. having a buckle or other fastener. **2.** a razor strop. **3.** a piece of material that passes over the shoulder and supports a garment. —v.t. **strapped, strap·ping 1.** fasten or bind with a strap. **2.** beat with a strap. **3.** embarrass financially. **4.** strop. [Var. of STROP] —**strap'less** adj.

strap·hang·er (STRAP HANG ər) n. a standee on a subway or bus; also, one who uses public transportation.

strap·ping (STRAP ing) adj. robust.

stra·ta (STRAY tə) a plural of STRATUM.

strat·a·gem (STRAT ə jəm) n. **1.** a maneuver designed to deceive or outwit an enemy in war. **2.** a device for obtaining advantage; trick. [< F *stratagème*]

strat·e·gy (STRAT i jee) n. pl. **·ties 1.** the science and art of conducting a military campaign on a broad scale. Compare TACTICS. **2.** the use of stratagem or artifice. **3.** a plan for achieving some end. [< Gk. *strategia* generalship] —**stra·te·gic** (strə TEE jik) *adj.* —**stra·te′gi·cal·ly** *adv.* — **strat·e·gist** (STRAT i jist) *n.*

strat·i·fy (STRAT ə FĪ) *v.* **-fied, ·fy·ing** *v.t.* **1.** form or arrange in strata. —*v.i.* **2.** form in strata. [< NL *stratificare*] —**strat′i·fi·ca′ tion** *n.*

strat·o·sphere (STRAT ə SFER) *n. Meteorol.* the portion of the atmosphere beginning at a height of about seven miles and characterized by a uniform temperature. —**strat′o·spher′ic** (STRAT ə SFER ik) *adj.*

stra·tum (STRAY təm) *n. pl.* **·ta** (-tə) or **·tums 1.** a natural or artificial layer, bed, or thickness. **2.** *Geol.* a more or less homogeneous layer of rock. **3.** something corresponding to a layer or grade: the lowest social *stratum.* [< NL]

straw (straw) *n.* **1.** a slender tube of paper, glass, etc., used to suck up a beverage. **2.** stems or stalks of grain collectively, after the grain has been thrashed out. —**the last straw** the final test of patience or endurance: from the phrase **the straw that broke the camel's back.** —**clutch (grasp, catch,** etc.) **at a straw** (at straws) in desperation, try any solution or expedient. —*adj.* **1.** like or of straw. **2.** of no value; worthless; sham. **3.** yellowish. [ME]

straw·ber·ry (STRAW BER ee) *n. pl.* **·ries 1.** the edible fruit of a stemless perennial herb of the rose family. **2.** the plant bearing this fruit. [ME]

strawberry blond a person having reddish blond hair.

straw vote an unofficial vote or poll.

stray (stray) *v.i.* **1.** wander from the proper course; straggle; roam. **2.** wander about; rove. **3.** digress. **4.** deviate from right or goodness. [ME *strayen*] —*adj.* **1.** having strayed; straying. **2.** irregular; occasional; casual; unrelated. —*n.* **1.** a domestic animal that has strayed. **2.** a person who is lost or wanders aimlessly.

streak (streek) *n.* **1.** a long, narrow, somewhat irregularly shaped mark, line, or stripe. **2.** a vein, tendency, or trace: a *streak* of meanness. **3.** *Informal* a run; spell: a winning *streak.* **4.** a layer or strip. [ME *streke*] —*v.t.* **1.** mark with a streak; form streaks in or on; stripe. —*v.i.* **2.** form a streak or streaks. **3.** move at great speed. **4.** make a sudden dash in public while naked, usu. as a prank. —**streak′er** *n.*

streak·y (STREE kee) *adj.* **streak·i·er, streak·i·est 1.** marked with or occurring in streaks. **2.** of variable quality or character.

stream (streem) *n.* **1.** a current or flow of water or other fluid. **2.** anything continuously flowing, moving, or passing, as people. **3.** a small river. **4.** anything issuing out or flowing from a source. —*v.i.* **1.** pour forth or issue in a stream. **2.** pour forth a stream. **3.** move in continuous succession. **4.** float with a waving movement, as a flag. —*v.t.* **5.** emit or exude. [ME *streem*]

stream·er (STREE mər) *n.* **1.** something that streams forth. **2.** an object that waves or hangs extended, as a long, narrow flag.

stream·line (STREEM LĪN) *n.* any shape or contour designed to offer minimum resistance to a flow of air or water. —*v.t.* **·lined, ·lin·ing 1.** design with a streamlined shape. **2.** make more simple, efficient, or up to date. —**stream′lined′** *adj.*

street (street) *n.* a thoroughfare in a city or town, with buildings on one or both sides; also, the roadway for vehicles, between sidewalks. [ME]

street·car (STREET KAHR) *n.* a public passenger car of an electric railway that runs on tracks set into the streets.

street people people without permanent homes, who spend much of their time on city streets; the homeless.

street·walk·er (STREET WAW kər) *n.* a prostitute who solicits in the streets. — **street′walk′ing** *n.*

strength (strength) *n.* **1.** muscular power; vigor. **2.** durability; toughness. **3.** power in general, or a source of power. **4.** vigor or force. **5.** available numerical force in a military unit or other organization. **6.** the degree of intensity or concentration, as of a color, odor, etc. **7.** potency, as of a drug. — **on the strength of** based on or dependent on. [ME *strengthe*]

strength·en (STRENGK thən) *v.t.* **1.** make strong or stronger. **2.** encourage; hearten. —*v.i.* **3.** become or grow strong or stronger.

stren·u·ous (STREN yoo əs) *adj.* **1.** necessitating or characterized by strong effort or exertion. **2.** vigorously active or zealous. [< L *strenuus*] —**stren′u·ous·ly** *adv.*

strep·to·coc·cus (STREP tə KOK əs) *n. pl.* **·coc·ci** (-KOK sī) any of a genus of bacteria, grouped in long chains, including species causing many diseases. [< NL] — **strep′to·coc′cal** (-KOK əl) *adj.*

strep·to·my·cin (SREP tə MĪ sin) *n.* an antibiotic isolated from a moldlike organism. [< NL *Streptomyces*]

stress (stres) *n.* **1.** special weight, importance, or significance. **2.** *Mech.* **a** a force exerted between contiguous portions of a body or bodies and usu. expressed in pounds per square inch. **b** a force that tends to produce deformation in a body. **3.** influence exerted forcibly; pressure. **4.** emotional or intellectual strain or tension. **5.** the relative force with which a sound, syllable, or word is uttered. [ME *stresse*] —*v.t.* **1.** subject to stress. **2.** put emphasis on; accent. —**stress′ful** *adj.* —**stress′less** *adj.*

-stress *suffix of nouns* feminine form of -STER: *songstress*

stretch (strech) *v.t.* **1.** extend or draw out, as to full length or width. **2.** extend or draw out forcibly, esp. beyond normal or proper limits. **3.** put forth, hold out, or extend: often with *out.* —*v.i.* **4.** reach or extend over an area or from one place to another. **5.** become extended, esp. beyond normal or proper limits. **6.** extend one's body or limbs, esp. to relieve stiffness. **7.** lie down: usu. with *out.* [ME *strecchen*] —*n.* **1.** the act of stretching, or the state of being stretched. **2.** extent or reach of that which stretches. **3.** a continuous extent of space or time. **4.** in racing, the final portion of a race, called the **homestretch** or **backstretch. 5.** *Slang* a term of imprisonment. —*adj.* of a cloth or garment, made elastic. —**stretch′a•ble** *adj.*

stretch•er (STRECH ər) *n.* **1.** one who or that which stretches. **2.** any device for stretching, as for loosening the fit of shoes, for drying curtains, etc. **3.** a frame, as of stretched canvas, for carrying the wounded, sick, or dead; a litter. [ME]

strew (stroo) *v.t.* **strewed, strewn** or **strewed, strew•ing 1.** spread about loosely or at random; scatter; sprinkle. **2.** cover with something scattered or sprinkled. **3.** be scattered over (a surface). [ME *strewen*]

stri•a (STRĪ ə) *n. pl.* **stri•ae** (-ee) **1.** a distinctive streak, stripe, or band. **2.** *Geol.* a small groove, channel, or ridge on a rock surface, due to the action of glacier ice. [< L, furrow]

stri•ate (STRĪ it) *adj.* **1.** having fine linear markings; striped or grooved. **2.** constituting a stria or striae. Also **stri•at•ed** (STRĪ ay tid) —*v.t.* (STRĪ ayt) •**at•ed,** •**at•ing** mark with striae. [< L *striatus* grooved] —**stri•a′tion** *n.*

strick•en (STRIK ən) a past participle of STRIKE. —*adj.* **1.** strongly affected or af-

flicted, esp. by a disease; overcome. **2.** wounded, esp. by a weapon.

strict (strikt) *adj.* •**er,** •**est 1.** observing or enforcing rules exactly; severe. **2.** containing exact or severe rules. **3.** rigorously enforced and observed. **4.** complete; absolute: *strict* attention. [< L *strictus* drawn tight] —**strict′ly** *adv.* —**strict′ ness** *n.*

stric•ture (STRIK chər) *n.* **1.** a severe criticism. **2.** *Pathol.* an abnormal contraction of a duct or channel. [ME]

stride (strīd) *n.* **1.** a long and sweeping or measured step. **2.** the space passed over by such a step. —**hit one's stride** attain one's normal speed or effectiveness. —**make rapid strides** make quick progress. —**take (something) in one's stride** do or react to (something) without undue effort or disturbance. —*v.* **strode, strid•den** (STRID n), **strid•ing** *v.i.* **1.** walk with long steps. —*v.t.* **2.** walk through, along, etc. with long steps. **3.** pass over with a single stride. [ME *striden*]

stri•dent (STRĪD nt) *adj.* having or making a high, harsh sound; shrill; grating. [< L *stridere* make a harsh noise] —**stri′den•cy** *n.* —**stri′dent•ly** *adv.*

strife (strīf) *n.* **1.** angry contention; fighting. **2.** any contest for advantage or superiority. [ME *strif*]

strike (strīk) *v.* **struck, struck** or **strick•en, strik•ing** *v.t.* **1.** come into violent contact with; hit. **2.** hit with a blow; smite. **3.** deal (a blow etc.). **4.** cause to hit forcibly: He *struck* his hand on the table. **5.** attack; assault. **6.** remove, separate, or take off by or as by a blow or stroke: with *off, from,* etc.: *Strike* it from the record. **7.** ignite (a match etc.); also, produce (a light etc.) thus. **8.** form by stamping, printing, etc. **9.** indicate (a specified time) by the sound of a stroke, bell, etc. **10.** reach, touch, or affect suddenly or in a specified manner. **11.** come upon; find. **12.** occur to: An idea *strikes* me. **13.** impress in a specified manner: He *strikes* me as an ardent feminist. **14.** attract the attention of; impress. **15.** lower or haul down, as a sail or flag. **16.** cease working at in order to compel compliance to a demand, etc. **17.** make; arrive at: *strike* a bargain. —*v.i.* **18.** come into violent contact; hit. **19.** deal or aim a blow or blows. **20.** make an assault or attack. **21.** make a sound by or as by means of a blow or blows. **22.** ignite. **23.** run aground, as on a reef or shoal. **24.** come suddenly or unexpectedly; chance: with *on* or *upon*. **25.** cease work in order to enforce demands etc. **26.** snatch at or swallow the lure: said of fish. —**strike camp** take down the tents of a camp. —**strike down 1.** fell with a blow. **2.** affect disastrously; incapacitate completely. —**strike dumb** astonish; amaze. —**strike home 1.** deal an effective blow. **2.** have telling effect. —**strike it rich** come into wealth. —**strike out 1.** make a start: *strike out* on one's own. **2.** in baseball: **a** put out (the batter) by pitching three strikes. **b** be put out because of having three strikes counted against one. —**strike up 1.** begin to play, sing, or sound. **2.** start up; begin. [ME *striken*] —*n.* **1.** an act of striking or hitting; a blow. **2.** in baseball, a pitched ball counted against a batter, because swung at and missed, not swung at when it is within the strike zone, batted foul, etc. **3.** in bowling, the knocking down by a player of all the pins with the first bowl in any frame. **4.** disadvantage; handicap: The plan had three *strikes* against it from the start. **5.** the quitting of work by a body of workers to enforce demands. **6.** a new or unexpected discovery, as of oil or ore. **7.** an air attack on a surface target. **8.** in fishing, a bite. —**strik′- er** *n.*

strike·bound (STRĪK BOWND) *adj.* closed or immobilized by a labor strike.

strike·break·er (STRĪK BRAY kər) *n.* one who takes the place of a worker on strike or who supplies workers to take the place of strikers. —**strike′break′ing** *n.*

strike·out (STRĪK OWT) *n.* in baseball, an instance of striking out.

strik·ing (STRĪ king) *adj.* notable; impressive.

string (string) *n.* **1.** a slender line or strip, as of twine, cloth, leather, etc., thinner than a cord and thicker than a thread. **2.** the cord of a bow. **3.** prepared wire or catgut for musical instruments. **4.** a stringlike organ, object, or formation. **5.** a connected series or succession, as of things, acts, or events, sometimes implying unusual length: a *string* of lies. **6.** *pl.* stringed instruments, esp. those of an orchestra. **7.** *Usu. pl.* a condition or restriction attached to a proposition or gift. —**pull strings** manipulate or influence others to gain some advantage. — *v.* **strung, string·ing** *v.t.* **1.** thread, as beads, on or as on a string. **2.** fit with a string or strings, as a guitar. **3.** cover, drape, or

adorn with things attached to a string or strings. **4.** arrange or extend in a line or series. **5.** remove the strings from (vegetables). **6.** kill by hanging: usu. with *up.* **7.** *Slang* fool or deceive; hoax: often with *along.* —*v.i.* **8.** extend, stretch, or proceed in a line or series. **9.** form into strings. — **string along** *Informal* **1.** keep waiting. **2.** deceive; cheat. [ME]

string bean 1. any of several varieties of beans cultivated for their edible pods. **2.** the complete pod itself.

stringed instrument a musical instrument that produces its tones by means of one or more vibrating strings, as a violin, cello, etc.

strin·gent (STRIN jənt) *adj.* **1.** severe, as regulations; strict. **2.** hampered by obstructions or scarcity of money. **3.** convincing; forcible. [< L *stringere* draw tight] — **strin′gen·cy** *n.* —**strin′gent·ly** *adv.*

string·er (STRING ər) *n.* **1.** *Archit.* a heavy timber, generally horizontal, supporting other members of a structure. **2.** a lengthwise timber on which rails are laid. **3.** one having a specified rank, as on a team: a second *stringer.* **4.** a correspondent for an out-of-town correspondent newspaper, wire service, etc., usu. working part-time.

string·y (STRING ee) *adj.* **string·i·er, string·i·est 1.** containing fibrous strings. **2.** forming in strings; ropy. **3.** having tough sinews. —**string′i·ness** *n.*

strip¹ (strip) *n.* **1.** a narrow piece, comparatively long, as of cloth, tape, land, etc. **2.** an airplane landing strip. —*v.t.* **stripped, strip·ping** cut or tear into strips. [ME]

strip² *v.* **stripped** or **stript, strip·ping** *v.t.* **1.** pull the covering, clothing, etc. from. **2.** pull off (the covering or clothing). **3.** rob or plunder. **4.** make bare or empty. **5.** remove; take away; divest. **6.** *Mech.* damage or break the teeth, thread, etc. of (a gear, bolt, or the like). —*v.i.* **7.** remove one's clothing; undress; also, perform a striptease. [ME *stripen*] —**strip′per** *n.*

stripe¹ (strīp) *n.* **1.** a line, band, or strip of color, material, etc. different from that of the adjacent surface. **2.** a piece of material or braid on the sleeve of a uniform to indicate rank, service, etc.; chevron. —*v.t.* **striped, strip·ing** mark with a stripe or stripes. [< MDu.] —**striped** *adj.*

stripe² *n.* a blow struck with a whip or rod, as in flogging. [ME]

strip·ling (STRIP ling) *n.* a youth.

strip mining the mining of coal by stripping off soil to expose and dig out a vein.

strip•tease (STRIP TEEZ) *n.* in burlesque etc., a gradual disrobing to musical accompaniment. —*v.i.* perform a striptease. — **strip′teas′er** *n.*

strive (strīv) *v.i.* **strove** or **strived, striv•en** (STRIV ən) or **strived, striv•ing 1.** make earnest effort. **2.** engage in strife. [ME *striven*]

strobe (strohb) *n. Informal* **1.** an electronic tube producing intense, very brief flashes of light: also **strobe light. 2.** a stroboscope.

stro•bo•scope (STROH bə SKOHP) *n.* an instrument for observing the motion of a body or object by rendering it visible only at intervals or at certain points of its path. [< Gk. *strόbos* whirling + -SCOPE] — **stro′•bo•scop′ic** (STROH bə SKOP ik) *adj.*

strode (strohd) past tense of STRIDE.

stroke (strohk) *n.* **1.** the act or movement of striking; impact. **2.** a single movement, as of the hand, arm, or some instrument, by which something is made or done. **3.** a blow, or any ill effect caused as if by a blow. **4.** an attack of paralysis or apoplexy. **5.** a blow or the sound of a blow of a striking mechanism, as of a clock. **6.** a sudden or brilliant act; coup: a *stroke* of wit. **7.** a pulsation, as of the heart. **8.** a mark or dash of a pen or tool. **9.** a light, caressing movement; a stroking. **10.** a manner or technique of swimming. [ME *strok*] —*v.t.* **stroked, strok•ing 1.** pass the hand over gently or caressingly, or with light pressure. **2.** hit with a stroke of the arm, propel with a racket, etc.

stroll (strohl) *v.i.* **1.** walk in a leisurely or idle manner; saunter. **2.** wander; roam. —*v.t.* **3.** walk idly or wander over or through. — **stroll** *n.*

stroll•er (STROH lər) *n.* **1.** one who strolls. **2.** a light, often collapsible carriage in which a small child may sit upright.

strong (strawng) *adj.* •er, •est **1.** powerful in physique; muscular; vigorous. **2.** healthy; robust. **3.** morally powerful; firm; resolute; courageous. **4.** especially competent or able in a specified subject or field: *strong* in mathematics. **5.** solidly made or constituted. **6.** powerful as a combatant. **7.** having (a specified) numerical force: an army 20,000 *strong.* **8.** capable of exerting influence, authority, etc.: a *strong* government. **9.** sound: a *strong* bank. **10.** powerful in effect: *strong* poison. **11.** concentrated; not

diluted or weak: *strong* coffee. **12.** intense in degree or quality; not faint or mild. **13.** firm; forceful: a *strong* voice. **14.** distinct; marked: a *strong* resemblance. **15.** moving with great force: said of a wind, stream, or tide. —*adv.* in a strong manner; so as to be strong. [ME *strang*]

strong•arm (STRAWNG AHRM) *adj.* violent; having and depending on physical power. —*v.t.* use force upon; assault or coerce.

strong•hold (STRAWNG HOHLD) *n.* **1.** a strongly fortified place; fortress. **2.** a place of security or refuge.

strong•man (STRAWNG MAN) *n. pl.* •men a political leader or dictator willing and able to use extralegal force, esp. military force.

strong•mind•ed (STRAWNG MIN did) *adj.* having a determined, vigorous mind.

strong-willed (STRAWNG WILD) *adj.* having a strong will; obstinate.

stron•ti•um (STRON shəm) *n.* a hard metallic element (symbol Sr) of the calcium group. [< NL]

strontium 90 *Physics* a radioactive isotope of strontium.

strop (strop) *n.* **1.** a strip of leather, canvas, etc., on which to sharpen a razor. **2.** a strap. [ME] —*v.t.* **stropped, strop•ping** sharpen on a strop.

strove (strohv) a past tense of STRIVE.

struck (struk) past tense and a past participle of STRIKE. —*adj.* closed down or affected by a strike, as a factory.

struc•ture (STRUK chər) *n.* **1.** that which is constructed; a combination of related parts, as a building or machine. **2.** the position and arrangement of parts, as of an organism, molecule, etc. **3.** the manner of construction or organization. [ME] —*v.t.* •tured, •tur•ing form into an organized structure; build; organize. —**struc′tur•al** *adj.* — **struc′tur•al•ly** *adv.*

stru•del (STROOD l) *n.* a kind of pastry made of a thin sheet of dough, spread with fruit or cheese, nuts, etc., rolled, and baked. [< G, lit., whirlpool]

strug•gle (STRUG əl) *n.* **1.** a violent effort or series of efforts; a labored contest. **2.** conflict; strife; battle. —*v.i.* •gled, •gling **1.** contend with an adversary; fight. **2.** put forth violent efforts; strive. [ME *struglen*] —**strug′gler** *n.*

strum (strum) *v.t. & v.i.* **strummed, strum•ming 1.** play (a stringed instrument) with the fingers or by brushing a pick over the strings. **2.** play (a tune) in this manner. —*n.* the act of strumming; also, a particular rhythmical pattern of strumming.

strum•pet (STRUM pit) *n.* a whore. [ME]

strung (strung) past tense, past participle of STRING.

strung-out (STRUNG OWT) *Slang* **1.** incapacitated from drug abuse. **2.** physically or emotionally exhausted.

strut (strut) *n.* **1.** a proud or pompous step or walk. **2.** a member in a framework, designed to relieve weight or pressure in the direction of its length. —*v.* **strut•ted, strut•ting** *v.i.* **1.** walk with a strut. —*v.t.* **2.** support with or as with struts. [ME *strouten*] —**strut'ter** *n.*

stub (stub) *n.* **1.** any short projecting part or piece, as the stump of a tree. **2.** a short or broken remnant, as of a pencil, cigarette, etc. **3.** the detachable portion of a theater ticket, bank check, etc. **4.** anything blunt, short, or stumpy, as a pen with a broad point. [ME *stubbe*] —*v.t.* **stubbed, stub•bing** strike, as the toe, against something hard.

stub•ble (STUB əl) *n.* **1.** the stubs of grain stalks, sugar cane, etc., covering a field after the crop has been cut. **2.** any surface or growth resembling stubble, as short bristly hair. [ME *stuble*] —**stub'bly** *adj.*

stub•born (STUB ərn) *adj.* **1.** inflexible; unreasonably obstinate. **2.** difficult to handle, manage, or work with; resistant. **3.** determined and persistent: *stubborn* fighting. [ME *stuborn*] —**stub'born•ly** *adv.* —**stub'born•ness** *n.*

stub•by (STUB ee) *adj.* **•bi•er, •bi•est 1.** short, stiff, and bristling: a *stubby* beard. **2.** resembling or of the nature of a stub: a *stubby* pencil. **3.** stocky; thickset. —**stub'bi•ness** *n.*

stuc•co (STUK oh) *n. pl.* **•coes** or **•cos 1.** a plaster or cement used for the external coating of buildings. **2.** ornamental work made from stucco: also **stuc'co•work'**. [< Ital.] —*v.t.* **•coed, •co•ing** apply stucco to; decorate with stucco.

stuck (stuk) past tense, past participle of STICK.

stuck-up (STUK UP) *adj. Informal* conceited; snobbish.

stud[1] (stud) *n.* **1.** a short intermediate post, as in a building frame, to which laths are nailed. **2.** a knob, round-headed nail, or small protuberant ornament. **3.** a removable button used to fasten a shirt front etc.

[ME *stode*] —*v.t.* **stud•ded, stud•ding 1.** set thickly with small points, projections, or knobs. **2.** be scattered or strewn over. **3.** support or strengthen by means of studs or upright props.

stud[2] *n.* **1.** a studhorse or other male animal used for breeding purposes. **2.** stud poker. —**at** (or **in) stud** of a male animal, used or available for breeding purposes. [ME *stod*] —*adj.* **1.** of or pertaining to a stud. **2.** kept for breeding purposes.

stud•book (STUD buuk) *n.* an official record of the pedigree of thoroughbred stock.

stud•ding (STUD ing) *n.* **1.** in construction, studs or joists collectively. **2.** the material from which studs are made.

stu•dent (STOOD nt) *n.* **1.** one engaged in a course of study, esp. in a school. **2.** one who makes a thorough study of a particular subject. [ME]

student body all the students attending a school.

stud•horse (STUD hors) *n.* a stallion kept for breeding.

stud•ied (STUD eed) *adj.* **1.** deliberately designed or undertaken: a *studied* insult. **2.** lacking freshness, naturalness, or spontaneity. —**stud'ied•ly** *adv.*

stu•di•o (STOO dee oh) *n. pl.* **•os 1.** the workroom of an artist, photographer, etc. **2.** a place where motion pictures are filmed. **3.** a room or rooms where radio or television programs are broadcast or recorded. [< Ital.]

studio couch a backless couch, with a bedframe underneath that may be drawn out to form a bed.

stu•di•ous (STOO dee əs) *adj.* **1.** given to study. **2.** earnest in effort. —**stu'di•ous•ly** *adv.* —**stu'di•ous•ness** *n.*

stud poker a game of poker in which one or more cards are dealt face down and the rest face up.

stud•y (STUD ee) *v.* **stud•ied, stud•y•ing** *v.t.* **1.** apply the mind in acquiring a knowledge of. **2.** examine; scrutinize. **3.** give thought and attention to. —*v.i.* **4.** apply the mind in acquiring knowledge. **5.** follow a regular course of instruction. [ME *studie*] —*n. pl.* **stud•ies 1.** the act of studying; the process of acquiring information. **2.** something to be studied; a branch of knowledge. **3.** in art, a first sketch, exercise, etc. **4.** a carefully elaborated literary treatment of a subject. **5.** a room devoted to study, reading, etc.

stuff (stuf) v.t. **1.** fill completely; cram full. **2.** plug. **3.** force or cram; pack. **4.** fill or expand with padding, as a cushion. **5.** fill (a fowl, roast, etc.) with stuffing. **6.** in taxidermy, fill the skin of (a bird, animal, etc.) with a material preparatory to mounting. **7.** fill or cram with food. **8.** put fraudulent votes into (a ballot box). —v.i. **9.** eat to excess. [ME *stuffen*] —n. **1.** the material out of which something may be shaped or made; the fundamental element of anything. **2.** *Informal* one's possessions: all my *stuff*. **3.** a worthless collection of things; rubbish. **4.** woven material, esp. of wool; also, any textile fabric. **5.** *Informal* any unspecified or vaguely defined substance, activity, etc.

stuffed shirt a pompous, self-satisfied person.

stuff·ing (STUF ing) n. **1.** the material with which anything is stuffed. **2.** a mixture, as of bread crumbs with meat and seasoning, used in stuffing fowl etc.

stuff·y (STUF ee) adj. **stuff·i·er, stuff·i·est 1.** badly ventilated. **2.** impeding respiration. **3.** pompous; smug. **4.** old-fashioned; strait-laced. —**stuff'i·ly** adv. —**stuff'i·ness** n.

stul·ti·fy (STUL tə fī) v.t. **·fied, ·fy·ing 1.** cause to appear absurd or foolish. **2.** make worthless or ineffectual. [< LL *stultificare* make foolish] —**stul'ti·fi·ca'tion** n.

stum·ble (STUM bəl) v.i. **·bled, ·bling 1.** miss one's step in walking or running; trip. **2.** walk or proceed unsteadily. **3.** speak, read, etc. falteringly. **4.** happen upon something by chance: with *across, on, upon*, etc. [ME *stumblen*] —n. **1.** the act of stumbling. **2.** a blunder; false step. —**stum'bler** n.

stumbling block any obstacle or hindrance.

stump (stump) n. **1.** the portion of a tree trunk left standing when the tree is felled. **2.** the part of anything, as of a limb, tooth, pencil, etc., that remains when the main part has been removed; stub. **3.** *pl. Informal* legs. **4.** a place or platform from which a political speech is made. **5.** a heavy step; a clump; also, the sound made by such a step. —**take the stump** electioneer in a political campaign. [ME *stumpe*] —adj. **1.** being or resembling a stump; stumpy. **2.** of or pertaining to political oratory or campaigning: a *stump* speaker. —v.t. **1.** reduce to a stump. **2.** remove stumps from (land). **3.** canvass (a district) by making political speeches. **4.** bring to a halt by real or fan-

cied obstacles; baffle. —v.i. **5.** walk heavily, noisily, and stiffly. **6.** go about making political speeches. —**stump'er** n.

stump·y (STUM pee) adj. **stump·i·er, stump·i·est 1.** full of stumps. **2.** like a stump; short and thick. —**stump'i·ness** n.

stun (stun) v.t. **stunned, stun·ning 1.** render unconscious or incapable of action by a blow, fall, etc. **2.** astonish; astound. **3.** daze or overwhelm by loud or explosive noise. [ME *stunen*]

stung (stung) past tense, past participle of STING.

stunk (stungk) past participle and alternative past tense of STINK.

stun·ner (STUN ər) n. **1.** one who or that which stuns. **2.** *Informal* a person of extraordinary beauty, excellence, etc.

stun·ning (STUN ing) adj. **1.** rendering unconscious. **2.** impressively beautiful etc. —**stun'ning·ly** adv.

stunt[1] (stunt) v.t. check the natural development of; dwarf; cramp. —n. a check in growth, progress, or development. [ME, stubborn] —**stunt'ed** adj.

stunt[2] n. a sensational feat, as of bodily skill. —v.i. perform stunts.

stu·pe·fy (STOO pə fī) v.t. **·fied, ·fy·ing 1.** dull the senses or faculties of; stun or make numb. **2.** amaze; astound. [< MF *stupefier*] —**stu'pe·fied** adj.

stu·pen·dous (stoo PEN dəs) adj. **1.** highly impressive; astonishing. **2.** of prodigious size or bulk. [< L *stupendus* astonished] —**stu·pen'dous·ly** adv.

stu·pid (STOO pid) adj. **1.** very slow of apprehension or understanding. **2.** marked by or resulting from lack of understanding, reason, or wit; senseless. **3.** tedious; dull. [< MF *stupide*] —n. *Informal* a stupid person. —**stu·pid'i·ty** n. —**stu'pid·ly** adv.

stu·por (STOO pər) n. **1.** a condition in which the senses and faculties are suspended or greatly dulled, as by drugs or liquor. **2.** mental dullness; stupidity. [ME] —**stu'por·ous** adj.

stur·dy (STUR dee) adj. **·di·er, ·di·est 1.** rugged and strong; hardy. **2.** firm and unyielding; resolute; courageous. [ME *stourdi* brave] —**stur'di·ly** adv. —**stur'di·ness** n.

stur·geon (STUR jən) n. a fish of northern regions, valued as a source of caviar. [ME]

stut·ter (STUT ər) v.t. & v.i. utter or speak with spasmodic repetition, blocking, and prolongation of sounds, esp. those at the beginning of a word. [ME *stutten*] —*n.* the act or habit of stuttering. —**stut′ter·er** *n.* —**stut′ter·ing** *n.*

sty[1] (stī) *n. pl.* **sties** a pen for swine. [ME] —*v.t. & v.i.* **stied, sty·ing** keep or live in a sty.

sty[2] *n. pl.* **sties** *Pathol.* a small, inflamed swelling of a gland on the edge of the eyelid. Also **stye.** [< *Obs. styan*]

styg·i·an (STIJ ee ən) *adj. Often cap.* infernal; dark and gloomy. [< L *stygius* < Greek mythology, *Styx*, a river of Hades]

style (stīl) *n.* **1.** manner of expressing thought, in writing or speaking. **2.** a particular or characteristic mode of composition, construction, etc.: the Gothic *style.* **3.** the manner in which some action or work is performed. **4.** a good or suitable manner of expression or performance. **5.** a mode of conduct; a way of living: live in makeshift *style.* **6.** a fashionable manner or appearance: live in *style.* **7.** a particular fashion in clothing. **8.** the conventions of design, usage, punctuation, etc. observed by a publisher or printer. **9.** stylus. **10.** *Bot.* the prolongation of a carpel or ovary, bearing the stigma. [ME] —*v.t.* **styled, styl·ing 1.** name; give a title to. **2.** make consistent in typography, spelling, punctuation, etc. **3.** give form, fashion, or style to.

style book a book containing rules of spelling, punctuation, typography, etc., used by printers, editors, etc.

styl·ish (STĪ lish) *adj.* having style or fashionableness in clothes, etc. —**styl′ish·ly** *adv.*

styl·ist (STĪ list) *n.* one who is a master of literary or rhetorical style. —**sty·lis′tic** *adj.* —**sty·lis′ti·cal·ly** *adv.*

styl·ize (STĪ līz) *v.t.* **·ized, ·iz·ing** make conform to a distinctive mode or style; conventionalize.

sty·lus (STĪ ləs) *n. pl.* **·lus·es** or **·li** (-lī) **1.** a pointed instrument used for writing or marking on wax, making stencils, etc. **2.** the needle of a record player or of a recording instrument. Also called *style.* [< L]

sty·mie (STĪ mee) *v.t.* **·mied, ·my·ing 1.** block or hinder; thwart. **2.** baffle or perplex.

styp·tic (STIP tik) *adj.* stopping hemorrhage or bleeding. Also **styp′ti·cal.** [ME] —*n.* a styptic substance or agent. Also **styptic pencil.**

sua·sion (SWAY zhən) *n.* persuasion. [ME]

suave (swahv) *adj.* **suav·er, suav·est** smoothly pleasant and ingratiating; blandly polite; urbane. [< F] —**suave′ly** *adv.* —**suave′·ness** *n.*

sub (sub) *n. Informal* short for any of various words beginning with *sub-,* as: **a** substitute. **b** submarine.

sub·a·tom·ic (SUB ə TOM ik) *adj.* within the atom: *subatomic* particle.

sub·con·scious (sub KON shəs) *adj.* **1.** not clearly or wholly conscious. **2.** *Psychol.* denoting the subconscious. —*n. Psychol.* the portion of mental activity not directly in the focus of consciousness but sometimes susceptible to recall. —**sub·con′scious·ly** *adv.*

sub·con·ti·nent (sub KON tn ənt) *n. Geog.* a great land mass forming part of a continent, as India.

sub·con·tract (sub KON trakt) *n.* a secondary contract assigning part or all of the work to another party. —*v.t. & v.i.* (SUB kən TRAKT) make a subcontract (for). —**sub·con′trac·tor** *n.*

sub·crit·i·cal (sub KRIT i kəl) *adj. Physics* of or containing fissionable material in a quantity not sufficient to start or sustain a chain reaction: *subcritical* mass.

sub·cu·ta·ne·ous (SUB kyoo TAY nee əs) *adj.* situated or applied beneath the skin. [< LL *subcutaneus*]

sub·di·vide (SUB di VĪD) *v.t. & v.i.* **·vid·ed, ·vid·ing 1.** divide (a part) again. **2.** divide (land) into lots for sale. [ME] —**sub·di·vi·sion** (SUB di VIZH ən) *n.*

sub·due (səb DOO) *v.t.* **·dued, ·du·ing 1.** conquer; subjugate; vanquish. **2.** bring under control; curb; tame. **3.** reduce the intensity of; soften. [ME *subduen*]

sub·fam·i·ly (sub FAM ə lee) *n. pl.* **·lies 1.** *Biol.* a division of plants or animals next below a family but above a genus. **2.** *Ling.* a division of languages below a family and above a branch.

sub·hu·man (sub HYOO mən) *adj.* **1.** less than or imperfectly human. **2.** below the level of *Homo sapiens.*

sub·ject (SUB jikt) *adj.* **1.** under the control or power of another. **2.** liable to be affected by: with *to*: *subject* to disease. **3.** likely to bring about or incur: with *to*: *subject* to severe criticism. **4.** dependent on: with *to*: a treaty *subject* to ratification. —*n.* **1.** one who is under the governing power of another, esp. of a monarch. **2.** a person or thing used or treated in a specified way: the *subject* of an experiment. **3.** a topic or theme, as of a discussion. **4.** a branch of learning or course of study. **5.** *Gram.* the word, phrase, or clause of a sentence about which something is stated or asked in the predicate. [ME] —*v.t.* (səb JEKT) **1.** bring under control. **2.** cause to undergo some experience or action: *subject* one to torture. —**sub·jec'tion** *n.*

sub·jec·tive (səb JEK tiv) *adj.* **1.** of, existing within, or resulting from an individual's own thoughts, emotions, interests, etc.; personal. **2.** *Gram.* designating the nominative case. —**sub·jec'tive·ly** *adv.* —**sub·jec·tiv·i·ty** (SUB jek TIV i tee) *n.*

sub·ju·gate (SUB jə GAYT) *v.t.* •**gat·ed,** •**gat·ing** conquer or make subservient. [ME *subjugaten*] —**sub'ju·ga'tion** *n.*

sub·junc·tive (səb JUNGK tiv) *Gram. adj.* of or pertaining to the mood of the verb expressing possibility, desire, supposition, etc. In the sentence: "If I were you, I'd do it," *were* is in the subjunctive. —*n.* **1.** the subjunctive mood. **2.** a verb form in this mood. [< LL *subjunctivus* subordinated]

sub·lease (SUB lees) *n.* a lease granted by a tenant. —*v.t.* (sub LEES) •**leased,** •**leas·ing** obtain or let (property) on a sublease. —**sub·les·see** (SUB le SEE) **sub·les·sor** (SUB le SOR) *n.*

sub·let (sub LET) *v.t.* •**let,** •**let·ting 1.** sublease (property) to another. **2.** subcontract (work).

sub·li·mate (SUB lə MAYT) *v.* •**mat·ed,** •**mat·ing** *v.t.* **1.** *Chem.* convert (a solid substance) directly to the gaseous state. **2.** *Psychol.* convert the energy of (instinctual drives) into acceptable social manifestations. **3.** divert the expression of (a desire or impulse) to a form that is considered more socially acceptable. —*v.i.* **4.** undergo sublimation. —*n.* the product or act of sublimation. [ME] —**sub'li·ma'tion** *n.*

sub·lime (sə BLĪM) *adj.* noble; exalted; grand. —*n.* that which is sublime: often with *the.* —*v.t. & v.i.* •**limed,** •**lim·ing** *Chem.* sublimate. [ME *sublimen*] —**sub·lime'ly** *adv.* —**sub·lime'ness** *n.*

sub·lim·i·nal (sub LIM ə nl) *adj. Psychol.* perceived below the threshold of consciousness: a *subliminal* image. [< *sub-* below + L *limen* threshold] —**sub·lim'i·nal·ly** *adv.*

sub·ma·rine (SUB mə REEN) *adj.* existing, done, or operating beneath the surface of the sea: *submarine* life. —*n.* **1.** a ship designed to operate below the surface of the sea. **2.** a hero sandwich.

sub·merge (səb MURJ) *v.t. & v.i.* •**merged,** •**merg·ing** plunge or sink beneath the surface of water. [< L *submergere* immerse] —**sub·mer'gence** *n.*

sub·merse (səb MURS) *v.t.* •**mersed,** •**mers·ing** submerge. [< L *submersus*] —**sub·mer'si·ble** *adj.* —**sub·mer·sion** (səb MUR zhən) *n.*

sub·mis·sion (səb MISH ən) *n.* **1.** the act of submitting or yielding to some power or authority. **2.** the act of presenting something for consideration, approval, etc.

sub·mis·sive (səb MIS iv) *adj.* yielding; obedient; docile. —**sub·mis'sive·ly** *adv.* —**sub·mis'sive·ness** *n.*

sub·mit (səb MIT) *v.* •**mit·ted,** •**mit·ting** *v.t.* **1.** present for consideration, decision, or approval. **2.** present as one's opinion; suggest. —*v.i.* **3.** give up; surrender. [ME *submitten*] —**sub·mit'tal** *n.*

sub·or·di·nate (sə BOR dn it) *adj.* **1.** of a lower class, rank, grade, etc. **2.** unimportant; minor. **3.** *Gram.* of or designating a clause connected with and dependent upon another clause. —*n.* a subordinate person or thing. —*v.t.* •**nat·ed,** •**nat·ing** (sə BOR dn AYT) **1.** make subordinate. **2.** hold as of less importance. [ME] —**sub·or'di·nate·ly** *adv.* —**sub·or'di·na'tion** *n.*

sub·orn (sə BORN) *v.t.* bribe or otherwise influence (a person) to commit a criminal act, esp. perjury. [< MF *suborner*] —**sub·or·na·tion** (SUB or NAY shən) *n.* —**sub·orn'er** *n.*

sub·plot (SUB PLOT) *n.* a plot subordinate to the principal one in a novel, play, etc.

sub·poe·na (sə PEE nə) *n.* a judicial writ requiring a person to appear in court to give testimony. —*v.t.* summon by subpoena. [ME *suppena*]

sub ro·sa (sub ROH zə) *Latin* confidentially; in secret.

sub·scribe (səb SKRĪB) *v.i.* •**scribed,** •**scrib·ing 1.** agree to receive and pay for issues of a magazine, a service, etc.: with *to.* **2.** give one's assent or approval; support: with *to.* [ME *subscriben*] —**sub·scrib'er** *n.*

sub·script (SUB skript) *adj.* written below and to the right or left. —*n.* **1.** a subscript character. **2.** *Math.* a subscript character that indicates a specific operation or characteristic. [< L *subscriptus* written under]

sub·scrip·tion (səb SKRIP shən) *n.* **1.** an agreement to pay for the receipt of a magazine, book, etc.; also, the amount to be paid.

2. a fund, as for a charity, raised by contributions.

sub·se·quent (SUB si kwənt) *adj.* following in time, place, etc.; coming after. [ME] — **sub′se·quent·ly** *adv.*

sub·ser·vi·ent (səb SUR vee ənt) *adj.* **1.** being of service; useful. **2.** servile; obsequious. [< L *subservire* serve under] — **sub·ser′vi·ence** *n.* —**sub·ser′vi·ent·ly** *adv.*

sub·side (səb SĪD) *v.i.* •**sid·ed**, •**sid·ing 1.** become calm or quiet; abate. **2.** sink to a lower level or to the bottom; settle. [< L *subsidere* settle] —**sub·sid·ence** (səb SĪD ns) *n.*

sub·sid·i·ar·y (səb SID ee ER ee) *adj.* **1.** giving aid or support; helpful. **2.** subordinate; secondary. **3.** of or relating to a subsidy. [< L *subsidiarius*] —*n. pl.* •**ar·ies 1.** one who gives aid or support. **2.** a company owned and controlled by another.

sub·si·dize (SUB si DĪZ) *v.t.* •**dized**, •**diz·ing** aid or support with a subsidy. — **sub′si·di·za′tion** *n.* —**sub′si·diz′er** *n.*

sub·si·dy (SUB si dee) *n. pl.* •**dies** financial aid, as that granted by a government to private enterprise or to another government. [ME]

sub·sist (səb SIST) *v.i.* **1.** continue to exist; persist. **2.** manage to live: often with *on* or *by: subsist* on vegetables. [< LL *subsistere* exist]

sub·sis·tence (səb SIS təns) *n.* **1.** continued existence. **2.** means of support; sustenance; livelihood. —**sub·sis′tent** *adj.*

sub·soil (SUB soil) *n.* the stratum of earth next beneath the surface soil.

sub·son·ic (sub SON ik) *adj. Aeron.* having a speed less than that of sound.

sub·stance (SUB stəns) *n.* **1.** the basic material of which anything consists. **2.** any type of matter of a specific chemical composition. **3.** density; body. **4.** a substantial quality; solidity: There is no *substance* to his remarks. **5.** the essential part of anything; essence; the gist. **6.** material wealth; property. [ME]

sub·stand·ard (sub STAN dərd) *adj.* below the standard or norm; nonstandard.

sub·stan·tial (səb STAN shəl) *adj.* **1.** solid; strong; firm. **2.** of real worth and importance; valuable. **3.** considerable; ample; great: *substantial* progress. **4.** possessed of wealth and influence. **5.** of or pertaining to substance; material; not imaginary. **6.** nourishing: a *substantial* lunch. [ME *sub-*

stancial] —**sub·stan′ti·al′i·ty** *n.* — **sub·stan′tial·ly** *adv.*

sub·stan·ti·ate (səb STAN shee AYT) *v.t.* •**at·ed**, •**at·ing 1.** prove with evidence; verify. **2.** give substance to; embody. [< NL *substantiatus*] —**sub·stan′ti·a′tion** *n.*

sub·stan·tive (SUB stən tiv) *n. Gram.* a noun, or any word or phrase that functions as a noun. —*adj.* **1.** *Gram.* capable of being used as a noun. **2.** having substance or reality; lasting. [ME]

sub·sti·tute (SUB sti TOOT) *v.* •**tut·ed**, •**tut·ing** *v.t.* **1.** put (someone or something) in the place of another. —*v.i.* **2.** act as a substitute. —*n.* a person or thing acting or used in place of another. [ME] — **sub′sti·tu′tion** *n.*

sub·stra·tum (sub STRAY təm) *n. pl.* •**ta** (-tə), •**tums 1.** an underlying stratum or layer, as of earth or rock. **2.** foundation; basis. [< NL]

sub·struc·ture (sub STRUK chər) *n.* the groundwork or foundation of a building etc.

sub·sume (səb SOOM) *v.t.* •**sumed**, •**sum·ing** include within a larger class or general category. [< NL *subsumere*]

sub·tend (səb TEND) *v.t. Geom.* extend under or opposite to, as the side of a triangle opposite to an angle. [< L *subtendere* stretch beneath]

sub·ter·fuge (SUB tər FYOOJ) *n.* any stratagem to avoid unpleasantness or difficulty. [< LL *subterfugium*]

sub·ter·ra·ne·an (SUB tə RAY nee əm) *adj.* **1.** situated below the surface of the earth; underground. **2.** hidden or secret.

sub·ti·tle (SUB TĪT L) *N.* **1. a secondary or explanatory title of a book, play, etc. 2.** in foreign-language motion pictures or television, a running translation of the dialogue, usu. appearing at the bottom of the screen.

sub·tle (SUT l) *adj.* **1.** cunning or crafty; sly. **2.** keen; discriminating. **3.** of delicate texture; refined; elusive. **4.** ingenious; clever. [ME *sutil*] —**sub′tly** *adv.*

sub·tle·ty (SUT l tee) *n. pl.* •**ties 1.** the state or quality of being subtle. **2.** something subtle, as a fine distinction.

sub·tract (səb TRAKT) *v.t. & v.i.* take away or deduct, as one quantity from another. [< L *subtractus* withdrawn] —**sub·trac′tion** *n.*

sub·tra·hend (SUB trə HEND) *n. Math.* a number to be subtracted from another.

sub·trop·i·cal (sub TROP i kəl) *adj.* of or

pertaining to regions adjacent to the Torrid Zone.

sub•urb (SUB urb) *n. Often pl.* an area, esp. a residential district, lying on the outskirts of a city. [ME] **—sub•ur•ban** (sə BUR bən) *adj.*

sub•ur•ban•ite (sə BUR bə NĪT) *n.* a resident of a suburb.

sub•ur•bi•a (sə BUR bee ə) *n.* suburbs or suburbanites collectively.

sub•ven•tion (səb VEN shən) *n.* a grant of money; subsidy. [ME]

sub•ver•sion (səb VUR zhən) *n.* the act of undermining or overthrowing a government or other institution.

sub•ver•sive (səb VUR siv) *adj.* tending to subvert or overthrow, as a government. — *n.* one who subverts a government etc.

sub•vert (səb VURT) *v.t.* **1.** overthrow or destroy. **2.** undermine the morals etc. of; corrupt. [ME *subverten* overturn]

sub•way (SUB way) *n.* an underground electric railroad, esp. one within a city.

suc•ceed (sək SEED) *v.i.* **1.** accomplish what is attempted or intended; be successful. **2.** come next in order; follow. **3.** come after another into office, etc.; be the successor: often with *to.* —*v.t.* **4.** follow. **5.** be the successor of. [ME *succeden*]

suc•cess (sək SES) *n.* **1.** a favorable or desired outcome. **2.** a person, enterprise, etc., that succeeds. **3.** attainment of wealth etc. [< L *successus*] **—suc•cess'ful** *adj.* **—suc•cess'ful•ly** *adv.*

suc•ces•sion (sək SESH ən) *n.* **1.** the act of following in order. **2.** a series; sequence. **3.** the act or right of succeeding another to an office, rank, etc.

suc•ces•sive (sək SES iv) *adj.* following in sequence; consecutive. **—suc•ces'sive•ly** *adv.*

suc•ces•sor (sək SES ər) *n.* one who or that which succeeds or follows.

suc•cinct (sək SINGKT) *adj.* brief and to the point; terse; concise. [ME] **—suc•cinct'ly** *adv.* **—suc•cinct'ness** *n.*

suc•cor (SUK ər) *n.* help or relief rendered to someone in danger or distress. [ME *succur*] —*v.t.* assist; help; aid.

suc•cu•bus (SUK yə bəs) *n. pl.* **•bi** (-BĪ) **1.** in folklore, a female demon that has sexual intercourse with sleeping men. **2.** any evil spirit. [ME]

suc•cu•lent (SUK yə lənt) *adj.* **1.** juicy. **2.** *Bot.* juicy or fleshy, as the tissues of certain plants. [< L *suculentus*] **—suc'cu•lence** *n.* **—suc'cu•lent•ly** *adv.*

suc•cumb (sə KUM) *v.i.* **1.** give way; yield. **2.** die. [< F *succomber*]

such (such) *adj.* **1.** of that kind; of the same or like kind: *such* people; shirts *such* as these. **2.** being the same as what has been indicated: There are no *such* things. **3.** of extreme degree, size, etc.: It was *such* a load. **—as such 1.** as being what is indicated or implied: An executive, *as such*, must take responsibility. **2.** in or by itself: Clothes, *as such*, do not make the man. **—such as 1.** for example: He raises livestock, *such as* cows and sheep. **2.** of a particular kind of degree: The outcome of the trial was *such as* might be expected. —*pron.* **1.** such a person or thing: She is the friend of *such* as are in trouble. **2.** the same; the aforesaid: *Such* being the case, we agreed. —*adv.* so: He has *such* awful manners. [ME]

such•like (SUCH LĪK) *adj.* of a like or similar kind. —*pron.* persons or things of such a kind.

suck (suk) *v.t.* **1.** draw into the mouth by creating a partial vacuum with the lips and tongue. **2.** draw in or take up in a manner resembling this; absorb. **3.** draw liquid from with the mouth. **4.** hold in the mouth and consume: *suck* candy. —*v.i.* **5.** draw in liquid, air, etc. by suction. **6.** suckle. —*n.* the act of sucking; suction. [ME *souken*]

suck•er (SUK ər) *n.* **1.** one who or that which sucks. **2.** *Zool.* an organ by which an animal adheres to other bodies by suction. **3.** *Informal* one who is easily deceived; a gull or dupe. **4.** *Informal* a lollipop. **5.** *Bot.* a shoot arising from an underground stem or root. [ME]

suck•le (SUK əl) *v.* **•led, •ling** *v.t.* **1.** give milk to from the breast; nurse. **2.** bring up; nourish. —*v.i.* **3.** drink milk from the breast: also *suck.* [ME *sucklen*]

suck•ling (SUK ling) *n.* **1.** an unweaned mammal. **2.** an infant. [ME]

su•crose (SOO krohs) *n. Biochem.* the sugar obtained from the sugarcane, sugar beet, etc. [< F *sucre* sugar]

suc•tion (SUK shən) *n.* **1.** the act or process of sucking. **2.** the force produced by a partial vacuum in a space connected with a liquid or gas under pressure. [< L *sugere* suck]

sud•den (SUD n) *adj.* **1.** happening or come upon without warning; unexpected: *sudden* downpours. **2.** quick; hasty: *sudden* decisions. **3.** sharp; abrupt: *sudden* turns in the road. **—all of a sudden** without warning; unexpectedly. [ME *sodain*] **—sud′den·ly** *adv.* **—sud′den·ness** *n.*

sudden infant death syndrome (SIDS) see CRIB DEATH.

su·dor·if·ic (soo də RIF ik) *Med. adj.* causing perspiration. **—n.** a medicine that causes sweating. [< NL *sudorificus*]

suds (sudz) *n.* (*construed as pl.*) **1.** soapy water, or bubbles and froth on its surface. **2.** foam. **3.** *Slang* beer. **—suds′y** *adj.* **suds· i·er, suds·i·est**

sue (soo) *v.* **sued, su·ing** *v.t.* **1.** take action against in a court of law. **—v.i. 2.** take legal action. **3.** appeal; plead: with *for*: *sue* for peace. [ME *suen*]

suede (swayd) *n.* **1.** a leather having a soft napped finish. **2.** a woven or knitted fabric finished to resemble this. [< F *gants de Suède* Swedish gloves]

su·et (SOO it) *n.* the hard fat of cattle and sheep, used in cooking and making tallow. [ME *sewet*]

suf·fer (SUF ər) *v.i.* **1.** feel pain or distress. **2.** sustain loss or injury. **—v.t. 3.** experience; undergo: *suffer* setbacks. **4.** bear; endure: *suffer* more pain. **5.** allow; permit: I cannot *suffer* interruption. [ME *sufferen*] **—suf′fer·a·ble** *adj.* **—suf′fer·a·bly** *adv.*

suf·fer·ance (SUF ər əns) *n.* **1.** permission implied by failure to prohibit; passive consent. **2.** capacity to endure suffering.

suf·fer·ing (SUF ər ing) *n.* the state of anguish or pain of one who suffers; misery; hardship.

suf·fice (sə FĪS) *v.i.* **-ficed, -fic·ing** be sufficient or adequate; enough. [ME *sufficen*]

suf·fi·cient (sə FISH ənt) *adj.* being all that is needed; adequate; enough. [ME] **— suf·fi′cien·cy** *n.* **—suf·fi′cient·ly** *adv.*

suf·fix (SUF iks) *n. Gram.* an addition to the end of a word to form a derivative of that word. [< NL *suffixum*]

suf·fo·cate (SUF ə KAYT) *v.* **-cat·ed, -cat·ing** *v.t.* **1.** kill by stopping one's breathing; smother. **2.** stifle or extinguish, as a fire. **—v.i. 3.** die from suffocation. [< L *suffocatus* choked] **—suf′fo·cat′ing·ly** *adv.* **—suf′fo·ca′tion** *n.*

suf·frage (SUF rij) *n.* **1.** the right or privilege of voting; franchise. **2.** the act or process of voting. [ME] **—suf′fra·gist** *n.*

suf·fra·gette (SUF rə JET) *n.* formerly, a woman who advocated or agitated for female suffrage.

suf·fuse (sə FYOOZ) *v.t.* **-fused, -fus·ing** overspread, as with a vapor or color. [< L *suffusus* poured beneath] **—suf·fu·sion** (sə FYOO zhən) *n.* **—suf·fu·sive** (sə FYOO siv) *adj.*

sug·ar (SHUUG ər) *n. Biochem.* **a** a sweet carbohydrate obtained from the juice of various plants, as from the sugarcane, the sugar beet, and the sugar maple. **♦** Collateral adjective: *saccharine.* **b** any of a large class of similar carbohydrates, widely distributed in plants and animals. **—v.t. 1.** sweeten, cover, or coat with sugar. **2.** make agreeable. **—v.i. 3.** make maple sugar. **4.** form sugar. [ME *sugre*] **—sug′ared** *adj.*

sugar beet a sugar-producing species of beet.

sug·ar·cane (SHUUG ər KAYN) *n.* a tall tropical grass grown as a major source of sugar.

sug·ar·coat (SHUUG ər KOHT) *v.t.* **1.** cover with sugar. **2.** make appear attractive or less distasteful, as with flattery.

sugar maple a maple yielding a sap from which maple sugar is made.

sug·ar·y (SHUUG ə ree) *adj.* **1.** containing much sugar; sweet. **2.** insincerely or cloyingly sweet. **—sug′ar·i·ness** *n.*

sug·gest (səg JEST) *v.t.* **1.** put forward for consideration etc.; propose. **2.** bring or call to mind, as by association; connote. **3.** give a hint of; intimate: The simple house *suggested* a modest income. [< L *suggestus* suggested]

sug·gest·i·ble (səg JES tə bəl) *adj.* **1.** that can be suggested. **2.** easily led; yielding: a *suggestible* patient. **—sug·gest′i·bil′i·ty** *n.*

sug·ges·tion (səg JES chən) *n.* **1.** the act of suggesting. **2.** something suggested. **3.** a hint; trace.

sug·ges·tive (səg JES tiv) *adj.* **1.** tending to suggest; hinting at: with *of*: clothing *suggestive* of another era. **2.** hinting at something indecent or improper; provocative.

su·i·cide (SOO ə SID) *n.* **1.** the intentional taking of one's own life. **2.** self-inflicted ruin, as in business or politics. **3.** one who has taken his or her own life. [< NL *suicidium*] **—su′i·ci′dal** *adj.*

su·i gen·e·ris (SOO ee JEN ər is) *Latin* one of a kind; unique.

suit (soot) *n.* **1.** a set of clothing consisting of a coat and trousers or skirt intended to be worn together. **2.** any of the four sets of playing cards in a deck, as the spades or diamonds. **3.** *Law* a proceeding in a court of law to recover a right or claim. **4.** courtship. **—follow suit** do the same as another. — *v.t.* **1.** meet the requirements of. **2.** please; satisfy. **3.** accommodate; adapt. [ME *siute* sequence]

suit·a·ble (SOO tə bəl) *adj.* appropriate to a particular occasion, condition, etc.; proper. **—suit′a·bil′i·ty, suit′a·ble·ness** *n.* — **suit′a·bly** *adv.*

suit·case (SOOT KAYS) *n.* a rectangular valise.

suite (sweet) *n.* **1.** a number of connected rooms. **2.** a set of matching furniture for a given room. **3.** a company of attendants or followers; retinue. **4.** *Music* a form of instrumental composition varying freely in construction. [< F]

suit·or (SOO tər) *n.* a man who courts a woman; wooer. [ME *seutor* follower]

su·ki·ya·ki (SOO kee YAH kee) *n.* a Japanese dish of thinly sliced meat and vegetables cooked in soy sauce and sake. [< Japanese]

sul·fa drug (SUL fə) *Chem.* any of a large group of organic compounds effective in treating certain bacterial infections.

sul·fa·nil·a·mide (SUL fə NIL ə MID) *n. Chem.* a colorless sulfur-containing compound used in treating various bacterial infections.

sul·fur (SUL fər) *n.* a pale yellow, non-metallic element (symbol S) existing in several forms, of which the best known is a crystalline solid that burns with a blue flame and a suffocating odor. Also **sul′phur.** [ME *sulphur* brimstone]

sul·fu·ric (sul FYUUR ik) *adj. Chem.* pertaining to or derived from sulfur, esp. in its higher valence.

sulfuric acid *Chem.* a colorless, exceedingly corrosive, oily liquid: also called *oil of vitriol.*

sul·fu·rous (SUL fər əs) *adj.* **1.** pertaining to or derived from sulfur, esp. in its lower valence. **2.** fiery; hellish. Also **sul′phu·rous.**

sulk (sulk) *v.i.* be sulky or morose. —*n. Often pl.* a sulky mood or humor. [Back formation of SULKY]

sulk·y¹ (SUL kee) *adj.* **sulk·i·er, sulk·i·est** sullenly cross; doggedly or resentfully ill-humored. [? < *Obs. sulke* sluggish] — **sulk′i·ly** *adv.* —**sulk′i·ness** *n.*

sulk·y² *n. pl.* **sulk·ies** a light, two-wheeled, one-horse vehicle for one person.

sul·len (SUL ən) *adj.* **1.** obstinately and gloomily ill-humored; morose; glum; melancholy. **2.** depressing; somber: *sullen clouds.* [ME *solain*] **—sul′len·ly** *adv.* — **sul′len·ness** *n.*

sul·ly (SUL ee) *v.* **·lied, ·ly·ing** *v.t.* **1.** mar the brightness or purity of; soil; defile; tarnish. —*v.i.* **2.** become soiled or tarnished. —*n.* a stain; spot; blemish.

sul·tan (SUL tn) *n.* a ruler or sovereign, esp. of a Muslim country. [< Arabic *sultān*] — **sul·tan·ate** (SUL tn AYT) *n.*

sul·tan·a (sul TAN ə) *n.* **1.** a sultan's wife, daughter, sister, or mother: also **sul·tan·ess** (SUL tn is). **2.** a variety of raisin.

sul·try (SUL tree) *adj.* **·tri·er, ·tri·est 1.** oppressively hot and humid; sweltering. **2.** showing or suggesting passion; sensual. [< *Obs. sulter* swelter] **—sul′tri·ly** *adv.* — **sul′tri·ness** *n.*

sum (sum) *n.* **1.** the result obtained by addition. **2.** the whole amount; entirety: the *sum* of our efforts. **3.** an amount of money. **4.** a problem in arithmetic. **5.** the gist or essence; pith. —*v.t.* **summed, sum·ming 1.** present in brief; recapitulate: usu. with *up.* **2.** add into one total: often with *up.* [ME *summe* highest]

su·mac (SOO mak) *n.* **1.** any of various woody plants or small trees having clusters of small berries and yielding a resinous or milky substance. **2.** the poison sumac.

sum·ma·rize (SUM ə RIZ) *v.t.* **·rized, ·riz·ing** make a summary of; sum up. — **sum′ma·ri·za′tion** *n.*

sum·ma·ry (SUM ə ree) *adj.* **1.** giving the main points; concise. **2.** performed without ceremony or delay: a *summary* execution. —*n. pl.* **·ries** a brief account of the main points; précis; abstract. [ME] — **sum·ma·ri·ly** (sə MAIR ə lee) *adv.*

sum·ma·tion (sə MAY shən) *n.* **1.** the act or operation of obtaining a sum; the computation of an aggregate sum; addition. **2.** the closing part of a talk or argument in which the main points are reviewed.

sum·mer (SUM ər) *n.* the warmest season of the year, occurring between spring and autumn. ♦ Collateral adjective: *estival.* [ME *sumer*] —*v.i.* pass the summer. —*adj.* of, pertaining to, or occurring in summer.

sum·mer·time (SUM ər TIM) *n.* the summer season.

sum·mit (SUM it) *n.* **1.** the highest part; top. **2.** the highest degree; maximum. **3.** the highest level of government: a meeting at the *summit.* —*adj.* of or characterized by diplomacy at the highest level: a *summit* meeting. [ME *somete*] **—sum·mit·ry** (SUM i tree) *n.* the act or practice of holding a summit meeting; such meetings collectively.

sum·mon (SUM ən) *v.t.* **1.** order to come; send for. **2.** call together; cause to convene, as a legislative assembly. **3.** order (a person) to appear in court by a summons. **4.** call forth; arouse: usu. with *up: summon up courage.* [ME *sumonen*] **—sum′mon·er** *n.*

sum·mons (SUM ənz) *n. pl.* **sum·mon·ses 1.** a call to attend or act at a particular place or time. **2.** *Law* a notice or citation to appear in court.

sump (sump) *n.* a pit for collecting sewage, water, oil, etc. [ME *sompe* swamp]

sump·tu·ous (SUMP choo əs) *adj.* **1.** costly and magnificent. **2.** luxurious; lavish. [< MF *sumptueux*] **—sump′tu·ous·ly** *adv.* **—sump′tu·ous·ness** *n.*

sun (sun) *n.* **1.** the star that is the main source of radiant energy in the solar system and about which the earth and other planets revolve. ◆ Collateral adjective: *solar.* **2.** any star that is the center of a planetary system. **3.** sunshine. [ME] **—v. sunned, sun·ning** *v.t.* **1.** expose to the rays of the sun. **2.** warm or dry in the sun. **—v.i. 3.** bask in the sun. **—sun′less** *adj.* **—sun′less·ness** *n.*

sun·bathe (SUN BAYTH) *v.i.* **-bathed, -bath·ing** bask in the sun. **—sun′ bath′ing** *n.*

sun·beam (SUN BEEM) *n.* a ray of sunlight.

Sun·belt (SUN BELT) *n.* the southern part of the U.S. from Virginia to southern California.

sun·bon·net (SUN BON it) *n.* a broad-brimmed bonnet that shields the face and neck from the sun.

sun·burn (SUN BURN) *n.* inflammation of the skin from exposure to the sun. **—v.t. & v.i. ·burned** or **·burnt, ·burn·ing** affect or be affected with sunburn.

sun·dae (SUN day) *n.* a refreshment of ice cream, whipped cream, syrup, etc.

Sun·day (SUN day) *n.* the first day of the week and the Sabbath for most Christians. [ME *sunnenday*]

Sunday school a school, usu. part of a religious institution, in which religious instruction is given on Sunday, esp., to the young; also, the teachers and pupils collectively.

sun·der (SUN dər) *v.t. & v.i.* make or become divided; disunite; separate. [ME *sundren*]

sun·di·al (SUN DI əl) *n.* a device that shows the time by the shadow of a pointer thrown on a dial.

sun·down (SUN DOWN) *n.* sunset.

sun·dries (SUN dreez) *n.pl.* a number of small, miscellaneous items. [pl. of SUNDRY]

sun·dry (SUN dree) *adj.* of an indefinite small number; various; miscellaneous. **—pron.** an indeterminate number. [ME]

sung (sung) a past tense and past participle of SING.

sunk (sungk) past participle and a past tense of SINK.

sunk·en (SUNG kən) *adj.* **1.** deeply depressed or fallen in; hollow: *sunken* cheeks. **2.** located beneath the surface of the ground or the water: *sunken* treasure. **3.** at a lower level: *sunken* gardens.

sun·lamp (SUN LAMP) *n.* an ultraviolet lamp used for therapeutic treatments or to acquire a suntan.

sun·light (SUN LIT) *n.* the light of the sun.

sun·lit (SUN lit) *adj.* lighted by the sun.

sun·ny (SUN ee) *adj.* **·ni·er, ·ni·est 1.** filled with sunshine. **2.** of or like the sun. **3.** bright; genial; cheery: a *sunny* smile. **—sun′ni·ness** *n.*

sunny side 1. the side facing the sun. **2.** the cheerful view of any situation.

sun·rise (SUN RĪZ) *n.* **1.** the daily first appearance of the sun above the horizon. **2.** the time at which the sun rises.

sun·set (SUN SET) *n.* **1.** the daily descent of the sun below the horizon. **2.** the time when the sun sets.

sun·shade (SUN SHAYD) *n.* something used as protection from the sun, as a parasol.

sun·shine (SUN SHIN) *n.* the shining light of the sun; direct sunlight. **—sunshine law** a law requiring a government agency to make public its records etc.

sun·spot (SUN SPOT) *n. Astron.* one of many dark irregular spots appearing periodically on the sun's surface.

sun·stroke (SUN STROHK) *n. Pathol.* illness caused by overexposure to the sun, often marked by fever.

sun·tan (SUN TAN) *n.* a bronze-colored condition of the skin, produced by exposure to the sun. **—sun′tanned′** *adj.*

sun·up (SUN UP) *n.* sunrise.

sup[1] (sup) *v.t. & v.i.* **supped, sup·ping** sip. [ME *suppen*] **—n.** a sip.

sup[2] *v.i.* **supped, sup·ping** eat supper; dine. [ME *soupen*]

su·per (SOO pər) *n. Informal* a superintendent; a supernumerary. **—adj.** *Informal* excellent; outstanding; first-rate.

super- *prefix* **1.** above; over: *superstructure.* **2.** higher or greater than; superior: *supersonic, superhighway.* **3.** excessively: *supersaturate.* **4.** extra; additional: *supertax.* [< L *super* above, beyond]

In the list below *super-* denotes excess or superiority, as *supercritical* excessively critical, *superexcellence* superior excellence.

su·per·an·nu·at·ed (SOO pər AN yoo AY tid) *adj.* **1.** retired with a pension on account of age. **2.** too old to work. **3.** outdated; obsolete. [< Med.L *superannatus* more than a year old]

su·perb (sə PURB) *adj.* **1.** magnificent; majestic; imposing. **2.** luxurious; rich and costly. **3.** very good; excellent. [< L *superbus* superior] **—su·perb'ness** *n.*

superachievement
superacid
superacute
superadaptable
superadequate
superaffluence
superagency
superalkaline
superambitious
superangelic
superarduous
superarrogant
superattraction
superattractive
superbenefit
superblunder
superbold
superbomb
superbrave
superbusy
supercandid
supercapable
supercaution

superceremonious
supercivilized
supercolossal
supercomplex
supercompression
superconfident
superconservative
supercool
supercordial
supercritic
supercritical
supercultivated
supercurious
supercynical
superdanger
superdelicate
superdemand
superdesirous
superdevilish
superdevotion
superdifficult
superdividend
supereffective

su·per·charge (SOO pər CHAHRJ) *v.t.* •**charged,** •**charg·ing** adapt (an engine) to develop more power by fitting with a supercharger.[1]

su·per·charg·er (SOO pər CHAHR jər) *n.* *Mech.* a compressor for supplying air or combustible mixture to an internal-combustion engine at a pressure greater than that developed by the suction of the pistons alone.

su·per·cil·i·ous (SOO pər SIL ee əs) *adj.* exhibiting haughty contempt or indifference; arrogant. [< L *superciliosus*] **—**

su'per·cil'i·ous·ly *adv.* **—su'per·cil' i·ous·ness** *n.*

su·per·e·go (SOO pər EE goh) *n. Psychoanal.* the part of the psyche that acts to secure the conformity of the ego to parental, social, and moral standards.

su·per·e·ro·gate (SOO pər ER ə GAYT) *v.i.* •**gat·ed,** •**gat·ing** do more than is required or ordered. [< LL *supererogatus* overpaid] **—su'per·er'o·ga'tion** *n.*

su·per·fi·cial (SOO pər FISH əl) *adj.* **1.** of or situated near the surface: a *superficial* wound. **2.** without depth or thoroughness; shallow: a *superficial* writer. [ME] **— su·per·fi·ci·al·i·ty** (SOO pər FISH ee AL i tee) *n.* **—su'per·fi'·cial·ly** *adv.*

su·per·flu·i·ty (SOO pər FLOO i tee) *n. pl.* •**ties 1.** the state of being superfluous. **2.** that which is superfluous. **3.** superabundance; plenty. [ME *superfluitee*]

su·per·flu·ous (suu PUR floo əs) *adj.* **1.** excessively abundant; surplus. **2.** unnecessary; uncalled for; irrelevant: a *superfluous* question. **—su·per'flu·ous·ly** *adv.*

su·per·hu·man (SOO pər HYOO mən) *adj.* **1.** beyond human power or understanding; divine. **2.** beyond normal human ability or skill. **—su'per·hu'man·ly** *adv.*

superelastic
superelegance
supereloquent
supereminence
supereminent
superemphasis
superendurance
superesthetic
superethical
superexacting
superexalt
superexcellence
superexcellent
superexcited
superexpenditure
superexpressive
superexquisite
superfeminine
superfervent
superfine
superfluid
superfolly
superformal

superformidable
superfriendly
supergallant
supergenerosity
superglorious
supergovernment
superhandsome
superhearty
superheat
superhero
superheroic
superimportant
superimproved
superincentive
superindependent
superindignant
superindividualist
superinduce
superinduction
superindulgence
superindustrious
superinfluence
superingenious

su·per·im·pose (SOO pər im POHZ) *v.t.* •**posed,** •**pos·ing** lay or impose upon something else. **—su·per·im·po·si·tion** (SOO pər IM pə ZISH ən) *n.*

su·per·in·ten·dent (SOO pər in TEN dənt)

n. **1.** a person in charge of an office, staff, etc. **2.** a person responsible for maintenance and repair in an office or apartment building. [< Med.L]

su·pe·ri·or (sə PEER ee ər) *adj.* **1.** higher or greater in amount, value, rank, etc.: a *superior* force, a *superior* wine, a *superior* officer. **2.** indifferent to; unaffected by: with *to*: *superior* to envy. **3.** haughty; arrogant; disdainful: a *superior* attitude. —*n.* **1.** one who surpasses another in rank or excellence. **2.** the head of a convent or monastery. [ME] —**su·pe·ri·or·i·ty** (sə PEER ee OR i tee) *n.*

su·per·la·tive (sə PUR lə tiv) *adj.* **1.** surpassing all others; supreme. **2.** *Gram.* expressing the highest degree of comparison of adjectives or adverbs. [ME] —*n.* **1.** that which is superlative. **2.** *Gram.* **a** the highest degree of comparison of the adjective or adverb. **b** any word or phrase in this degree. —**su·per′la·tive·ly** *adv.* —**su·per′la·tive·ness** *n.*

su·per·man (SOO pər MAN) *n. pl.* **·men** a person possessing superhuman powers. [Trans. of G *Übermensch*]

su·per·mar·ket (SOO pər MAHR kit) *n.* a large self-service store selling food and household supplies.

su·per·nat·u·ral (SOO pər NACH ər əl) *adj.* **1.** relating to that which cannot be explained by known laws of nature. **2.** believed to be caused by a divine power. [< Med.L *supernaturalis*] —*n.* that which is supernatural. —**su′per·nat′u·ral·ism** *n.* —**su′per·nat′u·ral·ly** *adv.*

superinitiative
superinjustice
superinquisitive
superinsistent
superintellectual
superlaborious
superlenient
superlie
superliner
superloyal
superlucky
superluxurious
supermarvelous
supermasculine
supermediocre
supermodest
supermoisten
supermorose
supermundane
supernotable

superoffensive
superofficious
superordinary
superorganize
superpatient
superpatriotic
superpatriotism
superphysical
superpious
superpolite
superpositive
superpraise
superprecise
superpressure
superproduce
superprosperous
superpure
superradical
superrational
superrefined

superobese
superobjectionable
superobstinate

superrespectable
superresponsible
superreward

su·per·nu·mer·ar·y (SOO pər NOO mə RER ee) *adj.* beyond a customary or necessary number; extra; superfluous. [< LL *supernumerarius*] —*n. pl.* **·ar·ies 1.** a supernumerary person or thing. **2.** a performer without a speaking part, usu. employed for crowd scenes.

su·per·pose (SOO pər POHZ) *v.t.* **·posed,** **·pos·ing** lay over or upon something else. [< F *superposer*] —**su·per·po·si·tion** (SOO pər pə ZISH ən) *n.*

su·per·pow·er (SOO pər POW ər) *n.* a nation able to dominate world affairs through superior economic and military strength.

su·per·script (SOO pər SKRIPT) *adj.* written above or overhead. —*n.* **1.** a superscript character. **2.** *Math.* a character written above and to the right or left of a term to indicate a specific operation or characteristic of the term.

su·per·sede (SOO pər SEED) *v.t.* **·sed·ed,** **·sed·ing 1.** take the place of; succeed. **2.** replace as outdated, useless, etc. [< L *supersedere* sit upon or above]

su·per·son·ic (SOO pər SON ik) *adj.* of or characterized by a speed greater than that of sound.

su·per·sti·tion (SOO pər STISH ən) *n.* a belief founded on irrational feelings, esp. of fear, and marked by a trust in charms, omens, the supernatural, etc.; also, any rite or practice inspired by such belief. [ME *superstiction*] —**su′per·sti′tious** *adj.* **su′per·sti′tious·ly** *adv.*

su·per·struc·ture (SOO pər STRUK chər) *n.* **1.** the part of a building above the foundation. **2.** any structure built on something else. **3.** *Naut.* the part of a ship's structure above the main deck.

su·per·vene (SOO pər VEEN) *v.i.* **·vened,** **·ven·ing** happen as something extra or unexpected. [< L *supervenire*] —**su·per·ven·ient** (SOO pər VEEN yənt) *adj.* —**su·per·ven·tion** (SOO pər VEEN shən) *n.*

superrighteous
superromantic
supersacrifice
supersafe
supersalesman
supersarcastic
supersatisfaction
supersaturate

superstate
superstratum
superstrength
superstrenuous
superstrict
superstrong
superstylish
supersubtle

supersaturation
superscholarly
superscientific
supersensitive
supersentimental
superserious
supersimplify
supersize
supersized
supersmart
supersolemn
superspecialize
superspeed
superspirituality
superstar

supersurprise
supersweet
supertanker
supertension
superthankful
superthorough
superugly
superurgent
supervigilant
supervigorous
supervirulent
supervital
superwise
superworldly
superzealous

su·per·vise (SOO pər VīZ) v.t. **·vised,
·vis·ing** have charge of; oversee. [< Med.L
supervisus overseen] **—su·per·vi·sion**
(SOO pər VIZH ən) n. **—su′per·vi′sor** n.
—su′per·vi′so·ry adj.

su·pine (soo PĪN) adj. **1.** lying on the back
with the face turned upward. **2.** inactive;
indolent; listless. [< L *supinus*] **—
su·pine′ly** adv. **—su·pine′ness** n.

sup·per (SUP ər) n. the last meal of the day;
the evening meal. [ME]

sup·plant (sə PLANT) v.t. **1.** take the place
of; displace. **2.** take the place of (someone)
by scheming, treachery, etc. [ME *sup-
planten*]

sup·ple (SUP əl) adj. **·pler, ·plest 1.** easily
bent; flexible; pliant. **2.** showing adaptability of mind. [ME *souple*] **—sup·ply**
(SUP lee), **sup′ple·ly** adv. **—sup′
ple·ness** n.

sup·ple·ment (SUP lə mənt) v.t. make additions to; provide for what is lacking in. **—**n.
something that supplements; esp., an addition to a publication. **—sup′ple·men′tal,
sup′ple·men′ta·ry** adj.

sup·pli·ant (SUP lee ənt) adj. supplicating.
—n. one who supplicates. Also **sup·pli·
cant** (SUP li kənt). [ME] **—sup′pli·
ant·ly** adv.

sup·pli·cate (SUP li KAYT) v. **·cat·ed,
·cat·ing** v.t. **1.** ask for humbly and earnestly. **2.** beg something of; beseech; entreat. **—**v.i. **3.** make a humble request.
[ME] **—sup′pli·ca′tion** n. **—sup·pli·
ca·to·ry** (SUP li kə TOR ee) adj.

sup·ply (sə PLĪ) v.t. **·plied, ·ply·ing 1.** give
or furnish (something desirable). **2.** furnish
with what is needed: *supply* an army with
guns. **3.** provide for adequately; satisfy:
supply a demand. **4.** make good or compensate for (a loss or deficiency). [ME *suplien*]

—n. pl. **·plies 1.** an amount sufficient for a
given use; quantity on hand. **2.** Usu. pl.
food, clothing, or other stores reserved for
distribution, as for an army. **3.** the act of
supplying.

sup·port (sə PORT) v.t. **1.** bear the weight
of; hold up. **2.** provide with money, food,
etc.; maintain. **3.** verify (a statement etc.);
corroborate. **4.** give approval or assistance
to; uphold. **5.** tolerate: I cannot *support*
such insolence. **6.** carry on; keep up: *support* a war. **7.** act in a subordinate role to (a
star) in a play or film. [ME *supporten*] **—**n.
1. the act of supporting, or the state of being
supported. **2.** one who or that which supports. **3.** subsistence.

sup·port·a·ble (sə POR tə bəl) adj. capable
of being endured; bearable.

sup·port·er (sə POR tər) n. **1.** one who supports, aids, or approves; esp., an adherent: a
supporter of equal rights for women. **2.** an
elastic or other support for some part of the
body.

sup·por·tive (sə POR tiv) adj. **1.** serving to
support. **2.** providing emotional support, as
with sympathy, advice, and encouragement.

sup·pose (sə POHZ) v. **·posed, ·pos·ing**
v.t. **1.** believe probable; think. **2.** assume as
true for the sake of argument: *Suppose* she
is late. **3.** expect or require: used in the
passive: He is *supposed* to be on time. **4.**
imply; presuppose. **—**v.i. **5.** conjecture.
[ME *supposen*] **—sup·pos′a·ble** adj.

sup·posed (sə POHZD) adj. accepted as
genuine or true, often erroneously. **—
sup·pos′ed·ly** adv.

sup·po·si·tion (SUP ə ZISH ən) n. **1.** the act
of supposing. **2.** that which is supposed;
hypothesis. [ME] **—sup′po·si′tion·al**
adj. **—sup′po·si′tion·al·ly** adv.

sup·pos·i·to·ry (sə POZ i TOR ee) n. pl.
·ries Med. a small, solid medicated substance for insertion into the rectum or vagina. [ME]

sup·press (sə PRES) v.t. **1.** put an end to
forcibly; quell; crush. **2.** withhold from
knowledge or publication, as a book, news,
etc. **3.** repress, as a groan or sigh. **4.** check
or stop (a hemorrhage etc.) **5.** Psychoanal.
deliberately exclude (an idea, desire, etc.)
from one's consciousness. [ME *suppressen*]
—sup·press′i·ble adj. **—sup·pres·sion**
(sə PRESH ən) n.

sup·pu·rate (SUP yə RAYT) v.i. **·rat·ed,
·rat·ing** form or generate pus. [< L *sup-*

puratus] —sup′pu•ra′tion *n.* —sup′
pu•ra′tive *adj. & n.*

su•prem•a•cist (sə PREM ə sist) *n.* one who
believes in and advocates the supremacy of
a particular group or race of people.

su•prem•a•cy (sə PREM ə see) *n. pl.* •cies
1. the state of being supreme. 2. supreme
power or authority.

su•preme (sə PREEM) *adj.* 1. highest in
power or authority. 2. highest in degree,
importance, quality, etc.; utmost: *supreme*
devotion. 3. ultimate; last; final. [< L *su-
premus*] —su•preme′ly *adv.*

sur•cease (sur SEES) *n.* cessation; end. —
v.t. & v.i. •ceased, •ceas•ing cease; end.
[ME *sursesen*]

sur•charge (SUR CHAHRJ) *n.* 1. an additional amount charged; overcharge. 2. a
new valuation printed on a postage stamp.
—*v.t.* •charged, •charg•ing 1. overcharge; overload. 2. imprint a surcharge on
(a postage stamp). [ME *surchargen*]

sure (shuur) *adj.* sur•er, sur•est 1. free
from doubt; certain; positive. 2. confident:
with *of*: We are *sure* of the outcome. 3. not
liable to change; firm; stable. 4. bound to
happen; inevitable. 5. not liable to fail or
err; infallible: a *sure* sign of winter. 6. reliable; trustworthy. —for sure without a
doubt; unquestionably. —sure enough
Informal certainly; really. —to be sure indeed; certainly. —make sure make certain; secure. —*adv. Informal* certainly.
[ME *sur*] —sure′ness *n.*

sure•foot•ed (SHUUR FUUT id) *adj.* 1.
not liable to fall or stumble. 2. not liable to
fail or err.

sure•ly (SHUUR lee) *adv.* 1. certainly. 2.
securely; safely.

sure•ty (SHUUR i tee) *n. pl.* •ties 1. one
who agrees to be responsible for another,
as for another's debt. 2. a pledge or guarantee to secure against loss, damage, etc.;
security. 3. the state of being sure. [ME
surte]

surf (surf) *n.* the swell of the sea breaking on
a shore or reef; also, the sound or foam of
such a swell. —*v.i.* engage in surfing. —
surf′er *n.*

sur•face (SUR fis) *n.* 1. the exterior part or
face of anything. 2. a superficial aspect; outward appearance. [< F] —*adj.* 1. of, pertaining to, or on a surface. 2. superficial;
apparent.—*v.* •faced, •fac•ing *v.t.* 1. put a
surface on; esp., make smooth. —*v.i.* 2. rise
to the surface, as a submarine.

surf•board (SURF BORD) *n.* a long, narrow
board used in surfing.

sur•feit (SUR fit) *v.t.* feed or supply to excess; satiate. —*n.* 1. excess in eating or
drinking; overindulgence. 2. an excessive
quantity or supply. [ME *sorfete*]

surf•ing (SUR fing) *n.* a sport in which a
person on a surfboard rides the surf.

surge (surj) *v.i.* surged, surg•ing 1. move
with a heaving motion, as waves; swell. 2.
rise or increase suddenly. —*n.* 1. a large
swelling wave. 2. a heaving and rolling motion, as of waves. 3. a sudden, strong increase: a *surge* of electric power.

sur•geon (SUR jən) *n.* a physician who specializes in surgery. [ME *surgien*]

sur•ger•y (SUR jə ree) *n.* 1. the work of a
surgeon. 2. the branch of medicine concerned with the removal or repair of diseased or injured parts of the body. 3. *pl.*
•ger•ies a surgeon's operating room: She is
in *surgery*. [ME *surgerie*] —sur•gi•cal
(SUR ji kəl) *adj.* —sur′gi•cal•ly *adv.*

sur•ly (SUR lee) *adj.* sur•li•er, sur•li•est
characterized by rudeness or gruffness.
[Earlier *sirly* arrogant] —sur′li•ness *n.*

sur•mise (sər MĪZ) *v.t. & v.i.* •mised,
•mis•ing infer (something) on slight evidence; guess. [ME *surmisen accusé*] —*n.* a
conjecture; guess.

sur•mount (sər MOWNT) *v.t.* 1. overcome
(a difficulty etc.). 2. climb up and over (a
mountain or other height). 3. be above; top.
[ME *surmounten*] —sur•mount′a•ble
adj.

sur•name (SUR NAYM) *n.* a family name. —
v.t. •named, •nam•ing give or call by a
surname. [ME]

sur•pass (sər PAS) *v.t.* 1. go beyond or past
in degree or amount; excel. 2. go beyond
the reach or powers of; transcend. [< MF
surpasser] —sur•pass′a•ble *adj.*

sur•pass•ing (sər PAS ing) *adj.* superior; excellent; exceeding. —*adv.* extraordinarily.
—sur•pass′ing•ly *adv.*

sur•plice (SUR plis) *n. Eccl.* a loose white
outer vestment with full sleeves. [ME *sur-
plis*]

sur•plus (SUR plus) *adj.* being in excess of
what is used or needed. —*n.* 1. that which
remains over and above what has been used
or is required; excess. 2. assets in excess of
liabilities. [ME]

sur•prise (sər PRĪZ) *v.t.* •prised, •pris•ing
1. cause to feel wonder or astonishment;
amaze. 2. come upon suddenly or unexpec-

tedly; take unawares. **3.** attack or capture without warning. —*n.* **1.** the act of surprising, or the state of being surprised; astonishment. **2.** that which causes surprise, as a sudden and unexpected event, fact, or gift. —**take by surprise** come upon suddenly or unexpectedly. [ME]

sur·pris·ing (sər PRĪ zing) *adj.* causing surprise or wonder; amazing. —**sur·pris′ ·ing·ly** *adv.*

sur·re·al·ism (sə REE ə LIZ əm) *n.* a movement in literature and art of the 20th century stressing the nonrational or subconscious. [< F *surréalisme*] — **sur·re′al·ist** *adj. & n.* —**sur·re′al·is′tic** *adj.* —**sur·re′al·is′ti·cal·ly** *adv.*

sur·ren·der (sə REN dər) *v.t.* **1.** yield possession or control of under compulsion. **2.** give up; abandon, as hope. **3.** relinquish, esp. in favor of another. —*v.i.* **4.** give oneself up, as to an enemy in warfare. [ME *surrendren*] —*n.* the act of surrendering.

sur·rep·ti·tious (SUR əp TISH əs) *adj.* done or acting in a secret, sly manner. [ME] — **sur′rep·ti′tious·ly** *adv.* —**sur′rep·ti′ tious·ness** *n.*

sur·ro·gate (SUR ə GAYT) *n.* **1.** a substitute; deputy. **2.** a probate judge. [< L *surrogatus* substituted]

sur·round (sə ROWND) *v.t.* **1.** extend around; encircle; enclose. **2.** shut in or enclose so as to cut off retreat. [ME *surounden* submerge]

sur·round·ings (sə ROWN dingz) *n.pl.* environment; conditions of life.

sur·tax (SUR TAKS) *n.* a tax added to the usual tax.

sur·veil·lance (sər VAY ləns) *n.* **1.** close watch kept over one, as a suspect. **2.** supervision. [< F] —**sur·veil′lant** *adj. & n.*

sur·vey (sər VAY) *v.t.* **1.** look at in its entirety; view in a general way. **2.** look at carefully and minutely; scrutinize. **3.** determine accurately the area, contour, or boundaries of (land). —*v.i.* **4.** survey land. [ME *surveien*] —*n.* (SUR vay) **1.** the process of surveying land; also, a map, description, etc., of a surveyed area. **2.** a general or comprehensive view. **3.** a scrutinizing view; inspection.

sur·vey·ing (sər VAY ing) *n.* the science and art of determining the area and configuration of portions of the surface of the earth and representing them on maps. — **sur·vey′or** *n.*

sur·vive (sər VĪV) *v.* •**vived,** •**viv·ing** *v.i.* **1.** remain alive or in existence. —*v.t.* **2.** live or

exist beyond the death, occurrence, or end of; outlive; outlast. [ME] —**sur·viv′al** *n.* —**sur·viv′ing** *adj.* —**sur·vi′vor** *n.*

sus·cep·ti·ble (sə SEP tə bəl) *adj.* **1.** readily affected or influenced by; yielding easily to; open: usu. with *to* or *of.* **2.** impressionable. [< LL *susceptibilis* admitted] — **sus·cep′ti·bil′i·ty** *n.*

su·shi (SOO shee) *n.* vinegar-flavored rice usu. enclosed in a slice of raw fish. [< Jap.]

sus·pect (sə SPEKT) *v.t.* **1.** think (a person) guilty on little or no evidence. **2.** distrust; doubt. **3.** think possible; surmise. —*v.i.* **4.** have suspicions. —*adj.* viewed with suspicion; suspected. —*n.* (SUS pekt) one who is under suspicion, esp. for a crime. [ME]

sus·pend (sə SPEND) *v.t.* **1.** bar for a time from a privilege, office, or function as a punishment. **2.** cause to cease for a time; withhold temporarily. **3.** withhold or defer action on: *suspend* a sentence. **4.** hang from a support so as to allow free movement. — *v.i.* **5.** stop for a time. [ME *suspenden*]

sus·pend·ers (sə SPEN dərz) *n.pl.* a pair of straps worn over the shoulders for supporting the trousers.

sus·pense (sə SPENS) *n.* **1.** a state of excitement caused by uncertainty or insecurity. **2.** uncertain or doubtful condition. [ME] — **sus·pense′ful** *adj.*

sus·pen·sion (sə SPEN shən) *n.* **1.** the act of suspending, or the state of being suspended. **2.** *Physics* a uniform dispersion of small particles in a medium. **3.** any device from which something is suspended. **4.** *Mech.* in an automotive vehicle, a system of springs, torsion bars, etc. to protect the chassis from road shocks.

sus·pen·so·ry (sə SPEN sə ree) *adj.* suspending; sustaining; delaying. —*n. pl.* •**ries** a truss, bandage, or supporter.

sus·pi·cion (sə SPISH ən) *n.* **1.** the act of suspecting or the state of being suspected of something wrong without proof or clear evidence. **2.** any impression based on little or no proof. **3.** a trace or hint. [ME]

sus·pi·cious (sə SPISH əs) *adj.* **1.** inclined to suspect; distrustful. **2.** apt to arouse suspicion. **3.** indicating suspicion. —**sus·pi′ cious·ly** *adv.*

sus·tain (sə STAYN) *v.t.* **1.** keep from sinking or falling; uphold; support. **2.** endure; withstand. **3.** undergo or suffer, as loss or injury. **4.** keep up the spirits of; comfort. **5.** keep going; maintain; prolong. **6.** provide with food, drink, etc.; support. **7.** uphold or support as true or just. **8.** corroborate; confirm. [ME *sustenen*] **—sus·tain'a·ble** *adj.*

sus·te·nance (SUS tə nəns) *n.* **1.** the act of sustaining, or the state of being sustained; esp., maintenance of life. **2.** that which sustains or supports life; esp., food. **3.** means of support; livelihood. [ME *sustenauce*]

sut·tee (su TEE) *n.* the sacrifice of a Hindu widow on the funeral pyre of her husband. [< Skt. *satī* a good woman] **—sut·tee'ism** *n.*

su·ture (SOO chər) *n.* **1.** *Anat.* the interlocking of two bones at their edges, as in the skull. **2.** *Surg.* **a** the operation of uniting the edges of a cut or wound by or as by stitching. **b** the fastening used in this operation. **—***v.t.* **·tured, ·tur·ing** unite by means of sutures; sew together. [< L *sutura* seam]

svelte (sfelt) *adj.* slender; slim; willowy. [< F]

swab (swob) *n.* **1.** a small stick having a wad of cotton wound about one or both ends, used esp. for cleaning and for applying medication. **2.** a mop. **3.** *Slang* a sailor. **—***v.t.* **swabbed, swab·bing** use a swab on. Also *swob.* **—swab'·ber** *n.*

swag (swag) *n.* **1.** *Slang* property obtained by robbery or theft; plunder; booty. **2.** drapery, garland, etc., hanging in a loop between two points.

swage (swayj) *n.* a tool or form, often one of a pair, for shaping metal by hammering or pressure. **—***v.t.* **swaged, swag·ing** shape (metal) with or as with a swage. [ME, ornamental border]

swag·ger (SWAG ər) *v.i.* **1.** walk with a proud or insolent air; strut. **2.** boast; bluster. **—***n.* boastful manner or conduct. **—swag'ger·er** *n.* **—swag'ger·ing·ly** *adv.*

swagger stick a short, canelike stick carried by army officers.

Swa·hi·li (swah HEE lee) *n.* a Bantu language of East Africa.

swain (swayn) *n.* **1.** a youthful rustic. **2.** a lover. [ME *swein* servant]

swal·low¹ (SWOL oh) *v.t.* **1.** cause (food etc.) to pass from the mouth into the stomach. **2.** take in or engulf; absorb; envelop: often with *up.* **3.** put up with or endure. **4.** believe unquestioningly. **5.** refrain from expressing; suppress. **—***v.i.* **6.** perform the act or motions of swallowing. [ME *swalowen*] **—***n.* **1.** the amount swallowed at one time. **2.** the act of swallowing. **—swal'low·er** *n.*

swal·low² *n.* any of various small birds with short bills, long, pointed wings, and forked tails, noted for their swiftness of flight. [ME *swalowe*]

swam (swam) past tense of SWIM.

swa·mi (SWAH mee) *n. pl.* **·mies** a Hindu religious teacher. [< Skt. *svāmi* master]

swamp (swomp) *n.* a tract of lowland saturated with water; bog. [ME *sompe*] **—***v.t.* **1.** drench or submerge with water or other liquid. **2.** overwhelm with difficulties; crush. **3.** *Naut.* sink or fill (a vessel) with water. **—swamp'y** *adj.*

swan (swon) *n.* a large aquatic bird, noted for its white plumage and long, graceful neck. [ME]

swan dive a dive performed with head tilted back and arms extended until near the water.

swank (swangk) *adj.* ostentatiously fashionable; pretentious. Also **swank'y swank·i·er, swank·i·est —swank'i·ness** *n.*

swan song a last or dying work, as of a poet or composer: from the fable that the swan sings only before dying.

swap (swop) *v.t. & v.i.* **swapped, swap·ping** trade (one thing for another). [ME *swappen* strike] **—***n.* an exchange or trade. Also spelled *swop.*

sward (sword) *n.* land thickly covered with grass; turf. [ME]

swarm (sworm) *n.* **1.** a large number of bees, with a queen, leaving the hive at one time to start a new colony. **2.** a crowd or throng. **—***v.i.* **1.** leave the hive in a swarm: said of bees. **2.** come together, move, or occur in great numbers. **3.** be crowded; teem: with *with.* [ME]

swarth·y (SWOR thee) *adj.* **swarth·i·er, swarth·i·est** having a dark or sunburned complexion; tawny. **—swarth'i·ness** *n.*

swash·buck·ler (SWOSH BUK lər) *n.* a swaggering or boasting soldier; daredevil. **—swash'·buck'ling** *adj.*

swas·ti·ka (SWOS ti kə) *n.* **1.** a primitive religious ornament or symbol, consisting of a Greek cross with the ends of the arms bent at right angles. **2.** the symbol used as the emblem of the Nazis. [< Skt. *svastika*]

swat (swot) *v.t.* **swat·ted, swat·ting** hit with a sharp blow. **—***n.* a blow. **—swat'ter** *n.*

swatch (swoch) *n.* a sample of cloth.

swath (swoth) *n.* **1.** a row or line of grass, grain, etc., cut down by one sweep of a mowing device. **2.** the width of such a row. **3.** a narrow belt or track; strip. Also **swathe**.

—**cut a wide swath** make a fine impression or display. [ME]

swathe (swo*th*) *v.t.* **swathed, swath•ing 1.** bind or wrap, as in bandages. **2.** envelop; surround. [ME]

sway (sway) *v.i.* **1.** swing from side to side or to and fro; oscillate. **2.** bend or incline to one side; lean; veer. [ME *sweyen*] —*v.t.* **3.** cause to swing, bend, or incline. **4.** influence (a person, opinion, etc.). —*n.* **1.** power exercised in governing; dominion: hold *sway* over a nation. **2.** the act of swaying.

sway•back (SWAY BAK) *n.* a hollow or sagging condition of the back, as in a horse. — **sway′backed′** *adj.*

swear (swair) *v.* **swore, sworn, swear•ing** *v.i.* **1.** make a solemn affirmation with an appeal to God or one's honor. **2.** utter a solemn promise. **3.** use profanity; curse. — *v.t.* **4.** affirm or assert solemnly by appealing to God etc. **5.** vow. —**swear by 1.** appeal to by oath. **2.** have complete confidence in. —**swear in** administer a legal oath to. —**swear off** promise to renounce or give up: *swear off* whiskey. [ME *sweren*]

sweat (swet) *v.* **sweat or sweat•ed, sweat•ing** *v.i.* **1.** excrete moisture from the pores of the skin; perspire. **2.** exude moisture in drops; ooze. **3.** gather and condense moisture in drops, as a glass on its outer surface. **4.** *Informal* work hard; toil; drudge. —*v.t.* **5.** exude (moisture) from the pores. **6.** employ (people) to work for low wages and under unfavorable conditions. **7.** *Slang* extract (a confession etc.) from someone by force. —**sweat out** *Informal* wait through anxiously and helplessly. [ME *sweten*] —*n.* **1.** the moisture excreted from the sweat glands; perspiration. **2.** droplets of moisture exuded by something or collected on its surface. —**no sweat** *Informal* no difficulty whatever. —**sweat′i•ness** *n.* — **sweat′y** *adj.* **sweat•i•er, sweat•i•est**

sweat•er (SWET ər) *n.* a knitted garment for the upper part of the body.

sweat gland *Anat.* one of the numerous tiny glands beneath the skin that secrete sweat.

sweat•shirt (SWET SHURT) *n.* a heavy, collarless pullover worn to absorb sweat while exercising etc.

Swed•ish (SWEE dish) *adj.* pertaining to Sweden, its people, or its language. —*n.* **1.** the Germanic language of Sweden. **2.** the inhabitants of Sweden collectively.

sweep (sweep) *v.* **swept, sweep•ing** *v.t.* **1.** collect or remove with a broom, brush, etc. **2.** clear or clean with or as with a broom or brush: *sweep* a floor. **3.** touch or brush: Her dress *swept* the ground. **4.** pass over or through swiftly: Her eyes *swept* the sky. **5.** move, carry, bring, etc. with strong or continuous force: The flood *swept* the bridge away. —*v.i.* **6.** clean or brush a floor or other surface with a broom etc. **7.** move or go strongly and evenly, esp. with speed. **8.** extend with a long reach or curve: The road *sweeps* along the shore. [ME *swepen*] —*n.* **1.** the act of sweeping. **2.** a long stroke or movement: a *sweep* of the hand. **3.** a great victory or success, as in an election. **4.** the range or compass of a sweeping motion: the *sweep* of a searchlight. **5.** extent or expanse; stretch: a wide *sweep* of meadow. — **sweep′er** *n.*

sweep•ing (SWEE ping) *adj.* **1.** moving in a continuous motion. **2.** affecting a wide area; comprehensive: *sweeping* reforms. —*n.* **1.** the action of one who or that which sweeps. **2.** *pl.* things swept up; refuse. —**sweep′ing•ly** *adv.*

sweep•stakes (SWEEP STAYKS) *n.* (*construed as sing. or pl.*) **1.** a horse race etc. in which all the prize money may be won by one or by a few of the bettors. **2.** a lottery, drawing, etc. using this arrangement.

sweet (sweet) *adj.* **•er, •est 1.** having a flavor of or like that of sugar. **2.** not fermented or decaying; fresh. **3.** not sour or salty: *sweet* water. **4.** pleasing to the senses: a *sweet* sound. **5.** having gentle, pleasing, and winning qualities: a *sweet* child. **6.** not dry: said of wines. [ME *swete*] —*n.* **1.** *Chiefly pl.* a piece of candy. **2.** a sweetheart. —**sweet′ly** *adv.* —**sweet′ness** *n.*

sweet•bread (SWEET BRED) *n.* the pancreas (**stomach sweetbread**) or the thymus gland (**neck sweetbread** or **throat sweetbread**) of a calf or other animal, when used as food.

sweet•en (SWEET n) *v.t.* **1.** make sweet or sweeter. **2.** make more endurable. **3.** make pleasant or gratifying. —*v.i.* **4.** become sweet or sweeter. —**sweet′en•er** *n.* — **sweet′en•ing** *n.*

sweet•heart (SWEET HAHRT) *n.* a loved one; lover; darling.

sweet•ish (SWEE tish) *adj.* somewhat or rather sweet.

sweet potato 1. a perennial tropical vine with rose-violet or pink flowers and a fleshy, tuberous root. **2.** the root itself, eaten as a vegetable.

sweet tooth a fondness for sweets.

swell (swel) *v.t. & v.i.* **swelled, swelled** or **swol•len, swel•ling 1.** increase in size, as by inflation within; expand. **2.** increase in amount, degree, or intensity. **3.** curve out; bulge. **4.** become puffed with pride. [ME *swellen*] —*n.* **1.** an increase in size, amount, etc.; expansion. **2.** a long, continuous body of a wave; also, a rise in the land. **3.** a person of the fashionable set. —*adj. Informal* **1.** fashionable; smart. **2.** first-rate; distinctive.

swell•ing (SWEL ing) *n.* **1.** the act of increasing or expanding. **2.** *Pathol.* an abnormal enlargement of some part of the body. —*adj.* increasing; bulging.

swel•ter (SWEL tər) *v.i.* suffer or perspire from oppressive heat. [ME *sweltren*]

swel•ter•ing (SWEL tər ing) *adj.* very hot. —**swel´ter•ing•ly** *adv.*

swept (swept) past tense and past participle of SWEEP.]

swerve (swurv) *v.t. & v.i.* **swerved, swerv•ing** turn or cause to turn aside from a course or purpose; deflect. [ME *swerven*] —**swerve** *n.*

swift (swift) *adj.* **•er, •est 1.** moving with great speed; fast; fleet. **2.** happening quickly; a *swift* reply. —*n.* a small, swallowlike bird with long, narrow wings; esp., the **chimney swift**. [ME] —**swift´ly** *adv.* —**swift´•ness** *n.*

swig (swig) *Informal n.* a deep draft, as of liquor. —*v.t. & v.i.* **swigged, swig•ging** drink deeply or greedily.

swill (swil) *v.t. & v.i.* drink greedily or to excess. [ME *swilen*] —*n.* **1.** liquid food for animals, esp. for swine; slop. **2.** kitchen refuse; garbage. **3.** a deep draft of liquor.

swim (swim) *v.* **swam, swum, swim•ming** *v.i.* **1.** propel oneself through water by bodily movement. **2.** float on water or other liquid. **3.** move with a smooth or flowing motion. **4.** be flooded; overflow. **5.** be dizzy; reel. —*v.t.* **5.** traverse by swimming. [ME *swimmen*] —*n.* the action, pastime, or period of swimming. —**in the swim** in the current of affairs. —**swim•ming** *n.*

swim•ming•ly (SWIM ing lee) *adv.* successfully; very well.

swin•dle (SWIN dl) *v.* **•dled, •dling** *v.t.* **1.** cheat of money or property; defraud. **2.** obtain by such means. —*v.i.* **3.** practice fraud. —*n.* the act or an instance of swin-

dling; fraud. [Back formation < SWINDLER]

swin•dler (SWIN dlər) *n.* one who swindles or deceives. [< G *Schwindler* promoter]

swine (swīn) *n. pl.* **swine 1.** a domesticated pig. **2.** a brutal, vicious, or contemptible person. [ME] —**swin´ish** *adj.* —**swin´ish•ness** *n.*

swing (swing) *v.* **swung, swing•ing** *v.i.* **1.** move backward and forward rhythmically. **2.** move with an even, swaying motion. **3.** turn; pivot. **4.** be suspended. **5.** *Slang* be up-to-date and sophisticated. **6.** *Slang* engage in sexual promiscuity. —*v.t.* **7.** cause to move backward and forward. **8.** cause to move with an even, swaying motion. **9.** cause to turn. **10.** hang or suspend. **11.** *Informal* influence or win over. [ME *swingen*] —*n.* **1.** the act of swinging; also the distance covered. **2.** a free swaying motion. **3.** a seat hanging from ropes etc., on which one may move to and fro. **4.** a marked rhythm, as of poetry or music. **5.** a sweeping blow or stroke. **6.** in jazz, a development after about 1935, characterized by large bands, simple harmony, strong rhythms, etc. **8.** a trip; tour. —**in full swing** in full operation.

swing•er (SWING ər) *n.* **1.** a lively and up-to-date person. **2.** *Slang* a person who indulges in promiscuous sex.

swing shift a workshift from about 4 p.m. to midnight.

swipe (swīp) *v.t.* **swiped, swip•ing 1.** strike with a hard, sweeping blow. **2.** *Informal* steal; snatch. —*n.* a sweeping blow.

swirl (swurl) *v.t. & v.i.* move or cause to move in a whirling or twisting motion; whirl. —*n.* **1.** a whirling motion; eddy; whirl. **2.** a curl or twist; spiral. [ME]

swish (swish) *v.t. & v.i.* **1.** move through the air with a hissing, whistling sound, as a whip. **2.** rustle, as silk. **3.** exhibit effeminate behavior. —*n.* **1.** the sound of swishing. **2.** *Slang* an effeminate male homosexual. [Imit.]

switch (swich) *n.* **1.** a small flexible rod etc., used for whipping. **2.** a tress of false hair, used by women in building a coiffure. **3.** a mechanism for shifting a railway train from one track to another. **4.** a shift; change. **5.** *Electr.* a device to make, break, or divert a circuit. [< earlier *swits* rod] —*v.t.* **1.** whip with or as with a switch. **2.** change; shift. **3.** exchange: They *switched* plates. **4.** shift (a railroad car) to another track; shunt. **5.**

Electr. connect or disconnect with a switch: with *on* or *off*. —*v.i.* **6.** turn aside; change; shift. —**switch′er** *n.*

switch·board (SWICH BORD) *n.* a control panel for connecting and disconnecting electric circuits, as in a telephone exchange.

switch·yard (SWICH YAHRD) *n.* a railroad yard for assembly and disassembly of trains.

swiv·el (SWIV əl) *n.* a pivoted support on which a mechanism may be swung. —*v.t. & v.i.* **swiv·eled, swiv·el·ing** turn on or as on a swivel. [ME]

swivel chair a chair having a seat that turns horizontally on a swivel.

swob (swob) see SWAB.

swol·len (SWOH lən) a past participle of SWELL.

swoon (swoon) *v.i.* faint. [ME *swonen*] —*n.* a fainting fit. —**swoon′·ing·ly** *adv.*

swoop (swoop) *v.i.* **1.** drop or descend suddenly, as a bird pouncing on its prey. —*v.t.* **2.** take or seize suddenly: often with *up.* [ME *swopen*] —**swoop** *n.*

swop (swop) see SWAP.

sword (sord) *n.* **1.** a weapon, as a saber, consisting of a long blade fixed in a hilt. **2.** power; esp., military power. —**at swords′ points** mutually antagonistic, ready for a fight. —**put to the sword** kill with a sword. [ME]

swords·man (SORDZ mən) *n. pl.* **·men** a person skilled in the use of or armed with a sword. —**swords′man·ship** *n.*

swore (swor) past tense of SWEAR.

sworn (sworn) past participle of SWEAR.

swum (swum) past participle of SWIM.

swung (swung) past tense, past participle of SWING.

syb·a·rite (SIB ə RIT) *n.* one given to pleasure and luxury; hedonist. [< the notorious luxury of the Sybarites, in the ancient Greek city of Sybaris, in southern Italy] —**syb·a·rit·ic** (SIB ə RIT ik) *adj.* —**syb′a·rit′cal·ly** *adv.*

syc·o·phant (SIK ə fənt) *n.* a servile flatterer. [< L *sycophanta* informer] —**syc′o·phan·cy** *n.* —**syc′o·phan′tic** *adj.*

syl·lab·i·cate (si LAB i KAYT) *v.t.* **·cat·ed, ·cat·ing** syllabify. —**syl·lab′i·ca′tion** *n.*

syl·lab·i·fy (si LAB ə FI) *v.t.* **·fied, ·fy·ing** form or divide into syllables. —**syl·lab′i·fi·ca′tion** *n.*

syl·la·ble (SIL ə bəl) *n.* **1.** *Phonet.* a word or part of a word uttered in a single vocal impulse, usu. consisting of a vowel alone or with one or more consonants. **2.** a part of a written word corresponding to this. **3.** the least detail, mention, or trace. [ME *sillable*] —**syl·lab′ic** *adj.*

syl·la·bus (SIL ə bəs) *n. pl.* **·bus·es** or **·bi** (-BI) a concise statement of the main points of a course of study, subject, etc. [< NL, label for a scroll]

syl·lo·gism (SIL ə JIZ əm) *n. Logic* an argument consisting of two premises and a conclusion logically drawn from them. [< L *syllogismus*] —**syl′lo·gis′tic** *adj.* —**syl′lo·gis′ti·cal·ly** *adv.*

sylph (silf) *n.* **1.** an imaginary being inhabiting the air. **2.** a slender, graceful young woman. [< NL *sylphus*] —**sylph′like** *adj.*

syl·van (SIL vən) *adj.* **1.** of or located in a forest or woods. **2.** composed of or abounding in trees or woods. [< Med.L *silvanus*]

sym·bi·o·sis (SIM bee OH sis) *n. Biol.* the living together in mutually advantageous partnership of dissimilar organisms. [< NL] —**sym′bi·ot′ic** (-OT ik) *adj.* —**sym′bi·ot′i·cal·ly** *adv.*

sym·bol (SIM bəl) *n.* **1.** something chosen to represent something else; esp., an object used to typify a quality, abstract idea, etc.: The oak is a *symbol* of strength. **2.** a character, mark, etc. indicating something, as a quantity in mathematics. [ME]

sym·bol·ic (sim BOL ik) *adj.* **1.** of, pertaining to, or expressed by a symbol. **2.** serving as a symbol: with *of.* **3.** characterized by or involving the use of symbols: *symbolic* poetry. —**sym·bol′i·cal·ly** *adv.*

sym·bol·ism (SIM bə LIZ əm) *n.* **1.** representation by symbols. **2.** a system of symbols. **3.** symbolic character or meaning. **4.** the theory and practice of symbolists in literature and art.

sym·bol·ist (SIM bə list) *n.* an artist or writer skilled in the use of symbols.

sym·bol·ize (SIM bə LIZ) *v.* **·ized, ·iz·ing** *v.t.* **1.** be a symbol of; typify. **2.** represent by a symbol. —*v.i.* **3.** use symbols. —**sym′bol·i·za′tion** *n.*

sym·me·try (SIM i tree) *n. pl.* **·tries** **1.** an exact correspondence between the opposite halves of a figure, pattern, etc., on either side of an axis or center. **2.** beauty or harmony of form resulting from this. [< L *symmetria* balance] —**sym·met′ri·cal** *adj.*

sym·pa·thet·ic (SIM pə THET ik) *adj.* **1.** of, expressing, or proceeding from sympathy. **2.** being in accord or harmony; congenial:

with *to: sympathetic* to our plan. —
sym′pa·thet′i·cal·ly *adv.*

sym·pa·thize (SIM pə THIZ) *v.i.* •**thized,**
•**thiz·ing 1.** share or agree with the feelings
or ideas of another: with *with.* **2.** feel or
express compassion, as for another's sorrow: with *with.* —**sym′pa·thiz′er** *n.*

sym·pa·thy (SIM pə thee) *n. pl.* •**thies 1.**
the quality of being affected by the state of
another with feelings corresponding in
kind. **2.** a feeling or expression of compassion for another's sufferings; pity; commis-
eration. **3.** an agreement of affections,
inclinations, etc.; congeniality; accord. [< L
sympathia]

sym·pho·ny (SIM fə nee) *n. pl.* •**nies 1.**
Music a composition for orchestra, consisting usu. of four movements that are related
by structure, key, etc. **2.** a symphony orchestra. **3.** harmony, as of sounds, colors,
etc.: *symphony* in gray. [ME *symphonie*
concert] —**sym·phon·ic** (sim FON ik)
adj.

symphony orchestra a large orchestra
composed usu. of the string, brass, woodwind, and percussion sections needed to
present symphonic works.

sym·po·si·um (sim POH zee əm) *n. pl.*
•**si·ums** or •**si·a** (-zee ə) **1.** a meeting for
discussion of a particular subject. **2.** a collection of comments or opinions on a subject, esp. when published as a series of
essays or articles. [< L, drinking party] —
sym·po′si·ast (sim POH zee əst) *n.*

symp·tom (SIMP təm) *n.* **1.** a sign, token, or
indication. **2.** *Med.* any observable alteration in bodily functions indicating a disease. [ME] —**symp′to·mat′ic** *adj.* —
symp′to·mat′i·cal·ly *adv.*

syn·a·gogue (SIN ə GOG) *n.* **1.** a congregation of Jews assembled for religious instruction and observances. **2.** the place or
building for such an assembly. Also **syn′**
a·gog. [ME *synagoge*]

syn·apse (SIN aps) *n. Physiol.* the junction
point of two neurons, across which a nerve
impulse passes. Also called **syn·ap′sis.** [<
NL *synapsis* junction]

syn·chro·nize (SING krə NIZ) *v.* •**nized,**
•**niz·ing** *v.i.* **1.** occur at the same time; co-
incide. **2.** move or operate in unison. —*v.t.*
3. cause to operate in unison, agree in time,
etc. —**syn′chro·ni·za′tion** *n.*

syn·chro·nous (SING krə nəs) *adj.* **1.** occurring at the same time or rate. **2.** *Physics*
having the same period or rate of vibration,

as waves or electric currents. Also **syn′**
chro·nal. [< LL *synchronus*] —**syn′**
chro·nous·ly *adv.*

syn·co·pa·tion (SING kə PAY shən) *n. Music*
a the rhythmic placement of a tone on a
weak beat and continuing it through the
next strong beat. **b** any music featuring syn-
copation, as ragtime, jazz, etc.

syn·di·cate (SIN di kit) *n.* **1.** an association
of individuals united to negotiate some
business requiring capital. **2.** an agency that
sells articles etc. to a number of periodicals
for simultaneous publication. [< F *syndi-
cat*] —*v.* (SIN di KAYT) •**cat·ed,** •**cat·ing**
v.t. **1.** combine into or manage by a syndicate. **2.** sell (an article etc.) for publication
in many newspapers or magazines. —*v.i.* **3.**
form a syndicate.

syn·drome (SIN drohm) *n.* a set of symptoms indicating a disease, unfavorable social condition, etc. [< NL]

sy·nec·do·che (si NEK də kee) *n.* a figure of
speech in which a part is substituted for the
whole, as a *hand* for a *worker.* [< Med.L]

syn·er·gism (SIN ər JIZ əm) *n.* the joint action of people or different substances in
producing an effect greater than the sum of
the individual efforts or effects. [< NL *syn-
ergismus*] —**syn·er·gis·tic** (SIN ər JIS tik)
adj. —**syn·er·gy** *n. pl.* •**gies** combined action; cooperative action.

syn·od (SIN əd) *n.* **1.** an ecclesiastical council. **2.** any deliberative assembly. [ME] —
sy·nod·ic (si NOD ik) *adj.*

syn·o·nym (SIN ə nim) *n.* a word having the
same or almost the same meaning as some
other: opposed to *antonym.* [ME *sin-
onyme*] —**syn·on·y·mous** (si NON ə məs)
adj.

syn·op·sis (si NOP sis) *n. pl.* •**ses** (-seez) a
brief review or outline of a play, novel, etc.;
summary. [< LL] —**syn·op′tic** *adj.*

syn·tax (SIN taks) *n.* **1.** the arrangement and
relationship of words in sentences. **2.** the
branch of grammar dealing with this. [<
LL] —**syn·tac·tic** (sin TAK tik) or •**ti·cal**
adj.

syn·the·sis (SIN thə sis) *n. pl.* •**ses** (-SEEZ)
1. the assembling of separate or subordinate parts into a whole: opposed to *analysis.*
2. a complex whole composed of originally
separate parts. **3.** *Chem.* the building up of
compounds from a series of reactions involving elements, radicals, or similar compounds. [< L]

syn·the·size (SIN thə SIZ) *v.t.* •**sized,**

•siz•ing unite or produce by synthesis. —
syn′the•siz′er *n.* one who or that which
synthesizes, esp. an electronic instrument
for creating music.

syn•thet•ic (sin THET ik) *adj.* **1.** of or relating to synthesis. **2.** *Chem.* produced artificially by chemical synthesis rather than
occurring naturally. **3.** artificial; spurious.
—*n.* a product, esp. a fabric, produced by
chemical synthesis. —**syn•thet′i•cal•ly**
adv.

syph•i•lis (SIF ə lis) *n. Pathol.* an infectious
venereal and congenital disease caused by a
spirochete. [< NL, after *Syphilis*, a 1530
poem that provides an early account of the
disease] —**syph′i•lit′ic** *adj. & n.*

sy•ringe (si RINJ) *n.* **1.** *Med.* a device consisting of a nozzle and a rubber bulb or piston
into which a liquid may be drawn for ejection in a fine jet, used for cleaning wounds
etc. **2.** a hypodermic syringe. —*v.t.*
•**ringed, •ring•ing** spray, cleanse, inject,
etc. with a syringe.

syr•up (SIR əp) *n.* a thick, sweet liquid,
as the boiled juice of fruits, sugar cane, etc.
[ME *sirup*] —**syr′up•y** *adj.*

sys•tem (SIS təm) *n.* **1.** an arrangement of
parts, rules, principles, etc. into a unified
whole: a school *system*, the solar *system*, a
political *system*. **2.** *Physiol.* **a** a set of organs
acting together to perform a specific func-
tion: the nervous *system*. **b** the entire body
taken as a functional whole. **3.** a method or
plan; scheme. **4.** the quality of being orderly or methodical; orderliness. [< LL
systema]

sys•tem•at•ic (SIS tə MAT ik) *adj.* **1.** of, pertaining to, or of the nature of a system. **2.**
characterized by system or method; methodical. [< LL *systematicus*] Also **sys-
′tem•at′i•cal.** —**sys′•tem•at′i•cal•ly**
adv.

sys•tem•a•tize (SIS tə mə TĪZ) *v.t.* •**tized,
•tiz•ing** form into or arrange according to a
system. —**sys′tem•a•ti•za′tion** *n.*

sys•tem•ic (si STEM ik) *adj.* **1.** of or pertaining to a system. **2.** *Physiol.* of or affecting
the body as a whole: a *systemic* poison. —
sys•tem′i•cal•ly *adv.*

sys•to•le (SIS tə LEE) *n. Physiol.* the regular
contraction of the heart that impels the
blood outward. Compare DIASTOLE. [<
Gk., a contraction] —**sys•tol•ic** (si STOL
ik) *adj.*

T

t, T (tee) *n. pl.* **t's** or **ts, T's** or **Ts 1.** the twentieth letter of the English alphabet. **2.** the sound represented by the letter *t*. **3.** anything shaped like the letter T. —**to a T** or **to a tee** precisely; with exactness.

't contraction for IT, as in *'tis*.

tab (tab) *n.* **1.** a flap, strip, tongue, or appendage of something, as a garment. **2.** a small, projecting part used as an aid in filing papers, etc. **3.** *Informal* a bill. —**keep tab** or **tabs (on)** watch closely.

tab·by (TAB ee) *n. pl.* **·bies 1.** a brindled or striped cat. **2.** any domestic cat, esp. a female. **3.** any of various plain-woven fabrics, as a watered taffeta. —*adj.* **1.** having dark, wavy markings; brindled, as a cat. **2.** watered or mottled, as a fabric. [< F *tabis* < Arabic name for the quarter in Baghdad where the fabric was made]

tab·er·nac·le (TAB ər NAK əl) *n.* **1.** formerly, a tent or similar temporary shelter. **2.** the portable sanctuary used by the Israelites in the wilderness. **3.** any house of worship, esp. one of large size. **4.** *Eccl.* the ornamental receptacle for the consecrated Eucharistic elements. [ME] —*v.i. & v.t.* **·led, ·ling** dwell or place in or as in a tabernacle.

ta·ble (TAY bəl) *n.* **1.** an article of furniture with a flat horizontal top held up by one or more supports. **2.** the food served at a meal. **3.** the company of persons at a table. **4.** a collection of related numbers, values, signs, or items of any kind, arranged for reference, often in parallel columns. **5.** a summary statement; list: *table* of contents. — **turn the tables** thwart an opponent's action and turn the situation to one's own advantage. [ME] —*v.t.* **·bled, ·bling 1.** place on a table. **2.** postpone discussion of (a resolution, bill, etc.).

tab·leau (ta BLOH) *n. pl.* **·leaux** (-BLOH or -BLOHZ) or **·leaus** (-BLOHZ) **1.** any picture or picturesque representation; esp., a striking scene presented dramatically. **2.** a picturelike scene represented by silent and motionless persons standing in appropriate attitudes. [< F, picture]

tab·le d'hôte (TAB əl DOHT) *pl.* **tab·les d'hôte** (TAB əlz) a complete meal served at a restaurant or hotel for a fixed price. [< F, lit., table of the host]

ta·ble·spoon (TAY bəl SPOON) *n.* **1.** a large spoon used for serving food. **2.** also **ta'ble·spoon·ful** (-FUUL) a quantity equal to 3 teaspoonfuls.

tab·let (TAB lit) *n.* **1.** a pad, as of writing paper. **2.** a small, flat surface, esp. one designed for or containing an inscription or design. **3.** a definite portion of a drug etc. pressed into a solid form. **4.** a small, flat or nearly flat piece of some prepared substance, as chocolate or soap. [ME *tablett*]

table tennis a table game resembling tennis, played with a small plastic ball and wooden paddles.

ta·ble·ware (TAY bəl WAIR) *n.* dishes, knives, forks, spoons, etc. for table use, collectively.

tab·loid (TAB loid) *n.* a newspaper consisting of sheets half the size of those in an ordinary newspaper, in which the news is presented by means of pictures and concise reporting. —*adj.* **1.** compact; concise; condensed. **2.** sensational: *tabloid* journalism.

ta·boo (ta BOO) *n.* **1.** among primitive peoples, a religious and social rule forbidding mention of a certain thing, performance of a certain action, etc. **2.** the system or practice of such interdicts or prohibitions. **3.** any restriction or ban founded on custom. —*adj.* **1.** consecrated or prohibited by taboo. **2.** banned or forbidden by social convention. —*v.t.* place under taboo. Also **ta·bu'.** [< Tongan *tabu*]

tab·u·lar (TAB yə lər) *adj.* **1.** pertaining to or consisting of a table or list. **2.** computed from or with a mathematical table. **3.** having a flat surface; tablelike. —**tab'u·lar·ly** *adv.*

tab·u·late (TAB yə LAYT) *v.t.* **·lat·ed, ·lat·ing** arrange in a table or list. [< L *tabula* tablet] —**tab'u·la'tion** *n.*

ta·chom·e·ter (ta KOM i tər) *n.* **1.** an instrument for measuring speed and velocity. **2.** a device for indicating the speed of rotation of an engine etc.

tach·y·car·di·a (TAK i KAHR dee ə) *n. Pathol.* an abnormally rapid heartbeat. [< NL]

tac·it (TAS it) *adj.* **1.** existing or implied

without being directly stated. **2.** silent. [< L *tacitus* silent] —**tac′it·ly** *adv.*

tac·i·turn (TAS i TURN) *adj.* habitually silent or reserved. [< F *taciturne*] —**tac′i·turn′i·ty** *n.*

tack¹ (tak) *n.* **1.** a small sharp-pointed nail, commonly with tapering sides and a flat head. **2.** *Naut.* **a** the direction in which a vessel sails, considered in relation to the position of its sails. **b** the distance or the course run at one time in such direction. **c** the act of tacking. **d** a course sailed obliquely against the wind. **3.** a course of action. **4.** in sewing, a large, temporary stitch. [ME *tak* nail] —*v.t.* **1.** fasten or attach with tacks. **2.** sew with tacks. **3.** attach as supplementary; append. **4.** *Naut.* navigate (a vessel) by making a series of tacks. —*v.i.* **5.** *Naut.* change a ship's course. **6.** change one's course of action; veer. — **tack′er** *n.*

tack² *n.* food in general.

tack·le (TAK əl) *n.* **1.** a system of ropes and pulleys used for hoisting or moving objects. **2.** a winch, together with ropes and hooks. **3.** equipment; gear: fishing *tackle*. **4.** in football: **a** the act of tackling. **b** either of two linemen usu. stationed between a guard and an end. **5.** a ship's rigging. [ME *takel*] —*v.t.* **·led, ·ling 1.** deal with; undertake to master, accomplish, or solve. **2.** in football, seize and stop (an opponent carrying the ball). —*v.i.* **3.** in football, make a tackle. — **tack′ler** *n.*

tack·y¹ (TAK ee) *adj.* **tack·i·er, tack·i·est** adhesive; sticky. —**tack′i·ness** *n.*

tack·y² *adj.* **tack·i·er, tack·i·est** shabby; neglected; shoddy. —**tack′i·ness** *n.*

ta·co (TAH koh) *n.* a fried tortilla filled with meat, cheese, etc. [< Am.Sp.]

tact (takt) *n.* intuitive ability to avoid offending. [< F] —**tact′ful** *adj.* —**tact′ful·ly** *adv.* —**tact′ful·ness** *n.* —**tact′less** *adj.* — **tact′less·ly** *adv.* —**tact′·less·ness** *n.*

tac·tics (TAK tiks) *n.* **1.** *(construed as sing.)* the art of handling a military force, esp. in battle: also **tac′tic. 2.** *(construed as pl.)* any maneuvering to gain an objective. [< NL *tactica* tactics] —**tac·ti·cian** (tak TISH ən) *n.* —**tac′ti·cal** *adj.* —**tac′ti·cal·ly** *adv.*

tac·tile (TAK til) *adj.* pertaining to or perceptible through the sense of touch. [< F] Also **tac′tu·al** (TAK choo əl).

tad (tad) *n. Informal* **1.** a little child. **2.** a bit.

tad·pole (TAD pohl) *n.* the aquatic larva of a

frog or toad: also called *polliwog*. [ME *taddepol*]

taf·fe·ta (TAF i tə) *n.* a plain-woven, somewhat stiff fabric of silk, rayon, etc. [ME]

taf·fy (TAF ee) *n.* a candy made of boiled sugar or molasses and butter: also called *toffee.*

tag¹ (tag) *n.* **1.** a label, tacked on or attached loosely. **2.** a loose, ragged edge of anything; tatter. **3.** a nickname or epithet. [ME *tagge*] —*v.* **tagged, tag·ging** *v.t.* **1.** supply with a tag. **2.** follow closely or persistently. —*v.i.* **3.** follow closely: often with *along* or *after.*

tag² *v.t.* **tagged, tag·ging 1.** in baseball, touch (a player) with the ball or with the hand or glove in which the ball is held. **2.** overtake and touch, as in the game of tag. —*n.* **1.** in baseball, the act or instance of tagging a player, esp. a base runner, in order to retire the player. **2.** a children's game in which a player who is touched or caught tries to touch or catch another.

Ta·ga·log (tə GAH ləg) *n.* **1.** a member of a Malay people native to the Philippines, esp. Luzon. **2.** the official language of the Philippines.

tag end 1. a loose end or tag of cloth, yarn, etc. **2.** the last part of anything.

t'ai chi (TĪ JEE) a Chinese system of exercise consisting of slow rhythmic movements. Short for **t'ai chi ch'uan** (CHWAHN). Also **tai chi.** [< Chinese]

tail (tayl) *n.* **1.** the hindmost part or rear end of an animal, esp. when prolonged beyond the rest of the body as a distinct, flexible member. **2.** any terminal extension of the main part of an object. **3.** the bottom, back, or inferior portion of anything. **4.** the reverse side of a coin. **5.** *pl.* a man's full-dress suit. **6.** one who follows or closely watches someone. —*v.t.* **1.** furnish with a tail. **2.** *Informal* follow secretly; shadow. —*v.i.* **3.** extend or proceed in a line. **4.** *Informal* follow close behind. —*adj.* **1.** rearmost; hindmost. **2.** coming from behind; following: a *tail* wind. [ME] —**tail′less** *adj.*

tail·gate (TAYL GAYT) *n.* a hinged or vertically sliding gate closing the back end of a truck, wagon, etc. —*v.t. & v.i.* **·gat·ed, ·gat·ing** drive too close behind (another vehicle) for safety.

tail·ing (TAY ling) *n.* **1.** *pl.* refuse or residue from grain after milling, or from ground ore after washing. **2.** the inner, covered portion of a projecting brick or stone in a wall.

tai·lor (TAY lər) *n.* one who makes to order

or repairs people's outer garments. [ME] —*v.i.* **1.** do a tailor's work. —*v.t.* **2.** fit with garments. **3.** make by tailoring. **4.** make or adapt for a specific purpose.

tai·lored (TAY lərd) *adj.* **1.** characterized by simple, severe style: said esp. of women's clothes. **2.** made by a tailor.

tail·piece (TAYL pees) *n.* **1.** any end piece or appendage. **2.** in a violin, cello, etc., a piece of ebony to which the lower ends of the strings are attached. **3.** *Printing* an ornamental design on the lower blank portion of a page.

tail·pipe (TAYL PĪP) an exhaust pipe on an automobile, truck, etc.

tail·spin (TAYL SPIN) *n.* *Aeron.* the descent of a stalled airplane along a tight helical path at a steep angle.

taint (taynt) *v.t.* **1.** imbue with something offensive, poisonous, or corrupt; infect with decay. **2.** corrupt morally. —*v.i.* **3.** be or become tainted. [< ME *tainten* color] —*n.* **1.** a trace or germ of decay. **2.** a moral stain; disgrace.

take (tayk) *v.* **took, tak·en, tak·ing** *v.t.* **1.** lay hold of; grasp. **2.** get possession of; seize, capture, catch, or win. **3.** choose; select. **4.** buy, rent, or hire. **5.** assume the occupancy or responsibilities of: *take* office. **6.** bring or accept as one's own or into some relation to oneself: She *took* a lover. **7.** impose upon onself: *take* a vow. **8.** remove or carry off: with *away*. **9.** steal. **10.** subtract or deduct. **11.** undergo: *take* a beating. **12.** accept passively: *take* an insult. **13.** become affected with: He *took* cold. **14.** affect. **15.** captivate; charm or delight. **16.** react to: How did he *take* the news? **17.** undertake to deal with: *take* an examination. **18.** consider; deem. **19.** understand; comprehend. **20.** carry with one. **21.** lead: This road *takes* you away from town. **22.** escort; conduct: Who *took* him home? **23.** receive into the body, as by eating: *take* medicine. **24.** admit or accommodate. **25.** perform, as an action: *take* a stride. **26.** avail oneself of (an opportunity etc.). **27.** put into effect; adopt: *take* measures. **28.** use up, need, or require: The piano *takes* too much space. **29.** travel by means of: *take* a train. **30.** ascertain or obtain by measuring, computing, etc.: *take* a census. **31.** adopt or copy. **32.** experience; feel: *take* pride. **33.** *Informal* cheat; deceive. —*v.i.* **34.** get possession. **35.** engage; catch, as mechanical parts. **36.** begin to grow; germinate. **37.** have the intended effect: The vaccination *took*. **38.** detract: with *from*. **39.** make one's way; go. —**take after 1.** resemble. **2.** follow as an example. —**take amiss** be offended by. —**take at one's word** believe. —**take back 1.** regain. **2.** retract. —**take down 1.** pull down or dismantle; disassemble. **2.** humble. **3.** write down; make a record of. —**take heart** gain courage or confidence. —**take in 1.** admit; receive. **2.** lessen in size or scope. **3.** include; embrace. **4.** understand; comprehend. **5.** receive into one's home for pay, as boarders or roomers. **6.** *Informal* cheat or deceive. —**take in vain** use profanely or blasphemously, as the name of a deity. —**take it** endure hardship, abuse, etc. —**take it out on** *Informal* vent one's anger, frustration, etc. on. —**take off 1.** remove, as a coat. **2.** deduct. **3.** *Informal* mimic; burlesque. **4.** rise from the ground or water in starting a flight, as an airplane. **5.** *Informal* leave; depart. —**take on 1.** hire; employ. **2.** undertake to deal with; handle. —**take out 1.** extract; remove. **2.** obtain from the proper authority, as a license or patent. **3.** lead, escort, or date. —**take over** assume control. —**take place** happen. —**take stock 1.** make an inventory. **2.** estimate probability, position, etc.; consider. —**take the field** begin a campaign or game. —**take to 1.** have recourse to; go to: *take* to one's bed. **2.** develop the practice of, or an addiction to: She *took* to drink. **3.** become fond of. —**take to heart** be deeply affected by. —**take up 1.** make smaller or less; shorten or tighten. **2.** accept as stipulated: *take up* an option. **3.** begin or begin again. **4.** occupy, engage, or consume, as space or time. **5.** acquire an interest in or devotion to: *take up* a cause. —**take up with** *Informal* become friendly with. [ME *taken* grasp] —*n.* **1.** the act of taking, or that which is taken. **2.** an uninterrupted run of a camera or recording apparatus in making a motion picture, sound recording, etc. **3.** a quantity collected at one time: the *take* of fish. **4.** *Informal* money collected, as the receipts of a sporting event. —**on the take** *Slang* accepting bribes; corrupt.

take-home pay (TAYK HOHM) the net wages or salary after deductions.

take·off (TAYK AWF) *n.* **1.** the act of rising or leaping from the ground to begin flight. **2.** a satirical imitation; caricature.

take·o·ver (TAYK oh vər) *n.* an assuming or seizure of control, ownership, or rule.

tak·ing (TAY king) *adj.* fascinating; captivating. —*n.* **1.** the act of one who takes. **2.** The thing or things taken. **3.** *pl.* receipts. —**tak′ing·ly** *adv.*

tale (tayl) *n.* **1.** that which is told or related; a story. **2.** a piece of gossip. **3.** a lie; falsehood. [ME]

tal·ent (TAL ənt) *n.* **1.** a special aptitude for some work or activity. **2.** people of skill or ability, collectively. **3.** an ancient weight and denomination of money. [ME] —**tal·ent·ed** (TAL ən tid) *adj.*

talent scout one whose business is to discover talented people, as actors, athletes, etc.

tal·is·man (TAL is mən) *n. pl.* •**mans** a magic charm or amulet. [< F]

talk (tawk) *v.i.* **1.** express thoughts in audible words; communicate by speech. **2.** make a speech. **3.** communicate by means other than speech: *talk* with one's eyes. **4.** speak irrelevantly; chatter. **5.** confer; consult. **6.** gossip. **7.** give incriminating information, as to the police; inform. —*v.t.* **8.** express in words; utter. **9.** use in speaking; converse in: *talk* Spanish. **10.** converse about; discuss: *talk* business. **11.** influence by talking: *talk* one into doing something. —**talk back** answer impudently. —**talk big** *Slang* brag; boast. —**talk down** direct (an aircraft) to a landing by giving instructions to the pilot over the radio. —**talk down to** speak to in a condescending manner. —**talk shop** talk about one's work. —**talk up** promote; praise; extol. [ME *talken*] —*n.* **1.** the act of talking;.conversation; speech. **2.** a speech or lecture. **3.** report; rumor. **4.** mere words; verbiage. **5.** a language, dialect, or jargon: baseball *talk.*

talk·a·tive (TAW kə tiv) *adj.* given to much talking. —**talk′a·tive·ness** *n.*

tall (tawl) *adj.* •**er,** •**est 1.** having more than average height; high or lofty. **2.** having specified height. **3.** extravagant; unbelievable: a *tall* story. —*adv.* proudly: stand *tall.* [ME]

tal·lith (TAH lis) *n. pl.* **tal·li·thim** (tah LEE sim) a fringed scarf worn around the shoulders by some Jewish men when praying. [< Hebrew, cloak]

tal·low (TAL oh) *n.* a mixture of the harder animal fats, refined for use in candles, soaps, etc. [ME *talow*] —*v.t.* smear with tallow.

tal·ly (TAL ee) *n. pl.* •**lies 1.** a piece of wood on which notches are cut as marks of number. **2.** a score or mark. **3.** a reckoning; account. **4.** a counterpart; duplicate. **5.** a label; tag. [ME *talye* rod] —*v.* •**lied,** •**ly·ing** *v.t.* **1.** score on a tally; record. **2.** reckon; count; estimate: often with *up.* —*v.i.* **3.** correspond; fit: The stories *tally.* **4.** keep score. —**tal′li·er** *n.*

Tal·mud (TAHL muud) *n.* the body of Jewish civil and religious law (and related commentaries) not included in the Pentateuch. [< Hebrew *talmūdh* instruction] —**Tal·mud′ic** or •**i·cal** *adj.* —**Tal′mud·ist** *n.*

tal·on (TAL ən) *n.* the claw of a bird or other animal, esp. of a bird of prey. [ME]

ta·lus (TAY ləs) *n. pl.* •**li** (-lī) **1.** *Anat.* the bone of the foot just above the heel bone: also called *anklebone.* [< L] **2.** *Geol. pl.* •**lus·es** the sloping mass of rock fragments below a cliff. [< F]

ta·ma·le (tə MAH lee) *n.* a Mexican dish made of crushed corn and meat with red pepper, cooked in corn husks. [< Am.Sp. *tamales,* pl. of *tamal* tamale]

tam·bour (TAM buur) *n.* **1.** a drum. **2.** a round frame on which material for embroidering may be stretched. [< MF, drum] —*v.t. & v.i.* embroider on a tambour.

tam·bou·rine (TAM bə REEN) *n.* a musical instrument like the head of a drum, with jingles in the rim, played by striking it with the hand. [< MF *tambourin*]

tame (taym) *adj.* **tam·er, tam·est 1.** having lost its native wildness or shyness; domesticated. **2.** in agriculture, cultivated. **3.** docile; tractable. **4.** uninteresting; dull. [ME] —*v.t.* **tamed, tam·ing 1.** domesticate. **2.** bring into subjection or obedience. **3.** tone down; soften. —**tame′a·ble** or **tam′a·ble** *adj.* —**tame′ness** *n.* —**tam′er** *n.*

Tam·il (TAM əl) *n.* **1.** one of an ancient Dravidian people, and still the most numerous of the inhabitants of southern India and northern Sri Lanka. **2.** their language.

tamp (tamp) *v.t.* force down or pack closer by firm, repeated blows.

tam·per (TAM pər) *v.i.* **1.** meddle; interfere: usu. with *with.* **2.** make changes, esp. so as to damage or corrupt: with *with.*

tam·pi·on (TAM pee ən) *n. Mil.* a stopper, as a plug put into the mouth of a cannon. [ME *tampyon* bung]

tam·pon (TAM pon) *n. Med.* a plug of cotton or lint, esp. for absorbing menstrual flow.

[< F] —*v.t.* plug up, as a wound, with a tampon.

tan (tan) *v.* **tanned, tan•ning** *v.t.* **1.** convert (hides) into leather by treating with tannin. **2.** turn brown, as the skin, by exposure to sunlight. **3.** *Informal* thrash; whip. —*v.i.* **4.** become tanned, as hides or the skin. [ME *tannen*] —*n.* **1.** a yellowish brown color tinged with red. **2.** a brown coloring of the skin, resulting from exposure to the sun. —*adj.* **tan•ner, tan•nest** of the color tan; light brown.

tan•bark (TAN BAHRK) *n.* **1.** the bark of certain trees, esp. oak or hemlock, containing tannin and used in tanning leather. **2.** a surface covered with pieces of tanbark, esp. a circus ring

tan•dem (TAN dəm) *adv.* one in front of or behind another. —*n.* **1.** two or more horses harnessed in single file. **2.** a two-wheeled carriage drawn by a tandem of horses. **3.** a bicycle with seats for two persons, one behind the other: also **tandem bicycle.** —*adj.* arranged in tandem. [< L, at last]

tang (tang) *n.* **1.** a penetrating taste, flavor, or odor. **2.** a slender shank or tongue, as at the end of a sword blade or chisel, for inserting in a handle. [ME]

tan•gent (TAN jənt) *adj.* being in contact at a single point or along a line; touching. —*n.* **1.** *Geom.* a straight line, curve, or surface touching but not intersecting another curve or surface. **2.** *Trig.* a function of an acute angle, equal to the ratio of the side opposite the angle to the side adjacent to the angle when the angle is included in a right triangle. —**go off on a tangent** digress. [< L, touching] —**tan•gen•tial** (tan JEN shəl) *adj.* —**tan•gen'tial•ly** *adv.* —**tan•gen•cy** (TAN jən see) *n.*

tan•gi•ble (TAN jə bəl) *adj.* **1.** perceptible by touch; also, within reach by touch. **2.** definite; real. **3.** *Law* able to be bought, sold, used, etc.; material. [< LL *tangibilis*] —*n.* **1.** that which is tangible. **2.** *pl.* material assets. —**tan'gi•bly** *adv.*

tan•gle (TANG gəl) *v.* **•gled, •gling** *v.t.* **1.** twist or involve in a confused and not readily separable mass. **2.** ensnare; enmesh. —*v.i.* **3.** be or become entangled. —**tangle with** *Informal* come to blows with; argue. [ME *tanglen*] —*n.* **1.** a confused intertwining; snarl. **2.** a state of confusion or complication.

tan•go (TANG goh) *n. pl.* **•gos** any of several Latin-American dances characterized by deliberate gliding steps and low dips; also, the music for such a dance. —*v.i.* dance the tango. [< Am.Sp.]

tang•y (TANG ee) *adj.* **tang•i•er, tang•i•est** having a tang in taste or odor; pungent. —**tang'i•ness** *n.*

tank (tangk) *n.* **1.** a large vessel, basin, or receptacle for holding a fluid. **2.** *Mil.* a heavily armored combat vehicle, moving on caterpillar treads. [< Pg. *tanque* pool] —*v.t.* place or store in a tank.

tan•kard (TANG kərd) *n.* a large, one-handled drinking cup, often with a cover. [ME]

tank•er (TANG kər) *n.* a cargo vessel built for the transport of liquids, esp. oil and gasoline.

tank•ful (TANGK fuul) *n.* the amount a tank can hold.

tan•ner•y (TAN ə ree) *n. pl.* **•ner•ies** a place where leather is tanned.

tan•nic (TAN ik) *adj.* pertaining to or derived from tannin or tanbark.

tannic acid *n. Chem.* any of a group of astringent compounds, used in inks, dyeing, and tanning. Also **tan'nin.**

tan•ning (TAN ing) *n.* **1.** the art or process of converting hides into leather. **2.** a bronzing, as of the skin. **3.** *Informal* a thrashing.

tan•ta•lize (TAN tl IZ) *v.t.* **•lized, •liz•ing** tease or torment by repeated frustration. [< *Tantalus* in Greek mythology, a king punished by being made to stand in water that receded when he tried to drink, and under fruit-laden branches that rose out of reach when he was hungry] —**tan'ta•liz•ing** (TAN tl I zing *adj.* —**tan'ta•l•iz'•ing•ly** *adv.*

tan•ta•mount (TAN tə MOWNT) *adj.* having equivalent value or effect: with *to.* [< AF *tant amunter* amount to as much]

tan•trum (TAN trəm) *n.* a burst of ill temper.

Tao•ism (DOW iz əm) *n.* a religion of China, founded by Lao-tse, who taught that happiness could be acquired through obedience to man's nature in accordance with the **Tao** (dow), the basic principle of nature. [< Chinese] —**Tao'ist** *adj. & n.*

tap[1] (tap) *n.* **1.** an arrangement for drawing out liquid, as beer from a cask; a faucet or cock; spigot. **2.** a plug to close an opening in a cask or other vessel. **3.** liquor drawn from a tap. **4.** a tool for cutting internal screw threads. **5.** a point of connection for an electrical circuit. **7.** a connection, often a secret one, on a telephone line, gas line, etc. —**on**

tap 1. contained in a cask. 2. available; ready. —*v.t.* **tapped, tap•ping** 1. provide with a tap or spigot. 2. pierce or open so as to draw liquid from. 3. draw (liquid) from a container. 4. make connection with, often secretly: *tap* a telephone wire. 5. make an internal screw thread in with a tap. [ME *tappen*]

tap² *v.* **tapped, tap•ping** *v.t.* 1. touch or strike gently. 2. make or produce by tapping. 3. select, as for membership. —*v.i.* 4. strike a light blow or blows, as with the finger tip. —*n.* 1. a gentle or playful blow; also, the sound made by such a blow. 2. a metal plate affixed to a shoe sole or heel. [ME *tappe*]

tape (tayp) *n.* 1. a narrow strip of strong woven fabric. 2. any long, narrow, flat strip of paper, metal, etc. 3. a magnetic tape. 4. a tape measure. —*v.t.* **taped, tap•ing** 1. wrap or secure with tape. 2. measure with or as with a tapeline. 3. record on magnetic tape. [ME]

tape deck 1. a tape recorder. 2. a self-contained device for playing back sound recorded on a cassette or magnetic tape: also **tape player**.

tape measure a tape for measuring distances.

ta•per (TAY pər) *n.* 1. a small candle. 2. a burning wick or the like, giving slight illumination. 3. a gradual diminution of size in an elongated object. [ME] —*v.t. & v.i.* 1. make or become smaller or thinner toward one end. 2. lessen gradually; diminish: with *off.*

tape-re•cord (TAYP ri KORD) *v.t.* record by tape recorder. —**tape recording**

tape recorder a device that converts sound into magnetic patterns stored on a tape, reversing the process for playback.

tap•es•try (TAP ə stree) *n. pl.* **•tries** a woven, ornamental fabric, used for hangings. [ME *tapistry*] —*v.t.* **•tried, •try•ing** hang or adorn with tapestry.

tape•worm (TAYP WURM) *n.* any of various worms with ribbonlike bodies, parasitic on the intestines of vertebrates.

tap•root (TAP ROOT) *n. Bot.* the principal descending root of a plant.

taps (taps) *n. (construed as sing. or pl.)* a military signal by bugle, sounded at night as an order to extinguish lights, and sometimes played after a burial.

tar¹ (tahr) *n.* a dark, oily, viscid mixture obtained by the distillation of wood, coal, etc.

[ME *tarr*] —*v.t.* **tarred, tar•ring** cover with or as with tar. —**tar and feather** smear (a person) with tar and then cover with feathers as a punishment.

tar² *n. Informal* a sailor.

ta•ran•tu•la (tə RAN chə lə) *n. pl.* **•las** or **•lae** (-lee) 1. a large, hairy spider of southern Europe. 2. any of various related spiders. [< Med.L]

tar•dy (TAHR dee) *adj.* **•di•er, •di•est** 1. not on time; late. 2. moving slowly. [< L *tardus* slow] —**tar′di•ness** *n.*

tare (tair) *n.* an allowance made to a buyer of goods by deducting from the gross weight of a purchase the weight of the container. —*v.t.* **tared, tar•ing** determine the tare. [< MF, discard]

tar•get (TAHR git) *n.* 1. an object that is shot at, as in rifle or archery practice. 2. anything that is shot at. 3. a person or thing made an object of attack, effort, or attention. —**on target** 1. headed or aimed so as to hit a target. 2. well directed; to the point. [ME]

tar•iff (TA rif) *n.* 1. a schedule of articles of merchandise with the rates of duty to be paid for their importation or exportation. 2. a duty, or duties collectively. 3. any schedule of charges. [< Arabic *ta′rifah* information] —*v.t.* fix a price or tariff on.

tar•nish (TAHR nish) *v.t.* 1. dim the luster of. 2. stain; disgrace. —*v.i.* 3. lose luster, as by oxidation. —*n.* 1. loss of luster. 2. a stain. 3. the thin film of color on the exposed surface of a metal or mineral. [< MF *ternir* deaden]

tar•ot (TA roh) *n.* one of a set of playing cards used for telling fortunes. [< MF]

tar•pau•lin (tahr PAW lin) *n.* a waterproof canvas used to cover merchandise, athletic fields, etc. Also **tarp.**

tar•ry¹ (TAR ee) *v.i.* **•ried, •ry•ing** 1. put off going or coming; linger. 2. remain in the same place, esp. longer than one expected. [ME *taryen* delay] —*n.* sojourn; stay. —**tar′ri•er** *n.*

tar•ry² (TAHR ee) *adj.* **•ri•er, •ri•est** covered with tar; like tar.

tar•sus (TAHR səs) *n. pl.* **•si** (-sī) *Anat.* the ankle; in people, the group of seven bones of which it is composed. [< NL] —**tar′sal** (-səl) *adj.*

tart¹ (tahrt) *adj.* 1. having a sharp, sour taste. 2. severe; cutting; caustic: a *tart* remark. [ME] —**tart′ly** *adv.* —**tart′ness** *n.*

tart² *n.* 1. a small pastry shell with fruit or

custard filling. **2.** *Slang* a promiscuous woman; prostitute. [ME *tarte*, prostitute]

tar·tan (TAHR tn) *n.* a woolen fabric having varicolored lines or stripes at right angles, forming a distinctive pattern, the characteristic dress of the Scottish Highlanders. [< MF *tertaine*, a woolen cloth] —**tar·tan** *adj.*

tar·tar¹ (TAHR tər) *n.* **1.** an acid substance deposited from grape juice during fermentation as a pinkish sediment. **2.** *Dent.* a yellowish incrustation on the teeth. [ME] —**tar·tar·ic** (tahr TAR ik) *adj.*

tar·tar² *n.* a person of intractable or savage temper. [ME]

task (task) *n.* **1.** a specific amount of labor or study imposed by authority or required by duty or necessity. **2.** a specific military mission. [ME] —**take to task** reprove; admonish. —*v.t.* overtax with labor; burden.

task force 1. *Mil.* a temporary group of units assigned to accomplish a specific mission. **2.** any temporary group of specialists assigned to accomplish a specific task.

task·mas·ter (TASK MAS tər) *n.* one who assigns tasks, esp. severe ones.

tas·sel (TAS əl) *n.* **1.** a dangling ornament for curtains, cushions, etc., consisting of a tuft of loose threads or cords. **2.** any of various similar objects, as the silk of an ear of corn. [ME] —*v.* •**seled, •sel·ing** *v.t.* **1.** provide or adorn with tassels. **2.** remove the tassels from (corn). —*v.i.* **3.** put forth tassels, as corn.

taste (tayst) *v.* **tast·ed, tast·ing** *v.t.* **1.** perceive the flavor of (something) by taking into the mouth or touching with the tongue. **2.** eat or drink a little of. **3.** test the quality of (a product) thus: *Her business is tasting tea.* —*v.i.* **4.** have specified flavor: *Sugar tastes sweet.* **5.** have experience: with *of: taste of great sorrow.* [ME *tasten*] —*n.* **1.** *Physiol.* any of the four fundamental sensations—salt, sweet, bitter, or sour—excited by the action of the gustatory nerves. **2.** a small quantity tasted. **3.** a slight experience or sample of anything. **4.** special fondness and appreciation: *a taste for music.* **5.** the faculty of discerning and appreciating what is beautiful or correct, as in art, clothes, etc. **6.** individual preference.

taste·ful (TAYST fəl) *adj.* **1.** conforming to taste. **2.** possessing good taste. —**taste'ful·ness** *n.*

taste·less (TAYST lis) *adj.* **1.** flavorless; in-

sipid. **2.** lacking, or showing a lack of, good taste. —**taste'less·ness** *n.*

tast·y (TAY stee) *adj.* **tast·i·er, tast·i·est** having a fine flavor; savory. —**tast'i·ness** *n.*

tat (tat) *v.t. & v.i.* **tat·ted, tat·ting** make (tatting or an article of tatting).

ta·ta·mi (tə TAH mee) *n. pl.* •**mi, •mis** a mat, usu. of straw, used as floor covering. [< Jap.]

tat·ter (TAT ər) *n.* **1.** a torn and hanging shred; rag. **2.** *pl.* ragged clothing. [ME] —*v.t.* **1.** make ragged; tear into tatters. —*v.t.* **2.** become ragged. —**tat'tered** *adj.*

tat·ting (TAT ing) *n.* a lacelike threadwork; also, the act or process of making it.

tat·tle (TAT l) *v.* **·tled, ·tling** *v.i.* **1.** prate; chatter. **2.** tell tales about others. —*v.t.* **3.** reveal by gossiping. —*n.* idle talk or gossip. [< MDu. *tatelen*] —**tat'tler, tat·tle·tale** (TAT l TAYL) *n.*

tat·too¹ (ta TOO) *v.t.* •**tooed, •too·ing 1.** prick and mark (the skin) with indelible pigments. **2.** make (a design etc.) in this way. —*n. pl.* •**toos** a pattern or picture so made. [< Polynesian] —**tat·too'er** *n.* —**tat·too'ing** *n.*

tat·too² *n. pl.* •**toos 1.** a continuous beating or drumming. **2.** *Mil.* a signal on a bugle at night to go to quarters. [< Du. *tap toe!* taps shut!]

tau (tow) *n.* the nineteenth letter in the Greek alphabet (Τ, τ), corresponding to the *t.*

taught (tawt) past tense, past participle of TEACH.

taunt (tawnt) *n.* a sarcastic, biting speech or remark; scornful reproach. —*v.t.* reproach or tease with taunts; mock; upbraid. —**taunt'er** *n.* —**taunt'ing·ly** *adv.*

taut (tawt) *adj.* **1.** stretched tight; not loose or slack. **2.** tense; tight: *taut muscles.* [ME *tought*] —**taut'ness** *n.*

tau·tol·o·gy (taw TOL ə jee) *n. pl.* •**gies** repetition of the same idea in different words; pleonasm. [< LL *tautologia*] —**tau·to·log·i·cal** (TAWT l OJ i kəl) *adj.*

tav·ern (TAV ərn) *n.* **1.** a place licensed to retail liquors to be drunk on the premises. **2.** an inn. [ME *taverne*]

taw·dry (TAW dree) *adj.* •**dri·er, •dri·est** showy and cheap. [< *St. Audrey's lace,* a type of lace sold at St. Audrey's Fair at Ely, England] —**taw'dri·ness** *n.*

taw·ny (TAW nee) *adj.* •**ni·er, •ni·est** tan-colored; brownish yellow. [ME *tauny*]

tax (taks) *n.* **1.** a compulsory contribution

levied on persons, property, or business for the support of government. **2.** any proportionate assessment, as on the members of a society. **3.** a heavy demand; onerous duty; burden. —*v.t.* **1.** impose a tax on. **2.** impose a burden on: He *taxes* my patience. **3.** accuse; charge: usu. with *with.* [ME *taxen*] — **tax′a•ble** *adj.*

tax•a•tion (tak SAY shən) *n.* **1.** the act of taxing. **2.** a tax.

tax•i (TAK see) *n. pl.* **tax•is** a taxicab. —*v.* **tax•ied, tax•i•ing** or **tax•y•ing** *v.i.* **1.** ride in a taxicab. **2.** move along the ground, as an airplane before taking off. —*v.t.* **3.** cause (an airplane) to taxi.

tax•i•cab (TAK see KAB) *n.* an automobile available for hire, usu. fitted with a device for measuring distance traveled and computing fares, a **taximeter** (TAK see MEE tər).

tax•i•der•my (TAK si DUR mee) *n.* the art of stuffing and mounting the skins of dead animals for preservation or exhibition. [< Gk. *taxis* arrangement + *derma* skin] —**tax′ i•der′mist** *n.*

tax•on•o•my (tak SON ə mee) *n.* **1.** the laws and principles of classification. **2.** *Biol.* the systematic arrangement of plant and animal organisms according to established criteria. [< F *taxonomie*] —**tax•o•nom•ic** (TAK sə NOM ik) *adj.* —**tax•on′o•mist** *n.*

tea (tee) *n.* **1.** an Asian shrub having leathery, toothed leaves and white or pink flowers. **2.** the prepared leaves of this plant, or an infusion of them used as a beverage. **3.** a social gathering at which tea is served. [< dial. Chinese *t'e*]

tea ceremony a ritual preparation and serving of tea, practiced by the Japanese.

teach (teech) *v.* **taught, teach•ing** *v.t.* **1.** impart knowledge to by lessons; give instruction to. **2.** give instruction in. **3.** train by practice or exercise. —*v.i.* **4.** follow the profession of teaching. **5.** impart knowledge or skill. [ME *techen*]

teach•er (TEE chər) *n.* one who teaches; esp., one whose occupation is to teach others.

teach•ing (TEE ching) *n.* **1.** the act or occupation of a teacher. **2.** that which is taught.

tea•cup (TEE KUP) *n.* **1.** a small cup suitable for serving tea. **2.** as much as a teacup will hold, usu. four fluid ounces: also **tea′cup• ful′** (-FUUL).

team (teem) *n.* **1.** two or more beasts of burden harnessed together. **2.** a group of

people working, playing, or competing together. [ME *teme*] —*v.t.* **1.** harness together in a team. —*v.i.* **2.** form a team.

team•mate (TEEM MAYT) *n.* a fellow player on a team.

team•ster (TEEM stər) *n.* one who drives a truck as an occupation.

team•work (TEEM WURK) *n.* concerted action or effort by the members of a group to achieve some common end.

tear[1] (tair) *v.* **tore, torn, tear•ing** *v.t.* **1.** pull apart, as cloth; rip; rend. **2.** make by rending or tearing: *tear* a hole. **3.** injure or lacerate, as skin. **4.** divide; disrupt. —*v.i.* **5.** become torn or rent. **6.** move with haste and energy. —**tear into** *Informal* charge into or attack without restraint. [ME *teren*] —*n.* **1.** a fissure made by tearing; a rent; also, an act of tearing. **2.** *Informal* a spree; frolic. **3.** a rushing motion.

tear[2] (teer) *n.* **1.** a drop of the liquid secreted by the lachrymal gland, serving to moisten the eye, and stimulated to a flow by emotional distress. **2.** something resembling or suggesting a tear. —**in tears** weeping; crying. [ME *teer*] —*v.i.* shed or fill with tears. —**tear′y** *adj.* **tear•i•er, tear•i•est**

tear•drop (TEER DROP) *n.* a tear, or a tear-shaped object.

tear•ful (TEER fəl) *adj.* **1.** weeping abundantly. **2.** causing tears. —**tear′ful•ly** *adv.*

tear gas (teer) any of various chemicals that provoke a copious flow of tears, with irritation of the eyes.

tear•jerk•er (TEER JUR kər) *n. Informal* a story, play, etc. full of sentimental sadness.

tea•room (TEE ROOM) *n.* a restaurant serving tea and other refreshments.

tease (teez) *v.* **teased, teas•ing** *v.t.* **1.** annoy or harass with jokes, mocking remarks, demands, etc.; pester. **2.** scratch or dress in order to raise the nap, as cloth with teasels. **3.** comb (hair) so as to form fluffy layers. —*v.i.* **4.** annoy a person in a facetious or petty manner. [ME *tesen*] —*n.* one who or that which teases. —**teas′ing•ly** *adv.*

tea•spoon (TEE SPOON) *n.* **1.** a small spoon used for stirring tea etc. **2.** as much as a teaspoon will hold: also **tea′spoon•ful′** (-FUUL).

teat (teet) *n.* the protuberance on a breast or udder, through which the milk is drawn; nipple. [ME *tete*]

tech•ni•cal (TEK ni kəl) *adj.* **1.** pertaining to some particular art, science, or trade. **2.** peculiar to or used in a specialized field of knowledge. **3.** of or pertaining to the mechanical arts. **4.** considered in terms of an accepted body of rules: a *technical* defeat. —**tech′ni·cal·ly** *adv.*

tech·ni·cal·i·ty (TEK ni KAL i tee) *n. pl.* **·ties 1.** the state of being technical. **2.** a technical point peculiar to some profession, trade, etc. **3.** a petty distinction; quibble.

technical knockout in boxing, a victory awarded when the referee considers that one fighter is unable to continue.

tech·ni·cian (tek NISH ən) *n.* one skilled in handling instruments or in performing tasks requiring specialized training.

tech·nique (tek NEEK) *n.* working methods or manner of performance.

tech·nol·o·gy (tek NOL ə jee) *n. pl.* **·gies 1.** the application of science and of technical advances in industry, the arts, etc. **2.** the means by which material things are produced, as in a particular civilization. —**tech·no·log·i·cal** (TEK nə LOJ i kəl) *adj.* —**tech·nol′o·gist** *n.*

tec·ton·ics (tek TON iks) *n. (construed as sing.)* **1.** the science and art of construction, esp. of buildings. **2.** the geology of earth structures. —**tec·ton′ik** *adj.* [< LL *tectonicus* pertaining to construction]

te·di·ous (TEE dee əs) *adj.* causing weariness; boring. [ME] —**te′di·ous·ly** *adv.*

te·di·um (TEE dee əm) *n.* the state of being tiresome or wearisome; tediousness. [< L *taedium* disgust]

tee (tee) *n.* **1.** a small peg with a concave top on which a golf ball is placed in making the first play to a hole. **2.** a designated area within which the golf tee must be placed. —*v.t. & v.i.* **teed, tee·ing** place (the golf ball) on a tee. —**tee off** strike (the golf ball) in starting play.

teem[1] (teem) *v.i.* be full to overflowing; abound. [ME *temen*] —**teem′ing** *adj.*

teem[2] *v.i.* come down heavily; pour: said of rain. [ME *temen*]

teen·age (TEEN AYJ) *adj.* of, pertaining to, or characteristic of a teenager. —**teen′ag′er** *n.* a person between the ages of 13 through 19.

teens (teenz) *n.pl.* **1.** the numbers that end in *-teen.* **2.** the teenage years.

tee·ny (TEE nee) *adj.* **·ni·er, ·ni·est** tiny.

tee·pee (TEE pee) see TEPEE.

tee·ter (TEE tər) *v.i.* **1.** walk or move with a tottering motion. **2.** seesaw; waver; vacil-

late. —*v.t.* **3.** cause to teeter. [ME *titeren* totter] —*n.* **1.** an oscillating motion. **2.** a seesaw.

teeth (teeth) plural of TOOTH.

teethe (teeth) *v.i.* **teethed, teeth·ing** cut or develop teeth.

teeth·ing ring (TEETH ing) a ring of hard rubber, plastic, etc. for a teething baby to bite on. Also **teeth′er.**

tee·to·tal·er (tee TOHT lər) *n.* one who abstains totally from alcoholic drinks. —**tee·to′tal** *adj.* —**tee·to′tal·ism** *n.*

tel·e·cast (TEL i KAST) *v.t. & v.i.* **·cast** or **·cast·ed, ·cast·ing** broadcast by television. —*n.* a program broadcast by television. —**tel′e·cast′er** *n.*

tel·e·com·mu·ni·ca·tions (TEL i kə MYOO ni KAY shənz) *n. (construed as sing.)* the art and science of communicating at a distance, as in radio, television, telephony, etc. Also **tel′e·com·mu′ni·ca′tion.**

tel·e·gram (TEL i GRAM) *n.* a message sent by telegraph.

tel·e·graph (TEL i GRAF) *n.* any of various devices or systems using a code, esp. one using coded impulses transmitted by wire or radio. —*v.t.* **1.** send (a message) by telegraph. **2.** communicate with by telegraph. —*v.i.* **3.** transmit a message by telegraph. —**te·leg·ra·pher** (tə LEG rə fər) *n.* —**te·leg·ra·phy** (tə LEG rə fee) *n.* —**tel·e·graph·ic** (TEL i GRAF ik) *adj.*

te·lem·e·try (tə LEM i tree) *n.* the theory and practice of using electronic devices for transmitting information, esp. in relation to rockets, space probes, etc.

te·lep·a·thy (tə LEP ə thee) *n.* the supposed communication of one mind with another at a distance by other than normal sensory means. —**tel·e·path·ic** (TEL ə PATH ik) *adj.* —**te·lep′a·thist** *n.*

tel·e·phone (TEL ə FOHN) *n.* a device or system for transmitting sound over a wire or other communication channel. —*v.* **·phoned, ·phon·ing** *v.t.* **1.** communicate with by telephone. **2.** send by telephone, as a message. —*v.i.* **3.** communicate by telephone. —**tel·e·phon·ic** (TEL ə FON ik) *adj.*

te·leph·o·ny (tə LEF ə nee) *n.* the construction or operation of telephones.

tel·e·pho·to (TEL ə FOH toh) *adj.* **1.** designating a lens system of a camera that produces a large image of a distant object. **2.** pertaining to telephotography.

tel·e·pho·tog·ra·phy (TEL ə fə TOG rə

fee) *n.* photography of distant objects, as with a telephoto lens.

tel·e·scope (TEL ə SKOHP) *n.* an optical instrument for enlarging the image of a distant object. —*v.* **·scoped, ·scop·ing** *v.t.* **1.** drive or slide together so that one part fits into another. —*v.i.* **2.** crash into one another, as railroad cars. **3.** collapse on itself. —**tel·e·scop·ic** (TEL ə SKOP ik) *adj.*

tel·e·vise (TEL ə VĪZ) *v.t. & v.i.* **·vised, ·vis·ing** transmit or receive by television.

tel·e·vi·sion (TEL ə VIZH ən) *n.* **1.** the transmission of continuous visual images as a series of electrical impulses or a modulated carrier wave, restored to visual form on the cathode-ray screen of a receiver, often with accompanying sound. **2.** the television broadcasting industry. **3.** a television receiving set. Also called *TV.*

tell (tel) *v.* **told, tell·ing** *v.t.* **1.** relate in detail; narrate, as a story. **2.** communicate. **3.** reveal: *tell* secrets. **4.** decide; ascertain. **5.** express in words: *tell* a lie. **6.** give a command to; order. **7.** let know; inform. —*v.i.* **8.** give an account. **9.** serve as indication or evidence: with *of.* **10.** produce a marked effect: Every death *told.* —**all told** in all. —**tell off** *Informal* reprimand severely. —**tell on 1.** tire; weary. **2.** inform against. [ME *tellen*]

tell·er (TEL ər) *n.* **1.** one who relates or informs. **2.** a person who receives or pays out money, as in a bank. **3.** a person appointed to collect and count ballots.

tell·ing (TEL ing) *adj.* producing a great effect; impressive. —**tell′ing·ly** *adv.*

tell·tale (TEL TAYL) *n.* **1.** a tattler. **2.** that which reveals or discloses information. **3.** an instrument or device for providing or recording information. —*adj.* that reveals or discloses what is not to be known.

te·mer·i·ty (tə MER i tee) *n.* reckless boldness; rashness. [ME *temeryte*]

tem·per (TEM pər) *n.* **1.** a disposition to become angry. **2.** frame of mind; mood. **3.** composure of mind; self-command. **4.** *Metall.* the condition of a metal as regards hardness and elasticity, esp. when due to heating and sudden cooling. —*v.t.* **1.** bring to a state of moderation or suitability, as by addition of another quality; moderate. **2.** bring (clay etc.) to the proper consistency etc. by moistening and working. **3.** *Metall.* bring (metal) to a required hardness and elasticity by heating and sudden cooling.

—*v.i.* **4.** be or become tempered. [ME *temperen*]

tem·per·a (TEM pər ə) *n.* a painting medium consisting of an emulsion prepared from water and egg yolks, glue, gum, casein, etc.; also, a method of painting with such a medium. [< Ital.]

tem·per·a·ment (TEM prə mənt) *n.* **1.** the physical and mental peculiarities of an individual; nature. **2.** an intense, moody, and often rebellious nature. [ME]

tem·per·a·men·tal (TEM prə MEN tl) *adj.* **1.** of or pertaining to temperament. **2.** sensitive; easily excited. —**tem′per·a·men′tal·ly** *adv.*

tem·per·ance (TEM pər əns) *n.* **1.** the state or quality of being temperate; habitual moderation. **2.** the principle or practice of abstinence from intoxicants. [ME *temperaunce*]

tem·per·ate (TEM pər it) *adj.* **1.** observing moderation in the indulgence of an appetite, esp. in the use of intoxicating liquors. **2.** moderate as regards temperature. **3.** characterized by moderation; not excessive. —**tem′per·ate·ly** *adv.* —**tem′per·ate·ness** *n.*

Temperate Zones see under ZONE.

tem·per·a·ture (TEM pər ə chər) *n.* **1.** condition as regards heat or cold. **2.** the degree of heat in a body or substance, as measured on the graduated scale of a thermometer. **3.** an excess of body temperature; fever. [< L *temperatura* moderation]

tem·pered (TEM pərd) *adj.* **1.** having temper or a specified disposition: used mainly in compounds: *quick-tempered.* **2.** having the desired degree of hardness and elasticity.

tem·pest (TEM pist) *n.* **1.** a violent storm. **2.** a violent commotion; tumult. —**tempest in a teapot** an uproar over a trivial matter. [ME *tempeste*]

tem·pes·tu·ous (tem PES choo əs) *adj.* stormy; turbulent; violent. —**tem·pes′tu·ous·ness** *n.*

tem·plate (TEM plit) *n.* a pattern or gauge, as of metal, used as a guide in shaping something.

tem·ple¹ (TEM pəl) *n.* **1.** an edifice consecrated to the worship of one or more deities. **2.** in the U.S., a Reform or Conservative synagogue. **3.** a large building used for a special purpose. [ME]

tem·ple² *n.* the region on each side of the head above the cheek bone. [ME]

tem·po (TEM poh) *n. pl.* **·pos** or **·pi** (-pee) 1. *Music* relative speed at which a composition is rendered. 2. characteristic manner or rhythm. [< Ital.]

tem·po·ral (TEM pər əl) *adj.* 1. pertaining to affairs of the present life; earthly. 2. pertaining or related to time. [ME]

tem·po·ra·ry (TEM pə RER ee) *adj.* lasting or intended to be used for a short time only; transitory. [< L *temporarius*] —**tem'po·rar'i·ly** *adv.*

tem·po·rize (TEM pə RĪZ) *v.i.* **·rized, ·riz·ing** 1. act evasively so as to gain time or put off decision. 2. give real or apparent compliance. [< MF *temporiser* delay] —**tem'·po·riz'er** *n.*

tempt (tempt) *v.t.* 1. attempt to persuade (a person) to do something evil or unwise. 2. be attractive to; invite. 3. provoke or risk provoking: *tempt* fate. [ME] —**tempt'er** *n.* —**tempt'ress** *n.fem.*

temp·ta·tion (tem TAY shən) *n.* 1. the act of tempting, or the state of being tempted. 2. that which tempts. [ME *temptacion*]

tempt·ing (TEMP ting) *adj.* alluring; attractive; seductive. —**tempt'ing·ly** *adv.*

tem·pu·ra (TEM pə rə) *n.* seafood or vegetables dipped in batter and deep-fried. [< Jap.]

ten (ten) *n.* the sum of nine and one: a cardinal number written 10, X. [ME *tene*] —**ten** *adj.* **—tenth** (tenth) *adj. & n.*

ten·a·ble (TEN ə bəl) *adj.* capable of being held, maintained, or defended. [< F] —**ten'a·bil'i·ty** *n.*

te·na·cious (tə NAY shəs) *adj.* 1. having great cohesiveness of parts; tough. 2. holding or tending to hold strongly, as opinions, rights, etc. 3. strongly retentive, as memory. [< L *tenax* tending to hold fast] —**te·na'cious·ly** *adv.* —**te·nac·i·ty** (tə NAS i tee) *n.*

ten·an·cy (TEN ən see) *n. pl.* **·cies** 1. a holding of lands, houses, offices, etc.; occupancy. 2. the period of holding lands, houses, etc.

ten·ant (TEN ənt) *n.* 1. one who holds or possesses lands or property by the payment of rent or other fee. 2. a dweller in any place; an occupant. [ME *tenaunt*] —**ten'ant·less** *adj.*

tenant farmer one who farms another's land and pays rent, usu. in a share of the crops.

Ten Commandments the set of precepts given by God to Moses.

tend[1] (tend) *v.i.* 1. have an aptitude, ten-

dency, or disposition; incline. 2. have influence toward a specified result. 3. go in a certain direction. [ME *tenden*]

tend[2] *v.t.* 1. attend to the needs or requirements of; take care of. 2. watch over; look after. —*v.i.* 3. give attention or care: with *to.*

ten·den·cy (TEN dən see) *n. pl.* **·cies** 1. an inclination toward some purpose, end, or result; bent; aptitude. 2. an inclination to act or think in a particular way. 3. a course; direction. [< Med.L *tendentia*]

ten·den·tious (ten DEN shəs) *adj.* having a tendency to favor a particular point of view; biased. [See TENDENCY.] —**ten·den'tious·ness** *n.*

ten·der[1] (TEN dər) *adj.* **·er, ·est** 1. yielding easily to force that tends to crush, bruise, break, or injure. 2. easily chewed or cut: said of food. 3. delicate or weak; not strong, rough, or hardy. 4. youthful and delicate. 5. kind; affectionate; gentle. 6. capable of arousing sensitive feelings; touching: *tender* memories. 7. painful if touched. 8. requiring delicate treatment; ticklish; touchy. —*v.t.* make tender; soften. [ME] —**ten'der·ly** *adv.* —**ten'der·ness** *n.*

ten·der[2] *v.t.* present for acceptance, as a resignation; offer. —*n.* 1. the act of tendering; an offer. 2. that which is offered as payment: legal *tender.* [< AF *tendre* extend] —**ten'der·er** *n.*

tend·er[3] *n.* 1. *Naut.* a a vessel used to bring supplies, passengers, etc. back and forth between a larger vessel and shore. b a vessel that services another at sea. 2. a vehicle attached to the rear of a steam locomotive to carry fuel and water. [ME]

ten·der·foot (TEN dər FUUT) *n. pl.* **·foots** or **·feet** (-FEET) 1. in the West, one not yet inured to the hardships of the plains, the mining camp, etc. 2. any inexperienced person.

ten·der·heart·ed (TEN dər HAHR tid) *adj.* compassionate; kind. —**ten'der·heart'ed·ly** *adv.*

ten·der·ize (TEN də RĪZ) *v.t.* **·ized, ·iz·ing** make tender, as meat. —**ten'der·iz·er** *n.*

ten·der·loin (TEN dər LOIN) *n.* 1. the tender part of the loin of beef, pork, etc., lying close to the backbone. 2. an urban district noted for its night life, crime, etc.

ten·don (TEN dən) *n. Anat.* one of the bands of tough connective tissue forming the termination of a muscle and serving to transmit its force to some other part; sinew. [< Med.L]

ten·dril (TEN dril) n. Bot. one of the organs that serve a climbing plant as a means of attachment to a wall, tree trunk, or other surface.

ten·e·ment (TEN ə mənt) n. 1. an urban apartment building or rooming house that is poorly constructed or maintained, typically overcrowded and often part of a slum. [ME, a holding]

ten·et (TEN it) n. an opinion, principle, dogma, etc., believed or maintained as true. [< L, he holds]

ten·fold (TEN FOHLD) adj. 1. consisting of ten parts. 2. ten times as many or as great. —adv. in tenfold measure: penalized tenfold.

ten·nis (TEN is) n. a game played by striking a ball back and forth with rackets over a net stretched between two equal areas that together constitute a court. [ME tenys]

ten·on (TEN ən) n. a projection on the end of a timber etc., for inserting in a socket to form a joint. —v.t. 1. form a tenon on. 2. join by a mortise and tenon. [ME]

ten·or (TEN ər) n. 1. the adult male voice intermediate in range between baritone and alto; also, a singer having such a voice, or a part to be sung by it. 2. Music an instrument playing the part intermediate between the bass and the alto. 3. general purport, tendency, or character. [< ME] —adj. having the part or range of a tenor.

tense[1] (tens) adj. **tens·er, tens·est** 1. stretched tight; taut. 2. under mental or nervous strain; strained. [< L tensus] —v.t. & v.i. **tensed, tens·ing** make or become strained or drawn tight. —**tense'ly** adv.

tense[2] n. a form of a verb that relates it to time viewed as past, present, or future. [ME tens time]

ten·sile (TEN səl) adj. 1. of or pertaining to tension. 2. capable of being drawn out or extended. [< NL tensilis] —**ten·sil'i·ty** n.

tensile strength Physics the resistance of a material to longitudinal stress.

ten·sion (TEN shən) n. 1. the act of stretching or the condition of being stretched tight. 2. mental strain; intense nervous anxiety. 3. any strained relation, as between governments. 4. Physics stress on a material caused by a force pulling or stretching in one direction. [< MF] —**ten'sion·al** adj.

tent (tent) n. a shelter of canvas or the like,

supported by poles and fastened by cords to pegs driven into the ground. [ME tente]

ten·ta·cle (TEN tə kəl) n. 1. Zool. a protruding flexible process or appendage of invertebrate animals, functioning as an organ of touch or motion. 2. Bot. a sensitive glandular hair, as on the leaves of some plants. [< NL tentaculum]

ten·ta·tive (TEN tə tiv) adj. provisional or conjectural; subject to change; experimental. [< Med.L tentativus tried] —**ten'ta·tive·ly** adv. —**ten'ta·tive·ness** n.

ten·ter·hook (TEN tər HUUK) n. a sharp hook for holding cloth while it is being stretched on a drying frame (a **tenter**). —**be on tenterhooks** be in a state of anxiety or suspense.

ten·u·ous (TEN yoo əs) adj. 1. thin; slim; delicate; also, weak; flimsy; unsubstantial. 2. having slight density; rare. [< L tenuis] —**ten'u·ous·ly** adv. —**ten'u·ous·ness** n.

ten·ure (TEN yər) n. 1. the holding or use of land, office, etc., or the state of being held. 2. the term during which a thing is held. 3. permanent status granted to an employee, usu. after a trial period. [ME]

te·pee (TEE pee) n. a conical tent of Native Americans, usu. covered with skins: also spelled teepee. [< Dakota tipi]

tep·id (TEP id) adj. 1. moderately warm; lukewarm, as a liquid. 2. characterized by lack of enthusiasm: tepid praise. [ME] —**tep'id·ness** n. **tep'id·ly** adv.

te·qui·la (tə KEE lə) n. a Mexican alcoholic liquor made from the agave plant. [after Tequila, Mexico]

ter·a·tism (TER ə TIZ əm) n. 1. worship of the monstrous. 2. Biol. a monstrosity.

ter·cen·te·nar·y (TUR sen TEN ə ree) adj. of or pertaining to a period of 300 years or to a 300th anniversary. —n. pl. **·nar·ies** a 300th anniversary. Also tricentennial.

ter·gi·ver·sate (TUR JI vər SAYT) v.i. **·sat·ed, ·sat·ing** 1. be evasive; equivocate. 2. change sides, attitudes, etc. [< L tergiversatus turned about] —**ter'gi·ver·sa'tion** n. —**ter'gi·ver·sa'tor** n.

term (turm) n. 1. a word or expression used to designate some definite thing. 2. any word or expression conveying some thought: speak in general terms. 3. pl. conditions or stipulations: terms of sale. 4. pl. mutual relations: usu. preceded by on or upon: They were on friendly terms. 5. Math. a quantity that is part of a fraction, algebraic expression, progression, etc. 6.

Logic either the subject or predicate of a proposition. **7.** a fixed period or definite length of time, as one of the periods of the school year. **8.** *Law* a prescribed period during which a court may hold a session. **9.** *Med.* the time for childbirth. —**in terms of** with reference to; concerning. —**bring to terms** persuade or force to accede or agree. —**come to terms** reach an agreement. [ME *terme* limit] —*v.t.* designate by means of a term; name or call.

ter·mi·na·ble (TUR mə nə bəl) *adj.* that may be terminated; limitable; not perpetual. —**ter′mi·na·bly** *adv.*

ter·mi·nal (TUR mə nl) *adj.* **1.** of, pertaining to, or forming a boundary, limit, or end. **2.** ending in death: said of a disease. —*n.* **1.** that which terminates; a terminating point or part; end. **2.** *Electr.* a point at which a circuit element, as a battery, resistor, transistor, etc., may be connected to other elements. **3.** a railroad station, yard, etc. taken together. [ME] —**ter′mi·nal·ly** *adv.*

ter·mi·nate (TUR mə NAYT) *v.* •**nat·ed,** •**nat·ing** *v.t.* **1.** put an end or stop to. **2.** form the conclusion of; finish. **3.** bound or limit. —*v.i.* **4.** have or come to an end. [< L *terminatus* ended]

ter·mi·na·tion (TUR mə NAY shən) *n.* **1.** the act of setting bounds or ending. **2.** that which bounds or limits; close; end. [ME *terminacion*]

ter·mi·nol·o·gy (TUR mə NOL ə jee) *n. pl.* •**gies** the technical terms used in a science, trade, etc.; nomenclature. [< Med.L *terminus* term + -LOGY]

ter·mi·nus (TUR mə nəs) *n. pl.* •**ni** (-NI) or **nus·es 1.** the final point or goal; end. **2.** either end of a railway. [< L, boundary]

ter·mite (TUR mīt) *n.* any of various small, social insects that are destructive of wood: also, loosely, *white ant.* [< NL *Termes*]

ter·na·ry (TUR nə ree) *adj.* formed or consisting of three; grouped in threes. —*n. pl.* •**ries** a group of three; triad. [ME]

terp·si·cho·re·an (TURP si kə REE ən) *adj.* of or relating to dancing. —*n.* a dancer. [after *Terpsichore,* Greek muse of dancing]

ter·race (TER is) *n.* **1.** a raised, level space, as of lawn, having one or more vertical or sloping sides. **2.** a raised level supporting a row of houses, or the houses occupying such a position. **3.** an unroofed, usu. paved area near a house. **4.** an open balcony or gallery; also, a flat roof. [< MF] —*v.t.*

•**raced,** •**rac·ing** form into or provide with a terrace or terraces.

ter·ra cot·ta (TER ə KOT ə) **1.** a hard, durable clay, reddish brown in color and usu. unglazed, used as a structural material and in pottery, tiles, etc. **2.** its brownish orange color. [< Ital., lit., baked earth] —**terra-cotta** *adj.*

ter·ra fir·ma (FUR mə) dry land. [< NL, lit., solid ground]

ter·rain (tə RAYN) *n.* a piece or plot of ground; esp., a region or territory viewed with regard to its fitness for some use. [< F]

ter·rar·i·um (tə RAIR ee əm) *n. pl.* •**rar·i·ums** or •**rar·i·a** (-RAIR ee ə) an enclosure for keeping land animals, plants, etc. [< NL]

ter·raz·zo (tə RAZ oh) *n.* a flooring made of marble chips set in cement. [< Ital., lit., terrace]

ter·res·tri·al (tə RES tree əl) *adj.* **1.** of or consisting of earth or land. **2.** *Biol.* living on or growing in the earth or land. **3.** worldly; mundane. [ME]

ter·ri·ble (TER ə bəl) *adj.* **1.** exciting terror; appalling. **2.** characterized by excess; severe; extreme. **3.** inspiring awe. **4.** extremely bad; horrible. [ME] —**ter′ri·bly** *adv.*

ter·rif·ic (tə RIF ik) *adj.* **1.** extreme; intense; tremendous. **2.** wonderful; great; splendid. **3.** arousing great terror or fear. [< L *terrificus* frightening] —**ter·rif′i·cal·ly** *adv.*

ter·ri·fy (TER ə FI) *v.t.* •**fied,** •**fy·ing** fill with terror. [< L *terrificare*]

ter·ri·to·ri·al (TER i TOR ee əl) *adj.* **1.** of or pertaining to a territory or territories. **2.** limited to or within the jurisdiction of a particular territory or region. —**ter′ri·to′ri·al·ism** *n.*

ter·ri·to·ry (TER i TOR ee) *n. pl.* •**ries 1.** the domain over which a sovereign state exercises jurisdiction. **2.** any considerable tract of land; a region. **3.** a sphere of activity. **4.** an area assigned for a special purpose. **5.** *cap.* a region having some self-government but not having the status of a state, as American Samoa. [ME]

ter·ror (TER ər) *n.* **1.** an overwhelming impulse of fear; extreme dread. **2.** a person or thing that causes extreme fear. **3.** *Informal* an intolerable person or thing. [ME]

ter·ror·ism (TER ə RIZ əm) *n.* **1.** the act of terrorizing or the state of being terrorized. **2.** threats or acts of violence, esp. as a means of intimidating or coercing. —**ter′ror·ist** *n. & adj.*

ter·ror·ize (TER ə RĪZ) *v.t.* **-ized, -iz·ing 1.** reduce to a state of terror; terrify. **2.** coerce through intimidation. —**ter′ror·i·za′tion** *n.*

ter·ry cloth (TER ee) *n.* a pile fabric in which the loops are uncut.

terse (turs) *adj.* **ters·er, ters·est** short and to the point; concise. [< L *tersus* clean] —**terse′ly** *adv.* —**terse′ness** *n.*

ter·ti·ar·y (TUR shee ER ee) *adj.* third in point of time, number, degree, etc. [< Med.L *tertiarius*]

test (test) *v.t.* **1.** subject to an examination to determine certain characteristics; try. —*v.i.* **2.** show specific qualities or properties under a trial. —*n.* **1.** an examination or trial. **2.** a series of questions, problems, etc., intended to measure knowledge, aptitudes, etc.

tes·ta·ment (TES tə mənt) *n.* **1.** *Law* a will: chiefly in **last will and testament. 2.** *cap.* one of the two volumes of the Bible, distinguished as the *Old* and the *New Testament.* **3.** a statement of beliefs; credo. **4.** evidence; proof. [ME] —**tes′ta·men′ta·ry** *adj.*

tes·tate (TES tayt) *adj.* having made a will before death. [ME]

tes·ta·tor (TES tay tər) *n.* **1.** the maker of a will. **2.** one who has died leaving a will. [< L] —**tes·ta·trix** (te STAY triks) *n.fem. pl.* **tes·ta·tri·ces** (te STAY trə SEEZ)

tes·ti·cle (TES ti kəl) *n.* *Biol.* one of the two male sex glands enclosed in the scrotum and in which the spermatozoa and certain secretions are formed: also called *testis.* [ME *testicule*]

tes·ti·fy (TES tə FĪ) *v.* **-fied, -fy·ing** *v.i.* **1.** make solemn declaration of truth or fact. **2.** *Law* give testimony; bear witness. **3.** serve as evidence or indication: The woman's rags *testified* to her poverty. —*v.t.* **4.** bear witness to; affirm positively. **5.** be evidence or indication of. [ME *testifien*]

tes·ti·mo·ni·al (TES tə MOH nee əl) *n.* **1.** a formal token or statement of regard. **2.** a written acknowledgment of worth; also, a letter of recommendation. —*adj.* pertaining to or constituting testimony or a testimonial.

tes·ti·mo·ny (TES tə MOH nee) *n. pl.* **-nies 1.** a statement or affirmation of a fact, as before a court. **2.** evidence; proof; also, the aggregate of proof offered in a case. **3.** the act of testifying. [ME]

tes·tis (TES tis) *n. pl.* **-tes** (-teez) testicle. [< L]

tes·tos·ter·one (tes TOS tə ROHN) *n. Biochem.* a male sex hormone.

test tube a glass tube, open at one end, used in making chemical or biological tests.

tes·ty (TES tee) *adj.* **-ti·er, -ti·est** irritable in manner or disposition; touchy. [ME *testif* willful] —**tes′ti·ly** *adv.* —**tes′ti·ness** *n.*

tet·a·nus (TET nəs) *n. Pathol.* an acute disease characterized by rigid spasmodic contraction of various voluntary muscles, esp. those of the neck and jaw. [ME]

tête-à-tête (TAYT ə TAYT) *adj.* confidential, as between two persons only. —*n. pl.* **tête-à-têtes** a private chat. —*adv.* in or as in intimate conversation. [< F, lit., head to head]

teth·er (TETH ər) *n.* **1.** something used to check or confine, as a rope for fastening an animal. **2.** the range, scope, or limit of one's powers or field of action. [ME] —*v.t.* fasten or confine by a tether.

tet·rad (TE trad) *n.* a group or collection of four. [< Gk. *tetras* group of four]

te·tral·o·gy (te TRAL ə jee) *n. pl.* **-gies** a series of four related dramatic, operatic, or literary works. [< Gk. *tetralogía*]

te·tram·e·ter (te TRAM i tər) *n.* in prosody, a line of verse consisting of four metrical feet. [< L *tetrametrus*]

text (tekst) *n.* **1.** the body of matter on a written or printed page, as distinguished from notes, commentary, illustrations, etc. **2.** the actual or original words of an author. **3.** a written or printed version of the matter of an author's works: the folio *text* of Shakespeare. **4.** a verse of Scripture, esp. when used as the basis of a sermon. **5.** any subject of discourse; a topic. **6.** a textbook. [ME] —**tex·tu·al** (TEKS choo əl) *adj.*

text·book (TEKST buuk) *n.* a book used for instruction in a particular area of study.

tex·tile (TEKS tīl) *adj.* **I.** pertaining to weaving or woven fabrics. **2.** such as may be woven; manufactured by weaving. [< L *textilis* woven] —*n.* **1.** a woven fabric. **2.** material, as yarn, capable of being woven.

tex·ture (TEKS chər) *n.* **1.** the arrangement or character of the threads, etc., of a woven fabric. **2.** the structure, composition, or appearance of something, as of the surface of a painting. [ME] —**tex′·tur·al, tex′tured** *adj.*

thal·a·mus (THAL ə məs) *n. pl.* **-mi** (-MĪ) *Anat.* a large mass of gray matter at the base of the brain, the center for transmission of sensory impulses to the cerebral cortex. [< NL]

tha·lid·o·mide (thə LID ə MID) *n. Chem.* an organic compound, originally a mild sedative, later found to cause serious malformations in newborn children of mothers who had taken it during pregnancy.

than (*th*an) *conj.* **1.** when, as, or if compared with: after an adjective or adverb to express comparison between what precedes and what follows: She is stronger *than* I (am). **2.** except; but: used after *other, else,* etc.: no other *than* you. [ME]

thank (thangk) *v.t.* **1.** express gratitude to. **2.** hold responsible; blame: often used ironically. [ME]

thank·ful (THANGK fəl) *adj.* **1.** appreciative of favors received; grateful. **2.** expressing thanks. —**thank'ful·ness** *n.*

thank·less (THANGK lis) *adj.* **1.** not showing gratitude; ungrateful. **2.** not likely to gain thanks; unappreciated. —**thank'less·ness** (-nis) *n.*

thanks (thangks) *n.pl.* expressions of gratitude; grateful acknowledgment. —*interj.* thank you. —**thanks to 1.** thanks be given to. **2.** because of.

thanks·giv·ing (THANGKS GIV ing) *n.* **1.** the act of giving thanks, as to God; an expression of gratitude. **2.** a public celebration in recognition of divine favor. **3.** *cap.* in the U.S. a day in November, in Canada a day in October, set apart as an annual festival of thanksgiving: also **Thanksgiving Day.**

that (*th*at) *pl. for adj. and pron. def. 1* **those** (*th*ohz) *adj.* **1.** pertaining to some person or thing previously mentioned or understood. **2.** denoting something more remote, or something contrasted with another thing: distinguished from *this:* This house is brown; *that* one is red. —*pron.* **1.** as a demonstrative, the person or thing implied, mentioned, or understood; the person or thing there, or as distinguished from one already designated: *That* is the dress I like; Keep these and discard *those.* **2.** as a relative pronoun, who, whom, or which: the dress *that* I saw; the physician *that* I consulted. —*adv.* **1.** to an extent: I can't see *that* far. **2.** in such a manner or degree; so: He's *that* simple, he can hardly think. —*conj.* **1.** as a fact: introducing a fact: I tell you *that* it is so. **2.** as a result: introducing a result, consequence, or effect: He bled so profusely *that* he died. **3.** at which time;

when: It was only yesterday *that* I saw her. **4.** for the reason that; because. **5.** introducing an exclamation: O *that* he would come. —**so that 1.** to the end that. **2.** with the result that. [ME]

thatch (thach) *n.* **1.** a covering of reeds, straw, etc., arranged on a roof so as to shed water. **2.** any material used for such a covering. —*v.t.* cover with or as with thatch. [ME *thacchen* cover] —**thatch'er** *n.*

thaw (thaw) *v.i.* **1.** melt or dissolve; become liquid or semiliquid, as snow or ice. **2.** rise in temperature so as to melt ice and snow. **3.** become less cold and unsociable. —*v.t.* **4.** cause to thaw. [ME *thawen*] —*n.* **1.** the process or action of becoming less aloof or less hostile. **2.** a period in which weather warms, enabling ice to thaw. **3.** the process of thawing.

the[1] (*th*ə, thee) *definite article or adj.* The is opposed to the indefinite article *a* or *an,* and is used, esp. before nouns, to render the modified word more particular or individual. It is used specifically: **1.** when reference is made to a particular person, thing, or group: He left the room. **2.** to give an adjective substantive force, or render a notion abstract: *the* doing of the deed; *the* quick and *the* dead. **3.** before a noun to make it generic: *The* dog is a friend of children. **4.** with the force of a possessive pronoun: She kicked me in *the* (my) leg. [ME]

the[2] *adv.* by that much; by so much; this extent: used to modify words in the comparative degree: *the* more, *the* merrier. [ME]

the·a·ter (THEE ə tər) *n.* **1.** a building especially adapted to present dramas, operas, motion pictures, etc.; playhouse. **2.** the theatrical world and everything relating to it. **3.** a room or hall for lectures, demonstrations, etc. **4.** any place or region that is the scene of events: a *theater* of operations in war. [ME *theatre*]

the·a·ter·go·er (THEE ə tər GOH ər) *n.* one who goes often or regularly to the theater.

the·at·ri·cal (thee A tri kəl) *adj.* **1.** pertaining to the theater. **2.** designed for show or effect; showy. Also **the·at'ric.** —**the·at'ri·cal·ness** *n.* —**the·at'ri·cal·ly** *adv.*

the·at·rics (thee A triks) *n. (construed as sing.)* **1.** the staging of plays. **2.** an overly dramatic presentation.

thee (thee) *pron.* **1.** the objective case of the pronoun *thou.* **2.** thou: used by some

Quakers with a verb in the third person singular: *Thee* knows my mind. [ME]

theft (theft) *n.* the act or crime of thieving; larceny. [ME]

their (thair) *pronominal adj.* the possessive case of the pronoun *they*, used attributively: *their* homes. [ME]

theirs (thairz) *pron.* 1. the possessive case of the pronoun *they*, used predicatively: That house is *theirs*. 2. the one or ones belonging or relating to them: our country and *theirs*.

the·ism (THEE iz əm) *n.* 1. the belief in, or in the existence of, God, a god, or gods. 2. belief in one god; monotheism. —**the'ist** *n.*

them (them) *pron.* the objective case of the pronoun *they*. [ME *theym*]

theme (theem) *n.* 1. a topic to be discussed or developed in speech or writing; a subject of discourse. 2. a brief composition, esp. one written as an exercise as part of a course of instruction. 3. *Music* a melody that forms the basis of a composition. [ME *teme*] —**the·mat·ic** (thi MAT ik) *adj.* —**the·mat'i·cal·ly** *adv.*

them·selves (thəm SELVZ) *pron.* a form of the third person plural pronoun, used: 1. as a reflexive or as object of a preposition in a reflexive sense: They laughed at *themselves*. 2. as an intensive form of *they*: They *themselves* are at fault. 3. as a designation of a normal or usual state: They were not *themselves* then.

then (then) *adv.* 1. at that time. 2. soon or immediately afterward. 3. at another time: often following *now, at first*, etc. 4. for that reason; as a consequence. 5. in that case. —*adj.* being or acting in, or belonging to, that time: the *then* secretary of state. —*n.* a specific time already mentioned or understood; that time. [ME]

thence (thens) *adv.* 1. from that place. 2. from the circumstance, fact, or cause; therefore. 3. from that time; after that time. [ME *thannes*]

thence·forth (THens FORTH) *adv.* from that time on; thereafter.

the·oc·ra·cy (thee OK rə see) *n. pl.* •**cies** 1. a state, political unit, or group of people that claims a deity as its ruler. 2. government of a state by a priesthood claiming divine authority, as in the Papacy. [< Gk. *theokratía*] —**the·o·crat** (THEE ə KRAT) *n.* —**the·o·crat·ic** (THEE ə KRAT ik) *adj.*

the·o·lo·gi·an (THEE ə LOH jən) *n.* one versed in theology.

the·ol·o·gy (thee OL ə jee) *n. pl.* •**gies** 1.

the study of religion. 2. a body of doctrines as set forth by a particular church or religious group. [ME *theologie*] —**the·o·log·i·cal** (THEE ə LOJ i kəl) *adj.*

the·o·rem (THEE ər əm) *n.* 1. a proposition demonstrably true or acknowledged as such. 2. *Math.* **a** a proposition setting forth something to be proved. **b** a proposition that has been proved or assumed to be true. [< LL *theōrēma* subject]

the·o·ret·i·cal (THEE ə RET i kəl) *adj.* 1. of, relating to, or consisting of theory. 2. relating to knowledge or science without reference to its application. 3. existing only in theory; hypothetical. —**the'o·ret'i·cal·ly** *adv.*

the·o·re·ti·cian (THEE ər i TISH ən) *n.* one who deals with theory rather than with the practical aspects of a subject.

the·o·rize (THEE ə RĪZ) *v.i.* •**rized,** •**riz·ing** form or express theories; speculate. —**the'o·rist** *n.*

the·o·ry (THEE ə ree) *n. pl.* •**ries** 1. a speculative or conjectural view of something. 2. fundamental principles underlying a science, art, etc.: music *theory, theory* of equations. 3. abstract knowledge of any art as opposed to the practice of it. 4. suppositions derived from evidence and intended to serve as an explanation for phenomena: the quantum *theory*. [< LL *theōria* view]

ther·a·peu·tic (THER ə PYOO tik) *adj.* 1. having healing qualities; curative. 2. pertaining to therapeutics. [< NL *therapeuticus*] —**ther'a·peu'ti·cal·ly** *adv.*

ther·a·peu·tics (THER ə PYOO tiks) *n.* (*construed as sing.*) the branch of medical science dealing with the treatment of disease.

ther·a·py (THER ə pee) *n. pl.* •**pies** a treatment, activity, etc. intended to remedy or alleviate a disorder or undesirable condition. —**ther'a·pist** *n.*

there (thair) *adv.* 1. in, at, or about that place: opposed to *here*; also used to indicate or emphasize: John *there* is a good student. 2. to, toward, or into that place; thither. 3. at that stage or point of action or time. —*n.* that place: Are you from *there*? —*interj.* an exclamation of triumph, relief, etc.: *There!* It's finished. [ME]

there·a·bout (THAIR ə BOWT) *adv.* near that number, quantity, degree, place, or time. Also **there'a·bouts'**.

there·af·ter (THair AF tər) *adv.* afterward; from that time on.

there·by (*THAir* BĪ) *adv.* **1.** through the agency of that. **2.** connected with that.

there·for (*THAir* FOR) *adv.* for this, that, or it.

there·fore (*THAIR* FOR) *adv. & conj.* for that or this reason; consequently.

there·from (*THAir* FRUM) *adv.* from this, that, or it.

there·in (*th*air IN) *adv.* **1.** in that place. **2.** in that time, matter, or respect.

there·of (*THAir* UV) *adv.* **1.** of or relating to this, that, or it. **2.** from or because of this or that cause.

there·on (*THAir* ON) *adv.* **1.** on this, that, or it. **2.** thereupon.

there's (*th*airz) **1.** there is. **2.** there has.

there·to (*THAir* TOO) *adv.* **1.** to this, that, or it. **2.** in addition. Also **there·un·to** (*THAir* un TOO).

there·up·on (*THAIR* ə PON) *adv.* **1.** upon that; upon it. **2.** following upon or in consequence of that. **3.** immediately following; at once.

there·with (*THAir* WITH) *adv.* **1.** with this, that, or it. **2.** immediately afterward.

ther·mal (THUR məl) *adj.* **1.** pertaining to, determined by, or measured by heat. **2.** caused by, using, or producing heat. **3.** hot or warm. [< Gk. *thermē*] Also **ther'mic.** —**ther'mal·ly** *adv.*

ther·mo·cou·ple (THUR mə KUP əl) *n.* a device for temperature measurement that depends on the electric current or potential produced when joined conductors of two different metals have their ends at different temperatures.

ther·mo·dy·nam·ics (THUR moh dī NAM iks) *n. (construed as sing.)* the branch of physics dealing with the relations between heat and other forms of energy. —**ther'mo·dy·nam'ic** *adj.* —**ther'mo·dy·nam' i·cist** *n.*

ther·mom·e·ter (thər MOM i tər) *n.* an instrument for measuring temperature, usu. a graduated glass tube with a bulb containing a liquid, as mercury or alcohol, that expands or contracts as the temperature rises or falls. —**ther·mo·met·ric** (THUR mə ME trik) *adj.*

ther·mo·nu·cle·ar (THUR moh NOO klee ər) *adj. Physics* pertaining to or characterized by reactions involving the fusion of atomic nuclei at very high temperatures, esp. in stars and in the hydrogen bomb.

ther·mo·plas·tic (THUR mə PLAS tik) *adj.* able to be molded when heated. —*n.* a thermoplastic substance.

ther·mos (THUR məs) a bottle that keeps the contents hot or cold. Also **thermos bottle.** [< *Thermos* a former trademark]

ther·mo·set·ting (THUR moh SET ing) *adj.* having the property of assuming a fixed shape after being molded under heat, as certain plastics and resins.

ther·mo·stat (THUR mə STAT) *n.* a device for the automatic regulation of temperature. —**ther'·mo·stat'ic** *adj.* —**ther'mo·stat'i·cal·ly** *adv.*

the·sau·rus (thi SOR əs) *n. pl.* **·sau·rus·es, ·sau·ri** (-SOR ī) a book of words, esp., synonyms and antonyms, usu. arranged in categories. [< NL]

these (*th*eez) *adj. & pron.* plural of THIS.

the·sis (THEE sis) *n. pl.* **·ses** (-seez) **1.** a proposition or premise. **2.** a formal proposition, advanced and defended by argumentation. **3.** a formal treatise on a particular subject; esp., a dissertation presented for an academic degree. [ME]

Thes·pi·an (THES pee ən) Also **thespian.** *adj.* of or relating to drama; dramatic; tragic. —*n.* an actor or actress. [after *Thespis,* Greek poet and actor, 6th c. B.C.]

the·ta (THAY tə) *n.* **1.** the eighth letter in the Greek alphabet (θ, ϑ, Θ). **2.** *Math.* a symbol for an angle of unknown value.

they (*th*ay) *pron.pl., possessive* **their** or **theirs,** *objective* **them 1.** the nominative plural of *he, she,* and *it,* used of the persons, beings, or things previously mentioned or understood. **2.** people in general: *They* say this is her best book. [ME]

they'd (*th*ayd) **1.** they had. **2.** they would.

they'll (*th*ayl) they will.

they're (*th*air) they are.

they've (*th*ayv) they have.

thick (thik) *adj.* **·er, ·est 1.** having relatively large depth or extent from one surface to its opposite; not thin. **2.** having a specified dimension of this kind, whether great or small: an inch *thick.* **3.** arranged compactly; close. **4.** abundant with objects; abounding. **5.** having considerable density or consistency; heavy. **6.** having the component particles closely packed together, as smoke, fog, etc. **7.** dull; stupid. **8.** indistinct; muffled: a *thick* voice. **9.** *Informal* very friendly; intimate. **10.** disagreeably excessive. —*adv.* **·er, ·est** so as to be thick; thickly: bread sliced *thick.* —**lay it on thick** *Informal* **1.** overstate; exaggerate. **2.** flatter excessively. —n. 1. the thickest part. 2. the most intense time or place of anything: the *thick* of the fight. —**through thick and thin** through good times and bad; loyally. [ME *thikke*] —**thick′ly** adv. —**thick′ness** n.

thick·en (THIK ən) v.t. & v.i. 1. make or become thick or thicker. 2. make or become more intricate or intense. —**thick′·en·er** n.

thick·en·ing (THIK ə ning) n. 1. the act of making or becoming thick. 2. something added to a liquid to thicken it. 3. a thickened place or part.

thick·et (THIK it) n. a thick, dense growth, as of underbrush. [OE *thiccet*]

thick·set (THIK SET) adj. 1. having a short, thick body; stout. 2. planted closely together.

thick-skinned (THIK SKIND) adj. 1. having a thick skin. 2. insensitive to criticism or insults.

thick-wit·ted (THIK WIT id) adj. stupid; obtuse; dense.

thief (theef) n. pl. **thieves** (theevz) one who takes something belonging to another; one who steals. [ME]

thieve (theev) v.t. **thieved, thiev·ing** v.t. 1. steal. —v.i. 2. be a thief. [OE *thēofian*] —**thiev·er·y** (THEE və ree) n. —**thiev′ish** adj. —**thiev′ish·ly** adv. —**thiev′·ish·ness** n.

thigh (thī) n. the part of the limb between the hip and the knee of man, or the corresponding portion in other animals. [ME *thī*]

thigh·bone (THĪ BOHN) n. the femur.

thim·ble (THIM bəl) n. a caplike cover worn in sewing to protect the end of the finger that pushes the needle. [ME *thymbyl* thumb of a glove] —**thim·ble·ful** (THIM bəl FUUL) n.

thin (thin) adj. **thin·ner, thin·nest** 1. having opposite surfaces relatively close to each other; being of little depth or width; not thick. 2. lacking roundness or plumpness of figure; slender. 3. having the parts or particles scattered or diffused; sparse. 4. having little substance: *thin* clothing. 5. having little or no consistency, as a liquid. 6. having little volume or richness, as a voice. 7. having little intensity; pale. 8. feeble; superficial. —adv. **thin·ner, thin·est** so as to be thin; thinly. [ME *thinne*] —v.t. & v.i. **thinned, thin·ning** make or become thin or thinner. —**thin′-**

ly adv. —**thin′ner** n. —**thin′·ness** n.

thine (thīn) pron. 1. the possessive case of the pronoun *thou*, used predicatively: It is *thine*, not mine. 2. the one or ones belonging or relating to thee, used before a vowel or h: *thine* eyes; *thine* honor. 3. that which belongs to thee: *Thine* is the power. [ME]

thing (thing) n. 1. that which exists as a separate entity; an inanimate object. 2. that which is designated, as contrasted with the word or symbol used to denote it. 3. a matter or circumstance; affair; concern: *Things* have changed. 4. an act or deed; transaction. 5. a statement; utterance: say the right *thing*. 6. a quality; attribute; characteristic. 7. an organic being: usu. with a qualifying word: Every living *thing* dies. 8. an object that is not or cannot be described or particularized. 9. pl. possessions. —**do (one's) thing** Informal follow one's special interest. —**see things** Informal have hallucinations. [ME]

think (thingk) v. **thought, think·ing** v.t. 1. produce or form in the mind; conceive mentally. 2. examine in the mind; determine by reasoning: *think* a plan through. 3. believe; consider. 4. remember; recollect: I cannot *think* what he said. —v.i. 5. use the mind in exercising judgment, forming ideas, etc.; reason. 6. have a particular opinion or feeling. —**think better of** 1. abandon or change a course of action. 2. form a better opinion of. —**think fit (proper, right,** etc.) regard as worth doing. —**think nothing of** 1. consider of no importance; ignore. 2. consider easy to do. —**think of** 1. remember. 2. invent; imagine. 3. have a specified opinion or attitude toward. 4. be considerate of. —**think out (or through)** devise, invent, or solve by thinking. —**think over** reflect upon. —**think the world of** 1. have a high opinion of. 2. love very much. —**think twice** consider carefully. —**think up** devise, arrive at, or invent by thinking. —n. Informal an act of thinking; a thought. [ME *thinken*] —**think′a·ble** adj. —**think′er** n.

think tank an institute or group for theoretical study, often combining fields or disciplines.

thin-skinned (THIN SKIND) adj. 1. having a thin skin. 2. easily hurt; sensitive.

third (thurd) adj. 1. next after the second: the ordinal of *three*. 2. being one of three equal parts. —n. 1. that which follows the second. **2.** one of three equal parts. **3.** *Mech.* the forward gear with the third highest ratio in an automobile transmission. —*adv.* in the third order, rank, or place: also **third′ly.** [ME *thridde*]

third class 1. in the U.S. postal system, a classification of mail that includes all miscellaneous printed matter but not newspapers and periodicals legally entered as second class. **2.** a classification of accommodations on some ships and trains, usu. the cheapest and least luxurious available. —**third-class** (THURD KLAS) *adj. & adv.*

third degree severe or brutal examination of a prisoner by the police for the purpose of securing information.

third estate the third political class of a kingdom, following the nobility and the clergy; the commoners.

third-rate (THURD RAYT) *adj.* **1.** of the third rate or class. **2.** of poor quality; inferior.

Third World 1. any or all of the developing countries in the world. **2.** those nations not politically aligned with any world power. Also **third world.**

thirst (thurst) *n.* **1.** an uncomfortable feeling of dryness in the throat and mouth. **2.** the physiological condition that produces this feeling. **3.** any longing or craving. —*v.i.* **1.** be thirsty. **2.** have an eager desire or craving. [ME] —**thirst′i·ly** *adv.* —**thirst′i·ness** *n.* —**thirst′y** *adj.* **thirst·i·er, thirst·i·est**

thir·teen (THUR TEEN) *n.* the sum of twelve and one: a cardinal number written 13, XIII. [ME *thrittene*] —**thir·teen** *adj.* —**thir′·teenth′** *adj. & n.*

thir·ty (THUR tee) *n. pl.* **·ties** the sum of twenty and ten: a cardinal number written 30, XXX. [ME *thritty*] —**thir·ty** *adj.* —**thir′ti·eth** *adj. & n.*

this (this) *pl. for adj. and for pron. def* **2 these** (theez) *adj.* **1.** that is near or present, either actually or in thought: *This* house is for sale. **2.** that is understood or has just been mentioned: *These* offenses justified my revenge. **3.** denoting something nearer than or contrasted with something else: distinguished from *that*: *This* tree is still alive, but *that* one is dead. —*pron.* **1.** the person or thing near or present, being understood or just mentioned. **2.** the person or thing nearer than or contrasted with something else: opposed to *that*: *These* are better than

those. **3.** the idea, statement, etc. about to be made clear: I will say *this*: he is a hard worker. —*adv.* to this degree: I was not expecting you *this* soon. [ME]

this·tle (THIS əl) *n.* **1.** a prickly plant with cylindrical or globular heads of purple flowers. **2.** any of several other prickly plants. [ME *thistel*]

thith·er (thith ər) *adv.* to or toward that place; in that direction. —*adj.* situated or being on the other side; farther: the *thither* bank of the river. [ME]

tho (thoh) see THOUGH.

thong (thong) *n.* a narrow strip of leather, as for tying or fastening. [ME]

tho·rax (THOR aks) *n. pl.* **tho·rax·es** or **tho·ra·ces** (THOR ə SEEZ) *Anat.* the part of the body between the neck and the abdomen, enclosed by the ribs and containing the lungs, heart, etc.; the chest. [ME] —**tho·rac·ic** (thaw RAS ik) *adj.*

thorn (thorn) *n.* **1.** a sharp-pointed spine on a branch. **2.** any of various thorn-bearing shrubs or trees. **3.** anything or anyone that causes discomfort, pain, or annoyance. [ME] —**thorn′i·ness** *n.* —**thorn′·less** *adj.* —**thorn′y** *adj.* **thorn·i·er, thorn·i·est**

thor·ough (THUR oh) *adj.* **1.** carried to completion. **2.** marked by careful attention; persevering; painstaking. **3.** completely; through and through. [ME] —**thor′ough·ly** *adv.* —**thor′·ough·ness** *n.*

thor·ough·bred (THUR oh BRED) *n.* pure and unmixed stock: said of horses. —*adj.* bred from pure stock.

thor·ough·fare (THUR oh FAIR) *n.* a road or street through which the public has unobstructed passage; highway. [ME *thurghfare*]

thor·ough·go·ing (THUR oh GOH ing) *adj.* **1.** characterized by extreme thoroughness or efficiency. **2.** unmitigated.

those (thohz) *adj. & pron.* plural of THAT. [ME]

thou (thow) *pron., possessive* **thy** or **thine,** *objective* **thee;** *pl. nominative* **you, ye,** *possessive* **your** or **yours,** *objective* **you, ye** *Archaic* the nominative singular pronoun of the second person: replaced by singular *you*, and no longer used except in religious, elevated, or poetic language. [ME]

though (thoh) *conj.* **1.** notwithstanding the fact that. **2.** conceding or granting that; even if. **3.** and yet; still; however: I am well, *though* I do not feel very strong. **4.** notwithstanding what has been done or said; nevertheless. Also spelled tho. [ME *thoh*]

thought[1] (thawt) *n.* **1.** the act or process of thinking. **2.** the product of thinking; an idea. **3.** intellectual activity of a specific kind: Greek *thought*. **4.** consideration; attention. **5.** intention or plan. **6.** expectation. [ME *thoght*]

thought[2] past tense, past participle of THINK.

thought·ful (THAWT fəl) *adj.* **1.** full of thought; meditative. **2.** showing, characterized by, or promotive of thought. **3.** attentive; careful; considerate. —**thought'ful·ly** *adv.* —**thought'ful·ness** *n.*

thought·less (THAWT lis) *adj.* **1.** showing lack of thought or care; heedless. **2.** inconsiderate. —**thought'less·ly** *adv.* —**thought'·less·ness** *n.*

thou·sand (THOW zənd) *n.* the product of ten and a hundred; ten hundreds, written as 1000 or M: a cardinal number. [ME] —**thou·sand** *adj.* —**thou'sandth** *adj. & n.*

thrall (thrawl) *n.* **1.** a person in bondage; slave. **2.** the condition of bondage. [ME] —**thrall'dom** (-dəm) *n.*

thrash (thrash) *v.t.* **1.** beat as if with a flail; flog; whip. **2.** defeat utterly. —*v.i.* **3.** move or swing about with flailing, violent motions. —**thrash out** discuss fully. [ME *thrasshen* thresh] —**thrash'er** *n.*

thrash·ing (THRASH ing) *n.* a beating or whipping.

thread (thred) *n.* **1.** a very slender cord composed of two or more filaments, as of cotton, or silk, twisted together; also, such twisted fibers used in sewing. **2.** a filament of any ductile substance, as of metal, glass, etc. **3.** anything conceived of as serving to give sequence to the whole. **4.** *Mech.* the spiral ridge of a screw. [ME *thred*] —*v.t.* **1.** pass a thread through the eye of (a needle). **2.** arrange or string on a thread, as beads. **3.** cut a thread on or in, as a screw. **4.** make (one's way) carefully.

thread·bare (THRED BAIR) *adj.* **1.** worn so that the threads show, as a rug or garment. **2.** clad in worn garments. **3.** commonplace; hackneyed. —**thread'bare'ness** *n.*

threat (thret) *n.* **1.** a declaration of an intention to inflict injury or pain. **2.** an indication of impending danger or harm. **3.** a person or thing regarded as endangering the lives, peace of mind, etc. of others; menace. [ME *thret*]

threat·en (THRET n) *v.t.* **1.** utter threats against. **2.** be menacing or dangerous to. **3.** be ominous or portentous of. —*v.i.* **4.** utter threats. **5.** have a menacing aspect. [ME *thretnen*] —**threat'en·ing·ly** *adv.*

threatened species a species held to be endangered in its range.

three (three) *n.* the sum of two and one: a cardinal number written 3, III. [ME] —**three** *adj.*

three-base hit (THREE BAYS) a triple.

3-D (THREE DEE) *adj.* three-dimensional. —*n.* a three-dimensional appearance.

three-di·men·sion·al (THREE di MEN shə nl) *adj.* **1.** giving the illusion of depth. **2.** existing in three dimensions.

three·fold (THREE FOHLD) *n.* an amount or number three times as great as a given unit. —*adj.* **1.** consisting of three parts. **2.** three times as many or as great. —*adv.* trebly.

three-ply (THREE PLĪ) *adj.* consisting of three thicknesses, strands, layers, etc.

three·score (THREE SKOR) *adj.* sixty.

three·some (THREE səm) *n.* **1.** a group of three. **2.** that which is played by three persons.

thresh (thresh) *v.t. & v.i.* beat stalks of (ripened grain) with a flail or machine so as to separate the grain from the straw or husks. [ME *thresshen*]

thresh·er (THRESH ər) *n.* one who or that which threshes; esp., a machine for threshing.

thresh·old (THRESH ohld) *n.* **1.** the plank or stone lying under the door of a building. **2.** the entrance or beginning of anything. **3.** *Physiol. & Psychol.* **a** the point at which a stimulus just produces a response. **b** the minimum degree of stimulation necessary for conscious perception: the *threshold* of pain. [ME *thresshold*]

threw (throo) past tense of THROW.

thrice (thrīs) *adv.* **1.** three times. **2.** in a threefold manner. **3.** extremely; very. [ME *thries*]

thrift (thrift) *n.* care and wisdom in the management of one's resources; frugality. [ME] —**thrift'i·ly** *adv.* —**thrift'i·ness** *n.* —**thrift'y** *adj.* **thrift·i·er, thrift·i·est**

thrill (thril) *v.t.* **1.** cause to feel a sudden wave of emotion; move to great or tingling excitement. **2.** cause to vibrate or tremble. —*v.i.* **3.** feel a sudden wave of emotion or excitement. —*n.* something that thrills or excites. [ME *thirlen* pierce] —**thrill'ing** *adj.* —**thrill'ing·ly** *adv.*

thrill·er (THRIL ər) n. 1. one who or that which thrills. 2. a suspenseful book, motion picture, etc.

thrive (thrīv) v.i. **thrived** or **throve, thrived** or **thriv·en** (THRIV ən), **thriv·ing** 1. prosper; be successful. 2. grow with vigor; flourish. [ME *thriven*]

throat (throht) n. 1. the passage leading from the back of the mouth to the stomach and lungs. 2. the front of the neck, extending from below the chin to the collarbones. 3. any narrow passage resembling the throat. —**jump down one's throat** *Informal* criticize or berate one severely. —**ram (something) down one's throat** *Informal* force one to accept or hear something against his will. [ME *throte*]

throat·y (THROH tee) adj. **throat·i·er, throat·i·est** uttered deep in the throat; guttural. —**throat'i·ly** adv. —**throat'i·ness** n.

throb (throb) v.i. **throbbed, throb·bing** 1. beat rapidly or violently, as the heart from exertion or excitement. 2. pulsate. 3. feel or show great emotion. [ME *throbben*] —n. a pulsation or beat. —**throb'bing·ly** adv.

throe (throh) n. 1. a violent pang or pain. 2. pl. any agonizing or violent activity. [ME *throwe*]

throm·bo·sis (throm BOH sis) n. pl. **·ses** (-SEEZ) *Pathol.* local coagulation of blood in the heart or blood vessels, forming an obstruction to circulation. [< NL] —**throm·bot·ic** (throm BOT ik) adj.

throm·bus (THROM bəs) n. pl. **·bi** (-BI) *Pathol.* a blood clot formed in thrombosis. [< NL]

throne (throhn) n. 1. the chair of state occupied by a sovereign or some other dignitary. 2. royal estate or dignity; sovereign power. [ME] —v.t. & v.i. **throned, thron·ing** place or sit on a throne.

throng (throng) n. 1. a multitude of people crowded closely together. 2. any numerous collection. [ME] —v.t. 1. crowd into; jam. 2. press or crowd upon. —v.i. 3. collect or move in a throng.

throt·tle (THROT l) n. *Mech.* **a** a valve controlling the supply of steam or vaporized fuel to an engine: also **throttle valve. b** the lever that operates the throttle: also **throttle lever.** —v. **·tled, ·tling** v.t. 1. strangle or choke. 2. silence, stop, or suppress by or as by choking. 3. *Mech.* **a** reduce or shut off the flow of steam or fuel (in an engine). **b** reduce the speed of by means of a throttle.

—v.i. 4. choke. [ME *throtelen*] —**throt' tler** n.

through (throo) prep. 1. into one side, end, or point, and out of the other. 2. covering, entering, or penetrating all parts of; throughout. 3. from the first to the last of; during the time or period of. 4. in the midst of; among. 5. by way of. 6. by means of. 7. on account of. —adv. 1. from one end, side, surface, etc. to or beyond another. 2. from beginning to end. 3. to a termination or conclusion, esp. a successful one. —**through and through** totally; completely. —adj. 1. going from beginning to end without stops or with very few stops. 2. extending from one side or surface to another. 3. unobstructed; open; clear. 4. arrived at an end; finished. Also, informally, spelled *thru*. [ME]

through·out (throo OWT) adv. through or in every part. —prep. all through; everywhere in.

through·way (THROO way) see THRUWAY.

throve (throhv) a past tense of THRIVE.

throw (throh) v. **threw, thrown, throw·ing** v.t. 1. launch through the air by means of a sudden straightening or whirling of the arm. 2. propel or hurl. 3. put hastily or carelessly. 4. direct or project (light, a glance, etc.). 5. bring to a specified condition or state by or as by throwing: *throw* the enemy into a panic. 6. cause to fall; overthrow: The horse *threw* its rider. 7. in wrestling, force the shoulders of (an opponent) to the ground. 8. cast (dice). 9. lose purposely, as a race. 10. move, as a lever or switch. 11. give (a party etc.). 12. in card games, play or discard. —v.i. 13. cast or fling something. —**throw away 1.** discard. 2. waste; squander. —**throw cold water on** discourage. —**throw in 1.** cause (gears or a clutch) to mesh or engage. 2. contribute; add. 3. join with others. —**throw in the towel** (or **sponge**) *Informal* accept defeat; surrender. —**throw oneself at** strive to gain the affections or love of. —**throw oneself into** engage or take part in vigorously. —**throw oneself on** (or **upon**) entrust oneself to; rely on. —**throw open** free from restrictions or obstacles. —**throw the book at** *Informal* 1. sentence to the maximum penalty. 2. reprimand or castigate severely. —**throw out 1.** put forth; emit. 2. cast out or aside; discard; reject. 3. confuse; disconcert; distract. —**throw (something) up to (someone)** *In-*

formal mention or repeat as a reproach. — **throw together** put together hastily or roughly. —**throw up 1.** construct hastily. **2.** give up; relinquish. **3.** vomit. [ME *throwen* twist] —*n.* **1.** an act of throwing or hurling; a fling. **2.** the distance over which a missile may be thrown: a stone's *throw.* **3.** a cast of dice, or the resulting number. **4.** a bedspread or coverlet; also, a woman's scarf.

throw·a·way (THROH ə WAY) *adj.* **1.** designed to be discarded after use; disposable. **2.** presented with no emphasis: a *throwaway* line. —*n.* something free handed out for advertising or propaganda purposes.

throw·back (THROH BAK) *n.* reversion to an ancestral type or condition; also, an example of such reversion.

thru (throo) see THROUGH.

thrum (thrum) *v.* **thrummed, thrum·ming** *v.t.* **1.** play on or finger (a stringed instrument) idly and without expression. **2.** drum or tap monotonously or listlessly. —*v.i.* **3.** play a stringed instrument idly. —*n.* any monotonous sound.

thrust (thrust) *v.* **thrust, thrust·ing** *v.t.* **1.** push or shove with force or sudden impulse. **2.** pierce or stab, as with a sword or dagger. **3.** put (a person) forcibly into some condition or situation. **4.** put in; interpose. —*v.i.* **5.** make a sudden push against something. **6.** force oneself on or ahead; push one's way: with *through, into, on,* etc. [ME *thrusten*] —*n.* **1.** a sudden, forcible push, esp. with a pointed weapon. **2.** a vigorous attack. **3.** *Mech.* the driving force exerted by a steam engine, motor, propeller, jet engine, etc. **4.** the salient force or meaning of something or someone. —**thrust'er** *n.*

thru·way (THROO WAY) *n.* a long-distance express highway: also spelled *throughway.*

thud (thud) *n.* **1.** a dull, heavy sound, as of a hard body striking a comparatively soft surface. **2.** the blow causing such a sound. — *v.i.* **thud·ded, thud·ding** make a thud. [ME *thudden* strike]

thug (thug) *n.* a vicious ruffian. [< Hind. *thag* rogue] —**thug'gish** *adj.*

thumb (thum) *n.* **1.** the short, thick digit next to the forefinger of a hand. **2.** the division in a glove or mitten that covers the thumb. — **all thumbs** clumsy with the hands. — **thumbs down** no; nix. —**under one's thumb** under one's influence or power. — *v.t.* **1.** press, rub, soil, or wear with the thumb in handling, as the pages of a book. **2.** run through the pages of (a book, manuscript, etc.) rapidly and perfunctorily. **3.** solicit (a ride in an automobile) by signaling with the thumb. —*v.i.* **4.** hitchhike. — **thumb one's nose** show defiance or disgust by or as by raising the thumb to the nose with the fingers extended. [ME]

thumb·nail (THUM NAYL) *n.* the nail of the thumb. —*adj.* brief and concise.

thumb·screw (THUM SKROO) *n.* **1.** a screw to be turned by thumb and fingers. **2.** an instrument of torture for compressing the thumb.

thumb·tack (THUM TAK) *n.* a broad-headed tack that may be pushed in with the thumb.

thump (thump) *n.* **1.** a blow with a blunt or heavy object. **2.** the sound made by such a blow; a dull thud. —*v.t.* **1.** beat or strike so as to make a heavy thud or thuds. **2.** *Informal* beat severely. —*v.i.* **3.** make a thump or thumps; pound or throb.

thump·ing (THUM ping) *adj.* **1.** that thumps. **2.** huge; whopping.

thun·der (THUN dər) *n.* **1.** the sound that accompanies lightning, caused by the sudden heating and expansion of the air along the path of the electrical discharge. **2.** any loud or booming noise. [ME *thonder*] — *v.i.* **1.** give forth a peal of thunder. **2.** make a noise like thunder. —*v.t.* **3.** utter or express with a noise like thunder. —**thun'der·er** *n.*

thun·der·bolt (THUN dər BOHLT) *n.* an electric discharge accompanied by a clap of thunder.

thun·der·clap (THUN dər KLAP) *n.* a sharp, violent detonation of thunder.

thun·der·cloud (THUN dər KLOWD) *n.* a dark cloud highly charged with electricity.

thun·der·head (THUN dər HED) *n. Meteorol.* a rounded, dark cloud, often developing into a thundercloud.

thun·der·ous (THUN dər əs) *adj.* producing a noise like thunder. —**thun'der·ous·ly** *adv.*

thun·der·storm (THUN dər STORM) *n.* a local storm with lightning and thunder.

thun·der·struck (THUN dər STRUK) *adj.* amazed, astonished, or confounded, as with fear, surprise, etc.

Thurs·day (THURZ day) *n.* the fifth day of the week. [ME]

thus (*thus*) *adv.* **1.** in this, that, or the following manner. **2.** to such degree or extent;

so. **3.** in these circumstances or conditions; therefore. [ME]

thwack (thwak) *v.t.* strike with something flat; whack. —*n.* a blow with a flat or blunt instrument. —**thwack′er** *n.*

thwart (thwort) *v.t.* prevent the accomplishment of, as by interposing an obstacle; also, prevent (one) from accomplishing something; foil; frustrate; balk. —*n.* a rower's seat extending across a boat. —*adj.* lying, moving, or extending across something; transverse. —*adv. & prep.* across. [ME *thwert* across]

thy (thī) *pronominal adj.* the possessive case of the pronoun *thou*, used attributively: *Thy* kingdom come. [ME]

thyme (tīm) *n.* a small shrubby plant, having aromatic leaves and used in cookery. [ME]

thy·mus (THĪ məs) *n. Anat.* a glandular organ of man and some other vertebrates, found behind the top of the breastbone. [< NL]

thy·roid (THĪ roid) *adj. Physiol.* relating or pertaining to the thyroid cartilage or the thyroid gland. —*n.* the thyroid cartilage or gland. [< NL *thyroides*]

thyroid cartilage *Anat.* the largest cartilage of the larynx, composed of two blades whose juncture in front forms the Adam's apple.

thyroid gland *Anat.* an endocrine gland situated in front of and on each side of the trachea, and secreting thyroxin, important in the regulation of metabolism and body growth.

thy·rox·ine (thī ROK sən) *n. Biochem.* an amino acid that is the hormone of the thyroid gland. Also **thy·rox′in.**

thy·self (*thī* SELF) *pron.* a form of the second person singular pronouns *thee* and *thou*, used: **1.** as a reflexive: Know *thyself.* **2.** as an emphatic or intensive form: I love thee for *thyself.*

ti (tee) *n. Music* the seventh tone of the diatonic scale in solmization.

ti·ar·a (tee AR ə) *n.* an ornamental, semicircular headdress worn by women for formal occasions. [< L]

tib·i·a (TIB ee ə) *n. pl.* **tib·i·ae** (TIB ee EE) or **tib·i·as** *Anat.* the shinbone. [< L] —**tib′i·al** *adj.*

tic (tik) *n.* an involuntary spasm or twitching of muscles, usu. of the face. [< F]

tick¹ (tik) *n.* **1.** a light, recurring sound made by a clock or similar mechanism. **2.** a mark, as a dot or dash, used in checking off something. —*v.i.* **1.** make a recurrent clicking sound, as a running clock. —*v.t.* **2.** mark or check with ticks. [ME]

tick² *n.* one of numerous blood-sucking arachnids that attack the skin of man, horses, sheep, etc. [ME *teke*]

tick³ *n.* **1.** the outer covering of a mattress or pillow. **2.** ticking. [ME *tikke* case]

tick·er (TIK ər) *n.* **1.** one who or that which ticks. **2.** a telegraphic instrument that records stock quotations on a paper ribbon. **3.** *Slang* the heart.

tick·et (TIK it) *n.* **1.** a card showing that the holder is entitled to something, as transportation, admission, etc. **2.** a label or tag. **3.** a certificate or license. **4.** in politics: **a** a list of candidates of a single party on a ballot. **b** the group of candidates running for the offices of a party. **5.** a summons, as for a traffic violation. —*v.t.* **1.** affix a ticket to; label. **2.** present or furnish with a ticket or tickets. [< MF *etiquet*]

tick·ing (TIK ing) *n.* a strong cotton or linen fabric, used for mattress covers, awnings, etc.

tick·le (TIK əl) *v.* **·led, ·ling** *v.t.* **1.** touch or scratch (someone) so as to produce a sensation resulting in spasmodic laughter or twitching; titillate. **2.** amuse or entertain; delight. —*v.i.* **3.** have or experience a thrilling or tingling sensation. [ME *tikelen*] —*n.* the act of tickling or of being tickled; also the sensation produced.

tick·lish (TIK lish) *adj.* **1.** sensitive to tickling. **2.** liable to be upset or easily offended. **3.** attended with risk; difficult; delicate. —**tick′lish·ness** *n.*

tick-tack-toe (TIK tak TOH) *n.* a game for two players who alternately put circles or crosses in the spaces of a figure containing nine squares, each player trying to complete one row before the opponent does. Also **tic-tac-toe.**

tid·al wave (TĪD l) **1.** any great incoming rise of waters along a shore, caused by windstorms at sea or by excessively high tides. **2.** a tsunami.

tid·bit (TID bit) *n.* a choice bit, as of food. Also, *titbit.*

tid·dly·winks (TID lee WINGCKS) *n.* a game in which the players attempt to snap little disks of plastic from a plane surface into a cup. Also **tid·dle·dy·winks** (TID l dee WINGCKS).

tide (tīd) *n.* **1.** the periodic rise and fall of the surface waters of the oceans, caused by the attraction of moon and sun. **2.** anything that rises and falls like the tide; also, the time at which something is most flourishing. **3.** season; time; esp., a season of the ecclesiastical year: used chiefly in combination: *Christmastide.* [ME, time] —*v.* **tid•ed, tid•ing** *v.i.* **1.** ebb and flow like the tide. —*v.t.* **2.** help along: with *over:* Charity *tided* us over the depression. —**tid'al** *adj.*

tide•land (TĪD LAND) *n.* land alternately covered and uncovered by the tide.

tide•wa•ter (TĪD WAW tər) *n.* **1.** water that inundates land at high tide. **2.** any area, as a seacoast, whose waters are affected by tides.

ti•dings (TĪ dingz) *n.* (*sometimes construed as sing.*) a report; news. [ME]

ti•dy (TĪ dee) *adj.* **•di•er •di•est 1.** marked by neatness and order; trim. **2.** moderately large; considerable: a *tidy* sum. [ME *tidi* in good condition] —*v.t.* & *v.i.* **•died, •dy•ing** make (things) tidy; put (things) in order. —**ti'di•ness** *n.*

tie (tī) *v.* **tied, ty•ing** *v.t.* **1.** fasten with cord, rope, etc. **2.** draw the parts of together or into place by a cord or band fastened with a knot. **3.** form a knot in, as string. **4.** fasten, attach, or join in any way. **5.** restrain or confine; bind. **6.** in sports, games, etc., equal (a competitor) in score or achievement. —*v.i.* **7.** make a connection. **8.** make the same score; be equal. —**tie down** hinder; restrict. —**tie in** have a certain relationship or connection; often with *with.* — **tie up 1.** fasten with rope, string, etc. **2.** moor (a vessel). **3.** block; hinder. **4.** have or be already committed, in use, etc., so as to be unavailable. —*n.* **1.** a string, cord, etc., with which something is tied. **2.** any obligation. **3.** an exact equality in number, as of a score, votes, etc.; esp., a contest that neither side wins; a draw. **4.** a necktie. **5.** a structural member fastening parts of a framework together and receiving tensile stress. **6.** one of a set of timbers laid crosswise on the ground as supports for railroad tracks. [ME *teigh* rope]

tie-dye (TĪ DI) *v.t.* **-dyed, -dy•ing** dye (fabric) after tying parts together so that only the exposed parts absorb the dye. —*n.* the method of dyeing fabrics this way; also **tie-dye•ing.**

tie-in (TĪ IN) *n.* a connection; relation.

tier (teer) *n.* a rank or row of things, as seats, placed one above another. [< OF *tire* row] —*v.t.* & *v.i.* place or rise in tiers.

tie-up (TĪ UP) *n.* a situation in which progress or operation is impossible; gridlock.

tiff (tif) *n.* **1.** a peevish display of irritation; pet; huff. **2.** a light quarrel; spat. —*v.i.* be in or have a tiff.

ti•ger (TĪ gər) *n.* **1.** a large carnivorous feline of Asia, with vertical black wavy stripes on a tawny body. **2.** a fierce ,or courageous person. [ME *tigre*] —**ti'gress** *n.fem.*

tight (tīt) *adj.* **•er, •est 1.** so closely held together or constructed so as to be impervious to fluids, air, etc. **2.** firmly fixed or fastened in place; secure. **3.** fully stretched; taut. **4.** closely drawn, packed, fastened, etc. **5.** strict; stringent. **6.** fitting closely; esp., fitting too closely. **7.** difficult to cope with; troublesome. **8.** parsimonious; tightfisted. **9.** *Slang* drunk; tipsy. **10.** *Econ.* **a** difficult to obtain. **b** straitened from lack of money or commodities: a *tight* market. **11.** neat; tidy. —*adv.* **1.** firmly; securely. **2.** closely; with much constriction. —**sit tight** refrain from taking action. [ME] —**tight'ly** *adv.* — **tight'ness** *n.*

tight•en (TĪT n) *v.t.* & *v.i.* make or become tight or tighter. —**tight'en•er** *n.*

tight•fist•ed (TĪT FIS tid) *adj.* stingy; parsimonious.

tight•lipped (TĪT LIPT) *adj.* **1.** having the lips held tightly together. **2.** unwilling to talk; reticent or secretive.

tight•rope (TĪT ROHP) *n.* a rope stretched tight above the ground for acrobatic performances.

tights (tīts) *n.pl.* a tightly fitting garment, commonly for the legs and lower torso, worn by dancers, acrobats, etc.

tight•wad (TĪT wod) *n. Informal* a parsimonious person; miser.

til•de (TIL də) *n.* a sign used, esp. in Spanish over *n* as in *Señor,* to indicate the palatal nasal sound (roughly equivalent in *Señor* to *ny*). [< Sp.]

tile (tīl) *n.* **1.** a thin piece of baked clay, asbestos, linoleum, etc., used for covering roofs, floors, or walls and as an ornament. **2.** a short earthenware pipe, used in forming sewers. —*v.t.* **tiled, til•ing** cover with tiles. [ME] —**til'er** *n.*

till¹ (til) *v.t.* & *v.i.* work (soil) for the production of crops, as by plowing and sowing; cultivate. [ME *tilien*] —**till'a•ble** *adj.*

till² *prep.* & *conj.* until. [ME]

till³ *n.* a drawer or tray in which money or valuables are kept, as at a bank, store, etc. [ME *tylle* drawer]

till·age (TIL ij) *n.* the cultivation of land.

till·er¹ (TIL ər) *n.* one who or that which tills.

till·er² *n. Naut.* a lever to turn a rudder when steering. [ME, beam]

tilt (tilt) *v.t.* 1. cause to rise at one end or side; slant; tip. 2. aim or thrust, as a lance. —*v.i.* 3. tip; slant; lean. 4. engage in a joust. [ME *tilten*] —*n.* 1. a slant; slope. 2. the act of tipping, or the state of being tipped. 3. a medieval sport in which mounted knights, charging with lances, tried to unseat each other; joust. 4. a quarrel. —**at full tilt** at full speed. —**tilt′er** *n.*

tim·ber (TIM bər) *n.* 1. wood for building or structural purposes. 2. growing or standing trees; also, woodland. 3. a single piece of prepared wood for use in a structure. [ME] —*v.t.* provide or shore with timber. —**tim′bered** *adj.*

tim·ber·land (TIM bər LAND) *n.* land covered with forests.

timber line the upper limit of tree growth on mountains and in arctic regions.

tim·bre (TAM bər) *n.* the quality of a sound distinguishing one vowel from another or the tone of one musical instrument from another; tone color. [ME *tymbre*]

time (tīm) *n.* 1. continuous existence, comprising the past, present, and future. 2. finite existence; duration: a short *time* ago. 3. a system of measuring duration: daylight *time,* lunar *time.* 4. a definite portion of duration; esp., a specific hour, day, season, year, etc.: The *time* is 2:35. Autumn is my favorite *time.* 5. the moment or period in which something takes place: at the *time* of their marriage. 6. leisure: no *time* to rest. 7. an instance or occasion of recurrence or repetition: next *time;* three *times* a day. 8. a fit or proper moment or occasion: This is the *time* to be born. 9. a period considered with reference to one's personal experience: have a good *time.* 10. an era; period; age: ancient *times;* the *time* of Henry VIII. 11. *Usu. pl.* a period having some specific quality: *Times* are hard. 12. *Music* meter, tempo, or the duration of a note. —**ahead of time** before the time stated or due; early. —**at the same time** 1. at the same moment or period. 2. despite that; nevertheless. —**at times** now and then; occasionally. —**behind the times** old-fashioned. —**for the time being** temporarily. —**from time to time** now and then; occasionally. —**in good time** 1. quickly;

fast. 2. at the appropriate time; when properly due. —**in the nick of time** at just the critical moment. —**in time** 1. before it is too late. 2. ultimately. 3. in the proper rhythm, tempo, etc. —**on time** promptly. —**time and again** frequently; repeatedly: also **time after time.** —**keep time** 1. indicate time correctly, as a clock. 2. make rhythmic movements in unison with others. —*adj.* 1. of or pertaining to time. 2. devised so as to operate at a specified time: a *time* bomb. 3. paid for in installments or at a future date. —*v.t.* **timed, tim·ing** 1. regulate as to time. 2. cause to correspond in time: They *timed* their steps to the music. 3. arrange the time or occasion for. 4. mark the rhythm or measure of. 5. establish the speed or duration of: *time* a race. [ME] —**tim′er** *n.*

time·card (TĪM KAHRD) *n.* a card for recording the time of arrival and departure of an employee.

time clock a clock equipped for automatically recording times of arrival and departure.

time exposure *Photog.* 1. a film exposure made for a relatively long interval. 2. a picture made by such an exposure.

time-hon·ored (TĪM ON ərd) *adj.* observed or honored because of long usage or existence.

time·keep·er (TĪM KEE pər) *n.* one who declares the time in a race, game, etc., or records the hours worked by employees.

time·less (TĪM lis) *adj.* 1. independent of or unaffected by time; unending; eternal. 2. not limited to any special time. —**time′less·ness** *n.*

time·ly (TĪM lee) *adj.* **·li·er, ·li·est** being or occurring at a suitable time; opportune. —*adv.* opportunely. —**time′li·ness** *n.*

time-out (TĪM OWT) *n.* in sports, a short recess requested by a team during play. Also **time out.**

time·piece (TĪM PEES) *n.* something that records or measures time, as a clock.

times (tīmz) *prep.* multiplied by: three *times* three is nine. [ME]

time·ta·ble (TĪM TAY bəl) *n.* a schedule of the times at which certain things are to take place, as arrivals and departures of trains, times of high and low tides, etc.

time-test·ed (TĪM TES tid) *adj.* having worth proved by use over an extended period. [ME]

time•worn (TĪM worn) *adj.* **1.** showing the ravages of time. **2.** trite; overused.

tim•id (TIM id) *adj.* **•er, •est 1.** shrinking from danger or risk; fearful. **2.** lacking self-confidence; shy. **3.** characterized by fear or shyness: a *timid* voice. [< L *timidus* fearful] **—ti•mid′i•ty, tim′id•ness** *n.* **—tim′id•ly** *adv.*

tim•or•ous (TIM ər əs) *adj.* **1.** fearful of danger; timid. **2.** indicating or produced by fear. [ME] **—tim′or•ous•ness** *n.*

tim•pa•ni (TIM pə nee) *n. (construed as sing. or pl.)* kettledrums: also spelled *tympani*. [< Ital. *timpano*] **—tim′pa•nist** *n.*

tin (tin) *n.* **1.** a white metallic element (symbol Sn) of low tensile strength. **2.** tin plate. **3.** a container or box made of tin or tin plate. **—v.t.** **tinned, tin•ning 1.** coat or cover with tin. **2.** pack or put up in tins. [ME] **—tin** *adj.*

tinc•ture (TINGK chər) *n.* **1.** a solution, usu. in alcohol, of some medicinal substance: *tincture* of iodine. **2.** a tinge of color; tint. **3.** a slight additional flavor, quality, etc. **—v.t. •tured, •tur•ing** impart a slight hue or tinge to. [ME]

tin•der (TIN dər) *n.* any readily combustible substance that will ignite on contact with a spark. [ME] **—tin′der•y** *adj.*

tin•der•box (TIN dər BOKS) *n.* **1.** a portable metallic box containing tinder. **2.** anything highly flammable, explosive, touchy, etc.

tine (tīn) *n.* a spike or prong, as of a fork or of an antler. [ME *tyne*] **—tined** *adj.*

tin•foil (TIN FOIL) *n.* tin or an alloy of tin made into thin sheets for use as wrapping material etc.

tinge (tinj) *v.t.* **tinged, tinge•ing or ting•ing 1.** add a faint trace of color; tint. **2.** impart a slight characteristic quality of some other element to. [< L *tingere* dye] **—n. 1.** a faint trace of added color. **2.** a quality or peculiar characteristic imparted to something.

tin•gle (TING gəl) *v.* **•gled, •gling** *v.i.* **1.** experience a prickly, stinging sensation, as from cold or from a sharp blow. **2.** cause such a sensation. **—v.t.** cause to tingle. [ME *tinglen*] **—tin•gle** *n.* **—tin′gly** *adj.*

tin•ker (TING kər) *n.* **1.** an itinerant mender of domestic tin utensils, as pots and pans. **2.** loosely, one who does repairing work of any kind. **3.** a clumsy worker; botcher. [ME *tinkere* tin worker] **—v.i. 1.** work as a tinker. **2.** work in a clumsy fashion.

3. putter; fuss. **—v.t. 4.** mend as a tinker. **5.** repair inexpertly. **—tink′er•er** *n.*

tin•kle (TING kəl) *v.t. & v.i.* **•kled, •kling** produce or cause to produce slight, sharp, metallic sounds, as from a bell. [ME *tinklen*]

tin•ny (TIN ee) *adj.* **•ni•er, •ni•est 1.** pertaining to, composed of, or abounding in tin. **2.** resembling tin in lack of durability. **3.** having a thin sound. **—tin′ni•ness** *n.*

tin-plate (TIN PLAYT) *v.t.* **-plat•ed, -plat•ing** plate with tin.

tin plate sheet iron or steel plated with tin.

tin•sel (TIN səl) *n.* **1.** very thin, glittering bits of cheap metals used as decoration. **2.** a yarn containing gold or silver thread. **3.** anything sparkling and showy, with little real worth. [< MF *estincelle* spark] **—adj. 1.** made of, resembling, or covered with tinsel. **2.** superficially brilliant; tawdry.

tin•smith (TIN SMITH) *n.* one who works with tin or tin plate.

tint (tint) *n.* **1.** a variety of color; esp., a slight admixture of a different color; tinge. **2.** a gradation of a color made by mixture with white. **3.** any pale or delicate hue. **—v.t.** give a tint to; tinge. **—tint′er** *n.*

tin•tin•nab•u•la•tion (TIN ti NAB yə LAY shən) *n.* the pealing, tinkling, or ringing of bells. [< L *tintinnabulum* bell]

tin•ware (TIN WAIR) *n.* articles made of tin plate.

ti•ny (TĪ nee) *adj.* **•ni•er, •ni•est** very small; minute. [ME *tine* very small]

tip¹ (tip) *n.* a slanting position; tilt. **—v.t. & v.i.** **tipped, tip•ping 1.** lean or cause to lean by lowering or raising one end or side; tilt. **2.** overturn or topple. **—tip′per** *n.*

tip² *n.* **1.** a small gift of money for services rendered. **2.** a friendly, helpful hint. **—v.** **tipped, tip•ping** *v.t.* **1.** give a small gratuity to. **2.** give secret information to. **—v.i. 3.** give tips. **—tip′per** *n.*

tip³ *n.* **1.** the point of anything tapering; end: the *tip* of the tongue. **2.** a piece or part made to form the end of anything. **3.** the top or summit, as of a mountain. **—v.t.** **tipped, tip•ping 1.** furnish with a tip. **2.** form the tip of. **3.** cover or adorn the tip of. [ME *tipen*]

tip⁴ *v.t.* **tipped, tip•ping** strike lightly, or with something light; tap. **—n.** a tap; light blow. [ME]

tip-off (TIP AWF) *n. Informal* a hint or warning.

tip•ple (TIP əl) *v.t. & v.i.* **•pled, •pling**

drink (alcoholic beverages) frequently and habitually. —n. alcoholic liquor. —**tip′pler** n.

tip·ster (TIP stər) n. one who sells tips, as for betting on a race.

tip·sy (TIP see) adj. •si·er, •si·est 1. partially intoxicated; high. 2. apt to tip over; shaky; also, crooked; askew. —**tip′si·ness** n.

tip·toe (TIP TOH) v.i. •toed, •toe·ing walk on the tips of the toes; go in a stealthy or quiet manner. —n. the tip of a toe. —**on tiptoe** 1. on one's tiptoes. 2. eagerly expectant. 3. stealthily; quietly.

tip·top (TIP TOP) n. 1. the highest point; the very top. 2. Informal the highest quality or degree. —adj. (TIP TOP) 1. located at the very top. 2. Informal excellent. —**tip′top′** adv.

ti·rade (TĪ rayd) n. a prolonged outpouring of denunciation. [< F]

tire¹ (tīr) v. tired, tir·ing v.t. 1. reduce the strength of, as by toil; fatigue. 2. reduce the interest or patience of. —v.i. 3. become weary or exhausted. 4. lose patience, interest, etc. [ME]

tire² n. 1. a hollow inflatable structure, as of rubber, forming the outer part of the wheel of a vehicle. 2. a band or hoop of metal or rubber fixed tightly around the rim of a wheel. —v.t. tired, tir·ing furnish with a tire; put a tire on.

tired (tīrd) adj. weary; exhausted; fatigued. —**tired′ly** adv. —**tired′ness** n.

tire·less (TĪR lis) adj. not yielding to fatigue; untiring. —**tire′less·ly** adv.

tire·some (TĪR səm) adj. causing one to tire; tedious. —**tire′some·ness** n.

'tis (tiz) it is.

tis·sue (TISH oo) n. 1. Biol. an aggregate of cells with a particular function: connective tissue. 2. light, absorbent paper used as a disposable handkerchief etc. 3. very thin paper for wrapping and protecting things: also **tissue paper.** 4. a connected series; chain: a tissue of lies. 5. any light or gauzy textile fabric. [ME tissu]

ti·tan (TĪT n) n. a person of gigantic size, strength, ability, etc. [< Titan, one of a race of giant gods in Greek mythology]

ti·tan·ic (tī TAN ik) adj. of great size, strength, ability, etc.

tit·bit (TIT BIT) n. Chiefly Brit. tidbit.

tit for tat retaliation in kind.

tithe (tīth) n. 1. a tenth part of one's income, esp. when donated to a church. 2. the tenth part of anything. —v.t. tithed, tith·ing give or pay a tithe, or tenth part of. [ME tithen] —**tith′er** n.

ti·tian (TISH ən) n. a reddish yellow color. [after Titian, 1477?–1576, Venetian painter] —adj. having this color.

tit·il·late (TIT l AYT) v.t. •lat·ed, •lat·ing 1. cause a tickling sensation in. 2. excite pleasurably in any way. [< L titillatus tickled] —**tit′il·la′tion** n. —**tit′il·la′tive** adj.

tit·i·vate (TIT ə VAYT) v.t. & v.i. •vat·ed, •vat·ing put on decorative touches; dress up: also spelled tittivate. —**tit′i·va′tion** n.

ti·tle (TĪT l) n. 1. the name of a work, as of a book, play, or song. 2. a name of an office or rank: the title of duke, the heavyweight title. 3. a characteristic or descriptive name; epithet. 4. Law the means whereby one has the just possession of property; also, the legal evidence of one's right of property. [ME] —v.t. •tled, •tling give a name or title to; call.

ti·tled (TĪT ld) adj. having a title, esp. of nobility.

title page a page containing the title of a work and the names of its author and publisher.**tit·ter** (TIT ər) v.i. laugh in a half-smothered way, as from nervousness or in ridicule; snicker; giggle. —n. the act of tittering. —**tit′ter·er** n. —**tit′ter·ing·ly** adv.

tit·ti·vate (TIT ə VAYT) see TITIVATE.

tit·tle (TIT l) n. the smallest bit. [ME titel]

tit·tle-tat·tle (TIT l TAT l) n. foolish or idle talk; gossip. —v.i. •tled, •tling talk foolishly or idly; gossip.

tit·u·lar (TICH ə lər) adj. 1. existing in name only; nominal. 2. of, pertaining to, or like a title. 3. bestowing or taking title. [< L titulus title] —**tit′u·lar·ly** adv.

tiz·zy (TIZ ee) n. pl. •zies Slang a bewildered or excited state of mind.

TNT (TEE EN TEE) trinitrotoluene.

to (too) prep. 1. in a direction toward or terminating in: going to town. 2. opposite, in contact with, or near: face to face. 3. intending or aiming at: Come to my rescue. 4. resulting in: frozen to death. 5. belonging or used in connection with: the key to the door. 6. accompanied by: march to the beat. 7. in honor of: Drink to her health. 8. in comparison with: four quarts to the gallon. 9. approaching a limit; until: five minutes to one. 10. as far as: a miser to the end. 11. in respect of; concerning: blind to her charms. 12. in close application toward:

buckle down *to* work. **13.** for: The contest is open *to* everyone. **14.** by: known *to* the world. **15.** from the point of view of: It seems *to* me. **16.** about; involved in: That's all there is *to* it. ♦ *To* also serves to indicate the infinitive, and is often used for it: You may come if you care *to*. —*adv.* **1.** to or toward something. **2.** in a direction, position, or state understood or implied; esp., shut or closed: Pull the door *to*. **3.** into a normal condition; into consciousness: She soon came *to*. **4.** *Naut.* with head *to* the wind: said of a sailing vessel. [ME]

toad (tohd) *n.* **1.** a tailless, jumping amphibian resembling the frog but without teeth in the upper jaw and resorting to water only to breed. **2.** a lizard, the horned toad. **3.** any person regarded with scorn or contempt. [ME *tode*]

toad·stool (TOHD stool) *n.* a mushroom, esp. a poisonous one.

toad·y (TOH dee) *n. pl.* **toad·ies** a fawning, servile person. —*v.t. & v.i.* **toad·ied, toad·y·ing** act the toady (to). —**toad'y·ish** *adj.* —**toad'y·ism** *n.*

to-and-fro (TOO ən FROH) *adj.* moving back and forth.

toast[1] (tohst) *v.t.* **1.** brown (sliced bread) by heat. **2.** warm thoroughly. —*v.i.* **3.** become warm or toasted. [ME *tosten* parch] —*n.* sliced bread browned by heat.

toast[2] *n.* **1.** the act of drinking to someone's health or to some sentiment. **2.** a person or sentiment named in so drinking. —*v.t.* **1.** drink to the health of or in honor of. —*v.i.* **2.** drink a toast.

toast·er[1] (TOH stər) *n.* a device for making toast.

toast·er[2] *n.* one who proposes a toast.

toast·mas·ter (TOHST MAS tər) *n.* a person who, at public dinners, announces the toasts, calls upon the various speakers, etc. —**toast·mis·tress** (TOHST MIS tris) *n.fem.*

to·bac·co (tə BAK oh) *n. pl.* **·cos** or **·coes 1.** an annual plant of the genus *Nicotiana*. **2.** its leaves prepared in various ways, as for smoking, chewing, etc. **3.** the various products prepared from tobacco leaves, as cigarettes, cigars, etc. [< Sp. *tabaco*]

to·bac·co·nist (tə BAK ə nist) *n.* a dealer in tobacco.

to·bog·gan (tə BOG ən) *n.* a light sledlike vehicle, consisting of a long thin board curved up at the forward end. [< Micmac *topagan*] —*v.i.* **1.** coast on a toboggan. **2.**

move downward swiftly: Wheat prices *tobogganed*. —**to·bog'gan·er** *n.*

toc·ca·ta (tə KAH tə) *n. Music* a free composition for a keyboard instrument. [< Ital., lit., touched]

toc·sin (TOK sin) *n.* **1.** a signal sounded on a bell. **2.** an alarm bell. [< MF]

to·day (tə DAY) *adv.* **1.** on or during this present day. **2.** at the present time; nowadays. —*n.* the present day, time, or age. [ME]

tod·dle (TOD l) *v.i.* **·dled, ·dling** walk unsteadily and with short steps, as a little child. —*n.* the act of toddling. —**tod'dler** *n.*

tod·dy (TOD ee) *n. pl.* **·dies** a drink made with spirits, hot water, sugar, and a slice of lemon. [< Hind. *tādi*]

to-do (tə DOO) *n. Informal* confusion or bustle; fuss. [ME]

toe (toh) *n.* **1.** one of the digits of the foot. **2.** the forward part of the foot. **3.** the portion of a shoe, sock, etc. that covers the toes. **4.** the lower end or projection of something. —**on one's toes** alert; wide-awake. —**tread on (someone's) toes** trespass on (someone's) feelings, opinions, prejudices, etc. [ME] —*v.* **toed, toe·ing** *v.t.* **1.** touch or kick with the toes. —*v.i.* **2.** point the toes in a specified direction: *toe* out. —**toe the mark** (or line) abide by the rules; conform. —**toe'less** *adj.*

toed (tohd) *adj.* having toes: chiefly in combination: *two-toed*.

toe dance a dance performed on tiptoe. —**toe-dance** (TOH DANS) *v.i.* **·danced, ·danc·ing** —**toe' danc'er**

toe·hold (TOH HOHLD) *n.* **1.** a small space that supports the toes in climbing. **2.** any means of entrance or support; a footing.

toe·nail (TOH NAYL) *n.* a nail growing on the toe.

tof·fee (TAW fee) *n.* taffy. Also **tof'fy.**

togs (togz) *n.pl.* clothes; outfit. —*v.t.* **togged, tog·ging** dress; clothe. [ME]

to·ga (TOH gə) *n. pl.* **·gas** the loose, draped outer garment worn in public by a citizen of ancient Rome. [< L] —**to·gaed** (TOH gəd) *adj.*

to·geth·er (tə GETH ər) *adv.* **1.** into union or contact with each other. **2.** in the same place or at the same spot. **3.** at the same moment of time; simultaneously. **4.** without cessation. **5.** with one another; mutually. [ME]

tog·gle (TOG əl) *n.* a pin or short rod attached in the middle, as to a rope, and designed to be passed through a hole or eye and turned; a type of button. —*v.t.* **•gled, •gling** fix, fasten, or furnish with a toggle.

toggle switch *Electr.* a lever for opening or closing an electric circuit.

toil[1] (toil) *n.* **1.** fatiguing work; labor. **2.** any oppressive task. —*v.i.* **1.** work arduously. **2.** progress with slow and labored steps. [ME] —**toil′er** *n.*

toil[2] *n. Usu. pl.* something that binds or ensnares, as a net. [< F *toile*]

toi•let (TOI let) *n.* **1.** a room with a washbowl, water closet, etc.: also called *bathroom.* **2.** a fixture flushed by water, into which one urinates or defecates: also called **toilet bowl. 3.** the act of dressing and grooming oneself; toilette. [< F *toilette* small cloth]

toi•let•ry (TOI li tree) *n. pl.* **•ries** an article used in making one's toilet, as soap, comb, etc.

toi•lette (twah LET) *n.* **1.** the act or process of grooming oneself, usu. including bathing and hairdressing. **2.** a person's actual dress or style of dress. [< F]

toil•some (TOIL səm) *adj.* accomplished with fatigue; involving toil. —**toil′some•ly** *adv.*

toil•worn (TOIL WORN) *adj.* exhausted by toil; showing the effects of toil.

to•ken (TOH kən) *n.* **1.** anything indicative of some other thing; a visible sign. **2.** a symbol. **3.** a memento; souvenir. **4.** a characteristic mark or feature. **5.** a piece of metal issued by a transportation company and good for one fare. —*adj.* serving as a token; slight; minimal. [ME]

to•ken•ism (TOH kə NIZ əm) *n.* the policy of attempting to meet certain conditions by symbolic or partial efforts.

told (tohld) past tense, past participle of TELL.

tol•er•a•ble (TOL ər ə bəl) *adj.* **1.** fairly good; not bad. **2.** endurable. **3.** allowable; permissible. —**tol′er•a•bly** *adv.*

tol•er•ance (TOL ər əns) *n.* **1.** the character, state, or quality of being tolerant; esp., freedom from bigotry or prejudice. **2.** the act of enduring, or the capacity for endurance. **3.** a small permissible allowance for variations from the specified weight, dimensions, etc.

tol•er•ant (TOL ər ənt) *adj.* **1.** disposed to tolerate beliefs, views, etc. **2.** indulgent; liberal. —**tol′er•ant•ly** *adv.*

tol•er•ate (TOL ə RAYT) *v.t.* **•at•ed, •at•ing**

1. allow to be or be done without active opposition. **2.** concede, as the right to opinions or participation. **3.** bear, sustain, endure, or be capable of enduring. [< L *toleratus* endured] —**tol′er•a′tion** *n.*

toll[1] (tohl) *n.* **1.** a charge for some privilege granted or service rendered, as passage on a bridge. **2.** something taken like a toll; price: The train wreck took a heavy *toll* of lives. **3.** a charge for a long-distance telephone call. [ME]

toll[2] *v.t.* **1.** cause (a bell) to sound slowly and at regular intervals. **2.** announce by tolling, as a death or funeral. **3.** call or summon by tolling. —*v.i.* **4.** sound slowly and at regular intervals. [ME *tollen* entice] —*n.* the act or sound of tolling a bell.

toll•gate (TOHL GAYT) *n.* a gate at which a toll is paid.

tom (tom) *n.* the male of various animals, esp. the cat. [after *Tom,* a personal name]

Tom (tom) *Slang* an Uncle Tom: a contemptuous term. —*v.i.* **Tommed, Tom•ming** behave as an Uncle Tom.

tom•a•hawk (TOM ə HAWK) *n.* **1.** an axlike weapon formerly used by Native Americans. **2.** any similar weapon, tool, etc. [< Algonquian *tamahaac* hatchet] —*v.t.* strike or kill with a tomahawk.

to•ma•to (tə MAY toh) *n. pl.* **•toes 1.** the edible fruit, yellow or red when ripe, of a perennial plant cultivated as a vegetable. **2.** the plant itself. [< Nahuatl *tomatl*]

tomb (toom) *n.* **1.** a place for the burial of the dead, as a vault or grave. **2.** a monument for commemorating a dead person. [ME *tombe*]

tom•boy (TOM BOI) *n.* a girl who prefers boyish activities, dress, etc. —**tom′boy′ ish** *adj.* —**tom′boy′ish•ness** *n.*

tomb•stone (TOOM STOHN) *n.* a stone, usu. inscribed, marking a place of burial.

tom•cat (TOM KAT) *n.* a male cat.

tome (tohm) *n.* a volume; esp., a large book. [< F]

tom•fool•er•y (TOM FOO lə ree) *n. pl.* **•er•ies 1.** silly or foolish behavior. **2.** worthless or trivial stuff; frippery. Also **tom′fool′ ish•ness.**

tom•my•rot (TOM ee ROT) *n.* nonsense.

to•mor•row (tə MOR oh) *adv.* on or for the next day after today. —*n.* **1.** the next day after today; the morrow. **2.** some time in the future. [ME *to morowe* to morrow]

tom-tom (TOM TOM) *n.* a drum of Asian or

Native American origin, played with the hands. [< Hind. *tamtam*]

ton (tun) *n.* **1.** any of several large measures of weight; esp.: **a** the **short ton** of 2000 pounds, commonly used in the U.S. and Canada. **b** the **long ton** of 2240 pounds, used in Great Britain. **2.** a unit for reckoning the displacement or weight of vessels, 35 cubic feet of sea water weighing one long ton: called in full a **displacement ton. 3.** a unit for reckoning the freight-carrying capacity of a ship, usu. equivalent to 40 cubic feet of space: called in full a **shipping ton** or **measurement ton 4.** a metric ton. [ME]

to·nal·i·ty (toh NAL i tee) *n. pl.* **·ties 1.** *Music* the relationship of tones; key. **2.** the general color scheme or collective tones of a painting.

tone (tohn) *n.* **1.** sound in relation to quality, volume, and duration. **2.** a sound having a definite pitch. **3.** *Music* **a** the timbre, or characteristic sound, of a voice, instrument, etc. **b** a full interval of a diatonic scale. **4.** a prevailing disposition; mood. **5.** characteristic style or tendency. **6.** style or distinction; elegance. **7.** vocal inflection as expressive of feeling: a *tone* of pity. **8.** a shade, hue, tint, or degree of a particular color. **9.** *Physiol.* **a** the general condition of the body. **b** firmness and resilience, as of a muscle. —*v.t.* **toned, ton·ing 1.** give tone to. **2.** modify in tone. —**tone down 1.** subdue the tone of (a painting). **2.** moderate in quality or tone. —**tone up 1.** raise in quality or strength. **2.** gain in vitality. [ME] —**to′nal** *adj.*

tone-deaf (TOHN DEF) *adj.* unable to perceive fine distinctions in pitch, as musical intervals. —**tone′deaf′ness** *n.*

tone·less (TOHN lis) *adj.* **1.** having no tone; without tone. **2.** lacking spirit; listless.

tong (tong) *n.* a Chinese secret society or fraternal association. [< Chinese *t'ang* meeting place]

tongs (tongz) *n. (usually construed as pl.)* an implement for grasping, holding, or lifting objects, consisting usu. of a pair of pivoted levers. [ME *tonge*]

tongue (tung) *n.* **1.** a freely moving organ situated in the mouth of most vertebrates, serving in mammals as an organ of taste and in man also as an organ of speech. **2.** an animal's tongue, as of beef, prepared as food. **3.** the power of speech: lose one's *tongue.* **4.** manner or style of speaking: a

smooth *tongue.* **5.** utterance. **6.** a language, vernacular, or dialect. **7.** anything resembling an animal tongue in shape or function. **8.** a jet of flame. **9.** a projecting edge or tenon of a board for insertion into a corresponding groove of another board, thus forming a **tongue-and-groove joint.** —**on the tip of one's tongue** on the verge of being recalled. —**hold one's tongue** keep silent. —**(with) tongue in cheek** with ironic or facetious intent. [ME *tunge*] —*v.t. & v.i.* **tongued, tongu·ing 1.** *Music* separate the tones played on (a wind instrument) by means of the tongue. **2.** touch or lap with the tongue. —**tongue′less** *adj.*

tongued (tungd) *adj.* **1.** having a tongue or tongues. **2.** having or characterized by a (specified kind of) tongue: *sharp-tongued.*

tongue-lash·ing (TUNG LASH ing) *n.* a severe reprimand; scolding.

tongue-tied (TUNG TID) *adj.* speechless or halting in speech, as from an impediment, shyness, etc.

tongue twister a word or phrase difficult to say quickly, as "Miss Smith's fish-sauce shop."

ton·ic (TON ik) *adj.* **1.** having power to invigorate or build up; bracing. **2.** pertaining to tone or tones. **3.** *Music* pertaining to or in the key of the keynote. —*n.* **1.** a medicine that gradually restores the normal tone of organs. **2.** something imparting animation, vigor, or tone. **3.** *Music* the basic tone of a key or mode. **4.** quinine water. [< Gk. *tonikós* sound]

to·night (tə NIT) *adv.* in or during the present or coming night. —*n.* **1.** the night that follows this day. **2.** the present night. [ME *to night*]

ton·nage (TUN ij) *n.* **1.** the capacity of a merchant vessel expressed in units of 100 cubic feet. **2.** the total carrying capacity of vessels, esp. of a country's merchant marine. **3.** a tax levied on vessels at a given rate per ton. **4.** total weight in tons, as of materials produced or transported. [ME, tax]

ton·sil (TON sal) *n. Anat.* one of two oval organs situated on either side of the passage from the mouth to the pharynx. [< L *tonsillae* tonsils] —**ton′sil·lar** *adj.*

ton·sil·lec·to·my (TON sə LEK tə mee) *n. pl.* **·mies** *Surg.* removal of a tonsil or tonsils.

ton·sil·li·tis (TON sə LI tis) *n. Pathol.* inflammation of the tonsils.

ton·so·ri·al (TON SOR ee əl) *adj.* pertaining

to a barber or barbering: chiefly in the humorous term **tonsorial artist,** a barber. [< L *tonsorius*]

ton•sure (TON shər) *n.* **1.** the cutting of the hair of the head; the shaving of the head or crown of the head, as of a priest or monk. **2.** the part of a priest's or monk's head left bare by shaving. —*v.t.* **•sured, •sur•ing** shave the head of. [ME]

ton•y (TOH nee) *adj.* **ton•i•er, ton•i•est** *Informal* fashionable; stylish.

too (too) *adv.* **1.** in addition; likewise; also. **2.** in excessive quantity or degree. **3.** very; extremely: That's not *too* likely. **4.** indeed: You are *too*! [ME]

took (tuuk) past tense of TAKE.

tool (tool) *n.* **1.** an implement, as a hammer, saw, or chisel, used chiefly in manual work. **2.** a power-driven apparatus, as a lathe, used for cutting and shaping the parts of a machine. **3.** the cutting or shaping part of such an apparatus. **4.** a person used to carry out the designs of others; a dupe. **5.** any instrument or means necessary to one's profession or trade: Words are the writer's *tools*. —*v.t.* **1.** shape, mark, or ornament with a tool. **2.** provide with tools. **3.** ornament or impress designs upon (leather etc.) with a roller bearing a pattern. [ME]

tool•ing (TOO ling) *n.* **1.** ornamentation or work done with tools; esp., stamped or gilded ornamental designs on leather. **2.** the application of a tool or tools to any work.

tool•mak•er (TOOL MAY kər) *n.* a maker of tools.

toot (toot) *v.t. & v.i.* **1.** blow (a horn, whistle, etc.), esp. with short blasts. **2.** sound (a blast, toot, etc.). —*n.* **1.** a short note or blast on or as on a horn. **2.** *Informal* a spree; esp., a drinking spree.

tooth (tooth) *n. pl.* **teeth 1.** one of the hard structures in the mouth of most vertebrates, used for seizing and chewing food, as weapons, etc. **2.** one of various hard bodies of the oral or gastric regions of invertebrates. **3.** something resembling a tooth in form or use; esp., a projecting point or cog. —**armed to the teeth** heavily armed. —**in the teeth of** directly against, counter to, or in defiance of. —**get one's teeth into** achieve a solid grip or grasp of. —**show one's teeth** display a disposition to fight; threaten. —**tooth and nail** with all possible strength and effort; fiercely: fight *tooth and nail.* —*v.t.* **toothed, tooth•ing 1.** supply with teeth, as a rake or saw. **2.** give a

serrated edge to; indent. —*v.i.* **3.** become interlocked, as gearwheels. [ME] —**tooth' less** *adj.*

tooth•ache (TOOTH AYK) *n.* a pain in a tooth or teeth.

tooth•brush (TOOTH BRUSH) *n.* a small brush used for cleaning the teeth.

toothed (tootht) *adj.* **1.** having teeth. **2.** having or characterized by a specified kind or number of teeth: *sharp-toothed.*

tooth•pick (TOOTH PIK) *n.* a small sliver of wood, plastic, etc., used for removing particles of food from between the teeth.

tooth•some (TOOTH səm) *adj.* **1.** having a pleasant taste. **2.** attractive; voluptuous. —**tooth'some•ness** *n.*

tooth•y (TOO thee) *adj.* **tooth•i•er, tooth•i•est 1.** having large or prominent teeth. **2.** displaying the teeth: a *toothy* smile.

top[1] (top) *n.* **1.** the uppermost or highest part, end, side, or surface of anything. **2.** the end or part regarded as the higher or upper extremity: the *top* of the street. **3.** a lid or cover: a bottle *top*. **4.** the crown of the head. **5.** *pl.* the leafy part of a plant producing root vegetables. **6.** the highest or most prominent place or rank. **7.** one who is highest in rank or position. **8.** the highest or loudest pitch: at the *top* of his voice. **9.** the best part. —**blow one's top** *Informal* break out in a rage; flare up. —**on top 1.** at the highest point or position. **2.** in a situation of dominance or power. **3.** highly successful. —**on top of 1.** in addition to. **2.** conversant with (a problem etc.). **3.** in complete control of. —*adj.* **1.** of or pertaining to the top. **2.** forming or comprising the top. **3.** highest in rank or quality; chief: *top* authors. **4.** greatest in amount or degree: *top* prices. —*v.t.* **topped, top•ping 1.** remove the top of; prune. **2.** provide with a top, cap, etc. **3.** form the top of. **4.** reach or pass over the top of; surmount. **5.** surpass or exceed. —**top off** complete or finish with a crowning touch. [ME]

top[2] *n.* a toy with a point on which it is made to spin. [ME]

top-draw•er (TOP DROR) *adj.* of the highest standing, merit, excellence, etc.

top dressing *n.* a dressing of manure etc. spread over the surface of a field.

tope (tohp) *v.t.* **toped, top•ing** drink (alcoholic beverages) excessively and frequently.

top•er (TOH pər) *n.* a habitual drunkard.

top•flight (TOP FLIT) *adj.* of the highest quality; superior.

top hat a man's hat with a tall, cylindrical crown and a narrow brim.

top·heav·y (TOP HEV ee) *adj.* **-heav·i·er, -heav·i·est** having the upper part too heavy for the lower part. —**top'·heav'i·ness** *n.*

to·pi (toh PEE) *n.* a helmet made of pith, worn as protection against the sun: also called *topee* and *pith helmet*. [< Hind.]

top·ic (TOP ik) *n.* **1.** a subject of discourse or of a treatise. **2.** any matter treated of in speech or writing; a theme for discussion. [< L *topica* topics]

top·i·cal (TOP i kəl) *adj.* **1.** pertaining to a topic. **2.** belonging to a place or spot; local. **3.** pertaining to matters of present interest. —**top·i·cal·i·ty** (TOP i KAL i tee) *n.*

top·less (TOP lis) *adj.* **1.** lacking a top. **2.** nude above the waist. **3.** featuring entertainers or waitresses who are nude above the waist: *topless* bar. —**top'less·ness** *n.*

top·mast (TOP MAST) *n.* *Naut.* the mast next above the lower mast.

top·most (TOP MOHST) *adj.* highest.

top·notch (TOP NOCH) *adj.* excellent.

to·pog·ra·phy (tə POG rə fee) *n. pl.* **·phies 1.** the detailed description of places. **2.** the art of representing on a map the physical features of a place. **3.** the physical features, collectively, of a region. **4.** surveying with reference to the physical features of a region. —**to·pog'ra·pher** *n.* —**top·o·graph·ic** (TOP ə GRAF ik) or **·i·cal** *adj.*

top·ping (TOP ing) *n.* **1.** that which forms the top of anything. **2.** a sauce, garnish, etc. put on a cake, portion of food, etc.

top·ple (TOP əl) *v.* **·pled, ·pling** *v.t.* **1.** push and cause to fall; overturn. —*v.i.* **2.** fall.

tops (tops) *adj.* excellent; first-rate.

top-se·cret (TOP SEE krit) *adj.* denoting the highest category of security classification.

top·side (TOP SID) *n.* *Naut.* the portion of a ship above the main deck. —*adv.* to or on the upper parts of a ship.

top·soil (TOP SOIL) *n.* the surface soil of land.

top·sy-tur·vy (TOP see TUR vee) *adj.* **1.** turned upside down. **2.** in disorder. —*adv.* **1.** with the top where the bottom should be. **2.** in reverse order. —*n.* confusion; disorder; chaos. —**top'sy-tur'vi·ness** *n.*

toque (tohk) *n.* a close-fitting, brimless hat worn by women. [< F]

To·rah (TOH rə) *n.* in Judaism, the Penta-

teuch; also, the scroll containing this. [< Hebrew]

torch (torch) *n.* **1.** a source of light, as from flaming material fixed at the end of a handle. **2.** anything that illuminates: the *torch* of science. **3.** a portable device giving off an intensely hot flame and used for burning off paint, melting solder, etc. [ME *torche*]

torch·bear·er (TORCH BAIR ər) *n.* **1.** one who carries a torch. **2.** one who imparts knowledge, truth, etc.

torch·light (TORCH LIT) *n.* the light of a torch.

torch song a popular love song expressing sadness and hopeless love.

tore (tor) past tense of TEAR¹.

tor·e·a·dor (TOR ee ə DOR) *n.* a bullfighter. [< Sp.]

to·ri·i (TOR ee EE) *n.* the gateway of a Shinto temple, consisting of two uprights with two straight crosspieces. [< Jap.]

tor·ment (TOR ment) *n.* **1.** intense bodily pain or mental anguish; agony; torture. **2.** one who or that which torments. —*v.t.* (tor MENT) **1.** subject to intense physical or mental suffering. **2.** harass. [ME] —**tor·men'tor** or **tor·ment'er** *n.*

torn (torn) past participle of TEAR¹.

tor·na·do (tor NAY doh) *n. pl.* **·does** or **·dos** *Meteorol.* a whirling wind of exceptional violence, accompanied by a funnel-shaped cloud. [< Sp. *tronada* thunderstorm]

tor·pe·do (tor PEE doh) *n. pl.* **·does** an explosive, self-propelled underwater projectile, used to destroy enemy ships. —*v.t.* **·doed, ·do·ing** sink, damage, or wreck with or as with a torpedo. [< L, lit., numbness]

tor·pid (TOR pid) *adj.* **1.** inactive; dormant; numb. **2.** sluggish; apathetic; dull. [< L *torpidus*] —**tor·pid'i·ty, tor'pid·ness** *n.* —**tor'pid·ly** *adv.*

tor·por (TOR pər) *n.* **1.** complete or partial insensibility; stupor. **2.** apathy. [< L] —**tor'po·rif'ic** *adj.*

torque (tork) *n.* *Mech.* anything that causes or tends to cause torsion in a body. [< L *torquere* twist]

tor·rent (TOR ənt) *n.* **1.** a violent, onrushing flow, as of water. **2.** any abundant or tumultuous flow: a *torrent* of abuse. [< F] —**tor·ren·tial** (taw REN shəl) *adj.*

tor·rid (TOR id) *adj.* **1.** receiving the full force of the sun's heat. **2.** very hot; scorching; burning. **3.** impassioned; ardent. [< L *torridus*]

Torrid Zone see under ZONE.

tor·sion (TOR shən) n. 1. the act of twisting, or the state of being twisted. 2. Mech. deformation of a body, as a thread or rod, by twisting around its length as an axis. 3. the force with which a twisted cord or cable tends to return to its former position. [ME *torcion* twisting one's bowels] —**tor′sion·al** adj. —**tor′·sion·al·ly** adv.

tor·so (TOR soh) n. pl. ·**sos** 1. the trunk of a human body. 2. a sculptured representation of a human body without the head or limbs. [< Ital.]

tort (tort) n. Law any private or civil wrong by act or omission for which a civil suit can be brought, but not including breach of contract. [ME, injury]

torte (tort) n. a rich cake made with butter, eggs, and often fruit and nuts. [< G]

tor·til·la (tor TEE yə) n. a flat cake made of coarse cornmeal baked on a hot sheet of iron or a slab of stone. [< Sp.]

tor·toise (TOR təs) n. 1. a turtle, esp. a terrestrial one. 2. a slow-moving person or thing. [ME *tortuca*]

tor·tu·ous (TOR choo əs) adj. 1. consisting of irregular bends or turns; twisting. 2. not straightforward; devious. [ME] —**tor·tu·os·i·ty** (TOR choo OS i tee) n. —**tor′·tu·ous·ly** adv. —**tor′tu·ous·ness** n.

tor·ture (TOR chər) n. 1. infliction of or subjection to extreme physical pain. 2. great mental suffering; agony. 3. something that causes extreme pain. [< F] —v.t. ·**tured**, ·**tur·ing** 1. inflict extreme pain upon, as from cruelty. 2. cause to suffer agony, extreme discomfort, etc. 3. twist or turn into an abnormal form, meaning, etc. —**tor′tur·er** n. —**tor′tur·ous** adj.

To·ry (TOR ee) n. pl. ·**ries** 1. a member of an English political party, since about 1832 called the Conservative Party. 2. one who at the period of the American Revolution supported the British. 3. (also **to′ry**) one having very conservative beliefs, esp. in politics. [< Irish *tóraighe* bandit] —**To·ry·ism** (TOR ee IZ əm) n.

toss (taws) v.t. 1. throw, pitch, or fling about. 2. agitate; disturb. 3. throw with the hand, esp. with the palm of the hand upward. 4. lift with a quick motion, as the head. —v.i. 5. be flung to and fro, as a ship in a storm. 6. throw oneself from side to side restlessly, as in sleep. —**toss off** 1. drink at one draft. 2. utter, write, or do in an offhand manner. —n. 1. the act of tossing. 2. a quick upward or

backward movement, as of the head. 3. a tossup or wager.

toss·up (TAWS UP) n. 1. the throwing up of a coin to decide a bet, etc. 2. an even chance.

tot[1] (tot) n. 1. a little child. 2. a small amount or portion, as of liquor.

tot[2] v.t. **tot·ted, tot·ting** total.

to·tal (TOHT l) n. the whole sum or amount. —adj. 1. constituting or comprising a whole. 2. complete; absolute: a *total* loss. [ME] —v. **·taled, ·tal·ing** v.t. 1. ascertain the total of. 2. come to or reach as a total. 3. *Slang* wreck (a car) completely. —v.i. 4. amount. —**to′tal·ly** adv.

to·tal·i·tar·i·an (toh TAL i TAIR ee ən) adj. designating or characteristic of a government controlled exclusively by one party or faction and maintained by political suppression. —n. an adherent of totalitarian government. —**to·tal′i·tar′i·an·ism** n.

to·tal·i·ty (toh TAL i tee) n. pl. ·**ties** 1. an aggregate of parts or individuals. 2. the state of being total.

to·tal·i·za·tor (TOHT l ə ZAY tər) n. a parimutuel machine: also **to′tal·iz′er** (TOHT l I zər).

tote (toht) v.t. **tot·ed, tot·ing** 1. carry about. 2. haul, as supplies. —n. 1. the act of toting. 2. a load or haul. —**tot′er** n.

tote bag a large bag for carrying books or other items.

tote board *Informal* an apparatus at a racetrack, showing the betting odds, money bet, and results of races; totalizator.

to·tem (TOH təm) n. 1. an animal, plant, or other natural object believed to be ancestrally related to a tribe, clan, etc. 2. the representation of this. [< Algonquian] —**to·tem′ic** adj. —**to′tem·ism** n.

totem pole 1. a tall post or pole carved or painted with totemic images, often erected outside a dwelling by Native Americans of the NW coast. 2. an order of rank; hierarchy.

tot·ter (TOT ər) v.i. 1. walk feebly and unsteadily. 2. shake or sway, as if about to fall. [ME *toteren*] —n. the act or condition of tottering. —**tot′ter·y** adj.

touch (tuch) v.t. 1. place the hand, finger, etc. in contact with. 2. be in or come into contact with. 3. bring into contact with something else. 4. strike lightly. 5. border on; adjoin. 6. come to; reach. 7. color slightly; tinge. 8. affect injuriously; taint: vegetables *touched* by frost. 9. affect the emotions of; move, esp. to pity, gratitude, etc. **10.** use or partake of: *I will not touch this food.* —*v.i.* **11.** touch someone or something. **12.** come into or be in contact. —**touch at** stop briefly at (a port or place) in the course of a journey or voyage. —**touch off 1.** cause to explode; fire. **2.** cause to happen or occur. —**touch on** (or **upon**) **1.** relate to; concern. **2.** treat briefly or in passing. —**touch up** improve or alter by slight additions or corrections. [ME *touchen*] —*n.* **1.** the act or process of touching. **2.** the state of being touched. **3.** *Physiol.* the sense by which external objects are perceived through direct contact with any part of the body. ◆ Collateral adjective: *tactile.* **4.** the sensation conveyed by touching something: *a smooth touch.* **5.** a stroke; hit; blow. **6.** a perceptible effect or influence: *He felt the touch of her wit.* **7.** a light stroke or mark. **8.** a slight detail or improvement: *finishing touches.* **9.** the distinctive style of an artist. **10.** a trace; tinge: *a touch* of irony. **11.** a slight attack or twinge: *a touch* of rheumatism. **12.** a small quantity; a dash. **13.** close communication or contact: *keep in touch with someone.* **14.** *Music* the manner in which a player presses the keyboard. —**touch'a•ble** *adj.*

touch and go an uncertain or precarious situation. —**touch-and-go** (TUCH ən GOH) *adj.*

touch•back (TUCH BAK) *n.* in football, a play in which a player grounds the ball behind the player's own goal line.

touch•down (TUCH DOWN) *n.* in football, a scoring play, worth six points, in which the ball is held on or over the opponent's goal line.

tou•ché (too SHAY) *interj.* an acknowledgment that one's opponent has made a hit in fencing or has made a valid criticism in a discussion. [< F, *touched*]

touched (tucht) *adj.* **1.** emotionally moved. **2.** slightly unbalanced in mind.

touch•ing (TUCH ing) *adj.* appealing to the sympathies or emotions. —*prep.* with regard to; concerning. —**touch'ing•ly** *adv.*

touch•stone (TUCH STOHN) *n.* a criterion or standard by which the qualities of something are tested.

touch•y (TUCH ee) *adj.* **touch•i•er, touch•i•est 1.** likely to take offense easily; irritable. **2.** risky; delicate: *a touchy subject.* —**touch'i•ness** *n.*

tough (tuf) *adj.* **•er, •est 1.** capable of sustaining great tension or strain without breaking. **2.** firm and resilient. **3.** not easily separated, softened, etc.: *tough meat.* **4.** possessing great physical, moral, or intellectual endurance. **5.** unmanageably rough, unruly, or vicious. **6.** difficult to accomplish; laborious. **7.** severe; rigorous. [ME] —*n.* a lawless person; a rowdy; ruffian. —**tough' ness** *n.*

tough•en (TUF ən) *v.t. & v.i.* make or become tough or tougher.

tou•pee (too PAY) *n.* a man's wig worn to cover baldness or a bald spot. [< F *toupet* tuft of hair]

tour (tuur) *n.* **1.** a trip, as for inspection or sightseeing, or for presenting a performance. **2.** a turn or shift, as of service. —*v.t. & v.i.* go on a tour (of). [ME]

tour de force (TUUR də FORS) *French* a feat of remarkable strength or skill.

tour•ist (TUUR ist) *n.* one who makes a pleasure trip. —*adj.* in tourist-class accommodations.

tourist class the least costly class of accommodations on a ship or plane.

tour•na•ment (TUUR nə mənt) *n.* **1.** any contest of skill involving a number of competitors and a series of games: *a chess tournament.* **2.** In medieval times, a pageant in which two opposing parties of men in armor contended on horseback in mock combat. [ME *tornement*]

tour•ney (TUUR nee) *n.* a tournament. —*v.i.* take part in a tournament; tilt. [ME *tourneie*]

tour•ni•quet (TUR ni kit) *n. Surg.* a bandage, etc., for stopping the flow of blood through an artery by compression. [< F]

tou•sle (TOW zəl) *v.t.* **•sled, •sling** disarrange or disorder, as the hair or dress. [ME *touselen*]

tout (towt) *Informal v.t. & v.i.* **1.** seek patronage, votes, etc. **2.** advertise or praise excessively. **3.** in horse racing, provide information about (a horse), usu. for a fee. **4.** spy on (a horse in training) to gain betting information. [ME *tuten* peer] —*n.* one who touts. —**tout'er** *n.*

tout de suite (toot SWEET) *French* immediately.

tow[1] (tow) *n.* coarse, short hemp or flax fiber prepared for spinning. [ME]

tow[2] (toh) *v.t.* pull or drag, as by a rope, chain, etc. [ME *towen*] —*n.* **1.** the act of towing, or the state of being towed. **2.** that which is towed. **3.** a towline. —**take in tow** take charge of.

to•ward (tord) *prep.* **1.** in the direction of; facing. **2.** with respect to; regarding: his attitude *toward* children. **3.** in anticipation of; for: an effort *toward* peace. **4.** approaching in time; about: arriving *toward* evening. Also **to•wards** (tordz). [ME]

tow•el (TOW əl) *n.* a cloth or paper for drying anything by wiping. —*v.t.* **tow•eled, tow•el•ing** wipe or dry with a towel. [ME]

tow•el•ing (TOW ə ling) *n.* cloth used for towels.

tow•er (TOW ər) *n.* **1.** a tall, usu. narrow structure, sometimes part of a larger building. **2.** any similar tall structure or object, often erected for a specific use: a water *tower*. [ME *tour*] —*v.i.* rise or stand like a tower. —**tow'ered** *adj.*

tow•er•ing (TOW ər ing) *adj.* **1.** like a tower; lofty. **2.** unusually high or great; outstanding. **3.** intense.

tow•head (TOH HED) *n.* a head of very light-colored hair; also, a person having such hair. [< TOW¹ + HEAD] —**tow'head'ed** *adj.*

tow•line (TOH LIN) *n.* a heavy rope or cable used in towing.

town (town) *n.* **1.** any considerable collection of dwellings and other buildings, larger than a village but smaller than a city. **2.** the inhabitants of such a community. **3.** a township (def. 1). **4.** any closely settled urban district. —**on the town** *Informal* on a round of pleasure. —**go to town** *Informal* act with speed and efficiency; be successful. [ME *toun* enclosure]

town meeting an assembly of qualified voters for the purpose of transacting town business.

town•ship (TOWN SHIP) *n.* **1.** a territorial subdivision of a county with certain corporate powers of municipal government. **2.** a unit of area in surveys of U.S. public lands, normally six miles square.

towns•peo•ple (TOWNZ PEE pəl) *n.pl.* people who live in towns or in a particular town or city. Also **towns•folk** (TOWNZ FOHK).

tow•path (TOH PATH) *n.* a path along a river or canal used by draft animals, etc. for towing boats.

tox•e•mi•a (tok SEE mee ə) *n. Pathol.* blood poisoning. [< NL] —**tox•e•mic** (tok SEE mik) *adj.*

tox•ic (TOK sik) *adj.* of or caused by poison; poisonous. [< LL *toxicus*] —**tox•ic•i•ty** (tok SIS i tee) *n.*

tox•i•col•o•gy (TOK si KOL ə jee) *n.* the science that treats of the origin, properties, etc., of poisons. —**tox•i•co•log•i•cal** (TOK si kə LOJ i kəl) *adj.* —**tox'i•col'o•gist** *n.*

tox•in (TOK sin) *n.* **1.** a poisonous compound developed by animal, vegetable, or bacterial organisms and acting as a causative agent in many diseases. **2.** any toxic matter generated in living or dead organisms.

toy (toi) *n.* **1.** a plaything. **2.** any object of little importance or value; a trifle. **3.** a small ornament or trinket. [ME *toye*] —*v.i.* trifle; play. —*adj.* made to be used as or resembling a toy.

trace¹ (trays) *n.* **1.** a mark left by some past event or agent. **2.** a barely detectable quantity; touch. —*v.t.* **traced, trac•ing 1.** follow the tracks, course, or development of. **2.** follow (tracks etc.). **3.** discover by examination or investigation; determine. **4.** copy (a drawing etc.) on a superimposed transparent sheet. **5.** form (letters etc.) with careful strokes. [ME *tracen*] — **trace'a•bil'i•ty** *n.* —**trace'a•ble** *adj.*

trace² *n.* one of two side straps or chains for connecting the collar of a harness with a vehicle. —**kick over the traces** throw off control; become unmanageable. —*v.t.* **traced, trac•ing** fasten with or as with traces.

trac•er (TRAY sər) *n.* **1.** one of various instruments used in tracing drawings etc. **2.** an inquiry forwarded from one point to another, to trace missing mail. **3.** a radioactive substance introduced into the body for the purpose of following the processes of metabolism, the course of a disease, etc.

tra•che•a (TRAY kee ə) *n. pl.* **•che•ae** (-kee I) or **•che•as** *Anat.* the duct by which air passes out of the larynx: also called *windpipe*. [ME *trache*] —**tra'che•al** *adj.*

tra•che•os•to•my (TRAY kee OS tə mee) *n. pl.* **•mies** *Surg.* an opening made into the trachea from the outside of the neck, to facilitate breathing.

tra•che•ot•o•my (TRAY kee OT ə mee) *n. pl.* **•mies** *Surg.* the operation of cutting into the trachea.

trac•ing (TRAY sing) *n.* **1.** a copy made by tracing on transparent paper. **2.** a record made by an automatically registering instrument.

track (trak) *n.* **1.** a mark or trail left by the passage of anything. **2.** any regular path; course. **3.** any kind of racetrack; also, sports performed on such a course. **4.** a set of rails or a rail on which trains etc. may travel. **5. a** a groove on a phonograph record. **b** one of the parallel recording paths of a magnetic tape. **c** a data-recording path on a computer disk, tape, or drum. —**keep track of 1.** keep in touch with. **2.** follow the development of. **3.** be aware of; remember. —**in one's tracks** right where one is. —**lose track of** fail to keep in touch with. —**make tracks** hurry; run away in haste. [ME *trak*] —*v.t.* **1.** follow the tracks of; trail. **2.** discover, pursue, or follow by means of marks or indications. **3.** make tracks upon or with. —**track'a•ble** *adj.* —**track'er** *n.* —**track'less** *adj.*

track record a record of performance.

tract[1] (trakt) *n.* **1.** an extended area of land. **2.** *Anat.* an extensive region of the body, esp. one comprising a system of parts or organs: the alimentary *tract.* [< L *tractus* stretch]

tract[2] *n.* a treatise or pamphlet on a religious or political subject. [ME *tracte*]

trac•ta•ble (TRAK tə bəl) *adj.* **1.** easily led or controlled; docile. **2.** readily worked or handled; malleable. [< L *tractabilis* workable] —**tract'a•bil'i•ty** *n.* —**tract'a•bly** *adv.*

trac•tion (TRAK shən) *n.* **1.** the act of drawing over a surface. **2.** the state of being drawn, or the power employed. **3.** adhesive or rolling friction, as of wheels on a track. [< L *tractus* pulled]

trac•tor (TRAK tər) *n.* **1.** a powerful, motor-driven vehicle used to draw a plow etc. **2.** an automotive vehicle with a driver's cab, used to haul trailers. [< NL]

trade (trayd) *n.* **1.** a business; esp., a skilled handicraft. **2.** mercantile traffic; commerce. **3.** an exchange, as in barter, buying and selling, etc. **4.** a firm's customers. **5.** customary pursuit; occupation. —*v.* **trad•ed, trad•ing** *v.t.* **1.** exchange for something comparable; barter. —*v.i.* **2.** engage in commerce or in business. **3.** make an exchange. —**trade on** make advantageous use of. [ME]

trade-in (TRAYD IN) *n.* something given or accepted in part payment for something else.

trade journal a periodical publishing news and discussions of a particular trade or business.

trade•mark (TRAYD MAHRK) *n.* **1.** a name, design, etc., officially registered and used by merchants and manufacturers to distinguish their goods from goods made or sold by others. **2.** any distinctive characteristic. —*v.t.* **1.** label with a trademark. **2.** register as a trademark.

trade name 1. the name by which an article, process, service, or the like is designated in trade. **2.** a style or name of a business house.

trad•er (TRAY dər) *n.* **1.** one who trades. **2.** any vessel employed in trade.

trades•peo•ple (TRAYDZ PEE pəl) *n.pl.* people engaged in trade; esp., shopkeepers.

trade union a labor union of workers in a particular craft.

trade wind *Meteorol.* either of two steady winds blowing in the same course toward the equator, one from the northeast on the north side of the equator, the other from the southeast on the south side.

tra•di•tion (trə DISH ən) *n.* **1.** the knowledge, doctrines, customs, and practices transmitted from generation to generation; also, the transmission of such knowledge, doctrines, etc. **2.** the historic conceptions and usages of a school of art, literature, etc. **3.** a custom so long continued that it has almost the force of a law. [ME *tradicioun*] —**tra•di'tion•al** *adj.* —**tra•di'tion•al•ism** *n.* —**tra•di'tion•al•ist** *n.*

tra•duce (trə DOOS) *v.t.* **-duced, -duc•ing** defame; slander. [< L *traducere*] —**tra•duc'er** *n.*

traf•fic (TRAF ik) *n.* **1.** the movement or passage of vehicles, pedestrians, ships, etc. along a route; also, the vehicles, pedestrians, etc. **2.** buying and selling; trade. **3.** the business of transportation; also, the freight or passengers carried. **4.** the messages, signals, etc. handled by a communications system. **5.** unlawful or improper trade. [< MF *trafique*] —*v.i.* **-ficked, -fick•ing 1.** engage in buying and selling; do business, esp., illegally: with *in.* **2.** have dealings: with *with.* —**traf'fick•er** *n.*

tra•ge•di•an (trə JEE dee ən) *n.* **1.** an actor in tragedy. **2.** a writer of tragedies. [< MF *tragedien*]

tra•ge•di•enne (trə JEE dee EN) *n.* an actress of tragedy. [< F]

trag•e•dy (TRAJ i dee) *n. pl.* **-dies 1.** a calamitous or fatal event or course of events; disaster. **2.** a form of drama in which the protagonist comes to disaster through a character flaw or is crushed by social and psychological forces. [ME *tragedie*]

trag•ic (TRAJ ik) *adj.* **1.** involving death,

trail

calamity, or suffering. **2.** pertaining to or having the nature of tragedy. **3.** appropriate to or like tragedy, esp. in drama. Also **trag′i•cal.** [< L *tragicus* of tragedy] **—trag′i•cal•ly** *adv.*

trail (trayl) *v.t.* **1.** draw along lightly over a surface; also, drag or draw after: *trail* a robe. **2.** follow the track of; track. **3.** follow or lag behind, esp. in a race. **—v.i. 4.** hang or float loosely so as to drag along a surface. **5.** grow along the ground or over rocks, bushes, etc. in a loose, creeping way. **6.** follow behind loosely; stream. **7.** lag behind; straggle. [ME *trailen* pull] **—n. 1.** a path or track made by the passage of persons or animals. **2.** the tracks or other traces of an animal followed by a hunter. **3.** anything drawn behind or in the wake of something.

trail•blaz•er (TRAYl BLAY zər) *n.* **1.** one who blazes a trail. **2.** a pioneer in any field.

trail•er (TRAY lər) *n.* **1.** one who or that which trails. **2.** a vehicle drawn by another having motive power. **3.** a vehicle drawn by a car or truck and used as a dwelling. **4.** a short motion-picture film made up of scenes from a coming feature picture, used for advertising.

train (trayn) *n.* **1.** a continuous line of coupled railway cars. **2.** a set of connected things; series; sequence. **3.** a retinue. **4.** an extension of a dress skirt, trailing behind the wearer. **5.** a succession or line of vehicles, people, or animals en route. **—v.t. 1.** make proficient or qualified by instruction, drill, etc.; educate. **2.** make obedient or capable of performing tricks, as an animal. **3.** bring into a required physical condition by diet and exercise. **4.** develop into a fixed shape: *train* a plant on a trellis. **5.** aim, as a gun. **—v.i. 6.** undergo a course of training. [ME] **—train′a•ble** *adj.* **—train′er** *n.* **—train′ing** *n.*

train•ee (tray NEE) *n.* one who undergoes training.

traipse (trayps) *v.i.* **traipsed, traips•ing** *Informal* walk about in an idle or aimless manner.

trait (trayt) *n.* a distinguishing feature or quality of character. [< MF]

trai•tor (TRAY tər) *n.* one who betrays a trust; esp., one who commits treason. [ME *traitre*] **—trai′tor•ous** *adj.*

tra•jec•to•ry (trə JEK tə ree) *n. pl.* **•ries** the path described by an object moving in space; esp., the path of a projectile. [< NL *trajectoria*]

tram•mel (TRAM əl) *n. Usu. pl.* that which limits freedom or activity; an impediment; hindrance. [ME *tramayle* net] **—v.t. trammeled, tram•mel•ing 1.** hinder or obstruct; restrict. **2.** entangle in or as in a snare.

tramp (tramp) *v.i.* **1.** walk or hike. **2.** walk heavily or firmly. **—v.t. 3.** walk or wander through. **4.** walk on heavily; trample. [ME *trampen*] **—n. 1.** a poor wanderer; a vagrant; vagabond. **2.** a heavy, continued tread. **3.** the sound of heavy marching or walking. **4.** a long walk; hike. **5.** a steamer that picks up freight wherever it can be obtained: also **tramp steamer. 6.** a sexually promiscuous woman.

tram•ple (TRAM pəl) *v.* **•pled, •pling** *v.t.* **1.** tread on heavily or ruthlessly. **—v.i. 2.** tread heavily. **—n.** the act or sound of trampling.

tram•po•line (TRAM pə LEEN) *n.* a section of strong canvas stretched on a frame, on which an acrobat, athlete, etc. may bound or spring. [< Ital. *trampolino* springboard]

trance (trans) *n.* **1.** a condition characterized by the absence of conscious control over one's actions, as in hypnosis. **2.** a dreamlike, bewildered state; daze. **3.** a state of deep abstraction. [ME *traunce*] **—v.t. tranced, tranc•ing** put into or as into a trance.

tran•quil (TRANG kwil) *adj.* **1.** free from mental agitation or disturbance; calm. **2.** quiet and motionless. [< L *tranquillus*] **—tran•quil′li•ty** (trang KWIL i tee) or **tran•quil′i•ty** *n.* **—tran′quil•ly** *adv.*

tran•quil•ize (TRANG kwə LIZ) *v.t. & v.i.* **•ized, •iz•ing** make or become tranquil. Also **tran′quil•lize** *n.*

tran•quil•iz•er (TRANG kwə LI zər) *n.* **1.** one who or that which tranquilizes. **2.** *Med.* a drug able to reduce nervous tension. Also **tran′quil•liz′er.**

trans- *prefix* **1.** across; beyond; on the other side of:

transalpine	trans-Canadian
transarctic	transcontinental
transatlantic	transdesert
transborder	transequatorial
transfrontier	transpacific
transisthmian	transpolar
transoceanic	trans-Siberian

2. through: **transpierce 3.** into another state: **transform, transliterate 4.** surpassing; transcending; beyond:

transconscious　　**transmundane**
transhuman　　　　**transnational**
transmaterial　　　**transphysical**
transmental　　　　**transrational**
[< L *trans* across, beyond, over]

trans·act (tran ZAKT) *v.t.* carry through; accomplish; do. [< L *transactus* accomplished] —**trans·ac'tor** *n.*

trans·ac·tion (tran ZAK shən) *n.* **1.** the act of transacting, or the state of being transacted. **2.** something transacted; esp., a business deal. **3.** *pl.* published reports, as of a society. —**trans·ac'tion·al** *adj.*

tran·scend (tran SEND) *v.t.* **1.** rise above in excellence or degree. **2.** overstep or exceed as a limit. [ME] —**tran·scen'dent** *adj.* —**tran·scen'dence, tran·scen'den·cy** *n.*

tran·scen·den·tal (TRAN sen DEN tl) *adj.* **1.** of very high degree; transcendent. **2.** beyond or contrary to common sense or experience.

tran·scen·den·tal·ism (TRAN sen DEN tl IZ əm) *n.* **1.** *Philos.* any of several doctrines holding that reality is essentially mental or spiritual in nature. **2.** the state or quality of being transcendental. —**tran'scen·den'tal·ist** *n. & adj.*

tran·scribe (tran SKRĪB) *v.t.* •**scribed,** •**scrib·ing 1.** copy or recopy in handwriting or typewriting. **2.** *Telecom.* make a recording of (a radio program). **3.** adapt (a musical composition) for a change of instrument or voice. [< L *transcribere* copy off] —**tran·scrib'er** *n.*

tran·script (TRAN skript) *n.* **1.** an exact copy. **2.** an official record. **3.** an official report of a student's academic record.

tran·scrip·tion (tran SKRIP shən) *n.* **1.** the act of transcribing. **2.** a copy; transcript. **3.** *Telecom.* a recording of a performance made for a later radio broadcast. **4.** *Music* the adaptation of a composition for some other instrument or voice.

tran·sect (tran SEKT) *v.t.* cut across; dissect transversely. —**tran·sec·tion** (tran SEK shən) *n.*

tran·sept (TRAN sept) *n. Archit.* one of the side projections between the nave and choir of a cross-shaped church. [< NL *transeptum*]

trans·fer (trans FUR) *v.* •**ferred,** •**fer·ring** *v.t.* **1.** carry or cause to pass from one person or place to another. **2.** make over possession of to another. **3.** convey (a drawing) from one surface to another. —*v.i.* **4.** transfer oneself. **5.** be transferred. **6.** change to

another bus, school, etc. [ME *transferren*] —*n.* (TRANS fər) **1.** the act of transferring, or the state of being transferred: also **trans·fer·al** or **trans·fer·ral** (trans FUR əl). **2.** that which is transferred, as a design. **3.** a ticket entitling a passenger to change to another public vehicle. —**trans·fer'a·bil'i·ty** *n.* —**trans·fer'a·ble** *adj.* —**trans·fer'ence** *n.*

trans·fig·ure (trans FIG yər) *v.t.* •**ured,** •**ur·ing 1.** change the outward form or appearance of. **2.** make glorious; idealize. [ME *transfiguren* change shape] —**trans·fig'u·ra'tion** *n.*

trans·fix (trans FIKS) *v.t.* •**fixed, •fix·ing 1.** pierce through; impale. **2.** fix in place by impaling. **3.** make motionless, as with horror, awe, etc. [< L *transfixus* pierced through]

trans·form (trans FORM) *v.t.* **1.** change the form, appearance, character, or condition of. **2.** *Electr.* change the potential or flow of (a current), as with a transformer. —*v.i.* **3.** be or become changed. [ME *transformen* change shape]

trans·for·ma·tion (TRANS fər MAY shən) *n.* **1.** any change. **2.** the act of transforming, or the state of being transformed. **3.** *Ling.* a change from one construction to another, considered more or less equivalent, according to the syntactic laws of a language, as, in English, from active to passive. —**trans'for·ma'tion·al** *adj.*

trans·form·er (trans FOR mər) *n.* **1.** one who or that which transforms. **2.** *Electr.* a device for altering the ratio of current to voltage in AC circuits.

trans·fuse (trans FYOOZ) *v.t.* •**fused,** •**fus·ing 1.** pour from one vessel to another. **2.** cause to be imparted or instilled. **3.** *Med.* transfer (blood) from one person or animal to another. [ME *transfusen* transfer] —**trans·fus'i·ble** *adj.* —**trans·fu'sion** (trans FYOO zhən) *n.*

trans·gress (trans GRES) *v.t. & v.i.* **1.** break (a law, oath, etc.). **2.** pass beyond or over (limits); exceed; trespass. [< L *transgressus* stepped across] —**trans·gres'sion** (-GRESH ən) *n.* —**trans·gres'sor** *n.*

tran·sient (TRAN shənt) *adj.* **1.** passing away quickly; of short duration. **2.** not permanent; temporary. —*n.* one who or that which is transient; esp., a lodger or boarder who remains for a short time. [< L *transiens* passing] —**tran'sien·cy** *n.* —**tran'sient·ly** *adv.*

tran·sis·tor (tran ZIS tər) n. *Electronics* a miniature device for control and amplification of current flow, made of semiconducting materials. [< TRANS(FER) + (RES)ISTOR]

tran·sis·tor·ize (tran ZIS tə RĪZ) v.t. •ized, •iz·ing equip with transistors.

tran·sit (TRAN sit) n. 1. the act of passing over or through; passage. 2. the act of carrying across or through; conveyance. 3. a transition or change. 4. a surveying instrument for measuring horizontal and vertical angles. —v.t. pass through or across. [ME]

tran·si·tion (tran ZISH ən) n. 1. the act or state of passing from one place, condition, or action to another; change. 2. the time, period, or place of such passage. 3. a sentence, musical passage, etc. that leads from one subject or theme to another. —**tran·si′tion·al** adj. —**tran·si′tion·al·ly** adv.

tran·si·tive (TRAN si tiv) adj. 1. *Gram.* of a transitive verb or verbs. 2. capable of passing. —n. *Gram.* a transitive verb. [< LL *transitivus*] —**tran′si·tive·ly** adv.

transitive verb a verb that requires a direct object to complete its meaning.

tran·si·to·ry (TRAN si TOR ee) adj. existing for a short time only. [ME *transitorie*] —**tran′si·to′ri·ness** n.

trans·late (trans LAYT) v. •lat·ed, •lat·ing v.t. 1. express in another language. 2. explain in other words; interpret. 3. change into another form; transform. —v.i. 4. act as translator. 5. admit of translation: This book *translates* easily. [ME *translaten*] —**trans·lat′a·ble** adj. —**trans·la′tor** n.

trans·la·tion (trans LAY shən) n. 1. the act of translating, or the state of being\translated. 2. a work translated into another language, a version.

trans·lit·er·ate (trans LIT ə RAYT) v.t. •at·ed, •at·ing represent (a letter or word) by the alphabetic characters of another language. —**trans·lit′er·a′tion** n.

trans·lu·cent (trans LOO sənt) adj. allowing the passage of light, but not permitting a clear view of any object. [< L *translucere* shine through] —**trans·lu′cen·cy** n.

trans·mi·grate (trans MĪ grayt) v.i. •grat·ed, •grat·ing migrate from one place or condition to another. [ME] —**trans′mi·gra′tion** n.

trans·mis·sion (trans MISH ən) n. 1. the act of transmitting, or the state of being transmitted. 2. that which is transmitted, as a

radio broadcast. 3. *Mech.* a a device that transmits power from the engine of an automobile to the driving wheels. b the gears for changing speed.

trans·mit (trans MIT) v.t. •mit·ted, •mit·ting 1. send from one place or person to another. 2. pass on by heredity. 3. pass on or communicate (news, information, etc.). 4. *Telecom.* send out by means of electromagnetic waves. [ME *transmitten*] —**trans·mis·si·ble** (trans MIS ə bəl) adj. —**trans·mis′si·bil′i·ty** n. —**trans·mit′al** n. —**trans·mit′ta·ble** adj.

trans·mit·ter (trans MIT ər) n. 1. one who or that which transmits. 2. a telegraphic sending instrument. 3. the part of a telephone that converts sound waves into electrical waves. 4. *Telecom.* the part of a radio or television system that generates, modulates, and transmits electromagnetic waves to the antenna.

trans·mute (trans MYOOT) v.t. •mut·ed, •mut·ing change in nature, form, or quality; transform. [ME] —**trans·mut′a·bil′i·ty** n. —**trans·mut′a·ble** adj.

tran·som (TRAN səm) n. 1. a small window above a door or window, usu. hinged to a horizontal crosspiece; also, the crosspiece. 2. a horizontal construction dividing a window. [ME *traunsom*]

trans·par·en·cy (trans PAR ən see) n. pl. •cies 1. the quality of being transparent. 2. something transparent, as a slide.

trans·par·ent (trans PAR ənt) adj. 1. admitting the passage of light and permitting a clear view of objects beyond. 2. easy to understand; obvious. 3. without guile; candid. 4. diaphanous; sheer. [ME] —**trans·par′ent·ly** adv.

tran·spire (tran SPĪR) v. •spired, •spir·ing v.t. 1. give off (waste products) from the surface of the body, leaves, etc.; exhale. —v.i. 2. give off waste products, as the surface of the body, leaves, etc. 3. become known. 4. happen; occur. [< MF *transpirer*] —**tran·spi·ra·tion** (TRAN spə RAY shən) n.

trans·plant (trans PLANT) v.t. 1. remove and plant in another place. 2. remove and settle or establish for residence in another place. 3. *Surg.* transfer (tissue or organ) from the original site to another part of the same individual or to another individual. —n. (TRANS PLANT) 1. that which is transplanted. 2. the act of transplanting. [ME] —**trans′plan·ta′tion** n.

trans·port (trans PORT) v.t. 1. carry or convey from one place to another. **2.** carry away with emotion. **3.** carry into banishment, esp. beyond the sea. [ME *transporten*] —*n.* (TRANS port) **1.** a vessel used to transport troops, military supplies, etc. **2.** an aircraft used to transport passengers, mail, etc. **3.** a state of ecstasy. **4.** the act of transporting. —**trans·port'a·bil'i·ty** *n.* —**trans·port'a·ble** *adj.*

trans·por·ta·tion (TRANS pər TAY shən) *n.* **1.** the act of transporting, or the state of being transported. **2.** a means of transporting, as a vehicle. **3.** a charge for conveyance.

trans·pose (trans POHZ) *v.t.* **·posed, ·pos·ing 1.** reverse the order or change the place of. **2.** *Music* change the key of (a chord, melody, or composition). —*v.i.* **3.** *Music* play in another key. [ME *transposen*] —**trans·pos'a·ble** *adj.* —**trans·po·si·tion** (TRANS pə ZISH ən) *n.*

trans·sex·u·al (trans SEK shoo əl) *n.* one whose sex has been altered by surgery and hormone treatment. —*adj.* of, pertaining to, or characteristic of transsexuals.

tran·sub·stan·ti·a·tion (TRAN səb STAN shee AY shən) *n.* *Theol.* the doctrine that the substance of the eucharistic elements is converted into the body and blood of Christ. [ME *transubstanciacioun*]

trans·verse (trans VURS) *adj.* lying or being across or from side to side. [< L *transversus*] —*n.* that which is transverse. —**trans·verse'ly** *adv.*

trans·ves·tite (trans VES tīt) *n.* one who wears the clothes of the opposite sex. [< G *Transvestit*] —**trans·ves·tism** (trans VES tiz əm) *n.*

trap[1] (trap) *n.* **1.** a device for catching game or other animals. **2.** anything by which a person may be betrayed or taken unawares. **3.** *Mech.* a U- or S-bend in a pipe etc. that prevents a return flow, as of noxious gas. **4.** in trapshooting, a contrivance for hurling objects into the air for shooting at. **5.** in golf, an obstacle or hazard: a sand *trap.* **6.** a light, two-wheeled carriage suspended by springs. **7.** *pl.* percussion instruments. —*v.* **trapped, trap·ping** *v.t.* **1.** catch in a trap; ensnare. **2.** stop or hold (a gas, liquid, etc.) by some obstruction. **3.** provide with a trap. —*v.i.* **4.** set traps for game. **5.** be a trapper. [ME *trappe*]

trap[2] *n.* *Geol.* a dark, fine-grained igneous rock, as basalt, etc. Also **trap'rock'**. [< Sw. *trapp* stair]

trap·door (TRAP DOR) *n.* a door to cover an opening, as in a floor or roof.

tra·peze (tra PEEZ) *n.* a short swinging bar, suspended by two ropes, used by gymnasts. [< F *trapèze*]

trap·e·zoid (TRAP ə ZOID) *n.* *Geom.* a four-sided figure of which two sides are parallel. [< NL *trapezoides*] —**trap'e·zoi'dal** *adj.*

trap·per (TRAP ər) *n.* one who traps animals for their pelts.

trap·pings (TRAP ingz) *n.pl.* adornments of any kind; embellishments. [ME]

trap·shoot·ing (TRAP shoo ting) *n.* the sport of shooting clay pigeons sent up from spring traps. —**trap'shoot'er** *n.*

trash (trash) *n.* **1.** worthless or waste matter; rubbish. **2.** a despicable or worthless person; such persons collectively. —*v.t.* **1.** strip of leaves; prune. **2.** *Slang* **a** vandalize or destroy. **b** disparage. [ME *trasches* rubbish] —**trash'i·ness** *n.* —**trash'y** *adj.* **trash·i·er, trash·i·est**

trau·ma (TROW mə) *n. pl.* **·mas** or **·ma·ta** (-mə tə) **1.** *Pathol.* any injury to the body caused by shock, violence, etc. **2.** *Psychiatry* a severe emotional shock. [< Gk. *traûma* wound] —**trau·mat·ic** (trə MAT ik) *adj.*

tra·vail (trə VAYL) *v.i.* **1.** toil; labor. **2.** suffer the pangs of childbirth. —*n.* **1.** strenuous physical or mental labor. **2.** labor in childbirth. [ME]

trav·el (TRAV əl) *v.* **·eled, ·el·ing** *v.i.* **1.** go from one place to another. **2.** proceed; advance. **3.** pass or be transmitted, as light, sound, etc. **4.** *Mech.* move in a fixed path, as part of a mechanism. —*v.t.* **5.** move or journey across or through; traverse. —*n.* **1.** the act of traveling. **2.** *pl.* a trip or journey. **3.** a movement or progress of any kind. **4.** *Mech.* **a** the full course of a moving part in one direction. **b** length of stroke, as of a piston. [ME] —**trav'el·er** *n.*

trav·erse (trə VURS) *v.t.* **·ersed, ·ers·ing 1.** pass over, across, or through. **2.** move back and forth over or along. **3.** turn (a gun, lathe, etc.) to right or left; swivel. —*n.* (TRAV ərs) a part, as of a machine or structure, placed across or traversing another, as a crosspiece, crossbeam, transom, etc. —*adj.* (TRAV ərs) transverse; lying or being across. [ME *traversen* cross] —**trav·ers'a·ble** *adj.* —**trav·er'sal** *n.*

trav·es·ty (TRAV ə stee) *n. pl.* **·ties** a grotesque imitation; burlesque. —*v.t.* **·tied,**

•ty•ing make a travesty on; parody. [< F *travesti* disguised]

trawl (trawl) *n.* **1.** a fishing line having many baited hooks. **2.** a fishing net shaped like a flattened bag, for towing on the bottom of the ocean by a boat. —*v.t. & v.i.* fish or catch with a trawl. [< MDu. *tragel* dragnet] —**trawl′er** *n.*

tray (tray) *n.* a flat receptacle with a low rim, used to carry, hold, or display articles. [ME]

treach•er•ous (TRECH ər əs) *adj.* **1.** traitorous; perfidious; disloyal. **2.** having a deceptive appearance; unreliable. —**treach′ •er•ous•ly** *adv.* —**treach′er•ous•ness** *n.*

treach•er•y (TRECH ə ree) *n. pl.* **•er•ies** violation of allegiance, confidence, or faith; treason. [ME *trecherie*]

tread (tred) *v.* **trod,** **trod•den** or **trod,** **tread•ing** *v.t.* **1.** step or walk on, over, or along. **2.** press with the feet; trample. **3.** accomplish in walking or in dancing: *tread* a measure. —*v.i.* **4.** step or walk. **5.** trample: usu. with *on.* —*n.* **1.** the act, manner, or sound of treading or walking. **2.** the horizontal part of a step in a staircase. **3.** a part that makes contact with the ground, as of a wheel, tire, or shoe. [ME *treden*]

trea•dle (TRED l) *n.* a lever operated by the foot, usu. to cause rotary motion. —*v.i.* **•led,** **•ling** work a treadle. [ME *tredel* step]

tread•mill (TRED mil.) *n.* **1.** a mechanism rotated by the walking motion of one or more persons or by an animal or animals. **2.** any wearisome or monotonous work, activity, routine, etc.

trea•son (TREE zən) *n.* betrayal of one's sovereign or government. [ME *treisoun*]

trea•son•a•ble (TREE zə nə bəl) *adj.* of, involving, or characteristic of treason. Also **trea′son•ous.**

treas•ure (TREZH ər) *n.* **1.** riches accumulated or possessed. **2.** one who or that which is regarded as valuable, precious, or rare. —*v.t.* **•ured,** **•ur•ing** **1.** lay up in store; accumulate. **2.** retain carefully, as in the mind. **3.** set a high value upon; prize. [ME *tresor*]

treas•ur•er (TREZH ər ər) *n.* an officer who has charge of funds or revenues.

trea•sure-trove (TREZH ər TROHV) *n.* **1.** *Law* any treasure found hidden somewhere, the owner being unknown. **2.** any discovery that proves valuable. [ME]

treas•ur•y (TREZH ə ree) *n. pl.* **•ur•ies** **1.** the place where private or public funds or revenues are received, kept, and disbursed.

2. any public or private funds or revenues. **3.** a place where treasures are kept.

treat (treet) *v.t.* **1.** conduct oneself toward in a specified manner. **2.** look upon or regard in a specified manner: They *treat* the matter as a joke. **3.** subject to chemical or physical action, as for altering or improving. **4.** give medical or surgical attention to. **5.** deal with or develop (a subject). **6.** pay for the entertainment, food, or drink of: —*v.i.* **7.** handle a subject in writing or speaking: usu. with *of.* **8.** pay for another's entertainment or food. —*n.* **1.** something that gives unusual pleasure. **2.** entertainment furnished to another. [ME *treten*]

trea•tise (TREE tis) *n.* a formal written account of some subject. [ME *tretis*]

treat•ment (TREET mənt) *n.* **1.** the act, manner, or process of treating. **2.** the care of an illness by drugs, surgery, etc.

trea•ty (TREE tee) *n. pl.* **•ties** a formal agreement or compact between two or more states; also, the document containing such an agreement or compact. [ME *trete*]

tre•ble (TREB əl) *v.t. & v.i.* **•led,** **•ling** multiply by three; triple. —*adj.* **1.** threefold; triple. **2.** soprano. —*n.* **1.** *Music* a soprano voice, part, or instrument; also, the singer or player taking this part. **2.** high, piping sound. [ME] —**treb′ly** *adv.*

tree (tree) *n.* **1.** a perennial woody plant having usu. a single self-supporting trunk of considerable height, with branches and foliage growing at some distance above the ground. ♦ Collateral adjective: *arboreal.* **2.** something resembling a tree in form or outline; esp., a diagram showing family descent. —**up a tree** *Informal* in a position from which there is no retreat; cornered; also, in an embarrassing position. —*v.t.* **treed, tree•ing** **1.** force to climb or take refuge in a tree: *tree* a fugitive. **2.** *Informal* get the advantage of; corner. [ME]

tree•top (TREE TOP) *n.* the highest part of a tree.

tre•foil (TREE foil) *n.* **1.** any of a genus of plants having three-lobed leaves. **2.** a three-lobed architectural ornamentation. [ME]

trek (trek) *v.i.* **trekked, trek•king** travel, esp. slowly or arduously. —*n.* **1.** in South Africa, a journey or any part of it; esp., an organized migration. **2.** a slow or arduous journey. [< Afrikaans]

trel•lis (TREL is) *n.* **1.** a lattice of wood, metal, or other material, used as a screen or a support for vines, etc. **2.** a summerhouse, archway, etc., made from or consisting of such a structure. —*v.t.* **1.** interlace so as to form a trellis. **2.** furnish with or fasten on a trellis. [ME *trelis*]

trem·ble (TREM bəl) *v.i.* **·bled, ·bling 1.** shake, as with fear or weakness. **2.** have slight, irregular vibratory motion: The earth *trembled*. **3.** feel anxiety or fear. —*n.* the act or state of trembling. [ME *tremblen*] — **trem′bling·ly** *adv.* —**trem′·bly** *adj.*

tre·men·dous (tri MEN dəs) *adj.* **1.** extraordinarily large; vast. **2.** amazing; wonderful. **3.** causing astonishment by its magnitude, force, etc. [< L *tremendus*]

trem·or (TREM ər) *n.* **1.** a quick, vibratory movement; a shaking: earth *tremors*. **2.** any quivering or trembling, as of the body or limbs. [ME]

trem·u·lous (TREM yə ləs) *adj.* **1.** characterized or affected by trembling: *tremulous* speech. **2.** showing timidity or fear. — **trem′u·lous·ly** *adv.* —**trem′u·lous·ness** *n.*

trench (trench) *n.* **1.** a long, narrow excavation in the ground; ditch. **2.** a long irregular ditch, lined with a parapet of the excavated earth, to protect troops. [ME *trenche*] — *v.t.* **1.** dig a trench or trenches in. **2.** fortify with trenches. —*v.i.* **3.** dig trenches. **4.** cut; carve. —**trench′er** *n.*

trench·ant (TREN chənt) *adj.* **1.** cutting; incisive; keen. **2.** forceful; vigorous; effective. **3.** clearly defined; distinct. [ME *trenchaunt*] —**trench′an·cy** *n.*

trench·er·man (TREN chər mən) *n. pl.* **·men** a hearty eater.

trend (trend) *n.* a general course, inclination, or direction. —*v.i.* have or take a particular trend. [ME *trenden* turn]

trend·y (TREN dee) *adj.* **trend·i·er, trend·i·est** forming or following a fashionable trend. —**trend′i·ness** *n.*

trep·i·da·tion (TREP i DAY shən) *n.* **1.** a state of agitation or alarm. **2.** an involuntary trembling. [< L *trepidatus* trembled]

tres·pass (TRES pəs) *v.i.* **1.** commit an offense against another. **2.** intrude offensively; encroach; esp., enter wrongfully upon another's land. —*n.* **1.** any offense done to another. **2.** unlawful entry on another's land. [ME *trespas*] —**tres′pass·er** *n.*

tress (tres) *n.* **1.** a lock of human hair. **2.** *pl.* the hair of a woman or girl, esp. when worn loose. [ME *tresse*]

tres·tle (TRES əl) *n.* **1.** a beam or bar sup-

ported by four legs, for bearing platforms, etc. **2.** an open framework for supporting a railway bridge etc. [ME *trestel* crossbeam]

trey (tray) *n.* a card, domino, or die having three spots. [ME, three]

tri·ad (TRĪ ad) *n.* **1.** a group of three persons or things. **2.** *Music* a chord of three tones. [< Gk. *triás* three]

tri·al (trīl) *n.* **1.** the examination of the facts in a case before a court of law. **2.** the act of testing or proving by experience or use. **3.** the state of being tried or tested, as by suffering: hour of *trial*. **4.** an attempt or effort to do something; a try. —**on trial** in the process of being tried or tested. —*adj.* **1.** of or pertaining to a trial or trials. **2.** made, used, or performed in the course of trying or testing.

trial balloon any tentative plan or scheme advanced to test public reaction.

tri·an·gle (TRĪ ANG gəl) *n.* **1.** *Geom.* a plane figure bounded by three sides and having three angles. **2.** something resembling such a figure in shape or arrangement. **3.** a situation involving three persons. [ME] — **tri·an′gu·lar** (trī ANG gyə lər) *adj.*

tri·an·gu·late (trī ANG gyə LAYT) *v.t.* **·lat·ed, ·lat·ing 1.** divide into triangles. **2.** survey or determine a position using the principles of trigonometry. —*adj.* (trī ANG gyə lit) of or marked with triangles. — **tri·an′gu·la′tion** *n.*

tribe (trīb) *n.* **1.** a group of people, esp. a primitive or nomadic people, usu. characterized by common ancestry and customs. **2.** *Biol.* a group of plants or animals of indefinite rank. [ME] —**tri′bal** *adj.* —**tri′bal·ly** *adv.*

trib·u·la·tion (TRIB yə LAY shən) *n.* a condition of affliction and distress; suffering; also, that which causes it. [ME *tribulacion*]

tri·bu·nal (trī BYOON l) *n.* **1.** a court of justice. **2.** the seat set apart for judges etc. [< L, judgment seat]

trib·une (TRIB yoon) *n.* **1.** in Roman history, a magistrate chosen by the plebeians to protect them against patrician oppression. **2.** any champion of the people. [ME]

trib·u·tar·y (TRIB yə TER ee) *adj.* **1.** contributory: a *tributary* stream. **2.** offered or due as tribute: a *tributary* payment. **3.** paying tribute, as a state. —*n. pl.* **·tar·ies 1.** a person or state paying tribute. **2.** a stream flowing into a larger stream or body of water. [ME]

trib·ute (TRIB yoot) *n.* **1.** a speech, compliment, gift, etc. given as a sign of admiration, gratitude, or respect. **2.** payment by one state or ruler to another as a sign of submission or as the price of peace and protection. [ME *tribut* payment]

trice (trīs) *n.* an instant: now only in the phrase **in a trice.** [ME *tryse*]

tri·cen·ten·ni·al (TRĪ sen TEN ee əl) *adj. & n.* tercentenary.

tri·ceps (TRĪ seps) *n. Anat.* a large muscle at the back of the upper arm. [< NL]

trick (trik) *n.* **1.** a device for getting an advantage by deception; ruse. **2.** a practical joke; prank. **3.** a particular habit or manner; trait. **4.** a peculiar skill or knack. **5.** an act of legerdemain or magic. **6.** in card games, all the cards played in one round. —*v.t.* **1.** deceive or cheat; delude. **2.** dress or array: with *up* or *out*. [ME *trik*]

trick·er·y (TRIK ə ree) *n. pl.* **·er·ies** the practice of tricks; artifice; wiles.

trick·le (TRIK əl) *v.* **·led, ·ling** *v.i.* **1.** flow drop by drop or in a very thin stream. **2.** move slowly or bit by bit. —*v.t.* **3.** cause to trickle. [ME *triklen*] —*n.* **1.** the act or state of trickling. **2.** any slow and irregular movement.

trick·ster (TRIK stər) *n.* one who plays tricks; a cheat.

trick·y (TRIK ee) *adj.* **trick·i·er, trick·i·est** disposed to or characterized by trickery; deceitful; wily. —**trick′i·ly** *adv.* — **trick′i·ness** *n.*

tri·corn (TRĪ korn) *n.* a hat with the brim turned up on three sides. —*adj.* having three hornlike projections or corners. [< F *tricorne*]

tri·cy·cle (TRĪ si kəl) *n.* a three-wheeled vehicle; esp., such a vehicle with pedals.

tri·dent (TRĪD nt) *n.* a three-pronged fork. —*adj.* having three teeth or prongs: also **tri·den·tate** (trī DEN tayt).

tried (trīd) past tense, past participle of TRY. —*adj.* tested; trustworthy.

tri·en·ni·al (trī EN ee əl) *adj.* **1.** taking place every third year. **2.** lasting three years. —*n.* a third anniversary. —**tri·en′ni·al·ly** *adv.*

tri·fle (TRĪ fəl) *v.* **·fled, ·fling** *v.i.* **1.** treat something as of no value or importance; dally: with *with*. **2.** act or speak frivolously. **3.** play; toy. **4.** idle. —*v.t.* **5.** pass (time) in an idle and purposeless way. —*n.* anything of very little value or importance. —**a trifle** slightly: *a trifle short.* [ME *trufle*] —**tri′fler** *n.*

tri·fling (TRĪ fling) *adj.* **1.** frivolous. **2.** insignificant. —**tri′fling·ly** *adv.*

tri·fo·cal (trī FOH kəl) *adj.* **1.** having three focal lengths. **2.** *Optics* describing eyeglasses or a lens ground in three segments, for near, intermediate, and far vision. —*n. pl.* eyeglasses having trifocal lenses.

trig·ger (TRIG ər) *n.* **1.** the device pressed or squeezed to fire a firearm. **2.** any lever, release, etc. that begins a process or operation. —**quick on the trigger 1.** quick to shoot. **2.** quick to act; alert. [< Du. *trekker*] —*v.t.* cause to begin; initiate.

trig·o·nom·e·try (TRIG ə NOM i tree) *n.* the branch of mathematics that deals with the relations of the sides and angles of triangles. [< NL *trigonometria*] —**trig·o·no·met·ric** (TRIG ə nə ME trik) *adj.*

tri·lat·er·al (trī LAT ər əl) *adj.* having three sides. [< L *trilaterus*] —**tri·lat′er·al·ly** *adv.*

trill (tril) *v.t.* **1.** sing or play in a tremulous tone. **2.** *Phonet.* articulate with a trill. —*v.i.* **3.** give forth a tremulous sound. **4.** *Music* execute a trill. [ME *trillen*] —*n.* **1.** a tremulous utterance; warble. **2.** *Music* a rapid alternation of two tones a tone apart. **3.** *Phonet.* a rapid vibration of the tongue or uvula in the articulation of *r* in certain languages. [< Ital. *trillo*]

tril·lion (TRIL yən) *n.* **1.** a thousand billions, written as 1 followed by 12 zeros: a cardinal number: called a billion in Great Britain. **2.** *Brit.* a million billions, written as 1 followed by 18 zeros: a cardinal number. [< F] —**tril·ion** *adj.* —**tril′lionth** *adj. & n.*

tril·o·gy (TRIL ə jee) *n. pl.* **·gies** a group of three literary or dramatic compositions, each complete in itself, but continuing the same general subject. [< Gk. *trilogía*]

trim (trim) *v.* **trimmed, trim·ming** *v.t.* **1.** make neat by clipping. **2.** remove by cutting: usu. with *off* or *away*. **3.** put ornaments on; decorate. **4.** *Naut.* **a** adjust (sails) for sailing. **b** balance (a ship or aircraft) by adjusting cargo etc. —*v.i.* **5.** act so as to appear to favor both sides in a controversy. [ME *trimmen* prepare] —*n.* **1.** state of readiness or fitness. **2.** *Naut.* fitness for sailing. **3.** moldings, etc., as about the doors of a building. **4.** ornament; trimming. —*adj.* **trim·mer, trim·mest 1.** neat; orderly. **2.** compact; well-proportioned. —*adv.* in a trim manner: also **trim′ly.** —**trim′·mer** *n.* —**trim′ness** *n.*

tri·ma·ran (TRĪ mə RAN) *n.* a sailing vessel having three hulls.

trim·e·ter (TRIM ə tər) *n.* in prosody, a line of verse consisting of three metrical feet. —*adj.* consisting of three metrical feet. [< L *trimetrus* in three measures]

trim·ming (TRIM ing) *n.* **1.** something added for ornament. **2.** *pl.* fittings, as the hardware of a house. **3.** *pl.* the usual or proper accompaniments of an article or food. **4.** *pl.* that which is removed by trimming. **5.** *Informal* a defeat; a thrashing.

tri·ni·tro·tol·u·ene (trī NI troh TOL yoo EEN) *n. Chem.* a high explosive, used in warfare and as a blasting agent: also called *TNT.*

trin·i·ty (TRIN i tee) *n. pl.* **·ties** any union of three parts or elements in one; a trio. [ME *trinite*]

Trin·i·ty *n. Theol.* a threefold personality existing in the one divine being or substance; the union in one God of Father, Son, and Holy Spirit.

trin·ket (TRING kit) *n.* **1.** any small ornament, as of jewelry. **2.** a trivial object.

tri·o (TREE oh) *n. pl.* **tri·os 1.** any three things grouped or associated together. **2.** *Music* **a** a composition for three performers. **b** a group of three musicians that plays trios. [< F]

trip (trip) *n.* **1.** a journey or voyage. **2.** a misstep or stumble. **3.** an active, nimble step or movement. **4.** *Mech.* a device that triggers or releases a moving part or parts. **5.** a blunder; mistake. **6.** *Slang* the taking of a psychedelic drug, or the resulting mental experience. —*v.t.* & *v.i.* **tripped, tripping 1.** stumble or cause to stumble. **2.** move or perform quickly with light or small steps. **3.** commit or expose in an error. **4.** *Mech.* trigger or release. [ME *trippen*]

tri·par·tite (trī PAHR tīt) *adj.* **1.** divided into three parts or divisions; threefold: a *tripartite* leaf. **2.** pertaining to or concluded between three parties: a *tripartite* agreement. [ME]

tripe (trīp) *n.* **1.** a part of the stomach of a ruminant, used for food. **2.** *Slang* anything worthless; nonsense. [ME]

tri·ple (TRIP əl) *v.* **·pled, ·pling** *v.t.* **1.** make threefold in number or quantity. — *v.i.* **2.** be or become three times as many or as large. **3.** in baseball, hit a triple. —*adj.* **1.** consisting of three things or of three parts; threefold. **2.** multiplied by three. —*n.* **1.** a set or group of three. **2.** in baseball, a hit that enables the batter to reach third base. [ME] —**trip′ly** *adv.*

triple play in baseball, a play in which three putouts are made.

tri·plet (TRIP lit) *n.* **1.** a group of three of a kind. **2.** one of three children born at one birth. **3.** a group of three rhymed lines. **4.** *Music* a group of three equal notes performed in the time of two.

triple threat in football, a player expert at kicking, running, and passing.

trip·li·cate (TRIP li kit) *adj.* threefold; made in three copies. —*n.* one of three identical things. —*v.t.* **·cat·ed, ·cat·ing** (TRIP li KAYT) make three times as much or as many. [ME]

tri·pod (TRĪ pod) *n.* **1.** a stool etc. having three feet or legs. **2.** a three-legged stand for supporting a camera, transit, etc. [< L *tripus*]

trip·per (TRIP ər) *n.* **1.** one who trips. **2.** *Mech.* a trip or tripping mechanism.

trip·ping (TRIP ing) *adj.* nimble. —**trip′·ping·ly** *adv.*

trip·tych (TRIP tik) *n.* a triple picture or carving on three hinged panels, often depicting a religious subject. [< Gk. *tríptychos* having three folds]

tri·reme (TRĪ reem) *n.* an ancient Greek or Roman warship with three banks of oars. [< L *triremis*]

trite (trīt) *adj.* **trit·er, trit·est** made commonplace by repetition. [< L *tritus* rubbed] —**trite′ly** *adv.* —**trite′ness** *n.*

tri·umph (TRĪ əmf) *v.i.* **1.** win a victory; be victorious. **2.** rejoice over a victory; exult. —*n.* **1.** exultation over victory. **2.** the condition of being victorious; victory. [ME *triumphe*] —**tri·um·phal** (trī UM fəl), **tri·um·phant** (trī UM fənt) *adj.* — **tri·um′phant·ly** *adv.*

tri·um·vi·rate (trī UM vər it) *n.* a group of three men who exercise authority or control together. [< L *triumviratus*]

triv·et (TRIV it) *n.* a stand, esp., with three legs, for holding a hot dish or pot. [ME *trevet*]

triv·i·a (TRIV ee ə) *n.pl.* unimportant matters. [< NL]

triv·i·al (TRIV ee əl) *adj.* **1.** of little value or importance; trifling; insignificant. **2.** such as is found everywhere or every day; commonplace. **3.** occupied with trifles. [ME] — **triv′i·al·ly** *adv.*

triv·i·al·i·ty (TRIV ee AL i tee) *n. pl.* **·ties 1.** the state or quality of being trivial: also **triv'i·al·ness** (-əl nis) **2.** a trivial matter.

tro·che (TROH kee) *n.* a medicated lozenge, usu. circular. [ME *trocis* wheels]

tro·chee (TROH kee) *n.* **1.** in prosody, a metrical foot consisting of one long or accented syllable followed by one short or unaccented syllable. (). **2.** a line of verse made up of or characterized by such feet. [< F *trochée*] —**tro·cha·ic** (troh KAY ik) *adj.*

trod (trod) past tense and a past participle of TREAD.

trod·den (TROD n) a past participle of TREAD.

trog·lo·dyte (TROG lə DIT) *n.* **1.** a cave dweller. **2.** a hermit. **3.** a brutal or savage person. [< L *troglodytae* cave dwellers] —**trog'lo·dyt·ic** (-DIT ik) or **·i·cal** *adj.*

troi·ka (TROI kə) *n.* **1.** a Russian vehicle drawn by a team of three horses driven abreast. **2.** a ruling body of three. **3.** a group of three. [< Russian *tróika*]

troll¹ (trohl) *v.t. & v.i.* **1.** fish (for) with a moving line or lure. **2.** sing (parts of a round) in succession. **3.** roll or cause to roll; revolve. [ME *trollen*] —*n.* **1.** a round. **2.** in fishing, a spoon or other lure. —**troll'er** *n.*

troll² *n.* in Scandinavian folklore, a giant; later, a mischievous dwarf. [< Norw.]

trol·ley (TROL ee) *n. pl.* **·leys 1.** a streetcar: also **trolley car. 2.** a device that maintains contact with a conductor to convey current to an electric vehicle. **3.** a small truck or car for conveying material, as in a factory, mine, etc. —*v.t. & v.i.* convey or travel by trolley.

trol·lop (TROL əp) *n.* **1.** a slovenly woman. **2.** a prostitute.

trom·bone (trom BOHN) *n.* a brass instrument larger and lower in pitch than the trumpet: a **slide trombone** changes pitch by means of a U-shaped slide that can lengthen or shorten the air column: a **valve trombone** changes pitch by means of valves. [< Ital.] —**trom·bon'ist** *n.*

troop (troop) *n.* **1.** an assembled company; gathering. **2.** *Usu. pl.* a body of soldiers. **3.** the cavalry unit corresponding to a company of infantry. **4.** a body of Boy Scouts or Girl Scouts. —*v.i.* move along or gather as a troop or as a crowd. [< MF *trope*]

troop·er (TROO pər) *n.* **1.** a cavalryman. **2.** a mounted policeman. **3.** a state policeman.

trope (trohp) *n.* **1.** the figurative use of a word. **2.** loosely, a figure of speech. [< L *tropus*]

troph·ic (TROHF ik) *adj.* pertaining to nutrition and its processes. [< F *trophique*]

tro·phy (TROH fee) *n. pl.* **·phies** something symbolizing victory or success; as: **a** a cup etc. awarded for an achievement. **b** a mounted fish. **c** a weapon etc. captured from an enemy. [< F *trophée*]

trop·ic (TROP ik) *n.* **1.** *Geog.* either of two parallels of latitude 23°27' north and south of the equator, on which the sun is seen in the zenith on the days of its greatest declination, called respectively **tropic of Cancer** and **tropic of Capricorn. 2.** *pl.* the regions of the earth's surface between the tropics of Cancer and Capricorn. [ME *tropik*] —**trop'i·cal** *adj.*

trop·o·sphere (TROHP ə SFEER) *n. Meteorol.* the region of the atmosphere beneath the stratosphere, characterized by turbulence and by decreasing temperature with increasing altitude. —**trop·o·spher·ic** (TROHP ə SFER ik) *adj.*

trot (trot) *n.* **1.** a gait of a four-footed animal, esp. a horse, in which diagonal pairs of legs are moved almost simultaneously; also, the sound of this gait. **2.** a moderately rapid run. **3.** *Slang* a pony (def. 3). —*v.i.* **trot·ted, trot·ting** *v.i.* **1.** go at a trot. **2.** hurry. —*v.t.* **3.** ride at a trotting gait. —**trot out** bring forth for inspection, approval, etc. [ME *trotten*]

troth (trawth) *n.* **1.** good faith; fidelity. **2.** the act of pledging fidelity; esp., betrothal. [ME *trowthe* truth]

trot·ter (TROT ər) *n.* one who or that which trots; esp., a horse trained to trot for speed.

trou·ba·dour (TROO bə DOR) *n.* **1.** a class of lyric poets flourishing in southern France, northern Italy, and eastern Spain during the 12th and 13th centuries. **2.** a singer, esp., of love songs. [< F]

trou·ble (TRUB əl) *n.* **1.** the state of being distressed in mind; worry. **2.** a difficulty, perplexity or annoyance. **3.** effort; pains: Take the *trouble* to do it right. **4.** a diseased condition: lung *trouble.* —*v.* **·led, ·ling** *v.t.* **1.** distress mentally; worry. **2.** agitate or disturb. **3.** inconvenience. **4.** cause physical pain or discomfort to. —*v.i.* **5.** take pains; bother. **6.** worry. [ME *troublen*] —**troub'ling** *adj.*

troub·le·shoot·er (TRUB əl SHOO tər) *n.* one who locates difficulties and seeks to remove them, esp., in machine operations, industrial processes, etc. —**troub'le-shoot'ing** n.

troub·le·some (TRUB əl səm) adj. **1.** causing trouble; burdensome; trying. **2.** marked by violence; tumultuous. **3.** agitated or disturbed. —**troub'le·some·ly** adv.

trough (trawf) n. **1.** a long, narrow, open receptacle for conveying a fluid or for holding food or water for animals. **2.** a long, narrow channel or depression. [ME]

trounce (trowns) v.t. **trounced, trounc·ing 1.** beat severely; punish. **2.** defeat decisively.

troupe (troop) n. a company of actors or other performers. —v.i. **trouped, troup·ing** travel as one of a theatrical company. [< F] —**troup'er** n.

trou·sers (TROW zərz) n. (construed as pl.) a garment, esp. for men and boys, divided so as to make a separate covering for each leg and usu. extending from the waist to the ankles.

trous·seau (TROO soh) n. pl. **·seaux** (-sohz) or **·seaus** a bride's outfit, esp. of clothing and linens. [< F]

trow·el (TROW əl) n. **1.** a flat-bladed implement with an offset handle, used to smooth plaster, mortar, etc. **2.** a small concave scoop with a handle, used in digging about small plants. —v.t. **·eled, ·el·ing** apply, form, or dig with a trowel. [ME, ladle]

troy (troi) n. a system of weights (**troy weight**) in which 12 ounces make a pound, used by jewelers in England and the U.S. Also **troy weight.** [ME troye, after Troyes, France]

tru·ant (TROO ənt) n. one who neglects duty; esp., a student who stays away from school without permission. —adj. **1.** being truant; idle. **2.** relating to or characterizing a truant. [ME] —**tru·an·cy** (TROO ən see) n.

truce (troos) n. **1.** an agreement between belligerents for a temporary suspension of hostilities; an armistice. **2.** temporary cessation of any conflict. [ME trewes agreements]

truck¹ (truk) n. **1.** an automotive vehicle designed to carry loads, freight, etc. **2.** a two-wheeled barrowlike vehicle or a flat frame with wheels, used for moving barrels, boxes, etc. by hand. **3.** one of the pivoting sets of wheels on a railroad car or engine. —v.t. **1.** carry on a truck. —v.i. **2.** carry goods on a truck. **3.** drive a truck. —**truck'er** n.

truck² v.t. & v.i. exchange or barter; also,

peddle. [ME trukken] —n. **1.** commodities for sale. **2.** garden produce for market. **3.** barter. **4.** Informal dealings: I will have no truck with him. —**truck'er** n.

truck farm a farm on which vegetables are produced for market. —**truck farming.**

truck·le (TRUK əl) v.i. **·led, ·ling** yield meanly or weakly: with to.

truc·u·lent (TRUK yə lənt) adj. **1.** of savage character; cruel; belligerent. **2.** scathing; harsh; violent: said of writing or speech. [< L truculentus fierce] —**truc'u·lence, truc'u·len·cy** n. —**truc'u·lent·ly** adv.

trudge (truj) v.i. **trudged, trudg·ing** walk wearily or laboriously; plod. —n. a tiresome walk or tramp. —**trudg'er** n.

true (troo) adj. **tru·er, tru·est 1.** faithful to fact or reality; not false. **2.** being real or natural; genuine: true grit. **3.** faithful; steadfast. **4.** conforming to an existing type or pattern; exact: a true copy. **5.** legitimate. **6.** truthful; honest. —n. correct position: out of true. —adv. **1.** in truth; truly. **2.** in a true and accurate manner: The wheel runs true. —v.t. **trued, tru·ing** bring to conformity with a standard; adjust. [ME trewe] —**true'ness** n. —**tru'ly** adv.

true-blue (TROO BLOO) adj. loyal; faithful; genuine.

truf·fle (TRUF əl) n. an edible fleshy underground fungus. [< Du. truffele]

tru·ism (TROO iz əm) n. an obvious or self-evident truth.

trump (trump) n. **1.** in various card games, a card of the suit selected to rank above all others temporarily. **2.** Usu. pl. the suit thus determined. —v.t. **1.** top (another card) with a trump. **2.** surpass; excel; beat. —v.i. **3.** play a trump. —**trump up** make up for a dishonest purpose.

trump·er·y (TRUM pə ree) n. pl. **·er·ies 1.** worthless finery. **2.** rubbish; nonsense. **3.** deceit; trickery. [ME tromperie deceit]

trum·pet (TRUM pit) n. **1.** a brass wind instrument with a flaring bell and a long metal tube. **2.** something resembling a trumpet in form. **3.** a penetrating sound like that of a trumpet. [ME trumpette] —v.t. **1.** proclaim by or as by a trumpet; publish widely. —v.i. **2.** blow a trumpet or give forth a sound as if from a trumpet. —**trum'pet·er** n.

trun·cate (TRUNG kayt) v.t. **·cat·ed, ·cat·ing** cut the top or end from. —adj. **1.** truncated. **2.** Biol. ending abruptly, as though cut or broken squarely off. [< L *truncatus* lopped off] —**trun·ca'tion** *n.*

trun·ca·ted (TRUNG kay tid) *adj.* cut off; shortened.

trun·cheon (TRUN chən) *n.* a short, heavy stick; club. [ME *tronchoun*]

trun·dle (TRUN dl) *n.* **1.** a small, broad wheel, as of a caster. **2.** the act, motion, or sound of trundling. **3.** a trundle bed. —*v.t. & v.i.* **·dled, ·dling 1.** roll along. **2.** rotate.

trundle bed a bed with a low frame resting on casters, for rolling under another bed.

trunk (trungk) *n.* **1.** the main stem of a tree. **2.** a large case for carrying clothes etc., as for a journey. **3.** a large compartment of an automobile for storing luggage etc., usu. at the rear. **4.** the human body, apart from the head, neck, and limbs; torso. **5.** the main body, line, or stem of anything. **6.** a long nasal appendage, as of an elephant. **7.** *pl.* a close-fitting garment covering the loins, worn by male swimmers. [ME *tronke*] — *adj.* of a trunk or main body.

truss (trus) *n.* **1.** *Med.* a bandage or support for a rupture. **2.** a braced framework of ties, beams, or bars, as for the support of a roof, bridge, etc. —*v.t.* **1.** tie or bind; fasten. **2.** support by a truss; brace, as a roof. **3.** fasten the wings of (a fowl) before cooking. [ME *trussen*]

trust (trust) *n.* **1.** confident reliance on the integrity, honesty, or justice of another; faith. **2.** something committed to one's care; a charge; responsibility. **3.** the state of receiving an important charge; responsibility: a position of *trust.* **4.** business credit. **5.** custody; care; keeping. **6.** *Law* **a** a legal title to property held for the benefit of another. **b** the property or thing held. **7.** a combination of business firms that controls production and price of some commodity or service and thus lessens competition; monopoly. **8.** confident expectation; belief; hope. [ME] —*v.t.* **1.** have trust in; rely on. **2.** commit to the care of another; entrust. **3.** commit something to the care of: with *with.* **4.** allow to do something without fear. **5.** expect with confidence or with hope. **6.** believe. —*v.i.* **7.** place trust or confidence; rely: with *in.* **8.** hope: with *for.* —**trust to** depend on; confide in. —*adj.* held in trust: *trust* money.

trust company an institution that manages trusts and lends money.

trus·tee (tru STEE) *n.* **1.** one who holds property in trust. **2.** one of a body of persons who manage the affairs of a college, church, foundation, etc.

trus·tee·ship (tru STEE ship) *n.* **1.** the post or function of a trustee. **2.** supervision and control of a trust territory; also, the territory so controlled.

trust·ful (TRUST fəl) *adj.* disposed to trust. —**trust'ful·ness** *n.*

trust·ing (TRUS ting) *adj.* trustful. —**trust'ing·ly** *adv.*

trust territory a dependent area administered by a nation under the authority of the United Nations.

trust·wor·thy (TRUST WUR thee) *adj.* worthy of confidence; reliable. —**trust'wor'thi·ness** *n.*

trust·y (FRUS tee) *adj.* **trust·i·er, trust·i·est 1.** faithful to duty or trust. **2.** staunch; firm. —*n. pl.* **trust·ies** a trustworthy person; esp., a convict who has been found reliable and to whom special liberties are granted. —**trust'i·ness** *n.*

truth (trooth) *n. pl.* **truths** (troothz) **1.** the state or character of being true; conformity to fact or reality. **2.** conformity to rule, standard, pattern, or ideal. **3.** steadfastness; fidelity. **4.** that which is true; a statement or belief that corresponds to the reality. **5.** fact; reality. **6.** a disposition to tell only what is true; veracity. [ME]

truth·ful (TROOTH fəl) *adj.* **1.** habitually telling the truth. **2.** conforming to fact or reality; true. —**truth'ful·ly** *adv.* —**truth'·ful·ness** *n.*

try (trī) *v.* **tried, try·ing** *v.t.* **1.** make an attempt to do or accomplish; endeavor. **2.** make experimental use or application of. **3.** *Law* subject to a judicial trial. **4.** subject to a test; put to proof. **5.** put severe strain on or trouble greatly. **6.** extract by rendering or melting; refine. —*v.i.* **7.** make an attempt. —**try on** put on (a garment) to test for fit or appearance. —**try out** attempt to qualify: She *tried out* for the soccer team. [ME *trien*] —*n. pl.* **tries** the act of trying; trial; experiment.

try·ing (TRĪ ing) *adj.* testing severely; hard to endure.

try·out (TRĪ owt) *n.* a test of ability.

tryst (trist) *n.* **1.** an appointment, as between lovers, to meet at a set time and place; also, the meeting. **2.** the meeting place agreed on; rendezvous: also **tryst'ing place.** [ME] —**tryst'er** *n.*

tsar (zahr) *n.* see CZAR.

tset·se (TSET see) *n.* **1.** a small bloodsucking fly of southern Africa, whose bite transmits disease in cattle, horses, etc. **2.** a related species that transmits the causative agent of sleeping sickness. Also **tset·se fly.** [< Afrikaans]

T-shirt (TEE SHURT) *n.* **1.** a cotton undershirt with short sleeves. **2.** a similar outer garment. Also **tee-shirt.**

tsu·na·mi (tsuu NAH mee) *n.* an extensive ocean wave caused by an undersea earthquake: also called *tidal wave.* [< Japanese, lit., harbor wave]

tub (tub) *n.* **1.** a broad, open-topped vessel with handles on the sides. **2.** a bathtub. **3.** the amount that a tub contains. [ME *tubbe*] —*v.t. & v.i.* **tubbed, tub·bing** wash, bathe, or place in a tub.

tu·ba (TOO bə) *n. pl.* **·bas** a bass brass instrument whose pitch is varied by means of valves. [< L, trumpet]

tub·by (TUB ee) *adj.* **·bi·er, ·bi·est** short and fat.

tube (toob) *n.* **1.** a long, hollow, cylindrical body of metal, glass, rubber, etc., generally used for the conveyance of something through it; pipe. **2.** an electron tube. **3.** a cylinder for containing paints, toothpaste, glue, etc. **4.** *Zool.* any elongated hollow part or organ: a bronchial *tube.* **5.** a subway or tunnel. —**the tube** *Informal* **1.** a television set. **2.** television. [< F] —*v.t.* **tubed, tub·ing 1.** fit or furnish with a tube. **2.** enclose in a tube or tubes. **3.** make tubular. —**tub·al** (TOO bəl) *adj.*

tu·ber (TOO bər) *n.* **1.** *Bot.* a short, thickened portion of an underground stem, as in the potato. **2.** *Anat.* a swelling or prominence; tubercle. [< L, lump]

tu·ber·cle (TOO bər kəl) *n.* **1.** a small, rounded nodule, as on the skin or on a root of a plant. **2.** *Pathol.* a small, abnormal knob or swelling in an organ; esp., the lesion of tuberculosis. [< L *tuberculum*]

tubercle bacillus the rod-shaped bacterium that causes tuberculosis in people.

tu·ber·cu·lar (tuu BUR kyə lər) *adj.* **1.** covered with tubercles. **2.** of or affected with tuberculosis. —*n.* one affected with tuberculosis.

tu·ber·cu·lo·sis (tuu BUR kyə LOH sis) *n. Pathol.* **1.** a communicable disease caused by infection with the tubercle bacillus, characterized by the formation of tubercles within some organ or tissue. **2.** this disease affecting the lungs: also called *TB* and, formerly, *consumption.* [< NL] —**tu·ber′cu·lous** *adj.*

tu·ber·ous (TOO bər əs) *adj.* bearing or resembling tubers. Also **tu·ber·ose** (TOO bə ROHS).

tub·ing (TOO bing) *n.* **1.** tubes collectively. **2.** a piece of tube or material for tubes.

tu·bu·lar (TOO byə lər) *adj.* **1.** having the form of a tube. **2.** made up of or provided with tubes. [< NL *tubularis*]

tu·bule (TOO byool) *n.* a small tube.

tuck (tuk) *v.t.* **1.** fold under; press in the ends or edges of. **2.** wrap or cover snugly. **3.** thrust or press into a close place; cram; hide. **4.** make folds in. [ME *tuken* pull up sharply] —*n.* **1.** a fold stitched into a garment for a better fit or for decoration. **2.** any tucked piece or part.

tuck·er (TUK ər) *v.t. Informal* weary completely; exhaust.

Tues·day (TOOZ day) *n.* the third day of the week. [ME *tiwesday*]

tuft (tuft) *n.* a bunch or cluster of small, flexible parts, as hair, grass, feathers, or threads held or tied together at the base. [ME] —*v.t.* **1.** separate or form into tufts. **2.** cover or adorn with tufts. —*v.i.* **3.** form tufts.

tug (tug) *v.* **tugged, tug·ging** *v.t.* **1.** pull at with effort; strain at. **2.** pull, draw, or drag with effort. **3.** tow with a tugboat. —*v.i.* **4.** pull strenuously: *tug* at an oar. **5.** strive; toil. [ME *tuggen*] —*n.* **1.** an act of tugging; a violent pull. **2.** a strenuous contest. **3.** a tugboat.

tug·boat (TUG BOHT) *n.* a small, ruggedly built vessel designed for towing: also called *tug.*

tug of war 1. a contest in which teams at opposite ends of a rope try to outpull each other. **2.** a hard struggle for supremacy.

tu·i·tion (too ISH ən) *n.* **1.** the charge or payment for instruction, esp. formal instruction. **2.** teaching; instruction. [ME *tuicioun* protection]

tu·la·re·mi·a (TOO lə REE mee ə) *n.* a disease of rodents, esp. rabbits, that may be transmitted to people: also called *rabbit fever.* [< NL, after *Tulare* County, California, where first found]

tu·lip (TOO lip) *n.* **1.** any of numerous hardy, bulbous herbs cultivated for their bell-shaped flowers. **2.** a bulb or flower of this plant. [< Persian *tulbent* turban]

tulle (tool) *n.* a fine, open-meshed silk, used for veils etc. [< F, after *Tulle,* France]

tum·ble (TUM bəl) *v.* **·bled, ·bling** *v.i.* **1.**

roll or toss about. **2.** perform acrobatic feats, as somersaults etc. **3.** fall violently or awkwardly. **4.** move in a careless manner; stumble. —*v.t.* **5.** toss carelessly; cause to fall. **6.** throw into disorder or confusion; disturb; rumple. [ME *tumblen*] —*n.* **1.** the act of tumbling; a fall. **2.** a state of disorder or confusion.

tum·ble-down (TUM bəl DOWN) *adj.* rickety, as if about to fall in pieces; dilapidated.

tum·bler (TUM blər) *n.* **1.** a drinking glass with a flat bottom. **2.** one who or that which tumbles; esp., a gymnast. **3.** in a lock, a part that secures a bolt until raised by the key.

tum·ble·weed (TUM bəl WEED) *n.* a plant that breaks from the root and is driven by the wind.

tum·brel (TUM brəl) *n.* **1.** a farmer's cart, esp. one for carrying and dumping dung. **2.** a cart in which prisoners were taken to the guillotine during the French Revolution. Also **tum'bril.** [ME *tombrel*]

tu·mes·cent (too MES ənt) *adj.* **1.** becoming swollen. **2.** bombastic. [< L *tumescere* swell up] —**tu·mes'cence** *n.*

tu·mid (TOO mid) *adj.* **1.** swollen; enlarged, as a part of the body. **2.** inflated or pompous in style. [< L *tumidus* swollen] —**tu·mid'i·ty** *n.* —**tu'mid·ly** *adv.*

tu·mor (TOO mər) *n.* *Pathol.* a local swelling on or in any part of the body, esp. from some abnormal growth of tissue. [< L]

tu·mult (TOO məlt) *n.* **1.** the commotion, disturbance, or agitation of a crowd; uproar. **2.** any violent commotion or agitation, as of the mind. [ME *tumulte*]

tu·mul·tu·ous (too MUL choo əs) *adj.* **1.** characterized by tumult; disorderly. **2.** causing or affected by tumult; agitated or disturbed. —**tu·mul'tu·ous·ly** *adv.*

tun (tun) *n.* **1.** a large cask. **2.** a measure of capacity, usu. equal to 252 gallons. [ME *tunne*] —*v.t.* **tunned, tun·ning** put into a cask or tun.

tun·dra (TUN drə) *n.* a treeless, often marshy plain of the arctic north. [< Russ. *túndra*]

tune (toon) *n.* **1.** a melody or air. **2.** the proper pitch or, loosely, the proper key. **3.** concord or unison. **4.** suitable temper or humor. [ME] —*v.* **tuned, tun·ing** *v.t.* **1.** adjust the pitch of to a standard. **2.** adapt to a particular tone, expression, or mood. **3.** bring into harmony. **4.** adjust (an engine etc.) to proper working order. —*v.i.* **5.** be in harmony. —**tune in** adjust a radio receiver

to the frequency of (a station, broadcast, etc.). —**tune out 1.** adjust a radio receiver to exclude (interference, a station, etc.). **2.** exclude from one's attention; deliberately ignore. —**tun'a·ble** *adj.*

tune·ful (TOON fəl) *adj.* **1.** melodious; musical. **2.** producing musical sounds.

tune·less (TOON lis) *adj.* **1.** not making music; silent. **2.** lacking in rhythm, melody, etc.

tun·er (TOO nər) *n.* **1.** one who or that which tunes. **2.** a radio receiver without amplifiers.

tune-up (TOON UP) *n.* an adjustment to bring an engine etc. into proper working order.

tu·nic (TOO nik) *n.* **1.** in ancient Greece and Rome, a garment reaching to the knees. **2.** a modern outer garment, as a blouse or jacket. [< L *tunica* coat]

tun·ing fork a fork-shaped metal instrument that produces a tone of definite pitch when struck.

tun·nel (TUN əl) *n.* an underground passageway, as for a railway or a mine. [ME *tonel*] —*v.t.* **tun·neled, tun·nel·ing** *v.t.* **1.** make a tunnel through. —*v.i.* **2.** make a tunnel. —**tun'nel·er** *n.*

tur·ban (TUR bən) *n.* **1.** an Oriental head covering consisting of a sash twisted about the head or about a cap. **2.** any similar headdress. [< Persian *dulband*] —**tur'baned** *adj.*

tur·bid (TUR bid) *adj.* **1.** opaque or cloudy, as a liquid with a suspension of foreign particles. **2.** thick and dense, like heavy smoke or fog. **3.** being in a state of confusion. [< L *turbidus* confused] —**tur·bid'i·ty** *n.*

tur·bine (TUR bin) *n.* a motor mounted on a shaft and provided with a series of curved vanes driven by steam, water, gas, or other fluid under pressure. [< F]

tur·bo·jet engine (TUR boh JET) *n.* *Aeron.* a type of jet engine using a gas turbine to drive an air compressor.

tur·bo·prop (TUR boh PROP) *n.* *Aeron.* a turbojet engine connecting directly with a propeller.

tur·bot (TUR bət) *n. pl.* **·bot** or **·bots** a large European flatfish, used for food. [ME]

tur·bu·lent (TUR byə lənt) *adj.* **1.** being in violent agitation or commotion. **2.** having a tendency to disturb or throw into confusion. [< L *turbulentus*] —**tur'bu·lence, tur'bu·len·cy** *n.*

tu·reen (tuu REEN) *n.* a deep, covered

dish, as for holding soup to be served. [< F *terrine*]

turf (turf) *n.* **1.** grass with its matted roots filling the upper layer of soil; sod. **2.** peat (def. 2). **3.** *Slang* the neighborhood or area held and defended by a person or group. — **the turf 1.** a racetrack for horses. **2.** the sport of racing horses. [ME]

tur·gid (TUR jid) *adj.* **1.** unnaturally swollen, as by air or liquid. **2.** bombastic; inflated. [< L *turgidus* swollen] — **tur·gid′i·ty, tur′gid·ness** *n.* —**tur′gid·ly** *adv.*

tur·gor (TUR gər) *n.* the state of being turgid.

Turk (turk) *n.* a native or inhabitant of Turkey. —**Young Turk** a member of an insurgent group in Turkey in the early 20th century. —**young Turk** any person actively encouraging radical reform of an institution.

tur·key (TUR kee) *n.* **1.** a large American bird, having a naked head and extensible tail; esp., the American domesticated turkey, used for food. **2.** *Slang* a person or play that is a failure. —**talk turkey** discuss in a practical and direct manner.

Turk·ish (TUR kish) *adj.* of or pertaining to Turkey or the Turks. —*n.* the language of Turkey.

Turkish bath a bath with steam rooms, massage, and showers.

Turkish towel a heavy, rough towel with loose, uncut pile. Also **turkish towel.**

tur·moil (TUR moil) *n.* confused motion; disturbance; tumult.

turn (turn) *v.t.* **1.** cause to rotate, as about an axis. **2.** change the position or direction of. **3.** move so that the other side is visible: *turn* a page. **4.** reverse the arrangement or order of. **5.** go around: *turn* a corner. **6.** ponder: often with *over.* **7.** sprain or strain: *turn* one's ankle. **8.** nauseate (the stomach). **9.** cause to go away: *turn* a beggar from one's door. **10.** give graceful or finished form to: *turn* a phrase. **11.** perform by revolving: *turn* somersaults. **12.** bend, curve, fold or twist. **13.** change or transform: *turn* water into wine. **14.** exchange for an equivalent: *turn* stocks into cash. **15.** cause to become as specified: Dye *turned* the liquid green. **16.** make sour or rancid. **17.** deflect or divert: *turn* a blow. **18.** repel: *turn* a charge of troops etc. —*v.i.* **19.** move around an axis; rotate; revolve. **20.** move partially on or as if on an axis: He *turned* and ran. **21.** change

position; also, roll from side to side. **22.** reverse position; become inverted. **23.** change or reverse direction or flow: We *turned* North. The tide has *turned.* **24.** depend; hinge: with *on* or *upon.* **25.** whirl, as the head. **26.** become nauseated, as the stomach. **27.** become transformed: The water *turned* to ice. **28.** become as specified: Her hair *turned* gray. **29.** become sour, rancid, or fermented. —**turn against** become or cause to become opposed or hostile to. —**turn down** reject or refuse, as a request; also, refuse the request etc. of. — **turn in 1.** deliver; hand over. **2.** *Informal* go to bed. —**turn loose** set free. —**turn off** lose or cause to lose interest. —**turn on 1.** *Slang* take or experience the effects of taking a psychedelic drug, as marijuana. **2.** *Slang* evoke in (someone) a rapt response. **3.** become hostile to. —**turn out 1.** turn inside out. **2.** eject or expel. **3.** produce; make. **4.** come or go out, as for duty or service. **5.** prove (to be). **6.** become or result. —**turn over 1.** hand over; transfer or relinquish. **2.** do business to the amount of. **3.** invest and get back (capital). —**turn up 1.** find or be found. **2.** appear; arrive. [ME *turnen*] —*n.* **1.** the act of turning, or the state of being turned. **2.** a change to another direction, motion, or position. **3.** a deviation from a course; change in trend. **4.** a rotation or revolution. **5.** a bend, as in a road. **6.** a regular time or chance in some succession: It's my *turn* to play. **7.** a round; spell: a *turn* at singing. **8.** characteristic form or style: the *turn* of a phrase. **9.** tendency; direction: The talk took a serious *turn.* **10.** a deed performed: a good *turn.* **11.** a walk, drive, or trip to and fro: a *turn* in the park. **12.** a round in a coil etc.; also, a twist. **13.** *Informal* a shock to the nerves, as from alarm. — **at every turn** on every occasion; constantly. —**by turns 1.** in alternation or sequence. **2.** at intervals. —**in turn** one after another; in proper order or sequence. — **out of turn** not in proper order or sequence. —**to a turn** just right: said esp. of cooked food. —**take turns** act, play, etc. one after another in proper order.

turn·a·bout (TURN ə bowt) *n.* the act of reversing one's direction, opinion, etc.

turn·coat (TURN koht) *n.* one who goes over to the opposite side or party; renegade.

turn·ing (TUR ning) *n.* **1.** the art of shaping wood, metal, etc. on a lathe. **2.** any deviation from a straight or customary course; a winding; bend. **3.** the point where a road forks.

turning point the point of a decisive change in direction of action; crisis.

turn·off (TURN AWF) *n.* **1.** a road or way branching off from a main thoroughfare. **2.** *Slang* anything or anyone that causes one to lost interest or sympathy.

turn·out (TURN OWT) *n.* **1.** an act of turning out or coming forth. **2.** persons in attendance. **3.** a quantity produced; output. **4.** array; equipment; outfit.

turn·o·ver (TURN OH vər) *n.* **1.** the act or process of turning over; an upset. **2.** the rate at which persons hired within a given period are replaced by others; also, the number of persons hired. **3.** a change or revolution. **4.** a small pie or tart made by covering half of a crust with filling and turning the other half over on top. **5.** the amount of business accomplished, or of work achieved. —*adj.* **1.** designed for turning over or reversing. **2.** capable of being turned over or folded down.

turn·pike (TURN PĪK) *n.* **1.** a highway, esp. one maintained by tolls. **2.** a tollgate. [ME *turnepike* revolving frame]

turn·stile (TURN STĪL) *n.* a gate with revolving arms admitting one person at a time.

turn·ta·ble (TURN TAY bəl) *n.* **1.** a rotating disk, as one that carries a phonograph record. **2.** a rotating platform arranged to turn a section of a drawbridge, a locomotive, etc.

tur·pen·tine (TUR pən TĪN) *n.* an oil distilled from the resin of several coniferous trees. —**oil of turpentine** the colorless essential oil formed when turpentine is distilled with steam; chiefly used to thin paint: also called **spirits of turpentine.** [ME] — *v.t.* **·tined, ·tin·ing** put turpentine with or upon; saturate with turpentine.

tur·pi·tude (TUR pī TOOD) *n.* inherent baseness; vileness; depravity. [< MF]

tur·quoise (TUR kwoiz) *n.* **1.** a blue or green mineral, colored by copper, valued as a gemstone. **2.** a light greenish blue: also **turquoise blue.** [< F]

tur·ret (TUR it) *n.* **1.** *Mil.* **a** a rotating armored housing containing guns and forming part of a warship or of a fort. **b** a similar structure in a tank or airplane. **2.** *Archit.* a small tower rising above a larger structure, as on a castle. **3.** *Mech.* in a lathe, a rotating cylinder for holding tools: also **tur'ret·head'.** [ME *touret*] —**tur'ret·ed** *adj.*

tur·tle (TUR tl) *n.* **1.** any of numerous reptiles having a horny, toothless beak, and a stout body enclosed within a shell. **2.** the flesh of certain varieties of turtle, served as food. [< F *tortue* tortoise] —*v.i.* **·tled, ·tling** hunt or catch turtles.

tur·tle·neck (TUR tl NEK) *n.* **1.** a high collar that fits snugly about the neck, usu. rolled or turned over double, used esp. on sweaters. **2.** a sweater having such a collar.

tusk (tusk) *n.* **1.** a long, pointed tooth, as in the elephant. **2.** a sharp, toothlike projection. [ME] —*v.t.* **1.** gore with the tusks. **2.** root up with the tusks. —**tusked** *adj.* —**tusk'less** *adj.*

tus·sle (TUS əl) *v.t. & v.i.* **·sled, ·sling** fight or struggle in a vigorous, determined way; scuffle; wrestle. [ME *tussillen*] —*n.* a disorderly struggle, as in sport; scuffle.

tu·te·lage (TOOT l ij) *n.* **1.** the state of being under a tutor or guardian. **2.** the act or office of a guardian; guardianship. **3.** the act of tutoring; instruction. [< L *tutela* guardian]

tu·te·lar·y (TOOT l ER ee) *adj.* **1.** invested with guardianship. **2.** pertaining to a guardian.

tu·tor (TOO tər) *n.* **1.** one who instructs another; a private teacher. **2.** a college teacher below the rank of instructor. **3.** a guardian of a minor. [ME] —*v.t.* **1.** act as tutor to; instruct; train. **2.** have the guardianship of. —**tu·to·ri·al** (too TOR ee əl) *adj.*

tut·ti-frut·ti (TOO tee FROO tee) *n.* a confection made with a mixture of fruits. [< Ital., lit., all fruits]

tu·tu (TOO too) *n. French* a short, full skirt consisting of many layers of sheer fabric, worn by ballet dancers.

tux·e·do (tuk SEE doh) *n. pl.* **·dos 1.** a man's semiformal dinner coat without tails: also called *dinner jacket.* **2.** the suit of which the coat is a part. [After *Tuxedo* Park, N.Y.]

TV (TEE VEE) *n.* television. —**TV dinner** a quick-frozen dinner.

twad·dle (TWOD l) *v.t. & v.i.* **·dled, ·dling** talk foolishly. —*n.* silly, senseless talk. —**twad'dler** *n.*

twang (twang) *v.t. & v.i.* **1.** make or cause to make a sharp, vibrant sound. **2.** utter or speak nasally. —*n.* **1.** a sharp, vibrating sound, as of a string plucked. **2.** a sharp, nasal one, as of the voice. —**twang'y** *adj.*

tweak (tweek) *v.t.* pinch and twist sharply; twitch. —*n.* a pinch or jerk.

tweed (tweed) *n.* **1.** a soft woolen fabric, often woven in two or more colors. **2.** *pl.* clothing of tweed.

tweed·y (TWEE dee) *adj.* **tweed·i·er, tweed·i·est 1.** like tweed. **2.** given to wearing tweed. **3.** informal.

'tween (tween) *prep.* contraction of BE-TWEEN.

tweet (tweet) *v.i.* utter a thin, chirping note. —*n.* a twittering or chirping.

tweet·er (TWEE tər) *n. Electronics* a small loudspeaker used to reproduce high-pitched sounds. [< TWEET]

tweeze (tweez) *v.t.* **tweezed, tweez·ing** *Informal* handle, pluck, etc. with tweezers. [Back formation < TWEEZERS]

tweez·ers (TWEE zərz) *n. (construed as sing. or pl.)* small pincers for grasping and holding small objects. Also **pair of tweezers.** [< F *étuis* cases]

twelve (twelv) *n.* the sum of eleven and one: a cardinal number written 12, XII. [ME] — **twelfth** (twelfth) *adj. & n.* —**twelve** *adj.*

twelve-tone (TWELV TOHN) *adj. Music* **1.** of a composition in which the tones of the chromatic scale are arranged in an arbitrary series. **2.** in 20th c. music, using or composed in a freely chromatic style.

twen·ty (TWEN tee) *n. pl.* **·ties** the sum of nineteen and one: a cardinal number written 20, XX. [ME] —**twen'ti·eth** *adj. & n.* —**twen'ty** *adj.*

twen·ty-one (TEN tee WUN) *n.* a card game in which the object is to draw cards whose value will equal or approach twenty-one without exceeding that amount: also called *blackjack.*

twice (twīs) *adv.* **1.** two times. **2.** in double measure; doubly. [ME *twies*]

twice-told (TWĪS TOHLD) *adj.* told more than once.

twid·dle (TWID l) *v.* **·dled, ·dling** *v.t.* **1.** twirl idly; toy or play with. —*v.i.* **2.** revolve or twirl. **3.** toy with something idly. — **twiddle one's thumbs** rotate one's thumbs idly around one another; do nothing. —*n.* a gentle twirling. —**twid'·dler** *n.*

twig (twig) *n.* a small shoot or branch of a tree. [ME] —**twig'like** *adj.* —**twig'gy** *adj.* **·gi·er, ·gi·est** resembling a twig.

twi·light (TWĪ LĪT) *n.* **1.** the faint light in the sky when the sun is below the horizon, esp. in the evening; also, the period during which this light is prevalent. **2.** any faint light. **3.** a condition following the waning of

past glory, achievement, etc. [ME] — **twi·light** *adj.*

twill (twil) *n.* **1.** a weave characterized by diagonal ribs or lines in fabrics. **2.** a fabric woven with a twill. [ME *twyll*] —*v.t.* weave (cloth) so as to produce diagonal lines or ribs on the surface. —**twilled** *adj.*

twin (twin) *n.* **1.** one of two young produced at the same birth. **2.** the counterpart of another. [ME] —*adj.* **1.** being a twin or twins. **2.** consisting of, forming, or being one of a pair of similar and closely related objects. —*v.* **twinned, twin·ning** *v.i.* **1.** bring forth twins. **2.** be matched or equal; agree. —*v.t.* **3.** bring forth as twins. **4.** couple; match.

twine (twīn) *v.* **twined, twin·ing** *v.t.* **1.** twist together, as threads. **2.** form by such twisting. **3.** coil or wrap about something. —*v.i.* **4.** interlace. **5.** proceed in a winding course; meander. —*n.* a string composed of two or more strands twisted together; loosely, any small cord. [ME] —**twin'er** *n.*

twinge (twinj) *n.* **1.** a sharp local pain. **2.** a mental or emotional pang. —*v.t. & v.i.* **twinged, twing·ing** affect with or suffer a sudden pain or twinge. [ME *twengen*]

twin·kle (TWING kəl) *v.i.* **·kled, ·kling 1.** shine with fitful gleams, as a star. **2.** be bright, as with amusement: Her eyes *twinkled.* **3.** move rapidly to and fro; flicker: *twinkling* feet. [ME *twinklen*] —*n.* **1.** an intermittent gleam of light; sparkle; glimmer. **2.** a wink or sparkle of the eye. **3.** an instant; a twinkling. —**twin'kler** *n.*

twin·kling (TWING kling) *n.* **1.** the act of sparkling. **2.** a wink. **3.** a moment.

twirl (twurl) *v.t. & v.i.* whirl. —*n.* **1.** a whirling motion. **2.** a quick twisting action, as of the fingers. **3.** a curl; coil. —**twirl'er** *n.* **1.** a person or thing that twirls. **2.** in baseball, a pitcher.

twist (twist) *v.t.* **1.** wind (strands etc.) around each other. **2.** form by such winding: *twist* thread. **3.** give spiral form to, as by turning at either end. **4.** force out of natural shape; distort or contort. **5.** distort the meaning of. **6.** cause to revolve or rotate. —*v.i.* **7.** become twisted. **8.** move in a winding course. **9.** squirm; writhe. [ME *twisten*] —*n.* **1.** the act, manner, or result of twisting or turning on an axis. **2.** the state of being twisted. **3.** a curve; turn; bend. **4.** a wrench; strain, as of a joint or limb. **5.** a distortion or variation of: a *twist* of meaning. **6.** thread or cord made of tightly twisted strands; also, one of the strands. **7.** a twisted roll or loaf of bread. **8.** a type of tobacco twisted in the form of a rope.

twist·er (TWIS tər) *n.* **1.** one who or that which twists. **2.** *Informal* a tornado.

twit (twit) *v.t.* **twit·ted, twit·ting** taunt, reproach, or annoy by reminding of a mistake, fault, etc. [ME *atwiten* reproach] —**twit** *n. Informal* an annoying or insignificant person.

twitch (twich) *v.t. & v.i.* pull or move with a sudden jerk. [ME *twicchen*] —*n.* **1.** a sudden involuntary contraction of a muscle. **2.** a sudden, sharp pull or jerk.

twit·ter (TWIT ər) *v.i.* **1.** utter a series of light chirping or trembling notes, as a bird. **2.** titter. **3.** be excited; tremble. [ME *twiteren*] —*n.* **1.** the act of twittering. **2.** a twittering sound. **3.** a state of nervous agitation. —**twit′·ter·er** *n.* —**twit′ter·y** *adj.*

'twixt (twikst) *prep.* contraction of betwixt.

two (too) *n.* **1.** the sum of one and one: a cardinal number written 2, II. **2.** a couple; pair. —**put two and two together** reach the obvious conclusion. [ME] —**two** *adj.*

two-bit (TOO BIT) *adj. Slang* **1.** costing twenty-five cents. **2.** cheap; smalltime.

two bits *Slang* twenty-five cents.

two-faced (TOO FAYST) *adj.* **1.** having two faces. **2.** hypocritical or deceitful.

two-fist·ed (TOO FIS tid) *adj.* vigorous and aggressive.

two·fold (TOO FOHLD) —*adj.* **1.** consisting of two parts. **2.** twice as many or as great; double. —*adv.* doubly.

two-hand·ed (TOO HAN did) *adj.* **1.** requiring both hands at once. **2.** constructed for use by two persons. **3.** ambidextrous. **4.** having two hands.

two-ply (TOO PLĪ) *adj.* made of two strands, layers, or thicknesses of material.

two·some (TOO səm) *n.* **1.** two persons together; a couple. **2.** a match with one player on each side.

two-time (TOO TĪM) *v.t.* **-timed, -tim·ing** *Informal* be unfaithful to in love; deceive. —**two′-tim′er** *n.*

two-way (TOO WAY) *adj.* characterized by or permitting movement in two directions or use in two ways.

ty·coon (tī KOON) *n.* a wealthy and powerful industrial or business leader. [< Japanese *taikun* mighty lord]

tyke (tīk) *n.* **1.** a small child. **2.** a mongrel dog.

tym·pa·ni (TIM pə nee) see TIMPANI.

tympanic membrane *Anat.* the membrane

separating the middle ear from the external ear: also called *eardrum.* [See TYMPANUM]

tym·pa·nist (TIM pə nist) *n.* one who plays the drums in an orchestra.

tym·pa·num (TIM pə nəm) *n. pl.* **·nums** or **·na** (-nə) **1.** *Anat.* **a** the middle ear. **b.** the tympanic membrane. **2.** a drumlike membrane or part. [< L] —**tym·pan·ic** (tim PAN ik) *adj.*

type (tīp) *n.* **1.** class; category; kind; sort. **2.** one who or that which has the characteristics of a group or class; embodiment. **3.** *Printing* a block, usu. of metal, bearing on its upper surface a letter or character in relief for use in printing. **4.** printed or typewritten characters. **5.** *Informal* a person. [< LL *typus*] —*v.* **typed, typ·ing** *v.t.* **1.** typewrite (something). **2.** determine the type of; identify: *type* a blood sample. **3.** represent; typify. —*v.i.* **4.** typewrite.

type·cast (TĪP KAST) *v.t.* **·cast, ·cast·ing** cast, as an actor, in a role suited to his appearance, personality, etc.

type·face (TĪP FAYS) *n. Printing* the design of all the characters in a set of type.

type·set·ter (TĪP SET ər) *n.* **1.** one who sets type. **2.** a machine for composing type. —**type′set′ting** *n.*

type·write (TĪP RĪT) *v.t. & v.i.* **·wrote, ·writ·ten, ·writ·ing** write with a typewriter: also *type.*

type·writ·er (TĪP RĪ tər) *n.* a machine with a keyboard that produces printed characters by impressing type upon paper through an inked ribbon.

ty·phoid (TĪ foid) *n.* typhoid fever.

typhoid fever *Pathol.* an acute, infectious fever caused by a bacterium (the **typhoid bacillus**) and characterized by severe intestinal disturbances and red spots on the chest and abdomen.

ty·phoon (tī FOON) *n. Meteorol.* a hurricane originating over tropical waters in the western Pacific and the China Sea. [< Chinese *taai fung* big wind]

ty·phus (TĪ fəs) *n. Pathol.* an acute, contagious disease, marked by high fever, eruption of red spots, and cerebral disorders. Also **typhus fever.** [< NL] —**ty·phous** (TĪ fəs) *adj.*

typ·i·cal (TIP i kəl) *adj.* **1.** characteristic of a type; constituting a type; representative. **2.** conforming to the essential features of a type; serving to distinguish a type. [< Med.L *typicalis*] —**typ′i·cal·ly** *adv.* —**typ′i·cal·ness** *n.*

typ·i·fy (TIP ə fī) *v.t.* **·fied, ·fy·ing 1.** represent by a type; signify, as by an image or token. **2.** constitute a type or serve as a characteristic example of.

typ·ist (TĪ pist) *n.* one who operates a typewriter.

ty·po (TĪ poh) *n. pl.* **·pos** *Informal* a typographical error.

ty·pog·ra·phy (tī POG rə fee) *n. pl.* **·phies 1.** the arrangement of composed type. **2.** the style and appearance of printed matter. **3.** the act or art of composing and printing from type. —**ty·pog′ra·pher** *n.* —**ty·po·graph·ic** (TĪ pə GRAF ik) or **·i·cal** *adj.* —**ty′·po·graph′i·cal·ly** *adv.*

ty·ran·ni·cal (ti RAN i kəl) *adj.* of or characteristic of a tyrant; harsh; despotic. —**ty·ran′ni·cal·ly** *adv.*

tyr·an·nize (TIR ə NĪZ) *v.* **·nized, ·niz·ing**

v.i. **1.** exercise power cruelly or unjustly. **2.** rule as a tyrant. —*v.t.* **3.** treat tyrannically.

ty·ran·no·saur (ti RAN ə SOR) *n.* a huge carnivorous dinosaur of North America that walked on its hind legs. [< NL *Tyrannosaurus*]

tyr·an·ny (TIR ə nee) *n. pl.* **·nies 1.** absolute power arbitrarily or unjustly exercised; despotism. **2.** a tyrannical act. **3.** the authority, government, or rule of a tyrant. [ME *tyrannie*] —**tyr·an·nous** (TIR ə nəs) *adj.* —**tyr′an·nous·ly** *adv.*

tyr·ant (TĪ rənt) *n.* **1.** one who rules oppressively or cruelly; a despot. **2.** one who exercises absolute power without legal warrant. [ME *tirant*]

ty·ro (TĪ roh) *n. pl.* **·ros** a beginner; novice. [< Med.L]

tzar (zahr) see CZAR.

U

u, U (yoo) *n. pl.* **u's, us, U's** or **Us 1.** the twenty-first letter of the English alphabet. **2.** any sound represented by the letter *u.* — *symbol* **1.** anything shaped like a U. **2.** *Chem.* uranium (symbol U).

u·biq·ui·tous (yoo BIK wi təs) *adj.* existing or seeming to exist everywhere at once; omnipresent. —**u·biq'ui·tous·ly** *adv.* — **u·biq'ui·tous·ness, u·biq'ui·ty** *n.* [< L *ubique* everywhere]

ud·der (UD ər) *n.* a large hanging gland, secreting milk and provided with teats for the suckling of offspring, as in cows. [ME *uddre*]

UFO (YOO EF OH) *n. pl.* **UFO's** or **UFOs** unidentified flying object.

ug·ly (UG lee) *adj.* **·li·er, ·li·est 1.** displeasing to the eye. **2.** repulsive to the moral sense. **3.** bad in character or consequences, as a rumor, wound, etc. **4.** mean; hostile. [ME] —**ug'li·ness** *n.*

u·kase (yoo KAYS) *n.* an official decree. [< Russian *ukáz*]

u·ku·le·le (yoo kə LAY lee) *n.* a small guitarlike musical instrument having four strings. [< Hawaiian]

ul·cer (UL sər) *n.* **1.** *Pathol.* an open sore on a surface of the body. **2.** a corroding fault or vice. [ME] —**ul'cer·ous** *adj.*

ul·cer·ate (UL sə RAYT) *v.t. & v.i.* **·at·ed, ·at·ing** make or become affected with ulcers. —**ul'cer·a'tion** *n.*

ul·na (UL nə) *n. pl.* **·nae** (-nee) or **·nas** *Anat.* **1.** the inner bone of the two long bones of the forearm, located on the same side as the little finger. **2.** the corresponding bone in the forelimb of other vertebrates. [< NL] —**ul'nar** *adj.*

ul·te·ri·or (ul TEER ee ər) *adj.* **1.** intentionally hidden: *ulterior* motives. **2.** more remote: *ulterior* considerations. **3.** lying beyond or on the farther side. [< L, farther]

ul·ti·mate (UL tə mit) *adj.* **1.** beyond which there is no other; last of a series; final. **2.** not susceptible of further analysis; fundamental. **3.** most distant; extreme. [< LL *ultimatus* last] —*n.* **1.** the final result; last step; conclusion. **2.** a fundamental or final fact. —**ul'ti·mate·ly** *adv.*

ul·ti·ma·tum (UL tə MAY təm) *n. pl.* **·tums** or **·ta** (-tə) a final statement, as concerning terms, conditions, or concessions; esp., in diplomatic negotiations, the final terms offered. [< NL]

ul·tra (UL trə) *adj.* going beyond the bounds of moderation; extreme. —*n.* one who goes to extreme. [< ULTRA-]

ultra- *prefix* **1.** on the other side of; beyond: **ultragalactic, ultralunar, ultramicroscopic. 2.** excessively; extremely: **ultra-ambitious, ultraconservative, ultrafashionable, ultramodern, ultranationalistic, ultraorthodox.**

ultrahigh frequency *Telecom.* a band of wave frequencies between 300 and 3000 megahertz.

ul·tra·ma·rine (UL trə mə REEN) *n.* **1.** a deep blue, permanent pigment. **2.** a deep blue. —*adj.* **1.** being beyond or across the sea. **2.** of the color ultramarine. [< Med.L *ultramarinus* coming from beyond the sea]

ul·tra·son·ic (UL trə SON ik) *adj. Physics* designating sound waves having a frequency above the limits of human hearing.

ul·tra·vi·o·let (UL trə VĪ ə lit) *adj. Physics* of wavelengths, lying beyond the violet end of the visible spectrum.

ul·u·late (YOOL yə LAYT) *v.i.* **·lat·ed, ·lat·ing** howl, hoot, or wail. [< L *ululatus* howled] —**ul'u·la'tion** *n.*

um·bel (UM bəl) *n. Bot.* a flower cluster spreading outward from a small area at the top of the main stem. [< NL *umbella*]

um·ber (UM bər) *n.* **1.** a brown earth containing iron and used as a pigment. **2.** the color of such a pigment. [ME *umbre*] — *adj.* of the color umber; brownish. —*v.t.* color with umber.

umbilical cord *Anat.* **1.** a ropelike tissue connecting the navel of the fetus with the placenta. Also **umbilical. 2.** *Slang* the cable conveying power to a spacecraft before launching; a similar cable for supplying and tethering a space walker.

um·bil·i·cus (um BIL i kəs) *n. pl.* **·bil·i·ci** (-BIL i sī) *Anat.* the navel. [< L] — **um·bil'i·cal** *adj.*

um·bra (UM brə) *n. pl.* **·bras, ·brae** (-bree) **1.** a shadow or dark area. **2.** *Astron.* in a solar eclipse, the part of the shadow cast by the moon on the earth within which the sun is entirely hidden. [< L]

um•brage (UM brij) *n.* **1.** resentment: now usu. in **take umbrage. 2.** that which gives shade, as a leafy tree. **3.** shade. [ME] —**um•bra•geous** (um BRAY jəs) *adj.*

um•brel•la (um BREL ə) *n.* a shade, usu. round and usu. collapsible, used as a protection against rain or sun. [< Ital. < Ital. *ombrella*]

um•laut (UUM lowt) *n.* **1.** *Ling.* the change in a vowel caused by its partial assimilation to a vowel in the following syllable. **2.** in German, the two dots (̈) put over a vowel thus changed. [< G]

um•pire (UM pīr) *n.* **1.** in certain sports, a person who enforces rules and settles disputed points. **2.** a person called upon to settle a disagreement in opinion. [ME *oumpere*] —*v.t. & v.i.* **•pired, •pir ing** decide as umpire; act as umpire (of or in).

un-¹ *prefix* not; opposed to: *unintentional.*

un-² *prefix* reverse; remove: *untie, unarm.* The list starting below contains self-explanatory words formed with *un-¹* and *un-².*

unabashed	unaided
unabated	unaimed
unabetted	unalarmed
unacademic	unalike
unaccented	unalleviated
unacceptable	unallowable
unaccepted	unalloyed
unacclimated	unalterable
unaccommodating	unaltered
unaccounted	unambiguous
unaccredited	unambitious
unacknowledged	unamplified
unacquainted	unamusing
unadaptable	unanimated
unadjustable	unannounced
unadjusted	unanswerable
unadorned	unanswered
unadulterated	unanticipated
unadvertised	unapologetic
unadvisable	unappalled
unaffiliated	unappealing
unafraid	unappeasable
unaggressive	unappeased

un•a•ble (un AY bəl) *adj.* **1.** lacking the power or resources; not able. **2.** lacking mental capacity; incompetent.

un•a•bridged (UN ə BRIJD) *adj.* not shortened or abridged: an *unabridged* dictionary.

un•ac•com•pa•nied (UN ə KUM pə NEED)

adj. **1.** without an escort or companion. **2.** *Music* without an accompanist.

un•ac•com•plished (UN ə KOM plisht) *adj.* **1.** incomplete; unfinished. **2.** lacking accomplishments.

un•ac•count•a•ble (UN ə KOWN tə bəl) *adj.* **1.** impossible to be accounted for; inexplicable. **2.** remarkable; extraordinary. **3.** not accountable; irresponsible. —**un'ac•count'a•bly** *adv.*

un•ac•cus•tomed (UN ə KUS təmd) *adj.* **1.** not accustomed. **2.** not familiar; strange.

un•ad•vised (UN əd VĪZD) *adj.* **1.** not advised. **2.** rash or imprudent. —**un•ad•vis•ed•ly** (UN əd VĪ zid lee) *adv.*

un•af•fect•ed (UN ə FEK tid) *adj.* **1.** not showing affectation; sincere. **2.** not influenced or changed. —**un'af•fect'ed•ly** *adv.*

un•al•ien•a•ble (un AYL yə nə bəl) *adj.* inalienable.

un•a•ligned (UN ə LĪND) *adj.* **1.** not in a line. **2.** nonaligned.

un-A•mer•i•can (UN ə MER i kən) *adj.* not consistent with the character, ideals, or objectives of the U.S.

u•nan•i•mous (yoo NAN ə məs) *adj.* **1.** sharing the same views or sentiments. **2.** showing or resulting from the assent of all. [< L *unanimus*] —**u•na•nim•i•ty** (YOO nə NIM i tee) *n.* —**u•nan'i•mous•ly** *adv.*

unappetizing	unavailable
unappreciated	unavenged
unappreciative	unavowed
unappropriate	unawakened
unapproved	unawed
unartistic	unbaked
unashamed	unbaptized
unasked	unbeatable
unaspiring	unbeaten
unassailed	unbefitting
unassignable	unbeseeming
unassigned	unbeloved
unassumed	unbesought
unattainable	unbespoken
unattained	unblamable
unattempted	unblamed
unattended	unbleached
unattested	unblemished
unattractive	unboastful
unauthentic	unborrowed
unauthenticated	unbought
unauthorized	unboxed
unavailability	unbraid

un•ap•proach•a•ble (UN ə PROH chə bəl)

adj. **1.** not easy to know; aloof. **2.** inaccessible. —**un'ap·proach'a·ble·ness** *n.*

un·arm (un AHRM) *v.t.* deprive of weapons; disarm. —**un·armed'** *adj.*

un·as·sail·a·ble (UN ə SAY lə bəl) *adj.* **1.** not capable of being disproved; incontrovertible. **2.** proof against attack or destruction; impregnable. —**un'as·sail'a·bly** *adv.*

un·as·sum·ing (UN ə SOO ming) *adj.* modest.

un·at·tached (UN ə TACHT) *adj.* **1.** not attached. **2.** not engaged or married.

un·a·vail·ing (UN ə VAY ling) *adj.* futile; ineffective. —**un'a·vail'ing·ly** *adv.*

un·a·void·a·ble (UN ə VOI də bəl) *adj.* that cannot be avoided; inevitable. —**un'a·void'a·bil'i·ty** *n.* —**un'a·void'a·bly** *adv.*

un·a·ware (UN ə WAIR) *adj.* not aware. —*adv.* unawares.

un·a·wares (UN ə WAIRZ) *adv.* **1.** without warning. **2.** inadvertently.

un·bal·ance (un BAL əns) *v.t.* **·anced, ·anc·ing** **1.** deprive of balance. **2.** disturb or derange, as the mind. —*n.* the state or condition of being unbalanced.

un·bal·anced (un BAL ənst) *adj.* **1.** not in a state of balance. **2.** in bookkeeping, not adjusted so as to balance. **3.** lacking mental balance; erratic.

un·bear·a·ble (un BAIR ə bəl) *adj.* that cannot be tolerated. —**un'bear'a·ble·ness** *n.* —**un'bear'a·bly** *adv.*

un·be·com·ing (UN bi KUM ing) *adj.* **1.** not becoming; not suited. **2.** not befitting. **3.** not decorous; improper.

un·be·knownst (UN bi NOHNST) *adj.* unknown: used with *to.*

un·be·lief (UN bi LEEF) *n.* incredulity; doubt.

un·be·liev·ing (UN bi LEE ving) *adj.* doubting; skeptical. —**un'be·liev'ing·ness** *n.*

unbranched
unbranded
unbreakable
unbreached
unbreachable
unbridgeable
unbridged
unbrotherly
unbruised
unbrushed
unburied
unburned

uncaught
unceasing
uncelebrated
uncensored
uncertified
unchained
unchallenged
unchangeable
unchanged
unchanging
unchaperoned
uncharged
uncharted

unburnt
unbusinesslike
unbutton
uncage
uncalculating
uncanceled
uncandid
uncared-for
uncarpeted
uncatalogued

unchaste
unchastened
unchastised
unchecked
uncheerful
unchewed
unchilled
unchivalrous
unchosen
unchristened

un·bend (un BEND) *v.t. & v.i.* **·bent, ·bend·ing** **1.** relax, as from tension, exertion, or formality. **2.** straighten (something bent or curved).

un·bend·ing (un BEN ding) *adj.* **1.** not bending easily; stiff. **2.** unyielding, as in character. —**un·bend'ing·ly** *adv.* —**un·bend'ing·ness** *n.*

un·bi·ased (un BĪ əst) *adj.* having no bias; impartial.

un·bid·den (un BID n) *adj.* **1.** not invited. **2.** not called forth: *unbidden* thoughts.

un·bind (un BĪND) *v.t.* **·bound, ·bind·ing** free from bindings; undo; release. [ME *unbinden*]

un·blush·ing (un BLUSH ing) *adj.* **1.** not blushing. **2.** immodest; shameless.

un·bolt (un BOHLT) *v.t.* release, as a door, by withdrawing a bolt; unlock.

un·bolt·ed[1] (un BOHL tid) *adj.* not fastened by bolts.

un·bolt·ed[2] *adj.* not sifted: *unbolted* flour.

un·bos·om (un BUUZ əm) *v.t.* **1.** reveal, as one's thoughts or secrets. —*v.i.* **2.** say what is troubling one; tell one's thoughts, feelings, etc.

un·bound·ed (un BOWN did) *adj.* **1.** of unlimited extent. **2.** not restrained.

un·bowed (un BOWD) *adj.* **1.** not bent or bowed. **2.** not subdued.

un·bri·dled (un BRĪD ld) *adj.* **1.** having no bridle on: an *unbridled* horse. **2.** without restraint: an *unbridled* tongue.

un·bro·ken (un BROH kən) *adj.* **1.** not broken; whole. **2.** uninterrupted; smooth: *unbroken* sleep. **3.** not broken to harness or service, as a horse.

unclaimed
unclarified
unclassed
unclassifiable
unclassified
uncleaned
uncleansed
uncleared
unclipped

uncomplaisant
uncomplaisantly
uncompleted
uncompliant
uncomplicated
uncomplimentary
uncomplying
uncompounded
uncomprehended

unclog	uncomprehending
unclouded	uncompressed
uncluttered	uncompromised
uncoagulated	unconcealed
uncoated	unconceded
uncocked	unconcluded
uncoerced	uncondemned
uncollected	uncondensed
uncolored	unconfined
uncombed	unconfirmed
uncombined	unconfused
uncomforted	uncongealed
uncomforting	uncongenial
uncomplaining	unconnected

un•bur•den (un BUR dn) *v.t.* **1.** free from a burden. **2.** relieve oneself of (fears, worries, etc.).

un•caged (un KAYJD) *adj.* **1.** not locked up in a cage; free. **2.** set free from constraint; freed .

un•called-for (un KAWLD for) *adj.* not justified; improper or unnecessary.

un•can•ny (un KAN ee) *adj.* **1.** strange and without explanation. **2.** so good as to seem almost supernatural in origin: *uncanny accuracy.* **—un•can'ni•ly** *adv.* **—un•can'ni•ness** *n.*

un•cer•e•mo•ni•ous (UN ser ə MOH nee əs) *adj.* abrupt; discourteous. **—un'cer•e•mo'ni•ous•ly** *adv.*

un•cer•tain (un SUR tn) *adj.* **1.** that cannot be predicted with certainty; doubtful. **2.** not having certain knowledge or conviction. **3.** not capable of being relied on. **4.** not exactly known.

un•cer•tain•ty (un SUR tn tee) *n. pl.* **•ties 1.** the state of being uncertain; doubt. **2.** a doubtful matter.

un•char•i•ta•ble (un CHAR i tə bəl) *adj.* not charitable; harsh in judgment.

un•cial (UN shəl) *adj.* pertaining to or consisting of a form of letters found in manuscripts from the 3rd to the 9th century, and resembling rounded modern capitals. [< LL *uncialis* inch-high] **—un•cial** *n.*

un•civ•il (un SIV əl) *adj.* discourteous.

un•clad (un KLAD) *adj.* naked.

unconquerable	unconvincing
unconquered	uncooked
unconscientious	uncooperative
unconsecrated	uncoordinated
unconsidered	uncorrected
unconsoled	uncorroborated
unconsolidated	uncorrupted
unconstant	uncorruptness
unconstituted	uncountable

unconstrained	uncourteous
unconstricted	uncovered
unconsumed	uncrate
uncontaminated	uncredited
uncontemplated	uncritical
uncontending	uncross
uncontested	uncrowded
uncontradictable	uncrushable
uncontradicted	uncrystallized
uncontrite	uncultivated
uncontrolled	uncultured
uncontroverted	uncurable
uncontrovertible	uncurbed
unconvinced	uncurdled

un•cle (UNG kəl) *n.* the brother of one's father or mother; also, the husband of one's aunt. [ME]

un•clean (un KLEEN) *adj.* **•er, •est 1.** not clean; foul. **2.** characterized by impure thoughts. **3.** ceremonially impure.

un•clean•ly (un KLEN lee) *adj.* unclean. **—** *adv.* in an unclean manner. **—un•clean'li•ness** *n.*

un•clear (un KLEER) *adj.* **1.** not clear. **2.** confused or muddled: *unclear* reasoning. **—un•clear'ly** *adv.*

Uncle Sam the personification of the government or people of the U.S.

Uncle Tom *Offensive* an African American who is eager to receive the approval of white people. [After the chief character in *Uncle Tom's Cabin* by Harriet Beecher Stowe] **—Uncle Tom'ism**

un•cloak (un KLOHK) *v.t.* **1.** remove the cloak or covering from. **2.** unmask; expose.

un•clothe (un KLOTH) *v.t.* **•clothed** or **•clad** (-KLAD), **•cloth•ing 1.** undress. **2.** uncover.

un•coil (un KOIL) *v.t. & v.i.* unwind or become unwound.

un•com•fort•a•ble (un KUMF tə bəl) *adj.* **1.** not at ease; feeling discomfort. **2.** causing physical or mental uneasiness. **—un•com'fort•a•ble•ness** *n.* **—un•com'fort•a•bly** *adv.*

un•com•mit•ted (UN kə MIT id) *adj.* not committed; esp., not pledged to a particular action, viewpoint, etc.

un•com•mon (un KOM ən) *adj.* not common or usual; remarkable. **—un•com'•mon•ly** *adv.*

un•com•mu•ni•ca•tive (UN kə MYOO ni kə tiv) *adj.* not communicative; reserved. **—un'com•mu'ni•ca•tive•ness** *n.*

un•com•pro•mis•ing (un KOM prə MĪ zing) *adj.* making or admitting of no compromise; inflexible. **—un·com'pro·mis' ing·ly** adv.

uncured	undemocratic
uncurl	undemonstrable
uncushioned	undenominational
uncustomary	undependable
undamaged	undepreciated
undated	underived
undebatable	underogatory
undeceived	undescribable
undecipherable	undeserved
undeciphered	undeservedly
undeclared	undeserving
undecomposed	undesignated
undecorated	undesisting
undefeated	undespairing
undefended	undetachable
undefiled	undetached
undefinable	undetectable
undefined	undetected
undelayed	undetectible
undelineated	undetermined
undeliverable	undeterred
undelivered	undeveloped
undemanding	undeviating

un·con·cern (UN kən SURN) n. absence of concern or anxiety; indifference.

un·con·cerned (UN kən SURND) adj. not concerned or anxious; indifferent. **—un·con·cern·ed·ly** (UN kən SUR nid lee) adj.

un·con·di·tion·al (UN kən DISH ə nl) adj. not limited by conditions; absolute. **—un'con·di'tion·al·ly** adv.

un·con·di·tioned (UN kən DISH ənd) adj. 1. not restricted; unconditional; absolute. 2. Psychol. not acquired; natural.

un·con·scion·a·ble (un KON shə nə bəl) adj. 1. going beyond reasonable bounds; not justified. 2. not governed by conscience; unscrupulous. **—un·con'scion· a·bly** adv.

un·con·scious (un KON shəs) adj. 1. temporarily deprived of consciousness. 2. unaware: with of: unconscious of her charm. 3. not produced by conscious effort. —n. Psychoanal. the area of the psyche that is not in the immediate field of awareness. **—un·con'scious·ly** adv.

un·con·sti·tu·tion·al (UN kon sti TOO shə nl) adj. contrary to the constitution of a state. **—un'con·sti·tu'tion·al'i·ty** n.

un·con·ven·tion·al (un kən VEN shə nl) adj. 1. not adhering to conventions. 2. not usual or ordinary. **—un'con·ven'tion·al' i·ty** n.

un·count·ed (un KOWN tid) adj. 1. not counted. 2. beyond counting.

un·cou·ple (un KUP əl) v.t. & v.i. •led, •ling disconnect or become disconnected.

un·couth (un KOOTH) adj. 1. rough; crude. 2. awkward or odd; ungainly. [ME] **—un·couth'·ness** n.

un·cov·er (un KUV ər) v.t. 1. remove the covering from. 2. make known; disclose. — v.i. 3. raise or remove the hat, as in respect.

unc·tion (UNGK shən) n. 1. exaggerated earnestness. 2. Eccl. a ceremonial anointing with oil, as the sacramental rite of anointing those in danger of death: also called **extreme unction.** 3. the act of anointing. [ME unctioun]

undifferentiated	undisputed
undiffused	undisseminated
undigested	undissolved
undignified	undistilled
undiluted	undistinguishable
undiminished	undistinguished
undiplomatic	undistributed
undiscerned	undisturbed
undiscernible	undiversified
undiscerning	undivided
undisciplined	undivulged
undisclosed	undomesticated
undisconcerted	undoubting
undiscouraged	undramatic
undiscovered	undramatically
undiscriminating	undrape
undiscussed	undreamed
undisguised	undreamt
undisillusioned	undressed
undismayed	undried
undismissed	undrinkable
undispatched	undutiful
undispensed	undyed

unc·tu·ous (UNGK choo əs) adj. 1. characterized by affected emotion; unduly suave. 2. greasy; slippery to the touch. [ME] — **unc'tu·ous·ly** adv. **—unc'tu·ous·ness** n.

un·daunt·ed (un DAWN tid) adj. not daunted or intimidated; fearless.

un·de·ceive (UN di SEEV) v.t. •ceived, •ceiv·ing free from deception.

un·de·ni·a·ble (UN di NĪ ə bəl) adj. 1. that cannot be denied; obviously correct. 2. unquestionably good; excellent. **—un'de·ni' a·bly** adv.

un·der (UN dər) prep. 1. beneath, so as to have something directly above; covered by. 2. in a place lower than; under the hill. 3. beneath the guise or assumption of: under a false name. 4. less than in number, degree, etc.: *under* 10 tons. **5.** lower in rank or position. **6.** dominated by; subordinate to. **7.** subject to the guidance or direction of. **8.** with the liability of incurring: *under* penalty of death. **9.** being the subject of: *under* treatment. **10.** during the period of; in the reign of. **11.** in conformity to. — *adv.* **1.** in or into a position below something; underneath. **2.** in or into a lower degree or rank. **3.** so as to be covered or hidden. **4.** so as to be less than the required amount. —**go under** fail, as a business. —*adj.* **1.** situated or moving under something else; lower or lowermost. **2.** *Zool.* ventral. **3.** lower in rank; subordinate. **4.** insufficient.

under- *combining form* **1.** below in position; on the underside: **underlip, undersole. 2.** below a surface: **underflooring, underpainting. 3.** inferior in rank or importance; subordinate: **undertreasurer. 4.** insufficient or insufficiently; less than is usual or proper: **underdone, underpopulated. 5.** subdued; hidden: **underemphasis, underplot.**

unearned	unenforced
uneaten	unengaged
uneconomic	unengaging
uneconomical	unenjoyable
unedifying	unenlightened
uneducable	unenlivened
uneducated	unenriched
uneffaced	unentangled
uneliminated	unenterprising
unembarrassed	unentertaining
unembellished	unenthusiastic
unemotional	unentitled
unemphatic	unenviable
unenclosed	unenvied
unencumbered	unequipped
unendangered	unerasable
unendearing	unescapable
unending	unessential
unendorsed	unestablished
unendowed	unesthetic
unendurable	unethical
unenduring	unexacting
unenforceable	unexaggerated

un·der·a·chieve (UN dər ə CHEEV) *v.i.* **·chieved, ·chiev·ing** fail to achieve the level of accomplishment suggested by intelligence test scores or abilities. — **un′der·a·chieve′ment** *n.* —**un′der·a·chiev′er** *n.*

un·der·age (UN dər AYJ) *adj.* not of age; immature.

un·der·arm (UN dər AHRM) *adj.* situated, placed, executed, or used under the arm. — *n.* armpit. —*adv.* in an underarm manner.

un·der·brush (UN dər BRUSH) *n.* small trees and shrubs growing beneath forest trees; undergrowth.

un·der·car·riage (UN dər KAR ij) *n.* **1.** the framework supporting the body of a structure, as an automobile. **2.** the principal landing gear of an aircraft.

un·der·clothes (UN dər KLOHZ) *n.pl.* clothes to be worn next to the skin. Also **un′der·cloth′ing** (-KLOH thing).

un·der·coat (UN dər KOHT) *n.* **1.** a coat worn under another coat. **2.** underfur. **3.** a layer of paint, varnish, etc. beneath another layer: also **un′der·coat′ing.** —*v.t.* provide with an undercoat (def. 3).

un·der·cov·er (UN dər KUV ər) *adj.* in secret; esp., engaged in spying or secret investigation.

un·der·cur·rent (UN dər KUR ənt) *n.* **1.** a current, as of water or air, below another or below the surface. **2.** a hidden drift or tendency, as of popular sentiments.

un·der·cut (UN dər KUT) *v.t.* **·cut, ·cut·ting 1.** cut under. **2.** cut away a lower portion of. **3.** work or sell for lower payment than (a rival). **4.** in sports, strike (a ball) so as to give it a backspin. **5.** lessen or destroy the effectiveness of; undermine.

unexalted	unfading
unexamined	unfaltering
unexcavated	unfashionable
unexcelled	unfastened
unexceptional	unfathomable
unexchangeable	unfearing
unexcited	unfeasible
unexciting	unfed
unexcluded	unfelt
unexcused	unfeminine
unexecuted	unfenced
unexercised	unfermented
unexpired	unfertile
unexplainable	unfetter
unexplained	unfilial
unexploded	unfilled
unexploited	unfilmed
unexplored	unfiltered
unexposed	unfired
unexpressed	unfittingly
unexpurgate	unflagging
unextended	unflattering
unextinguish	unflavored

un·der·de·vel· (UN dər di VEL əpt) *adj.* **1.** not suffi developed. **2.** below

119°
119°
119°
119°
119°

a normal or adequate standard in the development of industry, resources, etc.

un•der•dog (UN dər DAWG) n. 1. one who is at a disadvantage in a struggle. 2. one who is victimized or downtrodden by society.

un•der•done (UN dər DUN) adj. not fully cooked.

un•der•es•ti•mate (UN dər ES tə MAYT) v.t. •mat•ed, •mat•ing put too low an estimate on. —**un'der•es'ti•mate** (-mit) n. —**un'der•es'ti•ma'tion** n.

un•der•ex•pose (UN dər ik SPOHZ) v.t. •posed, •pos•ing Photog. expose (a film) less than is required for proper development. —**un•der•ex•po•sure** (UN dər ik SPOH zhər) n. [ME undergon]

un•der•foot (UN dər FUUT) adv. 1. beneath the feet; down on the ground. 2. in the way. —adj. in a position to be stepped on.

un•der•fur (UN dər FUR) n. the coat of dense, fine hair forming the main part of a pelt.

un•der•go (UN dər GOH) v.t. •went, •gone, •go•ing 1. be subjected to. 2. endure. [ME undergon]

un•der•grad•u•ate (UN dər GRAJ ə wit) n. a student in a college or university who has not received a bachelor's degree.

un•der•ground (UN dər GROWND) adj. 1. situated, done, or operating beneath the surface of the ground. 2. done in secret; clandestine. 3. of a group, movement, or activity that is experimental, unconventional, or radical: underground press, underground movie. —n. 1. that which is beneath the surface of the ground. 2. a group secretly organized to oppose those in control of a government or country. —adv. 1. beneath the surface of the ground. 2. secretly.

unflickering	unfruitful
unforbearing	unfulfilled
unforbidden	unfurnished
unforced	ungallant
unforseeable	ungarnished
unforeseen	ungathered
unforetold	ungenerous
unforfeited	ungentle
unforged	ungentlemanly
unforgetting	ungently
unforgivable	ungifted
unforgiven	unglazed
unforgiving	unglue
unforgotten	ungoverned
unformulated	ungraceful

unforsaken	ungraded
unfortified	ungrained
unfought	ungrammatical
unfound	ungratified
unframed	ungrudging
unfree	unguided
unfreeze	unhackneyed
unfrequented	unhailed

un•der•growth (UN dər GROHTH) n. a growth of smaller plants among larger ones in a forest.

un•der•hand (UN dər HAND) adj. 1. done or acting in a secret manner; sly. 2. in sports, underarm. —adv. 1. slyly. 2. underarm.

un•der•hand•ed (UN dər HAN did) adj. 1. underhand. 2. short-handed. —**un'der•hand'ed•ly** adv. —**un'der•hand'ed•ness** n.

un•der•lay (UN dər LAY) v.t. •laid, •lay•ing 1. place (one thing) under another. 2. furnish with a base or lining.

un•der•lie (UN dər LĪ) v.t. •lay, •lain, •ly•ing 1. lie below or under. 2. be the basis or support of: the principle that underlies a scheme. [ME underlyen]

un•der•line (UN dər LĪN) v.t. •lined, •lin•ing 1. mark with a line underneath. 2. emphasize.

un•der•ling (UN dər ling) n. a subordinate; inferior.

un•der•mine (UN dər MĪN) v.t. •mined, •min•ing 1. excavate beneath; dig a mine or passage under. 2. weaken by wearing away at the base. 3. weaken or impair secretly or by degrees: undermine one's health.

un•der•neath (UN dər NEETH) adv. 1. in a place below. 2. on the lower side. —prep. 1. beneath; under; below. 2. under the form or appearance of. 3. under the authority of. —adj. lower. —n. the lower part or side. [ME undernethe]

un•der•nour•ished (UN dər NUR isht) adj. provided with too little nourishment for proper health and growth.

un•der•pin•ning (UN dər PIN ing) n. 1. material or framework used to support a wall or building from below. 2. pl. underlying causes or principles.

unhampered	unhoused
unharassed	unhung
unharbored	unhurried
unhardened	unhurt
unharmed	unhygienic
unharmful	unhyphenated
unharmonious	unidentified

unharnessed
unharvested
unhatched
unhealed
unhealthful
unheated
unheeded
unhelpful
unheralded
unheroic
unhesitating
unhindered
unhistorical
unhonored
unhoped
unhostile

unidiomatic
unilluminated
unillustrated
unimaginable
unimaginative
unimagined
unimitated
unimpaired
unimpassioned
unimpeded
unimportant
unimposing
unimpressed
unimpressionable
unimpressive
unimproved

un·der·priv·i·leged (UN dər PRIV lijd) *adj.* not privileged to enjoy certain material or social benefits because of poverty, illiteracy, etc.

un·der·rate (UN dər RAYT) *v.t.* **·rat·ed,** **·rat·ing** rate too low; underestimate.

un·der·score (UN dər SKOR) *v.t.* **·scored,** **·scor·ing 1.** put a line under. **2.** emphasize. —*n.* a line drawn beneath a word, etc., as for emphasis.

un·der·sea (UN dər SEE) *adj.* existing, carried on, or adapted for use beneath the surface of the sea. —*adv.* beneath the surface of the sea: also **un·der·seas** (UN dər SEEZ).

un·der·sell (UN dər SEL) *v.t.* **·sold,** **·sell·ing 1.** sell at a lower price than. **2.** sell for less than the real value.

un·der·shirt (UN dər SHURT) *n.* a garment worn beneath a shirt, generally of cotton.

un·der·shot (UN dər SHOT) *adj.* **1.** propelled by water that flows underneath: said of a water wheel. **2.** projecting, as the lower jaw or teeth.

un·der·side (UN dər ID) *n.* the lower or under side or surface.

un·der·signed (UN dər SIND) *adj.* having one's signature at the foot of a document. —*n.* (UN dər SIND) the subscriber or subscribers to a document: with *the.*

un·der·stand (UN dər STAND) *v.* **·stood,** **·stand·ing** *v.t.* **1.** come to know the meaning or import of; apprehend. **2.** comprehend the nature or character of. **3.** have comprehension or mastery of. **4.** be aware of; realize. **5.** have been told. **6.** infer the meaning of. **7.** accept as a condition or stipulation. **8.** supply in thought when unexpressed. **9.** be in agreement with; be privately in sympathy with. —*v.i.* **10.** have

understanding; comprehend. **11.** be informed; believe. [ME *understanden*] — **un'·der·stand'a·ble** *adj.* —**un'der· stand'a·bly** *adv.*

uninaugurated
unincorporated
uninfected
uninfested
uninflected
uninfluenced
uninfluential
uninformative
uninformed
uninhabitable
uninhabited
uninhibited
uninitiated
uninjured
uninspired
uninspiring
uninstructed
uninstructive
uninsurable
uninsured
unintellectual
unintelligent
unintelligibility

unintelligible
unintended
unintentional
uninterested
uninteresting
uninterpreted
uninterrupted
unintimidated
uninventive
uninvested
uninvited
uninviting
uninvolved
unjoined
unjointed
unjudicial
unjustifiable
unkindliness
unknowing
unlabeled
unladylike
unlamented
unlaundered

un·der·stand·ing (UN dər STAN ding) *n.* **1.** the act of one who understands or the resulting state; comprehension. **2.** the sum of the mental powers by which knowledge is acquired, retained, and extended. **3.** the facts or elements of a case as apprehended by any one individual. **4.** an informal or confidential compact; also, the thing agreed on. **5.** an arrangement or settlement of differences. —*adj.* **1.** possessing comprehension and good sense. **2.** tolerant or sympathetic.

un·der·state (UN dər STAYT) *v.* **·stat·ed,** **·stat·ing** *v.t.* **1.** state with less force than the truth warrants or allows. **2.** state, as a number or dimension, as less than the true one. —*v.i.* **3.** make an understatement.

un·der·state·ment (UN dər STAYT mənt) *n.* a statement deliberately restrained in tone.

un·der·stood (UN dər STUUD) *past tense, past participle of* UNDERSTAND. —*adj.* **1.** assumed; agreed upon by all. **2.** assumed when unexpressed, as the subject of a sentence.

un·der·stud·y (UN dər STUD ee) *v.t. & v.i.* **·stud·ied, ·stud·y·ing** study (a part) in order to be able, if necessary, to take the place of the performer playing it. —*n. pl.*

•**stud•ies** a performer prepared to take the place of another in a given role if called on.

un•der•take (UN dər TAYK) *v.t.* •**took,** •**tak•en, tak•ing 1.** take upon oneself; agree or attempt to do; begin. **2.** contract to do; pledge oneself to. **3.** guarantee or promise. **4.** take under charge or guidance.

unleased	unmapped
unleavened	unmarked
unlessened	unmarketable
unlet	unmarred
unlevel	unmarriageable
unlicensed	unmarried
unlighted	unmatched
unlikable	unmeant
unlikeable	unmeasurable
unliquefied	unmeasured
unliquidated	unmechanical
unlit	unmelodious
unlively	unmelted
unlocked	unmendable
unlovable	unmentioned
unloved	unmerited
unloving	unmethodical
unmagnified	unmilitary
unmanageable	unmilled
unmanful	unmingled
unmanned	unmirthful
unmannered	unmistaken
unmanufactured	unmixed

un•der•tak•er *n.* **1.** (UN dər TAY kər) a funeral director. **2.** (UN dər TAY kər) one who undertakes something.

un•der•tak•ing *n.* (UN dər TAY king) **1.** something undertaken; a task. **2.** an engagement, promise, or guaranty. **3.** the business of an undertaker.

un•der•tone (UN dər TOHN) *n.* **1.** a subdued voice or a whisper. **2.** a subdued shade of a color. **3.** an implicit meaning or suggestion.

un•der•tow (UN dər TOH) *n.* the seaward undercurrent below the surf.

un•der•val•ue (UN dər VAL yoo) *v.t.* •**ued,** •**u•ing** value too lightly.

un•der•wa•ter (UN dər WAW tər) *adj. & adv.* below the surface of a body of water; also, below the waterline of a ship.

un•der•way (UN dər WAY) *adv.* in progress; into operation.

un•der•world (UN dər WURLD) *n.* **1.** in mythology, the abode of the dead. **2.** the part of society engaged in crime or vice; esp., organized criminals.

un•der•write (UN dər RĪT) *v.t.* •**wrote,** •**writ•ten, writ•ing 1.** write beneath; sub-

scribe. **2.** in finance, execute and deliver (insurance on specified property); insure; assume (a risk) by way of insurance. **3.** engage to buy, at a determined price and time, all or part of the stock in (a new enterprise or company) that is not subscribed for by the public. **4.** assume financial responsibility for, as an enterprise. —**un'der• writ'er** *n.*

unmodified	unnoticeable
unmoistened	unnoticed
unmold	unobjectionable
unmolested	unobliging
unmollified	unobscured
unmortgaged	unobservant
unmotivated	unobserved
unmounted	unobserving
unmourned	unobstructed
unmovable	unobtainable
unmoved	unobtrusive
unmoving	unobtrusiveness
unmusical	unoffending
unmuzzle	unoffered
unmystified	unofficial
unnamable	unoiled
unnamed	unopened
unnaturalized	unopposed
unnavigable	unoppressed
unneeded	unordained
unneedful	unoriginal
unnegotiable	unorthodox
unneighborly	unostentatious

un•de•sir•a•ble (UN di ZĪR ə bəl) *adj.* not desirable; objectionable. —*n.* an objectionable person. —**un'de•sir'a•bil'i•ty** *n.*

un•do (un DOO) *v.t.* •**did, •done, •do•ing 1.** cause to be as if never done; reverse; annul. **2.** loosen or untie, as a knot etc. **3.** unfasten and open, as a parcel. **4.** bring to ruin; destroy. [ME] —**un•do'a•ble** *adj.*

un•do•ing (un DOO ing) *n.* **1.** the reversing or annulling of what has been done. **2.** a bringing to destruction; ruin; also, the cause of ruin.

un•done (un DUN) *adj.* **1.** not done. **2.** untied; unfastened. **3.** ruined.

un•doubt•ed (un DOW tid) *adj.* accepted as beyond question, beyond doubt. —**un• doubt'ed•ly** *adv.*

un•dress (un DRES) *v.t.* •**dressed, •dress•ing 1.** divest of clothes; strip. —*v.i.* **2.** remove one's clothing. —*n.* **1.** casual or ordinary attire, as distinguished from formal dress. **2.** dress not designed for wearing in public; negligee.

un•due (un DOO) *adj.* **1.** excessive; disproportionate. **2.** not due; not yet demandable. **3.** inappropriate; improper.

un•du•late (UN jə LAYT) *v.t. & v.i.* **•lat•ed, •lat•ing 1.** move or cause to move like a wave or in waves. **2.** have or cause to have a wavy appearance. —*adj.* (UN jə lit) **1.** having a wavy margin, as a leaf. **2.** having wave-like markings, as of color: also **un•du•lat•ed** (UN jə LAY tid). [< L *undulatus*]

un•du•la•tion (UN jə LAY shən) *n.* **1.** the act of undulating. **2.** a waving or sinuous motion or appearance. **3.** a wave. — **un•du•la•to•ry** (UN jə lə TOR ee) *adj.*

unostentatiously	unperplexed
unowned	unpersuadable
unpacified	unpersuaded
unpaid	unpersuasive
unpainful	unperturbed
unpainted	unphilosophical
unpaired	unpicked
unpalatable	unpierced
unpardonable	unpile
unparted	unpin
unpasteurized	unpitied
unpatented	unpitying
unpatriotic	unplaced
unpaved	unplagued
unpeaceful	unplanned
unpedigreed	unplanted
unpeg	unpleasing
unpensioned	unpledged
unpeopled	unplowed
unperceived	unplucked
unperceiving	unplug
unperfected	unpoetic
unperformed	unpolarized

un•du•ly (un DOO lee) *adv.* **1.** excessively. **2.** unjustly.

un•dy•ing (un DI ing) *adj.* everlasting.

un•earth (un URTH) *v.t.* **1.** dig up; bring to light. **2.** discover. [ME *unerthen*]

un•earth•ly (un URTH lee) *adj.* **1.** not earthly; sublime. **2.** weird; terrifying; supernatural. **3.** ridiculous. —**un•earth′li•ness** *n.*

un•eas•y (un EE zee) *adj.* **•eas•i•er, •eas•i•est 1.** lacking ease, assurance, or security; disturbed. **2.** not affording ease or rest. **3.** showing embarrassment; strained. —**un•eas′i•ly** *adv.* —**un•eas′i•ness** *n.* [ME *unesy*]

un•em•ploy•a•ble (UN em PLOI ə bəl) *adj.* not employable. —*n.* a person who cannot be employed.

un•em•ployed (UN em PLOID) *adj.* **1.** out

of work. **2.** not being put to use. —*n.* (*construed as pl.*) jobless people: *the unemployed.* —**un′em•ploy′ment** *n.*

un•e•qual (un EE kwəl) *adj.* **1.** not having equal extension, duration, ability, etc. **2.** inadequate for the purpose: with *to.* **3.** varying; irregular. **4.** not balanced; not symmetrical. —**un•e′qual•ly** *adv.*

un•e•qualed (un EE kwəld) *adj.* not equaled or matched; supreme.

un•e•quiv•o•cal (un i KWIV ə kwəl) *adj.* understandable in only one way. — **un′e•quiv′o•cal•ly** *adv.*

un•err•ing (un ER ing) *adj.* **1.** making no mistakes; not erring. **2.** certain; accurate. —**un•err′ing•ly** *adv.*

UNESCO (yoo NES koh) *United Nations Educational, Scientific and Cultural Organization.*

un•e•ven (un EE vən) *adj.* **1.** not even, smooth, parallel, or level; rough. **2.** not divisible by two without remainder; odd: said of numbers. **3.** not uniform; variable; spasmodic. —**un•e′ven•ness** *n.*

un•e•vent•ful (UN i VENT fəl) *adj.* lacking noteworthy events; quiet. —**un′e•vent′ ful•ly** *adv.*

unpolished	unprofitable
unpolitical	unprogressive
unpolluted	unprohibited
unpopulated	unpromising
unposed	unprompted
unpredictable	unpronounced
unpremeditated	unpropitious
unpreoccupied	unproportioned
unprepared	unprotected
unprepossessing	unproved
unprescribed	unproven
unpresentable	unprovoked
unpreserved	unpublishable
unpressed	unpublished
unpretentious	unpunishable
unpretentiousness	unpunished
unprevailing	unpurified
unpreventable	unquenchable
unprivileged	unquotable
unproductive	unratified

un•ex•cep•tion•a•ble (UN ik SEP shə nə bəl) *adj.* that cannot be objected to. — **un′ex•cep′tion•a•bly** *adv.*

un•ex•pect•ed (UN ik SPEK tid) *adj.* not expected; unforeseen. —**un′ex•pect′ ed•ly** *adv.*

un•fail•ing (un FAY ling) *adj.* **1.** giving or constituting a supply that never fails; inexhaustible. **2.** not falling short of need, hope, or expectation. **3.** sure; infallible.

un·fair (un FAIR) *adj.* **1.** not fair or just. **2.** dishonest; fraudulent.

un·faith·ful (un FAYTH fəl) *adj.* **1.** not having kept faith; unworthy of trust. **2.** not true to marriage vows; adulterous. **3.** not accurate or exact. **—un·faith'ful·ly** *adv.*

un·fa·mil·iar (UN fə MIL yər) *adj.* **1.** not having acquaintance: with *with.* **2.** not known or recognizable. **—un'fa·mil'i·ar'i·ty** (UN fə MIL ee AR i tee) *n.*

un·fast·en (un FAS ən) *v.t. & v.i.* untie or become untied; loosen; open. [ME *unfastnen*]

un·fa·vor·a·ble (un FAY və rə bəl) *adj.* not favorable; adverse. **—un·fa'vor·a·bly** *adv.*

un·feel·ing (un FEE ling) *adj.* **1.** not sympathetic; cruel. **2.** devoid of feeling or sensation. **—un·feel'ing·ly** *adv.*

un·feigned (un FAYND) *adj.* sincere; genuine. **—un·feign·ed·ly** (un FAY nid lee) *adv.*

un·fix (un FIKS) *v.t.* **1.** unfasten. **2.** unsettle.

un·flap·pa·ble (un FLAP ə bəl) *adj.* imperturbable. **—un·flap'pa·bil'i·ty**

unravaged	unrefined
unreachable	unreflecting
unreached	unrefreshed
unreadable	unrefreshing
unrealistic	unregarded
unrealizable	unregistered
unrealized	unregretted
unreasoned	unregulated
unrebuked	unrehearsed
unreceptive	unrelated
unreciprocated	unrelaxed
unreclaimed	unreliable
unrecognizable	unrelieved
unrecognized	unrelished
unrecompensed	unremarkable
unreconcilable	unremarked
unreconciled	unremedied
unrecorded	unremembered
unrecoverable	unremitted
unrecruited	unremorseful
unrectified	unremovable
unredeemed	unremoved
unredressed	unremunerated

un·fledged (un FLEJD) *adj.* **1.** not yet fledged, as a young bird. **2.** immature; inexperienced.

un·flinch·ing (un FLIN ching) *adj.* not shrinking from danger etc.; brave.

un·fold (un FOHLD) *v.t.* **1.** open or spread

out (something folded). **2.** make clear by detailed explanation. **3.** evolve; develop. **—v.i. 4.** become opened. **5.** become manifest. [ME *unfolden*]

un·for·get·ta·ble (UN fər GET ə bəl) *adj.* memorable. **—un'for·get'ta·bly** *adv.*

un·formed (un FORMD) *adj.* **1.** devoid of shape or form. **2.** not fully developed in character. **3.** unorganized.

un·for·tu·nate (un FOR chə nit) *adj.* **1.** not fortunate or happy; unsuccessful. **2.** causing or attended by ill fortune; disastrous. **—** *n.* one who is unfortunate. **—un·for'tu·nate·ly** *adv.*

un·found·ed (un FOWN did) *adj.* **1.** having no foundation; groundless. **2.** not established. **—un·found'ed·ness** *n.*

un·friend·ly (un FREND lee) *adj.* **1.** unkindly disposed; inimical; hostile. **2.** not favorable or propitious. **—un·friend'li·ness** *n.*

un·frock (un FROK) *v.t.* **1.** depose, as a priest, from ecclesiastical rank. **2.** divest of a frock or gown.

un·furl (un FURL) *v.t. & v.i.* **1.** spread open, as a flag. **2.** spread out; expand.

un·gain·ly (un GAYN lee) *adj.* **·li·er, ·li·est** lacking grace; awkward. **—un·gain'li·ness** *n.*

un·god·ly (un GOD lee) *adj.* **·li·er, ·li·est 1.** having no reverence for God; impious. **2.** wicked. **3.** outrageous. **—un·god'li·ness** *n.*

un·gra·cious (un GRAY shəs) *adj.* **1.** lacking in graciousness of manner. **2.** not pleasing; offensive. [ME] **—un·gra'cious·ness** *n.*

un·grate·ful (un GRAYT fəl) *adj.* **1.** not feeling or showing gratitude. **2.** disagreeable. **—un·grate'·ful·ly** *adv.*

unremunerative	unresisting
unrendered	unresolved
unrenewed	unrespectable
unrenounced	unresponsive
unrenowned	unrested
unrented	unresting
unrepaid	unrestrainable
unrepairable	unrestricted
unrepaired	unretentive
unrepealed	unretracted
unrepentant	unreturned
unrepenting	unrevealed
unreplaced	unrevenged
unreplenished	unreversed
unreported	unrevised
unrepresentative	unrevoked
unrepresented	unrewarded

unrepressed   **unrhythmical**
unrequested   **unrightful**
unrequited   **unripened**
unresigned   **unroasted**
unresistant   **unrobe**

un·guard·ed (un GAHR did) *adj.* **1.** being without protection. **2.** characterized by lack of caution or discretion. **—un·guard'·ed·ness** *n.*

un·guent (UNG gwənt) *n.* an ointment or salve. [ME]

un·gu·late (UNG gyə lit) *adj.* **1.** having hoofs. **2.** designating a large group of hoofed mammals, including the horse, hog, and all the ruminants. [< LL *ungulatus* hoofed] **—***n.* a hoofed mammal.

un·hal·lowed (un HAL ohd) *adj.* **1.** not consecrated or made holy. **2.** wicked.

un·hand (un HAND) *v.t.* release from the hand; let go.

un·hand·y (un HAN dee) *adj.* **·hand·i·er, ·hand·i·est 1.** inconvenient. **2.** clumsy; lacking in manual skill. **—un·hand'i·ness** *n.*

un·hap·py (un HAP ee) *adj.* **·pi·er, ·pi·est 1.** sad; miserable; depressed. **2.** unfortunate. **3.** not tactful or appropriate. **—un·hap'pi·ness** *n.*

un·hinge (un HINJ) *v.t.* **·hinged, ·hing·ing 1.** take from the hinges. **2.** detach; dislodge. **3.** unsettle, as the mind.

un·hitch (un HICH) *v.t.* set loose; detach.

un·ho·ly (un HOH lee) *adj.* **·li·er, ·li·est 1.** not sacred or hallowed. **2.** lacking purity; wicked; sinful. **3.** *Informal* dreadful. [ME] **—un·ho'li·ness** *n.*

unromantic	**unscheduled**
unroof	**unscholarly**
unrounded	**unschooled**
unruled	**unscientific**
unsafe	**unscientifically**
unsaid	**unscoured**
unsalable	**unscraped**
unsalaried	**unscratched**
unsalted	**unscreened**
unsanctified	**unsealed**
unsanctioned	**unseasoned**
unsanitary	**unseated**
unsated	**unseaworthy**
unsatisfactorily	**unseconded**
unsatisfactory	**unsecured**
unsatisfied	**unseeded**
unsatisfying	**unseeing**
unsatisfyingly	**unseen**
unsaved	**unsegmented**
unscaled	**unselected**

unscanned   **unselective**
unscarred   **unsensitive**
unscented   **unsent**

u·ni·cam·er·al (YOO ni KAM ər əl) *adj.* consisting of but one legislative chamber.

UNICEF (YOO nə SEF) United Nations Children's Fund. [orig. *United Nations Children's Emergency Fund*]

u·ni·cel·lu·lar (YOO nə SEL yə lər) *adj.* *Biol.* consisting of a single cell, as a protozoan.

u·ni·corn (YOO ni KORN) *n.* a mythical horselike animal with one horn. [ME *unicorne*]

un·i·den·ti·fied flying object (UN i DEN tə FID) any of various objects alleged to have been seen flying in the sky and believed by some to come from outer space. Abbr. *UFO.*

u·ni·form (YOO nə FORM) *adj.* **1.** being always the same or alike, as in form, quality, degree, etc.; not varying. **2.** agreeing or identical with each other; alike. **—***n.* **1.** a distinctive form of dress worn by members of the same organization or service, as soldiers, sailors, etc. **2.** a single suit of such clothes. **—***v.t.* **1.** put into or clothe with a uniform. **2.** make uniform. [< MF *uniforme*]

u·ni·form·i·ty (YOO nə FOR mi tee) *n. pl.* **·ties 1.** the state or quality of being uniform; also, an instance of it. **2.** conformity, as in opinions or religion. **3.** monotony; sameness.

u·ni·fy (YOO nə FI) *v.t. & v.i.* **·fied, ·fy·ing** combine into a unit; become or cause to be one. [< LL *unificare*] **—u'ni·fi·ca'tion** *n.* **—u'ni·fi'er** *n.*

unsentimental	**unsigned**
unserved	**unsilenced**
unserviceable	**unsimilar**
unsevered	**unsized**
unsewn	**unslaked**
unshadowed	**unsmiling**
unshaken	**unsmilingly**
unshapely	**unsmoked**
unshared	**unsocial**
unshaven	**unsoftened**
unshed	**unsoiled**
unshelled	**unsold**
unsheltered	**unsoldierly**
unshielded	**unsolicited**
unshod	**unsolicitous**
unshorn	**unsoluble**
unshrinkable	**unsolvable**
unshrinking	**unsolved**

unshrunk	unsoothed
unsifted	unsorted

u·ni·lat·er·al (YOO nə LAT ər əl) *adj.* **1.** of, pertaining to, or existing on one side only. **2.** made, undertaken, done, or signed by only one of two or more people or parties. **3.** one-sided. —**u'ni·lat'er·al·ly** *adv.*

un·im·peach·a·ble (UN im PEE chə bəl) *adj.* not to be called into question as regards truth etc. —**un'im·peach'a·bly** *adv.*

un·ion (YOON yən) *n.* **1.** the act of uniting, or the state of being united; also, that which is so formed. **2.** a joining of nations, states, parties, etc. for some mutual interest or purpose. **3.** the joining of two persons in marriage; also, the state of wedlock. **4.** a labor union. **5.** *Mech.* a device for connecting parts of machinery; esp., a connection for pipes or rods. **6.** a device emblematic of union, used in a flag or emblem. —**the Union** the U.S.; esp., the Federal government during the Civil War. [ME]

un·ion·ism (YOON yə NIZ əm) *n.* **1.** the principle of combining for unity of purpose and action. **2.** the principle or the support of labor unions. —**un'ion·ist** *n.*

un·ion·ize (YOON yə NIZ) *v.* -**ized, ·izing** *v.t.* **1.** cause to join, or to organize into a union, esp. a labor union. **2.** make conform to the rules etc. of a union. —*v.i.* **3.** become a member of or organize a labor union. —**un'ion·i·za'tion** *n.*

Union Jack the British national flag.

union shop an industrial establishment that hires only members of a labor union or those who promise to join a union within a specified time.

u·nique (yoo NEEK) *adj.* **1.** being the only one of its kind; sole. **2.** having no equal or like. **3.** loosely, unusual, rare, or notable. [< F] —**u·nique'ness** *n.*

unsought	unstick
unsounded	unstigmatized
unsown	unstinted
unspecified	unstitched
unspelled	unstoppable
unspent	unstrained
unspilled	unstressed
unspiritual	unstructured
unspoiled	unstuffed
unspoken	unsubdued
unsportsmanlike	unsubmissive
unspotted	unsubscribed
unsprung	unsubsidized
unstained	unsubstantiated
unstalked	unsuccessful

unstamped	unsuited
unstandardized	unsullied
unstarched	unsunk
unstated	unsupervised
unstatesmanlike	unsupportable
unsteadfast	unsupportably
unstemmed	unsupported
unsterile	unsuppressed
unsterilized	unsure

u·ni·sex (YOO nə SEKS) *adj.* for or appropriate to both sexes: *unisex* fashions.

u·ni·sex·u·al (YOO nə SEK shoo əl) *adj.* of only one sex; also, having sexual organs of one sex only.

u·ni·son (YOO nə sən) *n.* **1.** a sounding of the same words, tones, etc. simultaneously: with *in:* They answered in *unison.* **2.** complete accord or agreement. **3.** *Music* a state in which instruments or voices perform identical parts simultaneously, in the same or different octaves. [< MF]

u·nit (YOO nit) *n.* **1.** a single person or thing regarded as an individual but belonging to an entire group. **2.** a subdivision of a similar but larger body or group. **3.** a piece of equipment, usu. part of a larger object and having a specific function. **4.** a standard quantity; measure. **5.** *Math.* a quantity whose measure is represented by the number 1; a least whole number.

U·ni·tar·i·an (yoo ni TAIR ee ən) *n.* a member of a religious denomination that emphasizes complete freedom of religious opinion. —**U'ni·tar'i·an·ism** *n.*

u·ni·tar·y (YOO ni TER ee) *adj.* **1.** of or pertaining to a unit. **2.** characterized by or based on unity. **3.** having the nature of a unit; whole.

u·nite (yoo NĪT) *v.* **u·nit·ed, u·nit·ing** *v.t.* **1.** join together so as to form a whole; combine. **2.** bring into close connection, as by legal, physical, social, or other tie. **3.** join in marriage. **4.** attach permanently or solidly; bond. —*v.i.* **5.** become or be merged into one; combine. **6.** join together for action; concur. [ME *uniten*] —**u·nit'ed** *adj.*

United Nations an organization of sovereign states, having its permanent headquarters in New York City since 1951.

unsurmountable	untaken
unsurpassable	untalented
unsurpassed	untamable
unsurprised	untameable
unsusceptible	untanned
unsuspected	untapped
unsuspicious	untarnished

unsustainable	untasted
unsustained	untaxable
unswayed	untaxed
unsweetened	unteachable
unswept	untechnical
unswerving	untempered
unsymmetrical	untenanted
unsymmetrically	untended
unsympathetic	untested
unsympathetically	untethered
unsystematic	unthanked
unsystematically	untheatrical
unsystematized	unthought
untack	unthoughtful
untactful	unthriftiness
untactfully	unthrifty
untainted	unthrone

u•ni•ty (YOO ni tee) *n. pl.* **•ties 1.** the state or fact of being one. **2.** something that is wholly united and complete within itself. **3.** a state or quality of mutual understanding and harmony. **4.** the harmonious agreement of parts or elements into one united whole. **5.** singleness or constancy of purpose, action, etc. **6.** in art and literature, the arrangement of parts into a whole exhibiting oneness of purpose, spirit, and style. **7.** *Math.* **a** the number one. **b** a quantity, such as 1, that leaves any number unchanged under multiplication. [ME *unite*]

u•ni•valve (YOO ni valv) *adj.* having only one valve, as a mollusk. —*n.* **1.** a mollusk having a univalve shell. **2.** a shell of a single piece.

u•ni•ver•sal (YOO nə VUR səl) *adj.* **1.** of, pertaining to, or typical of all or the whole. **2.** including, involving, intended for, or applicable to all. **3.** of, pertaining to, or occurring throughout the universe. —*n.* any general or universal notion, condition, principle, etc. —**u'ni•ver'sal•ly** *adv.*

u•ni•ver•sal•i•ty (YOO nə vər SAL i tee) *n. pl.* **•ties 1.** the state or quality of being universal. **2.** unrestricted fitness or adaptability. **3.** an all-embracing range of knowledge, abilities, etc.

u•ni•verse (YOO nə vurs) *n.* **1.** the aggregate of all existing things; the whole creation embracing all celestial bodies and all of space; the cosmos. **2.** the whole world, esp. with reference to all its creatures. [ME]

untilled	untuned
untinge	untuneful
untiring	unturned
untiringly	untwisted

untitled	untypical
untouched	untypically
untraceable	unusable
untraced	unutilizable
untracked	unuttered
untractable	unvaccinated
untrained	unvacillating
untransferable	unvalidated
untransferred	unvanquished
untranslatable	unvaried
untranslated	unventilated
untransmitted	unverifiable
untraversed	unverified
untrimmed	unversed
untrod	unvexed
untroubled	unvisited
untrustful	unvitiated
untrustworthy	unvocal
untufted	unvocally
untunable	unwakened

u•ni•ver•si•ty (YOO nə VUR si tee) *n. pl.* **•ties 1.** an institution that includes schools for graduate or professional study, as well as an undergraduate division, and grants master's and doctor's degrees. **2.** the faculty and students of a university. **3.** the buildings and grounds of a university. [ME *universite*]

un•kempt (un KEMPT) *adj.* not combed; not clean or neat; untidy. [< UN-[1] + *KEMPT combed*]

un•kind (un KĪND) *adj.* showing a lack of kindness. —**un•kind'ly** *adj. & adv.*

un•known (un NOHN) *adj.* **1.** not known or apprehended; not recognized, as a fact or person. **2.** not ascertained, discovered, or established. —*n.* an unknown person or quantity.

un•law•ful (un LAW fəl) *adj.* **1.** contrary to or in violation of law; illegal. **2.** born out of wedlock. —**un•law'ful•ly** *adv.*

un•learn•ed (un LUR nid) *adj.* **1.** not possessed of or characterized by learning; illiterate; ignorant. **2.** unworthy of or unlike a learned man. **3.** (un LURND) not acquired by learning or study.

un•leash (un LEESH) *v.t.* set free from or as from a leash.

un•less (un LES) *conj.* if it be not a fact that; except that: *Unless we persevere, we shall lose.* [ME *on less*]

unwalled	unwincing
unwanted	unwinking
unwarlike	unwisdom
unwarmed	unwished
unwarped	unwithered
unwarranted	unwithering

unwashed
unwasted
unwatched
unwavering
unweakened
unweaned
unwearable
unweary
unweathered
unweave
unwed
unwedded
unweeded
unwelcome
unwelded
unwetted
unwhetted
unwifely

unwitnessed
unwomanly
unwon
unwooded
unwooed
unworkable
unworked
unworkmanlike
unworn
unworried
unworshiped
unwoven
unwrinkled
unyielding
unyouthful
unyouthfully
unzealous
unzip

un·let·tered (un LET ərd) *adj.* uneducated; illiterate.

un·like (un LĪK) *adj.* having little or no resemblance; different. —*prep.* dissimilar to or different from. —**un·like′ness** *n.*

un·like·ly (un LĪK lee) *adj.* **1.** not likely; improbable. **2.** not inviting or promising success. —*adv.* improbably. —**un·like′-li·ness, un·like′li·hood** *n.*

un·lim·ber (un LIM bər) *v.t. & v.i.* prepare for action.

un·lim·it·ed (un LIM i tid) *adj.* **1.** having no limits in space, number, or time. **2.** not limited by restrictions. **3.** not limited by qualifications; undefined.

un·load (un LOHD) *v.t.* **1.** remove the load or cargo from. **2.** take off or discharge (cargo etc.). **3.** relieve of something burdensome or oppressive. **4.** withdraw the charge of ammunition from. **5.** dispose of. —*v.i.* **6.** discharge freight, cargo, or other burden.

un·loose (un LOOS) *v.t.* **·loosed, ·loos·ing** release from fastenings; set loose or free.

un·luck·y (un LUK ee) *adj.* **·luck·i·er, ·luck·i·est 1.** not favored by luck. **2.** resulting in or attended by ill luck. **3.** ill-omened. —**un·luck′i·ly** *adv.* —**un·luck′i·ness** *n.*

un·man (un MAN) *v.t.* **·manned, ·man·ning 1.** cause to lose courage or fortitude; dishearten. **2.** render unmanly or effeminate. **3.** deprive of virility; castrate.

un·man·ly (un MAN lee) *adj.* **·li·er, ·li·est 1.** not masculine or virile; effeminate. **2.** not brave; cowardly. —**un·man′li·ness** *n.*

un·man·ner·ly (un′MAN ər lee) *adj.* lacking manners; rude. —*adv.* impolitely; rudely. —**un·man′ner·li·ness** *n.*

un·men·tion·a·ble (un MEN shə nə bəl) *adj.* not proper or fit to be mentioned or discussed. —**un·men′tion·a·bly** *adv.*

un·mind·ful (un MĪND fəl) *adj.* neglectful; inattentive; careless. —**un·mind′ful·ly** *adv.* —**un·mind′ful·ness** *n.*

un·mis·tak·a·ble (UN mi STAY kə bəl) *adj.* that cannot be mistaken; evident; clear. —**un′mis·tak′a·bly** *adv.*

un·mit·i·gat·ed (un MIT ə GAY tid) *adj.* **1.** not mitigated or lightened in effect. **2.** absolute: an *unmitigated* rogue.

un·mor·al (un MOR əl) *adj.* having no moral sense; neither moral nor immoral. —**un·mor′al·ly** *adv.*

un·nat·u·ral (un NACH ər əl) *adj.* **1.** contrary to the laws of nature. **2.** monstrous; inhuman. **3.** not having, or inconsistent with, those attitudes, feelings, etc. considered normal; abnormal. **4.** artificial; affected. —**un·nat′u·ral·ly** *adv.*

un·nec·es·sar·y (un NES ə SER ee) *adj.* not required or necessary; not essential. —**un·nec′es·sar′i·ly** *adv.*

un·nerve (un NURV) *v.t.* **·nerved, ·nerv·ing** deprive of strength, firmness, selfcontrol, or courage; unman.

un·par·al·leled (un PAR ə LELD) *adj.* without parallel; not matched; unprecedented.

un·pleas·ant (un PLEZ ənt) *adj.* disagreeable; objectionable; not pleasing. —**un·pleas′ant·ness** *n.*

un·plumbed (un PLUMD) *adj.* not explored fully.

un·pop·u·lar (un POP yə lər) *adj.* having no popularity; generally disliked or condemned. —**un·pop′u·lar′i·ty** *n.*

un·prec·e·dent·ed (un PRES i DEN tid) *adj.* being without precedent.

un·prej·u·diced (un PREJ ə dist) *adj.* **1.** free from prejudice or bias; impartial. **2.** not impaired, as a right.

un·prin·ci·pled (un PRIN sə pəld) *adj.* lacking in moral principles.

un·pro·fes·sion·al (UN prə FESH ə nl) *adj.* **1.** having no profession or no professional status. **2.** violating the rules or ethical code of a profession.

un·qual·i·fied (un KWOL ə FĪD) *adj.* **1.** being without the proper qualifications. **2.** without limitation or restrictions; absolute. —**un·qual′i·fied′ly** *adv.*

un·ques·tion·a·ble (un KWES chə nə bəl) *adj.* being beyond a doubt; indisputable. —**un·ques′tion·a·bly** *adv.*

un·quote (un KWOHT) *v.t. & v.i.*
·quot·ed, ·quot·ing close (a quotation).

un·rav·el (un RAV əl) *v.* **·eled, ·el·ing** *v.t.*
1. separate the threads of, as a knitted arti·
cle. **2.** free from entanglement; explain, as a
mystery or a plot. —*v.i.* **3.** become unrav·
eled.

un·read (un RED) *adj.* **1.** not informed by
reading; ignorant. **2.** not read.

un·read·y (un RED ee) *adj.* **1.** being with·
out readiness or alertness. **2.** not in a condi·
tion to act effectively. —**un·read'i·ness** *n.*

un·rea·son·a·ble (un REE zə nə bəl) *adj.*
1. acting without or contrary to reason. **2.**
not according to reason; irrational. **3.** im·
moderate; exorbitant. —**un·rea'son·a·**
ble·ness *n.* —**un·rea'son·a·bly** *adv.*

un·rea·son·ing (un REE zə ning) *adj.* not
accompanied by reason or control.

un·re·con·struct·ed (UN ree kən STRUK
tid) *adj.* **1.** not reconstructed. **2.** not recon·
ciled to or accepting changes in social or
political attitudes, policies, etc.

un·re·gen·er·ate (UN ri JEN ər it) *adj.* **1.**
not having been changed spiritually; not
reconciled to God. **2.** sinful; wicked. —
un're·gen'er·a·cy *n.* —**un're·gen'er·**
ate·ly *adv.*

un·re·lent·ing (UN ri LEN ting) *adj.* **1.** not
relenting; pitiless; inexorable. **2.** not dimin·
ishing, or not changing, in pace, effort,
speed, etc. —**un·re·lent'ing·ly** *adv.*

un·re·mit·ting (UN ri MIT ing) *adj.* not re·
laxing or stopping; incessant. —**un're·**
mit'ting·ly *adv.*

un·re·served (UN ri ZURVD) *adj.* **1.** given
or done without reserve. **2.** having no re·
serve of manner; informal; open. —
un·re·serv·ed·ly (UN ri ZUR vid lee) *adv.*

un·rest (un REST) *n.* **1.** restlessness, esp. of
the mind. **2.** trouble; turmoil, esp. with re·
gard to public or political conditions and
suggesting premonitions of revolt.

un·right·eous (un RĪ chəs) *adj.* **1.** not righ·
teous; wicked; sinful. **2.** contrary to justice;
not fair. —**un·right'eous·ness** *n.*

un·ruf·fled (un RUF əld) *adj.* not disturbed
or agitated emotionally; calm.

un·ru·ly (un ROO lee) *adj.* **·li·er, ·li·est**
disposed to resist rule or discipline; intract·
able. —**un·ru'li·ness** *n.*

un·sat·u·rat·ed (un SACH ə RAY tid) *adj.*
Chem. **1.** able to absorb or dissolve more of
something. **2.** capable of uniting with addi·
tional elements or radicals.

un·sa·vor·y (un SAY və ree) *adj.* **1.** having a
disagreeable taste or odor. **2.** suggesting
something disagreeable or offensive; also,
morally bad. —**un·sa'vor·i·ness** *n.*

un·scathed (un SKAYTHD) *adj.* not in·
jured.

un·scram·ble (un SKRAM bəl) *v.t.* **·bled,**
·bling resolve the confused condition
of.

un·scru·pu·lous (un SKROO pyə ləs) *adj.*
having no scruples or morals. —**un·scru'**
pu·lous·ly *adv.* —**un·scru'pu·lous·ness**
n.

un·sea·son·a·ble (un SEE zə nə bəl) *adj.* **1.**
not being in or characteristic of the season.
2. inappropriate; ill-timed. —**un·sea'son·**
a·bly *adv.*

un·seat (un SEET) *v.t.* **1.** remove from a
seat or fixed position. **2.** unhorse. **3.** deprive
of office or rank; depose.

un·seem·ly (un SEEM lee) *adj.* **·li·er,**
·li·est not seemly or proper; indecent. —
adv. in an unseemly fashion. —**un·seem'**
li·ness *n.*

un·set·tle (un SET l) *v.* **·tled, ·tling** *v.t.* **1.**
change or move from a fixed or settled con·
dition. **2.** confuse; disturb. —*v.i.* **3.** become
unsteady.

un·shack·le (un SHAK əl) *v.t.* **·led, ·ling**
free from or as from shackles.

un·sheathe (un SHEETH) *v.t.* **·sheathed,**
·sheath·ing take from or as from a sheath;
bare.

un·sight·ly (un SĪT lee) *adj.* **·li·er, ·li·est**
offensive to the sight. —**un·sight'li·ness**
n.

un·skilled (un SKILD) *adj.* **1.** exhibiting
lack of skill or dexterity. **2.** not requiring
special skill or training.

un·skill·ful (un SKIL fəl) *adj.* not skillful;
awkward; bungling. —**un·skill'ful·ly** *adv.*

un·snarl (un SNAHRL) *v.t.* untangle.

un·so·cia·ble (un SOH shə bəl) *adj.* **1.** not
sociable; not inclined to seek the society of
others. **2.** not encouraging social inter·
course. —**un·so'cia·ble·ness** *n.* —**un·**
so'cia·bly *adv.*

un·so·phis·ti·cat·ed (UN sə FIS ti KAY tid)
adj. not sophisticated; artless; simple. —
un'so·phis'ti·cat'ed·ness *n.*

un·sound (un SOWND) *adj.* lacking in
soundness; not strong, healthy, valid, etc.
—**un·sound'ly** *adv.* —**un·sound'ness** *n.*

un·spar·ing (un SPAIR ing) *adj.* **1.** not spar·
ing or saving; lavish; liberal. **2.** showing no
mercy. —**un·spar'ing·ly** *adv.*

un·speak·a·ble (un SPEE kə bəl) *adj.* **1.**

that cannot be expressed. **2.** extremely bad or objectionable. —**un·speak'a·bly** adv.

un·sta·ble (un STAY bəl) adj. **1.** lacking in stability or firmness. **2.** having no fixed purposes; inconstant. **3.** Chem. readily decomposable, as certain compounds. —**un·sta' ble·ness** n. —**un·sta'bly** adv.

un·stead·y (un STED ee) adj. ·**stead·i·er**, ·**stead·i·est 1.** not steady or firm; shaky. **2.** not regular or constant; wavering. **3.** inconstant and erratic in behavior, habits, etc. — **un·stead'i·ly** adv. —v. ·**tead·ied**, ·**stead·y·ing** make unsteady.

un·strung (un STRUNG) adj. **1.** having the strings removed or relaxed. **2.** unnerved; emotionally upset; weakened.

un·stud·ied (un STUD eed) adj. **1.** not planned. **2.** not stiff or artificial; natural. **3.** not acquainted through study: with in.

un·sub·stan·tial (UN səb STAN shəl) adj. **1.** lacking solidity or strength. **2.** having no valid basis. **3.** having no bodily existence; fanciful. —**un'sub·stan'tial·ly** adv.

un·suit·a·ble (un SOO tə bəl) adj. not suitable. —**un'suit·a·bil'i·ty** n. —**un·suit' a·bly** adv.

un·sung (un SUNG) adj. **1.** not celebrated in song or poetry; obscure. **2.** not yet sung.

un·tan·gle (un TANG gəl) v.t. ·**gled**, ·**gling 1.** free from entanglement or snarls. **2.** clear up; resolve.

un·taught (un TAWT) adj. **1.** not instructed; ignorant. **2.** acquired without training or instruction; natural.

un·ten·a·ble (un TEN ə bəl) adj. that cannot be maintained or defended. — **un·ten'a·bil'i·ty**, **un·ten'a·ble·ness** n.

un·think·a·ble (un THING kə bəl) adj. not imaginable. —**un·think'a·bly** adv.

un·think·ing (un THING king) adj. **1.** not having the power of thought. **2.** thoughtless; careless; heedless; inconsiderate. — **un·think'ing·ly** adv.

un·ti·dy (un TĪ dee) adj. ·**di·er**, ·**di·est** showing lack of tidiness. [ME] —**un·ti' di·ly** adv. —**un·ti'di·ness** n.

un·tie (un TĪ) v. ·**tied**, ·**ty·ing** v.t. **1.** loosen or undo, as a knot. **2.** free from restraint. — v.i. **3.** become untied. [ME untyen]

un·til (un TIL) prep. **1.** up to the time of; till: We will wait until midnight. **2.** before: used with a negative: The music doesn't begin until nine. —conj. **1.** to the time when: until I die. **2.** to the place or degree that: Walk east until you reach the river. [ME]

un·time·ly (un TĪM lee) adj. ·**li·er**, ·**li·est**

1. before the proper or expected time; premature. **2.** ill-timed. —adv. prematurely. —**un·time'li·ness** n.

un·to (UN too) prep. **1.** to. **2.** until. [ME]

un·told (un TOHLD) adj. **1.** that cannot be revealed or described. **2.** that cannot be numbered or estimated. **3.** not told.

un·touch·a·ble (un TUCH ə bəl) adj. **1.** inaccessible or forbidden to the touch; out of reach. **2.** intangible; unapproachable. **3.** unpleasant or dangerous to touch. —n. in India, a member of the lowest caste, whose touch is considered defilement by Hindús of high caste.

un·to·ward (un TORD) adj. **1.** causing hindrance; vexatious. **2.** perverse. **3.** not seemly. —**un·to'ward·ness** n.

un·true (un TROO) adj. ·**tru·er**, ·**tru·est 1.** not true; not corresponding with fact. **2.** not conforming to rule or standard. **3.** disloyal.

un·truth (un TROOTH) n. pl. ·**truths** (-TROOTHZ) **1.** the quality or character of being untrue. **2.** a lie. —**un·truth'ful** adj. —**un·truth'ful·ness** n.

un·tu·tored (un TOO tərd) adj. **1.** having had no tutor or teacher. **2.** naive; simple.

un·u·su·al (un YOO zhoo əl) adj. not usual, common, or ordinary. —**un·u'su·al·ly** adv.

un·ut·ter·a·ble (un UT ər ə bəl) adj. too great or deep for verbal expression; inexpressible. —**un·ut'ter·a·bly** adv.

un·var·nished (un VAHR nisht) adj. **1.** having no covering of varnish. **2.** having no embellishment; plain.

un·veil (un VAYL) v.t. **1.** remove the veil from; reveal. —v.i. **2.** remove one's veil; reveal oneself.

un·voiced (un VOIST) adj. **1.** not expressed. **2.** Phonet. a voiceless. b rendered voiceless.

un·war·y (un WAIR ee) adj. not careful or cautious; rash; careless. —**un·war'i·ly** adv.

un·whole·some (un HOHL səm) adj. **1.** harmful to physical or mental health. **2.** not sound in condition; diseased or decayed. **3.** morally bad; pernicious. —**un·whole' some·ly** adv.

un·wield·y (un WEEL dee) adj. moved or managed with difficulty, as from great size or awkward shape; bulky; clumsy. — **un·wield'i·ness** n.

un·wind (un WĪND) v. ·**wound** (-WOWND), ·**wind·ing** v.t. **1.** reverse the winding of; wind off; uncoil. **2.** disentangle. —*v.i:* **3.** become unwound.

un·wise (un WĪZ) *adj.* •**wis·er,** •**wis·est** showing lack of wisdom; imprudent; foolish. —**un·wise'ly** *adv.*

un·wit·ting (un WIT ing) *adj.* **1.** having no knowledge or consciousness of a thing in question. **2.** unintentional. —**un·wit'ting·ly** *adv.*

un·wont·ed (un WAWN tid) *adj.* not according to habit or custom; unusual.

un·wor·thy (un WUR *thee*) *adj.* •**thi·er,** •**thi·est 1.** not deserving: usu., with *of.* **2.** not befitting or becoming: often with *of.* **3.** lacking worth or merit. —**un·wor'thi·ness** *n.*

un·wound (un WOWND) past tense, past participle of UNWIND.

up (up) *adv.* **1.** from a lower to a higher place, level, position, etc. **2.** in, on, or to a higher place, position, etc. **3.** toward that which is figuratively or conventionally higher; as: **a** to or at a higher price. **b** to or at a higher place, rank, etc. **c** to or at a greater size or amount: swell *up.* **d** to or at a place that is regarded as higher: Go *up* north. **e** above the surface or horizon. **f** from an earlier to a later period. **g** to a source, conclusion, etc.: Follow *up* this lead. **4.** to a vertical position; standing; also, out of bed. **5.** so as to be compact or secure: Tie *up* the boxes. **6.** so as to be even with in space, time, etc.: *up* to date. **7.** in or into an excited state or some specific action: They were stirred *up* to mutiny. **8.** in or into view or existence: draw *up* a will. **9.** in or into prominence; under consideration: *up* for debate. **10.** in or into a place of safekeeping; aside: Fruits are put *up* in jars. **11.** at an end: Your time is *up.* **12.** completely; totally: The house was burned *up.* **13.** in baseball and cricket, at bat. **14.** in tennis and other sports: **a** in the lead; ahead. **b** apiece; alike: said of a score. **15.** running for as a candidate. ♦ In informal usage *up* is often added to a verb without affecting the meaning of the sentence: light *up* a room. —**be up against** *Informal* meet with; confront. —**be up against it** be in difficulty. —**be up on** (or *in*) be well informed in or skilled at something. —**be up to 1.** be doing or plotting. **2.** be equal to; be capable of. **3.** be incumbent upon; be dependent upon: It's *up* to her to save us. —*adj.* **1.** moving, sloping, or directed upward. **2.** going on; taking place: What's *up?* **3.** rising, risen, overflowing, or at flood. **4.** in an active or excited state. —**up and around** sufficiently recovered to walk. —*prep.* **1.** from a lower to a higher point or place of, on, or along. **2.** toward a higher condition or rank on or in. **3.** to or at a point farther above or along: *up* the road. **4.** toward the interior of (a country). **5.** toward the source of (a river). **6.** at, on, or near the height or top of. —*n.* **1.** a rise or ascent. **2.** a period of prosperity etc.: chiefly in the phrase **ups and downs.** —**be on the up and up** *Informal* be honest. —*v.* **upped, up·ping** *v.t.* **1.** increase. **2.** put or take up. —*v.i.* **3.** rise. [ME]

up-and-com·ing (UP ən KUM ing) *adj.* enterprising; energetic; promising.

up-and-down (UP ən DOWN) *adj.* **1.** alternately rising and falling; fluctuating; varying. **2.** vertical; perpendicular.

up·beat (UP BEET) *n. Music* the relatively unaccented beat that precedes the downbeat. —*adj.* optimistic.

up·braid (up BRAYD) *v.t.* **1.** scold or reprove. —*v.i.* **2.** utter reproaches. [ME] —**up·braid'er** *n.*

up·bring·ing (UP BRING ing) *n.* the rearing and training received during childhood.

up·chuck (UP CHUK) *Informal v.t. & v.i.* vomit.

up·com·ing (UP KUM ing) *adj.* coming soon; about to appear.

up·coun·try (UP KUN tree) *n.* country remote from the coast or from lowlands; inland country. —*adj. & adv.* in, toward, or characteristic of inland places.

up·grade (UP GRAYD) *n.* an upward incline or slope. —*v.t.* (up GRAYD) •**grad·ed,** •**grad·ing** raise to a higher grade, rank, post, etc.

up·heav·al (up HEE vəl) *n.* **1.** the act of upheaving, or the state of being upheaved. **2.** a violent disturbance or change.

up·heave (up HEEV) *v.* •**heaved** or •**hove,** •**heav·ing** *v.t.* **1.** heave or raise up. —*v.i.* **2.** be raised or lifted.

up·hill (UP HIL) *adv.* up or as up a hill or an ascent; against difficulties. —*adj.* **1.** going up an ascent; sloping upward. **2.** attended with difficulty or exertion. **3.** at a high place. —*n.* (UP HIL) an upward slope.

up·hold (up HOHLD) *v.t.* •**held,** •**hold·ing 1.** hold up; raise. **2.** keep from falling. **3.** support; agree with; encourage.

up·hol·ster (up HOHL stər) *v.t.* fit, as furniture, with coverings, cushioning, etc. —**up·hol'ster·er** *n.*

up·hol·ster·y (up HOHL stə ree) n. pl.
·ster·ies 1. fabric and fittings used in upholstering. **2.** the act, art, or business of
upholstering.

up·keep (UP KEEP) n. the act or state of
maintaining something; also, the cost of
maintenance.

up·land (UP lənd) n. **1.** the higher portions
of a region, district, farm, etc. **2.** the country
in the interior. —**up·land** adj.

up·lift (up LIFT) v.t. **1.** raise; elevate. **2.** put
on a higher plane, mentally or morally. —n.
(UP LIFT) **1.** the act of raising, or the fact of
being raised. **2.** mental or spiritual stimulation or elevation. **3.** a movement aiming to
improve the condition of the underprivi-
leged.

up·most (UP MOHST adj. uppermost.

up·on (ə PON) prep. on. [ME]

up·per (UP ər) adj. **1.** higher in place. **2.**
farther inland. **3.** higher in station, rank,
etc.; superior. —n. **1.** that part of a boot or
shoe above the sole; the vamp. **2.** Slang any
of various drugs that stimulate the central
nervous system.

upper case Printing the capital letters of the
alphabet. —**up′per·case′** adj.

upper class the socially or economically superior group in society. —**up′per-class′**
adj.

up·per·cut (UP ər KUT) n. in boxing, a
swinging blow upward, delivered under or
inside the opponent's guard. —v.t. & v.i.
·cut, ·cut·ting strike with an uppercut.

up·per·most (UP ər MOHST) adj. **1.** highest
in place, rank, authority, influence, etc. **2.**
first to come into the mind. Also upmost. —
adv. in the highest place, rank, authority,
etc.

up·pish (UP ish) adj. Informal arrogant;
pretentious; condescending. Also **up·pi·ty**
(UP i tee).

up·right (UP RĪT) adj. **1.** being in a vertical
position; straight up; erect. **2.** just and honest. —n. **1.** something having a vertical position, as an upright piano. **2.** in football,
one of the goal posts. —adv. in an upright
position; vertically. [ME] —**up′right′ly**
adv.

upright piano a piano having strings arranged vertically in a rectangular case.

up·ris·ing (UP RĪ zing) n. **1.** the act of rising.
2. a revolt or insurrection. **3.** an ascent;
slope.

up·roar (UP ROR) n. a violent disturbance,
noise, or tumult. [< Du. oproer revolt]

up·roar·i·ous (up ROR ee əs) adj. **1.** accompanied by or making an uproar. **2.** loud
and noisy; tumultuous. **3.** very funny.

up·root (up ROOT) v.t. **1.** tear up or remove
by or as if by the roots. **2.** destroy utterly;
eradicate.

up·scale (UP SKAYL) adj. Informal above
average in income and education: an up-
scale audience.

up·set (up SET) v. **·set, ·set·ting** v.t. **1.**
overturn. **2.** throw into confusion or disorder. **3.** disconcert, derange, or disquiet. **4.**
defeat, esp. unexpectedly. —v.i. **5.** become
overturned. —adj. **1.** tipped or turned over.
2. mentally or physically disturbed or ill. **3.**
confused; disordered. —n. (UP SET) **1.** the
act of upsetting, or the state of being upset.
2. an unexpected defeat. **3.** a mental or
physical disturbance or disorder.

up·shot (UP SHOT) n. **1.** the final outcome;
result. **2.** the gist.

up·side (UP SĪD) n. **1.** the upper side or part.
2. an upward trend.

upside down 1. with the upper side down.
2. in disorder. —**up′side-down′** adj.

up·si·lon (YOOP sə LON) n. the twentieth
letter and sixth vowel in the Greek alphabet
(Y, υ).

up·stage (UP STAYJ) adj. of the back half
of a stage. —adv. toward or on the back of
a stage. —v.t. **·staged, ·stag·ing 1.** steal
a scene from. **2.** behave snobbishly toward.

up·stairs (UP STAIRZ) adj. pertaining to an
upper floor. —n. an upper floor; esp., the
part of a building above the ground floor. —
adv. in, to, or toward an upper story. —**kick
upstairs** promote to a position with a
higher title but less power.

up·stand·ing (up STAN ding) adj. **1.** honest; upright; straightforward. **2.** standing
up; erect.

up·start (UP STAHRT) adj. **1.** suddenly
raised to prominence, wealth, or power. **2.**
characteristic of an upstart; vulgar; pretentious. —n. one who has suddenly risen to a
position of wealth or importance and become arrogant.

up·stream (UP STREEM) adv. toward or at
the source or upper part of a stream; against
the current.

up·surge (UP SURJ) n. a rapid or sudden
rise. —v.i. (up SURJ) **·surged, ·surg·ing**
rise suddenly.

up·swing (UP SWING) n. **1.** a swinging upward. **2.** an improvement. —v.i. (up

SWING) **•swung, •swing•ing** make an up-swing.

up•take (UP TAYK) *n.* the act of lifting or taking up. —**quick on the uptake** comprehending rapidly.

up-to-date (UP tə DAYT) *adj.* **1.** having the latest information, improvements, etc. **2.** modern in manner, fashion, or style.

up•ward (UP wərd) *adv.* **1.** in, to, or toward a higher place or position. **2.** to or toward the source, origin, etc. **3.** toward a higher rank, amount, age, etc. **4.** toward that which is better, nobler, etc. **5.** in excess; more. Also **up'wards.** —*adj.* in, on, turned, or directed toward a higher place. —**up'ward•ly** *adj.*

u•ra•ni•um (yuu RAY nee əm) *n.* a heavy, white, radioactive, metallic element (symbol U), used as a source of atomic energy.

U•ra•nus (YUUR ə nəs) *n.* the third largest planet of the solar system and seventh in order from the sun.

ur•ban (UR bən) *adj.* **1.** pertaining to, characteristic of, including, or constituting a city. **2.** situated or dwelling in a city. [< L *urbanus*]

ur•bane (ur BAYN) *adj.* characterized by or having refinement or elegance, esp. in manner; suave. [< MF *urbain*]

ur•ban•i•ty (ur BAN i tee) *n. pl.* **•ties 1.** the character or quality of being urbane; refined or elegant courtesy. **2.** *pl.* amenities or courtesies. [< L *urbanitas*]

ur•ban•ize (UR bə NIZ) *v.t.* **•ized, •iz•ing** render urban, as in character or manner. —**ur'ban•i•za'tion** *n.*

urban renewal the planned upgrading of a deteriorating urban area.

ur•chin (UR chin) *n.* **1.** a roguish, mischievous child. **2.** a sea urchin. [ME]

Ur•du (UUR doo) *n.* a language that is spoken by Muslims in Pakistan. [< Persian *urdū camp*]

u•re•a (yuu REE ə) *n. Biochem.* a colorless nitrogenous compound, found in urine and also made synthetically, used in medicine and in the making of plastics and fertilizers. [< NL]

u•re•mi•a (yuu REE mee ə) *n. Pathol.* a condition of the blood resulting from retention of constituents ordinarily excreted by the kidneys. [< NL] —**u•re'mic** *adj.*

u•re•ter (yuu REE tər) *n. Anat.* the duct by which urine passes from the kidney to the bladder. [< NL]

u•re•thra (yuu REE thrə) *n. Anat.* the duct by which urine is discharged from the bladder of most mammals, and which, in males, carries the seminal discharge. [< LL] —**u•re'thral** *adj.*

urge (urj) *v.t.* **urged, urg•ing 1.** drive or force forward; impel; push. **2.** plead with or entreat earnestly. **3.** press or argue the doing, consideration, or acceptance of. **4.** move or force to some course or action. **5.** stimulate or excite. [< L *urgere*] —*n.* **1.** a strong impulse. **2.** the act of urging, or the state of being urged.

ur•gent (UR jənt) *adj.* **1.** characterized by urging or importunity; requiring prompt attention; pressing. **2.** eagerly importunate or insistent. [ME] —**ur'gen•cy** *n.* —**ur'gent•ly** *adv.*

u•ric (YUUR ik) *adj.* of, pertaining to, or derived from urine.

uric acid *Biochem.* a colorless acid found in small quantities in the urine of people and animals and the chief constituent of excreta of birds and reptiles.

u•ri•nal (YUUR ə nl) *n.* **1.** an upright wall fixture with facilities for flushing, for men's use in urination; also, the room containing such a fixture. **2.** a glass receptacle for urine.

u•ri•nar•y (YUUR ə NER ee) *adj.* of or involved in the production and excretion of urine.

u•ri•nate (YUUR ə NAYT) *v.i.* **•nat•ed, •nat•ing** void or pass urine. —**u'ri•na'tion** *n.*

u•rine (YUUR in) *n.* a liquid containing body wastes, secreted by the kidneys. [ME]

urn (urn) *n.* **1.** a rounded or angular vase having a foot, variously used in antiquity as a receptacle for the ashes of the dead, a water vessel, etc. **2.** a vessel for preserving the ashes of the dead. **3.** a vase-shaped receptacle having a faucet and designed for keeping tea, coffee, etc. hot. [ME *urne*]

u•rol•o•gy (yuu ROL ə jee) *n.* the branch of medicine that deals with the urine and the genitourinary tract. —**u•rol'o•gist** *n.*

ur•sine (UR SIN) *adj.* pertaining to or like a bear. [< L *ursinus*]

us (us) *pron.* the objective case of *we.* [ME]

us•a•ble (YOO zə bəl) *adj.* **1.** capable of being used. **2.** that can be used conveniently.

us•age (YOO sij) *n.* **1.** the manner of using or treating a person or thing; treatment; also, the act of using. **2.** customary or habitual practice, esp. in the way words are used.

use (yooz) *v.* **used, us•ing** *v.t.* **1.** employ for the accomplishment of a purpose; make use of. **2.** put into practice or employ habitually; make a practice of. **3.** expend the whole of; consume: often with *up*. **4.** conduct oneself toward; treat: *use* one badly. **5.** make familiar by habit or practice; inure: now only in the past participle: She is *used* (*pr.* yoost) to cold climates. **6.** partake of: He does not *use* tobacco. —*v.i.* **7.** do something customarily or habitually: now only in the past tense as an auxiliary: I *used* (*pr.* yoost) to go there. — *n.* [ME *usen*] (yoos) **1.** the act of using: made good *use* of her time. **2.** the condition of being used: Is this form still in *use?* **3.** the right to use: the *use* of her car. **4.** the ability to use: the *use* of one's leg. **5.** adaptability for a purpose; usefulness: a new *use* for this product. **6.** the way or manner of using: the correct *use* of the machine. **7.** custom; habit; practice: long *use* shows us. —**have no use for 1.** have no need of. **2.** dislike; want nothing to do with. —**us′er** (YOO zər n.

use·ful (YOOS fəl) *adj.* serviceable; serving a use or purpose, esp. a valuable one. — **use′ful·ly** *adv.* —**use′ful·ness** n.

use·less (YOOS lis) *adj.* **1.** being of no use; not capable of serving any beneficial purpose. **2.** futile; in vain. —**use′less·ly** *adv.* —**use′·less·ness** n.

us·er-friend·ly (YOO zər FREND lee) *adj.* Computers. easy to operate: a *user-friendly* keyboard.

ush·er (USH ər) n. **1.** one who acts as doorkeeper, as of a court or other assembly room. **2.** an officer who walks before a person of rank. **3.** one who conducts persons to seats, as in a church or theater. —*v.t.* **1.** act as an usher to; escort; conduct. **2.** precede as a harbinger; be a forerunner of: usu. with *in*. [ME *ussher*]

u·su·al (YOO zhoo əl) *adj.* such as occurs in the ordinary course of events; frequent; common. [ME] —**u′su·al·ly** *adv.*

u·su·ri·ous (yoo ZHUUR ee əs) *adj.* practicing or having the nature of usury.

u·surp (yoo SURP) *v.t.* **1.** seize and hold (the office, rights, or powers of another) without right or legal authority; take possession of by force. **2.** take arrogantly, as if by right. — *v.i.* encroach: with *on* or *upon.* [ME] — **u·sur·pa·tion** n. (YOO sər PAY shən) — **u·surp′er** n.

u·su·ry (YOO zhə ree) n. pl. **·ries 1.** the act or practice of exacting an illegal rate of interest. **2.** a premium paid for the use of

money beyond the rate of interest established by law. [ME *usurie*] —**u′su·rer** n.

u·ten·sil (yoo TEN səl) n. a vessel, tool, implement, etc., serving a useful purpose, esp. for domestic use. [ME]

u·ter·ine (YOO tər in) *adj.* **1.** pertaining to the uterus. **2.** born of the same mother, but having a different father. [ME]

u·ter·us (YOO tər əs) n. pl. **u·ter·i** (YOO tə RI), **u·ter·us·es** *Anat.* the organ of a female mammal in which the young are protected and developed before birth; the womb. [< L]

u·til·i·tar·i·an (yoo TIL i TAIR ee ən) *adj.* **1.** relating to utility; esp., placing utility above beauty or the amenities of life. **2.** pertaining to or advocating utilitarianism. —*n.* **1.** an advocate of utilitarianism. **2.** one devoted to mere material utility.

u·til·i·tar·i·an·ism (yoo TIL i TAIR ee ə NIZ əm) n. **1.** *Philos.* the ethical theory that the greatest human happiness determines the highest moral good. **2.** devotion to mere material interests.

u·til·i·ty (yoo TIL i tee) n. pl. **·ties 1.** fitness for some desirable, practical purpose; also, that which is necessary. **2.** fitness to supply the natural needs of man. **3.** a public service, as gas, water, etc.; also, a company supplying such service. [ME *utilite*]

u·til·ize (YOOT l IZ) *v.t.* **·ized, ·iz·ing** make useful; turn to practical account; make use of. —**u′til·i·za′tion** n.

ut·most (UT MOHST) *adj.* **1.** of the highest degree or the largest amount or number; greatest. **2.** being at the farthest limit or point. —*n.* the greatest possible extent; the most possible. Also *uttermost.* [ME]

u·to·pi·a (yoo TOH pee ə) n. **1.** any state, condition, or place of ideal perfection. **2.** a visionary, impractical scheme for social improvement. [After *Utopia*, an imaginary island having a perfect social and political life, in Sir Thomas More's *Utopia*] —**u·to′pi·an** *adj. & n.* —**u·to′pi·an·ism** n.

ut·ter¹ (UT ər) *v.t.* give out or send forth with audible sound; say. [ME *uttren*] —**ut′ter·a·ble** *adj.* —**ut′ter·er** n.

ut·ter² *adj.* **1.** absolute; total. **2.** being or done without conditions or qualifications; final; absolute. [ME]

ut·ter·ance (UT ər əns) n. **1.** the act of uttering; vocal expression; also, the power of speech. **2.** a thing uttered or expressed.

ut·ter·ly (UT ər lee) *adv.* thoroughly; entirely.

ut•ter•most (UT ər MOHST) *adj. & n.* utmost.

U-turn (YOO TURN) *n.* a continuous turn that reverses the direction of a vehicle on a road.

u•vu•la (YOO vyə lə) *n. pl.* **•las** or **•lae** (-LEE) *Anat.* the pendent fleshy portion of the soft palate. [ME]

u•vu•lar (YOO vyə lər) *adj.* **1.** pertaining to or of the uvula. **2.** *Phonet.* produced by vibration of, or with the back of the tongue near or against, the uvula. —*n. Phonet.* a uvular sound.

ux•o•ri•ous (uk SOR ee əs) *adj.* fatuously or foolishly devoted to one's wife. [< L *uxorius*] —**ux•o′ri•ous•ness** *n.*

V

v, V (vee) *n. pl.* **v's** or **vs, V's** or **Vs 1.** the twenty-second letter of the English alphabet. **2.** the sound represented by the letter *v.* **3.** anything shaped like a V. —*symbol* the Roman numeral five.

va•can•cy (VAY kən see) *n. pl.* **•cies 1.** the state of being vacant; emptiness. **2.** that which is vacant; empty space. **3.** an unoccupied post, place, or office.

va•cant (VAY kənt) *adj.* **1.** containing or holding nothing; esp., devoid of occupants; empty. **2.** occupied with nothing; not in use; free. **3.** being or appearing without intelligence; inane. **4.** having no incumbent; unfilled: a *vacant* office. **5.** devoid of thought. [ME]

va•cate (VAY kayt) *v.t.* **•cat•ed, •cat•ing 1.** make vacant; leave. **2.** set aside; annul. **3.** give up (a position or office); quit.

va•ca•tion (vay KAY shən) *n.* **1.** an interlude, usu. of several days or weeks, from one's customary duties, as for recreation or rest. **2.** the intermission of the course of studies in an educational institution. —*v.i.* take a vacation. [ME *vacacioun*] —**va•ca′tion•er, va•ca′tion•ist** *n.*

vac•ci•nate (VAK sə NAYT) *v.t. & v.i.* **•nat•ed, •nat•ing** *Med.* inoculate with a vaccine as a preventive measure; esp., inoculate against smallpox. —**vac′ci•na′tion** *n.*

vac•cine (vak SEEN) *n.* any preparation containing bacteria or viruses so treated as to give immunity from specific diseases when injected into the subject. [< L *vaccinus* of or from cows]

vac•il•late (VAS ə LAYT) *v.i.* **•lat•ed, •lat•ing 1.** sway one way and the other; totter. **2.** fluctuate. **3.** waver in mind; be irresolute. [< L *vacillatus* wavered] —**vac•il•lant** (VAS ə lənt) *adj.* —**vac′il•la′tion** *n.*

va•cu•i•ty (va KYOO i tee) *n. pl.* **•ties 1.** the state of being a vacuum; emptiness. **2.** vacant space; a void. **3.** lack of intelligence or thought. **4.** an inane or idle thing or statement. [< L *vacuitas*]

vac•u•ous (VAK yoo əs) *adj.* **1.** having no contents; empty. **2.** lacking intelligence; blank. [< L *vacuus*] —**vac′u•ous•ness** *n.*

vac•u•um (VAK yoo əm) *n. pl.* **•u•ums** or **•u•a** (-yoo ə) **1.** a space absolutely devoid of matter. **2.** a space from which air or other gas has been exhausted to a very high degree. **3.** a void. **4.** a vacuum cleaner. —*adj.* **1.** of, or used in the production of, a vacuum. **2.** exhausted or partly exhausted of gas, air, or vapor. **3.** operated by suction to produce a vacuum. —*v.t. & v.i.* clean with a vacuum cleaner. [< L, empty]

vacuum bottle a thermos bottle.

vacuum cleaner a machine for cleaning carpets, furnishings, etc. by suction.

vacuum tube *Electronics* **1.** a glass tube exhausted of air to a high degree and containing electrodes between which electric discharges may be passed. **2.** an electron tube.

vag•a•bond (VAG ə BOND) *n.* **1.** one who wanders from place to place without visible means of support; tramp. **2.** a wanderer; nomad. —*adj.* **1.** pertaining to a vagabond; nomadic. **2.** having no definite residence; wandering; aimless. [ME]

va•gar•y (VAY gə ee) *n. pl.* **•gar•ies** a wild fancy; extravagant notion. [< L *vagari* wander]

va•gi•na (və JĪ nə) *n. pl.* **•nas** or **•nae** (-nee) *Anat.* the canal leading from the external genital orifice in female mammals to the uterus. [< NL] —**vag•i•nal** (VAJ ə nl) *adj.*

va•grant (VAY grənt) *n.* a person without a settled home; vagabond; tramp. —*adj.* **1.** wandering about as a vagrnt. **2.** of or pertaining to a wanderer; nomadic. **3.** having a wandering course. [ME *vagraunt* wandering] —**va′gran•cy** *n.*

vague (vayg) *adj.* **va•guer, va•guest 1.** lacking definiteness or precision; unclear. **2.** shadowy; hazy. [< MF] —**vague′ly** *adv.* —**vague′ness** *n.*

vain (vayn) *adj.* **•er, •est 1.** filled with or showing undue admiration for oneself, one's appearance, etc.; conceited. **2.** unproductive; fruitless. **3.** having no real basis; empty: *vain* hopes. **4.** ostentatious; showy. —**in vain** to no purpose; without effect. [ME] —**vain′ly** *adv.*

val•ance (VAL əns) *n.* **1.** a hanging drapery, as from the framework of a bed to the floor. **2.** a short drapery, board, or plate across the top of a window. [ME]

vale (vayl) *n.* a valley. [ME]

val·e·dic·tion (VAL i DIK shən) *n.* **1.** an act of bidding farewell. **2.** a valedictory. [< L *valedictus* bade farewell]

val·e·dic·to·ri·an (VAL i dik TOR ee ən) *n.* a student who delivers a valedictory at graduating exercises, usu. the graduating student ranking highest in scholarship.

val·e·dic·to·ry (VAL i DIK tə ree) *adj.* pertaining to a leavetaking. —*n. pl.* **·ries** a parting address.

va·lence (VAY ləns) *n. Chem.* the combining capacity of an element or radical expressed as the number of atoms of hydrogen (or its equivalent) with which an atom of the element or radical can combine, or which it can replace. Also **va'len·cy.** [< LL *valentia* power]

val·en·tine (VAL ən TIN) *n.* **1.** a greeting card or token of affection sent on Saint Valentine's Day. **2.** a sweetheart.

val·et (va LAY) *n.* **1.** a gentleman's personal servant. **2.** one who performs personal services for patrons at a hotel. —*v.t. & v.i.* serve or act as a valet. [< F]

val·iant (VAL yənt) *adj.* **1.** strong and courageous. **2.** performed with valor; heroic. [ME *valiaunt*] —**val'iant·ly** *adv.*

val·id (VAL id) *adj.* **1.** based on evidence that can be supported; convincing; sound. **2.** legally binding; effective; warranted. [< MF *valide*] —**va·lid·i·ty** (və LID i tee) *n.*

val·i·date (VAL i DAYT) *v.t.* **·dat·ed, ·dat·ing 1.** make valid; ratify and confirm. **2.** declare legally valid; legalize. —**val'i·da'tion** *n.*

va·lise (və LEES) *n.* a suitcase. [< F]

val·ley (VAL ee) *n. pl.* **·leys 1.** a depression of the earth's surface, as one through which a stream flows; level or low land between mountains, hills, or high lands. **2.** any depression or hollow like a valley. [ME *valey*]

val·or (VAL ər) *n.* courage; personal bravery. [ME] —**val'or·ous** *adj.*

val·u·a·ble (VAL yoo ə bəl) *adj.* **1.** costly. **2.** having material value. **3.** useful. **4.** highly esteemed; worthy. —*n. usu. pl.* an article of worth or value, as a piece of jewelry. —**val'u·a·bly** *adv.*

val·u·a·tion (VAL yoo AY shən) *n.* **1.** the act of valuing. **2.** estimated worth or value.

val·ue (VAL yoo) *n.* **1.** the desirability or worth of a thing; intrinsic worth; utility. **2.** *Often pl.* something regarded as desirable, worthy, or right, as a belief, standard, or moral precept. **3.** the rate at which a commodity is potentially exchangeable for others; worth in money; market price. **4.** a bargain. **5.** attributed or assumed valuation; esteem or regard. **6.** exact meaning. **7.** *Music* the relative length of a tone or note. **8.** *Math.* the quantity, magnitude, or number represented by an algebraic symbol or expression. **9.** in the graphic arts, the relation of the elements of a picture, as light and shade, to one another. —*v.t.* **·ued, ·u·ing 1.** estimate the value or worth of; appraise. **2.** regard highly; esteem; prize. **3.** place a relative estimate of value or desirability upon. **4.** give a (specified) value to. [ME] —**val'ue·less** *adj.*

value added tax a tax added to a product or commodity at each stage of its production or distribution, based on its increased value at that stage. Abbr. **VAT**

val·ued (VAL yood) *adj.* **1.** highly esteemed. **2.** having a (specified) value.

value judgment a subjective estimate of the quality, goodness, etc. of a person or or thing.

valve (valv) *n.* **1.** *Mech.* any contrivance or arrangement that regulates the amount and direction of flow, as of a liquid. **2.** *Anat.* a structure, as in the heart, enabling flow of a fluid in one direction only. **3.** *Zool.* one of the parts of a shell, as of a mollusk. **4.** a device in certain brass instruments for lengthening the air column and lowering the pitch of the instrument's scale. —*v.t.* **valved, valv·ing** furnish with or control by a valve or valves. [ME] —**valve'less** *adj.*

vamp¹ (vamp) *n.* **1.** the piece forming the upper front part of a boot or shoe. **2.** something added to give an old thing a new appearance. **3.** *Music* a simple improvised accompaniment. [ME *vampe* sock] —*v.t.* **1.** provide with a vamp. **2.** repair or patch. **3.** *Music* improvise an accompaniment to. —*v.i.* **4.** *Music* improvise accompaniments.

vamp² *v.t. & v.i.* seduce or try to seduce (a man) by feminine charms. —*n.* a seductive woman. [Short for VAMPIRE]

vam·pire (VAM pīr) *n.* **1.** in folklore, a corpse that rises from its grave at night to suck the blood of the living. **2.** one who victimizes persons of the opposite sex; esp., a woman who exploits or degrades her lovers. **3.** a tropical American bat that feeds on the blood of animals; usu. **vampire bat.** [< F] —**vam·pir·ism** (VAM pīr iz əm) *n.*

van¹ (van) *n.* a large covered vehicle, as a

truck, for transporting furniture, livestock, etc. [Short for CARAVAN]

van² *n.* **1.** the portion of an army, fleet, etc., that is nearest or in advance of the front. **2.** the vanguard of a movement. [Short for VANGUARD]

van·dal (VAN dl) *n.* one who vandalizes. —*adj.* wantonly destructive. [< L *Vandalii* the Germanic people who overran much of Europe and North Africa in the 4th and 5th centuries and sacked Rome in 455]

van·dal·ize (VAN dl īz) *v.t.* **·ized, ·iz·ing** destroy or deface (property) willfully. —**van'dal·ism** *n.*

vane (vayn) *n.* **1.** a movable thin plate of metal or wood that indicates the direction of the wind; weather vane. **2.** an arm or blade extending from a rotating shaft, as of a windmill, propeller, turbine, etc. **3.** *Ornithol.* the web of a feather. [ME] —**vaned** *adj.*

van·guard (VAN GAHRD) *n.* **1.** the advance guard of an army; van. **2.** those in the forefront of a movement, as in art etc. [ME *vantgard*]

va·nil·la (və NIL ə) *n.* **1.** a flavoring extract made from the podlike seed capsules of a climbing tropical orchid. **2.** the seed capsule of this plant: also **vanilla bean.** [< NL]

van·ish (VAN ish) *v.i.* **1.** disappear from sight; fade away; depart. **2.** pass out of existence. [ME *vanisshen*]

vanishing point in perspective, the point at which parallel lines appear to converge.

van·i·ty (VAN i tee) *n. pl.* **·ties 1.** the condition or character of being vain; conceit. **2.** ambitious display; ostentation. **3.** the quality or state of being fruitless, useless, etc. **4.** that which is vain or unsubstantial. **5.** a bag or box containing cosmetics, comb, mirror, etc.: also **vanity case. 6.** a dressing table. [ME *vanite*]

van·quish (VANG kwish) *v.t.* defeat; overcome; conquer. [ME *venquissen*] —**van'quish·a·ble** *adj.* —**van'quish·er** *n.*

van·tage (VAN tij) *n.* **1.** a position or condition that gives one an advantage: also **vantage ground 2.** a strategic position affording perspective; point of view: also **vantage point.** [ME]

vap·id (VAP id) *adj.* flat or flavorless; dull; insipid. [< L *vapidus*] —**va·pid·i·ty** (va PID i tee) *n.* —**vap'id·ly** *adv.*

va·por (VAY pər) *n.* **1.** moisture in the air; esp., light mist. **2.** any light, cloudy sub-

stance in the air, as fumes. **3.** any substance in the gaseous state that is usu. a liquid or solid. [ME *vapour*] —*v.t. & v.i.* vaporize. —**va'por·ish** *adj.*

va·por·ize (VAY pə RĪZ) *v.t. & v.i.* **·ized, ·iz·ing** convert or be converted into vapor. —**va'por·iz'er** *n.*

va·por·ous (VAY pər əs) *adj.* **1.** of or like vapor; foggy; misty. **2.** full of or producing vapors. **3.** diaphanous; ethereal. —**va'por·ous·ness** *n.*

vapor pressure *Physics* the pressure of a confined vapor in equilibrium with its liquid at any specific temperature. Also **vapor tension.**

var·i·a·ble (VAIR ee ə bəl) *adj.* **1.** having the capacity of varying; mutable. **2.** having a tendency to change; not constant. **3.** having no definite value as regards quantity.[ME] —*n.* **1.** that which varies or is subject to change. **2.** *Math.* a quantity susceptible of fluctuating in value or magnitude under different conditions. —**var'i·a·bil'i·ty** *n.* —**var'i·a·bly** *adv.*

var·i·ance (VAIR ee əns) *n.* **1.** the act of varying, or the state of being variant; difference; discrepancy. **2.** dissension; discord. —**at variance 1.** of things, disagreeing or conflicting. **2.** of people, in a state of dissension or discord.

var·i·ant (VAIR ee ənt) *adj.* **1.** having or showing variation; differing. **2.** tending to vary; changing. **3.** restless; fickle; inconstant. —*n.* a thing that differs from another in form only; esp., a different spelling or pronunciation of a word. [ME]

var·i·a·tion (VAIR ee AY shən) *n.* **1.** the act, process, state, or result of varying; diversity. **2.** the extent to which a thing varies. **3.** a repetition with its essential features intact and other features modified. **4.** *Music* a modification of a basic theme. **5.** *Biol.* deviation from the type or parent form.

var·i·col·ored (VAIR i KUL ərd) *adj.* variegated in color; of various colors.

var·i·cose (VAR i KOHS) *adj.* *Pathol.* abnormally dilated, as veins. [< L *varicosus* suffering from dilated veins]

var·ied (VAIR eed) *adj.* **1.** consisting of differing parts; diverse. **2.** partially or repeatedly altered, modified, etc. **3.** varicolored.

var·i·e·gate (VAIR ee ə GAYT) *v.t.* **·gat·ed, ·gat·ing 1.** make with different colors or tints; dapple; spot; streak. **2.** make varied; diversify. [< LL *variegatus* diversified] —**var'i·e·ga'ted** *adj.* —**var'i·e·ga'tion** *n.*

va·ri·e·ty (və RĪ i tee) *n. pl.* •**ties** **1.** the state or character of being various or varied; diversity. **2.** a collection of diverse things. **3.** the possession of different characteristics by one individual. **4.** a limited class of things that differ in certain common peculiarities from a larger class to which they belong. **5.** *Biol.* an individual or a group that differs from the type species in certain characters; a subdivision of a species. [< MF *variété*] —**va·ri′e·tal** (-təl) *adj.*

variety show a theatrical show consisting of a series of short, diversified acts.

var·i·o·rum (VAIR ee OR əm) *n.* an edition containing various versions of a text, usu. with notes and comments by various editors. Also **variorum edition.** [< L *editio cum notis variorum* an edition with the notes of various persons] —*adj.* related to such an edition.

var·i·ous (VAIR ee əs) *adj.* **1.** characteristically different from one another; diverse. **2.** more than one; several. **3.** many-sided; varying. **4.** having a diversity of appearance; variegated. [< L *varius*] —**var′i·ous·ly** *adv.*

var·nish (VAHR nish) *n.* **1.** a solution of certain gums or resins in alcohol, linseed oil, etc., used to produce a shining, transparent coat on a surface; also, the coat itself or the surface. **2.** a product resembling varnish. **3.** superficial polish or politeness. [ME *vernisch*] —*v.t.* **1.** cover with varnish. **2.** give a glossy appearance to; polish. **3.** hide by a deceptive covering; gloss over.

var·si·ty (VAHR si tee) *n. pl.* •**ties** a first-string team representing a school, college, in sports. [Alter. of UNIVERSITY]

var·y (VAIR ee) *v.* **var·ied, var·y·ing** *v.t.* **1.** change the form, nature, etc. of; modify. **2.** cause to be different from one another. **3.** impart variety to; diversify. —*v.i.* **4.** become changed in form, nature, etc. **5.** be diverse; differ. **6.** deviate: with *from.* [ME *varien*]

vas·cu·lar (VAS kyə lər) *adj. Biol.* **a** of or containing ducts that transport body liquids, as blood, lymph, etc. **b** richly supplied with blood vessels. [< NL *vascularis*]

vas def·er·ens (VAS DEF ə RENZ) *Anat.* the duct by which semen is conveyed from a testicle. [< NL, lit., vessel for leading off]

vase (vays, vayz) *n.* a decorative container used as an ornament or for holding flowers. [< F]

va·sec·to·my (va SEK tə mee) *n. pl.* •**mies**

Surg. removal of a portion of the vas deferens, esp. as a sterilization procedure.

vas·sal (VAS əl) *n.* **1.** in the feudal system, one who held land of a lord by a feudal tenure. **2.** a servant, slave, or bondman. [ME]

vast (vast) *adj.* •**er,** •**est 1.** of great extent or size; immense. **2.** very great in number, quantity, degree, intensity, etc. [< L *vastus*] —**vast′ly** *adv.* —**vast′ness** *n.*

vat (vat) *n.* a large vessel, tub, etc. for holding liquids. —*v.t.* **vat·ted, vat·ting** put into or treat in a vat. [ME]

vaude·ville (VAWD vil) *n.* a miscellaneous theatrical entertainment, as a variety show. [< F]

vault[1] (vawlt) *n.* **1.** an arched structure, as a ceiling or roof. **2.** any vaultlike covering, as the sky. **3.** an underground room or compartment covered by a vault, esp. when used for storage. **4.** a strongly protected place for keeping valuables, as in a bank. **5.** a burial chamber. [ME *voute*] —*v.t.* **1.** cover with or as with a vault. **2.** construct in the form of a vault.

vault[2] *v.t. & v.i.* leap or leap over, esp. with a boost from a pole or the hands. [< MF *volter*] —*n.* a leap or bound.

vaunt (vawnt) *v.t. & v.i.* boast of (something); brag. —*n.* a boastful assertion. [ME *vaunten*] —**vaunt′ing·ly** *adv.*

veal (veel) *n.* the flesh of a calf considered as food. [ME *veel*]

vec·tor (VEK tər) *n.* **1.** *Math.* a physical quantity that has magnitude and direction in space. **2.** *Med.* a carrier of disease microorganisms from one host to another. [< NL]

veer (veer) *v.i.* **1.** *Naut.* turn to another course. **2.** change direction by a clockwise motion, as the wind. **3.** change direction; shift. —*v.t.* **4.** change the direction of. [< MF *virer*] —*n.* a change in direction; swerve.

veg·e·ta·ble (VEJ tə bəl) *n.* **1.** the edible part of any plant, raw or cooked. **2.** any member of the vegetable kingdom; plant. —*adj.* **1.** pertaining to plants, esp. garden or farm vegetables. **2.** derived from, of the nature of, or resembling plants. **3.** made from or consisting of vegetables. [ME]

veg·e·tar·i·an (VEJ I TAIR ee ƏN) *ADJ.* pertaining to or advocating a diet containing no meat. —*n.* one who eats no meat. —**veg′e·tar′i·an·ism** *n.*

veg·e·tate (VEJ i TAYT) *v.i.* •**tat·ed,**

•tat•ing **1.** grow, as a plant. **2.** live in a monotonous, passive way. [< Med.L *vegetatus* grown] —**veg′e•ta′tive** *adj.*

veg•e•ta•tion (VEJ i TAY shən) *n.* **1.** the process of vegetating. **2.** plant life in the aggregate.

ve•he•ment (VEE ə mənt) *adj.* **1.** impetuous or passionate; ardent. **2.** forceful or energetic; violent. [< MF] —**ve′he•mence** *n.* —**ve′he•ment•ly** *adv.*

ve•hi•cle (VEE i kəl) *n.* **1.** any contrivance fitted with wheels or runners for carrying something; a conveyance, as a car or sled. **2.** a liquid, as oil, with which pigments are mixed in painting. **3.** anything by means of which something else, as power, thought, etc., is transmitted or communicated. **4.** a play, motion picture, etc. that permits a performer to display particular talents. [< F *véhicule*] —**ve•hic•u•lar** (vee HIK yə lər) *adj.*

veil (vayl) *n.* **1.** a thin fabric worn over the face or head for concealment, protection, or ornament. **2.** any piece of fabric used to conceal something; curtain. **3.** anything that conceals. —**take the veil** become a nun. [ME *veile*] —*v.t.* **1.** cover with a veil. **2.** hide; disguise.

vein (vayn) *n.* **1.** *Anat.* one of the tubular vessels that convey blood to the heart. **2.** *Entomol.* one of the radiating supports of an insect's wing. **3.** *Bot.* one of the slender vascular bundles that form the framework of a leaf. **4.** in mining, a lode. **5.** a long, irregular, colored streak, as in wood, marble, cheese, etc. **6.** a distinctive trait, tendency, or disposition. **7.** a temporary state of mind; mood. [ME *veine*] —*v.t.* **1.** furnish or fill with veins. **2.** streak or ornament with veins. —**veined** *adj.*

ve•lar (VEE lər) *adj.* **1.** of or pertaining to a velum, esp. to the soft palate. **2.** *Phonet.* formed with the back of the tongue touching or near the soft palate, as (k) in *cool,* (g) in *go.* [< NL *velaris*] —*n. Phonet.* a velar consonant.

Vel•cro (VEL kroh) *n.* a fabric made in opposing strips for use as a fastener for clothing etc., one strip having tiny loops and the other having tiny hooks so they can be fastened and unfastened by pressing together or pulling apart: a trade name. [< F *vel(ours) cro(ché)* hooked velvet]

veld (velt) *n.* in South Africa, open country or grassland. Also **veldt.** [< Afrikaans]

vel•lum (VEL əm) *n.* **1.** fine parchment made from the skins of calves. **2.** a manuscript written on such parchment. **3.** paper made to resemble parchment. [ME *velim*]

ve•loc•i•pede (və LOS ə PEED) *n.* a bicycle or tricycle. [< F *vélocipède*]

ve•loc•i•ty (və LOS i tee) *n. pl.* **•ties 1.** the state of moving swiftly; speed. **2.** the rate of motion. [< MF *velocité*]

ve•lour (və LUUR) *n.* a soft, velvetlike fabric. [< F *velours* velvet]

ve•lum (VEE ləm) *n. pl.* **•la** (-lə) **1.** *Biol.* a thin membranous covering or partition. **2.** *Anat.* the soft palate. [< NL]

vel•vet (VEL vit) *n.* **1.** a fabric having on one side a thick, short, smooth pile, formed either of loops (**pile velvet**) or of single threads (**cut velvet**). **2.** anything resembling such a fabric in softness, smoothness, etc. **3.** the furry skin covering a growing antler. —*adj.* **1.** made of velvet. **2.** velvety. [ME *veluet*]

vel•vet•y (VEL vi tee) *adj.* smooth and soft like velvet.

ve•nal (VEEN l) *adj.* **1.** ready to sell honor or principle, or to accept a bribe; mercenary. **2.** subject to or characterized by corruption. [< L *venalis* for sale] —**ve•nal•i•ty** (vee NAL i tee) *n.* —**ve′nal•ly** *adv.*

vend (vend) *v.t.* **1.** sell. **2.** utter (an opinion); publish. —*v.i.* **3.** be a vendor. **4.** be sold. [< L *vendere* sell] —**vend′or** or **vend′er** *n.*

ven•det•ta (ven DET ə) *n.* a feud, esp. between families. [< Ital.]

ve•neer (və NEER) *n.* **1.** a thin layer, as of choice wood, upon a commoner surface. **2.** a mere show or pleasing appearance. [< G *Furnier* veneer] —*v.t.* **1.** cover (a surface) with veneer. **2.** conceal with an attractive or deceptive surface.

ven•er•a•ble (VEN ər ə bəl) *adj.* meriting or commanding veneration; worthy of reverence: now usu. implying age. [ME] —**ven′er•a•bly** *adv.*

ven•er•ate (VEN ə RAYT) *v.t.* **•at•ed, •at•ing** regard with respect and deference; revere. [< L *veneratus* charmed] —**ven′er•a′tion** *n.*

ve•ne•re•al (və NEER ee əl) *adj.* **1.** pertaining to or proceeding from sexual intercourse. **2.** communicated by sexual relations. **3.** of or pertaining to venereal disease. [ME *venereall*]

venereal disease *Pathol.* any of several diseases communicated by sexual intercourse, as syphilis and gonorrhea.

venge•ance (VEN jəns) *n.* the act of reveng-

ing; retribution for a wrong or injury. —
with a vengeance with great force or violence. [ME]

venge·ful (VENJ fəl) *adj.* **1.** seeking to inflict vengeance; vindictive. **2.** serving to inflict vengeance. —**venge'ful·ly** *adv.* —
venge'ful·ness *n.*

ve·ni·al (VEE nee əl) *adj.* **1.** *Theol.* that may
be easily pardoned or forgiven: distinguished from *mortal: a venial* sin. **2.** excusable; pardonable. [ME] —**ve'ni·al'i·ty** *n.*

ven·i·son (VEN ə sən) *n.* deer flesh used for
food. [ME *venaison*]

ven·om (VEN əm) *n.* **1.** the poisonous liquid
secreted by certain animals, as serpents and
scorpions, and introduced into the victim
by a bite or sting. **2.** malice; malignity; spite.
[ME *venim*]

ven·om·ous (VEN ə məs) *adj.* **1.** having
glands secreting venom. **2.** poisonous; malignant; spiteful. —**ven'om·ous·ly** *adv.*

ve·nous (VEE nəs) *adj.* **1.** of, pertaining to,
or marked with veins. **2.** *Physiol.* designating the blood carried by the veins. [< L
venosus]

vent (vent) *n.* **1.** an opening, commonly
small, for the passage of liquids, gases, etc.
2. utterance; expression: chiefly in the
phrase **give vent to. 3.** *Zool.* the anus. —
v.t. **1.** relieve or give expression to. **2.** permit to escape from an opening. [ME *venten*]

ven·ti·late (VEN tl AYT) *v.t.* **·lat·ed,
·lat·ing 1.** produce a free circulation of air
in; admit fresh air into. **2.** provide with a
vent. **3.** expose to examination and discussion. **4.** *Physiol.* oxygenate, as blood. [ME
ventilatten blow away] —**ven'ti·la'tion** *n.*
—**ven'ti·la'tor** *n.*

ven·tral (VEN trəl) *adj. Anat.* **a** of, pertaining to, or situated on or near the abdomen.
b on or toward the lower or anterior part of
the body. [< L *ventralis*] —**ven'tral·ly**
adv.

ven·tri·cle (VEN tri kəl) *n. Anat.* **1.** one of
the two lower chambers of the heart, from
which blood is forced into the arteries. **2.**
any of various cavities in the body, as of the
brain, the spinal cord, etc. [ME] —
ven·tric·u·lar (ven TRIK yə lər) *adj.*

ven·tril·o·quism (ven TRIL ə KWIZ əm) *n.*
the art of speaking in such a manner that
the sounds seem to come from some source
other than the person speaking. Also **ven·
tril'o·quy** (-kwee). —**ven·tril'o·quist** *n.*
[< LL *ventriloquus* ventriloquist]

ven·ture (VEN chər) *v.* **·tured, ·tur·ing**
v.t. **1.** expose to chance or risk; bet. **2.** run
the risk of; brave. **3.** express at the risk of
denial or refutation: *venture* a suggestion.
—*v.i.* **4.** take a risk; dare. **5.** dare to go. [ME
venturen] —*n.* **1.** an undertaking attended
with risk or danger; esp., a business investment. **2.** that which is ventured. —**at a
venture** at random. —**ven'tur·er** *n.*

ven·ture·some (VEN chər səm) *adj.* **1.**
bold; daring. **2.** risky. —**ven'ture·some·
ness** *n.*

ven·tur·ous (VEN chər əs) *adj.* venturesome. —**ven'tur·ous·ness** *n.*

ven·ue (VEN yoo) *n. Law* the place where a
crime is committed or a cause of action
arises; also, the county or political division
from which the jury must be summoned
and in which the trial must be held. —
change of venue the change of the place
of trial. [ME *venyw* a coming]

Ve·nus (VEE nəs) *n.* the planet of the solar
system second in order from the sun. [ME
< *Venus,* Roman goddess of love and
beauty]

ve·rac·i·ty (və RAS i tee) *n. pl.* **·ties 1.**
truthfulness; honesty. **2.** agreement with
truth; accuracy. **3.** *pl.* **·ties** that which is
true; truth. [< Med.L *veracitas*] —
ve·ra·cious (və RAY shəs) *adj.*

ve·ran·da (və RAN də) *n.* an open, usu.
roofed balcony along the outside of a building. [< Hindi *varanda*]

verb (vurb) *n. Gram.* the part of speech that
expresses existence, action, or occurrence,
as the words *be, collide, think.* [ME *verbe*]

ver·bal (VUR bəl) *adj.* **1.** of, pertaining to, or
connected with words. **2.** expressed orally;
not written: a *verbal* contract. **3.** having
word corresponding with word; literal: a
verbal translation. **4.** *Gram.* **a** partaking of
the nature of or derived from a verb. **b** used
to form verbs. [< LL *verbalis*] —*n. Gram.*
a verb form that functions as a noun (**verbal noun**) or adjective: *Flying* is fun. She
invented a *flying* machine. —**ver'bal·ly**
adv.

ver·bal·ize (VUR bə LĪZ) *v.* **·ized, ·iz·ing**
v.t. **1.** express in words. **2.** *Gram.* make a
verb of; change into a verb. —*v.i.* **3.** speak
or write verbosely. **4.** express oneself in
words. —**ver'bal·i·za'tion** *n.*

ver·ba·tim (vər BAY tim) *adj. & adv.* in the
exact words; word for word. [ME]

ver·bi·age (VUR bee ij) *n.* excess of words;
wordiness. [< F]

ver·bose (vər BOHS) *adj.* using or containing a wearisome and unnecessary number of words; wordy. [< L *verbosus*] —**ver·bose′ly** *adv.* —**ver·bos·i·ty** (vər BOS i tee) *n.*

verb phrase *Gram.* a finite verb form consisting of a principal verb and an auxiliary or auxiliaries.

ver·dant (VUR dnt) *adj.* **1.** green with vegetation. **2.** unsophisticated; inexperienced. —**ver′dan·cy** *n.*

ver·dict (VUR dikt) *n.* **1.** the decision of a jury in an action. **2.** a conclusion; judgment. [ME]

ver·dure (VUR jər) *n.* greenness of growing vegetation; also, such vegetation. [ME]

verge¹ (vurj) *n.* **1.** the extreme edge of something; brink. **2.** a rod, wand, or staff as a symbol of authority or emblem of office. [ME] —*v.i.* **verged, verg·ing 1.** come near; approach; border: usu. with *on.* **2.** form the limit or verge.

verge² *v.i.* **verged, verg·ing** slope; tend; incline. [< L *vergere* incline]

ver·i·fy (VER ə FI) *v.t.* **·fied, ·fy·ing 1.** prove to be true or accurate; substantiate; confirm. **2.** test or ascertain the accuracy of truth of. **3.** *Law* **a** affirm under oath. **b** add a confirmation to. [ME *verifien*] —**ver′i·fi′a·bil′i·ty** *n.* —**ver′i·fi′a·ble** *adj.* —**ver′i·fi′a·bly** *adv.* —**ver′i·fi·ca′tion** *n.*

ver·i·si·mil·i·tude (VER ə si MIL i tood) *n.* **1.** the appearance of truth. **2.** that which resembles truth. [< L *verisimilitudo*]

ver·i·ta·ble (VER i tə bəl) *adj.* properly so called; unquestionable: a *veritable* villain. [ME] —**ver′i·ta·bly** *adv.*

ver·i·ty (VER i tee) *n.* **1.** the quality of being correct of true. **2.** *pl.* **·ties** a true or established statement, principle, etc.; a fact; truth. [ME *verite*]

ver·mic·u·lar (vər MIK yə lər) *adj.* **1.** having the form or motion of a worm. **2.** like the wavy tracks of a worm. [< Med.L *vermicularis*]

ver·mi·form (VUR mə FORM) *adj.* resembling a worm in shape. [< Med.L *vermiformis*]

vermiform appendix *Anat.* a slender, wormlike vestigial structure, protruding from the large intestine in man and certain other mammals.

ver·mi·fuge (VUR mə FYOOJ) *n.* any remedy that destroys intestinal worms. [< L *vermis* worm + *fugare* put to flight]

ver·mil·ion (vər MIL yən) *n.* **1.** a brilliant red pigment. **2.** the color of the pigment, an intense orange red. [ME *vermilioun*] —*adj.* of this color. —*v.t.* color with or as with vermilion.

ver·min (VUR min) *n. pl.* **ver·min 1.** collectively, objectionable small animals or parasitic insects, as lice, worms, rats, etc. **2.** a repulsive human being. [ME]

ver·mouth (vər MOOTH) *n.* a liqueur made from white wine flavored with aromatic herbs. [< F *vermout*]

ver·nac·u·lar (vər NAK yə lər) *n.* **1.** the native language of a locality. **2.** the everyday speech of the people, as opposed to the literary language. **3.** the vocabulary or jargon of a particular profession or trade. —*adj.* **1.** originating in or belonging to one's native land; indigenous: said of a language, idiom, etc. **2.** using everyday speech rather than the literary language. [< L *vernaculus* native]

ver·nal (VUR nl) *adj.* **1.** of or pertaining to spring. **2.** youthful; fresh. [< L *vernalis* of spring]

vernal equinox see under EQUINOX.

ver·sa·tile (VUR sə tl) *adj.* **1.** having an aptitude for various occupations; many-sided. **2.** having several different uses. **3.** capable of turning freely. [< F] —**ver′sa·til′i·ty** *n.*

verse (vurs) *n.* **1.** a single metrical or rhythmical line. **2.** poetry: distinguished from *prose.* **3.** a poem. **4.** one of the short divisions of a chapter of the Bible. **5.** a stanza. [ME *vers*]

versed (vurst) *adj.* thoroughly acquainted; adept; proficient: with *in.* [< L *versatus* occupied]

ver·si·fy (VUR sə FI) *v.t. & v.i.* **·fied, ·fy·ing** write or narrate in verse. [ME *versifien*] —**ver′si·fi·ca′tion** *n.* —**ver′si·fi′er** *n.*

ver·sion (VUR zhən) *n.* **1.** a description or account as modified by a particular point of view. **2.** a translation, esp. of the Bible. [< MF]

ver·so (VUR soh) *n. pl.* **·sos 1.** a left-hand page, as of a book: opposed to *recto.* **2.** the reverse of a coin or medal. [< L *verso (folio)* a turned (leaf)]

ver·sus (VUR soh) *prep.* **1.** in law and sports, against. **2.** considered as the alternative of: free trade *versus* tariffs. [ME]

ver·te·bra (VUR tə brə) *n. pl.* **·brae** (-bree) or **·bras** *Anat.* any of the segmented bones of the spinal column in man and the higher vertebrates. [< L] —ver·te·bral (vər TEE brəl) adj.

ver·te·brate (VUR tə brit) adj. 1. having a backbone or spinal column. 2. pertaining to or characteristic of vertebrates. [< L vertebratus jointed] —n. any of a primary division of animals having a segmented spinal column, as fishes, birds, reptiles, and mammals.

ver·tex (VUR teks) n. pl. ·tex·es or ·ti·ces (-tə SEEZ) 1. the highest point of anything; apex; top. 2. Geom. a the point of intersection of the sides of an angle. b the point of a triangle opposite to, and farthest from, the base. [< L, whirl]

ver·ti·cal (VUR ti kəl) adj. 1. perpendicular to the plane of the horizon; extending up and down; upright: opposed to horizontal. 2. of or at the vertex or highest point. [< LL verticalis] —n. a vertical line, plane, or circle. —ver·ti·cal'i·ty n.

ver·tig·i·nous (vər TIJ ə nəs) adj. 1. causing or affected by vertigo. 2. turning round; whirling. [< L vertiginosus] —ver·tig'i·nous·ly adv.

ver·ti·go (VUR ti GOH) n. pl. ·goes or ver·tig·i·nes (vər TIJ ə NEEZ) Pathol. a sensation of dizziness. [< L]

verve (vurv) n. enthusiasm; energy; vigor. [< F]

ver·y (VER ee) adv. in a high degree; extremely. —adj. 1. absolute; actual; simple: the very truth. 2. identical: my very words. 3. the (thing) itself; even: The very stones cry out. [ME]

very high frequency Telecom. any frequency between 30 and 300 megahertz. Abbr. VHF.

very low frequency Telecom. any frequency between 10 and 30 kilohertz. Abbr. VLF.

ves·i·cle (VES i kəl) n. 1. any small bladderlike cavity, cell, or cyst. 2. Pathol. a blister. [< L vesica bladder]

ves·per (VES pər) n. 1. a bell that calls to vespers. 2. an evening service, prayer, or song. [ME] —adj. of evening or vespers: also ves'per·al.

ves·pers (VES pərz) n. (construed as sing. or pl.) Often cap. Eccl. a service of worship in the evening. [< F vespres]

ves·sel (VES əl) n. 1. a hollow receptacle, esp. one capable of holding a liquid, as a pitcher. 2. a ship or boat. 3. Anat. a duct or canal for transporting a body fluid, as a vein. [ME]

vest (vest) n. a short, sleeveless garment, buttoning in front, commonly worn underneath a jacket. [< F veste] —v.t. 1. confer (ownership, authority, etc.) upon some person or persons: usu. with in. 2. place ownership or authority with (a person or persons). 3. clothe, as with vestments. [ME vesten]

ves·tal (VES tl) n. one of the virgin priestesses of Vesta, Roman goddess of the hearth. Also vestal virgin. —adj. chaste; pure.

vest·ed (VES tid) adj. 1. Law fixed; established; permanent. 2. dressed; robed, esp. in church vestments.

vested interest 1. a strong commitment to a system or institution whose existence serves one's self-interest. 2. Usu. pl. a financially powerful or influential group.

ves·ti·bule (VES tə BYOOL) n. 1. an entrance hall; lobby. 2. Anat. any of several chambers or channels adjoining or communicating with others. [< L vestibulum entrance] —ves·tib·u·lar (ves TIB yə lər) adj.

ves·tige (VES tij) n. 1. a trace of something absent or lost. 2. Biol. a small or degenerate part or organ that is well developed and functional in earlier forms of organisms. [< F] —ves·tig·i·al (ve STIJ ee əl) adj. —ves·tig'i·al·ly adv.

vest·ment (VEST mənt) n. 1. an article of dress; esp., a robe of office. 2. Eccl. one of the ritual garments of the clergy. [ME vestement]

ves·try (VES tree) n. pl. ·tries 1. a room, as in a church, where vestments and sacred vessels are kept: often called sacristy. 2. in the Anglican Church, a body administering the affairs of a parish. [ME vestrie]

ves·try·man (VES tree mən) n. pl. ·men a member of a vestry.

vet¹ (vet) n. Informal a veterinarian. —v.t. vet·ted, vet·ting examine carefully and critically for faults or errors: She vetted my manuscript.

vet² n. Informal a veteran.

vet·er·an (VET ər ən) n. 1. one who is much experienced in an activity, job, or skill. 2. a former member of the armed forces. [< L veteranus]

vet·er·i·nar·i·an (VET ər ə NAIR ee ən) n. a practitioner of veterinary medicine or surgery.

vet·er·i·nar·y (VET ər ə NER ee) adj. pertaining to the diseases or injuries of animals and to their medical treatment. —n. pl.

•nar•ies a veterinarian. [< L *veterinarius* of beasts of burden]

ve•to (VEE toh) *v.t.* •toed, •to•ing 1. refuse executive approval of (a bill passed by a legislative body). 2. forbid or prohibit authoritatively. —*n. pl.* •toes 1. the prerogative of a chief executive to refuse to approve a legislative enactment; also, the exercise of such a prerogative. 2. any authoritative prohibition. [< L, I forbid]

vex (veks) *v.t.* 1. irritate; annoy. 2. trouble or afflict. [ME *vexen*] —vexed *adj.*

vex•a•tion (vek SAY shən) *n.* 1. the act of vexing, or the state of being vexed. 2. that which vexes. —vex•a'tious *adj.*

vi•a (VĪ ə) *prep.* by way of; by a route passing through. [< L, by way of]

vi•a•ble (VĪ ə bəl) *adj.* 1. capable of developing normally, as a newborn infant, a seed, etc. 2. workable; practicable. [< F] — vi'a•bil'i•ty *n.*

vi•a•duct (VĪ ə DUKT) *n.* a bridgelike structure, esp. a large one of arched masonry, to carry a roadway over a ravine. [< L *via* way + (AQUE)DUCT]

vi•al (VĪ əl) *n.* a small bottle for liquids. — *v.t.* vi•aled, •vi•al•ing put or keep in or as in a vial. [ME *fiole*]

vi•and (VĪ ənd) *n.* 1. an article of food, esp. meat. 2. *pl.* victuals; provisions; food. [ME]

vi•brant (VĪ brənt) *adj.* 1. vibrating. 2. throbbing; pulsing. 3. rich and resonant, as a sound. 4. energetic; vigorous. 5. *Phonet.* voiced. —*n. Phonet.* a voiced sound. —vi'bran•cy *n.* —vi'brant•ly *adv.*

vi•brate (VĪ brayt) *v.* •brat•ed, •brat•ing *v.i.* 1. move back and forth rapidly; quiver. 2. move or swing back and forth, as a pendulum. 3. sound; resound. 4. be emotionally moved; thrill. —*v.t.* 5. cause to quiver or tremble. 6. cause to move back and forth. 7. send forth (sound etc.) by vibration. [< L *vibratus* shaken] — vi•bra•to•ry (VĪ brə TOR ee) *adj.*

vi•bra•tion (vī BRAY shən) *n.* 1. the act of vibrating, or the state of being vibrated. 2. *Physics* a any physical process characterized by cyclic variations in amplitude, intensity, or the like, as wave motion or an electric field. b a single complete oscillation. 3. a general feeling assumed to flow from a person or situation.

vi•bra•tor (VĪ bray tər) *n.* 1. that which vibrates. 2. an electrically operated massaging apparatus.

vic•ar (VIK ər) *n.* 1. in the Anglican Church,

the priest of a chapel, mission, or other dependent congregation. 2. in the Roman Catholic Church, a substitute or representative of an ecclesiastical person. 3. one authorized to perform functions in the stead of another; substitute. [ME]

vic•ar•age (VIK ər ij) *n.* the benefice or residence of a vicar.

vi•car•i•ous (vī KAIR ee əs) *adj.* 1. made or performed by substitution: a *vicarious* sacrifice. 2. enjoyed, felt, etc. by imagined participation in an experience not one's own: *vicarious* gratification. 3. acting for another. [< L *vicarius*] —vi•car'i•ous•ly *adv.* —vi•car'i•ous•ness *n.*

vice¹ (vīs) *n.* 1. an immoral habit or trait. 2. habitual immorality; corruption; evil. 3. something that mars; a blemish or imperfection. [ME]

vice² *prep.* instead of; in the place of. [< L]

vice- *combining form* acting as substitute or deputy for.

vice-admiral *Naval* a commissioned officer ranking next below an admiral.

vice-consul one who exercises consular authority in the place of a consul.

vi•cen•ni•al (vī SEN ee əl) *adj.* 1. occurring once in twenty years. 2. lasting or existing twenty years.

vice president an officer ranking next below a president. —vice-pres•i•den•cy (VĪS PREZ əd ən see) *n.* —vice-pres•i•den'tial (VĪS PREZ ə DEN chəl) *adj.*

vice•roy (VĪS roi) *n.* one who rules a country, colony, or province by authority of the sovereign. [< MF]

vice squad a police division charged with combatting prostitution, gambling, etc.

vice ver•sa (VĪS VUR sə) with the order changed; conversely. [< L]

vi•chys•soise (VISH ee SWAHZ) *n.* a potato cream soup, usu. served cold. [< F]

vi•cin•i•ty (vi SIN i tee) *n. pl.* •ties 1. a region adjacent or near; neighborhood. 2. nearness in space or relationship; proximity. [< MF *vicinité*]

vi•cious (VISH əs) *adj.* 1. malicious; spiteful. 2. violent; fierce. 3. corrupt. 4. morally injurious; vile. 5. unruly or dangerous. 6. leading from bad to worse, as due to problems that augment each other: a *vicious* circle. [ME] —vi'cious•ness *n.*

vi•cis•si•tude (vi SIS i TOOD) *n.* 1. *pl.* irregular changes or variations, as of fortune: the *vicissitudes* of life. 2. a change; esp., a complete change. **3.** alternating change or succession, as of the seasons. [< MF]

vic•tim (VIK tim) *n.* **1.** one who is killed, injured, or subjected to suffering. **2.** one who is swindled or tricked; dupe. [< L *victima*]

vic•tim•ize (VIK tə MĪZ) *v.t.* **•ized, •iz•ing** make a victim of, esp. by defrauding; cheat. —**vic'tim•i•za'tion** *n.* —**vic'tim•iz'er** *n.*

vic•tor (VIK tər) *n.* **1.** one who vanquishes an enemy. **2.** one who wins any struggle or contest. [ME]

Vic•to•ri•an (vik TOR ee ən) *adj.* **1.** of or relating to Queen Victoria or to her reign. **2.** pertaining to English-speaking culture during Queen Victoria's reign (1837–1901). **3.** prudish; conventional. —*n.* a contemporary of Queen Victoria. —**Vic'to'ri•an•ism** (vik TOR ee ə NIZ əm) *n.*

vic•to•ri•ous (vik TOR ee əs) *adj.* **1.** having won victory; triumphant. **2.** relating to or characterized by victory.

vic•to•ry (VIK tə ree) *n. pl.* **•ries** the overcoming of an enemy, opponent, or any difficulty; triumph. [ME]

vict•ual (VIT l) *n.* **1.** food. **2.** *pl.* food for human beings, as prepared for eating. Also *vittles*. [ME *vitaille*] —*v.t.* **•ualed, •ual•ing** furnish with victuals.

vi•de•li•cet (vi DEL ə sit) *adv.* to wit; that is to say; namely. Abbr. *viz.* [< L]

vid•e•o (VID ee OH) *adj.* **1.** of or pertaining to television, esp. to the picture. **2.** producing a signal convertible into a television picture. —*n.* television; a movie etc. available as a videocassette. [< L, I see]

vid•e•o•tape (VID ee oh TAYP) *n.* a recording of a television program on magnetic tape. Also **videocassette.** —*v.t.* **•taped, •tap•ing** make such a recording.

vie (vī) *v.i.* **vied, vy•ing** strive for superiority; compete: with *with* or *for.* [< MF *envier* challenge]

view (vyoo) *n.* **1.** the act of seeing; survey; inspection. **2.** mental examination or inspection. **3.** power or range of vision. **4.** that which is seen; outlook; prospect. **5.** a representation of a scene; esp., a landscape. **6.** the object of action; aim; intention; purpose. **7.** manner of looking at things; opinion; judgment. **8.** a general summary or account. —**in view 1.** in range of vision. **2.** under consideration. **3.** as a goal or end. —**in view of** in consideration of. —**on view** open to public inspection. —**with a view to 1.** with the aim or purpose of. **2.** with a

hope of. [ME *vewe*] —*v.t.* **1.** look at; see; examine. **2.** survey mentally; consider.

view•less (VYOO lis) *adj.* **1.** devoid of a view or prospect. **2.** having no views or opinions.

view•point (VYOO point) *n.* **1.** a mental attitude. **2.** a place affording a view.

vig•il (VIJ əl) *n.* **1.** the act of staying awake in order to observe, protect, etc.; watch. **2.** *Eccl.* **a** the eve of a holy day. **b** *pl.* religious devotions on such an eve. [ME *vigile*]

vig•i•lance (VIJ ə ləns) *n.* watchfulness in guarding against danger; alertness.

vig•i•lant (VIJ ə lənt) *adj.* characterized by vigilance; watchful; heedful. [ME] —**vig'i•lant•ly** *adv.*

vig•i•lan•te (vij ə LAN tee) *n.* one of a group whose members take the law into their own hands. [< Sp., watchman] —**vig•i•lan•tism** (vij ə LAN tiz əm) *n.* the summary action resorted to by vigilantes.

vi•gnette (vin YET) *n.* **1.** a short, subtle literary description. **2.** a decorative design placed on or before the title page of a book, at the end or beginning of a chapter, etc. **3.** an engraving, photograph, etc. having a background that shades off gradually. [< F] —*v.t.* **•gnet•ted, •gnet•ting 1.** make with a gradually shaded background, as a photograph. **2.** ornament with vignettes. **3.** depict in a vignette. —**vi•gnet'tist** *n.*

vig•or (VIG ər) *n.* active strength or force, physical or mental; vitality; energy; intensity. [ME]

vig•or•ous (VIG ər əs) *adj.* **1.** full of physical or mental vigor; robust. **2.** done with or showing vigor; forceful. —**vig'or•ous•ly** *adv.*

Vi•king (VĪ king) *n.* one of the Scandinavian pirates of the 8th to 10th c. Also **vi'king** a pirate. [< ON *vikingr*]

vile (vīl) *adj.* **vil•er, vil•est 1.** morally base; shamefully wicked. **2.** loathsome; disgusting. **3.** degrading; ignominious: *vile* treatment. **4.** flagrantly bad or inferior. **5.** unpleasant; disagreeable. [ME] —**vile'ly** *adv.*

vil•i•fy (VIL ə FĪ) *v.t.* **•fied, •fy•ing 1.** abuse; malign; slander. **2.** make base; degrade. [ME] —**vil'i•fi•ca'tion** *n.*

vil•la (VIL ə) *n.* a comfortable or luxurious house in the country, at a resort, etc. [< Ital.]

vil•lage (VIL ij) *n.* **1.** a collection of houses in a rural district. **2.** in some states, a municipality smaller than a city. **3.** any comparatively small community. **4.** the inhabitants of a village, collectively. [ME]

vil·lag·er (VIL i jər) *n.* one who lives in a village.

vil·lain (VIL ən) *n.* **1.** a wicked, malevolent person. **2.** such a person represented as a leading character in a novel, play, etc. **3.** a rogue; scoundrel: often used humorously. [ME *vilein*] —**vil′lain·ous** *adj.*

vil·lain·y (VIL ə nee) *n. pl.* **·lain·ies 1.** the quality of being villainous. **2.** conduct characteristic of a villain.

vim (vim) *n.* force or vigor; energy; spirit. [< L, power]

vin·ai·grette (VIN ə GRET) *n.* **1.** a small ornamental box or bottle, used for holding smelling salts or the like. **2.** vinaigrette sauce. [< F]

vinaigrette sauce a sauce made from vinegar, oil, herbs, etc.

vin·ci·ble (VIN sə bəl) *adj.* conquerable. [< L *vincibilis*] —**vin′ci·bil′i·ty** *n.*

vin·di·cate (VIN də KAYT) *v.t.* **·cat·ed, ·cat·ing 1.** clear of accusation, censure, suspicion, etc. **2.** support or maintain, as a right or claim. **3.** serve to justify. [< L *vindicatus* avenged] —**vin′di·ca′tor** *n.*

vin·di·ca·tion (VIN də KAY shən) *n.* **1.** the act of vindicating, or the state of being vindicated. **2.** justification; defense.

vin·dic·a·to·ry (VIN di kə TOR ee) *adj.* **1.** serving to vindicate. **2.** punitive; avenging.

vin·dic·tive (vin DIK tiv) *adj.* revengeful or spiteful. —**vin·dic′tive·ness** *n.*

vine (vīn) *n.* **1.** any of a group of plants having a slender, flexible stem that may twine about a support or clasp it by means of tendrils etc.; also, the stem itself. **2.** a grape plant. [ME]

vin·e·gar (VIN i gər) *n.* an acid liquid obtained by the fermentation of wine etc. and used as a condiment and preservative. [ME *vinegre*] —**vin′e·gar·y** *adj.*

vine·yard (VIN yərd) *n.* an area planted with grape plants. [ME]

vin·tage (VIN tij) *n.* **1.** the yield of a vineyard or wine-producing district for one season; also, the wine produced from this yield. **2.** the type popular at a particular time of the past: *a joke of ancient vintage.* [ME] —*adj.* **1.** of exceptional quality or excellence. **2.** of a good year; also, of time past.

vint·ner (VINT nər) *n.* a person who makes or sells wine.

vi·nyl (VĪN l) *n.* any of various tough plastics, used for coatings etc.

vi·o·la·ble (VĪ ə lə bəl) *adj.* capable of being violated. —**vi′o·la·bil′i·ty** *n.*

vi·o·late (VĪ ə LAYT) *v.t.* **·lat·ed, ·lat·ing 1.** break or infringe, as a law, oath, etc. **2.** profane, as a holy place. **3.** break in upon; disturb. **4.** ravish; rape. **5.** do violence to; outrage. [ME] —**vi′o·la′tion** *n.*

vi·o·lence (VĪ ə ləns) *n.* **1.** the quality or state of being violent; intensity; fury. **2.** an instance of violent action, treatment, etc. **3.** violent or abusive exercise or power; injury; outrage. —**do violence to 1.** injure or damage by rough or abusive treatment. **2.** distort the meaning of. [ME]

vi·o·lent (VĪ ə lənt) *adj.* **1.** proceeding from or marked by great physical force or roughness. **2.** caused by or exhibiting intense excitement; passionate; fierce. **3.** characterized by intensity of any kind; extreme: *violent* heat. **4.** marked by undue exercise of force; harsh: take *violent* measures. **5.** resulting from unusual force or injury: a *violent* death. [ME]

vi·o·let (VĪ ə lit) *n.* **1.** one of a widely distributed genus of herbs bearing usu. purplish blue flowers. **2.** a deep bluish purple color. —*adj.* bluish purple. [ME]

vi·o·lin (vī ə LIN) *n.* a musical instrument having four strings and a wood sounding box, held against the shoulder and played by means of a bow: also called *fiddle.* [< Ital. *violino*] —**vi′o·lin′ist** *n.*

vi·o·lon·cel·lo (VEE ə lən CHEL oh) *n. pl.* **·los** cello. [< Ital.]

VIP (VEE Ī PEE) *n. pl.* **VIPs** a *very imp*ortant *p*erson.

vi·per (VĪ pər) *n.* **1.** a venomous snake. **2.** a treacherous or spiteful person. [< MF *vipere*]

vi·per·ous (VĪ pər əs) *adj.* **1.** snakelike. **2.** venomous; malicious.

vi·ra·go (vi RAH goh) *n. pl.* **·goes** or **·gos** a noisy, sharp-tongued woman; scold. [ME]

vi·ral (VĪ rəl) *adj.* of, pertaining to, caused by, or of the nature of a virus.

vir·gin (VUR jin) *n.* a person, esp. a girl or woman, who has never had sexual intercourse. [ME] —*adj.* **1.** being a virgin. **2.** pertaining or suited to a virgin; chaste: maidenly. **3.** uncorrupted; pure; undefiled. **4.** not hitherto used or processed: *virgin* soil, *virgin* wool. —**vir·gin·al** (VUR jə nl) *adj.* pertaining to or characteristic of a virgin; chaste. —**vir·gin·i·ty** (vər JIN i tee) *n. pl.* **·ties** the state or condition of being a virgin.

vir•gule (VUR gyool) *n.* slash (def. 2). [< F]

vir•i•des•cent (VIR i DES ənt) *adj.* slightly green. [< LL *viridescere* become green] — **vir′i•des′cence** *n.*

vir•ile (VIR əl) *adj.* **1.** having the characteristics of adult manhood; masculine. **2.** having qualities considered typically masculine; vigorous; forceful. **3.** capable of procreation. [< MF *viril*] —**vi•ril•i•ty** (və RIL i tee) *n.*

vi•rol•o•gy (vī ROL ə jee) *n.* the scientific study of viruses, esp. in their relation to disease. —**vi•rol′o•gist** *n.*

vir•tu•al (VUR choo əl) *adj.* having the effect but not the actual form of what is specified. [ME]

vir•tu•al•ly (VUR choo ə lee) *adv.* in effect; for all practical purposes.

vir•tue (VUR choo) *n.* **1.** the quality of moral righteousness or excellence. **2.** the practice of moral duties and abstinence from vice. **3.** chastity; virginity. **4.** a particular type of moral excellence. **5.** any admirable quality, or trait. **6.** inherent or essential quality, power, etc. —**by** (or **in**) **virtue of** by or through the fact, quality, force, or authority of. —**make a virtue of necessity** seem to do freely or from principle what is or must be done. [ME *vertu*]

vir•tu•os•i•ty (VUR choo OS i tee) *n. pl.* **•ties** the skill of a virtuoso.

vir•tu•o•so (VUR choo OH soh) *n. pl.* **•sos** or **•si** (-see) a master of technique, as a skilled musician. [< Ital.]

vir•tu•ous (VUR choo əs) *adj.* **1.** characterized by, exhibiting, or having the nature of virtue. **2.** chaste. —**vir′tu•ous•ly** *adv.* —**vir′tu•ous•ness** *n.*

vir•u•lent (VIR yə lənt) *adj.* **1.** extremely harmful. **2.** bitterly rancorous; acrimonious. **3.** *Med.* actively poisonous or infective; malignant. **4.** *Bacteriol.* having the power to injure an organism by invasion of tissue and generation of internal toxins, as certain microorganisms. [ME] —**vir′u•lence** *n.* —**vir′u•lent•ly** *adv.*

vi•rus (VĪ rəs) *n.* **1.** any of a class of ultramicroscopic pathogenic agents, typically inert except when in contact with certain living cells. **2.** *Informal* an illness caused by such an agent. [< L, poison]

vi•sa (VEE zə) *n.* an official endorsement, as on a passport, certifying that it has been found correct and that the bearer may proceed. —*v.t.* **•saed, •sa•ing 1.** put a visa on (a passport). **2.** give a visa to. [< F]

vis•age (VIZ ij) *n.* the face or facial expression of a person; countenance. [ME]

vis-à-vis (VEE zə VEE) *n. pl.* **vis-à-vis 1.** one of two persons or things that face each other from opposite sides. **2.** a person face to face with another. —*adj.* face-to-face: a *vis-à-vis* discussion. —*adv.* face to face. —*prep.* **1.** face to face with. **2.** in relation to. [< F, face to face]

vis•cer•a (VIS ə rə) *n.pl., sing.* **vis•cus** (VIS kəs) *Anat.* the internal organs, esp. the abdominal organs. [< L, pl. of *viscus* flesh] —**vis′cer•al** *adj.*

vis•cid (VIS id) *adj.* sticky or adhesive; viscous. [< LL *viscidus*] —**vis•cid′i•ty** *n.*

vis•cos•i•ty (vi SKOS i tee) *n. pl.* **•ties 1.** the state, quality, property, or degree of being viscous. **2.** *Physics* the resistance of a fluid to flow freely because of the friction of its molecules.

vis•count (VĪ KOWNT) *n.* in England, a title of nobility ranking between earl and baron. [ME *viscounte*]

vis•count•ess (VĪ KOWN tis) *n.* **1.** the wife of a viscount. **2.** a woman holding a rank equivalent to viscount in her own right.

vis•cous (VIS kəs) *adj.* **1.** glutinous; sticky. **2.** *Physics* characterized by or having viscosity. [ME *viscouse*] —**vis′cous•ly** *adv.* —**vis′cous•ness** *n.*

vis•cus (VIS kəs) singular of VISCERA.

vise (vīs) *n.* a clamping device, usu. of two jaws made to be closed together with a screw, lever, etc., used for grasping and holding objects being worked on. [< MF *vis*] —*v.t.* **vised, vis•ing** hold, force, or squeeze in or as in a vise.

vis•i•bil•i•ty (VIZ ə BIL i tee) *n.* **1.** condition, capability, or degree of being visible. **2.** the clarity of unaided vision as affected by distance, atmospheric conditions, etc.

vis•i•ble (VIZ ə bəl) *adj.* **1.** perceivable by the eye; capable of being seen. **2.** apparent; observable; evident. [ME] —**vis′i•bly** *adv.*

vi•sion (VIZH ən) *n.* **1.** the faculty or sense of sight. **2.** understanding, esp. of what lies in the future; foresight. **3.** insight; imagination. **4.** a mental representation of or as of objects, scenes, etc., as in a religious revelation, dream, etc. **5.** something vividly imagined. **6.** something or someone very beautiful or pleasing. [ME] —*v.t.* envision.

vi•sion•ar•y (VIZH ə NER ee) *adj.* **1.** not founded on fact; imaginary. **2.** affected by or tending toward impractical idealism or fantasies; dreamy; impractical. **3.** having or

of the nature of apparitions, dreams, etc. —
n. pl. **•ar•ies 1.** one who has visions. **2.** a
dreamer; an impractical schemer or ideal-
ist.

vis•it (VIZ it) *v.t.* **1.** go or come to see (a
person). **2.** go or come to (a place etc.), as
for touring etc. **3.** be a guest of; stay with
temporarily. **4.** go or come to for professional purposes. **5.** come upon or afflict. **6.**
inflict (punishment, wrath, etc.). —*v.i.* **7.**
make a visit; pay a call or calls. **8.** chat or
converse casually. [ME *visiten*] —*n.* **1.** the
act of visiting a person or place. **2.** a chat. **3.**
a personal call for the discharge of an official or professional duty. —**vis′i•tor** *n.*

vis•it•ant (VIZ i tənt) *n.* **1.** a pilgrim. **2.** a
visitor, esp. from the spirit world. **3.** a migratory bird stopping at a particular region.

vis•i•ta•tion (VIZ i TAY shən) *n.* **1.** a visit,
esp. a formal one. **2.** in Biblical and religious use, a visiting of blessing or affliction.
—**vis′i•ta′tion•al** *adj.*

vi•sor (VĪ zər) *n.* **1.** a projecting piece at the
front of a cap etc., serving as a shade for the
eyes. **2.** in armor, the movable front piece of
a helmet. **3.** a movable piece or part serving
as a shield against glare etc., as on the windshield of an automobile. [ME *viser*]

vis•ta (VIS tə) *n.* **1.** a view or prospect, as
along an avenue; an outlook. **2.** a mental
view embracing a series of events. [<
Ital.]

vis•u•al (VIZH oo əl) *adj.* **1.** of or pertaining
to the sense of sight. **2.** visible. **3.** produced
or induced by mental images. [ME] —**vis′
u•al•ly** *adv.*

visual aid Often *pl.* in teaching, a device or
method designed to convey information
through the sense of sight, as motion pictures, charts, etc.

vis•u•al•ize (VIZH oo ə LĪZ) *v.t. & v.i.* •ized,
•iz•ing form a mental image (of). —
vis′u•al•i•za′tion *n.*

vi•tal (VĪT l) *adj.* **1.** necessary; essential. **2.** of
or pertaining to life. **3.** essential to or supporting life. **4.** affecting the course of life or
existence, esp. so as to be dangerous or
fatal: a *vital* error. **5.** energetic; forceful;
dynamic. [ME] —**vi′tal•ly** *adv.*

vi•tal•ism (VĪT l IZ əm) *n.* *Biol.* the doctrine
that life and its phenomena arose from a
hypothetical **vital force** (or **vital principle**). —**vi′tal•ist** *n.*

vi•tal•i•ty (vī TAL i tee) *n. pl.* **•ties 1.** the
state or quality of being vital. **2.** vital or life-
giving force, principle, etc. **3.** vigor; energy;

animation. **4.** power of continuing in force
or effect.

vi•tal•ize (VĪT l Iz) *v.t.* •ized, •iz•ing make
vital; endow with life or energy.

vi•tals (VĪT lz) *n.pl.* the parts or organs necessary to life.

vital signs the body temperature, rate of
breathing, pulse rate, and often the blood
pressure of a person.

vital statistics quantitative data relating to
aspects and conditions of human life.

vi•ta•min (VĪ tə min) *n.* any of a group of
complex organic substances found in food
and essential for health and growth.

vi•ti•ate (VISH ee AYT) *v.t.* •at•ed, •at•ing
1. impair the use or value of; spoil. **2.** debase or corrupt. **3.** render legally ineffective. [< L *vitiatus* spoiled] —**vi′ti•a′tion**
n.

vit•i•cul•ture (VIT i KUL chər) *n.* the study
and art of grapes and their cultivation. [< L
vitis vine + CULTURE] —**vit′i•cul′tur•ist**
n.

vit•re•ous (VI tree əs) *adj.* **1.** pertaining to,
obtained from, or like glass. **2.** pertaining to
the vitreous humor. [< L *vitreus*]

vitreous humor *Anat.* the transparent, jellylike material that fills the eyeball.

vit•ri•fy (VI trə FĪ) *v.t. & v.i.* •fied, •fy•ing
change into glass or a vitreous substance;
make or become vitreous. [< F *vitrifier*] —
vit′ri•fi•ca′tion *n.*

vit•ri•ol (VI tree əl) *n.* anything sharp or
caustic, esp. criticism. [ME]

vit•ri•ol•ic (VI tree OL ik) *adj.* corrosive,
burning, or caustic, as criticism.

vit•tles (VIT lz) *n.pl.* victuals.

vi•tu•per•ate (vī TOO pə RAYT) *v.t.* •at•ed,
•at•ing find fault with abusively; rail at; berate; scold. [< L *vituperatus* blamed] —
vi•tu′per•a′tion *n.* —**vi•tu•per•a•tive**
(vī TOO pər ə tiv) *adj.*

vi•va (VEE və) *interj.* an acclamation or salute: *Viva* Pavarotti! [< Ital., long live]

vi•va•cious (vi VAY shəs) *adj.* lively; active.
—**vi•va′cious•ly** *adv.* —**vi•vac•i•ty** (vi
VAS i tee) *n.*

vi•var•i•um (vī VAIR ee əm) *n. pl.*
•var•i•ums or •var•i•a (-VAIR ee ə) a place
for keeping or raising live animals, fish, or
plants, as a park, pond, aquarium, cage, etc.
[< L]

vi•va vo•ce (VĪ və VOH see) *Latin* by word
of mouth; orally.

viv•id (VIV id) *adj.* **1.** very bright; intense:
said of colors. **2.** producing or evoking life-

like imagery, freshness, etc.: *vivid* prose. **3.** clearly felt or strongly expressed, as emotions. **4.** full of life and vigor. **5.** clearly seen in the mind, as a memory. **6.** clearly perceived by the eye. [< L *vividus*] —**viv′id·ly** *adv.* —**viv′id·ness** *n.*

viv·i·fy (VIV ə FI) *v.t.* **·fied, ·fy·ing 1.** give life to; animate; vitalize. **2.** make more vivid or striking. [< MF *vivifier*] —**viv′i·fi·ca′ tion** *n.*

vi·vip·a·rous (vi VIP ər əs) *adj. Zool.* bringing forth living young, as most mammals. [< L *viviparus*] —**vi·vip′a·rous·ly** *adv.* —**vi·vip′a·rous·ness** *n.*

viv·i·sect (VIV ə SEKT) *v.t. & v.i.* dissect or operate upon (a living animal) for the purpose of research or study.

viv·i·sec·tion (VIV ə SEK shən) *n.* the act of vivisecting; experimentation on living animals by means of operations. —**viv′i·sec′ tion·ist** *n.*

vix·en (VIK sən) *n.* **1.** a female fox. **2.** an ill-tempered or quarrelsome woman; shrew. [ME] —**vix′en·ish, vix′en·ly** *adj.*

vi·zier (vi ZEER) *n.* formerly, a high official of some Muslim countries; esp., a minister of state. [< Turkish *vezir*]

vo·ca·ble (VOH kə bəl) *n.* **1.** a spoken or written word considered only as a sequence of sounds or letters, without regard to its meaning. **2.** a vocal sound. —*adj.* capable of being spoken. [< MF]

vo·cab·u·lar·y (voh KAB yə LER ee) *n. pl.* **·lar·ies 1.** a list of words, esp. one arranged in alphabetical order and defined or translated; glossary. **2.** all the words of a language. **3.** a sum or aggregate of the words used by a particular person, class, etc., or employed in some specialized field of knowledge. [< MF *vocabulaire*]

vo·cal (VOH kəl) *adj.* **1.** of, pertaining to, or for the voice. **2.** having voice. **3.** concerned in the production of voice: the *vocal* organs. **4.** freely expressing oneself in speech. [ME] —**vo′cal·ly** *adv.*

vocal cords two membranous bands in the larynx having edges that, when drawn tense, are caused to vibrate by the passage of air from the lungs.

vo·cal·ic (voh KAL ik) *adj.* consisting of, like, or relating to vowel sounds.

vo·cal·ist (VOH kə list) *n.* a singer.

vo·cal·ize (VOH kə LIZ) *v.* **·ized, ·iz·ing** *v.t.* **1.** make vocal; utter, say, or sing. **2.** provide a voice for; render articulate. **3.** *Phonet.* a change (a consonant) to a vowel

by some shift in the articulatory process. **b** voice. —*v.i.* **4.** produce sounds with the voice, as in speaking or singing. —**vo′cal·i·za′tion** *n.* —**vo′cal·iz′er** *n.*

vo·ca·tion (voh KAY shən) *n.* **1.** a stated or regular occupation; a calling. **2.** a call to or fitness for a certain career. [ME *vocacioun*] —**vo·ca′tion·al** *adj.* —**vo·ca′tion·al·ly** *adv.*

vocational school a school, usu. on the secondary level, that trains students for special trades.

voc·a·tive (VOK ə tiv) *Gram. adj.* in some inflected languages, denoting the case of a noun, pronoun, or adjective used in direct address. —*n.* **1.** the vocative case. **2.** a word in this case. [ME]

vo·cif·er·ate (voh SIF ə RAYT) *v.t. & v.i.* **·at·ed, ·at·ing** cry out with a loud voice; shout. [< L *vociferatus* shouted] —**vo·cif′er·a′tion** *n.*

vo·cif·er·ous (voh SIF ər əs) *adj.* making or characterized by a loud outcry; clamorous; noisy. —**vo·cif′er·ous·ness** *n.*

vod·ka (VOD kə) *n.* a colorless alcoholic liquor distilled from grain or potatoes. [< Russ. *vódka*]

vogue (vohg) *n.* **1.** the prevalent way or fashion; mode. **2.** popular favor; general acceptance. [< MF]

voice (vois) *n.* **1.** the sound produced by the vocal organs of a person or animal. **2.** the power or faculty of vocal utterance; speech. **3.** a sound suggesting vocal utterance: the *voice* of the wind. **4.** opinion or choice expressed; also, the means, medium, or agency of expression. **5.** *Phonet.* the sound produced by vibration of the vocal cords in the production of most vowels and certain consonants. **6.** the condition or effectiveness of the voice for singing or speaking: in good *voice*, in poor *voice*. **7.** *Gram.* the relation of the action expressed by the verb to the subject: **active** and **passive voice.** —**in voice** in proper condition for singing. —**with one voice** in accord; unanimously. [ME] —*v.t.* **voiced, voic·ing 1.** put into speech; utter. **2.** *Music* regulate the tone of, as the pipes of an organ. **3.** *Phonet.* pronounce (as a consonant) with voice.

voice box the larynx.

voiced (voist) *adj.* **1.** expressed by voice. **2.** *Phonet.* uttered with vibration of the vocal cords, as (b), (v), (z).

voice·less (VOIS lis) *adj.* **1.** having no voice, speech, or vote. **2.** *Phonet.* produced without voice, as (p), (f), (s). —**voice′•less•ly** adv. —**voice′less•ness** n.

void (void) adj. **1.** no longer having force or validity, as a contract, license, etc.; 'nvalid; null. **2.** destitute; clear or free: with of: That argument is void of reason. **3.** not occupied by matter; empty. **4.** unoccupied, as a house or room. **5.** producing no effect; useless. [ME voide] —n. **1.** an empty space; vacuum. **2.** empty condition or feeling; blank. —v.t. **1.** make void or of no effect; invalidate. **2.** empty or remove (contents); evacuate, as urine.

void•a•ble (VOI də bəl) adj. **1.** capable of being made void. **2.** that may be evacuated.

void•ance (VOID ns) n. **1.** the act of voiding, evacuating, ejecting, or emptying. **2.** the state or condition of being void; vacancy.

vo•lant (VOH lənt) adj. **1.** flying, or able to fly. **2.** nimble. [< MF]

vol•a•tile (VOL ə tl) adj. **1.** evaporating rapidly at ordinary temperatures on exposure to the air. **2.** capable of being vaporized. **3.** easily influenced; changeable. **4.** transient; ephemeral. [< F] —**vol′a•til′i•ty** n.

vol•a•til•ize (VOL ə tl Iz) v.t. & v.i. •ized, •iz•ing **1.** make or become volatile. **2.** pass off or cause to pass off in vapor; evaporate.

vol•can•ic (vol KAN ik) adj. **1.** of, pertaining to, or characteristic of a volcano or volcanoes. **2.** produced by or emitted from a volcano. **3.** eruptive. —**vol•can′i•cal•ly** adv.

vol•can•ism (VOL kə NIZ əm) n. the conditions and phenomena associated with volcanoes or volcanic action. Also vulcanism.

vol•ca•no (vol KAY noh) n. pl. •noes or •nos Geol. **1.** an opening in the crust of the earth from which steam, hot gases, ashes, etc. are expelled, forming a conical hill or mountain with a central crater. **2.** the formation itself. [< Ital.]

vol•can•ol•o•gy (VOL kə NOL ə jee) n. the scientific study of volcanoes. Also vulcanology. —**vol′can•ol′o•gist** n. Also vulcanologist.

vo•li•tion (voh LISH ən) n. **1.** the act or faculty of willing; exercise of the will. **2.** that which is willed or determined upon. [< Med.L] —**vo•li′tion•al** adj. —**vo•li′tion•al•ly** adv.

vol•ley (VOL ee) n. pl. •leys **1.** a simultaneous discharge of many missiles; also, the missiles so discharged. **2.** any discharge of many things at once: a volley of oaths. **3.** in tennis, a return of the ball before it

touches the ground. **4.** in soccer, a kick given the ball before its rebound. [< MF volee flight] —v.t. & v.i. •leyed, •ley•ing **1.** discharge or be discharged in a volley. **2.** in tennis, return (the ball) by a volley. **3.** in soccer, kick (the ball) before its rebound.

vol•ley•ball (VOL ee BAWL) n. a game in which two teams strike a large ball with the hands back and forth over a high net; also, the ball used.

volt¹ (vohlt) n. the unit of electromotive force, or the difference of potential, which when steadily applied against a resistance of one ohm will produce a current of one ampere. [after Alessandro Volta, Italian physicist]

volt² n. **1.** a gait in which a horse moves partially sidewise round a center. **2.** in fencing, a sudden leap to avoid a thrust. [< F volte turn]

volt•age (VOHL tij) n. electromotive force expressed in volts.

vol•ta•ic (vol TAY ik) adj. pertaining to electricity developed through chemical action or contact.

voltaic cell Electr. a primary cell.

volt-am•me•ter (VOHLT AM MEE tər) n. an instrument for measuring voltage or amperage.

volt-am•pere (VOHLT AM peer) n. the rate of work in an electric circuit when the current is one ampere and the potential one volt, equivalent to one watt.

volte-face (volt FAHS) n. pl. **volte-face** about-face (def. 2). [< F]

volt-me•ter (VOHLT MEE tər) n. an instrument for determining the voltage between any two points.

vol•u•ble (VOL yə bəl) adj. **1.** having a flow of words or fluency in speaking; garrulous. **2.** turning readily or easily; apt or formed to roll. [< L volubilis] —**vol′u•bil′i•ty** n. —**vol′u•bly** adv.

vol•ume (VOL yəm) n. **1.** a collection of sheets of paper bound together; book. **2.** a separately bound part of a work. **3.** sufficient matter to fill a volume. **4.** quantity of sound or tone; loudness. **5.** a large quantity; a considerable amount. **6.** space occupied in three dimensions, as measured by cubic units. —**speak volumes** be full of meaning; express a great deal. [ME]

vol•u•met•ric (VOL yə ME trik) adj. of or pertaining to measurement of substances by comparison of volumes. —**vol′u•met′ri•cal•ly** adv.

vo·lu·mi·nous (və LOO mə nəs) *adj.* **1.** having great quantity or volume. **2.** consisting of or capable of filling several volumes. **3.** writing or having written much; productive. **4.** having coils, folds, windings, etc. — **vo·lu'mi·nous·ly** *adv.*

vol·un·tar·y (VOL ən TER ee) *adj.* **1.** proceeding from free choice; intentional; volitional. **2.** effected by choice or volition. **3.** supported by private funds. [ME] —*n. pl.* **·tar·ies** an organ solo, often improvised, played before, during, or after a service. — **vol'un·tar'i·ly** *adv.* —**vol·un·ta·rism** (VOL ən tə RIZ əm) *n.*

vol·un·teer (VOL ən TEER) *n.* one who enters into any service, esp. military service or a hazardous undertaking, of his or her own free will. —*adj.* **1.** pertaining to or composed of volunteers. **2.** springing up naturally or spontaneously, as from fallen or self-sown seed. [< F *volontaire*] —*v.t.* **1.** offer to give or do. —*v.i.* **2.** act as a volunteer; enlist.

vo·lup·tu·ar·y (və LUP choo ER ee) *adj.* pertaining to or promoting sensual indulgence and luxurious pleasures. [< LL *voluptuarius*] —*n. pl.* **·ar·ies** one addicted to sensual pleasures; a sensualist.

vo·lup·tu·ous (və LUP choo əs) *adj.* **1.** of, pertaining to, or causing sensuous gratification; sensuous; luxurious. **2.** devoted to the enjoyment of pleasures or luxuries; sensual. **3.** having a full and beautiful form: a *voluptuous* woman. [ME] —**vo·lup'tu·ous·ly** *adv.* —**vo·lup'tu·ous·ness** *n.*

vo·lute (və LOOT) *n.* **1.** *Archit.* a spiral, scroll-like ornament. **2.** *Zool.* one of the whorls or turns of a spiral shell. [< L *voluta* scroll] —*adj.* **1.** rolled up; forming spiral curves. **2.** having a spiral form, as a machine part. —**vo·lut'ed** *adv.* —**vo·lu'tion** *n.*

vom·it (VOM it) *v.t. & v.i.* **1.** throw up or eject (the contents of the stomach) through the mouth. **2.** eject (matter) with violence from any hollow place. [ME *vomiten*] —*n.* matter ejected from the stomach in vomiting.

voo·doo (VOO doo) *n. pl.* **·doos 1.** a primitive religion of West Indians, characterized by belief in sorcery and the use of charms, fetishes, etc. **2.** one who practices voodoo. **3.** a voodoo charm or fetish. —*v.t.* **·dooed, ·doo·ing** put a spell upon after the manner of a voodoo. [< Creole] —*adj.* pertaining to the practice of voodoo. —**voo·doo·ism** (VOO doo IZ əm) *n.*

vo·ra·cious (və RAY shəs) *adj.* **1.** eating with greediness; ravenous. **2.** greedy; rapacious. **3.** ready to swallow up or engulf. **4.** insatiable; immoderate. [< L *vorare* devour] — **vo·ra'cious·ly** *adv.* —**vo·rac·i·ty** (vaw RAS i tee) *n.*

vor·tex (VOR teks) *n. pl.* **·tex·es** or **·ti·ces** (-tə SEEZ) **1.** a mass of whirling gas or liquid, esp. when sucked spirally toward a central axis; whirlwind; whirlpool. **2.** any action or state of affairs that is similar to a vortex in violence, force, etc. [< L] —**vor·ti·cal** (VOR ti kəl) *adj.* —**vor'ti·cal·ly** *adv.*

vo·ta·ry (VOH tə ree) *n. pl.* **·ries 1.** one bound by a vow or promise, as a nun. **2.** one devoted to some particular worship, pursuit, study, etc. —*adj.* consecrated by a vow or promise; votive. [< L *votum* vow]

vote (voht) *n.* **1.** a formal expression of will or opinion in regard to some question submitted for decision, as in electing officers, passing resolutions, etc. **2.** that by which such choice is expressed, as a show of hands, or ballot. **3.** the result of an election. **4.** the number of votes cast; also, votes collectively. **5.** the right to vote. **6.** a voter or group of voters. [ME] —*v.* **vot·ed, vot·ing** *v.t.* **1.** enact or determine by vote. **2.** cast one's vote for. **3.** declare by general agreement. —*v.i.* **4.** cast one's vote. —**vote down** defeat or suppress by voting against. —**vote in** elect.

vo·tive (VOH tiv) *adj.* dedicated by a vow; performed in fulfillment of a vow. —**vo'tive·ly** *adv.* —**vo'tive·ness** *n.*

vouch (vowch) *v.i.* **1.** give one's assurance or guarantee; bear witness: with *for.* **2.** serve as assurance or proof: with *for.* —*v.t.* **3.** bear witness to; attest or affirm. **4.** substantiate. [ME *vouchen*] —*n.* a declaration that attests.

vouch·er (VOW chər) *n.* **1.** a document that serves to attest an alleged act, esp. the payment or receipt of money. **2.** one who vouches for another; a witness.

vouch·safe (vowch SAYF) *v.t. & v.i.* **·safed, ·saf·ing** grant (something), as with condescension; permit; deign. —**vouch·safe' ment** *n.*

vow (vow) *n.* **1.** a solemn promise to or as to God; pledge. **2.** a pledge of faithfulness. **3.** a solemn and emphatic affirmation. —**take vows** enter a religious order. —*v.t.* **1.** promise solemnly, esp. to a deity. **2.** declare with assurance or solemnity. **3.** make a solemn promise or threat to do, inflict, etc. — *v.i.* **4.** make a vow. [ME *vowe*]

vow·el (VOW əl) *n.* **1.** *Phonet.* a speech sound produced by the relatively unimpeded passage of breath through the mouth. **2.** a letter representing such a sound, as *a,e,i,o,u,* and sometimes *w* and *y.* [ME] —*adj.* pertaining to a vowel.

vox po·pu·li (VOKS POP yə LI) *Latin* the voice of the people; popular opinion.

voy·age (VOI ij) *n.* **1.** a journey by water, esp. a long one. **2.** any journey or expedition. [ME] —*v.* •**aged,** •**ag·ing** *v.i.* **1.** make a voyage; journey by water. —*v.t.* **2.** travel over. —**voy′ag·er** *n.*

vo·ya·geur (VWAH yah ZHUR) *n. pl.* •**geurs** (-ZHURZ) a Canadian boatman, woodsman, and guide in remote areas. [< F, traveler]

vo·yeur (vwah YUR) *n.* one who derives sexually gratification from seeing sexual acts and organs. [< F] —**vo·yeur′ism** *n.*

vul·can·ism VUL kə NIZ əm) *n.* volcanism.

vul·can·ite (VUL kə NIT) *n.* a dark, hard variety of rubber obtained by vulcanizing.

vul·can·ize (VUL kə NIZ) *v.t.* •**ized,** •**iz·ing** treat (crude rubber) with sulfur or sulfur compounds in varying proportions and at different temperatures, thereby increasing its strength and elasticity. —**vul′can·iz′a·ble** *adj.* —**vul′can·i·za′tion** *n.*

vul·can·ol·o·gy (VUL kə NOL ə jee) *n.* volcanology. —**vul′can·ol′o·gist** *n.* volcanologist.

vul·gar (VUL gər) *ädj.* **1.** lacking in refinement or good taste; crude; boorish; also, obscene; indecent. **2.** of, pertaining to, or characteristic of the people at large, as distinguished from the privileged or educated classes; popular; common. **3.** written in or

translated into the common language or vulgate; vernacular. [ME] —**vul′gar·ly** *adv.* —**vul′gar·ness** *n.*

vul·gar·i·an (vul GAIR ee ən) *n.* a person of vulgar tastes or manners.

vul·gar·ism (VUL gə RIZ əm) *n.* **1.** vulgarity. **2.** a nonstandard or unrefined word, phrase, or expression.

vul·gar·i·ty (vul GAR i tee) *n. pl.* •**ties 1.** the quality or character of being vulgar. **2.** something vulgar, as an action, word, etc.

vul·gar·ize (VUL gə RIZ) *v.t.* •**ized,** •**iz·ing** **1.** make vulgar. **2.** popularize. —**vul′gar·i·za′tion** *n.*

Vulgar Latin see under LATIN.

Vul·gate (VUL gayt) *n.* a Latin version of the Bible, translated between A.D. 383 and 405, now revised and used as the authorized version by Roman Catholics. [< LL *vulgata (editio)* the popular (edition)] —*adj.* pertaining to the Vulgate.

vul·gate *adj.* common; popular; generally accepted. —*n.* **1.** everyday speech. **2.** any commonly accepted text.

vul·ner·a·ble (VUL nər ə bəl) *adj.* **1.** capable of being hurt or damaged. **2.** liable to attack; assailable. **3.** in contract bridge, having won one game of a rubber, and thus receiving increased penalties and increased bonuses. [< LL *vulnerabilis*] —**vul′·ner·a·bil′i·ty** *n.* —**vul′·ner·a·bly** *adv.*

vul·ture (VUL chər) *n.* any of various large birds having the head and neck naked or partly naked, and feeding mostly on carrion. [ME] —**vul·tur·ine** (VUL chə RIN) *adj.*

vul·va (VUL və) *n. pl.* •**vae** (-vee) *Anat.* the external genital parts of the female. [< NL] —**vul′val, vul′var** *adj.*

vy·ing (VĪ ing) present participle of VIE.

W

w, W (DUB əl YOO) *n. pl.* **w's** or **ws, W's** or **Ws 1.** the twenty-third letter of the English alphabet. **2.** the sound represented by the letter *w.*

wack•y (WAK ee) *adj.* **wack•i•er, wack•i•est** *Slang* extremely irrational or impractical; erratic; screwy.

wad (wod) *n.* **1.** a small compact mass of any soft or flexible substance: a *wad* of cotton. **2.** *Informal* a roll of banknotes; also, wealth. [< Med.L *wadda* batting] —*v.t.* **wad•ded, wad•ding** press or roll into a wad.

wad•ding (WOD ing) *n.* **1.** wads collectively. **2.** any substance used as material for wads.

wad•dle (WOD l) *v.i.* **•dled, •dling** walk with short steps, swaying from side to side. [ME] —*n.* a clumsy, rocking walk. —**wad′ dler** *n.* —**wad′dly** *adj.*

wade (wayd) *v.* **wad•ed, wad•ing** *v.i.* **1.** walk through water, mud, sand, etc. **2.** proceed slowly or laboriously: *wade* through a book. —*v.t.* **3.** pass or cross, as a river, by wading. —**wade in** (or **into**) attack or begin vigorously. [ME *waden*]

wa•di (WAH dee) *n. pl.* **•dies** in northern Africa, the bed or channel of a stream that is usu. dry except in the rainy season; also, a stream flowing through such a channel. [< Arabic *wādī*]

wa•fer (WAY fər) *n.* **1.** a very thin, crisp cooky or cracker; also, a small disk of candy. **2.** *Eccl.* a small, flat disk of unleavened bread used in the Eucharist. [ME]

waf•fle[1] (WOF əl) *n.* a batter cake baked between two hinged metal griddles marked with regular indentations (**waffle iron**). [< Du. *wafel*]

waf•fle[2] *v.i.* **•fled, •fling** *Informal* talk indecisively; vacillate.

waft (waft) *v.t.* **1.** carry or bear gently over air or water; float. **2.** convey as if on air or water. —*v.i.* **3.** float, as on the wind. —*n.* **1.** a light breeze; gust; puff. **2.** an odor, sound, etc., carried through the air. **3.** a wafting or waving motion.

wag[1] (wag) *v.t. & v.i.* **wagged, wag•ging 1.** move or cause to move quickly from side to side or up and down, as a dog's tail; swing. **2.** move (the tongue) in idle chatter or gossip. —*n.* the act or motion of wagging. [ME *waggen*]

wag[2] *n.* a humorous fellow; wit; joker. —**wag′gish** *adj.* —**wag′gish•ness** *n.*

wage (wayj) *v.t.* **waged, wag•ing** engage in; carry on: *wage* war. [ME, pledge] —*n.* **1.** *Usu.* payment for work done. **2.** *pl.* recompense; reward: the *wages* of crime.

wage earner one who works for wages.

wa•ger (WAY jər) *v.t. & v.i.* bet. —*n.* a bet. [ME, pledge] —**wa′ger•er** *n.*

wage scale a scale of wages paid to workers in a factory, industry, etc.

wag•ger•y (WAG ə ree) *n. pl.* **•ger•ies 1.** mischievous jocularity; drollery. **2.** a jest; joke.

wag•gle (WAG əl) *v.t. & v.i.* **•gled, •gling** move or cause to move with rapid to-and-fro motions; wag. —*n.* this movement. —**wag′gly** *adj.* unsteady.

wag•on (WAG ən) *n.* **1.** any of various four-wheeled horse-drawn vehicles used for carrying goods. **2.** a child's four-wheeled toy cart. **3.** a station wagon. —**on the wagon** *Slang* abstaining from alcoholic beverages. —**fix** (**someone's**) **wagon** *Slang* punish; get even with. [< Du. *wagen*]

wag•on•er (WAG ə nər) *n.* one whose work is driving wagons.

wagon train a train of covered wagons traveling together.

waif (wayf) *n.* **1.** a homeless, neglected wanderer, esp. a child; a stray. **2.** anything, as a stray cat, that is found and unclaimed. [ME]

wail (wayl) *v.i.* **1.** make a sad, melancholy sound, as in grief or pain. **2.** make a sound like a wail: The wind *wailed* through the night. [ME *weilen*] —*n.* a prolonged, mournful sound. —**wail′er** *n.* —**wail′ful** *adj.*

wain•scot (WAYN skət) *n.* **1.** a facing for inner walls, usu. of paneled wood. **2.** the lower part of an inner wall when finished differently from the rest. [ME] —*v.t.* **•scot•ed, •scot•ing** face or panel with wainscot.

wain•scot•ing (WAYN skoh ting) *n.* material for a wainscot; also, a wainscot.

waist (wayst) *n.* **1.** the part of the body between the chest and the hips. **2.** the middle part of any object, esp. if narrower than the ends. **3.** that part of a woman's dress covering the body from the waistline to the shoulders; a bodice. [ME *wast*]

waist·band (WAYST BAND) *n.* a band at the top of a skirt or trousers that encircles the waist.

waist·coat (WES kət) *n. Chiefly Brit.* a vest.

waist·line (WAYST LIN) *n.* the narrowest part of a person's waist.

wait (wayt) *v.i.* **1.** remain in expectation or readiness: with *for, until,* etc.: *wait* for a train. **2.** remain temporarily neglected or undone: Dinner will have to *wait.* —*v.t.* **3.** remain in expectation of: *wait* one's turn. — **wait on** (or **upon**) **1.** act as a servant to. **2.** serve (a customer). **3.** call upon; visit. — **wait up** put off going to bed until someone returns home etc. [ME *waiten*] —*n.* the act or period of waiting. —**lie in wait** hide in order to attack or trap; set an ambush: often with *for.*

wait·er (WAY tər) *n.* a person, esp. a man, who serves food and drink in a restaurant. [ME] —*v.i.* work or serve as a waiter.

waiting room a room for those waiting, as at an airport, in a doctor's office, etc.

wait·ress (WAY tris) *n.* a woman who serves food and drink in a restaurant. —*v.i.* work or serve as a waitress.

waive (wayv) *v.t.* **waived, waiv·ing 1.** *Law* give up or relinquish (a claim, right, etc.). **2.** put off; postpone; delay. [ME *weyven* abandon]

waiv·er (WAY vər) *n. Law* an intentional relinquishment of a claim, right, etc.; also, the instrument of such relinquishment. [< AF *weyver*]

wake[1] (wayk) *v.* **waked** or **woke, waked** or **wok·en, wak·ing** *v.i.* **1.** emerge from sleep. **2.** be or remain awake. **3.** become active or alert. **4.** rouse from sleep; awake. **5.** stir up; excite. [ME *waken*] —*n.* a watch or vigil over a corpse before burial.

wake[2] *n.* **1.** the track left by a vessel passing through the water. **2.** the area behind any moving thing. —**in the wake of 1.** following close behind. **2.** as a result of. [< MDu. *wake*]

wake·ful (WAYK fəl) *adj.* **1.** unable to sleep. **2.** watchful; alert. —**wake′ful·ly** *adv.* — **wake′ful·ness** *n.*

wak·en (WAY kən) *v.t. & v.i.* wake. [ME *waknen*]

wale (wayl) *n.* **1.** a welt (def. 3). **2.** *Naut.* outer planking running fore and aft on a vessel. **3.** a ridge on the surface of corduroy or other fabric. [ME] —*v.t.* **waled, wal-**

·ing raise wales on by striking, as with a lash; beat.

walk (wawk) *v.i.* **1.** advance on foot at a moderate pace. **2.** act or live in some manner: *walk* in peace. **3.** in baseball, achieve first base as a result of having been pitched four balls. —*v.t.* **4.** pass through, over, or across at a walk: *walk* the floor. **5.** cause to go at a walk: *walk* a horse. **6.** accompany on a walk: I'll *walk* you home. **7.** in baseball, allow to advance to first base by pitching four balls. —**walk off 1.** depart, esp. abruptly or without warning. **2.** get rid of (fat etc.) by walking. —**walk off with 1.** win. **2.** steal. — **walk out** go out on strike. —**walk out on** forsake; desert. —**walk over** defeat easily; overwhelm. [ME *walken*] —*n.* **1.** the act or manner of walking. **2.** chosen profession or sphere of activity: the various *walks* of life. **3.** distance walked; also, as indicated by the time required: an hour's *walk.* **4.** a path or area for walking. **5.** in baseball, a base on balls. —**walk′er** *n.*

walk·a·way (WAWK ə WAY) *n.* a contest won easily or without opposition: also called *walkover.*

walk·ie-talk·ie (WAW kee TAW kee) *n.* a portable two-way radio: also **walk′y-talk′y.**

walking papers *Informal* a notice of dismissal from employment etc.

walking stick 1. a staff or cane. **2.** any of various insects having legs, body, and wings resembling a twig.

walk-on (WAWK ON) *n.* a performer having a very small part; also, the part.

walk·out (WAWK OWT) *n.* a strike by workers.

walk·o·ver (WAWK OH vər) *n.* **1.** a walkaway. **2.** in racing, a running or trotting of a course by a lone starter.

walk-up (WAWK UP) *n.* an apartment or an apartment house having no elevator. —*adj.* located above the ground floor in an apartment house that has no elevator.

wall (wawl) *n.* **1.** a continuous structure that encloses, protects, or divides an area. ◆ Collateral adjective: *mural.* **2.** something suggesting a wall: a *wall* of bayonets. — **drive or push to the wall** force (one) to an extremity. [ME] —*v.t.* provide, surround, block, etc. with or as with a wall: with *up* or *in.*

wall·board (WAWL BORD) *n.* a structural material, as of wood pulp, pressed into large sheets and used to cover interior walls.

wal·let (WOL it) *n.* a pocketbook for holding paper money, cards, etc.: also called *bill-fold*. [ME *walet*]

wall·eye (WAWL ī) *n.* **1. a** an outward turning eye. **b** a whitish eye. **2.** a fish with prominent eyes: also **walleyed pike.** —**wall′eyed′** *adj.*

wall·flow·er (WAWL FLOW ər) *n.* a shy or unpopular person who remains on the sidelines at a dance or other social activity.

wal·lop (WOL əp) *v.t.* **1.** beat soundly; thrash. **2.** *Informal* hit hard; sock. **3.** *Informal* defeat soundly. [ME *walopen*] —*n.* a severe blow.

wal·lop·ing (WOL ə ping) *Informal adj.* very large; whopping. —*n.* a severe beating.

wal·low (WOL oh) *v.i.* **1.** roll about in mud, etc.: thrash about; flounder. **2.** involve oneself fully; revel: with *in*. [ME *walwe*] —*n.* a muddy or dusty hole in which animals wallow. —**wal′low·er** *n.*

wall·pa·per (WAWL PAY pər) *n.* paper for covering walls and ceilings. —*v.t.* cover with wallpaper.

Wall Street 1. a street in the financial district of New York City. **2.** the world of U.S. finance.

wal·nut (WAWL nut) *n.* **1.** any of various trees of the North Temperate Zone, valued for their timber and edible nuts. **2.** the wood or nut of any of these trees. **3.** a dark brown color. [ME]

wal·rus (WAWL rəs) *n. pl.* **·rus·es** or **·rus** a large marine mammal of arctic seas, having flippers, projecting ivory tusks, and a thick neck. [< Du., lit., whale horse]

waltz (wawlts) *n.* **1.** a dance for couples in ¾ time. **2.** the music for such a dance. [< G *Walzer* a waltz] —*v.i.* **1.** dance a waltz. **2.** move lightly and freely. —*v.t.* **3.** cause to waltz. —**waltz′er** *n.*

wam·pum (WOM pəm) *n.* **1.** beads made from shells, formerly used as currency by North American Indians. **2.** *Informal* money. [< Algonquian *wampum (peage)*, lit., a white string (of beads)]

wan (won) *adj.* **wan·ner, wan·nest 1.** pale, as from sickness or anxiety; pallid. **2.** indicating illness, unhappiness, etc.: a *wan* smile. [ME] —**wan′ly** *adv.* —**wan′ness** *n.*

wand (wond) *n.* **1.** a slender rod used by a magician. **2.** a rod symbolic of authority or an office. [ME]

wan·der (WON dər) *v.i.* **1.** move or travel about without destination or purpose;

roam; rove. **2.** go casually or indirectly; stroll. **3.** twist or meander. **4.** stray. **5.** deviate in conduct or opinion; go astray. —*v.t.* **6.** roam through or across. [ME *wandren*] —**wan′der·er** *n.*

wan·der·lust (WON dər LUST) *n.* a strong impulse to travel. [< G]

wane (wayn) *v.i.* **waned, wan·ing 1.** diminish gradually in size, brilliance, or strength. **2.** draw to an end. [ME *wanen*] —*n.* the act of waning; a gradual decrease. —**on the wane** gradually decreasing.

wan·gle (WANG gəl) *v.* **·gled, ·gling** *v.t.* **1.** obtain or accomplish by indirect or irregular methods: *wangle* an introduction. **2.** manipulate, esp. dishonestly. —*v.i.* **3.** resort to indirect, irregular, or dishonest methods. —**wan′gler** *n.*

want (wont) *v.t.* **1.** feel a desire or wish for. **2.** be deficient in; lack. **3.** require; need. —*v.i.* **4.** have a need: usu. with *for*. **5.** be needy or destitute. [ME *wante* lack] —*n.* a lack; scarcity; shortage. **2.** privation; poverty. **3.** something lacking; need.

want ad a classified advertisement for something wanted, as hired help, a job, a lodging, etc.

want·ing (WON ting) *adj.* **1.** missing; lacking. **2.** not up to standard; deficient. —*prep.* without; lacking.

wan·ton (WON tn) *adj.* **1.** licentious; lustful. **2.** unjust; malicious. **3.** of abundant growth; rank. [ME *wantowen* undisciplined] —*v.i.* act wantonly. —*n.* a licentious person, esp. a woman. —**wan′·ton·ly** *adv.* —**wan′ton·ness** *n.*

war (wor) *n.* **1.** an armed conflict between nations or states. **2.** any conflict or struggle; hostility. **3.** the science of military operations. [ME *werre*] —*v.i.* **warred, war·ring 1.** wage war. **2.** be in conflict; contend.

war·ble (WOR bəl) *v.t. & v.i.* **·bled, ·bling** sing with trills and quavers. [ME *werble* tune] —*n.*

war·bler (WOR blər) *n.* **1.** one who or that which warbles. **2.** any of various small songbirds.

war cry 1. a rallying cry used by combatants in a war. **2.** a slogan or motto used to rally support for a political cause etc.; watchword.

ward (word) *n.* **1. a** a division of a hospital. **b** a large room in a hospital for a number of patients. **2.** an administrative or electoral division of a city. **3.** *Law* a person, often a minor, who is in the charge of a guardian. **4.** the act of guarding or the state of being guarded; custody; also **ward′•ship.** [ME *warde*] —*v.t.* repel or turn aside, as a blow: usu., with *off*.

-ward *suffix* toward; in the direction of: *upward, homeward*. Also **-wards.** [ME]

war dance among certain primitive tribes, a ceremonial dance before going to war or in celebration of a victory.

war•den (WOR dn) *n.* **1.** the chief officer of a prison. **2.** any of various supervisors: air-raid *warden*. [ME *wardein*]

ward heeler a hanger-on of a political boss.

ward•robe (WOR drohb) *n.* **1.** all the garments belonging to any one person. **2.** a cabinet for clothes. **3.** a stock of theatrical costumes. [ME *warderobe*]

ward•room (WORD room) *n.* on a warship, the recreation area and dining room for commissioned officers.

ware (wair) *n.* **1.** manufactured articles of the same kind: used in combination: *glassware*. **2.** *pl.* goods; merchandise. **3.** pottery. [ME]

ware•house (WAIR hows) *n.* a storehouse for goods. —*v.t.* (WAIR howz) **•housed, •hous•ing 1.** store in a warehouse. **2.** *Informal* confine (the mentally ill) for long-term custodial care in an institution that offers little or no medical treatment.

war•fare (WOR fair) *n.* **1.** the waging of war. **2.** struggle; strife.

war•head (WOR hed) *n. Mil.* the nose section of a guided missile, bomb, etc., containing the explosive.

war horse 1. *Informal* a veteran of many struggles or conflicts. **2.** a horse used in combat; charger.

war•like (WOR lĭk) *adj.* **1.** disposed to engage in war; belligerent. **2.** relating to, used in, or suggesting war; martial. **3.** threatening war; hostile.

war•lock (WOR lok) *n.* a male wizard or sorcerer. [ME *warloghe* devil]

warm (worm) *adj.* **•er, •est 1.** moderately hot. **2.** preserving body heat: a *warm* coat. **3.** affectionate; loving. **4.** excited; agitated; also, vehement; passionate: a *warm* temper. **5.** suggesting warmth, friendliness, etc.: *warm* tones. **6.** recently made; fresh: a *warm* trail. **7.** close to discovering something. **8.** uncomfortable; unpleasant. [ME *werm*] —*v.t.* **1.** heat slightly. **2.** make ardent or enthusiastic. **3.** fill with kindly feelings. —*v.i.* **4.** become warm. **5.** become

ardent or enthusiastic: often with *to*. **6.** become kindly disposed or friendly: with *to* or *toward*. —**warm up 1.** warm. **2.** exercise before a game etc. **3.** run an engine until it reaches operating temperature. —**warm′ ly** *adv.* —**warm′ness** *n.*

warm-blood•ed (WORM BLUD id) *adj.* **1.** *Zool.* preserving a uniform body temperature, as mammals. **2.** enthusiastic; ardent; passionate.

warm•heart•ed (WORM HAHR tid) *adj.* kind; affectionate.

warming pan a long-handled, covered metal pan containing hot coals, formerly used to warm a bed.

war•mon•ger (WOR mung gər) *n.* one who propagates warlike ideas. —**war′ •mon′ger•ing** *adj. & n.*

warmth (wormth) *n.* **1.** the state or quality of being warm. **2.** enthusiasm; fervor. **3.** affection or kindness.

warm•up (WORM UP) *n.* the act of one who or that which warms up.

warn (worn) *v.t.* **1.** make aware of possible harm; caution. **2.** advise; admonish. **3.** give notice in advance. [ME *warnen*]

warn•ing (WOR ning) *n.* **1.** the act of one who warns. **2.** that which warns or admonishes. —*adj.* serving as a warning. —**warn′ ing•ly** *adv.* [ME]

warp (worp) *v.t.* **1.** turn or twist out of shape. **2.** turn from a correct course. **3.** *Naut.* move (a vessel) by hauling on a rope fastened to a pier or anchor. —*v.i.* **4.** become turned or twisted out of shape. [ME *warpen* throw] —*n.* **1.** a bend, twist, or distortion, esp. in wood. **2.** a mental or moral deviation; bias. **3.** the lengthwise threads in a fabric or on a loom. [ME] —**warp′er** *n.*

war paint paint applied to faces and bodies by primitive peoples in token of going to war.

war•path (WOR path) *n.* the route taken by American Indians going to war. —**on the warpath 1.** on a warlike expedition. **2.** ready for a fight; angry.

war•plane (WOR playn) *n.* an airplane equipped for fighting.

war•rant (WOR ənt) *n.* **1.** *Law* a judicial writ or order authorizing arrest, search, seizure, etc. **2.** something that assures or attests. **3.** that which gives authority for some act; sanction: justification. **4.** a certificate of appointment given to warrant officers. [ME *warant*] —*v.t.* **1.** guarantee. **2.** be sufficient grounds for; justify. **3.** give legal authority;

authorize. 4. say confidently. —war′rant-
•a•ble adj. —war′rant•er n.
warrant officer Mil. an officer ranking
above an enlisted person but below a commissioned officer.
war•ran•ty (WOR ən tee) n. pl. •ties 1. Law
a an assurance that facts regarding property, insurance risks, etc. are as they are
stated to be. b a covenant securing a title of
ownership. 2. a guarantee (def. 1). [ME
warantie]
war•ren (WOR ən) n. 1. a place where rabbits are kept and bred. 2. an enclosure for
keeping small game. 3. a crowded apartment house or area. [ME warenne]
war•ri•or (WOR ee ər) n. a person engaged
in or experienced in warfare. [ME wer-
rieour]
war•ship (WOR SHIP) n. any vessel used in
naval combat.
wart (wort) n. 1. a small, usu. hard bump on
the skin. 2. a hard protuberance on a plant.
3. any unattractive feature or characteristic. [ME] —wart′less adj.
war•time (WOR TĪM) n. a time of war. —
war•time adj.
war•y (WAIR ee) adj. war•i•er, war•i•est
carefully watching and guarding; cautious.[ME ware] —war′i•ly adv. —war′
i•ness n.
was (wuz, woz) first and third person singular, past indicative of BE. [ME]
wash (wosh) v.t. 1. cleanse with water or
other liquid. 2. purify from defilement or
guilt. 3. wet or cover with liquid. 4. flow
against or over: a beach washed by the
ocean. 5. remove by the action of water:
with away, off, out, etc. 6. purify, as gas, by
passing through a liquid. 7. coat with a thin
layer of color or metal. —v.i. 8. wash oneself. 9. wash clothes. 10. withstand the effects of washing: That fabric will wash. 11.
Informal undergo testing successfully: That
excuse won't wash. 12. flow with a lapping
sound, as waves. 13. be removed or eroded
by the action of water: with away, off, out,
etc. —wash out Informal fail. [ME
washen] —n. 1. the act of washing. 2.
clothes etc. to be washed at one time; laundry. 3. a preparation used in washing or
coating, as: a a mouthwash. b water color
spread on a picture. 4. churned air, water,
or other fluid resulting from the passage of
an object through it. 5. a the breaking of a
wave on the shore. b the flow of water over a
surface, as over an oar.

wash•a•ble (WOSH ə bəl) adj. that may be
washed without fading or injury. —n. pl.
washable fabrics or garments.
wash-and-wear (WOSH ən WAIR) adj.
needing little or no ironing after washing: a
wash-and-wear dress.
wash•board (WOSH BORD) n. a corrugated
board for scrubbing clothes during washing.
wash•bowl (WOSH BOHL) n. a basin or
bowl for washing the hands and face. Also
wash′ba′sin (-BAY sən).
wash•cloth (WOSH KLAWTH) n. a small
cloth for washing the body.
washed-out (WOSHT OWT) adj. 1. faded,
as from many washings. 2. Informal exhausted; worn-out; wan.
washed-up (WOSHT UP) adj. Informal no
longer successful, popular, etc.; finished.
wash•er (WOSH ər) n. 1. one who or that
which washes. 2. Mech. a small, flat disk
placed beneath a nut or at an axle bearing or
joint, to serve as a cushion, prevent leakage,
or relieve friction. 3. a washing machine.
wash•ing (WOSH ing) n. 1. the act of one
who or that which washes. 2. laundry to be
washed. 3. matter removed in washing.
washing machine a machine for washing
laundry.
wash•out (WOSH OWT) n. 1. the erosion of
earth by the action of water; also, the excavation thus made; a gully or gulch. 2. Informal a complete failure. 3. Informal a person
who has failed a course of study.
wash•rag (WOSH RAG) n. washcloth.
wash•room (WOSH ROOM) n. a lavatory.
wash•stand (WOSH STAND) n. a stand for a
washbowl, pitcher, etc.
wash•tub (WOSH TUB) n. a tub for washing
laundry.
wash•y (WOSH ee) adj. wash•i•er, wash•
i•est 1. overly diluted; weak. 2. faded; wan.
—wash′i•ness n.
was•n't (WUZ ənt) was not.
wasp (wosp) n. any of numerous stinging
insects. [ME waspe]
WASP (wosp) n. Contemptuous a white Protestant American of English or northern European descent. Also Wasp. [< white
Anglo-Saxon Protestant]
wasp•ish (WOS pish) adj. 1. irritable; bad-
tempered; irascible. 2. having a slender
build. —wasp′ish•ly adv. —wasp′ish•
ness n.
wasp•y (WOS pee) adj. wasp•i•er, wasp•
i•est like a wasp; waspish.

was·sail (WOS əl) n. **1.** an ancient toast to someone's health. **2.** the liquor, as spiced ale, prepared for a wassail. **3.** a festivity at which healths are drunk; revel. —v.i. **1.** take part in a wassail; carouse. —v.t. **2.** drink the health of; toast. [ME *was-hail* be in good health] —**was'sail·er** n.

Was·ser·mann test (WOS ər mən) a diagnostic test for syphilis. [after August von *Wassermann*, 1866—1925, German bacteriologist]

wast (wost) archaic second person singular, past indicative of BE: used with *thou*.

wast·age (WAY stij) n. **1.** loss by wear, waste, etc. **2.** something lost in this way.

waste (wayst) v. **wast·ed, wast·ing** v.t. **1.** use or expend needlessly or carelessly; squander. **2.** wear away; consume, as one's strength. **3.** fail to take advantage of, as of an opportunity. **4.** destroy; devastate. **5.** Slang murder; kill. —v.i. **6.** become weak or unhealthy: often with *away*. [ME *wasten*] — n. **1.** the act of wasting, or the state of being wasted. **2.** a wasteland. **3.** a gradual decrease by use, wear, etc. **4.** garbage, rubbish, or other discarded material. **5.** matter, as urine, that is excreted by the body. —**lay waste** destroy. [ME *waste* desert] —adj. **1.** cast aside as worthless; discarded. **2.** excreted, as urine. **3.** uncultivated or uninhabited; barren. [ME] —**wast'er** n.

waste·bas·ket (WAYST BAS kit) n. a receptacle for wastepaper and other waste. Also **wastepaper basket**.

waste·ful (WAYST fəl) adj. prone to or characterized by waste. —**waste'ful·ly** adv. —**waste'ful·ness** n.

waste·land (WAYST LAND) n. **1.** a barren or desolate land. **2.** an intellectually barren period or locality.

waste·pa·per (WAYST PAY pər) n. paper thrown away as worthless.

waste product useless material left over after the completion of a manufacturing process, digestion, etc.

wast·ing (WAY sting) adj. **1.** producing emaciation; enfeebling. **2.** laying waste; devastating.

wast·rel (WAY strəl) n. **1.** a spendthrift. **2.** an idler; loafer.

watch (woch) v.i. **1.** look attentively. **2.** wait expectantly: with *for*. **3.** do duty as a guard or sentinel. **4.** go without sleep; keep vigil. —v.t. **5.** look at steadily and attentively; observe. **6.** be alert for: *watch* one's opportunity. **7.** keep watch over; guard; tend. —

watch out be on one's guard. [ME *wacchen*] —n. **1.** the act of watching; close and continuous attention. **2.** a small timepiece worn or carried on the person. **3.** a watchman; guard. **4.** the period during which a guard is on duty. **5.** Naut. **a** a period of time, usu. four hours, during which a part of a ship's crew is on duty. **b** the crew on duty during such a period. —**watch'er** n.

watch·band (WOCH BAND) n. a band to fasten a watch on the wrist.

watch·dog (WOCH DAWG) n. **1.** a dog kept to guard property. **2.** one who acts as a vigilant guardian.

watch·ful (WOCH fəl) adj. vigilant. —**watch'·ful·ly** adv. —**watch'ful·ness** n.

watch·mak·er (WOCH MAY kər) n. one who makes or repairs watches. —**watch'mak'ing** n.

watch·man (WOCH mən) n. pl. **·men** one who keeps watch; a guard.

watch·tow·er (WOCH TOW ər) n. a tower on which a sentinel is stationed.

watch·word (WOCH WURD) n. **1.** a password. **2.** a rallying cry or maxim.

wa·ter (WAW tər) n. **1.** the tasteless and odorless liquid compound of hydrogen and oxygen, H_2O. **2.** any body of water, as a lake, river, or a sea. **3.** any one of the liquid secretions of the body, as perspiration, tears, urine, etc. **4.** the transparency or luster of a precious stone or a pearl. —**hold water** be valid or effective. [ME] —v.t. **1.** pour water on; moisten; sprinkle. **2.** provide with water for drinking. **3.** dilute with water: often with *down*. **4.** give an undulating sheen to the surface of (silk etc.). **5.** enlarge the number of shares of (a stock company) without increasing the paid-in capital in proportion. **6.** irrigate. —v.i. **7.** secrete saliva or tears. **8.** drink water. —**wa'ter·er** n.

wa·ter·bed (WAW tər BED) n. a bed having a mattress consisting of a plastic bag filled with water.

wa·ter·borne (WAW tər BORN) adj. **1.** floating on water. **2.** transported or carried by water.

water buffalo a large buffalo of Asia, India, and the Philippines, having a very wide spread of horns, and often domesticated for use as a draft animal: also called *water ox*.

water closet a toilet.

water color 1. a paint made by mixing water with a pigment. **2.** a painting done in water colors. —**wa'ter·col'or** adj. —**wa'ter·col'or·ist** n.

wa·ter-cool (WAW tər KOOL) v.t. cool by means of circulating water. —**wa'ter-cooled'** adj.

water cooler an apparatus for cooling and dispensing drinking water.

wa·ter·course (WAW tər KORS) n. 1. a stream of water; river; brook. 2. the channel of a stream or canal.

wa·ter·fall (WAW tər FAWL) n. a steep fall of water, as of a stream over a precipice; cascade.

wa·ter·fowl (WAW tər FOWL) n. pl. **·fowl** or **·fowls** a water bird; esp., a swimming game bird.

wa·ter·front (WAW tər FRUNT) n. 1. real property abutting on or overlooking a natural body of water. 2. that part of a town fronting on a body of water, esp. the area containing wharves, docks, etc.

water gap a deep ravine in a mountain ridge, giving passage to a stream.

Wa·ter·gate (WAW tər GAYT) n. any scandal involving criminal abuse of power by government officials. [after *Watergate*, a building complex in Washington, D.C., where a break-in occurred at Democratic Party headquarters in 1972]

water hole a small pond, esp. one used by animals as a drinking place.

wa·ter·ing place (WAW tər ing) a health resort having mineral springs.

water level 1. the level of still water in the sea or other body of water. 2. *Geol.* a water table. 3. *Naut.* a ship's water line.

water line 1. *Naut.* the part of a ship's hull corresponding to the water level at various loads: also called *water level.* 2. a line corresponding to the height to which water has risen or may rise.

wa·ter·logged (WAW tər LAWGD) adj. thoroughly filled or soaked with water.

Wa·ter·loo (WAW tər LOO) n. a final and decisive defeat: usu. in the phrase **meet one's Waterloo.** [after Napoleon's defeat at *Waterloo*, Belgium]

water main a large conduit for carrying water.

wa·ter·mark (WAW tər MAHRK) n. 1. a mark showing the extent to which water rises. 2. a mark or design impressed on paper that is visible when the paper is held up to the light. —v.t. 1. impress (paper) with a watermark. 2. impress as a watermark.

wa·ter·mel·on (WAW tər MEL ən) n. the large, edible fruit of a trailing plant of the gourd family, containing red or pink pulp and a watery juice; also, the plant.

water ox a water buffalo.

water pipe 1. a hookah. 2. a conduit for water.

water polo a game in which two teams of swimmers push or throw a buoyant ball toward opposite goals.

water power the power of rushing or falling water, as applied to the driving of machinery. Also **wa'ter·pow'er.**

wa·ter·proof (WAW tər PROOF) adj. permitting no water to enter or pass through; esp., treated with some substance that resists the passage of water. —v.t. render waterproof.

wa·ter·shed (WAW tər SHED) n. 1. the line of separation between two contiguous drainage valleys; divide. 2. the region from which a river receives its supply of water. 3. a crucial dividing point or line.

wa·ter·ski (WAW tər SKEE) v.i. **-skied, -ski·ing** glide over water on water skis, while being towed by a motorboat. — **water ski** a ski used in planing over water while being towed by a speedboat. —**wa'ter-ski'er** n. —**wa'ter·ski'ing** n.

water softener a substance added to water to counteract the effect of its mineral content.

wa·ter·sol·u·ble (WAW tər SOL yə bəl) adj. capable of dissolving in water.

wa·ter·spout (WAW tər SPOWT) n. 1. a moving, whirling column of spray and mist, generated at sea or on other large bodies of water. 2. a pipe for the free discharge of water.

water table *Geol.* the surface marking the upper level of a water-saturated zone beneath the ground: also called *water level.*

wa·ter·tight (WAW tər TlT) adj. 1. so closely made that water cannot enter or leak through. 2. having no loopholes; foolproof: *watertight* tax laws.

water tower an elevated tank for water storage.

water vapor the vapor of water, esp. when below the boiling point, as in the atmosphere.

wa·ter·way (WAW tər WAY) n. a river, channel, canal, etc. used as a means of travel.

water wheel a wheel turned by flowing water, used to provide power.

water wings an inflatable device used to keep one afloat while swimming or learning to swim.

wa·ter·works (WAW tər WURKS) *n.* (*construed as sing. or pl.*) a system of machines, buildings, etc. for supplying a city with water.

wa·ter·y (WAW tə ree) *adj.* **1.** of or relating to water. **2.** saturated or filled with water. **3.** diluted; thin: *watery* soup. **4.** pale; weak: *watery* colors. —**wa'ter·i·ness** *n.*

watt (wot) *n.* the practical unit of electric power, equivalent to the power developed when one ampere flows through a resistance of one ohm. [after James *Watt*, 1736—1819, Scottish inventor]

watt·age (WOT ij) *n.* **1.** amount of electric power in terms of watts. **2.** the amount of power needed to operate an appliance or device.

watt-hour (WOT OWR) *n.* electrical energy equivalent to one watt acting for one hour.

wat·tle (WOT l) *n.* **1.** a structure of rods or twigs woven together. **2.** a fleshy process hanging from the throat of a bird or snake. [ME *wattel*] —*v.t.* **·tled, ·tling 1.** weave or twist, as twigs, into a network. **2.** form, as baskets, by intertwining flexible twigs.

wave (wayv) *v.* **waved, wav·ing** *v.i.* **1.** move freely back and forth or up and down, as a flag in the wind. **2.** express farewell, hello, etc. by moving one's hand or arm up and down. **3.** have an undulating shape or form: Her hair *waves*. —*v.t.* **4.** cause to wave: *wave* a banner. **5.** form with an undulating surface or outline. **6.** signal or express by waving something: *wave* farewell. [ME *waven*] —*n.* **1.** a ridge or undulation moving on the surface of a liquid. **2.** one of a series of curves: *waves* of grain. **3.** something that comes, like a wave, with great volume or power: a *wave* of enthusiasm. **4.** one of a series, as of events, occurring together: the first *wave* of Marines. **5.** a wavelike tress or curl of hair. **6.** a sweeping or undulating motion, as with the hand. **7.** *Physics* one of the periodic vibratory impulses produced by a disturbance in and propagated through an elastic medium, as sound. —**wave'·less** *adj.*

wave·length (WAYV LENGKTH) *n. Physics* the distance, measured along the line of progression, between two points representing similar phases of two consecutive waves.

wave·let (WAYV lit) *n.* a little wave.

wa·ver (WAY vər) *v.i.* **1.** move one way and the other; sway. **2.** be uncertain or undecided; vacillate. **3.** falter. **4.** flicker; gleam. **5.** quaver; tremble. [ME] —*n.* a wavering. —**wa'ver·er** *n.* —**wa'ver·ing·ly** *adv.*

wav·y (WAY vee) *adj.* **wav·i·er, wav·i·est** undulatory; waving: *wavy* hair. —**wav'i·ly** *adv.* —**wav'i·ness** *n.*

wax¹ (waks) *n.* **1.** beeswax. **2.** any of various natural substances similar to fats, but harder and less greasy. **3.** a solid mineral substance resembling wax, as paraffin. **4.** earwax. [ME *wex*] —*v.t.* coat or treat with wax.

wax² *v.i.* **waxed, waxed** (*Poetic* **wax·en**), **wax·ing 1.** become larger gradually: said esp. of the moon as it approaches fullness. **2.** become: *wax* angry. [ME *waxen* grow]

wax·en (WAK sən) *adj.* **1.** resembling, made of, or treated with wax. **2.** pale; pallid: a *waxen* complexion.

wax paper paper coated or treated with wax and used to retain or protect against moisture. Also **waxed paper.**

wax·work (WAKS wurk) *n.* **1.** a work produced in wax; esp., ornaments or life-size figures of wax. **2.** *pl.* an exhibition of wax figures of famous or notorious persons.

wax·y (WAK see) *adj.* **wax·i·er, wax·i·est** of, like, or covered with wax. —**wax'i·ness** *n.*

way (way) *n.* **1.** a manner or method of doing something; procedure. **2.** direction; route: Which is the *way* to town? **3.** a path or track. **4.** space or room to advance or work: Make *way* for her. **5.** distance in general: a little *way* off: often, loosely, **ways. 6.** headway; progress. **7.** a customary or usual manner of living, speaking, behaving, etc. **8.** a specific detail; respect; particular: He erred in two *ways*. **9.** a course of life or experience: the *way* of sin. **10.** condition: He's in a bad *way*. **11.** the range of one's observation: An accident threw it in his *way*. **12.** *Naut. pl.* a tilted framework of timbers upon which a ship slides when launched. **13.** *Law* a right of way. —**by the way** in passing; incidentally. —**by way of 1.** with the purpose of; to serve as: *by way of* introduction. **2.** through; via. —**give way 1.** break down; collapse. **2.** yield. —**under way** in motion; making progress. —*adv.* away; very much or very far. [ME]

way·far·ing (WAY FAIR ing) *adj. & n.* journeying; being on the road. —**way'far'er** *n.*

way·lay (WAY LAY) *v.t.* **·laid, ·lay·ing 1.** lie in ambush for and attack, as in order to rob. **2.** accost on the way. —**way'lay'er** *n.*

way-out (WAY OWT) *adj. Informal* unusual; unconventional.

-ways *suffix of adverbs* in a (specified) manner, direction, or position: *always, sideways:* often equivalent to *-wise.*

ways and means in legislation, methods of raising funds for the use of the government.

way-side (WAY SID) *n.* the side or edge of a road or highway.

way station any station between principal stations, esp. on a railroad.

way-ward (WAY wərd) *adj.* **1.** headstrong or disobedient; willful. **2.** unpredictable; erratic; capricious. [ME] **—way′ward•ly** *adv.* **—way′ward•ness** *n.*

way-worn (WAY WORN) *adj.* fatigued by travel.

we (wee) *pron.pl., possessive* **ours**, *objective* **us**; the nominative plural pronoun of *I*, used by a group, by an individual when part of a group, by an editor or other writer to give his or her words an impersonal character, or by a sovereign on formal occasions. [ME]

weak (week) *adj.* **•er, •est 1.** lacking in physical strength or energy. **2.** insufficiently resisting stress: a *weak* link. **3.** lacking in strength of will or stability of character; pliable. **4.** ineffectual, as from deficient supply: *weak* artillery support. **5.** lacking in power: a *weak* voice. **6.** lacking the usual strength: *weak* tea. **7.** lacking the ability to function properly: a *weak* heart. **8.** showing or resulting from poor judgment: a *weak* plan. **9.** unable to convince: a *weak* argument. **10.** lacking in influence or authority. **11.** *Phonet.* unstressed; unaccented, as a syllable or sound. [ME *weik*] **—weak′ly** *adv.* **—weak′ness** *n.*

Weak as a combining form has the meaning lacking in strength of intensity, as in:

weak-backed	weak-tasting
weak-limbed	weak-tinted
weak-muscled	weak-voiced
weak-stemmed	weak-willed

weak•en (WEE kən) *v.t. & v.i.* make or become weak or weaker. **—weak′en•er** *n.*

weak-kneed (WEEK NEED) *adj.* **1.** weak in the knees. **2.** without resolution or purpose; spineless.

weak•ling (WEEK ling) *n.* a person who is physically or morally weak.

weak•ly (WEEK lee) *adj.* **•li•er, •li•est** sickly; feeble; weak. **—adv.** in a weak manner.

weak-mind•ed (WEEK MĪN did) *adj.* **1.**

indecisive; weak-willed. **2.** feeble-minded. **—weak′mind′ed•ness** *n.*

weak•ness (WEEK nis) *n.* **1.** the state or quality of being weak. **2.** a defect or weak point; fault. **3.** a penchant or fondness: with *for:* a *weakness* for sweets.

weal¹ (weel) *n.* a sound or healthy state; prosperity; welfare. [ME *wele*]

weal² *n.* welt (def.3).

wealth (welth) *n.* **1.** great abundance of valuable possessions; riches. **2.** *Econ.* all objects having a monetary value. **3.** a great amount: a *wealth* of learning. [ME *welth*]

wealth•y (WEL thee) *adj.* **wealth•i•er, wealth•i•est** possessing wealth; affluent. **—wealth′i•ness** *n.*

wean (ween) *v.t.* **1.** accustom (the young of any mammal) to food other than its mother's milk. **2.** remove from former habits or associations: usu. with *from.* [ME *wenen*]

weap•on (WEP ən) *n.* **1.** any implement for fighting or warfare. **2.** any means used in a struggle or contest. [ME *wepen*] **—weap′on•less** *adj.*

weap•on•ry (WEP ən ree) *n.* weapons collectively.

wear (wair) *v.* **wore, worn, wear•ing** *v.t.* **1.** carry or have on the person as a garment, ornament, etc. **2.** have in one's appearance; exhibit: She *wears* a scowl. **3.** bear habitually in a specified manner: He *wears* his hair long. **4.** display or fly: A ship *wears* its colors. **5.** impair, waste, or consume by use. **6.** cause by rubbing, use, etc.: *wear* a hole in a coat. **7.** exhaust; weary. **—v.i. 8.** be impaired gradually by use, rubbing, etc. **9.** withstand the effects of use, wear, etc.: The skirt *wears* well. **10.** become as specified from use or attrition: Our patience is *wearing* thin. **11.** pass gradually or tediously: with *on* or *away.* **—wear out 1.** make or become worthless by use. **2.** waste gradually; use up: He *wears out* shoes quickly. **3.** tire. [ME *weren* damage] **—n. 1.** the act of wearing, or the state of being worn. **2.** clothing: summer *wear.* **3.** the destructive effect of use, work, or time. **4.** capacity for resistance to use or impairment; durability. **—wear′a•bil′i•ty** *n.* **—wear′a•ble** *adj.* **—wear′er** *n.*

wear and tear loss by ordinary use.

wear•ing (WAIR ing) *adj.* **1.** fatiguing; exhausting. **2.** made to be worn: *wearing* apparel. **—wear′ing•ly** *adv.*

wea•ri•some (WEER ee səm) *adj.* causing

fatigue; tiresome or tedious. —**wea′ri•some•ly** adv. —**wea′ri•some•ness** n.

wea•ry (WEER ee) adj. •**ri•er, •ri•est** 1. tired; fatigued. 2. discontented or vexed: often with of: weary of life. 3. wearisome. [ME wery] —v.t. & v.i. •**ried, •ry•ing** make or become weary; tire. —**wea′ri•ly** adv. —**wea′ri•ness** n.

wea•sel (WEE zəl) n. 1. any of certain small, slender, predacious carnivores having brownish fur that in northern regions turns white in winter. 2. a sneaky, treacherous person. [ME wesele] —v.i. •**seled, •sel•ing** speak or act evasively etc.

weath•er (WETH ər) n. 1. atmospheric condition as regards temperature, moisture, winds, and other meteorological phenomena. 2. bad weather; storm. —**under the weather** Informal 1. ailing; ill. 2. somewhat drunk. [ME weder] —v.t. 1. expose to the action of the weather. 2. dry, discolor, etc. by action of the weather. 3. pass through and survive, as a crisis. 4. Naut. pass to windward of. —v.i. 5. undergo changes resulting from exposure to the weather. 6. resist the action of the weather. —**weath′ered** adj.

weath•er-beat•en (WETH ər BEET ən) adj. bearing or showing the effects of exposure to weather.

weath•er•cast•er (WETH ər KAS tər) n. a person who reads news of the weather on radio or television.

weath•er•cock (WETH ər KOK) n. a weather vane in the form of a rooster.

weath•er•man (WETH ər MAN) n. pl. •**men** n. 1. a meteorologist. 2. a weathercaster.

weather map a map or chart indicating weather conditions for a given region and time.

weath•er•proof (WETH ər PROOF) adj. capable of withstanding rough weather without much damage. —v.t. make weatherproof.

weather strip a narrow strip of material placed over or in crevices, as at windows, to keep out drafts, rain, etc. Also **weather stripping.**

weath•er•strip (WETH ər STRIP) v.t. -**stripped, -strip•ping** equip or fit with weather strips.

weather vane a vane (def. 1).

weave (weev) v. **wove** or for def. 8 **weaved, wo•ven** or **wove, weav•ing** v.t. 1. produce, as a textile, by interlacing threads or yarns, esp. in a loom. 2. form by interlacing strands, strips, twigs, etc.: weave a basket. 3. produce by combining details or elements: weave a story. 4. twist into, about, or through: weave ribbons through one's hair. 5. make or effect by moving in a zigzag course: weave one's way through a crowd. —v.i. 6. make cloth, baskets, etc. by weaving. 7. become woven or interlaced. 8. move in a zigzag path. —n. a particular style of weaving. [ME weven] —**weav′er** n.

web (web) n. 1. any fabric, structure, etc. woven of or as of interlaced strands. 2. the network of threads spun by a spider. 3. any complex network: a web of highways. 4. anything artfully contrived into a trap: a web of espionage. 5. Zool. a membrane connecting the digits of an animal, as in aquatic birds. 6. Ornithol. the series of barbs on either side of the shaft of a feather: also called vane. [ME]

webbed (webd) adj. 1. having a web. 2. having the digits united by a membrane, as the foot of a goose or duck.

web•bing (WEB ing) n. 1. a woven strip of strong fiber, used for safety belts etc. 2. any structure or material forming a web.

web-foot•ed (WEB FUUT íd) adj. having the toes connected by a membrane, as in many aquatic animals and birds.

wed (wed) v. **wed•ded** or **wed, wed•ding** v.t. 1. take as one's husband or wife; marry. 2. unite or give in marriage. 3. join closely. —v.i. 4. marry. [ME wedde pledge]

we'd (weed) 1. we had. 2. we would.

wed•ding (WED ing) n. the ceremony or celebration of a marriage. [ME]

wedge (wej) n. 1. a V-shaped piece of wood, metal, etc., used to split wood, raise weights, etc. 2. anything resembling a wedge, as a piece of pie etc. 3. anything serving to divide or disrupt. [ME wegge] —v.t. **wedged, wedg•ing** 1. force apart or split with or as with a wedge. 2. compress or fix in place with a wedge. 3. crowd or squeeze into a small space.

wed•lock (WED LOK) n. the state or relationship of being married; matrimony. [ME wedlok]

Wednes•day (WENZ day) n. the fourth day of the week. [ME Wednesdai]

wee (wee) adj. **we•er, we•est** 1. very small; tiny. 2. very early: the wee hours. [ME we]

weed (weed) n. any common, unsightly, or troublesome plant that grows in abundance. —v.t. 1. pull up and remove weeds from. **2.** remove (anything regarded as harmful or undersirable): with *out* **3.** rid of anything harmful or undesirable. —*v.i.* **4.** remove weeds. [ME *wede*] —**weed'er** *n.* —**weed'less** *adj.*

weeds (weedz) *n.pl.* a widow's mourning garb. [ME *wede* garment]

weed•y (WEE dee) *adj.* **weed•i•er, weed•i•est 1.** full of weeds. **2.** of or like weeds. **3.** scrawny; gawky. —**weed'i•ness** *n.*

week (week) *n.* **1.** a period of seven days; esp., such a period beginning with Sunday. **2.** the period of time within a week devoted to work: a 35-hour *week.* [ME *weke*]

week•day (WEEK DAY) *n.* any day of the week except Sunday and, often, Saturday.

week•end (WEEK END) *n.* the end of the week; esp., the time from Friday evening or Saturday to the following Monday morning. —*v.i.* pass the weekend. —**week'end'er** *n.* **1.** one who goes on a weekend vacation. **2.** a suitcase carrying clothing etc. sufficient for a weekend.

week•ly (WEEK lee) *adv.* once a week. —*adj.* **1.** of or pertaining to a week or to week-days. **2.** done or occurring once a week. —*n. pl.* **•lies** a publication issued once a week.

weep (weep) *v.* **wept, weep•ing** *v.i.* **1.** show grief, pain, etc. by shedding tears. **2.** mourn; lament: with *for.* **3.** ooze or shed liquid in drops. —*v.t.* **4.** shed (tears etc.). [ME *wepen*] —**weep'er** *n.*

weep•ing (WEE ping) *adj.* **1.** crying; tearful. **2.** having slim, pendulous branches.

weeping willow a willow having long, slender, pendulous branches.

weep•y (WEE pee) *adj.* **weep•i•er, weep•i•est 1.** tearful. **2.** sad or sentimental.

wee•vil (WEE vəl) *n.* any of numerous small beetles, feeding principally on beans and seeds, esp. the *boll weevil.* [ME *wevel*] —**wee'vil•y** *adj.* infested with weevils.

weft (weft) *n.* the cross threads in a web of cloth; woof. [ME]

weigh (way) *v.t.* **1.** determine the weight of, as by measuring on a scale or holding in the hand. **2.** measure (an amount of something) according to weight: with *out.* **3.** consider carefully: *weigh* a proposal. **4.** press down by heaviness; oppress: with *down.* —**weigh anchor** *Naut.* heave up a ship's anchor in preparation for sailing. —*v.i.* **5.** have a specified weight. **6.** have influence or importance. **7.** be burdensome or oppressive: with *on* or *upon:* It *weighs* on my mind. —**weigh in** of a

boxer, jockey, etc., be weighed before a contest. [ME *weghen*]

weight (wayt) *n.* **1.** any amount of heaviness, expressed indefinitely or in standard units. **2.** *Physics* the measure of the force with which bodies tend toward the center of the earth or other celestial body, equal to the mass of the body multiplied by the acceleration of local gravitation. **3.** any object or mass that weighs a specific amount. **4.** an object of known mass used to determine weight on a balance. **5.** any mass used to hold something down. **6.** burden; oppressiveness: the *weight* of care. **7.** influence; importance; consequence. —**carry weight** be of importance or significance. —**pull one's weight** do one's share. [ME] —*v.t.* **1.** add weight to; make heavy. **2.** oppress or burden.

weight•less (WAYT lis) *adj.* **1.** having or seeming to have no weight. **2.** experiencing little or no gravitational pull. —**weight'less•ness** *n.*

weight•y (WAY tee) *adj.* **weight•i•er, weight•i•est 1.** having great weight. **2.** of great importance or seriousness; grave; significant: a *weighty* decision. —**weight'i•ly** *adv.* —**weight'i•ness** *n.*

weir (weer) *n.* **1.** an obstruction or dam placed in a stream to raise or divert the water. **2.** a series of wattled enclosures in a stream to catch fish. [ME *were*]

weird (weerd) *adj.* **•er, •est 1.** concerned with the unnatural or with witchcraft; mysterious. **2.** strange; bizarre; odd. [ME] —**weird'ly** *adv.* —**weird'ness** *n.*

weird•o (WEER doh) *n. pl.* **weird•os** *Informal* a bizarre or freakish person or thing.

welch (welch) *v.i. Informal* welsh.

wel•come (WEL kəm) *adj.* **1.** admitted gladly; received cordially: a *welcome* guest. **2.** producing satisfaction or pleasure: pleasing: *welcome* news. **3.** made free to use or enjoy: Feel *welcome* to try it. —**you are** (or **you're**) **welcome** you are under no obligation: a conventional response to an expression of thanks. —*n.* the act of bidding or making welcome; a hearty greeting. —*v.t.* **•comed, •com•ing 1.** give a welcome to; greet hospitably. **2.** receive with pleasure. —*interj.* a greeting expressing pleasure at the arrival of a guest. [ME] —**wel'come•ness** *n.* —**wel'com•er** *n.*

weld (weld) *v.t.* **1.** unite, as two pieces of metal, by the application of heat along the area of contact. **2.** bring into close association or connection. —*v.i.* **3.** be capable of being welded. —*n.* the act of welding metal; also, the seam so formed. —**weld′a·ble** *adj.* —**weld′er** *n.*

wel·fare (WEL FAIR) *n.* **1.** the condition of faring well; prosperity. **2.** aid, as money, food, or clothing given to those in need. —**on welfare** receiving aid from a government because of need. [ME *wel fare* fare well]

welfare state a government that assumes a large measure of responsibility for the social welfare of its citizens.

well[1] (wel) *n.* **1.** a hole or shaft sunk into the earth to obtain water, oil, gas, etc. **2.** a spring of water; a fountain. **3.** a source of continued supply: a *well* of learning. **4.** a vessel used to hold a supply of liquid. **5.** *Archit.* a vertical opening descending through floors: an elevator *well.* —*v.t. & v.i.* pour forth; gush. [ME *welle* bubble up]

well[2] *adv.* **bet·ter, best 1.** satisfactorily; favorably: I hope everything goes *well.* **2.** in a good or correct manner; expertly: speak *well.* **3.** suitably; with reason or propriety: I cannot *well* remain here. **4.** in a successful or prosperous manner: He lives *well.* **5.** intimately: How *well* do you know them? **6.** to a considerable extent or degree: *well* aware. **7.** completely; wholly: Mix it *well.* **8.** far; at some distance: He lagged *well* behind us. **9.** kindly; generously; graciously. —**as well 1.** also; in addition. **2.** with equal effect or consequence: He might just *as well* have kept it. —**as well as 1.** as satisfactorily as. **2.** to the same degree as. **3.** in addition to. —*adj.* **1.** in good health. **2.** satisfactory; right: All is *well.* **3.** prosperous; comfortable. [ME] —*interj.* an exclamation used to express surprise, expectation, doubt, etc., or to preface a remark.

Well, as a combining form, has the meanings:

1. completely; extensively:

well-accustomed	well-deserved
well-authenticated	well-educated
well-hidden	well-pleased
well-liked	well-stocked

2. correctly; satisfactorily; skillfully:

well-behaved	well-mannered
well-built	well-planned
well-chosen	well-seasoned
well-dressed	well-trained
well-formed	well-worded
well-made	well-written

we'll (weel) **1.** we will. **2.** we shall.

well-ap·point·ed (WEL ə POIN tid) *adj.* properly equipped; excellently furnished.

well-bal·anced (WEL BAL ənst) *adj.* **1.** evenly balanced or proportioned. **2.** sensible; sane; sound.

well-be·ing (WEL BEE ing) *n.* a condition of health, happiness, or prosperity; welfare.

well-born (WEL BORN) *adj.* of good birth or ancestry.

well-bred (WEL BRED) *adj.* **1.** characterized by or showing good breeding; polite. **2.** of good stock, as an animal.

well-dis·posed (WEL di SPOHZD) *adj.* disposed or inclined to be kind, favorable, etc.

well-done (WEL DUN) *adj.* **1.** satisfactorily accomplished. **2.** thoroughly cooked, as meat.

well-fa·vored (WEL FAY vərd) *adj.* handsome; good-looking.

well-fed (WEL FED) *adj.* plump; fat.

well-fixed (WEL FIKST) *adj. Informal* affluent; well-to-do.

well-found·ed (WEL FOWN did) *adj.* based on fact, sound evidence, etc.: *well-founded* suspicions.

well-groomed (WEL GROOMD) *adj.* carefully dressed, combed, etc.

well-ground·ed (WEL GROWN did) *adj.* **1.** thoroughly schooled in the elements of a subject. **2.** well-founded.

well-head (WEL HED) *n.* **1.** a natural source supplying water to a spring or well. **2.** any source or fountainhead. **3.** the top of a well, as of an oil well.

well-heeled (WEL HEELD) *adj. Informal* plentifully supplied with money.

well-in·formed (WEL in FORMD) *adj.* having much information about a subject or a wide range of subjects, esp. of current events.

well-in·ten·tioned (WEL in TEN shənd) *adj.* having good intentions; well-meant.

well-known (WEL NOHN) *adj.* **1.** widely known; famous. **2.** thoroughly or fully known.

well-mean·ing (WEL MEE ning) *adj.* **1.** having good intentions. **2.** done with or characterized by good intentions: also **well-meant** (WEL MENT).

well-nigh (WEL NI) *adv.* very nearly; almost.

well-off (WEL AWF) *adj.* in comfortable or favorable circumstances; fortunate.

well-pre·served (WEL pri ZURVD) *adj.* showing few signs of age.

well-read (WEL RED) *adj.* having wide knowledge from reading much.

well-round·ed (WEL ROWN did) *adj.* **1.** having or displaying diverse knowledge, interests, etc. **2.** wide in scope; comprehensive: a *well-rounded* program. **3.** fully formed or developed: a *well-rounded* figure.

well-spo·ken (WEL SPOH kən) *adj.* **1.** fitly or excellently said. **2.** refined in speech and manners.

well·spring (WEL SPRING) *n.* **1.** the source of a stream or spring; fountainhead. **2.** a source of continual supply.

well-thought-of (WEL THAWT UV) *adj.* in good repute; esteemed; respected.

well-to-do (WEL tə DOO) *adj.* prosperous; affluent.

well-turned (WEL TURND) *adj.* **1.** pleasing in shape. **2.** aptly constructed: a *well-turned* phrase.

well-wish·er (WEL WISH ər) *n.* one who wishes well, as to another.

welsh (welsh, welch) *v.i. Informal* avoid paying a debt, fulfilling an obligation, etc.: often with *on*. Also *welch.* **—welsh′ er** *n.*

Welsh rabbit a dish of melted, seasoned cheese served hot over toast. Also **Welsh rarebit.**

welt (welt) *n.* **1.** a strip of material applied to a seam. **2.** a strip of leather set between the upper of a shoe and its outer sole. **3.** a stripe raised on the skin by a blow: also called *wale, weal.* [ME *welte*] **—v.t. 1.** sew a welt on or in. **2.** beat severely.

wel·ter (WEL tər) *v.i.* **1.** roll about; wallow. **2.** lie or be soaked in some fluid, as blood. [ME] **—n. 1.** a rolling movement, as of waves. **2.** a commotion; turmoil.

wel·ter·weight (WEL tər WAYT) *n.* a boxer or wrestler weighing up to 147 pounds.

wen (wen) *n. Pathol.* any benign tumor of the skin, esp. of the scalp. [ME]

wench (wench) *n.* **1.** formerly, a young woman; girl. **2.** formerly, a female servant. [ME *wenchel* child]

wend (wend) *v.* **wen·ded** (*Archaic* went), **wend·ing** *v.t.* **1.** direct or proceed on (one's course or way). **—v.i. 2.** travel; proceed; go. [ME *wenden*]

went (went) an archaic past tense and past participle of *wend,* now used as past tense of GO.

wept (wept) past tense, past participle of WEEP.

were (wur) plural and second person singular past indicative, and past subjunctive singular and plural, of BE. [ME]

we're (weer) we are.

were·n't (WUR ənt) were not.

were·wolf (WAIR WUULF) *n. pl.* **·wolves** (-WUULVZ) in folklore, a human being transformed into a wolf or one having power to assume the form of a wolf at will. Also **wer′wolf′.** [ME]

wert (wurt) archaic second person singular, past tense of both indicative and subjunctive of BE used with *thou.*

west (west) *n.* **1.** the direction of the sun in relation to an observer on earth at sunset. **2.** one of the four cardinal points of the compass, directly opposite *east.* **3.** *Sometimes cap.* any region west of a specified point. — **the West 1.** the countries lying west of Asia and Turkey; the Occident. **2.** the western hemisphere. **3.** the part of the U.S. lying west of the Mississippi River. **—adj. 1.** to, toward, facing, or in the west. **2.** coming from the west. **—adv.** in or toward the west. [ME]

west·bound (WEST BOWND) *adj.* going westward.

west·er·ly (WES tər lee) *adj.* **1.** in, toward, or pertaining to the west. **2.** from the west, as a wind. **—n. pl. ·lies** a wind or storm from the west. **—adv.** toward or from the west.

west·ern (WES tərn) *adj.* **1.** to, toward, or in the west. **2.** native to or inhabiting the west. **3.** *Sometimes cap.* of or like the west or the West. **—n.** a type of fiction or motion picture about cowboy and pioneer life in the western U.S.

West·ern·er (WES tər nər) *n.* one who lives in or comes from the western U.S.

Western Hemisphere see under HEMI-SPHERE.

west·ern·ize (WES tər NIZ) *v.t.* **·ized, ·iz·ing** make western in characteristics, habits, etc. **—west′ern·i·za′tion** *n.*

west·ward (WEST wərd) *adv.* toward the west: also **west′wards. —adj.** to, toward, facing, or in the west.

wet (wet) *adj.* **wet·ter, wet·test 1.** covered or saturated with water or other liquid. **2.** not yet dry: *wet* paint. **3.** marked by showers or by heavy rainfall; rainy. **4.** favoring or permitting the manufacture and sale of alcoholic beverages: a *wet* county. **—all wet**

Informal completely mistaken. **—wet be-hind the ears** inexperienced or unsophisticated. [ME *wett*] **—n. 1.** water; moisture; wetness. **2.** showery or rainy weather; rain. **—v.t. & v.i. wet** or **wet•ted, wet•ting** make or become wet. **—wet one's whistle** *Informal* take a drink. **—wet′ly** *adv.* **—wet′ness** *n.* **—wet′ter** *n.*

wet•back (WET BAK) *n. Offensive* a Mexican laborer who enters the U.S. illegally, as by swimming or wading across the Rio Grande]

wet blanket one who has a discouraging effect on enthusiasm, activity, etc.

weth•er (WETH ər) *n.* a castrated ram. [ME]

wet nurse a woman who is hired to suckle the child of another woman.

wet-nurse (WET NURS) *v.t.* **-nursed, -nurs•ing 1.** act as a wet nurse to. **2.** attend to with painstaking care.

wet suit a skintight rubber suit worn by skin divers for warmth.

wetting agent *Chem.* any of a class of substances that, by reducing surface tension, enable a liquid to spread more readily over a solid surface.

we've (weev) we have.

whack (hwak) *v.t. & v.i.* strike sharply; beat; hit. **—n. 1.** a sharp, resounding stroke or blow. **2.** *Slang* a share; portion. **—out of whack** *Informal* out of alignment; not in working condition.

whack•ing (HWAK ing) *Informal adj.* strikingly large; whopping.

whale[1] (hwayl) *n. pl.* **whales, whale 1.** a large marine mammal of fishlike form. **2.** *Informal* something extremely good or large: a *whale* of a party. [ME] **—v.i. whaled, whal•ing** engage in the hunting of whales.

whale[2] *v.t.* **whaled, whal•ing** *Informal* strike hard; flog.

whale•boat (HWAYL BOHT) *n.* a long, deep rowboat formerly used in whaling.

whale•bone (HWAYL BOHN) *n.* **1.** the horny substance from the upper jaw of certain whales; baleen. **2.** a strip of whalebone, formerly used in stiffening corsets etc.

whal•er (HWAY lər) *n.* **1.** a person or vessel engaged in whaling. **2.** a whaleboat.

whal•ing (HWAY ling) *n.* the industry of capturing whales.

wham•my (HWAM ee) *n. pl.* **•mies** *Informal* a jinx; hex.

wharf (hworf) *n. pl.* **wharves** (hworvz) or

wharfs a dock or pier where ships load and unload. [ME]

what (hwot, hwut) *pron.* **1.** which specific thing or things, action, etc.: *What* does he do? I don't know *what* to do. **2.** that which: He knew *what* he wanted. **—adj. 1.** in interrogative construction: **a** asking for information that will specify the person or thing qualified by it; which: *What* book will you review? **b** how much: *What* money has he? **2.** how surprising, ridiculous, great, etc.: *What* nerve! **3.** whatever: *What* money he had left was soon spent. **—adv. 1.** in what respect; to what extent: *What* does it matter? **2.** for what reason; why: with *for*: *What* are you saying that *for*? **—conj.** *Informal* that: used only in negative expressions: I don't doubt but *what* he will come. [ME]

what•ev•er (hwut EV ər) *pron.* **1.** the whole that; anything that; no matter what: often added for emphasis to a negative assertion: *whatever* makes life dear; I do not want anything *whatever*. **2.** what: usually interrogative: *Whatever* were you saying?

what•not (HWOT NOT) *n.* **1.** an ornamental set of shelves for holding bric-a-brac. **2.** a nondescript thing.

what•so•ev•er (WHUT soh EV ər) *adj. & pron.* an intensive form of *whatever*. Also *Poetic* **what•so•e'er** (HWUT soh AIR).

wheat (hweet) *n.* **1.** the grain of a cereal grass, providing a flour used for bread, pastries, etc. **2.** the plant producing this grain. [ME *whete*]

wheat germ the embryo of the wheat kernel, used as a source of vitamins.

whee•dle (HWEED l) *v.* **•dled, •dling** *v.t.* **1.** try to persuade by flattery, cajolery, etc.; coax. **2.** obtain by coaxing. **—v.i. 3.** use flattery or cajolery. **—whee′dler** *n.* **—whee′dling•ly** *adv.*

wheel (hweel) *n.* **1.** a circular rim and hub connected by spokes or a disk, capable of rotating on a central axis, as in vehicles and machines. **2.** an instrument or device having a wheel or wheels as its distinguishing characteristic, as a steering wheel, water wheel, spinning wheel, etc. **3.** anything resembling or suggestive of a wheel; any circular object or formation. **4.** an old instrument of torture to which the victim was tied. **5.** a turning; rotation; revolution. **6.** *pl.* a moving force: the *wheels* of democracy. [ME *whele*] **—v.t. 1.** move or convey on wheels. **2.** cause to turn on or as on an axis; pivot or revolve. **3.** perform with a circular movement. —*v.i.* **4.** turn on or as on an axis; rotate or revolve. **5.** take a new direction or course of action: often with *about.* **6.** move in a circular or spiral course. **7.** move on wheels.

wheel·bar·row (HWEEL BAR oh) *n.* a box-like vehicle ordinarily with one wheel and two handles, for moving small loads.

wheel·base (HWEEL BAYS) *n.* the distance between the front and rear axles, as in an automobile.

wheel·chair (HWEEL CHAIR) *n.* a mobile chair mounted between large wheels, for the use of persons who cannot walk.

wheel·er (HWEE lər) *n.* **1.** one who wheels. **2.** something furnished with a wheel or wheels: used in combination: a *two-wheeler.*

wheel·er-deal·er (HWEE lər DEE lər) *n. Informal* one who makes shrewd deals, esp. in business and politics.

wheel horse **1.** a horse harnessed nearest the wheels of a vehicle when there is a leader in front. **2.** a person who does the heaviest work or assumes the greatest responsibility.

wheel·wright (HWEEL RĪT) *n.* one whose business is making or repairing wheels.

wheeze (hweez) *v.t. & v.i.* **wheezed, wheez·ing** breathe or utter with a husky, whistling sound. [ME *whesen*] —*n.* a wheezing sound. —**wheez′er** *n.*

wheez·y (HWEE zee) *adj.* **wheez·i·er, wheez·i·est** affected with or characterized by wheezing. —**wheez′i·ness** *n.*

whelk (hwelk) *n.* any of various large marine mollusks having whorled shells, esp. the common whelk, used for food. [ME *welke*]

whelp (hwelp) *n.* **1.** one of the young of a dog, wolf, lion, or other beast. **2.** a young fellow: a contemptuous term. [ME] —*v.t. & v.i.* give birth (to): said of dogs, lions, etc.

when (hwen) *adv.* at what or which time: *When* did you arrive? —*conj.* **1.** at what or which time: They watched until midnight, *when* they fell asleep. **2.** as soon as: He laughed *when* he heard it. **3.** although: She drives *when* she might ride. **4.** at the time that; while: *when* we were young. **5.** if; considering that: How can I buy it *when* I have no money? —*pron.* what time: since *when.* —*n.* the time; date. [ME *whenne*]

whence (hwens) *adv.* from what place or source: *Whence* came you? —*conj.* from what or which place, source, or cause; from which: the place *whence* these sounds arise. [ME *whennes*]

when·ev·er (hwen EV ər) *conj.* at whatever time: Please call *whenever* your plane arrives.

where (hwair) *adv.* **1.** at or in what place or situation: *Where* is my book? **2.** to what place or end: *Where* are you going? **3.** from what place: *Where* did you get that hat? **4.** to a place or situation in or to which: Let us go *where* the mountains are. —*conj.* **1.** at which place: Let us go home, *where* we can relax. **2.** with the condition that. —*pron.* **1.** the place in which: That is *where* she lived. **2.** the point at which: That's *where* you are wrong. [ME]

where·a·bouts (HWAIR ə BOWTS) *adv.* near what place; about where: *Whereabouts* do they intend to put the dump? Also **whereabout.** —*n. (construed as sing. or pl.)* the place in or near which a person or thing is: I don't know his *whereabouts.*

where·as (hwair AZ) *conj.* **1.** since the facts are such as they are. **2.** the fact being that; when in truth: implying opposition to a previous statement. [ME *wheras*] —*n.* *pl.* **where·as·es** a clause or item beginning with the word "whereas."

where·by (hwair BĪ) *adv.* **1.** by means of which; through which: the gate *whereby* he entered. **2.** by what; how. [ME *wherby*]

where·fore (HWAIR FOR) *adv.* for that reason; why. —*n.* a statement providing a reason: the whys and *wherefores.*

where·in (hwair IN) *adv.* **1.** in what: *Wherein* is the error? **2.** in which: a marriage *wherein* there is discord.

where·so·ev·er (HWAIR soh EV ər) *conj.* in or to whatever place; wherever.

where·up·on (HWAIR ə PON) *conj.* upon which or what; in consequence of which; after which: *whereupon* they left the meeting.

wher·ev·er (hwair EV ər) *adv. & conj.* in, at, or to whatever place; wheresoever.

where·with·al (HWAIR with AWL) *n.* the necessary means or resources, esp. money.

wher·ry (HWER ee) *n. pl.* **·ries** a light rowboat. [ME *whery*] —*v.t. & v.i.* **·ried, ·ry·ing** transport in or use a wherry.

whet (hwet) *v.t.* **whet·ted, whet·ting** **1.** sharpen, as a knife, by friction. **2.** make more keen or eager; stimulate, as the appetite. [ME *whetten*] —*n.* **1.** the act of whetting. **2.** something that whets.

wheth·er (HWET͟H ər) *conj.* **1.** if it be the

case that: Tell me *whether* you are considering our plan. **2.** in either case; introducing alternative: I don't care *whether* you stay or go. **—whether or no** (or **not**) in any case. [ME]

whet•stone (HWET STOHN) *n.* a stone for sharpening knives, axes, etc.

whey (hway) *n.* a clear liquid that separates from the curd when milk is curdled, as in making cheese. [ME *wheye*] **—whey'ey, whey'ish** *adj.*

which (hwich) *pron.* **1.** what one or ones: *Which* are his? **2.** the thing designated; that: the story *which* we preferred. **—adj.** **1.** being one or more of several alternatives: *Which* way are you going? **2.** this: during *which* time. [ME]

which•ev•er (hwich EV ər) *pron.* any one that; no matter which: take *whichever* you like. **—adj.** no matter which: take *whichever* book you like best. [ME]

whiff (hwif) *n.* **1.** a slight gust of air. **2.** a gust of odor: a *whiff* of onions. **3.** a single expulsion or inhalation of breath. **—v.t. & v.i. 1.** exhale or inhale in whiffs. **2.** smell or sniff. **—whiff'er** *n.*

whif•fle•tree (HWIF əl TREE) *n.* a horizontal crossbar to which the ends of the traces of a harness are attached.

while (hwīl) *n.* **1.** a short time; also, any period of time: Stay and rest a *while.* **2.** time or pains expended: worth one's *while.* **—all the while** all along. **—conj. 1.** during the time that; as long as. **2.** at the same time that: *While* she found fault, she also praised. **3.** whereas: This man is short, *while* that one is tall. [ME] **—v.t. whiled, whil•ing** cause (time) to pass lightly and pleasantly: usu. with *away.*

whim (hwim) *n.* a sudden or unexpected notion or fanciful idea; caprice.

whim•per (HWIM pər) *v.i.* **1.** cry or whine with plaintive broken sounds. **—v.t. 2.** utter with a whimper. **—n.** a low, broken, whining cry; whine. **—whim'•per•er** *n.* **— whim'per•ing** *n.*

whim•si•cal (HWIM zi kəl) *adj.* **1.** having eccentric ideas; capricious. **2.** oddly constituted; fantastic. **—whim'si•cal'i•ty** (-KAL i tee) *n.* **—whim'si•cal•ly** (-kə lee) *adv.*

whim•sy (HWIM zee) *n. pl.* **•sies 1.** a whim. **2.** fanciful humor, as in a literary work.

whine (hwīn) *v.* **whined, whin•ing** *v.i.* **1.** utter a sound expressive of grief, peevishness, etc. **2.** complain in a tiresome or childish way. **—v.t. 3.** utter with a whine. [ME

whinen] **—n.** the act or sound of whining. **—whin'er** *n.* **—whin'ing•ly** *adv.* **— whin'y** *adj.*

whin•ny (HWIN ee) *v.* **•nied, •ny•ing** *v.i.* **1.** neigh, esp. in a low or gentle way. **—v.t. 2.** express with a whinny. **—n. pl. •nies** a neigh.

whip (hwip) *v.* **whipped** or **whipt, whip•ping** *v.t.* **1.** strike with a lash, rod, strap, etc. **2.** drive with lashes. **3.** cause to move like a whip: The wind *whipped* the trees. **4.** beat, as eggs or cream, to a froth. **5.** seize, move, jerk, throw, etc. with a sudden motion. **6.** wrap (rope, cable, etc.) with light line so as to prevent chafing or wear. **7.** sew, as a flat seam, with a loose overhand stitch. **8.** *Informal* defeat. **—v.i. 9.** go, come, move, or turn suddenly and quickly. **10.** thrash about in a manner suggestive of a whip. **—whip up 1.** excite; arouse. **2.** *Informal* prepare quickly, as a meal. **—n. 1.** a lash attached to a handle, used for driving draft animals or for administering punishment. **2.** a stroke, blow, or lashing motion. **3.** a member of a legislative body who enforces party discipline and looks after party interests. **4.** a kind of dessert, whipped to a froth. [ME *whippe*] **—whip'per** *n.*

whip hand an instrument or means of mastery; an advantageous or controlling position.

whip•lash (HWIP LASH) *n.* **1.** the lash of a whip. **2.** a whiplash injury.

whiplash injury an injury to the neck caused by a sudden jolting, as in an automobile collision.

whip•per•snap•per (HWIP ər SNAP ər) *n.* a pretentious but insignificant person, esp. a young one.

whip•ping (HWIP ing) *n.* **1.** the act of one who or that which whips; esp., a flogging. **2.** a material used to whip or lash parts together.

whipping boy a scapegoat.

whip•poor•will (HWIP ər WIL) *n.* a small nocturnal bird, common in the eastern U.S. [Imit. of its cry]

whip•saw (HWIP SAW) *n.* a long, narrow, tapering saw, mounted in a wooden frame. **—v.t. •sawed, •sawed** or **•sawn, •saw•ing 1.** saw with a whipsaw. **2.** defeat by the joint action of two opponents, or in two opposite ways at once.

whir (hwur) *v.t. & v.i.* **whirred, whir•ring** fly, move, or whirl with a buzzing sound.

[ME *quirren*] —*n.* the sound made in whirring.

whirl (hwurl) *v.i.* **1.** turn or revolve rapidly, as about a center. **2.** move or go swiftly. **3.** have a sensation of spinning: My head is *whirling.* —*v.t.* **4.** cause to turn or revolve rapidly. [ME *whirlen* revolve] —*n.* **1.** a swift rotating motion. **2.** a state of confusion; turmoil. **3.** a rapid succession of events, social activities, etc. **4.** *Informal* an attempt.

whirl·i·gig (HWUR li GIG) *n.* **1.** any toy or small device that rotates rapidly on an axis. **2.** anything that whirls. [ME *whirlegigge*]

whirl·pool (HWURL POOL) *n.* **1.** a vortex where water moves with a whirling motion. **2.** anything resembling the motion of a whirlpool.

whirl·wind (HWURL WIND) *n.* a funnel-shaped column of air, with a rapid, upward spiral motion. —*adj.* extremely swift or impetuous: a *whirlwind* courtship. [ME]

whisk (hwisk) *v.t.* **1.** sweep with light movements, as of a small broom. **2.** beat with a quick movement, as eggs, etc. —*v.i.* **3.** move quickly and lightly. —*n.* **1.** a sudden, sweeping movement. **2.** a little broom or brush. **3.** a small instrument for rapidly whipping (cream etc.) to a froth or for blending ingredients in cooking. [ME *wysk* sweeping movement]

whisk broom a small, short-handled broom for brushing clothing, etc.

whisk·er (HWIS kər) *n.* **1.** *pl.* the beard, esp. its side parts. **2.** a hair from the beard. **3.** one of the long, bristly hairs on the sides of the mouth of some animals. —**whisk'ered** *adj.*

whis·key (HWIS kee) *n. pl.* **·keys** **1.** an alcoholic liquor obtained by the distillation of certain fermented grains. **2.** a drink of whiskey. —**whis'ky** Scotch or Canadian whiskey. [Short for *usquebaugh* < Irish, water of life]

whis·per (HWIS pər) *n.* **1.** a low, soft, breathy voice. **2.** a low, rustling sound. **3.** a whispered utterance; hint; insinuation. —*v.i.* **1.** speak in a whisper. **2.** talk cautiously or furtively; plot or gossip. **3.** make a low, rustling sound. —*v.t.* **4.** utter in a whisper. [ME *whisperen*] —**whis'per·ing** *adj. & n.*

whist (hwist) *n.* a game of cards, the forerunner of bridge, played by four persons.

whis·tle (HWIS əl) *v.* **·tled,** **·tling** *v.i.* **1.** make a shrill sound by sending the breath through the teeth or through a small opening formed by the mouth. **2.** emit a shrill cry, as some birds and animals. **3.** cause a shrill sound by swift passage through the air, as wind etc. **4.** blow or sound a whistle. —*v.t.* **5.** produce (a tune) by whistling. **6.** call, manage, or direct by whistling. [ME *whistlen*] —*n.* **1.** a device for producing a shrill sound by forcing a current of air etc. through a narrowed opening. **2.** a whistling sound. **3.** the act of whistling. —**wet one's whistle** *Informal* take a drink. —**whist'ler** *n.*

whistle-blower (HWIS əl BLOH ər) *n.* a person who makes public disclosure of wrongdoing by another person.

whistle stop **1.** a small station at which a train stops only on signal. **2.** a small town. **3.** a brief stop during a tour, esp. by a candidate for office.

whit (hwit) *n.* a small particle; bit: not a *whit* less.

white (hwīt) *adj.* **whit·er,** **whit·est** **1.** having the color of milk, new snow, etc. **2.** very light in color. **3.** bloodless; ashen: *white* with rage. **4.** not intentionally wicked: a *white* lie. **5.** free from stain; innocent. **6.** blank; unmarked by ink. **7.** belonging to a racial group characterized by light-colored skin; Caucasian. **8.** of, pertaining to, or controlled by white people. **9.** *Slang* honorable; honest. [ME] —*n.* **1.** the color seen when light is reflected without sensible absorption of any of the visible rays of the spectrum; the color of new snow. **2.** the white or light-colored part of something, as the albumen of egg. **3.** one who has light-colored skin. —*v.t.* **whit·ed,** **whit·ing** whiten. —**white'ly** *adv.* —**white'ness** *n.*

white ant loosely, a termite.

white blood cell a white or colorless corpuscle; leucocyte. Also **white corpuscle.**

white·cap (HWĪT KAP) *n.* a wave with a crest of foam.

white-collar (HWĪT KOL ər) *adj.* designating clerical, professional, and other nonmanual workers.

white dwarf *Astron.* a star of low luminosity, small size, and great density.

white elephant **1.** a rare, pale gray variety of Asian elephant held sacred by the Burmese and Siamese. **2.** anything rare but expensive to keep. **3.** any burdensome possession.

white flag **1.** a flag of truce. **2.** a white flag hoisted as a signal of surrender.

white gold gold alloyed with another metal to give it a whitish appearance.

white goods household linens, such as sheets, towels, etc.

white·head (HWĪT HED) *n.* a white nodule on the skin containing secretions of an oil gland.

white heat 1. the temperature at which a body becomes incandescent. **2.** great excitement, intense emotion, etc. —**white hot** (HWĪT HOT) *adj.*

White House, the 1. the official residence of the President of the U.S., at Washington, D.C. **2.** the executive branch of the U.S. government; also the **Oval Office**.

white matter *Anat.* the portion of the brain and spinal cord composed mainly of nerve fibers, giving it a white appearance.

white meat the light-colored meat or flesh of animals, as veal or the breast of turkey.

whit·en (HWĪT n) *v.t. & v.i.* make or become white; blanch; bleach. —**whit'en·er** *n.*

white pine 1. a pine widely distributed in eastern North America, with soft, bluish green leaves in clusters of five. **2.** the light, soft wood of this tree.

white sale a sale of sheets, towels, etc. at reduced prices.

white sauce a sauce made of butter, flour, milk, etc., used for vegetables, meats, and fish.

white slave a woman forced into or held in prostitution. —**white slaver** —**white slavery**

white·wash (HWĪT WOSH) *n.* **1.** a mixture of slaked lime and water, sometimes with salt, whiting, and glue added, used for whitening walls etc. **2.** a covering up of reprehensible actions. **3.** *Informal* in sports, a defeat in which the loser fails to score. — *v.t.* **1.** coat with whitewash. **2.** cover up; hide. **3.** *Informal* in sports, defeat without allowing the losing side to score. —**white' ·wash'er** *n.*

white water rapids in a river.

whith·er (HWITH ər) *adv.* **1.** to what place? Where? **2.** to what point, end, extent, etc.? —*conj.* to which or whatever place, end, etc. [ME]

whit·ing[1] (HWĪ ting) *n.* a pure white chalk, powdered and washed, used in making putty and whitewash, as a pigment, and for polishing.

whit·ing[2] *n.* any of several unrelated light or silvery food fishes. [ME]

whit·ish (HWĪ tish) *adj.* somewhat white or, esp., very light gray. —**whit'ish·ness** *n.*

whit·low (HWIT loh) *n. Pathol.* an inflammatory tumor, esp. on the last joint of a finger; a felon. [ME *whitflowe*]

whit·tle (HWIT l) *v.* **·tled, ·tling** *v.t.* **1.** cut or shave bits from (wood, a stick, etc.). **2.** make or shape by carving or whittling. **3.** reduce by or as by cutting away a little at a time. —*v.i.* **4.** whittle wood. [ME] —**whit' tler** *n.*

whiz (hwiz) *v.* **whizzed, whiz·zing** *v.i.* **1.** make a high-pitched humming or hissing sound while passing through the air. **2.** move or pass with such a sound. **3.** move rapidly: She *whizzed* by. —*v.t.* **3.** cause to whiz. —*n. pl.* **whiz·zes 1.** a whizzing sound. **2.** *Informal* any person or thing of extraordinary excellence or ability.

who (hoo) *pron. possessive case* **whose;** *objective case* **whom 1.** which or what person or persons: *Who* said that? I know *who* he is. *Whom* did you give it to? **2.** that: Did you see the person *who* left? **3.** he, she, or they that; whoever: *Who* steals my purse steals trash. [ME]

who·dun·it (hoo DUN it) *n. Informal* a detective story, movie, or play.

who·ev·er (hoo EV ər) *pron.* anyone that; who; no matter who. [ME]

whole (hohl) *adj.* **1.** containing all the parts necessary to make up a total; entire. **2.** having all the essential or original parts intact. **3.** in sound health; hale. **4.** constituting the full extent or amount; entire. **5.** *Math.* of or relating to an integer. —*n.* **1.** all the parts making up a thing; totality. **2.** an organization of parts making a unity. —**on the whole** taking everything into consideration. [ME *hole*] —**whole'ness** *n.*

whole blood blood as taken directly from the body, esp. that used in transfusions.

whole·heart·ed (HOHL HAHR tid) *adj.* done or experienced with earnestness, sincerity, etc.; earnest. —**whole'heart'ed·ly** *adv.*

whole note *Music* a note having a time value equal to four quarter notes.

whole number *Math.* an integer.

whole·sale (HOHL SAYL) *n.* the sale of goods for resale: distinguished from *retail.* —*adj.* **1.** pertaining to the sale of goods at wholesale. **2.** made or done on a large scale or indiscriminately: *wholesale* murder. —*adv.* **1.** in bulk or quantity. **2.** without discrimination; indiscriminately. [ME] —*v.t. & v.i.* **·saled, ·sal·ing** sell at wholesale. —**whole'sal'er** *n.*

whole·some (HOHL səm) *adj.* **1.** tending to promote health. **2.** favorable to virtue and well-being. **3.** indicative of health: *wholesome* red cheeks: **4.** free from danger or risk. [ME *holsom*] **—whole′some·ly** *adv.* **—whole′·some·ness** *n.*

whole-wheat (HOHL HWEET) *adj.* made from the entire wheat kernel.

who'll (hool) **1.** who will. **2.** who shall.

whol·ly (HOH lee) *adv.* **1.** completely; totally. **2.** exclusively; only.

whom (hoom) *pron.* the objective case of WHO: *Whom* did you see?

whom·ev·er (hoom EV ər), **whom·so·ev·er** (HOOM soh EV ər) objective cases of WHOEVER, WHOSOEVER.

whoop (huup) *v.i.* **1.** utter loud cries. **2.** hoot, as an owl. **3.** inhale loudly, as after a fit of coughing. **—***v.t.* **4.** utter with whoops. **5.** call, urge, chase, etc. with whoops. [ME *whopen*] **—***n.* the cry, shout, or sound of one who or that which whoops. **—***interj.* an exclamation of joy, enthusiasm, etc.

whooping cough (HUUP ing) *Pathol.* a respiratory disease affecting children, marked in its final stage by violent coughing.

whop·per (HWOP ər) *n. Informal* something large or remarkable; esp., a big falsehood.

whop·ping (HWOP ing) *adj.* unusually large; great.

whore (hor) *n.* a prostitute. [ME] **—***v.i.* **whored, whor·ing 1.** have illicit sexual intercourse, esp. with a prostitute. **2.** be a whore. **—whor′ish** *adj.* **—whor′ish·ly** *adv.* **—whor′ish·ness** *n.*

whorl (hworl) *n.* **1.** a set of leaves etc. radiating from a common center. **2.** a spiral curve or convolution, as of a shell or of the ridges of a fingerprint. [ME *whorle*] **—whorled** *adj.*

whose (hooz) *pron.* the possessive case of WHO and often of WHICH. [ME *whos*]

whose·so·ev·er (HOOZ soh EV ər) the possessive case of WHOSOEVER.

who·so·ev·er (HOO soh EV ər) *pron.* any person whatever; who; whoever.

why (hwī) *adv.* for what cause, purpose, or reason. **—***n. pl.* **whys 1.** an explanatory cause. **2.** a puzzling problem; riddle; enigma. **—***interj.* an expletive, sometimes denoting surprise: *Why,* if it isn't Mrs. Jones! [ME]

wick (wik) *n.* a twist of fibers that draws fuel to a flame. [ME *wicke*]

wick·ed (WIK id) *adj.* **·er, ·est 1.** evil in principle and practice; vicious; sinful. **2.** mischievous; roguish. **3.** noxious; pernicious. **4.** troublesome; painful. **5.** *Slang* done with great skill: a *wicked* game. [ME *wikked*] **—wick′ed·ly** *adv.* **—wick′ed·ness** *n.*

wick·er (WIK ər) *adj.* made of twigs etc. **—***n.* **1.** a pliant young shoot or rod; twig. **2.** wickerwork. [ME]

wick·er·work (WIK ər WURK) *n.* work woven of twigs etc.; basketwork.

wick·et (WIK it) *n.* **1.** a small door or gate, esp. one that is part of a larger entrance. **2.** a small gate in a canal lock that regulates the flow of water. **3.** in cricket, three posts with two crosspieces laid over the top; also, the playing field: a sticky *wicket*. **4.** in croquet, a wire arch. [ME *wiket*]

wick·i·up (WIK ee UP) *n.* **1.** a hut of nomadic Indians of the SW U.S., consisting of a frame covered with grass, brush, etc. **2.** any crude hut. [< Algonquian *wikiyap*]

wide (wid) *adj.* **wid·er, wid·est 1.** having relatively great extent between sides; broad. **2.** extended in every direction; spacious: a *wide* expanse. **3.** having a specified degree of width: an inch *wide*. **4.** distant from the desired point: *wide* of the mark. **5.** having intellectual breadth; liberal: a man of *wide* views. **6.** fully open: *wide* eyes. [ME] **—***n.* **1.** in cricket, a ball bowled beyond the batsman's reach. **2.** breadth of extent; also, a broad, open space. **—***adv.* **1.** to a great distance; extensively. **2.** far from the mark. **3.** fully: *wide* open. **—wide′ly** *adv.* **—wide′·ness** *n.*

wide-an·gle (WĪD ANG gəl) *adj. Photog.* of or pertaining to a lens having an angle of view wider than that of the ordinary lens.

wide-a·wake (WĪD ə WAYK) *adj.* **1.** fully awake. **2.** marked by vigilance; keen.

wide-eyed (WĪD ID) *adj.* with the eyes wide open, as in wonder or surprise.

wid·en (WĪD n) *v.t. & v.i.* make or become wide or wider. **—wid′en·er** *n.*

wide-o·pen (WĪD OH pən) *adj.* **1.** opened wide. **2.** lacking laws or failing to enforce laws that regulate gambling etc.: a *wide-open* county.

wide·spread (WĪD SPRED) *adj.* **1.** extending over a large space or territory. **2.** occurring or accepted among many people; general: a *widespread* belief.

wid·ow (WID oh) *n.* **1.** a woman whose husband is dead and who has not married again. **2.** in some card games, an additional hand dealt to the table; also, a kitty. **3.** *Printing* an incomplete line of type at the top of a page or column. [ME *widewe*] —*v.t.* make a widow of; deprive of a husband. —**wid'ow·hood** *n.*

wid·ow·er (WID oh ər) *n.* a man whose wife is dead and who has not married again. [ME]

width (width) *n.* **1.** dimension or measurement of an object taken from side to side. **2.** the state or fact of being wide; breadth. **3.** something that has width; esp., one of the several pieces of material used in making a garment.

wield (weeld) *v.t.* **1.** handle, as a weapon or instrument, esp. with full command and effect. **2.** exercise (authority, power, etc.). [ME *welden* control] —**wield'er** *n.*

wield·y (WEEL dee) *adj.* **wield·i·er, wield·i·est** easily handled or managed; manageable.

wie·ner (WEE nər) *n.* **1.** a sausage made of beef and pork. **2.** frankfurter. [Short for G *Wiener Wurst* Viennese sausage]

wife (wīf) *n. pl.* **wives** (wīvz) a married woman. [ME *wif*] —**wife·hood** (WĪF huud) *n.* —**wife'ly** *adj.*

wig (wig) *n.* an artificial covering of hair for the head.

wig·gle (WIG əl) *v.t. & v.i.* **·gled, ·gling** move or cause to move quickly and irregularly from side to side; squirm; wriggle. [ME *wiglen*] —**wig'gle** *n.* —**wig'gly** *adj.* **·gli·, ·gli·est**

wig·gler (WIG lər) *n.* **1.** one who or that which wiggles. **2.** the larva of a mosquito.

wig·wag (WIG WAG) *v.t. & v.i.* **·wagged, ·wag·ging** send (a message) by moving hand flags, lights, etc. according to a code. —*n.* the act of wigwagging; also, a message so sent. —**wig'wag'ger** *n.*

wig·wam (WIG wom) *n.* a dwelling or lodge of the North American Indians, commonly an arch-shaped framework of poles covered with bark, hides, etc. [< Algonquian (Ojibwa) *wikwam* house]

wild (wīld) *adj.* **·er, ·est 1.** not domesticated or tamed. **2.** growing or produced without care or cultivation. **3.** uninhabited and uncultivated: *wild* prairies. **4.** living in a primitive or savage way; uncivilized. **5.** boisterous; unruly. **6.** stormy; turbulent: a *wild* night, a *wild* crowd. **7.** showing reckless want of judgment; extravagant: *wild* speculation. **8.** fantastically irregular or disordered; odd in arrangement or effect: a *wild* imagination, *wild* dress. **9.** being or going far from the proper course; erratic: a *wild* guess. **10.** in some card games, having (a card's) value arbitrarily determined by the dealer or holder. [ME *wilde*] —*n. Often pl.* an uninhabited and uncultivated place; wilderness: the *wilds* of Africa. —*adv.* in a wild manner: without control. —**wild'ly** *adv.* —**wild'·ness** *n.*

wild·cat (WĪLD KAT) *n.* **1.** any of various wild felines. **2.** an aggressive quick-tempered person, esp. a woman. **3.** a successful oil well drilled in an area previously unproductive. **4.** a tricky or unsound business venture; esp., a worthless mine. —*adj.* **1.** financially unsound or risky. **2.** illegal. —*v.t. & v.i.* **·cat·ted, ·cat·ting** drill for oil in (an area of unknown productivity).

wildcat strike a strike unauthorized by regular union procedure.

wild·cat·ter (WĪLD KAT ər) *n.* **1.** a promoter of mines of doubtful value. **2.** one who develops oil wells in unproved territory.

wil·de·beest (WIL də BEEST) *n.* gnu. [< Afrikaans *wildebees*]

wil·der·ness (WIL dər nis) *n.* an uninhabited, uncultivated, or barren region. [ME]

wild·fire (WĪLD FIR) *n.* a raging, destructive fire: now generally in the phrase **spread like wildfire.**

wild·flow·er (WĪLD FLOW ər) *n.* any uncultivated flowering plant; also, the flower of such a plant. Also **wild flower.**

wild·fowl (WĪLD FOWL) *n.* a game bird, esp. a wild duck or goose.

wild-goose chase (WĪLD GOOS) **1.** an absurd pursuit of the unknown or unattainable. **2.** a hopeless undertaking.

wild·life (WĪLD LIF) *n.* living things that are not human or domesticated, esp. those that are hunted for sport, food, or profit.

wild oat 1. *Usually pl.* an uncultivated grass, esp. a common species of Europe. **2.** *pl.* indiscretions of youth: usu. in the expression **sow one's wild oats.**

wild pitch in baseball, an error charged to a pitcher for throwing a pitch that the catcher cannot be expected to catch.

wild rice the grain of a tall aquatic grass of North America.

wild·wood (WĪLD WUUD) *n.* a forest.

wile (wīl) *n.* **1.** a means of cunning deception; also, any beguiling trick or artifice. **2.** craftiness; cunning. [ME] —*v.t.* **wiled,**

wil·ing 1. lure, beguile, or mislead. **2.** pass divertingly, as time: usu. with *away*.

wil·ful (WIL fəl) see WILLFUL.

will¹ (wil) *n.* **1.** the power of conscious, deliberate action or choice. **2.** the act or experience of exercising this power. **3.** strong determination; also, self-control. **4.** that which is wanted, chosen, or determined upon: What is your *will*? **5.** *Law* the legal document declaring a person's intentions as to the disposal of his or her estate after death. [ME *wille*] —*v.* willed, will·ing *v.t.* **1.** decide upon; choose. **2.** determine upon as an action or course. **3.** give, devise, or bequeath by a will. —*v.i.* **4.** exercise the will. —**will'a·ble** *adj.*

will² *v.* present: *1st & 2nd person sing.* **will;** *Archaic 2nd person sing.* **wilt;** past: **would;** *1st & Archaic 2nd person sing.* **wouldst;** an auxiliary verb used to express: **1.** futurity: They *will* arrive by dark. **2.** willingness: Why *will* you not tell the truth? **3.** capability or capacity: The ship *will* survive any storm. **4.** custom or habit: He *will* sit for hours and brood. **5.** probability or inference: I expect this *will* be the main street. —*v.t. & v.i.* wish or have a wish; desire: As you *will*. [ME *willen*]

willed (wild) *adj.* having a will, esp. one of a given character: usu. in combination: *strong-willed*.

will·ful (WIL fəl) *adj.* **1.** determined to have one's own way; headstrong. **2.** resulting from the exercise of one's own will; voluntary; intentional. Also *wilful*. [ME] —**will'ful·ly** *adv.* —**will'ful·ness** *n.*

will·ing (WIL ing) *adj.* **1.** having the mind favorably disposed. **2.** answering to demand or requirement; compliant. **3.** gladly offered or done; hearty. **4.** of or pertaining to the power of choice; volitional. —**will'ing·ly** *adv.* —**will'ing·ness** *n.*

will-o'-the-wisp (WIL ə *th*ə WISP) *n.* **1.** ignis fatuus. **2.** any elusive or deceptive object. —*adj.* deceptive; fleeting; misleading. [Earlier *Will* (William) *with the wisp*]

wil·low (WIL oh) *n.* **1.** any of various shrubs and trees having smooth, often supple branches. **2.** the soft white wood of the willow. [ME *wilwe*] —**wil'low·like** *adj.*

wil·low·y (WIL ə wee) *adj.* **·low·i·er, ·low·i·est 1.** abounding in willows. **2.** having supple grace of form or carriage.

will·pow·er (WIL POW ər) *n.* ability to control oneself; strength or firmness of mind.

wil·ly-nil·ly (WIL ee NIL ee) *adv.* **1.** slop-

pily. **2.** willingly or unwillingly. —*adj.* **1.** sloppy. **2.** vacillating. [Earlier *will ye, nill ye* whether you will or not]

wilt¹ (wilt) *v.i.* **1.** lose freshness; droop or wither. **2.** lose energy and vitality; become faint. —*v.t.* **3.** cause to droop or wither. **4.** cause to lose energy and vitality. [ME *welken*] —*n. Bot.* any of several plant diseases marked by a wilting of the leaves.

wilt² archaic second person singular, present tense of WILL²: used with *thou*.

wil·y (WĪ lee) *adj.* **wil·i·er, wil·i·est** full of or characterized by wiles; sly; cunning. —**wi'li·ness** *n.*

wim·ple (WIM pəl) *n.* a cloth worn by women over the head and under the chin, now used only by nuns. [ME] —*v.* **·pled, ·pling** *v.t.* **1.** cover or clothe with a wimple; veil. —*v.i.* **2.** lie in plaits or folds.

win (win) *v.* **won, win·ning** *v.i.* **1.** gain a victory. **2.** succeed in an effort or endeavor. —*v.t.* **3.** gain victory in; succeed in: *win* an argument. **4.** gain by effort, as in a competition or contest: *win* a gold medal. **5.** obtain the good will or favor of: She *won* him over. **6.** secure the love of; gain in marriage: He wooed and *won* her. **7.** capture; take possession of. **8.** earn, as a living. [ME *winnen*] —*n.* **1.** a victory; success. **2.** profit; winnings. **3.** the first position in a race.

wince (wins) *v.i.* **winced, winc·ing** shrink back or start aside, as from a blow or pain; flinch. [ME *winsen*] —*n.*

winch (winch) *n.* **1.** a device used for hoisting, as on a crane, having usu. one or more hand cranks geared to a drum. **2.** a crank with a handle, used to impart motion to a grindstone or the like. [ME *winche*] —**winch'er** *n.*

wind¹ (wind) *n.* **1.** a movement of air. **2.** air pervaded by a scent: The deer got *wind* of the hunter. **3.** a suggestion or intimation: get *wind* of a plot. **4.** the power of breathing; breath. **5.** idle chatter. **6.** *pl.* the wind instruments of an orchestra. **7.** the gaseous product of indigestion; flatulence. —**in the wind** impending. —*v.t.* **wind·ed, wind·ing 1.** follow by scent. **2.** exhaust the breath of, as by running. **3.** enable to recover breath by resting. **4.** expose to the wind, as in ventilating.

wind² (wīnd) *v.* **wound, wind·ing** *v.t.* **1.** coil (thread, rope, etc.) around some object. **2.** cover with something by coiling or wrapping: *wind* a spool with thread. **3.** renew the motion of, as a clock, by coiling a spring etc.

4. cause to turn and twist. **5.** make (one's way) by a twisting course. **6.** introduce deviously; insinuate: He *wound* himself into my confidence. **7.** raise or hoist, as by means of a windlass. —*v.i.* **8.** move in a twisting course; meander. **9.** coil or twine about some object. **10.** proceed carefully or deviously. —**wind up 1.** bring to conclusion or settlement. **2.** in baseball, swing the arm preparatory to pitching. [ME *winden*] —*n.* the act of winding, or the condition of being wound; a winding, turn, or twist. —**wind′er** *n.*

wind•age (WIN dij) *n.* **1.** the rush of air caused by the rapid passage of an object. **2.** the deflection of an object, as a bullet, from its natural course because of wind pressure.

wind•bag (WIND BAG) *n. Informal* a wordy talker.

wind•break (WIND BRAYK) *n.* something, as a hedge or fence, that protects from the force of the wind.

wind•burn (WIND BURN) *n.* irritation of the skin, produced by exposure to wind. —**wind′burned′** *adj.*

wind•chill factor (WIND CHIL.) the temperature of still air adjusted for the chilling effect of wind.

wind•fall (WIND FAWL) *n.* **1.** an unexpected or sudden gain. **2.** something, as ripening fruit, brought down by the wind.

wind•ing (WĪN ding) *n.* **1.** the act or condition of one who or that which winds. **2.** a bend or turn, or a series of them. —*adj.* **1.** turning spirally about an axis or core. **2.** having bends or turns. —**wind′ing•ly** *adv.*

winding sheet (WĪN ding) the sheet that wraps a corpse.

wind instrument (WIND) a musical instrument whose sounds are produced by vibrations of air blown into it.

wind•jam•mer (WIND JAM ər) *n.* **1.** *Naut.* a merchant sailing vessel. **2.** a member of its crew.

wind•lass (WIND ləs) *n.* a device for hauling or lifting, esp. one consisting of a drum, turned by a crank, on which the hoisting rope winds. [ME *windelas*] —*v.t. & v.i.* raise or haul with a windlass.

wind•mill (WIND MIL) *n.* a mill that operates by the action of the wind against slats or sails attached to a horizontal axis. [ME]

win•dow (WIN doh) *n.* **1.** an opening in the wall of a building to admit light and air, commonly equipped with movable sashes that enclose one or more panes of glass. **2.** a

windowpane. **3.** anything resembling or suggesting a window. —*v.t.* provide with a window or windows. [ME *windowe*]

window dressing *n.* **1.** the art of displaying merchandise in a store window. **2.** anything created to make something else seem better than it really is. —**win′dow dress′er** *n.*

win•dow•pane (WIN doh PAYN) *n.* a sheet of glass for a window.

win•dow•shop (WIN doh SHOP) *v.i.* **-shopped, -shop•ping** look at goods in store windows without buying them. —**win′dow-shop′per** *n.*

wind•pipe (WIND PĪP) *n.* trachea.

wind•row (WIND ROH) *n.* **1.** a long row of hay or grain raked together to dry. **2.** a windswept line of dust, surf, leaves, etc. —*v.t.* rake or shape into a windrow.

wind•shield (WIND SHEELD) *n.* a transparent screen in front of the occupants of an automobile or truck that protects against wind and weather.

wind•sock (WIND SOK) *n. Meteorol.* a conical bag mounted at an airport etc. to indicate the direction of the wind. Also **wind sleeve.**

wind•storm (WIND STORM) *n.* a violent wind with little or no precipitation.

wind tunnel (wind) *Aeron.* a large cylindrical structure in which the aerodynamic properties of airplane models, airfoils, etc. can be observed under the effects of artificially produced winds.

wind•up (WĪND UP) *n.* **1.** the act of concluding or closing; conclusion; finish. **2.** in baseball, the swing of the arm preparatory to pitching the ball.

wind•ward (WIND wərd) *adj.* moving toward or situated on the side facing the wind. —*n.* the direction from which the wind blows. —*adv.* toward the wind. Opposed to *leeward.*

wind•y (WIN dee) *adj.* **wind•i•er, wind•i•est 1.** having or exposed to much wind. **2.** long-winded; verbose; bombastic. [ME] —**wind′i•ly** *adv.* —**wind′i•ness** *n.*

wine (wīn) *n.* **1.** the fermented juice of the grape, commonly used as a beverage and in cooking. **2.** the fermented juice of some other fruit or plant. **3.** a dark purplish red, the color of certain wines. [ME] —*v.t. & v.i.* wined, win•ing entertain with or drink wine. —**wine and dine** entertain or feed in a lavish way.

wine cellar a storage place for wines; also, the wines stored.

wine-col·ored (WĪN KUL ərd) *adj.* having the color of red wine; dark purplish red.

wine·grow·er (WĪN GROH ər) *n.* one who cultivates a vineyard and makes wine. —**wine′grow′ing** *adj. & n.*

wine press *n.* an apparatus or a place where the juice of grapes is expressed. Also **wine presser.**

win·er·y (WĪ nə ree) *n. pl.* **·er·ies** an establishment for making wine.

wing (wing) *n.* **1.** an organ of flight; esp., one of a pair of movable appendages of a bird, bat, or insect. **2.** anything resembling a wing, as in form, function, or position. **3.** the act or means of flying; flight. **4.** either of two opposed groups in a political or other organization: the left *wing.* **5.** *Archit.* an extension of a building. **6.** *Aeron.* one of the main sustaining surfaces of an airplane. **7.** in a theater, one of the two sides of the stage not seen by an audience. **8.** *Mil.* the right or left section of a military force. **9.** a tactical and administrative unit of the U.S. Air Force. **10.** *Slang* an arm, esp. in baseball. **11.** in hockey, a position on either side of the center. —**on** (or **upon**) **the wing 1.** in flight. **2.** departing; also, journeying. —**under one's wing** under one's protection. [ME *winge*] —*v.t.* **1.** pass over or through in flight. **2.** accomplish by flying. **3.** cause to go swiftly; speed. **4.** wound in the wing or arm. —*v.i.* **5.** fly; soar. —**wing it** *Informal* improvise. —**wing′less** *adj.*

wing chair a large upholstered arm chair with high back and side pieces.

winged (wingd) *adj.* **1.** having wings. **2.** swift. **3.** (WING id) lofty.

wing·spread (WING SPRED) *n.* the distance between the tips of the fully extended wings of a bird, insect, or airplane. Also **wing′span** (-SPAN).

wink (wingk) *v.i.* **1.** close and open the eye or eyelids quickly. **2.** move one eyelid as a sign. **3.** pretend not to see: usu. with *at.* **4.** flicker; twinkle. —*v.t.* **5.** close and open (the eye or eyelids) quickly. [ME *winken*] —*n.* **1.** the act of winking. **2.** a short time. **3.** a twinkle; gleam. **4.** a hint conveyed by winking.

win·ner (WIN ər) *n.* one who or that which wins; victor.

win·ning (WIN ing) *adj.* **1.** successful in competition. **2.** charming; attractive; winsome. —*n.* **1.** the act of one who wins. **2.** *Usu. pl.* that which is won; esp. money won in gambling.

win·now (WIN oh) *v.t.* **1.** separate (grain)

from (chaff). **2.** select or sort: often with *out.* —*v.i.* **3.** separate grain from chaff. —*n.* any device used in winnowing grain. [ME *winewen*] —**win′now·er** *n.*

win·some (WIN səm) *adj.* charming or pleasing; attractive. [ME *winsum*] —**win′·some·ly** *adv.* —**win′some·ness** *n.*

win·ter (WIN tər) *n.* **1.** the coldest season of the year, occurring between autumn and spring. **2.** a period of time marked by coldness, cheerlessness, or lack of life: the *winter* of my life. —*v.i.* **1.** pass the winter. —*v.t.* **2.** care for, feed, or protect during the winter: *winter* animals. —*adj.* **1.** of or taking place in winter: *winter* sports. **2.** suitable to or characteristic of winter. [ME]

win·ter·green (WIN tər GREEN) *n.* **1.** a small evergreen plant of North America, bearing aromatic oval leaves that yield an oil (**oil of wintergreen**) used as a flavor. **2.** the flavor of this oil.

win·ter·ize (WIN tə RĪZ) *v.t.* **·ized, ·iz·ing** prepare or equip (engines etc.) for winter.

win·ter·kill (WIN tər KIL) *v.t. & v.i.* die or kill by exposure to extreme cold: said of plants and grains.

win·try (WIN tree) *adj.* **·tri·er, ·tri·est** of or like winter; cold; frosty. Also **win·ter·y** (WIN tə ree). [< OE *wintrig*] —**win′tri·ness** *n.*

win·y (WĪ nee) *adj.* **win·i·er, win·i·est** having the taste or qualities of wine.

wipe (wīp) *v.t.* **wiped, wip·ing 1.** clean or dry by rubbing, usu. with some soft, absorbent material. **2.** remove by or as if by rubbing: usu. with *away* or *off.* **3.** apply by wiping: usu. with *on.* **4.** draw or pass across. —**wipe out** remove or destroy utterly. [ME *wipen*] —*n.* the act of wiping or rubbing. —**wip′er** *n.*

wire (wīr) *n.* **1.** a strand of ductile metal. **2.** something made of wire, as a fence, a snare, etc. **3.** a telegraph or telephone cable. **4.** the telegraph system: sent by *wire.* **5.** a telegram. [ME] —*v.* **wired, wir·ing** *v.t.* **1.** fasten with wire. **2.** furnish or equip with wiring. **3.** transmit or send by electric telegraph: *wire* an order. **4.** send a telegram to. —*v.i.* **5.** telegraph. —**wire·less** (WĪR lis) *adj.*

wire service a news agency that collects and distributes news to subscribing newspapers, radio stations, etc.

wire·tap·ping (WĪR TAP ing) *n.* the act, process, or practice of tapping telephone or telegraph wires for the purpose of secretly

securing information: also called *wiretap.*
—**wire′tap′** *v.t. & v.i.* **•tapped, •tap•ping**
—**wire′tap′per** *n.*

wir•ing (WĪR ing) *n.* an entire system of
wire installed for the distribution of electric
power.

wir•y (WĪR ee) *adj.* **wir•i•er, wir•i•est 1.**
tough and sinewy. **2.** like wire; stiff. —**wir′**
i•ly *adv.* —**wir′i•ness** *n.*

wis•dom (WIZ dəm) *n.* **1.** knowledge; learning. **2.** practical judgment; insight; common
sense. [ME]

wisdom tooth the last molar tooth on either
side of the upper and lower jaws in humans.

wise[1] (wīz) *adj.* **wis•er, wis•est 1.** possessed
of or marked by wisdom. **2.** sagacious;
shrewd; crafty. **3.** *Slang* aware of; onto: *wise*
to his motives. **4.** *Slang* arrogant or sarcastic. [ME *wis*] —**wise′ly** *adv.*

wise[2] *n.* way of doing; manner; method:
chiefly in such phrases as **in any wise, in
no wise,** etc. [ME]

-wise *suffix of adverbs* in a (specified) way or
manner: *nowise, likewise:* often equivalent
to *-ways.*

wise•a•cre (WĪZ AY kər) *n.* one who affects
great wisdom. [< MDu. *wijsseger* sooth-
sayer]

wise•crack (WĪZ KRAK) *Informal n.* a facetious or supercilious remark. —*v.i.* utter a
wisecrack. —**wise′crack′er** *n.*

wise guy 1. a cocky, conceited person; smart
aleck. **2.** a gangster, esp. in organized
crime.

wish (wish) *n.* **1.** a desire or longing, usu. for
some definite thing. **2.** an expression of
such a desire. **3.** something wished for. —
v.t. **1.** have a desire or longing for; want. **2.**
invoke upon or for someone: I *wished* him
good luck. **3.** request or entreat; also, command: I *wish* you would be quiet. —*v.i.* **4.**
have or feel a desire; yearn; long: usu. with
for. **5.** make or express a wish. [ME *wiss-
hen*]

wish•ful (WISH fəl) *adj.* having a wish or
desire; full of longing. —**wish′ful•ly** *adv.*
—**wish′ful•ness** *n.*

wish•y-wash•y (WISH ee WOSH ee) *adj.*
lacking character or resolution; indecisive;
weak.

wisp (wisp) *n.* **1.** a small bunch, as of hair. **2.** a
small bit: *a wisp* of vapor. [ME] —**wisp′y**
adj. **wisp•i•er, wisp•i•est.**

wist (wist) past tense, past participle of WIT[2].

wis•te•ri•a (wi STEER ee ə) *n.* any of various woody twining shrubs with clusters of

blue, purple, or white flowers. Also
wis•tar′i•a (wi STEER ee ə). [< NL]

wist•ful (WIST fəl) *adj.* wishful; longing;
yearning. —**wist′ful•ly** *adv.* —**wist′ful•**
ness *n.*

wit[1] (wit) *n.* **1.** the power of knowing, perceiving, or judging. **2.** *pl.* the faculties of
perception and understanding. **3.** *pl.* one's
sanity: out of her *wits.* **4.** the perception and
expression of amusing relations among
ideas. **5.** one who is cleverly amusing. [ME]

wit[2] *v.t. & v.i.* **wist, wit•ting** present indicative: I **wot,** thou **wost,** he **wot,** we, you,
they **wot** or **wite** *Archaic* be or become
aware (of); learn; know. [ME *witen* know]
—**to wit** that is to say; namely.

witch (wich) *n.* **1.** a woman who practices
sorcery or is believed to have supernatural
powers, esp. to work evil, and usu. by association with evil spirits or the devil. **2.** an
ugly, malignant old woman; hag. **3.** a be-
witching woman. [ME *wicche*]

witch•craft (WICH KRAFT) *n.* **1.** the practices or powers of witches or wizards: also
called *black magic.* **2.** extraordinary influence or fascination.

witch doctor a person in a primitive society
who uses magic to exorcise evil spirits as a
means of curing sickness.

witch•er•y (WICH ə ree) *n. pl.* **•er•ies 1.**
witchcraft. **2.** power to charm; fascination.

witch hazel 1. a shrub with several branching trunks and small yellow flowers. **2.** an
ointment and extract derived from the bark
and dried leaves of this shrub.

witch hunt an intensive investigation of persons ostensibly to uncover subversive or
disloyal activities, but intended to harass
political or ideological opponents. —
witch-hunt (WICH HUNT) *v.t.* subject to a
witch hunt. —**witch hunt•er** *n.*

with (with) *prep.* **1.** in the company of. **2.**
next to; beside: Walk *with* me. **3.** having: a
hat *with* a feather. **4.** characterized by: the
house *with* green shutters. **5.** among:
counted *with* the others. **6.** in the course of:
We forget *with* time. **7.** separated from:
dispense *with* luxury. **8.** against: struggle
with an adversary. **9.** in the opinion of: That
is all right *with* me. **10.** because of: faint
with hunger. **11.** in possession of: Leave the
key *with* the janitor. **12.** by means of: write
with a pencil. **13.** by adding: trimmed *with*
lace. **14.** in spite of: *With* all her money, she
could not buy health. **15.** at the same time
as: go to bed *with* the chickens. **16.** in the

same direction as: drift *with* the crowd. **17.** in regard to: I am angry *with* them. **18.** onto; to: Join this tube *with* that one. **19.** in proportion to: His fame grew *with* his deeds. **20.** of the same opinion as: I'm *with* you to the end. **21.** compared to: Consider this book *with* that one. **22.** immediately after: *With* that, he slammed the door. **23.** having received or been granted: *With* your consent I'll go. [ME, against]

with- *combining form* **1.** against: *withstand.* **2.** back; away: *withhold.*

with·al (with AWL) *adv.* with the rest; in addition. —*prep.* with: used after its object: a bow to shoot *withal.* [ME *with al* with all]

with·draw (with DRAW) *v.* **·drew, ·drawn, ·draw·ing** *v.t.* **1.** draw or take away; remove. **2.** take back, as a promise. —*v.i.* **3.** draw back; retire. —**with·draw′al** *n.*

with·drawn (with DRAWN) *adj.* lacking in emotional responsiveness.

with·er (WITH ər) *v.i.* **1.** become limp or dry, as a plant deprived of moisture. **2.** waste, as flesh. **3.** droop or languish. —*v.t.* **4.** cause to become limp or dry. **5.** abash, as by a scornful glance. [ME]

with·ers (WITH ərz) *n. pl.* the highest part of the back of the horse between the shoulder blades.

with·hold (with HOHLD) *v.t.* **·held, ·hold·ing 1.** hold back; restrain. **2.** keep back; decline to grant. **3.** deduct (taxes, social security payments, etc.) from one's wages. [ME *withholden*] —**with·hold′er** *n.*

withholding tax a part of an employee's earnings that is deducted as an installment on income tax and paid directly to the tax authorities.

with·in (with IN) *prep.* **1.** in the inner part of; inside. **2.** in the limits, range, or compass of: *within* two hours. **3.** in the reach, limit, or scope of: *within* my power. —*n.* the inside: a revolt from *within.* —*adv.* **1.** inside. **2.** indoors. **3.** inside one's mind, heart, or body. [ME *withinne*]

with·out (with OWT) *prep.* **1.** not having; lacking: They are *without* a home. **2.** in the absence of: We must manage *without* help. **3.** free from: *without* fear. **4.** at, on, or to the outside of: **5.** with avoidance of: He listened *without* paying attention. [ME *withoute*] —*adv.* **1.** in or on the outer part. **2.** out of doors.

with·stand (with STAND) *v.t.* **·stood,** **·stand·ing** oppose or resist successfully. [ME *withstanden*]

wit·less (WIT lis) *adj.* lacking in wit; foolish. [ME] —**wit′less·ly** *adv.* —**wit′less· ness** *n.*

wit·ness (WIT nis) *n.* **1.** a person who has seen or knows something, and is therefore competent to give evidence concerning it; a spectator. **2.** that which serves as evidence or proof. *Law* **a** one who has knowledge of facts relating to a case and is subpoenaed to testify. **b** a person who testifies to the genuineness of another's signature. **4.** an attestation to a fact or an event; testimony: usu. in the phrase **bear witness.** [ME *witnesse* knowledge] —*v.t.* **1.** see or know by personal experience. **2.** serve as evidence of. **3.** give testimony to. **4.** be the site or scene of: This spot has *witnessed* many heinous crimes. **5.** *Law* sign (an instrument) as a witness.

wit·ted (WIT id) *adj.* having (a specified kind of) wit or wits: used in combination: *quick-witted, slow-witted.*

wit·ti·cism (WIT ə SIZ əm) *n.* a witty remark.

wit·ting (WIT ing) *adj.* intentional; deliberate. [ME *witing*] —**wit′ting·ly** *adv.*

wit·ty (WIT ee) *adj.* **·ti·er, ·ti·est** cleverly amusing. [ME, wise] —**wit′ti·ly** *adv.* —**wit′ti·ness** *n.*

wives (wīvz) plural of WIFE.

wiz·ard (WIZ ərd) *n.* **1.** a male witch; sorcerer. **2.** a very skillful or clever person: a *wizard* with machinery. Also *wiz.* [ME *wisard*] —**wiz·ard·ry** (WIZ ər dree) *n.*

wiz·ened (WIZ ənd) *adj.* shrunken; withered; dried up.

wob·ble (WOB əl) *v.* **·bled, ·bling** *v.i.* **1.** move or sway unsteadily. **2.** show indecision; vacillate. —*v.t.* **3.** cause to wobble. [< LG *wabbeln*] —*n.* an unsteady motion. —**wob′bler** *n.* —**wob′bling·ly** *adv.* —**wob′bly** *adj.* **·bli·er, ·bli·est**

woe (woh) *n.* **1.** overwhelming sorrow; grief. **2.** great trouble or calamity; disaster. [ME *wo*] —*interj.* Alas!

woe·be·gone (WOH bi GAWN) *adj.* overcome with woe; mournful; sorrowful. [ME *wo begon*]

woe·ful (WOH fəl) *adj.* **1.** accompanied by or causing woe; direful. **2.** expressive of sorrow; doleful. **3.** paltry; miserable; mean. —**woe′ful·ly** *adv.* —**woe′ful·ness** *n.*

wok (wok) *n.* a bowl-shaped pan used in Chinese cooking. [< Cantonese *wôk*]

woke (wohk) past tense of WAKE[1].

wok•en (WOH kən) a past participle of WAKE[1].

wolf (wuulf) *n. pl.* **wolves** (wuulvz) **1.** any of numerous carnivorous mammals related to the dog. **2.** any ravenous, cruel, or rapacious person. **3.** *Informal* a man who flirts with many women. —**cry wolf** give a false alarm. [ME] —*v.t.* devour ravenously; gulp down. —**wolf'ish** *adj.* —**wolf'ish•ly** *adv.* —**wolf'ish•ness** *n.*

wol•ver•ine (WUUL və REEN) *n.* a rapacious carnivore of northern forests, with stout body and limbs and bushy tail.

wolves (wuulvz) plural of WOLF.

wom•an (WUUM ən) *n. pl.* **wom•en** (WIM in) **1.** an adult human female. **2.** women collectively. **3.** womanly character; femininity. **4.** a female servant. [ME] —**wóm'an•hood** *n.* —**wom'an•li•ness** *n.* —**wom'an•ly** *adj.*

wom•an•ish (WUUM ə nish) *adj.* **1.** characteristic of a woman; womanly. **2.** effeminate; unmanly. —**wom'an•ish•ly** *adv.* —**wom'an•ish•ness** *n.*

wom•an•ize (WUUM ə NĪZ) *v.* •**ized,** •**iz•ing** *v.t.* **1.** make effeminate or womanish. —*v.i.* **2.** habitually pursue sexual relationships with women; philander. —**wom'an•iz'er** *n.*

wom•an•kind (WUUM ən KĪND) *n.* women collectively; the female sex.

womb (woom) *n.* **1.** the uterus. **2.** the place where anything is engendered or brought into life. [ME]

wom•en (WIM in) plural of WOMAN.

wom•en•folk (WIM in FOHK) *n. (construed as pl.)* women collectively. Also **wom'en•folks'.**

won (wun) past tense, past participle of WIN.

won•der (WUN dər) *n.* **1.** a feeling of mingled surprise and curiosity; astonishment. **2.** that which causes wonder; a strange thing; a miracle. [ME] —*v.i.* **2.** be curious and doubtful about. —*v.i.* **2.** be filled with wonder; marvel. **3.** be doubtful; want to know. —**won'der•er** *n.* —**won'der•ing** *adj.* —**won'der•ing•ly** *adv.*

won•der•ful (WUN dər fəl) *adj.* astonishing; incredible; marvelous. —**won'der•ful•ly** *adv.* —**won'der•ful•ness** *n.*

won•der•land (WUN dər LAND) *n.* a real or imaginary place that is full of wonders.

won•der•ment (WUN dər mənt) *n.* **1.** the emotion of wonder; surprise. **2.** something wonderful; a marvel.

won•drous (WUN drəs) *adj.* wonderful; marvelous. —**won'•drous•ly** *adv.* —**won'drous•ness** *n.*

wont (wawnt) *adj.* accustomed; used: He is *wont* to smoke after dinner. [ME *woned*] —*n.* customary practice; habit.

won't (wohnt) will not.

wont•ed (WAWN tid) *adj.* customary; habitual. —**wont'ed•ness** *n.*

woo (woo) *v.t.* **1.** seek the love of, esp. in order to marry; court. **2.** entreat earnestly; try to win over. —*v.i.* **3.** pay court. [ME *wowen*]

wood (wuud) *n.* **1.** the hard, fibrous material beneath the bark of a tree or shrub. **2.** lumber; timber; firewood. **3.** *Often pl.* a large, dense growth of trees; forest; grove. **4.** something made of wood, as a golf club. **5.** *pl.* a rural district; backwoods. [ME] —*adj.* **1.** made of wood. **2.** made for using or holding wood. **3.** living or growing in woods. —**wood'ed** *adj.*

wood alcohol methanol.

wood•block (WUUD BLOK) *n.* **1.** a block of wood prepared for engraving. **2.** a woodcut.

wood•craft (WUUD KRAFT) *n.* **1.** skill in things pertaining to woodland life, as hunting and trapping. **2.** skill in woodwork or in constructing articles of wood.

wood•cut (WUUD KUT) *n.* **1.** a carved block of wood from which prints are made. **2.** a print from such a block. Also called *woodblock.*

wood•cut•ter (WUUD KUT ər) *n.* one who cuts or chops wood. —**wood'cut'ting** *n.*

wood•en (WUUD n) *adj.* **1.** made of wood. **2.** stiff; clumsy; awkward. **3.** dull; spiritless. —**wood'en•ly** *adv.* —**wood'en•ness** *n.*

wood•land (WUUD LAND) *n.* land covered with woods or trees. —*adj.* (WUUD lənd) belonging to or dwelling in the woods.

wood nymph a nymph of the forest; dryad.

wood•peck•er (WUUD PEK ər) *n.* any of various birds having stiff tail feathers, strong claws, and a hard, sharp bill for drilling holes in trees.

wood•pile (WUUD PĪL) *n.* a stack of split logs, for burning.

wood pulp wood reduced to pulp, used for making paper.

woods•man (WUUDZ mən) *n. pl.* •**men 1.** a woodcutter. **2.** one who works or lives in a forest. **3.** a person skilled in woodcraft. Also **wood'man.**

woods•y (WUUD zee) *adj.* **woods•i•er,**

woods•i•est of, like, or dwelling in the woods.

wood•wind (WUUD WIND) *n. Music* **1.** one of a group of wind instruments, as a clarinet, flute, etc. **2.** *pl.* the section of an orchestra made up of such instruments.

wood•work (WUUD WURK) *n.* **1.** the wooden parts of any structure, esp. interior wooden parts, as moldings or doors. **2.** work made of wood. **—wood′work•er** *n.* **—wood′•work′ing** *n.*

wood•y (WUUD ee) *adj.* **wood•i•er, wood•i•est** **1.** of the nature of or containing wood. **2.** of or like wood. **3.** covered with woods. **—wood′i•ness** *n.*

woof (wuuf) *n.* **1.** the weft; the threads carried back and forth across the fixed threads of the warp in a loom. **2.** the texture of a fabric. [ME *oof*]

woof•er (WUUF ər) *n. Electronics* a loudspeaker used to reproduce low frequencies. Compare TWEETER.

wool (wuul) *n.* **1.** the fleece of sheep and some allied animals. **2.** material or garments made of wool. **3.** any substance resembling wool. *—adj.* woolen. [ME *wolle*]

wool•en (WUUL ən) *adj.* **1.** made of or like wool. **2.** of wool or its manufacture. *—n.* **1.** any cloth or clothing made of wool. **2.** *pl.* **woolens** (WUUL ənz) garments made of wool. [ME *wollen*]

wool•gath•er•ing (WUUL GATH ər ing) *n.* idle daydreaming. **—wool′gath′er•er** *n.* **—wool′gath′er** *v.i.*

wool•ly (WUUL ee) *adj.* **•li•er, •li•est** **1.** made of, covered with, or resembling wool. **2.** lacking clearness; fuzzy; blurry. **3.** rough and exciting: usu. in the phrase **wild and woolly.** *—n. pl.* **•lies** a knitted undergarment made of wool. Also **wool′y. —wool′•li•ness** *n.*

wooz•y (WOO zee) *adj.* **wooz•i•er, wooz•i•est** befuddled, esp. with drink; dazed. **—wooz′i•ly** *adv.* **—wooz′i•ness** *n.*

word (wurd) *n.* **1.** a linguistic form that can meaningfully be spoken. **2.** the letters or characters that stand for such a linguistic form. **3.** *Usu. pl.* conversation; talk: a person of few *words.* **4.** a brief remark. **5.** a communication or message; information: Send us *word.* **6.** a command, signal, or direction: Give the *word* to begin. **7.** a promise: a woman of her *word.* **8.** a watchword. **9.** *pl.* language used in anger: They had *words.* **—in a word** in short; briefly. **—the Word** the Scriptures. **—break one's**

word violate one's promise. **—eat one's words** retract something that one has said. **—mince words** be evasive. **—word for word** in exactly the same words; verbatim. [ME] *—v.t.* express in words.

word•age (WUR dij) *n.* **1.** words collectively. **2.** the number of words used in a piece of writing.

word•ing (WUR ding) *n.* the style used to express something in words; phraseology.

word•less (WURD lis) *adj.* having no words; inarticulate; silent. [ME] **—word′less•ly** *adv.* **—word′less•ness** *n.*

word processing the use of a computer program to write, edit, and print out letters, reports, books, etc.

word•y (WUR dee) *adj.* **word•i•er, word•i•est** using or containing too many words; verbose. [ME] **—word′i•ly** *adv.* **—word′i•ness** *n.*

wore (wor) past tense of WEAR.

work (wurk) *n.* **1.** continued exertion directed to some end; labor. **2.** one's job or occupation. **3.** employment: look for *work.* **4.** a place of employment: Was she at home or at *work?* **5.** something to be done; task. **6.** that which is produced by thought and effort, as a building, book, song, etc. **7.** a feat or deed. **8. works** (*construed as sing. or pl.*) **a** an industrial plant. **b** running gear or machinery, as of a watch. **c** *Informal* the whole of anything: the whole *works.* **9.** *Physics* a transference of energy from one body to another resulting in the motion or displacement of the body acted upon, expressed as the product of the force and the amount of displacement in the line of its action. [ME *werk*] *—v.* **worked** (for *v.t.* senses 9 *and* 11 **wrought**), **work•ing** *v.i.* **1.** perform work; labor; toil. **2.** be employed in some trade or business. **3.** perform a function; operate: The machine *works* well. **4.** prove effective; succeed: His stratagem *worked.* **5.** move or progress gradually or with difficulty: He *worked* up in his profession. **6.** become as specified, as by gradual motion: The bolts *worked* loose. **7.** undergo kneading, hammering, etc.; be shaped: Copper *works* easily. **8.** ferment. *—v.t.* **9.** cause or bring about: They *wrought* miracles. **10.** direct the operation of: *work* a machine. **11.** make, shape, or decorate by toil or skill: That factory *wrought* fine products. **12.** prepare, as by manipulating, hammering, etc.: He *worked* the dough too long. **13.** cause to be productive, as by toil: *work* a mine. **14.** cause to do work: He *worked* his employees too hard. **15.** cause to be as specified, usu. with effort: We *worked* the tiny battery into position. **16.** make or achieve by effort: He *worked* his way through the narrow tunnel. **17.** solve, as a problem in arithmetic. **18.** cause to move: *work* one's jaws. **19.** excite; provoke: He *worked* himself into a passion. **20.** influence or manage, as by insidious means; lead. **—work off** get rid of, as extra weight by exercise. **—work on** (or **upon**) try to influence or persuade. **—work out 1.** make its way out or through. **2.** effect by work or effort; accomplish. **3.** develop; form, as a plan. **4.** solve. **5.** prove effective or successful. **6.** result as specified: It *worked out* badly. **7.** exercise; train. **8.** pay out (a debt) by performing work. **—work over 1.** do over; revise. **2.** *Informal* beat up severely. **—work up 1.** excite; rouse. **2.** form or shape by working; develop. [ME *werken*]

work·a·ble (WUR kə bəl) *adj.* **1.** capable of being worked. **2.** capable of being put into effect, as a plan; practicable. **— work′a·bil′i·ty, work′a·ble·ness** *n.*

work·a·day (WUR kə DAY) *adj.* **1.** of, pertaining to, or suitable for working days; everyday. **2.** commonplace; prosaic. [ME *werkeday*]

work·a·hol·ic (WURK ə HAW lik) *n.* a person seemingly addicted to working.

work·bench (WURK BENCH) *n.* a table for work, as that of a carpenter or machinist.

work·book (WURK BUUK) *n.* a booklet based on a course of study and containing problems and exercises.

work·day (WURK DAY) *n.* **1.** a day in which work is done; a day not a holiday. **2.** the part of the day spent in work.

work·er (WUR kər) *n.* **1.** one who does work for a living; esp., a laborer. **2.** a sexually undeveloped insect in a colony, as an ant or bee.

work·horse (WURK HORS) *n.* **1.** a horse used for pulling loads. **2.** a tireless worker.

work·house (WURK HOWS) *n.* a house of correction for those who are convicted of minor offenses.

work·ing (WUR king) *adj.* **1.** that works. **2.** engaged actively in some employment. **3.** that performs a function; that upon which further work may be based: a *working* model; a *working* hypothesis. **4.** relating to or used in work. **—n. 1.** the act of one who

works. **2.** a manner of functioning. **3.** *Usu. pl.* the part of a mine or quarry where excavation is going on.

working capital 1. the part of the finances of a business available for its operation. **2.** current assets minus current liabilities.

work·ing·man (WUR king MAN) *n. pl.* **•men** a man who works for wages, esp. in manual work.

work·ing·wom·an (WUR king WUUM ən) *n. pl.* **•wom·en** a woman who works for wages.

work load the amount of work apportioned to a person, machine, or department over a given period.

work·man (WURK mən) *n. pl.* **•men 1.** one whose job involves manual labor. **2.** a male worker.

work·man·like (WURK mən LIK) *adj.* skillfully done; well-made. **—work′man·ly** *adv.*

work·man·ship (WURK mən SHIP) *n.* **1.** the art or skill of a workman, or the quality of work. **2.** something made or produced.

work·out (WURK OWT) *n.* **1.** a test, trial, practice performance, etc. **2.** any activity involving considerable effort; esp., running, calisthenics, or other physical exercise.

work·shop (WURK SHOP) *n.* **1.** a building or room where any work is carried on; workroom. **2.** a seminar for discussing or studying a subject, solving problems, etc.

work·week (WURK WEEK) *n.* the number of hours worked in a week; also, the number of working hours in a week.

world (wurld) *n.* **1.** the earth. **2.** a part of the earth: the Old *World.* **3.** the universe. **4.** a division of existing things belonging to the earth: the animal *world.* **5.** the human inhabitants of the earth; humankind. **6.** a definite class of people having certain interests or activities in common: the scientific *world.* **7.** a sphere or domain: the *world* of letters. **8.** secular, social, or public life; worldly matters or aims. **9.** a great quantity or number: a *world* of troubles. **10.** any condition or state: the *world* of the future. **—world-class** *adj.* being of the highest caliber in the world: a *world-class* swimmer. **—for all the world** in every respect. **—on top of the world** elated. **—out of this world** extraordinarily good. [ME]

world·ly (WURLD lee) *adj.* **•li·er, ·li·est 1.** of or devoted to this world and its concerns rather than religious or spiritual matters;

earthly; secular. **2.** sophisticated; worldly-wise. —**world'li•ness** n.

world•ly•wise (WURLD lee WĪZ) adj. wise in the ways and affairs of the world; sophisticated.

world•wide (WURL WĪD) adj. extended throughout the world.

worm (wurm) n. **1.** a small, limbless invertebrate with an elongated, soft body. ◆ Collateral adjective: *vermicular.* **2.** loosely, any small, creeping animal having a slender body and short or undeveloped limbs, as an insect larva. **3.** a despicable, groveling, or abject person. **4.** something like a worm in appearance or movement. **5.** pl. an intestinal disorder due to the presence of parasitic worms. [ME] —v.t. **1.** insinuate (oneself or itself) in a wormlike manner: with *in* or *into.* **2.** draw forth by artful means, as a secret: with *out.* **3.** free from intestinal worms. —v.i. **4.** move or progress slowly and stealthily. **5.** insinuate oneself by artful means: with *into.*

worm-eat•en (WURM EET n) adj. **1.** eaten or bored through by worms. **2.** worn-out or decayed, as by time.

worm gear Mech. a gear formed by a toothed wheel (**worm wheel**) meshed to a rotating threaded screw (**worm screw**).

worm•hole (WURM HOHL) n. the hole made by a worm, as in wood.

worm•wood (WURM WUUD) n. **1.** any of various European herbs or small shrubs, esp. a common species that is aromatic and bitter and is used in making absinthe. **2.** that which embitters or makes bitter; bitterness. [ME *wormwode*]

worm•y (WUR mee) adj. **worm•i•er, worm•i•est 1.** infested with or injured by worms. **2.** of or like a worm. —**worm'i•ness** n.

worn (worn) past participle of WEAR. —ADJ. affected by use or any continuous action; as: **a** threadbare: a *worn* suit. **b** exhausted, as from worry, anxiety, etc.: a *worn* face. **c** hackneyed: a *worn* phrase.

worn-out (WORN OWT) adj. **1.** used until without value or effectiveness. **2.** thoroughly tired; exhausted.

wor•ri•some (WUR ee səm) adj. **1.** causing worry or anxiety. **2.** given to worry. —**wor'•ri•some•ly** adv.

wor•ry (WUR ee) v. **•ried, •ry•ing** v.i. **1.** be uneasy in the mind; fret. **2.** pull or tear at something with the teeth: with *at.* —v.t. **3.** cause to feel uneasy in the mind; trouble. **4.**

bother; pester. **5.** of a a dog etc., bite, shake, or tear with the teeth. [ME *worien*] —n. pl. **•ries 1.** a state of anxiety or vexation. **2.** something that causes anxiety. —**wor'ri•er** n. —**wor'less** adj.

worse (wurs) comparative of BAD, BADLY, and ILL. —ADJ. **1.** bad, harmful, or ill in a greater degree. **2.** in a less favorable condition or situation. [ME *werse*] —n. something worse. —adv. in a worse manner.

wors•en (WUR sən) v.t. & v.i. make or become worse.

wor•ship (WUR ship) n. **1.** the adoration, homage, or veneration given to a deity. **2.** the expression of such adoration; esp. religious services and prayer. **3.** excessive or ardent devotion or admiration. **4.** Chiefly Brit. a title of honor in addressing persons of rank or station: with *your, his,* etc. [ME *worshipe*] —v. **wor•shiped, wor•ship•ing** v.t. **1.** show religious worship to. **2.** have an intense admiration or devotion for. —v.i. **3.** perform acts of worship. —**wor'ship•er** n.

wor•ship•ful (WUR ship fəl) adj. giving or feeling reverence or adoration.

worst (wurst) superlative of BAD, BADLY, and ILL. —ADJ. bad, ill, evil, harmful, etc., in the highest degree. [ME *worste*] —n. that which is worst. —**at worst** by the most pessimistic estimate. —**if (the) worst comes to (the) worst** if the worst imaginable thing comes to pass. —**get the worst of it** be defeated or put at a disadvantage. —adv. in the worst manner or degree. —v.t. get the better of; defeat.

wors•ted (WUUS tid) n. **1.** woolen yarn spun from fibers combed parallel and twisted hard. **2.** a fabric made from this. [ME *worstede* < former name of a town in England] —adj. made from worsted.

wort (wurt) n. **1.** a plant or herb: usu. in combination: *liverwort.* **2.** the unfermented infusion of malt that becomes beer when fermented. [ME]

worth (wurth) n. **1.** value or excellence of any kind. **2.** the exchangeable or market value of anything. **3.** the quality that makes one deserving of esteem. **4.** wealth. **5.** the amount of something that can be had for a specific sum: fifty cents' *worth* of candy. —adj. **1.** equal in value to. **2.** deserving of: be *worth* seeing. **3.** having possessions to the value of: They are *worth* millions. —**for all**

it is worth to the utmost. —**for all one is worth** with every effort possible. [ME]

worth·less (WURTH lis) *adj.* having no worth or value. —**worth'less·ly** *adv.* — **worth'less·ness** *n.*

worth·while (WURTH HWĪL) *adj.* sufficiently important to be worth one's time, effort, or money. —**worth'while'ness** *n.*

wor·thy (WUR thee) *adj.* ·thi·er, ·thi·est **1.** deserving of respect or honor; meritorious. **2.** possessing worth or value. —*n. pl.* ·thies a person of great worth or importance. [ME] —**wor'thi·ly** *adv.* —**wor'thi·ness** *n.*

-worthy *combining form* **1.** meriting or deserving: *trustworthy.* **2.** valuable as: *newsworthy.* **3.** fit for: *seaworthy.*

wot (wot) present tense, first and third person singular, of WIT[2].

would (wuud) past tense of WILL, chiefly used as an auxiliary expressing a wide range of conditions, as preference, expectation, request, etc. [ME *wolde*]

would-be (WUUD BEE) *adj.* **1.** desiring or professing to be: *a would-be poet.* **2.** intended to be: *a would-be act of generosity.* [ME]

would·n't (WUUD nt) would not.

wound[1] (woond) *n.* **1.** a hurt or injury to the body, usu. one in which the skin is cut or torn, as a stab. **2.** any injury to feelings, honor, etc. [ME] —*v.t. & v.i.* inflict a wound (upon); hurt.

wound[2] (wownd) past tense, past participle of WIND[2].

wove (wohv) past tense, alternative past participle of WEAVE.

wo·ven (WOH vən) a past participle of WEAVE.

wow (wow) *Informal interj.* an exclamation of wonder, surprise, pleasure, pain, etc. —*n.* something that is extraordinarily successful, amusing, etc. —*v.t.* excite to enthusiastic approval: *wowed the audience.*

wrack (rak) *n.* **1.** ruin; destruction: chiefly in the phrase **wrack and ruin. 2.** a wrecked ship; wreckage. **3.** marine vegetation cast ashore by the sea, as seaweed. [ME]

wraith (rayth) *n.* an apparition of a person; ghost.

wran·gle (RANG gəl) *v.* ·gled, ·gling *v.i.* **1.** argue or dispute noisily; brawl. —*v.t.* **2.** argue; debate. **3.** herd or round up (livestock). [ME *wranglen*] —*n.* an angry dispute. —**wran'gler** *n.*

·rap (rap) *v.* **wrapped** or **wrapt, wrap·**

ping *v.t.* **1.** surround and cover. **2.** cover with paper etc., folded about and secured. **3.** obscure; blot out. —*v.i.* **4.** be or become twined or coiled: with *about, around,* etc. —**wrap up 1.** conclude; end. **2.** summarize. [ME *wrappen*] —*n.* **1.** an article of dress drawn about a person. **2.** *pl.* outer garments collectively, as cloaks, scarfs, etc.

wrap·a·round (RAP ə ROWND) *adj.* **1.** designating a garment open down to the hem and made to fit by being wrapped around the body. **2.** encircling or overlapping: a *wraparound* windshield.

wrap·per (RAP ər) *n.* **1.** that in which something has been wrapped. **2.** a dressing gown; negligee. **3.** one who wraps.

wrap·ping (RAP ing) *n. Often pl.* something in which an object is wrapped.

wrap-up (RAP UP) *n.* a concluding statement; summary.

wrath (rath) *n.* extreme or violent rage. [ME] —**wrath'ful** *adj.* —**wrath'·ful·ly** *adv.* —**wrath'ful·ness** *n.*

wreak (reek) *v.t.* **1.** inflict or exact, as vengeance. **2.** give free expression to (anger, hatred, etc.); vent. [ME *wreken*]

wreath (reeth) *n. pl.* **wreaths** (reethz) **1.** a band or circle of flowers or greenery. **2.** anything having a shape suggesting this. [ME *wrethe*]

wreathe (reeth) *v.* **wreathed, wreath·ing** *v.t.* **1.** form into a wreath, as by twisting or twining. **2.** adorn or encircle with or as with wreaths. **3.** envelop; cover: *His face was wreathed* in smiles. —*v.i.* **4.** take the form of a wreath.

wreck (rek) *v.t.* **1.** cause the destruction of; damage badly. **2.** affect disastrously; ruin. **3.** tear down, as a building. —*v.t.* **4.** suffer wreck; be ruined. —*n.* **1.** that which has been ruined or destroyed. **2.** the accidental destruction of a ship; also, the ship so destroyed. **3.** one who is unsound or ruined. [ME *wrek*]

wreck·age (REK ij) *n.* **1.** the act of wrecking or the state of being wrecked. **2.** remains of a wreck; debris.

wreck·er (REK ər) *n.* **1.** one who or that which wrecks. **2.** one employed in tearing down and removing old buildings. **3.** a person, train, car, or machine that clears away wrecks. **4.** a person or boat employed to recover disabled vessels or wrecked cargoes.

wren (ren) *n.* any of numerous small birds

having short, rounded wings and a short tail. [ME *wrenne*]

wrench (rench) *n.* **1.** a violent twist. **2.** an injury, as to the back, caused by a violent twist or jerk; sprain. **3.** any sudden and violent emotion or grief. **4.** any perversion or distortion of an original meaning. **5.** any of various tools for twisting or turning bolts, nuts, pipe, etc. —*v.t.* **1.** twist violently. **2.** injure by a sudden, violent twist; sprain. **3.** distort, as a meaning. **4.** move or force with great effort. —*v.i.* **5.** give a twist or wrench. [ME *wrenchen*]

wrest (rest) *v.t.* **1.** pull or force away. **2.** turn from the true meaning; distort. **3.** seize forcibly. **4.** extract by toil and effort: *wrest* a living from barren soil. [ME *wresten*] —*n.* an act of wresting. —**wrest′er** *n.*

wres·tle (RES əl) *v.* **·tled, ·tling** *v.i.* **1.** engage in wrestling. **2.** struggle, as for mastery; contend. —*v.t.* **3.** engage in a wrestling match with. **4.** struggle or scuffle with. [ME *wrestlen*] —*n.* **1.** a wrestling match. **2.** any hard struggle. —**wres′tler** *n.*

wres·tling (RES ling) *n.* a sport in which a contestant endeavors to pin the other contestant's shoulders to the mat.

wretch (rech) *n.* **1.** a base, vile, or contemptible person. **2.** a miserable or pitiable person. [ME *wrecche* outcast]

wretch·ed (RECH id) *adj.* **·er, ·est 1.** sunk in dejection; profoundly unhappy. **2.** causing misery or grief. **3.** unsatisfactory or worthless in ability or quality. **4.** despicable; contemptible. [ME *wrecchede*] —**wretch′ed·ly** *adv.* —**wretch′·ed·ness** *n.*

wrig·gle (RIG əl) *v.* **·gled, ·gling** *v.i.* **1.** twist in a sinuous manner; squirm. **2.** proceed as by twisting or crawling. **3.** make one's way by evasive or indirect means. —*v.t.* **4.** cause to wriggle. —*n.* the motion of wriggling. [ME *wrigglen*] —**wrig′gly** *adj.* **·gli·er, ·gli·est**

wrig·gler (RIG lər) *n.* **1.** one who or that which wriggles. **2.** a mosquito larva.

wright (rīt) *n.* one who constructs, contrives, or creates: used chiefly in compounds: *playwright.* [ME]

wring (ring) *v.t.* **wrung, wring·ing 1.** squeeze or compress by twisting. **2.** squeeze or press out, as water, by twisting. **3.** extort; acquire by extortion. **4.** distress; torment. **5.** twist or wrest violently. [ME *wringen*] —*n.* the act of wringing.

wring·er (RING ər) *n.* **1.** a device with rollers for squeezing out water from wet laundry. **2.** a person or thing that wrings. **3.** an ordeal: put them through the *wringer.* [ME]

wrin·kle[1] (RING kəl) *n.* a small crease or fold, as on the skin or other smooth surface. [ME] —*v.t. & v.i.* **·kled, ·kling** make wrinkles in or become wrinkled. —**wrin′kly** *adj.* (RING klee) **·kli·er, ·kli·est**

wrin·kle[2] *Informal* a curious or ingenious method, idea, device, etc.

wrist (rist) *n.* the joint of the arm between the hand and the forearm. [ME]

wrist watch a watch worn on a band or strap around the wrist.

writ[1] (rit) *n.* **1.** *Law* a legal document ordering a person to do or not to do some act. **2.** that which is written: now chiefly in **Holy Writ,** the Bible. [ME]

writ[2] archaic past tense and past participle of WRITE.

write (rīt) *v.* **wrote** (*Archaic*) **writ, writ·ten** or (*Archaic*) **writ, writ·ing** *v.t.* **1.** trace or inscribe (words, numbers, etc.) on a surface, as with a pencil. **2.** describe in writing. **3.** communicate (with) by letter. **4.** be the author or composer of. **5.** draw up; draft: *write* a check. **6.** cover or fill with writing: *write* two full pages. **7.** leave marks or evidence of: Anxiety is *written* on their faces. —*v.i.* **8.** trace or inscribe words etc. on a surface. **9.** communicate in writing. **10.** be engaged in the occupation of a writer or author. —**write in** cast (a vote) for one not listed on a ballot. —**write off 1.** remove or cancel (debts etc.) from an account. **2.** acknowledge the loss or failure of. **3.** reduce the estimated value of. —**write up** describe in writing. [ME *writen*]

write-in (RĪT IN) *n.* a vote for a person not on a ballot. —*adj.* of such a person or vote: a *write-in* candidate.

write-off (RĪT AWF) *n.* **1.** a cancellation. **2.** an amount canceled or noted as a loss.

writ·er (RĪ tər) *n.* one who writes, esp. as a profession.

writer's cramp *Pathol.* cramp in the fingers and hand, caused by excessive writing.

write-up (RĪT UP) *n.* a written description.

writhe (rīth) *v.* **writhed, writh·ing** *v.t.* **1.** cause to twist or bend; distort. —*v.i.* **2.** twist or distort the body, face, etc., as in pain. **3.** suffer acutely, as from embarrassment, anguish, etc. [ME *writhen*] —**writh′er** *n.*

writ·ing (RĪ ting) *n.* **1.** the act of one who writes. **2.** handwriting; penmanship. **3.**

something written; esp., a novel, play, or other literary production. **4.** the profession or occupation of a writer. **5.** the practice, art, form, or style of literary composition.

writ·ten (RIT n) past participle of WRITE.

wrong (rawng) *adj.* **1.** not correct; mistaken; erroneous: a *wrong* estimate. **2.** not suitable; inappropriate; improper: the *wrong* clothes. **3.** not working or acting properly or satisfactorily: Something is *wrong* with the lock. **4.** intended to be unseen: the *wrong* side of the cloth. **5.** not desired or intended: the *wrong* road. **6.** not morally right, proper, or just. **7.** unsatisfactory: the *wrong* reply. **—go wrong 1.** make a mistake; err. **2.** turn out badly; go astray. **—adv.** in a wrong direction, place, or manner; erroneously. **—n.** that which is wrong, as an evil or unjust action. **—in the wrong** mistaken; wrong; at fault. [ME] **—v.t. 1.** inflict injury or injustice upon. **2.** impute evil to unjustly; malign. **—wrong′er** *n.* **—wrong′ly** *adv.* **—wrong′ness** *n.*

wrong·do·er (RAWNG DOO ər) *n.* one who does wrong; esp. a sinner. **—wrong′do′ing** *n.*

wrong·ful (RAWNG fəl) *adj.* **1.** unfair; injurious; unjust. **2.** unlawful; illegal. **—wrong′·ful·ly** *adv.* **—wrong′ful·ness** *n.*

wrong-head·ed (RAWNG HED id) *adj.* stubbornly or perversely erring in judgment, action, etc. **—wrong′-head′ed·ly** *adv.* **—wrong′-head′ed·ness** *n.*

wrote (roht) past tense of WRITE.

wroth (rawth) *adj.* angry; furious. [ME]

wrought (rawt) a past tense and past participle of WORK. **—adj. 1.** beaten or hammered into shape by tools: *wrought* gold. **2.** made; fashioned; formed. [ME *wroght*] **—wrought-up** perturbed; agitated.

wrought iron commercially pure iron that is easily forged and welded into various shapes.

wrung (rung) past tense, past participle of WRING.

wry (rī) *adj.* **wri·er, wri·est 1.** twisted; contorted; askew: a *wry* smile. **2.** perverse, ironic, or bitter: *wry* humor. **—wry′ly** *adv.* **—wry′ness** *n.*

wurst (wuurst) *n.* sausage. [< G]

X

x, X (eks) *n. pl.* **x's** or **xs, X's** or **Xs** 1. the twenty-fourth letter of the English alphabet. 2. the sounds represented by the letter. 3. anything shaped like an X. 4. an unknown quantity, factor, result, etc. —*symbol* 1. the Roman numeral ten. 2. a mark shaped like an X, representing the signature of one who cannot write. 3. a symbol used to indicate a kiss. —*v.t.* **x-ed** or **x'd** (ekst), **x-ing** or **x'ing** (EK sing) 1. indicate or mark with an *x*. 2. cancel: with *out*.

X-ax·is (EKS AK sis) *n. pl.* **x-ax·es** (EKS AK seez) the horizontal axis in a graph; the abscissa.

X chromosome *n. Genetics* one of the two types of chromosomes that determine the sex of an offspring.

xe·bec (ZEE bek) *n.* a small, three-masted Mediterranean vessel, formerly used by pirates: also spelled *zebec.* [Earlier *chebec*]

xeno- *combining form* strange; foreign; alien: *xenophobia.* [< Gk. *xénos* stranger]

xe·non (ZEE non) *n.* a heavy, gaseous element (symbol Xe) occurring in extremely small quantities in the atmosphere and freezing at a very low temperature. [< Gk. *xénon* strange]

xen·o·pho·bi·a (ZEN ə FOH bee ə) *n.* hatred or distrust of foreigners or strangers. —**xen'o·phobe'** *n.* —**xen'o·pho'bic** *adj.*

xero- *combining form* dry; dryness. [< Gk. *xērós* dry]

xe·rog·ra·phy (zi ROG rə fee) *n.* a method of copying in which a negatively charged ink powder is sprayed on a positively charged metal plate, from which it is trans-

ferred to the printing surface by electrostatic attraction. —**xe·ro·graph·ic** (ZEER ə GRAF ik) *adj.* —**xe·rog'raph·i·cal·ly** *adv.*

xe·roph·i·lous (zi ROF ə ləs) *adj. Biol.* growing in or adapted to dry, hot climates.

xe·ro·phyte (ZEER ə FIT) *n. Bot.* a plant adapted to dry conditions of air and soil. —**xe·ro·phyt·ic** (ZEER ə FIT ik) *adj.*

Xer·ox (ZEER oks) *n.* a xerographic process for reproducing printed or pictorial matter: a trade name. —*v.t.* reproduce by Xerox. Also **xer'ox.**

xi (zī) *n.* the fourteenth letter in the Greek alphabet (Ξ, ξ), equivalent to the English *x*.

Xmas Christmas: popular abbreviation.

X-rat·ed (EKS RAY tid) *adj.* of a motion picture, characterized by explicit sexuality.

x-ray (EKS RAY) *v.t.* examine, photograph, diagnose, or treat with X-rays. —*n.* a picture made with x-rays: also **x-ray photograph.**

x-rays (EKS RAYZ) *n.* a form of electromagnetic radiation of extremely short wavelength, emitted from a substance when it is bombarded by a stream of electrons, and able to penetrate many solids.

xy·lem (ZĪ ləm) *n. Bot.* a woody tissue that is part of the water-transporting system in higher plants. [< G]

xy·lo·phone (ZĪ lə FOHN) *n.* a musical instrument consisting of a row of wooden bars graduated in length to form a chromatic scale, and sounded by being struck with mallets. —**xy·lo·phon·ist** (ZĪ lə FOH nist) *n.*

Y

y, Y (wī) *n. pl.* **y's** or **ys, Y's** or **Ys 1.** the twenty-fifth letter of the English alphabet. **2.** the sounds represented by the letter *y*. **3.** anything shaped like a **Y**, as: **a** a pipe coupling, connection, etc. **b** a forked piece serving as a rest or support. —*symbol Chem.* yttrium (symbol Y).

yacht (yot) *n.* a vessel specially built or fitted for racing or for cruising. —*v.i.* cruise, race, or sail in a yacht. [< obs. Du. *jaght*]

yachts·man (YOTS mən) *n. pl.* •**men** a person who owns or sails a yacht.

yachts·wom·an (YOTS wuum ən) *n. pl.* •**wom·en** a woman who owns or sails a yacht.

ya·hoo (YAH hoo) *n.* **1.** any low, vicious person. **2.** an awkward person; bumpkin; yokel. **3.** a boor; philistine. [after the Yahoos, a brutish people in Jonathan Swift's *Gulliver's Travels*]

Yah·weh (YAH we) in the Old Testament, Jehovah, the God of Israel. Also **Yah·ve, Yah·veh.**

yak¹ (yak) *n.* a large, long-haired ox of Tibet and central Asia, often used as a beast of burden. [< Tibetan *gyag*]

yak² *v.i.* **yakked, yak·king** *Slang* chatter noisily or constantly.

yam (yam) *n.* **1.** the fleshy, edible, tuberous root of any of various climbing tropical plants. **2.** a variety of the sweet potato. [< Pg. *inhame*]

yam·mer (YAM ər) *Informal v.t. & v.i.* complain or utter peevishly. [ME *yomeren* murmur] —*n.* the act of yammering. —**yam'mer·er** *n.*

yang (yahng) *n.* in Chinese philosophy and art, the male element, source of life and heat. Compare **YIN.** [< Chinese]

yank (yangk) *v.t. & v.i.* jerk or pull suddenly. —*n.* a sudden pull.

Yank (yangk) *n. Informal* Yankee.

Yan·kee (YANG kee) *n.* **1.** originally, a native or inhabitant of New England. **2.** a Northerner, esp. a Union soldier during the Civil War. **3.** any citizen of the U.S.: a chiefly foreign usage.

yap (yap) *n.* **1.** *Slang* foolish talk; jabber. **2.** a bark or yelp. **3.** *Slang* the mouth. —*v.t.* **~apped, yap·ping 1.** *Slang* talk idly or ~tily; jabber. **2.** bark or yelp.

yard¹ (yahrd) *n.* **1.** a standard measure of length equal to 3 feet, 36 inches, or 0.914 meter. **2.** *Naut.* a spar supporting a square sail. [ME *yerd* rod]

yard² *n.* **1.** a tract of ground adjacent to a residence or other building. **2.** an outdoor space used for a specific purpose: *shipyard.* **3.** an area where railroad trains are made up, stored, or repaired. [ME *yerd* enclosure]

yard·age (YAHR dij) *n.* the amount or length of something expressed in yards.

yard·arm (YAHRD ahrm) *n. Naut.* either end of a yard of a square sail.

yard goods cloth that is sold by the yard.

yard·stick (YAHRD stik) *n.* **1.** a graduated measuring stick one yard in length. **2.** any measure or standard of comparison.

yar·mul·ke (YAHR məl kə) *n.* a skullcap worn by Jewish males, as during prayer. Also **yar'mul·ka.** [< Yiddish]

yarn (yahrn) *n.* **1.** any spun, threadlike material prepared for use in weaving, knitting, etc. **2.** a story, esp. of adventure or of doubtful truth. [ME]

yaw (yaw) *v.i.* (of a ship or aircraft) fail to hold a straight course; turn from side to side. —*v.t.* cause to yaw. —*n.* a yawing movement or course.

yawl (yawl) *n.* **1.** a fore-and-aft rigged, two-masted vessel. **2.** a ship's small boat. [< LG *jolle*]

yawn (yawn) *v.i.* **1.** open the mouth wide, usu. involuntarily, as a result of drowsiness, fatigue, or boredom. **2.** be or stand wide open: A chasm *yawned* before us. [ME *yenen*] —*n.* **1.** the act of yawning. **2.** the act of opening wide. **3.** *Informal* something quite boring. Also **yawner.** —**yawn'er** *n.*

yawp (yawp) *v.i.* **1.** bark or yelp. **2.** *Slang* talk loudly; talk foolishly. [ME *yolpen*] —*n.* **1.** a bark or yelp. **2.** *Slang* noisy, foolish speech. Also **yaup.** —**yawp'er** *n.*

yaws (yawz) *n.* (*construed as sing.*) *Pathol.* an infectious, nonvenereal disease, caused by a spirochete and resembling syphilis. [< Carib]

y-ax·is (WĪ ak sis) *n. pl.* **y-ax·es** (WĪ ak seez) the vertical axis in a graph or coordinate system; the ordinate.

Y chromosome *n. Genetics* one of the two

types of chromosomes that determine the sex of an offspring.

y·clept (ee KLEPT) *adj. Archaic* called; named. Also **y·cleped'**. [ME]

ye (yee) *pron. Archaic* you. [ME]

yea (yay) *adv.* **1.** yes; indeed. **2.** not only so, but more so: There were fifty, *yea*, a hundred archers. —*n.* an affirmative vote or voter. [ME *ye*]

year (yeer) *n.* **1.** the period of time in which the earth completes one revolution around the sun, consisting of 365 or 366 days divided into 12 months and now reckoned as beginning January 1 and ending December 31; also, a similar period in other calendars. **2.** the period of time during which a planet revolves once around the sun. **3.** a specific period of time, usu. less than a year, given over to some special work or activity: the school *year*. **4.** *pl.* age, esp. old age: active for his *years*. **5.** *pl.* time: in *years* gone by and *years* to come. —**year in, year out** from one year to the next; continually. [ME *yere*]

year·book (YEER buuk) *n.* **1.** a book published annually, presenting information about the previous year. **2.** a high school or college annual recording esp. senior class activities.

year·ling (YEER ling) *n.* a young animal past its first year and not yet two years old. [ME] —*adj.* being a year old.

year·long (YEER LAWNG) *adj.* lasting for a year.

year·ly (YEER lee) *adj.* **1.** occurring, done, payable, seen, etc. once a year; annual: a *yearly* physical. **2.** continuing or lasting for a year: a *yearly* subscription. —*adv.* once a year; annually. —*n.* a publication appearing once a year. [ME *yeerly*]

yearn (yurn) *v.i.* **1.** desire something earnestly; long: with *for*. **2.** be deeply moved; feel sympathy. [ME *yernen*]

yearn·ing (YUR ning) *n.* a strong emotion of longing or desire, esp. with tenderness. [ME] —**yearn'ing·ly** *adv.*

year-round (YEER ROWND) *adj.* open, operating, or continuing for the entire year: a *year-round* resort.

yeast (yeest) *n.* **1.** a fungus that ferments carbohydrates. **2.** a commercial preparation containing yeast cells, used in leavening bread and in brewing. **3.** froth or spume. **4.** ferment or agitation. [ME *yest*]

yeast·y (YEE stee) *adj.* **yeast·i·er, yeast·i·est** **1.** of, resembling, or containing

yeast. **2.** frothy; foamy. **3.** restless; unsettled. **4.** light or unsubstantial. —**yeast'i·ness** *n.*

yell (yel) *v.t. & v.i.* shout; scream; roar; also, cheer. [ME *yellen*] —*n.* **1.** a sharp, loud cry, as of pain or anger. **2.** a rhythmic cheer shouted in unison by cheerleaders etc.

yel·low (YEL oh) *adj.* •**er,** •**est** **1.** having the color of ripe lemons or sunflowers. **2.** changed to a sallow color by age, sickness, etc.: a paper *yellow* with age. **3.** having a yellowish complexion. **4.** sensational, esp. offensively so: said of newspapers: *yellow* journalism. **5.** *Informal* cowardly. [ME *yelwe*] —*n.* **1.** the color of the spectrum between green and orange. **2.** the yolk of an egg. —*v.t. & v.i.* make or become yellow. —**yel'low·ish** *adj.* —**yel'low·ness** *n.*

yel·low-bel·lied (YEL oh BEL eed) *adj.* **1.** *Slang* cowardly; yellow. **2.** having a yellow underside, as a bird.

yellow fever *Pathol.* an infectious intestinal disease caused by a virus transmitted by a mosquito. Also called **yellow jack**.

yellow jacket any of various wasps having bright yellow markings.

yelp (yelp) *v.t. & v.i.* utter or express with a sharp, shrill cry or bark, as a dog. [ME *yelpen* boast] —**yelp** *n.* —**yelp'er** *n.*

yen (yen) *n. pl.* **yen** an ardent longing or desire. —*v.i.* yenned, yen·ning yearn; long. [< Japanese]

yeo·man (YOH mən) *n. pl.* •**men** **1.** a naval petty officer who performs clerical duties. **2.** formerly, an attendant or servant in the service of a nobleman or of royalty. **3.** formerly, a freeholder next below the gentry who owned a small landed estate or farm. [ME *yoman*]

yeo·man·ly (YOH mən lee) *adj.* brave; rugged; staunch. —*adv.* bravely.

yeoman of the guard a member of the special bodyguard of the English royal household: also called *beefeater*.

yeo·man·ry (YOH mən ree) *n.* the collective body of yeomen (def. 3).

yep (yep) *adv. Informal* yes.

yes (yes) *adv.* as you say; truly; just so: a reply of affirmation or consent: opposed to *no*. —*n. pl.* **yes·es** **1.** a reply in the affirmative. **2.** an affirmative vote or voter: often *aye*. —*v.t.* yessed, yes·sing give an affirmative reply to. [ME]

ye·shi·va (yə SHEE və) *n.* In Judaism: **a** an orthodox rabbinical seminary. **b** a Hebrew day school. **c** a school of Talmudic studies. Also **ye•shi'vah.** [< Hebrew]

yes-man (YES MAN *n. pl.* **-men** one who agrees without criticism; sycophant.

yes•ter•day (YES tər DAY) *n.* **1.** the day preceding today. **2.** the near past. —*adv.* **1.** on the day before today. **2.** at a recent time. [ME *yisterday*]

yes•ter•year (YES tər YEER) *n.* **1.** last year. **2.** the recent past.

yet (yet) *adv.* **1.** in addition; besides. **2.** in continuance of a previous state or condition; still: I can hear him *yet.* **3.** at the present time; now: Don't go *yet.* **4.** after all the time that has or had elapsed: Are you ready *yet*? **5.** up to the present time; before: He has never *yet* lied to me. **6.** than that which has been previously affirmed: It was hot yesterday; today it is hotter *yet.* **7.** nevertheless: It was hot, *yet* not unpleasant. —**as yet** up to now. [ME] —*conj.* nevertheless; notwithstanding; but.

yet•i (YET ee) *n.* the abominable snowman. [< Tibetan]

yew (yoo) *n.* **1.** any of several evergreen trees or shrubs, having a red berrylike fruit. **2.** the hard, fine-grained, durable wood of the common yew. [ME *ew*]

Yid•dish (YID ish) *n.* a High German language now spoken primarily by Jewish emigrants from eastern Europe. [< Yiddish *yidish*] —*adj.* of, pertaining to, or characteristic of Yiddish.

yield (yeeld) *v.t.* **1.** give forth; produce: *yield* a large crop. **2.** give in return, as for investment. **3.** give up; relinquish: often with *up*: *yield* a fortress. **4.** concede or grant: *yield* precedence. —*v.i.* **5.** provide a return; produce. **6.** give up; surrender. **7.** give way, as to pressure or force. **8.** assent or comply, as under compulsion. **9.** give place, as through inferiority or weakness: with *to*: We will *yield* to them in nothing. [ME *yielden*] —*n.* **1.** the amount yielded; product. **2.** the profit derived from invested capital. —**yield'er** *n.*

yield•ing (YEEL ding) *adj.* disposed to yield; flexible; obedient.

yin (yin) *n.* in Chinese philosophy and art, the female element, which stands for darkness, cold, and death. Compare YANG. [< Chinese]

yo•del (YOHD l) *n.* a melody sung to meaningless syllables, with abrupt changes from natural to falsetto tones. —*v.t. & v.i.* **•led, •del•ing** sing (a yodel). [< G *jod-* —**yo'del•er** *n.*

yo•ga (YOH gə) *n.* **1.** a Hindu discipline aimed at spiritual insight through meditation and exercises. **2.** a related system of exercises, the purpose of which is to achieve both physical and spiritual well-being. [< Skt.] —**yo•gic** (YOH gik) *adj.*

yo•gi (YOH gee) *n. pl.* **•gis** one who practices yoga. Also **yo•gin** (YOH gin).

yo•gurt (YOH gərt) *n.* a thick, curdled milk treated with bacteria. Also **yo'ghurt, yo' •ghourt.** [< Turkish *yōgurt*]

yoke (yohk) *n. pl.* **yokes 1.** a curved timber with attachments used for coupling draft animals, as oxen. **2.** any of various similar contrivances, as a frame fitted for a person's shoulders and designed to carry a burden at either end. **3.** *pl.* **yoke** a pair of draft animals coupled with a yoke. **4.** an oppressive force or influence: under the *yokes* of tyrants. **5.** that which binds or connects; bond: the *yoke* of love. **6.** a part of a garment designed to support a pleated or gathered part, as at the hips or shoulders. [ME *yok*] —*v.* **yoked, yok•ing** *v.t.* **1.** put a yoke upon. **2.** join; couple; link. **3.** secure (a draft animal) to a plow etc.; also, secure a draft animal to (a plow etc.). —*v.i.* **4.** be joined or linked.

yo•kel (YOH kəl) *n.* a country bumpkin: a contemptuous term. —**yo'kel•ish** *adj.*

yolk (yohk) *n.* the yellow portion of an egg. [ME *yolke*]

Yom Kip•pur (yawm KIP ər) the Jewish Day of Atonement, marked by prayer and fasting for 24 hours. [< Hebrew]

yon•der (YON dər) *adj.* being at a distance indicated. —*adv.* in that place; there. [ME]

yore (yor) *n.* time long past: in days of *yore.* [ME]

York•shire pudding (YORK shər) a batter pudding usu. baked with roasting meat. [after *Yorkshire*, England]

you (yoo) *pron., possessive* **yours 1.** the nominative and objective singular and plural pronoun of the second person, used in addressing one or more: This one is *yours.* **2.** an indefinite pronoun equivalent to *one*: *You* learn by trying. [ME]

you'd (yood) **1.** you had. **2.** you would.

you'll (yool) you will.

young (yung) *adj.* **young•er** (YUNG gər), **young•est** (YUNG gist) **1.** being in the early period of life or growth; not old. **2.** not having progressed far; newly formed: The day was *young.* **3.** pertaining to youth or early life. **4.** full of vigor or freshness. **5.**

being without experience; immature. [ME *yong*] —*n.* **1.** young persons as a group; youth. **2.** offspring, esp. of animals. —**young'ish** *adj.*

young blood 1. youthful people. **2.** fresh ideas, enthusiasm, etc.

young•ster (YUNG stər) *n.* a young person; a child or youth.

your (yuur) *pronominal adj.* a form of possessive case of *you*, used attributively: *your* fate. [ME]

you're (yuur) you are.

yours (yuurz) *pron.* **1.** the possessive case of the pronoun *you*, used predicatively: This mistake is *yours*. **2.** the one or ones belonging or relating to you: a home as quiet as *yours*. [ME]

your•self (yuur SELF) *pron. pl.* **•selves** (-SELVZ) a form of the second person pronoun, used: **1.** as a reflexive or as object of a preposition in a reflexive sense: Did you hurt *yourself?* Look at *yourself.* **2.** as an intensive form of *you:* You said so *yourself.* **3.** as a designation of a normal or usual state: Why can't you be *yourself?*

youth (yooth) *n. pl.* **youths** (yoothz) **1.** the state or condition of being young. **2.** the period of life between childhood and adulthood; adolescence. **3.** any early period or stage. **4.** a young person, esp. a young man;

also, young persons collectively. [ME *youthe*]

youth•ful (YOOTH fəl) *adj.* **1.** having youth; being still young. **2.** characteristic of youth; fresh; vigorous. **3.** of or pertaining to youth. **4.** not far advanced; early; new. —**youth'ful•ly** *adv.* —**youth'ful•ness** *n.*

you've (yoov) you have.

yowl (yowl) *v.i.* utter a loud, prolonged wailing cry. —*n.* such a cry. [ME *yowlen*]

yo-yo (YOH yoh) *n. pl.* **-yos 1.** a wheellike toy with a string wound about it in a deep groove, commonly attached to the operator's finger and spun up and down by manipulating the string. **2.** *Slang* a stupid person.

yuc•ca (YUK ə) *n.* any of various plants of the southern U.S., Mexico, and Central America, having a woody stem that bears a large cluster of white, bell-shaped flowers. [< NL]

yule (yool) *n.* Christmas. [ME *yol*]

yule log a large log made the foundation of the Christmas Eve fire.

yule•tide (YOOL TID) *n.* the Christmas season.

yum•my (YUM ee) *adj.* **•mi•er, •mi•est** delicious; delectable.

yurt (yuurt) *n.* a portable tent made of felt laid on a framework of branches, used by nomads in central Asia. [< Russ.]

Z

z, Z (zee) *n. pl.* **z's** or **zs, Z's** or **Zs 1.** the twenty-sixth letter of the English alphabet. **2.** the sound represented by the letter *z.* — *symbol* **1.** *Physics* atomic number. **2.** *Electr.* impedance.

za•ny (ZAY nee) *adj.* **za•ni•er, za•ni•est** odd and comical; outlandish. — *n. pl.* **•nies 1.** a simpleton; buffoon; fool. **2.** in old comic plays, one who imitated the other performers, esp. the clown, with ludicrous failure. [< Ital. *zanni* in early Italian comedy, a masked clown]

zap (zap) *v.* **zapped, zap•ping** *Informal v.t.* **1.** hit or kill, by or as if by shooting. **2.** skip over quickly and suddenly: I *zap* all TV commercials. — *v.i.* **3.** move quickly; zip.

zeal (zeel) *n.* enthusiastic devotion; ardor; fervor. [ME *zele*]

zeal•ot (ZEL ət) *n.* **1.** an immoderate partisan; a fanatic. **2.** one who is zealous. [< LL *zelotes*] —**zeal•ot•ry** (ZEL ə tree) *n.* excessive zeal; fanaticism.

zeal•ous (ZEL əs) *adj.* filled with or incited by zeal; enthusiastic. —**zeal′ous•ly** *adv.* —**zeal′ous•ness** *n.*

ze•bec (ZEE bek) see XEBEC.

ze•bra (ZEE brə) *n.* any of various African mammals resembling the ass, having a light-colored body fully marked with dark bands. [< Pg.]

zebra crossing a street crossing marking with white stripes. Also **zebra.**

zeit•geist (TSĪT GĪST) *n.* the spirit of the time; the intellectual and moral tendencies that characterize any age or epoch. [< G *Zeitgeist*]

Zen (zen) a form of Buddhism stressing enlightenment through intuition and contemplation rather than formal study of scripture. Also **Zen.** [< Japanese *zen* religious meditation]

ze•nith (ZEE nith) *n.* **1.** the point of the celestial sphere that is exactly overhead and is opposite to the nadir. **2.** the highest or culminating point; peak: the *zenith* of her career. [ME *senith*]

zeph•yr (ZEF ər) *n.* **1.** any soft, gentle wind. **2.** *cap.* the west wind. **3.** a lightweight yarn or fabric. [ME *Zephirus* west wind]

zep•pe•lin (ZEP ə lin) *n.* Often *cap.* a large dirigible having a rigid, cigar-shaped body.

[after Count Ferdinand von *Zeppelin,* 1838—1917, German general]

ze•ro (ZEER oh) *n. pl.* **•ros** or **•roes 1.** the numeral or symbol 0; a cipher. **2.** *Math.* **a** a cardinal number indicating the absence of quantity. **b** the point at which a continuous function changes its sign from plus to minus, or vice versa. **3.** the point on a scale, as of a thermometer, from which measures are counted. **4.** the lowest point. **5.** nothing. — *v.t.* **•roed, •ro•ing** adjust (instruments) to an arbitrary zero point for synchronized readings. —**zero in on 1.** adjust the sight of (a gun) by calibrated results of firings. **2.** focus on. — *adj.* without value or appreciable change. [< Ital.]

ze•ro-base budgeting (ZEE roh BAYS) budgeting in which expenditures are freshly justified, instead of being derived from previous budgets.

zero hour 1. the hour appointed for the start of a military operation. **2.** any critical moment.

zest (zest) *n.* **1.** keen enjoyment; gusto: often with *for:* a *zest* for reading. **2.** that which imparts such excitement and relish. [< F *zeste* lemon peel (for flavoring)] —**zest′ful, zest′y** *adj.* **zest•i•er, zest•i•est** —**zest′ful•ly** *adv.* —**zest′ful•ness** *n.*

ze•ta (ZAY tə) *n.* the sixth letter (Z, ζ) in the Greek alphabet, corresponding to English *z.* [< Gk. *zēta*]

zig•zag (ZIG ZAG) *n.* **1.** a series of short, sharp turns or angles in alternating directions. **2.** something characterized by such angles, as a path or pattern. [< F] —*adj.* having or proceeding in a zigzag. —*adv.* in a zigzag manner. —*v.t. & v.i.* **•zagged, •zag•ging** form or move in zigzags. —**zig′zag•ger** *n.*

zilch (zilch) *n. Slang* nothing; zero: He knew *zilch.*

zil•lion (ZIL yən) *n. Informal* a large, indefinite number. [after *million*]

zinc (zingk) *n.* a bluish-white metallic element (symbol Zn), widely used in industry, medicine, and the arts. — *v.t.* **zincked** or **zinced** (zingkt), **zinck•ing** or **zinc•ing** (ZING king) coat with zinc; galvanize. [< G *Zink*] —**zinck′y, zinc′y, zink′y** *adj.*

zinc ointment a medicated ointment, used to treat skin disorders.

zinc oxide *Chem.* a white powdery compound, used as a pigment and as a mild antiseptic and astringent.

zin•fan•del (ZIN fən DEL) *n.* **1.** a dry red wine made in California. **2.** the grape from which it is made.

zing (zing) *n.* **1.** a high-pitched buzzing or humming sound. **2.** energy; vitality; vigor. —*v.i.* make a shrill, humming sound.

Zi•on (ZĪ ən) **1.** a hill in Jerusalem, the site of the temple and the royal residence of David and his successors, regarded by Jews as a symbol of Jewish national culture, government, and religion. **2.** the Jewish people. **3.** any place or community considered to be especially under God's rule. **4.** the heavenly Jerusalem; heaven. [< Hebrew *tsiyōn*]

Zi•on•ism (ZĪ ə NIZ əm) *n.* before the creation of modern Israel, a movement to establish a national homeland for Jews in Palestine; afterward, a movement in support of the social, economic, and cultural development of Israel. —**Zi′on•ist** *adj.* & *n.*

zip (zip) *n.* **1.** a sharp, hissing sound, as of a bullet passing through the air. **2.** *Informal* energy; vitality; vim. —*v.* **zipped, zip•ping** *v.t.* **1.** fasten or unfasten with a zipper. **2.** convey with speed and energy. —*v.i.* **2.** *Informal* be very energetic. **3.** move with great speed.

zip code a numerical code for zones or regions, devised by the U.S. Post Office to aid in the distribution of domestic mail. Also **ZIP code.** [< *zone improvement plan*]

zip•per (ZIP ər) *n.* a fastener having two rows of interlocking teeth that may be closed or separated by a sliding device, used on clothing, boots, etc.: also called *slide fastener.*

zip•py (ZIP ee) *adj.* •**pi•er,** •**pi•est** *Informal* lively; energetic.

zith•er (ZITH ər) *n.* a simple form of stringed instrument, having a flat sounding board and from thirty to forty strings that are played by plucking with a plectrum. [< G] —**zith′er•ist** *n.*

zo•di•ac (ZOH dee AK) *n.* **1.** an imaginary belt encircling the heavens and extending about 8° on each side of the ecliptic within which are the apparent orbits of the moon, sun, and larger planets. It is divided into twelve parts (**signs of the zodiac**) that formerly corresponded to twelve constella-

tions bearing the same names. **2.** a figure or diagram representing this belt and its signs, used in astrology. [ME *zodiaque*] —**zo•di•a•cal** (zoh DĪ ə kəl) *adj.*

zom•bie (ZOM bee) *n.* **1.** a corpse reactivated by sorcery, but still dead. **2.** *Informal* a person whose behavior is considered to resemble the behavior of such a corpse. **3.** a large, strong cocktail made from several kinds of rum, fruit juices, and liqueur. Also **zom′bi.** [< West African] —**zom′bi•ism** *n.* —**zom′bie•like′** *adj.*

zone (zohn) *n.* **1.** an area, tract, or section distinguished from other or adjacent areas by some special quality or purpose: enterprise *zone*; end *zone*. **2.** *Usu. cap.* any of five divisions of the earth's surface, enclosed between two parallels of latitude and named for the prevailing climate: the **Torrid Zone,** extending on each side of the equator 23° 27′; the **Temperate Zones,** included between the parallels 23° 27′ and 66° ƒ 33′ on both sides of the equator; and the **Frigid Zones,** within the parallels 66° 33′ and the poles. [< L *zona* belt] —*v.t.* **zoned, zon•ing 1.** divide into zones. **2.** designate (an area, etc.) as a zone or part of a zone.

zonked (zongkt) *adj. Slang* drunk or drugged. Also **zonked out.**

zoo (zoo) *n.* a park in which wild animals are kept for exhibition. Also **zoological garden.**

zoo- *combining form* animal; animal kingdom: *zoology.* Also **zo-.** [< Gk. *zōion*]

zo•o•ge•og•ra•phy (ZOH ə jee OG rə fee) *n.* the study of the distribution of animals and of the relations between animal groups and their environment. —**zo′o•ge•og′ra•pher** *n.*

zo•ol•o•gy (zoh OL ə jee) *n.* the science dealing with animals, their structure, functions, development, evolution, and classification. —**zo•o•log•i•cal** (ZOH ə LOJ ə kəl) *adj.* —**zo•ol•o•gist** (zoh OL ə jist) *n.*

zoom (zoom) *v.i.* **1.** move quickly with a low-pitched but loud buzzing sound: the truck *zoomed* by us. **2.** climb sharply, as in an airplane. —*v.t.* **3.** cause to zoom. —*n.* the act of zooming.

zoom lens *Photog.* a lens, used chiefly on television and motion picture cameras, that enables the size of the image to be varied continuously without loss of focus.

zo•o•mor•phism (ZOH ə MOR fiz əm) *n.* the

conception, symbolization, or representation of a man or a god in the form of an animal.

zo·o·phyte (ZOH ə FĪT) *n.* an invertebrate animal resembling a plant, as a coral. — **zo·o·phyt·ic** (ZOH ə FĪT ik) *adj.*

Zo·ro·as·tri·an·ism (ZOR oh AS tree ə NIZ əm) *n.* the religious system founded by the Persian religious teacher Zoroaster, which recognizes two creative powers, one good and the other evil, includes the belief in life after death, and teaches the final triumph of good over evil. —**Zo′ro·as′tri·an** *n. & adj.*

Zou·ave (zoo AHV) *n.* **1.** a lightly armed French soldier wearing a brilliant Oriental uniform, originally an Algerian recruit. **2.** in the American Civil War, a member of a volunteer regiment assuming the name and part of the dress of the French Zouaves. [< F]

zuc·chi·ni (zoo KEE nee) *n. pl.* **·ni, ·nis** a cucumber-shaped green summer squash. [< Ital., pl. of *zucchino* squash]

zwie·back (ZWĪ BAK) *n.* bread baked and then sliced and toasted. [< G, twice-baked]

zy·gote (ZĪ goht) *n. Biol.* the cell formed by the union of two gametes. [< Gk. *zygōtós* yoked] —**zy·got·ic** (zī GOT ik) *adj.*

zymo- *combining form* fermentation: *zymurgy.* [< Gk. *zymē* leaven]

zy·mol·o·gy (zī MOL ə jee) *n.* the study of fermentation and the action of enzymes. — **zy·mol′o·gist** *n.*

zy·mur·gy (ZĪ mur jee) *n.* a branch of chemistry treating of processes in which fermentation takes place, as brewing or winemaking.

opers

![] HarperPaperbacks

Have all the information you need at your fingertips with these handy reference guides!

❏ **American Slang** 109284-3 ....$5.99

❏ **Spell It Right!** 100814-1..$4.99

❏ **Punctuate It Right!** 100813-3 ....$4.99

❏ **Errors in English and Ways to Correct Them** 100815-X............$4.99

❏ **Speed Reading** 109301-7 ....$4.99

❏ **Writing That Works** 109381-5 ....$4.99

❏ **The Concise Roget's International Thesaurus** 100709-9 ....$4.99

❏ **Letters for All Occasions** 109283-5 ....$5.99

❏ **The Resume Writer's Handbook** 109300-9 ....$4.99

❏ **The Crossword Puzzle Dictionary** 100038-8 ....$5.99

❏ **Revised Funk & Wagnalls Standard Dictionary** 100708-0 ......$4.99

❏ **Collins French-English Dictionary** 100244-5...............................$4.99

❏ **Collins German-English Dictionary** 100243-7 ....$4.99

❏ **Collins Italian-English Dictionary** 100246-1 ....$4.99

❏ **Collins Spanish-English Dictionary** 100245-3 ....$4.99

*Add $1.00 per title to U.S. price for sales in Canada.

MAIL TO: HarperCollins Publishers
         P.O. Box 588 Dunmore, PA 18512-0588
         OR CALL: (800) 331-3761 (Visa/Mastercard)
Yes, please send me the books I have checked:

SUBTOTAL ....$_____

POSTAGE AND HANDLING ....$ 2.00_____

SALES TAX (Add applicable sales tax) ....$_____

Name_____

Address_____

City_____

State_____Zip_____

*Order 4 or more titles and postage and handling is free! Order less than 4
books, please include $2.00 postage & handling. Remit in U.S. funds. Do not
send cash.

Allow up to 6 weeks for delivery. (Valid in U.S. & Canada.)
Prices subject to change.   HO961

dyelogy

IDEAL FOR HOME, SCHOOL OR OFFICE

FUNK & WAGNALLS brings you the expertise and superior quality of nearly a century of distinguished reference book publishing.

FUNK & WAGNALLS STANDARD DICTIONARY offers more information than any other paperback dictionary available:

- *Over 75,000 entries*
- *Authoritative etymologies*
- *New entries such as AIDS, African American, fax, fungible, gridlock and many more*
- *Clear and concise definitions*
- *Preferred U.S. spellings of every entry*
- *New foolproof, at-a-glance pronunciation system*
- *Sample phrases and sentences provide guidance for correct usage*

DESIGNED FOR EASY READING!

Revised and updated!

00708

0 99455 00499 2

ISBN 0-06-100708-0

U.S. $4.99
CAN. $5.99